D0771870

SportingNews
BOOKS

BASEBALL
REGISTER

2005 EDITION

EDITED BY: Tom Gatto. **STATS, Inc. EDITOR:** Tony Nistler.
CONTRIBUTING EDITORS: Shawn Reid, Dave Sloan
COVER DESIGN AND PAGE LAYOUT BY: Chad Painter / TSN.

ON THE COVER: Ichiro Suzuki by Albert Dickson / TSN; Curt Schilling by Robert Seale / TSN; Albert Pujols by Albert Dickson / TSN; Barry Bonds by Bob Leverone / TSN. **ON THE SPINE:** Randy Johnson by John Cordes for TSN.

Major league statistics compiled by STATS, Inc., a News Corporation company, 8130 Lehigh Avenue, Morton Grove, IL 60053. STATS is a trademark of Sports Team Analysis and Tracking Systems, Inc.

Minor league statistics provided by SportsTicker.

Copyright ©2004 by the Sporting News, a division of Vulcan Sports Media, Inc.,
10176 Corporate Square Drive, Suite 200, St. Louis, MO 63132-2924. All rights reserved. Printed in the U.S.A.

No part of the *Baseball Register* may be reproduced or transmitted in any form or by any means, electronic or mechanical, including photocopy, recording or any information storage and retrieval system now known or to be invented, without permission in writing from the publisher, except by a reviewer who wishes to quote brief passages in connection with a review written for inclusion in a magazine, newspaper or broadcast.

SPORTING NEWS is a registered trademark of the Sporting News.

ISBN: 0-89204-745-3

10 9 8 7 6 5 4 3 2 1

CONTENTS

The Cardinals Larry Walker tries to avoid the tag of Red Sox catcher Jason Varitek in Game 3 of the World Series. Boston went on to a four-game sweep of St. Louis. It was the first world title for the Red Sox since 1918.

EXPLANATION OF FOOTNOTES
AND ABBREVIATIONS

Note for statistical comparisons: Player strikes forced the cancellation of games in the 1972 season (10 days missed), the 1981 season (50 days missed), the 1994 season (52 days missed) and the 1995 season (18 games missed).

Positions are listed in descending order of games played; because of limited space, pinch-hitter and pinch-runner are listed in the regular-season section only if a player did not play a defensive position.

* Led league. For fielding statistics, the player led the league at the position shown.
• Tied for league lead. For fielding statistics, the player tied for the league lead at the position shown.
† Led league, but number indicated is total figure for two or more positions.
‡ Tied for league lead, but number indicated is total figure for two or more positions.
§ Led or tied for league lead, but total figure is divided between two different teams.
... Statistic unavailable, inapplicable, unofficial or mathematically impossible to calculate.
— Manager statistic inapplicable.

LEAGUES: A.A., Am. Assoc.—American Association. **A.L.**—American. **App., Appal.**—Appalachian. **Ar., Ariz.**—Arizona. **Atl.**—Atlantic. **Cal., Calif.**—California. **Car., Caro.**—Carolina. **DSL**—Dominican Summer. **East.**—Eastern. **Fla. St., Florida St., FSL**—Florida State. **GCL**—Gulf Coast. **GSL**—Gulf States. **In.-Am.**—Inter-American. **Int'l., I.L.**—International. **J.P., Jap. Pac., Jp. Pac.**—Japan Pacific. **Jp. Cen., Jp. Cn.**—Japan Central. **Jp. East**—Japan East. **Jp. West**—Japan West. **Mex.**—Mexican. **Mex. Cen.**—Mexican Center. **Mid., Midw.**—Midwest. **Miss.-O.V.**—Mississippi-Ohio Valley. **N.L.**—National. **North., Nor.**—Northern. **N'West, NW**—Northwest. **NYP, NY-P, NY-Penn**—New York-Pennsylvania. **Pac. Coast, PCL**—Pacific Coast. **Pio.**—Pioneer. **S. Atl., SAL**—South Atlantic. **Soph.**—Sophomore. **Sou., South.**—Southern. **Taiw.**—Taiwan. **Tex.**—Texas. **Tex.-La.**—Texas-Louisiana. **VSL**—Venezuelan Summer. **West.**—Western. **W. Car., W. Caro.**—Western Carolinas.

TEAMS: Aguas.—Aguascalientes. **Alb./Colon., Alb./Colonie**—Albany/Colonie. **Ariz.**—Arizona. **Ariz. D-backs**—Arizona League Diamondbacks. **Belling.**—Bellingham. **Birm.**—Birmingham. **Brevard Co.**—Brevard County. **Cant./Akr.**—Canton/Akron. **Ced. Rap.**—Cedar Rapids. **Cent. Ore.**—Central Oregon. **Central Vall.**—Central Valley. **Char., Charl.**—Charleston. **Chatt.**—Chattanooga. **Chiba Lot.**—Chiba Lotte. **Ciu. Juarez**—Ciudad Juarez. **Colo. Spr., Colo. Springs**—Colorado Springs. **Dall./Fort W.**—Dallas/Fort Worth. **Day. Beach.**—Daytona Beach. **Dm., Dom.**—Dominican. **Dom. B. Jays**—Dominican Blue Jays. **Dom. Orioles/WS**—Dominican Orioles/White Sox. **Elizabeth.**—Elizabethton. **Estadio Quis.**—Estadio Quisqueya. **Eve.**—Everett. **Fort Lauder., Fort Laud.**—Fort Lauderdale. **Fukuoka**—Fukuoka Daiei. **GC**—Gulf Coast. **GC Astros-Or.**—Gulf Coast Astros-Orange. **GC Royals-Bl.**—Gulf Coast Royals-Blue. **GC Whi. Sox**—Gulf Coast White Sox. **Grays Har.**—Grays Harbor. **Greens.**—Greensboro. **Greenw.**—Greenwood. **Guana.**—Guanajuato. **Hunting.**—Huntington. **Jacksonv.**—Jacksonville. **Johns. City**—Johnson City. **Kane Co.**—Kane County. **Lake Charl.**—Lake Charles. **Matt.**—Mattoon. **M.C., Mex. City**—Mexico City. **Med. Hat.**—Medicine Hat. **Monc.**—Monclova. **Montgom.**— Montgomery. **Niag. F., Niag. Falls**—Niagara Falls. **Okla. City**—Oklahoma City. **Pan. City**—Panama City. **Phoe.**—Phoenix. **Pomp. Beach**—Pompano Beach. **Pres. Lions**—President Lions. **Prin. Will., Prin. William**—Prince William. **Ral./Dur.**—Raleigh/Durham. **Rancho Cuca.**—Rancho Cucamonga. **Rocky Mount.**—Rocky Mountain. **Salt.**—Saltillo. **Salt.-Monc.**—Saltillo-Monclova. **San. Dom., San. Domingo**—Santo Domingo. **San Bern.**—San Bernardino. **San Fran.**—San Francisco. **Scran./W.B.**—Scranton/Wilkes-Barre. **S.C.**—South Carolina. **S.F. de Mac.**—San Francisco de Macoris. **San Luis Pot.**—San Luis Potosi. **Sonoma Co.**—Sonoma County. **S. Oregon**—Southern Oregon. **Spartan.**—Spartanburg. **St. Cath., St. Cathar.**—St. Catharines. **St. Peters., St. Pete.**—St. Petersburg. **States.**—Statesville. **Stock.**—Stockton. **T.-C.**—Tri-Cities. **Vanc.**—Vancouver. **Ven.**—Venezuelan. **Vent. Co.**—Ventura County. **W. Mich.**—West Michigan. **Win.-Salem, Winst.-Salem**—Winston-Salem. **Wis. Rap., Wis. Rapids**—Wisconsin Rapids. **W.P. Beach**—West Palm Beach. **W.Va.**—West Virgina. **Yuc.**—Yucatan.

STATISTICS: A—assists. **AB**—at-bats. **Avg.**—average (average allowed for pitchers). **BB**—bases on balls. **CG**—complete games. **CS**—caught stealing. **E**—errors. **ER**—earned runs. **ERA**—earned run average. **G**—games. **GDP**—grounded into double play. **GS**—games started. **H**—hits. **HBP**—hit by pitch. **Hld.**—holds. **HR**—home runs. **IBB**—intentional bases on balls. **IP**—innings pitched. **L**—losses. **OBP**—on-base percentage. **OPS**—on-base percentage plus slugging percentage. **Pct.**—winning percentage. **PO**—putouts. **Pos.**—position. **R**—runs. **RBI**—runs batted in. **SB**—stolen bases. **ShO**—shutouts. **SLG**—slugging percentage. **SO**—strikeouts. **Sv.**—saves. **Sv.Opp.**—save opportunities. **W**—wins. **WHIP**—walks plus hits divided by innings pitched. **2B**—doubles. **3B**—triples.

A

AARDSMA, DAVID   P

PERSONAL: Born December 27, 1981, in Denver, Colo. ... 6-5/200. ... Throws right, bats right. ... Full name: David A. Aardsma. ... High school: Cherry Creek (Denver). ... College: Penn State, then Rice.
TRANSACTIONS/CAREER NOTES: Selected by San Francisco Giants organization in first round (22nd pick overall) of 2003 free-agent draft.
CAREER HITTING: 0-for-0 (.000), 0 R, 0 2B, 0 3B, 0 HR, 0 RBI.

Year Team (League)	W	L	Pct.	ERA	WHIP	G	GS	CG	ShO	Hld.	Sv.-Opp.	IP	H	R	ER	HR	BB-IBB	SO	Avg.
2003—San Jose (California)	1	1	.500	1.96	1.15	18	0	0	0	...	8-...	18.1	14	4	4	2	7-0	28	.212
2004—San Francisco (N.L.)	1	0	1.000	6.75	2.81	11	0	0	0	1	0-1	10.2	20	8	8	1	10-0	5	.417
—Fresno (PCL)	6	4	.600	3.09	1.37	44	0	0	0	...	11-...	55.1	46	21	19	2	30-3	53	.223
Major League totals (1 year)	**1**	**0**	**1.000**	**6.75**	**2.81**	**11**	**0**	**0**	**0**	**1**	**0-1**	**10.2**	**20**	**8**	**8**	**1**	**10-0**	**5**	**.417**

ABBOTT, PAUL   P

PERSONAL: Born September 15, 1967, in Van Nuys, Calif. ... 6-2/203. ... Throws right, bats right. ... Full name: Paul David Abbott. ... High school: Sunny Hills (Fullerton, Calif.).
TRANSACTIONS/CAREER NOTES: Selected by Minnesota Twins organization in third round of 1985 free-agent draft. ... On disabled list (March 28-June 5 and August 14-September 1, 1992). ... Released by Twins (March 2, 1993). ... Signed by Cleveland Indians organization (March 27, 1993). ... Signed as a free agent by Kansas City Royals organization (November 21, 1993). ... On disabled list (March 18-May 25 and June 16-30, 1994). ... Released by Royals (June 30, 1994). ... Signed by Chicago Cubs organization (March 17, 1995). ... Signed as a free agent by San Diego Padres organization (November 29, 1995). ... Signed as a free agent by Seattle Mariners organization (January 10, 1997). ... Released by Mariners (December 14, 1998). ... Re-signed by Mariners (January 21, 1999). ... On disabled list (April 1-28, 2001); included rehabilitation assignment to Tacoma. ... On disabled list (May 6, 2002-remainder of season); included rehabilitation assignments to San Bernardino and Tacoma. ... Released by Mariners (November 19, 2002). ... Signed by Arizona Diamondbacks organization (February 10, 2003). ... Traded by Diamondbacks to Kansas City Royals for P Aric LeClair (August 8, 2003). ... Signed as a free agent by Tampa Bay Devil Rays (November 14, 2003). ... Released by Devil Rays (June 3, 2004). ... Signed by Philadelphia Phillies organization (June 7, 2004). ... Released by Phillies (September 8, 2004).
CAREER HITTING: 5-for-20 (.250), 2 R, 1 2B, 0 3B, 0 HR, 2 RBI.

Year Team (League)	W	L	Pct.	ERA	WHIP	G	GS	CG	ShO	Hld.	Sv.-Opp.	IP	H	R	ER	HR	BB-IBB	SO	Avg.
1985—Elizabethton (Appal.)	1	5	.167	6.94	1.86	10	10	1	0	...	0-...	35.0	33	32	27	3	32-0	34	.237
1986—Kenosha (Midw.)	6	10	.375	4.50	1.79	25	15	1	0	...	0-...	98.0	102	62	49	13	73-3	73	.267
1987—Kenosha (Midw.)	13	6	.684	3.65	1.41	26	25	1	0	...	0-...	145.1	102	78	59	11	103-0	138	.203
1988—Visalia (Calif.)	11	9	.550	4.18	1.65	28	28	4	2	...	0-...	172.1	141	95	80	9	143-5	205	.222
1989—Orlando (Sou.)	9	3	.750	4.37	1.31	17	17	1	0	...	0-...	90.2	71	48	44	6	48-0	102	.210
1990—Portland (PCL)	5	14	.263	4.56	1.50	23	23	4	1	...	0-...	128.1	110	75	65	9	82-0	129	.230
—Minnesota (A.L.)	0	5	.000	5.97	1.88	7	7	0	0	0	0-0	34.2	37	24	23	0	28-0	25	.282
1991—Portland (PCL)	2	3	.400	3.89	1.45	8	8	1	1	...	0-...	44.0	36	19	19	2	28-0	40	.224
—Minnesota (A.L.)	3	1	.750	4.75	1.56	15	3	0	0	0	0-0	47.1	38	27	25	5	36-1	43	.232
1992—Portland (PCL)	4	1	.800	2.33	1.32	7	7	0	0	...	0-...	46.1	30	13	12	2	31-0	46	.188
—Minnesota (A.L.)	0	0	...	3.27	1.55	6	0	0	0	0	0-0	11.0	12	4	4	1	5-0	13	.279
1993—Cant./Akr. (Eastern)	4	5	.444	4.06	1.33	13	12	1	0	...	0-...	75.1	72	34	34	4	28-2	86	.253
—Cleveland (A.L.)	0	1	.000	6.38	1.64	5	5	0	0	0	0-0	18.1	19	15	13	5	11-1	7	.260
—Charlotte (Int'l)	0	1	.000	6.63	1.68	4	4	0	0	...	0-...	19.0	25	16	14	4	7-0	12	.313
1994—Omaha (Am. Assoc.)	4	1	.800	4.87	1.78	15	10	0	0	...	0-...	57.1	57	32	31	8	45-0	48	.266
1995—Iowa (Am. Assoc.)	7	7	.500	3.67	1.46	46	11	0	0	...	0-...	115.1	104	50	47	12	64-4	127	.242
1996—Las Vegas (PCL)	4	2	.667	4.18	1.39	28	0	0	0	...	7-...	28.0	27	14	13	4	12-4	37	.252
1997—Tacoma (PCL)	8	4	.667	4.13	1.16	17	14	3	0	...	0-...	93.2	80	48	43	11	29-1	117	.228
—Ariz. Mariners (Ariz.)	0	0	...	0.93	0.72	3	3	0	0	...	0-...	9.2	0	2	1	0	7-0	13	.000
1998—Ariz. Mariners (Ariz.)	0	0	...	0.00	0.33	1	0	0	0	...	0-...	3.0	1	0	0	0	0-0	6	.091
—Tacoma (PCL)	1	0	1.000	1.20	0.93	3	3	0	0	...	0-...	15.0	9	2	2	2	5-0	20	.176
—Seattle (A.L.)	3	1	.750	4.01	1.38	4	4	0	0	0	0-0	24.2	24	11	11	2	10-0	22	.255
1999—Tacoma (PCL)	1	1	.500	6.43	1.79	2	2	0	0	...	0-...	14.0	21	11	10	1	4-0	10	.375
—Seattle (A.L.)	6	2	.750	3.10	1.13	25	7	0	0	3	0-2	72.2	50	31	25	9	32-3	68	.193
2000—Seattle (A.L.)	9	7	.563	4.22	1.36	35	27	0	0	4	0-0	179.0	164	89	84	23	80-4	100	.243
2001—Tacoma (PCL)	0	0	...	0.00	1.25	1	1	0	0	...	0-...	4.0	1	0	0	0	4-0	4	.077
—Seattle (A.L.)	17	4	.810	4.25	1.42	28	27	1	0	0	0-0	163.0	145	79	77	21	87-5	118	.238
2002—Seattle (A.L.)	1	3	.250	11.96	2.28	7	5	0	0	0	0-0	26.1	40	36	35	5	20-0	22	.351
—San Bernardino (Calif.)	0	0	...	0.00	1.00	1	1	0	0	...	0-...	5.0	3	0	0	0	2-0	5	.188
—Tacoma (PCL)	0	1	.000	6.23	1.85	2	2	0	0	...	0-...	8.2	13	10	6	3	3-0	8	.342
2003—Tucson (PCL)	3	4	.429	3.95	1.40	11	8	1	1	...	0-...	54.2	63	29	24	3	12-0	50	.285
—Kansas City (A.L.)	1	2	.333	5.29	1.53	10	8	0	0	0	0-0	47.2	47	29	28	8	26-2	32	.257
2004—Tampa Bay (A.L.)	2	5	.286	6.70	1.62	10	9	0	0	0	0-0	47.0	49	39	35	4	27-0	25	.257
—Philadelphia (N.L.)	1	6	.143	6.24	1.80	10	10	0	0	0	0-0	49.0	57	37	34	14	31-1	21	.291
—Scran./W.B. (I.L.)	1	2	.333	6.15	1.63	5	5	1	0	...	0-...	26.1	26	18	18	4	17-0	19	.265
American League totals (11 years)	**42**	**31**	**.575**	**4.82**	**1.47**	**152**	**102**	**1**	**0**	**7**	**0-2**	**671.2**	**625**	**384**	**360**	**87**	**362-16**	**475**	**.246**
National League totals (1 year)	**1**	**6**	**.143**	**6.24**	**1.80**	**10**	**10**	**0**	**0**	**0**	**0-0**	**49.0**	**57**	**37**	**34**	**14**	**31-1**	**21**	**.291**
Major League totals (11 years)	**43**	**37**	**.538**	**4.92**	**1.49**	**162**	**112**	**1**	**0**	**7**	**0-2**	**720.2**	**682**	**421**	**394**	**101**	**393-17**	**496**	**.250**

DIVISION SERIES RECORD

Year Team (League)	W	L	Pct.	ERA	WHIP	G	GS	CG	ShO	Hld.	Sv.-Opp.	IP	H	R	ER	HR	BB-IBB	SO	Avg.
2000—Seattle (A.L.)	1	0	1.000	1.59	1.41	1	1	0	0	0	0-0	5.2	5	2	1	0	3-0	1	.250
2001—Seattle (A.L.)	0	0	...	24.00	4.67	1	1	0	0	0	0-0	3.0	9	8	8	3	5-0	3	.529
Division series totals (2 years)	**1**	**0**	**1.000**	**9.35**	**2.54**	**2**	**2**	**0**	**0**	**0**	**0-0**	**8.2**	**14**	**10**	**9**	**3**	**8-0**	**4**	**.378**

CHAMPIONSHIP SERIES RECORD

Year Team (League)	W	L	Pct.	ERA	WHIP	G	GS	CG	ShO	Hld.	Sv.-Opp.	IP	H	R	ER	HR	BB-IBB	SO	Avg.
2000—Seattle (A.L.)	0	1	.000	5.40	1.20	1	1	0	0	0	0-0	5.0	3	3	3	1	3-0	3	.167
2001—Seattle (A.L.)	0	0	...	0.00	1.60	1	1	0	0	0	0-0	5.0	0	0	0	0	8-0	2	.000
Champ. series totals (2 years)	**0**	**1**	**.000**	**2.70**	**1.40**	**2**	**2**	**0**	**0**	**0**	**0-0**	**10.0**	**3**	**3**	**3**	**1**	**11-0**	**5**	**.100**

ABREU, BOBBY — OF

PERSONAL: Born March 11, 1974, in Aragua, Venezuela. ... 6-0/211. ... Bats left, throws right. ... Full name: Bob Kelly Abreu. ... Name pronounced: ah-BRAY-you.

TRANSACTIONS/CAREER NOTES: Signed as a non-drafted free agent by Houston Astros organization (August 21, 1990). ... On disabled list (May 25-July 1, 1997); included rehabilitation assignments to Jackson and New Orleans. ... Selected by Tampa Bay Devil Rays in first round (sixth pick overall) of expansion draft (November 18, 1997). ... Traded by Devil Rays to Philadelphia Phillies for SS Kevin Stocker (November 18, 1997).

2004 GAMES PLAYED BY POSITION (MLB): OF-158.

									BATTING											FIELDING	
Year Team (League)	Pos.	G	AB	R	H	2B	3B	HR	RBI	BB	SO	HBP	GDP	SB-CS	Avg.	OBP	SLG	OPS		E	Avg.
1991—GC Astros (GCL)	SS-OF	56	183	21	55	7	3	0	20	17	27	1	3	10-6	.301	.358	.372	.729		5	.943
1992—Asheville (S. Atl.)	OF	135	480	81	140	21	4	8	48	63	79	3	5	15-11	.292	.375	.402	.777		11	.943
1993—Osceola (Fla. St.)	OF	129	474	62	134	21	17	5	55	51	90	1	8	10-14	.283	.352	.430	.782		8	.961
1994—Jackson (Texas)	OF	118	400	61	121	25	9	16	73	42	81	3	2	12-10	.303	.368	.530	.898		4	.967
1995—Tucson (PCL)	OF-2B	114	415	72	126	24	17	10	75	67	120	1	6	16-14	.304	.395	.516	.911		7	.970
1996—Tucson (PCL)	OF-DH	132	484	86	137	14	16	13	68	83	111	2	5	24-18	.283	.389	.459	.847		7	.969
—Houston (N.L.)	OF	15	22	1	5	1	0	0	1	2	3	0	1	0-0	.227	.292	.273	.564		0	1.000
1997—Houston (N.L.)	OF	59	188	22	47	10	2	3	26	21	48	1	0	7-2	.250	.329	.372	.701		2	.978
—Jackson (Texas)	OF	3	12	2	2	1	0	0	0	1	5	0	0	0-0	.167	.231	.250	.481		0	1.000
—New Orleans (A.A.)	OF	47	194	25	52	9	4	2	22	21	49	0	4	7-4	.268	.335	.387	.721		1	.990
1998—Philadelphia (N.L.)	OF	151	497	68	155	29	6	17	74	84	133	0	6	19-10	.312	.409	.497	.906		8	.973
1999—Philadelphia (N.L.)	OF-DH	152	546	118	183	35	•11	20	93	109	113	3	13	27-9	.335	.446	.549	.995		3	.989
2000—Philadelphia (N.L.)	OF	154	576	103	182	42	10	25	79	100	116	1	12	28-8	.316	.416	.554	.970		4	.989
2001—Philadelphia (N.L.)	OF	•162	588	118	170	48	4	31	110	106	137	1	13	36-14	.289	.393	.543	.936		8	.976
2002—Philadelphia (N.L.)	OF	157	572	102	176	*50	6	20	85	104	117	3	11	31-12	.308	.413	.521	.934		5	.983
2003—Philadelphia (N.L.)	OF	158	577	99	173	35	1	20	101	109	126	2	13	22-9	.300	.409	.468	.877		6	.981
2004—Philadelphia (N.L.)	OF	159	574	118	173	47	1	30	105	127	116	5	5	40-5	.301	.428	.544	.971		6	.982
Major League totals (9 years)		1167	4140	749	1264	297	41	166	674	762	909	16	74	210-69	.305	.412	.517	.929		42	.982

DIVISION SERIES RECORD

									BATTING										
Year Team (League)	Pos.	G	AB	R	H	2B	3B	HR	RBI	BB	SO	HBP	GDP	SB-CS	Avg.	OBP	SLG	OPS	E	Avg.
1997—Houston (N.L.)		3	3	0	1	0	0	0	0	0	2	0	0	1-0	.333	.333	.333	.667	...	...

ALL-STAR GAME RECORD

	G	AB	R	H	2B	3B	HR	RBI	BB	SO	HBP	GDP	SB-CS	Avg.	OBP	SLG	OPS	E	Avg.
All-Star Game totals (1 year)	1	1	0	0	0	0	0	0	0	1	0	0	0-0	.000	.000	.000	.000	0	...

ACEVEDO, JOSE — P

PERSONAL: Born December 18, 1977, in Santo Domingo, Dominican Republic. ... 6-0/185. ... Throws right, bats right. ... Full name: Jose Omar Acevedo. ... Name pronounced: AH-ceh-vedo. ... Cousin of Juan Marichal, pitcher with three major league teams (1960-75).

TRANSACTIONS/CAREER NOTES: Signed as non-drafted free agent by Cincinnati Reds organization (December 7, 1996). ... On disabled list (August 7, 2003-remainder of season).

CAREER HITTING: 7-for-93 (.075), 2 R, 2 2B, 0 3B, 0 HR, 4 RBI.

Year Team (League)	W	L	Pct.	ERA	WHIP	G	GS	CG	ShO	Hld.	Sv.-Opp.	IP	H	R	ER	HR	BB-IBB	SO	Avg.
1997—Char., W.Va. (SAL)	3	3	.500	3.92	1.22	15	8	0	0	...	0-...	57.1	61	29	25	8	9-0	34	.268
1998—Char., W.Va. (SAL)	9	9	.500	3.91	1.32	25	25	2	0	...	0-...	158.2	169	74	69	9	40-0	132	.275
1999—Clinton (Midw.)	8	6	.571	3.77	1.21	24	24	1	1	...	0-...	133.2	119	65	56	14	43-0	136	.236
2000—Dayton (Midw.)	11	5	.688	3.89	1.33	25	23	0	0	...	0-...	141.0	135	74	61	16	53-0	123	.247
2001—Chattanooga (Southern)	4	4	.500	3.69	1.19	16	11	0	0	...	0-...	78.0	68	34	32	6	25-1	82	.239
—Cincinnati (N.L.)	5	7	.417	5.44	1.41	18	18	0	0	0	0-0	96.0	101	61	58	17	34-2	68	.272
2002—Cincinnati (N.L.)	4	2	.667	7.23	1.69	6	5	0	0	0	0-0	23.2	28	21	19	8	12-0	14	.292
—Louisville (Int'l)	12	7	.632	3.20	1.16	23	23	0	0	...	0-...	154.2	146	61	55	16	34-0	128	.250
2003—Louisville (Int'l)	6	2	.750	3.43	1.30	29	3	0	0	...	0-...	60.1	56	26	23	5	20-1	57	.246
—Cincinnati (N.L.)	2	0	1.000	2.67	0.85	5	4	1	0	0	0-0	27.0	17	8	8	3	6-1	23	.183
2004—Cincinnati (N.L.)	5	12	.294	5.94	1.48	39	27	0	0	2	0-0	157.2	188	108	104	30	45-8	117	.292
Major League totals (4 years)	16	21	.432	5.59	1.42	68	54	1	0	2	0-0	304.1	334	198	189	58	97-11	222	.277

ADAMS, MIKE — P

PERSONAL: Born July 29, 1978, in Corpus Christi, Texas. ... 6-5/190. ... Throws right, bats right. ... Full name: Jon Michael Adams. ... College: Texas A&M-Kingsville.

TRANSACTIONS/CAREER NOTES: Signed as a non-drafted free agent by Milwaukee Brewers organization (May 15, 2001).

CAREER HITTING: 0-for-0 (.000), 0 R, 0 2B, 0 3B, 0 HR, 0 RBI.

Year Team (League)	W	L	Pct.	ERA	WHIP	G	GS	CG	ShO	Hld.	Sv.-Opp.	IP	H	R	ER	HR	BB-IBB	SO	Avg.
2001—Ogden (Pio.)	2	2	.500	2.81	1.00	23	0	0	0	...	12-...	32.0	26	10	10	4	6-1	44	.220
2002—Beloit (Midw.)	0	0	...	2.93	0.98	11	0	0	0	...	5-...	15.1	13	6	5	1	2-0	21	.228
—High Desert (Calif.)	2	1	.667	2.57	1.14	10	0	0	0	...	5-...	14.0	9	6	4	2	7-0	23	.173
—Huntsville (Southern)	1	0	1.000	3.38	1.39	13	0	0	0	...	1-...	18.2	14	11	7	3	12-0	11	.209
2003—Huntsville (Southern)	3	7	.300	3.15	1.22	45	2	0	0	...	14-...	74.1	58	30	26	6	33-1	83	.208
2004—Indianapolis (Int'l)	2	0	1.000	2.61	0.87	10	2	0	0	...	0-...	31.0	23	10	9	3	4-0	37	.209
—Milwaukee (N.L.)	2	3	.400	3.40	1.21	46	0	0	0	12	0-5	53.0	50	21	20	5	14-2	39	.248
Major League totals (1 year)	2	3	.400	3.40	1.21	46	0	0	0	12	0-5	53.0	50	21	20	5	14-2	39	.248

ADAMS, RUSS — SS

PERSONAL: Born August 30, 1980, in Laurinburg, N.C. ... 6-1/180. ... Bats left, throws right. ... Full name: Russ Moore Adams. ... High school: Scotland (Laurinburg, N.C.). ... College: North Carolina.

TRANSACTIONS/CAREER NOTES: Selected by Toronto Blue Jays organization in first round (14th pick overall) of 2002 free-agent draft.

2004 GAMES PLAYED BY POSITION (MLB): SS—21.

									BATTING										FIELDING	
Year Team (League)	Pos.	G	AB	R	H	2B	3B	HR	RBI	BB	SO	HBP	GDP	SB-CS	Avg.	OBP	SLG	OPS	E	Avg.
2002—Auburn (NY-Penn)	SS	30	113	25	40	7	3	0	16	24	11	1	1	13-1	.354	.464	.469	.933	5	.963
—Dunedin (Fla. St.)	SS	37	147	23	34	4	2	1	12	18	17	2	1	5-2	.231	.321	.306	.628	9	.947
2003—Dunedin (Fla. St.)	SS	68	258	50	72	9	5	3	16	38	27	6	5	9-2	.279	.380	.388	.768	19	.941

Year	Team (League)	Pos.	G	AB	R	H	2B	3B	HR	RBI	BB	SO	HBP	GDP	SB-CS	Avg.	OBP	SLG	OPS	E	Avg.
—	New Haven (East.)	SS	65	271	42	75	10	4	4	26	30	37	0	5	8-1	.277	.349	.387	.736	16	.944
2004—	Syracuse (Int'l)	SS-DH	122	483	58	139	37	3	5	54	45	62	5	9	6-2	.288	.351	.408	.753	33	.939
—	Toronto (A.L.)	SS	22	72	10	22	2	1	4	10	5	5	1	3	1-0	.306	.359	.528	.887	5	.936
	Major League totals (1 year)		22	72	10	22	2	1	4	10	5	5	1	3	1-0	.306	.359	.528	.887	5	.936

ADAMS, TERRY — P

PERSONAL: Born March 6, 1973, in Mobile, Ala. ... 6-3/220. ... Throws right, bats right. ... Full name: Terry Wayne Adams. ... High school: Mary G. Montgomery (Semmes, Ala.).

TRANSACTIONS/CAREER NOTES: Selected by Chicago Cubs organization in fourth round of 1991 free-agent draft. ... On disabled list (June 21-September 21, 1993). ... On disabled list (March 26-May 8 and June 19-July 4, 1999) ... Traded by Cubs with P Chad Ricketts and a player to be named to Los Angeles Dodgers for P Ismael Valdes and 2B Eric Young (December 12, 1999). ... Signed as a free agent by Philadelphia Phillies (January 17, 2002). ... On restricted list (May 26-27, 2003). ... On disabled list (August 27-September 11, 2003). ... Signed as a free agent by Toronto Blue Jays (January 7, 2004). ... Traded by Blue Jays to Boston Red Sox for 3B John Hattig (July 24, 2004).

CAREER HITTING: 4-for-78 (.051), 2 R, 1 2B, 0 3B, 0 HR, 2 RBI.

Year	Team (League)	W	L	Pct.	ERA	WHIP	G	GS	CG	ShO	Hld.	Sv.-Opp.	IP	H	R	ER	HR	BB-IBB	SO	Avg.
1991—	Huntington (Appal.)	0	9	.000	5.77	2.24	14	13	0	0	...	0-...	57.2	67	56	37	1	62-0	52	.293
1992—	Peoria (Midw.)	7	12	.368	4.41	1.46	25	25	3	1	...	0-...	157.0	144	95	77	7	86-0	96	.251
1993—	Daytona (Fla. St.)	3	5	.375	4.97	1.71	13	13	0	0	...	0-...	70.2	78	47	39	2	43-0	35	.288
1994—	Daytona (Fla. St.)	9	10	.474	4.38	1.58	39	7	0	0	...	7-...	84.1	87	47	41	5	46-3	64	.266
1995—	Orlando (Sou.)	2	3	.400	1.43	1.04	37	0	0	0	...	19-...	37.2	23	9	6	2	16-1	26	.177
—	Iowa (Am. Assoc.)	0	0	...	0.00	0.79	7	0	0	0	...	5-...	6.1	3	0	0	0	2-0	10	.130
—	Chicago (N.L.)	1	1	.500	6.50	1.78	18	0	0	0	0	1-1	18.0	22	15	13	0	10-1	15	.289
1996—	Chicago (N.L.)	3	6	.333	2.94	1.32	69	0	0	0	11	4-8	101.0	84	36	33	6	49-6	78	.231
1997—	Chicago (N.L.)	2	9	.182	4.62	1.77	74	0	0	0	11	18-22	74.0	91	43	38	3	40-6	64	.306
1998—	Chicago (N.L.)	7	7	.500	4.33	1.56	63	0	0	0	13	1-7	72.2	72	39	35	7	41-3	73	.255
—	Iowa (PCL)	0	0	...	0.00	1.00	3	0	0	0	...	0-...	4.0	1	1	0	0	3-0	5	.077
1999—	West Tenn (Sou.)	0	0	...	16.88	2.63	2	1	0	0	...	0-...	2.2	5	6	5	0	2-0	2	.417
—	Chicago (N.L.)	6	3	.667	4.02	1.35	52	0	0	0	3	13-18	65.0	60	33	29	9	28-2	57	.245
2000—	Los Angeles (N.L.)	6	9	.400	3.52	1.41	66	0	0	0	15	2-7	84.1	80	42	33	6	39-0	56	.245
2001—	Los Angeles (N.L.)	12	8	.600	4.33	1.36	43	22	0	0	4	0-1	166.1	172	84	80	9	54-1	141	.267
2002—	Philadelphia (N.L.)	7	9	.438	4.35	1.39	46	19	0	0	12	0-1	136.2	132	76	66	9	58-5	96	.255
2003—	Philadelphia (N.L.)	1	4	.200	2.65	1.34	66	0	0	0	16	0-0	68.0	68	22	20	1	23-4	51	.268
2004—	Toronto (A.L.)	4	4	.500	3.98	1.65	42	0	0	0	2	3-6	43.0	49	20	19	4	22-2	35	.290
—	Boston (A.L.)	2	0	1.000	6.00	1.52	19	0	0	0	1	0-0	27.0	35	19	18	6	6-1	21	.321
	American League totals (1 year)	6	4	.600	4.76	1.60	61	0	0	0	3	3-6	70.0	84	39	37	10	28-3	56	.302
	National League totals (9 years)	45	56	.446	3.97	1.43	497	41	0	0	85	39-65	786.0	781	390	347	50	342-28	631	.260
	Major League totals (10 years)	51	60	.459	4.04	1.44	558	41	0	0	88	42-71	856.0	865	429	384	60	370-31	687	.263

ADKINS, JON — P

PERSONAL: Born August 30, 1977, in Huntington, W.Va. ... 5-11/210. ... Throws right, bats left. ... Full name: Jonathan Scott Adkins. ... High school: Wayne (W. Va.). ... College: Oklahoma State.

TRANSACTIONS/CAREER NOTES: Selected by Oakland Athletics organization in ninth round of 1998 free-agent draft. ... Traded by A's to Chicago White Sox for 2B Ray Durham and cash considerations (July 25, 2002).

CAREER HITTING: 0-for-0 (.000), 0 R, 0 2B, 0 3B, 0 HR, 0 RBI.

Year	Team (League)	W	L	Pct.	ERA	WHIP	G	GS	CG	ShO	Hld.	Sv.-Opp.	IP	H	R	ER	HR	BB-IBB	SO	Avg.
1999—	Modesto (Calif.)	9	5	.643	4.76	1.40	26	15	0	0	...	1-...	102.0	113	65	54	6	30-1	93	.276
2000—	Ariz. A's (Ariz.)	1	1	.500	3.00	1.20	4	2	0	0	...	0-...	15.0	15	6	5	1	3-0	17	.234
—	Sacramento (PCL)	0	1	.000	9.00	1.75	1	1	0	0	...	0-...	4.0	6	4	4	2	1-0	2	.333
—	Modesto (Calif.)	5	2	.714	1.81	1.17	9	7	1	0	...	0-...	49.2	41	17	10	1	17-0	38	.225
2001—	Midland (Texas)	8	8	.500	4.46	1.33	24	24	1	1	...	0-...	137.1	147	71	68	9	36-1	74	.273
—	Sacramento (PCL)	1	0	1.000	4.26	1.97	3	2	0	0	...	0-...	12.2	17	9	6	1	8-0	7	.333
2002—	Modesto (Calif.)	0	1	.000	8.10	1.80	1	1	0	0	...	0-...	6.2	11	7	6	0	1-0	4	.379
—	Sacramento (PCL)	7	6	.538	6.03	1.77	20	20	0	0	...	0-...	97.0	139	74	65	9	33-0	76	.338
—	Charlotte (Int'l)	4	2	.667	3.69	1.27	8	7	1	0	...	0-...	46.1	47	20	19	4	12-0	31	.260
2003—	Charlotte (Int'l)	7	8	.467	3.96	1.25	26	19	1	1	...	1-...	122.2	119	65	54	11	34-1	59	.254
—	Chicago (A.L.)	0	0	...	4.82	1.61	4	0	0	0	0	0-0	9.1	8	5	5	1	7-0	3	.250
2004—	Chicago (A.L.)	2	3	.400	4.65	1.53	50	0	0	0	5	0-0	62.0	75	35	32	13	20-3	44	.305
	Major League totals (2 years)	2	3	.400	4.67	1.54	54	0	0	0	5	0-0	71.1	83	40	37	14	27-3	47	.299

AFFELDT, JEREMY — P

PERSONAL: Born June 6, 1979, in Phoenix, Ariz. ... 6-4/215. ... Throws left, bats left. ... Full name: Jeremy David Affeldt. ... Name pronounced: AFF-felt. ... High school: Northwest Christian (Spokane, Wash.).

TRANSACTIONS/CAREER NOTES: Selected by Kansas City Royals organization in third round of 1997 free-agent draft. ... On disabled list (June 9-August 1, 2002); included rehabilitation assignment to Wichita. ... On disabled list (April 20-May 6, 2003; and June 27-August 21, 2004); included rehabilitation assignment to Omaha.

CAREER HITTING: 2-for-6 (.333), 0 R, 0 2B, 0 3B, 0 HR, 2 RBI.

Year	Team (League)	W	L	Pct.	ERA	WHIP	G	GS	CG	ShO	Hld.	Sv.-Opp.	IP	H	R	ER	HR	BB-IBB	SO	Avg.
1997—	GC Royals (GCL)	2	0	1.000	4.50	1.38	10	9	0	0	...	0-...	40.0	34	24	20	3	21-0	36	.243
1998—	Lansing (Midw.)	0	3	.000	9.53	2.29	6	3	0	0	...	0-...	17.0	27	21	18	1	12-0	8	.355
—	GC Royals (GCL)	4	3	.571	2.89	1.32	12	9	0	0	...	0-...	56.0	50	24	18	1	24-0	67	.243
1999—	Char., W.Va. (SAL)	7	7	.500	3.83	1.53	27	24	2	1	...	0-...	143.1	140	78	61	4	80-0	111	.261
2000—	Wilmington (Caro.)	5	15	.250	4.09	1.47	27	26	0	0	...	0-...	147.1	158	87	67	7	59-0	92	.275
2001—	Wichita (Texas)	10	6	.625	3.90	1.37	25	25	0	0	...	0-...	145.1	153	74	63	9	46-0	128	.276
2002—	Kansas City (A.L.)	3	4	.429	4.64	1.57	34	7	0	0	1	0-1	77.2	85	41	40	8	37-4	67	.274
—	Wichita (Texas)	0	0	...	1.50	0.67	3	3	0	0	...	0-...	6.0	1	1	1	0	3-0	3	.059
2003—	Kansas City (A.L.)	7	6	.538	3.93	1.30	36	18	0	0	3	4-4	126.0	126	58	55	12	38-1	98	.261
2004—	Omaha (PCL)	0	0	...	0.00	0.50	4	0	0	0	...	3-...	4.0	2	0	0	0	0-0	5	.154
—	Kansas City (A.L.)	3	4	.429	4.95	1.61	38	8	0	0	0	13-17	76.1	91	49	42	6	32-2	49	.302
	Major League totals (3 years)	13	14	.481	4.40	1.46	108	33	0	0	4	17-22	280.0	302	148	137	26	107-7	214	.276

AGUILA, CHRIS — OF

PERSONAL: Born February 23, 1979, in Redwood City, Calif. ... 5-11/180. ... Bats right, throws right. ... Full name: Christopher Louis Aguila. ... High school: McQueen (Reno, Nev.).

TRANSACTIONS/CAREER NOTES: Selected by Florida Marlins organization in third round of 1997 free-agent draft.

2004 GAMES PLAYED BY POSITION (MLB): OF—20.

Year	Team (League)	Pos.	G	AB	R	H	2B	3B	HR	RBI	BB	SO	HBP	GDP	SB-CS	Avg.	OBP	SLG	OPS	E	Avg.
1997—GC Marlins (GCL)		3B	46	157	12	34	7	0	1	17	21	49	1	3	2-1	.217	.309	.280	.590	22	.843
1998—GC Marlins (GCL)		3B	51	171	29	46	12	3	4	29	19	49	2	4	6-2	.269	.349	.444	.793	15	.850
1999—Kane Co. (Midw.)		OF	122	430	74	105	21	7	15	78	40	127	9	9	14-4	.244	.320	.430	.750	5	.977
2000—Brevard County (FSL)		OF	136	518	68	125	27	3	9	56	37	105	1	11	8-8	.241	.292	.357	.649	5	.985
2001—Brevard County (FSL)		OF	73	272	44	75	15	3	10	34	21	54	2	7	8-4	.276	.328	.463	.791	3	.984
—Portland (East.)		OF	64	241	25	62	16	1	4	29	18	50	3	4	5-7	.257	.312	.382	.694	3	.969
2002—Portland (East.)		OF	130	429	62	126	28	4	6	46	48	101	4	8	14-8	.294	.369	.420	.788	3	.988
2003—GC Marlins (GCL)		OF	1	4	1	3	0	0	1	2	0	1	0	0	0-0	.750	.750	1.500	2.250	0	...
—Carolina (Southern)		OF	93	337	58	108	21	3	11	55	36	67	2	6	6-2	.320	.384	.499	.883	2	.989
2004—Albuquerque (PCL)		OF-DH	97	330	61	103	23	2	11	56	37	82	2	8	8-3	.312	.380	.494	.870	3	.986
—Florida (N.L.)		OF	29	45	10	10	2	1	3	5	2	12	0	0	0-0	.222	.255	.511	.766	2	.909
Major League totals (1 year)			29	45	10	10	2	1	3	5	2	12	0	0	0-0	.222	.255	.511	.766	2	.909

AINSWORTH, KURT — P

PERSONAL: Born September 9, 1978, in Baton Rouge, La. ... 6-3/208. ... Throws right, bats right. ... Full name: Kurt Harold Ainsworth. ... High school: Catholic (Baton Rouge, La.). ... College: LSU.

TRANSACTIONS/CAREER NOTES: Selected by San Francisco Giants organization in first round (24th pick overall) of 1999 free-agent draft. ... On disabled list (May 31-June 21, 2003); included rehabilitation assignment to Fresno. ... Traded by Giants with Ps Damian Moss and Ryan Hannaman to Baltimore Orioles for P Sidney Ponson (July 31, 2003).

CAREER HITTING: 2-for-28 (.071), 1 R, 1 2B, 0 3B, 0 HR, 0 RBI.

Year	Team (League)	W	L	Pct.	ERA	WHIP	G	GS	CG	ShO	Hld.	Sv.-Opp.	IP	H	R	ER	HR	BB-IBB	SO	Avg.
1999—Salem-Keizer (N'west)		3	3	.500	1.61	1.16	10	10	1	0	...	0-...	44.2	34	8	8	1	18-0	64	.211
2000—Shreveport (Texas)		10	9	.526	3.30	1.27	28	28	0	0	...	0-...	158.0	138	67	58	12	63-3	130	.233
2001—Fresno (PCL)		10	9	.526	5.07	1.30	27	26	0	0	...	0-...	149.0	139	91	84	22	54-1	157	.247
—San Francisco (N.L.)		0	0	...	13.50	2.50	2	0	0	0	0	0-0	2.0	3	3	3	1	2-0	3	.333
2002—Fresno (PCL)		8	6	.571	3.41	1.24	20	19	1	0	...	0-...	116.0	101	49	44	7	43-0	119	.238
—San Francisco (N.L.)		1	2	.333	2.10	1.32	6	4	0	0	0	0-0	25.2	22	7	6	1	12-0	15	.237
2003—San Francisco (N.L.)		5	4	.556	3.82	1.39	11	11	0	0	0	0-0	66.0	66	31	28	7	26-0	48	.262
—Fresno (PCL)		0	0	...	4.50	2.00	1	1	0	0	0	0-...	2.0	2	1	1	0	2-0	1	.250
—Baltimore (A.L.)		0	1	.000	11.57	3.00	3	0	0	0	0	0-0	2.1	6	3	3	1	1-0	4	.429
2004—Baltimore (A.L.)		0	1	.000	9.68	1.92	7	7	0	0	0	0-0	30.2	39	34	33	6	20-0	30	.320
—Ottawa (Int'l)		0	0	...	9.00	2.00	1	1	0	0	0	0-...	4.0	7	4	4	1	1-0	6	.412
—Aberdeen (NY-P)		0	1	.000	1.35	0.75	2	2	0	0	...	0-...	6.2	2	1	1	0	3-0	8	.095
American League totals (2 years)		0	2	.000	9.82	2.00	10	7	0	0	0	0-0	33.0	45	37	36	7	21-0	24	.331
National League totals (3 years)		6	6	.500	3.56	1.40	19	15	0	0	0	0-0	93.2	91	41	37	9	40-0	66	.257
Major League totals (4 years)		6	8	.429	5.19	1.56	29	22	0	0	0	0-0	126.2	136	78	73	16	61-0	90	.278

ALEXANDER, MANNY — 2B/SS

PERSONAL: Born March 20, 1971, in San Pedro de Macoris, Dominican Republic. ... 5-10/180. ... Bats right, throws right. ... Full name: Manuel Alexander.

TRANSACTIONS/CAREER NOTES: Signed as a non-drafted free agent by Baltimore Orioles organization (February 4, 1988). ... On disabled list (March 25-May 2, 1995). ... Traded by Orioles with IF Scott McClain to New York Mets for P Hector Ramirez (March 22, 1997). ... On disabled list (June 13-July 10 and August 1-11, 1997). ... Traded by Mets to Chicago Cubs (August 14, 1997), completing deal in which Mets traded OF Lance Johnson and two players to be named to Cubs for OF Brian McRae and Ps Mel Rojas and Turk Wendell (August 8, 1997); Mets traded P Mark Clark to Cubs as part of deal (August 11, 1997). ... Traded by Cubs to Boston Red Sox for OF Damon Buford (December 10, 1999). ... On disabled list (September 29, 2000-remainder of season). ... Signed as a free agent by Seattle Mariners organization (February 16, 2001). ... Signed as a free agent by New York Yankees organization (February 4, 2002). ... Released by Yankees (March 13, 2002). ... Acquired by Milwaukee Brewers organization from Cordoba of the Mexican League (August 10, 2002). ... Traded by Brewers to Texas Rangers for cash (March 25, 2003). ... Career major league pitching: 0-0, 67.50 ERA, 1 G, 0.2 IP, 1 H, 5 R, 5 ER, 4 BB, 0 SO.

2004 GAMES PLAYED BY POSITION (MLB): 2B—11, SS—7, 3B—3.

Year	Team (League)	Pos.	G	AB	R	H	2B	3B	HR	RBI	BB	SO	HBP	GDP	SB-CS	Avg.	OBP	SLG	OPS	E	Avg.
1988—				Did not play.																	
1989—Bluefield (Appal.)		SS	65	274	49	85	13	2	2	34	20	49	3	2	19-8	.310	.361	.394	.755	32	.908
1990—Wausau (Midw.)		SS	44	152	16	27	3	1	0	11	12	41	1	2	8-3	.178	.238	.211	.449	11	.938
1991—Hagerstown (East.)		SS	3	9	3	3	1	0	0	2	1	3	1	0	0-0	.333	.417	.444	.861	0	1.000
—Frederick (Carolina)		SS	134	548	81	143	17	3	3	42	44	68	2	4	47-14	.261	.318	.319	.637	32	.951
1992—Hagerstown (East.)		SS	127	499	69	129	23	8	2	41	25	62	6	10	43-12	.259	.300	.349	.648	36	.929
—Rochester (Int'l)		SS	6	24	3	7	1	0	0	3	1	3	0	0	0-2	.292	.320	.333	.653	1	.974
—Baltimore (A.L.)		SS	4	5	1	1	0	0	0	0	0	3	0	0	0-0	.200	.200	.200	.400	0	1.000
1993—Rochester (Int'l)		SS	120	471	55	115	23	8	6	51	22	60	4	11	19-7	.244	.283	.365	.648	18	.966
—Baltimore (A.L.)		DH	3	0	1	0	0	0	0	0	0	0	0	0	0-0	...	.000	...	...	...	...
1994—Rochester (Int'l)		SS-2B	111	426	63	106	23	6	6	39	16	67	3	7	30-8	.249	.278	.373	.651	33	.939
1995—Baltimore (A.L.)		2-S-3-DH	94	242	35	57	9	1	3	23	20	30	2	2	11-4	.236	.294	.318	.612	10	.969
1996—Baltimore (A.L.)		S-2-3-O-P-DH	54	68	6	7	0	0	0	4	3	27	0	2	3-3	.103	.141	.103	.244	5	.936
1997—New York (N.L.)		2-S-3	54	149	26	37	9	3	2	15	9	38	1	3	11-0	.248	.291	.389	.680	4	.979
—St. Lucie (Fla. St.)		SS	1	4	0	1	0	0	0	0	0	1	0	0	0-0	.250	.250	.500	.750	0	1.000
—Chicago (N.L.)		SS-2B	33	99	11	29	5	1	1	7	8	16	2	3	2-1	.293	.346	.374	.720	7	.949
1998—Chicago (N.L.)		S-2-3-DH-O	108	264	34	60	10	1	5	25	18	66	1	6	4-1	.227	.277	.330	.606	7	.970
1999—Chicago (N.L.)		S-3-2-OF	90	177	17	48	11	2	0	15	10	38	0	1	4-0	.271	.309	.356	.664	7	.954
2000—Boston (A.L.)		3-S-2-OF	101	194	30	41	4	3	4	19	13	41	0	0	2-0	.211	.261	.325	.586	6	.962
2001—Tacoma (PCL)		2-S-3-OF	97	344	46	97	26	2	8	51	14	55	2	6	5-9	.282	.311	.439	.750	13	.961
2002—Indianapolis (Int'l)		3B-SS	22	85	11	25	6	1	1	7	4	17	0	2	5-3	.294	.326	.424	.749	3	.944
2003—Oklahoma (PCL)		S-2-3-DH	120	450	52	116	17	4	6	48	30	75	4	11	27-10	.258	.309	.349	.658	15	.973
2004—Oklahoma (PCL)		SS	93	361	65	104	29	4	10	49	27	45	1	6	8-4	.288	.338	.474	.811	18	.965
—Texas (A.L.)		2B-SS-3B	21	21	3	5	2	0	0	3	1	7	0	0	0-0	.238	.273	.333	.606	3	.914
American League totals (6 years)			277	530	76	111	15	4	7	49	37	108	2	4	16-7	.209	.264	.292	.556	25	.960
National League totals (3 years)			285	689	88	174	33	7	8	62	45	158	4	13	21-2	.253	.301	.356	.657	25	.965
Major League totals (9 years)			562	1219	164	285	48	11	15	111	82	266	6	17	37-9	.234	.285	.328	.613	50	.963

A

Year Team (League)	Pos.	G	AB	R	H	2B	3B	HR	RBI	BB	SO	HBP	GDP	SB-CS	Avg.	OBP	SLG	OPS	E	Avg.
									DIVISION SERIES RECORD											
1996—Baltimore (A.L.)	DH	3	0	2	0	0	0	0	0	0	0	0	0	0-0	...	...	...	...	...	...
1998—Chicago (N.L.)	SS	2	5	0	0	0	0	0	0	0	1	0	0	0-0	.000	.000	.000	.000	0	1.000
Division series totals (2 years)		5	5	2	0	0	0	0	0	0	1	0	0	0-0	.000	.000	.000	.000	0	1.000

ALFARO, JASON — 3B

PERSONAL: Born November 29, 1977, in San Antonio, Texas. ... 5-10/185. ... Bats right, throws right. ... High school: Western Hills (Benbrook, Texas). ... Junior college: Hill (Texas).

TRANSACTIONS/CAREER NOTES: Selected by Houston Astros organization in 22nd round of 1997 free-agent draft.

2004 GAMES PLAYED BY POSITION (MLB): SS—3.

Year Team (League)	Pos.	G	AB	R	H	2B	3B	HR	RBI	BB	SO	HBP	GDP	SB-CS	Avg.	OBP	SLG	OPS	E	Avg.
							BATTING												FIELDING	
1997—GC Astros (GCL)	3B-SS-2B-P	34	102	8	27	5	0	2	13	8	14	1	2	6-0	.265	.324	.373	.697	10	.907
1998—GC Astros (GCL)	SS	47	178	20	43	8	0	1	18	11	24	0	5	5-5	.242	.286	.303	.589	15	.921
1999—Michigan (Midw.)	SS-3B	118	473	74	128	25	4	5	50	23	62	1	10	5-5	.271	.302	.372	.674	23	.950
2000—Kissimmee (Fla. St.)	SS-3B-2B	117	460	58	115	20	1	7	41	25	63	1	15	2-6	.250	.287	.343	.631	28	.946
2001—Round Rock (Texas)	2-0-S-3-P	87	284	26	69	16	2	2	29	7	40	2	13	2-1	.243	.264	.335	.599	9	.963
2002—Round Rock (Texas)	3-0-2-S	124	455	71	143	36	2	16	74	50	75	11	13	11-9	.314	.393	.508	.901	11	.964
2003—Round Rock (Texas)	3B-OF	22	81	6	12	3	0	0	9	5	20	0	1	0-1	.148	.198	.185	.383	6	.882
—New Orleans (PCL)	3B-SS-OF	105	361	45	107	20	4	9	49	30	53	3	14	2-3	.296	.354	.449	.802	14	.959
2004—New Orleans (PCL)	S-3-0-2	126	465	62	151	32	0	13	67	26	58	4	11	3-6	.325	.363	.477	.836	14	.946
—Houston (N.L.)	SS	7	11	1	2	0	0	0	0	0	5	0	1	0-0	.182	.182	.182	.364	0	1.000
Major League totals (1 year)		7	11	1	2	0	0	0	0	0	5	0	1	0-0	.182	.182	.182	.364	0	1.000

ALFONSECA, ANTONIO — P

PERSONAL: Born April 16, 1972, in La Romana, Dominican Republic. ... 6-5/250. ... Throws right, bats right. ... Name pronounced: al-fon-SAY-kah.

TRANSACTIONS/CAREER NOTES: Signed as non-drafted free agent by Montreal Expos organization (July 3, 1989). ... Selected by Florida Marlins organization from Expos organization in Rule 5 minor league draft (December 13, 1993). ... On disabled list (May 15-June 15, 1995). ... On disabled list (July 12-September 3, 1996). ... On disabled list (May 14-31, 1998). ... Traded by Marlins with P Matt Clement to Chicago Cubs for Ps Julian Tavarez, Jose Cueto and Dontrelle Willis and C Ryan Jorgensen (March 27, 2002). ... On disabled list (March 21-May 5, 2003); included rehabilitation assignment to Iowa. ... On suspended list (September 5-12, 2003). ... Signed as a free agent by Atlanta Braves (December 23, 2003).

HONORS: Named N.L. Fireman of the Year by THE SPORTING NEWS (2000).

CAREER HITTING: 2-for-13 (.154), 0 R, 0 2B, 0 3B, 0 HR, 2 RBI.

Year Team (League)	W	L	Pct.	ERA	WHIP	G	GS	CG	ShO	Hld.	Sv.-Opp.	IP	H	R	ER	HR	BB-IBB	SO	Avg.
1990—DSL Expos (DSL)	3	5	.375	3.60	1.53	13	13	1	0	...	0-...	60.0	60	29	24	...	32-...	19	...
1991—GC Expos (GCL)	3	3	.500	3.88	1.39	11	10	0	0	...	0-...	51.0	46	33	22	2	25-0	38	.240
1992—GC Expos (GCL)	3	4	.429	3.68	1.36	12	10	1	1	...	0-...	66.0	55	31	27	0	35-0	62	.233
1993—Jamestown (NYP)	2	2	.500	6.15	1.57	15	4	0	0	...	1-...	33.2	31	26	23	3	22-1	29	.250
1994—Kane County (Midwest)	6	5	.545	4.07	1.15	32	9	0	0	...	0-...	86.1	78	43	39	5	21-1	74	.234
1995—Portland (East.)	9	3	.750	3.64	1.28	19	17	1	0	...	0-...	96.1	81	43	39	6	42-1	75	.229
1996—Charlotte (Int'l)	4	4	.500	5.53	1.51	14	13	0	0	...	1-...	71.2	86	47	44	8	22-0	51	.296
1997—Charlotte (Int'l)	7	2	.778	4.32	1.34	46	0	0	0	...	7-...	58.1	58	34	28	8	20-3	45	.264
—Florida (N.L.)	1	3	.250	4.91	1.79	17	0	0	0	0	0-2	25.2	36	16	14	3	10-3	19	.324
1998—Florida (N.L.)	4	6	.400	4.08	1.51	58	0	0	0	9	8-14	70.2	75	36	32	10	33-9	46	.281
1999—Florida (N.L.)	4	5	.444	3.24	1.39	73	0	0	0	5	21-25	77.2	79	28	28	4	29-6	46	.274
2000—Florida (N.L.)	5	6	.455	4.24	1.51	68	0	0	0	0	* 45-49	70.0	82	35	33	7	24-3	47	.291
2001—Florida (N.L.)	4	4	.500	3.06	1.35	58	0	0	0	0	28-34	61.2	68	24	21	6	15-3	40	.281
2002—Chicago (N.L.)	2	5	.286	4.00	1.47	66	0	0	0	0	19-28	74.1	73	34	33	5	36-3	61	.257
2003—Iowa (PCL)	0	1	.000	4.91	1.90	3	0	0	0	...	0-...	3.2	6	2	2	0	1-0	5	.353
—Chicago (N.L.)	3	1	.750	5.83	1.51	60	0	0	0	9	0-4	66.1	76	43	43	7	27-3	51	.290
2004—Atlanta (N.L.)	6	4	.600	2.57	1.34	79	0	0	0	13	0-1	73.2	71	24	21	5	28-5	45	.255
Major League totals (8 years)	29	34	.460	3.89	1.47	479	0	0	0	36	121-157	520.0	560	240	225	47	202-35	355	.278

Year Team (League)	W	L	Pct.	ERA	WHIP	G	GS	CG	ShO	Hld.	Sv.-Opp.	IP	H	R	ER	HR	BB-IBB	SO	Avg.
						DIVISION SERIES RECORD													
1997—Florida (N.L.)	Did not play.																		
2003—Chicago (N.L.)	0	0	...	0.00	1.00	1	0	0	0	0	0-0	1.0	1	0	0	0	0-0	0	.250
2004—Atlanta (N.L.)	1	0	1.000	4.91	1.09	4	0	0	0	0	0-0	3.2	2	2	2	0	2-0	0	.154
Division series totals (2 years)	1	0	1.000	3.86	1.07	5	0	0	0	0	0-0	4.2	3	2	2	0	2-0	0	.176

Year Team (League)	W	L	Pct.	ERA	WHIP	G	GS	CG	ShO	Hld.	Sv.-Opp.	IP	H	R	ER	HR	BB-IBB	SO	Avg.
						CHAMPIONSHIP SERIES RECORD													
1997—Florida (N.L.)	Did not play.																		
2003—Chicago (N.L.)	0	0	...	0.00	1.71	3	0	0	0	0	0-0	2.1	2	0	0	0	2-1	0	.333

Year Team (League)	W	L	Pct.	ERA	WHIP	G	GS	CG	ShO	Hld.	Sv.-Opp.	IP	H	R	ER	HR	BB-IBB	SO	Avg.
						WORLD SERIES RECORD													
1997—Florida (N.L.)	0	0	...	0.00	1.11	3	0	0	0	0	0-0	6.1	6	0	0	0	1-0	5	.250

ALFONZO, EDGARDO — 3B

PERSONAL: Born November 8, 1973, in Soapire, Venezuela. ... 5-11/226. ... Bats right, throws right. ... Full name: Edgardo Antonio Alfonzo. ... High school: Cecilio Acosta (Venezuela).

TRANSACTIONS/CAREER NOTES: Signed as non-drafted free agent by New York Mets organization (February 19, 1991). ... On disabled list (August 11, 1995-remainder of season; and May 4-19, 1998). ... On disabled list (June 14-July 3, 2001); included rehabilitation assignment to Norfolk. ... On disabled list (August 4-24, 2002). ... Signed as a free agent by San Francisco Giants (December 15, 2002).

RECORDS: Shares major league record for runs scored, 9-inning game (6, August 30, 1999).

2004 GAMES PLAYED BY POSITION (MLB): 3B—129, 2B—5.

Year Team (League)	Pos.	G	AB	R	H	2B	3B	HR	RBI	BB	SO	HBP	GDP	SB-CS	Avg.	OBP	SLG	OPS	E	Avg.
							BATTING												FIELDING	
1991—GC Mets (GCL)	2B-3B-SS	54	175	29	58	8	4	0	27	34	12	2	1	6-4	.331	.433	.423	.856	9	.958

Year — Team (League)	Pos.	G	AB	R	H	2B	3B	HR	RBI	BB	SO	HBP	GDP	SB-CS	Avg.	OBP	SLG	OPS	E	Avg.
1992— St. Lucie (Fla. St.)	2B	4	5	0	0	0	0	0	0	0	0	0	0	0-0	.000	.000	.000	.000	0	1.000
—Pittsfield (NYP)	SS	74	298	44	106	13	5	1	44	18	31	0	6	7-5	.356	.388	.443	.830	26	.933
1993— St. Lucie (Fla. St.)	SS	128	494	75	145	18	3	11	86	57	51	5	13	26-16	.294	.366	.409	.775	29	.954
1994— Binghamton (East.)	2B-SS-1B	127	498	89	146	34	2	15	75	64	55	0	9	14-11	.293	.369	.460	.829	27	.958
1995— New York (N.L.)	3B-2B-SS	101	335	26	93	13	5	4	41	12	37	1	7	1-1	.278	.301	.382	.683	7	.973
1996— New York (N.L.)	2B-3B-SS	123	368	36	96	15	2	4	40	25	56	0	8	2-0	.261	.304	.345	.649	11	.973
1997— New York (N.L.)	3B-SS-2B	151	518	84	163	27	2	10	72	63	56	5	4	11-6	.315	.391	.432	.823	12	.970
1998— New York (N.L.)	3B-SS	144	557	94	155	28	2	17	78	65	77	3	11	8-3	.278	.355	.427	.782	9	.976
1999— New York (N.L.)	2B	158	628	123	191	41	1	27	108	85	85	3	14	9-2	.304	.385	.502	.886	5	.993
2000— New York (N.L.)	2B-DH	150	544	109	176	40	2	25	94	95	70	5	12	3-2	.324	.425	.542	.967	10	.985
2001— New York (N.L.)	2B	124	457	64	111	22	0	17	49	51	62	5	7	5-0	.243	.322	.403	.725	7	.987
—Norfolk (Int'l)	2B	2	8	0	0	0	0	0	0	0	0	0	1	0-0	.000	.000	.000	.000	0	1.000
2002— New York (N.L.)	3B	135	490	78	151	26	0	16	56	62	55	7	5	6-0	.308	.391	.459	.851	12	.969
2003— San Francisco (N.L.)	3B-2B	142	514	56	133	25	2	13	81	58	41	4	14	5-2	.259	.334	.391	.726	11	.968
2004— San Francisco (N.L.)	3B-2B	139	519	66	150	26	1	11	77	46	40	5	15	1-1	.289	.350	.407	.757	14	.961
Major League totals (10 years)		1367	4930	736	1419	263	17	144	696	562	579	38	97	51-17	.288	.362	.436	.797	98	.978

DIVISION SERIES RECORD

Year — Team (League)	Pos.	G	AB	R	H	2B	3B	HR	RBI	BB	SO	HBP	GDP	SB-CS	Avg.	OBP	SLG	OPS	E	Avg.
1999— New York (N.L.)	2B	4	16	6	4	1	0	3	6	3	2	0	0	0-0	.250	.368	.875	1.243	0	1.000
2000— New York (N.L.)	2B	4	18	1	5	2	0	1	5	1	2	0	0	0-1	.278	.316	.556	.871	0	1.000
2003— San Francisco (N.L.)	3B	4	17	3	9	4	0	0	5	1	1	0	0	0-0	.529	.556	.765	1.320	0	1.000
Division series totals (3 years)		12	51	10	18	7	0	4	16	5	5	0	0	0-1	.353	.411	.725	1.136	0	1.000

CHAMPIONSHIP SERIES RECORD

Year — Team (League)	Pos.	G	AB	R	H	2B	3B	HR	RBI	BB	SO	HBP	GDP	SB-CS	Avg.	OBP	SLG	OPS	E	Avg.
1999— New York (N.L.)	2B	6	27	2	6	4	0	0	1	1	9	0	0	0-0	.222	.250	.370	.620	1	.971
2000— New York (N.L.)	2B	5	18	5	8	1	1	0	4	4	1	1	0	0-0	.444	.565	.611	1.176	0	1.000
Champ. series totals (2 years)		11	45	7	14	5	1	0	5	5	10	1	0	0-0	.311	.392	.467	.859	1	.979

WORLD SERIES RECORD

Year — Team (League)	Pos.	G	AB	R	H	2B	3B	HR	RBI	BB	SO	HBP	GDP	SB-CS	Avg.	OBP	SLG	OPS	E	Avg.
2000— New York (N.L.)	2B	5	21	1	3	0	0	1	1	1	5	1	0	0-0	.143	.217	.143	.360	0	1.000

ALL-STAR GAME RECORD

		G	AB	R	H	2B	3B	HR	RBI	BB	SO	HBP	GDP	SB-CS	Avg.	OBP	SLG	OPS	E	Avg.
All-Star Game totals (1 year)		1	2	0	0	0	0	0	0	0	1	0	0	0-0	.000	.000	.000	.000	0	1.000

ALLEN, CHAD — OF

PERSONAL: Born February 6, 1975, in Dallas, Texas. ... 6-1/200. ... Bats right, throws right. ... Full name: John Chad Allen. ... High school: Duncanville (Texas). ... College: Texas A&M.

TRANSACTIONS/CAREER NOTES: Selected by Cincinnati Reds organization in 38th round of 1993 free-agent draft; did not sign. ... Selected by Minnesota Twins organization in fourth round of 1996 free-agent draft. ... On disabled list (June 4-19 and August 15, 2001-remainder of season). ... Signed as a free agent by Baltimore Orioles organization (March 27, 2002). ... Released by Orioles (April 16, 2002). ... Signed by Cleveland Indians organization (May 13, 2002). ... Released by Indians (September 30, 2002). ... Signed by Florida Marlins organization (November 25, 2002). ... Refused assignment to minors and became a free agent (September 29, 2003). ... Signed by Texas Rangers organization (November 26, 2003). ... Refused minor league assignment and became a free agent (October 9, 2004).

2004 GAMES PLAYED BY POSITION (MLB): OF—13, DH—5.

Year — Team (League)	Pos.	G	AB	R	H	2B	3B	HR	RBI	BB	SO	HBP	GDP	SB-CS	Avg.	OBP	SLG	OPS	E	Avg.
1996— Fort Wayne (Midw.)	OF	7	21	2	9	0	0	0	2	3	2	0	0	1-1	.429	.480	.429	.909	0	1.000
1997— Fort Myers (FSL)	OF	105	401	66	124	18	4	3	45	40	51	2	9	27-15	.309	.373	.397	.770	5	.977
—New Britain (East.)	OF	30	115	20	29	9	1	4	18	9	21	0	3	2-0	.252	.304	.452	.756	1	.973
1998— New Britain (East.)	OF	137	504	70	132	31	7	8	82	51	78	6	19	21-9	.262	.334	.399	.733	4	.980
1999— Minnesota (A.L.)	OF-DH	137	481	69	133	21	3	10	46	37	89	2	10	14-7	.277	.330	.395	.725	7	.975
2000— Salt Lake (PCL)	OF	96	389	71	121	21	5	9	67	31	72	1	13	10-2	.311	.363	.460	.823	1	.993
—Minnesota (A.L.)	OF	15	50	2	15	3	0	0	7	3	14	1	1	0-2	.300	.345	.360	.705	0	1.000
2001— Minnesota (A.L.)	OF-DH	57	175	20	46	13	2	4	20	19	37	0	7	1-2	.263	.333	.429	.762	2	.968
—Edmonton (PCL)	OF	6	22	4	8	2	0	1	1	4	1	1	0	2-0	.364	.481	.591	1.072	0	1.000
2002— Rochester (Int'l)	OF	8	32	1	7	2	1	0	1	0	6	0	...	0-0	.219	.219	.344	.563	0	1.000
—Buffalo (Int'l)	OF	70	279	45	84	20	1	10	62	15	34	2	...	0-1	.301	.340	.487	.828	0	1.000
—Cleveland (A.L.)	OF	5	10	0	1	1	0	0	0	0	2	0	1	0-0	.100	.100	.200	.300	0	1.000
2003— Florida (N.L.)	OF-DH	12	24	2	5	1	1	0	0	0	5	1	1	0-0	.208	.240	.333	.573	0	1.000
—Albuquerque (PCL)	OF	91	337	45	109	30	2	8	53	18	48	6	10	11-10	.323	.364	.496	.860	1	.993
2004— Oklahoma (PCL)	OF-DH-1B	93	386	75	138	28	3	7	70	31	72	5	9	18-2	.358	.407	.500	.907	1	.993
—Texas (A.L.)	OF-DH	20	58	4	14	4	1	0	6	2	13	0	1	0-1	.241	.262	.345	.607	0	1.000
American League totals (5 years)		234	774	95	209	42	6	14	79	61	155	3	20	15-12	.270	.324	.394	.718	9	.977
National League totals (1 year)		12	24	2	5	1	1	0	0	0	5	1	1	0-0	.208	.240	.333	.573	0	1.000
Major League totals (6 years)		246	798	97	214	43	7	14	79	61	160	4	21	15-12	.268	.321	.392	.714	9	.978

ALMANZA, ARMANDO — P

PERSONAL: Born October 26, 1972, in El Paso, Texas. ... 6-3/240. ... Throws left, bats left. ... Full name: Armando N. Almanza. ... High school: Bel Air (El Paso, Texas). ... Junior college: New Mexico J.C. (Hobbs, N.M.).

TRANSACTIONS/CAREER NOTES: Selected by St. Louis Cardinals organization in 21st round of 1993 free-agent draft. ... Traded by Cardinals with P Braden Looper and SS Pablo Ozuna to Florida Marlins for SS Edgar Renteria (December 14, 1998). ... On disabled list (March 30-May 21, 2002); included rehabilitation assignment to Jupiter. ... On disabled list (August 21, 2003-remainder of season). ... Signed as a free agent by Atlanta Braves (December 22, 2003). ... On disabled list (March 31-May 11, 2004); included rehabilitation assignments to Greenville and Richmond.

CAREER HITTING: 0-for-4 (.000), 0 R, 0 2B, 0 3B, 0 HR, 0 RBI.

Year — Team (League)	W	L	Pct.	ERA	WHIP	G	GS	CG	ShO	Hld.	Sv.-Opp.	IP	H	R	ER	HR	BB-IBB	SO	Avg.
1993— Ariz. Cardinals (Ariz.)	4	1	.800	3.21	1.24	20	4	0	0	...	0-...	42.0	38	19	15	2	14-0	56	.236
—Johnson City (App.)	1	1	.500	4.15	2.08	3	3	0	0	...	0-...	4.1	6	2	2	1	3-0	4	.333
1994— Madison (Midw.)							Did not play.												
1995— Savannah (S. Atl.)	3	9	.250	3.92	1.37	20	20	0	0	...	0-...	108.0	108	62	47	13	40-1	72	.255
1996— Peoria (Midw.)	8	6	.571	2.76	1.32	52	1	0	0	...	0-...	62.0	50	27	19	2	32-5	67	.216

Year—Team (League)	W	L	Pct.	ERA	WHIP	G	GS	CG	ShO	Hld.	Sv.-Opp.	IP	H	R	ER	HR	BB-IBB	SO	Avg.
1997— Prince William (Caro.)	2	3	.400	1.67	1.08	58	0	0	0	...	36-...	64.2	38	18	12	3	32-1	83	.172
1998— Arkansas (Texas)	4	1	.800	3.31	1.38	28	0	0	0	...	8-...	32.2	27	13	12	2	18-0	46	.225
— Memphis (PCL)	3	1	.750	3.03	1.51	31	0	0	0	...	1-...	35.2	35	13	12	1	19-1	45	.246
1999— Calgary (PCL)	2	2	.500	10.90	2.71	15	0	0	0	...	0-...	17.1	29	27	21	3	18-0	20	.363
— Portland (East.)	0	1	.000	3.97	0.79	10	0	0	0	...	3-...	11.1	5	5	5	1	4-0	20	.139
— Florida (N.L.)	0	1	.000	1.72	1.09	14	0	0	0	3	0-0	15.2	8	4	3	1	9-1	20	.154
2000— Florida (N.L.)	4	2	.667	4.86	1.75	67	0	0	0	13	0-4	46.1	38	27	25	7	43-6	46	.228
2001— Florida (N.L.)	2	2	.500	4.83	1.46	52	0	0	0	12	0-2	41.0	34	24	22	8	26-1	45	.230
2002— Jupiter (FSL)	0	0	...	0.00	0.60	6	5	0	0	...	0-...	6.2	1	0	0	0	3-0	6	.050
— Florida (N.L.)	3	2	.600	4.34	1.29	51	0	0	0	12	2-4	45.2	36	22	22	8	23-1	57	.224
2003— Florida (N.L.)	4	5	.444	6.08	1.67	51	0	0	0	6	0-2	50.1	59	37	34	10	25-2	49	.296
2004— Greenville (Sou.)	0	3	.000	8.10	2.25	5	2	0	0	...	0-...	6.2	12	6	6	0	3-0	5	.429
— Atlanta (N.L.)	1	1	.500	6.17	1.37	13	0	0	0	1	0-...	11.2	9	8	8	3	7-2	13	.200
— Richmond (Int'l)	1	1	.500	3.55	1.62	20	0	0	0	...	1-...	25.1	26	13	10	1	15-0	20	.255
Major League totals (6 years)	**14**	**13**	**.519**	**4.87**	**1.50**	**248**	**0**	**0**	**0**	**46**	**2-12**	**210.2**	**184**	**122**	**114**	**33**	**133-13**	**230**	**.238**

ALMANZAR, CARLOS P

PERSONAL: Born November 6, 1973... 6-2/200. ... Throws right, bats right. ... Full name: Carlos Manuel Almanzar.

TRANSACTIONS/CAREER NOTES: Signed as non-drafted free agent by Toronto Blue Jays organization (December 10, 1990). ... Traded by Blue Jays with P Woody Williams and OF Peter Tucci to San Diego Padres for P Joey Hamilton (December 13, 1998). ... On disabled list (April 24-May 27, 1999); included rehabilitation assignment to Las Vegas. ... Traded by Padres to New York Yankees for P David Lee (March 25, 2001). ... Signed as a free agent by Colorado Rockies organization (January 20, 2002). ... Claimed on waivers by Cincinnati Reds (March 30, 2002). ... On disabled list (June 11, 2002-remainder of season); included rehabilitation assignment to Louisville. ... Signed as a free agent by Texas Rangers organization (October 30, 2003). ... On suspended list (September 22-26, 2004).

CAREER HITTING: 0-for-4 (.000), 0 R, 0 2B, 0 3B, 0 HR, 0 RBI.

Year—Team (League)	W	L	Pct.	ERA	WHIP	G	GS	CG	ShO	Hld.	Sv.-Opp.	IP	H	R	ER	HR	BB-IBB	SO	Avg.
1991— Dom. B. Jays (DSL)	3	1	.750	2.83	1.34	6	6	1	0	...	0-...	35.0	36	17	11	...	11-...	20	...
1992— Dom. B. Jays (DSL)	10	0	1.000	2.01	1.13	13	11	2	1	...	1-...	67.0	45	26	15	...	31-...	60	...
1993— Dom. B. Jays (DSL)	5	2	.714	3.38	1.33	16	9	0	0	...	2-...	69.1	60	35	26	...	32-...	59	...
1994— Medicine Hat (Pio.)	7	4	.636	2.87	1.19	14	14	0	0	...	0-...	84.2	82	38	27	2	19-0	77	.255
1995— Knoxville (Southern)	3	12	.200	3.99	1.39	35	19	0	0	...	2-...	126.1	144	77	56	10	32-1	93	.287
1996— Knoxville (Southern)	7	8	.467	4.85	1.47	54	0	0	0	...	9-...	94.2	106	58	51	13	33-6	105	.280
1997— Knoxville (Southern)	1	1	.500	4.91	1.36	21	0	0	0	...	8-...	25.2	30	14	14	2	5-1	25	.300
— Syracuse (Int'l)	5	1	.833	1.41	0.75	32	0	0	0	...	3-...	51.0	30	9	8	2	8-0	47	.170
— Toronto (A.L.)	0	1	.000	2.70	0.60	4	0	0	0	0	0-0	3.1	1	1	1	1	1-0	4	.091
1998— Toronto (A.L.)	2	2	.500	5.34	1.47	25	0	0	0	1	0-3	28.2	34	18	17	4	8-2	20	.286
— Syracuse (Int'l)	3	6	.333	2.31	1.13	30	0	0	0	...	10-...	50.2	44	21	13	7	13-2	53	.229
1999— San Diego (N.L.)	0	0	...	7.47	1.69	28	0	0	0	0	0-0	37.1	48	32	31	6	15-2	30	.316
— Las Vegas (PCL)	1	3	.250	9.53	1.76	11	3	0	0	...	0-...	22.2	32	25	24	11	8-1	18	.337
2000— San Diego (N.L.)	4	5	.444	4.39	1.41	62	0	0	0	8	0-3	69.2	73	35	34	12	25-2	56	.266
— Las Vegas (PCL)	0	0	...	4.50	1.50	4	0	0	0	...	0-...	6.0	9	4	3	1	0-0	7	.321
2001— New York (A.L.)	0	1	.000	3.38	1.50	10	0	0	0	0	0-2	10.2	14	4	4	2	2-1	6	.333
— Columbus (Int'l)	2	1	.667	2.43	1.26	35	0	0	0	...	18-...	33.1	36	10	9	2	6-2	26	.279
2002— Louisville (Int'l)	1	0	1.000	2.74	1.13	21	0	0	0	...	11-...	23.0	21	7	7	0	5-0	19	.247
— Cincinnati (N.L.)	0	1	.000	2.31	0.94	8	1	0	0	0	0-0	11.2	6	4	3	0	5-1	7	.158
2003— Louisville (Int'l)	2	2	.500	3.50	1.08	42	0	0	0	...	23-...	46.1	47	19	18	2	3-0	54	.251
2004— Texas (A.L.)	7	3	.700	3.72	1.17	67	0	0	0	20	0-2	72.2	66	32	30	8	19-4	44	.244
American League totals (4 years)	**9**	**7**	**.563**	**4.06**	**1.26**	**106**	**0**	**0**	**0**	**21**	**0-7**	**115.1**	**115**	**55**	**52**	**15**	**30-7**	**74**	**.260**
National League totals (3 years)	**4**	**6**	**.400**	**5.16**	**1.45**	**98**	**1**	**0**	**0**	**8**	**0-3**	**118.2**	**127**	**71**	**68**	**18**	**45-5**	**93**	**.274**
Major League totals (7 years)	**13**	**13**	**.500**	**4.62**	**1.35**	**204**	**1**	**0**	**0**	**29**	**0-10**	**234.0**	**242**	**126**	**120**	**33**	**75-12**	**167**	**.267**

ALOMAR, ROBERTO 2B

PERSONAL: Born February 5, 1968, in Ponce, Puerto Rico. ... 6-0/190. ... Bats both, throws right. ... Full name: Roberto Velazquez Alomar. ... Name pronounced: AL-loh-mar. ... Son of Sandy Alomar, coach, Colorado Rockies, and infielder with six major league teams (1964-78); brother of Sandy Alomar Jr., catcher with Chicago White Sox in 2004.

TRANSACTIONS/CAREER NOTES: Signed as non-drafted free agent by San Diego Padres organization (February 16, 1985). ... Traded by Padres with OF Joe Carter to Toronto Blue Jays for 1B Fred McGriff and SS Tony Fernandez (December 5, 1990). ... On suspended list (May 23-24, 1995). ... Signed as a free agent by Baltimore Orioles (December 21, 1995). ... On suspended list (April 1-7, 1997). ... On disabled list (July 30-August 26, 1997; and July 19-August 4, 1998). ... Signed as a free agent by Cleveland Indians (December 1, 1998). ... Traded by Indians with P Mike Bacsik and OF Danny Peoples to New York Mets for OF Matt Lawton, OF Alex Escobar, P Jerrod Riggan and two players to be named (December 11, 2001); Indians acquired P Billy Traber and 1B Earl Snyder to complete deal (December 13, 2001). ... Traded by Mets to Chicago White Sox for P Edwin Almonte (July 1, 2003). ... Signed as a free agent by Arizona Diamondbacks (January 7, 2004). ... On disabled list (April 21-June 21, 2004); included rehabilitation assignment to Tucson. ... Traded by Diamondbacks to Chicago White Sox for a player to be named (August 5, 2004).

HONORS: Won A.L. Gold Glove at second base (1991-96 and 1998-2001).

2004 GAMES PLAYED BY POSITION (MLB): 2B—41, DH—6.

Year—Team (League)	Pos.	G	AB	R	H	2B	3B	HR	RBI	BB	SO	HBP	GDP	SB-CS	Avg.	OBP	SLG	OPS	E	Avg.
1985— Char., S.C. (SAL)	2B-SS	137	546	89	160	14	3	0	54	61	73	0	9	36-19	.293	.362	.330	.691	36	.947
1986— Reno (Calif.)	2B	90	356	53	123	16	4	4	49	32	38	3	7	14-8	.346	.397	.447	.844	18	.963
1987— Wichita (Texas)	2B-SS	130	536	88	171	41	4	12	68	49	74	2	6	43-15	.319	.374	.478	.851	36	.932
1988— Las Vegas (PCL)	2B	9	37	5	10	1	0	2	14	1	4	0	0	3-0	.270	.282	.459	.742	1	.981
— San Diego (N.L.)	2B	143	545	84	145	24	6	9	41	47	83	3	15	24-6	.266	.328	.382	.709	16	.981
1989— San Diego (N.L.)	2B	158	623	82	184	27	1	7	56	53	76	1	10	42-17	.295	.347	.376	.723	* 28	.967
1990— San Diego (N.L.)	2B-SS	147	586	80	168	27	5	6	60	48	72	2	16	24-7	.287	.340	.381	.721	‡ 19	.974
1991— Toronto (A.L.)	2B	161	637	88	188	41	11	9	69	57	86	4	5	53-11	.295	.354	.436	.791	15	.981
1992— Toronto (A.L.)	2B-DH	152	571	105	177	27	8	8	76	87	52	5	8	49-9	.310	.405	.427	.832	5	.993
1993— Toronto (A.L.)	2B	153	589	109	192	35	6	17	93	80	67	5	13	55-15	.326	.408	.492	.900	14	.980
1994— Toronto (A.L.)	2B	107	392	78	120	25	4	8	38	51	41	2	9	19-8	.306	.386	.452	.838	4	.991
1995— Toronto (A.L.)	2B	130	517	71	155	24	7	13	66	47	45	0	16	30-3	.300	.354	.449	.803	4	.993
1996— Baltimore (A.L.)	2B-DH	153	588	132	193	43	4	22	94	90	65	1	14	17-6	.328	.411	.527	.938	11	.985
1997— Baltimore (A.L.)	2B-DH	112	412	64	137	23	2	14	60	40	43	3	10	9-3	.333	.390	.500	.890	6	.988

Year Team (League)	Pos.	G	AB	R	H	2B	3B	HR	RBI	BB	SO	HBP	GDP	SB-CS	Avg.	OBP	SLG	OPS	E	Avg.
1998— Baltimore (A.L.)	2B-DH	147	588	86	166	36	1	14	56	59	70	2	11	18-5	.282	.347	.418	.765	11	.985
1999— Cleveland (A.L.)	2B-DH	159	563	* 138	182	40	3	24	120	99	96	7	13	37-6	.323	.422	.533	.955	6	.992
2000— Cleveland (A.L.)	2B	155	610	111	189	40	2	19	89	64	82	6	19	39-4	.310	.378	.475	.853	15	.980
2001— Cleveland (A.L.)	2B	157	575	113	193	34	12	20	100	80	71	4	9	30-6	.336	.415	.541	.956	5	.993
2002— New York (N.L.)	2B	149	590	73	157	24	4	11	53	57	83	1	12	16-4	.266	.331	.376	.708	11	.983
2003— New York (N.L.)	2B	73	263	34	69	17	1	2	22	29	40	2	8	6-0	.262	.336	.357	.693	6	.981
— Chicago (A.L.)	2B	67	253	42	64	11	1	3	17	30	37	1	9	6-2	.253	.330	.340	.670	3	.990
2004— Tucson (PCL)	2B	2	5	2	2	0	0	0	1	2	0	0	0	0-0	.400	.500	.400	.900	0	1.000
— Arizona (N.L.)	2B-DH	38	110	14	34	5	2	3	16	12	18	1	2	0-2	.309	.382	.473	.855	3	.971
— Chicago (A.L.)	2B-DH	18	61	4	11	1	0	1	8	2	13	0	2	0-0	.180	.203	.246	.449	1	.982
American League totals (13 years)		1671	6356	1141	1967	380	61	172	886	786	768	40	143	362-78	.309	.385	.470	.854	100	.987
National League totals (6 years)		708	2717	367	757	124	19	38	248	246	372	10	63	112-36	.279	.339	.380	.719	83	.976
Major League totals (17 years)		2379	9073	1508	2724	504	80	210	1134	1032	1140	50	206	474-114	.300	.371	.443	.814	183	.983

DIVISION SERIES RECORD

Year Team (League)	Pos.	G	AB	R	H	2B	3B	HR	RBI	BB	SO	HBP	GDP	SB-CS	Avg.	OBP	SLG	OPS	E	Avg.
1996— Baltimore (A.L.)	2B	4	17	2	5	0	0	1	4	2	3	0	0	0-0	.294	.350	.471	.821	0	1.000
1997— Baltimore (A.L.)	2B	4	10	1	3	2	0	0	2	1	1	0	0	0-0	.300	.364	.500	.864	0	1.000
1999— Cleveland (A.L.)	2B	5	19	4	7	4	0	0	3	2	3	0	0	2-0	.368	.409	.579	.988	1	.964
2001— Cleveland (A.L.)	2B	5	21	3	4	3	0	0	3	2	5	0	2	0-0	.190	.261	.333	.594	0	1.000
Division series totals (4 years)		18	67	10	19	9	0	1	12	7	12	0	2	2-0	.284	.342	.463	.805	1	.986

CHAMPIONSHIP SERIES RECORD

Year Team (League)	Pos.	G	AB	R	H	2B	3B	HR	RBI	BB	SO	HBP	GDP	SB-CS	Avg.	OBP	SLG	OPS	E	Avg.
1991— Toronto (A.L.)	2B	5	19	3	9	0	0	4	2	3	0	0	0	2-0	.474	.524	.474	.997	0	1.000
1992— Toronto (A.L.)	2B	6	26	4	11	1	0	2	4	2	1	0	2	5-0	.423	.464	.692	1.157	0	1.000
1993— Toronto (A.L.)	2B	6	24	3	7	1	0	0	1	4	3	0	1	4-0	.292	.393	.333	.726	0	1.000
1996— Baltimore (A.L.)	2B	5	23	2	5	2	0	0	1	0	4	0	0	0-0	.217	.208	.304	.513	2	.953
1997— Baltimore (A.L.)	2B	6	22	2	4	0	0	1	7	3	0	0	2	0-0	.182	.379	.318	.697	2	.931
Champ. series totals (5 years)		28	114	14	36	4	0	3	15	15	14	0	5	11-0	.316	.392	.430	.822	4	.975

WORLD SERIES RECORD

Year Team (League)	Pos.	G	AB	R	H	2B	3B	HR	RBI	BB	SO	HBP	GDP	SB-CS	Avg.	OBP	SLG	OPS	E	Avg.
1992— Toronto (A.L.)	2B	6	24	3	5	1	0	0	3	3	3	0	1	3-0	.208	.296	.250	.546	0	1.000
1993— Toronto (A.L.)	2B	6	25	5	12	2	1	0	6	2	3	0	1	4-2	.480	.519	.640	1.159	2	.938
World series totals (2 years)		12	49	8	17	3	1	0	9	5	6	0	2	7-2	.347	.407	.449	.856	2	.959

ALL-STAR GAME RECORD

		G	AB	R	H	2B	3B	HR	RBI	BB	SO	HBP	GDP	SB-CS	Avg.	OBP	SLG	OPS	E	Avg.
All-Star Game totals (12 years)		12	30	5	7	0	0	2	3	2	1	0	0	5-0	.233	.281	.433	.715	1	.971

ALOMAR JR., SANDY   C

PERSONAL: Born June 18, 1966, in Salinas, Puerto Rico. ... 6-5/235. ... Bats right, throws right. ... Full name: Santos Alomar Jr... ... Name pronounced: AL-uh-mar. ... High school: Luis Munoz Rivera (Salinas, Puerto Rico). ... Son of Sandy Alomar, coach, Colorado Rockies, and infielder with six major league teams (1964-78); brother of Roberto Alomar, second baseman with Arizona Diamondbacks and Chicago White Sox in 2004.

TRANSACTIONS/CAREER NOTES: Signed as a non-drafted free agent by San Diego Padres organization (October 21, 1983). ... Traded by Padres with OF Chris James and 3B Carlos Baerga to Cleveland Indians for OF Joe Carter (December 6, 1989). ... On disabled list (May 15-June 17 and July 29, 1991-remainder of season); included reha-bilitation assignments to Colorado Springs. ... On disabled list (May 2-18, 1992). ... On suspended list (July 29-August 2, 1992). ... On disabled list (May 1-August 7, 1993); included rehabilitation assignment to Charlotte. ... On disabled list (April 24-May 11, 1994). ... On disabled list (April 19-June 29, 1995); included rehabilitation assignment to Canton/Akron. ... On disabled list (May 11-September 6, 1999); included rehabilitation assignments to Akron and Buffalo. ... On disabled list (April 19-May 8, 2000). ... Signed as a free agent by Chicago White Sox (December 18, 2000). ... On disabled list (August 8-September 18, 2001). ... On disabled list (June 13-July 1, 2002); included rehabilitation assignment to Charlotte. ... Traded by White Sox to Colorado Rockies for P Enemencio Pacheco (July 29, 2002). ... Signed as a free agent by Chicago White Sox (December 20, 2002). ... On disabled list (May 31-June 23, 2003); included rehabilitation assignment to Charlotte. ... On disabled list (August 16-September 1, 2004).

RECORDS: Shares major league record for most doubles, game (4, June 6, 1997).

HONORS: Named Minor League co-Player of the Year by THE SPORTING NEWS (1988). ... Named Minor League Player of the Year by THE SPORTING NEWS (1989). ... Named A.L. Rookie Player of the Year by THE SPORTING NEWS (1990). ... Named A.L. Rookie of the Year by Baseball Writers' Association of America (1990). ... Won A.L. Gold Glove at catcher (1990).

2004 GAMES PLAYED BY POSITION (MLB): C—49, DH—1.

Year Team (League)	Pos.	G	AB	R	H	2B	3B	HR	RBI	BB	SO	HBP	GDP	SB-CS	Avg.	OBP	SLG	OPS	E	Avg.
1984— Spokane (N'west)	C-1B	59	219	13	47	5	0	0	21	13	20	1	7	3-0	.215	.260	.237	.497	8	.985
1985— Char., S.C. (SAL)	C-OF	100	352	38	73	7	0	3	43	31	30	3	9	3-1	.207	.276	.253	.529	18	.979
1986— Beaumont (Texas)	C	100	346	36	83	15	1	4	27	15	35	1	16	2-6	.240	.271	.324	.595	18	.969
1987— Wichita (Texas)	C	103	375	50	115	19	1	8	65	21	37	5	12	1-5	.307	.346	.427	.772	15	.978
1988— Las Vegas (PCL)	C-OF	93	337	59	100	9	5	16	71	28	35	4	11	1-1	.297	.354	.496	.849	14	.978
— San Diego (N.L.)	C	1	1	0	0	0	0	0	0	0	1	0	0	0-0	.000	.000	.000	.000	...	.000
1989— Las Vegas (PCL)	C-OF	131	523	88	160	33	8	13	101	42	58	2	23	3-1	.306	.358	.474	.832	12	.984
— San Diego (N.L.)	C	7	19	1	4	1	0	1	6	3	3	0	1	0-0	.211	.318	.421	.739	0	1.000
1990— Cleveland (A.L.)	C	132	445	60	129	26	2	9	66	25	46	2	10	4-1	.290	.326	.418	.744	* 14	.981
1991— Cleveland (A.L.)	DH-C	51	184	10	40	9	0	0	7	8	24	4	4	0-4	.217	.264	.266	.530	4	.987
— Colo. Springs (PCL)	C	12	35	5	14	2	0	1	10	5	0	0	0	0-0	.400	.463	.543	1.006	1	.833
1992— Cleveland (A.L.)	C-DH	89	299	22	75	16	0	2	26	13	32	5	7	3-3	.251	.293	.324	.618	2	.996
1993— Cleveland (A.L.)	C	64	215	24	58	7	1	6	32	11	28	6	3	3-1	.270	.318	.395	.713	6	.984
— Charlotte (Int'l)	C	12	44	8	16	5	0	1	8	1	5	8	1	0-0	.364	.440	.545	.985	0	1.000
1994— Cleveland (A.L.)	C	80	292	44	84	15	1	14	43	25	31	2	7	8-4	.288	.347	.490	.837	2	.996
1995— Cant./Akr. (Eastern)	C-DH	6	15	3	6	1	0	1	1	1	1	0	1	0-0	.400	.438	.467	.904	1	.958
— Cleveland (A.L.)	C	66	203	32	61	6	0	10	35	7	26	3	8	3-1	.300	.332	.478	.810	2	.995
1996— Cleveland (A.L.)	C-1B	127	418	53	110	23	0	11	50	19	42	3	20	1-0	.263	.299	.397	.696	9	.988
1997— Cleveland (A.L.)	C-DH	125	451	63	146	37	0	21	83	19	48	3	16	0-2	.324	.354	.545	.900	* 12	.985
1998— Cleveland (A.L.)	C-DH	117	409	45	96	26	2	6	44	18	45	3	15	0-3	.235	.270	.352	.622	6	.992
1999— Cleveland (A.L.)	C-DH	37	137	19	42	13	0	6	25	4	23	0	1	0-1	.307	.322	.533	.855	7	.974
— Akron (Eastern)	DH-C	10	29	8	9	0	0	1	6	3	2	0	0	1-0	.310	.344	.414	.767	1	.929
— Buffalo (Int'l)	C-DH	10	33	9	9	2	1	2	10	6	3	1	1	0-0	.273	.400	.576	.976	3	.921
2000— Cleveland (A.L.)	C-DH	97	356	44	103	16	2	7	42	16	41	4	9	2-2	.289	.324	.404	.728	8	.989
2001— Chicago (A.L.)	C	70	220	17	54	8	1	4	21	12	17	2	6	1-2	.245	.288	.345	.634	4	.990

Year	Team (League)	Pos.	G	AB	R	H	2B	3B	HR	RBI	BB	SO	HBP	GDP	SB-CS	Avg.	OBP	SLG	OPS	E	Avg.
2002—Chicago (A.L.)		C	51	167	21	48	10	1	7	25	5	14	1	5	0-0	.287	.309	.485	.794	2	.994
—Charlotte (Int'l)		C	3	8	0	1	0	0	0	0	0	0	0	1	0-0	.125	.125	.125	.250	0	1.000
—Colorado (N.L.)		C	38	116	8	31	4	0	0	12	4	19	0	6	0-0	.267	.292	.302	.593	0	1.000
2003—Charlotte (Int'l)		C-DH	5	15	2	4	0	0	0	1	1	1	0	2	0-0	.267	.313	.267	.579	0	1.000
—Chicago (A.L.)		C	75	194	22	52	12	0	5	26	4	17	0	4	0-0	.268	.281	.407	.689	1	.997
2004—Chicago (A.L.)		C-DH	50	146	15	35	4	0	2	14	11	13	2	4	0-0	.240	.298	.308	.606	3	.990
American League totals (15 years)			1231	4136	491	1133	228	10	110	539	197	447	40	119	25-24	.274	.311	.414	.725	82	.989
National League totals (3 years)			46	136	9	35	5	0	1	18	7	23	0	7	0-0	.257	.294	.316	.610	0	1.000
Major League totals (17 years)			1277	4272	500	1168	233	10	111	557	204	470	40	126	25-24	.273	.310	.411	.721	82	.989

DIVISION SERIES RECORD

Year	Team (League)	Pos.	G	AB	R	H	2B	3B	HR	RBI	BB	SO	HBP	GDP	SB-CS	Avg.	OBP	SLG	OPS	E	Avg.
1995—Cleveland (A.L.)		C	3	11	1	2	1	0	0	1	0	1	0	0	0-0	.182	.182	.273	.455	0	1.000
1996—Cleveland (A.L.)		C	4	16	0	2	0	0	0	3	0	2	0	0	0-1	.125	.125	.125	.250	1	.978
1997—Cleveland (A.L.)		C	5	19	4	6	1	0	2	5	0	2	0	0	0-0	.316	.316	.684	1.000	1	.967
1998—Cleveland (A.L.)		C	4	13	2	3	3	0	0	2	1	4	0	3	0-0	.231	.286	.462	.747	1	.967
1999—Cleveland (A.L.)		C	5	14	1	2	0	0	0	1	2	6	0	0	0-0	.143	.235	.143	.378	1	.971
Division series totals (5 years)			21	73	8	15	5	0	2	12	3	15	0	3	0-1	.205	.234	.356	.590	4	.975

CHAMPIONSHIP SERIES RECORD

Year	Team (League)	Pos.	G	AB	R	H	2B	3B	HR	RBI	BB	SO	HBP	GDP	SB-CS	Avg.	OBP	SLG	OPS	E	Avg.
1995—Cleveland (A.L.)		C	5	15	0	4	1	1	0	1	1	1	0	0	0-0	.267	.313	.467	.779	1	.971
1997—Cleveland (A.L.)		C	6	24	3	3	0	0	1	4	1	3	0	1	0-0	.125	.160	.250	.410	0	1.000
1998—Cleveland (A.L.)		C	5	16	1	1	0	0	0	0	0	2	1	0	0-0	.063	.118	.063	.180	2	.938
Champ. series totals (3 years)			16	55	4	8	1	1	1	5	2	6	1	1	0-0	.145	.190	.255	.444	3	.974

WORLD SERIES RECORD

Year	Team (League)	Pos.	G	AB	R	H	2B	3B	HR	RBI	BB	SO	HBP	GDP	SB-CS	Avg.	OBP	SLG	OPS	E	Avg.
1995—Cleveland (A.L.)		C	5	15	0	3	2	0	0	1	0	2	0	0	0-0	.200	.200	.333	.533	0	1.000
1997—Cleveland (A.L.)		C	7	30	5	11	1	0	2	10	2	3	0	2	0-0	.367	.406	.600	1.006	0	1.000
World series totals (2 years)			12	45	5	14	3	0	2	11	2	5	0	2	0-0	.311	.340	.511	.852	0	1.000

ALL-STAR GAME RECORD

			G	AB	R	H	2B	3B	HR	RBI	BB	SO	HBP	GDP	SB-CS	Avg.	OBP	SLG	OPS	E	Avg.
All-Star Game totals (6 years)			6	12	2	5	0	0	1	3	0	0	0	1	0-0	.417	.417	.667	1.083	0	1.000

ALOU, MOISES   OF

PERSONAL: Born July 3, 1966, in Atlanta, Ga. ... 6-3/220. ... Bats right, throws right. ... Full name: Moises Rojas Alou. ... Name pronounced: MOY-zes ah-LOO. ... High school: C.E.E. (Santo Domingo, Dominican Republic). ... Junior college: Canada College (Calif.). ... Son of Felipe Alou, manager, San Francisco Giants, and outfielder with six major league teams (1958-1974); nephew of Jesus Alou, outfielder with four major league teams (1963-75 and 1978-79); nephew of Matty Alou, outfielder with six major league teams (1960-74).

TRANSACTIONS/CAREER NOTES: Selected by Pittsburgh Pirates organization in first round (second pick overall) of January 1986 free-agent draft. ... Traded by Pirates to Montreal Expos (August 16, 1990), completing deal in which Expos traded P Zane Smith to Pirates for P Scott Ruskin, SS Willie Greene and a player to be named (August 8, 1990). ... On disabled list (March 19, 1991-entire season; July 7-27, 1992; September 18, 1993-remainder of season; August 18-September 5 and September 11, 1995-remainder of season). ... On disabled list (July 8-23, 1996). ... On suspended list (August 23-27, 1996). ... Signed as a free agent by Florida Marlins (December 12, 1996). ... Traded by Marlins to Houston Astros for Ps Oscar Henriquez and P Manuel Barrios and a player to be named (November 11, 1997); Marlins acquired P Mark Johnson to complete deal (December 16, 1997). ... On disabled list (April 3, 1999-entire season; April 27-May 14, 2000; and March 29-April 16, 2001). ... Signed as a free agent by Chicago Cubs (December 19, 2001). ... On disabled list (March 31-April 15, 2002); included rehabilitation assignment to Daytona.

2004 GAMES PLAYED BY POSITION (MLB): OF—154, DH—1.

Year	Team (League)	Pos.	G	AB	R	H	2B	3B	HR	RBI	BB	SO	HBP	GDP	SB-CS	Avg.	OBP	SLG	OPS	E	Avg.
1986—Watertown (NYP)		OF	69	254	30	60	9	8	6	35	22	72	1	5	14-8	.236	.300	.406	.705	7	.952
1987—Macon (S. Atl.)		OF	4	8	1	1	0	0	0	0	2	4	0	0	0-0	.125	.300	.125	.425	0	1.000
—Watertown (NYP)		OF	39	117	20	25	6	2	4	8	16	36	4	0	6-3	.214	.324	.402	.725	2	.957
1988—Augusta (S. Atl.)		OF	105	358	58	112	23	5	7	62	51	84	5	5	24-12	.313	.399	.464	.863	9	.962
1989—Salem (Caro.)		OF	86	321	50	97	29	2	14	53	35	69	3	6	12-5	.302	.374	.536	.910	10	.947
—Harrisburg (East.)		OF	54	205	36	60	5	2	3	19	17	38	0	1	8-4	.293	.344	.380	.724	2	.978
1990—Harrisburg (East.)		OF	36	132	19	39	12	2	3	22	16	21	1	5	7-4	.295	.373	.485	.858	1	.990
—Buffalo (A.A.)		OF	75	271	38	74	4	6	5	31	30	43	2	...	9-4	.273	.345	.387	.733	8	.957
—Pittsburgh (N.L.)		OF	2	5	0	1	0	0	0	0	0	0	0	1	0-0	.200	.200	.200	.400	0	1.000
—Indianapolis (A.A.)		OF	15	55	6	12	1	0	0	6	3	7	0	...	4-3	.218	.254	.236	.491	0	1.000
—Montreal (N.L.)		OF	14	15	4	3	0	1	0	0	0	3	0	0	0-0	.200	.200	.333	.533	0	1.000
1991—Montreal (N.L.)				Did not play.																	
1992—Montreal (N.L.)		OF	115	341	53	96	28	2	9	56	25	46	1	5	16-2	.282	.328	.455	.783	4	.978
1993—Montreal (N.L.)		OF	136	482	70	138	29	6	18	85	38	53	5	9	17-6	.286	.340	.483	.824	4	.985
1994—Montreal (N.L.)		OF	107	422	81	143	31	5	22	78	42	63	2	7	7-6	.339	.397	.592	.989	3	.986
1995—Montreal (N.L.)		OF	93	344	48	94	22	0	14	58	29	56	9	9	4-3	.273	.342	.459	.801	3	.981
1996—Montreal (N.L.)		OF	143	540	87	152	28	2	21	96	49	83	2	15	9-4	.281	.339	.457	.797	3	.989
1997—Florida (N.L.)		OF	150	538	88	157	29	5	23	115	70	85	4	13	9-5	.292	.373	.493	.866	3	.989
1998—Houston (N.L.)		OF-DH	159	584	104	182	34	5	38	124	84	87	5	14	11-3	.312	.399	.582	.981	5	.980
1999—Houston (N.L.)				Did not play.																	
2000—Houston (N.L.)		OF-DH	126	454	82	161	28	2	30	114	52	45	2	21	3-3	.355	.416	.623	1.039	6	.970
2001—Houston (N.L.)		OF-DH	136	513	79	170	31	1	27	108	57	57	3	18	5-1	.331	.396	.554	.949	2	.991
2002—Daytona (Fla. St.)		OF	2	8	0	5	1	0	0	2	1	1	0	0	0-0	.625	.667	.750	1.417	0	1.000
—Chicago (N.L.)		OF-DH	132	484	50	133	23	1	15	61	47	61	0	15	8-0	.275	.337	.419	.757	2	.991
2003—Chicago (N.L.)		OF-DH	151	565	83	158	35	1	22	91	63	67	7	16	3-1	.280	.357	.462	.819	6	.972
2004—Chicago (N.L.)		OF-DH	155	601	106	176	36	3	39	106	68	80	10	12	3-0	.293	.361	.557	.919	6	.969
Major League totals (13 years)			1619	5888	935	1764	354	34	278	1092	624	786	40	155	95-34	.300	.367	.513	.880	49	.982

DIVISION SERIES RECORD

Year	Team (League)	Pos.	G	AB	R	H	2B	3B	HR	RBI	BB	SO	HBP	GDP	SB-CS	Avg.	OBP	SLG	OPS	E	Avg.
1997—Florida (N.L.)		OF	3	14	1	3	1	0	0	1	0	3	0	1	0-0	.214	.214	.286	.500	0	1.000
1998—Houston (N.L.)		OF	4	16	0	3	0	0	0	0	0	2	0	1	0-0	.188	.188	.188	.375	0	1.000
2001—Houston (N.L.)		OF	3	12	0	2	1	0	0	1	0	1	0	0	0-0	.167	.167	.250	.417	0	1.000
2003—Chicago (N.L.)		OF	5	20	3	10	1	0	0	3	1	4	0	1	1-0	.500	.524	.550	1.074	0	1.000
Division series totals (4 years)			15	62	4	18	3	0	0	5	1	10	0	3	1-0	.290	.302	.339	.640	0	1.000

CHAMPIONSHIP SERIES RECORD

Year Team (League)	Pos.	G	AB	R	H	2B	3B	HR	RBI	BB	SO	HBP	GDP	SB-CS	Avg.	OBP	SLG	OPS	E	Avg.
1997— Florida (N.L.)	OF	5	15	0	1	1	0	0	5	1	3	0	1	0-0	.067	.125	.133	.258	0	1.000
2003— Chicago (N.L.)	OF	7	29	4	9	1	0	2	5	2	1	0	2	0-0	.310	.355	.552	.907	0	1.000
Champ. series totals (2 years)		12	44	4	10	2	0	2	10	3	4	0	3	0-0	.227	.277	.409	.686	0	1.000

WORLD SERIES RECORD

Year Team (League)	Pos.	G	AB	R	H	2B	3B	HR	RBI	BB	SO	HBP	GDP	SB-CS	Avg.	OBP	SLG	OPS	E	Avg.
1997— Florida (N.L.)	OF	7	28	6	9	2	0	3	9	3	6	0	0	1-0	.321	.387	.714	1.101	0	1.000

ALL-STAR GAME RECORD

	G	AB	R	H	2B	3B	HR	RBI	BB	SO	HBP	GDP	SB-CS	Avg.	OBP	SLG	OPS	E	Avg.
All-Star Game totals (5 years)	5	9	1	4	1	0	0	1	0	3	0	0	0-0	.444	.444	.556	1.000	0	1.000

ALVAREZ, ABE — P

PERSONAL: Born October 17, 1982, in Los Angeles, Calif. ... 6-2/190. ... Throws left, bats left. ... Full name: Abraham Alvarez. ... High school: Fontana (Calif.). ... College: Long Beach State.
TRANSACTIONS/CAREER NOTES: Selected by Boston Red Sox organization in second round of 2003 free-agent draft.
CAREER HITTING: 0-for-0 (.000), 0 R, 0 2B, 0 3B, 0 HR, 0 RBI.

Year Team (League)	W	L	Pct.	ERA	WHIP	G	GS	CG	ShO	Hld.	Sv.-Opp.	IP	H	R	ER	HR	BB-IBB	SO	Avg.
2003— Lowell (NY-Penn)	0	0	...	0.00	0.58	9	9	0	0	...	0-...	19.0	9	2	0	0	2-1	19	.138
2004— Boston (A.L.)	0	1	.000	9.00	2.60	1	1	0	0	0	0-0	5.0	8	5	5	2	5-0	2	.400
— Portland (East.)	10	9	.526	3.59	1.21	26	26	0	0	...	0-...	135.1	132	65	54	13	32-0	108	.252
Major League totals (1 year)	0	1	.000	9.00	2.60	1	1	0	0	0	0-0	5.0	8	5	5	2	5-0	2	.400

ALVAREZ, TONY — OF

PERSONAL: Born May 10, 1979, in Caracas, Venezuela. ... 6-1/202. ... Bats right, throws right. ... Full name: Antonio Enrique Alvarez.
TRANSACTIONS/CAREER NOTES: Signed as a non-drafted free agent by Pittsburgh Pirates organization (September 27, 1995).
2004 GAMES PLAYED BY POSITION (MLB): OF—16.

Year Team (League)	Pos.	G	AB	R	H	2B	3B	HR	RBI	BB	SO	HBP	GDP	SB-CS	Avg.	OBP	SLG	OPS	E	Avg.
1996— Dom. Pirates (DSL)	3B	39	109	12	15	2	0	1	9	8	12	...	...	6-...	.138	...	.183	...	15	.892
1997— Guacara 1 (VSL)		38	91	15	20	3	0	0	6	9	10	...	...	3-...	.220	...	.253	...	...	...
1998— GC Pirates (GCL)		50	190	27	47	13	1	4	29	13	24	3	4	19-1	.247	.299	.389	.688	14	.941
1999— Williamsport (NYP)	C	58	196	44	63	14	1	7	45	21	36	16	2	38-9	.321	.418	.510	.929	21	.871
2000— Hickory (S. Atl.)	1B-OF	118	442	75	126	25	4	15	77	39	93	15	8	52-21	.285	.357	.462	.819	14	.951
2001— Lynchburg (Caro.)	OF	25	93	10	32	4	0	2	11	7	11	0	2	7-3	.344	.390	.452	.842	3	.893
— Altoona (East.)	2B-OF	67	254	34	81	16	1	6	25	9	30	7	6	17-11	.319	.359	.461	.820	4	.968
2002— Altoona (East.)	OF	125	507	79	161	37	1	15	59	27	71	9	6	29-18	.318	.361	.483	.844	6	.978
— Pittsburgh (N.L.)	OF	14	26	8	8	2	0	1	2	3	5	0	0	1-0	.308	.379	.500	.879	0	1.000
2003— Nashville (PCL)	OF-DH	106	349	50	104	27	3	9	53	28	69	9	8	22-9	.298	.361	.470	.831	3	.984
2004— Nashville (PCL)	OF-DH	99	335	59	97	12	1	14	48	35	63	6	6	19-12	.290	.365	.457	.822	3	.980
— Pittsburgh (N.L.)	OF	24	38	5	8	2	0	1	8	4	7	1	1	0-0	.211	.289	.342	.631	0	1.000
Major League totals (2 years)		38	64	11	16	4	0	2	10	7	12	1	1	1-0	.250	.324	.406	.731	0	1.000

ALVAREZ, WILSON — P

PERSONAL: Born March 24, 1970, in Maracaibo, Venezuela. ... 6-1/255. ... Throws left, bats left. ... Full name: Wilson Eduardo Alvarez.
TRANSACTIONS/CAREER NOTES: Signed as non-drafted free agent by Texas Rangers organization (September 23, 1986). ... Traded by Rangers with IF Scott Fletcher and OF Sammy Sosa to Chicago White Sox for OF Harold Baines and IF Fred Manrique (July 29, 1989). ... Traded by White Sox with P Danny Darwin and P Roberto Hernandez to San Francisco Giants for SS Michael Caruso, OF Brian Manning, P Lorenzo Barcelo, P Keith Foulke, P Bobby Howry and P Ken Vining (July 31, 1997). ... Signed as a free agent by Tampa Bay Devil Rays (December 3, 1997). ... On disabled list (May 21-July 6, 1998; April 12-29 and July 24-August 8, 1999; March 25, 2000-entire season; March 23, 2001-entire season; April 15-May 31 and July 15-August 5, 2002). ... Released by Devil Rays (September 30, 2002). ... Signed by Los Angeles Dodgers organization (January 16, 2003).
CAREER HITTING: 13-for-93 (.140), 6 R, 0 2B, 0 3B, 0 HR, 1 RBI.

Year Team (League)	W	L	Pct.	ERA	WHIP	G	GS	CG	ShO	Hld.	Sv.-Opp.	IP	H	R	ER	HR	BB-IBB	SO	Avg.
1987— Gastonia (S. Atl.)	1	5	.167	6.47	1.94	8	6	0	0	...	0-...	32.0	39	24	23	5	23-0	19	.312
— GC Rangers (GCL)	2	5	.286	5.24	1.39	10	10	0	0	...	0-...	44.2	41	29	26	6	21-0	46	.246
1988— Gastonia (S. Atl.)	4	11	.267	2.98	1.28	23	23	1	0	...	0-...	127.0	113	63	42	5	49-1	134	.233
— Oklahoma City (A.A.)	1	1	.500	3.78	1.38	5	3	0	0	...	0-...	16.2	17	8	7	2	6-0	9	.274
1989— Charlotte (Fla. St.)	7	4	.636	2.11	1.10	13	13	3	2	...	0-...	81.0	68	29	19	2	21-0	51	.227
— Tulsa (Texas)	2	2	.500	2.06	1.17	7	7	1	1	...	0-...	48.0	40	14	11	1	16-3	29	.227
— Texas (A.L.)	0	1	.000	...	...	1	1	0	0	0	0-0	.0	3	3	3	2	2-0	0	1.000
— Birmingham (Southern)	2	1	.667	3.03	1.35	6	6	0	0	...	0-...	35.2	32	12	12	1	16-0	18	.246
1990— Vancouver (PCL)	7	7	.500	6.00	1.89	17	15	1	0	...	0-...	75.0	91	54	50	7	51-0	35	.314
— Birmingham (Southern)	5	1	.833	4.27	1.49	7	7	1	0	...	0-...	46.1	44	24	22	4	25-0	36	.246
1991— Birmingham (Southern)	10	6	.625	1.83	1.20	23	23	3	2	...	0-...	152.1	109	46	31	6	74-0	165	.200
— Chicago (A.L.)	3	2	.600	3.51	1.30	10	9	2	1	0	0-0	56.1	47	26	22	9	29-0	32	.230
1992— Chicago (A.L.)	5	3	.625	5.20	1.67	34	9	0	0	3	1-1	100.1	103	64	58	12	65-2	66	.272
1993— Chicago (A.L.)	15	8	.652	2.95	1.40	31	31	1	1	0	0-0	207.2	168	78	68	14	* 122-8	155	.230
— Nashville (A.A.)	0	1	.000	2.84	1.42	1	1	0	0	...	0-...	6.1	7	7	2	0	2-0	8	.241
1994— Chicago (A.L.)	12	8	.600	3.45	1.29	24	24	2	1	0	0-0	161.2	147	72	62	16	62-1	108	.241
1995— Chicago (A.L.)	8	11	.421	4.32	1.44	29	29	3	0	0	0-0	175.0	171	96	84	21	93-4	118	.258
1996— Chicago (A.L.)	15	10	.600	4.22	1.44	35	35	0	0	0	0-0	217.1	216	106	102	21	97-3	181	.258
1997— Chicago (A.L.)	9	8	.529	3.03	1.24	22	22	2	1	0	0-0	145.2	126	61	49	9	55-1	110	.232
— San Francisco (N.L.)	4	3	.571	4.48	1.36	11	11	0	0	0	0-0	66.1	54	36	33	9	36-3	69	.224
1998— Tampa Bay (A.L.)	6	14	.300	4.73	1.39	25	25	0	0	0	0-0	142.2	130	78	75	18	68-0	107	.239
— GC Devil Rays (GCL)	0	0	...	0.00	1.00	1	1	0	0	0	0-...	3.0	2	0	0	0	1-0	4	.200
— St. Pete. (FSL)	0	1	.000	27.00	4.20	1	1	0	0	0	0-...	1.2	5	5	5	1	2-0	2	.500
— Durham (Int'l)	0	0	...	3.86	1.29	1	1	0	0	0	0-...	4.2	4	2	2	0	2-0	6	.235
1999— Tampa Bay (A.L.)	9	9	.500	4.22	1.49	28	28	1	0	0	0-0	160.0	159	92	75	22	79-1	128	.260
2000— St. Pete. (FSL)	0	0	...	0.00	0.00	1	1	0	0	0	0-...	4.0	0	0	0	0	0-0	2	.000

Year Team (League)	W	L	Pct.	ERA	WHIP	G	GS	CG	ShO	Hld.	Sv.-Opp.	IP	H	R	ER	HR	BB-IBB	SO	Avg.
2001— Durham (Int'l)	1	1	.500	3.00	1.44	4	4	0	0	...	0-...	18.0	20	8	6	2	6-0	16	.282
— Orlando (Sou.)	1	3	.250	4.43	1.48	5	5	0	0	...	0-...	20.1	24	10	10	2	6-0	18	.286
2002— Tampa Bay (A.L.)	2	3	.400	5.28	1.55	23	10	0	0	2	1-1	75.0	80	47	44	13	36-3	56	.272
— Orlando (Sou.)	1	0	1.000	1.13	1.00	2	2	0	0	...	0-...	8.0	6	1	1	0	2-0	7	.222
2003— Las Vegas (PCL)	5	1	.833	1.34	0.90	8	8	0	0	...	0-...	47.0	36	9	7	1	6-0	33	.216
— Los Angeles (N.L.)	6	2	.750	2.37	1.08	21	12	1	1	1	1-1	95.0	80	27	25	5	23-1	82	.231
2004— Los Angeles (N.L.)	7	6	.538	4.03	1.16	40	15	0	0	2	1-2	120.2	109	56	54	12	31-2	102	.244
American League totals (11 years)	84	77	.522	4.01	1.43	262	223	11	4	5	2-2	1441.2	1350	723	642	157	708-23	1061	.249
National League totals (3 years)	17	11	.607	3.57	1.18	72	38	1	1	3	2-3	282.0	243	119	112	26	90-6	253	.235
Major League totals (13 years)	101	88	.534	3.94	1.39	334	261	12	5	8	4-5	1723.2	1593	842	754	183	798-29	1314	.247

DIVISION SERIES RECORD

Year Team (League)	W	L	Pct.	ERA	WHIP	G	GS	CG	ShO	Hld.	Sv.-Opp.	IP	H	R	ER	HR	BB-IBB	SO	Avg.
1997— San Francisco (N.L.)	0	1	.000	6.00	1.67	1	1	0	0	0	0-0	6.0	6	4	4	1	4-0	4	.261
2004— Los Angeles (N.L.)	0	1	.000	10.80	1.20	2	0	0	0	0	0-0	3.1	4	4	4	1	0-0	4	.286
Division series totals (2 years)	0	2	.000	7.71	1.50	3	1	0	0	0	0-0	9.1	10	8	8	2	4-0	8	.270

CHAMPIONSHIP SERIES RECORD

Year Team (League)	W	L	Pct.	ERA	WHIP	G	GS	CG	ShO	Hld.	Sv.-Opp.	IP	H	R	ER	HR	BB-IBB	SO	Avg.
1993— Chicago (A.L.)	1	0	1.000	1.00	1.00	1	1	0	0	0	0-0	9.0	7	1	1	0	2-0	6	.226

ALL-STAR GAME RECORD

	W	L	Pct.	ERA	WHIP	G	GS	CG	ShO	Hld.	Sv.-Opp.	IP	H	R	ER	HR	BB-IBB	SO	Avg.
All-Star Game totals (1 year)	0	0	...	0.00	0.00	1	0	0	0	1	0-0	1.0	0	0	0	0	0-0	0	.000

AMEZAGA, ALFREDO — SS/3B

PERSONAL: Born January 16, 1978, in Obregon, Mexico. ... 5-10/165. ... Bats both, throws right. ... Name pronounced: ah-mezz-ah-guh. ... High school: Miami Senior (Miami). ... Junior college: St. Petersburg (Fla.).

TRANSACTIONS/CAREER NOTES: Selected by Colorado Rockies organization in 36th round of 1997 free-agent draft; did not sign. ... Selected by Colorado Rockies organization in 44th round of 1998 free-agent draft; did not sign. ... Selected by Anaheim Angels organization in 13th round of 1999 free-agent draft.

2004 GAMES PLAYED BY POSITION (MLB): SS—32, 3B—26, 2B—16, DH—1.

Year Team (League)	Pos.	G	AB	R	H	2B	3B	HR	RBI	BB	SO	HBP	GDP	SB-CS	Avg.	OBP	SLG	OPS	E	Avg.
1999— Butte (Pio.)	2B-SS	8	34	11	10	2	0	0	5	5	5	1	0	6-2	.294	.400	.353	.753	0	1.000
— Boise (N'west)	2B-SS	48	205	52	66	6	4	2	29	23	29	5	7	14-3	.322	.402	.420	.821	12	.953
2000— Lake Elsinore (Calif.)	2B-SS	108	420	90	117	13	4	4	44	63	70	4	4	73-21	.279	.374	.357	.731	22	.961
2001— Arkansas (Texas)	SS	70	285	50	89	10	5	4	21	22	55	4	0	24-15	.312	.370	.425	.794	13	.964
— Salt Lake (PCL)	SS	49	200	28	50	5	4	1	16	14	45	3	2	9-6	.250	.307	.330	.637	11	.954
2002— Salt Lake (PCL)	SS-2B	128	518	77	130	25	7	6	51	45	100	8	15	23-14	.251	.317	.361	.678	24	.962
— Anaheim (A.L.)	SS-DH	12	13	3	7	1	0	0	2	0	1	0	1	1-0	.538	.538	.692	1.231	0	1.000
2003— Salt Lake (PCL)	SS-2B-DH	75	317	55	110	20	5	3	45	20	39	4	3	14-8	.347	.391	.470	.861	9	.982
— Anaheim (A.L.)	SS-3B-DH	37	105	15	22	3	2	2	7	9	23	1	2	2-2	.210	.278	.333	.612	5	.962
2004— Salt Lake (PCL)	SS	32	135	15	35	5	2	2	14	13	18	1	2	7-0	.259	.329	.370	.699	7	.961
— Anaheim (A.L.)	SS-3-2-DH	73	93	12	15	2	0	0	11	3	24	3	2	3-2	.161	.212	.247	.459	3	.978
Major League totals (3 years)		122	211	30	44	7	2	4	20	12	48	4	5	6-4	.209	.264	.318	.582	8	.972

DIVISION SERIES RECORD

Year Team (League)	Pos.	G	AB	R	H	2B	3B	HR	RBI	BB	SO	HBP	GDP	SB-CS	Avg.	OBP	SLG	OPS	E	Avg.
2004— Anaheim (A.L.)	2B	2	2	0	0	0	0	0	0	0	0	0	0	0-0	.000	.000	.000	.000	0	1.000

ANDERSON, BRIAN — P

PERSONAL: Born April 26, 1972, in Portsmouth, Va. ... 6-1/185. ... Throws left, bats right. ... Full name: Brian James Anderson. ... High school: Geneva (Ohio). ... College: Wright State.

TRANSACTIONS/CAREER NOTES: Selected by California Angels organization in first round (third pick overall) of 1993 free-agent draft. ... On disabled list (May 7-June 7, 1994); included rehabilitation assignment to Lake Elsinore. ... On disabled list (May 6-June 20, 1995); included rehabilitation assignment to Lake Elsinore. ... Traded by Angels to Cleveland Indians for Ps Jason Grimsley and Pep Harris (February 15, 1996). ... On disabled list (July 5-August 12, 1997); included rehabilitation assignment to Buffalo. ... Selected by Arizona Diamondbacks in first round (second pick overall) of expansion draft (November 18, 1997). ... On disabled list (April 12-May 2 and June 3-July 1, 2001); included rehabilitation assignments to Tucson. ... Signed as a free agent by Indians (December 23, 2002). ... Traded by Indians with a player to be named and cash to Kansas City Royals for OF Trey Dyson and P Kieran Mattison (August 25, 2003).

HONORS: Named A.L. Rookie Pitcher of the Year by THE SPORTING NEWS (1994).

CAREER HITTING: 35-for-255 (.137), 15 R, 5 2B, 3 3B, 1 HR, 10 RBI.

Year Team (League)	W	L	Pct.	ERA	WHIP	G	GS	CG	ShO	Hld.	Sv.-Opp.	IP	H	R	ER	HR	BB-IBB	SO	Avg.
1993— Midland (Texas)	0	1	.000	3.38	1.50	2	2	0	0	...	0-...	10.2	16	5	4	2	0-0	9	.340
— Vancouver (PCL)	0	1	.000	12.38	2.38	2	2	0	0	...	0-...	8.0	13	12	11	3	6-0	2	.394
— California (A.L.)	0	0	...	3.97	1.15	4	1	0	0	0	0-0	11.1	11	5	5	1	2-0	4	.256
1994— California (A.L.)	7	5	.583	5.22	1.45	18	18	0	0	0	0-0	101.2	120	63	59	13	27-0	47	.300
— Lake Elsinore (Calif.)	0	1	.000	3.00	0.50	2	2	0	0	...	0-...	12.0	6	4	4	1	0-0	9	.146
1995— California (A.L.)	6	8	.429	5.87	1.40	18	17	1	0	0	0-0	99.2	110	66	65	24	30-2	45	.282
— Lake Elsinore (Calif.)	1	1	.500	1.93	0.79	3	3	0	0	...	0-...	14.0	10	3	3	0	1-0	13	.204
1996— Buffalo (A.A.)	11	5	.688	3.59	1.20	19	19	2	0	...	0-...	128.0	125	57	51	14	28-0	85	.253
— Cleveland (A.L.)	3	1	.750	4.91	1.40	10	9	0	0	1	0-...	51.1	58	29	28	9	14-1	21	.296
1997— Buffalo (A.A.)	7	1	.875	3.05	1.09	15	15	1	1	...	0-...	85.2	78	33	29	13	15-0	60	.238
— Cleveland (A.L.)	4	2	.667	4.69	1.38	8	8	0	0	0	0-0	48.0	55	28	25	7	11-0	22	.301
1998— Arizona (N.L.)	12	13	.480	4.33	1.18	32	32	2	1	0	0-0	208.0	221	109	100	39	24-2	95	.274
1999— Arizona (N.L.)	8	2	.800	4.57	1.32	31	19	2	1	1	1-2	130.0	144	69	66	18	28-3	75	.279
— Tucson (PCL)	0	1	.000	5.40	1.50	2	2	0	0	...	0-...	6.2	9	5	4	1	1-0	8	.333
2000— Arizona (N.L.)	11	7	.611	4.05	1.24	33	32	2	0	...	0-...	213.1	226	101	96	38	39-7	104	.275
2001— Arizona (N.L.)	4	9	.308	5.20	1.40	29	22	1	0	0	0-1	133.1	156	93	77	25	30-2	55	.295
— Tucson (PCL)	1	0	1.000	1.50	0.75	2	2	0	0	...	0-...	12.0	7	2	2	0	2-0	8	.167
2002— Arizona (N.L.)	6	11	.353	4.79	1.32	35	24	0	0	1	0-0	156.0	174	86	83	23	32-3	81	.284
2003— Cleveland (A.L.)	9	10	.474	3.71	1.31	25	24	0	0	0	0-0	148.0	162	88	61	21	32-3	72	.282
— Kansas City (A.L.)	5	1	.833	3.99	1.23	7	7	0	0	0	0-0	49.2	50	22	22	6	11-0	15	.272
2004— Kansas City (A.L.)	6	12	.333	5.64	1.63	35	26	0	0	0	0-0	166.0	217	123	104	33	53-4	70	.320
American League totals (7 years)	40	39	.506	4.92	1.43	125	110	5	2	3	0-0	675.2	783	424	369	114	180-10	296	.295
National League totals (5 years)	41	42	.494	4.52	1.28	160	129	7	2	2	1-3	840.2	921	458	422	143	153-17	410	.280
Major League totals (12 years)	81	81	.500	4.69	1.34	285	239	12	4	5	1-3	1516.1	1704	882	791	257	333-27	706	.287

DIVISION SERIES RECORD

Year Team (League)	W	L	Pct.	ERA	WHIP	G	GS	CG	ShO	Hld.	Sv.-Opp.	IP	H	R	ER	HR	BB-IBB	SO	Avg.
1999— Arizona (N.L.)	0	0	...	2.57	1.00	1	1	0	0	0	0-0	7.0	7	2	2	1	0-0	4	.250
2001— Arizona (N.L.)	0	0	...	2.25	0.75	2	0	0	0	1	0-0	4.0	3	1	1	1	0-0	3	.214
Division series totals (2 years)	0	0	...	2.45	0.91	3	1	0	0	1	0-0	11.0	10	3	3	2	0-0	7	.238

CHAMPIONSHIP SERIES RECORD

Year Team (League)	W	L	Pct.	ERA	WHIP	G	GS	CG	ShO	Hld.	Sv.-Opp.	IP	H	R	ER	HR	BB-IBB	SO	Avg.
1997— Cleveland (A.L.)	1	0	1.000	1.42	0.63	3	0	0	0	0	0-0	6.1	1	1	1	0	3-1	7	.048
2001— Arizona (N.L.)	1	0	1.000	2.70	1.50	1	0	0	0	0	0-0	3.1	4	1	1	0	1-0	0	.308
Champ. series totals (2 years)	2	0	1.000	1.86	0.93	4	0	0	0	0	0-0	9.2	5	2	2	0	4-1	7	.147

WORLD SERIES RECORD

Year Team (League)	W	L	Pct.	ERA	WHIP	G	GS	CG	ShO	Hld.	Sv.-Opp.	IP	H	R	ER	HR	BB-IBB	SO	Avg.
1997— Cleveland (A.L.)	0	0	...	2.45	0.55	3	0	0	0	2	1-1	3.2	2	1	1	0	0-0	2	.154
2001— Arizona (N.L.)	0	1	.000	3.38	1.50	1	1	0	0	0	0-0	5.1	5	2	2	1	3-0	1	.238
World series totals (2 years)	0	1	.000	3.00	1.11	4	1	0	0	2	1-1	9.0	7	3	3	1	3-0	3	.206

ANDERSON, GARRET   OF

PERSONAL: Born June 30, 1972, in Los Angeles, Calif. ... 6-3/225. ... Bats left, throws left. ... Full name: Garret Joseph Anderson. ... High school: John F. Kennedy (Granada Hills, Calif.).

TRANSACTIONS/CAREER NOTES: Selected by California Angels organization in fourth round of 1990 free-agent draft. ... Angels franchise renamed Anaheim Angels for 1997 season. ... On disabled list (April 22-June 10, 2004); included rehabilitation assignment to Rancho Cucamonga.

HONORS: Named A.L. Rookie Player of the Year by THE SPORTING NEWS (1995).

2004 GAMES PLAYED BY POSITION (MLB): OF—94, DH—18.

Year Team (League)	Pos.	G	AB	R	H	2B	3B	HR	RBI	BB	SO	HBP	GDP	SB-CS	Avg.	OBP	SLG	OPS	E	Avg.
1990— Ariz. Angels (Ariz.)	OF	32	127	5	27	2	0	0	14	2	24	2	3	3-0	.213	.231	.228	.460	2	.965
— Boise (N'west)	OF	25	83	11	21	3	1	1	8	4	18	0	3	0-1	.253	.284	.349	.633	2	.950
1991— Quad City (Midw.)	OF	105	392	40	102	22	2	2	42	20	89	0	16	5-6	.260	.295	.342	.637	10	.943
1992— Palm Springs (Calif.)	OF	81	322	46	104	15	2	1	62	21	61	1	9	1-1	.323	.366	.391	.758	6	.959
— Midland (Texas)	OF	39	146	16	40	5	0	2	19	9	30	0	8	2-1	.274	.316	.349	.665	1	.986
1993— Vancouver (PCL)	OF-1B	124	467	57	137	34	4	4	71	31	95	0	15	3-4	.293	.334	.409	.743	2	.991
1994— Vancouver (PCL)	OF-DH-1B	123	505	75	162	42	6	12	102	28	93	1	7	3-3	.321	.356	.499	.855	2	.990
— California (A.L.)	OF	5	13	0	5	0	0	0	1	0	2	0	0	0-0	.385	.385	.385	.769	0	1.000
1995— California (A.L.)	OF-DH	106	374	50	120	19	1	16	69	19	65	1	8	6-2	.321	.352	.505	.857	5	.978
— Vancouver (PCL)	OF-DH	14	61	9	19	7	0	0	12	5	14	0	3	0-0	.311	.364	.426	.790	1	.957
1996— California (A.L.)	OF-DH	150	607	79	173	33	2	12	72	27	84	0	22	7-9	.285	.314	.405	.719	7	.979
1997— Anaheim (A.L.)	OF-DH	154	624	76	189	36	3	8	92	30	70	2	20	10-4	.303	.334	.409	.743	3	.992
1998— Anaheim (A.L.)	OF	156	622	62	183	41	7	15	79	29	80	1	13	8-3	.294	.325	.455	.780	6	.983
1999— Anaheim (A.L.)	OF-DH	157	620	88	188	36	2	21	80	34	81	0	15	3-4	.303	.336	.469	.806	3	.993
2000— Anaheim (A.L.)	OF-DH-1B	159	647	92	185	40	3	35	117	24	87	0	21	7-6	.286	.307	.519	.827	4	.990
2001— Anaheim (A.L.)	OF-DH	161	672	83	194	39	2	28	123	27	100	0	12	13-6	.289	.314	.478	.792	2	.994
2002— Anaheim (A.L.)	OF-DH	158	638	93	195	•56	3	29	123	30	80	0	11	6-4	.306	.332	.539	.871	2	.994
2003— Anaheim (A.L.)	OF-DH	159	638	80	201	•49	4	29	116	31	83	0	15	6-3	.315	.345	.541	.885	1	.997
2004— Rancho Cuca. (Calif.)	OF	3	9	1	4	0	0	1	1	1	1	0	0	0-0	.444	.500	.778	1.278	0	1.000
— Anaheim (A.L.)	OF-DH	112	442	57	133	20	1	14	75	29	75	1	3	2-1	.301	.343	.446	.789	2	.991
Major League totals (11 years)		1477	5897	760	1766	369	28	207	947	280	807	5	140	68-42	.299	.329	.477	.806	35	.989

DIVISION SERIES RECORD

Year Team (League)	Pos.	G	AB	R	H	2B	3B	HR	RBI	BB	SO	HBP	GDP	SB-CS	Avg.	OBP	SLG	OPS	E	Avg.
2002— Anaheim (A.L.)	OF	4	18	5	7	2	0	1	4	1	3	0	1	0-0	.389	.421	.667	1.088	0	1.000
2004— Anaheim (A.L.)	OF	3	13	1	2	0	0	0	0	0	3	0	0	0-0	.154	.154	.154	.308	0	1.000
Division series totals (2 years)		7	31	6	9	2	0	1	4	1	6	0	1	0-0	.290	.313	.452	.764	0	1.000

CHAMPIONSHIP SERIES RECORD

Year Team (League)	Pos.	G	AB	R	H	2B	3B	HR	RBI	BB	SO	HBP	GDP	SB-CS	Avg.	OBP	SLG	OPS	E	Avg.
2002— Anaheim (A.L.)	OF	5	20	3	5	1	0	1	3	1	0	0	0	0-1	.250	.286	.450	.736	0	1.000

WORLD SERIES RECORD

Year Team (League)	Pos.	G	AB	R	H	2B	3B	HR	RBI	BB	SO	HBP	GDP	SB-CS	Avg.	OBP	SLG	OPS	E	Avg.
2002— Anaheim (A.L.)	OF	7	32	3	9	1	0	0	6	0	3	0	1	0-0	.281	.281	.313	.594	1	.947

ALL-STAR GAME RECORD

		G	AB	R	H	2B	3B	HR	RBI	BB	SO	HBP	GDP	SB-CS	Avg.	OBP	SLG	OPS	E	Avg.
All-Star Game totals (2 years)		2	8	1	3	1	0	1	3	0	1	0	0	0-0	.375	.375	.875	1.250	0	...

ANDERSON, JASON   P

PERSONAL: Born June 9, 1979, in Danville, Ill. ... 6-0/188. ... Throws right, bats left. ... Full name: Jason R. Anderson. ... High school: Danville (Ill.). ... College: Illinois.

TRANSACTIONS/CAREER NOTES: Selected by Kansas City Royals organization in sixth round of 1997 free-agent draft; did not sign. ... Selected by New York Yankees in 10th round of 2000 free-agent draft. ... Traded by Yankees with Ps Ryan Bicondoa and Anderson Garcia to New York Mets for P Armando Benitez (July 18, 2003). ... Claimed on waivers by Cleveland Indians (April 8, 2004). ... Claimed on waivers by Yankees (June 1, 2004).

CAREER HITTING: 0-for-0 (.000), 0 R, 0 2B, 0 3B, 0 HR, 0 RBI.

Year Team (League)	W	L	Pct.	ERA	WHIP	G	GS	CG	ShO	Hld.	Sv.-Opp.	IP	H	R	ER	HR	BB-IBB	SO	Avg.
2000— Staten Island (NY-P)	6	5	.545	4.03	1.36	15	15	0	0	...	0-...	80.1	84	41	36	1	25-0	73	.273
2001— Greensboro (S. Atl.)	7	9	.438	3.76	1.34	23	19	1	0	...	1-...	124.1	127	68	52	9	40-1	101	.267
— Staten Island (NY-P)	5	1	.833	1.70	0.92	7	7	0	0	...	0-...	47.2	32	9	9	2	12-0	56	.190
2002— Tampa (FSL)	4	2	.667	4.07	1.23	12	3	0	0	...	1-...	24.1	27	13	11	2	3-0	22	.281
— Norwich (East.)	1	1	.500	0.93	0.98	16	0	0	0	...	2-...	19.1	14	2	2	1	5-1	21	.212
— Columbus (Int'l)	5	1	.833	3.15	1.08	26	0	0	0	...	7-...	34.1	26	13	12	3	11-0	28	.211
2003— Columbus (Int'l)	0	0	...	0.00	0.65	6	0	0	0	...	3-...	7.2	3	0	0	0	2-0	13	.115
— New York (A.L.)	1	0	1.000	4.79	1.79	22	0	0	0	0	0-0	20.2	23	13	11	3	14-4	9	.280
— Norfolk (Int'l)	1	3	.250	2.70	1.07	10	5	0	0	...	4-...	23.1	18	8	7	3	7-0	9	.214
— New York (N.L.)	0	0	...	5.06	1.41	6	0	0	0	0	0-0	10.2	10	6	6	2	5-1	7	.256

Year Team (League)	W	L	Pct.	ERA	WHIP	G	GS	CG	ShO	Hld.	Sv.-Opp.	IP	H	R	ER	HR	BB-IBB	SO	Avg.
2004—Cleveland (A.L.)	0	0	...	45.00	5.00	1	0	0	0	...	0-0	1.0	1	5	5	1	4-1	1	.250
—Buffalo (Int'l)	2	1	.667	2.76	1.04	9	0	0	0	...	1-...	16.1	15	5	5	1	2-1	11	.254
—Columbus (Int'l)	1	3	.250	4.63	1.34	36	0	0	0	...	1-...	44.2	48	24	23	4	12-0	38	.264
American League totals (2 years)	1	0	1.000	6.65	1.94	23	0	0	0	0	0-0	21.2	24	18	16	4	18-5	10	.279
National League totals (1 year)	0	0	...	5.06	1.41	6	0	0	0	0	0-0	10.2	10	6	6	2	5-1	7	.256
Major League totals (2 years)	1	0	1.000	6.12	1.76	29	0	0	0	0	0-0	32.1	34	24	22	6	23-6	17	.272

ANDERSON, JIMMY   P

PERSONAL: Born January 22, 1976, in Portsmouth, Va. ... 6-1/210. ... Throws left, bats left. ... Full name: James Drew Anderson. ... High school: Western Branch (Chesapeake, Va.).

TRANSACTIONS/CAREER NOTES: Selected by Pittsburgh Pirates organization in ninth round of 1994 free-agent draft. ... Released by Pirates (December 16, 2002). ... Signed by Cincinnati Reds organization (January 15, 2003). ... Refused minor league assignment and became a free agent (July 1, 2003). ... Signed by San Francisco Giants organization (July 9, 2003). ... Released by Giants (August 21, 2003). ... Signed as a free agent by Chicago Cubs organzation (December 19, 2003). ... Traded by Cubs to Boston Red Sox for P Andy Shipman and a player to be named (July 2, 2004). ... Traded by Red Sox to Cubs for a player to be named (July 31, 2004).

CAREER HITTING: 23-for-170 (.135), 11 R, 3 2B, 0 3B, 0 HR, 6 RBI.

Year Team (League)	W	L	Pct.	ERA	WHIP	G	GS	CG	ShO	Hld.	Sv.-Opp.	IP	H	R	ER	HR	BB-IBB	SO	Avg.
1994—GC Pirates (GCL)	5	1	.833	1.60	1.10	10	10	0	0	...	0-...	56.1	35	21	10	1	27-0	66	.177
1995—Augusta (S. Atl.)	4	2	.667	1.53	1.07	14	14	0	0	...	0-...	76.2	51	15	13	1	31-0	75	.190
—Lynchburg (Carolina)	1	5	.167	4.13	1.47	10	9	0	0	...	0-...	52.1	56	29	24	1	21-1	32	.280
1996—Lynchburg (Carolina)	5	3	.625	1.93	1.10	11	11	1	1	...	0-...	65.1	51	25	14	2	21-0	56	.211
—Carolina (Southern)	8	5	.615	3.34	1.40	17	16	0	0	...	0-...	97.0	92	40	36	3	44-3	79	.253
1997—Carolina (Southern)	2	1	.667	1.46	1.01	4	4	0	0	...	0-...	24.2	16	6	4	1	9-0	23	.184
—Calgary (PCL)	7	6	.538	5.68	1.83	21	21	0	0	...	0-...	103.0	124	78	65	9	64-3	71	.305
1998—Nashville (PCL)	9	10	.474	5.02	1.75	35	17	0	0	...	0-...	123.2	144	87	69	8	72-6	63	.301
1999—Nashville (PCL)	11	2	.846	3.84	1.45	21	21	1	0	...	0-...	133.2	153	67	57	5	41-0	93	.289
—Pittsburgh (N.L.)	2	1	.667	3.99	1.40	13	4	0	0	0	0-0	29.1	25	15	13	2	16-2	13	.234
2000—Pittsburgh (N.L.)	5	11	.313	5.25	1.58	27	26	1	0	0	0-0	144.0	169	94	84	13	58-2	73	.294
—Nashville (PCL)	0	0	...	4.15	1.69	2	2	0	0	...	0-...	13.0	18	6	6	0	4-0	7	.360
—Altoona (East.)	1	0	1.000	0.00	0.89	1	1	0	0	...	0-...	9.0	7	1	0	0	1-0	6	.212
2001—Pittsburgh (N.L.)	9	17	.346	5.10	1.53	34	34	1	0	0	0-0	206.1	232	123	117	15	83-14	89	.287
2002—Pittsburgh (N.L.)	8	13	.381	5.44	1.64	28	25	1	0	0	0-0	140.2	167	91	85	20	63-5	47	.299
2003—Louisville (Int'l)	6	1	.857	3.12	1.20	9	9	0	0	...	0-...	60.2	61	26	21	2	14-0	30	.265
—Cincinnati (N.L.)	1	5	.167	8.84	1.91	8	7	0	0	0	0-0	38.2	60	39	38	8	14-1	13	.359
—Fresno (PCL)	1	4	.200	6.44	1.80	8	8	0	0	...	0-...	43.1	65	36	31	3	15-0	17	.351
2004—Chicago (N.L.)	0	0	...	4.66	1.24	7	0	0	0	0	1-1	9.2	9	5	5	0	3-0	3	.243
—Boston (A.L.)	0	0	...	6.00	2.17	5	0	0	0	0	0-0	6.0	10	4	4	0	3-0	3	.400
—Pawtucket (Int'l)	0	0	...	5.40	1.20	1	0	0	0	...	0-...	1.2	1	1	1	0	1-0	1	.167
—Iowa (PCL)	6	5	.545	4.28	1.51	16	15	0	0	...	0-...	94.2	108	54	45	7	35-1	42	.292
American League totals (1 year)	0	0	...	6.00	2.17	5	0	0	0	0	0-0	6.0	10	4	4	0	3-0	3	.400
National League totals (6 years)	25	47	.347	5.41	1.58	117	96	3	0	0	1-1	568.2	662	367	342	58	237-24	238	.294
Major League totals (6 years)	25	47	.347	5.42	1.59	122	96	3	0	0	1-1	574.2	672	371	346	58	240-24	241	.295

ANDERSON, MARLON   2B/OF

PERSONAL: Born January 6, 1974, in Montgomery, Ala. ... 5-11/200. ... Bats left, throws right. ... Full name: Marlon Ordell Anderson. ... High school: Prattville (Ala.). ... College: South Alabama.

TRANSACTIONS/CAREER NOTES: Selected by Philadelphia Phillies organization in second round of 1995 free-agent draft; choice received from St. Louis Cardinals as part of compensation for Cardinals signing Type A free-agent P Danny Jackson. ... Signed as a free agent by Tampa Bay Devil Rays (January 16, 2003). ... On suspended list (July 29-August 1, 2003). ... Signed as a free agent by St. Louis Cardinals (January 9, 2004).

2004 GAMES PLAYED BY POSITION (MLB): 2B—37, OF—36, 1B—2, DH—1.

Year Team (League)	Pos.	G	AB	R	H	2B	3B	HR	RBI	BB	SO	HBP	GDP	SB-CS	Avg.	OBP	SLG	OPS	E	Avg.
1995—Batavia (NY-Penn)	2B	74	312	52	92	13	4	3	40	15	20	4	2	22-8	.295	.331	.391	.722	14	.965
1996—Clearwater (FSL)	2B	60	257	37	70	10	3	2	22	14	18	2	4	26-1	.272	.315	.358	.673	16	.958
—Reading (East.)	2B	75	314	38	86	14	3	3	28	26	44	1	5	17-9	.274	.330	.366	.697	18	.957
1997—Reading (East.)	2B	137	553	88	147	18	6	10	62	42	77	10	8	27-15	.266	.328	.374	.703	29	.961
1998—Scran./W.B. (I.L.)	2B	136	575	104	176	32	14	16	86	28	77	7	11	24-12	.306	.343	.494	.837	28	.959
—Philadelphia (N.L.)	2B	17	43	4	14	3	0	1	4	1	6	0	0	2-0	.326	.333	.465	.798	1	.978
1999—Philadelphia (N.L.)	2B	129	452	48	114	26	4	5	54	24	61	2	6	13-2	.252	.292	.361	.652	11	.979
2000—Scran./W.B. (I.L.)	2B	103	397	57	121	18	8	8	53	39	43	5	2	24-10	.305	.370	.451	.821	14	.969
—Philadelphia (N.L.)	2B	41	162	10	37	8	1	1	15	12	22	0	5	2-2	.228	.282	.309	.590	2	.989
2001—Philadelphia (N.L.)	2B	147	522	69	153	30	2	11	61	35	74	2	12	8-5	.293	.337	.421	.758	12	.982
2002—Philadelphia (N.L.)	2B	145	539	64	139	30	6	8	48	42	71	5	16	5-1	.258	.315	.380	.696	* 20	.970
2003—Tampa Bay (A.L.) 2B-DH-OF	145	482	59	130	27	3	6	67	41	60	3	6	19-3	.270	.328	.376	.703	15	.973
2004—St. Louis (N.L.) 2B-OF-1B-DH	113	253	31	60	12	0	8	28	12	38	1	5	6-2	.237	.269	.379	.649	7	.961
American League totals (1 year)		145	482	59	130	27	3	6	67	41	60	3	6	19-3	.270	.328	.376	.703	15	.973
National League totals (6 years)		592	1971	226	517	109	13	34	210	126	272	10	44	36-12	.262	.307	.383	.690	53	.977
Major League totals (7 years)		737	2453	285	647	136	16	40	277	167	332	13	50	55-15	.264	.311	.381	.693	68	.976

DIVISION SERIES RECORD

Year Team (League)	Pos.	G	AB	R	H	2B	3B	HR	RBI	BB	SO	HBP	GDP	SB-CS	Avg.	OBP	SLG	OPS	E	Avg.
2004—St. Louis (N.L.)	PH	3	3	0	0	0	0	0	0	0	1	0	0	0-0	.000	.000	.000	.000	0	...

CHAMPIONSHIP SERIES RECORD

Year Team (League)	Pos.	G	AB	R	H	2B	3B	HR	RBI	BB	SO	HBP	GDP	SB-CS	Avg.	OBP	SLG	OPS	E	Avg.
2004—St. Louis (N.L.)	2B	5	3	1	1	1	0	0	1	1	1	0	0	0-0	.333	.600	.667	1.267	0	...

WORLD SERIES RECORD

Year Team (League)	Pos.	G	AB	R	H	2B	3B	HR	RBI	BB	SO	HBP	GDP	SB-CS	Avg.	OBP	SLG	OPS	E	Avg.
2004—St. Louis (N.L.)	2B-DH	4	6	0	1	1	0	0	0	0	1	0	0	0-0	.167	.167	.333	.500	0	1.000

ANKIEL, RICK — P

PERSONAL: Born July 19, 1979, in Fort Pierce, Fla. ... 6-1/215. ... Throws left, bats left. ... Full name: Richard Alexander Ankiel. ... Name pronounced: ann-KEEL. ... High school: Port St. Lucie (Fla.).

TRANSACTIONS/CAREER NOTES: Selected by St. Louis Cardinals organization in second round of 1997 free-agent draft. ... On disabled list (March 29-June 5, 2002). ... On disabled list (March 25-September 1, 2004); included rehabilitation assignments to Palm Beach and Memphis.

HONORS: Named Minor League Player of the Year by THE SPORTING NEWS (1999). ... Named N.L. Rookie Pitcher of the Year by THE SPORTING NEWS (2000).

CAREER HITTING: 18-for-87 (.207), 9 R, 1 2B, 1 3B, 2 HR, 9 RBI.

Year Team (League)	W	L	Pct.	ERA	WHIP	G	GS	CG	ShO	Hld.	Sv.-Opp.	IP	H	R	ER	HR	BB-IBB	SO	Avg.
1998—Peoria (Midw.)	3	0	1.000	2.06	0.77	7	7	0	0	...	0-...	35.0	15	8	8	0	12-0	41	.134
—Prince William (Caro.)	9	6	.600	2.79	1.02	21	21	1	0	...	0-...	126.0	91	46	39	8	38-0	181	.205
1999—Arkansas (Texas)	6	0	1.000	0.91	0.83	8	8	1	1	...	0-...	49.1	25	6	5	2	16-0	75	.145
—Memphis (PCL)	7	3	.700	3.16	1.35	16	16	0	0	...	0-...	88.1	73	37	31	7	46-1	119	.223
—St. Louis (N.L.)	0	1	.000	3.27	1.21	9	5	0	0	0	1-1	33.0	26	12	12	2	14-0	39	.215
2000—St. Louis (N.L.)	11	7	.611	3.50	1.30	31	30	0	0	1	0-0	175.0	137	80	68	21	90-2	194	.219
2001—St. Louis (N.L.)	1	2	.333	7.13	2.08	6	6	0	0	0	0-0	24.0	25	21	19	7	25-0	27	.275
—Memphis (PCL)	0	2	.000	20.77	4.62	3	3	0	0	...	0-...	4.1	3	10	10	0	17-0	4	.200
—Johnson City (App.)	5	3	.625	1.33	0.68	41	14	1	0	...	0-...	87.2	42	20	13	1	18-0	158	.140
2002—Peoria (Midw.)			Did not play.																
—St. Louis (N.L.)			Did not play.																
2003—Tennessee (Sou.)	2	6	.250	6.29	1.70	20	10	1	0	...	0-...	54.1	45	42	38	5	49-1	64	.232
2004—Palm Beach (FSL)	0	1	.000	2.08	0.58	3	3	0	0	...	0-...	8.2	5	4	2	0	0-0	11	.167
—Tennessee (Sou.)	1	0	1.000	0.00	0.56	2	2	0	0	...	0-...	9.0	3	1	0	0	2-0	7	.100
—Memphis (PCL)	1	0	1.000	0.00	0.17	1	1	0	0	...	0-...	6.0	1	1	0	0	0-0	5	.053
—St. Louis (N.L.)	1	0	1.000	5.40	1.10	5	0	0	0	2	0-0	10.0	10	6	6	2	1-0	9	.256
Major League totals (4 years)	13	10	.565	3.90	1.36	51	41	0	0	3	1-1	242.0	198	119	105	32	130-2	269	.226

DIVISION SERIES RECORD

Year Team (League)	W	L	Pct.	ERA	WHIP	G	GS	CG	ShO	Hld.	Sv.-Opp.	IP	H	R	ER	HR	BB-IBB	SO	Avg.
2000—St. Louis (N.L.)	0	0	...	13.50	3.75	1	1	0	0	0	0-0	2.2	4	4	4	0	6-0	3	.400

CHAMPIONSHIP SERIES RECORD

Year Team (League)	W	L	Pct.	ERA	WHIP	G	GS	CG	ShO	Hld.	Sv.-Opp.	IP	H	R	ER	HR	BB-IBB	SO	Avg.
2000—St. Louis (N.L.)	0	0	...	20.25	4.50	2	1	0	0	0	0-0	1.1	1	3	3	0	5-0	2	.333

APPIER, KEVIN — P

PERSONAL: Born December 6, 1967, in Lancaster, Calif. ... 6-2/215. ... Throws right, bats right. ... Full name: Robert Kevin Appier. ... Name pronounced: APE-ee-er. ... High school: Antelope Valley (Lancaster, Calif.). ... College: Fresno State.

TRANSACTIONS/CAREER NOTES: Selected by Kansas City Royals organization in first round (ninth pick overall) of 1987 free-agent draft. ... On disabled list (July 26-August 12, 1995). ... On disabled list (March 20-September 1, 1998); included rehabilitation assignments to Gulf Coast Royals, Lansing, Wichita and Omaha. ... Traded by Royals to Oakland Athletics for Ps Blake Stein, Jeff D'Amico and Brad Rigby (July 31, 1999). ... On disabled list (April 25-May 13, 2000). ... Signed as a free agent by New York Mets (December 11, 2000). ... Traded by Mets to Anaheim Angels for 1B Mo Vaughn (December 27, 2001). ... On disabled list (April 20-May 7, 2003). ... Released by Angels (July 30, 2003). ... Signed by Kansas City Royals (August 6, 2003). ... On disabled list (August 26, 2003-remainder of season). ... On disabled list (March 26-April 17 and April 24, 2004-July 15, 2004); included rehabilitation assignments to Wichita and Omaha. ... On voluntarily retired list (July 15-November 1, 2004).

HONORS: Named A.L. Rookie Pitcher of the Year by THE SPORTING NEWS (1990).

CAREER HITTING: 8-for-83 (.096), 4 R, 0 2B, 0 3B, 0 HR, 4 RBI.

Year Team (League)	W	L	Pct.	ERA	WHIP	G	GS	CG	ShO	Hld.	Sv.-Opp.	IP	H	R	ER	HR	BB-IBB	SO	Avg.
1987—Eugene (N'west)	5	2	.714	3.04	1.43	15	15	0	0	...	0-...	77.0	81	43	26	2	29-0	72	.263
1988—Baseball City (FSL)	10	9	.526	2.75	1.17	24	24	1	0	...	0-...	147.1	134	58	45	1	39-5	112	.244
—Memphis (Sou.)	2	0	1.000	1.83	0.92	3	3	0	0	...	0-...	19.2	11	5	4	0	7-0	18	.164
1989—Omaha (Am. Assoc.)	8	8	.500	3.95	1.32	22	22	3	2	...	0-...	139.0	141	70	61	6	42-1	109	.259
—Kansas City (A.L.)	1	4	.200	9.14	2.12	6	5	0	0	0	0-0	21.2	34	22	22	3	12-1	10	.374
1990—Omaha (Am. Assoc.)	2	0	1.000	1.50	1.00	3	3	0	0	...	0-...	18.0	15	3	3	0	3-0	17	.231
—Kansas City (A.L.)	12	8	.600	2.76	1.25	32	24	3	3	0	0-0	185.2	179	67	57	13	54-2	127	.252
1991—Kansas City (A.L.)	13	10	.565	3.42	1.28	34	31	6	3	1	0-0	207.2	205	97	79	13	61-3	158	.255
1992—Kansas City (A.L.)	15	8	.652	2.46	1.13	30	30	3	0	0	0-0	208.1	167	59	57	10	68-5	150	.217
1993—Kansas City (A.L.)	18	8	.692	2.56	1.11	34	34	5	1	0	0-0	238.2	183	74	68	8	81-3	186	.212
1994—Kansas City (A.L.)	7	6	.538	3.83	1.29	23	23	1	0	0	0-0	155.0	137	68	66	11	63-7	145	.240
1995—Kansas City (A.L.)	15	10	.600	3.89	1.21	31	31	4	1	0	0-0	201.1	163	90	87	14	80-1	185	.221
1996—Kansas City (A.L.)	14	11	.560	3.62	1.26	32	32	5	1	0	0-0	211.1	192	87	85	17	75-2	207	.245
1997—Kansas City (A.L.)	9	13	.409	3.40	1.23	34	34	4	1	0	0-0	235.2	215	96	89	24	74-2	196	.243
1998—GC Royals (GCL)	0	1	.000	2.70	1.20	1	1	0	0	...	0-...	3.1	3	3	1	0	1-0	2	.214
—Lansing (Midw.)	0	0	...	2.25	1.00	1	1	0	0	...	0-...	4.0	4	1	1	0	0-0	5	.267
—Wichita (Texas)	0	1	.000	6.00	1.67	1	1	0	0	...	0-...	6.0	8	4	4	1	2-0	1	.348
—Omaha (PCL)	3	2	.600	7.03	1.66	6	6	0	0	...	0-...	32.0	41	25	25	7	12-1	22	.301
—Kansas City (A.L.)	1	2	.333	7.80	1.73	3	3	0	0	0	0-0	15.0	21	13	13	3	5-1	9	.339
1999—Kansas City (A.L.)	9	9	.500	4.87	1.45	22	22	1	0	0	0-0	140.1	153	81	76	18	51-3	78	.279
—Oakland (A.L.)	7	5	.583	5.77	1.60	12	12	0	0	0	0-0	68.2	77	50	44	9	33-1	53	.280
2000—Oakland (A.L.)	15	11	.577	4.52	1.55	31	31	1	1	0	0-0	195.1	200	109	98	23 *	102-10	129	.262
2001—New York (N.L.)	11	10	.524	3.57	1.19	33	33	1	1	0	0-0	206.2	181	89	82	22	64-4	172	.237
2002—Anaheim (A.L.)	14	12	.538	3.92	1.32	32	32	0	0	0	0-0	188.1	191	89	82	23	64-4	132	.267
2003—Anaheim (A.L.)	7	7	.500	5.63	1.52	19	19	0	0	0	0-0	92.2	105	60	58	17	36-4	50	.279
—Kansas City (A.L.)	1	2	.333	4.26	1.16	4	4	0	0	0	0-0	19.0	15	9	9	4	7-0	5	.217
2004—Kansas City (A.L.)	0	1	.000	13.50	2.50	2	2	0	0	0	0-0	4.0	7	8	6	0	3-0	2	.368
—Wichita (Texas)	0	0	...	4.91	1.57	4	4	0	0	...	0-...	14.2	19	9	8	1	4-0	3	.306
—Omaha (PCL)	0	0	...	6.75	2.25	1	1	0	0	...	0-...	4.0	7	3	3	1	2-0	2	.438
American League totals (15 years)	158	127	.554	3.75	1.30	381	369	33	11	1	0-0	2388.2	2244	1079	996	210	869-47	1822	.248
National League totals (1 year)	11	10	.524	3.57	1.19	33	33	1	1	0	0-0	206.2	181	89	82	22	64-4	172	.237
Major League totals (16 years)	169	137	.552	3.74	1.29	414	402	34	12	1	0-0	2595.1	2425	1168	1078	232	933-51	1994	.247

DIVISION SERIES RECORD

Year Team (League)	W	L	Pct.	ERA	WHIP	G	GS	CG	ShO	Hld.	Sv.-Opp.	IP	H	R	ER	HR	BB-IBB	SO	Avg.
2000—Oakland (A.L.)	0	1	.000	3.48	1.55	2	1	0	0	0	0-0	10.1	10	4	4	1	6-1	13	.250
2002—Anaheim (A.L.)	0	0	...	5.40	1.60	1	1	0	0	0	0-0	5.0	5	3	3	1	3-0	3	.250
Division series totals (2 years)	0	1	.000	4.11	1.57	3	2	0	0	0	0-0	15.1	15	7	7	2	9-1	16	.250

CHAMPIONSHIP SERIES RECORD

Year Team (League)	W	L	Pct.	ERA	WHIP	G	GS	CG	ShO	Hld.	Sv.-Opp.	IP	H	R	ER	HR	BB-IBB	SO	Avg.
2002— Anaheim (A.L.)	0	1	.000	3.48	1.35	2	2	0	0	0	0-0	10.1	10	4	4	0	4-0	3	.278

WORLD SERIES RECORD

Year Team (League)	W	L	Pct.	ERA	WHIP	G	GS	CG	ShO	Hld.	Sv.-Opp.	IP	H	R	ER	HR	BB-IBB	SO	Avg.
2002— Anaheim (A.L.)	0	0	...	11.37	2.21	2	2	0	0	0	0-0	6.1	9	8	8	4	5-1	4	.333

ALL-STAR GAME RECORD

	W	L	Pct.	ERA	WHIP	G	GS	CG	ShO	Hld.	Sv.-Opp.	IP	H	R	ER	HR	BB-IBB	SO	Avg.
All-Star Game totals (1 year)	0	0	...	0.00	0.00	1	0	0	0	0	0-0	2.0	0	0	0	0	0-0	1	.000

AQUINO, GREG   P

PERSONAL: Born January 11, 1978, in Palenque, Dominican Republic. ... 6-1/188. ... Throws right, bats right. ... Full name: Gregori Emilio Aquino. ... High school: Americo Lugo (Santo Domingo, D.R.).

TRANSACTIONS/CAREER NOTES: Signed as a non-drafted free agent by Arizona Diamondbacks organization (November 8, 1995). ... Played four seasons as an infielder in Diamondbacks organization (1996-99).

CAREER HITTING: 0-for-1 (.000), 0 R, 0 2B, 0 3B, 0 HR, 0 RBI.

Year Team (League)	W	L	Pct.	ERA	WHIP	G	GS	CG	ShO	Hld.	Sv.-Opp.	IP	H	R	ER	HR	BB-IBB	SO	Avg.
1999— Ariz. D'backs (Ariz.)	1	2	.333	3.79	1.58	13	2	0	0	...	0-...	19.0	17	11	8	0	13-0	20	.246
2000— South Bend (Mid.)	5	7	.417	4.46	1.47	29	18	0	0	...	0-...	119.0	119	67	59	9	56-0	93	.260
2001— Lancaster (Calif.)	2	5	.286	8.14	1.98	25	4	0	0	...	0-...	42.0	59	40	38	7	24-0	39	.331
— Yakima (N'west)	4	2	.667	3.30	1.14	8	8	0	0	...	0-...	46.1	39	18	17	2	14-1	39	.229
2002— Yakima (N'west)	1	1	.500	2.06	1.23	6	6	0	0	...	0-...	35.0	26	9	8	0	17-0	34	.213
— Lancaster (Calif.)	4	1	.800	3.67	1.39	8	8	0	0	...	0-...	49.0	50	20	20	3	18-0	50	.267
2003— El Paso (Texas)	7	3	.700	3.46	1.43	20	20	0	0	...	0-...	106.2	115	43	41	5	38-1	91	.278
2004— Tucson (PCL)	1	3	.250	6.37	1.72	21	2	0	0	...	1-...	29.2	33	25	21	2	18-0	19	.270
— Arizona (N.L.)	0	2	.000	3.06	1.16	34	0	0	0	1	16-19	35.1	24	15	12	4	17-2	26	.194
Major League totals (1 year)	0	2	.000	3.06	1.16	34	0	0	0	1	16-19	35.1	24	15	12	4	17-2	26	.194

ARDOIN, DANNY   C

PERSONAL: Born July 8, 1974, in Ville Platte, La. ... 6-0/218. ... Bats right, throws right. ... Full name: Daniel Wayne Ardoin. ... Name pronounced: ar-DWAH. ... High school: Sacred Heart (Ville Platte, La.). ... College: McNeese State.

TRANSACTIONS/CAREER NOTES: Selected by Boston Red Sox organization in 41st round of 1993 free-agent draft; did not sign. ... Selected by Cleveland Indians organization in 39th round of 1994 free-agent draft; did not sign. ... Selected by Oakland Athletics organization in fifth round of 1995 free-agent draft. ... On disabled list (July 27-August 4, 1998). ... Traded by A's to Minnesota Twins for 1B/OF Mario Valdez (July 31, 2000). ... Signed as a free agent by Kansas City Royals organization (December 22, 2001). ... Released by Royals (May 16, 2002). ... Signed as a free agent by Texas Rangers organization (May 17, 2002).

2004 GAMES PLAYED BY POSITION (MLB): C—6.

Year Team (League)	Pos.	G	AB	R	H	2B	3B	HR	RBI	BB	SO	HBP	GDP	SB-CS	Avg.	OBP	SLG	OPS	E	
1995— S. Oregon (N'west)	C	58	175	28	41	9	1	2	23	31	50	9	2	2-1	.234	.370	.331	.701	14	.971
1996— Modesto (California)	3B-C-1B	91	317	55	83	13	3	6	34	47	81	9	9	5-7	.262	.371	.379	.749	21	.968
1997— Visalia (Calif.)	3B-C-1B-OF	43	145	16	34	7	1	3	19	21	39	4	3	0-1	.234	.347	.359	.706	5	.987
— Huntsville (Sou.)	3B-C	57	208	26	48	10	1	4	23	17	38	3	7	2-3	.231	.296	.346	.642	10	.972
1998— Huntsville (Sou.)	C-1B-OF	109	363	67	90	21	0	16	62	62	87	7	10	8-4	.248	.367	.438	.805	12	.982
1999— Vancouver (PCL)	C-3B-1B	109	336	53	85	13	2	8	46	50	78	9	12	3-3	.253	.364	.375	.739	10	.984
2000— Sacramento (PCL)	C-1B-3B	67	234	42	65	16	1	6	34	34	72	8	5	6-0	.278	.385	.432	.817	8	.980
— Modesto (California)	C	4	10	1	3	1	0	0	2	0	4	1	0	0-0	.300	.364	.400	.764	1	.960
— Salt Lake (PCL)	C	3	9	1	2	0	0	0	0	3	4	0	0	0-0	.222	.417	.222	.639	0	1.000
— Minnesota (A.L.)	C	15	32	4	4	1	0	1	5	8	10	0	0	0-0	.125	.300	.250	.550	1	.989
2001— Edmonton (PCL)	C-OF	88	302	37	77	18	1	5	37	22	81	1	8	2-6	.255	.304	.371	.675	6	.989
2002— Omaha (PCL)	C-1B	25	77	10	16	3	0	3	10	11	25	0	0	1-0	.208	.297	.364	.660	3	.984
— Tulsa (Texas)	C	8	21	1	3	0	0	0	0	4	9	0	1	0-0	.143	.280	.143	.423	1	1.000
— Oklahoma (PCL)	C-OF	33	106	10	24	5	0	2	11	10	31	2	2	0-0	.226	.303	.330	.633	4	.984
2003— Oklahoma (PCL)	C-3B-DH	74	239	35	58	11	2	7	35	21	58	3	9	0-2	.243	.311	.393	.704	10	.973
2004— Texas (A.L.)	C	6	8	1	1	0	0	0	1	3	2	0	0	0-0	.125	.364	.125	.489	1	.958
— Oklahoma (PCL)	C	68	237	50	73	12	0	10	44	41	66	8	9	1-1	.308	.422	.485	.907	11	.976
Major League totals (2 years)		21	40	5	5	1	0	1	6	11	12	0	0	0-0	.125	.314	.225	.539	2	.982

ARMAS, TONY   P

PERSONAL: Born April 29, 1978, in Puerto Piritu, Venezuela. ... 6-3/225. ... Throws right, bats right. ... Full name: Antonio Jose Armas. ... Name pronounced: ar-MUS. ... Son of Tony Armas, outfielder with four major league teams (1976-89); nephew of Marcos Armas, outfielder with Oakland Athletics (1993).

TRANSACTIONS/CAREER NOTES: Signed as a non-drafted free agent by New York Yankees organization (August 16, 1994). ... Traded by Yankees with a player to be named to Boston Red Sox for C Mike Stanley and SS Randy Brown (August 13, 1997); Red Sox acquired P Jim Mecir to complete deal (September 29, 1997). ... Traded by Red Sox to Montreal Expos (December 18, 1997), completing deal in which Red Sox traded P Carl Pavano and a player to be named to Expos for P Pedro Martinez (November 18, 1997). ... On disabled list (April 1-28 and July 19-September 6, 2000); included rehabilitation assignments to Jupiter and Ottawa. ... On disabled list (July 27-August 19, 2002; and April 21, 2003-remainder of season). ... On disabled list (March 26-May 31, 2004); included rehabilitation assignments to Brevard County and Edmonton. ... Expos franchise transferred to Washington, D.C., for 2005 season.

CAREER HITTING: 16-for-157 (.102), 4 R, 1 2B, 1 3B, 0 HR, 7 RBI.

Year Team (League)	W	L	Pct.	ERA	WHIP	G	GS	CG	ShO	Hld.	Sv.-Opp.	IP	H	R	ER	HR	BB-IBB	SO	Avg.
1995— GC Yankees (GCL)	0	1	.000	0.64	1.29	5	4	0	0	...	0-...	14.0	12	9	1	1	6-0	13	.226
1996— Oneonta (N.Y.-Penn)	1	1	.500	5.74	1.60	3	3	0	0	...	0-...	15.2	14	12	10	1	11-0	14	.230
— GC Yankees (GCL)	4	1	.800	3.15	1.18	8	7	0	0	...	1-...	45.2	41	18	16	1	13-0	45	.236
1997— Greensboro (S. Atl.)	5	2	.714	1.05	0.95	9	9	2	1	...	0-...	51.2	36	13	6	3	13-0	64	.190
— Tampa (FSL)	3	1	.750	3.33	1.28	9	9	0	0	...	0-...	46.0	43	23	17	1	16-3	26	.257
— Sarasota (Florida State)	2	1	.667	6.62	1.70	3	3	0	0	...	0-...	17.2	18	13	13	2	12-0	9	.281
1998— Jupiter (FSL)	12	8	.600	2.88	1.30	27	27	1	1	...	0-...	153.1	140	63	49	11	59-0	136	.244
1999— Harrisburg (Eastern)	9	7	.563	2.89	1.19	24	24	2	1	...	0-...	149.2	123	62	48	10	55-0	106	.226
— Montreal (N.L.)	0	1	.000	1.50	1.67	1	1	0	0	...	0-0	6.0	8	4	1	0	2-1	2	.320
2000— Jupiter (FSL)	0	0	...	0.00	0.86	1	1	0	0	...	0-...	4.2	4	0	0	0	0-0	8	.222
— Ottawa (Int'l)	1	2	.333	3.79	1.37	4	4	0	0	...	0-...	19.0	22	11	8	3	4-0	12	.286
— Montreal (N.L.)	7	9	.438	4.36	1.31	17	17	0	0	...	0-0	95.0	74	49	46	10	50-2	59	.218

Year Team (League)	W	L	Pct.	ERA	WHIP	G	GS	CG	ShO	Hld.	Sv.-Opp.	IP	H	R	ER	HR	BB-IBB	SO	Avg.
2001— Montreal (N.L.)	9	14	.391	4.03	1.38	34	34	0	0	0	0-0	196.2	180	101	88	18	91-6	176	.247
2002— Montreal (N.L.)	12	12	.500	4.44	1.38	29	29	0	0	0	0-0	164.1	149	87	81	22	78-12	131	.243
2003— Montreal (N.L.)	2	1	.667	2.61	1.06	5	5	0	0	0	0-0	31.0	25	9	9	4	8-0	23	.225
2004— Brevard County (FSL)	0	1	.000	6.75	1.29	3	3	0	0	...	0-...	9.1	5	7	7	1	7-0	7	.179
— Edmonton (PCL)	0	0	...	1.80	1.20	2	2	0	0	...	0-...	10.0	11	4	2	0	1-0	8	.268
— Montreal (N.L.)	2	4	.333	4.88	1.54	16	16	0	0	0	0-0	72.0	66	41	39	13	45-6	54	.247
Major League totals (6 years)	32	41	.438	4.21	1.37	102	102	0	0	0	0-0	565.0	502	291	264	67	274-27	445	.241

ARROYO, BRONSON   P

PERSONAL: Born February 24, 1977, in Key West, Fla. ... 6-5/190. ... Throws right, bats right. ... Full name: Bronson Anthony Arroyo. ... Name pronounced: ah-ROY-yoh. ... High school: Hernando (Fla.).

TRANSACTIONS/CAREER NOTES: Selected by Pittsburgh Pirates organization in third round of 1995 free-agent draft. ... Claimed on waivers by Boston Red Sox (February 4, 2003).

CAREER HITTING: 4-for-54 (.074), 2 R, 2 2B, 0 3B, 0 HR, 1 RBI.

Year Team (League)	W	L	Pct.	ERA	WHIP	G	GS	CG	ShO	Hld.	Sv.-Opp.	IP	H	R	ER	HR	BB-IBB	SO	Avg.
1995— GC Pirates (GCL)	5	4	.556	4.26	1.32	13	9	0	0	...	1-...	61.1	72	39	29	4	9-0	48	.277
1996— Augusta (S. Atl.)	8	6	.571	3.52	1.17	26	26	0	0	...	0-...	135.2	123	64	53	11	36-0	107	.242
1997— Lynchburg (Carolina)	12	4	.750	3.31	1.17	24	24	3	1	...	0-...	160.1	154	69	59	17	33-0	121	.250
1998— Carolina (Southern)	9	8	.529	5.46	1.65	23	22	1	0	...	0-...	127.0	158	91	77	18	51-0	90	.310
1999— Altoona (East.)	15	4	.789	3.65	1.47	25	25	2	1	...	0-...	153.0	167	73	62	15	58-1	100	.280
— Nashville (PCL)	0	2	.000	10.38	2.46	3	3	0	0	...	0-...	13.0	22	15	15	1	10-0	11	.367
2000— Nashville (PCL)	8	2	.800	3.65	1.21	13	13	1	0	...	0-...	88.2	82	43	36	7	25-3	52	.251
— Pittsburgh (N.L.)	2	6	.250	6.40	1.73	20	12	0	0	0	0-0	71.2	88	61	51	10	36-6	50	.302
— Lynchburg (Carolina)	0	0	...	3.86	1.43	1	1	0	0	...	0-...	7.0	8	3	3	0	2-0	3	.267
2001— Pittsburgh (N.L.)	5	7	.417	5.09	1.51	24	13	1	0	2	0-0	88.1	99	54	50	12	34-6	39	.289
— Nashville (PCL)	6	2	.750	3.93	1.18	9	9	2	1	...	0-...	66.1	63	32	29	6	15-1	49	.247
2002— Nashville (PCL)	8	6	.571	2.96	1.08	22	21	3	2	...	0-...	143.0	126	57	47	10	28-1	116	.236
— Pittsburgh (N.L.)	2	1	.667	4.00	1.67	9	4	0	0	1	0-0	27.0	30	14	12	1	15-3	22	.283
2003— Pawtucket (Int'l)	12	6	.667	3.43	1.10	24	24	1	1	...	0-...	149.2	148	66	57	9	23-0	155	.252
— Boston (A.L.)	0	0	...	2.08	0.81	6	0	0	0	0	1-1	17.1	10	5	4	0	4-2	14	.164
2004— Boston (A.L.)	10	9	.526	4.03	1.22	32	29	0	0	0	0-0	178.2	171	99	80	17	47-3	142	.249
American League totals (2 years)	10	9	.526	3.86	1.18	38	29	0	0	0	1-1	196.0	181	104	84	17	51-5	156	.242
National League totals (3 years)	9	14	.391	5.44	1.61	53	29	1	0	3	0-0	187.0	217	129	113	23	85-15	111	.294
Major League totals (5 years)	19	23	.452	4.63	1.39	91	58	1	0	3	1-1	383.0	398	233	197	40	136-20	267	.267

DIVISION SERIES RECORD

Year Team (League)	W	L	Pct.	ERA	WHIP	G	GS	CG	ShO	Hld.	Sv.-Opp.	IP	H	R	ER	HR	BB-IBB	SO	Avg.
2004— Boston (A.L.)	0	0	...	3.00	0.83	1	1	0	0	0	0-0	6.0	3	2	2	1	2-0	7	.143

CHAMPIONSHIP SERIES RECORD

Year Team (League)	W	L	Pct.	ERA	WHIP	G	GS	CG	ShO	Hld.	Sv.-Opp.	IP	H	R	ER	HR	BB-IBB	SO	Avg.
2003— Boston (A.L.)	0	0	...	2.70	1.20	3	0	0	0	0	0-0	3.1	2	1	1	1	2-0	5	.167
2004— Boston (A.L.)	0	0	...	15.75	2.50	3	1	0	0	1	0-0	4.0	8	7	7	2	2-0	3	.421
Champ. series totals (2 years)	0	0	...	9.82	1.91	6	1	0	0	1	0-0	7.1	10	8	8	3	4-0	8	.323

WORLD SERIES RECORD

Year Team (League)	W	L	Pct.	ERA	WHIP	G	GS	CG	ShO	Hld.	Sv.-Opp.	IP	H	R	ER	HR	BB-IBB	SO	Avg.
2004— Boston (A.L.)	0	0	...	6.75	1.88	2	0	0	0	1	0-0	2.2	4	2	2	0	1-0	4	.333

ASHBY, ANDY   P

PERSONAL: Born July 11, 1967, in Kansas City, Mo. ... 6-1/202. ... Throws right, bats right. ... Full name: Andrew Jason Ashby. ... High school: Park Hill (Kansas City, Mo.). ... Junior college: Crowder (Mo.).

TRANSACTIONS/CAREER NOTES: Signed as a non-drafted free agent by Philadelphia Phillies organization (May 4, 1986). ... On disabled list (April 27-August 11, 1992); included rehabilitation assignments to Scranton/Wilkes-Barre. ... Selected by Colorado Rockies in first round (25th pick overall) of expansion draft (November 17, 1992). ... Traded by Rockies to San Diego Padres (July 27, 1993), completing deal in which Padres traded Ps Bruce Hurst and Greg W. Harris to Rockies for C Brad Ausmus, P Doug Bochtler and a player to be named (July 26, 1993). ... On disabled list (June 6-22, June 29-July 15 and July 27-September 1, 1996; May 20-June 15, 1997; and June 7-24, 1999). ... Traded by Padres to Phillies for Ps Carlton Loewer, Steve Montgomery and Adam Eaton (November 10, 1999). ... On disabled list (June 12-27, 2000). ... Traded by Phillies to Atlanta Braves for Ps Bruce Chen and Jimmy Osting (July 12, 2000). ... Signed as a free agent by Los Angeles Dodgers (December 6, 2000). ... On disabled list (April 16, 2001-remainder of season). ... Signed as a free agent by Padres organization (March 18, 2004).

CAREER HITTING: 70-for-521 (.134), 26 R, 13 2B, 2 3B, 1 HR, 26 RBI.

Year Team (League)	W	L	Pct.	ERA	WHIP	G	GS	CG	ShO	Hld.	Sv.-Opp.	IP	H	R	ER	HR	BB-IBB	SO	Avg.
1986— Bend (N'west)	1	2	.333	4.95	1.50	16	6	0	0	...	2-...	60.0	56	40	33	3	34-1	45	...
1987— Spartanburg (SAL)	4	6	.400	5.60	1.73	13	13	1	0	...	0-...	64.1	73	45	40	8	38-2	52	.284
— Utica (N.Y.-Penn)	3	7	.300	4.05	1.53	13	13	0	0	...	0-...	60.0	56	38	27	3	36-3	51	.250
1988— Spartanburg (SAL)	1	1	.500	2.70	1.20	3	3	0	0	...	0-...	16.2	13	7	5	0	7-0	16	.213
— Batavia (N.Y.-Penn)	3	1	.750	1.61	0.92	6	6	2	1	...	0-...	44.2	25	11	8	3	16-0	32	.161
1989— Spartanburg (SAL)	5	9	.357	2.87	1.35	17	17	3	1	...	0-...	106.2	95	48	34	8	49-0	100	.234
— Clearwater (Fla. St.)	1	4	.200	1.24	1.12	6	6	2	1	...	0-...	43.2	28	9	6	0	21-0	44	.185
1990— Reading (East.)	10	7	.588	3.42	1.30	23	23	4	1	...	0-...	139.2	134	65	53	3	48-0	94	.253
1991— Scran./W.B. (I.L.)	11	11	.500	3.46	1.26	26	26	6	3	...	0-...	161.1	144	78	62	12	60-2	113	.235
— Philadelphia (N.L.)	1	5	.167	6.00	1.43	8	8	0	0	0	0-0	42.0	41	28	28	5	19-0	26	.256
1992— Philadelphia (N.L.)	1	3	.250	7.54	1.70	10	8	0	0	0	0-0	37.0	42	31	31	6	21-0	24	.290
— Scran./W.B. (I.L.)	0	3	.000	3.00	1.12	7	7	1	0	...	0-...	33.0	23	13	11	4	14-0	18	.202
1993— Colorado (N.L.)	0	4	.000	8.50	2.24	20	9	0	0	0	1-1	54.0	89	54	51	5	32-4	33	.377
— Colo. Springs (PCL)	4	2	.667	4.10	1.37	7	6	1	0	...	0-...	41.2	45	25	19	2	12-0	35	.276
— San Diego (N.L.)	3	6	.333	5.48	1.49	12	12	0	0	0	0-0	69.0	79	46	42	14	24-1	44	.295
1994— San Diego (N.L.)	6	11	.353	3.40	1.14	24	24	4	0	0	0-0	164.1	145	75	62	16	43-12	121	.233
1995— San Diego (N.L.)	12	10	.545	2.94	1.26	31	•31	2	2	0	0-0	192.2	180	79	63	17	62-3	150	.253
1996— San Diego (N.L.)	9	5	.643	3.23	1.20	24	24	1	0	0	0-0	150.2	147	60	54	17	34-1	85	.259
1997— San Diego (N.L.)	9	11	.450	4.13	1.28	30	30	2	0	0	0-0	200.2	207	108	92	17	49-2	144	.266
1998— San Diego (N.L.)	17	9	.654	3.34	1.24	33	33	5	1	0	0-0	226.2	223	90	84	23	58-8	151	.259
1999— San Diego (N.L.)	14	10	.583	3.80	1.25	31	31	4	* 3	0	0-0	206.0	204	95	87	26	54-4	132	.258
2000— Philadelphia (N.L.)	4	7	.364	5.68	1.49	16	16	1	0	0	0-0	101.1	113	75	64	17	38-5	51	.288

Year — Team (League)	W	L	Pct.	ERA	WHIP	G	GS	CG	ShO	Hld.	Sv.-Opp.	IP	H	R	ER	HR	BB-IBB	SO	Avg.
—Atlanta (N.L.)	8	6	.571	4.13	1.29	15	15	2	1	0	0-0	98.0	103	49	45	12	23-4	55	.271
2001—Los Angeles (N.L.)	2	0	1.000	3.86	1.29	2	2	0	0	0	0-0	11.2	14	5	5	2	1-0	7	.292
2002—Los Angeles (N.L.)	9	13	.409	3.91	1.34	30	30	0	0	0	0-0	181.2	179	85	79	20	65-3	107	.261
2003—Los Angeles (N.L.)	3	10	.231	5.18	1.47	21	12	0	0	0	0-0	73.0	90	42	42	8	17-2	41	.311
2004—San Diego (N.L.)	0	0	...	0.00	0.50	2	0	0	0	0	0-0	2.0	1	0	0	0	0-0	2	.143
Major League totals (14 years)	98	110	.471	4.12	1.32	309	285	21	7	0	1-1	1810.2	1857	922	829	205	540-49	1173	.268

DIVISION SERIES RECORD

Year — Team (League)	W	L	Pct.	ERA	WHIP	G	GS	CG	ShO	Hld.	Sv.-Opp.	IP	H	R	ER	HR	BB-IBB	SO	Avg.
1996—San Diego (N.L.)	0	0	...	6.75	1.50	1	1	0	0	0	0-0	5.1	7	4	4	1	1-0	5	.304
1998—San Diego (N.L.)	0	0	...	6.75	1.75	1	1	0	0	0	0-0	4.0	6	3	3	0	1-0	4	.353
2000—Atlanta (N.L.)	0	0	...	2.45	1.09	2	0	0	0	0	0-0	3.2	1	1	1	0	3-2	5	.083
Division series totals (3 years)	0	0	...	5.54	1.46	4	2	0	0	0	0-0	13.0	14	8	8	1	5-2	14	.269

CHAMPIONSHIP SERIES RECORD

Year — Team (League)	W	L	Pct.	ERA	WHIP	G	GS	CG	ShO	Hld.	Sv.-Opp.	IP	H	R	ER	HR	BB-IBB	SO	Avg.
1998—San Diego (N.L.)	0	0	...	2.08	1.23	2	2	0	0	0	0-0	13.0	14	3	3	1	2-0	5	.280

WORLD SERIES RECORD

Year — Team (League)	W	L	Pct.	ERA	WHIP	G	GS	CG	ShO	Hld.	Sv.-Opp.	IP	H	R	ER	HR	BB-IBB	SO	Avg.
1998—San Diego (N.L.)	0	1	.000	13.50	4.13	1	1	0	0	0	0-0	2.2	10	7	4	1	1-0	1	.588

ALL-STAR GAME RECORD

	W	L	Pct.	ERA	WHIP	G	GS	CG	ShO	Hld.	Sv.-Opp.	IP	H	R	ER	HR	BB-IBB	SO	Avg.
All-Star Game totals (2 years)	0	0	...	6.75	1.50	2	0	0	0	0	0-0	1.1	1	1	1	1	1-0	0	.200

ASTACIO, PEDRO — P

PERSONAL: Born November 28, 1969, in Hato Mayor, Dominican Republic. ... 6-2/210. ... Throws right, bats right. ... Full name: Pedro Julio Astacio. ... Name pronounced: ah-STAH-see-oh. ... High school: Pilar Rondon (Dominican Republic).

TRANSACTIONS/CAREER NOTES: Signed as a non-drafted free agent by Los Angeles Dodgers organization (November 21, 1987). ... Traded by Dodgers to Colorado Rockies for 2B Eric Young (August 19, 1997). ... Traded by Rockies to Houston Astros for P Scott Elarton and a player to be named (July 31, 2001); Rockies acquired P Garrett Gentry to complete deal (September 27, 2001). ... On disabled list (August 29, 2001-remainder of season). ... Signed as a free agent by New York Mets (January 16, 2002). ... On disabled list (March 21-April 24 and May 22, 2003-remainder of season); included rehabilitation assignment to St. Lucie. ... Signed as a free agent by Boston Red Sox organization (June 30, 2004). ... On suspended list (September 29-October 2, 2004).

CAREER HITTING: 84-for-635 (.132), 28 R, 8 2B, 1 3B, 0 HR, 27 RBI.

Year — Team (League)	W	L	Pct.	ERA	WHIP	G	GS	CG	ShO	Hld.	Sv.-Opp.	IP	H	R	ER	HR	BB-IBB	SO	Avg.
1988—Dom. Dodgers (DSL)	4	2	.667	2.08	1.28	8	7	1	...	...	0-...	47.2	43	21	11	...	18-...	20	...
1989—GC Dodgers (GCL)	7	3	.700	3.17	1.16	12	12	1	1	...	0-...	76.2	77	30	27	3	12-0	52	.258
1990—Vero Beach (FSL)	1	5	.167	6.32	1.64	8	8	0	0	...	0-...	47.0	54	39	33	3	23-0	41	.286
—Yakima (N'west)	2	0	1.000	1.74	0.63	3	3	0	0	...	0-...	20.2	9	8	4	0	4-0	22	.123
—Bakersfield (California)	5	2	.714	2.77	1.17	10	7	1	0	...	0-...	52.0	46	22	16	3	15-1	34	.238
1991—Vero Beach (FSL)	5	3	.625	1.67	0.88	9	9	3	1	...	0-...	59.1	44	19	11	0	8-0	45	.209
—San Antonio (Texas)	4	11	.267	4.78	1.60	19	19	2	1	...	0-...	113.0	142	67	60	9	39-3	62	.318
1992—Albuquerque (PCL)	6	6	.500	5.47	1.61	24	15	1	0	...	0-...	98.2	115	68	60	8	44-1	66	.293
—Los Angeles (N.L.)	5	5	.500	1.98	1.22	11	11	4	4	0	0-0	82.0	80	23	18	1	20-4	43	.255
1993—Los Angeles (N.L.)	14	9	.609	3.57	1.25	31	31	3	2	0	0-0	186.1	165	80	74	14	68-5	122	.239
1994—Los Angeles (N.L.)	6	8	.429	4.29	1.27	23	23	3	1	0	0-0	149.0	142	77	71	18	47-4	108	.252
1995—Los Angeles (N.L.)	7	8	.467	4.24	1.27	48	11	1	1	2	0-1	104.0	103	53	49	12	29-5	80	.261
1996—Los Angeles (N.L.)	9	8	.529	3.44	1.29	35	32	0	0	0	0-0	211.2	207	86	81	18	67-9	130	.261
1997—Los Angeles (N.L.)	7	9	.438	4.10	1.29	26	24	2	1	0	0-0	153.2	151	75	70	15	47-0	115	.256
—Colorado (N.L.)	5	1	.833	4.25	1.29	7	7	0	0	0	0-0	48.2	49	23	23	9	14-0	51	.262
1998—Colorado (N.L.)	13	14	.481	6.23	1.52	35	34	0	0	0	0-0	209.1	245	*160	*145	*39	74-0	170	.294
1999—Colorado (N.L.)	17	11	.607	5.04	1.44	34	34	7	0	0	0-0	232.0	258	140	130	*38	75-6	210	.285
2000—Colorado (N.L.)	12	9	.571	5.27	1.50	32	32	3	0	0	0-0	196.1	217	119	115	30	77-5	193	.281
2001—Colorado (N.L.)	6	13	.316	5.49	1.43	22	22	4	1	0	0-0	141.0	151	91	86	21	50-3	125	.276
—Houston (N.L.)	2	1	.667	3.14	1.19	4	4	0	0	0	0-0	28.2	30	10	10	1	4-0	19	.280
2002—New York (N.L.)	12	11	.522	4.79	1.33	31	31	3	1	0	0-0	191.2	192	106	102	*32	63-5	152	.262
2003—St. Lucie (Fla. St.)	0	2	.000	2.08	1.00	4	4	0	0	...	0-...	17.1	15	6	4	0	3-0	15	.231
—New York (N.L.)	3	2	.600	7.36	1.77	7	7	0	0	0	0-0	36.2	47	30	30	8	18-1	20	.311
2004—GC Red Sox (GCL)	1	0	1.000	0.00	0.90	2	1	0	0	0	0-...	4.2	4	3	0	0	0-0	6	.211
—Portland (East.)	0	0	...	0.00	1.00	1	1	0	0	0	0-...	4.0	3	0	0	0	1-0	4	.214
—Pawtucket (Int'l)	0	1	.000	2.89	1.07	2	2	0	0	0	0-...	9.1	9	4	3	1	1-0	7	.250
—Boston (A.L.)	0	0	...	10.38	2.08	5	1	0	0	0	0-0	8.2	13	10	10	2	5-0	6	.342
American League totals (1 year)	0	0	...	10.38	2.08	5	1	0	0	0	0-0	8.2	13	10	10	2	5-0	6	.342
National League totals (12 years)	118	109	.520	4.58	1.36	346	303	30	11	2	0-1	1971.0	2037	1073	1004	258	653-47	1538	.269
Major League totals (13 years)	118	109	.520	4.61	1.37	351	304	30	11	2	0-1	1979.2	2050	1083	1014	260	658-47	1544	.269

DIVISION SERIES RECORD

Year — Team (League)	W	L	Pct.	ERA	WHIP	G	GS	CG	ShO	Hld.	Sv.-Opp.	IP	H	R	ER	HR	BB-IBB	SO	Avg.
1995—Los Angeles (N.L.)	0	0	...	0.00	0.30	3	0	0	0	0	0-0	3.1	1	0	0	0	0-0	5	.091
1996—Los Angeles (N.L.)	0	0	...	0.00	0.00	1	0	0	0	0	0-0	1.2	0	0	0	0	0-0	1	.000
Division series totals (2 years)	0	0	...	0.00	0.20	4	0	0	0	0	0-0	5.0	1	0	0	0	0-0	6	.063

ATCHISON, SCOTT — P

PERSONAL: Born March 29, 1976, in Denton, Texas. ... 6-2/180. ... Throws right, bats right. ... Full name: Scott Barhan Atchison. ... High school: McCullough (Granbury, Texas). ... College: Texas Christian.

TRANSACTIONS/CAREER NOTES: Selected by Seattle Mariners organization in 36th round of 1994 free-agent draft; did not sign. ... Selected by Mariners organization in 49th round of 1998 free-agent draft.

CAREER HITTING: 0-for-0 (.000), 0 R, 0 2B, 0 3B, 0 HR, 0 RBI.

Year — Team (League)	W	L	Pct.	ERA	WHIP	G	GS	CG	ShO	Hld.	Sv.-Opp.	IP	H	R	ER	HR	BB-IBB	SO	Avg.
1999—Wisconsin (Midw.)	4	5	.444	3.42	1.13	15	13	0	0	...	0-...	81.2	67	34	31	4	25-1	85	.228
2000—Tacoma (PCL)	1	1	.500	3.81	1.08	5	5	0	0	...	0-...	26.0	22	11	11	3	6-0	18	.227
—Lancaster (Calif.)	5	5	.500	3.69	1.41	18	18	1	0	...	0-...	97.2	117	58	40	10	21-0	77	.289

Year Team (League)	W	L	Pct.	ERA	WHIP	G	GS	CG	ShO	Hld.	Sv.-Opp.	IP	H	R	ER	HR	BB-IBB	SO	Avg.
2001—San Antonio (Texas)	9	10	.474	4.24	1.46	24	24	1	0	...	0-...	136.0	171	84	64	11	28-0	83	.315
2002—Tacoma (PCL)	5	10	.333	4.63	1.24	27	21	1	1	...	2-...	124.1	123	68	64	13	31-0	112	.256
2003—Tacoma (PCL)	6	9	.400	4.31	1.39	39	7	0	0	...	1-...	108.2	114	57	52	8	37-2	83	.269
2004—Tacoma (PCL)	5	3	.625	4.15	1.40	40	1	0	0	...	7-...	69.1	71	35	32	8	26-2	76	.266
—Seattle (A.L.)	2	3	.400	3.52	1.40	25	0	0	0	2	0-0	30.2	29	12	12	4	14-2	36	.250
Major League totals (1 year)	2	3	.400	3.52	1.40	25	0	0	0	2	0-0	30.2	29	12	12	4	14-2	36	.250

ATKINS, GARRETT — 3B

PERSONAL: Born December 12, 1979, in Orange, Calif. ... 6-3/210. ... Bats right, throws right. ... Full name: Garrett Bernard Atkins. ... High school: University (Irvine, Calif.). ... College: UCLA.

TRANSACTIONS/CAREER NOTES: Selected by New York Mets organization in 10th round of 1997 free-agent draft; did not sign. ... Selected by Colorado Rockies organization in fifth round of 2000 free-agent draft.

2004 GAMES PLAYED BY POSITION (MLB): 3B—4, 1B—3, OF—3.

Year Team (League)	Pos.	G	AB	R	H	2B	3B	HR	RBI	BB	SO	HBP	GDP	SB-CS	Avg.	OBP	SLG	OPS	E	Avg.
2000—Portland (N'west)	1B-3B	69	251	34	76	12	0	7	47	45	48	2	3	2-0	.303	.411	.434	.846	6	.983
2001—Salem (Caro.)	1B-3B	135	465	70	151	43	5	5	67	74	98	8	8	6-4	.325	.421	.471	.892	7	.995
2002—Carolina (Southern)	3B-1B	128	510	71	138	27	3	12	61	59	77	2	12	6-6	.271	.345	.406	.751	19	.951
2003—Colo. Springs (PCL) 3B-DH-1B		118	439	80	140	30	1	13	67	45	52	3	9	2-4	.319	.382	.481	.863	20	.942
—Colorado (N.L.)	3B	25	69	6	11	2	0	0	4	3	14	1	1	0-0	.159	.205	.188	.394	6	.850
2004—Colo. Springs (PCL) 3B-1B-DH		122	445	88	163	43	3	15	94	57	45	4	20	0-0	.366	.434	.578	1.012	21	.933
—Colorado (N.L.) 3B-1B-OF		15	28	3	10	2	0	1	8	4	3	0	0	0-0	.357	.424	.536	.960	0	1.000
Major League totals (2 years)		40	97	9	21	4	0	1	12	7	17	1	1	0-0	.216	.274	.289	.562	6	.919

AURILIA, RICH — SS

PERSONAL: Born September 2, 1971, in Brooklyn, N.Y. ... 6-1/189. ... Bats right, throws right. ... Full name: Richard Santo Aurilia. ... Name pronounced: uh-REEL-yuh. ... High school: Xaverian (Brooklyn, N.Y.). ... College: St. John's.

TRANSACTIONS/CAREER NOTES: Selected by Texas Rangers organization in 24th round of 1992 free-agent draft. ... Traded by Rangers with IF/OF Desi Wilson to San Francisco Giants for P John Burkett (December 24, 1994). ... On disabled list (September 24, 1996-remainder of season; July 4-20, 1998; May 20-June 4, 2002; and August 4-19, 2003). ... Signed as a free agent by Seattle Mariners (January 9, 2004). ... Traded by Mariners to San Diego Padres for a player to be named (July 19, 2004).

2004 GAMES PLAYED BY POSITION (MLB): SS—79, 3B—29, 2B—7, 1B—1.

Year Team (League)	Pos.	G	AB	R	H	2B	3B	HR	RBI	BB	SO	HBP	GDP	SB-CS	Avg.	OBP	SLG	OPS	E	Avg.
1992—Butte (Pio.)	SS	59	202	37	68	11	3	3	30	42	18	0	2	13-9	.337	.447	.465	.913	14	.943
1993—Charlotte (Fla. St.)	SS	122	440	80	136	16	5	5	56	75	57	3	9	15-18	.309	.408	.402	.810	24	.964
1994—Tulsa (Texas)	SS	129	458	67	107	18	6	12	57	53	74	4	8	10-13	.234	.315	.378	.693	24	.962
1995—Shreveport (Texas)	SS	64	226	29	74	17	1	4	42	27	26	1	8	10-3	.327	.398	.465	.863	14	.962
—Phoenix (PCL)	SS	71	258	42	72	12	0	5	34	35	29	0	4	2-2	.279	.361	.384	.745	9	.975
—San Francisco (N.L.)	SS	9	19	4	9	3	0	2	4	1	2	0	1	1-0	.474	.476	.947	1.424	0	1.000
1996—Phoenix (PCL)	SS-2B	7	30	9	13	7	0	0	4	2	3	0	1	1-1	.433	.469	.667	1.135	1	.972
—San Francisco (N.L.)	SS-2B	105	318	27	76	7	1	3	26	25	52	1	1	4-1	.239	.295	.296	.590	10	.975
1997—San Francisco (N.L.)	SS	46	102	16	28	8	0	5	19	8	15	0	3	1-1	.275	.321	.500	.821	3	.979
—Phoenix (PCL)	SS	8	34	9	10	2	0	1	5	5	4	0	1	2-1	.294	.385	.441	.826	0	1.000
1998—San Francisco (N.L.)	SS	122	413	54	110	27	2	9	49	31	62	2	3	3-3	.266	.316	.407	.726	10	.979
1999—San Francisco (N.L.)	SS	152	558	68	157	23	1	22	80	43	71	5	16	2-3	.281	.336	.444	.780	28	.957
2000—San Francisco (N.L.)	SS	141	509	67	138	24	2	20	79	54	90	0	15	1-2	.271	.339	.444	.783	21	.967
2001—San Francisco (N.L.)	SS	156	636	114	206	37	5	37	97	47	83	0	14	1-3	.324	.369	.572	.941	17	.975
2002—San Francisco (N.L.)	SS	133	538	76	138	35	2	15	61	37	90	4	15	1-2	.257	.305	.413	.718	11	.980
2003—San Francisco (N.L.)	SS-DH	129	505	65	140	26	1	13	58	36	82	1	18	2-2	.277	.325	.410	.735	13	.974
2004—Seattle (A.L.)	SS	73	261	27	63	13	0	4	28	22	43	2	10	1-0	.241	.304	.337	.641	3	.990
—San Diego (N.L.) 3B-2B-SS-1B		51	138	22	35	8	2	2	16	15	28	2	2	0-0	.254	.331	.384	.715	7	.937
American League totals (1 year)		73	261	27	63	13	0	4	28	22	43	2	10	1-0	.241	.304	.337	.641	3	.990
National League totals (10 years)		1044	3736	513	1037	198	16	128	489	297	575	15	88	16-17	.278	.331	.442	.773	120	.971
Major League totals (10 years)		1117	3997	540	1100	211	16	132	517	319	618	17	98	17-17	.275	.329	.435	.764	123	.973

DIVISION SERIES RECORD

Year Team (League)	Pos.	G	AB	R	H	2B	3B	HR	RBI	BB	SO	HBP	GDP	SB-CS	Avg.	OBP	SLG	OPS	E	Avg.
2000—San Francisco (N.L.)	SS	4	15	0	2	1	0	0	0	0	3	0	0	0-0	.133	.133	.200	.333	1	.955
2002—San Francisco (N.L.)	SS	5	21	4	5	1	0	2	7	1	5	0	0	0-0	.238	.273	.571	.844	0	1.000
2003—San Francisco (N.L.)	SS	4	15	4	2	1	0	0	1	3	3	0	0	0-0	.133	.278	.200	.478	2	.926
Division series totals (3 years)		13	51	8	9	3	0	2	8	4	11	0	0	0-0	.176	.236	.353	.589	3	.958

CHAMPIONSHIP SERIES RECORD

Year Team (League)	Pos.	G	AB	R	H	2B	3B	HR	RBI	BB	SO	HBP	GDP	SB-CS	Avg.	OBP	SLG	OPS	E	Avg.
2002—San Francisco (N.L.)	SS	5	15	4	5	1	0	2	5	2	2	1	0	0-0	.333	.421	.800	1.221	1	.955

WORLD SERIES RECORD

Year Team (League)	Pos.	G	AB	R	H	2B	3B	HR	RBI	BB	SO	HBP	GDP	SB-CS	Avg.	OBP	SLG	OPS	E	Avg.
2002—San Francisco (N.L.)	SS	7	32	5	8	2	0	2	5	1	9	0	0	0-0	.250	.273	.500	.773	0	1.000

ALL-STAR GAME RECORD

		G	AB	R	H	2B	3B	HR	RBI	BB	SO	HBP	GDP	SB-CS	Avg.	OBP	SLG	OPS	E	Avg.
All-Star Game totals (1 year)		1	2	0	0	0	0	0	0	0	0	0	0	0-0	.000	.000	.000	.000	0	1.000

AUSMUS, BRAD — C

PERSONAL: Born April 14, 1969, in New Haven, Conn. ... 5-11/190. ... Bats right, throws right. ... Full name: Bradley David Ausmus. ... Name pronounced: AHHS-muss. ... High school: Cheshire (Conn.). ... College: Dartmouth.

TRANSACTIONS/CAREER NOTES: Selected by New York Yankees organization in 48th round of 1987 free-agent draft. ... Selected by Colorado Rockies in third round (54th pick overall) of expansion draft (November 17, 1992). ... Traded by Rockies with P Doug Bochtler and a player to be named to San Diego Padres for Ps Bruce Hurst and Greg W. Harris (July 26, 1993); Padres acquired P Andy Ashby to complete deal (July 27, 1993). ... Traded by Padres with SS Andujar Cedeno and P Russ Spear to Detroit Tigers for C John Flaherty and SS Chris Gomez (June 18, 1996). ... On suspended list (September 4-5, 1996). ... Traded by Tigers with Ps Jose Lima, C.J. Nitkowski and Trever Miller and IF Daryle Ward to Houston Astros for OF Brian L. Hunter, IF Orlando Miller, Ps Doug Brocail and Todd Jones and cash considerations (December 10, 1996). ...

Traded by Astros with P C.J. Nitkowski to Tigers for C Paul Bako, Ps Dean Crow, Mark Persails and Brian Powell and 3B Carlos Villalobos (January 14, 1999). ... Traded by Tigers with Ps Doug Brocail and Nelson Cruz to Astros for C Mitch Meluskey, P Chris Holt and OF Roger Cedeno (December 11, 2000).
HONORS: Won N.L. Gold Glove at catcher (2001 and 2002).
2004 GAMES PLAYED BY POSITION (MLB): C—128.

Year	Team (League)	Pos.	G	AB	R	H	2B	3B	HR	RBI	BB	SO	HBP	GDP	SB-CS	Avg.	OBP	SLG	OPS	E	Avg.
1988—	GC Yankees (GCL)	C	43	133	22	34	2	0	0	15	11	25	2	4	5-2	.256	.320	.271	.590	9	.979
—	Oneonta (N.Y.-PENN.)	C	2	4	0	1	0	0	0	0	0	2	0	1	0-0	.250	.250	.250	.500	0	...
1989—	Oneonta (N.Y.-Penn.)	3B-C	52	165	29	43	6	0	1	18	22	28	0	2	6-4	.261	.348	.315	.663	7	.984
1990—	Prince Will. (Car.)	C	107	364	46	86	12	2	0	27	32	73	3	7	2-8	.236	.303	.280	.583	5	.993
1991—	Prince Will. (Car.)	C	63	230	28	70	14	3	2	30	24	37	0	2	17-6	.304	.366	.417	.783	5	.990
—	Alb./Colon. (East.)	C	67	229	36	61	9	2	1	29	27	36	1	8	14-3	.266	.345	.336	.681	4	.992
1992—	Alb./Colon. (East.)	C	5	18	0	3	0	1	0	1	2	3	0	1	2-1	.167	.250	.278	.528	1	.970
—	Columbus (Int'l)	C-OF	111	364	48	88	14	3	2	35	40	56	1	14	19-5	.242	.317	.313	.630	9	.988
1993—	Colo. Springs (PCL)	C	76	241	31	65	10	4	2	33	27	41	1	6	10-6	.270	.342	.369	.711	6	.987
—	San Diego (N.L.)	C	49	160	18	41	8	1	5	12	6	28	0	2	2-0	.256	.283	.413	.696	8	.975
1994—	San Diego (N.L.)	C-1B	101	327	45	82	12	1	7	24	30	63	1	8	5-1	.251	.314	.358	.672	7	.991
1995—	San Diego (N.L.)	C-1B	103	328	44	96	16	4	5	34	31	56	2	6	16-5	.293	.353	.412	.765	6	.992
1996—	San Diego (N.L.)	C	50	149	16	27	4	0	1	13	13	27	3	4	1-4	.181	.261	.228	.489	6	.982
—	Detroit (A.L.)	C	75	226	30	56	12	0	4	22	26	45	2	4	3-4	.248	.328	.354	.682	4	.992
1997—	Houston (N.L.)	C	130	425	45	113	25	1	4	44	38	78	3	8	14-6	.266	.326	.358	.684	7	.992
1998—	Houston (N.L.)	C	128	412	62	111	10	4	6	45	53	60	3	18	10-3	.269	.356	.357	.713	7	.992
1999—	Detroit (A.L.)	C	127	458	62	126	25	6	9	54	51	71	14	11	12-9	.275	.365	.415	.779	2	.998
2000—	Detroit (A.L.)	C-2B-3B-1B	150	523	75	139	25	3	7	51	69	79	6	19	11-5	.266	.357	.365	.722	8	.992
2001—	Houston (N.L.)	C	128	422	45	98	23	4	5	34	30	64	1	13	4-1	.232	.284	.341	.625	3	.997
2002—	Houston (N.L.)	C	130	447	57	115	19	3	6	50	38	71	6	30	2-3	.257	.322	.353	.675	3	.997
2003—	Houston (N.L.)	C	143	450	43	103	12	2	4	47	46	66	4	8	5-3	.229	.303	.291	.594	3	.997
2004—	Houston (N.L.)	C	129	403	38	100	14	1	5	31	33	56	2	13	2-2	.248	.306	.325	.631	5	.995
American League totals (3 years)			352	1207	167	321	62	9	20	127	146	195	22	34	26-18	.266	.354	.382	.736	14	.994
National League totals (10 years)			1091	3523	413	886	143	21	48	334	318	569	25	110	61-28	.251	.316	.345	.661	55	.993
Major League totals (12 years)			1443	4730	580	1207	205	30	68	461	464	764	47	144	87-46	.255	.326	.354	.680	69	.993

DIVISION SERIES RECORD

Year	Team (League)	Pos.	G	AB	R	H	2B	3B	HR	RBI	BB	SO	HBP	GDP	SB-CS	Avg.	OBP	SLG	OPS	E	Avg.
1997—	Houston (N.L.)	C	2	5	1	2	1	0	0	2	0	1	0	1	0-0	.400	.400	.600	1.000	0	1.000
1998—	Houston (N.L.)	C	4	9	0	2	0	0	0	0	0	4	0	0	0-0	.222	.222	.222	.444	0	1.000
2001—	Houston (N.L.)	C	3	8	1	2	0	0	1	2	0	0	0	1	0-0	.250	.250	.625	.875	0	1.000
2004—	Houston (N.L.)	C	5	9	3	3	0	1	1	3	3	3	0	0	0-0	.333	.500	.667	1.167	0	1.000
Division series totals (4 years)			14	31	5	9	1	0	2	5	3	8	0	2	0-0	.290	.353	.516	.869	0	1.000

CHAMPIONSHIP SERIES RECORD

Year	Team (League)	Pos.	G	AB	R	H	2B	3B	HR	RBI	BB	SO	HBP	GDP	SB-CS	Avg.	OBP	SLG	OPS	E	Avg.
2004—	Houston (N.L.)	C	7	19	0	2	0	0	0	2	8	0	0	0-0	.105	.190	.105	.296	0	1.000

ALL-STAR GAME RECORD

	G	AB	R	H	2B	3B	HR	RBI	BB	SO	HBP	GDP	SB-CS	Avg.	OBP	SLG	OPS	E	Avg.
All-Star Game totals (1 year)	1	1	0	0	0	0	0	0	0	0	0	0	0-0	.000	.000	.000	.000	0	1.000

AYALA, LUIS — P

PERSONAL: Born January 12, 1978, in Los Mochis, Mexico. ... 6-2/186. ... Throws right, bats right. ... Full name: Luis Ignacio Ayala. ... Name pronounced: eye-YA-lah.
TRANSACTIONS/CAREER NOTES: Contract purchased by Colorado Rockies organization from Saltillo of the Mexican League (October 14, 1999). ... Loaned by Rockies organization to Saltillo (April 13, 2000-entire season). ... Contract sold by Rockies to Saltillo (May 15, 2001). ... Contract purchased by Montreal Expos from Saltillo (August 13, 2002). ... Signed as a free agent by Arizona Diamondbacks organization (October 23, 2002). ... Selected by Montreal Expos from Diamondbacks organization in Rule 5 major league draft (December 16, 2002). ... On disabled list (June 22-July 21, 2003); included rehabilitation assignment to GCL Expos. ... Expos franchise transferred to Washington, D.C., for 2005 season.
CAREER HITTING: 3-for-10 (.300), 0 R, 1 2B, 0 3B, 0 HR, 0 RBI.

Year	Team (League)	W	L	Pct.	ERA	WHIP	G	GS	CG	ShO	Hld.	Sv.-Opp.	IP	H	R	ER	HR	BB-IBB	SO	Avg.
2001—	Salem (Caro.)	0	1	.000	4.05	1.80	13	0	0	0	...	7-...	13.1	19	10	6	0	5-0	10	.358
2002—	Ottawa (Int'l)	0	0	...	3.52	1.43	6	0	0	0	...	0-...	7.2	7	3	3	1	4-0	6	.250
2003—	GC Expos (GCL)	0	0	...	0.00	1.09	2	0	0	0	...	0-...	3.2	2	0	0	0	2-0	2	.154
—	Montreal (N.L.)	10	3	.769	2.92	1.10	65	0	0	0	19	5-8	71.0	65	27	23	8	13-3	46	.244
2004—	Montreal (N.L.)	6	12	.333	2.69	1.18	81	0	0	0	21	2-7	90.1	92	30	27	6	15-2	63	.268
Major League totals (2 years)		16	15	.516	2.79	1.15	146	0	0	0	40	7-15	161.1	157	57	50	14	28-5	109	.258

BACKE, BRANDON — P

PERSONAL: Born April 5, 1978, in Galveston, Texas. ... 6-0/180. ... Throws right, bats right. ... Full name: Brandon Allen Backe. ... Name pronounced: back-EE. ... High school: Ball (Galveston, Texas). ... Junior college: Galveston (Texas).
TRANSACTIONS/CAREER NOTES: Selected by Milwaukee Brewers organization in 36th round of 1996 free-agent draft; did not sign. ... Selected by Tampa Bay Devil Rays organization in 18th round of 1998 free-agent draft. ... Played three seasons as an outfielder in Devil Rays organization (1998-2000). ... Traded by Devil Rays to Houston Astros for IF Geoff Blum (December 14, 2003).
CAREER HITTING: 5-for-16 (.313), 4 R, 0 2B, 0 3B, 1 HR, 6 RBI.

Year	Team (League)	W	L	Pct.	ERA	WHIP	G	GS	CG	ShO	Hld.	Sv.-Opp.	IP	H	R	ER	HR	BB-IBB	SO	Avg.
2001—	Char., S.C. (SAL)	2	1	.667	2.92	0.97	16	0	0	0	...	7-...	24.2	17	8	8	2	7-1	20	.200
—	Bakersfield (California)	1	0	1.000	1.09	0.85	17	0	0	0	...	3-...	24.2	13	7	3	1	8-0	33	.149
—	Orlando (Sou.)	1	0	1.000	5.73	1.41	14	0	0	0	...	0-...	22.0	20	14	14	1	11-0	20	.253
2002—	Orlando (Sou.)	4	6	.400	4.68	1.39	20	14	3	1	...	2-...	92.1	91	58	48	9	37-1	45	.256
—	Tampa Bay (A.L.)	0	0	...	6.92	1.69	9	0	0	0	0	0-...	13.0	15	10	10	3	7-0	6	.288
2003—	Durham (Int'l)	2	0	.667	4.64	1.40	16	2	0	0	...	0-...	33.0	33	21	17	1	13-0	27	.250
—	Tampa Bay (A.L.)	1	1	.500	5.44	1.46	28	0	0	0	5	0-...	44.2	40	28	27	6	25-1	36	.247
2004—	New Orleans (PCL)	6	5	.545	2.80	1.29	19	9	0	0	...	0-...	64.1	57	26	20	7	26-1	74	.241
—	Houston (N.L.)	5	3	.625	4.30	1.52	33	9	0	0	3	0-0	67.0	75	33	32	10	27-4	54	.290
American League totals (2 years)		1	1	.500	5.77	1.51	37	0	0	0	5	0-0	57.2	55	38	37	9	32-1	42	.257
National League totals (1 year)		5	3	.625	4.30	1.52	33	9	0	0	3	0-0	67.0	75	33	32	10	27-4	54	.290
Major League totals (3 years)		6	4	.600	4.98	1.52	70	9	0	0	8	0-0	124.2	130	71	69	19	59-5	96	.275

Year Team (League)	W	L	Pct.	ERA	WHIP	G	GS	CG	ShO	Hld.	Sv.-Opp.	IP	H	R	ER	HR	BB-IBB	SO	Avg.
2004— Houston (N.L.)	1	0	1.000	3.00	1.17	1	1	0	0	...	0-0	6.0	5	2	2	1	2-1	5	.227

CHAMPIONSHIP SERIES RECORD

Year Team (League)	W	L	Pct.	ERA	WHIP	G	GS	CG	ShO	Hld.	Sv.-Opp.	IP	H	R	ER	HR	BB-IBB	SO	Avg.
2004— Houston (N.L.)	0	0	...	2.84	0.79	2	2	0	0	0	0-0	12.2	6	4	4	1	4-0	10	.140

BACSIK, MIKE — P

PERSONAL: Born November 11, 1977, in Dallas, Texas. ... 6-3/190. ... Throws left, bats left. ... Full name: Michael J. Bacsik. ... High school: Duncanville (Texas). ... Son of Mike Bacsik, pitcher with Texas Rangers and Minnesota Twins (1975-80).

TRANSACTIONS/CAREER NOTES: Selected by Cleveland Indians organization in 18th round of 1996 free-agent draft. ... Traded by Indians with 2B Roberto Alomar and OF Danny Peoples to New York Mets for OFs Matt Lawton and Alex Escobar, P Jerrod Riggan and two players to be named December 11, 2001); Indians acquired P Billy Traber and 1B Earl Snyder to complete deal (December 13, 2001). ... Signed as free agent by Texas Rangers organization (December 21, 2003).

CAREER HITTING: 2-for-21 (.095), 0 R, 1 2B, 0 3B, 0 HR, 2 RBI.

Year Team (League)	W	L	Pct.	ERA	WHIP	G	GS	CG	ShO	Hld.	Sv.-Opp.	IP	H	R	ER	HR	BB-IBB	SO	Avg.
1996— Burlington (Appalachian) ..	4	2	.667	2.20	0.90	13	13	1	0	...	0-...	69.2	49	23	17	3	14-0	61	.189
1997— Columbus (S. Atl.)	4	14	.222	5.44	1.51	28	28	0	0	...	0-...	139.0	163	94	84	16	47-1	100	.293
1998— Kinston (Caro.)	10	9	.526	2.88	1.11	27	27	1	0	...	0-...	165.2	147	64	53	17	37-3	128	.239
1999— Akron (East.)	11	11	.500	4.64	1.41	26	26	1	0	...	0-...	149.1	164	84	77	24	47-0	84	.281
2000— Kinston (Caro.)	3	6	.333	4.57	1.23	11	11	0	0	...	0-...	65.0	72	36	33	4	8-0	56	.281
— Akron (East.)	7	1	.875	2.78	1.07	11	11	1	1	...	0-...	71.1	61	23	22	3	15-0	44	.231
— Buffalo (Int'l)	0	3	.000	5.59	1.31	5	5	0	0	...	0-...	29.0	31	20	18	7	7-0	9	.270
2001— Buffalo (Int'l)	12	5	.706	3.26	1.15	21	20	2	0	...	0-...	121.1	115	47	44	13	25-0	81	.244
— Akron (East.)	1	1	.500	1.98	0.88	4	4	1	1	...	0-...	27.1	21	7	6	2	3-0	19	.208
— Cleveland (A.L.)	0	0	...	9.00	1.78	3	0	0	0	0	0-0	9.0	13	10	9	0	3-1	4	.325
2002— Norfolk (Int'l)	5	5	.500	3.74	1.47	25	14	1	1	...	0-...	108.1	134	48	45	13	25-0	75	.312
— New York (N.L.)	3	2	.600	4.37	1.47	11	9	1	0	0	0-0	55.2	63	29	27	8	19-3	30	.289
2003— New York (N.L.)	1	2	.333	10.19	2.04	5	3	0	0	0	0-0	17.2	28	21	20	5	8-0	12	.368
— Norfolk (Int'l)	2	9	.182	4.97	1.40	22	21	0	0	...	0-...	117.2	129	70	65	13	34-1	62	.288
2004— Texas (A.L.)	1	1	.500	4.60	1.09	3	3	0	0	0	0-0	15.2	16	8	8	2	1-0	6	.267
— Oklahoma (PCL)	8	6	.571	4.55	1.36	34	9	0	0	...	0-...	95.0	106	58	48	16	23-1	50	.286
American League totals (2 years)	1	1	.500	6.20	1.34	6	3	0	0	0	0-0	24.2	29	18	17	2	4-1	10	.290
National League totals (2 years)	4	4	.500	5.77	1.61	16	12	1	0	0	0-0	73.1	91	50	47	13	27-3	42	.310
Major League totals (4 years)	5	5	.500	5.88	1.54	22	15	1	0	0	0-0	98.0	120	68	64	15	31-4	52	.305

BAEK, CHA SEUNG — P

PERSONAL: Born May 29, 1980, in Pusan, South Korea. ... 6-4/190. ... Throws right, bats right. ... High school: Pusan (Pusan, South Korea).

TRANSACTIONS/CAREER NOTES: Signed as a non-drafted free agent by Seattle Mariners organization (September 25, 1998).

CAREER HITTING: 0-for-0 (.000), 0 R, 0 2B, 0 3B, 0 HR, 0 RBI.

Year Team (League)	W	L	Pct.	ERA	WHIP	G	GS	CG	ShO	Hld.	Sv.-Opp.	IP	H	R	ER	HR	BB-IBB	SO	Avg.
1999— Ariz. Mariners (Ariz.)	3	0	1.000	3.67	1.33	8	4	0	0	...	0-...	27.0	30	13	11	2	6-0	25	.283
2000— Wisconsin (Midw.)	8	5	.615	3.95	1.36	24	24	0	0	...	0-...	127.2	137	71	56	13	36-0	99	.275
2001— San Bernardino (Calif.)	1	0	1.000	3.43	0.90	5	4	0	0	...	0-...	21.0	17	10	8	2	2-0	16	.224
2003— Inland Empire (Calif.)	5	1	.833	3.65	1.13	13	10	0	0	...	1-...	56.2	55	27	23	3	9-0	50	.249
— San Antonio (Texas)	3	3	.500	2.57	1.18	9	9	0	0	...	0-...	56.0	49	18	16	2	17-1	46	.238
2004— Ariz. Mariners (Ariz.)	0	0	...	1.29	0.57	2	2	0	0	...	0-...	7.0	3	2	1	0	1-0	5	.125
— San Antonio (Texas)	0	0	...	0.00	0.40	1	1	0	0	...	0-...	5.0	2	0	0	0	2-0	5	.125
— Tacoma (PCL)	5	4	.556	4.21	1.50	14	14	0	0	...	0-...	72.2	85	41	34	7	24-0	56	.290
— Seattle (A.L.)	2	4	.333	5.52	1.48	7	5	0	0	0	0-0	31.0	35	23	19	5	11-1	20	.278
Major League totals (1 year)	2	4	.333	5.52	1.48	7	5	0	0	0	0-0	31.0	35	23	19	5	11-1	20	.278

BAERGA, CARLOS — 1B

PERSONAL: Born November 4, 1968, in San Juan, Puerto Rico. ... 5-11/215. ... Bats both, throws right. ... Full name: Carlos Obed Baerga. ... Name pronounced: by-AIR-ga. ... High school: Barbara Ann Rooshart (Rio Piedras, Puerto Rico).

TRANSACTIONS/CAREER NOTES: Signed as non-drafted free agent by San Diego Padres organization (November 4, 1985). ... Traded by Padres with C Sandy Alomar and OF Chris James to Cleveland Indians for OF Joe Carter (December 6, 1989). ... Traded by Indians with IF Alvaro Espinoza to New York Mets for IFs Jose Vizcaino and Jeff Kent (July 29, 1996). ... Signed as a free agent by St. Louis Cardinals (January 27, 1999). ... Released by Cardinals (March 17, 1999). ... Signed by Cincinnati Reds organization (March 23, 1999). ... Released by Reds (June 4, 1999). ... Signed by San Diego Padres organization (June 6, 1999). ... Traded by Padres to Indians for cash considerations (August 16, 1999). ... Signed as a free agent by Tampa Bay Devil Rays organization (February 24, 2000). ... Contract voided (March 21, 2000). ... Signed by Seattle Mariners organization (January 19, 2001). ... Released by Mariners (March 30, 2001). ... Signed by Boston Red Sox organization (December 18, 2001). ... On disabled list (July 2-26, 2002). ... Signed as a free agent by Arizona Diamondbacks organization (January 31, 2003). ... On disabled list (June 10-July 19, 2004); included rehabilitation assignment to Tucson.

2004 GAMES PLAYED BY POSITION (MLB): 1B—6, DH—2.

								BATTING										FIELDING	
Year Team (League)	Pos.	G	AB	R	H	2B	3B	HR	RBI	BB	SO	HBP	GDP	SB-CS	Avg.	OBP	SLG	OPS	E	Avg.
1986— Char., S.C. (SAL)	2B-SS	111	378	57	102	14	4	7	41	26	60	5	4	6-1	.270	.321	.384	.705	27	.943
1987— Char., S.C. (SAL)	2B-SS	134	515	83	157	23	9	7	50	38	107	12	10	26-21	.305	.365	.425	.790	36	.943
1988— Wichita (Texas)	2B-SS	122	444	67	121	28	1	12	65	31	83	9	8	4-4	.273	.331	.421	.752	33	.943
1989— Las Vegas (PCL)	3B	132	520	63	143	28	2	10	74	30	98	6	10	6-6	.275	.319	.394	.713	32	.916
1990— Cleveland (A.L.) 2B-3B-SS		108	312	46	81	17	2	7	47	16	57	4	4	0-2	.260	.300	.394	.694	17	.935
— Colo. Springs (PCL)	3B	12	50	11	19	2	1	1	11	5	4	0	4	1-0	.380	.436	.520	.956	4	.925
1991— Cleveland (A.L.) 2B-3B-SS		158	593	80	171	28	2	11	69	48	74	6	12	3-2	.288	.346	.398	.744	27	.959
1992— Cleveland (A.L.)	2B-DH	161	657	92	205	32	1	20	105	35	76	13	15	10-2	.312	.354	.455	.809	19	.979
1993— Cleveland (A.L.)	2B-DH	154	624	105	200	28	6	21	114	34	68	6	17	15-4	.321	.355	.486	.840	17	.979
1994— Cleveland (A.L.)	2B-DH	103	442	81	139	32	2	19	80	10	45	6	10	8-2	.314	.333	.525	.858	* 15	.973
1995— Cleveland (A.L.)	2B-DH	135	557	87	175	28	2	15	90	35	31	3	15	11-2	.314	.355	.452	.807	19	.973
1996— Cleveland (A.L.)	2B	100	424	54	113	25	0	10	55	16	25	7	15	1-1	.267	.302	.396	.698	15	.971
— New York (N.L.)	1B-3B-2B	26	83	5	16	3	0	2	11	5	2	2	8	0-0	.193	.253	.301	.554	4	.966
1997— New York (N.L.)	2B	133	467	53	131	25	1	9	52	20	54	4	13	2-6	.281	.311	.396	.707	14	.978

Year	Team (League)	Pos.	G	AB	R	H	2B	3B	HR	RBI	BB	SO	HBP	GDP	SB-CS	Avg.	OBP	SLG	OPS	E	Avg.
1998— New York (N.L.)	2B	147	511	46	136	27	1	7	53	24	55	6	21	0-1	.266	.303	.364	.667	9	.986
1999— Indianapolis (Int'l)	3B-2B-1B-DH	52	221	32	64	10	0	3	27	10	18	1	11	2-1	.290	.321	.376	.696	6	.975
—Las Vegas (PCL)	3B-2B	21	91	15	26	7	0	2	9	9	5	1	2	0-0	.286	.356	.429	.785	5	.919
—San Diego (N.L.)	2B-3B-1B-DH	33	80	6	20	1	0	2	5	6	14	2	2	1-0	.250	.318	.338	.656	2	.962
—Cleveland (A.L.)	3B-2B-DH	22	57	4	13	0	0	1	5	4	10	0	3	1-1	.228	.274	.281	.555	1	.976
2000—					Did not play.																
2001— Samsung (Korean)		120	18	33	...		4	17	10	12		...	...-...	.275	...	.375	...	...	...		
—Long Island (Atl.)		53	203	38	64	9	3	9	44	19	24	...		3-...	.315	...	.522	...	...	...	
2002— Boston (A.L.)	DH-2B-3B	73	182	17	52	11	0	2	19	7	20	2	6	6-0	.286	.316	.379	.695	1	.983
2003— Arizona (N.L.)	1B-2B-DH-3B	105	207	31	71	13	0	4	39	18	20	2	6	1-1	.343	.396	.464	.859	3	.986
2004— Tucson (PCL)	DH	1	4	1	1	1	0	0	0	0	0	0	0	0-0	.250	.250	.500	.750	0	...
—Arizona (N.L.)	1B-DH	79	85	6	20	2	0	2	11	6	12	3	7	0-0	.235	.309	.329	.638	0	1.000
American League totals (9 years)		1014	3848	566	1149	201	15	106	584	205	406	47	97	55-16	.299	.338	.441	.779	131	.971
National League totals (6 years)		523	1433	147	394	71	2	26	171	79	157	18	57	4-8	.275	.318	.382	.699	32	.981
Major League totals (13 years)		1537	5281	713	1543	272	17	132	755	284	563	65	154	59-24	.292	.332	.425	.757	163	.974

DIVISION SERIES RECORD

Year	Team (League)	Pos.	G	AB	R	H	2B	3B	HR	RBI	BB	SO	HBP	GDP	SB-CS	Avg.	OBP	SLG	OPS	E	Avg.
1995— Cleveland (A.L.)	2B	3	14	2	4	1	0	1	1	0	1	1	0	0-0	.286	.333	.357	.690	1	.929

CHAMPIONSHIP SERIES RECORD

Year	Team (League)	Pos.	G	AB	R	H	2B	3B	HR	RBI	BB	SO	HBP	GDP	SB-CS	Avg.	OBP	SLG	OPS	E	Avg.
1995— Cleveland (A.L.)	2B	6	25	3	10	0	0	1	4	2	3	0	0	0-0	.400	.444	.520	.964	0	1.000

WORLD SERIES RECORD

Year	Team (League)	Pos.	G	AB	R	H	2B	3B	HR	RBI	BB	SO	HBP	GDP	SB-CS	Avg.	OBP	SLG	OPS	E	Avg.
1995— Cleveland (A.L.)	2B	6	26	1	5	0	0	0	4	1	1	0	1	0-0	.192	.222	.269	.491	1	.975

ALL-STAR GAME RECORD

		G	AB	R	H	2B	3B	HR	RBI	BB	SO	HBP	GDP	SB-CS	Avg.	OBP	SLG	OPS	E	Avg.
All-Star Game totals (3 years)		3	6	3	4	2	0	0	1	0	1	0	0	0-1	.667	.667	1.000	1.667	0	1.000

BAEZ, DANYS — P

PERSONAL: Born September 10, 1977, in Pinar del Rio, Cuba. ... 6-3/225. ... Throws right, bats right. ... Name pronounced: DAN-ees BUY-ez.

TRANSACTIONS/CAREER NOTES: Signed as a non-drafted free agent by Cleveland Indians organization (November 5, 1999). ... Signed as a free agent by Tampa Bay Devil Rays (January 6, 2004).

CAREER HITTING: 0-for-3 (.000), 0 R, 0 2B, 0 3B, 0 HR, 0 RBI.

Year	Team (League)	W	L	Pct.	ERA	WHIP	G	GS	CG	ShO	Hld.	Sv.-Opp.	IP	H	R	ER	HR	BB-IBB	SO	Avg.
2000— Kinston (Caro.)	2	2	.500	4.71	1.31	9	9	0	0	...	0-...	49.2	45	29	26	5	20-0	56	.236
—Akron (East.)	4	9	.308	3.68	1.27	18	18	0	0	...	0-...	102.2	98	46	42	6	32-0	77	.259
2001— Buffalo (Int'l)	2	0	1.000	3.20	1.07	16	0	0	0	...	3-...	25.1	19	9	9	2	9-0	30	.200
—Akron (East.)	0	0	...	0.00	0.50	1	0	0	0	...	0-...	2.0	1	0	0	0	0-0	2	.143
—Cleveland (A.L.)	5	3	.625	2.50	1.07	43	0	0	0	14	0-1	50.1	34	22	14	5	20-4	52	.191
2002— Cleveland (A.L.)	10	11	.476	4.41	1.46	39	26	1	0	0	6-8	165.1	160	84	81	14	82-5	130	.256
2003— Cleveland (A.L.)	2	9	.182	3.81	1.16	73	0	0	0	5	25-35	75.2	65	36	32	9	23-0	66	.229
2004— Tampa Bay (A.L.)	4	4	.500	3.57	1.31	62	0	0	0	1	30-33	68.0	60	31	27	6	29-4	52	.237
Major League totals (4 years)	21	27	.438	3.86	1.32	217	26	1	0	20	61-77	359.1	319	173	154	34	154-13	300	.238

DIVISION SERIES RECORD

Year	Team (League)	W	L	Pct.	ERA	WHIP	G	GS	CG	ShO	Hld.	Sv.-Opp.	IP	H	R	ER	HR	BB-IBB	SO	Avg.
2001— Cleveland (A.L.)	0	0	...	2.45	1.09	3	0	0	0	0	0-0	3.2	4	1	1	0	0-0	6	.267

BAGWELL, JEFF — 1B

PERSONAL: Born May 27, 1968, in Boston, Mass. ... 6-0/215. ... Bats right, throws right. ... Full name: Jeffrey Robert Bagwell. ... Name pronounced: BAG-well. ... High school: Xavier (Middletown, Conn.). ... College: Hartford.

TRANSACTIONS/CAREER NOTES: Selected by Boston Red Sox organization in fourth round of 1989 free-agent draft. ... Traded by Red Sox to Houston Astros for P Larry Andersen (August 31, 1990). ... On disabled list (July 31-September 1, 1995); included rehabilitation assignment to Jackson. ... On disabled list (May 13-28, 1998).

RECORDS: Shares major league records for most doubles, game (4, June 14, 1996), and most bases on balls, game (6, August 20, 1999, 16 innings).

HONORS: Named N.L. Rookie Player of the Year by THE SPORTING NEWS (1991). ... Named N.L. Rookie of the Year by Baseball Writers' Association of America (1991). ... Named Major League Player of the Year by THE SPORTING NEWS (1994). ... Named N.L. Most Valuable Player by Baseball Writers' Association of America (1994). ... Won N.L. Gold Glove at first base (1994).

2004 GAMES PLAYED BY POSITION (MLB): 1B—152, DH—2.

Year	Team (League)	Pos.	G	AB	R	H	2B	3B	HR	RBI	BB	SO	HBP	GDP	SB-CS	Avg.	OBP	SLG	OPS	E	Avg.
1989— GC Red Sox (GCL)	2B-3B	5	19	3	6	1	0	0	3	3	0	0	1	0-0	.316	.409	.368	.778	2	.875
—Winter Haven (FSL)	2B-3B-1B	64	210	27	65	13	2	2	19	23	25	3	7	1-1	.310	.384	.419	.803	12	.931
1990— New Britain (East.)	3B	136	481	63	160	34	7	4	61	73	57	7	15	5-7	.333	.423	.457	.881	34	.914
1991— Houston (N.L.)	1B	156	554	79	163	26	4	15	82	75	116	13	12	7-4	.294	.387	.437	.824	12	.991
1992— Houston (N.L.)	1B	•162	586	87	160	34	6	18	96	84	97	12	17	10-6	.273	.368	.444	.812	7	.995
1993— Houston (N.L.)	1B	142	535	76	171	37	4	20	88	62	73	3	20	13-4	.320	.388	.516	.903	9	.993
1994— Houston (N.L.)	1B-OF	110	400	*104	147	32	2	39	*116	65	65	4	12	15-4	.368	.451	*.750	1.201	§9	.991
1995— Houston (N.L.)	1B	114	448	88	130	29	0	21	87	79	102	6	9	12-5	.290	.399	.496	.894	9	.994
—Jackson (Texas)	1B-DH	4	12	0	2	0	0	0	0	3	2	1	0	0-0	.167	.375	.167	.542	0	1.000
1996— Houston (N.L.)	1B	*162	568	111	179	*48	2	31	120	135	114	10	15	21-7	.315	.451	.570	1.021	*16	.989
1997— Houston (N.L.)	1B-DH	*162	566	109	162	40	2	43	135	127	122	16	10	31-10	.286	.425	.592	1.017	11	.993
1998— Houston (N.L.)	1B	147	540	124	164	33	1	34	111	109	90	7	14	19-7	.304	.424	.557	.981	7	.995
1999— Houston (N.L.)	1B-DH	•162	562	*143	171	35	0	42	126	*149	127	11	18	30-11	.304	.454	.591	1.045	8	.994
2000— Houston (N.L.)	1B-DH	159	590	*152	183	37	1	47	132	107	116	15	19	9-6	.310	.424	.615	1.039	9	.994
2001— Houston (N.L.)	1B	161	600	126	173	43	4	39	130	106	135	6	20	11-3	.288	.397	.568	.966	12	.992
2002— Houston (N.L.)	1B-DH	158	571	94	166	33	2	31	98	110	130	10	16	7-3	.291	.401	.518	.919	7	.995
2003— Houston (N.L.)	1B	160	605	109	168	28	2	39	100	88	119	6	25	11-4	.278	.373	.524	.897	9	.995
2004— Houston (N.L.)	1B-DH	156	572	104	152	29	2	27	89	96	131	8	12	6-4	.266	.377	.465	.842	9	.995
Major League totals (14 years)		2111	7697	1506	2289	484	32	446	1510	1383	1537	127	219	202-78	.297	.408	.542	.951	129	.993

DIVISION SERIES RECORD

Year Team (League)	Pos.	G	AB	R	H	2B	3B	HR	RBI	BB	SO	HBP	GDP	SB-CS	Avg.	OBP	SLG	OPS	E	Avg.
1997—Houston (N.L.)	1B	3	12	0	1	0	0	0	1	5	0	0		0-0	.083	.154	.083	.237	2	.920
1998—Houston (N.L.)	1B	4	14	0	2	0	0	0	4	1	6	1	0	0-0	.143	.250	.143	.393	0	1.000
1999—Houston (N.L.)	1B	4	13	3	2	0	0	0	0	5	4	1	0	0-0	.154	.421	.154	.575	0	1.000
2001—Houston (N.L.)	1B	3	7	0	3	0	0	0	0	5	1	0	0	0-1	.429	.667	.429	1.095	0	1.000
2004—Houston (N.L.)	1B	5	22	5	7	2	0	2	5	3	3	0	1	0-0	.318	.400	.682	1.082	1	.981
Division series totals (5 years)		19	68	8	15	2	0	2	9	15	19	2	1	0-1	.221	.376	.338	.715	3	.983

CHAMPIONSHIP SERIES RECORD

Year Team (League)	Pos.	G	AB	R	H	2B	3B	HR	RBI	BB	SO	HBP	GDP	SB-CS	Avg.	OBP	SLG	OPS	E	Avg.
2004—Houston (N.L.)	1B	7	27	1	7	2	0	0	3	4	5	0	1	1-1	.259	.355	.333	.688	0	1.000

ALL-STAR GAME RECORD

		G	AB	R	H	2B	3B	HR	RBI	BB	SO	HBP	GDP	SB-CS	Avg.	OBP	SLG	OPS	E	Avg.
All-Star Game totals (4 years)		4	12	1	3	0	0	0	0	0	4	0	0	0-0	.250	.250	.250	.500	0	1.000

BAJENARU, JEFF   P

PERSONAL: Born March 21, 1978, in Pomona, Calif. ... 6-1/190. ... Throws right, bats right. ... Full name: Jeffrey Michael Bajenaru. ... Name pronounced: Bah-juh-NAIR-oh. ... High school: Ayala (Chino Hills, Calif.). ... College: Oklahoma.

TRANSACTIONS/CAREER NOTES: Selected by Oakland Athletics organization in 13th round of 1998 free-agent draft; did not sign. ... Selected by Chicago White Sox organization in 36th round of 1999 free-agent draft.

CAREER HITTING: 0-for-0 (.000), 0 R, 0 2B, 0 3B, 0 HR, 0 RBI.

Year Team (League)	W	L	Pct.	ERA	WHIP	G	GS	CG	ShO	Hld.	Sv.-Opp.	IP	H	R	ER	HR	BB-IBB	SO	Avg.
2000—Bristol (Appalachian)	1	1	.500	3.77	1.05	12	0	0	0	...	5-...	14.1	10	6	6	2	5-0	31	.179
—Winston-Salem (Caro.)	2	0	1.000	4.38	0.97	10	0	0	0	...	2-...	12.1	7	6	6	1	5-0	15	.167
2001—Birmingham (Southern)	0	0	...	0.00	1.62	2	0	0	0	...	0-...	4.1	4	0	0	0	3-0	5	.222
—Winston-Salem (Caro.)	2	4	.333	3.35	1.31	35	0	0	0	...	10-...	40.1	32	16	15	3	21-2	51	.216
2003—Birmingham (Southern)	4	2	.667	3.20	1.25	50	0	0	0	...	14-...	64.2	53	29	23	2	28-3	62	.225
2004—Birmingham (Southern)	2	0	1.000	1.34	0.89	32	0	0	0	...	12-...	33.2	19	9	5	3	11-0	51	.158
—Charlotte (Int'l)	1	2	.333	1.80	0.75	16	0	0	0	...	10-...	20.0	12	6	4	2	3-0	16	.171
—Chicago (A.L.)	0	1	.000	10.80	2.52	9	0	0	0	...	0-0	8.1	15	10	10	0	6-1	8	.405
Major League totals (1 year)	0	1	.000	10.80	2.52	9	0	0	0	...	0-0	8.1	15	10	10	0	6-1	8	.405

BAKO, PAUL   C

PERSONAL: Born June 20, 1972, in Lafayette, La. ... 6-2/215. ... Bats left, throws right. ... Full name: Gabor Paul Bako II. ... Name pronounced: BAH-koh. ... High school: Lafayette (La.). ... College: Southwestern Louisiana.

TRANSACTIONS/CAREER NOTES: Selected by Cincinnati Reds organization in fifth round of 1993 free-agent draft. ... Traded by Reds with P Donne Wall to Detroit Tigers for OF Melvin Nieves (November 11, 1997). ... Traded by Tigers with Ps Dean Crow, Mark Persails and Brian Powell and 3B Carlos Villalobos to Houston Astros for C Brad Ausmus and P C.J. Nitkowski (January 14, 1999). ... Traded by Astros to Florida Marlins for cash (April 11, 2000). ... Claimed on waivers by Atlanta Braves (July 21, 2000). ... Traded by Braves with P Jose Cabrera to Milwaukee Brewers for C Henry Blanco (March 20, 2002). ... On disabled list (June 9-24, 2002). ... Traded by Brewers to Chicago Cubs for a player to be named (November 26, 2002); Brewers acquired IF Ryan Gripp to complete deal (December 16, 2002).

2004 GAMES PLAYED BY POSITION (MLB): C—47.

Year Team (League)	Pos.	G	AB	R	H	2B	3B	HR	RBI	BB	SO	HBP	GDP	SB-CS	Avg.	OBP	SLG	OPS	E	Avg.
1993—Billings (Pio.)	C-1B	57	194	34	61	11	0	4	30	22	37	1	5	5-1	.314	.382	.433	.815	6	.984
1994—Win.-Salem (Car.)	C	90	289	29	59	9	1	3	26	35	81	4	6	2-2	.204	.299	.273	.572	15	.977
1995—Win.-Salem (Car.)	C	82	249	29	71	11	2	7	27	42	66	1	6	3-1	.285	.389	.430	.819	6	.989
1996—Chattanooga (Sou.)	C	110	360	53	106	27	0	8	48	48	93	5	5	1-0	.294	.381	.436	.817	13	.984
1997—Indianapolis (A.A.)	C	104	321	34	78	14	1	8	43	34	81	2	7	0-5	.243	.316	.368	.683	6	.991
1998—Toledo (Int'l)	C	13	48	5	14	3	1	1	6	1	13	0	1	0-0	.292	.300	.458	.758	1	.988
—Detroit (A.L.)	C	96	305	23	83	12	1	3	30	23	82	0	3	1-1	.272	.319	.348	.667	6	.989
1999—New Orleans (PCL)	C	12	47	2	9	3	1	1	4	1	11	0	1	0-0	.191	.208	.362	.570	1	.984
—Houston (N.L.)	C	73	215	16	55	14	1	2	17	26	57	0	4	1-1	.256	.332	.358	.690	6	.988
2000—Houston (N.L.)	C	1	2	0	0	0	0	0	0	0	1	0	0	0-0	.000	.000	.000	.000	0	1.000
—Florida (N.L.)	C	56	161	10	39	6	1	0	14	22	48	1	4	0-0	.242	.335	.292	.627	3	.991
—Atlanta (N.L.)	C-1B	24	58	8	11	4	0	2	6	5	15	0	2	0-0	.190	.254	.362	.616	1	.992
2001—Atlanta (N.L.)	C	61	137	19	29	10	1	2	15	20	34	0	3	1-0	.212	.312	.343	.655	3	.991
2002—Milwaukee (N.L.)	C	87	234	24	55	8	1	4	20	20	46	0	4	0-2	.235	.295	.329	.624	4	.991
2003—Chicago (N.L.)	C	70	188	19	43	13	3	0	17	22	47	1	2	0-1	.229	.311	.330	.641	6	.987
2004—Chicago (N.L.)	C	49	138	13	28	8	0	1	10	15	29	2	4	1-0	.203	.288	.283	.571	4	.989
American League totals (1 year)		96	305	23	83	12	1	3	30	23	82	0	3	1-1	.272	.319	.348	.667	6	.989
National League totals (6 years)		421	1133	109	260	63	7	11	99	130	277	4	23	3-4	.229	.310	.327	.636	27	.990
Major League totals (7 years)		517	1438	132	343	75	8	14	129	153	359	4	26	4-5	.239	.312	.331	.643	33	.990

DIVISION SERIES RECORD

Year Team (League)	Pos.	G	AB	R	H	2B	3B	HR	RBI	BB	SO	HBP	GDP	SB-CS	Avg.	OBP	SLG	OPS	E	Avg.
2000—Atlanta (N.L.)	C	2	1	0	0	0	0	0	0	0	1	0	0	0-0	.000	.000	.000	.000	1	.800
2001—Atlanta (N.L.)	C	3	7	1	2	0	1	0	3	1	0	0	0	0-0	.286	.375	.857	1.232	0	1.000
2003—Chicago (N.L.)	C	3	4	0	0	0	0	0	1	2	2	0	0	0-0	.000	.333	.000	.333	0	1.000
Division series totals (3 years)		8	12	1	2	0	1	0	4	3	3	0	0	0-0	.167	.333	.500	.833	1	.976

CHAMPIONSHIP SERIES RECORD

Year Team (League)	Pos.	G	AB	R	H	2B	3B	HR	RBI	BB	SO	HBP	GDP	SB-CS	Avg.	OBP	SLG	OPS	E	Avg.
2001—Atlanta (N.L.)	C	3	3	0	0	0	0	0	0	0	0	0	0	0-0	.000	.000	.000	.000	0	1.000
2003—Chicago (N.L.)	C	6	16	4	4	1	0	0	1	1	7	0	0	0-0	.250	.294	.313	.607	0	1.000
Champ. series totals (2 years)		9	19	4	4	1	0	0	1	1	7	0	0	0-0	.211	.250	.263	.513	0	1.000

BALDELLI, ROCCO   OF

PERSONAL: Born September 25, 1981, in Woonsocket, R.I. ... 6-4/187. ... Bats right, throws right. ... Full name: Rocco Daniel Baldelli. ... High school: Bishop Hendrickson (Warwick, R.I.).

TRANSACTIONS/CAREER NOTES: Selected by Tampa Bay Devil Rays organization in first round (sixth pick overall) of 2000 free-agent draft. ... On disabled list (August 14-September 1, 2004).

2004 GAMES PLAYED BY POSITION (MLB): OF—124, DH—13.

													BATTING								FIELDING	
Year	Team (League)	Pos.	G	AB	R	H	2B	3B	HR	RBI	BB	SO	HBP	GDP	SB-CS	Avg.	OBP	SLG	OPS		E	Avg.
2000—	Princeton (Appal.)	OF-3B	60	232	33	50	9	2	3	25	12	56	5	3	11-3	.216	.269	.310	.579		4	.966
2001—	Char., S.C. (SAL)	OF	113	406	58	101	23	6	8	55	23	89	11	7	25-9	.249	.303	.394	.697		9	.964
2002—	Bakersfield (Calif.)	OF	77	312	63	104	19	1	14	51	18	63	7	2	21-6	.333	.382	.535	.917		3	.975
—	Orlando (South.)	OF	17	70	10	26	3	1	2	13	5	11	2	1	3-2	.371	.413	.529	.941		1	.967
—	Durham (Int'l)	OF	23	96	13	28	6	1	3	7	0	23	0	1	2-5	.292	.292	.469	.760		0	1.000
2003—	Tampa Bay (A.L.)	OF-DH	156	637	89	184	32	8	11	78	30	128	8	10	27-10	.289	.326	.416	.742		5	.989
2004—	Tampa Bay (A.L.)	OF-DH	136	518	79	145	27	3	16	74	30	88	8	12	17-4	.280	.326	.436	.762		8	.978
	Major League totals (2 years)		292	1155	168	329	59	11	27	152	60	216	16	22	44-14	.285	.326	.425	.751		13	.984

BALDWIN, JAMES   P

PERSONAL: Born July 15, 1971, in Southern Pines, N.C. ... 6-3/235. ... Throws right, bats right. ... Full name: James J. Baldwin Jr.. ... High school: Pinecrest (Southern Pines, N.C.).

TRANSACTIONS/CAREER NOTES: Selected by Chicago White Sox organization in fourth round of 1990 free-agent draft. ... On disabled list (August 3-19, 1994). ... On disabled list (March 23-April 21, 2001); included rehabilitation assignment to Charlotte. ... Traded by White Sox to Los Angeles Dodgers for Ps Onan Masaoka and Gary Majewski and OF Jeff Barry (July 26, 2001). ... Signed as a free agent by Seattle Mariners (February 1, 2002). ... Signed as a free agent by Kansas City Royals organization (January 23, 2003). ... Refused minor league assignment and became a free agent (June 4, 2003). ... Signed by Minnesota Twins organization (June 10, 2003). ... Refused minor league assignment and became a free agent (August 17, 2003). ... Signed by New York Mets organization (February 9, 2004). ... Refused minor league assignment and became a free agent (May 20, 2004). ... Signed by Detroit Tigers organization (June 6, 2004).

HONORS: Named A.L. Rookie Pitcher of the Year by THE SPORTING NEWS (1996).

CAREER HITTING: 4-for-43 (.093), 1 R, 1 2B, 1 3B, 0 HR, 2 RBI.

Year	Team (League)	W	L	Pct.	ERA	WHIP	G	GS	CG	ShO	Hld.	Sv.-Opp.	IP	H	R	ER	HR	BB-IBB	SO	Avg.
1990—	GC White Sox (GCL)	1	6	.143	4.10	1.34	9	7	0	0		0-...	37.1	32	29	17	1	18-0	32	.225
1991—	GC White Sox (GCL)	3	1	.750	2.12	0.94	6	6	0	0		0-...	34.0	16	8	8	0	16-0	48	.140
—	Utica (N.Y.-Penn)	1	4	.200	5.30	1.79	7	7	1	0		0-...	37.1	40	26	22	0	27-0	23	.267
1992—	South Bend (Mid.)	9	5	.643	2.42	1.18	21	21	1	1		0-...	137.2	118	53	37	6	45-0	137	.228
—	Sarasota (Florida State)	1	2	.333	2.87	1.01	6	6	1	0		0-...	37.2	31	13	12	2	7-0	39	.225
1993—	Birmingham (Southern)	8	5	.615	2.25	1.14	17	17	4	0		0-...	120.0	94	48	30	4	43-0	107	.219
—	Nashville (A.A.)	5	4	.556	2.61	1.14	10	10	1	0		0-...	69.0	43	21	20	5	36-0	61	.180
1994—	Nashville (A.A.)	12	6	.667	3.72	1.40	26	26	2	0		0-...	162.0	144	75	67	14	83-1	156	.237
1995—	Chicago (A.L.)	0	1	.000	12.89	2.80	6	4	0	0	0	0-0	14.2	32	22	21	6	9-1	10	.444
—	Nashville (A.A.)	5	9	.357	5.85	1.72	18	18	0	0		0-...	95.1	120	76	62	27	44-1	89	.302
1996—	Nashville (A.A.)	1	1	.500	0.64	0.64	2	2	1	0		0-...	14.0	5	1	1	0	4-0	15	.116
—	Chicago (A.L.)	11	6	.647	4.42	1.33	28	28	0	0	0	0-0	169.0	168	88	83	24	57-3	127	.257
1997—	Chicago (A.L.)	12	•15	.444	5.27	1.44	32	32	1	0	0	0-0	200.0	205	128	117	19	83-3	140	.262
1998—	Chicago (A.L.)	13	6	.684	5.32	1.48	37	34	1	0	0	0-1	159.0	176	103	94	18	60-2	108	.278
1999—	Chicago (A.L.)	12	13	.480	5.10	1.51	35	33	1	0	0	0-0	199.1	219	119	113	34	81-1	123	.278
2000—	Chicago (A.L.)	14	7	.667	4.65	1.37	29	28	2	1	0	0-0	178.0	185	96	92	34	59-3	116	.272
2001—	Charlotte (Int'l)	1	0	1.000	5.25	1.17	2	2	0	0		0-...	12.0	12	7	7	2	2-0	11	.273
—	Chicago (A.L.)	7	5	.583	4.61	1.54	17	16	2	1	0	0-...	95.2	109	56	49	15	38-0	42	.286
—	Los Angeles (N.L.)	3	6	.333	4.20	1.35	12	12	0	0	0	0-...	79.1	82	39	37	10	25-1	53	.274
2002—	Seattle (A.L.)	7	10	.412	5.28	1.52	30	23	0	0	0	0-...	150.0	179	95	88	26	49-2	88	.298
2003—	Omaha (PCL)	3	2	.600	4.08	1.30	8	8	0	0		0-...	46.1	48	25	21	8	13-0	24	.265
—	Rochester (Int'l)	0	2	.000	2.43	0.90	5	5	0	0		0-...	29.2	25	11	8	2	3-0	18	.225
—	Minnesota (A.L.)	0	1	.000	5.40	1.67	10	0	0	0	1	1-2	15.0	21	10	9	6	4-1	7	.333
2004—	Norfolk (Int'l)	3	2	.600	2.90	1.26	5	5	0	0	0	0-...	31.0	34	11	10	3	5-0	24	.281
—	New York (N.L.)	0	2	.000	15.00	3.00	2	2	0	0	0	0-0	6.0	13	10	10	3	5-1	1	.448
—	Toledo (International)	5	7	.417	3.74	1.12	18	16	3	0	0	1-...	115.2	110	52	48	12	20-3	61	.255
	American League totals (9 years)	76	64	.543	5.08	1.47	224	188	7	2	1	1-3	1180.2	1294	717	666	182	440-16	761	.278
	National League totals (2 years)	3	8	.273	4.96	1.46	14	14	0	0	0	0-0	85.1	95	49	47	13	30-2	54	.290
	Major League totals (10 years)	79	72	.523	5.07	1.47	238	202	7	2	1	1-3	1266.0	1389	766	713	195	470-18	815	.279

DIVISION SERIES RECORD

Year	Team (League)	W	L	Pct.	ERA	WHIP	G	GS	CG	ShO	Hld.	Sv.-Opp.	IP	H	R	ER	HR	BB-IBB	SO	Avg.
2000—	Chicago (A.L.)	0	0		1.50	1.00	1	1	0	0		0-0	6.0	3	1	1		3-0	2	.150

ALL-STAR GAME RECORD

	W	L	Pct.	ERA	WHIP	G	GS	CG	ShO	Hld.	Sv.-Opp.	IP	H	R	ER	HR	BB-IBB	SO	Avg.
All-Star Game totals (1 year)	1	0	1.000	9.00	2.00	1	0	0	0	0	0-0	1.0	2	1	1	1	0-0	0	.400

BALFOUR, GRANT   P

PERSONAL: Born December 30, 1977, in Sydney, Australia. ... 6-2/188. ... Throws right, bats right. ... Full name: Grant Robert Balfour. ... High school: William Clarke College (Kellyville, New South Wales, Australia).

TRANSACTIONS/CAREER NOTES: Signed as non-drafted free agent by Minnesota Twins organization (January 19, 1997). ... On disabled list (April 4-May 14 and July 26-August 17, 2004).

CAREER HITTING: 0-for-0 (.000), 0 R, 0 2B, 0 3B, 0 HR, 0 RBI.

Year	Team (League)	W	L	Pct.	ERA	WHIP	G	GS	CG	ShO	Hld.	Sv.-Opp.	IP	H	R	ER	HR	BB-IBB	SO	Avg.
1997—	GC Twins (GCL)	2	4	.333	3.76	1.39	13	12	0	0		0-...	67.0	73	31	28	1	20-0	43	.292
1998—	Elizabethton (Appal.)	7	2	.778	3.36	1.25	13	13	0	0		0-...	77.2	70	36	29	1	27-0	75	.240
1999—	Quad City (Midw.)	8	5	.615	3.53	1.12	19	14	0	0		1-...	91.2	66	39	36	7	37-0	95	.204
2000—	Fort Myers (Fla. St.)	8	5	.615	4.25	1.40	35	10	0	0		0-...	89.0	91	46	42	8	34-2	90	.263
2001—	New Britain (East.)	2	1	.667	1.08	0.96	35	0	0	0		13-...	50.0	26	6	6	1	22-2	72	.149
—	Minnesota (A.L.)	0	0	...	13.50	2.25	2	0	0	0	0	0-0	2.2	3	4	4	2	3-0	2	.333

Year Team (League)	W	L	Pct.	ERA	WHIP	G	GS	CG	ShO	Hld.	Sv.-Opp.	IP	H	R	ER	HR	BB-IBB	SO	Avg.
— Edmonton (PCL)	2	2	.500	5.51	1.71	11	0	0	0	...	0-...	16.1	18	11	10	2	10-1	17	.305
2002— Edmonton (PCL)	2	4	.333	4.16	1.26	58	0	0	0	...	8-...	71.1	60	34	33	3	30-1	88	.231
2003— Rochester (Int'l)	5	2	.714	2.41	0.90	21	11	0	0	...	5-...	71.0	48	21	19	6	16-0	87	.188
— Minnesota (A.L.)	1	0	1.000	4.15	1.42	17	1	0	0	1	0-1	26.0	23	12	12	4	14-2	30	.235
2004— Minnesota (A.L.)	4	1	.800	4.35	1.42	36	0	0	0	4	0-1	39.1	35	19	19	4	21-1	42	.238
Major League totals (3 years)	5	1	.833	4.63	1.46	55	1	0	0	5	0-2	68.0	61	35	35	10	38-3	74	.240

DIVISION SERIES RECORD

Year Team (League)	W	L	Pct.	ERA	WHIP	G	GS	CG	ShO	Hld.	Sv.-Opp.	IP	H	R	ER	HR	BB-IBB	SO	Avg.
2004— Minnesota (A.L.)	0	0	...	0.00	0.00	2	0	0	0	0	0-0	2.2	0	0	0	0	0-0	2	.000

BARAJAS, ROD — C

PERSONAL: Born September 5, 1975, in Ontario, Calif. ... 6-2/220. ... Bats right, throws right. ... Full name: Rodrigo Richard Barajas. ... Name pronounced: bar-AH-hoss. ... High school: Sante Fe Springs (Calif.). ... Junior college: Cerritos (Calif.).

TRANSACTIONS/CAREER NOTES: Signed as a non-drafted free agent by Arizona Diamondbacks organization (January 23, 1996). ... Loaned by Diamondbacks organization to Oakland Athletics organization (April 5-June 16, 1996). ... On disabled list (April 7-28 and July 5-23, 2003); included rehabilitation assignments to Tucson and Lancaster. ... Signed as a free agent by Texas Rangers organization (January 15, 2004).

2004 GAMES PLAYED BY POSITION (MLB): C—105, 1B—2.

Year Team (League)	Pos.	G	AB	R	H	2B	3B	HR	RBI	BB	SO	HBP	GDP	SB-CS	Avg.	OBP	SLG	OPS	E	Avg.
1996— Visalia (Calif.)	C	27	74	6	12	3	0	0	8	7	21	1	3	0-0	.162	.244	.203	.447	0	1.000
— Lethbridge (Pio.)	C-1B	51	175	47	59	9	3	10	50	12	24	2	6	2-1	.337	.378	.594	.973	5	.986
1997— High Desert (Calif.)	C-1B	57	199	24	53	11	0	7	30	8	41	1	7	0-2	.266	.297	.427	.724	3	.993
1998— High Desert (Calif.)	C	113	442	67	134	26	0	23	81	25	81	7	13	1-1	.303	.345	.518	.863	14	.983
1999— El Paso (Texas)	C-DH-1B	127	510	77	162	41	2	14	95	24	73	8	8	2-0	.318	.354	.488	.842	14	.985
— Arizona (N.L.)	C	5	16	3	4	1	0	1	3	1	1	0	0	0-0	.250	.294	.500	.794	0	1.000
2000— Tucson (PCL)	C-1B-3B	110	416	43	94	25	0	13	75	14	65	5	13	4-3	.226	.253	.380	.633	14	.980
— Arizona (N.L.)	C	5	13	1	3	0	0	1	3	0	4	0	0	0-0	.231	.231	.462	.692	0	1.000
2001— Arizona (N.L.)	C	51	106	9	17	3	0	3	9	4	26	0	0	0-0	.160	.191	.274	.464	1	.995
— Tucson (PCL)	1B-C	45	162	23	52	13	0	9	32	9	23	3	2	3-1	.321	.366	.568	.934	3	.990
2002— Arizona (N.L.)	C-1B	70	154	12	36	10	0	3	23	10	25	3	4	1-0	.234	.288	.357	.645	1	.997
— Tucson (PCL)	C-1B	5	16	2	7	1	0	1	1	1	2	0	0	0-0	.438	.471	.688	1.158	0	1.000
2003— Tucson (PCL)	C-DH	4	16	3	7	1	0	1	4	1	1	0	0	0-0	.438	.471	.688	1.158	0	1.000
— Lancaster (Calif.)	C-DH	3	12	2	5	0	0	0	3	1	2	0	0	0-0	.417	.462	.417	.878	0	1.000
— Arizona (N.L.)	C	80	220	19	48	15	0	3	28	14	43	1	6	0-0	.218	.265	.327	.592	0	1.000
2004— Texas (A.L.)	C-1B	108	358	50	89	26	1	15	58	13	63	3	3	0-1	.249	.276	.453	.728	7	.990
American League totals (1 year)		108	358	50	89	26	1	15	58	13	63	3	3	0-1	.249	.276	.453	.728	7	.990
National League totals (5 years)		211	509	44	108	29	0	11	66	29	99	4	10	1-0	.212	.257	.334	.591	2	.998
Major League totals (6 years)		319	867	94	197	55	1	26	124	42	162	7	13	1-1	.227	.265	.383	.648	9	.995

DIVISION SERIES RECORD

Year Team (League)	Pos.	G	AB	R	H	2B	3B	HR	RBI	BB	SO	HBP	GDP	SB-CS	Avg.	OBP	SLG	OPS	E	Avg.
2001— Arizona (N.L.)	C	1	0	0	0	0	0	0	0	0	0	0	0	0-0	...	...	...	...	0	...
2002— Arizona (N.L.)	C	2	4	1	1	0	0	1	1	0	1	0	0	0-0	.250	.250	1.000	1.250	0	1.000
Division series totals (2 years)		3	4	1	1	0	0	1	1	0	1	0	0	0-0	.250	.250	1.000	1.250	0	1.000

CHAMPIONSHIP SERIES RECORD

Year Team (League)	Pos.	G	AB	R	H	2B	3B	HR	RBI	BB	SO	HBP	GDP	SB-CS	Avg.	OBP	SLG	OPS	E	Avg.
2001— Arizona (N.L.)		Did not play.																		

WORLD SERIES RECORD

Year Team (League)	Pos.	G	AB	R	H	2B	3B	HR	RBI	BB	SO	HBP	GDP	SB-CS	Avg.	OBP	SLG	OPS	E	Avg.
2001— Arizona (N.L.)	C	2	5	1	2	0	0	1	1	0	0	0	0	0-0	.400	.400	1.000	1.400	0	1.000

BARD, JOSH — C

PERSONAL: Born March 30, 1978, in Ithaca, N.Y. ... 6-3/215. ... Bats both, throws right. ... Full name: Joshua David Bard. ... Name pronounced: baahrd. ... High school: Cherry Creek (Englewood, Colo.). ... College: Texas Tech.

TRANSACTIONS/CAREER NOTES: Selected by Minnesota Twins organization in 35th round of 1996 free-agent draft; did not sign. ... Selected by Colorado Rockies organization in third round of 1999 free-agent draft. ... Traded by Rockies with OF Jody Gerut to Cleveland Indians for OF Jacob Cruz (June 2, 2001). ... On disabled list (March 28-July 5, 2004); included rehabilitation assignments to Akron and Buffalo.

2004 GAMES PLAYED BY POSITION (MLB): C—7.

Year Team (League)	Pos.	G	AB	R	H	2B	3B	HR	RBI	BB	SO	HBP	GDP	SB-CS	Avg.	OBP	SLG	OPS	E	Avg.
2000— Salem (Caro.)	C	93	309	40	88	17	0	2	25	32	33	1	6	3-1	.285	.352	.359	.711	10	.987
— Colo. Springs (PCL)	C	4	17	0	4	0	0	0	1	0	2	0	0	0-0	.235	.235	.235	.471	1	.923
2001— Carolina (Southern)	C	35	124	14	32	13	0	1	24	19	23	1	1	0-1	.258	.359	.387	.746	2	.993
— Akron (East.)	C	51	194	26	54	11	0	4	25	16	27	2	4	0-0	.278	.338	.397	.735	4	.986
— Mahoning Valley (NY-P)	C	13	44	7	12	4	0	2	8	6	2	1	1	0-1	.273	.373	.500	.873	3	.769
— Buffalo (Int'l)	DH	1	4	0	0	0	0	0	0	0	1	0	0	0-0	.000	.000	.000	.000	...	...
2002— Buffalo (Int'l)	C	94	344	36	102	26	2	6	53	20	45	0	13	0-0	.297	.332	.436	.768	11	.984
— Cleveland (A.L.)	C	24	90	9	20	5	0	3	12	4	13	0	6	0-0	.222	.255	.378	.633	2	.988
2003— Buffalo (Int'l)	C-DH	35	115	14	38	7	0	5	21	14	17	1	5	1-2	.330	.408	.522	.929	1	.995
— Cleveland (A.L.)	C-DH	91	303	25	74	13	1	8	36	22	53	0	9	0-2	.244	.293	.373	.666	5	.991
2004— Akron (East.)	DH-C	10	30	5	5	1	0	0	5	7	5	0	2	0-0	.167	.324	.200	.524	0	1.000
— Buffalo (Int'l)	C-DH	40	156	25	41	10	0	4	18	11	23	0	7	0-0	.263	.310	.404	.713	3	.988
— Cleveland (A.L.)	C	7	19	5	8	2	0	1	4	3	0	0	0	0-0	.421	.478	.684	1.162	0	1.000
Major League totals (3 years)		122	412	39	102	20	1	12	52	29	66	0	15	0-2	.248	.294	.388	.683	7	.991

BARMES, CLINT — SS/2B

PERSONAL: Born March 6, 1979, in Vincennes, Ind. ... 6-0/175. ... Bats right, throws right. ... Full name: Clint Harold Barmes. ... College: Indiana State.

TRANSACTIONS/CAREER NOTES: Selected by Colorado Rockies in 10th round of 2000 free-agent draft.

2004 GAMES PLAYED BY POSITION (MLB): 2B—9, SS—9.

Year Team (League)	Pos.	G	AB	R	H	2B	3B	HR	RBI	BB	SO	HBP	GDP	SB-CS	Avg.	OBP	SLG	OPS	E	Avg.
2000— Portland (N'west)	SS-OF	45	181	37	51	6	4	2	16	18	28	5	1	12-9	.282	.361	.392	.753	12	.934
— Asheville (S. Atl.)	2B-SS-3B-OF	19	81	11	14	4	0	0	4	10	13	1	3	4-1	.173	.269	.222	.491	2	.977
2001— Asheville (S. Atl.)	SS	74	285	40	74	14	1	5	24	17	37	7	6	21-7	.260	.314	.368	.683	22	.943
— Salem (Caro.)	SS	38	121	17	30	3	3	0	9	15	20	4	5	4-1	.248	.350	.322	.672	13	.934
2002— Carolina (Southern)	SS	103	438	62	119	23	2	15	60	31	72	9	3	15-11	.272	.329	.436	.765	33	.940
2003— Colo. Springs (PCL)	SS-2B	136	493	63	136	35	1	7	54	22	63	9	9	12-7	.276	.316	.394	.709	29	.951
— Colorado (N.L.)	SS	12	25	2	8	3	0	0	2	0	10	2	0	0-0	.320	.357	.400	.757	2	.958
2004— Colo. Springs (PCL)	SS-2B-DH	125	533	104	175	42	2	16	51	28	61	15	5	20-8	.328	.376	.505	.881	20	.964
— Colorado (N.L.)	2B-SS	20	71	14	20	3	1	2	10	3	10	1	2	0-1	.282	.320	.437	.757	2	.980
Major League totals (2 years)		32	96	16	28	5	1	2	12	3	20	3	2	0-1	.292	.330	.427	.757	4	.973

BARRETT, MICHAEL   C

PERSONAL: Born October 22, 1976, in Atlanta, Ga. ... 6-3/210. ... Bats right, throws right. ... Full name: Michael Patrick Barrett. ... High school: Pace Academy (Atlanta).
TRANSACTIONS/CAREER NOTES: Selected by Montreal Expos organization in first round (28th pick overall) of 1995 free-agent draft. ... On disabled list (June 24-July 11, 1999); included rehabilitation assignment to Ottawa. ... On disabled list (July 27-September 10, 2003); included rehabilitation assignment to Edmonton. ... Traded by Expos to Oakland Athletics for P Brett Price (December 15, 2003). ... Traded by Athletics to Chicago Cubs for C Damian Miller (December 16, 2003).
2004 GAMES PLAYED BY POSITION (MLB): C—130.

Year Team (League)	Pos.	G	AB	R	H	2B	3B	HR	RBI	BB	SO	HBP	GDP	SB-CS	Avg.	OBP	SLG	OPS	E	Avg.
1995— GC Expos (GCL)	3B-SS	50	183	22	57	13	4	0	19	15	19	0	1	7-6	.311	.362	.426	.788	25	.893
— Vermont (N.Y.-Penn.)	SS	3	10	0	1	0	0	0	1	1	1	0	0	0-0	.100	.167	.100	.267	0	1.000
1996— Delmarva (S. Atl.)	C-DH-3B	129	474	57	113	29	4	4	62	18	42	9	9	5-11	.238	.277	.342	.618	15	.978
1997— W.P. Beach (FSL)	C-DH	119	423	52	120	30	0	8	61	36	49	5	11	7-4	.284	.340	.411	.751	13	.982
1998— Harrisburg (East.)	C-3B-DH	120	453	78	145	32	2	19	87	27	43	2	16	7-6	.320	.358	.525	.883	12	.981
— Montreal (N.L.)	3B-C	8	23	3	7	2	0	1	2	3	6	1	0	0-0	.304	.407	.522	.929	3	.929
1999— Montreal (N.L.)	3B-C-SS	126	433	53	127	32	3	8	52	32	39	3	18	0-2	.293	.345	.436	.782	14	.973
— Ottawa (Int'l)	3B	2	7	1	3	0	0	0	2	1	0	0	0	0-1	.429	.500	.429	.929	1	.800
2000— Ottawa (Int'l)	3B-C	31	120	21	43	7	0	2	19	13	10	2	5	1-0	.358	.430	.467	.896	5	.945
— Montreal (N.L.)	3B-C	89	271	28	58	15	1	1	22	23	35	1	7	0-1	.214	.277	.288	.565	15	.949
2001— Montreal (N.L.)	C	132	472	42	118	33	2	6	38	25	54	2	14	2-1	.250	.289	.367	.655	7	.993
2002— Montreal (N.L.)	C-1B	117	376	41	99	20	1	12	49	40	65	1	14	6-3	.263	.332	.418	.749	9	.989
2003— Edmonton (PCL)	C	2	6	2	2	1	0	0	0	0	2	0	0	1-0	.333	.333	.500	.833	0	1.000
— Montreal (N.L.)	C	70	226	33	47	9	2	10	30	21	37	2	6	0-0	.208	.280	.398	.678	1	.998
2004— Chicago (N.L.)	C	134	456	55	131	32	6	16	65	36	64	5	13	1-4	.287	.337	.489	.826	6	.994
Major League totals (7 years)		676	2257	255	587	143	15	54	258	177	300	15	72	9-11	.260	.316	.409	.724	55	.987

BARTLETT, JASON   SS

PERSONAL: Born October 30, 1979, in Mountain View, Calif. ... 6-0/180. ... Bats right, throws right. ... Full name: Jason Alan Bartlett. ... High school: St. Mary's (Lodi, Calif.). ... College: Oklahoma.
TRANSACTIONS/CAREER NOTES: Selected by San Diego Padres organization in 13th round of 2001 free-agent draft. ... Traded by Padres to Minnesota Twins for OF Brian Buchanan (July 12, 2002).
2004 GAMES PLAYED BY POSITION (MLB): SS—5, 2B—1, DH—1.

Year Team (League)	Pos.	G	AB	R	H	2B	3B	HR	RBI	BB	SO	HBP	GDP	SB-CS	Avg.	OBP	SLG	OPS	E	Avg.
2001— Eugene (Northwest)	SS	68	267	49	80	12	4	3	37	28	47	4	6	12-4	.300	.371	.408	.779	17	.946
2002— Lake Elsinore (Calif.)	SS	75	308	57	77	14	4	1	33	32	53	5	7	24-5	.250	.329	.331	.660	22	.929
— Fort Myers (FSL)	SS-3B-2B	39	145	24	38	7	0	2	9	17	24	2	1	11-2	.262	.341	.352	.693	7	.949
2003— New Britain (East.)	SS	139	548	96	162	31	8	8	48	58	67	20	7	41-24	.296	.380	.425	.805	20	.969
2004— GC Twins (GCL)	SS	5	14	1	5	1	0	0	1	0	3	1	0	0-0	.357	.400	.429	.829	2	.846
— Rochester (Int'l)	SS-2B-DH	67	269	54	89	15	7	3	29	33	37	7	1	7-3	.331	.415	.472	.873	19	.946
— Minnesota (A.L.)	SS-2B-DH	8	12	2	1	0	0	0	1	1	1	0	0	2-0	.083	.154	.083	.237	2	.895
Major League totals (1 year)		8	12	2	1	0	0	0	1	1	1	0	0	2-0	.083	.154	.083	.237	2	.895

BARTOSH, CLIFF   P

PERSONAL: Born September 5, 1979, in West, Texas. ... 6-2/180. ... Throws left, bats left. ... Full name: Clifford Paul Bartosh. ... High school: Duncanville (Texas).
TRANSACTIONS/CAREER NOTES: Selected by San Diego Padres organization in 29th round of 1998 free-agent draft. ... Claimed on waivers by Detroit Tigers (October 31, 2003). ... Claimed on waivers by Cleveland Indians (December 8, 2003).
CAREER HITTING: 0-for-0 (.000), 0 R, 0 2B, 0 3B, 0 HR, 0 RBI.

Year Team (League)	W	L	Pct.	ERA	WHIP	G	GS	CG	ShO	Hld.	Sv.-Opp.	IP	H	R	ER	HR	BB-IBB	SO	Avg.
1998— Ariz. Padres (Ariz.)	3	2	.600	3.48	1.34	13	5	0	0	...	0-...	44.0	43	23	17	2	16-0	43	.257
1999— Fort Wayne (Midw.)	5	12	.294	4.44	1.43	35	20	1	1	...	0-...	129.2	136	76	64	14	49-0	100	.270
2000— Fort Wayne (Midw.)	8	4	.667	3.04	1.22	50	4	0	0	...	1-...	77.0	50	40	26	6	44-3	94	.178
2001— Lake Elsinore (Calif.)	6	2	.750	1.58	1.18	38	0	0	0	...	10-...	45.2	42	17	8	2	12-5	66	.237
— Mobile (Sou.)	1	2	.333	3.97	1.46	20	0	0	0	...	2-...	22.2	20	12	10	5	13-1	20	.233
2002— Mobile (Sou.)	2	4	.333	3.18	1.22	62	0	0	0	...	25-...	70.2	54	28	25	4	32-5	70	.211
2003— Portland (PCL)	2	5	.286	4.29	1.25	64	0	0	0	...	10-...	71.1	67	36	34	4	22-1	51	.249
2004— Buffalo (Int'l)	0	3	.000	2.80	0.96	28	0	0	0	...	3-...	35.1	26	11	11	3	8-2	46	.202
— Cleveland (A.L.)	1	0	1.000	4.66	1.71	34	0	0	0	3	0-2	19.1	22	10	10	4	11-0	25	.275
Major League totals (1 year)	1	0	1.000	4.66	1.71	34	0	0	0	3	0-2	19.1	22	10	10	4	11-0	25	.275

BATISTA, MIGUEL   P

PERSONAL: Born February 19, 1971, in Santo Domingo, Dominican Republic. ... 6-1/197. ... Throws right, bats right. ... Full name: Miguel Jerez Batista. ... Name pronounced: bah-TEESE-tah. ... High school: Nuevo Horizondes (San Pedro de Macoris, Dominican Republic).
TRANSACTIONS/CAREER NOTES: Signed as non-drafted free agent by Montreal Expos organization (February 29, 1988). ... Selected by Pittsburgh Pirates from Expos organization in Rule 5 major league draft (December 9, 1991). ... Returned to Expos organization (April 23, 1992). ... Released by Expos (November 18, 1994). ... Signed by Florida Marlins organization (December 9, 1994). ... Claimed on waivers by Chicago Cubs (December 17, 1996). ... Traded by Cubs to Expos for OF Henry Rodriguez (December 12, 1997). ... On disabled list (July 16-August 10, 1999); included rehabilitation assignment to Ottawa. ... Traded by Expos to Kansas City Royals for P Brad Rigby (April 25,

2000). ... Signed as a free agent by Arizona Diamondbacks organization (November 3, 2000). ... On suspended list (May 23-June 2, 2003). ... Signed as a free agent by Toronto Blue Jays (December 18, 2003).

CAREER HITTING: 21-for-224 (.094), 16 R, 4 2B, 0 3B, 2 HR, 5 RBI.

Year— Team (League)	W	L	Pct.	ERA	WHIP	G	GS	CG	ShO	Hld.	Sv.-Opp.	IP	H	R	ER	HR	BB-IBB	SO	Avg.
1989— DSL Expos (DSL)	1	7	.125	4.24	1.56	13	11	0	0	...	0-...	68.0	56	46	32	...	50-...	60	...
1990— GC Expos (GCL)	4	3	.571	2.06	1.27	9	6	0	0	...	0-...	39.1	33	16	9	0	17-0	21	.226
— Rockford (Midwest)	0	1	.000	8.76	1.70	3	2	0	0	...	0-...	12.1	16	13	12	2	5-0	7	.302
1991— Rockford (Midwest)	11	5	.688	4.04	1.37	23	23	2	1	...	0-...	133.2	126	74	60	1	57-0	90	.245
1992— Pittsburgh (N.L.)	0	0	...	9.00	3.50	1	0	0	0	0	0-0	2.0	4	2	2	1	3-0	1	.400
— W.P. Beach (FSL)	7	7	.500	3.79	1.36	24	24	1	0	...	0-...	135.1	130	69	57	3	54-1	92	.251
1993— Harrisburg (Eastern)	13	5	.722	4.34	1.60	26	26	0	0	...	0-...	141.0	139	79	68	11	86-0	91	.263
1994— Harrisburg (Eastern)	0	1	.000	2.38	1.50	3	3	0	0	...	0-...	11.1	8	3	3	0	9-0	5	.200
1995— Charlotte (Int'l)	6	12	.333	4.80	1.53	34	18	0	0	...	0-...	116.1	118	79	62	11	60-2	58	.260
1996— Charlotte (Int'l)	4	3	.571	5.38	1.71	47	2	0	0	...	4-...	77.0	93	57	46	4	39-0	56	.303
— Florida (N.L.)	0	0	...	5.56	1.41	9	0	0	0	0	0-...	11.1	9	8	7	0	7-2	6	.231
1997— Iowa (Am. Assoc.)	9	4	.692	4.20	1.27	31	14	2	2	...	0-...	122.0	117	60	57	19	38-1	95	.252
— Chicago (N.L.)	0	5	.000	5.70	1.65	11	6	0	0	0	0-0	36.1	36	24	23	4	24-2	27	.267
1998— Montreal (N.L.)	3	5	.375	3.80	1.53	56	13	0	0	3	0-0	135.0	141	66	57	12	65-7	92	.274
1999— Montreal (N.L.)	8	7	.533	4.88	1.51	39	17	2	1	0	1-1	134.2	146	88	73	10	58-2	95	.280
— Ottawa (Int'l)	0	0	.000	2.25	0.88	3	3	0	0	...	0-...	8.0	3	2	2	1	4-0	7	.115
2000— Montreal (N.L.)	0	1	.000	14.04	2.64	4	0	0	0	0	0-2	8.1	19	14	13	2	3-0	7	.452
— Kansas City (A.L.)	2	6	.250	7.74	1.75	14	9	0	0	0	0-0	57.0	66	54	49	17	34-2	30	.292
— Omaha (PCL)	2	2	.500	6.04	1.48	18	1	0	0	...	3-...	28.1	35	20	19	6	7-0	27	.302
2001— Arizona (N.L.)	11	8	.579	3.36	1.24	48	18	0	0	4	0-0	139.1	113	57	52	13	60-2	90	.226
2002— Arizona (N.L.)	8	9	.471	4.29	1.31	36	29	1	0	2	0-0	184.2	172	99	88	12	70-3	112	.245
2003— Arizona (N.L.)	10	9	.526	3.54	1.33	36	29	2	1	0	0-0	193.1	197	85	76	13	60-3	142	.267
2004— Toronto (A.L.)	10	13	.435	4.80	1.52	38	31	2	1	0	5-5	198.2	206	115	106	22	•96-1	104	.273
American League totals (2 years)	12	19	.387	5.46	1.57	52	40	2	1	0	5-5	255.2	272	169	155	39	130-3	134	.277
National League totals (9 years)	40	44	.476	4.16	1.40	240	112	5	2	9	1-3	845.0	837	443	391	67	350-21	572	.262
Major League totals (10 years)	52	63	.452	4.46	1.44	292	152	7	3	9	6-8	1100.2	1109	612	546	106	480-24	706	.265

DIVISION SERIES RECORD

Year— Team (League)	W	L	Pct.	ERA	WHIP	G	GS	CG	ShO	Hld.	Sv.-Opp.	IP	H	R	ER	HR	BB-IBB	SO	Avg.
2001— Arizona (N.L.)	1	0	1.000	2.70	0.60	2	1	0	0	0	0-0	6.2	3	2	2	1	1-0	4	.136
2002— Arizona (N.L.)	0	1	.000	9.82	2.18	1	1	0	0	0	0-0	3.2	5	4	4	0	3-0	1	.357
Division series totals (2 years)	1	1	.500	5.23	1.16	3	2	0	0	0	0-0	10.1	8	6	6	1	4-0	5	.222

CHAMPIONSHIP SERIES RECORD

Year— Team (League)	W	L	Pct.	ERA	WHIP	G	GS	CG	ShO	Hld.	Sv.-Opp.	IP	H	R	ER	HR	BB-IBB	SO	Avg.
2001— Arizona (N.L.)	0	1	.000	5.14	1.00	2	1	0	0	0	0-0	7.0	5	4	4	2	2-0	3	.185

WORLD SERIES RECORD

Year— Team (League)	W	L	Pct.	ERA	WHIP	G	GS	CG	ShO	Hld.	Sv.-Opp.	IP	H	R	ER	HR	BB-IBB	SO	Avg.
2001— Arizona (N.L.)	0	0	...	0.00	1.25	2	1	0	0	0	0-0	8.0	5	0	0	0	5-0	6	.192

BATISTA, TONY — 3B

PERSONAL: Born December 9, 1973, in Puerto Plata, Dominican Republic. ... 6-0/208. ... Bats right, throws right. ... Full name: Leocadio Francisco Batista. ... Name pronounced: bah-TEESE-tah.

TRANSACTIONS/CAREER NOTES: Signed as non-drafted free agent by Oakland Athletics organization (February 8, 1991). ... On disabled list (August 27-September 12, 1997); included rehabilitation assignment to Edmonton. ... Selected by Arizona Diamondbacks in first round (27th pick overall) of expansion draft (November 18, 1997). ... Traded by Diamondbacks with P John Frascatore to Toronto Blue Jays for P Dan Plesac (June 12, 1999). ... Claimed on waivers by Baltimore Orioles (June 25, 2001). ... Signed as a free agent by Montreal Expos (January 6, 2004). ... Expos franchise transferred to Washington, D.C., for 2005 season.

RECORDS: Shares major league record for strikeouts, 9-inning game (5, August 31, 2004).

2004 GAMES PLAYED BY POSITION (MLB): 3B—155.

Year Team (League)	Pos.	G	AB	R	H	2B	3B	HR	RBI	BB	SO	HBP	GDP	SB-CS	Avg.	OBP	SLG	OPS	E	Avg.
1991— Dom. Athletics (DSL)		46	166	16	31	5	1	2	15	23	16	...	...	4-...	.187	...	.265	...	...	...
1992— Ariz. A's (Ariz.)	2B-SS-OF	45	167	32	41	6	2	0	22	15	29	2	4	1-0	.246	.315	.305	.621	8	.960
1993— Ariz. A's (Ariz.)	2B-3B-SS	24	104	21	34	6	2	2	17	6	14	0	1	6-2	.327	.357	.481	.838	3	.967
— Tacoma (PCL)	OF	4	12	1	2	1	0	0	1	1	4	1	0	0-0	.167	.286	.250	.536	0	1.000
1994— Modesto (California)	2B-SS	119	466	91	131	26	3	17	68	54	108	4	10	7-7	.281	.359	.459	.819	30	.949
1995— Huntsville (Sou.)	SS-2B	120	419	55	107	23	1	16	61	29	98	2	8	7-8	.255	.305	.430	.734	29	.949
1996— Edmonton (PCL)	SS	57	205	33	66	17	4	8	40	15	30	2	8	2-1	.322	.372	.561	.933	8	.973
— Oakland (A.L.)	2B-3B-SS-DH	74	238	38	71	10	2	6	25	19	49	1	2	7-3	.298	.350	.433	.783	5	.983
1997— Oakland (A.L.)	SS-3B-2B-DH	68	188	22	38	10	1	4	18	14	31	2	8	2-2	.202	.265	.330	.594	8	.971
— Edmonton (PCL)	SS-DH	33	124	25	39	10	1	3	21	17	18	1	4	2-2	.315	.396	.484	.880	6	.952
1998— Arizona (N.L.)	2B-SS-3B	106	293	46	80	16	1	18	41	18	52	3	7	1-1	.273	.318	.519	.836	6	.982
1999— Arizona (N.L.)	SS	44	144	16	37	5	0	5	21	16	17	2	1	2-0	.257	.335	.396	.731	4	.979
— Toronto (A.L.)	SS	98	375	61	107	25	1	26	79	22	79	4	11	2-0	.285	.328	.565	.893	12	.975
2000— Toronto (A.L.)	3B	154	620	96	163	32	2	41	114	35	121	6	15	5-4	.263	.307	.519	.827	17	.963
2001— Toronto (A.L.)	3B	72	271	29	56	11	1	13	45	13	66	4	2	0-1	.207	.251	.399	.649	10	.953
— Baltimore (A.L.)	DH-3B-SS	84	308	41	82	15	5	12	42	19	47	0	7	5-1	.266	.305	.468	.773	6	.965
2002— Baltimore (A.L.)	3B-DH	161	615	60	150	36	1	31	87	50	107	11	13	5-4	.244	.309	.457	.766	16	.962
2003— Baltimore (A.L.)	3B-DH	161	631	76	148	20	1	26	99	28	102	5	20	4-3	.235	.270	.393	.663	20	.950
2004— Montreal (N.L.)	3B	157	606	76	146	30	2	32	110	26	78	4	14	14-6	.241	.272	.455	.728	19	.954
American League totals (7 years)		872	3246	453	815	160	14	159	504	200	602	33	78	30-18	.251	.299	.456	.755	94	.965
National League totals (3 years)		307	1043	138	263	51	3	55	172	60	147	9	22	17-7	.252	.294	.465	.759	29	.969
Major League totals (9 years)		1179	4289	591	1078	211	17	214	681	260	749	42	100	47-25	.251	.298	.458	.756	123	.966

ALL-STAR GAME RECORD

	G	AB	R	H	2B	3B	HR	RBI	BB	SO	HBP	GDP	SB-CS	Avg.	OBP	SLG	OPS	E	Avg.
All-Star Game totals (2 years)	2	4	1	1	0	0	0	1	0	2	0	0	0-0	.250	.250	.250	.500	0	1.000

B

BAUER, RICK   P

PERSONAL: Born January 10, 1977, in Garden Grove, Calif. ... 6-6/223. ... Throws right, bats right. ... Full name: Richard Edward Bauer. ... Name pronounced: BOW-er. ... High school: Centennial (Meridian, Idaho). ... Junior college: Treasure Valley (Ore.) Community College.

TRANSACTIONS/CAREER NOTES: Selected by Baltimore Orioles organization in fifth round of 1997 free-agent draft. ... On disabled list (June 15-July 3, 2004); included rehabilitation assignments to Bowie and Ottawa.

CAREER HITTING: 0-for-0 (.000), 0 R, 0 2B, 0 3B, 0 HR, 0 RBI.

Year Team (League)	W	L	Pct.	ERA	WHIP	G	GS	CG	ShO	Hld.	Sv.-Opp.	IP	H	R	ER	HR	BB-IBB	SO	Avg.
1997—Bluefield (Appalachian)	8	3	.727	2.86	1.08	13	13	0	0	...	0-...	72.1	58	31	23	1	20-0	67	.218
—Delmarva (S.Atl.)	0	0	...	0.00	0.50	1	0	0	0	...	1-...	2.0	0	0	0	0	1-0	2	.000
1998—Delmarva (S.Atl.)	5	8	.385	4.73	1.45	22	22	1	0	...	0-...	118.0	127	69	62	11	44-0	81	.285
1999—Frederick (Caro.)	10	9	.526	4.56	1.40	26	26	4	0	...	0-...	152.0	159	85	77	17	54-2	123	.273
2000—Bowie (East.)	6	8	.429	5.30	1.50	26	23	1	0	...	1-...	129.0	154	89	76	16	39-1	87	.293
—Frederick (Caro.)	0	1	.000	5.21	1.37	3	3	0	0	...	0-...	19.0	20	13	11	1	6-0	15	.278
2001—Bowie (East.)	2	6	.250	3.54	1.02	9	9	2	0	...	0-...	61.0	52	27	24	8	10-0	34	.227
—Rochester (Int'l)	10	4	.714	3.89	1.30	19	18	1	1	...	0-...	113.1	119	63	49	10	28-0	89	.263
—Baltimore (A.L.)	0	5	.000	4.64	1.33	6	6	0	0	0	0-0	33.0	35	22	17	7	9-0	16	.265
2002—Baltimore (A.L.)	6	7	.462	3.98	1.43	56	1	0	0	12	1-5	83.2	84	41	37	12	36-4	45	.268
—Rochester (Int'l)	0	1	.000	6.75	1.50	1	1	0	0	...	0-...	4.0	4	3	3	2	2-0	1	.267
2003—Ottawa (Int'l)	3	1	.750	2.45	1.20	7	7	0	0	...	0-...	36.2	31	10	10	1	13-0	21	.235
—Baltimore (A.L.)	0	0	...	4.55	1.34	35	0	0	0	3	0-1	61.1	58	36	31	5	24-3	43	.256
2004—Bowie (East.)	0	0	...	0.00	0.67	1	1	0	0	...	0-...	3.0	2	0	0	0	0-0	1	.200
—Ottawa (Int'l)	3	5	.375	4.00	1.40	11	11	0	0	...	0-...	63.0	69	28	28	3	19-0	42	.285
—Baltimore (A.L.)	2	1	.667	4.70	1.29	23	2	0	0	0	0-1	53.2	49	31	28	4	20-0	37	.238
Major League totals (4 years)	8	13	.381	4.39	1.36	120	9	0	0	15	1-7	231.2	226	130	113	28	89-7	141	.257

BAUTISTA, DANNY   OF

PERSONAL: Born May 24, 1972, in Santo Domingo, Dominican Republic. ... 5-11/225. ... Bats right, throws right. ... Full name: Daniel Bautista. ... Name pronounced: BAW-tee-sta.

TRANSACTIONS/CAREER NOTES: Signed as non-drafted free agent by Detroit Tigers organization (June 24, 1989). ... Traded by Tigers to Atlanta Braves for OF Anton French (May 31, 1996). ... On disabled list (June 28, 1996-remainder of season). ... On disabled list (March 23-April 23, 1997); included rehabilitation assignment to Richmond. ... On disabled list (April 17-May 7 and August 25-September 17, 1998); included rehabilitation assignment to Greenville. ... Released by Braves (April 2, 1999). ... Signed by Florida Marlins organization (April 8, 1999). ... Traded by Marlins to Arizona Diamondbacks for IF Andy Fox (June 10, 2000). ... On disabled list (May 23, 2002-remainder of season). ... On disabled list (June 19-July 23, 2003); included rehabilitation assignment to Tucson.

RECORDS: Shares major league record for most strikeouts, 9-inning game (5, May 28, 1995).

2004 GAMES PLAYED BY POSITION (MLB): OF—137, DH—1.

Year Team (League)	Pos.	G	AB	R	H	2B	3B	HR	RBI	BB	SO	HBP	GDP	SB-CS	Avg.	OBP	SLG	OPS	E	Avg.
1989—		Did not play.																		
1990—Bristol (Appal.)	OF	27	95	9	26	3	0	2	12	8	21	0	1	2-3	.274	.330	.368	.699	0	1.000
1991—Fayetteville (SAL)	OF	69	234	21	45	6	4	1	30	21	65	1	8	7-7	.192	.259	.265	.524	4	.973
1992—Fayetteville (SAL)	OF	121	453	59	122	22	0	5	52	29	76	5	9	18-20	.269	.319	.351	.670	6	.974
1993—London (East.)	OF	117	424	55	121	21	1	6	48	32	69	2	8	28-12	.285	.334	.382	.716	3	.989
—Detroit (A.L.)	OF-DH	17	61	6	19	3	0	1	9	1	10	0	1	3-1	.311	.317	.410	.727	0	1.000
1994—Detroit (A.L.)	OF-DH	31	99	12	23	4	1	4	15	3	18	0	3	1-2	.232	.255	.414	.669	0	1.000
—Toledo (Int'l)	OF	27	98	7	25	7	0	2	14	6	23	0	2	2-3	.255	.292	.388	.680	1	.982
1995—Detroit (A.L.)	OF	89	271	28	55	9	0	7	27	12	68	0	4	4-1	.203	.237	.314	.550	2	.988
—Toledo (Int'l)	OF	18	58	6	14	3	0	0	4	1	10	3	1	1-2	.241	.290	.293	.583	2	.943
1996—Detroit (A.L.)	OF-DH	25	64	12	16	2	0	2	8	9	15	0	1	1-2	.250	.342	.375	.717	1	.974
—Atlanta (N.L.)	OF	17	20	1	3	0	0	0	1	2	5	1	0	0-0	.150	.261	.150	.411	0	1.000
1997—Richmond (Int'l)	OF-DH	46	170	28	48	10	3	2	28	19	30	1	9	1-0	.282	.356	.412	.768	1	.984
—Atlanta (N.L.)	OF	64	103	14	25	3	2	3	9	5	24	1	3	2-0	.243	.282	.398	.680	1	.984
1998—Atlanta (N.L.)	OF-DH	82	144	17	36	11	0	3	17	7	21	0	4	1-0	.250	.281	.389	.670	2	.959
—Greenville (Sou.)	OF	2	6	1	2	0	0	1	2	1	1	0	0	0-0	.333	.429	.833	1.262	0	1.000
1999—Calgary (PCL)	OF-DH	38	135	25	43	8	1	8	28	11	18	1	1	3-3	.319	.374	.570	.945	3	.969
—Florida (N.L.)	OF	70	205	32	59	10	1	5	24	4	30	1	5	3-0	.288	.303	.420	.723	3	.979
2000—Florida (N.L.)	OF	44	89	9	17	4	0	4	12	5	20	0	1	1-0	.191	.234	.371	.605	1	.980
—Arizona (N.L.)	OF	87	262	45	83	16	7	7	47	20	30	3	10	5-2	.317	.366	.511	.877	2	.987
2001—Arizona (N.L.)	OF	100	222	26	67	11	2	5	26	14	31	1	7	3-2	.302	.346	.437	.783	0	1.000
2002—Arizona (N.L.)	OF	40	154	22	50	5	2	6	23	11	21	0	4	4-2	.325	.367	.500	.867	1	.985
2003—El Paso (Texas)	OF	2	7	1	1	0	0	0	1	1	2	0	0	0-0	.143	.250	.143	.393	0	1.000
—Tucson (PCL)	OF	8	24	4	9	1	1	1	4	2	2	0	2	1-1	.375	.423	.625	1.048	0	1.000
—Arizona (N.L.)	OF	88	284	29	78	16	3	4	36	21	54	4	7	3-2	.275	.330	.394	.724	5	.961
2004—Arizona (N.L.)	OF-DH	141	539	64	154	27	1	11	65	35	66	4	20	6-2	.286	.332	.401	.733	4	.986
American League totals (4 years)		162	495	58	113	18	1	14	59	25	111	0	11	9-6	.228	.265	.354	.618	3	.990
National League totals (9 years)		733	2022	259	572	103	18	48	260	124	298	15	64	28-10	.283	.327	.423	.749	19	.982
Major League totals (12 years)		895	2517	317	685	121	19	62	319	149	409	15	75	37-16	.272	.315	.409	.724	22	.984

DIVISION SERIES RECORD

Year Team (League)	Pos.	G	AB	R	H	2B	3B	HR	RBI	BB	SO	HBP	GDP	SB-CS	Avg.	OBP	SLG	OPS	E	Avg.
1997—Atlanta (N.L.)	OF	3	3	0	1	0	0	0	2	0	1	0	0	0-0	.333	.333	.333	.667	0	...
1998—Atlanta (N.L.)	OF	2	2	1	1	1	0	0	0	0	0	0	0	0-0	.500	.500	1.000	1.500	0	1.000
2001—Arizona (N.L.)	OF	3	6	0	0	0	0	0	1	0	1	0	0	0-0	.000	.000	.000	.000	0	1.000
Division series totals (3 years)		8	11	1	2	1	0	0	3	0	2	0	0	0-0	.182	.182	.273	.455	0	1.000

CHAMPIONSHIP SERIES RECORD

Year Team (League)	Pos.	G	AB	R	H	2B	3B	HR	RBI	BB	SO	HBP	GDP	SB-CS	Avg.	OBP	SLG	OPS	E	Avg.
1997—Atlanta (N.L.)	OF	2	4	0	1	0	0	0	1	0	1	0	0	0-0	.250	.250	.250	.500	0	1.000
1998—Atlanta (N.L.)	OF	5	5	0	0	0	0	0	0	0	1	0	0	0-0	.000	.000	.000	.000	1	.667
2001—Arizona (N.L.)	OF	2	4	1	1	0	0	0	1	1	0	0	0	0-0	.250	.400	.250	.650	0	1.000
Champ. series totals (3 years)		9	13	1	2	0	0	0	2	1	2	0	0	0-0	.154	.214	.154	.368	1	.889

Year Team (League)	Pos.	G	AB	R	H	2B	3B	HR	RBI	BB	SO	HBP	GDP	SB-CS	Avg.	OBP	SLG	OPS	E	Avg.
													WORLD SERIES RECORD						
2001— Arizona (N.L.)	DH-OF	5	12	1	7	2	0	0	7	1	1	0	0	0-0	.583	.615	.750	1.365	0	1.000

BAUTISTA, DENNY — P

PERSONAL: Born August 23, 1980, in Sanchez, Dominican Republic. ... 6-5/170. ... Throws right, bats right. ... Full name: Denny M. Bautista.

TRANSACTIONS/CAREER NOTES: Signed as a non-drafted free agent by Florida Marlins organization (April 11, 2000). ... Traded by Marlins with P Don Levinski to Baltimore Orioles for OF/1B Jeff Conine (August 31, 2003). ... Traded by Orioles to Kansas City Royals for P Jason Grimsley (June 21, 2004).

CAREER HITTING: 0-for-0 (.000), 0 R, 0 2B, 0 3B, 0 HR, 0 RBI.

Year Team (League)	W	L	Pct.	ERA	WHIP	G	GS	CG	ShO	Hld.	Sv.-Opp.	IP	H	R	ER	HR	BB-IBB	SO	Avg.
2000— GC Marlins (GCL)	6	2	.750	2.43	1.05	11	11	2	0	...	0-...	63.0	49	24	17	1	17-1	58	.209
— Utica (N.Y.-Penn)	0	0	...	3.60	1.20	1	1	0	0	...	0-...	5.0	4	3	2	0	2-0	5	.222
2001— Utica (N.Y.-Penn)	3	1	.750	2.08	0.79	7	7	0	0	...	0-...	39.0	25	16	9	0	6-0	31	.174
— Kane County (Midwest)	3	1	.750	4.35	1.45	8	7	0	0	...	0-...	39.1	43	21	19	2	14-0	20	.281
2002— Jupiter (FSL)	4	6	.400	4.99	1.36	19	15	0	0	...	0-...	88.1	80	52	49	6	40-0	79	.242
2003— Jupiter (FSL)	8	4	.667	3.21	1.23	14	14	0	0	...	0-...	84.0	68	32	30	2	35-0	77	.219
— Carolina (Southern)	4	5	.444	3.71	1.50	11	11	0	0	...	0-...	53.1	45	33	22	5	35-0	61	.226
2004— Baltimore (A.L.)	0	0	...	36.00	4.00	2	0	0	0	0	0-0	2.0	6	8	8	1	2-0	1	.545
— Bowie (East.)	3	5	.375	4.74	1.45	14	13	0	0	...	0-...	62.2	58	37	33	5	33-1	72	.243
— Wichita (Texas)	4	3	.571	2.54	1.22	12	12	2	0	...	0-...	81.2	68	32	23	3	32-0	73	.227
— Kansas City (A.L.)	0	4	.000	6.51	1.77	5	5	0	0	0	0-0	27.2	38	20	20	2	11-1	18	.333
Major League totals (1 year)	0	4	.000	8.49	1.92	7	5	0	0	0	0-0	29.2	44	28	28	3	13-1	19	.352

BAUTISTA, JOSE — OF/3B

PERSONAL: Born October 19, 1980, in Santo Domingo, Dominican Republic. ... 6-0/192. ... Bats right, throws right. ... Full name: Jose Antonio Bautista. ... High school: Instituto San Juan Bautista (Santo Domingo, D.R.). ... Junior college: Chipola (Fla.).

TRANSACTIONS/CAREER NOTES: Selected by Pittsburgh Pirates organization in 20th round of 2000 free-agent draft. ... Selected by Baltimore Orioles from Pirates organization in Rule 5 major league draft (December 15, 2003). ... Claimed on waivers by Tampa Bay Devil Rays (June 3, 2004). ... Traded by Devil Rays to Kansas City Royals for cash (June 28, 2004). ... Traded by Royals to New York Mets for C Justin Huber (July 30, 2004). ... Traded by Mets with IF Ty Wigginton and P Matt Peterson to Pittsburgh Pirates for P Kris Benson and IF Jeff Keppinger (July 30, 2004).

2004 GAMES PLAYED BY POSITION (MLB): OF—27, 3B—17, DH—3.

Year Team (League)	Pos.	G	AB	R	H	2B	3B	HR	RBI	BB	SO	HBP	GDP	SB-CS	Avg.	OBP	SLG	OPS	E	Avg.
											BATTING								**FIELDING**	
2001— Williamsport(P)	3B-OF	62	220	43	63	10	3	5	30	21	41	6	5	8-1	.286	.364	.427	.792	8	.927
2002— Hickory (S. Atl.)	3B-SS	129	438	72	132	26	3	14	57	67	104	8	12	3-2	.301	.402	.470	.872	24	.918
2003— GC Pirates (GCL)	3B	7	23	5	8	1	0	1	3	4	7	0	0	0-0	.348	.429	.522	.950	1	.929
— Lynchburg (Caro.)	3B-2B	51	165	28	40	14	2	4	20	27	48	3	1	1-5	.242	.359	.424	.783	10	.936
2004— Baltimore (A.L.)	OF-3B-DH	16	11	3	3	0	0	0	0	1	3	0	0	0-0	.273	.333	.273	.606	0	1.000
— Tampa Bay (A.L.)	OF-3B-DH	12	12	1	2	0	0	0	1	3	1	0	0	0-1	.167	.333	.167	.500	1	1.000
— Kansas City (A.L.)	3B-OF	13	25	1	5	1	0	0	1	1	12	0	0	0-0	.200	.231	.240	.471	1	.957
— Pittsburgh (N.L.)	OF	23	40	1	8	2	0	0	0	2	18	0	1	0-0	.200	.238	.250	.488	3	.864
American League totals (1 year)		41	48	5	10	1	0	0	2	5	22	0	0	0-1	.208	.283	.229	.512	1	.971
National League totals (1 year)		23	40	1	8	2	0	0	0	2	18	0	1	0-0	.200	.238	.250	.488	3	.864
Major League totals (1 year)		64	88	6	18	3	0	0	2	7	40	0	1	0-1	.205	.263	.239	.502	4	.929

BAY, JASON — OF

PERSONAL: Born September 20, 1978, in Trail, British Columbia. ... 6-2/200. ... Bats right, throws right. ... Full name: Jason Raymond Bay. ... High school: J. Lloyd Crowe Secondary (Trail, B.C.). ... College: Gonzaga.

TRANSACTIONS/CAREER NOTES: Selected by Montreal Expos in 22nd round of 2000 free-agent draft. ... Traded by Expos with P Jim Serrano to New York Mets for SS Lou Collier (March 27, 2002). ... Traded by Mets with Ps Bobby M. Jones and Josh Reynolds to San Diego Padres for Ps Steve Reed and Jason Middlebrook (July 31, 2002). ... Traded by Padres with P Oliver Perez and a player to be named to Pittsburgh Pirates for OF Brian Giles (August 27, 2003); Pirates obtained P Cory Stewart to complete deal (October 2, 2003). ... On disabled list (March 26-May 7, 2004); included rehabilitation assignment to Nashville.

HONORS: Named N.L. Rookie Player of the Year by THE SPORTING NEWS (2004). ... Named N.L. Rookie of the Year by Baseball Writers' Association of America (2004).

2004 GAMES PLAYED BY POSITION (MLB): OF—119.

Year Team (League)	Pos.	G	AB	R	H	2B	3B	HR	RBI	BB	SO	HBP	GDP	SB-CS	Avg.	OBP	SLG	OPS	E	Avg.
											BATTING								**FIELDING**	
2000— Vermont (N.Y.-Penn.)	OF	35	135	17	41	5	0	2	12	11	25	1	2	17-4	.304	.358	.385	.743	0	1.000
2001— Jupiter (FSL)	OF-2B	38	123	12	24	4	1	1	10	18	26	2	4	10-3	.195	.306	.268	.574	1	.963
— Clinton (Midw.)	OF	87	318	67	115	20	4	13	61	48	62	4	4	15-2	.362	.449	.572	1.021	3	.984
2002— St. Lucie (Fla. St.)	OF	69	261	48	71	12	2	9	54	34	54	5	4	22-2	.272	.363	.437	.800	6	.950
— Binghamton (East.)	OF	34	107	17	31	4	2	4	19	15	23	3	2	13-3	.290	.383	.477	.859	2	.956
— Mobile (Sou.)	OF	23	81	16	25	5	2	4	12	13	22	1	0	4-2	.309	.411	.568	.978	0	1.000
2003— San Diego (N.L.)	OF	3	8	2	2	1	0	1	2	1	1	1	0	0-0	.250	.400	.750	1.150	0	1.000
— Portland (PCL)	OF	91	307	64	93	11	1	20	59	55	71	5	3	23-4	.303	.410	.541	.951	1	.995
— Pittsburgh (N.L.)	OF	27	79	13	23	6	1	3	12	18	28	0	0	3-1	.291	.423	.506	.929	1	.976
2004— Nashville (PCL)	OF	4	10	3	4	2	0	1	3	3	5	0	0	0-0	.400	.538	.900	1.438	0	1.000
— Pittsburgh (N.L.)	OF	120	411	61	116	24	4	26	82	41	129	10	9	4-6	.282	.358	.550	.907	2	.991
Major League totals (2 years)		150	498	76	141	31	5	30	96	60	158	11	9	7-7	.283	.369	.546	.916	3	.989

BECK, ROD — P

PERSONAL: Born August 3, 1968, in Burbank, Calif. ... 6-1/230. ... Throws right, bats right. ... Full name: Rodney Roy Beck. ... High school: Grant (Van Nuys, Calif.).

TRANSACTIONS/CAREER NOTES: Selected by Oakland Athletics organization in 13th round of 1986 free-agent draft. ... Traded by A's to San Francisco Giants for P Charlie Corbell (March 23, 1988). ... On disabled list (April 6-30, 1994). ... Signed as a free agent by Chicago Cubs (January 15, 1998). ... On disabled list (May 17-July 21, 1999); included rehabilitation assignment to Iowa. ... Traded by Cubs to Boston Red Sox for P Mark Guthrie and a player to be named (August 31, 1999); Cubs acquired 3B Cole Liniak to complete deal (September 1, 1999). ... On disabled list (March 18-June 13 and July 3-22, 2000); included rehabilitation assignment to Pawtucket. ... Signed as a free agent by Cubs organization (December 28, 2002). ... Released by Cubs (June 1, 2003). ... Signed by San Diego Padres (June 2, 2003). ... On restricted list (March 15-April 20, 2004). ... Released by Padres (August 17, 2004).

CAREER HITTING: 4-for-19 (.211), 0 R, 0 2B, 0 3B, 0 HR, 1 RBI.

B

Year	Team (League)	W	L	Pct.	ERA	WHIP	G	GS	CG	ShO	Hld.	Sv.-Opp.	IP	H	R	ER	HR	BB-IBB	SO	Avg.
1986—	Medford (N'west)	1	3	.250	5.23	1.78	13	6	0	0	...	1-...	32.2	47	25	19	4	11-1	21	...
1987—	Medford (N'west)	5	8	.385	5.18	1.43	17	12	2	0	...	0-...	92.0	106	74	53	5	26-0	69	.270
1988—	Clinton (Midw.)	12	7	.632	3.00	1.15	28	23	5	1	...	0-...	177.0	177	68	59	11	27-2	123	.263
1989—	San Jose (California)	11	2	.846	2.40	1.20	13	13	4	0	...	0-...	97.1	91	29	26	5	26-0	88	.245
	— Shreveport (Texas)	7	3	.700	3.55	1.25	16	14	4	1	...	0-...	99.0	108	45	39	6	16-3	74	.275
1990—	Shreveport (Texas)	10	3	.769	2.23	1.10	14	14	2	1	...	0-...	93.0	85	26	23	4	17-1	71	.248
	— Phoenix (PCL)	4	7	.364	4.93	1.54	12	12	2	0	...	0-...	76.2	100	51	42	8	18-1	43	.313
1991—	Phoenix (PCL)	4	3	.571	2.02	0.97	23	5	3	0	...	6-...	71.1	56	18	16	3	13-2	35	.216
	— San Francisco (N.L.)	1	1	.500	3.78	1.26	31	0	0	0	1	1-1	52.1	53	22	22	4	13-2	38	.273
1992—	San Francisco (N.L.)	3	3	.500	1.76	0.84	65	0	0	0	4	17-23	92.0	62	20	18	4	15-2	87	.190
1993—	San Francisco (N.L.)	3	1	.750	2.16	0.88	76	0	0	0	0	48-52	79.1	57	20	19	11	13-4	86	.201
1994—	San Francisco (N.L.)	2	4	.333	2.77	1.27	48	0	0	0	0	28-28	48.2	49	17	15	10	13-2	39	.261
1995—	San Francisco (N.L.)	5	6	.455	4.45	1.38	60	0	0	0	0	33-43	58.2	60	31	29	7	21-3	42	.267
1996—	San Francisco (N.L.)	0	9	.000	3.34	1.06	63	0	0	0	0	35-42	62.0	56	23	23	9	10-2	48	.238
1997—	San Francisco (N.L.)	7	4	.636	3.47	1.07	73	0	0	0	1	37-45	70.0	67	31	27	7	8-2	53	.249
1998—	Chicago (N.L.)	3	4	.429	3.02	1.32	81	0	0	0	1	51-58	80.1	86	33	27	11	20-4	81	.269
1999—	Chicago (N.L.)	2	4	.333	7.80	1.80	31	0	0	0	1	7-11	30.0	41	26	26	5	13-3	13	.331
	— Iowa (PCL)	0	0	...	0.00	0.50	2	0	0	0	...	0-...	2.0	1	0	0	0	0-0	2	.143
	— Boston (A.L.)	0	1	.000	1.93	1.00	12	0	0	0	2	3-4	14.0	9	3	3	0	5-0	12	.184
2000—	Pawtucket (Int'l)	1	0	1.000	0.00	0.67	3	0	0	0	...	0-...	6.0	4	0	0	0	0-0	7	.182
	— Boston (A.L.)	3	0	1.000	3.10	1.13	34	0	0	0	7	0-3	40.2	34	15	14	2	12-1	35	.222
2001—	Boston (A.L.)	6	4	.600	3.90	1.30	68	0	0	0	15	6-11	80.2	77	42	35	15	28-6	63	.252
2003—	Iowa (PCL)	1	1	.500	0.59	1.00	21	0	0	0	...	4-...	30.2	25	3	2	2	7-0	26	.227
	— San Diego (N.L.)	3	2	.600	1.78	1.02	36	0	0	0	1	20-20	35.1	25	7	7	4	11-2	32	.197
2004—	San Diego (N.L.)	0	2	.000	6.38	1.50	26	0	0	0	5	0-...	24.0	27	18	17	8	9-0	15	.278
American League totals (3 years)		9	5	.643	3.46	1.22	114	0	0	0	24	9-18	135.1	120	60	52	17	45-7	110	.236
National League totals (11 years)		29	40	.420	3.27	1.15	590	0	0	0	14	277-323	632.2	583	248	230	80	146-26	534	.244
Major League totals (13 years)		38	45	.458	3.30	1.16	704	0	0	0	38	286-341	768.0	703	308	282	97	191-33	644	.243

DIVISION SERIES RECORD

Year	Team (League)	W	L	Pct.	ERA	WHIP	G	GS	CG	ShO	Hld.	Sv.-Opp.	IP	H	R	ER	HR	BB-IBB	SO	Avg.
1997—	San Francisco (N.L.)	0	0	...	0.00	0.75	1	0	0	0	0	0-0	1.1	1	0	0	0	0-0	1	.250
1998—	Chicago (N.L.)	0	0	...	16.20	4.20	1	0	0	0	0	0-0	1.2	5	3	3	1	2-1	1	.500
1999—	Boston (A.L.)	0	0	...	0.00	1.00	2	0	0	0	0	0-0	2.0	2	0	0	0	0-0	2	.250
Division series totals (3 years)		0	0	...	5.40	2.00	4	0	0	0	0	0-0	5.0	8	3	3	1	2-1	4	.364

CHAMPIONSHIP SERIES RECORD

Year	Team (League)	W	L	Pct.	ERA	WHIP	G	GS	CG	ShO	Hld.	Sv.-Opp.	IP	H	R	ER	HR	BB-IBB	SO	Avg.
1999—	Boston (A.L.)	0	1	.000	27.00	3.00	2	0	0	0	0	0-0	.2	2	2	2	2	0-0	1	.500

ALL-STAR GAME RECORD

		W	L	Pct.	ERA	WHIP	G	GS	CG	ShO	Hld.	Sv.-Opp.	IP	H	R	ER	HR	BB-IBB	SO	Avg.
All-Star Game totals (2 years)		0	0	...	3.38	1.13	2	0	0	0	0	0-0	2.2	3	1	1	0	0-0	2	.300

BECKETT, JOSH   P

PERSONAL: Born May 15, 1980, in Spring, Texas. ... 6-5/222. ... Throws right, bats right. ... Full name: Joshua Patrick Beckett. ... High school: Spring (Texas).
TRANSACTIONS/CAREER NOTES: Selected by Florida Marlins organization in first round (second pick overall) of 1999 free-agent draft. ... On disabled list (April 29-May 14, June 5-July 16 and August 23-September 11, 2002); included rehabilitation assignments to GCL Marlins and Jupiter. ... On disabled list (May 8-July 1, 2003); included rehabilitation assignments to Jupiter and Carolina. ... On disabled list (May 31-June 17, June 18-July 5 and July 6-30, 2004).
HONORS: Named Minor League Player of the Year by THE SPORTING NEWS (2001).
CAREER HITTING: 17-for-128 (.133), 6 R, 5 2B, 0 3B, 0 HR, 5 RBI.

Year	Team (League)	W	L	Pct.	ERA	WHIP	G	GS	CG	ShO	Hld.	Sv.-Opp.	IP	H	R	ER	HR	BB-IBB	SO	Avg.
2000—	Kane County (Midwest)	2	3	.400	2.12	1.01	13	12	0	0	...	0-...	59.1	45	18	14	4	15-0	61	.214
2001—	Brevard County (FSL)	6	0	1.000	1.23	0.72	13	12	0	0	...	0-...	65.2	32	13	9	0	15-0	101	.145
	— Portland (East.)	8	1	.889	1.82	0.93	13	13	0	0	...	0-...	74.1	50	16	15	8	19-0	102	.191
	— Florida (N.L.)	2	2	.500	1.50	1.04	4	4	0	0	0	0-0	24.0	14	9	4	3	11-0	24	.161
2002—	Florida (N.L.)	6	7	.462	4.10	1.27	23	21	0	0	0	0-0	107.2	93	56	49	13	44-2	113	.232
	— GC Marlins (GCL)	0	0	...	4.50	1.50	1	1	0	0	0	0-...	4.0	5	2	2	0	1-0	7	.294
	— Jupiter (FSL)	1	0	1.000	0.00	0.83	1	1	0	0	0	0-...	6.0	4	0	0	0	1-0	12	.174
2003—	Jupiter (FSL)	0	0	...	0.00	0.70	1	1	0	0	0	0-0	3.0	2	0	0	0	0-0	5	.182
	— Carolina (Southern)	0	0	...	4.50	1.00	1	1	0	0	0	0-...	4.0	4	2	2	1	0-0	7	.267
	— Florida (N.L.)	9	8	.529	3.04	1.32	24	23	0	0	0	0-0	142.0	132	54	48	9	56-4	152	.246
2004—	Florida (N.L.)	9	9	.500	3.79	1.22	26	26	1	1	0	0-0	156.2	137	72	66	16	54-3	152	.235
Major League totals (4 years)		26	26	.500	3.49	1.26	77	74	1	1	0	0-0	430.1	376	191	167	41	165-9	441	.234

DIVISION SERIES RECORD

Year	Team (League)	W	L	Pct.	ERA	WHIP	G	GS	CG	ShO	Hld.	Sv.-Opp.	IP	H	R	ER	HR	BB-IBB	SO	Avg.
2003—	Florida (N.L.)	0	1	.000	1.29	1.00	1	1	0	0	0	0-0	7.0	2	1	1	0	5-1	9	.087

CHAMPIONSHIP SERIES RECORD

Year	Team (League)	W	L	Pct.	ERA	WHIP	G	GS	CG	ShO	Hld.	Sv.-Opp.	IP	H	R	ER	HR	BB-IBB	SO	Avg.
2003—	Florida (N.L.)	1	0	1.000	3.26	0.67	3	2	1	1	0	0-0	19.1	11	7	7	3	2-0	19	.162

WORLD SERIES RECORD

Year	Team (League)	W	L	Pct.	ERA	WHIP	G	GS	CG	ShO	Hld.	Sv.-Opp.	IP	H	R	ER	HR	BB-IBB	SO	Avg.
2003—	Florida (N.L.)	1	1	.500	1.10	0.80	2	2	1	1	0	0-0	16.1	8	2	2	0	5-0	19	.148

BEDARD, ERIK   P

PERSONAL: Born March 6, 1979, in Navan, Ontario. ... 6-1/189. ... Throws left, bats left. ... Full name: Erik Joseph Bedard. ... Junior college: Norwalk (Conn.) Community College.
TRANSACTIONS/CAREER NOTES: Selected by Baltimore Orioles organization in sixth round of 1999 free-agent draft. ... On disabled list (March 28-September 1, 2003); included minor league rehabilitation assignment to GCL Orioles.
CAREER HITTING: 0-for-4 (.000), 0 R, 0 2B, 0 3B, 0 HR, 0 RBI.

Year	Team (League)	W	L	Pct.	ERA	WHIP	G	GS	CG	ShO	Hld.	Sv.-Opp.	IP	H	R	ER	HR	BB-IBB	SO	Avg.
1999—GC Orioles (GCL)		2	1	.667	1.86	1.14	8	6	0	0	...	0-...	29.0	20	7	6	1	13-0	41	.192
2000—Delmarva (S.Atl.)		9	4	.692	3.57	1.20	29	22	1	1	...	2-...	111.0	98	48	44	2	35-0	131	.233
2001—GC Orioles (GCL)		0	0	.000	3.00	1.17	2	2	0	0	...	0-...	6.0	4	2	2	0	3-0	7	.200
—Frederick (Caro.)		9	2	.818	2.15	0.98	17	17	0	0	...	0-...	96.1	68	27	23	4	26-0	130	.198
2002—Bowie (East.)		6	3	.667	1.97	1.06	13	12	0	0	...	0-...	68.2	43	18	15	0	30-0	66	.176
—Baltimore (A.L.)		0	0	...	13.50	3.00	2	0	0	0	0	0-0	.2	2	1	1	0	0-0	1	.500
2003—GC Orioles (GCL)		0	0	...	1.13	0.80	3	3	0	0	...	0-...	8.0	4	1	1	0	2-0	11	.154
—Aberdeen (NY-P)		0	0	...	2.35	1.00	2	2	0	0	...	0-...	7.2	7	2	2	0	1-0	13	.233
—Frederick (Caro.)		0	1	.000	7.36	1.60	1	1	0	0	...	0-...	3.2	5	3	3	1	1-0	2	.357
2004—Ottawa (Int'l)		0	1	.000	7.20	2.20	2	2	0	0	...	0-...	5.0	8	4	4	1	3-0	3	.348
—Baltimore (A.L.)		6	10	.375	4.59	1.60	27	26	0	0	0	0-0	137.1	149	83	70	13	71-1	121	.270
Major League totals (2 years)		6	10	.375	4.63	1.61	29	26	0	0	0	0-0	138.0	151	84	71	13	71-1	122	.272

BEIMEL, JOE   P   B

PERSONAL: Born April 19, 1977, in St. Marys, Pa. ... 6-3/217. ... Throws left, bats left. ... Full name: Joseph Ronald Beimel. ... Name pronounced: BYE-muhl. ... High school: St. Mary's Area (St. Mary's, Pa.). ... College: Duquesne.

TRANSACTIONS/CAREER NOTES: Selected by Texas Rangers organiztion in 26th round of 1996 free-agent draft; did not sign. ... Selected by Pittsburgh Pirates organization in 18th round of 1998 free-agent draft. ... Released by Pirates (March 31, 2004). ... Signed by Minnesota Twins organization (April 11, 2004). ... Refused minor league assignment and became a free agent (October 9, 2004).

CAREER HITTING: 10-for-41 (.244), 3 R, 1 2B, 0 3B, 0 HR, 1 RBI.

Year	Team (League)	W	L	Pct.	ERA	WHIP	G	GS	CG	ShO	Hld.	Sv.-Opp.	IP	H	R	ER	HR	BB-IBB	SO	Avg.
1998—Erie (N.Y.-Penn)		1	4	.200	6.32	1.66	17	6	0	0	...	0-...	47.0	56	39	33	6	22-0	37	.296
1999—Hickory (S. Atl.)		5	11	.313	4.43	1.45	29	22	0	0	...	0-...	130.0	146	81	64	12	43-0	102	.289
2000—Lynchburg (Carolina)		10	6	.625	3.36	1.28	18	18	2	1	...	0-...	120.2	111	49	45	6	44-1	82	.247
—Altoona (East.)		1	6	.143	4.16	1.48	10	10	1	0	...	0-...	62.2	72	38	29	8	21-0	28	.288
2001—Pittsburgh (N.L.)		7	11	.389	5.23	1.56	42	15	0	0	0	0-0	115.1	131	72	67	12	49-4	58	.290
2002—Pittsburgh (N.L.)		2	5	.286	4.64	1.56	53	8	0	0	5	0-1	85.1	88	49	44	9	45-12	53	.267
2003—Pittsburgh (N.L.)		1	3	.250	5.05	1.64	69	0	0	0	12	0-5	62.1	69	35	35	7	33-6	42	.299
2004—Rochester (Int'l)		2	4	.333	6.97	1.73	49	1	0	0	0	2-...	62.0	83	54	48	12	24-1	44	.322
—Minnesota (A.L.)		0	0	...	43.20	6.00	3	0	0	0	0	0-0	1.2	8	8	8	1	2-0	2	.615
American League totals (1 year)		0	0	...	43.20	6.00	3	0	0	0	0	0-0	1.2	8	8	8	1	2-0	2	.615
National League totals (3 years)		10	19	.345	5.00	1.58	164	23	0	0	17	0-6	263.0	288	156	146	28	127-22	153	.284
Major League totals (4 years)		10	19	.345	5.24	1.61	167	23	0	0	17	0-6	264.2	296	164	154	29	129-22	155	.288

BELL, DAVID   3B

PERSONAL: Born September 14, 1972, in Cincinnati, Ohio. ... 5-10/181. ... Bats right, throws right. ... Full name: David Michael Bell. ... High school: Moeller (Cincinnatl). ... Son of Buddy Bell, third baseman with four major league teams (1972-89) and manager with Detroit Tigers (1996-98) and Colorado Rockies (2000-02); brother of Mike Bell, third baseman with Cincinnati Reds (2000); and grandson of Gus Bell, outfielder with four major league teams (1950-64).

TRANSACTIONS/CAREER NOTES: Selected by Cleveland Indians organization in seventh round of 1990 free-agent draft. ... Traded by Indians with C Pepe McNeal and P Rick Heiserman to St. Louis Cardinals for P Ken Hill (July 27, 1995). ... On disabled list (April 29-June 30, 1997); included rehabilitation assignments to Arkansas and Louisville. ... Claimed on waivers by Indians (April 14, 1998). ... Traded by Indians to Seattle Mariners for 2B Joey Cora (August 31, 1998). ... Traded by Mariners to San Francisco Giants for SS Desi Relaford and cash (January 25, 2002). ... Signed as a free agent by Philadelphia Phillies (November 24, 2002). ... On disabled list (July 11-September 23, 2003).

2004 GAMES PLAYED BY POSITION (MLB): 3B—142.

Year	Team (League)	Pos.	G	AB	R	H	2B	3B	HR	RBI	BB	SO	HBP	GDP	SB-CS	Avg.	OBP	SLG	OPS	E	Avg.
1990—GC Indians (GCL)		3B	30	111	18	29	5	1	0	13	10	8	4	5	1-1	.261	.341	.324	.666	7	.919
—Burlington (Appal.)		3B	12	42	4	7	1	1	0	2	2	5	1	1	2-1	.167	.217	.238	.455	3	.921
1991—Columbus (S. Atl.)		3B	136	491	47	113	24	1	5	63	37	50	5	22	3-2	.230	.287	.314	.601	31	.920
1992—Kinston (Caro.)		3B	123	464	52	117	17	2	6	47	54	66	1	13	2-4	.252	.327	.336	.663	20	.946
1993—Cant./Akr. (Eastern)		3B-2B-SS	129	483	69	141	20	2	9	60	43	54	3	12	3-4	.292	.350	.398	.747	21	.950
1994—Charlotte (Int'l)		3B-SS-2B	134	481	66	141	17	4	18	88	41	54	9	9	2-5	.293	.355	.457	.812	20	.956
1995—Buffalo (A.A.)		3B-SS-2B	70	254	34	69	11	1	8	34	22	37	4	...	0-3	.272	.336	.417	.753	11	.952
—Cleveland (A.L.)		3B	2	2	0	0	0	0	0	0	0	0	0	0	0-0	.000	.000	.000	.000	0	1.000
—Louisville (A.A.)		2B	18	76	9	21	3	1	1	9	2	10	3	...	4-0	.276	.321	.382	.703	1	.989
—St. Louis (N.L.)		2B-3B	39	144	13	36	7	2	2	19	4	25	2	0	1-2	.250	.278	.368	.646	7	.964
1996—St. Louis (N.L.)		3B-2B-SS	62	145	12	31	6	0	1	9	10	22	1	3	1-1	.214	.268	.276	.543	5	.969
—Louisville (A.A.)		2B-3B-SS	42	136	9	24	5	1	0	7	7	15	0	4	1-2	.176	.217	.228	.445	5	.973
1997—St. Louis (N.L.)		3B-2B-SS	66	142	9	30	7	2	1	12	10	28	0	2	1-0	.211	.261	.310	.571	8	.949
—Arkansas (Texas)		3B-2B	9	32	3	7	2	0	1	3	2	2	0	1	0-0	.219	.265	.375	.640	1	.947
—Louisville (A.A.)		2-3-S-DH	6	22	3	5	0	0	0	1	4	0	6	1	0-0	.227	.250	.364	.614	1	.941
1998—St. Louis (N.L.)		3B-2B	4	9	0	2	1	0	0	0	0	3	0	0	0-0	.222	.222	.333	.556	0	1.000
—Cleveland (A.L.)		2-3-S-1	107	340	37	89	21	2	10	41	22	54	2	8	0-4	.262	.306	.424	.730	9	.983
—Seattle (A.L.)		2-3-1-OF	21	80	11	26	8	0	0	8	5	8	0	3	0-0	.325	.365	.425	.790	1	.991
1999—Seattle (A.L.)		2B-1B-SS	157	597	92	160	31	2	21	78	58	90	2	7	7-4	.268	.331	.432	.763	17	.978
2000—Seattle (A.L.)		3-2-1-S-DH	133	454	57	112	24	2	11	47	42	66	6	11	2-3	.247	.316	.381	.697	15	.963
2001—Seattle (A.L.)		3B-1B	135	470	62	122	28	0	15	64	28	59	3	8	2-1	.260	.303	.415	.718	14	.962
2002—San Francisco (N.L.)		3-2-S-1	154	552	82	144	29	2	20	73	54	80	9	18	1-2	.261	.333	.429	.762	12	.971
2003—Philadelphia (N.L.)		3B-2B	85	297	32	58	14	0	4	37	41	40	4	7	0-0	.195	.296	.283	.579	8	.968
2004—Philadelphia (N.L.)		3B	143	533	67	155	33	1	18	77	57	75	6	14	1-1	.291	.363	.458	.821	24	.943
American League totals (5 years)			555	1943	259	509	112	6	57	238	155	277	13	37	11-12	.262	.318	.414	.731	56	.974
National League totals (7 years)			553	1822	215	456	97	7	46	227	176	273	22	44	5-6	.250	.320	.387	.707	64	.960
Major League totals (10 years)			1108	3765	474	965	209	13	103	465	331	550	35	81	16-18	.256	.319	.401	.720	120	.968

DIVISION SERIES RECORD

Year	Team (League)	Pos.	G	AB	R	H	2B	3B	HR	RBI	BB	SO	HBP	GDP	SB-CS	Avg.	OBP	SLG	OPS	E	Avg.
2000—Seattle (A.L.)		3B	3	11	0	4	1	0	0	1	2	2	0	0	0-0	.364	.462	.455	.916	0	1.000
2001—Seattle (A.L.)		3B	5	16	2	5	1	0	1	2	1	6	0	0	0-0	.313	.333	.563	.896	0	1.000
2002—San Francisco (N.L.)		3B	5	16	3	3	0	0	0	1	3	4	0	0	0-0	.188	.316	.188	.503	1	.944
Division series totals (3 years)			13	43	5	12	2	0	1	4	6	12	0	0	0-0	.279	.360	.395	.755	1	.969

CHAMPIONSHIP SERIES RECORD																			
Year Team (League)	Pos.	G	AB	R	H	2B	3B	HR	RBI	BB	SO	HBP	GDP	SB-CS	Avg.	OBP	SLG	OPS	E	Avg.
2000— Seattle (A.L.)	3B	5	18	0	4	0	0	0	0	0	0	0	0	0-0	.222	.222	.222	.444	0	1.000
2001— Seattle (A.L.)	3B	5	16	1	3	0	0	0	4	0	3	0	0	0-0	.188	.188	.188	.375	1	.923
2002— San Francisco (N.L.)	3B	5	17	4	7	1	0	1	1	2	3	0	0	0-0	.412	.474	.647	1.121	0	1.000
Champ. series totals (3 years)		15	51	5	14	1	0	1	5	2	6	0	0	0-0	.275	.302	.353	.655	1	.974

WORLD SERIES RECORD																			
Year Team (League)	Pos.	G	AB	R	H	2B	3B	HR	RBI	BB	SO	HBP	GDP	SB-CS	Avg.	OBP	SLG	OPS	E	Avg.
2002— San Francisco (N.L.)	3B	7	23	4	7	0	0	1	4	5	4	1	1	0-1	.304	.448	.435	.883	2	.889

BELL, HEATH — P

PERSONAL: Born September 29, 1977, in Oceanside, Calif. ... 6-2/244. ... Throws right, bats right. ... Full name: Heath Justin Bell. ... High school: Rancho Santiago (Calif.). ... Junior college: Santa Ana (Calif.).

TRANSACTIONS/CAREER NOTES: Selected by Tampa Bay Devil Rays organization in 69th round of 1997 free-agent draft; did not sign. ... Signed as a non-drafted free agent by New York Mets organization (June 16, 1998).

CAREER HITTING: 0-for-1 (.000), 0 R, 0 2B, 0 3B, 0 HR, 0 RBI.

Year Team (League)	W	L	Pct.	ERA	WHIP	G	GS	CG	ShO	Hld.	Sv.-Opp.	IP	H	R	ER	HR	BB-IBB	SO	Avg.
1998— Kingsport (Appalachian)	1	0	1.000	2.54	1.11	22	0	0	0	...	8-...	46.0	40	15	13	5	11-0	61	.231
1999— Capital City (S. Atl.)	1	7	.125	2.60	1.03	55	0	0	0	...	25-...	62.1	47	23	18	3	17-0	68	.203
2000— St. Lucie (Fla. St.)	5	1	.833	2.55	1.07	48	0	0	0	...	23-...	60.0	43	19	17	4	21-2	75	.201
2001— Binghamton (Eastern)	3	1	.750	6.02	1.65	43	0	0	0	...	4-...	61.1	82	44	41	13	19-3	55	.320
2002— Norfolk (Int'l)	3	4	.429	4.26	1.48	22	0	0	0	...	5-...	31.2	38	15	15	2	9-1	28	.302
— Binghamton (Eastern) ...	1	0	1.000	1.18	0.74	24	0	0	0	...	6-...	38.0	22	6	5	0	6-0	49	.168
2003— Norfolk (Int'l)	2	3	.400	4.71	1.25	40	0	0	0	...	3-...	49.2	54	26	26	4	8-0	54	.284
2004— Binghamton (Eastern)	0	0	...	0.00	1.00	1	0	0	0	...	0-...	2.0	2	0	0	0	0-0	0	.250
— Norfolk (Int'l)	3	1	.750	3.23	1.19	45	0	0	0	...	16-...	55.2	42	21	20	4	24-2	69	.210
— New York (N.L.)	0	2	.000	3.33	1.15	17	0	0	0	1	0-1	24.1	22	9	9	5	6-0	27	.253
Major League totals (1 year)	0	2	.000	3.33	1.15	17	0	0	0	1	0-1	24.1	22	9	9	5	6-0	27	.253

BELL, ROB — P

PERSONAL: Born January 17, 1977, in Newburgh, N.Y. ... 6-5/225. ... Throws right, bats right. ... Full name: Robert Allen Bell. ... High school: Marlboro (N.Y.) Central.

TRANSACTIONS/CAREER NOTES: Selected by Atlanta Braves organization in third round of 1995 free-agent draft. ... Traded by Braves with OF Michael Tucker and P Denny Neagle to Cincinnati Reds for 2B Bret Boone and P Mike Remlinger (November 10, 1998). ... Traded by Reds to Texas Rangers for OF Ruben Mateo and 3B Edwin Encarnacion (June 15, 2001). ... Released by Rangers (March 12, 2003). ... Signed by Tampa Bay Devil Rays organization (March 17, 2003).

CAREER HITTING: 5-for-60 (.083), 2 R, 2 2B, 0 3B, 0 HR, 0 RBI.

Year Team (League)	W	L	Pct.	ERA	WHIP	G	GS	CG	ShO	Hld.	Sv.-Opp.	IP	H	R	ER	HR	BB-IBB	SO	Avg.
1995— GC Braves (GCL)	1	6	.143	6.88	1.53	10	8	0	0	...	0-...	34.0	38	29	26	2	14-0	33	.279
1996— Eugene (N'west)	5	6	.455	5.11	1.46	16	16	0	0	...	0-...	81.0	89	49	46	5	29-1	74	.282
1997— Macon (S. Atl.)	14	7	.667	3.68	1.26	27	27	1	0	...	0-...	146.2	144	72	60	15	41-1	140	.258
1998— Danville (Caro.)	7	9	.438	3.28	1.21	28	28	2	0	...	0-...	178.1	169	79	65	8	46-0	197	.252
1999— Chattanooga (Southern)	3	6	.333	3.13	1.28	12	12	1	1	...	0-...	72.0	75	30	25	7	17-0	68	.276
— GC Reds (GCL)	0	0	...	1.13	0.38	2	2	0	0	...	0-...	8.0	3	1	1	0	0-0	11	.120
2000— Cincinnati (N.L.)	7	8	.467	5.00	1.45	26	26	1	0	0	0-0	140.1	130	84	78	32	73-6	112	.243
— Louisville (Int'l)	4	0	1.000	3.73	1.17	6	6	0	0	0	0-0	41.0	35	18	17	6	13-0	47	.224
2001— Cincinnati (N.L.)	0	5	.000	5.48	1.42	9	9	0	0	0	0-0	44.1	46	28	27	9	17-1	33	.275
— Louisville (Int'l)	2	2	.500	3.33	1.33	5	4	0	0	0	0-0	27.0	32	10	10	4	4-0	26	.288
— Texas (A.L.)	5	5	.500	7.18	1.68	18	18	0	0	0	0-0	105.1	130	87	84	23	47-0	64	.310
2002— Oklahoma (PCL)	5	1	1.000	4.06	1.26	12	11	2	2	...	0-...	75.1	70	36	34	10	25-0	55	.247
— Texas (A.L.)	4	3	.571	6.22	1.57	17	15	0	0	0	0-0	94.0	113	69	65	16	35-0	70	.296
— Tulsa (Texas)	1	0	1.000	0.00	0.50	1	1	0	0	...	0-...	8.0	4	0	0	0	0-0	5	.154
2003— Durham (Int'l)	6	4	.600	4.02	1.20	12	12	0	0	...	0-...	71.2	72	33	32	10	15-1	48	.260
— Tampa Bay (A.L.)	5	4	.556	5.52	1.41	19	18	0	0	0	0-0	101.0	103	64	62	15	39-1	44	.263
2004— Durham (Int'l)	5	0	1.000	1.69	0.96	7	7	0	0	...	0-...	37.1	28	7	7	3	8-0	35	.209
— Tampa Bay (A.L.)	8	8	.500	4.46	1.32	24	19	1	0	0	0-0	123.0	121	71	61	16	41-0	57	.253
American League totals (4 years)	22	20	.524	5.78	1.49	78	70	1	0	0	0-0	423.1	467	291	272	70	162-1	235	.279
National League totals (2 years)	7	13	.350	5.12	1.44	35	35	1	0	0	0-0	184.2	176	112	105	41	90-7	145	.251
Major League totals (5 years)	29	33	.468	5.58	1.47	113	105	2	0	0	0-0	608.0	643	403	377	111	252-8	380	.271

BELLHORN, MARK — 2B/3B

PERSONAL: Born August 23, 1974, in Boston, Mass. ... 6-1/205. ... Bats both, throws right. ... Full name: Mark Christian Bellhorn. ... High school: Oviedo (Fla.). ... College: Auburn.

TRANSACTIONS/CAREER NOTES: Selected by Oakland Athletics organization in second round of 1995 free-agent draft. ... Traded by A's to Chicago Cubs for IF Adam Morrissey (November 2, 2001). ... Traded by Cubs to to Colorado Rockies for IF Jose Hernandez (June 20, 2003). ... On disabled list (August 1-23, 2003); included rehabilitation assignment to Colorado Springs. ... Traded by Rockies to Boston Red Sox for a player to be named (December 15, 2003). ... On disabled list (August 2-20, 2004); included rehabilitation assignment to Pawtucket.

2004 GAMES PLAYED BY POSITION (MLB): 2B—124, 3B—16, SS—1, DH—1.

Year Team (League)	Pos.	G	AB	R	H	2B	3B	HR	RBI	BB	SO	HBP	GDP	SB-CS	Avg.	OBP	SLG	OPS	E	Avg.
1995— Modesto (California)	SS	56	229	35	59	12	0	6	31	27	52	4	9	5-2	.258	.346	.389	.735	21	.927
1996— Huntsville (Sou.)	IF	131	468	84	117	24	5	10	71	73	124	4	7	19-2	.250	.353	.387	.740	32	.945
1997— Edmonton (PCL)	2-S-3-DH	70	241	54	79	18	3	11	46	64	59	2	4	6-6	.328	.472	.564	1.037	13	.957
— Oakland (A.L.)	3-2-DH-S	68	224	33	51	9	1	6	19	32	70	0	1	7-1	.228	.324	.357	.681	9	.956
1998— Edmonton (PCL)	3-2-DH-S-1	87	309	57	77	20	4	10	44	62	90	6	8	6-2	.249	.384	.437	.820	11	.965
— Oakland (A.L.)	3-S-DH-2	11	12	1	1	1	0	0	1	3	4	1	0	2-0	.083	.313	.167	.479	0	1.000
1999— Ariz. A's (Ariz.)	2B-DH	12	43	11	10	3	0	0	5	11	9	0	1	0-0	.233	.389	.302	.691	0	1.000
— Midland (Texas)	2B	17	57	12	17	3	0	2	8	11	13	0	2	1-0	.298	.412	.456	.868	2	.973
2000— Sacramento (PCL)	3-2-S-1	117	436	111	116	17	11	24	73	94	121	5	5	20-5	.266	.399	.521	.920	15	.945
— Oakland (A.L.)	2-3-SS	9	13	2	2	0	0	0	0	2	6	0	0	0-0	.154	.267	.154	.421	0	1.000
2001— Sacramento (PCL)	OF-2-S-3	43	156	30	42	6	0	12	36	22	60	4	0	3-0	.269	.370	.538	.908	2	.985

Year	Team (League)	Pos.	G	AB	R	H	2B	3B	HR	RBI	BB	SO	HBP	GDP	SB-CS	Avg.	OBP	SLG	OPS	E	Avg.
—Oakland (A.L.)		2-3-S-DH-OF	38	74	11	10	1	2	1	4	7	37	0	1	0-0	.135	.210	.243	.453	5	.932
2002—Chicago (N.L.)		2-3-1-S-OF	146	445	86	115	24	4	27	56	76	144	6	6	7-5	.258	.374	.512	.886	11	.977
2003—Chicago (N.L.)		3B	51	139	15	29	7	1	2	22	29	46	1	2	3-3	.209	.341	.317	.658	6	.938
—Colo. Springs (PCL)		3B-2B	16	54	11	21	5	1	4	16	11	10	0	0	2-0	.389	.485	.741	1.226	1	.981
—Colorado (N.L.)		2-3-S-OF-1	48	110	12	26	3	0	0	4	21	32	2	1	2-3	.236	.368	.264	.632	3	.974
2004—Pawtucket (Int'l)		2B	2	6	1	1	1	0	0	0	0	2	0	0	0-0	.167	.167	.333	.500	0	1.000
—Boston (A.L.)		2-3-S-DH	138	523	93	138	37	3	17	82	88 *	177	5	8	6-1	.264	.373	.444	.817	14	.977
American League totals (5 years)			264	846	140	202	48	6	24	106	132	294	6	10	15-2	.239	.344	.395	.739	28	.969
National League totals (2 years)			245	694	113	170	34	5	29	82	126	222	9	9	12-11	.245	.366	.434	.800	20	.971
Major League totals (7 years)			509	1540	253	372	82	11	53	188	258	516	15	19	27-13	.242	.354	.412	.767	48	.970

DIVISION SERIES RECORD

Year	Team (League)	Pos.	G	AB	R	H	2B	3B	HR	RBI	BB	SO	HBP	GDP	SB-CS	Avg.	OBP	SLG	OPS	E	Avg.
2004—Boston (A.L.)		2B	3	11	2	1	0	0	0	5	4	0	0	0-0	.091	.375	.091	.466	0	1.000

CHAMPIONSHIP SERIES RECORD

Year	Team (League)	Pos.	G	AB	R	H	2B	3B	HR	RBI	BB	SO	HBP	GDP	SB-CS	Avg.	OBP	SLG	OPS	E	Avg.
2004—Boston (A.L.)		2B	7	26	3	5	2	0	2	4	5	11	0	1	0-0	.192	.323	.500	.823	0	1.000

WORLD SERIES RECORD

Year	Team (League)	Pos.	G	AB	R	H	2B	3B	HR	RBI	BB	SO	HBP	GDP	SB-CS	Avg.	OBP	SLG	OPS	E	Avg.
2004—Boston (A.L.)		2B	4	10	3	3	1	0	1	4	5	2	1	1	0-0	.300	.563	.700	1.263	1	.938

BELLIARD, RONNIE — 2B/3B

PERSONAL: Born April 7, 1975, in Bronx, N.Y. ... 5-8/197. ... Bats right, throws right. ... Full name: Ronald Belliard. ... Name pronounced: BELL-ee-yard. ... High school: Central (Miami).
TRANSACTIONS/CAREER NOTES: Selected by Milwaukee Brewers organization in eighth round of 1994 free-agent draft. ... On disabled list (August 8-September 30, 2001). ... On disabled list (June 2-23, 2003); included rehabilitation assignment to Colorado Springs. ... Released by Rockies (November 20, 2003). ... Signed by Cleveland Indians (December 26, 2003).
2004 GAMES PLAYED BY POSITION (MLB): 2B—151, DH—1.

Year	Team (League)	Pos.	G	AB	R	H	2B	3B	HR	RBI	BB	SO	HBP	GDP	SB-CS	Avg.	OBP	SLG	OPS	E	Avg.
1994—Ariz. Brewers (Ariz.)		2B-3B-SS	39	143	32	42	7	3	0	27	14	25	3	3	7-0	.294	.366	.385	.751	12	.935
1995—Beloit (Midw.)		2B-3B	130	461	76	137	28	5	13	76	36	67	7	10	16-12	.297	.356	.464	.821	26	.956
1996—El Paso (Texas)		2B-DH	109	416	73	116	20	8	3	57	60	51	4	11	26-10	.279	.373	.387	.760	16	.972
1997—Tucson (PCL)		2B-SS	118	443	80	125	35	4	4	55	61	69	11	13	10-7	.282	.379	.406	.785	26	.959
1998—Louisville (Int'l)		2B-SS	133	507	114	163	36	7	14	73	69	77	8	17	33-12	.322	.408	.503	.911	14	.979
—Milwaukee (N.L.)		2B	8	5	1	1	0	0	0	0	0	0	0	0	0-0	.200	.200	.200	.400	0	...
1999—Louisville (Int'l)		2B	29	108	14	26	4	0	1	8	14	13	1	3	12-2	.241	.331	.306	.636	3	.975
—Milwaukee (N.L.)		2B-3B-SS	124	457	60	135	29	4	8	58	64	59	0	16	4-5	.295	.379	.429	.808	13	.978
2000—Milwaukee (N.L.)		2B	152	571	83	150	30	9	8	54	82	84	3	12	7-5	.263	.354	.389	.743	* 19	.976
2001—Milwaukee (N.L.)		2B	101	364	69	96	30	3	11	36	35	65	5	5	5-2	.264	.335	.453	.788	5	.990
2002—Milwaukee (N.L.)		2B-3B	104	289	30	61	13	0	3	26	18	46	1	9	2-3	.211	.257	.287	.544	10	.963
2003—Colo. Springs (PCL)		2B	6	19	2	5	1	0	0	0	0	1	0	0	0-0	.263	.263	.316	.579	0	1.000
—Colorado (N.L.)		2B	116	447	73	124	31	2	8	50	49	71	2	7	7-2	.277	.351	.409	.760	15	.973
2004—Cleveland (A.L.)		2B-DH	152	599	78	169	48	1	12	70	60	98	2	18	3-2	.282	.348	.426	.774	14	.981
American League totals (1 year)			152	599	78	169	48	1	12	70	60	98	2	18	3-2	.282	.348	.426	.774	14	.981
National League totals (6 years)			605	2133	316	567	133	18	38	224	248	325	11	49	25-17	.266	.343	.398	.741	62	.977
Major League totals (7 years)			757	2732	394	736	181	19	50	294	308	423	13	67	28-19	.269	.344	.404	.749	76	.978

ALL-STAR GAME RECORD

	G	AB	R	H	2B	3B	HR	RBI	BB	SO	HBP	GDP	SB-CS	Avg.	OBP	SLG	OPS	E	Avg.
All-Star Game totals (1 year)	1	1	0	0	0	0	0	0	0	1	0	0	0-0	.000	.000	.000	.000	0	1.000

BELTRAN, CARLOS — OF

PERSONAL: Born April 24, 1977, in Manati, Puerto Rico. ... 6-1/190. ... Bats both, throws right. ... Full name: Carlos Ivan Beltran. ... Name pronounced: BELL-tron. ... High school: Fernando Callejas (Manati, Puerto Rico).
TRANSACTIONS/CAREER NOTES: Selected by Kansas City Royals organization in second round of 1995 free-agent draft. ... On disabled list (July 4-September 4, 2000); included rehabilitation assignments to GCL Royals, Wilmington and Omaha. ... On disabled list (March 21-April 18, 2003); included rehabilitation assignment to Wichita. ... Traded by Royals to Houston Astros as part of three-team deal in which Royals received C John Buck and cash from Astros and P Mike Wood and 3B Mark Teahen from Oakland Athletics and A's acquired P Octavio Dotel from Astros (June 24, 2003).
HONORS: Named A.L. Rookie Player of the Year by THE SPORTING NEWS (1999). ... Named A.L. Rookie of the Year by Baseball Writers' Association of America (1999).
2004 GAMES PLAYED BY POSITION (MLB): OF—158.

Year	Team (League)	Pos.	G	AB	R	H	2B	3B	HR	RBI	BB	SO	HBP	GDP	SB-CS	Avg.	OBP	SLG	OPS	E	Avg.
1995—GC Royals (GCL)		OF	52	180	29	50	9	0	0	23	13	30	3	1	5-3	.278	.332	.328	.659	2	.977
1996—Lansing (Midw.)		OF	11	42	3	6	2	0	0	0	1	11	0	0	1-0	.143	.163	.190	.353	2	.938
—Spokane (N'west)		OF	59	215	29	58	8	3	7	29	31	65	0	4	10-2	.270	.359	.433	.791	7	.938
1997—Wilmington (Caro.)		OF	120	419	57	96	15	4	11	46	46	96	4	10	17-7	.229	.311	.363	.673	8	.968
1998—Wilmington (Caro.)		OF	52	192	32	53	14	0	5	32	25	39	2	2	11-7	.276	.364	.427	.791	2	.983
—Wichita (Texas)		OF	47	182	50	64	13	3	14	44	23	30	1	4	7-1	.352	.427	.687	1.114	4	.960
—Kansas City (A.L.)		OF	14	58	12	16	5	3	0	7	3	12	1	2	3-0	.276	.317	.466	.783	1	.978
1999—Kansas City (A.L.)		OF-DH	156	663	112	194	27	7	22	108	46	123	4	17	27-8	.293	.337	.454	.791	* 12	.972
2000—Kansas City (A.L.)		OF-DH	98	372	49	92	15	4	7	44	35	69	0	12	13-0	.247	.309	.366	.675	6	.975
—GC Royals (GCL)		DH	1	4	3	2	1	0	1	1	1	0	0	0	0-0	.500	.600	1.500	2.100	...	...
—Wilmington (Caro.)		OF	3	13	2	4	0	1	2	6	0	5	0	0	0-0	.308	.308	.923	1.231	0	1.000
—Omaha (PCL)		OF	5	18	4	6	1	0	2	2	3	3	1	0	1-0	.333	.455	.722	1.177	0	1.000
2001—Kansas City (A.L.)		OF-DH	155	617	106	189	32	12	24	101	52	120	5	7	31-1	.306	.362	.514	.876	5	.988
2002—Kansas City (A.L.)		OF-DH	* 162	637	114	174	44	7	29	105	71	135	4	12	35-7	.273	.346	.501	.847	7	.983
2003—Wichita (Texas)		OF-DH	3	9	3	3	2	0	0	1	2	3	0	0	1-0	.333	.455	.556	1.010	0	1.000
—Kansas City (A.L.)		OF-DH	141	521	102	160	14	10	26	100	72	81	2	8	41-4	.307	.389	.522	.911	5	.987
2004—Kansas City (A.L.)		OF	69	266	51	74	19	2	15	51	37	44	2	4	14-3	.278	.367	.534	.901	3	.985
—Houston (N.L.)		OF	90	333	70	86	17	7	23	53	55	57	5	4	28-0	.258	.368	.559	.926	5	.977
American League totals (7 years)			795	3134	546	899	156	45	123	516	316	584	18	62	164-23	.287	.352	.483	.835	39	.982
National League totals (1 year)			90	333	70	86	17	7	23	53	55	57	5	4	28-0	.258	.368	.559	.926	5	.977
Major League totals (7 years)			885	3467	616	985	173	52	146	569	371	641	23	66	192-23	.284	.353	.490	.844	44	.981

B

DIVISION SERIES RECORD

Year	Team (League)	Pos.	G	AB	R	H	2B	3B	HR	RBI	BB	SO	HBP	GDP	SB-CS	Avg.	OBP	SLG	OPS	E	Avg.
2004— Houston (N.L.)		OF	5	22	9	10	2	0	4	9	1	4	1	0	2-0	.455	.500	1.091	1.591	0	1.000

CHAMPIONSHIP SERIES RECORD

Year	Team (League)	Pos.	G	AB	R	H	2B	3B	HR	RBI	BB	SO	HBP	GDP	SB-CS	Avg.	OBP	SLG	OPS	E	Avg.
2004— Houston (N.L.)		OF	7	24	12	10	1	0	4	5	8	4	0	0	4-0	.417	.563	.958	1.521	0	1.000

ALL-STAR GAME RECORD

	G	AB	R	H	2B	3B	HR	RBI	BB	SO	HBP	GDP	SB-CS	Avg.	OBP	SLG	OPS	E	Avg.
All-Star Game totals (1 year)	1	2	1	1	0	0	0	0	0	0	0	0	0-0	.500	.500	.500	1.000	0	...

B

BELTRAN, FRANCIS   P

PERSONAL: Born November 29, 1979, in Santo Domingo, Dominican Republic. ... 6-6/230. ... Throws right, bats right. ... Full name: Francis Lebron Beltran. ... Name pronounced: bell-TRON.

TRANSACTIONS/CAREER NOTES: Signed as a non-drafted free agent by Chicago Cubs organization (November 15, 1996). ... Traded by Cubs with SS Alex S. Gonzalez and IF Brendan Harris to Montreal Expos as part of four-team deal in which Cubs acquired SS Nomar Garciaparra and OF Matt Murton from Red Sox, Red Sox acquired SS Orlando Cabrera from Expos and 1B Doug Mientkiewicz from Twins, and Twins acquired P Justin Jones from Cubs (July 31, 2004). ... On disabled list (August 25-September 9, 2004).

CAREER HITTING: 1-for-4 (.250). 0 R, 0 2B, 0 3B, 0 HR, 0 RBI.

Year	Team (League)	W	L	Pct.	ERA	WHIP	G	GS	CG	ShO	Hld.	Sv.-Opp.	IP	H	R	ER	HR	BB-IBB	SO	Avg.
1997— Ariz. Cubs (Ariz.)		0	1	.000	3.42	1.48	16	0	0	0	...	1-...	23.2	27	18	9	1	8-0	17	.276
1998— Ariz. Cubs (Ariz.)		1	1	.500	5.55	1.77	12	5	0	0	...	0-...	35.2	49	23	22	1	14-1	26	.343
1999— Ariz. Cubs (Ariz.)		0	1	.000	0.00	0.56	7	7	0	0	...	2-...	10.2	5	3	0	0	1-0	8	.139
— Eugene (N'west)		0	2	.000	8.36	1.96	16	0	0	0	...	0-...	28.0	41	32	26	2	14-0	28	.331
2000— Lansing (Midw.)		1	1	.500	9.68	2.43	16	0	0	0	...	0-...	17.2	24	22	19	0	19-0	16	.338
— Eugene (N'west)		2	2	.500	2.68	1.10	25	0	0	0	...	8-...	43.2	28	16	13	1	20-2	52	.178
2001— Daytona (Fla. St.)		6	9	.400	5.00	1.40	21	18	0	0	...	0-...	95.1	93	62	53	10	40-1	72	.251
2002— West Tenn. (Sou.)		2	2	.500	2.59	1.13	39	0	0	0	...	23-...	41.2	28	14	12	2	19-2	43	.192
— Chicago (N.L.)		0	0	...	7.50	2.50	11	0	0	0	0	0-0	12.0	14	11	10	2	16-1	11	.311
2003— Iowa (PCL)		6	2	.750	2.96	1.30	31	2	0	0	...	4-...	48.2	46	17	16	2	19-3	33	.247
2004— Chicago (N.L.)		2	2	.500	4.63	1.40	34	0	0	0	5	0-0	35.0	27	19	18	8	22-0	40	.214
— Iowa (PCL)		0	0	...	2.84	0.95	6	0	0	0	...	4-...	6.1	5	2	2	1	1-0	6	.208
— Edmonton (PCL)		0	0	...	1.50	1.00	6	0	0	0	...	3-...	6.0	4	1	1	0	2-0	8	.190
— Montreal (N.L.)		0	0	...	7.53	1.74	11	0	0	0	0	1-1	14.1	20	12	12	3	5-1	8	.333
Major League totals (2 years)		2	2	.500	5.87	1.70	56	0	0	0	5	1-1	61.1	61	42	40	13	43-2	59	.264

BELTRAN, RIGO   P

PERSONAL: Born November 13, 1969, in Tijuana, Mexico. ... 5-11/200. ... Throws left, bats left. ... Full name: Rigoberto Beltran. ... Name pronounced: REE-go. ... High school: Point Loma (San Diego). ... College: Wyoming.

TRANSACTIONS/CAREER NOTES: Selected by St. Louis Cardinals organization in 26th round of 1991 free-agent draft. ... Traded by Cardinals to New York Mets for P Juan Acevedo (March 29, 1998). ... Traded by Mets with OFs Brian McRae and Thomas Johnson and a player to be named to Colorado Rockies for OF Darryl Hamilton and P Chuck McElroy (July 31, 1999); Rockies acquired OF Carlos Mendoza to complete deal (April 5, 2000). ... Signed as a free agent by Philadelphia Phillies organization (November 16, 2000). ... Signed by Hiroshima of the Japan Central League (2002). ... Signed as a free agent by Baltimore Orioles organization (November 4, 2002). ... Signed as a free agent by Cincinnati Reds organization (December 19, 2003). ... Released by Reds (2004). ... Signed by Montreal Expos organization (March 26, 2004). ... On disabled list (April 29-June 4, 2004). ... Expos franchise transferred to Washington, D.C., for 2005 season.

CAREER HITTING: 2-for-11 (.182). 1 R, 1 2B, 0 3B, 0 HR, 0 RBI.

Year	Team (League)	W	L	Pct.	ERA	WHIP	G	GS	CG	ShO	Hld.	Sv.-Opp.	IP	H	R	ER	HR	BB-IBB	SO	Avg.
1991— Hamilton (N.Y.-Penn.)		5	2	.714	2.63	1.25	21	4	0	0	...	0-...	48.0	41	17	14	4	19-0	69	.229
1992— Savannah (S. Atl.)		6	1	.857	2.17	0.94	13	13	2	1	...	0-...	83.0	38	20	20	4	40-0	106	.140
— St. Pete. (FSL)		0	0	...	0.00	1.00	2	2	0	0	...	0-...	8.0	6	0	0	0	2-0	3	.222
1993— Arkansas (Texas)		5	5	.500	3.25	1.26	18	16	0	0	...	0-...	88.2	74	39	32	8	38-1	82	.227
1994— Arkansas (Texas)		4	0	1.000	0.64	0.54	4	4	1	1	...	0-...	28.0	12	2	2	2	3-0	21	.132
— Louisville (A.A.)		11	11	.500	5.07	1.55	23	23	1	0	...	0-...	138.1	147	82	78	15	68-2	87	.274
1995— Louisville (A.A.)		8	9	.471	5.21	1.47	24	24	0	0	...	0-...	129.2	156	81	75	12	34-0	92	.297
1996— Louisville (A.A.)		8	6	.571	4.35	1.20	38	16	3	1	...	0-...	130.1	132	67	63	17	24-1	132	.257
1997— Louisville (A.A.)		5	2	.714	2.32	1.21	9	8	1	0	...	0-...	54.1	45	17	14	7	21-0	46	.221
— St. Louis (N.L.)		1	2	.333	3.48	1.18	35	4	0	0	2	1-1	54.1	47	25	21	3	17-0	50	.237
1998— Norfolk (Int'l)		6	5	.545	4.29	1.53	36	11	0	0	...	0-...	94.1	104	51	45	16	40-1	98	.279
— New York (N.L.)		0	0	...	3.38	1.25	7	0	0	0	0	0-0	8.0	6	3	3	1	4-0	5	.214
1999— Norfolk (Int'l)		2	1	.667	1.61	1.25	21	0	0	0	...	0-...	22.1	16	5	4	1	12-1	27	.203
— New York (N.L.)		1	1	.500	3.48	1.35	21	0	0	0	0	0-0	31.0	30	15	12	5	12-2	35	.250
— Colo. Springs (PCL)		1	0	1.000	2.25	2.13	6	0	0	0	...	0-...	8.0	12	3	2	1	5-1	12	.343
— Colorado (N.L.)		0	0	...	7.36	2.45	12	0	0	0	1	0-0	11.0	20	9	9	2	7-1	15	.385
2000— Colo. Springs (PCL)		6	10	.375	5.90	1.56	25	21	1	1	...	0-...	125.0	132	85	82	15	63-0	95	.272
— Colorado (N.L.)		0	0	...	40.50	6.75	1	1	0	0	0	0-0	1.1	6	6	6	2	3-0	1	.600
2001— Scran./W.B. (I.L.)		2	5	.286	2.96	1.11	37	1	0	0	...	2-...	115.2	87	40	38	10	41-6	113	.211
2003— Ottawa (Int'l)		5	4	.556	2.71	1.10	31	13	2	1	...	1-...	103.0	77	33	31	3	41-3	69	.213
2004— Montreal (N.L.)		0	0	...	13.50	1.50	2	0	0	0	0	0-0	.2	1	1	1	0	0-0	0	.333
— Edmonton (PCL)		3	2	.600	3.64	1.27	25	8	0	0	...	3-...	64.1	65	27	26	5	17-1	52	.267
Major League totals (5 years)		2	3	.400	4.40	1.44	78	5	0	0	3	1-1	106.1	110	59	52	13	43-3	106	.268

BELTRE, ADRIAN   3B

PERSONAL: Born April 7, 1979, in Santo Domingo, Dominican Republic. ... 5-11/220. ... Bats right, throws right. ... Full name: Adrian Perez Beltre. ... Name pronounced: BELL-tray. ... High school: Liceo Maximo Gomez (Santo Domingo, Dominican Republic).

TRANSACTIONS/CAREER NOTES: Signed as a non-drafted free agent by Los Angeles Dodgers (July 7, 1994). ... On disabled list (May 28-June 17, 2000). ... On disabled list (March 23-May 12, 2001); included rehabilitation assignments to Vero Beach and Las Vegas.

2004 GAMES PLAYED BY POSITION (MLB): 3B—155, SS—1.

Year	Team (League)	Pos.	G	AB	R	H	2B	3B	HR	RBI	BB	SO	HBP	GDP	SB-CS	Avg.	OBP	SLG	OPS	E	Avg.
															BATTING					**FIELDING**	
1995— Dom. Dodgers (DSL)		3B	62	218	56	67	15	3	8	40	54	26	...	...	2-1	.307	...	.514	...	19	.920

Year Team (League)	Pos.	G	AB	R	H	2B	3B	HR	RBI	BB	SO	HBP	GDP	SB-CS	Avg.	OBP	SLG	OPS	E	Avg.
1996—Savannah (S. Atl.)	3B-2B	68	244	48	75	14	3	16	59	35	46	7	7	4-3	.307	.406	.586	.992	19	.912
—San Bern. (Calif.)	3B-DH	63	238	40	62	13	1	10	40	19	44	5	3	3-4	.261	.322	.450	.772	7	.953
1997—Vero Beach (FSL)	3B-OF	123	435	95	138	24	2	26	104	67	66	6	9	25-9	.317	.407	.561	.967	37	.895
1998—San Antonio (Texas)	3B-DH	64	246	49	79	21	2	13	56	39	37	2	3	20-4	.321	.411	.581	.992	17	.910
—Los Angeles (N.L.)	3B-SS	77	195	18	42	9	0	7	22	14	37	3	4	3-1	.215	.278	.369	.648	13	.926
1999—Los Angeles (N.L.)	3B	152	538	84	148	27	5	15	67	61	105	6	4	18-7	.275	.352	.428	.780	•29	.932
2000—Los Angeles (N.L.)	3B-SS	138	510	71	148	30	2	20	85	56	80	2	13	12-5	.290	.360·	.475	.835	23	.944
2001—Vero Beach (FSL)	3B	3	9	0	4	1	0	0	1	2	1	1	0	0-0	.444	.583	.556	1.139	0	1.000
—Las Vegas (PCL)	3B	2	5	2	3	1	0	1	2	2	0	0	0	0-0	.600	.714	1.400	2.114	1	.833
—Los Angeles (N.L.)	3B-SS	126	475	59	126	22	4	13	60	28	82	5	9	13-4	.265	.310	.411	.720	16	.953
2002—Los Angeles (N.L.)	3B	159	587	70	151	26	5	21	75	37	96	4	17	7-5	.257	.303	.426	.729	20	.954
2003—Los Angeles (N.L.)	3B-SS	158	559	50	134	30	2	13	80	37	103	5	13	2-2	.240	.290	.424	.714	19	.957
2004—Los Angeles (N.L.)	3B-SS	156	598	104	200	32	0	*48	121	53	87	2	15	7-2	.334	.388	.629	1.017	10	.978
Major League totals (7 years)		966	3462	456	949	176	18	147	510	286	590	27	75	62-26	.274	.332	.463	.794	130	.951

DIVISION SERIES RECORD

Year Team (League)	Pos.	G	AB	R	H	2B	3B	HR	RBI	BB	SO	HBP	GDP	SB-CS	Avg.	OBP	SLG	OPS	E	Avg.
2004—Los Angeles (N.L.)	3B	4	15	1	4	0	0	0	1	0	3	0	0	0-0	.267	.250	.267	.517	0	1.000

BENITEZ, ARMANDO — P

PERSONAL: Born November 3, 1972, in Ramon Santana, Dominican Republic. ... 6-4/229. ... Throws right, bats right. ... Full name: Armando German Benitez. ... Name pronounced: buh-NEE-tezz.

TRANSACTIONS/CAREER NOTES: Signed as a non-drafted free agent by Baltimore Orioles organization (April 1, 1990). ... On disabled list (April 20-August 26, 1996); included rehabilitation assignments to Bowie and GCL Orioles. ... On suspended list (May 20-28, 1998). ... Traded by Orioles to New York Mets for C Charles Johnson (December 1, 1998). ... Traded by Mets to New York Yankees for Ps Jason Anderson, Ryan Bicondoa and Anderson García (July 18, 2003). ... Traded by Yankees to Seattle Mariners for P Jeff Nelson (August 6, 2003). ... Signed as a free agent by Florida Marlins (January 6, 2004). ... On disabled list (July 23-August 12, 2004).

HONORS: Named N.L. co-Reliever of the Year by THE SPORTING NEWS (2001).

CAREER HITTING: 0-for-8 (.000), 0 R, 0 2B, 0 3B, 0 HR, 2 RBI.

Year Team (League)	W	L	Pct.	ERA	WHIP	G	GS	CG	ShO	Hld.	Sv.-Opp.	IP	H	R	ER	HR	BB-IBB	SO	Avg.
1990—Dominican Orioles/W.S. (DSL)	3	1	.750	2.72	1.37	19	0	0	0	...	8-...	43.0	39	23	13	...	20-...	34	...
1991—GC Orioles (GCL)	3	2	.600	2.72	1.27	14	3	0	0	...	0-...	36.1	35	16	11	2	11-0	33	.252
1992—Bluefield (Appalachian)	1	2	.333	4.31	1.85	25	0	0	0	...	5-...	31.1	35	31	15	1	23-0	37	.276
1993—Albany (S. Atl.)	5	1	.833	1.52	0.94	40	0	0	0	...	14-...	53.1	31	10	9	2	19-0	83	.168
—Frederick (Caro.)	3	0	1.000	0.66	0.80	12	0	0	0	...	4-...	13.2	7	1	1	0	4-0	29	.149
1994—Bowie (East.)	8	4	.667	3.14	1.12	53	0	0	0	...	16-...	71.2	41	29	25	6	39-0	106	.160
—Baltimore (A.L.)	0	0	...	0.90	1.20	3	0	0	0	0	0-0	10.0	8	1	1	0	4-0	14	.216
1995—Baltimore (A.L.)	1	5	.167	5.66	1.55	44	0	0	0	6	2-5	47.2	37	33	30	8	37-2	56	.213
—Rochester (Int'l)	2	2	.500	1.25	0.78	17	0	0	0	...	8-...	21.2	10	4	3	2	7-0	37	.135
1996—Baltimore (A.L.)	1	0	1.000	3.77	0.91	18	0	0	0	1	4-5	14.1	7	6	6	2	6-0	20	.143
—Bowie (East.)	0	0	...	4.50	1.17	4	4	0	0	...	0-...	6.0	7	3	3	0	0-0	8	.304
—GC Orioles (GCL)	1	0	1.000	0.00	0.50	1	0	0	0	...	0-...	2.0	1	0	0	0	0-0	5	.143
—Rochester (Int'l)	0	0	...	2.25	1.00	2	0	0	0	...	0-...	4.0	3	1	1	1	1-0	5	.188
1997—Baltimore (A.L.)	4	5	.444	2.45	1.25	71	0	0	0	20	9-10	73.1	49	22	20	7	43-5	106	.191
1998—Baltimore (A.L.)	5	6	.455	3.82	1.27	71	0	0	0	3	22-26	68.1	48	29	29	10	39-2	87	.199
1999—New York (N.L.)	4	3	.571	1.85	1.04	77	0	0	0	17	22-28	78.0	40	17	16	4	41-4	128	.148
2000—New York (N.L.)	4	4	.500	2.61	1.01	76	0	0	0	0	41-46	76.0	39	24	22	10	38-2	106	.148
2001—New York (N.L.)	6	4	.600	3.77	1.30	73	0	0	0	0	43-46	76.1	59	32	32	12	40-6	93	.214
2002—New York (N.L.)	1	0	1.000	2.27	1.05	62	0	0	0	0	33-37	67.1	46	20	17	8	25-0	79	.190
2003—New York (N.L.)	3	3	.500	3.10	1.32	45	0	0	0	0	21-28	49.1	41	18	17	5	24-1	50	.223
—New York (N.L.)	1	1	.500	1.93	1.50	9	0	0	0	4	0-0	9.1	8	4	2	0	6-1	10	.235
—Seattle (A.L.)	0	0	...	3.14	1.47	15	0	0	0	1	0-1	14.1	10	5	5	1	11-1	15	.189
2004—Florida (N.L.)	2	2	.500	1.29	0.82	64	0	0	0	0	•47-51	69.2	36	11	10	6	21-4	62	.152
American League totals (6 years)	12	17	.414	3.53	1.32	231	0	0	0	35	37-47	237.1	167	100	93	28	146-11	308	.198
National League totals (6 years)	20	16	.556	2.46	1.08	397	0	0	0	17	207-236	416.2	261	122	114	45	189-17	518	.177
Major League totals (11 years)	32	33	.492	2.85	1.17	628	0	0	0	52	244-283	654.0	428	222	207	73	335-28	826	.185

DIVISION SERIES RECORD

Year Team (League)	W	L	Pct.	ERA	WHIP	G	GS	CG	ShO	Hld.	Sv.-Opp.	IP	H	R	ER	HR	BB-IBB	SO	Avg.
1996—Baltimore (A.L.)	2	0	1.000	2.25	0.75	3	0	0	0	0	0-1	4.0	1	1	1	1	2-0	6	.083
1997—Baltimore (A.L.)	0	0	...	3.00	1.67	3	0	0	0	2	0-0	3.0	3	1	1	1	2-0	4	.250
1999—New York (N.L.)	0	0	...	0.00	1.29	2	0	0	0	0	0-1	2.1	2	0	0	0	1-1	2	.250
2000—New York (N.L.)	1	0	1.000	6.00	1.67	2	0	0	0	0	0-1	3.0	4	2	2	1	1-1	3	.308
Division series totals (4 years)	3	0	1.000	2.92	1.30	10	0	0	0	2	0-3	12.1	10	4	4	3	6-2	15	.222

CHAMPIONSHIP SERIES RECORD

Year Team (League)	W	L	Pct.	ERA	WHIP	G	GS	CG	ShO	Hld.	Sv.-Opp.	IP	H	R	ER	HR	BB-IBB	SO	Avg.
1996—Baltimore (A.L.)	0	0	...	7.71	2.57	3	0	0	0	0	1-2	2.1	3	2	2	2	3-1	2	.300
1997—Baltimore (A.L.)	0	2	.000	12.00	2.33	4	0	0	0	0	0-1	3.0	3	4	4	2	4-0	6	.250
1999—New York (N.L.)	0	0	...	1.35	0.75	5	0	0	0	0	1-1	6.2	3	1	1	0	2-0	9	.136
2000—New York (N.L.)	0	0	...	0.00	1.67	3	0	0	0	0	1-1	3.0	3	2	0	0	2-0	2	.231
Champ. series totals (4 years)	0	2	.000	4.20	1.53	15	0	0	0	0	3-5	15.0	12	9	7	4	11-1	19	.211

WORLD SERIES RECORD

Year Team (League)	W	L	Pct.	ERA	WHIP	G	GS	CG	ShO	Hld.	Sv.-Opp.	IP	H	R	ER	HR	BB-IBB	SO	Avg.
2000—New York (N.L.)	0	0	...	3.00	1.67	3	0	0	0	0	1-2	3.0	3	1	1	0	2-0	2	.250

BENNETT, GARY — C

PERSONAL: Born April 17, 1972, in Waukegan, Ill. ... 6-0/208. ... Bats right, throws right. ... Full name: Gary David Bennett. ... High school: Waukegan East (Ill.).

TRANSACTIONS/CAREER NOTES: Selected by Philadelphia Phillies organization in 11th round of 1990 free-agent draft (June 4, 1990). ... Signed as a free agent by Boston Red Sox organization (February 10, 1997). ... Signed as a free agent by Philadelphia Phillies organization (December 27, 1997). ... Traded by Phillies to New York Mets for C Todd Pratt (July 23, 2001). ... Traded by Mets to Colorado Rockies for a player to be named (August 24, 2001); Mets acquired OF Endy Chavez to complete deal (December 27, 2001). ... Signed as a free agent by San Diego Padres (December 23, 2002). ... On disabled list (April 17-May 23, 2003). ... Signed as a free agent by Milwaukee Brewers organization (December 22, 2003). ... Refused minor league assignment and became a free agent (October 14, 2004).

2004 GAMES PLAYED BY POSITION (MLB): C—75.

B

Year	Team (League)	Pos.	G	AB	R	H	2B	3B	HR	RBI	BB	SO	HBP	GDP	SB-CS	Avg.	OBP	SLG	OPS	E	Avg.
														BATTING						FIELDING	
1990— Martinsville (App.)	C	16	52	3	14	2	1	0	10	4	15	0	0	0-1	.269	.316	.346	.662	3	.965
1991— Martinsville (App.)	C	41	136	15	32	7	0	1	16	17	26	5	5	0-1	.235	.340	.309	.648	2	.994
1992— Batavia (NY-Penn)	C	47	146	22	30	2	0	0	12	15	27	2	2	2-1	.205	.288	.219	.508	2	.994
1993— Spartanburg (SAL)	C	42	126	18	32	4	1	0	15	12	22	1	2	0-2	.254	.321	.302	.623	2	.992
— Clearwater (FSL)	C	17	55	5	18	0	0	1	6	3	10	1	0	0-1	.327	.373	.382	.755	0	1.000
1994— Clearwater (FSL)	C	19	55	6	13	3	0	0	10	8	6	0	1	0-0	.236	.328	.291	.619	1	.991
— Reading (East.)	C	63	208	13	48	9	0	3	22	14	26	0	6	0-1	.231	.276	.317	.593	2	.995
1995— Reading (East.)	C-DH	86	271	27	64	11	0	4	40	22	36	3	12	0-0	.236	.299	.321	.620	4	.994
— Scran./W.B. (I.L.)	C	7	20	1	3	0	0	0	1	2	2	0	0	0-0	.150	.227	.150	.377	0	1.000
— Philadelphia (N.L.)		1	1	0	0	0	0	0	0	0	1	0	0	0-0	.000	.000	.000	.000	...	...
1996— Scran./W.B. (I.L.)	C	91	286	37	71	15	1	8	37	24	43	3	10	1-0	.248	.310	.392	.702	7	.988
— Philadelphia (N.L.)	C	6	16	0	4	0	0	0	1	2	6	0	0	0-0	.250	.333	.250	.583	0	1.000
1997— Pawtucket (Int'l)	C-1B	71	224	16	48	7	1	4	22	18	39	2	10	1-1	.214	.278	.308	.586	8	.986
1998— Scran./W.B. (I.L.)	C-DH-1B	86	282	33	72	18	0	10	40	25	41	2	6	0-0	.255	.316	.426	.742	1	.998
— Philadelphia (N.L.)	C	9	31	4	9	0	0	0	3	5	5	0	1	0-0	.290	.378	.290	.669	0	1.000
1999— Philadelphia (N.L.)	C	36	88	7	24	4	0	1	21	4	11	0	7	0-0	.273	.298	.352	.650	4	.971
2000— Scran./W.B. (I.L.)	C	92	317	47	97	24	0	12	52	40	44	7	9	1-0	.306	.393	.495	.889	2	.996
— Philadelphia (N.L.)	C	31	74	8	18	5	0	2	5	13	15	2	0	0-0	.243	.371	.392	.763	1	.995
2001— Philadelphia (N.L.)	C	26	75	8	16	3	1	1	6	9	19	0	1	0-0	.213	.294	.320	.614	2	.987
— New York (N.L.)		1	1	0	1	0	0	0	0	0	0	0	0	0-0	1.000	1.000	1.000	2.000	...	...
— Norfolk (Int'l)	C-3B	20	67	7	20	5	0	2	14	4	12	1	0	0-0	.299	.342	.463	.805	0	1.000
— Colorado (N.L.)	C	19	55	7	15	3	0	1	4	3	5	1	0	0-0	.273	.317	.382	.698	0	1.000
2002— Colorado (N.L.)	C	90	291	26	77	10	2	4	26	15	45	6	10	1-3	.265	.314	.354	.668	4	.992
2003— San Diego (N.L.)	C	96	307	26	73	15	0	2	42	24	48	2	8	3-0	.238	.296	.306	.602	2	.996
2004— Milwaukee (N.L.)	C	75	219	18	49	14	0	3	20	22	32	2	9	1-0	.224	.297	.329	.626	3	.993
Major League totals (9 years)		390	1158	104	286	54	3	14	128	97	187	13	36	5-3	.247	.310	.335	.645	16	.993

BENNETT, JEFF   P

PERSONAL: Born June 10, 1980, in Donelson, Tenn. ... 6-3/206. ... Throws right, bats right. ... Full name: David Jeffrey Bennett. ... High school: Gordonsville (Tenn.).

TRANSACTIONS/CAREER NOTES: Selected by Pittsburgh Pirates oganization in 19th round of 1998 free-agent draft. ... Selected by Milwaukee Brewers from Pirates organization in Rule 5 major league draft (December 15, 2003).

CAREER HITTING: 0-for-2 (.000), 0 R, 0 2B, 0 3B, 0 HR, 0 RBI.

Year	Team (League)	W	L	Pct.	ERA	WHIP	G	GS	CG	ShO	Hld.	Sv.-Opp.	IP	H	R	ER	HR	BB-IBB	SO	Avg.
1998— GC Pirates (GCL)	2	4	.333	4.63	1.35	13	11	0	0	...	0-...	46.2	50	29	24	4	13-0	18	.265
1999— GC Pirates (GCL)	3	4	.429	4.23	1.39	8	8	0	0	...	0-...	44.2	53	27	21	1	9-0	28	.296
— Hickory (S. Atl.)	2	2	.500	5.91	1.63	8	6	0	0	...	0-...	35.0	48	25	23	5	9-0	16	.322
2000— Hickory (S. Atl.)	10	13	.435	4.40	1.37	27	27	1	0	...	0-...	171.2	189	116	84	14	47-1	126	.276
2001— Lynchburg (Carolina)	11	10	.524	3.42	1.21	25	25	2	1	...	0-...	166.0	171	78	63	14	30-1	98	.268
— Altoona (East.)	0	1	.000	3.86	1.57	1	1	0	0	...	0-...	7.0	9	3	3	0	2-0	6	.300
2002— Lynchburg (Carolina)	10	6	.625	3.62	1.34	24	20	0	0	...	0-...	124.1	137	64	50	7	30-0	90	.280
2003— Altoona (East.)	4	4	.500	2.72	1.14	33	2	0	0	...	1-...	59.2	45	22	18	2	23-3	62	.201
— Nashville (PCL)	1	3	.250	6.56	1.63	9	5	0	0	...	0-...	23.1	26	21	17	4	12-0	16	.277
2004— Milwaukee (N.L.)	1	5	.167	4.79	1.46	60	0	0	0	8	0-1	71.1	78	43	38	12	26-2	45	.278
Major League totals (1 year)	1	5	.167	4.79	1.46	60	0	0	0	8	0-1	71.1	78	43	38	12	26-2	45	.278

BENOIT, JOAQUIN   P

PERSONAL: Born July 26, 1977, in Santiago, Dominican Republic. ... 6-3/220. ... Throws right, bats right. ... Full name: Joaquin Antonio Benoit. ... Name pronounced: ben-WAH.

TRANSACTIONS/CAREER NOTES: Signed as a non-drafted free agent by Texas Rangers organization (May 20, 1996). ... On disabled list (June 1-22, 2003); included rehabilitation assignment to Oklahoma. ... On disabled list (August 23-September 7, 2004); included rehabilitation assignment to Frisco.

CAREER HITTING: 0-for-8 (.000), 1 R, 0 2B, 0 3B, 0 HR, 0 RBI.

Year	Team (League)	W	L	Pct.	ERA	WHIP	G	GS	CG	ShO	Hld.	Sv.-Opp.	IP	H	R	ER	HR	BB-IBB	SO	Avg.
1996— Dom. Rangers (DSL)	6	5	.545	2.28	1.15	14	13	2	1	...	0-...	75.0	63	26	19	...	23-...	63	...
1997— GC Rangers (GCL)	3	3	.500	2.05	1.16	10	10	1	0	...	0-...	44.0	40	14	10	0	11-0	38	.244
1998— Savannah (S. Atl.)	4	3	.571	3.83	1.21	15	1	0	0	...	0-...	80.0	79	41	34	8	18-0	68	.252
1999— Charlotte (Fla. St.)	7	4	.636	5.31	1.59	22	22	0	0	...	0-...	105.0	117	67	62	5	50-0	83	.283
2000— Tulsa (Texas)	4	4	.500	3.83	1.25	16	16	0	0	...	0-...	82.1	73	40	35	6	30-0	72	.237
2001— Tulsa (Texas)	1	0	1.000	3.32	1.34	4	4	0	0	...	0-...	21.2	23	8	8	1	6-0	23	.264
— Oklahoma (PCL)	9	5	.643	4.19	1.42	24	24	1	1	...	0-...	131.0	113	63	61	14	73-0	142	.234
— Texas (A.L.)	0	0	...	10.80	2.20	1	1	0	0	0	0-...	5.0	8	6	6	3	3-0	4	.364
2002— Oklahoma (PCL)	8	4	.667	3.56	1.13	16	16	0	0	...	0-...	98.2	74	42	39	8	37-0	103	.204
— Texas (A.L.)	4	5	.444	5.31	1.76	17	13	0	0	0	1-1	84.2	91	51	50	6	58-2	59	.272
— Charlotte (Fla. St.)	0	0	...	0.00	0.80	1	1	0	0	0	0-...	5.0	1	0	0	0	3-0	8	.059
2003— Oklahoma (PCL)	2	1	.667	3.82	1.20	6	6	0	0	...	0-...	33.0	28	17	14	3	11-0	31	.231
— Texas (A.L.)	8	5	.615	5.49	1.43	25	17	0	0	0	0-0	105.0	99	67	64	23	51-0	87	.246
2004— Frisco (Texas)	0	0	...	0.00	...	1	1	0	0	0	0-...	2.0	0	0	0	0	0-0	6	.000
— Texas (A.L.)	3	5	.375	5.68	1.40	28	15	0	0	0	0-0	103.0	113	67	65	19	31-0	95	.279
Major League totals (4 years)	15	15	.500	5.59	1.53	71	46	0	0	0	1-1	297.2	311	191	185	51	143-2	245	.267

BENSON, KRIS   P

PERSONAL: Born November 7, 1974, in Superior, Wis. ... 6-4/195. ... Throws right, bats right. ... Full name: Kristin James Benson. ... High school: Spayberry (Marietta, Ga.). ... College: Clemson.

TRANSACTIONS/CAREER NOTES: Selected by Pittsburgh Pirates organization in first round (first pick overall) of 1996 free-agent draft. ... On disabled list (March 31, 2001-entire season). ... On disabled list (March 22-May 13, 2002); included rehabilitation assignments to Nashville and Altoona. ... On disabled list (July 28, 2003-remainder of season). ... Traded by Pirates with IF Jeff Keppinger to New York Mets for 3B Ty Wigginton, IF Jose Bautista and P Matt Peterson (July 30, 2004).

CAREER HITTING: 31-for-258 (.120), 18 R, 6 2B, 0 3B, 0 HR, 14 RBI.

Year Team (League)	W	L	Pct.	ERA	WHIP	G	GS	CG	ShO	Hld.	Sv.-Opp.	IP	H	R	ER	HR	BB-IBB	SO	Avg.
1997—Lynchburg (Carolina)	5	2	.714	2.58	1.04	10	10	0	0	...	0-...	59.1	49	20	17	1	13-0	72	.221
—Carolina (Southern)	3	5	.375	4.98	1.65	14	14	0	0	...	0-...	68.2	81	49	38	11	32-1	66	.289
1998—Nashville (PCL)	8	10	.444	5.37	1.36	28	28	1	1	...	0-...	156.0	162	102	93	26	50-5	129	.260
1999—Pittsburgh (N.L.)	11	14	.440	4.07	1.36	31	31	2	0	0	0-0	196.2	184	105	89	16	83-5	139	.249
2000—Pittsburgh (N.L.)	10	12	.455	3.85	1.34	32	32	2	1	0	0-0	217.2	206	104	93	24	86-5	184	.249
2001—Pittsburgh (N.L.)	Did not play.																		
2002—Nashville (PCL)	0	2	.000	1.53	0.91	4	4	0	0	...	0-...	17.2	8	4	3	1	8-0	25	.133
—Altoona (East.)	1	0	1.000	1.29	0.71	1	1	0	0	...	0-...	7.0	5	1	1	1	0-0	7	.208
—Pittsburgh (N.L.)	9	6	.600	4.70	1.55	25	25	0	0	0	0-0	130.1	152	76	68	18	50-8	79	.295
2003—Pittsburgh (N.L.)	5	9	.357	4.97	1.55	18	18	0	0	0	0-0	105.0	127	67	58	14	36-4	68	.295
2004—Pittsburgh (N.L.)	8	8	.500	4.22	1.37	20	20	0	0	0	0-0	132.1	137	69	62	7	44-5	83	.272
—New York (N.L.)	4	4	.500	4.50	1.21	11	11	1	1	0	0-0	68.0	65	37	34	8	17-3	51	.244
Major League totals (5 years)	47	53	.470	4.28	1.40	137	137	5	2	0	0-0	850.0	871	458	404	87	316-30	604	.266

BENTZ, CHAD — P

PERSONAL: Born May 5, 1980, in Seward, Alaska. ... 6-2/215. ... Throws left, bats right. ... Full name: Chad Robert Bentz. ... High school: Juneau-Douglas (Alaska). ... College: Long Beach State.

TRANSACTIONS/CAREER NOTES: Selected by New York Yankees organization in 34th round of 1999 free-agent draft; did not sign. ... Selected by Montreal Expos organization in seventh round of 2001 free-agent draft. ... Montreal franchise transferred to Washington, D.C., for 2005 season.

CAREER HITTING: 1-for-2 (.500), 0 R, 0 2B, 0 3B, 0 HR, 0 RBI.

Year Team (League)	W	L	Pct.	ERA	WHIP	G	GS	CG	ShO	Hld.	Sv.-Opp.	IP	H	R	ER	HR	BB-IBB	SO	Avg.
2001—Vermont (NY-P)	1	3	.250	4.91	1.36	8	8	0	0	...	0-...	36.2	39	23	20	2	11-0	38	.264
2002—Brevard County (FSL)	0	1	.000	3.64	1.48	23	0	0	0	...	5-...	29.2	30	14	12	1	14-2	34	.259
2003—Harrisburg (Eastern)	1	4	.200	2.55	1.31	52	0	0	0	...	16-...	84.2	72	31	24	4	39-2	56	.241
2004—Montreal (N.L.)	0	3	.000	5.86	1.66	36	0	0	0	5	0-0	27.2	23	19	18	5	23-3	18	.228
—Edmonton (PCL)	0	0	...	3.60	1.60	5	0	0	0	...	0-...	5.0	5	2	2	1	3-0	2	.278
—Harrisburg (Eastern)	0	1	.000	8.59	1.77	5	1	0	0	...	1-...	7.1	5	7	7	2	8-0	2	.200
Major League totals (1 year)	0	3	.000	5.86	1.66	36	0	0	0	5	0-0	27.2	23	19	18	5	23-3	18	.228

BERG, DAVE — OF

PERSONAL: Born September 3, 1970, in Roseville, Calif. ... 5-11/185. ... Bats right, throws right. ... Full name: David Scott Berg. ... High school: Roseville (Calif.). ... College: Miami (Fla.).

TRANSACTIONS/CAREER NOTES: Selected by California Angels organization in 32nd round of 1990 free-agent draft; did not sign. ... Selected by Florida Marlins organization in 38th round of 1993 free-agent draft. ... On disabled list (April 2-25, 2000); included rehabilitation assignment to Brevard County. ... Signed as a free agent by Toronto Blue Jays organization (January 12, 2002). ... On disabled list (June 28-July 28, 2003); included rehabilitation assignment to Syracuse.

2004 GAMES PLAYED BY POSITION (MLB): OF—31, DH—7, 1B—7, 2B—4, 3B—3.

Year Team (League)	Pos.	G	AB	R	H	2B	3B	HR	RBI	BB	SO	HBP	GDP	SB-CS	Avg.	OBP	SLG	OPS	E	Avg.
1993—Elmira (N.Y.-Penn)	2B-3B-OF	75	281	37	74	13	1	4	28	34	37	8	8	7-4	.263	.356	.359	.715	20	.925
1994—Kane Co. (Midw.)	2B-3B	121	437	80	117	27	8	9	53	54	80	8	10	8-6	.268	.354	.428	.782	17	.948
1995—Brevard County (FSL)	2B-3B-SS	114	382	71	114	18	1	3	39	68	61	8	9	9-4	.298	.407	.374	.781	26	.951
1996—Portland (East.)	3B-SS	109	414	64	125	28	5	9	73	42	60	5	10	17-7	.302	.368	.459	.827	26	.951
1997—Charlotte (Int'l)	2B-3B-SS	117	424	76	125	26	6	9	47	55	71	3	13	16-7	.295	.377	.448	.825	22	.954
1998—Florida (N.L.)	2B-3B-SS	81	182	18	57	11	0	2	21	26	46	0	1	3-0	.313	.393	.407	.800	7	.969
1999—Florida (N.L.)	S-2-3B-OF	109	304	42	87	18	1	3	25	27	59	2	7	2-2	.286	.348	.382	.730	8	.974
2000—Brevard County (FSL)	2B-3B-SS	3	11	2	3	0	0	0	2	1	3	1	1	0-1	.273	.385	.273	.657	0	1.000
—Florida (N.L.)	SS-3B-2B	82	210	23	53	14	1	1	21	25	46	5	5	3-0	.252	.340	.343	.683	6	.964
2001—Florida (N.L.)	2B-SS-3B	82	215	26	52	12	1	4	16	14	39	2	3	0-1	.242	.292	.363	.655	6	.961
2002—Toronto (A.L.)	2-B-S-O-1-D	109	374	42	101	26	2	4	39	26	57	5	6	0-2	.270	.322	.382	.704	10	.974
2003—Syracuse (Int'l)	2B-3B-DH	6	20	3	5	1	0	0	4	1	2	1	0	0-0	.250	.318	.300	.618	0	1.000
—Toronto (A.L.)	2-3-DH-O-1-S	61	161	26	41	6	1	4	18	11	34	0	7	0-1	.255	.301	.379	.679	5	.966
2004—Toronto (A.L.)	O-DH-1-2-3	58	154	13	39	4	0	3	23	4	27	2	4	0-1	.253	.278	.338	.615	5	.953
American League totals (3 years)		228	689	81	181	36	3	11	80	41	118	7	17	0-4	.263	.307	.372	.679	20	.969
National League totals (4 years)		354	911	109	249	55	3	10	83	92	190	9	16	8-3	.273	.343	.373	.716	31	.968
Major League totals (7 years)		582	1600	190	430	91	6	21	163	133	308	16	33	8-7	.269	.328	.373	.700	51	.968

BERGER, BRANDON — OF

PERSONAL: Born February 21, 1975, in Covington, Ky. ... 5-11/205. ... Bats right, throws right. ... Full name: Brandon Charles Berger. ... High school: Beechwood (Fort Mitchell, Ky.). ... College: Eastern Kentucky.

TRANSACTIONS/CAREER NOTES: Selected by Chicago White Sox organization in 41st round of 1993 free-agent draft; did not sign. ... Selected by Kansas City Royals organization in 14th round of 1996 free-agent draft.

2004 GAMES PLAYED BY POSITION (MLB): OF—11.

Year Team (League)	Pos.	G	AB	R	H	2B	3B	HR	RBI	BB	SO	HBP	GDP	SB-CS	Avg.	OBP	SLG	OPS	E	Avg.
1996—Spokane (N'west)	OF	71	283	46	87	12	1	13	58	31	64	2	7	17-5	.307	.376	.495	.871	6	.967
1997—Lansing (Midw.)	OF	107	393	64	115	22	6	12	73	42	79	7	8	13-1	.293	.368	.471	.838	3	.979
1998—Wilmington (Caro.)	P-OF	110	338	53	75	18	3	8	50	53	94	5	11	13-3	.222	.332	.364	.696	2	.986
1999—Wilmington (Caro.)	OF	119	450	73	132	27	4	16	73	45	93	8	3	29-7	.293	.363	.478	.841	5	.964
2000—Wichita (Texas)	OF	27	86	9	14	2	0	3	8	7	27	2	2	6-1	.163	.240	.291	.530	0	1.000
—Wilmington (Caro.)	OF	102	379	63	108	18	4	15	71	40	71	17	8	12-4	.285	.376	.472	.848	3	.983
2001—Wichita (Texas)	OF	120	454	98	140	28	3	40	118	43	91	14	9	14-6	.308	.383	.648	1.031	4	.971
—Kansas City (A.L.)	OF-DH	6	16	4	5	1	1	2	2	2	2	0	0	0-0	.313	.389	.875	1.264	0	1.000
2002—Omaha (PCL)	OF-1B	68	261	34	76	16	1	13	47	25	43	5	4	11-2	.291	.363	.510	.873	4	.975
—Kansas City (A.L.)	OF-DH-1B	51	134	16	27	5	1	6	17	8	32	2	2	1-0	.201	.255	.388	.643	0	1.000
2003—Kansas City (A.L.)	OF-DH	13	32	3	7	0	0	3	3	5	4	0	0	0-0	.219	.324	.219	.543	0	1.000
—Omaha (PCL)	OF-DH-1B	62	226	43	61	16	3	12	53	31	58	6	5	6-1	.270	.367	.527	.894	4	.966
2004—Kansas City (A.L.)	OF	11	35	5	7	2	0	0	2	0	11	0	1	1-1	.200	.200	.257	.457	0	1.000
—Wichita (Texas)	OF-DH	70	267	42	75	18	2	12	50	34	40	2	6	3-2	.281	.360	.498	.859	2	.974
—Omaha (PCL)	OF-DH	39	146	25	34	9	0	14	37	19	22	2	5	1-1	.233	.327	.582	.910	1	.983
Major League totals (4 years)		81	217	28	46	8	2	8	24	15	45	2	3	2-1	.212	.268	.378	.646	0	1.000

B

BERGERON, PETER   OF

PERSONAL: Born November 9, 1977, in Greenfield, Mass. ... 6-0/190. ... Bats left, throws right. ... Full name: Peter Francis Bergeron. ... Name pronounced: BERR-jer-ron. ... High school: Greenfield (Mass.).

TRANSACTIONS/CAREER NOTES: Selected by Los Angeles Dodgers organization in fourth round of 1996 free-agent draft. ... Traded by Dodgers with 2B Wilton Guerrero, P Ted Lilly and 1B Jonathan Tucker to Montreal Expos for P Carlos Perez, SS Mark Grudzielanek and OF Hiram Bocachica (July 31, 1998). ... On disabled list (April 19-May 24, 2004); included rehabilitation assignment to Brevard County. ... Traded by Expos to Milwaukee Brewers for P Jason Childers and OF Jason Belcher (June 7, 2004).

2004 GAMES PLAYED BY POSITION (MLB): OF—11.

												BATTING								FIELDING	
Year Team (League)	Pos.	G	AB	R	H	2B	3B	HR	RBI	BB	SO	HBP	GDP	SB-CS	Avg.	OBP	SLG	OPS		E	Avg.
1996— Yakima (N'west)	OF	61	232	36	59	5	3	5	21	28	59	0	2	13-9	.254	.335	.366	.701		1	.990
1997— Savannah (S. Atl.)	OF	131	492	89	138	18	5	5	36	67	110	2	5	32-21	.280	.367	.368	.735		4	.984
— San Bern. (Calif.)	OF	2	8	1	2	0	0	0	1	0	2	0	0	2-0	.250	.250	.250	.500		0	1.000
1998— San Antonio (Texas)	OF	109	416	81	132	17	8	8	54	61	69	2	2	33-9	.317	.406	.454	.861		2	.992
— Harrisburg (East.)	OF	34	134	22	33	8	4	0	9	17	26	0	0	8-3	.246	.331	.366	.697		0	1.000
1999— Harrisburg (East.)	OF-DH	42	162	29	53	14	2	4	18	24	29	0	0	9-7	.327	.407	.512	.920		1	.986
— Ottawa (Int'l)	OF-DH	58	194	36	61	12	3	3	20	23	40	1	1	14-8	.314	.386	.454	.840		2	.973
— Montreal (N.L.)	OF	16	45	12	11	2	0	0	1	9	5	0	0	0-0	.244	.370	.289	.659		1	.967
2000— Montreal (N.L.)	OF	148	518	80	127	25	7	5	31	58	100	0	4	11-13	.245	.320	.349	.669		5	.985
2001— Montreal (N.L.)	OF	102	375	53	79	11	4	3	16	28	87	5	5	10-7	.211	.275	.285	.560		1	.996
— Ottawa (Int'l)	OF	52	206	29	49	5	3	0	8	20	42	1	1	15-7	.238	.307	.291	.598		2	.983
2002— Montreal (N.L.)	OF	31	123	24	23	3	2	0	7	22	44	0	0	10-3	.187	.310	.244	.554		2	.974
— Ottawa (Int'l)	OF	104	340	51	99	9	4	1	29	39	65	1	1	7-7	.291	.364	.350	.714		3	.984
2003— Edmonton (PCL)	OF	110	388	62	117	19	7	1	32	37	64	1	3	12-3	.302	.360	.394	.754		5	.981
2004— Montreal (N.L.)	OF	11	42	2	9	0	0	0	1	2	16	0	0	0-1	.214	.250	.214	.464		2	.913
— Brevard County (FSL)	OF	4	17	3	3	0	1	0	0	2	2	0	0	3-0	.176	.176	.294	.471		0	1.000
— Edmonton (PCL)	OF	11	41	8	21	4	1	1	5	3	1	0	2	2-0	.512	.545	.732	1.277		0	1.000
— Indianapolis (Int'l)	OF	82	318	46	87	10	8	3	22	20	40	1	2	12-7	.274	.318	.384	.701		3	.983
Major League totals (5 years)		308	1103	171	249	41	13	8	56	119	252	5	9	31-24	.226	.303	.308	.612		11	.984

BERGMAN, DUSTY   P

PERSONAL: Born February 1, 1978, in Carson City, Nev. ... 6-5/200. ... Throws left, bats left. ... Full name: Dustin Michael Bergman. ... High school: Carson City (Nev.). ... College: Hawaii.

TRANSACTIONS/CAREER NOTES: Selected by Anaheim Angels organization in sixth round of 1999 free-agent draft.

CAREER HITTING: 0-for-0 (.000), 0 R, 0 2B, 0 3B, 0 HR, 0 RBI.

Year Team (League)	W	L	Pct.	ERA	WHIP	G	GS	CG	ShO	Hld.	Sv.-Opp.	IP	H	R	ER	HR	BB-IBB	SO	Avg.
1999— Boise (N'west)	5	5	.500	6.54	1.61	15	15	0	0	...	0-...	74.1	102	58	54	12	18-2	46	.320
2000— Cedar Rapids (Midw.)	4	15	.211	3.90	1.43	28	25	6	1	...	0-...	163.2	174	102	71	12	60-0	108	.267
— Lake Elsinore (Calif.)	0	1	.000	2.25	1.00	1	1	0	0	...	0-...	4.0	3	4	1	0	1-0	3	.176
2001— Arkansas (Texas)	7	13	.350	5.11	1.62	27	25	1	0	...	0-...	153.1	196	100	87	10	53-0	83	.314
2002— Arkansas (Texas)	5	0	1.000	2.41	1.00	35	0	0	0	...	3-...	56.0	48	21	15	3	8-0	38	.230
— Salt Lake (PCL)	1	1	.500	6.44	1.47	21	0	0	0	...	1-...	29.1	34	25	21	7	9-0	26	.291
2003— Salt Lake (PCL)	0	1	.000	20.25	4.50	1	0	0	0	...	1-...	1.1	5	5	3	0	1-0	0	.714
— Arkansas (Texas)	6	5	.545	3.79	1.36	50	10	0	0	...	0-...	109.1	116	54	46	7	33-3	82	.273
2004— Anaheim (A.L.)	0	0	...	13.50	2.50	1	0	0	0	0	0-0	2.0	4	3	3	0	1-0	1	.444
— Salt Lake (PCL)	1	2	.333	2.85	1.31	45	0	0	0	...	1-...	72.2	82	35	23	2	13-0	54	.280
Major League totals (1 year)	0	0	...	13.50	2.50	1	0	0	0	0	0-0	2.0	4	3	3	0	1-0	1	.444

BERKMAN, LANCE   OF

PERSONAL: Born February 10, 1976, in Waco, Texas. ... 6-1/220. ... Bats both, throws left. ... Full name: William Lance Berkman. ... High school: Canyon (New Braunfels, Texas). ... College: Rice.

TRANSACTIONS/CAREER NOTES: Selected by Houston Astros organization in first round (16th pick overall) of 1997 free-agent draft.

2004 GAMES PLAYED BY POSITION (MLB): OF—160, 1B—4.

												BATTING								FIELDING	
Year Team (League)	Pos.	G	AB	R	H	2B	3B	HR	RBI	BB	SO	HBP	GDP	SB-CS	Avg.	OBP	SLG	OPS		E	Avg.
1997— Kissimmee (Fla. St.)	OF-DH	53	184	31	54	10	0	12	35	37	38	2	2	2-1	.293	.417	.543	.961		0	1.000
1998— Jackson (Texas)	OF-DH	122	425	82	130	34	0	24	89	85	82	4	12	6-4	.306	.424	.555	.979		4	.980
— New Orleans (PCL)	OF	17	59	14	16	4	0	6	13	12	16	2	1	0-0	.271	.411	.644	1.055		0	1.000
1999— New Orleans (PCL)	OF-1B	64	226	42	73	20	0	8	49	39	47	0	10	7-1	.323	.419	.518	.937		4	.972
— Houston (N.L.)	OF-1B	34	93	10	22	2	0	4	15	12	21	0	2	5-1	.237	.321	.387	.708		2	.956
2000— New Orleans (PCL)	OF-1B	31	112	18	37	4	2	6	27	31	20	1	7	4-4	.330	.479	.563	1.042		2	.982
— Houston (N.L.)	OF-1B	114	353	76	105	28	1	21	67	56	73	1	6	6-2	.297	.388	.561	.949		6	.968
2001— Houston (N.L.)	OF	156	577	110	191	* 55	5	34	126	92	121	13	8	7-9	.331	.430	.620	1.051		6	.981
2002— Houston (N.L.)	OF	158	578	106	169	35	2	42	* 128	107	118	4	10	8-4	.292	.405	.578	.982		7	.977
2003— Houston (N.L.)	OF	153	538	110	155	35	4	25	93	107	108	9	10	5-3	.288	.412	.515	.927		3	.989
2004— Houston (N.L.)	OF-1B	160	544	104	172	40	3	30	106	127	101	10	10	9-7	.316	.450	.566	1.016		2	.992
Major League totals (6 years)		775	2683	516	814	195	17	156	535	501	542	37	46	40-26	.303	.416	.563	.980		26	.981

DIVISION SERIES RECORD

Year Team (League)	Pos.	G	AB	R	H	2B	3B	HR	RBI	BB	SO	HBP	GDP	SB-CS	Avg.	OBP	SLG	OPS	E	Avg.
2001— Houston (N.L.)	OF	3	12	0	2	0	0	0	0	0	4	0	2	0-0	.167	.167	.167	.333	0	1.000
2004— Houston (N.L.)	OF	5	22	5	9	1	0	1	3	3	6	0	0	0-1	.409	.480	.591	1.071	1	.800
Division series totals (2 years)		8	34	5	11	1	0	1	3	3	10	0	2	0-1	.324	.378	.441	.820	1	.909

CHAMPIONSHIP SERIES RECORD

Year Team (League)	Pos.	G	AB	R	H	2B	3B	HR	RBI	BB	SO	HBP	GDP	SB-CS	Avg.	OBP	SLG	OPS	E	Avg.
2004— Houston (N.L.)	OF	7	24	7	7	2	0	3	9	5	4	0	0	1-0	.292	.400	.750	1.150	0	1.000

ALL-STAR GAME RECORD

		G	AB	R	H	2B	3B	HR	RBI	BB	SO	HBP	GDP	SB-CS	Avg.	OBP	SLG	OPS	E	Avg.
All-Star Game totals (3 years)		3	7	0	2	0	0	0	2	0	0	0	0	1-0	.286	.286	.286	.571	0	1.000

BERNERO, ADAM P

PERSONAL: Born November 28, 1976, in Los Gatos, Calif. ... 6-4/210. ... Throws right, bats right. ... Full name: Adam Gino Bernero. ... Name pronounced: bur-NAIR-o. ... High school: John F. Kennedy (Sacramento, Calif.). ... College: Armstrong Atlantic State (Ga.).

TRANSACTIONS/CAREER NOTES: Selected by Chicago White Sox organization in 24th round of 1994 free-agent draft; did not sign. ... Selected by Colorado Rockies organization in 38th round of 1996 free-agent draft; did not sign. ... Signed as a non-drafted free agent by Detroit Tigers organization (May 21, 1999). ... Traded by Tigers to Colorado Rockies for C Ben Petrick (July 13, 2003). ... On disabled list (April 3-June 30, 2004); included rehabilitation assignments to Tulsa and Colorado Springs. ... Refused minor league assignment and became a free agent (October 6, 2004).

CAREER HITTING: 0-for-15 (.000), 2 R, 0 2B, 0 3B, 0 HR, 0 RBI.

Year Team (League)	W	L	Pct.	ERA	WHIP	G	GS	CG	ShO	Hld.	Sv.-Opp.	IP	H	R	ER	HR	BB-IBB	SO	Avg.
1999—West. Mich. (Mid.)	8	4	.667	2.54	1.02	15	15	2	1	...	0-...	95.2	75	36	27	8	23-0	80	.210
2000—Jacksonville (Southern)	2	5	.286	2.79	1.27	10	10	0	0	...	0-...	61.1	54	26	19	6	24-0	46	.237
—Toledo (International)	3	1	.750	2.47	0.93	7	7	1	1	...	0-...	47.1	34	16	13	5	10-0	37	.201
—Detroit (A.L.)	0	1	.000	4.19	1.34	12	4	0	0	1	0-0	34.1	33	18	16	3	13-1	20	.270
2001—Toledo (International)	6	11	.353	5.13	1.61	26	25	1	0	...	0-...	140.1	172	90	80	13	54-0	99	.303
—Detroit (A.L.)	0	0	...	7.30	1.38	5	0	0	0	0	0-0	12.1	13	13	10	4	4-0	8	.260
2002—Toledo (International)	2	2	.500	1.58	1.04	9	9	2	1	...	0-...	57.0	46	13	10	2	13-0	49	.223
—Detroit (A.L.)	4	7	.364	6.20	1.56	28	11	0	0	0	0-0	101.2	128	74	70	17	31-1	69	.309
2003—Detroit (A.L.)	1	12	.077	6.08	1.44	18	17	0	0	0	0-0	100.2	104	68	68	14	41-0	54	.267
—Colorado (N.L.)	0	2	.000	5.23	1.41	31	0	0	0	5	0-2	32.2	33	22	19	5	13-1	26	.266
2004—Tulsa (Texas)	1	0	1.000	0.00	0.50	1	1	0	0	...	0-...	6.0	2	0	0	0	1-1	3	.105
—Colo. Springs (PCL)	3	2	.600	3.17	1.39	9	8	0	0	...	0-...	48.1	57	23	17	0	10-0	48	.294
—Colorado (N.L.)	1	1	.500	5.57	1.64	16	2	0	0	1	0-1	32.1	36	20	20	7	17-2	21	.283
American League totals (4 years)	5	20	.200	5.93	1.47	63	32	0	0	1	0-0	249.0	278	173	164	38	89-2	151	.285
National League totals (2 years)	1	3	.250	5.40	1.52	47	2	0	0	6	0-3	65.0	69	42	39	12	30-3	47	.275
Major League totals (5 years)	6	23	.207	5.82	1.48	110	34	0	0	7	0-3	314.0	347	215	203	50	119-5	198	.283

BERROA, ANGEL SS

PERSONAL: Born January 27, 1978, in Santo Domingo, Dominican Republic. ... 6-0/175. ... Bats right, throws right. ... Full name: Angel Maria Berroa.

TRANSACTIONS/CAREER NOTES: Signed as a non-drafted free agent by Oakland Athletics organization (August 14, 1997). ... Traded by A's with C A.J. Hinch and cash to Kansas City Royals as part of three-team deal in which Royals received P Roberto Hernandez from Tampa Devil Rays, A's received P Cory Lidle from Devil Rays and OF Johnny Damon, IF Mark Ellis and player to be named or cash from Royals and Devil Rays received OF Ben Grieve and a player to be named or cash from A's (January 8, 2001). ... On disabled list (April 16-May 1, 2004); included rehabilitation assignment to Wichita.

HONORS: Named A.L. Rookie of the Year by Baseball Writers' Association of America (2003).

2004 GAMES PLAYED BY POSITION (MLB): SS—133.

Year Team (League)	Pos.	G	AB	R	H	2B	3B	HR	RBI	BB	SO	HBP	GDP	SB-CS	Avg.	OBP	SLG	OPS	E	Avg.
1998—Dom. Athletics (DSL)		58	196	51	48	7	4	8	37	25	37	...	...	4-...	.245	...	.444	...	...	...
1999—Ariz. A's (Ariz.)	2-3-SS-OF	46	169	42	49	11	4	2	24	16	26	7	1	11-4	.290	.371	.438	.809	18	.925
—Midland (Texas)	SS	4	17	3	1	1	0	0	0	0	2	0	0	0-0	.059	.059	.118	.176	2	.889
2000—Visalia (Calif.)	SS	129	429	61	119	25	6	10	63	30	70	10	10	11-9	.277	.337	.434	.770	54	.909
2001—Wilmington (Caro.)	SS	51	199	43	63	18	4	6	25	9	41	14	7	10-6	.317	.382	.538	.920	17	.933
—Wichita (Texas)	SS	80	304	63	90	20	4	8	42	17	55	22	6	15-6	.296	.373	.467	.840	13	.965
—Kansas City (A.L.)	SS	15	53	8	16	2	0	0	4	3	10	0	2	2-0	.302	.339	.340	.679	3	.953
2002—Omaha (PCL)	SS	77	297	37	64	11	4	8	35	15	84	11	5	6-4	.215	.277	.360	.637	16	.956
—Kansas City (A.L.)	SS	20	75	8	17	7	1	0	5	7	10	1	1	3-0	.227	.301	.347	.648	4	.964
2003—Kansas City (A.L.)	SS	158	567	92	163	28	7	17	73	29	100	18	13	21-5	.287	.338	.452	.789	24	.968
2004—Wichita (Texas)	SS	11	51	8	16	1	0	3	10	2	8	0	0	3-2	.314	.340	.510	.849	1	1.000
—Kansas City (A.L.)	SS	134	512	72	134	27	6	8	43	23	87	12	10	14-8	.262	.308	.385	.693	28	.955
Major League totals (4 years)		327	1207	180	330	64	14	25	125	62	207	31	26	40-13	.273	.323	.412	.735	59	.962

BETANCOURT, RAFAEL P

PERSONAL: Born April 29, 1975, in Cumana, Venezuela. ... 6-2/200. ... Throws right, bats right. ... Full name: Rafael Jose Betancourt. ... High school: A.J.S. (Cumana, Venezuela). ... College: Isaac Newton College (Venezuela).

TRANSACTIONS/CAREER NOTES: Signed as a non-drafted free agent by Boston Red Sox organization (September 6, 1993). ... Played three seasons as an infielder in Red Sox organization (1994-96). ... Contract purchased from Red Sox organization by Yokohama of the Japan Central League (November 18, 1999). ... Signed as a free agent by Red Sox organization (December 13, 2000). ... Signed as a free agent by Cleveland Indians organization (February 6, 2003). ... On disabled list (June 26-July 11, 2004); included rehabilitation assignment to Akron.

CAREER HITTING: 0-for-0 (.000), 0 R, 0 2B, 0 3B, 0 HR, 0 RBI.

Year Team (League)	W	L	Pct.	ERA	WHIP	G	GS	CG	ShO	Hld.	Sv.-Opp.	IP	H	R	ER	HR	BB-IBB	SO	Avg.
1997—Michigan (Midw.)	0	3	.000	1.95	0.87	27	0	0	0	...	11-...	32.1	26	9	7	2	2-0	52	.213
1998—GC Red Sox (GCL)	0	2	.000	7.20	1.40	4	3	0	0	...	0-...	5.0	6	5	4	1	1-0	4	.300
—Sarasota (Florida State)	3	1	.750	3.54	1.00	20	0	0	0	...	2-...	28.0	22	12	11	2	6-0	33	.212
—Trenton (East.)	0	0	...	6.75	1.29	7	0	0	0	...	0-...	9.1	9	7	7	0	3-0	9	.237
1999—Sarasota (Florida State)	0	0	...	0.00	0.86	6	0	0	0	...	4-...	7.0	5	0	0	0	1-0	6	.208
—Trenton (East.)	6	2	.750	3.62	1.10	39	0	0	0	...	13-...	54.2	50	24	22	7	10-0	57	.248
2001—Trenton (East.)	0	1	.000	5.63	1.29	16	0	0	0	...	4-...	24.0	28	16	15	0	3-0	27	.295
2003—Akron (East.)	0	0	...	1.39	1.01	31	0	0	0	...	16-...	45.1	33	10	7	0	13-2	75	.195
—Buffalo (Int'l)	0	0	...	4.05	1.20	4	0	0	0	...	1-...	6.2	6	3	3	1	2-0	6	.240
—Cleveland (A.L.)	2	2	.500	2.13	1.05	33	0	0	0	4	1-3	38.0	27	11	9	5	13-2	36	.196
2004—Akron (East.)	0	0	...	0.00	1.00	1	0	0	0	...	0-...	1.0	0	0	0	0	1-0	2	.000
—Cleveland (A.L.)	5	6	.455	3.92	1.34	68	0	0	0	12	4-11	66.2	71	32	29	7	18-6	76	.268
Major League totals (2 years)	7	8	.467	3.27	1.23	101	0	0	0	16	5-14	104.2	98	43	38	12	31-8	112	.243

BETEMIT, WILSON SS

PERSONAL: Born July 28, 1980, in Santo Domingo, Dominican Republic. ... 6-3/190. ... Bats both, throws right. ... Name pronounced: BET-a-mitt.

TRANSACTIONS/CAREER NOTES: Signed as a non-drafted free agent by Atlanta Braves organization (July 28, 1996).

Year	Team (League)	Pos.	G	AB	R	H	2B	3B	HR	RBI	BB	SO	HBP	GDP	SB-CS	Avg.	OBP	SLG	OPS	FIELDING E	Avg.
																			BATTING		
1997—	GC Braves (GCL)	SS	32	113	12	24	6	1	0	15	9	32	0	3	0-0	.212	.270	.283	.554	20	.856
1998—	GC Braves (GCL)	SS	51	173	23	38	8	4	5	16	20	49	0	1	6-5	.220	.301	.399	.699	20	.908
1999—	Danville (Appal.)	SS	67	259	39	83	18	2	5	53	27	63	1	4	6-3	.320	.383	.463	.846	33	.899
2000—	Jamestown (N.Y.-Penn.)	SS	69	269	54	89	15	2	5	37	30	37	1	4	3-4	.331	.393	.457	.851	29	.910
2001—	Myrtle Beach (Caro.)	SS	84	318	38	88	20	1	7	43	23	71	1	8	8-5	.277	.324	.412	.736	23	.944
	—Greenville (Sou.)	SS	47	183	22	65	14	0	5	19	12	36	1	4	6-2	.355	.394	.514	.908	9	.954
	—Atlanta (N.L.)	SS	8	3	1	0	0	0	0	0	2	3	0	0	1-0	.000	.400	.000	.400	0	...
2002—	GC Braves (GCL)	SS	7	19	2	5	4	0	0	2	5	2	0	0	1-0	.263	.417	.474	.890	2	.867
	—Richmond (Int'l)	SS	93	343	43	84	17	1	8	34	34	82	1	7	8-5	.245	.312	.370	.683	21	.946
2003—	Richmond (Int'l)	3B-DH-SS	127	478	55	125	23	13	8	65	38	115	0	8	8-5	.262	.315	.414	.729	28	.902
2004—	Richmond (Int'l)	3B-SS	105	356	48	99	24	2	13	59	32	99	0	17	3-3	.278	.336	.466	.802	16	.938
	—Atlanta (N.L.)	SS-3B	22	47	2	8	0	0	0	3	4	16	0	0	0-1	.170	.231	.170	.401	3	.943
	Major League totals (2 years)		30	50	3	8	0	0	0	3	6	19	0	0	1-1	.160	.246	.160	.406	3	.943

DIVISION SERIES RECORD

Year	Team (League)	Pos.	G	AB	R	H	2B	3B	HR	RBI	BB	SO	HBP	GDP	SB-CS	Avg.	OBP	SLG	OPS	E	Avg.
2004—	Atlanta (N.L.)	...	1	0	0	0	0	0	0	0	0	0	0	0	0-0	...	...	...	...	0	...

BIDDLE, ROCKY — P

PERSONAL: Born May 21, 1976, in Las Vegas, Nev. ... 6-3/221. ... Throws right, bats right. ... Full name: Lee Francis Biddle. ... High school: Temple City (Calif.). ... College: Long Beach State.

TRANSACTIONS/CAREER NOTES: Selected by San Diego Padres organization in 25th round of 1994 free-agent draft; did not sign. ... Selected by Chicago White Sox organization in supplemental round ("sandwich" pick between first and second rounds, 51st pick overall) of free-agent draft (June 3, 1997); pick received as compensation for failure to sign 1996 first-round pick P Bobby Seay. ... On disabled list (September 21, 2001-remainder of season). ... On disabled list (March 22-May 3, 2002); included rehabilitation assignment to Charlotte. ... Traded by White Sox with P Orlando Hernandez, 3B/OF Jeff Liefer and cash to Montreal Expos for P Bartolo Colon and 2B/SS Jorge Nunez (January 15, 2003). ... Expos transferred to Washington, D.C., for 2005 season. ... Released by Washington (November 8, 2004).

CAREER HITTING: 0-for-13 (.000), 0 R, 0 2B, 0 3B, 0 HR, 0 RBI.

Year	Team (League)	W	L	Pct.	ERA	WHIP	G	GS	CG	ShO	Hld.	Sv.-Opp.	IP	H	R	ER	HR	BB-IBB	SO	Avg.
1997—	Hickory (S. Atl.)	0	1	.000	4.64	1.50	13	0	0	0	...	1-...	21.1	22	18	11	2	10-0	25	.265
1998—	Winston-Salem (Caro.)	4	5	.444	4.57	1.66	16	16	0	0	...	0-...	82.2	92	55	42	7	45-0	72	.280
	—Ariz. White Sox (Ariz.)	1	0	1.000	3.94	1.44	5	2	0	0	...	0-...	16.0	15	9	7	2	8-0	18	.242
1999—	Winston-Salem (Caro.)			Did not play.																
2000—	Birmingham (Southern)	11	6	.647	3.08	1.31	23	23	2	2	...	0-...	146.1	138	63	50	10	54-0	118	.250
	—Chicago (A.L.)	1	2	.333	8.34	1.72	4	4	0	0	0	0-0	22.2	31	25	21	5	8-0	7	.326
2001—	Chicago (A.L.)	7	8	.467	5.39	1.47	30	21	0	0	1	0-3	128.2	137	87	77	16	52-3	85	.272
2002—	Charlotte (Int'l)	0	0	...	1.29	0.71	2	2	0	0	...	0-...	7.0	4	1	1	0	1-0	9	.160
	—Chicago (A.L.)	3	4	.429	4.06	1.43	44	7	0	0	4	0-...	77.2	72	42	35	13	39-4	64	.245
2003—	Montreal (N.L.)	5	8	.385	4.65	1.55	73	0	0	0	4	34-41	71.2	71	43	37	10	40-5	54	.254
2004—	Montreal (N.L.)	4	8	.333	6.92	1.65	47	9	0	0	1	11-15	78.0	98	69	60	15	31-3	51	.307
	American League totals (3 years)	11	14	.440	5.23	1.48	78	32	0	0	5	1-6	229.0	240	154	133	34	99-7	156	.269
	National League totals (2 years)	9	16	.360	5.83	1.60	120	9	0	0	5	45-56	149.2	169	112	97	25	71-8	105	.283
	Major League totals (5 years)	20	30	.400	5.47	1.53	198	41	0	0	10	46-62	378.2	409	266	230	59	170-15	261	.274

BIERBRODT, NICK — P

PERSONAL: Born May 16, 1978, in Tarzana, Calif. ... 6-5/214. ... Throws left, bats left. ... Full name: Nicholas Raymond Bierbrodt. ... Name pronounced: BEER-brot. ... High school: Millikan (Long Beach, Calif.).

TRANSACTIONS/CAREER NOTES: Selected by Arizona Diamondbacks organization in first round (30th pick overall) of 1996 free-agent draft. ... On disabled list (March 23-April 19, 2001); included rehabilitation assignment to El Paso. ... Traded by Diamondbacks with OF Jason Conti to Tampa Bay Devil Rays for P Albie Lopez and C Mike Difelice (July 25, 2001). ... On disabled list (June 7, 2002-remainder of season). ... On suspended list (May 2-5, 2003). ... Claimed on waivers by Cleveland Indians (June 11, 2003). ... Signed as a free agent by Boston Red Sox (January 15, 2004). ... Refused minor league assignment and became a free agent (March 20, 2004). ... Signed by Texas Rangers organization (March 22, 2004). ... Released by Rangers (July 29, 2004). ... Signed by Cincinnati Reds organization (August 6, 2004).

CAREER HITTING: 4-for-8 (.500), 3 R, 1 2B, 0 3B, 0 HR, 0 RBI.

Year	Team (League)	W	L	Pct.	ERA	WHIP	G	GS	CG	ShO	Hld.	Sv.-Opp.	IP	H	R	ER	HR	BB-IBB	SO	Avg.
1996—	Ariz. D'backs (Ariz.)	1	1	.500	1.66	1.00	8	8	0	0	...	0-...	38.0	25	9	7	1	13-0	46	.188
	—Lethbridge (Pio.)	2	0	1.000	0.50	0.94	3	3	0	0	...	0-...	18.0	12	4	1	0	5-0	23	.185
1997—	South Bend (Mid.)	2	4	.333	4.04	1.51	15	15	0	0	...	0-...	75.2	77	43	34	4	37-0	64	.266
1998—	High Desert (Calif.)	8	7	.533	3.40	1.43	24	23	1	0	...	0-...	129.2	122	66	49	7	64-0	88	.254
1999—	El Paso (Texas)	5	6	.455	4.62	1.51	14	14	2	1	...	0-...	76.0	78	45	39	3	37-0	55	.266
	—Tucson (PCL)	1	4	.200	7.27	2.01	11	11	0	0	...	0-...	43.1	57	42	35	9	30-0	43	.324
2000—	Tucson (PCL)	2	1	.667	4.82	1.45	4	3	0	0	...	0-...	18.2	13	10	10	3	14-0	11	.213
	—Ariz. D'backs (Ariz.)	0	0	...	4.50	1.13	4	3	0	0	...	0-...	8.0	4	4	4	0	5-0	10	.143
	—El Paso (Texas)	1	3	.250	7.13	1.73	7	7	0	0	...	0-...	35.1	37	30	28	1	24-0	36	.272
2001—	El Paso (Texas)	2	1	.667	1.37	0.97	4	4	0	0	...	0-...	19.2	13	3	3	1	6-0	18	.186
	—Tucson (PCL)	4	1	.800	2.18	1.26	7	6	0	0	...	0-...	45.1	48	15	11	0	9-1	56	.281
	—Arizona (A.L.)	2	2	.500	8.22	1.78	5	5	0	0	...	0-0	23.0	29	21	21	6	12-0	17	.305
	—Tampa Bay (A.L.)	3	4	.429	4.55	1.60	11	11	0	0	...	0-0	61.1	71	38	31	11	27-1	56	.285
2002—	Char., S.C. (SAL)	0	0	...	1.40	1.40	1	1	0	0	...	0-...	5.0	5	4	2	0	2-0	2	.238
2003—	Tampa Bay (A.L.)	0	2	.000	9.68	2.32	13	5	0	0	...	0-0	35.1	59	41	38	7	23-0	20	.376
	—Cleveland (A.L.)	0	0	...	6.75	1.13	5	0	0	0	...	0-...	8.0	5	6	6	0	4-0	9	.185
	—Buffalo (Int'l)	2	2	.500	3.00	1.50	16	1	0	0	...	0-...	27.0	22	10	9	1	18-2	31	.222
2004—	Frisco (Texas)	1	2	.333	4.68	1.60	5	5	0	0	...	0-...	25.0	29	14	13	1	11-2	21	.293
	—Texas (A.L.)	1	1	.500	5.82	1.94	4	4	0	0	...	0-...	17.0	14	11	11	1	19-0	16	.246
	—Oklahoma (PCL)	1	3	.250	7.30	1.95	5	5	0	0	...	0-...	24.2	26	21	20	5	22-0	26	.274
	American League totals (3 years)	4	7	.364	6.36	1.82	33	20	0	0	...	0-0	121.2	149	96	86	24	73-4	95	.304
	National League totals (1 year)	2	2	.500	8.22	1.78	5	5	0	0	...	0-0	23.0	29	21	21	6	12-0	17	.305
	Major League totals (3 years)	6	9	.400	6.66	1.82	38	25	0	0	...	0-0	144.2	178	117	107	30	85-4	112	.304

BIGBIE, LARRY — OF

PERSONAL: Born November 4, 1977, in Hobart, Ind. ... 6-4/207. ... Bats left, throws right. ... Full name: Larry Robert Bigbie. ... High school: Hobart (Ind.). ... College: Ball State.

TRANSACTIONS/CAREER NOTES: Selected by Baltimore Orioles organization in first round (21st pick overall) of 1999 free-agent draft; pick received from Texas Rangers as part of compensation for signing of Type A free-agent 1B Rafael Palmeiro. ... On disabled list (May 22-July 27, 2003); included rehabilitation assignments to Ottawa and GCL Orioles. ... On disabled list (August 16-September 1, 2004); included rehabilitation assignment to Frederick.

2004 GAMES PLAYED BY POSITION (MLB): OF—134, DH—2.

			BATTING																	FIELDING	
Year	Team (League)	Pos.	G	AB	R	H	2B	3B	HR	RBI	BB	SO	HBP	GDP	SB-CS	Avg.	OBP	SLG	OPS	E	Avg.
1999—	Bluefield (Appal.)	OF	8	30	3	8	0	0	0	4	3	8	1	1	1-3	.267	.343	.267	.610	0	1.000
—	Delmarva (S. Atl.)	OF	43	165	18	46	7	3	2	27	29	42	0	4	3-1	.279	.381	.394	.775	3	.950
2000—	Frederick (Carolina)	OF	55	201	33	59	11	0	2	28	23	34	0	3	7-3	.294	.360	.378	.738	3	.975
—	Bowie (East.)	OF	31	112	11	27	6	0	0	5	11	28	0	3	3-0	.241	.309	.295	.604	0	1.000
2001—	Bowie (East.)	OF	71	262	41	77	13	3	8	33	40	54	0	5	10-7	.294	.386	.458	.844	4	.972
—	Baltimore (A.L.)	OF	47	131	15	30	6	0	2	11	17	42	0	2	4-1	.229	.318	.321	.638	0	1.000
—	Rochester (Int'l)	OF	10	42	5	13	4	0	1	2	3	8	0	0	1-1	.310	.356	.476	.832	0	1.000
2002—	Rochester (Int'l)	OF	98	348	42	105	23	2	2	35	35	79	1	9	7-3	.302	.363	.397	.760	2	.990
—	Baltimore (A.L.)	OF	16	34	1	6	1	0	0	3	1	11	0	1	1-0	.176	.194	.206	.400	0	1.000
2003—	GC Orioles (GCL)	OF	2	6	1	2	1	0	0	0	0	1	0	0	0-0	.333	.333	.500	.833	0	1.000
—	Ottawa (Int'l)	OF-DH	30	117	23	41	14	4	3	21	14	31	1	1	0-0	.350	.421	.615	1.036	1	.974
—	Baltimore (A.L.)	OF	83	287	43	87	15	1	9	31	29	60	0	2	7-1	.303	.365	.456	.821	1	.994
2004—	Frederick (Carolina)	OF	1	5	2	2	0	0	2	2	0	1	0	0	0-0	.400	.400	1.600	2.000	1	...
—	Baltimore (A.L.)	OF-DH	139	478	76	134	23	1	15	68	45	113	1	7	8-3	.280	.341	.427	.768	2	.993
Major League totals (4 years)			285	930	135	257	45	2	26	113	92	226	1	12	20-5	.276	.340	.413	.753	3	.995

BIGGIO, CRAIG — OF

PERSONAL: Born December 14, 1965, in Smithtown, N.Y. ... 5-11/185. ... Bats right, throws right. ... Full name: Craig Alan Biggio. ... Name pronounced: BIDG-ee-oh. ... High school: Kings Park (N.Y.). ... College: Seton Hall.

TRANSACTIONS/CAREER NOTES: Selected by Houston Astros organization in first round (22nd pick overall) of 1987 free-agent draft. ... On disabled list (August 2, 2000-remainder of season).

RECORDS: Shares major league record for grounding into fewest double plays, season; minimum 150 games played (0, 1997).

HONORS: Won N.L. Gold Glove at second base (1994-97).

2004 GAMES PLAYED BY POSITION (MLB): OF—149, DH—1.

			BATTING																	FIELDING	
Year	Team (League)	Pos.	G	AB	R	H	2B	3B	HR	RBI	BB	SO	HBP	GDP	SB-CS	Avg.	OBP	SLG	OPS	E	Avg.
1987—	Asheville (S. Atl.)	C-OF	64	216	59	81	17	2	9	49	39	33	2	5	31-10	.375	.471	.597	1.068	2	.995
1988—	Tucson (PCL)	C-OF	77	281	60	90	21	4	3	41	40	39	3	2	19-4	.320	.408	.456	.863	6	.983
—	Houston (N.L.)	C	50	123	14	26	6	1	3	5	7	29	0	1	6-1	.211	.254	.350	.603	3	.991
1989—	Houston (N.L.)	C-OF	134	443	64	114	21	2	13	60	49	64	6	7	21-3	.257	.336	.402	.738	9	.989
1990—	Houston (N.L.)	C-OF	150	555	53	153	24	2	4	42	53	79	3	11	25-11	.276	.342	.348	.689	13	.982
1991—	Houston (N.L.)	2B-C-OF	149	546	79	161	23	4	4	46	53	71	2	2	19-6	.295	.358	.374	.731	11	.989
1992—	Houston (N.L.)	2B	• 162	613	96	170	32	3	6	39	94	95	7	5	38-15	.277	.378	.369	.747	12	.984
1993—	Houston (N.L.)	2B	155	610	98	175	41	5	21	64	77	93	10	10	15-17	.287	.373	.474	.847	14	.982
1994—	Houston (N.L.)	2B	114	437	88	139	* 44	5	6	56	62	58	8	5	* 39-4	.318	.411	.483	.893	7	.988
1995—	Houston (N.L.)	2B	141	553	* 123	167	30	2	22	77	80	85	22	6	33-8	.302	.406	.483	.889	10	.986
1996—	Houston (N.L.)	2B	• 162	605	113	174	24	4	15	75	75	72	27	10	25-7	.288	.386	.415	.801	10	.988
1997—	Houston (N.L.)	2B-DH	• 162	619	* 146	191	37	8	22	81	84	107	34	0	47-10	.309	.415	.501	.916	18	.979
1998—	Houston (N.L.)	2B-DH	160	646	123	210	* 51	2	20	88	64	113	23	10	50-8	.325	.403	.503	.906	15	.980
1999—	Houston (N.L.)	2B-OF-DH	160	639	123	188	* 56	0	16	73	88	107	11	5	28-14	.294	.386	.457	.843	12	.985
2000—	Houston (N.L.)	2B	101	377	67	101	13	5	8	35	61	73	16	10	12-2	.268	.388	.393	.780	6	.987
2001—	Houston (N.L.)	2B-DH	155	617	118	180	35	3	20	70	66	100	28	11	7-4	.292	.382	.455	.838	11	.984
2002—	Houston (N.L.)	2B-OF	145	577	96	146	36	3	15	58	50	111	17	15	16-2	.253	.330	.404	.734	8	.988
2003—	Houston (N.L.)	OF	153	628	102	166	44	2	15	62	57	116	27	4	8-4	.264	.350	.412	.763	1	.997
2004—	Houston (N.L.)	OF-DH	156	633	100	178	47	0	24	63	40	94	15	8	7-2	.281	.337	.469	.806	9	.966
Major League totals (17 years)			2409	9221	1603	2639	564	51	234	994	1060	1467	256	120	396-118	.286	.373	.435	.807	169	.985

DIVISION SERIES RECORD

Year	Team (League)	Pos.	G	AB	R	H	2B	3B	HR	RBI	BB	SO	HBP	GDP	SB-CS	Avg.	OBP	SLG	OPS	E	Avg.
1997—	Houston (N.L.)	2B	3	12	0	1	0	0	0	0	1	0	0	0	0-0	.083	.154	.083	.237	1	.923
1998—	Houston (N.L.)	2B	4	11	3	2	1	0	0	1	4	4	2	0	0-0	.182	.471	.273	.743	1	.950
1999—	Houston (N.L.)	2B	4	19	1	2	0	0	0	0	1	5	0	0	0-0	.105	.150	.105	.255	0	1.000
2001—	Houston (N.L.)	2B	3	12	0	2	0	0	0	0	0	1	0	0	0-0	.167	.167	.167	.333	0	1.000
2004—	Houston (N.L.)	OF	5	20	5	8	2	0	1	4	2	4	0	1	1-0	.400	.455	.650	1.105	0	1.000
Division series totals (5 years)			19	74	9	15	3	0	1	5	8	14	2	1	1-0	.203	.298	.284	.581	2	.973

CHAMPIONSHIP SERIES RECORD

Year	Team (League)	Pos.	G	AB	R	H	2B	3B	HR	RBI	BB	SO	HBP	GDP	SB-CS	Avg.	OBP	SLG	OPS	E	Avg.
2004—	Houston (N.L.)	OF	7	32	3	6	1	0	1	1	0	4	0	0	0-1	.188	.188	.313	.500	0	1.000

ALL-STAR GAME RECORD

		G	AB	R	H	2B	3B	HR	RBI	BB	SO	HBP	GDP	SB-CS	Avg.	OBP	SLG	OPS	E	Avg.
All-Star Game totals (7 years)		7	15	2	1	0	0	1	1	0	5	1	0	0-0	.067	.125	.267	.392	1	.957

BLACKLEY, TRAVIS — P

PERSONAL: Born November 4, 1982, in Melbourne, Australia. ... 6-3/190. ... Throws left, bats left. ... Full name: Travis Jarrod Blackley. ... High school: Cheltenham Secondary (Victoria, Australia).

TRANSACTIONS/CAREER NOTES: Signed as a non-drafted free agent by Seattle Mariners organization (October 29, 2000).

CAREER HITTING: 0-for-0 (.000), 0 R, 0 2B, 0 3B, 0 HR, 0 RBI.

Year	Team (League)	W	L	Pct.	ERA	WHIP	G	GS	CG	ShO	Hld.	Sv.-Opp.	IP	H	R	ER	HR	BB-IBB	SO	Avg.
2001—	Everett (Northwest)	6	1	.857	3.32	1.13	14	14	0	0	...	0-...	78.2	60	34	29	7	29-0	90	.211
2002—	San Bernardino (Calif.)	5	9	.357	3.49	1.20	21	20	1	0	...	0-...	121.1	102	52	47	11	44-0	152	.227
2003—	San Antonio (Texas)	17	3	.850	2.61	1.15	27	27	0	0	...	0-...	162.1	125	55	47	11	62-0	144	.215
2004—	Seattle (A.L.)	1	3	.250	10.04	2.19	6	6	0	0	0	0-0	26.0	35	31	29	9	22-0	16	.321
—	Tacoma (PCL)	8	6	.571	3.83	1.33	19	18	2	2	...	0-...	110.1	100	49	47	14	47-0	80	.249
Major League totals (1 year)		1	3	.250	10.04	2.19	6	6	0	0	0	0-0	26.0	35	31	29	9	22-0	16	.321

BLAKE, CASEY — 3B

PERSONAL: Born August 23, 1973, in Des Moines, Iowa. ... 6-2/210. ... Bats right, throws right. ... Full name: William Casey Blake. ... High school: Indianola (Iowa). ... College: Wichita State.

TRANSACTIONS/CAREER NOTES: Selected by Philadelphia Phillies organization in 11th round of 1992 free-agent draft; did not sign. ... Selected by New York Yankees organization in 45th round of 1995 free-agent draft; did not sign. ... Selected by Toronto Blue Jays organization in seventh round of 1996 free-agent draft. ... Claimed on waivers by Minnesota Twins (May 23, 2000). ... Claimed on waivers by Baltimore Orioles (September 21, 2001). ... Claimed on waivers by Twins (October 12, 2001). ... Released by Twins (October 14, 2002). ... Signed by Cleveland Indians organization (December 18, 2002).

2004 GAMES PLAYED BY POSITION (MLB): 3B—152, 1B—8.

Year	Team (League)	Pos.	G	AB	R	H	2B	3B	HR	RBI	BB	SO	HBP	GDP	SB-CS	Avg.	OBP	SLG	OPS	E	Avg.
1996—Hagerstown (SAL)	3B-1B-OF	48	172	29	43	13	1	2	18	11	40	7	3	5-3	.250	.318	.372	.690	12	.906
1997—Dunedin (Fla. St.)	3B-SS	129	449	56	107	21	0	7	39	48	91	6	5	19-9	.238	.319	.332	.651	39	.895
1998—Dunedin (Fla. St.)	3B	88	340	62	119	28	3	11	65	30	81	9	5	9-6	.350	.409	.547	.956	16	.939
—Knoxville (Southern)	3B	45	172	41	64	15	4	7	38	22	25	2	6	10-0	.372	.442	.628	1.070	11	.913
1999—Syracuse (Int'l)	3B-SS-DH	110	387	69	95	16	2	22	75	61	82	7	10	9-5	.245	.357	.468	.824	10	.963
—Toronto (A.L.)	3B	14	39	6	10	2	0	1	1	2	7	0	1	0-0	.256	.293	.385	.677	0	1.000
—St. Catharines (NY-Penn.)	3B	1	3	0	2	0	0	0	0	1	0	0	0	0-0	.667	.750	.667	1.417	0	1.000
2000—Syracuse (Int'l)	3B-SS	30	106	10	23	6	1	2	7	8	23	3	2	0-3	.217	.291	.349	.640	2	.971
—Salt Lake (PCL)	3B-SS-1B	80	293	59	93	22	2	12	52	39	59	6	4	7-2	.317	.406	.529	.935	14	.934
—Minnesota (A.L.)	3B-DH-1B	7	16	1	3	2	0	0	1	3	7	1	1	0-0	.188	.333	.313	.646	0	1.000
2001—Edmonton (PCL)	3-1-2-S-OF	94	375	64	116	24	6	10	49	34	66	6	11	14-3	.309	.376	.485	.861	11	.961
—Minnesota (A.L.)	3B-DH-1B	13	22	1	7	1	0	0	2	3	8	0	0	1-0	.318	.400	.364	.764	1	.955
—Baltimore (A.L.)	1B-DH	6	15	2	2	0	0	1	2	1	4	0	0	2-0	.133	.188	.333	.521	1	.967
2002—Edmonton (PCL)	3-2-1B-OF	126	482	87	149	25	3	19	58	54	78	6	11	24-9	.309	.383	.492	.874	12	.969
—Minnesota (A.L.)	3B-1B-DH	9	20	2	4	1	0	0	1	2	7	0	0	0-0	.200	.273	.250	.523	2	.920
2003—Cleveland (A.L.)	3B-1B	152	557	80	143	35	0	17	67	38	109	10	11	7-9	.257	.312	.411	.723	19	.965
2004—Cleveland (A.L.)	3B-1B	152	587	93	159	36	3	28	88	68	139	9	19	5-8	.271	.354	.486	.839	26	.940
Major League totals (6 years)		353	1256	185	328	77	3	47	162	117	281	20	32	15-17	.261	.331	.439	.770	49	.955

BLALOCK, HANK   3B

PERSONAL: Born November 21, 1980, in San Diego, Calif. ... 6-1/200. ... Bats left, throws right. ... Full name: Hank Joe Blalock. ... Name pronounced: BLAY-lock. ... High school: Rancho Bernardo (San Diego).

TRANSACTIONS/CAREER NOTES: Selected by Texas Rangers organization in third round of 1999 free-agent draft.

2004 GAMES PLAYED BY POSITION (MLB): 3B—159.

Year	Team (League)	Pos.	G	AB	R	H	2B	3B	HR	RBI	BB	SO	HBP	GDP	SB-CS	Avg.	OBP	SLG	OPS	E	Avg.
1999—GC Rangers (GCL)	3B	51	191	34	69	17	6	3	38	25	23	1	7	3-2	.361	.428	.560	.988	12	.914
—Savannah (S. Atl.)	3B	7	25	3	6	1	0	1	2	1	3	1	0	0-0	.240	.286	.400	.686	5	.762
2000—Savannah (S. Atl.)	3B	139	512	66	153	32	2	10	77	62	53	5	13	31-8	.299	.373	.428	.801	20	.942
2001—Tulsa (Texas)	3B	68	272	50	89	18	4	11	61	39	38	2	5	3-3	.327	.413	.544	.957	8	.953
—Charlotte (Fla. St.)	3B	63	237	46	90	19	1	7	47	26	31	1	6	7-4	.380	.437	.557	.994	7	.963
2002—Texas (A.L.)	3B	49	147	16	31	8	0	3	17	20	43	1	2	0-0	.211	.306	.327	.632	6	.943
—Oklahoma (PCL)	3B-2B	95	387	63	119	32	1	8	62	34	61	1	9	2-1	.307	.363	.457	.821	16	.938
2003—Texas (A.L.)	3B-2B	143	567	89	170	33	3	29	90	44	97	1	16	2-3	.300	.350	.522	.872	16	.957
2004—Texas (A.L.)	3B	159	624	107	172	38	3	32	110	75	149	6	13	2-2	.276	.355	.500	.855	17	.957
Major League totals (3 years)		351	1338	212	373	79	6	64	217	139	289	8	31	4-5	.279	.347	.490	.837	39	.956

ALL-STAR GAME RECORD

	G	AB	R	H	2B	3B	HR	RBI	BB	SO	HBP	GDP	SB-CS	Avg.	OBP	SLG	OPS	E	Avg.
All-Star Game totals (2 years)	2	3	1	1	0	0	1	2	0	0	0	0	0-0	.333	.333	1.333	1.667	0	...

BLANCO, ANDRES   SS

PERSONAL: Born April 11, 1984, in Carabobo, Venezuela. ... 5-10/155. ... Bats both, throws right. ... Full name: Andres Eloy Blanco. ... High school: El Carmen (Venezuela).

TRANSACTIONS/CAREER NOTES: Signed as a non-drafted free agent by Kansas City Royals organization (August 2, 2000).

2004 GAMES PLAYED BY POSITION (MLB): SS—19.

Year	Team (League)	Pos.	G	AB	R	H	2B	3B	HR	RBI	BB	SO	HBP	GDP	SB-CS	Avg.	OBP	SLG	OPS	E	Avg.
2002—GC Royals (GCL)	SS	52	193	27	48	8	0	0	14	15	29	4	2	16-4	.249	.315	.290	.605	13	.945
—Wilmington (Caro.)	SS	5	13	2	4	1	0	0	0	1	4	0	0	0-0	.308	.357	.385	.742	2	.926
2003—Wilmington (Caro.)	SS	113	394	61	96	11	3	0	25	44	50	8	9	13-7	.244	.330	.287	.617	26	.947
2004—Kansas City (A.L.)	SS	19	60	9	19	2	2	0	5	5	6	1	0	1-2	.317	.379	.417	.795	4	.959
—Wichita (Texas)	SS	93	324	34	80	10	2	0	21	18	44	7	14	7-6	.247	.299	.290	.575	21	.951
Major League totals (1 year)		19	60	9	19	2	2	0	5	5	6	1	0	1-2	.317	.379	.417	.795	4	.959

BLANCO, HENRY   C

PERSONAL: Born August 29, 1971, in Caracas, Venezuela. ... 5-11/224. ... Bats right, throws right. ... Full name: Henry Ramon Blanco. ... Name pronounced: BLAHN-ko. ... High school: Antonio Jose de Sucre (Venezuela).

TRANSACTIONS/CAREER NOTES: Signed as non-drafted free agent by Los Angeles Dodgers organization (November 12, 1989). ... On disabled list (March 22-July 29, 1998); included rehabilitation assignment to San Bernardino. ... Signed as a free agent by Colorado Rockies organization (December 18, 1998). ... Traded by Rockies with P Jamey Wright to Milwaukee Brewers as part of three-way deal in which Rockies acquired 3B Jeff Cirillo, P Scott Karl and cash from Brewers, Oakland Athletics acquired P Justin Miller and cash from Rockies and Brewers acquired P Jimmy Haynes from A's (December 13, 1999). ... On disabled list (April 14-May 2, 2000); included rehabilitation assignment to Indianapolis. ... Traded by Brewers to Atlanta Braves for C Paul Bako and P Jose Cabrera (March 20, 2002). ... On disabled list (August 12-27, 2002). ... Signed as a free agent by Minnesota Twins (December 18, 2003).

2004 GAMES PLAYED BY POSITION (MLB): C—114.

Year	Team (League)	Pos.	G	AB	R	H	2B	3B	HR	RBI	BB	SO	HBP	GDP	SB-CS	Avg.	OBP	SLG	OPS	E	Avg.
1990—GC Dodgers (GCL)	3B	60	178	23	39	8	0	1	19	26	41	1	6	7-2	.219	.316	.281	.597	11	.941
1991—Vero Beach (FSL)	3B-SS	5	7	0	1	0	0	0	0	2	0	0	0	0-0	.143	.333	.143	.476	0	1.000
—Great Falls (Pio.)	3B-1B	62	216	35	55	7	1	5	28	27	39	1	5	3-6	.255	.336	.366	.702	8	.960
1992—Bakersfield (Calif.)	3B	124	401	42	94	21	2	5	52	51	91	9	10	10-6	.234	.328	.334	.662	14	.959
1993—San Antonio (Texas)	3B-1B-SS	117	374	33	73	19	1	10	42	29	80	4	7	3-3	.195	.260	.332	.591	16	.952
1994—San Antonio (Texas)	3B-1B-P	132	405	36	93	23	2	6	38	53	67	2	12	6-6	.230	.320	.341	.660	21	.924

Year	Team (League)	Pos.	G	AB	R	H	2B	3B	HR	RBI	BB	SO	HBP	GDP	SB-CS	Avg.	OBP	SLG	OPS	E	Avg.
1995— San Antonio (Texas)	3B-C	88	302	37	77	18	4	12	48	29	52	4	4	1-1	.255	.328	.460	.789	11	.964
— Albuquerque (PCL)	3B-1B-OF	29	97	11	22	4	1	2	13	10	23	0	3	0-0	.227	.294	.351	.644	2	.988
1996— San Antonio (Texas)	C-3B	92	307	39	82	14	1	5	40	28	38	0	8	2-3	.267	.324	.368	.692	13	.979
— Albuquerque (PCL)	C	2	6	1	1	0	0	0	0	0	3	0	0	0-0	.167	.167	.167	.333	0	1.000
1997— Albuquerque (PCL) C-1-DH-OF	91	294	38	92	20	1	6	47	37	63	1	7	7-4	.313	.388	.449	.837	3	.996
— Los Angeles (N.L.)	3B-1B	3	5	1	2	0	0	1	1	0	1	0	0	0-0	.400	.400	1.000	1.400	0	1.000
1998— San Bern. (Calif.)	C-DH	7	19	5	6	1	0	2	3	4	6	0	2	1-0	.316	.435	.684	1.119	0	1.000
— Albuquerque (PCL)	C-DH	48	134	19	36	11	0	4	23	22	27	0	5	2-0	.269	.367	.440	.807	4	.985
1999— Colo. Springs (PCL)	C	15	57	8	19	4	0	3	12	1	12	0	1	0-1	.333	.339	.561	.900	1	.990
— Colorado (N.L.)	C-OF	88	263	30	61	12	3	6	28	34	38	1	4	1-1	.232	.320	.369	.689	5	.992
2000— Milwaukee (N.L.)	C	93	284	29	67	24	0	7	31	36	60	0	9	0-3	.236	.318	.394	.712	5	.991
— Indianapolis (Int'l)	DH	1	3	1	1	1	0	0	0	1	0	0	1	0-0	.333	.500	.667	1.167	...	...
2001— Milwaukee (N.L.)	C	104	314	33	66	18	3	6	31	34	72	2	10	3-1	.210	.290	.344	.634	6	.992
2002— Atlanta (N.L.)	C	81	221	17	45	9	1	6	22	20	51	1	5	0-2	.204	.267	.335	.602	3	.993
2003— Atlanta (N.L.)	C	55	151	11	30	8	0	1	13	10	21	1	3	0-0	.199	.252	.272	.523	1	.996
2004— Minnesota (A.L.)	C	114	315	36	65	19	1	10	37	21	56	3	8	0-3	.206	.260	.368	.628	7	.991
American League totals (1 year)		114	315	36	65	19	1	10	37	21	56	3	8	0-3	.206	.260	.368	.628	7	.991
National League totals (6 years)		424	1238	121	271	71	7	27	126	134	243	5	31	4-7	.219	.295	.353	.648	20	.992
Major League totals (7 years)		538	1553	157	336	90	8	37	163	155	299	8	39	4-10	.216	.288	.356	.644	27	.992

DIVISION SERIES RECORD

Year	Team (League)	Pos.	G	AB	R	H	2B	3B	HR	RBI	BB	SO	HBP	GDP	SB-CS	Avg.	OBP	SLG	OPS	E	Avg.
2002— Atlanta (N.L.)	C	2	6	0	1	0	0	0	0	0	2	0	0	0-0	.167	.167	.167	.333	0	1.000
2004— Minnesota (A.L.)	C	4	8	1	2	0	0	1	2	0	2	0	1	0-0	.250	.222	.625	.847	1	.957
Division series totals (2 years)		6	14	1	3	0	0	1	2	0	4	0	1	0-0	.214	.200	.429	.629	1	.970

BLANTON, JOE — P

PERSONAL: Born December 11, 1980, in Bowling Green, Ky. ... 6-3/225. ... Throws right, bats right. ... Full name: Joseph Matthew Blanton. ... High school: Franklin-Simpson (Franklin, Ky.). ... College: Kentucky.

TRANSACTIONS/CAREER NOTES: Selected by Oakland Athletics organization in first round (24th pick overall) of 2002 free-agent draft; pick received as compensation for New York Yankees signing Type A free-agent 1B Jason Giambi.

CAREER HITTING: 0-for-0 (.000), 0 R, 0 2B, 0 3B, 0 HR, 0 RBI.

Year	Team (League)	W	L	Pct.	ERA	WHIP	G	GS	CG	ShO	Hld.	Sv.-Opp.	IP	H	R	ER	HR	BB-IBB	SO	Avg.
2002— Vancouver (N'west)	1	1	.500	3.14	0.91	4	2	0	0	...	0-...	14.1	11	5	5	0	2-0	15	.216
— Modesto (Calif.)	0	1	.000	7.50	2.33	2	1	0	0	...	0-...	6.0	8	6	5	1	6-0	6	.296
2003— Kane County (Midwest)	8	7	.533	2.57	0.97	21	21	2	2	...	0-...	133.0	110	47	38	6	19-0	144	.219
— Midland (Texas)	3	1	.750	1.26	0.79	7	5	1	0	...	1-...	35.2	21	6	5	1	7-0	30	.174
2004— Sacramento (PCL)	11	8	.579	4.19	1.32	28	26	1	0	...	0-...	176.1	199	101	82	13	34-2	143	.284
— Oakland (A.L.)	0	0	...	5.63	1.00	3	0	0	0	0	0-0	8.0	6	5	5	1	2-0	6	.214
Major League totals (1 year)	0	0	...	5.63	1.00	3	0	0	0	0	0-0	8.0	6	5	5	1	2-0	6	.214

BLOOMQUIST, WILLIE — 3B/SS

PERSONAL: Born November 27, 1977, in Bremerton, Wash. ... 5-11/185. ... Bats right, throws right. ... Full name: William Paul Bloomquist. ... High school: South Kitsap (Port Orchard, Wash.). ... College: Arizona State.

TRANSACTIONS/CAREER NOTES: Selected by Seattle Mariners organization in eighth round of 1996 free-agent draft; did not sign. ... Selected by Mariners organization in third round of 1999 free-agent draft. ... On disabled list (May 2-21, 2004); included rehabilitation assignment to Tacoma.

2004 GAMES PLAYED BY POSITION (MLB): 3B—31, SS—20, 1B—19, OF—9, DH—6, 2B—1.

Year	Team (League)	Pos.	G	AB	R	H	2B	3B	HR	RBI	BB	SO	HBP	GDP	SB-CS	Avg.	OBP	SLG	OPS	E	Avg.
									BATTING											FIELDING	
1999— Everett (N'west)	2B-OF	42	178	35	51	10	3	2	27	22	25	1	1	17-5	.287	.366	.410	.776	7	.954
2000— Lancaster (Calif.)	2B-SS	64	256	63	97	19	6	2	51	37	27	0	3	22-12	.379	.456	.523	.979	12	.961
— Tacoma (PCL)	2B	51	191	17	43	5	1	1	23	7	28	0	3	5-0	.225	.249	.277	.526	3	.987
2001— San Antonio (Texas)	2B-SS	123	491	59	125	23	2	0	28	28	55	1	11	34-9	.255	.294	.310	.603	24	.959
2002— Tacoma (PCL)	OF-2-3-SS	104	337	47	91	14	3	6	47	29	44	3	5	20-10	.270	.331	.383	.713	12	.961
— Seattle (A.L.)	OF-2B-DH	12	33	11	15	4	0	0	7	5	2	0	0	3-1	.455	.526	.576	1.102	0	1.000
2003— Seattle (A.L.)	3-S-DH-O-2-1	89	196	30	49	7	2	1	14	19	39	1	6	4-1	.250	.317	.321	.638	4	.975
2004— Tacoma (PCL)	SS-OF	3	12	2	5	0	0	1	3	0	2	0	0	1-0	.417	.417	.667	1.083	0	1.000
— Seattle (A.L.)	3-S-1-O-DH-2	93	188	27	46	10	0	2	18	10	48	0	2	13-2	.245	.283	.330	.613	10	.956
Major League totals (3 years)		194	417	68	110	21	2	3	39	34	89	1	8	20-4	.264	.319	.345	.665	14	.966

BLUM, GEOFF — 2B/3B

PERSONAL: Born April 26, 1973, in Redwood City, Calif. ... 6-3/200. ... Bats both, throws right. ... Full name: Geoffrey Edward Blum. ... Name pronounced: bluhm. ... High school: Chino (Calif.). ... College: California.

TRANSACTIONS/CAREER NOTES: Selected by Montreal Expos organization in seventh round of 1994 free-agent draft. ... Traded by Expos to Houston Astros for 3B Chris Truby (March 12, 2002). ... Traded by Astros to Tampa Bay Devil Rays for P Brandon Backe (December 14, 2003).

2004 GAMES PLAYED BY POSITION (MLB): 3B—59, 2B—52, OF—7, DH—2, 1B—2, SS—1.

Year	Team (League)	Pos.	G	AB	R	H	2B	3B	HR	RBI	BB	SO	HBP	GDP	SB-CS	Avg.	OBP	SLG	OPS	E	Avg.
									BATTING											FIELDING	
1994— Vermont (N.Y.-Penn.)	SS	63	241	48	83	15	1	3	38	33	21	3	4	5-5	.344	.428	.452	.880	15	.948
1995— W.P. Beach (FSL)	2B-3B-SS	125	457	54	120	20	2	1	62	34	61	3	12	6-7	.263	.313	.322	.635	18	.963
1996— Harrisburg (East.)		120	396	47	95	22	1	1	41	59	51	3	11	6-7	.240	.341	.313	.654	9	.984
1997— Ottawa (Int'l)	2B-3B-SS	118	407	59	101	21	2	3	35	52	73	3	6	14-6	.248	.333	.332	.665	17	.969
1998— Ottawa (Int'l)	2B	8	23	1	4	0	0	1	1	3	6	0	0	0-0	.174	.269	.174	.443	0	1.000
— GC Expos (GCL)	2B	5	18	0	3	1	1	0	1	1	4	0	0	0-0	.167	.211	.333	.544	0	1.000
— Jupiter (FSL)	2B-3B-SS	17	58	13	16	6	0	0	5	13	14	1	0	1-0	.276	.411	.379	.790	2	.976
— Harrisburg (East.)	2-3-S-1	39	139	25	43	12	3	6	21	17	24	4	3	2-1	.309	.400	.568	.968	3	.986
1999— Ottawa (Int'l)	S-2-1-3-DH	77	268	43	71	14	1	10	37	37	39	2	5	6-1	.265	.350	.437	.787	12	.965
— Montreal (N.L.)	SS-2B	45	133	21	32	7	2	8	18	17	25	0	3	1-0	.241	.327	.504	.830	10	.929
2000— Montreal (N.L.)	3-S-2-1	124	343	40	97	20	2	11	45	26	60	3	4	1-4	.283	.335	.449	.784	9	.974
2001— Montreal (N.L.)	3-OF-2-1-S	148	453	57	107	25	0	9	50	43	94	10	12	9-5	.236	.313	.351	.664	8	.980

Year Team (League)	Pos.	G	AB	R	H	2B	3B	HR	RBI	BB	SO	HBP	GDP	SB-CS	Avg.	OBP	SLG	OPS	E	Avg.
2002— Houston (N.L.) 3-OF-S-2-1		130	368	45	104	20	4	10	52	49	70	1	8	2-0	.283	.367	.440	.807	8	.972
2003— Houston (N.L.) 3-2-S-1-OF		123	420	51	110	19	0	10	52	20	50	2	15	0-0	.262	.295	.379	.674	7	.975
2004— Tampa Bay (A.L.) 3-2-O-DH-1-S		112	339	38	73	21	0	8	35	24	58	0	4	2-3	.215	.266	.348	.614	10	.970
American League totals (1 year)		112	339	38	73	21	0	8	35	24	58	0	4	2-3	.215	.266	.348	.614	10	.970
National League totals (5 years)		570	1717	214	450	91	8	48	217	155	299	16	42	13-9	.262	.326	.408	.734	42	.971
Major League totals (6 years)		682	2056	252	523	112	8	56	252	179	357	16	46	15-12	.254	.316	.398	.715	52	.971

BOCACHICA, HIRAM — OF

PERSONAL: Born March 4, 1976, in Ponce, Puerto Rico. ... 5-11/180. ... Bats right, throws right. ... Full name: Hiram Colon Bocachica. ... Name pronounced: hear-ram bow-ka-cheeka. ... High school: Rexville (Bayamon, Puerto Rico).

TRANSACTIONS/CAREER NOTES: Selected by Montreal Expos organization in first round (21st pick overall) of 1994 free-agent draft. ... Traded by Expos with P Carlos Perez and SS Mark Grudzielanek to Los Angeles Dodgers for 2B Wilton Guerrero, P Ted Lilly, OF Peter Bergeron and 1B Jonathan Tucker (July 31, 1998). ... On disabled list (July 9-26, 2001). ... Traded by Dodgers to Detroit Tigers for P Tom Farmer and a player to be named (July 25, 2002); Dodgers acquired P Jason Frasor to complete deal (September 18, 2002). ... Signed as a free agent by Seattle Mariners organization (January 16, 2004). ... Refused minor league assignment and became a free agent (October 11, 2004).

2004 GAMES PLAYED BY POSITION (MLB): OF—44, DH—3.

Year Team (League)	Pos.	G	AB	R	H	2B	3B	HR	RBI	BB	SO	HBP	GDP	SB-CS	Avg.	OBP	SLG	OPS	E	Avg.
1994— GC Expos (GCL)	SS	43	168	31	47	9	0	5	16	15	42	2	1	11-4	.280	.346	.423	.769	23	.896
1995— Albany (S. Atl.)	2B-SS	96	380	65	108	20	10	2	30	52	78	8	4	47-17	.284	.381	.405	.786	58	.881
1996— W.P. Beach (FSL)	DH-SS	71	267	50	90	17	5	2	26	34	47	6	6	21-3	.337	.419	.461	.880	24	.833
— GC Expos (GCL)	DH	9	32	11	8	3	0	0	2	5	3	1	0	2-1	.250	.368	.344	.712	...	...
1997— Harrisburg (East.)	SS-2B-DH	119	443	82	123	19	3	11	35	41	98	13	3	29-12	.278	.354	.409	.763	32	.909
1998— Harrisburg (East.)	OF-DH	80	296	39	78	18	4	4	27	21	61	11	1	20-8	.264	.334	.392	.726	10	.946
— Ottawa (Int'l)	OF	12	41	5	8	3	1	0	5	6	14	1	1	2-0	.195	.313	.317	.630	0	1.000
— Albuquerque (PCL)	OF	26	101	16	24	7	1	4	16	13	24	6	1	5-3	.238	.358	.446	.804	2	.976
1999— San Antonio (Texas)	2B-DH	123	477	84	139	22	10	11	60	60	71	13	5	30-15	.291	.382	.449	.831	31	.946
2000— Albuquerque (PCL)	2B	124	482	99	155	38	4	23	84	40	100	15	7	10-14	.322	.390	.560	.950	23	.963
— Los Angeles (N.L.)	2B	8	10	2	3	0	0	0	0	0	2	0	0	0-0	.300	.300	.300	.600	0	1.000
2001— Los Angeles (N.L.) 2B-OF-3B		75	133	15	31	11	1	2	9	9	33	1	1	4-1	.233	.287	.376	.663	7	.919
2002— Los Angeles (N.L.)	OF-DH	49	65	12	14	3	0	4	9	5	19	0	1	1-1	.215	.271	.446	.718	1	.960
— Detroit (A.L.) OF-2B-DH		34	103	14	23	4	0	4	8	5	22	0	2	3-2	.223	.259	.379	.638	2	.969
2003— Detroit (A.L.)	OF	6	22	1	1	1	0	0	0	0	7	0	0	0-0	.045	.045	.091	.136	0	1.000
— Toledo (Int'l) OF-2-3-DH		95	322	48	78	19	3	12	37	24	57	10	5	11-6	.242	.313	.432	.745	11	.954
2004— Tacoma (PCL) OF-DH-1B		40	136	22	39	5	1	10	25	17	36	8	2	12-3	.287	.393	.559	.951	4	.953
— Seattle (A.L.) .... OF-DH		50	90	9	22	5	0	3	6	12	27	1	1	5-4	.244	.337	.400	.737	0	1.000
American League totals (3 years)		90	215	24	46	10	0	7	14	17	56	1	3	7-6	.214	.274	.358	.632	2	.986
National League totals (3 years)		132	208	29	48	14	1	6	18	14	54	1	2	5-2	.231	.283	.394	.677	8	.935
Major League totals (5 years)		222	423	53	94	24	1	13	32	31	110	2	5	12-8	.222	.278	.376	.654	10	.963

BOEHRINGER, BRIAN — P

PERSONAL: Born January 8, 1970, in St. Louis, Mo. ... 6-2/196. ... Throws right, bats both. ... Full name: Brian Edward Boehringer. ... Name pronounced: BOH-ring-uhr. ... High school: Northwest (House Springs, Mo.). ... College: UNLV.

TRANSACTIONS/CAREER NOTES: Selected by Houston Astros organization in 10th round of 1990 free-agent draft; did not sign. ... Selected by Chicago White Sox organization in fourth round of 1991 free-agent draft. ... Traded by White Sox to New York Yankees for P Paul Assenmacher (March 21, 1994). ... On disabled list (May 27-August 19, 1997); included rehabilitation assignments to GCL Yankees and Tampa. ... Selected by Tampa Bay Devil Rays in second round (30th pick overall) of expansion draft (November 18, 1997). ... Traded by Devil Rays with SS Andy Sheets to San Diego Padres for C John Flaherty (November 18, 1997). ... On disabled list (August 14, 1999-remainder of season). ... On disabled list (April 21-May 24 and July 4, 2000-remainder of season); included rehabilitation assignment to Rancho Cucamonga. ... On disabled list (December 14, 2000). ... Traded by Yankees to San Francisco Giants for C Bobby Estalella and P Joe Smith (July 5, 2001). ... Signed as a free agent by Pittsburgh Pirates organization (January 25, 2002). ... On disabled list (June 2, 2004-remainder of season).

CAREER HITTING: 2-for-31 (.065), 0 R, 1 2B, 0 3B, 0 HR, 2 RBI.

Year Team (League)	W	L	Pct.	ERA	WHIP	G	GS	CG	ShO	Hld.	Sv.-Opp.	IP	H	R	ER	HR	BB-IBB	SO	Avg.
1991— Utica (N.Y.-Penn)	1	1	.500	2.37	1.16	4	4	0	0	...	0-...	19.0	14	8	5	0	8-0	19	.206
1992— South Bend (Mid.)	6	7	.462	4.38	1.47	15	15	2	0	...	0-...	86.1	87	52	42	5	40-0	59	.264
— GC White Sox (GCL)	1	1	.500	1.50	0.92	2	2	0	0	...	0-...	12.0	9	3	2	0	2-0	8	.214
1993— Sarasota (Florida State)	10	4	.714	2.80	1.29	18	17	3	0	...	0-...	119.0	103	47	37	2	51-2	92	.237
— Birmingham (Southern)	2	1	.667	3.54	1.35	7	7	1	0	...	0-...	40.2	41	20	16	3	14-0	29	.265
1994— Alb./Colon. (East.)	10	11	.476	3.62	1.29	27	27	5	1	...	0-...	171.2	165	85	69	10	57-1	145	.256
1995— New York (A.L.)	0	3	.000	13.75	2.60	7	3	0	0	0	0-1	17.2	24	27	27	5	22-1	10	.320
— Columbus (Int'l)	8	6	.571	2.77	1.27	17	17	3	0	...	0-...	104.0	101	39	32	6	31-1	58	.254
1996— Columbus (Int'l)	11	7	.611	4.00	1.38	25	25	3	1	...	0-...	153.0	155	79	68	13	56-1	132	.263
— New York (A.L.)	2	4	.333	5.44	1.45	15	3	0	0	4	0-1	46.1	46	28	28	6	21-2	37	.260
1997— New York (A.L.)	3	2	.600	2.63	1.48	34	0	0	0	5	0-3	48.0	39	16	14	4	32-6	53	.225
— GC Yankees (GCL)	0	0	...	0.00	0.50	1	1	0	0	...	0-...	2.0	1	0	0	0	0-0	2	.143
— Tampa (FSL)	0	1	.000	5.00	1.56	3	3	0	0	...	0-...	9.0	9	5	5	1	5-0	8	.265
1998— San Diego (N.L.)	5	2	.714	4.36	1.57	56	1	0	0	7	0-1	76.1	75	38	37	10	45-4	67	.257
1999— San Diego (N.L.)	6	5	.545	3.24	1.40	33	11	0	0	3	0-2	94.1	97	38	34	10	35-4	64	.267
2000— San Diego (N.L.)	0	3	.000	5.74	1.79	7	3	0	0	0	0-...	15.2	18	15	10	4	10-0	9	.286
— Rancho Cuca. (Calif.)	0	0	.000	5.40	1.80	4	2	0	0	...	0-...	5.0	8	3	3	0	1-0	5	.381
2001— San Diego (N.L.)	0	1	.000	3.12	1.36	22	0	0	0	1	1-1	34.2	35	15	12	3	12-0	33	.255
— San Francisco (N.L.)	0	3	.000	4.19	1.43	29	0	0	0	2	1-1	34.1	32	20	16	4	17-5	27	.239
2002— Pittsburgh (N.L.)	4	4	.500	3.39	1.23	70	0	0	0	28	1-6	79.2	65	30	30	5	33-6	65	.229
2003— Pittsburgh (N.L.)	5	4	.556	5.49	1.51	62	0	0	0	15	0-3	62.1	64	39	38	11	30-3	47	.267
2004— Pittsburgh (N.L.)	1	1	.500	4.62	1.74	21	0	0	0	0	0-2	25.1	27	14	13	2	17-3	20	.293
American League totals (4 years)	5	10	.333	4.97	1.57	78	6	0	0	10	1-6	146.2	144	86	81	18	87-9	133	.256
National League totals (7 years)	21	22	.488	4.13	1.46	278	15	0	0	56	2-16	388.0	378	194	178	46	187-25	299	.257
Major League totals (10 years)	26	32	.448	4.36	1.49	356	21	0	0	66	3-22	534.2	522	280	259	64	274-34	432	.257

DIVISION SERIES RECORD

Year Team (League)	W	L	Pct.	ERA	WHIP	G	GS	CG	ShO	Hld.	Sv.-Opp.	IP	H	R	ER	HR	BB-IBB	SO	Avg.
1996— New York (A.L.)	1	0	1.000	6.75	3.75	2	0	0	0	...	0-0	1.1	3	2	1	0	2-0	0	.375
1997— New York (A.L.)	0	0	...	0.00	1.20	1	0	0	0	...	0-0	1.2	1	0	0	1	1-0	2	.143
1998— San Diego (N.L.)	Did not play.																		
Division series totals (2 years)	1	0	1.000	3.00	2.33	3	0	0	0	...	0-0	3.0	4	2	1	1	3-0	2	.267

CHAMPIONSHIP SERIES RECORD

Year Team (League)	W	L	Pct.	ERA	WHIP	G	GS	CG	ShO	Hld.	Sv.-Opp.	IP	H	R	ER	HR	BB-IBB	SO	Avg.
1998— San Diego (N.L.)	0	0	...	0.00	1.33	3	0	0	0	0	0-0	3.0	3	0	0	0	1-0	1	.273

WORLD SERIES RECORD

Year Team (League)	W	L	Pct.	ERA	WHIP	G	GS	CG	ShO	Hld.	Sv.-Opp.	IP	H	R	ER	HR	BB-IBB	SO	Avg.
1996— New York (A.L.)	0	0	...	5.40	1.00	2	0	0	0	0	0-0	5.0	5	5	3	2	0-0	5	.250
1998— San Diego (N.L.)	0	0	...	9.00	3.00	2	0	0	0	0	0-0	2.0	4	2	2	1	2-0	3	.364
World series totals (2 years)	**0**	**0**	**...**	**6.43**	**1.57**	**4**	**0**	**0**	**0**	**0**	**0-0**	**7.0**	**9**	**7**	**5**	**3**	**2-0**	**8**	**.290**

BONDERMAN, JEREMY — P

PERSONAL: Born October 28, 1982, in Kennewick, Wash. ... 6-2/210. ... Throws right, bats right. ... Full name: Jeremy Allen Bonderman. ... High school: Pasco (Wash.).

TRANSACTIONS/CAREER NOTES: Selected by Oakland Athletics in first round (26th pick overall) of 2001 free-agent draft; pick received as compensation for New York Mets signing free-agent P Kevin Appier. ... Traded by A's to Detroit Tigers (August 22, 2002), completing three-team deal in which Tigers acquired 1B Carlos Pena, P Franklyn German and a player to be named from A's, A's acquired P Ted Lilly, OF John-Ford Griffin and P Jason Arnold from New York Yankees and Yankees acquired P Jeff Weaver from Tigers (July 6, 2002).

CAREER HITTING: 0-for-9 (.000), 0 R, 0 2B, 0 3B, 0 HR, 0 RBI.

Year Team (League)	W	L	Pct.	ERA	WHIP	G	GS	CG	ShO	Hld.	Sv.-Opp.	IP	H	R	ER	HR	BB-IBB	SO	Avg.
2002— Modesto (Calif.)	9	8	.529	3.61	1.27	25	25	1	0	...	0-...	144.2	129	77	58	15	55-1	160	.233
—Lakeland (Fla. St.)	0	1	.000	6.00	1.25	2	2	1	0	...	0-...	12.0	11	8	8	3	4-0	10	.262
2003— Detroit (A.L.)	6	19	.240	5.56	1.55	33	28	0	0	0	0-0	162.0	193	118	100	23	58-2	108	.294
2004— Detroit (A.L.)	11	13	.458	4.89	1.31	33	32	2	•2	0	0-0	184.0	168	101	100	24	73-5	168	.242
Major League totals (2 years)	**17**	**32**	**.347**	**5.20**	**1.42**	**66**	**60**	**2**	**2**	**0**	**0-0**	**346.0**	**361**	**219**	**200**	**47**	**131-7**	**276**	**.267**

BONDS, BARRY — OF

PERSONAL: Born July 24, 1964, in Riverside, Calif. ... 6-2/228. ... Bats left, throws left. ... Full name: Barry Lamar Bonds. ... High school: Serra (San Mateo, Calif.). ... College: Arizona State. ... Son of Bobby Bonds, outfielder with eight major league teams (1968-81); and coach with Cleveland Indians (1984-87) and San Francisco Giants (1993-96).

TRANSACTIONS/CAREER NOTES: Selected by San Francisco Giants organization in second round of June 1982 free-agent draft; did not sign. ... Selected by Pittsburgh Pirates organization in first round (sixth pick overall) of June 1985 free-agent draft. ... On disabled list (June 15-July 4, 1992). ... Signed as a free agent by Giants (December 8, 1992). ... On suspended list (August 14-16, 1998). ... On disabled list (April 18-June 9, 1999).

RECORDS: Holds major league records for most home runs, season (73, 2001); highest slugging percentage, season (.863, 2001); highest on-base percentage, season (.609, 2004); most bases on balls, season (232, 2004); and most intentional bases on balls, season (120, 2004). ... Holds major league record for most bases on balls, career (2,302), and most intentional bases on balls, career (604).

HONORS: Named Major League Player of the Year by THE SPORTING NEWS (1990, 2001 and 2004). ... Named N.L. Player of the Year by THE SPORTING NEWS (1990 and 1991). ... Named N.L. Most Valuable Player by Baseball Writers' Association of America (1990, 1992-93 and 2001-04). ... Won N.L. Gold Glove as outfielder (1990-94 and 1996-98).

2004 GAMES PLAYED BY POSITION (MLB): OF—133, DH—7.

Year Team (League)	Pos.	G	AB	R	H	2B	3B	HR	RBI	BB	SO	HBP	GDP	SB-CS	Avg.	OBP	SLG	OPS	E	Avg.
1985— Prince Will. (Car.)	OF	71	254	49	76	16	4	13	37	37	52	0	3	15-3	.299	.383	.547	.930	5	.976
1986— Hawaii (PCL)	OF	44	148	30	46	7	2	7	37	33	31	2	1	16-5	.311	.435	.527	.963	2	.983
—Pittsburgh (N.L.)	OF	113	413	72	92	26	3	16	48	65	102	2	4	36-7	.223	.330	.416	.746	5	.983
1987— Pittsburgh (N.L.)	OF	150	551	99	144	34	9	25	59	54	88	3	4	32-10	.261	.329	.492	.821	5	.986
1988— Pittsburgh (N.L.)	OF	144	538	97	152	30	5	24	58	72	82	2	3	17-11	.283	.368	.491	.859	6	.980
1989— Pittsburgh (N.L.)	OF	159	580	96	144	34	6	19	58	93	93	1	9	32-10	.248	.351	.426	.777	6	.984
1990— Pittsburgh (N.L.)	OF	151	519	104	156	32	3	33	114	93	83	3	8	52-13	.301	.406 *	.565	.970	6	.983
1991— Pittsburgh (N.L.)	OF	153	510	95	149	28	5	25	116	107	73	4	8	43-13	.292 *	.410	.514	.924	3	.991
1992— Pittsburgh (N.L.)	OF	140	473	* 109	147	36	5	34	103	* 127	69	5	9	39-8	.311 *	.456 *	.624	1.080	3	.991
1993— San Francisco (N.L.)	OF	159	539	129	181	38	4	* 46	* 123	126	79	2	11	29-12	.336 *	.458 *	.677	1.136	5	.984
1994— San Francisco (N.L.)	OF	112	391	89	122	18	1	37	81	* 74	43	6	3	29-9	.312	.426	.647	1.073	3	.986
1995— San Francisco (N.L.)	OF	144	506	109	149	30	7	33	104	* 120	83	5	12	31-10	.294 *	.432	.577	1.009	6	.980
1996— San Francisco (N.L.)	OF	158	517	122	159	27	3	42	129	* 151	76	1	11	40-7	.308	.461	.615	1.076	6	.984
1997— San Francisco (N.L.)	OF	159	532	123	155	26	5	40	101	* 145	87	8	13	37-8	.291	.446	.585	1.031	5	.984
1998— San Francisco (N.L.)	OF	156	552	120	167	44	7	37	122	130	92	8	15	28-12	.303	.438	.609	1.047	5	.984
1999— San Francisco (N.L.)	OF-DH	102	355	91	93	20	2	34	83	73	62	3	6	15-2	.262	.389	.617	1.006	3	.984
2000— San Francisco (N.L.)	OF	143	480	129	147	28	4	49	106	* 117	77	3	6	11-3	.306	.440	.688	1.127	3	.989
2001— San Francisco (N.L.)	OF-DH	153	476	129	156	32	2	* 73	137	* 177	93	9	5	13-3	.328 *	.515 *	.863 *	1.379	6	.977
2002— San Francisco (N.L.)	OF-DH	143	403	117	149	31	2	46	110	* 198	47	9	4	9-2	.370 *	.582 *	.799	1.381	8	.968
2003— San Francisco (N.L.)	OF-DH	130	390	111	133	22	1	45	90	* 148	58	10	7	7-0	.341 *	.529 *	.749	1.278	2	.992
2004— San Francisco (N.L.)	OF-DH	147	373	129	135	27	3	45	101	* 232	41	9	5	6-1	.362 *	.609 *	.812 *	1.422	4	.983
Major League totals (19 years)		**2716**	**9098**	**2070**	**2730**	**563**	**77**	**703**	**1843**	**2302**	**1428**	**93**	**143**	**506-141**	**.300**	**.443**	**.611**	**1.053**	**90**	**.984**

DIVISION SERIES RECORD

Year Team (League)	Pos.	G	AB	R	H	2B	3B	HR	RBI	BB	SO	HBP	GDP	SB-CS	Avg.	OBP	SLG	OPS	E	Avg.
1997— San Francisco (N.L.)	OF	3	12	0	3	2	0	0	2	0	3	0	0	1-0	.250	.231	.417	.647	0	1.000
2000— San Francisco (N.L.)	OF	4	17	2	3	1	1	0	1	3	4	0	0	1-0	.176	.300	.353	.653	0	1.000
2002— San Francisco (N.L.)	OF	5	17	5	5	0	0	3	4	4	1	0	0	0-1	.294	.409	.824	1.233	1	.909
2003— San Francisco (N.L.)	OF	4	9	3	2	1	0	0	2	8	0	0	0	1-0	.222	.556	.333	.889	0	1.000
Division series totals (4 years)		**16**	**55**	**10**	**13**	**4**	**1**	**3**	**9**	**15**	**8**	**0**	**0**	**3-1**	**.236**	**.384**	**.509**	**.893**	**1**	**.968**

CHAMPIONSHIP SERIES RECORD

Year Team (League)	Pos.	G	AB	R	H	2B	3B	HR	RBI	BB	SO	HBP	GDP	SB-CS	Avg.	OBP	SLG	OPS	E	Avg.
1990— Pittsburgh (N.L.)	OF	6	18	4	3	0	0	1	1	6	5	0	0	2-0	.167	.375	.167	.542	0	1.000
1991— Pittsburgh (N.L.)	OF	7	27	1	4	1	0	0	0	2	4	0	1	3-0	.148	.207	.185	.392	1	.938
1992— Pittsburgh (N.L.)	OF	7	23	5	6	1	0	1	2	6	4	1	0	1-0	.261	.433	.435	.868	0	1.000
2002— San Francisco (N.L.)	OF	5	11	5	3	0	1	1	6	10	2	0	0	0-0	.273	.591	.727	1.318	0	1.000
Champ. series totals (4 years)		**25**	**79**	**15**	**16**	**2**	**1**	**3**	**9**	**24**	**15**	**1**	**1**	**6-0**	**.203**	**.390**	**.329**	**.720**	**1**	**.982**

WORLD SERIES RECORD

Year Team (League)	Pos.	G	AB	R	H	2B	3B	HR	RBI	BB	SO	HBP	GDP	SB-CS	Avg.	OBP	SLG	OPS	E	Avg.
2002— San Francisco (N.L.)	OF	7	17	8	8	2	0	4	6	13	3	0	0	0-0	.471	.700	1.294	1.994	1	.909

ALL-STAR GAME RECORD

	G	AB	R	H	2B	3B	HR	RBI	BB	SO	HBP	GDP	SB-CS	Avg.	OBP	SLG	OPS	E	Avg.
All-Star Game totals (12 years)	12	29	5	6	3	0	2	7	4	5	0	0	1-1	.207	.294	.517	.811	0	1.000

BONG, JUNG KEUN   P

PERSONAL: Born July 15, 1980, in Seoul, South Korea. ... 6-3/215. ... Throws left, bats left. ... Full name: Jung Keun Bong.
TRANSACTIONS/CAREER NOTES: Signed as a non-drafted free agent by Atlanta Braves organization (November 6, 1997). ... Traded by Braves with P Bubba Nelson to Cincinnati Reds for P Chris Reitsma (March 26, 2004).
CAREER HITTING: 0-for-11 (.000), 0 R, 0 2B, 0 3B, 0 HR, 0 RBI.

Year Team (League)	W	L	Pct.	ERA	WHIP	G	GS	CG	ShO	Hld.	Sv.-Opp.	IP	H	R	ER	HR	BB-IBB	SO	Avg.
1998— GC Braves (GCL)	1	1	.500	1.49	0.93	11	10	0	0	...	0-...	48.1	31	9	8	2	14-0	56	.195
1999— Macon (S. Atl.)	6	5	.545	3.98	1.48	26	20	0	0	...	1-...	108.2	111	61	48	8	50-0	100	.266
2000— Macon (S. Atl.)	7	7	.500	4.23	1.46	20	19	0	0	...	0-...	112.2	119	65	53	4	45-0	90	.275
— Myrtle Beach (Caro.)	3	1	.750	2.18	0.97	7	6	0	0	...	0-...	41.1	33	14	10	1	7-0	37	.220
2001— Myrtle Beach (Caro.)	13	9	.591	3.00	1.18	28	28	0	0	...	0-...	168.0	151	67	56	7	47-0	145	.245
2002— Greenville (Sou.)	7	8	.467	3.25	1.48	27	17	0	0	...	2-...	122.0	136	59	44	6	45-1	107	.286
— Atlanta (N.L.)	0	1	.000	7.50	1.67	1	1	0	0	0	0-0	6.0	8	5	5	0	2-0	4	.320
2003— Richmond (Int'l)	1	2	.333	5.56	1.20	3	3	0	0	...	0-...	11.1	11	7	7	1	3-0	15	.239
— Atlanta (N.L.)	6	2	.750	5.05	1.53	44	0	0	0	2	1-3	57.0	56	32	32	8	31-6	47	.267
2004— Cincinnati (N.L.)	1	1	.500	4.70	1.76	3	3	0	0	0	0-0	15.1	17	13	8	3	10-0	11	.270
— GC Reds (GCL)	0	0	...	12.00	1.70	2	2	0	0	...	0-...	3.0	3	5	4	0	2-0	3	.231
— Louisville (Int'l)	8	8	.500	5.82	1.58	19	19	0	0	...	0-...	94.1	118	66	61	13	31-0	65	.313
Major League totals (3 years)	7	4	.636	5.17	1.58	48	4	0	0	2	1-3	78.1	81	50	45	11	43-6	62	.272

BOONE, AARON   3B

PERSONAL: Born March 9, 1973, in La Mesa, Calif. ... 6-2/200. ... Bats right, throws right. ... Full name: Aaron John Boone. ... High school: Villa Park (Calif.). ... College: USC. ... Son of Bob Boone, catcher with three major league teams (1972-90) and manager of Kansas City Royals (1995-97) and Cincinnati Reds (2001-03); brother of Bret Boone, second baseman, Seattle Mariners; grandson of Ray Boone, infielder with six major league teams (1948-60).
TRANSACTIONS/CAREER NOTES: Selected by California Angels organization in 43rd round of 1991 free-agent draft; did not sign. ... Selected by Cincinnati Reds organization in third round of 1994 free-agent draft. ... On disabled list (July 10, 2000-remainder of season). ... On disabled list (May 15-June 15, August 15-September 1 and September 24, 2001-remainder of season); included rehabilitation assignment to Louisville. ... Traded by Reds to New York Yankees for Ps Brandon Claussen and Charlie Manning and cash (July 31, 2003). ... Released by Yankees (February 26, 2004). ... Signed by Cleveland Indians (June 26, 2004). ... On disabled list (June 26, 2004-remainder of season).

Year Team (League)	Pos.	G	AB	R	H	2B	3B	HR	RBI	BB	SO	HBP	GDP	SB-CS	Avg.	OBP	SLG	OPS	E	Avg.
1994— Billings (Pio.)	3B-1B	67	256	48	70	15	5	7	55	36	35	3	7	6-3	.273	.362	.453	.815	18	.924
1995— Chattanooga (Sou.)	3B	23	66	6	15	3	0	0	3	5	12	0	5	2-0	.227	.274	.273	.547	6	.875
— Win.-Salem (Car.)	3B	108	395	61	103	19	1	14	50	43	77	9	4	11-7	.261	.345	.420	.765	21	.940
1996— Chattanooga (Sou.)	3B-SS-DH	136	548	86	158	44	7	17	95	38	77	5	5	21-10	.288	.338	.487	.825	22	.945
1997— Indianapolis (A.A.)	3B-SS-2B	131	476	79	138	30	4	22	75	40	81	1	11	12-4	.290	.344	.508	.853	24	.941
— Cincinnati (N.L.)	3B-2B	16	49	5	12	1	0	0	5	2	5	0	1	1-0	.245	.275	.265	.540	3	.917
1998— Cincinnati (N.L.)	3B-2B-SS	58	181	24	51	13	2	2	28	15	36	5	3	6-1	.282	.350	.409	.759	8	.944
— Indianapolis (Int'l)	3B-2B-SS	87	332	56	80	18	1	7	38	31	71	8	6	17-5	.241	.316	.364	.680	19	.943
1999— Cincinnati (N.L.)	3B-SS	139	472	56	132	26	5	14	72	30	79	8	8	17-6	.280	.330	.445	.775	15	.958
— Indianapolis (Int'l)	3B-SS	11	41	6	14	2	1	0	7	3	4	2	1	2-2	.341	.388	.439	.827	3	.930
2000— Cincinnati (N.L.)	3B	84	291	44	83	18	0	12	43	24	52	10	5	6-1	.285	.356	.471	.826	8	.965
2001— Cincinnati (N.L.)	3B	103	381	54	112	26	2	14	62	29	71	8	6	6-3	.294	.351	.483	.834	19	.936
— Louisville (Int'l)	3B	1	4	0	1	0	0	0	0	0	0	0	0	0-0	.250	.250	.250	.500	0	1.000
2002— Cincinnati (N.L.)	3B-SS	•162	606	83	146	38	2	26	87	56	111	10	9	32-8	.241	.314	.439	.753	22	.956
2003— Cincinnati (N.L.)	3B-2B-SS	106	403	61	110	19	3	18	65	35	74	5	6	15-3	.273	.339	.469	.808	17	.956
— New York (A.L.)	3B	54	189	31	48	13	0	6	31	11	30	3	7	8-0	.254	.302	.418	.720	6	.961
2004— Cleveland (A.L.)		Did not play.																		
American League totals (1 year)		54	189	31	48	13	0	6	31	11	30	3	7	8-0	.254	.302	.418	.720	6	.961
National League totals (7 years)		668	2383	327	646	141	14	86	362	191	428	46	39	83-22	.271	.334	.450	.785	92	.953
Major League totals (7 years)		722	2572	358	694	154	14	92	393	202	458	49	46	91-22	.270	.332	.448	.780	98	.953

DIVISION SERIES RECORD

Year Team (League)	Pos.	G	AB	R	H	2B	3B	HR	RBI	BB	SO	HBP	GDP	SB-CS	Avg.	OBP	SLG	OPS	E	Avg.
2003— New York (A.L.)	3B	4	15	1	3	1	0	0	0	0	3	0	0	1-0	.200	.200	.267	.467	0	1.000

CHAMPIONSHIP SERIES RECORD

Year Team (League)	Pos.	G	AB	R	H	2B	3B	HR	RBI	BB	SO	HBP	GDP	SB-CS	Avg.	OBP	SLG	OPS	E	Avg.
2003— New York (A.L.)	3B	7	17	2	3	0	0	1	2	1	6	1	0	1-1	.176	.263	.353	.616	2	.857

WORLD SERIES RECORD

Year Team (League)	Pos.	G	AB	R	H	2B	3B	HR	RBI	BB	SO	HBP	GDP	SB-CS	Avg.	OBP	SLG	OPS	E	Avg.
2003— New York (A.L.)	3B	6	21	1	3	0	0	1	2	0	6	0	0	0-0	.143	.136	.286	.422	3	.850

ALL-STAR GAME RECORD

	G	AB	R	H	2B	3B	HR	RBI	BB	SO	HBP	GDP	SB-CS	Avg.	OBP	SLG	OPS	E	Avg.
All-Star Game totals (1 year)	1	1	0	0	0	0	0	0	0	0	0	0	0-0	.000	.000	.000	.000	0	...

BOONE, BRET   2B

PERSONAL: Born April 6, 1969, in El Cajon, Calif. ... 5-10/190. ... Bats right, throws right. ... Full name: Bret Robert Boone. ... High school: El Dorado (Yorba Linda, Calif.). ... College: USC. ... Son of Bob Boone, catcher with three major league teams (1972-90) and manager of Kansas City Royals (1995-97) and Cincinnati Reds (2001-03); brother of Aaron Boone, third baseman, Cleveland Indians; grandson of Ray Boone, major league infielder with six teams (1948-60).
TRANSACTIONS/CAREER NOTES: Selected by Minnesota Twins organization in 28th round of 1987 free-agent draft; did not sign. ... Selected by Seattle Mariners organization in fifth round of 1990 free-agent draft. ... Traded by Mariners with P Erik Hanson to Cincinnati Reds for P Bobby Ayala and C Dan Wilson (November 2, 1993). ... On disabled list (April 1-16, 1996). ... Traded by Reds with P Mike Remlinger to Atlanta Braves for Ps Denny Neagle and Rob Bell and OF Michael Tucker (November 10, 1998). ... Traded by Braves with OF/1B Ryan Klesko and P Jason Shiell to San Diego Padres for 2B Quilvio Veras, 1B Wally Joyner and OF Reggie Sanders (December 22, 1999). ... On disabled list (August 27, 2000-remainder of season). ... Signed as a free agent by Mariners (December 22, 2000).
HONORS: Won N.L. Gold Glove at second base (1998). ... Won A.L. Gold Glove at second base (2002-04).
2004 GAMES PLAYED BY POSITION (MLB): 2B—148.

Year Team (League)	Pos.	G	AB	R	H	2B	3B	HR	RBI	BB	SO	HBP	GDP	SB-CS	Avg.	OBP	SLG	OPS	E	Avg.
									BATTING										**FIELDING**	
1990— Peninsula (Caro.)	2B	74	255	42	68	13	2	8	38	47	57	1	1	5-2	.267	.383	.427	.810	19	.951
1991— Jacksonville (Sou.)	2B-3B	139	475	64	121	18	1	19	75	72	123	5	21	9-9	.255	.357	.417	.774	21	.970
1992— Calgary (PCL)	2B-SS	118	439	73	138	26	5	13	73	60	88	5	12	17-12	.314	.398	.485	.883	10	.984
— Seattle (A.L.)	2B-3B	33	129	15	25	4	0	4	15	4	34	1	4	1-1	.194	.224	.318	.542	6	.966
1993— Calgary (PCL)	2B	71	274	48	91	18	3	8	56	28	58	1	7	3-8	.332	.388	.507	.896	8	.976
— Seattle (A.L.)	2B-DH	76	271	31	68	12	2	12	38	17	52	4	6	2-3	.251	.301	.443	.743	3	.991
1994— Cincinnati (N.L.)	2B-3B	108	381	59	122	25	2	12	68	24	74	8	10	3-4	.320	.368	.491	.858	12	.975
1995— Cincinnati (N.L.)	2B	138	513	63	137	34	2	15	68	41	84	6	14	5-1	.267	.326	.429	.755	4	.994
1996— Cincinnati (N.L.)	2B	142	520	56	121	21	3	12	69	31	100	3	9	3-2	.233	.275	.354	.629	6	.991
1997— Cincinnati (N.L.)	2B	139	443	40	99	25	1	7	46	45	101	4	11	5-5	.223	.298	.332	.630	2	.997
— Indianapolis (A.A.)	2B	3	7	1	2	1	0	0	1	2	2	0	0	1-0	.286	.444	.429	.873	0	1.000
1998— Cincinnati (N.L.)	2B	157	583	76	155	38	1	24	95	48	104	4	23	6-4	.266	.324	.458	.782	9	.988
1999— Atlanta (N.L.)	2B	152	608	102	153	38	1	20	63	47	112	5	11	14-9	.252	.310	.416	.726	13	.982
2000— San Diego (N.L.)	2B	127	463	61	116	18	2	19	74	50	97	5	11	8-4	.251	.326	.421	.747	15	.977
2001— Seattle (A.L.)	2B-DH	158	623	118	206	37	3	37	*141	40	110	9	11	5-5	.331	.372	.578	.950	10	.986
2002— Seattle (A.L.)	2B-DH	155	608	88	169	34	3	24	107	53	102	6	11	12-5	.278	.339	.462	.801	7	.989
2003— Seattle (A.L.)	2B	159	622	111	183	35	5	35	117	68	125	7	17	16-3	.294	.366	.535	.902	7	.990
2004— Seattle (A.L.)	2B	148	593	74	149	30	0	24	83	56	135	3	18	10-5	.251	.317	.423	.740	14	.978
American League totals (6 years)		729	2846	437	800	152	13	136	501	238	558	30	67	46-22	.281	.339	.487	.826	47	.985
National League totals (7 years)		963	3511	457	903	199	12	109	483	286	672	35	89	44-29	.257	.316	.414	.730	61	.987
Major League totals (13 years)		1692	6357	894	1703	351	25	245	984	524	1230	65	156	90-51	.268	.327	.447	.773	108	.986

DIVISION SERIES RECORD

Year Team (League)	Pos.	G	AB	R	H	2B	3B	HR	RBI	BB	SO	HBP	GDP	SB-CS	Avg.	OBP	SLG	OPS	E	Avg.
1995— Cincinnati (N.L.)	2B	3	10	4	3	1	0	1	1	1	3	0	0	1-0	.300	.364	.700	1.064	0	1.000
1999— Atlanta (N.L.)	2B	4	19	3	9	1	0	0	1	0	4	0	1	1-0	.474	.474	.526	1.000	0	1.000
2001— Seattle (A.L.)	2B	5	21	1	2	0	0	0	0	1	11	0	1	1-0	.095	.136	.095	.232	1	.960
Division series totals (3 years)		12	50	8	14	2	0	1	2	2	18	0	2	3-0	.280	.308	.380	.688	1	.984

CHAMPIONSHIP SERIES RECORD

Year Team (League)	Pos.	G	AB	R	H	2B	3B	HR	RBI	BB	SO	HBP	GDP	SB-CS	Avg.	OBP	SLG	OPS	E	Avg.
1995— Cincinnati (N.L.)	2B	4	14	1	3	0	0	0	1	1	2	0	2	0-0	.214	.267	.214	.481	0	1.000
1999— Atlanta (N.L.)	2B	6	22	2	4	1	0	0	1	1	7	1	0	2-1	.182	.250	.227	.477	0	1.000
2001— Seattle (A.L.)	2B	5	19	2	6	0	0	2	6	2	2	0	0	0-0	.316	.381	.632	1.013	0	1.000
Champ. series totals (3 years)		15	55	5	13	1	0	2	7	4	11	1	2	2-1	.236	.300	.364	.664	0	1.000

WORLD SERIES RECORD

Year Team (League)	Pos.	G	AB	R	H	2B	3B	HR	RBI	BB	SO	HBP	GDP	SB-CS	Avg.	OBP	SLG	OPS	E	Avg.
1999— Atlanta (N.L.)	2B	4	13	1	7	4	0	0	3	1	3	0	0	0-1	.538	.571	.846	1.418	0	1.000

ALL-STAR GAME RECORD

		G	AB	R	H	2B	3B	HR	RBI	BB	SO	HBP	GDP	SB-CS	Avg.	OBP	SLG	OPS	E	Avg.
All-Star Game totals (2 years)		2	4	0	0	0	0	0	0	0	1	0	0	0-0	.000	.000	.000	.000	0	1.000

BORCHARD, JOE   OF

PERSONAL: Born November 25, 1978, in Panorama City, Calif. ... 6-5/220. ... Bats both, throws right. ... Full name: Joseph Edward Borchard. ... Name pronounced: BORE-churd. ... High school: Camarillo (Calif.). ... College: Stanford.

TRANSACTIONS/CAREER NOTES: Selected by Baltimore Orioles organization in 20th round of 1997 free-agent draft; did not sign. ... Selected by Chicago White Sox organization in first round (12th pick overall) of 2000 free-agent draft.

2004 GAMES PLAYED BY POSITION (MLB): OF—56, DH—4.

Year Team (League)	Pos.	G	AB	R	H	2B	3B	HR	RBI	BB	SO	HBP	GDP	SB-CS	Avg.	OBP	SLG	OPS	E	Avg.
									BATTING										**FIELDING**	
2000— Ariz. White Sox (Ariz.)	OF	7	29	3	12	4	0	0	8	4	4	0	0	0-0	.414	.485	.552	1.037	0	1.000
— Win.-Salem (Car.)	OF	14	52	7	15	3	0	2	7	6	9	2	0	0-0	.288	.377	.462	.839	0	1.000
— Birmingham (Sou.)	OF	6	22	3	5	0	1	0	3	3	8	0	1	0-0	.227	.308	.318	.626	1	.875
2001— Birmingham (Sou.)	OF	133	515	95	152	27	1	27	98	67	158	10	13	5-4	.295	.384	.509	.892	12	.965
2002— Win.-Salem (Car.)	OF	2	3	1	0	0	0	0	0	0	6	0	0	0-0	.000	.667	.000	.667	0	1.000
— Charlotte (Int'l)	OF	117	438	62	119	35	2	20	59	49	139	4	11	2-4	.272	.349	.498	.847	3	.990
— Chicago (A.L.)	OF	16	36	5	8	0	0	2	5	1	14	0	0	0-0	.222	.243	.389	.632	0	1.000
2003— Chicago (A.L.)	OF	16	49	5	9	1	0	1	5	5	18	0	0	0-1	.184	.246	.265	.511	0	1.000
— Charlotte (Int'l)	OF	114	435	62	110	20	2	13	53	27	103	8	14	2-4	.253	.307	.398	.705	5	.985
2004— Charlotte (Int'l)	OF-DH	82	301	44	80	21	0	16	48	30	68	2	7	4-3	.266	.333	.495	.828	4	.980
— Chicago (A.L.)	OF-DH	63	201	26	35	4	1	9	20	19	57	1	4	1-0	.174	.249	.338	.587	3	.972
Major League totals (3 years)		95	286	36	52	5	1	12	30	25	89	1	4	1-1	.182	.248	.332	.580	3	.981

BORDERS, PAT   C

PERSONAL: Born May 14, 1963, in Columbus, Ohio. ... 6-2/200. ... Bats right, throws right. ... Full name: Patrick Lance Borders. ... High school: Lake Wales (Fla.).

TRANSACTIONS/CAREER NOTES: Selected by Toronto Blue Jays organization in sixth round of June 1982 free-agent draft. ... On disabled list (July 5-August 19, 1988); included rehabilitation assignment to Syracuse. ... Signed as a free agent by Kansas City Royals (April 10, 1995). ... Traded by Royals to Houston Astros for a player to be named (August 12, 1995); Royals acquired P Rick Huisman to complete deal (August 17, 1995). ... On suspended list (September 8-14, 1995). ... Signed as a free agent by St. Louis Cardinals organization (January 10, 1996). ... Traded by Cardinals to California Angels for P Ben VanRyn (June 15, 1996). ... Traded by Angels to Chicago White Sox for P Robert Ellis (July 27, 1996). ... Signed as a free agent by Cleveland Indians organization (December 13, 1996). ... Released by Indians (August 30, 1999). ... Signed by Blue Jays (August 31, 1999). ... Signed as a free agent by Tampa Bay Devil Rays (January 27, 2000). ... Traded by Devil Rays to Seattle Mariners for cash (August 27, 2001). ... Signed as a free agent by Texas Rangers organization (February 2, 2002). ... Released by Rangers (April 2, 2002). ... Signed by Mariners organization (April 8, 2002). ... Traded by Mariners to Minnesota Twins for OF B.J. Garbe (August 31, 2004). ... Refused minor league assignment and became a free agent (October 15, 2004).

2004 GAMES PLAYED BY POSITION (MLB): C—38.

Year Team (League)	Pos.	G	AB	R	H	2B	3B	HR	RBI	BB	SO	HBP	GDP	SB-CS	Avg.	OBP	SLG	OPS	E	Avg.
									BATTING										**FIELDING**	
1982— Medicine Hat (Pio.)	3B	61	217	30	66	12	2	5	33	24	52	2	...	1-2	.304	.377	.447	.824	25	.826
1983— Florence (S. Atl.)	3B	131	457	62	125	31	4	5	54	46	116	1	...	4-1	.274	.341	.392	.732	41	.881
1984— Florence (S. Atl.)	3B-1B-OF	131	467	69	129	32	5	12	85	56	109	1	6	3-4	.276	.353	.443	.796	25	.967

Year	Team (League)	Pos.	G	AB	R	H	2B	3B	HR	RBI	BB	SO	HBP	GDP	SB-CS	Avg.	OBP	SLG	OPS	E	Avg.
1985—	Kinston (Caro.)	1B	127	460	43	120	16	1	10	60	45	116	1	11	6-5	.261	.327	.365	.692	20	.978
1986—	Florence (S. Atl.)	C-OF	16	40	8	15	7	0	3	9	2	9	0	0	0-0	.375	.405	.775	1.180	0	1.000
	— Knoxville (Southern)	C-1B	12	34	3	12	1	0	2	5	1	6	0	2	0-3	.353	.371	.559	.930	3	.943
	— Kinston (Caro.)	C-1B-OF	49	174	24	57	10	0	6	26	10	42	1	5	0-0	.328	.366	.489	.854	7	.971
1987—	Dunedin (Fla. St.)	1B	3	11	0	4	0	0	0	1	0	3	0	0	0-0	.364	.364	.364	.727	0	1.000
	— Knoxville (Southern)	C	94	349	44	102	14	1	11	51	20	56	2	13	2-5	.292	.332	.433	.764	12	.976
1988—	Toronto (A.L.)	2B-3B-DH-C	56	154	15	42	6	3	5	21	3	24	0	5	0-0	.273	.285	.448	.733	7	.970
	— Syracuse (Int'l)	C	35	120	11	29	8	0	3	14	16	22	0	1	0-0	.242	.326	.383	.709	2	.991
1989—	Toronto (A.L.)	DH-C	94	241	22	62	11	1	3	29	11	45	1	7	2-1	.257	.290	.349	.639	6	.980
1990—	Toronto (A.L.)	DH-C	125	346	36	99	24	2	15	49	18	57	0	17	0-1	.286	.319	.497	.816	4	.993
1991—	Toronto (A.L.)	C	105	291	22	71	17	0	5	36	11	45	1	8	0-0	.244	.271	.354	.625	4	.993
1992—	Toronto (A.L.)	C	138	480	47	116	26	2	13	53	33	75	2	11	1-1	.242	.290	.385	.676	8	.991
1993—	Toronto (A.L.)	C	138	488	38	124	30	0	9	55	20	66	2	18	2-2	.254	.285	.371	.656	* 13	.986
1994—	Toronto (A.L.)	C	85	295	24	73	13	1	3	26	15	50	0	7	1-1	.247	.284	.329	.613	8	.988
1995—	Kansas City (A.L.)	C-DH	52	143	14	33	8	1	4	13	7	22	0	1	0-0	.231	.267	.385	.651	0	1.000
	— Houston (N.L.)	C	11	35	1	4	0	0	0	0	2	7	0	2	0-0	.114	.162	.114	.276	1	.987
1996—	St. Louis (N.L.)	C-1B	26	69	3	22	3	0	0	4	1	14	0	1	0-1	.319	.329	.362	.691	3	.977
	— California (A.L.)	C	19	57	6	13	3	0	2	8	3	11	0	1	0-1	.228	.267	.386	.653	2	.984
	— Chicago (A.L.)	C-DH	31	94	6	26	1	0	3	6	5	18	0	2	0-0	.277	.313	.383	.696	3	.982
1997—	Cleveland (A.L.)	C	55	159	17	47	7	1	4	15	9	27	2	5	0-2	.296	.341	.428	.769	0	1.000
1998—	Cleveland (A.L.)	C-3B	54	160	12	38	6	0	0	6	10	40	2	3	0-2	.238	.289	.275	.564	8	.974
1999—	Buffalo (Int'l)	C-DH	55	198	17	47	7	0	5	23	12	31	3	5	0-1	.237	.290	.348	.638	5	.986
	— Cleveland (A.L.)	C-3B	6	20	2	6	0	1	0	3	0	3	0	0	0-1	.300	.300	.400	.700	2	.943
	— Toronto (A.L.)	DH-C	6	14	1	3	0	0	1	3	1	2	0	0	0-0	.214	.267	.429	.695	0	1.000
2000—	Durham (Int'l)	C-1B	96	348	44	95	16	0	12	55	20	66	1	8	7-2	.273	.311	.422	.733	3	.995
2001—	Durham (Int'l)	C-1B	87	313	26	74	15	1	2	28	16	61	2	14	3-2	.236	.278	.310	.588	4	.989
	— Tacoma (PCL)	C	3	11	2	3	0	0	1	2	1	1	1	0	0-0	.273	.385	.545	.930	0	1.000
	— Seattle (A.L.)	C	5	6	1	3	0	0	0	1	0	1	0	0	0-0	.500	.500	.500	1.000	1	.923
2002—	Tacoma (PCL)	C-3B-1B	92	317	42	84	16	1	12	27	11	47	0	6	3-2	.265	.289	.435	.724	5	.992
	— Seattle (A.L.)	DH-C	4	4	0	2	1	0	0	1	0	1	0	0	0-0	.500	.500	.750	1.250	0	1.000
2003—	Tacoma (PCL)	C-DH-1B	79	293	36	92	27	1	12	51	20	54	4	12	1-2	.314	.363	.536	.898	6	.987
	— Seattle (A.L.)	C-3B-DH	12	14	1	2	1	0	0	1	1	5	0	0	0-0	.143	.200	.214	.414	0	1.000
2004—	Seattle (A.L.)	C	19	53	6	10	2	0	1	5	1	12	0	2	1-1	.189	.204	.283	.487	1	.992
	— Tacoma (PCL)	C	36	137	16	35	5	1	5	13	3	28	3	4	0-1	.255	.287	.416	.703	1	.996
	— Minnesota (A.L.)	C	19	42	3	12	4	0	0	5	0	10	1	0	2-0	.286	.302	.381	.683	3	.968
	American League totals (16 years)		1023	3061	273	782	160	12	68	335	148	514	11	87	9-13	.255	.291	.382	.673	70	.987
	National League totals (2 years)		37	104	4	26	3	0	0	4	3	21	0	3	0-1	.250	.271	.279	.550	4	.980
	Major League totals (16 years)		1060	3165	277	808	163	12	68	339	151	535	11	90	9-14	.255	.290	.379	.669	74	.987

DIVISION SERIES RECORD

Year	Team (League)	Pos.	G	AB	R	H	2B	3B	HR	RBI	BB	SO	HBP	GDP	SB-CS	Avg.	OBP	SLG	OPS	E	Avg.
2004—	Minnesota (A.L.)	C	2	2	0	0	0	0	0	0	0	1	0	0	0-0	.000	.000	.000	.000	0	1.000

CHAMPIONSHIP SERIES RECORD

Year	Team (League)	Pos.	G	AB	R	H	2B	3B	HR	RBI	BB	SO	HBP	GDP	SB-CS	Avg.	OBP	SLG	OPS	E	Avg.
1989—	Toronto (A.L.)	C	1	1	0	1	0	0	0	1	0	0	0	0	0-0	1.000	1.000	1.000	2.000	0	1.000
1991—	Toronto (A.L.)	C	5	19	0	5	1	0	0	2	0	0	0	2	0-0	.263	.263	.316	.579	2	.955
1992—	Toronto (A.L.)	C	6	22	3	7	0	0	1	3	1	1	0	0	0-0	.318	.320	.455	.775	1	.976
1993—	Toronto (A.L.)	C	6	24	1	6	1	0	0	3	0	6	0	0	1-0	.250	.250	.292	.542	0	1.000
	Champ. series totals (4 years)		18	66	4	19	2	0	1	9	1	7	0	2	1-0	.288	.290	.364	.653	3	.977

WORLD SERIES RECORD

Year	Team (League)	Pos.	G	AB	R	H	2B	3B	HR	RBI	BB	SO	HBP	GDP	SB-CS	Avg.	OBP	SLG	OPS	E	Avg.
1992—	Toronto (A.L.)	C	6	20	2	9	3	0	1	3	2	1	0	0	0-0	.450	.500	.750	1.250	1	.981
1993—	Toronto (A.L.)	C	6	23	2	7	0	0	0	1	2	1	0	1	0-0	.304	.360	.304	.664	1	.981
	World series totals (2 years)		12	43	4	16	3	0	1	4	4	2	0	1	0-0	.372	.426	.512	.937	2	.981

BORKOWSKI, DAVE   P

PERSONAL: Born February 7, 1977, in Detroit, Mich. ... 6-1/200. ... Throws right, bats right. ... Full name: David Richard Borkowski. ... Name pronounced: boar-cow-ski. ... High school: Sterling Heights (Mich.).

TRANSACTIONS/CAREER NOTES: Selected by Detroit Tigers organization in 11th round of 1995 free-agent draft. ... On disabled list (July 7, 2001-remainder of season). ... Released by Tigers (November 5, 2001). ... Re-signed by Tigers organization (November 7, 2001). ... Released by Tigers (April 27, 2003). ... Signed by Baltimore Orioles organization (May 2, 2003).

CAREER HITTING: 0-for-3 (.000), 0 R, 0 2B, 0 3B, 0 HR, 1 RBI.

Year	Team (League)	W	L	Pct.	ERA	WHIP	G	GS	CG	ShO	Hld.	Sv.-Opp.	IP	H	R	ER	HR	BB-IBB	SO	Avg.
1995—	GC Tigers (GCL)	3	2	.600	2.96	1.03	10	10	1	0	...	0-...	51.2	45	24	17	2	8-0	36	.227
	— Lakeland (Fla. St.)	1	0	1.000	0.00	0.60	1	1	0	0	...	0-...	5.0	2	0	0	0	1-0	3	.125
1996—	Fayetteville (S. Atl.)	10	10	.500	3.33	1.19	27	27	5	0	...	0-...	178.1	158	85	66	7	54-0	117	.239
1997—	West. Mich. (Mid.)	15	3	.833	3.46	1.06	25	25	4	2	...	0-...	164.0	143	79	63	15	31-0	104	.228
1998—	Jacksonville (Southern) ...	16	7	.696	4.63	1.44	28	28	3	1	...	0-...	178.2	204	99	92	25	54-0	97	.291
1999—	Toledo (International)	6	8	.429	3.50	1.29	19	19	3	0	...	0-...	126.0	119	59	49	16	43-0	94	.251
	— Detroit (A.L.)	2	6	.250	6.10	1.64	17	12	0	0	0	0-0	76.2	86	58	52	10	40-0	50	.283
2000—	Toledo (International)	3	1	.750	4.40	1.23	8	8	0	0	...	0-...	47.0	44	27	23	9	14-0	29	.239
	— Detroit (A.L.)	0	1	.000	21.94	3.38	2	1	0	0	0	0-0	5.1	11	13	13	2	7-1	1	.423
	— GC Tigers (GCL)	0	0		2.25	0.88	3	3	0	0	...	0-...	8.0	7	3	2	0	0-0	6	.219
	— Lakeland (Fla. St.)	0	1	.000	8.59	2.05	2	2	0	0	...	0-...	7.1	11	7	7	1	4-0	5	.355
2001—	Toledo (International)	1	2	.333	3.54	1.11	18	0	0	0	...	1-...	28.0	22	14	11	1	9-1	22	.214
	— Detroit (A.L.)	0	2	.000	6.37	1.52	15	0	0	0	0	0-0	29.2	30	21	21	5	15-3	30	.261
2002—	GC Tigers (GCL)	0	0		8.44	1.69	3	2	0	0	...	0-...	5.1	9	5	5	2	0-0	4	.360
	— Erie (East.)	0	2	.000	7.56	1.68	2	2	0	0	...	0-...	8.1	12	7	7	1	2-0	6	.343
2003—	Erie (East.)	0	1	.000	3.38	1.50	6	0	0	0	...	0-...	8.0	10	4	3	0	2-2	4	.333
	— Bowie (East.)	6	7	.462	3.29	1.20	24	19	2	0	...	0-...	120.1	126	50	44	11	22-1	66	.271
2004—	Ottawa (Int'l)	6	9	.400	4.85	1.46	16	16	0	0	...	0-...	85.1	99	53	46	6	26-0	56	.294
	— Baltimore (A.L.)	3	4	.429	5.14	1.43	17	8	0	0	1	0-1	56.0	65	37	32	6	15-1	45	.289
	Major League totals (4 years)	5	13	.278	6.33	1.60	51	21	0	0	1	0-1	167.2	192	129	118	23	77-5	126	.287

B

BORLAND, TOBY   P

PERSONAL: Born May 29, 1969, in Quitman, La. ... 6-6/214. ... Throws right, bats right. ... Full name: Toby Shawn Borland. ... High school: Quitman (La.).

TRANSACTIONS/CAREER NOTES: Selected by Philadelphia Phillies organization in 27th round of 1987 free-agent draft. ... On disabled list (June 14-July 8, 1995); included rehabilitation assignment to Scranton/Wilkes-Barre. ... Traded by Phillies with P Ricardo Jordan to New York Mets for 1B Rico Brogna (November 27, 1996). ... Traded by Mets to Boston Red Sox for P Rick Trlicek (May 12, 1997). ... Signed as a free agent by Cincinnati Reds organization (November 27, 1997). ... Released by Reds (March 5, 1998). ... Signed by Phillies organization (March 6, 1998). ... Released by Phillies (July 6, 1998). ... Signed by Florida Marlins organization (July 14, 1998). ... Signed as a free agent by Anaheim Angels organization (November 23, 1998). ... Signed as a free agent by Marlins organization (November 20, 2001). ... On disabled list (May 15, 2003-remainder of season).

CAREER HITTING: 1-for-12 (.083), 1 R, 0 2B, 0 3B, 0 HR, 2 RBI.

Year	Team (League)	W	L	Pct.	ERA	WHIP	G	GS	CG	ShO	Hld.	Sv.-Opp.	IP	H	R	ER	HR	BB-IBB	SO	Avg.
1988—	Martinsville (App.)	2	3	.400	4.04	1.45	34	0	0	0	...	12-...	49.0	42	26	22	1	29-1	43	.233
1989—	Spartanburg (SAL)	4	5	.444	2.97	1.46	47	0	0	0	...	9-...	66.2	62	29	22	3	35-1	48	.248
1990—	Clearwater (Fla. St.)	1	2	.333	2.26	1.32	44	0	0	0	...	5-...	59.2	44	21	15	1	35-4	44	.209
—	Reading (East.)	4	1	.800	1.44	1.08	14	0	0	0	...	0-...	25.0	16	6	4	1	11-1	26	.186
1991—	Reading (East.)	8	3	.727	2.70	1.62	59	0	0	0	...	24-...	76.2	68	31	23	2	56-5	72	.232
1992—	Scran./W.B. (I.L.)	0	1	.000	7.24	1.87	27	0	0	0	...	1-...	27.1	25	23	22	2	26-3	25	.253
—	Reading (East.)	2	4	.333	3.43	1.69	32	0	0	0	...	5-...	42.0	39	23	16	2	32-3	45	.244
1993—	Reading (East.)	2	2	.500	2.52	1.08	44	0	0	0	...	13-...	53.2	38	17	15	2	20-1	74	.194
—	Scran./W.B. (I.L.)	2	4	.333	5.76	1.72	26	0	0	0	...	1-...	29.2	31	20	19	4	20-3	26	.279
1994—	Reading (East.)	4	1	.800	1.68	1.06	27	1	0	0	...	4-...	53.2	36	12	10	2	21-7	61	.191
—	Philadelphia (N.L.)	1	0	1.000	2.36	1.31	24	0	0	0	0	1-1	34.1	31	10	9	1	14-3	26	.248
1995—	Philadelphia (N.L.)	1	3	.250	3.77	1.59	50	0	0	0	11	6-9	74.0	81	37	31	3	37-7	59	.277
—	Scran./W.B. (I.L.)	0	0	...	0.00	0.97	8	0	0	0	...	1-...	11.1	5	0	0	0	6-1	15	.128
1996—	Philadelphia (N.L.)	7	3	.700	4.07	1.39	69	0	0	0	10	0-2	90.2	83	51	41	9	43-3	76	.239
1997—	New York (N.L.)	0	1	.000	6.08	1.88	13	0	0	0	1	1-2	13.1	11	9	9	1	14-0	7	.220
—	Boston (A.L.)	0	0	...	13.50	3.90	3	0	0	0	0	0-0	3.1	6	5	5	1	7-0	1	.400
—	Pawtucket (Int'l)	2	0	1.000	3.99	1.58	28	2	0	0	...	2-...	47.1	50	22	21	5	25-3	46	.269
1998—	Reading (East.)	1	3	.250	9.64	2.46	8	0	0	0	...	3-...	9.1	18	12	10	4	5-0	13	.400
—	Scran./W.B. (I.L.)	2	0	.000	5.68	1.34	13	0	0	0	...	5-...	12.2	14	8	8	1	3-0	15	.298
—	Philadelphia (N.L.)	0	0	...	5.00	1.44	6	0	0	0	0	0-0	9.0	8	5	5	1	5-0	9	.242
—	Charlotte (Int'l)	3	0	1.000	2.70	1.47	19	0	0	0	...	1-...	36.2	33	12	11	3	21-1	26	.244
1999—	Edmonton (PCL)	2	1	.667	7.00	2.00	21	0	0	0	...	0-...	27.0	31	24	21	5	23-2	34	.292
2000—	Erie (East.)	1	3	.250	4.50	1.58	9	1	0	0	...	1-...	12.0	12	8	6	0	7-0	12	.250
2001—	Salt Lake (PCL)	7	3	.700	2.30	1.10	45	1	0	0	...	3-...	74.1	53	25	19	2	29-0	92	.198
—	Anaheim (A.L.)	0	1	.000	10.80	2.70	2	0	0	0	0	0-1	3.1	8	5	4	1	1-0	5	.471
2002—	Calgary (PCL)	5	2	.714	2.96	1.21	56	0	0	0	...	14-...	70.0	55	24	23	2	30-3	75	.216
—	Florida (N.L.)	1	0	1.000	5.27	1.39	15	0	0	0	1	0-0	13.2	14	8	8	3	5-0	11	.269
2003—	Albuquerque (PCL)	1	1	.500	3.72	1.20	9	0	0	0	...	3-...	9.2	6	5	4	1	6-0	12	.176
—	Florida (N.L.)	0	0	...	1.86	1.14	7	0	0	0	0	0-0	9.2	3	3	2	0	8-1	4	.097
2004—	Florida (N.L.)	1	1	.500	5.40	1.64	18	0	0	0	3	0-1	18.1	18	11	11	3	12-5	18	.254
—	Albuquerque (PCL)	4	2	.667	2.29	0.92	34	0	0	0	...	11-...	39.1	24	10	10	2	12-2	38	.182
American League totals (2 years)		0	1	.000	12.15	3.30	5	0	0	0	0	0-1	6.2	14	10	9	2	8-0	6	.438
National League totals (8 years)		11	8	.579	3.97	1.47	202	0	0	0	26	8-15	263.0	249	134	116	21	138-19	210	.249
Major League totals (9 years)		11	9	.550	4.17	1.52	207	0	0	0	26	8-16	269.2	263	144	125	23	146-19	211	.254

BOROWSKI, JOE   P

PERSONAL: Born May 4, 1971, in Bayonne, N.J. ... 6-2/225. ... Throws right, bats right. ... Full name: Joseph Thomas Borowski. ... Name pronounced: bor-OW-ski. ... High school: Marist (Bayonne, N.J.). ... College: Rutgers.

TRANSACTIONS/CAREER NOTES: Selected by Chicago White Sox organization in 32nd round of 1989 free-agent draft. ... Traded by White Sox to Baltimore Orioles for IF Pete Rose II (March 21, 1991). ... Traded by Orioles with P Rachaad Stewart to Atlanta Braves for P Kent Mercker (December 17, 1995). ... Claimed on waivers by New York Yankees (September 15, 1997). ... On disabled list (August 24-September 8, 1998). ... Claimed on waivers by Milwaukee Brewers (December 4, 1998). ... Signed as a free agent by Cincinnati Reds organization (November 9, 1999). ... Released by Reds (April 14, 2000). ... Signed by Chicago Cubs organization (December 11, 2000). ... On disabled list (June 5, 2004-remainder of season); included rehabilitation assignment to Iowa.

CAREER HITTING: 2-for-9 (.222), 1 R, 0 2B, 0 3B, 0 HR, 0 RBI.

Year	Team (League)	W	L	Pct.	ERA	WHIP	G	GS	CG	ShO	Hld.	Sv.-Opp.	IP	H	R	ER	HR	BB-IBB	SO	Avg.
1990—	GC White Sox (GCL)	2	8	.200	5.58	1.61	12	11	0	0	...	0-...	61.1	74	47	38	3	25-0	67	.289
1991—	Kane County (Midwest)	7	2	.778	2.56	1.27	49	0	0	0	...	13-...	81.0	60	26	23	2	43-2	76	.207
1992—	Frederick (Caro.)	5	6	.455	3.70	1.51	48	0	0	0	...	10-...	80.1	71	40	33	3	50-3	85	.238
1993—	Frederick (Caro.)	1	1	.500	3.61	1.57	42	2	0	0	...	11-...	62.1	61	30	25	5	37-0	70	.258
—	Bowie (East.)	3	0	1.000	0.00	1.25	9	0	0	0	...	0-...	17.2	11	0	0	0	11-3	17	.180
1994—	Bowie (East.)	3	4	.429	1.91	1.21	49	0	0	0	...	14-...	66.0	52	14	14	3	28-3	73	.213
1995—	Rochester (Int'l)	1	3	.250	4.04	1.40	28	0	0	0	...	6-...	35.2	32	16	16	3	18-2	32	.256
—	Bowie (East.)	2	2	.500	3.92	1.11	16	0	0	0	...	7-...	20.2	16	9	9	2	7-1	32	.211
—	Baltimore (A.L.)	0	0	...	1.23	1.23	6	0	0	0	0	0-0	7.1	5	1	1	0	4-0	3	.192
1996—	Richmond (Int'l)	1	5	.167	3.71	1.35	34	0	0	0	...	7-...	53.1	42	25	22	4	30-1	40	.226
—	Atlanta (N.L.)	2	4	.333	4.85	1.77	22	0	0	0	1	0-0	26.0	33	15	14	4	13-4	15	.324
1997—	Atlanta (N.L.)	2	2	.500	3.75	1.79	20	0	0	0	2	0-0	24.0	27	11	10	2	16-4	6	.287
—	Richmond (Int'l)	1	2	.333	3.58	1.35	21	0	0	0	...	2-...	37.2	32	16	15	3	19-2	34	.234
—	New York (A.L.)	0	1	.000	9.00	3.00	1	0	0	0	0	0-0	2.0	2	2	2	0	4-1	2	.250
1998—	Columbus (Int'l)	3	3	.500	2.93	1.43	45	0	0	0	...	4-...	73.2	66	25	24	6	39-1	67	.243
—	New York (A.L.)	1	0	1.000	6.52	1.55	8	0	0	0	0	0-0	9.2	11	7	7	0	4-0	7	.289
1999—	Louisville (Int'l)	6	2	.750	5.46	1.55	58	0	0	0	...	4-...	89.0	94	59	54	7	44-3	70	.275
2000—	Newark (Atl.)	6	3	.667	5.50	1.62	28	0	0	0	...	0-...	37.2	44	23	23	5	17-...	39	...
—	Monterrey (Mex.)	4	2	.667	3.19	1.16	12	5	0	0	...	1-...	42.1	31	15	15	0	18-...	44	...
2001—	Iowa (PCL)	8	7	.533	2.62	1.03	39	12	1	1	...	1-...	110.0	87	35	32	10	26-3	131	.216
—	Chicago (N.L.)	0	1	.000	32.40	5.40	1	1	0	0	0	0-0	1.2	6	6	6	1	3-0	1	.667
2002—	Chicago (N.L.)	4	4	.500	2.73	1.18	73	0	0	0	12	2-6	95.2	84	31	29	10	29-6	97	.239
2003—	Chicago (N.L.)	2	2	.500	2.63	1.05	68	0	0	0	1	33-37	68.1	53	23	20	8	19-1	66	.207
2004—	Chicago (N.L.)	2	4	.333	8.02	1.97	22	0	0	0	0	9-11	21.1	27	19	19	3	15-2	11	.303
—	Iowa (PCL)	0	3	.000	8.22	1.70	7	3	0	0	...	0-...	7.2	9	8	7	1	4-0	2	.290
American League totals (3 years)		1	1	.500	4.74	1.58	15	0	0	0	0	0-0	19.0	18	10	10	0	12-1	12	.250
National League totals (6 years)		12	17	.414	3.72	1.37	206	1	0	0	16	44-54	237.0	230	105	98	25	95-17	202	.255
Major League totals (8 years)		13	18	.419	3.80	1.39	221	1	0	0	16	44-54	256.0	248	115	108	25	107-18	214	.255

DIVISION SERIES RECORD

Year — Team (League)	W	L	Pct.	ERA	WHIP	G	GS	CG	ShO	Hld.	Sv.-Opp.	IP	H	R	ER	HR	BB-IBB	SO	Avg.
2003— Chicago (N.L.)	0	0		0.00	0.50	2	0	0	0	0	1-1	2.0	1	0	0	0	0-0	5	.143

CHAMPIONSHIP SERIES RECORD

Year — Team (League)	W	L	Pct.	ERA	WHIP	G	GS	CG	ShO	Hld.	Sv.-Opp.	IP	H	R	ER	HR	BB-IBB	SO	Avg.
2003— Chicago (N.L.)	1	0	1.000	1.59	1.41	3	0	0	0	0	0-1	5.2	5	2	1	0	3-1	1	.227

BOTTALICO, RICKY   P

PERSONAL: Born August 26, 1969, in New Britain, Conn. ... 6-0/215. ... Throws right, bats left. ... Full name: Richard Paul Bottalico. ... Name pronounced: bo-TAL-e-koh. ... High school: South Catholic (Hartford, Conn.). ... College: Central Connecticut State.

TRANSACTIONS/CAREER NOTES: Signed as a non-drafted free agent by Philadelphia Phillies organization (July 21, 1991). ... On disabled list (April 24-July 1, 1998); included rehabilitation assignment to Scranton/Wilkes-Barre. ... On suspended list (August 25-28, 1998). ... Traded by Phillies with P Garrett Stephenson to St. Louis Cardinals for OF Ron Gant and Ps Jeff Brantley and Cliff Politte (November 19, 1998). ... Signed as a free agent by Kansas City Royals (January 27, 2000). ... Signed as a free agent by Phillies (December 15, 2000). ... On disabled list (June 29-July 20, 2001); included rehabilitation assignment to Reading. ... On disabled list (June 23, 2002-remainder of season). ... Signed as a free agent by Arizona Diamondbacks organization (January 30, 2003). ... Refused minor league assignment and became a free agent (September 30, 2003). ... Signed as a free agent by New York Mets organization (February 9, 2004). ... Released by Mets (April 3, 2004). ... Re-signed by Mets organization (April 18, 2004).

CAREER HITTING: 2-for-17 (.118), 1 R, 2 2B, 0 3B, 0 HR, 1 RBI.

Year — Team (League)	W	L	Pct.	ERA	WHIP	G	GS	CG	ShO	Hld.	Sv.-Opp.	IP	H	R	ER	HR	BB-IBB	SO	Avg.
1991— Martinsville (App.)	3	2	.600	4.09	1.36	7	6	2	1		0-...	33.0	32	20	15	2	13-0	38	.248
— Spartanburg (SAL)	2	0	1.000	0.00	0.40	2	2	0	0		0-...	15.0	4	0	0	0	2-0	11	.082
1992— Spartanburg (SAL)	5	10	.333	2.41	1.25	42	11	1	0		13-...	119.2	94	41	32	6	56-0	118	.216
1993— Clearwater (Fla. St.)	1	0	1.000	2.75	1.22	13	0	0	0		4-...	19.2	19	6	6	0	5-0	19	.257
— Reading (East.)	3	3	.500	2.25	1.24	49	0	0	0		20-...	72.0	63	22	18	4	26-3	65	.236
1994— Scran./W.B. (I.L.)	3	1	.750	8.87	2.42	19	0	0	0		3-...	22.1	32	27	22	4	22-2	22	.327
— Reading (East.)	2	2	.500	2.53	0.91	38	0	0	0		22-...	42.2	29	13	12	6	10-0	51	.190
— Philadelphia (N.L.)	0	0		0.00	1.33	3	0	0	0		0-...	3.0	3	0	0	0	1-0	3	.250
1995— Philadelphia (N.L.)	5	3	.625	2.46	1.05	62	0	0	0	20	1-5	87.2	50	25	24	7	42-3	87	.167
1996— Philadelphia (N.L.)	4	5	.444	3.19	1.03	61	0	0	0		34-38	67.2	47	24	24	6	23-2	74	.197
1997— Philadelphia (N.L.)	2	5	.286	3.65	1.49	69	0	0	0		34-41	74.0	68	31	30	7	42-4	89	.245
1998— Philadelphia (N.L.)	1	5	.167	6.44	1.82	39	0	0	0	3	6-7	43.1	54	31	31	7	25-5	27	.305
— Scran./W.B. (I.L.)	1	0	1.000	2.92	1.38	10	5	0	0		1-...	12.1	8	4	4	1	9-0	4	.190
1999— St. Louis (N.L.)	3	7	.300	4.91	1.80	68	0	0	0	8	20-28	73.1	83	45	40	8	49-1	66	.284
2000— Kansas City (A.L.)	9	6	.600	4.83	1.46	62	0	0	0	1	16-23	72.2	65	40	39	12	41-3	56	.239
2001— Philadelphia (N.L.)	3	4	.429	3.90	1.24	66	0	0	0	22	3-7	67.0	58	31	29	11	25-2	57	.241
— Reading (East.)	0	1	.000	1.80	0.80	3	3	0	0		0-...	5.0	3	2	1	1	1-0	5	.167
2002— Philadelphia (N.L.)	0	3	.000	4.61	1.68	30	0	0	0	15	0-1	27.1	33	16	14	3	13-2	24	.300
2003— Arizona (N.L.)	1	0	1.000	5.40	3.00	2	0	0	0	1	0-0	1.2	3	1	1	0	2-1	2	.375
— Tucson (PCL)	2	2	.500	3.66	1.40	31	0	0	0		0-...	39.1	39	24	16	4	16-1	28	.258
2004— Norfolk (Int'l)	0	0		0.00	1.50	5	0	0	0		0-...	7.1	7	1	0	0	4-0	8	.233
— New York (N.L.)	3	2	.600	3.38	1.27	60	0	0	0	12	0-4	69.1	54	30	26	3	34-7	61	.215
American League totals (1 year)	9	6	.600	4.83	1.46	62	0	0	0	1	16-23	72.2	65	40	39	12	41-3	56	.239
National League totals (10 years)	22	34	.393	3.83	1.38	460	0	0	0	81	98-131	514.1	453	234	219	52	256-27	490	.238
Major League totals (11 years)	31	40	.437	3.96	1.39	522	0	0	0	82	114-154	587.0	518	274	258	64	297-30	546	.238

ALL-STAR GAME RECORD

	W	L	Pct.	ERA	WHIP	G	GS	CG	ShO	Hld.	Sv.-Opp.	IP	H	R	ER	HR	BB-IBB	SO	Avg.
All-Star Game totals (1 year)	0	0		0.00	0.00	1	0	0	0	0	0-0	1.0	0	0	0	0	0-0	1	.000

BOWEN, ROB   C

PERSONAL: Born February 24, 1981, in Bedford, Texas. ... 6-3/216. ... Bats both, throws right. ... Full name: Robert McClure Bowen. ... High school: Homestead (Fort Wayne, Ind.).

TRANSACTIONS/CAREER NOTES: Selected by Minnesota Twins organization in second round of 1999 free-agent draft.

2004 GAMES PLAYED BY POSITION (MLB): C—15, DH—1.

Year — Team (League)	Pos.	G	AB	R	H	2B	3B	HR	RBI	BB	SO	HBP	GDP	SB-CS	Avg.	OBP	SLG	OPS	E	Avg.
1999— GC Twins (GCL)	C	29	77	10	20	4	0	0	11	20	15	0	0	2-2	.260	.400	.312	.712	8	.959
2000— Elizabethton (App.)	C	21	73	17	21	3	0	4	19	11	18	0	0	0-0	.288	.381	.874	3		.983
2001— Quad City (Midw.)	C	106	385	47	98	18	2	18	70	37	112	2	11	4-0	.255	.321	.452	.773	6	.993
2002— Fort Myers (FSL)	C-1B	100	342	52	63	12	1	10	49	38	69	5	12	1-0	.184	.272	.313	.585	12	.981
— Quad City (Midw.)	C	5	21	1	4	1	0	0	2	2	4	0	0	0-0	.190	.261	.238	.499	0	1.000
2003— New Britain (East.)	C	42	134	17	41	13	0	1	16	13	24	2	0	0-0	.306	.376	.425	.801	2	.992
— Rochester (Int'l)	C-DH	30	105	14	27	7	0	6	17	11	25	1	3	0-0	.257	.333	.495	.829	1	.995
— Minnesota (A.L.)		7	10	1	1	0	0	0	1	0	4	0	1	0-0	.100	.091	.100	.191	1	.944
2004— Minnesota (A.L.)	C-DH	17	27	1	3	0	0	1	2	4	10	0	1	0-0	.111	.226	.222	.448	1	.985
— New Britain (East.)	C-DH	77	249	28	49	10	0	9	24	31	76	3	3	3-0	.197	.292	.345	.638	8	.985
Major League totals (2 years)		24	37	1	4	0	0	1	3	4	14	0	2	0-0	.108	.190	.189	.380	2	.976

BOYD, JASON   P

PERSONAL: Born February 23, 1973, in St. Clair, Ill. ... 6-3/175. ... Throws right, bats right. ... Full name: Jason Pernell Boyd. ... High school: Edwardsville (Ill.). ... Junior college: John A. Logan (Ill.).

TRANSACTIONS/CAREER NOTES: Selected by Philadelphia Phillies organization in eighth round of 1994 free-agent draft. ... Selected by Arizona Diamondbacks in first round (23rd pick overall) of expansion draft (November 18, 1997). ... On disabled list (May 22, 1998-remainder of season). ... Traded by Diamondbacks to Pittsburgh Pirates (August 25, 1999), completing deal in which Pirates traded 2B Tony Womack to Diamondbacks for OF Paul Weichard and a player to named (February 26, 1999). ... Claimed on waivers by Milwaukee Brewers (March 29, 2000). ... Claimed on waivers by Philadelphia Phillies (March 31, 2000). ... On disabled list (March 25-May 4 and June 15-August 15, 2000); included rehabilitation assignments to Clearwater and Scranton/Wilkes-Barre. ... Signed as a free agent by San Diego Padres organization (December 6, 2001). ... Released by Padres (August 4, 2002). ... Signed by Boston Red Sox organization (August 16, 2002). ... Signed as a free agent by Cleveland Indians organization (November 21, 2002). ... On suspended list (June 27-30, 2003). ... On disabled list (August 16-September 1, 2003). ... Claimed on waivers by Pirates (October 1, 2003).

CAREER HITTING: 0-for-1 (.000), 0 R, 0 2B, 0 3B, 0 HR, 0 RBI.

Year — Team (League)	W	L	Pct.	ERA	WHIP	G	GS	CG	ShO	Hld.	Sv.-Opp.	IP	H	R	ER	HR	BB-IBB	SO	Avg.
1994— Martinsville (App.)	3	7	.300	4.17	1.41	14	13	1	0		0-...	69.0	65	46	32	6	32-0	45	.242
1995— Piedmont (S. Atl.)	6	8	.429	3.58	1.29	26	24	1	0		0-...	151.0	151	77	60	8	44-0	129	.259

Year	Team (League)	W	L	Pct.	ERA	WHIP	G	GS	CG	ShO	Hld.	Sv.-Opp.	IP	H	R	ER	HR	BB-IBB	SO	Avg.
1996— Clearwater (Fla. St.)	11	8	.579	3.90	1.29	26	26	2	0	...	0-...	161.2	160	75	70	12	49-1	120	.261
1997— Reading (East.)	10	6	.625	4.82	1.53	48	7	0	0	...	0-...	115.2	113	65	62	16	64-7	98	.259
1998— Tucson (PCL)	2	2	.500	6.23	1.94	15	0	0	0	...	0-...	21.2	28	22	15	4	14-1	13	.298
1999— Tucson (PCL)	6	5	.545	4.52	1.36	44	0	0	0	...	5-...	75.2	76	42	38	6	27-2	60	.263
— Nashville (PCL)	0	0	...	0.00	0.43	5	0	0	0	...	0-...	4.2	2	0	0	0	0-0	2	.143
— Pittsburgh (N.L.)	0	0	...	3.38	1.31	4	0	0	0	0	0-0	5.1	5	2	2	0	2-0	4	.250
2000— Clearwater (Fla. St.)	1	0	1.000	2.38	1.32	6	3	0	0	...	0-...	11.1	11	4	3	0	4-0	12	.250
— Scran./W.B. (I.L.)	1	0	1.000	1.72	1.40	11	2	0	0	...	0-...	15.2	8	3	3	0	14-0	10	.157
— Philadelphia (N.L.)	0	1	.000	6.55	1.83	30	0	0	0	2	0-1	34.1	39	28	25	2	24-4	32	.293
2001— Scran./W.B. (I.L.)	2	7	.222	1.97	1.11	52	0	0	0	...	12-...	59.1	44	17	13	4	22-1	66	.205
2002— Portland (PCL)	0	1	.000	1.04	1.00	19	0	0	0	...	4-...	26.0	19	4	3	2	7-0	22	.216
— San Diego (N.L.)	1	0	1.000	7.94	1.69	23	0	0	0	4	0-3	28.1	33	29	25	6	15-1	18	.300
— Pawtucket (Int'l)	1	0	1.000	3.94	1.38	9	0	0	0	...	1-...	16.0	13	7	7	3	9-0	15	.213
2003— Buffalo (Int'l)	1	0	1.000	1.23	1.00	9	0	0	0	...	3-...	14.2	12	3	2	0	2-0	14	.222
— Cleveland (A.L.)	3	1	.750	4.30	1.22	44	0	0	0	8	0-1	52.1	38	25	25	4	26-1	31	.200
2004— Pittsburgh (N.L.)	1	0	1.000	5.54	1.62	12	0	0	0	0	0-0	13.0	13	9	8	4	8-1	12	.260
— Nashville (PCL)	1	3	.250	3.86	1.59	11	0	0	0	...	0-...	16.1	23	7	7	2	3-1	11	.333
American League totals (1 year)	3	1	.750	4.30	1.22	44	0	0	0	8	0-1	52.1	38	25	25	4	26-1	31	.200
National League totals (4 years)	2	1	.667	6.67	1.72	69	0	0	0	6	0-4	81.0	90	68	60	12	49-6	66	.288
Major League totals (5 years)	5	2	.714	5.74	1.52	113	0	0	0	14	0-5	133.1	128	93	85	16	75-7	97	.254

BRADFORD, CHAD   P

PERSONAL: Born September 14, 1974, in Jackson, Miss. ... 6-5/203. ... Throws right, bats right. ... Full name: Chadwick Lee Bradford. ... High school: Byram (Jackson, Miss.). ... College: Southern Mississippi.

TRANSACTIONS/CAREER NOTES: Selected by Chicago White Sox organization in 34th round of 1994 free-agent draft; did not sign. ... Selected by White Sox organization in 13th round of 1996 free-agent draft. ... Traded by White Sox to Oakland Athletics for a player to be named (December 7, 2000); White Sox acquired C Miguel Olivo to complete deal (December 13, 2000). ... On disabled list (August 8-23, 2004); included rehabilitation assignment to Sacramento.

CAREER HITTING: 0-for-0 (.000), 0 R, 0 2B, 0 3B, 0 HR, 0 RBI.

Year	Team (League)	W	L	Pct.	ERA	WHIP	G	GS	CG	ShO	Hld.	Sv.-Opp.	IP	H	R	ER	HR	BB-IBB	SO	Avg.
1996— Hickory (S. Atl.)	0	2	.000	0.90	0.93	28	0	0	0	...	18-...	30.0	21	7	3	1	7-1	27	.194
1997— Winston-Salem (Caro.)	3	7	.300	3.95	1.39	46	0	0	0	...	15-...	54.2	51	30	24	2	25-5	43	.239
1998— Birmingham (Southern) ...	1	1	.500	2.60	1.21	10	0	0	0	...	1-...	17.1	13	6	5	2	8-0	14	.203
— Calgary (PCL)	4	1	.800	1.94	1.20	29	0	0	0	...	0-...	51.0	50	12	11	3	11-2	27	.260
— Chicago (A.L.)	2	1	.667	3.23	1.11	29	0	0	0	9	1-3	30.2	27	16	11	0	7-0	11	.229
1999— Charlotte (Int'l)	9	3	.750	1.94	1.05	47	0	0	0	...	5-...	74.1	63	19	16	2	15-0	56	.231
— Chicago (A.L.)	0	0	...	19.64	3.82	3	0	0	0	0	0-0	3.2	9	8	8	1	5-0	0	.474
2000— Charlotte (Int'l)	2	4	.333	1.51	0.93	55	0	0	0	...	10-...	53.2	38	18	9	2	12-1	42	.200
— Chicago (A.L.)	1	0	1.000	1.98	1.02	12	0	0	0	2	0-0	13.2	13	4	3	0	1-1	9	.255
2001— Sacramento (PCL)	0	0	...	0.38	0.72	12	0	0	0	...	2-...	23.2	15	2	1	0	2-0	24	.181
— Oakland (A.L.)	2	1	.667	2.70	1.28	35	0	0	0	4	1-4	36.2	41	12	11	6	6-0	34	.281
2002— Oakland (A.L.)	4	2	.667	3.11	1.15	75	0	0	0	24	2-5	75.1	73	29	26	2	14-5	56	.253
2003— Oakland (A.L.)	7	4	.636	3.04	1.26	72	0	0	0	23	2-5	77.0	67	28	26	7	30-9	62	.236
2004— Sacramento (PCL)	0	0	...	0.00	0.50	2	0	0	0	...	0-...	2.0	1	0	0	0	0-0	3	.143
— Oakland (A.L.)	5	7	.417	4.42	1.27	68	0	0	0	14	1-4	59.0	51	32	29	5	24-9	34	.234
Major League totals (7 years)	21	15	.583	3.47	1.24	294	0	0	0	76	7-21	296.0	281	129	114	21	87-24	206	.250

DIVISION SERIES RECORD

Year	Team (League)	W	L	Pct.	ERA	WHIP	G	GS	CG	ShO	Hld.	Sv.-Opp.	IP	H	R	ER	HR	BB-IBB	SO	Avg.
2000— Chicago (A.L.)	0	0	...	0.00	3.00	1	0	0	0	0	0-1	.2	2	0	0	0	0-0	0	.667
2001— Oakland (A.L.)	0	0	...	0.00	0.00	1	0	0	0	0	0-0	1.0	0	0	0	0	0-0	1	.000
2002— Oakland (A.L.)	0	0	...	0.00	0.33	2	0	0	0	0	0-0	3.0	1	0	0	0	0-0	1	.111
2003— Oakland (A.L.)	0	0	...	0.00	1.64	4	0	0	0	0	0-0	3.2	4	0	0	0	2-2	5	.286
Division series totals (4 years)	0	0	...	0.00	1.08	8	0	0	0	0	0-1	8.1	7	0	0	0	2-2	7	.241

BRADLEY, MILTON   OF

PERSONAL: Born April 15, 1978, in Harbor City, Calif. ... 6-0/205. ... Bats both, throws right. ... Full name: Milton Obelle Bradley. ... High school: Polytechnic (Long Beach, Calif.).
TRANSACTIONS/CAREER NOTES: Selected by Montreal Expos organization in second round of 1996 free-agent draft. ... Traded by Expos to Cleveland Indians for P Zach Day (July 31, 2001). ... On disabled list (May 2-June 4 and August 14-30, 2002); included rehabilitation assignments to Buffalo and Akron. ... On disabled list (April 23-May 8 and August 15, 2003-remainder of season). ... Traded by Indians to Los Angeles Dodgers for OF Franklin Gutierrez and a player to be named (April 3, 2004); Indians received P Andrew Brown to complete deal (May 19, 2004). ... On suspended list (September 29, 2004-remainder of season).
2004 GAMES PLAYED BY POSITION (MLB): OF—138.

Year	Team (League)	Pos.	G	AB	R	H	2B	3B	HR	RBI	BB	SO	HBP	GDP	SB-CS	Avg.	OBP	SLG	OPS	E	Avg.
1996— GC Expos (GCL)	OF	32	112	18	27	7	1	1	12	13	15	1	2	7-7	.241	.320	.348	.669	3	.949
1997— Vermont (N.Y.-Penn.)	OF	50	200	29	60	7	5	3	30	17	34	0	6	7-7	.300	.352	.430	.782	4	.967
— GC Expos (GCL)	OF	9	25	6	5	2	0	1	2	4	4	1	0	2-2	.200	.333	.400	.733	1	.938
1998— Cape Fear (S. Atl.)	OF	75	281	54	85	21	4	6	50	23	57	4	7	13-8	.302	.360	.470	.830	3	.968
— Jupiter (FSL)	OF	67	261	55	75	14	1	5	34	30	42	5	3	17-9	.287	.369	.406	.775	1	.993
1999— Harrisburg (East.)	OF	87	346	62	114	22	5	12	50	33	61	4	5	14-10	.329	.391	.526	.917	5	.971
2000— Ottawa (Int'l)	OF	88	342	58	104	20	1	6	29	45	56	1	5	10-15	.304	.385	.421	.806	3	.987
— Montreal (N.L.)	OF	42	154	20	34	8	1	2	15	14	32	1	3	2-1	.221	.288	.325	.613	2	.979
2001— Montreal (N.L.)	OF	67	220	19	49	16	3	1	19	19	62	1	6	7-4	.223	.288	.336	.624	2	.988
— Ottawa (Int'l)	OF	35	136	21	37	7	2	2	13	23	30	2	...	14-1	.272	.383	.397	.780	3	.966
— Buffalo (Int'l)	OF	30	114	18	29	3	0	5	15	19	31	0	...	9-2	.254	.361	.412	.773	0	1.000
— Cleveland (A.L.)	OF-DH	10	18	3	4	1	0	0	1	1	1	0	1	1-1	.222	.300	.278	.578	1	.929
2002— Cleveland (A.L.)	OF-DH	98	325	48	81	18	3	9	38	32	58	0	12	6-3	.249	.317	.406	.723	4	.982
— Buffalo (Int'l)	OF	6	23	3	6	0	0	0	3	3	5	0	0	2-1	.261	.321	.261	.582	0	1.000
— Akron (East.)	OF	3	11	1	3	1	0	0	1	1	1	0	0	0-1	.273	.333	.364	.697	0	1.000
2003— Cleveland (A.L.)	OF-DH	101	377	61	121	34	2	10	56	64	73	5	10	17-7	.321	.421	.501	.923	2	.992
2004— Los Angeles (N.L.)	OF	141	516	72	138	24	0	19	67	71	123	6	12	15-11	.267	.362	.424	.786	8	.977
American League totals (3 years)		209	720	112	206	53	5	19	94	98	134	5	23	24-11	.286	.373	.453	.826	7	.986
National League totals (3 years)		250	890	111	221	48	4	22	101	104	217	8	21	24-16	.248	.332	.385	.717	12	.980
Major League totals (5 years)		459	1610	223	427	101	9	41	195	202	351	13	44	48-27	.265	.350	.416	.766	19	.983

DIVISION SERIES RECORD

Year	Team (League)	Pos.	G	AB	R	H	2B	3B	HR	RBI	BB	SO	HBP	GDP	SB-CS	Avg.	OBP	SLG	OPS	E	Avg.
2004—Los Angeles (N.L.)		OF	4	11	1	3	1	0	1	1	5	2	0	1	2-0	.273	.500	.636	1.136	0	1.000

BRAGG, DARREN — OF

PERSONAL: Born September 7, 1969, in Waterbury, Conn. ... 5-9/180. ... Bats left, throws right. ... Full name: Darren William Bragg. ... High school: Taft (Watertown, Conn.). ... College: Georgia Tech.

TRANSACTIONS/CAREER NOTES: Selected by Seattle Mariners organization in 22nd round of 1991 free-agent draft. ... Traded by Mariners to Boston Red Sox for P Jamie Moyer (July 30, 1996). ... Signed as a free agent by St. Louis Cardinals (January 12, 1999). ... On disabled list (August 3, 1999-remainder of season). ... Released by Cardinals (December 16, 1999). ... Signed by Colorado Rockies (February 1, 2000). ... Released by Rockies (July 24, 2000). ... Signed by New York Mets organization (January 9, 2001). ... Claimed on waivers by New York Yankees (June 12, 2001). ... Signed as a free agent by Mets organization (January 15, 2002). ... Released by Mets (April 1, 2002). ... Signed by Atlanta Braves organization (April 2, 2002). ... Signed as a free agent by Yankees organization (January 28, 2004). ... Released by Yankees (July 2, 2004). ... Signed by San Diego Padres (July 4, 2004). ... Refused minor league assignment and became a free agent (July 20, 2004). ... Signed by Cincinnati Reds organization (July 30, 2004).

2004 GAMES PLAYED BY POSITION (MLB): OF—26.

									BATTING											FIELDING	
Year	Team (League)	Pos.	G	AB	R	H	2B	3B	HR	RBI	BB	SO	HBP	GDP	SB-CS	Avg.	OBP	SLG	OPS	E	Avg.
1991—Peninsula (Caro.)		2B-OF	69	237	42	53	14	0	3	29	66	72	2	8	21-9	.224	.395	.321	.716	4	.978
1992—Peninsula (Caro.)		OF	135	428	83	117	29	5	9	58	105	76	5	8	44-19	.273	.418	.428	.846	4	.986
1993—Jacksonville (Sou.)		P	131	451	74	119	26	3	11	46	81	82	7	12	19-11	.264	.382	.408	.790	10	.970
1994—Calgary (PCL)		OF	126	500	112	175	33	6	17	85	68	72	6	11	28-12	.350	.430	.542	.972	7	.980
—Seattle (A.L.)		DH-OF	8	19	4	3	1	0	0	2	2	5	0	0	0-0	.158	.238	.211	.449	0	1.000
1995—Seattle (A.L.)		OF-DH	52	145	20	34	5	1	3	12	18	37	4	2	9-0	.234	.331	.345	.676	1	.989
—Tacoma (PCL)		OF-DH	53	212	24	65	13	3	4	31	23	39	0	3	10-3	.307	.373	.453	.826	4	.968
1996—Seattle (A.L.)		OF	69	195	36	53	12	1	7	25	33	35	2	2	8-5	.272	.376	.451	.827	1	.992
—Tacoma (PCL)		OF	20	71	17	20	8	0	3	8	14	14	2	1	1-0	.282	.414	.521	.935	0	1.000
—Boston (A.L.)		OF	58	222	38	56	14	1	3	22	36	39	2	3	6-4	.252	.357	.365	.722	2	.986
1997—Boston (A.L.)		OF-3B	153	513	65	132	35	2	9	57	61	102	3	16	10-6	.257	.337	.386	.723	5	.987
1998—Boston (A.L.)		OF-DH	129	409	51	114	29	3	8	57	42	99	6	16	5-3	.279	.351	.423	.774	1	.996
1999—St. Louis (N.L.)		OF	93	273	38	71	12	1	6	26	44	67	3	5	3-0	.260	.369	.377	.746	3	.982
2000—Colorado (N.L.)		OF	71	149	16	33	7	1	3	21	17	41	0	3	4-1	.221	.296	.342	.638	0	1.000
2001—Norfolk (Int'l)		OF	32	99	22	33	4	0	4	7	23	22	2	...	5-2	.333	.468	.495	.963	0	1.000
—New York (N.L.)		OF	18	57	4	15	6	0	0	5	4	23	1	0	3-2	.263	.323	.368	.691	0	1.000
—New York (A.L.)		OF	5	4	1	1	1	0	0	0	1	0	0	0	0-0	.250	.250	.500	.750	0	1.000
—Columbus (Int'l)		OF	53	199	30	58	11	2	7	21	27	51	1	0	3-2	.291	.379	.472	.851	0	1.000
2002—Richmond (Int'l)		OF	22	75	15	22	5	0	1	8	20	15	0	0	4-2	.293	.442	.400	.842	0	1.000
—Atlanta (N.L.)		OF-DH	109	212	34	57	15	2	3	15	24	52	2	4	5-2	.269	.347	.401	.748	3	.971
2003—Atlanta (N.L.)		OF	104	162	21	39	5	1	0	9	13	38	2	1	2-1	.241	.305	.284	.589	1	.988
2004—Columbus (Int'l)		OF-DH	70	273	41	77	21	3	6	37	29	45	0	6	7-2	.282	.367	.469	.835	1	.991
—San Diego (N.L.)			9	7	2	1	0	0	0	0	2	2	0	0	0-0	.143	.333	.143	.476	0	...
—Louisville (Int'l)		OF	13	46	4	11	1	0	2	4	5	13	0	2	1-0	.239	.314	.391	.705	0	1.000
—Cincinnati (N.L.)		OF	38	94	11	18	3	1	4	9	8	29	0	2	1-0	.191	.255	.372	.627	1	.984
American League totals (6 years)			474	1507	215	393	97	8	30	175	192	318	17	39	38-18	.261	.347	.395	.743	10	.990
National League totals (6 years)			442	954	126	234	48	6	16	85	112	252	8	15	18-6	.245	.328	.358	.687	8	.984
Major League totals (11 years)			916	2461	341	627	145	14	46	260	304	570	25	54	56-24	.255	.340	.381	.721	18	.988

DIVISION SERIES RECORD

Year	Team (League)	Pos.	G	AB	R	H	2B	3B	HR	RBI	BB	SO	HBP	GDP	SB-CS	Avg.	OBP	SLG	OPS	E	Avg.
1998—Boston (A.L.)		OF	3	12	0	1	0	0	0	0	0	5	0	1	0-0	.083	.083	.083	.167	0	1.000
2002—Atlanta (N.L.)		OF	4	3	0	0	0	0	0	0	0	0	0	1	0-0	.000	.000	.000	.000	0	...
2003—Atlanta (N.L.)		OF	2	5	0	0	0	0	0	1	0	1	0	0	0-0	.000	.000	.000	.000	0	1.000
Division series totals (3 years)			9	20	0	1	0	0	0	1	0	6	0	2	0-0	.050	.050	.050	.100	0	1.000

BRANYAN, RUSSELL — 3B/1B

PERSONAL: Born December 19, 1975, in Warner Robins, Ga. ... 6-3/195. ... Bats left, throws right. ... Full name: Russell Oles Branyan. ... Name pronounced: BRAN-yen. ... High school: Stratford Academy (Warner Robins, Ga.).

TRANSACTIONS/CAREER NOTES: Selected by Cleveland Indians organization in seventh round of 1994 free-agent draft. ... Traded by Indians to Cincinnati Reds for OF Ben Broussard (June 7, 2002). ... On disabled list (March 18-May 29 and August 13-28, 2003); included rehabilitation assignments to Louisville. ... Signed as a free agent by Atlanta Braves organization (January 21, 2004). ... Traded by Braves to Indians for P Scott Sturkie (April 25, 2004). ... Traded by Indians to Milwaukee Brewers for future considerations (July 25, 2004).

2004 GAMES PLAYED BY POSITION (MLB): 3B—44, 1B—2.

									BATTING											FIELDING	
Year	Team (League)	Pos.	G	AB	R	H	2B	3B	HR	RBI	BB	SO	HBP	GDP	SB-CS	Avg.	OBP	SLG	OPS	E	Avg.
1994—Burlington (Appal.)		3B	55	171	21	36	10	0	5	13	25	64	4	3	4-2	.211	.323	.357	.680	21	.851
1995—Columbus (S. Atl.)		3B	76	277	46	71	8	6	19	55	27	120	3	6	1-1	.256	.326	.534	.860	26	.856
1996—Columbus (S. Atl.)		3B-DH	130	482	102	129	20	4	40	106	62	166	5	4	7-4	.268	.355	.575	.930	44	.885
1997—Kinston (Caro.)		3B-DH	83	297	59	86	26	2	27	75	52	94	5	9	3-1	.290	.398	.663	1.062	21	.897
—Akron (East.)		3B-DH	41	137	26	32	4	0	12	30	28	56	2	1	0-0	.234	.369	.526	.895	11	.921
1998—Akron (East.)		3B-DH	43	163	35	48	11	3	16	46	35	58	0	2	1-1	.294	.417	.693	1.110	7	.932
—Cleveland (A.L.)		3B	1	4	0	0	0	0	0	0	0	2	0	0	0-0	.000	.000	.000	.000	0	1.000
1999—Buffalo (Int'l)		3B	109	395	51	82	11	1	30	67	52	187	4	5	8-3	.208	.305	.468	.773	23	.921
—Cleveland (A.L.)		3B-DH	11	38	4	8	2	0	1	6	3	19	1	0	0-0	.211	.286	.342	.628	1	.960
2000—Buffalo (Int'l)		3B-OF	64	229	46	56	9	2	21	60	28	93	2	2	1-1	.245	.330	.576	.906	9	.942
—Cleveland (A.L.) OF-DH-3B			67	193	32	46	7	2	16	38	22	76	4	2	0-0	.238	.327	.544	.871	3	.954
2001—Cleveland (A.L.) 3B-OF-DH			113	315	48	73	16	2	20	54	38	132	3	2	1-1	.232	.316	.486	.802	14	.931
2002—Cleveland (A.L.) OF-3B-DH			50	161	16	33	4	0	8	17	17	65	0	3	1-2	.205	.278	.379	.657	2	.976
—Cincinnati (N.L.)		OF-1-3-DH	84	217	34	53	9	1	16	39	34	86	2	2	3-1	.244	.349	.516	.865	6	.977
2003—Louisville (Int'l) DH-3-OF-1			14	49	5	16	5	0	1	3	9	15	1	0	0-0	.327	.441	.490	.930	1	.968
—Cincinnati (N.L.) 3-OF-1-DH			74	176	22	38	12	0	9	26	27	69	1	1	0-0	.216	.322	.438	.759	3	.985
2004—Richmond (Int'l)		OF	11	28	5	5	0	0	1	4	13	11	1	0	1-0	.179	.452	.286	.738	0	1.000
—Buffalo (Int'l) 1-3-OF-DH			82	313	58	90	16	2	25	75	42	102	5	5	5-2	.288	.374	.591	.965	6	.964
—Milwaukee (N.L.)		3B-1B	51	158	21	37	11	1	11	27	20	68	2	1	1-0	.234	.324	.525	.849	5	.964
American League totals (5 years)			242	711	100	160	29	4	45	115	80	294	8	7	2-3	.225	.307	.467	.774	20	.947
National League totals (3 years)			209	551	77	128	32	2	36	92	81	223	5	4	4-1	.232	.333	.494	.827	14	.977
Major League totals (7 years)			451	1262	177	288	61	6	81	207	161	517	13	11	6-4	.228	.319	.479	.797	34	.965

Year	Team (League)	Pos.	G	AB	R	H	2B	3B	HR	RBI	BB	SO	HBP	GDP	SB-CS	Avg.	OBP	SLG	OPS	E	Avg.
2001—Cleveland (A.L.)		OF	2	3	1	1	0	0	0	0	0	1	0	0	0-0	.333	.333	.333	.667	0	...

BRAZELL, CRAIG — 1B

PERSONAL: Born May 10, 1980, in Montgomery, Ala. ... 6-3/211. ... Bats left, throws right. ... Full name: Craig Walter Brazell. ... High school: Jefferson Davis (Montgomery, Ala.).

TRANSACTIONS/CAREER NOTES: Selected by New York Mets organization in fifth round of 1998 free-agent draft.

2004 GAMES PLAYED BY POSITION (MLB): 1B—7.

Year	Team (League)	Pos.	G	AB	R	H	2B	3B	HR	RBI	BB	SO	HBP	GDP	SB-CS	Avg.	OBP	SLG	OPS	E	Avg.
1998—GC Mets (GCL)	1B-C	13	47	6	14	3	1	1	6	2	13	1	0	0-0	.298	.340	.468	.808	1	.983
1999—Kingsport (Appalachian)	1B	59	221	27	85	16	1	6	39	7	34	8	5	6-5	.385	.422	.548	.969	4	.986
2000—Capital City (SAL)		112	406	35	98	28	0	8	57	15	82	9	6	3-3	.241	.279	.369	.648	18	.973
2001—Capital City (SAL)		83	331	51	102	25	5	19	72	15	74	5	3	0-3	.308	.343	.586	.929	6	.989
2002—St. Lucie (Fla. St.)	1B	100	402	38	107	25	3	16	82	13	78	6	7	2-1	.266	.292	.463	.755	13	.987
—Binghamton (East.)	1B	35	130	14	40	8	0	6	19	1	28	6	2	0-2	.308	.343	.508	.851	7	.972
2003—Binghamton (East.)	1B	111	432	58	126	23	2	17	76	23	97	6	4	2-1	.292	.331	.472	.803	11	.989
—Norfolk (Int'l)	1B	12	46	4	12	3	0	0	1	1	8	1	0	1-0	.261	.292	.326	.618	0	1.000
2004—Norfolk (Int'l) 1B-OF-DH		121	475	66	126	22	2	23	67	21	99	3	5	1-2	.265	.300	.465	.761	9	.989
—New York (N.L.)	1B	24	34	3	9	2	0	1	3	1	7	0	1	0-0	.265	.286	.412	.697	1	.974
Major League totals (1 year)		24	34	3	9	2	0	1	3	1	7	0	1	0-0	.265	.286	.412	.697	1	.974

BRAZELTON, DEWON — P

PERSONAL: Born June 16, 1980, in Tullahoma, Tenn. ... 6-4/214. ... Throws right, bats right. ... Full name: Dewon Cortez Brazelton. ... Name pronounced: de-wan bra-zel-ton. ... College: Middle Tennessee State.

TRANSACTIONS/CAREER NOTES: Selected by Tampa Bay Devil Rays organization in first round (third pick overall) of 2001 free-agent draft.

CAREER HITTING: 0-for-2 (.000), 0 R, 0 2B, 0 3B, 0 HR, 0 RBI.

Year	Team (League)	W	L	Pct.	ERA	WHIP	G	GS	CG	ShO	Hld.	Sv.-Opp.	IP	H	R	ER	HR	BB-IBB	SO	Avg.
2002—Orlando (Sou.)	5	9	.357	3.33	1.34	26	26	1	0	...	0-...	146.0	129	69	54	7	67-1	109	.241
—Durham (Int'l)	1	0	1.000	0.00	1.20	1	1	0	0	...	0-...	5.0	5	0	0	0	1-0	6	.263
—Tampa Bay (A.L.)	0	1	.000	4.85	1.38	2	2	0	0	0	0-...	13.0	12	7	7	3	6-0	5	.279
2003—Durham (Int'l)	2	2	.500	4.21	1.30	5	5	0	0	...	0-...	25.2	23	14	12	1	11-0	18	.235
—Tampa Bay (A.L.)	1	6	.143	6.89	1.66	10	10	0	0	0	0-...	48.1	57	49	37	9	23-1	24	.292
—Bakersfield (California)	1	5	.167	5.26	1.60	9	9	0	0	...	0-...	49.2	62	33	29	4	19-0	42	.298
—Orlando (Sou.)	2	0	1.000	2.53	1.50	2	2	0	0	...	0-...	10.2	8	6	3	0	8-0	5	.200
2004—Durham (Int'l)	4	4	.500	4.71	1.53	10	10	0	0	...	0-...	49.2	61	35	26	0	15-0	38	.299
—Tampa Bay (A.L.)	6	8	.429	4.77	1.44	22	21	0	0	0	0-0	120.2	121	71	64	12	53-2	64	.260
Major League totals (3 years)	7	15	.318	5.34	1.49	34	33	0	0	0	0-0	182.0	190	127	108	24	82-3	93	.270

BRAZOBAN, YHENCY — P

PERSONAL: Born June 11, 1980, in Santo Domingo, Dominican Republic. ... 6-1/170. ... Throws right, bats right. ... Full name: Yhency Jose Brazoban.

TRANSACTIONS/CAREER NOTES: Signed as a non-drafted free agent by New York Yankees organization (July 10, 1997). ... Played five seasons as an outfielder in Yankees organization (1998-2002). ... Traded by Yankees with Ps Jeff Weaver and Brandon Wheedon and cash to Los Angeles Dodgers for P Kevin Brown (December 13, 2003).

CAREER HITTING: 0-for-1 (.000), 0 R, 0 2B, 0 3B, 0 HR, 0 RBI.

Year	Team (League)	W	L	Pct.	ERA	WHIP	G	GS	CG	ShO	Hld.	Sv.-Opp.	IP	H	R	ER	HR	BB-IBB	SO	Avg.
2002—GC Yankees (GCL)	0	0	...	4.50	1.17	6	0	0	0	...	0-...	6.0	3	3	3	0	4-0	11	.136
2003—Trenton (East.)	2	2	.500	7.81	1.70	20	0	0	0	...	3-...	27.2	33	25	24	5	14-1	19	.314
—GC Yankees (GCL)	0	0	...	6.00	2.00	3	0	0	0	...	0-...	3.0	5	3	2	0	1-1	5	.385
—Tampa (FSL)	0	2	.000	2.83	1.36	24	0	0	0	...	15-...	28.2	27	13	9	0	12-2	34	.245
2004—Jacksonville (Southern)	4	4	.500	2.65	1.18	37	0	0	0	...	13-...	51.0	38	18	15	4	22-1	61	.210
—Las Vegas (PCL)	2	0	1.000	2.19	1.22	10	0	0	0	...	1-...	12.1	14	3	3	1	1-0	17	.286
—Los Angeles (N.L.)	6	2	.750	2.48	1.22	31	0	0	0	5	0-0	32.2	25	9	9	2	15-2	27	.219
Major League totals (1 year)	6	2	.750	2.48	1.22	31	0	0	0	5	0-0	32.2	25	9	9	2	15-2	27	.219

Year	Team (League)	W	L	Pct.	ERA	WHIP	G	GS	CG	ShO	Hld.	Sv.-Opp.	IP	H	R	ER	HR	BB-IBB	SO	Avg.
2004—Los Angeles (N.L.)	0	0	...	3.00	1.00	2	0	0	0	0	0-0	3.0	1	1	1	0	2-0	2	.100

BRITO, JUAN — C

PERSONAL: Born November 7, 1977, in Santiago Rodriguez, Dominican Republic. ... 5-11/205. ... Bats right, throws right. ... Full name: Juan Ramon Brito. ... High school: Liceo JuanPablo Duarte (Dominican Republic).

TRANSACTIONS/CAREER NOTES: Signed as a non-drafted free agent by Kansas City Royals organization (November 13, 1996). ... Signed as a free agent by Arizona Diamondbacks organization (January 21, 2004). ... Refused minor league assignment and became a free agent (October 13, 2004).

2004 GAMES PLAYED BY POSITION (MLB): C—54.

Year	Team (League)	Pos.	G	AB	R	H	2B	3B	HR	RBI	BB	SO	HBP	GDP	SB-CS	Avg.	OBP	SLG	OPS	E	Avg.
1997—GC Royals (GCL)	C	25	70	14	22	4	0	3	15	5	5	1	1	0-0	.314	.368	.500	.868	3	.980
1998—Lansing (Midw.)	C	63	212	16	52	7	0	0	22	17	41	2	6	2-2	.245	.305	.278	.583	6	.989
1999—Wilmington (Caro.)	C	14	46	3	13	1	0	0	1	1	11	0	1	0-0	.283	.298	.304	.602	2	.984
—Char., W.Va. (SAL)	C-1B	61	208	14	50	6	0	0	19	11	37	1	8	1-2	.240	.282	.269	.551	5	.991
—Omaha (PCL)	C	2	7	1	2	2	0	0	0	0	2	0	0	0-0	.286	.286	.571	.857	0	1.000
—Wichita (Texas)	C	4	11	0	1	0	0	0	0	2	3	0	2	0-0	.091	.231	.091	.322	0	1.000
2000—Wichita (Texas)	C	34	105	9	27	2	0	0	10	11	15	1	4	2-1	.257	.328	.276	.604	2	.990
—Wilmington (Caro.)	C	22	54	4	12	4	0	0	9	8	7	0	2	1-0	.222	.317	.296	.614	4	.972
—Omaha (PCL)	C	17	49	8	14	1	0	1	2	3	10	0	1	1-1	.286	.327	.367	.694	0	1.000
2001—Wichita (Texas)	C-OF	70	236	22	63	10	0	4	28	17	29	0	9	3-3	.267	.315	.360	.675	2	.996
2002—Omaha (PCL)	C	3	9	1	2	0	0	1	1	0	1	0	0	0-0	.222	.300	.333	.633	0	1.000
—Wichita (Texas)	C	89	302	40	77	11	0	7	38	21	46	1	9	1-1	.255	.303	.361	.664	5	.992

B

– 57 –

Year	Team (League)	Pos.	G	AB	R	H	2B	3B	HR	RBI	BB	SO	HBP	GDP	SB-CS	Avg.	OBP	SLG	OPS	E	Avg.
— Kansas City (A.L.)		C	9	23	1	7	2	0	0	1	0	3	0	2	0-0	.304	.304	.391	.696	1	.978
2003— Omaha (PCL)		C	36	122	14	29	2	0	2	12	3	25	1	4	0-2	.238	.262	.303	.565	0	1.000
2004— Tucson (PCL)		C	34	102	22	32	5	2	3	16	6	25	1	3	1-0	.314	.358	.490	.848	1	.995
— Arizona (N.L.)		C	54	171	17	35	7	0	3	12	9	41	1	6	1-0	.205	.246	.298	.544	4	.990
American League totals (1 year)			9	23	1	7	2	0	0	1	0	3	0	2	0-0	.304	.304	.391	.696	1	.978
National League totals (1 year)			54	171	17	35	7	0	3	12	9	41	1	6	1-0	.205	.246	.298	.544	4	.990
Major League totals (2 years)			63	194	18	42	9	0	3	13	9	44	1	8	1-0	.216	.252	.309	.562	5	.989

BROCAIL, DOUG — P

PERSONAL: Born May 16, 1967, in Clearfield, Pa. ... 6-5/235. ... Throws right, bats left. ... Full name: Douglas Keith Brocail. ... Name pronounced: broh-KALE. ... High school: Lamar (Colo.). ... Junior college: Lamar (Colo.) Community College.

TRANSACTIONS/CAREER NOTES: Selected by San Diego Padres organization in first round (12th pick overall) of January 1986 free-agent draft. ... On disabled list (April 2-June 28, 1994); included rehabilitation assignments to Wichita and Las Vegas. ... Traded by Padres with OFs Phil Plantier and Derek Bell, P Pedro Martinez and IF Craig Shipley and SS Ricky Gutierrez to Houston Astros for 3B Ken Caminiti, OF Steve Finley, SS Andujar Cedeno, 1B Roberto Petagine, P Brian Williams and a player to be named (December 28, 1994); Padres acquired P Sean Fesh to complete deal (May 1, 1995). ... On disabled list (May 11-August 15, 1996); included rehabilitation assignments to Jackson and Tucson. ... Traded by Astros with OF Brian L. Hunter, IF Orlando Miller, P Todd Jones and cash to Detroit Tigers for C Brad Ausmus, Ps Jose Lima, C.J. Nitkowski and Trever Miller and 1B Daryle Ward (December 10, 1996). ... On suspended list (June 10-13, 1998). ... On disabled list (August 9-24, 1998). ... On suspended list (April 28-May 1, 2000). ... On disabled list (August 14-September 1 and September 29, 2000-remainder of season). ... Traded by Tigers with C Brad Ausmus and P Nelson Cruz to Astros for C Mitch Meluskey, P Chris Holt and OF Roger Cedeno (December 11, 2000). ... On disabled list (March 31, 2001-entire season); included rehabilitation assignments to New Orleans and Round Rock. ... On disabled list (March 22, 2002-entire season). ... Signed as a free agent by Texas Rangers organization (February 18, 2004). ... On disabled list (May 9-June 7 and July 25-August 9, 2004); included rehabilitation assignments to Oklahoma and Frisco. ... On suspended list (September 26-October 2, 2004).

CAREER HITTING: 11-for-67 (.164), 9 R, 0 2B, 1 3B, 0 HR, 1 RBI.

Year	Team (League)	W	L	Pct.	ERA	WHIP	G	GS	CG	ShO	Hld.	Sv.-Opp.	IP	H	R	ER	HR	BB-IBB	SO	Avg.
1986— Spokane (N'west)	5	4	.556	3.81	1.62	16	15	0	0	...	0-...	85.0	85	52	36	4	53-1	77	...
1987— Char., S.C. (SAL)	2	6	.250	4.09	1.32	19	18	0	0	...	0-...	92.1	94	51	42	6	28-0	68	.263
1988— Char., S.C. (SAL)	8	6	.571	2.69	1.23	22	13	5	0	...	2-...	107.0	107	40	32	3	25-0	107	.257
1989— Wichita (Texas)	5	9	.357	5.21	1.54	23	22	1	1	...	0-...	134.2	158	88	78	11	50-4	95	.292
1990— Wichita (Texas)	2	2	.500	4.33	1.48	12	9	0	0	...	0-...	52.0	53	30	25	7	24-0	27	.265
1991— Wichita (Texas)	10	7	.588	3.87	1.30	34	16	3	3	...	6-...	146.1	147	77	63	15	43-3	108	.259
1992— Las Vegas (PCL)	10	10	.500	3.97	1.45	29	25	4	0	...	0-...	172.1	187	82	76	7	63-5	103	.285
— San Diego (N.L.)	0	0	...	6.43	1.57	3	3	0	0	0	0-0	14.0	17	10	10	2	5-0	15	.298
1993— Las Vegas (PCL)	1	2	.667	3.68	1.27	10	8	0	0	...	1-...	51.1	51	26	21	4	14-0	32	.254
— San Diego (N.L.)	4	13	.235	4.56	1.44	24	24	0	0	0	0-0	128.1	143	75	65	16	42-4	70	.283
1994— Wichita (Texas)	0	0	...	0.00	1.00	2	0	0	0	...	0-...	4.0	3	1	0	0	1-0	2	.200
— Las Vegas (PCL)	0	0	...	7.11	1.82	7	3	0	0	...	0-...	12.2	21	12	10	1	2-0	8	.375
— San Diego (N.L.)	0	0	...	5.82	1.53	12	0	0	0	...	0-1	17.0	21	13	11	1	5-3	11	.304
1995— Houston (N.L.)	6	4	.600	4.19	1.41	36	7	0	0	1	1-1	77.1	87	40	36	10	22-2	39	.280
— Tucson (PCL)	1	0	1.000	3.86	1.35	3	3	0	0	...	0-...	16.1	18	9	7	1	4-0	16	.269
1996— Houston (N.L.)	1	5	.167	4.58	1.53	23	4	0	0	1	0-0	53.0	58	31	27	7	23-1	34	.289
— Jackson (Texas)	0	0	...	0.00	0.50	2	2	0	0	...	0-...	4.0	1	0	0	0	1-0	5	.077
— Tucson (PCL)	0	1	.000	7.36	1.77	5	1	0	0	...	0-...	7.1	12	6	6	1	1-0	4	.375
1997— Detroit (A.L.)	3	4	.429	3.23	1.41	61	0	0	0	16	2-9	78.0	74	31	28	10	36-4	60	.256
1998— Detroit (A.L.)	5	2	.714	2.73	1.04	60	0	0	0	11	0-1	62.2	47	23	19	2	18-3	55	.211
1999— Detroit (A.L.)	4	4	.500	2.52	1.04	70	0	0	0	23	2-4	82.0	60	23	23	7	25-1	78	.206
2000— Detroit (A.L.)	5	4	.556	4.09	1.40	49	0	0	0	19	0-5	50.2	57	25	23	5	14-2	41	.285
2001— New Orleans (PCL)	0	0	...	0.00	1.29	2	0	0	0	...	0-...	2.1	2	0	0	0	1-0	2	.222
— Round Rock (Texas)	0	0	...	0.00	0.00	1	1	0	0	...	0-...	1.0	0	0	0	0	0-0	1	.000
2002— Houston (N.L.)			Did not play.																
2004— Oklahoma (PCL)	2	0	1.000	4.19	1.14	12	0	0	0	1	0-...	19.1	20	9	9	1	2-0	19	.263
— Frisco (Texas)	0	0	...	2.08	0.46	1	1	0	0	...	0-...	4.1	2	1	1	1	0-0	6	.143
— Texas (A.L.)	4	1	.800	4.13	1.41	43	0	0	0	4	1-1	52.1	54	29	24	2	20-1	43	.269
American League totals (5 years)	21	15	.583	3.23	1.24	283	4	0	0	73	5-20	325.2	292	131	117	26	113-11	277	.243
National League totals (5 years)	11	22	.333	4.63	1.48	98	38	0	0	1	1-2	289.2	326	169	149	36	97-10	169	.285
Major League totals (10 years)	32	37	.464	3.89	1.35	381	42	0	0	74	6-22	615.1	618	300	266	62	210-21	446	.263

BROOKS, FRANK — P

PERSONAL: Born September 6, 1978, in Brooklyn, N.Y. ... 6-1/200. ... Throws left, bats left. ... Full name: Frank J. Brooks. ... High school: Sheepshead Bay (Brooklyn, N.Y.). ... College: St. Peter's.

TRANSACTIONS/CAREER NOTES: Selected by Philadelphia Phillies organization in 13th round of 1999 free-agent draft. ... Traded by Phillies to Pittsburgh Pirates for P Mike Williams and cash (July 20, 2003). ... Selected by New York Mets from Pirates organization in Rule 5 major league draft (December 15, 2003). ... Traded by Mets to Oakland Athletics for a player to be named (December 15, 2003). ... Claimed on waivers by Boston Red Sox (March 18, 2004). ... Returned to Pirates organization (March 31, 2004).

CAREER HITTING: 0-for-1 (.000), 0 R, 0 2B, 0 3B, 0 HR, 0 RBI.

Year	Team (League)	W	L	Pct.	ERA	WHIP	G	GS	CG	ShO	Hld.	Sv.-Opp.	IP	H	R	ER	HR	BB-IBB	SO	Avg.
1999— Batavia (N.Y.-Penn)	7	3	.700	2.91	1.25	16	12	1	1	...	0-...	77.1	64	26	25	2	33-0	58	.232
2000— Piedmont (S. Atl.)	14	8	.636	3.44	1.19	29	27	3	2	...	0-...	177.2	152	78	68	17	60-0	138	.236
2001— Clearwater (Fla. St.)	5	10	.333	4.71	1.52	37	15	0	0	...	1-...	112.2	113	70	59	18	58-2	92	.262
2002— Clearwater (Fla. St.)	3	5	.375	3.46	1.56	35	0	0	0	...	7-...	39.0	34	18	15	2	27-3	33	.233
— Reading (East.)	1	1	.500	3.10	1.41	17	1	0	0	...	2-...	29.0	29	11	10	1	12-0	23	.266
2003— Reading (East.)	3	4	.429	2.30	0.90	34	0	0	0	...	9-...	58.2	40	16	15	5	13-1	71	.194
— Altoona (East.)	0	0	...	7.71	1.29	1	0	0	0	...	0-...	2.1	3	2	2	1	0-0	4	.300
— Nashville (PCL)	2	0	1.000	2.54	1.16	16	0	0	0	...	0-...	28.1	22	9	8	2	11-2	22	.218
2004— Nashville (PCL)	6	3	.667	4.10	1.24	42	8	0	0	...	2-...	83.1	81	42	38	13	22-0	55	.255
— Pittsburgh (N.L.)	0	1	.000	4.67	1.27	11	1	0	0	0	0-0	17.1	13	10	9	5	9-2	18	.203
Major League totals (1 year)	0	1	.000	4.67	1.27	11	1	0	0	0	0-0	17.1	13	10	9	5	9-2	18	.203

BROUSSARD, BEN — 1B/OF

PERSONAL: Born September 24, 1976, in Beaumont, Texas. ... 6-2/220. ... Bats left, throws left. ... Full name: Benjamin Isaac Broussard. ... Name pronounced: brew-SARD. ... College: McNeese State.

TRANSACTIONS/CAREER NOTES: Selected by Cincinnati Reds organization in second round of 1999 free-agent draft. ... Traded by Reds to Cleveland Indians for 3B Russell Branyan (June 7, 2002). ... On disabled list (March 21-April 6, 2003); included rehabilitation assignment to Buffalo.

2004 GAMES PLAYED BY POSITION (MLB): 1B—133.

Year	Team (League)	Pos.	G	AB	R	H	2B	3B	HR	RBI	BB	SO	HBP	GDP	SB-CS	Avg.	OBP	SLG	OPS	E	Avg.
1999—Billings (Pio.)	1B-OF	38	145	39	59	11	2	14	48	34	30	4	0	1-0	.407	.527	.800	1.327	5	.963
—Clinton (Midw.)	1B-OF	5	20	8	11	4	1	2	6	3	4	0	0	0-0	.550	.609	1.150	1.759	2	.926
—Chattanooga (Sou.)	1B-OF	35	127	26	27	5	0	8	21	11	41	3	0	1-0	.213	.291	.441	.732	2	.987
2000—Chattanooga (Sou.)	1B-OF	87	286	64	73	8	4	14	51	72	78	6	6	15-2	.255	.413	.458	.871	10	.958
2001—Mudville California (Calif.)	1B	30	102	14	25	5	0	5	21	16	31	4	2	0-0	.245	.360	.441	.801	2	.992
—Chattanooga (Sou.)	1B-OF	100	353	81	113	27	0	23	69	61	69	8	5	10-3	.320	.428	.592	1.020	8	.990
2002—Louisville (Int'l)	1B	57	187	31	51	14	1	11	30	31	50	9	...	4-1	.273	.396	.535	.930	2	.995
—Buffalo (Int'l)	OF-1B	42	153	30	37	8	0	5	21	24	30	3	...	0-0	.242	.354	.392	.746	3	.975
—Cleveland (A.L.)	OF-1B-DH	39	112	10	27	4	0	4	9	7	25	1	3	0-0	.241	.292	.384	.676	2	.974
2003—Buffalo (Int'l)	1B-DH	32	120	17	30	2	1	3	15	9	29	1	1	3-0	.250	.303	.358	.661	2	.990
—Cleveland (A.L.)	1B	116	386	53	96	21	3	16	55	32	75	5	6	5-2	.249	.312	.443	.755	9	.991
2004—Cleveland (A.L.)	1B	139	418	57	115	28	5	17	82	52	95	12	7	4-2	.275	.370	.488	.858	6	.994
Major League totals (3 years)		294	916	120	238	53	8	37	146	91	195	18	16	9-4	.260	.337	.456	.793	17	.992

BROWER, JIM — P

PERSONAL: Born December 29, 1972, in Edina, Minn. ... 6-3/215. ... Throws right, bats right. ... Full name: James Robert Brower. ... Name pronounced: BROW-er. ... High school: Minnetonka (Minn.). ... College: Minnesota.

TRANSACTIONS/CAREER NOTES: Selected by Texas Rangers organization in sixth round of 1994 free-agent draft (June 2, 1994). ... Released by Rangers (April 15, 1998). ... Signed by Cleveland Indians organization (April 18, 1998). ... Traded by Indians with P Robert Pugmire to Cincinnati Reds for C Eddie Taubensee (November 16, 2000). ... Traded by Reds to Montreal Expos for P Bruce Chen (June 14, 2002). ... Traded by Expos with a player to be named to San Francisco Giants for P Livan Hernandez, 3B/C Edwards Guzman and cash (March 24, 2003); Giants acquired P Matt Blank to complete deal (April 30, 2003).

CAREER HITTING: 12-for-57 (.211), 9 R, 1 2B, 0 3B, 0 HR, 4 RBI.

Year	Team (League)	W	L	Pct.	ERA	WHIP	G	GS	CG	ShO	Hld.	Sv.-Opp.	IP	H	R	ER	HR	BB-IBB	SO	Avg.
1994—Hudson Valley (NY-Penn.)	2	1	.667	3.20	1.02	4	4	1	0	...	0-...	19.2	14	10	7	0	6-0	15	.189
—Char., S.C. (SAL)	7	3	.700	1.72	0.99	12	12	3	2	...	0-...	78.2	52	18	15	2	26-1	84	.186
1995—Charlotte (Fla. St.)	7	10	.412	3.89	1.34	27	27	2	1	...	0-...	173.2	170	93	75	16	62-1	110	.256
1996—Charlotte (Fla. St.)	9	8	.529	3.79	1.30	23	21	2	0	...	0-...	145.0	148	67	61	11	40-0	86	.267
—Tulsa (Texas)	3	2	.600	3.78	1.35	5	5	1	1	...	0-...	33.1	35	16	14	4	10-0	16	.273
1997—Tulsa (Texas)	5	12	.294	5.21	1.41	23	23	1	0	...	0-...	140.0	156	99	81	13	42-1	103	.286
—Oklahoma City (A.A.)	2	1	.667	7.23	2.04	4	3	0	0	...	0-...	18.2	30	17	15	3	8-0	7	.370
1998—Akron (East.)	13	5	.722	3.01	1.16	23	23	0	0	...	0-...	155.2	142	60	52	9	38-0	91	.246
1999—Buffalo (Int'l)	11	11	.500	4.73	1.39	27	27	0	0	...	0-0	160.0	164	101	84	23	59-6	76	.270
—Cleveland (A.L.)	3	1	.750	4.56	1.44	9	2	0	0	0	0-0	25.2	27	13	13	8	10-1	18	.270
2000—Buffalo (Int'l)	9	4	.692	3.11	1.21	16	15	1	0	...	0-...	101.1	99	41	35	7	24-1	68	.253
—Cleveland (A.L.)	2	3	.400	6.24	1.79	17	11	0	0	0	0-0	62.0	80	45	43	11	31-1	32	.309
2001—Louisville (Int'l)	1	0	1.000	4.09	1.27	2	2	0	0	...	0-...	11.0	12	5	5	1	2-0	11	.273
—Cincinnati (N.L.)	7	10	.412	3.97	1.38	46	10	0	0	2	1-2	129.1	119	65	57	17	60-5	94	.247
2002—Cincinnati (N.L.)	2	0	1.000	3.89	1.22	22	0	0	0	0	0-...	39.1	38	18	17	2	10-1	24	.260
—Montreal (N.L.)	1	2	.333	4.83	1.49	30	0	0	0	6	0-1	41.0	39	22	22	5	22-1	33	.245
2003—San Francisco (N.L.)	8	5	.615	3.96	1.29	51	5	0	0	2	2-3	100.0	90	48	44	8	39-2	65	.249
2004—San Francisco (N.L.)	7	7	.500	3.29	1.35	*89	0	0	0	24	1-5	93.0	90	42	34	6	36-2	63	.259
American League totals (2 years)	5	4	.556	5.75	1.69	26	13	0	0	0	0-0	87.2	107	58	56	19	41-2	50	.298
National League totals (4 years)	25	24	.510	3.89	1.35	238	15	0	0	34	4-11	402.2	376	195	174	38	167-11	279	.251
Major League totals (6 years)	30	28	.517	4.22	1.41	264	28	0	0	34	4-11	490.1	483	253	230	57	208-13	329	.260

DIVISION SERIES RECORD

Year	Team (League)	W	L	Pct.	ERA	WHIP	G	GS	CG	ShO	Hld.	Sv.-Opp.	IP	H	R	ER	HR	BB-IBB	SO	Avg.
2003—San Francisco (N.L.)	0	0	...	6.00	2.67	2	0	0	0	0	0-0	3.0	5	3	2	0	3-1	3	.357

BROWN, ADRIAN — OF

PERSONAL: Born February 7, 1974, in McComb, Miss. ... 6-0/200. ... Bats both, throws right. ... Full name: Adrian Demond Brown. ... High school: McComb (Miss.).

TRANSACTIONS/CAREER NOTES: Selected by Pittsburgh Pirates organization in 48th round of 1992 free-agent draft. ... Loaned by Pirates organization to Lethbridge of Pioneer League (June 11-September 19, 1993). ... On disabled list (June 13-July 4 and July 6-August 7, 2000); included rehabilitation assignments to Altoona and Nashville. ... On disabled list (April 17, 2001-remainder of season); included rehabilitation assignments to Altoona, Lynchburg and Williamsport. ... Released by Pirates (October 10, 2002). ... Signed by Tampa Bay Devil Rays organization (November 6, 2002). ... Selected by Boston Red Sox from Devil Rays organization in Rule 5 major league draft (December 16, 2002). ... Offered back to Devil Rays (March 26, 2003); Devil Rays declined offer. ... Signed as a free agent by Kansas City Royals organization (January 21, 2004).

2004 GAMES PLAYED BY POSITION (MLB): OF—5.

Year	Team (League)	Pos.	G	AB	R	H	2B	3B	HR	RBI	BB	SO	HBP	GDP	SB-CS	Avg.	OBP	SLG	OPS	E	Avg.
1992—GC Pirates (GCL)	1B-OF	39	121	11	31	2	2	0	12	0	12	2	3	8-4	.256	.268	.306	.574	1	.985
1993—Lethbridge (Pio.)	OF	69	282	47	75	12	9	3	27	17	34	5	8	22-7	.266	.319	.404	.723	1	.992
1994—Augusta (S. Atl.)	OF	79	308	41	80	17	1	1	18	14	38	0	2	19-12	.260	.292	.331	.623	2	.985
1995—Augusta (S. Atl.)	OF	76	287	64	86	15	4	4	31	33	23	1	2	25-14	.300	.372	.422	.793	7	.950
—Lynchburg (Caro.)	OF	54	215	30	52	5	2	1	14	12	20	1	3	11-6	.242	.284	.298	.582	2	.983
1996—Lynchburg (Caro.)	OF	52	215	39	69	9	3	4	25	14	24	2	1	18-9	.321	.368	.447	.814	2	.981
—Carolina (Southern)	OF	84	341	48	101	11	3	3	25	25	40	1	4	27-11	.296	.345	.372	.718	2	.990
1997—Carolina (Southern)	OF	37	145	29	44	4	4	2	15	18	12	2	1	9-5	.303	.388	.428	.815	3	.956
—Pittsburgh (N.L.)	OF	48	147	17	28	6	0	1	10	13	18	4	3	8-4	.190	.273	.252	.524	1	.987
—Calgary (PCL)	OF	62	248	53	79	10	1	1	19	27	38	0	9	20-4	.319	.383	.379	.762	1	.993
1998—Nashville (PCL)	OF	85	311	58	90	12	5	3	27	28	38	0	7	25-7	.289	.346	.389	.735	5	.977
—Pittsburgh (N.L.)	OF	41	152	20	43	4	1	0	5	9	18	0	3	4-0	.283	.323	.322	.645	2	.977
1999—Pittsburgh (N.L.)	OF	116	226	34	61	5	2	4	17	33	39	1	5	5-3	.270	.364	.363	.727	4	.966
—Nashville (PCL)	OF	17	56	10	18	3	1	0	4	11	8	0	0	6-1	.321	.433	.411	.844	5	.969
2000—Pittsburgh (N.L.)	OF	104	308	64	97	18	3	4	28	29	34	0	1	13-1	.315	.373	.432	.805	4	.976
—Altoona (East.)	OF	2	5	1	0	0	0	0	0	3	1	0	0	0-0	.000	.375	.000	.375	0	1.000
—Nashville (PCL)	OF	8	26	3	6	1	0	0	2	2	4	1	0	3-0	.231	.310	.269	.580	0	1.000
2001—Pittsburgh (N.L.)	OF	8	31	3	6	0	0	1	2	3	3	0	1	2-1	.194	.265	.290	.555	0	1.000

Year	Team (League)	Pos.	G	AB	R	H	2B	3B	HR	RBI	BB	SO	HBP	GDP	SB-CS	Avg.	OBP	SLG	OPS	E	Avg.
— Altoona (East.)		DH	7	30	7	10	1	1	0	1	1	7	0	0	1-2	.333	.344	.433	.777	...	...
— Lynchburg (Caro.)		DH	4	18	2	6	0	0	0	1	1	3	1	0	2-0	.333	.400	.333	.733	...	...
— Williamsport (N.Y.-Penn.) .		DH	4	18	4	6	0	1	0	4	1	2	0	0	2-0	.333	.368	.444	.813	...	...
2002— Pittsburgh (N.L.)		OF	91	208	20	45	10	2	1	21	19	34	1	5	10-6	.216	.284	.298	.582	3	.974
— Nashville (PCL)		OF	51	184	36	62	7	1	3	16	23	18	0	3	22-6	.337	.409	.435	.843	2	.975
2003— Pawtucket (Int'l)		OF-DH	122	482	81	136	16	3	5	32	48	81	0	10	34-11	.282	.347	.359	.706	5	.983
— Boston (A.L.)		OF	9	15	2	3	0	0	0	1	1	4	0	0	2-0	.200	.250	.200	.450	0	1.000
2004— Kansas City (A.L.)		OF	5	11	0	3	0	0	0	0	0	2	0	0	0-0	.273	.273	.273	.545	0	1.000
— Omaha (PCL)		OF-DH	114	444	69	118	17	7	7	51	57	74	0	7	28-4	.266	.347	.383	.730	3	.987
American League totals (2 years)			14	26	2	6	0	0	0	1	1	6	0	0	2-0	.231	.259	.231	.490	0	1.000
National League totals (6 years)			408	1072	158	280	43	8	11	83	106	146	6	18	42-15	.261	.330	.347	.677	14	.976
Major League totals (8 years)			422	1098	160	286	43	8	11	84	107	152	6	18	44-15	.260	.328	.344	.673	14	.977

DIVISION SERIES RECORD

Year	Team (League)	Pos.	G	AB	R	H	2B	3B	HR	RBI	BB	SO	HBP	GDP	SB-CS	Avg.	OBP	SLG	OPS	E	Avg.
2003— Boston (A.L.)		OF-DH	4	2	0	0	0	0	0	0	0	1	0	0	0-0	.000	.000	.000	.000	0	...

BROWN, DEE — OF

PERSONAL: Born March 27, 1978, in Bronx, N.Y. ... 6-0/225. ... Bats left, throws right. ... Full name: Dermal Bram Brown. ... High school: Marlboro (N.Y.) Central.

TRANSACTIONS/CAREER NOTES: Selected by Kansas City Royals organization in first round (14th pick overall) of 1996 free-agent draft. ... On disabled list (June 17-July 27, 2001); included rehabilitation assignment to Omaha. ... On disabled list (May 28-July 19, 2003); included rehabilitation assignments to AZL Royals and Omaha. ... On disabled list (August 10-September 3, 2004); included rehabilitation assignment to Omaha. ... Refused minor league assignment and became a free agent (October 6, 2004).

2004 GAMES PLAYED BY POSITION (MLB): OF—53, DH—1.

Year	Team (League)	Pos.	BATTING																	FIELDING	
			G	AB	R	H	2B	3B	HR	RBI	BB	SO	HBP	GDP	SB-CS	Avg.	OBP	SLG	OPS	E	Avg.
1996— GC Royals (GCL)		DH	7	20	1	1	1	0	0	1	0	6	1	0	0-2	.050	.095	.100	.195	...	...
1997— Spokane (N'west)		OF	73	298	67	97	20	6	13	73	38	65	2	5	17-4	.326	.404	.564	.968	7	.921
1998— Wilmington (Caro.)		OF	128	442	64	114	30	2	10	58	53	115	7	12	26-10	.258	.347	.403	.749	13	.908
— Kansas City (A.L.)		DH-OF	5	3	2	0	0	0	0	0	0	1	0	0	0-0	.000	.000	.000	.000	0	1.000
1999— Wilmington (Caro.)		OF-DH	61	221	49	68	10	2	13	46	44	56	4	10	20-7	.308	.431	.548	.979	2	.979
— Wichita (Texas)		OF	65	235	58	83	14	3	12	56	35	41	3	2	10-8	.353	.440	.591	1.031	5	.958
— Kansas City (A.L.)		OF-DH	12	25	1	2	0	0	0	0	2	7	0	0	0-0	.080	.148	.080	.228	1	.929
2000— Omaha (PCL)		OF	125	479	76	129	25	6	23	70	37	112	3	14	20-3	.269	.324	.491	.814	7	.966
— Kansas City (A.L.)		OF	15	25	4	4	1	0	0	4	3	9	0	0	0-0	.160	.250	.200	.450	0	1.000
2001— Kansas City (A.L.)		OF-DH	106	380	39	93	19	0	7	40	22	81	1	12	5-3	.245	.286	.350	.636	2	.988
— Omaha (PCL)		OF	10	37	5	11	0	0	2	6	3	5	1	0	0-0	.297	.357	.459	.817	1	.950
2002— Omaha (PCL)		OF	121	458	66	126	23	1	17	75	44	111	6	12	10-4	.275	.344	.441	.785	5	.968
— Kansas City (A.L.)		OF-DH	16	51	5	12	3	1	1	7	4	20	0	1	0-0	.235	.291	.392	.683	1	.923
2003— Royals-1 (Ariz.)		OF	2	7	4	5	2	0	0	3	0	2	1	0	0-0	.714	.750	1.000	1.750	0	1.000
— Omaha (PCL)		OF-DH	12	47	6	13	2	0	2	9	4	9	1	2	1-0	.277	.340	.447	.788	1	.955
— Kansas City (A.L.)		OF-DH	50	132	16	30	7	0	2	14	8	37	2	0	1-1	.227	.280	.326	.605	1	.985
2004— Wichita (Texas)		OF-DH	61	241	42	73	19	2	12	50	24	38	2	4	1-4	.303	.367	.548	.914	1	.989
— Omaha (PCL)		OF-DH	10	40	2	5	0	0	2	5	0	12	0	3	0-0	.125	.125	.275	.400	1	.875
— Kansas City (A.L.)		OF-DH	59	195	19	49	7	0	4	24	11	50	1	1	2-2	.251	.293	.349	.642	3	.970
Major League totals (7 years)			263	811	86	190	37	1	14	89	50	205	4	13	8-6	.234	.281	.334	.615	8	.978

BROWN, JAMIE — P

PERSONAL: Born March 31, 1977, in Meridian, Miss. ... 6-2/200. ... Throws right, bats right. ... Full name: Jamie Monroe Brown. ... High school: West Lauderdale (Collinsville, Miss.). ... Junior college: Meridian (Miss.) Community College.

TRANSACTIONS/CAREER NOTES: Selected by Cleveland Indians organization in 34th round of 1995 free-agent draft; did not sign. ... Selected by Cleveland Indians organization in 21st round of 1996 free-agent draft. ... On disabled list (September 4, 2000-remainder of season). ... On disabled list (March 25-April 18 and May 8-September 1, 2001). ... Released by Indians (September 1, 2001). ... Re-signed by Indians organization (October 9, 2001). ... Traded by Indians to Boston Red Sox for IF Angel Santos (June 22, 2002).

CAREER HITTING: 0-for-0 (.000), 0 R, 0 2B, 0 3B, 0 HR, 0 RBI.

Year	Team (League)	W	L	Pct.	ERA	WHIP	G	GS	CG	ShO	Hld.	Sv.-Opp.	IP	H	R	ER	HR	BB-IBB	SO	Avg.
1997— Watertown (N.Y.-Penn.)		10	2	.833	3.08	1.11	13	13	1	0	...	0-...	73.0	66	35	25	6	15-0	57	.235
1998— Kinston (Caro.)		11	9	.550	3.81	1.19	27	27	2	0	...	0-...	172.2	162	91	73	12	44-1	148	.250
— Akron (East.)		1	0	1.000	2.57	0.86	1	1	0	0	...	0-...	7.0	5	2	2	1	1-0	5	.192
1999— Akron (East.)		5	9	.357	4.57	1.30	23	23	1	0	...	0-...	138.0	140	72	70	11	39-1	98	.271
— Buffalo (Int'l)		1	0	1.000	5.40	1.80	1	0	0	0	...	0-...	5.0	8	4	3	0	1-0	2	.400
2000— Akron (East.)		7	6	.538	4.38	1.25	17	17	1	0	...	0-...	96.2	95	49	47	12	26-0	57	.251
2001— Akron (East.)		1	1	.500	5.03	1.47	4	4	0	0	...	0-...	19.2	22	11	11	2	7-0	12	.278
2002— Akron (East.)		9	5	.643	2.78	1.11	18	17	0	0	...	0-...	103.2	98	41	32	5	17-0	72	.249
2003— Buffalo (Int'l)		4	4	.500	3.52	1.01	13	10	0	0	...	0-...	61.1	45	26	24	4	17-1	26	.206
— Pawtucket (Int'l)		4	1	.800	2.26	0.87	18	3	0	0	...	1-...	51.2	40	17	13	1	5-1	39	.209
2004— Boston (A.L.)		0	0	...	5.87	2.48	4	0	0	0	0	0-0	7.2	15	7	5	1	4-0	6	.417
— Pawtucket (Int'l)		4	6	.400	4.82	1.14	23	20	2	1	...	0-...	127.0	128	76	68	21	17-0	92	.257
Major League totals (1 year)		0	0	...	5.87	2.48	4	0	0	0	0	0-0	7.2	15	7	5	1	4-0	6	.417

BROWN, KEVIN — P

PERSONAL: Born March 14, 1965, in McIntyre, Ga. ... 6-4/220. ... Throws right, bats right. ... Full name: James Kevin Brown. ... High school: Wilkinson County (Irwinton, Ga.). ... College: Georgia Tech.

TRANSACTIONS/CAREER NOTES: Selected by Texas Rangers organization in first round (fourth pick overall) of June 1986 free-agent draft. ... On disabled list (August 14-29, 1990; and March 27-April 11, 1993). ... Signed as a free agent by Baltimore Orioles (April 9, 1995). ... On disabled list (June 23-July 17, 1995). ... Signed as a free agent by Florida Marlins (December 22, 1995). ... On disabled list (May 13-28, 1996). ... Traded by Marlins to San Diego Padres for Ps Rafael Medina and Steve Hoff and 1B Derrek Lee (December 15, 1997). ... Signed as a free agent by Los Angeles Dodgers (December 12, 1998). ... On disabled list (April 9-25, 2000; March 24-April 10, May 30-June 24 and July 16-August 28, 2001). ... On disabled list (April 14-30 and May 27-August 15, 2002); included rehabilitation assignment to Las Vegas. ... On disabled list (July 4-19, 2003). ... Traded by Dodgers to New York Yankees for Ps Jeff Weaver, Yhency Brazoban and Brandon Wheedon and cash (December 13, 2003). ... On disabled list (June 10-July 30, 2004); included rehabilitation assignments to Trenton, Columbus and Staten Island.

HONORS: Named N.L. Pitcher of the Year by THE SPORTING NEWS (1998).

CAREER HITTING: 63-for-493 (.128), 20 R, 9 2B, 0 3B, 2 HR, 29 RBI.

Year Team (League)	W	L	Pct.	ERA	WHIP	G	GS	CG	ShO	Hld.	Sv.-Opp.	IP	H	R	ER	HR	BB-IBB	SO	Avg.
1986— GC Rangers (GCL)	0	0	...	6.00	1.50	3	0	0	0	...	0-...	6.0	7	4	4	0	2-0	1	.292
— Tulsa (Texas)	0	0	...	4.50	1.40	3	2	0	0	...	0-...	10.0	9	7	5	0	5-0	10	.220
— Texas (A.L.)	1	0	1.000	3.60	1.20	1	1	0	0	0	0-0	5.0	6	2	2	0	0-0	4	.316
1987— Tulsa (Texas)	1	4	.200	7.29	1.69	8	8	0	0	0	0-...	42.0	53	36	34	3	18-1	26	.308
— Oklahoma City (A.A.)	0	5	.000	10.73	2.01	5	5	0	0	...	0-...	24.1	32	32	29	2	17-0	9	.311
— Charlotte (Fla. St.)	0	2	.000	2.72	1.38	6	6	1	0	...	0-...	36.1	33	14	11	1	17-0	21	.248
1988— Tulsa (Texas)	12	10	.545	3.51	1.35	26	26	5	0	...	0-...	174.1	174	94	68	5	61-1	118	.261
— Texas (A.L.)	1	1	.500	4.24	1.76	4	4	1	0	0	0-0	23.1	33	15	11	2	8-0	12	.330
1989— Texas (A.L.)	12	9	.571	3.35	1.24	28	28	7	0	0	0-0	191.0	167	81	71	10	70-2	104	.234
1990— Texas (A.L.)	12	10	.545	3.60	1.31	26	26	6	2	0	0-0	180.0	175	84	72	13	60-3	88	.255
1991— Texas (A.L.)	9	12	.429	4.40	1.53	33	33	0	0	0	0-0	210.2	233	116	103	17	90-5	96	.284
1992— Texas (A.L.)	•21	11	.656	3.32	1.27	35	35	11	1	0	0-0	*265.2	*262	117	98	11	76-2	173	.260
1993— Texas (A.L.)	15	12	.556	3.59	1.30	34	34	12	3	0	0-0	233.0	228	105	93	14	74-5	142	.252
1994— Texas (A.L.)	7	9	.438	4.82	1.58	26	•25	3	0	0	0-0	170.0	*218	109	91	18	50-3	123	.314
1995— Texas (A.L.)	10	9	.526	3.60	1.18	26	26	3	1	0	0-0	172.1	155	73	69	10	48-1	117	.241
1996— Florida (N.L.)	17	11	.607	*1.89	0.94	32	32	5	*3	0	0-0	233.0	187	60	49	8	33-2	159	.220
1997— Florida (N.L.)	16	8	.667	2.69	1.18	33	33	6	2	0	0-0	237.1	214	77	71	10	66-7	205	.240
1998— San Diego (N.L.)	18	7	.720	2.38	1.07	36	•35	7	3	1	0-0	257.0	225	77	68	8	49-4	257	.235
1999— Los Angeles (N.L.)	18	9	.667	3.00	1.07	35	•35	5	1	0	0-0	252.1	210	99	84	19	59-1	221	.222
2000— Los Angeles (N.L.)	13	6	.684	*2.58	0.99	33	33	5	0	0	0-0	230.0	181	76	66	21	47-1	216	.213
2001— Los Angeles (N.L.)	10	4	.714	2.65	1.14	20	19	1	0	0	0-0	115.2	94	41	34	8	38-2	104	.224
2002— Los Angeles (N.L.)	3	4	.429	4.81	1.43	17	10	0	0	1	0-0	63.2	68	36	34	9	23-1	58	.274
— Las Vegas (PCL)	1	0	1.000	1.86	0.93	2	2	0	0	...	0-...	9.2	6	2	2	0	3-0	7	.182
2003— Los Angeles (N.L.)	14	9	.609	2.39	1.14	32	32	0	0	0	0-0	211.0	184	67	56	11	56-2	185	.236
2004— Trenton (East.)	0	1	.000	13.50	3.50	1	1	0	0	...	0-...	2.0	7	5	3	0	0-0	0	.500
— Columbus (Int'l)	0	0	...	4.50	1.50	1	1	0	0	...	0-...	4.0	5	2	2	1	1-0	3	.313
— Staten Island (NY-P)	0	1	.000	3.00	1.17	1	1	0	0	...	0-...	6.0	6	4	2	0	1-0	6	.240
— New York (A.L.)	8	6	.625	4.09	1.27	22	22	0	0	0	0-0	132.0	132	65	60	14	35-0	83	.262
American League totals (10 years)	98	79	.554	3.81	1.34	235	234	43	7	0	0-0	1583.0	1609	767	670	109	511-21	942	.264
National League totals (8 years)	109	58	.653	2.60	1.08	238	229	29	10	2	0-0	1600.0	1363	533	462	94	371-20	1405	.230
Major League totals (18 years)	207	137	.602	3.20	1.21	473	463	72	17	2	0-0	3183.0	2972	1300	1132	203	882-41	2347	.247

DIVISION SERIES RECORD

Year Team (League)	W	L	Pct.	ERA	WHIP	G	GS	CG	ShO	Hld.	Sv.-Opp.	IP	H	R	ER	HR	BB-IBB	SO	Avg.
1997— Florida (N.L.)	0	0	...	1.29	0.57	1	1	0	0	0	0-0	7.0	4	1	1	1	0-0	5	.167
1998— San Diego (N.L.)	1	0	1.000	0.61	0.82	2	2	0	0	0	0-0	14.2	5	1	1	0	7-0	21	.109
2004— New York (A.L.)	1	0	1.000	1.50	1.33	1	1	0	0	0	0-0	6.0	8	1	1	1	0-0	1	.348
Division series totals (3 years)	2	0	1.000	0.98	0.87	4	4	0	0	0	0-0	27.2	17	3	3	2	7-0	27	.183

CHAMPIONSHIP SERIES RECORD

Year Team (League)	W	L	Pct.	ERA	WHIP	G	GS	CG	ShO	Hld.	Sv.-Opp.	IP	H	R	ER	HR	BB-IBB	SO	Avg.
1997— Florida (N.L.)	2	0	1.000	4.20	1.40	2	2	1	0	0	0-0	15.0	16	7	7	2	5-0	11	.276
1998— San Diego (N.L.)	1	1	.500	2.61	0.87	2	1	1	1	0	0-1	10.1	5	3	3	1	4-0	12	.143
2004— New York (A.L.)	0	1	.000	21.60	3.90	2	2	0	0	0	0-0	3.1	9	9	8	2	4-0	2	.500
Champ. series totals (3 years)	3	2	.600	5.65	1.50	6	5	2	1	0	0-1	28.2	30	19	18	5	13-0	25	.270

WORLD SERIES RECORD

Year Team (League)	W	L	Pct.	ERA	WHIP	G	GS	CG	ShO	Hld.	Sv.-Opp.	IP	H	R	ER	HR	BB-IBB	SO	Avg.
1997— Florida (N.L.)	0	2	.000	8.18	1.82	2	2	0	0	0	0-0	11.0	15	10	10	1	5-0	6	.375
1998— San Diego (N.L.)	0	1	.000	4.40	1.40	2	2	0	0	0	0-0	14.1	14	7	7	0	6-2	13	.259
World series totals (2 years)	0	3	.000	6.04	1.58	4	4	0	0	0	0-0	25.1	29	17	17	1	11-2	19	.309

ALL-STAR GAME RECORD

Year Team (League)	W	L	Pct.	ERA	WHIP	G	GS	CG	ShO	Hld.	Sv.-Opp.	IP	H	R	ER	HR	BB-IBB	SO	Avg.
All-Star Game totals (5 years)	1	0	1.000	1.93	1.07	5	1	0	0	...	0-0	4.2	2	1	1	0	3-0	2	.133

BRUNEY, BRIAN — P

PERSONAL: Born February 17, 1982, in Astoria, Ore. ... 6-3/226. ... Throws right, bats right. ... Full name: Brian Anthony Bruney. ... High school: Warrenton (Ore.).
TRANSACTIONS/CAREER NOTES: Selected by Arizona Diamondbacks organization in 12th round of 2000 free-agent draft. ... On disabled list (May 27-July 6, 2004); included rehabilitation assignment to Tucson.
CAREER HITTING: 0-for-0 (.000), 0 R, 0 2B, 0 3B, 0 HR, 0 RBI.

Year Team (League)	W	L	Pct.	ERA	WHIP	G	GS	CG	ShO	Hld.	Sv.-Opp.	IP	H	R	ER	HR	BB-IBB	SO	Avg.
2000— Ariz. D'backs (Ariz.)	4	1	.800	6.48	2.00	20	2	0	0	...	2-...	25.0	21	23	18	2	29-0	24	.221
2001— South Bend (Mid.)	1	4	.200	4.13	1.32	26	0	0	0	...	8-...	32.2	24	19	15	1	19-2	40	.205
— Yakima (N'west)	1	2	.333	5.14	1.43	15	0	0	0	...	2-...	21.0	19	14	12	2	11-0	28	.226
2002— South Bend (Mid.)	4	3	.571	1.68	1.12	37	0	0	0	...	10-...	48.1	37	15	9	1	17-4	57	.210
— El Paso (Texas)	0	2	.000	2.92	1.22	10	0	0	0	...	0-...	12.1	11	5	4	1	4-1	14	.268
2003— El Paso (Texas)	0	2	.000	2.59	1.34	28	0	0	0	...	14-...	31.1	29	17	9	1	13-2	28	.234
— Tucson (PCL)	3	1	.750	2.81	1.31	32	0	0	0	...	12-...	32.0	24	12	10	0	18-0	32	.207
2004— Tucson (PCL)	2	0	1.000	1.18	1.00	38	0	0	0	...	5-...	38.0	18	8	5	1	20-1	42	.141
— Arizona (N.L.)	3	4	.429	4.31	1.50	30	0	0	0	3	0-1	31.1	20	16	15	2	27-5	34	.189
Major League totals (1 year)	3	4	.429	4.31	1.50	30	0	0	0	3	0-1	31.1	20	16	15	2	27-5	34	.189

BRUNTLETT, ERIC — SS

PERSONAL: Born March 29, 1978, in Lafayette, Ind. ... 6-0/190. ... Bats right, throws right. ... Full name: Eric Kevin Bruntlett. ... High school: William Henry Harrison (West Lafayette, Indiana). ... College: Stanford.
TRANSACTIONS/CAREER NOTES: Selected by Los Angeles Dodgers organization in 72nd round of 1996 free-agent draft; did not sign. ... Selected by Houston Astros in ninth round of 2000 free-agent draft.
2004 GAMES PLAYED BY POSITION (MLB): SS—33, 2B—5, OF—2.

Year	Team (League)	Pos.	G	AB	R	H	2B	3B	HR	RBI	BB	SO	HBP	GDP	SB-CS	Avg.	OBP	SLG	OPS	E	Avg.
2000—	Martinsville (App.)	SS-OF	50	172	40	47	11	4	1	21	30	22	11	2	14-1	.273	.413	.401	.814	12	.944
2001—	Round Rock (Texas)	SS	123	503	84	134	23	3	3	40	50	76	8	7	23-7	.266	.340	.342	.682	23	.956
	—New Orleans (PCL)	SS	5	16	3	2	0	0	0	1	2	1	0	1	0-0	.125	.222	.125	.347	0	1.000
2002—	Round Rock (Texas)	SS-2B	116	464	81	123	21	2	2	48	56	61	10	17	35-12	.265	.351	.332	.683	19	.966
	—New Orleans (PCL)	SS-2B	18	68	9	14	3	0	0	1	10	10	0	3	1-1	.206	.308	.250	.558	6	.941
2003—	New Orleans (PCL)	SS-2B-OF	84	324	48	84	10	0	2	27	35	51	3	3	9-4	.259	.332	.309	.641	13	.967
	—Houston (N.L.)	SS-2B-OF-3B	31	54	3	14	3	0	1	4	0	10	0	1	0-0	.259	.255	.370	.625	1	.981
2004—	New Orleans (PCL)	SS-OF-2B	86	332	50	83	12	4	6	37	35	72	7	10	14-4	.250	.331	.364	.695	12	.970
	—Houston (N.L.)	SS-2B-OF	45	52	14	13	2	0	4	8	7	13	0	0	4-0	.250	.328	.519	.847	3	.947
	Major League totals (2 years)		76	106	17	27	5	0	5	12	7	23	0	1	4-0	.255	.293	.443	.736	4	.964

DIVISION SERIES RECORD

Year	Team (League)	Pos.	G	AB	R	H	2B	3B	HR	RBI	BB	SO	HBP	GDP	SB-CS	Avg.	OBP	SLG	OPS	E	Avg.
2004—	Houston (N.L.)	SS	2	1	0	0	0	0	0	0	0	0	0	0	0-0	.000	.500	.000	.500	0	1.000

CHAMPIONSHIP SERIES RECORD

Year	Team (League)	Pos.	G	AB	R	H	2B	3B	HR	RBI	BB	SO	HBP	GDP	SB-CS	Avg.	OBP	SLG	OPS	E	Avg.
2004—	Houston (N.L.)	SS	4	2	0	0	0	0	0	0	0	0	0	0	0-0	.000	.000	.000	.000	0	...

BUCHANAN, BRIAN — OF

PERSONAL: Born July 21, 1973, in Miami, Fla. ... 6-4/230. ... Bats right, throws right. ... Full name: Brian James Buchanan. ... High school: Fairfax (Va.). ... College: Virginia.

TRANSACTIONS/CAREER NOTES: Selected by New York Yankees organization in first round (24th pick overall) of 1994 free-agent draft. ... Traded by Yankees with Ps Eric Milton and Danny Mota, SS Cristian Guzman and cash to Minnesota Twins for 2B Chuck Knoblauch (February 6, 1998). ... On disabled list (June 29-July 14, 2001). ... On disabled list (April 4-19, 2002); included rehabilitation assignment to Edmonton. ... Traded by Twins to San Diego Padres for SS Jason Bartlett (July 12, 2002). ... On disabled list (May 29-June 23, 2004); included rehabilitation assignment to Lake Elsinore. ... Refused minor league assignment and became a free agent (August 24, 2004). ... Signed by New York Mets (August 25, 2004).

2004 GAMES PLAYED BY POSITION (MLB): OF—18, 1B—4.

Year	Team (League)	Pos.	G	AB	R	H	2B	3B	HR	RBI	BB	SO	HBP	GDP	SB-CS	Avg.	OBP	SLG	OPS	E	Avg.
1994—	Oneonta (N.Y.-Penn.)	OF	50	177	28	40	9	2	4	26	24	53	6	2	5-3	.226	.335	.367	.702	0	1.000
1995—	Greensboro (S. Atl.)	OF	23	96	19	29	3	0	3	12	9	17	1	1	7-1	.302	.368	.427	.795	1	.970
1996—	Tampa (Fla. St.)	OF	131	526	65	137	22	4	10	58	37	108	10	14	23-8	.260	.321	.375	.695	6	.969
1997—	Norwich (East.)	OF	116	470	75	145	25	2	10	69	32	85	11	11	11-9	.309	.362	.434	.796	8	.962
	—Columbus (Int'l)	OF	18	61	8	17	1	0	4	7	4	11	3	3	2-1	.279	.348	.492	.840	1	.947
1998—	Salt Lake (PCL)	OF	133	500	74	139	29	3	17	82	36	90	9	7	14-2	.278	.337	.450	.787	8	.969
1999—	Salt Lake (PCL)	OF	107	391	67	116	24	1	10	60	28	85	9	14	11-2	.297	.355	.440	.795	4	.980
2000—	Salt Lake (PCL)	OF-1B	95	364	82	108	20	1	27	103	41	75	3	16	5-1	.297	.363	.580	.942	4	.980
	—Minnesota (A.L.)	OF-DH	30	82	10	19	3	0	1	8	8	22	1	1	0-2	.232	.301	.305	.606	0	1.000
2001—	Minnesota (A.L.)	OF-DH	69	197	28	54	12	0	10	32	19	58	2	2	1-1	.274	.342	.487	.830	2	.973
2002—	Minnesota (A.L.)	OF-DH	44	135	19	34	5	1	5	15	6	33	2	4	2-1	.252	.294	.415	.709	0	1.000
	—Edmonton (PCL)	OF	1	3	0	0	0	0	0	0	0	0	0	0	0-0	.000	.000	.000	.000	0	...
	—San Diego (N.L.)	1B-OF	48	92	12	27	5	0	6	13	9	26	1	2	0-1	.293	.363	.543	.906	1	.990
2003—	San Diego (N.L.)	OF-1B	115	198	29	52	10	2	8	29	24	51	3	8	6-2	.263	.346	.455	.801	2	.990
2004—	Lake Elsinore (Calif.)	1B-DH-OF	4	10	1	3	2	0	0	1	1	3	1	0	0-0	.300	.417	.500	.917	0	1.000
	—Portland (PCL)	1B-DH	12	42	9	15	8	0	2	12	9	7	1	1	0-0	.357	.481	.690	1.171	0	.983
	—San Diego (N.L.)	OF-1B	38	60	7	12	2	0	2	6	6	19	1	2	0-0	.200	.279	.333	.613	0	1.000
	—New York (N.L.)	1B	2	3	0	0	0	0	0	0	1	1	0	0	0-0	.000	.250	.000	.250	0	1.000
	American League totals (3 years)		143	414	57	107	20	1	16	55	33	113	5	9	3-4	.258	.319	.428	.746	2	.987
	National League totals (3 years)		203	353	48	91	17	2	16	48	40	97	5	12	6-3	.258	.338	.453	.792	3	.991
	Major League totals (5 years)		346	767	105	198	37	3	32	103	73	210	10	21	9-7	.258	.328	.439	.767	5	.990

BUCK, JOHN — C

PERSONAL: Born July 7, 1980, in Kemmerer, Wyo. ... 6-3/210. ... Bats right, throws right. ... Full name: Johnathan R. Buck. ... High school: Taylorsville (Utah).

TRANSACTIONS/CAREER NOTES: Selected by Houston Astros organization in seventh round of 1998 free-agent draft. ... Traded by Astros with cash to Kansas City Royals as part of three-team deal in which Astros acquired OF Carlos Beltran from Royals, Royals acquired P Mike Wood and 3B Mark Teahen from Oakland Athletics and Athletics acquired P Octavio Dotel from Astros (June 24, 2004).

2004 GAMES PLAYED BY POSITION (MLB): C—68, DH—3.

Year	Team (League)	Pos.	G	AB	R	H	2B	3B	HR	RBI	BB	SO	HBP	GDP	SB-CS	Avg.	OBP	SLG	OPS	E	Avg.
1998—	GC Astros (GCL)	C	36	126	24	36	9	0	3	15	13	22	2	0	2-2	.286	.362	.429	.790	4	.983
1999—	Auburn (NY-Penn)	C	63	233	36	57	17	0	3	29	25	48	5	7	7-1	.245	.328	.356	.685	16	.974
	—Michigan (Midw.)	C	4	10	1	1	1	0	0	0	2	3	0	0	0-0	.100	.250	.200	.450	0	1.000
2000—	Michigan (Midw.)	C	109	390	57	110	33	0	10	71	55	81	5	8	2-4	.282	.374	.444	.817	15	.982
2001—	Lexington (S.Atl.)	C	122	443	72	122	24	1	22	73	37	84	12	8	4-9	.275	.345	.483	.828	6	.995
2002—	Round Rock (Texas)	C	120	448	48	118	29	3	12	89	31	93	6	11	2-3	.263	.314	.422	.736	8	.990
2003—	New Orleans (PCL)	C	78	274	32	70	18	2	2	39	14	53	4	11	1-0	.255	.301	.358	.659	3	.993
2004—	New Orleans (PCL)	C-DH	65	227	31	68	11	0	12	35	21	39	4	13	0-1	.300	.368	.507	.864	11	.971
	—Kansas City (A.L.)	C-DH	71	238	36	56	9	0	12	30	15	79	0	6	1-1	.235	.280	.424	.704	3	.992
	Major League totals (1 year)		71	238	36	56	9	0	12	30	15	79	0	6	1-1	.235	.280	.424	.704	3	.992

BUEHRLE, MARK — P

PERSONAL: Born March 23, 1979, in St. Charles, Mo. ... 6-2/220. ... Throws left, bats left. ... Full name: Mark Anthony Buehrle. ... Name pronounced: BURR-lee. ... High school: Francis Howell North (St. Charles, Mo.). ... Junior college: Jefferson (Mo.).

TRANSACTIONS/CAREER NOTES: Selected by Chicago White Sox organization in 38th round of 1998 free-agent draft.

CAREER HITTING: 2-for-18 (.111), 1 R, 0 2B, 0 3B, 0 HR, 1 RBI.

Year	Team (League)	W	L	Pct.	ERA	WHIP	G	GS	CG	ShO	Hld.	Sv.-Opp.	IP	H	R	ER	HR	BB-IBB	SO	Avg.
1999—	Burlington (Midw.)	7	4	.636	4.10	1.23	20	14	1	1	...	3-...	98.2	105	49	45	8	16-1	91	.271
2000—	Birmingham (Southern)	8	4	.667	2.28	0.94	16	16	1	1	...	0-...	118.2	95	37	30	8	17-0	68	.222
	—Chicago (A.L.)	4	1	.800	4.21	1.44	28	3	0	0	3	0-2	51.1	55	27	24	5	19-1	37	.272

Year	Team (League)	W	L	Pct.	ERA	WHIP	G	GS	CG	ShO	Hld.	Sv.-Opp.	IP	H	R	ER	HR	BB-IBB	SO	Avg.
2001—Chicago (A.L.)		16	8	.667	3.29	1.07	32	32	4	2	0	0-0	221.1	188	89	81	24	48-2	126	.230
2002—Chicago (A.L.)		19	12	.613	3.58	1.24	34	34	5	2	0	0-0	239.0	236	102	95	25	61-7	134	.260
2003—Chicago (A.L.)		14	14	.500	4.14	1.35	35	35	2	0	0	0-0	230.1	250	124	106	22	61-2	119	.278
2004—Chicago (A.L.)		16	10	.615	3.89	1.26	35	•35	4	1	0	0-0	*245.1	257	119	106	33	51-2	165	.271
Major League totals (5 years)		69	45	.605	3.76	1.24	164	139	15	5	3	0-2	987.1	986	461	412	109	240-14	581	.261

DIVISION SERIES RECORD

Year	Team (League)	W	L	Pct.	ERA	WHIP	G	GS	CG	ShO	Hld.	Sv.-Opp.	IP	H	R	ER	HR	BB-IBB	SO	Avg.
2000—Chicago (A.L.)		0	0	...	0.00	6.00	1	0	0	0	0	0-0	.1	2	0	0	0	0-0	1	.667

ALL-STAR GAME RECORD

		W	L	Pct.	ERA	WHIP	G	GS	CG	ShO	Hld.	Sv.-Opp.	IP	H	R	ER	HR	BB-IBB	SO	Avg.
All-Star Game totals (1 year)		0	0	...	4.50	1.00	1	0	0	0	0	0-0	2.0	2	1	1	0	0-0	2	.250

BUKVICH, RYAN — P

PERSONAL: Born May 13, 1978, in Naperville, Ill. ... 6-2/250. ... Throws right, bats right. ... Full name: Ryan Adrien Bukvich. ... Name pronounced: BUCK-vich. ... High school: Northwest Rankin (Brandon, Miss.). ... College: Mississippi.

TRANSACTIONS/CAREER NOTES: Selected by Kansas City Royals organization in 11th round of 2000 free-agent draft. ... Traded by Royals with P Darrell May to San Diego Padres for OF Terrence Long, P Dennis Tankersley and cash (November 8, 2004).

CAREER HITTING: 0-for-0 (.000), 0 R, 0 2B, 0 3B, 0 HR, 0 RBI.

Year	Team (League)	W	L	Pct.	ERA	WHIP	G	GS	CG	ShO	Hld.	Sv.-Opp.	IP	H	R	ER	HR	BB-IBB	SO	Avg.
2000—Spokane (N'west)		2	0	1.000	0.64	1.00	10	0	0	0	...	2-...	14.0	5	1	1	0	9-0	15	.111
—Char., W.Va. (SAL)		0	0	...	1.88	0.91	11	0	0	0	...	4-...	14.1	6	3	3	0	7-0	17	.128
—Wilmington (Caro.)		0	1	.000	18.00	4.00	2	0	0	0	...	0-...	2.0	3	4	4	0	5-2	3	.375
2001—Wilmington (Caro.)		0	1	.000	1.72	1.25	37	0	0	0	...	13-...	57.2	41	16	11	1	31-0	80	.194
—Wichita (Texas)		0	0	...	3.75	0.92	7	0	0	0	...	0-...	12.0	9	6	5	2	2-0	14	.200
2002—Wichita (Texas)		1	1	.500	1.31	0.93	23	0	0	0	...	8-...	34.1	17	8	5	0	15-1	47	.145
—Omaha (PCL)		1	0	1.000	0.00	0.80	12	0	0	0	...	8-...	13.2	4	0	0	0	7-0	17	.093
—Kansas City (A.L.)		1	0	1.000	6.12	1.80	26	0	0	0	5	0-1	25.0	26	19	17	2	19-3	20	.277
2003—Kansas City (A.L.)		1	0	1.000	9.58	2.03	9	0	0	0	0	0-0	10.1	12	11	11	2	9-0	8	.293
—Omaha (PCL)		1	2	.333	4.91	1.70	34	0	0	0	...	5-...	36.2	39	21	20	2	25-0	44	.273
2004—Kansas City (A.L.)		0	0	...	3.68	1.50	9	0	0	0	1	1-1	7.1	4	3	3	0	7-0	7	.182
—Omaha (PCL)		3	4	.429	4.37	1.33	38	0	0	0	...	7-...	47.1	33	25	23	4	30-0	60	.193
Major League totals (3 years)		2	0	1.000	6.54	1.80	44	0	0	0	6	1-2	42.2	42	33	31	4	35-3	35	.268

BULLINGER, KIRK — P

PERSONAL: Born October 28, 1969, in New Orleans, La. ... 6-2/170. ... Throws right, bats right. ... Full name: Kirk Matthew Bullinger. ... High school: Archbishop Rummel (Metairie, La.). ... College: Southeastern Louisiana. ... Brother of Jim Bullinger, pitcher with three major league teams (1992-1998).

TRANSACTIONS/CAREER NOTES: Selected by St. Louis Cardinals in 32nd round of 1992 free-agent draft. ... Traded by Cardinals organization with OF DaRond Stovall and P Bryan Eversgerd to Montreal Expos for P Ken Hill (April 5, 1995). ... Signed as a free agent by Boston Red Sox organization (December 14, 1998). ... Signed as a free agent by Philadelphia Phillies organization (January 29, 2000). ... On disabled list (April 11-June 20, 2000); included rehabilitation assignments to Reading and GCL Phillies. ... Refused minor league assignment and became a free agent (October 2, 2000). ... Signed by Cleveland Indians organization (February 8, 2001). ... Released by Indians (April 23, 2001). ... Contract purchased by Chicago White Sox organization from Somerset of the independent Atlantic League (June 6, 2001). ... Signed as a free agent by Houston Astros organization (December 21, 2001).

CAREER HITTING: 0-for-4 (.000), 0 R, 0 2B, 0 3B, 0 HR, 0 RBI.

Year	Team (League)	W	L	Pct.	ERA	WHIP	G	GS	CG	ShO	Hld.	Sv.-Opp.	IP	H	R	ER	HR	BB-IBB	SO	Avg.
1992—Hamilton (N.Y.-Penn.)		2	2	.500	1.11	0.80	35	0	0	0	...	2-...	48.2	24	7	6	0	15-4	61	.140
1993—Springfield (Mid.)		1	3	.250	2.28	0.92	50	0	0	0	...	33-...	51.1	26	19	13	5	21-1	72	.144
1994—St. Pete. (FSL)		2	0	1.000	1.17	1.06	39	0	0	0	...	6-...	53.2	37	16	7	0	20-5	50	.191
1995—Harrisburg (Eastern)		5	3	.625	2.42	1.28	56	0	0	0	...	7-...	67.0	61	22	18	4	25-5	42	.242
1996—Ottawa (Int'l)		2	1	.667	3.52	1.24	10	0	0	0	...	0-...	15.1	10	6	6	3	9-1	9	.189
—Harrisburg (Eastern)		3	4	.429	1.97	1.40	47	0	0	0	...	22-...	45.2	46	16	10	5	18-3	29	.271
1997—Harrisburg (Eastern)		3	0	1.000	2.67	1.04	21	0	0	0	...	6-...	27.0	22	9	8	4	6-0	21	.224
—W.P. Beach (FSL)		2	0	1.000	0.00	0.82	2	0	0	0	...	0-...	3.2	3	0	0	0	0-0	7	.200
—Ottawa (Int'l)		3	4	.429	1.71	0.85	22	0	0	0	...	5-...	31.2	17	7	6	0	10-0	15	.160
1998—GC Expos (GCL)		0	0	...	0.00	0.50	2	0	0	0	...	0-...	4.0	2	0	0	0	0-0	7	.143
—Jupiter (FSL)		0	0	...	5.40	1.10	8	0	0	0	...	0-...	10.0	9	7	6	1	2-0	12	.225
—Ottawa (Int'l)		0	0	...	1.06	1.29	13	0	0	0	...	3-...	17.0	16	2	2	0	6-1	7	.246
—Montreal (N.L.)		1	0	1.000	9.00	2.00	8	0	0	0	0	0-1	7.0	14	8	7	1	0-0	2	.400
1999—Trenton (East.)		1	1	.500	0.53	0.65	17	0	0	0	...	10-...	17.0	6	2	1	1	5-1	16	.111
—Pawtucket (Int'l)		0	2	.000	2.39	1.33	35	0	0	0	...	15-...	37.2	37	14	10	3	13-4	27	.259
—Boston (A.L.)		0	0	...	4.50	2.00	4	0	0	0	2	0-0	2.0	2	1	1	0	2-0	0	.286
2000—Philadelphia (N.L.)		0	0	...	5.40	1.20	3	0	0	0	1	0-0	3.1	4	2	2	0	2-0	4	.308
—Scran./W.B. (I.L.)		0	1	.000	0.72	1.16	26	0	0	0	...	12-...	25.0	19	4	2	0	10-2	16	.224
—Reading (East.)		0	0	...	0.00	1.33	2	1	0	0	...	0-...	3.0	3	0	0	0	1-0	1	.300
—GC Phillies (GCL)		0	0	...	0.00	0.00	1	1	0	0	...	0-...	1.0	0	0	0	0	0-0	1	.000
2001—Akron (East.)		0	1	.000	4.91	1.64	3	0	0	0	...	1-...	3.2	5	2	2	0	1-1	4	.357
—Charlotte (Int'l)		0	3	.000	3.58	1.29	36	0	0	0	...	5-...	50.1	44	23	20	5	21-6	34	.247
2002—New Orleans (PCL)		4	1	.800	2.75	0.96	55	0	0	0	...	4-...	75.1	61	25	23	6	11-4	46	.223
2003—New Orleans (PCL)		3	3	.500	1.94	1.10	55	0	0	0	...	20-...	65.0	56	18	14	3	14-4	46	.230
—Houston (N.L.)		0	0	...	6.75	1.00	7	0	0	0	1	0-0	8.0	7	6	6	2	1-0	5	.219
2004—New Orleans (PCL)		3	1	.750	3.00	1.10	28	0	0	0	...	14-...	30.0	24	10	10	3	9-2	14	.226
—Houston (N.L.)		1	0	1.000	6.16	1.50	27	0	0	0	1	1-2	30.2	36	22	21	6	10-2	11	.286
American League totals (1 year)		0	0	...	4.50	2.00	4	0	0	0	2	0-0	2.0	2	1	1	0	2-0	0	.286
National League totals (4 years)		2	0	1.000	6.61	1.47	45	0	0	0	3	1-3	49.0	61	38	36	8	11-2	22	.296
Major League totals (5 years)		2	0	1.000	6.53	1.49	49	0	0	0	5	1-3	51.0	63	39	37	8	13-2	22	.296

BUMP, NATE — P

PERSONAL: Born July 24, 1976, in Towanda, Pa. ... 6-2/196. ... Throws right, bats left. ... Full name: Nathan Louis Bump. ... College: Penn State.

TRANSACTIONS/CAREER NOTES: Selected by Boston Red Sox organization in 23rd round of 1997 free-agent draft; did not sign. ... Selected by San Francisco Giants organization in first round (25th pick overall) of 1998 free-agent draft. ... Traded by Giants with P Jason Grilli to Florida Marlins for P Livan Hernandez (July 24, 1999).

CAREER HITTING: 0-for-5 (.000), 0 R, 0 2B, 0 3B, 0 HR, 0 RBI.

Year	Team (League)	W	L	Pct.	ERA	WHIP	G	GS	CG	ShO	Hld.	Sv.-Opp.	IP	H	R	ER	HR	BB-IBB	SO	Avg.
1998—Salem-Keizer (N'west)		0	0	...	0.00	1.00	2	2	0	0	...	0-...	8.0	5	0	0	0	3-0	8	.192
—San Jose (California)		6	1	.857	1.75	0.99	11	11	0	0	...	0-...	61.2	37	13	12	2	24-0	61	.175
1999—Shreveport (Texas)		4	10	.286	3.31	1.27	17	17	1	1	...	0-...	92.1	85	40	34	9	32-0	59	.242
—Portland (East.)		2	6	.250	6.07	1.60	8	8	0	0	...	0-...	43.0	57	38	29	3	12-0	33	.311
2000—Portland (East.)		8	9	.471	4.57	1.46	26	26	3	1	...	0-...	149.2	169	85	76	16	49-1	98	.287
2001—Portland (East.)		4	5	.444	5.27	1.19	11	8	0	0	...	0-...	54.2	55	41	32	10	10-0	41	.259
2002—Portland (East.)		7	6	.538	3.38	1.09	20	20	3	0	...	0-...	127.2	110	56	48	5	29-0	81	.227
2003—Albuquerque (PCL)		6	5	.545	4.43	1.32	15	15	0	0	...	0-...	85.1	89	48	42	4	24-1	52	.267
—Florida (N.L.)		4	0	1.000	4.71	1.49	32	0	0	0	...	6	0-0	36.1	34	21	19	3	20-0	17	.248
2004—Albuquerque (PCL)		0	0	...	1.39	0.62	3	2	0	0	...	0-...	13.0	7	2	2	0	1-0	12	.159
—Florida (N.L.)		2	4	.333	5.01	1.60	50	2	0	0	...	5	1-4	73.2	86	46	41	7	32-8	44	.297
Major League totals (2 years)		6	4	.600	4.91	1.56	82	2	0	0	11	1-4	110.0	120	67	60	10	52-8	61	.281

CHAMPIONSHIP SERIES RECORD

Year	Team (League)	W	L	Pct.	ERA	WHIP	G	GS	CG	ShO	Hld.	Sv.-Opp.	IP	H	R	ER	HR	BB-IBB	SO	Avg.
2003—Florida (N.L.)		0	0	...	6.00	1.00	2	0	0	0	0	0-0	3.0	3	2	2	1	0-0	3	.250

BURBA, DAVE   P

PERSONAL: Born July 7, 1966, in Dayton, Ohio. ... 6-4/255. ... Throws right, bats right. ... Full name: David Allen Burba. ... Name pronounced: BUR-ba. ... High school: Kenton Ridge (Springfield, Ohio). ... College: Ohio State.

TRANSACTIONS/CAREER NOTES: Selected by Seattle Mariners organization in second round of 1987 free-agent draft. ... Traded by Mariners with Ps Bill Swift and Mike Jackson to San Francisco Giants for OF Kevin Mitchell and P Mike Remlinger (December 11, 1991). ... Traded by Giants with OF Darren Lewis and P Mark Portugal to Cincinnati Reds for OF Deion Sanders, Ps John Roper, Ricky Pickett and Scott Service and IF Dave McCarty (July 21, 1995). ... On disabled list (August 7-27, 1997). ... Traded by Reds to Cleveland Indians for 1B Sean Casey (March 30, 1998). ... Signed as a free agent by Texas Rangers (Decemer 19, 2001). ... Released by Rangers (July 29, 2002). ... Signed by Indians organization (August 7, 2002). ... Released by Indians (May 3, 2003). ... Signed by Milwaukee Brewers organization (May 4, 2003). ... Traded by Brewers to Giants for P Josh Habel (September 2, 2004).

CAREER HITTING: 26-for-194 (.134), 10 R, 1 2B, 0 3B, 3 HR, 12 RBI.

Year	Team (League)	W	L	Pct.	ERA	WHIP	G	GS	CG	ShO	Hld.	Sv.-Opp.	IP	H	R	ER	HR	BB-IBB	SO	Avg.
1987—Bellingham (N'west)		3	1	.750	1.93	0.99	5	5	0	0	...	0-...	23.1	20	10	5	0	3-0	24	.213
—Salinas (Calif.)		1	6	.143	4.61	1.50	9	9	0	0	...	0-...	54.2	53	31	28	3	29-0	46	.252
1988—San Bernardino (Calif.)		5	7	.417	2.68	1.40	20	20	0	0	...	0-...	114.0	106	41	34	4	54-1	102	.252
1989—Williamsport (Eastern)		11	7	.611	3.16	1.23	25	25	5	1	...	0-...	156.2	138	69	55	7	55-0	89	.236
1990—Calgary (PCL)		10	6	.625	4.67	1.49	31	18	1	0	...	2-...	113.2	124	64	59	11	45-0	47	.282
—Seattle (A.L.)		0	0	...	4.50	1.25	6	0	0	0	0	0-0	8.0	8	6	4	0	2-0	4	.267
1991—Seattle (A.L.)		2	2	.500	3.68	1.31	22	2	0	0	0	1-1	36.2	34	16	15	6	14-3	16	.245
—Calgary (PCL)		6	4	.600	3.53	1.53	23	9	0	0	...	4-...	71.1	82	35	28	4	27-0	42	.294
1992—San Francisco (N.L.)		2	7	.222	4.97	1.57	23	11	0	0	0	0-0	70.2	80	43	39	4	31-2	47	.287
—Phoenix (PCL)		5	5	.500	4.72	1.48	13	13	0	0	...	0-...	74.1	86	40	39	5	24-2	44	.295
1993—San Francisco (N.L.)		10	3	.769	4.25	1.38	54	5	0	0	10	0-0	95.1	95	49	45	14	37-5	88	.265
1994—San Francisco (N.L.)		3	6	.333	4.38	1.41	57	0	0	0	11	0-3	74.0	59	39	36	5	45-3	84	.221
1995—San Francisco (N.L.)		4	2	.667	4.98	1.45	37	0	0	0	5	0-1	43.1	38	26	24	5	25-2	46	.235
—Cincinnati (N.L.)		6	2	.750	3.27	1.23	15	9	1	1	0	0-0	63.1	52	24	23	4	26-1	50	.223
1996—Cincinnati (N.L.)		11	13	.458	3.83	1.42	34	33	0	0	0	0-0	195.0	179	96	83	18	97-9	148	.244
1997—Cincinnati (N.L.)		11	10	.524	4.73	1.44	30	27	2	0	0	0-0	160.0	157	88	84	22	73-10	131	.255
1998—Cleveland (A.L.)		15	10	.600	4.11	1.37	32	31	0	0	1	0-0	203.2	210	100	93	30	69-4	132	.269
1999—Cleveland (A.L.)		15	9	.625	4.25	1.40	34	34	1	0	0	0-0	220.0	211	113	104	30	96-3	174	.254
2000—Cleveland (A.L.)		16	6	.727	4.47	1.52	32	32	0	0	0	0-0	191.1	199	99	95	19	91-2	180	.267
2001—Cleveland (A.L.)		10	10	.500	6.21	1.61	32	27	1	0	0	0-0	150.2	188	112	104	16	54-2	118	.306
2002—Texas (A.L.)		4	5	.444	5.42	1.48	23	18	1	0	0	0-1	111.1	125	71	67	13	40-3	70	.279
—Akron (East.)		0	0	...	0.00	0.64	1	1	0	0	...	0-...	4.2	2	0	0	0	1-0	1	.133
—Cleveland (A.L.)		1	0	1.000	4.50	1.38	12	3	0	0	1	0-1	34.0	30	20	17	3	17-0	25	.236
2003—Buffalo (Int'l)		1	3	.250	2.05	1.00	4	4	0	0	...	0-...	22.0	18	6	5	2	5-0	10	.228
—Indianapolis (Int'l)		5	4	.556	5.33	1.60	10	9	0	0	...	0-...	50.2	65	37	30	4	16-0	34	.316
—Milwaukee (N.L.)		1	1	.500	3.53	1.41	17	2	0	0	0	0-0	43.1	42	19	17	5	19-2	35	.250
2004—Milwaukee (N.L.)		3	1	.750	4.08	1.23	45	0	0	0	3	2-4	70.2	63	36	32	6	24-2	47	.237
—San Francisco (N.L.)		1	0	1.000	5.68	1.42	6	0	0	0	1	0-1	6.1	7	4	4	1	2-0	3	.280
American League totals (7 years)		63	42	.600	4.70	1.45	193	147	3	0	1	1-3	955.2	1005	537	499	117	383-17	719	.270
National League totals (8 years)		52	45	.536	4.24	1.40	318	87	3	1	30	2-9	822.0	772	424	387	84	379-36	679	.248
Major League totals (15 years)		115	87	.569	4.49	1.43	511	234	6	1	31	3-12	1777.2	1777	961	886	201	762-53	1398	.260

DIVISION SERIES RECORD

Year	Team (League)	W	L	Pct.	ERA	WHIP	G	GS	CG	ShO	Hld.	Sv.-Opp.	IP	H	R	ER	HR	BB-IBB	SO	Avg.
1995—Cincinnati (N.L.)		1	0	1.000	0.00	3.00	1	0	0	0	0	0-0	1.0	2	0	0	0	1-0	0	.400
1998—Cleveland (A.L.)		1	0	1.000	5.06	1.13	1	0	0	0	0	0-0	5.1	4	3	3	0	2-0	4	.222
1999—Cleveland (A.L.)		0	0	...	0.00	0.50	1	1	0	0	0	0-0	4.0	1	0	0	0	1-0	0	.083
2001—Cleveland (A.L.)		0	0	...	0.00	0.00	1	0	0	0	0	0-0	1.0	0	0	0	0	0-0	1	.000
Division series totals (4 years)		2	0	1.000	2.38	0.97	4	1	0	0	0	0-0	11.1	7	3	3	0	4-0	5	.184

CHAMPIONSHIP SERIES RECORD

Year	Team (League)	W	L	Pct.	ERA	WHIP	G	GS	CG	ShO	Hld.	Sv.-Opp.	IP	H	R	ER	HR	BB-IBB	SO	Avg.
1995—Cincinnati (N.L.)		0	0	...	0.00	1.91	2	0	0	0	0	0-0	3.2	3	0	0	0	4-1	0	.231
1998—Cleveland (A.L.)		1	0	1.000	3.00	1.33	3	0	0	0	0	0-0	6.0	3	4	2	0	5-0	8	.136
Champ. series totals (2 years)		1	0	1.000	1.86	1.55	5	0	0	0	0	0-0	9.2	6	4	2	0	9-1	8	.171

BURKE, CHRIS   2B/SS

PERSONAL: Born March 11, 1980, in Louisville, Ky. ... 5-11/180. ... Bats right, throws right. ... Full name: Christopher A. Burke. ... High school: St.Xavier (Louisville). ... College: Tennessee.

TRANSACTIONS/CAREER NOTES: Selected by Houston Astros organization in first round (10th pick overall) of 2001 free-agent draft.

2004 GAMES PLAYED BY POSITION (MLB): 2B—7.

Year Team (League)	Pos.	G	AB	R	H	2B	3B	HR	RBI	BB	SO	HBP	GDP	SB-CS	Avg.	OBP	SLG	OPS	E	Avg.
										BATTING									FIELDING	
2001— Michigan (Midw.)	SS	56	233	47	70	11	6	3	17	26	31	3	3	21-8	.300	.376	.438	.814	17	.931
2002— Round Rock (Texas)	2B-SS	136	481	66	127	19	8	3	37	39	61	10	8	16-15	.264	.330	.356	.686	23	.965
2003— Round Rock (Texas) 2B-SS-OF		137	549	88	165	23	8	3	41	57	57	14	8	34-10	.301	.379	.388	.767	21	.969
2004— New Orleans (PCL)	2B	123	483	93	152	33	6	16	52	55	76	13	7	37-14	.315	.396	.507	.888	11	.975
— Houston (N.L.)	2B	17	17	2	1	0	0	0	0	3	3	0	0	0-0	.059	.200	.059	.259	0	1.000
Major League totals (1 year)		17	17	2	1	0	0	0	0	3	3	0	0	0-0	.059	.200	.059	.259	0	1.000

BURKE, JAMIE   C

PERSONAL: Born September 24, 1971, in Roseburg, Ore. ... 6-0/220. ... Bats right, throws right. ... Full name: James Eugene Burke. ... High school: Roseburg (Ore.). ... College: Oregon State.

TRANSACTIONS/CAREER NOTES: Selected by California Angels organization in ninth round of 1993 free-agent draft. ... Angels franchise renamed Anaheim Angels for 1997 season. ... Signed as a free agent by Chicago White Sox organization (January 27, 2003).

2004 GAMES PLAYED BY POSITION (MLB): C—45, DH—3, 3B—2, 1B—2, OF—2.

Year Team (League)	Pos.	G	AB	R	H	2B	3B	HR	RBI	BB	SO	HBP	GDP	SB-CS	Avg.	OBP	SLG	OPS	E	Avg.
										BATTING									FIELDING	
1993— Boise (N'west)	3B	66	226	32	68	11	1	1	30	39	28	5	4	2-3	.301	.412	.372	.783	18	.873
1994— Cedar Rap. (Midw.)	3B-1B	127	469	57	124	24	1	1	47	40	64	12	15	6-8	.264	.333	.326	.659	22	.973
1995— Lake Elsinore (Calif.)	3B-1B	106	365	47	100	15	6	2	56	32	53	9	12	6-4	.274	.344	.364	.708	22	.949
1996— Midland (Texas) 3B-C-1B-OF		45	144	24	46	8	2	2	16	20	22	2	1	1-1	.319	.410	.444	.854	5	.968
— Vancouver (PCL)	3B-C-OF	41	156	12	39	5	0	1	14	7	18	1	5	2-1	.250	.283	.301	.584	5	.952
1997— Midland (Texas) 3B-C-1B-OF		116	428	77	141	44	3	6	72	40	46	8	12	2-3	.329	.395	.488	.883	27	.956
— Vancouver (PCL)	3B-C	8	27	4	8	1	0	0	3	3	2	1	1	0-0	.296	.387	.333	.720	3	.923
1998— Vancouver (PCL)	3B-C-1B	61	162	16	35	6	0	2	14	13	25	6	7	0-1	.216	.295	.290	.585	5	.985
— Midland (Texas)	3B	12	41	7	10	1	0	0	4	7	4	0	4	0-0	.244	.354	.268	.622	3	.870
1999— Edmonton (PCL) 2-B-P-C-1		46	149	29	50	9	0	3	16	23	18	3	2	0-1	.336	.434	.456	.891	5	.958
2000— Edmonton (PCL)	2B-3B	75	263	25	63	12	0	0	17	19	42	5	5	1-1	.240	.301	.285	.586	6	.980
2001— Salt Lake (PCL) C-3B-1B-OF		61	215	25	47	10	3	0	27	19	28	5	6	1-0	.219	.292	.293	.585	5	.988
— Anaheim (A.L.)	C-DH-1B	9	5	1	1	0	0	0	0	0	2	0	0	0-0	.200	.200	.200	.400	0	1.000
2002— Salt Lake (PCL)	C-3B-1B	88	316	47	96	12	4	8	44	20	37	4	9	1-3	.304	.350	.443	.793	13	.974
2003— Charlotte (Int'l) C-DH-1B-3B		94	323	47	104	13	0	6	50	20	39	4	9	1-1	.322	.363	.418	.781	6	.990
— Chicago (A.L.)	C-DH-1B	6	8	0	3	0	0	0	2	0	0	0	1	0-0	.375	.375	.375	.750	0	1.000
2004— Charlotte (Int'l)	C-DH	37	134	12	31	6	0	2	12	9	15	2	4	0-0	.231	.286	.321	.607	2	.993
— Chicago (A.L.)	C-DH-3-1-O	57	120	22	40	9	0	0	15	10	13	1	3	0-0	.333	.386	.408	.795	3	.987
Major League totals (3 years)		72	133	23	44	9	0	0	17	10	15	1	3	0-0	.331	.379	.398	.778	3	.988

BURKS, ELLIS   DH

PERSONAL: Born September 11, 1964, in Vicksburg, Miss. ... 6-2/205. ... Bats right, throws right. ... Full name: Ellis Rena Burks. ... High school: Everman (Texas). ... Junior college: Ranger (Texas).

TRANSACTIONS/CAREER NOTES: Selected by Boston Red Sox organization in first round (20th pick overall) of January 1983 free-agent draft. ... On disabled list (March 26-April 12, 1988). ... On disabled list (June 15-August 1, 1989); included rehabilitation assignment to Pawtucket. ... On disabled list (June 25, 1992-remainder of season). ... Signed as a free agent by Chicago White Sox (January 4, 1993). ... Signed as a free agent by Colorado Rockies (November 30, 1993). ... On disabled list (May 18-July 31, 1994); included rehabilitation assignment to Colorado Springs. ... On disabled list (April 17-May 5, 1995); included rehabilitation assignment to Colorado Springs. ... On disabled list (June 28-July 29, 1997). ... Traded by Rockies to San Francisco Giants for OF Darryl Hamilton, P James Stoops and a player to be named (July 31, 1998); Rockies acquired P Jason Brester to complete deal (August 17, 1998). ... On disabled list (June 9-26, 1999; and May 9-24, 2000). ... Signed as a free agent by Cleveland Indians (November 19, 2000). ... On disabled list (July 16-August 1, 2001). ... On disabled list (June 8, 2003-remainder of season). ... Signed as a free agent by Red Sox (February 6, 2004). ... On disabled list (April 26-September 23, 2004). ... Announced retirement (November 1, 2004).

HONORS: Won A.L. Gold Glove as outfielder (1990).

2004 GAMES PLAYED BY POSITION (MLB): DH—9.

Year Team (League)	Pos.	G	AB	R	H	2B	3B	HR	RBI	BB	SO	HBP	GDP	SB-CS	Avg.	OBP	SLG	OPS	E	Avg.
										BATTING									FIELDING	
1983— Elmira (N.Y.-Penn)	OF	53	174	30	42	9	0	2	23	17	43	1	...	9-0	.241	.313	.328	.640	2	.979
1984— Winter Haven (FSL)	OF	112	375	52	96	15	4	6	43	42	68	5	8	29-8	.256	.337	.365	.703	5	.977
1985— New Britain (East.)	OF	133	476	66	121	25	7	10	61	42	85	3	5	17-14	.254	.316	.399	.715	8	.975
1986— New Britain (East.)	OF	124	462	70	126	20	3	14	55	44	75	2	4	31-9	.273	.337	.420	.757	5	.985
1987— Pawtucket (Int'l)	OF	11	40	11	9	3	1	3	6	7	7	0	1	1-0	.225	.340	.575	.915	0	1.000
— Boston (A.L.)	DH-OF	133	558	94	152	30	2	20	59	41	98	2	1	27-6	.272	.324	.441	.765	4	.988
1988— Boston (A.L.)	DH-OF	144	540	93	159	37	5	18	92	62	89	3	8	25-9	.294	.367	.481	.848	9	.977
1989— Boston (A.L.)	DH-OF	97	399	73	121	19	6	12	61	36	52	5	8	21-5	.303	.365	.471	.836	6	.977
— Pawtucket (Int'l)	OF	5	21	4	3	1	0	0	0	2	3	0	2	0-0	.143	.217	.190	.408	0	1.000
1990— Boston (A.L.)	DH-OF	152	588	89	174	33	8	21	89	48	82	1	18	9-11	.296	.349	.486	.835	2	.994
1991— Boston (A.L.)	DH-OF	130	474	56	119	33	3	14	56	39	81	6	7	6-11	.251	.314	.422	.736	2	.993
1992— Boston (A.L.)	OF-DH	66	235	35	60	8	3	8	30	25	48	1	5	5-2	.255	.327	.417	.744	2	.984
1993— Chicago (A.L.)	OF	146	499	75	137	24	4	17	74	60	97	4	11	6-9	.275	.352	.441	.793	6	.982
1994— Colorado (N.L.)	OF	42	149	33	48	8	3	13	24	16	39	0	3	3-1	.322	.388	.678	1.066	3	.964
— Colo. Springs (PCL)	OF	2	8	4	4	1	0	1	2	2	1	0	1	0-0	.500	.600	1.000	1.600	0	1.000
1995— Colo. Springs (PCL)	OF-DH	8	29	9	9	2	1	2	6	4	7	0	1	0-0	.310	.394	.655	1.049	0	1.000
— Colorado (N.L.)	OF	103	278	41	74	10	6	14	49	39	72	2	7	7-3	.266	.359	.496	.856	5	.970
1996— Colorado (N.L.)	OF	156	613	* 142	211	45	8	40	128	61	114	6	19	32-6	.344	.408	* .639	1.047	5	.983
1997— Colorado (N.L.)	OF	119	424	91	123	19	2	32	82	47	75	3	17	7-2	.290	.363	.571	.934	4	.982
1998— Colorado (N.L.)	OF	100	357	54	102	22	5	16	54	39	80	2	10	3-7	.286	.355	.510	.865	5	.975
— San Francisco (N.L.)	OF	42	147	22	45	6	1	5	22	19	31	3	2	8-1	.306	.387	.463	.850	1	.989
1999— San Francisco (N.L.)	OF-DH	120	390	73	110	19	0	31	96	69	86	6	11	7-5	.282	.394	.569	.964	2	.991
2000— San Francisco (N.L.)	OF-DH	122	393	74	135	21	5	24	96	56	49	1	10	5-1	.344	.419	.606	1.025	4	.982
2001— Cleveland (A.L.)	DH-OF	124	439	83	123	29	4	28	74	62	85	5	16	5-1	.280	.369	.542	.911	0	1.000
2002— Cleveland (A.L.)	DH-OF	138	518	92	156	28	0	32	91	44	108	6	13	2-3	.301	.362	.541	.903	0	1.000
2003— Cleveland (A.L.)	DH-OF	55	198	27	52	11	1	6	28	27	46	3	4	1-1	.263	.360	.419	.779	0	1.000
2004— Pawtucket (Int'l)	DH	1	2	1	0	0	0	0	0	0	1	0	0	0-0	...	.333	...	.333	0	...
— Boston (A.L.)	DH	11	33	6	6	0	0	1	1	3	8	1	1	2-0	.182	.270	.273	.543	0	...
American League totals (11 years)		1196	4481	723	1259	252	33	177	655	447	794	37	92	109-58	.281	.349	.470	.819	31	.985
National League totals (7 years)		804	2751	530	848	150	30	175	551	346	546	23	79	72-26	.308	.387	.575	.962	29	.980
Major League totals (18 years)		2000	7232	1253	2107	402	63	352	1206	793	1340	60	171	181-84	.291	.363	.510	.874	60	.983

B

DIVISION SERIES RECORD

Year — Team (League)	Pos.	G	AB	R	H	2B	3B	HR	RBI	BB	SO	HBP	GDP	SB-CS	Avg.	OBP	SLG	OPS	E	Avg.
1995— Colorado (N.L.)	OF	2	6	1	2	1	0	0	2	0	1	0	0	0-0	.333	.286	.500	.786	1	.800
2000— San Francisco (N.L.)	OF	4	13	2	3	1	0	1	4	4	2	0	0	0-0	.231	.412	.538	.950	0	1.000
2001— Cleveland (A.L.)	DH	5	19	4	6	1	0	1	1	1	3	0	0	0-0	.316	.350	.526	.876	...	...
Division series totals (3 years)		11	38	7	11	3	0	2	7	5	6	0	0	0-0	.289	.364	.526	.890	1	.941

CHAMPIONSHIP SERIES RECORD

Year — Team (League)	Pos.	G	AB	R	H	2B	3B	HR	RBI	BB	SO	HBP	GDP	SB-CS	Avg.	OBP	SLG	OPS	E	Avg.
1988— Boston (A.L.)	OF	4	17	2	4	1	0	0	1	0	3	0	0	0-0	.235	.235	.294	.529	0	1.000
1990— Boston (A.L.)	OF	4	15	1	4	2	0	0	0	1	1	0	0	1-0	.267	.313	.400	.713	0	1.000
1993— Chicago (A.L.)	OF	6	23	4	7	1	0	1	3	3	5	1	1	0-1	.304	.407	.478	.886	0	1.000
Champ. series totals (3 years)		14	55	7	15	4	0	1	4	4	9	1	1	1-1	.273	.333	.400	.733	0	1.000

ALL-STAR GAME RECORD

	G	AB	R	H	2B	3B	HR	RBI	BB	SO	HBP	GDP	SB-CS	Avg.	OBP	SLG	OPS	E	Avg.
All-Star Game totals (1 year)	1	2	0	1	0	1	0	0	0	1	0	0	0-0	.500	.500	1.500	2.000	1	1.000

BURNETT, A.J.   P

PERSONAL: Born January 3, 1977, in North Little Rock, Ark. ... 6-4/230. ... Throws right, bats right. ... Full name: Allan James Burnett. ... High school: Central Arkansas Christian (North Little Rock, Ark.).

TRANSACTIONS/CAREER NOTES: Selected by New York Mets organization in eighth round of 1995 free-agent draft. ... Traded by Mets with P Jesus Sanchez and OF Robert Stratton to Florida Marlins for P Al Leiter and 2B Ralph Milliard (February 6, 1998). ... On disabled list (March 17-July 20, 2000); included rehabilitation assignments to Brevard County and Calgary. ... On disabled list (March 23-May 7, 2001); included rehabilitation assignment to Brevard County. ... On disabled list (August 19-September 14, 2002; and April 26, 2003-remainder of season). ... On disabled list (March 26-June 3, 2004); included rehabilitation assignments to Jupiter and Albuquerque.

CAREER HITTING: 24-for-185 (.130), 9 R, 4 2B, 1 3B, 2 HR, 7 RBI.

Year — Team (League)	W	L	Pct.	ERA	WHIP	G	GS	CG	ShO	Hld.	Sv.-Opp.	IP	H	R	ER	HR	BB-IBB	SO	Avg.
1995— GC Mets (GCL)	2	3	.400	4.28	1.49	9	8	1	0	...	0-...	33.2	27	16	16	2	23-0	26	.231
1996— Kingsport (Appalachian)	4	0	1.000	3.88	1.47	12	12	0	0	...	0-...	58.0	31	26	25	0	54-0	68	.171
1997— GC Mets (GCL)	0	1	.000	3.18	1.41	3	2	0	0	...	0-...	11.1	8	8	4	0	8-0	15	.182
— Pittsfield (N.Y.-Penn.)	3	1	.750	4.70	1.43	20	9	0	0	...	0-...	44.0	28	26	23	3	35-0	48	.188
1998— Kane County (Midwest)	10	4	.714	1.97	1.00	20	20	0	0	...	0-...	119.0	74	27	26	3	45-0	186	.179
1999— Portland (East.)	6	12	.333	5.52	1.68	26	23	0	0	...	0-...	120.2	132	91	74	15	71-0	121	.281
— Florida (N.L.)	4	2	.667	3.48	1.50	7	7	0	0	0	0-0	41.1	37	23	16	3	25-2	33	.242
2000— Brevard County (FSL)	0	0	...	3.68	1.36	2	2	0	0	...	0-...	7.1	4	3	3	0	6-0	6	.160
— Calgary (PCL)	0	0	...	0.00	0.60	1	1	0	0	...	0-...	5.0	0	0	0	0	3-0	6	.000
— Florida (N.L.)	3	7	.300	4.79	1.50	13	13	0	0	0	0-0	82.2	80	46	44	8	44-3	57	.259
2001— Brevard County (FSL)	0	0	...	1.93	0.86	2	2	0	0	...	0-...	9.1	4	2	2	0	4-0	10	.129
— Florida (N.L.)	11	12	.478	4.05	1.32	27	27	2	1	0	0-0	173.1	145	82	78	20	83-3	128	.231
2002— Florida (N.L.)	12	9	.571	3.30	1.19	31	29	7	*5	0	0-1	204.1	153	84	75	12	90-5	203	.209
2003— Florida (N.L.)	0	2	.000	4.70	1.57	4	4	0	0	0	0-0	23.0	18	13	12	2	18-2	21	.217
2004— Jupiter (FSL)	0	0	...	0.00	1.00	1	1	0	0	...	0-...	4.0	2	1	0	0	2-0	4	.143
— Albuquerque (PCL)	0	0	...	10.80	2.70	1	1	0	0	...	0-...	3.1	7	4	4	1	2-0	6	.412
— Florida (N.L.)	7	6	.538	3.68	1.17	20	19	1	0	0	0-0	120.0	102	50	49	9	38-0	113	.231
Major League totals (6 years)	37	38	.493	3.83	1.29	102	99	10	6	0	0-1	644.2	535	298	274	54	298-15	555	.228

BURNETT, SEAN   P

PERSONAL: Born September 17, 1982, in Dunedin, Fla. ... 5-11/190. ... Throws left, bats left. ... Full name: Sean Richard Burnett. ... High school: Wellington Community High (Fla.).

TRANSACTIONS/CAREER NOTES: Selected by Pittsburgh Pirates organization in first round (19th pick overall) of 2000 free-agent draft. ... On disabled list (August 22, 2004-remainder of season).

CAREER HITTING: 0-for-23 (.000), 0 R, 0 2B, 0 3B, 0 HR, 0 RBI.

Year — Team (League)	W	L	Pct.	ERA	WHIP	G	GS	CG	ShO	Hld.	Sv.-Opp.	IP	H	R	ER	HR	BB-IBB	SO	Avg.
2000— GC Pirates (GCL)	2	1	.667	4.06	1.10	8	6	0	0	...	0-...	31.0	31	17	14	0	3-0	24	.250
2001— Hickory (S. Atl.)	11	8	.579	2.62	1.22	26	26	1	0	...	0-...	161.1	164	63	47	11	33-0	134	.265
2002— Lynchburg (Carolina)	13	4	.765	1.80	0.97	26	26	2	0	...	0-...	155.1	118	46	31	4	33-0	96	.210
2003— Altoona (East.)	14	6	.700	3.21	1.17	27	27	2	1	...	0-...	159.2	158	60	57	2	29-1	86	.265
2004— Nashville (PCL)	1	5	.167	5.36	1.60	10	10	0	0	...	0-...	47.0	58	29	28	5	17-2	25	.319
— Pittsburgh (N.L.)	5	5	.500	5.02	1.59	13	13	1	1	0	0-0	71.2	86	41	40	9	28-2	30	.301
Major League totals (1 year)	5	5	.500	5.02	1.59	13	13	1	1	0	0-0	71.2	86	41	40	9	28-2	30	.301

BURNITZ, JEROMY   OF

PERSONAL: Born April 15, 1969, in Westminster, Calif. ... 6-0/213. ... Bats left, throws right. ... Full name: Jeromy Neal Burnitz. ... Name pronounced: ber-NITS. ... High school: Conroe (Texas). ... College: Oklahoma State.

TRANSACTIONS/CAREER NOTES: Selected by Milwaukee Brewers organization in 24th round of 1987 free-agent draft; did not sign. ... Selected by New York Mets organization in first round (17th pick overall) of 1990 free-agent draft. ... Traded by Mets with P Joe Roa to Cleveland Indians for Ps Paul Byrd, Jerry DiPoto and Dave Mlicki and a player to be named (November 18, 1994); Mets acquired 2B Jesus Azuaje to complete deal (December 6, 1994). ... Traded by Indians to Milwaukee Brewers for 3B/1B Kevin Seitzer (August 31, 1996). ... On disabled list (July 18-August 20, 1999). ... Traded by Brewers with P Jeff D'Amico, IF Lou Collier and OF/1B Mark Sweeney to Mets as part of three-team deal in which Brewers acquired P Glendon Rusch and IF Lenny Harris from Mets and OF Alex Ochoa from Rockies, Rockies acquired IFs Todd Zeile, OF Benny Agbayani and cash from Rockies, and Mets acquired 1B/OF Ross Gload and Craig House from Rockies (January 21, 2002). ... On disabled list (April 23-May 23, 2003); included rehabilitation assignment to Binghamton. ... Traded by Mets to Los Angeles Dodgers for IF Victor Diaz and Ps Joselo Diaz and Kole Strayhorn (July 14, 2003). ... Signed as a free agent by Colorado Rockies (January 9, 2004).

2004 GAMES PLAYED BY POSITION (MLB): OF—143, DH—3.

Year — Team (League)	Pos.	G	AB	R	H	2B	3B	HR	RBI	BB	SO	HBP	GDP	SB-CS	Avg.	OBP	SLG	OPS	E	Avg.
1990— Pittsfield (N.Y.-Penn.)	OF	51	173	37	52	6	5	6	22	45	39	3	3	12-5	.301	.444	.497	.942	0	1.000
— St. Lucie (Fla. St.)	OF	11	32	6	5	1	0	0	3	7	12	4	0	1-0	.156	.372	.188	.560	0	1.000
1991— Williamsport (East.)	OF	135	457	80	103	16	10	31	85	104	127	4	7	31-13	.225	.368	.508	.876	11	.958
1992— Tidewater (Int'l)	OF	121	445	56	108	21	3	8	40	33	84	3	7	30-7	.243	.298	.357	.655	8	.967
1993— Norfolk (Int'l)	OF	65	255	33	58	15	3	8	44	25	53	2	6	10-7	.227	.298	.404	.702	1	.993
— New York (N.L.)	OF	86	263	49	64	10	6	13	38	38	66	1	2	3-6	.243	.339	.475	.814	4	.977

Year	Team (League)	Pos.	G	AB	R	H	2B	3B	HR	RBI	BB	SO	HBP	GDP	SB-CS	Avg.	OBP	SLG	OPS	E	Avg.
1994—New York (N.L.)	OF		45	143	26	34	4	0	3	15	23	45	1	2	1-1	.238	.347	.329	.676	2	.970
—Norfolk (Int'l)	OF-DH		85	314	58	75	15	5	14	49	49	82	1	0	18-6	.239	.340	.452	.792	4	.979
1995—Buffalo (A.A.)	OF		128	443	72	126	26	7	19	85	50	83	3	6	13-5	.284	.359	.503	.862	5	.981
—Cleveland (A.L.)	OF-DH		9	7	4	4	1	0	0	0	0	0	0	0	0-0	.571	.571	.714	1.286	0	1.000
1996—Cleveland (A.L.)	OF-DH		71	128	30	36	10	0	7	26	25	31	2	3	2-1	.281	.406	.523	.930	1	1.000
—Milwaukee (A.L.)	OF		23	72	8	17	4	0	2	14	8	16	2	1	2-0	.236	.321	.375	.696	1	.975
1997—Milwaukee (A.L.)	OF		153	494	85	139	37	8	27	85	75	111	5	8	20-13	.281	.382	.553	.934	7	.975
1998—Milwaukee (N.L.)	OF		161	609	92	160	28	1	38	125	70	158	4	9	7-4	.263	.339	.499	.838	9	.972
1999—Milwaukee (N.L.)	OF-DH		130	467	87	126	33	2	33	103	91	124	16	11	7-3	.270	.402	.561	.963	5	.982
2000—Milwaukee (N.L.)	OF-DH		161	564	91	131	29	2	31	98	99	121	14	12	6-4	.232	.356	.456	.811	7	.979
2001—Milwaukee (N.L.)	OF		154	562	104	141	32	4	34	100	80	150	5	8	0-4	.251	.347	.504	.851	6	.981
2002—New York (N.L.)	OF-DH		154	479	65	103	15	0	19	54	58	135	10	11	10-7	.215	.311	.365	.677	9	.966
2003—Binghamton (East.)	OF		3	13	1	3	0	0	1	3	0	4	0	0	1-0	.231	.231	.462	.692	0	1.000
—New York (N.L.)	OF		65	234	38	64	18	0	18	45	21	55	4	4	1-4	.274	.344	.581	.925	2	.986
—Los Angeles (N.L.)	OF		61	230	25	47	4	0	13	32	14	57	1	1	4-0	.204	.252	.391	.643	5	.946
2004—Colorado (N.L.)	OF-DH		150	540	94	153	30	4	37	110	58	124	5	7	5-6	.283	.356	.559	.916	7	.974
American League totals (3 years)			256	701	127	196	52	8	36	125	108	158	9	12	24-14	.280	.382	.531	.912	8	.978
National League totals (9 years)			1167	4091	671	1023	203	19	239	720	552	1035	61	67	44-39	.250	.345	.484	.830	56	.975
Major League totals (12 years)			1423	4792	798	1219	255	27	275	845	660	1193	70	79	68-53	.254	.351	.491	.842	64	.976

ALL-STAR GAME RECORD

	G	AB	R	H	2B	3B	HR	RBI	BB	SO	HBP	GDP	SB-CS	Avg.	OBP	SLG	OPS	E	Avg.
All-Star Game totals (1 year)	1	2	1	1	1	0	0	0	0	0	0	0	0-0	.500	.500	1.000	1.500	0	...

BURRELL, PAT   OF

PERSONAL: Born October 10, 1976, in Eureka Springs, Ark. ... 6-4/223. ... Bats right, throws right. ... Full name: Patrick Brian Burrell. ... Name pronounced: BURL. ... High school: Bellarmine Prep (San Jose, Calif.). ... College: Miami (Fla.).
TRANSACTIONS/CAREER NOTES: Selected by Boston Red Sox organization in 43rd round of 1995 free-agent draft; did not sign. ... Selected by Philadelphia Phillies organization in first round (first pick overall) of 1998 free-agent draft. ... On disabled list (August 4-September 3, 2004); included rehabilitation assignment to Reading.
2004 GAMES PLAYED BY POSITION (MLB): OF—122.

											BATTING									FIELDING	
Year	Team (League)	Pos.	G	AB	R	H	2B	3B	HR	RBI	BB	SO	HBP	GDP	SB-CS	Avg.	OBP	SLG	OPS	E	Avg.
1998—Clearwater (FSL)	1B		37	132	29	40	7	1	7	30	27	22	0	3	2-0	.303	.416	.530	.946	1	.995
1999—Reading (East.)	1B-OF		117	417	84	139	28	6	28	90	79	103	0	13	3-1	.333	.438	.631	1.068	12	.985
—Scran./W.B. (I.L.)	1B-OF		10	33	4	5	0	0	1	4	4	8	1	0	0-1	.152	.263	.242	.506	0	1.000
2000—Scran./W.B. (I.L.)	1B		40	143	31	42	15	1	4	25	32	36	0	1	1-1	.294	.420	.497	.917	2	.987
—Philadelphia (N.L.)	1B-OF-DH		111	408	57	106	27	1	18	79	63	139	1	5	0-0	.260	.359	.463	.822	8	.986
2001—Philadelphia (N.L.)	OF		155	539	70	139	29	2	27	89	70	162	5	12	2-1	.258	.346	.469	.816	7	.972
2002—Philadelphia (N.L.)	OF		157	586	96	165	39	2	37	116	89	153	3	16	1-0	.282	.376	.544	.920	6	.979
2003—Philadelphia (N.L.)	OF-DH		146	522	57	109	31	4	21	64	72	142	4	18	0-0	.209	.309	.404	.713	6	.976
2004—Reading (East.)	OF		4	15	2	3	0	0	2	4	3	7	0	0	0-0	.200	.333	.600	.933	1	.923
—Philadelphia (N.L.)	OF		127	448	66	115	17	0	24	84	78	130	4	10	2-0	.257	.365	.455	.821	4	.983
Major League totals (5 years)			696	2503	346	634	143	9	127	432	372	726	15	61	5-1	.253	.351	.470	.821	31	.980

BURROUGHS, SEAN   3B

PERSONAL: Born September 12, 1980, in Atlanta, Ga. ... 6-2/200. ... Bats left, throws right. ... Full name: Sean Patrick Burroughs. ... High school: Wilson (Long Beach, Calif.). ... Son of Jeff Burroughs, outfielder with five major league teams (1970-85).
TRANSACTIONS/CAREER NOTES: Selected by San Diego Padres organization in first round (ninth pick overall) of 1998 free-agent draft. ... On disabled list (May 29-July 15, 2002); included rehabilitation assignment to Portland.
2004 GAMES PLAYED BY POSITION (MLB): 3B—125.

											BATTING									FIELDING	
Year	Team (League)	Pos.	G	AB	R	H	2B	3B	HR	RBI	BB	SO	HBP	GDP	SB-CS	Avg.	OBP	SLG	OPS	E	Avg.
1999—Rancho Cuca. (Calif.)	3B		6	23	3	10	3	0	1	5	3	3	1	1	0-1	.435	.519	.696	1.214	0	1.000
—Fort Wayne (Midw.)	3B		122	426	65	153	30	3	5	80	74	59	14	10	17-15	.359	.464	.479	.943	37	.898
2000—Mobile (Sou.)	3B		108	392	46	114	29	4	2	42	58	45	3	10	6-8	.291	.383	.401	.783	16	.947
2001—Portland (PCL)	3B		104	394	60	127	28	1	9	55	37	54	4	13	9-2	.322	.386	.467	.853	10	.964
2002—San Diego (N.L.)	3B-2B		63	192	18	52	5	1	1	11	12	30	1	6	2-0	.271	.317	.323	.640	8	.949
—Portland (PCL)	2B-3B		50	179	29	54	16	2	2	23	21	16	3	5	1-0	.302	.380	.447	.827	6	.969
2003—San Diego (N.L.)	3B		146	517	62	148	27	6	7	58	44	75	11	13	7-2	.286	.352	.402	.755	12	.966
2004—San Diego (N.L.)	3B		130	523	76	156	23	3	2	47	31	52	9	6	5-4	.298	.348	.365	.713	14	.957
Major League totals (3 years)			339	1232	156	356	55	10	10	116	87	157	21	25	14-6	.289	.345	.374	.719	34	.959

BUSH, DAVID   P

PERSONAL: Born November 9, 1979, in Pittsburgh, Pa. ... 6-2/212. ... Throws right, bats right. ... Full name: David T. Bush. ... High school: Conestoga (Berwyn, Pa.). ... College: Wake Forest.
TRANSACTIONS/CAREER NOTES: Selected by Tampa Bay Devil Rays organization in fourth round of 2001 free-agent draft; did not sign. ... Selected by Toronto Blue Jays organization in second round of 2002 free-agent draft.
CAREER HITTING: 0-for-2 (.000), 0 R, 0 2B, 0 3B, 0 HR, 0 RBI.

Year	Team (League)	W	L	Pct.	ERA	WHIP	G	GS	CG	ShO	Hld.	Sv.-Opp.	IP	H	R	ER	HR	BB-IBB	SO	Avg.
2002—Auburn (N.Y.-Penn)	1	1	.500	2.82	0.90	18	0	0	0	...	10-...	22.1	13	9	7	1	7-2	39	.159
—Dunedin (Fla. St.)	0	1	.000	2.03	0.90	7	0	0	0	...	0-...	13.1	10	3	3	1	2-0	9	.222
2003—Dunedin (Fla. St.)	7	3	.700	2.81	0.95	14	14	0	0	...	0-...	77.0	64	29	24	6	9-0	75	.223
—New Haven (East.)	7	3	.700	2.78	1.14	14	14	1	0	...	0-...	81.0	73	26	25	4	19-1	73	.239
2004—Syracuse (Int'l)	6	6	.500	4.06	1.28	16	16	2	1	...	0-...	99.2	108	52	45	7	20-1	88	.276
—Toronto (A.L.)	5	4	.556	3.69	1.23	16	16	1	1	0	0-0	97.2	95	47	40	11	25-2	64	.255
Major League totals (1 year)	5	4	.556	3.69	1.23	16	16	1	1	0	0-0	97.2	95	47	40	11	25-2	64	.255

BUSH, HOMER — 2B

PERSONAL: Born November 12, 1972, in East St. Louis, Ill. ... 5-10/180. ... Bats right, throws right. ... Full name: Homer Giles Bush. ... High school: East St. Louis (Ill.).

TRANSACTIONS/CAREER NOTES: Selected by San Diego Padres organization in seventh round of 1991 free-agent draft. ... Traded by Padres with OF Gordon Amerson, a player to be named and the rights to P Hideki Irabu to New York Yankees for OF Ruben Rivera, P Rafael Medina and cash (April 22, 1997); Yankees acquired OF Vernon Maxwell to complete deal (June 9, 1997). ... Traded by Yankees with Ps David Wells and Graeme Lloyd to Toronto Blue Jays for P Roger Clemens (February 18, 1999). ... On disabled list (April 11-May 14, 1999); included rehabilitation assignment to Dunedin. ... On disabled list (May 22-June 6 and July 31, 2000-remainder of season). ... On disabled list (April 5-May 18 and June 26-August 1, 2001); included rehabilitation assignments to Dunedin and Syracuse. ... Released by Blue Jays (May 10, 2002). ... Signed by Florida Marlins (May 21, 2002). ... Released by Marlins (September 1, 2002). ... Signed by Padres organization (December 13, 2002). ... On voluntarily retired list (February 24, 2003-January 23, 2004). ... Signed by New York Yankees organization (January 23, 2004).

2004 GAMES PLAYED BY POSITION (MLB): 2B—4, DH—2.

Year	Team (League)	Pos.	G	AB	R	H	2B	3B	HR	RBI	BB	SO	HBP	GDP	SB-CS	Avg.	OBP	SLG	OPS	E	Avg.
1991—	Ariz. Padres (Ariz.)	3B	32	127	16	41	3	2	0	16	4	33	1	2	11-7	.323	.348	.378	.726	10	.895
1992—	Char., S.C. (SAL)	2B	108	367	37	86	10	5	0	18	13	85	1	3	14-11	.234	.265	.289	.554	34	.935
1993—	Waterloo (Midw.)	2B	130	472	63	152	19	3	5	51	19	87	1	10	39-14	.322	.349	.407	.756	38	.930
1994—	Rancho Cuca. (Calif.)	2B	39	161	37	54	10	3	0	16	9	29	4	2	9-2	.335	.383	.435	.818	7	.961
—	Wichita (Texas)	2B	59	245	35	73	11	4	3	14	10	39	3	6	20-7	.298	.333	.412	.746	8	.967
1995—	Memphis (Sou.)	2B-DH	108	432	53	121	12	5	5	37	15	83	2	6	34-12	.280	.307	.366	.673	16	.969
1996—	Las Vegas (PCL)	2B-DH	32	116	24	42	11	1	2	3	3	33	2	2	3-5	.362	.388	.526	.914	5	.969
1997—	Las Vegas (PCL)	2B-DH	38	155	25	43	10	1	3	14	7	40	2	1	5-1	.277	.310	.413	.722	4	.978
—	Columbus (Int'l)	2B	74	275	36	68	10	3	2	26	25	56	1	6	12-7	.247	.308	.327	.635	9	.978
—	New York (A.L.)	2B	10	11	2	4	0	0	0	3	0	0	0	0	0-0	.364	.364	.364	.727	2	.913
1998—	New York (A.L.)	2-DH-3-SS	45	71	17	27	3	0	1	5	5	19	0	1	6-3	.380	.421	.465	.886	2	.974
1999—	Toronto (A.L.)	2B-SS	128	485	69	155	26	4	5	55	21	82	6	9	32-8	.320	.353	.421	.774	16	.976
—	Dunedin (Fla. St.)	2B-DH	4	14	3	5	2	0	0	0	1	1	1	1	1-0	.357	.438	.500	.938	0	1.000
2000—	Toronto (A.L.)	2B	76	297	38	64	8	0	1	18	18	60	5	10	9-4	.215	.271	.253	.524	6	.986
2001—	Toronto (A.L.)	2B	78	271	32	83	11	1	3	27	8	50	6	2	13-4	.306	.336	.387	.723	4	.990
—	Dunedin (Fla. St.)	2B	4	17	4	6	0	0	0	2	2	3	0	0	1-0	.353	.421	.353	.774	0	1.000
—	Syracuse (Int'l)	2B	9	32	11	8	2	0	0	3	3	6	2	1	0-0	.250	.342	.313	.655	0	1.000
2002—	Toronto (A.L.)	2B-DH	23	78	9	18	2	0	1	2	2	12	2	2	2-0	.231	.268	.295	.563	1	.990
—	Florida (N.L.)	2B-SS	40	54	7	12	0	0	0	5	3	13	0	0	2-1	.222	.263	.222	.485	1	.962
2004—	New York (A.L.)	2B-DH	9	7	2	0	0	0	0	0	0	2	1	1	1-0	.000	.125	.000	.125	0	1.000
—	Columbus (Int'l)	3-2-S-DH-O	63	233	35	64	15	0	2	18	11	41	2	3	2-3	.275	.312	.365	.677	5	.974
	American League totals (7 years)		369	1220	169	351	50	5	11	110	54	225	20	25	63-19	.288	.326	.364	.690	31	.982
	National League totals (1 year)		40	54	7	12	0	0	0	5	3	13	0	0	2-1	.222	.263	.222	.485	1	.962
	Major League totals (7 years)		409	1274	176	363	50	5	11	115	57	238	20	25	65-20	.285	.324	.358	.682	32	.981

DIVISION SERIES RECORD

Year	Team (League)	Pos.	G	AB	R	H	2B	3B	HR	RBI	BB	SO	HBP	GDP	SB-CS	Avg.	OBP	SLG	OPS	E	Avg.
1998—	New York (A.L.)	DH	1	0	0	0	0	0	0	0	0	0	0	0	1-0	...	...	...	...		

CHAMPIONSHIP SERIES RECORD

Year	Team (League)	Pos.	G	AB	R	H	2B	3B	HR	RBI	BB	SO	HBP	GDP	SB-CS	Avg.	OBP	SLG	OPS	E	Avg.
1998—	New York (A.L.)	DH	2	0	1	0	0	0	0	0	0	0	0	0	1-0	...	...	...	...		

WORLD SERIES RECORD

Year	Team (League)	Pos.	G	AB	R	H	2B	3B	HR	RBI	BB	SO	HBP	GDP	SB-CS	Avg.	OBP	SLG	OPS	E	Avg.
1998—	New York (A.L.)	DH	2	0	0	0	0	0	0	0	0	0	0	0	0-0	...	...	...	...		

BYNUM, MIKE — P

PERSONAL: Born March 20, 1978, in Tampa, Fla. ... 6-4/197. ... Throws left, bats left. ... Full name: Michael Alan Bynum. ... Name pronounced: BI-num. ... High school: Middleburg (Fla.). ... College: North Carolina.

TRANSACTIONS/CAREER NOTES: Selected by Boston Red Sox organization in 32nd round of 1996 free-agent draft; did not sign. ... Selected by San Diego Padres organization in first round (19th pick overall) of 1999 free-agent draft.

CAREER HITTING: 3-for-18 (.167), 0 R, 0 2B, 0 3B, 0 HR, 0 RBI.

Year	Team (League)	W	L	Pct.	ERA	WHIP	G	GS	CG	ShO	Hld.	Sv.-Opp.	IP	H	R	ER	HR	BB-IBB	SO	Avg.
1999—	Idaho Falls (Pioneer)	1	0	1.000	0.00	0.65	5	3	0	0	...	0-...	17.0	7	0	0	0	4-0	21	.127
—	Rancho Cuca. (Calif.)	3	1	.750	3.29	1.12	7	7	0	0	...	0-...	38.1	35	17	14	1	8-0	44	.238
2000—	Rancho Cuca. (Calif.)	9	6	.600	3.00	1.21	21	21	0	0	...	0-...	126.0	101	55	42	4	51-0	129	.224
—	Mobile (Sou.)	3	1	.750	2.91	1.38	6	6	0	0	...	0-...	34.0	31	12	11	2	16-0	27	.252
2001—	Mobile (Sou.)	2	7	.222	5.02	1.48	16	15	0	0	...	0-...	84.1	90	53	47	14	35-0	69	.279
2002—	Mobile (Sou.)	4	0	1.000	0.82	0.73	6	5	0	0	...	0-...	33.0	17	5	3	0	7-0	29	.150
—	Portland (PCL)	3	2	.600	3.51	1.05	7	7	0	0	...	0-...	41.0	36	19	16	6	7-0	35	.235
—	San Diego (N.L.)	1	0	1.000	5.27	1.64	14	3	0	0	...	0-0	27.1	33	16	16	3	15-2	17	.308
2003—	Portland (PCL)	7	12	.368	4.81	1.50	24	23	0	0	...	0-0	125.1	130	76	67	11	60-2	106	.271
—	San Diego (N.L.)	1	4	.200	8.75	1.64	13	5	0	0	...	0-0	36.0	44	35	35	14	15-0	35	.297
2004—	Portland (PCL)	6	6	.500	3.19	1.40	62	0	0	0	...	6-...	79.0	72	33	28	6	44-8	75	.243
—	San Diego (N.L.)	0	1	.000	54.00	6.00	2	0	0	0	...	0-0	.2	1	4	4	0	3-0	0	.333
	Major League totals (3 years)	2	5	.286	7.73	1.73	29	8	0	0	...	0-0	64.0	78	55	55	17	33-2	52	.302

BYRD, MARLON — OF

PERSONAL: Born August 30, 1977, in Boynton Beach, Fla. ... 6-0/229. ... Bats right, throws right. ... Full name: Marlon Jerrard Byrd. ... High school: Sprayberry (Marietta, Ga.). ... Junior college: Georgia Perimeter.

TRANSACTIONS/CAREER NOTES: Selected by Philadelphia Phillies organization in 10th round of 1999 free-agent draft. ... On disabled list (April 14-29, 2003); included rehabilitation assignment to Reading.

2004 GAMES PLAYED BY POSITION (MLB): OF—92.

Year	Team (League)	Pos.	G	AB	R	H	2B	3B	HR	RBI	BB	SO	HBP	GDP	SB-CS	Avg.	OBP	SLG	OPS	E	Avg.
1999—	Batavia (NY-Penn)	OF	65	243	40	72	7	6	13	50	28	70	5	3	8-2	.296	.376	.535	.911	7	.926
2000—	Piedmont (S. Atl.)	OF	133	515	104	159	29	13	17	93	51	110	10	7	41-5	.309	.379	.515	.893	4	.980
2001—	Reading (East.)	OF	137	510	108	161	22	8	28	89	52	93	11	7	32-5	.316	.386	.555	.941	2	.994

Year	Team (League)	Pos.	G	AB	R	H	2B	3B	HR	RBI	BB	SO	HBP	GDP	SB-CS	Avg.	OBP	SLG	OPS	E	Avg.
2002—Scran./W.B. (I.L.)		OF	136	538	103	160	37	7	15	63	46	98	11	5	15-1	.297	.362	.476	.838	8	.975
—Philadelphia (N.L.)		OF	10	35	2	8	2	0	1	1	8	0	0	0	0-2	.229	.250	.371	.621	0	1.000
2003—Scran./W.B. (I.L.)		OF	1	4	1	3	1	0	0	0	0	1	0	0	0-0	.750	.750	1.000	1.750	0	1.000
—Reading (East.)		OF	3	16	3	5	0	0	1	3	0	3	0	1	0-0	.313	.313	.500	.813	1	.800
—Philadelphia (N.L.)		OF	135	495	86	150	28	4	7	45	44	94	7	8	11-1	.303	.366	.418	.784	5	.984
2004—Scran./W.B. (I.L.)		OF	37	152	13	40	11	1	2	17	10	18	4	5	2-3	.263	.323	.388	.712	2	.980
—Philadelphia (N.L.)		OF	106	346	48	79	13	2	5	33	22	68	7	10	2-2	.228	.287	.321	.608	2	.990
Major League totals (3 years)			251	876	136	237	43	6	13	79	67	170	14	18	13-5	.271	.331	.378	.709	7	.987

BYRD, PAUL — P

PERSONAL: Born December 3, 1970, in Louisville, Ky. ... 6-1/190. ... Throws right, bats right. ... Full name: Paul Gregory Byrd. ... High school: St. Xavier (Louisville, Ky.). ... College: LSU.

TRANSACTIONS/CAREER NOTES: Selected by Cincinnati Reds organization in 13th round of 1988 free-agent draft; did not sign. ... Selected by Cleveland Indians organization in fourth round of 1991 free-agent draft. ... Traded by Indians with Ps Dave Mlicki and Jerry DiPoto and a player to be named to New York Mets for OF Jeromy Burnitz and P Joe Roa (November 18, 1994); Mets acquired 2B Jesus Azuaje to complete deal (December 6, 1994). ... On disabled list (March 22-June 9, 1996); included rehabilitation assignment to Norfolk. ... Traded by Mets with a player to be named to Atlanta Braves for P Greg McMichael (November 25, 1996); Braves acquired P Andy Zwirchitz to complete deal (May 25, 1997). ... Claimed on waivers by Philadelphia Phillies (August 14, 1998). ... On disabled list (July 27, 2000-remainder of season). ... Traded by Phillies to Kansas City Royals for P Jose Santiago (June 5, 2001). ... On disabled list (September 22, 2001-remainder of season). ... Signed as a free agent by Braves (December 17, 2002). ... On disabled list (March 21, 2003-entire season); included rehabilitation assignment to Greenville (April 5-6). ... On disabled list (March 26-June 19, 2004); included rehabilitation assignments to Greenville and Richmond.

CAREER HITTING: 22-for-141 (.156), 11 R, 0 2B, 0 3B, 0 HR, 10 RBI.

Year	Team (League)	W	L	Pct.	ERA	WHIP	G	GS	CG	ShO	Hld.	Sv.-Opp.	IP	H	R	ER	HR	BB-IBB	SO	Avg.
1991—Kinston (Caro.)	4	3	.571	3.16	1.21	14	11	0	0	...	0-...	62.2	40	27	22	7	36-0	62	.181
1992—Cant./Akr. (Eastern)	14	6	.700	3.01	1.29	24	24	4	0	...	0-...	151.1	122	68	51	4	75-2	118	.216
1993—Charlotte (Int'l)	7	4	.636	3.89	1.36	14	14	1	1	...	0-...	81.0	80	43	35	9	30-0	54	.257
—Cant./Akr. (Eastern)	0	0	...	3.60	1.00	2	1	0	0	...	0-...	10.0	7	4	4	1	3-0	5	.189
1994—Cant./Akr. (Eastern)	5	9	.357	3.81	1.34	21	20	4	1	...	0-...	139.1	135	70	59	10	52-3	106	.255
—Charlotte (Int'l)	2	2	.500	3.93	1.20	9	4	0	0	...	1-...	36.2	33	19	16	5	11-1	15	.250
1995—Norfolk (Int'l)	3	5	.375	2.79	1.06	22	10	1	0	...	6-...	87.0	71	29	27	6	21-0	61	.227
—New York (N.L.)	2	0	1.000	2.05	1.14	17	0	0	0	...	0-0	22.0	18	6	5	1	7-1	26	.222
1996—Norfolk (Int'l)	2	0	1.000	3.52	1.04	5	0	0	0	...	1-...	7.2	4	3	3	0	4-1	8	.148
—New York (N.L.)	1	2	.333	4.24	1.48	38	0	0	0	3	0-2	46.2	48	22	22	7	21-4	31	.265
1997—Atlanta (N.L.)	4	4	.500	5.26	1.42	31	4	0	0	1	0-0	53.0	47	34	31	6	28-4	37	.235
—Richmond (Int'l)	2	1	.667	3.18	0.88	3	3	0	0	...	0-...	17.0	14	6	6	2	1-0	14	.230
1998—Richmond (Int'l)	5	5	.500	3.69	1.25	17	17	2	0	...	0-...	102.1	92	44	42	9	36-2	84	.241
—Atlanta (N.L.)	0	0	...	13.50	2.50	1	0	0	0	0	0-0	2.0	4	3	3	0	1-0	1	.400
—Philadelphia (N.L.)	5	2	.714	2.29	1.05	8	8	2	1	0	0-0	55.0	41	16	14	6	17-1	38	.204
1999—Philadelphia (N.L.)	15	11	.577	4.60	1.38	32	32	1	0	0	0-0	199.2	205	119	102	34	70-2	106	.265
2000—Philadelphia (N.L.)	2	9	.182	6.51	1.49	17	15	0	0	0	0-0	83.0	89	67	60	17	35-2	53	.271
—Scran./W.B. (I.L.)	2	0	1.000	1.73	1.00	3	3	2	0	...	0-...	26.0	20	6	5	2	6-0	10	.215
2001—Clearwater (Fla. St.)	0	3	.000	3.42	1.23	4	4	0	0	...	0-...	23.2	24	10	9	1	5-0	17	.267
—Scran./W.B. (I.L.)	1	3	.250	3.65	1.11	5	5	0	0	...	0-...	37.0	34	18	15	4	7-0	35	.239
—Philadelphia (N.L.)	0	1	.000	8.10	1.40	3	1	0	0	0	0-0	10.0	10	9	9	1	4-0	3	.278
—Kansas City (A.L.)	6	6	.500	4.05	1.41	16	15	1	0	0	0-0	93.1	110	45	42	11	22-1	49	.298
2002—Kansas City (A.L.)	17	11	.607	3.90	1.15	33	33	*7	2	0	0-0	228.1	224	111	99	36	38-1	129	.256
2003—Greenville (Sou.)	0	0	...	8.31	2.10	1	1	0	0	...	0-...	4.1	8	6	4	1	1-0	3	.364
2004—Greenville (Sou.)	1	1	.500	7.11	1.42	3	3	0	0	...	0-...	12.2	13	10	10	2	5-0	8	.271
—Richmond (Int'l)	0	1	.000	7.71	1.07	1	1	0	0	...	0-...	4.2	3	4	4	0	2-0	5	.167
—Atlanta (N.L.)	8	7	.533	3.94	1.24	19	19	0	0	0	0-0	114.1	123	57	50	18	19-0	79	.270
American League totals (2 years)	23	17	.575	3.95	1.22	49	48	8	2	0	0-0	321.2	334	156	141	47	60-2	178	.268
National League totals (8 years)	37	36	.507	4.55	1.34	166	79	3	1	7	0-2	585.2	585	333	296	90	202-14	374	.258
Major League totals (9 years)	60	53	.531	4.33	1.30	215	127	11	3	7	0-2	907.1	919	489	437	137	262-16	552	.262

DIVISION SERIES RECORD

Year	Team (League)	W	L	Pct.	ERA	WHIP	G	GS	CG	ShO	Hld.	Sv.-Opp.	IP	H	R	ER	HR	BB-IBB	SO	Avg.
2004—Atlanta (N.L.)	0	1	.000	6.35	1.94	2	0	0	0	0	0-0	5.2	8	4	4	1	3-1	3	.364

BYRNES, ERIC — OF

PERSONAL: Born February 16, 1976, in Redwood City, Calif. ... 6-2/210. ... Bats right, throws right. ... Full name: Eric James Byrnes. ... Name pronounced: burns. ... High school: St. Francis (Mountain View, Calif.). ... College: UCLA.

TRANSACTIONS/CAREER NOTES: Selected by Los Angeles Dodgers organization in 38th round of 1994 free-agent draft; did not sign. ... Selected by Houston Astros organization in fourth round of 1997 free-agent draft; did not sign. ... Selected by Oakland Athletics organization in eighth round of 1998 free-agent draft.

2004 GAMES PLAYED BY POSITION (MLB): OF—141, DH—1.

Year	Team (League)	Pos.	G	AB	R	H	2B	3B	HR	RBI	BB	SO	HBP	GDP	SB-CS	Avg.	OBP	SLG	OPS	E	Avg.
1998—S. Oregon (N'west)	OF	42	169	36	53	10	2	7	31	16	16	2	3	6-1	.314	.378	.521	.898	1	.986
—Visalia (Calif.)	OF	29	108	26	46	9	2	4	21	18	15	1	2	11-1	.426	.504	.657	1.161	3	.952
1999—Modesto (California)	OF	96	365	86	123	28	1	6	66	58	37	9	14	28-8	.337	.433	.468	.901	6	.960
—Midland (Texas)	OF	43	164	25	39	14	0	1	22	17	32	3	5	6-3	.238	.316	.341	.657	5	.923
2000—Midland (Texas)	OF	67	259	49	78	25	2	5	30	43	38	1	5	21-11	.301	.395	.471	.866	2	.983
—Sacramento (PCL)	OF	67	243	55	81	23	1	9	47	31	30	2	3	12-5	.333	.410	.547	.957	2	.980
—Oakland (A.L.)	OF-DH	10	10	5	3	0	0	0	0	0	1	1	0	2-1	.300	.364	.300	.664	0	1.000
2001—Sacramento (PCL)	OF	100	415	81	120	23	2	20	51	33	66	5	10	25-3	.289	.343	.499	.842	5	.973
—Oakland (A.L.)	OF-DH	19	38	9	9	1	0	3	5	4	6	1	0	1-0	.237	.326	.500	.826	1	.933
2002—Sacramento (PCL)	OF	31	119	16	31	7	0	4	16	7	15	0	2	5-1	.261	.302	.420	.722	2	.971
—Oakland (A.L.)	OF-DH	90	94	24	23	4	2	3	11	4	17	3	3	3-0	.245	.291	.426	.717	1	.982
2003—Oakland (A.L.)	OF-DH	121	414	64	109	27	9	12	51	42	71	2	3	10-2	.263	.333	.459	.792	2	.991
2004—Oakland (A.L.)	OF-DH	143	569	91	161	39	3	20	73	46	111	12	11	17-1	.283	.347	.467	.814	3	.989
Major League totals (5 years)		383	1125	193	305	71	14	38	140	96	206	19	17	33-4	.271	.336	.460	.797	7	.988

DIVISION SERIES RECORD

Year Team (League)	Pos.	G	AB	R	H	2B	3B	HR	RBI	BB	SO	HBP	GDP	SB-CS	Avg.	OBP	SLG	OPS	E	Avg.
2001— Oakland (A.L.)		2	2	0	0	0	0	0	0	0	1	0	0	0-0	.000	.000	.000	.000	...	...
2002— Oakland (A.L.)	OF	2	1	0	0	0	0	0	0	0	1	0	0	0-0	.000	.000	.000	.000	0	1.000
2003— Oakland (A.L.)	OF	5	13	2	6	1	0	0	2	0	5	0	0	1-0	.462	.462	.538	1.000	0	1.000
Division series totals (3 years)		9	16	2	6	1	0	0	2	0	7	0	0	1-0	.375	.375	.438	.813	0	1.000

CABRERA, DANIEL   P

PERSONAL: Born May 28, 1981, in San Pedro de Macoris, Dominican Republic. ... 6-7/230. ... Throws right, bats right. ... Full name: Daniel Alberto Cabrera.
TRANSACTIONS/CAREER NOTES: Signed as non-drafted free agent by Baltimore Orioles organization (March 15, 1999).
CAREER HITTING: 0-for-4 (.000), 0 R, 0 2B, 0 3B, 0 HR, 0 RBI.

Year Team (League)	W	L	Pct.	ERA	WHIP	G	GS	CG	ShO	Hld.	Sv.-Opp.	IP	H	R	ER	HR	BB-IBB	SO	Avg.
2001— GC Orioles (GCL)	2	3	.400	5.53	1.72	12	7	0	0	...	0-...	40.2	31	29	25	1	39-2	36	.215
2002— Bluefield (Appalachian)	5	2	.714	3.28	1.28	12	12	0	0	...	0-...	60.1	52	25	22	0	25-0	69	.234
2003— Delmarva (S.Atl.)	5	9	.357	4.24	1.46	26	26	1	0	...	0-...	125.1	105	74	59	6	78-0	120	.225
2004— Bowie (East.)	0	1	.000	2.63	0.84	5	5	0	0	...	0-...	27.1	11	10	8	1	12-0	35	.118
— Baltimore (A.L.)	12	8	.600	5.00	1.58	28	27	1	1	0	1-1	147.2	145	85	82	14	89-2	76	.259
Major League totals (1 year)	12	8	.600	5.00	1.58	28	27	1	1	0	1-1	147.2	145	85	82	14	89-2	76	.259

CABRERA, FERNANDO   P

PERSONAL: Born November 16, 1981, in Toja Baja, Puerto Rico. ... 6-4/170. ... Throws right, bats right. ... Full name: Fernando Jose Cabrera. ... High school: Discipulous (Toa Baja, P.R.).
TRANSACTIONS/CAREER NOTES: Selected by Cleveland Indians organization in 10th round of 1999 free-agent draft.
CAREER HITTING: 0-for-0 (.000), 0 R, 0 2B, 0 3B, 0 HR, 0 RBI.

Year Team (League)	W	L	Pct.	ERA	WHIP	G	GS	CG	ShO	Hld.	Sv.-Opp.	IP	H	R	ER	HR	BB-IBB	SO	Avg.
2000— Burlington (Appalachian) ..	3	7	.300	4.61	1.23	13	13	0	0	...	0-...	68.1	64	42	35	4	20-0	50	.252
2001— Columbus (S. Atl.)	5	6	.455	3.61	1.33	20	20	0	0	...	0-...	94.2	89	49	38	7	37-1	96	.242
2002— Kinston (Caro.)	6	8	.429	3.52	1.12	21	21	0	0	...	0-...	110.0	83	48	43	7	40-2	107	.206
— Akron (East.)	1	2	.333	5.33	1.41	7	4	0	0	...	1-...	27.0	26	16	16	1	12-0	29	.252
2003— Akron (East.)	9	4	.692	2.97	1.25	36	15	0	0	...	5-...	109.0	96	41	36	8	40-0	115	.237
2004— Buffalo (Int'l)	4	3	.571	3.79	1.32	45	0	0	0	...	5-...	76.0	57	37	32	9	43-3	93	.208
— Cleveland (A.L.)	0	0	...	3.38	0.75	4	0	0	0	0	0-0	5.1	3	3	2	0	1-0	6	.167
Major League totals (1 year)	0	0	...	3.38	0.75	4	0	0	0	0	0-0	5.1	3	3	2	0	1-0	6	.167

CABRERA, JOLBERT   3B/OF

PERSONAL: Born December 8, 1972, in Cartagena, Colombia. ... 6-1/195. ... Bats right, throws right. ... Full name: Jolbert Alexis Cabrera. ... Name pronounced: HOLE-bert kah-brair-RAH. ... High school: Confenalco (Cartagena, Colombia). ... Brother of Orlando Cabrera, shortstop with Montreal Expos and Boston Red Sox in 2004.
TRANSACTIONS/CAREER NOTES: Signed as a non-drafted free agent by Montreal Expos organization (July 3, 1990). ... Loaned by Expos organization to San Bernardino of the California League (July 27-September 1, 1994). ... Signed as a free agent by Cleveland Indians organization (January 19, 1998). ... On disabled list (March 28-May 2, 2002); included rehabilitation assignment to Buffalo. ... Traded by Indians to Los Angeles Dodgers for P Lance Caraccioli (July 22, 2002). ... Traded by Dodgers to Seattle Mariners for Ps Aaron Looper and Ryan Ketchner (April 3, 2004).
2004 GAMES PLAYED BY POSITION (MLB): 3B—36, 1B—23, OF—23, 2B—18, SS—14, DH—5.

Year Team (League)	Pos.	G	AB	R	H	2B	3B	HR	RBI	BB	SO	HBP	GDP	SB-CS	Avg.	OBP	SLG	OPS	E	Avg.
1990— Dom. Expos (DSL)	SS	29	115	31	36	3	2	0	12	14	10	...	...	14-...	.313	...	.374	...	...	...
1991— Sumter (S. Atl.)	SS	101	324	33	66	4	0	1	20	19	62	4	5	10-11	.204	.255	.225	.480	28	.934
1992— Albany (S. Atl.)	SS	118	377	44	86	9	2	0	23	34	77	1	8	22-11	.228	.294	.263	.556	35	.927
1993— Burlington (Midw.)	SS	128	507	62	129	24	2	0	38	39	93	7	13	31-11	.254	.314	.310	.624	36	.929
1994— W.P. Beach (FSL)	SS	83	266	32	54	4	0	0	13	14	48	8	4	7-10	.203	.264	.218	.482	26	.933
— San Bern. (Calif.)	SS	30	109	14	27	5	1	0	11	14	24	0	1	2-2	.248	.328	.312	.640	7	.950
— Harrisburg (East.)	SS	3	2	0	0	0	0	0	0	0	1	0	0	0-0	.000	.000	.000	.000	0	1.000
1995— W.P. Beach (FSL)	2B-3B-SS	103	357	62	102	23	2	1	25	38	61	8	3	19-12	.286	.364	.370	.733	29	.938
— Harrisburg (East.)	SS	9	35	4	10	2	0	0	1	1	3	0	1	3-1	.286	.306	.343	.648	2	.935
1996— Harrisburg (East.)	3B-SS-OF	107	354	40	85	18	2	3	29	23	63	1	9	10-5	.240	.285	.328	.613	25	.951
1997— Harrisburg (East.)	2B-SS-OF	48	171	28	43	9	0	2	11	28	28	1	4	5-4	.251	.360	.339	.699	9	.951
— Ottawa (Int'l)	2-3-SS-OF	68	191	28	54	10	4	0	12	11	31	0	5	15-5	.283	.320	.377	.697	7	.962
1998— Cleveland (A.L.)	SS	1	2	0	0	0	0	0	0	0	1	0	0	0-0	.000	.000	.000	.000	0	1.000
— Buffalo (Int'l)	2B-SS-OF	129	494	94	157	24	1	10	45	68	71	13	10	25-15	.318	.412	.431	.844	27	.956
1999— Cleveland (A.L.)	OF-2B-DH	30	37	6	7	1	0	0	0	1	8	1	1	3-0	.189	.231	.216	.447	1	.968
— Buffalo (Int'l)	OF-SS-2-3	71	279	44	74	13	4	0	27	26	43	2	8	20-4	.265	.327	.341	.667	6	.975
2000— Buffalo (Int'l)	OF-SS-2B	20	74	18	25	6	1	3	11	5	8	1	0	2-1	.338	.383	.568	.950	0	1.000
— Cleveland (A.L.)	OF-2-S-DH	100	175	27	44	3	1	2	15	8	15	2	1	6-4	.251	.290	.314	.605	1	.993
2001— Cleveland (A.L.)	O-2-3-S-DH	141	287	50	75	16	3	1	38	16	41	6	4	10-4	.261	.312	.348	.660	6	.973
2002— Buffalo (Int'l)	OF-S-3-1-2	23	91	16	26	5	0	0	7	9	10	1	3	4-2	.286	.353	.341	.694	0	1.000
— Cleveland (A.L.)	OF-2B-DH	38	72	5	8	1	0	0	7	5	13	1	3	1-1	.111	.177	.125	.302	0	1.000
— Las Vegas (PCL)	OF-3-SS-2	27	102	22	35	8	1	2	11	14	18	1	3	2-3	.343	.417	.500	.917	2	.969
— Los Angeles (N.L.)	OF-3B-2B	10	12	3	4	1	0	0	1	2	2	0	0	0-0	.333	.429	.417	.845	0	1.000
2003— Los Angeles (N.L.)	OF-3-SS-2	128	347	43	98	32	2	6	37	17	62	10	10	6-4	.282	.332	.438	.770	5	.984
2004— Seattle (A.L.)	3-1-O-2-S-DH	113	359	38	97	19	2	6	47	16	70	8	13	10-3	.270	.312	.384	.696	5	.985
American League totals (6 years)		423	932	126	231	40	6	9	107	46	148	18	22	30-12	.248	.294	.333	.626	14	.984
National League totals (2 years)		138	359	46	102	33	2	6	38	19	64	10	10	6-4	.284	.335	.437	.772	5	.984
Major League totals (7 years)		561	1291	172	333	73	8	15	145	65	212	28	32	36-16	.258	.305	.362	.667	19	.984

DIVISION SERIES RECORD

Year Team (League)	Pos.	G	AB	R	H	2B	3B	HR	RBI	BB	SO	HBP	GDP	SB-CS	Avg.	OBP	SLG	OPS	E	Avg.
2001— Cleveland (A.L.)	OF	2	1	1	1	0	0	0	1	0	0	1	0	0-0	1.000	1.000	1.000	2.000	0	...

CABRERA, MIGUEL   OF

PERSONAL: Born April 18, 1983, in Maracay, Venezuela. ... 6-2/210. ... Bats right, throws right. ... Full name: Jose Miguel Torres Cabrera.
TRANSACTIONS/CAREER NOTES: Signed as a non-drafted free agent by Florida Marlins organization (July 2, 1999).
2004 GAMES PLAYED BY POSITION (MLB): OF—158, DH—1.

Year — Team (League)	Pos.	G	AB	R	H	2B	3B	HR	RBI	BB	SO	HBP	GDP	SB-CS	Avg.	OBP	SLG	OPS	E	Avg.
								BATTING											FIELDING	
2000— GC Marlins (GCL)	SS	57	219	38	57	10	2	2	22	23	46	6	7	1-0	.260	.344	.352	.696	13	.950
— Utica (N.Y.-Penn)	SS-2B-3B	8	32	3	8	2	0	0	6	2	6	0	0	0-0	.250	.294	.313	.607	4	.902
2001— Kane Co. (Midw.)	SS-3B	110	422	61	113	19	4	7	66	37	76	2	10	3-0	.268	.328	.382	.709	32	.931
2002— Jupiter (FSL)	3B-SS	124	489	77	134	43	1	9	75	38	85	9	19	10-1	.274	.333	.421	.754	17	.941
2003— Carolina (Southern)	3B-OF-DH	69	266	46	97	29	3	10	59	31	49	2	8	9-4	.365	.429	.609	1.038	15	.926
— Florida (N.L.)	OF-3B	87	314	39	84	21	3	12	62	25	84	2	12	0-2	.268	.325	.468	.793	4	.978
2004— Florida (N.L.)	OF-DH	160	603	101	177	31	1	33	112	68	148	6	20	5-2	.294	.366	.512	.879	9	.968
Major League totals (2 years)		247	917	140	261	52	4	45	174	93	232	8	32	5-4	.285	.352	.497	.850	13	.972

DIVISION SERIES RECORD

Year — Team (League)	Pos.	G	AB	R	H	2B	3B	HR	RBI	BB	SO	HBP	GDP	SB-CS	Avg.	OBP	SLG	OPS	E	Avg.
2003— Florida (N.L.)	3B	4	14	1	4	2	0	0	3	1	6	0	0	0-0	.286	.333	.429	.762	1	.900

CHAMPIONSHIP SERIES RECORD

Year — Team (League)	Pos.	G	AB	R	H	2B	3B	HR	RBI	BB	SO	HBP	GDP	SB-CS	Avg.	OBP	SLG	OPS	E	Avg.
2003— Florida (N.L.)	OF-3B-SS	7	30	9	10	0	0	3	6	2	6	1	1	0-0	.333	.394	.633	1.027	0	1.000

WORLD SERIES RECORD

Year — Team (League)	Pos.	G	AB	R	H	2B	3B	HR	RBI	BB	SO	HBP	GDP	SB-CS	Avg.	OBP	SLG	OPS	E	Avg.
2003— Florida (N.L.)	OF	6	24	1	4	0	0	1	3	1	7	0	1	0-0	.167	.200	.292	.492	1	.938

ALL-STAR GAME RECORD

	G	AB	R	H	2B	3B	HR	RBI	BB	SO	HBP	GDP	SB-CS	Avg.	OBP	SLG	OPS	E	Avg.
All-Star Game totals (1 year)	1	2	0	0	0	0	0	0	0	1	0	0	0-0	.000	.000	.000	.000	0	1.000

CABRERA, ORLANDO — SS

PERSONAL: Born November 2, 1974, in Cartagena, Colombia. ... 5-10/190. ... Bats right, throws right. ... Full name: Orlando Luis Cabrera. ... Name pronounced: kah-BRAY-rah. ... Brother of Jolbert Cabrera, infielder/outfielder, Seatle Mariners.

TRANSACTIONS/CAREER NOTES: Signed as a non-drafted free agent by Montreal Expos organization (June 1, 1993). ... On disabled list (August 9, 1999-remainder of season). ... On disabled list (July 15-August 15, 2000); included rehabilitation assignment to Ottawa. ... Traded by Expos to Boston Red Sox as part of four-team deal in which Expos acquired SS Alex S. Gonzalez, P Francis Beltran and IF Brendan Harris from Cubs, Cubs acquired SS Nomar Garciaparra and Matt Murton from Red Sox, Red Sox acquired 1B Doug Mientkiewicz from Twins and Twins acquired P Justin Jones from Cubs (July 31, 2004).

HONORS: Won N.L. Gold Glove at shortstop (2001).

2004 GAMES PLAYED BY POSITION (MLB): SS—158.

Year — Team (League)	Pos.	G	AB	R	H	2B	3B	HR	RBI	BB	SO	HBP	GDP	SB-CS	Avg.	OBP	SLG	OPS	E	Avg.
								BATTING											FIELDING	
1993— Dom. Expos (DSL)	IF	38	122	24	42	6	1	1	17	18	11	...	...	14-...	.344	...	.434	...	3	.982
1994— GC Expos (GCL)	2B-SS-OF	22	73	13	23	4	1	0	11	5	8	0	2	6-0	.315	.359	.397	.756	4	.941
1995— Vermont (N.Y.-Penn.)	2B-SS	65	248	37	70	12	5	3	33	16	28	1	3	15-8	.282	.323	.407	.731	17	.950
— W.P. Beach (FSL)	SS	3	5	0	1	0	0	0	0	0	1	0	0	0-0	.200	.200	.200	.400	1	.833
1996— Delmarva (S. Atl.)	2B-SS	134	512	86	129	28	4	14	65	54	63	5	4	51-18	.252	.327	.404	.731	27	.953
1997— W.P. Beach (FSL)	SS-DH-2B	69	279	56	77	19	2	5	26	27	33	0	1	32-12	.276	.340	.412	.752	20	.927
— Harrisburg (East.)	SS-2B	35	133	34	41	13	2	5	20	15	18	0	0	7-2	.308	.378	.549	.927	5	.966
— Ottawa (Int'l)	SS-2B	31	122	17	32	5	2	2	14	7	16	2	0	8-1	.262	.306	.385	.691	3	.979
— Montreal (N.L.)	SS-2B	16	18	4	4	0	0	0	2	1	3	0	1	1-2	.222	.263	.222	.485	1	.963
1998— Ottawa (Int'l)	SS-2B	66	272	31	63	9	4	0	26	28	27	0	8	19-9	.232	.298	.294	.592	12	.963
— Montreal (N.L.)	SS-2B	79	261	44	73	16	5	3	22	18	27	0	6	6-2	.280	.325	.414	.739	7	.978
1999— Montreal (N.L.)	SS	104	382	48	97	23	5	8	39	18	38	3	9	2-2	.254	.279	.403	.696	10	.979
2000— Montreal (N.L.)	SS-2B	125	422	47	100	25	1	13	55	25	28	1	12	4-4	.237	.279	.393	.673	10	.981
— Ottawa (Int'l)	SS	2	6	1	4	0	0	0	2	0	1	0	1	1-0	.667	.750	.667	1.417	0	1.000
2001— Montreal (N.L.)	SS	•162	626	64	173	41	6	14	96	43	54	4	15	19-7	.276	.324	.428	.752	11	.986
2002— Montreal (N.L.)	SS	153	563	64	148	43	1	7	56	48	53	2	16	25-7	.263	.321	.380	.701	*29	.962
2003— Montreal (N.L.)	SS	162	626	95	186	47	2	17	80	52	64	1	18	24-2	.297	.347	.460	.807	18	.975
2004— Montreal (N.L.)	SS	103	390	41	96	19	2	4	31	28	31	2	12	12-3	.246	.298	.336	.634	7	.984
— Boston (A.L.)	SS	58	228	33	67	19	1	6	31	11	23	1	4	4-1	.294	.320	.465	.785	8	.966
American League totals (1 year)		58	228	33	67	19	1	6	31	11	23	1	4	4-1	.294	.320	.465	.785	8	.966
National League totals (8 years)		904	3288	407	877	214	22	66	381	233	298	13	89	93-29	.267	.315	.405	.721	93	.977
Major League totals (8 years)		962	3516	440	944	233	23	72	412	244	321	14	93	97-30	.268	.316	.409	.725	101	.976

DIVISION SERIES RECORD

Year — Team (League)	Pos.	G	AB	R	H	2B	3B	HR	RBI	BB	SO	HBP	GDP	SB-CS	Avg.	OBP	SLG	OPS	E	Avg.
2004— Boston (A.L.)	SS	3	13	1	2	1	0	0	3	2	2	0	0	0-0	.154	.267	.231	.497	0	1.000

CHAMPIONSHIP SERIES RECORD

Year — Team (League)	Pos.	G	AB	R	H	2B	3B	HR	RBI	BB	SO	HBP	GDP	SB-CS	Avg.	OBP	SLG	OPS	E	Avg.
2004— Boston (A.L.)	SS	7	29	5	11	2	0	0	5	3	5	0	1	1-0	.379	.424	.448	.873	0	1.000

WORLD SERIES RECORD

Year — Team (League)	Pos.	G	AB	R	H	2B	3B	HR	RBI	BB	SO	HBP	GDP	SB-CS	Avg.	OBP	SLG	OPS	E	Avg.
2004— Boston (A.L.)	SS	4	17	3	4	1	0	0	3	3	1	1	0	0-0	.235	.381	.294	.675	0	1.000

CAIRO, MIGUEL — 2B

PERSONAL: Born May 4, 1974, in Anaco, Venezuela. ... 6-1/208. ... Bats right, throws right. ... Full name: Miguel Jesus Cairo. ... Name pronounced: KI-row. ... High school: Escuela Anaco (Anaco, Venezuela).

TRANSACTIONS/CAREER NOTES: Signed as a non-drafted free agent by Los Angeles Dodgers organization (September 20, 1990). ... Traded by Dodgers with 3B Willis Otanez to Seattle Mariners for 3B Mike Blowers (November 29, 1995). ... Traded by Mariners with P Bill Risley to Toronto Blue Jays for Ps Edwin Hurtado and Paul Menhart (December 18, 1995). ... Traded by Blue Jays to Chicago Cubs for P Jason Stevenson (November 20, 1996). ... Selected by Tampa Bay Devil Rays in first round (eighth pick overall) of expansion draft (November 18, 1997). ... On disabled list (April 24-May 17 and July 26-August 11, 1999); included rehabilitation assignments to Orlando and St. Petersburg. ... Released by Devil Rays (November 27, 2000). ... Signed by Oakland Athletics organization (January 7, 2001). ... Traded by A's to Chicago Cubs for 3B/1B Eric Hinske (March 28, 2001). ... Claimed on waivers by St. Louis Cardinals (August 10, 2001). ... On disabled list (June 19-July 29, 2003); included rehabilitation assignment to Memphis. ... Signed as a free agent by New York Yankees (December 19, 2003).

2004 GAMES PLAYED BY POSITION (MLB): 2B—113, 3B—8, SS—3, 1B—1.

Year	Team (League)	Pos.	G	AB	R	H	2B	3B	HR	RBI	BB	SO	HBP	GDP	SB-CS	Avg.	OBP	SLG	OPS	E	Avg.
1991— Dom. Dodgers (DSL)	....	IF	57	203	16	45	5	1	0	17	0	17	...	...	8-...	.222	...	.256	...	...	...
1992— GC Dodgers (GCL)		3B-SS	21	76	10	23	5	2	0	9	2	6	2	1	1-0	.303	.333	.421	.754	4	.953
— Vero Beach (FSL)	....	2B-3B	36	125	7	28	0	0	0	7	11	12	0	3	5-3	.224	.285	.224	.509	10	.935
1993— Vero Beach (FSL)	......	2B-3B-SS	90	346	50	109	10	1	1	23	28	22	7	2	23-16	.315	.378	.358	.736	18	.959
1994— Bakersfield (Calif.)	....	2B-SS	133	533	76	155	23	4	2	48	34	37	6	9	44-23	.291	.338	.360	.698	28	.958
1995— San Antonio (Texas)	....	2B-SS-DH	107	435	53	121	20	1	1	41	26	31	5	6	33-16	.278	.323	.336	.659	23	.958
1996— Syracuse (Int'l)	....	2B-3B-SS	120	465	71	129	14	4	3	48	26	44	8	5	27-9	.277	.323	.344	.667	23	.955
— Toronto (A.L.)		2B	9	27	5	6	2	0	0	1	2	9	1	1	0-0	.222	.300	.296	.596	0	1.000
1997— Iowa (Am. Assoc.)	....	2B-SS	135	569	82	159	35	4	5	46	24	54	6	9	40-15	.279	.314	.381	.695	20	.969
— Chicago (N.L.)	....	2B-SS	16	29	7	7	1	0	0	1	2	3	1	0	0-0	.241	.313	.276	.588	0	1.000
1998— Tampa Bay (A.L.)		2B-DH	150	515	49	138	26	5	5	46	24	44	6	9	19-8	.268	.307	.367	.674	16	.978
1999— Tampa Bay (A.L.)		2B-DH	120	465	61	137	15	5	3	36	24	46	7	13	22-7	.295	.335	.368	.703	9	.986
— Orlando (South.)	....	2B	3	13	1	5	2	0	0	1	0	1	0	0	0-1	.385	.385	.538	.923	0	1.000
— St. Pete. (FSL)	....	2B	3	13	2	5	0	0	0	0	1	2	0	0	1-1	.385	.429	.385	.813	1	.958
2000— Tampa Bay (A.L.)		2B-DH	119	375	49	98	18	2	1	34	29	34	2	7	28-7	.261	.314	.328	.642	9	.983
2001— Iowa (PCL)	....	2B-SS-3B	34	123	22	37	7	1	3	14	8	11	1	3	3-4	.301	.348	.447	.796	3	.978
— Chicago (N.L.)	....	3B-2B-SS	66	123	20	35	3	1	2	9	16	21	0	3	2-1	.285	.364	.374	.738	7	.917
— St. Louis (N.L.)	....	OF-2-3-S-1	27	33	5	11	5	0	1	7	2	2	0	1	0-0	.333	.371	.576	.947	1	.929
2002— St. Louis (N.L.)	....	O-2-3-S-1-DH	108	184	28	46	9	2	2	23	13	36	3	5	1-1	.250	.307	.353	.660	4	.963
2003— Memphis (PCL)	....	2B-DH	3	13	2	3	1	0	0	0	0	3	0	0	0-0	.231	.231	.308	.538	0	1.000
— St. Louis (N.L.)	....	2-0-3-SS-1	92	261	41	64	15	2	5	32	13	30	6	6	4-1	.245	.289	.375	.665	6	.972
2004— New York (A.L.)	....	2-3-SS-1	122	360	48	105	17	5	6	42	18	49	14	7	11-3	.292	.346	.417	.763	8	.984
American League totals (5 years)			**520**	**1742**	**212**	**484**	**78**	**17**	**15**	**159**	**97**	**182**	**30**	**37**	**80-25**	**.278**	**.324**	**.368**	**.692**	**42**	**.983**
National League totals (4 years)			**309**	**630**	**101**	**163**	**33**	**5**	**10**	**72**	**46**	**92**	**10**	**15**	**7-3**	**.259**	**.315**	**.375**	**.689**	**18**	**.961**
Major League totals (9 years)			**829**	**2372**	**313**	**647**	**111**	**22**	**25**	**231**	**143**	**274**	**40**	**52**	**87-28**	**.273**	**.322**	**.370**	**.691**	**60**	**.979**

DIVISION SERIES RECORD

Year	Team (League)	Pos.	G	AB	R	H	2B	3B	HR	RBI	BB	SO	HBP	GDP	SB-CS	Avg.	OBP	SLG	OPS	E	Avg.
2001— St. Louis (N.L.)	....	OF	3	5	0	1	0	0	0	0	0	1	0	0	1-0	.200	.200	.200	.400	0	1.000
2002— St. Louis (N.L.)	....	3B	2	4	2	4	1	0	0	3	0	0	1	0	0-1	1.000	1.000	1.250	2.250	0	1.000
2004— New York (A.L.)	....	2B	4	14	3	3	1	0	0	1	2	5	0	0	0-0	.214	.313	.286	.598	0	1.000
Division series totals (3 years)			**9**	**23**	**5**	**8**	**2**	**0**	**0**	**4**	**2**	**6**	**1**	**0**	**1-1**	**.348**	**.423**	**.435**	**.858**	**0**	**1.000**

CHAMPIONSHIP SERIES RECORD

Year	Team (League)	Pos.	G	AB	R	H	2B	3B	HR	RBI	BB	SO	HBP	GDP	SB-CS	Avg.	OBP	SLG	OPS	E	Avg.
2002— St. Louis (N.L.)	....	3B	3	13	2	5	0	0	1	2	0	2	0	0	0-0	.385	.385	.615	1.000	0	1.000
2004— New York (A.L.)	....	2B	7	25	4	7	3	0	0	2	2	4	4	0	1-0	.280	.419	.400	.819	0	1.000
Champ. series totals (2 years)			**10**	**38**	**6**	**12**	**3**	**0**	**1**	**2**	**2**	**6**	**4**	**0**	**1-0**	**.316**	**.409**	**.474**	**.883**	**0**	**1.000**

CALERO, KIKO   P

PERSONAL: Born January 9, 1975, in Santurce, Puerto Rico. ... 6-1/180. ... Throws right, bats right. ... Full name: Enrique Nomar Calero. ... High school: University Gardens (P.R.). ... College: St. Thomas (Fla.).

TRANSACTIONS/CAREER NOTES: Selected by Kansas City Royals organization in 27th round of 1996 free-agent draft. ... Signed as a free agent by St. Louis Cardinals organization (December 3, 2002). ... On disabled list (August 7-September 4, 2004); included rehabilitation assignments to Memphis.

CAREER HITTING: 1-for-5 (.200), 1 R, 0 2B, 0 3B, 0 HR, 1 RBI.

Year	Team (League)	W	L	Pct.	ERA	WHIP	G	GS	CG	ShO	Hld.	Sv.-Opp.	IP	H	R	ER	HR	BB-IBB	SO	Avg.
1996— Spokane (N'west)	....	4	2	.667	2.52	1.27	17	11	0	0	...	1-...	75.0	77	34	21	5	18-0	61	.265
1997— Wichita (Texas)	....	11	9	.550	4.44	1.28	23	22	2	0	...	0-...	127.2	120	78	63	15	44-0	100	.248
1998— Lansing (Midw.)	....	1	0	1.000	3.78	1.56	4	4	0	0	...	0-...	16.2	19	7	7	1	7-0	10	.284
— Wichita (Texas)	....	1	0	1.000	9.64	2.07	3	3	0	0	...	0-...	14.0	23	16	15	2	6-0	5	.359
— Wilmington (Caro.)	....	7	3	.700	2.86	1.28	17	17	0	0	...	0-...	97.2	74	33	31	7	51-1	90	.213
1999— Wichita (Texas)	....	9	3	.750	4.11	1.55	26	23	1	1	...	1-...	129.1	143	67	59	14	57-3	92	.279
2000— Wichita (Texas)	....	10	7	.588	3.63	1.35	28	25	0	0	...	0-...	153.2	141	74	62	16	66-0	130	.251
2001— Wichita (Texas)	....	14	5	.737	3.33	1.29	27	19	0	0	...	1-...	124.1	110	57	46	10	51-1	94	.237
2002— Wichita (Texas)	....	1	0	1.000	2.25	0.94	5	2	0	0	...	0-...	16.0	10	5	4	2	5-0	15	.172
— Omaha (PCL)	....	7	7	.500	3.44	1.17	20	18	0	0	...	0-...	125.2	112	52	48	11	35-1	109	.244
2003— St. Louis (N.L.)	....	1	1	.500	2.82	1.28	26	1	0	0	1	1-4	38.1	29	12	12	5	20-2	51	.212
2004— Memphis (PCL)	....	0	0	...	2.49	1.22	12	3	0	0	...	1-...	25.1	20	8	7	3	11-2	33	.222
— St. Louis (N.L.)	....	3	1	.750	2.78	0.82	41	0	0	0	12	2-3	45.1	27	14	14	5	10-1	47	.176
Major League totals (2 years)		**4**	**2**	**.667**	**2.80**	**1.03**	**67**	**1**	**0**	**0**	**13**	**3-7**	**83.2**	**56**	**26**	**26**	**10**	**30-3**	**98**	**.193**

DIVISION SERIES RECORD

Year	Team (League)	W	L	Pct.	ERA	WHIP	G	GS	CG	ShO	Hld.	Sv.-Opp.	IP	H	R	ER	HR	BB-IBB	SO	Avg.
2004— St. Louis (N.L.)	....	0	0	...	0.00	0.00	1	0	0	0	0	0-0	1.0	0	0	0	0	0-0	2	.000

CHAMPIONSHIP SERIES RECORD

Year	Team (League)	W	L	Pct.	ERA	WHIP	G	GS	CG	ShO	Hld.	Sv.-Opp.	IP	H	R	ER	HR	BB-IBB	SO	Avg.
2004— St. Louis (N.L.)	....	0	0	...	3.86	1.29	5	0	0	0	2	0-1	7.0	8	3	3	1	1-0	7	.296

WORLD SERIES RECORD

Year	Team (League)	W	L	Pct.	ERA	WHIP	G	GS	CG	ShO	Hld.	Sv.-Opp.	IP	H	R	ER	HR	BB-IBB	SO	Avg.
2004— St. Louis (N.L.)	....	0	0	...	13.50	4.50	2	0	0	0	0	0-0	1.1	2	2	2	0	4-0	0	.400

CALI, CARMEN   P

PERSONAL: Born November 2, 1978, in Cleveland, Ohio. ... 5-10/185. ... Throws left, bats left. ... Full name: Carmen S. Cali. ... High school: Naples (Fla.). ... College: Florida Atlantic.

TRANSACTIONS/CAREER NOTES: Selected by St. Louis Cardinals organization in 10th round of 2000 free-agent draft.

CAREER HITTING: 0-for-0 (.000), 0 R, 0 2B, 0 3B, 0 HR, 0 RBI.

Year	Team (League)	W	L	Pct.	ERA	WHIP	G	GS	CG	ShO	Hld.	Sv.-Opp.	IP	H	R	ER	HR	BB-IBB	SO	Avg.
2000— New Jersey (N.Y.-Penn.)	...	2	7	.222	4.89	1.40	14	14	0	0	...	0-...	70.0	68	45	38	3	30-0	55	.261
2001— Peoria (Midw.)	....	7	3	.700	6.00	1.71	39	6	0	0	...	1-...	48.0	53	40	32	4	29-0	47	.275
— Potomac (Caro.)	....	1	0	1.000	2.19	1.46	12	0	0	0	...	0-...	12.1	12	4	3	1	6-1	9	.279

Year Team (League)	W	L	Pct.	ERA	WHIP	G	GS	CG	ShO	Hld.	Sv.-Opp.	IP	H	R	ER	HR	BB-IBB	SO	Avg.
2002—Potomac (Caro.)	2	2	.500	4.11	1.49	29	0	0	0	...	0-...	35.0	31	18	16	1	21-2	24	.248
—Peoria (Midw.)	1	1	.500	1.78	1.42	24	0	0	0	...	2-...	35.1	36	17	7	0	14-0	27	.259
2003—Palm Beach (FSL)	2	1	.667	4.99	1.48	62	0	0	0	...	3-...	70.1	72	49	39	2	32-6	70	.265
2004—Tennessee (Sou.)	1	2	.333	2.91	1.34	38	0	0	0	...	14-...	46.1	43	19	15	3	19-3	47	.246
—Memphis (PCL)	1	1	.500	2.70	1.05	17	0	0	0	...	3-...	20.0	17	6	6	4	4-0	20	.227
—St. Louis (N.L.)	0	0	...	8.59	2.59	10	0	0	0	0	0-0	7.1	13	7	7	1	6-1	8	.394
Major League totals (1 year)	0	0	...	8.59	2.59	10	0	0	0	0	0-0	7.1	13	7	7	1	6-1	8	.394

CALLAWAY, MICKEY — P

PERSONAL: Born May 13, 1975, in Memphis, Tenn. ... 6-2/215. ... Throws right, bats right. ... Full name: Michael C. Callaway. ... High school: Germantown (Tenn.). ... College: Mississippi.

TRANSACTIONS/CAREER NOTES: Selected by San Francisco Giants organization in 16th round of 1993 free-agent draft; did not sign. ... Selected by Tampa Bay Devil Rays organization in seventh round of 1996 free-agent draft. ... Loaned by Devil Rays organization to Seattle Mariners organization (April 2-July 21, 1998). ... On disabled list (June 19-July 6, 1999; and May 22-June 5, 2000). ... Traded by Devil Rays to Anaheim Angels for SS/2B Wilmy Caceres (December 17, 2001). ... On disabled list (June 6-July 23, 2003); included rehabilitation assignment to Salt Lake. ... Released by Angels (July 29, 2003). ... Signed by Texas Rangers organization (August 7, 2003). ... On disabled list (April 14-August 16 and August 22, 2004-remainder of season); included rehabilitation assignments to Frisco and Oklahoma. ... Refused minor league assignment and became a free agent (October 15, 2004).

CAREER HITTING: 2-for-3 (.667), 0 R, 0 2B, 0 3B, 0 HR, 1 RBI.

Year Team (League)	W	L	Pct.	ERA	WHIP	G	GS	CG	ShO	Hld.	Sv.-Opp.	IP	H	R	ER	HR	BB-IBB	SO	Avg.
1996—Butte (Pio.)	6	2	.750	3.71	1.51	16	11	0	0	...	0-...	63.0	70	37	26	5	25-0	57	.288
1997—St. Pete. (FSL)	11	7	.611	3.22	1.18	28	28	3	0	...	0-...	170.2	162	74	61	9	39-0	109	.250
1998—Orlando (Sou.)	5	6	.455	4.42	1.64	18	17	0	0	...	0-...	89.2	103	56	44	8	44-0	57	.289
—Durham (Int'l)	5	3	.625	4.53	1.38	9	8	0	0	...	0-...	47.2	49	27	24	6	17-0	19	.258
1999—Orlando (Sou.)	1	1	.500	4.50	1.70	2	2	0	0	...	0-...	10.0	15	6	5	1	2-0	7	.357
—Durham (Int'l)	7	1	.875	4.20	1.40	15	15	0	0	...	0-...	81.1	86	45	38	5	28-0	56	.277
—Tampa Bay (A.L.)	1	2	.333	7.45	2.28	5	4	0	0	0	0-0	19.1	30	20	16	2	14-1	11	.357
2000—Durham (Int'l)	11	6	.647	5.29	1.71	26	20	0	0	...	0-...	117.1	151	88	69	11	50-2	64	.313
2001—Durham (Int'l)	11	7	.611	3.07	1.20	29	21	2	1	...	0-...	129.0	131	50	44	9	24-0	81	.265
—Tampa Bay (A.L.)	0	0	...	7.20	1.00	2	0	0	0	0	0-0	5.0	3	4	4	2	2-0	2	.167
2002—Salt Lake (PCL)	9	2	.818	1.68	1.11	17	14	1	0	...	0-...	91.1	79	26	17	7	22-0	75	.229
—Anaheim (A.L.)	2	1	.667	4.19	1.22	6	6	0	0	0	0-0	34.1	31	20	16	4	11-0	23	.235
2003—Salt Lake (PCL)	1	0	1.000	2.95	1.30	7	4	0	0	...	0-...	21.1	22	8	7	1	6-0	10	.286
—Anaheim (A.L.)	1	4	.200	6.81	1.90	17	4	0	0	0	0-0	38.1	57	32	29	7	16-1	22	.345
—Oklahoma (PCL)	2	0	1.000	1.59	1.20	4	4	0	0	...	0-...	17.0	16	6	3	0	5-0	9	.254
—Texas (A.L.)	0	3	.000	6.45	1.57	6	3	0	0	0	0-0	22.1	27	18	16	0	14-0	19	.314
2004—Frisco (Texas)	2	0	1.000	0.00	0.58	2	2	0	0	...	0-...	12.0	3	0	0	0	4-0	9	.086
—Texas (A.L.)	0	1	.000	7.94	2.21	4	3	0	0	0	0-0	11.1	18	10	10	2	7-0	9	.367
Major League totals (5 years)	4	11	.267	6.27	1.71	40	20	0	0	0	0-0	130.2	166	104	91	17	58-2	86	.311

CALLOWAY, RON — OF

PERSONAL: Born September 4, 1976, in San Jose, Calif. ... 6-1/198. ... Bats left, throws left. ... Full name: Ronald Isiah Calloway. ... High school: James Lick (San Jose, Calif.). ... Junior college: Canada College (Calif.).

TRANSACTIONS/CAREER NOTES: Selected by Arizona Diamondbacks organization in eighth round of 1997 free-agent draft. ... Traded by Diamondbacks to Montreal Expos (July 5, 1999), completing deal in which Expos traded C John Pachot to Diamondbacks for future considerations (May 21, 1999). ... Expos franchise transferred to Washington, D.C., for 2005 season.

2004 GAMES PLAYED BY POSITION (MLB): OF—20.

Year Team (League)	Pos.	G	AB	R	H	2B	3B	HR	RBI	BB	SO	HBP	GDP	SB-CS	Avg.	OBP	SLG	OPS	E	Avg.
1997—Lethbridge (Pio.)	OF	43	148	23	37	5	0	0	9	14	29	3	4	5-8	.250	.323	.284	.607	3	.954
—South Bend (Mid.)	OF	9	25	3	7	1	0	0	1	2	8	0	1	1-0	.280	.333	.320	.653	2	.846
1998—High Desert (Calif.)	OF	44	156	30	44	8	2	3	27	12	38	2	3	2-4	.282	.337	.417	.754	4	.946
—South Bend (Mid.)	OF	69	251	29	66	12	2	3	33	25	50	2	6	6-5	.263	.331	.363	.694	6	.944
1999—High Desert (Calif.)	OF	60	196	41	62	14	1	3	23	30	34	2	3	22-7	.316	.412	.444	.856	3	.962
—El Paso (Texas)	OF	11	32	4	7	0	0	0	1	7	7	0	0	1-2	.219	.359	.219	.578	0	1.000
—Jupiter (FSL)	OF	54	211	30	57	8	4	3	25	15	45	2	9	5-6	.270	.325	.389	.713	0	1.000
2000—Jupiter (FSL)	OF	135	530	78	147	24	6	6	65	55	89	4	13	34-14	.277	.346	.379	.725	2	.994
2001—Harrisburg (East.)	OF	74	279	48	92	22	4	9	47	24	46	3	2	25-7	.330	.385	.534	.919	4	.969
—Ottawa (Int'l)	OF	61	239	27	63	12	0	10	35	16	64	6	6	11-1	.264	.323	.439	.763	5	.959
2002—Ottawa (Int'l)	OF	128	447	72	118	21	5	14	60	44	89	6	18	16-12	.264	.335	.427	.762	3	.988
2003—Montreal (N.L.)	OF	126	340	36	81	17	1	9	52	20	80	2	13	9-2	.238	.282	.374	.656	3	.983
2004—Montreal (N.L.)	OF	46	84	4	14	2	0	1	10	5	22	0	3	2-0	.167	.211	.226	.437	0	1.000
—Edmonton (PCL)	OF-DH	59	223	36	63	17	1	5	46	34	39	4	10	13-5	.283	.385	.435	.820	2	.982
Major League totals (2 years)		172	424	40	95	19	1	10	62	25	102	2	16	11-2	.224	.268	.344	.612	3	.985

CAMERON, MIKE — OF

PERSONAL: Born January 8, 1973, in LaGrange, Ga. ... 6-2/200. ... Bats right, throws right. ... Full name: Michael Terrance Cameron. ... High school: La Grange (Ga.).

TRANSACTIONS/CAREER NOTES: Selected by Chicago White Sox organization in 18th round of 1991 free-agent draft. ... Traded by White Sox to Cincinnati Reds for 1B/3B Paul Konerko (November 11, 1998). ... Traded by Reds with Ps Brett Tomko and Jake Meyer and IF Antonio Perez to Seattle Mariners for OF Ken Griffey Jr. (February 10, 2000). ... Signed as a free agent by New York Mets (December 23, 2003).

RECORDS: Shares major league record for most home runs, game (4, May 2, 2002).

HONORS: Won A.L. Gold Glove as outfielder (2001 and 2003).

2004 GAMES PLAYED BY POSITION (MLB): OF—135.

Year Team (League)	Pos.	G	AB	R	H	2B	3B	HR	RBI	BB	SO	HBP	GDP	SB-CS	Avg.	OBP	SLG	OPS	E	Avg.
1991—GC Whi. Sox (GCL)	OF	44	136	20	30	3	0	0	11	17	29	4	3	13-2	.221	.325	.243	.567	3	.951
1992—Utica (N.Y.-Penn)	OF	26	87	15	24	1	4	2	12	11	26	0	0	3-7	.276	.354	.448	.802	0	1.000
—South Bend (Mid.)	OF	35	114	19	26	8	1	1	9	10	37	4	0	2-3	.228	.310	.342	.652	3	.957
1993—South Bend (Mid.)	OF	122	411	52	98	14	5	0	30	27	101	6	8	19-10	.238	.292	.297	.589	4	.985
1994—Prince Will. (Car.)	OF	131	468	86	116	15	17	6	48	60	101	8	6	22-10	.248	.343	.391	.734	6	.979
1995—Birmingham (Sou.)	OF	107	350	64	87	20	5	11	60	54	104	6	9	21-12	.249	.355	.429	.784	4	.985

C

Year Team (League)	Pos.	G	AB	R	H	2B	3B	HR	RBI	BB	SO	HBP	GDP	SB-CS	Avg.	OBP	SLG	OPS	E	Avg.
—Chicago (A.L.)	OF	28	38	4	7	2	0	1	2	3	15	0	0	0-0	.184	.244	.316	.560	0	1.000
1996—Birmingham (Sou.)	OF-DH	123	473	120	142	34	12	28	77	71	117	12	5	39-15	.300	.402	.600	1.002	7	.973
—Chicago (A.L.)	OF-DH	11	11	1	1	0	0	0	0	1	3	0	0	0-1	.091	.167	.091	.258	0	1.000
1997—Nashville (A.A.)	OF-DH	30	120	21	33	7	3	6	17	18	31	3	1	4-2	.275	.378	.533	.911	1	.985
—Chicago (A.L.)	OF-DH	116	379	63	98	18	3	14	55	55	105	5	8	23-2	.259	.356	.433	.789	5	.985
1998—Chicago (A.L.)	OF	141	396	53	83	16	5	8	43	37	101	6	6	27-11	.210	.285	.336	.621	4	.988
1999—Cincinnati (N.L.)	OF	146	542	93	139	34	9	21	66	80	145	6	4	38-12	.256	.357	.469	.825	8	.979
2000—Seattle (A.L.)	OF	155	543	96	145	28	4	19	78	78	133	9	10	24-7	.267	.365	.438	.803	6	.985
2001—Seattle (A.L.)	OF-DH	150	540	99	144	30	5	25	110	69	155	10	13	34-5	.267	.353	.480	.832	6	.986
2002—Seattle (A.L.)	OF-DH	158	545	84	130	26	5	25	80	79	176	7	8	31-8	.239	.340	.442	.782	5	.988
2003—Seattle (A.L.)	OF	147	534	74	135	31	5	18	76	70	137	5	13	17-7	.253	.344	.431	.774	4	.992
2004—New York (N.L.)	OF	140	493	76	114	30	1	30	76	57	143	8	5	22-6	.231	.319	.479	.798	8	.978
American League totals (8 years)		906	2986	474	743	151	27	110	444	392	825	42	58	156-41	.249	.341	.428	.769	30	.988
National League totals (2 years)		286	1035	169	253	64	10	51	142	137	288	14	9	60-18	.244	.339	.473	.812	16	.979
Major League totals (10 years)		1192	4021	643	996	215	37	161	586	529	1113	56	67	216-59	.248	.340	.440	.780	46	.986

DIVISION SERIES RECORD

Year Team (League)	Pos.	G	AB	R	H	2B	3B	HR	RBI	BB	SO	HBP	GDP	SB-CS	Avg.	OBP	SLG	OPS	E	Avg.
2000—Seattle (A.L.)	OF	3	12	2	3	0	0	0	2	0	0	1	1	1-0	.250	.308	.250	.558	0	1.000
2001—Seattle (A.L.)	OF	5	18	2	4	3	0	1	3	2	7	1	0	0-1	.222	.333	.556	.889	0	1.000
Division series totals (2 years)		8	30	4	7	3	0	1	5	2	7	2	1	1-1	.233	.324	.433	.757	0	1.000

CHAMPIONSHIP SERIES RECORD

Year Team (League)	Pos.	G	AB	R	H	2B	3B	HR	RBI	BB	SO	HBP	GDP	SB-CS	Avg.	OBP	SLG	OPS	E	Avg.
2000—Seattle (A.L.)	OF	6	18	3	2	0	0	1	2	7	7	0	0	1-0	.111	.200	.111	.311	0	1.000
2001—Seattle (A.L.)	OF	5	17	3	3	2	0	0	4	4	1	1	1	0-0	.176	.364	.294	.658	0	1.000
Champ. series totals (2 years)		11	35	6	5	2	0	1	6	11	1	1	1-0	.143	.286	.200	.486	0	1.000

ALL-STAR GAME RECORD

	G	AB	R	H	2B	3B	HR	RBI	BB	SO	HBP	GDP	SB-CS	Avg.	OBP	SLG	OPS	E	Avg.
All-Star Game totals (1 year)	1	3	0	1	1	0	0	0	0	1	0		0-0	.333	.333	.667	1.000	0	1.000

CAMP, SHAWN — P

PERSONAL: Born November 18, 1975, in Fairfax, Va. ... 6-1/200. ... Throws right, bats right. ... Full name: Shawn Anthony Camp. ... High school: James W. Robinson Jr. Secondary School (Fairfax, Va.). ... College: George Mason.

TRANSACTIONS/CAREER NOTES: Selected by San Diego Padres organization in 16th round of 1997 free-agent draft. ... Traded by Padres with OF Shawn Gilbert to Pittsburgh Pirates for OF Emil Brown (July 10, 2001). ... Signed as a free agent by Kansas City Royals organization (October 29, 2003).

CAREER HITTING: 0-for-0 (.000), 0 R, 0 2B, 0 3B, 0 HR, 0 RBI.

Year Team (League)	W	L	Pct.	ERA	WHIP	G	GS	CG	ShO	Hld.	Sv.-Opp.	IP	H	R	ER	HR	BB-IBB	SO	Avg.
1997—Idaho Falls (Pioneer)	2	1	.667	5.51	1.68	30	0	0	0	...	12-...	32.2	41	22	20	3	14-0	41	.311
1998—Clinton (Midw.)	3	5	.375	2.62	1.24	47	0	0	0	...	13-...	55.0	48	19	16	0	20-4	62	.232
1999—Rancho Cuca. (Calif.)	1	5	.167	3.95	1.41	53	0	0	0	...	6-...	66.0	68	37	29	4	25-3	78	.271
2000—Rancho Cuca. (Calif.)	1	0	1.000	1.45	0.80	14	0	0	0	...	6-...	18.2	10	3	3	0	5-0	18	.154
—Mobile (Sou.)	3	3	.500	2.43	1.30	45	0	0	0	...	1-...	59.1	47	23	16	4	30-2	53	.217
2001—Portland (PCL)	1	0	1.000	0.00	0.43	4	1	0	0	...	0-...	7.0	2	0	0	0	1-0	6	.095
—Mobile (Sou.)	6	2	.750	4.44	1.25	35	1	0	0	...	0-...	48.2	46	24	24	2	15-1	55	.261
—Altoona (East.)	4	0	1.000	4.24	1.41	8	3	0	0	...	0-...	23.1	25	14	11	3	8-1	19	.278
—Nashville (PCL)	0	0		2.12	1.12	11	0	0	0	...	0-...	17.0	11	4	4	1	8-1	15	.190
2002—Nashville (PCL)	4	1	.800	3.24	1.11	39	0	0	0	...	2-...	58.1	50	22	21	5	15-3	59	.239
2003—Nashville (PCL)	0	1	.000	4.98	1.50	33	1	0	0	...	0-...	43.1	50	26	24	2	15-2	36	.289
—Altoona (East.)	0	2	.000	4.34	1.28	18	0	0	0	...	0-...	29.0	26	14	14	2	11-0	35	.236
2004—Omaha (PCL)	1	1	.500	5.32	1.45	15	0	0	0	...	1-...	22.0	26	14	13	2	6-0	21	.289
—Kansas City (A.L.)	2	2	.500	3.92	1.35	42	0	0	0	5	2-3	66.2	74	37	29	10	16-1	51	.285
Major League totals (1 year)	2	2	.500	3.92	1.35	42	0	0	0	5	2-3	66.2	74	37	29	10	16-1	51	.285

CANTU, JORGE — 2B/3B

PERSONAL: Born January 30, 1982, in Reynosa, Mexico. ... 6-1/184. ... Bats right, throws right. ... Full name: Jorge Luis Cantu. ... High school: Sharyland (McAllen, Texas).

TRANSACTIONS/CAREER NOTES: Signed as a non-drafted free agent by Tampa Bay Devil Rays organization (July 2, 1998).

2004 GAMES PLAYED BY POSITION (MLB): 2B—33, 3B—11, DH—4, SS—1.

Year Team (League)	Pos.	G	AB	R	H	2B	3B	HR	RBI	BB	SO	HBP	GDP	SB-CS	Avg.	OBP	SLG	OPS	E	Avg.
1999—Hudson Valley (NY-Penn.) .	SS	72	281	33	73	17	2	1	33	20	59	2	8	3-4	.260	.313	.345	.658	25	.928
2000—Char., S.C. (SAL)	SS-2B	46	186	25	56	13	2	2	24	10	39	3	3	3-3	.301	.345	.425	.770	17	.928
—St. Pete. (FSL)	SS	36	130	18	38	5	2	1	14	3	13	1	3	4-2	.292	.313	.385	.698	8	.944
2001—Orlando (South.)	SS	130	512	58	131	26	3	4	45	17	93	8	13	4-9	.256	.287	.342	.629	26	.948
2002—Orlando (South.)	SS-3B-2B	131	512	50	124	31	1	3	43	23	74	4	13	2-6	.242	.278	.324	.602	41	.931
2003—Orlando (South.)	3B-SS-2B	43	158	15	34	10	3	3	17	9	27	1	3	0-3	.215	.259	.335	.594	6	.940
—Durham (Int'l)	SS-3B	60	200	26	59	16	1	4	30	8	21	2	5	2-1	.295	.319	.445	.764	12	.949
2004—Durham (Int'l)	2-S-3-DH	95	368	57	111	33	1	22	80	16	64	4	11	3-0	.302	.335	.576	.904	15	.964
—Tampa Bay (A.L.)	2-3-DH-S	50	173	25	52	20	1	2	17	9	44	2	5	0-0	.301	.341	.462	.803	8	.956
Major League totals (1 year)		50	173	25	52	20	1	2	17	9	44	2	5	0-0	.301	.341	.462	.803	8	.956

CAPELLAN, JOSE — P

PERSONAL: Born January 13, 1981, in Cotui, Dominican Republic. ... 6-4/235. ... Throws right, bats right. ... Full name: Jose Francisco Capellan.

TRANSACTIONS/CAREER NOTES: Signed as a non-drafted free agent by Atlanta Braves organization (August 6, 1998).

CAREER HITTING: 0-for-2 (.000), 0 R, 0 2B, 0 3B, 0 HR, 0 RBI.

Year Team (League)	W	L	Pct.	ERA	WHIP	G	GS	CG	ShO	Hld.	Sv.-Opp.	IP	H	R	ER	HR	BB-IBB	SO	Avg.
2001—Danville (Appalachian)	0	0		1.72	1.02	3	3	0	0	...	0-...	15.2	12	7	3	1	4-0	25	.200
2003—GC Braves (GCL)	0	1	.000	2.65	1.53	5	5	0	0	...	0-...	17.0	18	7	5	0	8-0	17	.277
—Rome (S. Atl.)	1	2	.333	3.80	1.31	14	12	1	0	...	0-...	47.1	43	23	20	2	19-0	32	.253
2004—Myrtle Beach (Caro.)	5	1	.833	1.94	0.82	8	8	1	0	...	0-...	46.1	27	11	10	0	11-0	62	.168

Year	Team (League)	W	L	Pct.	ERA	WHIP	G	GS	CG	ShO	Hld.	Sv.-Opp.	IP	H	R	ER	HR	BB-IBB	SO	Avg.
	— Greenville (Sou.)	5	1	.833	2.50	1.43	9	8	0	0	...	0-...	50.1	53	15	14	1	19-0	53	.270
	— Richmond (Int'l)	4	2	.667	2.51	1.12	7	7	0	0	...	0-...	43.0	33	13	12	0	15-1	37	.214
	— Atlanta (N.L.)	0	1	.000	11.25	2.38	3	2	0	0	0	0-0	8.0	14	10	10	2	5-0	4	.400
Major League totals (1 year)		0	1	.000	11.25	2.38	3	2	0	0	0	0-0	8.0	14	10	10	2	5-0	4	.400

CAPUANO, CHRIS — P

PERSONAL: Born August 19, 1978, in Springfield, Mass. ... 6-3/210. ... Throws left, bats left. ... Full name: Christopher Frank Capuano. ... Name pronounced: cap-u-ON-o. ... High school: Cathedral (West Springfield, Mass.). ... College: Duke.

TRANSACTIONS/CAREER NOTES: Selected by Pittsburgh Pirates organization in 45th round of 1996 free-agent draft; did not sign. ... Selected by Arizona Diamondbacks organization in eighth round of 1999 free-agent draft. ... Traded by Diamondbacks with SS Craig Counsell, 2B Junior Spivey, 1B Lyle Overbay, C Chad Moeller and P Jorge de la Rosa to Milwaukee Brewers for 1B Richie Sexson, P Shane Nance and a player to be named (December 1, 2003); Diamondbacks acquired OF Noochie Varner to complete deal (December 15, 2003). ... On disabled list (April 19-May 26, May 27-June 12 and August 25, 2004-remainder of season); included rehabilitation assignments to Beloit, High Desert and Indianapolis.

CAREER HITTING: 6-for-38 (.158), 0 R, 2 2B, 0 3B, 0 HR, 2 RBI.

Year	Team (League)	W	L	Pct.	ERA	WHIP	G	GS	CG	ShO	Hld.	Sv.-Opp.	IP	H	R	ER	HR	BB-IBB	SO	Avg.
2000—	South Bend (Mid.)	10	4	.714	2.21	1.11	18	18	0	0	...	0-...	101.2	68	35	25	2	45-0	105	.193
2001—	El Paso (Texas)	10	11	.476	5.31	1.63	28	28	2	2	...	0-...	159.1	184	109	94	13	75-0	167	.290
2002—	Tucson (PCL)	4	1	.800	2.72	1.13	6	6	0	0	...	0-...	36.1	30	12	11	1	11-0	29	.227
2003—	Tucson (PCL)	9	5	.643	3.34	1.23	23	23	0	0	...	0-...	142.2	133	66	53	9	43-2	108	.250
	— Arizona (N.L.)	2	4	.333	4.64	1.15	9	5	0	0	1	0-0	33.0	27	19	17	3	11-1	23	.233
2004—	Beloit (Midw.)	0	0	...	3.38	1.50	1	1	0	0	...	0-...	2.2	3	1	1	1	1-0	4	.300
	— Indianapolis (Int'l)	0	1	.000	8.31	1.73	2	2	0	0	...	0-...	8.2	10	9	8	1	5-0	9	.294
	— High Desert (Calif.)	0	1	.000	27.00	4.50	1	1	0	0	...	0-...	2.0	6	6	6	1	3-0	2	.600
	— Milwaukee (N.L.)	6	8	.429	4.99	1.45	17	17	0	0	0	0-0	88.1	91	55	49	18	37-1	80	.269
Major League totals (2 years)		8	12	.400	4.90	1.37	26	22	0	0	1	0-0	121.1	118	74	66	21	48-2	103	.260

CARPENTER, CHRIS — P

PERSONAL: Born April 27, 1975, in Exeter, N.H. ... 6-6/230. ... Throws right, bats right. ... Full name: Christopher John Carpenter. ... High school: Trinity (Manchester, N.H.).

TRANSACTIONS/CAREER NOTES: Selected by Toronto Blue Jays organization in first round (15th pick overall) of 1993 free-agent draft. ... On disabled list (June 3-28, 1999); included rehabilitation assignment to St. Catharines. ... On disabled list (April 2-20, April 22-June 21 and August 14, 2002-remainder of season); included rehabilitation assignments to Tennessee (May 23-June 12) and Syracuse (June 13-18). ... Released by Blue Jays (October 9, 2002). ... Signed by St. Louis Cardinals (December 13, 2002). ... On disabled list (March 27, 2003-entire season); included rehabilitation assignments to Palm Beach and Tennessee.

HONORS: Named N.L. Comeback Player of the Year by THE SPORTING NEWS (2004).

CAREER HITTING: 7-for-73 (.096), 2 R, 0 2B, 0 3B, 0 HR, 1 RBI.

Year	Team (League)	W	L	Pct.	ERA	WHIP	G	GS	CG	ShO	Hld.	Sv.-Opp.	IP	H	R	ER	HR	BB-IBB	SO	Avg.
1994—	Medicine Hat (Pio.)	6	3	.667	2.76	1.36	15	15	0	0	...	0-...	84.2	76	40	26	3	39-0	80	.243
1995—	Dunedin (Fla. St.)	3	5	.375	2.17	1.34	15	15	0	0	...	0-...	99.1	83	29	24	3	50-0	56	.229
	— Knoxville (Southern)	3	7	.300	5.18	1.59	12	12	0	0	...	0-...	64.1	71	47	37	3	31-1	53	.284
1996—	Knoxville (Southern)	7	9	.438	3.94	1.47	28	28	1	0	...	0-...	171.1	161	94	75	13	91-4	150	.250
1997—	Syracuse (Int'l)	4	9	.308	4.50	1.38	19	19	3	2	...	0-...	120.0	113	64	60	16	53-0	97	.257
	— Toronto (A.L.)	3	7	.300	5.09	1.78	14	13	1	1	0	0-0	81.1	108	55	46	7	37-0	55	.325
1998—	Toronto (A.L.)	12	7	.632	4.37	1.36	33	24	1	0	0	0-0	175.0	177	97	85	18	61-1	136	.265
1999—	Toronto (A.L.)	9	8	.529	4.38	1.50	24	24	4	1	0	0-0	150.0	177	81	73	16	48-1	106	.294
	— St. Catharines (NY-Penn.)	0	0	...	4.50	1.50	1	1	0	0	0	0-0	4.0	5	2	2	0	1-0	6	.294
2000—	Toronto (A.L.)	10	12	.455	6.26	1.64	34	27	2	0	0	0-0	175.1	204	*130	*122	30	83-1	113	.290
2001—	Toronto (A.L.)	11	11	.500	4.09	1.41	34	34	3	2	0	0-0	215.2	229	112	98	29	75-5	157	.274
2002—	Toronto (A.L.)	4	5	.444	5.28	1.58	13	13	1	0	0	0-0	73.1	89	45	43	11	27-0	45	.306
	— Tennessee (Sou.)	0	1	.000	8.20	1.82	5	5	0	0	...	0-...	18.2	26	18	17	5	8-0	9	.338
	— Syracuse (Int'l)	0	1	.000	4.50	1.67	1	1	0	0	...	0-...	6.0	8	3	3	1	2-0	6	.320
2003—	Palm Beach (FSL)	0	1	.000	1.29	1.00	4	4	0	0	...	0-...	7.0	6	3	1	1	1-0	6	.222
	— Memphis (PCL)	0	0	...	5.40	1.60	3	3	0	0	...	0-...	8.1	11	5	5	0	2-0	4	.333
	— Tennessee (Sou.)	0	1	.000	13.50	2.70	1	1	0	0	...	0-...	3.1	7	5	5	1	2-0	2	.438
2004—	St. Louis (N.L.)	15	5	.750	3.46	1.14	28	28	1	0	0	0-0	182.0	169	75	70	24	38-2	152	.245
American League totals (6 years)		49	50	.495	4.83	1.51	152	135	12	5	0	0-0	870.2	984	520	467	111	331-8	612	.287
National League totals (1 year)		15	5	.750	3.46	1.14	28	28	1	0	0	0-0	182.0	169	75	70	24	38-2	152	.245
Major League totals (7 years)		64	55	.538	4.59	1.45	180	163	13	5	0	0-0	1052.2	1153	595	537	135	369-10	764	.280

CARRARA, GIOVANNI — P

PERSONAL: Born March 4, 1968, in Anzoategui, Venezuela. ... 6-2/230. ... Throws right, bats right. ... Full name: Giovanni Jimenez Carrara. ... Name pronounced: ka-rah-rah.

TRANSACTIONS/CAREER NOTES: Signed as a non-drafted free agent by Toronto Blue Jays organization (January 23, 1990). ... Claimed on waivers by Cincinnati Reds (July 3, 1996). ... Signed as a free agent by Baltimore Orioles organization (November 12, 1996). ... Released by Orioles (May 14, 1997). ... Signed by Reds organization (May 17, 1997). ... Played for Seibu Lions of Japan Pacific League (1998). ... Signed by Reds organization (December 23, 1998). ... Signed as a free agent by Colorado Rockies organization (December 1, 1999). ... On disabled list (August 3-September 4, 2000); included rehabilitation assignment to Colorado Springs. ... Signed as a free agent by Los Angeles Dodgers organization (January 4, 2001). ... On disabled list (August 11-September 1, 2002). ... Released by Dodgers (March 26, 2003). ... Signed by Seattle Mariners (March 28, 2003). ... Signed as a free agent by Cleveland Indians organization (December 19, 2003). ... Released by Indians (March 27, 2004). ... Signed by Chicago Cubs organization (March 28, 2003). ... Released by Cubs (May 31, 2004). ... Signed by Dodgers organization (June 1, 2003).

CAREER HITTING: 3-for-30 (.100), 2 R, 0 2B, 0 3B, 0 HR, 0 RBI.

Year	Team (League)	W	L	Pct.	ERA	WHIP	G	GS	CG	ShO	Hld.	Sv.-Opp.	IP	H	R	ER	HR	BB-IBB	SO	Avg.
1990—	Dom. B. Jays (DSL)	2	2	.500	2.62	1.35	15	14	4	0	...	0-...	86.0	88	31	25		28-...	55	
1991—	St. Catharines (NY-Penn.)	5	2	.714	1.71	0.97	15	13	2	2	...	0-...	89.2	66	26	17	5	21-0	83	.200
1992—	Dunedin (Fla. St.)	0	1	.000	4.63	1.41	5	4	0	0	...	0-...	23.1	22	13	12	1	11-0	16	.250
	— Myrtle Beach (SAL)	11	7	.611	3.14	1.22	22	16	1	1	...	0-...	100.1	86	40	35	12	36-0	100	.231
1993—	Dunedin (Fla. St.)	6	11	.353	3.45	1.39	27	24	1	0	...	0-...	140.2	136	69	54	14	59-0	108	.258
1994—	Knoxville (Southern)	13	7	.650	3.89	1.32	26	26	1	0	...	0-...	164.1	158	85	71	16	59-0	96	.251
1995—	Syracuse (Int'l)	7	7	.500	3.96	1.31	21	21	0	0	...	0-...	131.2	116	72	58	11	56-2	81	.232
	— Toronto (A.L.)	2	4	.333	7.21	1.83	12	7	1	0	0	0-0	48.2	64	46	39	10	25-1	27	.322
1996—	Toronto (A.L.)	0	1	.000	11.40	2.33	11	0	0	0	0	0-1	15.0	23	19	19	5	12-2	10	.359
	— Syracuse (Int'l)	4	4	.500	3.58	1.30	9	6	1	0	...	0-...	37.2	37	16	15	2	12-1	28	.253
	— Indianapolis (A.A.)	4	0	1.000	0.76	0.71	9	6	1	0	...	1-...	47.2	25	6	4	2	9-0	45	.152

C

Year	Team (League)	W	L	Pct.	ERA	WHIP	G	GS	CG	ShO	Hld.	Sv.-Opp.	IP	H	R	ER	HR	BB-IBB	SO	Avg.
	—Cincinnati (N.L.)	1	0	1.000	5.87	1.91	8	5	0	0	0	0-0	23.0	31	17	15	6	13-1	13	.323
1997—	Rochester (Int'l)	4	2	.667	4.44	1.31	8	8	1	0	...	0-...	46.2	45	23	23	4	16-0	48	.259
	—Indianapolis (A.A.)	12	5	.706	3.51	1.34	19	18	2	0	...	0-...	120.2	111	50	47	12	51-3	105	.247
	—Cincinnati (N.L.)	0	1	.000	7.84	1.94	2	2	0	0	0	0-0	10.1	14	9	9	4	6-1	5	.333
1998—	Seibu (Jp. East.)	2	0	1.000	4.50	1.13	4	0	0	0	...	0-...	8.0	8	4	4	...	1-...	8	...
	—Seibu (Jap. Pac.)	1	2	.333	4.91	1.47	33	5	0	0	...	1-...	73.1	68	44	40		40-...	50	...
1999—	Indianapolis (Int'l)	12	7	.632	3.47	1.28	39	21	2	1	...	0-...	158.0	144	68	61	20	58-3	114	.246
2000—	Colo. Springs (PCL)	7	2	.778	3.26	1.23	18	15	0	0	...	0-...	96.2	89	39	35	8	30-1	89	.245
	—Colorado (N.L.)	0	1	.000	12.83	2.40	8	0	0	0	0	0-1	13.1	21	19	19	5	11-2	15	.356
2001—	Las Vegas (PCL)	1	2	.333	3.10	1.24	6	6	0	0	...	0-...	29.0	27	10	10	5	9-0	35	.248
	—Los Angeles (N.L.)	6	1	.857	3.16	1.14	47	3	0	0	9	0-3	85.1	73	30	30	12	24-3	70	.231
2002—	Los Angeles (N.L.)	6	3	.667	3.28	1.27	63	1	0	0	14	1-6	90.2	83	34	33	14	32-4	56	.243
2003—	Seattle (A.L.)	2	0	1.000	6.83	1.86	23	0	0	0	4	0-0	29.0	40	22	22	6	14-0	13	.333
	—Tacoma (PCL)	1	1	.500	4.23	1.30	18	0	0	0	...	1-...	27.2	28	14	13	2	9-0	27	.264
2004—	Iowa (PCL)	1	2	.333	3.81	1.31	20	0	0	0	...	1-...	28.1	29	12	12	3	8-1	23	.279
	—Las Vegas (PCL)	0	1	.000	2.51	1.33	11	0	0	0	...	2-...	14.1	11	4	4	1	8-2	15	.208
	—Los Angeles (N.L.)	5	2	.714	2.18	1.23	42	0	0	0	6	2-3	53.2	46	15	13	1	20-3	48	.228
American League totals (3 years)		4	5	.444	7.77	1.92	46	7	1	0	4	0-1	92.2	127	87	80	21	51-3	50	.332
National League totals (6 years)		18	8	.692	3.88	1.35	170	11	0	0	29	3-13	276.1	268	124	119	42	106-14	207	.254
Major League totals (8 years)		22	13	.629	4.85	1.50	216	18	1	0	33	3-14	369.0	395	211	199	63	157-17	257	.274

DIVISION SERIES RECORD

Year	Team (League)	W	L	Pct.	ERA	WHIP	G	GS	CG	ShO	Hld.	Sv.-Opp.	IP	H	R	ER	HR	BB-IBB	SO	Avg.
2004—	Los Angeles (N.L.)	0	0	...	9.00	2.50	3	0	0	0	0	0-0	2.0	4	2	2	1	1-0	1	.444

C

CARRASCO, D.J. P

PERSONAL: Born April 12, 1977, in Safford, Ariz. ... 6-1/215. ... Throws right, bats right. ... Full name: Daniel Carrasco. ... Junior college: Pima (Ariz.) Community College.
TRANSACTIONS/CAREER NOTES: Selected by Baltimore Orioles organization in 20th round of 1997 free-agent draft. ... Released by Orioles (June 14, 1998). ... Signed by Cleveland Indians organization (June 18, 1998). ... Released by Indians (August 21, 1998). ... Signed by Pittsburgh Pirates organization (March 29, 1999). ... Selected by Kansas City Royals from Pirates organization in Rule 5 major league draft (December 16, 2002).
CAREER HITTING: 0-for-2 (.000), 0 R, 0 2B, 0 3B, 0 HR, 0 RBI.

Year	Team (League)	W	L	Pct.	ERA	WHIP	G	GS	CG	ShO	Hld.	Sv.-Opp.	IP	H	R	ER	HR	BB-IBB	SO	Avg.
1998—	Watertown (N.Y.-Penn.)	1	1	.500	5.40	1.58	13	1	0	0	...	2-...	31.2	36	23	19	3	14-0	38	.281
1999—	Williamsport (N.Y.-Penn.)	4	2	.667	2.96	1.28	18	4	0	0	...	0-...	51.2	43	20	17	2	23-0	49	.236
	—Lynchburg (Carolina)	0	1	.000	6.35	2.12	2	0	0	0	...	0-...	5.2	9	8	4	0	3-0	4	.360
2000—	Hickory (S. Atl.)	5	4	.556	1.34	1.36	27	0	0	0	...	6-...	40.1	35	10	6	0	20-1	40	.236
	—Lynchburg (Carolina)	1	0	1.000	3.48	1.55	8	0	0	0	...	2-...	10.1	8	5	4	1	8-0	10	.222
	—Altoona (East.)	1	1	.500	8.36	2.07	9	0	0	0	...	0-...	14.0	16	14	13	0	13-0	10	.296
2001—	Lynchburg (Carolina)	4	0	1.000	1.50	0.89	22	0	0	0	...	7-...	36.0	18	7	6	0	14-1	40	.145
	—Altoona (East.)	2	2	.500	4.14	1.59	27	1	0	0	...	1-...	37.0	34	22	17	2	25-2	35	.239
2002—	Lynchburg (Carolina)	4	4	.500	1.61	0.96	55	0	0	0	...	29-...	72.2	52	18	13	1	18-1	83	.205
2003—	Kansas City (A.L.)	6	5	.545	4.82	1.52	50	2	0	0	6	2-5	80.1	82	44	43	8	40-4	57	.271
2004—	Omaha (PCL)	2	1	.667	3.20	1.38	32	1	0	0	...	3-...	56.1	60	22	20	2	18-0	50	.278
	—Kansas City (A.L.)	2	2	.500	4.84	1.58	30	0	0	0	4	0-3	35.1	41	22	19	5	15-3	22	.287
Major League totals (2 years)		8	7	.533	4.82	1.54	80	2	0	0	10	2-8	115.2	123	66	62	13	55-7	79	.276

CARROLL, JAMEY 2B/3B

PERSONAL: Born February 18, 1974, in Evansville, Ind. ... 5-9/170. ... Bats right, throws right. ... Full name: Jamey Blake Carroll. ... High school: Castle (Newburgh, Ind.). ... College: Evansville.
TRANSACTIONS/CAREER NOTES: Selected by Montreal Expos organization in 14th round of 1996 free-agent draft.
2004 GAMES PLAYED BY POSITION (MLB): 2B—51, 3B—13, SS—10, OF—2.

Year	Team (League)	Pos.	G	AB	R	H	2B	3B	HR	RBI	BB	SO	HBP	GDP	SB-CS	Avg.	OBP	SLG	OPS	E	Avg.
1996—	Vermont (N.Y.-Penn.)	SS-2B-3B	54	203	40	56	6	1	0	17	29	25	0	1	16-11	.276	.363	.315	.679	9	.960
1997—	W.P. Beach (FSL)	SS-2B	121	407	56	99	19	1	0	38	43	48	4	4	17-11	.243	.319	.295	.614	22	.951
1998—	Jupiter (FSL)	2B-SS	55	222	40	58	5	0	0	14	24	26	5	2	11-4	.261	.345	.284	.629	6	.977
	—Harrisburg (East.)	2B-SS	75	261	43	66	11	3	0	20	41	29	5	4	11-5	.253	.365	.318	.683	17	.953
1999—	Harrisburg (East.)	2B-SS	141	561	78	164	34	5	5	63	48	58	5	13	21-10	.292	.351	.398	.749	14	.979
2000—	Ottawa (Int'l)	2B-3B-SS	91	349	53	97	17	2	2	23	33	32	2	9	6-3	.278	.342	.355	.697	13	.967
	—Harrisburg (East.)	3B-2B-SS	45	169	23	49	5	3	0	18	12	13	0	5	8-2	.290	.335	.355	.690	6	.960
2001—	Ottawa (Int'l)	2B-SS-3B	83	267	26	64	8	2	0	16	18	41	2	8	5-5	.240	.292	.285	.576	9	.972
2002—	Harrisburg (East.)	2B	3	9	1	4	0	0	0	1	3	0	1	0	0-0	.444	.583	.444	1.028	0	1.000
	—Ottawa (Int'l)	3B-2B-SS	117	421	57	118	19	2	8	49	37	39	3	8	6-10	.280	.342	.392	.734	7	.983
	—Montreal (N.L.)	3B-SS-2B	16	71	16	22	5	3	1	6	4	12	0	1	1-0	.310	.347	.507	.854	4	.925
2003—	Montreal (N.L.)	3-S-2-DH	105	227	31	59	10	1	1	10	19	39	3	10	5-2	.260	.323	.326	.649	5	.976
2004—	Montreal (N.L.)	2-3-S-OF	102	218	36	63	14	2	0	16	32	21	1	3	5-1	.289	.378	.372	.750	3	.988
Major League totals (3 years)			223	516	83	144	29	6	2	32	55	72	4	14	11-3	.279	.350	.370	.720	12	.977

CARTER, LANCE P

PERSONAL: Born December 18, 1974, in Bradenton, Fla. ... 6-1/190. ... Throws right, bats right. ... Full name: Lance David Carter. ... High school: Manatee (Bradenton, Fla.). ... Junior college: Manatee (Fla.) Community College.
TRANSACTIONS/CAREER NOTES: Selected by Minnesota Twins organization in 41st round of 1993 free-agent draft; did not sign. ... Selected by Kansas City Royals organization in 21st round of 1994 free-agent draft. ... Signed as a free agent by Tampa Bay Devil Rays organization (January 22, 2002).
CAREER HITTING: 0-for-0 (.000), 0 R, 0 2B, 0 3B, 0 HR, 0 RBI.

Year	Team (League)	W	L	Pct.	ERA	WHIP	G	GS	CG	ShO	Hld.	Sv.-Opp.	IP	H	R	ER	HR	BB-IBB	SO	Avg.
1994—	Eugene (N'west)	1	0	1.000	5.47	1.56	8	7	0	0	...	0-...	26.1	26	17	16	2	15-0	23	.265
	—GC Royals (GCL)	3	0	1.000	0.29	0.71	5	5	0	0	...	0-...	31.0	19	1	1	1	3-0	36	.179
1995—	Springfield (Mid.)	9	5	.643	3.99	1.26	27	24	1	1	...	0-...	137.2	151	77	61	14	22-0	118	.276
1996—	Wilmington (Caro.)	3	6	.333	6.34	1.50	16	12	0	0	...	0-...	65.1	81	50	46	8	17-2	49	.298
1997—	Kingsport (Appalachian)	Did not play.																		

Year Team (League)	W	L	Pct.	ERA	WHIP	G	GS	CG	ShO	Hld.	Sv.-Opp.	IP	H	R	ER	HR	BB-IBB	SO	Avg.
1998— Lansing (Midw.)	3	1	.750	0.67	1.07	15	2	0	0	...	2-...	40.1	34	6	3	0	9-1	37	.231
— Wilmington (Caro.)	1	4	.200	3.29	1.23	28	1	0	0	...	5-...	52.0	50	21	19	5	14-1	61	.262
1999— Wichita (Texas)	5	2	.714	0.78	1.09	44	0	0	0	...	13-...	69.2	49	10	6	1	27-5	77	.195
— Kansas City (A.L.)	0	1	.000	5.06	1.13	6	0	0	0	0	0-0	5.1	3	3	3	2	3-0	3	.167
2000— Omaha (PCL)	2	8	.200	4.95	1.39	34	6	0	0	...	5-...	76.1	88	46	42	13	18-1	51	.295
2001—					Did not play.														
2002— Durham (Int'l)	12	2	.857	2.80	0.93	33	18	2	1	...	1-...	132.0	111	43	41	15	12-0	90	.230
— Tampa Bay (A.L.)	2	0	1.000	1.33	0.98	8	0	0	0	0	2-2	20.1	15	3	3	2	5-1	14	.203
2003— Tampa Bay (A.L.)	7	5	.583	4.33	1.15	62	0	0	0	2	26-33	79.0	72	39	38	12	19-6	47	.242
2004— Tampa Bay (A.L.)	3	3	.500	3.47	1.24	56	0	0	0	7	0-1	80.1	77	32	31	12	23-2	36	.252
Major League totals (4 years)	12	9	.571	3.65	1.17	132	0	0	0	9	28-36	185.0	167	77	75	28	50-9	100	.240

CASEY, SEAN — 1B

PERSONAL: Born July 2, 1974, in Willingboro, N.J. ... 6-4/225. ... Bats left, throws right. ... Full name: Sean Thomas Casey. ... Name pronounced: KAY-see. ... High school: Upper St. Clair (Pittsburgh). ... College: Richmond.

TRANSACTIONS/CAREER NOTES: Selected by Cleveland Indians organization in second round of 1995 free-agent draft. ... Traded by Indians to Cincinnati Reds for P Dave Burba (March 30, 1998). ... On disabled list (April 2-May 5, 1998); included rehabilitation assignment to Indianapolis. ... On disabled list (April 2-19, 2000). ... On disabled list (July 23-August 9 and September 10, 2002-remainder of season); included rehabilitation assignment to Louisville. ... On suspended list (July 2-4, 2003). ... On disabled list (June 28-July 14, 2004).

2004 GAMES PLAYED BY POSITION (MLB): 1B—145, DH—1.

Year Team (League)	Pos.	G	AB	R	H	2B	3B	HR	RBI	BB	SO	HBP	GDP	SB-CS	Avg.	OBP	SLG	OPS	E	Avg.
1995— Watertown (N.Y.-Penn.)	1B	55	207	26	68	18	0	2	37	18	21	1	6	3-0	.329	.380	.444	.824	8	.985
1996— Kinston (Caro.)	1B-DH	92	344	62	114	31	3	12	57	36	47	6	5	1-1	.331	.402	.544	.946	6	.991
1997— Akron (East.)	1B-DH	62	241	38	93	19	1	10	66	23	34	5	5	0-1	.386	.448	.598	1.046	5	.988
— Buffalo (A.A.)	DH-1B	20	72	12	26	7	0	5	18	9	11	1	0	0-0	.361	.439	.667	1.106	0	1.000
— Cleveland (A.L.)	1B	6	10	1	2	0	0	0	1	1	2	1	0	0-0	.200	.333	.200	.533	0	1.000
1998— Cincinnati (N.L.)	1B	96	302	44	82	21	1	7	52	43	45	3	11	1-1	.272	.365	.417	.782	4	.994
— Indianapolis (Int'l)	1B-DH	27	95	14	31	8	1	1	13	14	10	1	0	0-0	.326	.418	.463	.881	2	.991
1999— Cincinnati (N.L.)	1B-DH	151	594	103	197	42	3	25	99	61	88	9	15	0-2	.332	.399	.539	.938	6	.995
2000— Cincinnati (N.L.)	1B	133	480	69	151	33	2	20	85	52	80	7	16	1-0	.315	.385	.517	.902	6	.995
2001— Cincinnati (N.L.)	1B-DH	145	533	69	165	40	0	13	89	43	63	9	16	3-1	.310	.369	.458	.827	7	.994
2002— Cincinnati (N.L.)	1B-DH	120	425	56	111	25	0	6	42	43	47	5	11	2-1	.261	.334	.362	.696	7	.993
— Louisville (Int'l)	DH	2	8	2	4	0	0	1	3	1	0	0	0	0-0	.500	.556	.875	1.431	...	...
2003— Cincinnati (N.L.)	1B-DH	147	573	71	167	19	3	14	80	51	58	2	19	4-0	.291	.350	.408	.758	6	.996
2004— Cincinnati (N.L.)	1B-DH	146	571	101	185	44	2	24	99	46	36	10	16	2-0	.324	.381	.534	.915	6	.994
American League totals (1 year)		6	10	1	2	0	0	0	1	1	2	1	0	0-0	.200	.333	.200	.533	0	1.000
National League totals (7 years)		938	3478	513	1058	224	11	109	546	339	417	45	104	13-5	.304	.371	.469	.840	44	.994
Major League totals (8 years)		944	3488	514	1060	224	11	109	547	340	419	46	104	13-5	.304	.370	.468	.839	44	.994

ALL-STAR GAME RECORD

	G	AB	R	H	2B	3B	HR	RBI	BB	SO	HBP	GDP	SB-CS	Avg.	OBP	SLG	OPS	E	Avg.
All-Star Game totals (2 years)	2	2	0	0	0	0	0	0	0	1	0	0	0-0	.000	.000	.000	.000	0	1.000

CASH, KEVIN — C

PERSONAL: Born December 6, 1977, in Tampa, Fla. ... 6-0/185. ... Bats right, throws right. ... Full name: Kevin Forrest Cash. ... College: Florida State.

TRANSACTIONS/CAREER NOTES: Signed as a non-drafted free agent by Toronto Blue Jays organization (August 7, 1999). ... On disabled list (May 24-June 10, 2004).

2004 GAMES PLAYED BY POSITION (MLB): C—60.

Year Team (League)	Pos.	G	AB	R	H	2B	3B	HR	RBI	BB	SO	HBP	GDP	SB-CS	Avg.	OBP	SLG	OPS	E	Avg.
2000— Hagerstown (SAL)	C	59	196	28	48	10	1	10	27	22	54	1	7	5-3	.245	.323	.459	.782	10	.974
2001— Dunedin (Fla. St.)	C	105	371	55	105	27	0	12	66	43	80	8	11	4-3	.283	.369	.453	.822	12	.979
2002— Tennessee (Sou.)		55	213	38	59	15	1	8	44	36	44	1	4	5-2	.277	.381	.469	.850	4	.983
— Syracuse (Int'l)	C	67	236	27	52	18	0	10	26	25	72	2	3	0-1	.220	.299	.424	.723	4	.989
— Toronto (A.L.)	C	7	14	1	2	0	0	0	0	1	4	0	1	0-0	.143	.200	.143	.343	1	.968
2003— Syracuse (Int'l)	C-DH-3B	93	326	37	88	28	2	8	37	29	81	2	14	1-0	.270	.331	.442	.772	1	.998
— Toronto (A.L.)	C	34	106	10	15	3	0	1	8	4	22	1	6	0-0	.142	.179	.198	.377	1	.995
2004— Toronto (A.L.)	C	60	181	18	35	9	0	4	21	10	59	4	3	0-0	.193	.249	.309	.558	2	.994
Major League totals (3 years)		101	301	29	52	12	0	5	29	15	85	5	10	0-0	.173	.222	.262	.485	4	.993

CASTILLA, VINNY — 3B

PERSONAL: Born July 4, 1967, in Oaxaca, Mexico. ... 6-1/205. ... Bats right, throws right. ... Full name: Vinicio Soria Castilla. ... Name pronounced: cas-TEE-yah. ... High school: Instituto Carlos Gracida (Oaxaca, Mexico). ... College: Benito Suarez (Mexico).

TRANSACTIONS/CAREER NOTES: Contract sold by Saltillo to Atlanta Braves organization (March 19, 1990). ... Selected by Colorado Rockies in second round (40th pick overall) of expansion draft (November 17, 1992). ... On disabled list (May 20-June 4, 1993). ... Traded by Rockies to Tampa Bay Devil Rays for P Rolando Arrojo and IF Aaron Ledesma (December 13, 1999). ... On disabled list (March 25-April 11, June 14-July 3 and July 30-September 4, 2000); included rehabilitation assignment to Durham. ... Released by Devil Rays (May 10, 2001). ... Signed by Houston Astros (May 15, 2001). ... Signed as a free agent by Braves (December 11, 2001). ... Signed as a free agent by Rockies (December 11, 2003).

2004 GAMES PLAYED BY POSITION (MLB): 3B—148.

Year Team (League)	Pos.	G	AB	R	H	2B	3B	HR	RBI	BB	SO	HBP	GDP	SB-CS	Avg.	OBP	SLG	OPS	E	Avg.
1987— Saltillo (Mex.)	3B	13	27	0	5	2	0	0	1	0	5	...	...	0-0	.185	...	.259	...	1	.976
1988— Salt.-Monc. (Mex.)	SS	50	124	22	30	2	2	5	18	8	29	...	...	1-4	.242	...	.411	...	13	.924
1989— Saltillo (Mex.)	3B-SS	128	462	70	142	25	13	10	58	33	70	...	...	11-12	.307	...	.483	...	34	.950
1990— Sumter (S. Atl.)	SS	93	339	47	91	15	2	9	53	28	54	8	8	2-5	.268	.334	.404	.738	23	.952
— Greenville (Sou.)	SS	46	170	20	40	5	1	4	16	13	23	2	7	4-4	.235	.296	.347	.643	7	.971
1991— Greenville (Sou.)	SS	66	259	34	70	17	3	7	44	9	35	2	4	0-1	.270	.296	.440	.736	11	.965
— Richmond (Int'l)	SS	67	240	25	54	7	4	7	36	14	32	3	4	1-1	.225	.271	.375	.646	12	.962
— Atlanta (N.L.)	SS	12	5	1	1	0	0	0	0	0	2	0	0	0-0	.200	.200	.200	.400	0	1.000

C

Year Team (League)	Pos.	G	AB	R	H	2B	3B	HR	RBI	BB	SO	HBP	GDP	SB-CS	Avg.	OBP	SLG	OPS	E	Avg.
1992— Richmond (Int'l)	SS	127	449	49	113	29	1	7	44	21	68	4	19	1-2	.252	.288	.367	.655	31	.944
—Atlanta (N.L.)	3B-SS	9	16	1	4	1	0	0	1	1	4	1	0	0-0	.250	.333	.313	.646	1	.933
1993— Colorado (N.L.)	SS	105	337	36	86	9	7	9	30	13	45	2	10	2-5	.255	.283	.404	.686	11	.975
1994— Colorado (N.L.)	S-2-3-1	52	130	16	43	11	1	3	18	7	23	0	3	2-1	.331	.357	.500	.857	2	.986
—Colo. Springs (PCL)	3B-2B-SS	22	78	13	19	6	1	1	11	7	11	1	6	0-0	.244	.303	.385	.688	3	.964
1995— Colorado (N.L.)	3B-SS	139	527	82	163	34	2	32	90	30	87	4	15	2-8	.309	.347	.564	.911	15	.959
1996— Colorado (N.L.)	3B	160	629	97	191	34	0	40	113	35	88	5	20	7-2	.304	.343	.548	.892	20	.960
1997— Colorado (N.L.)	3B	159	612	94	186	25	2	40	113	44	108	8	17	2-4	.304	.356	.547	.904	21	.954
1998— Colorado (N.L.)	3B-SS	•162	645	108	206	28	4	46	144	40	89	6	24	5-9	.319	.362	.589	.951	13	.970
1999— Colorado (N.L.)	3B	158	615	83	169	24	1	33	102	53	75	1	15	2-3	.275	.331	.478	.809	19	.954
2000— Tampa Bay (A.L.)	3B	85	331	22	73	9	1	6	42	14	41	3	9	1-2	.221	.254	.308	.562	8	.967
—Durham (Int'l)	3B	2	8	1	3	1	0	1	3	0	1	0	0	0-0	.375	.375	.875	1.250	0	1.000
2001— Tampa Bay (A.L.)	3B	24	93	7	20	6	0	2	9	3	22	1	3	0-0	.215	.247	.344	.592	5	.934
—Houston (N.L.)	3B-SS	122	445	62	120	28	1	23	82	32	86	3	19	1-4	.270	.320	.492	.812	12	.963
2002— Atlanta (N.L.)	3B	143	543	56	126	23	2	12	61	22	69	7	22	4-1	.232	.268	.348	.616	6	.982
2003— Atlanta (N.L.)	3B	147	542	65	150	28	3	22	76	26	86	3	22	1-2	.277	.310	.461	.771	19	.955
2004— Colorado (N.L.)	3B	148	583	93	158	43	3	35	*131	51	113	6	22	0-0	.271	.332	.535	.867	6	.987
American League totals (2 years)		109	424	29	93	15	1	8	51	17	63	4	12	1-2	.219	.253	.316	.569	13	.959
National League totals (13 years)		1516	5629	794	1603	288	26	295	961	354	875	46	189	28-39	.285	.329	.502	.832	145	.966
Major League totals (14 years)		1625	6053	823	1696	303	27	303	1012	371	938	50	201	29-41	.280	.324	.489	.813	158	.966

DIVISION SERIES RECORD

Year Team (League)	Pos.	G	AB	R	H	2B	3B	HR	RBI	BB	SO	HBP	GDP	SB-CS	Avg.	OBP	SLG	OPS	E	Avg.
1995— Colorado (N.L.)	3B	4	15	3	7	1	0	3	6	0	1	1	1	0-0	.467	.500	1.133	1.633	1	.941
2001— Houston (N.L.)	3B	3	11	1	3	0	0	1	1	0	3	0	1	0-0	.273	.273	.545	.818	0	1.000
2002— Atlanta (N.L.)	3B	5	18	5	7	0	0	1	4	2	2	0	0	0-0	.389	.450	.556	1.006	0	1.000
2003— Atlanta (N.L.)	3B	5	16	0	4	0	0	0	1	3	6	0	0	0-0	.250	.368	.250	.618	2	.895
Division series totals (4 years)		17	60	9	21	1	0	5	12	5	12	1	2	0-0	.350	.409	.617	1.026	3	.952

ALL-STAR GAME RECORD

	G	AB	R	H	2B	3B	HR	RBI	BB	SO	HBP	GDP	SB-CS	Avg.	OBP	SLG	OPS	E	Avg.
All-Star Game totals (2 years)	2	4	0	0	0	0	0	0	0	1	0	0	0-0	.000	.000	.000	.000	0	1.000

CASTILLO, ALBERTO — C

PERSONAL: Born February 10, 1970, in San Juan de la Maguana, Dominican Republic. ... 6-0/216. ... Bats right, throws right. ... Full name: Alberto Terrero Castillo. ... Name pronounced: cas-TEE-oh. ... High school: Mercedes Maria Mateo (Dominican Republic).

TRANSACTIONS/CAREER NOTES: Signed as a non-drafted free agent by New York Mets organization (April 15, 1987). ... Signed as a free agent by Philadelphia Phillies organization (November 5, 1998). ... Selected by St. Louis Cardinals from Phillies organization in Rule 5 major league draft (December 14, 1998). ... Traded by Cardinals with Ps Lance Painter and Matt DeWitt to Toronto Blue Jays for Ps Pat Hentgen and Paul Spoljaric (November 11, 1999). ... Released by Blue Jays (December 12, 2001). ... Signed by New York Yankees organization (December 21, 2001). ... Released by Yankees (October 10, 2002). ... Signed by San Francisco Giants organization (March 14, 2003). ... Loaned to Mexico City Reds of the Mexican League (March 15, 2003). ... On disabled list (July 27-August 27, 2003); included rehabilitation assignment to Fresno. ... Released by Giants (March 17, 2004). ... Signed by Kansas City Royals organization (March 22, 2004).

2004 GAMES PLAYED BY POSITION (MLB): C—29.

Year Team (League)	Pos.	BATTING																	FIELDING	
		G	AB	R	H	2B	3B	HR	RBI	BB	SO	HBP	GDP	SB-CS	Avg.	OBP	SLG	OPS	E	Avg.
1987— Kingsport (Appalachian)	C	7	9	1	1	0	0	0	0	5	3	0	0	1-0	.111	.429	.111	.540	0	1.000
1988— GC Mets (GCL)	C	22	68	7	18	4	0	0	10	4	4	2	3	2-0	.265	.312	.324	.635	1	.993
—Kingsport (Appalachian)	C	24	75	7	22	3	0	1	14	15	14	0	1	0-1	.293	.407	.373	.780	5	.973
1989— Kingsport (Appalachian)	C-1B	27	74	15	19	4	0	3	12	11	14	1	2	2-1	.257	.360	.432	.793	1	.994
—Pittsfield (N.Y.-Penn.)	C	34	123	13	29	8	0	1	13	7	26	1	3	2-0	.236	.278	.325	.603	2	.991
1990— Columbia (S. Atl.)	C	30	103	8	24	4	3	1	14	10	21	0	1	1-1	.233	.296	.359	.655	5	.977
—Pittsfield (N.Y.-Penn.)	C-1B-OF	58	187	19	41	8	1	4	24	26	35	5	7	3-3	.219	.327	.337	.664	9	.980
—St. Lucie (Fla. St.)	C	3	11	4	4	0	0	0	1	3	1	1	0	0-0	.364	.417	.636	1.053	0	1.000
1991— Columbia (S. Atl.)	C	90	267	35	74	20	3	3	47	43	44	5	6	6-6	.277	.382	.408	.791	15	.982
1992— St. Lucie (Fla. St.)	C	60	162	11	33	6	0	3	17	16	37	2	4	0-0	.204	.280	.296	.577	12	.967
1993— St. Lucie (Fla. St.)	C	105	333	37	86	21	0	5	42	28	46	3	5	0-2	.258	.315	.366	.682	12	.983
1994— Binghamton (East.)	C-1B	90	315	33	78	14	0	7	42	41	46	0	11	1-3	.248	.333	.359	.692	6	.991
1995— Norfolk (Int'l)	C-DH	69	217	23	58	13	1	4	31	26	32	1	6	2-3	.267	.346	.392	.737	7	.987
—New York (N.L.)	C	13	29	2	3	0	0	0	0	3	9	1	0	0-0	.103	.212	.103	.316	2	.974
1996— New York (N.L.)	C	6	11	1	4	0	0	0	0	0	4	0	0	0-0	.364	.364	.364	.727	0	1.000
—Norfolk (Int'l)	C	113	341	34	71	12	1	11	39	39	67	4	3	2-2	.208	.295	.346	.641	8	.990
1997— New York (N.L.)	C	35	59	3	12	1	0	0	2	9	16	0	1	0-1	.203	.304	.220	.525	2	.987
—Norfolk (Int'l)	C-OF	34	83	4	18	1	0	1	8	17	16	0	3	1-0	.217	.347	.265	.612	7	.968
1998— New York (N.L.)	C-DH	38	83	13	17	4	0	2	7	9	17	1	1	0-2	.205	.290	.325	.616	2	.990
—Norfolk (Int'l)	C-OF	21	49	4	9	2	0	1	6	11	12	0	0	0-0	.184	.333	.286	.619	1	.991
1999— St. Lucie (N.L.)	C	93	255	21	67	8	0	4	31	24	48	2	6	0-0	.263	.326	.341	.667	5	.991
2000— Toronto (A.L.)	C	66	185	14	39	7	0	1	16	21	36	0	3	0-0	.211	.287	.265	.552	3	.993
2001— Toronto (A.L.)	C	66	131	9	26	4	0	1	7	7	30	3	2	1-1	.198	.255	.252	.507	4	.989
2002— Toronto (A.L.)	C	15	37	3	5	1	1	0	4	1	12	0	2	0-0	.135	.158	.216	.374	1	.990
—Columbus (Int'l)	C	30	91	7	25	7	0	0	8	9	8	2	3	1-0	.275	.350	.352	.701	4	.984
2003— Fresno (PCL)	C	12	34	2	8	1	0	0	7	8	8	0	1	0-0	.235	.381	.265	.646	1	1.000
—San Francisco (N.L.)	C	11	15	2	3	1	0	0	1	3	5	0	0	0-0	.200	.200	.467	.667	1	.975
2004— Omaha (PCL)	C-DH-1B	48	161	15	41	9	0	1	15	20	20	3	8	0-0	.255	.348	.329	.677	5	.985
—Kansas City (A.L.)	C	29	89	12	24	6	0	1	11	14	10	0	1	0-2	.270	.365	.371	.736	1	.995
American League totals (4 years)		176	442	38	94	18	1	3	35	43	88	3	8	1-3	.213	.285	.278	.563	9	.992
National League totals (6 years)		196	452	42	106	14	0	7	49	39	99	4	10	1-3	.235	.306	.312	.618	12	.989
Major League totals (10 years)		372	894	80	200	32	1	10	84	88	187	7	18	2-6	.224	.296	.295	.591	21	.990

CASTILLO, FRANK — P

PERSONAL: Born April 1, 1969, in El Paso, Texas. ... 6-1/198. ... Throws right, bats right. ... Full name: Frank Anthony Castillo. ... Name pronounced: cas-TEE-yoh. ... High school: Eastwood (El Paso, Texas).

TRANSACTIONS/CAREER NOTES: Selected by Chicago Cubs organization in sixth round of 1987 free-agent draft. ... On disabled list (August 11-27, 1991). ... On suspended list (September 20-24, 1993). ... On disabled list (March 20-May 12, 1994); included rehabilitation assignments to Daytona, Orlando and Iowa. ... Traded by Cubs to Colorado Rockies for P Matt Pool (July 15, 1997). ... Signed as a free agent by Detroit Tigers (December 11, 1997). ... On disabled list (March 24-April 28, 1998); included rehabilitation assignment to Lakeland. ... Signed as a free agent by Arizona Diamondbacks organization (January 12, 1999). ... Released by Diamondbacks (March 27, 1999). ... Signed by Pittsburgh Pirates organization (April 20, 1999). ... Signed as a free agent by Toronto Blue Jays organization (December 21, 1999). ... On disabled list (August 14-September 16, 2000). ... Signed as a free agent by Boston Red Sox (December 7, 2000). ... On disabled list (June 29-August 8, 2001); included rehabilitation assignment to Pawtucket. ... On suspended list (May 17-22 and July 1-5, 2002). ... Released by Red Sox (March 26, 2003). ... Signed by Oakland Athletics organization (April 9, 2003). ... Released by A's (June 9, 2003). ... Signed by Atlanta Braves organization (August 16, 2003). ... Released by Braves (September 2, 2003). ... Signed as a free agent by Red Sox organization (February 18, 2004).

CAREER HITTING: 37-for-337 (.110), 7 R, 0 2B, 0 3B, 0 HR, 13 RBI.

Year Team (League)	W	L	Pct.	ERA	WHIP	G	GS	CG	ShO	Hld.	Sv.-Opp.	IP	H	R	ER	HR	BB-IBB	SO	Avg.
1987— Wytheville (Appal.)	10	1	.909	2.29	1.18	12	12	5	0	...	0-...	90.1	86	31	23	4	21-0	83	.252
— Geneva (N.Y.-Penn)	1	0	1.000	0.00	0.67	1	1	0	0	...	0-...	6.0	3	1	0	0	1-0	6	.136
1988— Peoria (Midw.)	6	1	.857	0.71	0.69	9	8	2	2	...	0-...	51.0	25	5	4	1	10-0	58	.143
1989— Winston-Salem (Caro.)	9	6	.600	2.51	1.10	18	18	8	1	...	0-...	129.1	118	42	36	5	24-1	114	.240
— Charlotte (Sou.)	3	4	.429	3.84	1.25	10	10	4	0	...	0-...	68.0	73	35	29	7	12-3	43	.277
1990— Charlotte (Sou.)	6	6	.500	3.88	1.26	18	18	4	1	...	0-...	111.1	113	54	48	8	27-4	112	.265
1991— Iowa (Am. Assoc.)	3	1	.750	2.52	1.08	4	4	1	1	...	0-...	25.0	20	7	7	0	7-0	20	.225
— Chicago (N.L.)	6	7	.462	4.35	1.25	18	18	4	0	0	0-0	111.2	107	56	54	5	33-2	73	.252
1992— Chicago (N.L.)	10	11	.476	3.46	1.18	33	33	0	0	0	0-0	205.1	179	91	79	19	63-6	135	.232
1993— Chicago (N.L.)	5	8	.385	4.84	1.42	29	25	2	0	0	0-0	141.1	162	83	76	20	39-4	84	.293
1994— Daytona (Fla. St.)	0	1	.000	4.50	1.75	1	1	0	0	...	0-...	4.0	7	3	2	0	0-0	1	.368
— Orlando (Sou.)	1	0	1.000	1.29	0.71	1	1	0	0	...	0-...	7.0	4	2	1	0	1-0	2	.167
— Iowa (Am. Assoc.)	4	2	.667	3.27	1.02	11	11	0	0	...	0-...	66.0	57	30	24	9	10-0	64	.228
— Chicago (N.L.)	2	1	.667	4.30	1.30	4	4	1	0	0	0-0	23.0	25	13	11	3	5-0	19	.278
1995— Chicago (N.L.)	11	10	.524	3.21	1.23	29	29	2	2	0	0-0	188.0	179	75	67	22	52-4	135	.248
1996— Chicago (N.L.)	7	•16	.304	5.28	1.40	33	33	1	1	0	0-0	182.1	209	112	107	28	46-4	139	.288
1997— Chicago (N.L.)	6	9	.400	5.42	1.60	20	19	0	0	0	0-0	98.0	113	64	59	9	44-1	67	.292
— Colorado (N.L.)	6	3	.667	5.42	1.53	14	14	0	0	0	0-0	86.1	107	57	52	16	25-3	59	.308
1998— Lakeland (Fla. St.)	1	0	1.000	0.00	0.40	1	1	0	0	...	0-...	5.0	2	0	0	0	0-0	4	.125
— Detroit (A.L.)	3	9	.250	6.83	1.67	27	19	0	0	0	1-1	116.0	150	91	88	17	44-0	81	.316
1999— Nashville (PCL)	7	5	.583	4.68	1.43	19	19	0	0	...	0-...	119.1	139	72	62	15	32-4	90	.290
2000— Toronto (A.L.)	10	5	.667	3.59	1.22	25	24	0	0	0	0-0	138.0	112	58	55	18	56-0	104	.220
2001— Boston (A.L.)	10	9	.526	4.21	1.27	26	26	0	0	0	0-0	136.2	138	72	64	14	35-2	89	.260
— Pawtucket (Int'l)	0	0	...	0.00	0.91	2	2	0	0	...	0-...	7.2	7	1	0	0	0-0	3	.250
2002— Boston (A.L.)	6	15	.286	5.07	1.42	36	23	0	0	0	1-2	163.1	174	101	92	19	58-6	112	.274
2003— Sacramento (PCL)	5	4	.556	4.13	1.40	19	16	0	0	...	0-...	96.0	104	47	44	12	34-2	59	.280
— Richmond (Int'l)	0	1	.000	1.50	1.50	4	3	0	0	...	0-...	18.0	23	5	3	1	4-0	14	.307
2004— Boston (A.L.)	0	0	...	0.00	2.00	2	0	0	0	0	0-0	1.0	1	0	0	0	0-0	0	.333
— Pawtucket (Int'l)	10	9	.526	4.38	1.21	27	25	0	0	...	0-...	168.1	169	87	82	28	34-0	123	.260
American League totals (5 years)	29	38	.433	4.85	1.39	116	92	0	0	0	2-3	555.0	575	322	299	68	194-8	386	.267
National League totals (7 years)	53	65	.449	4.39	1.34	180	175	10	3	0	0-0	1036.0	1081	551	505	122	307-24	711	.269
Major League totals (12 years)	82	103	.443	4.55	1.36	296	267	10	3	0	2-3	1591.0	1656	873	804	190	501-32	1097	.268

CASTILLO, JOSE — 2B

PERSONAL: Born March 19, 1981, in Las Mercedes, Venezuela. ... 6-1/200. ... Bats right, throws right.

TRANSACTIONS/CAREER NOTES: Signed as a non-drafted free agent by Pittsburgh Pirates organization (July 2, 1997).

2004 GAMES PLAYED BY POSITION (MLB): 2B—123, SS—2.

Year Team (League)	Pos.	G	AB	R	H	2B	3B	HR	RBI	BB	SO	HBP	GDP	SB-CS	Avg.	OBP	SLG	OPS	E	Avg.
1999— GC Pirates (GCL)	SS-2B	47	173	27	46	9	0	4	30	11	23	3	4	8-0	.266	.316	.387	.703	18	.923
2000— Hickory (S. Atl.)	SS	125	529	95	158	32	8	16	72	29	107	10	10	16-12	.299	.346	.480	.826	60	.908
2001— Lynchburg (Caro.)	SS	125	485	57	119	20	7	7	49	21	94	9	9	23-10	.245	.288	.359	.647	37	.939
2002— Lynchburg (Caro.)	SS	134	503	82	151	25	2	16	81	49	95	11	18	27-14	.300	.370	.453	.823	33	.951
2003— Altoona (East.)	2B-SS	126	498	68	143	24	6	5	66	40	81	3	18	19-10	.287	.339	.390	.728	23	.963
2004— Pittsburgh (N.L.)	2B-SS	129	383	44	98	15	2	8	39	23	92	1	12	3-2	.256	.298	.368	.666	11	.980
Major League totals (1 year)		129	383	44	98	15	2	8	39	23	92	1	12	3-2	.256	.298	.368	.666	11	.980

CASTILLO, LUIS — 2B

PERSONAL: Born September 12, 1975, in San Pedro de Macoris, Dominican Republic. ... 5-11/190. ... Bats both, throws right. ... Full name: Luis Antonio Castillo. ... Name pronounced: ca-STEE-yo. ... High school: Colegio San Benito Abad (San Pedro de Macoris, Dominican Republic). ... College: San Benito Abad (D.R.).

TRANSACTIONS/CAREER NOTES: Signed as a non-drafted free agent by Florida Marlins organization (August 19, 1992). ... On disabled list (May 7-22, 1997). ... On disabled list (April 16-May 5, 2000); included rehabilitation assignment to Calgary.

HONORS: Won N.L. Gold Glove at second base (2003 and 2004).

2004 GAMES PLAYED BY POSITION (MLB): 2B—148.

Year Team (League)	Pos.	G	AB	R	H	2B	3B	HR	RBI	BB	SO	HBP	GDP	SB-CS	Avg.	OBP	SLG	OPS	E	Avg.
1993— Dom. Marlins (DSL)	IF	69	266	48	75	7	1	4	31	36	22	...	...	21-...	.282	...	.361	...	20	.943
1994— GC Marlins (GCL)	2B-SS	57	216	49	57	8	0	0	16	37	36	1	1	31-12	.264	.371	.301	.672	9	.972
1995— Kane Co. (Midw.)	2B	89	340	71	111	4	4	0	23	55	50	0	1	41-18	.326	.419	.362	.781	17	.962
1996— Portland (East.)	2B	109	420	83	133	15	7	1	35	66	68	2	2	51-28	.317	.411	.393	.804	14	.975
— Florida (N.L.)	2B	41	164	26	43	2	1	1	8	14	46	0	0	17-4	.262	.320	.305	.625	3	.986
1997— Florida (N.L.)	2B	75	263	27	63	8	0	0	8	27	53	· 0	6	16-10	.240	.310	.270	.580	9	.971
— Charlotte (Int'l)	2B	37	130	25	46	5	0	1	16	16	22	0	2	8-6	.354	.425	.392	.817	5	.970
1998— Charlotte (Int'l)	2B	100	381	74	109	11	2	0	15	75	68	0	6	41-15	.286	.403	.325	.728	16	.970
— Florida (N.L.)	2B	44	153	21	31	3	2	1	10	22	33	1	1	3-0	.203	.307	.268	.575	7	.970
1999— Florida (N.L.)	2B	128	487	76	147	23	4	0	28	67	85	0	3	50-17	.302	.384	.366	.750	15	.976
2000— Florida (N.L.)	2B	136	539	101	180	17	3	2	17	78	86	0	11	* 62-22	.334	.418	.388	.806	11	.983
— Calgary (PCL)	2B	4	13	4	4	1	0	1	0	4	2	0	0	1-0	.308	.471	.538	1.009	1	.944
2001— Florida (N.L.)	2B	134	537	76	141	16	10	2	45	67	90	1	6	33-16	.263	.344	.341	.685	* 13	.980
2002— Florida (N.L.)	2B	146	606	86	185	18	5	2	39	55	76	2	7	* 48-15	.305	.364	.361	.726	13	.981

Year Team (League)	Pos.	G	AB	R	H	2B	3B	HR	RBI	BB	SO	HBP	GDP	SB-CS	Avg.	OBP	SLG	OPS	E	Avg.
2003—Florida (N.L.)	2B	152	595	99	187	19	6	6	39	63	60	2	7	21-19	.314	.381	.397	.778	10	.986
2004—Florida (N.L.)	2B	150	564	91	164	12	7	2	47	75	68	1	15	21-4	.291	.373	.348	.720	6	.991
Major League totals (9 years)		1006	3908	603	1141	118	38	16	241	468	597	7	56	271-107	.292	.368	.354	.722	87	.982

DIVISION SERIES RECORD

Year Team (League)	Pos.	G	AB	R	H	2B	3B	HR	RBI	BB	SO	HBP	GDP	SB-CS	Avg.	OBP	SLG	OPS	E	Avg.
2003—Florida (N.L.)	2B	4	17	2	5	3	0	0	1	3	3	0	0	0-0	.294	.400	.471	.871	0	1.000

CHAMPIONSHIP SERIES RECORD

Year Team (League)	Pos.	G	AB	R	H	2B	3B	HR	RBI	BB	SO	HBP	GDP	SB-CS	Avg.	OBP	SLG	OPS	E	Avg.
2003—Florida (N.L.)	2B	7	28	3	6	1	0	0	2	5	2	0	0	2-0	.214	.333	.250	.583	0	1.000

WORLD SERIES RECORD

Year Team (League)	Pos.	G	AB	R	H	2B	3B	HR	RBI	BB	SO	HBP	GDP	SB-CS	Avg.	OBP	SLG	OPS	E	Avg.
2003—Florida (N.L.)	2B	6	26	1	4	0	0	0	1	0	7	0	0	1-1	.154	.154	.154	.308	0	1.000

ALL-STAR GAME RECORD

	G	AB	R	H	2B	3B	HR	RBI	BB	SO	HBP	GDP	SB-CS	Avg.	OBP	SLG	OPS	E	Avg.
All-Star Game totals (2 years)	2	4	0	0	0	0	0	0	0	0	0	0	0-0	.000	.000	.000	.000	0	1.000

CASTRO, JUAN — 3B/SS

C

PERSONAL: Born June 20, 1972, in Los Mochis, Mexico. ... 5-11/195. ... Bats right, throws right. ... Full name: Juan Gabriel Castro. ... Name pronounced: KASS-tro. ... High school: CBTIS 43 (Los Mochis, Mexico).

TRANSACTIONS/CAREER NOTES: Signed as a non-drafted free agent by Los Angeles Dodgers organization (June 13, 1991). ... On disabled list (June 5-August 1, 1997). ... Traded by Dodgers to Cincinnati Reds for a player to be named and cash (April 1, 2000); Dodgers acquired P Kenny Lutz to complete deal (June 8, 2000). ... On disabled list (March 27-June 1, 2002); included rehabilitation assignments to Louisville. ... On disabled list (March 25-April 14, 2003); included rehabilitation assignment to Louisville. ... On disabled list (June 1-22, 2004); included rehabilitation assignment to Louisville.

2004 GAMES PLAYED BY POSITION (MLB): 3B—78, SS—31, 2B—12, 1B—4.

Year Team (League)	Pos.	G	AB	R	H	2B	3B	HR	RBI	BB	SO	HBP	GDP	SB-CS	Avg.	OBP	SLG	OPS	E	Avg.
1991—Great Falls (Pio.)	2B-SS	60	217	36	60	4	2	1	27	33	31	0	2	7-6	.277	.369	.327	.696	21	.921
1992—Bakersfield (Calif.)	SS	113	446	56	116	15	4	4	42	37	64	1	7	14-11	.260	.314	.339	.652	38	.928
1993—San Antonio (Texas)	2B-SS	118	424	55	117	23	8	7	41	30	40	2	14	12-11	.276	.325	.417	.742	28	.945
1994—San Antonio (Texas)	SS	123	445	55	128	25	4	4	44	31	66	1	9	4-7	.288	.334	.389	.723	29	.951
1995—Albuquerque (PCL)	SS-2B	104	341	51	91	18	4	3	43	20	42	0	11	4-4	.267	.307	.370	.677	14	.973
—Los Angeles (N.L.)	3B-SS	11	4	0	1	0	0	0	0	1	1	0	0	0-0	.250	.400	.250	.650	0	1.000
1996—Albuquerque (PCL)	3B-SS-2B	17	56	12	21	4	2	1	8	6	7	1	0	1-1	.375	.444	.571	1.016	2	.962
—Los Angeles (N.L.)	SS-3-2-OF	70	132	16	26	5	3	0	5	10	27	0	3	1-0	.197	.254	.280	.534	3	.979
1997—Los Angeles (N.L.)	SS-2B-3B	40	75	3	11	3	1	0	4	7	20	0	2	0-0	.147	.220	.213	.433	1	.990
—Albuquerque (PCL)	SS-2B	27	101	11	31	5	2	1	11	4	20	0	5	1-0	.307	.327	.455	.783	9	.928
1998—Los Angeles (N.L.)	SS-2B-3B	89	220	25	43	7	0	2	14	15	37	0	5	0-0	.195	.245	.255	.499	10	.965
1999—Albuquerque (PCL)	SS-3-2-DH	116	423	52	116	25	4	7	51	34	70	0	14	2-3	.274	.325	.402	.727	19	.956
—Los Angeles (N.L.)	2B-SS	2	1	0	0	0	0	0	0	1	0	0	0	0-0	.000	.000	.000	.000	0	1.000
2000—Louisville (Int'l)	SS-2B-3B	19	60	9	19	5	1	2	10	12	12	0	3	0-1	.317	.425	.533	.958	4	.956
—Cincinnati (N.L.)	SS-2B-3B	82	224	20	54	12	2	4	23	14	33	0	9	0-2	.241	.283	.366	.649	2	.993
2001—Cincinnati (N.L.)	SS-2-3-1	96	242	27	54	10	0	3	13	13	50	0	9	0-0	.223	.261	.302	.562	8	.970
2002—Louisville (Int'l)	SS-2B	5	17	2	3	0	0	0	2	1	3	0	0	0-0	.176	.222	.176	.399	1	.962
—Cincinnati (N.L.)	SS-2-3-1	54	82	5	18	3	0	2	11	7	18	0	0	0-0	.220	.278	.329	.607	3	.971
2003—Louisville (Int'l)	SS	9	32	3	7	0	0	1	5	2	3	0	2	0-1	.219	.257	.313	.570	2	.950
—Cincinnati (N.L.)	2-3-SS-1	113	320	28	81	14	1	9	33	18	58	0	7	2-3	.253	.290	.388	.678	5	.987
2004—Louisville (Int'l)	SS-2B-3B	5	18	1	3	1	0	0	3	1	2	0	0	0-0	.167	.200	.222	.422	1	.955
—Cincinnati (N.L.)	3-SS-2-1	111	299	36	73	21	2	5	26	14	51	0	11	1-0	.244	.277	.378	.655	8	.973
Major League totals (10 years)		668	1599	160	361	75	9	25	129	99	296	0	46	4-5	.226	.269	.331	.600	40	.979

DIVISION SERIES RECORD

Year Team (League)	Pos.	G	AB	R	H	2B	3B	HR	RBI	BB	SO	HBP	GDP	SB-CS	Avg.	OBP	SLG	OPS	E	Avg.
1996—Los Angeles (N.L.)	2B	2	5	0	1	1	0	0	1	1	1	0	0	0-0	.200	.333	.400	.733	0	1.000

CASTRO, RAMON — C

PERSONAL: Born March 1, 1976, in Vega Baja, Puerto Rico. ... 6-3/235. ... Bats right, throws right. ... Full name: Ramon Abraham Castro. ... Name pronounced: RA-mon. ... High school: Lino P. Rivera (Vega Baja, Puerto Rico).

TRANSACTIONS/CAREER NOTES: Selected by Houston Astros organization in first round (17th pick overall) of 1994 free-agent draft. ... Traded by Astros to Florida Marlins for P Jay Powell and C Scott Makarewicz (July 6, 1998). ... On disabled list (May 17-June 8, 2002; and June 2, 2004-remainder of season). ... Refused minor league assignment and became a free agent (October 8, 2004).

2004 GAMES PLAYED BY POSITION (MLB): C—31.

Year Team (League)	Pos.	G	AB	R	H	2B	3B	HR	RBI	BB	SO	HBP	GDP	SB-CS	Avg.	OBP	SLG	OPS	E	Avg.
1994—GC Astros (GCL)	C	37	123	17	34	7	0	3	14	17	14	2	4	5-5	.276	.373	.407	.780	4	.983
1995—Kissimmee (Fla. St.)	C	36	120	6	25	5	0	0	8	6	21	1	1	0-0	.208	.250	.250	.500	7	.967
—Auburn (NY-Penn)	C	63	224	40	67	17	0	9	49	24	27	0	6	0-1	.299	.358	.496	.854	2	.994
1996—Quad City (Midw.)	C	96	314	38	78	15	0	7	43	31	61	2	12	2-0	.248	.317	.363	.680	10	.987
1997—Kissimmee (Fla. St.)	C	115	410	53	115	22	1	8	65	53	73	2	17	1-0	.280	.357	.398	.755	6	.992
1998—Jackson (Texas)	C	48	168	27	43	6	0	8	25	13	31	4	3	0-1	.256	.324	.435	.759	10	.974
—Portland (East.)	C	31	88	9	22	3	0	3	11	8	21	0	3	0-0	.250	.306	.386	.692	5	.946
1999—Calgary (PCL)	C-DH	97	349	43	90	22	0	15	61	24	64	2	11	0-0	.258	.307	.450	.757	7	.989
—Florida (N.L.)	C	24	67	4	12	4	0	2	4	10	14	0	1	0-0	.179	.282	.328	.610	1	.992
2000—Florida (N.L.)	C	67	218	44	73	22	0	14	45	16	38	0	5	0-0	.335	.380	.628	1.009	4	.990
—Florida (N.L.)	C	50	138	10	33	4	0	2	14	16	36	1	1	0-0	.239	.318	.312	.630	6	.990
2001—Florida (N.L.)	C	7	11	0	2	0	0	0	1	1	1	0	0	0-0	.182	.250	.182	.432	0	1.000
—Calgary (PCL)	C	108	390	81	131	33	0	27	90	38	74	1	11	1-1	.336	.393	.628	1.021	7	.989

Year	Team (League)	Pos.	G	AB	R	H	2B	3B	HR	RBI	BB	SO	HBP	GDP	SB-CS	Avg.	OBP	SLG	OPS	E	Avg.
2002—Florida (N.L.)	C-DH	54	101	11	24	4	0	6	18	14	24	0	4	0-0	.238	.322	.455	.777	0	1.000
2003—Florida (N.L.)	C-DH	40	53	6	15	2	0	5	8	4	11	0	0	0-0	.283	.333	.604	.937	1	.982
2004—Florida (N.L.)	C	32	96	9	13	3	0	3	8	11	30	1	1	0-0	.135	.231	.260	.492	2	.990
Major League totals (6 years)		207	466	40	99	17	0	18	53	56	116	2	7	0-0	.212	.296	.365	.661	10	.988

CASTRO, RAMON A. 3B

PERSONAL: Born October 23, 1979, in Valencia, Venezuela. ... 6-0/195. ... Bats right, throws right. ... Full name: Ramon Alfredo Castro.
TRANSACTIONS/CAREER NOTES: Signed as a non-drafted free agent by Atlanta Braves organization (July 9, 1996). ... Signed as a free agent by Oakland Athletics organization (November 17, 2003).
2004 GAMES PLAYED BY POSITION (MLB): 3B—6, SS—1, DH—1.

									BATTING											FIELDING	
Year	Team (League)	Pos.	G	AB	R	H	2B	3B	HR	RBI	BB	SO	HBP	GDP	SB-CS	Avg.	OBP	SLG	OPS	E	Avg.
1997—Eugene (Northwest)	SS	71	226	20	45	8	3	1	23	24	56	6	5	7-1	.199	.290	.274	.564	27	.916
1998—Eugene (Northwest)	2B-3B-SS	74	296	33	77	10	1	3	33	22	49	5	1	8-1	.260	.320	.331	.651	25	.908
1999—Macon (S. Atl.)	2-SS-3-OF	105	350	32	91	12	4	3	33	24	55	2	4	13-5	.260	.310	.343	.652	13	.955
2000—Myrtle Beach (Caro.)	SS-2B-1B	108	385	52	97	20	3	5	44	44	76	12	4	13-5	.252	.346	.358	.705	15	.966
2001—Greenville (Sou.)	SS-2B-3B	76	261	35	80	19	5	6	31	25	56	9	5	5-8	.307	.383	.487	.869	9	.971
—Richmond (Int'l)	SS-2B-3B	36	135	14	30	8	2	1	15	7	30	1	5	1-2	.222	.266	.333	.599	4	.972
2002—Richmond (Int'l)	2B-SS	39	121	22	28	7	1	6	14	14	22	6	1	4-3	.231	.340	.455	.795	5	.969
—GC Braves (GCL)	3B-2B-SS	9	32	3	8	0	0	1	4	3	6	1	1	2-0	.250	.333	.344	.677	2	.917
—Greenville (Sou.)	SS-3B	56	210	47	68	17	2	5	22	39	44	9	3	14-8	.324	.446	.495	.941	6	.973
2003—Richmond (Int'l)	SS-2B-3B	33	84	11	13	2	0	0	8	10	22	0	2	0-0	.155	.242	.179	.421	3	.967
—Greenville (Sou.)	3-SS-2-1	66	204	33	59	9	1	5	20	27	39	2	1	4-5	.289	.376	.417	.793	12	.936
2004—Sacramento (PCL)	SS-2B-3B	40	123	15	28	8	2	1	16	15	20	2	4	2-2	.228	.317	.350	.657	7	.953
—Oakland (A.L.)	3B-SS-DH	9	15	2	2	1	0	0	3	1	3	0	1	0-0	.133	.188	.200	.388	0	1.000
—Midland (Texas)	3B-2B-SS	28	93	16	23	2	3	0	12	12	18	4	1	3-2	.247	.348	.333	.657	5	.951
Major League totals (1 year)		9	15	2	2	1	0	0	3	1	3	0	1	0-0	.133	.188	.200	.388	0	1.000

CATALANOTTO, FRANK OF

PERSONAL: Born April 27, 1974, in Smithtown, N.Y. ... 5-11/195. ... Bats left, throws right. ... Full name: Frank John Catalanotto. ... Name pronounced: ca-tal-a-NAH-tow. ... High school: Smithtown (N.Y.) East. ... College: Post C.W. (N.Y.).
TRANSACTIONS/CAREER NOTES: Selected by Detroit Tigers organization in 10th round of 1992 free-agent draft. ... Selected by Oakland Athletics from Tigers organization in Rule 5 major league draft (December 9, 1996). ... Returned to Tigers organization (March 21, 1997). ... Traded by Tigers with Ps Justin Thompson, P Francisco Cordero and Alan Webb, OF Gabe Kapler and C Bill Haselman to Texas Rangers for OF Juan Gonzalez, P Danny Patterson and C Gregg Zaun (November 2, 1999). ... On disabled list (April 22-May 15, 2000); included rehabilitation assignment to Oklahoma (May 12-15). ... On disabled list (May 11-June 28 and August 17, 2002-remainder of season); included rehabilitation assignment to Tulsa. ... Signed as a free agent by Toronto Blue Jays (December 30, 2002). ... On disabled list (May 20-June 8, June 18-July 20 and August 21, 2004-remainder of season).
2004 GAMES PLAYED BY POSITION (MLB): OF—41, DH—29.

									BATTING											FIELDING	
Year	Team (League)	Pos.	G	AB	R	H	2B	3B	HR	RBI	BB	SO	HBP	GDP	SB-CS	Avg.	OBP	SLG	OPS	E	Avg.
1992—Bristol (Appal.)	2B	21	50	6	10	2	0	0	4	8	8	0	0	0-1	.200	.310	.240	.550	2	.875
1993—Bristol (Appal.)	2B	55	199	37	61	9	5	3	22	15	19	3	3	3-6	.307	.364	.447	.811	10	.957
1994—Fayetteville (SAL)	2B	119	458	72	149	24	8	3	56	37	54	3	4	4-5	.325	.379	.432	.811	15	.973
1995—Jacksonville (Sou.)	2B	134	491	66	111	19	5	8	48	49	56	9	9	13-8	.226	.306	.334	.640	18	.974
1996—Jacksonville (Sou.)	2B	132	497	105	148	34	6	17	67	74	69	11	8	15-14	.298	.398	.493	.891	22	.968
1997—Toledo (Int'l)	2-3-0-1	134	500	75	150	32	3	16	68	47	80	10	9	12-11	.300	.368	.472	.840	18	.966
—Detroit (A.L.)	2B-DH	13	26	2	8	2	0	0	3	3	7	0	0	0-0	.308	.379	.385	.764	0	1.000
1998—Detroit (A.L.)	2-DH-1-3	89	213	23	60	13	2	6	25	12	39	4	4	3-2	.282	.325	.446	.771	3	.986
—Toledo (Int'l)	1B-2B-DH	28	105	20	35	6	3	4	28	14	21	7	2	0-0	.333	.438	.562	.999	2	.989
1999—Detroit (A.L.)	2-1-3-DH	100	286	41	79	19	0	11	35	15	49	6	5	3-4	.276	.327	.458	.785	5	.986
2000—Texas (A.L.)	2-DH-1-O	103	282	55	82	13	2	10	42	33	36	6	5	6-2	.291	.375	.457	.832	9	.969
—Oklahoma (PCL)	2B-OF	3	11	2	3	0	0	0	1	0	4	1	0	0-0	.273	.333	.273	.606	0	1.000
2001—Texas (A.L.)	O-2-3-DH-1	133	463	77	153	31	5	11	54	39	55	8	3	15-5	.330	.391	.490	.882	4	.985
2002—Texas (A.L.)	OF-2-1-DH	68	212	42	57	16	3	3	23	25	27	8	3	9-5	.269	.364	.443	.808	2	.990
—Tulsa (Texas)	1B-2B-OF	4	16	1	2	0	1	0	3	1	1	1	3	0-0	.125	.222	.250	.472	0	1.000
2003—Toronto (A.L.)	OF-DH-1B	133	489	83	146	34	6	13	59	35	62	6	9	2-2	.299	.351	.472	.823	3	.983
2004—Toronto (A.L.)	OF-DH	75	249	27	73	19	1	1	26	17	33	4	7	1-0	.293	.344	.390	.734	2	.971
Major League totals (8 years)		714	2220	350	658	147	22	55	267	179	308	45	38	39-20	.296	.358	.457	.815	28	.982

CEDENO, ROGER OF

PERSONAL: Born August 16, 1974, in Valencia, Venezuela. ... 6-1/205. ... Bats both, throws right. ... Full name: Roger Leandro Cedeno. ... Name pronounced: sid-AIN-yo.
TRANSACTIONS/CAREER NOTES: Signed as a non-drafted free agent by Los Angeles Dodgers organization (March 28, 1991). ... On disabled list (March 25-April 17 and August 25, 1997-remainder of season); included rehabilitation assignment to Albuquerque. ... On disabled list (March 22-April 24, 1998); included rehabilitation assignment to Vero Beach. ... Traded by Dodgers with C Charles Johnson to New York Mets for C Todd Hundley and P Arnold Gooch (December 1, 1998). ... Traded by Mets with Ps Octavio Dotel and Kyle Kessel to Houston Astros for P Mike Hampton and OF Derek Bell (December 23, 1999). ... On Houston disabled list (May 26-August 18, 2000); included rehabilitation assignment to New Orleans. ... Traded by Astros with C Mitch Meluskey and P Chris Holt to Detroit Tigers for C Brad Ausmus and Ps Doug Brocail and Nelson Cruz (December 11, 2000). ... Signed as a free agent by Mets (December 17, 2001). ... Traded by Mets to St. Louis Cardinals for IF Wilson Delgado and C Chris Widger (April 4, 2004). ... On disabled list (April 11-May 13, 2004); included rehabilitation assignment to Memphis. ... On suspended list (July 15-17, 2004).
2004 GAMES PLAYED BY POSITION (MLB): OF—54, DH—1.

									BATTING											FIELDING	
Year	Team (League)	Pos.	G	AB	R	H	2B	3B	HR	RBI	BB	SO	HBP	GDP	SB-CS	Avg.	OBP	SLG	OPS	E	Avg.
1991—Dom. Dodgers (DSL)	OF	58	209	25	50	1	1	0	7	0	0	...	...	26-13	.239	...	.254	...	...	...
1992—Great Falls (Pio.)	OF	69	256	60	81	6	5	2	27	51	53	2	4	40-9	.316	.431	.402	.833	8	.937
1993—San Antonio (Texas)	OF	122	465	70	134	12	8	4	30	45	90	1	5	28-20	.288	.353	.374	.726	9	.961
—Albuquerque (PCL)	OF	6	18	1	4	1	1	0	4	4	3	0	0	0-1	.222	.333	.389	.722	1	.923
1994—Albuquerque (PCL)	OF	104	383	84	123	18	5	4	49	51	57	0	4	30-13	.321	.395	.426	.820	8	.962
1995—Albuquerque (PCL)	OF-DH	99	367	67	112	19	9	2	44	53	56	2	5	23-18	.305	.393	.422	.815	3	.985
—Los Angeles (N.L.)	OF	40	42	6	10	2	0	0	3	8	10	0	1	1-0	.238	.283	.286	.568	1	.977

C

Year	Team (League)	Pos.	G	AB	R	H	2B	3B	HR	RBI	BB	SO	HBP	GDP	SB-CS	Avg.	OBP	SLG	OPS	E	Avg.
1996—	Los Angeles (N.L.)	OF	86	211	26	52	11	1	2	18	24	47	1	0	5-1	.246	.326	.336	.663	2	.983
	—Albuquerque (PCL)	OF	33	125	16	28	2	3	1	10	15	22	0	2	6-5	.224	.307	.312	.619	0	1.000
1997—	Albuquerque (PCL)	OF	29	113	21	40	4	4	2	9	22	16	1	1	5-5	.354	.463	.513	.977	2	.964
	—Los Angeles (N.L.)	OF	80	194	31	53	10	2	3	17	25	44	3	1	9-1	.273	.362	.392	.753	2	.987
1998—	Vero Beach (FSL)	OF	6	21	5	9	0	1	1	6	5	5	0	2	1-0	.429	.538	.667	1.205	1	.933
	—Los Angeles (N.L.)	OF	105	240	33	58	11	1	2	17	27	57	0	1	8-2	.242	.317	.321	.638	2	.978
1999—	New York (N.L.)	OF-2B	155	453	90	142	23	4	4	36	60	100	3	5	66-17	.313	.396	.408	.804	3	.989
2000—	Houston (N.L.)	OF	74	259	54	73	2	5	6	26	43	47	0	6	25-11	.282	.383	.398	.781	3	.978
	—New Orleans (PCL)	OF	6	20	2	7	0	1	0	3	2	5	0	0	1-1	.350	.391	.450	.841	0	1.000
2001—	Detroit (A.L.)	OF-DH	131	523	79	153	14	11	6	48	36	83	2	5	55-15	.293	.337	.396	.733	12	.953
2002—	New York (N.L.)	OF	149	511	65	133	19	2	7	41	42	92	2	10	25-4	.260	.318	.346	.664	8	.966
2003—	New York (N.L.)	OF	148	484	70	129	25	4	7	37	38	86	1	8	14-9	.267	.320	.378	.698	3	.987
2004—	Memphis (PCL)	OF	7	23	3	5	0	0	0	1	2	6	0	0	0-0	.217	.280	.217	.497	0	1.000
	—St. Louis (N.L.)	OF-DH	95	200	22	53	9	2	3	23	19	41	0	5	5-1	.265	.327	.375	.702	0	1.000
	American League totals (1 year)		131	523	79	153	14	11	6	48	36	83	2	5	55-15	.293	.337	.396	.733	12	.953
	National League totals (9 years)		932	2594	395	703	112	21	34	218	281	524	10	37	158-46	.271	.343	.370	.713	24	.982
	Major League totals (10 years)		1063	3117	474	856	126	32	40	266	317	607	12	42	213-61	.275	.342	.374	.716	36	.977

DIVISION SERIES RECORD

Year	Team (League)	Pos.	G	AB	R	H	2B	3B	HR	RBI	BB	SO	HBP	GDP	SB-CS	Avg.	OBP	SLG	OPS	E	Avg.
1999—	New York (N.L.)	OF	4	7	1	2	0	0	0	2	1	1	0	1	1-0	.286	.333	.286	.619	0	1.000
2004—	St. Louis (N.L.)		2	2	0	1	0	0	0	0	0	0	0	0	0-0	.500	.500	.500	1.000	0	—
	Division series totals (2 years)		6	9	1	3	0	0	0	2	1	1	0	1	1-0	.333	.364	.333	.697	0	1.000

CHAMPIONSHIP SERIES RECORD

Year	Team (League)	Pos.	G	AB	R	H	2B	3B	HR	RBI	BB	SO	HBP	GDP	SB-CS	Avg.	OBP	SLG	OPS	E	Avg.
1999—	New York (N.L.)	OF	5	12	2	6	1	0	0	1	0	1	0	0	2-1	.500	.500	.583	1.083	0	1.000
2004—	St. Louis (N.L.)	OF	6	6	1	1	0	0	0	1	0	2	0	0	0-0	.167	.167	.167	.333	0	—
	Champ. series totals (2 years)		11	18	3	7	1	0	0	2	0	3	0	0	2-1	.389	.389	.444	.833	0	1.000

WORLD SERIES RECORD

Year	Team (League)	Pos.	G	AB	R	H	2B	3B	HR	RBI	BB	SO	HBP	GDP	SB-CS	Avg.	OBP	SLG	OPS	E	Avg.
2004—	St. Louis (N.L.)	OF	3	4	1	1	0	0	0	0	0	1	0	0	0-0	.250	.250	.250	.500	0	—

CEPICKY, MATT   OF

PERSONAL: Born November 10, 1977, in St. Louis, Mo. ... 6-2/215. ... Bats left, throws right. ... Full name: Matthew William Cepicky. ... Name pronounced: suh-PICK-ee. ... High school: Vianney (Kirkwood, Mo.). ... College: Southwest Missouri State. ... Cousin of Scott Cepicky, first baseman in Chicago White Sox organization (1989-94).

TRANSACTIONS/CAREER NOTES: Selected by Montreal Expos organization in fourth round of 1999 free-agent draft.

2004 GAMES PLAYED BY POSITION (MLB): OF—11, DH—2.

Year	Team (League)	Pos.	G	AB	R	H	2B	3B	HR	RBI	BB	SO	HBP	GDP	SB-CS	Avg.	OBP	SLG	OPS	E	Avg.
																	BATTING			FIELDING	
1999—	Vermont (N.Y.-Penn.)	OF	74	323	50	99	15	5	12	53	20	49	1	6	10-9	.307	.349	.495	.844	1	.986
2000—	Jupiter (FSL)	OF	131	536	61	160	32	7	5	88	24	64	2	9	32-13	.299	.328	.412	.740	4	.983
2001—	Harrisburg (East.)	OF	122	459	59	121	23	8	15	77	21	97	2	6	5-12	.264	.296	.447	.743	3	.986
2002—	Harrisburg (East.)	OF	109	419	54	116	25	2	16	76	33	94	2	14	7-1	.277	.327	.461	.787	2	.988
	—Montreal (N.L.)	OF	32	74	7	16	3	0	3	15	4	21	0	0	0-0	.216	.256	.378	.635	0	1.000
2003—	Montreal (N.L.)	OF	5	8	0	2	1	0	0	0	0	2	0	0	0-0	.250	.250	.375	.625	0	1.000
	—Edmonton (PCL)	OF-DH-1B	122	442	61	133	23	4	7	64	31	82	4	12	7-2	.301	.349	.419	.767	11	.948
2004—	Montreal (N.L.)	OF-DH	32	60	4	13	4	0	1	3	1	18	0	1	1-0	.217	.230	.333	.563	0	1.000
	—Edmonton (PCL)	OF-DH-1B	82	312	51	84	15	3	15	67	18	75	0	4	2-1	.269	.305	.481	.786	4	.975
	Major League totals (3 years)		69	142	11	31	8	0	4	18	5	41	0	1	1-0	.218	.245	.359	.604	0	1.000

CERDA, JAIME   P

PERSONAL: Born October 26, 1978, in Fresno, Calif. ... 6-0/175. ... Throws left, bats left. ... Full name: Jaime M. Cerda. ... Name pronounced: SER-da. ... Junior college: Fresno City (Calif.).

TRANSACTIONS/CAREER NOTES: Selected by New York Mets organization in 23rd round of 1998 free-agent draft. ... Traded by Mets to Kansas City Royals for P Shawn Sedlacek (January 26, 2004).

CAREER HITTING: 0-for-2 (.000), 0 R, 0 2B, 0 3B, 0 HR, 0 RBI.

Year	Team (League)	W	L	Pct.	ERA	WHIP	G	GS	CG	ShO	Hld.	Sv.-Opp.	IP	H	R	ER	HR	BB-IBB	SO	Avg.
1999—		Did not play.																		
2000—	Pittsfield (N.Y.-Penn.)	4	1	.800	0.57	0.83	20	1	0	0	...	5-...	47.0	33	6	3	0	6-1	51	.198
2001—	St. Lucie (Fla. St.)	2	1	.667	0.97	0.93	28	0	0	0	...	6-...	55.2	40	8	6	3	12-0	53	.204
	—Binghamton (Eastern)	1	0	1.000	3.10	1.13	12	0	0	0	...	3-...	20.1	17	7	7	1	6-0	22	.233
	—Norfolk (Int'l)	0	0	...	3.86	0.86	3	0	0	0	...	0-...	4.2	2	2	2	0	2-0	4	.125
2002—	Binghamton (Eastern)	5	1	.833	2.27	0.98	14	0	0	0	...	1-...	31.2	21	8	8	0	10-0	33	.193
	—Norfolk (Int'l)	0	0	...	0.43	0.81	12	0	0	0	...	1-...	21.0	10	2	1	0	7-1	17	.143
	—New York (N.L.)	0	0	...	2.45	1.44	32	0	0	0	4	0-0	25.2	22	7	7	0	14-0	21	.232
2003—	Norfolk (Int'l)	3	0	1.000	1.67	1.20	22	0	0	0	...	0-...	32.1	29	7	6	3	10-1	35	.246
	—New York (N.L.)	1	1	.500	5.85	1.61	27	0	0	0	2	0-1	32.1	32	21	21	4	20-1	19	.267
2004—	Omaha (PCL)	0	0	...	3.00	1.83	6	0	0	0	...	0-...	6.0	8	2	2	0	3-0	2	.348
	—Kansas City (A.L.)	1	4	.200	3.15	1.55	53	0	0	0	12	2-3	45.2	41	21	16	1	30-3	33	.244
	American League totals (1 year)	1	4	.200	3.15	1.55	53	0	0	0	12	2-3	45.2	41	21	16	1	30-3	33	.244
	National League totals (2 years)	1	1	.500	4.34	1.52	59	0	0	0	6	0-1	58.0	54	28	28	4	34-1	40	.251
	Major League totals (3 years)	2	5	.286	3.82	1.53	112	0	0	0	18	2-4	103.2	95	49	44	5	64-4	73	.248

CHACIN, GUSTAVO   P

PERSONAL: Born December 4, 1980, in Maracaibo, Venezuela. ... 5-11/193. ... Throws left, bats left. ... Full name: Gustavo G. Adolfo Chacin.

TRANSACTIONS/CAREER NOTES: Signed as a non-drafted free agent by Toronto Blue Jays organization (July 3, 1998).

CAREER HITTING: 0-for-0 (.000), 0 R, 0 2B, 0 3B, 0 HR, 0 RBI.

Year Team (League)	W	L	Pct.	ERA	WHIP	G	GS	CG	ShO	Hld.	Sv.-Opp.	IP	H	R	ER	HR	BB-IBB	SO	Avg.
1998— Dom. B. Jays (DSL)	3	2	.600	2.70	1.17	9	6	2	2	...	0-...	36.2	28	12	11	...	15-...	56	...
1999— Medicine Hat (Pio.)	4	3	.571	3.09	1.42	15	9	0	0	...	1-...	64.0	68	33	22	6	23-0	50	.281
2000— Dunedin (Fla. St.)	9	5	.643	4.02	1.58	25	21	0	0	...	0-...	127.2	138	69	57	14	64-0	77	.269
— Tennessee (Sou.)	0	2	.000	12.60	3.20	2	2	0	0	...	0-...	5.0	10	7	7	1	6-0	5	.417
2001— Tennessee (Sou.)	11	8	.579	3.98	1.26	25	23	1	1	...	0-...	140.1	138	66	62	17	39-0	86	.257
2002— Tennessee (Sou.)	6	5	.545	4.66	1.59	35	13	1	0	...	1-...	119.2	131	73	62	12	59-0	68	.282
2003— New Haven (East.)	3	4	.429	4.15	1.54	46	2	0	0	...	2-...	69.1	78	39	32	1	29-1	55	.283
2004— Syracuse (Int'l)	2	0	1.000	2.31	1.63	2	2	0	0	...	0-...	11.2	16	4	3	0	3-0	14	.327
— New Hampshire (East.)	16	2	.889	2.92	1.14	25	25	0	0	...	0-...	141.2	113	53	46	15	49-0	109	.215
— Toronto (A.L.)	1	1	.500	2.57	0.79	2	2	0	0	...	0-0	14.0	8	4	4	0	3-0	6	.167
Major League totals (1 year)	1	1	.500	2.57	0.79	2	2	0	0	...	0-0	14.0	8	4	4	0	3-0	6	.167

CHACON, SHAWN   P

PERSONAL: Born December 23, 1977, in Anchorage, Alaska. ... 6-3/212. ... Throws right, bats right. ... Full name: Shawn Anthony Chacon. ... Name pronounced: chah-CONE. ... High school: Greeley (Colo.) Central.

TRANSACTIONS/CAREER NOTES: Selected by Colorado Rockies organization in third round of 1996 free-agent draft. ... On disabled list (May 10-June 6, 2002); included rehabilitation assignment to Colorado Springs. ... On disabled list (June 30-July 19 and August 18, 2003-remainder of season); included rehabilitation assignment to Colorado Springs.

CAREER HITTING: 20-for-128 (.156), 9 R, 3 2B, 0 3B, 1 HR, 8 RBI.

Year Team (League)	W	L	Pct.	ERA	WHIP	G	GS	CG	ShO	Hld.	Sv.-Opp.	IP	H	R	ER	HR	BB-IBB	SO	Avg.
1996— Ariz. Rockies (Ariz.)	1	2	.333	1.60	1.08	11	11	1	0	...	0-...	56.1	46	17	10	1	15-0	64	.209
— Portland (N'west)	0	2	.000	6.86	1.68	4	4	0	0	...	0-...	19.2	24	18	15	2	9-0	17	.293
1997— Asheville (S. Atl.)	11	7	.611	3.89	1.35	28	27	1	0	...	0-...	162.0	155	80	70	13	63-1	149	.252
1998— Salem (Caro.)	0	4	.000	5.30	1.50	12	12	0	0	...	0-...	56.0	53	35	33	5	31-0	54	.245
1999— Salem (Caro.)	5	5	.500	4.13	1.43	12	12	0	0	...	0-...	72.0	69	44	33	3	34-0	66	.250
2000— Carolina (Southern)	10	10	.500	3.16	1.36	27	27	4	3	...	0-...	173.2	151	71	61	10	85-1	172	.236
2001— Colo. Springs (PCL)	2	0	1.000	2.25	1.04	4	4	0	0	...	0-...	24.0	18	6	6	3	7-0	28	.207
— Colorado (N.L.)	6	10	.375	5.06	1.53	27	27	0	0	0	0-0	160.0	157	96	90	26	87-10	134	.260
2002— Colorado (N.L.)	5	11	.313	5.73	1.53	21	21	0	0	0	0-0	119.1	122	84	76	25	60-3	67	.264
— Colo. Springs (PCL)	2	0	1.000	4.79	1.60	4	4	0	0	...	0-...	20.2	23	12	11	3	10-0	15	.291
2003— Colo. Springs (PCL)	0	0	...	6.00	1.70	1	0	0	0	...	0-...	3.0	5	2	2	1	0-0	2	.385
— Colorado (N.L.)	11	8	.579	4.60	1.33	23	23	0	0	0	0-0	137.0	124	73	70	12	58-4	93	.243
2004— Colorado (N.L.)	1	9	.100	7.11	1.94	66	0	0	0	0	35-44	63.1	71	52	50	12	52-7	52	.282
Major League totals (4 years)	23	38	.377	5.37	1.52	137	71	0	0	0	35-44	479.2	474	305	286	75	257-24	346	.259

CHAVEZ, ENDY   OF

PERSONAL: Born February 7, 1978, in Valencia, Venezuela. ... 5-10/189. ... Bats left, throws left. ... Full name: Endy DeJesus Chavez. ... Name pronounced: shah-VEZ. ... High school: Liceo Bataila Carabobo (Venezuela).

TRANSACTIONS/CAREER NOTES: Signed as a non-drafted free agent by New York Mets organization (April 29, 1996). ... Selected by Kansas City Royals from Mets organization in Rule 5 major league draft (December 11, 2000). ... Returned to Mets organization (March 30, 2001). ... Traded by Mets to Royals for OF Michael Curry (March 30, 2001). ... Claimed on waivers by Detroit Tigers (December 20, 2001). ... Claimed on waivers by Mets (February 1, 2002). ... Claimed on waivers by Montreal Expos (February 22, 2002).

2004 GAMES PLAYED BY POSITION (MLB): OF—127.

Year Team (League)	Pos.	G	AB	R	H	2B	3B	HR	RBI	BB	SO	HBP	GDP	SB-CS	Avg.	OBP	SLG	OPS	E	Avg.
1996— Dom. Mets (DSL)	OF	48	164	42	58	11	1	7	29	22	16	...	...	3-...	.354	...	.561	...	3	.963
1997— GC Mets (GCL)	OF	33	119	26	33	6	3	0	15	20	10	0	2	1-2	.277	.379	.378	.757	2	.967
— Kingsport (Appalachian)	OF	19	73	16	22	4	0	0	4	13	10	0	2	5-2	.301	.407	.356	.763	2	.957
1998— Kingsport (Appalachian)	OF	33	114	26	33	8	4	0	16	17	17	0	1	10-5	.289	.373	.430	.803	2	.941
1999— Capital City (SAL)	OF	73	253	40	64	8	1	0	15	34	36	0	3	20-12	.253	.340	.292	.633	5	.967
— St. Lucie (Fla. St.)	OF	45	183	33	57	8	3	2	18	22	22	0	5	9-3	.311	.383	.421	.804	2	.980
2000— St. Lucie (Fla. St.)	OF	111	433	84	129	20	2	1	43	47	48	0	3	38-16	.298	.364	.360	.725	5	.980
2001— Wichita (Texas)	OF	43	168	27	50	6	1	1	13	16	13	0	1	11-6	.298	.353	.363	.716	1	.990
— Kansas City (A.L.)	OF	29	77	4	16	2	0	0	5	3	8	0	3	0-2	.208	.238	.234	.471	0	1.000
— Omaha (PCL)	OF	23	104	18	35	6	0	0	4	4	13	0	1	4-3	.337	.333	.394	.728	0	1.000
2002— Ottawa (Int'l)	OF	103	405	67	139	28	5	4	41	33	37	0	8	21-13	.343	.392	.467	.858	4	.985
— Montreal (N.L.)	OF	36	125	20	37	8	5	1	9	5	16	0	0	3-5	.296	.321	.464	.785	1	.989
2003— Montreal (N.L.)	OF	141	483	66	121	25	5	5	47	31	59	0	7	18-7	.251	.294	.354	.648	3	.990
2004— Edmonton (PCL)	OF	14	61	9	21	3	2	0	7	7	7	0	0	5-2	.344	.406	.459	.865	0	1.000
— Montreal (N.L.)	OF	132	502	65	139	20	6	5	34	30	40	1	6	32-7	.277	.318	.371	.688	5	.984
American League totals (1 year)		29	77	4	16	2	0	0	5	3	8	0	3	0-2	.208	.238	.234	.471	0	1.000
National League totals (3 years)		309	1110	151	297	53	16	11	90	66	115	1	13	53-19	.268	.308	.374	.682	9	.987
Major League totals (4 years)		338	1187	155	313	55	16	11	95	69	123	1	16	53-21	.264	.303	.365	.668	9	.988

CHAVEZ, ERIC   3B

PERSONAL: Born December 7, 1977, in Los Angeles, Calif. ... 6-1/206. ... Bats left, throws right. ... Full name: Eric Cesar Chavez. ... Name pronounced: shah-VEZ. ... High school: Mount Carmel (San Diego).

TRANSACTIONS/CAREER NOTES: Selected by Oakland Athletics organization in first round (10th pick overall) of 1996 free-agent draft. ... On disabled list (August 21-September 19, 1999); included rehabilitation assignment to Vancouver. ... On disabled list (June 2-July 9, 2004); included rehabilitation assignment to Sacramento.

HONORS: Won A.L. Gold Glove at third base (2001-04).

2004 GAMES PLAYED BY POSITION (MLB): 3B—125, OF—1.

Year Team (League)	Pos.	G	AB	R	H	2B	3B	HR	RBI	BB	SO	HBP	GDP	SB-CS	Avg.	OBP	SLG	OPS	E	Avg.
1997— Visalia (Calif.)	3B-DH	134	520	67	141	30	3	18	100	37	91	2	20	13-7	.271	.321	.444	.765	32	.917
1998— Huntsville (Sou.)	3B-DH	88	335	66	110	27	1	22	86	42	61	1	6	12-4	.328	.402	.612	1.014	14	.935
— Edmonton (PCL)	3B-DH	47	194	38	63	18	0	11	40	12	32	1	4	2-3	.325	.364	.588	.951	7	.935
— Oakland (A.L.)	3B	16	45	6	14	4	1	0	6	3	5	0	1	1-1	.311	.354	.444	.799	0	1.000

Year	Team (League)	Pos.	G	AB	R	H	2B	3B	HR	RBI	BB	SO	HBP	GDP	SB-CS	Avg.	OBP	SLG	OPS	E	Avg.
1999— Oakland (A.L.)	3B-DH-SS	115	356	47	88	21	2	13	50	46	56	0	7	1-1	.247	.333	.427	.760	9	.961
2000— Oakland (A.L.)	3B-SS-DH	153	501	89	139	23	4	26	86	62	94	1	9	2-2	.277	.355	.495	.850	18	.951
2001— Oakland (A.L.)	3-S-DH-1	151	552	91	159	43	0	32	114	41	99	4	7	8-2	.288	.338	.540	.878	12	.972
2002— Oakland (A.L.)	3B-DH-OF	153	585	87	161	31	3	34	109	65	119	4	8	8-3	.275	.348	.513	.860	17	.961
2003— Oakland (A.L.)	3B	156	588	94	166	39	5	29	101	62	89	1	14	8-3	.282	.350	.514	.864	14	.971
2004— Sacramento (PCL)	DH-3B	3	13	2	4	1	0	0	0	1	2	0	0	0-0	.308	.357	.385	.742	0	...
— Oakland (A.L.)	3B-OF	125	475	87	131	20	0	29	77	* 95	99	3	21	6-3	.276	.397	.501	.898	13	.968
Major League totals (7 years)		869	3102	501	858	181	15	163	543	374	561	10	67	34-15	.277	.354	.502	.856	83	.965

DIVISION SERIES RECORD

Year	Team (League)	Pos.	G	AB	R	H	2B	3B	HR	RBI	BB	SO	HBP	GDP	SB-CS	Avg.	OBP	SLG	OPS	E	Avg.
2000— Oakland (A.L.)	3B	5	21	4	7	3	0	0	4	0	5	0	1	0-0	.333	.333	.476	.810	0	1.000
2001— Oakland (A.L.)	3B	5	21	0	3	1	0	0	0	0	5	0	1	0-0	.143	.143	.190	.333	1	.938
2002— Oakland (A.L.)	3B	5	21	3	8	0	0	1	5	2	1	0	0	0-0	.381	.435	.524	.959	0	1.000
2003— Oakland (A.L.)	3B	5	22	1	1	1	0	0	0	1	3	0	0	1-0	.045	.087	.091	.178	2	.867
Division series totals (4 years)		20	85	8	19	5	0	1	9	3	14	0	2	1-0	.224	.250	.318	.568	3	.949

CHAVEZ, RAUL — C

PERSONAL: Born March 18, 1973, in Valencia, Venezuela. ... 5-11/215. ... Bats right, throws right. ... Full name: Raul Alexander Chavez.

TRANSACTIONS/CAREER NOTES: Signed as a non-drafted free agent by Houston Astros organization (January 10, 1990). ... Traded by Astros with P Dave Veres to Montreal Expos for 3B Sean Berry (December 20, 1995). ... Traded by Expos to Seattle Mariners for OF Robert Perez (May 8, 1998). ... Signed as a free agent by Astros organization (January 5, 2000).

2004 GAMES PLAYED BY POSITION (MLB): C—61.

Year	Team (League)	Pos.	G	AB	R	H	2B	3B	HR	RBI	BB	SO	HBP	GDP	SB-CS	Avg.	OBP	SLG	OPS	E	Avg.
1990— GC Astros (GCL)	2B-3B-SS	48	155	23	50	8	1	0	23	7	12	2	7	5-3	.323	.358	.387	.745	9	.954
1991— Burlington (Midw.)	3B-SS	114	420	54	108	17	0	3	41	25	65	10	13	1-4	.257	.312	.319	.631	41	.914
1992— Asheville (S. Atl.)	C	95	348	37	99	22	1	2	40	16	39	4	11	1-0	.284	.320	.371	.691	13	.976
1993— Osceola (Fla. St.)	C	58	197	13	45	5	1	0	16	8	19	1	12	1-1	.228	.261	.264	.525	5	.986
1994— Jackson (Texas)	C	89	251	17	55	7	0	1	22	17	41	2	5	1-0	.219	.273	.259	.532	9	.986
1995— Jackson (Texas)	C	58	188	16	54	8	0	4	25	8	17	3	7	0-4	.287	.323	.394	.717	5	.987
— Tucson (PCL)	C	32	103	14	27	5	0	0	10	8	13	2	7	0-1	.262	.325	.311	.635	5	.980
1996— Ottawa (Int'l)	C	60	198	15	49	10	0	2	24	11	31	1	7	0-2	.247	.290	.328	.619	4	.990
— Montreal (N.L.)	C	3	5	1	1	0	0	0	0	1	1	0	1	1-0	.200	.333	.200	.533	0	1.000
1997— Ottawa (Int'l)	C-DH	92	310	31	76	17	0	4	46	18	42	4	9	1-3	.245	.293	.339	.631	15	.978
— Montreal (N.L.)	C	13	26	0	7	0	0	0	2	0	5	0	0	1-0	.269	.259	.269	.528	0	1.000
1998— Ottawa (Int'l)	C	11	31	2	7	0	0	0	1	5	5	0	1	0-0	.226	.333	.226	.559	0	1.000
— Tacoma (PCL)	C-DH	76	233	27	52	6	0	4	34	22	41	4	7	1-2	.223	.294	.300	.595	6	.990
— Seattle (A.L.)	C	1	1	0	0	0	0	0	0	0	0	0	0	0-0	.000	.000	.000	.000	0	1.000
1999— Tacoma (PCL)	C-DH-2-3-S-1	102	354	39	95	20	1	3	40	28	63	6	11	1-3	.268	.331	.356	.687	10	.987
2000— New Orleans (PCL)	C	99	303	31	74	13	0	2	36	34	44	4	12	3-0	.244	.325	.307	.632	8	.987
— Houston (N.L.)	C	14	43	3	11	2	0	1	5	3	6	0	5	0-0	.256	.298	.372	.670	1	.986
2001— New Orleans (PCL)	C-3B-1B	85	278	38	84	17	0	8	40	19	34	7	9	1-1	.302	.361	.450	.810	5	.992
2002— New Orleans (PCL)	C	111	373	24	85	10	0	3	36	21	50	7	11	3-4	.228	.278	.279	.557	7	.991
— Houston (N.L.)	C	2	4	1	1	1	0	0	0	0	1	0	1	0-0	.250	.500	.500	1.000	0	1.000
2003— New Orleans (PCL)	C-3B-DH	101	355	47	97	28	1	6	47	13	43	11	11	0-2	.273	.315	.408	.724	11	.977
— Houston (N.L.)	C	19	37	5	10	1	1	1	4	1	6	0	3	0-0	.270	.289	.432	.722	0	1.000
2004— Houston (N.L.)	C	64	162	9	34	8	0	0	23	10	38	0	1	0-1	.210	.256	.259	.515	4	.991
American League totals (1 year)		1	1	0	0	0	0	0	0	0	0	0	0	0-0	.000	.000	.000	.000	0	1.000
National League totals (6 years)		115	277	19	64	12	1	2	34	16	56	1	18	2-1	.231	.274	.303	.577	5	.992
Major League totals (7 years)		116	278	19	64	12	1	2	34	16	56	1	18	2-1	.230	.273	.302	.575	5	.992

DIVISION SERIES RECORD

Year	Team (League)	Pos.	G	AB	R	H	2B	3B	HR	RBI	BB	SO	HBP	GDP	SB-CS	Avg.	OBP	SLG	OPS	E	Avg.
2004— Houston (N.L.)	C	2	5	1	3	0	0	1	1	0	0	0	0	0-0	.600	.600	1.200	1.800	1	.941

CHAMPIONSHIP SERIES RECORD

Year	Team (League)	Pos.	G	AB	R	H	2B	3B	HR	RBI	BB	SO	HBP	GDP	SB-CS	Avg.	OBP	SLG	OPS	E	Avg.
2004— Houston (N.L.)	C	2	4	0	1	0	0	0	0	0	1	0	1	0-0	.250	.250	.250	.500	0	1.000

CHEN, BRUCE — P

PERSONAL: Born June 19, 1977, in Panama City, Panama. ... 6-1/210. ... Throws left, bats left. ... Full name: Bruce Kastulo Chen. ... High school: Instituto Panamericano (Panama). ... College: Institute of Panama.

TRANSACTIONS/CAREER NOTES: Signed as a non-drafted free agent by Atlanta Braves organization (July 1, 1993). ... Traded by Braves with P Jimmy Osting to Philadelphia Phillies for P Andy Ashby (July 12, 2000). ... Traded by Phillies with P Adam Walker to New York Mets for Ps Turk Wendell and Dennis Cook (July 27, 2001). ... Traded by Mets with P Dicky Gonzalez, IF Luis Figueroa and a player to be named to Montreal Expos for Ps Scott Strickland and Phil Seibel and OF Matt Watson (April 5, 2002); Expos acquired P Saul Rivera to complete deal (July 14, 2002). ... Traded by Expos to Cincinnati Reds for P Jim Brower (June 14, 2002). ... Released by Reds (March 10, 2003). ... Signed by Houston Astros organization (March 14, 2003). ... Claimed on waivers by Boston Red Sox (May 7, 2003). ... Signed as a free agent by Toronto Blue Jays organization (November 26, 2003). ... Traded by Blue Jays to Baltimore Orioles for future considerations (May 1, 2004).

CAREER HITTING: 13-for-111 (.117), 4 R, 1 2B, 0 3B, 0 HR, 3 RBI.

Year	Team (League)	W	L	Pct.	ERA	WHIP	G	GS	CG	ShO	Hld.	Sv.-Opp.	IP	H	R	ER	HR	BB-IBB	SO	Avg.
1994— GC Braves (GCL)	1	4	.200	3.80	1.05	9	7	0	0	...	1-...	42.2	42	21	18	2	3-0	26	.244
1995— Danville (Appalachian)	4	4	.500	3.97	1.38	14	13	1	0	...	0-...	70.1	78	42	31	3	19-1	56	.276
1996— Eugene (N'west)	4	1	.800	2.27	1.04	11	8	0	0	...	0-...	35.2	23	13	9	1	14-0	55	.173
1997— Macon (S. Atl.)	12	7	.632	3.51	1.12	28	28	1	1	...	0-...	146.1	120	67	57	19	44-0	182	.222
1998— Greenville (Sou.)	13	7	.650	3.29	1.11	24	23	1	0	...	0-...	139.1	106	57	51	12	48-0	164	.209
— Richmond (Int'l)	2	1	.667	1.88	1.50	4	4	0	0	...	0-...	24.0	17	5	5	1	19-0	29	.205
— Atlanta (N.L.)	2	0	1.000	3.98	1.57	4	4	0	0	0	0-0	20.1	23	9	9	3	9-1	17	.288
1999— Richmond (Int'l)	6	3	.667	3.81	1.27	14	14	0	0	...	0-...	78.0	73	36	33	10	26-0	90	.251
— Atlanta (N.L.)	2	2	.500	5.47	1.27	16	7	0	0	0	0-0	51.0	38	32	31	11	27-3	45	.208

Year	Team (League)	W	L	Pct.	ERA	WHIP	G	GS	CG	ShO	Hld.	Sv.-Opp.	IP	H	R	ER	HR	BB-IBB	SO	Avg.
2000—Atlanta (N.L.)		4	0	1.000	2.50	1.36	22	0	0	0	0	0-0	39.2	35	15	11	4	19-2	32	.232
—Richmond (Int'l)		1	0	1.000	0.00	1.00	1	1	0	0	...	0-...	6.0	5	0	0	0	1-0	6	.238
—Philadelphia (N.L.)		3	4	.429	3.63	1.14	15	15	0	0	0	0-0	94.1	81	39	38	14	27-2	80	.232
2001—Philadelphia (N.L.)		4	5	.444	5.00	1.40	16	16	0	0	0	0-0	86.1	90	53	48	19	31-4	79	.262
—Reading (East.)		1	0	1.000	0.00	0.50	1	1	0	0	...	0-...	6.0	3	0	0	0	0-0	7	.136
—Scran./W.B. (I.L.)		1	0	1.000	3.86	1.02	3	3	0	0	...	0-...	18.2	14	8	8	2	5-0	14	.212
—New York (N.L.)		3	2	.600	4.68	1.41	11	11	0	0	0	0-0	59.2	56	37	31	10	28-0	47	.255
2002—New York (N.L.)		0	0	...	0.00	1.50	1	0	0	0	0	0-0	.2	1	0	0	0	0-0	0	.333
—Montreal (N.L.)		2	3	.400	6.99	1.88	15	5	0	0	0	0-0	37.1	47	29	29	9	23-3	43	.303
—Cincinnati (N.L.)		0	2	.000	4.31	1.44	39	1	0	0	4	0-0	39.2	37	24	19	7	20-2	37	.243
2003—Houston (N.L.)		0	0	...	6.00	1.83	11	0	0	0	1	0-0	12.0	14	8	8	2	8-1	8	.311
—Boston (A.L.)		0	1	.000	5.11	1.14	5	2	0	0	0	0-0	12.1	12	8	7	4	2-0	12	.255
—Pawtucket (Int'l)		5	5	.500	4.24	1.10	16	15	1	1	...	1-...	85.0	80	44	40	12	15-1	73	.244
2004—Syracuse (Int'l)		0	1	.000	8.71	2.13	3	3	0	0	...	0-...	10.1	17	12	10	4	5-1	8	.354
—Ottawa (Int'l)		4	3	.571	3.22	1.21	22	17	1	1	...	0-...	95.0	85	41	34	12	30-1	108	.235
—Baltimore (A.L.)		2	1	.667	3.02	1.15	8	7	1	0	0	0-0	47.2	39	19	16	7	16-0	32	.220
American League totals (2 years)		2	2	.500	3.45	1.15	13	9	1	0	0	0-0	60.0	51	27	23	11	18-0	44	.228
National League totals (6 years)		20	18	.526	4.57	1.39	150	59	0	0	5	0-0	441.0	422	246	224	79	192-18	388	.251
Major League totals (7 years)		22	20	.524	4.44	1.36	163	68	1	0	5	0-0	501.0	473	273	247	90	210-18	432	.248

DIVISION SERIES RECORD

Year	Team (League)	W	L	Pct.	ERA	WHIP	G	GS	CG	ShO	Hld.	Sv.-Opp.	IP	H	R	ER	HR	BB-IBB	SO	Avg.
1999—Atlanta (N.L.)	Did not play.																			

CHAMPIONSHIP SERIES RECORD

Year	Team (League)	W	L	Pct.	ERA	WHIP	G	GS	CG	ShO	Hld.	Sv.-Opp.	IP	H	R	ER	HR	BB-IBB	SO	Avg.
1999—Atlanta (N.L.)	Did not play.																			

WORLD SERIES RECORD

Year	Team (League)	W	L	Pct.	ERA	WHIP	G	GS	CG	ShO	Hld.	Sv.-Opp.	IP	H	R	ER	HR	BB-IBB	SO	Avg.
1999—Atlanta (N.L.)	Did not play.																			

CHEN, CHIN-FENG   OF

PERSONAL: Born October 28, 1977, in Tainan City, Taiwan. ... 6-1/189. ... Bats right, throws right.
TRANSACTIONS/CAREER NOTES: Signed as a non-drafted free agent by Los Angeles Dodgers organization (January 5, 1999).
2004 GAMES PLAYED BY POSITION (MLB): OF—3.

Year	Team (League)	Pos.	G	AB	R	H	2B	3B	HR	RBI	BB	SO	HBP	GDP	SB-CS	Avg.	OBP	SLG	OPS	E	Avg.
1999—San Bern. (Calif.)		OF	131	510	98	161	22	10	31	123	75	129	5	7	31-7	.316	.404	.580	.984	6	.971
2000—San Antonio (Texas)		OF	133	516	66	143	27	3	6	67	61	131	3	7	23-15	.277	.355	.376	.731	3	.988
2001—Vero Beach (FSL)		OF	62	235	38	63	15	3	5	41	28	56	6	3	2-0	.268	.359	.421	.781	0	1.000
—Jacksonville (Sou.)		OF	66	224	47	70	16	2	17	50	41	65	2	7	5-4	.313	.422	.629	1.051	3	.966
2002—Las Vegas (PCL)		1B-OF	137	511	90	145	26	4	26	84	58	160	0	19	1-0	.284	.352	.503	.855	11	.988
—Los Angeles (N.L.)		OF	3	5	1	0	0	0	0	0	1	3	0	0	0-0	.000	.167	.000	.167	0	1.000
2003—Los Angeles (N.L.)		OF	1	1	0	0	0	0	0	0	0	0	0	0	0-0	.000	.000	.000	.000	0	—
—Las Vegas (PCL)		OF-1B-DH	133	474	84	133	30	5	26	86	59	106	2	15	6-4	.281	.360	.530	.889	11	.963
2004—Las Vegas (PCL)		OF-DH-1B	81	308	59	89	19	6	20	65	35	78	2	4	6-2	.289	.359	.584	.943	4	.971
—Los Angeles (N.L.)		OF	8	8	1	0	0	0	0	0	2	3	0	1	0-0	.000	.200	.000	.200	0	1.000
Major League totals (3 years)			12	14	2	0	0	0	0	0	3	6	0	1	0-0	.000	.176	.000	.176	0	1.000

CHOATE, RANDY   P

PERSONAL: Born September 5, 1975, in San Antonio, Texas. ... 6-2/195. ... Throws left, bats left. ... Full name: Randol Doyol Choate. ... Name pronounced: chote. ... High school: Winston Churchill (San Antonio). ... College: Florida State.
TRANSACTIONS/CAREER NOTES: Selected by New York Yankees organization in fifth round of 1997 free-agent draft. ... Traded by Yankees with 1B Nick Johnson and OF Juan Rivera to Montreal Expos for P Javier Vazquez (December 16, 2003). ... Traded by Expos to Arizona Diamondbacks for P John Patterson (March 27, 2004).
CAREER HITTING: 0-for-5 (.000), 0 R, 0 2B, 0 3B, 0 HR, 0 RBI.

Year	Team (League)	W	L	Pct.	ERA	WHIP	G	GS	CG	ShO	Hld.	Sv.-Opp.	IP	H	R	ER	HR	BB-IBB	SO	Avg.
1997—Oneonta (N.Y.-Penn)		5	1	.833	1.73	0.98	10	10	0	0	...	0-...	62.1	49	12	12	1	12-1	61	.216
1998—Tampa (FSL)		1	8	.111	5.27	1.50	13	13	0	0	...	0-...	70.0	83	57	41	6	22-2	55	.290
—Greensboro (S. Atl.)		1	5	.167	3.00	1.36	8	8	1	0	...	0-...	39.0	46	21	13	1	7-0	32	.293
1999—Tampa (FSL)		2	2	.500	4.50	1.50	47	0	0	0	...	1-...	50.0	51	25	25	4	24-5	62	.263
2000—Columbus (Int'l)		2	0	1.000	2.04	1.36	33	0	0	0	...	1-...	35.1	34	8	8	2	14-3	37	.254
—New York (A.L.)		0	1	.000	4.76	1.29	22	0	0	0	2	0-0	17.0	14	10	9	3	8-0	12	.215
2001—New York (A.L.)		3	1	.750	3.35	1.26	37	0	0	0	3	0-0	48.1	34	21	18	0	27-2	35	.202
—Columbus (Int'l)		1	1	.500	2.08	2.31	4	0	0	0	...	0-...	4.1	7	1	1	0	3-0	4	.389
2002—Columbus (Int'l)		3	2	.600	1.72	1.09	31	0	0	0	...	1-...	36.2	25	8	7	0	15-1	32	.189
—New York (A.L.)		0	0	...	6.04	1.48	18	0	0	0	0	0-0	22.1	18	18	15	1	15-0	17	.217
2003—New York (A.L.)		0	0	...	7.36	2.18	5	0	0	0	0	0-0	3.2	7	3	3	0	1-0	1	.467
—Columbus (Int'l)		3	5	.375	3.91	1.40	54	3	0	0	...	1-...	71.1	75	35	31	4	24-3	56	.271
2004—Tucson (PCL)		0	0	...	5.68	1.42	15	0	0	0	...	1-...	12.2	10	8	8	1	8-1	7	.222
—Arizona (N.L.)		2	4	.333	4.62	1.58	74	0	0	0	11	0-2	50.2	52	26	26	1	28-11	49	.267
American League totals (4 years)		3	2	.600	4.43	1.36	82	0	0	0	5	0-0	91.1	73	52	45	4	51-2	64	.221
National League totals (1 year)		2	4	.333	4.62	1.58	74	0	0	0	11	0-2	50.2	52	26	26	1	28-11	49	.267
Major League totals (5 years)		5	6	.455	4.50	1.44	156	0	0	0	16	0-2	142.0	125	78	71	5	79-13	113	.238

DIVISION SERIES RECORD

Year	Team (League)	W	L	Pct.	ERA	WHIP	G	GS	CG	ShO	Hld.	Sv.-Opp.	IP	H	R	ER	HR	BB-IBB	SO	Avg.
2000—New York (A.L.)		0	0	...	6.75	0.75	1	0	0	0	0	0-0	1.1	0	1	1	0	1-0	1	.000
2001—New York (A.L.)	Did not play.																			

CHAMPIONSHIP SERIES RECORD

Year	Team (League)	W	L	Pct.	ERA	WHIP	G	GS	CG	ShO	Hld.	Sv.-Opp.	IP	H	R	ER	HR	BB-IBB	SO	Avg.
2000—New York (A.L.)		0	0	...	0.00	0.00	1	0	0	0	0	0-0	.1	0	0	0	0	0-0	1	.000
2001—New York (A.L.)	Did not play.																			

WORLD SERIES RECORD

Year	Team (League)	W	L	Pct.	ERA	WHIP	G	GS	CG	ShO	Hld.	Sv.-Opp.	IP	H	R	ER	HR	BB-IBB	SO	Avg.
2000—New York (A.L.)	Did not play.																			
2001—New York (A.L.)		0	0	...	2.45	2.18	2	0	0	0	0	0-0	3.2	7	4	1	0	1-1	2	.350

CHOI, HEE SEOP — 1B

PERSONAL: Born March 16, 1979, in Chun-Nam, South Korea. ... 6-5/240. ... Bats left, throws left. ... Name pronounced: hee sop choy. ... High school: Kwang-Ju Jae (Kwang-Ju, Korea). ... College: Korea University.

TRANSACTIONS/CAREER NOTES: Signed as a non-drafted free agent by Chicago Cubs organization (March 8, 1999). ... On disabled list (June 8-30, 2003); included rehabilitation assignment to Iowa. ... Traded by Cubs with P Mike Nannini to Florida Marlins for 1B Derrek Lee (November 25, 2003). ... Traded by Marlins with Ps Brad Penny and Bill Murphy to Los Angeles Dodgers for C Paul Lo Duca, P Guillermo Mota and OF Juan Encarnacion (July 30, 2004).

2004 GAMES PLAYED BY POSITION (MLB): 1B—112.

Year Team (League)	Pos.	G	AB	R	H	2B	3B	HR	RBI	BB	SO	HBP	GDP	SB-CS	Avg.	OBP	SLG	OPS	E	Avg.
1999— Lansing (Midw.)	1B	79	290	71	93	18	6	18	70	50	68	2	8	2-1	.321	.422	.610	1.032	18	.976
2000— Daytona (Fla. St.)	1B	96	345	60	102	25	6	15	70	37	78	6	7	4-1	.296	.369	.533	.902	4	.995
— West Tenn (Sou.)	1B	36	122	25	37	9	0	10	25	25	38	0	5	3-1	.303	.419	.623	1.042	1	.997
2001— Iowa (PCL)	1B	77	266	38	61	11	0	13	45	34	67	0	5	5-1	.229	.313	.417	.730	3	.995
2002— Iowa (PCL)	1B	135	478	94	137	24	3	26	97	95	119	6	6	3-2	.287	.406	.513	.919	12	.990
— Chicago (N.L.)	1B	24	50	6	9	1	0	2	4	7	15	0	2	0-0	.180	.281	.320	.601	2	.983
2003— Iowa (PCL)	1B	18	66	12	17	4	1	6	16	9	19	1	2	0-1	.258	.351	.621	.972	0	1.000
— Chicago (N.L.)	1B	80	202	31	44	17	0	8	28	37	71	4	2	1-1	.218	.350	.421	.771	5	.991
2004— Florida (N.L.)	1B	95	281	48	76	16	1	15	40	52	78	3	4	1-0	.270	.388	.495	.882	8	.990
— Los Angeles (N.L.)	1B	31	62	5	10	5	0	0	6	11	18	1	2	0-0	.161	.289	.242	.531	1	.994
Major League totals (3 years)		230	595	90	139	39	1	25	78	107	182	8	10	2-1	.234	.356	.429	.784	16	.990

DIVISION SERIES RECORD

Year Team (League)	Pos.	G	AB	R	H	2B	3B	HR	RBI	BB	SO	HBP	GDP	SB-CS	Avg.	OBP	SLG	OPS	E	Avg.
2004— Los Angeles (N.L.)		1	1	0	0	0	0	0	0	0	0	0	0	0-0	.000	.000	.000	.000	0	...

CHRISTIANSEN, JASON — P

PERSONAL: Born September 21, 1969, in Omaha, Neb. ... 6-5/241. ... Throws left, bats right. ... Full name: Jason Samuel Christiansen. ... High school: Elkhorn (Neb.). ... Junior college: Iowa Western Community College.

TRANSACTIONS/CAREER NOTES: Signed as a non-drafted free agent by Pittsburgh Pirates organization (July 5, 1991). ... On disabled list (March 31-June 19, 1997). ... On disabled list (May 7-28, July 29-August 21 and August 24-September 23, 1999); included rehabilitation assignments to Altoona and Nashville. ... Traded by Pirates to St. Louis Cardinals for SS Jack Wilson (July 30, 2000). ... On disabled list (March 23-May 7, 2001); included rehabilitation assignment to Memphis. ... Traded by Cardinals to San Francisco Giants for P Kevin Joseph and a player to be named or cash (July 31, 2001). ... On disabled list (April 16, 2002-remainder of season). ... On disabled list (March 25-June 3, 2003); included rehabilitation assignments to San Jose and Fresno. ... On disabled list (June 19-July 6, 2004).

CAREER HITTING: 1-for-10 (.100), 0 R, 0 2B, 0 3B, 0 HR, 1 RBI.

Year Team (League)	W	L	Pct.	ERA	WHIP	G	GS	CG	ShO	Hld.	Sv.-Opp.	IP	H	R	ER	HR	BB-IBB	SO	Avg.
1991— GC Pirates (GCL)	1	0	1.000	0.00	0.63	6	0	0	0	...	1-...	8.0	4	0	0	0	1-0	8	.143
— Welland (N.Y.-Penn)	0	1	.000	2.53	1.27	8	1	0	0	...	0-...	21.1	15	9	6	1	12-1	17	.208
1992— Augusta (S. Atl.)	1	0	1.000	1.80	1.00	10	0	0	0	...	2-...	20.0	12	4	4	0	8-0	21	.194
— Salem (Caro.)	3	1	.750	3.24	1.38	38	0	0	0	...	2-...	50.0	47	20	18	7	22-2	59	.254
1993— Salem (Caro.)	1	1	.500	3.15	1.01	57	0	0	0	...	4-...	71.1	48	30	25	5	24-2	70	.190
— Carolina (Southern)	0	0	...	0.00	1.50	2	0	0	0	...	0-...	2.2	3	0	0	0	1-0	2	.273
1994— Carolina (Southern)	2	1	.667	2.09	1.14	28	0	0	0	...	2-...	38.2	30	10	9	2	14-1	43	.216
— Buffalo (A.A.)	3	1	.750	2.41	1.04	33	0	0	0	...	0-...	33.2	19	9	9	3	16-0	39	.168
1995— Pittsburgh (N.L.)	1	3	.250	4.15	1.47	63	0	0	0	12	0-4	56.1	49	28	26	5	34-9	53	.234
1996— Pittsburgh (N.L.)	3	3	.500	6.70	1.69	33	0	0	0	2	0-2	44.1	56	34	33	7	19-2	38	.311
— Calgary (PCL)	1	0	1.000	3.27	0.91	2	2	0	0	...	0-...	11.0	9	4	4	1	1-0	10	.237
1997— Carolina (Southern)	0	1	.000	4.20	1.47	8	1	0	0	...	1-...	15.0	17	7	7	1	5-0	25	.293
— Pittsburgh (N.L.)	3	0	1.000	2.94	1.60	39	0	0	0	8	0-...	33.2	37	11	11	2	17-3	37	.274
1998— Pittsburgh (N.L.)	3	3	.500	2.51	1.21	60	0	0	0	15	6-10	64.2	51	22	18	2	27-7	71	.216
1999— Pittsburgh (N.L.)	2	3	.400	4.06	1.27	39	0	0	0	7	3-5	37.2	26	17	17	2	22-4	35	.197
— Altoona (East.)	0	0	...	0.00	0.67	2	1	0	0	...	0-...	3.0	1	0	0	0	1-0	2	.100
— Nashville (PCL)	0	0	...	0.00	0.00	2	0	0	0	...	0-...	2.0	0	0	0	0	0-0	1	.000
2000— Pittsburgh (N.L.)	2	8	.200	4.97	1.39	44	0	0	0	13	1-3	38.0	28	22	21	2	25-4	41	.207
— St. Louis (N.L.)	1	0	1.000	5.40	1.50	21	0	0	0	9	0-1	10.0	13	7	6	1	2-1	12	.317
2001— Memphis (PCL)	0	0	...	2.25	1.13	7	1	0	0	...	0-...	8.0	9	2	2	0	0-0	9	.281
— St. Louis (N.L.)	1	1	.500	4.66	1.29	30	0	0	0	4	3-3	19.1	15	10	10	4	10-1	19	.211
— San Francisco (N.L.)	1	0	1.000	1.59	1.12	25	0	0	0	7	0-1	17.0	14	3	3	1	5-0	12	.241
2002— San Francisco (N.L.)	0	1	.000	5.40	1.60	6	0	0	0	0	0-...	5.0	6	3	3	1	2-0	1	.316
2003— San Jose (California)	0	0	...	1.93	1.70	5	1	0	0	...	0-...	4.2	5	1	1	0	3-0	2	.313
— Fresno (PCL)	0	0	...	5.40	1.20	4	1	0	0	...	0-...	5.0	5	3	3	0	1-0	2	.263
— San Francisco (N.L.)	0	0	...	5.19	1.38	40	0	0	0	7	0-1	26.0	25	15	15	3	11-0	22	.243
2004— San Francisco (N.L.)	4	3	.571	4.50	1.67	60	0	0	0	8	3-6	36.0	34	20	18	3	26-1	22	.250
Major League totals (10 years)	21	25	.457	4.20	1.43	460	0	0	0	92	16-38	388.0	354	192	181	33	200-32	363	.243

DIVISION SERIES RECORD

Year Team (League)	W	L	Pct.	ERA	WHIP	G	GS	CG	ShO	Hld.	Sv.-Opp.	IP	H	R	ER	HR	BB-IBB	SO	Avg.
2000— St. Louis (N.L.)	0	0	...	0.00	0.00	1	0	0	0	0	0-0	.1	0	0	0	0	0-0	0	.000
2003— San Francisco (N.L.)	0	0	...	...	...	1	0	0	0	0	0-0	.0	1	0	0	0	0-0	1	1.000
Division series totals (2 years)	0	0	...	0.00	3.00	2	0	0	0	0	0-0	.1	1	0	0	0	0-0	0	.500

CHAMPIONSHIP SERIES RECORD

Year Team (League)	W	L	Pct.	ERA	WHIP	G	GS	CG	ShO	Hld.	Sv.-Opp.	IP	H	R	ER	HR	BB-IBB	SO	Avg.
2000— St. Louis (N.L.)	0	0	...	0.00	0.00	2	0	0	0	0	0-0	2.0	0	0	0	0	0-0	1	.000

CHULK, VINNIE — P

PERSONAL: Born December 19, 1978, in Miami, Fla. ... 6-2/195. ... Throws right, bats right. ... Full name: Charles Vincent Chulk. ... College: St. Thomas (Fla.).

CAREER HITTING: 0-for-0 (.000), 0 R, 0 2B, 0 3B, 0 HR, 0 RBI.

Year Team (League)	W	L	Pct.	ERA	WHIP	G	GS	CG	ShO	Hld.	Sv.-Opp.	IP	H	R	ER	HR	BB-IBB	SO	Avg.
2000— Medicine Hat (Pio.)	2	4	.333	3.80	1.38	14	13	0	0	...	0-...	68.2	75	36	29	5	20-0	51	.277
2001— Syracuse (Int'l)	1	0	1.000	1.50	1.50	5	0	0	0	...	0-...	6.0	5	1	1	0	4-0	3	.238
— Dunedin (Fla. St.)	1	2	.333	3.12	1.47	16	1	0	0	...	1-...	34.2	38	16	12	2	13-1	50	.271

Year	Team (League)	W	L	Pct.	ERA	WHIP	G	GS	CG	ShO	Hld.	Sv.-Opp.	IP	H	R	ER	HR	BB-IBB	SO	Avg.
— Tennessee (Sou.)	2	5	.286	3.14	0.98	24	1	0	0	...	2-...	43.0	34	15	15	5	8-1	43	.227
2002— Tennessee (Sou.)	13	5	.722	2.96	1.22	25	24	0	0	...	1-...	152.0	133	55	50	12	53-0	108	.236
— Syracuse (Int'l)	0	1	.000	5.79	2.57	2	1	0	0	...	0-...	4.2	6	3	3	0	6-0	2	.316
2003— Syracuse (Int'l)	8	10	.444	4.22	1.37	23	21	1	0	...	0-...	119.1	118	70	56	14	46-0	90	.256
— Toronto (A.L.)	0	0	...	5.06	1.69	3	0	0	0	0	0-1	5.1	6	3	3	0	3-0	2	.273
2004— Syracuse (Int'l)	4	2	.667	2.83	1.33	18	0	0	0	...	3-...	28.2	27	13	9	5	11-2	26	.252
— Toronto (A.L.)	1	3	.250	4.66	1.54	47	0	0	0	13	2-5	56.0	59	30	29	6	27-1	44	.271
Major League totals (2 years)	1	3	.250	4.70	1.55	50	0	0	0	13	2-6	61.1	65	33	32	6	30-1	46	.271

CHURCH, RYAN — OF

PERSONAL: Born October 14, 1978, in Santa Barbara, Calif. ... 6-1/190. ... Bats left, throws left. ... Full name: Ryan Matthew Church. ... High school: Lompoc (Calif.). ... College: Nevada.

TRANSACTIONS/CAREER NOTES: Selected by Cleveland Indians organization in 14th round of 2000 free-agent draft. ... Traded by Indians with SS Maicer Izturis to Montreal Expos for P Scott Stewart (January 5, 2004).

2004 GAMES PLAYED BY POSITION (MLB): OF—18.

												BATTING						FIELDING		
Year	Team (League)	Pos.	G	AB	R	H	2B	3B	HR	RBI	BB	SO	HBP	GDP	SB-CS	Avg.	OBP	SLG	OPS	E	Avg.
2000— Mahoning Valley (NY-P)	OF	73	272	51	81	16	5	10	65	38	49	8	4	11-4	.298	.396	.504	.899	3	.973
2001— Columbus (S. Atl.)	OF	101	363	64	104	23	3	17	76	54	79	6	6	4-6	.287	.385	.507	.892	3	.987
— Kinston (Caro.)	OF	24	83	16	20	7	0	5	15	18	23	1	1	1-0	.241	.379	.506	.885	2	.947
2002— Kinston (Caro.)	OF	53	181	30	59	12	1	10	30	31	51	4	3	4-4	.326	.433	.569	1.002	3	.965
— Akron (East.)	OF	71	291	39	86	17	4	12	51	12	58	2	8	1-0	.296	.325	.505	.830	1	.993
2003— Akron (East.)	OF	99	371	47	97	17	3	13	52	32	64	4	17	4-3	.261	.325	.429	.754	6	.977
2004— Edmonton (PCL)	OF-DH	98	347	74	120	29	8	17	79	51	62	4	4	0-1	.346	.430	.622	1.041	2	.990
— Montreal (N.L.)	OF	30	63	6	11	1	0	1	6	7	16	0	3	0-0	.175	.257	.238	.495	0	1.000
Major League totals (1 year)		30	63	6	11	1	0	1	6	7	16	0	3	0-0	.175	.257	.238	.495	0	1.000

CINTRON, ALEX — SS

PERSONAL: Born December 17, 1978, in Humacao, Puerto Rico. ... 6-2/199. ... Bats both, throws right. ... Full name: Alexander Cintron. ... Name pronounced: SIN-tron. ... High school: Mech-Tech (Caguas, Puerto Rico).

TRANSACTIONS/CAREER NOTES: Selected by Arizona Diamondbacks organization in 36th round of 1997 free-agent draft.

2004 GAMES PLAYED BY POSITION (MLB): SS—133, 2B—19, 3B—1.

												BATTING						FIELDING		
Year	Team (League)	Pos.	G	AB	R	H	2B	3B	HR	RBI	BB	SO	HBP	GDP	SB-CS	Avg.	OBP	SLG	OPS	E	Avg.
1997— Arizl. D'backs (Ariz.)	SS	43	152	23	30	6	1	0	20	21	32	2	3	1-4	.197	.301	.250	.551	15	.931
— Lethbridge (Pio.)	SS	1	3	0	1	0	0	0	0	0	0	0	0	0-0	.333	.333	.333	.667	1	.857
1998— Lethbridge (Pio.)	SS	67	258	41	68	11	4	3	34	20	32	2	8	8-4	.264	.319	.372	.691	27	.921
1999— High Desert (Calif.)	SS	128	499	78	153	25	4	3	64	19	65	3	14	15-8	.307	.333	.391	.724	28	.950
2000— El Paso (Texas)	SS	125	522	83	157	30	6	4	59	29	56	2	22	9-9	.301	.336	.404	.740	32	.950
2001— Tucson (PCL)	SS-2B	107	425	53	124	24	3	3	35	15	48	2	12	9-6	.292	.315	.384	.698	32	.950
— Arizona (N.L.)	SS	8	7	0	2	0	1	0	0	0	0	0	0	0-0	.286	.286	.571	.857	0	1.000
2002— Tucson (PCL)	SS-2B	85	351	53	113	22	3	4	35	11	33	2	8	9-5	.322	.345	.436	.781	14	.960
— Arizona (N.L.) 2B-3B-SS	38	75	11	16	6	0	0	4	12	13	0	2	0-0	.213	.322	.293	.615	1	.989
2003— Tucson (PCL)	SS-2B	26	107	21	42	11	2	2	21	8	6	0	1	1-0	.393	.435	.589	1.024	4	.970
— Arizona (N.L.) SS-3B-2B	117	448	70	142	26	6	13	51	29	33	2	7	2-3	.317	.359	.489	.848	11	.976
2004— Arizona (N.L.) 2B-3B-3B	154	564	56	148	31	7	4	49	31	59	2	11	3-3	.262	.301	.363	.665	17	.973
Major League totals (4 years)		317	1094	137	308	63	14	17	104	72	105	4	20	5-6	.282	.326	.411	.738	29	.975

DIVISION SERIES RECORD

Year	Team (League)	Pos.	G	AB	R	H	2B	3B	HR	RBI	BB	SO	HBP	GDP	SB-CS	Avg.	OBP	SLG	OPS	E	Avg.
2002— Arizona (N.L.)	3B	2	0	0	0	0	0	0	0	0	0	0	0	0-0	...	...	...	...	0	...

CIRILLO, JEFF — 3B/1B

PERSONAL: Born September 23, 1969, in Pasadena, Calif. ... 6-1/200. ... Bats right, throws right. ... Full name: Jeffrey Howard Cirillo. ... Name pronounced: suh-RILL-oh. ... High school: Providence (Burbank, Calif.). ... College: USC.

TRANSACTIONS/CAREER NOTES: Selected by Chicago Cubs organization in 37th round of 1987 free-agent draft; did not sign. ... Selected by Milwaukee Brewers organization in 11th round of 1991 free-agent draft. ... Traded by Brewers with P Scott Karl and cash to Colorado Rockies as part of three-team deal in which Brewers acquired P Jamey Wright and C Henry Blanco from Rockies and P Jimmy Haynes from Oakland Athletics, and A's acquired P Justin Miller and cash from Rockies (December 13, 1999). ... On disabled list (April 27-May 13, 2001); included rehabilitation assignment to Colorado Springs. ... Traded by Rockies to Seattle Mariners for Ps Jose Paniagua, Denny Stark and Brian Fuentes (December 15, 2001). ... On disabled list (July 24-August 19, 2003); included rehabilitation assignment to AZL Mariners. ... Traded by Mariners with P Brian Sweeney and cash to San Diego Padres for P Kevin Jarvis, IF Dave Hansen, C Wiki Gonzalez and OF Vince Faison (January 6, 2004). ... On disabled list (April 2-May 11, 2004); included rehabilitation assignment to Portland. ... Released by Padres (August 4, 2004).

2004 GAMES PLAYED BY POSITION (MLB): 3B—11, 1B—10, 2B—4, OF—1.

												BATTING						FIELDING		
Year	Team (League)	Pos.	G	AB	R	H	2B	3B	HR	RBI	BB	SO	HBP	GDP	SB-CS	Avg.	OBP	SLG	OPS	E	Avg.
1991— Helena (Pio.)	3B-OF	70	286	60	100	16	2	10	51	31	28	4	11	3-1	.350	.418	.524	.942	15	.921
1992— Stockton (Calif.)	3B	7	27	2	6	1	0	0	5	2	0	2	2	0-0	.222	.323	.259	.582	0	1.000
— Beloit (Midw.)	2B-3B	126	444	65	135	27	3	9	71	84	85	6	7	21-12	.304	.417	.439	.856	26	.942
1993— El Paso (Texas)	2B-3B	67	249	53	85	16	2	9	41	26	37	5	5	2-3	.341	.410	.530	.940	9	.962
— New Orleans (A.A.) 3B-2B-SS	58	215	31	63	13	2	3	32	29	33	3	7	2-1	.293	.385	.414	.799	5	.974
1994— New Orleans (A.A.) 3-2B-S-DH	61	236	45	73	18	2	10	46	28	39	2	9	4-0	.309	.386	.530	.915	8	.963
— Milwaukee (A.L.)	3B-2B	39	126	17	30	9	0	3	12	11	16	2	4	0-1	.238	.309	.381	.690	3	.965
1995— Milwaukee (A.L.)	3-2-1-SS	125	328	57	91	19	4	9	39	47	42	4	8	7-2	.277	.371	.442	.813	15	.958
1996— Milwaukee (A.L.)	3-DH-1-2	158	566	101	184	46	5	15	83	58	69	7	14	4-9	.325	.391	.504	.894	‡18	.952
1997— Milwaukee (A.L.)	3B-DH	154	580	74	167	46	2	10	82	60	74	14	13	4-3	.288	.367	.426	.793	17	.963
1998— Milwaukee (N.L.)	3B-1B	156	604	97	194	31	1	14	68	79	88	4	26	10-4	.321	.402	.445	.847	11	.979
1999— Milwaukee (N.L.)	3B	157	607	98	198	35	1	15	88	75	83	5	15	7-4	.326	.401	.461	.862	15	.967
2000— Colorado (N.L.)	3B	157	598	111	195	53	2	11	115	67	72	6	19	3-4	.326	.392	.477	.869	15	.964
2001— Colorado (N.L.)	3B	138	528	72	165	26	4	17	83	43	63	5	15	12-2	.313	.364	.489	.853	7	.982
— Colo. Springs (PCL)	3B	1	4	2	3	1	0	0	3	1	0	0	0	0-0	.750	.800	1.000	1.800	0	1.000
2002— Seattle (A.L.)	3B-1B	146	485	51	121	20	0	6	54	31	67	9	12	8-4	.249	.302	.328	.629	9	.976

C

Year	Team (League)	Pos.	G	AB	R	H	2B	3B	HR	RBI	BB	SO	HBP	GDP	SB-CS	Avg.	OBP	SLG	OPS	E	Avg.
2003—Ariz. Mariners (Ariz.)	DH-3B	6	20	2	6	0	0	0	0	4	1	1	1	0-1	.300	.440	.300	.740	0	1.000
—Inland Empire (Calif.)	3B-DH	5	15	1	3	1	0	0	1	3	1	0	1	0-0	.200	.333	.267	.600	1	.833
—Tacoma (PCL)	3B-DH	5	17	7	6	3	0	2	6	3	3	1	0	0-0	.353	.476	.882	1.359	0	1.000
—Seattle (A.L.)	3B-DH-1B	87	258	24	53	11	0	2	23	24	32	5	6	1-1	.205	.284	.271	.555	4	.978
2004—Portland (PCL)	3-2-S-DH-1-O	7	23	3	8	3	0	0	2	5	1	0	1	1-0	.348	.464	.478	.943	1	.960
—San Diego (N.L.)	3-1-2-OF	33	75	12	16	3	0	1	7	5	14	0	0	0-0	.213	.259	.293	.553	2	.979
American League totals (6 years)		709	2343	324	646	151	11	45	293	231	300	41	57	24-20	.276	.348	.407	.755	66	.964
National League totals (5 years)		641	2412	390	768	148	8	58	361	269	320	20	75	32-14	.318	.387	.459	.845	50	.973
Major League totals (11 years)		1350	4755	714	1414	299	19	103	654	500	620	61	132	56-34	.297	.368	.433	.801	116	.969

ALL-STAR GAME RECORD

	G	AB	R	H	2B	3B	HR	RBI	BB	SO	HBP	GDP	SB-CS	Avg.	OBP	SLG	OPS	E	Avg.
All-Star Game totals (2 years)	2	2	0	0	0	0	0	0	0	1	0	0	0-0	.000	.000	.000	.000	0	1.000

CLARK, BRADY — OF

PERSONAL: Born April 18, 1973, in Portland, Ore. ... 6-2/202. ... Bats right, throws right. ... Full name: Brady William Clark. ... High school: Sunset (Beaverton, Ore.). ... College: San Diego.

TRANSACTIONS/CAREER NOTES: Signed as a non-drafted free agent by Cincinnati Reds organization (January 13, 1996). ... Released by Reds (April 10, 1996). ... Re-signed by Reds organization (February 15, 1997). ... Traded by Reds to New York Mets (September 9, 2002), completing deal in which Reds traded P Pedro Feliciano, OF Elvin Andujar and two players to be named to Mets for P Shawn Estes (August 15, 2002); Mets acquired OF Raul Gonzalez as part of deal (August 20, 2002). ... Claimed on waivers by Milwaukee Brewers (January 21, 2003). ... On disabled list (March 21-April 15, 2003); included rehabilitation assignment to Indianapolis.

2004 GAMES PLAYED BY POSITION (MLB): OF—133.

												BATTING								FIELDING	
Year	Team (League)	Pos.	G	AB	R	H	2B	3B	HR	RBI	BB	SO	HBP	GDP	SB-CS	Avg.	OBP	SLG	OPS	E	Avg.
1997—Burlington (Midw.)		OF	126	459	108	149	29	7	11	63	76	71	4	10	31-18	.325	.423	.490	.913	4	.986
1998—Chattanooga (Sou.)		OF	64	222	41	60	13	1	2	16	31	34	4	11	12-4	.270	.370	.365	.735	1	.993
1999—Chattanooga (Sou.)		OF-3B	138	506	103	165	37	4	17	75	89	58	2	6	25-17	.326	.425	.516	.941	5	.981
2000—Louisville (Int'l)		OF	132	487	90	148	41	6	16	79	72	51	9	14	12-8	.304	.397	.511	.908	6	.981
—Cincinnati (N.L.)		OF	11	11	1	3	1	0	0	2	0	2	0	0	0-0	.273	.273	.364	.636	0	1.000
2001—Louisville (Int'l)		OF	49	167	24	44	5	1	2	18	18	17	6	5	6-2	.263	.354	.341	.695	2	.981
—Cincinnati (N.L.)		OF-DH	89	129	22	34	3	0	6	18	22	16	1	6	4-1	.264	.373	.426	.799	1	.981
2002—Cincinnati (N.L.)		OF	51	66	6	10	3	0	0	9	6	9	1	2	1-2	.152	.233	.197	.430	1	.938
—Louisville (Int'l)		OF-3B	25	109	17	33	7	0	1	17	3	9	2	3	0-2	.303	.328	.395	.722	3	.955
—New York (N.L.)		OF	10	12	3	5	1	0	0	1	1	2	0	0	0-0	.417	.462	.500	.962	0	1.000
2003—Indianapolis (Int'l)		OF-DH	9	34	4	9	3	0	0	3	2	6	0	3	1-0	.265	.306	.353	.658	0	1.000
—Milwaukee (N.L.)		OF	128	315	33	86	21	1	6	40	21	40	9	12	13-2	.273	.330	.403	.733	5	.973
2004—Milwaukee (N.L.)		OF	138	353	41	99	18	1	7	46	53	48	9	9	15-8	.280	.385	.397	.782	4	.984
Major League totals (5 years)			427	886	106	237	47	2	19	116	103	117	20	29	33-13	.267	.353	.389	.742	11	.979

CLARK, HOWIE — 1B/OF

PERSONAL: Born February 13, 1974, in San Diego, Calif. ... 5-11/180. ... Bats left, throws right. ... Full name: Howard Roddy Clark. ... High school: Huntington Beach (Calif.).

TRANSACTIONS/CAREER NOTES: Selected by Baltimore Orioles organization in 27th round of 1992 free-agent draft. ... Signed as a free agent by Orioles organization (October 8, 2001). ... Signed as a free agent by Toronto Blue Jays organization (November 5, 2002).

2004 GAMES PLAYED BY POSITION (MLB): OF—19, 1B—11, DH—4, 2B—1, 3B—1.

												BATTING								FIELDING	
Year	Team (League)	Pos.	G	AB	R	H	2B	3B	HR	RBI	BB	SO	HBP	GDP	SB-CS	Avg.	OBP	SLG	OPS	E	Avg.
1992—GC Orioles (GCL)	2B-3B-1B	43	138	12	33	7	1	0	6	12	21	2	2	1-2	.239	.309	.304	.614	7	.948
1993—Albany (S. Atl.)	2B	7	17	2	4	0	0	0	1	0	3	0	1	1-0	.235	.235	.235	.471	2	.833
—Bluefield (Appal.)	2B-OF-1B	58	180	29	53	10	1	3	30	26	34	4	4	2-2	.294	.388	.411	.799	10	.900
1994—Albany (S. Atl.)	1B-2B	108	353	56	95	22	7	2	47	51	58	7	7	5-4	.269	.371	.388	.759	14	.978
—Frederick (Carolina)	2B	7	14	1	2	1	0	0	0	0	2	0	1	0-0	.143	.143	.286	.429	0	1.000
1995—High Desert (Calif.)	3-2-O-S-C-1	100	329	50	85	20	2	5	40	32	51	4	4	12-6	.258	.329	.377	.706	21	.920
1996—Bowie (East.)	2-O-3-S-C-1	127	449	55	122	29	3	4	52	59	54	2	8	2-8	.272	.354	.376	.730	14	.975
1997—Bowie (East.)	3B-2B-1B	105	314	39	90	16	0	9	37	32	38	1	5	2-2	.287	.351	.424	.775	20	.909
1998—Bowie (East.)	OF-2-1-3	88	276	37	79	16	4	9	45	29	42	3	7	1-1	.286	.359	.442	.801	6	.954
—Rochester (Int'l)	1B-2B-3B	30	95	13	22	4	1	3	8	9	11	0	2	1-2	.232	.298	.389	.688	2	.983
1999—Bowie (East.)	2B-1B-OF-C	39	126	17	37	6	0	2	12	10	12	3	0	2-0	.294	.360	.389	.749	0	1.000
—Rochester (Int'l)	OF-2-3-1	79	279	33	82	19	4	6	28	34	24	1	8	1-2	.294	.370	.455	.825	2	.988
2000—Bowie (East.)	OF-1B	13	53	11	18	6	0	1	9	3	6	1	1	0-0	.340	.379	.509	.889	0	1.000
—Rochester (Int'l)	2-OF-3-1	54	189	25	54	10	0	3	21	26	14	1	4	3-1	.286	.373	.386	.760	5	.966
2001—Yucatan (Mex.)		121	493	68	164	42	7	5	64	43	47	...	...	5-4	.333	...	.477	...	2	.993
—Chico (West.)		4	15	3	8	1	0	0	0	1	1	...	...	0-...	.533	...	.667	...	...	...
2002—Rochester (Int'l)	O-1-2-3	108	418	57	129	21	4	7	43	41	28	2	11	3-4	.309	.369	.428	.797	8	.976
—Baltimore (A.L.)	DH-OF-1B	14	53	3	16	5	0	0	4	3	6	2	5	0-0	.302	.362	.396	.758	0	1.000
2003—Syracuse (Int'l)	2-O-1-DH-3	66	252	29	65	14	1	4	30	21	20	3	3	1-0	.258	.316	.369	.685	9	.970
—Toronto (A.L.)	3-DH-O-2-1-S	38	70	9	25	3	1	0	7	3	6	2	3	0-1	.357	.400	.429	.829	2	.959
2004—Toronto (A.L.)	O-1-DH-2-3	40	115	17	25	6	0	3	12	13	15	0	2	0-0	.217	.292	.348	.640	1	.993
—Syracuse (Int'l)	O-2-3-1-DH	72	256	43	80	14	2	6	32	40	18	3	3	1-0	.313	.407	.453	.860	10	.986
Major League totals (3 years)		92	238	29	66	14	1	3	23	19	27	4	10	0-1	.277	.338	.382	.721	3	.986

CLARK, JERMAINE — OF/2B

PERSONAL: Born September 29, 1976, in Berkeley, Calif. ... 5-10/170. ... Bats left, throws right. ... Full name: Jermaine Marcel Clark. ... High school: Will C. Wood (Vacaville, Calif.). ... College: San Francisco.

TRANSACTIONS/CAREER NOTES: Selected by Los Angeles Dodgers organization in 44th round of 1994 free-agent draft; did not sign. ... Selected by Seattle Mariners organization in fifth round of 1997 free-agent draft. ... Selected by Detroit Tigers from Mariners organization in Rule 5 major league draft (December 11, 2000). ... Returned to Mariners (April 19, 2001). ... Traded by Mariners with P Derrick Van Dusen to Texas Rangers for P Ismael Valdes (August 18, 2002). ... Claimed on waivers by San Diego Padres (April 30, 2003). ... Traded by Padres to Rangers for cash (July 9, 2003). ... Signed as a free agent by Cincinnati Reds organization (January 9, 2004).

2004 GAMES PLAYED BY POSITION (MLB): OF—8, 2B—2.

Year	Team (League)	Pos.	G	AB	R	H	2B	3B	HR	RBI	BB	SO	HBP	GDP	SB-CS	Avg.	OBP	SLG	OPS	E	Avg.
											BATTING									FIELDING	
1997—	Everett (N'west)	2B-3B	59	199	42	67	13	2	3	29	34	31	3	1	22-3	.337	.437	.467	.904	9	.957
1998—	Wisconsin (Midw.)	2B-OF	123	448	81	145	24	13	6	55	57	64	2	3	40-14	.324	.402	.475	.877	14	.970
1999—	Lancaster (Calif.)	2B	126	502	112	158	27	8	6	61	58	80	2	10	33-15	.315	.386	.436	.822	10	.983
2000—	New Haven (East.)	2B	133	447	80	131	23	9	2	44	87	69	14	7	38-8	.293	.421	.398	.819	13	.977
2001—	Detroit (A.L.)	DH	3	0	1	0	0	0	0	0	0	0	0	0	0-0	...	...	...	...	...	...
	— Tacoma (PCL)	2B	74	216	35	54	7	3	1	26	27	39	3	6	13-2	.250	.340	.324	.664	6	.980
2002—	Tacoma (PCL)	2B-SS	108	368	47	98	14	4	6	36	62	59	2	...	29-14	.266	.370	.375	.745	8	.982
	— Oklahoma (PCL)	2B-OF	13	57	13	17	2	1	1	4	7	11	0	...	6-2	.298	.375	.421	.796	1	.982
2003—	San Diego (N.L.)	OF	1	2	0	0	0	0	0	0	1	0	1	0	0-0	.000	.000	.000	.000	0	1.000
	— Portland (PCL)	OF-2-S-3	50	160	27	40	2	2	4	10	22	24	1	1	14-3	.250	.342	.363	.705	4	.968
	— Oklahoma (PCL)	OF-2B	49	171	24	38	6	4	6	24	16	26	1	3	11-1	.222	.291	.409	.700	2	.981
	— Texas (A.L.)	OF-2B-DH	24	46	2	8	2	0	0	6	6	4	0	1	2-1	.174	.264	.217	.482	0	1.000
2004—	Cincinnati (N.L.)	2B	14	30	4	4	1	0	0	2	1	8	2	0	1-0	.133	.212	.167	.379	0	1.000
	— Louisville (Int'l)	OF-2-3-DH	115	398	77	113	15	5	10	52	63	54	7	4	24-9	.284	.386	.422	.808	2	.992
	American League totals (2 years)		27	46	3	8	2	0	0	6	6	4	0	1	2-1	.174	.264	.217	.482	0	1.000
	National League totals (2 years)		15	32	4	4	1	0	0	3	1	9	2	0	1-1	.125	.194	.156	.351	0	1.000
	Major League totals (3 years)		42	78	7	12	3	0	0	9	7	13	2	1	3-2	.154	.236	.192	.428	0	1.000

CLARK, TONY — 1B

PERSONAL: Born June 15, 1972, in Newton, Kan. ... 6-7/245. ... Bats both, throws right. ... Full name: Anthony Christopher Clark. ... High school: Valhalla (El Cajon, Calif.), then Christian (El Cajon, Calif.). ... College: San Diego State.

TRANSACTIONS/CAREER NOTES: Selected by Detroit Tigers organization in first round (second pick overall) of 1990 free-agent draft. ... On disabled list (May 26-June 10, 1999); included rehabilitation assignment to Toledo. ... On Detroit disabled list (May 13-June 12, July 15-September 1 and September 19, 2000-remainder of season); included rehabilitation assignments to Toledo. ... Claimed on waivers by Boston Red Sox (November 20, 2001). ... Signed as a free agent by New York Mets organization (February 20, 2003). ... Signed as a free agent by New York Yankees (January 12, 2004).

2004 GAMES PLAYED BY POSITION (MLB): 1B—99, DH—1.

Year	Team (League)	Pos.	G	AB	R	H	2B	3B	HR	RBI	BB	SO	HBP	GDP	SB-CS	Avg.	OBP	SLG	OPS	E	Avg.
											BATTING									FIELDING	
1990—	Bristol (Appal.)	OF	25	73	2	12	2	0	1	8	6	28	1	0	0-0	.164	.238	.233	.470	0	1.000
1991—	Niagara Falls (N.Y.-Penn.) .		Did not play.																		
1992—	Niagara Falls (N.Y.-Penn.) .	OF	27	85	12	26	9	0	5	17	9	34	0	0	1-0	.306	.372	.588	.961	0	1.000
1993—	Lakeland (Fla. St.)	OF	36	117	14	31	4	1	1	22	18	32	0	1	0-1	.265	.358	.342	.700	2	.944
1994—	Trenton (East.)	DH-1B	107	394	50	110	25	0	21	86	40	113	1	9	0-4	.279	.346	.503	.848	13	.977
	— Toledo (Int'l)	1B-DH	25	92	10	24	4	0	2	13	12	25	0	1	2-0	.261	.340	.370	.709	0	1.000
1995—	Toledo (Int'l)	1B-DH	110	405	50	98	17	2	14	63	52	129	3	8	0-2	.242	.330	.398	.728	13	.981
	— Detroit (A.L.)	1B	27	101	10	24	5	1	3	11	8	30	0	2	0-0	.238	.294	.396	.690	4	.985
1996—	Toledo (Int'l)	1B-DH	55	194	42	58	7	1	14	36	31	58	0	3	1-1	.299	.396	.562	.957	3	.993
	— Detroit (A.L.)	1B-DH	100	376	56	94	14	0	27	72	29	127	0	7	0-1	.250	.299	.503	.802	6	.993
1997—	Detroit (A.L.)	1B-DH	159	580	105	160	28	3	32	117	93	144	3	11	1-3	.276	.376	.500	.876	10	.993
1998—	Detroit (A.L.)	1B-DH	157	602	84	175	37	0	34	103	63	128	3	16	3-3	.291	.358	.522	.880	13	.991
1999—	Detroit (A.L.)	1B-DH	143	536	74	150	29	0	31	99	64	133	6	14	2-1	.280	.361	.507	.869	10	.992
	— Toledo (Int'l)	1B	1	3	0	0	0	0	0	0	1	1	0	0	0-0	.000	.250	.000	.250	0	1.000
2000—	Detroit (A.L.)	1B-DH	60	208	32	57	14	0	13	37	24	51	0	10	0-0	.274	.349	.529	.878	4	.993
	— Toledo (Int'l)	1B	6	22	1	2	0	0	1	2	1	1	0	0	0-0	.091	.130	.273	.403	0	1.000
2001—	Detroit (A.L.)	1B-DH	126	428	67	123	29	3	16	75	62	108	1	14	0-1	.287	.374	.481	.856	3	.996
2002—	Boston (A.L.)	1B-DH	90	275	25	57	12	1	3	29	21	57	1	11	0-0	.207	.265	.291	.556	6	.992
2003—	St. Lucie (Fla. St.)	1B	1	4	0	1	0	0	0	0	0	1	0	0	0-0	.250	.250	.250	.500	1	1.000
	— New York (N.L.)	1B-OF	125	254	29	59	13	0	16	43	24	73	1	8	0-0	.232	.300	.472	.772	4	.992
2004—	New York (A.L.)	1B-DH	106	253	37	56	12	0	16	49	26	92	2	6	0-0	.221	.297	.459	.755	4	.994
	American League totals (9 years)		968	3359	490	896	180	8	175	592	390	870	16	91	6-9	.267	.343	.481	.825	60	.992
	National League totals (1 year)		125	254	29	59	13	0	16	43	24	73	1	8	0-0	.232	.300	.472	.772	4	.992
	Major League totals (10 years)		1093	3613	519	955	193	8	191	635	414	943	17	99	6-9	.264	.340	.481	.821	64	.992

DIVISION SERIES RECORD

Year	Team (League)	Pos.	G	AB	R	H	2B	3B	HR	RBI	BB	SO	HBP	GDP	SB-CS	Avg.	OBP	SLG	OPS	E	Avg.
2004—	New York (A.L.)	1B	1	1	0	0	0	0	0	0	0	1	0	0	0-0	.000	.000	.000	.000	0	1.000

CHAMPIONSHIP SERIES RECORD

Year	Team (League)	Pos.	G	AB	R	H	2B	3B	HR	RBI	BB	SO	HBP	GDP	SB-CS	Avg.	OBP	SLG	OPS	E	Avg.
2004—	New York (A.L.)	1B	5	21	0	3	1	0	0	1	0	9	0	0	0-0	.143	.143	.190	.333	1	.976

ALL-STAR GAME RECORD

	G	AB	R	H	2B	3B	HR	RBI	BB	SO	HBP	GDP	SB-CS	Avg.	OBP	SLG	OPS	E	Avg.
All-Star Game totals (1 year)	1	1	0	0	0	0	0	0	0	1	0	0	0-0	.000	.000	.000	.000	...	...

CLAUSSEN, BRANDON — P

PERSONAL: Born May 1, 1979, in Rapid City, S.D. ... 6-1/200. ... Throws left, bats right. ... Full name: Brandon Allen Falker Claussen. ... Name pronounced: CLAW-sin. ... High school: Goddard (Roswell, N.M.). ... Junior college: Howard (Texas).

TRANSACTIONS/CAREER NOTES: Selected by New York Yankees oranization in 34th round of 1998 free-agent draft. ... Traded by Yankees with P Charlie Manning and cash to Cincinnati Reds with for 3B Aaron Boone (July 31, 2003).

CAREER HITTING: 3-for-23 (.130), 1 R, 0 2B, 0 3B, 0 HR, 1 RBI.

Year	Team (League)	W	L	Pct.	ERA	WHIP	G	GS	CG	ShO	Hld.	Sv.-Opp.	IP	H	R	ER	HR	BB-IBB	SO	Avg.
1999—	GC Yankees (GCL)	0	1	.000	3.18	0.79	2	2	0	0	...	0-...	11.1	7	4	4	2	2-0	16	.175
	— Staten Island (NY-P)	6	4	.600	3.38	1.14	12	12	1	0	...	0-...	72.0	70	30	27	4	12-2	89	.253
	— Greensboro (S. Atl.)	0	1	.000	10.50	1.67	1	1	1	0	...	0-...	6.0	8	7	7	1	2-0	5	.296
2000—	Greensboro (S. Atl.)	8	5	.615	4.05	1.38	17	17	1	0	...	0-...	97.2	91	49	44	9	44-0	98	.251
	— Tampa (FSL)	2	5	.286	3.10	1.26	9	9	1	1	...	0-...	52.1	49	24	18	2	17-0	44	.245
2001—	Tampa (FSL)	5	2	.714	2.73	1.07	8	8	0	0	...	0-...	56.0	47	21	17	2	13-0	69	.224
	— Norwich (East.)	9	2	.818	2.13	1.19	21	21	1	1	...	0-...	131.0	101	42	31	6	55-0	151	.210
2002—	Columbus (Int'l)	2	8	.200	3.28	1.40	15	15	0	0	...	0-...	93.1	85	47	34	4	46-3	73	.242
2003—	Tampa (FSL)	2	0	1.000	1.64	0.86	4	4	0	0	...	0-...	22.0	16	5	4	0	3-0	26	.198
	— New York (N.L.)	1	0	1.000	1.42	1.42	1	1	0	0	0	0-...	6.1	7	1	1	1	1-0	5	.296
	— Columbus (Int'l)	2	1	.667	2.75	1.03	11	11	1	0	...	0-...	68.2	53	28	21	4	18-0	39	.213
	— Louisville (Int'l)	0	1	.000	7.47	1.47	3	3	0	0	...	0-...	15.2	17	13	13	3	6-0	16	.293

C

Year Team (League)	W	L	Pct.	ERA	WHIP	G	GS	CG	ShO	Hld.	Sv.-Opp.	IP	H	R	ER	HR	BB-IBB	SO	Avg.
2004— Louisville (Int'l)	8	6	.571	4.66	1.45	18	18	0	0	...	0-...	100.1	98	56	52	10	47-0	111	.256
— Cincinnati (N.L.)	2	8	.200	6.14	1.74	14	14	0	0	...	0-0	66.0	80	50	45	9	35-2	45	.299
American League totals (1 year)	1	0	1.000	1.42	1.42	1	1	0	0	0	0-0	6.1	8	2	1	1	1-0	5	.296
National League totals (1 year)	2	8	.200	6.14	1.74	14	14	0	0	0	0-0	66.0	80	50	45	9	35-2	45	.299
Major League totals (2 years)	3	8	.273	5.72	1.71	15	15	0	0	0	0	72.1	88	52	46	10	36-2	50	.298

CLAYTON, ROYCE — SS

PERSONAL: Born January 2, 1970, in Burbank, Calif. ... 6-0/185. ... Bats right, throws right. ... Full name: Royce Spencer Clayton. ... High school: St. Bernard (Playa del Ray, Calif.).

TRANSACTIONS/CAREER NOTES: Selected by San Francisco Giants organization in first round (15th pick overall) of 1988 free-agent draft; pick received as compensation for Cincinnati Reds signing Type B free-agent OF Eddie Milner. ... Traded by Giants with a player to be named to St. Louis Cardinals for Ps Allen Watson, Rich DeLucia and Doug Creek (December 14, 1995); Cardinals acquired 2B Chris Wimmer to complete deal (January 16, 1996). ... On disabled list (June 24-July 9, 1998). ... Traded by Cardinals with P Todd Stottlemyre to Texas Rangers for P Darren Oliver, 3B Fernando Tatis and a player to be named (July 31, 1998); Cardinals acquired OF Mark Little to complete deal (August 9, 1998). ... On disabled list (May 1-21, 1999); included rehabilitation assignment to Oklahoma. ... Traded by Rangers to Chicago White Sox for Ps Aaron Myette and Brian Schmack (December 14, 2000). ... Released by White Sox (September 8, 2002). ... Signed by Milwaukee Brewers (December 11, 2002). ... Signed as a free agent by Colorado Rockies organization (January 5, 2004).

2004 GAMES PLAYED BY POSITION (MLB): SS—144.

Year Team (League)	Pos.	G	AB	R	H	2B	3B	HR	RBI	BB	SO	HBP	GDP	SB-CS	Avg.	OBP	SLG	OPS	E	Avg.
1988— Everett (N'west)	SS	60	212	35	55	4	0	3	29	27	54	3	8	10-4	.259	.348	.321	.669	35	.873
1989— Clinton (Midw.)	SS	104	385	39	91	13	3	0	24	39	101	4	9	28-16	.236	.309	.286	.595	31	.943
— San Jose (Calif.)	SS	28	92	5	11	2	0	0	4	13	27	1	5	10-1	.120	.236	.141	.377	8	.939
1990— San Jose (Calif.)	SS	123	460	80	123	15	10	7	71	68	98	4	13	33-15	.267	.364	.389	.753	37	.938
1991— Shreveport (Texas)	SS	126	485	84	136	22	8	5	68	61	104	3	7	36-10	.280	.361	.390	.751	29	.950
— San Francisco (N.L.)	SS	9	26	0	3	1	0	0	2	1	6	0	1	0-0	.115	.148	.154	.302	3	.880
1992— San Francisco (N.L.)	SS-3B	98	321	31	72	7	4	4	24	26	63	0	11	8-4	.224	.281	.308	.589	11	.973
— Phoenix (PCL)	SS	48	192	30	46	6	2	3	18	17	25	0	8	15-6	.240	.300	.339	.639	7	.973
1993— San Francisco (N.L.)	SS	153	549	54	155	21	5	6	70	38	91	5	16	11-10	.282	.331	.372	.702	27	.963
1994— San Francisco (N.L.)	SS	108	385	38	91	14	6	3	30	30	74	3	7	23-3	.236	.295	.327	.623	14	.973
1995— San Francisco (N.L.)	SS	138	509	56	124	29	3	5	58	38	109	3	7	24-9	.244	.298	.342	.640	20	.969
1996— St. Louis (N.L.)	SS	129	491	64	136	20	4	6	35	33	89	1	13	33-15	.277	.321	.372	.692	15	.972
1997— St. Louis (N.L.)	SS	154	576	75	153	39	5	9	61	33	109	3	19	30-10	.266	.306	.398	.704	19	.973
1998— St. Louis (N.L.)	SS	90	355	59	83	19	1	4	29	40	51	2	10	19-6	.234	.313	.327	.640	13	.970
— Texas (A.L.)	SS	52	186	30	53	12	1	5	24	13	32	1	6	5-5	.285	.330	.441	.771	7	.972
1999— Texas (A.L.)	SS	133	465	69	134	21	5	14	52	39	100	4	6	8-6	.288	.346	.445	.792	* 25	.961
— Oklahoma (PCL)	SS	2	7	1	1	0	0	0	1	3	3	0	0	0-0	.143	.400	.143	.543	0	1.000
2000— Texas (A.L.)	SS	148	513	70	124	21	5	14	54	42	92	3	21	11-7	.242	.301	.384	.685	16	.977
2001— Chicago (A.L.)	SS	135	433	62	114	21	4	9	60	33	72	3	16	10-7	.263	.315	.393	.708	7	.988
2002— Chicago (A.L.)	SS	112	342	51	86	14	2	7	35	20	67	3	7	5-1	.251	.295	.366	.661	5	.989
2003— Milwaukee (N.L.)	SS	146	483	49	110	16	1	11	39	49	92	3	25	5-2	.228	.301	.333	.634	14	.977
2004— Colorado (N.L.)	SS	146	574	95	160	36	4	8	54	48	125	4	13	10-5	.279	.338	.397	.735	9	.986
American League totals (5 years)		580	1939	282	511	89	17	49	225	147	363	14	56	39-26	.264	.317	.403	.720	60	.977
National League totals (10 years)		1171	4269	521	1087	202	33	56	402	336	809	24	122	163-64	.255	.311	.357	.667	145	.972
Major League totals (14 years)		1751	6208	803	1598	291	50	105	627	483	1172	38	178	202-90	.257	.313	.371	.684	205	.974

DIVISION SERIES RECORD

Year Team (League)	Pos.	G	AB	R	H	2B	3B	HR	RBI	BB	SO	HBP	GDP	SB-CS	Avg.	OBP	SLG	OPS	E	Avg.
1996— St. Louis (N.L.)	SS	2	6	1	2	0	0	0	0	3	1	0	0	0-1	.333	.556	.333	.889	0	1.000
1998— Texas (A.L.)	SS	3	9	0	2	0	0	0	0	0	4	0	1	0-0	.222	.222	.222	.444	1	.929
1999— Texas (A.L.)	SS	3	10	0	0	0	0	0	0	0	1	0	0	0-0	.000	.000	.000	.000	0	1.000
Division series totals (3 years)		8	25	1	4	0	0	0	0	3	6	0	1	0-1	.160	.250	.160	.410	1	.973

CHAMPIONSHIP SERIES RECORD

Year Team (League)	Pos.	G	AB	R	H	2B	3B	HR	RBI	BB	SO	HBP	GDP	SB-CS	Avg.	OBP	SLG	OPS	E	Avg.
1996— St. Louis (N.L.)	SS	5	20	4	7	0	0	0	1	1	4	0	0	1-1	.350	.381	.350	.731	2	.913

ALL-STAR GAME RECORD

	G	AB	R	H	2B	3B	HR	RBI	BB	SO	HBP	GDP	SB-CS	Avg.	OBP	SLG	OPS	E	Avg.
All-Star Game totals (1 year)	1	1	0	0	0	0	0	0	0	1	0	0	0-0	.000	.000	.000	.000	0	1.000

CLEMENS, ROGER — P

PERSONAL: Born August 4, 1962, in Dayton, Ohio. ... 6-4/235. ... Throws right, bats right. ... Full name: William Roger Clemens. ... High school: Spring Woods (Houston). ... College: Texas.

TRANSACTIONS/CAREER NOTES: Selected by New York Mets organization in 12th round of June 1981 free-agent draft; did not sign. ... Selected by Boston Red Sox organization in first round (19th pick overall) of June 1983 free-agent draft. ... On disabled list (July 8-August 3 and August 21, 1985-remainder of season). ... On suspended list (April 26-May 3, 1991). ... On disabled list (June 19-July 16, 1993); included rehabilitation assignment to Pawtucket. ... On disabled list (April 16-June 2, 1995); included rehabilitation assignments to Sarasota and Pawtucket. ... Signed as a free agent by Toronto Blue Jays (December 13, 1996). ... Traded by Blue Jays to New York Yankees for Ps David Wells and Graeme Lloyd and 2B Homer Bush (February 18, 1999). ... On disabled list (April 28-May 21, 1999; and June 15-July 2, 2000). ... On disabled list (July 13-August 7, 2002); included rehabilitation assignments to Tampa and Norwich. ... Signed as a free agent by Houston Astros (January 19, 2004).

RECORDS: Shares major league record for most strikeouts, nine-inning game (20, April 29, 1986; and September 18, 1996).

HONORS: Named Major League Player of the Year by THE SPORTING NEWS (1986). ... Named A.L. Pitcher of the Year by THE SPORTING NEWS (1986, 1991, 1997, 1998 and 2001). ... Named A.L. Most Valuable Player by Baseball Writers' Association of America (1986). ... Named A.L. Cy Young Award winner by Baseball Writers' Association of America (1986, 1987, 1991, 1997, 1998 and 2001). ... Named N.L. Cy Young Award winner by Baseball Writers' Association of America (2004).

CAREER HITTING: 16-for-92 (.174), 3 R, 3 2B, 0 3B, 0 HR, 8 RBI.

Year Team (League)	W	L	Pct.	ERA	WHIP	G	GS	CG	ShO	Hld.	Sv.-Opp.	IP	H	R	ER	HR	BB-IBB	SO	Avg.
1983— Winter Haven (FSL)	3	1	.750	1.24	0.76	4	4	3	1	...	0-...	29.0	22	4	4	0	0-0	36	.206
— New Britain (East.)	4	1	.800	1.38	0.83	7	7	1	1	...	0-...	52.0	31	8	8	1	12-0	59	.167
1984— Pawtucket (Int'l)	2	3	.400	1.93	1.14	7	6	3	1	...	0-...	46.2	39	12	10	3	14-0	50	.228
— Boston (A.L.)	9	4	.692	4.32	1.31	21	20	5	1	0	0-0	133.1	146	67	64	13	29-3	126	.271
1985— Boston (A.L.)	7	5	.583	3.29	1.22	15	15	3	1	0	0-0	98.1	83	38	36	5	37-0	74	.228
1986— Boston (A.L.)	* 24	4	* .857	* 2.48	0.97	33	33	10	1	0	0-0	254.0	179	77	70	21	67-0	238	.195

Year	Team (League)	W	L	Pct.	ERA	WHIP	G	GS	CG	ShO	Hld.	Sv.-Opp.	IP	H	R	ER	HR	BB-IBB	SO	Avg.
1987— Boston (A.L.)		•20	9	.690	2.97	1.18	36	36	*18	*7	0	0-0	281.2	248	100	93	19	83-4	256	.235
1988— Boston (A.L.)		18	12	.600	2.93	1.06	35	35	*14	*8	0	0-0	264.0	217	93	86	17	62-4	*291	.220
1989— Boston (A.L.)		17	11	.607	3.13	1.22	35	35	8	3	0	0-0	253.1	215	101	88	20	93-5	230	.231
1990— Boston (A.L.)		21	6	.778	*1.93	1.08	31	31	7	•4	0	0-0	228.1	193	59	49	7	54-3	209	.228
1991— Boston (A.L.)		18	10	.643	*2.62	1.05	35	*35	13	*4	0	0-0	*271.1	219	93	79	15	65-12	*241	.221
1992— Boston (A.L.)		18	11	.621	*2.41	1.07	32	32	11	*5	0	0-0	246.2	203	80	66	11	62-5	208	.224
1993— Boston (A.L.)		11	14	.440	4.46	1.26	29	29	2	1	0	0-0	191.2	175	99	95	17	67-4	160	.244
—Pawtucket (Int'l)		0	0	...	0.00	1.36	1	1	0	0	...	0-...	3.2	1	0	0	0	4-0	8	.091
1994— Boston (A.L.)		9	7	.563	2.85	1.14	24	24	3	1	0	0-0	170.2	124	62	54	15	71-1	168	.204
1995— Sarasota (Florida State)		0	0	...	0.00	0.50	1	1	0	0	...	0-...	4.0	1	0	0	0	2-0	7	.000
—Pawtucket (Int'l)		0	0	...	0.00	0.80	1	1	0	0	...	0-...	5.0	1	0	0	0	3-0	5	.063
—Boston (A.L.)		10	5	.667	4.18	1.44	23	23	0	0	0	0-0	140.0	141	70	65	15	60-0	132	.259
1996— Boston (A.L.)		10	13	.435	3.63	1.33	34	34	6	2	0	0-0	242.2	216	106	98	19	106-2	*257	.237
1997— Toronto (A.L.)		*21	7	.750	*2.05	1.03	34	34	•9	•3	0	0-0	•264.0	204	65	60	9	68-1	*292	.213
1998— Toronto (A.L.)		•20	6	.769	*2.65	1.10	33	33	5	3	0	0-0	234.2	169	78	69	11	88-0	*271	.198
1999— New York (A.L.)		14	10	.583	4.60	1.47	30	30	1	1	0	0-0	187.2	185	101	96	20	90-0	163	.261
2000— New York (A.L.)		13	8	.619	3.70	1.31	32	32	1	0	0	0-0	204.1	184	96	84	26	84-0	188	.236
2001— New York (A.L.)		20	3	.870	3.51	1.26	33	33	0	0	0	0-0	220.1	205	94	86	19	72-1	213	.246
2002— New York (A.L.)		13	6	.684	4.35	1.31	29	29	0	0	0	0-0	180.0	172	94	87	18	63-6	192	.250
—Tampa (FSL)		1	0	1.000	5.40	1.40	1	1	0	0	0	0-...	5.0	5	3	3	1	2-0	6	.263
—Norwich (East.)		0	1	.000	1.29	0.71	1	1	0	0	0	...	7.0	5	1	1	0	0-0	7	.200
2003— New York (A.L.)		17	9	.654	3.91	1.21	33	33	1	1	0	0-0	211.2	199	99	92	24	58-1	190	.247
2004— Houston (N.L.)		18	4	.818	2.98	1.16	33	33	0	0	0	0-0	214.1	169	76	71	15	79-5	218	.217
American League totals (20 years)		310	160	.660	3.19	1.18	607	606	117	46	0	0-0	4278.2	3677	1672	1517	321	1379-52	4099	.231
National League totals (1 year)		18	4	.818	2.98	1.16	33	33	0	0	0	0-0	214.1	169	76	71	15	79-5	218	.217
Major League totals (21 years)		328	164	.667	3.18	1.18	640	639	117	46	0	0-0	4493.0	3846	1748	1588	336	1458-57	4317	.230

DIVISION SERIES RECORD

Year	Team (League)	W	L	Pct.	ERA	WHIP	G	GS	CG	ShO	Hld.	Sv.-Opp.	IP	H	R	ER	HR	BB-IBB	SO	Avg.
1995— Boston (A.L.)		0	0	...	3.86	0.86	1	1	0	0	0	0-0	7.0	5	3	3	0	1-0	5	.192
1999— New York (A.L.)		1	0	1.000	0.00	0.71	1	1	0	0	0	0-0	7.0	3	0	0	0	2-0	2	.125
2000— New York (A.L.)		0	2	.000	8.18	1.91	2	2	0	0	0	0-0	11.0	13	10	10	1	8-1	10	.302
2001— New York (A.L.)		0	1	.000	5.40	1.56	2	2	0	0	0	0-0	8.1	9	5	5	1	4-0	6	.265
2002— New York (A.L.)		0	0	...	6.35	1.94	1	1	0	0	0	0-0	5.2	8	4	4	1	3-0	5	.348
2003— New York (A.L.)		1	0	1.000	1.29	0.86	1	1	0	0	0	0-0	7.0	5	1	1	0	1-0	6	.192
2004— Houston (N.L.)		1	0	1.000	3.00	1.67	2	2	0	0	0	0-0	12.0	12	5	4	1	8-0	12	.267
Division series totals (7 years)		3	3	.500	4.19	1.41	10	10	0	0	0	0-0	58.0	55	28	27	5	27-1	46	.249

CHAMPIONSHIP SERIES RECORD

Year	Team (League)	W	L	Pct.	ERA	WHIP	G	GS	CG	ShO	Hld.	Sv.-Opp.	IP	H	R	ER	HR	BB-IBB	SO	Avg.
1986— Boston (A.L.)		1	1	.500	4.37	1.28	3	3	0	0	0	0-0	22.2	22	12	11	1	7-0	17	.244
1988— Boston (A.L.)		0	0	...	3.86	0.86	1	1	0	0	0	0-0	7.0	6	3	3	1	0-0	8	.231
1990— Boston (A.L.)		0	1	.000	3.52	1.57	2	2	0	0	0	0-0	7.2	7	3	3	0	5-0	4	.259
1999— New York (A.L.)		0	1	.000	22.50	4.00	1	1	0	0	0	0-0	2.0	6	5	5	1	2-0	2	.462
2000— New York (A.L.)		1	0	1.000	0.00	0.33	1	1	1	1	0	0-0	9.0	1	0	0	0	2-0	15	.036
2001— New York (A.L.)		0	0	...	0.00	1.00	1	1	0	0	0	0-0	5.0	1	0	0	0	4-0	7	.063
2003— New York (A.L.)		1	0	1.000	5.00	1.44	2	2	0	0	0	0-0	9.0	11	6	5	2	2-0	8	.297
2004— Houston (N.L.)		1	1	.500	4.15	0.92	2	2	0	0	0	0-0	13.0	10	6	6	3	2-0	9	.217
Champ. series totals (8 years)		4	4	.500	3.94	1.17	13	13	1	1	0	0-0	75.1	64	35	33	8	24-0	70	.226

WORLD SERIES RECORD

Year	Team (League)	W	L	Pct.	ERA	WHIP	G	GS	CG	ShO	Hld.	Sv.-Opp.	IP	H	R	ER	HR	BB-IBB	SO	Avg.
1986— Boston (A.L.)		0	0	...	3.18	1.32	2	2	0	0	0	0-0	11.1	9	5	4	0	6-0	11	.225
1999— New York (A.L.)		1	0	1.000	1.17	0.78	1	1	0	0	0	0-0	7.2	4	1	1	0	2-0	4	.154
2000— New York (A.L.)		1	0	1.000	0.00	0.25	1	1	0	0	0	0-0	8.0	2	0	0	0	0-0	9	.074
2001— New York (A.L.)		1	0	1.000	1.35	1.05	2	2	0	0	0	0-0	13.1	10	2	2	0	4-0	19	.204
2003— New York (A.L.)		0	0	...	3.86	1.14	1	1	0	0	0	0-0	7.0	8	3	3	1	0-0	5	.286
World series totals (5 years)		3	0	1.000	1.90	0.95	7	7	0	0	0	0-0	47.1	33	11	10	1	12-0	48	.194

ALL-STAR GAME RECORD

	W	L	Pct.	ERA	WHIP	G	GS	CG	ShO	Hld.	Sv.-Opp.	IP	H	R	ER	HR	BB-IBB	SO	Avg.
All-Star Game totals (9 years)	1	1	.500	4.50	1.00	9	3	0	0	0	0-0	12.0	11	9	6	3	1-0	9	.239

CLEMENT, MATT   P

PERSONAL: Born August 12, 1974, in Butler, Pa. ... 6-3/210. ... Throws right, bats right. ... Full name: Matthew Paul Clement. ... Name pronounced: klah-MENT. ... High school: Butler (Pa.).

TRANSACTIONS/CAREER NOTES: Selected by San Diego Padres organization in third round of 1993 free-agent draft. ... Traded by Padres with OF Eric Owens and P Omar Ortiz to Florida Marlins for OFs Mark Kotsay and Cesar Crespo (March 28, 2001). ... Traded by Marlins with P Antonio Alfonseca to Chicago Cubs for Ps Julian Tavarez, Jose Cueto and Dontrelle Willis and C Ryan Jorgensen (March 27, 2002).

CAREER HITTING: 32-for-342 (.094), 21 R, 5 2B, 1 3B, 0 HR, 12 RBI.

Year	Team (League)	W	L	Pct.	ERA	WHIP	G	GS	CG	ShO	Hld.	Sv.-Opp.	IP	H	R	ER	HR	BB-IBB	SO	Avg.
1994— Spokane (N'west)		1	1	.500	6.14	2.59	2	2	0	0	...	0-...	7.1	8	7	5	0	11-0	4	.296
—Ariz. Padres (Ariz.)		8	5	.615	4.43	1.22	13	13	0	0	...	0-...	67.0	65	38	33	0	17-0	76	.248
1995— Rancho Cuca. (Calif.)		3	4	.429	4.24	1.92	12	12	0	0	...	0-...	57.1	61	37	27	1	49-0	33	.295
—Idaho Falls (Pioneer)		6	3	.667	4.33	1.27	14	14	0	0	...	0-...	81.0	61	53	39	3	42-0	65	.214
1996— Clinton (Midw.)		8	3	.727	2.80	1.22	16	16	1	1	...	0-...	96.1	66	31	30	3	52-0	109	.191
—Rancho Cuca. (Calif.)		4	5	.444	5.59	1.54	11	11	0	0	...	0-...	56.1	61	40	35	8	26-0	75	.280
1997— Rancho Cuca. (Calif.)		6	3	.667	1.60	1.04	14	14	2	0	...	0-...	101.0	74	30	18	3	31-1	109	.202
—Mobile (Sou.)		6	5	.545	2.56	1.31	13	13	1	1	...	0-...	88.0	83	37	25	4	32-0	92	.249
1998— Las Vegas (PCL)		10	9	.526	3.98	1.41	27	27	1	0	...	0-...	171.2	157	94	76	12	85-2	160	.245
—San Diego (N.L.)		2	0	1.000	4.61	1.61	4	2	0	0	0	0-0	13.2	15	8	7	0	7-1	13	.283
1999— San Diego (N.L.)		10	12	.455	4.48	1.53	31	31	0	0	0	0-0	180.2	190	106	90	18	86-2	135	.273

Year Team (League)	W	L	Pct.	ERA	WHIP	G	GS	CG	ShO	Hld.	Sv.-Opp.	IP	H	R	ER	HR	BB-IBB	SO	Avg.
2000— San Diego (N.L.)	13	17	.433	5.14	1.56	34	34	0	0	0	0-0	205.0	194	131	117	22	* 125-4	170	.248
2001— Florida (N.L.)	9	10	.474	5.05	1.52	31	31	0	0	0	0-0	169.1	172	102	95	15	85-2	134	.268
2002— Chicago (N.L.)	12	11	.522	3.60	1.20	32	32	3	2	0	0-0	205.0	162	84	82	18	85-7	215	.215
2003— Chicago (N.L.)	14	12	.538	4.11	1.23	32	32	2	1	0	0-0	201.2	169	100	92	22	79-2	171	.227
2004— Chicago (N.L.)	9	13	.409	3.68	1.28	30	30	0	0	0	0-0	181.0	155	79	74	23	77-4	190	.229
Major League totals (7 years)	69	75	.479	4.34	1.38	194	192	5	3	0	0-0	1156.1	1057	610	557	118	544-22	1028	.243

DIVISION SERIES RECORD

Year Team (League)	W	L	Pct.	ERA	WHIP	G	GS	CG	ShO	Hld.	Sv.-Opp.	IP	H	R	ER	HR	BB-IBB	SO	Avg.
2003— Chicago (N.L.)	0	1	.000	7.71	2.57	1	1	0	0	0	0-0	4.2	8	4	4	1	4-0	3	.381

CHAMPIONSHIP SERIES RECORD

Year Team (League)	W	L	Pct.	ERA	WHIP	G	GS	CG	ShO	Hld.	Sv.-Opp.	IP	H	R	ER	HR	BB-IBB	SO	Avg.
2003— Chicago (N.L.)	1	0	1.000	3.52	0.91	1	1	0	0	0	0-0	7.2	5	3	3	0	2-0	3	.192

CLOSSER, J.D.　　　　C

PERSONAL: Born January 15, 1980, in Beech Grove, Ind. ... 5-10/176. ... Bats both, throws right. ... Full name: Jeffrey Darrin Closser. ... High school: Monroe Central (Parker City, Ind.).

TRANSACTIONS/CAREER NOTES: Selected by Arizona Diamondbacks organization in fifth round of 1998 free-agent draft. ... Traded by Diamondbacks with OF Jack Cust to Colorado Rockies for P Mike Myers (January 7, 2002).

2004 GAMES PLAYED BY POSITION (MLB): C—32.

Year Team (League)	Pos.	G	AB	R	H	2B	3B	HR	RBI	BB	SO	HBP	GDP	SB-CS	Avg.	OBP	SLG	OPS	E	FIELDING Avg.
1998— Ariz. D'backs (Ariz.)	C-1B	45	150	26	47	13	2	4	21	37	36	2	3	3-2	.313	.453	.507	.959	13	.965
— South Bend (Mid.)	C	4	14	3	3	1	0	0	2	2	7	0	0	0-0	.214	.313	.286	.598	0	1.000
1999— South Bend (Mid.)	C	52	174	29	42	8	0	3	27	34	37	1	3	0-1	.241	.363	.339	.702	12	.951
— Missoula (Pio.)	C	76	275	73	89	22	0	10	54	71	57	2	8	9-3	.324	.458	.513	.970	21	.964
2000— South Bend (Mid.)	C-1B	101	331	54	74	19	1	8	37	60	61	3	7	6-2	.224	.347	.360	.706	12	.979
2001— Lancaster (Calif.)	C-OF	128	468	85	136	26	6	21	87	65	106	2	4	6-7	.291	.377	.506	.883	16	.981
2002— Carolina (Southern)	C	95	315	43	89	27	1	13	62	44	69	0	7	9-3	.283	.369	.498	.868	12	.977
2003— Tulsa (Texas)	C-OF	110	410	62	116	28	5	13	54	47	79	3	10	3-2	.283	.359	.471	.829	18	.976
2004— Colo. Springs (PCL)	C-DH	83	298	53	89	19	1	7	54	41	47	2	3	0-2	.299	.384	.440	.820	10	.983
— Colorado (N.L.)	C	36	113	5	36	6	0	1	10	6	22	2	3	0-0	.319	.364	.398	.762	3	.986
Major League totals (1 year)		36	113	5	36	6	0	1	10	6	22	2	3	0-0	.319	.364	.398	.762	3	.986

COLBRUNN, GREG　　　　1B

PERSONAL: Born July 26, 1969, in Fontana, Calif. ... 6-0/215. ... Bats right, throws right. ... Full name: Gregory Joseph Colbrunn. ... Name pronounced: COAL-brun. ... High school: Fontana (Calif.).

TRANSACTIONS/CAREER NOTES: Selected by Montreal Expos organization in sixth round of 1987 free-agent draft. ... On disabled list (August 2-18, 1992); included rehabilitation assignment to Indianapolis. ... On disabled list (April 5-21, 1993); included rehabilitation assignment to West Palm Beach. ... On disabled list (July 12, 1993-remainder of season); included rehabilitation assignment to Ottawa. ... Claimed on waivers by Florida Marlins (October 7, 1993). ... On disabled list (April 9-May 27, and July 15-30, 1994); included rehabilitation assignments to Brevard County and Edmonton. ... On disabled list (July 24-August 8, 1996). ... Signed as a free agent by Minnesota Twins organization (January 24, 1997). ... Traded by Twins to Atlanta Braves for a player to be named (August 14, 1997); Twins acquired OF Marc Lewis to complete deal (October 1, 1997). ... Signed as a free agent by Colorado Rockies organization (December 23, 1997). ... Traded by Rockies to Braves for Ps David Cortes and Mike Porzio and a player to be named (July 30, 1998); Rockies acquired P Anthony Briggs to complete deal (September 9, 1998). ... Signed as a free agent by Arizona Diamondbacks (November 17, 1998). ... On disabled list (June 6-25 and June 27-August 17, 2001); included rehabilitation assignment to Tucson. ... On disabled list (March 22-April 10 and July 18-August 2, 2002); included rehabilitation assignment to Tucson. ... Signed as a free agent by Seattle Mariners (January 3, 2003). ... On disabled list (June 9-28 and July 3, 2003-remainder of season); included rehabilitation assignments to Tacoma and Everett. ... Traded by Mariners with cash to Diamondbacks for OF Quinton McCracken (December 15, 2003). ... On disabled list (May 16-June 21 and June 29-September 15, 2004); included rehabilitation assignment to Tucson.

2004 GAMES PLAYED BY POSITION (MLB): DH—2, 1B—2.

Year Team (League)	Pos.	G	AB	R	H	2B	3B	HR	RBI	BB	SO	HBP	GDP	SB-CS	Avg.	OBP	SLG	OPS	E	FIELDING Avg.
1988— Rockford (Midwest)	C	115	417	55	111	18	2	7	46	22	60	11	5	5-3	.266	.318	.369	.687	15	.978
1989— W.P. Beach (FSL)	C	59	228	20	54	8	0	0	25	6	29	2	5	3-1	.237	.261	.272	.532	5	.988
— Jacksonville (Sou.)	C	55	178	21	49	11	1	3	18	13	33	2	9	0-1	.275	.330	.399	.729	4	.988
1990— Jacksonville (Sou.)	C	125	458	57	138	29	1	13	76	38	78	6	8	1-2	.301	.358	.454	.812	15	.981
1991—								Did not play.												
1992— Indianapolis (A.A.)	1B	57	216	32	66	19	1	11	48	7	41	3	7	1-0	.306	.333	.556	.889	4	.992
— Montreal (N.L.)	1B	52	168	12	45	8	0	2	18	6	34	2	1	3-2	.268	.294	.351	.646	3	.992
1993— W.P. Beach (FSL)	1B	8	31	6	12	2	1	1	5	4	1	0	2	0-0	.387	.457	.613	1.070	1	.988
— Montreal (N.L.)	1B	70	153	15	39	9	0	4	23	6	33	1	4	4-2	.255	.282	.392	.674	2	.995
— Ottawa (Int'l)	1B	6	22	4	6	1	0	0	8	1	2	0	1	1-0	.273	.292	.318	.610	0	1.000
1994— Florida (N.L.)	1B	47	155	17	47	10	0	6	31	9	27	2	3	1-1	.303	.345	.484	.829	4	.988
— Brevard County (FSL)	DH-1B	7	11	3	6	2	0	1	2	1	0	0	0	0-0	.545	.583	1.000	1.583	1	.944
— Edmonton (PCL)	1B-DH	7	17	2	4	0	0	1	2	0	1	1	1	0-0	.235	.278	.412	.690	1	.967
1995— Florida (N.L.)	1B	138	528	70	146	22	1	23	89	22	69	6	15	11-3	.277	.311	.453	.763	5	.996
1996— Florida (N.L.)	1B	141	511	60	146	26	2	16	69	25	76	14	22	4-5	.286	.333	.438	.772	6	.995
1997— Minnesota (A.L.)	1B-DH	70	217	24	61	14	0	5	26	8	38	1	7	1-2	.281	.307	.415	.722	6	.988
— Atlanta (N.L.)	1B-DH	28	54	3	15	3	0	2	9	2	11	1	1	0-0	.278	.316	.444	.760	1	.984
1998— Colorado (N.L.) 1B-OF-DH-C		62	122	12	38	8	2	2	13	8	23	1	1	3-3	.311	.359	.459	.818	2	.992
— Atlanta (N.L.)	1B-OF	28	44	6	13	3	0	1	10	2	11	3	0	1-0	.295	.367	.432	.799	0	1.000
1999— Arizona (N.L.) 1B-3B-DH		67	135	20	44	5	3	5	24	12	23	4	3	1-1	.326	.392	.519	.911	1	.996
2000— Arizona (N.L.) 1B-DH-3B		116	329	48	103	22	1	15	57	43	45	10	13	0-1	.313	.405	.523	.928	8	.989
2001— Arizona (N.L.)	1B-3B	59	97	12	28	8	0	4	18	9	14	4	5	0-0	.289	.373	.495	.868	3	.988
— Tucson (PCL)	1B	5	13	1	5	1	0	0	4	2	0	0	1	0-0	.385	.467	.462	.928	0	1.000
2002— Tucson (PCL)	1B-3B	6	25	6	9	3	0	2	7	3	3	0	1	0-0	.360	.429	.720	1.149	1	.960
— Arizona (N.L.) 1B-3B-DH		72	171	30	57	16	2	10	27	13	19	0	5	0-0	.333	.378	.626	1.004	2	.993
2003— Tacoma (PCL)	DH-1B	3	11	3	3	0	0	1	2	1	1	0	0	0-0	.273	.333	.545	.879	0	1.000
— Everett (N'west)	DH	1	3	0	2	1	0	0	1	0	0	0	0	0-0	.667	.750	1.000	1.750	0	1.000
— Seattle (A.L.)	1B-DH	22	58	7	16	1	0	3	7	4	16	0	0	0-1	.276	.323	.483	.805	1	.989

Year Team (League)	Pos.	G	AB	R	H	2B	3B	HR	RBI	BB	SO	HBP	GDP	SB-CS	Avg.	OBP	SLG	OPS	E	Avg.
2004— Tucson (PCL)	DH-1B	3	10	1	3	1	0	1	5	0	2	0	0	0-0	.300	.300	.700	1.000	0	1.000
— Arizona (N.L.)	DH-1B	20	27	1	3	0	0	0	1	1	5	0	0	0-0	.111	.143	.111	.254	0	1.000
American League totals (2 years)		92	275	31	77	15	1	8	33	12	54	1	10	1-3	.280	.310	.429	.739	7	.988
National League totals (12 years)		900	2494	306	724	140	11	90	389	158	390	48	70	28-18	.290	.341	.464	.805	37	.993
Major League totals (13 years)		992	2769	337	801	155	12	98	422	170	444	49	80	29-21	.289	.338	.460	.799	44	.992

DIVISION SERIES RECORD

Year Team (League)	Pos.	G	AB	R	H	2B	3B	HR	RBI	BB	SO	HBP	GDP	SB-CS	Avg.	OBP	SLG	OPS	E	Avg.
1997— Atlanta (N.L.)		1	1	0	1	0	0	0	2	0	0	0	0	0-0	1.000	1.000	1.000	2.000	...	...
1998— Atlanta (N.L.)		2	2	0	0	0	0	0	0	0	0	0	0	0-0	.000	.000	.000	.000	...	...
1999— Arizona (N.L.)	1B	2	5	1	2	1	0	1	2	2	2	1	0	0-0	.400	.625	1.200	1.825	0	1.000
2001— Arizona (N.L.)	1B	4	6	0	2	0	0	0	1	1	0	0	1	0-0	.333	.429	.333	.762	0	1.000
2002— Arizona (N.L.)	1B	1	3	1	0	0	0	0	0	1	1	0	0	0-0	.000	.250	.000	.250	0	1.000
Division series totals (5 years)		10	17	2	5	1	0	1	5	4	3	1	1	0-0	.294	.455	.529	.984	0	1.000

CHAMPIONSHIP SERIES RECORD

Year Team (League)	Pos.	G	AB	R	H	2B	3B	HR	RBI	BB	SO	HBP	GDP	SB-CS	Avg.	OBP	SLG	OPS	E	Avg.
1997— Atlanta (N.L.)		3	3	0	2	0	0	0	0	0	0	0	0	0-0	.667	.667	.667	1.333	...	...
1998— Atlanta (N.L.)		6	6	0	2	0	0	0	0	0	2	0	0	0-0	.333	.333	.333	.667	...	...
2001— Arizona (N.L.)		1	1	0	0	0	0	0	0	0	0	0	0	0-0	.000	.000	.000	.000	...	...
Champ. series totals (3 years)		10	10	0	4	0	0	0	0	0	2	0	0	0-0	.400	.400	.400	.800	...	...

WORLD SERIES RECORD

Year Team (League)	Pos.	G	AB	R	H	2B	3B	HR	RBI	BB	SO	HBP	GDP	SB-CS	Avg.	OBP	SLG	OPS	E	Avg.
2001— Arizona (N.L.)	1B	1	5	2	2	0	0	0	1	1	1	0	0	0-0	.400	.500	.400	.900	0	1.000

COLLIER, LOU   OF

PERSONAL: Born August 21, 1973, in Chicago, Ill. ... 5-10/190. ... Bats right, throws right. ... Full name: Louis Keith Collier. ... High school: Vocational (Chicago). ... Junior college: Triton (Ill.).

TRANSACTIONS/CAREER NOTES: Selected by Pittsburgh Pirates organization in 31st round of 1992 free-agent draft. ... On disabled list (May 22-June 7, 1998); included rehabilitation assignment to Lynchburg. ... Claimed on waivers by Milwaukee Brewers (December 18, 1998). ... Traded by Brewers with P Jeff D'Amico, OF Jeromy Burnitz and OF/1B Mark Sweeney to New York Mets as part of three-team deal in which Brewers acquired P Glendon Rusch and IF Lenny Harris from Mets and OF Alex Ochoa from Rockies, Rockies acquired 1B/3B Todd Zeile, OF Benny Agbayani and cash from Mets and Mets acquired 1B/OF Ross Gload and P Craig House from Rockies (January 21, 2002). ... Traded by Mets to Montreal Expos for P Jimmy Serrano and OF Jason Bay (March 26, 2002). ... Released by Expos (September 30, 2002). ... Signed by Boston Red Sox organization (March 21, 2003). ... Signed as a free agent by Philadelphia Phillies organization (December 17, 2003).

2004 GAMES PLAYED BY POSITION (MLB): OF—8, 3B—1.

									BATTING										FIELDING	
Year Team (League)	Pos.	G	AB	R	H	2B	3B	HR	RBI	BB	SO	HBP	GDP	SB-CS	Avg.	OBP	SLG	OPS	E	Avg.
1993— Welland (N.Y.-Penn.)	SS	50	201	35	61	6	2	1	19	12	31	5	2	8-7	.303	.356	.368	.724	27	.887
1994— Augusta (S. Atl.)	SS	85	318	48	89	17	4	7	40	25	53	8	4	32-10	.280	.345	.425	.769	34	.915
— Salem (Caro.)	SS	43	158	25	42	4	1	6	16	15	29	6	4	5-8	.266	.348	.418	.766	11	.946
1995— Lynchburg (Caro.)	SS	114	399	68	110	19	3	4	38	51	60	7	13	31-11	.276	.365	.368	.734	35	.937
1996— Carolina (Southern)	SS-DH	119	443	76	124	20	3	3	49	48	73	7	11	29-9	.280	.355	.359	.714	30	.943
1997— Calgary (PCL)	SS-2B-DH	112	397	65	131	31	5	1	48	37	47	6	13	12-7	.330	.393	.441	.834	34	.937
— Pittsburgh (N.L.)	SS	18	37	3	5	0	0	0	3	1	11	0	1	1-0	.135	.158	.135	.293	0	1.000
1998— Pittsburgh (N.L.)	SS	110	334	30	82	13	6	2	34	31	70	6	8	2-2	.246	.316	.338	.655	18	.960
— Lynchburg (Caro.)	SS	5	18	4	3	2	0	0	2	2	1	0	0	0-0	.167	.286	.278	.563	4	.840
1999— Milwaukee (N.L.)	S-OF-3-2	74	135	18	35	9	0	2	21	14	32	0	2	3-2	.259	.325	.370	.695	5	.951
— Louisville (Int'l)	3B-SS-OF	27	91	25	35	10	4	4	11	15	14	1	2	6-3	.385	.472	.626	1.099	3	.962
2000— Indianapolis (Int'l)	OF-2B-3B	17	56	7	14	4	1	0	12	11	9	1	1	2-2	.250	.371	.357	.729	3	.933
— Huntsville (Sou.)	3-OF-2-SS	50	172	29	46	4	2	2	29	30	44	1	5	7-3	.267	.374	.349	.723	8	.929
— Milwaukee (N.L.)	OF-3B	14	32	9	7	1	0	1	2	6	4	0	1	0-0	.219	.333	.344	.677	0	1.000
2001— Indianapolis (Int'l)	OF-2B-3B	86	312	48	90	17	2	14	36	24	64	7	6	9-3	.288	.350	.490	.840	6	.976
— Milwaukee (N.L.)	OF-3B-DH	50	127	19	32	8	1	2	14	17	30	1	0	5-1	.252	.340	.378	.718	4	.948
2002— Montreal (N.L.)	OF-2B-3B	13	11	3	1	1	0	0	0	1	3	1	0	0-0	.091	.231	.182	.413	0	1.000
— Ottawa (Int'l)	OF-3-2-S-1	89	307	48	97	26	6	6	52	37	69	6	9	5-2	.316	.394	.498	.893	14	.932
2003— Boston (A.L.)	3B-OF	4	1	0	0	0	0	0	0	0	0	0	0	0-1	.000	.000	.000	.000	0	1.000
— Pawtucket (Int'l)	O-S-DH-3-1	103	392	58	115	19	4	14	69	32	94	8	13	8-7	.293	.354	.469	.823	7	.971
2004— Scran./W.B. (I.L.)	O-3-DH-1	101	387	62	126	26	3	14	66	34	82	4	8	14-3	.326	.383	.517	.900	14	.933
— Philadelphia (N.L.)	OF-3B	32	36	7	10	1	0	1	4	5	10	1	2	1-0	.278	.381	.389	.770	0	1.000
American League totals (1 year)		4	1	0	0	0	0	0	0	0	0	0	0	0-1	.000	.000	.000	.000	0	1.000
National League totals (7 years)		311	712	89	172	33	7	8	78	75	160	9	14	12-5	.242	.318	.341	.659	27	.962
Major League totals (8 years)		315	713	89	172	33	7	8	78	75	160	9	14	12-6	.241	.317	.341	.658	27	.962

COLOME, JESUS   P

PERSONAL: Born December 23, 1977, in San Pedro de Macoris, Dominican Republic. ... 6-4/205. ... Throws right, bats right. ... Full name: Jesus Colome De La Cruz. ... Name pronounced: hay-soos cal-um-ay.

TRANSACTIONS/CAREER NOTES: Signed as a non-drafted free agent by Oakland Athletics organization (September 29, 1996). ... Traded by A's with a player to be named to Tampa Bay Devil Rays for Ps Jim Mecir and Todd Belitz (July 28, 2000). ... On disabled list (September 14, 2004-remainder of season).

CAREER HITTING: 0-for-1 (.000), 0 R, 0 2B, 0 3B, 0 HR, 0 RBI.

Year Team (League)	W	L	Pct.	ERA	WHIP	G	GS	CG	ShO	Hld.	Sv.-Opp.	IP	H	R	ER	HR	BB-IBB	SO	Avg.
1997— Dominican Athletics (DSL)	9	3	.750	2.70	1.06	18	7	3	0	...	0-...	90.0	73	33	27		22-...	55	...
1998— Ariz. A's (Ariz.)	2	5	.286	3.18	1.11	12	11	0	0	...	0-...	56.2	47	27	20	1	16-0	62	.228
1999— Modesto (Calif.)	8	4	.667	3.36	1.44	31	22	0	0	...	1-...	128.2	125	63	48	6	60-2	127	.256
2000— Midland (Texas)	9	4	.692	3.59	1.35	20	20	0	0	...	0-...	110.1	99	62	44	10	50-0	95	.239
— Orlando (Sou.)	1	2	.333	6.75	1.70	3	3	0	0	...	0-...	14.2	18	12	11	2	7-0	9	.290
2001— Durham (Int'l)	0	3	.000	6.23	1.62	13	0	0	0	...	0-...	17.1	22	13	12	1	6-0	18	.319
— Tampa Bay (A.L.)	2	3	.400	3.33	1.27	30	0	0	0	6	0-0	48.2	37	22	18	8	25-4	31	.208
2002— Tampa Bay (A.L.)	2	7	.222	8.27	2.15	32	0	0	0	3	0-5	41.1	56	41	38	6	33-5	33	.341
— Durham (Int'l)	2	2	.500	2.17	1.07	18	0	0	0	...	1-...	29.0	18	8	7	1	13-0	30	.176
2003— Tampa Bay (A.L.)	3	7	.300	4.50	1.55	54	0	0	0	11	2-8	74.0	69	37	37	9	46-5	69	.247
2004— Durham (Int'l)	2	1	.667	3.52	1.40	18	0	0	0	...	2-...	30.2	27	12	12	0	16-0	17	.243
— Tampa Bay (A.L.)	2	2	.500	3.27	1.11	33	0	0	0	8	3-4	41.1	28	16	15	4	18-1	40	.193
Major League totals (4 years)	9	19	.321	4.73	1.52	149	0	0	0	28	5-17	205.1	190	116	108	27	122-15	173	.248

COLON, BARTOLO — P

PERSONAL: Born May 24, 1973, in Altamira, Dominican Republic. ... 5-11/250. ... Throws right, bats right. ... Name pronounced: bar-TOE-loh ko-LONE.

TRANSACTIONS/CAREER NOTES: Signed as a non-drafted free agent by Cleveland Indians organization (June 26, 1993). ... On disabled list (April 16-May 12, 2000); included rehabilitation assignment to Buffalo. ... On suspended list (July 28-August 2, 2001). ... Traded by Indians with future considerations to Montreal Expos for 1B Lee Stevens, SS Brandon Phillips, P Cliff Lee and OF Grady Sizemore (June 27, 2002); Expos acquired P Tim Drew to complete deal (June 28, 2002). ... Traded by Expos with 2B/SS Jorge Nunez to Chicago White Sox for P Orlando Hernandez, P Rocky Biddle, 3B/OF Jeff Liefer and cash (January 15, 2003). ... On suspended list (May 21-27, 2003). ... Signed as a free agent by Anaheim Angels (December 10, 2003).

CAREER HITTING: 9-for-76 (.118), 1 R, 0 2B, 0 3B, 0 HR, 4 RBI.

Year — Team (League)	W	L	Pct.	ERA	WHIP	G	GS	CG	ShO	Hld.	Sv.-Opp.	IP	H	R	ER	HR	BB-IBB	SO	Avg.
1993— Santiago (DSL)	6	1	.857	2.59	1.17	11	10	2	1	...	1-...	66.0	44	24	19		33-...	48	
1994— Burlington (Appalachian)	7	4	.636	3.14	1.36	12	12	0	0	...	0-...	66.0	46	32	23	3	44-0	84	.192
1995— Kinston (Caro.)	13	3	.813	1.96	1.01	21	21	0	0	...	0-...	128.2	91	31	28	8	39-0	152	.202
1996— Cant./Akr. (Eastern)	2	2	.500	1.74	1.11	13	12	0	0	...	0-...	62.0	44	17	12	2	25-0	56	.196
— Buffalo (A.A.)	0	0	...	6.00	1.60	8	0	0	0	...	0-...	15.0	16	10	10	2	8-0	19	.271
1997— Cleveland (A.L.)	4	7	.364	5.65	1.62	19	17	1	0	0	0-0	94.0	107	66	59	12	45-1	66	.286
— Buffalo (A.A.)	7	1	.875	2.22	1.20	10	10	1	1	...	0-...	56.2	45	15	14	4	23-0	54	.221
1998— Cleveland (A.L.)	14	9	.609	3.71	1.39	31	31	6	2	0	0-0	204.0	205	91	84	15	79-5	158	.260
1999— Cleveland (A.L.)	18	5	.783	3.95	1.27	32	32	1	1	0	0-0	205.0	185	97	90	24	76-5	161	.242
2000— Cleveland (A.L.)	15	8	.652	3.88	1.39	30	30	2	1	0	0-0	188.0	163	86	81	21	98-4	212	.233
— Buffalo (Int'l)	1	0	1.000	1.80	1.20	1	1	0	0	...	0-...	5.0	6	1	1	0	0-0	4	.286
2001— Cleveland (A.L.)	14	12	.538	4.09	1.39	34	34	1	0	0	0-0	222.1	220	106	101	26	90-2	201	.261
2002— Cleveland (A.L.)	10	4	.714	2.55	1.16	16	16	4	2	0	0-0	116.1	104	37	33	11	31-1	75	.245
— Montreal (N.L.)	10	4	.714	3.31	1.32	17	17	4	1	0	0-0	117.0	115	48	43	9	39-4	74	.259
2003— Chicago (A.L.)	15	13	.536	3.87	1.20	34	34	•9	0	0	0-0	242.0	223	107	104	30	67-3	173	.248
2004— Anaheim (A.L.)	18	12	.600	5.01	1.37	34	34	0	0	0	0-0	208.1	215	122	116	38	71-1	158	.265
American League totals (8 years)	108	70	.607	4.06	1.34	230	228	24	6	0	0-0	1480.0	1422	712	668	177	557-22	1204	.254
National League totals (1 year)	10	4	.714	3.31	1.32	17	17	4	1	0	0-0	117.0	115	48	43	9	39-4	74	.259
Major League totals (8 years)	118	74	.615	4.01	1.34	247	245	28	7	0	0-0	1597.0	1537	760	711	186	596-26	1278	.254

DIVISION SERIES RECORD

Year — Team (League)	W	L	Pct.	ERA	WHIP	G	GS	CG	ShO	Hld.	Sv.-Opp.	IP	H	R	ER	HR	BB-IBB	SO	Avg.
1997— Cleveland (A.L.)	Did not play.																		
1998— Cleveland (A.L.)	0	0		1.59	1.41	1	1	0	0	0	0-0	5.2	5	1	1	1	3-1	3	.250
1999— Cleveland (A.L.)	0	1	.000	9.00	1.67	2	2	0	0	0	0-0	9.0	11	9	9	3	4-0	12	.306
2001— Cleveland (A.L.)	1	1	.500	1.84	1.23	2	2	0	0	0	0-0	14.2	12	3	3	0	6-0	13	.231
2004— Anaheim (A.L.)	0	0		4.50	1.67	1	1	0	0	0	0-0	6.0	7	3	3	1	3-0	3	.304
Division series totals (4 years)	1	2	.333	4.08	1.44	6	6	0	0	0	0-0	35.1	35	16	16	5	16-1	31	.267

CHAMPIONSHIP SERIES RECORD

Year — Team (League)	W	L	Pct.	ERA	WHIP	G	GS	CG	ShO	Hld.	Sv.-Opp.	IP	H	R	ER	HR	BB-IBB	SO	Avg.
1997— Cleveland (A.L.)	Did not play.																		
1998— Cleveland (A.L.)	1	0	1.000	1.00	0.89	1	1	1	0	0	0-0	9.0	4	1	1	0	4-0	3	.148

WORLD SERIES RECORD

Year — Team (League)	W	L	Pct.	ERA	WHIP	G	GS	CG	ShO	Hld.	Sv.-Opp.	IP	H	R	ER	HR	BB-IBB	SO	Avg.
1997— Cleveland (A.L.)	Did not play.																		

ALL-STAR GAME RECORD

	W	L	Pct.	ERA	WHIP	G	GS	CG	ShO	Hld.	Sv.-Opp.	IP	H	R	ER	HR	BB-IBB	SO	Avg.
All-Star Game totals (1 year)	1	0	1.000	27.00	3.00	1	0	0	0	0	0-0	1.0	2	3	3	1	1-0	1	.400

COLON, ROMAN — P

PERSONAL: Born August 13, 1979, in Montecristi, Dominican Republic. ... 6-6/225. ... Throws right, bats right. ... Full name: Roman Benedicto Colon.

TRANSACTIONS/CAREER NOTES: Signed as a non-drafted free agent by Atlanta Braves organization (August 14, 1995).

CAREER HITTING: 0-for-0 (.000), 0 R, 0 2B, 0 3B, 0 HR, 0 RBI.

Year — Team (League)	W	L	Pct.	ERA	WHIP	G	GS	CG	ShO	Hld.	Sv.-Opp.	IP	H	R	ER	HR	BB-IBB	SO	Avg.
1997— GC Braves (GCL)	3	4	.429	4.29	1.52	14	12	0	0	...	0-...	63.0	68	47	30	2	28-0	44	.270
1998— Danville (Appalachian)	1	7	.125	5.77	1.64	13	13	0	0	...	0-...	73.1	92	59	47	7	28-0	53	.302
1999— Jamestown (N.Y.-Penn.)	7	5	.583	4.54	1.32	15	15	1	0	...	0-...	77.1	77	48	39	4	25-0	61	.258
2001— Macon (S. Atl.)	7	7	.500	3.59	1.27	23	21	0	0	...	0-...	128.0	136	69	51	9	26-0	91	.271
2002— Myrtle Beach (Caro.)	9	8	.529	3.53	1.28	26	26	1	0	...	0-...	163.0	170	81	64	8	38-1	94	.269
2003— Greenville (Sou.)	11	3	.786	3.36	1.28	39	12	1	0	...	2-...	107.0	104	48	40	9	33-3	58	.261
2004— Richmond (Int'l)	4	1	.800	3.65	1.27	51	0	0	0	...	0-...	74.0	72	33	30	4	22-1	64	.258
— Greenville (Sou.)	1	0	1.000	0.00	0.33	3	0	0	0	...	0-...	3.0	1	0	0	0	0-0	5	.091
— Atlanta (N.L.)	2	1	.667	3.32	1.37	18	0	0	0	0	0-1	19.0	18	9	7	0	8-1	15	.254
Major League totals (1 year)	2	1	.667	3.32	1.37	18	0	0	0	0	0-1	19.0	18	9	7	0	8-1	15	.254

COLYER, STEVE — P

PERSONAL: Born February 22, 1979, in St. Louis, Mo. ... 6-4/205. ... Throws left, bats left. ... Full name: Stephen Edward Colyer. ... Name pronounced: call-yer. ... High school: Fort Zumwalt South (O'Fallon, Mo.). ... Junior college: Meramec (Mo.).

TRANSACTIONS/CAREER NOTES: Selected by Los Angeles Dodgers organization in supplemental round ("sandwich pick" between second and third round) of 1997 free-agent draft; pick received as part of compensation for St. Louis Cardinals signing Type C free agent 2B Delino DeShields. ... Traded by Dodgers with a player to be named to Detroit Tigers for OF Cody Ross (April 1, 2004).

CAREER HITTING: 0-for-0 (.000), 0 R, 0 2B, 0 3B, 0 HR, 0 RBI.

Year — Team (League)	W	L	Pct.	ERA	WHIP	G	GS	CG	ShO	Hld.	Sv.-Opp.	IP	H	R	ER	HR	BB-IBB	SO	Avg.
1998— Yakima (N'west)	2	2	.500	4.96	1.65	15	12	0	0	...	0-...	65.1	72	46	36	2	36-0	75	.277
1999— San Bernardino (Calif.)	7	9	.438	4.70	1.59	27	25	1	0	...	0-...	145.2	145	82	76	12	86-0	131	.269
2000— Vero Beach (FSL)	5	7	.417	5.76	1.73	26	18	1	0	...	0-...	95.1	97	74	61	9	68-0	80	.272
2001— Vero Beach (FSL)	4	8	.333	3.96	1.48	24	24	0	0	...	0-...	120.1	101	62	53	16	77-0	118	.234
2002— Jacksonville (Southern)	5	4	.556	3.45	1.44	59	0	0	0	...	21-...	62.2	50	29	24	6	40-3	68	.214
2003— Las Vegas (PCL)	2	3	.400	3.21	1.38	44	0	0	0	...	23-...	47.2	44	18	17	1	22-0	50	.243
— Los Angeles (N.L.)	0	0	...	2.75	1.58	13	0	0	0	0	0-0	19.2	22	6	6	0	9-0	16	.297

Year Team (League)	W	L	Pct.	ERA	WHIP	G	GS	CG	ShO	Hld.	Sv.-Opp.	IP	H	R	ER	HR	BB-IBB	SO	Avg.
2004—Toledo (International)	2	1	.667	4.21	1.99	25	0	0	0	...	0-...	25.2	26	13	12	2	25-1	23	.265
—Detroit (A.L.)	1	0	1.000	6.47	1.78	41	0	0	0	4	0-0	32.0	33	24	23	8	24-1	31	.270
American League totals (1 year)	1	0	1.000	6.47	1.78	41	0	0	0	4	0-0	32.0	33	24	23	8	24-1	31	.270
National League totals (1 year)	0	0	...	2.75	1.58	13	0	0	0	0	0-0	19.2	22	6	6	0	9-0	16	.297
Major League totals (2 years)	1	0	1.000	5.05	1.70	54	0	0	0	4	0-0	51.2	55	30	29	8	33-1	47	.281

CONINE, JEFF — OF/1B

PERSONAL: Born June 27, 1966, in Tacoma, Wash. ... 6-1/220. ... Bats right, throws right. ... Full name: Jeffrey Guy Conine. ... Name pronounced: COH-nine. ... High school: Eisenhower (Rialto, Calif.). ... College: UCLA.

TRANSACTIONS/CAREER NOTES: Selected by Kansas City Royals organization in 58th round of 1987 free-agent draft. ... Selected by Florida Marlins in first round (22nd pick overall) of expansion draft (November 17, 1992). ... Traded by Marlins to Royals for P Blaine Mull (November 20, 1997). ... On disabled list (March 25-May 5 and July 27-August 19, 1998); included rehabilitation assignment to Omaha. ... Traded by Royals to Baltimore Orioles for P Chris Fussell (April 2, 1999). ... On disabled list (June 15-August 7, 2002). ... Traded by Orioles to Marlins for Ps Denny Bautista and Don Levinski (August 31, 2003).

2004 GAMES PLAYED BY POSITION (MLB): OF—83, 1B—57.

Year Team (League)	Pos.	G	AB	R	H	2B	3B	HR	RBI	BB	SO	HBP	GDP	SB-CS	Avg.	OBP	SLG	OPS	E	Avg.
1988—Baseball City (FSL)	3B-1B	118	415	63	113	23	9	10	59	46	77	0	6	26-12	.272	.342	.443	.785	22	.970
1989—Baseball City (FSL)	1B	113	425	68	116	12	7	14	69	40	91	3	14	32-13	.273	.338	.433	.771	18	.980
1990—Memphis (Sou.)	3B-1B	137	487	89	156	37	8	15	95	94	88	1	10	21-6	.320	.425	.522	.947	22	.983
—Kansas City (A.L.)	1B	9	20	3	5	2	0	0	2	2	5	0	1	0-0	.250	.318	.350	.668	1	.977
1991—Omaha (A.A.)	1B-OF	51	171	23	44	9	1	3	15	26	39	1	3	0-6	.257	.359	.374	.733	7	.984
1992—Omaha (A.A.)	1B-OF	110	397	69	120	24	5	20	72	54	67	2	6	4-5	.302	.383	.539	.922	6	.993
—Kansas City (A.L.)	OF-1B	28	91	10	23	5	2	0	9	8	23	0	1	0-0	.253	.313	.352	.665	0	1.000
1993—Florida (N.L.)	OF-1B *	162	595	75	174	24	3	12	79	52	135	5	14	2-2	.292	.351	.403	.754	2	.995
1994—Florida (N.L.)	OF-1B	115	451	60	144	27	6	18	82	40	92	1	8	1-2	.319	.373	.526	.898	6	.986
1995—Florida (N.L.)	OF-1B	133	483	72	146	26	2	25	105	66	94	1	13	2-0	.302	.379	.520	.899	6	.981
1996—Florida (N.L.)	OF-1B	157	597	84	175	32	2	26	95	62	121	4	17	1-4	.293	.360	.484	.844	8	.985
1997—Florida (N.L.)	1B-OF	151	405	46	98	13	1	17	61	57	89	2	11	2-0	.242	.337	.405	.742	8	.992
1998—Kansas City (A.L.)	OF-1B-DH	93	309	30	79	26	0	8	43	26	68	2	8	3-0	.256	.312	.417	.729	1	.996
—Omaha (PCL)	DH-OF	2	9	0	0	0	0	0	0	0	3	0	0	0-0	.000	.000	.000	.000	0	1.000
1999—Baltimore (A.L.)	1-DH-O-3	139	444	54	129	31	1	13	75	30	40	3	12	0-3	.291	.335	.453	.787	7	.992
2000—Baltimore (A.L.)	3-1-DH-O	119	409	53	116	20	2	13	46	36	53	2	14	4-3	.284	.341	.438	.779	15	.969
2001—Baltimore (A.L.)	1-O-3-DH	139	524	75	163	23	2	14	97	64	75	5	12	12-8	.311	.386	.443	.829	4	.995
2002—Baltimore (A.L.)	1B-DH-OF	116	451	44	123	26	4	15	63	25	66	2	10	8-0	.273	.307	.448	.755	10	.990
2003—Baltimore (A.L.)	1B-OF-3B	124	493	75	143	33	3	15	80	37	60	5	14	5-0	.290	.338	.460	.799	9	.992
—Florida (N.L.)		25	84	13	20	3	0	5	15	13	10	0	2	0-0	.238	.337	.464	.789	0	1.000
2004—Florida (N.L.)	OF-1B	140	521	55	146	35	1	14	83	48	78	2	15	5-5	.280	.340	.432	.772	5	.993
American League totals (8 years)		767	2741	344	781	166	14	78	415	228	390	19	72	32-14	.285	.339	.441	.780	47	.990
National League totals (7 years)		883	3136	405	903	160	15	117	520	338	619	15	80	13-13	.288	.356	.460	.817	35	.990
Major League totals (14 years)		1650	5877	749	1684	326	29	195	935	566	1009	34	152	45-27	.287	.348	.451	.799	82	.990

DIVISION SERIES RECORD

Year Team (League)	Pos.	G	AB	R	H	2B	3B	HR	RBI	BB	SO	HBP	GDP	SB-CS	Avg.	OBP	SLG	OPS	E	Avg.
1997—Florida (N.L.)	1B	3	11	3	4	1	0	0	1	1	0	0	0	0-0	.364	.417	.455	.871	1	.964
2003—Florida (N.L.)	OF	4	15	2	4	0	0	0	2	1	0	0	0	0-0	.267	.353	.267	.620	0	1.000
Division series totals (2 years)		7	26	5	8	1	0	0	3	2	1	0	0	0-0	.308	.379	.346	.725	1	.973

CHAMPIONSHIP SERIES RECORD

Year Team (League)	Pos.	G	AB	R	H	2B	3B	HR	RBI	BB	SO	HBP	GDP	SB-CS	Avg.	OBP	SLG	OPS	E	Avg.
1997—Florida (N.L.)	1B	6	18	1	2	0	0	0	1	1	4	0	1	0-0	.111	.158	.111	.269	0	1.000
2003—Florida (N.L.)	OF	7	24	4	11	1	1	1	3	4	2	0	0	0-0	.458	.500	.708	1.208	1	.875
Champ. series totals (2 years)		13	42	5	13	1	1	1	4	5	6	0	1	0-0	.310	.367	.452	.820	1	.979

WORLD SERIES RECORD

Year Team (League)	Pos.	G	AB	R	H	2B	3B	HR	RBI	BB	SO	HBP	GDP	SB-CS	Avg.	OBP	SLG	OPS	E	Avg.
1997—Florida (N.L.)	1B	6	13	1	3	0	0	0	2	0	0	0	1	0-0	.231	.231	.231	.462	0	1.000
2003—Florida (N.L.)	DH-OF	6	21	4	7	1	0	0	0	3	2	0	0	0-0	.333	.417	.381	.798	0	1.000
World series totals (2 years)		12	34	5	10	1	0	0	2	3	2	0	1	0-0	.294	.351	.324	.675	0	1.000

ALL-STAR GAME RECORD

	G	AB	R	H	2B	3B	HR	RBI	BB	SO	HBP	GDP	SB-CS	Avg.	OBP	SLG	OPS	E	Avg.
All-Star Game totals (1 year)	1	1	1	1	0	0	1	1	0	0	0	0	0-0	1.000	1.000	4.000	5.000	...	...

CONTI, JASON — OF

PERSONAL: Born January 27, 1975, in Pittsburgh, Pa. ... 5-11/180. ... Bats left, throws right. ... Full name: Stanley Jason Conti. ... Name pronounced: CON-tie. ... High school: Seneca Valley (Harmony, Pa.). ... College: Pittsburgh.

TRANSACTIONS/CAREER NOTES: Selected by Arizona Diamondbacks organization in 32nd round of 1996 free-agent draft. ... Loaned by Diamondbacks organization to Texas Rangers organization (April 1-September 14, 1998). ... Traded by Diamondbacks with P Nick Bierbrodt to Tampa Bay Devil Rays for P Albie Lopez and C Mike DiFelice (July 25, 2001). ... Traded by Devil Rays to Milwaukee Brewers for C Javier Valentin (March 24, 2003). ... Signed as a free agent by Rangers organization (November 26, 2003).

2004 GAMES PLAYED BY POSITION (MLB): OF—21.

Year Team (League)	Pos.	G	AB	R	H	2B	3B	HR	RBI	BB	SO	HBP	GDP	SB-CS	Avg.	OBP	SLG	OPS	E	Avg.
1996—Lethbridge (Pio.)	OF	63	226	63	83	15	1	4	49	30	29	6	3	30-7	.367	.449	.496	.945	4	.955
1997—South Bend (Mid.)	OF	117	458	78	142	22	10	3	43	45	99	11	10	30-18	.310	.383	.421	.804	5	.981
—High Desert (Calif.)	OF	14	59	15	21	5	1	2	8	10	12	1	0	1-2	.356	.457	.576	1.033	5	.853
1998—Tulsa (Texas)	OF	130	530	125	167	31	12	15	67	63	96	9	5	19-13	.315	.396	.504	.899	5	.976
1999—Tucson (PCL)	OF	133	520	100	151	23	8	9	57	55	89	5	4	22-7	.290	.360	.417	.777	8	.974
2000—Tucson (PCL)	OF	93	383	75	117	20	5	11	57	23	57	5	6	11-3	.305	.349	.470	.819	10	.951
—Arizona (N.L.)	OF	47	91	11	21	4	3	1	15	7	30	1	2	3-0	.231	.293	.374	.667	1	.983
2001—Tucson (PCL)	OF	92	362	68	120	23	6	9	52	33	54	12	2	2-5	.331	.402	.503	.905	2	.991
—Arizona (N.L.)	OF	5	4	1	1	0	0	0	0	1	2	0	0	0-0	.250	.400	.250	.650	0	...
—Durham (Int'l)	OF	38	157	24	48	12	0	5	18	9	31	1	0	3-1	.306	.347	.478	.825	1	.987
2002—Tampa Bay (A.L.)	OF	78	222	26	57	15	2	3	21	18	55	1	5	4-2	.257	.315	.383	.698	6	.966
2003—Indianapolis (Int'l)	OF-DH	121	456	57	113	17	3	10	40	24	120	8	6	13-8	.248	.295	.364	.659	7	.976

Year	Team (League)	Pos.	G	AB	R	H	2B	3B	HR	RBI	BB	SO	HBP	GDP	SB-CS	Avg.	OBP	SLG	OPS	E	Avg.
	— Milwaukee (N.L.)	OF	30	48	3	11	2	0	2	7	2	18	0	1	0-1	.229	.255	.396	.651	3	.909
2004	— Texas (A.L.)	OF	22	55	6	10	3	0	4	5	19	0	0	0-2	.182	.250	.236	.486	0	1.000
	— Oklahoma (PCL)	OF-DH	104	421	63	138	26	5	8	61	33	84	5	8	5-1	.328	.381	.470	.851	5	.979
	American League totals (2 years)		100	277	32	67	18	2	3	25	23	74	1	5	4-4	.242	.302	.354	.656	6	.973
	National League totals (3 years)		82	143	15	33	6	3	3	22	10	50	1	3	3-1	.231	.284	.378	.661	4	.956
	Major League totals (5 years)		182	420	47	100	24	5	6	47	33	124	2	8	7-5	.238	.296	.362	.658	10	.968

CONTRERAS, JOSE — P

PERSONAL: Born December 6, 1971, in Havana, Cuba. ... 6-4/224. ... Throws right, bats right.
TRANSACTIONS/CAREER NOTES: Signed as a free agent by New York Yankees (February 6, 2003). ... On disabled list (June 7-August 24, 2003); included rehabilitation assignment to Tampa. ... Traded by Yankees with cash to Chicago White Sox for P Esteban Loaiza (July 31, 2003).
CAREER HITTING: 0-for-11 (.000), 0 R, 0 2B, 0 3B, 0 HR, 0 RBI.

Year	Team (League)	W	L	Pct.	ERA	WHIP	G	GS	CG	ShO	Hld.	Sv.-Opp.	IP	H	R	ER	HR	BB-IBB	SO	Avg.
2003	— Columbus (Int'l)	2	0	1.000	1.20	0.80	3	3	0	0	...	0-...	15.0	10	2	2	1	2-0	18	.189
	— Trenton (East.)	0	0	...	0.00	1.80	1	1	0	0	...	0-...	1.2	1	0	0	0	2-0	3	.167
	— Tampa (FSL)	0	0	...	4.50	1.75	1	1	0	0	...	0-...	4.0	4	2	2	0	3-0	5	.286
	— Staten Island (NY-P)	0	0	...	0.00	0.29	1	1	0	0	...	0-...	7.0	2	0	0	0	0-0	15	.087
	— New York (A.L.)	7	2	.778	3.30	1.15	18	9	0	0	1	0-1	71.0	52	27	26	4	30-1	72	.202
2004	— Columbus (Int'l)	2	0	1.000	3.29	1.17	2	2	0	0	...	0-...	13.2	11	5	5	2	5-0	19	.216
	— New York (A.L.)	8	5	.615	5.64	1.41	18	18	0	0	0	0-0	95.2	93	66	60	22	42-1	82	.250
	— Chicago (A.L.)	5	4	.556	5.30	1.54	13	13	0	0	0	0-0	74.2	73	48	44	9	42-0	68	.256
	Major League totals (2 years)	20	11	.645	4.85	1.38	49	40	0	0	1	0-1	241.1	218	141	130	35	114-2	222	.239

CHAMPIONSHIP SERIES RECORD

Year	Team (League)	W	L	Pct.	ERA	WHIP	G	GS	CG	ShO	Hld.	Sv.-Opp.	IP	H	R	ER	HR	BB-IBB	SO	Avg.
2003	— New York (A.L.)	0	1	.000	5.79	1.71	4	0	0	0	2	0-1	4.2	6	3	3	0	2-0	7	.316

WORLD SERIES RECORD

Year	Team (League)	W	L	Pct.	ERA	WHIP	G	GS	CG	ShO	Hld.	Sv.-Opp.	IP	H	R	ER	HR	BB-IBB	SO	Avg.
2003	— New York (A.L.)	0	1	.000	5.68	1.58	4	0	0	0	0	0-0	6.1	5	4	4	0	5-0	10	.227

COOK, AARON — P

PERSONAL: Born February 8, 1979, in Ft. Campbell, Ky. ... 6-3/205. ... Throws right, bats right. ... Full name: Aaron Lane Cook. ... High school: Hamilton (Ohio).
TRANSACTIONS/CAREER NOTES: Selected by Colorado Rockies organization in second round of 1997 free-agent draft. ... On disabled list (August 8, 2004-remainder of season).
CAREER HITTING: 10-for-74 (.135), 4 R, 0 2B, 0 3B, 0 HR, 5 RBI.

Year	Team (League)	W	L	Pct.	ERA	WHIP	G	GS	CG	ShO	Hld.	Sv.-Opp.	IP	H	R	ER	HR	BB-IBB	SO	Avg.
1997	— Ariz. Rockies (Ariz.)	1	3	.250	3.13	1.41	9	8	0	0	...	0-...	46.0	48	27	16	1	17-0	35	.261
1998	— Portland (N'west)	5	8	.385	4.88	1.59	15	15	1	0	...	0-...	79.1	87	50	43	4	39-0	38	.275
1999	— Asheville (S. Atl.)	4	12	.250	6.44	1.64	25	24	2	0	...	0-...	121.2	157	99	87	17	42-0	73	.310
2000	— Asheville (S. Atl.)	10	7	.588	2.96	1.07	21	21	4	2	...	0-...	142.2	130	54	47	10	23-0	118	.241
	— Salem (Caro.)	1	6	.143	5.44	1.49	7	7	1	0	...	0-...	43.0	52	33	26	4	12-0	37	.297
2001	— Salem (Caro.)	11	11	.500	3.08	1.26	27	27	0	0	...	0-...	155.0	157	73	53	4	38-0	122	.263
2002	— Carolina (Southern)	7	2	.778	1.42	0.97	14	14	2	2	...	0-...	95.0	73	24	15	4	19-0	58	.213
	— Colo. Springs (PCL)	4	4	.500	3.78	1.32	10	10	1	0	...	0-0	64.1	67	40	27	6	18-0	32	.264
	— Colorado (N.L.)	2	1	.667	4.54	1.51	5	5	0	0	1	0-0	35.2	41	18	18	4	13-0	14	.295
2003	— Colo. Springs (PCL)	1	1	.500	2.25	0.90	2	2	1	0	...	0-0	16.0	10	4	4	2	4-0	12	.175
	— Colorado (N.L.)	4	6	.400	6.02	1.75	43	16	1	0	1	0-0	124.0	160	89	83	8	57-7	43	.317
2004	— Colo. Springs (PCL)	3	1	.750	2.74	0.91	7	7	1	1	...	0-0	46.0	34	15	14	1	8-0	25	.206
	— Colorado (N.L.)	6	4	.600	4.28	1.56	16	16	1	0	0	0-0	96.2	112	47	46	7	39-5	40	.294
	Major League totals (3 years)	12	11	.522	5.16	1.65	68	37	2	0	2	0-0	256.1	313	154	147	19	109-12	97	.306

COOPER, BRIAN — P

PERSONAL: Born August 19, 1974, in Hollywood, Calif. ... 6-1/185. ... Throws right, bats right. ... Full name: Brian John Cooper. ... High school: Glendora (Calif.). ... College: USC.
TRANSACTIONS/CAREER NOTES: Selected by Philadelphia Phillies organization in 39th round of 1994 free-agent draft; did not sign. ... Selected by California Angels organization in fourth round of 1995 free-agent draft. ... Angels franchise renamed Anaheim Angels for 1997 season. ... Traded by Angels to Toronto Blue Jays for DH/1B Brad Fullmer (January 17, 2002). ... Released by Blue Jays (September 30, 2002). ... Signed by Chicago White Sox organization (January 27, 2003). ... Signed as a free agent by San Francisco Giants organization (December 6, 2003).
CAREER HITTING: 0-for-7 (.000), 0 R, 0 2B, 0 3B, 0 HR, 0 RBI.

Year	Team (League)	W	L	Pct.	ERA	WHIP	G	GS	CG	ShO	Hld.	Sv.-Opp.	IP	H	R	ER	HR	BB-IBB	SO	Avg.
1995	— Boise (N'west)	3	2	.600	3.92	1.32	13	11	0	0	...	1-...	62.0	60	31	27	5	22-1	66	.260
1996	— Lake Elsinore (Calif.)	7	9	.438	4.21	1.33	26	23	1	1	...	0-...	162.1	177	100	76	17	39-0	155	.277
1997	— Lake Elsinore (Calif.)	7	3	.700	3.54	1.18	17	17	1	0	...	0-...	117.0	111	56	46	7	27-0	104	.246
1998	— Midland (Texas)	8	10	.444	7.13	1.69	32	24	5	0	...	1-...	161.2	215	138	128	35	59-1	141	.320
1999	— Erie (East.)	10	5	.667	3.30	1.11	22	22	6	0	...	0-...	158.0	146	61	58	17	29-0	143	.246
	— Edmonton (PCL)	2	1	.667	3.77	1.29	5	5	0	0	...	0-...	31.0	30	17	13	0	10-0	32	.256
	— Anaheim (A.L.)	1	1	.500	4.88	1.48	5	5	0	0	0	0-0	27.2	23	15	15	3	18-0	15	.228
2000	— Edmonton (PCL)	3	7	.300	7.23	1.72	11	11	1	0	...	0-...	61.0	87	51	49	12	18-0	37	.331
	— Anaheim (A.L.)	4	8	.333	5.90	1.61	15	15	1	1	0	0-0	87.0	105	66	57	18	35-1	36	.300
	— Lake Elsinore (Calif.)	0	0	...	0.00	0.86	1	1	0	0	...	0-...	7.0	4	1	0	0	2-0	3	.167
2001	— Salt Lake (PCL)	12	8	.600	4.63	1.38	28	28	1	0	...	0-...	173.0	181	98	89	26	58-0	109	.273
	— Anaheim (A.L.)	0	1	.000	2.63	1.02	7	1	0	0	0	0-0	13.2	10	5	4	2	4-0	7	.200
2002	— Syracuse (Int'l)	9	9	.500	5.09	1.43	27	25	1	0	...	0-...	155.2	176	98	88	19	46-1	71	.289
	— Toronto (A.L.)	0	1	.000	14.04	2.16	2	2	0	0	0	0-0	8.1	14	13	13	5	4-0	3	.400
2003	— Charlotte (Int'l)	15	9	.625	3.98	1.30	28	28	2	0	...	0-...	174.1	195	91	77	18	35-2	106	.286
2004	— San Francisco (N.L.)	0	2	.000	8.78	1.50	5	2	0	0	0	0-0	13.1	15	13	13	4	5-1	7	.288
	— Fresno (PCL)	0	0	...	2.08	1.15	4	4	0	0	...	0-...	21.2	16	5	5	3	6-0	15	.205
	American League totals (4 years)	5	11	.313	5.86	1.56	29	23	1	1	0	0-0	136.2	152	99	89	28	61-1	61	.284
	National League totals (1 year)	0	2	.000	8.78	1.50	5	2	0	0	0	0-0	13.1	15	13	13	4	5-1	7	.288
	Major League totals (5 years)	5	13	.278	6.12	1.55	34	25	1	1	0	0-0	150.0	167	112	102	32	66-2	68	.284

C

CORA, ALEX — 2B

PERSONAL: Born October 18, 1975, in Caguas, Puerto Rico. ... 6-0/180. ... Bats left, throws right. ... Full name: Jose Alexander Cora. ... High school: Bautista (Caguas, Puerto Rico). ... College: Miami (Fla.). ... Brother of Joey Cora, second baseman with four major league teams (1987-98), and coach, Chicago White Sox.

TRANSACTIONS/CAREER NOTES: Selected by Minnesota Twins organization in 12th round of 1993 free-agent draft; did not sign. ... Selected by Los Angeles Dodgers organization in third round of 1996 free-agent draft. ... On disabled list (March 25-June 27, 1999); included rehabilitation assignment to Albuquerque.

2004 GAMES PLAYED BY POSITION (MLB): 2B—138.

Year	Team (League)	Pos.	G	AB	R	H	2B	3B	HR	RBI	BB	SO	HBP	GDP	SB-CS	Avg.	OBP	SLG	OPS	E	Avg.
1996—	Vero Beach (FSL)	SS-OF	61	214	26	55	5	4	0	26	12	36	3	1	5-5	.257	.306	.318	.623	16	.940
1997—	San Antonio (Texas)	SS	127	448	52	105	20	4	3	48	25	60	3	17	12-9	.234	.279	.317	.596	20	.968
1998—	Albuquerque (PCL)	2B-SS	81	299	42	79	17	5	5	45	15	38	3	1	10-7	.264	.303	.405	.708	18	.957
	— Los Angeles (N.L.)	SS-2B	29	33	1	4	0	1	0	0	2	8	1	0	0-0	.121	.194	.182	.376	2	.965
1999—	Albuquerque (PCL)	SS-2B-DH	80	302	51	93	11	7	4	37	12	37	8	8	9-5	.308	.348	.430	.778	12	.968
	— Los Angeles (N.L.)	SS-2B	11	30	2	5	1	0	0	3	0	4	1	1	0-0	.167	.194	.200	.394	2	.943
2000—	Albuquerque (PCL)	SS	30	110	18	41	8	3	0	20	7	10	2	1	5-3	.373	.417	.500	.917	7	.959
	— Los Angeles (N.L.)	SS-2B	109	353	39	84	18	6	4	32	26	53	7	6	4-1	.238	.302	.357	.658	12	.973
2001—	Los Angeles (N.L.)	SS-2B	134	405	38	88	18	3	4	29	31	58	8	16	0-2	.217	.285	.306	.591	20	.962
2002—	Los Angeles (N.L.)	SS-2B	115	258	37	75	14	4	5	28	26	38	7	3	7-2	.291	.371	.434	.805	7	.977
2003—	Los Angeles (N.L.)	2B-SS	148	477	39	119	24	3	4	34	16	59	10	5	4-2	.249	.287	.338	.625	15	.979
2004—	Los Angeles (N.L.)	2B	138	405	47	107	9	4	10	47	47	41	18	9	3-4	.264	.364	.380	.745	8	.987
	Major League totals (7 years)		684	1961	203	482	84	21	27	173	148	261	52	40	18-11	.246	.314	.351	.666	66	.975

DIVISION SERIES RECORD

Year	Team (League)	Pos.	G	AB	R	H	2B	3B	HR	RBI	BB	SO	HBP	GDP	SB-CS	Avg.	OBP	SLG	OPS	E	Avg.
2004—	Los Angeles (N.L.)	2B	4	15	1	2	0	1	0	1	0	3	1	2	0-0	.133	.188	.267	.454	0	1.000

CORCORAN, ROY — P

PERSONAL: Born May 11, 1980, in Baton Rouge, La. ... 5-10/170. ... Throws right, bats right. ... Full name: Roy Elliot Corcoran. ... High school: Silliman Institute (Clinton, Louisiana). ... College: LSU.

TRANSACTIONS/CAREER NOTES: Signed as a non-drafted free agent by Montreal Expos organization (June 15, 2001).

CAREER HITTING: 0-for-1 (.000), 0 R, 0 2B, 0 3B, 0 HR, 0 RBI.

Year	Team (League)	W	L	Pct.	ERA	WHIP	G	GS	CG	ShO	Hld.	Sv.-Opp.	IP	H	R	ER	HR	BB-IBB	SO	Avg.
2001—	Jupiter (FSL)	0	0	...	0.00	1.00	1	0	0	0	...	0-...	2.0	0	0	0	0	2-0	0	.000
	— GC Expos (GCL)	2	0	1.000	1.56	0.81	13	0	0	0	...	2-...	17.1	12	4	3	2	2-0	21	.185
2002—	Clinton (Midw.)	3	4	.429	4.16	1.33	48	1	0	0	...	11-...	80.0	82	51	37	5	24-1	106	.253
2003—	Brevard County (FSL)	5	3	.625	1.91	0.91	28	0	0	0	...	12-...	33.0	19	8	7	1	11-1	35	.171
	— Harrisburg (Eastern)	1	1	.500	0.38	0.89	14	0	0	0	...	3-...	23.2	14	4	1	0	7-1	26	.167
	— Montreal (N.L.)	0	0	...	1.23	1.36	5	0	0	0	0	0-0	7.1	7	2	1	0	3-0	2	.250
	— Edmonton (PCL)	0	0	...	0.00	0.00	2	0	0	0	0	0-0	2.0	0	0	0	0	0-0	1	.000
2004—	Montreal (N.L.)	0	0	...	6.75	2.25	5	0	0	0	0	0-0	5.1	7	4	4	0	5-0	4	.304
	— Edmonton (PCL)	6	1	.857	3.05	1.42	30	0	0	0	...	5-...	44.1	39	16	15	0	24-1	35	.245
	Major League totals (2 years)	0	0	...	3.55	1.74	10	0	0	0	0	0-0	12.2	14	6	5	0	8-0	6	.275

CORDERO, CHAD — P

PERSONAL: Born March 18, 1982, in Upland, Calif. ... 6-0/198. ... Throws right, bats right. ... Full name: Chad Patrick Cordero. ... High school: Don Lugo (Chino, Calif.). ... College: Cal State Fullerton.

TRANSACTIONS/CAREER NOTES: Selected by San Diego Padres organization in 26th round of 2000 free-agent draft; did not sign. ... Selected by Montreal Expos organization in first round (20th pick overall) of 2003 free-agent draft. ... Expos franchise moved to Washington, D.C., for 2005 season.

CAREER HITTING: 0-for-2 (.000), 0 R, 0 2B, 0 3B, 0 HR, 0 RBI.

Year	Team (League)	W	L	Pct.	ERA	WHIP	G	GS	CG	ShO	Hld.	Sv.-Opp.	IP	H	R	ER	HR	BB-IBB	SO	Avg.
2003—	Brevard County (FSL)	1	1	.500	2.05	1.03	19	0	0	0	...	6-...	26.1	17	8	6	1	10-0	17	.198
	— Montreal (N.L.)	1	0	1.000	1.64	0.64	12	0	0	0	1	1-1	11.0	4	2	2	1	3-1	12	.111
2004—	Montreal (N.L.)	7	3	.700	2.94	1.34	69	0	0	0	8	14-18	82.2	68	28	27	8	43-4	83	.222
	Major League totals (2 years)	8	3	.727	2.79	1.26	81	0	0	0	9	15-19	93.2	72	30	29	9	46-5	95	.210

CORDERO, FRANCISCO — P

PERSONAL: Born May 11, 1975, in Santo Domingo, Dominican Republic. ... 6-2/235. ... Throws right, bats right. ... Full name: Francisco Javier Cordero. ... Name pronounced: cor-DAIR-oh. ... High school: Colegio Luz de Arroyo Hondo (Dominican Republic).

TRANSACTIONS/CAREER NOTES: Signed as a non-drafted free agent by Detroit Tigers organization (June 18, 1994). ... Traded by Tigers with Ps Justin Thompson and Alan Webb, OF Gabe Kapler, C Bill Haselman and 2B Frank Catalanotto to Texas Rangers for OF Juan Gonzalez, P Danny Patterson and C Gregg Zaun (November 2, 1999). ... On disabled list (March 23-June 19 and June 26, 2001-remainder of season); included rehabilitation assignment to Oklahoma. ... On disabled list (June 25-July 27, 2002); included rehabilitation assignment to Oklahoma.

CAREER HITTING: 0-for-1 (.000), 0 R, 0 2B, 0 3B, 0 HR, 0 RBI.

Year	Team (League)	W	L	Pct.	ERA	WHIP	G	GS	CG	ShO	Hld.	Sv.-Opp.	IP	H	R	ER	HR	BB-IBB	SO	Avg.
1994—	Dominican Tigers (DSL)	4	3	.571	3.90	1.53	12	12	0	0	...	0-...	60.0	65	47	26	0	27-...	36	...
1995—	Fayetteville (S. Atl.)	0	3	.000	6.30	1.90	4	4	0	0	...	0-...	20.0	26	16	14	1	12-0	19	.342
	— Jamestown (N.Y.-Penn.)	4	7	.364	5.22	1.51	15	14	0	0	...	0-...	88.0	96	62	51	3	37-0	54	.282
1996—	Fayetteville (S. Atl.)	0	0	...	2.57	1.14	2	1	0	0	...	0-...	7.0	2	2	2	0	6-0	7	.095
	— Jamestown (N.Y.-Penn.)	0	0	...	0.82	0.64	2	2	0	0	...	0-...	11.0	5	1	1	0	2-0	10	.135
1997—	West. Mich. (Mid.)	6	1	.857	0.99	0.94	50	0	0	0	...	35-...	54.1	36	13	6	2	15-2	67	.193
1998—	Jacksonville (Southern)	1	1	.500	4.86	1.68	17	0	0	0	...	8-...	16.2	19	12	9	1	9-0	18	.284
1999—	Jacksonville (Southern)	4	1	.800	1.38	1.09	47	0	0	0	...	27-...	52.1	35	9	8	3	22-0	58	.183
	— Detroit (A.L.)	2	2	.500	3.32	1.95	20	0	0	0	6	0-0	19.0	19	7	7	2	18-2	19	.284
2000—	Texas (A.L.)	1	2	.333	5.35	1.75	56	0	0	0	4	0-3	77.1	87	51	46	11	48-3	49	.285
	— Oklahoma (PCL)	0	0	...	4.15	2.31	3	0	0	0	...	1-...	4.1	7	3	2	0	3-0	5	.350
2001—	Oklahoma (PCL)	0	1	.000	0.59	0.72	12	0	0	0	...	6-...	15.1	8	2	1	0	3-0	20	.148
	— Texas (A.L.)	0	1	.000	3.86	2.14	3	0	0	0	1	0-0	2.1	3	1	1	0	2-1	1	.300
2002—	Texas (A.L.)	2	0	1.000	1.79	1.01	39	0	0	0	1	10-12	45.1	33	12	9	4	13-1	41	.204
	— Oklahoma (PCL)	0	2	.000	5.84	1.78	11	1	0	0	...	2-...	12.1	15	14	8	2	7-1	21	.278
2003—	Texas (A.L.)	5	8	.385	2.94	1.31	73	0	0	0	18	15-25	82.2	70	33	27	4	38-6	90	.230
2004—	Texas (A.L.)	3	4	.429	2.13	1.28	67	0	0	0	0	49-54	71.2	60	19	17	1	32-2	79	.226
	Major League totals (6 years)	13	17	.433	3.23	1.42	258	0	0	0	30	74-94	298.1	272	123	107	20	151-15	279	.244

C

CORDERO, WIL — 1B

PERSONAL: Born October 3, 1971, in Mayaguez, Puerto Rico. ... 6-2/232. ... Bats right, throws right. ... Full name: Wilfredo Nieva Cordero. ... Name pronounced: cor-DARE-oh. ... High school: Centro de Servicios Education de Mayaguez (Puerto Rico).

TRANSACTIONS/CAREER NOTES: Signed as a non-drafted free agent by Montreal Expos organization (May 24, 1988). ... Traded by Expos with P Bryan Eversgerd to Boston Red Sox for Ps Rheal Cormier and Shayne Bennett and 1B Ryan McGuire (January 10, 1996). ... On disabled list (May 21-August 12, 1996); included rehabilitation assignments to GCL Red Sox and Pawtucket. ... Released by Red Sox (September 28, 1997). ... Signed by Chicago White Sox (March 23, 1998). ... Signed as a free agent by Cleveland Indians (February 3, 1999). ... On disabled list (June 9-September 8, 1999); included rehabilitation assignment to Akron. ... Signed as a free agent by Pittsburgh Pirates (December 14, 1999). ... Traded by Pirates to Indians for OF Alex Ramirez and IF Enrique Wilson (July 28, 2000). ... On suspended list (September 19-23, 2000). ... On disabled list (June 11-26, 2001). ... Released by Indians (April 29, 2002). ... Signed by Expos (May 12, 2002). ... On disabled list (August 1-16, 2002). ... Signed as a free agent by Florida Marlins (February 6, 2004). ... On disabled list (May 17-September 7, 2004); included rehabilitation assignment to Jupiter.

2004 GAMES PLAYED BY POSITION (MLB): 1B—13, OF—3.

Year Team (League)	Pos.	G	AB	R	H	2B	3B	HR	RBI	BB	SO	HBP	GDP	SB-CS	Avg.	OBP	SLG	OPS	E	Avg.
1988—Jamestown (N.Y.-Penn.) ...	SS	52	190	18	49	3	0	2	22	15	44	4	2	3-3	.258	.322	.305	.628	31	.886
1989—W.P. Beach (FSL)	SS	78	289	37	80	12	2	6	29	33	58	3	6	2-5	.277	.355	.394	.749	29	.922
—Jacksonville (Sou.)	SS	39	121	9	26	6	1	3	17	12	33	0	3	1-2	.215	.284	.355	.639	7	.957
1990—Jacksonville (Sou.)	SS	131	444	63	104	18	4	7	40	56	122	5	5	9-4	.234	.326	.340	.666	41	.928
1991—Indianapolis (A.A.)	SS	98	360	48	94	16	4	11	52	26	89	3	4	9-3	.261	.315	.419	.734	27	.943
1992—Indianapolis (A.A.)	SS	52	204	32	64	11	1	6	27	24	54	0	7	6-7	.314	.384	.466	.850	12	.949
—Montreal (N.L.)	SS-2B	45	126	17	38	4	1	2	8	9	31	1	3	0-0	.302	.353	.397	.750	8	.947
1993—Montreal (N.L.)	SS-3B	138	475	56	118	32	2	10	58	34	60	7	12	12-3	.248	.308	.387	.695	36	.937
1994—Montreal (N.L.)	SS	110	415	65	122	30	3	15	63	41	62	6	8	16-3	.294	.363	.489	.853	22	.952
1995—Montreal (N.L.)	SS-OF	131	514	64	147	35	2	10	49	36	88	9	11	9-5	.286	.341	.420	.761	22	.953
1996—Boston (A.L.) 2B-DH-1B	59	198	29	57	14	0	3	37	11	31	2	8	2-1	.288	.330	.404	.734	10	.951
—GC Red Sox (GCL)	DH-2B	3	10	1	3	0	0	1	3	0	2	0	1	0-0	.300	.273	.600	.873	0	1.000
—Pawtucket (Int'l)	2B-DH	4	10	2	3	1	0	1	2	2	3	0	1	0-0	.300	.417	.700	1.117	0	1.000
1997—Boston (A.L.) OF-DH-2B	140	570	82	160	26	3	18	72	31	122	4	11	1-3	.281	.320	.432	.752	2	.992
1998—Birmingham (Sou.)	1B-DH	11	35	6	10	2	0	2	11	7	3	0	1	0-0	.286	.405	.514	.919	1	.989
—Chicago (A.L.)	1B-OF	96	341	58	91	18	2	13	49	22	66	3	7	2-1	.267	.314	.446	.759	7	.991
1999—Cleveland (A.L.)	OF-DH	54	194	35	58	15	0	8	32	15	37	6	7	2-0	.299	.364	.500	.864	1	.981
—Akron (East.)	OF-DH	3	11	2	4	2	0	0	0	0	3	1	1	0-0	.364	.417	.545	.962	0	...
2000—Pittsburgh (N.L.)	OF-DH	89	348	46	98	24	3	16	51	25	58	4	11	1-2	.282	.336	.506	.842	2	.983
—Cleveland (A.L.)	OF	38	148	18	39	11	2	0	17	7	18	3	7	0-0	.264	.310	.365	.675	0	1.000
2001—Cleveland (A.L.) OF-1B-DH	89	268	30	67	11	1	4	21	22	50	4	8	0-0	.250	.313	.343	.656	2	.992
2002—Cleveland (A.L.)	OF-1B	6	18	1	4	0	0	0	1	0	3	0	1	0-0	.222	.222	.222	.444	0	1.000
—Montreal (N.L.) OF-1B-DH	66	143	21	39	9	0	6	29	17	26	2	3	2-0	.273	.349	.462	.811	2	.983
2003—Montreal (N.L.) 1B-DH-OF	130	436	57	121	27	0	16	71	49	90	4	11	1-1	.278	.354	.450	.803	5	.996
2004—Jupiter (FSL)	DH-1B	3	8	3	4	0	0	2	5	1	1	0	0	0-0	.500	.556	1.250	1.806	0	1.000
—Florida (N.L.)	1B-OF	27	66	6	13	3	0	1	6	3	19	2	2	1-0	.197	.250	.288	.538	1	.991
American League totals (7 years)		482	1737	253	476	95	8	46	229	108	327	22	49	7-5	.274	.322	.417	.740	22	.987
National League totals (8 years)		736	2523	332	696	164	11	76	335	214	434	35	61	42-14	.276	.339	.440	.779	98	.969
Major League totals (13 years)		1218	4260	585	1172	259	19	122	564	322	761	57	110	49-19	.275	.332	.431	.763	120	.975

DIVISION SERIES RECORD

Year Team (League)	Pos.	G	AB	R	H	2B	3B	HR	RBI	BB	SO	HBP	GDP	SB-CS	Avg.	OBP	SLG	OPS	E	Avg.
1999—Cleveland (A.L.)	DH-OF	3	9	3	5	0	0	1	2	1	2	0	0	0-0	.556	.600	.889	1.489	0	1.000
2001—Cleveland (A.L.)	OF	1	1	0	0	0	0	0	0	0	0	0	0	0-0	.000	.000	.000	.000	0	1.000
Division series totals (2 years)		4	10	3	5	0	0	1	2	1	2	0	0	0-0	.500	.545	.800	1.345	0	1.000

ALL-STAR GAME RECORD

		G	AB	R	H	2B	3B	HR	RBI	BB	SO	HBP	GDP	SB-CS	Avg.	OBP	SLG	OPS	E	Avg.
All-Star Game totals (1 year)		1	2	0	0	0	0	0	0	0	0	1	0	0-0	.000	.000	.000	.000	0	1.000

COREY, MARK — P

PERSONAL: Born November 16, 1974, in Coudersport, Pa. ... 6-3/225. ... Throws right, bats right. ... Full name: Mark Franklin Corey. ... High school: Austin Area (Austin, Pa.). ... College: Edinboro (Pa.).

TRANSACTIONS/CAREER NOTES: Selected by Cincinnati Reds organization in fourth round of 1995 free-agent draft. ... Traded by Reds to New York Mets for IF Ralph Milliard (February 4, 1999). ... On disabled list (June 27-July 12, 2002); included rehabilitation assignment to Norfolk. ... Traded by Mets with OFs Jay Payton and Robert Stratton to Colorado Rockies for P John Thomson and OF Mark Little (July 31, 2002). ... Signed as a free agent by Pittsburgh Pirates organization (December 25, 2002). ... Refused minor league assignment and became a free agent (October 14, 2004).

CAREER HITTING: 0-for-3 (.000), 0 R, 0 2B, 0 3B, 0 HR, 0 RBI.

Year Team (League)	W	L	Pct.	ERA	WHIP	G	GS	CG	ShO	Hld.	Sv.-Opp.	IP	H	R	ER	HR	BB-IBB	SO	Avg.
1995—Princeton (Appalachian)	1	1	.500	3.68	1.23	4	3	0	0	...	0-...	14.2	12	7	6	1	6-0	8	.218
1996—			Did not play.																
1997—Char., W.Va. (SAL)	8	13	.381	4.57	1.55	26	26	1	0	...	0-...	136.0	169	87	69	7	42-3	97	.311
1998—Burlington (Midw.)	12	6	.667	2.44	1.15	20	20	6	2	...	0-...	140.0	125	55	38	9	36-0	109	.236
—Chattanooga (Southern)	0	4	.000	8.20	1.82	6	6	0	0	...	0-...	26.1	32	25	24	6	16-1	6	.302
—Indianapolis (Int'l)	0	1	.000	4.50	1.17	1	1	0	0	...	0-...	6.0	4	3	3	1	3-0	2	.200
1999—Binghamton (Eastern)	7	13	.350	5.40	1.54	29	27	0	0	...	0-...	155.0	175	108	93	18	64-0	111	.282
2000—Binghamton (Eastern)	0	0	...	1.05	1.01	14	2	0	0	...	0-...	25.2	15	5	3	0	11-0	19	.170
—Norfolk (Int'l)	3	7	.300	6.79	1.71	20	11	0	0	...	1-...	63.2	80	52	48	11	29-1	43	.307
2001—Binghamton (Eastern)	1	2	.333	1.80	1.00	25	0	0	0	17-...		35.0	23	10	7	1	12-0	50	.189
—Norfolk (Int'l)	8	2	.800	1.47	1.25	28	0	0	0	10-...		36.2	24	7	6	1	22-0	42	.197
—New York (N.L.)	0	0	...	16.20	4.80	2	0	0	0	0-0		1.2	5	3	3	0	3-1	3	.500
2002—Norfolk (Int'l)	3	1	.750	1.03	0.80	25	0	0	0	7-...		26.1	14	3	3	1	7-1	37	.157
—New York (N.L.)	0	3	.000	4.50	1.80	12	0	0	0	0-0		10.0	10	7	5	2	8-1	9	.250
—St. Lucie (Fla. St.)	0	0	...	0.00	0.00	1	0	0	0	0-...		2.0	0	0	0	0	0-0	3	.000
—Colorado (N.L.)	0	0	...	12.00	2.50	14	0	0	0	1	0-0	12.0	22	16	16	7	8-1	12	.400
2003—Nashville (PCL)	1	3	.250	4.34	1.20	46	0	0	0	30-...		45.2	37	23	22	5	18-2	63	.214
—Pittsburgh (N.L.)	1	2	.333	5.34	1.32	22	0	0	0	0-0		30.1	29	19	18	2	11-1	27	.252
2004—Nashville (PCL)	1	4	.200	4.42	1.42	34	0	0	0	16-...		38.2	40	21	19	4	15-1	39	.265
—Pittsburgh (N.L.)	1	2	.333	4.54	1.63	31	0	0	0	0-1		35.2	39	20	18	3	19-3	28	.275
Major League totals (4 years)	2	7	.222	6.02	1.72	81	0	0	0	7	0-1	89.2	105	65	60	14	49-7	79	.290

CORMIER, LANCE   P

PERSONAL: Born August 19, 1980, in Lafayette, La. ... 6-1/192. ... Throws right, bats right. ... Full name: Lance Robert Cormier. ... High school: Lafayette (La.). ... College: Alabama.

TRANSACTIONS/CAREER NOTES: Selected by Cincinnati Reds organization in 40th round of 1998 free-agent draft; did not sign. ... Selected by Houston Astros organization in 10th round of 2001 free-agent draft; did not sign. ... Selected by Arizona Diamondbacks organization in fourth round of 2002 free-agent draft.

CAREER HITTING: 2-for-8 (.250), 1 R, 1 2B, 0 3B, 0 HR, 1 RBI.

Year — Team (League)	W	L	Pct.	ERA	WHIP	G	GS	CG	ShO	Hld.	Sv.-Opp.	IP	H	R	ER	HR	BB-IBB	SO	Avg.
2002— Yakima (N'west)	0	0	...	27.00	4.00	1	0	0	0	...	0-...	1.0	4	4	3	0	0-0	3	.500
— South Bend (Mid.)	3	0	1.000	2.93	1.12	11	3	0	0	...	1-...	27.2	29	9	9	1	2-0	17	.259
2003— Lancaster (Calif.)	6	5	.545	3.82	1.25	15	15	0	0	...	0-...	94.1	102	55	40	6	16-1	59	.280
— Tucson (PCL)	1	1	.500	2.60	1.12	5	4	0	0	...	0-...	27.2	26	10	8	1	5-0	11	.260
— El Paso (Texas)	2	3	.400	6.10	1.96	9	8	0	0	...	0-...	41.1	59	33	28	3	22-0	26	.337
2004— El Paso (Texas)	2	3	.400	2.29	1.32	10	8	0	0	...	0-...	63.0	66	19	16	3	17-0	58	.277
— Tucson (PCL)	3	3	.500	2.68	1.33	8	8	2	1	...	0-...	50.1	50	17	15	0	17-1	37	.260
— Arizona (N.L.)	1	4	.200	8.14	1.92	17	5	0	0	2	0-0	45.1	62	42	41	13	25-2	24	.333
Major League totals (1 year)	1	4	.200	8.14	1.92	17	5	0	0	2	0-0	45.1	62	42	41	13	25-2	24	.333

CORMIER, RHEAL   P

PERSONAL: Born April 23, 1967, in Moncton, New Brunswick. ... 5-10/195. ... Throws left, bats left. ... Full name: Rheal Paul Cormier. ... Name pronounced: ree-AL cor-MEE-ay. ... High school: Polyvalente Louis J. Robichaud. ... Junior college: Rhode Island Community College.

TRANSACTIONS/CAREER NOTES: Selected by St. Louis Cardinals organization in sixth round of 1988 free-agent draft. ... On disabled list (August 12-September 7, 1993). ... On disabled list (April 28-May 13 and May 21-August 3, 1994); included rehabilitation assignments to Arkansas and Louisville. ... Traded by Cardinals with OF Mark Whiten to Boston Red Sox for 3B Scott Cooper, P Cory Bailey and a player to be named (April 8, 1995). ... Traded by Red Sox with 1B Ryan McGuire and P Shayne Bennett to Montreal Expos for SS Wil Cordero and P Bryan Eversgerd (Jauary 10, 1996). ... On disabled list (August 26-September 10, 1996). ... Signed as a free agent by Cleveland Indians organization (December 18, 1997). ... Signed as a free agent by Red Sox organization (January 5, 1999). ... On suspended list (May 7-10, 1999). ... Signed as a free agent by Philadelphia Phillies (November 29, 2000). ... On disabled list (August 10-29, 2001); included rehabilitation assignment to Reading.

CAREER HITTING: 36-for-191 (.188), 15 R, 4 2B, 1 3B, 0 HR, 12 RBI.

Year — Team (League)	W	L	Pct.	ERA	WHIP	G	GS	CG	ShO	Hld.	Sv.-Opp.	IP	H	R	ER	HR	BB-IBB	SO	Avg.
1989— St. Pete. (FSL)	12	7	.632	2.23	1.03	26	26	4	1	...	0-...	169.2	141	63	42	9	33-2	122	.225
1990— Arkansas (Texas)	5	12	.294	5.04	1.34	22	21	3	1	...	0-...	121.1	133	81	68	9	30-2	102	.273
— Louisville (A.A.)	1	1	.500	2.25	0.88	4	4	0	0	...	0-...	24.0	18	8	6	1	3-0	9	.202
1991— Louisville (A.A.)	7	9	.438	4.23	1.34	21	21	3	3	...	0-...	127.2	140	64	60	5	31-1	74	.286
— St. Louis (N.L.)	4	5	.444	4.12	1.21	11	10	2	0	...	0-0	67.2	74	35	31	5	8-1	38	.277
1992— St. Louis (N.L.)	10	10	.500	3.68	1.22	31	30	3	0	...	0-0	186.0	194	83	76	15	33-2	117	.269
— Louisville (A.A.)	0	1	.000	6.75	2.00	1	1	0	0	...	0-...	4.0	8	4	3	0	0-0	1	.400
1993— St. Louis (N.L.)	7	6	.538	4.33	1.31	38	21	1	0	...	0-0	145.1	163	80	70	18	27-3	75	.284
1994— St. Louis (N.L.)	3	2	.600	5.45	1.18	7	7	0	0	...	0-0	39.2	40	24	24	6	7-0	26	.256
— Arkansas (Texas)	1	0	1.000	1.93	0.96	2	2	0	0	...	0-...	9.1	9	2	2	0	0-0	11	.257
— Louisville (A.A.)	1	2	.333	4.50	1.32	3	3	1	0	...	0-...	22.0	21	11	11	3	8-1	13	.250
1995— Boston (A.L.)	7	5	.583	4.07	1.41	48	12	0	0	9	0-2	115.0	131	60	52	12	31-2	69	.294
1996— Montreal (N.L.)	7	10	.412	4.17	1.29	33	27	1	1	0	0-0	159.2	165	80	74	16	41-3	100	.270
1997— Montreal (N.L.)	0	1	.000	33.75	3.75	1	1	0	0	0	0-0	1.1	4	5	5	1	1-0	0	.500
1998— Akron (East.)	0	0	...	6.52	1.76	3	3	0	0	...	0-...	9.2	15	7	7	3	2-0	6	.366
1999— Boston (A.L.)	2	0	1.000	3.69	1.25	60	0	0	0	15	0-3	63.1	61	34	26	4	18-2	39	.246
2000— Boston (A.L.)	3	3	.500	4.61	1.33	64	0	0	0	9	0-2	68.1	74	40	35	7	17-2	43	.275
2001— Philadelphia (N.L.)	5	6	.455	4.21	1.29	60	0	0	0	12	1-6	51.1	49	26	24	5	17-4	37	.247
— Reading (East.)	0	0	...	0.00	0.50	1	1	0	0	...	0-...	2.0	0	0	0	0	1-0	2	.000
2002— Philadelphia (N.L.)	5	6	.455	5.25	1.55	54	0	0	0	9	0-3	60.0	61	38	35	6	32-6	49	.266
2003— Philadelphia (N.L.)	8	0	1.000	1.70	0.93	65	0	0	0	14	1-4	84.2	54	18	16	4	25-2	67	.182
2004— Philadelphia (N.L.)	4	5	.444	3.56	1.19	84	0	0	0	28	0-7	81.0	70	32	32	7	26-6	46	.237
American League totals (3 years)	12	8	.600	4.12	1.35	172	12	0	0	33	0-7	246.2	266	134	113	23	66-6	151	.276
National League totals (10 years)	53	51	.510	3.97	1.24	384	96	7	1	63	2-20	876.2	874	421	387	83	217-27	555	.260
Major League totals (13 years)	65	59	.524	4.01	1.27	556	108	7	1	96	2-27	1123.1	1140	555	500	106	283-33	706	.264

DIVISION SERIES RECORD

Year — Team (League)	W	L	Pct.	ERA	WHIP	G	GS	CG	ShO	Hld.	Sv.-Opp.	IP	H	R	ER	HR	BB-IBB	SO	Avg.
1995— Boston (A.L.)	0	0	...	13.50	4.50	2	0	0	0	0	0-0	.2	2	1	1	0	1-0	2	.500
1999— Boston (A.L.)	0	0	...	0.00	0.75	2	0	0	0	0	0-0	4.0	2	0	0	0	1-0	4	.154
Division series totals (2 years)	0	0	...	1.93	1.29	4	0	0	0	0	0-0	4.2	4	1	1	0	2-0	6	.235

CHAMPIONSHIP SERIES RECORD

Year — Team (League)	W	L	Pct.	ERA	WHIP	G	GS	CG	ShO	Hld.	Sv.-Opp.	IP	H	R	ER	HR	BB-IBB	SO	Avg.
1999— Boston (A.L.)	0	0	...	0.00	1.64	4	0	0	0	0	0-0	3.2	3	0	0	0	3-1	4	.200

CORNEJO, NATE   P

PERSONAL: Born September 24, 1979, in Wellington, Kan. ... 6-5/245. ... Throws right, bats right. ... Full name: Nathan J. Cornejo. ... Name pronounced: cor-NAY-ho. ... High school: Wellington (Kan.). ... Son of Mardie Cornejo, pitcher with New York Mets (1978).

TRANSACTIONS/CAREER NOTES: Selected by Detroit Tigers organization in supplemental round ("sandwich pick" between first and second round, 34th pick overall) of free-agent draft (June 2, 1998); pick received as part of compensation for Arizona Diamondbacks signing Type A free-agent P Willie Blair. ... On disabled list (May 3, 2004-remainder of season); included rehabilitation assignment to Toledo.

CAREER HITTING: 0-for-4 (.000), 0 R, 0 2B, 0 3B, 0 HR, 0 RBI.

Year — Team (League)	W	L	Pct.	ERA	WHIP	G	GS	CG	ShO	Hld.	Sv.-Opp.	IP	H	R	ER	HR	BB-IBB	SO	Avg.
1998— GC Tigers (GCL)	1	0	1.000	1.26	0.98	5	0	0	0	...	1-...	14.1	12	2	2	0	2-0	9	.218
1999— West. Mich. (Mid.)	9	11	.450	3.71	1.37	28	28	4	1	...	0-...	174.2	173	87	72	4	67-0	125	.265
2000— Lakeland (Fla. St.)	5	5	.500	3.04	1.27	12	12	1	0	...	0-...	77.0	67	37	26	5	31-0	60	.234
— Jacksonville (Southern)	5	7	.417	4.61	1.46	16	16	0	0	...	0-...	91.2	91	52	47	6	43-1	60	.271
2001— Erie (East.)	12	3	.800	2.68	1.19	19	19	3	1	...	0-...	124.1	107	47	37	12	41-0	105	.229
— Toledo (International)	4	0	1.000	2.12	1.04	4	4	0	0	...	0-...	29.2	24	8	7	1	7-0	22	.229

C

Year	Team (League)	W	L	Pct.	ERA	WHIP	G	GS	CG	ShO	Hld.	Sv.-Opp.	IP	H	R	ER	HR	BB-IBB	SO	Avg.
	—Detroit (A.L.)	4	4	.500	7.38	2.13	10	10	0	0	0	0-0	42.2	63	38	35	10	28-4	22	.344
2002—	Toledo (International)	9	8	.529	4.42	1.47	21	20	1	0	...	0-...	132.1	163	72	65	11	31-1	86	.307
	—Detroit (A.L.)	1	5	.167	5.04	1.62	9	9	1	0	0	0-0	50.0	63	33	28	6	18-0	23	.303
2003—	Detroit (A.L.)	6	17	.261	4.67	1.51	32	32	2	0	0	0-0	194.2	236	111	101	18	58-8	46	.307
2004—	Detroit (A.L.)	1	3	.250	8.42	2.06	5	5	0	0	0	0-0	25.2	42	25	24	4	11-1	12	.375
	—Toledo (International)	0	0	...	4.15	1.50	4	3	0	0	0	0-...	8.2	11	4	4	2	2-0	8	.314
	Major League totals (4 years)	12	29	.293	5.41	1.66	56	56	3	0	0	0-0	313.0	404	207	188	38	115-13	103	.318

CORREIA, KEVIN — P

PERSONAL: Born August 24, 1980, in San Diego, Calif. ... 6-3/200. ... Throws right, bats right. ... Full name: Kevin John Correia. ... College: Cal-Poly SLO.

TRANSACTIONS/CAREER NOTES: Selected by St. Louis Cardinals organization in 23rd round of 2001 free-agent draft; did not sign. ... Selected by San Francisco Giants organization in fourth round of 2002 free-agent draft.

CAREER HITTING: 3-for-16 (.188), 2 R, 1 2B, 0 3B, 0 HR, 2 RBI.

Year	Team (League)	W	L	Pct.	ERA	WHIP	G	GS	CG	ShO	Hld.	Sv.-Opp.	IP	H	R	ER	HR	BB-IBB	SO	Avg.
2002—	Salem-Keizer (N'west)	2	2	.500	4.54	1.35	10	8	0	0	...	0-...	37.2	37	20	19	1	14-0	31	.257
2003—	Norwich (East.)	6	6	.500	3.65	1.27	16	14	0	0	...	0-...	86.1	80	38	35	3	30-0	73	.248
	—Fresno (PCL)	1	0	1.000	2.84	0.95	3	3	0	0	...	0-...	19.0	16	8	6	3	2-0	23	.222
	—San Francisco (N.L.)	3	1	.750	3.66	1.50	10	7	0	0	0	0-0	39.1	41	16	16	6	18-1	28	.275
2004—	Fresno (PCL)	3	7	.300	4.53	1.45	29	16	0	0	...	0-...	105.1	118	61	53	12	35-3	70	.284
	—San Francisco (N.L.)	0	1	.000	8.05	1.84	12	1	0	0	0	0-0	19.0	25	20	17	3	10-0	14	.333
	Major League totals (2 years)	3	2	.600	5.09	1.61	22	8	0	0	0	0-0	58.1	66	36	33	9	28-1	42	.295

C

COTA, HUMBERTO — C

PERSONAL: Born February 7, 1979, in San Luis Rio Colorado, Mexico. ... 6-0/210. ... Bats right, throws right. ... Full name: Humberto Figueroa Cota. ... Name pronounced: KOH-ta. ... High school: Preparatoria Abierta.

TRANSACTIONS/CAREER NOTES: Signed as a non-drafted free agent by Atlanta Braves organization (December 22, 1995). ... Loaned by Braves organization to Mexico City Tigers of the Mexican League (June 23-September 23, 1996); did not play. ... Released by Braves (January 27, 1997). ... Signed by Tampa Bay Devil Rays organization (May 22, 1997). ... Traded by Devil Rays with C Joe Oliver to Pittsburgh Pirates for OF Jose Guillen and P Jeff Sparks (July 23, 1999). ... On disabled list (May 28-August 2, 2004); included rehabilitation assignment to Nashville.

2004 GAMES PLAYED BY POSITION (MLB): C—24.

Year	Team (League)	Pos.	G	AB	R	H	2B	3B	HR	RBI	BB	SO	HBP	GDP	SB-CS	Avg.	OBP	SLG	OPS	E	Avg.
																			FIELDING	
1996—	M.C. Tigers (Mex.)		Did not play.																		
1997—	GC Devil Rays (GCL)	C	44	133	14	32	6	1	2	20	17	27	3	1	3-1	.241	.333	.346	.679	5	.985
	—Hudson Valley (NY-Penn.) .	C	3	9	0	2	0	0	0	2	0	1	0	0	0-0	.222	.222	.222	.444	0	1.000
1998—	Princeton (Appal.)	C	67	245	48	76	13	4	15	61	32	59	6	3	4-4	.310	.399	.580	.978	12	.973
1999—	Char., S.C. (SAL)	C-1B	85	336	42	94	21	1	9	61	20	51	2	...	1-1	.280	.320	.429	.748	7	.986
	—Hickory (S. Atl.)	C	37	133	28	36	11	2	2	20	21	20	0	...	3-1	.271	.365	.429	.794	2	.992
2000—	Altoona (East.)	C-1B	112	429	49	112	20	1	8	44	21	80	3	8	6-4	.261	.297	.368	.665	17	.973
2001—	Nashville (PCL)	C	111	377	61	112	22	2	14	72	25	74	8	8	7-2	.297	.351	.477	.829	8	.986
	—Pittsburgh (N.L.)	C	7	9	0	2	0	0	0	1	0	5	0	0	0-0	.222	.222	.222	.444	0	1.000
2002—	Nashville (PCL)	C-1B	118	404	51	108	27	1	9	54	31	106	5	11	5-8	.267	.321	.406	.727	4	.994
	—Pittsburgh (N.L.)	C	7	17	2	5	1	0	0	0	1	4	0	0	0-0	.294	.333	.353	.686	0	1.000
2003—	Pittsburgh (N.L.)	C	10	16	1	4	1	0	0	1	1	5	0	0	0-0	.250	.294	.313	.607	0	1.000
	—Nashville (PCL)	C-DH	62	200	23	41	9	0	8	27	20	59	2	4	2-0	.205	.284	.370	.654	0	1.000
2004—	Nashville (PCL)	C-DH	8	27	4	7	0	0	1	2	3	7	0	3	0-0	.259	.333	.370	.704	0	1.000
	—Pittsburgh (N.L.)	C	36	66	10	15	1	1	5	8	3	20	1	1	0-0	.227	.271	.500	.771	1	.991
	Major League totals (4 years)		60	108	13	26	3	1	5	10	5	34	1	1	0-0	.241	.281	.426	.707	1	.994

COTTS, NEAL — P

PERSONAL: Born March 25, 1980, in Belleville, Ill. ... 6-2/200. ... Throws left, bats left. ... Full name: Neal James Cotts. ... High school: Lebanon (Ill). ... College: Illinois State.

TRANSACTIONS/CAREER NOTES: Selected by Oakland Athletics organization in second round of 2001 free-agent draft. ... Traded by Athletics with OF Dayton Holt to Chicago White Sox (December 16, 2002), completing deal in which White Sox traded Ps Keith Foulke and Joe Valentine and C Mark Johnson to Athletics for P Billy Koch and two players to be named (December 3, 2002).

CAREER HITTING: 1-for-1 (1.000), 0 R, 1 2B, 0 3B, 0 HR, 0 RBI.

Year	Team (League)	W	L	Pct.	ERA	WHIP	G	GS	CG	ShO	Hld.	Sv.-Opp.	IP	H	R	ER	HR	BB-IBB	SO	Avg.
2001—	Vancouver (N'west)	1	0	1.000	3.09	1.17	9	7	0	0	...	0-...	35.0	28	14	12	2	13-0	44	.215
	—Visalia (Calif.)	3	2	.600	2.32	1.35	7	7	0	0	...	0-...	31.0	27	14	8	0	15-0	34	.225
2002—	Modesto (Calif.)	12	6	.667	4.12	1.53	28	28	0	0	...	0-...	137.2	123	72	63	5	87-0	178	.239
2003—	Chicago (A.L.)	1	1	.500	8.10	2.40	4	4	0	0	0	0-0	13.1	15	12	12	1	17-0	10	.294
	—Birmingham (Southern)	9	7	.563	2.16	1.14	21	21	0	0	...	0-...	108.1	67	32	26	2	56-1	133	.178
2004—	Chicago (A.L.)	4	4	.500	5.65	1.39	56	1	0	0	4	0-2	65.1	61	45	41	13	30-2	58	.247
	Major League totals (2 years)	5	5	.500	6.06	1.56	60	5	0	0	4	0-2	78.2	76	57	53	14	47-2	68	.255

COUNSELL, CRAIG — SS

PERSONAL: Born August 21, 1970, in South Bend, Ind. ... 6-0/184. ... Bats left, throws right. ... Full name: Craig John Counsell. ... High school: Whitefish Bay (Milwaukee). ... College: Notre Dame.

TRANSACTIONS/CAREER NOTES: Selected by Colorado Rockies organization in 11th round of 1992 free-agent draft. ... On disabled list (May 1-July 15 and July 18-September 3, 1996). ... Traded by Rockies to Florida Marlins for P Mark Hutton (July 27, 1997). ... On disabled list (August 4, 1998-remainder of season). ... Traded by Marlins to Los Angeles Dodgers for a player to be named (June 15, 1999); Marlins acquired P Ryan Moskau to complete deal (July 15, 1999). ... Released by Dodgers (March 15, 2000). ... Signed by Arizona Diamondbacks organization (March 20, 2000). ... On disabled list (August 9, 2002-remainder of season). ... On disabled list (May 7-July 7, 2003); included rehabilitation assignment to Tucson. ... Traded by Diamondbacks with 2B Junior Spivey, 1B Lyle Overbay, C Chad Moeller and Ps Chris Capuano and Jorge de la Rosa to Milwaukee Brewers for 1B Richie Sexson, P Shane Nance and a player to be named (December 1, 2003); Diamondbacks acquired OF Noochie Varner to complete deal (December 15, 2003).

2004 GAMES PLAYED BY POSITION (MLB): SS—129, 3B—1.

Year Team (League)	Pos.	G	AB	R	H	2B	3B	HR	RBI	BB	SO	HBP	GDP	SB-CS	Avg.	OBP	SLG	OPS	E	Avg.
												BATTING							FIELDING	
1992— Bend (N'west)	2B-SS	18	61	11	15	6	1	0	8	9	10	1	2	1-2	.246	.352	.377	.729	2	.967
1993— Central Valley (Cal.)	SS	131	471	79	132	26	3	5	59	95	68	3	8	14-8	.280	.401	.380	.781	35	.944
1994— New Haven (East.)	2B-SS	83	300	47	84	20	1	5	37	37	32	5	6	4-1	.280	.366	.403	.770	27	.931
1995— Colo. Springs (PCL)	SS	118	399	60	112	22	6	5	53	34	47	2	12	10-2	.281	.336	.404	.739	30	.950
— Colorado (N.L.)	SS	3	1	0	0	0	0	0	0	1	0	0	0	0-0	.000	.500	.000	.500	0	1.000
1996— Colo. Springs (PCL) 2B-3B-SS		25	75	17	18	3	0	2	10	24	7	0	2	4-3	.240	.424	.360	.784	4	.961
1997— Colo. Springs (PCL)	2B-SS	96	376	77	126	31	6	5	63	45	38	6	6	12-2	.335	.409	.489	.898	9	.981
— Colorado (N.L.)		1	0	0	0	0	0	0	0	0	0	0	0	0-0	...	.000	...	...		.989
— Florida (N.L.)	2B	51	164	20	49	9	2	1	16	18	17	3	5	1-1	.299	.376	.396	.773	3	.989
1998— Florida (N.L.)	2B	107	335	43	84	19	5	4	40	51	47	4	5	3-0	.251	.356	.373	.729	5	.991
1999— Florida (N.L.)	2B	37	66	4	10	1	0	0	2	5	10	0	1	0-0	.152	.211	.167	.378	1	.980
— Los Angeles (N.L.)	2B	50	108	20	28	6	0	0	9	9	14	0	1	1-0	.259	.311	.315	.626	1	.993
2000— Tucson (PCL) 2B-3B-SS		50	198	45	69	14	3	3	27	22	20	1	1	4-1	.348	.413	.495	.908	4	.981
— Arizona (N.L.) 2B-3B-SS		67	152	23	48	8	1	2	11	20	18	2	4	3-3	.316	.400	.421	.821	6	.957
2001— Arizona (N.L.)	S-2-3-1B	141	458	76	126	22	3	4	38	61	76	2	9	6-8	.275	.359	.362	.721	8	.985
2002— Arizona (N.L.)	3B-SS-2B	112	436	63	123	22	1	2	51	45	52	1	10	7-5	.282	.348	.351	.699	8	.979
2003— Tucson (PCL) 2B-SS-3B		5	23	8	10	2	0	0	2	1	3	0	0	0-0	.435	.458	.522	.980	1	.963
— Arizona (N.L.)	3-SS-2-1	89	303	40	71	6	3	3	21	41	32	2	4	11-4	.234	.328	.304	.631	3	.989
2004— Milwaukee (N.L.)	SS-3B	140	473	59	114	19	5	2	23	59	88	5	5	17-4	.241	.330	.315	.645	9	.983
Major League totals (9 years)		798	2496	348	653	112	20	18	211	310	354	19	44	49-25	.262	.345	.344	.689	44	.984

DIVISION SERIES RECORD

Year Team (League)	Pos.	G	AB	R	H	2B	3B	HR	RBI	BB	SO	HBP	GDP	SB-CS	Avg.	OBP	SLG	OPS	E	Avg.
1997— Florida (N.L.)	2B	3	5	0	2	1	0	0	1	1	0	0	0	0-0	.400	.500	.600	1.100	1	.875
2001— Arizona (N.L.)	2B	5	16	2	3	0	0	1	3	2	2	0	1	0-0	.188	.278	.375	.653	0	1.000
Division series totals (2 years)		8	21	2	5	1	0	1	4	3	2	0	1	0-0	.238	.333	.429	.762	1	.963

CHAMPIONSHIP SERIES RECORD

Year Team (League)	Pos.	G	AB	R	H	2B	3B	HR	RBI	BB	SO	HBP	GDP	SB-CS	Avg.	OBP	SLG	OPS	E	Avg.
1997— Florida (N.L.)	2B	5	14	0	6	0	0	0	3	3	0	0	0	0-0	.429	.529	.429	.958	1	.941
2001— Arizona (N.L.)	2B-SS	5	21	5	8	3	0	0	4	0	3	0	0	1-0	.381	.381	.524	.905	0	1.000
Champ. series totals (2 years)		10	35	5	14	3	0	0	6	3	6	0	0	1-0	.400	.447	.486	.933	1	.972

WORLD SERIES RECORD

Year Team (League)	Pos.	G	AB	R	H	2B	3B	HR	RBI	BB	SO	HBP	GDP	SB-CS	Avg.	OBP	SLG	OPS	E	Avg.
1997— Florida (N.L.)	2B	7	22	4	4	1	0	0	2	6	5	0	0	1-0	.182	.345	.227	.572	1	.971
2001— Arizona (N.L.)	2B	6	24	1	2	0	0	1	1	0	7	1	0	0-0	.083	.120	.208	.328	0	1.000
World series totals (2 years)		13	46	5	6	1	0	1	3	6	12	1	0	1-0	.130	.241	.217	.458	1	.984

CRAIN, JESSE — P

PERSONAL: Born July 5, 1981, in Toronto, Ontario. ... 6-1/205. ... Throws right, bats right. ... Full name: Jesse Alan Crain. ... High school: Fairview (Colo.). ... College: Houston.
TRANSACTIONS/CAREER NOTES: Selected by Minnesota Twins organization in second round of 2002 free-agent draft.
CAREER HITTING: 0-for-0 (.000), 0 R, 0 2B, 0 3B, 0 HR, 0 RBI.

Year Team (League)	W	L	Pct.	ERA	WHIP	G	GS	CG	ShO	Hld.	Sv.-Opp.	IP	H	R	ER	HR	BB-IBB	SO	Avg.
2002— Elizabethton (Appal.)	2	1	.667	0.57	0.70	9	0	0	0	...	2-...	15.2	4	2	1	0	7-3	18	.082
— Quad City (Midw.)	1	1	.500	1.50	0.83	9	0	0	0	...	1-...	12.0	6	3	2	0	4-0	11	.154
2003— Fort Myers (Fla. St.)	2	1	.667	2.84	0.79	10	0	0	0	...	0-...	19.0	10	6	6	0	5-0	25	.154
— New Britain (East.)	1	1	.500	0.69	0.59	22	0	0	0	...	9-...	39.0	13	4	3	0	10-1	56	.099
— Rochester (Int'l)	3	1	.750	3.12	1.31	23	0	0	0	...	10-...	26.0	24	10	9	0	10-1	33	.245
2004— Rochester (Int'l)	3	2	.600	2.49	1.09	41	0	0	0	...	19-...	50.2	38	20	14	5	17-2	64	.208
— Minnesota (A.L.)	3	0	1.000	2.00	1.07	22	0	0	0	2	0-1	27.0	17	6	6	2	12-1	14	.179
Major League totals (1 year)	3	0	1.000	2.00	1.07	22	0	0	0	2	0-1	27.0	17	6	6	2	12-1	14	.179

DIVISION SERIES RECORD

Year Team (League)	W	L	Pct.	ERA	WHIP	G	GS	CG	ShO	Hld.	Sv.-Opp.	IP	H	R	ER	HR	BB-IBB	SO	Avg.
2004— Minnesota (A.L.)	0	0	...	0.00	3.00	1	0	0	0	0	0-0	.1	1	0	0	0	0-0	0	.500

CRAWFORD, CARL — OF

PERSONAL: Born August 5, 1981, in Houston, Texas. ... 6-2/219. ... Bats left, throws left. ... Full name: Carl Demonte Crawford. ... High school: Jefferson Davis (Houston).
TRANSACTIONS/CAREER NOTES: Selected by Tampa Bay Devil Rays organization in second round of 1999 free-agent draft. ... On suspended list (July 19-22, 2003).
2004 GAMES PLAYED BY POSITION (MLB): OF—145, DH—5.

Year Team (League)	Pos.	G	AB	R	H	2B	3B	HR	RBI	BB	SO	HBP	GDP	SB-CS	Avg.	OBP	SLG	OPS	E	Avg.
												BATTING							FIELDING	
1999— Princeton (Appal.)	OF	60	260	62	83	14	4	0	25	13	47	1	5	17-2	.319	.350	.404	.754	8	.934
2000— Char., S.C. (SAL)	OF	135	564	99	170	21	11	6	57	32	102	3	1	55-9	.301	.342	.410	.751	8	.968
2001— Orlando (South.)	OF	132	537	64	147	24	3	4	51	36	90	4	3	36-20	.274	.323	.352	.675	6	.981
2002— Durham (Int'l)	OF	85	353	59	105	17	9	7	52	20	69	2	5	26-8	.297	.335	.456	.791	1	.994
— Tampa Bay (A.L.)	OF	63	259	23	67	11	6	2	30	9	41	3	0	9-5	.259	.290	.371	.661	1	.994
2003— Tampa Bay (A.L.)	OF-DH	151	630	80	177	18	9	5	54	26	102	1	5	* 55-10	.281	.309	.362	.671	3	.992
2004— Tampa Bay (A.L.)	OF-DH	152	626	104	185	26	* 19	11	55	35	81	1	2	* 59-15	.296	.331	.450	.781	2	.994
Major League totals (3 years)		366	1515	207	429	55	34	18	139	70	224	5	7	123-30	.283	.315	.400	.715	6	.993

ALL-STAR GAME RECORD

	G	AB	R	H	2B	3B	HR	RBI	BB	SO	HBP	GDP	SB-CS	Avg.	OBP	SLG	OPS	E	Avg.
All-Star Game totals (1 year)	1	2	0	0	0	0	0	0	0	1	0	0	0-0	.000	.000	.000	.000	0	1.000

CREDE, JOE — 3B

PERSONAL: Born April 26, 1978, in Jefferson City, Mo. ... 6-1/200. ... Bats right, throws right. ... Full name: Joseph Crede. ... Name pronounced: CREE-dee. ... High school: Fatima (Westphalia, Mo.).
TRANSACTIONS/CAREER NOTES: Selected by Chicago White Sox organization in fifth round of 1996 free-agent draft.
HONORS: Named Carolina League Most Valuable Player (1998). ... Named Southern League Most Valuable Player (2000).
2004 GAMES PLAYED BY POSITION (MLB): 3B—144.

Year	Team (League)	Pos.	G	AB	R	H	2B	3B	HR	RBI	BB	SO	HBP	GDP	SB-CS	Avg.	OBP	SLG	OPS	E	Avg.
1996— GC Whi. Sox (GCL)	3B	56	221	30	66	17	1	4	32	9	41	2	8	1-1	.299	.326	.439	.765	25	.857
1997— Hickory (S. Atl.)	3B	113	402	45	109	25	0	5	62	24	83	5	6	3-1	.271	.319	.371	.689	33	.905
1998— Win.-Salem (Car.)	3B	137	492	92	155	32	3	20	88	53	98	12	10	9-7	.315	.387	.514	.902	30	.929
1999— Birmingham (Sou.)	3B	74	291	37	73	14	1	4	42	22	47	1	15	2-6	.251	.303	.347	.650	20	.910
2000— Birmingham (Sou.)	3B	138	533	84	163	35	0	21	94	56	111	15	18	3-4	.306	.384	.490	.874	19	.942
—Chicago (A.L.)	3B-DH	7	14	2	5	1	0	0	3	0	3	0	0	0-0	.357	.333	.429	.762	1	.933
2001— Charlotte (Int'l)	3B	124	463	67	128	34	1	17	65	46	88	7	5	2-1	.276	.349	.464	.813	20	.946
—Chicago (A.L.)	3B	17	50	1	11	1	1	0	7	3	11	1	1	1-0	.220	.273	.280	.553	0	1.000
2002— Charlotte (Int'l)	3B	95	359	57	112	21	0	24	65	26	48	4	8	0-1	.312	.359	.571	.930	15	.944
—Chicago (A.L.)	3B	53	200	28	57	10	0	12	35	8	40	0	1	0-2	.285	.311	.515	.826	8	.938
2003— Chicago (A.L.)	3B	151	536	68	140	31	2	19	75	32	75	6	11	1-1	.261	.308	.433	.741	14	.964
2004— Chicago (A.L.)	3B	144	490	67	117	25	0	21	69	34	81	10	14	1-2	.239	.299	.418	.717	12	.965
Major League totals (5 years)		372	1290	166	330	68	3	52	189	77	210	17	27	3-5	.256	.304	.434	.738	35	.962

CRESPO, CESAR — SS/2B

PERSONAL: Born May 23, 1979, in Rio Piedras, Puerto Rico. ... 5-11/170. ... Bats both, throws right. ... Full name: Cesar Antonio Crespo. ... Name pronounced: cress-po. ... High school: Notre Dame (Caguas, Puerto Rico). ... Brother of Felipe Crespo, infielder/outfielder with three major league teams (1996-2001).

TRANSACTIONS/CAREER NOTES: Selected by New York Mets organization in third round of 1997 free-agent draft. ... Traded by Mets to Florida Marlins (September 12, 1998), completing deal in which Marlins traded OF Robert Stratton to Mets for a player to be named (March 20, 1998). ... Traded by Marlins with OF Mark Kotsay to San Diego Padres for OF Eric Owens and Ps Matt Clement and Omar Ortiz (March 28, 2001). ... Traded by Padres to Boston Red Sox for IF Luis Cruz (December 16, 2002).

2004 GAMES PLAYED BY POSITION (MLB): SS—27, OF—19, 2B—11.

Year	Team (League)	Pos.	G	AB	R	H	2B	3B	HR	RBI	BB	SO	HBP	GDP	SB-CS	Avg.	OBP	SLG	OPS	E	Avg.
1998— Capital City (SAL)	2B-SS	116	428	61	108	18	4	6	48	44	114	3	6	47-14	.252	.326	.355	.681	27	.948
1999— Brevard County (FSL)	2B	115	427	63	122	17	2	6	40	62	86	1	4	22-8	.286	.376	.377	.753	22	.958
2000— Portland (East.)	2B-SS-OF	134	482	96	124	21	6	9	60	77	118	2	8	41-15	.257	.359	.382	.740	15	.958
2001— Portland (PCL)	2-OF-S-3	78	273	46	71	18	3	8	29	39	66	1	4	23-3	.260	.354	.436	.789	4	.986
—San Diego (N.L.)	2-OF-3-S	55	153	27	32	6	0	4	12	25	50	0	2	6-2	.209	.320	.327	.647	4	.976
2002— Portland (PCL)	2-OF-S-3	92	322	43	83	17	2	9	37	50	78	3	5	21-7	.258	.363	.407	.769	12	.967
—San Diego (N.L.)	OF-2-3-S	25	29	5	5	2	0	0	0	3	6	0	0	3-2	.172	.250	.241	.491	1	.923
2003— Pawtucket (Int'l) O-2-DH-3-S	132	465	69	124	31	3	9	58	40	93	0	14	13-8	.267	.323	.404	.727	15	.958
2004— Boston (A.L.)	SS-OF-2B	52	79	6	13	2	1	0	2	0	20	0	1	2-0	.165	.165	.215	.380	3	.969
—Pawtucket (Int'l)	SS-2B	55	221	30	60	13	3	4	19	21	53	0	2	10-2	.271	.333	.412	.745	9	.965
American League totals (1 year)		52	79	6	13	2	1	0	2	0	20	0	1	2-0	.165	.165	.215	.380	3	.969
National League totals (2 years)		80	182	32	37	8	0	4	12	28	56	0	2	9-4	.203	.310	.313	.623	5	.972
Major League totals (3 years)		132	261	38	50	10	1	4	14	28	76	0	3	11-4	.192	.270	.284	.553	8	.971

CRESSEND, JACK — P

PERSONAL: Born May 13, 1975, in New Orleans, La. ... 6-1/195. ... Throws right, bats right. ... Full name: John Baptiste Cressend. ... High school: Mandeville (La.). ... College: Tulane.

TRANSACTIONS/CAREER NOTES: Signed as a non-drafted free agent by Boston Red Sox organization (July 24, 1996). ... Claimed on waivers by Minnesota Twins (April 22, 1999). ... On disabled list (June 8-September 30, 2002); included rehabilitation assignments to GCL Twins and Fort Myers. ... Claimed on waivers by Cleveland Indians (October 17, 2002).

CAREER HITTING: 0-for-0 (.000), 0 R, 0 2B, 0 3B, 0 HR, 0 RBI.

Year	Team (League)	W	L	Pct.	ERA	WHIP	G	GS	CG	ShO	Hld.	Sv.-Opp.	IP	H	R	ER	HR	BB-IBB	SO	Avg.
1996— Lowell (NY-Penn)	3	2	.600	2.36	1.18	9	8	0	0	...	0-...	45.2	37	15	12	0	17-1	57	.226
1997— Sarasota (Florida State)	8	11	.421	3.80	1.32	28	25	2	1	...	0-...	165.2	163	98	70	15	56-1	149	.252
1998— Trenton (East.)	10	11	.476	4.34	1.49	29	29	1	1	...	0-...	149.1	168	86	72	13	55-0	130	.293
1999— Trenton (East.)	1	0	1.000	7.20	1.73	3	3	0	0	...	0-...	15.0	19	12	12	3	7-0	11	.302
—New Britain (East.)	7	10	.412	4.34	1.39	25	24	2	2	...	0-...	145.0	152	79	70	10	50-0	125	.269
2000— Salt Lake (PCL)	4	4	.500	3.44	1.46	54	1	0	0	...	8-...	86.1	87	40	33	3	39-4	87	.261
—Minnesota (A.L.)	0	0	...	5.27	1.90	11	0	0	0	...	0-0	13.2	20	8	8	0	6-0	6	.364
2001— Edmonton (PCL)	2	2	.500	3.50	1.44	12	0	0	0	...	1-...	18.0	19	12	7	2	7-2	9	.284
—Minnesota (A.L.)	3	2	.600	3.67	1.17	44	0	0	0	5	0-2	56.1	50	24	23	6	16-0	40	.237
2002— Minnesota (A.L.)	0	1	.000	5.91	1.84	23	0	0	0	...	0-0	32.0	40	25	21	6	19-4	22	.305
—GC Twins (GCL)	0	0	...	7.11	1.74	3	3	0	0	...	0-...	6.1	10	7	5	0	1-0	8	.357
—Fort Myers (Fla. St.)	1	0	1.000	3.60	1.20	3	1	0	0	...	0-...	5.0	4	2	2	0	2-0	5	.211
2003— Kinston (Caro.)	0	1	.000	12.46	2.10	2	0	0	0	...	0-...	4.1	9	6	6	1	0-0	4	.429
—Akron (East.)	2	0	1.000	0.00	1.10	8	0	0	0	...	1-...	16.0	15	4	0	0	2-0	9	.234
—Buffalo (Int'l)	1	0	1.000	1.23	0.90	8	0	0	0	...	0-...	14.2	7	2	2	0	6-0	12	.149
—Cleveland (A.L.)	2	1	.667	2.51	1.14	33	0	0	0	5	0-1	43.0	40	12	12	1	9-1	28	.252
2004— Cleveland (A.L.)	0	1	.000	6.32	2.04	11	0	0	0	...	0-0	15.2	22	11	11	4	10-2	8	.333
—Buffalo (Int'l)	10	1	.909	5.13	1.58	24	4	0	0	...	1-...	52.2	73	30	30	7	10-0	41	.333
Major League totals (5 years)	5	5	.500	4.20	1.44	122	0	0	0	12	0-3	160.2	172	80	75	17	60-7	104	.277

CRISP, COCO — OF

PERSONAL: Born November 1, 1979, in Los Angeles, Calif. ... 6-0/185. ... Bats both, throws right. ... Full name: Covelli Loyce Crisp. ... Junior college: Los Angeles Pierce.

TRANSACTIONS/CAREER NOTES: Selected by St. Louis Cardinals organization in seventh round of 1999 free-agent draft. ... Traded by Cardinals to Cleveland Indians (August 6, 2002), completing deal in which Cardinals traded 1B Luis Garcia and a player to be named to Indians for P Chuck Finley (July 19, 2002).

2004 GAMES PLAYED BY POSITION (MLB): OF—128, DH—6.

Year	Team (League)	Pos.	G	AB	R	H	2B	3B	HR	RBI	BB	SO	HBP	GDP	SB-CS	Avg.	OBP	SLG	OPS	E	Avg.
1999— Johnson City (App.)	2B	65	229	55	59	5	4	3	22	44	41	2	0	27-5	.258	.379	.354	.733	24	.912
2000— New Jersey (N.Y.-Penn.) ...	OF-2B	36	134	18	32	5	0	0	14	11	22	1	1	25-3	.239	.301	.276	.577	2	.972
—Peoria (Midw.)	OF	27	98	14	27	9	0	0	7	16	15	0	1	7-3	.276	.377	.367	.745	0	1.000

Year	Team (League)	Pos.	G	AB	R	H	2B	3B	HR	RBI	BB	SO	HBP	GDP	SB-CS	Avg.	OBP	SLG	OPS	E	Avg.
2001—Potomac (Caro.)	OF	139	530	80	162	23	3	11	47	52	64	1	8	39-21	.306	.368	.423	.791	6	.975
2002—New Haven (East.)	OF	89	355	61	107	16	1	9	47	36	56	0	...	26-10	.301	.365	.428	.793	4	.985
—Akron (East.)	OF	7	32	9	13	1	0	1	4	3	3	0	...	4-0	.406	.457	.531	.988	0	1.000
—Cleveland (A.L.)	OF	32	127	16	33	9	2	1	9	11	19	0	0	4-1	.260	.314	.386	.700	1	.988
—Buffalo (Int'l)	OF	4	21	3	5	1	0	0	2	0	2	0	2	1-0	.238	.238	.286	.524	0	1.000
2003—Buffalo (Int'l)	OF	56	225	42	81	19	6	1	24	26	24	5	5	20-8	.360	.434	.511	.945	3	.982
—Cleveland (A.L.)	OF-DH	99	414	55	110	15	6	3	27	23	51	0	4	15-9	.266	.302	.353	.655	1	.995
2004—Cleveland (A.L.)	OF-DH	139	491	78	146	24	2	15	71	36	69	0	8	20-13	.297	.344	.446	.790	4	.986
Major League totals (3 years)		270	1032	149	289	48	10	20	107	70	139	0	12	39-23	.280	.324	.401	.725	6	.990

CROSBY, BOBBY — SS

PERSONAL: Born January 12, 1980, in Lakewood, Calif. ... 6-3/195. ... Bats right, throws right. ... Full name: Robert Edward Crosby. ... High school: La Quinta (Westminster, Calif.). ... College: Cal State Long Beach. ... Son of Ed Crosby, infielder with three major league teams (1970-76).

TRANSACTIONS/CAREER NOTES: Selected by Anaheim Angels organization in 34th round of 1998 free-agent draft; did not sign. ... Selected by Oakland Athletics organization in first round (25th pick overall) of 2001 free-agent draft.

HONORS: Named A.L. Rookie Player of the Year by THE SPORTING NEWS (2004). ... Named A.L. Rookie of the Year by Baseball Writers' Association of America (2004).

2004 GAMES PLAYED BY POSITION (MLB): SS—151.

											BATTING									FIELDING	
Year	Team (League)	Pos.	G	AB	R	H	2B	3B	HR	RBI	BB	SO	HBP	GDP	SB-CS	Avg.	OBP	SLG	OPS	E	Avg.
2001—Modesto (California)	SS	11	38	7	15	5	0	1	3	3	8	0	1	0-0	.395	.439	.605	1.044	4	.889
2002—Modesto (California)	SS	73	280	47	86	17	2	2	38	33	43	7	5	5-0	.307	.393	.404	.796	19	.938
—Midland (Texas)	SS	59	228	31	64	16	0	7	31	19	41	0	9	9-2	.281	.335	.443	.778	13	.952
2003—Sacramento (PCL)	SS-DH	127	465	86	143	32	6	22	90	63	110	7	16	24-4	.308	.395	.544	.939	15	.973
—Oakland (A.L.)	SS-DH	11	12	1	0	0	0	0	0	1	5	1	0	0-0	.000	.143	.000	.143	2	.889
2004—Oakland (A.L.)	SS	151	545	70	130	34	1	22	64	58	141	9	20	7-3	.239	.319	.426	.744	19	.975
Major League totals (2 years)		162	557	71	130	34	1	22	64	59	146	10	20	7-3	.233	.315	.417	.731	21	.973

CROSBY, BUBBA — OF

PERSONAL: Born August 11, 1976, in Houston, Texas. ... 5-11/185. ... Bats left, throws left. ... Full name: Richard Stephen Crosby. ... High school: Bellaire (Texas). ... College: Rice.

TRANSACTIONS/CAREER NOTES: Selected by Los Angeles Dodgers organization in first round (23rd pick overall) in 1998 free-agent draft. ... Traded by Dodgers with P Scott Proctor to New York Yankees for IF Robin Ventura (July 31, 2003).

2004 GAMES PLAYED BY POSITION (MLB): OF—45, DH—2.

											BATTING									FIELDING	
Year	Team (League)	Pos.	G	AB	R	H	2B	3B	HR	RBI	BB	SO	HBP	GDP	SB-CS	Avg.	OBP	SLG	OPS	E	Avg.
1998—San Bern. (Calif.)	OF	56	199	25	43	9	2	0	14	17	38	0	3	3-5	.216	.274	.281	.555	1	.990
1999—San Bern. (Calif.)	OF	96	371	53	110	21	3	1	37	42	71	6	6	19-8	.296	.376	.377	.754	5	.975
2000—Vero Beach (FSL)	OF	73	274	50	73	13	8	8	51	31	41	7	9	27-10	.266	.355	.460	.814	4	.969
—San Bern. (Calif.)		3	12	2	3	0	0	0	2	0	4	0	1	1-0	.250	.250	.250	.500	...	...
2001—Las Vegas (PCL)	OF	13	42	5	9	2	1	0	5	1	8	0	0	1-1	.214	.233	.310	.542	0	1.000
—Jacksonville (Sou.)	OF	107	384	68	116	22	5	6	47	37	60	8	7	22-6	.302	.369	.432	.802	3	.985
2002—Las Vegas (PCL)	OF	73	279	26	73	12	1	9	36	19	47	2	3	3-1	.262	.312	.409	.721	2	.989
—Jacksonville (Sou.)	OF	38	150	14	39	6	2	2	20	11	23	2	2	7-3	.260	.317	.367	.684	0	1.000
2003—Las Vegas (PCL)	OF-DH	76	277	57	100	24	8	12	57	25	47	3	6	8-0	.361	.410	.635	1.046	1	.991
—Los Angeles (N.L.)	OF	9	12	0	1	0	0	0	1	0	3	0	0	0-0	.083	.083	.083	.167	1	.667
—Columbus (Int'l)	OF	16	63	9	19	2	1	2	8	6	12	1	0	3-0	.302	.366	.460	.827	0	1.000
2004—Columbus (Int'l)	OF-DH	33	116	18	32	5	2	1	15	14	26	4	2	3-3	.276	.365	.379	.744	0	1.000
—New York (A.L.)	OF-DH	55	53	8	8	2	0	2	7	2	13	1	0	2-0	.151	.196	.302	.498	1	.973
American League totals (1 year)		55	53	8	8	2	0	2	7	2	13	1	0	2-0	.151	.196	.302	.498	1	.973
National League totals (1 year)		9	12	0	1	0	0	0	1	0	3	0	0	0-0	.083	.083	.083	.167	1	.667
Major League totals (2 years)		64	65	8	9	2	0	2	8	2	16	1	0	2-0	.138	.176	.262	.438	2	.950

DIVISION SERIES RECORD

Year	Team (League)	Pos.	G	AB	R	H	2B	3B	HR	RBI	BB	SO	HBP	GDP	SB-CS	Avg.	OBP	SLG	OPS	E	Avg.
2004—New York (A.L.)	OF	2	0	0	0	0	0	0	0	0	0	0	0	0-0	...	...	...	...	0	...

CHAMPIONSHIP SERIES RECORD

Year	Team (League)	Pos.	G	AB	R	H	2B	3B	HR	RBI	BB	SO	HBP	GDP	SB-CS	Avg.	OBP	SLG	OPS	E	Avg.
2004—New York (A.L.)	OF	1	0	1	0	0	0	0	0	0	0	0	0	0-0	...	...	...	...	0	...

CROWELL, JIM — P

PERSONAL: Born May 14, 1974, in Minneapolis, Minn. ... 6-4/225. ... Throws left, bats right. ... Full name: James Everett Crowell. ... High school: Valparaiso (Ind.). ... College: Indianapolis.

TRANSACTIONS/CAREER NOTES: Signed as a non-drafted free agent by Cleveland Indians organization (June 17, 1995). ... Traded by Indians with Ps Danny Graves and Scott Winchester and IF Damian Jackson to Cincinnati Reds for P John Smiley and IF Jeff Branson (July 31, 1997). ... Released by Reds (July 11, 2000). ... Signed by St. Louis Cardinals organization (July 22, 2000). ... Released by Cardinals (October 12, 2000). ... Re-signed by Cardinals organization (November 16, 2000). ... Released by Cardinals (March 30, 2001). ... Signed by San Diego Padres organization (April 23, 2001). ... Released by Padres (July 2, 2001). ... Contract purchased by Philadelphia Phillies organization from Atlantic City of the independent Atlantic League (August 18, 2002).

CAREER HITTING: 0-for-2 (.000), 0 R, 0 2B, 0 3B, 0 HR, 0 RBI.

Year	Team (League)	W	L	Pct.	ERA	WHIP	G	GS	CG	ShO	Hld.	Sv.-Opp.	IP	H	R	ER	HR	BB-IBB	SO	Avg.
1995—Watertown (N.Y.-Penn.)	5	2	.714	2.86	1.36	12	9	0	0	...	0-...	56.2	50	22	18	1	27-1	48	.237
1996—Columbus (S. Atl.)	7	10	.412	4.14	1.40	28	28	3	0	...	0-...	165.1	163	89	76	16	69-0	104	.264
1997—Kinston (Caro.)	9	4	.692	2.37	1.07	17	17	0	0	...	0-...	114.0	96	41	30	4	26-0	94	.227
—Akron (East.)	1	0	1.000	4.50	1.33	3	3	0	0	...	0-...	18.0	13	12	9	2	11-0	7	.197
—Chattanooga (Southern)	2	1	.667	2.84	1.26	3	3	0	0	...	0-...	19.0	19	6	6	2	5-0	14	.279
—Indianapolis (A.A.)	1	1	.500	2.75	1.37	3	3	1	1	...	0-...	19.2	19	7	6	1	8-0	6	.253
—Cincinnati (N.L.)	0	1	.000	9.95	2.68	2	1	0	0	0	0-0	6.1	12	7	7	2	5-0	3	.414
1998—Chattanooga (Southern)	0	4	.000	8.51	2.26	5	5	0	0	...	0-...	24.1	38	27	23	2	17-0	10	.349
—Char., W.Va. (SAL)	0	4	.000	13.20	2.47	5	5	0	0	...	0-...	15.0	28	23	22	1	9-0	9	.400

Year	Team (League)	W	L	Pct.	ERA	WHIP	G	GS	CG	ShO	Hld.	Sv.-Opp.	IP	H	R	ER	HR	BB-IBB	SO	Avg.
	— Indianapolis (Int'l)	0	0	...	6.75	1.75	1	1	0	0	...	0-...	4.0	7	3	3	0	0-0	2	.368
1999—	Chattanooga (Southern)	10	5	.667	5.10	1.74	27	27	0	0	...	0-...	148.1	173	98	84	12	85-0	80	.293
2000—	Chattanooga (Southern)	0	0	...	5.90	1.97	23	0	0	0	...	0-...	29.0	35	23	19	3	22-2	20	.289
	— Arkansas (Texas)	1	1	.500	5.40	1.60	12	0	0	0	...	1-...	15.0	16	10	9	1	8-1	10	.276
2001—	Portland (PCL)	0	0	...	5.49	1.88	11	2	0	0	...	0-...	19.2	22	15	12	3	15-0	7	.293
	— Mobile (Sou.)	1	0	1.000	2.08	1.38	5	0	0	0	...	0-...	4.1	2	1	1	0	4-0	0	.154
2003—	Scran./W.B. (I.L.)	0	8	.000	4.12	1.60	54	0	0	0	...	9-...	54.2	63	31	25	5	23-5	42	.289
2004—	Philadelphia (N.L.)	0	0	...	3.00	2.00	4	0	0	0	0	0-0	3.0	6	2	1	0	0-0	1	.333
	— Scran./W.B. (I.L.)	7	3	.700	2.40	1.18	48	0	0	0	...	16-...	63.2	61	22	17	6	14-4	44	.250
	Major League totals (2 years)	0	1	.000	7.71	2.46	6	1	0	0	0	0-0	9.1	18	9	8	2	5-0	4	.383

CROZIER, ERIC   1B

PERSONAL: Born August 11, 1978, in Columbus, Ohio. ... 6-4/200. ... Bats left, throws left. ... Full name: Eric Le Roi Crozier. ... High school: Independence (Columbus, Ohio). ... College: Norfolk State.

TRANSACTIONS/CAREER NOTES: Selected by Cleveland Indians organization in 41st round of 2000 free-agent draft. ... Traded by Indians to Toronto Blue Jays for DH Josh Phelps (August 6, 2004).

2004 GAMES PLAYED BY POSITION (MLB): DH—8, 1B—5.

								BATTING											FIELDING	
Year	Team (League)	Pos.	G	AB	R	H	2B	3B	HR	RBI	BB	SO	HBP	GDP	SB-CS	Avg.	OBP	SLG	OPS	E	Avg.
2000—	Mahoning Valley (NY-P)	OF-1B	52	179	31	38	9	0	4	24	30	61	0	3	4-2	.212	.324	.330	.653	3	.984
2001—	Columbus (S. Atl.)	OF-1B	67	221	41	52	9	2	4	19	37	84	1	3	5-3	.235	.346	.348	.695	5	.976
2002—	Kinston (Caro.)	1B-OF	72	258	40	84	16	2	9	55	42	57	4	4	4-3	.326	.423	.508	.931	2	.996
	— Akron (East.)	1B-OF	43	142	19	42	8	1	1	13	21	50	3	0	1-0	.296	.398	.387	.785	1	.997
2003—	Akron (East.)	1B-OF	108	347	52	85	10	3	19	52	51	92	3	4	5-3	.245	.344	.455	.799	12	.986
2004—	Buffalo (Int'l)	1B-OF-DH	84	296	55	88	21	0	20	53	36	67	1	8	5-1	.297	.375	.571	.944	6	.989
	— Syracuse (Int'l)	1B-DH	25	94	12	26	8	0	1	16	16	27	2	2	3-2	.277	.393	.394	.775	4	.983
	— Toronto (A.L.)	DH-1B	14	33	5	5	2	0	2	4	6	19	0	0	0-0	.152	.282	.394	.676	1	.972
	Major League totals (1 year)		14	33	5	5	2	0	2	4	6	19	0	0	0-0	.152	.282	.394	.676	1	.972

CRUCETA, FRANCISCO   P

PERSONAL: Born July 4, 1981, in La Vega, Dominican Republic. ... 6-2/180. ... Throws right, bats right. ... Full name: Francisco Alberto Cruceta.

TRANSACTIONS/CAREER NOTES: Signed as a non-drafted free agent by Los Angeles Dodgers organization (May 20, 1999). ... Traded by Dodgers with Ps Terry Mulholland and Ricardo Rodriguez to Cleveland Indians for P Paul Shuey (July 28, 2002).

CAREER HITTING: 0-for-0 (.000), 0 R, 0 2B, 0 3B, 0 HR, 0 RBI.

Year	Team (League)	W	L	Pct.	ERA	WHIP	G	GS	CG	ShO	Hld.	Sv.-Opp.	IP	H	R	ER	HR	BB-IBB	SO	Avg.
2002—	South Georgia (S.Atl.)	8	5	.615	2.80	1.17	20	20	3	2	...	0-...	112.2	98	42	35	7	34-0	111	.231
	— Kinston (Caro.)	2	0	1.000	2.50	1.41	7	7	0	0	...	0-...	39.2	31	13	11	2	25-1	37	.217
2003—	Akron (East.)	13	9	.591	3.09	1.27	27	25	6	0	...	0-...	163.1	141	70	56	7	66-0	134	.232
2004—	Akron (East.)	4	8	.333	5.28	1.38	15	15	1	0	...	0-...	88.2	89	58	52	11	33-0	45	.261
	— Buffalo (Int'l)	6	5	.545	3.25	1.37	14	14	1	0	...	0-...	83.0	78	35	30	6	36-0	62	.252
	— Cleveland (A.L.)	0	1	.000	9.39	1.83	2	2	0	0	...	0-0	7.2	10	9	8	1	4-0	9	.303
	Major League totals (1 year)	0	1	.000	9.39	1.83	2	2	0	0	0	0-0	7.2	10	9	8	1	4-0	9	.303

CRUZ, DEIVI   SS

PERSONAL: Born November 6, 1972, in Nizao de Bani, Dominican Republic. ... 6-0/207. ... Bats right, throws right. ... Full name: Deivi Garcia Cruz. ... Name pronounced: DAY-vee. ... High school: Liceo Aliro Paulino Nizao (Dominican Republic).

TRANSACTIONS/CAREER NOTES: Signed as a non-drafted free agent by San Francisco Giants organization (April 23, 1993). ... Selected by Los Angeles Dodgers from Giants organization in Rule 5 major league draft (December 9, 1996). ... Traded by Dodgers with OF Juan Hernaiz to Detroit Tigers for 2B Jeff Berblinger (December 9, 1996). ... On disabled list (March 20-April 27, 1998); included rehabilitation assignments to Lakeland and Toledo. ... On disabled list (June 8-July 18, 2001); included rehabilitation assignment to Erie. ... Signed as a free agent by San Diego Padres (January 30, 2002). ... Signed as a free agent by Baltimore Orioles (December 15, 2002). ... Signed as a free agent by Tampa Bay Devil Rays organization (January 7, 2004). ... Released by Devil Rays (March 24, 2004). ... Signed by San Francisco Giants organization (March 30, 2004).

2004 GAMES PLAYED BY POSITION (MLB): SS—104, 2B—2, 3B—1.

								BATTING											FIELDING	
Year	Team (League)	Pos.	G	AB	R	H	2B	3B	HR	RBI	BB	SO	HBP	GDP	SB-CS	Avg.	OBP	SLG	OPS	E	Avg.
1993—	Ariz. Giants (Ariz.)	3B-SS-1B	28	82	8	28	3	0	0	15	4	5	0	3	3-0	.341	.368	.378	.746	2	.972
1994—	Ariz. Giants (Ariz.)	3B-SS	18	53	10	16	8	0	0	5	5	3	1	1	0-1	.302	.367	.453	.819	1	.980
1995—	Burlington (Midw.)	2B-3B-SS	16	58	2	8	1	0	1	9	4	7	0	1	1-1	.138	.194	.207	.400	2	.969
	— Bellingham (N'west)	2B-3B	62	223	32	66	17	0	3	28	19	21	0	5	6-3	.296	.348	.413	.761	10	.947
1996—	Burlington (Midw.)	SS-3B	127	517	72	152	27	2	9	64	35	49	4	20	12-5	.294	.342	.406	.748	13	.979
1997—	Detroit (A.L.)	SS	147	436	35	105	26	0	2	40	14	55	0	9	3-6	.241	.263	.314	.577	13	.979
1998—	Lakeland (Fla. St.)	SS	2	9	0	0	0	0	0	1	0	1	0	0	0-0	.000	.000	.000	.000	0	1.000
	— Toledo (Int'l)	SS	2	9	1	1	1	0	0	2	2	3	0	0	0-0	.111	.273	.222	.495	0	1.000
	— Detroit (A.L.)	SS	135	454	52	118	22	3	5	45	13	55	3	11	3-4	.260	.284	.355	.639	11	.983
1999—	Detroit (A.L.)	SS	155	518	64	147	35	0	13	58	12	57	4	10	1-4	.284	.302	.427	.729	12	.983
2000—	Detroit (A.L.)	SS	156	583	68	176	46	5	10	82	13	43	4	25	1-4	.302	.318	.449	.767	13	.982
2001—	Detroit (A.L.)	SS-3B	110	414	39	106	28	1	7	52	17	46	4	13	4-1	.256	.291	.379	.670	17	.964
	— Erie (East.)	SS-3B	4	12	2	5	1	0	1	3	0	0	0	1	1-0	.417	.417	.750	1.167	1	.929
2002—	San Diego (N.L.)	SS-1B	151	514	49	135	28	2	7	47	22	58	3	20	2-3	.263	.294	.366	.660	15	.973
2003—	Baltimore (A.L.)	SS-DH	152	548	61	137	24	2	14	65	13	49	2	13	1-2	.250	.269	.378	.647	16	.975
2004—	Fresno (PCL)	SS	12	42	5	13	3	0	1	6	3	2	0	1	0-0	.310	.348	.452	.800	1	.976
	— San Francisco (N.L.)	SS-2B-3B	127	397	46	116	30	2	7	55	17	32	3	11	1-3	.292	.322	.431	.752	8	.980
	American League totals (6 years)		855	2953	319	789	181	11	51	342	82	305	17	81	13-21	.267	.289	.388	.677	82	.979
	National League totals (2 years)		278	911	95	251	58	4	14	102	39	90	6	31	3-6	.276	.306	.394	.700	23	.976
	Major League totals (8 years)		1133	3864	414	1040	239	15	65	444	121	395	23	112	16-27	.269	.293	.389	.682	105	.978

CRUZ, JACOB   OF

PERSONAL: Born January 28, 1973, in Oxnard, Calif. ... 6-0/210. ... Bats left, throws left. ... High school: Channel Islands (Oxnard, Calif.). ... College: Arizona State.

TRANSACTIONS/CAREER NOTES: Selected by California Angels organization in 45th round of 1991 free-agent draft; did not sign. ... Selected by San Francisco Giants organization in supplemental round ("sandwich pick" between first and second round; 32nd pick overall) of free-agent draft (June 2, 1994); pick received as part of compensation for Texas Rangers signing Type A free agent 1B Will Clark. ... Traded by Giants with P Steve Reed to Cleveland Indians for Ps Jose Mesa and Alvin Morman and IF Shawon Dunston (July 24, 1998). ... On disabled list (March 30-April 29 and August 3, 1999-remainder of season); included rehabilitation assignment to Buffalo. ... On disabled list (April 30, 2000-remainder of season). ... Traded by Indians to Colorado Rockies for C Josh Bard and OF Jody Gerut (June 2, 2001). ... On disabled list (July 17-August 17, 2001); included rehabilitation assignment to Colorado Springs. ... Released by Rockies (November 30, 2001). ... Signed by Detroit Tigers organization (December 21, 2001). ... On disabled list (June 1-18 and June 23, 2002-remainder of season); included rehabilitation assignment to Toledo. ... Released by Tigers (October 3, 2002). ... Signed by Cincinnati Reds organization (January 10, 2003). ... Refused minor league assignment and became a free agent (October 7, 2004).

2004 GAMES PLAYED BY POSITION (MLB): OF—29, 1B—6, DH—2.

										BATTING								FIELDING	
Year Team (League)	Pos.	G	AB	R	H	2B	3B	HR	RBI	BB	SO	HBP	GDP	SB-CS	Avg.	OBP	SLG	OPS	E	Avg.
1994—San Jose (Calif.)	OF	31	118	14	29	7	0	0	12	9	22	2	6	0-2	.246	.305	.305	.610	2	.957
1995—Shreveport (Texas)	OF	127	458	88	136	33	1	13	77	57	72	8	15	9-8	.297	.383	.459	.841	1	.996
1996—Phoenix (PCL)	OF-DH	121	435	60	124	26	4	7	75	62	77	10	16	5-9	.285	.378	.411	.790	3	.989
—San Francisco (N.L.)	OF	33	77	10	18	3	0	3	10	12	24	2	2	0-1	.234	.352	.390	.741	1	.977
1997—Phoenix (PCL)	OF-DH	127	493	97	178	45	3	12	95	64	64	3	11	18-3	.361	.434	.538	.971	8	.970
—San Francisco (N.L.)	OF	16	25	3	4	1	0	0	3	3	4	0	3	0-0	.160	.241	.200	.441	1	.933
1998—Fresno (PCL)	OF-DH	89	342	60	102	17	3	18	62	46	57	8	9	12-5	.298	.393	.523	.916	6	.963
—San Francisco (N.L.)		3	3	0	0	0	0	0	0	0	2	0	0	0-0	.000	.000	.000	.000	0	...
—Buffalo (Int'l)	OF	43	169	32	56	8	2	13	36	13	26	1	3	2-3	.331	.380	.633	1.014	4	.949
—Cleveland (A.L.)		1	1	0	0	0	0	0	0	0	1	0	0	0-0	.000	.000	.000	.000	0	...
1999—Buffalo (Int'l)	OF-DH	54	202	29	55	7	2	7	31	21	39	3	7	4-2	.272	.348	.431	.779	4	.953
—Cleveland (A.L.)	OF-DH	32	88	14	29	5	1	3	17	5	13	1	4	0-2	.330	.368	.511	.880	0	1.000
2000—Cleveland (A.L.)	OF-DH	11	29	3	7	3	0	0	5	5	4	1	0	1-0	.241	.361	.345	.706	0	1.000
2001—Cleveland (A.L.)	OF	28	68	12	15	4	0	3	11	5	23	3	3	0-2	.221	.303	.412	.714	1	.976
—Colorado (N.L.)	OF	44	76	7	16	1	0	1	7	10	27	1	1	0-2	.211	.303	.263	.567	2	.931
—Colo. Springs (PCL)	OF	20	86	18	28	5	2	6	25	1	23	1	2	1-0	.326	.337	.640	.977	0	1.000
2002—Detroit (A.L.)	DH-OF-1B	35	88	12	24	3	1	2	6	13	20	3	2	3-1	.273	.377	.398	.775	1	.976
—Toledo (Int'l)	OF	11	43	6	7	1	1	0	5	8	14	1	3	1-0	.163	.302	.233	.534	0	1.000
2003—Louisville (Int'l)	OF-1B-DH	36	132	25	46	8	0	7	29	14	22	1	5	3-0	.348	.409	.568	.977	5	.953
2004—Louisville (Int'l)	OF-1B-DH	17	54	12	17	4	0	3	7	10	10	0	2	0-0	.315	.415	.556	.971	0	1.000
—Cincinnati (N.L.)	OF-1B-DH	96	147	22	33	8	0	3	28	16	43	4	5	0-0	.224	.317	.340	.658	0	...
American League totals (5 years)		107	274	41	75	15	2	8	39	28	61	8	9	4-5	.274	.354	.431	.784	2	.986
National League totals (5 years)		192	328	42	71	13	0	7	48	41	100	7	11	0-3	.216	.314	.320	.634	4	.970
Major League totals (8 years)		299	602	83	146	28	2	15	87	69	161	15	20	4-8	.243	.332	.370	.702	6	.979

CRUZ, JUAN   P

PERSONAL: Born October 15, 1978, in Bonao, Dominican Republic. ... 6-2/165. ... Throws right, bats right. ... Full name: Juan Carlos Cruz.

TRANSACTIONS/CAREER NOTES: Signed as a non-drafted free agent by Chicago Cubs organization (July 4, 1997). ... On disabled list (August 10-25, 2002). ... Traded by Cubs with P Steve Smyth to Atlanta Braves for P Andy Pratt and IF Richard Lewis (March 25, 2004).

CAREER HITTING: 8-for-47 (.170), 2 R, 1 2B, 1 3B, 0 HR, 2 RBI.

Year Team (League)	W	L	Pct.	ERA	WHIP	G	GS	CG	ShO	Hld.	Sv.-Opp.	IP	H	R	ER	HR	BB-IBB	SO	Avg.
1998—Ariz. Cubs (Ariz.)	2	4	.333	6.10	1.81	12	6	0	0	...	0-...	41.1	61	48	28	2	14-0	36	.326
1999—Eugene (N'west)	5	6	.455	5.94	1.62	15	15	0	0	...	0-...	80.1	97	59	53	11	33-0	65	.297
2000—Lansing (Midw.)	5	5	.500	3.28	1.41	17	17	2	1	...	0-...	96.0	75	50	35	6	60-0	106	.215
—Daytona (Fla. St.)	3	0	1.000	3.25	1.08	8	7	1	0	...	0-...	44.1	30	22	16	5	18-0	54	.186
2001—West Tenn (Sou.)	9	6	.600	4.01	1.38	23	23	0	0	...	0-...	121.1	107	56	54	6	60-0	137	.238
—Chicago (N.L.)	3	1	.750	3.22	1.28	8	8	0	0	0	0-0	44.2	40	16	16	4	17-1	39	.244
2002—Chicago (N.L.)	3	11	.214	3.98	1.47	45	9	0	0	3	1-4	97.1	84	56	43	11	59-4	81	.241
2003—Iowa (PCL)	4	0	1.000	1.95	0.90	9	9	0	0	...	0-...	50.2	37	12	11	1	11-0	47	.207
—Chicago (N.L.)	2	7	.222	6.05	1.54	25	6	0	0	1	0-1	61.0	66	44	41	7	28-0	65	.275
2004—Atlanta (N.L.)	6	2	.750	2.75	1.24	50	0	0	0	2	0-0	72.0	59	24	22	7	30-1	70	.224
Major League totals (4 years)	14	21	.400	3.99	1.39	128	23	0	0	6	1-5	275.0	249	140	122	29	134-6	255	.245

DIVISION SERIES RECORD

Year Team (League)	W	L	Pct.	ERA	WHIP	G	GS	CG	ShO	Hld.	Sv.-Opp.	IP	H	R	ER	HR	BB-IBB	SO	Avg.
2003—Chicago (N.L.)	0	0	...	0.00	1.00	1	0	0	0	0	0-0	1.0	0	0	0	0	1-0	2	.000
2004—Atlanta (N.L.)	0	0	...	9.82	2.73	3	0	0	0	0	0-0	3.2	6	4	4	0	4-0	4	.353
Division series totals (2 years)	0	0	...	7.71	2.36	4	0	0	0	0	0-0	4.2	6	4	4	0	5-0	6	.300

CRUZ JR., JOSE   OF

PERSONAL: Born April 19, 1974, in Arroyo, Puerto Rico. ... 6-0/210. ... Bats both, throws right. ... Full name: Jose L. Cruz Jr.. ... High school: Bellaire (Houston). ... College: Rice. ... Son of Jose Cruz, outfielder with three major league teams (1970-88); nephew of Hector Cruz, outfielder/third baseman with four major league teams (1973, 1975-82); and nephew of Tommy Cruz, outfielder with two major league teams (1973-77).

TRANSACTIONS/CAREER NOTES: Selected by Atlanta Braves organization in 15th round of 1992 free-agent draft; did not sign. ... Selected by Seattle Mariners organization in first round (third pick overall) of 1995 free-agent draft. ... Traded by Mariners to Toronto Blue Jays for Ps Mike Timlin and Paul Spoljaric (July 31, 1997). ... On disabled list (June 24-July 9, 1999); included rehabilitation assignment to Syracuse. ... On disabled list (May 6-21, 2001; and August 10-September 15, 2002). ... Signed as a free agent by San Francisco Giants (January 28, 2003). ... Signed as a free agent by Tampa Bay Devil Rays (December 17, 2003).

HONORS: Won N.L. Gold Glove as outfielder (2003).

2004 GAMES PLAYED BY POSITION (MLB): OF—152.

										BATTING								FIELDING	
Year Team (League)	Pos.	G	AB	R	H	2B	3B	HR	RBI	BB	SO	HBP	GDP	SB-CS	Avg.	OBP	SLG	OPS	E	Avg.
1995—Everett (N'west)	OF	3	11	6	5	0	0	0	2	3	3	0	0	1-0	.455	.571	.455	1.026	0	1.000
—Riverside (Calif.)	OF	35	144	34	37	7	1	7	29	24	50	0	1	3-1	.257	.359	.465	.824	3	.961
1996—Lancaster (Calif.)	OF-DH	53	203	38	66	17	1	6	43	39	33	0	4	7-1	.325	.423	.507	.931	1	.986
—Port City (Sou.)	OF-DH	47	181	39	51	10	2	3	31	27	38	0	8	5-0	.282	.373	.409	.782	1	.990
—Tacoma (PCL)	OF	22	76	15	18	1	2	6	15	18	12	0	2	1-1	.237	.383	.539	.922	0	1.000
1997—Tacoma (PCL)	OF-DH	50	190	33	51	16	2	6	30	34	44	1	4	3-0	.268	.382	.468	.851	0	1.000
—Seattle (A.L.)	OF	49	183	28	49	12	1	12	34	13	45	0	3	1-0	.268	.315	.541	.856	3	.966
—Toronto (A.L.)	OF	55	212	31	49	7	0	14	34	28	72	0	4	6-2	.231	.316	.462	.778	2	.981
1998—Toronto (A.L.)	OF	105	352	55	89	14	3	11	42	57	99	0	0	11-4	.253	.354	.403	.757	4	.985

Year Team (League)	Pos.	G	AB	R	H	2B	3B	HR	RBI	BB	SO	HBP	GDP	SB-CS	Avg.	OBP	SLG	OPS	E	Avg.
—Syracuse (Int'l)	OF	40	141	29	42	14	1	7	23	32	32	0	2	8-4	.298	.425	.560	.986	1	.991
1999— Toronto (A.L.)	OF	106	349	63	84	19	3	14	45	64	91	0	6	14-4	.241	.358	.433	.791	3	.990
—Syracuse (Int'l)	OF-DH	31	103	17	19	3	1	3	14	28	20	0	3	5-0	.184	.356	.320	.676	0	1.000
2000— Toronto (A.L.)	OF	•162	603	91	146	32	5	31	76	71	129	2	11	15-5	.242	.323	.466	.789	3	.993
2001— Toronto (A.L.)	OF-DH	146	577	92	158	38	4	34	88	45	138	1	8	32-5	.274	.326	.530	.857	3	.990
2002— Toronto (A.L.)	OF-DH	124	466	64	114	26	5	18	70	51	106	0	8	7-1	.245	.317	.438	.754	2	.992
2003— San Francisco (N.L.)	OF	158	539	90	135	26	1	20	68	102	121	0	14	5-8	.250	.366	.414	.779	2	.994
2004— Tampa Bay (A.L.)	OF	153	545	76	132	25	8	21	78	76	117	2	6	11-6	.242	.333	.433	.766	10	.970
American League totals (7 years)		900	3287	500	821	173	29	155	467	405	797	5	44	97-27	.250	.331	.462	.792	30	.985
National League totals (1 year)		158	539	90	135	26	1	20	68	102	121	0	14	5-8	.250	.366	.414	.779	2	.994
Major League totals (8 years)		1058	3826	590	956	199	30	175	535	507	918	5	58	102-35	.250	.336	.455	.791	32	.987

DIVISION SERIES RECORD

Year Team (League)	Pos.	G	AB	R	H	2B	3B	HR	RBI	BB	SO	HBP	GDP	SB-CS	Avg.	OBP	SLG	OPS	E	Avg.
2003— San Francisco (N.L.)	OF	4	11	0	0	0	0	0	0	2	4	0	0	0-0	.000	.154	.000	.154	1	.938

CUBILLAN, DARWIN — P

PERSONAL: Born November 15, 1972, in Bobures, Venezuela. ... 6-2/170. ... Throws right, bats right. ... Full name: Darwin Harrikson Salom Cubillan. ... Name pronounced: coo-BEE-yan.

TRANSACTIONS/CAREER NOTES: Signed as a non-drafted free agent by New York Yankees organization (June 28, 1993). ... Signed as a free agent by Toronto Blue Jays organization (November 12, 1999). ... Traded by Blue Jays with 2B/SS Michael Young to Texas Rangers for P Esteban Loaiza (July 19, 2000). ... Traded by Rangers to Montreal Expos for P Mike Johnson (May 8, 2001). ... Released by Expos (July 7, 2002). ... Signed by Baltimore Orioles organization (July 12, 2002).

CAREER HITTING: 0-for-1 (.000), 0 R, 0 2B, 0 3B, 0 HR, 0 RBI.

Year Team (League)	W	L	Pct.	ERA	WHIP	G	GS	CG	ShO	Hld.	Sv.-Opp.	IP	H	R	ER	HR	BB-IBB	SO	Avg.
1993— Dom. Yankees (DSL)	0	2	.000	9.45	3.30	4	2	0	0	...	0-...	6.2	8	9	7		14-...	3	...
1994— GC Yankees (GCL)	4	2	.667	2.35	1.06	13	8	1	1		0-...	57.1	45	16	15	1	16-0	48	.225
— Greensboro (S. Atl.)	0	0		18.00	4.00	1	0	0	0		0-...	2.0	6	5	4	1	2-0	1	.462
1995— Greensboro (S. Atl.)	5	5	.500	3.62	1.28	22	14	1	1		0-...	97.0	86	50	39	5	38-1	78	.237
1996—				Did not play.															
1997— GC Yankees (GCL)	0	0		0.00	1.20	1	1	0	0		0-...	1.2	1	0	0	0	1-0	2	.167
1998— Tampa (FSL)	9	2	.818	4.71	1.77	45	1	0	0		1-...	65.0	79	45	34	3	36-9	70	.298
1999— Tampa (FSL)	7	4	.636	2.51	1.18	55	0	0	0		3-...	75.1	57	27	21	6	32-6	76	.210
2000— Syracuse (Int'l)	3	1	.750	0.55	0.83	24	0	0	0		6-...	32.2	14	2	2	0	13-1	41	.130
— Toronto (A.L.)	1	0	1.000	8.04	1.98	7	0	0	0		0-...	15.2	20	14	14	5	11-0	14	.317
— Oklahoma (PCL)	0	0		1.08	0.78	8	0	0	0		2-...	16.2	9	2	2	0	4-0	12	.158
— Texas (A.L.)	0	0		10.70	2.60	13	0	0	0		0-0	17.2	32	22	21	4	14-0	13	.400
2001— Oklahoma (PCL)	1	1	.500	10.38	2.46	9	0	0	0		2-...	13.0	20	16	15	4	12-0	8	.351
— Ottawa (Int'l)	2	2	.500	5.28	1.50	17	4	0	0		0-...	30.2	31	22	18	2	15-1	29	.267
— Montreal (N.L.)	0	0		4.10	1.63	29	0	0	0	1	0-0	26.1	31	13	12	1	12-1	19	.295
2002— Ottawa (Int'l)	1	1	.500	3.50	1.36	29	0	0	0		6-...	36.0	28	16	14	4	21-0	35	.219
2003— Ottawa (Int'l)	5	6	.455	3.21	1.20	65	0	0	0		20-...	73.0	57	29	26	6	34-6	77	.213
2004— Baltimore (A.L.)	0	0		5.40	2.00	10	0	0	0		0-1	10.0	13	7	6	3	7-0	8	.302
— Ottawa (Int'l)	3	4	.429	4.59	1.35	51	0	0	0		24-...	51.0	52	26	26	7	17-1	53	.269
American League totals (2 years)	1	0	1.000	8.52	2.24	27	0	0	0		0-1	43.1	65	43	41	12	32-0	35	.349
National League totals (1 year)	0	0		4.10	1.63	29	0	0	0		0-0	26.1	31	13	12	1	12-1	19	.295
Major League totals (3 years)	1	0	1.000	6.85	2.01	56	0	0	0		0-1	69.2	96	56	53	13	44-1	54	.330

CUDDYER, MICHAEL — 3B/2B

PERSONAL: Born March 27, 1979, in Norfolk, Va. ... 6-2/222. ... Bats right, throws right. ... Full name: Michael Brent Cuddyer. ... Name pronounced: cuh-DIE-er. ... High school: Great Bridge (Chesapeake, Va.).

TRANSACTIONS/CAREER NOTES: Selected by Minnesota Twins organization in first round (ninth pick overall) of 1997 free-agent draft.

2004 GAMES PLAYED BY POSITION (MLB): 2B—48, 3B—43, OF—15, 1B—10, DH—5.

Year Team (League)	Pos.	G	AB	R	H	2B	3B	HR	RBI	BB	SO	HBP	GDP	SB-CS	Avg.	OBP	SLG	OPS	E	Avg.
1998— Fort Wayne (Midw.)	2B-SS	129	497	82	137	37	7	12	81	61	107	10	13	16-7	.276	.364	.451	.814	61	.907
1999— Fort Myers (FSL)	3B	130	466	87	139	24	4	16	82	76	91	10	20	14-4	.298	.403	.470	.873	28	.921
2000— New Britain (East.)	3B	138	490	72	129	30	8	6	61	55	93	12	16	5-4	.263	.351	.394	.745	34	.903
2001— New Britain (East.)	3B-1B-OF	141	509	95	153	36	3	30	87	75	106	6	6	5-9	.301	.395	.560	.955	28	.963
— Minnesota (A.L.)	1B-3B-DH	8	18	1	4	2	0	0	1	2	6	0	1	1-0	.222	.300	.333	.633	1	.975
2002— Edmonton (PCL)	OF-1B-3B	86	330	70	102	16	9	20	53	36	79	3	9	12-7	.309	.379	.573	.973	7	.970
— Minnesota (A.L.)	OF-3-1-DH	41	112	12	29	7	0	4	13	8	30	1	3	2-0	.259	.311	.429	.740	1	.990
2003— GC Twins (GCL)	DH-OF	2	5	1	4	0	0	0	3	1	0	1	0	0-1	.800	.857	1.400	2.257	0	1.000
— Rochester (Int'l)	O-2-DH-3-1	53	186	25	57	17	0	3	34	25	49	1	4	5-4	.306	.381	.441	.827	1	.993
— Minnesota (A.L.)	O-3-1-DH-2	35	102	14	25	1	3	4	8	12	19	0	6	1-1	.245	.325	.431	.756	1	.985
2004— Minnesota (A.L.)	2-3-O-1-DH	115	339	49	89	22	1	12	45	37	74	3	8	5-5	.263	.339	.440	.779	10	.968
Major League totals (4 years)		199	571	76	147	32	4	20	67	59	129	4	18	9-6	.257	.330	.433	.763	13	.975

DIVISION SERIES RECORD

Year Team (League)	Pos.	G	AB	R	H	2B	3B	HR	RBI	BB	SO	HBP	GDP	SB-CS	Avg.	OBP	SLG	OPS	E	Avg.
2002— Minnesota (A.L.)	OF	5	13	1	5	1	0	0	1	3	3	0	0	0-0	.385	.500	.462	.962	0	1.000
2003— Minnesota (A.L.)	DH	1	4	0	1	0	0	0	1	0	3	0	0	0-0	.250	.250	.250	.500	0	...
2004— Minnesota (A.L.)	2B-1B	4	15	1	7	0	0	0	2	0	3	0	0	0-2	.467	.467	.467	.933	0	1.000
Division series totals (3 years)		10	32	2	13	1	0	0	4	3	9	0	0	0-2	.406	.457	.438	.895	0	1.000

CHAMPIONSHIP SERIES RECORD

Year Team (League)	Pos.	G	AB	R	H	2B	3B	HR	RBI	BB	SO	HBP	GDP	SB-CS	Avg.	OBP	SLG	OPS	E	Avg.
2002— Minnesota (A.L.)	OF	3	5	0	1	0	0	0	0	1	1	0	0	0-0	.200	.333	.200	.533	0	1.000

CUMMINGS, MIDRE — OF

PERSONAL: Born October 14, 1971, in St. Croix, Virgin Islands. ... 6-0/195. ... Bats left, throws right. ... Full name: Midre Almeric Cummings. ... Name pronounced: MEE-dray. ... High school: Miami Edison Senior.

TRANSACTIONS/CAREER NOTES: Selected by Minnesota Twins organization in supplemental round ("sandwich pick" between first and second round, 29th pick overall) of 1990 free-agent draft; pick received as part of compensation for Boston Red Sox signing Type A free-agent P Jeff Reardon. ... Traded by Twins with P Denny Neagle to Pittsburgh Pirates for P John Smiley (March 17, 1992). ... Claimed on waivers by Philadelphia Phillies (July 8, 1997). ... Released by Phillies (February 24, 1998). ... Signed by Cincinnati Reds organization (February 27, 1998). ... Claimed on waivers by Boston Red Sox (March 19, 1998). ... On disabled list (July 29-September 7, 1998). ... Released by Red Sox (March 30, 1999). ... Signed by Twins organization (May 14, 1999). ... Traded by Twins to Red Sox for IF Hector De Los Santos (August 31, 2000). ... Signed as a free agent by Arizona Diamondbacks organization (December 15, 2000). ... Signed as a free agent by Milwaukee Brewers organization (February 8, 2002). ... Signed as a free agent by Chicago Cubs organization (January 13, 2003). ... Signed as a free agent by Tampa Bay Devil Rays organization (February 13, 2004). ... Released by Devil Rays (October 13, 2004).

2004 GAMES PLAYED BY POSITION (MLB): DH—12, OF—2.

Year	Team (League)	Pos.	G	AB	R	H	2B	3B	HR	RBI	BB	SO	HBP	GDP	SB-CS	Avg.	OBP	SLG	OPS	E	Avg.
1990— GC Twins (GCL)		OF	47	177	28	56	3	4	5	28	13	32	2	1	14-9	.316	.362	.463	.826	6	.926
1991— Kenosha (Midw.)		OF	106	382	59	123	20	4	4	54	22	66	6	7	28-10	.322	.367	.427	.793	13	.930
1992— Salem (Caro.)		OF	113	420	55	128	20	5	14	75	35	67	4	2	23-9	.305	.361	.476	.838	6	.964
1993— Carolina (Southern)		OF	63	237	33	70	17	2	6	26	14	23	1	3	5-3	.295	.337	.460	.797	4	.964
— Buffalo (A.A.)		OF	60	232	36	64	12	1	9	21	22	45	0	4	5-1	.276	.336	.453	.789	2	.978
— Pittsburgh (N.L.)		OF	13	36	5	4	1	0	0	3	4	9	0	1	0-0	.111	.200	.139	.339	0	1.000
1994— Buffalo (A.A.)		OF	49	183	23	57	12	4	2	22	13	26	2	11	5-0	.311	.360	.454	.814	0	1.000
— Pittsburgh (N.L.)		OF	24	86	11	21	4	0	1	12	4	18	1	0	0-0	.244	.278	.326	.603	2	.962
1995— Pittsburgh (N.L.)		OF	59	152	13	37	7	1	2	15	13	30	0	1	1-0	.243	.303	.342	.645	1	.988
— Calgary (PCL)		OF	45	159	19	44	9	1	1	16	6	27	2	1	1-1	.277	.302	.365	.667	6	.943
1996— Calgary (PCL)		OF-DH	97	368	63	112	24	3	8	55	21	60	1	6	6-4	.304	.341	.451	.792	5	.974
— Pittsburgh (N.L.)		OF	24	85	11	19	3	1	3	7	0	16	0	0	0-0	.224	.224	.388	.612	1	.980
1997— Pittsburgh (N.L.)		OF	52	106	11	20	6	2	3	8	8	26	1	1	0-0	.189	.246	.368	.614	0	1.000
— Philadelphia (N.L.)		OF	63	208	24	63	16	4	1	23	23	30	0	2	2-3	.303	.372	.433	.805	1	.991
1998— Boston (A.L.)		DH-OF	67	120	20	34	8	0	5	15	17	19	2	2	3-3	.283	.372	.475	.847	1	.941
1999— New Britain (East.)		OF	24	93	28	35	7	0	2	15	17	14	2	1	3-1	.376	.474	.516	.990	0	1.000
— Salt Lake (PCL)		OF-DH	69	261	50	84	19	4	13	68	23	43	3	5	4-4	.322	.382	.575	.957	5	.954
— Minnesota (A.L.)		DH-OF	16	38	1	10	0	0	1	9	3	7	0	0	2-0	.263	.310	.342	.652	0	1.000
2000— Minnesota (A.L.)		OF-DH	77	181	28	50	10	4	4	22	11	25	3	4	0-0	.276	.328	.398	.726	0	1.000
— Boston (A.L.)		OF-DH	21	25	1	7	0	0	0	2	6	3	0	1	0-0	.280	.419	.280	.699	0	1.000
2001— Arizona (N.L.)		OF	20	20	1	6	1	0	0	1	0	4	0	2	0-0	.300	.286	.350	.636	0	1.000
— Tucson (PCL)		OF-1B	77	263	38	87	23	9	5	38	24	49	0	4	2-3	.331	.383	.544	.926	2	.985
2002— Indianapolis (Int'l)		OF	11	39	7	12	2	0	3	8	2	4	0	2	1-1	.308	.341	.590	.931	0	1.000
2003— Iowa (PCL)		OF-DH	114	385	53	98	22	2	19	54	40	86	4	10	1-3	.255	.328	.470	.798	2	.987
2004— Durham (Int'l)		DH-OF-1B	119	414	83	118	26	3	27	89	86	107	3	6	13-2	.285	.408	.558	.966	1	.983
— Tampa Bay (A.L.)		DH-OF	22	54	10	15	4	0	2	7	5	12	2	0	1-0	.278	.361	.463	.824	0	1.000
American League totals (4 years)			203	418	60	116	22	0	12	55	42	66	7	7	6-3	.278	.353	.416	.769	1	.989
National League totals (6 years)			255	693	76	170	38	8	10	69	52	133	2	7	3-3	.245	.297	.367	.664	5	.986
Major League totals (10 years)			458	1111	136	286	60	8	22	124	94	199	9	14	9-6	.257	.319	.385	.704	6	.987

DIVISION SERIES RECORD

Year	Team (League)	Pos.	G	AB	R	H	2B	3B	HR	RBI	BB	SO	HBP	GDP	SB-CS	Avg.	OBP	SLG	OPS	E	Avg.
1998— Boston (A.L.)			3	3	0	0	0	0	0	0	0	0	0	0	0-0	.000	.000	.000	.000	...	...
2001— Arizona (N.L.)			2	0	1	0	0	0	0	0	0	0	0	0	0-1	...	...	...	...	...	...
Division series totals (2 years)			5	3	1	0	0	0	0	0	0	0	0	0	0-1	.000	.000	.000	.000	...	...

CHAMPIONSHIP SERIES RECORD

Year	Team (League)	Pos.	G	AB	R	H	2B	3B	HR	RBI	BB	SO	HBP	GDP	SB-CS	Avg.	OBP	SLG	OPS	E	Avg.
2001— Arizona (N.L.)			1	1	0	0	0	0	0	0	0	0	0	0	0-0	.000	.000	.000	.000	...	...

WORLD SERIES RECORD

Year	Team (League)	Pos.	G	AB	R	H	2B	3B	HR	RBI	BB	SO	HBP	GDP	SB-CS	Avg.	OBP	SLG	OPS	E	Avg.
2001— Arizona (N.L.)		DH	2	0	2	0	0	0	0	0	0	0	0	0	0-0	...	...	...	...	...	...

CUNNANE, WILL   P

PERSONAL: Born April 24, 1974, in Suffern, N.Y. ... 6-1/200. ... Throws right, bats right. ... Full name: William Joseph Cunnane. ... Name pronounced: COO-nayn. ... High school: Clarkstown North (New City, N.Y.).

TRANSACTIONS/CAREER NOTES: Signed as a non-drafted free agent by Florida Marlins organization (August 18, 1992). ... Selected by San Diego Padres from Marlins organization in Rule 5 major league draft (December 9, 1996). ... On disabled list (March 29-June 21, 1998); included rehabilitation assignment to Las Vegas. ... Traded by Padres to Milwaukee Brewers for OF Chad Green (December 20, 2000), completing deal in which Brewers traded SS Santiago Perez and a player to be named later or cash to San Deigo Padres for P Brandon Kolb (December 1, 2000). ... Signed as a free agent by Chicago Cubs organization (December 17, 2001). ... Released by Cubs (May 12, 2003). ... Signed by Atlanta Braves organization (July 2, 2003).

CAREER HITTING: 7-for-35 (.200), 6 R, 1 2B, 1 3B, 0 HR, 4 RBI.

Year	Team (League)	W	L	Pct.	ERA	WHIP	G	GS	CG	ShO	Hld.	Sv.-Opp.	IP	H	R	ER	HR	BB-IBB	SO	Avg.
1993—GC Marlins (GCL)		3	3	.500	2.70	1.25	16	9	0	0	...	2-...	66.2	75	32	20	1	8-0	64	.269
1994—Kane County (Midwest)		11	3	.786	1.43	0.96	32	16	5	4	...	1-...	138.2	110	27	22	2	23-4	106	.217
1995—Portland (East.)		9	2	.818	3.67	1.31	21	21	1	1	...	0-...	117.2	120	48	48	10	34-1	83	.264
1996—Portland (East.)		10	12	.455	3.74	1.23	25	25	4	0	...	0-...	151.2	156	73	63	15	30-6	101	.263
1997—San Diego (N.L.)		6	3	.667	5.81	1.78	54	0	0	0	4	0-2	91.1	114	69	59	11	49-3	79	.305
1998—Las Vegas (PCL)		1	2	.333	5.25	1.78	33	0	0	0	...	4-...	36.0	45	26	21	4	19-4	30	.310
—San Diego (N.L.)		0	0	...	6.00	1.67	3	0	0	0	...	0-0	3.0	4	2	2	1	1-1	1	.308
1999—Las Vegas (PCL)		2	1	.667	0.98	1.25	28	0	0	0	11	11-...	36.2	30	5	4	0	16-2	54	.214
—San Diego (N.L.)		2	1	.667	5.23	1.48	24	0	0	0	5	0-0	31.0	34	19	18	8	12-3	22	.293
2000—San Diego (N.L.)		2	2	.500	4.23	1.46	27	3	0	0	1	0-0	38.1	35	21	18	2	21-0	34	.241
—Las Vegas (PCL)		7	4	.636	3.98	1.25	17	17	1	1	...	0-...	97.1	96	46	43	7	26-0	97	.257
2001—Milwaukee (N.L.)		0	3	.000	5.40	1.70	31	1	0	0	1	0-0	51.2	66	34	31	6	22-6	37	.320
—Indianapolis (Int'l)		0	1	.000	3.86	1.33	7	3	0	0	...	1-...	23.1	25	10	10	2	6-1	25	.278
2002—Iowa (PCL)		4	1	.800	2.20	1.22	43	0	0	0	...	2-...	73.2	67	23	18	3	23-3	69	.245
—Chicago (N.L.)		1	1	.500	5.47	1.52	16	0	0	0	...	0-1	26.1	27	16	16	5	13-1	30	.270
2003—Iowa (PCL)		0	1	.000	2.20	1.50	12	0	0	0	...	0-...	16.1	17	5	4	0	8-3	16	.274
—Richmond (Int'l)		1	0	1.000	0.00	0.60	15	0	0	0	...	2-...	21.0	11	2	0	0	2-0	19	.159
—Atlanta (N.L.)		2	2	.500	2.70	1.00	20	0	0	0	5	3-3	20.0	14	6	6	2	6-2	20	.189
2004—Atlanta (N.L.)		1	1	.500	7.30	1.78	9	0	0	0	0	0-1	12.1	18	10	10	3	4-1	11	.346
—Richmond (Int'l)		1	7	.125	5.23	1.72	35	2	0	0	...	2-...	43.0	52	27	25	4	22-1	42	.304
Major League totals (8 years)		13	12	.520	5.26	1.61	184	12	0	0	17	3-7	274.0	312	177	160	38	128-17	234	.289

DIVISION SERIES RECORD

Year	Team (League)	W	L	Pct.	ERA	WHIP	G	GS	CG	ShO	Hld.	Sv.-Opp.	IP	H	R	ER	HR	BB-IBB	SO	Avg.
2003—Atlanta (N.L.)		0	0	...	5.40	1.80	2	0	0	0	0	0-0	1.2	3	2	1	1	0-0	2	.333

C

CUST, JACK — OF

PERSONAL: Born January 16, 1979, in Flemington, N.J. ... 6-1/231. ... Bats left, throws right. ... Full name: John Joseph Cust. ... High school: Immaculata (Somerville, N.J.).
TRANSACTIONS/CAREER NOTES: Selected by Arizona Diamondbacks organization in first round (30th pick overall) of 1997 free-agent draft. ... Traded by Diamondbacks with C J.D. Closser to Colorado Rockies for P Mike Myers (January 7, 2002). ... Traded by Rockies to Baltimore Orioles for OF/1B Chris Richard (March 11, 2003).

Year Team (League)	Pos.	G	AB	R	H	2B	3B	HR	RBI	BB	SO	HBP	GDP	SB-CS	Avg.	OBP	SLG	OPS	E	Avg.
1997—Ariz. D'backs (Ariz.)	OF	35	121	26	37	11	1	3	33	31	39	0	4	2-0	.306	.447	.488	.935	5	.902
1998—South Bend (Mid.)	OF	16	62	5	15	3	0	0	4	5	20	0	0	0-1	.242	.294	.290	.584	4	.975
—Lethbridge (Pio.)	OF	73	223	75	77	20	2	11	56	86	71	4	3	15-8	.345	.530	.601	1.131	0	1.000
1999—High Desert (Calif.)	OF	125	455	107	152	43	3	32	112	96	145	2	5	1-4	.334	.450	.651	1.100	12	.922
2000—El Paso (Texas)	OF	129	447	100	131	32	6	20	75	117	150	2	10	12-9	.293	.440	.526	.966	11	.944
2001—Tucson (PCL)	OF	135	442	81	123	24	2	27	79	102	160	5	10	6-3	.278	.415	.525	.940	11	.948
—Arizona (N.L.)	OF	3	2	0	1	0	0	0	0	1	0	0	0	0-0	.500	.667	.500	1.167	0	...
2002—Colo. Springs (PCL)	OF	105	359	74	95	24	0	23	55	83	121	5	5	6-3	.265	.407	.524	.930	6	.961
—Colorado (N.L.)	OF	35	65	8	11	2	0	1	8	12	32	0	0	0-1	.169	.295	.246	.541	1	.960
2003—Ottawa (Int'l)	OF-DH	97	333	55	95	18	1	9	58	80	94	0	9	5-2	.285	.422	.426	.848	3	.978
—Baltimore (A.L.)	DH-OF	27	73	7	19	7	0	4	11	10	25	1	0	0-0	.260	.357	.521	.878	0	1.000
2004—Baltimore (A.L.)	PH	1	1	0	0	0	0	0	0	0	1	0	0	0-0	.000	.000	.000	.000	0	...
—Ottawa (Int'l)	DH-OF	102	344	55	81	15	1	17	55	65	127	2	6	4-0	.235	.358	.433	.791	2	.966
American League totals (2 years)		28	74	7	19	7	0	4	11	10	26	1	0	0-0	.257	.353	.514	.866	0	1.000
National League totals (2 years)		38	67	8	12	2	0	1	8	13	32	0	3	0-1	.179	.309	.254	.562	1	.960
Major League totals (4 years)		66	141	15	31	9	0	5	19	23	58	1	3	0-1	.220	.331	.390	.721	1	.964

DAIGLE, CASEY — P

PERSONAL: Born April 4, 1981, in Lake Charles, La. ... 6-5/217. ... Throws right, bats right. ... Full name: Sean Casey Daigle. ... High school: Sulphur (La.).
TRANSACTIONS/CAREER NOTES: Selected by Arizona Diamondbacks organization in suplemental round ("sandwich pick" between first and second rounds, 31st pick overall) of 1999 free-agent draft; pick received as compensation for Los Angeles Dodgers signing Type A free-agent OF Devon White.

CAREER HITTING: 2-for-17 (.118), 2 R, 2 2B, 0 3B, 0 HR, 0 RBI.

Year Team (League)	W	L	Pct.	ERA	WHIP	G	GS	CG	ShO	Hld.	Sv.-Opp.	IP	H	R	ER	HR	BB-IBB	SO	Avg.
2000—Missoula (Pio.)	3	5	.375	4.90	1.72	15	15	0	0	...	0-...	82.2	88	57	45	4	54-0	56	.271
2001—South Bend (Midw.)	10	10	.500	4.12	1.43	28	27	2	1	...	0-...	164.0	180	100	75	11	55-0	85	.279
2002—Lancaster (Calif.)	4	10	.286	5.09	1.47	21	21	0	0	...	0-...	122.0	137	82	69	19	42-0	85	.285
—El Paso (Texas)	3	2	.600	3.25	1.24	7	7	2	0	...	0-...	44.1	46	19	16	5	9-0	29	.275
2003—El Paso (Texas)	11	11	.500	4.59	1.53	29	27	1	0	...	0-...	176.1	219	108	90	9	51-1	115	.304
2004—Arizona (N.L.)	2	3	.400	7.16	1.84	10	10	0	0	0	0-0	49.0	63	41	39	9	27-3	17	.320
—Tucson (PCL)	4	9	.308	6.88	1.77	18	15	0	0	...	0-...	100.2	154	85	77	21	24-0	51	.348
Major League totals (1 year)	2	3	.400	7.16	1.84	10	10	0	0	0	0-0	49.0	63	41	39	9	27-3	17	.320

DALLIMORE, BRIAN — 2B/3B

PERSONAL: Born November 15, 1973, in Las Vegas, Nev. ... 6-1/180. ... Bats right, throws right. ... Full name: Brian Scott Dallimore. ... High school: Clark (Las Vegas). ... College: Stanford.
TRANSACTIONS/CAREER NOTES: Selected by Florida Marlins organization in 37th round of 1995 free-agent draft; did not sign. ... Selected by Houston Astros organization in ninth round of 1996 free-agent draft. ... Traded by Astros to Arizona Diamondbacks for C Joshua McAfee (April 20, 2000). ... Signed as a free agent by San Francisco Giants organization (December 16, 2002).
2004 GAMES PLAYED BY POSITION (MLB): 2B—9, 3B—6.

Year Team (League)	Pos.	G	AB	R	H	2B	3B	HR	RBI	BB	SO	HBP	GDP	SB-CS	Avg.	OBP	SLG	OPS	E	Avg.
1996—Auburn (NY-Penn)	3B-2B-SS	74	290	50	77	17	3	5	30	18	38	10	5	7-5	.266	.326	.397	.723	24	.911
1997—Quad City (Midw.)	SS-3B-2B	130	492	80	128	23	3	6	48	38	76	20	19	24-8	.260	.335	.356	.691	46	.915
—Kissimmee (Fla. St.)	2B	1	3	0	0	0	0	0	0	0	2	0	0	0-0	.000	.000	.000	.000	0	1.000
1998—Kissimmee (Fla. St.)	3B-2B	62	240	34	61	11	1	0	19	19	42	5	6	7-5	.254	.321	.308	.629	9	.958
1999—Kissimmee (Fla. St.)	2B-3B-OF	19	74	12	20	2	0	0	3	4	10	3	1	2-1	.270	.329	.297	.627	6	.910
—Jackson (Texas)	2-OF-3-S	70	251	38	67	13	1	5	19	16	44	10	12	13-3	.267	.335	.386	.721	15	.943
2000—Round Rock (Texas)	SS	5	11	1	2	1	0	1	3	1	3	0	0	0-0	.182	.250	.545	.795	2	.667
—El Paso (Texas)	3-2-S-OF	107	356	50	99	16	1	4	53	25	56	6	13	17-3	.278	.332	.362	.694	22	.936
2001—El Paso (Texas)	3B-2B	127	517	74	169	38	6	8	67	30	56	13	9	11-13	.327	.378	.470	.848	25	.939
2002—Tucson (PCL)	3-2-OF-S	122	419	62	123	26	2	6	50	28	72	9	10	13-4	.294	.346	.408	.754	13	.958
2003—Fresno (PCL)	2B	91	330	53	116	16	2	4	46	37	37	10	6	6-4	.352	.427	.448	.875	10	.975
2004—Fresno (PCL)	2-3-S-O-DH	111	432	72	140	21	4	8	67	40	53	15	13	9-2	.324	.396	.447	.842	15	.967
—San Francisco (N.L.)	2B-3B	20	43	8	12	2	0	1	7	4	7	1	0	0-1	.279	.347	.395	.742	2	.950
Major League totals (1 year)		20	43	8	12	2	0	1	7	4	7	1	0	0-1	.279	.347	.395	.742	2	.950

D'AMICO, JEFF — P

PERSONAL: Born December 27, 1975, in St. Petersburg, Fla. ... 6-7/255. ... Throws right, bats right. ... Full name: Jeffrey Charles D'Amico. ... Name pronounced: duh-MEEK-oh. ... High school: Northeast (St. Petersburg, Fla.).
TRANSACTIONS/CAREER NOTES: Selected by Milwaukee Brewers organization in first round (23rd pick overall) of 1993 free-agent draft. ... On disabled list (July 28-September 2, 1997; and January 14, 1998-entire season). ... On disabled list (March 29-September 25, 1999; included rehabilitation assignments to Beloit, Huntsville and Louisville. ... On disabled list (June 6-30, 2000). ... On disabled list (April 23-September 1, 2001; included rehabilitation assignments to Beloit and Huntsville. ... Traded by Brewers with OF Jeromy Burnitz, IF Lou Collier, OF/1B Mark Sweeney and cash to New York Mets as part of three-team deal in which Brewers acquired P Glendon Rusch and IF Lenny Harris from Mets and OF Alex Ochoa from Rockies, Mets acquired 1B/OF Ross Gload and P Craig House from Rockies, and Rockies acquired IF Todd Zeile, OF Benny Agbayani and cash from Mets (January 21, 2002). ... Signed as a free agent by Pittsburgh Pirates organization (January 17, 2003). ... Released by PIrates (October 2, 2003). ... Signed by Cleveland Indians organization (January 5, 2004). ... On disabled list (May 11-June 26, 2004); included rehabilitation assignments to Lake County and Buffalo. ... Released by Indians (June 26, 2004).

CAREER HITTING: 15-for-148 (.101), 7 R, 2 2B, 1 3B, 2 HR, 5 RBI.

Year Team (League)	W	L	Pct.	ERA	WHIP	G	GS	CG	ShO	Hld.	Sv.-Opp.	IP	H	R	ER	HR	BB-IBB	SO	Avg.
1994—Ariz. Brewers (Ariz.)	Did not play.																		
1995—Beloit (Midw.)	13	3	.813	2.39	1.01	21	20	3	1	...	0-...	132.0	102	40	35	7	31-2	119	.211
1996—El Paso (Texas)	5	4	.556	3.19	1.06	13	13	3	0	...	0-...	96.0	89	42	34	10	13-0	76	.241

Year	Team (League)	W	L	Pct.	ERA	WHIP	G	GS	CG	ShO	Hld.	Sv.-Opp.	IP	H	R	ER	HR	BB-IBB	SO	Avg.
	— Milwaukee (A.L.)	6	6	.500	5.44	1.38	17	17	0	0		0-0	86.0	88	53	52	21	31-0	53	.267
1997—	Milwaukee (A.L.)	9	7	.563	4.71	1.34	23	23	1	1	0	0-0	135.2	139	81	71	25	43-2	94	.264
	— Beloit (Midw.)	0	0	...	0.00	0.33	1	1	0	0		0-...	3.0	0	0	0	0	1-0	7	.000
1998—	Milwaukee (A.L.)	Did not play.																		
1999—	Beloit (Midw.)	1	0	1.000	0.00	1.00	2	2	0	0		0-...	8.0	7	0	0	0	1-0	6	.233
	— Huntsville (Southern)	0	0	...	36.00	3.50	1	1	0	0		0-...	2.0	6	8	8	3	1-0	2	.500
	— Louisville (Int'l)	0	0	...	13.50	2.40	1	1	0	0		0-...	3.1	6	5	5	0	2-0	1	.400
	— Milwaukee (N.L.)	0	0	...	0.00	1.00	1	0	0	0	0	0-0	1.0	1	0	0	0	0-0	1	.250
2000—	Indianapolis (Int'l)	1	1	.500	3.16	1.15	6	6	0	0	0	0-...	31.1	25	11	11	6	11-0	20	.219
	— Milwaukee (N.L.)	12	7	.632	2.66	1.16	23	23	1	1	0	0-0	162.1	143	55	48	14	46-5	101	.238
2001—	Milwaukee (N.L.)	2	4	.333	6.08	1.61	10	10	0	0	0	0-0	47.1	60	42	32	11	16-4	32	.306
	— Beloit (Midw.)	0	0	...	5.40	1.44	2	2	0	0		0-...	8.1	11	6	5	1	1-0	6	.306
	— Huntsville (Southern)	1	0	1.000	2.57	0.71	1	1	0	0		0-...	7.0	3	2	2	2	2-0	5	.130
2002—	New York (N.L.)	6	10	.375	4.94	1.30	29	22	1	1	0	0-0	145.2	152	84	80	20	37-8	101	.267
2003—	Pittsburgh (N.L.)	9	*16	.360	4.77	1.40	29	29	2	1	0	0-0	175.1	204	104	93	23	42-6	100	.291
2004—	Cleveland (A.L.)	1	2	.333	7.63	1.66	7	7	0	0	0	0-0	30.2	45	29	26	6	6-0	16	.333
	— Lake County (S.Atl.)	0	0	...	0.00	0.50	2	1	0	0	0	0-...	2.0	1	0	0	0	0-0	1	.143
	— Buffalo (Int'l)	0	0	...	10.45	2.03	3	3	0	0	0	0-...	10.1	18	12	12	3	3-0	5	.391
American League totals (3 years)		16	15	.516	5.31	1.39	47	47	1	1	0	0-0	252.1	272	163	149	52	80-2	163	.274
National League totals (5 years)		29	37	.439	4.28	1.32	92	84	4	3	0	0-0	531.2	560	285	253	68	141-23	335	.270
Major League totals (8 years)		45	52	.464	4.61	1.34	139	131	5	4	0	0-0	784.0	832	448	402	120	221-25	498	.272

DAMON, JOHNNY — OF

PERSONAL: Born November 5, 1973, in Fort Riley, Kan. ... 6-2/190. ... Bats left, throws left. ... Full name: Johnny David Damon. ... Name pronounced: DAY-mun. ... High school: Dr. Phillips (Orlando).

TRANSACTIONS/CAREER NOTES: Selected by Kansas City Royals organization in supplemental round ("sandwich pick" between first and second round, 35th pick overall) of 1992 free-agent draft; pick received as part of compensation for San Diego Padres signing Type A free-agent IF Kurt Stillwell. ... On suspended list (September 5-7, 1997). ... Traded by Royals with IF Mark Ellis and a player to be named to Oakland Athletics as part of three-team deal in which Royals acquired P Roberto Hernandez from Tampa Bay Devil Rays, A's acquired P Cory Lidle from Devil Rays, Royals acquired C A.J. Hinch, IF Angel Berroa and cash from A's and Devil Rays acquired OF Ben Grieve and a player to be named later or cash from A's (January 8, 2001). ... Signed as a free agent by Boston Red Sox (December 21, 2001).

RECORDS: Shares major league record for most doubles, game (4, July 18, 2000).

2004 GAMES PLAYED BY POSITION (MLB): OF—148, DH—1.

							BATTING												FIELDING	
Year	Team (League)	Pos.	G	AB	R	H	2B	3B	HR	RBI	BB	SO	HBP	GDP	SB-CS	Avg.	OBP	SLG	OPS	E	Avg.
1992—	GC Royals (GCL)	OF	50	192	58	67	12	9	4	24	31	21	4	1	33-6	.349	.449	.568	1.017	1	.988
	— Baseball City (FSL)	OF	1	1	0	0	0	0	0	0	0	0	0	0	0-0	.000	.000	.000	.000	0	...
1993—	Rockford (Midwest)	OF	127	511	82	148	25	13	5	50	52	83	6	4	59-18	.290	.360	.419	.779	6	.977
1994—	Wilmington (Caro.)	OF	119	472	96	149	25	13	6	75	62	55	8	4	44-9	.316	.399	.462	.861	3	.989
1995—	Wichita (Texas)	OF-DH	111	423	83	145	15	9	16	54	67	35	2	3	26-15	.343	.434	.534	.968	5	.984
	— Kansas City (A.L.)	OF	47	188	32	53	11	5	3	23	12	22	1	2	7-0	.282	.324	.441	.765	1	.991
1996—	Kansas City (A.L.)	OF-DH	145	517	61	140	22	5	6	50	31	64	3	4	25-5	.271	.313	.368	.680	6	.983
1997—	Kansas City (A.L.)	OF-DH	146	472	70	130	12	8	8	48	42	70	3	3	16-10	.275	.338	.386	.723	4	.988
1998—	Kansas City (A.L.)	OF	161	642	104	178	30	10	18	66	58	84	4	4	26-12	.277	.339	.439	.779	4	.990
1999—	Kansas City (A.L.)	OF-DH	145	583	101	179	39	9	14	77	67	60	3	13	36-6	.307	.379	.477	.856	4	.987
2000—	Kansas City (A.L.)	OF-DH	159	655	*136	214	42	10	16	88	65	60	1	7	*46-9	.327	.382	.495	.877	5	.986
2001—	Oakland (A.L.)	OF	155	644	108	165	34	4	9	49	61	70	5	7	27-12	.256	.324	.363	.687	3	.991
2002—	Boston (A.L.)	OF-DH	154	623	118	178	34	*11	14	63	65	70	6	4	31-6	.286	.356	.443	.799	1	.997
2003—	Boston (A.L.)	OF-DH	145	608	103	166	32	6	12	67	68	74	2	5	30-6	.273	.345	.405	.750	1	.997
2004—	Boston (A.L.)	OF-DH	150	621	123	189	35	6	20	94	76	71	2	8	19-8	.304	.380	.477	.857	5	.986
Major League totals (10 years)			1407	5553	956	1592	291	74	120	625	545	635	30	57	263-74	.287	.351	.431	.782	34	.990

DIVISION SERIES RECORD

Year	Team (League)	Pos.	G	AB	R	H	2B	3B	HR	RBI	BB	SO	HBP	GDP	SB-CS	Avg.	OBP	SLG	OPS	E	Avg.
2001—	Oakland (A.L.)	OF	5	22	3	9	2	1	0	0	1	1	0	0	2-0	.409	.435	.591	1.026	0	1.000
2003—	Boston (A.L.)	OF	5	19	2	6	2	0	1	3	2	1	1	1	2-0	.316	.409	.579	.988	0	1.000
2004—	Boston (A.L.)	OF	3	15	4	7	1	0	0	0	1	2	0	0	3-0	.467	.500	.533	1.033	0	1.000
Division series totals (3 years)			13	56	9	22	5	1	1	3	4	4	1	1	7-0	.393	.443	.571	1.014	0	1.000

CHAMPIONSHIP SERIES RECORD

Year	Team (League)	Pos.	G	AB	R	H	2B	3B	HR	RBI	BB	SO	HBP	GDP	SB-CS	Avg.	OBP	SLG	OPS	E	Avg.
2003—	Boston (A.L.)	OF	5	20	1	4	1	0	0	1	3	3	0	1	1-0	.200	.304	.250	.554	0	1.000
2004—	Boston (A.L.)	OF	7	35	5	6	0	0	2	7	2	8	0	1	2-1	.171	.216	.343	.559	0	1.000
Champ. series totals (2 years)			12	55	6	10	1	0	2	8	5	11	0	2	3-1	.182	.250	.309	.559	0	1.000

WORLD SERIES RECORD

Year	Team (League)	Pos.	G	AB	R	H	2B	3B	HR	RBI	BB	SO	HBP	GDP	SB-CS	Avg.	OBP	SLG	OPS	E	Avg.
2004—	Boston (A.L.)	OF	4	21	4	6	2	1	1	2	0	1	0	1	0-0	.286	.286	.619	.905	0	1.000

ALL-STAR GAME RECORD

	G	AB	R	H	2B	3B	HR	RBI	BB	SO	HBP	GDP	SB-CS	Avg.	OBP	SLG	OPS	E	Avg.
All-Star Game totals (1 year)	1	3	1	1	0	0	0	0	0	1	0	0	1-0	.333	.333	.333	.667	0	1.000

DARENSBOURG, VIC — P

PERSONAL: Born November 13, 1970, in Los Angeles, Calif. ... 5-10/180. ... Throws left, bats left. ... Full name: Victor Anthony Darensbourg. ... Name pronounced: darens-berg. ... High school: Westchester (Los Angeles). ... College: Lewis-Clark (Idaho) State.

TRANSACTIONS/CAREER NOTES: Signed as a non-drafted free agent by Florida Marlins organization (June 11, 1992). ... On disabled list (August 20-September 17, 2001). ... Traded by Marlins with C Charles Johnson, OF Preston Wilson and 2B Pablo Ozuna to Colorado Rockies for P Mike Hampton, OF Juan Pierre and cash (November 16, 2002). ... Released by Rockies (July 10, 2003). ... Signed by Montreal Expos organization (July 28, 2003). ... Signed as a free agent by Chicago White Sox organization (January 16, 2004). ... Released by White Sox (July 1, 2004). ... Signed by New York Mets organization (July 15, 2004). ... Refused minor league assignment and became a free agent (October 12, 2004).

CAREER HITTING: 2-for-18 (.111), 0 R, 0 2B, 0 3B, 0 HR, 0 RBI.

Year Team (League)	W	L	Pct.	ERA	WHIP	G	GS	CG	ShO	Hld.	Sv.-Opp.	IP	H	R	ER	HR	BB-IBB	SO	Avg.
1992— GC Marlins (GCL)	2	1	.667	0.64	0.93	8	4	0	0	...	2-...	42.0	28	5	3	1	11-2	37	.190
1993— Kane County (Midwest)	9	1	.900	2.14	1.21	46	0	0	0	...	16-...	71.1	58	17	17	3	28-3	89	.221
—High Desert (Calif.)	0	0	...	0.00	0.00	1	0	0	0	...	0-...	1.0	0	0	0	0	0-0	1	.000
1994— Portland (East.)	10	7	.588	3.81	1.38	35	21	1	1	...	4-...	149.0	146	76	63	18	60-3	103	.264
1995— Florida (N.L.)			Did not play.																
1996— Brevard County (FSL)	0	0	...	0.00	0.67	2	0	0	0	...	0-...	3.0	1	0	0	0	1-0	5	.111
—Charlotte (Int'l)	1	5	.167	3.69	1.47	47	0	0	0	...	7-...	63.1	61	30	26	7	32-3	66	.253
1997— Charlotte (Int'l)	4	2	.667	4.38	1.50	27	0	0	0	...	2-...	24.2	22	12	12	4	15-3	21	.242
1998— Florida (N.L.)	0	7	.000	3.68	1.15	59	0	0	0	13	1-2	71.0	52	29	29	5	30-6	74	.207
1999— Florida (N.L.)	0	1	.000	8.83	2.05	56	0	0	0	10	0-1	34.2	50	36	34	3	21-1	16	.340
—Calgary (PCL)	0	0	...	4.63	1.11	9	0	0	0	...	1-...	11.2	13	6	6	0	0-0	12	.289
2000— Florida (N.L.)	5	3	.625	4.06	1.44	56	0	0	0	3	0-1	62.0	61	32	28	7	28-1	59	.260
2001— Florida (N.L.)	1	2	.333	4.25	1.27	58	0	0	0	11	1-3	48.2	52	24	23	4	10-6	33	.277
2002— Florida (N.L.)	1	2	.333	6.14	1.80	42	0	0	0	3	0-0	48.1	61	34	33	10	26-4	33	.305
2003— Colorado (N.L.)	0	0	...	0.00	1.71	3	0	0	0	0	0-0	2.1	4	1	0	0	0-0	0	.333
—Colo. Springs (PCL)	2	2	.500	3.57	1.30	20	0	0	0	...	0-...	22.2	24	13	9	1	5-1	15	.273
—Edmonton (PCL)	1	1	.500	1.98	1.40	11	0	0	0	...	0-...	13.2	12	3	3	0	7-0	11	.235
—Montreal (N.L.)	0	0	...	10.80	2.10	6	0	0	0	0	0-0	6.2	13	8	8	2	1-0	4	.406
2004— Charlotte (Int'l)	3	3	.500	2.64	1.11	24	0	0	0	...	0-...	30.2	25	10	9	1	9-2	33	.229
—Chicago (A.L.)	0	0	...	0.00	1.50	2	0	0	0	...	0-...	1.1	1	0	0	0	1-0	0	.333
—Norfolk (Int'l)	1	1	.500	3.18	1.10	18	0	0	0	...	0-...	22.2	13	9	8	1	12-2	21	.169
—New York (N.L.)	0	1	.000	7.94	2.12	5	0	0	0	...	0-...	5.2	10	5	5	1	2-0	1	.435
American League totals (1 year)	0	0	...	0.00	1.50	2	0	0	0	...	0-0	1.1	1	0	0	0	1-0	0	.333
National League totals (7 years)	7	16	.304	5.16	1.51	285	0	0	0	40	2-7	279.1	303	169	160	32	118-18	220	.278
Major League totals (7 years)	7	16	.304	5.13	1.51	287	0	0	0	40	2-7	280.2	304	169	160	32	119-18	220	.279

DAUBACH, BRIAN — 1B/OF

PERSONAL: Born February 11, 1972, in Belleville, Ill. ... 6-1/230. ... Bats left, throws right. ... Full name: Brian Michael Daubach. ... Name pronounced: DAW-back. ... High school: Belleville (Ill.) West.

TRANSACTIONS/CAREER NOTES: Selected by New York Mets organization in 17th round of 1990 free-agent draft. ... Signed as a free agent by Florida Marlins organization (November 7, 1996). ... Released by Marlins (November 19, 1998). ... Signed by Boston Red Sox organization (December 18, 1998). ... On disabled list (August 15-September 2, 2001); included rehabilitation assignments to Pawtucket and Lowell. ... Signed as a free agent by Chicago White Sox organization (January 27, 2003). ... Released by White Sox (December 10, 2003). ... Signed by Red Sox organization (December 28, 2003).

2004 GAMES PLAYED BY POSITION (MLB): 1B—14, OF—7.

											BATTING								FIELDING	
Year Team (League)	Pos.	G	AB	R	H	2B	3B	HR	RBI	BB	SO	HBP	GDP	SB-CS	Avg.	OBP	SLG	OPS	E	Avg.
1990— GC Mets (GCL)	1B	45	152	26	41	8	4	1	19	22	41	2	2	2-1	.270	.363	.395	.758	7	.976
1991— Kingsport (Appalachian)	1B	65	218	30	53	9	1	7	42	33	64	6	1	1-3	.243	.355	.390	.745	9	.986
1992— Pittsfield (N.Y.-Penn.)	1B	72	260	26	63	15	2	2	40	30	61	3	5	4-0	.242	.323	.338	.662	12	.982
1993— Capital City (SAL)	1B-OF	102	379	50	106	19	3	7	72	52	84	5	14	6-1	.280	.368	.401	.769	5	.989
1994— St. Lucie (Fla. St.)	1B	129	450	52	123	30	2	6	74	58	120	5	3	14-9	.273	.360	.389	.749	12	.991
1995— Binghamton (East.)	3B-1B	135	469	61	115	25	2	10	72	51	104	7	5	6-2	.245	.324	.371	.695	10	.992
—Norfolk (Int'l)	1B	2	7	0	0	0	0	0	0	1	0	0	0	0-0	.000	.125	.000	.125	0	1.000
1996— Binghamton (East.)	3B-1B	122	436	80	129	24	1	22	76	74	103	7	8	7-9	.296	.403	.507	.910	11	.991
—Norfolk (Int'l)	1B	17	54	7	11	2	0	0	6	6	14	0	1	1-1	.204	.279	.241	.519	0	1.000
1997— Charlotte (Int'l)	1B	136	461	66	128	40	2	21	93	65	126	6	7	1-8	.278	.367	.510	.877	8	.991
1998— Charlotte (Int'l)	1B-OF	140	497	102	157	45	4	35	124	80	114	15	15	9-3	.316	.421	.634	1.055	3	.992
—Florida (N.L.)	1B	10	15	0	3	1	0	0	3	1	5	1	0	0-0	.200	.294	.267	.561	0	1.000
1999— Boston (A.L.)	1-DH-O-3	110	381	61	112	33	3	21	73	36	92	3	5	0-1	.294	.360	.562	.921	8	.983
—Pawtucket (Int'l)	DH-1-O-3	9	31	4	9	2	0	1	6	6	8	2	0	0-0	.290	.436	.452	.888	1	.971
2000— Boston (A.L.)	1-DH-F-3	142	495	55	123	32	2	21	76	44	130	6	6	1-1	.248	.315	.448	.764	3	.996
2001— Boston (A.L.)	1B-OF	122	407	54	107	28	3	22	71	53	108	5	10	1-0	.263	.350	.509	.859	11	.988
—Pawtucket (Int'l)	DH	1	4	0	1	0	0	0	0	0	0	0	0	0-0	.250	.250	.250	.500	...	...
—Lowell (NY-Penn)	1B	1	2	0	0	0	0	0	0	1	1	0	0	0-0	.000	.333	.000	.333	1	1.000
2002— Boston (A.L.)	1B-OF-DH	137	444	62	118	24	2	20	78	51	126	7	10	2-1	.266	.348	.464	.812	5	.991
2003— Chicago (A.L.)	1B-DH-OF	95	183	26	42	11	0	6	21	34	54	1	3	1-0	.230	.352	.388	.740	2	.993
2004— Boston (A.L.)	1B-OF	30	75	9	17	8	0	2	8	10	21	1	1	0-0	.227	.326	.413	.739	2	.983
—Pawtucket (Int'l)	1-DH-O-3	93	336	63	92	23	0	21	81	71	93	3	1	0-1	.274	.403	.530	.933	5	.992
American League totals (6 years)		636	1985	267	519	136	10	92	327	228	531	23	35	5-3	.261	.342	.479	.821	31	.990
National League totals (1 year)		10	15	0	3	1	0	0	3	1	5	1	0	0-0	.200	.294	.267	.561	0	1.000
Major League totals (7 years)		646	2000	267	522	137	10	92	330	229	536	24	35	5-3	.261	.342	.478	.819	31	.990

DIVISION SERIES RECORD

											BATTING								FIELDING	
Year Team (League)	Pos.	G	AB	R	H	2B	3B	HR	RBI	BB	SO	HBP	GDP	SB-CS	Avg.	OBP	SLG	OPS	E	Avg.
1999— Boston (A.L.)	DH-1B	4	16	3	4	2	0	1	2	2	7	0	0	0-0	.250	.250	.563	.813	0	1.000

CHAMPIONSHIP SERIES RECORD

											BATTING								FIELDING	
Year Team (League)	Pos.	G	AB	R	H	2B	3B	HR	RBI	BB	SO	HBP	GDP	SB-CS	Avg.	OBP	SLG	OPS	E	Avg.
1999— Boston (A.L.)	DH-1B	5	17	2	3	1	0	1	3	1	4	0	1	0-0	.176	.222	.412	.634	0	...

DAVANON, JEFF — OF

PERSONAL: Born December 8, 1973, in San Diego, Calif. ... 6-0/200. ... Bats both, throws right. ... Full name: Jeffrey Graham DaVanon. ... Name pronounced: duh-VAN-un. ... High school: Bellaire (Texas). ... College: San Diego State. ... Son of Jerry DaVanon, infielder with five major league teams (1969-77).

TRANSACTIONS/CAREER NOTES: Selected by Oakland Athletics organization in 26th round of 1995 free-agent draft. ... Traded by A's with P Elvin Nina and OF Nathan Haynes to Anaheim Angels for P Omar Olivares and 2B Randy Velarde (July 29, 1999). ... On disabled list (March 20, 2000-entire season). ... On disabled list (July 24-August 10, 2004); included rehabilitation assignment to Salt Lake.

2004 GAMES PLAYED BY POSITION (MLB): OF—81, DH—19.

											BATTING								FIELDING	
Year Team (League)	Pos.	G	AB	R	H	2B	3B	HR	RBI	BB	SO	HBP	GDP	SB-CS	Avg.	OBP	SLG	OPS	E	Avg.
1995— S. Oregon (N'west)	OF	57	167	29	42	6	2	1	17	34	49	0	1	6-5	.252	.376	.329	.706	8	.864
1996— W. Mich. (Mid.)	2B-1B-OF	89	289	43	70	13	4	2	33	49	66	1	6	5-7	.242	.353	.336	.689	2	.976

Year	Team (League)	Pos.	G	AB	R	H	2B	3B	HR	RBI	BB	SO	HBP	GDP	SB-CS	Avg.	OBP	SLG	OPS	E	Avg.
1997— Visalia (Calif.)	OF	119	408	70	104	17	3	6	38	81	101	0	7	23-14	.255	.377	.355	.732	10	.948
1998— Modesto (California)	OF	84	301	66	101	17	4	5	60	59	69	1	4	33-10	.336	.439	.468	.907	13	.902
1999— Midland (Texas)	OF-DH	100	374	87	128	29	11	11	60	53	68	4	6	18-10	.342	.424	.567	.991	7	.960
— Edmonton (PCL)	OF-DH	34	132	35	43	8	3	6	19	20	27	1	1	11-4	.326	.416	.568	.984	0	1.000
— Anaheim (A.L.)	OF-DH	7	20	4	4	0	1	1	4	2	7	0	0	0-1	.200	.273	.450	.723	0	1.000
2000— Anaheim (A.L.)					Did not play.															
2001— Salt Lake (PCL)	OF	69	256	46	80	19	8	10	48	32	57	3	4	8-3	.313	.390	.566	.956	1	.992
— Anaheim (A.L.)	OF-DH	40	88	7	17	2	1	5	9	11	29	0	1	1-3	.193	.280	.409	.689	1	.980
2002— Salt Lake (PCL)	OF-DH	16	30	3	5	3	0	1	4	2	6	0	0	1-0	.167	.219	.367	.585	0	1.000
— Salt Lake (PCL)	OF	25	100	21	33	10	1	5	18	17	24	1	1	5-3	.330	.429	.600	1.029	2	.962
— Ariz. Angels (Ariz.)	OF	5	15	5	10	6	1	0	4	5	2	0	0	2-0	.667	.714	1.200	1.914	0	1.000
2003— Salt Lake (PCL)	OF-DH	16	60	11	18	4	1	2	14	9	9	1	1	4-1	.300	.400	.500	.900	2	.933
— Anaheim (A.L.)	OF-DH	123	330	56	93	16	1	12	43	42	59	1	6	17-5	.282	.360	.445	.805	4	.983
2004— Salt Lake (PCL)	OF	3	8	4	5	0	0	1	1	2	0	0	0	1-1	.625	.700	1.000	1.700	0	1.000
— Anaheim (A.L.)	OF-DH	108	285	41	79	11	4	7	34	46	54	0	2	18-3	.277	.372	.418	.790	1	.993
Major League totals (5 years)		294	753	111	198	32	7	26	94	103	155	1	9	37-12	.263	.348	.428	.776	6	.987

DIVISION SERIES RECORD

Year	Team (League)	Pos.	G	AB	R	H	2B	3B	HR	RBI	BB	SO	HBP	GDP	SB-CS	Avg.	OBP	SLG	OPS	E	Avg.
2004— Anaheim (A.L.)	OF	3	10	1	2	0	0	0	0	2	1	0	0	0-1	.200	.333	.200	.533	0	1.000

DAVIS, BEN — C

PERSONAL: Born March 10, 1977, in Chester, Pa. ... 6-4/225. ... Bats both, throws right. ... Full name: Mark Christopher Davis. ... High school: Malvern (Pa.) Prep.

TRANSACTIONS/CAREER NOTES: Selected by San Diego Padres organization in first round (second pick overall) of 1995 free-agent draft. ... On disabled list (August 13-September 1, 2000). ... Traded by Padres with P Wascar Serrano and SS Alex Arias to Seattle Mariners for P Brett Tomko, C Tom Lampkin and SS Ramon Vazquez (December 11, 2001). ... Traded by Mariners with RHP Freddy Garcia to Chicago White Sox for C Miguel Olivo, OF Jeremy Reed and SS Michael Morse (June 27, 2004).

2004 GAMES PLAYED BY POSITION (MLB): C—67.

											BATTING									FIELDING	
Year	Team (League)	Pos.	G	AB	R	H	2B	3B	HR	RBI	BB	SO	HBP	GDP	SB-CS	Avg.	OBP	SLG	OPS	E	Avg.
1995— Idaho Falls (Pio.)	C	52	197	36	55	8	3	5	46	17	36	1	3	0-0	.279	.338	.426	.764	6	.985
1996— Rancho Cuca. (Calif.)	C-DH	98	353	35	71	10	1	6	41	31	89	0	8	1-1	.201	.264	.286	.550	9	.987
1997— Rancho Cuca. (Calif.)	C-DH-1B	122	474	67	132	30	1	17	76	28	107	2	11	3-1	.278	.320	.454	.773	14	.987
1998— Mobile (Sou.)	C-DH	116	433	65	124	29	2	14	75	42	60	6	11	4-2	.286	.352	.460	.812	6	.994
— San Diego (N.L.)	C	1	1	0	0	0	0	0	0	0	0	0	0	0-0	.000	.000	.000	.000	0	1.000
1999— Las Vegas (PCL)	C	58	201	27	62	18	1	7	44	24	41	2	5	4-1	.308	.384	.512	.897	4	.992
— San Diego (N.L.)	C	76	266	29	65	14	1	5	30	25	70	0	9	2-1	.244	.307	.361	.668	7	.986
2000— Las Vegas (PCL)	C	59	221	38	58	16	1	7	40	38	43	1	5	5-2	.262	.373	.439	.812	7	.986
— San Diego (N.L.)	C-DH	43	130	12	29	6	0	3	14	14	35	0	2	1-1	.223	.297	.338	.635	1	.996
2001— San Diego (N.L.)	C-1B	138	448	56	107	20	0	11	57	66	112	4	13	4-4	.239	.337	.357	.694	9	.990
2002— Seattle (A.L.)	C-1B	80	228	24	59	10	1	7	43	18	58	2	6	1-1	.259	.313	.404	.717	1	.998
2003— Seattle (A.L.)	C-DH	80	246	25	58	18	0	6	42	18	61	0	5	0-0	.236	.284	.382	.666	4	.991
2004— Seattle (A.L.)	C	14	33	1	3	0	0	0	2	3	9	0	3	0-0	.091	.162	.091	.253	0	1.000
— Tacoma (PCL)	C	39	141	18	35	9	0	4	15	15	29	0	1	1-0	.248	.321	.397	.718	1	.997
— Chicago (A.L.)	C	54	160	21	37	9	0	6	16	9	40	1	2	1-1	.231	.276	.400	.676	3	.991
American League totals (3 years)		228	667	71	157	37	1	19	103	48	168	3	16	2-2	.235	.286	.379	.665	8	.994
National League totals (4 years)		258	845	97	201	40	1	19	101	105	217	4	24	7-6	.238	.322	.355	.677	17	.990
Major League totals (7 years)		486	1512	168	358	77	2	38	204	153	385	7	40	9-8	.237	.306	.366	.672	25	.992

DAVIS, DOUG — P

PERSONAL: Born September 21, 1975, in Sacramento, Calif. ... 6-4/213. ... Throws left, bats right. ... Full name: Douglas P. Davis. ... High school: Northgate (Walnut Creek, Calif.). ... Junior college: San Francisco (Calif.) City College.

TRANSACTIONS/CAREER NOTES: Selected by Texas Rangers organization in 10th round of 1996 free-agent draft. ... Claimed on waivers by Toronto Blue Jays (April 30, 2003). ... Refused minor league assignment and became a free agent (July 11, 2003). ... Signed by Milwaukee Brewers organization (July 14, 2003). ... Selected by Los Angeles Dodgers organization in 31st round of 1993 free-agent draft; did not sign.

CAREER HITTING: 3-for-88 (.034), 0 R, 0 2B, 0 3B, 0 HR, 0 RBI.

Year	Team (League)	W	L	Pct.	ERA	WHIP	G	GS	CG	ShO	Hld.	Sv.-Opp.	IP	H	R	ER	HR	BB-IBB	SO	Avg.
1996— GC Rangers (GCL)	3	1	.750	1.90	1.27	8	7	0	0	...	0-...	42.2	28	13	9	0	26-1	49	.193
1997— GC Rangers (GCL)	3	1	.750	1.71	1.38	4	4	0	0	...	0-...	21.0	14	5	4	0	15-0	27	.200
— Charlotte (Fla. St.)	5	3	.625	3.10	1.26	9	8	1	0	...	0-...	49.1	29	19	17	2	33-1	52	.175
1998— Charlotte (Fla. St.)	11	7	.611	3.24	1.31	27	27	1	1	...	0-...	155.1	129	69	56	8	74-0	173	.225
1999— Tulsa (Texas)	4	4	.500	2.42	1.21	12	12	1	0	...	0-...	74.1	65	26	20	9	25-0	79	.235
— Oklahoma (PCL)	7	0	1.000	3.00	1.38	13	11	0	0	...	0-...	78.0	77	27	26	4	31-0	74	.263
— Texas (A.L.)	0	0	...	33.75	4.50	2	0	0	0	0	0-0	2.2	12	10	10	3	0-0	3	.600
2000— Oklahoma (PCL)	8	3	.727	2.84	1.38	12	12	2	0	...	0-...	69.2	62	32	22	8	34-1	53	.248
— Texas (A.L.)	7	6	.538	5.38	1.69	30	13	1	0	2	0-3	98.2	109	61	59	14	58-3	66	.288
2001— Texas (A.L.)	11	10	.524	4.45	1.55	30	30	1	0	0	0-0	186.0	220	103	92	14	69-1	115	.295
— Oklahoma (PCL)	2	0	1.000	2.87	0.89	2	2	0	0	...	0-...	15.2	10	5	5	1	4-0	14	.189
2002— Texas (A.L.)	3	5	.375	4.98	1.49	10	10	1	1	0	0-...	59.2	67	36	33	7	22-0	28	.290
— Oklahoma (PCL)	4	3	.571	4.99	1.32	9	9	0	0	...	0-...	61.1	70	38	34	7	11-0	48	.290
2003— Oklahoma (PCL)	3	0	1.000	3.25	1.10	4	4	0	0	...	0-...	27.2	29	10	10	3	1-0	18	.271
— Texas (A.L.)	0	0	...	12.00	2.67	1	1	0	0	0	0-0	3.0	4	4	4	2	4-0	2	.308
— Toronto (A.L.)	4	6	.400	5.00	1.78	12	11	0	0	0	0-0	54.0	70	33	30	8	26-1	25	.318
— Huntsville (Southern)	1	0	1.000	3.00	1.30	1	1	0	0	...	0-...	6.0	5	2	2	0	3-0	6	.227
— Indianapolis (Int'l)	1	2	.333	4.15	1.20	5	5	0	0	...	0-...	34.2	33	16	16	2	10-0	19	.250
— Milwaukee (N.L.)	3	2	.600	2.58	1.34	8	8	0	0	...	0-0	52.1	49	18	15	8	21-0	35	.247
2004— Milwaukee (N.L.)	12	12	.500	3.39	1.31	34	34	0	0	0	0-0	207.1	192	84	78	14	79-3	166	.247
American League totals (5 years)	25	27	.481	5.08	1.64	85	65	3	1	2	0-3	404.0	482	247	228	46	179-5	239	.300
National League totals (2 years)	15	14	.517	3.22	1.31	42	42	0	0	0	0-0	259.2	241	102	93	22	100-3	201	.247
Major League totals (6 years)	40	41	.494	4.35	1.51	127	107	4	1	2	0-3	663.2	723	349	321	68	279-8	440	.280

DAVIS, JASON   P

PERSONAL: Born May 8, 1980, in Chattanooga, Tenn. ... 6-6/210. ... Throws right, bats right. ... Full name: Jason Thomas Davis. ... College: Cleveland State.
TRANSACTIONS/CAREER NOTES: Selected by Cleveland Indians organization in 21st round of 1999 free-agent draft.
CAREER HITTING: 1-for-7 (.143), 1 R, 0 2B, 0 3B, 1 HR, 1 RBI.

Year Team (League)	W	L	Pct.	ERA	WHIP	G	GS	CG	ShO	Hld.	Sv.-Opp.	IP	H	R	ER	HR	BB-IBB	SO	Avg.
2000— Burlington (Appalachian) ..	4	4	.500	4.40	1.42	10	10	0	0	...	0-...	45.0	48	27	22	5	16-0	35	.276
2001— Columbus (S. Atl.)	14	6	.700	2.70	1.24	27	27	1	1	...	0-...	160.0	147	72	48	9	51-1	115	.243
2002— Kinston (Caro.)	3	6	.333	4.15	1.38	17	17	1	1	...	0-...	99.2	107	64	46	7	31-2	68	.272
— Akron (East.)	6	2	.750	3.51	1.34	10	10	0	0	...	0-...	59.0	63	26	23	2	16-0	45	.278
— Cleveland (A.L.)	1	0	1.000	1.84	1.09	3	2	0	0	0	0-0	14.2	12	3	3	1	4-0	11	.218
2003— Cleveland (A.L.)	8	11	.421	4.68	1.32	27	27	1	0	0	0-0	165.1	172	101	86	25	47-4	85	.273
2004— Buffalo (Int'l)	3	2	.600	3.00	1.31	9	9	0	0	...	0-...	54.0	53	26	18	4	18-1	39	.261
— Cleveland (A.L.)	2	7	.222	5.51	1.74	26	19	0	0	1	0-0	114.1	148	81	70	13	51-1	72	.311
Major League totals (3 years)	**11**	**18**	**.379**	**4.86**	**1.47**	**56**	**48**	**1**	**0**	**1**	**0-0**	**294.1**	**332**	**185**	**159**	**39**	**102-5**	**168**	**.286**

DAVIS, J.J.   OF

PERSONAL: Born October 25, 1978, in Glendora, Calif. ... 6-5/250. ... Bats right, throws right. ... Full name: Jerry C. Davis. ... High school: Baldwin Park (Calif.).
TRANSACTIONS/CAREER NOTES: Selected by Pittsburgh Pirates organization in first round (eighth pick overall) of 1997 free-agent draft. ... On disabled list (May 19-June 25 and July 15, 2004-remainder of season); included rehabilitation assignment to Nashville.
2004 GAMES PLAYED BY POSITION (MLB): OF—17.

Year Team (League)	Pos.	G	AB	R	H	2B	3B	HR	RBI	BB	SO	HBP	GDP	SB-CS	Avg.	OBP	SLG	OPS	E	Avg.
1997— GC Pirates (GCL)	OF	45	165	19	42	10	2	1	18	14	44	2	4	0-0	.255	.315	.358	.673	0	1.000
— Erie (N.Y.-Penn)	DH	4	13	1	1	0	0	0	0	0	4	0	0	0-0	.077	.077	.077	.154	...	...
1998— Augusta (S. Atl.)	OF	30	106	11	21	6	0	4	11	3	24	0	4	1-1	.198	.220	.368	.588	3	.923
— Erie (N.Y.-Penn)	OF	52	196	25	53	12	2	8	39	20	54	2	3	4-1	.270	.341	.474	.815	7	.932
1999— Hickory (S. Atl.)	OF	86	317	58	84	26	1	19	65	44	99	4	3	2-5	.265	.360	.533	.893	4	.950
2000— Lynchburg (Caro.)	OF	130	485	77	118	36	1	20	80	52	171	4	11	9-4	.243	.319	.445	.765	18	.925
2001— Altoona (East.)	OF	67	228	21	57	13	3	4	26	21	79	2	1	2-5	.250	.317	.386	.703	0	1.000
— GC Pirates (GCL)	OF	4	17	3	8	1	0	2	6	1	2	0	1	0-0	.471	.500	.882	1.382	1	.667
2002— Altoona (East.)	OF	101	348	51	100	17	3	20	62	33	101	3	3	7-4	.287	.351	.526	.877	6	.971
— Pittsburgh (N.L.)	OF	9	10	1	1	0	0	0	0	1	4	1	1	0-0	.100	.182	.100	.282	0	1.000
2003— Nashville (PCL)	OF-DH	122	426	68	121	29	4	26	67	35	85	4	11	23-6	.284	.342	.554	.896	9	.964
— Pittsburgh (N.L.)	OF	19	35	1	7	0	0	1	4	3	13	0	0	0-1	.200	.263	.286	.549	0	1.000
2004— Pittsburgh (N.L.)	OF	25	35	4	5	1	0	0	3	4	10	0	0	2-0	.143	.225	.171	.396	2	.895
— Nashville (PCL)	OF-DH	27	84	11	21	6	1	8	17	3	28	0	0	3-0	.250	.270	.631	.901	0	1.000
Major League totals (3 years)		**53**	**80**	**6**	**13**	**1**	**0**	**1**	**7**	**7**	**27**	**1**	**1**	**2-1**	**.163**	**.236**	**.213**	**.448**	**2**	**.944**

DAWLEY, JOE   P

PERSONAL: Born September 19, 1971, in Riverside, Calif. ... 6-4/205. ... Throws right, bats right. ... Full name: Joseph Thomas Dawley. ... Junior college: Riverside (Calif.) Community College.
TRANSACTIONS/CAREER NOTES: Selected by Baltimore Orioles organization in 28th round of 1992 free-agent draft. ... Released by Orioles (July 9, 1995). ... Signed as a free agent by Atlanta Braves organization (September 19, 1998). ... Signed as a free agent by Kansas City Royals (October 29, 2003). ... Claimed on waivers by Cleveland Indians (May 19, 2004). ... On disabled list (June 6, 2004-remainder of season); included rehabilitation assignments to Buffalo and Akron. ... Refused minor league assignment and became a free agent (October 14, 2004).
CAREER HITTING: 0-for-1 (.000), 0 R, 0 2B, 0 3B, 0 HR, 0 RBI.

Year Team (League)	W	L	Pct.	ERA	WHIP	G	GS	CG	ShO	Hld.	Sv.-Opp.	IP	H	R	ER	HR	BB-IBB	SO	Avg.
1993— Bluefield (Appalachian)	3	1	.750	3.52	1.57	20	0	0	0	...	3-...	30.2	34	20	12	1	14-3	30	.272
1994— Bluefield (Appalachian)	1	2	.333	5.70	1.61	11	2	0	0	...	2-...	23.2	20	18	15	2	18-0	18	.222
— Albany (S. Atl.)	0	0	...	6.14	1.91	5	0	0	0	...	0-...	7.1	7	6	5	0	7-1	4	.250
1995— Frederick (Caro.)	1	2	.333	6.34	1.93	24	0	0	0	...	1-...	32.2	41	28	23	4	22-1	29	.301
— Palm Springs (West.)	1	0	1.000	3.86	1.32	15	0	0	0	...	0-...	28.0	28	14	12	2	9-0	20	.241
1996— Palm Springs (West.)	2	1	.667	1.59	1.29	27	0	0	0	...	4-...	34.0	26	14	6	3	18-1	29	.205
1997— Chico (West.)	1	4	.200	4.39	1.46	41	0	0	0	...	14-...	41.0	42	24	20	2	18-2	51	.256
1998— Chico (West.)	2	4	.333	3.35	1.63	45	0	0	0	...	26-...	43.0	43	22	16	2	27-2	36	.261
1999— Richmond (Int'l)	0	3	.000	5.18	1.38	7	7	1	0	...	0-...	40.0	43	26	23	5	12-0	31	.274
— Greenville (Sou.)	5	3	.625	4.03	1.23	26	11	0	0	...	0-...	91.2	76	54	41	5	37-3	89	.224
2000— Did not play.																			
2001— Myrtle Beach (Caro.)	1	0	1.000	1.80	0.40	5	0	0	0	...	0-...	10.0	4	2	2	0	0-0	16	.118
— Richmond (Int'l)	1	0	1.000	2.84	0.63	3	0	0	0	...	0-...	6.1	3	2	2	1	1-0	5	.143
— Greenville (Sou.)	7	5	.583	3.04	1.11	22	21	1	0	...	0-...	127.1	95	50	43	15	46-0	130	.207
2002— Richmond (Int'l)	9	7	.563	2.63	1.06	24	23	1	1	...	0-...	140.1	113	44	41	10	36-0	136	.220
— Atlanta (N.L.)	0	0	...	0.00	0.00	1	0	0	0	0	0-0	.1	0	0	0	0	0-0	1	.000
2003— Richmond (Int'l)	3	5	.375	3.34	1.24	46	4	0	0	...	23-...	56.2	47	25	21	4	23-1	73	.221
— Atlanta (N.L.)	0	0	...	18.00	2.57	5	0	0	0	0	0-0	7.0	15	14	14	3	3-0	8	.405
2004— Omaha (PCL)	1	2	.333	3.19	1.10	9	3	0	0	...	0-...	31.0	26	14	11	1	8-0	29	.222
— Buffalo (Int'l)	0	0	...	0.00	0.88	1	1	0	0	...	0-...	5.2	4	3	0	0	1-0	7	.190
— Cleveland (A.L.)	0	0	...	5.40	1.68	2	2	0	0	0	0-...	8.1	7	5	5	1	7-0	8	.233
— Akron (East.)	0	1	.000	...	...	1	1	0	0	...	0-...	...	3	3	3	0	1-0	0	1.000
American League totals (1 year)	**0**	**0**	**...**	**5.40**	**1.68**	**2**	**2**	**0**	**0**	**0**	**0-0**	**8.1**	**7**	**5**	**5**	**1**	**7-0**	**8**	**.233**
National League totals (2 years)	**0**	**0**	**...**	**17.18**	**2.45**	**6**	**0**	**0**	**0**	**0**	**0-0**	**7.1**	**15**	**14**	**14**	**3**	**3-0**	**9**	**.395**
Major League totals (3 years)	**0**	**0**	**...**	**10.91**	**2.04**	**8**	**2**	**0**	**0**	**0**	**0-0**	**15.2**	**22**	**19**	**19**	**4**	**10-0**	**17**	**.324**

DAY, ZACH   P

PERSONAL: Born June 15, 1978, in Cincinnati, Ohio. ... 6-4/216. ... Throws right, bats right. ... Full name: Stephen Zachary Day. ... High school: La Salle (Cincinnati). ... College: Cincinnati.
TRANSACTIONS/CAREER NOTES: Selected by New York Yankees organization in fifth round of 1996 free-agent draft. ... Traded by Yankees to Cleveland Indians with P Jake Westbrook (July 24, 2000), completing deal in which Indians traded OF David Justice to Yankees for OF Ricky Ledee and two players to be named (June 29, 2000). ... Traded

D

by Indians to Montreal Expos for OF Milton Bradley (July 31, 2001). ... On disabled list (May 29-July 26, 2003); includes rehabilitation assignments to GCL Expos and Brevard County. ... On disabled list (July 6-22 and August 2, 2004-remainder of season). ... Expos franchise transferred to Washington, D.C., for 2005 season.

CAREER HITTING: 4-for-82 (.049), 4 R, 0 2B, 0 3B, 1 HR, 3 RBI.

Year Team (League)	W	L	Pct.	ERA	WHIP	G	GS	CG	ShO	Hld.	Sv.-Opp.	IP	H	R	ER	HR	BB-IBB	SO	Avg.
1996— GC Yankees (GCL)	5	2	.714	5.61	1.31	7	5	0	0	...	0-...	33.2	41	26	21	3	3-0	23	.311
1997— Oneonta (N.Y.-Penn)	7	2	.778	2.15	1.14	14	14	0	0	...	0-...	92.0	82	26	22	2	23-0	92	.240
1998— Tampa (FSL)	5	8	.385	5.49	1.74	18	17	0	0	...	0-...	100.0	142	89	61	5	32-4	69	.326
— Greensboro (S. Atl.)	1	2	.333	2.75	1.14	7	6	1	0	...	0-...	36.0	35	22	11	1	6-0	37	.245
1999— GC Yankees (GCL)	1	1	.500	3.78	1.44	5	4	0	0	...	0-...	16.2	20	10	7	1	4-0	17	.290
— Greensboro (S. Atl.)	0	1	.000	2.25	1.88	2	2	0	0	...	0-...	8.0	14	11	2	0	1-0	4	.359
2000— Greensboro (S. Atl.)	9	3	.750	1.90	1.21	13	13	1	1	...	0-...	85.1	72	29	18	6	31-0	101	.232
— Tampa (FSL)	2	4	.333	4.19	1.40	7	7	0	0	...	0-...	34.1	33	22	16	2	15-1	36	.246
— Akron (East.)	4	2	.667	3.52	1.28	8	8	0	0	...	0-...	46.0	38	20	18	1	21-0	43	.232
2001— Akron (East.)	9	10	.474	3.10	1.23	22	22	2	0	...	0-...	136.2	123	57	47	8	45-1	94	.237
— Buffalo (Int'l)	1	0	1.000	1.50	0.67	1	1	0	0	...	0-...	6.0	3	1	1	0	1-0	4	.143
— Ottawa (Int'l)	2	2	.500	7.43	1.73	6	5	0	0	...	0-...	26.2	38	23	22	2	8-0	15	.349
2002— Ottawa (Int'l)	5	6	.455	3.50	1.21	17	16	1	0	...	0-...	90.0	77	38	35	5	32-0	68	.231
— Montreal (N.L.)	4	1	.800	3.62	1.15	19	2	0	0	2	1-2	37.1	28	18	15	3	15-2	25	.207
2003— GC Expos (GCL)	0	0	...	3.86	1.70	1	1	0	0	...	0-...	2.1	3	3	1	0	1-0	3	.300
— Brevard County (FSL)	0	0	...	1.69	0.80	1	1	0	0	...	0-...	5.1	3	1	1	0	1-0	3	.167
— Montreal (N.L.)	9	8	.529	4.18	1.45	23	23	1	1	0	0-0	131.1	132	64	61	8	59-3	61	.262
2004— Montreal (N.L.)	5	10	.333	3.93	1.39	19	19	1	1	0	0-0	116.2	117	53	51	13	45-7	61	.265
Major League totals (3 years)	**18**	**19**	**.486**	**4.01**	**1.39**	**61**	**44**	**2**	**2**	**1-2**		**285.1**	**277**	**135**	**127**	**24**	**119-12**	**147**	**.256**

DEJEAN, MIKE   P

PERSONAL: Born September 28, 1970, in Baton Rouge, La. ... 6-2/219. ... Throws right, bats right. ... Full name: Michel Dwain DeJean. ... Name pronounced: DAY-zhan. ... High school: Walker (La.). ... College: Livingston University (Ala.).

TRANSACTIONS/CAREER NOTES: Selected by New York Yankees organization in 24th round of 1992 free-agent draft. ... Traded by Yankees with a player to be named to Colorado Rockies for C Joe Girardi (November 20, 1995). ... Rockies acquired P Steve Shoemaker to complete deal (December 6, 1995). ... On disabled list (July 18-August 8, 1997); included rehabilitation assignment to New Haven. ... On disabled list (September 2, 1998-remainder of season). ... On disabled list (August 14-September 1, 1999); included rehabilitation assignment to Colorado Springs. ... On disabled list (March 29-April 28 and July 25-August 15, 2000); included rehabilitation assignment to Colorado Springs. ... Traded by Rockies with P Mark Leiter and 2B/SS Elvis Pena to Milwaukee Brewers for Ps Juan Acevedo and Kane Davis and IF Jose Flores (April 4, 2001). ... Traded by Milwaukee Brewers to St. Louis Cardinals for two players to be named (August 22, 2003); Brewers acquired Ps Mike Crudale (August 27, 2003) and John Novinsky (September 10, 2003) to complete deal. ... Signed as a free agent by Baltimore Orioles (January 8, 2004). ... Traded by Orioles to New York Mets for OF Karim Garcia (July 19, 2004). ... On disabled list (August 30, 2004-remainder of season).

CAREER HITTING: 1-for-17 (.059), 0 R, 1 2B, 0 3B, 0 HR, 0 RBI.

Year Team (League)	W	L	Pct.	ERA	WHIP	G	GS	CG	ShO	Hld.	Sv.-Opp.	IP	H	R	ER	HR	BB-IBB	SO	Avg.
1992— Oneonta (N.Y.-Penn)	0	0	...	0.44	0.73	20	0	0	0	...	16-...	20.2	12	3	1	1	3-0	20	.160
1993— Greensboro (S. Atl.)	2	3	.400	5.00	1.67	20	0	0	0	...	9-...	18.0	22	12	10	1	8-2	16	.286
1994— Tampa (FSL)	0	2	.000	2.38	1.53	34	0	0	0	...	16-...	34.0	39	15	9	1	13-0	22	.283
— Albany (East.)	0	2	.000	4.38	1.50	16	0	0	0	...	4-...	24.2	22	14	12	1	15-3	13	.250
1995— Norwich (East.)	5	5	.500	2.99	1.17	59	0	0	0	...	20-...	78.1	58	29	26	5	34-2	57	.208
1996— Colo. Springs (PCL)	0	2	.000	5.13	1.81	30	0	0	0	...	1-...	40.1	52	24	23	3	21-3	31	.319
— New Haven (East.)	0	0	...	3.22	1.25	16	0	0	0	...	11-...	22.1	20	9	8	2	8-0	12	.247
1997— Colo. Springs (PCL)	0	1	.000	5.40	2.40	10	0	0	0	...	4-...	10.0	17	6	6	0	7-1	9	.405
— Colorado (N.L.)	5	0	1.000	3.99	1.45	55	0	0	0	13	2-4	67.2	74	34	30	4	24-2	38	.280
— New Haven (East.)	0	1	.000	6.00	1.67	2	0	0	0	...	0-...	3.0	3	2	2	0	2-0	2	.273
1998— Colorado (N.L.)	3	1	.750	3.03	1.37	59	1	0	0	11	2-3	74.1	78	29	25	4	24-1	27	.285
1999— Colorado (N.L.)	2	4	.333	8.41	1.89	56	0	0	0	9	0-4	61.0	83	61	57	13	32-8	31	.335
— Colo. Springs (PCL)	0	0	...	0.00	1.00	1	0	0	0	...	0-...	1.0	1	0	0	0	0-0	3	.333
2000— Colo. Springs (PCL)	1	1	.500	2.51	1.33	12	0	0	0	...	5-...	14.1	15	4	4	0	4-0	12	.273
— Colorado (N.L.)	4	4	.500	4.89	1.58	54	0	0	0	7	0-4	53.1	54	31	29	9	30-6	34	.269
2001— Milwaukee (N.L.)	4	2	.667	2.77	1.35	75	0	0	0	8	2-4	84.1	75	31	26	4	39-7	68	.236
2002— Milwaukee (N.L.)	1	5	.167	3.12	1.40	68	0	0	0	5	27-30	75.0	66	28	26	7	39-8	65	.237
2003— Milwaukee (N.L.)	4	7	.364	4.87	1.48	58	0	0	0	5	18-26	64.2	69	38	35	12	27-7	58	.271
— St. Louis (N.L.)	1	1	.500	4.00	1.61	18	0	0	0	5	1-1	18.0	17	8	8	1	12-0	13	.262
2004— Baltimore (A.L.)	0	5	.000	6.13	1.94	37	0	0	0	1	0-0	39.2	49	29	27	2	28-6	36	.308
— New York (N.L.)	0	0	...	1.69	1.22	17	0	0	0	2	0-0	21.1	21	5	4	0	5-2	24	.256
American League totals (1 year)	**0**	**5**	**.000**	**6.13**	**1.94**	**37**	**0**	**0**	**0**	**1**	**0-0**	**39.2**	**49**	**29**	**27**	**2**	**28-6**	**36**	**.308**
National League totals (8 years)	**24**	**24**	**.500**	**4.16**	**1.48**	**460**	**1**	**0**	**0**	**60**	**52-76**	**519.2**	**537**	**265**	**240**	**54**	**232-41**	**358**	**.270**
Major League totals (8 years)	**24**	**29**	**.453**	**4.30**	**1.51**	**497**	**1**	**0**	**0**	**61**	**52-76**	**559.1**	**586**	**294**	**267**	**56**	**260-47**	**394**	**.273**

DEJESUS, DAVID   OF

PERSONAL: Born December 20, 1979, in Brooklyn, N.Y. ... 6-0/175. ... Bats left, throws left. ... Full name: David Christopher DeJesus. ... High school: Manalapan (N.J.). ... College: Rutgers.

TRANSACTIONS/CAREER NOTES: Selected by New York Mets organization in 43rd round of 1997 free-agent draft; did not sign. ... Selected by Kansas City Royals organization in fourth round of 2000 free-agent draft.

2004 GAMES PLAYED BY POSITION (MLB): OF—94.

Year Team (League)	Pos.	G	AB	R	H	2B	3B	HR	RBI	BATTING BB	SO	HBP	GDP	SB-CS	Avg.	OBP	SLG	OPS	FIELDING E	Avg.
2002— Wilmington (Caro.)	OF	87	334	69	99	22	6	4	41	48	42	13	8	15-6	.296	.400	.434	.834	1	.994
— Wichita (Texas)	OF	25	79	7	20	5	2	2	15	8	10	5	3	3-1	.253	.347	.443	.790	1	.976
2003— Wichita (Texas)	OF	17	71	14	24	4	0	2	10	9	8	2	3	1-3	.338	.422	.479	.901	1	.980
— Omaha (PCL)	OF-DH	59	215	49	64	16	3	5	23	34	30	9	9	8-4	.298	.412	.470	.881	0	1.000
— Kansas City (A.L.)	OF	12	7	0	2	0	1	0	0	1	2	1	0	0-0	.286	.444	.571	1.016	0	1.000
2004— Omaha (PCL)	OF	50	197	38	62	14	4	6	16	21	30	7	5	7-6	.315	.400	.518	.918	1	.991
— Kansas City (A.L.)	OF	96	363	58	104	15	3	7	39	33	53	9	6	8-11	.287	.360	.402	.763	4	.984
Major League totals (2 years)		**108**	**370**	**58**	**106**	**15**	**4**	**7**	**39**	**34**	**55**	**10**	**6**	**8-11**	**.286**	**.362**	**.405**	**.768**	**4**	**.984**

DE LA ROSA, JORGE — P

PERSONAL: Born April 5, 1981, in Monterrey, Mexico. ... 6-1/190. ... Throws left, bats left. ... Full name: Jorge Alberto de la Rosa.

TRANSACTIONS/CAREER NOTES: Signed as a non-drafted free agent by Arizona Diamondbacks organization (March 20, 1998). ... Contract sold by Diamondbacks organization to Monterrey of the Mexican League (April 2, 2000). ... Contract purchased by Boston Red Sox organization from Monterrey (February 22, 2001). ... Traded with Ps Casey Fossum and Brandon Lyon and OF Mike Goss to Diamondbacks for P Curt Schilling (November 28, 2003). ... Traded with SS Craig Counsell, 2B Junior Spivey, 1B Lyle Overbay, C Chad Moeller and P Chris Capuano to Milwaukee Brewers for 1B Richie Sexson P Shane Nance and a player to be named (December 1, 2003); Diamondbacks acquired OF Noochie Varner to complete deal (December 15, 2003).

CAREER HITTING: 0-for-6 (.000), 0 R, 0 2B, 0 3B, 0 HR, 0 RBI.

Year — Team (League)	W	L	Pct.	ERA	WHIP	G	GS	CG	ShO	Hld.	Sv.-Opp.	IP	H	R	ER	HR	BB-IBB	SO	Avg.
1999— High Desert (Calif.)	0	0	...	0.00	1.00	2	0	0	0	...	0-...	3.0	1	0	0	0	2-0	3	.100
— Ariz. D'backs (Ariz.)	0	0	...	3.21	1.07	8	0	0	0	...	2-...	14.0	12	5	5	1	3-0	17	.226
— Missoula (Pio.)	0	1	.000	7.98	2.11	13	0	0	0	...	2-...	14.2	22	17	13	2	9-0	14	.333
2001— Sarasota (Florida State)	0	1	.000	1.21	0.84	12	0	0	0	...	2-...	29.2	13	7	4	0	12-0	27	.127
— Trenton (East.)	1	3	.250	5.84	2.05	29	0	0	0	...	0-...	37.0	56	35	24	4	20-1	27	.348
2002— Sarasota (Florida State)	7	7	.500	3.65	1.30	23	23	1	1	...	0-...	120.2	105	53	49	10	52-1	95	.231
— Trenton (East.)	1	2	.333	5.50	1.44	4	4	0	0	...	0-...	18.0	17	12	11	0	9-0	15	.239
2003— Portland (East.)	6	3	.667	2.80	1.23	22	20	0	0	...	1-...	99.2	87	39	31	6	36-0	102	.236
— Pawtucket (Int'l)	1	2	.333	3.75	1.63	5	5	0	0	...	0-...	24.0	27	14	10	0	12-0	17	.278
2004— Indianapolis (Int'l)	5	6	.455	4.52	1.35	20	20	0	0	...	0-...	85.2	80	45	43	9	36-1	86	.249
— Milwaukee (N.L.)	0	3	.000	6.35	1.90	5	5	0	0	...	0-0	22.2	29	20	16	1	14-0	5	.309
Major League totals (1 year)	0	3	.000	6.35	1.90	5	5	0	0	...	0-0	22.2	29	20	16	1	14-0	5	.309

DELGADO, CARLOS — 1B

PERSONAL: Born June 25, 1972, in Aguadilla, Puerto Rico. ... 6-3/230. ... Bats left, throws right. ... Full name: Carlos Juan Delgado. ... Name pronounced: del-GAH-doh. ... High school: Jose de Diego (Aguadilla, Puerto Rico).

TRANSACTIONS/CAREER NOTES: Signed as a non-drafted free agent by Toronto Blue Jays organization (October 9, 1988). ... On disabled list (March 15-April 24, 1998); included rehabilitation assignments to Dunedin and Syracuse. ... On disabled list (August 9-25, 2002). ... On disabled list (May 30-July 6, 2004); included rehabilitation assignments to Dunedin and Syracuse.

RECORDS: Shares major league record for most home runs, game (4, September 25, 2003).

HONORS: Named Major League Player of the Year by THE SPORTING NEWS (2000).

2004 GAMES PLAYED BY POSITION (MLB): 1B—120, DH—8.

Year — Team (League)	Pos.	G	AB	R	H	2B	3B	HR	RBI	BB	SO	HBP	GDP	SB-CS	Avg.	OBP	SLG	OPS	E	Avg.
1989— St. Catharines (NY-Penn.)	C	31	89	9	16	5	0	0	11	23	39	0	4	0-0	.180	.345	.236	.581	2	.974
1990— St. Catharines (NY-Penn.)	C	67	228	30	64	13	0	6	39	35	65	5	2	2-7	.281	.382	.417	.799	7	.987
1991— Myrtle Beach (SAL)	C	132	441	72	126	18	2	18	70	75	97	8	7	9-10	.286	.396	.458	.854	19	.976
— Syracuse (Int'l)	C	1	3	0	0	0	0	0	0	0	2	0	0	0-0	.000	.000	.000	.000	0	1.000
1992— Dunedin (Fla. St.)	C	133	485	83	157	30	2	30	100	59	91	6	8	2-5	.324	.402	.579	.982	11	.986
1993— Knoxville (Southern)	C	140	468	91	142	28	0	25	102	102	98	6	11	10-3	.303	.430	.524	.954	14	.983
— Toronto (A.L.)	DH-C	2	1	0	0	0	0	0	0	1	0	0	0	0-0	.000	.500	.000	.500	0	1.000
1994— Toronto (A.L.)	OF-C	43	130	17	28	2	0	9	24	25	46	3	5	1-1	.215	.352	.438	.791	2	.967
— Syracuse (Int'l)	DH-C-1B	85	307	52	98	11	0	19	58	42	58	3	3	1-0	.319	.404	.541	.945	7	.974
1995— Toronto (A.L.)	OF-DH-1B	37	91	7	15	3	0	3	11	6	26	0	1	0-0	.165	.212	.297	.509	0	1.000
— Syracuse (Int'l)	1B-OF	91	333	59	106	24	4	22	74	45	78	5	8	0-4	.318	.403	.610	1.013	4	.995
1996— Toronto (A.L.)	DH-1B	138	488	68	132	28	2	25	92	58	139	9	13	0-0	.270	.353	.490	.843	4	.983
1997— Toronto (A.L.)	1B-DH	153	519	79	136	42	3	30	91	64	133	8	6	0-3	.262	.350	.528	.878	12	.988
1998— Dunedin (Fla. St.)	DH-1B	4	16	4	5	1	0	2	7	2	4	0	1	0-0	.313	.389	.750	1.139	0	1.000
— Syracuse (Int'l)	1B	2	7	4	4	2	0	1	6	2	0	0	0	0-0	.571	.667	1.286	1.952	0	1.000
— Toronto (A.L.)	1B-DH	142	530	94	155	43	1	38	115	73	139	11	8	3-0	.292	.385	.592	.978	10	.990
1999— Toronto (A.L.)	1B-DH	152	573	113	156	39	0	44	134	86	141	15	11	1-1	.272	.377	.571	.948	* 14	.990
2000— Toronto (A.L.)	1B	• 162	569	115	196	* 57	1	41	137	123	104	15	12	0-1	.344	.470	.664	1.134	13	.991
2001— Toronto (A.L.)	1B	• 162	574	102	160	31	1	39	102	111	136	16	9	3-0	.279	.408	.540	.948	9	.994
2002— Toronto (A.L.)	1B-DH	143	505	103	140	34	2	33	108	102	126	13	8	0-0	.277	.406	.549	.955	12	.991
2003— Toronto (A.L.)	1B-DH	161	570	117	172	38	1	42	* 145	109	137	19	9	0-0	.302	.426	.593	1.019	10	.993
2004— Dunedin (Fla. St.)	1B	2	8	1	2	0	0	1	2	0	0	0	1	0-0	.250	.250	.625	.875	0	1.000
— Syracuse (Int'l)	1B	2	9	2	5	2	0	1	4	0	0	0	1	0-0	.556	.556	1.111	1.667	0	1.000
— Toronto (A.L.)	1B-DH	128	458	74	123	26	0	32	99	69	115	13	11	0-1	.269	.372	.535	.907	5	.996
Major League totals (12 years)		1423	5008	889	1413	343	11	336	1058	827	1242	122	93	9-7	.282	.392	.556	.949	91	.992

ALL-STAR GAME RECORD

	G	AB	R	H	2B	3B	HR	RBI	BB	SO	HBP	GDP	SB-CS	Avg.	OBP	SLG	OPS	E	Avg.
All-Star Game totals (2 years)	2	4	0	2	1	0	1	4	0	1	0	0	0-0	.500	.500	.750	1.250	0	1.000

DELGADO, WILSON — SS/2B

PERSONAL: Born July 15, 1972, in San Cristobal, Dominican Republic. ... 5-11/165. ... Bats both, throws right. ... Full name: Wilson Duran Delgado. ... Name pronounced: del-GAH-doh.

TRANSACTIONS/CAREER NOTES: Signed as non-drafted free agent by Seattle Mariners organization (October 29, 1992). ... Traded by Mariners with P Shawn Estes to San Francisco Giants for P Salomon Torres (May 21, 1995). ... Traded by Giants to New York Yankees for SS Juan Melo (March 23, 2000). ... Traded by Yankees to Kansas City Royals for SS Nick Ortiz (August 11, 2000). ... Granted free agency (October 9, 2001). ... Signed by St. Louis Cardinals organization (December 23, 2001). ... On Memphis disabled list (June 12-July 29, 2002). ... Traded by Cardinals to Anaheim Angels for cash (August 31, 2003). ... Refused minor league assignment and became a free agent (October 12, 2004).

2004 GAMES PLAYED BY POSITION (MLB): SS—39.

Year — Team (League)	Pos.	G	AB	R	H	2B	3B	HR	RBI	BB	SO	HBP	GDP	SB-CS	Avg.	OBP	SLG	OPS	E	Avg.
1993— Dom. Mariners (DSL)	IF	60	171	19	50	8	0	0	26	34	25		...	5-...	.292	...	.339	...	16	.938
1994— Ariz. Mariners (Ariz.)	2B-SS	39	149	30	56	5	4	0	10	15	24	1	2	13-5	.376	.436	.463	.899	10	.945
— Appleton (Midwest)	SS	9	31	2	6	0	0	0	0	0	8	0	2	0-0	.194	.194	.194	.387	1	.967
1995— Port City (Sou.)	SS	13	41	3	8	4	0	0	1	6	8	0	1	0-0	.195	.298	.293	.591	5	.917
— Wisconsin (Midw.)	SS	19	70	13	17	3	0	0	7	3	15	0		3-0	.243	.274	.286	.560	6	.940
— Burlington (Midw.)	SS	93	365	52	113	20	3	5	37	32	57	2		9-9	.310	.368	.422	.789	19	.956
— San Jose (Calif.)	SS	1	2	1	0	0	0	0	0	0	0	0		0-0	.000	.000	.000	.000	0	1.000
1996— San Jose (Calif.)	SS	121	462	59	124	19	6	2	54	48	89	2	8	8-2	.268	• .337	.348	.686	24	.957
— Phoenix (PCL)	SS	12	43	1	6	0	1	0	1	3	7	0	1	0-1	.140	.196	.186	.382	2	.975
— San Francisco (N.L.)	SS	6	22	3	8	0	0	0	2	1	5	2	1	1-0	.364	.440	.364	.804	2	.960

Year	Team (League)	Pos.	G	AB	R	H	2B	3B	HR	RBI	BB	SO	HBP	GDP	SB-CS	Avg.	OBP	SLG	OPS	E	Avg.
1997—San Francisco (N.L.)		2B-SS	8	7	1	1	1	0	0	0	0	2	0	0	0-0	.143	.143	.286	.429	0	1.000
—Phoenix (PCL)		SS-2B	119	416	47	120	22	4	9	59	24	70	1	9	9-3	.288	.326	.425	.751	18	.969
1998—Fresno (PCL)		SS	127	512	87	142	22	2	12	63	52	92	3	6	9-5	.277	.345	.398	.743	23	.962
—San Francisco (N.L.)		SS	10	12	1	2	1	0	0	1	1	3	0	0	0-0	.167	.231	.250	.481	0	1.000
1999—Fresno (PCL)		SS-2B-DH	57	213	28	64	10	3	1	33	18	35	0	8	4-2	.300	.355	.390	.745	15	.944
—San Francisco (N.L.)		SS-2B	35	71	7	18	2	1	0	3	5	9	1	2	1-0	.254	.312	.310	.622	5	.942
2000—New York (A.L.)		2B-SS-3B	31	45	6	11	1	0	1	4	5	9	0	1	1-0	.244	.314	.333	.647	3	.952
—Kansas City (A.L.)		2B-SS-3B	33	83	15	22	1	0	0	7	6	17	0	1	1-1	.265	.311	.277	.588	1	.993
2001—Omaha (PCL)		2B-3B-SS	76	255	24	63	11	2	4	30	16	43	1	10	8-3	.247	.293	.353	.646	11	.963
—Kansas City (A.L.)		SS-3B-2B	14	25	1	3	0	0	0	1	3	10	0	1	0-0	.120	.214	.120	.334	0	1.000
2002—Memphis (PCL)		SS	98	365	31	95	19	2	7	35	23	54	3	6	2-5	.260	.309	.381	.689	10	.977
—St. Louis (N.L.)		SS	12	20	2	4	2	0	2	5	0	6	0	0	0-0	.200	.200	.600	.800	0	1.000
2003—St. Louis (N.L.)		2B-3B-SS	43	77	8	13	3	0	0	3	3	10	1	4	0-0	.169	.207	.208	.415	1	.983
—Memphis (PCL)		SS-2B	26	86	11	20	2	0	2	12	10	15	0	2	2-1	.233	.313	.326	.638	3	.991
—Anaheim (A.L.)		3B-SS-2B	19	50	4	16	0	0	0	4	8	8	0	1	0-0	.320	.414	.320	.734	3	.951
2004—Norfolk (Int'l)		SS-2B	108	352	40	92	18	5	3	23	27	73	2	7	1-6	.261	.317	.366	.683	10	.978
—New York (N.L.)		SS	42	130	11	38	4	1	2	13	15	29	0	1	1-0	.292	.366	.385	.750	8	.957
American League totals (3 years)			97	203	26	52	2	0	1	16	22	44	0	4	2-1	.256	.326	.281	.607	7	.975
National League totals (7 years)			156	339	33	84	13	2	4	27	25	64	4	7	3-0	.248	.306	.333	.640	15	.961
Major League totals (9 years)			253	542	59	136	15	2	5	43	47	108	4	11	5-1	.251	.314	.314	.627	22	.967

DELLUCCI, DAVID — OF

PERSONAL: Born October 31, 1973, in Baton Rouge, La. ... 5-11/190. ... Bats left, throws left. ... Full name: David Michael Dellucci. ... Name pronounced: duh-LOO-chee. ... High school: Catholic (Baton Rouge, La.). ... College: Mississippi.

TRANSACTIONS/CAREER NOTES: Selected by Minnesota Twins in 11th round of 1994 free-agent draft; did not sign. ... Selected by Baltimore Orioles organization in 10th round of 1995 free-agent draft. ... Selected by Arizona Diamondbacks in second round (45th pick overall) of expansion draft (November 18, 1997). ... On disabled list (July 25, 1999-remainder of season). ... On disabled list (May 3-24, 2002); included rehabilitation assignment to Tucson. ... On disabled list (June 2-17, 2003). ... Traded by Diamondbacks with P Bret Prinz and C Jon-Mark Sprowl to New York Yankees for OF Raul Mondesi (July 29, 2003). ... On disabled list (August 28-September 27, 2003). ... Signed as a free agent by Texas Rangers (December 23, 2003).

2004 GAMES PLAYED BY POSITION (MLB): OF—94, DH—9.

Year	Team (League)	Pos.	G	AB	R	H	2B	3B	HR	RBI	BB	SO	HBP	GDP	SB-CS	Avg.	OBP	SLG	OPS	E	Avg.
1995—Bluefield (Appal.)		OF	20	69	11	23	5	1	2	12	6	7	1	1	3-1	.333	.390	.522	.911	2	.846
—Frederick (Carolina)		OF	28	96	16	27	3	0	1	10	12	10	3	3	1-2	.281	.378	.344	.722	1	.966
1996—Frederick (Carolina)		OF	59	185	33	60	11	1	4	28	38	34	0	2	5-6	.324	.438	.459	.897	3	.972
—Bowie (East.)		OF	66	251	27	73	14	1	2	33	28	56	1	4	2-7	.291	.363	.378	.741	3	.979
1997—Bowie (East.)		OF-DH	107	385	71	126	29	3	20	55	58	69	5	6	11-4	.327	.421	.574	.995	1	.994
—Baltimore (A.L.)		OF-DH	17	27	3	6	1	0	1	3	4	7	1	2	0-0	.222	.344	.370	.714	0	1.000
1998—Tucson (PCL)		OF	17	72	17	22	4	3	1	11	5	8	0	2	4-0	.306	.346	.486	.832	0	1.000
—Arizona (N.L.)		OF	124	416	43	108	19 *	12	5	51	33	103	3	6	3-5	.260	.318	.399	.717	3	.987
1999—Arizona (N.L.)		OF-DH	63	109	27	43	7	1	1	15	11	24	3	3	2-0	.395	.463	.505	.968	0	1.000
2000—Arizona (N.L.)		OF	34	50	2	15	3	0	0	2	4	9	0	1	0-2	.300	.352	.360	.712	0	1.000
—Tucson (PCL)		OF	33	122	16	28	6	3	3	17	13	15	0	0	4-0	.230	.301	.402	.703	2	.966
—Ariz. D'backs (Ariz.)		OF	2	6	0	2	1	0	0	2	0	1	0	0	0-0	.333	.333	.500	.833	0	...
—South Bend (Mid.)		OF	2	5	3	1	1	0	0	1	2	0	0	0	0-1	.200	.375	.400	.775	0	1.000
2001—Arizona (N.L.)		OF	115	217	28	60	10	2	6	40	22	52	2	2	2-1	.277	.349	.479	.828	1	.989
2002—Arizona (N.L.)		OF-DH	97	229	34	56	11	2	7	29	28	55	1	7	2-4	.245	.326	.402	.727	3	.967
—Tucson (PCL)		OF	4	15	2	2	1	0	0	2	2	4	0	0	0-0	.133	.235	.200	.435	0	1.000
2003—Arizona (N.L.)		OF	70	165	18	40	11	3	2	19	19	45	3	4	9-0	.242	.328	.382	.710	2	.976
—New York (A.L.)		OF-DH	21	51	8	9	1	0	1	4	4	13	2	2	3-0	.176	.263	.255	.518	0	1.000
2004—Texas (A.L.)		OF-DH	107	331	59	80	13	1	17	61	47	88	5	4	9-4	.242	.342	.441	.783	2	.989
American League totals (3 years)			145	409	70	95	15	1	19	68	55	108	8	8	12-4	.232	.333	.413	.746	2	.991
National League totals (6 years)			503	1186	152	322	61	20	25	156	117	288	12	23	18-12	.272	.341	.420	.761	9	.984
Major League totals (8 years)			648	1595	222	417	76	21	44	224	172	396	20	31	30-16	.261	.339	.418	.757	11	.986

DIVISION SERIES RECORD

Year	Team (League)	Pos.	G	AB	R	H	2B	3B	HR	RBI	BB	SO	HBP	GDP	SB-CS	Avg.	OBP	SLG	OPS	E	Avg.
2001—Arizona (N.L.)			2	0	0	0	0	0	0	0	0	0	0	0	0-0	...	...	...	...	0	...
2002—Arizona (N.L.)		OF	3	7	1	2	0	0	1	2	0	1	0	0	0-0	.286	.286	.714	1.000	0	1.000
2003—New York (A.L.)		DH	1	0	0	0	0	0	0	0	0	0	0	0	0-0	...	...	...	...	0	...
Division series totals (3 years)			6	7	1	2	0	0	1	2	0	1	0	0	0-0	.286	.286	.714	1.000	0	1.000

CHAMPIONSHIP SERIES RECORD

Year	Team (League)	Pos.	G	AB	R	H	2B	3B	HR	RBI	BB	SO	HBP	GDP	SB-CS	Avg.	OBP	SLG	OPS	E	Avg.
2001—Arizona (N.L.)			2	2	1	1	0	0	0	0	0	0	0	0	0-0	.500	.500	.500	1.000	...	...
2003—New York (A.L.)		DH-OF	3	3	2	1	0	0	0	0	1	1	0	0	1-0	.333	.500	.333	.833	0	...
Champ. series totals (2 years)			5	5	3	2	0	0	0	0	1	1	0	0	1-0	.400	.500	.400	.900	0	...

WORLD SERIES RECORD

Year	Team (League)	Pos.	G	AB	R	H	2B	3B	HR	RBI	BB	SO	HBP	GDP	SB-CS	Avg.	OBP	SLG	OPS	E	Avg.
2001—Arizona (N.L.)		OF	2	2	0	1	0	0	0	0	0	0	0	0	0-0	.500	.500	.500	1.000	0	1.000
2003—New York (A.L.)		OF-DH	4	2	1	0	0	0	0	0	0	0	0	0	0-0	.000	.000	.000	.000	0	1.000
World series totals (2 years)			6	4	1	1	0	0	0	0	0	0	0	0	0-0	.250	.250	.250	.500	0	1.000

DE LOS SANTOS, VALERIO — P

PERSONAL: Born October 6, 1972, in Las Matas, Dominican Republic. ... 6-2/211. ... Throws left, bats left. ... Full name: Valerio Lorenzo de los Santos.

TRANSACTIONS/CAREER NOTES: Signed as a non-drafted free agent by Milwaukee Brewers organization (January 26, 1993). ... On disabled list (April 29-September 23, 1999; April 4, 2001-remainder of season, and April 27-May 27, 2003). ... Traded by Brewers to Philadelphia Phillies for cash (September 2, 2003). ... Signed as a free agent by Toronto Blue Jays (December 27, 2003). ... On disabled list (June 6, 2004-remainder of season).

CAREER HITTING: 0-for-9 (.000), 0 R, 0 2B, 0 3B, 0 HR, 0 RBI.

Year	Team (League)	W	L	Pct.	ERA	WHIP	G	GS	CG	ShO	Hld.	Sv.-Opp.	IP	H	R	ER	HR	BB-IBB	SO	Avg.
1993—Dom. Brewers (DSL)		1	7	.125	6.50	2.01	19	6	1	0	...	0-...	63.2	91	57	46	...	37-...	39	
1994—Dom. Brewers (DSL)		7	6	.538	3.69	1.38	17	16	1	1	...	0-...	90.1	90	52	37	...	35-...	50	
1995—Ariz. Brewers (Ariz.)		4	6	.400	2.20	1.13	14	12	0	0	...	0-...	82.0	81	34	20	3	12-2	57	.258
1996—Beloit (Midw.)		10	8	.556	3.55	1.35	33	23	5	1	...	4-...	164.2	164	83	65	11	59-4	137	.257
1997—El Paso (Texas)		6	10	.375	5.75	1.61	26	16	1	0	...	2-...	114.1	146	83	73	6	38-2	61	.314

Year Team (League)	W	L	Pct.	ERA	WHIP	G	GS	CG	ShO	Hld.	Sv.-Opp.	IP	H	R	ER	HR	BB-IBB	SO	Avg.
1998—El Paso (Texas)	6	2	.750	3.92	1.59	42	4	0	0		10-...	66.2	81	34	29	2	25-1	62	.299
—Milwaukee (N.L.)	0	0	...	2.91	0.60	13	0	0	0	0	0-...	21.2	11	7	7	4	2-0	18	.151
—Louisville (Int'l)	0	0	...	3.60	0.80	5	0	0	0	0	0-...	5.0	4	2	2	0	0-0	0	.211
1999—Milwaukee (N.L.)	0	1	.000	6.48	2.28	7	0	0	0	0	0-0	8.1	12	6	6	1	7-0	5	.343
2000—Milwaukee (N.L.)	2	3	.400	5.13	1.43	66	2	0	0	9	0-1	73.2	72	43	42	15	33-7	70	.254
2001—Milwaukee (N.L.)	0	0	...	9.00	2.00	1	0	0	0	0	0-0	1.0	1	1	1	0	1-0	1	.250
2002—Indianapolis (Int'l)	1	0	1.000	0.00	1.00	2	0	0	0	0	0-...	2.0	1	0	0	0	1-0	1	.143
—Milwaukee (N.L.)	2	3	.400	3.12	1.18	51	0	0	0	7	0-...	57.2	42	21	20	4	26-3	38	.211
2003—Milwaukee (N.L.)	3	3	.500	4.13	1.25	45	0	0	0	11	1-4	48.0	38	24	22	8	22-0	35	.225
—Philadelphia (N.L.)	1	0	1.000	9.00	2.50	6	0	0	0	0	0-0	4.0	7	7	4	0	3-0	4	.389
2004—Toronto (A.L.)	0	0	...	6.17	1.80	17	0	0	0	0	0-1	11.2	11	8	8	0	10-2	10	.250
American League totals (1 year)	0	0	...	6.17	1.80	17	0	0	0	0	0-1	11.2	11	8	8	0	10-2	10	.250
National League totals (6 years)	8	10	.444	4.28	1.29	189	2	0	0	27	1-5	214.1	183	109	102	32	94-10	171	.234
Major League totals (7 years)	8	10	.444	4.38	1.32	206	2	0	0	27	1-6	226.0	194	117	110	32	104-12	181	.235

DEMPSTER, RYAN — P

PERSONAL: Born May 3, 1977, in Sechelt, British Columbia. ... 6-2/215. ... Throws right, bats right. ... Full name: Ryan Scott Dempster. ... High school: Elphinstone (Gibsons, B.C.).
TRANSACTIONS/CAREER NOTES: Selected by Texas Rangers organization in third round of 1995 free-agent draft. ... Traded by Rangers with a player to be named to Florida Marlins for P John Burkett (August 8, 1996); Marlins acquired P Rick Helling to complete deal (September 3, 1996). ... Traded by Marlins to Cincinnati Reds for OF Juan Encarnacion, OF/2B Wilton Guerrero and P Ryan Snare (July 11, 2002). ... On disabled list (May 23-June 7 and July 29, 2003-remainder of season); included rehabilitation assignment to Louisville. ... Released by Reds (November 4, 2003). ... Signed by Chicago Cubs (January 21, 2004). ... On disabled list (March 26-August 1, 2004); included rehabilitation assignments to Lansing and Iowa.
CAREER HITTING: 23-for-297 (.077), 12 R, 5 2B, 1 3B, 0 HR, 7 RBI.

Year Team (League)	W	L	Pct.	ERA	WHIP	G	GS	CG	ShO	Hld.	Sv.-Opp.	IP	H	R	ER	HR	BB-IBB	SO	Avg.
1995—GC Rangers (GCL)	3	1	.750	2.36	1.49	8	6	1	0	...	0-...	34.1	34	21	9	1	17-0	37	.254
—Hudson Valley (NY-Penn.)	1	0	1.000	3.18	1.41	1	1	0	0	...	0-...	5.2	7	2	2	0	1-0	6	.318
1996—Char., S.C. (SAL)	7	11	.389	3.30	1.23	23	23	2	0	...	0-...	144.1	120	71	53	13	58-1	141	.229
—Kane County (Midwest)	2	1	.667	2.73	1.37	4	4	1	1	...	0-...	26.1	18	10	8	0	18-0	16	.202
1997—Brevard County (FSL)	10	9	.526	4.90	1.43	28	26	2	1	...	0-...	165.1	190	100	90	19	46-1	131	.290
1998—Portland (East.)	4	3	.571	3.22	1.10	7	7	0	0	...	0-...	44.2	34	20	16	8	15-0	33	.214
—Florida (N.L.)	1	5	.167	7.08	2.01	14	11	0	0	0	0-1	54.2	72	47	43	6	38-1	35	.336
—Charlotte (Int'l)	3	1	.750	3.27	1.36	5	5	1	0	0	0-...	33.0	33	14	12	4	12-1	24	.270
1999—Calgary (PCL)	1	1	.500	4.99	1.30	5	5	0	0	0	0-...	30.2	30	17	17	6	10-1	29	.252
—Florida (N.L.)	7	8	.467	4.71	1.63	25	25	0	0	0	0-0	147.0	146	77	77	21	93-2	126	.262
2000—Florida (N.L.)	14	10	.583	3.66	1.36	33	33	2	1	0	0-0	226.1	210	102	92	30	97-7	209	.243
2001—Florida (N.L.)	15	12	.556	4.94	1.56	34	34	2	1	0	0-0	211.1	218	123	116	21	* 112-5	171	.269
2002—Florida (N.L.)	5	8	.385	4.79	1.50	18	18	3	0	0	0-0	120.1	126	66	64	12	55-1	87	.281
—Cincinnati (N.L.)	5	5	.500	6.19	1.58	15	15	1	0	0	0-0	88.2	102	61	†61	16	38-1	66	.293
2003—Louisville (Int'l)	1	1	.500	3.29	1.20	2	2	1	0	0	0-...	13.2	13	5	5	1	3-0	9	.255
—Cincinnati (N.L.)	3	7	.300	6.54	1.76	22	20	0	0	0	0-0	115.2	134	89	84	14	70-4	84	.293
2004—Lansing (Midw.)	0	0	...	1.96	1.20	5	5	0	0	0	0-...	18.1	20	5	4	0	2-0	21	.270
—Iowa (PCL)	1	1	.500	3.86	1.38	6	4	0	0	0	0-...	21.0	19	9	9	1	10-0	20	.244
—Chicago (N.L.)	1	1	.500	3.92	1.40	23	0	0	0	3	2-2	20.2	16	9	9	1	13-0	18	.208
Major League totals (7 years)	51	56	.477	4.99	1.56	184	156	8	2	3	2-3	984.2	1024	574	546	121	516-21	796	.271

DENNEY, KYLE — P

PERSONAL: Born July 27, 1977, in Prague, Okla. ... 6-2/195. ... Throws right, bats right. ... Full name: Kyle Dean Denney. ... High school: Prague (Okla.). ... College: Oklahoma.
CAREER HITTING: 0-for-0 (.000), 0 R, 0 2B, 0 3B, 0 HR, 0 RBI.

Year Team (League)	W	L	Pct.	ERA	WHIP	G	GS	CG	ShO	Hld.	Sv.-Opp.	IP	H	R	ER	HR	BB-IBB	SO	Avg.
1999—Burlington (Appalachian)	3	4	.429	3.44	1.21	12	3	0	0	...	1-...	34.0	26	17	13	7	15-0	37	.215
—Mahoning Valley (NY-P)	1	0	1.000	1.80	1.00	1	1	0	0	...	0-...	5.0	5	1	1	1	0-0	5	.313
2000—Columbus (S. Atl.)	8	6	.571	3.05	1.31	28	24	0	0	...	0-...	138.2	135	55	47	12	46-0	131	.255
2001—Kinston (Caro.)	5	3	.625	2.05	0.79	11	10	0	0	...	0-...	57.0	32	14	13	2	13-1	80	.159
2002—Kinston (Caro.)	7	6	.538	3.60	1.38	15	14	0	0	...	0-...	85.0	76	37	34	5	41-2	68	.242
—Akron (East.)	3	1	.750	1.56	0.81	6	5	0	0	...	0-...	34.2	23	7	6	2	5-0	32	.183
2003—Akron (East.)	7	3	.700	2.42	1.16	18	18	1	0	...	0-...	104.0	97	34	28	7	24-0	87	.244
—Buffalo (Int'l)	2	1	.667	5.28	1.47	6	6	0	0	...	0-...	30.2	35	18	18	4	10-2	26	.276
2004—Buffalo (Int'l)	10	5	.667	4.41	1.28	24	24	1	1	...	0-...	134.2	134	74	66	17	39-1	113	.251
—Cleveland (A.L.)	1	2	.333	9.56	2.50	4	4	0	0	0	0-0	16.0	32	17	17	3	8-0	13	.421
Major League totals (1 year)	1	2	.333	9.56	2.50	4	4	0	0	0	0-0	16.0	32	17	17	3	8-0	13	.421

DEPAULA, JORGE — P

PERSONAL: Born November 10, 1978, in Sabana Grande, Dominican Republic. ... 6-1/160. ... Throws right, bats right.
TRANSACTIONS/CAREER NOTES: Signed as a non-drafted free agent by Colorado Rockies organization (January 13, 1997). ... Traded by Rockies to New York Yankees (April 20, 2001), completing deal in which Yankees traded P Craig Dingman to Rockies for a player to be named (April 20, 2001). ... On disabled list (April 17, 2004-remainder of season).
CAREER HITTING: 0-for-0 (.000), 0 R, 0 2B, 0 3B, 0 HR, 0 RBI.

Year Team (League)	W	L	Pct.	ERA	WHIP	G	GS	CG	ShO	Hld.	Sv.-Opp.	IP	H	R	ER	HR	BB-IBB	SO	Avg.
1998—Ariz. Rockies (Ariz.)	5	5	.500	3.81	1.33	17	9	0	0	...	2-...	54.1	54	30	23	1	18-1	62	.252
1999—Portland (N'west)	6	6	.500	6.01	1.64	16	16	0	0	...	0-...	85.1	97	67	57	8	43-0	77	.290
2000—Asheville (S. Atl.)	8	13	.381	4.70	1.37	28	27	1	1	...	0-...	155.0	151	90	81	16	62-0	187	.260
2001—Asheville (S. Atl.)	1	1	.500	3.78	1.26	3	3	0	0	...	0-...	16.2	19	13	7	3	2-0	26	.268
—Greensboro (S. Atl.)	6	1	.857	2.75	1.01	8	8	0	0	...	0-...	55.2	35	19	17	2	21-0	67	.179
—Tampa (FSL)	9	5	.643	3.58	1.42	16	13	0	0	...	0-...	83.0	65	43	33	3	53-2	77	.212
2002—Norwich (East.)	14	6	.700	3.45	1.10	27	26	6	1	...	0-...	175.0	141	74	67	11	52-0	152	.221
2003—Columbus (Int'l)	10	11	.476	4.35	1.34	27	27	3	2	...	0-...	167.2	168	90	81	22	57-2	125	.262
—New York (A.L.)	0	0	...	0.79	0.35	4	1	0	0	0	0-0	11.1	3	1	1	0	1-0	7	.083
2004—New York (A.L.)	0	1	.000	5.00	1.44	3	1	0	0	0	0-0	9.0	9	6	5	2	4-0	2	.281
Major League totals (2 years)	0	1	.000	2.66	0.84	7	2	0	0	0	0-0	20.1	12	7	6	3	5-0	9	.176

DEROSA, MARK — 3B

PERSONAL: Born February 26, 1975, in Passaic, N.J. ... 6-1/205. ... Bats right, throws right. ... Full name: Mark Thomas DeRosa. ... High school: Bergen Catholic (Oradell, N.J.). ... College: Pennsylvania.

TRANSACTIONS/CAREER NOTES: Selected by Atlanta Braves organization in seventh round of 1996 free-agent draft. ... On disabled list (May 18-July 17, 2002); included rehabilitation assignment to Richmond and Myrtle Beach.

2004 GAMES PLAYED BY POSITION (MLB): 3B—72, SS—11, 2B—5, OF—3.

Year	Team (League)	Pos.	G	AB	R	H	2B	3B	HR	RBI	BB	SO	HBP	GDP	SB-CS	Avg.	OBP	SLG	OPS	E	Avg.
1996—Eugene (Northwest)		SS	70	255	43	66	13	1	2	28	38	48	5	10	3-4	.259	.363	.341	.705	24	.921
1997—Durham (Caro.)		SS	92	346	51	93	11	3	8	37	24	73	10	12	6-8	.269	.332	.387	.720	21	.948
1998—Greenville (Sou.)		SS	125	461	67	123	26	2	8	49	60	57	5	18	7-13	.267	.356	.384	.740	20	.964
—Atlanta (N.L.)		SS	5	3	2	1	0	0	0	0	0	1	0	0	0-0	.333	.333	.333	.667	0	1.000
1999—Richmond (Int'l)		SS-DH	105	364	41	99	16	2	1	40	21	49	5	5	7-6	.272	.317	.335	.652	20	.951
—Atlanta (N.L.)		SS	7	8	0	0	0	0	0	0	0	2	0	0	0-0	.000	.000	.000	.000	0	1.000
2000—Richmond (Int'l)		SS-2B-3B	101	370	62	108	22	3	3	35	38	36	3	13	13-4	.292	.359	.392	.751	19	.958
—Atlanta (N.L.)		SS	22	13	9	4	1	0	0	3	2	1	0	0	0-0	.308	.400	.385	.785	1	1.000
2001—Richmond (Int'l)		SS-3B-2B	49	186	31	55	18	0	2	17	17	22	1	6	7-3	.296	.351	.425	.776	4	.978
—Atlanta (N.L.)		S-2-DH-3-O	66	164	27	47	8	0	3	20	12	19	5	3	2-1	.287	.350	.390	.740	7	.966
2002—Atlanta (N.L.)		2-S-OF-3	72	212	24	63	9	2	5	23	12	24	3	5	2-3	.297	.339	.429	.768	6	.976
—Richmond (Int'l)		2B-SS	16	55	9	14	3	0	0	6	5	2	2	4	2-0	.255	.339	.309	.648	3	.952
—Myrtle Beach (Caro.)		2B	2	7	0	0	0	0	0	0	1	1	0	0	0-0	.000	.125	.000	.125	1	.889
2003—Atlanta (N.L.)		2-3-S-DH-O-1	103	266	40	70	14	0	6	22	16	49	5	6	1-0	.263	.316	.383	.699	6	.976
2004—Atlanta (N.L.)		3-S-2B-OF	118	309	33	74	16	0	3	31	23	53	3	6	1-3	.239	.293	.320	.614	12	.942
Major League totals (7 years)			393	975	135	259	48	2	17	99	65	149	16	20	6-7	.266	.318	.371	.690	31	.967

DIVISION SERIES RECORD

Year	Team (League)	Pos.	G	AB	R	H	2B	3B	HR	RBI	BB	SO	HBP	GDP	SB-CS	Avg.	OBP	SLG	OPS	E	Avg.
2001—Atlanta (N.L.)		SS	1	1	0	1	0	0	0	0	0	0	0	0	0-0	1.000	1.000	1.000	2.000	0	1.000
2002—Atlanta (N.L.)		2B	4	7	2	3	1	1	0	3	1	1	0	0	0-0	.429	.500	.857	1.357	0	1.000
2003—Atlanta (N.L.)		2B-3B	4	7	1	3	2	0	0	2	1	2	0	0	0-0	.429	.500	.714	1.214	0	1.000
Division series totals (3 years)			9	15	3	7	3	1	0	5	2	3	0	0	0-0	.467	.529	.800	1.329	0	1.000

CHAMPIONSHIP SERIES RECORD

Year	Team (League)	Pos.	G	AB	R	H	2B	3B	HR	RBI	BB	SO	HBP	GDP	SB-CS	Avg.	OBP	SLG	OPS	E	Avg.
2001—Atlanta (N.L.)		SS	4	4	0	0	0	0	0	0	0	0	0	0	0-0	.000	.000	.000	.000	0	1.000

DESSENS, ELMER — P

PERSONAL: Born January 13, 1971, in Hermosillo, Mexico. ... 5-10/198. ... Throws right, bats right. ... Full name: Elmer Dessens Jusaino. ... Name pronounced: duh-SENZ. ... High school: Carrera Technica (Hermosillo, Mexico).

TRANSACTIONS/CAREER NOTES: Signed as a non-drafted free agent by Pittsburgh Pirates organization (January 27, 1993). ... Loaned by Pirates organization to Mexico City Red Devils of the Mexican League for 1993 and 1994 seasons; returned to Pirates organization for 1995 season. ... Loaned by Pirates organization to Red Devils (May 7, 1996). ... Returned to Pirates organization (June 21, 1996). ... On disabled list (July 31-September 10, 1996); included rehabilitation assignment to Carolina. ... Loaned by Pirates to Red Devils (March 27-September 5, 1997). ... On disabled list (April 8-24, 1998); included rehabilitation assignment to Nashville. ... Released by Pirates (March 31, 1999). ... Signed as a free agent by Cincinnati Reds organization (December 15, 1999). ... On disabled list (August 2-27, 2002). ... Traded by Reds with cash to Arizona Diamondbacks as part of a four-team deal in which Reds acquired SS Felipe Lopez from Toronto Blue Jays, Blue Jays acquired a player to be named from Oakland Athletics and Athletics acquired 1B Erubiel Durazo from Diamondbacks (December 15, 2002); Blue Jays acquired P Jason Arnold to complete deal (December 16, 2002). ... Traded by Diamondbacks to Los Angeles Dodgers for OF Jereme Milons (August 19, 2004).

CAREER HITTING: 39-for-223 (.175), 12 R, 4 2B, 1 3B, 0 HR, 16 RBI.

Year	Team (League)	W	L	Pct.	ERA	WHIP	G	GS	CG	ShO	Hld.	Sv.-Opp.	IP	H	R	ER	HR	BB-IBB	SO	Avg.
1993—M.C. Red Devils (Mex.)	3	1	.750	2.35	1.17	14	0	0	0	...	2-...	30.2	31	8	8	2	5-...	16	...
1994—M.C. Red Devils (Mex.)	11	4	.733	2.04	1.20	37	15	4	1	...	3-...	127.2	121	37	29	5	32-...	51	...
1995—Carolina (Southern)	15	8	.652	2.49	1.26	27	27	1	0	...	0-...	152.0	170	62	42	10	21-3	68	.284
1996—Calgary (PCL)	2	2	.500	3.15	1.60	6	6	0	0	...	0-...	34.1	40	14	12	5	15-1	15	.305
—M.C. Red Devils (Mex.)	7	0	1.000	1.26	1.08	7	7	1	0	...	0-...	50.0	44	12	7	1	10-...	17	...
—Pittsburgh (N.L.)	0	2	.000	8.28	1.76	15	3	0	0	3	0-0	25.0	40	23	23	2	4-0	13	.385
—Carolina (Southern)	0	1	.000	5.40	1.63	5	1	0	0	...	0-...	11.2	15	8	7	1	4-0	7	.300
1997—M.C. Red Devils (Mex.)	16	5	.762	3.56	1.30	26	25	3	1	...	0-...	159.1	156	73	63	1	51-...	61	...
—Pittsburgh (N.L.)	0	0	...	0.00	0.60	3	0	0	0	0	0-0	3.1	2	0	0	0	0-0	2	.167
1998—Pittsburgh (N.L.)	2	6	.250	5.67	1.54	43	5	0	0	6	0-1	74.2	90	50	47	10	25-2	43	.300
—Nashville (PCL)	3	1	.750	3.30	1.27	6	5	0	0	...	0-...	30.0	32	12	11	2	6-1	13	.274
1999—Yomiuri (Jp. East.)	4	3	.571	2.08	0.96	15	14	2	...	...	0-...	95.0	67	26	22	...	24-...	58	...
—Yomiuri (Jp. Cen.)	0	1	.000	3.86	1.71	8	0	0	0	0	0-...	16.1	24	7	7	...	4-...	6	...
2000—Louisville (Int'l)	2	0	1.000	3.18	1.37	4	4	0	0	...	0-...	22.2	24	10	8	1	7-0	14	.270
—Cincinnati (N.L.)	11	5	.688	4.28	1.45	40	16	1	0	1	1-1	147.1	170	73	70	10	43-7	85	.296
2001—Cincinnati (N.L.)	10	14	.417	4.48	1.35	34	34	1	1	0	0-0	205.0	221	103	102	32	56-1	128	.279
2002—Cincinnati (N.L.)	7	8	.467	3.03	1.25	30	30	0	0	0	0-0	178.0	173	70	60	24	49-8	93	.257
2003—Arizona (N.L.)	8	8	.500	5.07	1.53	34	30	0	0	0	0-0	175.2	212	107	99	22	57-6	113	.299
2004—Arizona (N.L.)	1	6	.143	4.75	1.52	38	9	0	0	4	2-4	85.1	107	54	45	11	23-4	55	.301
—Los Angeles (N.L.)	1	0	1.000	3.20	1.22	12	1	0	0	0	0-1	19.2	16	7	7	4	8-0	18	.216
Major League totals (8 years)	40	49	.449	4.46	1.42	249	128	2	1	14	3-7	914.0	1031	487	453	115	265-28	550	.287

DIVISION SERIES RECORD

Year	Team (League)	W	L	Pct.	ERA	WHIP	G	GS	CG	ShO	Hld.	Sv.-Opp.	IP	H	R	ER	HR	BB-IBB	SO	Avg.
2004—Los Angeles (N.L.)	0	0	...	6.75	0.75	1	0	0	0	0	0-0	1.1	1	1	1	1	0-0	1	.200

DEVORE, DOUG — OF

PERSONAL: Born December 14, 1977, in Columbus, Ohio. ... 6-4/217. ... Bats left, throws left. ... Full name: Douglas Rinehart DeVore. ... High school: Coffman (Dublin, Ohio). ... College: Indiana.

TRANSACTIONS/CAREER NOTES: Selected by Cincinnati Reds organization in 35th round of 1996 free-agent draft; did not sign. ... Selected by Arizona Diamondbacks organization in 12th round of 1999 free-agent draft.

2004 GAMES PLAYED BY POSITION (MLB): OF—31.

Year Team (League)	Pos.	G	AB	R	H	2B	3B	HR	RBI	BATTING BB	SO	HBP	GDP	SB-CS	Avg.	OBP	SLG	OPS	FIELDING E	Avg.
1999— Missoula (Pio.)	OF	32	115	22	27	4	4	3	22	14	36	4	2	2-0	.235	.333	.417	.751	3	.929
2000— South Bend (Mid.)	OF	127	452	64	132	27	4	15	60	47	101	2	9	9-6	.292	.358	.469	.827	12	.941
2001— El Paso (Texas)	OF	128	476	67	140	32	11	15	74	46	118	4	7	11-3	.294	.358	.502	.861	12	.953
2002— Tucson (PCL)	OF	125	436	58	114	20	6	14	59	27	103	5	7	9-6	.261	.311	.431	.742	4	.968
2003— Tucson (PCL)	OF	134	462	74	135	29	7	14	75	44	95	3	11	5-7	.292	.357	.476	.833	8	.967
2004— Tucson (PCL)	OF-DH	61	234	32	63	13	0	14	43	21	67	0	3	3-2	.269	.328	.504	.832	4	.951
—Arizona (N.L.)	OF	50	107	5	24	3	2	3	13	7	31	0	1	1-1	.224	.272	.374	.646	0	1.000
Major League totals (1 year)		50	107	5	24	3	2	3	13	7	31	0	1	1-1	.224	.272	.374	.646	0	1.000

DIAZ, EINAR   C

PERSONAL: Born December 28, 1972, in Chiriqui, Panama. ... 5-10/200. ... Bats right, throws right. ... Full name: Einar Antonio Diaz. ... Name pronounced: AY-een-ar.
TRANSACTIONS/CAREER NOTES: Signed as a non-drafted free agent by Cleveland Indians organization (October 5, 1990). ... On disabled list (August 23-September 30, 2002); included rehabilitation assignment to Mahoning Valley. ... Traded by Indians with P Ryan Drese to Texas Rangers for 1B Travis Hafner and P Aaron Myette (December 6, 2002). ... Traded by Rangers with P Justin Echols and cash to Montreal Expos for IF Josh McKinley and P Chris Young (April 3, 2004).
2004 GAMES PLAYED BY POSITION (MLB): C—44, 3B—1.

Year Team (League)	Pos.	G	AB	R	H	2B	3B	HR	RBI	BATTING BB	SO	HBP	GDP	SB-CS	Avg.	OBP	SLG	OPS	FIELDING E	Avg.
1991— Dom. Inds. (DSL)		62	239	35	67	6	3	1	29	14	5	...	...	10-...	.280	...	.343	...	...	...
1992— Burlington (Appal.)	3B-SS	52	178	19	37	3	0	1	14	20	9	3	4	2-3	.208	.296	.242	.537	7	.959
1993— Burlington (Appal.)	3B-C	60	231	40	69	15	3	5	33	8	7	4	5	7-3	.299	.328	.455	.782	10	.974
—Columbus (S. Atl.)	C	1	5	0	0	0	0	0	0	0	1	0	1	0-0	.000	.000	.000	.000	0	1.000
1994— Columbus (S. Atl.)	3B-C	120	491	67	137	23	2	16	71	17	34	21	18	4-4	.279	.330	.432	.762	9	.991
1995— Kinston (Caro.)	C-3B-DH	104	373	46	98	21	0	6	43	12	29	8	6	3-6	.263	.297	.367	.665	7	.991
1996— Cant./Akr. (Eastern)	C-3B	104	395	47	111	26	2	3	35	12	22	9	11	3-2	.281	.317	.380	.696	15	.983
—Cleveland (A.L.)	C	4	1	0	0	0	0	0	0	0	0	0	0	0-0	.000	.000	.000	.000	1	1.000
1997— Buffalo (A.A.)	C-3B	109	336	40	86	18	2	3	31	18	34	5	12	2-6	.256	.302	.348	.650	19	.974
—Cleveland (A.L.)	C	5	7	1	1	1	0	0	1	0	2	0	0	0-0	.143	.143	.286	.429	1	.955
1998— Buffalo (Int'l)	C	115	415	62	130	21	3	8	63	21	33	6	8	3-3	.313	.354	.436	.790	12	.986
—Cleveland (A.L.)	C	17	48	8	11	1	0	2	9	3	2	2	2	0-0	.229	.286	.375	.661	3	.973
1999— Cleveland (A.L.)	C	119	392	43	110	21	1	3	32	23	41	5	10	11-4	.281	.328	.362	.690	10	.988
2000— Cleveland (A.L.)	C-3B	75	250	29	68	14	2	4	25	11	29	8	7	4-2	.272	.323	.392	.715	4	.994
2001— Cleveland (A.L.)	C-2B	134	487	54	121	34	1	4	56	17	44	16	11	1-2	.277	.328	.387	.714	8	.992
2002— Cleveland (A.L.)	C	102	320	34	66	19	0	2	16	17	27	6	13	0-1	.206	.258	.284	.542	8	.989
2003— Texas (A.L.)	C	101	334	30	86	14	1	4	35	9	32	10	12	3-1	.257	.294	.341	.635	8	.989
2004— Montreal (N.L.)	C-3B	55	139	9	31	6	1	1	11	11	10	4	6	2-0	.223	.293	.302	.595	3	.990
American League totals (8 years)		557	1789	199	463	104	5	19	174	80	177	47	55	19-10	.259	.306	.354	.661	42	.990
National League totals (1 year)		55	139	9	31	6	1	1	11	11	10	4	6	2-0	.223	.293	.302	.595	3	.990
Major League totals (9 years)		612	1928	208	494	110	6	20	185	91	187	51	61	21-10	.256	.305	.351	.656	45	.990

DIVISION SERIES RECORD

Year Team (League)	Pos.	G	AB	R	H	2B	3B	HR	RBI	BB	SO	HBP	GDP	SB-CS	Avg.	OBP	SLG	OPS	E	Avg.
1998— Cleveland (A.L.)		Did not play.																		
1999— Cleveland (A.L.)	C	2	1	0	0	0	0	0	0	0	0	0	0	0-0	.000	.000	.000	.000	0	1.000
2001— Cleveland (A.L.)	C	5	16	3	5	0	0	0	2	2	1	0	0	0-0	.313	.389	.313	.701	1	.982
Division series totals (2 years)		7	17	3	5	0	0	0	2	2	1	0	0	0-0	.294	.368	.294	.663	1	.983

CHAMPIONSHIP SERIES RECORD

Year Team (League)	Pos.	G	AB	R	H	2B	3B	HR	RBI	BB	SO	HBP	GDP	SB-CS	Avg.	OBP	SLG	OPS	E	Avg.
1998— Cleveland (A.L.)	C	4	4	0	0	0	0	0	0	0	1	0	0	0-0	.000	.000	.000	.000	0	1.000

DIAZ, FELIX   P

PERSONAL: Born July 27, 1980, in Las Mata de Farfan, Dominican Republic. ... 6-1/180. ... Throws right, bats right. ... Full name: Felix Antonio Diaz. ... High school: David Ortiz (Las Mata de Farfan, D.R.).
TRANSACTIONS/CAREER NOTES: Signed as a non-drafted free agent by San Francisco Giants organization (March 20, 1998). ... Traded by Giants with P Ryan Meaux to Chicago White Sox for OF Kenny Lofton (July 28, 2002).
CAREER HITTING: 0-for-1 (.000), 0 R, 0 2B, 0 3B, 0 HR, 0 RBI.

Year Team (League)	W	L	Pct.	ERA	WHIP	G	GS	CG	ShO	Hld.	Sv.-Opp.	IP	H	R	ER	HR	BB-IBB	SO	Avg.
2000— Ariz. Giants (Ariz.)	3	4	.429	4.16	1.15	11	11	0	0	...	0-...	62.2	56	35	29	0	16-0	58	.232
—Salem-Keizer (N'west)	0	1	.000	8.10	2.10	3	0	0	0	...	0-...	3.1	6	6	3	2	1-0	2	.400
2001— Hagerstown (S. Atl.)	1	4	.200	3.66	1.26	15	12	0	0	...	0-...	51.2	49	27	21	4	16-0	56	.245
2002— Shreveport (Texas)	3	5	.375	2.70	1.28	12	12	1	0	...	0-...	60.0	54	22	18	1	23-0	48	.240
—Birmingham (Southern)	4	0	1.000	3.48	1.06	7	6	0	0	...	0-...	31.0	25	14	12	4	8-0	30	.207
2003— Charlotte (Int'l)	5	7	.417	3.97	1.34	27	18	1	0	...	0-...	115.2	122	59	51	12	33-3	83	.270
2004— Charlotte (Int'l)	10	2	.833	2.97	1.03	19	17	0	0	...	0-...	115.0	95	41	38	14	24-0	96	.226
—Chicago (A.L.)	2	5	.286	6.75	1.58	18	7	0	0	0	0-0	49.1	62	38	37	13	16-1	33	.310
Major League totals (1 year)	2	5	.286	6.75	1.58	18	7	0	0	0	0-0	49.1	62	38	37	13	16-1	33	.310

DIAZ, MATT   OF

PERSONAL: Born March 3, 1978, in Portland, Ore. ... 6-1/206. ... Bats right, throws right. ... Full name: Matthew Edward Diaz. ... High school: Sante Fe (Fla.). ... College: Florida State.
TRANSACTIONS/CAREER NOTES: Selected by Tampa Bay Devil Rays organization in 17th round of 1999 free-agent draft.
2004 GAMES PLAYED BY POSITION (MLB): DH—4, OF—4.

Year Team (League)	Pos.	G	AB	R	H	2B	3B	HR	RBI	BATTING BB	SO	HBP	GDP	SB-CS	Avg.	OBP	SLG	OPS	FIELDING E	Avg.
1999— Hudson Valley (NY-Penn.)	OF	54	208	22	51	15	2	1	20	6	43	6	5	6-2	.245	.284	.351	.635	3	.972
2000— St. Pete. (FSL)	OF	106	392	37	106	21	3	6	53	11	54	11	21	2-3	.270	.305	.385	.691	10	.957
2001— Bakersfield (Calif.)	OF	131	524	79	172	40	2	17	81	24	73	14	11	11-5	.328	.370	.510	.880	10	.961
2002— Orlando (South.)	OF-1B	122	449	71	123	28	1	10	50	34	72	10	11	31-9	.274	.337	.408	.744	3	.987
2003— Orlando (South.)	OF	60	227	32	87	21	0	5	41	19	24	8	7	9-5	.383	.444	.542	.985	1	.994
—Tampa Bay (A.L.)	DH-OF	4	9	2	1	0	0	0	0	1	3	0	0	0-0	.111	.200	.111	.311	1	.857
—Durham (Int'l)	OF-DH	67	253	35	83	18	3	8	45	16	45	8	8	6-2	.328	.382	.518	.900	1	.993
2004— Durham (Int'l)	OF-DH	134	503	81	167	47	5	21	93	26	96	13	9	15-4	.332	.377	.571	.948	7	.974
—Tampa Bay (A.L.)	DH-OF	10	21	3	4	1	1	1	3	1	9	2	0	0-0	.190	.292	.476	.768	0	1.000
Major League totals (2 years)		14	30	5	5	1	1	1	3	2	12	2	0	0-0	.167	.265	.367	.631	1	.944

D

DIAZ, VICTOR — 2B

PERSONAL: Born December 10, 1981, in Santo Domingo, Dominican Republic. ... 6-0/200. ... Bats right, throws right. ... Full name: Victor Israel Diaz. ... High school: Roberto Clemente (Chicago). ... Junior college: Grayson County (Texas).

TRANSACTIONS/CAREER NOTES: Selected by Los Angeles Dodgers organization in 37th round of 2000 free-agent draft. ... Traded by Dodgers with Ps Kole Strayhorn and Jose Diaz to New York Mets for OF Jeromy Burnitz and cash (July 14, 2003).

2004 GAMES PLAYED BY POSITION (MLB): OF—14.

Year Team (League)	Pos.	G	AB	R	H	2B	3B	HR	RBI	BB	SO	HBP	GDP	SB-CS	Avg.	OBP	SLG	OPS	E	Avg.
2001— GC Dodgers (GCL)	2B-3B	53	195	36	69	22	2	3	31	16	23	6	3	6-3	.354	.414	.533	.947	12	.949
2002— South Georgia (S.Atl.)	3B-2B-1B	91	349	64	122	26	2	10	58	27	69	10	4	20-6	.350	.407	.521	.928	23	.903
— Jacksonville (Sou.)	1B-3B-2B	42	152	22	32	7	0	4	24	7	42	3	3	7-5	.211	.258	.336	.593	3	.989
2003— Jacksonville (Sou.)	2B	85	316	42	92	20	2	10	55	27	60	6	10	8-10	.291	.353	.462	.815	14	.962
— Binghamton (East.)	2B	45	175	29	62	11	0	6	23	8	32	1	3	7-5	.354	.382	.520	.902	6	.968
2004— Norfolk (Int'l)	OF-DH	141	528	81	154	31	1	24	94	31	133	5	12	6-8	.292	.332	.491	.816	9	.969
— New York (N.L.)	OF	15	51	8	15	3	0	3	8	1	15	1	3	0-0	.294	.321	.529	.850	2	.935
Major League totals (1 year)		15	51	8	15	3	0	3	8	1	15	1	3	0-0	.294	.321	.529	.850	2	.935

DICKEY, R.A. — P

PERSONAL: Born October 29, 1974, in Nashville, Tenn. ... 6-3/220. ... Throws right, bats right. ... Full name: Robert Alan Dickey. ... High school: Montgomery Bell Academy (Nashville, Tenn.). ... College: Tennessee.

TRANSACTIONS/CAREER NOTES: Selected by Detroit Tigers organization in 10th round of 1993 free-agent draft; did not sign. ... Selected by Texas Rangers organization in first round (18th pick overall) of 1996 free-agent draft. ... On disabled list (June 25-July 19 and July 30-August 23, 2004); included rehabilitation assignment to Frisco.

CAREER HITTING: 1-for-1 (1.000), 0 R, 0 2B, 0 3B, 0 HR, 0 RBI.

Year Team (League)	W	L	Pct.	ERA	WHIP	G	GS	CG	ShO	Hld.	Sv.-Opp.	IP	H	R	ER	HR	BB-IBB	SO	Avg.
1997— Charlotte (Fla. St.)	1	4	.200	6.94	1.80	8	6	0	0	...	0-...	35.0	51	32	27	8	12-1	32	.340
1998— Charlotte (Fla. St.)	1	5	.167	3.30	1.33	57	0	0	0	...	38-...	60.0	58	31	22	9	22-3	53	.249
1999— Tulsa (Texas)	6	7	.462	4.55	1.53	35	11	0	0	...	10-...	95.0	105	60	48	13	40-1	59	.282
— Oklahoma (PCL)	2	2	.500	4.37	1.32	6	2	0	0	...	0-...	22.2	23	12	11	1	7-1	17	.261
2000— Oklahoma (PCL)	8	9	.471	4.49	1.47	30	23	2	0	...	1-...	158.1	167	83	79	13	65-1	85	.281
2001— Oklahoma (PCL)	11	7	.611	3.75	1.28	24	24	3	0	...	1-...	163.0	164	77	68	14	45-1	120	.262
— Texas (A.L.)	0	1	.000	6.75	1.67	4	0	0	0	0	0-0	12.0	13	9	9	3	7-1	4	.283
2002— Oklahoma (PCL)	8	7	.533	4.09	1.45	37	19	1	0	...	0-...	154.0	176	81	70	8	47-5	109	.295
2003— Oklahoma (PCL)	1	1	.500	1.20	1.10	3	2	0	0	...	0-...	15.0	14	3	2	1	3-0	4	.259
— Texas (A.L.)	9	8	.529	5.09	1.48	38	13	1	1	3	1-1	116.2	135	68	66	16	38-5	94	.292
2004— Frisco (Texas)	1	1	.500	1.98	1.24	4	4	0	0	...	0-...	13.2	16	5	3	0	1-0	9	.286
— Texas (A.L.)	6	7	.462	5.61	1.62	25	15	0	0	...	1-1	104.1	136	77	65	17	33-1	57	.311
Major League totals (3 years)	15	16	.484	5.41	1.55	67	28	1	1	3	2-2	233.0	284	154	140	36	78-7	155	.300

DIFELICE, MIKE — C

PERSONAL: Born May 28, 1969, in Philadelphia, Pa. ... 6-2/205. ... Bats right, throws right. ... Full name: Michael William DiFelice. ... Name pronounced: DEE-fah-lease. ... High school: Bearden (Knoxville, Tenn.). ... College: Tennessee.

TRANSACTIONS/CAREER NOTES: Selected by St. Louis Cardinals organization in 11th round of 1991 free-agent draft. ... Selected by Tampa Bay Devil Rays in first round (20th pick overall) of expansion draft (November 18, 1997). ... Traded by Devil Rays with P Albie Lopez to Arizona Diamondbacks for OF Jason Conti and P Nick Bierbrodt (July 25, 2001). ... Released by Diamondbacks (September 4, 2001). ... Signed by Cardinals (November 20, 2001). ... Signed as a free agent by Kansas City Royals (January 9, 2003). ... On suspended list (September 4-6, 2003). ... Signed by Detroit Tigers (December 18, 2003). ... Released by Tigers (April 3, 2004). ... Re-signed by Tigers organization (April 13, 2004). ... Traded by Tigers to Chicago Cubs for a player to be named (August 31, 2004). ... Refused minor league assignment and became a free agent (October 12, 2004).

2004 GAMES PLAYED BY POSITION (MLB): C—16, DH—1.

Year Team (League)	Pos.	G	AB	R	H	2B	3B	HR	RBI	BB	SO	HBP	GDP	SB-CS	Avg.	OBP	SLG	OPS	E	Avg.
1991— Hamilton (N.Y.-Penn.)	C	43	157	10	33	5	0	4	15	9	40	1	3	1-5	.210	.257	.318	.576	9	.974
1992— Hamilton (N.Y.-Penn.)	C-1B	18	58	11	20	3	0	2	9	4	7	1	0	2-0	.345	.397	.500	.897	5	.969
— St. Pete. (FSL)	C	17	53	0	12	3	0	0	4	3	11	0	3	0-0	.226	.259	.283	.542	2	.977
1993— Springfield (Midw.)	C	8	20	5	7	1	0	0	3	2	3	1	0	0-1	.350	.435	.400	.835	1	1.000
— St. Pete. (FSL)	C	30	97	5	22	2	0	0	8	11	13	1	4	1-0	.227	.306	.247	.554	7	.964
1994— Arkansas (Texas)	C	71	200	19	50	11	2	2	15	12	48	2	9	0-1	.250	.296	.355	.651	6	.987
1995— Arkansas (Texas)	C	62	176	14	47	10	1	1	24	23	29	3	13	0-2	.267	.360	.352	.712	6	.984
— Louisville (A.A.)	C	21	63	8	17	4	0	0	3	5	11	0	4	1-0	.270	.324	.333	.657	2	.984
1996— Louisville (A.A.)	C	79	246	25	70	13	0	9	33	20	43	1	15	0-3	.285	.338	.447	.785	8	.984
— St. Louis (N.L.)	C	4	7	0	2	1	0	0	2	0	1	0	0	0-0	.286	.286	.429	.714	0	1.000
1997— Arkansas (Texas)	C-1B	93	260	16	62	10	1	4	30	19	61	3	11	1-1	.238	.297	.331	.628	6	.991
— Louisville (A.A.)	C	1	4	1	1	0	0	0	1	1	0	0	0	0-0	.250	.250	1.000	1.250	0	1.000
1998— Tampa Bay (A.L.)	C	84	248	17	57	12	3	6	23	15	56	1	12	0-0	.230	.274	.339	.613	4	.993
1999— Tampa Bay (A.L.)	C	51	179	21	55	11	0	6	27	8	23	3	1	0-0	.307	.346	.469	.815	5	.987
2000— Tampa Bay (A.L.)	C	60	204	23	49	13	1	6	27	19	40	0	8	0-0	.240	.280	.402	.682	8	.980
2001— Tampa Bay (A.L.)	C	48	149	13	31	5	1	2	9	8	39	3	3	1-1	.208	.259	.295	.555	6	.982
— Arizona (N.L.)	C	12	21	1	1	0	0	0	1	0	10	1	0	0-0	.048	.091	.048	.139	1	.982
— Tucson (PCL)	C-1B	7	26	6	9	0	0	1	2	3	6	0	2	0-0	.346	.414	.462	.875	3	.940
2002— St. Louis (N.L.)	C	70	174	17	40	11	0	4	19	17	42	1	4	0-0	.230	.297	.362	.660	3	.991
2003— Kansas City (A.L.)	C-DH	62	189	29	48	16	1	3	25	9	30	4	6	1-0	.254	.299	.397	.696	2	.994
2004— Detroit (A.L.)	C-DH	13	22	3	3	1	0	0	2	3	3	0	3	0-0	.136	.240	.227	.467	0	1.000
— Toledo (Int'l)	C-DH	64	237	20	64	14	0	5	36	14	37	1	7	1-0	.270	.311	.392	.703	4	.990
— Chicago (N.L.)	C	4	3	0	0	0	0	0	0	0	1	0	0	0-0	.000	.000	.000	.000	0	1.000
American League totals (6 years)		318	991	106	243	57	7	20	105	55	191	11	33	2-1	.245	.290	.377	.667	25	.988
National League totals (5 years)		183	465	34	105	22	1	8	52	36	115	5	15	1-1	.226	.286	.329	.615	10	.991
Major League totals (9 years)		501	1456	140	348	79	8	28	157	91	306	16	48	3-2	.239	.289	.362	.651	35	.989

D

Year	Team (League)	Pos.	G	AB	R	H	2B	3B	HR	RBI	BB	SO	HBP	GDP	SB-CS	Avg.	OBP	SLG	OPS	E	Avg.
2002— St. Louis (N.L.)			1	1	0	0	0	0	0	0	0	0	0	0	0-0	.000	.000	.000	.000	...	...

DINARDO, LENNY   P

PERSONAL: Born September 19, 1979, in Miami, Fla. ... 6-4/195. ... Throws left, bats left. ... Full name: Leonard Edward DiNardo. ... High school: Santa Fe (Alachua, Fla.). ... College: Stetson.

TRANSACTIONS/CAREER NOTES: Selected by Boston Red Sox organization in 10th round of 1998 free-agent draft; did not sign. ... Selected by New York Mets organization in third round of 2001 free-agent draft. ... Selected by Boston Red Sox from Mets organization in Rule 5 major league draft (December 15, 2003). ... On disabled list (April 4-19 and July 5-September 16, 2004); included rehabilitation assignments to GCL Red Sox, Sarasota, Portland and Pawtucket.

CAREER HITTING: 0-for-0 (.000), 0 R, 0 2B, 0 3B, 0 HR, 0 RBI.

Year	Team (League)	W	L	Pct.	ERA	WHIP	G	GS	CG	ShO	Hld.	Sv.-Opp.	IP	H	R	ER	HR	BB-IBB	SO	Avg.
2001— Brooklyn (NY-P)	1	2	.333	2.00	1.19	9	5	0	0	...	0-...	36.0	26	10	8	0	17-0	40	.200
2002— Capital City (S. Atl.)	5	5	.500	4.35	1.60	24	19	0	0	...	1-...	101.1	106	60	49	3	56-1	103	.274
2003— Binghamton (Eastern)	1	3	.250	3.60	1.20	7	7	1	0	...	0-...	40.0	35	19	16	3	13-0	36	.236
—St. Lucie (Fla. St.)	3	8	.273	2.01	0.92	19	13	1	0	...	1-...	85.0	64	27	19	1	14-0	93	.211
2004— Sarasota (Florida State) ...	0	0	...	0.00	0.67	1	1	0	0	...	0-...	3.0	2	0	0	0	0-0	2	.182
—Pawtucket (Int'l)	0	0	...	0.00	1.00	1	1	0	0	...	0-...	3.0	3	0	0	0	0-0	4	.250
—Boston (A.L.)	0	0	...	4.23	1.66	22	0	0	0	0	0-0	27.2	34	17	13	1	12-1	21	.298
—GC Red Sox (GCL)	0	0	...	0.00	1.00	2	1	0	0	0	0-...	3.0	3	0	0	0	0-0	5	.273
—Portland (East.)	1	0	1.000	9.53	1.59	3	0	0	0	0	0-...	5.2	8	6	6	1	1-0	4	.333
Major League totals (1 year)	0	0	...	4.23	1.66	22	0	0	0	0	0-0	27.2	34	17	13	1	12-1	21	.298

DINGMAN, CRAIG   P

PERSONAL: Born March 12, 1974, in Wichita, Kan. ... 6-4/215. ... Throws right, bats right. ... Full name: Craig Allen Dingman. ... High school: North (Wichita, Kan.). ... Junior college: Hutchinson (Kan.) Community College.

TRANSACTIONS/CAREER NOTES: Selected by New York Yankees organization in 36th round of 1993 free-agent draft. ... On disabled list (June 19, 1995-entire season). ... Traded by Yankees to Colorado Rockies for a player to be named later (March 29, 2001); Yankees acquired P Jorge DePaula to complete deal (April 20, 2001). ... On disabled list (April 9-24, 2001); included rehabilitation assignment to Colorado Springs. ... Signed as a free agent by Cincinnati Reds organization (December 21, 2001). ... Traded by Reds to Yankees for a player to be named (June 6, 2002). ... Signed as a free agent by Yucatan of the Mexican League (March 1, 2003). ... Contract purchased by Chicago Cubs from Cancun of the Mexican League (July 22, 2003). ... Signed as a free agent by Detroit Tigers organization (December 19, 2003).

CAREER HITTING: 0-for-0 (.000), 0 R, 0 2B, 0 3B, 0 HR, 0 RBI.

Year	Team (League)	W	L	Pct.	ERA	WHIP	G	GS	CG	ShO	Hld.	Sv.-Opp.	IP	H	R	ER	HR	BB-IBB	SO	Avg.
1994— GC Yankees (GCL)	0	5	.000	3.38	1.16	17	1	0	0	...	1-...	32.0	27	17	12	0	10-0	51	.239
1995—				Did not play.																
1996— Oneonta (N.Y.-Penn)	0	2	.000	2.04	0.74	20	0	0	0	...	9-...	35.1	17	11	8	0	9-0	52	.136
1997— Greensboro (S. Atl.)	2	0	1.000	1.91	0.94	30	0	0	0	...	19-...	33.0	19	7	7	0	12-0	41	.165
—Tampa (FSL)	0	4	.000	5.24	1.30	19	0	0	0	...	6-...	22.1	15	14	13	2	14-2	26	.195
1998— Tampa (FSL)	5	4	.556	2.93	1.23	50	0	0	0	...	7-...	70.2	48	29	23	8	39-9	95	.194
1999— Norwich (East.)	8	6	.571	1.57	0.91	55	0	0	0	...	9-...	74.1	56	16	13	2	12-2	90	.206
2000— Columbus (Int'l)	6	1	.857	3.05	1.09	47	2	0	0	...	1-...	73.2	60	31	25	5	20-2	65	.220
—New York (A.L.)	0	0	...	6.55	1.91	10	0	0	0	0	0-0	11.0	18	8	8	1	3-0	8	.375
2001— Colo. Springs (PCL)	3	5	.375	3.75	1.38	46	0	0	0	...	7-...	48.0	57	28	20	4	9-1	55	.294
—Colorado (N.L.)	0	0	...	13.50	1.91	7	0	0	0	0	1-1	7.1	11	11	11	4	3-2	2	.355
2002— Louisville (Int'l)	0	1	.000	4.15	1.27	22	0	0	0	...	0-...	26.0	20	12	12	3	13-0	26	.215
—Columbus (Int'l)	0	0	...	13.50	5.25	2	0	0	0	...	0-...	1.1	6	6	2	0	1-1	2	.545
2003— West Tenn (Sou.)	0	1	.000	6.00	1.80	4	0	0	0	...	0-...	6.0	6	4	4	2	5-1	5	.273
—Iowa (PCL)	1	0	1.000	2.00	1.20	11	0	0	0	...	0-...	18.0	14	4	4	0	7-0	12	.667
2004— Toledo (International)	1	2	.333	4.56	1.44	21	0	0	0	...	0-...	25.2	26	14	13	5	11-2	31	.260
—Detroit (A.L.)	2	2	.500	6.75	1.88	24	0	0	0	0	0-2	29.1	33	22	22	3	22-3	16	.295
American League totals (2 years)	2	2	.500	6.69	1.88	34	0	0	0	0	0-2	40.1	51	30	30	4	25-3	24	.319
National League totals (1 year)	0	0	...	13.50	1.91	7	0	0	0	0	1-1	7.1	11	11	11	4	3-2	2	.355
Major League totals (3 years)	2	2	.500	7.74	1.89	41	0	0	0	0	1-3	47.2	62	41	41	8	28-5	26	.325

DOBBS, GREG   3B

PERSONAL: Born July 2, 1978, in Los Angeles, Calif. ... 6-1/205. ... Bats left, throws right. ... Full name: Gregory Stuart Dobbs. ... High school: Canyon Springs (Calif). ... College: Oklahoma.

TRANSACTIONS/CAREER NOTES: Selected by Seattle Mariners organization in 52nd round of 1996 free-agent draft; did not sign. ... Selected by Houston Astros organiztion in 10th round of 1999 free-agent draft; did not sign. ... Signed as a non-drafted free agent by Seattle Mariners organization (May 28, 2001).

2004 GAMES PLAYED BY POSITION (MLB): 3B—14, DH—1.

Year	Team (League)	Pos.	G	AB	R	H	2B	3B	HR	RBI	BB	SO	HBP	GDP	SB-CS	Avg.	OBP	SLG	OPS	E	Avg.
2001— Everett (N'west)	1B-OF-3B	65	249	37	80	17	2	6	41	30	39	2	2	5-3	.321	.396	.478	.874	12	.972
—San Bern. (Calif.)	OF	3	13	2	5	1	0	1	3	0	4	0	0	0-0	.385	.357	.692	1.049	0	1.000
2002— Wisconsin (Midw.)	3B	86	320	43	88	16	2	10	48	31	50	1	6	13-3	.275	.338	.431	.769	23	.902
—San Antonio (Texas)	OF-1B	27	96	13	35	2	0	5	15	9	17	1	2	1-3	.365	.425	.542	.966	2	.964
2003— San Antonio (Texas)	3B	2	6	0	2	0	0	0	0	0	1	0	0	0-0	.333	.333	.667	1.000	0	1.000
2004— San Antonio (Texas)	3B	51	203	25	66	14	4	5	34	11	23	5	5	5-4	.325	.373	.507	.866	10	.918
—Tacoma (PCL)	3B-DH	67	255	28	69	9	2	8	31	5	36	1	10	4-3	.271	.286	.416	.699	13	.931
—Seattle (A.L.)	3B-DH	18	53	4	12	1	0	1	9	1	14	1	0	0-0	.226	.250	.302	.552	2	.929
Major League totals (1 year)		18	53	4	12	1	0	1	9	1	14	1	0	0-0	.226	.250	.302	.552	2	.929

DOHMANN, SCOTT   P

PERSONAL: Born February 13, 1978, in New Orleans, La. ... 6-1/181. ... Throws right, bats right. ... Full name: Christopher Scott Dohmann. ... High school: St. Thomas More Catholic (Lafayette, La.). ... College: Louisiana-Lafayette.

TRANSACTIONS/CAREER NOTES: Selected by Colorado Rockies in sixth round of 2000 free-agent draft.

CAREER HITTING: 0-for-1 (.000), 0 R, 0 2B, 0 3B, 0 HR, 0 RBI.

Year Team (League)	W	L	Pct.	ERA	WHIP	G	GS	CG	ShO	Hld.	Sv.-Opp.	IP	H	R	ER	HR	BB-IBB	SO	Avg.
2000—Portland (N'west)	2	1	.667	0.78	0.83	5	4	0	0	...	0-...	23.0	14	3	2	0	5-0	23	.177
—Asheville (S. Atl.)	1	5	.167	6.06	1.56	7	7	0	0	...	0-...	32.2	43	24	22	3	8-0	36	.319
2001—Asheville (S. Atl.)	11	13	.458	4.32	1.14	28	28	3	1	...	0-...	173.0	165	88	83	27	33-5	154	.251
2002—Salem (Caro.)	13	5	.722	4.23	1.19	28	28	0	0	...	0-...	170.1	149	85	80	22	53-0	131	.233
2003—Tulsa (Texas)	9	4	.692	4.13	1.31	50	4	0	0	...	4-...	93.2	94	47	43	11	29-2	102	.259
2004—Colo. Springs (PCL)	1	0	1.000	1.64	1.32	18	0	0	0	...	2-...	22.0	22	5	4	1	7-1	31	.250
—Colorado (N.L.)	0	3	.000	4.11	1.30	41	0	0	0	4	0-4	46.0	41	22	21	8	19-0	49	.236
Major League totals (1 year)	0	3	.000	4.11	1.30	41	0	0	0	4	0-4	46.0	41	22	21	8	19-0	49	.236

DOMINGUEZ, JUAN — P

PERSONAL: Born May 18, 1980, in Ensanchez Ramirez, Dominican Republic. ... 6-2/195. ... Throws right, bats right. ... Full name: Juan Ramon Dominguez.

TRANSACTIONS/CAREER NOTES: Signed as a non-drafted free agent by Texas Rangers organization (December 26, 1999). ... On disabled list (June 12-September 13 and September 19, 2004-remainder of season); included rehabilitation assignments to Oklahoma and Frisco.

CAREER HITTING: 0-for-0 (.000), 0 R, 0 2B, 0 3B, 0 HR, 0 RBI.

Year Team (League)	W	L	Pct.	ERA	WHIP	G	GS	CG	ShO	Hld.	Sv.-Opp.	IP	H	R	ER	HR	BB-IBB	SO	Avg.
2001—GC Rangers (GCL)	4	2	.667	4.01	1.17	11	9	1	1	...	0-...	58.1	56	29	26	4	12-0	55	.250
—Charlotte (Fla. St.)	1	0	1.000	3.60	1.00	2	0	0	0	...	0-...	5.0	4	2	2	1	1-0	5	.235
2002—Savannah (S. Atl.)	1	3	.250	2.16	1.07	16	9	0	0	...	1-...	66.2	50	23	16	4	21-1	70	.209
2003—Stockton (Calif.)	4	0	1.000	2.84	1.12	16	9	0	0	...	1-...	63.1	55	27	20	3	16-0	72	.226
—Oklahoma (PCL)	1	0	1.000	3.50	1.00	3	3	0	0	...	0-...	18.0	15	7	7	1	3-0	14	.227
—Frisco (Texas)	5	0	1.000	2.60	1.01	9	9	0	0	...	0-...	55.1	35	17	16	2	21-0	54	.178
—Texas (A.L.)	0	2	.000	7.16	1.71	6	3	0	0	...	0-0	16.1	16	14	13	5	12-0	13	.271
2004—Oklahoma (PCL)	5	1	.833	3.13	1.10	9	9	1	0	...	0-...	54.2	41	20	19	3	19-0	41	.205
—Frisco (Texas)	0	0	...	1.08	0.60	3	2	0	0	...	0-...	8.1	4	1	1	0	1-0	11	.143
—Texas (A.L.)	1	2	.333	3.91	1.30	4	4	0	0	0	0-0	23.0	25	11	10	2	5-0	14	.281
Major League totals (2 years)	1	4	.200	5.26	1.47	10	7	0	0	0	0-0	39.1	41	25	23	7	17-0	27	.277

DOMINIQUE, ANDY — C

PERSONAL: Born October 30, 1975, in Tarzana, Calif. ... 6-0/220. ... Bats right, throws right. ... Full name: Andrew John Dominique. ... High school: Alemany (Mission Hills, Calif.). ... College: Nevada-Reno.

TRANSACTIONS/CAREER NOTES: Selected by Philadelphia Phillies in 26th round of free-agent draft (June 4, 1997). ... Traded by Phillies to Boston Red Sox for future considerations (April 26, 2002).

2004 GAMES PLAYED BY POSITION (MLB): 1B—5, C—1.

Year Team (League)	Pos.	G	AB	R	H	2B	3B	HR	RBI	BB	SO	HBP	GDP	SB-CS	Avg.	OBP	SLG	OPS	E	Avg.
															BATTING				FIELDING	
1997—Batavia (NY-Penn)	1B	72	277	52	77	17	0	14	48	26	60	10	6	4-1	.278	.355	.491	.846	6	.990
1998—Piedmont (S. Atl.)	3B-1B	133	514	82	145	38	0	24	102	61	97	12	9	0-2	.282	.369	.496	.865	17	.961
1999—Clearwater (FSL)	C-1B	130	487	77	124	29	5	14	92	69	84	10	13	3-3	.255	.354	.421	.775	10	.984
2000—Reading (East.)	C-1B-3B	104	327	46	78	27	0	13	50	35	56	8	9	0-1	.239	.324	.440	.764	4	.994
2001—Reading (East.)	C-1B-3B	76	261	43	73	16	0	12	49	37	45	1	6	3-1	.280	.369	.479	.848	8	.985
—Scran./W.B. (I.L.)	1B-3B-C	40	135	16	23	6	0	3	18	12	34	1	4	0-0	.170	.243	.281	.525	5	.986
2002—Clearwater (FSL)	1B-OF	8	34	5	14	5	0	0	2	1	4	1	0	0-0	.412	.444	.559	1.003	0	1.000
—Trenton (East.)	1B-C	103	361	40	98	21	1	8	51	36	60	9	9	2-1	.271	.347	.402	.749	7	.991
2003—Portland (East.)	1B-C	32	97	18	35	7	0	3	21	16	15	3	1	0-0	.361	.454	.526	.980	3	.983
—Pawtucket (Int'l)	C-1B	79	289	42	88	18	0	13	57	22	45	7	10	2-1	.304	.364	.502	.866	3	.992
2004—Boston (A.L.)	1B-C	7	11	0	2	0	0	0	1	0	3	0	0	0-0	.182	.182	.182	.364	1	.964
—Pawtucket (Int'l)	DH-C-1B	111	419	54	112	28	0	15	69	55	87	8	11	0-2	.267	.360	.442	.791	6	.985
Major League totals (1 year)		7	11	0	2	0	0	0	1	0	3	0	0	0-0	.182	.182	.182	.364	1	.964

DONNELLY, BRENDAN — P

PERSONAL: Born July 4, 1971, in Washington, District of Columbia. ... 6-3/240. ... Throws right, bats right. ... Full name: Brendan Kevin Donnelly. ... High school: Sandia (Albuquerque, N.M.). ... Junior college: Mesa (Ari.) Community College. ... College: Mesa State (Colo.).

TRANSACTIONS/CAREER NOTES: Selected by Chicago White Sox organization in 27th round of 1992 free-agent draft. ... Released by White Sox (April 16, 1993). ... Signed by Chicago Cubs organization (June 16, 1993). ... Released by Cubs (March 29, 1994). ... Signed by Cincinnati Reds organization (March 4, 1995). ... Released by Reds (April 3, 1999). ... Contract purchased by Tampa Bay Devil Rays organization from Nashua of the independent Atlantic League (May 15, 1999). ... Released by Devil Rays (August 12, 1999). ... Signed by Pittsburgh Pirates organization (August 18, 1999). ... Released by Pirates (August 25, 1999). ... Signed by Toronto Blue Jays organization (August 26, 1999). ... Released by Blue Jays (July 28, 2000). ... Signed by Cubs organization (August 10, 2000). ... Signed as a free agent by Anaheim Angels organization (January 9, 2001). ... On disabled list (March 26-June 17, 2004); included rehabilitation assignments to Rancho Cucamonga and Salt Lake.

CAREER HITTING: 0-for-0 (.000), 0 R, 0 2B, 0 3B, 0 HR, 0 RBI.

Year Team (League)	W	L	Pct.	ERA	WHIP	G	GS	CG	ShO	Hld.	Sv.-Opp.	IP	H	R	ER	HR	BB-IBB	SO	Avg.
1992—GC White Sox (GCL)	0	3	.000	3.67	1.49	9	7	0	0	...	1-...	41.2	41	25	17	0	21-0	31	.256
1993—Geneva (N.Y.-Penn)	4	0	1.000	6.28	1.58	21	3	0	0	...	0-...	43.0	39	34	30	4	29-0	29	.242
1994—Ohio Valley (Fron.)	1	1	.500	2.57	1.21	10	0	0	0	...	0-...	14.0	13	5	4	1	4-0	20	.250
1995—Char., W.Va. (SAL)	1	1	.500	1.19	0.69	24	0	0	0	...	12-...	30.1	14	4	4	0	7-1	33	.139
—Winston-Salem (Caro.)	1	2	.333	1.02	0.96	23	0	0	0	...	2-...	35.1	20	6	4	1	14-2	32	.167
—Indianapolis (A.A.)	1	1	.500	23.63	3.38	3	0	0	0	...	0-...	2.2	7	8	7	2	2-0	1	.500
1996—Chattanooga (Southern)	1	2	.333	5.52	1.50	22	0	0	0	...	0-...	29.1	27	21	18	4	17-2	22	.237
1997—Chattanooga (Southern)	6	4	.600	3.27	1.31	62	0	0	0	...	6-...	82.2	71	43	30	6	37-4	64	.228
1998—Chattanooga (Southern)	2	5	.286	2.98	1.48	38	0	0	0	...	13-...	45.1	43	16	15	4	24-5	47	.247
—Indianapolis (Int'l)	4	1	.800	2.65	1.21	19	1	0	0	...	0-...	37.1	29	16	11	3	16-3	39	.212
1999—Nashua (Atl.)	0	0	...	3.00	1.33	3	0	0	0	...	0-...	3.0	1	1	1		3-...	4	...
—Durham (Int'l)	5	5	.500	3.05	1.15	37	1	0	0	...	2-...	62.0	53	23	21	5	18-1	61	.240
—Altoona (East.)	0	0	...	7.71	2.57	2	0	0	0	...	1-...	2.1	4	2	2	0	2-0	5	.571
—Syracuse (Int'l)	0	1	.000	2.89	1.29	5	0	0	0	...	0-...	9.1	8	4	3	1	4-1	9	.242
2000—Syracuse (Int'l)	4	6	.400	5.48	1.73	37	0	0	0	...	0-...	42.2	47	34	26	5	27-2	34	.278
—Iowa (PCL)	0	3	.000	7.56	1.86	9	0	0	0	...	0-...	16.2	25	19	14	3	6-1	14	.338
2001—Arkansas (Texas)	4	1	.800	2.48	1.17	27	0	0	0	...	12-...	29.0	21	8	8	2	13-1	37	.200
—Salt Lake (PCL)	5	1	.833	2.40	1.11	29	0	0	0	...	1-...	41.1	38	13	11	4	8-0	50	.245
2002—Salt Lake (PCL)	4	0	1.000	3.48	1.13	25	0	0	0	...	6-...	33.2	27	13	13	5	11-0	42	.213

D

Year Team (League)	W	L	Pct.	ERA	WHIP	G	GS	CG	ShO	Hld.	Sv.-Opp.	IP	H	R	ER	HR	BB-IBB	SO	Avg.
— Anaheim (A.L.)	1	1	.500	2.17	1.03	46	0	0	0	13	1-3	49.2	32	13	12	2	19-3	54	.184
2003— Anaheim (A.L.)	2	2	.500	1.58	1.07	63	0	0	0	29	3-5	74.0	55	14	13	2	24-1	79	.200
2004— Rancho Cuca. (Calif.)	0	0	...	0.00	1.33	2	0	0	0	...	0-...	3.0	3	0	0	0	1-0	5	.250
— Salt Lake (PCL)	0	0	...	7.71	1.71	3	0	0	0	...	0-...	2.1	2	2	2	0	2-0	6	.250
— Anaheim (A.L.)	5	2	.714	3.00	1.17	40	0	0	0	5	0-0	42.0	34	14	14	5	15-0	56	.224
Major League totals (3 years)	8	5	.615	2.12	1.08	149	0	0	0	47	4-8	165.2	121	41	39	9	58-4	189	.201

DIVISION SERIES RECORD

Year Team (League)	W	L	Pct.	ERA	WHIP	G	GS	CG	ShO	Hld.	Sv.-Opp.	IP	H	R	ER	HR	BB-IBB	SO	Avg.
2002— Anaheim (A.L.)	0	0	...	13.50	2.00	3	0	0	0	1	0-0	2.0	3	3	3	2	1-0	2	.333
2004— Anaheim (A.L.)	0	0	...	10.80	1.50	2	0	0	0	0	0-0	3.1	3	4	4	0	2-2	5	.231
Division series totals (2 years)	0	0	...	11.81	1.69	5	0	0	0	1	0-0	5.1	6	7	7	2	3-2	7	.273

CHAMPIONSHIP SERIES RECORD

Year Team (League)	W	L	Pct.	ERA	WHIP	G	GS	CG	ShO	Hld.	Sv.-Opp.	IP	H	R	ER	HR	BB-IBB	SO	Avg.
2002— Anaheim (A.L.)	0	0	...	8.10	0.90	3	0	0	0	2	0-0	3.1	3	3	3	0	0-0	5	.231

WORLD SERIES RECORD

Year Team (League)	W	L	Pct.	ERA	WHIP	G	GS	CG	ShO	Hld.	Sv.-Opp.	IP	H	R	ER	HR	BB-IBB	SO	Avg.
2002— Anaheim (A.L.)	1	0	1.000	0.00	0.65	5	0	0	0	1	0-0	7.2	1	0	0	0	4-0	6	.042

ALL-STAR GAME RECORD

Year Team (League)	W	L	Pct.	ERA	WHIP	G	GS	CG	ShO	Hld.	Sv.-Opp.	IP	H	R	ER	HR	BB-IBB	SO	Avg.
All-Star Game totals (1 year)	1	0	1.000	0.00	0.00	1	0	0	0	0	0-0	1.0	0	0	0	0	0-0	1	.000

DOTEL, OCTAVIO   P

PERSONAL: Born November 25, 1973, in Santo Domingo, Dominican Republic. ... 6-0/210. ... Throws right, bats right. ... Full name: Octavio Eduardo Dotel. ... Name pronounced: OC-tay-vee-oh dough-TEL. ... High school: Liceo Eansino Afuera (Dominican Republic).

TRANSACTIONS/CAREER NOTES: Signed as a non-drafted free agent by New York Mets organization (March 20, 1993). ... Traded by Mets with OF Roger Cedeno and P Kyle Kessel to Houston Astros for P Mike Hampton and OF Derek Bell (December 23, 1999). ... Traded by Astros to Oakland Athletics as part of three-team deal in which Astros acquired OF Carlos Beltran and cash from Kansas City Royals and Royals acquired C John Buck and cash from Astros and P Mike Wood and 3B Mark Teahen from Athletics (June 24, 2004).

CAREER HITTING: 5-for-74 (.068), 3 R, 0 2B, 0 3B, 0 HR, 1 RBI.

Year Team (League)	W	L	Pct.	ERA	WHIP	G	GS	CG	ShO	Hld.	Sv.-Opp.	IP	H	R	ER	HR	BB-IBB	SO	Avg.
1993— Dom. Mets (DSL)	6	2	.750	4.10	1.42	15	11	0	0	...	0-...	59.1	46	30	27	...	38-...	48	...
1994— Dom. Mets (DSL)	5	0	1.000	4.32	1.41	15	14	1	0	...	0-...	81.1	84	53	39	...	31-...	95	...
1995— GC Mets (GCL)	7	4	.636	2.18	0.87	13	12	2	0	...	0-...	74.1	48	23	18	0	17-1	86	.178
— St. Lucie (Fla. St.)	1	0	1.000	5.63	1.75	3	0	0	0	...	0-...	8.0	10	5	5	1	4-0	9	.323
1996— Capital City (S. Atl.)	11	3	.786	3.59	1.20	22	19	0	0	...	0-...	115.1	89	49	46	7	49-0	142	.212
1997— St. Lucie (Fla. St.)	5	2	.714	2.52	1.34	9	8	1	1	...	0-...	50.0	44	18	14	2	23-0	39	.235
— Binghamton (Eastern)	3	4	.429	5.98	1.87	12	12	0	0	...	0-...	55.2	66	50	37	5	38-1	40	.293
— GC Mets (GCL)	0	0	...	0.96	1.18	3	2	0	0	...	1-...	9.1	9	1	1	0	2-0	7	.250
1998— Binghamton (Eastern)	4	2	.667	1.97	0.95	10	10	2	1	...	0-...	68.2	41	19	15	4	24-1	82	.175
— Norfolk (Int'l)	8	6	.571	3.45	1.26	17	16	1	0	...	0-...	99.0	82	47	38	9	43-1	118	.221
1999— Norfolk (Int'l)	5	2	.714	3.84	1.22	13	13	1	0	...	0-...	70.1	52	33	30	9	34-1	90	.204
— New York (N.L.)	8	3	.727	5.38	1.38	19	14	0	0	...	0-...	85.1	69	52	51	12	49-1	85	.226
2000— Houston (N.L.)	3	7	.300	5.40	1.50	50	16	0	0	0	16-23	125.0	127	80	75	26	61-3	142	.265
2001— Houston (N.L.)	7	5	.583	2.66	1.20	61	4	0	0	14	2-4	105.0	79	35	31	5	47-2	145	.205
2002— Houston (N.L.)	6	4	.600	1.85	0.87	83	0	0	0	31	6-10	97.1	58	21	20	7	27-2	118	.173
2003— Houston (N.L.)	6	4	.600	2.48	0.97	76	0	0	0	33	4-6	87.0	53	25	24	9	31-2	97	.172
2004— Houston (N.L.)	0	4	.000	3.12	1.21	32	0	0	0	14-17	14-17	34.2	27	15	12	4	15-4	50	.213
— Oakland (A.L.)	6	2	.750	4.09	1.16	45	0	0	0	22-28	22-28	50.2	41	23	23	9	18-3	72	.220
American League totals (1 year)	6	2	.750	4.09	1.16	45	0	0	0	22-28	22-28	50.2	41	23	23	9	18-3	72	.220
National League totals (6 years)	30	27	.526	3.59	1.20	321	34	0	0	78	42-60	534.1	413	228	213	63	230-14	637	.213
Major League totals (6 years)	36	29	.554	3.63	1.20	366	34	0	0	78	64-88	585.0	454	251	236	72	248-17	709	.213

DIVISION SERIES RECORD

Year Team (League)	W	L	Pct.	ERA	WHIP	G	GS	CG	ShO	Hld.	Sv.-Opp.	IP	H	R	ER	HR	BB-IBB	SO	Avg.
1999— New York (N.L.)	0	0	...	54.00	9.00	1	0	0	0	0	0-0	.1	1	2	2	0	2-0	0	.500
2001— Houston (N.L.)	0	0	...	5.40	1.50	2	0	0	0	0	0-0	3.1	5	2	2	1	0-0	5	.333
Division series totals (2 years)	0	0	...	9.82	2.18	3	0	0	0	0	0-0	3.2	6	4	4	1	2-0	5	.353

CHAMPIONSHIP SERIES RECORD

Year Team (League)	W	L	Pct.	ERA	WHIP	G	GS	CG	ShO	Hld.	Sv.-Opp.	IP	H	R	ER	HR	BB-IBB	SO	Avg.
1999— New York (N.L.)	1	0	1.000	3.00	2.00	1	0	0	0	0	0-0	3.0	4	1	1	0	2-1	5	.333

DOUGLASS, SEAN   P

PERSONAL: Born April 28, 1979, in Lancaster, Calif. ... 6-6/210. ... Throws right, bats right. ... Full name: Sean R. Douglass. ... High school: Antelope Valley (Lancaster, Calif.).

TRANSACTIONS/CAREER NOTES: Selected by Baltimore Orioles organization in second round of 1997 free-agent draft. ... Claimed on waivers by Minnesota Twins (October 14, 2003). ... Claimed on waivers by Toronto Blue Jays (March 31, 2004). ... Refused minor league assignment and became a free agent (October 14, 2004).

CAREER HITTING: 0-for-0 (.000), 0 R, 0 2B, 0 3B, 0 HR, 0 RBI.

Year Team (League)	W	L	Pct.	ERA	WHIP	G	GS	CG	ShO	Hld.	Sv.-Opp.	IP	H	R	ER	HR	BB-IBB	SO	Avg.
1997— GC Orioles (GCL)	1	3	.250	6.11	1.64	9	1	0	0	...	0-...	17.2	20	14	12	2	9-0	10	.308
1998— Bluefield (Appalachian)	2	2	.500	3.23	1.11	10	0	0	0	...	0-...	53.0	45	20	19	6	14-0	62	.231
1999— Frederick (Caro.)	5	6	.455	3.32	1.63	16	16	1	0	...	0-...	97.2	101	48	36	9	58-0	161	.267
2000— Bowie (East.)	9	8	.529	4.02	1.31	27	27	2	0	...	0-...	159.0	174	88	71	17	34-1	105	.280
2001— Rochester (Int'l)	8	9	.471	3.49	1.36	27	27	0	0	...	0-...	162.1	160	79	63	13	61-0	156	.252
— Baltimore (A.L.)	2	1	.667	5.31	1.57	4	4	0	0	0	0-0	20.1	21	12	12	3	11-0	17	.259
2002— Rochester (Int'l)	4	6	.400	4.73	1.52	14	13	0	0	...	0-...	66.2	66	39	35	4	35-0	71	.256
— Baltimore (A.L.)	0	5	.000	6.08	1.74	15	8	0	0	0	0-0	53.1	58	41	36	10	35-2	44	.283
2003— Ottawa (Int'l)	10	8	.556	3.40	1.40	27	27	0	0	...	0-...	143.0	142	67	54	6	58-4	118	.256
— Baltimore (A.L.)	0	0	...	13.50	2.50	3	0	0	0	0	0-0	8.0	14	12	12	2	6-0	3	.378
2004— Syracuse (Int'l)	5	6	.455	4.75	1.45	18	18	1	0	...	0-...	89.0	92	53	47	7	37-0	74	.272
— Toronto (A.L.)	0	2	.000	6.28	1.68	14	3	0	0	0	0-0	38.2	37	27	27	6	28-4	36	.252
Major League totals (4 years)	2	8	.200	6.51	1.75	36	15	0	0	0	0-0	120.1	130	92	87	21	80-6	100	.277

DOWNS, SCOTT — P

PERSONAL: Born March 17, 1976, in Louisville, Ky. ... 6-2/190. ... Throws left, bats left. ... Full name: Scott Jeremy Downs. ... High school: Pleasure Ridge Park (Louisville, Ky.). ... College: Kentucky.

TRANSACTIONS/CAREER NOTES: Selected by Atlanta Braves organization in 12th round of 1994 free-agent draft; did not sign. ... Selected by Chicago Cubs organization in third round of 1997 free-agent draft. ... Traded by Cubs to Minnesota Twins (November 3, 1998), completing deal in which Twins traded P Mike Morgan to Cubs for cash and a player to be named (August 25, 1998). ... Traded by Twins with P Rick Aguilera to Cubs for Ps Kyle Lohse and Jason Ryan (May 21, 1999). ... Traded by Cubs to Montreal Expos for OF Rondell White (July 31, 2000). ... On disabled list (August 9, 2000-remainder of season; and March 23, 2001-entire season). ... On disabled list (March 27-June 10, 2002); included rehabilitation assignment to Brevard County and Ottawa.

CAREER HITTING: 3-for-44 (.068), 3 R, 0 2B, 0 3B, 0 HR, 1 RBI.

Year	Team (League)	W	L	Pct.	ERA	WHIP	G	GS	CG	ShO	Hld.	Sv.-Opp.	IP	H	R	ER	HR	BB-IBB	SO	Avg.
1997—	Williamsport (N.Y.-Penn.) .	0	2	.000	2.74	0.96	5	5	0	0	...	0-...	23.0	15	11	7	0	7-0	28	.181
—	Rockford (Midwest)	3	0	1.000	1.25	0.69	5	5	0	0	...	0-...	36.0	17	5	5	1	8-0	43	.144
1998—	Daytona (Fla. St.)	8	9	.471	3.90	1.45	27	27	2	0	...	0-...	161.2	179	83	70	12	55-0	117	.280
1999—	New Britain (East.)	0	0	...	8.69	2.19	6	3	0	0	...	0-...	19.2	33	21	19	5	10-1	22	.375
—	Fort Myers (Fla. St.)	0	1	.000	0.00	1.34	2	2	0	0	...	0-...	9.2	7	3	0	0	6-0	9	.184
—	Daytona (Fla. St.)	5	0	1.000	1.88	1.08	7	7	1	1	...	0-...	48.0	41	12	10	2	11-0	41	.237
—	West Tenn (Sou.)	8	1	.889	1.35	1.05	13	12	1	0	...	0-...	80.0	56	13	12	2	28-0	101	.194
2000—	Chicago (N.L.)	4	3	.571	5.17	1.64	18	18	0	0	0	0-0	94.0	117	59	54	13	37-1	63	.310
—	Montreal (N.L.)	0	0	...	9.00	2.67	1	1	0	0	0	0-0	3.0	5	3	3	0	3-0	1	.385
2001—	Montreal (N.L.)			Did not play.																
2002—	Brevard County (FSL)	0	0	...	3.00	1.00	7	0	0	0	...	1-...	9.0	7	3	3	0	2-0	7	.206
—	Ottawa (Int'l)	2	1	.667	5.79	1.46	17	0	0	0	...	0-...	23.1	31	21	15	6	3-0	15	.320
2003—	Montreal (N.L.)	0	1	.000	15.00	2.67	1	1	0	0	0	0-0	3.0	5	5	5	2	3-2	4	.357
—	Edmonton (PCL)	8	9	.471	4.29	1.30	21	21	3	0	...	0-...	121.2	119	67	58	13	39-0	54	.263
2004—	Edmonton (PCL)	10	6	.625	3.53	1.25	22	22	2	2	...	0-...	135.1	143	57	53	16	26-0	67	.274
—	Montreal (N.L.)	3	6	.333	5.14	1.62	12	12	1	1	0	0-0	63.0	79	47	36	9	23-2	38	.310
Major League totals (3 years)		7	10	.412	5.41	1.67	32	32	1	1	0	0-0	163.0	206	114	98	24	66-5	105	.312

DRANSFELDT, KELLY — SS/3B

PERSONAL: Born April 16, 1975, in Joliet, Ill. ... 6-2/195. ... Bats right, throws right. ... Full name: Kelly Daniel Dransfeldt. ... Name pronounced: DRANS-felt. ... High school: Morris (Ill.). ... College: Michigan.

TRANSACTIONS/CAREER NOTES: Selected by Minnesota Twins organization in seventh round of 1993 free-agent draft; did not sign. ... Selected by Texas Rangers organization in fourth round of 1996 free-agent draft. ... Signed as a free agent by Cincinnati Reds organization (November 19, 2002). ... Released by Reds (June 18, 2003). ... Signed by Boston Red Sox organization (June 25, 2003). ... Signed as a free agent by Chicago White Sox organization (January 21, 2004).

2004 GAMES PLAYED BY POSITION (MLB): SS—8, 3B—3, DH—1.

Year	Team (League)	Pos.	G	AB	R	H	2B	3B	HR	RBI	BB	SO	HBP	GDP	SB-CS	Avg.	OBP	SLG	OPS	E	Avg.
1996—	Hudson Valley (NY-Penn.) .	SS	75	284	42	67	17	1	7	29	27	76	4	2	13-4	.236	.308	.377	.685	21	.946
1997—	Charlotte (Fla. St.)	3B-SS	135	466	64	106	20	7	6	58	42	115	3	8	25-16	.227	.294	.339	.633	36	.943
1998—	Charlotte (Fla. St.)	SS	67	245	46	79	17	0	18	76	29	67	2	4	7-2	.322	.390	.612	1.002	19	.941
—	Tulsa (Texas)	SS	58	226	43	57	15	4	9	36	18	79	2	4	8-1	.252	.309	.473	.783	14	.950
1999—	Oklahoma (PCL) SS-2B-DH		102	359	55	85	21	2	10	44	24	108	...	...	6-3	.237	...	.390	...	19	.960
—	Texas (A.L.)	SS	16	53	3	10	1	0	1	5	3	12	0	2	0-0	.189	.232	.264	.496	3	.966
2000—	Oklahoma (PCL)	SS	117	441	60	109	22	3	8	42	38	123	4	7	10-5	.247	.311	.365	.676	22	.962
—	Texas (A.L.)	SS-2B	16	26	2	3	2	0	0	2	1	14	0	0	0-0	.115	.148	.192	.340	0	1.000
2001—	Oklahoma (PCL)	SS	143	551	76	138	29	5	9	63	50	116	3	9	12-9	.250	.313	.370	.683	24	.965
—	Texas (A.L.)	SS-3B	4	3	0	0	0	0	0	0	0	0	0	0	0-0	.000	.000	.000	.000	0	1.000
2002—	Oklahoma (PCL)	SS-2B	140	507	60	116	21	7	13	66	44	133	4	9	9-3	.229	.293	.375	.668	14	.978
2003—	Louisville (Int'l)	SS-3B	46	140	15	30	9	2	2	12	9	34	1	3	0-1	.214	.263	.350	.613	10	.947
—	Pawtucket (Int'l)	SS	66	214	29	45	11	1	6	34	16	53	3	5	0-1	.210	.274	.355	.629	10	.963
2004—	Chicago (A.L.) SS-3B-DH		15	30	5	10	0	0	0	4	0	6	0	0	0-0	.333	.333	.333	.667	1	.952
—	Charlotte (Int'l) 3B-SS-DH		88	305	34	76	18	6	5	30	15	63	3	8	5-2	.249	.287	.364	.651	7	.976
Major League totals (4 years)			51	112	10	23	3	0	1	11	4	32	0	2	0-0	.205	.233	.259	.492	4	.974

DREIFORT, DARREN — P

PERSONAL: Born May 3, 1972, in Wichita, Kan. ... 6-2/211. ... Throws right, bats right. ... Full name: Darren John Dreifort. ... Name pronounced: DRY-fort. ... High school: Wichita (Kan.) Heights. ... College: Wichita State.

TRANSACTIONS/CAREER NOTES: Selected by New York Mets organization in 11th round of 1990 free-agent draft; did not sign. ... Selected by Los Angeles Dodgers organization in first round (second pick overall) of 1993 free-agent draft. ... On disabled list (April 23, 1995-entire season). ... On disabled list (March 25-May 16, 1996); included rehabilitation assignment to Albuquerque. ... On disabled list (May 12-June 17, 1997); included rehabilitation assignment to Albuquerque. ... On disabled list (June 30, 2001-remainder of season; and March 19, 2002-entire season). ... On disabled list (May 29, 2003-remainder of season; and August 17, 2004-remainder of season).

CAREER HITTING: 44-for-239 (.184), 26 R, 10 2B, 0 3B, 6 HR, 23 RBI.

Year	Team (League)	W	L	Pct.	ERA	WHIP	G	GS	CG	ShO	Hld.	Sv.-Opp.	IP	H	R	ER	HR	BB-IBB	SO	Avg.
1994—	Los Angeles (N.L.)	0	5	.000	6.21	2.07	27	0	0	0	3	6-9	29.0	45	21	20	0	15-3	22	.357
—	San Antonio (Texas)	3	1	.750	2.80	1.39	8	8	0	0	...	0-...	35.1	36	14	11	0	13-0	32	.261
—	Albuquerque (PCL)	1	0	1.000	5.68	1.74	1	1	0	0	...	0-...	6.1	8	4	4	1	3-0	3	.348
1995—	Los Angeles (N.L.)			Did not play.																
1996—	Albuquerque (PCL)	5	6	.455	4.17	1.62	18	18	0	0	...	0-...	86.1	88	49	40	6	52-3	75	.272
—	Los Angeles (N.L.)	1	4	.200	4.94	1.48	19	0	0	0	1	0-2	23.2	23	13	13	2	12-4	24	.256
1997—	Los Angeles (N.L.)	5	2	.714	2.86	1.25	48	0	0	0	9	4-7	63.0	45	21	20	3	34-2	63	.202
—	Albuquerque (PCL)	0	0	...	1.59	0.53	2	2	0	0	...	0-...	5.2	2	1	1	1	1-0	3	.111
1998—	Los Angeles (N.L.)	8	12	.400	4.00	1.27	32	26	1	1	0	0-0	180.0	171	84	80	12	57-2	168	.256
1999—	Los Angeles (N.L.)	13	13	.500	4.79	1.42	30	29	1	1	0	0-0	178.2	177	105	95	28	76-2	140	.260
2000—	Los Angeles (N.L.)	12	9	.571	4.16	1.36	32	32	1	1	0	0-0	192.2	175	105	89	31	87-1	164	.238
2001—	Los Angeles (N.L.)	4	7	.364	5.13	1.44	16	16	0	0	0	0-0	94.2	89	62	54	11	47-0	91	.251
2002—	Los Angeles (N.L.)			Did not play.																
2003—	Los Angeles (N.L.)	4	4	.500	4.03	1.38	10	10	0	0	0	0-0	60.1	58	29	27	6	25-0	67	.250
2004—	Los Angeles (N.L.)	1	4	.200	4.44	1.56	60	0	0	0	6	15	1-4	50.2	43	25	25	5	36-2	63	.232
Major League totals (9 years)		48	60	.444	4.36	1.39	274	113	3	3	28	11-22	872.2	826	465	423	90	389-16	802	.251

D

Year	Team (League)	W	L	Pct.	ERA	WHIP	G	GS	CG	ShO	Hld.	Sv.-Opp.	IP	H	R	ER	HR	BB-IBB	SO	Avg.
1996— Los Angeles (N.L.)		0	0	...	0.00	0.00	1	0	0	0	0	0-0	.2	0	0	0	0	0-0	0	.000

DRESE, RYAN — P

PERSONAL: Born April 5, 1976, in San Francisco, Calif. ... 6-3/235. ... Throws right, bats right. ... Full name: Ryan Thomas Drese. ... Name pronounced: drees. ... High school: Bishop O'Dowd (Oakland). ... College: California.

TRANSACTIONS/CAREER NOTES: Selected by Oakland Athletics organization in fifth round of 1994 free-agent draft; did not sign. ... Selected by Athletics organization in 14th round of 1997 free-agent draft; did not sign. ... Selected by Cleveland Indians organization in fifth round of 1998 free-agent draft. ... Traded by Indians with C Einar Diaz to Texas Rangers for 1B Travis Hafner and P Aaron Myette (December 6, 2002).

CAREER HITTING: 2-for-7 (.286), 1 R, 1 2B, 0 3B, 0 HR, 0 RBI.

Year	Team (League)	W	L	Pct.	ERA	WHIP	G	GS	CG	ShO	Hld.	Sv.-Opp.	IP	H	R	ER	HR	BB-IBB	SO	Avg.
1998— Watertown (N.Y.-Penn.)	2	5	.286	4.07	1.29	9	9	0	0	...	0-...	42.0	40	21	19	1	14-0	40	.250
1999— Kinston (Caro.)	5	4	.556	4.93	1.41	15	15	1	0	...	0-...	69.1	46	47	38	2	52-0	81	.189
— Mahoning Valley (NY-P)	0	2	.000	2.65	0.88	5	5	0	0	...	0-...	17.0	8	6	5	1	7-0	26	.143
— Columbus (S. Atl.)	0	2	.000	4.50	1.08	2	2	0	0	...	0-...	12.0	9	6	6	2	4-0	15	.200
2000— Kinston (Caro.)	0	1	.000	3.86	1.29	1	1	0	0	...	0-...	2.1	2	1	1	0	1-0	4	.286
2001— Akron (East.)	5	7	.417	3.35	1.08	14	13	1	1	...	0-...	86.0	64	34	32	4	29-0	73	.215
— Buffalo (Int'l)	5	1	.833	4.01	1.27	11	10	0	0	...	0-...	60.2	60	28	27	7	17-0	52	.262
— Cleveland (A.L.)	1	2	.333	3.44	1.28	9	4	0	0	0	0-0	36.2	32	15	14	2	15-2	24	.242
2002— Cleveland (A.L.)	10	9	.526	6.55	1.73	26	26	1	0	0	0-0	137.1	176	104	100	15	62-1	102	.317
— Buffalo (Int'l)	1	0	1.000	1.64	0.91	3	3	0	0	...	0-...	22.0	16	4	4	1	4-0	16	.200
2003— Frisco (Texas)	1	1	.500	4.00	1.10	2	2	0	0	...	0-...	9.0	10	4	4	1	0-0	8	.278
— Oklahoma (PCL)	8	6	.571	4.65	1.50	20	20	0	0	...	0-...	122.0	143	70	63	8	39-1	68	.300
— Texas (A.L.)	2	4	.333	6.85	1.85	11	8	0	0	1	0-...	46.0	61	42	35	8	24-1	26	.314
2004— Oklahoma (PCL)	1	0	1.000	1.80	1.20	1	1	0	0	...	0-...	5.0	6	1	1	1	0-0	0	.300
— Texas (A.L.)	14	10	.583	4.20	1.40	34	33	2	0	0	0-0	207.2	233	104	97	16	58-6	98	.285
Major League totals (4 years)	27	25	.519	5.18	1.55	80	71	3	0	1	0-0	427.2	502	265	246	41	159-10	250	.296

DREW, J.D. — OF

PERSONAL: Born November 20, 1975, in Valdosta, Ga. ... 6-1/200. ... Bats left, throws right. ... Full name: David Jonathan Drew. ... High school: Lowndes County (Hahira, Ga.). ... College: Florida State. ... Brother of Tim Drew, pitcher with Atlanta Braves in 2004.

TRANSACTIONS/CAREER NOTES: Selected by San Francisco Giants organization in 20th round of 1994 free-agent draft; did not sign. ... Selected by Philadelphia Phillies organization in first round (second pick overall) of 1997 free-agent draft; did not sign. ... Selected by St. Louis Cardinals organization in first round (fifth pick overall) of 1998 free-agent draft. ... On disabled list (May 16-June 17, 1999); included rehabilitation assignment to Memphis. ... On disabled list (June 18-July 31, 2001); included rehabilitation assignment to Peoria. ... On disabled list (June 28-July 13, 2002). ... On disabled list (March 21-April 20 and August 9-September 1, 2003); included rehabilitation assignment to Palm Beach. ... Traded by Cardinals with OF/C Eli Marrero to Atlanta Braves for Ps Jason Marquis, Ray King and Adam Wainwright (December 14, 2003).

HONORS: Named College Player of the Year by THE SPORTING NEWS (1997).

2004 GAMES PLAYED BY POSITION (MLB): OF—142, DH—1.

Year	Team (League)	Pos.	G	AB	R	H	2B	3B	HR	RBI	BB	SO	HBP	GDP	SB-CS	Avg.	OBP	SLG	OPS	E	Avg.
1997— St. Paul (Nor.)		44	170	51	58	6	1	18	50	30	40	2	1	5-3	.341	.443	.706	1.149	...	...
1998— St. Paul (Nor.)		30	114	27	44	11	2	9	33	21	32	6	2	8-1	.386	.504	.754	1.258	...	...
— Arkansas (Texas)	OF	19	67	18	22	3	1	5	11	13	15	1	0	2-1	.328	.444	.627	1.071	1	.980
— Memphis (PCL)	OF	26	79	15	25	8	1	2	13	22	18	1	1	1-3	.316	.471	.519	.990	2	.966
— St. Louis (N.L.)	OF	14	36	9	15	3	1	5	13	4	10	0	4	0-0	.417	.463	.972	1.436	0	1.000
1999— St. Louis (N.L.)	OF	104	368	72	89	16	6	13	39	50	77	6	4	19-3	.242	.340	.424	.763	7	.972
— Memphis (PCL)	OF	25	87	11	26	5	1	2	15	8	20	2	0	6-1	.299	.371	.448	.819	0	1.000
2000— St. Louis (N.L.)	OF	135	407	73	120	17	2	18	57	67	99	6	3	17-9	.295	.401	.479	.880	9	.966
2001— St. Louis (N.L.)	OF	109	375	80	121	18	5	27	73	57	75	4	6	13-3	.323	.414	.613	1.027	6	.973
— Peoria (Midw.)	OF	3	11	3	6	2	0	0	0	1	0	0	1	0-0	.545	.583	.727	1.311	0	1.000
2002— St. Louis (N.L.)	OF	135	424	61	107	19	1	18	56	57	104	8	4	8-2	.252	.349	.429	.778	3	.987
2003— Palm Beach (FSL)	OF-DH	8	19	4	7	0	0	1	3	7	4	1	0	0-0	.368	.556	.526	1.082	0	1.000
— St. Louis (N.L.)	OF	100	287	60	83	13	3	15	42	36	48	3	6	2-2	.289	.374	.512	.886	1	.994
2004— Atlanta (N.L.)	OF-DH	145	518	118	158	28	8	31	93	118	116	5	7	12-3	.305	.436	.570	1.006	3	.990
Major League totals (7 years)		742	2415	473	693	114	26	127	373	389	529	32	34	71-22	.287	.391	.513	.904	29	.980

DIVISION SERIES RECORD

Year	Team (League)	Pos.	G	AB	R	H	2B	3B	HR	RBI	BB	SO	HBP	GDP	SB-CS	Avg.	OBP	SLG	OPS	E	Avg.
2000— St. Louis (N.L.)	OF	2	6	1	1	0	0	0	0	2	1	0	0	2-0	.167	.375	.167	.542	0	1.000
2001— St. Louis (N.L.)	OF	5	13	1	2	0	0	1	2	3	1	0	0	0-0	.154	.313	.385	.697	0	1.000
2002— St. Louis (N.L.)	OF	2	9	1	2	0	0	1	1	1	2	0	0	0-0	.222	.300	.556	.856	0	1.000
2004— Atlanta (N.L.)	OF	5	20	1	4	0	0	0	1	4	7	0	0	1-1	.200	.333	.200	.533	1	.889
Division series totals (4 years)		14	48	4	9	0	0	2	4	10	11	0	0	3-1	.188	.328	.313	.640	1	.964

CHAMPIONSHIP SERIES RECORD

Year	Team (League)	Pos.	G	AB	R	H	2B	3B	HR	RBI	BB	SO	HBP	GDP	SB-CS	Avg.	OBP	SLG	OPS	E	Avg.
2000— St. Louis (N.L.)	OF	5	12	2	4	1	0	0	1	0	3	0	0	0-0	.333	.333	.417	.750	0	1.000
2002— St. Louis (N.L.)	OF	5	13	1	5	0	0	1	1	1	2	0	1	0-0	.385	.429	.615	1.044	0	1.000
Champ. series totals (2 years)		10	25	3	9	1	0	1	2	1	5	0	1	0-0	.360	.385	.520	.905	0	1.000

DREW, TIM — P

PERSONAL: Born August 31, 1978, in Valdosta, Ga. ... 6-1/190. ... Throws right, bats right. ... Full name: Timothy Andrew Drew. ... High school: Lowndes County (Hahira, Ga.). ... Brother of J.D. Drew, outfielder with Atlanta Braves in 2004.

TRANSACTIONS/CAREER NOTES: Selected by Cleveland Indians organization in first round (28th pick overall) of 1997 free-agent draft. ... Traded by Indians to Montreal Expos (June 28, 2002), completing deal in which Indians traded P Bartolo Colon with future considerations to Expos for 1B Lee Stevens, SS Brandon Phillips, P Cliff Lee and OF Grady Sizemore (June 27, 2002). ... Signed as a free agent by Atlanta Braves organization (January 12, 2004). ... On disabled list (August 18-September 2, 2004); included rehabilitation assignment to Richmond. ... Refused minor league assignment and became a free agent (October 15, 2004).

CAREER HITTING: 0-for-7 (.000), 1 R, 0 2B, 0 3B, 0 HR, 0 RBI.

Year Team (League)	W	L	Pct.	ERA	WHIP	G	GS	CG	ShO	Hld.	Sv.-Opp.	IP	H	R	ER	HR	BB-IBB	SO	Avg.
1997— Burlington (Appalachian) ..	0	1	.000	6.17	1.71	4	4	0	0	...	0-...	11.2	16	15	8	0	4-0	14	.302
—Watertown (N.Y.-Penn.)	0	0		1.93	1.50	1	1	0	0	...	0-...	4.2	4	1	1	0	3-0	9	.235
1998— Columbus (S. Atl.)	4	3	.571	3.79	1.32	13	13	0	0	...	0-...	71.1	68	43	30	5	26-0	64	.247
—Kinston (Caro.)	3	8	.273	5.20	1.51	15	15	0	0	...	0-...	90.0	105	58	52	9	31-1	67	.302
1999— Kinston (Caro.)	13	5	.722	3.73	1.27	28	28	2	0	...	0-...	169.0	154	79	70	12	60-0	125	.243
2000— Akron (East.)	3	2	.600	2.42	1.08	9	9	0	0	...	0-...	52.0	41	19	14	1	15-0	22	.217
—Cleveland (A.L.)	1	0	1.000	10.00	2.78	3	3	0	0	0	0-...	9.0	17	12	10	1	8-0	5	.425
—Buffalo (Int'l)	7	8	.467	5.87	1.61	16	16	2	0	...	0-...	95.0	122	69	62	12	31-0	53	.312
2001— Cleveland (A.L.)	0	2	.000	7.97	1.91	8	6	0	0	0	0-0	35.0	51	39	31	9	16-0	15	.340
—Buffalo (Int'l)	8	6	.571	3.92	1.31	18	18	1	1	...	0-...	108.0	115	54	47	13	27-1	75	.268
2002— Buffalo (Int'l)	8	4	.667	3.27	1.24	15	15	2	2	...	0-...	96.1	96	43	35	6	23-1	43	...
—Ottawa (Int'l)	6	3	.667	2.87	1.19	13	13	0	0	...	0-...	84.2	77	31	27	5	24-2	29	...
—Montreal (N.L.)	1	0	1.000	2.81	0.88	7	1	0	0	1	2-3	16.0	12	8	5	1	2-0	10	.200
2003— Montreal (N.L.)	0	2	.000	12.46	2.31	6	1	0	0	0	0-0	8.2	12	12	12	3	8-1	3	.343
—Edmonton (PCL)	5	9	.357	7.23	1.70	27	15	0	0	...	2-...	93.1	128	80	75	10	35-2	54	.334
2004— Richmond (Int'l)	4	5	.444	3.31	1.42	19	13	0	0	...	1-...	81.2	92	35	30	5	24-1	44	.292
—Atlanta (N.L.)	0	0		4.50	1.63	11	0	0	0	0	0-0	16.0	21	11	8	2	5-0	7	.318
American League totals (2 years)	1	2	.333	8.39	2.09	11	9	0	0	0	0-0	44.0	68	51	41	10	24-0	20	.358
National League totals (3 years)	1	2	.333	5.53	1.48	24	2	0	0	1	2-3	40.2	45	31	25	6	15-1	20	.280
Major League totals (5 years)	2	4	.333	7.02	1.80	35	11	0	0	1	2-3	84.2	113	82	66	16	39-1	40	.322

DRISKILL, TRAVIS   P

PERSONAL: Born August 1, 1971, in Omaha, Neb. ... 6-0/215. ... Throws right, bats right. ... Full name: Travis Corey Driskill. ... High school: L.C. Anderson (Austin, Texas). ... College: Texas Tech.

TRANSACTIONS/CAREER NOTES: Selected by Houston Astros organization in 76th round of 1990 free-agent draft; did not sign. ... Selected by Cleveland Indians organization in fourth round of 1993 free-agent draft. ... Contract sold by Indians to Yakult of the Japan Central League (January 6, 1998). ... Signed as a free agent by Indians organization (August 3, 1998). ... Signed as a free agent by Astros organization (January 3, 2000). ... Signed as a free agent by Baltimore Orioles organization (November 16, 2001). ... Signed as a free agent by Colorado Rockies organization (December 17, 2003).

CAREER HITTING: 0-for-5 (.000), 1 R, 0 2B, 0 3B, 0 HR, 0 RBI.

Year Team (League)	W	L	Pct.	ERA	WHIP	G	GS	CG	ShO	Hld.	Sv.-Opp.	IP	H	R	ER	HR	BB-IBB	SO	Avg.
1993— Watertown (N.Y.-Penn.)	5	4	.556	4.14	1.32	21	8	0	0	...	3-...	63.0	62	38	29	4	21-0	53	.257
1994— Columbus (S. Atl.)	5	5	.500	2.52	1.26	62	0	0	0	...	35-...	64.1	51	25	18	2	30-4	88	.223
1995— Kinston (Caro.)	0	2	.000	2.74	0.96	15	0	0	0	...	0-...	23.0	17	7	7	2	5-1	24	.210
—Cant./Akr. (Eastern)	3	4	.429	4.66	1.40	33	0	0	0	...	4-...	46.1	46	24	24	3	19-1	39	.258
1996— Cant./Akr. (Eastern)	13	7	.650	3.61	1.35	29	24	4	2	...	0-...	172.0	169	89	69	8	63-0	148	.258
1997— Buffalo (A.A.)	8	7	.533	4.65	1.49	29	24	1	0	...	0-...	147.0	159	86	76	22	60-0	102	.277
1998— Yakult (Jp. East.)	1	6	.143	6.08	1.63	12	5	0	0	...	0-...	40.0	46	29	27	...	19-...	25	...
—Yakult (Jp. Cen.)	0	1	.000	4.80	1.80	7	3	0	0	...	0-...	15.0	21	9	8	...	6-...	7	...
—Akron (East.)	3	0	1.000	3.42	1.29	5	4	0	0	...	0-...	26.1	27	12	10	4	7-0	16	.270
—Buffalo (Int'l)	0	0		9.00	1.67	1	1	0	0	...	0-...	6.0	9	6	6	0	1-0	5	.333
1999— Buffalo (Int'l)	9	8	.529	4.83	1.35	31	18	0	0	...	0-...	132.1	146	78	71	21	32-2	90	.285
2000— New Orleans (PCL)	12	11	.522	4.01	1.37	28	28	2	1	...	0-...	179.1	201	101	80	15	45-0	113	.282
2001— New Orleans (PCL)	11	5	.688	3.78	1.16	28	28	1	0	...	0-...	178.2	175	83	75	21	33-2	145	.255
2002— Rochester (Int'l)	2	2	.500	1.64	0.82	4	4	1	1	...	0-...	22.0	17	8	4	1	1-0	15	.202
—Baltimore (A.L.)	8	8	.500	4.95	1.49	29	19	0	0	0	0-...	132.2	150	78	73	21	48-1	78	.284
2003— Baltimore (A.L.)	3	5	.375	6.00	1.48	20	0	0	0	0	1-1	48.0	62	35	32	8	9-2	33	.310
—Ottawa (Int'l)	4	0	1.000	2.84	1.00	9	9	0	0	...	0-...	50.2	46	17	16	2	6-0	36	.238
2004— Colorado (N.L.)	0	0		6.48	1.92	5	0	0	0	...	0-1	8.1	13	6	6	0	3-0	6	.361
—Colo. Springs (PCL)	5	5	.500	5.40	1.48	28	13	0	0	...	2-...	111.2	141	70	67	18	24-0	81	.311
American League totals (2 years)	11	13	.458	5.23	1.49	49	19	0	0	0	1-1	180.2	212	113	105	29	57-3	111	.291
National League totals (1 year)	0	0		6.48	1.92	5	0	0	0	0	0-1	8.1	13	6	6	0	3-0	6	.361
Major League totals (3 years)	11	13	.458	5.29	1.51	54	19	0	0	0	1-2	189.0	225	119	111	29	60-3	117	.294

D

DUBOIS, JASON   OF

PERSONAL: Born March 26, 1979, in Virginia Beach, Va. ... 6-5/220. ... Bats right, throws right. ... Full name: Jason Bradford Dubois. ... Name pronounced: do-BOYCE. ... High school: Frank W. Cox (Virginia Beach). ... College: Virginia Commonwealth.

TRANSACTIONS/CAREER NOTES: Selected by Chicago Cubs organization in 14th round of 2000 free-agent draft. ... Selected by Toronto Blue Jays from Cubs organization in Rule 5 major league draft (December 16, 2002). ... Returned to Cubs organization (March 15, 2003).

2004 GAMES PLAYED BY POSITION (MLB): OF—5, 1B—1.

Year Team (League)	Pos.	G	AB	R	H	2B	3B	HR	RBI	BB	SO	HBP	GDP	SB-CS	Avg.	OBP	SLG	OPS	E	Avg.
2001— Lansing (Midw.)	OF-1B	118	443	76	131	28	9	24	92	46	120	14	8	1-2	.296	.377	.562	.940	7	.973
2002— Daytona (Fla. St.)	OF	99	361	64	116	25	1	20	85	57	95	9	7	6-2	.321	.422	.562	.985	4	.975
2003— West Tenn (Sou.)	OF-1B	130	443	57	119	31	4	15	73	57	118	15	12	2-4	.269	.367	.458	.825	9	.970
2004— Iowa (PCL)	OF-1B-DH	109	385	75	121	26	1	31	99	41	97	7	10	2-0	.314	.388	.629	1.009	4	.987
—Chicago (N.L.)	OF-1B	20	23	2	5	0	1	1	5	1	7	0	0	0-0	.217	.240	.435	.675	0	1.000
Major League totals (1 year)		20	23	2	5	0	1	1	5	1	7	0	0	0-0	.217	.240	.435	.675	0	1.000

DUBOSE, ERIC   P

PERSONAL: Born May 15, 1976, in Bradenton, Fla. ... 6-3/216. ... Throws left, bats left. ... Full name: Eric Ladell DuBose. ... Name pronounced: dew-BOWES. ... High school: Patrician Academy (Butler, Ala.). ... College: Mississippi State.

TRANSACTIONS/CAREER NOTES: Selected by Los Angeles Dodgers organization in sixth round of 1994 free-agent draft; did not sign. ... Selected by Oakland Athletics organization in first round (21st pick overall) of 1997 free-agent draft; pick received as compensation for Baltimore Orioles signing Type A free-agent SS Mike Bordick. ... Claimed on waivers by Cleveland Indians organization (September 8, 2000). ... Claimed on waivers by Detroit Tigers (September 22, 2000). ... Released by Tigers (March 31, 2001). ... Signed by Baltimore Orioles organization (February 4, 2002). ... On disabled list (June 20, 2004-remainder of season).

CAREER HITTING: 0-for-2 (.000), 0 R, 0 2B, 0 3B, 0 HR, 0 RBI.

Year Team (League)	W	L	Pct.	ERA	WHIP	G	GS	CG	ShO	Hld.	Sv.-Opp.	IP	H	R	ER	HR	BB-IBB	SO	Avg.
1997— S. Oregon (N'west)	1	0	1.000	0.00	1.10	3	1	0	0	...	0-...	10.0	5	0	0	0	6-0	15	.152
—Visalia (Calif.)	1	3	.250	7.04	1.85	10	9	0	0	...	0-...	38.1	43	37	30	4	28-0	39	.270
1998— Visalia (Calif.)	6	1	.857	3.38	1.13	17	10	0	0	...	1-...	72.0	56	34	27	5	25-0	85	.212

Year	Team (League)	W	L	Pct.	ERA	WHIP	G	GS	CG	ShO	Hld.	Sv.-Opp.	IP	H	R	ER	HR	BB-IBB	SO	Avg.
	—Huntsville (Southern)	7	6	.538	2.70	1.44	14	14	1	1	...	0-...	83.1	86	37	25	2	34-1	66	.273
1999—	Midland (Texas)	4	2	.667	5.49	1.73	21	14	0	0	...	1-...	77.0	89	57	47	10	44-1	68	.293
2000—	Midland (Texas)	5	1	.833	4.13	1.52	18	0	0	0	...	0-...	28.1	25	16	13	1	18-2	20	.227
	—Visalia (Calif.)	0	1	.000	1.69	1.22	5	0	0	0	...	1-...	10.2	8	2	2	0	5-1	12	.200
2001—	....								Did not play.											
2002—	Rochester (Int'l)	0	0	...	27.00	9.00	1	0	0	0	...	0-...	.1	1	2	1	0	2-0	0	.333
	—Bowie (East.)	5	3	.625	2.51	1.04	41	0	0	0	...	3-...	64.2	46	21	18	2	21-0	66	.198
	—Baltimore (A.L.)	0	0	...	3.00	1.33	4	0	0	0	...	0-0	6.0	7	2	2	1	1-0	4	.304
2003—	Ottawa (Int'l)	9	5	.643	3.39	1.30	19	19	0	0	...	0-0	114.0	112	49	43	7	34-2	107	.261
	—Baltimore (A.L.)	3	6	.333	3.79	1.15	17	10	1	0	1	0-1	73.2	60	33	31	6	25-2	44	.222
2004—	Baltimore (A.L.)	4	6	.400	6.39	1.61	14	14	0	0	...	0-0	74.2	76	55	53	12	44-0	48	.263
	Major League totals (3 years)	**7**	**12**	**.368**	**5.02**	**1.38**	**35**	**24**	**1**	**0**	**1**	**0-1**	**154.1**	**143**	**90**	**86**	**19**	**70-2**	**96**	**.246**

DUCHSCHERER, JUSTIN   P

PERSONAL: Born November 19, 1977, in Aberdeen, S.D. ... 6-3/190. ... Throws right, bats right. ... Full name: Justin Craig Duchscherer. ... Name pronounced: DUKE-sher. ... High school: Coronado (Lubbock, Texas).

TRANSACTIONS/CAREER NOTES: Selected by Boston Red Sox organization in eighth round of 1996 free-agent draft. ... Traded by Red Sox to Texas Rangers for C Doug Mirabelli (June 12, 2001). ... Traded by Rangers to Oakland Athletics for P Luis Vizcaino (March 18, 2002).

CAREER HITTING: 0-for-0 (.000), 0 R, 0 2B, 0 3B, 0 HR, 0 RBI.

Year	Team (League)	W	L	Pct.	ERA	WHIP	G	GS	CG	ShO	Hld.	Sv.-Opp.	IP	H	R	ER	HR	BB-IBB	SO	Avg.
1996—	GC Red Sox (GCL)	0	2	.000	3.13	1.21	13	8	0	0	...	1-...	54.2	52	26	19	0	14-0	45	.249
1997—	GC Red Sox (GCL)	2	3	.400	1.81	1.14	10	8	0	0	...	0-...	44.2	34	18	9	0	17-0	59	.204
	—Michigan (Midw.)	1	1	.500	5.63	1.50	4	4	0	0	...	0-...	24.0	26	17	15	1	10-0	19	.274
1998—	Michigan (Midw.)	7	12	.368	4.79	1.49	30	26	0	0	...	0-...	142.2	166	87	76	9	47-3	106	.298
1999—	Augusta (S. Atl.)	4	0	1.000	0.22	0.71	6	6	0	0	...	0-...	41.0	21	1	1	0	8-0	39	.148
	—Sarasota (Florida State) ...	7	7	.500	4.49	1.17	20	18	0	0	...	0-...	112.1	101	62	56	14	30-0	105	.237
2000—	Trenton (East.)	7	9	.438	3.39	1.18	24	24	2	2	...	0-...	143.1	134	59	54	7	35-1	126	.246
2001—	Trenton (East.)	6	3	.667	2.44	0.86	12	12	1	1	...	0-...	73.2	49	25	20	6	14-1	69	.179
	—Tulsa (Texas)	4	0	1.000	2.08	1.13	6	6	1	0	...	0-...	43.1	39	14	10	3	10-0	55	.242
	—Texas (A.L.)	1	1	.500	12.27	1.91	5	2	0	0	0	0-0	14.2	24	20	20	5	4-0	11	.353
	—Oklahoma (PCL)	3	3	.500	2.84	1.14	7	7	1	1	...	0-...	50.2	48	20	16	6	10-0	52	.255
2002—	Sacramento (PCL)	2	4	.333	5.57	1.43	14	11	0	0	...	0-...	63.0	73	45	39	7	17-0	52	.283
2003—	Sacramento (PCL)	14	2	.875	3.25	1.10	24	23	0	0	...	0-...	155.0	151	59	56	12	18-0	117	.254
	—Oakland (A.L.)	1	1	.500	3.31	1.22	4	3	0	0	0	0-0	16.1	17	7	6	1	3-0	15	.262
2004—	Oakland (A.L.)	7	6	.538	3.27	1.21	53	0	0	0	6	0-2	96.1	85	37	35	13	32-6	59	.241
	Major League totals (3 years)	**9**	**8**	**.529**	**4.31**	**1.30**	**62**	**5**	**0**	**0**	**6**	**0-2**	**127.1**	**126**	**64**	**61**	**19**	**39-6**	**85**	**.259**

DUCKWORTH, BRANDON   P

PERSONAL: Born January 23, 1976, in Salt Lake City, Utah. ... 6-2/190. ... Throws right, bats right. ... Full name: Brandon J. Duckworth. ... High school: Kearns (Utah). ... College: Cal State Fullerton.

TRANSACTIONS/CAREER NOTES: Selected by Toronto Blue Jays organization in 30th round of 1995 free-agent draft; did not sign. ... Selected by Arizona Diamondbacks organization in 61st round of 1996 free-agent draft; did not sign. ... Signed as a non-drafted free agent by Philadelphia Phillies organization (August 13, 1997). ... On disabled list (March 21-April 20, 2003); included rehabilitation assignments to Clearwater and Reading. ... Traded by Phillies with Ps Taylor Buchholz and Ezequiel Astacio to Houston Astros for P Billy Wagner (November 3, 2003).

CAREER HITTING: 21-for-106 (.198), 6 R, 2 2B, 0 3B, 0 HR, 8 RBI.

Year	Team (League)	W	L	Pct.	ERA	WHIP	G	GS	CG	ShO	Hld.	Sv.-Opp.	IP	H	R	ER	HR	BB-IBB	SO	Avg.
1998—	Piedmont (S. Atl.)	9	8	.529	2.80	0.95	21	21	5	3	...	0-...	147.2	116	58	46	10	24-0	119	.215
	—Clearwater (Fla. St.)	6	2	.750	3.74	1.62	9	9	1	1	...	0-...	53.0	64	25	22	2	22-0	46	.306
1999—	Clearwater (Fla. St.)	11	5	.688	4.84	1.55	27	17	0	0	...	1-...	132.0	164	84	71	13	40-0	101	.301
2000—	Reading (East.)	13	7	.650	3.16	1.19	27	27	1	0	...	0-...	165.0	145	70	58	17	52-0	178	.233
2001—	Scran./W.B. (I.L.)	13	2	.867	2.63	1.07	22	20	2	1	...	0-...	147.0	122	46	43	14	36-2	150	.228
	—Philadelphia (N.L.)	3	2	.600	3.52	1.25	11	11	0	0	0	0-0	69.0	57	29	27	2	29-5	40	.234
2002—	Philadelphia (N.L.)	8	9	.471	5.41	1.45	30	29	0	0	0	0-0	163.0	167	103	98	26	69-5	167	.261
2003—	Clearwater (Fla. St.)	0	0	...	1.00	0.60	2	2	0	0	...	0-...	9.0	3	1	1	1	2-0	11	.100
	—Reading (East.)	0	0	...	4.50	0.50	1	1	0	0	...	0-...	2.0	1	1	1	1	0-0	2	.143
	—Scran./W.B. (I.L.)	2	1	.667	3.38	1.30	3	3	0	0	...	0-...	18.2	21	11	7	3	4-0	14	.280
	—Philadelphia (N.L.)	4	7	.364	4.94	1.53	24	18	0	0	0	0-0	93.0	98	58	51	12	44-3	68	.272
2004—	New Orleans (PCL)	5	5	.500	5.53	1.56	14	13	0	0	...	0-...	70.0	81	44	43	10	28-1	63	.286
	—Houston (N.L.)	1	2	.333	6.86	1.73	19	6	0	0	0	0-0	39.1	55	30	30	11	13-3	23	.337
	Major League totals (4 years)	**16**	**20**	**.444**	**5.09**	**1.46**	**84**	**64**	**0**	**0**	**0**	**0-0**	**364.1**	**377**	**220**	**206**	**51**	**155-16**	**298**	**.268**

DUNCAN, JEFF   OF

PERSONAL: Born December 9, 1978, in Harvey, Ill. ... 6-2/188. ... Bats left, throws left. ... Full name: Jeffrey Matthew Duncan. ... High school: Lemont (Ill.). ... College: Arizona State.

TRANSACTIONS/CAREER NOTES: Selected by Chicago Cubs organization in 41st round of 1997 free-agent draft; did not sign. ... Selected by New York Mets organization in seventh round of 2000 free-agent draft.

2004 GAMES PLAYED BY POSITION (MLB): OF—4.

Year	Team (League)	Pos.	G	AB	R	H	2B	3B	HR	RBI	BATTING BB	SO	HBP	GDP	SB-CS	Avg.	OBP	SLG	OPS	FIELDING E	Avg.
2000—	Pittsfield (N.Y.-Penn.)	OF	53	186	39	45	3	5	2	13	34	46	4	1	20-3	.242	.371	.344	.715	1	.990
2001—	Capital City (SAL)	OF	88	318	49	69	16	8	3	23	46	97	3	2	41-3	.217	.320	.346	.666	6	.959
2002—	St. Lucie (Fla. St.)	OF	29	102	20	35	5	0	2	10	24	15	1	4	10-1	.343	.472	.451	.923	2	.967
	—Capital City (SAL)	OF	40	150	33	59	13	3	4	17	18	34	3	1	15-3	.393	.468	.600	1.068	4	.882
2003—	Binghamton (East.)	OF	76	278	49	80	11	5	4	23	36	59	5	0	24-10	.288	.376	.406	.782	2	.987
	—Norfolk (Int'l)	OF	4	15	2	4	1	0	2	4	1	7	0	0	1-0	.267	.313	.733	1.046	0	1.000
	—New York (N.L.)	OF	56	139	13	27	0	2	1	10	17	41	2	1	4-2	.194	.291	.245	.536	0	1.000
2004—	New York (N.L.)	OF	13	15	2	1	0	0	0	1	1	5	0	0	3-0	.067	.125	.067	.192	0	1.000
	—Norfolk (Int'l)	OF	55	202	26	52	12	1	2	14	23	52	0	1	11-5	.257	.332	.356	.688	2	.972
	—Binghamton (East.)	OF	38	133	19	34	6	1	0	9	21	38	3	4	10-2	.256	.367	.316	.683	2	.972
	Major League totals (2 years)		**69**	**154**	**15**	**28**	**0**	**2**	**1**	**11**	**18**	**46**	**2**	**1**	**7-2**	**.182**	**.276**	**.227**	**.503**	**0**	**1.000**

DUNN, ADAM   OF

PERSONAL: Born November 9, 1979, in Houston, Texas. ... 6-6/240. ... Bats left, throws right. ... Full name: Adam Troy Dunn. ... High school: New Caney (Texas).
TRANSACTIONS/CAREER NOTES: Selected by Cincinnati Reds organization in second round of 1998 free-agent draft. ... On suspended list (June 20-22, 2003). ... On disabled list (August 16, 2003-remainder of season).
RECORDS: Holds major league record for most strikeouts, season (195, 2004). ... Shares major league record for most strikeouts, nine-inning game (5, August 20, 2002).
2004 GAMES PLAYED BY POSITION (MLB): OF—156, 1B—10, DH—1.

Year Team (League)	Pos.	G	AB	R	H	2B	3B	HR	RBI	BB	SO	HBP	GDP	SB-CS	Avg.	OBP	SLG	OPS	E	Avg.
1998— Billings (Pio.)	OF	34	125	26	36	3	1	4	13	22	33	3	3	4-2	.288	.404	.424	.828	6	.860
1999— Rockford (Midwest)	OF	93	313	62	96	16	2	11	44	46	64	10	6	21-9	.307	.409	.476	.885	8	.918
2000— Dayton (Midw.)	OF	122	420	101	118	29	1	16	79	100	101	12	10	24-5	.281	.428	.469	.897	9	.958
2001— Chattanooga (Sou.)	OF	39	140	30	48	9	0	12	31	24	31	3	1	6-3	.343	.449	.664	1.113	3	.961
— Louisville (Int'l)	OF	55	210	44	69	13	6	20	53	38	51	5	1	5-1	.329	.441	.676	1.117	5	.954
— Cincinnati (N.L.)	OF	66	244	54	64	18	1	19	43	38	74	4	4	4-2	.262	.371	.578	.949	2	.986
2002— Cincinnati (N.L.)	OF-1B-DH	158	535	84	133	28	2	26	71	128	170	9	8	19-9	.249	.400	.454	.854	15	.975
2003— Cincinnati (N.L.)	OF-1B-DH	116	381	70	82	12	1	27	57	74	126	10	4	8-2	.215	.354	.465	.819	11	.965
2004— Cincinnati (N.L.)	OF-1B-DH	161	568	105	151	34	0	46	102	108 *	195	5	8	6-1	.266	.388	.569	.956	8	.977
Major League totals (4 years)		501	1728	313	430	92	4	118	273	348	565	28	24	37-14	.249	.382	.512	.893	36	.974

ALL-STAR GAME RECORD

	G	AB	R	H	2B	3B	HR	RBI	BB	SO	HBP	GDP	SB-CS	Avg.	OBP	SLG	OPS	E	Avg.
All-Star Game totals (1 year)	1	1	0	0	0	0	0	0	1	0	0	0	0-0	.000	.500	.000	.500	0	...

DUNN, SCOTT   P

PERSONAL: Born May 23, 1978, in San Antonio, Texas. ... 6-3/200. ... Throws right, bats right. ... Full name: Scott Allen Dunn. ... High school: Winston Churchill (San Antonio). ... College: Texas.
TRANSACTIONS/CAREER NOTES: Selected by Florida Marlins organization in 26th round of 1996 free-agent draft; did not sign. ... Selected by Cincinnati Reds oganization in 10th round of 1999 free-agent draft. ... Traded by Reds to Chicago White Sox for IF D'Angelo Jimenez (July 6, 2003). ... Traded by White Sox with Ps Gary Glover and Tim Bittner to Anaheim Angels for Ps Scott Schoeneweis and Doug Nickle (July 30, 2003).
CAREER HITTING: 0-for-0 (.000), 0 R, 0 2B, 0 3B, 0 HR, 0 RBI.

Year Team (League)	W	L	Pct.	ERA	WHIP	G	GS	CG	ShO	Hld.	Sv.-Opp.	IP	H	R	ER	HR	BB-IBB	SO	Avg.
1999— Billings (Pio.)	1	3	.250	4.31	1.51	9	8	0	0	...	0-...	39.2	36	24	19	3	24-0	36	.240
2000— Clinton (Midw.)	11	3	.786	3.96	1.44	26	26	2	1	...	0-...	147.2	123	78	65	9	89-1	159	.228
2001— Mudville (Calif.)	5	3	.625	2.11	1.27	10	10	1	1	...	0-...	59.0	45	17	14	2	31-0	73	.208
— Chattanooga (Southern)	7	2	.778	4.12	1.70	17	17	0	0	...	0-...	98.1	96	51	45	10	71-0	87	.262
2002— Chattanooga (Southern)	5	7	.417	3.92	1.39	37	12	0	0	...	1-...	110.1	99	57	48	10	54-3	114	.245
2003— Chattanooga (Southern)	3	2	.600	3.79	1.17	31	0	0	0	...	8-...	40.1	31	21	17	3	16-2	54	.211
— Birmingham (Southern)	3	1	.750	1.69	1.22	8	0	0	0	...	1-...	10.2	8	2	2	0	5-2	14	.216
— Arkansas (Texas)	1	0	1.000	0.00	0.40	3	0	0	0	...	0-...	5.0	2	0	0	0	1-0	7	.125
— Salt Lake (PCL)	0	0	...	11.74	2.48	6	0	0	0	...	0-...	7.2	9	10	10	1	10-0	11	.273
2004— Salt Lake (PCL)	10	4	.714	3.21	1.43	46	6	0	0	...	1-...	89.2	72	36	32	6	56-0	84	.224
— Anaheim (A.L.)	0	0	...	9.00	2.67	3	0	0	0	...	0-0	3.0	7	3	3	0	1-0	2	.438
Major League totals (1 year)	0	0	...	9.00	2.67	3	0	0	0	...	0-0	3.0	7	3	3	0	1-0	2	.438

DURAZO, ERUBIEL   DH

PERSONAL: Born January 23, 1975, in Hermosillo, Mexico. ... 6-3/240. ... Bats left, throws left. ... Full name: Erubiel Durazo Cardenas. ... Name pronounced: eh-ROO-bee-el du-RAH-zo. ... High school: Amphitheater (Tucson, Ariz.). ... Junior college: Pima (Ariz.) Community College.
TRANSACTIONS/CAREER NOTES: Signed by Monterrey, Mexican League (1997). ... Contract sold by Monterrey to Arizona Diamondbacks organization (December 16, 1998). ... On disabled list (May 30-June 24, June 27-July 13 and August 20, 2000-remainder of season); included rehabilitation assignments to Tuscon and AZL Diamondbacks. ... On disabled list (August 15-September 1, 2001); included rehabilitation assignment to Tucson. ... On Arizona disabled list (March 22-May 16 and June 30-July 27, 2002); included rehabilitation assignments to Tucson and El Paso. ... Traded by Diamondbacks to Oakland Athletics as part of four-team deal in which Diamondbacks acquired P Elmer Dessens from Cincinnati Reds, Reds acquired SS Felipe Lopez from Toronto Blue Jays and Blue Jays acquired a player to be named from A's (December 15, 2002); Blue Jays acquired P Jason Arnold to complete deal (December 16, 2002).
2004 GAMES PLAYED BY POSITION (MLB): DH—132, 1B—4.

Year Team (League)	Pos.	G	AB	R	H	2B	3B	HR	RBI	BB	SO	HBP	GDP	SB-CS	Avg.	OBP	SLG	OPS	E	Avg.
1997— Monterrey (Mex.)	1B-OF	110	358	47	101	21	10	8	61	52	43	...	...	3-7	.282	...	.464	...	3	.994
1998— Monterrey (Mex.)	1B-OF	119	420	84	147	32	2	19	98	99	71	...	...	4-3	.350	...	.571	...	0	1.000
1999— El Paso (Texas)	1B	64	226	53	91	18	3	14	55	44	37	2	5	2-1	.403	.498	.695	1.193	10	.982
— Tucson (PCL)	1B-DH	30	118	27	48	7	0	10	28	14	18	1	0	1-0	.407	.470	.720	1.190	1	.996
— Arizona (N.L.)	1B	52	155	31	51	4	2	11	30	26	43	1	1	1-1	.329	.422	.594	1.015	0	1.000
2000— Arizona (N.L.)	1B	67	196	35	52	11	0	8	33	34	43	1	3	1-0	.265	.373	.444	.817	5	.989
— Tucson (PCL)	1B	13	43	9	18	6	0	3	10	6	7	0	0	0-0	.419	.490	.767	1.257	3	.957
— Ariz. D'backs (Ariz.)	1B	2	5	2	3	0	0	1	2	1	0	0	0	0-0	.600	.667	1.200	1.867	0	1.000
2001— Arizona (N.L.)	1B-DH-OF	92	175	34	47	11	0	12	38	28	49	2	1	0-0	.269	.372	.537	.909	2	.993
— Tucson (PCL)	1B	3	11	3	3	0	0	1	1	1	3	0	0	0-0	.273	.333	.545	.879	1	1.000
2002— Tucson (PCL)	1B	7	22	5	7	2	1	1	3	0	2	1	1	0-0	.318	.348	.636	.984	1	.971
— Arizona (N.L.)	1B-DH-OF	76	222	46	58	12	2	16	48	49	60	2	1	0-1	.261	.395	.550	.944	7	.984
— El Paso (Texas)	1B	5	14	5	7	3	0	2	7	4	1	0	1	0-0	.500	.611	1.143	1.754	0	1.000
2003— Oakland (A.L.)	DH-1B	154	537	92	139	29	0	21	77	100	105	2	11	1-1	.259	.374	.430	.804	6	.981
2004— Oakland (A.L.)	DH-1B	142	511	80	164	35	1	22	88	56	104	9	7	3-2	.321	.396	.523	.919	2	.882
American League totals (2 years)		296	1048	172	303	64	1	43	165	156	209	11	18	4-3	.289	.384	.475	.859	8	.976
National League totals (4 years)		287	748	146	208	38	4	47	149	137	195	6	6	2-2	.278	.390	.528	.918	14	.991
Major League totals (6 years)		583	1796	318	511	102	5	90	314	293	404	17	24	6-5	.285	.387	.497	.884	22	.988

DIVISION SERIES RECORD

Year Team (League)	Pos.	G	AB	R	H	2B	3B	HR	RBI	BB	SO	HBP	GDP	SB-CS	Avg.	OBP	SLG	OPS	E	Avg.
1999— Arizona (N.L.)	1B	2	7	1	1	0	0	1	1	1	0	0	1	0-0	.143	.250	.571	.821	0	1.000
2001— Arizona (N.L.)		1	1	0	0	0	0	0	0	0	0	0	0	0-0	.000	.000	.000	...	...	...
2002— Arizona (N.L.)	1B	2	4	0	0	0	0	0	0	1	0	0	0	0-0	.000	.200	.000	.200	0	1.000
2003— Oakland (A.L.)	DH	5	21	3	5	2	0	0	4	3	4	0	0	0-0	.238	.333	.333	.667	...	...
Division series totals (4 years)		10	33	4	6	2	0	1	5	5	4	0	1	0-0	.182	.289	.333	.623	0	1.000

Year Team (League)	Pos.	G	AB	R	H	2B	3B	HR	RBI	BB	SO	HBP	GDP	SB-CS	Avg.	OBP	SLG	OPS	E	Avg.
CHAMPIONSHIP SERIES RECORD																				
2001—Arizona (N.L.)	1B	2	3	1	1	0	0	1	2	0	1	0	0	0-0	.333	.333	1.333	1.667	0	1.000
WORLD SERIES RECORD																				
2001—Arizona (N.L.)	DH	4	11	0	4	1	0	0	1	3	4	0	0	0-0	.364	.500	.455	.955	...	...

DURBIN, CHAD — P

PERSONAL: Born December 3, 1977, in Spring Valley, Ill. ... 6-2/200. ... Throws right, bats both. ... Full name: Chad Griffin Durbin. ... High school: Woodlawn (Shreveport, La.).

TRANSACTIONS/CAREER NOTES: Selected by Kansas City Royals organization in third round of 1996 free-agent draft. ... Signed as a free agent by Cleveland Indians organization (February 14, 2003). ... Claimed on waivers by Arizona Diamondbacks (August 31, 2004). ... Refused minor league assignment and became a free agent (October 11, 2004).

CAREER HITTING: 0-for-2 (.000), 0 R, 0 2B, 0 3B, 0 HR, 0 RBI.

Year Team (League)	W	L	Pct.	ERA	WHIP	G	GS	CG	ShO	Hld.	Sv.-Opp.	IP	H	R	ER	HR	BB-IBB	SO	Avg.
1996—GC Royals (GCL)	3	2	.600	4.26	1.33	11	8	1	1	...	0-...	44.1	34	22	21	3	25-0	43	.213
1997—Lansing (Midw.)	5	8	.385	4.79	1.45	26	26	0	0	...	0-...	144.2	157	85	77	15	53-0	116	.277
1998—Wilmington (Caro.)	10	7	.588	2.93	1.25	26	26	0	0	...	0-...	147.2	126	57	48	10	59-3	162	.231
1999—Wichita (Texas)	8	10	.444	4.64	1.29	28	27	1	1	...	0-...	157.0	154	88	81	20	49-1	122	.258
—Kansas City (A.L.)	0	0	...	0.00	0.86	1	0	0	0	0	0-0	2.1	1	0	0	0	1-0	3	.125
2000—Kansas City (A.L.)	2	5	.286	8.21	1.85	16	16	0	0	0	0-0	72.1	91	71	66	14	43-1	37	.301
—Omaha (PCL)	4	4	.500	4.46	1.33	12	12	0	0	...	0-...	72.2	75	37	36	10	22-0	53	.269
2001—Omaha (PCL)	2	2	.500	3.33	1.04	5	5	0	0	...	0-...	27.0	22	11	10	4	6-0	35	.216
—Kansas City (A.L.)	9	16	.360	4.93	1.45	29	29	2	0	0	0-0	179.0	201	109	98	26	58-0	95	.288
2002—Kansas City (A.L.)	0	1	.000	11.88	2.04	2	2	0	0	0	0-0	8.1	13	11	11	3	4-0	5	.342
—Omaha (PCL)	0	1	.000	10.80	2.40	1	1	0	0	...	0-...	1.2	4	2	2	0	0-0	2	.444
—GC Royals (GCL)	0	0	...	0.00	0.83	3	3	0	0	...	0-...	6.0	4	0	0	0	1-0	5	.200
—Wichita (Texas)	0	0	...	5.06	1.69	3	1	0	0	...	0-...	5.1	5	4	3	1	4-0	6	.238
2003—Mahoning Valley (NY-P)	1	1	.500	2.25	1.00	2	2	0	0	...	0-...	12.0	9	4	3	1	3-0	8	.220
—Akron (East.)	2	0	1.000	1.50	0.70	3	3	0	0	...	0-...	12.0	7	2	2	1	1-0	11	.163
—Buffalo (Int'l)	3	6	.333	4.60	1.10	10	10	1	0	...	0-...	58.2	51	30	30	9	16-0	64	.233
—Cleveland (A.L.)	0	1	.000	7.27	2.42	3	1	0	0	0	0-0	8.2	18	12	7	2	3-0	8	.429
2004—Buffalo (Int'l)	3	3	.500	3.46	1.37	9	9	0	0	...	0-...	52.0	55	22	20	7	16-0	40	.271
—Cleveland (A.L.)	5	6	.455	6.66	1.69	17	8	1	0	0	0-0	51.1	63	40	38	10	24-3	38	.301
—Arizona (N.L.)	1	1	.500	8.68	2.14	7	0	0	0	1	0-0	9.1	9	10	9	1	11-0	10	.237
American League totals (6 years)	16	29	.356	6.15	1.61	68	56	3	0	0	0-0	322.0	387	243	220	55	133-4	186	.298
National League totals (1 year)	1	1	.500	8.68	2.14	7	0	0	0	1	0-0	9.1	9	10	9	1	11-0	10	.237
Major League totals (6 years)	17	30	.362	6.22	1.63	75	56	3	0	1	0-0	331.1	396	253	229	56	144-4	196	.297

DURBIN, J.D. — P

PERSONAL: Born February 24, 1982, in Portland, Ore. ... 6-0/200. ... Throws right, bats right. ... Full name: Joseph Adam Durbin.

TRANSACTIONS/CAREER NOTES: Selected by Minnesota Twins organization in second round of 2000 free-agent draft; pick received as part of compensation for Baltimore Orioles signing Type A free-agent P Mike Trombley.

CAREER HITTING: 0-for-0 (.000), 0 R, 0 2B, 0 3B, 0 HR, 0 RBI.

Year Team (League)	W	L	Pct.	ERA	WHIP	G	GS	CG	ShO	Hld.	Sv.-Opp.	IP	H	R	ER	HR	BB-IBB	SO	Avg.
2000—GC Twins (GCL)	0	0	...	0.00	1.00	2	0	0	0	...	0-...	2.0	2	0	0	0	0-0	4	.222
2001—Elizabethton (Appal.)	3	2	.600	1.87	1.19	8	7	0	0	...	0-...	33.2	23	13	7	2	17-0	39	.190
2002—Quad City (Midw.)	13	4	.765	3.19	1.21	27	27	0	0	...	0-...	161.0	144	66	57	14	51-1	163	.239
2003—Fort Myers (Fla. St.)	9	2	.818	3.09	1.09	14	14	0	0	...	0-...	87.1	73	35	30	3	22-0	69	.224
—New Britain (East.)	6	3	.667	3.14	1.38	14	14	2	0	...	0-...	94.2	102	39	33	10	29-0	70	.278
2004—New Britain (East.)	4	1	.800	2.52	1.31	13	13	0	0	...	0-...	64.1	62	21	18	4	22-0	53	.251
—Rochester (Int'l)	3	2	.600	4.54	1.82	7	7	0	0	...	0-...	35.2	49	27	18	4	16-0	38	.329
—Minnesota (A.L.)	0	1	.000	7.36	2.45	4	1	0	0	0	0-0	7.1	12	6	6	0	6-0	6	.387
Major League totals (1 year)	0	1	.000	7.36	2.45	4	1	0	0	0	0-0	7.1	12	6	6	0	6-0	6	.387

DURHAM, RAY — 2B

PERSONAL: Born November 30, 1971, in Charlotte, N.C. ... 5-8/196. ... Bats both, throws right. ... High school: Harding (Charlotte).

TRANSACTIONS/CAREER NOTES: Selected by Chicago White Sox organization in fifth round of 1990 free-agent draft. ... Traded by White Sox to Oakland Athletics for P Jon Adkins (July 25, 2002). ... Signed as a free agent by San Francisco Giants (December 7, 2002). ... On disabled list (May 11-26 and August 7-September 1, 2003). ... On disabled list (April 28-May 13 and May 23-June 15, 2004); included rehabilitation assignments to Fresno and San Jose.

2004 GAMES PLAYED BY POSITION (MLB): 2B—118.

Year Team (League)	Pos.	G	AB	R	H	2B	3B	HR	RBI	BB	SO	HBP	GDP	SB-CS	Avg.	OBP	SLG	OPS	E	Avg.
										BATTING									**FIELDING**	
1990—GC Whi. Sox (GCL)	2B-SS	35	116	18	32	3	3	0	13	15	36	4	0	23-9	.276	.375	.353	.728	15	.907
1991—Utica (N.Y.-Penn)	2B	39	142	29	36	2	7	0	17	25	44	2	0	12-1	.254	.371	.366	.737	12	.928
—GC Whi. Sox (GCL)	2B	6	23	3	7	1	0	0	4	3	5	0	0	5-1	.304	.385	.348	.732	0	1.000
1992—Sarasota (Fla. St.)	2B	57	202	37	55	6	3	0	7	32	36	10	2	28-8	.272	.398	.332	.729	10	.945
—GC Whi. Sox (GCL)	2B	5	13	3	7	2	0	0	2	3	1	0	0	1-0	.538	.625	.692	1.317	0	1.000
1993—Birmingham (Sou.)	2B	137	528	83	143	22	10	3	37	42	100	14	5	39-25	.271	.338	.367	.705	30	.945
1994—Nashville (A.A.)	2B	133	527	89	156	33	12	16	66	46	91	12	5	34-11	.296	.363	.495	.859	19	.973
1995—Chicago (A.L.)	2B-DH	125	471	68	121	27	6	7	51	31	83	6	8	18-5	.257	.309	.384	.693	15	.973
1996—Chicago (A.L.)	2B-DH	156	557	79	153	33	5	10	65	58	95	10	6	30-4	.275	.350	.406	.755	11	.984
1997—Chicago (A.L.)	2B-DH	155	634	106	172	27	5	11	53	61	96	6	14	33-16	.271	.337	.382	.719	* 18	.974
1998—Chicago (A.L.)	2B	158	635	126	181	35	8	19	67	73	105	6	5	36-9	.285	.363	.455	.818	18	.976
1999—Chicago (A.L.)	2B-DH	153	612	109	181	30	8	13	60	73	105	4	9	34-11	.296	.373	.435	.808	19	.974
2000—Chicago (A.L.)	2B	151	614	121	172	35	9	17	75	75	105	7	13	25-13	.280	.361	.450	.810	15	.980
2001—Chicago (A.L.)	2B-DH	152	611	104	163	42	10	20	65	64	110	4	10	23-10	.267	.337	.466	.804	10	.986
2002—Chicago (A.L.)	2B	96	345	71	103	20	2	9	48	49	59	5	13	20-5	.299	.390	.446	.836	15	.968

Year	Team (League)	Pos.	G	AB	R	H	2B	3B	HR	RBI	BB	SO	HBP	GDP	SB-CS	Avg.	OBP	SLG	OPS	E	Avg.
—Oakland (A.L.)	DH-2B	54	219	43	60	14	4	6	22	24	34	2	2	6-2	.274	.350	.457	.806	2	.967
2003—San Francisco (N.L.)	2B	110	410	61	117	30	5	8	33	50	82	3	4	7-7	.285	.366	.441	.807	5	.990
2004—San Jose (Calif.)	2B	1	3	0	1	0	0	0	0	0	0	0	0	0-0	.333	.333	.333	.667	0	1.000
—Fresno (PCL)	2B	5	14	4	8	0	1	1	5	2	2	1	0	0-1	.571	.647	.929	1.576	2	.944
—San Francisco (N.L.)	2B	120	471	95	133	28	8	17	65	57	60	6	6	10-4	.282	.364	.484	.848	16	.972
American League totals (8 years)		1200	4698	827	1306	263	57	112	506	508	792	50	80	225-75	.278	.352	.430	.782	123	.977
National League totals (2 years)		230	881	156	250	58	13	25	98	107	142	9	10	17-11	.284	.365	.464	.829	21	.980
Major League totals (10 years)		1430	5579	983	1556	321	70	137	604	615	934	59	90	242-86	.279	.354	.435	.789	144	.978

DIVISION SERIES RECORD

Year	Team (League)	Pos.	G	AB	R	H	2B	3B	HR	RBI	BB	SO	HBP	GDP	SB-CS	Avg.	OBP	SLG	OPS	E	Avg.
2000—Chicago (A.L.)	2B	3	10	2	2	1	0	1	1	3	3	0	2	0-0	.200	.385	.600	.985	0	1.000
2002—Oakland (A.L.)	DH	5	21	7	7	3	0	2	2	2	4	1	0	1-0	.333	.417	.762	1.179	0	...
2003—San Francisco (N.L.)	2B	4	17	2	4	0	0	0	0	1	5	1	0	0-0	.235	.316	.235	.551	0	1.000
Division series totals (3 years)		12	48	11	13	4	0	3	3	6	12	2	2	1-0	.271	.375	.542	.917	0	1.000

ALL-STAR GAME RECORD

		G	AB	R	H	2B	3B	HR	RBI	BB	SO	HBP	GDP	SB-CS	Avg.	OBP	SLG	OPS	E	Avg.
All-Star Game totals (2 years)		2	3	2	2	0	0	0	1	0	0	0	0	0-0	.667	.667	.667	1.333	0	1.000

DURRINGTON, TRENT   3B/2B

PERSONAL: Born August 27, 1975, in Sydney, Australia. ... 5-10/190. ... Bats right, throws right. ... Full name: Trent John Durrington. ... High school: The Southport School (Australia).

TRANSACTIONS/CAREER NOTES: Signed as a non-drafted free agent by California Angels organization (April 22, 1994). ... Angels franchise renamed Anaheim Angels for 1997 season. ... Released by Angels (August 29, 2000). ... Signed by Los Angeles Dodgers organization (December 27, 2000). ... Released by Dodgers (May 11, 2001). ... Signed by Angels organization (May 12, 2001). ... Signed as a free agent by Milwaukee Brewers organization (November 7, 2003). ... Career major league pitching: 0-0, 0.00 ERA, 1 G, 0.1 IP, 0 H, 0 R, 0 ER, 0 BB, 0 SO.

2004 GAMES PLAYED BY POSITION (MLB): 3B—11, 2B—6, P—1, DH—1.

											BATTING									FIELDING	
Year	Team (League)	Pos.	G	AB	R	H	2B	3B	HR	RBI	BB	SO	HBP	GDP	SB-CS	Avg.	OBP	SLG	OPS	E	Avg.
1994—Ariz. Angels (Ariz.)	2B-SS	16	52	13	14	3	0	1	2	11	16	1	1	5-1	.269	.406	.385	.791	5	.907
1995—Boise (N'west)	2B-SS	50	140	23	24	4	1	3	19	17	35	2	4	2-0	.171	.267	.279	.546	8	.959
1996—Boise (N'west)	2B-3B-SS	40	154	38	43	7	2	0	14	31	32	13	4	24-5	.279	.439	.351	.790	12	.946
—Cedar Rap. (Midw.)	2B	25	76	12	19	1	0	0	4	33	20	2	2	15-2	.250	.482	.263	.745	3	.969
1997—Lake Elsinore (Calif.)	2B-3B-OF	123	409	80	101	21	3	3	36	51	90	11	8	52-18	.247	.344	.335	.679	17	.969
1998—Midland (Texas)		112	351	62	79	10	1	1	30	50	74	17	5	24-12	.225	.346	.268	.614	13	.971
1999—Erie (East.)	2B	107	396	84	114	26	1	3	34	52	66	9	4	59-16	.288	.379	.381	.760	14	.974
—Anaheim (A.L.)	2B-DH	43	122	14	22	2	0	0	2	9	28	0	1	4-3	.180	.237	.197	.433	6	.966
2000—Edmonton (PCL)	2B-SS	28	105	19	23	4	1	3	14	16	25	1	0	8-6	.219	.325	.362	.687	2	.986
—Anaheim (A.L.)	2B	4	3	0	0	0	0	0	0	0	0	0	1	0-0	.000	.000	.000	.000	0	1.000
2001—Salt Lake (PCL)	2-OF-3-SS	39	122	20	40	11	4	3	21	11	24	...	...	7-4	.328	...	.557	...	4	.960
—Arkansas (Texas)	2-SS-3-OF	51	182	37	53	12	0	10	35	26	47	7	2	22-2	.291	.398	.522	.920	10	.949
—Las Vegas (PCL)	2B	22	55	10	12	4	1	1	2	8	19	...	...	3-1	.218	...	.382	...	2	.973
2002—Arkansas (Texas)	C-2-O-3-S	107	382	59	94	18	4	9	47	39	71	11	3	25-14	.246	.328	.385	.713	14	.969
—Salt Lake (PCL)	OF-2-3B-C	19	68	6	14	3	1	3	10	3	15	2	4	2-1	.206	.260	.412	.672	1	.984
2003—Salt Lake (PCL)	2-3-1-DH-O-C	117	447	81	136	27	5	7	54	61	75	6	6	35-8	.304	.390	.434	.824	10	.980
—Anaheim (A.L.)	2-3-DH-OF	12	14	5	2	0	0	0	1	3	0	0	0	1-1	.143	.294	.143	.437	0	1.000
2004—Indianapolis (Int'l)	2-3-O-DH-1	51	162	19	36	1	0	1	9	16	34	2	6	17-5	.222	.298	.247	.545	10	.945
—Milwaukee (N.L.)	3B-2B-P-DH	53	82	13	19	2	3	2	4	4	23	0	1	4-0	.232	.267	.402	.670	4	.907
American League totals (3 years)		59	139	19	24	2	0	0	3	12	28	0	2	5-4	.173	.238	.187	.425	6	.968
National League totals (1 year)		53	82	13	19	2	3	2	4	4	23	0	1	4-0	.232	.267	.402	.670	4	.907
Major League totals (4 years)		112	221	32	43	4	3	2	7	16	51	0	3	9-4	.195	.249	.267	.516	10	.957

DYE, JERMAINE   OF

PERSONAL: Born January 28, 1974, in Vacaville, Calif. ... 6-5/220. ... Bats right, throws right. ... Full name: Jermaine Terrell Dye. ... Name pronounced: ger-MAIN. ... High school: Will C. Wood (Vacaville, Calif.). ... Junior college: Cosumnes River (Calif.).

TRANSACTIONS/CAREER NOTES: Selected by Atlanta Braves organization in 17th round of 1993 free-agent draft. ... Traded by Braves with P Jamie Walker to Kansas City Royals for OF Michael Tucker and IF Keith Lockhart (March 27, 1997). ... On disabled list (April 17-May 3, 1997); included rehabilitation assignment to Omaha. ... On disabled list (July 10-August 13, 1997); included rehabilitation assignment to Omaha. ... On disabled list (March 23-May 8 and September 1, 1998-remainder of season); included rehabilitation assignment to Omaha. ... Traded by Royals to Colorado Rockies for SS Neifi Perez (July 25, 2001). ... Traded by Rockies to Oakland Athletics for OF Mario Encarnacion, 2B/SS Jose Ortiz and P Todd Belitz (July 25, 2001). ... On disabled list (March 22-April 26, 2002); included rehabilitation assignments to Sacramento and Modesto. ... On disabled list (April 25-May 30 and July 7-September 1, 2003); included rehabilitation assignments to Sacramento.

HONORS: Won A.L. Gold Glove as outfielder (2000).

2004 GAMES PLAYED BY POSITION (MLB): OF—134, DH—2.

											BATTING									FIELDING	
Year	Team (League)	Pos.	G	AB	R	H	2B	3B	HR	RBI	BB	SO	HBP	GDP	SB-CS	Avg.	OBP	SLG	OPS	E	Avg.
1993—GC Braves (GCL)	3B-OF	31	124	17	43	14	0	0	27	5	13	5	5	5-0	.347	.393	.460	.852	3	.948
—Danville (Appal.)	OF	25	94	6	26	6	1	2	12	8	10	0	2	19-1	.277	.327	.426	.752	2	.963
1994—Macon (S. Atl.)	OF	135	506	73	151	41	1	15	98	33	82	8	10	19-10	.298	.346	.472	.818	9	.969
1995—Greenville (Sou.)	OF	104	403	50	115	26	4	15	71	27	74	1	9	4-8	.285	.329	.481	.810	5	.981
1996—Richmond (Int'l)	OF	36	142	25	33	7	1	6	19	5	25	1	3	3-0	.232	.264	.423	.686	4	.955
—Atlanta (N.L.)	OF	98	292	32	82	16	0	12	37	8	67	3	11	1-4	.281	.304	.459	.763	8	.950
1997—Kansas City (A.L.)	OF	75	263	26	62	14	0	7	22	17	51	1	6	2-1	.236	.284	.369	.653	6	.984
—Omaha (A.A.)	OF-DH	39	144	21	44	6	0	10	25	9	25	1	3	0-2	.306	.348	.556	.904	0	1.000
1998—Omaha (PCL)	OF-1B-DH	41	157	29	47	8	0	12	35	19	29	1	8	7-0	.299	.374	.567	.941	1	.992
—Kansas City (A.L.)	OF	60	214	24	50	5	1	5	23	11	46	1	8	2-2	.234	.270	.336	.606	2	.987
1999—Kansas City (A.L.)	OF-DH	158	608	96	179	44	8	27	119	58	119	1	17	2-3	.294	.354	.526	.880	6	.984
2000—Kansas City (A.L.)	OF-DH	157	601	107	193	41	2	33	118	69	99	3	12	0-1	.321	.390	.561	.951	7	.976
2001—Kansas City (A.L.)	OF-DH	97	367	50	100	14	0	13	47	30	68	2	6	7-1	.272	.333	.417	.749	3	.984
—Oakland (A.L.)	OF	61	232	41	69	17	1	13	59	27	44	1	6	2-0	.297	.366	.547	.913	3	.971

Year Team (League)	Pos.	G	AB	R	H	2B	3B	HR	RBI	BB	SO	HBP	GDP	SB-CS	Avg.	OBP	SLG	OPS	E	Avg.
2002— Sacramento (PCL)	DH	4	16	3	3	2	0	0	1	2	2	0	1	0-0	.188	.278	.313	.590	...	...
— Modesto (California)	OF	2	8	1	4	3	0	0	2	0	0	0	0	0-0	.500	.500	.875	1.375	0	1.000
— Oakland (A.L.)	OF-DH	131	488	74	123	27	1	24	86	52	108	10	15	2-0	.252	.333	.459	.792	5	.972
2003— Sacramento (PCL)	DH-OF	13	49	9	14	2	0	2	9	11	11	0	1	0-0	.286	.417	.449	.866	0	1.000
— Oakland (A.L.)	OF-DH	65	221	28	38	6	0	4	20	25	42	3	11	1-0	.172	.261	.253	.514	0	1.000
2004— Oakland (A.L.)	OF-DH	137	532	87	141	29	4	23	80	49	128	4	16	4-2	.265	.329	.464	.793	2	.992
American League totals (8 years)		941	3526	533	955	197	17	149	574	338	705	30	93	22-10	.271	.336	.463	.799	34	.982
National League totals (1 year)		98	292	32	82	16	0	12	37	8	67	3	11	1-4	.281	.304	.459	.763	8	.950
Major League totals (9 years)		1039	3818	565	1037	213	17	161	611	346	772	33	104	23-14	.272	.334	.463	.797	42	.979

DIVISION SERIES RECORD

Year Team (League)	Pos.	G	AB	R	H	2B	3B	HR	RBI	BB	SO	HBP	GDP	SB-CS	Avg.	OBP	SLG	OPS	E	Avg.
1996— Atlanta (N.L.)	OF	3	11	1	2	0	0	1	1	0	6	0	0	1-0	.182	.182	.455	.636	0	1.000
2001— Oakland (A.L.)	OF	4	13	0	3	2	0	0	0	2	2	0	0	0-0	.231	.333	.385	.718	0	1.000
2002— Oakland (A.L.)	OF	5	20	3	8	2	0	1	1	1	5	0	0	0-0	.400	.429	.650	1.079	0	1.000
2003— Oakland (A.L.)	OF	4	13	2	3	0	0	1	3	0	2	1	0	0-0	.231	.286	.462	.747	0	1.000
Division series totals (4 years)		16	57	6	16	4	0	3	5	3	15	1	0	1-0	.281	.328	.509	.837	0	1.000

CHAMPIONSHIP SERIES RECORD

Year Team (League)	Pos.	G	AB	R	H	2B	3B	HR	RBI	BB	SO	HBP	GDP	SB-CS	Avg.	OBP	SLG	OPS	E	Avg.
1996— Atlanta (N.L.)	OF	7	28	2	6	1	0	0	4	1	7	0	0	0-1	.214	.226	.250	.476	0	1.000

WORLD SERIES RECORD

Year Team (League)	Pos.	G	AB	R	H	2B	3B	HR	RBI	BB	SO	HBP	GDP	SB-CS	Avg.	OBP	SLG	OPS	E	Avg.
1996— Atlanta (N.L.)	OF	5	17	0	2	0	0	1	1	1	0	0	0	0-0	.118	.167	.118	.284	1	.938

ALL-STAR GAME RECORD

		G	AB	R	H	2B	3B	HR	RBI	BB	SO	HBP	GDP	SB-CS	Avg.	OBP	SLG	OPS	E	Avg.
All-Star Game totals (1 year)		1	2	1	0	0	0	0	0	1	1	0	0	0-0	.000	.333	.000	.333	0	1.000

EASLEY, DAMION   2B/1B

PERSONAL: Born November 11, 1969, in New York, N.Y. ... 5-11/190. ... Bats right, throws right. ... Full name: Jacinto Damion Easley. ... High school: Lakewood (Calif.). ... Junior college: Long Beach (Calif.) City College.

TRANSACTIONS/CAREER NOTES: Selected by California Angels organization in 30th round of 1988 free-agent draft. ... On disabled list (June 19-July 4 and July 28, 1993-remainder of season; and May 30-June 17, 1994). ... On disabled list (April 1-May 10, 1996); included rehabilitation assignment to Vancouver. ... Traded by Angels to Detroit Tigers for P Greg Gohr (July 31, 1996). ... On disabled list (April 10-25 and May 9-June 2, 2000); included rehabilitation assignment to Toledo. ... On disabled list (April 17-June 1, 2002) included rehabilitation assignment to Toledo. ... Released by Tigers (March 28, 2003). ... Signed by Tampa Bay Devil Rays (April 2, 2003). ... Released by Devil Rays (June 4, 2003). ... Signed by Florida Marlins organization (January 8, 2004).

RECORDS: Shares major league record for most times hit by pitch, game (3, May 31, 1999; and July 16, 2002).

2004 GAMES PLAYED BY POSITION (MLB): 2B—25, 1B—18, SS—15, 3B—6, OF—5, DH—3.

Year Team (League)	Pos.	G	AB	R	H	2B	3B	HR	RBI	BB	SO	HBP	GDP	SB-CS	Avg.	OBP	SLG	OPS	E	Avg.
1989— Bend (N'west)	2B	36	131	34	39	5	1	4	21	25	21	4	1	9-4	.298	.425	.443	.868	22	.863
1990— Quad City (Midw.)	SS	103	365	59	100	19	3	10	56	41	60	8	8	25-8	.274	.358	.425	.783	41	.893
1991— Midland (Texas)	SS	127	452	73	115	24	5	6	57	58	67	7	12	23-9	.254	.347	.369	.716	47	.924
1992— Edmonton (PCL)	SS-3B	108	429	61	124	18	3	3	44	31	44	5	13	26-10	.289	.340	.366	.706	30	.943
— California (A.L.)	3B-SS	47	151	14	39	5	0	1	12	8	26	3	2	9-5	.258	.307	.311	.618	5	.964
1993— California (A.L.) 2B-3B-DH		73	230	33	72	13	2	2	22	28	35	3	5	6-6	.313	.392	.413	.805	6	.978
1994— California (A.L.)	3B-2B	88	316	41	68	16	1	6	30	29	48	4	8	4-5	.215	.288	.329	.617	7	.977
1995— California (A.L.)	2B-SS	114	357	35	77	14	2	4	35	32	47	6	11	5-2	.216	.288	.300	.588	10	.979
1996— Vancouver (PCL) SS-3B-2B		12	48	13	15	2	1	2	8	9	6	1	0	4-1	.313	.424	.521	.945	2	.958
— Midland (Texas)	3B-SS	4	14	1	6	2	0	0	2	0	0	0	0	1-0	.429	.429	.571	1.000	1	.944
— California (A.L.) S-2-3-DH-O		28	45	4	7	1	0	2	7	6	12	0	0	0-0	.156	.255	.311	.566	3	.954
— Detroit (A.L.) 2-S-3-DH		21	67	10	23	1	0	2	10	4	13	1	0	3-1	.343	.384	.448	.831	3	.958
1997— Detroit (A.L.) 2B-SS-DH		151	527	97	139	37	4	22	72	68	102	16	18	28-13	.264	.362	.471	.833	12	.982
1998— Detroit (A.L.) 2B-SS-DH		153	594	84	161	38	2	27	100	39	112	16	8	15-5	.271	.332	.478	.810	12	.985
1999— Detroit (A.L.)	2B-SS	151	549	83	146	30	1	20	65	51	124	19	15	11-3	.266	.346	.434	.779	8	.990
2000— Detroit (A.L.)	2B	126	464	76	120	27	2	14	58	55	79	11	11	13-4	.259	.350	.416	.766	6	.990
— Toledo (Int'l)	2B	4	13	3	3	1	0	1	4	4	2	0	0	0-0	.231	.474	.538	1.012	0	1.000
2001— Detroit (A.L.)	2B	154	585	77	146	27	7	11	65	52	90	13	10	10-5	.250	.323	.376	.699	14	.982
2002— Detroit (A.L.)	2B-DH	85	304	29	68	14	1	8	30	27	43	11	4	1-3	.224	.307	.355	.663	9	.980
— Toledo (Int'l)	2B	8	26	5	3	1	0	0	0	5	0	1	1	0-2	.115	.281	.154	.435	2	.949
2003— Tampa Bay (A.L.) 3B-DH-2B		36	107	8	20	3	1	1	7	2	18	0	3	0-0	.187	.202	.262	.464	4	.935
2004— Florida (N.L.) 2-1-S-3-O-DH		98	223	26	53	20	1	9	43	24	36	8	6	4-1	.238	.331	.457	.788	7	.974
American League totals (12 years)		1227	4296	591	1086	226	22	120	513	401	749	103	95	105-52	.253	.329	.399	.729	99	.982
National League totals (1 year)		98	223	26	53	20	1	9	43	24	36	8	6	4-1	.238	.331	.457	.788	7	.974
Major League totals (13 years)		1325	4519	617	1139	246	23	129	556	425	785	111	101	109-53	.252	.329	.402	.732	106	.982

ALL-STAR GAME RECORD

		G	AB	R	H	2B	3B	HR	RBI	BB	SO	HBP	GDP	SB-CS	Avg.	OBP	SLG	OPS	E	Avg.
All-Star Game totals (1 year)		1	1	1	1	0	0	0	0	0	0	0	0	0-0	1.000	1.000	1.000	2.000	0	...

EATON, ADAM   P

PERSONAL: Born November 23, 1977, in Seattle, Wash. ... 6-2/196. ... Throws right, bats right. ... Full name: Adam Thomas Eaton. ... High school: Snohomish (Wash.).

TRANSACTIONS/CAREER NOTES: Selected by Philadelphia Phillies organization in first round (11th pick overall) of 1996 free-agent draft. ... Traded by Phillies with Ps Carlton Loewer and Steve Montgomery to San Diego Padres for P Andy Ashby (November 10, 1999). ... On disabled list (July 6, 2001-remainder of season). ... On disabled list (March 27-September 1, 2002); included rehabilitation assignments to Lake Elsinore and Portland. ... On disabled list (May 5-20, 2003).

CAREER HITTING: 40-for-205 (.195), 22 R, 13 2B, 0 3B, 2 HR, 17 RBI.

Year Team (League)	W	L	Pct.	ERA	WHIP	G	GS	CG	ShO	Hld.	Sv.-Opp.	IP	H	R	ER	HR	BB-IBB	SO	Avg.
1997— Piedmont (S. Atl.)	5	6	.455	4.16	1.56	14	14	0	0	...	0-...	71.1	81	38	33	2	30-0	57	.287
1998— Clearwater (Fla. St.)	9	8	.529	4.44	1.51	24	23	1	0	...	0-...	131.2	152	68	65	9	47-1	89	.293
1999— Clearwater (Fla. St.)	5	5	.500	3.91	1.52	13	13	0	0	...	0-...	69.0	81	39	30	2	24-0	50	.293

Year	Team (League)	W	L	Pct.	ERA	WHIP	G	GS	CG	ShO	Hld.	Sv.-Opp.	IP	H	R	ER	HR	BB-IBB	SO	Avg.
	— Reading (East.)	5	4	.556	2.92	1.14	12	12	2	0	...	0-...	77.0	60	30	25	9	28-1	67	.214
	— Scran./W.B. (I.L.)	1	1	.500	3.00	1.10	3	3	0	0	...	0-...	21.0	17	10	7	1	6-0	10	.224
2000—	Mobile (Sou.)	4	1	.800	2.68	1.14	10	10	1	1	...	0-...	57.0	47	20	17	3	18-0	58	.219
	— San Diego (N.L.)	7	4	.636	4.13	1.44	22	22	0	0	0	0-0	135.0	134	63	62	14	61-3	90	.260
2001—	San Diego (N.L.)	8	5	.615	4.32	1.27	17	17	2	0	0	0-0	116.2	108	61	56	20	40-3	109	.241
2002—	Lake Elsinore (Calif.)	0	0	...	2.70	0.98	3	3	0	0	...	0-...	13.1	10	7	4	0	3-0	19	.196
	— Portland (PCL)	1	1	.500	2.92	0.97	2	2	0	0	...	0-...	12.1	9	9	4	3	3-0	6	.200
	— San Diego (N.L.)	1	1	.500	5.40	1.35	6	6	0	0	0	0-0	33.1	28	20	20	5	17-0	25	.235
2003—	San Diego (N.L.)	9	12	.429	4.08	1.32	31	31	1	0	0	0-0	183.0	173	91	83	20	68-6	146	.246
2004—	San Diego (N.L.)	11	14	.440	4.61	1.28	33	33	0	0	0	0-0	199.1	204	113	102	28	52-3	153	.266
Major League totals (5 years)		36	36	.500	4.36	1.33	109	109	3	0	0	0-0	667.1	647	348	323	87	238-15	523	.253

ECKSTEIN, DAVID — SS

PERSONAL: Born January 20, 1975, in Sanford, Fla. ... 5-7/165. ... Bats right, throws right. ... Full name: David Mark Eckstein. ... Name pronounced: eck-STYNE. ... High school: Seminole (Sanford, Fla.). ... College: Florida.

TRANSACTIONS/CAREER NOTES: Selected by Boston Red Sox organization in 19th round of 1997 free-agent draft. ... Claimed on waivers by Anaheim Angels (August 16, 2000). ... On disabled list (August 18-September 9, 2003).

2004 GAMES PLAYED BY POSITION (MLB): SS—138, DH—1.

							BATTING									FIELDING	
Year	Team (League)	Pos.	G	AB	R	H	2B	3B	HR	RBI	BB	SO	HBP	GDP	SB-CS	Avg.	OBP	SLG	OPS	E	Avg.
1997—	Lowell (NY-Penn)	2B	68	249	43	75	11	4	4	39	33	29	12	2	21-5	.301	.407	.426	.832	9	.971
1998—	Sarasota (Fla. St.)	2B-SS	135	503	99	154	29	4	3	58	87	51	22	8	45-16	.306	.428	.398	.826	8	.986
1999—	Trenton (East.)	2B	131	483	109	151	22	5	6	52	89	48	25	6	32-13	.313	.440	.416	.856	9	.985
2000—	Pawtucket (Int'l)	2B-SS	119	422	77	104	20	0	1	31	60	45	20	8	11-8	.246	.364	.301	.665	4	.992
	— Edmonton (PCL)	2B	15	52	17	18	8	0	3	8	9	1	5	0	5-3	.346	.485	.673	1.158	0	1.000
2001—	Anaheim (A.L.) SS-2B-DH		153	582	82	166	26	2	4	41	43	60	21	11	29-4	.285	.355	.357	.712	18	.969
2002—	Anaheim (A.L.)	SS-DH	152	608	107	178	22	6	8	63	45	44	27	7	21-13	.293	.363	.388	.752	14	.977
2003—	Anaheim (A.L.)	SS-DH	120	452	59	114	22	1	3	31	36	45	15	9	16-5	.252	.325	.325	.651	8	.984
2004—	Anaheim (A.L.)	SS-DH	142	566	92	156	24	1	2	35	42	49	13	11	16-5	.276	.339	.332	.671	6	.988
Major League totals (4 years)			567	2208	340	614	94	10	17	170	166	198	76	38	82-27	.278	.347	.353	.700	46	.979

DIVISION SERIES RECORD

Year	Team (League)	Pos.	G	AB	R	H	2B	3B	HR	RBI	BB	SO	HBP	GDP	SB-CS	Avg.	OBP	SLG	OPS	E	Avg.
2002—	Anaheim (A.L.)	SS	4	18	2	5	0	0	0	1	0	0	1	0	1-0	.278	.316	.278	.594	0	1.000
2004—	Anaheim (A.L.)	SS	3	12	2	4	0	0	0	0	1	1	0	0	0-0	.333	.333	.333	.667	1	.917
Division series totals (2 years)			7	30	4	9	0	0	0	1	1	1	1	0	1-0	.300	.323	.300	.623	1	.960

CHAMPIONSHIP SERIES RECORD

Year	Team (League)	Pos.	G	AB	R	H	2B	3B	HR	RBI	BB	SO	HBP	GDP	SB-CS	Avg.	OBP	SLG	OPS	E	Avg.
2002—	Anaheim (A.L.)	SS	5	21	1	6	0	0	0	2	2	1	0	0	0-0	.286	.318	.286	.604	1	.944

WORLD SERIES RECORD

Year	Team (League)	Pos.	G	AB	R	H	2B	3B	HR	RBI	BB	SO	HBP	GDP	SB-CS	Avg.	OBP	SLG	OPS	E	Avg.
2002—	Anaheim (A.L.)	SS	7	29	6	9	0	0	0	3	3	2	0	0	1-0	.310	.364	.310	.674	0	1.000

EDMONDS, JIM — OF

PERSONAL: Born June 27, 1970, in Fullerton, Calif. ... 6-1/212. ... Bats left, throws left. ... Full name: James Patrick Edmonds. ... Name pronounced: ED-muns. ... High school: Diamond Bar (Calif.).

TRANSACTIONS/CAREER NOTES: Selected by California Angels organization in seventh round of 1988 free-agent draft. ... On disabled list (May 26-June 10 and June 12-July 18, 1996); included rehabilitation assignment to Lake Elsinore. ... Angels franchise renamed Anaheim Angels for 1997 season. ... On disabled list (August 1-16, 1997). ... On disabled list (March 30-August 2, 1999); included rehabilitation assignment to Lake Elsinore. ... Traded by Angels to St. Louis Cardinals for 2B/SS Adam Kennedy and P Kent Bottenfield (March 23, 2000). ... On disabled list (June 1-16, 2002).

HONORS: Won A.L. Gold Glove as outfielder (1997-98). ... Won N.L. Gold Glove as outfielder (2000-04).

2004 GAMES PLAYED BY POSITION (MLB): OF—146, DH—1, 1B—1.

							BATTING									FIELDING	
Year	Team (League)	Pos.	G	AB	R	H	2B	3B	HR	RBI	BB	SO	HBP	GDP	SB-CS	Avg.	OBP	SLG	OPS	E	Avg.
1988—	Bend (N'west)	OF	35	122	23	27	4	0	0	13	20	44	0	2	4-0	.221	.329	.254	.583	1	.984
1989—	Quad City (Midw.)	OF	31	92	11	24	4	0	1	4	7	34	0	3	1-0	.261	.313	.337	.650	3	.942
1990—	Palm Springs (Calif.)	OF	91	314	36	92	18	6	3	56	27	75	2	10	5-2	.293	.351	.417	.768	10	.954
1991—	Palm Springs (Calif.)	OF	60	187	28	55	15	1	2	27	40	57	0	2	2-2	.294	.417	.417	.834	0	1.000
1992—	Midland (Texas)	OF	70	246	42	77	15	2	8	32	41	48	1	8	3-4	.313	.413	.488	.901	5	.967
	— Edmonton (PCL)	OF	50	194	37	58	15	2	6	36	14	55	0	2	3-1	.299	.343	.490	.833	1	.988
1993—	Vancouver (PCL)	OF	95	356	59	112	28	4	9	74	41	81	0	5	6-8	.315	.382	.492	.873	3	.983
	— California (A.L.)	OF	18	61	5	15	4	1	0	4	2	16	0	1	0-2	.246	.270	.344	.614	1	.981
1994—	California (A.L.)	OF-1B	94	289	35	79	13	1	5	37	30	72	1	3	4-2	.273	.343	.377	.720	3	.991
1995—	California (A.L.)	OF	141	558	120	162	30	4	33	107	51	130	5	10	1-4	.290	.352	.536	.888	1	.998
1996—	California (A.L.)	OF-DH	114	431	73	131	28	3	27	66	46	101	4	8	4-0	.304	.375	.571	.946	1	.997
	— Lake Elsinore (Calif.)	OF-DH	5	15	4	6	2	0	1	4	1	1	1	0	0-0	.400	.471	.733	1.204	0	1.000
1997—	Anaheim (A.L.) OF-1B-DH		133	502	82	146	27	0	26	80	60	80	4	8	5-7	.291	.368	.500	.868	5	.988
1998—	Anaheim (A.L.)	OF	154	599	115	184	42	1	25	91	57	114	1	16	7-5	.307	.368	.506	.874	5	.988
1999—	Lake Elsinore (Calif.)	DH	5	19	4	8	2	0	0	3	4	2	0	0	2-0	.421	.522	.526	1.048	0	
	— Anaheim (A.L.) OF-DH-1B		55	204	34	51	17	2	5	23	28	45	0	3	5-4	.250	.339	.426	.766	1	.993
2000—	St. Louis (N.L.)	OF-1B	152	525	129	155	25	0	42	108	103	167	6	5	10-3	.295	.411	.583	.994	4	.990
2001—	St. Louis (N.L.)	OF-1B	150	500	95	152	38	1	30	110	93	136	4	8	5-5	.304	.410	.564	.974	6	.983
2002—	St. Louis (N.L.)	OF	144	476	96	148	31	2	28	83	86	134	8	9	4-3	.311	.420	.561	.981	5	.986
2003—	St. Louis (N.L.)	OF-DH	137	447	89	123	32	2	39	89	77	127	4	11	1-3	.275	.385	.617	1.002	5	.986
2004—	St. Louis (N.L.) OF-DH-1B		153	498	102	150	38	3	42	111	101	150	5	4	8-3	.301	.418	.643	1.061	4	.988
American League totals (7 years)			709	2644	464	768	161	12	121	408	274	558	15	49	26-24	.290	.359	.498	.856	17	.992
National League totals (5 years)			736	2446	511	728	164	8	181	501	460	714	27	37	28-17	.298	.410	.593	1.003	24	.987
Major League totals (12 years)			1445	5090	975	1496	325	20	302	909	734	1272	42	86	54-41	.294	.384	.544	.928	41	.989

E

DIVISION SERIES RECORD

Year Team (League)	Pos.	G	AB	R	H	2B	3B	HR	RBI	BB	SO	HBP	GDP	SB-CS	Avg.	OBP	SLG	OPS	E	Avg.
2000—St. Louis (N.L.)	OF	3	14	5	8	4	0	2	7	1	2	0	0	1-0	.571	.600	1.286	1.886	0	1.000
2001—St. Louis (N.L.)	OF	5	17	3	4	1	0	2	3	3	6	0	0	0-0	.235	.350	.647	.997	0	1.000
2002—St. Louis (N.L.)	OF	3	11	1	3	0	0	1	2	2	4	0	0	0-1	.273	.385	.545	.930	0	1.000
2004—St. Louis (N.L.)	OF	4	15	1	4	0	0	1	2	1	9	0	0	0-1	.267	.313	.467	.779	0	1.000
Division series totals (4 years)		15	57	10	19	5	0	6	14	7	21	0	0	1-2	.333	.406	.737	1.143	0	1.000

CHAMPIONSHIP SERIES RECORD

Year Team (League)	Pos.	G	AB	R	H	2B	3B	HR	RBI	BB	SO	HBP	GDP	SB-CS	Avg.	OBP	SLG	OPS	E	Avg.
2000—St. Louis (N.L.)	OF	5	22	1	5	1	0	1	5	1	9	0	0	0-0	.227	.261	.409	.670	1	.933
2002—St. Louis (N.L.)	OF	5	20	2	8	2	0	1	4	2	5	0	0	0-0	.400	.455	.650	1.105	0	1.000
2004—St. Louis (N.L.)	OF	7	24	2	7	2	0	2	7	2	6	1	0	0-0	.292	.357	.625	.982	1	.952
Champ. series totals (3 years)		17	66	5	20	5	0	4	16	5	20	1	0	0-0	.303	.356	.561	.917	2	.957

WORLD SERIES RECORD

Year Team (League)	Pos.	G	AB	R	H	2B	3B	HR	RBI	BB	SO	HBP	GDP	SB-CS	Avg.	OBP	SLG	OPS	E	Avg.
2004—St. Louis (N.L.)	OF	4	15	2	1	0	0	0	0	1	6	0	0	0-0	.067	.125	.067	.192	0	1.000

ALL-STAR GAME RECORD

	G	AB	R	H	2B	3B	HR	RBI	BB	SO	HBP	GDP	SB-CS	Avg.	OBP	SLG	OPS	E	Avg.
All-Star Game totals (3 years)	3	5	0	2	0	0	0	0	0	2	0	0	0-0	.400	.400	.400	.800	0	1.000

EISCHEN, JOEY — P

PERSONAL: Born May 25, 1970, in West Covina, Calif. ... 6-0/214. ... Throws left, bats left. ... Full name: Joseph Raymond Eischen. ... Name pronounced: EYE-shen. ... High school: West Covina (Calif.). ... Junior college: Pasadena (Calif.) City College.

TRANSACTIONS/CAREER NOTES: Selected by Chicago White Sox organization in fifth round of 1988 free-agent draft; did not sign. ... Selected by Texas Rangers in fourth round of 1989 free-agent draft. ... Traded by Rangers with P Jonathan Hurst and a player to be named to Montreal Expos for P Dennis Boyd (July 21, 1991); Expos acquired P Travis Buckley to complete deal (September 1, 1991). ... Traded by Expos with OF Roberto Kelly to Los Angeles Dodgers for OF Henry Rodriguez and IF Jeff Treadway (May 23, 1995). ... Traded by Dodgers with P John Cummings to Detroit Tigers for OF Chad Curtis (July 31, 1996). ... Traded by Tigers with P Cam Smith to San Diego Padres for C Brian Johnson and P Willie Blair (December 17, 1996). ... Traded by Padres to Cincinnati Reds for a player to be named (March 16, 1997); Padres acquired IF Ray Brown to complete deal (March 19, 1997). ... On disabled list (March 25-April 26 and April 29-July 18, 1997); included rehabilitation assignment to Indianapolis. ... Signed as a free agent by New York Yankees organization (February 3, 1998). ... Released by Yankees (March 11, 1998). ... Signed by Reds (March 19, 1998). ... Released by Reds (March 12, 1999). ... Signed by Arizona Diamondbacks organization (March 18, 1999). ... Released by Diamondbacks (July 1, 1999). ... Signed as a free agent by Cleveland Indians organization (December 23, 1999). ... Released by Indians (April 29, 2000). ... Signed as a free agent by Expos organization (July 12, 2000). ... On disabled list (March 26-August 2, 2004); included rehabilitation assignments to GCL Expos and Brevard County.

CAREER HITTING: 4-for-23 (.174), 4 R, 1 2B, 0 3B, 0 HR, 0 RBI.

Year Team (League)	W	L	Pct.	ERA	WHIP	G	GS	CG	ShO	Hld.	Sv.-Opp.	IP	H	R	ER	HR	BB-IBB	SO	Avg.
1989—Butte (Pio.)	3	7	.300	5.30	1.67	12	12	0	0	...	0-...	52.2	50	45	31	4	38-0	57	.246
1990—Gastonia (S. Atl.)	3	7	.300	2.70	1.24	17	14	0	0	...	0-...	73.1	51	36	22	0	40-0	69	.195
1991—Charlotte (Fla. St.)	4	10	.286	3.41	1.42	18	18	1	0	...	0-...	108.1	99	59	41	5	55-1	80	.249
—W.P. Beach (FSL)	4	2	.667	5.17	1.54	8	8	1	0	...	0-...	38.1	35	27	22	3	24-0	26	.238
1992—W.P. Beach (FSL)	9	8	.529	3.08	1.24	27	26	3	0	...	0-...	169.2	128	68	58	5	83-2	167	.211
1993—Harrisburg (Eastern)	14	4	.778	3.62	1.53	20	20	0	0	...	0-...	119.1	122	62	48	11	60-0	110	.265
—Ottawa (Int'l)	2	2	.500	3.54	1.20	6	6	0	0	...	0-...	40.2	34	18	16	3	15-0	29	.230
1994—Ottawa (Int'l)	2	6	.250	4.94	1.52	48	2	0	0	...	2-...	62.0	54	38	34	7	40-4	57	.238
—Montreal (N.L.)	0	0	...	54.00	6.00	1	0	0	0	0	0-0	.2	4	4	4	0	0-0	1	.667
1995—Ottawa (Int'l)	2	1	.667	1.72	1.09	11	0	0	0	...	0-...	15.2	9	4	3	0	8-1	13	.173
—Los Angeles (N.L.)	0	0	...	3.10	1.48	17	0	0	0	1	0-0	20.1	19	9	7	1	11-1	15	.232
—Albuquerque (PCL)	3	0	1.000	0.00	0.67	13	0	0	0	...	2-...	16.1	8	0	0	0	3-0	14	.145
1996—Los Angeles (N.L.)	0	1	.000	4.78	1.57	28	0	0	0	0	0-0	43.1	48	25	23	4	20-4	36	.282
—Detroit (A.L.)	1	1	.500	3.24	1.64	24	0	0	0	1	0-2	25.0	27	11	9	3	14-3	15	.284
1997—Indianapolis (A.A.)	1	0	1.000	1.27	1.27	26	0	0	0	...	2-...	42.2	41	7	6	1	13-1	26	.261
—Cincinnati (N.L.)	0	0	...	6.75	2.25	1	0	0	0	0	0-0	1.1	2	2	1	0	1-0	2	.333
1998—Indianapolis (Int'l)	2	5	.286	4.54	1.39	61	0	0	0	...	2-...	73.1	73	42	37	9	29-3	60	.258
1999—Tucson (PCL)	1	3	.250	9.07	2.14	27	0	0	0	...	1-...	41.2	63	47	42	7	26-3	36	.350
—Adirondack (Nor.)	4	2	.667	3.71	1.31	7	7	1	0	...	0-...	48.0	52	22	20	1	11-...	49	...
2000—Buffalo (Int'l)	0	0	...	40.50	6.00	1	0	0	0	...	0-...	.2	4	3	3	0	0-0	0	.667
—Adirondack (Nor.)	7	1	.875	1.80	1.22	10	10	0	0	...	0-...	65.0	55	25	13	...	24-...	57	...
—Ottawa (Int'l)	0	4	.000	3.64	1.30	10	9	0	0	...	0-...	59.1	55	31	24	8	22-0	34	.250
2001—Ottawa (Int'l)	2	3	.400	2.24	1.01	34	1	0	0	...	7-...	52.1	42	16	13	6	11-0	54	.220
—Montreal (N.L.)	0	1	.000	4.85	1.52	24	0	0	0	2	0-2	29.2	29	17	16	4	16-1	19	.257
2002—Ottawa (Int'l)	1	0	1.000	0.00	0.79	11	0	0	0	...	4-...	14.0	8	4	0	0	3-0	15	.167
—Montreal (N.L.)	6	1	.857	1.34	1.14	59	0	0	0	11	2-3	53.2	43	11	8	1	18-5	51	.224
2003—Montreal (N.L.)	2	2	.500	3.06	1.32	70	0	0	0	15	1-4	53.0	57	27	18	7	13-1	40	.282
2004—GC Expos (GCL)	0	0	...	0.00	0.00	1	1	0	0	...	0-...	1.0	0	0	0	0	0-0	2	.000
—Brevard County (FSL)	0	0	...	0.00	1.00	4	0	0	0	...	0-...	6.0	5	4	0	0	1-0	7	.217
—Montreal (N.L.)	0	1	.000	3.93	1.31	24	0	0	0	2	0-1	18.1	16	10	8	2	8-2	17	.232
American League totals (1 year)	1	1	.500	3.24	1.64	24	0	0	0		0-2	25.0	27	11	9	3	14-3	15	.284
National League totals (8 years)	8	6	.571	3.47	1.38	221	0	0	0	32	3-10	220.1	218	105	85	19	87-14	181	.260
Major League totals (8 years)	9	7	.563	3.45	1.41	245	0	0	0	33	3-12	245.1	245	116	94	22	101-17	196	.262

ELARTON, SCOTT — P

PERSONAL: Born February 23, 1976, in Lamar, Colo. ... 6-8/240. ... Throws right, bats right. ... Full name: Vincent Scott Elarton. ... High school: Lamar (Colo.).

TRANSACTIONS/CAREER NOTES: Selected by Houston Astros organization in first round (25th pick overall) of 1994 free-agent draft. ... On disabled list (March 29-April 23, 2000); included rehabilitation assignments to New Orleans and Round Rock. ... On disabled list (July 17-31, 2001). ... Traded by Astros with a player to be named to Colorado Rockies for P Pedro Astacio and cash (July 31, 2001); Rockies acquired C Garrett Gentry to complete deal (September 27, 2001). ... On disabled list (July 31-September 4, 2001); included rehabilitation assignment to Colorado Springs. ... On disabled list (March 8, 2002-entire season). ... On disabled list (March 26-April 30, 2003); included rehabilitation assignment to Colorado Springs. ... Released by Rockies (May 20, 2004). ... Signed by Cleveland Indians organization (May 25, 2004).

CAREER HITTING: 22-for-160 (.138), 12 R, 2 2B, 0 3B, 0 HR, 3 RBI.

Year Team (League)	W	L	Pct.	ERA	WHIP	G	GS	CG	ShO	Hld.	Sv.-Opp.	IP	H	R	ER	HR	BB-IBB	SO	Avg.
1994—GC Astros (GCL)	4	0	1.000	0.00	0.50	5	5	0	0	...	0-...	28.0	9	0	0	0	5-0	28	.103
—Quad City (Midw.)	4	1	.800	3.29	1.10	9	9	0	0	...	0-...	54.2	42	23	20	4	18-0	42	.213

E

Year	Team (League)	W	L	Pct.	ERA	WHIP	G	GS	CG	ShO	Hld.	Sv.-Opp.	IP	H	R	ER	HR	BB-IBB	SO	Avg.
1995— Quad City (Midw.)	13	7	.650	4.45	1.47	26	26	0	0	...	0-...	149.2	149	86	74	12	71-2	112	.259
1996— Kissimmee (Fla. St.)	12	7	.632	2.92	1.21	27	27	3	1	...	0-...	172.1	154	67	56	13	54-0	130	.241
1997— Jackson (Texas)	7	4	.636	3.24	1.13	20	20	2	0	...	0-...	133.1	103	57	48	6	47-3	141	.210
— New Orleans (A.A.)	4	4	.500	5.33	1.26	9	9	0	0	...	0-...	54.0	51	36	32	5	17-1	50	.249
1998— New Orleans (PCL)	9	4	.692	4.01	1.22	14	14	2	1	...	0-...	92.0	71	42	41	6	41-3	100	.212
— Houston (N.L.)	2	1	.667	3.32	1.05	28	2	0	0	2	2-3	57.0	40	21	21	5	20-0	56	.196
1999— Houston (N.L.)	9	5	.643	3.48	1.24	42	15	0	0	5	1-4	124.0	111	55	48	8	43-0	121	.238
2000— New Orleans (PCL)	1	0	1.000	0.75	0.58	2	2	0	0	...	0-...	12.0	3	1	1	0	4-0	12	.081
— Round Rock (Texas)	1	0	1.000	2.84	1.11	1	1	0	0	...	0-...	6.1	7	2	2	1	0-0	7	.280
— Houston (N.L.)	17	7	.708	4.81	1.46	30	30	2	0	0	0-0	192.2	198	117	103	29	84-1	131	.263
2001— Houston (N.L.)	4	8	.333	7.14	1.60	20	20	0	0	0	0-0	109.2	126	88	87	26	49-1	76	.290
— Colo. Springs (PCL)	0	1	.000	7.04	1.83	2	2	0	0	0	0-0	7.2	14	6	6	2	0-0	8	.378
— Colorado (N.L.)	0	2	.000	6.65	1.30	4	4	0	0	0	0-0	23.0	20	17	17	8	10-1	11	.233
2002— Colorado (N.L.)				Did not play.															
2003— Colo. Springs (PCL)	6	8	.429	5.31	1.60	20	20	0	0	0	0-...	118.2	146	81	70	15	39-1	92	.298
— Colorado (N.L.)	4	4	.500	6.27	1.80	11	10	0	0	0	0-0	51.2	73	46	36	13	20-3	20	.329
2004— Colorado (N.L.)	0	6	.000	9.80	1.86	8	8	0	0	0	0-0	41.1	57	45	45	8	20-1	23	.328
— Buffalo (Int'l)	1	1	.500	3.15	1.20	3	3	1	1	0	0-...	20.0	19	7	7	1	5-0	10	.250
— Cleveland (A.L.)	3	5	.375	4.53	1.27	21	21	1	1	0	0-0	117.1	107	62	59	25	42-2	80	.240
American League totals (1 year)	3	5	.375	4.53	1.27	21	21	1	1	0	0-0	117.1	107	62	59	25	42-2	80	.240
National League totals (6 years)	36	33	.522	5.36	1.45	143	89	2	0	7	3-7	599.1	625	389	357	97	246-7	438	.267
Major League totals (6 years)	39	38	.506	5.22	1.42	164	110	3	1	7	3-7	716.2	732	451	416	122	288-9	518	.263

DIVISION SERIES RECORD

Year	Team (League)	W	L	Pct.	ERA	WHIP	G	GS	CG	ShO	Hld.	Sv.-Opp.	IP	H	R	ER	HR	BB-IBB	SO	Avg.
1998— Houston (N.L.)	0	1	.000	4.50	1.00	1	0	0	0	0	0-0	2.0	1	1	1	1	1-0	3	.167
1999— Houston (N.L.)	0	0	...	3.86	2.14	2	0	0	0	0	0-0	2.1	4	1	1	0	1-0	3	.400
Division series totals (2 years)	0	1	.000	4.15	1.62	3	0	0	0	0	0-0	4.1	5	2	2	1	2-0	6	.313

ELDRED, CAL   P

PERSONAL: Born November 24, 1967, in Cedar Rapids, Iowa. ... 6-4/240. ... Throws right, bats right. ... Full name: Calvin John Eldred. ... Name pronounced: EL-dred. ... High school: Urbana (Iowa) Community. ... College: Iowa.

TRANSACTIONS/CAREER NOTES: Selected by Milwaukee Brewers organization in first round (17th pick overall) of 1989 free-agent draft. ... On disabled list (May 15, 1995-remainder of season). ... On disabled list (March 29-July 14, 1996); included rehabilitation assignment to New Orleans. ... On disabled list (July 26, 1998-remainder of season). ... On disabled list (March 29-April 20 and July 2-August 15, 1999); included rehabilitation assignments to Huntsville and Louisville. ... Traded by Brewers with SS Jose Valentin to Chicago White Sox for Ps Jaime Navarro and John Snyder (January 12, 2000). ... On disabled list (July 15-September 27, 2000); included rehabilitation assignment to Charlotte. ... On disabled list (April 12, 2001-remainder of season). ... Signed as a free agent by St. Louis Cardinals organization (December 18, 2002).

HONORS: Named A.L. Rookie Pitcher of the Year by THE SPORTING NEWS (1992).

CAREER HITTING: 8-for-70 (.114), 7 R, 2 2B, 0 3B, 0 HR, 4 RBI.

Year	Team (League)	W	L	Pct.	ERA	WHIP	G	GS	CG	ShO	Hld.	Sv.-Opp.	IP	H	R	ER	HR	BB-IBB	SO	Avg.
1989— Beloit (Midw.)	2	1	.667	2.30	1.09	5	5	0	0	...	0-...	31.1	23	10	8	0	11-1	32	.202
1990— Stockton (Calif.)	4	2	.667	1.62	1.00	7	7	3	1	...	0-...	50.0	31	12	9	2	19-0	75	.177
— El Paso (Texas)	5	4	.556	4.49	1.57	19	19	0	0	...	0-...	110.1	126	61	55	9	47-0	93	.293
1991— Denver (Am. Assoc.)	13	9	.591	3.75	1.32	29	29	3	1	...	0-...	185.0	161	82	77	13	84-2	168	.239
— Milwaukee (A.L.)	2	0	1.000	4.50	1.63	3	3	0	0	0	0-0	16.0	20	9	8	2	6-0	10	.299
1992— Denver (Am. Assoc.)	10	6	.625	3.00	1.16	19	19	4	1	...	0-...	141.0	122	49	47	9	42-0	99	.237
— Milwaukee (A.L.)	11	2	.846	1.79	0.99	14	14	2	1	0	0-0	100.1	76	21	20	4	23-0	62	.207
1993— Milwaukee (A.L.)	16	16	.500	4.01	1.25	36	•36	8	1	0	0-0	* 258.0	232	120	115	32	91-5	180	.239
1994— Milwaukee (A.L.)	11	11	.500	4.68	1.35	25	•25	6	0	0	0-0	179.0	158	96	93	23	84-0	98	.236
1995— Milwaukee (A.L.)	1	1	.500	3.42	1.44	4	4	0	0	0	0-0	23.2	24	10	9	4	10-0	18	.261
1996— New Orleans (A.A.)	2	2	.500	3.34	1.27	6	6	0	0	...	0-...	32.1	24	12	12	2	17-0	30	.205
— Milwaukee (A.L.)	4	4	.500	4.46	1.42	15	15	0	0	0	0-0	84.2	82	43	42	8	38-0	50	.259
1997— Milwaukee (A.L.)	13	•15	.464	4.99	1.47	34	34	1	0	0	0-0	202.0	207	118	112	31	89-0	122	.266
1998— Milwaukee (A.L.)	4	8	.333	4.80	1.64	23	23	0	0	0	0-0	133.0	157	82	71	14	61-3	86	.297
1999— Huntsville (Southern)	0	1	.000	7.50	1.33	2	2	1	0	0	0-...	12.0	13	10	10	2	3-0	10	.260
— Louisville (Int'l)	0	1	.000	5.30	1.55	4	4	0	0	0	0-...	18.2	19	11	11	4	10-0	21	.250
— Milwaukee (A.L.)	2	8	.200	7.79	1.79	20	15	0	0	0	0-0	82.0	101	75	71	19	46-0	60	.297
2000— Chicago (A.L.)	10	2	.833	4.58	1.45	20	20	2	1	0	0-0	112.0	103	61	57	12	59-0	97	.244
— Charlotte (Int'l)	0	1	.000	7.20	0.80	2	2	0	0	...	0-...	5.0	4	4	4	2	0-0	1	.211
2001— Chicago (A.L.)	0	1	.000	13.50	2.50	2	2	0	0	0	0-0	6.0	12	9	9	1	3-1	6	.429
2003— St. Louis (N.L.)	7	4	.636	3.74	1.38	62	0	0	0	11	8-14	67.1	62	32	28	9	31-4	67	.248
2004— St. Louis (N.L.)	4	2	.667	3.76	1.31	52	0	0	0	9	1-3	67.0	71	31	28	11	17-1	54	.276
American League totals (9 years)	68	52	.567	4.26	1.34	153	153	19	4	0	0-0	981.2	914	487	465	117	403-6	643	.246
National League totals (4 years)	17	22	.436	5.10	1.56	157	38	0	0	20	9-17	349.1	391	220	198	53	155-8	267	.284
Major League totals (13 years)	85	74	.535	4.48	1.40	310	191	19	4	20	9-17	1331.0	1305	707	663	170	558-14	910	.257

DIVISION SERIES RECORD

Year	Team (League)	W	L	Pct.	ERA	WHIP	G	GS	CG	ShO	Hld.	Sv.-Opp.	IP	H	R	ER	HR	BB-IBB	SO	Avg.
2004— St. Louis (N.L.)	0	0	...	0.00	4.50	2	0	0	0	0	0-0	.2	1	0	0	0	2-0	0	.333

CHAMPIONSHIP SERIES RECORD

Year	Team (League)	W	L	Pct.	ERA	WHIP	G	GS	CG	ShO	Hld.	Sv.-Opp.	IP	H	R	ER	HR	BB-IBB	SO	Avg.
2004— St. Louis (N.L.)	0	0	...	0.00	3.00	1	0	0	0	0	0-0	.1	0	0	0	0	1-0	0	.000

WORLD SERIES RECORD

Year	Team (League)	W	L	Pct.	ERA	WHIP	G	GS	CG	ShO	Hld.	Sv.-Opp.	IP	H	R	ER	HR	BB-IBB	SO	Avg.
2004— St. Louis (N.L.)	0	0	...	10.80	2.40	2	0	0	0	0	0-0	1.2	4	2	2	0	0-0	2	.444

ELLIS, MARK   SS

PERSONAL: Born June 6, 1977, in Rapid City, S.D. ... 5-11/180. ... Bats right, throws right. ... Full name: Mark William Ellis. ... High school: Stevens (Rapid City, S.D.). ... College: Florida.

TRANSACTIONS/CAREER NOTES: Selected by Kansas City Royals organization in ninth round of 1999 free-agent draft. ... Traded by Royals with OF Johnny Damon and cash to Oakland Athletics as part of three-team deal in which Royals acquired P Roberto Hernandez from Tampa Bay Devil Rays, A's acquired P Cory Lidle from Devil Rays, Royals acquired C A.J. Hinch, IF Angel Berroa and cash from A's and Devil Rays received OF Ben Grieve and cash from A's (January 8, 2001). ... On disabled list (March 26, 2004-entire season).

Year	Team (League)	Pos.	G	AB	R	H	2B	3B	HR	RBI	BB	SO	HBP	GDP	SB-CS	Avg.	OBP	SLG	OPS	E	Avg.
1999— Spokane (N'west)		SS	71	281	67	92	14	0	7	47	47	40	3	1	21-7	.327	.424	.452	.876	16	.958
2000— Wilmington (Caro.)		2B-SS	132	484	83	146	27	4	6	62	78	72	7	11	25-7	.302	.404	.411	.815	31	.954
— Wichita (Texas)		2B	7	22	4	7	1	0	0	4	5	5	0	0	1-0	.318	.444	.364	.808	0	1.000
2001— Sacramento (PCL)		SS	132	472	71	129	38	0	10	53	54	78	5	13	21-7	.273	.351	.417	.768	19	.968
2002— Sacramento (PCL)		SS	21	84	14	25	10	1	0	5	6	13	4	1	4-0	.298	.372	.440	.813	3	.974
— Oakland (A.L.)		2-S-3-DH	98	345	58	94	16	4	6	35	44	54	4	3	4-2	.272	.359	.394	.753	11	.976
2003— Oakland (A.L.)		2B	154	553	78	137	31	5	9	52	48	94	7	7	6-2	.248	.313	.371	.684	14	.982
2004— Oakland (A.L.)			Did not play.																		
Major League totals (2 years)			252	898	136	231	47	9	15	87	92	148	11	10	10-4	.257	.331	.380	.711	25	.980

DIVISION SERIES RECORD

Year	Team (League)	Pos.	G	AB	R	H	2B	3B	HR	RBI	BB	SO	HBP	GDP	SB-CS	Avg.	OBP	SLG	OPS	E	Avg.
2002— Oakland (A.L.)		2B	5	19	1	7	2	0	1	4	1	2	0	0	0-0	.368	.400	.632	1.032	1	.960
2003— Oakland (A.L.)		2B	5	17	2	2	0	0	0	0	4	7	1	0	0-0	.118	.318	.118	.436	1	.964
Division series totals (2 years)			10	36	3	9	2	0	1	4	5	9	1	0	0-0	.250	.357	.389	.746	2	.962

ELLISON, JASON — OF

PERSONAL: Born April 4, 1978, in Quincy, Calif. ... 5-10/180. ... Bats right, throws right. ... Full name: Jason Jerome Ellison. ... High school: South Kitsap High (Port Orchar, Wash.). ... College: Lewis-Clark (Idaho) State.

TRANSACTIONS/CAREER NOTES: Selected by San Francisco Giants organization in 22nd round of 2000 free-agent draft.

2004 GAMES PLAYED BY POSITION (MLB): OF—4.

Year	Team (League)	Pos.	G	AB	R	H	2B	3B	HR	RBI	BB	SO	HBP	GDP	SB-CS	Avg.	OBP	SLG	OPS	E	Avg.
2000— Salem-Keizer (N'west)		OF	74	300	67	90	15	2	0	28	29	45	7	1	13-7	.300	.374	.363	.737	4	.976
2001— Hagerstown (SAL)		OF	130	494	95	144	38	3	6	55	71	68	10	6	19-15	.291	.388	.429	.817	5	.984
2002— San Jose (Calif.)		OF	81	322	40	87	13	0	5	40	25	37	2	10	9-9	.270	.325	.357	.682	4	.980
— Fresno (PCL)		OF	49	196	31	61	8	1	3	8	21	28	4	4	16-3	.311	.389	.408	.797	1	.992
2003— San Francisco (N.L.)		OF	7	10	1	1	0	0	0	0	0	1	0	0	0-0	.100	.100	.100	.200	0	1.000
— Fresno (PCL)		OF-DH	119	461	74	136	22	4	6	39	39	52	6	7	21-13	.295	.356	.399	.755	9	.974
2004— Fresno (PCL)		OF	125	505	90	159	32	7	9	40	40	66	3	8	27-12	.315	.368	.459	.827	6	.983
— San Francisco (N.L.)		OF	13	4	4	2	0	0	1	3	0	1	0	0	2-0	.500	.500	1.250	1.750	0	1.000
Major League totals (2 years)			20	14	5	3	0	0	1	3	0	2	0	0	2-0	.214	.214	.429	.643	0	1.000

EMBREE, ALAN — P

PERSONAL: Born January 23, 1970, in The Dalles, Ore. ... 6-2/190. ... Throws left, bats left. ... Full name: Alan Duane Embree. ... Name pronounced: EMM-bree. ... High school: Prairie (Vancouver, Wash.).

TRANSACTIONS/CAREER NOTES: Selected by Cleveland Indians organization in fifth round of 1989 free-agent draft. ... On disabled list (April 1-June 2 and June 2, 1993-remainder of season); included rehabilitation assignment to Canton/Akron. ... On disabled list (August 1-September 7, 1996); included rehabilitation assignment to Buffalo. ... Traded by Indians with OF Kenny Lofton to Atlanta Braves for OFs Marquis Grissom and David Justice (March 25, 1997). ... Traded by Braves to Arizona Diamondbacks for P Russ Springer (June 23, 1998). ... Traded by Diamondbacks to San Francisco Giants for OF Dante Powell (November 10, 1998). ... On disabled list (May 23-June 12, 2001); included rehabilitation assignment to Fresno. ... Traded by Giants to Chicago White Sox for P Derek Hasselhoff (June 29, 2001). ... Signed as a free agent by San Diego Padres (January 3, 2002). ... Traded by Padres with P Andy Shibilo to Boston Red Sox for Ps Brad Baker and Dan Giese (June 26, 2002). ... On disabled list (July 14-29, 2002). ... On disabled list (April 9-29, 2003); included rehabilitation assignment to Sarasota.

CAREER HITTING: 0-for-2 (.000), 0 R, 0 2B, 0 3B, 0 HR, 0 RBI.

Year	Team (League)	W	L	Pct.	ERA	WHIP	G	GS	CG	ShO	Hld.	Sv.-Opp.	IP	H	R	ER	HR	BB-IBB	SO	Avg.
1990— Burlington (Appalachian) ..		4	4	.500	2.64	1.43	15	15	0	0	...	0-...	81.2	87	36	24	3	30-0	58	.274
1991— Columbus (S. Atl.)		10	8	.556	3.59	1.31	27	26	3	1	...	0-...	155.1	126	80	62	4	77-1	137	.224
1992— Kinston (Caro.)		10	5	.667	3.30	1.20	15	15	1	0	...	0-...	101.0	89	48	37	10	32-0	115	.234
— Cant./Akr. (Eastern)		7	2	.778	2.28	1.13	12	12	0	0	...	0-...	79.0	61	24	20	2	28-1	56	.216
— Cleveland (A.L.)		0	2	.000	7.00	1.50	4	4	0	0	...	0-0	18.0	19	14	14	3	8-0	12	.271
1993— Cant./Akr. (Eastern)		0	0	...	3.38	1.13	1	1	0	0	...	0-0	5.1	3	2	2	0	3-0	4	.176
1994— Cant./Akr. (Eastern)		9	16	.360	5.50	1.57	30	27	2	1	...	0-...	157.0	183	106	96	15	64-3	81	.294
1995— Buffalo (A.A.)		3	4	.429	0.89	1.23	30	0	0	0	...	5-...	40.2	31	10	4	0	19-2	56	.211
— Cleveland (A.L.)		3	2	.600	5.11	1.58	23	0	0	0	6	1-1	24.2	23	16	14	2	16-0	23	.253
1996— Cleveland (A.L.)		1	1	.500	6.39	1.65	24	0	0	0	1	0-0	31.0	30	26	22	10	21-3	33	.259
— Buffalo (A.A.)		4	1	.800	3.93	1.17	20	0	0	0	...	5-...	34.1	26	16	15	1	14-0	46	.210
1997— Atlanta (N.L.)		3	1	.750	2.54	1.22	66	0	0	0	16	0-0	46.0	36	13	13	1	20-2	45	.221
1998— Atlanta (N.L.)		1	0	1.000	4.34	1.77	20	0	0	0	6	0-1	18.2	23	14	9	2	10-0	19	.307
— Arizona (N.L.)		3	2	.600	4.11	1.31	35	0	0	0	6	1-2	35.0	33	18	16	5	13-0	24	.248
1999— San Francisco (N.L.)		3	2	.600	3.38	1.16	68	0	0	0	22	0-3	58.2	42	22	22	4	26-2	53	.200
2000— San Francisco (N.L.)		3	5	.375	4.95	1.45	63	0	0	0	9	2-5	60.0	62	34	33	4	25-2	49	.274
2001— San Francisco (N.L.)		0	2	.000	11.25	2.20	22	0	0	0	0	0-1	20.0	34	26	25	7	10-2	25	.374
— Fresno (PCL)		1	0	1.000	1.13	0.75	7	0	0	0	...	1-...	8.0	5	3	1	0	1-0	6	.179
— Chicago (A.L.)		1	2	.333	5.03	1.12	39	0	0	0	9	0-2	34.0	31	21	19	7	7-0	34	.242
2002— San Diego (N.L.)		3	4	.429	1.26	1.12	36	0	0	0	9	0-2	28.2	23	7	4	2	9-2	38	.211
— Boston (A.L.)		1	2	.333	2.97	1.05	32	0	0	0	8	2-5	33.1	24	12	11	4	11-1	43	.203
2003— Sarasota (Florida State)		0	0	...	13.50	3.00	1	1	0	0	...	0-...	.2	2	1	1	0	0-0	2	.500
— Boston (A.L.)		4	1	.800	4.25	1.18	65	0	0	0	14	1-2	55.0	49	26	26	5	16-3	45	.241
2004— Boston (A.L.)		2	2	.500	4.13	1.15	71	0	0	0	20	0-1	52.1	49	28	24	7	11-1	37	.244
American League totals (7 years)		12	12	.500	4.71	1.27	258	4	0	0	58	4-11	248.1	225	143	130	38	90-8	227	.243
National League totals (6 years)		16	16	.500	4.11	1.37	310	0	0	0	69	3-14	267.0	253	134	122	27	113-10	253	.251
Major League totals (11 years)		28	28	.500	4.40	1.32	568	4	0	0	127	7-25	515.1	478	277	252	65	203-18	480	.247

DIVISION SERIES RECORD

Year	Team (League)	W	L	Pct.	ERA	WHIP	G	GS	CG	ShO	Hld.	Sv.-Opp.	IP	H	R	ER	HR	BB-IBB	SO	Avg.
1996— Cleveland (A.L.)		0	0	...	9.00	0.00	3	0	0	0	1	0-0	1.0	0	1	1	0	0-0	1	.000
2000— San Francisco (N.L.)		0	0	...	0.00	0.00	2	0	0	0	1	0-0	1.2	0	0	0	0	0-0	0	.000
2003— Boston (A.L.)		0	0	...	0.00	0.50	3	0	0	0	1	0-1	2.0	1	0	0	0	0-0	0	.000
2004— Boston (A.L.)		0	0	...	0.00	1.00	2	0	0	0	0	0-0	1.0	1	0	0	0	1-0	1	.000
Division series totals (4 years)		0	0	...	1.59	0.35	10	0	0	0	3	0-1	5.2	1	1	1	0	1-0	1	.059

E

Year	Team (League)	W	L	Pct.	ERA	WHIP	G	GS	CG	ShO	Hld.	Sv.-Opp.	IP	H	R	ER	HR	BB-IBB	SO	Avg.
1995—Cleveland (A.L.)		0	0	...	0.00	0.00	1	0	0	0	0	0-0	.1	0	0	0	0	0-0	1	.000
1997—Atlanta (N.L.)		0	0	...	0.00	1.00	1	0	0	0	0	0-0	1.0	1	0	0	0	1-0	1	.000
2003—Boston (A.L.)		1	0	1.000	0.00	0.64	5	0	0	0	0	0-0	4.2	3	0	0	0	0-0	1	.214
2004—Boston (A.L.)		0	0	...	3.86	2.14	6	0	0	0	0	0-0	4.2	9	2	2	0	1-1	2	.409
Champ. series totals (4 years)		1	0	1.000	1.69	1.31	13	0	0	0	0	0-0	10.2	12	2	2	0	2-1	5	.308

WORLD SERIES RECORD

Year	Team (League)	W	L	Pct.	ERA	WHIP	G	GS	CG	ShO	Hld.	Sv.-Opp.	IP	H	R	ER	HR	BB-IBB	SO	Avg.
1995—Cleveland (A.L.)		0	0	...	2.70	1.20	4	0	0	0	0	0-0	3.1	2	1	1	0	2-1	2	.182
2004—Boston (A.L.)		0	0	...	0.00	0.60	3	0	0	0	1	0-0	1.2	1	1	0	0	0-0	4	.167
World series totals (2 years)		0	0	...	1.80	1.00	7	0	0	0	1	0-0	5.0	3	2	1	0	2-1	6	.176

ENCARNACION, JUAN   OF

PERSONAL: Born March 8, 1976, in Las Matas de Farfan, Dominican Republic. ... 6-3/215. ... Bats right, throws right. ... Full name: Juan de Dios Encarnacion. ... Name pronounced: en-car-NAH-see-own. ... High school: Liceo Mercedes Maria Mateo (Las Matas de Faran, Dominican Republic).

TRANSACTIONS/CAREER NOTES: Signed as a non-drafted free agent by Detroit Tigers organization (December 27, 1992). ... On disabled list (March 20-April 29, 1998); included rehabilitation assignment to Lakeland. ... On suspended list (May 27-29, 2000). ... Traded by Tigers with P Luis Pineda to Cincinnati Reds for OF Dmitri Young (December 11, 2001). ... Traded by Reds with OF/2B Wilton Guerrero and P Ryan Snare to Florida Marlins for P Ryan Dempster (July 11, 2002). ... Traded by Marlins to Los Angeles Dodgers for OF Travis Ezi (December 13, 2003). ... On disabled list (July 4-19, 2004). ... Traded by Dodgers with C Paul Lo Duca and P Guillermo Mota to Marlins for Ps Brad Penny and Bill Murphy and 1B Hee Seop Choi (July 30, 2004).

2004 GAMES PLAYED BY POSITION (MLB): OF—133.

Year	Team (League)	Pos.	G	AB	R	H	2B	3B	HR	RBI	BB	SO	HBP	GDP	SB-CS	Avg.	OBP	SLG	OPS	E	Avg.
1993—Dom. Tigers (DSL)		OF	72	251	36	63	13	4	13	49	15	65	...	...	6-...	.251	...	.490	...	17	.879
1994—Bristol (Appal.)		OF	54	197	16	49	7	1	4	31	13	54	5	2	9-2	.249	.310	.355	.666	3	.968
—Fayetteville (SAL)		OF	24	83	6	16	1	1	1	4	8	36	1	2	1-1	.193	.272	.265	.537	2	.920
—Lakeland (Fla. St.)		OF	3	6	1	2	0	0	0	0	0	3	1	0	0-0	.333	.429	.333	.762	0	...
1995—Fayetteville (SAL)		OF	124	457	62	129	31	7	16	72	30	113	8	10	30-6	.282	.336	.486	.822	7	.956
1996—Lakeland (Fla. St.)		OF	131	499	54	120	31	2	15	58	24	104	12	10	11-5	.240	.290	.401	.691	6	.976
1997—Jacksonville (Sou.)		OF-DH	131	493	91	159	31	4	26	90	43	86	19	8	17-3	.323	.394	.560	.954	3	.987
—Detroit (A.L.)		OF	11	33	3	7	1	1	1	5	3	12	2	1	3-1	.212	.316	.394	.710	0	1.000
1998—Lakeland (Fla. St.)		OF	4	16	4	4	0	1	0	4	2	4	1	0	4-0	.250	.368	.375	.743	0	1.000
—Toledo (Int'l)		OF-DH	92	356	55	102	17	3	8	41	29	85	10	9	24-4	.287	.353	.419	.772	5	.973
—Detroit (A.L.)		OF-DH	40	164	30	54	9	4	7	21	7	31	1	2	7-4	.329	.354	.561	.915	1	.985
1999—Detroit (A.L.)		OF	132	509	62	130	30	6	19	74	14	113	9	12	33-12	.255	.287	.450	.736	9	.968
2000—Detroit (A.L.)		OF	141	547	75	158	25	6	14	72	29	90	7	15	16-4	.289	.330	.433	.764	5	.987
2001—Detroit (A.L.)		OF-DH	120	417	52	101	19	7	12	52	25	93	6	9	9-5	.242	.292	.408	.700	5	.977
2002—Cincinnati (N.L.)		OF	83	321	43	89	11	2	16	51	26	63	1	7	9-4	.277	.330	.474	.804	5	.977
—Florida (N.L.)		OF	69	263	34	69	11	3	8	34	20	50	3	11	12-5	.262	.317	.418	.735	1	.993
2003—Florida (N.L.)		OF	156	601	80	162	37	6	19	94	37	82	4	17	19-8	.270	.313	.446	.759	0	1.000
2004—Los Angeles (N.L.)		OF	86	324	42	76	18	1	13	43	21	53	4	9	3-3	.235	.289	.417	.705	4	.976
—Florida (N.L.)		OF	47	160	21	38	12	1	3	19	17	33	3	2	2-1	.238	.320	.381	.702	2	.980
American League totals (5 years)			444	1670	222	450	84	24	53	224	78	339	25	39	68-26	.269	.310	.444	.753	21	.979
National League totals (3 years)			443	1669	220	434	89	13	59	241	121	281	15	46	45-21	.260	.313	.435	.748	12	.988
Major League totals (8 years)			887	3339	442	884	173	37	112	465	199	620	40	85	113-47	.265	.311	.439	.751	33	.983

DIVISION SERIES RECORD

Year	Team (League)	Pos.	G	AB	R	H	2B	3B	HR	RBI	BB	SO	HBP	GDP	SB-CS	Avg.	OBP	SLG	OPS	E	Avg.
2003—Florida (N.L.)		OF	4	15	1	2	0	0	1	1	2	3	0	1	0-0	.133	.235	.333	.569	0	1.000

CHAMPIONSHIP SERIES RECORD

Year	Team (League)	Pos.	G	AB	R	H	2B	3B	HR	RBI	BB	SO	HBP	GDP	SB-CS	Avg.	OBP	SLG	OPS	E	Avg.
2003—Florida (N.L.)		OF	5	12	1	3	1	0	1	1	0	4	0	1	0-0	.250	.250	.583	.833	0	1.000

WORLD SERIES RECORD

Year	Team (League)	Pos.	G	AB	R	H	2B	3B	HR	RBI	BB	SO	HBP	GDP	SB-CS	Avg.	OBP	SLG	OPS	E	Avg.
2003—Florida (N.L.)		OF	6	11	1	2	0	0	0	1	1	5	0	0	0-0	.182	.231	.182	.413	0	1.000

ENNIS, JOHN   P

PERSONAL: Born October 17, 1979, in Montrose, Colo. ... 6-5/220. ... Throws right, bats right. ... Full name: John Wayne Ennis. ... High school: Monroe (Panorama City, Calif.).

TRANSACTIONS/CAREER NOTES: Selected by Atlanta Braves organization in 14th round of 1998 free-agent draft. ... Claimed on waivers by Detroit Tigers (August 20, 2003).

CAREER HITTING: 0-for-1 (.000), 0 R, 0 2B, 0 3B, 0 HR, 0 RBI.

Year	Team (League)	W	L	Pct.	ERA	WHIP	G	GS	CG	ShO	Hld.	Sv.-Opp.	IP	H	R	ER	HR	BB-IBB	SO	Avg.
1998—GC Braves (GCL)		0	3	.000	4.62	1.42	8	2	0	0	...	0-...	25.1	30	16	13	0	6-1	18	.288
1999—Danville (Appalachian)		4	3	.571	5.07	1.40	13	13	13	0	...	0-...	65.2	71	46	37	7	21-0	60	.272
2000—Macon (S. Atl.)		7	4	.636	2.55	1.03	18	16	0	0	...	0-...	98.2	77	37	28	5	25-0	105	.209
2001—Myrtle Beach (Caro.)		6	8	.429	3.58	1.13	25	25	1	0	...	0-...	138.1	111	63	55	12	45-0	144	.219
2002—Greenville (Sou.)		9	9	.500	4.18	1.30	26	26	0	0	...	0-...	148.2	131	79	69	7	62-0	103	.243
—Atlanta (N.L.)		0	0	...	4.50	2.00	1	1	0	0	0	0-...	4.0	5	2	2	0	3-0	1	.385
2003—Richmond (Int'l)		2	11	.154	5.56	1.60	28	15	0	0	...	0-...	100.1	121	70	62	11	37-1	76	.305
—Greenville (Sou.)		0	0	...	2.45	1.60	1	1	0	0	...	0-...	3.2	4	1	1	1	2-0	3	.286
—Toledo (International)		1	0	1.000	5.17	1.70	3	3	0	0	...	0-...	15.2	22	9	9	0	5-0	9	.355
2004—Toledo (International)		9	5	.643	3.59	1.32	38	13	0	0	...	10-...	102.2	100	49	41	10	36-3	77	.258
—Detroit (A.L.)		0	0	...	8.44	1.56	12	0	0	0	0	1-2	16.0	20	16	15	3	5-0	13	.290
American League totals (1 year)		0	0	...	8.44	1.56	12	0	0	0	0	1-2	16.0	20	16	15	3	5-0	13	.290
National League totals (1 year)		0	0	...	4.50	2.00	1	1	0	0	0	0-0	4.0	5	2	2	0	3-0	1	.385
Major League totals (2 years)		0	0	...	7.65	1.65	13	1	0	0	0	1-2	20.0	25	18	17	3	8-0	14	.305

E

ENSBERG, MORGAN — 3B

PERSONAL: Born August 26, 1975, in Hermosa Beach, Calif. ... 6-2/210. ... Bats right, throws right. ... Full name: Morgan Paul Ensberg. ... High school: Redondo Union (Redondo Beach, Calif.). ... College: USC.

TRANSACTIONS/CAREER NOTES: Selected by Seattle Mariners organization in 61st round of 1994 free-agent draft; did not sign. ... Selected by Houston Astros organization in ninth round of 1998 free-agent draft.

2004 GAMES PLAYED BY POSITION (MLB): 3B—118, SS—1.

Year Team (League)	Pos.	G	AB	R	H	2B	3B	HR	RBI	BB	SO	HBP	GDP	SB-CS	Avg.	OBP	SLG	OPS	E	Avg.
1998— Auburn (NY-Penn)	3B-SS	59	196	39	45	10	1	5	31	46	51	6	5	15-3	.230	.388	.367	.755	11	.927
1999— Kissimmee (Fla. St.)	3B-SS-1B	123	427	72	102	25	2	15	69	68	90	9	9	17-6	.239	.353	.412	.765	35	.900
2000— Round Rock (Texas)	3B	137	483	95	145	34	0	28	90	92	107	8	15	9-12	.300	.416	.545	.960	24	.942
—Houston (N.L.)	3B	4	7	0	2	0	0	0	0	0	1	0	0	0-0	.286	.286	.286	.571	1	.667
2001— New Orleans (PCL)	3B-SS	87	316	65	98	20	0	23	61	45	60	3	12	6-3	.310	.397	.592	.989	17	.929
2002— Houston (N.L.)	3B	49	132	14	32	7	2	3	19	18	25	3	8	2-0	.242	.346	.394	.740	8	.929
—New Orleans (PCL)	3B-1B	83	292	50	84	12	3	7	37	50	56	7	9	9-5	.288	.401	.421	.822	19	.926
2003— Houston (N.L.)	3B-DH	127	385	69	112	15	1	25	60	48	60	6	10	7-2	.291	.377	.530	.907	9	.967
2004— Houston (N.L.)	3B-SS	131	411	51	113	20	3	10	66	36	46	0	17	6-4	.275	.330	.411	.742	13	.949
Major League totals (4 years)		311	935	134	259	42	6	38	145	102	132	9	35	15-6	.277	.352	.457	.809	31	.952

DIVISION SERIES RECORD

Year Team (League)	Pos.	G	AB	R	H	2B	3B	HR	RBI	BB	SO	HBP	GDP	SB-CS	Avg.	OBP	SLG	OPS	E	Avg.
2004— Houston (N.L.)	3B	5	19	1	7	2	0	0	5	3	1	0	1	0-1	.368	.455	.474	.928	0	1.000

CHAMPIONSHIP SERIES RECORD

Year Team (League)	Pos.	G	AB	R	H	2B	3B	HR	RBI	BB	SO	HBP	GDP	SB-CS	Avg.	OBP	SLG	OPS	E	Avg.
2004— Houston (N.L.)	3B	7	22	2	3	0	0	1	2	1	3	2	1	0-1	.136	.240	.273	.513	0	1.000

ERICKSON, MATT — 3B

PERSONAL: Born July 30, 1975, in Appleton, Wis. ... 5-11/190. ... Bats left, throws right. ... High school: Appleton (Wis.) West. ... College: Arkansas.

TRANSACTIONS/CAREER NOTES: Selected by Milwaukee Brewers organization in 57th round of 1994 free-agent draft; did not sign. ... Selected by Florida Marlins organization in seventh round of 1997 free-agent draft. ... Signed as a free agent by Brewers organization (December 22, 2003).

2004 GAMES PLAYED BY POSITION (MLB): 2B—1, SS—1.

Year Team (League)	Pos.	G	AB	R	H	2B	3B	HR	RBI	BB	SO	HBP	GDP	SB-CS	Avg.	OBP	SLG	OPS	E	Avg.
1997— Utica (N.Y.-Penn)	3B-2B	69	238	44	78	10	0	5	44	48	36	11	7	9-3	.328	.455	.433	.888	11	.949
1998— Kane Co. (Midw.)	3B-2B-SS	124	441	83	143	32	2	4	64	72	62	18	8	17-7	.324	.436	.433	.869	21	.940
1999— Portland (East.)	2B	107	361	38	97	20	2	0	35	51	65	3	9	2-3	.269	.360	.335	.695	13	.974
2000— Portland (East.)	SS-3B-2B	100	335	56	101	23	4	2	41	59	62	9	9	8-3	.301	.416	.412	.828	10	.974
2001— Calgary (PCL)	2B-SS-3B	115	413	66	128	21	1	2	29	39	69	12	13	11-4	.310	.386	.380	.766	14	.972
2002— Calgary (PCL)	2-3-OF-S	108	379	63	109	30	2	1	27	31	63	11	11	15-4	.288	.359	.385	.744	10	.973
2003— Albuquerque (PCL)	3B-2B-OF	98	298	43	102	22	4	2	35	43	42	10	7	14-9	.342	.442	.463	.905	11	.958
2004— Milwaukee (N.L.)	2B-SS	4	6	0	1	0	0	0	0	0	1	0	0	0-0	.167	.167	.167	.333	0	1.000
—Indianapolis (Int'l)	2-3-S-DH	122	400	57	108	27	1	2	34	45	69	11	5	12-10	.270	.359	.358	.702	6	.986
Major League totals (1 year)		4	6	0	1	0	0	0	0	0	1	0	0	0-0	.167	.167	.167	.333	0	1.000

ERICKSON, SCOTT — P

PERSONAL: Born February 2, 1968, in Long Beach, Calif. ... 6-4/230. ... Throws right, bats right. ... Full name: Scott Gavin Erickson. ... High school: Homestead (Cupertino, Calif.). ... College: Arizona.

TRANSACTIONS/CAREER NOTES: Selected by New York Mets organization in 36th round of June 1986 free-agent draft; did not sign. ... Selected by Houston Astros organization in 34th round of 1987 free-agent draft; did not sign. ... Selected by Toronto Blue Jays organization in 44th round of 1988 free-agent draft; did not sign. ... Selected by Minnesota Twins organization in fourth round of 1989 free-agent draft. ... On disabled list (June 30-July 15, 1991; April 3-18, 1993 and May 15-31, 1994). ... Traded by Twins to Baltimore Orioles for P Scott Klingenbeck and a player to be named (July 7, 1995); Twins acquired OF Kimera Bartee to complete deal (September 18, 1995). ... On disabled list (March 28-May 4 and July 28, 2000-remainder of season); included rehabilitation assignments to Frederick and Bowie. ... On disabled list (April 1, 2001-entire season; and March 28, 2003-entire season). ... Signed as a free agent by New York Mets organization (February 5, 2004). ... On disabled list (April 4-June 30, 2004); included rehabilitation assignments to St. Lucie and Norfolk. ... Traded by Mets to Texas Rangers for a player to be named (July 31, 2004); Mets acquired IF Josh Hoffpauir to complete deal (September 17, 2004).

CAREER HITTING: 2-for-22 (.091), 4 R, 1 2B, 0 3B, 0 HR, 1 RBI.

Year Team (League)	W	L	Pct.	ERA	WHIP	G	GS	CG	ShO	Hld.	Sv.-Opp.	IP	H	R	ER	HR	BB-IBB	SO	Avg.
1989— Visalia (Calif.)	3	4	.429	2.97	1.28	12	12	2	0	...	0-...	78.2	79	29	26	3	22-0	59	.265
1990— Orlando (Sou.)	8	3	.727	3.03	0.98	15	15	3	1	...	0-...	101.0	75	38	34	3	24-0	69	.205
—Minnesota (A.L.)	8	4	.667	2.87	1.41	19	17	1	0	0	0-0	113.0	108	49	36	9	51-4	53	.256
1991— Minnesota (A.L.)	•20	8	.714	3.18	1.27	32	32	5	3	0	0-0	204.0	189	80	72	13	71-3	108	.248
1992— Minnesota (A.L.)	13	12	.520	3.40	1.32	32	32	5	3	0	0-0	212.0	197	86	80	18	83-3	101	.252
1993— Minnesota (A.L.)	8	* 19	.296	5.19	1.54	34	34	1	0	0	0-0	218.2	* 266	* 138	126	17	71-1	116	.305
1994— Minnesota (A.L.)	8	11	.421	5.44	1.61	23	23	2	1	0	0-0	144.0	173	95	87	15	59-0	104	.299
1995— Minnesota (A.L.)	4	6	.400	5.95	1.53	15	15	0	0	0	0-0	87.2	102	61	58	11	32-0	45	.291
—Baltimore (A.L.)	9	4	.692	3.89	1.34	17	16	7	2	0	0-0	108.2	111	47	47	7	35-0	61	.273
1996— Baltimore (A.L.)	13	12	.520	5.02	1.48	34	34	6	0	0	0-0	222.1	262	137	124	21	66-4	100	.297
1997— Baltimore (A.L.)	16	7	.696	3.69	1.26	34	33	3	2	0	0-0	221.2	218	100	91	16	61-5	131	.257
1998— Baltimore (A.L.)	16	13	.552	4.01	1.40	36	* 36	* 11	2	0	0-0	* 251.1	* 284	125	112	23	69-4	186	.281
1999— Baltimore (A.L.)	15	12	.556	4.81	1.49	34	34	6	* 3	0	0-0	230.1	244	127	123	27	* 99-4	106	.280
2000— Frederick (Caro.)	0	0	...	2.70	0.60	1	1	0	0	...	0-...	6.2	3	2	2	0	1-0	5	.130
—Bowie (East.)	0	0	...	0.00	0.57	1	1	0	0	...	0-...	7.0	4	0	0	0	0-0	5	.160
—Baltimore (A.L.)	5	8	.385	7.87	1.89	16	16	1	0	0	0-0	92.2	127	81	81	14	48-0	41	.331
2001— Baltimore (A.L.)							Did not play.												
2002— Baltimore (A.L.)	5	12	.294	5.55	1.62	29	28	3	1	0	0-0	160.2	192	109	99	20	68-2	74	.303
2004— St. Lucie (Fla. St.)	1	0	1.000	0.00	0.86	2	2	0	0	...	0-...	7.0	0	0	0	0	0-0	5	.222
—Norfolk (Int'l)	3	3	.500	4.50	1.31	8	8	0	0	...	0-...	52.0	56	30	26	5	12-0	30	.279
—New York (N.L.)	0	1	.000	7.88	2.38	2	2	0	0	0	0-0	8.0	15	9	7	1	4-0	3	.395
—Texas (A.L.)	1	3	.250	6.16	2.05	4	4	0	0	0	0-0	19.0	23	13	13	2	16-0	6	.307
—Oklahoma (PCL)	0	1	.000	9.82	2.36	2	2	0	0	...	0-...	11.0	17	13	12	1	9-0	11	.370
American League totals (13 years)	141	131	.518	4.52	1.45	359	354	51	17	0	0-0	2286.0	2496	1248	1149	213	829-30	1232	.281
National League totals (1 year)	0	1	.000	7.88	2.38	2	2	0	0	0	0-0	8.0	15	9	7	1	4-0	3	.395
Major League totals (13 years)	141	132	.516	4.54	1.46	361	356	51	17	0	0-0	2294.0	2511	1257	1156	214	833-30	1235	.282

DIVISION SERIES RECORD

Year Team (League)	W	L	Pct.	ERA	WHIP	G	GS	CG	ShO	Hld.	Sv.-Opp.	IP	H	R	ER	HR	BB-IBB	SO	Avg.
1996— Baltimore (A.L.)	0	0	...	4.05	1.20	1	1	0	0	0	0-0	6.2	6	3	3	1	2-0	6	.240
1997— Baltimore (A.L.)	1	0	1.000	4.05	1.35	1	1	0	0	0	0-0	6.2	7	3	3	0	2-0	6	.269
Division series totals (2 years)	1	0	1.000	4.05	1.28	2	2	0	0	0	0-0	13.1	13	6	6	1	4-0	12	.255

CHAMPIONSHIP SERIES RECORD

Year Team (League)	W	L	Pct.	ERA	WHIP	G	GS	CG	ShO	Hld.	Sv.-Opp.	IP	H	R	ER	HR	BB-IBB	SO	Avg.
1991— Minnesota (A.L.)	0	0	...	4.50	2.00	1	1	0	0	0	0-0	4.0	3	2	2	1	5-0	2	.214
1996— Baltimore (A.L.)	0	1	.000	2.38	1.59	2	2	0	0	0	0-0	11.1	14	9	3	3	4-0	8	.286
1997— Baltimore (A.L.)	1	0	1.000	4.26	1.26	2	2	0	0	0	0-0	12.2	15	7	6	2	1-0	6	.300
Champ. series totals (3 years)	1	1	.500	3.54	1.50	5	5	0	0	0	0-0	28.0	32	18	11	6	10-0	16	.283

WORLD SERIES RECORD

Year Team (League)	W	L	Pct.	ERA	WHIP	G	GS	CG	ShO	Hld.	Sv.-Opp.	IP	H	R	ER	HR	BB-IBB	SO	Avg.
1991— Minnesota (A.L.)	0	0	...	5.06	1.31	2	2	0	0	0	0-0	10.2	10	7	6	3	4-0	5	.233

ERSTAD, DARIN   1B

PERSONAL: Born June 4, 1974, in Jamestown, N.D. ... 6-2/210. ... Bats left, throws left. ... Full name: Darin Charles Erstad. ... Name pronounced: ER-stad. ... High school: Jamestown (N.D.). ... College: Nebraska.

TRANSACTIONS/CAREER NOTES: Selected by New York Mets organization in 13th round of 1992 free-agent draft; did not sign. ... Selected by California Angels organization in first round (first pick overall) of 1995 free-agent draft. ... Angels franchise renamed Anaheim Angels for 1997 season. ... On disabled list (August 4-19, 1998; and August 11-26, 1999). ... On disabled list (April 20-June 9 and August 7, 2003-remainder of season); included rehabilitation assignment to Salt Lake. ... On disabled list (May 9-June 14, 2004); included rehabilitation assignment to Salt Lake.

HONORS: Won A.L. Gold Glove as outfielder (2000 and 2002). ... Won A.L. Gold Glove at first base (2004).

2004 GAMES PLAYED BY POSITION (MLB): 1B—124.

Year Team (League)	Pos.	G	AB	R	H	2B	3B	HR	RBI	BB	SO	HBP	GDP	SB-CS	Avg.	OBP	SLG	OPS	E	Avg.
1995— Ariz. Angels (Ariz.)	OF	4	18	2	10	1	0	0	1	1	1	0	0	1-0	.556	.579	.611	1.190	0	1.000
— Lake Elsinore (Calif.)	OF	25	113	24	41	7	2	5	24	6	22	0	2	3-0	.363	.392	.593	.985	1	.985
1996— Vancouver (PCL)	OF-1B-DH	85	351	63	107	22	5	6	41	44	53	3	5	11-6	.305	.385	.447	.832	1	.995
— California (A.L.)	OF	57	208	34	59	5	1	4	20	17	29	0	3	3-3	.284	.333	.375	.708	3	.976
1997— Anaheim (A.L.)	1B-DH-OF	139	539	99	161	34	4	16	77	51	86	4	5	23-8	.299	.360	.466	.826	11	.990
1998— Anaheim (A.L.)	OF-1B-DH	133	537	84	159	39	3	19	82	43	77	6	2	20-6	.296	.353	.486	.839	3	.995
1999— Anaheim (A.L.)	1B-OF-DH	142	585	84	148	22	5	13	53	47	101	1	16	13-7	.253	.308	.374	.683	1	.999
2000— Anaheim (A.L.)	OF-DH-1B	157	*676	121	*240	39	6	25	100	64	82	1	8	28-8	.355	.409	.541	.951	3	.992
2001— Anaheim (A.L.)	OF-1B-DH	157	631	89	163	35	4	9	63	62	113	10	8	24-10	.258	.331	.360	.691	1	.998
2002— Anaheim (A.L.)	OF-1B-DH	150	625	99	177	28	4	10	73	27	67	2	9	23-3	.283	.313	.389	.702	1	.998
2003— Salt Lake (PCL)	OF	7	27	6	11	0	0	0	4	2	1	0	0	1-0	.407	.448	.407	.856	0	1.000
— Anaheim (A.L.)	OF	67	258	35	65	7	1	4	17	18	40	4	8	9-1	.252	.309	.333	.642	1	1.000
2004— Salt Lake (PCL)	1B	4	16	2	2	0	0	0	3	1	1	0	0	0-0	.125	.176	.125	.301	1	.963
— Anaheim (A.L.)	1B	125	495	79	146	29	1	7	69	37	74	4	9	16-1	.295	.346	.400	.746	4	.996
Major League totals (9 years)		1127	4554	724	1318	238	26	107	554	366	669	32	68	159-47	.289	.344	.424	.768	27	.995

DIVISION SERIES RECORD

Year Team (League)	Pos.	G	AB	R	H	2B	3B	HR	RBI	BB	SO	HBP	GDP	SB-CS	Avg.	OBP	SLG	OPS	E	Avg.
2002— Anaheim (A.L.)	OF	4	19	4	8	2	0	0	2	0	1	0	2	1-0	.421	.421	.526	.947	0	1.000
2004— Anaheim (A.L.)	1B	3	10	2	5	1	0	1	2	3	1	1	0	0-0	.500	.643	.900	1.543	0	1.000
Division series totals (2 years)		7	29	6	13	3	0	1	4	3	2	1	2	1-0	.448	.515	.655	1.170	0	1.000

CHAMPIONSHIP SERIES RECORD

Year Team (League)	Pos.	G	AB	R	H	2B	3B	HR	RBI	BB	SO	HBP	GDP	SB-CS	Avg.	OBP	SLG	OPS	E	Avg.
2002— Anaheim (A.L.)	OF	5	22	4	8	0	0	1	2	0	3	0	0	1-0	.364	.364	.500	.864	0	1.000

WORLD SERIES RECORD

Year Team (League)	Pos.	G	AB	R	H	2B	3B	HR	RBI	BB	SO	HBP	GDP	SB-CS	Avg.	OBP	SLG	OPS	E	Avg.
2002— Anaheim (A.L.)	OF	7	30	6	9	3	0	1	3	1	4	0	0	1-0	.300	.313	.500	.813	1	.955

ALL-STAR GAME RECORD

	G	AB	R	H	2B	3B	HR	RBI	BB	SO	HBP	GDP	SB-CS	Avg.	OBP	SLG	OPS	E	Avg.
All-Star Game totals (2 years)	2	4	1	0	0	0	0	1	0	0	0	0	0-0	.000	.000	.000	.000	0	1.000

ESCALONA, FELIX   SS

PERSONAL: Born March 12, 1979, in Puerto Cabello, Venezuela. ... 6-0/190. ... Bats right, throws right. ... Full name: Felix Eduardo Escalona.

TRANSACTIONS/CAREER NOTES: Signed as a non-drafted free agent by Houston Astros organization (October 2, 1995). ... Selected by San Francisco Giants from Astros organization in Rule 5 major league draft (December 13, 2001). ... Claimed on waivers by Tampa Bay Devil Rays (March 27, 2002). ... Claimed on waivers by Baltimore Orioles (May 19, 2003). ... Signed as a free agent by New York Yankees organization (February 4, 2004).

2004 GAMES PLAYED BY POSITION (MLB): SS—4, 3B—1.

Year Team (League)	Pos.	G	AB	R	H	2B	3B	HR	RBI	BB	SO	HBP	GDP	SB-CS	Avg.	OBP	SLG	OPS	E	Avg.
1996— GC Astros (GCL)	2B-3B	28	75	8	11	2	0	1	9	8	31	4	0	1-2	.147	.261	.213	.475	6	.924
1997— GC Astros (GCL)	2B	51	189	27	39	9	0	1	9	20	49	3	1	11-3	.206	.292	.270	.562	7	.969
— Kissimmee (Fla. St.)	2B	3	9	6	2	0	0	0	0	1	2	3	0	0-0	.222	.462	.222	.684	3	.833
1998— Kissimmee (Fla. St.)	3B	3	4	0	0	0	0	0	0	0	1	0	0	0-0	.000	.000	.000	.000	0	1.000
— Auburn (NY-Penn)	2B-3B-SS	51	149	22	31	5	0	1	17	11	33	6	4	4-2	.208	.282	.262	.544	14	.933
1999— Michigan (Midw.)	2B-3B-SS	116	396	78	114	29	4	6	47	29	60	17	4	7-7	.288	.360	.427	.786	21	.955
2000— Michigan (Midw.)	2B-SS	64	251	42	65	14	1	6	35	22	49	4	4	7-0	.259	.394	.721	.721	14	.953
— Kissimmee (Fla. St.)	2B-3B-SS	42	143	19	36	5	1	0	8	9	21	6	3	5-3	.252	.321	.301	.621	7	.955
2001— Lexington (S.Atl.)	2B-SS	130	536	92	155	42	2	16	64	30	85	16	8	46-12	.289	.342	.465	.807	23	.963
2002— Tampa Bay (A.L.)	S-2-3B	59	157	17	34	8	2	0	9	3	44	7	2	7-2	.217	.262	.293	.555	11	.949
2003— Orlando (South.)	S-2-3-DH	22	90	11	22	7	0	1	8	5	14	5	3	0-0	.244	.320	.356	.676	11	.896
— Tampa Bay (A.L.)	SS-2B-3B	10	27	2	5	2	0	0	2	2	6	0	1	1-0	.185	.241	.259	.501	0	1.000
— Bowie (East.)	2B	1	3	0	1	0	0	0	0	0	1	0	0	0-0	.333	.333	.333	.667	0	1.000
— Ottawa (Int'l)	2B-SS	9	30	5	7	2	0	0	5	1	5	2	0	2-0	.233	.303	.300	.603	2	.950
2004— Columbus (Int'l)	SS-3B-DH	130	447	79	138	32	1	7	59	31	56	18	19	2-4	.309	.373	.432	.804	23	.958
— New York (A.L.)	SS-3B	5	8	1	0	0	0	0	0	0	2	1	0	0-0	.000	.111	.000	.111	0	1.000
Major League totals (3 years)		74	192	20	39	10	2	0	11	5	52	8	2	8-2	.203	.252	.276	.528	11	.959

E

ESCOBAR, ALEX — OF

PERSONAL: Born September 6, 1978, in Valencia, Venezuela. ... 6-1/190. ... Bats right, throws right. ... Full name: Alexander Jose Escobar. ... Name pronounced: ess-COE-bar. ... High school: El Santuario (Valencia, Venezuela).

TRANSACTIONS/CAREER NOTES: Signed as a non-drafted free agent by New York Mets organization (July 1, 1995). ... Traded by Mets with OF Matt Lawton, P Jerrod Riggan and two players to be named to Cleveland Indians for 2B Roberto Alomar, P Mike Bacsik and OF Danny Peoples (December 11, 2001); Indians acquired P Billy Traber and 1B Earl Snyder to complete deal (December 13, 2001). ... On disabled list (March 30, 2002-entire season). ... Claimed on waivers by Chicago White Sox (August 17, 2004). ... On disabled list (August 17, 2004-remainder of season).

2004 GAMES PLAYED BY POSITION (MLB): OF—42, DH—3.

Year Team (League)	Pos.	G	AB	R	H	2B	3B	HR	RBI	BB	SO	HBP	GDP	SB-CS	Avg.	OBP	SLG	OPS	E	Avg.
1996— GC Mets (GCL)	SS-OF	24	75	15	27	4	0	0	10	4	9	3	0	7-1	.360	.410	.413	.823	3	.936
1997— Kingsport (Appalachian)	OF	10	36	6	7	3	0	0	3	3	8	0	3	1-0	.194	.250	.278	.528	2	.905
— GC Mets (GCL)	OF	26	73	12	18	4	1	1	11	10	17	1	1	0-0	.247	.341	.370	.711	1	.966
1998— Capital City (SAL)	OF	112	416	90	129	23	5	27	91	54	133	5	1	49-7	.310	.393	.584	.977	12	.941
1999— GC Mets (GCL)	OF	2	8	1	3	2	0	0	1	1	2	0	0	0-0	.375	.444	.625	1.069	0	1.000
— St. Lucie (Fla. St.)	OF	1	3	1	2	0	0	1	3	1	1	0	0	1-1	.667	.600	1.667	2.267	0	1.000
2000— Binghamton (East.)	OF	122	437	79	126	25	7	16	67	57	114	7	8	24-5	.288	.375	.487	.863	5	.983
2001— Norfolk (Int'l)	OF	111	397	55	106	21	4	12	52	35	146	3	10	18-3	.267	.327	.431	.758	5	.980
— New York (N.L.)	OF	18	50	3	10	1	0	3	8	3	19	0	1	1-0	.200	.245	.400	.645	2	.935
2002— Cleveland (A.L.)		Did not play.																		
2003— Buffalo (Int'l)	OF-DH	118	439	63	110	21	2	24	78	24	133	7	11	8-3	.251	.296	.472	.768	5	.975
— Cleveland (A.L.)	OF	28	99	16	27	2	0	5	14	7	33	1	0	1-0	.273	.324	.444	.769	2	.969
2004— Cleveland (A.L.)	OF-DH	46	152	20	32	8	2	1	12	23	42	1	1	1-1	.211	.318	.309	.627	1	.991
— Buffalo (Int'l)	OF-DH	16	63	10	18	5	0	4	10	4	15	2	0	0-1	.286	.348	.556	.903	0	1.000
American League totals (2 years)		74	251	36	59	10	2	6	26	30	75	2	1	2-1	.235	.320	.363	.683	3	.983
National League totals (1 year)		18	50	3	10	1	0	3	8	3	19	0	1	1-0	.200	.245	.400	.645	2	.935
Major League totals (3 years)		92	301	39	69	11	2	9	34	33	94	2	2	3-1	.229	.309	.369	.677	5	.976

ESCOBAR, KELVIM — P

PERSONAL: Born April 11, 1976, in La Guaira, Venezuela. ... 6-1/210. ... Throws right, bats right. ... Full name: Kelvim Jose Escobar.

TRANSACTIONS/CAREER NOTES: Signed as a non-drafted free agent by Toronto Blue Jays organization (July 9, 1992). ... On disabled list (April 16-May 6, 1998); included rehabilitation assignment to Syracuse. ... Signed as a free agent by Anaheim Angels (November 24, 2003).

CAREER HITTING: 1-for-16 (.063), 1 R, 0 2B, 0 3B, 0 HR, 1 RBI.

Year Team (League)	W	L	Pct.	ERA	WHIP	G	GS	CG	ShO	Hld.	Sv.-Opp.	IP	H	R	ER	HR	BB-IBB	SO	Avg.
1993— Dom. B. Jays (DSL)	2	1	.667	4.13	1.81	8	7	0	0		0-...	32.2	34	17	15	...	25-...	31	...
1994— GC Blue Jays (GCL)	4	4	.500	2.35	1.14	11	10	1	0		1-...	65.0	56	23	17	0	18-0	64	.237
1995— Dom. B. Jays (DSL)	0	1	.000	1.72	1.21	3	2	0	0		0-...	15.2	14	3	3	0	5-...	20	...
— Medicine Hat (Pio.)	3	3	.500	5.71	1.43	14	14	1	1		0-...	69.1	66	47	44	6	33-0	75	.253
1996— Dunedin (Fla. St.)	9	5	.643	2.69	1.21	18	18	1	0		0-...	110.1	101	44	33	5	33-0	113	.240
— Knoxville (Southern)	3	4	.429	5.33	1.57	10	10	0	0		0-...	54.0	61	36	32	7	24-0	44	.288
1997— Dunedin (Fla. St.)	0	1	.000	3.75	1.58	3	2	0	0		0-...	12.0	16	9	5	0	4-0	16	.327
— Knoxville (Southern)	2	1	.667	3.70	1.48	5	5	1	0		0-...	24.1	20	13	10	1	16-0	31	.222
— Toronto (A.L.)	3	2	.600	2.90	1.52	27	1	0	0	1	14-17	31.0	28	12	10	1	19-2	36	.237
1998— Toronto (A.L.)	7	3	.700	3.73	1.34	22	10	0	0	5	0-1	79.2	72	37	33	5	35-0	72	.238
— Syracuse (Int'l)	2	2	.500	3.77	1.26	13	10	0	0		1-...	59.2	51	26	25	7	24-0	64	.229
1999— Toronto (A.L.)	14	11	.560	5.69	1.63	33	30	1	0	0	0-0	174.0	203	118	110	19	81-2	129	.293
2000— Toronto (A.L.)	10	15	.400	5.35	1.51	43	24	3	1	3	2-3	180.0	186	118	107	26	85-3	142	.267
2001— Toronto (A.L.)	6	8	.429	3.50	1.15	59	11	1	1	13	0-0	126.0	93	51	49	8	52-5	121	.204
2002— Toronto (A.L.)	5	7	.417	4.27	1.53	76	0	0	0		38-46	78.0	75	39	37	8	44-6	85	.246
2003— Toronto (A.L.)	13	9	.591	4.29	1.18	41	26	1	1	0	4-5	180.1	189	94	86	15	78-3	159	.270
2004— Anaheim (A.L.)	11	12	.478	3.93	1.29	33	33	0	0	0	0-0	208.1	192	91	91	21	76-2	191	.244
Major League totals (8 years)	69	67	.507	4.45	1.43	334	134	6	3	22	58-72	1057.1	1038	560	523	105	470-23	935	.256

DIVISION SERIES RECORD

Year Team (League)	W	L	Pct.	ERA	WHIP	G	GS	CG	ShO	Hld.	Sv.-Opp.	IP	H	R	ER	HR	BB-IBB	SO	Avg.
2004— Anaheim (A.L.)	0	0	...	8.10	3.00	1	1	0	0	0	0-0	3.1	5	5	3	0	5-1	4	.333

ESTALELLA, BOBBY — C

PERSONAL: Born August 23, 1974, in Hialeah, Fla. ... 6-1/225. ... Bats right, throws right. ... Full name: Robert M. Estalella. ... Name pronounced: ES-ta-LAY-yuh. ... High school: Cooper City (Fla.). ... Junior college: Miami-Dade Community College South. ... Grandson of Bobby Estalella, outfielder with three major league teams (1935-36, 1939, 1941-45 and 1949).

TRANSACTIONS/CAREER NOTES: Selected by Philadelphia Phillies organization in 23rd round of 1992 free-agent draft. ... On disabled list (March 27-April 29, 1999); included rehabilitation assignments to Clearwater and Scranton/Wilkes-Barre. ... Traded by Phillies to San Francisco Giants for P Chris Brock (December 12, 1999). ... Traded by Giants with P Joe Smith to New York Yankees for P Brian Boehringer (July 5, 2001). ... Released by Yankees (March 27, 2002). ... Signed by Colorado Rockies organization (March 31, 2002). ... On disabled list (July 8, 2002-remainder of season; and August 11, 2003-remainder of season). ... Signed by Arizona Diamondbacks organization (February 13, 2004). ... Refused minor league assignment and became a free agent (May 12, 2004). ... Signed by Toronto Blue Jays organization (May 20, 2004). ... On disabled list (June 7, 2004-remainder of season). ... Refused minor league assignment and became a free agent (October 8, 2004).

2004 GAMES PLAYED BY POSITION (MLB): C—9, DH—2.

Year Team (League)	Pos.	G	AB	R	H	2B	3B	HR	RBI	BB	SO	HBP	GDP	SB-CS	Avg.	OBP	SLG	OPS	E	Avg.
1993— Martinsville (App.)	C	35	122	14	36	11	0	3	19	14	24	2	6	0-1	.295	.377	.459	.836	6	.975
— Clearwater (FSL)	C	11	35	4	8	0	0	0	4	2	3	0	1	0-0	.229	.270	.229	.499	0	1.000
1994— Spartanburg (SAL)	C	86	299	34	65	19	1	9	41	31	85	1	5	0-1	.217	.290	.378	.667	10	.985
— Clearwater (FSL)	C	13	46	3	12	1	0	2	9	3	17	0	1	0-0	.261	.300	.413	.713	1	.990
1995— Clearwater (FSL)	C	117	404	61	105	24	1	15	58	56	76	2	12	0-3	.260	.350	.436	.785	11	.987
— Reading (East.)	C	10	34	5	8	1	0	2	9	4	7	1	1	0-0	.235	.333	.441	.775	1	.986
1996— Reading (East.)	C	111	365	48	89	14	2	23	72	67	104	5	7	2-4	.244	.365	.482	.847	14	.984
— Scran./W.B. (I.L.)	C	11	36	7	9	3	0	3	8	5	10	0	1	0-0	.250	.341	.583	.925	2	.968
— Philadelphia (N.L.)	C	7	17	5	6	0	0	2	4	1	4	0	0	1-0	.353	.389	.706	1.095	0	1.000
1997— Scran./W.B. (I.L.)	C-DH	123	433	63	101	32	0	16	65	56	109	9	14	3-0	.233	.332	.418	.750	13	.986

E

Year	Team (League)	Pos.	G	AB	R	H	2B	3B	HR	RBI	BB	SO	HBP	GDP	SB-CS	Avg.	OBP	SLG	OPS	E	Avg.
	— Philadelphia (N.L.)	C	13	29	9	10	1	0	4	9	7	7	0	2	0-0	.345	.472	.793	1.265	0	1.000
1998— Scran./W.B. (I.L.)		C-DH	76	242	49	68	14	1	17	49	66	49	2	13	0-0	.281	.436	.558	.994	5	.990
	— Philadelphia (N.L.)	C	47	165	16	31	6	1	8	20	13	49	1	4	0-0	.188	.247	.382	.629	4	.988
1999— Clearwater (FSL)		C-DH	8	26	3	11	3	0	1	8	3	3	0	0	0-0	.423	.483	.654	1.137	1	.976
	— Scran./W.B. (I.L.)	C-DH	110	386	58	89	23	2	15	62	55	100	5	12	4-1	.231	.330	.417	.747	5	.993
	— Philadelphia (N.L.)	C	9	18	2	3	0	0	0	1	4	7	0	0	0-1	.167	.318	.167	.485	1	.976
2000— San Francisco (N.L.)		C	106	299	45	70	22	3	14	53	57	92	2	4	3-0	.234	.357	.468	.826	5	.993
2001— San Francisco (N.L.)		C	29	93	11	19	5	1	3	10	11	28	1	2	0-0	.204	.295	.376	.672	0	1.000
	— Fresno (PCL)	C-1B	6	22	3	7	1	0	1	4	1	9	0	1	0-0	.318	.348	.500	.848	0	1.000
	— Columbus (Int'l)	C-1B	48	171	26	44	10	1	10	38	21	45	2	7	0-2	.257	.340	.503	.843	2	.993
	— New York (A.L.)	C	3	4	1	0	0	0	0	0	1	2	1	0	0-0	.000	.333	.000	.333	0	1.000
2002— Colo. Springs (PCL)		C	23	79	16	23	9	0	6	20	11	20	0	0	0-0	.291	.374	.633	1.007	1	.995
	— Colorado (N.L.)	C	38	112	17	23	8	0	8	25	14	33	0	1	0-1	.205	.285	.491	.776	1	.995
2003— Colorado (N.L.)		C	46	140	17	28	7	0	7	21	19	55	1	4	2-0	.200	.294	.400	.694	4	.985
2004— Arizona (N.L.)		C	7	14	2	2	0	0	2	4	0	6	0	0	0-0	.143	.143	.571	.714	0	1.000
	— Syracuse (Int'l)	C-DH	6	24	3	6	0	0	2	3	1	6	0	0	0-0	.250	.280	.500	.780	0	1.000
	— Toronto (A.L.)	C-DH	5	13	1	3	0	0	0	0	3	5	1	1	0-0	.231	.412	.231	.643	0	1.000
American League totals (2 years)			8	17	2	3	0	0	0	0	4	7	2	1	0-0	.176	.391	.176	.568	0	1.000
National League totals (9 years)			302	887	124	192	49	5	48	147	126	283	5	17	6-2	.216	.313	.445	.759	15	.992
Major League totals (9 years)			310	904	126	195	49	5	48	147	130	290	7	18	6-2	.216	.315	.440	.755	15	.992

DIVISION SERIES RECORD

Year	Team (League)	Pos.	G	AB	R	H	2B	3B	HR	RBI	BB	SO	HBP	GDP	SB-CS	Avg.	OBP	SLG	OPS	E	Avg.
2000— San Francisco (N.L.)		C	4	12	1	1	0	0	0	1	0	2	0	0	0-0	.083	.083	.083	.167	0	1.000

ESTES, SHAWN — P

PERSONAL: Born February 18, 1973, in San Bernardino, Calif. ... 6-2/200. ... Throws left, bats right. ... Full name: Aaron Shawn Estes. ... Name pronounced: ES-tus. ... High school: Douglas (Minden, Nev.).

TRANSACTIONS/CAREER NOTES: Selected by Seattle Mariners organization in first round (11th pick overall) of 1991 free-agent draft. ... Traded by Mariners with IF Wilson Delgado to San Francisco Giants for P Salomon Torres (May 21, 1995). ... On disabled list (March 23-April 6, 1997). ... On disabled list (July 11-September 4, 1998); included rehabilitation assignments to Bakersfield and Fresno. ... On disabled list (March 29-April 17, 2000); included rehabilitation assignments to Fresno and San Jose. ... On disabled list (May 9-24 and August 23, 2001-remainder of season). ... Traded by Giants to New York Mets for OF Tsuyoshi Shinjo and SS Desi Relaford (December 16, 2001). ... Traded by Mets with cash to Cincinnati Reds for P Pedro Feliciano, OF Elvin Andujar and two players to be named (August 15, 2002); Mets acquired OF Raul Gonzalez (August 20, 2002) and OF Brady Clark (September 9, 2002) to complete deal. ... Signed as a free agent by Chicago Cubs (December 20, 2002). ... Signed as a free agent by Colorado Rockies organization (January 23, 2004).

CAREER HITTING: 75-for-459 (.163), 47 R, 14 2B, 1 3B, 4 HR, 28 RBI.

Year	Team (League)	W	L	Pct.	ERA	WHIP	G	GS	CG	ShO	Hld.	Sv.-Opp.	IP	H	R	ER	HR	BB-IBB	SO	Avg.
1991— Bellingham (N'west)		1	3	.250	6.88	2.41	9	9	0	0	...	0-...	34.0	27	33	26	2	55-0	35	.218
1992— Bellingham (N'west)		3	3	.500	4.32	1.68	15	15	0	0	...	0-...	77.0	84	55	37	6	45-0	77	.279
1993— Appleton (Midw.)		5	9	.357	7.24	1.92	19	18	0	0	...	0-...	83.1	108	85	67	3	52-1	65	.305
1994— Ariz. Mariners (Ariz.)		0	3	.000	3.15	1.10	5	5	0	0	...	0-...	20.0	16	9	7	0	6-0	31	.205
— Appleton (Midw.)		0	2	.000	4.58	1.83	5	4	0	0	...	0-...	19.2	19	13	10	1	17-0	28	.271
1995— Wisconsin (Midw.)		0	0	...	0.90	1.00	2	2	0	0	...	0-...	10.0	5	1	1	0	5-0	11	.156
— Burlington (Midw.)		0	0	...	4.11	1.63	4	4	0	0	...	0-...	15.1	13	8	7	2	12-0	22	.224
— San Jose (California)		5	2	.714	2.17	0.99	8	8	0	0	...	0-...	49.2	32	13	12	1	17-0	61	.188
— Shreveport (Texas)		2	0	1.000	2.01	1.07	4	4	0	0	...	0-...	22.1	14	5	5	1	10-0	18	.184
— San Francisco (N.L.)		0	3	.000	6.75	1.21	3	3	0	0	0	0-0	17.1	16	14	13	2	5-0	14	.229
1996— Phoenix (PCL)		9	3	.750	3.43	1.18	18	18	0	0	...	0-0	110.1	92	43	42	7	38-1	95	.228
— San Francisco (N.L.)		3	5	.375	3.60	1.46	11	11	0	0	0	0-0	70.0	63	30	28	2	39-3	60	.243
1997— San Francisco (N.L.)		19	5	.792	3.18	1.30	32	32	3	2	0	0-0	201.0	162	80	71	12	100-2	181	.223
1998— San Francisco (N.L.)		7	12	.368	5.06	1.54	25	25	1	1	0	0-0	149.1	150	89	84	14	80-6	136	.269
— Bakersfield (California)		0	0	...	0.00	0.92	1	1	0	0	...	0-...	4.1	3	0	0	0	1-0	5	.188
— Fresno (PCL)		1	0	1.000	1.80	1.20	1	1	0	0	...	0-...	5.0	3	1	1	0	3-0	6	.188
1999— San Francisco (N.L.)		11	11	.500	4.92	1.58	32	32	1	1	0	0-0	203.0	209	121	111	21	112-2	159	.268
2000— Fresno (PCL)		0	1	.000	9.00	2.33	1	1	0	0	...	0-...	3.0	5	3	3	2	2-0	2	.294
— San Jose (California)		1	0	1.000	0.00	0.43	1	1	0	0	...	0-...	7.0	2	0	0	0	1-0	11	.095
— San Francisco (N.L.)		15	6	.714	4.26	1.59	30	30	4	2	0	0-0	190.1	194	99	90	11	108-1	136	.275
2001— San Francisco (N.L.)		9	8	.529	4.02	1.43	27	27	0	0	0	0-0	159.0	151	78	71	11	77-7	109	.253
2002— New York (N.L.)		4	9	.308	4.55	1.50	23	23	1	1	0	0-0	132.2	133	70	67	12	66-9	92	.267
— Cincinnati (N.L.)		1	3	.250	7.71	1.96	6	6	0	0	0	0-0	28.0	38	24	24	1	17-0	17	.345
2003— Chicago (N.L.)		8	11	.421	5.73	1.74	29	28	1	1	0	0-0	152.1	182	113	97	20	83-1	103	.305
2004— Colorado (N.L.)		15	8	.652	5.84	1.62	34	34	1	0	0	0-0	202.0	223	* 133	* 131	30	105-5	117	.291
Major League totals (10 years)		92	81	.532	4.71	1.54	252	251	12	8	0	0-0	1505.0	1521	851	787	137	792-36	1124	.268

DIVISION SERIES RECORD

Year	Team (League)	W	L	Pct.	ERA	WHIP	G	GS	CG	ShO	Hld.	Sv.-Opp.	IP	H	R	ER	HR	BB-IBB	SO	Avg.
1997— San Francisco (N.L.)		0	0	...	15.00	3.00	1	1	0	0	0	0-0	3.0	5	5	5	1	4-0	3	.357
2000— San Francisco (N.L.)		0	0	...	6.00	2.00	1	1	0	0	0	0-0	3.0	3	2	2	0	3-0	3	.250
Division series totals (2 years)		0	0	...	10.50	2.50	2	2	0	0	0	0-0	6.0	8	7	7	1	7-0	6	.308

ALL-STAR GAME RECORD

	W	L	Pct.	ERA	WHIP	G	GS	CG	ShO	Hld.	Sv.-Opp.	IP	H	R	ER	HR	BB-IBB	SO	Avg.
All-Star Game totals (1 year)	0	1	.000	18.00	2.00	1	0	0	0	0	0-0	1.0	1	2	2	0	1-0	1	.250

ESTRADA, JOHNNY — C

PERSONAL: Born June 27, 1976, in Hayward, Calif. ... 5-11/209. ... Bats both, throws right. ... Full name: Johnny P. Estrada. ... High school: Roosevelt (Fresno, Calif.). ... Junior college: College of the Sequoias (Calif.).

TRANSACTIONS/CAREER NOTES: Selected by Houston Astros organization in 71st round of 1994 free-agent draft; did not sign. ... Selected by Philadelphia Phillies organization in 17th round of 1997 free-agent draft. ... Traded by Phillies to Atlanta Braves for P Kevin Millwood (December 20, 2002).

2004 GAMES PLAYED BY POSITION (MLB): C—133.

E

Year	Team (League)	Pos.	G	AB	R	H	2B	3B	HR	RBI	BB	SO	HBP	GDP	SB-CS	Avg.	OBP	SLG	OPS	E	Avg.
											BATTING									FIELDING	
1997—	Batavia (NY-Penn)	C-1B	58	223	28	70	17	2	6	43	9	15	1	9	0-0	.314	.336	.489	.825	0	1.000
1998—	Piedmont (S. Atl.)	C	77	303	33	94	14	2	7	44	6	19	5	11	0-1	.310	.331	.439	.770	6	.990
	—Clearwater (FSL)	C	37	117	8	26	8	0	0	13	5	7	0	2	0-0	.222	.250	.291	.541	5	.979
1999—	Clearwater (FSL)	C	98	346	35	96	15	0	9	52	14	26	2	12	1-0	.277	.303	.399	.702	5	.990
2000—	Reading (East.)	C	95	356	42	105	18	0	12	42	10	20	4	8	1-0	.295	.322	.447	.768	7	.990
2001—	Scran./W.B. (I.L.)	C	32	131	13	38	13	0	0	16	5	6	1	5	0-0	.290	.319	.389	.708	0	1.000
	—Philadelphia (N.L.)	C	89	298	26	68	15	0	8	37	16	32	4	15	0-0	.228	.273	.359	.632	4	.993
2002—	Scran./W.B. (I.L.)	C	118	434	49	121	27	0	11	67	26	53	5	19	1-0	.279	.322	.417	.739	4	.995
	—Philadelphia (N.L.)	C	10	17	0	2	1	0	0	2	2	2	0	0	0-0	.118	.211	.176	.387	1	1.000
2003—	Richmond (Int'l)	C-DH	106	354	40	116	29	0	10	66	30	30	12	11	0-0	.328	.393	.494	.887	4	.994
	—Atlanta (N.L.)	C	16	36	2	11	0	0	0	2	0	3	3	1	0-0	.306	.359	.306	.665	0	1.000
2004—	Atlanta (N.L.)	C	134	462	56	145	36	0	9	76	39	66	11	18	0-0	.314	.378	.450	.828	9	.989
	Major League totals (4 years)		249	813	84	226	52	0	17	117	57	103	18	34	0-0	.278	.336	.405	.741	13	.991

DIVISION SERIES RECORD

Year	Team (League)	Pos.	G	AB	R	H	2B	3B	HR	RBI	BB	SO	HBP	GDP	SB-CS	Avg.	OBP	SLG	OPS	E	Avg.
2004—	Atlanta (N.L.)	C	5	17	3	6	0	0	2	4	3	3	0	0	0-0	.353	.429	.706	1.134	0	1.000

ALL-STAR GAME RECORD

		G	AB	R	H	2B	3B	HR	RBI	BB	SO	HBP	GDP	SB-CS	Avg.	OBP	SLG	OPS	E	Avg.
All-Star Game totals (1 year)		1	2	0	0	0	0	0	0	0	1	0	0	0-0	.000	.000	.000	.000	0	1.000

ESTRELLA, LEO — P

PERSONAL: Born February 20, 1975, in Puerto Plata, Dominican Republic. ... 6-1/188. ... Throws right, bats right. ... Full name: Leoncio Ramirez Estrella. ... Name pronounced: LE-ON-cio es-TRAY-yah. ... High school: Liceo Padre Las Casas (Puerto Plata, Dominican Republic).

TRANSACTIONS/CAREER NOTES: Signed as a non-drafted free agent by New York Mets organization (October 12, 1993). ... Traded by Mets to Toronto Blue Jays for IF/OF Tony Phillips (July 31, 1998). ... Traded by Blue Jays with P Clayton Andrews to Cincinnati Reds for P Steve Parris (November 22, 2000). ... Claimed on waivers by New York Mets (June 14, 2001). ... Claimed on waivers by Reds (July 17, 2001). ... Signed as a free agent by Milwaukee Brewers organization (January 17, 2003). ... Traded by Brewers with P Wayne Franklin to San Francisco Giants for Ps Carlos Villanueva and Glenn Woolard (March 30, 2004).

CAREER HITTING: 0-for-0 (.000), 0 R, 0 2B, 0 3B, 0 HR, 0 RBI.

Year	Team (League)	W	L	Pct.	ERA	WHIP	G	GS	CG	ShO	Hld.	Sv.-Opp.	IP	H	R	ER	HR	BB-IBB	SO	Avg.
1994—	Dom. Mets (DSL)	5	0	1.000	3.47	1.79	30	0	0	0	...	3-...	36.1	33	28	14	...	32-...	20	...
1995—	Dom. Mets (DSL)	2	4	.333	5.44	1.72	12	8	0	0	...	0-...	43.0	61	37	26	...	13-...	32	...
1996—	Kingsport (Appalachian)	6	3	.667	3.88	1.34	15	7	1	0	...	0-...	58.0	54	32	25	3	24-0	52	.248
1997—	Pittsfield (N.Y.-Penn.)	7	6	.538	3.03	1.28	15	15	0	0	...	0-...	92.0	91	48	31	0	27-0	55	.253
1998—	Capital City (S. Atl.)	10	8	.556	3.93	1.20	20	20	3	0	...	0-...	119.0	120	66	52	10	23-0	97	.261
	—Hagerstown (S. Atl.)	1	3	.250	4.50	1.57	5	5	0	0	...	0-...	30.0	34	19	15	0	13-1	27	.304
1999—	Dunedin (Fla. St.)	14	7	.667	3.21	1.27	27	24	2	2	...	0-...	168.0	166	74	60	11	47-0	116	.267
2000—	Tennessee (Sou.)	5	5	.500	3.67	1.29	13	13	3	2	...	0-...	76.0	68	36	31	6	30-1	63	.246
	—Syracuse (Int'l)	5	4	.556	4.01	1.29	15	15	3	1	...	0-...	89.2	68	42	40	8	40-0	48	.215
	—Toronto (A.L.)	0	0	...	5.79	1.93	2	0	0	0	...	0-...	4.2	9	3	3	1	0-0	3	.450
2001—	Chattanooga (Southern) ...	0	1	.000	3.68	1.16	3	3	0	0	...	0-...	14.2	13	6	6	0	4-0	14	.241
	—Louisville (Int'l)	1	1	.500	4.88	1.50	34	5	0	0	...	1-...	62.2	67	36	34	8	27-0	37	.277
	—Norfolk (Int'l)	2	0	1.000	3.12	1.79	8	1	0	0	...	0-...	17.1	23	7	6	1	8-0	10	.354
2002—	West Tenn (Sou.)	2	2	.500	3.28	1.26	10	3	0	0	...	0-...	24.2	23	13	9	0	8-0	18	.250
	—Iowa (PCL)	0	0	...	5.91	1.59	8	0	0	0	...	1-...	10.2	10	8	7	0	7-0	9	.238
	—New Haven (East.)	2	2	.500	4.81	1.68	14	5	0	0	...	0-...	39.1	46	30	21	0	20-0	23	.289
2003—	Indianapolis (Int'l)	1	0	1.000	1.20	1.00	7	0	0	0	...	0-...	15.0	9	2	2	1	6-0	12	.170
	—Milwaukee (N.L.)	7	3	.700	4.36	1.45	58	0	0	0	9	3-8	66.0	75	32	32	10	21-5	25	.290
2004—	San Francisco (N.L.)	0	0		27.00	6.75	2	0	0	0	0	0-0	1.1	8	4	4	0	1-0	0	.727
	—Fresno (PCL)	0	8	.000	7.65	2.03	38	5	0	0	...	0-...	77.2	125	71	66	15	33-0	34	.368
	American League totals (1 year)	0	0	...	5.79	1.93	2	0	0	0	...	0-...	4.2	9	3	3	1	0-0	3	.450
	National League totals (2 years)	7	3	.700	4.81	1.56	60	0	0	0	9	3-8	67.1	83	36	36	10	22-5	25	.307
	Major League totals (3 years)	7	3	.700	4.78	1.58	62	0	0	0	9	3-8	72.0	92	39	39	11	22-5	28	.317

EVERETT, ADAM — SS

PERSONAL: Born February 5, 1977, in Austell, Ga. ... 6-0/170. ... Bats right, throws right. ... Full name: Jeffrey Adam Everett. ... High school: Harrison (Kennesaw, Ga.). ... College: South Carolina.

TRANSACTIONS/CAREER NOTES: Selected by Chicago Cubs organization in fourth round of 1995 free-agent draft; did not sign. ... Selected by Boston Red Sox organization in first round (12th pick overall) of 1998 free-agent draft. ... Traded by Red Sox with P Greg Miller to Houston Astros for OF Carl Everett (December 14, 1999). ... On disabled list (August 7-September 29, 2004).

2004 GAMES PLAYED BY POSITION (MLB): SS—99.

Year	Team (League)	Pos.	G	AB	R	H	2B	3B	HR	RBI	BB	SO	HBP	GDP	SB-CS	Avg.	OBP	SLG	OPS	E	Avg.
											BATTING									FIELDING	
1998—	Lowell (NY-Penn)	SS	21	71	11	21	6	2	0	9	11	13	3	2	2-1	.296	.407	.437	.844	9	.918
1999—	Trenton (East.)	SS	98	338	56	89	11	0	10	44	41	64	10	3	21-5	.263	.356	.385	.741	18	.959
2000—	New Orleans (PCL)	SS	126	453	82	111	25	2	5	37	75	100	11	6	13-4	.245	.363	.342	.705	25	.959
2001—	New Orleans (PCL)	SS	114	441	69	110	20	8	5	40	39	74	16	4	24-5	.249	.330	.365	.695	24	.956
	—Houston (N.L.)	SS	9	3	1	0	0	0	0	0	0	1	0	0	1-0	.000	.000	.000	.000	2	.667
2002—	Houston (N.L.)	SS	40	88	11	17	3	0	0	4	12	19	1	1	3-0	.193	.297	.227	.524	5	.962
	—New Orleans (PCL)	SS	88	345	51	95	16	7	2	25	24	59	6	3	12-3	.275	.331	.380	.710	7	.984
2003—	New Orleans (PCL)	SS-2B	25	100	23	25	6	1	1	9	7	16	1	1	3-1	.250	.306	.360	.666	2	.982
	—Houston (N.L.)	SS	128	387	51	99	18	3	8	51	28	59	9	7	8-1	.256	.320	.380	.700	17	.970
2004—	Houston (N.L.)	SS	104	384	66	105	15	2	8	31	17	56	9	4	13-2	.273	.317	.385	.703	10	.977
	Major League totals (4 years)		281	862	129	221	36	5	16	86	57	142	19	12	25-3	.256	.315	.365	.681	34	.970

DIVISION SERIES RECORD

Year	Team (League)	Pos.	G	AB	R	H	2B	3B	HR	RBI	BB	SO	HBP	GDP	SB-CS	Avg.	OBP	SLG	OPS	E	Avg.
2004—	Houston (N.L.)	SS	2	0	0	0	0	0	0	0	0	0	0	0	0-0	...	...	...	...	0	...

CHAMPIONSHIP SERIES RECORD

Year	Team (League)	Pos.	G	AB	R	H	2B	3B	HR	RBI	BB	SO	HBP	GDP	SB-CS	Avg.	OBP	SLG	OPS	E	Avg.
2004—	Houston (N.L.)	SS	3	1	0	0	0	0	0	0	0	0	0	0	0-0	.000	.000	.000	.000	0	1.000

E

EVERETT, CARL — OF

PERSONAL: Born June 3, 1971, in Tampa, Fla. ... 6-0/215. ... Bats both, throws right. ... Full name: Carl Edward Everett. ... High school: Hillsborough (Tampa).

TRANSACTIONS/CAREER NOTES: Selected by New York Yankees organization in first round (10th pick overall) of 1990 free-agent draft. ... Selected by Florida Marlins in second round (27th pick overall) of expansion draft (November 17, 1992). ... On disabled list (July 23-August 10, 1994). ... Traded by Marlins to New York Mets for 2B Quilvio Veras (November 29, 1994). ... On disabled list (April 12-27, 1996). ... Traded by Mets to Houston Astros for P John Hudek (December 22, 1997). ... On disabled list (July 16-August 6, 1999). ... Traded by Astros to Boston Red Sox for SS Adam Everett and P Greg Miller (December 14, 1999). ... On suspended list (July 24-August 5, 2000; and March 29-30, 2001). ... On Boston disabled list (June 22-July 28, 2001; included rehabilitation assignments to Sarasota and GCL Red Sox. ... Traded by Red Sox to Texas Rangers for P Darren Oliver (December 13, 2001). ... On disabled list (May 5-21 and June 3-July 2, 2002); included rehabilitation assignment to Charlotte. ... Traded by Rangers to Chicago White Sox for three players to be named (July 1, 2003); Rangers acquired Ps Frank Francisco and Josh Rupe and OF Anthony Webster to complete deal (July 24, 2003). ... Signed as a free agent by Montreal Expos (December 19, 2003). ... On disabled list (April 15-May 17 and May 30-June 16, 2004); included rehabilitation assignment to Brevard County. ... Traded by Expos to Chicago White Sox for Ps Jon Rauch and Gary Majewski (July 18, 2004).

2004 GAMES PLAYED BY POSITION (MLB): DH—44, OF—34.

Year	Team (League)	Pos.	G	AB	R	H	2B	3B	HR	RBI	BB	SO	HBP	GDP	SB-CS	Avg.	OBP	SLG	OPS	E	Avg.
1990—	GC Yankees (GCL)	OF	48	185	28	48	8	5	1	14	15	38	6	1	15-2	.259	.333	.373	.706	5	.932
1991—	Greensboro (S. Atl.)	OF	123	468	96	127	18	0	4	40	57	122	23	1	28-19	.271	.376	.335	.711	7	.974
1992—	Fort Laud. (FSL)	OF	46	183	30	42	8	2	2	9	12	40	4	1	11-3	.230	.291	.328	.619	3	.975
—	Prince Will. (Car.)	OF	6	22	7	7	0	0	4	9	5	7	0	0	1-0	.318	.444	.864	1.308	0	1.000
1993—	High Desert (Calif.)	OF	59	253	48	73	12	6	10	52	22	73	6	3	24-9	.289	.358	.502	.860	2	.985
—	Florida (N.L.)	OF	11	19	0	2	0	0	0	1	0	9	0	1	0-0	.105	.150	.105	.255	1	.857
—	Edmonton (PCL)	OF	35	136	28	42	13	4	6	16	19	45	2	1	12-1	.309	.401	.596	.997	2	.976
1994—	Edmonton (PCL)	OF-DH	78	321	63	108	17	2	11	47	19	65	4	7	16-13	.336	.380	.505	.884	2	.989
—	Florida (N.L.)	OF	16	51	7	11	1	0	2	6	3	15	0	0	4-0	.216	.259	.353	.612	0	1.000
1995—	New York (N.L.)	OF	79	289	48	75	13	1	12	54	39	67	2	11	2-5	.260	.352	.436	.788	3	.981
—	Norfolk (Int'l)	OF-SS-DH	67	260	52	78	16	4	6	35	20	47	4	2	12-6	.300	.358	.462	.819	0	1.000
1996—	New York (N.L.)	OF	101	192	29	46	8	1	1	16	21	53	4	4	6-0	.240	.326	.307	.633	7	.935
1997—	New York (N.L.)	OF	142	443	58	110	28	3	14	57	32	102	7	3	17-9	.248	.308	.420	.728	4	.971
1998—	Houston (N.L.)	OF	133	467	72	138	34	4	15	76	44	102	3	11	14-12	.296	.359	.482	.840	4	.987
1999—	Houston (N.L.)	OF-DH	123	464	86	151	33	3	25	108	50	94	11	5	27-7	.325	.398	.571	.969	6	.978
2000—	Boston (A.L.)	OF-DH	137	496	82	149	32	4	34	108	52	113	8	4	11-4	.300	.373	.587	.959	6	.980
2001—	Boston (A.L.)	OF-DH	102	409	61	105	24	4	14	58	27	104	13	3	9-2	.257	.323	.438	.761	5	.974
—	Sarasota (Fla. St.)	DH	2	7	0	3	0	0	0	0	2	0	0	0	0-0	.429	.556	.429	.984	...	...
—	GC Red Sox (GCL)	OF	3	10	2	2	0	0	0	2	1	3	0	0	0-0	.200	.273	.800	1.073	0	1.000
2002—	Texas (A.L.)	OF-DH	105	374	47	100	16	0	16	62	33	77	6	7	2-3	.267	.333	.439	.772	5	.969
—	Charlotte (Fla. St.)	OF	1	4	1	2	0	1	0	1	0	1	0	0	0-0	.500	.500	1.000	1.500	0	1.000
2003—	Texas (A.L.)	OF-DH	74	270	53	74	13	3	18	51	31	48	5	2	4-1	.274	.356	.544	.900	2	.986
—	Chicago (A.L.)	OF-DH	73	256	40	77	14	0	10	41	22	36	10	5	4-3	.301	.377	.473	.850	2	1.000
2004—	Brevard County (FSL)	OF-DH	5	15	2	6	1	0	0	3	2	3	0	0	0-0	.400	.444	.467	.911	0	1.000
—	Montreal (N.L.)	OF-DH	39	127	8	32	10	0	2	14	8	19	5	8	0-0	.252	.319	.378	.697	3	.955
—	Chicago (A.L.)	DH-OF	43	154	21	41	7	1	5	21	8	26	5	3	1-0	.266	.320	.422	.742	0	1.000
	American League totals (5 years)		534	1959	304	546	106	12	97	341	173	404	47	24	31-13	.279	.349	.494	.843	20	.979
	National League totals (8 years)		644	2052	308	565	127	12	71	331	198	461	32	42	71-33	.275	.346	.453	.799	31	.974
	Major League totals (12 years)		1178	4011	612	1111	233	24	168	672	371	865	79	66	102-46	.277	.348	.473	.820	51	.976

DIVISION SERIES RECORD

Year	Team (League)	Pos.	G	AB	R	H	2B	3B	HR	RBI	BB	SO	HBP	GDP	SB-CS	Avg.	OBP	SLG	OPS	E	Avg.
1998—	Houston (N.L.)	OF	4	13	1	2	0	0	0	0	4	0	1	0	0-0	.154	.154	.154	.308	0	1.000
1999—	Houston (N.L.)	OF	4	15	2	2	0	0	0	1	2	8	1	0	1-0	.133	.263	.133	.396	0	1.000
	Division series totals (2 years)		8	28	3	4	0	0	0	1	2	12	1	1	1-0	.143	.219	.143	.362	0	1.000

ALL-STAR GAME RECORD

		G	AB	R	H	2B	3B	HR	RBI	BB	SO	HBP	GDP	SB-CS	Avg.	OBP	SLG	OPS	E	Avg.
	All-Star Game totals (2 years)	2	3	0	0	0	0	0	1	1	0	0	0	0-0	.000	.250	.000	.250	0	1.000

EYRE, SCOTT — P

PERSONAL: Born May 30, 1972, in Inglewood, Calif. ... 6-1/210. ... Throws left, bats left. ... Full name: Scott Alan Eyre. ... Name pronounced: AIR. ... High school: Cyprus (Magna, Utah). ... Junior college: Southern Idaho.

TRANSACTIONS/CAREER NOTES: Selected by Texas Rangers organization in ninth round of 1991 free-agent draft. ... Traded by Rangers to Chicago White Sox for SS Esteban Beltre (March 28, 1994). ... On disabled list (August 31-September 26, 1999); included rehabilitation assignment to Charlotte. ... Traded by White Sox to Toronto Blue Jays for P Gary Glover (November 7, 2000). ... Claimed on waivers by San Francisco Giants (August 8, 2002). ... On disabled list (March 27-April 22, 2004); included rehabilitation assignment to Fresno.

CAREER HITTING: 2-for-9 (.222), 0 R, 0 2B, 0 3B, 0 HR, 0 RBI.

Year	Team (League)	W	L	Pct.	ERA	WHIP	G	GS	CG	ShO	Hld.	Sv.-Opp.	IP	H	R	ER	HR	BB-IBB	SO	Avg.
1992—	Butte (Pio.)	7	3	.700	2.90	1.36	15	14	2	1	...	0-...	80.2	71	30	26	6	39-0	94	.241
1993—	Char., S.C. (SAL)	11	7	.611	3.45	1.21	26	26	0	0	...	0-...	143.2	115	74	55	6	59-1	154	.220
1994—	South Bend (Mid.)	8	4	.667	3.47	1.30	19	18	2	0	...	0-...	111.2	108	56	43	7	37-0	111	.248
1995—	GC White Sox (GCL)	0	0	.000	2.30	1.02	9	9	0	0	...	0-...	27.1	16	7	7	0	12-0	40	.174
1996—	Birmingham (Southern)	12	7	.632	4.38	1.57	27	27	0	0	...	0-...	158.1	170	90	77	12	79-3	137	.277
1997—	Birmingham (Southern)	13	5	.722	3.84	1.30	22	22	0	0	...	0-...	126.2	110	61	54	14	55-2	127	.231
—	Chicago (A.L.)	4	4	.500	5.04	1.53	11	11	0	0	0	0-0	60.2	62	36	34	11	31-1	36	.267
1998—	Chicago (A.L.)	3	8	.273	5.38	1.66	33	17	0	0	0	0-0	107.0	114	78	64	24	64-0	73	.271
1999—	Charlotte (Int'l)	6	4	.600	3.82	1.43	12	11	0	0	...	0-0	68.1	75	32	29	3	23-1	63	.284
—	Chicago (A.L.)	1	1	.500	7.56	2.12	21	0	0	0	1	0-0	25.0	38	22	21	6	15-2	17	.339
2000—	Chicago (A.L.)	1	1	.500	6.63	2.16	13	1	0	0	0	0-0	19.0	29	15	14	3	12-0	16	.372
—	Charlotte (Int'l)	3	2	.600	3.00	1.10	47	0	0	0	...	12-...	48.0	33	18	16	1	20-3	46	.200
2001—	Syracuse (Int'l)	4	6	.400	3.18	1.17	62	2	0	0	...	0-...	79.1	67	30	28	8	26-4	96	.224
—	Toronto (A.L.)	1	2	.333	3.45	1.40	17	0	0	0	3	2-3	15.2	15	6	6	1	7-2	16	.263
2002—	Toronto (A.L.)	2	4	.333	4.97	1.55	49	3	0	0	12	0-1	63.1	69	37	35	4	29-7	51	.278
—	San Francisco (N.L.)	0	0	...	1.59	1.59	21	0	0	0	6	0-0	11.1	11	4	2	0	7-1	7	.256
2003—	San Francisco (N.L.)	2	1	.667	3.32	1.51	74	0	0	0	20	1-3	57.0	60	23	21	4	26-0	35	.268
2004—	Fresno (PCL)	0	0	...	0.00	1.67	3	0	0	0	...	0-...	3.0	3	0	0	0	2-0	1	.250
—	San Francisco (N.L.)	2	2	.500	4.10	1.33	83	0	0	0	23	1-5	52.2	43	26	24	8	27-3	49	.219
	American League totals (6 years)	12	20	.375	5.39	1.67	144	32	0	0	16	2-4	290.2	327	194	174	49	158-12	209	.285
	National League totals (3 years)	4	3	.571	3.50	1.44	178	0	0	0	49	2-8	121.0	114	53	47	12	60-4	91	.246
	Major League totals (8 years)	16	23	.410	4.83	1.60	322	32	0	0	65	4-12	411.2	441	247	221	61	218-16	300	.274

E

DIVISION SERIES RECORD

Year Team (League)	W	L	Pct.	ERA	WHIP	G	GS	CG	ShO	Hld.	Sv.-Opp.	IP	H	R	ER	HR	BB-IBB	SO	Avg.
2002— San Francisco (N.L.)	0	0	...	0.00	0.75	3	0	0	0	1	0-0	1.1	1	0	0	0	0-0	0	.200
2003— San Francisco (N.L.)	0	0	...	0.00	...	1	0	0	0	0	0-0	.1	0	0	0	0	0-0	0	.000
Division series totals (2 years)	0	0	...	0.00	0.60	4	0	0	0	1	0-0	1.2	1	0	0	0	0-0	0	.167

CHAMPIONSHIP SERIES RECORD

Year Team (League)	W	L	Pct.	ERA	WHIP	G	GS	CG	ShO	Hld.	Sv.-Opp.	IP	H	R	ER	HR	BB-IBB	SO	Avg.
2002— San Francisco (N.L.)	0	0	...	0.00	1.20	4	0	0	0	0	0-0	1.2	2	0	0	0	0-0	0	.286

WORLD SERIES RECORD

Year Team (League)	W	L	Pct.	ERA	WHIP	G	GS	CG	ShO	Hld.	Sv.-Opp.	IP	H	R	ER	HR	BB-IBB	SO	Avg.
2002— San Francisco (N.L.)	0	0	...	0.00	2.00	3	0	0	0	0	0-0	3.0	5	1	0	0	1-1	2	.385

FALKENBORG, BRIAN — P

PERSONAL: Born January 18, 1978, in Newport Beach, Calif. ... 6-6/190. ... Throws right, bats right. ... Full name: Brian Thomas Falkenborg. ... High school: Redmond (Wash.).

TRANSACTIONS/CAREER NOTES: Selected by Baltimore Orioles organization in second round of 1996 free-agent draft. ... On disabled list (March 23, 2000-entire season). ... Released by Orioles (December 19, 2000). ... Signed by Seattle Mariners organization (January 24, 2001). ... Signed as a free agent by Los Angeles Dodgers organization (November 10, 2003). ... On disabled list (April 5-24, 2004); included rehabilitation assignment to Las Vegas.

CAREER HITTING: 0-for-2 (.000), 1 R, 0 2B, 0 3B, 0 HR, 0 RBI.

Year Team (League)	W	L	Pct.	ERA	WHIP	G	GS	CG	ShO	Hld.	Sv.-Opp.	IP	H	R	ER	HR	BB-IBB	SO	Avg.
1996— GC Orioles (GCL)	0	3	.000	2.57	1.04	8	6	0	0	...	0-...	28.0	21	13	8	1	8-0	36	.196
— High Desert (Calif.)	0	0	...	0.00	1.00	1	0	0	0	...	0-...	1.0	1	0	0	0	0-0	1	.333
1997— Delmarva (S.Atl.)	7	9	.438	4.46	1.32	25	25	0	0	...	0-...	127.0	122	73	63	6	46-2	107	.253
— Bowie (East.)	0	1	.000	16.20	3.60	1	1	0	0	...	0-...	1.2	3	3	3	0	3-0	0	.375
1998— Frederick (Caro.)	5	5	.500	4.50	1.29	15	14	1	1	...	0-...	78.0	83	42	39	6	18-0	70	.267
1999— Bowie (East.)	3	6	.333	3.78	1.36	16	16	0	0	...	0-...	83.1	77	40	35	11	36-0	77	.242
— GC Orioles (GCL)	1	0	1.000	2.00	1.00	3	2	0	0	...	0-...	9.0	6	2	2	0	3-0	11	.176
— Baltimore (A.L.)	0	0	...	0.00	1.33	2	0	0	0	0	0-0	3.0	2	0	0	0	2-0	1	.200
2001— San Antonio (Texas)	5	6	.455	5.45	1.58	12	12	2	1	...	0-...	66.0	80	47	40	9	24-0	56	.305
— Tacoma (PCL)	2	4	.333	4.47	1.41	8	8	0	0	...	0-...	48.1	50	25	24	6	18-0	27	.273
2002— Tacoma (PCL)	4	4	.500	2.74	1.30	9	9	0	0	...	0-...	49.1	51	22	15	3	13-0	42	.267
2003— Tacoma (PCL)	4	2	.667	2.94	1.20	17	14	0	0	...	0-...	79.2	66	28	26	7	26-0	62	.221
2004— Los Angeles (N.L.)	1	0	1.000	7.53	1.95	6	0	0	0	0	0-0	14.1	19	14	12	2	9-0	11	.322
— Las Vegas (PCL)	4	6	.400	6.17	1.45	18	16	0	0	...	1-...	89.0	104	66	61	17	25-0	87	.286
American League totals (1 year)	0	0	...	0.00	1.33	2	0	0	0	0	0-0	3.0	2	0	0	0	2-0	1	.200
National League totals (1 year)	1	0	1.000	7.53	1.95	6	0	0	0	0	0-0	14.1	19	14	12	2	9-0	11	.322
Major League totals (2 years)	1	0	1.000	6.23	1.85	8	0	0	0	0	0-0	17.1	21	14	12	2	11-0	12	.304

FARNSWORTH, KYLE — P

PERSONAL: Born April 14, 1976, in Wichita, Kan. ... 6-4/240. ... Throws right, bats right. ... Full name: Kyle Lynn Farnsworth. ... High school: Milton (Alpharetta, Ga.). ... Junior college: Abraham Baldwin (Ga.).

TRANSACTIONS/CAREER NOTES: Selected by Chicago Cubs organization in 47th round of 1994 free-agent draft. ... On disabled list (April 10-June 4, 2002); included rehabilitation assignment to Iowa. ... On suspended list (June 26-28, 2003). ... On disabled list (August 28-September 12, 2004).

CAREER HITTING: 4-for-54 (.074), 3 R, 1 2B, 0 3B, 0 HR, 3 RBI.

Year Team (League)	W	L	Pct.	ERA	WHIP	G	GS	CG	ShO	Hld.	Sv.-Opp.	IP	H	R	ER	HR	BB-IBB	SO	Avg.
1995— GC Cubs (GCL)	3	2	.600	0.87	1.06	16	0	0	0	...	1-...	31.0	22	8	3	0	11-0	18	.214
1996— Rockford (Midwest)	9	6	.600	3.70	1.40	20	20	1	0	...	0-...	112.0	122	62	46	7	35-0	82	.274
1997— Daytona (Fla. St.)	10	10	.500	4.09	1.44	27	27	2	0	...	0-...	156.1	178	91	71	13	47-1	105	.286
1998— West Tenn (Sou.)	8	2	.800	2.77	1.12	13	13	0	0	...	0-...	81.1	70	32	25	6	21-0	73	.231
— Iowa (PCL)	5	9	.357	6.93	1.61	18	18	0	0	...	0-...	102.2	129	88	79	18	36-0	79	.309
1999— Iowa (PCL)	2	2	.500	3.20	1.19	6	6	0	0	...	0-...	39.1	38	16	14	5	9-0	29	.262
— Chicago (N.L.)	5	9	.357	5.05	1.48	27	21	1	1	0	0-0	130.0	140	80	73	28	52-1	70	.271
2000— Chicago (N.L.)	2	9	.182	6.43	1.82	46	5	0	0	6	1-6	77.0	90	58	55	14	50-8	74	.291
— Iowa (PCL)	0	2	.000	3.20	1.66	22	0	0	0	9	9-...	25.1	24	10	9	1	18-2	22	.250
2001— Chicago (N.L.)	4	6	.400	2.74	1.15	76	0	0	0	24	2-3	82.0	65	26	25	8	29-2	107	.213
2002— Chicago (N.L.)	4	6	.400	7.33	1.65	45	0	0	0	6	1-7	46.2	53	47	38	9	24-7	46	.293
— Iowa (PCL)	0	1	.000	6.00	1.00	2	0	0	0	...	0-...	3.0	3	2	2	1	0-0	2	.273
2003— Chicago (N.L.)	3	2	.600	3.30	1.17	77	0	0	0	19	0-3	76.1	53	31	28	6	36-1	92	.196
2004— Chicago (N.L.)	4	5	.444	4.73	1.50	72	0	0	0	18	0-4	66.2	67	39	35	10	33-1	78	.260
Major League totals (6 years)	22	37	.373	4.78	1.45	343	26	1	1	73	4-23	478.2	468	281	254	75	224-20	467	.254

DIVISION SERIES RECORD

Year Team (League)	W	L	Pct.	ERA	WHIP	G	GS	CG	ShO	Hld.	Sv.-Opp.	IP	H	R	ER	HR	BB-IBB	SO	Avg.
2003— Chicago (N.L.)	0	0	...	0.00	0.75	3	0	0	0	1	0-0	2.2	1	0	0	0	1-0	2	.111

CHAMPIONSHIP SERIES RECORD

Year Team (League)	W	L	Pct.	ERA	WHIP	G	GS	CG	ShO	Hld.	Sv.-Opp.	IP	H	R	ER	HR	BB-IBB	SO	Avg.
2003— Chicago (N.L.)	0	0	...	10.13	1.50	5	0	0	0	0	0-0	5.1	6	6	6	0	2-2	7	.300

FASSERO, JEFF — P

PERSONAL: Born January 5, 1963, in Springfield, Ill. ... 6-1/200. ... Throws left, bats left. ... Full name: Jeffrey Joseph Fassero. ... Name pronounced: fuh-SAIR-oh. ... High school: Griffin (Springfield, Ill.). ... College: Mississippi.

TRANSACTIONS/CAREER NOTES: Selected by St. Louis Cardinals organization in 22nd round of June 1984 free-agent draft. ... Selected by Chicago White Sox organization from Cardinals organization in Rule 5 minor league draft (December 5, 1989). ... Released by White Sox (April 3, 1990). ... Signed by Cleveland Indians organization (April 9, 1990). ... Signed as a free agent by Montreal Expos organization (January 3, 1991). ... On disabled list (July 24-August 11, 1994). ... Traded by Expos with P Alex Pacheco to Seattle Mariners for C Chris Widger and Ps Trey Moore and Matt Wagner (October 29, 1996). ... On disabled list (March 22-April 12, 1998). ... Traded by Mariners to Texas Rangers for a player to named (August 27, 1999); Mariners acquired OF Adrian Myers to complete deal (September 22, 1999). ... Signed as a free agent by Boston Red Sox (December 22, 1999). ... On disabled list (June 19-July 5, 2000). ... Signed as a free agent by Chicago Cubs (December 8, 2000). ... Traded by Cubs with cash to Cardinals for two players to be named (August 24, 2002); Cubs acquired Ps Jason Karnuth and Jared Blasdell to complete deal (September 24, 2002). ... On suspended list (May 2-4,

F

2003). ... Signed as a free agent by Colorado Rockies organization (January 13, 2004). ... Released by Rockies (September 24, 2004). ... Signed by Arizona Diamondbacks (September 29, 2004).

CAREER HITTING: 22-for-259 (.085), 19 R, 2 2B, 1 3B, 0 HR, 6 RBI.

Year Team (League)	W	L	Pct.	ERA	WHIP	G	GS	CG	ShO	Hld.	Sv.-Opp.	IP	H	R	ER	HR	BB-IBB	SO	Avg.
1984— Johnson City (App.)	4	7	.364	4.59	1.56	13	11	2	0	...	1-...	66.2	65	42	34	2	39-0	59	.261
1985— Springfield (Mid.)	4	8	.333	4.01	1.43	29	15	1	0	...	1-...	119.0	125	78	53	11	45-3	65	.262
1986— St. Pete. (FSL)	13	7	.650	2.45	1.20	26	26	6	1	...	0-...	176.0	156	63	48	5	56-4	112	.239
1987— Arkansas (Texas)	10	7	.588	4.10	1.55	28	27	2	1	...	0-...	151.1	168	90	69	16	67-7	118	.283
1988— Arkansas (Texas)	5	5	.500	3.58	1.77	70	1	0	0	...	17-...	78.0	97	48	31	1	41-13	72	.301
1989— Louisville (A.A.)	3	10	.231	5.22	1.63	22	19	0	0	...	0-...	112.0	136	79	65	13	47-1	73	.302
— Arkansas (Texas)	4	1	.800	1.64	1.00	6	6	2	1	...	0-...	44.0	32	11	8	1	12-0	38	.200
1990— Cant./Akr. (Eastern)	5	4	.556	2.80	1.40	61	0	0	0	...	6-...	64.1	66	24	20	5	24-6	61	.263
1991— Indianapolis (A.A.)	3	0	1.000	1.47	0.98	18	0	0	0	...	4-...	18.1	11	3	3	1	7-3	12	.177
— Montreal (N.L.)	2	5	.286	2.44	1.01	51	0	0	0	7	8-11	55.1	39	17	15	1	17-1	42	.196
1992— Montreal (N.L.)	8	7	.533	2.84	1.34	70	0	0	0	12	1-7	85.2	81	35	27	1	34-6	63	.249
1993— Montreal (N.L.)	12	5	.706	2.29	1.16	56	15	1	0	6	1-3	149.2	119	50	38	7	54-0	140	.216
1994— Montreal (N.L.)	8	6	.571	2.99	1.15	21	21	1	0	0	0-0	138.2	119	54	46	13	40-4	119	.229
1995— Montreal (N.L.)	13	14	.481	4.33	1.49	30	30	0	0	0	0-0	189.0	207	102	91	15	74-3	164	.283
1996— Montreal (N.L.)	15	11	.577	3.30	1.17	34	34	5	1	0	0-0	231.2	217	95	85	20	55-3	222	.244
1997— Seattle (A.L.)	16	9	.640	3.61	1.32	35	•35	2	1	0	0-0	234.1	226	108	94	21	84-6	189	.249
1998— Seattle (A.L.)	13	12	.520	3.97	1.29	32	32	7	0	0	0-0	224.2	223	115	99	33	66-2	176	.259
1999— Seattle (A.L.)	4	14	.222	7.38	1.88	30	24	0	0	2	0-0	139.0	188	123	114	34	73-3	101	.321
— Texas (A.L.)	1	0	1.000	5.71	1.73	7	3	0	0	0	0-0	17.1	20	12	11	1	10-0	13	.286
2000— Boston (A.L.)	8	8	.500	4.78	1.56	38	23	0	0	5	0-0	130.0	153	72	69	16	50-2	97	.296
2001— Chicago (A.L.)	4	4	.500	3.42	1.21	82	0	0	0	25	12-17	73.2	66	31	28	6	23-5	79	.235
2002— Chicago (N.L.)	5	6	.455	6.18	1.71	57	0	0	0	6	0-1	51.0	65	37	35	5	22-5	44	.313
— St. Louis (N.L.)	3	0	1.000	3.00	1.17	16	0	0	0	7	0-2	18.0	16	6	6	4	5-0	12	.232
2003— St. Louis (N.L.)	1	7	.125	5.68	1.64	62	6	0	0	11	3-6	77.2	93	51	49	17	34-4	59	.296
2004— Colorado (N.L.)	3	8	.273	5.51	1.62	40	12	0	0	2	0-0	111.0	136	73	68	9	44-5	59	.306
— Arizona (N.L.)	0	0	...	0.00	0.00	1	0	0	0	0	0-0	.0	0	0	0	0	0-0	1	.000
American League totals (4 years)	42	43	.494	4.67	1.47	142	117	9	1	7	0-0	745.1	810	430	387	105	283-13	576	.276
National League totals (10 years)	74	73	.503	3.71	1.32	520	118	8	1	76	25-47	1182.1	1158	551	488	98	402-36	1000	.255
Major League totals (14 years)	116	116	.500	4.09	1.38	662	235	17	2	83	25-47	1927.2	1968	981	875	203	685-49	1576	.263

DIVISION SERIES RECORD

Year Team (League)	W	L	Pct.	ERA	WHIP	G	GS	CG	ShO	Hld.	Sv.-Opp.	IP	H	R	ER	HR	BB-IBB	SO	Avg.
1997— Seattle (A.L.)	1	0	1.000	1.13	0.88	1	1	0	0	0	0-0	8.0	3	1	1	0	4-0	3	.120
1999— Texas (A.L.)	0	0	...	9.00	3.00	1	0	0	0	0	0-0	1.0	2	1	1	0	1-0	1	.400
2002— St. Louis (N.L.)	2	0	1.000	0.00	1.13	3	0	0	0	0	0-0	2.2	3	0	0	0	0-0	2	.300
Division series totals (3 years)	3	0	1.000	1.54	1.11	5	1	0	0	0	0-0	11.2	8	2	2	0	5-0	6	.200

CHAMPIONSHIP SERIES RECORD

Year Team (League)	W	L	Pct.	ERA	WHIP	G	GS	CG	ShO	Hld.	Sv.-Opp.	IP	H	R	ER	HR	BB-IBB	SO	Avg.
2002— St. Louis (N.L.)	0	0	...	0.00	0.00	1	0	0	0	0	0-0	.2	0	0	0	0	0-0	1	.000

FELICIANO, PEDRO — P

PERSONAL: Born August 25, 1976, in Rio Piedras, Puerto Rico. ... 5-10/185. ... Throws left, bats left. ... Full name: Pedro Juan Feliciano. ... High school: Jose S. Alegria (Dorado, Puerto Rico).

TRANSACTIONS/CAREER NOTES: Selected by Los Angeles Dodgers organization in 31st round of 1995 free-agent draft. ... Signed as a free agent by Cincinnati Reds organization (November 19, 2001). ... Traded by Reds with OF Elvin Andujar and two players to be named to New York Mets for P Shawn Estes and cash (August 15, 2002); Mets acquired OF Raul Gonzalez (August 20, 2002) and OF Brady Clark (September 9, 2002) to complete deal. ... Claimed on waivers by Detroit Tigers (October 11, 2002). ... Released by Tigers (December 16, 2002). ... Signed by Mets organization (January 13, 2003).

CAREER HITTING: 0-for-3 (.000), 0 R, 0 2B, 0 3B, 0 HR, 0 RBI.

Year Team (League)	W	L	Pct.	ERA	WHIP	G	GS	CG	ShO	Hld.	Sv.-Opp.	IP	H	R	ER	HR	BB-IBB	SO	Avg.
1995— Great Falls (Pio.)	0	0	...	13.50	2.85	6	0	0	0	...	0-...	6.2	12	12	10	0	7-1	9	.333
1996— Great Falls (Pio.)	2	3	.400	5.71	1.85	22	1	0	0	...	3-...	41.0	50	36	26	1	26-2	39	.291
1997— Savannah (S. Atl.)	3	7	.300	2.64	1.22	36	9	1	0	...	4-...	105.2	90	45	31	11	39-0	94	.230
— Vero Beach (FSL)	0	0	...	4.50	1.50	1	0	0	0	...	0-...	2.0	3	1	1	0	1-0	1	.429
1998— Vero Beach (FSL)	2	5	.286	4.61	1.43	22	10	0	0	...	2-...	68.1	68	44	35	8	30-1	51	.255
1999—				Did not play.															
2000— Vero Beach (FSL)	4	5	.444	3.82	1.63	25	2	0	0	...	0-...	61.1	76	31	26	4	24-1	48	.303
— San Antonio (Texas)	0	0	...	1.93	1.18	9	0	0	0	...	2-...	9.1	7	2	2	0	4-1	11	.226
— Albuquerque (PCL)	0	0	...	18.00	4.00	1	0	0	0	...	0-...	1.0	3	3	2	0	2-0	2	.375
2001— Jacksonville (Southern)	5	4	.556	1.94	0.86	54	0	0	0	...	17-...	60.1	41	14	13	3	11-1	55	.194
— Las Vegas (PCL)	0	1	.000	7.27	2.42	6	0	0	0	...	0-...	8.2	16	11	7	2	5-1	5	.390
2002— Chattanooga (Southern)	2	1	.667	2.56	1.14	28	0	0	0	...	4-...	38.2	33	14	11	1	11-1	26	.234
— Louisville (Int'l)	1	1	.500	3.04	1.46	20	0	0	0	...	0-...	26.2	35	10	9	3	4-0	19	.327
— Norfolk (Int'l)	0	0	...	7.00	1.67	5	0	0	0	...	0-...	9.0	14	7	7	1	1-0	5	.359
— New York (N.L.)	0	0	...	7.50	1.67	6	0	0	0	0	0-0	6.0	9	5	5	0	1-0	4	.360
2003— Norfolk (Int'l)	3	2	.600	3.97	1.10	15	0	0	0	...	1-...	22.2	20	10	10	3	6-1	18	.238
— New York (N.L.)	0	0	...	3.35	1.51	23	0	0	0	0	0-0	48.1	52	21	18	5	21-3	43	.269
2004— Norfolk (Int'l)	4	3	.571	5.30	1.40	32	0	0	0	...	2-...	35.2	35	25	21	4	15-1	25	.259
— New York (N.L.)	1	1	.500	5.40	1.42	22	0	0	0	2	0-0	18.1	14	12	11	2	12-0	14	.209
Major League totals (3 years)	1	1	.500	4.21	1.50	51	0	0	0	2	0-0	72.2	75	38	34	7	34-3	61	.263

FELIZ, PEDRO — 1B/3B

PERSONAL: Born April 27, 1975, in Azua, Dominican Republic. ... 6-1/205. ... Bats right, throws right. ... Full name: Pedro Julio Feliz. ... High school: Augustine de Chequer (Dominican Republic).

TRANSACTIONS/CAREER NOTES: Signed as a non-drafted free agent by San Francisco Giants organization (February 7, 1994).

2004 GAMES PLAYED BY POSITION (MLB): 1B—70, 3B—51, SS—20, OF—4.

Year Team (League)	Pos.	G	AB	R	H	2B	3B	HR	RBI	BB	SO	HBP	GDP	SB-CS	Avg.	OBP	SLG	OPS	E	Avg.
1994— Ariz. Giants (Ariz.)	3B	38	119	7	23	0	0	0	3	2	20	2	3	2-3	.193	.220	.193	.413	5	.953
1995— Bellingham (N'west)	3B-1B	43	113	14	31	2	1	0	16	7	33	0	2	1-1	.274	.311	.310	.621	2	.971

F

Year	Team (League)	Pos.	G	AB	R	H	2B	3B	HR	RBI	BB	SO	HBP	GDP	SB-CS	Avg.	OBP	SLG	OPS	E	Avg.
1996— Burlington (Midw.)	3B-1B	93	321	36	85	12	2	5	36	18	65	1	11	5-2	.265	.303	.361	.665	17	.937
1997— Bakersfield (Calif.)	3B	135	515	59	140	25	4	14	56	23	90	7	15	5-7	.272	.310	.417	.728	23	.950
1998— Shreveport (Texas)	3B	100	364	39	96	23	2	12	50	9	62	2	15	0-1	.264	.282	.437	.719	22	.926
— Fresno (PCL)	3B	3	7	1	3	1	0	1	3	0	1	0	0	0-0	.429	.500	1.000	1.500	0	1.000
1999— Shreveport (Texas)	3B	131	491	52	124	24	6	13	77	19	90	3	18	4-2	.253	.282	.405	.687	27	.934
2000— Fresno (PCL)	3B-SS	128	503	85	150	34	2	33	105	30	94	2	18	1-1	.298	.337	.571	.908	24	.939
— San Francisco (N.L.)	3B	8	7	1	2	0	0	0	0	0	1	0	0	0-0	.286	.286	.286	.571	0	…
2001— San Francisco (N.L.)	3B-DH	94	220	23	50	9	1	7	22	10	50	2	5	2-1	.227	.264	.373	.637	12	.908
2002— San Francisco (N.L.)	3B-SS-OF	67	146	14	37	4	1	2	13	6	27	0	2	0-0	.253	.281	.336	.617	3	.966
2003— San Francisco (N.L.)	3B-OF-1B	95	235	31	58	9	3	16	48	10	53	1	7	2-2	.247	.278	.515	.793	4	.982
2004— San Francisco (N.L.)	1B-3B-SS-OF	144	503	72	139	33	3	22	84	23	85	0	18	5-2	.276	.305	.485	.790	13	.983
Major League totals (5 years)		408	1111	141	286	55	8	47	167	49	216	3	32	9-5	.257	.288	.448	.736	32	.973

DIVISION SERIES RECORD

Year	Team (League)	Pos.	G	AB	R	H	2B	3B	HR	RBI	BB	SO	HBP	GDP	SB-CS	Avg.	OBP	SLG	OPS	E	Avg.
2002— San Francisco (N.L.)		1	1	0	0	0	0	0	0	0	1	0	0	0-0	.000	.000	.000	.000	…	…
2003— San Francisco (N.L.)		3	3	1	2	0	1	0	1	0	1	0	0	0-0	.667	.667	1.333	2.000	0	…
Division series totals (2 years)		4	4	1	2	0	1	0	1	0	2	0	0	0-0	.500	.500	1.000	1.500	0	…

CHAMPIONSHIP SERIES RECORD

Year	Team (League)	Pos.	G	AB	R	H	2B	3B	HR	RBI	BB	SO	HBP	GDP	SB-CS	Avg.	OBP	SLG	OPS	E	Avg.
2002— San Francisco (N.L.)		1	0	0	0	0	0	0	0	0	0	0	0	0-0	.000	.000	.000	.000	…	…

WORLD SERIES RECORD

Year	Team (League)	Pos.	G	AB	R	H	2B	3B	HR	RBI	BB	SO	HBP	GDP	SB-CS	Avg.	OBP	SLG	OPS	E	Avg.
2002— San Francisco (N.L.)	DH	3	5	0	0	0	0	0	0	0	2	0	0	0-0	.000	.000	.000	.000	…	…

FERNANDEZ, JARED — P

PERSONAL: Born February 2, 1972, in Salt Lake City, Utah. ... 6-1/235. ... Throws right, bats right. ... Full name: Jared Wade Fernandez. ... High school: Kearns (Utah). ... College: Fresno State.

TRANSACTIONS/CAREER NOTES: Signed as a non-drafted free agent by Boston Red Sox organization (June 23, 1994). ... Signed as a free agent by Cincinnati Reds organization (December 15, 2000). ... Released by Reds (December 15, 2002). ... Signed by Houston Astros organization (December 20, 2002).

CAREER HITTING: 2-for-21 (.095), 3 R, 0 2B, 0 3B, 0 HR, 1 RBI.

Year	Team (League)	W	L	Pct.	ERA	WHIP	G	GS	CG	ShO	Hld.	Sv.-Opp.	IP	H	R	ER	HR	BB-IBB	SO	Avg.
1994— Utica (N.Y.-Penn)	1	1	.500	3.60	1.70	21	1	0	0	…	4-…	30.0	43	18	12	4	8-2	24	.316
1995— Utica (N.Y.-Penn)	3	2	.600	1.89	1.03	5	5	1	0	…	0-…	38.0	30	11	8	2	9-1	23	.219
— Trenton (East.)	5	4	.556	3.90	1.37	11	10	1	0	…	0-…	67.0	64	32	29	4	28-1	40	.253
1996— Trenton (East.)	9	9	.500	5.08	1.50	30	29	3	0	…	0-…	179.0	185	115	101	19	83-5	94	.268
1997— Trenton (East.)	4	6	.400	5.41	1.68	21	16	1	0	…	0-…	121.1	138	90	73	12	66-0	73	.282
— Pawtucket (Int'l)	0	3	.000	5.79	1.71	11	11	0	0	…	0-…	60.2	76	45	39	7	28-1	33	.311
1998— Trenton (East.)	3	7	.300	5.25	1.55	36	7	0	0	…	1-…	118.1	132	80	69	8	51-3	70	.286
— Pawtucket (Int'l)	1	1	.500	4.74	1.34	5	2	0	0	…	0-…	24.2	26	16	13	5	7-0	15	.274
1999— Trenton (East.)	3	0	1.000	3.38	1.39	7	0	0	0	…	1-…	18.2	18	9	7	4	8-0	10	.250
— Pawtucket (Int'l)	12	9	.571	4.25	1.29	27	20	3	0	…	0-…	163.0	172	88	77	20	39-0	76	.273
2000— Pawtucket (Int'l)	10	4	.714	3.02	1.23	31	9	2	0	…	0-…	113.1	103	51	38	10	36-0	65	.248
2001— Louisville (Int'l)	10	9	.526	4.13	1.39	33	28	4	1	…	0-…	196.1	218	105	90	24	54-0	118	.281
— Cincinnati (N.L.)	0	1	.000	4.38	1.54	5	2	0	0	0	0-0	12.1	13	9	6	1	6-0	5	.265
2002— Louisville (Int'l)	12	5	.706	3.93	1.42	26	18	1	0	…	1-…	128.1	151	63	56	14	31-1	80	.298
— Cincinnati (N.L.)	1	3	.250	4.44	1.64	14	8	0	0	0	0-0	50.2	59	31	25	5	24-1	36	.294
2003— New Orleans (PCL)	7	10	.412	3.81	1.30	26	23	2	0	…	0-…	156.0	164	73	66	16	37-1	51	.270
— Houston (N.L.)	3	3	.500	3.99	1.28	12	6	0	0	0	0-0	38.1	37	17	17	2	12-2	19	.259
2004— Houston (N.L.)	0	0	…	54.00	11.00	2	1	0	0	0	0-0	1.0	6	6	6	0	5-0	0	.750
— New Orleans (PCL)	7	11	.389	4.77	1.30	35	28	3	0	…	0-…	196.1	209	120	104	27	46-2	98	.272
Major League totals (4 years)	4	7	.364	4.75	1.58	33	17	0	0	0	0-0	102.1	115	63	54	8	47-3	60	.287

FETTERS, MIKE — P

PERSONAL: Born December 19, 1964, in Van Nuys, Calif. ... 6-4/230. ... Throws right, bats right. ... Full name: Michael Lee Fetters. ... High school: Iolani (Honolulu, Hawaii). ... College: Pepperdine.

TRANSACTIONS/CAREER NOTES: Selected by Los Angeles Dodgers organization in 22nd round of June 1983 free-agent draft; did not sign. ... Selected by California Angels organization in supplemental round ("sandwich pick" between first and second round, 27th pick overall) of June 1986 free-agent draft; pick received as compensation for Baltimore Orioles signing Type A free-agent OF/IF Juan Beniquez. ... Traded by Angels with P Glenn Carter to Milwaukee Brewers for P Chuck Crim (December 10, 1991). ... On disabled list (May 3-19, 1992; and May 25-June 9, 1995). ... On disabled list (April 4-May 5, 1997); included rehabilitation assignment to Tucson. ... Traded by Brewers with Ps Ben McDonald and Ron Villone to Cleveland Indians for OF Marquis Grissom and P Jeff Juden (December 8, 1997). ... Traded by Indians to Oakland Athletics for P Steve Karsay (December 8, 1997). ... On disabled list (April 6-26, 1998). ... Traded by A's to Anaheim Angels for a player to be named and cash (August 10, 1998). ... Signed as a free agent by Baltimore Orioles organization (February 4, 1999). ... On disabled list (June 7-September 1, 1999); included rehabilitation assignment to Rochester. ... Signed as a free agent by Dodgers organization (December 15, 1999). ... On disabled list (May 4-26, 2000). ... On suspended list (July 21-22, 2000). ... On disabled list (June 20-July 5, 2001). ... Traded by Dodgers with P Adrian Burnside to Pittsburgh Pirates for P Terry Mulholland (July 31, 2001). ... Traded by Pirates to Arizona Diamondbacks for P Duaner Sanchez (July 6, 2002). ... Signed as a free agent by Minnesota Twins organization (January 27, 2003). ... On disabled list (April 5-20 and April 27, 2003-remainder of season). ... Signed as a free agent by Diamondbacks organization (June 20, 2004).

CAREER HITTING: 0-for-0 (.000), 0 R, 0 2B, 0 3B, 0 HR, 0 RBI.

Year	Team (League)	W	L	Pct.	ERA	WHIP	G	GS	CG	ShO	Hld.	Sv.-Opp.	IP	H	R	ER	HR	BB-IBB	SO	Avg.
1986— Salem (N'west)	4	2	.667	3.38	1.54	12	12	1	0	…	0-…	72.0	60	39	27	4	51-0	72	…
1987— Palm Springs (Calif.)	9	7	.563	3.57	1.54	19	19	2	0	…	0-…	116.0	106	62	46	2	73-0	105	.247
1988— Midland (Texas)	8	8	.500	5.92	1.61	20	20	2	0	…	0-…	114.0	116	78	75	10	67-3	101	.262
— Edmonton (PCL)	2	0	1.000	1.93	1.29	2	2	1	0	…	0-…	14.0	8	3	3	0	10-0	11	.170
1989— Edmonton (PCL)	12	8	.600	3.80	1.38	26	26	6	2	…	0-…	168.0	160	80	71	11	72-2	144	.257
— California (A.L.)	0	0	…	8.10	1.80	1	0	0	0	0	0-0	3.1	5	4	3	1	1-0	4	.333
1990— Edmonton (PCL)	1	1	.500	0.99	1.28	5	5	1	1	…	0-…	27.1	22	9	3	0	13-0	26	.218
— California (A.L.)	1	1	.500	4.12	1.43	26	2	0	0	1	1-1	67.2	77	33	31	9	20-0	35	.287
1991— Edmonton (PCL)	2	7	.222	4.87	1.49	11	11	1	0	…	0-…	61.0	65	39	33	5	26-0	43	.279
— California (A.L.)	2	5	.286	4.84	1.81	19	4	0	0	0	0-1	44.2	53	29	24	4	28-2	24	.305
1992— Milwaukee (A.L.)	5	1	.833	1.87	0.99	50	0	0	0	8	2-5	62.2	38	15	13	3	24-2	43	.185

– 144 –

Year	Team (League)	W	L	Pct.	ERA	WHIP	G	GS	CG	ShO	Hld.	Sv.-Opp.	IP	H	R	ER	HR	BB-IBB	SO	Avg.
1993— Milwaukee (A.L.)		3	3	.500	3.34	1.37	45	0	0	0	8	0-0	59.1	59	29	22	4	22-4	23	.278
1994— Milwaukee (A.L.)		1	4	.200	2.54	1.48	42	0	0	0	3	17-20	46.0	41	16	13	0	27-5	31	.243
1995— Milwaukee (A.L.)		0	3	.000	3.38	1.73	40	0	0	0	2	22-27	34.2	40	16	13	3	20-04	33	.286
1996— Milwaukee (A.L.)		3	3	.500	3.38	1.48	61	0	0	0	1	32-38	61.1	65	28	23	4	26-4	53	.274
1997— Tucson (PCL)		0	0	...	10.80	1.20	2	0	0	0	...	0-...	1.2	1	2	2	0	1-0	0	.167
— Milwaukee (A.L.)		1	5	.167	3.45	1.35	51	0	0	0	11	6-11	70.1	62	30	27	4	33-3	62	.244
1998— Oakland (A.L.)		1	6	.143	3.99	1.46	48	0	0	0	10	5-8	47.1	48	26	21	3	21-2	34	.258
— Anaheim (A.L.)		1	2	.333	5.56	1.59	12	0	0	0	1	0-1	11.1	14	8	7	2	4-0	9	.304
1999— Baltimore (A.L.)		1	0	1.000	5.81	1.84	27	0	0	0	2	0-3	31.0	35	23	20	5	22-2	22	.278
— Rochester (Int'l)		0	0	...	0.00	0.55	4	0	0	0	...	0-...	3.2	0	0	0	0	2-0	6	.000
2000— Los Angeles (N.L.)		6	2	.750	3.24	1.20	51	0	0	0	11	5-7	50.0	35	18	18	7	25-2	40	.205
2001— Los Angeles (N.L.)		2	1	.667	6.07	1.55	34	0	0	0	14	1-3	29.2	33	23	20	6	13-0	26	.273
— Pittsburgh (N.L.)		1	1	.500	4.58	1.64	20	0	0	0	0	8-9	17.2	16	9	9	1	13-1	11	.235
2002— Pittsburgh (N.L.)		1	0	1.000	3.26	1.42	32	0	0	0	11	0-1	30.1	25	13	11	3	18-1	29	.219
— Arizona (N.L.)		2	3	.400	5.11	1.91	33	0	0	0	5	0-1	24.2	28	18	14	1	19-5	24	.292
2003— Minnesota (A.L.)		0	0	...	0.00	0.50	5	0	0	0	0	0-0	6.0	2	0	0	0	1-0	1	.100
2004— Tucson (PCL)		0	0	...	4.50	1.50	7	0	0	0	...	1-...	8.0	11	5	4	0	1-0	10	.314
— Arizona (N.L.)		1	0	1.000	8.68	1.98	23	0	0	0	1	1-1	18.2	23	22	18	2	14-2	14	.299
American League totals (12 years)		19	33	.365	3.58	1.44	427	6	0	0	47	85-115	545.2	539	257	217	42	249-28	374	.263
National League totals (4 years)		12	8	.600	4.74	1.53	193	0	0	0	42	15-22	171.0	160	103	90	20	102-11	144	.247
Major League totals (16 years)		31	41	.431	3.86	1.47	620	6	0	0	89	100-137	716.2	699	360	307	62	351-39	518	.259

DIVISION SERIES RECORD

Year	Team (League)	W	L	Pct.	ERA	WHIP	G	GS	CG	ShO	Hld.	Sv.-Opp.	IP	H	R	ER	HR	BB-IBB	SO	Avg.
2002— Arizona (N.L.)		0	0	...	0.00	3.00	1	0	0	0	0	0-0	.2	1	0	0	0	1-0	1	.333

FICK, ROBERT — OF/1B

PERSONAL: Born March 15, 1974, in Torrance, Calif. ... 6-1/205. ... Bats left, throws right. ... Full name: Robert Charles Fick. ... High school: Newbury Park (Calif.). ... College: Cal State Northridge.

TRANSACTIONS/CAREER NOTES: Selected by Oakland Athletics organization in 45th round of 1992 free-agent draft; did not sign. ... Selected by Detroit Tigers organization in 43rd round of 1995 free-agent draft; did not sign. ... Selected by Tigers organization in fifth round of 1996 free-agent draft. ... On disabled list (March 31-September 7, 1999); included rehabilitation assignments to GCL Tigers, West Michigan and Toledo. ... On suspended list (May 23-26, 2000). ... On disabled list (July 6-September 1, 2000); included rehabilitation assignment to Toledo. ... On suspended list (September 22-27, 2001). ... Signed as a free agent by Atlanta Braves organization (January 6, 2003). ... On disabled list (April 13-29, 2003). ... Released by Braves (November 5, 2003). ... Signed by Tampa Bay Devil Rays (January 9, 2004). ... Released by Devil Rays (August 13, 2004). ... Signed by San Diego Padres organization (August 19, 2004).

2004 GAMES PLAYED BY POSITION (MLB): DH—34, OF—21, 1B—11, C—3.

Year	Team (League)	Pos.	G	AB	R	H	2B	3B	HR	RBI	BB	SO	HBP	GDP	SB-CS	Avg.	OBP	SLG	OPS	E	Avg.
										BATTING										FIELDING	
1996— Jamestown (N.Y.-Penn.)		C	43	133	18	33	6	0	1	14	12	25	0	4	3-1	.248	.306	.316	.622	3	.982
1997— W. Mich. (Mid.)		3B-C-1B	122	463	100	158	50	3	16	90	75	74	5	10	13-4	.341	.429	.566	.994	12	.989
1998— Jacksonville (Sou.)		C-1B-OF	130	515	101	164	47	6	18	114	71	83	6	8	8-4	.318	.401	.538	.939	9	.985
— Detroit (A.L.)		C-DH-1B	7	22	6	8	1	0	3	7	2	7	0	1	1-0	.364	.417	.818	1.235	1	.966
1999— GC Tigers (GCL)		DH-C-1B	3	9	2	3	1	0	0	2	2	0	0	0	1-0	.333	.455	.444	.899	0	1.000
— W. Mich. (Mid.)		DH-C-1B	3	11	2	3	0	0	0	0	2	2	0	0	1-0	.273	.385	.273	.657	2	.913
— Toledo (Int'l)		1-C-DH-3	14	48	11	15	0	1	2	8	8	5	1	0	1-0	.313	.414	.479	.893	5	.944
— Detroit (A.L.)		DH-C	15	41	6	9	0	0	3	10	7	6	0	1	1-0	.220	.327	.439	.766	1	1.000
2000— Detroit (A.L.)		1B-C-DH	66	163	18	41	7	2	3	22	22	39	1	4	2-1	.252	.340	.374	.715	5	.983
— Toledo (Int'l)		1B	17	68	5	10	5	0	1	7	6	13	2	0	1-0	.147	.234	.265	.498	0	1.000
2001— Detroit (A.L.)		C-1-DH-O	124	401	62	109	21	2	19	61	39	62	4	10	0-3	.272	.339	.476	.816	7	.989
2002— Detroit (A.L.)		OF-DH	148	556	66	150	36	2	17	63	46	90	7	17	0-1	.270	.331	.433	.764	*12	.963
2003— Atlanta (N.L.)		1B	126	409	52	110	26	1	11	80	42	47	2	9	1-0	.269	.335	.418	.753	14	.987
2004— Tampa Bay (A.L.)		DH-O-1-C	76	214	12	43	5	2	6	26	20	32	2	2	0-0	.201	.273	.327	.600	3	.977
— Portland (PCL)		1B-C	12	50	8	19	4	0	2	6	2	11	0	0	1-0	.380	.404	.580	.984	1	.990
— San Diego (N.L.)		1B	13	12	2	2	0	0	0	0	2	4	1	0	0-0	.167	.333	.167	.500	0	1.000
American League totals (6 years)			436	1397	170	360	70	8	51	189	136	236	14	35	4-5	.258	.327	.429	.755	28	.981
National League totals (2 years)			139	421	54	112	26	1	11	80	44	51	3	9	1-0	.266	.335	.411	.746	14	.987
Major League totals (7 years)			575	1818	224	472	96	9	62	269	180	287	17	44	5-5	.260	.329	.425	.753	42	.983

DIVISION SERIES RECORD

Year	Team (League)	Pos.	G	AB	R	H	2B	3B	HR	RBI	BB	SO	HBP	GDP	SB-CS	Avg.	OBP	SLG	OPS	E	Avg.
2003— Atlanta (N.L.)		1B	4	11	0	0	0	0	0	0	1	2	0	1	0-0	.000	.083	.000	.083	0	1.000

ALL-STAR GAME RECORD

		G	AB	R	H	2B	3B	HR	RBI	BB	SO	HBP	GDP	SB-CS	Avg.	OBP	SLG	OPS	E	Avg.
All-Star Game totals (1 year)		1	2	1	1	0	0	0	0	0	0	0	0	1-0	.500	.500	.500	1.000	0	1.000

FIELD, NATE — P

PERSONAL: Born December 11, 1975, in Denver, Colo. ... 6-2/200. ... Throws right, bats right. ... Full name: Nathan Patrick Field. ... College: Fort Hays State (Kan.).

TRANSACTIONS/CAREER NOTES: Signed as a non-drafted free agent by Montreal Expos organization (June 11, 1998). ... Released by Expos (March 29, 2000). ... Contract purchased by Kansas City Royals organization from Sioux City of the independent Northern League (June 29, 2000). ... Claimed on waivers by New York Yankees (June 12, 2002). ... Signed as a free agent by Royals organization (January 6, 2003). ... On disabled list (August 11, 2004-remainder of season).

CAREER HITTING: 0-for-0 (.000), 0 R, 0 2B, 0 3B, 0 HR, 0 RBI.

Year	Team (League)	W	L	Pct.	ERA	WHIP	G	GS	CG	ShO	Hld.	Sv.-Opp.	IP	H	R	ER	HR	BB-IBB	SO	Avg.
1998— Vermont (NY-P)		3	1	.750	3.09	1.23	25	0	0	0	...	2-...	35.0	32	16	12	1	11-0	39	.237
1999— Cape Fear (S. Atl.)		4	8	.333	5.40	1.49	42	0	0	0	...	2-...	65.0	75	49	39	8	22-2	55	.282
— Ottawa (Int'l)		0	0	...	3.00	2.67	2	0	0	0	...	0-...	3.0	4	1	1	0	4-0	4	.333
2000— Sioux City (Nor.)		3	0	1.000	1.93	1.37	11	0	0	0	...	0-...	23.1	17	10	5	...	15-...	19	...
— Char., W.Va. (SAL)		1	2	.333	2.23	1.18	17	0	0	0	...	0-...	36.1	28	10	9	2	15-0	31	.215
2001— Wichita (Texas)		4	2	.667	1.48	1.08	52	0	0	0	...	19-...	73.0	61	16	12	3	18-3	67	.222
2002— Omaha (PCL)		0	1	.000	3.31	1.84	18	0	0	0	...	7-...	16.1	22	10	6	0	8-0	13	.301
— Kansas City (A.L.)		0	0	...	9.00	2.20	5	0	0	0	0	0-0	5.0	8	5	5	2	3-1	3	.364
— Columbus (Int'l)		2	1	.667	6.75	1.73	21	0	0	0	...	0-...	38.2	46	30	29	6	21-1	25	.305

F

Year	Team (League)	W	L	Pct.	ERA	WHIP	G	GS	CG	ShO	Hld.	Sv.-Opp.	IP	H	R	ER	HR	BB-IBB	SO	Avg.
2003—Wichita (Texas)		1	0	1.000	3.60	1.40	15	0	0	0	...	3-...	20.0	20	9	8	2	8-1	20	.256
—Omaha (PCL)		2	2	.500	3.18	0.80	19	0	0	0	...	4-...	22.2	15	8	8	4	4-0	17	.188
—Kansas City (A.L.)		1	1	.500	4.15	1.52	19	0	0	0	2	0-0	21.2	19	10	10	3	14-1	19	.235
2004—Kansas City (A.L.)		2	3	.400	4.26	1.33	43	0	0	0	2	3-5	44.1	40	25	21	5	19-2	30	.241
Major League totals (3 years)		3	4	.429	4.56	1.45	67	0	0	0	4	3-5	71.0	67	40	36	10	36-4	52	.249

FIGGINS, CHONE — 3B/OF

PERSONAL: Born January 22, 1978, in Leary, Ga. ... 5-8/160. ... Bats both, throws right. ... Full name: Desmond DeChone Figgins. ... Name pronounced: shawn. ... High school: Brandon (Fla.).

TRANSACTIONS/CAREER NOTES: Selected by Colorado Rockies organization in fourth round of 1997 free-agent draft. ... Traded by Rockies to Anaheim Angels for OF Kimera Bartee (July 13, 2001).

2004 GAMES PLAYED BY POSITION (MLB): 3B—92, OF—57, 2B—20, SS—13, DH—1.

									BATTING								FIELDING		
Year	Team (League)	Pos.	G	AB	R	H	2B	3B	HR	RBI	BB	SO	HBP	GDP	SB-CS	Avg.	OBP	SLG	OPS	E	Avg.
1997—Ariz. Rockies (Ariz.)	SS	54	214	41	60	5	6	1	23	35	51	3	2	30-12	.280	.386	.374	.760	40	.865
1998—Portland (N'west)	SS	69	269	41	76	9	3	1	26	24	56	2	3	25-4	.283	.345	.349	.694	16	.947
1999—Salem (Caro.)	SS	123	444	65	106	12	3	0	22	41	86	3	5	27-13	.239	.306	.279	.585	45	.925
2000—Salem (Caro.)	2B	134	522	92	145	26	14	3	48	67	107	1	7	37-19	.278	.358	.398	.756	28	.955
2001—Carolina (Southern)	2B-SS	86	332	41	73	14	5	2	25	40	73	2	0	27-8	.220	.306	.310	.616	16	.963
—Arkansas (Texas)	2B-SS-3B	39	138	21	37	12	2	0	12	14	26	0	0	7-2	.268	.329	.384	.713	10	.945
2002—Salt Lake (PCL)	2B-SS	125	511	100	156	25	18	7	62	53	83	0	0	39-8	.305	.364	.466	.830	23	.964
—Anaheim (A.L.)	2B	15	12	6	2	1	0	0	1	0	5	0	1	2-1	.167	.167	.250	.417	1	.941
2003—Salt Lake (PCL)	2-S-OF-3	68	285	55	89	14	15	4	30	29	36	3	4	16-6	.312	.379	.509	.888	17	.949
—Anaheim (A.L.)	OF-2-S-DH	71	240	34	71	9	4	0	27	20	38	0	1	13-7	.296	.345	.367	.711	3	.985
2004—Anaheim (A.L.)	3-O-2-S-DH	148	577	83	171	22	17	5	60	49	94	0	6	34-13	.296	.350	.419	.770	15	.964
Major League totals (3 years)		234	829	123	244	32	21	5	88	69	137	0	8	49-21	.294	.346	.402	.748	19	.970

DIVISION SERIES RECORD

Year	Team (League)	Pos.	G	AB	R	H	2B	3B	HR	RBI	BB	SO	HBP	GDP	SB-CS	Avg.	OBP	SLG	OPS	E	Avg.
2002—Anaheim (A.L.)	DH	1	0	1	0	0	0	0	0	0	0	0	0	1-0	...	...	...	...	...	...
2004—Anaheim (A.L.)	2B-3B	3	14	0	2	0	0	0	0	0	5	1	0	1-0	.143	.200	.143	.343	2	.875
Division series totals (2 years)		4	14	1	2	0	0	0	0	0	5	1	0	2-0	.143	.200	.143	.343	2	.875

CHAMPIONSHIP SERIES RECORD

Year	Team (League)	Pos.	G	AB	R	H	2B	3B	HR	RBI	BB	SO	HBP	GDP	SB-CS	Avg.	OBP	SLG	OPS	E	Avg.
2002—Anaheim (A.L.)		3	1	2	1	0	0	0	0	0	0	0	0	0-0	1.000	1.000	1.000	2.000		

WORLD SERIES RECORD

Year	Team (League)	Pos.	G	AB	R	H	2B	3B	HR	RBI	BB	SO	HBP	GDP	SB-CS	Avg.	OBP	SLG	OPS	E	Avg.
2002—Anaheim (A.L.)		2	0	1	0	0	0	0	0	0	0	0	0	0-0	...	...	...	...		

FIGUEROA, NELSON — P

PERSONAL: Born May 18, 1974, in Brooklyn, N.Y. ... 6-1/178. ... Throws right, bats right. ... Full name: Nelson Walter Figueroa. ... Name pronounced: fig-uh-ROE-uh. ... High school: Abraham Lincoln (Brooklyn, N.Y.). ... College: Brandeis (Mass.).

TRANSACTIONS/CAREER NOTES: Selected by New York Mets organization in 30th round of 1995 free-agent draft. ... Traded by Mets with OF Bernard Gilkey and cash to Arizona Diamondbacks for P Willie Blair, C Jorge Fabregas and cash considerations (July 31, 1998). ... Traded by Diamondbacks with OF Travis Lee and Ps Omar Daal and Vicente Padilla to Philadelphia Phillies for P Curt Schilling (July 26, 2000). ... Claimed on waivers by Milwaukee Brewers (April 3, 2002). ... On disabled list (May 6-21, 2002). ... Released by Brewers (October 11, 2002). ... Signed by Pittsburgh Pirates organization (January 13, 2003). ... Released by Pirates (October 12, 2004).

CAREER HITTING: 10-for-56 (.179), 5 R, 1 2B, 0 3B, 0 HR, 5 RBI.

Year	Team (League)	W	L	Pct.	ERA	WHIP	G	GS	CG	ShO	Hld.	Sv.-Opp.	IP	H	R	ER	HR	BB-IBB	SO	Avg.
1995—Kingsport (Appalachian)	7	3	.700	3.07	1.03	12	12	2	2	...	0-...	76.1	57	31	26	3	22-1	79	.210
1996—Capital City (S. Atl.)	14	7	.667	2.04	0.96	26	25	8	4	...	0-...	185.1	119	55	42	10	58-1	200	.181
1997—Binghamton (Eastern)	5	11	.313	4.34	1.43	33	22	0	0	...	0-...	143.0	137	76	69	14	68-1	116	.257
1998—Binghamton (Eastern)	12	3	.800	4.66	1.43	21	21	3	2	...	0-...	123.2	133	73	64	19	44-2	116	.275
—Tucson (PCL)	2	2	.500	3.70	1.50	7	7	0	0	...	0-...	41.1	46	22	17	8	16-1	29	.288
1999—Tucson (PCL)	11	6	.647	3.94	1.32	24	21	1	1	...	0-...	128.0	128	59	56	16	41-0	106	.261
—Ariz. D'backs (Ariz.)	0	1	.000	0.00	1.00	1	1	0	0	...	0-...	3.0	3	1	0	0	0-0	2	.273
2000—Arizona (N.L.)	9	4	.692	2.81	1.15	17	16	1	0	...	0-...	112.0	101	41	35	9	28-2	78	.239
—Arizona (N.L.)	0	1	.000	7.47	1.40	3	3	0	0	...	0-0	15.2	17	13	13	4	5-0	7	.283
—Scran./W.B. (I.L.)	4	3	.571	3.78	1.22	8	8	1	0	...	0-0	50.0	50	28	21	9	11-0	35	.259
2001—Scran./W.B. (I.L.)	4	2	.667	2.47	1.05	13	12	3	0	...	0-0	87.1	74	33	24	6	18-2	74	.224
—Philadelphia (N.L.)	4	5	.444	3.94	1.48	19	13	0	0	0	0-0	89.0	95	40	39	8	37-3	61	.275
2002—Milwaukee (N.L.)	1	7	.125	5.03	1.43	30	11	0	0	1	0-0	93.0	96	59	52	18	37-6	51	.270
—Indianapolis (Int'l)	5	0	1.000	3.63	1.31	6	6	0	0	...	0-0	39.2	39	18	16	2	13-0	25	.253
2003—Nashville (PCL)	12	5	.706	2.97	1.20	23	23	3	1	...	0-0	151.1	144	54	50	11	37-5	121	.251
—Pittsburgh (N.L.)	2	1	.667	3.31	1.16	12	3	0	0	...	0-0	35.1	26	13	13	8	13-2	23	.207
2004—Nashville (PCL)	12	8	.600	4.20	1.34	25	23	4	1	...	0-0	152.1	168	79	71	20	36-1	129	.279
—Pittsburgh (N.L.)	0	3	.000	5.72	1.52	10	3	0	0	...	0-0	28.1	32	18	18	4	11-1	10	.302
Major League totals (5 years)	7	17	.292	4.65	1.42	74	33	0	0	1	0-0	261.1	268	143	135	42	103-12	152	.270

FIKAC, JEREMY — P

PERSONAL: Born April 8, 1975, in Shiner, Texas. ... 6-2/185. ... Throws right, bats right. ... Full name: Jeremy Joseph Fikac. ... Name pronounced: FEE-kotch. ... High school: Somerville (Texas). ... College: Texas State.

TRANSACTIONS/CAREER NOTES: Selected by San Diego Padres organization in 19th round of 1998 free-agent draft. ... Traded by Padres to Oakland Athletics for a player to be named (January 2, 2003). ... Signed as a free agent by Montreal Expos organization (December 26, 2003).

CAREER HITTING: 0-for-2 (.000), 0 R, 0 2B, 0 3B, 0 HR, 0 RBI.

Year	Team (League)	W	L	Pct.	ERA	WHIP	G	GS	CG	ShO	Hld.	Sv.-Opp.	IP	H	R	ER	HR	BB-IBB	SO	Avg.
1998—Idaho Falls (Pioneer)	2	0	1.000	2.25	0.95	12	0	0	0	...	1-...	20.0	11	6	5	0	8-1	19	.153
1999—Rancho Cuca. (Calif.)	8	3	.727	5.08	1.61	40	6	0	0	...	0-...	85.0	94	50	48	7	43-0	75	.283
2000—Rancho Cuca. (Calif.)	5	3	.625	1.80	0.93	61	0	0	0	...	20-...	75.0	46	19	15	2	24-0	101	.174

F

Year	Team (League)	W	L	Pct.	ERA	WHIP	G	GS	CG	ShO	Hld.	Sv.-Opp.	IP	H	R	ER	HR	BB-IBB	SO	Avg.
2001—Mobile (Sou.)		6	0	1.000	1.97	1.08	53	0	0	0	...	18-...	68.2	54	16	15	3	20-4	75	.219
—Portland (PCL)		0	0	...	3.00	1.00	1	0	0	0	...	0-...	3.0	3	1	1	0	0-0	3	.250
—San Diego (N.L.)		2	0	1.000	1.37	0.76	23	0	0	0	6	0-2	26.1	15	6	4	2	5-1	19	.165
2002—San Diego (N.L.)		4	7	.364	5.48	1.57	65	0	0	0	12	0-6	69.0	74	50	42	13	34-8	66	.267
—Mobile (Sou.)		1	0	1.000	3.00	1.67	3	0	0	0	...	1-...	3.0	5	1	1	0	0-0	0	.455
2003—Sacramento (PCL)		3	3	.500	2.25	0.90	42	0	0	0	...	4-...	56.0	40	19	14	4	13-1	50	.197
—Oakland (A.L.)		0	1	.000	4.50	1.56	14	0	0	0	2	0-0	16.0	14	8	8	4	11-1	9	.246
2004—Montreal (N.L.)		1	2	.333	5.40	1.56	19	0	0	0	2	0-0	25.0	26	16	15	5	13-4	22	.274
—Edmonton (PCL)		5	5	.500	5.88	1.60	28	0	0	0	...	1-...	41.1	45	30	27	9	21-1	34	.274
American League totals (1 year)		0	1	.000	4.50	1.56	14	0	0	0	2	0-0	16.0	14	8	8	4	11-1	9	.246
National League totals (3 years)		7	9	.438	4.56	1.39	107	0	0	0	20	0-8	120.1	115	72	61	20	52-13	107	.248
Major League totals (4 years)		7	10	.412	4.56	1.41	121	0	0	0	22	0-8	136.1	129	80	69	24	63-14	116	.248

FILE, BOB — P

PERSONAL: Born January 28, 1977, in Philadelphia, Pa. ... 6-4/215. ... Throws right, bats right. ... Full name: Robert Michael File. ... High school: Father Judge (Philadelphia). ... College: Philadelphia College of Textiles.

TRANSACTIONS/CAREER NOTES: Selected by Toronto Blue Jays organization in 19th round of 1998 free-agent draft. ... On disabled list (March 27-April 16 and April 24-May 22, 2002); included rehabilitation assignment to Dunedin. ... On disabled list (March 21-August 19, 2003); included rehabilitation assignments to Dunedin and Syracuse. ... On disabled list (March 26-May 14, 2004); included rehabilitation assignment to Syracuse.

CAREER HITTING: 0-for-1 (.000), 0 R, 0 2B, 0 3B, 0 HR, 0 RBI.

Year	Team (League)	W	L	Pct.	ERA	WHIP	G	GS	CG	ShO	Hld.	Sv.-Opp.	IP	H	R	ER	HR	BB-IBB	SO	Avg.
1998—Medicine Hat (Pio.)		2	1	.667	1.41	0.91	28	0	0	0	...	16-...	32.0	24	7	5	1	5-0	28	.211
1999—Dunedin (Fla. St.)		4	1	.800	1.70	0.83	47	0	0	0	...	26-...	53.0	30	13	10	2	14-0	48	.165
2000—Tennessee (Sou.)		4	3	.571	3.12	1.21	36	0	0	0	...	20-...	34.2	29	20	12	1	13-0	40	.215
—Syracuse (Int'l)		2	0	1.000	0.93	0.83	20	0	0	0	...	8-...	19.1	14	2	2	1	2-0	10	.212
2001—Tennessee (Sou.)		0	0	...	3.00	1.00	3	0	0	0	...	1-...	3.0	3	1	1	1	0-0	2	.300
—Toronto (A.L.)		5	3	.625	3.27	1.16	60	0	0	0	6	0-2	74.1	57	28	27	6	29-8	38	.220
—Syracuse (Int'l)		0	0	...	0.00	0.25	2	0	0	0	...	0-...	4.0	1	0	0	0	1-0	3	.083
2002—Dunedin (Fla. St.)		0	2	.000	11.12	2.82	4	3	0	0	...	0-...	5.2	13	9	7	0	3-0	1	.448
—Toronto (A.L.)		0	1	.000	18.90	3.00	5	0	0	0	1	0-0	3.1	8	7	7	0	2-0	2	.471
—Syracuse (Int'l)		0	0	...	5.94	1.49	33	0	0	0	...	2-...	36.1	39	29	24	2	15-1	23	.269
2003—Dunedin (Fla. St.)		0	0	...	0.00	1.00	3	2	0	0	...	0-...	3.0	3	1	1	0	0-0	0	.273
—Syracuse (Int'l)		0	0	...	4.22	1.10	11	0	0	0	...	0-...	10.2	10	5	5	0	7-0	11	.250
2004—Syracuse (Int'l)		3	3	.500	2.57	1.09	24	0	0	0	...	7-...	35.0	31	11	10	2	7-0	11	.237
—Toronto (A.L.)		1	0	1.000	4.81	1.69	24	0	0	0	2	0-0	33.2	45	19	18	4	12-2	15	.331
Major League totals (3 years)		6	4	.600	4.20	1.37	89	0	0	0	9	0-2	111.1	110	54	52	10	43-10	55	.267

FINLEY, STEVE — OF

PERSONAL: Born March 12, 1965, in Union City, Tenn. ... 6-2/194. ... Bats left, throws left. ... Full name: Steven Allen Finley. ... High school: Paducah (Ky.) Tilghman. ... College: Southern Illinois.

TRANSACTIONS/CAREER NOTES: Selected by Atlanta Braves organization in 11th round of June 1986 free-agent draft; did not sign. ... Selected by Baltimore Orioles organization in 13th round of 1987 free-agent draft. ... On disabled list (April 4-22, 1989). ... On disabled list (July 29-September 1, 1989); included rehabilitation assignment to Hagerstown. ... Traded by Orioles with Ps Pete Harnisch and Curt Schilling to Houston Astros for 1B Glenn Davis (January 10, 1991). ... On disabled list (April 25-May 14, 1993). ... On disabled list (June 13-July 3, 1994); included rehabilitation assignment to Jackson. ... Traded by Astros with 3B Ken Caminiti, SS Andujar Cedeno, 1B Roberto Petagine, P Brian Williams and a player to be named to San Diego Padres for OFs Phil Plantier and Derek Bell, Ps Pedro Martinez and P Doug Brocail, IF Craig Shipley and SS Ricky Gutierrez (December 28, 1994); Padres acquired P Sean Fesh to complete deal (May 1, 1995). ... On disabled list (April 20-May 6, 1997); included rehabilitation assignment to Rancho Cucamonga. ... Signed as a free agent by Arizona Diamondbacks (December 18, 1998). ... Traded by Diamondbacks with C Brent Mayne to Los Angeles Dodgers for C Koyie Hill, P Bill Murphy and OF Reggie Abercrombie (July 31, 2004). ... Career major league pitching: 0-0, 0.00 ERA, 1 G, 1.0 IP, 0 H, 0 ER, 1 BB, 0 SO.

HONORS: Won N.L. Gold Glove as outfielder (1995, 1996, 1999, 2000 and 2004).

2004 GAMES PLAYED BY POSITION (MLB): OF—158, DH—1.

Year	Team (League)	Pos.	G	AB	R	H	2B	3B	HR	RBI	BB	SO	HBP	GDP	SB-CS	Avg.	OBP	SLG	OPS	E	Avg.
1987—Newark (NY-Penn)	OF	54	222	40	65	13	2	3	33	22	24	2	4	26-5	.293	.359	.410	.769	4	.970
—Hagerstown (Car.)	OF	15	65	9	22	3	2	1	5	1	6	0	2	7-2	.338	.348	.492	.841	0	1.000
1988—Hagerstown (Car.)	OF	8	28	2	6	2	0	0	3	4	3	0	2	4-0	.214	.313	.286	.598	0	1.000
—Charlotte (Sou.)	OF	10	40	7	12	4	2	1	6	4	3	1	1	2-0	.300	.378	.575	.953	0	1.000
—Rochester (Int'l)	OF	120	456	61	143	19	7	5	54	28	55	0	4	20-11	.314	.352	.419	.771	12	.962
1989—Baltimore (A.L.)	DH-OF	81	217	35	54	5	2	2	25	15	30	1	3	17-3	.249	.298	.318	.616	2	.986
—Rochester (Int'l)	OF	7	25	2	4	0	0	0	2	1	5	0	0	3-0	.160	.192	.160	.352	0	1.000
—Hagerstown (East.)	OF	11	48	11	20	3	1	0	7	4	3	0	0	4-0	.417	.453	.521	.974	3	.925
1990—Baltimore (A.L.)	DH-OF	142	464	46	119	16	4	3	37	32	53	2	8	22-9	.256	.304	.328	.632	7	.977
1991—Houston (N.L.)	OF	159	596	84	170	28	10	8	54	42	65	2	8	34-18	.285	.331	.406	.737	5	.985
1992—Houston (N.L.)	OF	*162	607	84	177	29	13	5	55	58	63	3	10	44-9	.292	.355	.407	.762	3	.993
1993—Houston (N.L.)	OF	142	545	69	145	15	*13	8	44	28	65	3	8	19-6	.266	.304	.385	.689	4	.988
1994—Houston (N.L.)	OF	94	373	64	103	16	5	11	33	28	52	2	3	13-7	.276	.329	.434	.764	4	.982
—Jackson (Texas)	OF-DH	5	13	3	4	0	0	0	0	4	0	0	0	1-0	.308	.471	.308	.778	0	1.000
1995—San Diego (N.L.)	OF	139	562	104	167	23	8	10	44	59	62	3	8	36-12	.297	.366	.420	.786	7	.977
1996—San Diego (N.L.)	OF	161	655	126	195	45	9	30	95	56	87	4	20	22-8	.298	.354	.531	.885	7	.982
1997—San Diego (N.L.)	OF	143	560	101	146	26	5	28	92	43	92	3	10	15-3	.261	.313	.475	.788	4	.989
—Mobile (Sou.)	DH	1	4	1	2	0	0	1	2	1	2	0	0	0-0	.500	.600	1.250	1.850	...	...
—Rancho Cuca. (Calif.)	DH-OF	4	14	3	4	0	0	2	3	3	2	1	0	1-0	.286	.444	.714	1.159	0	...
1998—San Diego (N.L.)	OF	159	619	92	154	40	6	14	67	45	103	3	9	12-3	.249	.301	.401	.702	5	.981
1999—Arizona (N.L.)	OF-DH	156	590	100	156	32	10	34	103	63	94	3	4	8-4	.264	.361	.525	.886	2	.995
2000—Arizona (N.L.)	OF-DH	152	539	100	151	27	5	35	96	65	87	8	9	12-6	.280	.361	.544	.904	3	.992
2001—Arizona (N.L.)	OF	140	495	66	136	27	4	14	73	47	67	1	8	11-7	.275	.337	.430	.767	2	.994
2002—Arizona (N.L.)	OF	150	505	82	145	24	4	25	89	65	73	3	10	16-4	.287	.370	.499	.869	2	.994
2003—Arizona (N.L.)	OF	147	516	82	148	24	*10	22	70	57	94	6	6	15-8	.287	.363	.500	.863	5	.982
2004—Arizona (N.L.)	OF-DH	104	404	61	111	16	1	23	48	40	52	1	9	8-4	.275	.338	.490	.828	2	.991
—Los Angeles (N.L.)	OF	58	224	31	59	12	0	13	46	21	30	0	5	1-3	.263	.324	.491	.815	1	.993
American League totals (2 years)		223	681	81	173	21	6	5	62	47	83	3	11	39-12	.254	.302	.325	.627	9	.980
National League totals (14 years)		2066	7790	1246	2163	384	103	280	1009	717	1086	45	127	266-102	.278	.340	.461	.801	58	.988
Major League totals (16 years)		2289	8471	1327	2336	405	109	285	1071	764	1169	48	138	305-114	.276	.337	.450	.787	67	.987

F

DIVISION SERIES RECORD

Year Team (League)	Pos.	G	AB	R	H	2B	3B	HR	RBI	BB	SO	HBP	GDP	SB-CS	Avg.	OBP	SLG	OPS	E	Avg.
1996— San Diego (N.L.)	OF	3	12	0	1	0	0	0	1	0	4	1	0	1-0	.083	.154	.083	.237	0	1.000
1998— San Diego (N.L.)	OF	4	10	2	1	1	0	0	1	1	4	0	0	0-0	.100	.182	.200	.382	0	1.000
1999— Arizona (N.L.)	OF	4	13	0	5	1	0	0	5	3	1	0	1	0-0	.385	.500	.462	.962	0	1.000
2001— Arizona (N.L.)	OF	5	19	1	8	1	0	0	2	0	2	0	0	0-0	.421	.421	.474	.895	0	1.000
2002— Arizona (N.L.)	OF	3	9	1	2	0	0	0	1	2	2	0	0	1-0	.222	.333	.222	.556	0	1.000
2004— Los Angeles (N.L.)	OF	4	16	0	2	1	0	0	2	1	0	0	0	0-0	.125	.176	.188	.364	0	1.000
Division series totals (6 years)		23	79	4	19	4	0	0	12	7	13	1	1	2-0	.241	.307	.291	.598	0	1.000

CHAMPIONSHIP SERIES RECORD

Year Team (League)	Pos.	G	AB	R	H	2B	3B	HR	RBI	BB	SO	HBP	GDP	SB-CS	Avg.	OBP	SLG	OPS	E	Avg.
1998— San Diego (N.L.)	OF	6	21	3	7	1	0	0	2	6	2	0	1	1-0	.333	.481	.381	.862	0	1.000
2001— Arizona (N.L.)	OF	5	14	1	4	1	0	0	4	3	1	0	1	1-0	.286	.412	.357	.769	0	1.000
Champ. series totals (2 years)		11	35	4	11	2	0	0	6	9	3	0	1	2-0	.314	.455	.371	.826	0	1.000

WORLD SERIES RECORD

Year Team (League)	Pos.	G	AB	R	H	2B	3B	HR	RBI	BB	SO	HBP	GDP	SB-CS	Avg.	OBP	SLG	OPS	E	Avg.
1998— San Diego (N.L.)	OF	3	12	0	1	1	0	0	0	0	2	0	1	1-0	.083	.083	.167	.250	0	1.000
2001— Arizona (N.L.)	OF	7	19	5	7	0	0	1	2	4	5	0	0	0-1	.368	.478	.526	1.005	0	1.000
World series totals (2 years)		10	31	5	8	1	0	1	2	4	7	0	1	1-1	.258	.343	.387	.730	0	1.000

ALL-STAR GAME RECORD

		G	AB	R	H	2B	3B	HR	RBI	BB	SO	HBP	GDP	SB-CS	Avg.	OBP	SLG	OPS	E	Avg.
All-Star Game totals (2 years)		2	2	0	1	0	0	0	1	0	1	0		0-0	.500	.500	.500	1.000	0	1.000

FLAHERTY, JOHN — C

PERSONAL: Born October 21, 1967, in New York, N.Y. ... 6-1/200. ... Bats right, throws right. ... Full name: John Timothy Flaherty. ... High school: St. Joseph's Regional (Montvale, N.J.). ... College: George Washington.

TRANSACTIONS/CAREER NOTES: Selected by Boston Red Sox organization in 25th round of 1988 free-agent draft. ... Traded by Red Sox to Detroit Tigers for C Rich Rowland (April 1, 1994). ... Traded by Tigers with SS Chris Gomez to San Diego Padres for C Brad Ausmus, SS Andujar Cedeno and P Russ Spear (June 18, 1996). ... Traded by Padres to Tampa Bay Devil Rays for P Brian Boehringer and IF Andy Sheets (November 18, 1997). ... On disabled list (May 26-June 20, 1998); included rehabilitation assignment to Durham. ... Signed by New York Yankees organization (January 16, 2003).

2004 GAMES PLAYED BY POSITION (MLB): C—46.

									BATTING										FIELDING	
Year Team (League)	Pos.	G	AB	R	H	2B	3B	HR	RBI	BB	SO	HBP	GDP	SB-CS	Avg.	OBP	SLG	OPS	E	Avg.
1988— Elmira (N.Y.-Penn)	C	46	162	17	38	3	0	3	16	12	23	2	5	2-1	.235	.294	.309	.602	7	.975
1989— Winter Haven (FSL)	C-1B	95	334	31	87	14	2	4	28	20	44	3	19	1-0	.260	.306	.350	.657	9	.979
1990— Pawtucket (Int'l)	3B-C	99	317	35	72	18	0	4	32	24	43	2	11	1-1	.227	.284	.322	.606	10	.983
— Lynchburg (Caro.)	C	1	4	0	0	0	0	0	1	0	1	0	0	0-0	.000	.000	.000	.000	0	1.000
1991— New Britain (East.)	C	67	225	27	65	9	0	3	18	31	22	1	5	0-2	.289	.375	.369	.743	9	.970
— Pawtucket (Int'l)	C	45	156	18	29	7	0	3	13	15	14	0	1	0-1	.186	.257	.288	.546	9	.970
1992— Boston (A.L.)	C	35	66	3	13	2	0	0	2	3	7	0	0	0-0	.197	.229	.227	.456	2	.982
— Pawtucket (Int'l)	C	31	104	11	26	3	0	0	7	5	8	1	6	0-0	.250	.291	.279	.570	4	.978
1993— Pawtucket (Int'l)	C	105	365	29	99	22	0	6	35	26	41	5	9	0-2	.271	.327	.381	.707	10	.986
— Boston (A.L.)	C	13	25	3	3	2	0	0	2	2	6	1	0	0-0	.120	.214	.200	.414	0	1.000
1994— Toledo (Int'l)	C-DH	44	151	20	39	10	2	7	17	6	21	0	1	3-1	.258	.285	.490	.775	2	.994
— Detroit (A.L.)	C-DH	34	40	2	6	1	0	0	4	1	11	0	1	0-1	.150	.167	.175	.342	0	1.000
1995— Detroit (A.L.)	C	112	354	39	86	22	1	11	40	18	47	3	8	0-0	.243	.284	.404	.688 *	11	.982
1996— Detroit (A.L.)	C	47	152	18	38	12	0	4	23	8	25	1	5	1-0	.250	.290	.408	.698	5	.981
— San Diego (N.L.)	C	72	264	22	80	12	0	9	41	9	36	2	8	2-3	.303	.327	.451	.778	5	.990
1997— San Diego (N.L.)	C	129	439	38	120	21	1	9	46	33	62	0	11	4-4	.273	.323	.387	.710	11	.987
1998— Tampa Bay (A.L.)	C	91	304	21	63	11	0	3	24	22	46	1	9	0-5	.207	.261	.273	.534	4	.993
— Durham (Int'l)	DH-C	6	23	1	3	1	0	0	2	1	5	0	1	0-0	.130	.160	.174	.334	0	1.000
1999— Tampa Bay (A.L.)	C-DH	117	446	53	124	19	0	14	71	19	64	6	14	0-2	.278	.310	.415	.725	6	.993
2000— Tampa Bay (A.L.)	C	109	394	36	103	15	0	10	39	20	57	0	11	0-0	.261	.296	.376	.671	5	.993
2001— Tampa Bay (A.L.)	C	78	248	20	59	17	1	4	29	10	33	1	9	1-0	.238	.269	.363	.632	7	.986
2002— Tampa Bay (A.L.)	C	76	281	27	73	20	0	4	33	15	50	1	6	2-2	.260	.296	.374	.669	4	.992
2003— New York (A.L.)	C	40	105	16	28	8	0	4	14	4	19	1	6	0-0	.267	.297	.457	.754	2	.991
2004— New York (A.L.)	C	47	127	11	32	9	0	6	16	5	25	1	5	0-2	.252	.286	.465	.750	3	.989
American League totals (12 years)		799	2542	249	628	138	2	60	297	127	390	16	74	4-12	.247	.284	.374	.658	49	.989
National League totals (2 years)		201	703	60	200	33	1	18	87	42	98	2	19	6-7	.284	.324	.411	.736	16	.988
Major League totals (13 years)		1000	3245	309	828	171	3	78	384	169	488	18	93	10-19	.255	.293	.382	.675	65	.989

DIVISION SERIES RECORD

Year Team (League)	Pos.	G	AB	R	H	2B	3B	HR	RBI	BB	SO	HBP	GDP	SB-CS	Avg.	OBP	SLG	OPS	E	Avg.
1996— San Diego (N.L.)	C	2	4	0	0	0	0	0	0	1	0	0	0	0-0	.000	.000	.000	.000	0	1.000

WORLD SERIES RECORD

Year Team (League)	Pos.	G	AB	R	H	2B	3B	HR	RBI	BB	SO	HBP	GDP	SB-CS	Avg.	OBP	SLG	OPS	E	Avg.
2003— New York (A.L.)	C	1	2	0	0	0	0	0	0	0	0	0	0	0-0	.000	.000	.000	.000	0	1.000

FLORES, JOSE — 2B

PERSONAL: Born June 28, 1973, in New York, N.Y. ... 6-11/180. ... Bats right, throws right. ... Full name: Jose Carlos Flores. ... Name pronounced: FLOR-es. ... High school: Louis D. Brandeis (N.Y.). ... College: Texas.

TRANSACTIONS/CAREER NOTES: Selected by Philadelphia Phillies organization in 34th round of 1994 free-agent draft. ... Traded by Phillies to Seattle Mariners for SS Domingo Cedeno (July 7, 1999). ... Signed as a free agent by Milwaukee Brewers organization (January 8, 2001). ... Traded by Brewers with Ps Kane Davis and Juan Acevedo to Colorado Rockies for Ps Mark Leiter and Mike DeJean and SS Elvis Pena (April 4, 2001). ... Signed as a free agent by Oakland Athletics organization (October 26, 2001). ... Traded by A's to San Diego Padres for P Buddy Hernandez (December 16, 2002). ... Claimed on waivers by A's (March 17, 2003). ... Traded by A's to Los Angeles Dodgers for cash (March 11, 2004).

2004 GAMES PLAYED BY POSITION (MLB): 2B—1, 3B—1.

F

Year	Team (League)	Pos.	G	AB	R	H	2B	3B	HR	RBI	BB	SO	HBP	GDP	SB-CS	Avg.	OBP	SLG	OPS	E	Avg.
																			BATTING		FIELDING
1994—Batavia (NY-Penn)	SS-2B	68	229	41	58	7	3	0	16	41	31	6	3	23-8	.253	.378	.310	.688	20	.935
1995—Piedmont (S. Atl.)	3B-2B-SS	61	186	22	49	7	0	0	19	24	29	3	6	11-8	.263	.350	.301	.651	12	.937
—Clearwater (FSL)	3B-2B-SS	49	185	25	41	4	3	1	19	15	27	4	4	12-5	.222	.293	.292	.585	12	.938
1996—Clearwater (FSL)	SS-2B-3B	84	281	39	64	6	5	1	39	34	42	3	6	15-2	.228	.317	.295	.612	22	.948
—Scran./W.B. (I.L.)	2B-SS	26	70	10	18	1	0	0	3	12	10	2	2	0-1	.257	.376	.271	.648	4	.955
1997—Scran./W.B. (I.L.)	2B-3B-SS	71	204	32	51	14	1	1	18	28	51	2	2	3-1	.250	.343	.343	.686	11	.957
1998—Scran./W.B. (I.L.)	SS-3B-2B	98	345	53	104	18	2	6	34	49	45	2	7	12-6	.301	.389	.417	.807	14	.964
1999—Scran./W.B. (I.L.)	SS	64	228	35	56	6	2	0	18	37	43	7	1	13-3	.246	.368	.289	.657	11	.960
—Tacoma (PCL)	SS-3B	42	143	33	44	6	1	3	15	37	23	5	2	4-3	.308	.460	.427	.886	11	.947
2000—Tacoma (PCL)	SS-3B-2B	91	328	53	93	14	4	3	30	53	44	5	6	19-7	.284	.388	.378	.766	23	.930
—New Haven (East.)	SS	12	38	5	7	3	0	0	1	7	5	2	0	0-0	.184	.340	.263	.604	2	.960
2001—Colo. Springs (PCL) S-3-2-0-1		100	316	61	93	21	5	2	36	48	57	3	1	8-2	.294	.391	.411	.803	18	.950
2002—Sacramento (PCL) S-OF-2-3		95	363	64	111	19	1	2	38	56	53	3	11	16-4	.306	.397	.380	.777	15	.959
—Oakland (A.L.)	2B-SS-DH	7	3	2	0	0	0	0	0	1	0	1	0	1-1	.000	.400	.000	.400	0	1.000
2003—Sacramento (PCL) O-2-S-3-DH		107	370	72	101	12	2	2	38	62	48	3	16	16-2	.273	.377	.332	.709	18	.947
2004—Las Vegas (PCL) S-3-2-DH		99	319	64	100	20	1	7	51	49	30	4	6	6-2	.313	.407	.448	.855	14	.957
—Los Angeles (N.L.)	2B-3B	9	4	0	1	0	0	0	0	1	2	0	0	0-0	.250	.400	.250	.650	0	1.000
American League totals (1 year)		7	3	2	0	0	0	0	0	1	0	1	0	1-1	.000	.400	.000	.400	0	1.000
National League totals (1 year)		9	4	0	1	0	0	0	0	1	2	0	0	0-0	.250	.400	.250	.650	0	1.000
Major League totals (2 years)		16	7	2	1	0	0	0	0	2	2	1	0	1-1	.143	.400	.143	.543	0	1.000

FLORES, RANDY   P

PERSONAL: Born July 31, 1975, in Bellflower, Calif. ... 6-0/180. ... Throws left, bats left. ... Full name: Randy Alan Flores. ... High school: El Rancho (Pico Rivera, Calif.). ... College: USC.

TRANSACTIONS/CAREER NOTES: Selected by St. Louis Cardinals organization in 21st round of 1996 free-agent draft; did not sign. ... Selected by New York Yankees organization in ninth round of 1997 free-agent draft. ... Traded by Yankees with P Rosman Garcia to Texas Rangers (October 11, 2001), completing deal in which Rangers traded 2B Randy Velarde to Yankees for two players to be named (August 31, 2001). ... Claimed on waivers by Colorado Rockies (July 18, 2002). ... Signed as a free agent by Cardinals organization (November 21, 2003).

CAREER HITTING: 0-for-6 (.000), 0 R, 0 2B, 0 3B, 0 HR, 0 RBI.

Year	Team (League)	W	L	Pct.	ERA	WHIP	G	GS	CG	ShO	Hld.	Sv.-Opp.	IP	H	R	ER	HR	BB-IBB	SO	Avg.
1997—Oneonta (N.Y.-Penn)	4	4	.500	3.25	1.17	13	13	2	1	...	0-...	74.2	64	32	27	3	23-1	70	.229
1998—Tampa (FSL)	1	2	.333	6.46	1.86	5	5	0	0	...	0-...	23.2	28	23	17	2	16-2	15	.298
—Greensboro (S. Atl.)	12	7	.632	2.62	1.16	21	20	2	1	...	0-...	130.2	119	48	38	6	33-0	139	.243
1999—Norwich (East.)	0	1	.000	6.48	1.72	4	4	0	0	...	0-...	25.0	32	20	18	0	11-1	19	.302
—Tampa (FSL)	11	4	.733	2.87	1.16	21	20	1	1	...	0-...	135.0	118	56	43	4	38-0	99	.235
2000—Norwich (East.)	10	9	.526	2.94	1.39	31	20	3	0	...	1-...	141.0	138	64	46	8	58-1	97	.259
—Columbus (Int'l)	1	2	.333	7.33	2.14	4	4	0	0	...	0-...	23.1	43	21	19	3	7-0	16	.391
2001—Columbus (Int'l)	0	1	.000	4.76	1.24	3	0	0	0	...	0-...	5.2	5	4	3	1	2-0	4	.238
—Norwich (East.)	14	6	.700	2.78	1.38	25	25	3	2	...	0-...	158.2	156	64	49	13	63-0	115	.258
2002—Oklahoma (PCL)	1	1	.500	5.75	1.33	15	0	0	0	...	1-...	20.1	22	13	13	1	5-1	16	.268
—Texas (A.L.)	0	0	...	4.50	1.58	20	0	0	0	2	1-2	12.0	11	7	6	2	8-2	7	.268
—Colo. Springs (PCL)	2	2	.500	3.28	1.51	7	7	0	0	...	0-...	35.2	36	15	13	1	18-0	27	.269
—Colorado (N.L.)	0	2	.000	9.53	2.18	8	2	0	0	0	0-...	17.0	29	19	18	5	9-1	7	.382
2003—Colo. Springs (PCL)	10	8	.556	4.98	1.60	28	24	0	0	...	0-...	142.2	156	89	79	16	67-4	116	.279
2004—Memphis (PCL)	5	7	.417	3.82	1.31	36	15	1	1	...	2-...	122.2	115	60	52	10	46-1	99	.251
—St. Louis (N.L.)	1	0	1.000	1.93	1.14	9	1	0	0	0	0-0	14.0	13	3	3	0	3-1	7	.265
American League totals (1 year)	0	0	...	4.50	1.58	20	0	0	0	2	1-2	12.0	11	7	6	2	8-2	7	.268
National League totals (2 years)	1	2	.333	6.10	1.71	17	3	0	0	0	0-0	31.0	42	22	21	5	11-2	14	.336
Major League totals (2 years)	1	2	.333	5.65	1.67	37	3	0	0	2	1-2	43.0	53	29	27	7	19-4	21	.319

FLOYD, CLIFF   OF

PERSONAL: Born December 5, 1972, in Chicago, Ill. ... 6-4/230. ... Bats left, throws right. ... Full name: Cornelius Clifford Floyd. ... High school: Thornwood (South Holland, Ill.).

TRANSACTIONS/CAREER NOTES: Selected by Montreal Expos organization in first round (14th pick overall) of 1991 free-agent draft. ... On disabled list (May 16-September 11, 1995). ... Traded by Expos to Florida Marlins for OF Joe Orsulak and P Dustin Hermanson (March 26, 1997). ... On disabled list (May 9-24 and June 21-September 1, 1997); included rehabilitation assignment to Charlotte. ... On disabled list (March 30-April 27 and June 20-September 7, 1999); included rehabilitation assigment to Calgary. ... On disabled list (July 29-August 29, 2000). ... Traded by Marlins with P Claudio Vargas, OF/2B Wilton Guerrero, a player to be named and cash considerations to Expos for Ps Carl Pavano, Graeme Lloyd and Justin Wayne and IF Mike Mordecai (July 11, 2002); Expos acquired P Don Levinski to complete deal (August 5, 2002). ... Traded by Expos to Boston Red Sox for Ps Seung Song and Sun-Woo Kim (July 30, 2002). ... Signed as a free agent by New York Mets (December 20, 2002). ... On disabled list (August 19, 2003-remainder of season). ... On disabled list (April 12-May 13, 2004); included rehabilitation assignment to St. Lucie.

HONORS: Named Minor League Player of the Year by THE SPORTING NEWS (1993).

2004 GAMES PLAYED BY POSITION (MLB): OF—106, DH—1.

Year	Team (League)	Pos.	G	AB	R	H	2B	3B	HR	RBI	BB	SO	HBP	GDP	SB-CS	Avg.	OBP	SLG	OPS	E	Avg.
																			BATTING		FIELDING
1991—GC Expos (GCL)	1B	56	214	35	56	9	3	6	30	19	37	5	3	13-3	.262	.335	.416	.751	15	.970
1992—Albany (S. Atl.)	1B-OF	134	516	83	157	24	16	16	97	45	75	9	4	32-11	.304	.368	.506	.874	17	.964
—W.P. Beach (FSL)	OF	1	4	0	0	0	0	0	1	0	1	0	0	0-0	.000	.000	.000	.000	0	1.000
1993—Harrisburg (East.)	1B-OF	101	380	82	125	17	4	26	101	54	71	5	8	31-10	.329	.417	.600	1.017	19	.969
—Ottawa (Int'l)	1B	32	125	12	30	2	2	2	18	16	34	1	1	2-2	.240	.329	.336	.665	5	.983
—Montreal (N.L.)	1B	10	31	3	7	0	0	1	2	0	9	0	0	0-0	.226	.226	.323	.548	0	1.000
1994—Montreal (N.L.)	1B-OF	100	334	43	94	19	4	4	41	24	63	3	3	10-3	.281	.332	.398	.731	6	.990
1995—Montreal (N.L.)	1B-OF	29	69	6	9	1	0	1	8	7	22	1	1	3-0	.130	.221	.188	.409	3	.981
1996—Ottawa (Int'l) OF-3B-DH		20	76	7	23	3	1	1	8	7	20	1	0	2-2	.303	.368	.408	.777	2	.951
—Montreal (N.L.)	OF-1B	117	227	29	55	15	4	6	26	30	52	5	3	7-1	.242	.340	.423	.763	5	.957
1997—Florida (N.L.)	OF-1B	61	137	23	32	9	1	6	19	24	33	2	3	6-2	.234	.354	.445	.799	3	.971
—Charlotte (Int'l)	OF-1B	39	131	27	48	10	0	9	33	10	29	1	3	7-2	.366	.415	.649	1.064	1	.988
1998—Florida (N.L.)	OF-DH	153	588	85	166	45	3	22	90	47	112	3	10	27-14	.282	.337	.481	.818	7	.974
1999—Florida (N.L.)	OF-DH	69	251	37	76	19	1	11	49	30	47	2	8	5-6	.303	.379	.518	.897	6	.952
—Calgary (PCL)	OF	9	31	6	12	1	0	3	8	2	8	0	0	0-1	.387	.424	.710	1.134	0	1.000

F

Year Team (League)	Pos.	G	AB	R	H	2B	3B	HR	RBI	BB	SO	HBP	GDP	SB-CS	Avg.	OBP	SLG	OPS	E	Avg.
2000— Florida (N.L.)	OF-DH	121	420	75	126	30	0	22	91	50	82	8	4	24-3	.300	.378	.529	.906	9	.951
2001— Florida (N.L.)	OF-DH	149	555	123	176	44	4	31	103	59	101	10	9	18-3	.317	.390	.578	.968	8	.972
2002— Florida (N.L.)	OF-DH	84	296	49	85	20	0	18	57	58	68	7	0	10-5	.287	.414	.537	.952	3	.983
— Montreal (N.L.)	OF	15	53	7	11	2	0	3	4	3	10	1	0	1-0	.208	.263	.415	.678	1	.941
— Boston (A.L.)	OF-DH	47	171	30	54	21	0	7	18	15	28	2	6	4-0	.316	.374	.561	.935	1	.977
2003— New York (N.L.)	OF-DH	108	365	57	106	25	2	18	68	51	66	3	10	3-0	.290	.376	.518	.894	5	.971
2004— St. Lucie (Fla. St.)	OF	1	4	2	2	0	0	0	1	0	2	0	0	0-0	.500	.500	.500	1.000	0	1.000
— New York (N.L.)	OF-DH	113	396	55	103	26	0	18	63	47	103	11	8	11-4	.260	.352	.462	.814	2	.988
American League totals (1 year)		47	171	30	54	21	0	7	18	15	28	2	6	4-0	.316	.374	.561	.935	1	.977
National League totals (12 years)		1129	3722	592	1046	255	19	161	621	430	768	56	59	125-41	.281	.361	.490	.851	58	.977
Major League totals (12 years)		1176	3893	622	1100	276	19	168	639	445	796	58	65	129-41	.283	.362	.493	.854	59	.977

DIVISION SERIES RECORD

Year Team (League)	Pos.	G	AB	R	H	2B	3B	HR	RBI	BB	SO	HBP	GDP	SB-CS	Avg.	OBP	SLG	OPS	E	Avg.
1997— Florida (N.L.)	Did not play.																			

CHAMPIONSHIP SERIES RECORD

Year Team (League)	Pos.	G	AB	R	H	2B	3B	HR	RBI	BB	SO	HBP	GDP	SB-CS	Avg.	OBP	SLG	OPS	E	Avg.
1997— Florida (N.L.)	Did not play.																			

WORLD SERIES RECORD

Year Team (League)	Pos.	G	AB	R	H	2B	3B	HR	RBI	BB	SO	HBP	GDP	SB-CS	Avg.	OBP	SLG	OPS	E	Avg.
1997— Florida (N.L.)	DH	4	2	1	0	0	0	0	0	1	1	0	0	0-0	.000	.333	.000	.333	...	...

ALL-STAR GAME RECORD

	G	AB	R	H	2B	3B	HR	RBI	BB	SO	HBP	GDP	SB-CS	Avg.	OBP	SLG	OPS	E	Avg.
All-Star Game totals (1 year)	1	2	0	0	0	0	0	0	0	0	0	0	0-0	.000	.000	.000	.000	...	...

FLOYD, GAVIN   P

PERSONAL: Born January 27, 1983, in Annapolis, Md. ... 6-4/212. ... Throws right, bats right. ... Full name: Gavin Christopher Floyd. ... High school: Mount St. Joseph (Baltimore).

TRANSACTIONS/CAREER NOTES: Selected by Philadelphia Phillies organization in first round (fourth overall pick) of 2001 free-agent draft.

CAREER HITTING: 0-for-10 (.000), 0 R, 0 2B, 0 3B, 0 HR, 0 RBI.

Year Team (League)	W	L	Pct.	ERA	WHIP	G	GS	CG	ShO	Hld.	Sv.-Opp.	IP	H	R	ER	HR	BB-IBB	SO	Avg.
2002— Lakewood (S.Atl.)	11	10	.524	2.77	1.10	27	27	3	0	...	0-...	166.0	119	59	51	13	64-0	140	...
2003— Clearwater (Fla. St.)	7	8	.467	3.00	1.25	24	20	1	1	...	0-...	138.0	128	61	46	9	45-0	115	...
2004— Reading (East.)	6	6	.500	2.57	1.17	20	20	2	1	...	0-...	119.0	93	39	34	8	46-1	94	.212
— Scran./W.B. (I.L.)	1	3	.250	4.99	1.57	5	5	0	0	...	0-...	30.2	39	20	17	4	9-0	18	.312
— Philadelphia (N.L.)	2	0	1.000	3.49	1.45	6	4	0	0	0	0-0	28.1	25	11	11	1	16-0	24	.240
Major League totals (1 year)	2	0	1.000	3.49	1.45	6	4	0	0	0	0-0	28.1	25	11	11	1	16-0	24	.240

FOGG, JOSH   P

PERSONAL: Born December 13, 1976, in Lynn, Mass. ... 6-0/203. ... Throws right, bats right. ... Full name: Joshua Smith Fogg. ... High school: Cadinal Gibbons (Fort Lauderdale, Fla.). ... College: Florida.

TRANSACTIONS/CAREER NOTES: Selected by Chicago White Sox organization in third round of 1998 free-agent draft. ... Traded by White Sox with Ps Kip Wells and Sean Lowe to Pittsburgh Pirates for P Todd Ritchie and C Lee Evans (December 13, 2001). ... On disabled list (April 21-May 26, 2003); included rehabilitation assignment to Nashville.

CAREER HITTING: 19-for-153 (.124), 7 R, 1 2B, 0 3B, 0 HR, 5 RBI.

Year Team (League)	W	L	Pct.	ERA	WHIP	G	GS	CG	ShO	Hld.	Sv.-Opp.	IP	H	R	ER	HR	BB-IBB	SO	Avg.
1998— Ariz. White Sox (Ariz.)	1	0	1.000	0.00	0.25	2	0	0	0	...	0-...	4.0	0	0	0	0	1-0	5	.000
— Hickory (S. Atl.)	1	3	.250	2.18	1.19	8	8	0	0	...	0-...	41.1	36	17	10	4	13-0	29	.228
— Winston-Salem (Caro.)	0	1	.000	0.00	2.00	1	0	0	0	...	0-...	1.0	2	2	0	0	0-0	2	.333
1999— Winston-Salem (Caro.)	10	5	.667	2.96	1.22	17	17	1	1	...	0-...	103.1	93	44	34	3	33-0	109	.235
— Birmingham (Southern)	3	2	.600	5.89	1.53	10	10	0	0	...	0-...	55.0	66	37	36	8	18-0	40	.296
2000— Birmingham (Southern)	11	7	.611	2.57	1.22	27	27	2	0	...	0-...	192.1	190	68	55	7	44-2	136	.261
2001— Charlotte (Int'l)	4	7	.364	4.79	1.39	40	16	0	0	...	4-...	114.2	129	68	61	19	30-1	89	.283
— Chicago (A.L.)	0	0	...	2.03	0.98	11	0	0	0	0	2 0-0	13.1	10	3	3	0	3-1	17	.208
2002— Pittsburgh (N.L.)	12	12	.500	4.35	1.38	33	33	0	0	0	0-0	194.1	199	102	94	28	69-12	113	.267
2003— Nashville (PCL)	0	1	.000	5.40	1.30	2	2	0	0	...	0-...	10.0	12	6	6	1	1-0	7	.324
— Pittsburgh (N.L.)	10	9	.526	5.26	1.45	26	26	1	0	0	0-0	142.0	166	90	83	22	40-0	71	.293
2004— Pittsburgh (N.L.)	11	10	.524	4.64	1.45	32	32	0	0	0	0-0	178.1	193	98	92	17	66-8	82	.283
American League totals (1 year)	0	0	...	2.03	0.98	11	0	0	0	0	2 0-0	13.1	10	3	3	0	3-1	17	.208
National League totals (3 years)	33	31	.516	4.70	1.42	91	91	1	0	0	0-0	514.2	558	290	269	67	175-20	266	.280
Major League totals (4 years)	33	31	.516	4.64	1.41	102	91	1	0	2	0-0	528.0	568	293	272	67	178-21	283	.278

FOPPERT, JESSE   P

PERSONAL: Born July 10, 1980, in Reading, Pa. ... 6-6/210. ... Throws right, bats right. ... Full name: Jesse W. Foppert. ... College: San Francisco.

TRANSACTIONS/CAREER NOTES: Selected by San Francisco Giants organization in second round of 2001 free-agent draft. ... On disabled list (August 21, 2003-remainder of season; and March 31-August 18, 2004); included rehabilitation assignments to AZL Giants, San Jose and Fresno.

CAREER HITTING: 3-for-37 (.081), 3 R, 1 2B, 1 3B, 0 HR, 1 RBI.

Year Team (League)	W	L	Pct.	ERA	WHIP	G	GS	CG	ShO	Hld.	Sv.-Opp.	IP	H	R	ER	HR	BB-IBB	SO	Avg.
2001— Salem-Keizer (N'west)	8	1	.889	1.93	0.83	14	14	0	0	...	0-...	70.0	35	18	15	7	23-0	88	.150
2002— Shreveport (Texas)	3	3	.500	2.79	1.06	11	11	1	0	...	0-...	61.1	44	22	19	3	21-0	74	.199
— Fresno (PCL)	3	6	.333	3.99	1.34	14	14	0	0	...	0-...	79.0	71	37	35	12	35-0	109	.244
2003— Fresno (PCL)	0	0	...	1.80	0.60	1	1	0	0	...	0-...	5.0	3	1	1	0	0-0	9	.167
— San Jose (California)	0	1	.000	9.00	1.67	1	1	0	0	...	0-...	3.0	5	3	3	0	0-0	3	.385
— San Francisco (N.L.)	8	9	.471	5.03	1.55	23	21	0	0	1	0-0	111.0	103	69	62	16	69-4	101	.249
2004— Ariz. Giants (Ariz.)	0	0	...	9.00	3.00	1	1	0	0	...	0-0	1.0	3	1	1	0	0-0	2	.500
— San Jose (California)	0	0	...	1.93	0.86	4	4	0	0	...	0-0	9.1	4	2	2	1	4-0	11	.133
— Fresno (PCL)	0	2	.000	3.68	1.57	4	4	0	0	...	0-0	14.2	14	11	6	2	9-0	13	.241
— San Francisco (N.L.)	0	0	...	0.00	1.00	1	1	0	0	...	0-0	1.0	1	0	0	0	0-0	2	.250
Major League totals (2 years)	8	9	.471	4.98	1.54	24	21	0	0	1	0-0	112.0	104	69	62	16	69-4	103	.249

F

FORD, BEN — P

PERSONAL: Born August 15, 1975, in Cedar Rapids, Iowa. ... 6-7/225. ... Throws right, bats right. ... Full name: Benjamin Cooper Ford. ... High school: George Washington (Cedar Rapids, Iowa). ... Junior college: Indian Hills (Iowa) Community College.

TRANSACTIONS/CAREER NOTES: Selected by New York Yankees organization in 20th round of 1994 free-agent draft. ... Selected by Arizona Diamondbacks in first round (17th pick overall) of expansion draft (November 18, 1997). ... Traded by Diamondbacks with C Izzy Molina to Yankees for P Darren Holmes and cash (March 30, 1999). ... Traded by Yankees with P Oswaldo Mairena to Chicago Cubs for OF Glenallen Hill (July 21, 2000). ... Released by Cubs (November 27, 2000). ... Re-signed by Cubs (February 19, 2001). ... Signed as a free agent by Minnesota Twins organization (November 12, 2002). ... Signed by Milwaukee Brewers organization (May 19, 2003). ... On disabled list (May 16-July 2, 2004); included rehabilitation assignment to Indianapolis.

CAREER HITTING: 0-for-0 (.000), 0 R, 0 2B, 0 3B, 0 HR, 0 RBI.

Year Team (League)	W	L	Pct.	ERA	WHIP	G	GS	CG	ShO	Hld.	Sv.-Opp.	IP	H	R	ER	HR	BB-IBB	SO	Avg.
1994— GC Yankees (GCL)	2	2	.500	2.38	1.03	18	0	0	0	...	3-...	34.0	27	13	9	0	8-0	31	.209
1995— Oneonta (N.Y.-Penn)	5	0	1.000	0.87	1.06	29	0	0	0	...	0-...	52.0	39	23	5	1	16-0	50	.194
— Greensboro (S. Atl.)	0	0	...	5.14	1.29	7	0	0	0	...	0-...	7.0	4	4	4	1	5-1	8	.160
1996— Greensboro (S. Atl.)	2	6	.250	4.26	1.31	43	0	0	0	...	2-...	82.1	75	48	39	3	33-6	84	.243
1997— Tampa (FSL)	4	0	1.000	1.93	1.10	32	0	0	0	...	18-...	37.1	27	8	8	1	14-1	37	.205
— Norwich (East.)	4	3	.571	4.22	1.27	28	0	0	0	...	1-...	42.2	35	28	20	1	19-1	38	.222
1998— Tucson (PCL)	2	5	.286	4.35	1.48	48	0	0	0	0	13-...	68.1	68	41	33	6	33-5	63	.250
— Arizona (N.L.)	0	0	...	9.90	1.60	8	0	0	0	0	0-0	10.0	13	12	11	2	3-0	5	.295
1999— Columbus (Int'l)	6	3	.667	4.73	1.54	53	0	0	0	...	3-...	70.1	69	42	37	4	39-1	40	.258
2000— Columbus (Int'l)	3	0	1.000	3.07	1.39	20	2	0	0	...	0-...	44.0	37	15	15	3	24-0	41	.224
— New York (A.L.)	0	1	.000	9.00	1.91	4	2	0	0	0	0-0	11.0	14	11	11	1	7-0	5	.333
— Iowa (PCL)	1	3	.250	6.63	1.83	8	8	0	0	...	0-...	36.2	36	30	27	4	31-0	30	.261
2001— Ariz. Cubs (Ariz.)	0	1	.000	2.00	1.33	3	3	0	0	...	0-...	9.0	10	4	2	0	2-0	9	.270
— Iowa (PCL)	2	3	.400	5.79	1.71	5	5	0	0	...	0-...	23.1	31	15	15	3	9-0	16	.326
2002— Iowa (PCL)	6	11	.353	4.88	1.62	32	23	0	0	...	0-...	142.0	157	91	77	13	73-1	84	.284
2003— Indianapolis (Int'l)	5	4	.556	3.00	1.20	26	9	1	0	...	1-...	84.0	80	32	28	8	18-0	72	.254
2004— Indianapolis (Int'l)	2	2	.500	4.85	1.73	32	1	0	0	...	9-...	42.2	53	25	23	2	21-3	36	.317
— Milwaukee (N.L.)	1	1	.500	6.38	1.46	19	0	0	0	2	0-3	24.0	25	17	17	4	10-0	13	.269
American League totals (1 year)	0	1	.000	9.00	1.91	4	2	0	0	0	0-0	11.0	14	11	11	1	7-0	5	.333
National League totals (2 years)	1	1	.500	7.41	1.50	27	0	0	0	2	0-3	34.0	38	29	28	6	13-0	18	.277
Major League totals (3 years)	1	2	.333	7.80	1.60	31	2	0	0	2	0-3	45.0	52	40	39	7	20-0	23	.291

FORD, LEW — OF

PERSONAL: Born August 12, 1976, in Port Neches, Texas. ... 6-0/195. ... Bats right, throws right. ... Full name: Jon Lewis Ford. ... High school: Port Neches-Groves High (Texarkana, Texas). ... College: Dallas Baptist (Texas).

TRANSACTIONS/CAREER NOTES: Selected by Boston Red Sox organization in 12th round of 1999 free-agent draft. ... Traded by Red Sox to Minnesota Twins for P Hector Carrasco (September 10, 2000). ... On disabled list (July 14-September 2, 2003); included rehabilitation assignment to Rochester.

2004 GAMES PLAYED BY POSITION (MLB): OF—126, DH—26.

Year Team (League)	Pos.	G	AB	R	H	2B	3B	HR	RBI	BB	SO	HBP	GDP	SB-CS	Avg.	OBP	SLG	OPS	E	Avg.
1999— Lowell (NY-Penn)	OF	62	250	48	70	17	4	7	34	19	35	5	6	15-2	.280	.339	.464	.803	1	.993
2000— Augusta (S. Atl.)	OF	126	514	122	162	35	11	9	74	52	83	12	12	52-4	.315	.390	.479	.868	2	.994
2001— Fort Myers (FSL)	OF	67	265	42	79	15	2	2	24	21	30	12	3	19-9	.298	.373	.392	.766	1	.993
— New Britain (East.)	OF	62	252	30	55	9	3	7	25	20	35	6	4	5-5	.218	.289	.361	.650	3	.974
2002— New Britain (East.)	OF	93	373	81	116	27	2	15	51	49	47	8	5	17-5	.311	.401	.515	.916	3	.986
— Edmonton (PCL)	OF	47	193	40	64	11	2	5	24	13	21	6	2	11-1	.332	.390	.487	.877	5	.964
2003— Rochester (Int'l)	OF-DH	53	211	33	64	18	2	3	31	10	28	8	1	4-5	.303	.357	.450	.807	1	.990
— Minnesota (A.L.)	OF-DH	34	73	16	24	7	1	3	15	8	9	1	1	2-0	.329	.402	.575	.978	3	.923
2004— Rochester (Int'l)	OF	1	5	0	1	0	0	0	0	0	1	0	0	0-0	.200	.200	.200	.400	0	1.000
— Minnesota (A.L.)	OF-DH	154	569	89	170	31	4	15	72	67	75	13	15	20-2	.299	.381	.446	.827	4	.986
Major League totals (2 years)		188	642	105	194	38	5	18	87	75	84	14	16	22-2	.302	.383	.461	.845	7	.978

DIVISION SERIES RECORD

Year Team (League)	Pos.	G	AB	R	H	2B	3B	HR	RBI	BB	SO	HBP	GDP	SB-CS	Avg.	OBP	SLG	OPS	E	Avg.
2003— Minnesota (A.L.)		1	1	0	0	0	0	0	0	0	1	0	0	0-0	.000	.000	.000	.000	0	...
2004— Minnesota (A.L.)	DH-OF	3	11	1	3	1	0	0	2	0	2	2	0	1-1	.273	.385	.364	.748	0	1.000
Division series totals (2 years)		4	12	1	3	1	0	0	2	0	3	2	0	1-1	.250	.357	.333	.690	0	1.000

FORDYCE, BROOK — C

PERSONAL: Born May 7, 1970, in New London, Conn. ... 6-0/194. ... Bats right, throws right. ... Full name: Brook Alexander Fordyce. ... Name pronounced: four-DICE. ... High school: St. Bernard (Uncasville, Conn.).

TRANSACTIONS/CAREER NOTES: Selected by New York Mets organization in third round of 1989 free-agent draft. ... Claimed on waivers by Cleveland Indians (May 15, 1995). ... Signed as a free agent by Cincinnati Reds organization (December 7, 1995). ... On disabled list (July 16-August 5, 1997); included rehabilitation assignment to Indianapolis. ... On disabled list (July 13-August 12, 1998); included rehabilitation assignment to Indianapolis. ... Traded by Reds to Chicago White Sox for P Jake Meyer (March 25, 1999). ... On disabled list (March 25-May 23, 2000); included rehabilitation assignment to Charlotte. ... Traded by White Sox with Ps Miguel Felix, Juan Figueroa and Jason Lakman to Baltimore Orioles for C Charles Johnson and DH Harold Baines (July 29, 2000). ... Signed as a free agent by Tampa Bay Devil Rays (January 7, 2004).

2004 GAMES PLAYED BY POSITION (MLB): C—51, DH—1.

Year Team (League)	Pos.	G	AB	R	H	2B	3B	HR	RBI	BB	SO	HBP	GDP	SB-CS	Avg.	OBP	SLG	OPS	E	Avg.
1989— Kingsport (Appalachian)	3B-C-OF	69	226	45	74	15	0	9	38	30	26	1	3	10-6	.327	.405	.513	.919	4	.988
1990— Columbia (S. Atl.)	C	104	372	45	117	29	1	10	54	39	42	0	18	4-1	.315	.378	.478	.856	15	.977
1991— St. Lucie (Fla. St.)	C	115	406	42	97	19	3	7	55	37	50	4	7	4-5	.239	.305	.352	.657	13	.982
1992— Binghamton (East.)	C	118	425	59	118	30	0	11	61	37	78	4	13	1-2	.278	.337	.426	.763	3	.996
1993— Norfolk (Int'l)	C	116	409	33	106	21	2	2	41	26	62	5	10	2-2	.259	.307	.335	.642	8	.990
1994— Norfolk (Int'l)	C-DH	66	229	26	60	13	3	3	32	19	26	1	9	1-0	.262	.320	.384	.704	7	.981
1995— New York (N.L.)		4	2	1	1	1	0	0	0	1	0	0	0	0-0	.500	.667	1.000	1.667	...	...
— Buffalo (A.A.)	C-OF-DH	58	176	18	44	13	0	0	9	14	20	2	2	1-0	.250	.313	.324	.636	4	.991
1996— Indianapolis (A.A.)	C-DH-1B	107	374	48	103	20	3	16	64	25	56	1	5	2-1	.275	.319	.473	.793	4	.994
— Cincinnati (N.L.)	C	4	7	0	2	1	0	0	1	3	1	0	0	0-0	.286	.500	.429	.929	0	1.000
1997— Cincinnati (N.L.)	C-DH	47	96	7	20	5	0	1	8	8	15	0	0	2-0	.208	.267	.292	.558	3	.983

F

Year	Team (League)	Pos.	G	AB	R	H	2B	3B	HR	RBI	BB	SO	HBP	GDP	SB-CS	Avg.	OBP	SLG	OPS	E	Avg.
	—Indianapolis (A.A.)	C-DH	12	47	7	11	2	0	2	6	5	6	1	3	1-1	.234	.321	.404	.725	0	1.000
1998—	Cincinnati (N.L.)	C	57	146	8	37	9	0	3	14	11	28	0	2	0-1	.253	.306	.377	.682	7	.978
	—Indianapolis (Int'l)	C	6	24	4	6	1	0	2	3	1	2	0	1	0-0	.250	.280	.542	.822	0	1.000
1999—	Chicago (A.L.)	C	105	333	36	99	25	1	9	49	21	48	3	5	2-0	.297	.343	.459	.802	8	.987
2000—	Charlotte (Int'l)	C	17	67	9	16	5	0	2	12	8	13	0	2	0-1	.239	.316	.403	.719	0	1.000
	—Chicago (A.L.)	C	40	125	18	34	7	1	5	21	6	23	2	1	0-0	.272	.313	.464	.777	0	1.000
	—Baltimore (A.L.)	C	53	177	23	57	11	0	9	28	11	27	2	3	0-0	.322	.361	.537	.898	4	.988
2001—	Baltimore (A.L.)	C	95	292	30	61	18	0	5	19	21	56	3	7	1-2	.209	.268	.322	.590	10	.983
2002—	Baltimore (A.L.)	C	56	130	7	30	8	0	1	8	9	19	4	5	1-0	.231	.301	.315	.616	4	.986
2003—	Baltimore (A.L.)	C	108	348	28	95	12	2	6	31	19	44	1	10	2-3	.273	.311	.371	.682	3	.996
2004—	Tampa Bay (A.L.)	C-DH	54	151	14	31	6	0	2	9	9	34	2	3	0-0	.205	.259	.285	.544	3	.990
	American League totals (6 years)		511	1556	156	407	87	4	37	165	96	251	17	34	6-5	.262	.310	.394	.704	32	.989
	National League totals (4 years)		112	251	16	60	16	0	4	23	23	44	0	2	2-1	.239	.302	.351	.652	10	.980
	Major League totals (10 years)		623	1807	172	467	103	4	41	188	119	295	17	36	8-6	.258	.309	.388	.697	42	.988

FORTUNATO, BARTOLOME — P

PERSONAL: Born August 24, 1974, in Santo Domingo, Dominican Republic. ... 6-1/197. ... Throws right, bats right.

TRANSACTIONS/CAREER NOTES: Signed as a non-drafted free agent by Tampa Bay Devil Rays (August 15, 1996). ... Played three seasons as an outielder in Devil Rays organization (1997-99). ... Traded by Devil Rays with P Victor Zambrano to New York Mets for Ps Scott Kazmir and Jose Diaz (July 30, 2004).

CAREER HITTING: 0-for-0 (.000), 0 R, 0 2B, 0 3B, 0 HR, 0 RBI.

Year	Team (League)	W	L	Pct.	ERA	WHIP	G	GS	CG	ShO	Hld.	Sv.-Opp.	IP	H	R	ER	HR	BB-IBB	SO	Avg.
2000—	Princeton (Appalachian)	3	4	.429	4.63	1.61	17	5	0	0	...	1-...	46.2	56	31	24	4	19-0	51	.284
2001—	Hudson Valley (NY-Penn.)	2	5	.286	5.13	1.66	16	9	0	0	...	1-...	59.2	70	35	34	3	29-0	53	.299
2002—	Bakersfield (California)	2	4	.333	4.01	1.37	25	5	0	0	...	0-...	60.2	58	31	27	3	25-0	85	.251
	—Durham (Int'l)	1	0	1.000	4.15	1.85	2	0	0	0	...	0-...	4.1	6	3	2	1	2-0	0	.333
	—Orlando (Sou.)	3	0	1.000	2.10	1.05	10	2	0	0	...	0-...	25.2	16	7	6	2	11-1	34	.180
2003—	Durham (Int'l)	1	2	.333	3.32	1.20	5	4	0	0	...	0-...	21.2	15	11	8	3	11-0	20	.192
	—Orlando (Sou.)	4	2	.667	3.06	1.28	35	1	0	0	...	1-...	53.0	48	25	18	4	20-1	63	.242
2004—	Tampa Bay (A.L.)	0	0	...	3.68	1.64	3	0	0	0	0	0-0	7.1	10	3	3	1	2-0	5	.357
	—Durham (Int'l)	4	3	.571	2.42	1.10	34	0	0	0	...	9-...	44.2	28	14	12	4	21-1	54	.183
	—Norfolk (Int'l)	0	0	...	3.38	1.31	6	0	0	0	...	0-...	5.1	4	2	2	0	3-0	5	.211
	—New York (N.L.)	1	0	1.000	3.86	1.45	15	0	0	0	2	1-2	18.2	14	8	8	2	13-0	20	.203
	American League totals (1 year)	0	0	...	3.68	1.64	3	0	0	0	0	0-0	7.1	10	3	3	1	2-0	5	.357
	National League totals (1 year)	1	0	1.000	3.86	1.45	15	0	0	0	2	1-2	18.2	14	8	8	2	13-0	20	.203
	Major League totals (1 year)	1	0	1.000	3.81	1.50	18	0	0	0	2	1-2	26.0	24	11	11	3	15-0	25	.247

FOSSUM, CASEY — P

PERSONAL: Born January 9, 1978, in Cherry Hill, N.J. ... 6-1/160. ... Throws left, bats left. ... Full name: Casey Paul Fossum. ... High school: Midway (Waco, Texas). ... College: Texas A&M.

TRANSACTIONS/CAREER NOTES: Selected by Arizona Diamondbacks organization in sixth round of 1996 free-agent draft; did not sign. ... Selected by Boston Red Sox organization as "sandwich pick" between first and second round of 1999 free-agent draft; pick received as part of compensation for Arizona Diamondbacks signing Type A free-agent P Greg Swindell. ... On disabled list (June 8-July 17, 2003); included rehabilitation assignment to Portland, Maine. ... Traded by Red Sox with Ps Brandon Lyon and Jorge de la Rosa and a player to be named to Arizona Diamondbacks for P Curt Schilling (November 28, 2003); Diamondbacks acquired OF Michael Goss to complete deal (December 15, 2004). ... On disabled list (March 26-May 14, 2004); included rehabilitation assignments to El Paso and Tucson.

CAREER HITTING: 4-for-42 (.095), 3 R, 0 2B, 0 3B, 0 HR, 0 RBI.

Year	Team (League)	W	L	Pct.	ERA	WHIP	G	GS	CG	ShO	Hld.	Sv.-Opp.	IP	H	R	ER	HR	BB-IBB	SO	Avg.
1999—	Lowell (NY-Penn)	0	1	.000	1.26	0.77	5	5	0	0	...	0-...	14.1	6	2	2	1	5-0	16	.122
2000—	Sarasota (Florida State)	9	10	.474	3.44	1.23	27	27	3	3	...	0-...	149.1	147	71	57	7	36-0	143	.257
2001—	Trenton (East.)	3	7	.300	2.83	1.10	20	20	0	0	...	0-...	117.2	102	47	37	5	28-0	130	.231
	—Boston (A.L.)	3	2	.600	4.87	1.44	13	7	0	0	0	0-0	44.1	44	26	24	4	20-1	26	.259
2002—	Boston (A.L.)	5	4	.556	3.46	1.34	43	12	0	0	3	1-1	106.2	113	56	41	12	30-0	101	.268
	—Pawtucket (Int'l)	0	3	.000	3.96	1.60	5	3	1	0	...	0-...	25.0	34	15	11	1	6-0	28	.337
2003—	Portland (East.)	0	1	.000	6.75	2.00	3	2	0	0	...	0-...	4.0	5	3	3	1	3-0	7	.294
	—Pawtucket (Int'l)	1	0	1.000	3.46	1.20	5	4	0	0	...	1-...	13.0	11	5	5	1	5-0	14	.234
	—Boston (A.L.)	6	5	.545	5.47	1.47	19	14	0	0	1	1-1	79.0	82	55	48	9	34-0	63	.270
2004—	El Paso (Texas)	0	0	...	2.08	1.38	2	2	0	0	...	0-...	4.1	3	1	1	0	3-0	5	.188
	—Tucson (PCL)	2	0	1.000	0.00	0.93	3	3	0	0	...	0-...	15.0	11	2	0	0	3-0	16	.196
	—Arizona (N.L.)	4	15	.211	6.65	1.65	27	27	0	0	0	0-0	142.0	171	111	105	31	63-5	117	.302
	American League totals (3 years)	14	11	.560	4.42	1.40	75	33	0	0	3	2-2	230.0	239	137	113	25	84-1	190	.267
	National League totals (1 year)	4	15	.211	6.65	1.65	27	27	0	0	0	0-0	142.0	171	111	105	31	63-5	117	.302
	Major League totals (4 years)	18	26	.409	5.27	1.50	102	60	0	0	3	2-2	372.0	410	248	218	56	147-6	307	.280

FOULKE, KEITH — P

PERSONAL: Born October 19, 1972, in Rapid City, S.D. ... 6-0/210. ... Throws right, bats right. ... Full name: Keith Charles Foulke. ... Name pronounced: FOLK. ... High school: Hargrove (Huffman, Texas). ... College: Lewis-Clark (Idaho) State.

TRANSACTIONS/CAREER NOTES: Selected by San Francisco Giants organization in ninth round of 1994 free-agent draft. ... Traded by Giants with SS Mike Caruso, OF Brian Manning and Ps Lorenzo Barcelo, Bob Howry and Ken Vining to Chicago White Sox for Ps Wilson Alvarez, Danny Darwin and Roberto Hernandez (July 31, 1997). ... On disabled list (August 28, 1998-remainder of season). ... On suspended list (May 5-7, 2000). ... Traded by White Sox with C Mark Johnson, P Joe Valentine and cash to Oakland Athletics for P Billy Koch and two players to be named (December 3, 2002); White Sox acquired P Neal Cotts and OF Daylon Holt to complete deal (December 16, 2002). ... Signed as a free agent by Boston Red Sox (January 7, 2004). ... Selected by Detroit Tigers organiztion in 14th round of 1993 free-agent draft; did not sign.

CAREER HITTING: 2-for-16 (.125), 0 R, 0 2B, 0 3B, 0 HR, 0 RBI.

Year	Team (League)	W	L	Pct.	ERA	WHIP	G	GS	CG	ShO	Hld.	Sv.-Opp.	IP	H	R	ER	HR	BB-IBB	SO	Avg.
1994—	Everett (Northwest)	2	1	1.000	0.93	1.03	4	4	0	0	...	0-...	19.1	17	4	2	0	3-0	22	.233
1995—	San Jose (California)	13	6	.684	3.50	1.12	28	26	2	1	...	0-...	177.1	166	85	69	16	32-0	168	.247
1996—	Shreveport (Texas)	12	7	.632	2.76	1.01	27	27	4	2	...	0-...	182.2	149	61	56	16	35-0	129	.225
1997—	Phoenix (PCL)	5	4	.556	4.50	1.24	12	12	0	0	...	0-...	76.0	79	38	38	11	15-0	54	.270
	—San Francisco (N.L.)	1	5	.167	8.26	1.75	11	8	0	0	...	0-1	44.2	60	41	41	9	18-1	33	.324
	—Nashville (A.A.)	0	0	...	5.79	1.71	1	1	0	0	...	0-...	4.2	8	3	3	1	0-0	4	.400
	—Chicago (A.L.)	3	0	1.000	3.45	1.15	16	0	0	0	3-5	...	28.2	28	11	11	4	5-1	21	.255

F

Year	Team (League)	W	L	Pct.	ERA	WHIP	G	GS	CG	ShO	Hld.	Sv.-Opp.	IP	H	R	ER	HR	BB-IBB	SO	Avg.
1998— Chicago (A.L.)		3	2	.600	4.13	1.09	54	0	0	0	13	1-2	65.1	51	31	30	9	20-3	57	.213
1999— Chicago (A.L.)		3	3	.500	2.22	0.88	67	0	0	0	22	9-13	105.1	72	28	26	11	21-4	123	.188
2000— Chicago (A.L.)		3	1	.750	2.97	1.00	72	0	0	0	3	34-39	88.0	66	31	29	9	22-2	91	.207
2001— Chicago (A.L.)		4	9	.308	2.33	0.98	72	0	0	0	0	42-45	81.0	57	21	21	3	22-1	75	.199
2002— Chicago (A.L.)		2	4	.333	2.90	1.00	65	0	0	0	8	11-14	77.2	65	26	25	7	13-2	58	.225
2003— Oakland (A.L.)		9	1	.900	2.08	0.89	72	0	0	0	*	43-48	86.2	57	21	20	10	20-2	88	.184
2004— Boston (A.L.)		5	3	.625	2.17	0.94	72	0	0	0	0	32-39	83.0	63	22	20	8	15-5	79	.206
American League totals (8 years)		32	23	.582	2.66	0.97	490	0	0	0	51	175-205	615.2	459	191	182	61	138-20	592	.205
National League totals (1 year)		1	5	.167	8.26	1.75	11	8	0	0	0	0-1	44.2	60	41	41	9	18-1	33	.324
Major League totals (8 years)		33	28	.541	3.04	1.02	501	8	0	0	51	175-206	660.1	519	232	223	70	156-21	625	.214

DIVISION SERIES RECORD

Year	Team (League)	W	L	Pct.	ERA	WHIP	G	GS	CG	ShO	Hld.	Sv.-Opp.	IP	H	R	ER	HR	BB-IBB	SO	Avg.
2000— Chicago (A.L.)		0	1	.000	11.57	2.57	2	0	0	0	0	0-0	2.1	4	3	3	2	2-0	2	.400
2003— Oakland (A.L.)		0	1	.000	3.60	1.20	3	0	0	0	0	0-1	5.0	4	2	2	0	2-1	3	.211
2004— Boston (A.L.)		0	0	...	0.00	1.00	2	0	0	0	0	1-1	3.0	2	0	0	0	1-1	5	.182
Division series totals (3 years)		0	2	.000	4.35	1.45	7	0	0	0	0	1-2	10.1	10	5	5	2	5-2	10	.250

CHAMPIONSHIP SERIES RECORD

Year	Team (League)	W	L	Pct.	ERA	WHIP	G	GS	CG	ShO	Hld.	Sv.-Opp.	IP	H	R	ER	HR	BB-IBB	SO	Avg.
2004— Boston (A.L.)		0	0	...	0.00	1.17	5	0	0	0	0	1-1	6.0	1	0	0	0	6-0	6	.053

WORLD SERIES RECORD

Year	Team (League)	W	L	Pct.	ERA	WHIP	G	GS	CG	ShO	Hld.	Sv.-Opp.	IP	H	R	ER	HR	BB-IBB	SO	Avg.
2004— Boston (A.L.)		1	0	1.000	1.80	1.00	4	0	0	0	0	1-2	5.0	4	1	1	1	1-1	8	.200

ALL-STAR GAME RECORD

Year	Team (League)	W	L	Pct.	ERA	WHIP	G	GS	CG	ShO	Hld.	Sv.-Opp.	IP	H	R	ER	HR	BB-IBB	SO	Avg.
All-Star Game totals (1 year)		0	0	...	0.00	0.00	1	0	0	0	0	1-1	1.0	0	0	0	0	0-0	0	.000

FOX, ANDY   3B

PERSONAL: Born January 12, 1971, in Sacramento, Calif. ... 6-4/202. ... Bats left, throws right. ... Full name: Andrew Junipero Fox. ... High school: Christian Brothers (Sacramento).

TRANSACTIONS/CAREER NOTES: Selected by New York Yankees organization in second round of 1989 free-agent draft. ... Traded by Yankees to Arizona Diamondbacks for Ps Marty Janzen and Todd Erdos (March 8, 1998). ... On disabled list (August 28-September 11, 1999). ... On disabled list (March 23-April 17, 2000); included rehabilitation assignments to El Paso and Tucson. ... Traded by Diamondbacks to Florida Marlins for OF Danny Bautista (June 9, 2000). ... On disabled list (April 11-July 12, 2001); included rehabilitation assignments to Calgary. ... Signed as a free agent by Texas Rangers organization (November 17, 2003). ... Selected by Montreal Expos from Rangers organization in Rule 5 major league draft (December 15, 2003). ... Released by Expos (July 11, 2004). ... Signed by Rangers organization (July 14, 2004).

2004 GAMES PLAYED BY POSITION (MLB): 2B—6, 3B—5, SS—5, OF—2, DH—1, 1B—1.

									BATTING										FIELDING	
Year	Team (League)	Pos.	G	AB	R	H	2B	3B	HR	RBI	BB	SO	HBP	GDP	SB-CS	Avg.	OBP	SLG	OPS	E	Avg.
1989— GC Yankees (GCL)		3B	40	141	26	35	9	2	3	25	31	29	2	1	6-1	.248	.386	.404	.791	10	.920
1990— Greensboro (S. Atl.)		3B	134	455	68	99	19	4	9	55	92	132	4	14	26-5	.218	.353	.336	.689	45	.880
1991— Prince Will. (Car.)		3B	126	417	60	96	22	2	10	46	81	104	6	7	15-13	.230	.357	.365	.721	29	.920
1992— Prince Will. (Car.)		3B-SS	125	473	75	113	18	3	7	42	54	81	6	7	28-14	.239	.325	.334	.659	27	.937
1993— Alb./Colon. (East.)		3B	65	236	44	65	16	1	3	24	32	54	0	1	12-6	.275	.362	.390	.752	19	.917
1994— Alb./Colon. (East.)		3B-SS-2B	121	472	75	105	20	3	11	43	62	102	2	4	22-13	.222	.315	.347	.662	34	.916
1995— Norwich (East.)		SS	44	175	23	36	3	5	5	17	19	36	0	3	8-1	.206	.282	.366	.648	9	.958
— Columbus (Int'l)		3-S-OF-2	82	302	61	105	16	6	9	37	43	41	4	5	22-4	.348	.432	.530	.962	9	.970
1996— New York (A.L.)		2-3-S-DH-O	113	189	26	37	4	0	3	13	20	28	1	2	11-3	.196	.276	.265	.541	12	.955
1997— Columbus (Int'l)		3-2-S-O-DH	95	318	66	87	11	4	6	33	54	64	1	5	28-11	.274	.380	.390	.770	14	.959
— New York (A.L.)		3-2-S-DH-O	22	31	13	7	1	0	0	1	7	9	0	1	2-1	.226	.368	.258	.626	1	.980
1998— Arizona (N.L.)		2-0-3-1B	139	502	67	139	21	6	9	44	43	97	18	2	14-7	.277	.355	.396	.751	8	.984
1999— Arizona (N.L.)		SS-3B	99	274	34	70	12	2	6	33	33	61	9	1	4-1	.255	.351	.380	.731	14	.955
2000— El Paso (Texas)		3B-SS-OF	4	15	3	6	2	0	0	4	2	2	0	0	1-1	.400	.471	.533	1.004	2	.714
— Tucson (PCL)		2B-3B-SS	3	13	1	3	0	1	0	3	0	1	0	1	0-1	.231	.231	.385	.615	1	.917
— Arizona (N.L.)		3B-0F-1B	31	86	10	18	4	0	1	10	4	16	0	1	2-1	.209	.244	.291	.535	2	.962
— Florida (N.L.)		S-OF-3-2B	69	164	19	40	4	2	3	10	18	37	3	1	8-3	.244	.330	.348	.677	11	.938
2001— Florida (N.L.)		SS-3-2-OF	54	81	8	15	0	1	3	7	15	17	2	2	1-0	.185	.327	.321	.648	3	.957
— Calgary (PCL)		2-S-OF-3-1	11	42	10	18	2	1	2	8	3	2	1	1	1-1	.429	.478	.667	1.145	1	.971
2002— Florida (N.L.)		S-2-3B-OF	133	435	55	109	14	5	4	41	49	94	10	9	31-7	.251	.338	.333	.671	18	.966
2003— Florida (N.L.)		2-S-3-1-OF	70	108	12	21	5	1	0	8	7	29	4	2	1-2	.194	.269	.259	.528	4	.950
2004— Montreal (N.L.)		SS-2-3-1	34	43	2	4	0	0	1	1	0	16	0	1	0-0	.093	.093	.163	.256	0	1.000
— Oklahoma (PCL)		3-DH-1-O-S	34	125	22	37	10	0	1	12	14	25	4	0	1-2	.296	.385	.400	.785	6	.939
— Texas (A.L.)		2-3-OF-DH	12	12	2	1	0	0	0	0	1	3	0	0	0-0	.083	.154	.083	.237	0	1.000
American League totals (3 years)			147	232	41	45	5	0	3	14	28	40	1	3	13-4	.194	.284	.254	.538	13	.961
National League totals (7 years)			629	1693	207	416	60	17	27	154	169	367	46	22	61-21	.246	.330	.349	.679	60	.965
Major League totals (9 years)			776	1925	248	461	65	17	30	168	197	407	47	25	74-25	.239	.324	.338	.662	73	.964

DIVISION SERIES RECORD

Year	Team (League)	Pos.	G	AB	R	H	2B	3B	HR	RBI	BB	SO	HBP	GDP	SB-CS	Avg.	OBP	SLG	OPS	E	Avg.
1996— New York (A.L.)		DH	2	0	0	0	0	0	0	0	0	0	0	0	0-0	...	...	...	...	0	...
1997— New York (A.L.)		2B	2	0	0	0	0	0	0	0	0	0	0	0	0-0	...	...	...	...	0	...
1999— Arizona (N.L.)		SS	1	3	0	0	0	0	0	0	0	1	0	0	0-0	.000	.000	.000	.000	1	.750
Division series totals (3 years)			5	3	0	0	0	0	0	0	0	1	0	0	0-0	.000	.000	.000	.000	1	.750

CHAMPIONSHIP SERIES RECORD

Year	Team (League)	Pos.	G	AB	R	H	2B	3B	HR	RBI	BB	SO	HBP	GDP	SB-CS	Avg.	OBP	SLG	OPS	E	Avg.
1996— New York (A.L.)		DH	2	0	0	0	0	0	0	0	0	0	0	0	0-0	...	...	...	...	0	...

WORLD SERIES RECORD

Year	Team (League)	Pos.	G	AB	R	H	2B	3B	HR	RBI	BB	SO	HBP	GDP	SB-CS	Avg.	OBP	SLG	OPS	E	Avg.
1996— New York (A.L.)		2B-3B	4	0	1	0	0	0	0	0	0	0	0	0	0-0	...	...	...	...	0	1.000

F

FOX, CHAD   P

PERSONAL: Born September 3, 1970, in Houston, Texas. ... 6-3/209. ... Throws right, bats right. ... Full name: Chad Douglas Fox. ... High school: Westfield (Houston). ... College: Tarleton State (Texas).

TRANSACTIONS/CAREER NOTES: Selected by Cincinnati Reds organization in 23rd round of 1992 free-agent draft. ... Traded by Reds with a player to be named to Atlanta Braves for OF Mike Kelly (January 9, 1996); Braves acquired P Ray King to complete deal (June 11, 1996). ... On disabled list (July 16-September 3, 1996). ... Traded by Braves to Milwaukee Brewers for OF Gerald Williams (December 11, 1997). ... On disabled list (May 11-June 30, 1998); included rehabilitation assignment to Beloit. ... On disabled list (April 21, 1999-remainder of season; and March 28, 2000-entire season). ... On disabled list (March 30-May 31 and June 8, 2002-remainder of season); included rehabilitation assignment to Huntsville. ... Released by Brewers (October 15, 2002). ... Signed by Boston Red Sox (December 24, 2002). ... On disabled list (April 28-June 29, 2003); included rehabilitation assignments to Sarasota and Portland, Maine. ... Released by Red Sox (July 30, 2003). ... Signed by Florida Marlins organization (August 8, 2003). ... On disabled list (April 28, 2004-remainder of season).

CAREER HITTING: 0-for-7 (.000), 0 R, 0 2B, 0 3B, 0 HR, 0 RBI.

Year	Team (League)	W	L	Pct.	ERA	WHIP	G	GS	CG	ShO	Hld.	Sv.-Opp.	IP	H	R	ER	HR	BB-IBB	SO	Avg.
1992—	Princeton (Appalachian)	4	2	.667	4.74	1.80	15	8	0	0	...	0-...	49.1	55	43	26	2	34-1	37	.275
1993—	Char., W.Va. (SAL)	9	12	.429	5.37	1.73	27	26	0	0	...	0-...	135.2	138	100	81	7	97-0	81	.268
1994—	Winston-Salem (Caro.)	12	5	.706	3.86	1.38	25	25	1	0	...	0-...	156.1	121	77	67	18	94-0	137	.216
1995—	Chattanooga (Southern)	4	5	.444	5.06	1.60	20	17	0	0	...	0-...	80.0	76	49	45	2	52-1	56	.250
1996—	Richmond (Int'l)	3	10	.231	4.73	1.50	18	18	1	0	...	0-...	93.1	91	57	49	9	49-1	87	.261
1997—	Richmond (Int'l)	1	0	1.000	3.70	1.56	13	0	0	0	...	0-...	24.1	24	10	10	1	14-0	25	.273
—	Atlanta (N.L.)	0	1	.000	3.29	1.46	30	0	0	0	7	0-1	27.1	24	12	10	4	16-0	28	.231
1998—	Milwaukee (N.L.)	1	4	.200	3.95	1.33	49	0	0	0	20	0-2	57.0	56	27	25	4	20-0	64	.260
—	Beloit (Midw.)	0	1	.000	4.50	0.50	2	1	0	0	...	0-...	2.0	1	1	1	0	0-0	3	.167
1999—	Milwaukee (N.L.)	0	0	...	10.80	2.25	6	0	0	0	1	0-0	6.2	11	8	8	1	4-0	12	.355
2000—	Milwaukee (N.L.)			Did not play.																
2001—	Indianapolis (Int'l)	3	0	1.000	1.50	1.17	4	0	0	0	...	0-...	6.0	4	1	1	0	3-0	8	.190
—	Milwaukee (N.L.)	5	2	.714	1.89	1.20	65	0	0	0	20	2-4	66.2	44	16	14	6	36-7	80	.181
2002—	Huntsville (Southern)	0	1	.000	0.00	1.31	3	0	0	0	...	0-...	5.1	5	1	0	0	2-0	7	.263
—	Milwaukee (N.L.)	1	0	1.000	5.79	2.36	3	0	0	0	0	0-0	4.2	6	3	3	0	5-1	3	.316
2003—	Sarasota (Florida State)	0	0	...	4.50	1.50	2	1	0	0	...	0-...	2.0	2	1	1	0	1-0	1	.250
—	Pawtucket (Int'l)	0	0	...	13.50	3.00	1	0	0	0	...	0-...	1.1	3	3	2	1	1-0	2	.500
—	Portland (East.)	0	0	...	0.00	2.20	1	0	0	0	...	0-...	1.1	1	0	0	0	2-0	2	.200
—	Boston (A.L.)	1	2	.333	4.50	2.00	17	0	0	0	0	3-5	18.0	19	10	9	2	17-2	19	.264
—	Albuquerque (PCL)	0	0	...	3.86	2.10	3	0	0	0	...	0-...	2.1	4	1	1	0	1-0	5	.364
—	Florida (N.L.)	2	1	.667	2.13	1.18	21	0	0	0	7	0-0	25.1	16	6	6	1	14-2	27	.190
2004—	Florida (N.L.)	1	0	1.000	6.75	1.59	12	0	0	0	5	0-2	10.2	9	8	8	1	8-0	17	.225
	American League totals (1 year)	1	2	.333	4.50	2.00	17	0	0	0	0	3-5	18.0	19	10	9	2	17-2	19	.264
	National League totals (7 years)	9	9	.500	3.36	1.36	186	0	0	0	60	2-9	198.1	166	80	74	17	103-10	231	.226
	Major League totals (7 years)	10	11	.476	3.45	1.41	203	0	0	0	60	5-14	216.1	185	90	83	19	120-12	250	.229

DIVISION SERIES RECORD

Year	Team (League)	W	L	Pct.	ERA	WHIP	G	GS	CG	ShO	Hld.	Sv.-Opp.	IP	H	R	ER	HR	BB-IBB	SO	Avg.
2003—	Florida (N.L.)	0	0	...	1.80	1.20	3	0	0	0	1	0-0	5.0	3	1	1	0	3-2	3	.188

CHAMPIONSHIP SERIES RECORD

Year	Team (League)	W	L	Pct.	ERA	WHIP	G	GS	CG	ShO	Hld.	Sv.-Opp.	IP	H	R	ER	HR	BB-IBB	SO	Avg.
2003—	Florida (N.L.)	1	0	1.000	5.40	2.10	3	0	0	0	0	0-0	3.1	5	2	2	1	2-0	2	.333

WORLD SERIES RECORD

Year	Team (League)	W	L	Pct.	ERA	WHIP	G	GS	CG	ShO	Hld.	Sv.-Opp.	IP	H	R	ER	HR	BB-IBB	SO	Avg.
2003—	Florida (N.L.)	0	0	...	6.00	2.67	3	0	0	0	0	0-0	3.0	4	2	2	1	4-1	4	.364

FRANCIS, JEFF   P

PERSONAL: Born January 8, 1981, in Vancouver, British Columbia. ... 6-5/200. ... Throws left, bats left. ... Full name: Jeffrey William Francis. ... High school: North Delta Senior (Delta, B.C.). ... College: British Columbia.

TRANSACTIONS/CAREER NOTES: Selected by Colorado Rockies organization in first round (ninth pick overall) of 2002 free-agent draft.

CAREER HITTING: 0-for-10 (.000), 1 R, 0 2B, 0 3B, 0 HR, 0 RBI.

Year	Team (League)	W	L	Pct.	ERA	WHIP	G	GS	CG	ShO	Hld.	Sv.-Opp.	IP	H	R	ER	HR	BB-IBB	SO	Avg.
2002—	Tri-Cities (N'west)	0	0	...	0.00	0.84	4	3	0	0	...	0-...	10.2	5	0	0	0	4-0	16	.143
—	Asheville (S. Atl.)	0	0	...	1.80	1.00	4	4	0	0	...	0-...	20.0	16	6	4	2	4-0	23	.232
2003—	Visalia (Calif.)	12	9	.571	3.47	1.12	27	27	2	2	...	0-...	160.2	135	66	62	8	45-1	153	.229
2004—	Tulsa (Texas)	13	1	.929	1.98	0.84	17	17	1	1	...	0-...	113.2	73	26	25	9	22-0	147	.180
—	Colo. Springs (PCL)	3	2	.600	2.85	1.02	7	7	0	0	...	0-...	41.0	35	16	13	3	7-0	49	.230
—	Colorado (N.L.)	3	2	.600	5.15	1.50	7	7	0	0	0	0-0	36.2	42	22	21	8	13-1	32	.286
	Major League totals (1 year)	3	2	.600	5.15	1.50	7	7	0	0	0	0-0	36.2	42	22	21	8	13-1	32	.286

FRANCISCO, FRANK   P

PERSONAL: Born September 11, 1979, in Santo Domingo, Dominican Republic. ... 6-2/180. ... Throws right, bats right. ... Full name: Franklin Francisco.

TRANSACTIONS/CAREER NOTES: Signed as a non-drafted free agent by Boston Red Sox organization (December 15, 1996). ... Traded by Red Sox with P Byeong Hak An to Chicago White Sox for P Bob Howry (July 31, 2002). ... Traded by White Sox with OF Anthony Webster and P Josh Rupe to Texas Rangers (July 24, 2003), completing deal in which White Sox acquired OF Carl Everett for three players to be named (July 1, 2003). ... On suspended list (September 18, 2004-remainder of season).

CAREER HITTING: 0-for-0 (.000), 0 R, 0 2B, 0 3B, 0 HR, 0 RBI.

Year	Team (League)	W	L	Pct.	ERA	WHIP	G	GS	CG	ShO	Hld.	Sv.-Opp.	IP	H	R	ER	HR	BB-IBB	SO	Avg.
1999—	GC Red Sox (GCL)	2	4	.333	4.56	1.74	12	7	0	0	...	0-...	53.1	58	39	27	3	35-0	48	.275
2000—	GC Red Sox (GCL)	0	0	...	18.00	4.00	1	0	0	0	...	0-...	1.0	2	3	2	0	2-0	1	.400
2001—	Augusta (S. Atl.)	4	3	.571	2.91	1.03	37	0	0	0	...	2-...	68.0	40	25	22	3	30-0	90	.168
2002—	Trenton (East.)	2	2	.500	5.63	1.63	9	0	0	0	...	0-...	16.0	10	13	10	0	16-1	18	.172
—	Sarasota (Florida State)	1	5	.167	2.55	1.13	16	10	0	0	...	0-...	53.0	33	19	15	1	27-0	58	.185
—	Winston-Salem (Caro.)	0	4	.000	8.06	1.91	6	6	0	0	...	0-...	25.2	31	23	23	3	18-0	25	.310
2003—	Winston-Salem (Caro.)	7	3	.700	3.56	1.21	16	16	1	1	...	0-...	78.1	59	40	31	7	36-0	67	.207
—	Frisco (Texas)	2	3	.400	8.41	1.73	7	6	0	0	...	0-...	35.1	43	33	33	5	18-1	22	.305
2004—	Frisco (Texas)	1	3	.250	2.55	0.96	15	0	0	0	...	6-...	17.2	7	6	5	1	10-1	30	.119
—	Texas (A.L.)	5	1	.833	3.33	1.25	45	0	0	0	10	0-3	51.1	36	19	19	4	28-2	60	.198
	Major League totals (1 year)	5	1	.833	3.33	1.25	45	0	0	0	10	0-3	51.1	36	19	19	4	28-2	60	.198

FRANCO, JOHN

P

PERSONAL: Born September 17, 1960, in Brooklyn, N.Y. ... 5-10/185. ... Throws left, bats left. ... Full name: John Anthony Franco. ... High school: Lafayette (Brooklyn, N.Y.). ... College: St. John's.

TRANSACTIONS/CAREER NOTES: Selected by Los Angeles Dodgers organization in fifth round of June 1981 free-agent draft. ... Traded by Dodgers with P Brett Wise to Cincinnati Reds for IF Rafael Landestoy (May 9, 1983). ... Traded by Reds with OF Don Brown to New York Mets for Ps Randy Myers and Kip Gross (December 6, 1989). ... On disabled list (June 30-August 1 and August 26, 1992-remainder of season; April 17-May 7 and August 3-26, 1993). ... On disabled list (July 3-September 4, 1999); included rehabilitation assignment to Binghamton. ... On disabled list (March 21, 2002-entire season). ... On disabled list (March 28-May 30, 2003); included rehabilitation assignment to St. Lucie.

HONORS: Named N.L. Fireman of the Year by THE SPORTING NEWS (1988, 1990 and 1994).

CAREER HITTING: 3-for-34 (.088), 2 R, 0 2B, 0 3B, 0 HR, 1 RBI.

Year — Team (League)	W	L	Pct.	ERA	WHIP	G	GS	CG	ShO	Hld.	Sv.-Opp.	IP	H	R	ER	HR	BB-IBB	SO	Avg.
1981— Vero Beach (FSL)	7	4	.636	3.53	1.51	13	11	3	0	...	0-...	79.0	78	41	31	1	41-2	60	...
1982— Albuquerque (PCL)	1	2	.333	7.24	2.05	5	5	0	0	...	0-...	27.1	41	22	22	3	15-1	24	...
— San Antonio (Texas)	10	5	.667	4.96	1.74	17	17	3	0	...	0-...	105.1	137	70	58	11	46-1	76	...
1983— Albuquerque (PCL)	0	0	...	5.40	1.40	11	0	0	0	...	0-...	15.0	10	11	9	3	11-2	8	...
— Indianapolis (A.A.)	6	10	.375	4.85	1.65	23	18	2	0	...	2-...	115.0	148	69	62	10	42-3	54	...
1984— Wichita (Am. Assoc.)	1	0	1.000	5.79	1.29	6	0	0	0	...	0-...	9.1	8	6	6	1	4-0	11	.235
— Cincinnati (N.L.)	6	2	.750	2.61	1.39	54	0	0	0	1	4-9	79.1	74	28	23	3	36-4	55	.256
1985— Cincinnati (N.L.)	12	3	.800	2.18	1.24	67	0	0	0	11	12-15	99.0	83	27	24	5	40-8	61	.234
1986— Cincinnati (N.L.)	6	6	.500	2.94	1.33	74	0	0	0	1	29-38	101.0	90	40	33	7	44-12	84	.243
1987— Cincinnati (N.L.)	8	5	.615	2.52	1.26	68	0	0	0	0	32-41	82.0	76	26	23	6	27-6	61	.245
1988— Cincinnati (N.L.)	6	6	.500	1.57	1.01	70	0	0	0	0	* 39-42	86.0	60	18	15	3	27-3	46	.198
1989— Cincinnati (N.L.)	4	8	.333	3.12	1.40	60	0	0	0	0	32-39	80.2	77	35	28	3	36-8	60	.258
1990— New York (N.L.)	5	3	.625	2.53	1.29	55	0	0	0	0	* 33-39	67.2	66	22	19	4	21-2	56	.252
1991— New York (N.L.)	5	9	.357	2.93	1.43	52	0	0	0	0	30-35	55.1	61	27	18	2	18-4	45	.271
1992— New York (N.L.)	6	2	.750	1.64	1.06	31	0	0	0	0	15-17	33.0	24	6	6	1	11-2	20	.209
1993— New York (N.L.)	4	3	.571	5.20	1.79	35	0	0	0	0	10-17	36.1	46	24	21	6	19-3	29	.313
1994— New York (N.L.)	1	4	.200	2.70	1.32	47	0	0	0	0	* 30-36	50.0	47	20	15	2	19-0	42	.244
1995— New York (N.L.)	5	3	.625	2.44	1.26	48	0	0	0	0	29-36	51.2	48	17	14	4	17-2	41	.251
1996— New York (N.L.)	4	3	.571	1.83	1.39	51	0	0	0	0	28-36	54.0	54	15	11	2	21-0	48	.260
1997— New York (N.L.)	5	3	.625	2.55	1.15	59	0	0	0	0	36-42	60.0	49	18	17	3	20-2	53	.226
1998— New York (N.L.)	0	8	.000	3.62	1.47	61	0	0	0	0	38-46	64.2	66	28	26	4	29-7	59	.267
1999— New York (N.L.)	0	2	.000	2.88	1.45	46	0	0	0	1	19-21	40.2	40	14	13	1	19-1	41	.255
— Binghamton (Eastern)	0	0	...	0.00	0.00	1	1	0	0	...	0-...	1.1	0	0	0	0	0-0	1	.000
2000— New York (N.L.)	5	4	.556	3.40	1.29	62	0	0	0	20	4-4	55.2	46	24	21	6	26-6	56	.221
2001— New York (N.L.)	6	2	.750	4.05	1.39	58	0	0	0	17	2-7	53.1	55	25	24	8	19-2	50	.264
2002— New York (N.L.)	Did not play.																		
2003— St. Lucie (Fla. St.)	0	1	.000	6.23	1.60	4	3	0	0	0	0-...	4.1	6	3	3	1	1-0	5	.316
— Norfolk (Int'l)	0	0	...	0.00	1.20	2	0	0	0	0	0-...	1.2	1	0	0	0	1-0	2	.167
— New York (N.L.)	0	3	.000	2.62	1.40	38	0	0	0	4	2-3	34.1	35	11	10	5	13-2	16	.265
2004— New York (N.L.)	2	7	.222	5.28	1.52	52	0	0	0	11	0-1	46.0	46	28	27	6	24-2	36	.258
Major League totals (20 years)	**90**	**86**	**.511**	**2.84**	**1.32**	**1088**	**0**	**0**	**0**	**66**	**424-524**	**1230.2**	**1143**	**453**	**388**	**81**	**486-76**	**959**	**.248**

DIVISION SERIES RECORD

Year — Team (League)	W	L	Pct.	ERA	WHIP	G	GS	CG	ShO	Hld.	Sv.-Opp.	IP	H	R	ER	HR	BB-IBB	SO	Avg.
1999— New York (N.L.)	1	0	1.000	0.00	0.27	3	0	0	0	0	0-0	3.2	1	0	0	0	0-0	2	.091
2000— New York (N.L.)	0	0	...	0.00	0.50	2	0	0	0	0	1-1	2.0	1	0	0	0	0-0	2	.167
Division series totals (2 years)	**1**	**0**	**1.000**	**0.00**	**0.35**	**5**	**0**	**0**	**0**	**0**	**1-1**	**5.2**	**2**	**0**	**0**	**0**	**0-0**	**4**	**.118**

CHAMPIONSHIP SERIES RECORD

Year — Team (League)	W	L	Pct.	ERA	WHIP	G	GS	CG	ShO	Hld.	Sv.-Opp.	IP	H	R	ER	HR	BB-IBB	SO	Avg.
1999— New York (N.L.)	0	0	...	3.38	1.50	3	0	0	0	0	0-1	2.2	3	1	1	0	1-0	3	.333
2000— New York (N.L.)	0	0	...	6.75	1.88	3	0	0	0	2	0-0	2.2	3	2	2	0	2-0	2	.273
Champ. series totals (2 years)	**0**	**0**	**...**	**5.06**	**1.69**	**6**	**0**	**0**	**0**	**2**	**0-1**	**5.1**	**6**	**3**	**3**	**0**	**3-0**	**5**	**.300**

WORLD SERIES RECORD

Year — Team (League)	W	L	Pct.	ERA	WHIP	G	GS	CG	ShO	Hld.	Sv.-Opp.	IP	H	R	ER	HR	BB-IBB	SO	Avg.
2000— New York (N.L.)	1	0	1.000	0.00	0.90	4	0	0	0	1	0-0	3.1	3	0	0	0	0-0	1	.273

ALL-STAR GAME RECORD

	W	L	Pct.	ERA	WHIP	G	GS	CG	ShO	Hld.	Sv.-Opp.	IP	H	R	ER	HR	BB-IBB	SO	Avg.
All-Star Game totals (2 years)	**0**	**0**	**...**	**0.00**	**0.00**	**2**	**0**	**0**	**0**	**0**	**0-0**	**1.2**	**0**	**0**	**0**	**0**	**0-0**	**0**	**.000**

FRANCO, JULIO

1B

PERSONAL: Born August 23, 1958, in San Pedro de Macoris, Dominican Republic. ... 6-1/188. ... Bats right, throws right. ... Full name: Julio Cesar Franco. ... High school: Divine Providence (San Pedro de Macoris, Dominican Republic).

TRANSACTIONS/CAREER NOTES: Signed as a non-drafted free agent by Philadelphia Phillies organization (June 23, 1978). ... Traded by Phillies with 2B Manny Trillo, OF George Vukovich, P Jay Baller and C Jerry Willard to Cleveland Indians for OF Von Hayes (December 9, 1982). ... On disabled list (July 13-August 8, 1987). ... Traded by Indians to Texas Rangers for 1B Pete O'Brien, OF Oddibe McDowell and 2B Jerry Browne (December 6, 1988). ... On disabled list (March 28-April 19, May 4-June 1 and July 9, 1992-remainder of season). ... Signed as a free agent by Chicago White Sox (December 15, 1993). ... Signed by Chiba Lotte Marines of Japan Pacific League (December 28, 1994). ... Signed as a free agent by Indians (December 7, 1995). ... On disabled list (July 7-25 and August 4-30, 1996). ... Released by Indians (August 13, 1997). ... Signed by Milwaukee Brewers (August 13, 1997). ... Signed by Chiba (1998). ... Signed as a free agent by Tampa Bay Devil Rays organization (February 19, 1999). ... Loaned by Devil Rays organization to Mexico City Tigers of the Mexican League (March 29-September 18, 1999). ... Contract purchased by Atlanta Braves organization from Mexico City (August 31, 2001). ... On disabled list (August 17-September 1, 2003).

2004 GAMES PLAYED BY POSITION (MLB): 1B—84, DH—1.

Year — Team (League)	Pos.	G	AB	R	H	2B	3B	HR	RBI	BB	SO	HBP	GDP	SB-CS	Avg.	OBP	SLG	OPS	E	Avg.
1978— Butte (Pio.)	SS	47	141	34	43	5	2	3	28	17	30	1	...	4-3	.305	.381	.433	.814	25	.781
1979— Cen. Oregon (NWL)	SS	71	299	57	98	15	5	10	45	24	59	3	...	22-9	.328	.381	.512	.893	31	.921
1980— Peninsula (Caro.)	SS	140	555	105	178	25	6	11	99	33	66	8	...	44-12	.321	.361	.447	.808	42	.934
1981— Reading (East.)	SS	139	532	70	160	17	3	8	74	52	60	5	...	27-14	.301	.365	.389	.754	30	.958
1982— Okla. City (A.A.)	3B-SS	120	463	80	139	19	5	21	66	39	56	3	...	33-11	.300	.357	.499	.856	42	.930

F

Year	Team (League)	Pos.	G	AB	R	H	2B	3B	HR	RBI	BB	SO	HBP	GDP	SB-CS	Avg.	OBP	SLG	OPS	E	Avg.
— Philadelphia (N.L.)	3B-SS	16	29	3	8	1	0	0	3	2	4	0	1	0-2	.276	.323	.310	.633	0	1.000
1983—Cleveland (A.L.)	SS	149	560	68	153	24	8	8	80	27	50	2	21	32-12	.273	.306	.388	.693	28	.961
1984—Cleveland (A.L.)	SS-DH	160	* 658	82	188	22	5	3	79	43	68	6	23	19-10	.286	.331	.348	.679	* 36	.955
1985—Cleveland (A.L.) 2B-SS-DH		160	636	97	183	33	4	6	90	54	74	4	26	13-9	.288	.343	.381	.723	‡ 36	.950
1986—Cleveland (A.L.) 2B-SS-DH		149	599	80	183	30	5	10	74	32	66	0	28	10-7	.306	.338	.422	.760	19	.972
1987—Cleveland (A.L.) 2B-SS-DH		128	495	86	158	24	3	8	52	57	56	3	23	32-9	.319	.389	.428	.818	18	.964
1988—Cleveland (A.L.)	2B-DH	152	613	88	186	23	6	10	54	56	72	2	17	25-11	.303	.361	.409	.771	14	.982
1989—Texas (A.L.)	2B-DH	150	548	80	173	31	5	13	92	66	69	1	27	21-3	.316	.386	.462	.848	13	.980
1990—Texas (A.L.)	2B-DH	157	582	96	172	27	1	11	69	82	83	2	12	31-10	.296	.383	.402	.785	• 19	.975
1991—Texas (A.L.)	2B	146	589	108	201	27	3	15	78	65	78	3	13	36-9	* .341	.408	.474	.882	14	.979
1992—Texas (A.L.) DH-2B-OF		35	107	19	25	7	0	2	8	15	17	0	3	1-1	.234	.328	.355	.683	3	.927
1993—Texas (A.L.)	DH	144	532	85	154	31	3	14	84	62	95	1	16	9-3	.289	.360	.438	.798	...	...
1994—Chicago (A.L.)	DH-1B	112	433	72	138	19	2	20	98	62	75	5	14	8-1	.319	.406	.510	.916	3	.969
1995—Chiba Lotte (Jap. Pac.)	1B	127	474	60	145	25	3	10	58	...	...	...	...	11-...	.306	...	.435	...	...	...
1996—Cleveland (A.L.)	1B-DH	112	432	72	139	20	1	14	76	61	82	3	14	8-8	.322	.407	.470	.877	9	.990
1997—Cleveland (A.L.) DH-2B-1B		78	289	46	82	13	1	3	25	38	75	0	13	8-5	.284	.367	.367	.734	3	.983
— Milwaukee (A.L.)	DH-1B	42	141	22	34	3	0	4	19	31	41	1	4	7-1	.241	.373	.348	.720	1	.992
1998—Chiba Lotte (Jap. Pac.)		131	487	78	141	27	2	18	77	...	...	...	...	7-...	.290	...	.464	...	...	...
1999—Tigres (Mex.)	1B	93	326	90	138	22	6	14	77	80	44	...	...	9-1	.423	...	.656	...	2	.993
— Tampa Bay (A.L.)	1B	1	1	0	0	0	0	0	0	0	1	0	0	0-0	.000	.000	.000	.000	0	1.000
2000—Samsung (Korean)		132	477	...	156	...	...	22	110	...	...	...	...	0-...	.327	...	.465	...	...	...
2001—Tigres (Mex.) DH-1B-OF		110	407	90	178	34	5	18	90	50	56	...	...	15-6	.437	...	.678	...	5	.991
— Atlanta (N.L.)	1B	25	90	13	27	4	0	3	11	10	20	1	3	0-0	.300	.376	.444	.821	1	.995
2002—Atlanta (N.L.)	1B-DH	125	338	51	96	13	1	6	30	39	75	1	13	5-1	.284	.357	.382	.739	8	.990
2003—Atlanta (N.L.)	1B	103	197	28	58	12	2	5	31	25	43	0	8	0-1	.294	.372	.452	.824	1	.998
2004—Atlanta (N.L.)	1B-DH	125	320	37	99	18	3	6	57	36	65	1	10	4-2	.309	.378	.441	.818	2	.997
American League totals (15 years)		1875	7215	1101	2169	334	47	141	978	751	1002	33	254	260-99	.301	.366	.419	.785	216	.972
National League totals (5 years)		394	974	132	288	48	6	20	132	112	210	3	35	9-6	.296	.368	.419	.787	12	.994
Major League totals (20 years)		2269	8189	1233	2457	382	53	161	1110	863	1212	36	289	269-105	.300	.366	.419	.785	228	.977

DIVISION SERIES RECORD

Year	Team (League)	Pos.	G	AB	R	H	2B	3B	HR	RBI	BB	SO	HBP	GDP	SB-CS	Avg.	OBP	SLG	OPS	E	Avg.
1996—Cleveland (A.L.)	DH-1B	4	15	1	2	0	0	0	1	1	6	0	0	0-0	.133	.176	.133	.310	0	1.000
2001—Atlanta (N.L.)	1B	3	13	3	4	0	0	1	1	0	1	0	0	0-1	.308	.308	.538	.846	0	1.000
2002—Atlanta (N.L.)	1B	5	22	2	4	0	0	0	1	2	3	0	1	1-0	.182	.250	.182	.432	0	1.000
2003—Atlanta (N.L.)	1B	4	8	1	4	1	0	0	0	2	2	0	0	0-0	.500	.600	.625	1.225	0	1.000
2004—Atlanta (N.L.)	1B	3	4	0	0	0	0	0	0	0	1	0	0	0-0	.000	.000	.000	.000	0	1.000
Division series totals (5 years)		19	62	7	14	1	0	1	3	5	13	0	1	1-1	.226	.279	.290	.570	0	1.000

CHAMPIONSHIP SERIES RECORD

Year	Team (League)	Pos.	G	AB	R	H	2B	3B	HR	RBI	BB	SO	HBP	GDP	SB-CS	Avg.	OBP	SLG	OPS	E	Avg.
2001—Atlanta (N.L.)	1B	5	23	2	6	0	0	1	2	0	2	0	0	0-0	.261	.261	.391	.652	0	1.000

ALL-STAR GAME RECORD

			G	AB	R	H	2B	3B	HR	RBI	BB	SO	HBP	GDP	SB-CS	Avg.	OBP	SLG	OPS	E	Avg.
All-Star Game totals (2 years)			2	6	0	2	1	0	0	2	0	0	0	0	0-0	.333	.333	.500	.833	0	1.000

FRANKLIN, RYAN   P

PERSONAL: Born March 5, 1973, in Fort Smith, Ark. ... 6-3/180. ... Throws right, bats right. ... Full name: Ryan Ray Franklin. ... High school: Spiro (Okla.). ... Junior college: Seminole (Okla.).

TRANSACTIONS/CAREER NOTES: Selected by Toronto Blue Jays organization in 25th round of 1991 free-agent draft; did not sign. ... Selected by Seattle Mariners organization in 23rd round of 1992 free-agent draft. ... On disabled list (June 28-July 15, 2002); included rehabilitation assignment to Everett.

CAREER HITTING: 1-for-7 (.143), 1 R, 0 2B, 0 3B, 0 HR, 0 RBI.

Year	Team (League)	W	L	Pct.	ERA	WHIP	G	GS	CG	ShO	Hld.	Sv.-Opp.	IP	H	R	ER	HR	BB-IBB	SO	Avg.
1993—Bellingham (N'west)	5	3	.625	2.92	1.34	15	14	1	1	...	0-...	74.0	72	38	24	2	27-0	55	.250
1994—Appleton (Midw.)	9	6	.600	3.13	1.08	18	18	5	1	...	0-...	118.0	105	60	41	6	23-0	102	.234
— Riverside (California)	4	2	.667	3.06	1.12	8	8	1	1	...	0-...	61.2	61	26	21	5	8-0	35	.249
— Calgary (PCL)	0	0	...	7.94	1.76	1	1	0	0	...	0-...	5.2	9	6	5	2	1-0	2	.333
1995—Port City (Sou.)	6	10	.375	4.32	1.34	31	20	1	1	...	0-...	146.0	153	84	70	13	43-4	102	.274
1996—Port City (Sou.)	6	12	.333	4.01	1.23	28	27	2	0	...	0-...	182.0	186	99	81	23	37-0	127	.265
— Tacoma (PCL)	4	2	.667	3.03	0.99	11	8	2	2	...	0-...	59.1	45	22	20	4	14-1	49	.208
1997—Memphis (Sou.)	5	5	.500	4.18	1.34	14	14	0	0	...	0-...	90.1	97	48	42	11	24-1	59	.281
1998—Tacoma (PCL)	5	6	.455	4.51	1.41	34	16	1	0	...	1-...	127.2	148	75	64	18	32-2	90	.292
1999—Tacoma (PCL)	6	9	.400	4.71	1.29	29	19	2	1	...	0-...	135.2	142	81	71	17	33-1	94	.270
— Seattle (A.L.)	0	0	...	4.76	1.59	6	0	0	0	0	0-0	11.1	10	6	6	2	8-1	6	.238
2000—Tacoma (PCL)	11	5	.688	3.90	1.11	31	22	4	0	...	0-...	164.0	147	85	71	28	35-1	142	.240
2001—Seattle (A.L.)	5	1	.833	3.56	1.28	38	0	0	0	5	0-1	78.1	76	32	31	13	24-4	60	.250
— Tacoma (PCL)	0	0	...	0.00	0.55	1	0	0	0	...	0-...	3.2	2	0	0	0	0-0	3	.167
2002—Seattle (A.L.)	7	5	.583	4.02	1.17	41	12	0	0	3	0-1	118.2	117	62	53	14	22-1	65	.255
— Everett (Northwest)	0	0	...	0.00	0.75	1	1	0	0	...	0-...	2.2	2	1	0	0	0-0	1	.200
2003—Seattle (A.L.)	11	13	.458	3.57	1.23	32	32	2	1	0	0-0	212.0	199	93	84	34	61-3	99	.251
2004—Seattle (A.L.)	4	16	.200	4.90	1.42	32	32	1	0	0	0-0	200.1	224	116	109	33	61-1	104	.285
Major League totals (5 years)	27	35	.435	4.10	1.29	149	76	4	2	9	0-2	620.2	626	309	283	96	176-10	334	.263

FRANKLIN, WAYNE   P

PERSONAL: Born March 9, 1974, in Wilmington, Del. ... 6-2/204. ... Throws left, bats left. ... Full name: Gary Wayne Franklin. ... High school: Northeast (Md.). ... College: Maryland-Baltimore County.

TRANSACTIONS/CAREER NOTES: Selected by Los Angeles Dodgers organization in 36th round of 1996 free-agent draft. ... Selected by Houston Astros organization from Dodgers organization in Rule 5 minor league draft (December 14, 1998). ... Traded by Astros to Milwaukee Brewers (September 3, 2002), as part of deal in which Brewers traded IF Mark Loretta to Astros for two players to be named (August 31, 2002); Brewers acquired 2B Keith Ginter to complete deal (September 5, 2002). ... Traded by Brewers with P Leo Estrella to San Francisco Giants for Ps Carlos Villanueva and Glenn Woolard (March 30, 2004). ... On disabled list (July 29-August 18, 2004); included rehabilitation assignment to Fresno.

F

CAREER HITTING: 11-for-70 (.157), 3 R, 1 2B, 0 3B, 0 HR, 5 RBI.

Year — Team (League)	W	L	Pct.	ERA	WHIP	G	GS	CG	ShO	Hld.	Sv.-Opp.	IP	H	R	ER	HR	BB-IBB	SO	Avg.
1996— Yakima (N'west)	1	0	1.000	2.52	1.76	20	0	0	0	...	1-...	25.0	32	10	7	2	12-3	22	.311
1997— Savannah (S. Atl.)	5	3	.625	3.18	1.39	28	7	1	0	...	2-...	82.0	79	41	29	10	35-0	58	.246
— San Bernardino (Calif.) ...	0	0	...	0.00	1.00	1	0	0	0	...	0-...	2.0	2	0	0	0	0-0	1	.286
1998— Vero Beach (FSL)	9	3	.750	3.53	1.23	48	0	0	0	...	10-...	86.2	81	43	34	7	26-0	78	.243
1999— Kissimmee (Fla. St.)	3	0	1.000	1.53	0.96	12	0	0	0	...	1-...	17.2	11	4	3	0	6-0	22	.180
— Jackson (Texas)	3	1	.750	1.61	0.93	46	0	0	0	...	20-...	50.1	31	11	9	3	16-3	40	.178
2000— New Orleans (PCL)	3	3	.500	3.63	1.57	48	0	0	0	...	4-...	44.2	51	29	18	4	19-3	37	.279
— Houston (N.L.)	0	0	...	5.48	1.69	25	0	0	0	8	0-0	21.1	24	14	13	2	12-1	21	.282
2001— Houston (N.L.)	0	0	...	6.75	2.17	11	0	0	0	1	0-0	12.0	17	9	9	4	9-0	9	.333
— New Orleans (PCL)	2	1	.667	3.81	1.31	41	0	0	0	...	0-...	49.2	47	28	21	6	18-2	51	.244
2002— New Orleans (PCL)	13	9	.591	3.12	1.18	29	27	1	0	...	0-...	179.0	153	68	62	14	59-2	141	.235
— Milwaukee (N.L.)	2	1	.667	2.63	1.38	4	4	0	0	0	0-0	24.0	16	8	7	1	17-1	17	.188
2003— Milwaukee (N.L.)	10	.13	.435	5.50	1.52	36	34	1	1	0	0-0	194.2	201	* 129	• 119	36	94-2	116	.268
2004— Fresno (PCL)	0	2	.000	3.86	1.07	3	3	0	0	...	0-...	9.1	6	4	4	0	4-0	11	.182
— San Francisco (N.L.)	2	1	.667	6.39	1.52	43	2	0	0	5	0-1	50.2	55	37	36	11	22-2	40	.281
Major League totals (5 years)	14	15	.483	5.47	1.54	119	40	1	1	14	0-1	302.2	313	197	184	54	154-6	203	.268

FRASOR, JASON   P

PERSONAL: Born August 9, 1977, in Chicago, Ill. ... 5-10/170. ... Throws right, bats right. ... Full name: Jason Andrew Frasor. ... High school: Oak Forest (Ill.). ... College: Southern Illinois.

TRANSACTIONS/CAREER NOTES: Selected by Detroit Tigers organization in 33rd round of 1999 free-agent draft. ... Traded by Tigers to Los Angeles Dodgers (September 18, 2002), completing deal in which Tigers acquired OF Hiram Bocachica for P Tom Farmer and a player to be named (July 25, 2002). ... Traded by Dodgers to Toronto Blue Jays for OF Jayson Werth (March 29, 2004).

CAREER HITTING: 0-for-0 (.000), 0 R, 0 2B, 0 3B, 0 HR, 0 RBI.

Year — Team (League)	W	L	Pct.	ERA	WHIP	G	GS	CG	ShO	Hld.	Sv.-Opp.	IP	H	R	ER	HR	BB-IBB	SO	Avg.
1999— Oneonta (N.Y.-Penn)	3	3	.500	1.69	0.99	12	11	0	0	...	0-...	58.2	36	16	11	3	22-0	69	.176
— West. Mich. (Mid.)	2	1	.667	2.63	1.08	4	4	1	1	...	0-...	24.0	17	10	7	2	9-0	33	.198
2000— West. Mich. (Mid.)	5	3	.625	3.28	1.18	14	14	0	0	...	0-...	71.1	55	32	26	2	29-0	65	.208
2002— Lakeland (Fla. St.)	5	6	.455	3.54	1.35	24	24	0	0	...	0-...	117.0	112	54	46	10	46-1	87	.257
2003— Vero Beach (FSL)	0	0	1.000	1.85	0.82	15	0	0	0	...	6-...	24.1	16	7	5	0	4-0	36	.182
— Jacksonville (Southern)	1	0	1.000	2.95	1.28	35	0	0	0	...	17-...	36.2	33	14	12	2	14-0	50	.241
2004— Syracuse (Int'l)	0	0	...	2.25	1.50	3	0	0	0	...	0-...	4.0	1	1	1	0	5-0	6	.077
— Toronto (A.L.)	4	6	.400	4.08	1.46	63	0	0	0	8	17-19	68.1	64	31	31	4	36-3	54	.251
Major League totals (1 year)	4	6	.400	4.08	1.46	63	0	0	0	8	17-19	68.1	64	31	31	4	36-3	54	.251

FREDERICK, KEVIN   P

PERSONAL: Born November 4, 1976, in Evanston, Ill. ... 6-1/215. ... Throws right, bats left. ... Full name: Kevin Albert Francis Frederick. ... High school: Adlai E. Stevenson (Lincolnshire, Ill.). ... College: Creighton.

TRANSACTIONS/CAREER NOTES: Selected by Minnesota Twins organization in 17th round of 1997 free-agent draft; did not sign. ... Selected by Minnesota Twins organization in 34th round of 1998 free-agent draft. ... Claimed on waivers by Toronto Blue Jays (March 28, 2003).

CAREER HITTING: 0-for-0 (.000), 0 R, 0 2B, 0 3B, 0 HR, 0 RBI.

Year — Team (League)	W	L	Pct.	ERA	WHIP	G	GS	CG	ShO	Hld.	Sv.-Opp.	IP	H	R	ER	HR	BB-IBB	SO	Avg.
1998— Elizabethton (Appal.)	1	4	.200	4.25	1.28	17	0	0	0	...	1-...	29.2	28	21	14	4	10-1	46	.237
1999— GC Twins (GCL)	0	0	...	15.43	3.00	2	0	0	0	...	0-...	2.1	6	5	4	0	1-0	3	.500
2000— Quad City (Midw.)	5	0	1.000	2.35	1.24	27	0	0	0	...	4-...	46.0	34	17	12	1	23-4	51	.210
— Fort Myers (Fla. St.)	2	1	.667	2.70	1.13	19	0	0	0	...	3-...	30.0	20	11	9	0	14-1	37	.189
2001— Fort Myers (Fla. St.)	2	0	1.000	1.00	0.67	9	0	0	0	...	1-...	18.0	9	2	2	1	3-1	19	.145
— New Britain (East.)	6	2	.750	1.63	1.02	44	0	0	0	...	7-...	82.2	56	17	15	5	28-7	109	.195
2002— Edmonton (PCL)	3	6	.333	4.58	1.53	46	2	0	0	...	22-...	55.0	63	31	28	8	21-1	47	.289
— Minnesota (A.L.)	0	0	...	10.03	1.97	8	0	0	0	0	0-0	11.2	13	13	13	3	10-0	5	.283
2003— New Haven (East.)	2	2	.500	3.38	1.60	25	0	0	0	...	7-...	29.1	32	16	11	3	14-2	27	.271
— Syracuse (Int'l)	1	3	.250	8.06	2.00	24	0	0	0	...	2-...	25.2	40	28	23	5	12-3	20	.357
2004— New Hampshire (East.)	2	0	1.000	1.27	0.94	18	0	0	0	...	1-...	21.1	15	7	3	1	5-0	26	.190
— Syracuse (Int'l)	3	2	.600	0.99	0.99	20	0	0	0	...	5-...	27.1	18	6	3	2	9-0	26	.180
— Toronto (A.L.)	0	2	.000	6.59	1.67	22	0	0	0	3	0-1	28.2	32	21	21	4	16-1	22	.283
Major League totals (2 years)	0	2	.000	7.59	1.76	30	0	0	0	3	0-1	40.1	45	34	34	7	26-1	27	.283

FREEL, RYAN   3B/OF

PERSONAL: Born March 8, 1976, in Jacksonville, Fla. ... 5-10/180. ... Bats right, throws right. ... Full name: Ryan Paul Freel. ... High school: Englewood (Jacksonville). ... Junior college: Tallahassee (Fla.) Community College.

TRANSACTIONS/CAREER NOTES: Selected by St. Louis Cardinals organization in 14th round of 1994 free-agent draft; did not sign. ... Selected by Toronto Blue Jays organization in 10th round of 1995 free-agent draft. ... Signed as a free agent by Tampa Bay Devil Rays organization (November 8, 2001). ... Signed as a free agent by Cincinnati Reds organization (November 19, 2002). ... On disabled list (May 29-July 4, 2003).

2004 GAMES PLAYED BY POSITION (MLB): OF—89, 3B—56, 2B—15.

							BATTING										FIELDING	
Year — Team (League)	Pos.	G	AB	R	H	2B	3B	HR	RBI	BB	SO	HBP	GDP	SB-CS	Avg.	OBP	SLG	OPS	E	Avg.
1995— St. Catharines (NY-Penn.) .	2B	65	243	30	68	10	5	3	29	22	49	7	3	12-7	.280	.350	.399	.749	19	.940
1996— Dunedin (Fla. St.)	2B-3B	104	381	64	97	23	3	4	41	33	76	5	4	19-15	.255	.321	.362	.683	20	.959
1997— Knoxville (Southern)	SS	33	94	18	19	1	1	0	4	19	13	2	3	5-3	.202	.348	.234	.582	13	.913
— Dunedin (Fla. St.) 2-3-SS-OF	61	181	42	51	8	2	3	17	46	28	9	3	24-5	.282	.447	.398	.845	18	.910
1998— Knoxville (Southern) 2B-SS-OF	66	252	47	72	17	3	4	36	33	32	1	3	18-9	.286	.366	.425	.790	6	.982
— Syracuse (Int'l)	2B-OF	37	118	19	27	4	0	2	12	26	16	4	3	9-4	.229	.377	.314	.691	3	.962
1999— Knoxville (Southern)	OF	11	46	9	13	5	1	1	9	8	4	0	3	4-2	.283	.382	.500	.882	0	1.000
— Syracuse (Int'l)	OF-SS	20	77	15	23	3	2	1	11	8	13	4	3	10-3	.299	.393	.429	.822	1	.976
2000— Dunedin (Fla. St.)	OF	4	18	7	9	1	0	3	6	0	1	0	0	0-0	.500	.500	1.056	1.556	0	1.000
— Tennessee (Sou.)	OF-2B	12	44	11	13	3	1	0	8	8	6	1	0	2-3	.295	.400	.409	.809	0	1.000
— Syracuse (Int'l) 2-OF-3-SS	80	283	62	81	14	5	10	30	35	44	9	3	30-7	.286	.380	.477	.857	9	.957
2001— Toronto (A.L.)	2B-OF	9	22	1	6	1	0	0	3	1	4	1	0	2-1	.273	.333	.318	.652	1	.969

Year	Team (League)	Pos.	G	AB	R	H	2B	3B	HR	RBI	BB	SO	HBP	GDP	SB-CS	Avg.	OBP	SLG	OPS	E	Avg.
— Syracuse (Int'l)	OF-2-3-SS		85	319	60	83	21	3	5	33	42	42	7	8	22-9	.260	.357	.392	.749	9	.959
2002— Durham (Int'l)	2B-OF		119	448	65	117	27	4	8	48	38	51	14	10	37-10	.261	.337	.393	.730	7	.981
2003— Louisville (Int'l)	2-OF-3-DH		54	215	38	59	11	1	3	12	21	32	0	2	25-6	.274	.336	.377	.713	2	.990
— Cincinnati (N.L.)	OF-2B-3B		43	137	23	39	6	1	4	12	9	13	4	2	9-4	.285	.344	.431	.775	1	.990
2004— Cincinnati (N.L.)	OF-3B-2B		143	505	74	140	21	8	3	28	67	88	12	7	37-10	.277	.375	.368	.743	15	.963
American League totals (1 year)			9	22	1	6	1	0	0	3	1	4	1	0	2-1	.273	.333	.318	.652	1	.969
National League totals (2 years)			186	642	97	179	27	9	7	40	76	101	16	9	46-14	.279	.369	.382	.750	16	.968
Major League totals (3 years)			195	664	98	185	28	9	7	43	77	105	17	9	48-15	.279	.368	.380	.747	17	.968

FREEMAN, CHOO — OF

PERSONAL: Born October 20, 1979, in Pine Bluff, Ark. ... 6-2/200. ... Bats right, throws right. ... Full name: Raphael Freeman. ... High school: Dallas Christian.

TRANSACTIONS/CAREER NOTES: Selected by Colorado Rockies organization in supplemental round ("sandwich pick" between first and second rounds, 36th pick overall) of 1998 free-agent draft; pick received as part of compensation for Atlanta Braves signing Type A free-agent 1B Andres Galarraga.

2004 GAMES PLAYED BY POSITION (MLB): OF—41.

								BATTING												FIELDING	
Year	Team (League)	Pos.	G	AB	R	H	2B	3B	HR	RBI	BB	SO	HBP	GDP	SB-CS	Avg.	OBP	SLG	OPS	E	Avg.
1998— Ariz. Rockies (Ariz.)	OF		40	147	35	47	3	6	1	24	15	25	4	2	14-1	.320	.391	.442	.833	6	.880
1999— Asheville (S. Atl.)	OF		131	485	82	133	22	4	14	66	39	132	7	3	16-4	.274	.336	.423	.759	6	.975
2000— Salem (Caro.)	OF		127	429	73	114	18	7	5	54	37	104	4	4	16-8	.266	.326	.375	.702	8	.965
2001— Salem (Caro.)	OF		132	517	63	124	16	5	8	42	31	108	9	8	19-7	.240	.292	.337	.628	5	.979
2002— Carolina (Southern)	OF		124	430	81	125	18	6	12	64	64	101	6	15	15-13	.291	.400	.444	.844	6	.977
2003— Colo. Springs (PCL)	OF		103	327	44	83	9	4	7	36	23	71	7	7	2-8	.254	.315	.370	.685	12	.936
2004— Colo. Springs (PCL)	OF-DH		103	360	58	107	21	7	10	50	26	84	6	11	7-3	.297	.350	.478	.818	4	.983
— Colorado (N.L.)	OF		45	90	15	17	3	2	1	11	14	21	0	6	1-1	.189	.298	.300	.598	1	.986
Major League totals (1 year)			45	90	15	17	3	2	1	11	14	21	0	5	1-1	.189	.298	.300	.598	1	.986

FUENTES, BRIAN — P

PERSONAL: Born August 9, 1975, in Merced, Calif. ... 6-4/220. ... Throws left, bats left. ... Full name: Brian Christopher Fuentes. ... Name pronounced: foo-WHEN-tayz. ... High school: Merced (Calif.). ... Junior college: Merced (Calif.).

TRANSACTIONS/CAREER NOTES: Selected by Seattle Mariners organization in 25th round of 1995 free-agent draft. ... Traded by Mariners with Ps Jose Paniagua and Denny Stark to Colorado Rockies for 3B Jeff Cirillo (December 15, 2001). ... On disabled list (June 7-August 15, 2004); included rehabilitation assignment to Colorado Springs.

CAREER HITTING: 0-for-1 (.000), 0 R, 0 2B, 0 3B, 0 HR, 0 RBI.

Year	Team (League)	W	L	Pct.	ERA	WHIP	G	GS	CG	ShO	Hld.	Sv.-Opp.	IP	H	R	ER	HR	BB-IBB	SO	Avg.
1996— Everett (Northwest)	0	1	.000	4.39	1.35	13	2	0	0	...	0-	26.2	23	14	13	2	13-0	26	.230
1997— Wisconsin (Midw.)	6	7	.462	3.56	1.21	22	22	0	0	...	0-	118.2	84	52	47	6	59-0	153	.203
1998— Lancaster (Calif.)	7	7	.500	4.17	1.70	24	22	0	0	...	0-	118.2	121	73	55	8	81-0	137	.273
1999— New Haven (East.)	3	3	.500	4.95	1.65	15	14	0	0	...	0-	60.0	53	36	33	5	46-0	66	.255
2000— New Haven (East.)	7	12	.368	4.51	1.41	26	26	1	0	...	0-	139.2	127	80	70	7	70-0	152	.246
2001— Tacoma (PCL)	3	2	.600	2.94	1.15	35	0	0	0	...	6-	52.0	35	19	17	4	25-0	70	.206
— Seattle (A.L.)	1	1	.500	4.63	1.20	10	0	0	0	1	0-1	11.2	6	6	6	2	8-0	10	.171
2002— Colo. Springs (PCL)	3	3	.500	3.70	1.56	41	0	0	0	...	1-	48.2	44	25	20	0	32-1	61	.246
— Colorado (N.L.)	2	0	1.000	4.73	1.43	31	0	0	0	0	0-0	26.2	25	14	14	4	13-0	38	.250
2003— Colorado (N.L.)	3	3	.500	2.75	1.30	75	0	0	0	19	4-6	75.1	64	24	23	7	34-2	82	.231
2004— Colo. Springs (PCL)	0	0	...	0.00	0.80	5	5	0	0	...	0-	5.0	1	0	0	0	3-0	6	.063
— Colorado (N.L.)	2	4	.333	5.64	1.46	47	0	0	0	13	0-1	44.2	46	30	28	5	19-6	48	.269
American League totals (1 year)	1	1	.500	4.63	1.20	10	0	0	0	1	0-1	11.2	6	6	6	2	8-0	10	.171
National League totals (3 years)	7	7	.500	3.99	1.37	153	0	0	0	32	4-7	146.2	135	68	65	16	66-8	168	.246
Major League totals (4 years)	8	8	.500	4.04	1.36	163	0	0	0	33	4-8	158.1	141	74	71	18	74-8	178	.242

FULLMER, BRAD — DH

PERSONAL: Born January 17, 1975, in Chatsworth, Calif. ... 6-0/220. ... Bats left, throws right. ... Full name: Bradley Ryan Fullmer. ... High school: Montclair Prep (Van Nuys, Calif.).

TRANSACTIONS/CAREER NOTES: Selected by Montreal Expos organization in second round of 1993 free-agent draft. ... Traded by Expos to Toronto Blue Jays as part of three-team deal in which Expos acquired 1B Lee Stevens from Texas Rangers and Rangers acquired 1B/DH David Segui and cash from Blue Jays (March 16, 2000). ... Traded by Blue Jays to Anaheim Angels for P Brian Cooper (January 17, 2002). ... On disabled list (June 27, 2003-remainder of season). ... Released by Angels (October 15, 2003). ... Signed by Rangers (December 18, 2003). ... On disabled list (July 26, 2004-remainder of season). ... Traded by Rangers to San Diego Padres for IF Jake Gautreau (July 30, 2004). ... Trade rescinded by Padres (July 30, 2004).

2004 GAMES PLAYED BY POSITION (MLB): DH—66, 1B—4.

								BATTING												FIELDING	
Year	Team (League)	Pos.	G	AB	R	H	2B	3B	HR	RBI	BB	SO	HBP	GDP	SB-CS	Avg.	OBP	SLG	OPS	E	Avg.
1994—				Did not play.																	
1995— Albany (S. Atl.)	3B-1B		123	468	69	151	38	4	8	67	36	33	17	9	10-10	.323	.387	.472	.859	30	.918
1996— W.P. Beach (FSL)	1B-OF		102	380	52	115	29	1	5	63	32	43	11	9	4-6	.303	.367	.424	.790	7	.967
— Harrisburg (East.)	1B		24	98	11	27	4	1	4	14	3	8	2	3	0-0	.276	.311	.459	.770	2	.957
1997— Harrisburg (East.)	1B-OF-DH		94	357	60	111	24	2	19	62	30	25	7	11	6-4	.311	.372	.549	.921	6	.990
— Ottawa (Int'l)	1B-DH-OF		24	91	13	27	7	0	3	17	3	10	2	3	1-1	.297	.317	.473	.789	1	.995
— Montreal (N.L.)	1B-OF		19	40	4	12	2	0	3	8	2	7	1	0	0-0	.300	.349	.575	.924	2	.966
1998— Montreal (N.L.)	1B		140	505	58	138	44	2	13	73	39	70	2	12	6-6	.273	.327	.446	.773	* 17	.985
1999— Montreal (N.L.)	1B		100	347	38	96	34	2	9	47	22	35	2	14	2-3	.277	.321	.464	.785	7	.991
— Ottawa (Int'l)	1B-DH		39	142	31	45	9	0	11	32	12	16	3	3	2-2	.317	.380	.613	.992	2	.990
2000— Toronto (A.L.)	DH-1B		133	482	76	142	29	1	32	104	30	68	14	3	3-1	.295	.340	.558	.898	0	1.000
2001— Toronto (A.L.)	DH-1B		146	522	71	143	31	2	18	83	38	88	6	13	5-2	.274	.326	.444	.771	0	1.000
2002— Anaheim (A.L.)	DH-1B		130	429	75	124	35	6	19	59	32	44	15	7	10-3	.289	.357	.531	.888	1	.995
2003— Anaheim (A.L.)	DH-1B		63	206	32	63	9	2	9	35	26	31	2	4	5-4	.306	.387	.500	.887	0	1.000
2004— Texas (A.L.)	DH-1B		76	258	41	60	19	1	11	33	27	30	3	1	1-2	.233	.310	.442	.752	0	1.000
American League totals (5 years)			548	1897	295	532	123	12	89	314	153	261	32	45	24-12	.280	.341	.499	.840	1	.997
National League totals (3 years)			259	892	100	246	80	4	25	128	63	112	5	26	8-9	.276	.326	.459	.784	26	.987
Major League totals (8 years)			807	2789	395	778	203	16	114	442	216	373	37	71	32-21	.279	.336	.486	.822	27	.988

DIVISION SERIES RECORD

Year	Team (League)	Pos.	G	AB	R	H	2B	3B	HR	RBI	BB	SO	HBP	GDP	SB-CS	Avg.	OBP	SLG	OPS	E	Avg.
2002— Anaheim (A.L.)	DH		3	7	1	2	1	0	0	0	1	1	0	1	0-0	.286	.375	.429	.804	0	...

CHAMPIONSHIP SERIES RECORD

Year	Team (League)	Pos.	G	AB	R	H	2B	3B	HR	RBI	BB	SO	HBP	GDP	SB-CS	Avg.	OBP	SLG	OPS	E	Avg.
2002— Anaheim (A.L.)	DH		4	12	2	4	2	0	1	4	0	2	0	1	0-0	.333	.333	.750	1.083	0	...

F

Year Team (League)	Pos.	G	AB	R	H	2B	3B	HR	RBI	BB	SO	HBP	GDP	SB-CS	Avg.	OBP	SLG	OPS	E	Avg.
2002— Anaheim (A.L.)	DH	5	15	3	4	0	0	0	1	2	2	0	1	2-0	.267	.353	.267	.620	0	...

FULTZ, AARON — P

PERSONAL: Born September 4, 1973, in Memphis, Tenn. ... 6-0/205. ... Throws left, bats left. ... Full name: Richard Aaron Fultz. ... High school: Munford (Tenn.). ... Junior college: North Florida Community College.

TRANSACTIONS/CAREER NOTES: Selected by San Francisco Giants organization in sixth round of 1992 free-agent draft. ... Traded by Giants with SS Andres Duncan and P Greg Brummett to Minnesota Twins for P Jim Deshaies (August 28, 1993). ... Released by Twins (April 1, 1996). ... Signed by Giants organization (April 4, 1996). ... Signed as a free agent by Texas Rangers (December 31, 2002). ... On disabled list (June 23-July 11, 2003); included rehabilitation assignments to Oklahoma and Frisco. ... Refused minor league assignment and became a free agent (October 4, 2003). ... Signed by Twins organization (January 11, 2004). ... Claimed on waivers by Philadelphia Phillies (October 14, 2004).

CAREER HITTING: 4-for-12 (.333), 1 R, 0 2B, 0 3B, 0 HR, 0 RBI.

Year Team (League)	W	L	Pct.	ERA	WHIP	G	GS	CG	ShO	Hld.	Sv.-Opp.	IP	H	R	ER	HR	BB-IBB	SO	Avg.
1992— Ariz. Giants (Ariz.)	3	2	.600	2.13	1.24	14	14	0	0	...	0-...	67.2	51	24	16	0	33-0	72	.213
1993— Clinton (Midw.)	14	8	.636	3.41	1.32	26	25	2	1	...	0-...	148.0	132	63	56	8	64-2	144	.239
— Fort Wayne (Midw.)	0	0	...	9.00	2.50	1	1	0	0	...	0-...	4.0	10	4	4	0	0-0	3	.476
1994— Fort Myers (Fla. St.)	9	10	.474	4.33	1.50	28	28	3	0	...	0-...	168.1	193	95	81	9	60-5	132	.289
1995— Fort Myers (Fla. St.)	3	6	.333	3.25	1.28	21	21	2	2	...	0-...	122.0	115	52	44	10	41-1	127	.250
— New Britain (East.)	0	2	.000	6.60	1.33	3	3	0	0	...	0-...	15.0	11	12	11	1	9-0	12	.208
1996— San Jose (California)	9	5	.643	3.96	1.48	36	12	0	0	...	1-...	104.2	101	52	46	7	54-2	103	.262
1997— Shreveport (Texas)	6	3	.667	2.83	1.20	49	0	0	0	...	1-...	70.0	65	30	22	6	19-0	60	.247
1998— Shreveport (Texas)	5	7	.417	3.77	1.40	54	0	0	0	...	15-...	62.0	58	40	26	4	29-10	61	.252
— Fresno (PCL)	0	0	...	5.06	1.50	10	0	0	0	...	0-...	16.0	22	10	9	2	2-1	13	.333
1999— Fresno (PCL)	9	8	.529	4.98	1.40	37	20	1	0	...	0-...	137.1	141	87	76	32	51-1	151	.266
2000— San Francisco (N.L.)	5	2	.714	4.67	1.37	58	0	0	0	7	1-3	69.1	67	38	36	8	28-0	62	.263
2001— San Francisco (N.L.)	3	1	.750	4.56	1.28	66	0	0	0	12	1-2	71.0	70	40	36	9	21-3	67	.259
2002— San Francisco (N.L.)	2	2	.500	4.79	1.60	43	0	0	0	4	0-1	41.1	47	22	22	4	19-3	31	.294
— Fresno (PCL)	1	3	.250	3.18	1.28	17	0	0	0	...	4-...	22.2	18	8	8	1	11-2	22	.222
2003— Oklahoma (PCL)	0	0	...	27.00	3.00	1	0	0	0	...	0-...	1.0	2	3	3	2	1-0	2	.400
— Frisco (Texas)	0	0	...	9.00	2.00	1	0	0	0	...	0-...	1.0	2	1	1	0	0-0	0	.333
— Texas (A.L.)	1	3	.250	5.21	1.51	64	0	0	0	19	0-0	67.1	75	43	39	9	27-7	53	.287
2004— Rochester (Int'l)	0	0	...	0.00	1.32	7	0	0	0	...	0-...	8.1	6	1	0	0	5-0	5	.194
— Minnesota (A.L.)	3	3	.500	5.04	1.46	55	0	0	0	5	1-4	50.0	50	28	28	5	23-2	37	.267
American League totals (2 years)	4	6	.400	5.14	1.49	119	0	0	0	24	1-4	117.1	125	71	67	14	50-9	90	.279
National League totals (3 years)	10	5	.667	4.66	1.39	167	0	0	0	23	2-6	181.2	184	100	94	21	68-6	160	.269
Major League totals (5 years)	14	11	.560	4.85	1.43	286	0	0	0	47	3-10	299.0	309	171	161	35	118-15	250	.273

DIVISION SERIES RECORD

Year Team (League)	W	L	Pct.	ERA	WHIP	G	GS	CG	ShO	Hld.	Sv.-Opp.	IP	H	R	ER	HR	BB-IBB	SO	Avg.
2000— San Francisco (N.L.)	0	1	.000	6.75	2.25	1	0	0	0	0	0-0	1.1	3	1	1	0	0-0	0	.500
2002— San Francisco (N.L.)	0	0	...	...	...	2	0	0	0	0	0-0	.0	2	1	1	0	0-0	0	1.000
Division series totals (2 years)	0	1	.000	13.50	3.75	3	0	0	0	0	0-0	1.1	5	2	2	1	0-0	0	.625

CHAMPIONSHIP SERIES RECORD

Year Team (League)	W	L	Pct.	ERA	WHIP	G	GS	CG	ShO	Hld.	Sv.-Opp.	IP	H	R	ER	HR	BB-IBB	SO	Avg.
2002— San Francisco (N.L.)	0	0	...	0.00	0.00	1	0	0	0	0	0-0	.1	0	0	0	0	0-0	0	.000

WORLD SERIES RECORD

Year Team (League)	W	L	Pct.	ERA	WHIP	G	GS	CG	ShO	Hld.	Sv.-Opp.	IP	H	R	ER	HR	BB-IBB	SO	Avg.
2002— San Francisco (N.L.)	0	0	...	3.86	2.14	2	0	0	0	0	0-1	2.1	4	1	1	0	1-0	0	.400

FURCAL, RAFAEL — SS

PERSONAL: Born August 24, 1978, in Loma de Cabrera, Dominican Republic. ... 5-10/165. ... Bats both, throws right. ... Full name: Rafael Antoni Furcal. ... Name pronounced: fur-CALL. ... High school: Jose Cabrera (Loma De Cabrera, Dominican Republic).

TRANSACTIONS/CAREER NOTES: Signed as a non-drafted free agent by Atlanta Braves organization (November 9, 1996). ... On disabled list (June 13-29, 2000; and July 7, 2001-remainder of season).

RECORDS: Shares major league single-game record for most triples 3 (April 21, 2002).

HONORS: Named N.L. Rookie Player of the Year by THE SPORTING NEWS (2000). ... Named N.L. Rookie of the Year by Baseball Writers' Association of America (2000).

2004 GAMES PLAYED BY POSITION (MLB): SS—131, 2B—1.

Year Team (League)	Pos.	G	AB	R	H	2B	3B	HR	RBI	BB	SO	HBP	GDP	SB-CS	Avg.	OBP	SLG	OPS	E	Avg.
1997— GC Braves (GCL)	2B-OF	50	190	31	49	5	4	1	9	20	21	2	1	15-2	.258	.335	.342	.677	10	.961
1998— Danville (Appal.)	2B	66	268	56	88	15	4	0	23	36	29	3	2	60-15	.328	.412	.414	.827	14	.965
1999— Macon (S. Atl.)	SS	83	335	73	113	15	1	1	29	41	36	5	4	73-22	.337	.417	.397	.814	30	.912
— Myrtle Beach (Caro.)	SS	43	184	32	54	9	3	0	12	14	42	0	3	23-8	.293	.343	.375	.718	4	.975
2000— Greenville (Sou.)	SS	3	10	1	2	0	0	1	3	1	0	0	0	0-0	.200	.273	.500	.773	1	.889
— Atlanta (N.L.)	SS-2B	131	455	87	134	20	4	4	37	73	80	3	2	40-14	.295	.394	.382	.776	24	.958
2001— Atlanta (N.L.)	SS	79	324	39	89	19	4	4	30	24	56	1	5	22-6	.275	.323	.370	.692	11	.970
2002— Atlanta (N.L.)	SS-2B	154	636	95	175	31	8	8	47	43	114	3	8	27-15	.275	.323	.387	.710	27	.964
2003— Atlanta (N.L.)	SS	156	664	130	194	35	*10	15	61	60	76	3	1	25-2	.292	.352	.443	.794	31	.959
2004— Atlanta (N.L.)	SS-2B	143	563	103	157	24	5	14	59	58	71	1	9	29-6	.279	.345	.414	.758	24	.962
Major League totals (5 years)		663	2642	454	749	129	27	45	234	258	397	11	25	143-43	.283	.347	.404	.751	117	.962

DIVISION SERIES RECORD

Year Team (League)	Pos.	G	AB	R	H	2B	3B	HR	RBI	BB	SO	HBP	GDP	SB-CS	Avg.	OBP	SLG	OPS	E	Avg.
2000— Atlanta (N.L.)	2B-SS	3	11	2	1	0	0	0	0	3	0	0	0	1-1	.091	.286	.091	.377	1	.933
2002— Atlanta (N.L.)	SS	5	24	2	6	1	1	0	2	0	5	0	0	1-1	.250	.250	.375	.625	0	1.000
2003— Atlanta (N.L.)	SS	5	19	3	4	0	0	0	0	3	5	0	0	1-0	.211	.318	.211	.529	1	.968
2004— Atlanta (N.L.)	SS	5	21	5	8	0	1	2	4	3	3	1	0	3-0	.381	.480	.762	1.242	0	1.000
Division series totals (4 years)		18	75	12	19	1	2	2	6	9	13	1	0	6-2	.253	.341	.400	.741	2	.978

ALL-STAR GAME RECORD

	G	AB	R	H	2B	3B	HR	RBI	BB	SO	HBP	GDP	SB-CS	Avg.	OBP	SLG	OPS	E	Avg.
All-Star Game totals (1 year)	1	3	1	1	0	0	0	0	0	1	0	0	0-0	.333	.333	.333	.667	0	.500

GAGNE, ERIC   P

PERSONAL: Born January 7, 1976, in Montreal, Quebec. ... 6-2/234. ... Throws right, bats right. ... Full name: Eric Serge Gagne. ... Name pronounced: gahn-yay. ... High school: Polyvalente Edouard Montpetit (Montreal). ... Junior college: Seminole (Okla.).

TRANSACTIONS/CAREER NOTES: Selected by Chicago White Sox organization in 30th round of 1994 free-agent draft; did not sign. ... Signed as a non-drafted free agent by Los Angeles Dodgers organization (July 26, 1995).

HONORS: Named N.L. Reliever of the Year by THE SPORTING NEWS (2004). ... Named N.L. Cy Young Award winner by Baseball Writers' Association of America (2003).

CAREER HITTING: 12-for-86 (.140), 5 R, 2 2B, 1 3B, 1 HR, 3 RBI.

Year	Team (League)	W	L	Pct.	ERA	WHIP	G	GS	CG	ShO	Hld.	Sv.-Opp.	IP	H	R	ER	HR	BB-IBB	SO	Avg.
1996—Savannah (S. Atl.)		7	6	.538	3.28	1.19	23	21	1	1	...	0-...	115.1	94	48	42	11	43-1	131	.221
1997—	Did not play.																			
1998—Vero Beach (FSL)		9	7	.563	3.74	1.19	25	25	3	1	...	0-...	139.2	118	69	58	16	48-0	144	.225
1999—San Antonio (Texas)		12	4	.750	2.63	1.11	26	26	0	0	...	0-...	167.2	122	55	49	17	64-0	185	.201
—Los Angeles (N.L.)		1	1	.500	2.10	1.10	5	5	0	0	0	0-...	30.0	18	8	7	3	15-0	30	.175
2000—Albuquerque (PCL)		5	1	.833	3.88	1.28	9	9	0	0	0	0-...	55.2	56	30	24	8	15-0	59	.260
—Los Angeles (N.L.)		4	6	.400	5.15	1.64	20	19	0	0	0	0-0	101.1	106	62	58	20	60-1	79	.270
2001—Los Angeles (N.L.)		6	7	.462	4.75	1.25	33	24	0	0	0	0-0	151.2	144	90	80	24	46-1	130	.251
—Las Vegas (PCL)		3	0	1.000	1.52	0.97	4	4	0	0	0	0-...	23.2	15	4	4	2	8-0	31	.195
2002—Los Angeles (N.L.)		4	1	.800	1.97	0.86	77	0	0	0	1	52-56	82.1	55	18	18	6	16-4	114	.189
2003—Los Angeles (N.L.)		2	3	.400	1.20	0.69	77	0	0	0	0	* 55-55	82.1	37	12	11	2	20-2	137	.133
2004—Los Angeles (N.L.)		7	3	.700	2.19	0.91	70	0	0	0	0	45-47	82.1	53	24	20	5	22-3	114	.181
Major League totals (6 years)		24	21	.533	3.29	1.12	282	48	0	0	1	152-158	530.0	413	214	194	60	179-11	604	.214

DIVISION SERIES RECORD

Year	Team (League)	W	L	Pct.	ERA	WHIP	G	GS	CG	ShO	Hld.	Sv.-Opp.	IP	H	R	ER	HR	BB-IBB	SO	Avg.
2004—Los Angeles (N.L.)		0	0	...	0.00	0.67	2	0	0	0	0	0-0	3.0	1	0	0	0	1-0	3	.111

ALL-STAR GAME RECORD

	W	L	Pct.	ERA	WHIP	G	GS	CG	ShO	Hld.	Sv.-Opp.	IP	H	R	ER	HR	BB-IBB	SO	Avg.
All-Star Game totals (3 years)	0	1	.000	12.00	2.00	3	0	0	0	0	0-0	3.0	5	4	4	2	1-0	4	.357

GALARRAGA, ANDRES   1B

PERSONAL: Born June 18, 1961, in Caracas, Venezuela. ... 6-3/265. ... Bats right, throws right. ... Full name: Andres Jose Galarraga. ... Name pronounced: ON-dress Gahl-la-RAH-ga. ... High school: Enrique Felmi (Caracas, Venezuela).

TRANSACTIONS/CAREER NOTES: Signed as a non-drafted free agent by Montreal Expos organization (January 19, 1979). ... On disabled list (July 10-August 19 and August 20-September 4, 1986; and May 26-July 4, 1991). ... Traded by Expos to St. Louis Cardinals for P Ken Hill (November 25, 1991). ... On disabled list (April 8-May 22, 1992); included rehabilitation assignment to Louisville. ... Signed as a free agent by Colorado Rockies (November 16, 1992). ... On disabled list (May 10-27 and July 25-August 21, 1993). ... On disabled list (July 29, 1994-remainder of season). ... On suspended list (August 3-5, 1997). ... Signed as a free agent by Atlanta Braves (November 20, 1997). ... On suspended list (September 2-5, 1998). ... On disabled list (April 3, 1999-entire season). ... On suspended list (September 7-10, 2000). ... Signed as a free agent by Texas Rangers (December 8, 2000). ... Traded by Rangers to San Francisco Giants for Ps Erasmo Ramirez and Todd Ozias and IF Chris Magruder (July 24, 2001). ... Signed as a free agent by Expos (March 7, 2002). ... On disabled list (May 3-26, 2002). ... Signed as a free agent by Giants organization (January 29, 2003). ... Signed as a free agent by Anaheim Angels organization (August 4, 2004).

HONORS: Won N.L. Gold Glove at first base (1989-90). ... Named N.L. Comeback Player of the Year by THE SPORTING NEWS (1993 and 2000).

2004 GAMES PLAYED BY POSITION (MLB): DH—4, 1B—1.

Year	Team (League)	Pos.	G	AB	R	H	2B	3B	HR	RBI	BB	SO	HBP	GDP	SB-CS	Avg.	OBP	SLG	OPS	E	Avg.
1979—W.P. Beach (FSL)	1B	7	23	3	3	0	0	0	1	2	11	1	...	0-0	.130	.231	.130	.361	0	1.000
—Calgary (Pio.)	3B-C-1B	42	112	14	24	3	1	4	16	9	42	5	...	1-1	.214	.299	.366	.665	5	.977
1980—Calgary (Pio.)	3B-C-1B-OF	59	190	27	50	11	4	4	22	7	55	5	...	3-0	.263	.307	.426	.733	21	.942
1981—Jamestown (N.Y.-Penn.)	3B-C-1B	47	154	24	40	5	4	6	26	15	44	4	...	0-0	.260	.339	.461	.800	0	1.000
1982—W.P. Beach (FSL)	1B-OF	105	338	39	95	20	2	14	51	34	77	9	...	2-1	.281	.360	.476	.837	9	.982
1983—W.P. Beach (FSL)	3B-1B-OF	104	401	55	116	18	3	10	66	33	68	7	...	7-5	.289	.353	.424	.777	13	.986
1984—Jacksonville (Sou.)	1B	143	533	81	154	28	4	27	87	59	122	9	10	2-8	.289	.367	.508	.875	16	.989
1985—Indianapolis (A.A.)	1B-OF	121	439	75	118	15	8	25	87	45	103	7	12	3-0	.269	.344	.510	.854	14	.986
—Montreal (N.L.)	1B	24	75	9	14	1	0	2	4	3	18	1	0	1-2	.187	.228	.280	.508	1	.995
1986—Montreal (N.L.)	1B	105	321	39	87	13	0	10	42	30	79	3	8	6-5	.271	.338	.405	.743	4	.995
1987—Montreal (N.L.)	1B	147	551	72	168	40	3	13	90	41	127	10	11	7-10	.305	.361	.459	.821	10	.993
1988—Montreal (N.L.)	1B	157	609	99	* 184	* 42	8	29	92	39 *	153	10	12	13-4	.302	.353	.540	.893	15	.991
1989—Montreal (N.L.)	1B	152	572	76	147	30	1	23	85	48 *	158	13	12	12-5	.257	.327	.434	.761	11	.992
1990—Montreal (N.L.)	1B	155	579	65	148	29	0	20	87	40 *	169	4	14	10-1	.256	.306	.409	.715	10	.993
1991—Montreal (N.L.)	1B	107	375	34	82	13	2	9	33	23	86	2	6	5-6	.219	.268	.336	.604	9	.991
1992—St. Louis (N.L.)	1B	95	325	38	79	14	2	10	39	11	69	8	8	5-4	.243	.282	.391	.673	8	.991
—Louisville (A.A.)	1B	11	34	3	6	0	1	2	3	0	8	1	0	1-0	.176	.200	.412	.612	2	.971
1993—Colorado (N.L.)	1B	120	470	71	174	35	4	22	98	24	73	6	9	2-4	* .370	.403	.602	1.005	11	.990
1994—Colorado (N.L.)	1B	103	417	77	133	21	0	31	85	19	93	6	10	8-3	.319	.356	.592	.949	8	.992
1995—Colorado (N.L.)	1B	143	554	89	155	29	3	31	106	32 *	146	13	14	12-2	.280	.331	.511	.842	* 13	.991
1996—Colorado (N.L.)	1B-3B	159	626	119	190	39	3	* 47	* 150	40	157	17	6	18-8	.304	.357	.601	.958	14	.992
1997—Colorado (N.L.)	1B	154	600	120	191	31	3	41	* 140	54	141	17	16	15-8	.318	.389	.585	.974	* 15	.991
1998—Atlanta (N.L.)	1B-DH	153	555	103	169	27	1	44	121	63	146	25	8	7-6	.305	.397	.595	.991	11	.992
1999—Atlanta (N.L.)		Did not play.																		
2000—Atlanta (N.L.)	1B-DH	141	494	67	149	25	1	28	100	36	126	17	15	3-5	.302	.369	.526	.895	14	.988
2001—Texas (A.L.)	DH-1B	72	243	33	57	16	0	10	34	18	68	9	9	1-0	.235	.310	.424	.734	1	.995
—San Francisco (N.L.)	1B	49	156	17	45	12	1	7	35	13	49	3	3	0-3	.288	.351	.513	.863	5	.984
2002—Montreal (N.L.)	1B	104	292	30	76	12	0	9	40	30	81	9	8	2-2	.260	.344	.394	.738	13	.981
2003—San Francisco (N.L.)	1B-DH	110	272	36	82	15	0	12	42	19	61	2	9	1-3	.301	.352	.489	.841	3	.994
2004—Salt Lake (PCL)	DH-1B	25	102	10	31	3	0	4	19	6	24	1	7	0-0	.304	.342	.451	.793	0	1.000
—Anaheim (A.L.)	DH-1B	7	10	1	3	0	0	1	2	0	3	1	1	0-0	.300	.364	.600	.964	0	1.000
American League totals (2 years)		79	253	34	60	16	0	11	36	18	71	10	10	1-0	.237	.312	.431	.743	1	.995
National League totals (18 years)		2178	7843	1161	2273	428	32	388	1389	565	1932	168	169	127-81	.290	.348	.501	.849	175	.991
Major League totals (19 years)		2257	8096	1195	2333	444	32	399	1425	583	2003	178	179	128-81	.288	.347	.499	.846	176	.991

DIVISION SERIES RECORD

Year Team (League)	Pos.	G	AB	R	H	2B	3B	HR	RBI	BB	SO	HBP	GDP	SB-CS	Avg.	OBP	SLG	OPS	E	Avg.
1995— Colorado (N.L.)	1B	4	18	1	5	1	0	0	2	0	6	0	0	0-0	.278	.278	.333	.611	0	1.000
1998— Atlanta (N.L.)	1B	3	12	1	3	0	0	0	0	1	3	0	0	0-0	.250	.308	.250	.558	0	1.000
2000— Atlanta (N.L.)	1B	3	10	1	2	1	0	0	1	2	4	1	0	0-0	.200	.385	.300	.685	0	1.000
2003— San Francisco (N.L.)	1B	2	5	0	0	0	0	0	0	0	1	0	0	0-0	.000	.000	.000	.000	0	1.000
Division series totals (4 years)		12	45	3	10	2	0	0	3	3	14	1	0	0-0	.222	.286	.267	.552	0	1.000

CHAMPIONSHIP SERIES RECORD

Year Team (League)	Pos.	G	AB	R	H	2B	3B	HR	RBI	BB	SO	HBP	GDP	SB-CS	Avg.	OBP	SLG	OPS	E	Avg.
1998— Atlanta (N.L.)	1B	6	21	1	2	0	0	1	4	6	6	0	1	0-0	.095	.296	.238	.534	4	.949

ALL-STAR GAME RECORD

		G	AB	R	H	2B	3B	HR	RBI	BB	SO	HBP	GDP	SB-CS	Avg.	OBP	SLG	OPS	E	Avg.
All-Star Game totals (5 years)		5	8	0	1	0	0	0	0	0	2	0	1	0-0	.125	.125	.125	.250	0	1.000

GALLO, MIKE   P

PERSONAL: Born April 2, 1977, in Long Beach, Calif. ... 6-0/175. ... Throws left, bats left. ... Full name: Michael Dwain Gallo. ... College: Long Beach State.
TRANSACTIONS/CAREER NOTES: Selected by Houston Astros organization in fifth round of 1999 free-agent draft.
CAREER HITTING: 0-for-3 (.000), 0 R, 0 2B, 0 3B, 0 HR, 0 RBI.

Year Team (League)	W	L	Pct.	ERA	WHIP	G	GS	CG	ShO	Hld.	Sv.-Opp.	IP	H	R	ER	HR	BB-IBB	SO	Avg.
1999— Auburn (N.Y.-Penn)	1	0	1.000	1.23	1.36	3	3	0	0	...	0-...	14.2	13	4	2	0	7-0	11	.232
— Michigan (Midw.)	2	3	.400	5.85	1.65	12	12	0	0	...	0-...	60.0	76	47	39	6	23-0	32	.315
2000— Michigan (Midw.)	8	3	.727	4.86	1.44	24	13	0	0	...	0-...	90.2	104	58	49	6	27-1	56	.285
2001— Michigan (Midw.)	9	2	.818	3.84	1.21	44	0	0	0	...	4-...	84.1	83	38	36	4	19-1	67	.252
2002— Lexington (S.Atl.)	4	4	.500	1.83	1.08	42	2	0	0	...	8-...	88.1	69	29	18	6	26-4	93	.211
— Round Rock (Texas)	0	0	...	6.75	0.75	1	0	0	0	...	0-...	1.1	1	1	1	1	0-0	0	.200
2003— Round Rock (Texas)	1	1	.500	1.37	1.17	17	0	0	0	...	2-...	19.2	17	3	3	1	6-2	22	.246
— New Orleans (PCL)	3	0	1.000	2.08	0.92	16	0	0	0	...	0-...	17.1	13	4	4	0	3-0	11	.217
— Houston (N.L.)	1	0	1.000	3.00	1.27	32	0	0	0	6	0-1	30.0	28	10	10	3	10-2	16	.267
2004— New Orleans (PCL)	0	0	...	0.00	0.50	1	0	0	0	...	1-...	4.0	0	0	0	0	2-0	4	.000
— Houston (N.L.)	2	0	1.000	4.74	1.52	69	0	0	0	4	0-1	49.1	55	27	26	12	20-7	34	.284
Major League totals (2 years)	3	0	1.000	4.08	1.42	101	0	0	0	10	0-2	79.1	83	37	36	15	30-9	50	.278

DIVISION SERIES RECORD

Year Team (League)	W	L	Pct.	ERA	WHIP	G	GS	CG	ShO	Hld.	Sv.-Opp.	IP	H	R	ER	HR	BB-IBB	SO	Avg.
2004— Houston (N.L.)	0	0	...	4.50	2.00	3	0	0	0	0	0-0	2.0	3	1	1	0	1-0	4	.333

GARCIA, DANNY   2B

PERSONAL: Born April 12, 1980, in Riverside, Calif. ... 6-1/175. ... Bats right, throws right. ... Full name: Daniel Joseph Garcia. ... High school: J.W. North. ... College: Pepperdine.
TRANSACTIONS/CAREER NOTES: Selected by New York Mets organization in fifth round of 2001 free-agent draft.
2004 GAMES PLAYED BY POSITION (MLB): 2B—44.

Year Team (League)	Pos.	G	AB	R	H	2B	3B	HR	RBI	BB	SO	HBP	GDP	SB-CS	Avg.	OBP	SLG	OPS	E	Avg.
2001— Brooklyn N.Y.-Penn. (NY-P)	2B	15	56	10	18	2	0	1	6	4	10	2	0	3-2	.321	.387	.411	.798	3	.952
— Capital City (SAL)	2B-OF	30	103	25	31	12	1	2	16	15	18	6	0	7-3	.301	.409	.495	.905	11	.927
2002— St. Lucie (Fla. St.)	2B-SS-OF	122	432	69	118	34	5	4	52	53	77	15	9	13-6	.273	.369	.403	.772	21	.963
2003— Binghamton (East.)	2B-DH	32	117	22	39	12	1	3	22	10	20	3	2	2-2	.333	.391	.530	.921	4	.967
— Norfolk (Int'l)	2B-DH	101	388	45	102	23	3	4	54	22	60	9	3	11-1	.263	.313	.369	.682	13	.972
— New York (N.L.)	2B-OF	19	56	5	12	2	0	2	6	2	11	3	2	0-0	.214	.274	.357	.631	4	.950
2004— Norfolk (Int'l) 2-S-OF-3-1		63	242	28	63	14	1	2	19	15	35	7	5	9-5	.260	.322	.351	.673	16	.938
— New York (N.L.)	2B	58	138	23	32	7	1	3	17	22	34	9	1	3-0	.232	.371	.362	.733	6	.969
Major League totals (2 years)		77	194	28	44	9	1	5	23	24	45	12	3	3-0	.227	.345	.361	.706	10	.964

GARCIA, FREDDY   P

PERSONAL: Born June 10, 1975, in Caracas, Venezuela. ... 6-4/240. ... Throws right, bats right. ... Full name: Freddy Antonio Garcia.
TRANSACTIONS/CAREER NOTES: Signed as a non-drafted free agent by Houston Astros organization (October 21, 1993). ... Traded by Astros with SS Carlos Guillen and a player to be named to Seattle Mariners for P Randy Johnson (July 31, 1998); Mariners acquired P John Halama to complete deal (October 1, 1998). ... On disabled list (April 22-July 7, 2000); included rehabilitation assignments to Tacoma and Everett. ... Traded by Mariners with C Ben Davis to Chicago White Sox for C Miguel Olivo, OF Jeremy Reed and SS Michael Morse (June 27, 2004).
CAREER HITTING: 7-for-29 (.241), 0 R, 1 2B, 0 3B, 0 HR, 2 RBI.

Year Team (League)	W	L	Pct.	ERA	WHIP	G	GS	CG	ShO	Hld.	Sv.-Opp.	IP	H	R	ER	HR	BB-IBB	SO	Avg.
1994— Dom. Astros (DSL)	4	6	.400	5.29	1.39	16	15	0	0	...	0-...	85.0	80	61	50	...	38-...	68	...
1995— GC Astros (GCL)	6	3	.667	4.47	1.27	11	11	0	0	...	0-...	58.1	60	32	29	2	14-0	58	.261
1996— Quad City (Midw.)	5	4	.556	3.12	1.38	13	13	0	0	...	0-...	60.2	57	27	21	3	27-0	50	.247
1997— Kissimmee (Fla. St.)	10	8	.556	2.56	1.20	27	27	5	2	...	0-...	179.0	165	63	51	6	49-3	131	.242
1998— Jackson (Texas)	6	7	.462	3.24	1.27	19	19	2	0	...	0-...	119.1	94	48	43	8	58-0	115	.215
— New Orleans (PCL)	1	0	1.000	3.14	1.05	2	2	0	0	...	0-...	14.1	14	5	5	2	1-0	13	.255
— Tacoma (PCL)	3	1	.750	3.86	1.32	5	5	0	0	...	0-...	32.2	30	14	14	6	13-0	30	.246
1999— Seattle (A.L.)	17	8	.680	4.07	1.47	33	33	2	1	0	0-0	201.1	205	96	91	18	90-4	170	.263
2000— Seattle (A.L.)	9	5	.643	3.91	1.42	21	20	0	0	0	0-0	124.1	112	62	54	16	64-4	79	.241
— Everett (Northwest)	0	0	...	4.50	1.30	2	2	0	0	...	0-...	10.0	11	5	5	1	0-0	15	.262
— Tacoma (PCL)	1	0	1.000	2.57	1.00	1	1	0	0	...	0-...	7.0	5	2	2	2	2-0	11	.208
2001— Seattle (A.L.)	18	6	.750	* 3.05	1.12	34	34	4	3	0	0-0	* 238.2	199	88	81	16	69-6	163	.225
2002— Seattle (A.L.)	16	10	.615	4.39	1.30	34	34	4	0	0	0-0	223.2	227	110	109	30	63-3	181	.260
2003— Seattle (A.L.)	12	14	.462	4.51	1.33	33	33	1	0	0	0-0	201.1	196	109	101	31	71-2	144	.255
2004— Seattle (A.L.)	4	7	.364	3.20	1.20	15	15	1	0	0	0-0	107.0	96	39	38	8	32-1	82	.236
— Chicago (A.L.)	9	4	.692	4.46	1.24	16	16	0	0	0	0-0	103.0	96	53	51	14	32-2	102	.247
Major League totals (6 years)	85	54	.612	3.94	1.29	186	185	9	4	0	0-0	1199.1	1131	557	525	133	421-22	921	.248

G

DIVISION SERIES RECORD

Year Team (League)	W	L	Pct.	ERA	WHIP	G	GS	CG	ShO	Hld.	Sv.-Opp.	IP	H	R	ER	HR	BB-IBB	SO	Avg.
2000— Seattle (A.L.)	0	0	...	10.80	2.70	1	1	0	0	0	0-0	3.1	6	4	4	1	3-0	2	.375
2001— Seattle (A.L.)	1	1	.500	3.86	1.37	2	2	0	0	0	0-0	11.2	13	6	5	1	3-0	13	.277
Division series totals (2 years)	1	1	.500	5.40	1.67	3	3	0	0	0	0-0	15.0	19	10	9	2	6-0	15	.302

CHAMPIONSHIP SERIES RECORD

Year Team (League)	W	L	Pct.	ERA	WHIP	G	GS	CG	ShO	Hld.	Sv.-Opp.	IP	H	R	ER	HR	BB-IBB	SO	Avg.
2000— Seattle (A.L.)	2	0	1.000	1.54	1.20	2	2	0	0	0	0-0	11.2	10	2	2	0	4-0	11	.227
2001— Seattle (A.L.)	0	1	.000	3.68	1.50	1	1	0	0	0	0-0	7.1	7	3	3	0	4-0	6	.292
Champ. series totals (2 years)	2	1	.667	2.37	1.32	3	3	0	0	0	0-0	19.0	17	5	5	0	8-0	17	.250

ALL-STAR GAME RECORD

	W	L	Pct.	ERA	WHIP	G	GS	CG	ShO	Hld.	Sv.-Opp.	IP	H	R	ER	HR	BB-IBB	SO	Avg.
All-Star Game totals (2 years)	1	0	1.000	0.00	0.67	2	0	0	0	0	0-0	3.0	2	0	0	0	0-0	3	.182

GARCIA, JAIRO — P

PERSONAL: Born March 7, 1983, in Nizao, Dominican Republic. ... 6-0/164. ... Throws right, bats right. ... Full name: Jairo Paulino Garcia.

TRANSACTIONS/CAREER NOTES: Signed as a non-drafted free agent by Oakland Athletics organization (January 31, 2000).

CAREER HITTING: 0-for-0 (.000), 0 R, 0 2B, 0 3B, 0 HR, 0 RBI.

Year Team (League)	W	L	Pct.	ERA	WHIP	G	GS	CG	ShO	Hld.	Sv.-Opp.	IP	H	R	ER	HR	BB-IBB	SO	Avg.
2001— Ariz. A's (Ariz.)	4	2	.667	2.85	0.91	12	7	0	0	...	0-...	47.1	37	19	15	2	6-0	50	.214
2002— Ariz. A's (Ariz.)	2	1	.667	2.44	1.24	13	8	0	0	...	1-...	59.0	56	24	16	5	17-0	66	.258
— Vancouver (N'west)	0	3	.000	7.30	1.78	3	3	0	0	...	0-...	12.1	15	11	10	1	7-0	16	.300
2003— Kane County (Midwest)	0	1	.000	2.55	1.39	14	9	0	0	...	0-...	42.1	40	14	12	0	19-0	28	.250
2004— Kane County (Midwest)	1	0	1.000	0.30	0.73	25	0	0	0	...	16-...	30.0	16	2	1	0	6-2	49	.154
— Midland (Texas)	2	0	1.000	1.50	1.39	13	0	0	0	...	2-...	18.0	10	3	3	0	15-0	32	.161
— Sacramento (PCL)	1	2	.333	3.95	1.39	11	0	0	0	...	1-...	13.2	10	6	6	1	9-1	21	.208
— Oakland (A.L.)	0	0	...	12.71	2.47	4	0	0	0	0	0-0	5.2	5	8	8	3	9-0	5	.227
Major League totals (1 year)	0	0	...	12.71	2.47	4	0	0	0	0	0-0	5.2	5	8	8	3	9-0	5	.227

GARCIA, JESSE — SS/2B

PERSONAL: Born September 24, 1973, in Corpus Christi, Texas. ... 5-10/171. ... Bats right, throws right. ... Full name: Jesus Jesse Garcia. ... High school: Robstown (Texas). ... Junior college: Lee (Texas).

TRANSACTIONS/CAREER NOTES: Selected by Baltimore Orioles organization in 26th round of 1993 free-agent draft. ... Traded by Orioles for Atlanta Braves for IF Steve Sisco (December 18, 2000). ... Released by Braves (August 27, 2004).

2004 GAMES PLAYED BY POSITION (MLB): SS—25, 2B—11, 3B—3.

										BATTING									FIELDING	
Year Team (League)	Pos.	G	AB	R	H	2B	3B	HR	RBI	BB	SO	HBP	GDP	SB-CS	Avg.	OBP	SLG	OPS	E	Avg.
1993— GC Orioles (GCL) 2B-3B-SS		48	156	20	37	4	0	0	16	21	32	1	1	14-6	.237	.326	.263	.589	14	.934
1994— Bluefield (Appal.)			Did not play.																	
1995— Frederick (Carolina)	2B	124	365	52	82	11	3	3	27	49	75	9	5	5-10	.225	.329	.296	.625	28	.952
1996— High Desert (Calif.)	2B-SS	137	459	94	122	21	5	10	66	57	81	8	7	25-7	.266	.354	.399	.753	22	.968
1997— Bowie (East.) 2B-3B-SS		141	437	52	103	18	1	5	42	38	71	6	9	7-7	.236	.304	.316	.620	13	.981
1998— Bowie (East.) 2B-SS-OF		86	258	46	73	13	1	2	20	34	37	1	3	12-3	.283	.369	.364	.733	9	.973
— Rochester (Int'l)	2B	44	160	20	47	6	4	0	18	7	22	3	3	7-5	.294	.329	.381	.711	8	.969
1999— Baltimore (A.L.) ...SS-2B-3B-DH 17			29	6	6	0	0	2	2	3	0	1		0-0	.207	.258	.414	.672	0	1.000
— Rochester (Int'l)	SS-2B	62	220	25	56	10	2	2	23	11	21	0	5	9-6	.255	.289	.345	.634	15	.944
2000— Baltimore (A.L.)	2B-SS	14	17	2	1	0	0	0	0	2	2	0	0	0-0	.059	.158	.059	.217	0	1.000
— Rochester (Int'l)	SS-2B-3B	106	372	44	90	12	2	1	23	27	60	4	9	9-4	.242	.300	.293	.593	18	.963
2001— Richmond (Int'l)	SS-2B-3B	105	375	50	100	23	3	2	22	22	54	4	9	18-6	.267	.313	.357	.671	20	.955
— Atlanta (N.L.)	2B-SS	22	5	3	1	0	0	0	0	0	1	0	0	6-2	.200	.200	.200	.400	0	1.000
2002— Richmond (Int'l) 2B-SS-3B-OF		58	230	29	69	12	1	6	17	16	32	2	5	9-5	.300	.349	.439	.789	9	.966
— Atlanta (N.L.)	2B-SS-OF	39	61	6	12	1	0	0	5	0	14	0	1	0-1	.197	.197	.213	.410	1	.989
2003— Richmond (Int'l) S-2-O-3-DH		110	425	45	130	17	3	2	30	12	50	4	9	29-9	.306	.329	.374	.703	18	.956
— Atlanta (N.L.)	2B-SS-3B	13	10	6	4	0	1	0	2	0	1	0	0	0-1	.400	.400	.600	1.000	0	1.000
2004— Atlanta (N.L.)	SS-2B-3B	50	115	14	29	4	1	1	10	1	16	1	2	1-2	.252	.265	.330	.595	7	.953
— Richmond (Int'l)	2B-SS	20	78	6	17	2	0	0	2	4	13	1	3	0-2	.218	.265	.244	.509	5	.943
American League totals (2 years)		31	46	8	7	0	0	2	2	4	5	0	1	0-0	.152	.220	.283	.503	0	1.000
National League totals (4 years)		124	191	29	46	5	2	1	17	1	32	1	3	7-6	.241	.249	.304	.552	8	.969
Major League totals (6 years)		155	237	37	53	5	2	3	19	5	37	1	4	7-6	.224	.243	.300	.542	8	.975

DIVISION SERIES RECORD

Year Team (League)	Pos.	G	AB	R	H	2B	3B	HR	RBI	BB	SO	HBP	GDP	SB-CS	Avg.	OBP	SLG	OPS	E	Avg.
2003— Atlanta (N.L.)	2B	2	0	1	0	0	0	0	0	0	0	0	0	0-0	...	...	...	...	0	1.000

G

GARCIA, KARIM — OF

PERSONAL: Born October 29, 1975, in Ciudad Obregon, Mexico. ... 6-0/210. ... Bats left, throws left. ... Full name: Gustavo Karim Garcia. ... Name pronounced: ka-REEM. ... High school: Preparatoria Abierta (Ciudad Obregon, Mexico).

TRANSACTIONS/CAREER NOTES: Signed as a non-drafted free agent by Los Angeles Dodgers organization (July 16, 1992). ... On disabled list (September 1, 1997-remainder of season). ... Selected by Arizona Diamondbacks in first round (ninth pick overall) of expansion draft (November 18, 1997). ... Traded by Diamondbacks to Detroit Tigers for OF Luis Gonzalez (December 28, 1998). ... Traded by Tigers to Baltimore Orioles for future considerations (June 12, 2000). ... On suspended list (September 1-4, 2000). ... Released by Orioles (October 17, 2000). ... Signed by Cleveland Indians organization (December 22, 2000). ... Released by Indians (March 27, 2002). ... Signed by New York Yankees organization (April 2, 2002). ... Released by Yankees (July 2, 2002). ... Signed by Indians organization (July 12, 2002). ... On disabled list (May 8-June 23, 2003); included rehabilitation assignments to Buffalo. ... Traded by Indians with P Dan Miceli to New York Yankees for a player to be named (June 25, 2003). ... Signed as a free agent by New York Mets (January 26, 2004). ... On disabled list (June 24-July 9, 2004); included rehabilitation assignment to Binghamton. ... Traded by Mets to Orioles for P Mike DeJean (July 19, 2004). ... Released by Orioles (August 26, 2004).

HONORS: Named Minor League Player of the Year by THE SPORTING NEWS (1995).

2004 GAMES PLAYED BY POSITION (MLB): OF—70, 1B—1.

Year	Team (League)	Pos.	G	AB	R	H	2B	3B	HR	RBI	BB	SO	HBP	GDP	SB-CS	Avg.	OBP	SLG	OPS	E	Avg.
1993— Bakersfield (Calif.)		OF	123	460	61	111	20	9	19	54	37	109	2	5	5-3	.241	.299	.448	.747	13	.940
1994— Vero Beach (FSL)		OF	121	452	72	120	28	10	21	84	37	112	1	7	8-3	.265	.319	.511	.830	5	.980
1995— Albuquerque (PCL)		OF-DH	124	474	88	151	26	10	20	91	38	102	2	12	12-6	.319	.369	.542	.912	14	.932
— Los Angeles (N.L.)		OF	13	20	1	4	0	0	0	0	0	4	0	0	0-0	.200	.200	.200	.400	0	1.000
1996— Albuquerque (PCL)		OF-DH	84	327	54	97	17	10	13	58	29	67	1	9	6-4	.297	.353	.529	.882	13	.921
— San Antonio (Texas)		OF	35	129	21	32	6	1	5	22	9	38	0	1	1-1	.248	.297	.426	.723	2	.971
— Los Angeles (N.L.)		OF	1	1	0	0	0	0	0	0	0	1	0	0	0-0	.000	.000	.000	.000	0	...
1997— Albuquerque (PCL)		OF-DH	71	262	53	80	17	6	20	66	23	70	0	4	11-5	.305	.361	.645	1.006	5	.952
— Los Angeles (N.L.)		OF	15	39	5	5	0	0	1	8	6	14	0	0	0-0	.128	.239	.205	.444	0	1.000
1998— Arizona (N.L.)		OF	113	333	39	74	10	8	9	43	18	78	0	6	5-4	.222	.260	.381	.641	5	.975
— Tucson (PCL)		OF	27	106	21	33	4	2	10	27	15	24	0	2	5-1	.311	.393	.670	1.063	3	.958
1999— Detroit (A.L.)		OF-DH	96	288	38	69	10	3	14	32	20	67	0	2	2-4	.240	.288	.441	.729	7	.958
2000— Detroit (A.L.)		OF-DH	8	17	1	3	0	0	0	0	0	4	0	1	0-0	.176	.176	.176	.353	0	1.000
— Toledo (Int'l)		OF	40	155	31	46	6	2	15	38	11	32	3	...	2-1	.297	.349	.652	1.000	4	.956
— Rochester (Int'l)		OF	76	270	38	75	17	1	13	54	34	70	2	...	3-3	.278	.358	.493	.851	3	.977
— Baltimore (A.L.)		DH-OF	8	16	0	0	0	0	0	0	0	6	0	0	0-0	.000	.000	.000	.000	0	1.000
2001— Buffalo (Int'l)		OF-1B	125	462	73	122	16	4	31	85	44	106	1	9	4-4	.264	.326	.517	.843	7	.973
— Cleveland (A.L.)		OF-1B	20	45	8	14	3	0	5	9	3	13	1	1	0-0	.311	.360	.711	1.071	2	.917
2002— Columbus (Int'l)		OF-1B	74	288	44	78	16	3	12	49	20	48	0		1-5	.271	.316	.472	.788	2	.987
— New York (A.L.)		OF	2	5	1	1	0	0	0	0	0	1	0	0	0-0	.200	.200	.200	.400	0	1.000
— Buffalo (Int'l)		OF	23	91	16	36	7	2	3	22	9	6	0		0-1	.396	.450	.615	1.065	0	1.000
— Cleveland (A.L.)		OF	51	197	29	59	8	0	16	52	6	40	0	6	0-3	.299	.317	.584	.901	1	.990
2003— Cleveland (A.L.)		OF-DH	24	93	8	18	1	0	5	14	5	20	1	4	0-0	.194	.238	.366	.603	4	.905
— Buffalo (Int'l)		OF-DH	14	60	6	16	6	0	0	7	2	17	0	1	2-1	.267	.290	.367	.657	0	1.000
— New York (A.L.)		OF-DH	52	151	17	46	5	0	6	21	9	32	0	4	0-2	.305	.342	.457	.799	2	.981
2004— Binghamton (East.)		1B	3	12	1	1	1	0	0	3	1	2	0	0	0-0	.083	.143	.167	.310	1	.955
— New York (N.L.)		OF	62	192	24	45	7	2	7	22	10	35	0	6	3-0	.234	.272	.401	.673	3	.968
— Baltimore (A.L.)		OF-1B	23	66	9	14	0	0	3	11	4	15	0	1	0-0	.212	.247	.348	.595	0	1.000
American League totals (6 years)			284	878	111	224	27	3	49	139	47	198	2	19	2-9	.255	.291	.460	.751	16	.968
National League totals (5 years)			204	585	69	128	17	10	17	73	34	132	0	12	8-4	.219	.260	.369	.629	8	.975
Major League totals (10 years)			488	1463	180	352	44	13	66	212	81	330	2	31	10-13	.241	.279	.424	.703	24	.970

CHAMPIONSHIP SERIES RECORD

Year	Team (League)	Pos.	G	AB	R	H	2B	3B	HR	RBI	BB	SO	HBP	GDP	SB-CS	Avg.	OBP	SLG	OPS	E	Avg.
2003— New York (A.L.)		OF	5	16	1	4	0	0	0	3	2	4	1	0	0-0	.250	.368	.250	.618	0	1.000

WORLD SERIES RECORD

Year	Team (League)	Pos.	G	AB	R	H	2B	3B	HR	RBI	BB	SO	HBP	GDP	SB-CS	Avg.	OBP	SLG	OPS	E	Avg.
2003— New York (A.L.)		OF	5	14	1	4	0	0	0	0	0	3	0	0	0-0	.286	.286	.286	.571	0	1.000

GARCIA, ROSMAN — P

PERSONAL: Born January 3, 1979, in Maracay, Venezuela. ... 6-2/215. ... Throws right, bats right. ... Full name: Rosman Jose Garcia.
TRANSACTIONS/CAREER NOTES: Signed as a non-drafted free agent by New York Yankees organization (February 15, 1996). ... Traded by Yankees with P Randy Flores to Texas Rangers (October 11, 2001), completing deal in which Rangers traded 2B Randy Velarde to Yankees for two players to be named (August 31, 2001).
CAREER HITTING: 0-for-0 (.000), 0 R, 0 2B, 0 3B, 0 HR, 0 RBI.

Year	Team (League)	W	L	Pct.	ERA	WHIP	G	GS	CG	ShO	Hld.	Sv.-Opp.	IP	H	R	ER	HR	BB-IBB	SO	Avg.
1998— GC Yankees (GCL)		4	3	.571	2.55	1.18	12	12	0	0	...	0-...	67.0	70	38	19	1	9-0	47	.260
1999— Greensboro (S. Atl.)		2	3	.400	6.38	1.89	9	9	0	0	...	0-...	42.1	60	33	30	4	20-0	31	.331
— Staten Island (NY-P)		2	6	.250	4.26	1.44	18	10	0	0	...	1-...	69.2	86	40	33	3	14-2	40	.301
2000— Greensboro (S. Atl.)		6	6	.500	4.57	1.44	23	15	1	0	...	0-...	104.1	115	67	53	12	35-0	73	.280
— Tampa (FSL)		0	2	.000	5.50	1.22	4	3	0	0	...	1-...	18.0	18	13	11	1	4-0	6	.265
2001— Norwich (East.)		1	0	1.000	0.00	1.17	1	1	0	0	...	0-...	6.0	5	4	0	0	2-0	6	.200
— Tampa (FSL)		2	6	.250	3.47	1.31	26	7	0	0	...	1-...	59.2	56	30	23	2	22-6	42	.243
2002— Tulsa (Texas)		8	5	.615	3.01	1.43	53	0	0	0	...	6-...	74.2	75	34	25	1	32-9	38	.270
2003— Oklahoma (PCL)		1	2	.333	1.91	0.92	17	2	0	0	...	10-...	28.1	20	7	6	1	6-0	21	.196
— Texas (A.L.)		1	2	.333	6.02	1.86	46	0	0	0	7	0-2	46.1	63	33	31	4	23-0	25	.320
2004— Texas (A.L.)		0	0		5.40	2.10	4	0	0	0	0	0-0	6.2	9	5	4	1	5-0	5	.310
— Oklahoma (PCL)		4	6	.400	4.65	1.72	41	0	0	0	...	2-...	71.2	87	41	37	6	36-3	49	.307
Major League totals (2 years)		1	2	.333	5.94	1.89	50	0	0	0	7	0-2	53.0	72	38	35	5	28-0	30	.319

GARCIAPARRA, NOMAR — SS

PERSONAL: Born July 23, 1973, in Whittier, Calif. ... 6-0/190. ... Bats right, throws right. ... Full name: Anthony Nomar Garciaparra. ... Name pronounced: no-mar GARCIA-par-uh. ... High school: St. John Bosco (Bellflower, Calif.). ... College: Georgia Tech.
TRANSACTIONS/CAREER NOTES: Selected by Milwaukee Brewers organization in fifth round of 1991 free-agent draft; did not sign. ... Selected by Boston Red Sox organization in first round (12th pick overall) of 1994 free-agent draft. ... On disabled list (May 9-28, 1998; and May 12-27, 2000). ... On disabled list (March 21-July 29 and August 27, 2001-remainder of season); included rehabilitation assignment to Pawtucket. ... On disabled list (March 26-June 9, 2004); included rehabilitation assignment to Pawtucket. ... Traded by Red Sox with OF Matt Murton to Chicago Cubs as part of four-team deal in which Red Sox acquired SS Orlando Cabrera from Expos and 1B Doug Mientkiewicz from Twins, Expos acquired SS Alex S. Gonzalez, P Francis Beltran and IF Brendan Harris from Cubs, and Twins acquired P Justin Jones from Cubs (July 31, 2004).
HONORS: Named A.L. Rookie Player of the Year by THE SPORTING NEWS (1997). ... Named A.L. Rookie of the Year by Baseball Writers' Association of America (1997).
2004 GAMES PLAYED BY POSITION (MLB): SS—79, DH—1.

Year	Team (League)	Pos.	G	AB	R	H	2B	3B	HR	RBI	BB	SO	HBP	GDP	SB-CS	Avg.	OBP	SLG	OPS	E	Avg.
1994— Sarasota (Fla. St.)		SS	28	105	20	31	8	1	1	16	10	6	1	2	5-2	.295	.356	.419	.775	3	.974
1995— Trenton (East.)		SS	125	513	77	137	20	8	8	47	50	42	8	10	35-12	.267	.338	.384	.722	23	.963
1996— Pawtucket (Int'l)		SS	43	172	40	59	15	2	16	46	14	21	1	6	3-1	.343	.387	.733	1.120	5	.973
— GC Red Sox (GCL)		SS	5	14	4	4	2	1	0	5	1	0	1	1	0-0	.286	.375	.571	.946	1	.950
— Boston (A.L.)		SS-2B-DH	24	87	11	21	2	3	4	16	4	14	0	0	5-0	.241	.272	.471	.743	1	.989
1997— Boston (A.L.)		SS	153	* 684	122	* 209	44	* 11	30	98	35	92	6	9	22-9	.306	.342	.534	.875	21	.971
1998— Boston (A.L.)		SS	143	604	111	195	37	8	35	122	33	62	8	20	12-6	.323	.362	.584	.946	25	.962
1999— Boston (A.L.)		SS	135	532	103	190	42	4	27	104	51	39	6	11	14-3	* .357	.418	.603	1.022	17	.972

Year Team (League)	Pos.	G	AB	R	H	2B	3B	HR	RBI	BB	SO	HBP	GDP	SB-CS	Avg.	OBP	SLG	OPS	E	Avg.
2000— Boston (A.L.)	SS-DH	140	529	104	197	51	3	21	96	61	50	2	8	5-2	*.372	.434	.599	1.033	18	.971
2001— Pawtucket (Int'l)	SS	4	16	3	7	2	0	1	4	1	2	1	0	0-0	.438	.500	.750	1.250	1	.941
— Boston (A.L.)	SS	21	83	13	24	3	0	4	8	7	9	1	1	0-1	.289	.352	.470	.822	3	.968
2002— Boston (A.L.)	SS	156	635	101	197	•56	5	24	120	41	63	6	17	5-2	.310	.352	.528	.880	*25	.965
2003— Boston (A.L.)	SS	156	658	120	198	37	13	28	105	39	61	11	10	19-5	.301	.345	.524	.870	20	.971
2004— Pawtucket (Int'l)	SS	6	21	1	5	1	0	1	3	1	3	0	0	0-0	.238	.273	.429	.701	0	1.000
— Boston (A.L.)	SS-DH	38	156	24	50	7	3	5	21	8	16	4	4	2-0	.321	.367	.500	.867	6	.957
— Chicago (N.L.)	SS	43	165	28	49	14	0	4	20	16	14	2	6	2-1	.297	.364	.455	.819	3	.982
American League totals (9 years)		966	3968	709	1281	279	50	178	690	279	406	46	80	84-28	.323	.370	.553	.923	136	.969
National League totals (1 year)		43	165	28	49	14	0	4	20	16	14	2	6	2-1	.297	.364	.455	.819	3	.982
Major League totals (9 years)		1009	4133	737	1330	293	50	182	710	295	420	48	86	86-29	.322	.370	.549	.919	139	.969

DIVISION SERIES RECORD

Year Team (League)	Pos.	G	AB	R	H	2B	3B	HR	RBI	BB	SO	HBP	GDP	SB-CS	Avg.	OBP	SLG	OPS	E	Avg.
1998— Boston (A.L.)	SS	4	15	4	5	1	0	3	11	1	0	0	1	0-0	.333	.333	1.000	1.333	0	1.000
1999— Boston (A.L.)	SS	4	12	6	5	2	0	2	4	3	3	1	0	0-0	.417	.563	1.083	1.646	0	1.000
2003— Boston (A.L.)	SS	5	20	2	6	1	0	0	0	3	2	0	1	1-0	.300	.391	.350	.741	1	.958
Division series totals (3 years)		13	47	12	16	4	0	5	15	7	5	1	2	1-0	.340	.421	.745	1.166	1	.980

CHAMPIONSHIP SERIES RECORD

Year Team (League)	Pos.	G	AB	R	H	2B	3B	HR	RBI	BB	SO	HBP	GDP	SB-CS	Avg.	OBP	SLG	OPS	E	Avg.
1999— Boston (A.L.)	SS	5	20	2	8	2	0	2	5	2	2	0	0	1-0	.400	.455	.800	1.255	4	.833
2003— Boston (A.L.)	SS	7	29	2	7	0	1	0	1	2	8	0	1	0-0	.241	.290	.310	.601	1	.966
Champ. series totals (2 years)		12	49	4	15	2	1	2	6	4	10	0	1	1-0	.306	.358	.510	.869	5	.906

ALL-STAR GAME RECORD

	G	AB	R	H	2B	3B	HR	RBI	BB	SO	HBP	GDP	SB-CS	Avg.	OBP	SLG	OPS	E	Avg.
All-Star Game totals (5 years)	5	7	1	1	0	0	0	0	0	0	0	0	0-0	.143	.143	.143	.286	2	.778

GARLAND, JON   P

PERSONAL: Born September 27, 1979, in Valencia, Calif. ... 6-6/210. ... Throws right, bats right. ... Full name: Jon Steven Garland. ... High school: John F. Kennedy (Granada Hills, Calif.).

TRANSACTIONS/CAREER NOTES: Selected by Chicago Cubs organization in first round (10th pick overall) of 1997 free-agent draft. ... Traded by Cubs to Chicago White Sox for P Matt Karchner (July 29, 1998). ... On disabled list (August 19-September 3, 2000); included rehabilitation assignment to Birmingham.

CAREER HITTING: 1-for-10 (.100), 0 R, 0 2B, 0 3B, 0 HR, 0 RBI.

Year Team (League)	W	L	Pct.	ERA	WHIP	G	GS	CG	ShO	Hld.	Sv.-Opp.	IP	H	R	ER	HR	BB-IBB	SO	Avg.
1997— Ariz. Cubs (Ariz.)	3	2	.600	2.70	1.18	10	7	0	0	...	0-...	40.0	37	14	12	3	10-0	39	.247
1998— Rockford (Midwest)	4	7	.364	5.03	1.57	19	19	1	0	...	0-...	107.1	124	69	60	11	45-0	70	.301
— Hickory (S. Atl.)	1	4	.200	5.40	1.84	5	5	0	0	...	0-...	26.2	36	20	16	2	13-0	19	.333
1999— Winston-Salem (Caro.)	5	7	.417	3.33	1.24	19	19	2	1	...	0-...	119.0	109	57	44	7	39-2	84	.244
— Birmingham (Southern)	3	1	.750	4.38	1.46	7	7	0	0	...	0-...	39.0	39	22	19	4	18-0	27	.258
2000— Charlotte (Int'l)	9	2	.818	2.26	1.26	16	16	2	1	...	0-...	103.2	99	28	26	3	32-2	63	.251
— Chicago (A.L.)	4	8	.333	6.46	1.75	15	13	0	0	1	0-0	69.2	82	55	50	10	40-0	42	.292
— Birmingham (Southern)	0	0	...	0.00	0.83	1	1	0	0	...	0-...	6.0	4	0	0	0	1-0	10	.200
2001— Charlotte (Int'l)	0	3	.000	2.73	1.27	5	5	1	0	...	0-...	33.0	31	10	10	1	11-1	26	.261
— Chicago (A.L.)	6	7	.462	3.69	1.52	35	16	0	0	2	1-1	117.0	123	59	48	16	55-2	61	.277
2002— Chicago (A.L.)	12	12	.500	4.58	1.41	33	33	1	1	0	0-0	192.2	188	109	98	23	83-1	112	.258
2003— Chicago (A.L.)	12	13	.480	4.51	1.37	32	32	0	0	0	0-0	191.2	188	103	96	28	74-1	108	.260
2004— Chicago (A.L.)	12	11	.522	4.89	1.38	34	33	1	0	0	0-0	217.0	223	125	118	34	76-2	113	.269
Major League totals (5 years)	46	51	.474	4.68	1.44	149	127	2	1	3	1-1	788.0	804	451	410	111	328-6	436	.268

GATHRIGHT, JOEY   OF

PERSONAL: Born April 27, 1981, in Hattiesburg, Miss. ... 5-10/170. ... Bats left, throws right. ... Full name: Joey Renard Gathright. ... High school: Bonnabel (Kenner, La.).

TRANSACTIONS/CAREER NOTES: Selected by Tampa Bay Devil Rays organization in 32nd round of 2001 free-agent draft.

2004 GAMES PLAYED BY POSITION (MLB): OF—16, DH—1.

Year Team (League)	Pos.	G	AB	R	H	2B	3B	HR	RBI	BB	SO	HBP	GDP	SB-CS	Avg.	OBP	SLG	OPS	E	Avg.
2002— Char., S.C. (SAL)	OF	59	208	30	55	1	0	0	14	21	36	10	1	22-7	.264	.360	.269	.629	1	.992
2003— Bakersfield (Calif.)	OF	89	340	65	110	6	3	0	23	41	54	6	3	57-13	.324	.406	.359	.765	3	.981
— Orlando (South.)	OF	22	85	12	32	1	0	0	5	5	15	2	0	12-3	.376	.419	.388	.808	1	.983
2004— Montgm. (Sou.)	OF-DH	32	126	23	43	5	1	0	8	11	30	1	1	10-6	.341	.399	.397	.795	1	.985
— Tampa Bay (A.L.)	OF-DH	19	52	11	13	0	0	0	1	2	14	3	2	6-1	.250	.316	.250	.566	0	1.000
— Durham (Int'l)	OF	60	236	34	77	9	1	0	8	19	46	3	5	33-13	.326	.384	.373	.749	4	.968
Major League totals (1 year)		19	52	11	13	0	0	0	1	2	14	3	2	6-1	.250	.316	.250	.566	0	1.000

GAUDIN, CHAD   P

PERSONAL: Born March 24, 1983, in New Orleans, La. ... 5-11/165. ... Throws right, bats right. ... Full name: Chad Edward Gaudin. ... High school: Crescent City (Calif.).

TRANSACTIONS/CAREER NOTES: Selected by Tampa Bay Devil Rays organization in 34th round of 2001 free-agent draft.

CAREER HITTING: 0-for-1 (.000), 0 R, 0 2B, 0 3B, 0 HR, 0 RBI.

Year Team (League)	W	L	Pct.	ERA	WHIP	G	GS	CG	ShO	Hld.	Sv.-Opp.	IP	H	R	ER	HR	BB-IBB	SO	Avg.
2002— Char., S.C. (SAL)	4	6	.400	2.26	1.20	26	17	0	0	...	1-...	119.1	106	43	30	5	37-0	106	.244
2003— Bakersfield (California)	5	3	.625	2.13	1.07	14	14	1	0	...	0-...	80.1	63	23	19	2	23-0	70	.214
— Orlando (Sou.)	2	0	1.000	0.47	0.58	3	3	1	1	...	0-...	19.0	8	1	1	0	3-0	23	.131
— Tampa Bay (A.L.)	2	0	1.000	3.60	1.33	15	3	0	0	0	0-0	40.0	37	18	16	4	16-0	23	.240
2004— Durham (Int'l)	1	3	.250	4.72	1.36	17	7	0	0	...	2-...	47.2	48	26	25	8	17-0	52	.264
— Tampa Bay (A.L.)	1	2	.333	4.85	1.76	26	4	0	0	5	0-1	42.2	59	27	23	4	16-4	30	.337
Major League totals (2 years)	3	2	.600	4.25	1.55	41	7	0	0	5	0-1	82.2	96	45	39	8	32-4	53	.292

G

GEARY, GEOFF   P

PERSONAL: Born August 26, 1976, in Buffalo, N.Y. ... 6-0/167. ... Throws right, bats right. ... Full name: Geoffrey Michael Geary. ... High school: Grossmont (El Cajon, Calif.). ... College: Oklahoma.

TRANSACTIONS/CAREER NOTES: Selected by Milwaukee Brewers organization in 41st round of 1997 free-agent draft; did not sign. ... Selected by Philadelphia Phillies organization in 15th round of 1998 free-agent draft.

CAREER HITTING: 0-for-1 (.000), 0 R, 0 2B, 0 3B, 0 HR, 0 RBI.

Year	Team (League)	W	L	Pct.	ERA	WHIP	G	GS	CG	ShO	Hld.	Sv.-Opp.	IP	H	R	ER	HR	BB-IBB	SO	Avg.
1998—Batavia (N.Y.-Penn)		9	1	.900	1.60	0.97	16	15	1	1	...	0-...	95.1	78	20	17	6	14-0	101	.222
1999—Clearwater (Fla. St.)		10	5	.667	3.95	1.48	24	19	2	0	...	0-...	139.0	175	77	61	11	31-1	77	.310
2000—Reading (East.)		7	6	.538	4.11	1.26	22	22	1	0	...	0-...	129.1	141	66	59	15	22-0	112	.272
2001—Reading (East.)		9	7	.563	3.61	1.09	29	13	0	0	...	2-...	112.1	101	48	45	14	21-3	88	.245
—Scran./W.B. (I.L.)		0	3	.000	6.95	1.86	7	3	0	0	...	0-...	22.0	35	17	17	2	6-1	21	.376
2002—Scran./W.B. (I.L.)		4	2	.667	3.03	1.39	38	3	0	0	...	1-...	101.0	108	46	34	9	32-1	82	.277
2003—Scran./W.B. (I.L.)		9	4	.692	2.16	0.98	46	3	0	0	...	5-...	87.2	73	26	21	3	13-1	80	.229
—Philadelphia (N.L.)		0	0	...	4.50	1.83	5	0	0	0	0	0-0	6.0	8	3	3	0	3-0	3	.333
2004—Scran./W.B. (I.L.)		1	2	.333	2.31	1.41	21	0	0	0	...	10-...	23.1	20	7	6	1	13-4	23	.235
—Philadelphia (N.L.)		1	0	1.000	5.44	1.52	33	0	0	0	0	0-0	44.2	52	29	27	8	16-3	30	.292
Major League totals (2 years)		1	0	1.000	5.33	1.56	38	0	0	0	0	0-0	50.2	60	32	30	8	19-3	33	.297

GEORGE, CHRIS   P

PERSONAL: Born September 16, 1979, in Houston, Texas. ... 6-2/200. ... Throws left, bats left. ... Full name: Christopher Coleman George. ... High school: Klein (Texas).

TRANSACTIONS/CAREER NOTES: Selected by Kansas City Royals organization in supplemental round ("sandwich pick" between first and second rounds, 31st pick overall) of 1998 free-agent draft; pick received as part of compensation for Arizona Diamondbacks signing Type A free-agent IF Jay Bell. ... On disabled list (May 18-June 18, 2002); included rehabiltiation assignment to Omaha.

CAREER HITTING: 1-for-3 (.333), 0 R, 0 2B, 0 3B, 0 HR, 1 RBI.

Year	Team (League)	W	L	Pct.	ERA	WHIP	G	GS	CG	ShO	Hld.	Sv.-Opp.	IP	H	R	ER	HR	BB-IBB	SO	Avg.
1998—GC Royals (GCL)		0	1	.000	2.87	1.15	5	4	0	0	...	0-...	15.2	14	9	5	1	4-0	10	.233
1999—Wilmington (Caro.)		9	7	.563	3.60	1.34	27	27	0	0	...	0-...	145.0	142	65	58	8	53-0	142	.257
2000—Wichita (Texas)		8	5	.615	3.14	1.47	18	18	0	0	...	0-...	97.1	92	41	34	8	51-1	80	.253
—Omaha (PCL)		3	2	.600	4.84	1.50	8	8	0	0	...	0-...	44.2	47	29	24	8	20-0	27	.273
2001—Omaha (PCL)		11	3	.786	3.53	1.31	20	20	0	0	...	0-...	117.1	103	54	46	14	51-0	84	.237
—Kansas City (A.L.)		4	8	.333	5.59	1.36	13	13	1	0	0	0-0	74.0	83	48	46	14	18-0	32	.288
2002—Omaha (PCL)		6	12	.333	5.87	1.65	22	21	1	0	...	0-...	127.1	145	86	83	15	65-0	94	.287
—Kansas City (A.L.)		0	4	.000	5.60	1.65	6	6	0	0	0	0-0	27.1	37	17	17	2	8-0	13	.325
2003—Kansas City (A.L.)		9	6	.600	7.11	1.75	18	18	0	0	0	0-0	93.2	120	75	74	22	44-2	39	.309
—Omaha (PCL)		3	5	.375	7.29	1.70	10	10	0	0	...	0-...	54.1	71	49	44	8	22-0	28	.314
2004—Omaha (PCL)		8	6	.571	3.42	1.30	20	19	2	1	...	0-...	105.1	97	45	40	7	40-0	74	.251
—Kansas City (A.L.)		1	2	.333	7.23	2.01	10	7	0	0	0	0-0	42.1	60	39	34	1	25-1	15	.331
Major League totals (4 years)		14	20	.412	6.48	1.66	47	44	1	0	0	0-0	237.1	300	179	171	39	95-3	99	.309

GERMAN, ESTEBAN   3B/2B

PERSONAL: Born January 26, 1978, in Santo Domingo, Dominican Republic. ... 5-9/165. ... Bats right, throws right. ... Full name: Esteban German Guridi. ... Name pronounced: her-MAHN.

TRANSACTIONS/CAREER NOTES: Signed as a non-drafted free agent by Oakland Athletics organization (July 4, 1996). ... On disabled list (July 4-31, 2004); included rehabilitation assignment to Sacramento.

2004 GAMES PLAYED BY POSITION (MLB): 3B—15, 2B—10, DH—2.

Year	Team (League)	Pos.	G	AB	R	H	2B	3B	HR	RBI	BB	SO	HBP	GDP	SB-CS	Avg.	OBP	SLG	OPS	E	Avg.
1997—Dom. Athletics (DSL)			69	249	69	79	17	1	2	29	73	30	...	...	58-...	.317	...	.418	...	...	...
1998—Dom. Athletics (DSL)			10	32	9	10	1	1	0	4	7	2	...	...	1-...	.313	...	.406	...	...	...
—Ariz. A's (Ariz.)		2B	55	202	52	62	3	10	2	28	33	43	4	1	40-8	.307	.413	.451	.863	13	.940
1999—Modesto (California)		2B	128	501	107	156	16	12	4	52	102	128	5	3	40-16	.311	.428	.415	.843	38	.932
2000—Midland (Texas)		2B	24	75	13	16	1	0	1	6	18	21	2	1	5-3	.213	.379	.267	.646	5	.951
—Visalia (Calif.)		2B-SS	109	428	82	113	14	10	2	35	61	86	5	4	78-8	.264	.361	.357	.718	25	.953
2001—Midland (Texas)		2B	92	335	79	95	20	3	6	30	63	66	12	6	31-11	.284	.415	.415	.830	16	.963
—Sacramento (PCL)		2B	38	150	40	56	8	0	4	14	18	20	6	4	17-2	.373	.457	.507	.964	7	.962
2002—Sacramento (PCL)		2B	121	458	72	126	16	4	2	43	78	66	8	7	26-14	.275	.390	.341	.730	8	.986
—Oakland (A.L.)		2B	9	35	4	7	0	0	0	0	4	11	1	0	1-0	.200	.300	.200	.500	1	.978
2003—Sacramento (PCL)		2B	115	467	86	143	20	8	3	51	56	64	2	17	32-8	.306	.379	.403	.781	13	.976
—Oakland (A.L.)		2B	5	4	0	1	0	0	0	1	1	0	1	0	0-0	.250	.250	.250	.500	0	1.000
2004—Sacramento (PCL)		2B-SS-DH	55	231	33	76	8	4	2	29	19	28	3	6	18-2	.329	.380	.424	.804	9	.961
—Oakland (A.L.)		3B-2B-DH	31	60	9	15	1	1	0	7	4	13	0	1	0-1	.250	.297	.300	.597	2	.967
Major League totals (3 years)			45	99	13	23	1	1	0	8	8	25	1	2	1-1	.232	.296	.263	.559	3	.974

GERMAN, FRANKLYN   P

PERSONAL: Born January 20, 1980, in San Cristobal, Dominican Republic. ... 6-7/270. ... Throws right, bats right. ... Full name: Franklyn Miguel German. ... Name pronounced: her-MAHN.

TRANSACTIONS/CAREER NOTES: Signed as a non-drafted free agent by Oakland Athletics organization (July 2, 1996). ... Traded by A's with 1B Carlos Pena and a player to be named to Detroit Tigers as part of a three-team deal in which New York Yankees acquired P Jeff Weaver from Tigers and A's acquired Ps Ted Lilly and Jason Arnold and OF John-Ford Griffin from Yankees (July 6, 2002); Tigers acquired P Jeremy Bonderman to complete deal (August 22, 2002).

CAREER HITTING: 0-for-1 (.000), 0 R, 0 2B, 0 3B, 0 HR, 0 RBI.

Year	Team (League)	W	L	Pct.	ERA	WHIP	G	GS	CG	ShO	Hld.	Sv.-Opp.	IP	H	R	ER	HR	BB-IBB	SO	Avg.
1997—Dominican Athletics (DSL)		8	3	.727	2.33	1.09	13	13	5	...	...	0-...	89.0	66	33	23	...	31-...	80	...
1998—Ariz. A's (Ariz.)		2	1	.667	6.13	1.60	14	12	0	0	...	0-...	54.1	69	43	37	5	18-0	48	.317
1999—S. Oregon (N'west)		3	5	.375	5.99	1.82	15	15	0	0	...	0-...	73.2	89	52	49	10	45-1	58	.306
2000—Modesto (Calif.)		5	5	.500	5.50	1.74	17	14	0	0	...	0-...	72.0	88	55	44	4	37-0	52	.307
—Vancouver (N'west)		1	0	1.000	1.77	1.13	9	2	0	0	...	0-...	20.1	13	4	4	0	10-0	20	.173
2001—Visalia (Calif.)		2	4	.333	3.98	1.55	53	0	0	0	...	19-...	63.1	67	34	28	7	31-1	93	.262

G

Year	Team (League)	W	L	Pct.	ERA	WHIP	G	GS	CG	ShO	Hld.	Sv.-Opp.	IP	H	R	ER	HR	BB-IBB	SO	Avg.
2002—Midland (Texas)		1	1	.500	3.05	1.33	37	0	0	0	...	16-...	41.1	28	14	14	0	27-2	59	.194
—Toledo (International)		1	1	.500	1.59	0.97	23	0	0	0	...	13-...	22.2	15	4	4	0	7-0	31	.188
—Detroit (A.L.)		1	0	1.000	0.00	0.75	7	0	0	0	1	1-1	6.2	3	0	0	0	2-1	6	.150
2003—Toledo (International)		1	4	.200	2.45	1.00	24	0	0	0	...	4-...	29.1	21	9	8	2	9-1	32	.212
—Detroit (A.L.)		2	4	.333	6.04	2.06	45	0	0	0	4	5-7	44.2	47	32	30	5	45-3	41	.273
2004—Toledo (International)		3	5	.375	4.59	1.45	49	0	0	0	...	27-...	49.0	46	25	25	6	25-2	60	.246
—Detroit (A.L.)		1	0	1.000	7.36	1.91	16	0	0	0	1	0-1	14.2	17	15	12	4	11-1	8	.279
Major League totals (3 years)		4	4	.500	5.73	1.89	68	0	0	0	6	6-9	66.0	67	47	42	9	58-5	55	.265

GERMANO, JUSTIN   P

PERSONAL: Born August 6, 1982, in Pasadena, Calif. ... 6-1/190. ... Throws right, bats right. ... Full name: Justin William Germano.
TRANSACTIONS/CAREER NOTES: Selected by San Diego Padres organization in 13th round of 2000 free-agent draft.
CAREER HITTING: 0-for-7 (.000), 0 R, 0 2B, 0 3B, 0 HR, 0 RBI.

Year	Team (League)	W	L	Pct.	ERA	WHIP	G	GS	CG	ShO	Hld.	Sv.-Opp.	IP	H	R	ER	HR	BB-IBB	SO	Avg.
2000—Ariz. Padres (Ariz.)		5	5	.500	4.59	1.11	17	8	0	0	...	1-...	66.2	65	36	34	4	9-0	67	.249
2001—Fort Wayne (Midw.)		2	6	.250	4.98	1.48	13	13	0	0	...	0-...	65.0	80	47	36	7	16-1	55	.302
—Eugene (N'west)		6	5	.545	3.49	1.10	13	13	2	0	...	0-...	80.0	77	35	31	5	11-0	74	.246
2002—Fort Wayne (Midw.)		12	5	.706	3.18	1.19	24	24	1	0	...	0-...	155.2	166	63	55	14	19-2	119	.269
—Lake Elsinore (Calif.)		2	0	1.000	0.95	0.89	3	3	0	0	...	0-...	19.0	12	3	2	1	5-0	18	.174
2003—Lake Elsinore (Calif.)		9	5	.643	4.23	1.37	19	19	1	0	...	0-...	110.2	127	61	52	4	25-1	78	.287
—Mobile (Sou.)		2	5	.286	4.34	1.26	9	9	1	0	...	0-...	58.0	60	34	28	6	13-3	44	.268
2004—Mobile (Sou.)		2	1	.667	2.51	1.18	5	5	0	0	...	0-...	32.1	31	11	9	3	7-0	20	.258
—Portland (PCL)		9	5	.643	3.38	1.13	20	20	2	2	...	0-...	122.2	113	48	46	12	25-0	98	.241
—San Diego (N.L.)		1	2	.333	8.86	2.11	7	5	0	0	0	0-0	21.1	31	24	21	2	14-0	16	.341
Major League totals (1 year)		1	2	.333	8.86	2.11	7	5	0	0	0	0-0	21.1	31	24	21	2	14-0	16	.341

GERUT, JODY   OF

PERSONAL: Born September 18, 1977, in Elmhurst, Ill. ... 6-0/190. ... Bats left, throws left. ... Full name: Joseph Gerut. ... Name pronounced: GARE-et. ... High school: Willowbrook (Ill.). ... College: Stanford.
TRANSACTIONS/CAREER NOTES: Selected by Colorado Rockies organization in second round of 1998 free-agent draft. ... Traded by Rockies with C Josh Bard to Cleveland Indians for OF Jacob Cruz (June 1, 2001). ... On disabled list (September 19, 2004-remainder of season).
HONORS: Named A.L. Rookie Player of the Year by THE SPORTING NEWS (2003).
2004 GAMES PLAYED BY POSITION (MLB): OF—131, DH—1.

Year	Team (League)	Pos.	G	AB	R	H	2B	3B	HR	RBI	BB	SO	HBP	GDP	SB-CS	Avg.	OBP	SLG	OPS	E	Avg.
1999—Salem (Caro.)		OF	133	499	80	144	33	11	11	63	61	65	3	10	25-12	.289	.367	.465	.832	7	.970
2000—Carolina (Southern)		OF	109	362	48	103	32	3	3	57	76	54	2	9	18-11	.285	.405	.414	.819	4	.977
2002—Akron (East.)		OF	65	256	44	72	15	2	9	39	34	30	1	7	17-8	.281	.368	.461	.829	3	.979
—Buffalo (Int'l)		OF	55	183	31	59	7	2	1	21	23	20	1	6	3-5	.322	.401	.399	.800	1	.993
2003—Buffalo (Int'l)		OF-DH	17	65	13	18	5	0	5	19	11	11	0	1	4-0	.277	.377	.585	.961	0	1.000
—Cleveland (A.L.)		OF-DH	127	480	66	134	33	2	22	75	35	70	7	13	4-5	.279	.336	.494	.830	4	.984
2004—Cleveland (A.L.)		OF-DH	134	481	72	121	31	5	11	51	54	59	7	9	13-6	.252	.334	.405	.739	4	.986
Major League totals (2 years)			261	961	138	255	64	7	33	126	89	129	14	22	17-11	.265	.335	.450	.784	8	.985

GETTIS, BYRON   OF

PERSONAL: Born March 13, 1980, in Centreville, Ill. ... 6-0/240. ... Bats right, throws right. ... Full name: Byron Earl Gettis. ... High school: Cahokia (Ill.).
TRANSACTIONS/CAREER NOTES: Signed by Kansas City Royals organization as a non-drafted free agent (June 29, 1998). ... Claimed on waivers by Detroit Tigers (October 15, 2004).
2004 GAMES PLAYED BY POSITION (MLB): OF—21.

Year	Team (League)	Pos.	G	AB	R	H	2B	3B	HR	RBI	BB	SO	HBP	GDP	SB-CS	Avg.	OBP	SLG	OPS	E	Avg.
1998—GC Royals (GCL)		OF	27	88	11	19	2	0	0	4	4	20	0	2	0-0	.216	.247	.239	.486	0	1.000
1999—GC Royals (GCL)		OF-3B	28	95	20	30	6	2	5	21	17	21	3	2	3-2	.316	.424	.579	1.003	1	.972
—Char., W.Va. (SAL)		OF-1B	43	149	19	44	7	2	2	13	10	36	6	3	10-3	.295	.361	.409	.771	4	.947
2000—Wilmington (Caro.)		OF	30	97	13	15	2	0	0	10	13	33	2	1	2-1	.155	.265	.175	.441	1	.976
—Char., W.Va. (SAL)		OF	94	344	43	74	18	3	5	50	31	95	11	5	11-7	.215	.297	.328	.626	4	.979
2001—Burlington (Midw.)		OF	37	140	26	44	9	2	5	26	14	25	4	3	4-3	.314	.385	.514	.899	1	.990
—Wilmington (Caro.)		OF	82	303	34	76	21	2	6	51	20	70	12	7	4-5	.251	.321	.393	.714	5	.967
2002—Wilmington (Caro.)		OF	120	449	76	127	33	2	8	70	48	103	13	8	10-5	.283	.364	.419	.783	4	.981
2003—Wichita (Texas)		OF	140	510	80	154	31	4	16	103	55	110	13	11	15-11	.302	.377	.473	.849	6	.980
2004—Kansas City (A.L.)		OF	21	39	7	7	1	1	0	1	8	14	1	0	0-1	.179	.327	.256	.583	3	.930
—Omaha (PCL)		OF	51	179	23	46	7	0	4	19	33	61	0	4	4-1	.257	.366	.363	.729	3	.966
—Wichita (Texas)		OF	17	58	6	21	4	1	2	11	8	12	1	1	0-1	.362	.448	.569	1.008	2	.926
Major League totals (1 year)			21	39	7	7	1	1	0	1	8	14	1	0	0-1	.179	.327	.256	.583	3	.930

GIAMBI, JASON   1B/DH

PERSONAL: Born January 8, 1971, in West Covina, Calif. ... 6-3/230. ... Bats left, throws right. ... Full name: Jason Gilbert Giambi. ... Name pronounced: gee-OM-bee. ... High school: South Hills (West Covina, Calif.). ... College: Long Beach State. ... Brother of Jeremy Giambi, first baseman/outfielder with four major league teams (1998-2003).
TRANSACTIONS/CAREER NOTES: Selected by Milwaukee Brewers organization in 43rd round of 1989 free-agent draft; did not sign. ... Selected by Oakland Athletics organization in second round of 1992 free-agent draft. ... Signed as a free agent by New York Yankees (December 18, 2001). ... On disabled list (May 22-June 6 and July 26-September 14, 2004); included rehabilitation assignments to Tampa and Columbus.
HONORS: Named A.L. Most Valuable Player by Baseball Writers' Association of America (2000).
2004 GAMES PLAYED BY POSITION (MLB): 1B—47, DH—28.

Year	Team (League)	Pos.	G	AB	R	H	2B	3B	HR	RBI	BB	SO	HBP	GDP	SB-CS	Avg.	OBP	SLG	OPS	E	Avg.
1992—S. Oregon (N'west)		3B	13	41	9	13	3	0	3	13	9	6	0	0	1-1	.317	.440	.610	1.050	1	.962
1993—Modesto (California)		3B	89	313	72	91	16	2	12	60	73	47	10	12	2-3	.291	.436	.470	.906	19	.911
1994—Huntsville (Sou.)		3B-1B	56	193	31	43	9	0	6	30	27	31	2	8	0-0	.223	.319	.363	.681	11	.945

G

Year	Team (League)	Pos.	G	AB	R	H	2B	3B	HR	RBI	BB	SO	HBP	GDP	SB-CS	Avg.	OBP	SLG	OPS	E	Avg.
	—Tacoma (PCL)	3B-SS	52	176	28	56	20	0	4	38	25	32	0	1	1-0	.318	.388	.500	.888	8	.949
1995	—Edmonton (PCL)	3B-DH-1B	55	190	34	65	26	1	3	41	34	26	2	4	0-0	.342	.441	.537	.978	4	.938
	—Oakland (A.L.)	3B-1B-DH	54	176	27	45	7	0	6	25	28	31	3	4	2-1	.256	.364	.398	.761	4	.984
1996	—Oakland (A.L.)	1-OF-3-DH	140	536	84	156	40	1	20	79	51	95	5	15	0-1	.291	.355	.481	.836	11	.982
1997	—Oakland (A.L.)	OF-1B-DH	142	519	66	152	41	2	20	81	55	89	6	11	0-1	.293	.362	.495	.857	7	.987
1998	—Oakland (A.L.)	1B-DH	153	562	92	166	28	0	27	110	81	102	5	16	2-2	.295	.384	.489	.873	* 14	.990
1999	—Oakland (A.L.)	1B-DH-3B	158	575	115	181	36	1	33	123	105	106	7	11	1-1	.315	.422	.553	.975	7	.995
2000	—Oakland (A.L.)	1B-DH	152	510	108	170	29	1	43	137	* 137	96	9	9	2-0	.333	* .476	.647	1.123	6	.995
2001	—Oakland (A.L.)	1B-DH	154	520	109	178	* 47	2	38	120	* 129	83	13	17	2-0	.342	* .477	* .660	1.137	11	.992
2002	—New York (A.L.)	1B-DH	155	560	120	176	34	1	41	122	109	112	15	18	2-2	.314	.435	.598	1.034	4	.995
2003	—New York (A.L.)	1B-DH	156	535	97	134	25	0	41	107	* 129	* 140	21	9	2-1	.250	.423	.527	.939	4	.995
2004	—Tampa (Fla. St.)	1B	2	6	0	1	0	0	0	0	1	1	0	0	0-0	.167	.286	.167	.452	0	1.000
	—New York (A.L.)	1B-DH	80	264	33	55	9	0	12	40	47	62	8	5	0-1	.208	.342	.379	.720	4	.990
Major League totals (10 years)			1344	4757	851	1413	296	8	281	944	871	916	92	115	13-10	.297	.411	.540	.951	72	.992

DIVISION SERIES RECORD

Year	Team (League)	Pos.	G	AB	R	H	2B	3B	HR	RBI	BB	SO	HBP	GDP	SB-CS	Avg.	OBP	SLG	OPS	E	Avg.
2000	—Oakland (A.L.)	1B	5	14	2	4	0	0	0	1	7	2	0	0	1-0	.286	.500	.286	.786	1	.976
2001	—Oakland (A.L.)	1B	5	17	2	6	0	0	1	4	4	2	0	1	0-0	.353	.455	.529	.984	1	.982
2002	—New York (A.L.)	1B-DH	4	14	5	5	0	0	1	3	4	1	1	1	0-0	.357	.526	.571	1.098	0	1.000
2003	—New York (A.L.)	DH	4	16	1	4	2	0	0	2	2	5	0	0	0-0	.250	.333	.375	.708	0	...
Division series totals (4 years)			18	61	10	19	2	0	2	10	17	10	1	2	1-0	.311	.457	.443	.899	2	.984

CHAMPIONSHIP SERIES RECORD

Year	Team (League)	Pos.	G	AB	R	H	2B	3B	HR	RBI	BB	SO	HBP	GDP	SB-CS	Avg.	OBP	SLG	OPS	E	Avg.
2003	—New York (A.L.)	DH	7	26	4	6	0	0	3	3	4	7	0	0	0-0	.231	.333	.577	.910	0	...

WORLD SERIES RECORD

Year	Team (League)	Pos.	G	AB	R	H	2B	3B	HR	RBI	BB	SO	HBP	GDP	SB-CS	Avg.	OBP	SLG	OPS	E	Avg.
2003	—New York (A.L.)	DH-1B	6	17	2	4	1	0	1	4	3	1	1	1	0-0	.235	.409	.471	.880	0	1.000

ALL-STAR GAME RECORD

			G	AB	R	H	2B	3B	HR	RBI	BB	SO	HBP	GDP	SB-CS	Avg.	OBP	SLG	OPS	E	Avg.
All-Star Game totals (5 years)			5	8	4	3	0	0	1	1	1	3	0	0	0-0	.375	.444	.750	1.194	0	1.000

GIBBONS, JAY — OF

PERSONAL: Born March 2, 1977, in Rochester, Mich. ... 6-0/197. ... Bats left, throws left. ... Full name: Jay Jonathon Gibbons. ... High school: Mayfair (Lakewood, Calif.). ... College: Cal State Los Angeles.

TRANSACTIONS/CAREER NOTES: Selected by Toronto Blue Jays organization in 14th round of 1998 free-agent draft. ... Selected by Baltimore Orioles from Blue Jays organization in Rule 5 major league draft (December 11, 2000). ... On disabled list (August 5, 2001-remainder of season). ... On disabled list (May 26-June 14 and June 29-August 10, 2004); included rehabilitation assignments to Frederick and Bowie.

2004 GAMES PLAYED BY POSITION (MLB): OF—66, DH—16, 1B—14.

Year	Team (League)	Pos.	G	AB	R	H	2B	3B	HR	RBI	BB	SO	HBP	GDP	SB-CS	Avg.	OBP	SLG	OPS	E	Avg.
													BATTING							FIELDING	
1998	—Medicine Hat (Pio.)	1B	73	290	66	115	29	1	19	98	37	25	3	7	2-1	.397	.457	.700	1.157	6	.983
1999	—Hagerstown (SAL)	1B-OF	71	292	53	89	20	2	16	69	32	56	1	12	3-0	.305	.370	.551	.921	6	.975
	—Dunedin (Fla. St.)	1B	60	212	34	66	14	0	9	39	25	38	0	4	2-1	.311	.382	.505	.887	5	.991
2000	—Tennessee (Sou.)	1B-OF	132	474	85	152	38	1	19	75	61	67	10	10	3-1	.321	.404	.525	.929	8	.991
2001	—Baltimore (A.L.)	DH-OF-1B	73	225	27	53	10	0	15	36	17	39	4	7	0-1	.236	.301	.480	.781	0	1.000
2002	—Baltimore (A.L.)	OF-1B-DH	136	490	71	121	29	1	28	69	45	66	2	9	1-3	.247	.311	.482	.792	2	.995
2003	—Baltimore (A.L.)	OF-1B-DH	160	625	80	173	39	2	23	100	49	89	3	12	0-0	.277	.330	.456	.786	6	.985
2004	—Frederick (Carolina)	OF-DH	3	11	2	2	1	0	1	5	2	2	0	0	0-0	.182	.308	.545	.853	0	...
	—Bowie (East.)	OF-DH	5	15	3	1	0	0	0	1	2	2	0	1	0-0	.067	.167	.067	.233	0	1.000
	—Baltimore (A.L.)	OF-DH-1B	97	346	36	85	14	1	10	47	29	64	1	11	1-1	.246	.303	.379	.682	3	.988
Major League totals (4 years)			466	1686	214	432	92	4	76	252	140	258	10	39	2-6	.256	.315	.451	.766	11	.990

GIL, GERONIMO — C

PERSONAL: Born August 7, 1975, in Oaxaca, Mexico. ... 6-2/234. ... Bats right, throws right. ... Name pronounced: heel.

TRANSACTIONS/CAREER NOTES: Contract purchased by Los Angeles Dodgers organization from Mexico City Red Devils of the Mexican League (February 15, 1996). ... Traded by Dodgers with P Kris Foster to Baltimore Orioles for P Mike Trombley (July 31, 2001).

2004 GAMES PLAYED BY POSITION (MLB): C—11.

Year	Team (League)	Pos.	G	AB	R	H	2B	3B	HR	RBI	BB	SO	HBP	GDP	SB-CS	Avg.	OBP	SLG	OPS	E	Avg.
													BATTING							FIELDING	
1993	—M.C. R. Dev. (Mex.)	DH	1	1	0	0	0	0	0	0	0	1	...	...	0-0	.000	...	.000	...	...	...
1994						Did not play.															
1995	—M.C. R. Dev. (Mex.)	OF	4	7	1	2	0	0	0	0	0	1	...	...	0-0	.286	...	.286	...	0	1.000
1996	—Savannah (S. Atl.)	C	79	276	29	67	13	1	7	38	8	69	5	4	0-2	.243	.274	.373	.647	10	.983
1997	—Vero Beach (FSL)	C	66	213	30	53	13	1	6	24	15	41	4	5	3-0	.249	.310	.404	.714	13	.975
1998	—San Antonio (Texas)	C-1B-OF	75	241	27	70	17	3	6	29	15	43	0	8	2-1	.290	.329	.461	.790	9	.972
1999	—San Antonio (Texas)	3-C-1-OF	106	343	47	97	26	1	15	59	49	58	2	15	2-0	.283	.372	.496	.867	9	.986
2000	—San Antonio (Texas)	3-C-1-OF	100	352	42	100	19	1	11	58	33	65	6	8	3-2	.284	.351	.438	.789	8	.988
	—Albuquerque (PCL)	3B-C-OF	15	50	9	19	5	0	2	22	5	9	0	1	0-1	.380	.421	.600	1.021	3	.959
2001	—Las Vegas (PCL)	C-1B-SS	82	281	40	83	15	0	9	40	16	56	2	9	0-1	.295	.334	.445	.779	3	.995
	—Rochester (Int'l)	C	23	82	7	22	6	1	2	14	0	23	1	1	0-0	.268	.271	.439	.710	3	.986
	—Baltimore (A.L.)	C	17	58	3	17	2	0	0	6	5	7	2	1	0-0	.293	.369	.328	.697	2	.985
2002	—Baltimore (A.L.)	C	125	422	33	98	19	0	12	45	21	88	1	17	2-2	.232	.270	.363	.632	4	.995
2003	—Ottawa (Int'l)	C-DH-1B	36	134	15	47	10	0	1	17	7	28	2	2	0-3	.351	.386	.448	.834	2	.992
	—Baltimore (A.L.)	C	54	169	22	40	4	0	3	16	12	34	3	2	0-0	.237	.299	.314	.613	6	.984
2004	—Ottawa (Int'l)	C-DH-1B	106	375	55	97	24	0	6	34	32	67	6	12	2-1	.259	.327	.371	.698	9	.990
	—Baltimore (A.L.)	C	12	32	1	9	2	0	0	4	3	5	0	0	0-0	.281	.343	.344	.687	0	1.000
Major League totals (4 years)			208	681	59	164	27	0	15	71	41	134	6	20	2-2	.241	.289	.347	.636	12	.991

G

GIL, JERRY — SS

PERSONAL: Born October 14, 1982, in San Pedro de Macoris, Dominican Republic. ... 6-3/183. ... Bats right, throws right. ... Full name: Jerry Bienbenido Gil. ... High school: Colegio La Zafra (San Pedro de Macoris, D.R.).
TRANSACTIONS/CAREER NOTES: Signed as a non-drafted free agent by Arizona Diamondbacks organization (November 15, 1999).
2004 GAMES PLAYED BY POSITION (MLB): SS—28.

Year Team (League)	Pos.	G	AB	R	H	2B	3B	HR	RBI	BB	SO	HBP	GDP	SB-CS	Avg.	OBP	SLG	OPS	E	Avg.
2000— Missoula (Pio.)	SS	58	227	24	51	10	2	0	20	11	63	2	5	7-3	.225	.266	.286	.552	35	.891
2001— South Bend (Mid.)	SS	105	363	40	78	14	5	2	31	8	103	4	12	19-7	.215	.240	.298	.538	34	.937
2002— Lancaster (Calif.)	SS	10	37	4	8	0	0	1	4	1	11	0	0	1-1	.216	.237	.297	.534	5	.917
— Yakima (N'west)	SS-3B	65	224	21	56	11	2	2	28	6	47	2	6	14-1	.250	.274	.344	.617	23	.918
2003— South Bend (Mid.)	SS	116	429	52	111	16	6	4	58	10	90	2	7	19-10	.259	.275	.352	.627	32	.947
2004— Tucson (PCL)	SS	114	421	53	117	31	8	11	58	12	94	2	4	12-1	.278	.299	.468	.764	29	.946
— Arizona (N.L.)	SS	29	86	3	15	2	1	0	8	0	33	1	2	2-0	.174	.182	.221	.403	5	.955
Major League totals (1 year)		29	86	3	15	2	1	0	8	0	33	1	2	2-0	.174	.182	.221	.403	5	.955

GILES, BRIAN — OF

PERSONAL: Born January 20, 1971, in El Cajon, Calif. ... 5-10/205. ... Bats left, throws left. ... Full name: Brian Stephen Giles. ... Name pronounced: JYLES. ... High school: Granite Hills (El Cajon, Calif.). ... Brother of Marcus Giles, second baseman, Atlanta Braves.
TRANSACTIONS/CAREER NOTES: Selected by Cleveland Indians organization in 17th round of 1989 free-agent draft. ... On disabled list (June 1-July 7, 1998); included rehabilitation assignment to Buffalo. ... Traded by Indians to Pittsburgh Pirates for P Ricardo Rincon (November 18, 1998). ... On disabled list (April 11-May 7, 2003). ... Traded by Pirates to San Diego Padres for P Oliver Perez, OF Jason Bay and a player to be named (August 26, 2003); Padres acquired P Cory Stewart to complete deal (October 2, 2003).
2004 GAMES PLAYED BY POSITION (MLB): OF—159.

Year Team (League)	Pos.	G	AB	R	H	2B	3B	HR	RBI	BB	SO	HBP	GDP	SB-CS	Avg.	OBP	SLG	OPS	E	Avg.
1989— Burlington (Appal.)	OF	36	129	18	40	7	0	0	20	11	19	1	0	6-3	.310	.366	.364	.731	1	.982
1990— Watertown (N.Y.-Penn.)	OF	70	246	44	71	15	2	1	23	48	23	0	3	11-8	.289	.403	.378	.781	1	.991
1991— Kinston (Caro.)	OF	125	394	71	122	14	0	4	47	68	70	2	5	19-7	.310	.411	.376	.787	5	.975
1992— Cant./Akr. (Eastern)	OF	23	74	6	16	4	0	0	3	10	10	0	4	3-1	.216	.310	.270	.580	0	1.000
— Kinston (Caro.)	OF	42	140	28	37	5	1	3	18	30	21	1	5	3-5	.264	.398	.379	.776	1	.987
1993— Cant./Akr. (Eastern)	OF	123	425	64	139	17	6	6	64	57	43	4	9	18-12	.327	.409	.438	.847	5	.974
1994— Charlotte (Int'l)	OF	128	434	74	136	18	3	16	58	55	61	2	5	8-5	.313	.390	.479	.869	4	.985
1995— Buffalo (A.A.)	OF-DH	123	413	67	128	18	8	15	67	54	40	8	9	7-3	.310	.395	.501	.896	5	.981
— Cleveland (A.L.)	OF-DH	6	9	6	5	0	0	1	3	0	1	0	0	0-0	.556	.556	.889	1.444	0	1.000
1996— Buffalo (A.A.)	OF	83	318	65	100	17	6	20	64	42	29	2	4	1-0	.314	.395	.594	.989	2	.986
— Cleveland (A.L.)	DH-OF	51	121	26	43	14	1	5	27	19	13	0	6	3-0	.355	.434	.612	1.045	0	1.000
1997— Cleveland (A.L.)	OF-DH	130	377	62	101	15	3	17	61	63	50	1	10	13-3	.268	.368	.459	.827	6	.972
1998— Cleveland (A.L.)	OF-DH	112	350	56	94	19	0	16	66	73	75	3	7	10-5	.269	.396	.460	.856	5	.978
— Buffalo (Int'l)	OF-DH	13	46	5	11	2	0	2	7	6	8	0	2	0-0	.239	.327	.413	.740	1	.947
1999— Pittsburgh (N.L.)	OF-DH	141	521	109	164	33	3	39	115	95	80	3	14	6-2	.315	.418	.614	1.032	3	.990
2000— Pittsburgh (N.L.)	OF	156	559	111	176	37	7	35	123	114	69	7	15	6-0	.315	.432	.594	1.026	6	.982
2001— Pittsburgh (N.L.)	OF	160	576	116	178	37	7	37	95	90	67	4	10	13-6	.309	.404	.590	.994	10	.969
2002— Pittsburgh (N.L.)	OF	153	497	95	148	37	5	38	103	135	74	7	10	15-6	.298	.450	.622	1.072	7	.973
2003— Pittsburgh (N.L.)	OF	105	388	70	116	30	4	16	70	85	48	6	8	0-3	.299	.430	.521	.951	2	.992
— San Diego (N.L.)	OF	29	104	23	31	4	2	4	18	20	10	2	4	4-0	.298	.414	.490	.904	2	.966
2004— San Diego (N.L.)	OF	159	609	97	173	33	7	23	94	89	80	4	12	10-3	.284	.374	.475	.849	7	.979
American League totals (4 years)		299	857	150	243	48	4	39	157	155	139	4	23	26-8	.284	.391	.485	.876	11	.976
National League totals (6 years)		903	3254	621	986	211	35	192	618	628	428	33	73	54-20	.303	.417	.566	.983	37	.980
Major League totals (10 years)		1202	4111	771	1229	259	39	231	775	783	567	37	96	80-28	.299	.411	.550	.961	48	.979

DIVISION SERIES RECORD

Year Team (League)	Pos.	G	AB	R	H	2B	3B	HR	RBI	BB	SO	HBP	GDP	SB-CS	Avg.	OBP	SLG	OPS	E	Avg.
1996— Cleveland (A.L.)		1	1	0	0	0	0	0	0	0	1	0	0	0-0	.000	.000	.000	.000	...	...
1997— Cleveland (A.L.)	OF	3	7	0	1	0	0	0	0	0	1	0	0	0-0	.143	.143	.143	.286	0	1.000
1998— Cleveland (A.L.)	DH-OF	3	10	1	2	1	0	0	0	1	4	1	0	0-0	.200	.333	.300	.633	0	1.000
Division series totals (3 years)		7	18	1	3	1	0	0	0	1	6	1	0	0-0	.167	.250	.222	.472	0	1.000

CHAMPIONSHIP SERIES RECORD

Year Team (League)	Pos.	G	AB	R	H	2B	3B	HR	RBI	BB	SO	HBP	GDP	SB-CS	Avg.	OBP	SLG	OPS	E	Avg.
1997— Cleveland (A.L.)	OF	6	16	1	3	3	0	0	2	6	0	0	0	0-0	.188	.278	.375	.653	0	1.000
1998— Cleveland (A.L.)	OF	4	12	0	1	0	0	0	0	1	3	0	0	0-0	.083	.154	.083	.237	1	.875
Champ. series totals (2 years)		10	28	1	4	3	0	0	0	3	9	0	0	0-0	.143	.226	.250	.476	1	.941

WORLD SERIES RECORD

Year Team (League)	Pos.	G	AB	R	H	2B	3B	HR	RBI	BB	SO	HBP	GDP	SB-CS	Avg.	OBP	SLG	OPS	E	Avg.
1997— Cleveland (A.L.)	OF	5	4	1	2	1	0	0	2	4	1	0	0	0-1	.500	.750	.750	1.500	0	1.000

ALL-STAR GAME RECORD

	G	AB	R	H	2B	3B	HR	RBI	BB	SO	HBP	GDP	SB-CS	Avg.	OBP	SLG	OPS	E	Avg.
All-Star Game totals (2 years)	2	3	0	0	0	0	0	0	0	0	0	0	0-0	.000	.000	.000	.000	0	...

GILES, MARCUS — 2B

PERSONAL: Born May 18, 1978, in San Diego, Calif. ... 5-8/180. ... Bats right, throws right. ... Full name: Marcus William Giles. ... Name pronounced: JYLES. ... High school: Granite Hills (Calif.). ... Junior college: Grossmont (Calif.). ... Brother of Brian Giles, outfielder, San Diego Padres.
TRANSACTIONS/CAREER NOTES: Selected by Atlanta Braves organization in 53rd round of 1996 free-agent draft. ... On disabled list (May 29-July 16, 2002); included rehabilitation assignment to Richmond. ... On disabled list (May 16-July 15, 2004); included rehabilitation assignments to Rome and Myrtle Beach.
RECORDS: Shares major league record for most doubles, game (4, July 27, 2003).
2004 GAMES PLAYED BY POSITION (MLB): 2B—97.

G

Year Team (League)	Pos.	G	AB	R	H	2B	3B	HR	RBI	BB	SO	HBP	GDP	SB-CS	Avg.	OBP	SLG	OPS	E	Avg.
1997—Danville (Appal.)	2B	55	207	53	72	13	3	8	45	32	47	3	4	5-2	.348	.437	.556	.992	7	.962
1998—Macon (S. Atl.)	2B	135	505	111	166	38	3	37	108	85	103	10	15	12-5	.329	.433	.636	1.068	25	.954
1999—Myrtle Beach (Caro.)	2B	126	497	80	162	40	7	13	73	54	89	4	9	9-6	.326	.393	.513	.906	8	.985
2000—Greenville (Sou.)	2B	132	458	73	133	28	2	17	62	72	71	2	11	25-5	.290	.388	.472	.860	18	.973
2001—Richmond (Int'l) 2-SS-3-OF		67	252	48	84	19	1	6	44	22	48	2	4	13-5	.333	.387	.488	.875	8	.975
—Atlanta (N.L.)	2B	68	244	36	64	10	2	9	31	28	37	0	8	2-5	.262	.338	.430	.769	6	.978
2002—Atlanta (N.L.)	2B-3B	68	213	27	49	10	1	8	23	25	41	2	5	1-1	.230	.315	.399	.714	8	.972
—Richmond (Int'l)	2B-3B	31	115	25	37	6	0	3	16	13	15	0	1	3-0	.322	.385	.452	.837	3	.970
2003—Atlanta (N.L.)	2B	145	551	101	174	49	2	21	69	59	80	11	7	14-4	.316	.390	.526	.917	14	.982
2004—Rome (S. Atl.)	DH	1	2	0	0	0	0	0	0	2	0	0	0	0-0	...	.500	...	.500	0	...
—Myrtle Beach (Caro.) ...	2B-DH	4	13	1	1	1	0	0	2	1	4	0	0	0-0	.077	.133	.154	.287	0	1.000
—Atlanta (N.L.)	2B	102	379	61	118	22	2	8	48	36	70	9	6	17-4	.311	.378	.443	.821	12	.975
Major League totals (4 years)		383	1387	225	405	91	7	46	171	148	228	22	26	34-14	.292	.366	.467	.834	40	.978

DIVISION SERIES RECORD

Year Team (League)	Pos.	G	AB	R	H	2B	3B	HR	RBI	BB	SO	HBP	GDP	SB-CS	Avg.	OBP	SLG	OPS	E	Avg.
2001—Atlanta (N.L.)	2B	3	12	2	3	1	0	0	1	0	3	0	0	0-0	.250	.250	.333	.583	0	1.000
2002—Atlanta (N.L.)		3	2	0	1	0	0	0	0	0	0	0	0	0-0	.500	.500	.500	1.000	0	...
2003—Atlanta (N.L.)	2B	5	14	3	5	0	0	1	3	2	2	0	0	0-0	.357	.412	.571	.983	1	.955
2004—Atlanta (N.L.)	2B	5	24	1	3	0	0	0	1	0	6	0	0	1-0	.125	.125	.125	.250	0	1.000
Division series totals (4 years)		16	52	6	12	1	0	1	5	2	11	0	0	1-0	.231	.255	.308	.562	1	.988

CHAMPIONSHIP SERIES RECORD

Year Team (League)	Pos.	G	AB	R	H	2B	3B	HR	RBI	BB	SO	HBP	GDP	SB-CS	Avg.	OBP	SLG	OPS	E	Avg.
2001—Atlanta (N.L.)	2B	5	20	4	4	1	0	1	3	4	0	1	0-0	.200	.304	.400	.704	2	.917	

GINTER, KEITH — 3B/2B

PERSONAL: Born May 5, 1976, in Norwalk, Calif. ... 5-10/195. ... Bats right, throws right. ... Full name: Keith Michael Ginter. ... Name pronounced: GHIN-ter. ... High school: Fullerton Union (Fullerton, Calif.). ... College: Texas Tech.

TRANSACTIONS/CAREER NOTES: Selected by Houston Astros organization in 10th round of 1998 free-agent draft. ... Traded by Astros to Milwaukee Brewers (September 5, 2002), completing deal in which Brewers traded IF Mark Loretta to Astros for two players to be named (August 31, 2002); Brewers acquired P Wayne Franklin as part of deal (September 3, 2002). ... On disabled list (July 25-August 28, 2004); included rehabilitation assignment to Indianapolis.

2004 GAMES PLAYED BY POSITION (MLB): 2B—54, 3B—47, DH—2, OF—2.

Year Team (League)	Pos.	G	AB	R	H	2B	3B	HR	RBI	BB	SO	HBP	GDP	SB-CS	Avg.	OBP	SLG	OPS	E	Avg.
1998—Auburn (NY-Penn)	2B	71	241	55	76	22	1	8	41	60	68	7	1	10-7	.315	.461	.515	.976	8	.971
1999—Kissimmee (Fla. St.)	2B	103	376	66	99	15	4	13	46	61	90	12	7	9-10	.263	.381	.428	.810	21	.959
—Jackson (Texas)	2B	9	34	9	13	1	0	1	6	4	6	2	0	0-0	.382	.463	.500	.963	2	.956
2000—Round Rock (Texas)	2B	125	462	108	154	30	3	26	92	82	127	24	9	24-11	.333	.457	.580	1.037	17	.972
—Houston (N.L.)	2B	5	8	3	2	0	0	1	3	1	3	0	0	0-0	.250	.300	.625	.925	0	1.000
2001—New Orleans (PCL) 2B-OF-3B		132	457	76	123	31	5	16	70	61	147	23	6	8-6	.269	.380	.464	.844	12	.975
—Houston (N.L.)		1	1	0	0	0	0	0	0	0	0	0	0	0-0	.000	.000	.000	.000	...	...
2002—New Orleans (PCL) 2B-3B-OF		121	435	70	115	28	1	12	54	56	97	12	7	3-4	.264	.362	.416	.778	22	.952
—Houston (N.L.)	3B-SS	7	5	1	1	1	0	0	0	2	1	1	0	0-0	.200	.400	.400	.900	1	.909
—Milwaukee (N.L.)	3B	21	76	6	18	8	0	1	9	15	14	0	0	0-0	.237	.363	.382	.744	2	.961
2003—Milwaukee (N.L.) 2-3-SS-OF		127	358	51	92	15	2	14	44	37	87	17	8	1-1	.257	.352	.427	.779	8	.975
2004—Indianapolis (Int'l) 2B-3B-DH		4	14	3	3	2	0	1	3	1	4	0	0	0-0	.214	.267	.571	.838	0	1.000
—Milwaukee (N.L.) 2-3-DH-OF		113	386	47	101	23	2	19	60	37	100	6	9	8-1	.262	.333	.479	.812	9	.974
Major League totals (5 years)		274	834	108	214	47	4	35	115	92	205	24	17	9-2	.257	.344	.448	.793	20	.973

GINTER, MATT — P

PERSONAL: Born December 24, 1977, in Winchester, Ky. ... 6-1/220. ... Throws right, bats right. ... Full name: Matthew Shane Ginter. ... High school: George Rogers Clark (Winchester, Ky.). ... College: Mississippi State.

TRANSACTIONS/CAREER NOTES: Selected by New York Yankees organization in 17th round of 1996 free-agent draft; did not sign. ... Selected by Chicago White Sox organization in first round (22nd pick overall) of 1999 free-agent draft; pick received from New York Mets as compensation for signing Type A free-agent 3B Robin Ventura. ... Traded by White Sox to Mets for OF Timo Perez (March 27, 2004). ... On disabled list (September 11, 2004-remainder of season).

CAREER HITTING: 3-for-14 (.214), 1 R, 1 2B, 0 3B, 0 HR, 1 RBI.

Year Team (League)	W	L	Pct.	ERA	WHIP	G	GS	CG	ShO	Hld.	Sv.-Opp.	IP	H	R	ER	HR	BB-IBB	SO	Avg.
1999—Ariz. White Sox (Ariz.)	1	0	1.000	3.24	0.96	3	0	0	0	...	1-...	8.1	5	4	3	0	3-0	10	.172
—Burlington (Midw.)	4	2	.667	4.05	1.43	9	9	0	0	...	0-...	40.0	38	20	18	3	19-0	29	.253
2000—Birmingham (Southern)	11	8	.579	2.25	1.19	27	26	0	0	...	0-...	179.2	153	72	45	6	60-2	126	.233
—Chicago (A.L.)	1	0	1.000	13.50	2.68	7	0	0	0	0	0-1	9.1	18	14	14	5	7-0	6	.409
2001—Charlotte (Int'l)	2	3	.400	2.59	1.13	22	10	0	0	0	0-0	76.1	62	26	22	8	24-4	67	.219
—Chicago (A.L.)	1	1	1.000	5.22	1.21	20	0	0	0	0	0-0	39.2	34	23	23	2	14-2	24	.238
2002—Charlotte (Int'l)	1	0	1.000	3.94	1.88	13	0	0	0	0	0-0	16.0	20	8	7	3	10-1	9	.313
—Chicago (A.L.)	1	0	1.000	4.47	1.47	33	0	0	0	0	1-1	54.1	59	34	27	6	21-0	37	.278
2003—Chicago (A.L.)	0	0	...	13.50	0.90	3	0	0	0	0	0-0	3.1	2	5	5	1	1-0	0	.182
—Charlotte (Int'l)	3	5	.375	3.03	1.30	49	0	0	0	0	14-...	68.1	66	27	23	2	22-3	52	.249
2004—Norfolk (Int'l)	1	5	.167	2.95	0.98	11	11	0	0	0	0-0	64.0	55	26	21	4	8-1	49	.228
—New York (N.L.)	1	3	.250	4.54	1.47	15	14	0	0	0	0-0	69.1	82	41	35	8	20-5	38	.289
American League totals (4 years)	3	0	1.000	5.82	1.46	63	0	0	0	0	1-2	106.2	113	76	69	14	43-2	67	.276
National League totals (1 year)	1	3	.250	4.54	1.47	15	14	0	0	0	0-0	69.1	82	41	35	8	20-5	38	.289
Major League totals (5 years)	4	3	.571	5.32	1.47	78	14	0	0	0	1-2	176.0	195	117	104	22	63-7	105	.281

GIPSON, CHARLES — OF

PERSONAL: Born December 16, 1972, in Orange, Calif. ... 6-0/195. ... Bats right, throws right. ... Full name: Charles Wells Gipson. ... High school: Loara (Anaheim, Calif.). ... Junior college: Cypress (Calif.).

TRANSACTIONS/CAREER NOTES: Selected by Seattle Mariners organization in 63rd round of 1991 free-agent draft. ... On disabled list (July 11-September 1, 1999); included rehabilitation assignments to New Haven and Everett. ... Signed as a free agent by Chicago Cubs organization (January 21, 2003). ... Released by Cubs (March 29, 2003). ...

G

Signed by New York Yankees organization (April 17, 2003). ... Refused minor league assignment and became a free agent (September 29, 2003). ... Signed by Tampa Bay Devil Rays organization (February 13, 2004).

2004 GAMES PLAYED BY POSITION (MLB): SS—2, OF—2, DH—1.

									BATTING										FIELDING	
Year	Team (League)	Pos.	G	AB	R	H	2B	3B	HR	RBI	BB	SO	HBP	GDP	SB-CS	Avg.	OBP	SLG	OPS	E	Avg.
1992—	Ariz. Mariners (Ariz.)	SS	39	124	30	39	2	0	0	14	13	19	6	0	11-5	.315	.403	.331	.733	23	.876
1993—	Appleton (Midwest)	2B-SS-OF	109	348	53	89	13	1	0	20	61	76	27	3	21-15	.256	.405	.299	.704	28	.933
1994—	Riverside (Calif.)	OF	128	481	102	141	12	3	1	41	76	67	12	8	34-15	.293	.401	.337	.738	9	.972
1995—	Port City (Sou.)	2B-OF	112	391	36	87	11	2	0	29	30	66	8	13	10-12	.223	.291	.261	.552	6	.977
1996—	Port City (Sou.)	SS-OF	119	407	54	109	12	3	1	30	41	62	7	9	15-15	.268	.345	.319	.664	15	.961
1997—	Memphis (Sou.)	2-3-SS-OF	88	320	56	79	9	4	1	28	34	71	13	4	31-6	.247	.342	.309	.652	23	.939
—Tacoma (PCL)		2-3-SS-OF	11	35	5	11	2	0	0	5	4	3	1	0	0-1	.314	.400	.371	.771	3	.912
1998—	Seattle (A.L.)	OF-3B-DH	44	51	11	12	1	0	0	2	5	9	1	1	2-1	.235	.316	.255	.571	2	.957
—Tacoma (PCL)		2-3-SS-OF	75	278	39	67	16	2	0	11	27	50	6	17	14-11	.241	.322	.313	.634	11	.954
1999—	Seattle (A.L.)	O-3-DH-2-SS	55	80	16	18	5	0	0	9	6	13	1	2	3-4	.225	.287	.338	.625	3	.967
—Tacoma (PCL)		S-O-3-2-DH	47	174	26	52	6	3	0	21	14	24	3	5	18-4	.299	.361	.368	.729	9	.940
—New Haven (East.)		2-3-S-DH-OF	5	18	2	0	0	0	0	0	3	2	0	0	1-0	.000	.143	.000	.143	1	.944
—Everett (N'west)		SS	1	2	0	1	0	1	0	1	2	0	0	0	1-0	.500	.750	1.500	2.250	1	1.000
2000—	Seattle (A.L.)	O-3-SS-DH	59	29	7	9	1	1	0	3	4	9	0	0	2-3	.310	.394	.414	.808	0	1.000
—Tacoma (PCL)		O-3-S-2B	67	214	27	53	6	6	1	22	31	38	3	7	16-7	.248	.347	.346	.692	6	.971
2001—	Seattle (A.L.)	O-DH-3-S-2	94	64	16	14	2	0	0	5	4	20	2	2	1-1	.219	.282	.313	.594	2	.972
2002—	Seattle (A.L.)	OF-3B-DH	79	72	22	17	5	2	0	8	9	14	1	3	4-0	.236	.329	.361	.690	2	.972
2003—	New York (A.L.)	OF-DH	18	10	3	2	0	0	0	2	1	2	0	0	2-1	.200	.273	.200	.473	0	1.000
—Columbus (Int'l)		OF-3B-2B	31	120	17	33	6	1	0	9	9	18	5	1	5-6	.275	.351	.342	.692	3	.972
2004—	Tampa Bay (A.L.)	SS-OF-DH	5	4	1	2	0	0	0	0	0	1	0	0	1-0	.500	.500	.500	1.000	0	1.000
—Durham (Int'l)		O-3-2-S-DH	96	297	50	88	14	3	2	27	35	57	7	5	8-8	.296	.381	.384	.765	8	.966
Major League totals (7 years)			354	310	76	74	14	7	0	29	29	68	5	8	15-10	.239	.313	.329	.642	9	.972

DIVISION SERIES RECORD

Year	Team (League)	Pos.	G	AB	R	H	2B	3B	HR	RBI	BB	SO	HBP	GDP	SB-CS	Avg.	OBP	SLG	OPS	E	Avg.
2000—	Seattle (A.L.)			Did not play.																	
2001—	Seattle (A.L.)		1	1	0	0	0	0	0	0	0	0	0	0	0-0	.000	.000	.000	.000	...	...

CHAMPIONSHIP SERIES RECORD

Year	Team (League)	Pos.	G	AB	R	H	2B	3B	HR	RBI	BB	SO	HBP	GDP	SB-CS	Avg.	OBP	SLG	OPS	E	Avg.
2000—	Seattle (A.L.)	OF	2	0	0	0	0	0	0	0	0	0	0	0	0-0	...	...	...	...	0	...
2001—	Seattle (A.L.)	DH-OF	2	1	1	0	0	0	0	0	0	0	0	0	0-0	.000	.000	.000	.000	0	...
Champ. series totals (2 years)			4	1	1	0	0	0	0	0	0	0	0	0	0-0	.000	.000	.000	.000	0	...

GISSELL, CHRIS — P

PERSONAL: Born January 4, 1978, in Tacoma, Wash. ... 6-5/210. ... Throws right, bats right. ... Full name: Chris Odell Gissell. ... Name pronounced: gihs-ZELL. ... High school: Hudson's Bay (Vancouver, Wash.).

TRANSACTIONS/CAREER NOTES: Selected by Chicago Cubs organization in fourth round of 1996 free-agent draft. ... Signed as a free agent by Houston Astros organization (November 7, 2002). ... Released by Astros (March 29, 2003). ... Signed by Colorado Rockies organization (April 3, 2003). ... Signed as a free agent by San Francisco Giants organization (December 3, 2003). ... Released by Giants (April 3, 2004). ... Signed by Rockies organization (May 11, 2004). ... Refused minor league assignment and became a free agent (October 7, 2004).

CAREER HITTING: 0-for-1 (.000), 0 R, 0 2B, 0 3B, 0 HR, 0 RBI.

Year	Team (League)	W	L	Pct.	ERA	WHIP	G	GS	CG	ShO	Hld.	Sv.-Opp.	IP	H	R	ER	HR	BB-IBB	SO	Avg.
1996—GC Cubs (GCL)		4	2	.667	2.35	1.01	11	10	0	0	...	0-...	61.1	54	23	16	1	8-0	64	.232
1997—Rockford (Midwest)		6	11	.353	4.45	1.51	26	24	3	1	...	0-...	143.2	155	89	71	7	62-1	105	.275
1998—Rockford (Midwest)		3	0	1.000	0.80	1.25	5	5	0	0	...	0-...	33.2	27	8	3	0	15-0	23	.225
—Daytona (Fla. St.)		7	6	.538	4.17	1.38	22	21	1	0	...	0-...	136.0	149	80	63	12	38-1	123	.276
—West Tenn (Sou.)		0	1	.000	13.50	2.25	1	1	0	0	...	0-...	4.0	5	7	6	2	4-2	4	.294
1999—West Tenn (Sou.)		3	8	.273	5.99	1.87	20	18	0	0	...	0-...	97.2	121	76	65	10	62-3	57	.312
2000—West Tenn (Sou.)		7	5	.583	3.10	1.30	16	16	0	0	...	0-...	93.0	80	39	32	6	41-1	65	.233
2001—West Tenn (Sou.)		5	11	.313	4.51	1.39	28	27	0	0	...	0-...	159.2	159	91	80	13	63-0	136	.261
2002—Iowa (PCL)		8	12	.400	6.12	1.54	28	27	2	0	...	0-...	154.1	177	108	105	19	61-3	133	.290
2003—Colo. Springs (PCL)		8	4	.667	3.55	1.20	38	10	0	0	...	1-...	109.0	96	53	43	8	35-1	82	.232
2004—Colo. Springs (PCL)		14	2	.875	3.67	1.07	24	8	0	0	...	0-...	90.2	80	41	37	11	17-0	74	.233
—Colorado (N.L.)		0	1	.000	14.54	2.65	5	1	0	0	0	0-0	8.2	20	14	14	4	3-0	11	.465
Major League totals (1 year)		0	1	.000	14.54	2.65	5	1	0	0	0	0-0	8.2	20	14	14	4	3-0	11	.465

GLANVILLE, DOUG — OF

PERSONAL: Born August 25, 1970, in Hackensack, N.J. ... 6-2/174. ... Bats right, throws right. ... Full name: Douglas Metunwa Glanville. ... High school: Teaneck (N.J.). ... College: Pennsylvania.

TRANSACTIONS/CAREER NOTES: Selected by Chicago Cubs organization in first round (12th pick overall) of 1991 free-agent draft. ... Traded by Cubs to Philadelphia Phillies for 2B Mickey Morandini (December 23, 1997). ... Signed as a free agent by Texas Rangers (December 18, 2002). ... On disabled list (April 15-June 7, 2003); included rehabilitation assignments to Oklahoma and Frisco. ... Traded by Rangers to Chicago Cubs for OF Jason Fransz and cash (July 30, 2003). ... Signed as a free agent by Phillies (February 26, 2004).

2004 GAMES PLAYED BY POSITION (MLB): OF—68.

									BATTING										FIELDING	
Year	Team (League)	Pos.	G	AB	R	H	2B	3B	HR	RBI	BB	SO	HBP	GDP	SB-CS	Avg.	OBP	SLG	OPS	E	Avg.
1991—Geneva (NY-Penn)		OF	36	152	29	46	8	0	2	12	11	25	1	1	17-3	.303	.352	.395	.746	0	1.000
1992—Win.-Salem (Car.)		OF	120	485	72	125	18	4	4	36	40	78	4	6	32-9	.258	.318	.336	.654	7	.978
1993—Daytona (Fla. St.)		OF	61	239	47	70	10	1	2	21	28	24	3	2	18-15	.293	.374	.368	.742	7	.950
—Orlando (South.)		OF	73	296	42	78	14	4	9	40	12	41	1		15-7	.264	.292	.429	.721	5	.972
1994—Orlando (South.)		OF	130	483	53	127	22	2	5	52	24	49	5	7	26-20	.263	.301	.348	.648	3	.991
1995—Iowa (Am. Assoc.)		OF-DH	112	419	48	113	16	2	4	37	16	64	3	4	13-9	.270	.299	.346	.645	4	.982
1996—Iowa (Am. Assoc.)		OF-DH	90	373	53	115	23	3	3	34	12	35	2	2	15-10	.308	.331	.410	.741	3	.987
—Chicago (N.L.)		OF	49	83	10	20	5	1	1	10	3	11	0	0	2-0	.241	.264	.361	.626	1	.973
1997—Chicago (N.L.)		OF	146	474	79	142	22	5	4	35	24	46	1	9	19-11	.300	.333	.392	.726	3	.989
1998—Philadelphia (N.L.)		OF	158	*678	106	189	28	7	8	49	42	89	6	7	23-6	.279	.325	.376	.701	2	.995

Year Team (League)	Pos.	G	AB	R	H	2B	3B	HR	RBI	BB	SO	HBP	GDP	SB-CS	Avg.	OBP	SLG	OPS	E	Avg.
1999— Philadelphia (N.L.)	OF	150	628	101	204	38	6	11	73	48	82	6	9	34-2	.325	.376	.457	.833	8	.980
2000— Philadelphia (N.L.)	OF	154	637	89	175	27	6	8	52	31	76	2	11	31-8	.275	.307	.374	.681	4	.990
2001— Philadelphia (N.L.)	OF	153	634	74	166	24	3	14	55	19	91	4	7	28-6	.262	.285	.375	.660	4	.991
2002— Philadelphia (N.L.)	OF	138	422	49	105	16	3	6	29	25	57	2	5	19-2	.249	.292	.344	.636	0	1.000
2003— Oklahoma (PCL)	OF-DH	9	37	4	6	0	0	0	3	2	3	1	1	1-0	.162	.225	.162	.387	0	1.000
—Frisco (Texas)	OF	4	15	2	2	0	0	0	0	1	4	0	0	0-0	.133	.188	.133	.321	1	.875
—Texas (A.L.)	OF	52	195	22	53	5	0	4	14	6	25	0	2	4-0	.272	.294	.359	.653	0	1.000
—Chicago (N.L.)	OF	28	51	2	12	0	0	1	2	2	4	0	0	0-1	.235	.259	.294	.553	0	1.000
2004— Philadelphia (N.L.)	OF	87	162	21	34	1	1	2	14	8	21	0	5	8-0	.210	.244	.265	.510	0	1.000
American League totals (1 year)		52	195	22	53	5	0	4	14	6	25	0	2	4-0	.272	.294	.359	.653	0	1.000
National League totals (9 years)		1063	3769	531	1047	161	32	55	319	202	477	21	53	164-36	.278	.316	.381	.697	22	.990
Major League totals (9 years)		1115	3964	553	1100	166	32	59	333	208	502	21	55	168-36	.277	.315	.380	.695	22	.991

DIVISION SERIES RECORD

Year Team (League)	Pos.	G	AB	R	H	2B	3B	HR	RBI	BB	SO	HBP	GDP	SB-CS	Avg.	OBP	SLG	OPS	E	Avg.
2003— Chicago (N.L.)		2	1	1	0	0	0	0	0	0	0	0	1	0-0	.000	.000	.000	.000	0	...

CHAMPIONSHIP SERIES RECORD

Year Team (League)	Pos.	G	AB	R	H	2B	3B	HR	RBI	BB	SO	HBP	GDP	SB-CS	Avg.	OBP	SLG	OPS	E	Avg.
2003— Chicago (N.L.)	OF	1	1	0	1	0	1	0	0	0	0	0	0	0-0	1.000	1.000	3.000	4.000	0	...

GLAUS, TROY — 3B

PERSONAL: Born August 3, 1976, in Tarzana, Calif. ... 6-5/240. ... Bats right, throws right. ... Full name: Troy Edward Glaus. ... Name pronounced: gloss. ... High school: Carlsbad (Calif.). ... College: UCLA.

TRANSACTIONS/CAREER NOTES: Selected by San Diego Padres organization in second round of 1994 free-agent draft; did not sign. ... Selected by Anaheim Angels organization in first round (third pick overall) of 1997 free-agent draft. ... On disabled list (July 22-August 11, 2003); included rehabilitation assignment to Rancho Cucamonga. ... On disabled list (May 12-August 29, 2004); included rehabilitation assignment to Rancho Cucamonga.

2004 GAMES PLAYED BY POSITION (MLB): DH—39, 3B—19.

								BATTING												FIELDING	
Year Team (League)	Pos.	G	AB	R	H	2B	3B	HR	RBI	BB	SO	HBP	GDP	SB-CS	Avg.	OBP	SLG	OPS	E	Avg.
1998— Midland (Texas)	3B	50	188	51	58	11	2	19	51	39	41	2	4	4-2	.309	.430	.691	1.122	11	.925
—Vancouver (PCL)	3B	59	219	33	67	16	0	16	42	21	55	3	1	3-2	.306	.374	.598	.973	13	.932
—Anaheim (A.L.)	3B	48	165	19	36	9	0	1	23	15	51	0	3	1-0	.218	.280	.291	.571	7	.941
1999— Anaheim (A.L.)	3B-DH	154	551	85	132	29	0	29	79	71	143	6	9	5-1	.240	.331	.450	.781	19	.954
2000— Anaheim (A.L.)	3B-SS-DH	159	563	120	160	37	1	*47	102	112	163	2	14	14-11	.284	.404	.604	1.008	‡33	.934
2001— Anaheim (A.L.)	3B-SS-DH	161	588	100	147	38	2	41	108	107	158	6	16	10-3	.250	.367	.531	.898	19	.954
2002— Anaheim (A.L.)	3B-SS	156	569	99	142	24	1	30	111	88	144	6	12	10-3	.250	.352	.453	.805	20	.950
2003— Anaheim (A.L.)	3B-DH	91	319	53	79	17	2	16	50	46	73	1	8	7-2	.248	.343	.464	.807	16	.923
—Rancho Cuca. (Calif.)	DH	2	6	1	2	0	0	0	1	3	2	0	0	0-0	.333	.556	.333	.889	0	.000
2004— Rancho Cuca. (Calif.)	DH	5	15	4	3	0	0	2	4	6	5	0	0	0-0	.200	.429	.600	1.029	0	...
—Anaheim (A.L.)	DH-3B	58	207	47	52	11	1	18	42	31	52	3	6	2-3	.251	.355	.575	.930	2	.950
Major League totals (7 years)		827	2962	523	748	165	7	182	515	470	784	24	68	49-23	.253	.357	.497	.854	116	.944

DIVISION SERIES RECORD

Year Team (League)	Pos.	G	AB	R	H	2B	3B	HR	RBI	BB	SO	HBP	GDP	SB-CS	Avg.	OBP	SLG	OPS	E	Avg.
2002— Anaheim (A.L.)	3B	4	16	4	5	0	0	3	3	1	3	1	0	0-0	.313	.389	.875	1.264	1	.929
2004— Anaheim (A.L.)	DH	3	11	3	4	2	0	2	3	2	4	0	0	0-0	.364	.462	1.091	1.552	0	...
Division series totals (2 years)		7	27	7	9	2	0	5	6	3	7	1	0	0-0	.333	.419	.963	1.382	1	.929

CHAMPIONSHIP SERIES RECORD

Year Team (League)	Pos.	G	AB	R	H	2B	3B	HR	RBI	BB	SO	HBP	GDP	SB-CS	Avg.	OBP	SLG	OPS	E	Avg.
2002— Anaheim (A.L.)	3B	5	19	4	6	0	1	1	2	2	5	0	0	0-0	.316	.381	.579	.960	0	1.000

WORLD SERIES RECORD

Year Team (League)	Pos.	G	AB	R	H	2B	3B	HR	RBI	BB	SO	HBP	GDP	SB-CS	Avg.	OBP	SLG	OPS	E	Avg.
2002— Anaheim (A.L.)	3B	7	26	7	10	3	0	3	8	4	6	0	1	0-0	.385	.467	.846	1.313	1	.938

ALL-STAR GAME RECORD

	G	AB	R	H	2B	3B	HR	RBI	BB	SO	HBP	GDP	SB-CS	Avg.	OBP	SLG	OPS	E	Avg.
All-Star Game totals (3 years)	3	5	0	0	0	0	0	0	0	2	0	0	0-0	.000	.000	.000	.000	0	1.000

GLAVINE, TOM — P

PERSONAL: Born March 25, 1966, in Concord, Mass. ... 6-0/185. ... Throws left, bats left. ... Full name: Thomas Michael Glavine. ... Name pronounced: GLA-vin. ... High school: Billerica (Mass.). ... Brother of Mike Glavine, first baseman with New York Mets (2003).

TRANSACTIONS/CAREER NOTES: Selected by Atlanta Braves organization in second round of June 1984 free-agent draft. ... Signed as a free agent by New York Mets (December 5, 2002).

HONORS: Named N.L. Pitcher of the Year by THE SPORTING NEWS (1991 and 2000). ... Named N.L. Cy Young Award winner by Baseball Writers' Association of America (1991 and 1998).

CAREER HITTING: 210-for-1131 (.186), 80 R, 23 2B, 2 3B, 1 HR, 80 RBI.

Year Team (League)	W	L	Pct.	ERA	WHIP	G	GS	CG	ShO	Hld.	Sv.-Opp.	IP	H	R	ER	HR	BB-IBB	SO	Avg.
1984— GC Braves (GCL)	2	3	.400	3.34	1.30	8	7	0	0	...	0-...	32.1	29	17	12	0	13-0	34	.236
1985— Sumter (S. Atl.)	9	6	.600	2.35	1.11	26	26	2	1	...	0-...	168.2	114	58	44	6	73-0	174	.193
1986— Greenville (Sou.)	11	6	.647	3.41	1.37	22	22	2	1	...	0-...	145.1	129	62	55	14	70-3	114	.237
—Richmond (Int'l)	1	5	.167	5.63	1.68	7	7	1	1	...	0-...	40.0	40	29	25	4	27-0	12	.260
1987— Richmond (Int'l)	6	12	.333	3.35	1.32	22	22	4	1	...	0-...	150.1	142	70	56	15	56-3	91	.248
—Atlanta (N.L.)	2	4	.333	5.54	1.75	9	9	0	0	0	0-0	50.1	55	34	31	5	33-4	20	.279
1988— Atlanta (N.L.)	7	*17	.292	4.56	1.35	34	34	1	0	0	0-0	195.1	201	111	99	12	63-7	84	.270
1989— Atlanta (N.L.)	14	8	.636	3.68	1.14	29	29	6	4	0	0-0	186.0	172	88	76	20	40-8	90	.243
1990— Atlanta (N.L.)	10	12	.455	4.28	1.45	33	33	1	0	0	0-0	214.1	232	111	102	18	78-10	129	.281
1991— Atlanta (N.L.)	•20	11	.645	2.55	1.09	34	34	•9	1	0	0-0	246.2	201	83	70	17	69-6	192	.222
1992— Atlanta (N.L.)	•20	8	.714	2.76	1.19	33	33	7	•5	0	0-0	225.0	197	81	69	6	70-7	129	.235
1993— Atlanta (N.L.)	•22	6	.786	3.20	1.36	36	•36	4	2	0	0-0	239.1	236	91	85	16	90-7	120	.259
1994— Atlanta (N.L.)	13	9	.591	3.97	1.47	25	25	2	0	0	0-0	165.1	173	76	73	10	70-10	140	.268

G

Year	Team (League)	W	L	Pct.	ERA	WHIP	G	GS	CG	ShO	Hld.	Sv.-Opp.	IP	H	R	ER	HR	BB-IBB	SO	Avg.
1995—Atlanta (N.L.)		16	7	.696	3.08	1.25	29	29	3	1	0	0-0	198.2	182	76	68	9	66-0	127	.246
1996—Atlanta (N.L.)		15	10	.600	2.98	1.30	36	*36	1	0	0	0-0	235.1	222	91	78	14	85-7	181	.249
1997—Atlanta (N.L.)		14	7	.667	2.96	1.15	33	33	5	2	0	0-0	240.0	197	86	79	20	79-9	152	.226
1998—Atlanta (N.L.)		*20	6	.769	2.47	1.20	33	33	4	3	0	0-0	229.1	202	67	63	13	74-2	157	.238
1999—Atlanta (N.L.)		14	11	.560	4.12	1.46	35	•35	2	0	0	0-0	234.0	*259	115	107	18	83-14	138	.287
2000—Atlanta (N.L.)		*21	9	.700	3.40	1.19	35	•35	4	2	0	0-0	241.0	222	101	91	24	65-6	152	.244
2001—Atlanta (N.L.)		16	7	.696	3.57	1.41	35	•35	1	0	0	0-0	219.1	213	92	87	24	97-10	116	.261
2002—Atlanta (N.L.)		18	11	.621	2.96	1.28	36	•36	2	1	0	0-0	224.2	210	85	74	21	78-8	127	.252
2003—New York (N.L.)		9	14	.391	4.52	1.48	32	32	0	0	0	0-0	183.1	205	94	92	21	66-7	82	.288
2004—New York (N.L.)		11	14	.440	3.60	1.29	33	33	1	1	0	0-0	212.1	204	94	85	20	70-10	109	.252
Major League totals (18 years)		262	171	.605	3.44	1.30	570	570	53	23	0	0-0	3740.1	3583	1576	1429	288	1276-127	2245	.254

DIVISION SERIES RECORD

Year	Team (League)	W	L	Pct.	ERA	WHIP	G	GS	CG	ShO	Hld.	Sv.-Opp.	IP	H	R	ER	HR	BB-IBB	SO	Avg.
1995—Atlanta (N.L.)		0	0	...	2.57	0.86	1	1	0	0	0	0-0	7.0	5	3	2	1	1-0	3	.185
1996—Atlanta (N.L.)		1	0	1.000	1.35	1.20	1	1	0	0	0	0-0	6.2	5	1	1	0	3-0	7	.217
1997—Atlanta (N.L.)		1	0	1.000	4.50	1.67	1	1	0	0	0	0-0	6.0	5	3	3	0	5-0	4	.217
1998—Atlanta (N.L.)		0	0	...	1.29	0.57	1	1	0	0	0	0-0	7.0	3	1	1	0	1-0	8	.136
1999—Atlanta (N.L.)		0	0	...	3.00	1.33	1	1	0	0	0	0-0	6.0	5	2	2	0	3-0	6	.238
2000—Atlanta (N.L.)		0	1	.000	27.00	3.00	1	1	0	0	0	0-0	2.1	6	7	7	2	1-0	2	.500
2001—Atlanta (N.L.)		1	0	1.000	0.00	1.00	1	1	0	0	0	0-0	8.0	6	0	0	0	2-0	3	.222
2002—Atlanta (N.L.)		0	2	.000	15.26	3.13	2	2	0	0	0	0-0	7.2	17	13	13	1	7-3	4	.459
Division series totals (8 years)		3	3	.500	5.15	1.48	9	9	0	0	0	0-0	50.2	52	30	29	4	23-3	37	.271

CHAMPIONSHIP SERIES RECORD

Year	Team (League)	W	L	Pct.	ERA	WHIP	G	GS	CG	ShO	Hld.	Sv.-Opp.	IP	H	R	ER	HR	BB-IBB	SO	Avg.
1991—Atlanta (N.L.)		0	2	.000	3.21	1.29	2	2	0	0	0	0-0	14.0	12	5	5	1	6-2	11	.226
1992—Atlanta (N.L.)		0	2	.000	12.27	2.18	2	2	0	0	0	0-0	7.1	13	11	10	3	3-1	2	.382
1993—Atlanta (N.L.)		1	0	1.000	2.57	0.86	1	1	0	0	0	0-0	7.0	6	2	2	1	0-0	5	.222
1995—Atlanta (N.L.)		0	0	...	1.29	1.29	1	1	0	0	0	0-0	7.0	7	1	1	0	2-1	5	.292
1996—Atlanta (N.L.)		1	1	.500	2.08	0.77	2	2	0	0	0	0-0	13.0	10	3	3	2	0-0	9	.217
1997—Atlanta (N.L.)		1	1	.500	5.40	1.80	2	2	0	0	0	0-0	13.1	13	8	8	0	11-3	9	.271
1998—Atlanta (N.L.)		0	2	.000	2.31	1.89	2	2	0	0	0	0-0	11.2	13	4	3	1	9-0	8	.283
1999—Atlanta (N.L.)		1	0	1.000	0.00	1.14	1	1	0	0	0	0-0	7.0	7	0	0	0	1-0	8	.259
2001—Atlanta (N.L.)		1	1	.500	1.50	1.25	2	2	0	0	0	0-0	12.0	10	4	2	1	5-0	5	.217
Champ. series totals (9 years)		5	9	.357	3.31	1.39	15	15	0	0	0	0-0	92.1	91	40	34	8	37-7	62	.259

WORLD SERIES RECORD

Year	Team (League)	W	L	Pct.	ERA	WHIP	G	GS	CG	ShO	Hld.	Sv.-Opp.	IP	H	R	ER	HR	BB-IBB	SO	Avg.
1991—Atlanta (N.L.)		1	1	.500	2.70	1.13	2	2	1	0	0	0-0	13.1	8	6	4	2	7-0	8	.174
1992—Atlanta (N.L.)		1	1	.500	1.59	0.82	2	2	2	0	0	0-0	17.0	10	3	3	2	4-0	8	.175
1995—Atlanta (N.L.)		2	0	1.000	1.29	0.71	2	2	0	0	0	0-0	14.0	4	2	2	1	6-0	11	.087
1996—Atlanta (N.L.)		0	1	.000	1.29	1.00	1	1	0	0	0	0-0	7.0	4	2	1	0	3-0	8	.174
1999—Atlanta (N.L.)		0	0	...	5.14	1.00	1	1	0	0	0	0-0	7.0	7	5	4	3	0-0	3	.250
World series totals (5 years)		4	3	.571	2.16	0.91	8	8	3	0	0	0-0	58.1	33	18	14	8	20-0	38	.165

ALL-STAR GAME RECORD

		W	L	Pct.	ERA	WHIP	G	GS	CG	ShO	Hld.	Sv.-Opp.	IP	H	R	ER	HR	BB-IBB	SO	Avg.
All-Star Game totals (6 years)		0	1	.000	10.13	2.50	6	2	0	0	0	0-0	8.0	16	9	9	0	4-0	7	.421

GLOAD, ROSS — OF/1B

PERSONAL: Born April 5, 1976, in Brooklyn, N.Y. ... 6-0/185. ... Bats left, throws left. ... Full name: Ross Peter Gload. ... High school: East Hampton (N.Y.). ... College: South Florida.

TRANSACTIONS/CAREER NOTES: Selected by Florida Marlins organization in 13th round of 1997 free-agent draft. ... Traded by Marlins with P David Noyce to Chicago Cubs for OF Henry Rodriguez (July 31, 2000). ... Claimed on waivers by Colorado Rockies (September 12, 2001). ... Traded by Rockies with P Craig House to New York Mets as part of three-team deal in which Rockies acquired 1B/3B Todd Zeile, OF Benny Agbayani and cash from Mets, Mets acquired P Jeff D'Amico, OF Jeromy Burnitz, IF Lou Collier, OF/1B Mark Sweeney and cash from Brewers, and Brewers acquired P Glendon Rusch and IF Lenny Harris from Mets and OF Alex Ochoa from Rockies (January 21, 2002). ... Traded by Mets to Rockies for cash considerations (January 27, 2002). ... Traded by Rockies to Chicago White Sox for P Wade Parrish (March 27, 2003).

2004 GAMES PLAYED BY POSITION (MLB): 1B—42, OF—39, DH—13.

									BATTING											FIELDING	
Year	Team (League)	Pos.	G	AB	R	H	2B	3B	HR	RBI	BB	SO	HBP	GDP	SB-CS	Avg.	OBP	SLG	OPS	E	Avg.
1997—Utica (N.Y.-Penn)		1B	68	245	28	64	15	2	3	43	28	57	2	5	1-1	.261	.336	.376	.711	16	.973
1998—Kane Co. (Midw.)		1B	132	501	77	157	41	3	12	92	58	84	3	13	7-6	.313	.386	.479	.865	14	.989
1999—Brevard County (FSL)		1B	133	490	80	146	26	3	10	74	53	76	5	8	3-1	.298	.369	.424	.793	9	.993
2000—Portland (East.)		OF-1B	100	401	60	114	28	4	16	65	29	53	2	4	4-1	.284	.333	.494	.826	7	.986
—Iowa (PCL)		OF	28	104	24	42	10	2	14	39	9	13	1	2	1-1	.404	.452	.942	1.394	4	.917
—Chicago (N.L.)		OF-1B	18	31	4	6	0	1	1	3	3	10	0	1	0-0	.194	.257	.355	.612	0	1.000
2001—Iowa (PCL)		OF-1B	133	475	70	141	32	10	15	93	35	88	3	8	9-7	.297	.344	.501	.845	3	.994
2002—Colo. Springs (PCL)		1B-OF	104	442	69	139	28	6	16	71	18	59	1	4	9-4	.314	.338	.514	.852	11	.987
—Colorado (N.L.)		1B-OF	26	31	4	8	1	0	1	4	3	7	0	0	0-0	.258	.324	.387	.711	0	1.000
2003—Charlotte (Int'l)		1B-OF	133	508	72	160	40	6	18	70	29	60	1	12	6-3	.315	.349	.524	.873	8	.991
2004—Chicago (A.L.)		1B-OF-DH	110	234	28	75	16	0	7	44	20	37	2	11	0-3	.321	.375	.479	.853	3	.990
American League totals (1 year)			110	234	28	75	16	0	7	44	20	37	2	11	0-3	.321	.375	.479	.853	3	.990
National League totals (2 years)			44	62	8	14	1	1	2	7	6	17	0	1	0-0	.226	.290	.371	.661	0	1.000
Major League totals (3 years)			154	296	36	89	17	1	9	51	26	54	2	12	0-3	.301	.357	.456	.813	3	.991

GLOVER, GARY — P

PERSONAL: Born December 3, 1976, in Cleveland, Ohio. ... 6-5/220. ... Throws right, bats right. ... Full name: John Gary Glover. ... High school: DeLand (Fla.).

TRANSACTIONS/CAREER NOTES: Selected by Toronto Blue Jays organization in 15th round of 1994 free-agent draft. ... Traded by Blue Jays to Chicago White Sox for P Scott Eyre (November 7, 2000). ... Traded by White Sox with Ps Scott Dunn and Tim Bittner to Anaheim Angels for Ps Scott Schoeneweis and Doug Nickle (July 30, 2003). ... Signed as a free agent by Chicago Cubs organization (December 18, 2003). ... Released by Cubs (June 5, 2004). ... Signed by Minnesota Twins organization (June 7, 2004). ... Released by Twins (July 2, 2004). ... Signed by Milwaukee Brewers organization (July 12, 2004).

CAREER HITTING: 0-for-8 (.000), 0 R, 0 2B, 0 3B, 0 HR, 0 RBI.

Year — Team (League)	W	L	Pct.	ERA	WHIP	G	GS	CG	ShO	Hld.	Sv.-Opp.	IP	H	R	ER	HR	BB-IBB	SO	Avg.
1994— GC Blue Jays (GCL)	0	0	...	47.25	6.00	2	0	0	0	...	0-...	1.1	4	8	7	1	4-0	2	.500
1995— GC Blue Jays (GCL)	3	7	.300	4.91	1.41	12	10	2	0	...	0-...	62.1	62	48	34	4	26-0	46	.264
1996— Medicine Hat (Pio.)	3	12	.200	7.75	1.77	15	15	2	0	...	0-...	83.2	119	94	72	14	29-1	54	.322
1997— Hagerstown (S. Atl.)	6	17	.261	3.73	1.28	28	28	3	0	...	0-...	173.2	165	94	72	9	58-1	155	.245
1998— Knoxville (Southern)	0	5	.000	6.75	1.85	8	8	0	0	...	0-...	37.1	41	36	28	2	28-0	14	.277
— Dunedin (Fla. St.)	7	6	.538	4.28	1.40	19	18	0	0	...	0-...	109.1	117	66	52	8	36-0	88	.270
1999— Knoxville (Southern)	8	2	.800	3.56	1.13	13	13	1	0	...	0-...	86.0	70	39	34	5	27-0	77	.224
— Syracuse (Int'l)	4	6	.400	5.19	1.68	14	14	0	0	...	0-...	76.1	93	50	44	10	35-0	57	.301
— Toronto (A.L.)	0	0	...	0.00	1.00	1	0	0	0	0	0-0	1.0	0	0	0	0	1-0	0	.000
2000— Syracuse (Int'l)	9	9	.500	5.02	1.46	27	27	1	0	...	0-...	166.2	181	104	93	21	62-0	119	.274
2001— Chicago (A.L.)	5	5	.500	4.93	1.30	46	11	0	0	7	0-1	100.1	98	61	55	16	32-3	63	.252
— Charlotte (Int'l)	2	1	.667	1.88	0.68	6	6	1	1	...	0-...	38.1	21	8	8	3	5-0	29	.158
2002— Chicago (A.L.)	7	8	.467	5.20	1.36	41	22	0	0	2	1-1	138.1	136	86	80	21	52-1	70	.253
2003— Chicago (A.L.)	1	0	1.000	4.54	1.60	24	0	0	0	1	0-0	35.2	43	18	18	3	14-2	23	.305
— Anaheim (A.L.)	1	0	1.000	5.00	1.56	18	0	0	0	0	0-0	27.0	34	15	15	3	8-1	14	.315
2004— Iowa (PCL)	3	2	.600	7.92	1.86	20	1	0	0	...	0-...	30.2	43	29	27	8	14-0	18	.328
— Rochester (Int'l)	0	1	.000	8.44	2.00	5	4	0	0	...	0-...	16.0	27	15	15	6	5-0	8	.386
— Indianapolis (Int'l)	3	3	.500	3.98	1.43	8	6	0	0	...	0-...	40.2	47	19	18	1	11-0	18	.307
— Milwaukee (N.L.)	2	1	.667	3.50	1.44	4	3	0	0	0	0-0	18.0	18	9	7	2	8-1	8	.265
American League totals (4 years)	14	13	.519	5.01	1.38	130	33	0	0	10	1-2	302.1	311	180	168	43	107-7	170	.264
National League totals (1 year)	2	1	.667	3.50	1.44	4	3	0	0	0	0-0	18.0	18	9	7	2	8-1	8	.265
Major League totals (5 years)	16	14	.533	4.92	1.39	134	36	0	0	10	1-2	320.1	329	189	175	45	115-8	178	.264

GLYNN, RYAN — P

PERSONAL: Born November 1, 1974, in Portsmouth, Va. ... 6-3/200. ... Throws right, bats right. ... Full name: Ryan David Glynn. ... High school: Churchland (Portsmouth, Va.). ... College: Virginia Military.

TRANSACTIONS/CAREER NOTES: Selected by Texas Rangers organization in fourth round of 1995 free-agent draft. ... On disabled list (July 2-17 and August 12-29, 2000); included rehabilitation assignment to Oklahoma. ... On disabled list (June 1-July 1, 2001); included rehabilitation assignment to Oklahoma. ... Signed as a free agent by Milwaukee Brewers organization (January 11, 2002). ... Released by Brewers (June 6, 2002). ... Signed by Florida Marlins organization (June 14, 2002). ... Signed as a free agent by Atlanta Braves organization (January 14, 2003). ... Released by Braves (May 29, 2004). ... Signed by Toronto Blue Jays organization (June 1, 2004).

CAREER HITTING: 0-for-3 (.000), 0 R, 0 2B, 0 3B, 0 HR, 0 RBI.

Year — Team (League)	W	L	Pct.	ERA	WHIP	G	GS	CG	ShO	Hld.	Sv.-Opp.	IP	H	R	ER	HR	BB-IBB	SO	Avg.
1995— Hudson Valley (NY-Penn.) .	3	3	.500	4.70	1.64	9	8	0	0	...	0-...	44.0	56	27	23	0	16-1	21	.326
1996— Char., S.C. (SAL)	8	7	.533	4.54	1.46	19	19	2	1	...	0-...	121.0	118	70	61	10	59-2	72	.264
1997— Charlotte (Fla. St.)	8	7	.533	4.97	1.43	23	22	5	1	...	1-...	134.0	148	81	74	13	44-0	96	.284
— Tulsa (Texas)	1	1	.500	3.38	1.45	3	3	0	0	...	0-...	21.1	21	9	8	1	10-0	18	.266
1998— Tulsa (Texas)	9	6	.600	3.44	1.30	26	24	4	1	...	0-...	157.0	140	66	60	12	64-0	111	.240
1999— Oklahoma (PCL)	6	2	.750	3.39	1.30	16	16	2	1	...	0-...	90.1	81	46	34	7	36-...	55	...
— Texas (A.L.)	2	4	.333	7.24	1.94	13	10	0	0	0	0-0	54.2	71	46	44	10	35-0	39	.316
2000— Oklahoma (PCL)	4	2	.667	3.55	1.25	15	14	2	2	...	0-...	83.2	72	36	33	5	33-1	66	.235
— Texas (A.L.)	5	7	.417	5.58	1.67	16	16	0	0	0	0-0	88.2	107	65	55	15	41-2	33	.293
2001— Texas (A.L.)	1	5	.167	7.04	1.85	12	9	0	0	0	0-0	46.0	59	38	36	7	26-1	15	.309
— Oklahoma (PCL)	2	6	.250	6.49	1.62	13	13	1	0	...	0-...	79.0	87	62	57	10	41-0	52	.282
2002— Indianapolis (Int'l)	3	6	.333	5.23	1.59	12	11	0	0	...	0-...	63.2	75	48	37	7	26-0	36	.286
— Calgary (PCL)	5	5	.500	6.00	1.65	14	14	0	0	...	0-...	78.0	102	58	52	7	27-0	48	.312
2003— Richmond (Int'l)	6	5	.545	2.91	1.20	16	16	0	0	...	0-...	92.2	84	31	30	4	31-3	75	.244
2004— Richmond (Int'l)	1	1	.500	5.60	2.26	11	0	0	0	...	0-...	17.2	26	11	11	0	14-0	19	.351
— Syracuse (Int'l)	7	2	.778	3.40	1.25	16	16	1	1	...	0-...	92.2	82	38	35	7	34-0	75	.236
— Toronto (A.L.)	1	0	1.000	4.05	1.35	6	2	0	0	0	0-0	20.0	19	9	9	4	8-1	14	.250
Major League totals (4 years)	9	16	.360	6.19	1.75	47	37	0	0	0	0-0	209.1	256	158	144	36	110-4	101	.299

GOBBLE, JIMMY — P

PERSONAL: Born July 19, 1981, in Bristol, Tenn. ... 6-3/190. ... Throws left, bats left. ... Full name: Billy James Gobble. ... High school: John S. Battle (Bristol, Va.).

TRANSACTIONS/CAREER NOTES: Selected by Kansas City Royals organization in supplemental round ("sandwich" pick between first and second rounds, 43rd pick overall) of 1999 free-agent draft; Royals received pick as compensation for Detroit Tigers signing Type A free-agent 3B Dean Palmer.

CAREER HITTING: 0-for-2 (.000), 0 R, 0 2B, 0 3B, 0 HR, 0 RBI.

Year — Team (League)	W	L	Pct.	ERA	WHIP	G	GS	CG	ShO	Hld.	Sv.-Opp.	IP	H	R	ER	HR	BB-IBB	SO	Avg.
1999— GC Royals (GCL)	0	0	...	2.70	1.65	4	1	0	0	...	0-...	6.2	6	3	2	0	5-0	8	.222
2000— Char., W.Va. (SAL)	12	10	.545	3.66	1.23	25	25	3	2	...	0-...	145.0	144	75	59	10	34-0	115	.256
2001— Wilmington (Caro.)	10	6	.625	2.55	1.03	27	27	0	0	...	0-...	162.1	134	58	46	8	33-3	154	.226
2002— Wichita (Texas)	5	7	.417	3.38	1.30	13	13	0	0	...	0-...	69.1	71	29	26	3	19-2	52	.267
2003— Wichita (Texas)	12	8	.600	3.19	1.27	22	22	2	1	...	0-...	132.2	128	57	47	11	40-1	100	.254
— Kansas City (A.L.)	4	5	.444	4.61	1.35	9	9	0	0	0	0-0	52.2	56	32	27	8	15-0	31	.271
2004— Omaha (PCL)	3	1	.750	4.58	1.63	4	4	0	0	...	0-...	19.2	25	20	10	5	7-0	15	.298
— Kansas City (A.L.)	9	8	.529	5.35	1.35	25	24	1	0	0	0-0	148.0	157	94	88	24	43-0	49	.270
Major League totals (2 years)	13	13	.500	5.16	1.35	34	33	1	0	0	0-0	200.2	213	126	115	32	58-0	80	.270

GOMES, JONNY — OF/DH

PERSONAL: Born November 22, 1980, in San Francisco, Calif. ... 6-1/205. ... Bats right, throws right. ... Full name: Jonny Johnson Gomes. ... Junior college: Santa Rosa (Calif.).

TRANSACTIONS/CAREER NOTES: Selected by Tampa Bay Devil Rays organization in 18th round of 2001 free-agent draft.

2004 GAMES PLAYED BY POSITION (MLB): DH—4.

Year — Team (League)	Pos.	G	AB	R	H	2B	3B	HR	RBI	BB	SO	HBP	GDP	SB-CS	Avg.	OBP	SLG	OPS	E	Avg.
2001— Princeton (Appal.)	OF	62	206	58	60	11	2	16	44	33	73	26	1	15-4	.291	.442	.597	1.039	7	.936
2002— Bakersfield (Calif.)	OF	134	446	102	124	24	9	30	72	91	173	31	4	15-3	.278	.432	.574	1.006	7	.961
2003— Orlando (South.)	OF-DH	120	442	68	110	28	3	17	56	53	148	16	5	23-2	.249	.348	.441	.789	4	.977
— Durham (Int'l)	OF-DH	5	19	2	6	2	1	0	1	2	5	2	0	0-0	.316	.435	.526	.961	0	1.000

G

Year Team (League)	Pos.	G	AB	R	H	2B	3B	HR	RBI	BB	SO	HBP	GDP	SB-CS	Avg.	OBP	SLG	OPS	E	Avg.
—Tampa Bay (A.L.)	DH	8	15	1	2	1	0	0	0	0	6	1	0	0-0	.133	.188	.200	.388	0	...
2004—Tampa Bay (A.L.)	DH	5	14	0	1	0	0	0	1	1	6	0	0	0-0	.071	.133	.071	.205	0	...
—Durham (Int'l)	OF-DH	114	389	73	100	27	1	26	78	51	136	22	6	8-5	.257	.368	.532	.900	7	.962
Major League totals (2 years)		13	29	1	3	1	0	0	1	1	12	1	0	0-0	.103	.161	.138	.299	0	...

GOMEZ, ALEXIS — OF

PERSONAL: Born August 6, 1978, in Loma de Cabrera, Dominican Republic. ... 6-2/180. ... Bats left, throws left. ... Full name: Alexis De Jesus Gomez. ... High school: Liceo General Jose Cabrera (Loma de Cabrera, Dominican Republic).

TRANSACTIONS/CAREER NOTES: Signed as a non-drafted free agent by Kansas City Royals organization (February 21, 1997). ... Claimed on waivers by Detroit Tigers (October 1, 2004).

2004 GAMES PLAYED BY POSITION (MLB): OF—12, DH—1.

Year Team (League)	Pos.	G	AB	R	H	2B	3B	HR	RBI	BB	SO	HBP	GDP	SB-CS	Avg.	OBP	SLG	OPS	E	Avg.
1997—Dom. Royals (DSL)		64	248	51	87	12	9	0	42	33	52	...	...	9-...	.351	...	.472	...	...	...
1998—Dom. Royals (DSL)		67	233	51	66	11	3	1	34	50	46	...	...	17-...	.283	...	.369	...	...	...
1999—GC Royals (GCL)	OF	56	214	44	59	12	1	5	31	32	48	1	1	13-5	.276	.371	.411	.782	2	.986
2000—Wilmington (Caro.)	OF	121	461	63	117	13	4	1	33	45	121	2	8	21-10	.254	.322	.306	.628	14	.950
2001—Wilmington (Caro.)	OF	48	169	29	51	8	2	1	9	11	43	1	4	7-3	.302	.348	.391	.739	5	.957
—Wichita (Texas)	OF	83	342	55	96	15	6	4	34	27	70	4	4	16-10	.281	.337	.395	.732	6	.971
2002—Wichita (Texas)	OF	114	461	72	136	21	8	14	75	45	84	3	9	36-24	.295	.359	.466	.825	8	.967
—Kansas City (A.L.)	OF	5	10	0	2	0	0	0	0	0	2	0	0	0-0	.200	.200	.200	.400	0	1.000
2003—Omaha (PCL)	OF	121	457	49	123	23	8	8	58	26	92	1	12	4-5	.269	.307	.407	.714	9	.970
2004—Omaha (PCL)	OF	109	383	45	96	17	8	7	34	19	96	1	11	8-6	.251	.285	.392	.677	6	.971
—Kansas City (A.L.)	OF-DH	13	29	1	8	1	0	0	4	2	8	0	1	0-0	.276	.323	.310	.633	1	.955
Major League totals (2 years)		18	39	1	10	1	0	0	4	2	10	0	1	0-0	.256	.293	.282	.575	1	.963

GOMEZ, CHRIS — SS

PERSONAL: Born June 16, 1971, in Los Angeles, Calif. ... 6-1/188. ... Bats right, throws right. ... Full name: Christopher Cory Gomez. ... High school: Lakewood (Calif.). ... College: Long Beach State.

TRANSACTIONS/CAREER NOTES: Selected by California Angels organization in 37th round of 1989 free-agent draft; did not sign. ... Selected by Detroit Tigers organization in third round of 1992 free-agent draft. ... Traded by Tigers with C John Flaherty to San Diego Padres for C Brad Ausmus, SS Andujar Cedeno and P Russ Spear (June 18, 1996). ... On disabled list (June 2-July 31, 1999); included rehabilitation assignment to Las Vegas. ... On disabled list (June 22, 2000-remainder of season). ... Released by Padres (June 22, 2001). ... Signed by Tampa Bay Devil Rays organization (June 27, 2001). ... Released by Devil Rays (September 30, 2002). ... Signed by Minnesota Twins organization (January 2, 2003). ... On disabled list (June 7-July 5, 2003). ... Signed as a free agent by Toronto Blue Jays (January 7, 2004).

2004 GAMES PLAYED BY POSITION (MLB): SS—77, 1B—19, 3B—5, DH—5, 2B—3.

Year Team (League)	Pos.	G	AB	R	H	2B	3B	HR	RBI	BB	SO	HBP	GDP	SB-CS	Avg.	OBP	SLG	OPS	E	Avg.
1992—London (East.)	SS	64	220	20	59	13	2	1	19	20	34	3	11	1-3	.268	.337	.359	.697	14	.951
1993—Toledo (Int'l)	SS	87	277	29	68	12	2	0	20	23	37	3	4	6-2	.245	.308	.303	.611	16	.961
—Detroit (A.L.)	SS-2B-DH	46	128	11	32	7	1	0	11	9	17	1	2	2-2	.250	.304	.320	.625	5	.974
1994—Detroit (A.L.)	SS-2B	84	296	32	76	19	0	8	53	33	64	3	8	5-3	.257	.336	.402	.738	8	.978
1995—Detroit (A.L.)	SS-2B-DH	123	431	49	96	20	2	11	50	41	96	3	13	4-1	.223	.292	.355	.647	15	.974
1996—Detroit (A.L.)	SS	48	128	21	31	5	0	1	16	18	20	1	5	1-1	.242	.340	.305	.645	6	.970
—San Diego (N.L.)	SS	89	328	32	86	16	1	3	29	39	64	6	11	2-2	.262	.349	.345	.694	13	.967
1997—San Diego (N.L.)	SS	150	522	62	132	19	2	5	54	53	114	5	16	5-8	.253	.326	.326	.652	15	.978
1998—San Diego (N.L.)	SS	145	449	55	120	32	3	4	39	51	87	5	11	1-3	.267	.346	.379	.725	12	.980
1999—San Diego (N.L.)	SS	76	234	20	59	8	1	1	15	27	49	1	6	1-2	.252	.331	.308	.638	12	.961
—Las Vegas (PCL)	SS	10	27	3	9	1	0	0	4	2	6	1	1	0-0	.333	.400	.370	.770	2	.933
2000—San Diego (N.L.)	SS-2B	33	54	4	12	0	0	0	3	7	5	0	1	0-0	.222	.306	.222	.529	5	.933
2001—San Diego (N.L.)	SS-2B	40	112	6	21	3	0	0	7	9	14	0	1	1-0	.188	.244	.214	.458	6	.948
—Portland (PCL)	SS-2B	11	40	5	12	3	0	1	5	2	4	0	1	1-0	.300	.333	.450	.783	2	.959
—Durham (Int'l)	SS	23	93	16	28	5	1	4	17	11	11	0	5	1-1	.301	.375	.505	.880	2	.978
—Tampa Bay (A.L.)	SS	58	189	31	57	16	0	8	36	8	24	2	4	3-0	.302	.332	.513	.845	7	.968
2002—Tampa Bay (A.L.)	SS	130	461	51	122	31	3	10	46	21	58	7	8	1-3	.265	.305	.411	.715	12	.980
2003—Minnesota (A.L.)	2-3-SS-DH	58	175	14	44	9	3	1	15	7	13	0	10	2-1	.251	.279	.354	.633	3	.982
2004—Toronto (A.L.)	S-1-3-DH-2	109	341	41	96	11	1	3	37	28	41	2	4	3-2	.282	.337	.346	.683	12	.974
American League totals (8 years)		656	2149	250	554	118	10	42	264	165	333	19	54	21-13	.258	.314	.381	.695	68	.976
National League totals (6 years)		533	1699	179	430	78	7	13	147	186	333	17	50	10-15	.253	.331	.330	.661	63	.971
Major League totals (12 years)		1189	3848	429	984	196	17	55	411	351	666	36	104	31-28	.256	.322	.358	.680	131	.973

DIVISION SERIES RECORD

Year Team (League)	Pos.	G	AB	R	H	2B	3B	HR	RBI	BB	SO	HBP	GDP	SB-CS	Avg.	OBP	SLG	OPS	E	Avg.
1996—San Diego (N.L.)	SS	3	12	0	2	0	0	0	1	0	4	0	0	0-0	.167	.167	.167	.333	0	1.000
1998—San Diego (N.L.)	SS	4	11	1	3	0	0	0	0	4	1	0	0	0-0	.273	.467	.273	.739	1	.938
2003—Minnesota (A.L.)	2B	1	0	0	0	0	0	0	0	0	0	0	0	0-0	...	...	...	...	0	...
Division series totals (3 years)		8	23	1	5	0	0	0	1	4	5	0	0	0-0	.217	.333	.217	.551	1	.966

CHAMPIONSHIP SERIES RECORD

Year Team (League)	Pos.	G	AB	R	H	2B	3B	HR	RBI	BB	SO	HBP	GDP	SB-CS	Avg.	OBP	SLG	OPS	E	Avg.
1998—San Diego (N.L.)	SS	6	20	2	3	1	0	0	0	2	5	0	3	0-0	.150	.227	.200	.427	1	.950

WORLD SERIES RECORD

Year Team (League)	Pos.	G	AB	R	H	2B	3B	HR	RBI	BB	SO	HBP	GDP	SB-CS	Avg.	OBP	SLG	OPS	E	Avg.
1998—San Diego (N.L.)	SS	4	11	2	4	0	1	0	1	1	1	0	0	0-0	.364	.417	.545	.962	0	1.000

GONZALEZ, ADRIAN — 1B

PERSONAL: Born May 8, 1982, in San Diego, Calif. ... 6-2/220. ... Bats left, throws left. ... High school: Eastlake High (Chula Vista, California).

TRANSACTIONS/CAREER NOTES: Selected by Florida Marlins organization in first round (first pick overall) of 2000 draft. ... Traded by Marlins with P Ryan Snare and OF Will Smith to Texas Rangers for P Ugueth Urbina (July 11, 2003).

HONORS: Named Midwest League Most Valuable Player (2001).

G

2004 GAMES PLAYED BY POSITION (MLB): 1B—11, DH—1.

										BATTING									FIELDING	
Year	Team (League)	Pos.	G	AB	R	H	2B	3B	HR	RBI	BB	SO	HBP	GDP	SB-CS	Avg.	OBP	SLG	OPS	E	Avg.
2000—	GC Marlins (GCL)	1B	53	193	24	57	10	1	0	30	32	35	2	6	0-0	.295	.397	.358	.755	7	.986
—	Utica (N.Y.-Penn)	1B	8	29	7	9	3	0	0	3	7	6	0	0	0-0	.310	.444	.414	.858	2	.976
2001—	Kane Co. (Midw.)	1B	127	516	86	161	37	1	17	103	57	83	5	17	5-5	.312	.382	.486	.868	14	.988
2002—	Portland (East.)	1B	138	508	70	135	34	1	17	96	54	112	8	13	6-3	.266	.344	.437	.781	16	.987
2003—	Albuquerque (PCL)	1B	39	139	17	30	5	1	1	18	14	25	0	6	1-0	.216	.286	.288	.573	1	.997
—	Carolina (Southern)	1B	36	137	15	42	9	1	1	16	14	25	0	6	1-1	.307	.368	.409	.777	4	.987
—	Frisco (Texas)	1B	45	173	16	49	6	2	3	17	11	27	1	6	0-0	.283	.326	.393	.719	7	.983
2004—	Oklahoma (PCL)	1B	123	457	61	139	28	3	12	88	39	73	6	17	1-1	.304	.364	.457	.813	6	.995
—	Texas (A.L.)	1B-DH	16	42	7	10	3	0	1	7	2	6	0	0	0-0	.238	.273	.381	.654	1	.990
Major League totals (1 year)			16	42	7	10	3	0	1	7	2	6	0	0	0-0	.238	.273	.381	.654	1	.990

GONZALEZ, ALEX   SS

PERSONAL: Born February 15, 1977, in Cagua, Venezuela. ... 6-0/202. ... Bats right, throws right. ... Full name: Alexander Gonzalez. ... High school: Liceo Ramon Bastidas (Venezuela).

TRANSACTIONS/CAREER NOTES: Signed as a non-drafted free agent by Florida Marlins organization (April 18, 1994). ... On disabled list (July 28-September 1, 2000); included rehabilitation assignment to Brevard County. ... On disabled list (May 19, 2002-remainder of season); included rehabilitation assignments to GCL Marlins.I ... On suspended list (June 3-5, 2004).

2004 GAMES PLAYED BY POSITION (MLB): SS—158.

										BATTING									FIELDING	
Year	Team (League)	Pos.	G	AB	R	H	2B	3B	HR	RBI	BB	SO	HBP	GDP	SB-CS	Avg.	OBP	SLG	OPS	E	Avg.
1994—	Dom. Marlins (DSL)	SS	54	239	30	54	7	3	3	31	15	36	...	...	4-...	.226	...	.318	...	34	.914
1995—	Brevard County (FSL)	SS	17	59	6	12	2	1	0	8	1	14	1	2	1-1	.203	.230	.271	.501	8	.906
—	GC Marlins (GCL)	SS	53	187	30	55	7	4	2	30	19	27	2	2	11-2	.294	.358	.406	.765	17	.932
1996—	GC Marlins (GCL)	SS	10	41	6	16	3	0	0	6	2	4	0	1	1-0	.390	.419	.463	.882	5	.898
—	Kane Co. (Midw.)	SS	4	10	2	2	0	0	0	0	2	4	1	1	0-0	.200	.385	.200	.585	0	1.000
—	Portland (East.)	SS	11	34	4	8	0	1	0	1	2	10	1	2	0-0	.235	.297	.294	.591	7	.887
1997—	Portland (East.)	SS	133	449	69	114	16	4	19	65	27	83	7	7	4-7	.254	.305	.434	.739	37	.943
1998—	Charlotte (Int'l)	SS	108	422	71	117	20	10	10	51	28	80	6	4	4-7	.277	.330	.443	.773	20	.960
—	Florida (N.L.)	SS	25	86	11	13	2	0	3	7	9	30	1	2	0-0	.151	.240	.279	.519	2	.978
1999—	Florida (N.L.)	SS	136	560	81	155	28	8	14	59	15	113	12	13	3-5	.277	.308	.430	.739	27	.955
2000—	Florida (N.L.)	SS	109	385	35	77	17	4	7	42	13	77	2	7	7-1	.200	.229	.319	.548	19	.957
—	Brevard County (FSL)	SS	4	17	1	2	0	0	0	2	1	3	0	0	1-0	.118	.167	.118	.284	0	1.000
2001—	Florida (N.L.)	SS-C	145	515	57	129	36	1	9	48	30	107	10	13	2-2	.250	.303	.377	.680	26	.960
2002—	Florida (N.L.)	SS	42	151	15	34	7	1	2	18	12	32	4	2	3-1	.225	.296	.325	.620	3	.984
—	GC Marlins (GCL)	SS	5	12	0	2	1	0	0	1	0	5	0	1	0-0	.167	.154	.250	.404	1	.923
2003—	Florida (N.L.)	SS	150	528	52	135	33	6	18	77	33	106	13	8	0-4	.256	.313	.443	.756	16	.976
2004—	Florida (N.L.)	SS	159	561	67	130	30	3	23	79	27	126	4	17	3-1	.232	.270	.419	.689	16	.976
Major League totals (7 years)			766	2786	318	673	153	23	76	330	139	591	46	62	18-14	.242	.287	.395	.682	109	.967

DIVISION SERIES RECORD

Year	Team (League)	Pos.	G	AB	R	H	2B	3B	HR	RBI	BB	SO	HBP	GDP	SB-CS	Avg.	OBP	SLG	OPS	E	Avg.
2003—	Florida (N.L.)	SS	4	16	2	1	0	0	0	1	3	0	1	0-0	.063	.118	.063	.180	1	.929

CHAMPIONSHIP SERIES RECORD

Year	Team (League)	Pos.	G	AB	R	H	2B	3B	HR	RBI	BB	SO	HBP	GDP	SB-CS	Avg.	OBP	SLG	OPS	E	Avg.
2003—	Florida (N.L.)	SS	7	24	1	3	2	0	0	4	0	6	0	0	0-0	.125	.125	.208	.333	1	.970

WORLD SERIES RECORD

Year	Team (League)	Pos.	G	AB	R	H	2B	3B	HR	RBI	BB	SO	HBP	GDP	SB-CS	Avg.	OBP	SLG	OPS	E	Avg.
2003—	Florida (N.L.)	SS	6	22	3	6	2	0	1	2	0	7	0	1	0-1	.273	.273	.500	.773	0	1.000

ALL-STAR GAME RECORD

Year	Team (League)	Pos.	G	AB	R	H	2B	3B	HR	RBI	BB	SO	HBP	GDP	SB-CS	Avg.	OBP	SLG	OPS	E	Avg.
All-Star Game totals (1 year)		1	1	0	0	0	0	0	0	0	0	0	0	0-0	.000	.000	.000	.000	0	1.000

GONZALEZ, ALEX S.   SS

PERSONAL: Born April 8, 1973, in Miami, Fla. ... 6-0/200. ... Bats right, throws right. ... Full name: Alexander Scott Gonzalez. ... High school: Miami Killian.

TRANSACTIONS/CAREER NOTES: Selected by Toronto Blue Jays organization in 14th round of 1991 free-agent draft. ... On disabled list (April 29-May 27, 1994); included rehabilitation assignment to Syracuse. ... On disabled list (August 13-September 14, 1997; and May 17, 1999-remainder of season). ... On disabled list (July 7-22, 2000); included rehabilitation assignment to Syracuse. ... Traded by Blue Jays to Chicago Cubs for P Felix Heredia and a player to be named (December 10, 2001); Blue Jays acquired IF James Deschaine to complete deal (December 13, 2001). ... On disabled list (May 10-25, 2002). ... On disabled list (May 6-July 19, 2004); included rehabilitation assignment to Iowa. ... Traded by Cubs with P Francis Beltran and IF Brendan Harris to Montreal Expos as part of four-team deal in which Cubs acquired SS Nomar Garciaparra and OF Matt Murton from Red Sox, Red Sox acquired SS Orlando Cabrera from Expos and 1B Doug Mientkiewicz from Twins, and Twins acquired P Justin Jones from Cubs (July 31, 2004). ... Traded by Expos to San Diego Padres for a player to be named and cash (September 16, 2004).

RECORDS: Shares major league record for most strikeouts, game (6, September 9, 1998, 13 innings).

2004 GAMES PLAYED BY POSITION (MLB): SS—81.

										BATTING									FIELDING	
Year	Team (League)	Pos.	G	AB	R	H	2B	3B	HR	RBI	BB	SO	HBP	GDP	SB-CS	Avg.	OBP	SLG	OPS	E	Avg.
1991—	GC Jays (GCL)	SS	53	191	29	40	5	4	0	10	12	41	3	1	7-2	.209	.267	.277	.544	21	.915
1992—	Myrtle Beach (SAL)	SS	134	535	83	145	22	9	10	62	38	119	3	4	26-14	.271	.322	.402	.724	48	.932
1993—	Knoxville (Southern)	SS	142	561	93	162	29	7	16	69	39	110	6	9	38-13	.289	.339	.451	.790	30	.956
1994—	Toronto (A.L.)	SS	15	53	7	8	3	1	0	1	4	17	1	2	3-0	.151	.224	.245	.469	6	.918
—	Syracuse (Int'l)	SS-DH	110	437	69	124	22	4	12	57	53	92	1	9	23-6	.284	.361	.435	.796	31	.943
1995—	Toronto (A.L.) SS-3B-DH	111	367	51	89	19	4	10	42	44	114	1	7	4-4	.243	.322	.398	.720	19	.954
1996—	Toronto (A.L.)	SS	147	527	64	124	30	5	14	64	45	127	5	12	16-6	.235	.300	.391	.691	21	.973
1997—	Toronto (A.L.)	SS	126	426	46	102	23	2	12	35	34	94	5	9	15-6	.239	.302	.387	.689	8	.986
1998—	Toronto (A.L.)	SS	158	568	70	136	28	1	13	51	28	121	6	13	21-6	.239	.281	.361	.642	17	.976
1999—	Toronto (A.L.)	SS-DH	38	154	22	45	13	0	2	12	16	23	3	4	4-2	.292	.370	.416	.786	4	.980
2000—	Toronto (A.L.)	SS	141	527	68	133	31	2	15	69	43	113	4	14	4-4	.252	.313	.404	.717	16	.975
—	Syracuse (Int'l)	SS	1	5	0	0	0	0	0	0	2	0	0	0	0-0	.000	.000	.000	.000	0	1.000

G

Year Team (League)	Pos.	G	AB	R	H	2B	3B	HR	RBI	BB	SO	HBP	GDP	SB-CS	Avg.	OBP	SLG	OPS	E	Avg.
2001— Toronto (A.L.)	SS	154	636	79	161	25	5	17	76	43	149	7	16	18-11	.253	.303	.388	.692	10	.987
2002— Chicago (N.L.)	SS	142	513	58	127	27	5	18	61	46	136	3	11	5-3	.248	.312	.425	.737	21	.965
2003— Chicago (N.L.)	SS	152	536	71	122	37	0	20	59	47	123	6	17	3-3	.228	.295	.409	.704	10	.960
2004— Iowa (PCL)	SS	8	24	7	8	3	0	0	0	4	7	0	1	1-0	.333	.429	.458	.887	0	1.000
— Chicago (N.L.)	SS	37	129	15	28	10	0	3	8	4	26	0	1	1-1	.217	.241	.364	.605	5	.967
— Montreal (N.L.)	SS	35	133	19	32	7	0	4	16	8	32	1	1	1-1	.241	.289	.383	.672	6	.960
— San Diego (N.L.)	SS	11	23	2	4	1	1	0	3	2	6	0	0	0-0	.174	.240	.304	.544	0	1.000
American League totals (8 years)		890	3258	407	798	172	20	83	350	257	758	32	77	85-39	.245	.304	.386	.691	101	.975
National League totals (3 years)		377	1334	165	313	82	6	45	147	107	323	10	35	10-8	.235	.295	.406	.701	42	.973
Major League totals (11 years)		1267	4592	572	1111	254	26	128	497	364	1081	42	112	95-47	.242	.302	.392	.694	143	.975

DIVISION SERIES RECORD

Year Team (League)	Pos.	G	AB	R	H	2B	3B	HR	RBI	BB	SO	HBP	GDP	SB-CS	Avg.	OBP	SLG	OPS	E	Avg.
2003— Chicago (N.L.)	SS	5	12	1	3	0	0	0	1	2	3	0	0	0-1	.250	.357	.500	.857	0	1.000

CHAMPIONSHIP SERIES RECORD

Year Team (League)	Pos.	G	AB	R	H	2B	3B	HR	RBI	BB	SO	HBP	GDP	SB-CS	Avg.	OBP	SLG	OPS	E	Avg.
2003— Chicago (N.L.)	SS	7	28	5	8	2	0	3	7	2	7	0	0	0-0	.286	.333	.679	1.012	1	.968

GONZALEZ, DICKY   P

PERSONAL: Born December 21, 1978, in Bayamon, Puerto Rico. ... 5-11/170. ... Throws right, bats right. ... Full name: Dicky Angel Gonzalez. ... High school: Puig (Puerto Rico).

TRANSACTIONS/CAREER NOTES: Selected by New York Mets organization in 16th round of 1996 free-agent draft. ... Traded by Mets with P Bruce Chen, SS/2B Luis Figueroa and a player to be named to Montreal Expos for Ps Scott Strickland and Phil Seibel and OF Matt Watson (April 5, 2002); Expos acquired P Saul Rivera to complete deal (July 14, 2002). ... Claimed on waivers by Boston Red Sox (March 28, 2003). ... Signed as a free agent by Tampa Bay Devil Rays organization (November 24, 2003). ... Signed by Yakult of the Japan Central League (June 5, 2004).

CAREER HITTING: 2-for-20 (.100), 1 R, 0 2B, 0 3B, 0 HR, 0 RBI.

Year Team (League)	W	L	Pct.	ERA	WHIP	G	GS	CG	ShO	Hld.	Sv.-Opp.	IP	H	R	ER	HR	BB-IBB	SO	Avg.
1996— GC Mets (GCL)	4	2	.667	2.66	1.12	11	8	2	1	...	0-...	47.1	50	19	14	1	3-0	51	.266
— Kingsport (Appalachian)	1	0	1.000	1.80	0.80	1	1	0	0	...	0-...	5.0	4	2	1	0	0-0	7	.211
1997— Capital City (S. Atl.)	1	4	.200	4.94	1.37	10	7	1	0	...	0-...	47.1	50	28	26	8	15-0	49	.270
— Kingsport (Appalachian)	3	6	.333	4.36	1.21	12	12	1	0	...	0-...	66.0	70	38	32	7	14-0	76	.267
1998— St. Lucie (Fla. St.)	2	1	.667	3.09	1.26	8	8	0	0	...	0-...	46.2	46	22	16	8	13-0	23	.258
— Capital City (S. Atl.)	10	3	.769	3.31	1.06	18	18	1	0	...	0-...	111.1	104	57	41	9	14-1	107	.248
1999— St. Lucie (Fla. St.)	14	9	.609	2.83	1.10	25	25	3	0	...	0-...	168.2	156	66	53	11	30-1	143	.246
— Norfolk (Int'l)	0	1	.000	2.70	0.90	1	1	0	0	...	0-...	6.2	5	2	2	0	1-0	3	.227
2000— Binghamton (Eastern)	13	5	.722	3.84	1.12	26	25	2	1	...	0-...	147.2	130	75	63	14	36-0	138	.234
2001— Norfolk (Int'l)	6	5	.545	3.09	1.21	17	16	2	2	...	0-...	96.0	96	35	33	10	20-1	70	.268
— New York (N.L.)	3	2	.600	4.88	1.51	16	7	0	0	1	0-0	59.0	72	33	32	4	17-3	31	.306
2002— Norfolk (Int'l)	0	0	...	3.60	1.60	1	1	0	0	...	0-...	5.0	6	2	2	1	2-0	7	.286
— Ottawa (Int'l)	8	5	.615	3.76	1.42	22	22	0	0	...	0-...	119.2	137	59	50	10	33-2	72	.289
2003— Pawtucket (Int'l)	8	8	.500	4.04	1.40	27	25	1	0	...	0-...	151.2	180	77	68	13	29-1	104	.295
2004— Tampa Bay (A.L.)	0	0	...	6.14	1.50	4	0	0	0	0	0-0	7.1	9	5	5	1	2-0	7	.310
— Durham (Int'l)	1	2	.333	4.80	1.17	6	6	0	0	...	0-...	30.0	28	16	16	3	7-0	30	.252
American League totals (1 year)	0	0	...	6.14	1.50	4	0	0	0	0	0-0	7.1	9	5	5	1	2-0	7	.310
National League totals (1 year)	3	2	.600	4.88	1.51	16	7	0	0	1	0-0	59.0	72	33	32	4	17-3	31	.306
Major League totals (2 years)	3	2	.600	5.02	1.51	20	7	0	0	1	0-0	66.1	81	38	37	5	19-3	38	.307

GONZALEZ, EDGAR   P

PERSONAL: Born February 23, 1983, in Monterrey, Mexico. ... 6-0/215. ... Throws right, bats right. ... Full name: Edgar Gerardo Gonzalez.

TRANSACTIONS/CAREER NOTES: Signed as a non-drafted free agent by Arizona Diamondbacks organization (April 18, 2000). ... On suspended list for 2000 and 2001 seasons.

CAREER HITTING: 3-for-17 (.176), 1 R, 0 2B, 0 3B, 0 HR, 0 RBI.

Year Team (League)	W	L	Pct.	ERA	WHIP	G	GS	CG	ShO	Hld.	Sv.-Opp.	IP	H	R	ER	HR	BB-IBB	SO	Avg.
2002— South Bend (Mid.)	11	8	.579	2.91	1.16	23	23	4	2	...	0-...	151.1	141	66	49	4	34-0	110	.246
— Lancaster (Calif.)	3	0	1.000	0.78	1.17	4	4	0	0	...	0-...	23.0	24	7	2	1	3-0	21	.264
2003— El Paso (Texas)	2	2	.500	3.50	1.42	6	6	0	0	...	0-...	36.0	40	18	14	1	11-0	30	.282
— Tucson (PCL)	8	7	.533	3.75	1.19	20	19	1	0	...	0-...	129.2	126	65	54	4	28-0	69	.255
— Arizona (N.L.)	2	1	.667	4.91	1.91	9	2	0	0	...	0-1	18.1	28	10	10	3	7-2	14	.368
2004— Tucson (PCL)	5	5	.500	4.88	1.32	15	15	1	1	...	0-...	94.0	99	52	51	15	25-0	66	.277
— Arizona (N.L.)	0	9	...	9.32	1.94	10	10	0	0	...	0-0	46.1	72	49	48	15	18-4	31	.362
Major League totals (2 years)	2	10	.167	8.07	1.93	19	12	0	0	...	0-1	64.2	100	59	58	18	25-6	45	.364

GONZALEZ, JEREMI   P

PERSONAL: Born January 8, 1975, in Maracaibo, Venezuela. ... 6-0/220. ... Throws right, bats right. ... Full name: Geremis Segundo Gonzalez. ... High school: Colegro La Chinita (Maracaibo, Venezuela).

TRANSACTIONS/CAREER NOTES: Signed as a non-drafted free agent by Chicago Cubs organization (October 21, 1991). ... On disabled list (July 25, 1998-remainder of season). ... On disabled list (April 1, 1999-entire season); included rehabilitation assignments to Daytona, West Tenn and Iowa. ... On disabled list (March 28, 2000-remainder of season); included rehabilitation assignments to AZL Cubs and Lansing. ... Released by Cubs (March 13, 2001). ... Signed by Texas Rangers organization (December 18, 2001). ... Signed as a free agent by Tampa Bay Devil Rays organization (November 21, 2002).

CAREER HITTING: 10-for-78 (.128), 1 R, 1 2B, 0 3B, 0 HR, 3 RBI.

Year Team (League)	W	L	Pct.	ERA	WHIP	G	GS	CG	ShO	Hld.	Sv.-Opp.	IP	H	R	ER	HR	BB-IBB	SO	Avg.
1992— Ariz. Cubs (Ariz.)	0	5	.000	7.80	1.93	14	7	0	0	...	0-...	45.0	65	59	39	0	22-0	39	.325
1993— Huntington (Appal.)	3	9	.250	6.25	1.77	12	12	1	0	...	0-...	67.2	82	59	47	6	38-0	42	.300
1994— Peoria (Midw.)	1	7	.125	5.55	1.65	13	13	1	0	...	0-...	71.1	86	53	44	4	32-0	39	.306
— Williamsport (N.Y.-Penn.)	4	6	.400	4.24	1.39	16	12	1	1	...	1-...	80.2	83	46	38	6	29-0	64	.266
1995— Rockford (Midwest)	4	4	.500	5.10	1.39	12	12	1	0	...	0-...	65.1	63	43	37	4	28-0	36	.247
— Daytona (Fla. St.)	5	1	.833	1.22	1.06	19	2	0	0	...	4-...	44.1	34	15	6	0	13-1	30	.211
1996— Orlando (Sou.)	6	3	.667	3.34	1.27	17	14	0	0	...	0-...	97.0	95	39	36	8	28-1	85	.250
1997— Iowa (Am. Assoc.)	2	2	.500	3.48	1.10	10	10	1	1	...	0-...	62.0	47	27	24	8	21-0	58	.209

G

Year	Team (League)	W	L	Pct.	ERA	WHIP	G	GS	CG	ShO	Hld.	Sv.-Opp.	IP	H	R	ER	HR	BB-IBB	SO	Avg.
	— Chicago (N.L.)	11	9	.550	4.25	1.35	23	23	1	1	0	0-...	144.0	126	73	68	16	69-5	93	.236
1998	— Chicago (N.L.)	7	7	.500	5.32	1.50	20	20	1	1	0	0-...	110.0	124	72	65	13	41-5	70	.281
1999	— Daytona (Fla. St.)	0	0	...	0.00	0.43	2	2	0	0	0	0-...	4.2	2	0	0	0	0-0	4	.125
	— West Tenn (Sou.)	0	0	...	1.74	1.55	3	3	0	0	0	0-...	10.1	7	2	2	0	9-0	12	.200
	— Iowa (PCL)	0	1	.000	4.50	1.60	3	3	0	0	0	0-...	10.0	10	8	5	1	6-0	10	.270
2000	— Ariz. Cubs (Ariz.)	0	1	.000	2.70	1.00	4	4	0	0	0	0-...	10.0	8	3	3	0	2-0	15	.211
	— Lansing (Midw.)	0	0	...	0.00	0.00	1	1	0	0	0	0-...	.2	0	0	0	0	0-0	2	.000
2001	Did not play.																			
2002	— Oklahoma (PCL)	6	5	.545	3.33	1.36	46	5	0	0		14-...	92.0	86	40	34	8	39-5	93	.249
2003	— Durham (Int'l)	1	0	1.000	2.53	0.90	7	6	0	0		0-...	32.0	24	11	9	2	6-0	33	.202
	— Tampa Bay (A.L.)	6	11	.353	3.91	1.28	25	25	2	0	0	0-0	156.1	131	71	68	18	69-1	97	.228
2004	— Tampa Bay (A.L.)	0	5	.000	6.97	1.83	11	8	0	0	0	0-0	50.1	72	42	39	9	20-0	22	.346
	— Durham (Int'l)	4	2	.667	3.90	1.20	19	8	0	0	0	1-...	57.2	50	27	25	7	19-0	44	.233
	American League totals (2 years)	6	16	.273	4.66	1.41	36	33	2	0	0	0-0	206.2	203	113	107	27	89-1	119	.259
	National League totals (2 years)	18	16	.529	4.71	1.42	43	43	2	2	0	0-...	254.0	250	145	133	29	110-10	163	.256
	Major League totals (4 years)	24	32	.429	4.69	1.42	79	76	4	2	0	0-0	460.2	453	258	240	56	199-11	282	.258

GONZALEZ, JUAN   OF

PERSONAL: Born October 16, 1969, in Vega Baja, Puerto Rico. ... 6-3/220. ... Bats right, throws right. ... Full name: Juan Alberto Gonzalez. ... High school: Vega Baja (Puerto Rico).

TRANSACTIONS/CAREER NOTES: Signed as a non-drafted free agent by Texas Rangers organization (May 30, 1986). ... On disabled list (March 30-April 26, 1991; April 16-June 1 and July 27-August 16, 1995; May 8-June 1, 1996; and March 24-May 2, 1997). ... Traded by Rangers with P Danny Patterson and C Gregg Zaun to Detroit Tigers for Ps Justin Thompson, Francisco Cordero and Alan Webb, OF Gabe Kapler, C Bill Haselman and 2B Frank Catalanotto (November 2, 1999). ... On disabled list (July 8-26, 2000). ... Signed as a free agent by Cleveland Indians (January 9, 2001). ... Signed as a free agent by Rangers (January 8, 2002). ... On disabled list (April 9-May 17 and July 31, 2002-remainder of season). ... On disabled list (July 20, 2003-remainder of season). ... Signed as a free agent by Kansas City Royals (January 6, 2004). ... On disabled list (May 22, 2004-remainder of season); included rehabilitation assignment to AZL Royals.

HONORS: Named A.L. Most Valuable Player by Baseball Writers' Association of America (1996 and 1998).

2004 GAMES PLAYED BY POSITION (MLB): OF—29, DH—4.

Year	Team (League)	Pos.	G	AB	R	H	2B	3B	HR	RBI	BB	SO	HBP	GDP	SB-CS	Avg.	OBP	SLG	OPS	E	Avg.
1986	— GC Rangers (GCL)	OF	60	233	24	56	4	1	0	36	21	57	1	9	7-5	.240	.302	.266	.568	6	.941
1987	— Gastonia (S. Atl.)	OF	127	509	69	135	21	2	14	74	30	92	5	14	9-4	.265	.310	.397	.707	12	.953
1988	— Charlotte (Fla. St.)	OF	77	277	25	77	14	3	8	43	25	64	4	7	5-2	.256	.325	.415	.740	4	.973
1989	— Tulsa (Texas)	OF	133	502	73	147	30	7	21	85	31	98	9	8	1-8	.293	.342	.506	.848	9	.972
	— Texas (A.L.)	OF	24	60	6	9	3	0	1	7	6	17	0	4	0-0	.150	.227	.250	.477	2	.964
1990	— Okla. City (A.A.)	OF	128	496	78	128	29	4	29	101	32	109	1	11	2-2	.258	.300	.508	.808	8	.966
	— Texas (A.L.)	DH-OF	25	90	11	26	7	1	4	12	2	18	2	2	0-1	.289	.316	.522	.838	0	1.000
1991	— Texas (A.L.)	DH-OF	142	545	78	144	34	1	27	102	42	118	5	16	4-4	.264	.321	.479	.800	6	.981
1992	— Texas (A.L.)	OF-DH	155	584	77	152	24	2	* 43	109	35	143	5	10	0-1	.260	.304	.529	.833	10	.975
1993	— Texas (A.L.)	OF-DH	140	536	105	166	33	1	* 46	118	37	99	13	12	4-1	.310	.368	* .632	1.000	4	.985
1994	— Texas (A.L.)	OF	107	422	57	116	18	4	19	85	30	66	7	18	6-4	.275	.330	.472	.802	2	.991
1995	— Texas (A.L.)	DH-OF	90	352	57	104	20	2	27	82	17	66	0	15	0-0	.295	.324	.594	.917	0	1.000
1996	— Texas (A.L.)	OF-DH	134	541	89	170	33	2	47	144	45	82	3	10	2-0	.314	.368	.643	1.012	4	.988
1997	— Texas (A.L.)	DH-OF	133	533	87	158	24	3	42	131	33	107	3	10	0-0	.296	.335	.589	.924	4	.971
1998	— Texas (A.L.)	OF-DH	154	606	110	193	* 50	2	45	* 157	46	126	6	20	2-1	.318	.366	.630	.997	4	.982
1999	— Texas (A.L.)	OF-DH	144	562	114	183	36	1	39	128	51	105	4	10	3-3	.326	.378	.601	.980	4	.983
2000	— Detroit (A.L.)	OF-DH	115	461	69	133	30	2	22	67	32	84	2	13	1-2	.289	.337	.505	.842	1	.992
2001	— Cleveland (A.L.)	OF-DH	140	532	97	173	34	1	35	140	41	94	6	18	1-0	.325	.370	.590	.960	3	.987
2002	— Texas (A.L.)	OF-DH	70	277	38	78	21	1	8	35	17	56	1	11	2-0	.282	.324	.451	.776	1	.992
2003	— Texas (A.L.)	OF-DH	82	327	49	96	17	1	24	70	14	73	4	10	1-1	.294	.329	.572	.901	0	1.000
2004	— Kansas City (A.L.)	OF-DH	33	127	17	35	4	1	5	17	9	19	1	3	0-1	.276	.326	.441	.767	3	.948
	— Royals (Ariz.)	DH	9	26	6	9	4	0	0	5	6	8	0	1	0-0	.346	.455	.538	.993	0	1.000
	Major League totals (16 years)		1688	6555	1061	1936	388	25	434	1404	457	1273	62	184	26-19	.295	.343	.561	.904	46	.983

DIVISION SERIES RECORD

Year	Team (League)	Pos.	G	AB	R	H	2B	3B	HR	RBI	BB	SO	HBP	GDP	SB-CS	Avg.	OBP	SLG	OPS	E	Avg.
1996	— Texas (A.L.)	OF	4	16	5	7	0	0	5	9	3	2	0	0	0-0	.438	.526	1.375	1.901	0	1.000
1998	— Texas (A.L.)	OF	3	12	1	1	1	0	0	0	0	3	0	0	0-0	.083	.083	.167	.250	0	1.000
1999	— Texas (A.L.)	OF	3	11	1	2	0	0	1	1	1	3	0	1	0-0	.182	.250	.455	.705	0	1.000
2001	— Cleveland (A.L.)	OF	5	23	4	8	3	0	2	5	0	7	0	1	0-0	.348	.348	.739	1.087	0	1.000
	Division series totals (4 years)		15	62	11	18	4	0	8	15	4	15	0	2	0-0	.290	.333	.742	1.075	0	1.000

ALL-STAR GAME RECORD

		G	AB	R	H	2B	3B	HR	RBI	BB	SO	HBP	GDP	SB-CS	Avg.	OBP	SLG	OPS	E	Avg.
	All-Star Game totals (3 years)	3	5	0	0	0	0	0	1	1	2	0		0-0	.000	.143	.000	.143	0	1.000

GONZALEZ, LUIS   OF

PERSONAL: Born September 3, 1967, in Tampa, Fla. ... 6-2/200. ... Bats left, throws right. ... Full name: Luis Emilio Gonzalez. ... High school: Jefferson (Tampa). ... College: South Alabama.

TRANSACTIONS/CAREER NOTES: Selected by Houston Astros organization in fourth round of 1988 free-agent draft. ... On disabled list (August 29-September 13, 1991; and July 21-August 5, 1992). ... Traded by Astros with C Scott Servais to Chicago Cubs for C Rick Wilkins (June 28, 1995). ... Signed as a free agent by Astros (December 19, 1996). ... Signed as a free agent by Detroit Tigers (December 9, 1997). ... Traded by Tigers to Arizona Diamondbacks for OF Karim Garcia (December 28, 1998). ... On disabled list (August 2, 2004-remainder of season).

2004 GAMES PLAYED BY POSITION (MLB): OF—104, DH—1.

Year	Team (League)	Pos.	G	AB	R	H	2B	3B	HR	RBI	BB	SO	HBP	GDP	SB-CS	Avg.	OBP	SLG	OPS	E	Avg.
1988	— Asheville (S. Atl.)	3B	31	115	13	29	7	1	2	14	12	17	2	4	2-2	.252	.333	.383	.716	6	.931
	— Auburn (NY-Penn)	3B-SS-1B	39	157	32	49	10	3	5	27	12	19	1	1	2-0	.312	.354	.510	.864	13	.902
1989	— Osceola (Fla. St.)	DH	86	287	46	82	16	7	6	38	37	49	4	3	2-1	.286	.370	.453	.823	...	.000

Year Team (League)	Pos.	G	AB	R	H	2B	3B	HR	RBI	BB	SO	HBP	GDP	SB-CS	Avg.	OBP	SLG	OPS	E	Avg.
1990— Columbus (Southern)	3B-1B	138	495	86	131	30	6	24	89	54	100	6	6	27-9	.265	.337	.495	.832	23	.980
—Houston (N.L.)	3B-1B	12	21	1	4	2	0	0	2	5	0	0	0	0-0	.190	.261	.286	.547	0	1.000
1991—Houston (N.L.)	OF	137	473	51	120	28	9	13	69	40	101	8	9	10-7	.254	.320	.433	.753	5	.984
1992—Houston (N.L.)	OF	122	387	40	94	19	3	10	55	24	52	2	6	7-7	.243	.289	.385	.674	5	.993
—Tucson (PCL)	OF	13	44	11	19	4	2	1	9	5	7	1	0	4-1	.432	.490	.682	1.172	1	.963
1993—Houston (N.L.)	OF	154	540	82	162	34	3	15	72	47	83	10	9	20-9	.300	.361	.457	.818	8	.978
1994—Houston (N.L.)	OF	112	392	57	107	29	4	8	67	49	57	3	10	15-13	.273	.353	.429	.782	5	.991
1995—Houston (N.L.)	OF	56	209	35	54	10	4	6	35	18	30	3	8	1-3	.258	.322	.431	.753	2	.980
—Chicago (N.L.)	OF	77	262	34	76	19	4	7	34	39	33	3	8	5-5	.290	.384	.473	.858	4	.978
1996—Chicago (N.L.)	OF-1B	146	483	70	131	30	4	15	79	61	49	4	13	9-6	.271	.354	.443	.797	3	.988
1997—Houston (N.L.)	OF-1B	152	550	78	142	31	2	10	68	71	67	5	12	10-7	.258	.345	.376	.722	5	.982
1998—Detroit (A.L.)	OF-DH	154	547	84	146	35	5	23	71	57	62	8	9	12-7	.267	.340	.475	.816	3	.988
1999—Arizona (N.L.)	OF-DH	153	614	112	*206	45	4	26	111	66	63	7	13	9-5	.336	.403	.549	.952	5	.983
2000—Arizona (N.L.)	OF	•162	618	106	192	47	2	31	114	78	85	12	12	2-4	.311	.392	.544	.935	3	.990
2001—Arizona (N.L.)	OF	•162	609	128	198	36	7	57	142	100	83	14	14	1-1	.325	.429	.688	1.117	0	1.000
2002—Arizona (N.L.)	OF	148	524	90	151	19	3	28	103	97	76	5	12	9-2	.288	.400	.496	.896	4	.985
2003—Arizona (N.L.)	OF	156	579	92	176	46	4	26	104	94	67	3	19	5-3	.304	.402	.532	.934	3	.989
2004—Arizona (N.L.)	OF-DH	105	379	69	98	28	5	17	48	68	58	2	9	2-2	.259	.373	.493	.866	6	.965
American League totals (1 year)		154	547	84	146	35	5	23	71	57	62	8	9	12-7	.267	.340	.475	.816	3	.988
National League totals (14 years)		1854	6640	1045	1911	423	58	269	1101	854	909	81	154	105-74	.288	.372	.491	.863	52	.985
Major League totals (15 years)		2008	7187	1129	2057	458	63	292	1172	911	971	89	163	117-81	.286	.370	.489	.859	55	.986

DIVISION SERIES RECORD

Year Team (League)	Pos.	G	AB	R	H	2B	3B	HR	RBI	BB	SO	HBP	GDP	SB-CS	Avg.	OBP	SLG	OPS	E	Avg.
1997—Houston (N.L.)	OF	3	12	0	4	0	0	0	0	0	1	0	0	0-0	.333	.333	.333	.667	1	.933
1999—Arizona (N.L.)	OF	4	10	3	2	1	0	1	2	5	1	1	0	0-0	.200	.500	.600	1.100	0	1.000
2001—Arizona (N.L.)	OF	5	19	1	5	0	0	1	1	2	4	0	0	0-0	.263	.333	.421	.754	0	1.000
Division series totals (3 years)		12	41	4	11	1	0	2	3	7	6	1	0	0-0	.268	.388	.439	.827	1	.958

CHAMPIONSHIP SERIES RECORD

Year Team (League)	Pos.	G	AB	R	H	2B	3B	HR	RBI	BB	SO	HBP	GDP	SB-CS	Avg.	OBP	SLG	OPS	E	Avg.
2001—Arizona (N.L.)	OF	5	19	4	4	0	0	1	4	3	3	1	0	0-0	.211	.348	.368	.716	0	1.000

WORLD SERIES RECORD

Year Team (League)	Pos.	G	AB	R	H	2B	3B	HR	RBI	BB	SO	HBP	GDP	SB-CS	Avg.	OBP	SLG	OPS	E	Avg.
2001—Arizona (N.L.)	OF	7	27	4	7	2	0	1	5	1	11	2	1	0-0	.259	.333	.444	.778	0	1.000

ALL-STAR GAME RECORD

	G	AB	R	H	2B	3B	HR	RBI	BB	SO	HBP	GDP	SB-CS	Avg.	OBP	SLG	OPS	E	Avg.
All-Star Game totals (4 years)	4	6	0	3	1	0	0	0	0	0	0	0	0-0	.500	.500	.667	1.167	0	...

GONZALEZ, LUIS A.　　　　2B

PERSONAL: Born June 26, 1979, in Maracay, Venezuela. ... 5-11/170. ... Bats right, throws right. ... Full name: Luis Alberto Gonzalez.
TRANSACTIONS/CAREER NOTES: Signed as non-drafted free agent by Cleveland Indians organization (July 5, 1996). ... Selected by Colorado Rockies from Indians organization in Rule 5 major league draft (December 15, 2003).
2004 GAMES PLAYED BY POSITION (MLB): 2B—40, OF—29, 3B—18, SS—10, DH—1.

Year Team (League)	Pos.	G	AB	R	H	2B	3B	HR	RBI	BB	SO	HBP	GDP	SB-CS	Avg.	OBP	SLG	OPS	E	Avg.
1998—Columbus (S. Atl.)	SS	101	320	48	87	14	1	3	32	28	63	8	5	10-3	.272	.345	.350	.695	28	.940
1999—Kinston (Caro.)		1	1	0	0	0	0	0	0	0	0	0	0	0-0	.000	.000	.000	.000	...	...
—Columbus (S. Atl.)	SS-3B-2B	83	299	41	88	18	2	7	50	26	40	5	5	6-5	.294	.355	.438	.793	21	.931
2000—Kinston (Caro.)	2B-SS	79	284	32	70	11	0	2	33	21	54	6	6	6-6	.246	.310	.306	.616	12	.961
2001—Kinston (Caro.)	3B-2B-SS	52	183	31	59	14	0	5	19	14	36	8	1	3-5	.322	.391	.481	.872	9	.945
—Akron (East.)	2B-SS-3B	52	199	41	60	12	2	5	17	7	26	2	3	2-3	.302	.329	.457	.786	5	.987
2002—Buffalo (Int'l)	2B	6	19	0	2	0	0	0	1	1	4	1	1	0-0	.105	.190	.105	.296	1	.967
—Akron (East.)	2-3-S-O-F-1	73	263	42	70	10	3	6	24	12	37	5	6	4-0	.266	.304	.395	.700	8	.962
2003—Akron (East.)	1-2-0-3-S	116	431	72	137	22	4	7	62	46	41	6	17	1-0	.318	.385	.436	.821	9	.985
2004—Colorado (N.L.)	2-0-3-S-DH	102	322	42	94	17	2	12	40	15	67	4	5	1-5	.292	.330	.469	.799	2	.993
Major League totals (1 year)		102	322	42	94	17	2	12	40	15	67	4	5	1-5	.292	.330	.469	.799	2	.993

GONZALEZ, MIKE　　　　P

PERSONAL: Born May 23, 1978, in Corpus Christi, Texas. ... 6-2/205. ... Throws left, bats right. ... Full name: Michael Vela Gonzalez. ... High school: Harvest Christian Academy (Pasadena, Texas). ... Junior college: San Jacinto (Texas).
TRANSACTIONS/CAREER NOTES: Selected by Pittsburgh Pirates organization in 17th round of 1996 free-agent draft; did not sign. ... Selected by Pittsburgh Pirates organization in 30th round of 1997 free-agent draft. ... Traded by Pirates with P Scott Sauerbeck to Boston Red Sox for Ps Brandon Lyon and Anastacio Martinez (July 22, 2003). ... Traded by Red Sox with IF Freddy Sanchez to Pirates for Ps Jeff Suppan, Brandon Lyon and Anastacio Martinez (July 31, 2003).
CAREER HITTING: 1-for-1 (1.000), 0 R, 1 2B, 0 3B, 0 HR, 2 RBI.

Year Team (League)	W	L	Pct.	ERA	WHIP	G	GS	CG	ShO	Hld.	Sv.-Opp.	IP	H	R	ER	HR	BB-IBB	SO	Avg.
1997—GC Pirates (GCL)	2	0	1.000	2.48	1.00	7	3	0	0	...	0-...	29.0	21	9	8	0	8-0	33	.200
—Augusta (S. Atl.)	1	1	.500	1.86	0.98	4	3	0	0	...	0-...	19.1	11	5	4	1	8-0	22	.164
1998—Lynchburg (Carolina)	0	3	.000	6.67	1.87	7	7	0	0	...	0-...	28.1	40	21	21	5	13-0	22	.351
—Augusta (S. Atl.)	4	2	.667	2.84	1.36	11	9	0	0	...	0-...	50.2	43	24	16	2	26-0	72	.231
1999—Lynchburg (Carolina)	10	4	.714	4.02	1.44	20	20	0	0	...	0-...	112.0	98	55	50	10	63-0	119	.240
—Altoona (East.)	2	3	.400	8.10	1.99	7	5	0	0	...	0-...	26.2	34	25	24	4	19-0	31	.312
2000—GC Pirates (GCL)	1	0	1.000	4.50	2.00	2	1	0	0	...	0-...	6.0	8	6	3	1	4-0	7	.267
—Lynchburg (Carolina)	4	3	.571	4.66	1.63	12	10	0	0	...	0-...	56.0	57	34	29	6	34-0	53	.269
2001—Lynchburg (Carolina)	2	2	.500	2.93	1.14	14	2	0	0	...	0-...	30.2	28	14	10	3	7-1	32	.241
—Altoona (East.)	5	4	.556	3.71	1.34	14	14	1	1	...	0-...	87.1	81	38	36	5	36-0	66	.251
2002—GC Pirates (GCL)	2	0	1.000	0.00	0.60	2	2	0	0	...	0-...	13.1	5	1	0	0	3-0	14	.114
—Altoona (East.)	8	4	.667	3.80	1.45	16	16	0	0	...	0-...	85.1	77	38	36	4	47-2	65	.244
2003—Lynchburg (Carolina)	0	1	.000	5.14	1.71	5	2	0	0	...	0-...	7.0	7	9	4	0	5-0	9	.269
—Altoona (East.)	0	0	...	1.23	0.82	5	0	0	0	...	1-...	7.1	4	1	1	1	2-0	10	.154

G

Year	Team (League)	W	L	Pct.	ERA	WHIP	G	GS	CG	ShO	Hld.	Sv.-Opp.	IP	H	R	ER	HR	BB-IBB	SO	Avg.
	—Pawtucket (Int'l)	0	0	...	0.00	1.80	2	0	0	0	...	1-...	1.2	2	0	0	0	1-0	2	.286
	—Nashville (PCL)	0	0	...	4.50	1.30	7	0	0	0	...	2-...	10.0	9	5	5	0	4-1	10	.231
	—Pittsburgh (N.L.)	0	1	.000	7.56	1.56	16	0	0	0	3	0-0	8.1	7	7	7	4	6-0	6	.233
2004	—Nashville (PCL)	2	0	1.000	0.90	0.95	14	0	0	0	...	2-...	20.0	12	2	2	0	7-0	35	.185
	—Pittsburgh (N.L.)	3	1	.750	1.25	0.88	47	0	0	0	13	1-4	43.1	32	7	6	2	6-0	55	.201
	Major League totals (2 years)	3	2	.600	2.26	0.99	63	0	0	0	16	1-4	51.2	39	14	13	6	12-0	61	.206

GONZALEZ, RAUL — OF

PERSONAL: Born December 27, 1973, in Santurce, Puerto Rico. ... 5-9/190. ... Bats right, throws right. ... Full name: Victor Raul Gonzalez. ... High school: Gilberto Concepcion (Carolina, Puerto Rico).

TRANSACTIONS/CAREER NOTES: Selected by Kansas City Royals organization in 17th round of 1990 free-agent draft. ... Signed as a free agent by Boston Red Sox organization (November 18, 1998). ... Signed as a free agent by Chicago Cubs organization (November 18, 1999). ... Signed as a free agent by Cincinnati Reds organization (December 21, 2000). ... Traded by Reds to New York Mets (August 20, 2002), partially completing deal in which Mets traded P Shawn Estes and cash to Reds for P Pedro Feliciano, OF Elvin Andujar and two players to be named (August 15, 2002); Mets acquired OF Brady Clark to complete deal (September 9, 2002). ... Released by Mets (December 4, 2003). ... Re-signed by Mets organization (February 5, 2004). ... Released by Mets (May 17, 2004). ... Signed by Cleveland Indians organization (May 21, 2004).

2004 GAMES PLAYED BY POSITION (MLB): OF—4.

								BATTING										FIELDING	
Year	Team (League)	Pos.	G	AB	R	H	2B	3B	HR	RBI	BB	SO	HBP	GDP	SB-CS	Avg.	OBP	SLG	OPS	E	Avg.
1991	—GC Royals (GCL)	OF	47	160	24	47	5	3	0	17	19	21	0	4	3-4	.294	.365	.363	.727	4	.941
1992	—Appleton (Midwest)	OF	119	449	82	115	32	1	9	51	57	58	2	4	13-5	.256	.339	.392	.731	5	.981
1993	—Wilmington (Caro.)	OF	127	461	59	124	30	3	11	55	54	58	4	8	13-5	.269	.348	.419	.767	8	.969
1994	—Wilmington (Caro.)	OF	115	414	60	108	19	8	9	51	45	50	2	8	0-4	.261	.333	.411	.744	10	.941
1995	—Wichita (Texas)	OF	22	79	14	23	3	2	1	11	8	13	0	1	4-0	.291	.356	.456	.812	2	.957
	—Wilmington (Caro.)	OF	86	308	36	90	19	3	11	49	14	34	2	3	6-4	.292	.320	.481	.801	5	.966
1996	—Wichita (Texas)	OF	23	84	17	24	5	1	1	9	5	12	1	3	1-2	.286	.333	.405	.738	1	.969
1997	—Wichita (Texas)	OF	129	452	66	129	30	4	13	74	36	52	2	12	12-8	.285	.335	.456	.791	14	.926
1998	—Wichita (Texas)	OF	118	455	84	148	31	1	17	66	58	53	2	15	12-8	.325	.401	.510	.911	9	.957
1999	—Trenton (East.)	OF	127	505	80	169	33	4	18	103	51	71	3	14	12-3	.335	.394	.523	.917	2	.993
2000	—Iowa (PCL)	OF	69	241	35	64	13	1	4	33	21	20	2	6	5-5	.266	.328	.378	.706	3	.974
	—Chicago (N.L.)	OF	3	0	0	0	0	0	0	0	0	2	0	0	0-0	.000	.000	.000	.000	0	...
2001	—Louisville (Int'l)	OF	142	539	90	161	39	1	11	66	64	70	1	20	6-8	.299	.371	.436	.807	9	.973
	—Cincinnati (N.L.)	OF	11	14	0	3	0	0	0	0	1	3	0	0	0-0	.214	.267	.214	.481	0	1.000
2002	—Louisville (Int'l)	OF	114	432	91	144	27	2	13	69	61	59	4	15	9-8	.333	.416	.495	.911	8	.970
	—Cincinnati (N.L.)	OF	10	23	4	6	1	0	0	1	2	5	0	1	2-0	.261	.320	.304	.624	0	1.000
	—New York (N.L.)	OF	30	81	9	21	2	0	3	11	4	17	0	2	2-2	.259	.291	.395	.686	0	1.000
2003	—Norfolk (Int'l)	OF-DH	32	120	18	43	3	1	3	19	16	23	0	3	5-2	.358	.431	.475	.906	0	1.000
	—New York (N.L.)	OF	107	217	28	50	12	2	2	21	27	34	1	8	3-0	.230	.317	.332	.649	1	.993
2004	—Norfolk (Int'l)	OF-DH	18	65	5	17	6	1	1	6	6	9	4	1	1-2	.262	.333	.431	.764	0	1.000
	—Cleveland (A.L.)	OF	7	11	0	1	0	0	0	0	0	4	0	0	0-0	.091	.091	.091	.182	0	1.000
	—Buffalo (Int'l)	OF-DH	56	232	36	72	13	1	9	40	13	19	0	11	5-5	.310	.346	.491	.837	2	.984
	American League totals (1 year)		7	11	0	1	0	0	0	0	0	4	0	0	0-0	.091	.091	.091	.182	0	1.000
	National League totals (4 years)		161	337	41	80	15	2	5	33	34	61	1	11	7-2	.237	.307	.338	.646	1	.995
	Major League totals (5 years)		168	348	41	81	15	2	5	33	34	65	1	11	7-2	.233	.301	.330	.632	1	.995

GOOD, ANDREW — P

PERSONAL: Born September 19, 1979, in San Diego, Calif. ... 6-1/209. ... Throws right, bats right. ... Full name: Andrew Richard Good. ... High school: Rochester (Rochester Hills, Mich.).

TRANSACTIONS/CAREER NOTES: Selected by Arizona Diamondbacks organization in eighth round of 1998 free-agent draft. ... On disabled list (July 9, 2004-remainder of season); included rehabilitation assignments to Tucson and El Paso.

CAREER HITTING: 2-for-21 (.095), 0 R, 0 2B, 0 3B, 0 HR, 2 RBI.

Year	Team (League)	W	L	Pct.	ERA	WHIP	G	GS	CG	ShO	Hld.	Sv.-Opp.	IP	H	R	ER	HR	BB-IBB	SO	Avg.
1998	—Ariz. D'backs (Ariz.)	1	3	.250	4.28	1.57	9	8	0	0	...	0-...	33.2	46	25	16	1	7-0	25	.324
	—South Bend (Mid.)	0	1	.000	3.00	1.33	2	0	0	0	...	0-...	6.0	7	4	2	0	1-0	6	.280
1999	—South Bend (Mid.)	11	10	.524	4.10	1.31	27	27	0	0	...	0-...	153.2	160	80	70	9	42-0	146	.268
2001	—Lancaster (Calif.)	8	6	.571	4.80	1.33	19	18	0	0	...	0-...	101.1	108	63	54	12	27-0	104	.267
	—El Paso (Texas)	3	3	.400	5.88	1.75	10	9	0	0	...	0-...	56.2	79	44	37	2	20-0	46	.324
2002	—El Paso (Texas)	13	6	.684	3.54	1.10	28	27	2	1	...	0-...	178.0	170	89	70	21	26-0	127	.248
2003	—Arizona (N.L.)	4	2	.667	5.29	1.36	16	10	0	0	1	0-0	66.1	74	42	39	15	16-3	42	.281
	—Tucson (PCL)	4	4	.500	5.00	1.44	11	11	0	0	...	0-...	63.0	78	36	35	12	13-0	45	.300
2004	—Arizona (N.L.)	1	2	.333	5.31	1.38	17	2	0	0	0	0-0	40.2	43	25	24	8	13-0	26	.272
	—El Paso (Texas)	0	0	...	0.93	1.03	4	4	0	0	...	0-...	9.2	7	2	1	0	3-0	9	.212
	—Tucson (PCL)	3	2	.600	3.04	1.23	5	3	0	0	...	0-...	23.2	25	12	8	4	4-0	17	.266
	Major League totals (2 years)	5	4	.556	5.30	1.36	33	12	0	0	1	0-0	107.0	117	67	63	23	29-3	68	.278

GOODWIN, TOM — OF

PERSONAL: Born July 27, 1968, in Fresno, Calif. ... 6-0/195. ... Bats left, throws right. ... Full name: Thomas Jones Goodwin. ... High school: Central (Fresno, Calif.). ... College: Fresno State.

TRANSACTIONS/CAREER NOTES: Selected by Pittsburgh Pirates organization in sixth round of June 1986 free-agent draft; did not sign. ... Selected by Los Angeles Dodgers organization in first round (22nd pick overall) of 1989 free-agent draft. ... Claimed on waivers by Kansas City Royals (January 6, 1994). ... Traded by Royals to Texas Rangers for 3B Dean Palmer (July 25, 1997). ... On disabled list (June 11-27 and June 28-August 6, 1999); included rehabilitation assignment to Charlotte. ... Signed as a free agent by Colorado Rockies (December 9, 1999). ... Traded by Rockies with cash to Dodgers for OFs Todd Hollandsworth and Kevin Gibbs and P Randey Dorame (July 31, 2000). ... On disabled list (July 21-August 9, 2001); included rehabilitation assignment to Wilmington. ... Released by Dodgers (April 8, 2002). ... Signed by San Francisco Giants organization (April 17, 2002). ... Signed as a free agent by Chicago Cubs organization (January 16, 2003). ... On disabled list (July 23-August 19, 2003; and May 24-June 11, 2004).

2004 GAMES PLAYED BY POSITION (MLB): OF—28.

								BATTING										FIELDING	
Year	Team (League)	Pos.	G	AB	R	H	2B	3B	HR	RBI	BB	SO	HBP	GDP	SB-CS	Avg.	OBP	SLG	OPS	E	Avg.
1989	—Great Falls (Pio.)	OF	63	240	55	74	12	3	2	33	28	30	2	3	60-8	.308	.382	.408	.791	1	.986
1990	—Bakersfield (Calif.)	OF	32	134	24	39	6	2	0	13	11	22	0	0	22-4	.291	.345	.366	.710	0	1.000

G

Year	Team (League)	Pos.	G	AB	R	H	2B	3B	HR	RBI	BB	SO	HBP	GDP	SB-CS	Avg.	OBP	SLG	OPS	E	Avg.
	— San Antonio (Texas)	OF	102	428	76	119	15	4	0	28	38	72	1	3	60-11	.278	.336	.332	.668	3	.989
1991—	Albuquerque (PCL)	OF	132	509	84	139	19	4	1	45	59	83	2	5	48-22	.273	.349	.332	.681	3	.990
	— Los Angeles (N.L.)	OF	16	7	3	1	0	0	0	0	0	0	0	0	1-1	.143	.143	.143	.286	0	1.000
1992—	Albuquerque (PCL)	OF	82	319	48	96	10	4	2	28	37	47	1	3	27-10	.301	.372	.376	.748	1	.995
	— Los Angeles (N.L.)	OF	57	73	15	17	1	1	0	3	6	10	0	0	7-3	.233	.291	.274	.565	1	1.000
1993—	Los Angeles (N.L.)	OF	30	17	6	5	1	0	0	1	1	4	0	1	1-2	.294	.333	.353	.686	0	1.000
	— Albuquerque (PCL)	OF	85	289	48	75	5	5	1	28	30	51	2	1	21-5	.260	.329	.322	.651	2	.986
1994—	Kansas City (A.L.)	DH-OF	2	2	0	0	0	0	0	0	0	1	0	0	0-0	.000	.000	.000	.000	0	1.000
	— Omaha (A.A.)	OF	113	429	67	132	17	7	2	34	23	60	4	1	50-20	.308	.346	.394	.740	2	.993
1995—	Kansas City (A.L.)	OF-DH	133	480	72	138	16	3	4	28	38	72	5	7	50-18	.288	.346	.358	.704	3	.990
1996—	Kansas City (A.L.)	OF-DH	143	524	80	148	14	4	1	35	39	79	2	3	66-22	.282	.334	.330	.664	5	.984
1997—	Kansas City (A.L.)	OF	97	367	51	100	13	4	2	22	19	51	2	5	34-10	.272	.311	.346	.657	1	.996
	— Texas (A.L.)	OF	53	207	39	49	13	2	0	17	25	37	1	2	16-6	.237	.319	.319	.638	2	.986
1998—	Texas (A.L.)	OF-DH	154	520	102	151	13	3	2	33	73	90	2	2	38-20	.290	.378	.338	.716	3	.992
1999—	Texas (A.L.)	OF	109	405	63	105	12	6	3	33	40	61	0	7	39-11	.259	.324	.341	.664	3	.989
	— Charlotte (Fla. St.)	OF	3	11	2	4	1	0	0	0	1	4	0	1	0-0	.364	.417	.455	.871	0	1.000
2000—	Colorado (N.L.)	OF	91	317	65	86	8	8	5	47	50	76	1	9	39-7	.271	.368	.394	.763	3	.986
	— Los Angeles (N.L.)	OF	56	211	29	53	3	1	1	11	18	41	0	4	16-3	.251	.310	.289	.599	0	1.000
2001—	Los Angeles (N.L.)	OF	105	286	51	66	8	5	4	22	23	58	0	3	22-8	.231	.286	.336	.622	1	.994
	— Wilmington (S.Atl.)	OF	2	5	2	2	0	1	0	1	1	0	0	0	0-0	.400	.429	.800	1.229	0	1.000
2002—	Fresno (PCL)	OF	17	62	11	14	3	1	0	7	8	8	0	1	3-2	.226	.314	.306	.621	0	1.000
	— San Francisco (N.L.)	OF	78	154	23	40	5	2	1	17	14	25	0	3	16-2	.260	.321	.338	.659	1	.990
2003—	Chicago (N.L.)	OF	87	171	26	49	10	0	1	12	11	33	0	3	19-5	.287	.328	.363	.690	0	1.000
2004—	Chicago (N.L.)	OF	77	105	11	21	8	0	0	3	8	22	0	1	5-0	.200	.254	.276	.531	0	1.000
American League totals (6 years)			691	2505	407	691	81	22	12	168	234	391	12	26	243-87	.276	.339	.340	.679	17	.990
National League totals (8 years)			597	1341	229	338	44	17	12	116	131	269	1	18	126-31	.252	.317	.337	.654	5	.993
Major League totals (14 years)			1288	3846	636	1029	125	39	24	284	365	660	13	44	369-118	.268	.332	.339	.671	22	.991

DIVISION SERIES RECORD

Year	Team (League)	Pos.	G	AB	R	H	2B	3B	HR	RBI	BB	SO	HBP	GDP	SB-CS	Avg.	OBP	SLG	OPS	E	Avg.
1998—	Texas (A.L.)	OF	2	4	0	1	0	0	0	0	0	1	0	0	0-0	.250	.250	.250	.500	0	1.000
1999—	Texas (A.L.)	OF	3	7	0	1	0	0	0	0	0	1	0	0	0-0	.143	.143	.143	.286	0	1.000
2002—	San Francisco (N.L.)		2	2	0	0	0	0	0	0	0	2	0	0	0-0	.000	.000	.000	.000	0	...
2003—	Chicago (N.L.)		2	1	0	1	1	0	0	2	0	0	0	0	0-0	1.000	.500	2.000	2.500	0	...
Division series totals (4 years)			9	14	0	3	1	0	0	2	0	4	0	0	0-0	.214	.200	.286	.486	0	1.000

CHAMPIONSHIP SERIES RECORD

Year	Team (League)	Pos.	G	AB	R	H	2B	3B	HR	RBI	BB	SO	HBP	GDP	SB-CS	Avg.	OBP	SLG	OPS	E	Avg.
2002—	San Francisco (N.L.)	OF	2	3	0	0	0	0	0	0	0	2	0	0	0-0	.000	.000	.000	.000	0	1.000
2003—	Chicago (N.L.)	OF	5	4	1	1	0	1	0	0	0	3	0	0	0-0	.250	.250	.750	1.000	0	...
Champ. series totals (2 years)			7	7	1	1	0	1	0	0	0	5	0	0	0-0	.143	.143	.429	.571	0	1.000

WORLD SERIES RECORD

Year	Team (League)	Pos.	G	AB	R	H	2B	3B	HR	RBI	BB	SO	HBP	GDP	SB-CS	Avg.	OBP	SLG	OPS	E	Avg.
2002—	San Francisco (N.L.)	DH-OF	5	4	0	0	0	0	0	0	0	2	0	0	1-0	.000	.200	.000	.200	0	1.000

GORDON, TOM   P

PERSONAL: Born November 18, 1967, in Sebring, Fla. ... 5-10/190. ... Throws right, bats right. ... Full name: Thomas Gordon. ... High school: Avon Park (Fla.).

TRANSACTIONS/CAREER NOTES: Selected by Kansas City Royals organization in sixth round of June 1986 free-agent draft. ... On disabled list (August 12-September 1, 1992; and May 8-24, 1995). ... Signed as a free agent by Boston Red Sox (December 21, 1995). ... On disabled list (April 18-May 10 and June 12-September 27, 1999); included rehabilitation assignments to Trenton and Augusta. ... On disabled list (April 2, 2000-entire season). ... Signed as a free agent by Chicago Cubs (December 14, 2000). ... On disabled list (March 23-May 1, 2001); included rehabilitation assignments to Daytona and Iowa. ... On disabled list (March 28-July 2, 2002); included rehabilitation assignments to Daytona and Iowa. ... Traded by Cubs to Houston Astros for P Russ Rohlicek and two players to be named (August 22, 2002); Cubs acquired Ps Travis Anderson and Mike Nannini to complete deal (September 11, 2002). ... Signed as a free agent by Chicago White Sox (January 20, 2003). ... Signed as a free agent by New York Yankees (December 16, 2003).

HONORS: Named A.L. Rookie Pitcher of the Year by THE SPORTING NEWS (1989).

CAREER HITTING: 0-for-2 (.000), 0 R, 0 2B, 0 3B, 0 HR, 0 RBI.

Year	Team (League)	W	L	Pct.	ERA	WHIP	G	GS	CG	ShO	Hld.	Sv.-Opp.	IP	H	R	ER	HR	BB-IBB	SO	Avg.
1986—	GC Royals (GCL)	3	1	.750	1.02	1.23	9	7	2	1	...	0-...	44.0	31	12	5	0	23-1	47	.194
	— Omaha (Am. Assoc.)	0	0	...	47.25	6.00	1	0	0	0	...	0-...	1.1	6	7	7	0	2-0	3	.600
1987—	Eugene (N'west)	9	0	1.000	2.86	1.31	15	13	0	0	...	1-...	72.1	48	33	23	2	47-0	91	.183
	— Fort Myers (Fla. St.)	1	0	1.000	2.63	1.61	3	3	0	0	...	0-...	13.2	5	4	4	0	17-0	11	.122
1988—	Appleton (Midw.)	7	5	.583	2.06	0.95	17	17	5	1	...	0-...	118.0	69	30	27	3	43-1	172	.163
	— Memphis (Sou.)	6	0	1.000	0.38	0.70	6	6	2	2	...	0-...	47.1	16	3	2	1	17-0	62	.103
	— Omaha (Am. Assoc.)	3	0	1.000	1.33	1.28	3	3	0	0	...	0-...	20.1	11	3	3	0	15-0	29	.157
	— Kansas City (A.L.)	0	2	.000	5.17	1.47	5	2	0	0	2	0-0	15.2	16	9	9	1	7-0	18	.267
1989—	Kansas City (A.L.)	17	9	.654	3.64	1.28	49	16	1	1	3	1-7	163.0	122	67	66	10	86-4	153	.210
1990—	Kansas City (A.L.)	12	11	.522	3.73	1.49	32	32	6	1	0	0-0	195.1	192	99	81	17	99-1	175	.258
1991—	Kansas City (A.L.)	9	14	.391	3.87	1.37	45	14	1	0	4	1-4	158.0	129	76	68	16	87-6	167	.221
1992—	Kansas City (A.L.)	6	10	.375	4.59	1.45	40	11	0	0	0	0-2	117.2	116	67	60	9	55-4	98	.258
1993—	Kansas City (A.L.)	12	6	.667	3.58	1.30	48	14	2	0	1	1-6	155.2	125	65	62	11	77-5	143	.223
1994—	Kansas City (A.L.)	11	7	.611	4.35	1.44	24	24	0	0	0	0-0	155.1	136	79	75	15	87-3	126	.237
1995—	Kansas City (A.L.)	12	12	.500	4.43	1.55	31	31	2	0	0	0-0	189.0	204	110	93	12	89-4	119	.279
1996—	Boston (A.L.)	12	9	.571	5.59	1.64	34	34	4	1	0	0-0	215.2	249	143 *	134	28	105-5	171	.284
1997—	Boston (A.L.)	6	10	.375	3.74	1.28	42	25	2	1	0	11-13	182.2	155	85	76	10	78-1	159	.226
1998—	Boston (A.L.)	7	4	.636	2.72	1.01	73	0	0	0	0	* 46-47	79.1	55	24	24	2	25-1	78	.191
1999—	Boston (A.L.)	0	2	.000	5.60	1.64	21	0	0	0	1	11-13	17.2	17	11	11	2	12-2	24	.246
2000—	Boston (A.L.)			Did not play.																
2001—	Daytona (Fla. St.)	0	0	...	0.00	0.00	2	2	0	0	...	0-...	2.0	0	0	0	0	0-0	3	.000
	— Iowa (PCL)	0	0	...	0.00	1.00	2	2	0	0	...	0-...	2.0	1	0	0	0	1-0	2	.167
	— Chicago (N.L.)	1	2	.333	3.38	1.06	47	0	0	0	...	27-31	45.1	32	18	17	4	16-1	67	.188
2002—	Daytona (Fla. St.)	0	0	...	3.38	1.13	2	2	0	0	...	0-...	2.2	1	1	1	0	2-0	3	.100
	— Iowa (PCL)	0	0	...	16.20	2.40	2	0	0	0	...	1-...	1.2	1	4	3	0	3-0	0	.167

G

Year	Team (League)	W	L	Pct.	ERA	WHIP	G	GS	CG	ShO	Hld.	Sv.-Opp.	IP	H	R	ER	HR	BB-IBB	SO	Avg.
	—Chicago (N.L.)	1	1	.500	3.42	1.56	19	0	0	0	2	0-0	23.2	27	12	9	1	10-1	31	.293
	— Houston (N.L.)	0	2	.000	3.32	1.11	15	0	0	0	4	0-0	19.0	15	7	7	2	6-2	17	.217
2003—	Chicago (A.L.)	7	6	.538	3.16	1.19	66	0	0	0	7	12-17	74.0	57	29	26	4	31-3	91	.213
2004—	New York (A.L.)	9	4	.692	2.21	0.88	80	0	0	0	36	4-10	89.2	56	23	22	5	23-5	96	.180
	American League totals (14 years)	120	106	.531	4.02	1.38	590	203	18	4	55	87-119	1808.2	1629	887	807	142	861-44	1618	.240
	National League totals (2 years)	2	5	.286	3.38	1.20	81	0	0	0	6	27-31	88.0	74	37	33	7	32-4	115	.224
	Major League totals (16 years)	122	111	.524	3.99	1.37	671	203	18	4	61	114-150	1896.2	1703	924	840	149	893-48	1733	.239

DIVISION SERIES RECORD

Year	Team (League)	W	L	Pct.	ERA	WHIP	G	GS	CG	ShO	Hld.	Sv.-Opp.	IP	H	R	ER	HR	BB-IBB	SO	Avg.
1998—	Boston (A.L.)	0	1	.000	9.00	2.67	2	0	0	0	0	0-1	3.0	4	3	3	0	4-0	1	.333
1999—	Boston (A.L.)	0	0	...	4.50	1.00	2	0	0	0	0	0-0	2.0	1	1	1	1	1-0	3	.143
2004—	New York (A.L.)	0	0	...	4.91	0.55	3	0	0	0	1	0-0	3.2	2	2	2	0	0-0	3	.143
	Division series totals (3 years)	0	1	.000	6.23	1.38	7	0	0	0	1	0-1	8.2	7	6	6	1	5-0	7	.212

CHAMPIONSHIP SERIES RECORD

Year	Team (League)	W	L	Pct.	ERA	WHIP	G	GS	CG	ShO	Hld.	Sv.-Opp.	IP	H	R	ER	HR	BB-IBB	SO	Avg.
1999—	Boston (A.L.)	0	0	...	13.50	2.00	3	0	0	0	0	0-0	2.0	3	3	3	2	1-0	3	.333
2004—	New York (A.L.)	0	0	...	8.10	1.80	6	0	0	0	3	0-0	6.2	10	6	6	2	2-0	3	.357
	Champ. series totals (2 years)	0	0	...	9.35	1.85	9	0	0	0	3	0-0	8.2	13	9	9	4	3-0	6	.351

ALL-STAR GAME RECORD

		W	L	Pct.	ERA	WHIP	G	GS	CG	ShO	Hld.	Sv.-Opp.	IP	H	R	ER	HR	BB-IBB	SO	Avg.
	All-Star Game totals (2 years)	0	0	...	13.50	3.00	2	0	0	0	0	0-0	1.1	3	2	2	0	1-0	5	.500

GOSLING, MIKE   P

PERSONAL: Born September 23, 1980, in Madison, Wis. ... 6-0/210. ... Throws left, bats left. ... Full name: Michael F. Gosling. ... High school: East (Salt Lake City). ... College: Stanford.

TRANSACTIONS/CAREER NOTES: Selected by Minnesota Twins organization in 14th round of 1998 free-agent draft; did not sign. ... Selected by Arizona Diamondbacks organization in second round of 2001 free-agent draft.

CAREER HITTING: 0-for-6 (.000), 0 R, 0 2B, 0 3B, 0 HR, 0 RBI.

Year	Team (League)	W	L	Pct.	ERA	WHIP	G	GS	CG	ShO	Hld.	Sv.-Opp.	IP	H	R	ER	HR	BB-IBB	SO	Avg.
2002—	El Paso (Texas)	14	5	.737	3.13	1.27	27	27	2	2	...	0-...	166.2	149	66	58	7	62-4	115	.238
2003—	Tucson (PCL)	9	12	.429	5.61	1.80	26	26	0	0	...	0-...	136.1	190	106	85	13	56-0	89	.330
2004—	Tucson (PCL)	9	5	.643	5.82	1.66	24	21	0	0	...	0-...	128.1	160	101	83	16	53-0	67	.305
	— Arizona (N.L.)	1	1	.500	4.62	1.54	6	4	0	0	0	0-0	25.1	26	13	13	5	13-1	14	.274
	Major League totals (1 year)	1	1	.500	4.62	1.54	6	4	0	0	0	0-0	25.1	26	13	13	5	13-1	14	.274

GOTAY, RUBEN   2B

PERSONAL: Born December 25, 1982, in Rio Piedras, Puerto Rico. ... 5-11/160. ... Bats both, throws right. ... Full name: Ruben A. Gotay. ... High school: Dr. Santiago Veue Calzada (Fajardo, P.R.). ... Junior college: Indian Hills (Iowa) Community College.

TRANSACTIONS/CAREER NOTES: Selected by Kansas City Royals organization in 31st round of 2000 free-agent draft.

2004 GAMES PLAYED BY POSITION (MLB): 2B—42.

Year	Team (League)	Pos.	G	AB	R	H	2B	3B	HR	RBI	BB	SO	HBP	GDP	SB-CS	Avg.	OBP	SLG	OPS	E	Avg.
												BATTING								**FIELDING**	
2001—	GC Royals (GCL)	2B-3B	52	184	29	58	15	1	3	19	26	22	0	2	5-6	.315	.398	.457	.855	13	.937
2002—	Burlington (Midw.)	2B-3B	133	509	87	145	42	9	9	83	73	110	8	5	5-4	.285	.377	.456	.833	17	.974
2003—	Wilmington (Caro.)	2B	134	502	68	131	31	2	9	72	60	97	7	7	8-1	.261	.343	.384	.727	16	.973
2004—	Wichita (Texas)	2B-DH	106	405	71	117	22	6	9	68	51	60	6	9	9-10	.289	.373	.440	.806	15	.971
	— Kansas City (A.L.)	2B	44	152	17	41	7	3	1	16	9	36	2	4	0-1	.270	.315	.375	.690	3	.983
	Major League totals (1 year)		44	152	17	41	7	3	1	16	9	36	2	4	0-1	.270	.315	.375	.690	3	.983

GRABOW, JOHN   P

PERSONAL: Born November 4, 1978, in Arcadia, Calif. ... 6-2/210. ... Throws left, bats left. ... Full name: John William Grabow. ... High school: San Gabriel (Calif.).

TRANSACTIONS/CAREER NOTES: Selected by Pittsburgh Pirates organization in third round of 1997 free-agent draft.

CAREER HITTING: 0-for-1 (.000), 0 R, 0 2B, 0 3B, 0 HR, 0 RBI.

Year	Team (League)	W	L	Pct.	ERA	WHIP	G	GS	CG	ShO	Hld.	Sv.-Opp.	IP	H	R	ER	HR	BB-IBB	SO	Avg.
1997—	GC Pirates (GCL)	2	7	.222	4.57	1.57	11	8	0	0	...	0-...	45.1	57	32	23	0	14-0	28	.305
1998—	Augusta (S. Atl.)	6	3	.667	5.78	1.65	17	16	0	0	...	0-...	71.2	84	59	46	7	34-0	67	.294
1999—	Hickory (S. Atl.)	9	10	.474	3.80	1.18	26	26	0	0	...	0-...	156.1	152	82	66	16	32-0	164	.249
2000—	Altoona (East.)	8	7	.533	4.33	1.44	24	24	1	0	...	0-...	145.1	145	81	70	10	65-0	109	.259
2001—	GC Pirates (GCL)	0	1	.000	3.75	1.25	6	6	0	0	...	0-...	12.0	11	6	5	1	4-0	9	.244
	— Lynchburg (Carolina)	1	3	.250	6.38	1.85	7	7	0	0	...	0-...	36.2	42	30	26	3	26-0	35	.294
	— Altoona (East.)	2	5	.286	3.38	1.36	10	10	0	0	...	0-...	50.2	30	23	19	1	39-0	42	.175
2002—	Altoona (East.)	8	13	.381	5.47	1.56	28	27	1	1	...	0-...	146.1	181	94	89	10	47-0	95	.308
2003—	Altoona (East.)	6	1	.857	3.36	1.28	24	9	0	0	...	1-...	83.0	87	34	31	9	19-2	73	.281
	— Nashville (PCL)	0	2	.000	4.74	1.54	17	0	0	0	...	0-...	24.2	31	17	13	0	7-2	26	.298
	— Pittsburgh (N.L.)	0	0	...	3.60	1.20	5	0	0	0	0	0-0	5.0	6	3	2	0	0-0	9	.273
2004—	Pittsburgh (N.L.)	2	5	.286	5.11	1.77	68	0	0	0	11	1-7	61.2	81	39	35	8	28-7	64	.323
	Major League totals (2 years)	2	5	.286	5.00	1.73	73	0	0	0	11	1-7	66.2	87	42	37	8	28-7	73	.319

GRABOWSKI, JASON   OF

PERSONAL: Born May 24, 1976, in New Haven, Conn. ... 6-3/200. ... Bats left, throws right. ... Full name: Jason William Grabowski. ... High school: The Morgan School (Clinton, Conn.). ... College: Connecticut.

TRANSACTIONS/CAREER NOTES: Selected by New York Yankees organization in 17th round of 1994 free-agent draft; did not sign. ... Selected by Texas Rangers organization in second round of 1997 free-agent draft. ... Claimed on waivers by Seattle Mariners (December 18, 2000). ... Selected by Oakland Athletics from Mariners organization in Rule 5 major league draft (December 13, 2001). ... Traded by Athletics to Los Angeles Dodgers for cash (March 29, 2004).

2004 GAMES PLAYED BY POSITION (MLB): OF—31, DH—3, 1B—3.

G

Year	Team (League)	Pos.	G	AB	R	H	2B	3B	HR	RBI	BB	SO	HBP	GDP	SB-CS	Avg.	OBP	SLG	OPS	E	Avg.
1997— Pulaski (Appalachian)	C	50	174	36	51	14	0	4	24	40	32	0	2	6-1	.293	.423	.443	.866	8	.982
1998— Savannah (S. Atl.)	C-1B	104	352	63	95	13	6	14	52	57	93	1	7	16-9	.270	.372	.460	.832	6	.990
1999— Charlotte (Fla. St.)	3B-1B	123	434	68	136	31	6	12	87	65	66	5	8	13-10	.313	.407	.495	.903	27	.917
—Tulsa (Texas)	DH	2	6	1	1	0	0	0	0	2	2	0	0	0-0	.167	.375	.167	.542	...	...
2000— Tulsa (Texas)	3B	135	493	93	135	33	5	19	90	88	106	4	12	8-7	.274	.383	.477	.860	40	.898
2001— Tacoma (PCL)	3-OF-1-S	114	394	60	117	32	3	9	58	61	94	2	8	7-4	.297	.390	.462	.852	21	.942
2002— Sacramento (PCL)	OF-C-3-1	73	265	50	78	22	3	12	52	39	56	1	8	6-4	.294	.387	.536	.923	8	.962
—Oakland (A.L.)	OF	4	8	3	3	1	1	0	1	3	1	0	0	0-0	.375	.545	.750	1.295	0	1.000
2003— Ariz. A's (Ariz.)	DH	2	6	1	2	1	0	0	1	3	0	0	0	0-0	.333	.556	.500	1.056	0	.000
—Sacramento (PCL)	O-DH-C-1-3	67	250	44	73	13	2	9	40	31	46	0	6	7-2	.292	.364	.468	.832	5	.969
—Oakland (A.L.)	OF-3B-DH	8	8	0	0	0	0	0	0	1	5	0	0	0-0	.000	.111	.000	.111	0	1.000
2004— Los Angeles (N.L.)	OF-DH-1B	113	173	18	38	7	0	7	20	19	50	0	4	0-0	.220	.297	.382	.678	1	.978
American League totals (2 years)		12	16	3	3	1	1	0	1	4	6	0	0	0-0	.188	.350	.375	.725	0	1.000
National League totals (1 year)		113	173	18	38	7	0	7	20	19	50	0	4	0-0	.220	.297	.382	.678	1	.978
Major League totals (3 years)		125	189	21	41	8	1	7	21	23	56	0	4	0-0	.217	.302	.381	.683	1	.982

DIVISION SERIES RECORD

Year	Team (League)	Pos.	G	AB	R	H	2B	3B	HR	RBI	BB	SO	HBP	GDP	SB-CS	Avg.	OBP	SLG	OPS	E	Avg.
2004— Los Angeles (N.L.)		3	2	0	0	0	0	0	0	1	0	0	0	0-0	.000	.333	.000	.333	0	...

GRACESQUI, FRANKLYN — P

PERSONAL: Born August 20, 1979, in Santo Domingo, Dominican Republic. ... 6-5/210. ... Throws left, bats both. ... Full name: Franklyn Benjamin Gracesqui. ... High school: George Washington (Bronx, N.Y.).

TRANSACTIONS/CAREER NOTES: Selected by Toronto Blue Jays organization in 21st round of 1998 free-agent draft. ... Selected by Florida Marlins organization from Blue Jays organization in Rule 5 minor league draft (December 16, 2002).

CAREER HITTING: 0-for-0 (.000), 0 R, 0 2B, 0 3B, 0 HR, 0 RBI.

Year	Team (League)	W	L	Pct.	ERA	WHIP	G	GS	CG	ShO	Hld.	Sv.-Opp.	IP	H	R	ER	HR	BB-IBB	SO	Avg.
1998— St. Catharines (NY-Penn.)	1	1	1.000	6.61	1.71	11	0	0	0	...	0-...	16.1	16	12	12	2	12-0	19	.242
1999— St. Catharines (NY-Penn.)	2	3	.400	5.05	1.83	15	10	0	0	...	1-...	46.1	44	30	26	4	41-0	45	.253
2000— Medicine Hat (Pio.)	0	1	.000	2.63	1.50	8	4	0	0	...	0-...	24.0	15	11	7	1	21-0	20	.185
—Hagerstown (S. Atl.)	0	1	.000	4.91	1.77	3	1	0	0	...	0-...	7.1	4	4	4	1	9-0	6	.174
2001— Char., W.Va. (SAL)	2	8	.200	3.17	1.44	35	2	0	0	...	0-...	65.1	60	40	23	1	34-0	66	.245
—Dunedin (Fla. St.)	1	0	1.000	1.76	1.76	4	0	0	0	...	0-...	5.2	2	0	0	0	8-0	6	.125
2002— Tennessee (Sou.)	4	2	.667	4.64	1.73	41	0	0	0	...	0-...	42.2	40	26	22	3	34-0	48	.258
—Dunedin (Fla. St.)	2	1	.667	2.49	1.20	10	0	0	0	...	1-...	21.2	15	8	6	1	11-0	25	.192
2003— Carolina (Southern)	3	3	.500	2.48	1.50	44	0	0	0	...	5-...	58.0	44	19	16	0	43-1	75	.211
2004— GC Marlins (GCL)	0	1	.000	0.00	1.88	2	2	0	0	...	0-...	2.2	1	1	0	0	4-0	4	.111
—Florida (N.L.)	0	1	.000	11.25	2.25	7	0	0	0	...	1-1	4.0	6	5	5	0	3-0	1	.333
—Albuquerque (PCL)	1	0	1.000	3.27	1.32	19	0	0	0	...	0-...	22.0	10	9	8	2	19-0	16	.139
Major League totals (1 year)	0	1	.000	11.25	2.25	7	0	0	0	...	1-1	4.0	6	5	5	0	3-0	1	.333

GRAFFANINO, TONY — 2B

PERSONAL: Born June 6, 1972, in Amityville, N.Y. ... 6-1/190. ... Bats right, throws right. ... Full name: Anthony Joseph Graffanino. ... Name pronounced: graf-a-NEEN-oh. ... High school: East Islip (Islip Terrace, N.Y.).

TRANSACTIONS/CAREER NOTES: Selected by Atlanta Braves organization in 10th round of 1990 free-agent draft. ... Released by Braves (April 2, 1999). ... Signed by Tampa Bay Devil Rays organization (April 9, 1999). ... Traded by Devil Rays to Chicago White Sox for P Tanyon Sturtze (May 31, 2000). ... On disabled list (August 26-September 30, 2002). ... Signed as a free agent by Kansas City Royals (December 16, 2003). ... On disabled list (May 1-28 and August 1, 2004-remainder of season); included rehabilitation assignment to Omaha.

2004 GAMES PLAYED BY POSITION (MLB): 2B—75.

Year	Team (League)	Pos.	G	AB	R	H	2B	3B	HR	RBI	BB	SO	HBP	GDP	SB-CS	Avg.	OBP	SLG	OPS	E	Avg.
1990— Pulaski (Appalachian)	SS	42	131	23	27	5	1	0	11	26	17	2	3	6-3	.206	.344	.260	.603	24	.873
1991— Idaho Falls (Pio.)	SS	66	274	53	95	16	4	4	56	27	37	3	2	19-4	.347	.408	.478	.887	29	.912
1992— Macon (S. Atl.)	2B	112	400	50	96	15	5	10	31	50	84	8	6	9-6	.240	.333	.378	.711	17	.961
1993— Durham (Caro.)	2B	123	459	78	126	30	5	15	69	45	78	4	10	24-11	.275	.342	.460	.801	15	.968
1994— Greenville (Sou.)	2B-DH	140	440	66	132	28	3	7	52	50	53	2	8	29-7	.300	.372	.425	.797	14	.976
1995— Richmond (Int'l)	2B	50	179	20	34	6	0	4	17	15	49	1	4	2-2	.190	.254	.291	.544	4	.983
1996— Richmond (Int'l)	2B	96	353	57	100	29	2	7	33	34	72	3	3	11-7	.283	.350	.436	.787	10	.977
—Atlanta (N.L.)	2B	22	46	7	8	1	1	0	2	4	13	1	0	0-0	.174	.250	.239	.489	2	.969
1997— Atlanta (N.L.)	2-3-S-1	104	186	33	48	9	1	8	20	26	46	1	3	6-4	.258	.344	.446	.790	5	.982
1998— Atlanta (N.L.)	2B-SS-3B	105	289	32	61	14	1	5	24	24	68	2	7	1-4	.211	.275	.318	.594	11	.971
1999— Durham (Int'l)	2B-DH-3B	87	345	66	108	25	6	9	58	37	46	3	9	16-9	.313	.379	.499	.878	1	.998
—Tampa Bay (A.L.)	2-S-3-DH	39	130	20	41	9	4	2	19	9	22	1	1	3-2	.315	.364	.492	.857	5	.977
2000— Tampa Bay (A.L.)	2B-3B-SS	13	20	8	6	1	0	0	1	1	2	1	1	0-0	.300	.364	.350	.714	0	1.000
—Durham (Int'l)	SS-2-3-1	10	35	9	10	3	0	2	6	7	8	0	0	2-0	.286	.405	.543	.948	0	1.000
—Chicago (A.L.)	S-2-3-DH	57	148	25	40	5	1	2	16	21	25	1	1	7-4	.270	.363	.358	.721	6	.968
2001— Chicago (A.L.)	3-2-S-DH-0-1	74	145	23	44	9	0	2	15	16	29	1	4	4-1	.303	.370	.407	.777	7	.957
2002— Chicago (A.L.)	3B-2B-SS	70	229	35	60	12	4	6	31	22	38	2	2	2-1	.262	.329	.428	.757	10	.953
2003— Chicago (A.L.)	S-2-3-DH-1	90	250	51	65	15	3	7	23	24	37	3	1	8-0	.260	.331	.428	.759	8	.972
2004— Omaha (PCL)	2B-DH	4	14	2	3	0	0	1	2	3	5	0	0	0-0	.214	.353	.429	.782	0	1.000
—Kansas City (A.L.)	2B	75	278	37	73	11	0	3	26	27	38	3	5	10-2	.263	.332	.335	.667	5	.988
American League totals (6 years)		418	1200	199	329	62	12	22	131	120	191	12	15	34-10	.274	.344	.401	.745	41	.972
National League totals (3 years)		231	521	72	117	24	3	13	44	54	127	4	10	7-8	.225	.299	.357	.656	18	.975
Major League totals (9 years)		649	1721	271	446	86	15	35	175	174	318	16	25	41-18	.259	.330	.388	.718	59	.973

DIVISION SERIES RECORD

Year	Team (League)	Pos.	G	AB	R	H	2B	3B	HR	RBI	BB	SO	HBP	GDP	SB-CS	Avg.	OBP	SLG	OPS	E	Avg.
1997— Atlanta (N.L.)	2B	3	3	0	0	0	0	0	0	2	1	0	0	0-0	.000	.400	.000	.400	0	1.000
1998— Atlanta (N.L.)		1	0	0	0	0	0	0	0	0	0	0	0	0-0	...	...	...	...	0	...
2000— Chicago (A.L.)	3B	1	0	0	0	0	0	0	0	0	0	0	0	0-0	...	...	...	...	0	1.000
Division series totals (3 years)		5	3	0	0	0	0	0	0	2	1	0	0	0-0	.000	.400	.000	.400	0	1.000

G

Year Team (League)	Pos.	G	AB	R	H	2B	3B	HR	RBI	BB	SO	HBP	GDP	SB-CS	Avg.	OBP	SLG	OPS	E	Avg.
1997— Atlanta (N.L.)	2B	3	8	1	2	1	0	0	0	0	3	0	1	0-0	.250	.250	.375	.625	0	1.000
1998— Atlanta (N.L.)	2B	4	3	2	1	1	0	0	2	1	0	0	0	0-0	.333	.600	.667	1.267	0	1.000
Champ. series totals (2 years)		7	11	3	3	2	0	0	2	4	0	1	0-0	.273	.385	.455	.839	0	1.000

GRAMAN, ALEX — P

PERSONAL: Born November 17, 1977, in Huntingburg, Ind. ... 6-4/210. ... Throws left, bats left. ... Full name: Alex Joseph Graman. ... High school: Southridge (Huntingburg, Ind.). ... College: Indiana State.
TRANSACTIONS/CAREER NOTES: Selected by New York Yankees organization in third round of 1999 free-agent draft.
CAREER HITTING: 0-for-0 (.000), 0 R, 0 2B, 0 3B, 0 HR, 0 RBI.

Year Team (League)	W	L	Pct.	ERA	WHIP	G	GS	CG	ShO	Hld.	Sv.-Opp.	IP	H	R	ER	HR	BB-IBB	SO	Avg.
1999— Staten Island (NY-P)	6	3	.667	2.99	1.11	14	14	0	0	...	0-...	81.1	74	30	27	7	16-0	85	.244
2000— Tampa (FSL)	8	9	.471	3.65	1.24	28	28	3	1	...	0-...	143.0	120	64	58	6	58-1	111	.226
— Norwich (East.)	0	1	.000	11.81	1.88	1	1	0	0	...	0-...	5.1	6	7	7	3	4-0	3	.300
2001— Norwich (East.)	12	9	.571	3.52	1.41	28	28	1	0	...	0-...	166.1	174	83	65	10	60-0	138	.267
2002— Norwich (East.)	5	2	.714	2.88	1.18	8	8	2	1	...	0-...	50.0	46	19	16	2	13-0	31	.242
— Columbus (Int'l)	6	9	.400	4.65	1.44	20	20	1	0	...	0-...	124.0	141	74	64	11	37-3	98	.284
2003— Columbus (Int'l)	9	10	.474	4.48	1.39	26	26	0	0	...	0-...	142.2	135	77	71	14	63-0	110	.250
2004— New York (A.L.)	0	0	...	19.80	3.20	3	2	0	0	0	0-0	5.0	14	11	11	1	2-0	4	.500
— Columbus (Int'l)	11	6	.647	3.37	1.28	24	22	1	1	...	0-...	131.0	115	56	49	12	53-0	129	.235
Major League totals (1 year)	0	0	...	19.80	3.20	3	2	0	0	0	0-0	5.0	14	11	11	1	2-0	4	.500

GRANDERSON, CURTIS — OF

PERSONAL: Born March 16, 1981, in Blue Island, Ill. ... 6-1/185. ... Bats left, throws right. ... College: Illinois-Chicago.
TRANSACTIONS/CAREER NOTES: Selected by Detroit Tigers organization in third round of 2002 free-agent draft.
2004 GAMES PLAYED BY POSITION (MLB): OF—8.

Year Team (League)	Pos.	G	AB	R	H	2B	3B	HR	RBI	BB	SO	HBP	GDP	SB-CS	Avg.	OBP	SLG	OPS	E	Avg.
2002— Oneonta (N.Y.-Penn.)	OF	52	212	45	73	15	4	3	34	20	35	7	1	9-2	.344	.417	.495	.912	1	.989
2003— Lakeland (Fla. St.)	OF	127	476	71	136	29	10	11	51	49	91	12	5	10-7	.286	.365	.458	.823	5	.984
2004— Erie (East.)	OF	123	462	89	139	19	8	21	94	80	95	4	2	14-8	.301	.405	.513	.918	3	.991
— Detroit (A.L.)	OF	9	25	2	6	1	1	0	0	3	8	0	1	0-0	.240	.321	.360	.681	0	1.000
Major League totals (1 year)		9	25	2	6	1	1	0	0	3	8	0	1	0-0	.240	.321	.360	.681	0	1.000

GRAVES, DANNY — P

PERSONAL: Born August 7, 1973, in Saigon, Vietnam. ... 6-0/185. ... Throws right, bats right. ... Full name: Daniel Peter Graves. ... High school: Brandon (Fla.). ... College: Miami (Fla.).
TRANSACTIONS/CAREER NOTES: Selected by Cleveland Indians organization in fourth round of 1994 free-agent draft. ... Traded by Indians with Ps Jim Crowell and Scott Winchester and IF Damian Jackson to Cincinnati Reds for P John Smiley and IF Jeff Branson (July 31, 1997). ... On disabled list (August 19-September 3, 2004).
CAREER HITTING: 8-for-76 (.105), 5 R, 0 2B, 0 3B, 2 HR, 3 RBI.

Year Team (League)	W	L	Pct.	ERA	WHIP	G	GS	CG	ShO	Hld.	Sv.-Opp.	IP	H	R	ER	HR	BB-IBB	SO	Avg.
1995— Kinston (Caro.)	3	1	.750	0.82	0.95	38	0	0	0	...	21-...	44.0	30	11	4	0	12-2	46	.183
— Cant./Akr. (Eastern)	1	0	1.000	0.00	0.51	17	0	0	0	...	10-...	23.1	10	1	0	0	2-0	11	.133
— Buffalo (A.A.)	0	0	...	3.00	2.00	3	0	0	0	...	0-...	3.0	5	4	1	0	1-0	2	.333
1996— Buffalo (A.A.)	4	3	.571	1.48	1.03	43	0	0	0	...	19-...	79.0	57	14	13	1	24-2	46	.208
— Cleveland (A.L.)	2	0	1.000	4.55	1.31	15	0	0	0	0	0-1	29.2	29	18	15	2	10-0	22	.246
1997— Buffalo (A.A.)	2	3	.400	4.19	1.30	19	3	0	0	...	2-...	43.0	45	21	20	3	11-0	21	.276
— Cleveland (A.L.)	0	0	...	4.76	2.12	5	0	0	0	0	0-0	11.1	15	8	6	2	9-0	4	.326
— Indianapolis (A.A.)	1	0	1.000	3.09	1.03	11	0	0	0	...	5-...	11.2	7	4	4	1	5-0	5	.184
— Cincinnati (N.L.)	0	0	...	6.14	2.52	10	0	0	0	1	0-...	14.2	26	14	10	0	11-1	7	.413
1998— Indianapolis (Int'l)	1	0	1.000	1.93	1.29	13	0	0	0	...	0-...	14.0	15	3	3	0	3-0	11	.273
— Cincinnati (N.L.)	2	1	.667	3.32	1.28	62	0	0	0	6	8-8	81.1	76	31	30	6	28-4	44	.252
1999— Cincinnati (N.L.)	8	7	.533	3.08	1.25	75	0	0	0	0	27-36	111.0	90	42	38	10	49-4	69	.227
2000— Cincinnati (N.L.)	10	5	.667	2.56	1.35	66	0	0	0	0	30-35	91.1	81	31	26	8	42-7	53	.243
2001— Cincinnati (N.L.)	6	5	.545	4.15	1.26	66	0	0	0	0	32-39	80.1	83	41	37	7	18-6	49	.268
2002— Cincinnati (N.L.)	7	3	.700	3.19	1.26	68	0	0	0	0	32-39	98.2	99	37	35	7	25-9	58	.264
2003— Cincinnati (N.L.)	4	15	.211	5.33	1.45	30	26	2	1	0	2-2	169.0	204	108	100	30	41-6	60	.298
2004— Cincinnati (N.L.)	1	6	.143	3.95	1.32	68	0	0	1	0	41-50	68.1	77	39	30	12	13-6	40	.282
American League totals (2 years)	2	0	1.000	4.61	1.54	20	0	0	0	0	0-1	41.0	44	26	21	4	19-0	26	.268
National League totals (8 years)	38	42	.475	3.85	1.35	445	30	2	1	7	172-209	714.2	736	343	306	80	227-43	380	.269
Major League totals (9 years)	40	42	.488	3.89	1.36	465	30	2	1	7	172-210	755.2	780	369	327	84	246-43	406	.269

	W	L	Pct.	ERA	WHIP	G	GS	CG	ShO	Hld.	Sv.-Opp.	IP	H	R	ER	HR	BB-IBB	SO	Avg.
All-Star Game totals (1 year)	0	0	...	0.00	1.00	1	0	0	0	0	0-0	1.0	1	0	0	0	0-0	1	.250

ALL-STAR GAME RECORD

GREEN, ANDY — 3B/2B

PERSONAL: Born July 7, 1977, in Lexington, Ky. ... 5-9/180. ... Bats right, throws right. ... Full name: Andrew M. Green. ... High school: Lexington (Ky.) Christian Academy. ... College: Kentucky.
TRANSACTIONS/CAREER NOTES: Selected by Arizona Diamondbacks organization in 24th round of 2000 free-agent draft.
2004 GAMES PLAYED BY POSITION (MLB): 3B—18, 2B—14, OF—9.

Year Team (League)	Pos.	G	AB	R	H	2B	3B	HR	RBI	BB	SO	HBP	GDP	SB-CS	Avg.	OBP	SLG	OPS	E	Avg.
2000— South Bend (Mid.)	2B	3	9	1	0	0	0	0	0	0	1	2	0	0-0	.000	.182	.000	.182	0	1.000
— Missoula (Pio.)	2B-3B	23	83	10	19	2	1	0	16	12	9	2	1	8-3	.229	.324	.277	.601	5	.949
2001— South Bend (Mid.)	2B	128	477	76	143	18	6	5	59	59	50	1	7	51-15	.300	.379	.394	.773	16	.973
2002— Tucson (PCL)	2B	27	99	13	22	8	0	1	13	9	17	1	2	2-1	.222	.294	.333	.627	2	.980

G

Year	Team (League)	Pos.	G	AB	R	H	2B	3B	HR	RBI	BB	SO	HBP	GDP	SB-CS	Avg.	OBP	SLG	OPS	E	Avg.
	— Lancaster (Calif.)	2B	102	401	74	124	36	4	6	50	60	59	5	7	15-10	.309	.401	.464	.865	10	.979
2003	— El Paso (Texas)	2-S-O-3	126	490	70	148	38	2	2	51	38	51	13	6	17-9	.302	.366	.400	.766	21	.962
2004	— Tucson (PCL) 3-2-S-O-DH		77	309	56	101	31	3	9	45	34	45	3	3	10-4	.327	.394	.534	.923	11	.961
	— Arizona (N.L.)	3B-2B-OF	46	109	13	22	2	1	1	4	5	17	1	2	1-1	.202	.241	.266	.507	5	.946
	Major League totals (1 year)		46	109	13	22	2	1	1	4	5	17	1	2	1-1	.202	.241	.266	.507	5	.946

GREEN, NICK 2B

PERSONAL: Born September 10, 1978, in Pensacola, Fla. ... 6-0/178. ... Bats right, throws right. ... Full name: Nicholas Anthony Green. ... High school: Duluth (Ga.). ... Junior college: Georgia Perimeter.

TRANSACTIONS/CAREER NOTES: Selected by Atlanta Braves organization in 32nd round of 1998 free-agent draft. ... On disabled list (March 22-April 24, 2002).

2004 GAMES PLAYED BY POSITION (MLB): 2B—75, 3B—5, OF—1.

Year	Team (League)	Pos.	G	AB	R	H	2B	3B	HR	RBI	BB	SO	HBP	GDP	SB-CS	Avg.	OBP	SLG	OPS	E	Avg.
												BATTING								**FIELDING**	
1999	— Jamestown (N.Y.-Penn.) ...	2B	73	273	52	81	15	0	11	41	26	66	4	4	14-4	.297	.363	.473	.835	15	.955
	— Macon (S. Atl.)	2B	3	10	1	2	0	0	1	3	0	4	0	0	1-0	.200	.200	.500	.700	0	1.000
2000	— Macon (S. Atl.)	SS-2B	91	339	47	83	19	4	11	43	22	75	5	4	10-4	.245	.296	.422	.718	37	.911
	— Myrtle Beach (Caro.)	SS-2B	27	91	13	22	6	0	1	6	10	23	3	0	3-2	.242	.337	.341	.677	9	.890
2001	— Richmond (Int'l)	2B	2	5	0	1	0	0	0	1	0	3	0	0	0-0	.200	.200	.200	.400	1	.833
	— Myrtle Beach (Caro.)	2B-SS	80	297	49	79	18	1	10	42	32	70	7	2	9-2	.266	.348	.434	.782	13	.958
2002	— Greenville (Sou.)	2B-SS	94	355	49	85	16	2	15	50	36	92	8	4	2-5	.239	.321	.423	.743	14	.962
2003	— Richmond (Int'l)	2B-SS	124	399	40	99	26	1	11	51	26	79	7	7	7-5	.248	.303	.401	.704	20	.961
2004	— Richmond (Int'l)	2B-3B	22	77	8	29	4	1	0	11	6	9	4	2	0-3	.377	.443	.455	.871	3	.969
	— Atlanta (N.L.)	2B-3B-OF	95	264	40	72	15	3	3	26	12	63	4	0	1-2	.273	.312	.386	.698	8	.977
	Major League totals (1 year)		95	264	40	72	15	3	3	26	12	63	4	0	1-2	.273	.312	.386	.698	8	.977

DIVISION SERIES RECORD

Year	Team (League)	Pos.	G	AB	R	H	2B	3B	HR	RBI	BB	SO	HBP	GDP	SB-CS	Avg.	OBP	SLG	OPS	E	Avg.
2004	— Atlanta (N.L.)		2	0	0	0	0	0	0	0	0	0	0	0	0-0	...	...	...	...	0	...

GREEN, SHAWN 1B/OF

PERSONAL: Born November 10, 1972, in Des Plaines, Ill. ... 6-4/200. ... Bats left, throws left. ... Full name: Shawn David Green. ... High school: Tustin (Calif.).

TRANSACTIONS/CAREER NOTES: Selected by Toronto Blue Jays organization in first round (16th pick overall) of 1991 free-agent draft; pick received as compensation for San Francisco Giants signing Type A free-agent P Bud Black. ... Traded by Blue Jays with 2B Jorge Nunez to Los Angeles Dodgers for OF Raul Mondesi and P Pedro Borbon (November 8, 1999).

RECORDS: Shares major league single-game records for most home runs, game (4, May 23, 2002); and most runs scored, game (6, May 23, 2002).

HONORS: Won A.L. Gold Glove as outfielder (1999).

2004 GAMES PLAYED BY POSITION (MLB): 1B—111, OF—52, DH—3.

Year	Team (League)	Pos.	G	AB	R	H	2B	3B	HR	RBI	BB	SO	HBP	GDP	SB-CS	Avg.	OBP	SLG	OPS	E	Avg.
												BATTING								**FIELDING**	
1992	— Dunedin (Fla. St.)	OF	114	417	44	114	21	3	1	49	28	66	4	9	22-9	.273	.319	.345	.665	5	.974
1993	— Knoxville (Southern)	OF	99	360	40	102	14	2	4	34	26	72	5	6	4-9	.283	.339	.367	.706	8	.956
	— Toronto (A.L.)	OF-DH	3	6	0	0	0	0	0	0	0	1	0	0	0-0	.000	.000	.000	.000	0	1.000
1994	— Syracuse (Int'l)	OF-DH	109	433	82	149	27	3	13	61	40	54	4	5	19-7	.344	.401	.510	.912	1	.996
	— Toronto (A.L.)	OF	14	33	1	3	1	0	0	1	1	8	0	1	1-0	.091	.118	.121	.239	0	1.000
1995	— Toronto (A.L.)	OF	121	379	52	109	31	4	15	54	20	68	3	4	1-2	.288	.326	.509	.835	6	.973
1996	— Toronto (A.L.)	OF-DH	132	422	52	118	32	3	11	45	33	75	8	9	5-1	.280	.342	.448	.790	2	.992
1997	— Toronto (A.L.)	OF-DH	135	429	57	123	22	4	16	53	36	99	1	4	14-3	.287	.340	.469	.809	3	.984
1998	— Toronto (A.L.)	OF	158	630	106	175	33	4	35	100	50	142	5	6	35-12	.278	.334	.510	.844	7	.979
1999	— Toronto (A.L.)	OF	153	614	134	190	*45	0	42	123	66	117	11	13	20-7	.309	.384	.588	.972	1	.997
2000	— Los Angeles (N.L.)	OF	•162	610	98	164	44	4	24	99	90	121	8	18	24-5	.269	.367	.472	.839	6	.980
2001	— Los Angeles (N.L.)	OF-1B	161	619	121	184	31	4	49	125	72	107	5	10	20-4	.297	.372	.598	.970	6	.982
2002	— Los Angeles (N.L.)	OF-DH	158	582	110	166	31	1	42	114	93	112	5	26	8-5	.285	.385	.558	.944	2	.994
2003	— Los Angeles (N.L.)	OF-DH	160	611	84	171	49	2	19	85	68	112	6	16	6-2	.280	.355	.460	.814	5	.982
2004	— Los Angeles (N.L.) 1B-OF-DH		157	590	92	157	28	1	28	86	71	114	8	17	5-2	.266	.352	.459	.811	7	.993
	American League totals (7 years)		716	2513	402	718	164	15	119	376	206	510	28	37	76-25	.286	.344	.505	.849	19	.986
	National League totals (5 years)		798	3012	505	842	183	12	162	509	394	566	32	89	63-18	.280	.366	.510	.876	26	.989
	Major League totals (12 years)		1514	5525	907	1560	347	27	281	885	600	1076	60	126	139-43	.282	.357	.508	.864	45	.988

DIVISION SERIES RECORD

Year	Team (League)	Pos.	G	AB	R	H	2B	3B	HR	RBI	BB	SO	HBP	GDP	SB-CS	Avg.	OBP	SLG	OPS	E	Avg.
2004	— Los Angeles (N.L.)	1B	4	16	3	4	0	0	3	3	0	3	0	0	0-0	.250	.250	.813	1.063	0	1.000

ALL-STAR GAME RECORD

		G	AB	R	H	2B	3B	HR	RBI	BB	SO	HBP	GDP	SB-CS	Avg.	OBP	SLG	OPS	E	Avg.
All-Star Game totals (2 years)		2	4	0	2	0	0	0	0	0	1	0	0	1-0	.500	.500	.500	1.000	0	1.000

G

GREENE, KHALIL SS

PERSONAL: Born October 21, 1979, in Butler, Pa. ... 5-11/210. ... Bats right, throws right. ... Full name: Khalil Thabit Greene. ... High school: Key West (Fla.). ... College: Clemson.

TRANSACTIONS/CAREER NOTES: Selected by Chicago Cubs organization in 14th round of 2001 free-agent draft; did not sign. ... Selected by San Diego Padres organization in first round (13th pick overall) of 2002 free-agent draft.

2004 GAMES PLAYED BY POSITION (MLB): SS—136.

Year	Team (League)	Pos.	G	AB	R	H	2B	3B	HR	RBI	BB	SO	HBP	GDP	SB-CS	Avg.	OBP	SLG	OPS	E	Avg.
												BATTING								**FIELDING**	
2002	— Eugene (Northwest)	SS	10	37	5	10	1	0	0	6	5	6	3	1	0-0	.270	.368	.297	.697	3	.900
	— Lake Elsinore (Calif.) SS-2B-3B		46	183	33	58	9	1	9	32	12	33	4	7	0-0	.317	.368	.525	.893	9	.947
2003	— Mobile (Sou.)	SS-DH	59	229	20	63	17	2	3	20	16	55	2	7	2-3	.275	.327	.406	.733	9	.949
	— Portland (PCL)	SS	76	319	42	92	19	0	10	47	20	52	11	3	5-4	.288	.346	.442	.788	11	.967
	— San Diego (N.L.)	SS	20	65	8	14	4	1	2	6	4	19	1	3	0-1	.215	.271	.400	.671	3	.963
2004	— San Diego (N.L.)	SS	139	484	67	132	31	4	15	65	53	94	8	9	4-2	.273	.349	.446	.795	20	.965
	Major League totals (2 years)		159	549	75	146	35	5	17	71	57	113	9	12	4-3	.266	.340	.441	.781	23	.965

GREENE, TODD   C

PERSONAL: Born May 8, 1971, in Augusta, Ga. ... 5-10/208. ... Bats right, throws right. ... Full name: Todd Anthony Greene. ... High school: Evans (Ga.). ... College: Georgia Southern.

TRANSACTIONS/CAREER NOTES: Selected by Atlanta Braves organization in 27th round of 1989 free-agent draft; did not sign. ... Selected by California Angels organization in 12th round of 1993 free-agent draft. ... Angels franchise renamed Anaheim Angels for 1997 season. ... On disabled list (August 20, 1997-remainder of season). ... On disabled list (March 19-August 5, 1998); included rehabilitation assignments to Lake Elsinore and Vancouver. ... On suspended list (May 13-16, 1999). ... Released by Angels (March 29, 2000). ... Signed by Toronto Blue Jays organization (April 10, 2000). ... On disabled list (June 7-23, 2000); included rehabilitation assignment to Dunedin. ... Released by Blue Jays (March 28, 2001). ... Signed by New York Yankees organization (April 5, 2001). ... Released by Yankees (March 26, 2002). ... Signed by Los Angeles Dodgers organization (April 2, 2002). ... Released by Dodgers (May 15, 2002). ... Signed by Texas Rangers (May 16, 2002). ... On disabled list (April 30-May 15, 2003); included rehabilitation assignment to Frisco (May 12-15). ... Signed as a free agent by Colorado Rockies organization (December 22, 2003). ... On disabled list (August 8-September 1, 2004); included rehabilitation assignment to Colorado Springs.

2004 GAMES PLAYED BY POSITION (MLB): C—53.

										BATTING									FIELDING	
Year Team (League)	Pos.	G	AB	R	H	2B	3B	HR	RBI	BB	SO	HBP	GDP	SB-CS	Avg.	OBP	SLG	OPS	E	Avg.
1993—Boise (N'west)	OF	76	305	55	82	15	3	15	71	34	44	9	3	4-3	.269	.356	.485	.841	3	.979
1994—Lake Elsinore (Calif.)	C-1B-OF	133	524	98	158	39	2	35	124	64	96	4	12	10-3	.302	.378	.584	.962	15	.979
1995—Midland (Texas)	C-DH	82	318	59	104	19	1	26	57	17	55	5	6	3-5	.327	.365	.638	1.004	3	.992
— Vancouver (PCL)	C-DH	43	168	28	42	3	1	14	35	11	36	4	3	1-0	.250	.308	.530	.838	1	.995
1996—Vancouver (PCL)	C-DH	60	223	27	68	18	0	5	33	16	36	1	6	0-2	.305	.347	.453	.800	3	.988
— California (A.L.)	C-DH	29	79	9	15	1	0	2	9	4	11	1	4	2-0	.190	.238	.278	.517	0	1.000
1997—Anaheim (A.L.)	C-DH	34	124	24	36	6	0	9	24	7	25	0	1	2-0	.290	.328	.556	.885	0	1.000
— Vancouver (PCL)	C-DH-1-OF	64	260	51	92	22	0	25	75	20	31	5	6	5-1	.354	.408	.727	1.135	3	.992
1998—Lake Elsinore (Calif.)	DH-1B	12	44	9	10	2	0	1	6	4	7	0	1	1-0	.227	.286	.341	.627	2	.833
— Vancouver (PCL)	DH-1-C-OF	30	108	16	30	12	0	7	20	12	17	3	2	1-0	.278	.360	.583	.943	1	.990
— Anaheim (A.L.)	OF-DH-1B	29	71	3	18	4	0	1	7	2	20	0		0-0	.254	.274	.352	.626	0	1.000
1999—Anaheim (A.L.)	DH-OF-C	97	321	36	78	20	0	14	42	12	63	3	8	1-4	.243	.275	.436	.711	2	.980
— Edmonton (PCL)	DH-OF	19	74	10	18	6	0	5	14	0	12	1	4	0-0	.243	.253	.527	.780	0	1.000
2000—Syracuse (Int'l)	OF-C	24	91	14	27	3	0	7	14	6	16	0	3	1-0	.297	.337	.560	.897	1	.970
— Toronto (A.L.)	DH-C-OF	34	85	11	20	2	0	5	10	5	18	0	4	0-0	.235	.278	.435	.713	0	1.000
— Dunedin (Fla. St.)	OF	5	20	2	4	1	0	1	4	2	4	1	0	0-0	.200	.304		.704	0	1.000
2001—Columbus (Int'l)	C-OF	34	131	16	33	8	0	6	17	4	19	1	3	3-2	.252	.279	.450	.730	4	.982
— New York (A.L.)	C-DH	35	96	9	20	4	0	1	11	3	21	1	3	0-0	.208	.240	.281	.521	0	1.000
2002—Las Vegas (PCL)	C-1B-OF	32	125	27	44	12	0	11	41	3	21	3	...	0-0	.352	.373	.712	1.085	2	.989
— Texas (A.L.)	C-1-DH-OF	42	112	15	30	5	0	10	19	2	23	1	4	0-0	.268	.282	.580	.862	3	.985
— Oklahoma (PCL)	C-OF-1B	39	152	21	46	9	0	6	29	9	27	1	...	2-0	.303	.339	.480	.820	2	.991
2003—Frisco (Texas)	C-1B	3	9	3	3	0	0	2	4	2	2	0	1	0-0	.333	.455	1.000	1.455	0	1.000
— Texas (A.L.)	C-DH-1B	62	205	25	47	10	1	10	20	2	47	2	2	0-0	.229	.243	.434	.677	4	.988
2004—Colo. Springs (PCL)	C-1B	4	12	2	4	1	0	1	4	1	3	0	0	0-0	.333	.385	.667	1.051	0	1.000
— Colorado (N.L.)	C	75	195	23	55	14	0	10	35	13	38	0	9	0-0	.282	.325	.508	.833	3	.989
American League totals (8 years)		362	1093	132	264	52	1	52	142	37	228	8	26	5-4	.242	.270	.434	.704	9	.992
National League totals (1 year)		75	195	23	55	14	0	10	35	13	38	0	9	0-0	.282	.325	.508	.833	3	.989
Major League totals (9 years)		437	1288	155	319	66	1	62	177	50	266	8	35	5-4	.248	.279	.445	.724	12	.992

DIVISION SERIES RECORD

Year Team (League)	Pos.	G	AB	R	H	2B	3B	HR	RBI	BB	SO	HBP	GDP	SB-CS	Avg.	OBP	SLG	OPS	E	Avg.
2001— New York (A.L.)		Did not play.																		

CHAMPIONSHIP SERIES RECORD

Year Team (League)	Pos.	G	AB	R	H	2B	3B	HR	RBI	BB	SO	HBP	GDP	SB-CS	Avg.	OBP	SLG	OPS	E	Avg.
2001— New York (A.L.)	C	1	1	0	0	0	0	0	0	0	0	0	0	0-0	.000	.000	.000	.000	0	1.000

WORLD SERIES RECORD

Year Team (League)	Pos.	G	AB	R	H	2B	3B	HR	RBI	BB	SO	HBP	GDP	SB-CS	Avg.	OBP	SLG	OPS	E	Avg.
2001— New York (A.L.)	C	1	2	1	1	1	0	0	0	0	0	0	1	0-0	.500	.500	1.000	1.500	0	1.000

GREGG, KEVIN   P

PERSONAL: Born June 20, 1978, in Corvallis, Ore. ... 6-6/220. ... Throws right, bats right. ... Full name: Kevin Marschall Gregg. ... High school: Corvallis (Ore.).

TRANSACTIONS/CAREER NOTES: Selected by Oakland Athletics organization in 15th round of 1996 free-agent draft. ... Signed as a free agent by Anaheim Angels organization (November 19, 2002).

CAREER HITTING: 0-for-0 (.000), 0 R, 0 2B, 0 3B, 0 HR, 0 RBI.

Year Team (League)	W	L	Pct.	ERA	WHIP	G	GS	CG	ShO	Hld.	Sv.-Opp.	IP	H	R	ER	HR	BB-IBB	SO	Avg.
1996—Ariz. A's (Ariz.)	3	3	.500	3.10	1.25	11	9	0	0	...	0-...	40.2	30	14	14	1	21-0	48	.208
1997—Visalia (Calif.)	6	8	.429	5.70	1.65	25	24	0	0	...	0-...	115.1	116	81	73	8	74-0	136	.258
1998—Modesto (Calif.)	8	7	.533	3.81	1.49	30	24	0	0	...	1-...	144.0	139	72	61	7	76-2	141	.254
1999—Visalia (Calif.)	4	4	.500	3.80	1.30	13	11	1	1	...	1-...	64.0	60	34	27	3	23-0	48	.249
— Midland (Texas)	4	7	.364	3.74	1.16	16	16	2	0	...	0-...	91.1	75	45	38	7	31-1	66	.221
— Vancouver (PCL)	1	0	1.000	3.60	1.60	1	1	0	0	...	0-...	5.0	6	2	2	0	2-0	4	.316
2000—Midland (Texas)	5	14	.263	6.40	1.73	28	27	0	0	...	0-...	140.2	171	120	100	18	73-0	97	.304
2001—Midland (Texas)	5	5	.500	4.54	1.57	44	1	0	0	...	1-...	81.1	88	48	41	5	40-4	72	.274
2002—Midland (Texas)	3	3	.500	4.30	1.30	11	4	0	0	...	0-...	37.2	31	20	18	3	18-0	45	.221
— Visalia (Calif.)	2	1	.667	2.08	0.98	3	3	0	0	...	0-...	17.1	8	5	4	0	9-0	11	.140
— Sacramento (PCL)	2	5	.286	7.52	1.79	16	8	0	0	...	0-...	58.2	82	56	49	7	23-0	45	.332
2003—Arkansas (Texas)	4	3	.571	3.53	1.19	15	11	2	0	...	0-...	66.1	60	29	26	2	19-0	60	.241
— Salt Lake (PCL)	7	4	.636	4.03	1.18	15	15	0	0	...	0-...	91.2	90	47	41	10	18-0	75	.256
— Anaheim (A.L.)	2	0	1.000	3.28	1.05	5	3	0	0	0	0-0	24.2	18	9	9	3	8-0	14	.205
2004—Anaheim (A.L.)	5	2	.714	4.21	1.30	55	0	0	0	3	1-2	87.2	86	43	41	6	28-3	84	.255
Major League totals (2 years)	7	2	.778	4.01	1.25	60	3	0	0	3	1-2	112.1	104	52	50	9	36-3	98	.245

DIVISION SERIES RECORD

Year Team (League)	W	L	Pct.	ERA	WHIP	G	GS	CG	ShO	Hld.	Sv.-Opp.	IP	H	R	ER	HR	BB-IBB	SO	Avg.
2004—Anaheim (A.L.)	0	0	...	0.00	2.00	1	0	0	0	0	0-0	2.0	3	0	0	0	1-0		.333

G

GREINKE, ZACK P

PERSONAL: Born October 21, 1983, in Orlando, Fla. ... 6-2/200. ... Throws right, bats right. ... Full name: Donald Zackary Greinke. ... High school: Apopka (Fla.).
TRANSACTIONS/CAREER NOTES: Selected by Kansas City Royals organization in first round (sixth pick overall) of 2002 free-agent draft.
HONORS: Named Minor League Player of the Year by THE SPORTING NEWS (2003).
CAREER HITTING: 0-for-2 (.000), 0 R, 0 2B, 0 3B, 0 HR, 0 RBI.

Year Team (League)	W	L	Pct.	ERA	WHIP	G	GS	CG	ShO	Hld.	Sv.-Opp.	IP	H	R	ER	HR	BB-IBB	SO	Avg.
2002— GC Royals (GCL)	0	0	...	1.93	1.29	3	3	0	0	...	0-...	4.2	3	1	1	0	3-0	4	.200
— Spokane (N'west)	0	0	...	7.71	1.93	2	2	0	0	...	0-...	4.2	9	4	4	0	0-0	5	.391
— Wilmington (Caro.)	0	0	...	0.00	0.50	1	0	0	0	...	0-...	2.0	1	0	0	0	0-0	0	.167
2003— Wilmington (Caro.)	11	1	.917	1.14	0.79	14	14	3	1	...	0-...	87.0	56	16	11	5	13-0	78	.178
— Wichita (Texas)	4	3	.571	3.23	1.19	9	9	0	0	...	0-...	53.0	58	20	19	5	5-2	34	.286
2004— Omaha (PCL)	1	1	.500	2.51	1.08	6	6	0	0	...	0-...	28.2	25	8	8	2	6-0	23	.225
— Kansas City (A.L.)	8	11	.421	3.97	1.17	24	24	0	0	0	0-0	145.0	143	64	64	26	26-3	100	.256
Major League totals (1 year)	**8**	**11**	**.421**	**3.97**	**1.17**	**24**	**24**	**0**	**0**	**0**	**0-0**	**145.0**	**143**	**64**	**64**	**26**	**26-3**	**100**	**.256**

GREISINGER, SETH P

PERSONAL: Born July 29, 1975, in Kansas City, Kan. ... 6-3/195. ... Throws right, bats right. ... Full name: Seth Adam Greisinger. ... Name pronounced: gri-sing-er. ... High school: McLean (Va.). ... College: Virginia.
TRANSACTIONS/CAREER NOTES: Selected by Cleveland Indians organization in seventh round of 1993 free-agent draft; did not sign. ... Selected by Detroit Tigers organization in first round (sixth pick overall) of 1996 free-agent draft. ... On disabled list (March 26, 1999-entire season); included rehabilitation assignments to Lakeland and Toledo. ... On disabled list (March 13, 2000-entire season; and March 30, 2001-entire sesaon). ... Refused minor league assignment and became a free agent (October 7, 2002). ... Re-signed by Tigers organization (December 19, 2002). ... Signed as a free agent by Minnesota Twins organization (November 22, 2003).
CAREER HITTING: 1-for-4 (.250), 0 R, 0 2B, 0 3B, 0 HR, 1 RBI.

Year Team (League)	W	L	Pct.	ERA	WHIP	G	GS	CG	ShO	Hld.	Sv.-Opp.	IP	H	R	ER	HR	BB-IBB	SO	Avg.
1997— Jacksonville (Southern)	10	6	.625	5.20	1.55	28	28	1	0	...	0-...	159.1	194	103	92	29	53-0	105	.301
1998— Toledo (International)	3	4	.429	2.91	1.23	10	10	0	0	...	0-...	58.2	50	21	19	5	22-0	37	.229
— Detroit (A.L.)	6	9	.400	5.12	1.46	21	21	0	0	0	0-0	130.0	142	79	74	17	48-2	66	.282
1999— Lakeland (Fla. St.)	0	0	...	3.86	0.64	1	1	0	0	...	0-...	4.2	2	2	2	1	1-0	2	.125
— Toledo (International)	0	1	.000	5.87	1.57	2	2	0	0	...	0-...	7.2	9	5	5	0	3-0	4	.300
2000— Detroit (A.L.)				Did not play.															
2001— Detroit (A.L.)				Did not play.															
2002— Erie (East.)	2	0	1.000	1.29	1.00	4	4	0	0	...	0-...	21.0	12	4	3	1	9-0	21	.160
— Detroit (A.L.)	2	2	.500	6.21	1.57	8	8	0	0	0	0-0	37.2	46	26	26	4	13-2	14	.303
— Toledo (International)	1	1	.500	4.11	1.43	3	3	0	0	...	0-...	15.1	15	8	7	0	7-0	11	.278
2003— Toledo (International)	6	9	.400	3.97	1.30	25	21	2	1	...	0-...	136.0	154	77	60	16	23-3	80	.285
2004— Minnesota (A.L.)	2	5	.286	6.18	1.63	12	9	0	0	0	0-0	51.0	68	40	35	12	15-1	36	.319
— Rochester (Int'l)	5	5	.500	4.96	1.52	13	13	0	0	...	0-...	74.1	94	44	41	10	19-0	44	.319
Major League totals (3 years)	**10**	**16**	**.385**	**5.56**	**1.52**	**41**	**38**	**0**	**0**	**0**	**0-0**	**218.2**	**256**	**145**	**135**	**33**	**76-5**	**116**	**.295**

GRIEVE, BEN OF

PERSONAL: Born May 4, 1976, in Arlington, Texas. ... 6-4/216. ... Bats left, throws right. ... Full name: Benjamin Grieve. ... Name pronounced: greev. ... High school: James W. Martin (Arlington, Texas). ... Son of Tom Grieve, outfielder with four major league teams (1970-79).
TRANSACTIONS/CAREER NOTES: Selected by Oakland Athletics organization in first round (second pick overall) of 1994 free-agent draft. ... Traded by Athletics with cash to Tampa Bay Devil Rays as part of three-team deal in which Kansas City Royals acquired P Roberto Hernandez from Devil Rays, Athletics acquired P Cory Lidle from Devil Rays, Athletics acquired OF Johnny Damon, IF Mark Ellis and cash from Royals and Royals acquired C A.J. Hinch, IF Angel Berroa and cash from Athletics (January 8, 2001). ... On disabled list (April 18-May 22 and July 18, 2003-remainder of season). ... Signed as a free agent by Milwaukee Brewers (December 23, 2003). ... Traded by Brewers to Chicago Cubs for a player to be named and cash (August 31, 2004); Brewers acquired P Andy Pratt to complete deal (September 2, 2004).
HONORS: Named Minor League Player of the Year by THE SPORTING NEWS (1997). ... Named A.L. Rookie Player of the Year by THE SPORTING NEWS (1998). ... Named A.L. Rookie of the Year by Baseball Writers' Association of America (1998).
2004 GAMES PLAYED BY POSITION (MLB): OF—69, DH—1.

Year Team (League)	Pos.	G	AB	R	H	2B	3B	HR	RBI	BB	SO	HBP	GDP	SB-CS	Avg.	OBP	SLG	OPS	E	Avg.
1994— S. Oregon (N'west)	OF	72	252	44	83	13	0	7	50	51	48	10	6	2-2	.329	.456	.464	.920	6	.959
1995— W. Mich. (Mid.)	OF	102	371	53	97	16	1	4	62	60	75	8	10	11-3	.261	.371	.342	.713	8	.942
— Modesto (California)	OF	28	107	17	28	5	0	2	14	14	15	0	3	2-0	.262	.341	.364	.706	2	.951
1996— Modesto (California)	OF-DH	72	281	61	100	20	1	11	51	38	52	1	5	8-7	.356	.430	.552	.982	5	.956
— Huntsville (Sou.)	OF-DH	63	232	34	55	8	1	8	32	35	53	2	3	0-3	.237	.338	.384	.722	4	.953
1997— Huntsville (Sou.)	OF-DH	100	372	100	122	29	2	24	108	81	75	9	8	5-1	.328	.455	.610	1.065	8	.961
— Edmonton (PCL)	OF	27	108	27	46	11	1	7	28	12	16	1	4	0-1	.426	.484	.741	1.224	2	.964
— Oakland (A.L.)	OF	24	93	12	29	6	0	3	24	13	25	1	1	0-0	.312	.402	.473	.875	0	1.000
1998— Oakland (A.L.)	OF-DH	155	583	94	168	41	2	18	89	85	123	9	18	2-2	.288	.386	.458	.844	2	.993
1999— Oakland (A.L.)	OF-DH	148	486	80	129	21	0	28	86	63	108	8	17	4-0	.265	.358	.481	.840	3	.988
2000— Oakland (A.L.)	OF-DH	158	594	92	166	40	1	27	104	73	130	3	32	3-0	.279	.359	.487	.845	3	.988
2001— Tampa Bay (A.L.)	OF-DH	154	542	72	143	30	2	11	72	87	159	8	13	7-1	.264	.372	.387	.760	4	.984
2002— Tampa Bay (A.L.)	OF-DH	136	482	62	121	30	0	19	64	69	121	8	15	8-2	.251	.353	.432	.784	4	.988
2003— Tampa Bay (A.L.)	DH-OF	55	165	28	38	7	0	4	17	32	41	6	3	0-0	.230	.371	.345	.716	1	.947
2004— Milwaukee (N.L.)	OF-DH	108	234	28	61	15	0	7	29	39	65	0	4	0-0	.261	.364	.415	.778	4	.964
— Chicago (N.L.)	OF	15	16	2	4	2	0	1	6	0	5	2	0	0-0	.250	.316	.563	.878	0	1.000
American League totals (7 years)		**830**	**2945**	**440**	**794**	**175**	**5**	**110**	**456**	**422**	**707**	**43**	**99**	**24-5**	**.270**	**.368**	**.444**	**.812**	**16**	**.988**
National League totals (1 year)		**123**	**250**	**30**	**65**	**17**	**0**	**8**	**35**	**39**	**70**	**2**	**4**	**0-0**	**.260**	**.361**	**.424**	**.785**	**4**	**.965**
Major League totals (8 years)		**953**	**3195**	**470**	**859**	**192**	**5**	**118**	**491**	**461**	**777**	**45**	**103**	**24-5**	**.269**	**.367**	**.443**	**.810**	**20**	**.986**

DIVISION SERIES RECORD

Year Team (League)	Pos.	G	AB	R	H	2B	3B	HR	RBI	BB	SO	HBP	GDP	SB-CS	Avg.	OBP	SLG	OPS	E	Avg.
2000— Oakland (A.L.)	OF	5	17	1	2	0	0	0	2	3	7	0	2	0-0	.118	.250	.118	.368	0	1.000

ALL-STAR GAME RECORD

		G	AB	R	H	2B	3B	HR	RBI	BB	SO	HBP	GDP	SB-CS	Avg.	OBP	SLG	OPS	E	Avg.
All-Star Game totals (1 year)		1	0	0	0	0	0	0	0	1	0	0	0	0-0	...	1.000	...	1.000	...	...

G

GRIFFEY JR., KEN — OF

PERSONAL: Born November 21, 1969, in Donora, Pa. ... 6-3/205. ... Bats left, throws left. ... Full name: George Kenneth Griffey Jr.. ... High school: Moeller (Cincinnati). ... Son of Ken Griffey, special consultant to general manager, Cincinnati Reds, and outfielder with four major league teams (1973-91).

TRANSACTIONS/CAREER NOTES: Selected by Seattle Mariners organization in first round (first pick overall) of 1987 free-agent draft. ... On disabled list (July 24-August 20, 1989; June 9-25, 1992; and June 20-July 13, 1996). ... On disabled list (May 27-August 15, 1995); included rehabilitation assignment to Tacoma. ... Traded by Mariners to Cincinnati Reds for Ps Brett Tomko and Jake Meyer, OF Mike Cameron and IF Antonio Perez (February 10, 2000). ... On disabled list (April 29-June 15, 2001; and April 7-May 24 and June 24-July 22, 2002). ... On disabled list (April 6-May 13 and July 18, 2003-remainder of season). ... On disabled list (July 11-August 3 and August 12, 2004-remainder of season).

HONORS: Named Major League Player of the Year by THE SPORTING NEWS (1997). ... Named A.L. Most Valuable Player by Baseball Writers' Association of America (1997). ... Won A.L. Gold Glove as outfielder (1990-99).

2004 GAMES PLAYED BY POSITION (MLB): OF—77, DH—1.

Year Team (League)	Pos.	G	AB	R	H	2B	3B	HR	RBI	BB	SO	HBP	GDP	SB-CS	Avg.	OBP	SLG	OPS	E	Avg.
																		BATTING		FIELDING
1987— Bellingham (N'west)	OF	54	182	43	57	9	1	14	40	44	42	0	2	13-6	.313	.445	.604	1.049	1	.992
1988— San Bern. (Calif.)	OF	58	219	50	74	13	3	11	42	34	39	2	3	32-9	.338	.431	.575	1.007	2	.987
— Vermont (East.)	OF	17	61	10	17	5	1	2	10	5	12	2	3	4-2	.279	.353	.492	.845	1	.977
1989— Seattle (A.L.)	DH-OF	127	455	61	120	23	0	16	61	44	83	2	4	16-7	.264	.329	.420	.748	• 10	.969
1990— Seattle (A.L.)	OF	155	597	91	179	28	7	22	80	63	81	2	12	16-11	.300	.366	.481	.847	7	.980
1991— Seattle (A.L.)	DH-OF	154	548	76	179	42	1	22	100	71	82	1	10	18-6	.327	.399	.527	.926	4	.989
1992— Seattle (A.L.)	OF-DH	142	565	83	174	39	4	27	103	44	67	5	15	10-5	.308	.361	.535	.896	1	.997
1993— Seattle (A.L.)	OF-DH-1B	156	582	113	180	38	3	45	109	96	91	6	14	17-9	.309	.408	.617	1.025	3	.991
1994— Seattle (A.L.)	OF-DH	111	433	94	140	24	4	* 40	90	56	73	2	9	11-3	.323	.402	.674	1.076	4	.983
1995— Seattle (A.L.)	OF-DH	72	260	52	67	7	0	17	42	52	53	1	4	4-2	.258	.379	.481	.860	2	.990
— Tacoma (PCL)	DH	1	3	0	0	0	0	0	0	0	1	0	0	0-0	.000	.000	.000	.000	...	...
1996— Seattle (A.L.)	OF-DH	140	545	125	165	26	2	49	140	78	104	7	7	16-1	.303	.392	.628	1.020	4	.990
1997— Seattle (A.L.)	OF-DH	157	608	* 125	185	34	3	* 56	* 147	76	121	8	12	15-4	.304	.382	* .646	1.028	6	.985
1998— Seattle (A.L.)	OF-DH-1B	161	633	120	180	33	3	* 56	146	76	121	7	14	20-5	.284	.365	.611	.977	5	.988
1999— Seattle (A.L.)	OF-DH	160	606	123	173	26	3	* 48	134	91	108	7	8	24-7	.285	.384	.576	.960	9	.978
2000— Cincinnati (N.L.)	OF	145	520	100	141	22	3	40	118	94	117	9	7	6-4	.271	.387	.556	.942	5	.987
2001— Cincinnati (N.L.)	OF-DH	111	364	57	104	20	2	22	65	44	72	4	8	2-0	.286	.365	.533	.898	3	.985
2002— Cincinnati (N.L.)	OF	70	197	17	52	8	0	8	23	28	39	3	6	1-2	.264	.358	.426	.784	3	.971
2003— Cincinnati (N.L.)	OF-DH	53	166	34	41	12	1	13	26	27	44	6	3	1-0	.247	.370	.566	.936	1	.989
2004— Cincinnati (N.L.)	OF-DH	83	300	49	76	18	0	20	60	44	67	2	8	1-0	.253	.351	.513	.864	1	.994
American League totals (11 years)		1535	5832	1063	1742	320	30	398	1152	747	984	47	109	167-60	.299	.380	.569	.948	55	.986
National League totals (5 years)		462	1547	257	414	80	6	103	292	237	339	24	32	11-6	.268	.369	.527	.896	13	.986
Major League totals (16 years)		1997	7379	1320	2156	400	36	501	1444	984	1323	71	141	178-66	.292	.377	.560	.937	68	.986

DIVISION SERIES RECORD

Year Team (League)	Pos.	G	AB	R	H	2B	3B	HR	RBI	BB	SO	HBP	GDP	SB-CS	Avg.	OBP	SLG	OPS	E	Avg.
1995— Seattle (A.L.)	OF	5	23	9	9	0	0	5	7	2	4	1	0	1-0	.391	.444	1.043	1.488	0	1.000
1997— Seattle (A.L.)	OF	4	15	0	2	0	0	0	2	1	3	0	0	2-0	.133	.188	.133	.321	0	1.000
Division series totals (2 years)		9	38	9	11	0	0	5	9	3	7	1	0	3-0	.289	.349	.684	1.033	0	1.000

CHAMPIONSHIP SERIES RECORD

Year Team (League)	Pos.	G	AB	R	H	2B	3B	HR	RBI	BB	SO	HBP	GDP	SB-CS	Avg.	OBP	SLG	OPS	E	Avg.
1995— Seattle (A.L.)	OF	6	21	2	7	2	0	1	2	4	4	0	0	2-1	.333	.440	.571	1.011	1	.929

ALL-STAR GAME RECORD

	G	AB	R	H	2B	3B	HR	RBI	BB	SO	HBP	GDP	SB-CS	Avg.	OBP	SLG	OPS	E	Avg.
All-Star Game totals (8 years)	8	23	4	10	2	0	1	5	2	4	0	0	1-0	.435	.480	.652	1.132	1	.900

GRIFFITHS, JEREMY — P

PERSONAL: Born March 22, 1978, in Fairview, Ohio. ... 6-6/235. ... Throws right, bats right. ... Full name: Jeremy Richard Griffiths. ... High school: Avon Lake (Ohio). ... College: Toledo.

TRANSACTIONS/CAREER NOTES: Selected by New York Mets organization in third round of 1999 free-agent draft. ... Traded by Mets with P David Weathers to Houston Astros for OF Richard Hidalgo (June 17, 2004).

CAREER HITTING: 0-for-10 (.000), 0 R, 0 2B, 0 3B, 0 HR, 0 RBI.

Year Team (League)	W	L	Pct.	ERA	WHIP	G	GS	CG	ShO	Hld.	Sv.-Opp.	IP	H	R	ER	HR	BB-IBB	SO	Avg.
1999— Kingsport (Appalachian)	3	5	.375	3.30	1.36	14	14	1	0	...	0-...	76.1	68	40	28	6	36-1	74	.243
2000— Capital City (S. Atl.)	7	12	.368	4.34	1.24	26	26	0	0	...	0-...	128.2	120	78	62	12	39-0	138	.242
2001— St. Lucie (Fla. St.)	7	8	.467	3.75	1.22	23	20	2	0	...	0-...	132.0	126	63	55	9	35-1	95	.253
— Binghamton (Eastern)	2	0	1.000	0.69	0.92	2	2	1	0	...	0-...	13.0	8	3	1	0	4-0	12	.174
2002— Binghamton (Eastern)	8	6	.571	3.89	1.38	27	26	2	0	...	0-...	152.2	157	75	66	12	54-0	126	.272
2003— Norfolk (Int'l)	7	6	.538	2.74	1.04	21	19	1	0	...	1-...	115.0	94	43	35	6	26-0	78	.224
— New York (N.L.)	1	4	.200	7.02	1.85	9	6	0	0	0	0-0	41.0	57	34	32	5	19-2	25	.328
2004— Norfolk (Int'l)	5	2	.714	3.47	1.31	13	13	0	0	0	0-0	70.0	63	30	27	6	29-1	31	.254
— Houston (N.L.)	0	0	...	10.38	1.62	1	1	0	0	0	0-0	4.1	4	5	5	1	3-0	5	.235
— New Orleans (PCL)	3	6	.333	5.85	1.51	15	14	0	0	...	0-...	80.0	95	55	52	9	26-1	58	.300
Major League totals (2 years)	1	4	.200	7.35	1.83	10	7	0	0	0	0-0	45.1	61	39	37	6	22-2	30	.319

GRILLI, JASON — P

PERSONAL: Born November 11, 1976... 6-4/185. ... Throws right, bats right. ... Full name: Jason Michael Grilli. ... High school: C.W. Baker (Baldwinsville, N.Y.). ... College: Seton Hall. ... Son of Steve Grilli, pitcher with two major league teams (1975-79).

TRANSACTIONS/CAREER NOTES: Selected by New York Yankees organization in 24th round of 1994 free-agent draft; did not sign. ... Selected by San Francisco Giants organization in first round (fourth pick overall) of 1997 free-agent draft. ... Traded by Giants with P Nate Bump to Florida Marlins for P Livan Hernandez (July 24, 1999). ... Selected by Chicago White Sox from Florida Marlins organization in Rule 5 major league draft (December 15, 2003).

CAREER HITTING: 3-for-9 (.333), 1 R, 0 2B, 0 3B, 1 HR, 3 RBI.

Year Team (League)	W	L	Pct.	ERA	WHIP	G	GS	CG	ShO	Hld.	Sv.-Opp.	IP	H	R	ER	HR	BB-IBB	SO	Avg.
1998— Shreveport (Texas)	7	10	.412	3.79	1.22	21	21	3	0	...	0-...	123.1	113	60	52	11	37-0	100	.245
— Fresno (PCL)	2	3	.400	5.14	1.60	8	8	0	0	...	0-...	42.0	49	30	24	7	18-0	37	.290

G

Year	Team (League)	W	L	Pct.	ERA	WHIP	G	GS	CG	ShO	Hld.	Sv.-Opp.	IP	H	R	ER	HR	BB-IBB	SO	Avg.
1999—	Fresno (PCL)	7	5	.583	5.54	1.62	19	19	1	0	...	0-...	100.2	124	69	62	22	39-0	76	.302
	—Calgary (PCL)	1	5	.167	7.68	1.93	8	8	0	0	...	0-...	41.0	56	48	35	7	23-0	27	.316
2000—	Calgary (PCL)	1	4	.200	7.19	1.96	8	8	0	0	...	0-...	41.1	58	37	33	4	23-0	21	.335
	—Florida (N.L.)	1	0	1.000	5.40	1.95	1	1	0	0	0	0-0	6.2	11	4	4	0	2-0	3	.379
2001—	Florida (N.L.)	2	2	.500	6.08	1.54	6	5	0	0	0	0-0	26.2	30	18	18	6	11-0	17	.297
	—Calgary (PCL)	1	2	.333	4.02	1.40	8	8	0	0	0	0-0	47.0	46	26	21	4	20-0	35	.256
	—GC Marlins (GCL)	0	0	...	0.00	0.50	2	2	0	0	0	0-...	4.0	2	0	0	0	0-0	6	.143
	—Brevard County (FSL)	2	0	1.000	1.98	1.24	3	3	0	0	0	0-...	13.2	12	4	3	0	5-0	14	.231
	—Portland (East.)	0	1	.000	2.25	0.75	1	1	0	0	0	0-...	4.0	3	1	1	1	0-0	3	.200
2002—	Calgary (PCL)	0	1	.000	1.59	1.06	1	1	0	0	0	0-...	5.2	3	1	1	0	3-0	8	.158
2004—	Charlotte (Int'l)	9	9	.500	4.83	1.45	25	25	2	1		0-...	152.2	163	95	82	22	68-0	101	.276
	—Chicago (A.L.)	2	3	.400	7.40	1.60	8	8	1	0	0	0-0	45.0	52	38	37	11	20-0	26	.294
	American League totals (1 year)	2	3	.400	7.40	1.60	8	8	1	0	0	0-0	45.0	52	38	37	11	20-0	26	.294
	National League totals (2 years)	3	2	.600	5.94	1.62	7	6	0	0	0	0-0	33.1	41	22	22	6	13-0	20	.315
	Major League totals (3 years)	5	5	.500	6.78	1.61	15	14	1	0	0	0-0	78.1	93	60	59	17	33-0	46	.303

GRIMSLEY, JASON — P

PERSONAL: Born August 7, 1967, in Cleveland, Texas. ... 6-3/205. ... Throws right, bats right. ... Full name: Jason Alan Grimsley. ... High school: Tarkington (Cleveland, Texas).

TRANSACTIONS/CAREER NOTES: Selected by Philadelphia Phillies organization in 10th round of June 1985 free-agent draft. ... On disabled list (June 6-August 22, 1991); included rehabilitation assignments to Scranton/Wilkes-Barre. ... Traded by Phillies to Houston Astros for P Curt Schilling (April 2, 1992). ... On disabled list (May 14-June 14, 1992). ... Released by Astros (March 30, 1993). ... Signed by Cleveland Indians organization (April 7, 1993). ... Traded by Indians with P Pep Harris to California Angels for P Brian Anderson (February 15, 1996). ... Signed as a free agent by Detroit Tigers organization (January 17, 1997). ... Released by Tigers (March 20, 1997). ... Signed by Milwaukee Brewers (April 3, 1997). ... Traded by Brewers to Kansas City Royals for P Jamie Brewington (July 29, 1997). ... Signed as a free agent by Indians organization (January 8, 1998). ... Signed as a free agent by New York Yankees organization (January 26, 1999). ... On suspended list (August 11-15, 1999). ... Released by Yankees (November 20, 2000). ... Signed by Royals (January 19, 2001). ... On disabled list (June 4-22, 2002); included rehabilitation assignment to Wichita. ... Traded by Royals to Baltimore Orioles for P Denny Bautista (June 17, 2004).

CAREER HITTING: 4-for-39 (.103), 3 R, 0 2B, 0 3B, 0 HR, 2 RBI.

Year	Team (League)	W	L	Pct.	ERA	WHIP	G	GS	CG	ShO	Hld.	Sv.-Opp.	IP	H	R	ER	HR	BB-IBB	SO	Avg.
1985—	Bend (N'west)	0	1	.000	13.50	3.26	6	1	0	0	...	0-...	11.1	12	21	17	0	25-0	10	...
1986—	Utica (N.Y.-Penn)	1	10	.091	6.40	2.16	14	14	3	0	...	0-...	64.2	63	61	46	3	77-0	46	.251
1987—	Spartanburg (SAL)	7	4	.636	3.16	1.28	23	9	3	0	...	0-...	88.1	59	48	31	4	54-2	98	.190
1988—	Clearwater (Fla. St.)	4	7	.364	3.73	1.15	16	15	2	0	...	0-...	101.1	80	48	42	2	37-1	90	.217
	—Reading (East.)	1	3	.250	7.17	1.55	5	4	0	0	...	0-...	21.1	20	19	17	1	13-1	14	.247
1989—	Reading (East.)	11	8	.579	2.98	1.34	26	26	8	2	...	0-...	172.0	121	65	57	13	109-4	134	.202
	—Philadelphia (N.L.)	1	3	.250	5.89	2.07	4	4	0	0	0	0-0	18.1	19	13	12	2	19-1	7	.268
1990—	Scran./W.B. (I.L.)	8	5	.615	3.93	1.47	22	22	0	0	...	0-...	128.1	111	68	56	7	78-1	99	.236
	—Philadelphia (N.L.)	3	2	.600	3.30	1.57	11	11	0	0	0	0-0	57.1	47	21	21	1	43-0	41	.227
1991—	Philadelphia (N.L.)	1	7	.125	4.87	1.56	12	12	0	0	0	0-0	61.0	54	34	33	4	41-3	42	.242
	—Scran./W.B. (I.L.)	2	3	.400	4.35	1.65	9	9	0	0	...	0-...	51.2	48	28	25	3	37-2	43	.254
1992—	Tucson (PCL)	8	7	.533	5.05	1.66	26	20	0	0	...	0-...	124.2	152	79	70	4	55-0	90	.308
1993—	Charlotte (Int'l)	6	6	.500	3.39	1.38	28	19	3	1	...	0-...	135.1	138	64	51	10	49-1	102	.263
	—Cleveland (A.L.)	3	4	.429	5.31	1.70	10	6	0	0	1	0-0	42.1	52	26	25	3	20-1	27	.302
1994—	Charlotte (Int'l)	7	0	1.000	3.42	1.06	10	10	2	0	...	0-...	71.0	58	36	27	10	17-0	60	.218
	—Cleveland (A.L.)	5	2	.714	4.57	1.51	14	13	1	0	0	0-0	82.2	91	47	42	7	34-1	59	.283
1995—	Cleveland (A.L.)	0	0	...	6.09	2.03	15	2	0	0	0	1-1	34.0	37	24	23	4	32-1	25	.289
	—Buffalo (A.A.)	5	3	.625	2.91	1.18	10	10	2	0	...	0-...	68.0	61	26	22	4	19-0	40	.236
1996—	Vancouver (PCL)	2	0	1.000	1.20	0.73	2	2	1	0	...	0-...	15.0	8	2	2	0	3-0	11	.163
	—California (A.L.)	5	7	.417	6.84	1.72	35	20	2	1	0	0-0	130.1	150	110	99	14	74-5	82	.286
1997—	Tucson (PCL)	5	10	.333	5.70	1.63	36	10	0	0	...	4-...	85.1	96	70	54	6	43-2	65	.278
	—Omaha (Am. Assoc.)	1	5	.167	6.68	2.10	7	6	0	0	...	0-...	31.0	36	26	23	3	29-0	22	.293
1998—	Buffalo (Int'l)	6	3	.667	3.76	1.50	52	0	0	0	...	0-...	88.2	76	40	37	10	57-3	68	.234
1999—	New York (A.L.)	7	2	.778	3.60	1.41	55	0	0	0	8	1-4	75.0	66	39	30	7	40-5	49	.231
2000—	New York (A.L.)	3	2	.600	5.04	1.47	63	4	0	0	4	1-4	96.1	100	58	54	10	42-1	53	.268
2001—	Kansas City (A.L.)	1	5	.167	3.02	1.23	73	0	0	0	26	0-7	80.1	71	32	27	8	28-5	61	.242
2002—	Kansas City (A.L.)	4	7	.364	3.91	1.42	70	0	0	0	13	1-3	71.1	64	32	31	4	37-8	59	.236
	—Wichita (Texas)	0	0	...	9.00	2.00	1	1	0	0	0	0-0	1.0	1	1	1	0	1-0	0	.250
2003—	Kansas City (A.L.)	2	6	.250	5.16	1.65	76	0	0	0	28	0-7	75.0	88	47	43	6	36-5	58	.299
2004—	Kansas City (A.L.)	3	3	.500	3.38	1.46	32	0	0	0	5	0-3	26.2	24	11	10	1	15-3	18	.238
	—Baltimore (A.L.)	2	4	.333	4.21	1.57	41	0	0	0	12	0-6	36.1	37	25	17	3	20-3	21	.261
	American League totals (10 years)	35	42	.455	4.81	1.54	484	45	3	1	97	4-35	750.1	780	451	401	67	378-38	512	.268
	National League totals (3 years)	5	12	.294	4.35	1.63	27	27	0	0	0	0-0	136.2	120	68	66	7	103-4	90	.240
	Major League totals (13 years)	40	54	.426	4.74	1.56	511	72	3	1	97	4-35	887.0	900	519	467	74	481-42	602	.264

DIVISION SERIES RECORD

Year	Team (League)	W	L	Pct.	ERA	WHIP	G	GS	CG	ShO	Hld.	Sv.-Opp.	IP	H	R	ER	HR	BB-IBB	SO	Avg.
1999—	New York (A.L.)	Did not play.																		
2000—	New York (A.L.)	Did not play.																		

CHAMPIONSHIP SERIES RECORD

Year	Team (League)	W	L	Pct.	ERA	WHIP	G	GS	CG	ShO	Hld.	Sv.-Opp.	IP	H	R	ER	HR	BB-IBB	SO	Avg.
1999—	New York (A.L.)	Did not play.																		
2000—	New York (A.L.)	0	0		0.00	5.00	2	0	0	0	0	0-0	1.0	2	0	0	0	3-0	1	.400

WORLD SERIES RECORD

Year	Team (League)	W	L	Pct.	ERA	WHIP	G	GS	CG	ShO	Hld.	Sv.-Opp.	IP	H	R	ER	HR	BB-IBB	SO	Avg.
1999—	New York (A.L.)	0	0		0.00	1.71	1	0	0	0	0	0-0	2.1	2	0	0	0	2-0	0	.250
2000—	New York (A.L.)	Did not play.																		

GRISSOM, MARQUIS — OF

PERSONAL: Born April 17, 1967, in Atlanta, Ga. ... 5-11/208. ... Bats right, throws right. ... Full name: Marquis Deon Grissom. ... Name pronounced: mar-KEESE. ... High school: Lakeshore (College Park, Ga.). ... College: Florida A&M.

TRANSACTIONS/CAREER NOTES: Selected by Montreal Expos organization in third round of 1988 free-agent draft. ... On disabled list (May 29-June 30, 1990); included rehabilitation assignment to Indianapolis. ... Traded by Expos to Atlanta Braves for OFs Roberto Kelly and Tony Tarasco and P Esteban Yan (April 6, 1995). ... Traded by Braves with OF Dave Justice to Cleveland Indians for OF Kenny Lofton and P Alan Embree (March 25, 1997). ... On disabled list (April 22-May 5, 1997). ... Traded by Indians with P Jeff Juden to Milwaukee Brewers for Ps Ben McDonald, Mike Fetters and Ron Villone (December 8, 1997). ... Traded by Brewers with a player to be named to Los Angeles

G

Dodgers for OF Devon White (February 25, 2001); Dodgers acquired P Rudy Lugo to complete deal (June 1, 2001). ... On suspended list (July 18-24, 2001). ... Signed as a free agent by San Francisco Giants (December 7, 2002).

HONORS: Won N.L. Gold Glove as outfielder (1993-96).

2004 GAMES PLAYED BY POSITION (MLB): OF—142.

Year	Team (League)	Pos.	G	AB	R	H	2B	3B	HR	RBI	BB	SO	HBP	GDP	SB-CS	Avg.	OBP	SLG	OPS	E	Avg.
1988—	Jamestown (N.Y.-Penn.) ...	OF	74	291	69	94	14	7	8	39	35	39	2	2	23-7	.323	.393	.502	.895	3	.978
1989—	Jacksonville (Sou.)	OF	78	278	43	83	15	4	3	31	24	31	7	1	24-6	.299	.365	.414	.779	3	.980
	— Indianapolis (A.A.)	OF	49	187	28	52	10	4	2	21	14	23	0	2	16-4	.278	.327	.406	.733	0	1.000
	— Montreal (N.L.)	OF	26	74	16	19	2	0	1	2	12	21	0	1	1-0	.257	.360	.324	.685	2	.943
1990—	Montreal (N.L.)	OF	98	288	42	74	14	2	3	29	27	40	0	3	22-2	.257	.320	.351	.670	2	.988
	— Indianapolis (A.A.)	OF	5	22	3	4	0	0	2	3	0	5	0	0	1-0	.182	.182	.455	.636	0	1.000
1991—	Montreal (N.L.)	OF	148	558	73	149	23	9	6	39	34	89	1	8	* 76-17	.267	.310	.373	.683	6	.984
1992—	Montreal (N.L.)	OF	159	* 653	99	180	39	6	14	66	42	81	5	12	* 78-13	.276	.322	.418	.741	7	.983
1993—	Montreal (N.L.)	OF	157	630	104	188	27	2	19	95	52	76	3	9	53-10	.298	.351	.438	.789	7	.984
1994—	Montreal (N.L.)	OF	110	475	96	137	25	4	11	45	41	66	1	10	36-6	.288	.344	.427	.771	5	.985
1995—	Atlanta (N.L.)	OF	139	551	80	142	23	3	12	42	47	61	3	8	29-9	.258	.317	.376	.693	2	.994
1996—	Atlanta (N.L.)	OF	158	671	106	207	32	10	23	74	41	73	3	12	28-11	.308	.349	.489	.838	1	.997
1997—	Cleveland (A.L.)	OF	144	558	74	146	27	6	12	66	43	89	6	12	22-13	.262	.317	.396	.713	3	.992
1998—	Milwaukee (N.L.)	OF	142	542	57	147	28	1	10	60	24	78	2	12	13-8	.271	.304	.382	.685	3	.991
1999—	Milwaukee (N.L.)	OF	154	603	92	161	27	1	20	83	49	109	0	12	24-6	.267	.320	.415	.734	5	.987
2000—	Milwaukee (N.L.)	OF	146	595	67	145	18	2	14	62	39	99	0	9	20-10	.244	.288	.351	.640	3	.992
2001—	Los Angeles (N.L.)	OF-DH	135	448	56	99	17	1	21	60	16	107	2	12	7-5	.221	.250	.404	.654	0	1.000
2002—	Los Angeles (N.L.)	OF	111	343	57	95	21	4	17	60	22	68	2	6	5-1	.277	.321	.510	.831	4	.978
2003—	San Francisco (N.L.)	OF	149	587	82	176	33	3	20	79	20	82	2	14	11-3	.300	.322	.468	.790	8	.977
2004—	San Francisco (N.L.)	OF	145	562	78	157	26	2	22	90	37	83	1	22	3-1	.279	.323	.450	.773	2	.994
	American League totals (1 year)		144	558	74	146	27	6	12	66	43	89	6	12	22-13	.262	.317	.396	.713	3	.992
	National League totals (15 years)		1977	7580	1105	2076	355	50	213	886	503	1133	25	150	406-102	.274	.319	.418	.737	57	.988
	Major League totals (16 years)		2121	8138	1179	2222	382	56	225	952	546	1222	31	162	428-115	.273	.319	.417	.736	60	.988

DIVISION SERIES RECORD

Year	Team (League)	Pos.	G	AB	R	H	2B	3B	HR	RBI	BB	SO	HBP	GDP	SB-CS	Avg.	OBP	SLG	OPS	E	Avg.
1995—	Atlanta (N.L.)	OF	4	21	5	11	2	0	3	4	0	3	0	0	2-1	.524	.524	1.048	1.571	0	1.000
1996—	Atlanta (N.L.)	OF	3	12	2	1	0	0	0	0	1	2	0	0	1-0	.083	.154	.083	.237	1	.800
1997—	Cleveland (A.L.)	OF	5	17	3	4	0	1	0	0	1	2	0	0	0-1	.235	.278	.353	.631	0	1.000
2003—	San Francisco (N.L.)	OF	4	14	1	2	0	0	0	1	2	5	0	0	0-1	.143	.250	.143	.393	1	.889
	Division series totals (4 years)		16	64	11	18	2	1	3	5	4	12	0	0	3-3	.281	.324	.484	.808	2	.946

CHAMPIONSHIP SERIES RECORD

Year	Team (League)	Pos.	G	AB	R	H	2B	3B	HR	RBI	BB	SO	HBP	GDP	SB-CS	Avg.	OBP	SLG	OPS	E	Avg.
1995—	Atlanta (N.L.)	OF	4	19	2	5	0	1	0	0	1	4	0	0	0-0	.263	.300	.368	.668	1	.889
1996—	Atlanta (N.L.)	OF	7	35	7	10	1	0	1	3	0	8	0	0	2-0	.286	.286	.400	.686	1	.944
1997—	Cleveland (A.L.)	OF	6	23	2	6	0	0	1	4	1	9	0	0	3-0	.261	.292	.391	.683	0	1.000
	Champ. series totals (3 years)		17	77	11	21	1	1	2	7	2	21	0	0	5-0	.273	.291	.390	.681	2	.951

WORLD SERIES RECORD

Year	Team (League)	Pos.	G	AB	R	H	2B	3B	HR	RBI	BB	SO	HBP	GDP	SB-CS	Avg.	OBP	SLG	OPS	E	Avg.
1995—	Atlanta (N.L.)	OF	6	25	3	9	1	0	0	1	1	3	1	1	3-1	.360	.407	.400	.807	0	1.000
1996—	Atlanta (N.L.)	OF	6	27	4	12	2	1	0	5	1	2	0	0	1-0	.444	.464	.593	1.057	1	.875
1997—	Cleveland (A.L.)	OF	7	25	5	9	1	0	0	2	4	4	0	1	0-0	.360	.448	.400	.848	1	.950
	World series totals (3 years)		19	77	12	30	4	1	0	8	6	9	1	2	4-1	.390	.440	.468	.908	2	.951

ALL-STAR GAME RECORD

		G	AB	R	H	2B	3B	HR	RBI	BB	SO	HBP	GDP	SB-CS	Avg.	OBP	SLG	OPS	E	Avg.
	All-Star Game totals (2 years)		2	4	1	1	0	0	1	1	1	1	0	0	0-0	.250	.400	1.000	1.400	0	1.000

GROOM, BUDDY   P

PERSONAL: Born July 10, 1965, in Dallas, Texas. ... 6-2/203. ... Throws left, bats left. ... Full name: Wedsel Gary Groom. ... High school: Red Oak (Texas). ... College: Mary Hardin-Baylor.

TRANSACTIONS/CAREER NOTES: Selected by Chicago White Sox organization in 12th round of 1987 free-agent draft. ... Selected by Detroit Tigers organization from White Sox organization in Rule 5 minor league draft (December 3, 1990). ... Traded by Tigers to Florida Marlins for a player to be named (August 7, 1995); Tigers acquired P Mike Myers to complete deal (August 9, 1995). ... Signed as a free agent by Oakland Athletics organization (November 27, 1995). ... Signed as a free agent by Baltimore Orioles (December 21, 1999).

CAREER HITTING: 0-for-0 (.000), 0 R, 0 2B, 0 3B, 0 HR, 0 RBI.

Year	Team (League)	W	L	Pct.	ERA	WHIP	G	GS	CG	ShO	Hld.	Sv.-Opp.	IP	H	R	ER	HR	BB-IBB	SO	Avg.
1987—	GC White Sox (GCL)	1	0	1.000	0.75	1.17	4	1	0	0	...	1-...	12.0	12	1	1	0	2-0	8	.273
	— Daytona Beach (FSL)	7	2	.778	3.59	1.37	11	10	2	0	...	0-...	67.2	60	30	27	4	33-1	29	.236
1988—	Tampa (FSL)	13	10	.565	2.54	1.19	27	27	8	0	...	0-...	195.0	181	69	55	7	51-1	118	.247
1989—	Birmingham (Southern)	13	8	.619	4.52	1.49	26	26	3	1	...	0-...	167.1	172	101	84	13	78-1	94	.270
1990—	Birmingham (Southern)	6	8	.429	5.07	1.59	20	20	0	0	...	0-...	115.1	135	81	65	10	48-1	66	.290
1991—	Toledo (International)	2	5	.286	4.32	1.33	24	6	0	0	...	1-...	75.0	75	39	36	7	25-2	49	.264
	— London (East.)	7	1	.875	3.48	1.22	11	7	0	0	...	0-...	51.2	51	20	20	7	12-1	39	.248
1992—	Toledo (International)	7	7	.500	2.80	1.14	16	16	1	0	...	0-...	109.1	102	41	34	8	23-1	71	.248
	— Detroit (A.L.)	0	5	.000	5.82	1.81	12	7	0	0	0	1-2	38.2	48	28	25	4	22-4	15	.320
1993—	Toledo (International)	9	3	.750	2.74	1.25	16	15	0	0	...	0-...	102.0	98	34	31	5	30-1	78	.254
	— Detroit (A.L.)	0	2	.000	6.14	1.66	19	3	0	0	1	0-0	36.2	48	25	25	4	13-5	15	.322
1994—	Toledo (International)	0	0	...	2.25	0.50	5	0	0	0	...	0-...	4.0	2	1	1	0	0-0	6	.154
	— Detroit (A.L.)	0	1	.000	3.94	1.38	40	0	0	0	11	1-1	32.0	31	14	14	4	13-2	27	.256
1995—	Detroit (A.L.)	1	3	.250	7.52	1.99	23	4	0	0	0	1-3	40.2	55	35	34	6	26-4	23	.322
	— Toledo (International)	2	3	.400	1.91	1.06	6	5	1	0	...	0-...	33.0	31	14	7	4	4-0	24	.244
	— Florida (N.L.)	1	2	.333	7.20	2.13	14	0	0	0	0	0-0	15.0	26	12	12	2	6-0	12	.400
1996—	Oakland (A.L.)	5	0	1.000	3.84	1.54	72	0	0	0	10	2-4	77.1	85	37	33	8	34-3	57	.281
1997—	Oakland (A.L.)	2	2	.500	5.15	1.53	78	0	0	0	12	3-5	64.2	75	38	37	9	24-1	45	.292
1998—	Oakland (A.L.)	3	1	.750	4.24	1.43	75	0	0	0	16	0-6	57.1	62	30	27	4	20-1	36	.274

G

Year	Team (League)	W	L	Pct.	ERA	WHIP	G	GS	CG	ShO	Hld.	Sv.-Opp.	IP	H	R	ER	HR	BB-IBB	SO	Avg.
1999—	Oakland (A.L.)	3	2	.600	5.09	1.43	76	0	0	0	27	0-3	46.0	48	29	26	1	18-5	32	.274
2000—	Baltimore (A.L.)	6	3	.667	4.85	1.42	70	0	0	0	27	4-11	59.1	63	37	32	5	21-2	44	.275
2001—	Baltimore (A.L.)	1	4	.200	3.55	1.11	66	0	0	0	16	11-13	66.0	64	28	26	4	9-0	54	.252
2002—	Baltimore (A.L.)	3	2	.600	1.60	0.90	70	0	0	0	19	2-4	62.0	44	11	11	4	12-3	48	.196
2003—	Baltimore (A.L.)	1	3	.250	5.36	1.59	60	0	0	0	16	1-3	45.1	58	27	27	7	14-2	34	.309
2004—	Baltimore (A.L.)	4	1	.800	4.78	1.58	60	0	0	0	8	0-2	52.2	67	30	28	6	16-1	32	.309
	American League totals (13 years)	29	29	.500	4.58	1.46	725	15	0	0	163	26-57	678.2	748	369	345	66	242-33	462	.281
	National League totals (1 year)	1	2	.333	7.20	2.13	14	0	0	0	0	0-0	15.0	26	12	12	2	6-0	12	.400
	Major League totals (13 years)	30	31	.492	4.63	1.47	739	15	0	0	163	26-57	693.2	774	381	357	68	248-33	474	.284

GROSS, GABE   OF

PERSONAL: Born October 21, 1979, in Baltimore, Md. ... 6-3/209. ... Bats left, throws right. ... Full name: Gabriel Jordan Gross. ... High school: Northview (Dothan, Ala.). ... College: Auburn.

TRANSACTIONS/CAREER NOTES: Selected by Toronto Blue Jays organization in first round (15th pick overall) of 2001 free-agent draft.

2004 GAMES PLAYED BY POSITION (MLB): OF—38, DH—7.

Year	Team (League)	Pos.	G	AB	R	H	2B	3B	HR	RBI	BB	SO	HBP	GDP	SB-CS	Avg.	OBP	SLG	OPS	E	Avg.
2001—	Dunedin (Fla. St.)	OF	35	126	23	38	9	2	4	15	26	29	2	2	4-2	.302	.426	.500	.926	3	.930
—	Tennessee (Sou.)	OF	11	41	8	10	1	0	3	11	6	12	3	1	0-1	.244	.373	.488	.860	0	1.000
2002—	Tennessee (Sou.)	OF	112	403	57	96	17	5	10	54	53	71	5	4	8-2	.238	.333	.380	.712	2	.991
2003—	New Haven (East.)	OF	84	310	52	99	23	3	7	51	52	53	5	9	3-2	.319	.423	.481	.903	3	.980
—	Syracuse (Int'l)	OF	53	182	22	48	16	2	5	23	31	56	3	2	1-1	.264	.380	.456	.836	2	.985
2004—	Syracuse (Int'l)	DH-OF	103	377	52	111	29	2	9	54	53	81	1	8	4-5	.294	.381	.454	.833	3	.957
—	Toronto (A.L.)	OF-DH	44	129	18	27	4	0	3	16	19	31	0	1	2-2	.209	.311	.310	.621	0	1.000
	Major League totals (1 year)		44	129	18	27	4	0	3	16	19	31	0	1	2-2	.209	.311	.310	.621	0	1.000

GRUDZIELANEK, MARK   2B

PERSONAL: Born June 30, 1970, in Milwaukee, Wis. ... 6-1/190. ... Bats right, throws right. ... Full name: Mark James Grudzielanek. ... Name pronounced: grud-zuh-LAN-nick. ... High school: J.M. Hanks (El Paso, Texas). ... Junior college: Trinidad State (Colo.).

TRANSACTIONS/CAREER NOTES: Selected by New York Mets organization in 17th round of 1989 free-agent draft; did not sign. ... Selected by Montreal Expos organization in 11th round of 1991 free-agent draft. ... Traded by Expos with P Carlos Perez and OF Hiram Bocachica to Los Angeles Dodgers for 2B Wilton Guerrero, P Ted Lilly, OF Peter Bergeron and 1B Jonathan Tucker (July 31, 1998). ... On disabled list (June 12-July 6, 1999); included rehabilitation assignment to San Bernardino. ... On disabled list (June 12-28, 2001). ... Traded by Dodgers with 1B Eric Karros and cash to Chicago Cubs for C Todd Hundley and OF Chad Hermansen (December 4, 2002). ... On disabled list (August 3-September 2, 2003); included rehabilitation assignment to Iowa. ... On disabled list (April 10-June 19, 2004); included rehabilitation assignment to Iowa.

2004 GAMES PLAYED BY POSITION (MLB): 2B—76.

Year	Team (League)	Pos.	G	AB	R	H	2B	3B	HR	RBI	BB	SO	HBP	GDP	SB-CS	Avg.	OBP	SLG	OPS	E	Avg.
1991—	Jamestown (N.Y.-Penn.) ...	SS	72	275	44	72	9	3	2	32	18	43	3	6	14-4	.262	.311	.338	.649	23	.933
1992—	Rockford (Midwest)	SS	128	496	64	122	12	5	5	54	22	59	5	10	25-4	.246	.285	.321	.605	41	.919
1993—	W.P. Beach (FSL)	2-3-SS-OF	86	300	41	80	11	6	1	34	14	42	7	6	17-10	.267	.315	.353	.668	13	.949
1994—	Harrisburg (East.)	3B-SS	122	488	92	157	37	3	11	66	43	66	8	15	32-10	.322	.382	.477	.860	23	.958
1995—	Montreal (N.L.)	SS-3B-2B	78	269	27	66	12	2	1	20	14	47	7	7	8-3	.245	.300	.316	.616	10	.967
—	Ottawa (Int'l)	SS	49	181	26	54	9	1	1	22	10	17	4	6	12-1	.298	.342	.376	.717	14	.939
1996—	Montreal (N.L.)	SS	153	657	99	201	34	4	6	49	26	83	9	10	33-7	.306	.340	.397	.737	27	.959
1997—	Montreal (N.L.)	SS	156	* 649	76	177	* 54	3	4	51	23	76	10	13	25-9	.273	.307	.384	.690	* 32	.955
1998—	Montreal (N.L.)	SS	105	396	51	109	15	1	8	41	21	50	9	11	11-5	.275	.323	.379	.702	23	.950
—	Los Angeles (N.L.)	SS	51	193	11	51	6	0	2	21	5	23	2	7	7-0	.264	.286	.326	.612	† 10	.962
1999—	Los Angeles (N.L.)	SS	123	488	72	159	23	5	7	46	31	65	10	13	6-6	.326	.376	.436	.812	13	.973
—	San Bern. (Calif.)	SS	4	16	2	4	0	0	0	0	0	1	0	1	0-2	.250	.250	.250	.500	0	1.000
2000—	Los Angeles (N.L.)	2B-SS	148	617	101	172	35	6	7	49	45	81	9	16	12-3	.279	.335	.389	.724	17	.976
2001—	Los Angeles (N.L.)	2B	133	539	83	146	21	3	13	55	28	83	11	9	4-4	.271	.317	.393	.711	10	.984
2002—	Los Angeles (N.L.)	2B-DH	150	536	56	145	23	0	9	50	22	89	3	17	4-1	.271	.301	.364	.665	7	.989
2003—	Iowa (PCL)	2B-DH	2	10	1	5	0	0	0	1	1	1	0	0	0-0	.500	.545	.500	1.045	0	1.000
—	Chicago (N.L.)	2B	121	481	73	151	38	1	3	38	30	64	11	12	6-2	.314	.366	.416	.782	8	.986
2004—	Iowa (PCL)	2B-DH	8	28	6	7	3	0	2	4	0	4	0	1	0-0	.250	.250	.571	.821	0	1.000
—	Chicago (N.L.)	2B	81	257	32	79	12	1	6	23	15	32	1	7	1-1	.307	.347	.432	.779	5	.985
	Major League totals (10 years)		1299	5082	681	1456	273	26	66	443	260	693	82	122	117-41	.287	.330	.389	.719	162	.972

DIVISION SERIES RECORD

Year	Team (League)	Pos.	G	AB	R	H	2B	3B	HR	RBI	BB	SO	HBP	GDP	SB-CS	Avg.	OBP	SLG	OPS	E	Avg.
2003—	Chicago (N.L.)	2B	5	20	2	3	0	0	0	0	3	4	0	1	0-0	.150	.261	.150	.411	0	1.000

CHAMPIONSHIP SERIES RECORD

Year	Team (League)	Pos.	G	AB	R	H	2B	3B	HR	RBI	BB	SO	HBP	GDP	SB-CS	Avg.	OBP	SLG	OPS	E	Avg.
2003—	Chicago (N.L.)	2B	7	30	2	6	1	1	0	3	0	5	0	0	0-0	.200	.200	.300	.500	2	.956

ALL-STAR GAME RECORD

	G	AB	R	H	2B	3B	HR	RBI	BB	SO	HBP	GDP	SB-CS	Avg.	OBP	SLG	OPS	E	Avg.
All-Star Game totals (1 year)	1	1	0	0	0	0	0	0	0	0	0	0	0-0	.000	.000	.000	.000	0	...

GRYBOSKI, KEVIN   P

PERSONAL: Born November 15, 1973, in Wilkes-Barre, Pa. ... 6-5/225. ... Throws right, bats right. ... Full name: Kevin John Gryboski. ... Name pronounced: gri-BOS-ski. ... College: Wilkes University (Pa.).

TRANSACTIONS/CAREER NOTES: Selected by Cincinnati Reds organization in 16th round of 1994 free-agent draft; did not sign. ... Selected by Seattle Mariners organization in 16th round of 1995 free-agent draft. ... Traded by Mariners to Atlanta Braves for P Elvis Perez (January 18, 2002). ... On disabled list (July 24-August 20, 2002); included rehabilitation assignment to Macon. ... On disabled list (August 28-September 20, 2003).

CAREER HITTING: 0-for-1 (.000), 0 R, 0 2B, 0 3B, 0 HR, 0 RBI.

Year	Team (League)	W	L	Pct.	ERA	WHIP	G	GS	CG	ShO	Hld.	Sv.-Opp.	IP	H	R	ER	HR	BB-IBB	SO	Avg.
1995—	Everett (Northwest)	1	5	.167	3.50	1.25	25	0	0	0	...	2-...	36.0	27	18	14	2	18-2	25	.206
1996—	Wisconsin (Midw.)	10	5	.667	4.74	1.50	32	21	3	0	...	1-...	138.2	146	90	73	7	62-2	100	.270

Year	Team (League)	W	L	Pct.	ERA	WHIP	G	GS	CG	ShO	Hld.	Sv.-Opp.	IP	H	R	ER	HR	BB-IBB	SO	Avg.
1997— Lancaster (Calif.)		0	7	.000	9.89	2.06	21	15	0	0	...	0-...	67.1	113	82	74	13	26-0	41	.383
1998— Lancaster (Calif.)		5	5	.500	2.65	1.25	37	3	0	0	...	8-...	85.0	75	35	25	4	31-1	73	.240
— Orlando (Sou.)		0	0	...	9.00	1.80	2	0	0	0	...	0-...	5.0	8	5	5	1	1-0	4	.364
1999— New Haven (East.)		2	5	.286	2.89	1.40	47	0	0	0	...	10-...	62.1	67	27	20	5	20-4	41	.283
2000— New Haven (East.)		2	2	.500	2.50	1.28	16	0	0	0	...	9-...	18.0	15	5	5	0	8-1	20	.221
— Tacoma (PCL)		2	2	.500	4.83	1.66	31	0	0	0	...	2-...	41.0	45	23	22	3	23-4	35	.288
2001— Tacoma (PCL)		2	5	.286	3.90	1.38	58	0	0	0	...	22-...	60.0	64	29	26	8	19-2	50	.277
2002— Richmond (Int'l)		1	0	1.000	1.29	1.14	7	0	0	0	...	3-...	7.0	7	1	1	0	1-0	5	.250
— Atlanta (N.L.)		2	1	.667	3.48	1.68	57	0	0	0	11	0-2	51.2	50	20	20	6	37-5	33	.256
— Macon (S. Atl.)		0	0	...	0.00	1.00	2	1	0	0	...	0-...	2.0	1	0	0	0	1-0	2	.167
2003— Atlanta (N.L.)		6	4	.600	3.86	1.51	64	0	0	0	12	0-4	44.1	44	22	19	3	23-6	32	.272
2004— Atlanta (N.L.)		3	2	.600	2.84	1.52	69	0	0	0	16	2-4	50.2	54	22	16	2	23-4	24	.280
Major League totals (3 years)		**11**	**7**	**.611**	**3.38**	**1.57**	**190**	**0**	**0**	**0**	**39**	**2-10**	**146.2**	**148**	**64**	**55**	**11**	**83-15**	**89**	**.269**

DIVISION SERIES RECORD

Year	Team (League)	W	L	Pct.	ERA	WHIP	G	GS	CG	ShO	Hld.	Sv.-Opp.	IP	H	R	ER	HR	BB-IBB	SO	Avg.
2002— Atlanta (N.L.)		0	0	...	0.00	1.09	3	0	0	0	0	0-0	3.2	2	0	0	0	2-1	3	.154
2003— Atlanta (N.L.)		0	0	...	3.00	1.33	5	0	0	0	2	0-0	3.0	2	1	1	0	2-1	4	.222
2004— Atlanta (N.L.)		0	0	...	2.08	0.92	5	0	0	0	0	0-0	4.1	3	1	1	0	1-0	3	.200
Division series totals (3 years)		**0**	**0**	**...**	**1.64**	**1.09**	**13**	**0**	**0**	**0**	**2**	**0-0**	**11.0**	**7**	**2**	**2**	**0**	**5-2**	**10**	**.189**

GUARDADO, EDDIE   P

PERSONAL: Born October 2, 1970, in Stockton, Calif. ... 6-0/205. ... Throws left, bats right. ... Full name: Edward Adrian Guardado. ... Name pronounced: gwar-DAH-doe. ... High school: Franklin (Stockton, Calif.). ... Junior college: San Joaquin Delta (Calif.).

TRANSACTIONS/CAREER NOTES: Selected by Minnesota Twins organization in 21st round of 1990 free-agent draft. ... On disabled list (May 22-June 28, 1999); included rehabilitation assignment to New Britain. ... On disabled list (June 5-20, 2001). ... Signed by Seattle Mariners (December 16, 2003). ... On dsabled list (August 1, 2004-remainder of season).

CAREER HITTING: 0-for-1 (.000), 0 R, 0 2B, 0 3B, 0 HR, 0 RBI.

Year	Team (League)	W	L	Pct.	ERA	WHIP	G	GS	CG	ShO	Hld.	Sv.-Opp.	IP	H	R	ER	HR	BB-IBB	SO	Avg.
1991— Elizabethton (Appal.)		8	4	.667	1.86	1.07	14	13	3	1	...	0-...	92.0	67	30	19	5	31-0	106	.199
1992— Kenosha (Midw.)		5	10	.333	4.37	1.35	18	18	2	1	...	0-...	101.0	106	57	49	5	30-0	103	.274
— Visalia (Calif.)		7	0	1.000	1.64	1.16	7	7	1	1	...	0-...	49.1	47	13	9	1	10-0	39	.258
1993— Nashville (Sou.)		4	0	1.000	1.24	0.96	10	10	2	2	...	0-...	65.1	53	10	9	1	10-0	57	.221
— Minnesota (A.L.)		3	8	.273	6.18	1.68	19	16	0	0	0	0-0	94.2	123	68	65	13	36-2	46	.319
1994— Salt Lake (PCL)		12	7	.632	4.83	1.47	24	24	2	0	...	0-...	151.0	171	90	81	23	51-0	87	.290
— Minnesota (A.L.)		0	2	.000	8.47	1.76	4	4	0	0	0	0-0	17.0	26	16	16	3	4-0	8	.351
1995— Minnesota (A.L.)		4	9	.308	5.12	1.58	51	5	0	0	5	2-5	91.1	99	54	52	13	45-2	71	.280
1996— Minnesota (A.L.)		6	5	.545	5.25	1.28	* 83	0	0	0	18	4-7	73.2	61	45	43	12	33-4	74	.228
1997— Minnesota (A.L.)		0	4	.000	3.91	1.35	69	0	0	0	13	1-1	46.0	45	23	20	7	17-2	54	.251
1998— Minnesota (A.L.)		3	1	.750	4.52	1.43	79	0	0	0	16	0-0	65.2	66	34	33	10	28-6	53	.265
1999— Minnesota (A.L.)		2	5	.286	4.50	1.29	63	0	0	0	15	2-4	48.0	37	24	24	6	25-4	50	.222
— New Britain (East.)		0	0	...	1.93	0.64	3	0	0	0	...	0-...	4.2	3	1	1	0	0-0	5	.176
2000— Minnesota (A.L.)		7	4	.636	3.94	1.30	70	0	0	0	8	9-11	61.2	55	27	27	14	25-3	52	.238
2001— Minnesota (A.L.)		7	1	.875	3.51	1.05	67	0	0	0	14	12-14	66.2	47	27	26	5	23-4	67	.197
2002— Minnesota (A.L.)		1	3	.250	2.93	1.05	68	0	0	0	0	* 45-51	67.2	53	22	22	9	18-2	70	.215
2003— Minnesota (A.L.)		3	5	.375	2.89	0.98	66	0	0	0	0	41-45	65.1	50	22	21	7	14-2	60	.207
2004— Seattle (A.L.)		2	2	.500	2.78	0.99	41	0	0	0	0	18-25	45.1	31	14	14	8	14-0	45	.194
Major League totals (12 years)		**38**	**49**	**.437**	**4.40**	**1.31**	**680**	**25**	**0**	**0**	**89**	**134-167**	**743.0**	**693**	**376**	**363**	**107**	**282-31**	**650**	**.248**

DIVISION SERIES RECORD

Year	Team (League)	W	L	Pct.	ERA	WHIP	G	GS	CG	ShO	Hld.	Sv.-Opp.	IP	H	R	ER	HR	BB-IBB	SO	Avg.
2002— Minnesota (A.L.)		0	0	...	13.50	3.00	2	0	0	0	0	1-1	2.0	5	3	3	1	1-0	1	.455
2003— Minnesota (A.L.)		0	0	...	9.00	2.50	2	0	0	0	0	1-1	2.0	5	2	2	1	0-0	2	.455
Division series totals (2 years)		**0**	**0**	**...**	**11.25**	**2.75**	**4**	**0**	**0**	**0**	**0**	**2-2**	**4.0**	**10**	**5**	**5**	**2**	**1-0**	**3**	**.455**

CHAMPIONSHIP SERIES RECORD

Year	Team (League)	W	L	Pct.	ERA	WHIP	G	GS	CG	ShO	Hld.	Sv.-Opp.	IP	H	R	ER	HR	BB-IBB	SO	Avg.
2002— Minnesota (A.L.)		0	0	...	0.00	1.00	1	0	0	0	0	1-1	1.0	0	0	0	0	1-0	2	.000

ALL-STAR GAME RECORD

		W	L	Pct.	ERA	WHIP	G	GS	CG	ShO	Hld.	Sv.-Opp.	IP	H	R	ER	HR	BB-IBB	SO	Avg.
All-Star Game totals (2 years)		0	0	...	9.00	2.00	2	0	0	0	0	0-0	1.0	2	1	1	0	0-0	2	.400

GUERRERO, VLADIMIR   OF

PERSONAL: Born February 9, 1976, in Nizao Bani, Dominican Republic. ... 6-3/220. ... Bats right, throws right. ... Full name: Vladimir Alvino Guerrero. ... Name pronounced: guh-RAR-oh. ... Brother of Wilton Guerrero, infielder/outfielder with Kansas City Royals in 2004.

TRANSACTIONS/CAREER NOTES: Signed as a non-drafted free agent by Montreal Expos organization (March 1, 1993). ... On disabled list (March 30-May 2, June 5-21 and July 12-27, 1997); included rehabilitation assignment to West Palm Beach. ... On suspended list (March 30-April 3, 2003). ... On disabled list (June 5-July 21, 2003); included rehabilitation assignment to Brevard County. ... Signed as a free agent by Anaheim Angels (January 14, 2004).

HONORS: Named Minor League Player of the Year by THE SPORTING NEWS (1996). Named A.L. Most Valuable Player by Baseball Writers' Association of America. (2004)

2004 GAMES PLAYED BY POSITION (MLB): OF—143, DH—13.

Year	Team (League)	Pos.	G	AB	R	H	2B	3B	HR	RBI	BB	SO	HBP	GDP	SB-CS	Avg.	OBP	SLG	OPS	E	Avg.
1993— Dom. Expos (DSL)		OF	34	105	19	35	4	0	1	14	8	13	...	...	4-...	.333	...	.400	...	5	.943
1994— Dom. Expos (DSL)		OF	25	92	34	39	11	0	12	35	21	6	...	...	5-...	.424	...	.935	...	2	.957
— GC Expos (GCL)		OF	37	137	24	43	13	3	5	25	11	18	2	0	0-7	.314	.366	.562	.928	1	.986
1995— Albany (S. Atl.)		OF	110	421	77	140	21	10	16	63	30	45	7	8	12-7	.333	.383	.544	.927	11	.953
1996— W.P. Beach (FSL)		OF	20	80	16	29	8	0	5	18	3	10	1	1	2-2	.363	.388	.650	1.038	3	.917
— Harrisburg (East.)		OF	118	417	84	150	32	8	19	78	51	42	9	8	17-10	.360	.438	.612	1.050	8	.961
— Montreal (N.L.)		OF	9	27	2	5	0	0	1	1	0	3	0	1	0-0	.185	.185	.296	.481	0	1.000
1997— W.P. Beach (FSL)		OF	3	10	0	4	2	0	0	2	1	0	0	1	1-0	.400	.455	.600	1.055	0	1.000
— Montreal (N.L.)		OF	90	325	44	98	22	2	11	40	19	39	7	11	3-4	.302	.350	.483	.833	* 12	.929

Year	Team (League)	Pos.	G	AB	R	H	2B	3B	HR	RBI	BB	SO	HBP	GDP	SB-CS	Avg.	OBP	SLG	OPS	E	Avg.
1998— Montreal (N.L.)	OF	159	623	108	202	37	7	38	109	42	95	7	15	11-9	.324	.371	.589	.960	* 17	.951
1999— Montreal (N.L.)	OF	160	610	102	193	37	5	42	131	55	62	7	18	14-7	.316	.378	.600	.978	* 19	.948
2000— Montreal (N.L.)	OF-DH	154	571	101	197	28	11	44	123	58	74	8	15	9-10	.345	.410	.664	1.074	• 10	.969
2001— Montreal (N.L.)	OF	159	599	107	184	45	4	34	108	60	88	9	24	37-16	.307	.377	.566	.943	12	.965
2002— Montreal (N.L.)	OF	161	614	106	* 206	37	2	39	111	84	70	6	20	40-* 20	.336	.417	.593	1.010	* 10	.969
2003— Brevard County (FSL)	OF-DH	3	6	2	3	0	0	1	1	0	0	1	0	0-0	.500	.571	1.000	1.571	0	1.000
— Montreal (N.L.)	OF	112	394	71	130	20	3	25	79	63	53	6	18	9-5	.330	.426	.586	1.012	7	.970
2004— Anaheim (A.L.)	OF-DH	156	612	* 124	206	39	2	39	126	52	74	8	19	15-3	.337	.391	.598	.989	9	.973
American League totals (1 year)		156	612	124	206	39	2	39	126	52	74	8	19	15-3	.337	.391	.598	.989	9	.973
National League totals (8 years)		1004	3763	641	1215	226	34	234	702	381	484	50	122	123-71	.323	.390	.588	.978	87	.959
Major League totals (9 years)		1160	4375	765	1421	265	36	273	828	433	558	58	141	138-74	.325	.390	.589	.979	96	.961

DIVISION SERIES RECORD

Year	Team (League)	Pos.	G	AB	R	H	2B	3B	HR	RBI	BB	SO	HBP	GDP	SB-CS	Avg.	OBP	SLG	OPS	E	Avg.
2004— Anaheim (A.L.)	OF	3	12	1	2	0	0	1	6	2	4	0	0	0-0	.167	.286	.417	.702	0	1.000

ALL-STAR GAME RECORD

	G	AB	R	H	2B	3B	HR	RBI	BB	SO	HBP	GDP	SB-CS	Avg.	OBP	SLG	OPS	E	Avg.
All-Star Game totals (5 years)	5	10	2	3	0	0	0	0	0	1	0	0	0-0	.300	.300	.300	.600	0	1.000

GUERRERO, WILTON — 2B/3B

PERSONAL: Born October 24, 1974, in Don Gregorio, Dominican Republic. ... 6-0/175. ... Bats both, throws right. ... Full name: Wilton Alvaro Guerrero. ... Name pronounced: guh-RAR-oh. ... High school: Escuela Primaria Don Gregorio (Dominican Republic). ... Brother of Vladimir Guerrero, outfielder, Anaheim Angels.

TRANSACTIONS/CAREER NOTES: Signed as a non-drafted free agent by Los Angeles Dodgers organization (October 8, 1991). ... On suspended list (June 2-9, 1997). ... Traded by Dodgers with P Ted Lilly, OF Peter Bergeron and 1B Jonathan Tucker to Montreal Expos for P Carlos Perez, SS Mark Grudzielanek and OF Hiram Bocachica (July 31, 1998). ... Signed as a free agent by Cincinnati Reds (January 9, 2001). ... Traded by Reds with OF Juan Encarnacion and P Ryan Snare to Florida Marlins for P Ryan Dempster (July 11, 2002). ... Traded by Marlins with OF Cliff Floyd, P Claudio Vargas, a player to be named and cash considerations to Expos for Ps Carl Pavano, Graeme Lloyd and Justin Wayne and IF Mike Mordecai (July 11, 2002); Expos acquired P Don Levinski to complete deal (August 6, 2002). ... Released by Expos (October 10, 2002). ... Signed by Reds organization (December 24, 2002). ... Signed as a free agent by Kansas City Royals organization (December 9, 2003). ... Refused minor league assignment and became a free agent (October 15, 2004).

2004 GAMES PLAYED BY POSITION (MLB): 2B—8, SS—3, OF—3, 3B—2, DH—2, 1B—2.

									BATTING										FIELDING	
Year	Team (League)	Pos.	G	AB	R	H	2B	3B	HR	RBI	BB	SO	HBP	GDP	SB-CS	Avg.	OBP	SLG	OPS	E	Avg.
1992— Dom. Dodgers (DSL)	SS	61	225	52	87	7	4	0	38	34	21			15-	.387		.453		21	.938
1993— Great Falls (Pio.)	SS	66	256	44	76	5	1	0	21	24	33	3	5	20-8	.297	.364	.324	.688	21	.925
— Dom. Dodgers (DSL)	SS	8	31	6	11	0	1	0	4	4	3	...	...	2-	.355	...	.419	...	1	.971
1994— Vero Beach (FSL)	SS	110	402	55	118	11	4	1	32	29	71	1	2	23-20	.294	.341	.348	.689	17	.960
1995— San Antonio (Texas)	SS	95	382	53	133	13	6	0	26	24	63	1	10	21-22	.348	.390	.414	.804	19	.953
— Albuquerque (PCL)	SS-OF	14	49	10	16	1	1	0	2	1	7	0	1	2-3	.327	.340	.388	.728	9	.852
1996— Albuquerque (PCL)	2B-SS	98	425	79	146	17	12	2	38	26	48	1	6	26-15	.344	.383	.454	.837	19	.963
— Los Angeles (N.L.)	OF	5	2	1	0	0	0	0	0	0	2	0	0	0-0	.000	.000	.000	.000	0	...
1997— Los Angeles (N.L.)	2B-SS	111	357	39	104	10	9	4	32	8	52	0	7	6-5	.291	.305	.403	.709	4	.990
— Albuquerque (PCL)	SS-2B	10	45	9	18	0	1	0	5	2	3	0	1	3-0	.400	.417	.444	.861	5	.915
1998— Los Angeles (N.L.)	2B-SS-OF	64	180	21	51	4	3	0	7	4	33	1	3	5-2	.283	.299	.339	.638	7	.959
— Albuquerque (PCL)	2B-OF-DH	30	121	15	36	3	2	1	10	9	12	1	2	11-3	.298	.351	.380	.731	1	.990
— Montreal (N.L.)	2B	52	222	29	63	10	6	2	20	10	30	0	1	3-0	.284	.313	.410	.723	6	.975
1999— Montreal (N.L.)	2B-OF-DH	132	315	42	92	15	3	2	31	13	38	2	4	7-6	.292	.324	.403	.727	12	.939
2000— Montreal (N.L.)	OF-DH-2B	127	288	30	77	7	2	2	23	19	41	0	6	8-1	.267	.312	.326	.638	4	.967
2001— Louisville (Int'l)	2B-SS-OF	54	227	23	69	14	2	0	28	12	30	1	4	12-5	.304	.342	.383	.725	8	.963
— Cincinnati (N.L.)	S-2-O-3-DH	60	142	16	48	5	1	1	8	3	17	0	1	5-2	.338	.352	.408	.760	5	.956
2002— Cincinnati (N.L.)	2B-SS-3B	59	78	9	19	1	1	0	4	6	13	0	1	2-1	.244	.298	.282	.580	2	.962
— Montreal (N.L.)	OF-2B-3B	44	62	3	12	1	0	0	1	1	19	0	1	5-0	.194	.206	.210	.416	1	.974
2003— Louisville (Int'l)	O-2-S-3-DH	126	476	68	132	20	1	1	29	26	58	1	5	30-9	.277	.315	.330	.645	7	.979
2004— Omaha (PCL)	2-DH-S-O	72	282	30	92	14	4	3	40	8	33	2	8	12-8	.326	.349	.436	.785	10	.957
— Kansas City (A.L.)	S-2-O-3-DH-1	24	32	7	7	0	1	0	1	0	4	0	1	1-0	.219	.219	.281	.500	1	.970
American League totals (1 year)		24	32	7	7	0	1	0	1	0	4	0	1	1-0	.219	.219	.281	.500	1	.970
National League totals (7 years)		654	1646	190	466	53	29	11	126	64	245	3	24	41-17	.283	.310	.371	.681	41	.969
Major League totals (8 years)		678	1678	197	473	53	30	11	127	64	249	3	25	42-17	.282	.308	.369	.677	42	.969

GUERRIER, MATT — P

PERSONAL: Born August 2, 1978, in Cleveland, Ohio. ... 6-3/185. ... Throws right, bats right. ... Full name: Matthew Olson Guerrier. ... High school: Shaker Heights (Ohio). ... College: Kent State.

TRANSACTIONS/CAREER NOTES: Selected by Kansas City Royals organization in 33rd round of 1996 free-agent draft; did not sign. ... Selected by Chicago White Sox organization in 10th round of 1999 free-agent draft. ... Traded by White Sox to Pittsburgh Pirates for P Damaso Marte and IF Edwin Yan (March 27, 2002). ... Claimed on waivers by Minnesota Twins (November 20, 2003).

CAREER HITTING: 0-for-1 (.000), 0 R, 0 2B, 0 3B, 0 HR, 0 RBI.

Year	Team (League)	W	L	Pct.	ERA	WHIP	G	GS	CG	ShO	Hld.	Sv.-Opp.	IP	H	R	ER	HR	BB-IBB	SO	Avg.
1999— Bristol (Appalachian)	5	0	1.000	1.05	1.25	21	0	0	0	...	10-...	25.2	18	9	3	1	14-2	37	.196
— Winston-Salem (Caro.)	0	0	...	5.40	0.90	4	0	0	0	...	2-...	3.1	3	2	2	0	0-0	5	.214
2000— Winston-Salem (Caro.)	0	3	.000	1.30	1.07	30	0	0	0	...	19-...	34.2	25	13	5	0	12-0	35	.194
— Birmingham (Southern)	3	1	.750	2.70	1.24	23	0	0	0	...	7-...	23.1	17	9	7	1	12-1	19	.207
2001— Birmingham (Southern)	11	3	.786	3.10	1.19	15	15	1	1	...	0-...	98.2	85	42	34	8	32-1	75	.237
— Charlotte (Int'l)	7	1	.875	3.54	1.14	12	12	3	0	...	0-...	81.1	75	33	32	7	18-0	43	.250
2002— Nashville (PCL)	7	12	.368	4.59	1.28	27	26	2	1	...	0-...	157.0	154	88	80	20	47-3	130	.253
2003— Nashville (PCL)	4	6	.400	4.53	1.20	20	19	0	0	...	0-...	105.1	108	56	53	15	18-1	78	.262
2004— Rochester (Int'l)	5	10	.333	3.19	1.11	24	23	0	0	...	0-...	144.0	135	65	51	15	25-0	97	.248
— Minnesota (A.L.)	0	1	.000	5.68	1.47	9	2	0	0	0	0-0	19.0	22	13	12	5	6-0	11	.293
Major League totals (1 year)	0	1	.000	5.68	1.47	9	2	0	0	0	0-0	19.0	22	13	12	5	6-0	11	.293

G

GUIEL, AARON — OF

PERSONAL: Born October 5, 1972, in Vancouver, British Columbia. ... 5-10/200. ... Bats left, throws right. ... Full name: Aaron Colin Guiel. ... Name pronounced: GUY-el. ... High school: Woodlands Senior (B.C.). ... Junior college: Kwantlen (B.C.).

TRANSACTIONS/CAREER NOTES: Selected by California Angels organization in 21st round of 1992 free-agent draft. ... Traded by Angels to San Diego Padres for C Angelo Encarnacion (August 25, 1997). ... Signed as a free agent by Oakland Athletics organization (March 18, 2000). ... Released by A's (March 30, 2000). ... Signed by Kansas City Royals organization (June 13, 2000). ... On disabled list (May 13-July 17, 2004); included rehabilitation assignments to AZL Royals and Omaha.

2004 GAMES PLAYED BY POSITION (MLB): OF—39, DH—2.

									BATTING											FIELDING	
Year	Team (League)	Pos.	G	AB	R	H	2B	3B	HR	RBI	BB	SO	HBP	GDP	SB-CS	Avg.	OBP	SLG	OPS	E	Avg.
1993—Boise (N'west)		2B-OF	35	104	24	31	6	4	2	12	26	21	4	1	3-0	.298	.455	.490	.946	12	.874
1994—Cedar Rap. (Midw.)		2B	127	454	84	122	30	1	18	82	64	93	6	7	21-7	.269	.364	.458	.822	32	.944
1995—Lake Elsinore (Calif.)		2B	113	409	73	110	25	7	7	58	69	96	7	7	7-6	.269	.380	.416	.796	22	.958
1996—Midland (Texas)		3B-2B-OF	129	439	72	118	29	7	10	48	56	71	10	6	11-7	.269	.364	.435	.799	28	.933
1997—Midland (Texas)		OF-3B-2B	116	419	91	138	37	7	22	85	59	94	18	9	14-10	.329	.431	.609	1.039	8	.953
—Mobile (Sou.)		OF	8	26	9	10	2	0	1	9	5	4	1	0	1-0	.385	.500	.577	1.077	0	1.000
1998—Ariz. Padres (Ariz.)		OF	8	16	8	8	3	1	1	6	5	5	3	0	1-1	.500	.667	1.000	1.667	0	1.000
—Las Vegas (PCL)		OF-3B	60	183	33	57	15	4	5	31	28	51	4	4	5-1	.311	.410	.519	.929	4	.947
1999—Las Vegas (PCL)		OF	84	257	46	63	25	2	12	39	44	86	5	6	5-4	.245	.362	.498	.861	5	.944
2000—Oaxaca (Mex.)			56	192	55	70	11	1	22	62	52	35	...		7-5	.365	...	.776	...	4	...
—Omaha (PCL)		OF	73	258	47	74	15	2	13	40	35	54	8	3	6-0	.287	.389	.512	.900	4	.977
2001—Omaha (PCL)		OF	121	442	78	118	27	3	21	73	51	92	13	12	6-4	.267	.355	.484	.840	6	.973
2002—Omaha (PCL)		OF	61	215	44	76	11	1	9	50	29	34	8	4	8-1	.353	.443	.540	.983	3	.977
—Kansas City (A.L.)		OF-DH	70	240	30	56	13	0	4	38	19	61	4	3	1-5	.233	.296	.338	.633	6	.952
2003—Omaha (PCL)		OF	52	190	38	53	9	2	8	30	33	43	9	3	3-0	.279	.408	.474	.881	5	.962
—Kansas City (A.L.)		OF-DH	99	354	63	98	30	0	15	52	27	63	13	3	3-5	.277	.346	.489	.835	3	.985
2004—Royals (Ariz.)		DH	4	17	3	8	1	0	2	5	0	2	1	0	0-0	.471	.500	.882	1.382	0	1.000
—Wichita (Texas)		OF	6	20	7	5	0	0	0	0	8	6	3	0	2-0	.250	.516	.250	.766	1	.933
—Omaha (PCL)		OF-DH	30	116	29	36	6	0	10	30	21	33	6	1	0-2	.310	.438	.621	1.058	4	.980
—Kansas City (A.L.)		OF-DH	42	135	15	21	4	0	5	13	17	42	3	3	1-1	.156	.263	.296	.559	3	.966
Major League totals (3 years)			211	729	108	175	47	0	24	103	63	166	20	9	5-11	.240	.314	.403	.717	12	.971

GUILLEN, CARLOS — SS/3B

PERSONAL: Born September 30, 1975, in Maracay, Venezuela. ... 6-1/204. ... Bats both, throws right. ... Full name: Carlos Alfonso Guillen. ... Name pronounced: GEY-un.

TRANSACTIONS/CAREER NOTES: Signed as a non-drafted free agent by Houston Astros organization (September 19, 1992). ... Traded by Astros with P Freddy Garcia and a player to be named to Seattle Mariners for P Randy Johnson (July 31, 1998); Mariners acquired P John Halama to complete deal (October 1, 1998). ... On disabled list (April 7, 1999-remainder of season). ... On disabled list (April 13-28, 2000); included rehabilitation assignment to Tacoma. ... On disabled list (July 29-August 23, 2003); included rehabilitation assignment to Tacoma. ... Traded by Mariners to Detroit Tigers for IFs Ramon Santiago and Juan Gonzalez (January 8, 2004).

2004 GAMES PLAYED BY POSITION (MLB): SS—135.

									BATTING											FIELDING	
Year	Team (League)	Pos.	G	AB	R	H	2B	3B	HR	RBI	BB	SO	HBP	GDP	SB-CS	Avg.	OBP	SLG	OPS	E	Avg.
1993—Dom. Astros (DSL)		IF	18	56	12	14	4	2	0	8	8	12	...	...	0-...	.250	...	.393	...	2	.956
1994—					Did not play.																
1995—GC Astros (GCL)			30	105	17	31	4	2	2	15	9	17	1	0	17-1	.295	.350	.429	.779	...	...
1996—Quad City (Midw.)		SS	29	112	23	37	7	1	3	17	16	25	0	1	13-6	.330	.405	.491	.896	9	.929
1997—Jackson (Texas)		SS-DH	115	390	47	99	16	1	10	39	38	78	2	9	6-5	.254	.322	.377	.699	35	.932
—New Orleans (A.A.)		SS	3	13	3	4	1	0	0	0	0	4	0	0	0-0	.308	.308	.385	.692	1	1.000
1998—New Orleans (PCL)		SS	100	374	67	109	18	4	12	51	31	61	5	...	3-4	.291	.350	.457	.807	26	.943
—Tacoma (PCL)		2B	24	92	8	21	1	1	1	4	9	17	0	...	1-2	.228	.297	.293	.591	2	.982
—Seattle (A.L.)		2B	10	39	9	13	1	1	0	5	3	9	0	0	2-0	.333	.381	.410	.791	0	1.000
1999—Seattle (A.L.)		SS-2B	5	19	2	3	0	0	1	3	1	6	0	1	0-0	.158	.200	.316	.516	1	.964
2000—Seattle (A.L.)		3B-SS	90	288	45	74	15	2	7	42	28	53	2	6	1-3	.257	.324	.396	.720	21	.921
—Tacoma (PCL)		3B-SS	24	87	19	26	4	1	2	11	12	17	1	3	4-1	.299	.386	.437	.823	6	.926
2001—Seattle (A.L.)		SS-DH	140	456	72	118	21	4	5	53	53	89	1	9	4-1	.259	.333	.355	.689	10	.980
2002—Seattle (A.L.)		SS-DH	134	475	73	124	24	6	9	56	46	91	1	8	4-5	.261	.326	.394	.719	18	.966
2003—Tacoma (PCL)		2B	4	14	2	5	1	0	2	4	0	1	1	2	0-0	.357	.400	.857	1.257	0	1.000
—Seattle (A.L.)		SS-3B-DH	109	388	63	107	19	3	7	52	52	64	1	12	4-4	.276	.359	.394	.753	14	.963
2004—Detroit (A.L.)		SS	136	522	97	166	37	10	20	97	52	87	2	12	12-5	.318	.379	.542	.921	17	.974
Major League totals (7 years)			624	2187	361	605	117	26	49	308	235	399	7	48	27-18	.277	.346	.421	.767	81	.966

DIVISION SERIES RECORD

Year	Team (League)	Pos.	G	AB	R	H	2B	3B	HR	RBI	BB	SO	HBP	GDP	SB-CS	Avg.	OBP	SLG	OPS	E	Avg.
2000—Seattle (A.L.)			1	1	0	1	0	0	0	1	0	0	0	0	0-0	1.000	1.000	1.000	2.000	...	...
2001—Seattle (A.L.)					Did not play.																

CHAMPIONSHIP SERIES RECORD

Year	Team (League)	Pos.	G	AB	R	H	2B	3B	HR	RBI	BB	SO	HBP	GDP	SB-CS	Avg.	OBP	SLG	OPS	E	Avg.
2000—Seattle (A.L.)		3B	2	5	1	1	0	0	1	2	2	2	0	0	0-1	.200	.429	.800	1.229	0	1.000
2001—Seattle (A.L.)		SS	3	8	1	2	0	0	0	0	1	0			0-0	.250	.250	.250	.500	0	1.000
Champ. series totals (2 years)			5	13	2	3	0	0	1	2	2	3	0	0	0-1	.231	.333	.462	.795	0	1.000

GUILLEN, JOSE — OF

PERSONAL: Born May 17, 1976, in San Cristobal, Dominican Republic. ... 5-11/190. ... Bats right, throws right. ... Full name: Jose Manuel Guillen. ... Name pronounced: GHEE-yen.

TRANSACTIONS/CAREER NOTES: Signed as a non-drafted free agent by Pittsburgh Pirates organization (August 19, 1992). ... Traded by Pirates with P Jeff Sparks to Tampa Bay Devil Rays for Cs Joe Oliver and Humberto Cota (July 23, 1999). ... On disabled list (March 28-April 12, 2000). ... On disabled list (May 17-June 24 and June 25-July 30, 2001); included rehabilitation assignments to Durham. ... Released by Devil Rays (November 27, 2001). ... Signed by Arizona Diamondbacks (December 18, 2001). ... Released by Diamondbacks (July 22, 2002). ... Signed by Colorado Rockies organization (July 29, 2002). ... Released by Rockies (August 1, 2002). ... Signed by Cincinnati Reds organization (August 20, 2002). ... Released by Reds (March 12, 2003). ... Re-signed by Reds organization (March 13, 2003). ... Traded by Reds to Oakland Athletics for Ps Aaron Harang, Joe Valentine and Jeff Bruksch (July 30, 2003). ... On suspended list (September 4-6, 2003). ... Signed as a free agent by Anaheim Angels (December 20, 2003). ... On Anaheim suspended list (September 26, 2004-remainder of season).

2004 GAMES PLAYED BY POSITION (MLB): OF—136, DH—10.

Year	Team (League)	Pos.	G	AB	R	H	2B	3B	HR	RBI	BB	SO	HBP	GDP	SB-CS	Avg.	OBP	SLG	OPS	E	FIELDING Avg.
1993— Dom. Pirates (DSL)	OF	63	234	39	53	3	4	11	41	21	55	...	...	10-...	.227	...	.415	...	7	.947
1994— GC Pirates (GCL)	OF	30	110	17	29	4	1	4	11	7	15	6	0	2-1	.264	.341	.427	.769	2	.970
1995— Erie (N.Y.-Penn)	OF	66	258	41	81	17	1	12	46	10	44	12	5	1-5	.314	.367	.527	.894	13	.900
— Augusta (S. Atl.)	OF	10	34	6	8	1	1	2	6	2	9	2	0	0-0	.235	.316	.500	.816	0	1.000
1996— Lynchburg (Caro.)	OF-DH	136	528	78	170	30	0	21	94	20	73	13	16	24-13	.322	.357	.498	.855	13	.949
1997— Pittsburgh (N.L.)	OF	143	498	58	133	20	5	14	70	17	88	8	16	1-2	.267	.300	.412	.712	9	.963
1998— Pittsburgh (N.L.)	OF	153	573	60	153	38	2	14	84	21	100	6	7	3-5	.267	.298	.414	.712	10	.968
1999— Pittsburgh (N.L.)	OF	40	120	18	32	6	0	1	18	10	21	0	7	1-0	.267	.321	.342	.662	3	.952
— Nashville (PCL)	OF-DH	35	132	28	44	10	0	5	22	8	21	2	4	0-1	.333	.378	.523	.900	4	.939
— Durham (Int'l)	OF	9	34	8	13	1	0	3	12	7	7	0	2	0-1	.382	.476	.676	1.153	0	1.000
— Tampa Bay (A.L.)	OF	47	168	24	41	10	0	2	13	10	36	7	9	0-0	.244	.312	.339	.651	3	.966
2000— Durham (Int'l)	OF	19	78	20	33	8	2	9	31	8	11	1	2	0-1	.423	.477	.923	1.400	3	.912
— Tampa Bay (A.L.)	OF	105	316	40	80	16	5	10	41	18	65	13	6	3-1	.253	.320	.430	.750	4	.978
2001— Tampa Bay (A.L.)	OF-DH	41	135	14	37	5	0	3	11	6	26	3	2	2-3	.274	.317	.378	.695	3	.969
— Durham (Int'l)	OF	33	119	18	35	9	0	7	29	3	28	0	3	0-0	.294	.306	.546	.853	1	.982
2002— Arizona (N.L.)	OF-DH	54	131	13	30	4	0	4	15	7	25	2	7	3-4	.229	.277	.351	.628	0	1.000
— Colo. Springs (PCL)	OF	5	17	2	7	3	0	0	5	1	2	1	1	0-1	.412	.474	.588	1.062	0	1.000
— Louisville (Int'l)	OF	8	29	4	9	4	0	2	8	0	5	0	1	0-0	.310	.310	.655	.966	0	1.000
— Cincinnati (N.L.)	OF	31	109	12	27	3	0	4	16	7	18	1	6	1-1	.248	.299	.385	.684	1	.979
2003— Louisville (Int'l)	OF	4	15	4	5	1	0	0	3	1	3	0	1	1-0	.333	.353	.400	.753	0	1.000
— Cincinnati (N.L.)	OF	91	315	52	106	21	1	23	63	17	63	9	8	1-3	.337	.385	.629	1.013	8	.957
— Oakland (A.L.)	OF-DH	45	170	25	45	7	1	8	23	7	32	5	8	0-0	.265	.311	.459	.770	4	.942
2004— Anaheim (A.L.)	OF-DH	148	565	88	166	28	3	27	104	37	92	15	14	5-4	.294	.352	.497	.849	6	.979
American League totals (5 years)			386	1354	191	369	66	9	50	192	78	251	43	39	10-8	.273	.331	.445	.776	20	.972
National League totals (5 years)			512	1746	213	481	92	8	60	266	79	315	26	51	10-15	.275	.315	.440	.755	31	.966
Major League totals (8 years)			898	3100	404	850	158	17	110	458	157	566	69	90	20-23	.274	.322	.443	.764	51	.969

DIVISION SERIES RECORD

Year	Team (League)	Pos.	G	AB	R	H	2B	3B	HR	RBI	BB	SO	HBP	GDP	SB-CS	Avg.	OBP	SLG	OPS	E	Avg.
2003— Oakland (A.L.)	OF	4	11	1	5	1	0	0	1	3	2	0	0	0-0	.455	.571	.545	1.117	0	1.000

GUTHRIE, JEREMY — P

PERSONAL: Born April 8, 1979, in Roseburg, Ore. ... 6-1/200. ... Throws right, bats right. ... Full name: Jeremy S. Guthrie. ... High school: Ashland (Ore.). ... College: Stanford.

TRANSACTIONS/CAREER NOTES: Selected by New York Mets organization in 15th round of 1997 free-agent draft; did not sign. ... Selected by Pittsburgh Pirates organization in third round of 2001 free-agent draft; did not sign. ... Selected by Cleveland Indians organization in first round (22nd pick overall) of 2002 free-agent draft.

CAREER HITTING: 0-for-0 (.000), 0 R, 0 2B, 0 3B, 0 HR, 0 RBI.

Year	Team (League)	W	L	Pct.	ERA	WHIP	G	GS	CG	ShO	Hld.	Sv.-Opp.	IP	H	R	ER	HR	BB-IBB	SO	Avg.
2003— Akron (East.)	6	2	.750	1.44	0.93	10	9	2	2	...	0-...	62.2	44	11	10	0	14-0	35	.196
— Buffalo (Int'l)	4	9	.308	6.52	1.64	18	18	1	0	...	0-...	96.2	129	75	70	15	30-1	62	.321
2004— Buffalo (Int'l)	1	2	.333	7.91	2.12	4	4	0	0	...	0-...	19.1	23	19	17	0	18-0	10	.303
— Akron (East.)	8	8	.500	4.21	1.43	23	21	1	0	...	0-...	130.1	145	76	61	16	42-0	94	.277
— Cleveland (A.L.)	0	0	...	4.63	1.29	6	0	0	0	0	0-0	11.2	9	6	6	1	6-0	7	.214
Major League totals (1 year)	0	0	...	4.63	1.29	6	0	0	0	0	0-0	11.2	9	6	6	1	6-0	7	.214

GUTIERREZ, RICKY — 2B

PERSONAL: Born May 23, 1970, in Miami, Fla. ... 6-1/190. ... Bats right, throws right. ... Full name: Ricardo Gutierrez. ... Name pronounced: goo-tee-AIR-ezz. ... High school: American (Hialeah, Fla.).

TRANSACTIONS/CAREER NOTES: Selected by Baltimore Orioles organization in supplemental round ("sandwich pick" between first and second round, 28th pick overall) of 1988 free-agent draft; pick received as compensation for Orioles failing to sign 1987 first-round pick P Brad DuVall. ... Traded by Orioles to San Diego Padres (September 4, 1992), completing deal in which Padres traded P Craig Lefferts to Orioles for P Erik Schullstrom and a player to be named (August 31, 1992). ... Traded by Padres with OF Phil Plantier, OF Derek Bell, Ps Pedro Martinez and Doug Brocail and IF Craig Shipley to Houston Astros for 3B Ken Caminiti, OF Steve Finley, SS Andujar Cedeno, 1B Robert Petagine, P Brian Williams and a player to be named (December 28, 1994); Padres acquired P Sean Fesh to complete deal (May 1, 1995). ... On disabled list (March 31-May 6, 1997); included rehabilitation assignment to New Orleans. ... On disabled list (April 28-June 7 and July 10-August 9, 1999); included rehabilitation assignments to Jackson and New Orleans. ... Signed as a free agent by Chicago Cubs (December 20, 1999). ... On disabled list (May 25-June 23, 2000); included rehabilitation assignment to Daytona. ... Signed as a free agent by Cleveland Indians (December 19, 2001). ... On disabled list (June 14-July 2 and August 15, 2002-remainder of season). ... On disabled list (March 29-June 24 and July 13, 2003-remainder of season); included rehabilitation assignment to Buffalo. ... Traded by Indians to New York Mets for a player to be named (March 29, 2004). ... Released by Mets (May 21, 2004). ... Signed by Cubs organization (June 14, 2004). ... Traded by Cubs to Boston Red Sox for a player to be named or cash (July 21, 2004).

2004 GAMES PLAYED BY POSITION (MLB): 2B—32, SS—6, 3B—2.

Year	Team (League)	Pos.	G	AB	R	H	2B	3B	HR	RBI	BB	SO	HBP	GDP	SB-CS	Avg.	OBP	SLG	OPS	E	FIELDING Avg.
1988— Bluefield (Appal.)	SS	62	208	35	51	8	2	2	19	44	40	5	4	5-3	.245	.383	.332	.715	34	.890
1989— Frederick (Carolina)	SS	127	456	48	106	16	2	3	41	39	89	3	12	15-10	.232	.294	.296	.590	34	.943
1990— Frederick (Carolina)	SS	112	425	54	117	16	4	1	46	38	59	6	11	12-6	.275	.341	.339	.680	26	.948
— Hagerstown (East.)	SS	20	64	4	15	0	1	0	6	3	8	0	2	2-0	.234	.265	.266	.530	4	.944
1991— Hagerstown (East.)	SS	84	292	47	69	6	4	0	30	57	52	1	8	11-0	.236	.363	.284	.647	22	.941
— Rochester (Int'l)	3B-SS	49	157	23	48	5	3	0	15	24	27	0	3	4-1	.306	.396	.376	.771	8	.960
1992— Rochester (Int'l)	2B-SS	125	431	54	109	9	3	0	41	53	77	0	12	14-12	.253	.331	.288	.619	15	.973
— Las Vegas (PCL)	SS	3	6	0	1	0	0	0	1	0	3	0	0	0-0	.167	.250	.167	.417	0	1.000
1993— Las Vegas (PCL)	2B-SS	5	24	4	10	4	0	0	4	0	4	0	0	4-0	.417	.417	.583	1.000	2	.926
— San Diego (N.L.)	SS-2-0-3	133	438	76	110	10	5	5	26	50	97	5	7	4-3	.251	.334	.331	.665	14	.973
1994— San Diego (N.L.)	SS-2B	90	275	27	66	11	2	1	28	32	54	2	8	2-6	.240	.321	.305	.626	22	.931
1995— Houston (N.L.)	SS-3B	52	156	22	43	6	0	0	12	10	33	1	4	5-0	.276	.321	.314	.636	8	.956
— Tucson (PCL)	SS-DH	64	236	46	71	12	4	1	26	28	28	3	6	9-7	.301	.379	.398	.777	6	.977
1996— Houston (N.L.)	SS-3B-2B	89	218	28	62	8	1	1	15	23	42	3	4	6-1	.284	.359	.344	.703	12	.951
1997— New Orleans (A.A.)	SS	7	27	2	5	1	0	0	4	3	6	1	0	0-1	.185	.233	.222	.456	1	.971
— Houston (N.L.)	SS-3B-2B	102	303	33	79	14	4	3	34	21	50	2	17	5-2	.261	.315	.363	.678	8	.974
1998— Houston (N.L.)	SS	141	491	55	128	24	3	2	46	54	84	6	20	13-7	.261	.337	.334	.671	15	.976

Year	Team (League)	Pos.	G	AB	R	H	2B	3B	HR	RBI	BB	SO	HBP	GDP	SB-CS	Avg.	OBP	SLG	OPS	E	Avg.
1999—Houston (N.L.)	SS-3B		85	268	33	70	7	5	1	25	37	45	2	9	2-5	.261	.354	.336	.690	9	.971
—Jackson (Texas)	SS-DH		4	12	4	4	1	0	0	1	4	3	0	0	0-1	.333	.500	.417	.917	0	1.000
—New Orleans (PCL)	SS		4	14	0	3	0	0	0	1	2	3	0	2	0-0	.214	.313	.214	.527	3	.875
2000—Chicago (N.L.)	SS		125	449	73	124	19	2	11	56	66	58	7	10	8-2	.276	.375	.401	.775	7	.986
—Daytona (Fla. St.)	SS		4	10	0	4	1	0	0	1	2	2	0	1	1-0	.400	.500	.500	1.000	3	.727
2001—Chicago (N.L.)	SS		147	528	76	153	23	3	10	66	40	56	10	13	4-3	.290	.345	.402	.746	16	.971
2002—Cleveland (A.L.)	2B-DH		94	353	38	97	13	0	4	38	20	48	7	14	0-1	.275	.325	.346	.671	11	.976
2003—Buffalo (Int'l)	3-S-2-DH		16	65	8	19	2	1	0	5	4	5	1	2	4-1	.292	.338	.354	.692	0	1.000
—Cleveland (A.L.)	SS-3B		16	50	2	13	3	0	0	3	3	5	1	1	0-0	.260	.309	.320	.629	3	.942
2004—New York (N.L.)	2B-3B		24	63	2	11	2	0	0	5	6	8	1	3	0-0	.175	.257	.206	.463	1	.987
—Daytona (Fla. St.)	DH-2B-SS		4	13	1	1	0	0	0	3	1	3	2	1	0-0	.077	.235	.077	.312	0	1.000
—Iowa (PCL)	SS-2B-3B		21	68	5	25	5	0	0	10	6	10	0	1	0-1	.368	.419	.441	.860	2	.974
—Boston (A.L.)	2B-SS		21	40	6	11	1	0	0	3	2	6	0	2	1-0	.275	.310	.300	.610	1	.982
American League totals (3 years)			131	443	46	121	17	0	4	44	25	59	8	17	1-1	.273	.322	.339	.661	15	.973
National League totals (10 years)			988	3189	425	846	124	25	34	313	339	527	40	95	49-29	.265	.341	.352	.692	112	.969
Major League totals (12 years)			1119	3632	471	967	141	25	38	357	364	586	48	112	50-30	.266	.338	.350	.689	127	.970

DIVISION SERIES RECORD

Year	Team (League)	Pos.	G	AB	R	H	2B	3B	HR	RBI	BB	SO	HBP	GDP	SB-CS	Avg.	OBP	SLG	OPS	E	Avg.
1997—Houston (N.L.)	SS		3	8	0	1	0	0	0	0	2	1	0	0	0-0	.125	.300	.125	.425	0	1.000
1998—Houston (N.L.)	SS		4	10	1	3	0	0	0	0	3	7	1	0	1-0	.300	.500	.300	.800	0	1.000
1999—Houston (N.L.)	SS		3	10	0	0	0	0	0	0	2	5	0	1	0-0	.000	.167	.000	.167	1	.952
Division series totals (3 years)			10	28	1	4	0	0	0	0	7	13	1	1	1-0	.143	.333	.143	.476	1	.980

GUZMAN, CRISTIAN — SS

PERSONAL: Born March 21, 1978, in Santo Domingo, Dominican Republic. ... 6-0/205. ... Bats both, throws right. ... Full name: Christian Antonio Guzman. ... Name pronounced: GOOZ-mahn.

TRANSACTIONS/CAREER NOTES: Signed as a non-drafted free agent by New York Yankees organization (August 24, 1994). ... Traded by Yankees with Ps Eric Milton and Danny Mota, OF Brian Buchanan and cash to Minnesota Twins for 2B Chuck Knoblauch (February 6, 1998). ... On disabled list (May 27-June 11, 1999). ... On suspended list (September 10-13, 1999). ... On disabled list (July 13-August 17, 2001); included rehabilitation assignment to GCL Twins.

2004 GAMES PLAYED BY POSITION (MLB): SS—145.

							BATTING													FIELDING	
Year	Team (League)	Pos.	G	AB	R	H	2B	3B	HR	RBI	BB	SO	HBP	GDP	SB-CS	Avg.	OBP	SLG	OPS	E	Avg.
1995—Dom. Yankees (DSL)	SS		46	160	24	43	6	5	3	20	12	23	...		11-...	.269	...	.425	...	13	.935
1996—GC Yankees (GCL)	SS		42	170	37	50	8	2	1	21	10	31	3	2	7-6	.294	.341	.382	.723	20	.890
1997—Greensboro (S. Atl.)	SS		124	495	68	135	21	4	4	52	17	105	10	3	23-12	.273	.309	.356	.665	37	.936
—Tampa (Fla. St.)	SS		4	14	4	4	0	0	0	1	1	1	0	0	0-1	.286	.333	.286	.619	2	.889
1998—New Britain (East.)	SS		140	566	68	157	29	5	1	40	21	111	1	13	23-14	.277	.304	.352	.655	32	.952
1999—Minnesota (A.L.)	SS		131	420	47	95	12	3	1	26	22	90	3	5	9-7	.226	.267	.276	.543	24	.959
2000—Minnesota (A.L.)	SS-DH		156	631	89	156	25	*20	8	54	46	101	2	5	28-10	.247	.299	.388	.687	22	.967
2001—Minnesota (A.L.)	SS		118	493	80	149	28	*14	10	51	21	78	5	6	25-8	.302	.337	.477	.814	* 21	.959
—GC Twins (GCL)	SS		5	16	4	4	0	1	0	0	2	4	1	1	0-1	.250	.368	.375	.743	0	1.000
2002—Minnesota (A.L.)	SS-DH		148	623	80	170	31	6	9	59	17	79	2	12	12-13	.273	.292	.385	.677	12	.981
2003—Minnesota (A.L.)	SS		143	534	78	143	15	*14	3	53	30	79	5	4	18-9	.268	.311	.365	.676	11	.980
2004—Minnesota (A.L.)	SS		145	576	84	158	31	4	8	46	30	64	1	15	10-5	.274	.309	.384	.693	12	.983
Major League totals (6 years)			841	3277	458	871	142	61	39	289	166	491	18	47	102-52	.266	.303	.382	.685	102	.972

DIVISION SERIES RECORD

Year	Team (League)	Pos.	G	AB	R	H	2B	3B	HR	RBI	BB	SO	HBP	GDP	SB-CS	Avg.	OBP	SLG	OPS	E	Avg.
2002—Minnesota (A.L.)	SS		5	21	5	6	2	0	1	2	2	4	0	0	2-0	.286	.348	.524	.872	1	.923
2003—Minnesota (A.L.)	SS		4	13	1	2	0	0	0	0	1	2	0	0	0-0	.154	.214	.154	.368	0	1.000
2004—Minnesota (A.L.)	SS		4	15	2	5	0	0	0	0	2	3	0	0	1-0	.333	.412	.333	.745	1	.964
Division series totals (3 years)			13	49	8	13	2	0	1	2	5	9	0	0	3-0	.265	.333	.367	.701	2	.966

CHAMPIONSHIP SERIES RECORD

Year	Team (League)	Pos.	G	AB	R	H	2B	3B	HR	RBI	BB	SO	HBP	GDP	SB-CS	Avg.	OBP	SLG	OPS	E	Avg.
2002—Minnesota (A.L.)	SS		5	18	1	3	1	0	0	0	0	3	1	0	0-0	.167	.211	.222	.433	1	.962

ALL-STAR GAME RECORD

		G	AB	R	H	2B	3B	HR	RBI	BB	SO	HBP	GDP	SB-CS	Avg.	OBP	SLG	OPS	E	Avg.
All-Star Game totals (1 year)		1	1	0	0	0	0	0	0	0	1	0	0	0-0	.000	.000	.000	.000	0	...

GUZMAN, FREDDY — OF

PERSONAL: Born January 20, 1981, in Santo Domingo, Dominican Republic. ... 5-10/165. ... Bats both, throws right. ... Full name: Freddy Antonio Guzman.
TRANSACTIONS/CAREER NOTES: Signed as a non-drafted free agent by San Diego Padres organization (April 17, 2000).
2004 GAMES PLAYED BY POSITION (MLB): OF—17.

							BATTING													FIELDING	
Year	Team (League)	Pos.	G	AB	R	H	2B	3B	HR	RBI	BB	SO	HBP	GDP	SB-CS	Avg.	OBP	SLG	OPS	E	Avg.
2001—Idaho Falls (Pio.)	2B		12	46	11	16	4	1	0	5	2	10	1	1	5-0	.348	.388	.478	.866	4	.932
2002—Lake Elsinore (Calif.)	OF-2B-3B		21	81	13	21	3	0	1	6	8	12	0	1	14-4	.259	.326	.333	.659	7	.865
—Fort Wayne (Midw.)	OF		47	190	35	53	7	5	0	18	18	37	0	3	39-7	.279	.341	.368	.710	6	.950
—Eugene (Northwest)	OF		21	80	14	18	2	1	0	8	7	15	2	0	16-1	.225	.293	.275	.568	3	.921
2003—Lake Elsinore (Calif.)	OF		70	281	64	80	12	3	2	22	40	60	2	1	49-10	.285	.375	.370	.745	5	.962
—Mobile (Sou.)	OF		46	177	30	48	5	2	1	11	26	34	1	0	38-7	.271	.368	.339	.707	2	.984
—Portland (PCL)	OF		2	10	1	3	0	0	0	0	0	1	0	0	3-0	.300	.300	.300	.600	0	1.000
2004—Mobile (Sou.)	OF-DH		35	138	21	39	5	2	1	7	16	28	1	2	17-5	.283	.359	.370	.724	1	.989
—Portland (PCL)	OF		66	264	48	77	12	4	1	19	30	46	1	1	48-5	.292	.365	.379	.742	3	.983
—San Diego (N.L.)	OF		20	76	8	16	3	0	0	5	3	13	1	0	5-2	.211	.250	.250	.500	2	.960
Major League totals (1 year)			20	76	8	16	3	0	0	5	3	13	1	0	5-2	.211	.250	.250	.500	2	.960

G

HAFNER, TRAVIS — DH/1B

PERSONAL: Born June 3, 1977, in Jamestown, N.D. ... 6-3/240. ... Bats left, throws right. ... Full name: Travis Lee Hafner. ... Name pronounced: HAF-ner. ... Junior college: Cowley County (Kan.) Community College.

TRANSACTIONS/CAREER NOTES: Selected by Texas Rangers organization in 31st round of 1996 free-agent draft. ... Traded by Rangers with P Aaron Myette to Cleveland Indians for C Einar Diaz and P Ryan Drese (December 6, 2002). ... On disabled list (May 10-26, 2003); included rehabilitation assignment to Buffalo.

2004 GAMES PLAYED BY POSITION (MLB): DH—128, 1B—11.

													BATTING							FIELDING	
Year	Team (League)	Pos.	G	AB	R	H	2B	3B	HR	RBI	BB	SO	HBP	GDP	SB-CS	Avg.	OBP	SLG	OPS	E	Avg.
1997— GC Rangers (GCL)		1B-OF	55	189	38	54	14	0	5	24	24	45	3	3	7-2	.286	.375	.439	.814	3	.991
1998— Savannah (S. Atl.)		3B-1B-OF	123	405	62	96	15	4	16	84	68	139	6	8	7-3	.237	.351	.412	.764	12	.980
1999— Savannah (S. Atl.)		3B-1B	134	480	94	140	30	4	28	111	67	151	11	11	5-4	.292	.387	.546	.933	15	.984
2000— Charlotte (Fla. St.)		1B-3B	122	436	90	151	34	1	22	109	67	86	18	9	0-4	.346	.447	.580	1.027	13	.978
2001— Tulsa (Texas)		1B	88	323	59	91	25	0	20	74	59	82	4	10	3-1	.282	.396	.545	.941	5	.993
2002— Oklahoma (PCL)		1B	110	401	79	137	22	1	21	77	79	76	12	9	2-1	.342	.463	.559	1.022	4	.993
— Texas (A.L.)		DH-1B	23	62	6	15	4	1	1	6	8	15	0	0	0-1	.242	.329	.387	.716	1	.909
2003— Buffalo (Int'l)		1B-DH	29	100	15	27	4	0	2	10	25	26	1	2	2-1	.270	.421	.370	.791	3	.986
— Cleveland (A.L.)		DH-1B	91	291	35	74	19	3	14	40	22	81	10	7	2-1	.254	.327	.485	.812	6	.985
2004— Cleveland (A.L.)		DH-1B	140	482	96	150	41	3	28	109	68	111	17	11	3-2	.311	.410	.583	.993	0	1.000
Major League totals (3 years)			254	835	137	239	64	7	43	155	98	207	27	18	5-4	.286	.376	.534	.911	7	.986

HAIRSTON, SCOTT — 2B

PERSONAL: Born May 25, 1980, in Fort Worth, Texas. ... 6-0/188. ... Bats right, throws right. ... Full name: Scott Alexander Hairston. ... High school: Canyon del Oro (Tucson, Ariz.). ... Junior college: Central Arizona. ... Son of Jerry Hairston, outfielder with two major league teams (1973-77 and 1981-89); brother of Jerry Hairston Jr., infielder/outfielder, Baltimore Orioles; nephew of John Hairston, catcher/outfielder with Chicago Cubs (1969); grandson of Sam Hairston, catcher with Chicago White Sox (1951).

TRANSACTIONS/CAREER NOTES: Selected by Chicago White Sox organization in 18th round of 1999 free-agent draft; did not sign. ... Selected by Arizona Diamondbacks in third round of 2001 free-agent draft.

2004 GAMES PLAYED BY POSITION (MLB): 2B—85, OF—3.

													BATTING							FIELDING	
Year	Team (League)	Pos.	G	AB	R	H	2B	3B	HR	RBI	BB	SO	HBP	GDP	SB-CS	Avg.	OBP	SLG	OPS	E	Avg.
2001— Missoula (Pio.)		2B	74	291	81	101	16	6	14	65	38	50	7	5	2-2	.347	.432	.588	1.020	21	.935
2002— South Bend (Mid.)		2B-3B	109	394	79	131	35	4	16	72	58	74	10	11	9-3	.332	.426	.563	.990	28	.944
— Lancaster (Calif.)		2B-3B	18	79	20	32	11	1	6	26	6	16	0	4	1-0	.405	.442	.797	1.239	2	.952
2003— El Paso (Texas)		2B	88	337	53	93	21	7	10	47	30	80	6	10	6-2	.276	.345	.469	.814	15	.960
— Tucson (PCL)			1	0	0	0	0	0	0	1	0	0	0	0	0-0	.000	.000	.000	.000	...	...
2004— Tucson (PCL)		2B-OF-DH	28	115	29	36	8	3	5	20	11	21	1	1	0-3	.313	.375	.565	.935	6	.940
— Arizona (N.L.)		2B-OF	101	339	39	84	15	6	13	29	21	88	1	4	3-3	.248	.293	.442	.735	11	.972
Major League totals (1 year)			101	339	39	84	15	6	13	29	21	88	1	4	3-3	.248	.293	.442	.735	11	.972

HAIRSTON JR., JERRY — OF

PERSONAL: Born May 29, 1976, in Naperville, Ill. ... 5-10/183. ... Bats right, throws right. ... Full name: Jerry Wayne Hairston Jr. ... High school: Naperville (Ill.) North. ... College: Southern Illinois. ... Son of Jerry Hairston, outfielder with two major league teams (1973-77 and 1981-89); brother of Scott Hairston, second baseman, Arizona Diamondbacks; nephew of John Hairston, catcher/outfielder with Chicago Cubs (1969); grandson of Sam Hairston, catcher with Chicago White Sox (1951).

TRANSACTIONS/CAREER NOTES: Selected by Baltimore Orioles organization in 42nd round of 1995 free-agent draft; did not sign. ... Selected by Orioles organization in 11th round of 1997 free-agent draft. ... On disabled list (May 21-September 4, 2003); included rehabilitation assignment to Bowie and Aberdeen. ... On disabled list (March 26-May 11 and August 18, 2004-remainder of season); included rehabilitation assignment to Bowie.

2004 GAMES PLAYED BY POSITION (MLB): OF—52, DH—21, 2B—12, 3B—1.

													BATTING							FIELDING	
Year	Team (League)	Pos.	G	AB	R	H	2B	3B	HR	RBI	BB	SO	HBP	GDP	SB-CS	Avg.	OBP	SLG	OPS	E	Avg.
1997— Bluefield (Appal.)		SS	59	221	44	73	13	4	2	36	21	29	10	4	13-9	.330	.409	.452	.862	14	.949
1998— Frederick (Carolina)		2B-SS	80	293	56	83	22	3	5	33	28	32	12	4	13-7	.283	.366	.430	.796	24	.943
— Bowie (East.)		2B-SS	55	221	42	72	12	3	5	37	20	25	5	5	6-4	.326	.393	.475	.868	5	.980
— Baltimore (A.L.)		2B	6	7	2	0	0	0	0	0	0	1	0	0	0-0	.000	.000	.000	.000	2	.750
1999— Rochester (Int'l)		2B-SS	107	413	65	120	24	5	7	48	30	50	19	9	19-10	.291	.363	.424	.787	16	.968
— Baltimore (A.L.)		2B	50	175	26	47	12	1	4	17	11	24	3	2	9-4	.269	.323	.417	.740	0	1.000
2000— Baltimore (A.L.)		2B	49	180	27	46	5	0	5	19	21	22	6	8	8-5	.256	.353	.367	.719	5	.981
— Rochester (Int'l)		2B-SS	58	201	43	59	15	1	4	21	29	32	5	2	6-4	.294	.392	.438	.830	11	.963
— GC Orioles (GCL)		2B	4	10	3	3	2	0	0	3	3	2	2	0	4-0	.300	.500	.500	1.000	0	1.000
— Frederick (Carolina)		2B	2	8	1	3	2	0	0	1	1	0	0	0	0-0	.375	.444	.625	1.069	0	1.000
2001— Baltimore (A.L.)		2B	159	532	63	124	25	5	8	47	44	73	13	12	29-11	.233	.305	.344	.649	19	.976
2002— Baltimore (A.L.)		2B	122	426	55	114	23	3	5	32	34	55	7	5	21-6	.268	.329	.376	.705	11	.982
2003— Bowie (East.)		2B-DH	6	20	4	6	1	0	1	2	1	4	2	0	0-0	.300	.391	.500	.891	1	.941
— Aberdeen (NY-P)		2B-DH	2	3	2	1	0	0	0	0	3	0	0	0	1-0	.333	.667	.333	1.000	0	1.000
— Baltimore (A.L.)		2B-DH	58	218	25	59	12	2	2	21	23	25	6	8	14-5	.271	.353	.372	.725	5	.980
2004— Bowie (East.)		2B	5	13	4	2	1	0	0	2	3	0	0	0	2-0	.154	.313	.231	.543	1	.929
— Baltimore (A.L.)		O-DH-2-3	86	287	43	87	19	1	2	24	29	29	3	3	13-8	.303	.378	.397	.775	2	.988
Major League totals (7 years)			530	1825	241	477	98	12	26	160	162	229	43	38	94-39	.261	.334	.371	.705	44	.981

HALAMA, JOHN — P

PERSONAL: Born February 22, 1972, in Brooklyn, N.Y. ... 6-5/215. ... Throws left, bats left. ... Full name: John Thadeuz Halama. ... Name pronounced: ha-LA-ma. ... High school: Bishop Ford (Brooklyn, N.Y.). ... College: St. Francis (N.Y.).

TRANSACTIONS/CAREER NOTES: Selected by Houston Astros organization in 23rd round of 1994 free-agent draft. ... Traded by Astros to Seattle Mariners (October 1, 1998), completing deal in which Mariners traded P Randy Johnson to Astros for SS Carlos Guillen, P Freddy Garcia and a player to be named (July 31, 1998). ... Signed as a free agent by Oakland Athletics (January 17, 2003). ... Signed as a free agent by Tampa Bay Devil Rays (November 14, 2003).

CAREER HITTING: 2-for-21 (.095), 2 R, 1 2B, 0 3B, 0 HR, 0 RBI.

Year	Team (League)	W	L	Pct.	ERA	WHIP	G	GS	CG	ShO	Hld.	Sv.-Opp.	IP	H	R	ER	HR	BB-IBB	SO	Avg.
1994— Auburn (N.Y.-Penn)		4	1	.800	1.29	0.82	6	3	0	0	...	1-...	28.0	18	5	4	1	5-0	27	.180
— Quad City (Midw.)		3	4	.429	4.56	1.58	9	9	1	1	...	0-...	51.1	63	31	26	2	18-1	37	.317
1995— Quad City (Midw.)		1	2	.333	2.02	1.12	55	0	0	0	...	2-...	62.1	48	16	14	7	22-1	56	.225

H

Year	Team (League)	W	L	Pct.	ERA	WHIP	G	GS	CG	ShO	Hld.	Sv.-Opp.	IP	H	R	ER	HR	BB-IBB	SO	Avg.
1996— Jackson (Texas)		9	10	.474	3.21	1.29	27	27	0	0	...	0-...	162.2	151	77	58	10	59-0	110	.248
1997— New Orleans (A.A.)		13	3	.813	2.58	1.06	26	24	1	0	...	0-...	171.0	150	57	49	9	32-1	126	.238
1998— Houston (N.L.)		1	1	.500	5.85	1.55	6	6	0	0	0	0-0	32.1	37	21	21	0	13-0	21	.296
— New Orleans (PCL)		12	3	.800	3.20	1.11	17	17	4	1	...	0-...	121.0	118	48	43	11	16-1	86	.255
1999— Seattle (A.L.)		11	10	.524	4.22	1.39	38	24	1	1	1	0-0	179.0	193	88	84	20	56-3	105	.282
2000— Seattle (A.L.)		14	9	.609	5.08	1.57	30	30	1	1	0	0-0	166.2	206	108	94	19	56-0	87	.308
2001— Seattle (A.L.)		10	7	.588	4.73	1.43	31	17	0	0	1	0-0	110.1	132	69	58	18	26-0	50	.296
— Tacoma (PCL)		2	0	1.000	0.47	0.47	3	3	1	1	...	0-...	19.0	9	2	1	1	0-0	22	.138
2002— Seattle (A.L.)		6	5	.545	3.56	1.44	31	10	0	0	0	0-0	101.0	112	45	40	9	33-5	70	.281
— Tacoma (PCL)		0	1	.000	6.14	1.36	2	2	0	0	...	0-...	14.2	19	11	10	0	1-1	9	.322
2003— Oakland (A.L.)		3	5	.375	4.22	1.41	35	13	0	0	3	0-0	108.2	117	68	51	18	36-2	51	.268
2004— Tampa Bay (A.L.)		7	6	.538	4.70	1.36	34	14	0	0	0	0-0	118.2	134	68	62	17	27-3	59	.284
American League totals (6 years)		51	42	.548	4.46	1.44	199	108	2	2	5	0-0	784.1	894	446	389	101	234-13	422	.288
National League totals (1 year)		1	1	.500	5.85	1.55	6	6	0	0	0	0-0	32.1	37	21	21	0	13-0	21	.296
Major League totals (7 years)		52	43	.547	4.52	1.44	205	114	2	2	5	0-0	816.2	931	467	410	101	247-13	443	.288

DIVISION SERIES RECORD

Year	Team (League)	W	L	Pct.	ERA	WHIP	G	GS	CG	ShO	Hld.	Sv.-Opp.	IP	H	R	ER	HR	BB-IBB	SO	Avg.
2000— Seattle (A.L.)		Did not play.																		
2001— Seattle (A.L.)		0	0	...	0.00	1.00	2	0	0	0	0	0-0	3.0	3	0	0	0	0-0	3	.300

CHAMPIONSHIP SERIES RECORD

Year	Team (League)	W	L	Pct.	ERA	WHIP	G	GS	CG	ShO	Hld.	Sv.-Opp.	IP	H	R	ER	HR	BB-IBB	SO	Avg.
2000— Seattle (A.L.)		0	0	...	2.89	1.61	2	2	0	0	0	0-0	9.1	10	3	3	0	5-0	3	.278
2001— Seattle (A.L.)		0	0	...	13.50	1.50	2	0	0	0	0	0-0	2.0	3	3	3	0	0-0	0	.333
Champ. series totals (2 years)		0	0	...	4.76	1.59	4	2	0	0	0	0-0	11.1	13	6	6	0	5-0	3	.289

HALL, BILL — 2B/SS

PERSONAL: Born December 28, 1979, in Nettleton, Miss. ... 6-0/195. ... Bats right, throws right. ... Full name: William Hall. ... High school: Nettleton (Miss.).
TRANSACTIONS/CAREER NOTES: Selected by Milwaukee Brewers organization in sixth round of 1998 free-agent draft.
2004 GAMES PLAYED BY POSITION (MLB): 2B—50, SS—37, 3B—11.

Year	Team (League)	Pos.	G	AB	R	H	2B	3B	HR	RBI	BB	SO	HBP	GDP	SB-CS	Avg.	OBP	SLG	OPS	E	Avg.
1998— Helena (Pio.)		SS	29	85	11	15	3	0	0	5	9	27	1	2	5-5	.176	.263	.212	.475	16	.876
1999— Ogden (Pio.)		SS	69	280	41	81	15	2	6	31	15	61	2	6	19-8	.289	.329	.421	.750	38	.894
2000— Beloit (Midw.)		SS	130	470	57	123	30	6	3	41	18	127	1	12	10-11	.262	.287	.370	.658	40	.939
2001— High Desert (Calif.)		SS	89	346	61	105	21	6	15	51	22	78	3	3	18-9	.303	.348	.529	.876	30	.929
— Huntsville (Sou.)		SS	41	160	14	41	8	1	3	14	5	46	0	5	5-3	.256	.279	.375	.654	15	.925
2002— Indianapolis (Int'l)		SS	134	465	35	106	20	1	4	31	25	105	4	12	17-10	.228	.272	.301	.573	41	.934
— Milwaukee (N.L.)		SS-3B	19	36	3	7	1	1	1	5	3	13	0	1	0-1	.194	.256	.361	.618	2	.951
2003— Indianapolis (Int'l)		2B-SS-OF	89	354	57	100	25	2	5	32	27	79	1	7	10-11	.282	.335	.407	.742	19	.957
— Milwaukee (N.L.)		2B-SS-3B	52	142	23	37	9	2	5	20	7	28	1	5	1-2	.261	.298	.458	.756	9	.948
2004— Milwaukee (N.L.)		2B-SS-3B	126	390	43	93	20	3	9	53	20	119	1	4	12-6	.238	.276	.374	.650	19	.956
Major League totals (3 years)			197	568	69	137	30	6	15	78	30	160	2	10	13-9	.241	.280	.394	.675	30	.953

HALL, TOBY — C

PERSONAL: Born October 21, 1975, in Tacoma, Wash. ... 6-3/240. ... Bats right, throws right. ... Full name: Toby Jason Hall. ... High school: El Dorado (Placentia, Calif.). ... College: UNLV.
TRANSACTIONS/CAREER NOTES: Selected by San Francisco Giants organization in 24th round of 1995 free-agent draft; did not sign. ... Selected by Tampa Bay Devil Rays organization in ninth round of 1997 free-agent draft.
2004 GAMES PLAYED BY POSITION (MLB): C—119.

Year	Team (League)	Pos.	G	AB	R	H	2B	3B	HR	RBI	BB	SO	HBP	GDP	SB-CS	Avg.	OBP	SLG	OPS	E	Avg.
1997— Hudson Valley (NY-Penn.)		C	55	200	25	50	3	0	1	27	13	33	1	3	0-0	.250	.295	.280	.575	3	.989
1998— Char., S.C. (SAL)		C	105	377	59	121	25	1	6	50	39	32	5	15	3-7	.321	.386	.440	.827	18	.979
1999— Orlando (South.)		C	46	173	20	44	7	0	9	34	4	10	1	7	1-1	.254	.269	.451	.720	4	.986
— St. Pete. (FSL)		C	56	212	24	63	13	1	4	36	17	9	2	7	0-2	.297	.350	.425	.775	4	.980
2000— Orlando (South.)		C	68	271	37	93	14	0	9	50	17	24	1	6	3-2	.343	.378	.494	.872	7	.984
— Durham (Int'l)		C	47	184	21	56	15	0	7	35	3	19	2	9	0-0	.304	.314	.500	.814	2	.993
— Tampa Bay (A.L.)		C	4	12	1	2	0	0	1	1	1	0	0	0	0-0	.167	.231	.417	.647	0	1.000
2001— Durham (Int'l)		C	94	373	59	125	28	1	19	72	29	22	3	15	1-3	.335	.385	.568	.953	6	.987
— Tampa Bay (A.L.)		C	49	188	28	56	16	0	4	30	4	16	3	5	2-2	.298	.321	.447	.768	5	.986
2002— Tampa Bay (A.L.)		C	85	330	37	85	19	1	6	42	17	27	1	14	0-1	.258	.293	.376	.669	6	.989
— Durham (Int'l)		C	22	92	13	32	4	0	2	20	3	10	4	3	0-0	.348	.382	.457	.839	1	.993
2003— Tampa Bay (A.L.)		C	130	463	50	117	23	0	12	47	23	40	7	14	0-1	.253	.295	.380	.675	9	.988
2004— Tampa Bay (A.L.)		C	119	404	35	103	21	0	8	60	24	41	5	20	0-2	.255	.300	.366	.666	6	.992
Major League totals (5 years)			387	1397	151	363	79	1	31	180	69	124	16	53	2-6	.260	.299	.384	.683	26	.989

HALLADAY, ROY — P

PERSONAL: Born May 14, 1977, in Denver, Colo. ... 6-6/230. ... Throws right, bats right. ... Full name: Harry Leroy Halladay. ... Name pronounced: HAL-luh-day. ... High school: Arvada (Colo.) West.
TRANSACTIONS/CAREER NOTES: Selected by Toronto Blue Jays organization in first round (17th pick overall) of 1995 free-agent draft. ... On disabled list (May 28-June 12 and July 17-September 21, 2004).
HONORS: Named A.L.Cy Young Award winner by Baseball Writers' Association of America (2003).
CAREER HITTING: 1-for-24 (.042), 2 R, 0 2B, 0 3B, 0 HR, 0 RBI.

Year	Team (League)	W	L	Pct.	ERA	WHIP	G	GS	CG	ShO	Hld.	Sv.-Opp.	IP	H	R	ER	HR	BB-IBB	SO	Avg.
1995— GC Blue Jays (GCL)		3	5	.375	3.40	1.01	10	8	0	0	...	0-...	50.1	35	25	19	4	16-0	48	.190
1996— Dunedin (Fla. St.)		15	7	.682	2.73	1.24	27	27	2	2	...	0-...	164.2	158	75	50	7	46-0	109	.251
1997— Knoxville (Southern)		2	3	.400	5.40	1.55	7	7	0	0	...	0-...	36.2	46	26	22	4	11-0	30	.305

H

Year	Team (League)	W	L	Pct.	ERA	WHIP	G	GS	CG	ShO	Hld.	Sv.-Opp.	IP	H	R	ER	HR	BB-IBB	SO	Avg.
	—Syracuse (Int'l)	7	10	.412	4.58	1.47	22	22	2	2	...	0-...	125.2	132	74	64	13	53-1	64	.276
1998—	Syracuse (Int'l)	9	5	.643	3.79	1.38	21	21	1	1	...	0-...	116.1	107	52	49	11	53-3	71	.246
	—Toronto (A.L.)	1	0	1.000	1.93	0.79	2	2	1	0	0	0-0	14.0	9	4	3	2	2-0	13	.176
1999—	Toronto (A.L.)	8	7	.533	3.92	1.57	36	18	1	1	2	1-1	149.1	156	76	65	19	79-1	82	.270
2000—	Toronto (A.L.)	4	7	.364	10.64	2.20	19	13	0	0	0	0-0	67.2	107	87	80	14	42-0	44	.357
	—Syracuse (Int'l)	2	3	.400	5.50	1.44	11	11	3	0	...	0-...	73.2	85	46	45	10	21-0	38	.290
2001—	Dunedin (Fla. St.)	0	1	.000	3.97	1.37	13	0	0	0	...	2-...	22.2	28	12	10	1	3-0	15	.304
	—Tennessee (Sou.)	2	1	.667	2.12	0.91	5	5	3	0	...	0-...	34.0	25	9	8	2	6-0	29	.202
	—Syracuse (Int'l)	1	0	1.000	3.21	0.86	2	2	0	0	...	0-...	14.0	12	5	5	2	0-0	13	.222
	—Toronto (A.L.)	5	3	.625	3.16	1.16	17	16	1	1	0	0-0	105.1	97	41	37	3	25-0	96	.241
2002—	Toronto (A.L.)	19	7	.731	2.93	1.19	34	34	2	1	0	0-0	* 239.1	223	93	78	10	62-6	168	.244
2003—	Toronto (A.L.)	* 22	7	.759	3.25	1.07	36	* 36	•9	•2	0	0-0	* 266.0	* 253	111	96	26	32-1	204	.247
2004—	Toronto (A.L.)	8	8	.500	4.20	1.35	21	21	1	1	0	0-0	133.0	140	66	62	13	39-1	95	.272
	Major League totals (7 years)	**67**	**39**	**.632**	**3.89**	**1.30**	**165**	**140**	**15**	**6**	**2**	**1-1**	**974.2**	**985**	**478**	**421**	**87**	**281-9**	**702**	**.260**

ALL-STAR GAME RECORD

		W	L	Pct.	ERA	WHIP	G	GS	CG	ShO	Hld.	Sv.-Opp.	IP	H	R	ER	HR	BB-IBB	SO	Avg.
	All-Star Game totals (1 year)	0	0	...	27.00	3.00	1	0	0	0	...	0-0	1.0	3	3	3	1	0-0	1	.500

HALSEY, BRAD — P

PERSONAL: Born February 14, 1981, in Houston, Texas. ... 6-1/180. ... Throws left, bats left. ... Full name: Bradford A. Halsey. ... High school: Westfield (Houston). ... College: Texas.

TRANSACTIONS/CAREER NOTES: Selected by New York Yankees organization in 19th round of 2000 free-agent draft; did not sign. ... Selected by New York Yankees organization in eighth round of 2002 free-agent draft.

CAREER HITTING: 1-for-2 (.500), 0 R, 0 2B, 0 3B, 0 HR, 0 RBI.

Year	Team (League)	W	L	Pct.	ERA	WHIP	G	GS	CG	ShO	Hld.	Sv.-Opp.	IP	H	R	ER	HR	BB-IBB	SO	Avg.
2002—	Staten Island (NY-P)	6	1	.857	1.93	1.00	11	10	0	0	...	0-...	56.0	39	15	12	0	17-0	53	.195
2003—	Tampa (FSL)	10	4	.714	3.43	1.31	14	13	1	0	...	0-...	84.0	96	36	32	3	14-0	56	.287
	—Trenton (East.)	7	5	.583	4.93	1.59	15	15	0	0	...	0-...	91.1	123	51	50	4	22-0	78	.325
2004—	Columbus (Int'l)	11	4	.733	2.63	1.15	24	23	3	2	...	0-...	144.0	128	46	42	8	37-0	109	.237
	—New York (A.L.)	1	3	.250	6.47	1.72	8	7	0	0	0	0-0	32.0	41	26	23	4	14-0	25	.306
	Major League totals (1 year)	**1**	**3**	**.250**	**6.47**	**1.72**	**8**	**7**	**0**	**0**	**0**	**0-0**	**32.0**	**41**	**26**	**23**	**4**	**14-0**	**25**	**.306**

HALTER, SHANE — 3B

PERSONAL: Born November 8, 1969, in LaPlata, Md. ... 6-0/195. ... Bats right, throws right. ... Full name: Shane David Halter. ... High school: Hooks (Texas). ... College: Texas.

TRANSACTIONS/CAREER NOTES: Selected by Cincinnati Reds organization in 16th round of 1990 free-agent draft; did not sign. ... Selected by Kansas City Royals organization in fifth round of 1991 free-agent draft. ... Loaned by Royals organization to Florida Marlins organization (April 11-May 7, 1996). ... Traded by Royals to New York Mets for OF Jonathan Guzman (March 23, 1999). ... Claimed on waivers by Detroit Tigers (March 13, 2000). ... Signed as a free agent by Anaheim Angels (January 15, 2004). ... On disabled list (June 14-July 6, 2004); included rehabilitation assignment to Rancho Cucamonga. ... Career major league pitching: 0-0, 0.00 ERA, 2 G, 1.0 IP, 1 H, 0 R, 0 ER, 1 BB, 0 SO.

2004 GAMES PLAYED BY POSITION (MLB): 3B—33, 2B—6, 1B—4, SS—3, DH—3.

Year	Team (League)	Pos.	G	AB	R	H	2B	3B	HR	RBI	BB	SO	HBP	GDP	SB-CS	Avg.	OBP	SLG	OPS	E	Avg.
1991—	Eugene (Northwest)	SS	64	236	41	55	9	1	1	18	49	60	3	3	12-6	.233	.370	.292	.663	21	.928
1992—	Appleton (Midwest)	SS	80	313	50	83	22	3	3	33	41	54	1	4	21-6	.265	.349	.383	.733	16	.959
	—Baseball City (FSL)	SS	44	117	11	28	1	0	1	14	24	31	0	4	5-5	.239	.359	.274	.632	6	.969
1993—	Wilmington (Caro.)	SS	54	211	44	63	8	5	5	32	27	55	2	3	5-4	.299	.377	.455	.832	15	.939
	—Memphis (Sou.)	SS	81	306	50	79	7	0	4	20	30	74	2	3	4-7	.258	.326	.320	.646	16	.959
1994—	Memphis (Sou.)	SS	129	494	61	111	23	1	6	35	39	102	3	10	10-14	.225	.282	.312	.594	29	.950
1995—	Omaha (A.A.)	SS-2B	124	392	42	90	19	3	8	39	40	97	0	6	2-3	.230	.300	.355	.655	19	.968
1996—	Omaha (A.A.)	O-3-S-2B	93	299	43	77	24	0	3	33	31	49	2	6	7-2	.258	.330	.368	.698	13	.940
	—Charlotte (Int'l)	O-2-3-DH-1	16	41	3	12	1	0	0	4	2	8	0	0	0-0	.293	.311	.317	.628	1	.962
1997—	Omaha (A.A.)	3-0-2-SS	14	49	10	13	1	1	2	9	6	10	1	1	0-0	.265	.345	.449	.794	2	.947
	—Kansas City (A.L.)	O-2-3-S-DH	74	123	16	34	5	1	2	10	10	28	2	1	4-3	.276	.341	.382	.723	1	.990
1998—	Kansas City (A.L.)	S-O-3-2-P-1	86	204	17	45	12	0	2	13	12	38	1	3	2-5	.221	.265	.309	.574	10	.964
	—Omaha (PCL)	S-2-1-3-OF	22	97	15	30	6	1	1	13	6	15	0	2	4-1	.309	.350	.423	.772	3	.973
1999—	Norfolk (Int'l)	S-O-2-3-C	127	474	77	130	22	3	6	35	60	90	0	10	19-17	.274	.354	.371	.725	20	.955
	—New York (N.L.)	OF-SS	7	0	0	0	0	0	0	0	0	0	0	0	0-0	...	...	...	...	0	...
2000—	Detroit (A.L.)	3-1-S-2-O-C-P	105	238	26	62	12	2	3	27	14	49	1	5	5-2	.261	.302	.366	.668	8	.979
2001—	Detroit (A.L.)	3-S-1-DH	136	450	53	128	32	7	12	65	37	100	7	14	3-3	.284	.344	.467	.811	26	.955
2002—	Detroit (A.L.)	S-3-O-2-DH-1	122	410	46	98	22	6	10	39	39	92	4	12	0-4	.239	.309	.395	.704	21	.958
2003—	Detroit (A.L.)	3-S-2-1-DH-O	114	360	33	78	5	2	12	30	27	77	0	11	2-3	.217	.269	.342	.611	9	.980
2004—	Rancho Cuca. (Calif.)	3B-1B-SS	5	19	4	4	1	0	0	1	2	4	1	1	2-0	.211	.318	.263	.581	0	1.000
	—Salt Lake (PCL)	O-S-2-1-3-DH	35	131	18	36	7	1	6	18	15	21	0	5	2-3	.275	.349	.481	.830	2	.985
	—Anaheim (A.L.)	3-2-1-S-DH	46	114	10	23	5	0	4	13	7	30	0	3	1-1	.202	.248	.351	.599	10	.910
	American League totals (7 years)		683	1899	201	468	93	18	45	197	146	414	15	49	17-21	.246	.303	.385	.688	85	.964
	National League totals (1 year)		7	0	0	0	0	0	0	0	0	0	0	0	0-0	...	...	...	...	0	...
	Major League totals (8 years)		690	1899	201	468	93	18	45	197	146	414	15	49	17-21	.246	.303	.385	.688	85	.964

HAMMOCK, ROBBY — C

PERSONAL: Born May 13, 1977, in Macon, Ga. ... 5-10/187. ... Bats right, throws right. ... Full name: Robert Wade Hammock. ... Name pronounced: HAM-uk. ... High school: South Cobb (Dacula, Ga.). ... College: Georgia.

TRANSACTIONS/CAREER NOTES: Selected by Florida Marlins organization in 66th round of 1995 free-agent draft; did not sign. ... Selected by Tampa Bay Devil Rays organization in 89th round of 1997 free-agent draft; did not sign. ... Selected by Arizona Diamondbacks organization in 23rd round of 1998 free-agent draft. ... On disabled list (April 1-20 and July 16-September 7, 2004); included rehabilitation assignments to Tucson and Lancaster.

2004 GAMES PLAYED BY POSITION (MLB): C—46, OF—12, 3B—1.

Year	Team (League)	Pos.	G	AB	R	H	2B	3B	HR	RBI	BB	SO	HBP	GDP	SB-CS	Avg.	OBP	SLG	OPS	E	Avg.
1998—	Lethbridge (Pio.)	C-3B	62	227	46	65	14	2	10	56	28	34	2	3	5-4	.286	.367	.498	.865	4	.990

Year	Team (League)	Pos.	G	AB	R	H	2B	3B	HR	RBI	BB	SO	HBP	GDP	SB-CS	Avg.	OBP	SLG	OPS	E	Avg.
1999— High Desert (Calif.)	C-OF-3B	114	379	80	126	20	7	9	72	47	63	2	8	3-6	.332	.403	.493	.897	18	.975
2000— High Desert (Calif.)	C-1B	40	136	25	48	15	1	3	23	27	24	1	5	3-3	.353	.455	.544	.999	11	.962
— El Paso (Texas)	C-3B-OF	45	140	22	35	5	1	1	15	11	25	1	1	1-2	.250	.305	.321	.627	2	.990
2001— South Bend (Mid.)	C-OF	34	125	16	31	3	2	2	14	14	21	0	2	5-6	.248	.324	.352	.676	2	.988
— El Paso (Texas)	3-1-OF-C	26	74	6	12	5	0	0	4	7	18	0	1	2-2	.162	.235	.230	.464	5	.948
— Lancaster (Calif.)	O-C-3-1-2	45	190	33	59	11	3	4	36	16	42	7	6	3-2	.311	.378	.463	.841	7	.966
2002— El Paso (Texas)	OF-C-3B	122	441	68	128	28	4	11	73	43	68	8	14	5-4	.290	.358	.447	.805	8	.986
2003— Tucson (PCL)	C-OF-1-3	33	116	14	31	6	2	2	17	11	24	0	2	1-0	.267	.321	.405	.726	5	.972
— Arizona (N.L.)	C-O-3-DH	65	195	30	55	10	2	8	28	17	44	2	5	3-2	.282	.343	.477	.820	7	.980
2004— Tucson (PCL)	C-DH	8	21	1	6	1	0	0	4	2	1	0	0	2-0	.286	.333	.333	.667	1	.968
— Lancaster (Calif.)	DH-C	2	9	2	6	2	0	0	3	1	1	0	0	0-0	.667	.700	.889	1.589	0	1.000
— Arizona (N.L.)	C-OF-3B	62	195	22	47	16	2	4	18	13	39	0	9	3-3	.241	.287	.405	.692	2	.994
Major League totals (2 years)		127	390	52	102	26	4	12	46	30	83	2	14	6-5	.262	.315	.441	.756	9	.987

HAMMOND, CHRIS — P

PERSONAL: Born January 21, 1966, in Atlanta, Ga. ... 6-1/210. ... Throws left, bats left. ... Full name: Chris Andrew Hammond. ... High school: Vestavia Hills (Birmingham, Ala.). ... Junior college: Gulf Coast (Fla.) Community College. ... Brother of Steve Hammond, outfielder with Kansas City Royals (1982).

TRANSACTIONS/CAREER NOTES: Selected by Cincinnati Reds organization in sixth round of January1986 free-agent draft. ... On disabled list (July 27-September 1, 1991). ... Traded by Reds to Florida Marlins for 3B Gary Scott and a player to be named (March 27, 1993); Reds acquired P Hector Carrasco to complete deal (September 10, 1993). ... On disabled list (June 11-August 3, 1994); included rehabilitation assignments to Portland and Brevard County. ... On disabled list (April 16-May 13 and August 3-19, 1995); included rehabilitation assignments to Brevard County and Charlotte. ... On disabled list (June 9-July 14, 1996); included rehabilitation assignments to Brevard County and Charlotte. ... Signed as a free agent by Boston Red Sox (December 17, 1996). ... On disabled list (June 30, 1997-remainder of season). ... Signed as a free agent by Kansas City Royals organization (January 12, 1998). ... Released by Royals (March 23, 1998). ... Signed by Marlins organization (March 27, 1998). ... Released by Marlins (June 2, 1998). ... Signed by Cleveland Indians organization (March 30, 2001). ... Released by Indians (July 3, 2001). ... Signed by Atlanta Braves organization (July 17, 2001). ... On suspended list (September 13-16, 2002). ... Signed as a free agent by New York Yankees (December 12, 2002). ... Traded by Yankees to Oakland Athletics for RHP Eduardo Sierra and SS J.T. Stotts (December 18, 2003). ... On disabled list (June 12-July 27, 2004); included rehabilitation assignment to Sacramento.

CAREER HITTING: 48-for-235 (.204), 30 R, 7 2B, 1 3B, 4 HR, 14 RBI.

Year	Team (League)	W	L	Pct.	ERA	WHIP	G	GS	CG	ShO	Hld.	Sv.-Opp.	IP	H	R	ER	HR	BB-IBB	SO	Avg.
1986— GC Reds (GCL)		3	2	.600	2.81	1.06	7	7	1	0	...	0-...	41.2	27	21	13	0	17-1	53	.172
— Tampa (FSL)		0	2	.000	3.32	1.75	5	5	0	0	...	0-...	21.2	25	8	8	0	13-1	5	.291
1987— Tampa (FSL)		11	11	.500	3.55	1.38	25	24	6	0	...	0-...	170.0	174	81	67	10	60-1	126	.258
1988— Chattanooga (Southern)		16	5	.762	1.72	1.12	26	26	4	2	...	0-...	182.2	127	48	35	2	77-3	127	.193
1989— Nashville (A.A.)		11	7	.611	3.38	1.53	24	24	3	1	...	0-...	157.1	144	69	59	7	96-1	142	.245
1990— Nashville (A.A.)		15	1	.938	2.17	1.21	24	24	5	3	...	0-...	149.0	118	43	36	7	63-1	149	.219
— Cincinnati (N.L.)		0	2	.000	6.35	2.21	3	3	0	0	0	0-0	11.1	13	9	8	2	12-1	4	.302
1991— Cincinnati (N.L.)		7	7	.500	4.06	1.40	20	18	0	0	0	0-0	99.2	92	51	45	4	48-3	50	.250
1992— Cincinnati (N.L.)		7	10	.412	4.21	1.38	28	26	0	0	0	0-0	147.1	149	75	69	13	55-6	79	.266
1993— Florida (N.L.)		11	12	.478	4.66	1.43	32	32	1	0	0	0-0	191.0	207	106	99	18	66-2	108	.277
1994— Florida (N.L.)		4	4	.500	3.07	1.39	13	13	1	1	0	0-0	73.1	79	30	25	5	23-1	40	.281
— Portland (East.)		0	0	...	0.00	0.00	1	1	0	0	...	0-...	2.0	0	0	0	0	0-0	2	.000
— Brevard County (FSL)		0	0	...	1.23	0.95	2	2	0	0	...	0-...	7.1	4	3	1	0	3-0	5	.160
1995— Brevard County (FSL)		0	0	...	0.00	0.75	1	1	0	0	...	0-...	4.0	3	1	0	0	0-0	4	.200
— Charlotte (Int'l)		0	0	...	0.00	1.25	1	1	0	0	...	0-...	4.0	3	1	0	0	2-0	3	.176
— Florida (N.L.)		9	6	.600	3.80	1.27	25	24	3	2	0	0-0	161.0	157	73	68	17	47-2	126	.256
1996— Florida (N.L.)		5	8	.385	6.56	1.62	38	9	0	0	5	0-0	81.0	104	65	59	14	27-3	50	.315
— Brevard County (FSL)		0	0	...	0.00	0.75	1	1	0	0	0	0-...	4.0	3	0	0	0	0-0	6	.214
— Charlotte (Int'l)		1	0	1.000	7.20	1.00	1	1	0	0	...	0-...	5.0	5	4	4	0	0-0	3	.250
1997— Boston (A.L.)		3	4	.429	5.92	1.65	29	8	0	0	4	1-2	65.1	81	45	43	5	27-4	48	.310
1998— Charlotte (Int'l)		1	3	.250	4.82	1.75	5	5	0	0	0	0-...	28.0	35	17	15	2	14-2	22	.315
— Florida (N.L.)		0	2	.000	6.59	2.05	3	3	0	0	0	0-0	13.2	20	11	10	3	8-0	8	.357
1999—	Did not play.																		
2000—	Did not play.																		
2001— Buffalo (Int'l)		7	3	.700	3.31	1.41	28	4	0	0	...	0-...	51.2	53	22	19	5	20-1	54	.261
— Richmond (Int'l)		3	1	.750	2.35	1.17	21	0	0	0	...	1-...	30.2	32	9	8	0	4-0	29	.281
2002— Atlanta (N.L.)		7	2	.778	0.95	1.11	63	0	0	0	17	0-2	76.0	53	15	8	1	31-9	63	.195
2003— New York (A.L.)		3	2	.600	2.86	1.21	62	0	0	0	17	1-4	63.0	65	23	20	5	11-0	45	.270
— Sacramento (PCL)		0	0	...	0.00	1.50	3	3	0	0	...	0-...	4.0	6	0	0	0	0-0	5	.353
— Oakland (A.L.)		4	1	.800	2.68	1.29	41	0	0	0	3	1-3	53.2	56	21	16	4	13-1	34	.277
American League totals (3 years)		10	7	.588	3.91	1.39	132	8	0	0	24	3-9	182.0	202	89	79	14	51-5	127	.287
National League totals (9 years)		50	53	.485	4.12	1.39	225	128	5	3	22	0-2	854.1	874	435	391	77	317-27	528	.267
Major League totals (12 years)		60	60	.500	4.08	1.39	357	136	5	3	46	3-11	1036.1	1076	524	470	91	368-32	655	.271

DIVISION SERIES RECORD

Year	Team (League)	W	L	Pct.	ERA	WHIP	G	GS	CG	ShO	Hld.	Sv.-Opp.	IP	H	R	ER	HR	BB-IBB	SO	Avg.
2002— Atlanta (N.L.)		0	0	...	6.75	1.88	3	0	0	0	0	0-0	2.2	2	2	2	0	3-1	2	.200

WORLD SERIES RECORD

Year	Team (League)	W	L	Pct.	ERA	WHIP	G	GS	CG	ShO	Hld.	Sv.-Opp.	IP	H	R	ER	HR	BB-IBB	SO	Avg.
2003— New York (A.L.)		0	0	...	0.00	1.00	1	0	0	0	0	0-0	2.0	2	2	0	0	0-0	0	.250

HAMMONDS, JEFFREY — OF

PERSONAL: Born March 5, 1971, in Scotch Plains, N.J. ... 6-0/222. ... Bats right, throws right. ... Full name: Jeffrey Bryan Hammonds. ... High school: Scotch Plains (N.J.)-Fanwood. ... College: Stanford. ... Brother of Reggie Hammonds, outfielder with Pittsburgh Pirates organization (1984-86).

TRANSACTIONS/CAREER NOTES: Selected by Toronto Blue Jays organization in ninth round of 1989 free-agent draft; did not sign. ... Selected by Baltimore Orioles organization in first round (fourth pick overall) of 1992 free-agent draft. ... On disabled list (August 8-September 1 and September 28, 1993-remainder of season); included rehabilitation assignment to Bowie. ... On disabled list (May 4-June 16, 1994; July 18-September 3, 1995; and August.17-September 22, 1996). ... On disabled list (June 3-July 11, 1998); included rehabilitation assignment to Bowie. ... Traded by Orioles to Cincinnati Reds for 3B/OF Willie Greene (August 10, 1998). ... Traded by Reds with P Stan Belinda to Colorado Rockies for OF Dante Bichette and cash (October 30, 1999). ... On disabled list (April 4-22, 2000). ... Signed as a free agent by Milwaukee Brewers (December 20, 2000). ... On disabled list (June 7, 2001-remainder of season); included rehabilitation assignment to AZL Brewers. ... On disabled list (April 15-June 4, 2003). ... Released by Brewers (June 4, 2003). ... Signed by San Francisco Giants organization (July 1, 2003). ... On disabled list (March 26-April 10, 2004). ... Released by Giants (June 3, 2003).

H

2004 GAMES PLAYED BY POSITION (MLB): OF—28.

| | | | | | | | | | | BATTING | | | | | | | | | FIELDING | |
Year Team (League)	Pos.	G	AB	R	H	2B	3B	HR	RBI	BB	SO	HBP	GDP	SB-CS	Avg.	OBP	SLG	OPS	E	Avg.
1992— Hagerstown (East.)		Did not play.																		
1993— Bowie (East.)	OF	24	92	13	26	3	0	3	10	9	18	2	1	4-3	.283	.356	.413	.769	0	1.000
— Rochester (Int'l)	OF	36	151	25	47	9	1	5	23	5	27	2	1	6-3	.311	.338	.483	.821	0	1.000
— Baltimore (A.L.)	OF-DH	33	105	10	32	8	0	3	19	2	16	0	3	4-0	.305	.312	.467	.779	2	.961
1994— Baltimore (A.L.)	OF	68	250	45	74	18	2	8	31	17	39	2	3	5-0	.296	.339	.480	.819	6	.962
1995— Baltimore (A.L.)	OF-DH	57	178	18	43	9	1	4	23	9	30	1	3	4-2	.242	.279	.371	.650	1	.989
— Bowie (East.)	OF-DH	9	31	7	12	3	1	1	11	10	7	0	0	3-0	.387	.524	.645	1.169	1	.923
1996— Baltimore (A.L.)	OF-DH	71	248	38	56	10	1	9	27	23	53	4	7	3-3	.226	.301	.383	.684	3	.980
— Rochester (Int'l)	OF-DH	34	125	24	34	4	2	3	19	19	19	1	2	3-1	.272	.365	.408	.773	1	.987
1997— Baltimore (A.L.)	OF-DH	118	397	71	105	19	3	21	55	32	73	3	6	15-1	.264	.323	.486	.809	5	.980
1998— Baltimore (A.L.)	OF-DH	63	171	36	46	12	1	6	28	26	38	3	2	7-2	.269	.369	.456	.826	2	.980
— Bowie (East.)	OF	3	6	4	2	0	0	0	0	2	2	1	0	3-1	.333	.556	.333	.889	0	1.000
— Cincinnati (N.L.)	OF	26	86	14	26	4	1	0	11	13	18	0	0	1-1	.302	.390	.372	.762	1	.985
1999— Cincinnati (N.L.)	OF	123	262	43	73	13	0	17	41	27	64	1	4	3-6	.279	.347	.523	.870	0	1.000
2000— Colorado (N.L.)	OF	122	454	94	152	24	2	20	106	44	83	5	11	14-7	.335	.395	.529	.924	2	.991
2001— Milwaukee (N.L.)	OF	49	174	20	43	11	1	6	21	14	42	4	2	5-3	.247	.314	.425	.740	2	.982
— Ariz. Brewers (Ariz.)	OF	1	3	0	1	0	0	0	0	0	0	0	0	0-0	.333	.333	.333	.667	0	...
2002— Milwaukee (N.L.)	OF	128	448	47	115	26	5	9	41	52	86	2	13	4-5	.257	.332	.397	.729	2	.992
2003— Milwaukee (N.L.)	OF	10	38	2	6	2	0	1	3	3	7	0	2	0-0	.158	.220	.289	.509	0	1.000
— Ariz. Giants (Ariz.)	OF	4	10	4	5	1	1	3	6	1	1	0	2	0-0	.500	.545	1.700	2.245	0	1.000
— Fresno (PCL)	OF-DH	11	36	7	12	1	0	2	2	3	3	0	1	1-0	.333	.385	.528	.912	0	1.000
— San Francisco (N.L.)	OF	36	94	20	26	10	0	3	10	13	21	1	1	1-0	.277	.370	.479	.849	0	1.000
2004— San Francisco (N.L.)	OF	40	95	14	20	5	0	3	6	15	22	3	2	1-0	.211	.336	.358	.694	0	1.000
American League totals (6 years)		410	1349	218	356	76	8	51	183	109	249	13	24	38-8	.264	.322	.446	.767	19	.976
National League totals (7 years)		534	1651	254	461	95	9	59	239	181	343	16	35	29-22	.279	.353	.455	.808	7	.992
Major League totals (12 years)		944	3000	472	817	171	17	110	422	290	592	29	59	67-30	.272	.339	.451	.790	26	.985

DIVISION SERIES RECORD

Year Team (League)	Pos.	G	AB	R	H	2B	3B	HR	RBI	BB	SO	HBP	GDP	SB-CS	Avg.	OBP	SLG	OPS	E	Avg.
1997— Baltimore (A.L.)	OF	4	10	3	1	1	0	0	2	2	2	0	1	1-0	.100	.250	.200	.450	0	1.000
2003— San Francisco (N.L.)	OF	3	5	1	2	0	0	0	0	1	0	1	0	0-0	.400	.571	.400	.971	0	1.000
Division series totals (2 years)		7	15	4	3	1	0	0	2	3	2	1	1	1-0	.200	.368	.267	.635	0	1.000

CHAMPIONSHIP SERIES RECORD

Year Team (League)	Pos.	G	AB	R	H	2B	3B	HR	RBI	BB	SO	HBP	GDP	SB-CS	Avg.	OBP	SLG	OPS	E	Avg.
1997— Baltimore (A.L.)	OF	5	3	0	0	0	0	0	0	1	2	0	0	1-0	.000	.250	.000	.250	0	1.000

ALL-STAR GAME RECORD

	G	AB	R	H	2B	3B	HR	RBI	BB	SO	HBP	GDP	SB-CS	Avg.	OBP	SLG	OPS	E	Avg.
All-Star Game totals (1 year)	1	1	0	0	0	0	0	0	0	0	0	0	0-0	.000	.000	.000	.000	...	...

HAMPTON, MIKE   P

PERSONAL: Born September 9, 1972, in Brooksville, Fla. ... 5-10/195. ... Throws left, bats right. ... Full name: Michael William Hampton. ... High school: Crystal River (Fla.).

TRANSACTIONS/CAREER NOTES: Selected by Seattle Mariners organization in sixth round of 1990 free-agent draft. ... Traded by Mariners with OF Mike Felder to Houston Astros for OF Eric Anthony (December 10, 1993). ... On disabled list (May 15-June 13, 1995; June 16-July 4, 1998). ... Traded by Astros with OF Derek Bell to New York Mets for OF Roger Cedeno and Ps Octavio Dotel and Kyle Kessel (December 23, 1999). ... Signed as a free agent by Colorado Rockies (December 9, 2000). ... On suspended list (October 3-8, 2001). ... Traded by Rockies with OF Juan Pierre and cash to Florida Marlins for C Charles Johnson, P Vic Darensbourg, OF Preston Wilson and 2B Pablo Ozuna (November 16, 2002). ... Traded by Marlins with cash to Atlanta Braves for Ps Tim Spooneybarger and Ryan Baker (November 18, 2002). ... On disabled list (March 28-April 19, 2003).

HONORS: Named N.L. Pitcher of the Year by THE SPORTING NEWS (1999). ... Won N.L. Gold Glove at pitcher (2003).

CAREER HITTING: 153-for-639 (.239), 84 R, 18 2B, 5 3B, 14 HR, 67 RBI.

Year Team (League)	W	L	Pct.	ERA	WHIP	G	GS	CG	ShO	Hld.	Sv.-Opp.	IP	H	R	ER	HR	BB-IBB	SO	Avg.
1990— Ariz. Mariners (Ariz.)	7	2	.778	2.66	1.43	14	13	0	0	...	0-...	64.1	52	32	19	0	40-0	59	.213
1991— San Bernardino (Calif.)	1	7	.125	5.25	1.60	18	15	1	1	...	0-...	73.2	71	58	43	3	47-1	57	.249
— Bellingham (N'west)	5	2	.714	1.58	1.02	9	9	0	0	...	0-...	57.0	32	15	10	0	26-0	65	.162
1992— San Bernardino (Calif.)	13	8	.619	3.12	1.35	25	25	6	2	...	0-...	170.0	163	75	59	8	66-1	132	.255
— Jacksonville (Southern)	0	1	.000	4.35	1.35	2	2	1	0	...	0-...	10.1	13	5	5	0	1-0	6	.317
1993— Seattle (A.L.)	1	3	.250	9.53	2.65	13	3	0	0	2	1-1	17.0	28	20	18	3	17-3	8	.368
— Jacksonville (Southern)	6	4	.600	3.71	1.19	15	14	1	0	...	0-...	87.1	71	43	36	3	33-1	84	.225
1994— Houston (N.L.)	2	1	.667	3.70	1.50	44	0	0	0	10	0-1	41.1	46	19	17	4	16-1	24	.282
1995— Houston (N.L.)	9	8	.529	3.35	1.26	24	24	0	0	0	0-0	150.2	141	73	56	13	49-3	115	.247
1996— Houston (N.L.)	10	10	.500	3.59	1.40	27	27	2	1	0	0-0	160.1	175	79	64	12	49-1	101	.280
1997— Houston (N.L.)	15	10	.600	3.83	1.32	34	34	7	2	0	0-0	223.0	217	105	95	16	77-2	139	.257
1998— Houston (N.L.)	11	7	.611	3.36	1.46	32	32	1	1	0	0-0	211.2	227	92	79	18	81-1	137	.278
1999— Houston (N.L.)	* 22	4	.846	2.90	1.28	34	34	3	2	0	0-0	239.0	206	86	77	12	101-2	177	.241
2000— New York (N.L.)	15	10	.600	3.14	1.35	33	33	3	1	0	0-0	217.2	194	89	76	10	99-5	151	.241
2001— Colorado (N.L.)	14	13	.519	5.41	1.58	32	32	2	1	0	0-0	203.0	236	138	122	31	85-7	122	.296
2002— Colorado (N.L.)	7	15	.318	6.15	1.79	30	30	0	0	0	0-0	178.2	228	* 135	122	24	91-4	74	.313
2003— Atlanta (N.L.)	14	8	.636	3.84	1.39	31	31	1	0	0	0-0	190.0	186	91	81	14	78-4	110	.255
2004— Atlanta (N.L.)	13	9	.591	4.28	1.53	29	29	1	0	0	0-0	172.1	198	86	82	15	65-3	87	.290
American League totals (1 year)	1	3	.250	9.53	2.65	13	3	0	0	2	1-1	17.0	28	20	18	3	17-3	8	.368
National League totals (11 years)	132	95	.581	3.94	1.43	350	306	20	8	10	0-1	1987.2	2054	993	871	169	791-33	1237	.270
Major League totals (12 years)	133	98	.576	3.99	1.44	363	309	20	8	12	1-2	2004.2	2082	1013	889	172	808-36	1245	.271

DIVISION SERIES RECORD

Year Team (League)	W	L	Pct.	ERA	WHIP	G	GS	CG	ShO	Hld.	Sv.-Opp.	IP	H	R	ER	HR	BB-IBB	SO	Avg.
1997— Houston (N.L.)	0	1	.000	11.57	2.14	1	1	0	0	0	0-0	4.2	2	6	6	1	8-0	2	.125
1998— Houston (N.L.)	0	0	...	1.50	0.50	1	1	0	0	0	0-0	6.0	2	1	1	0	1-0	2	.111
1999— Houston (N.L.)	0	0	...	3.86	1.00	1	1	0	0	0	0-0	7.0	6	3	3	1	1-0	9	.231
2000— New York (N.L.)	0	0	...	8.44	1.69	1	1	0	0	0	0-0	5.1	6	5	5	0	3-1	2	.273
2003— Atlanta (N.L.)	0	1	.000	4.26	1.34	2	2	0	0	0	0-0	12.2	11	6	6	1	6-0	16	.224
2004— Atlanta (N.L.)	0	0	...	2.45	1.09	2	1	0	0	0	0-0	7.1	4	2	2	2	4-0	6	.174
Division series totals (6 years)	0	3	.000	4.81	1.26	8	7	0	0	0	0-0	43.0	31	23	23	7	23-1	37	.201

H

Year	Team (League)	W	L	Pct.	ERA	WHIP	G	GS	CG	ShO	Hld.	Sv.-Opp.	IP	H	R	ER	HR	BB-IBB	SO	Avg.
	CHAMPIONSHIP SERIES RECORD																			
2000—New York (N.L.)		2	0	1.000	0.00	0.81	2	2	1	1	0	0-0	16.0	9	0	0	0	4-0	12	.158
	WORLD SERIES RECORD																			
2000—New York (N.L.)		0	1	.000	6.00	2.17	1	1	0	0	0	0-0	6.0	8	4	4	1	5-1	4	.320
	ALL-STAR GAME RECORD																			
All-Star Game totals (2 years)		0	0	...	0.00	0.60	2	0	0	0	0	0-0	1.2	1	1	0	0	0-0	0	.143

HANCOCK, JOSH — P

PERSONAL: Born April 11, 1978, in Cleveland, Miss. ... 6-3/205. ... Throws right, bats right. ... Full name: Joshua Morgan Hancock. ... High school: Vestavia Hills (Ala.). ... College: Auburn.

TRANSACTIONS/CAREER NOTES: Selected by Milwaukee Brewers organization in fourth round of 1996 free-agent draft; did not sign. ... Selected by Boston Red Sox organization in fifth round of 1998 free-agent draft. ... Traded by Red Sox to Philadelphia Phillies for 1B/OF Jeremy Giambi (December 15, 2002). ... Traded by Phillies with SS Anderson Machado to Cincinnati Reds for P Todd Jones (July 30, 2004).

CAREER HITTING: 2-for-17 (.118), 1 R, 0 2B, 0 3B, 0 HR, 1 RBI.

Year	Team (League)	W	L	Pct.	ERA	WHIP	G	GS	CG	ShO	Hld.	Sv.-Opp.	IP	H	R	ER	HR	BB-IBB	SO	Avg.
1998—GC Red Sox (GCL)		1	1	.500	3.38	0.90	5	1	0	0	...	0-...	13.1	9	5	5	1	3-0	21	.196
—Lowell (NY-Penn)		0	1	.000	2.25	2.25	1	1	0	0	...	0-...	4.0	5	2	1	0	4-0	4	.333
1999—Augusta (S. Atl.)		6	8	.429	3.80	1.43	25	25	0	0	...	0-...	139.2	154	79	59	12	46-0	106	.279
2000—Sarasota (Florida State)		5	10	.333	4.45	1.40	26	24	1	0	...	0-...	143.2	164	89	71	9	37-0	95	.286
2001—Trenton (East.)		8	6	.571	3.65	1.34	24	24	0	0	...	0-...	130.2	138	60	53	8	37-0	119	.273
2002—Trenton (East.)		3	4	.429	3.61	1.18	15	14	2	0	...	1-...	84.2	82	40	34	9	18-0	69	.250
—Pawtucket (Int'l)		4	2	.667	3.45	1.47	8	8	0	0	...	0-...	44.1	39	20	17	2	26-0	29	.235
—Boston (A.L.)		0	1	.000	3.68	0.95	3	1	0	0	0	0-0	7.1	5	3	3	1	2-0	6	.200
2003—Scran./W.B. (I.L.)		10	9	.526	3.86	1.20	28	27	2	2	0	0-...	165.2	147	78	71	14	46-1	122	.238
—Philadelphia (N.L.)		0	0	...	3.00	0.67	2	0	0	0	0	0-0	3.0	2	1	1	0	0-0	4	.182
2004—Scran./W.B. (I.L.)		8	7	.533	4.01	1.19	18	18	1	0	...	0-...	107.2	107	52	48	10	21-1	65	.263
—Philadelphia (N.L.)		0	1	.000	9.00	1.78	4	2	0	0	0	0-0	9.0	13	9	9	3	3-0	5	.333
—Cincinnati (N.L.)		5	1	.833	4.45	1.55	12	9	0	0	0	0-0	54.2	60	34	27	14	25-2	31	.273
American League totals (1 year)		0	1	.000	3.68	0.95	3	1	0	0	0	0-0	7.1	5	3	3	1	2-0	6	.200
National League totals (2 years)		5	2	.714	5.00	1.55	18	11	0	0	0	0-0	66.2	75	44	37	17	28-2	40	.278
Major League totals (3 years)		5	3	.625	4.86	1.49	21	12	0	0	0	0-0	74.0	80	47	40	18	30-2	46	.271

HANSEN, DAVE — 3B/1B

PERSONAL: Born November 24, 1968, in Long Beach, Calif. ... 6-0/195. ... Bats left, throws right. ... Full name: David Andrew Hansen. ... High school: Rowland (Long Beach, Calif.).

TRANSACTIONS/CAREER NOTES: Selected by Los Angeles Dodgers organization in second round of June 1986 free-agent draft. ... On disabled list (May 9-28, 1994). ... Signed as a free agent by Chicago Cubs organization (January 22, 1997). ... Signed by Hanshin Tigers of Japan Central League (November 7, 1997). ... Signed as a free agent by Dodgers (January 11, 1999). ... On disabled list (March 23-April 26, 2001); included rehabilitation assignment to Vero Beach. ... Signed as a free agent by San Diego Padres (December 10, 2002). ... Traded by Padres with RHP Kevin Jarvis, C Wiki Gonzalez and OF Vince Faison to Seattle Mariners for IF Jeff Cirillo and RHP Brian Sweeney (January 6, 2004). ... Traded by Mariners to Padres for P Jon Huber (July 30, 2004).

2004 GAMES PLAYED BY POSITION (MLB): 1B—14, 3B—8, DH—8.

Year	Team (League)	Pos.	G	AB	R	H	2B	3B	HR	RBI	BB	SO	HBP	GDP	SB-CS	Avg.	OBP	SLG	OPS	E	Avg.
1986—Great Falls (Pio.)	2B-3B-C-OF	61	204	39	61	7	3	1	36	27	28	0	6	9-3	.299	.381	.377	.758	7	.901
1987—Bakersfield (Calif.)	3B-OF	132	432	68	113	22	1	3	38	65	61	4	11	4-2	.262	.363	.338	.701	45	.860
1988—Vero Beach (FSL)	3B	135	512	68	149	28	6	7	81	56	46	4	9	2-2	.291	.360	.410	.770	18	.953
1989—San Antonio (Texas)	3B	121	464	72	138	21	4	6	52	50	44	2	18	3-2	.297	.365	.399	.763	16	.949
—Albuquerque (PCL)	3B	6	30	6	8	1	0	2	10	2	3	0	1	0-0	.267	.313	.500	.813	3	.786
1990—Albuquerque (PCL)	3B-SS-OF	135	487	90	154	20	3	11	92	90	54	3	12	9-4	.316	.419	.437	.857	26	.926
—Los Angeles (N.L.)	3B	5	7	0	1	0	0	0	1	0	3	0	0	0-0	.143	.143	.143	.286	1	.500
1991—Albuquerque (PCL)	3B-SS	68	254	42	77	11	1	5	40	49	33	0	7	4-3	.303	.406	.413	.820	6	.966
—Los Angeles (N.L.)	3B-SS	53	56	3	15	4	0	1	5	2	12	0	2	1-0	.268	.293	.393	.686	0	1.000
1992—Los Angeles (N.L.)	3B	132	341	30	73	11	0	6	22	34	49	1	9	0-2	.214	.286	.299	.585	8	.968
1993—Los Angeles (N.L.)	3B	84	105	13	38	3	0	4	30	21	13	0	0	0-1	.362	.465	.505	.969	3	.927
1994—Los Angeles (N.L.)	3B	40	44	3	15	3	0	0	5	5	5	0	0	0-0	.341	.408	.409	.817	1	.857
1995—Los Angeles (N.L.)	3B	100	181	19	52	10	1	1	14	28	28	1	4	0-0	.287	.384	.350	.743	7	.933
1996—Los Angeles (N.L.)	3B-1B	80	104	7	23	1	0	0	6	11	22	0	4	0-0	.221	.293	.231	.524	1	.988
1997—Chicago (N.L.)	3B-1B-2B	90	151	19	47	8	2	3	21	31	32	1	0	1-2	.311	.429	.450	.880	7	.929
1998—Hanshin (Jp. Cn.)	3B	121	400	42	101	13	1	11	55	42	89			0-...	.253	...	.373	...	...	...
1999—Los Angeles (N.L.)	1-3-DH-OF	100	107	14	27	8	1	2	17	26	20	2	2	0-0	.252	.404	.402	.806	3	.962
2000—Los Angeles (N.L.)	3-1-DH-OF	102	121	18	35	6	2	8	26	26	32	0	3	0-1	.289	.415	.570	.985	2	.973
2001—Vero Beach (FSL)	3B	3	9	1	0	0	0	0	0	1	2	0	0	0-0	.000	.100	.000	.100	0	1.000
—Los Angeles (N.L.)	1-3-SS-DH	92	140	13	33	10	0	2	20	32	29	0	3	0-1	.236	.371	.350	.721	6	.973
2002—Los Angeles (N.L.)	1B-3B-DH	96	120	15	35	6	0	2	17	14	22	0	2	1-0	.292	.363	.392	.755	2	.980
2003—San Diego (N.L.)	1-3-DH-2B	110	135	13	33	4	1	2	15	23	25	1	4	1-0	.244	.358	.333	.692	1	.993
2004—Seattle (A.L.)	DH-1B-3B	57	78	14	22	5	0	2	12	18	16	0	3	0-0	.282	.412	.423	.835	0	1.000
—San Diego (N.L.)	1B-3B	29	28	1	4	0	0	0	0	3	5	0	3	0-0	.143	.226	.143	.369	0	1.000
American League totals (1 year)		57	78	14	22	5	0	2	12	18	16	0	3	0-0	.282	.412	.423	.835	0	1.000
National League totals (14 years)		1113	1640	168	431	74	6	31	199	256	297	6	36	4-7	.263	.362	.372	.734	42	.966
Major League totals (14 years)		1170	1718	182	453	79	6	33	211	274	313	6	39	4-7	.264	.365	.374	.739	42	.967

Year	Team (League)	Pos.	G	AB	R	H	2B	3B	HR	RBI	BB	SO	HBP	GDP	SB-CS	Avg.	OBP	SLG	OPS	E	Avg.
	DIVISION SERIES RECORD																				
1995—Los Angeles (N.L.)		3	3	0	2	0	0	0	0	0	0	0	0	0-0	.667	.667	.667	1.333	...	...
1996—Los Angeles (N.L.)	3B	2	2	0	0	0	0	0	0	0	0	0	0	0-0	.000	.000	.000	.000	0	1.000
Division series totals (2 years)		5	5	0	2	0	0	0	0	0	0	0	0	0-0	.400	.400	.400	.800	0	1.000

H

HARANG, AARON P

PERSONAL: Born May 9, 1978, in San Diego, Calif. ... 6-7/240. ... Throws right, bats right. ... Full name: Aaron Michael Harang. ... Name pronounced: ha-RANG. ... High school: Patrick Henry (San Diego). ... College: San Diego State.

TRANSACTIONS/CAREER NOTES: Selected by Boston Red Sox organization in 22nd round of 1996 free-agent draft; did not sign. ... Selected by Texas Rangers organization in sixth round of 1999 free-agent draft. ... Traded by Rangers with P Ryan Cullen to Oakland Athletics for 2B Randy Velarde (December 12, 2000). ... Traded by Athletics with Ps Joe Valentine and Jeff Bruksch to Cincinnati Reds for OF Jose Guillen (July 30, 2003). ... On disabled list (June 2-26, 2004); included rehabilitation assignment to Louisville.

CAREER HITTING: 5-for-78 (.064), 1 R, 1 2B, 0 3B, 0 HR, 0 RBI.

Year Team (League)	W	L	Pct.	ERA	WHIP	G	GS	CG	ShO	Hld.	Sv.-Opp.	IP	H	R	ER	HR	BB-IBB	SO	Avg.
1999— Pulaski (Appalachian)	9	2	.818	2.30	1.03	16	10	1	1	...	1-...	78.1	64	22	20	5	17-1	87	.226
2000— Charlotte (Fla. St.)	13	5	.722	3.32	1.13	28	27	3	2	...	0-...	157.0	128	68	58	10	50-0	136	.220
2001— Midland (Texas)	10	8	.556	4.14	1.40	27	27	0	0	...	0-...	150.0	173	81	69	9	37-1	112	.285
2002— Midland (Texas)	2	0	1.000	1.08	1.14	3	3	0	0	...	0-...	16.2	12	3	2	0	7-0	21	.218
—Sacramento (PCL)	3	3	.500	3.26	1.29	8	8	0	0	...	0-...	38.2	41	17	14	0	9-0	39	.301
—Oakland (A.L.)	5	4	.556	4.83	1.57	16	15	0	0	0	0-0	78.1	78	44	42	7	45-2	64	.261
2003— Oakland (A.L.)	1	3	.250	5.34	1.65	7	6	0	0	0	0-0	30.1	41	19	18	5	9-0	16	.331
—Sacramento (PCL)	8	2	.800	2.71	1.10	12	12	0	0	...	0-...	69.2	62	24	21	5	17-0	60	.234
—Louisville (Int'l)	0	1	.000	15.00	2.30	1	1	0	0	...	0-...	3.0	5	5	5	1	2-0	4	.357
—Cincinnati (N.L.)	4	3	.571	5.28	1.26	9	9	0	0	0	0-0	46.0	48	28	27	6	10-0	26	.271
2004— Louisville (Int'l)	0	1	.000	12.00	4.00	1	1	0	0	...	0-...	3.0	9	8	4	1	3-0	3	.529
—Cincinnati (N.L.)	10	9	.526	4.86	1.43	28	28	1	1	0	0-0	161.0	177	90	87	26	53-5	125	.280
American League totals (2 years)	6	7	.462	4.97	1.59	23	21	0	0	0	0-0	108.2	119	63	60	12	54-2	80	.281
National League totals (2 years)	14	12	.538	4.96	1.39	37	37	1	1	0	0-0	207.0	225	118	114	32	63-5	151	.278
Major League totals (3 years)	20	19	.513	4.96	1.46	60	58	1	1	0	0-0	315.2	344	181	174	44	117-7	231	.279

HARDEN, RICH P

PERSONAL: Born November 30, 1981, in Victoria, British Columbia. ... 6-1/180. ... Throws right, bats left. ... Full name: James Richard Harden. ... High school: Claremont Secondary (Victoria, B.C.). ... Junior college: Central Arizona.

TRANSACTIONS/CAREER NOTES: Selected by Seattle Mariners organization in 38th round of 1999 free-agent draft; did not sign. ... Selected by Oakland Athletics organization in 17th round of 2000 free-agent draft.

CAREER HITTING: 0-for-5 (.000), 0 R, 0 2B, 0 3B, 0 HR, 0 RBI.

Year Team (League)	W	L	Pct.	ERA	WHIP	G	GS	CG	ShO	Hld.	Sv.-Opp.	IP	H	R	ER	HR	BB-IBB	SO	Avg.
2001— Vancouver (N'west)	2	4	.333	3.39	1.14	18	14	0	0	...	0-...	74.1	47	29	28	3	38-0	100	.179
2002— Visalia (Calif.)	4	3	.571	2.93	1.08	12	12	1	0	...	0-...	67.2	49	27	22	4	24-0	85	.201
—Midland (Texas)	8	3	.727	2.95	1.39	16	16	1	0	...	0-...	85.1	67	33	28	2	52-1	102	.217
2003— Midland (Texas)	2	0	1.000	0.00	0.00	2	2	0	0	...	0-...	13.0	0	0	0	0	0-0	17	.000
—Sacramento (PCL)	9	4	.692	3.15	1.21	16	14	0	0	...	0-...	88.2	72	34	31	6	35-0	91	.226
—Oakland (A.L.)	5	4	.556	4.46	1.50	15	13	0	0	0	0-0	74.2	72	38	37	5	40-1	67	.259
2004— Sacramento (PCL)	0	0	...	5.40	1.80	1	1	0	0	...	0-...	5.0	6	3	3	0	3-0	6	.300
—Oakland (A.L.)	11	7	.611	3.99	1.33	31	31	0	0	0	0-0	189.2	171	90	84	16	81-6	167	.242
Major League totals (2 years)	16	11	.593	4.12	1.38	46	44	0	0	0	0-0	264.1	243	128	121	21	121-7	234	.246

DIVISION SERIES RECORD

Year Team (League)	W	L	Pct.	ERA	WHIP	G	GS	CG	ShO	Hld.	Sv.-Opp.	IP	H	R	ER	HR	BB-IBB	SO	Avg.
2003— Oakland (A.L.)	1	1	.500	13.50	3.00	2	0	0	0	0	0-0	1.1	2	2	2	1	2-1	1	.333

HAREN, DANNY P

PERSONAL: Born September 17, 1980, in Monterey Park, Calif. ... 6-5/220. ... Throws right, bats right. ... Full name: Daniel John Haren. ... College: Pepperdine.

TRANSACTIONS/CAREER NOTES: Selected by St. Louis Cardinals organization in second round of 2001 free-agent draft.

CAREER HITTING: 2-for-37 (.054), 1 R, 2 2B, 0 3B, 0 HR, 1 RBI.

Year Team (League)	W	L	Pct.	ERA	WHIP	G	GS	CG	ShO	Hld.	Sv.-Opp.	IP	H	R	ER	HR	BB-IBB	SO	Avg.
2001— New Jersey (N.Y.-Penn.) ...	3	3	.500	3.10	1.05	12	8	0	0	...	1-...	52.1	47	22	18	6	8-0	57	.239
2002— Peoria (Midw.)	7	3	.700	1.95	0.99	14	14	1	0	...	0-...	101.2	89	32	22	6	12-0	89	.234
—Potomac (Caro.)	3	6	.333	3.62	1.18	14	14	1	0	...	0-...	92.0	90	43	37	8	19-2	82	.252
2003— Tennessee (Sou.)	6	0	1.000	0.82	0.76	8	8	0	0	...	0-...	55.0	36	8	5	2	6-0	49	.181
—Memphis (PCL)	2	1	.667	4.93	1.27	8	8	0	0	...	0-...	45.2	50	25	25	6	8-1	35	.272
—St. Louis (N.L.)	3	7	.300	5.08	1.46	14	14	0	0	0	0-0	72.2	84	44	41	9	22-0	43	.293
2004— Memphis (PCL)	11	4	.733	4.15	1.33	21	21	0	0	...	0-...	128.0	137	60	59	19	33-1	150	.276
—St. Louis (N.L.)	3	3	.500	4.50	1.35	14	5	0	0	0	0-0	46.0	45	23	23	4	17-2	32	.265
Major League totals (2 years)	6	10	.375	4.85	1.42	28	19	0	0	0	0-0	118.2	129	67	64	13	39-2	75	.282

DIVISION SERIES RECORD

Year Team (League)	W	L	Pct.	ERA	WHIP	G	GS	CG	ShO	Hld.	Sv.-Opp.	IP	H	R	ER	HR	BB-IBB	SO	Avg.
2004— St. Louis (N.L.)	1	0	1.000	0.00	1.00	1	0	0	0	0	0-0	2.0	1	0	0	0	1-0	3	.143

CHAMPIONSHIP SERIES RECORD

Year Team (League)	W	L	Pct.	ERA	WHIP	G	GS	CG	ShO	Hld.	Sv.-Opp.	IP	H	R	ER	HR	BB-IBB	SO	Avg.
2004— St. Louis (N.L.)	0	0	...	10.80	1.80	2	0	0	0	0	0-0	1.2	3	2	2	1	0-0	2	.375

WORLD SERIES RECORD

Year Team (League)	W	L	Pct.	ERA	WHIP	G	GS	CG	ShO	Hld.	Sv.-Opp.	IP	H	R	ER	HR	BB-IBB	SO	Avg.
2004— St. Louis (N.L.)	0	0	...	0.00	1.50	2	0	0	0	0	0-0	4.2	4	0	0	0	3-0	2	.222

HARIKKALA, TIM P

PERSONAL: Born July 15, 1971, in West Palm Beach, Fla. ... 6-2/185. ... Throws right, bats right. ... Full name: Timothy Allan Harikkala. ... Name pronounced: ha-RICK-a-la. ... High school: Lake Worth Christian (Lantana, Fla.). ... College: Florida Atlantic.

TRANSACTIONS/CAREER NOTES: Selected by Seattle Mariners organization in 34th round of 1992 free-agent draft. ... Signed as a free agent by Boston Red Sox organization (December 14, 1998). ... Signed as a free agent by Milwaukee Brewers organization (April 17, 2000). ... Signed as a free agent by Oaxaca of the Mexican League (April 2003). ... Contract purchased from Oaxaca by Baltimore Orioles organization (July 21, 2003). ... Signed as a free agent by Colorado Rockies organization (November 11, 2003). ... Claimed on waivers by Oakland Athletics (October 6, 2004).

CAREER HITTING: 0-for-3 (.000), 0 R, 0 2B, 0 3B, 0 HR, 0 RBI.

Year	Team (League)	W	L	Pct.	ERA	WHIP	G	GS	CG	ShO	Hld.	Sv.-Opp.	IP	H	R	ER	HR	BB-IBB	SO	Avg.
1992—	Bellingham (N'west)	2	0	1.000	2.70	1.59	15	2	0	0	...	1-...	33.1	37	15	10	2	16-0	18	.298
1993—	Bellingham (N'west)	1	0	1.000	1.13	0.63	4	0	0	0	...	0-...	8.0	3	1	1	0	2-0	12	.111
	Appleton (Midw.)	3	3	.500	6.52	1.60	15	4	0	0	...	0-...	38.2	50	30	28	3	12-2	33	.316
1994—	Appleton (Midw.)	8	3	.727	1.92	0.99	13	13	3	0	...	0-...	93.2	69	31	20	6	24-0	63	.204
	Riverside (California)	4	0	1.000	0.62	0.90	4	4	0	0	...	0-...	29.0	16	6	2	1	10-0	30	.165
	Jacksonville (Southern)	4	1	.800	3.98	1.64	9	9	0	0	...	0-...	54.1	70	30	24	4	19-0	22	.317
1995—	Seattle (A.L.)	0	0	...	16.20	2.40	1	0	0	0	0	0-0	3.1	7	6	6	1	1-0	1	.412
	Tacoma (PCL)	5	12	.294	4.24	1.41	25	24	4	1	...	0-...	146.1	151	78	69	13	55-3	73	.263
1996—	Tacoma (PCL)	8	12	.400	4.83	1.59	27	27	1	1	...	0-...	158.1	204	98	85	12	48-2	115	.312
	Seattle (A.L.)	0	1	.000	12.46	1.38	1	1	0	0	0	0-0	4.1	6	6	6	1	2-0	1	.250
1997—	Tacoma (PCL)	6	8	.429	6.43	1.85	21	21	0	0	...	0-...	113.1	160	93	81	11	50-2	86	.336
	Memphis (Sou.)	3	1	.750	3.74	1.28	5	5	1	0	...	0-...	33.2	39	18	14	3	4-0	26	.283
1998—	Orlando (Sou.)	5	7	.417	4.53	1.22	15	15	3	2	...	0-...	103.1	112	56	52	9	14-0	55	.279
	Tacoma (PCL)	2	3	.400	4.89	1.53	18	4	1	1	...	1-...	57.0	74	32	31	6	13-0	44	.307
1999—	Pawtucket (Int'l)	1	2	.333	5.40	1.70	14	1	0	0	...	0-...	30.0	44	19	18	2	7-1	19	.336
	Boston (A.L.)	1	1	.500	6.23	1.62	7	0	0	0	0	0-0	13.0	15	9	9	6	6-1	7	.306
2000—	Huntsville (Southern)	5	3	.625	2.98	1.28	22	4	0	0	...	0-...	48.1	54	20	16	1	8-0	34	.281
	Indianapolis (Int'l)	4	2	.667	4.52	1.38	14	10	0	0	...	0-...	63.2	73	36	32	5	15-0	22	.285
2001—	Indianapolis (Int'l)	11	10	.524	4.76	1.47	31	27	1	0	...	0-...	172.0	210	104	91	15	42-1	96	.304
2002—	Indianapolis (Int'l)	8	10	.444	3.50	1.20	31	20	1	0	...	0-...	162.0	172	76	63	8	23-1	90	.271
2003—	Ottawa (Int'l)	5	0	1.000	0.81	0.80	20	3	0	0	...	2-...	44.1	27	4	4	0	7-1	29	.176
2004—	Colo. Springs (PCL)	0	0	...	4.50	1.75	4	0	0	0	...	3-...	4.0	5	2	2	0	2-1	5	.263
	Colorado (N.L.)	6	6	.500	4.74	1.24	55	0	0	0	15	0-7	62.2	55	34	33	10	23-5	30	.235
American League totals (3 years)		1	2	.333	9.15	1.69	9	1	0	0	0	0-0	20.2	26	21	21	2	9-1	9	.317
National League totals (1 year)		6	6	.500	4.74	1.24	55	0	0	0	15	0-7	62.2	55	34	33	10	23-5	30	.235
Major League totals (4 years)		7	8	.467	5.83	1.36	64	1	0	0	15	0-7	83.1	81	55	54	12	32-6	39	.256

HARPER, TRAVIS — P

PERSONAL: Born May 21, 1976, in Harrisonburg, Va. ... 6-4/192. ... Throws right, bats left. ... Full name: Travis Boyd Harper. ... High school: Circleville (W. Va.). ... College: James Madison (Va.).

TRANSACTIONS/CAREER NOTES: Selected by New York Mets organization in 14th round of 1994 free-agent draft; did not sign. ... Selected by Boston Red Sox organization in third round of 1997 free-agent draft. ... Contract with Red Sox voided due to pre-existing injury (October 29, 1997). ... Signed by Tampa Bay Devil Rays organization (June 29, 1998).

CAREER HITTING: 0-for-0 (.000), 0 R, 0 2B, 0 3B, 0 HR, 0 RBI.

Year	Team (League)	W	L	Pct.	ERA	WHIP	G	GS	CG	ShO	Hld.	Sv.-Opp.	IP	H	R	ER	HR	BB-IBB	SO	Avg.
1998—	Hudson Valley (NY-Penn.) .	6	2	.750	1.92	1.03	13	10	0	0	...	0-...	56.1	38	14	12	2	20-0	81	.192
1999—	St. Pete. (FSL)	5	4	.556	3.43	1.29	14	14	0	0	...	0-...	81.1	82	36	31	4	23-0	79	.265
	Orlando (Sou.)	6	3	.667	5.38	1.38	14	14	1	1	...	0-...	72.0	73	45	43	10	26-0	68	.263
2000—	Orlando (Sou.)	3	1	.750	2.63	1.17	9	9	0	0	...	0-...	51.1	49	19	15	1	11-0	33	.255
	Durham (Int'l)	7	4	.636	4.24	1.19	17	17	0	0	...	0-...	104.0	98	53	49	15	26-1	48	.246
	Tampa Bay (A.L.)	1	2	.333	4.78	1.41	6	5	1	1	0	0-0	32.0	30	17	17	5	15-0	14	.244
2001—	Tampa Bay (A.L.)	0	2	.000	7.71	2.57	2	2	0	0	0	0-...	7.0	15	11	6	5	3-0	2	.455
	Durham (Int'l)	12	6	.667	3.70	1.14	25	25	1	1	...	0-...	155.2	140	70	64	25	38-0	115	.241
2002—	Durham (Int'l)	1	2	.333	6.98	1.76	4	4	0	0	...	0-...	19.1	31	15	15	5	3-0	17	.383
	Tampa Bay (A.L.)	5	9	.357	5.46	1.49	37	7	0	0	3	1-2	85.2	101	54	52	14	27-3	60	.289
2003—	Tampa Bay (A.L.)	4	8	.333	3.77	1.26	61	0	0	0	15	1-6	93.0	86	45	39	9	31-8	64	.252
2004—	Durham (Int'l)	1	0	1.000	3.52	1.30	2	1	0	0	...	0-...	7.2	10	3	3	1	0-0	5	.294
	Tampa Bay (A.L.)	6	2	.750	3.89	1.17	52	0	0	0	9	0-1	78.2	69	37	34	8	23-3	59	.234
Major League totals (5 years)		16	23	.410	4.49	1.35	158	14	1	1	27	2-9	296.1	301	164	148	41	99-14	199	.264

HARRIS, BRENDAN — 3B

PERSONAL: Born August 26, 1980, in Albany, N.Y. ... 6-1/200. ... Bats right, throws right. ... Full name: Brendan Michael Harris. ... High school: Queensbury (N.Y.). ... College: William & Mary (Va.).

TRANSACTIONS/CAREER NOTES: Selected by Chicago Cubs organization in fifth round of 2001 free-agent draft. ... Traded by Cubs with SS Alex S. Gonzalez and P Francis Beltran to Montreal Expos as part of four-team deal in which Cubs acquired SS Nomar Garciaparra and OF Matt Murton from Boston Red Sox, Red Sox acquired SS Orlando Cabrera from Expos and 1B Doug Mientkiewicz from Twins, and Twins acquired P Justin Jones from Cubs (July 31, 2004).

2004 GAMES PLAYED BY POSITION (MLB): 2B—11, 3B—7.

									BATTING										FIELDING		
Year	Team (League)	Pos.	G	AB	R	H	2B	3B	HR	RBI	BB	SO	HBP	GDP	SB-CS	Avg.	OBP	SLG	OPS	E	Avg.
2001—	Lansing (Midw.)	2B-3B-SS	32	113	25	31	5	1	4	22	17	26	2	4	5-1	.274	.370	.442	.813	4	.966
2002—	Daytona (Fla. St.)	3B-2B	110	425	82	140	35	6	13	54	43	57	4	7	16-4	.329	.395	.532	.926	16	.965
	West Tenn. (Sou.)	3B-2B	13	53	8	17	4	1	2	11	2	5	0	1	1-1	.321	.345	.547	.893	0	1.000
2003—	West Tenn. (Sou.)	3B-2B-SS	120	435	56	122	34	7	5	52	51	72	8	10	6-7	.280	.364	.425	.789	17	.939
2004—	Chicago (N.L.)	3B	3	9	0	2	1	0	0	1	1	1	0	0	0-0	.222	.300	.333	.633	1	.889
	Iowa (PCL)	2-S-3-DH	69	254	48	79	21	1	11	35	16	40	1	8	0-2	.311	.353	.531	.882	5	.983
	Edmonton (PCL)	3B	35	130	20	35	6	0	6	24	10	21	1	4	0-0	.269	.317	.454	.811	5	.943
	Montreal (N.L.)	2B-3B	20	50	4	8	2	0	1	2	2	11	1	0	0-0	.160	.208	.260	.468	2	.952
Major League totals (1 year)			23	59	4	10	3	0	1	3	3	12	1	0	0-0	.169	.222	.271	.493	3	.941

HARRIS, LENNY — OF

PERSONAL: Born October 28, 1964, in Miami, Fla. ... 5-10/234. ... Bats left, throws right. ... Full name: Leonard Anthony Harris. ... High school: Jackson (Miami). ... Junior college: Miami-Dade Community College North.

TRANSACTIONS/CAREER NOTES: Selected by Cincinnati Reds organization in fifth round of June 1983 free-agent draft. ... Loaned by Reds organization to Detroit Tigers organization (May 6-28, 1988). ... Traded by Reds with OF Kal Daniels to Los Angeles Dodgers for P Tim Leary and SS Mariano Duncan (July 18, 1989). ... Signed as a free agent by Reds (December 1, 1993). ... Traded by Reds to New York Mets for P John Hudek (July 3, 1998). ... Signed as a free agent by Colorado Rockies (November 9, 1998). ... Traded by Rockies to Arizona Diamondbacks for IF Belvani Martinez (August 31, 1999). ... Traded by Diamondbacks to Mets for P Bill Pulsipher (June 2, 2000). ... Traded by Mets with P Glendon Rusch to Milwaukee Brewers as part of three-team deal in which Brewers also acquired OF Alex Ochoa from Colorado Rockies, Mets acquired P Jeff D'Amico, OF Jeromy Burnitz, OF/1B Mark Sweeney and IF Lou Collier from Brewers and 1B/OF Ross Gload and P Craig House from Rockies, and Rockies acquired IF Todd

H

Zeile, OF Benny Agbayani and cash from Mets (January 21, 2002). ... Signed as a free agent by Chicago Cubs organization (January 8, 2003). ... Released by Cubs (August 2, 2003). ... Signed by Florida Marlins organization (August 8, 2003). ... Career major league pitching: 0-0, 0.00 ERA, 1 G, 1.0 IP, 0 H, 0 R, 0 ER, 0 BB, 1 SO.

2004 GAMES PLAYED BY POSITION (MLB): OF—14, 3B—3, DH—2.

Year Team (League)	Pos.	G	AB	R	H	2B	3B	HR	RBI	BB	SO	HBP	GDP	SB-CS	Avg.	OBP	SLG	OPS	E	Avg.
1983— Billings (Pio.)	3B	56	224	37	63	8	1	1	26	13	35	1	...	7-1	.281	.322	.339	.661	22	.854
1984— Cedar Rap. (Midw.)	3B	132	468	52	115	15	3	6	53	42	59	3	14	31-10	.246	.308	.329	.637	34	.903
1985— Tampa (Fla. St.)	3B	132	499	66	129	11	8	3	51	37	57	1	9	15-8	.259	.307	.331	.638	35	.913
1986— Vermont (East.)	3B-SS	119	450	68	114	17	2	10	52	29	38	6	9	36-10	.253	.303	.367	.670	28	.924
1987— Nashville (A.A.)	3B-SS	120	403	45	100	12	3	2	31	27	43	5	10	30-12	.248	.302	.308	.610	34	.908
1988— Nashville (A.A.)	2B-3B-SS	107	422	46	117	20	2	0	35	22	36	0	13	45-22	.277	.313	.334	.647	25	.947
— Glens Falls (East.)	2B	17	65	9	22	5	1	1	7	9	6	0	1	6-2	.338	.419	.492	.911	5	.947
— Cincinnati (N.L.)	2B-3B	16	43	7	16	1	0	0	8	5	4	0	0	4-1	.372	.420	.395	.815	1	.979
1989— Nashville (A.A.)	2B	8	34	6	9	2	0	3	6	0	5	0	0	0-2	.265	.265	.588	.853	0	1.000
— Cincinnati (N.L.)	2B-3B-SS	61	188	17	42	4	0	2	11	9	20	1	5	10-6	.223	.263	.277	.539	13	.946
— Los Angeles (N.L.)	2-3-S-OF	54	147	19	37	6	1	1	15	11	13	1	9	4-3	.252	.308	.327	.635	2	.978
1990— Los Angeles (N.L.)	2-3-S-OF	137	431	61	131	16	4	2	29	29	31	1	8	15-10	.304	.348	.374	.722	11	.969
1991— Los Angeles (N.L.)	2-3-S-OF	145	429	59	123	16	1	3	38	37	32	5	16	12-3	.287	.349	.350	.698	20	.949
1992— Los Angeles (N.L.)	2-3-O-SS	135	347	28	94	11	0	0	30	24	24	1	10	19-7	.271	.318	.303	.621	27	.943
1993— Los Angeles (N.L.)	2-3-S-OF	107	160	20	38	6	1	2	11	15	15	1	4	3-1	.238	.303	.325	.628	3	.982
1994— Cincinnati (N.L.)	3-1-O-2B	66	100	13	31	3	1	0	14	5	13	0	0	7-2	.310	.340	.360	.700	6	.903
1995— Cincinnati (N.L.)	3-1-O-2B	101	197	32	41	8	3	2	16	14	20	0	6	10-1	.208	.259	.310	.569	4	.982
1996— Cincinnati (N.L.)	O-3-1-2B	125	302	33	86	17	2	5	32	21	31	1	3	14-6	.285	.330	.404	.734	6	.978
1997— Cincinnati (N.L.)	O-2-3-1B	120	238	32	65	13	1	3	28	18	18	2	10	4-3	.273	.327	.374	.701	3	.983
1998— Cincinnati (N.L.)	OF-P-DH	57	122	12	36	8	0	0	10	8	9	1	8	1-3	.295	.338	.361	.699	3	.929
— New York (N.L.)	O-3-2-1B	75	168	18	39	7	0	6	17	9	12	1	5	5-2	.232	.272	.381	.653	2	.980
1999— Colorado (N.L.)	2-O-3-DH	91	158	15	47	12	0	0	13	6	6	0	7	1-1	.297	.323	.373	.697	9	.926
— Arizona (N.L.)	3B-OF	19	29	2	11	1	0	1	7	0	1	0	0	1-0	.379	.367	.517	.884	0	1.000
2000— Arizona (N.L.)	3B-OF	36	85	9	16	1	1	1	13	3	5	0	3	5-0	.188	.209	.259	.468	4	.909
— New York (N.L.)	3-0-1-2-DH	76	138	22	42	6	3	3	13	17	17	0	4	8-1	.304	.381	.457	.837	11	.904
2001— Milwaukee (N.L.)	3-0-1-DH-2	110	135	12	30	5	1	0	9	8	9	0	3	3-2	.222	.266	.274	.540	3	.943
2002— Milwaukee (N.L.)	O-3-1-DH	122	197	23	60	8	2	3	17	14	17	2	4	4-1	.305	.355	.411	.766	0	1.000
2003— Chicago (N.L.)	3B-1B-OF	75	131	11	24	3	0	1	7	13	20	0	1	1-0	.183	.255	.229	.484	3	.953
— Albuquerque (PCL)	1B-3B-DH	8	24	3	4	1	0	0	1	4	3	0	0	0-0	.167	.286	.208	.494	1	.979
— Florida (N.L.)	OF	13	14	3	4	0	0	0	1	3	1	0	1	0-0	.286	.412	.286	.697	0	1.000
2004— Florida (N.L.)	OF-3B-DH	79	95	7	20	5	0	1	17	3	8	0	2	0-0	.211	.232	.295	.527		
Major League totals (17 years)		1820	3854	455	1033	157	21	36	356	272	326	16	109	131-53	.268	.317	.348	.665	131	.959

DIVISION SERIES RECORD

Year Team (League)	Pos.	G	AB	R	H	2B	3B	HR	RBI	BB	SO	HBP	GDP	SB-CS	Avg.	OBP	SLG	OPS	E	Avg.
1999— Arizona (N.L.)	3B	2	2	0	0	0	0	0	0	0	0	0	0	0-0	.000	.000	.000	.000	0	...
2000— New York (N.L.)		2	2	1	0	0	0	0	0	0	0	0	0	1-0	.000	.000	.000	.000	0	...
2003— Florida (N.L.)		2	2	0	1	0	0	0	0	0	0	0	0	0-0	.500	.500	.500	1.000	0	...
Division series totals (3 years)		6	6	1	1	0	0	0	0	0	0	0	0	1-0	.167	.167	.167	.333	0	...

CHAMPIONSHIP SERIES RECORD

Year Team (League)	Pos.	G	AB	R	H	2B	3B	HR	RBI	BB	SO	HBP	GDP	SB-CS	Avg.	OBP	SLG	OPS	E	Avg.
1995— Cincinnati (N.L.)		3	2	0	2	0	0	0	1	0	0	0	0	1-0	1.000	1.000	1.000	2.000	...	...
2000— New York (N.L.)		2	1	0	0	0	0	0	0	0	1	0	0	0-0	.000	.000	.000	.000	...	...
2003— Florida (N.L.)		3	2	0	0	0	0	0	0	1	0	0	0	0-0	.000	.333	.000	.333	0	...
Champ. series totals (3 years)		8	5	0	2	0	0	0	1	1	1	0	0	1-0	.400	.500	.400	.900	0	...

WORLD SERIES RECORD

Year Team (League)	Pos.	G	AB	R	H	2B	3B	HR	RBI	BB	SO	HBP	GDP	SB-CS	Avg.	OBP	SLG	OPS	E	Avg.
2000— New York (N.L.)	DH	3	4	1	0	0	0	0	0	1	1	0	0	0-0	.000	.200	.000	.200	...	...

HARRIS, WILLIE — 2B/OF

PERSONAL: Born June 22, 1978, in Cairo, Ga. ... 5-9/170. ... Bats left, throws right. ... Full name: William Charles Harris. ... High school: Cairo (Ga.). ... College: Kennesaw State. ... Nephew of Ernest Riles, infielder with five major league teams (1985-1993).

TRANSACTIONS/CAREER NOTES: Selected by Pittsburgh Pirates organization in 28th round of 1996 free-agent draft; did not sign. ... Selected by Baltimore Orioles organization in 24th round of 1999 free-agent draft. ... Traded by Orioles to Chicago White Sox for OF Chris Singleton (January 29, 2002). ... On disabled list (May 22-June 16, 2003); included rehabilitation assignment to Charlotte.

2004 GAMES PLAYED BY POSITION (MLB): 2B—92, OF—30, DH—2.

Year Team (League)	Pos.	G	AB	R	H	2B	3B	HR	RBI	BB	SO	HBP	GDP	SB-CS	Avg.	OBP	SLG	OPS	E	Avg.
1999— Bluefield (Appal.)	2B	5	22	3	6	1	0	0	3	4	2	0	1	1-0	.273	.370	.318	.689	1	.966
— Delmarva (S. Atl.)	2B-OF	66	272	42	72	13	3	2	32	20	41	1	4	11-11	.265	.313	.357	.670	11	.965
2000— Delmarva (S. Atl.)	2B-SS-OF	133	474	106	130	27	10	6	60	89	89	9	3	38-15	.274	.396	.411	.807	19	.968
2001— Bowie (East.)	2B-OF	133	525	83	160	27	4	9	49	46	71	5	4	54-16	.305	.364	.423	.787	14	.974
— Baltimore (A.L.)	OF	24	24	3	3	1	0	0	0	0	7	0	0	0-0	.125	.125	.167	.292	0	1.000
2002— Charlotte (Int'l)	2B-OF	89	360	54	102	16	5	5	33	33	61	2	4	32-14	.283	.345	.397	.742	6	.986
— Chicago (A.L.)	2B-OF	49	163	14	38	4	0	2	12	9	21	0	3	8-0	.233	.270	.294	.565	3	.986
2003— Charlotte (Int'l)	2B-OF	28	100	22	38	6	1	6	13	17	20	0	0	9-3	.380	.470	.640	1.110	0	1.000
— Chicago (A.L.)	OF-2B	79	137	19	28	3	1	0	5	10	28	0	1	12-2	.204	.259	.241	.499	2	.984
2004— Chicago (A.L.)	2B-OF-DH	129	409	68	107	15	2	2	27	51	79	1	4	19-7	.262	.343	.323	.665	5	.989
Major League totals (4 years)		266	733	104	176	23	3	4	44	70	135	1	8	39-9	.240	.305	.296	.601	10	.988

HART, BO — 2B

PERSONAL: Born September 27, 1976, in Creswell, Ore. ... 5-11/175. ... Bats right, throws right. ... Full name: Bodhi J. Hart. ... College: Gonzaga.

TRANSACTIONS/CAREER NOTES: Selected by St. Louis Cardinals organization in 33rd round of 1999 free-agent draft.

2004 GAMES PLAYED BY POSITION (MLB): 2B—4, SS—1.

Year	Team (League)	Pos.	G	AB	R	H	2B	3B	HR	RBI	BB	SO	HBP	GDP	SB-CS	Avg.	OBP	SLG	OPS	E	Avg.
1999—New Jersey (N.Y.-Penn.)	SS-2B-3B	50	163	23	30	3	3	3	15	10	38	12	1	4-2	.184	.281	.294	.576	9	.957
2000—Potomac (Caro.)	2B-OF	75	273	42	70	25	4	0	20	23	42	13	2	9-6	.256	.342	.377	.719	13	.955
2001—Potomac (Caro.)	2B-3B-OF	81	279	48	85	23	3	5	34	17	69	15	3	16-7	.305	.375	.462	.837	6	.985
2002—New Haven (East.)	2B-SS	104	405	61	101	17	6	4	39	43	82	12	6	14-7	.249	.338	.351	.688	7	.985
2003—Memphis (PCL)	2-3-SS-DH	67	266	30	79	14	2	7	31	15	55	0	2	4-2	.297	.331	.444	.775	7	.973
— St. Louis (N.L.)	2B-SS	77	296	46	82	13	5	4	28	12	64	6	3	3-1	.277	.317	.395	.713	4	.989
2004— St. Louis (N.L.)	2B-SS	11	13	0	2	0	0	0	2	1	3	0	0	0-0	.154	.214	.154	.368	0	1.000
— Memphis (PCL)	2-S-3-DH	116	445	81	132	25	7	8	45	25	66	13	9	8-7	.297	.349	.438	.787	13	.976
Major League totals (2 years)		88	309	46	84	13	5	4	30	13	67	6	3	3-1	.272	.313	.385	.698	4	.989

HART, COREY — 3B

PERSONAL: Born March 24, 1982, in Bowling Green, Ky. ... 6-6/200. ... Bats right, throws right. ... Full name: Jon Corey Hart. ... High school: Greenwood (Bowling Green).
TRANSACTIONS/CAREER NOTES: Selected by Milwaukee Brewers organization in 11th round of 2000 free-agent draft.

Year	Team (League)	Pos.	G	AB	R	H	2B	3B	HR	RBI	BB	SO	HBP	GDP	SB-CS	Avg.	OBP	SLG	OPS	E	Avg.
2000—Ogden (Pio.)	1B	57	216	32	62	9	1	2	30	13	27	2	6	6-0	.287	.332	.366	.698	11	.978
2001—Ogden (Pio.)	1B-OF	69	262	53	89	18	1	11	62	26	47	2	4	14-1	.340	.395	.542	.937	9	.985
2002—High Desert (Calif.)	3B-1B	100	393	76	113	26	10	22	84	37	101	5	3	24-11	.288	.356	.573	.928	22	.959
—Huntsville (Sou.)	3B-1B	28	94	16	25	3	0	2	15	7	16	4	1	3-2	.266	.340	.362	.701	10	.906
2003—Huntsville (Sou.)	3B-OF	130	493	70	149	40	1	13	94	28	101	5	7	25-8	.302	.340	.467	.807	32	.897
2004—Milwaukee (N.L.)	PH	1	1	0	0	0	0	0	0	0	1	0	0	0-0	.000	.000	.000	.000	0	...
—Indianapolis (Int'l)	OF-DH-1B	121	440	68	124	29	8	15	67	42	92	3	6	17-7	.282	.344	.486	.823	9	.954
Major League totals (1 year)		1	1	0	0	0	0	0	0	0	1	0	0	0-0	.000	.000	.000	.000	0	...

HARVEY, KEN — 1B/DH

PERSONAL: Born March 1, 1978, in Los Angeles, Calif. ... 6-2/240. ... Bats right, throws right. ... Full name: Kenneth Eugene Harvey. ... High school: Beverly Hills (Calif.). ... College: Nebraska.
TRANSACTIONS/CAREER NOTES: Selected by Kansas City Royals organization in fifth round of 1999 free-agent draft. ... On disabled list (August 21-September 5, 2004).
2004 GAMES PLAYED BY POSITION (MLB): 1B—73, DH—41, OF—4.

Year	Team (League)	Pos.	G	AB	R	H	2B	3B	HR	RBI	BB	SO	HBP	GDP	SB-CS	Avg.	OBP	SLG	OPS	E	Avg.
1999—Spokane (N'west)	1B	56	204	49	81	17	0	8	41	23	30	8	3	7-1	.397	.477	.598	1.075	5	.984
2000—Wilmington (Caro.)	1B	46	164	20	55	10	0	4	25	14	29	7	4	0-2	.335	.411	.470	.880	3	.983
2001—Wilmington (Caro.)	1B	35	137	22	52	9	1	6	27	13	21	6	5	3-1	.380	.455	.591	1.046	3	.984
—Wichita (Texas)	1B-OF	79	314	54	106	20	3	9	63	18	60	4	12	3-0	.338	.380	.506	.878	5	.990
—Kansas City (A.L.)	1B-DH	4	12	1	3	1	0	0	2	0	4	0	...	0-1	.250	.250	.333	.583	0	1.000
2002—Omaha (PCL)	1B	128	488	75	135	30	1	20	75	42	87	8	22	8-3	.277	.342	.465	.807	15	.984
2003—Kansas City (A.L.)	1B-DH	135	485	50	129	30	0	13	64	29	94	5	15	2-3	.266	.313	.408	.721	11	.988
2004—Kansas City (A.L.)	1B-DH-OF	120	456	47	131	20	1	13	55	28	89	8	14	1-1	.287	.338	.421	.759	4	.994
Major League totals (3 years)		259	953	98	263	51	1	26	121	57	187	13	29	3-5	.276	.324	.413	.738	15	.990

ALL-STAR GAME RECORD

	G	AB	R	H	2B	3B	HR	RBI	BB	SO	HBP	GDP	SB-CS	Avg.	OBP	SLG	OPS	E	Avg.
All-Star Game totals (1 year)	1	1	0	0	0	0	0	0	0	1	0	0	0-0	.000	.000	.000	.000	0	...

HARVILLE, CHAD — P

PERSONAL: Born September 16, 1976, in Selmer, Tenn. ... 5-9/185. ... Throws right, bats right. ... Full name: Chad Ashley Harville. ... High school: Hardin County (Savannah, Tenn.). ... College: Memphis.
TRANSACTIONS/CAREER NOTES: Selected by Oakland Athletics organization in second round of 1997 free-agent draft. ... On disabled list (March 31-June 9, 2001); included rehabilitation assignments to Visalia and Modesto. ... Traded by A's to Houston Astros for RHP Kirk Saarloos (April 17, 2004). ... On disabled list (May 6-31, 2004); included rehabilitation assignment to Round Rock.
CAREER HITTING: 0-for-1 (.000), 0 R, 0 2B, 0 3B, 0 HR, 0 RBI.

Year	Team (League)	W	L	Pct.	ERA	WHIP	G	GS	CG	ShO	Hld.	Sv.-Opp.	IP	H	R	ER	HR	BB-IBB	SO	Avg.
1997—S. Oregon (N'west)	1	0	1.000	0.00	1.20	3	0	0	0	...	0-...	5.0	3	0	0	0	3-0	6	.176
—Visalia (Calif.)	0	0	...	5.79	2.04	14	0	0	0	...	0-...	18.2	25	14	12	2	13-1	24	.325
1998—Visalia (Calif.)	4	3	.571	3.00	1.30	24	7	0	0	...	4-...	69.0	59	25	23	0	31-0	76	.230
—Huntsville (Southern)	0	0	...	2.45	1.30	12	0	0	0	...	8-...	14.2	6	4	4	0	13-1	24	.122
1999—Midland (Texas)	2	0	1.000	2.01	0.99	17	0	0	0	...	7-...	22.1	13	6	5	1	9-0	35	.165
—Vancouver (PCL)	1	0	1.000	1.75	1.36	22	0	0	0	...	11-...	25.2	24	5	5	0	11-1	36	.240
—Oakland (A.L.)	0	2	.000	6.91	1.95	15	0	0	0	0	0-0	14.1	18	11	11	2	10-1	15	.310
2000—Sacramento (PCL)	5	3	.625	4.50	1.38	53	0	0	0	...	9-...	64.0	53	35	32	8	35-0	77	.222
2001—Modesto (Calif.)	0	0	...	3.00	0.67	2	1	0	0	...	0-...	3.0	2	1	0	0	0-0	3	.182
—Visalia (Calif.)	0	0	...	0.00	1.00	1	1	0	0	...	0-...	3.0	3	0	0	0	2-0	3	.250
—Sacramento (PCL)	5	2	.714	3.98	1.16	33	0	0	0	...	8-...	40.2	35	20	18	5	12-0	55	.230
—Oakland (A.L.)	0	0	...	0.00	0.67	3	0	0	0	1	0-0	3.0	2	0	0	0	0-0	2	.182
2002—Sacramento (PCL)	1	2	.333	5.40	1.50	24	0	0	0	...	5-...	30.0	32	19	18	5	21-0	26	.274
2003—Sacramento (PCL)	3	5	.375	2.05	1.10	48	0	0	0	...	18-...	57.0	42	16	13	5	21-2	57	.202
—Oakland (A.L.)	1	0	1.000	5.82	1.94	21	0	0	0	0	1-1	21.2	25	15	14	3	17-1	18	.294
2004—Oakland (A.L.)	0	0	...	3.38	1.13	3	0	0	0	1	0-0	2.2	2	1	1	0	1-0	0	.200
—Round Rock (Texas)	0	0	...	0.00	0.67	2	2	0	0	...	0-...	3.0	0	0	0	0	2-0	2	.000
—Houston (N.L.)	3	2	.600	4.75	1.51	56	0	0	0	3	0-4	53.0	54	35	28	8	26-2	46	.260
American League totals (4 years)	1	2	.333	5.62	1.80	42	0	0	0	2	1-1	41.2	47	27	26	5	28-2	35	.287
National League totals (1 year)	3	2	.600	4.75	1.51	56	0	0	0	3	0-4	53.0	54	35	28	8	26-2	46	.260
Major League totals (4 years)	4	4	.500	5.13	1.64	98	0	0	0	5	1-5	94.2	101	62	54	13	54-4	81	.272

H

DIVISION SERIES RECORD

Year Team (League)	W	L	Pct.	ERA	WHIP	G	GS	CG	ShO	Hld.	Sv.-Opp.	IP	H	R	ER	HR	BB-IBB	SO	Avg.
2004— Houston (N.L.)	0	0	...	0.00	0.00	1	0	0	0	0	0-0	.2	0	0	0	0	0-0	0	.000

CHAMPIONSHIP SERIES RECORD

Year Team (League)	W	L	Pct.	ERA	WHIP	G	GS	CG	ShO	Hld.	Sv.-Opp.	IP	H	R	ER	HR	BB-IBB	SO	Avg.
2004— Houston (N.L.)	0	0	...	13.50	3.00	3	0	0	0	0	0-0	1.1	3	2	2	1	1-0	3	.429

HASEGAWA, SHIGETOSHI   P

PERSONAL: Born August 1, 1968, in Kobe, Japan. ... 5-11/180. ... Throws right, bats right. ... Name pronounced: shig-eh-toe-shl hoss-eh-gawa. ... College: Ritsumeikan University (Japan).

TRANSACTIONS/CAREER NOTES: Signed as a non-drafted free agent by Anaheim Angels (January 9, 1997). ... On disabled list (May 20-June 29, 2001); included rehabilitation assignment to Rancho Cucamonga. ... Signed as a free agent by Seattle Mariners (January 23, 2002).

CAREER HITTING: 0-for-1 (.000), 0 R, 0 2B, 0 3B, 0 HR, 0 RBI.

Year Team (League)	W	L	Pct.	ERA	WHIP	G	GS	CG	ShO	Hld.	Sv.-Opp.	IP	H	R	ER	HR	BB-IBB	SO	Avg.
1991— Orix (Jap. Pac.)	12	9	.571	3.55	1.26	28	25	11	3	...	1-...	185.0	184	76	73	...	50-...	111	...
1992— Orix (Jap. Pac.)	6	8	.429	3.27	1.32	24	19	4	0	...	1-...	143.1	138	60	52	...	51-...	86	...
1993— Orix (Jap. Pac.)	12	6	.667	2.71	1.22	23	22	9	3	...	0-...	159.2	146	61	48	...	48-...	86	...
1994— Orix (Jap. Pac.)	11	9	.550	3.11	1.38	25	22	8	3	...	1-...	156.1	169	61	54	...	46-...	86	...
1995— Orix (Jap. Pac.)	12	7	.632	2.89	1.27	24	23	9	4	...	0-...	171.0	167	62	55	...	51-...	91	...
1996— Orix (Jap. Pac.)	4	6	.400	5.34	1.70	18	16	2	0	...	1-...	87.2	109	60	52	...	40-...	55	...
1997— Anaheim (A.L.)	3	7	.300	3.93	1.41	50	7	0	0	3	0-1	116.2	118	60	51	14	46-6	83	.269
1998— Anaheim (A.L.)	8	3	.727	3.14	1.21	61	0	0	0	10	5-7	97.1	86	37	34	14	32-2	73	.241
1999— Anaheim (A.L.)	4	6	.400	4.91	1.48	64	1	0	0	6	2-5	77.0	80	45	42	14	34-2	44	.276
2000— Anaheim (A.L.)	10	5	.667	3.48	1.44	66	0	0	0	19	9-18	95.2	100	42	37	11	38-6	59	.270
2001— Anaheim (A.L.)	5	6	.455	4.04	1.29	46	0	0	0	12	0-6	55.2	52	28	25	5	20-5	41	.248
— Rancho Cuca. (Calif.) ...	0	0	...	0.00	1.50	2	0	0	0	...	0-...	2.0	3	1	0	0	0-0	1	.375
2002— Seattle (A.L.)	8	3	.727	3.20	1.28	53	0	0	0	8	1-5	70.1	60	26	25	4	30-8	39	.238
2003— Seattle (A.L.)	2	4	.333	1.48	1.10	63	0	0	0	12	16-17	73.0	62	12	12	5	18-3	32	.235
2004— Seattle (A.L.)	4	6	.400	5.16	1.44	68	0	0	0	12	0-5	68.0	67	42	39	5	31-4	46	.260
Major League totals (8 years)	44	40	.524	3.65	1.34	471	8	0	0	82	33-64	653.2	625	292	265	72	249-36	417	.256

ALL-STAR GAME RECORD

	W	L	Pct.	ERA	WHIP	G	GS	CG	ShO	Hld.	Sv.-Opp.	IP	H	R	ER	HR	BB-IBB	SO	Avg.
All-Star Game totals (1 year)	0	0	...	54.00	6.00	1	0	0	0	0	0-0	.2	3	4	4	1	1-0	1	.600

HATTEBERG, SCOTT   1B

PERSONAL: Born December 14, 1969, in Salem, Ore. ... 6-1/210. ... Bats left, throws right. ... Full name: Scott Allen Hatteberg. ... Name pronounced: HATT-eh-berg. ... High school: Eisenhower (Yakima, Wash.). ... College: Washington State.

TRANSACTIONS/CAREER NOTES: Selected by Philadelphia Phillies organization in 12th round of 1988 free-agent draft; did not sign. ... Selected by Boston Red Sox organization in supplemental round ("sandwich pick" between first and second round, 43rd pick overall) of free-agent draft (June 3, 1991); pick received as part of compensation for Kansas City Royals signing Type A free-agent P Mike Boddicker. ... On disabled list (April 15-May 7 and May 17-August 16, 1999); included rehabilitation assignments to Pawtucket, GCL Red Sox and Sarasota. ... Traded by Red Sox to Colorado Rockies for 2B Pokey Reese (December 19, 2001). ... Signed as a free agent by Oakland Athletics (January 2, 2002).

2004 GAMES PLAYED BY POSITION (MLB): 1B—148, DH—2.

Year Team (League)	Pos.	G	AB	R	H	2B	3B	HR	RBI	BB	SO	HBP	GDP	SB-CS	Avg.	OBP	SLG	OPS	E	Avg.
1991— Winter Haven (FSL)	C	56	191	21	53	7	3	1	25	22	22	0	4	1-2	.277	.349	.361	.710	5	.983
— Lynchburg (Caro.)	C	8	25	4	5	1	0	0	2	7	6	0	0	0-0	.200	.375	.240	.615	0	1.000
1992— New Britain (East.)	C	103	297	28	69	13	2	1	30	41	49	2	6	1-3	.232	.327	.300	.626	11	.979
1993— New Britain (East.)	C	68	227	35	63	10	2	7	28	42	38	1	6	1-3	.278	.393	.432	.824	10	.978
— Pawtucket (Int'l)	C	18	53	6	10	0	0	1	2	6	12	1	5	0-0	.189	.283	.245	.529	5	.964
1994— New Britain (East.)	C	20	68	6	18	4	1	1	9	7	9	0	2	0-2	.265	.329	.397	.726	1	.993
— Pawtucket (Int'l)	C	78	238	26	56	14	0	7	19	32	49	3	14	2-1	.235	.332	.382	.714	7	.986
1995— Pawtucket (Int'l)	C-DH	85	251	36	68	15	1	7	27	40	39	4	8	2-0	.271	.376	.422	.798	8	.984
— Boston (A.L.)	C	2	2	1	1	0	0	0	0	0	0	0	1	0-0	.500	.500	.500	1.000	0	1.000
1996— Pawtucket (Int'l)	C-DH	90	287	52	77	16	0	12	49	58	66	2	6	1-1	.268	.391	.449	.841	6	.990
— Boston (A.L.)	C	10	11	3	2	1	0	0	0	3	2	0	2	0-0	.182	.357	.273	.630	0	1.000
1997— Boston (A.L.)	C-DH	114	350	46	97	23	1	10	44	40	70	2	11	0-0	.277	.354	.434	.788	11	.983
1998— Boston (A.L.)	C	112	359	46	99	23	1	12	43	43	58	5	11	0-0	.276	.359	.446	.804	5	.993
1999— Boston (A.L.)	C-DH	30	80	12	22	5	0	1	11	18	14	1	2	0-0	.275	.410	.375	.785	1	.993
— Pawtucket (Int'l)	C-DH	10	34	3	6	2	0	0	4	4	6	0	2	0-0	.176	.263	.235	.498	0	1.000
— GC Red Sox (GCL)	C-DH	6	15	4	6	2	0	1	6	7	1	0	1	0-0	.400	.591	.733	1.324	0	1.000
— Sarasota (Fla. St.)	C	1	1	0	1	0	0	0	1	0	0	1	0	0-0	1.000	1.000	1.000	2.000	0	1.000
2000— Boston (A.L.)	C-DH-3B	92	230	21	61	15	0	8	36	38	39	0	8	0-1	.265	.367	.435	.801	6	.981
2001— Boston (A.L.)	C-DH	94	278	34	68	19	0	3	25	33	26	4	7	1-1	.245	.332	.345	.678	4	.992
2002— Oakland (A.L.)	1B-DH	136	492	58	138	22	4	15	61	68	56	6	8	0-0	.280	.374	.433	.807	5	.994
2003— Oakland (A.L.)	1B-DH	147	541	63	137	34	0	12	61	66	53	9	14	0-0	.253	.342	.383	.725	10	.992
2004— Oakland (A.L.)	1B-DH	152	550	87	156	30	0	15	82	72	48	5	10	0-0	.284	.367	.420	.787	10	.993
Major League totals (10 years)		889	2893	371	781	172	6	76	363	381	366	32	74	1-4	.270	.359	.412	.771	52	.991

DIVISION SERIES RECORD

Year Team (League)	Pos.	G	AB	R	H	2B	3B	HR	RBI	BB	SO	HBP	GDP	SB-CS	Avg.	OBP	SLG	OPS	E	Avg.
1998— Boston (A.L.)	C	3	9	0	1	0	0	0	0	3	1	0	0	0-0	.111	.333	.111	.444	0	1.000
1999— Boston (A.L.)	C	1	1	1	1	0	0	0	1	0	0	0	0	0-0	1.000	1.000	1.000	2.000	0	1.000
2002— Oakland (A.L.)	1B	5	14	5	7	2	0	1	3	3	0	0	0	0-0	.500	.588	.857	1.445	1	.973
2003— Oakland (A.L.)	1B	5	17	3	3	0	0	0	0	5	3	0	0	0-0	.176	.364	.176	.540	0	1.000
Division series totals (4 years)		14	41	9	12	2	0	1	4	11	4	0	0	0-0	.293	.442	.415	.857	1	.990

CHAMPIONSHIP SERIES RECORD

Year Team (League)	Pos.	G	AB	R	H	2B	3B	HR	RBI	BB	SO	HBP	GDP	SB-CS	Avg.	OBP	SLG	OPS	E	Avg.
1999— Boston (A.L.)	C	3	1	0	0	0	0	0	0	0	1	0	0	0-0	.000	.000	.000	.000	0	...

HAWKINS, LATROY   P

PERSONAL: Born December 21, 1972, in Gary, Ind. ... 6-5/215. ... Throws right, bats right. ... High school: West Side (Gary, Ind.).

TRANSACTIONS/CAREER NOTES: Selected by Minnesota Twins organization in seventh round of 1991 free-agent draft. ... Signed as a free agent by Chicago Cubs (December 3, 2003). ... On suspended list (August 13-17, 2004).

CAREER HITTING: 0-for-5 (.000), 0 R, 0 2B, 0 3B, 0 HR, 0 RBI.

Year Team (League)	W	L	Pct.	ERA	WHIP	G	GS	CG	ShO	Hld.	Sv.-Opp.	IP	H	R	ER	HR	BB-IBB	SO	Avg.
1991— GC Twins (GCL)	4	3	.571	4.75	1.60	11	11	0	0	...	0-...	55.0	62	34	29	2	26-0	47	.281
1992— GC Twins (GCL)	3	2	.600	3.22	1.27	6	6	1	0	...	0-...	36.1	36	19	13	1	10-0	35	.243
— Elizabethton (Appal.)	0	1	.000	3.38	1.20	5	5	1	0	...	0-...	26.2	21	12	10	2	11-0	36	.202
1993— Fort Wayne (Midw.)	15	5	.750	2.06	0.96	26	23	4	3	...	0-...	157.1	110	53	36	5	41-0	179	.195
1994— Fort Myers (Fla. St.)	4	0	1.000	2.33	0.98	6	6	1	1	...	0-...	38.2	32	10	10	1	6-0	36	.224
— Nashville (Sou.)	9	2	.818	2.33	1.06	11	11	1	0	...	0-...	73.1	50	23	19	2	28-0	53	.191
— Salt Lake (PCL)	5	4	.556	4.08	1.53	12	12	1	0	...	0-...	81.2	92	42	37	8	33-0	37	.296
1995— Minnesota (A.L.)	2	3	.400	8.67	1.89	6	6	1	0	0	0-0	27.0	39	29	26	3	12-0	9	.339
— Salt Lake (PCL)	9	7	.563	3.55	1.32	22	22	4	1	...	0-...	144.1	150	63	57	7	40-1	74	.271
1996— Minnesota (A.L.)	1	1	.500	8.20	1.94	7	6	0	0	0	0-0	26.1	42	24	24	8	9-0	24	.372
— Salt Lake (PCL)	9	8	.529	3.92	1.23	20	20	4	1	...	0-...	137.2	138	66	60	11	31-3	99	.263
1997— Salt Lake (PCL)	9	4	.692	5.45	1.53	14	13	2	1	...	0-...	76.0	100	53	46	4	16-1	53	.311
— Minnesota (A.L.)	6	12	.333	5.84	1.75	20	20	0	0	0	0-0	103.1	134	71	67	19	47-0	58	.317
1998— Minnesota (A.L.)	7	14	.333	5.25	1.51	33	33	0	0	0	0-0	190.1	227	126	111	27	61-1	105	.299
1999— Minnesota (A.L.)	10	14	.417	6.66	1.71	33	33	1	0	0	0-0	174.1	238	* 136	* 129	29	60-2	103	.323
2000— Minnesota (A.L.)	2	5	.286	3.39	1.33	66	0	0	0	7	14-14	87.2	85	34	33	7	32-1	59	.256
2001— Minnesota (A.L.)	1	5	.167	5.96	1.91	62	0	0	0	1	28-37	51.1	59	34	34	3	39-3	36	.291
2002— Minnesota (A.L.)	6	0	1.000	2.13	0.97	65	0	0	0	13	0-3	80.1	63	23	19	5	15-1	63	.217
2003— Minnesota (A.L.)	9	3	.750	1.86	1.09	74	0	0	0	28	2-8	77.1	69	20	16	4	15-1	75	.239
2004— Chicago (N.L.)	5	4	.556	2.63	1.05	77	0	0	0	4	25-34	82.0	72	27	24	10	14-5	69	.233
American League totals (9 years)	44	57	.436	5.05	1.52	366	98	2	0	49	44-62	818.0	956	497	459	105	290-9	532	.293
National League totals (1 year)	5	4	.556	2.63	1.05	77	0	0	0	4	25-34	82.0	72	27	24	10	14-5	69	.233
Major League totals (10 years)	49	61	.445	4.83	1.48	443	98	2	0	53	69-96	900.0	1028	524	483	115	304-14	601	.288

DIVISION SERIES RECORD

Year Team (League)	W	L	Pct.	ERA	WHIP	G	GS	CG	ShO	Hld.	Sv.-Opp.	IP	H	R	ER	HR	BB-IBB	SO	Avg.
2002— Minnesota (A.L.)	0	0	...	0.00	0.00	3	0	0	0	1	0-0	2.1	0	0	0	0	0-0	5	.000
2003— Minnesota (A.L.)	1	0	1.000	6.00	1.67	3	0	0	0	1	0-0	3.0	5	3	2	0	0-0	5	.357
Division series totals (2 years)	1	0	1.000	3.38	0.94	6	0	0	0	2	0-0	5.1	5	3	2	0	0-0	10	.238

CHAMPIONSHIP SERIES RECORD

Year Team (League)	W	L	Pct.	ERA	WHIP	G	GS	CG	ShO	Hld.	Sv.-Opp.	IP	H	R	ER	HR	BB-IBB	SO	Avg.
2002— Minnesota (A.L.)	0	0	...	20.25	3.75	4	0	0	0	0	0-0	1.1	4	3	3	0	1-0	1	.571

HAWPE, BRAD   OF

PERSONAL: Born June 22, 1979, in Fort Worth, Texas. ... 6-3/200. ... Bats left, throws left. ... Full name: Bradley Bonte Hawpe. ... High school: Boswell (Fort Worth). ... College: LSU.

TRANSACTIONS/CAREER NOTES: Selected by Toronto Blue Jays organization in 46th round of 1997 free-agent draft; did not sign. ... Selected by Colorado Rockies organization in 11th round of 2000 free-agent draft.

2004 GAMES PLAYED BY POSITION (MLB): OF—34.

Year Team (League)	Pos.	G	AB	R	H	2B	3B	HR	RBI	BB	SO	HBP	GDP	SB-CS	Avg.	OBP	SLG	OPS	E	Avg.
2000— Portland (N'west)	OF-1B	62	205	38	59	19	2	7	29	40	51	2	1	2-0	.288	.398	.502	.900	5	.983
2001— Asheville (S. Atl.)	OF-1B	111	393	78	105	22	3	22	72	59	113	6	8	7-4	.267	.363	.506	.870	11	.981
2002— Salem (Caro.)	1B	122	450	87	156	38	2	22	97	81	84	2	7	1-1	.347	.447	.587	1.033	8	.994
2003— Tulsa (Texas)	OF-1B	93	346	52	96	27	0	17	68	31	84	1	5	1-3	.277	.338	.503	.841	6	.976
2004— Colo. Springs (PCL)	OF-DH	92	345	62	111	19	4	31	86	36	91	4	10	3-2	.322	.384	.652	1.035	3	.984
— Colorado (N.L.)	OF	42	105	12	26	3	2	3	9	11	34	1	4	1-1	.248	.322	.400	.722	1	.982
Major League totals (1 year)		42	105	12	26	3	2	3	9	11	34	1	4	1-1	.248	.322	.400	.722	1	.982

HAYNES, JIMMY   P

PERSONAL: Born September 5, 1972, in LaGrange, Ga. ... 6-4/220. ... Throws right, bats right. ... Full name: Jimmy Wayne Haynes. ... High school: Troup (La Grange, Ga.).

TRANSACTIONS/CAREER NOTES: Selected by Baltimore Orioles organization in seventh round of 1991 free-agent draft. ... Traded by Orioles with a player to be named to Oakland Athletics for OF Geronimo Berroa (June 27, 1997); A's acquired P Mark Seaver to complete deal (September 2, 1997). ... Traded by A's to Milwaukee Brewers as part of three-team deal in which A's received P Justin Miller and cash from Colorado Rockies, Brewers received P Jamey Wright and C Henry Blanco from Rockies and Rockies received 3B Jeff Cirillo, P Scott Karl and cash from Brewers (December 13, 1999). ... On disabled list (August 24-September 26, 2001). ... Signed as a free agent by Cincinnati Reds organization (January 11, 2002). ... On disabled list (April 18-May 27 and August 4, 2003-remainder of season); included rehabilitation assignments to Louisville and Dayton. ... Released by Reds (May 10, 2004). ... Signed by Detroit Tigers organization (May 18, 2004). ... Released by Tigers (June 20, 2004).

CAREER HITTING: 32-for-213 (.150), 16 R, 9 2B, 0 3B, 0 HR, 13 RBI.

Year Team (League)	W	L	Pct.	ERA	WHIP	G	GS	CG	ShO	Hld.	Sv.-Opp.	IP	H	R	ER	HR	BB-IBB	SO	Avg.
1991— GC Orioles (GCL)	3	2	.600	1.60	1.05	14	8	1	0	...	2-...	62.0	44	27	11	0	21-0	67	.190
1992— Kane County (Midwest)	7	11	.389	2.56	1.22	24	24	4	0	...	0-...	144.0	131	66	41	2	45-0	141	.236
1993— Frederick (Caro.)	12	8	.600	3.03	1.16	27	27	2	1	...	0-...	172.1	139	73	58	13	61-1	174	.217
1994— Bowie (East.)	13	8	.619	2.90	1.15	25	25	5	1	...	0-...	173.2	154	67	56	16	46-1	177	.238
— Rochester (Int'l)	1	0	1.000	6.75	1.95	3	3	0	0	...	0-...	13.1	20	12	10	3	6-0	14	.333
1995— Rochester (Int'l)	12	8	.600	3.29	1.26	26	25	3	1	...	0-...	167.0	162	77	61	16	49-0	140	.257
— Baltimore (A.L.)	2	1	.667	2.25	0.96	4	3	0	0	0	0-0	24.0	11	6	6	2	12-1	22	.136
1996— Baltimore (A.L.)	3	6	.333	8.29	2.02	26	11	0	0	0	1-1	89.0	122	84	82	14	58-1	65	.333
— Rochester (Int'l)	1	1	.500	5.65	1.71	5	5	0	0	...	0-...	28.2	31	19	18	5	18-0	24	.279
1997— Rochester (Int'l)	5	4	.556	3.44	1.41	16	16	2	1	...	0-...	102.0	89	49	39	9	55-0	113	.239
— Edmonton (PCL)	0	2	.000	4.85	1.58	5	5	0	0	...	0-...	29.2	36	22	16	4	11-0	24	.298
— Oakland (A.L.)	3	6	.333	4.42	1.55	13	13	0	0	0	0-0	73.1	74	38	36	7	40-1	65	.262
1998— Oakland (A.L.)	11	9	.550	5.09	1.63	33	33	1	1	0	0-0	194.1	229	124	110	25	88-4	134	.298
1999— Oakland (A.L.)	7	12	.368	6.34	1.68	30	25	0	0	0	0-0	142.0	158	112	100	21	80-3	93	.282

H

Year Team (League)	W	L	Pct.	ERA	WHIP	G	GS	CG	ShO	Hld.	Sv.-Opp.	IP	H	R	ER	HR	BB-IBB	SO	Avg.
2000— Milwaukee (N.L.)	12	13	.480	5.33	1.65	33	33	0	0	0	0-0	199.1	228	128	118	21	100-7	88	.295
2001— Milwaukee (N.L.)	8	17	.320	4.85	1.51	31	29	0	0	0	0-0	172.2	182	98	93	20	78-17	112	.279
2002— Cincinnati (N.L.)	15	10	.600	4.12	1.48	34	34	0	0	0	0-0	196.2	210	97	90	21	81-4	126	.278
2003— Dayton (Midw.)	1	0	1.000	0.00	0.60	1	1	0	0	...	0-...	7.0	2	1	0	0	2-0	6	.087
— Louisville (Int'l)	1	1	.500	2.53	1.20	2	2	0	0	...	0-...	10.2	10	4	3	1	3-0	7	.244
— Cincinnati (N.L.)	2	12	.143	6.30	1.86	18	18	1	0	0	0-0	94.1	118	74	66	14	57-3	49	.311
2004— Cincinnati (N.L.)	0	3	.000	9.60	2.20	5	4	0	0	0	0-0	15.0	26	17	16	3	7-0	8	.388
— Toledo (International)	0	1	.000	8.78	1.88	5	3	0	0	...	0-...	13.1	19	13	13	0	6-0	9	.328
American League totals (5 years)	26	34	.433	5.75	1.67	106	85	1	1	0	1-1	522.2	594	364	334	69	278-10	379	.289
National League totals (5 years)	37	55	.402	5.08	1.60	121	118	1	0	0	0-0	678.0	764	414	383	79	323-31	383	.291
Major League totals (10 years)	63	89	.414	5.37	1.63	227	203	2	1	0	1-1	1200.2	1358	778	717	148	601-41	762	.290

HEILMAN, AARON — P

PERSONAL: Born November 12, 1978, in Logansport, Ind. ... 6-5/220. ... Throws right, bats right. ... Full name: Aaron Michael Heilman. ... High school: Logansport (Ind.). ... College: Notre Dame.

TRANSACTIONS/CAREER NOTES: Selected by New York Yankees organization in 55th round of 1997 free-agent draft; did not sign. ... Selected by Minnesota Twins organization in supplemental round ("sandwich" pick between first and second rounds, 31st pick overall) of 2000 free-agent draft; did not sign; pick received as part of compensation for Baltimore Orioles signing Type A free-agent P Mike Trombley. ... Selected by New York Mets organization in first round (18th pick overall) of 2001 free-agent draft.

CAREER HITTING: 1-for-29 (.034), 1 R, 0 2B, 0 3B, 0 HR, 1 RBI.

Year Team (League)	W	L	Pct.	ERA	WHIP	G	GS	CG	ShO	Hld.	Sv.-Opp.	IP	H	R	ER	HR	BB-IBB	SO	Avg.
2001— St. Lucie (Fla. St.)	0	1	.000	2.35	1.02	7	7	0	0	...	0-...	38.1	26	11	10	0	13-0	39	.190
2002— Binghamton (Eastern)	4	4	.500	3.82	1.17	17	17	0	0	...	0-...	96.2	85	43	41	7	28-2	97	.237
— Norfolk (Int'l)	2	3	.400	3.28	1.18	10	7	0	0	...	0-...	49.1	42	18	18	3	16-1	35	.240
2003— Norfolk (Int'l)	6	4	.600	3.24	1.39	16	16	0	0	...	0-...	94.1	99	37	34	5	32-0	71	.274
— New York (N.L.)	2	7	.222	6.75	1.84	14	13	0	0	0	0-0	65.1	79	53	49	13	41-2	51	.300
2004— Norfolk (Int'l)	7	10	.412	4.33	1.46	26	26	1	0	...	0-...	151.2	156	88	73	15	66-0	123	.264
— New York (N.L.)	1	3	.250	5.46	1.43	5	5	0	0	0	0-0	28.0	27	17	17	4	13-0	22	.257
Major League totals (2 years)	3	10	.231	6.36	1.71	19	18	0	0	0	0-0	93.1	106	70	66	17	54-2	73	.288

HELMS, WES — 3B

PERSONAL: Born May 12, 1976, in Gastonia, N.C. ... 6-4/231. ... Bats right, throws right. ... Full name: Wesley Ray Helms. ... High school: Ashbrook (Gastonia, N.C.).

TRANSACTIONS/CAREER NOTES: Selected by Atlanta Braves organization in 10th round of 1994 free-agent draft. ... On disabled list (April 3-July 15 and September 5, 1999-remainder of season); included rehabilitation assignment to GCL Braves. ... On disabled list (August 10-September 10, 2002). ... Traded by Braves with P John Foster to Milwaukee Brewers for P Ray King (December 16, 2002). ... On disabled list (August 7-22, 2003); included rehabilitation assignment to Indianapolis. ... On disabled list (May 19-June 28, 2004); included rehabilitation assignment to Indianapolis.

2004 GAMES PLAYED BY POSITION (MLB): 3B—66, 1B—10.

Year Team (League)	Pos.	G	AB	R	H	2B	3B	HR	RBI	BB	SO	HBP	GDP	SB-CS	Avg.	OBP	SLG	OPS	E	Avg.
1994— GC Braves (GCL)	3B	56	184	22	49	15	1	4	29	22	36	4	3	6-1	.266	.355	.424	.779	20	.875
1995— Macon (S. Atl.)	3B	136	539	89	149	32	1	11	85	50	107	10	8	2-2	.276	.347	.401	.748	40	.900
1996— Durham (Caro.)	3B	67	258	40	83	19	2	13	54	12	51	7	7	1-1	.322	.367	.562	.929	15	.920
— Greenville (Sou.)	3B	64	231	24	59	13	2	4	22	13	48	4	6	2-1	.255	.306	.381	.687	12	.924
1997— Richmond (Int'l)	3B	32	110	11	21	4	0	3	15	10	34	5	4	1-1	.191	.286	.309	.595	9	.902
— Greenville (Sou.)	3B	86	314	50	93	14	1	11	44	33	50	6	14	3-4	.296	.371	.452	.823	11	.950
1998— Richmond (Int'l)	3B-DH	125	451	56	124	27	1	13	75	35	103	13	11	6-2	.275	.342	.426	.768	15	.952
— Atlanta (N.L.)	3B	7	13	2	4	1	0	1	2	0	4	0	0	0-0	.308	.308	.615	.923	1	.750
1999— GC Braves (GCL)	DH-1B	9	33	1	15	2	0	0	10	5	4	1	1	0-1	.455	.538	.515	1.054	0	1.000
— Greenville (Sou.)	1B	30	113	15	34	6	0	8	26	7	34	1	3	1-0	.301	.347	.566	.913	4	.984
2000— Richmond (Int'l)	3B	136	539	74	155	27	7	20	88	27	92	6	10	0-6	.288	.325	.475	.800	23	.933
— Atlanta (N.L.)	3B	6	5	0	1	0	0	0	0	0	2	0	0	0-0	.200	.200	.200	.400	1	.833
2001— Atlanta (N.L.)	1B-3B-OF	100	216	19	48	10	3	10	36	21	56	1	3	1-1	.222	.293	.435	.728	4	.992
2002— Atlanta (N.L.)	1B-3B-OF	85	210	20	51	16	0	6	22	11	57	3	5	1-1	.243	.283	.405	.687	5	.986
2003— Indianapolis (Int'l)	3B	2	5	0	2	0	0	0	0	1	1	0	0	0-0	.400	.500	.400	.900	0	1.000
— Milwaukee (N.L.)	3B	134	476	56	124	21	0	23	67	43	131	10	10	0-1	.261	.330	.450	.780	19	.945
2004— Indianapolis (Int'l)	3B-DH	6	19	4	6	1	0	0	1	3	4	0	0	0-0	.316	.409	.368	.778	2	.857
— Milwaukee (N.L.)	3B-1B	92	274	24	72	13	1	4	28	24	60	5	10	0-1	.263	.331	.361	.692	18	.925
Major League totals (6 years)		424	1194	130	300	61	4	44	155	99	310	19	28	2-4	.251	.315	.420	.734	48	.967

DIVISION SERIES RECORD

Year Team (League)	Pos.	G	AB	R	H	2B	3B	HR	RBI	BB	SO	HBP	GDP	SB-CS	Avg.	OBP	SLG	OPS	E	Avg.
2002— Atlanta (N.L.)	1B	1	0	0	0	0	0	0	0	0	0	0	0	0-0	...	...	...	...	0	...

HELTON, TODD — 1B

PERSONAL: Born August 20, 1973, in Knoxville, Tenn. ... 6-2/204. ... Bats left, throws left. ... Full name: Todd Lynn Helton. ... High school: Knoxville (Tenn.) Central. ... College: Tennessee.

TRANSACTIONS/CAREER NOTES: Selected by San Diego Padres organization in second round of 1992 free-agent draft; did not sign. ... Selected by Colorado Rockies organization in first round (eighth pick overall) of 1995 free-agent draft.

HONORS: Named N.L. Rookie Player of the Year by THE SPORTING NEWS (1998). ... Won N.L. Gold Glove at first base (2001, 2002 and 2004).

2004 GAMES PLAYED BY POSITION (MLB): 1B—153.

Year Team (League)	Pos.	G	AB	R	H	2B	3B	HR	RBI	BB	SO	HBP	GDP	SB-CS	Avg.	OBP	SLG	OPS	E	Avg.
1995— Asheville (S. Atl.)	DH-1B	54	201	24	51	11	1	1	15	25	32	1	7	1-1	.254	.339	.333	.673	4	.990
1996— New Haven (East.)	1B-DH	93	319	46	106	24	2	7	51	51	37	1	8	2-5	.332	.425	.486	.911	5	.994
— Colo. Springs (PCL)	1B-OF	21	71	13	25	4	1	2	13	11	12	0	3	0-0	.352	.439	.521	.960	2	.988
1997— Colo. Springs (PCL)	1B-OF-DH	99	392	87	138	31	2	16	88	61	68	0	10	3-1	.352	.434	.564	.997	9	.987
— Colorado (N.L.)	OF-1B	35	93	13	26	2	1	5	11	8	11	0	1	0-1	.280	.337	.484	.821	1	1.000
1998— Colorado (N.L.)	1B	152	530	78	167	37	1	25	97	53	54	6	15	3-3	.315	.380	.530	.911	7	.995
1999— Colorado (N.L.)	1B	159	578	114	185	39	5	35	113	68	77	6	14	7-6	.320	.395	.587	.981	9	.993
2000— Colorado (N.L.)	1B	160	580	138	*216	*59	2	42	*147	103	61	4	12	5-3	*.372	*.463	*.698	1.162	7	.995

H

Year Team (League)	Pos.	G	AB	R	H	2B	3B	HR	RBI	BB	SO	HBP	GDP	SB-CS	Avg.	OBP	SLG	OPS	E	Avg.
2001—Colorado (N.L.)	1B	159	587	132	197	54	2	49	146	98	104	5	14	7-5	.336	.432	.685	1.116	2	.999
2002—Colorado (N.L.)	1B	156	553	107	182	39	4	30	109	99	91	5	10	5-1	.329	.429	.577	1.006	7	.995
2003—Colorado (N.L.)	1B	160	583	135	209	49	5	33	117	111	72	2	19	0-4	.358	.458	.630	1.088	11	.993
2004—Colorado (N.L.)	1B	154	547	115	190	49	2	32	96	127	72	3	12	3-0	.347	.469	.620	1.088	4	.997
Major League totals (8 years)		1135	4051	832	1372	328	22	251	836	667	542	31	97	30-23	.339	.432	.616	1.048	47	.995

ALL-STAR GAME RECORD

	G	AB	R	H	2B	3B	HR	RBI	BB	SO	HBP	GDP	SB-CS	Avg.	OBP	SLG	OPS	E	Avg.
All-Star Game totals (5 years)	5	9	2	2	0	0	1	3	0	2	0	0	0-0	.222	.222	.556	.778	0	1.000

HENDRICKSON, BEN　　　　　P

PERSONAL: Born February 4, 1981, in St. Cloud, Minn. ... 6-4/190. ... Throws right, bats right. ... Full name: Benjamin J. Hendrickson. ... High school: Jefferson (Bloomington, Minn.).

TRANSACTIONS/CAREER NOTES: Selected by Milwaukee Brewers organization in 10th round of 1999 free-agent draft.

CAREER HITTING: 2-for-16 (.125), 0 R, 0 2B, 0 3B, 0 HR, 0 RBI.

Year Team (League)	W	L	Pct.	ERA	WHIP	G	GS	CG	ShO	Hld.	Sv.-Opp.	IP	H	R	ER	HR	BB-IBB	SO	Avg.
2000—Ogden (Pio.)	4	3	.571	5.68	1.56	13	7	0	0	...	1-...	50.2	50	37	32	7	29-0	48	.245
2001—Beloit (Midw.)	8	9	.471	2.84	1.46	25	25	1	0	...	0-...	133.1	122	58	42	3	72-0	133	.246
2002—High Desert (Calif.)	5	5	.500	2.55	1.25	14	14	0	0	...	0-...	81.1	61	31	23	3	41-0	70	.209
—Huntsville (Southern)	4	2	.667	2.97	1.32	13	13	0	0	...	0-...	69.2	57	31	23	2	35-0	50	.231
2003—Huntsville (Southern)	7	6	.538	3.45	1.40	17	16	0	0	...	0-...	78.1	82	35	30	6	28-0	56	.278
2004—Indianapolis (Int'l)	11	3	.786	2.02	1.12	21	21	2	2	...	0-...	125.0	114	32	28	6	26-0	93	.246
—Milwaukee (N.L.)	1	8	.111	6.22	1.68	10	9	0	0	0	0-0	46.1	58	33	32	6	20-1	29	.310
Major League totals (1 year)	1	8	.111	6.22	1.68	10	9	0	0	0	0-0	46.1	58	33	32	6	20-1	29	.310

HENDRICKSON, MARK　　　　　P

PERSONAL: Born June 23, 1974, in Mount Vernon, Wash. ... 6-9/230. ... Throws left, bats left. ... Full name: Mark Allan Hendrickson. ... High school: Mount Vernon (Wash.). ... College: Washington State.

TRANSACTIONS/CAREER NOTES: Selected by Atlanta Braves organization in 12th round of 1992 free-agent draft; did not sign. ... Selected by San Diego Padres organization in 21st round of 1993 free-agent draft; did not sign. ... Selected by Braves organization in 32nd round of 1994 free-agent draft; did not sign. ... Selected by Detroit Tigers organization in 16th round of 1995 free-agent draft; did not sign. ... Selected by Texas Rangers organization in 19th round of 1996 free-agent draft; did not sign. ... Selected by Toronto Blue Jays organization in 20th round of 1997 free-agent draft. ... Traded by Blue Jays to Tampa Bay Devil Rays as part of three-team deal in which Blue Jays acquired P Justin Speier from Colorado Rockies and Rockies acquired P Joe Kennedy from Devil Rays and a player to be named from Blue Jays (December 14, 2003); Rockies acquired P Sandy Nin to complete deal (December 15, 2003). ... Played as a forward for four NBA teams (1996-2000).

CAREER HITTING: 2-for-9 (.222), 1 R, 0 2B, 0 3B, 1 HR, 1 RBI.

Year Team (League)	W	L	Pct.	ERA	WHIP	G	GS	CG	ShO	Hld.	Sv.-Opp.	IP	H	R	ER	HR	BB-IBB	SO	Avg.
1998—Dunedin (Fla. St.)	4	3	.571	2.37	1.42	16	5	0	0	...	1-...	49.1	44	16	13	2	26-1	38	.249
1999—Knoxville (Southern)	2	7	.222	6.63	1.69	12	11	0	0	...	0-...	55.2	73	46	41	4	21-0	39	.319
2000—Dunedin (Fla. St.)	2	2	.500	5.61	1.79	12	12	1	0	...	0-...	51.1	63	34	32	7	29-0	38	.315
—Tennessee (Sou.)	3	1	.750	3.63	1.11	6	6	0	0	...	0-...	39.2	32	17	16	5	12-0	29	.216
2001—Syracuse (Int'l)	2	9	.182	4.66	1.34	38	6	0	0	...	0-...	73.1	80	43	38	13	18-1	33	.274
2002—Syracuse (Int'l)	7	5	.583	3.52	1.22	19	14	0	0	...	0-...	92.0	90	38	36	12	22-0	68	.254
—Toronto (A.L.)	3	0	1.000	2.45	1.01	16	4	0	0	1	0-1	36.2	25	11	10	1	12-3	21	.202
2003—Syracuse (Int'l)	0	0	...	4.50	1.50	1	1	0	0	...	0-...	6.0	8	4	3	1	1-0	5	.333
—Dunedin (Fla. St.)	1	0	1.000	1.59	1.60	1	1	0	0	...	0-...	5.2	5	2	1	0	4-0	3	.227
—Toronto (A.L.)	9	9	.500	5.51	1.56	30	30	1	0	0	0-0	158.1	207	111	97	24	40-3	76	.317
2004—Tampa Bay (A.L.)	10	15	.400	4.81	1.40	32	30	2	0	0	0-0	183.1	211	113	98	21	46-5	87	.285
Major League totals (3 years)	22	24	.478	4.88	1.43	78	64	3	1	1	0-1	378.1	443	235	205	46	98-11	184	.292

HENNESSEY, BRAD　　　　　P

PERSONAL: Born February 7, 1980, in Toledo, Ohio. ... 6-2/185. ... Throws right, bats right. ... Full name: Brad Martin Hennessey. ... High school: Whitmer (Toldeo). ... College: Youngstown State.

TRANSACTIONS/CAREER NOTES: Selected by San Francisco Giants organization in first round (21st pick overall) of 2001 free-agent draft.

CAREER HITTING: 3-for-13 (.231), 1 R, 0 2B, 0 3B, 0 HR, 2 RBI.

Year Team (League)	W	L	Pct.	ERA	WHIP	G	GS	CG	ShO	Hld.	Sv.-Opp.	IP	H	R	ER	HR	BB-IBB	SO	Avg.
2001—Salem-Keizer (N'west)	1	0	1.000	2.38	1.15	9	9	0	0	...	0-...	34.0	28	9	9	1	11-0	22	.224
2003—Hagerstown (S. Atl.)	3	9	.250	4.20	1.36	15	15	1	0	...	0-...	79.1	81	49	37	6	27-0	44	.265
2004—Norwich (East.)	5	5	.500	3.56	1.39	18	18	0	0	...	0-...	101.0	106	42	40	8	34-0	55	.272
—Fresno (PCL)	4	1	.800	2.02	1.15	5	5	0	0	...	0-...	35.2	26	8	8	2	15-0	16	.202
—San Francisco (N.L.)	2	2	.500	4.98	1.66	7	7	0	0	0	0-0	34.1	42	24	19	2	15-1	25	.294
Major League totals (1 year)	2	2	.500	4.98	1.66	7	7	0	0	0	0-0	34.1	42	24	19	2	15-1	25	.294

HENSLEY, MATT　　　　　P

PERSONAL: Born August 18, 1978, in San Diego CA, Calif. ... 6-2/220. ... Throws right, bats right. ... Full name: Matthew Davis Hensley. ... High school: Patrick Henry (San Diego). ... Junior college: Grossmont (Calif.).

TRANSACTIONS/CAREER NOTES: Selected by Anaheim Angels organization in 10th round of 2000 free-agent draft.

CAREER HITTING: 0-for-1 (.000), 0 R, 0 2B, 0 3B, 0 HR, 0 RBI.

Year Team (League)	W	L	Pct.	ERA	WHIP	G	GS	CG	ShO	Hld.	Sv.-Opp.	IP	H	R	ER	HR	BB-IBB	SO	Avg.
2000—Butte (Pio.)	1	2	.333	2.57	1.39	8	5	0	0	...	0-...	28.0	29	21	8	0	10-0	22	.242
—Cedar Rapids (Midw.)	2	2	.500	4.15	1.42	5	5	1	0	...	0-...	30.1	33	16	14	1	10-0	26	.287
—Lake Elsinore (Calif.)	0	0	...	0.00	1.00	1	0	0	0	...	0-...	1.0	1	0	0	0	0-0	2	.250
2001—Cedar Rapids (Midw.)	5	3	.625	3.64	1.38	11	11	1	0	...	0-...	71.2	80	42	29	10	19-0	63	.270
—Rancho Cuca. (Calif.)	2	7	.222	5.93	1.60	14	12	0	0	...	0-...	68.1	85	57	45	4	24-0	58	.306
2002—Rancho Cuca. (Calif.)	1	1	.500	5.40	1.67	12	2	0	0	...	0-...	31.2	42	21	19	3	11-0	27	.318
—Salt Lake (PCL)	7	5	.583	4.97	1.45	19	18	1	0	...	0-...	117.2	132	76	65	16	39-0	106	.288
2003—Salt Lake (PCL)	8	12	.400	4.89	1.53	27	27	1	0	...	0-...	158.1	194	105	86	16	49-0	85	.303
2004—Salt Lake (PCL)	1	3	.250	2.93	0.95	30	0	0	0	...	5-...	43.0	29	16	14	6	12-0	49	.185
—Anaheim (A.L.)	0	2	.000	4.88	1.41	16	0	0	0	0	0-0	27.2	32	15	15	5	7-1	30	.294
Major League totals (1 year)	0	2	.000	4.88	1.41	16	0	0	0	0	0-0	27.2	32	15	15	5	7-1	30	.294

H

HENTGEN, PAT — P

PERSONAL: Born November 13, 1968, in Detroit, Mich. ... 6-2/195. ... Throws right, bats right. ... Full name: Patrick George Hentgen. ... Name pronounced: HENT-gen. ... High school: Fraser (Mich.).

TRANSACTIONS/CAREER NOTES: Selected by Toronto Blue Jays organization in fifth round of June 1986 free-agent draft. ... On disabled list (August 13-September 29, 1992); included rehabilitation assignment to Syracuse. ... Traded by Blue Jays with P Paul Spoljaric to St. Louis Cardinals for Ps Lance Painter and Matt DeWitt and C Alberto Castillo (November 11, 1999). ... Signed as a free agent by Baltimore Orioles (December 19, 2000). ... On disabled list (May 17, 2001-remainder of season). ... On Baltimore disabled list (March 31-September 8, 2002); included rehabilitation assignments to GCL Orioles, Delmarva, Aberdeen, Bowie and Frederick. ... Signed as a free agent by Blue Jays (November 18, 2003). ... Announced retirement (July 24, 2004).

HONORS: Named A.L. Pitcher of the Year by THE SPORTING NEWS (1996). ... Named A.L. Cy Young Award winner by Baseball Writers' Association of America (1996).

CAREER HITTING: 9-for-84 (.107), 4 R, 0 2B, 0 3B, 0 HR, 0 RBI.

Year — Team (League)	W	L	Pct.	ERA	WHIP	G	GS	CG	ShO	Hld.	Sv.-Opp.	IP	H	R	ER	HR	BB-IBB	SO	Avg.
1986— St. Catharines (NY-Penn.) .	0	4	.000	4.50	1.70	13	11	0	0	...	1-...	40.0	38	27	20	3	30-1	30	.244
1987— Myrtle Beach (SAL)	11	5	.688	2.35	1.09	32	31	2	2	...	0-...	188.0	145	62	49	5	60-0	131	.214
1988— Dunedin (Fla. St.)	3	12	.200	3.45	1.35	31	30	0	0	...	0-...	151.1	139	80	58	10	65-1	125	.243
1989— Dunedin (Fla. St.)	9	8	.529	2.68	1.28	29	28	0	0	...	0-...	151.1	123	53	45	5	71-1	148	.225
1990— Knoxville (Southern)	9	5	.643	3.05	1.23	28	26	0	0	...	0-...	153.1	121	57	52	10	68-0	142	.218
1991— Syracuse (Int'l)	8	9	.471	4.47	1.38	31	28	1	0	...	0-...	171.0	146	91	85	17	90-1	155	.234
— Toronto (A.L.)	0	0	...	2.45	1.09	3	1	0	0	0	0-0	7.1	5	2	2	1	3-0	3	.208
1992— Toronto (A.L.)	5	2	.714	5.36	1.61	28	2	0	0	1	0-1	50.1	49	30	30	7	32-5	39	.254
— Syracuse (Int'l)	1	2	.333	2.66	1.13	4	4	0	0	...	0-...	20.1	15	6	6	1	8-0	17	.211
1993— Toronto (A.L.)	19	9	.679	3.87	1.34	34	32	3	0	0	0-0	216.1	215	103	93	27	74-0	122	.258
1994— Toronto (A.L.)	13	8	.619	3.40	1.24	24	24	6	3	0	0-0	174.2	158	74	66	21	59-1	147	.240
1995— Toronto (A.L.)	10	14	.417	5.11	1.62	30	30	2	0	0	0-0	200.2	*236	*129	*114	24	90-6	135	.290
1996— Toronto (A.L.)	20	10	.667	3.22	1.25	35	35	*10	•3	0	0-0	*265.2	238	105	95	20	94-3	177	.241
1997— Toronto (A.L.)	15	10	.600	3.68	1.23	35	•35	•9	•3	0	0-0	•264.0	253	116	108	31	71-2	160	.254
1998— Toronto (A.L.)	12	11	.522	5.17	1.56	29	29	0	0	0	0-0	177.2	208	109	102	28	69-1	94	.293
1999— Toronto (A.L.)	11	12	.478	4.79	1.46	34	34	1	0	0	0-0	199.0	225	115	106	32	65-1	118	.286
2000— St. Louis (N.L.)	15	12	.556	4.72	1.50	33	33	1	1	0	0-0	194.1	202	107	102	24	89-4	118	.276
2001— Baltimore (A.L.)	2	3	.400	3.47	1.12	9	9	1	0	0	0-0	62.1	51	25	24	7	19-3	33	.221
2002— GC Orioles (GCL)	0	0	...	0.00	0.67	1	1	0	0	0	0-...	3.0	2	0	0	0	0-0	3	.182
— Delmarva (S.Atl.)	0	1	.000	1.80	1.00	1	1	0	0	0	0-...	5.0	4	1	1	0	1-0	4	.235
— Aberdeen (NY-P)	1	1	.500	3.09	1.37	2	2	0	0	0	0-...	11.2	16	8	4	1	0-0	10	.314
— Bowie (East.)	0	0	...	1.50	1.17	1	1	0	0	0	0-...	6.0	5	2	1	0	2-0	3	.227
— Frederick (Caro.)	1	0	1.000	2.57	1.00	1	1	0	0	0	0-...	7.0	5	2	2	0	2-0	5	.208
— Baltimore (A.L.)	0	4	.000	7.77	1.86	4	4	0	0	0	0-...	22.0	31	20	19	6	10-0	11	.337
2003— Baltimore (A.L.)	7	8	.467	4.09	1.29	28	22	1	0	0	1-1	160.2	150	74	73	25	58-1	100	.247
2004— Toronto (A.L.)	2	9	.182	6.95	1.64	18	16	0	0	0	0-0	80.1	90	67	62	16	42-2	33	.283
American League totals (13 years)	116	100	.537	4.28	1.38	311	273	33	9	1	1-2	1881.0	1909	969	894	245	686-25	1172	.263
National League totals (1 year)	15	12	.556	4.72	1.50	33	33	1	1	0	0-0	194.1	202	107	102	24	89-4	118	.276
Major League totals (14 years)	131	112	.539	4.32	1.39	344	306	34	10	1	1-2	2075.1	2111	1076	996	269	775-29	1290	.264

DIVISION SERIES RECORD

Year — Team (League)	W	L	Pct.	ERA	WHIP	G	GS	CG	ShO	Hld.	Sv.-Opp.	IP	H	R	ER	HR	BB-IBB	SO	Avg.
2000— St. Louis (N.L.)							Did not play.												

CHAMPIONSHIP SERIES RECORD

Year — Team (League)	W	L	Pct.	ERA	WHIP	G	GS	CG	ShO	Hld.	Sv.-Opp.	IP	H	R	ER	HR	BB-IBB	SO	Avg.
1993— Toronto (A.L.)	0	1	.000	18.00	3.67	1	1	0	0	0	0-0	3.0	9	6	6	0	2-0	3	.529
2000— St. Louis (N.L.)	0	1	.000	14.73	3.27	1	1	0	0	0	0-0	3.2	7	6	6	0	5-0	2	.389
Champ. series totals (2 years)	0	2	.000	16.20	3.45	2	2	0	0	0	0-0	6.2	16	12	12	0	7-0	5	.457

WORLD SERIES RECORD

Year — Team (League)	W	L	Pct.	ERA	WHIP	G	GS	CG	ShO	Hld.	Sv.-Opp.	IP	H	R	ER	HR	BB-IBB	SO	Avg.
1993— Toronto (A.L.)	1	0	1.000	1.50	1.33	1	1	0	0	0	0-0	6.0	5	1	1	0	3-0	6	.227

ALL-STAR GAME RECORD

	W	L	Pct.	ERA	WHIP	G	GS	CG	ShO	Hld.	Sv.-Opp.	IP	H	R	ER	HR	BB-IBB	SO	Avg.
All-Star Game totals (2 years)	0	0	...	0.00	0.50	2	0	0	0	2	0-0	2.0	1	0	0	0	0-0	0	.167

HEREDIA, FELIX — P

PERSONAL: Born June 20, 1975, in Barahona, Dominican Republic. ... 6-0/180. ... Throws left, bats left. ... Full name: Felix Perez Heredla. ... Name pronounced: heh-RAY-dee-ah. ... High school: Escuela Dominical (Barahona, Dominican Republic).

TRANSACTIONS/CAREER NOTES: Signed as a non-drafted free agent by Florida Marlins organization (November 22, 1992). ... Traded by Marlins with P Steve Hoff to Chicago Cubs for 3B Kevin Orie and Ps Todd Noel and Justin Speier (July 31, 1998). ... On disabled list (August 21-September 5 and September 18-October 3, 2001). ... Traded by Cubs with a player to be named to Toronto Blue Jays for SS Alex Gonzalez (December 10, 2001); Blue Jays acquired IF James Deschaine to complete deal (December 13, 2001). ... Signed as a free agent by Cincinnati Reds organization (January 7, 2003). ... Claimed on waivers by New York Yankees (August 25, 2003). ... On disabled list (April 10-May 17, 2004); included rehabilitation assignment to Columbus.

CAREER HITTING: 4-for-15 (.267), 0 R, 0 2B, 0 3B, 0 HR, 1 RBI.

Year — Team (League)	W	L	Pct.	ERA	WHIP	G	GS	CG	ShO	Hld.	Sv.-Opp.	IP	H	R	ER	HR	BB-IBB	SO	Avg.
1993— GC Marlins (GCL)	5	1	.833	2.47	0.98	12	12	0	0	...	0-...	62.0	50	18	17	0	11-0	53	.238
1994— Kane County (Midwest)	4	5	.444	5.69	1.47	24	8	1	0	...	3-...	68.0	86	55	43	7	14-0	65	.305
1995— Brevard County (FSL)	6	4	.600	3.57	1.43	34	8	0	0	...	1-...	95.2	101	52	38	6	36-1	76	.271
1996— Portland (East.)	8	1	.889	1.50	1.05	55	0	0	0	...	5-...	60.0	48	11	10	3	15-2	42	.223
— Florida (N.L.)	1	1	.500	4.32	1.86	21	0	0	0	2	0-0	16.2	21	8	8	1	10-1	10	.313
1997— Florida (N.L.)	5	3	.625	4.29	1.46	56	0	0	0	7	0-1	56.2	53	30	27	3	30-1	54	.243
1998— Florida (N.L.)	0	3	.000	5.49	1.71	41	2	0	0	9	2-3	41.0	38	30	25	1	32-2	38	.241
— Chicago (N.L.)	3	0	1.000	4.08	1.42	30	0	0	0	8	0-2	17.2	19	9	8	1	6-1	16	.279
1999— Chicago (N.L.)	3	1	.750	4.85	1.56	69	0	0	0	12	1-7	52.0	56	35	28	7	25-2	50	.272
2000— Chicago (N.L.)	7	3	.700	4.76	1.35	74	0	0	0	12	2-5	58.2	46	31	31	6	33-4	52	.220
2001— Chicago (N.L.)	2	2	.500	6.17	1.74	48	0	0	0	8	0-3	35.0	45	27	24	6	16-1	28	.315
2002— Toronto (A.L.)	1	2	.333	3.61	1.47	53	0	0	0	7	0-2	52.1	51	29	21	9	26-3	31	.256
2003— Cincinnati (N.L.)	5	2	.714	3.00	1.24	57	0	0	0	7	1-4	72.0	61	27	24	9	28-5	41	.228
— New York (A.L.)	0	1	.000	1.20	1.20	12	0	0	0	1	0-1	15.0	13	5	2	1	5-2	4	.228

H

Year Team (League)	W	L	Pct.	ERA	WHIP	G	GS	CG	ShO	Hld.	Sv.-Opp.	IP	H	R	ER	HR	BB-IBB	SO	Avg.
2004—Columbus (Int'l)	0	0	...	0.00	0.82	3	0	0	0	...	0-...	3.2	2	0	0	0	1-0	5	.154
—Tampa (FSL)	0	0	...	1.80	1.40	2	2	0	0	...	0-...	5.0	4	1	1	0	3-0	3	.222
—Trenton (East.)	0	1	.000	5.40	1.40	3	1	0	0	...	0-...	5.0	7	6	3	0	0-0	8	.350
—New York (A.L.)	1	1	.500	6.28	1.66	47	0	0	0	5	0-1	38.2	44	28	27	5	20-0	25	.278
American League totals (3 years)	2	4	.333	4.25	1.50	112	0	0	0	13	0-4	106.0	108	62	50	11	51-5	60	.261
National League totals (7 years)	26	15	.634	4.50	1.48	396	2	0	0	65	6-25	349.2	339	197	175	34	180-17	289	.254
Major League totals (9 years)	28	19	.596	4.44	1.49	508	2	0	0	78	6-29	455.2	447	259	225	45	231-22	349	.255

DIVISION SERIES RECORD

Year Team (League)	W	L	Pct.	ERA	WHIP	G	GS	CG	ShO	Hld.	Sv.-Opp.	IP	H	R	ER	HR	BB-IBB	SO	Avg.
1997—Florida (N.L.)	Did not play.																		
1998—Chicago (N.L.)	0	0	...	54.00	6.00	1	0	0	0	0	0-0	.1	0	2	2	0	2-0	0	.000
2003—New York (A.L.)	0	0	...	0.00	1.00	1	0	0	0	0	0-0	2.0	1	0	0	0	1-1	1	.167
2004—New York (A.L.)	0	0	...	54.00	1.00	1	0	0	0	0	0-0	.1	0	2	2	0	0-0	0	.000
Division series totals (3 years)	0	0	...	13.50	1.50	3	0	0	0	0	0-0	2.2	1	4	4	0	3-1	1	.125

CHAMPIONSHIP SERIES RECORD

Year Team (League)	W	L	Pct.	ERA	WHIP	G	GS	CG	ShO	Hld.	Sv.-Opp.	IP	H	R	ER	HR	BB-IBB	SO	Avg.
1997—Florida (N.L.)	0	0	...	5.40	1.50	2	0	0	0	0	0-0	3.1	3	2	2	0	2-0	4	.250
2003—New York (A.L.)	0	0	...	3.38	1.13	5	0	0	0	0	0-0	2.2	0	1	1	0	3-1	3	.000
2004—New York (A.L.)	0	0	...	0.00	0.75	3	0	0	0	0	0-0	1.1	1	0	0	0	0-0	1	.250
Champ. series totals (3 years)	0	0	...	3.68	1.23	10	0	0	0	0	0-0	7.1	4	3	3	0	5-1	8	.174

WORLD SERIES RECORD

Year Team (League)	W	L	Pct.	ERA	WHIP	G	GS	CG	ShO	Hld.	Sv.-Opp.	IP	H	R	ER	HR	BB-IBB	SO	Avg.
1997—Florida (N.L.)	0	0	...	0.00	0.56	4	0	0	0	0	0-0	5.1	2	0	0	0	1-0	5	.111

HERGES, MATT — P

PERSONAL: Born April 1, 1970, in Champaign, Ill. ... 6-0/200. ... Throws right, bats left. ... Full name: Matthew Tyler Herges. ... Name pronounced: hur-JISS. ... High school: Centennial (Champaign, Ill.). ... College: Illinois State.

TRANSACTIONS/CAREER NOTES: Signed as a non-drafted free agent by Los Angeles Dodgers organization (June 13, 1992). ... Traded by Dodgers with IF Jorge Nunez to Montreal Expos for P Guillermo Mota and OF Wilkin Ruan (March 24, 2002). ... Traded by Expos to Pittsburgh Pirates for Ps Chris Young and Jon Searles (December 20, 2002). ... Released by Pirates (March 26, 2003). ... Signed by San Diego Padres organization (April 11, 2003). ... Traded by Padres to San Francisco Giants for P Clay Hensley and a player to be named or cash (July 13, 2003).

CAREER HITTING: 6-for-27 (.222), 0 R, 0 2B, 0 3B, 0 HR, 1 RBI.

Year Team (League)	W	L	Pct.	ERA	WHIP	G	GS	CG	ShO	Hld.	Sv.-Opp.	IP	H	R	ER	HR	BB-IBB	SO	Avg.
1992—Yakima (N'west)	2	3	.400	3.22	1.28	27	0	0	0	...	9-...	44.2	33	21	16	2	24-1	57	.199
1993—Bakersfield (California)	2	6	.250	3.69	1.39	51	0	0	0	...	2-...	90.1	70	49	37	6	56-6	84	.214
1994—Vero Beach (FSL)	8	9	.471	3.32	1.33	48	3	1	0	...	3-...	111.0	115	45	41	8	33-3	61	.268
1995—San Antonio (Texas)	0	3	.000	4.88	1.81	19	0	0	0	...	8-...	27.2	34	16	15	2	16-1	18	.306
—San Bernardino (Calif.)	5	2	.714	3.66	1.41	22	0	0	0	...	1-...	51.2	58	29	21	3	15-0	35	.275
1996—San Antonio (Texas)	3	2	.600	2.71	1.34	30	6	0	0	...	3-...	83.0	83	38	25	3	28-0	45	.261
—Albuquerque (PCL)	4	1	.800	2.60	1.36	10	4	2	1	...	0-...	34.2	33	11	10	2	14-0	15	.270
1997—Albuquerque (PCL)	8	8	.000	8.89	1.95	31	12	0	0	...	0-...	85.0	120	92	84	13	46-1	61	.340
—San Antonio (Texas)	0	1	.000	8.80	2.09	4	3	0	0	...	0-...	15.1	22	15	15	2	10-0	12	.355
1998—Albuquerque (PCL)	3	5	.375	5.71	1.72	34	8	0	0	...	0-...	88.1	115	64	56	9	37-1	75	.325
—San Antonio (Texas)	0	0	...	0.00	0.83	3	0	0	0	...	0-...	6.0	3	0	0	0	2-0	3	.158
1999—Albuquerque (PCL)	8	3	.727	4.73	1.39	21	21	2	0	...	0-...	131.1	135	82	69	17	47-0	88	.272
—Los Angeles (N.L.)	0	2	.000	4.07	1.32	17	0	0	0	1	0-2	24.1	24	13	11	5	8-0	18	.255
2000—Los Angeles (N.L.)	11	3	.786	3.17	1.27	59	4	0	0	4	1-3	110.2	100	43	39	7	40-5	75	.249
2001—Los Angeles (N.L.)	9	8	.529	3.44	1.44	75	0	0	0	15	1-8	99.1	97	39	38	8	46-12	66	.259
2002—Montreal (N.L.)	2	5	.286	4.04	1.64	62	0	0	0	9	6-14	64.2	80	33	29	10	26-8	50	.305
2003—Portland (PCL)	0	0	...	1.80	0.60	4	0	0	0	...	0-...	5.0	1	1	1	0	2-0	5	.063
—San Diego (N.L.)	2	2	.500	2.86	1.36	40	0	0	0	4	3-5	44.0	40	16	14	2	20-2	40	.244
—San Francisco (N.L.)	1	0	1.000	2.31	1.06	27	0	0	0	5	0-1	35.0	28	11	9	1	9-0	28	.219
2004—San Francisco (N.L.)	4	5	.444	5.23	1.70	70	0	0	0	5	23-31	65.1	90	44	38	8	21-4	39	.338
Major League totals (6 years)	29	25	.537	3.61	1.42	350	4	0	0	43	34-64	443.1	459	199	178	41	170-31	326	.272

DIVISION SERIES RECORD

Year Team (League)	W	L	Pct.	ERA	WHIP	G	GS	CG	ShO	Hld.	Sv.-Opp.	IP	H	R	ER	HR	BB-IBB	SO	Avg.
2003—San Francisco (N.L.)	0	0	...	0.00	0.69	3	0	0	0	0	0-0	4.1	1	0	0	0	2-0	5	.083

HERMANSEN, CHAD — OF

PERSONAL: Born September 10, 1977, in Salt Lake City, Utah. ... 6-2/190. ... Bats right, throws right. ... Full name: Chad Bruce Hermansen. ... High school: Green Valley (Henderson, Nev.).

TRANSACTIONS/CAREER NOTES: Selected by Pittsburgh Pirates organization in first round (10th pick overall) of 1995 free-agent draft. ... On disabled list (March 27-May 10, 2002); included rehabilitation assignment to Nashville. ... Traded by Pirates to Chicago Cubs for OF Darren Lewis (July 31, 2002). ... Traded by Cubs with C Todd Hundley to Los Angeles Dodgers for 1B Eric Karros, 2B Mark Grudzielanek and cash (December 4, 2002). ... On disabled list (March 30-May 16, 2003); included rehabilitation assignment to Vero Beach. ... Released by Dodgers (November 20, 2003). ... Signed Toronto Blue Jays organization (December 27, 2003).

2004 GAMES PLAYED BY POSITION (MLB): OF—4.

Year Team (League)	Pos.	G	AB	R	H	2B	3B	HR	RBI	BATTING BB	SO	HBP	GDP	SB-CS	Avg.	OBP	SLG	OPS	FIELDING E	Avg.
1995—GC Pirates (GCL)	SS	24	92	14	28	10	1	3	17	9	19	0	2	0-0	.304	.363	.533	.895	10	.884
—Erie (N.Y.-Penn)	SS	44	165	30	45	8	3	6	25	18	39	4	6	4-2	.273	.354	.467	.821	30	.839
1996—Augusta (S. Atl.)	SS-DH	62	226	41	57	11	3	14	41	38	65	8	1	11-3	.252	.377	.513	.891	25	.892
—Lynchburg (Caro.)	SS-DH	66	251	40	69	11	3	10	46	29	56	3	8	5-1	.275	.352	.462	.814	28	.897
1997—Carolina (Southern) O-S-2-DH		129	487	87	134	31	4	20	70	69	136	10	3	18-6	.275	.373	.478	.851	39	.891
1998—Nashville (PCL)	OF-2B	126	458	81	118	26	5	28	78	50	152	4	3	21-4	.258	.334	.520	.854	14	.942
1999—Nashville (PCL)	OF	125	496	89	134	27	3	32	97	35	119	4	9	19-9	.270	.321	.530	.851	3	.989
—Pittsburgh (N.L.)	OF	19	60	5	14	3	0	1	1	7	19	1	0	2-2	.233	.324	.333	.657	0	1.000
2000—Pittsburgh (N.L.)	OF	33	108	12	20	4	1	2	8	6	37	0	3	0-0	.185	.226	.296	.522	1	.979
—Nashville (PCL)	OF	78	294	47	66	12	1	11	38	25	89	9	2	16-4	.224	.304	.384	.688	4	.975

H

Year Team (League)	Pos.	G	AB	R	H	2B	3B	HR	RBI	BB	SO	HBP	GDP	SB-CS	Avg.	OBP	SLG	OPS	E	Avg.
2001—Nashville (PCL)	OF	123	447	75	110	22	6	17	64	41	154	5	5	22-5	.246	.315	.436	.751	4	.984
—Pittsburgh (N.L.)	OF	22	55	5	9	1	0	2	5	1	18	0	0	0-1	.164	.179	.291	.469	0	1.000
2002—Nashville (PCL)	OF	16	56	11	11	2	0	4	9	8	23	2	0	1-0	.196	.318	.446	.765	0	1.000
—Pittsburgh (N.L.)	OF	65	194	22	40	11	1	7	15	17	68	1	1	7-5	.206	.272	.381	.654	2	.982
—Chicago (N.L.)	OF	35	43	3	9	3	0	1	3	5	14	0	0	0-0	.209	.292	.349	.641	2	.895
2003—Vero Beach (FSL)	OF-DH	17	63	12	15	4	0	1	7	6	7	0	2	0-1	.238	.296	.349	.645	1	.952
—Las Vegas (PCL)	OF-DH-1B	68	235	43	83	15	1	9	31	19	38	2	4	4-1	.353	.405	.540	.945	1	.989
—Los Angeles (N.L.)	OF	11	25	2	4	1	0	0	2	2	9	0	0	0-0	.160	.222	.200	.422	0	1.000
2004—Toronto (A.L.)	OF	4	7	0	0	0	0	0	0	0	3	0	0	0-0	.000	.000	.000	.000	0	1.000
—Syracuse (Int'l)	DH-OF	42	146	18	35	9	1	6	18	16	52	0	1	0-0	.240	.307	.438	.746	0	1.000
American League totals (1 year)		4	7	0	0	0	0	0	0	0	3	0	0	0-0	.000	.000	.000	.000	0	1.000
National League totals (5 years)		185	485	49	96	23	2	13	34	38	165	2	4	9-8	.198	.258	.334	.592	5	.980
Major League totals (6 years)		189	492	49	96	23	2	13	34	38	168	2	4	9-8	.195	.255	.329	.584	5	.980

HERMANSON, DUSTIN — P

PERSONAL: Born December 21, 1972, in Springfield, Ohio. ... 6-2/200. ... Throws right, bats right. ... Full name: Dustin Michael Hermanson. ... High school: Kenton Ridge (Springfield, Ohio). ... College: Kent State.

TRANSACTIONS/CAREER NOTES: Selected by Pittsburgh Pirates organization in 39th round of 1991 free-agent draft; did not sign. ... Selected by San Diego Padres organization in first round (third pick overall) of 1994 free-agent draft. ... Traded by Padres to Florida Marlins for 2B Quilvio Veras (November 21, 1996). ... Traded by Marlins with OF Joe Orsulak to Montreal Expos for OF/1B Cliff Floyd (March 26, 1997). ... On disabled list (May 15-30, 1998). ... Traded by Expos with P Steve Kline to St. Louis Cardinals for 3B Fernando Tatis and P Britt Reames (December 14, 2000). ... Traded by Cardinals to Boston Red Sox for OF Rick Asadoorian and 1B Luis Garcia and Dustin Brisson (December 15, 2001). ... On disabled list (April 4-July 20 and July 21-August 22, 2002); included rehabilitation assignments to Pawtucket and GCL Red Sox (August 9-13). ... Signed as a free agent by Cardinals (January 20, 2003). ... Released by Cardinals (June 26, 2003). ... Signed by San Francisco Giants organization (July 11, 2003). ... On disabled list (August 24-September 9, 2003). ... On disabled list (April 21-May 8, 2004).

CAREER HITTING: 30-for-322 (.093), 14 R, 5 2B, 0 3B, 2 HR, 10 RBI.

Year Team (League)	W	L	Pct.	ERA	WHIP	G	GS	CG	ShO	Hld.	Sv.-Opp.	IP	H	R	ER	HR	BB-IBB	SO	Avg.
1994—Wichita (Texas)	1	0	1.000	0.43	0.90	16	0	0	0	...	8-...	21.0	13	1	1	0	6-2	30	.176
—Las Vegas (PCL)	0	0	...	6.14	1.50	7	0	0	0	...	3-...	7.1	6	5	5	1	5-0	6	.222
1995—Las Vegas (PCL)	0	1	.000	3.50	1.78	31	0	0	0	...	11-...	36.0	35	23	14	5	29-0	42	.245
—San Diego (N.L.)	3	1	.750	6.82	1.80	26	0	0	0	1	0-0	31.2	35	26	24	8	22-1	19	.280
1996—Las Vegas (PCL)	1	4	.200	3.13	1.48	42	0	0	0	...	21-...	46.0	41	20	16	3	27-7	54	.229
—San Diego (N.L.)	1	0	1.000	8.56	1.61	8	0	0	0	0	0-0	13.2	18	15	13	3	4-0	11	.340
1997—Montreal (N.L.)	8	8	.500	3.69	1.26	32	28	1	1	0	0-0	158.1	134	68	65	15	66-2	136	.234
1998—Montreal (N.L.)	14	11	.560	3.13	1.17	32	30	1	0	1	0-0	187.0	163	80	65	21	56-3	154	.234
1999—Montreal (N.L.)	9	14	.391	4.20	1.36	34	34	0	0	1	0-0	216.1	225	110	101	20	69-4	145	.271
2000—Montreal (N.L.)	12	14	.462	4.77	1.52	38	30	2	1	1	4-7	198.0	226	128	105	26	75-5	94	.290
2001—St. Louis (N.L.)	14	13	.519	4.45	1.39	33	33	0	0	0	0-0	192.1	195	106	95	34	73-3	123	.264
2002—Boston (A.L.)	1	1	.500	7.77	1.91	12	1	0	0	2	0-1	22.0	35	19	19	3	7-0	13	.354
—Pawtucket (Int'l)	0	1	.000	2.63	1.17	5	3	0	0	...	0-...	13.2	9	5	4	0	7-0	11	.191
—GC Red Sox (GCL)	0	0	...	9.00	2.50	1	1	0	0	...	0-...	2.0	5	3	2	0	0-0	1	.500
2003—St. Louis (N.L.)	1	2	.333	5.46	1.65	23	0	0	0	1	1-6	29.2	35	18	18	4	14-2	12	.315
—Fresno (PCL)	0	1	.000	4.85	1.20	4	4	0	0	...	0-...	26.0	29	16	14	2	3-1	17	.290
—San Francisco (N.L.)	2	1	.667	3.00	1.15	9	6	0	0	0	0-0	39.0	35	14	13	5	10-2	27	.238
2004—San Francisco (N.L.)	6	9	.400	4.53	1.36	47	18	0	0	1	17-20	131.0	132	71	66	15	46-5	102	.262
American League totals (1 year)	1	1	.500	7.77	1.91	12	1	0	0	2	0-1	22.0	35	19	19	3	7-0	13	.354
National League totals (9 years)	70	73	.490	4.25	1.36	282	179	4	2	5	22-33	1197.0	1198	636	565	151	435-27	823	.263
Major League totals (10 years)	71	74	.490	4.31	1.37	294	180	4	2	7	22-34	1219.0	1233	655	584	154	442-27	836	.265

DIVISION SERIES RECORD

Year Team (League)	W	L	Pct.	ERA	WHIP	G	GS	CG	ShO	Hld.	Sv.-Opp.	IP	H	R	ER	HR	BB-IBB	SO	Avg.
2001—St. Louis (N.L.)	0	0	...	0.00	0.00	1	0	0	0	1	0-0	3.0	0	0	0	0	0-0	0	.000
2003—San Francisco (N.L.)	0	0	...	0.00	2.00	1	0	0	0	0	0-0	1.0	1	0	0	0	1-0	0	.250
Division series totals (2 years)	0	0	...	0.00	0.50	2	0	0	0	1	0-0	4.0	1	0	0	0	1-0	0	.077

HERNANDEZ, ADRIAN — P

PERSONAL: Born March 25, 1975, in Havana, Cuba. ... 6-1/180. ... Throws right, bats right.

TRANSACTIONS/CAREER NOTES: Signed as a non-drafted free agent by New York Yankees organization (June 2, 2000). ... Signed as a free agent by Milwaukee Brewers organization (December 22, 2003).

CAREER HITTING: 0-for-4 (.000), 0 R, 0 2B, 0 3B, 0 HR, 0 RBI.

Year Team (League)	W	L	Pct.	ERA	WHIP	G	GS	CG	ShO	Hld.	Sv.-Opp.	IP	H	R	ER	HR	BB-IBB	SO	Avg.
2000—Tampa (FSL)	1	0	1.000	1.35	0.60	1	1	0	0	...	0-...	6.2	3	1	1	0	1-0	13	.130
—Norwich (East.)	5	1	.833	4.04	1.46	6	6	1	0	...	0-...	35.2	34	17	16	1	18-0	44	.248
—Columbus (Int'l)	2	1	.667	4.40	1.37	5	5	2	1	...	0-...	30.2	24	18	15	2	18-0	29	.218
2001—Columbus (Int'l)	8	7	.533	5.51	1.50	21	21	0	0	...	0-...	117.2	116	75	72	13	60-1	97	.265
—New York (A.L.)	0	3	.000	3.68	1.14	6	3	0	0	0	0-0	22.0	15	10	9	7	10-1	10	.190
2002—Columbus (Int'l)	6	7	.462	5.25	1.45	20	20	0	0	...	0-...	109.2	114	67	64	9	45-1	109	.270
—New York (A.L.)	0	1	.000	12.00	2.67	2	1	0	0	0	0-0	6.0	10	8	8	2	6-0	9	.357
2003—Tampa (FSL)	0	0	...	0.00	0.50	1	0	0	0	...	0-...	2.0	1	0	0	0	0-0	4	.167
—Trenton (East.)	0	0	...	3.86	1.50	1	1	0	0	...	0-...	4.2	5	4	2	0	2-0	7	.238
—Columbus (Int'l)	8	5	.615	3.21	1.40	32	9	0	0	...	1-...	101.0	92	47	36	6	49-4	103	.240
2004—Milwaukee (N.L.)	0	2	.000	8.44	2.13	6	1	0	0	0	0-1	16.0	20	18	15	1	14-0	14	.294
—Indianapolis (Int'l)	0	8	.000	5.72	1.59	20	15	0	0	...	0-...	94.1	111	61	60	9	39-2	83	.301
American League totals (2 years)	0	4	.000	5.46	1.46	8	4	0	0	0	0-0	28.0	25	18	17	9	16-1	19	.234
National League totals (1 year)	0	2	.000	8.44	2.13	6	1	0	0	0	0-1	16.0	20	18	15	1	14-0	14	.294
Major League totals (3 years)	0	6	.000	6.55	1.70	14	5	0	0	0	0-1	44.0	45	36	32	10	30-1	33	.257

HERNANDEZ, CARLOS — P

PERSONAL: Born April 22, 1980, in Guacara, Venezuela. ... 5-10/200. ... Throws left, bats both. ... Full name: Carlos E. Hernandez.

TRANSACTIONS/CAREER NOTES: Signed as non-drafted free agent by Houston Astros organization (April 23, 1997). ... On Houston disabled list (July 2-August 18, 2002); included rehabilitation assignments to New Orleans (August 2-4) and Round Rock (August 5-18). ... On disabled list (March 29, 2003-[need end]).

H

CAREER HITTING: 8-for-52 (.154), 3 R, 0 2B, 0 3B, 0 HR, 2 RBI.

Year	Team (League)	W	L	Pct.	ERA	WHIP	G	GS	CG	ShO	Hld.	Sv.-Opp.	IP	H	R	ER	HR	BB-IBB	SO	Avg.
1997—	VSL Astros (VSL)	5	1	.833	2.54	1.48	22	0	0	0	...	3-...	46.0	47	20	13	...	21-...	53	...
1998—	Dom. Astros (DSL).	2	0	1.000	1.46	1.14	17	0	0	0	...	9-...	24.2	16	4	4	...	12-...	33	...
1999—	Martinsville (App.)	5	1	.833	1.79	1.07	13	9	0	0	...	0-...	55.1	36	21	11	2	23-0	82	.184
2000—	Michigan (Midw.)	6	6	.500	3.82	1.40	22	22	2	1	...	0-...	110.2	92	57	47	8	63-0	115	.225
2001—	Round Rock (Texas)	12	3	.800	3.69	1.32	24	23	0	0	...	0-...	139.0	115	60	57	11	69-0	167	.228
—Houston (N.L.)		1	0	1.000	1.02	1.02	3	3	0	0	0	0-0	17.2	11	2	2	1	7-0	17	.177
2002—	Houston (N.L.)	7	5	.583	4.38	1.56	23	21	0	0	0	0-0	111.0	112	56	54	11	61-5	93	.261
—New Orleans (PCL)		0	0	...	0.00	0.67	1	1	0	0	...	0-...	3.0	1	0	0	0	1-0	2	.100
—Round Rock (Texas)		0	0	...	4.15	0.92	2	2	0	0	...	0-...	8.2	8	4	4	1	4-0	10	.138
2004—	New Orleans (PCL)	9	4	.692	3.60	1.26	23	23	0	0	...	0-...	127.2	115	54	51	9	46-1	81	.247
—Houston (N.L.)		1	3	.250	6.43	1.74	9	9	0	0	0	0-0	42.0	50	31	30	11	23-0	26	.303
Major League totals (3 years)		9	8	.529	4.54	1.55	35	33	0	0	0	0-0	170.2	173	89	86	23	91-5	136	.264

HERNANDEZ, JOSE — 2B/SS

PERSONAL: Born July 14, 1969, in Vega Alta, Puerto Rico. ... 6-1/190. ... Bats right, throws right. ... Full name: Jose Antonio Hernandez. ... Name pronounced: her-NAN-dezz. ... High school: Maestro Ladi (Vega Alta, Puerto Rico). ... College: Interamericana University (P.R.).

TRANSACTIONS/CAREER NOTES: Signed as a non-drafted free agent by Texas Rangers organization (January 13, 1987). ... Claimed on waivers by Cleveland Indians (April 3, 1992). ... Traded by Indians to Chicago Cubs for P Heathcliff Slocumb (June 1, 1993). ... Traded by Cubs with P Terry Mulholland to Atlanta Braves for Ps Micah Bowie and P Ruben Quevedo and a player to be named (July 31, 1999); Cubs acquired P Joey Nation to complete deal (August 24, 1999). ... Signed as a free agent by Milwaukee Brewers (December 16, 1999). ... On disabled list (August 10-September 1, 2000); included rehabilitation assignment to Indianapolis. ... Signed as a free agent by Colorado Rockies (January 24, 2003). ... Traded by Rockies to Chicago Cubs for IF Mark Bellhorn (June 20, 2003). ... Traded by Cubs with P Matt Bruback and a player to be named to Pittsburgh Pirates for 3B Aramis Ramirez, OF Kenny Lofton and cash (July 23, 2003); Pirates acquired IF Bobby Hill to complete deal (August 15, 2003). ... Released by Pirates (October 1, 2003). ... Signed by Los Angeles Dodgers organization (January 27, 2004).

2004 GAMES PLAYED BY POSITION (MLB): 2B—50, SS—13, 3B—12, OF—9, 1B—8.

Year	Team (League)	Pos.	G	AB	R	H	2B	3B	HR	RBI	BB	SO	HBP	GDP	SB-CS	Avg.	OBP	SLG	OPS	E	Avg.
1987—	GC Rangers (GCL)	SS	24	52	5	9	1	1	0	2	9	25	1	1	2-1	.173	.306	.231	.537	5	.932
1988—	GC Rangers (GCL)	SS	55	162	19	26	7	1	1	13	12	36	0	5	4-1	.160	.217	.235	.452	8	.958
1989—	Gastonia (S. Atl.) 2-3-SS-OF		91	215	35	47	7	6	1	16	33	67	0	3	9-2	.219	.323	.321	.644	17	.941
1990—	Charlotte (Fla. St.)	SS-OF	121	388	43	99	14	7	1	44	50	122	4	8	11-8	.255	.345	.335	.680	25	.958
1991—	Tulsa (Texas)	SS	91	301	36	72	17	4	1	20	26	75	1	6	4-3	.239	.298	.332	.630	15	.968
—Okla. City (A.A.)		SS	14	46	6	14	1	1	1	3	4	10	0	1	0-0	.304	.353	.435	.788	3	.962
—Texas (A.L.)		3B-SS	45	98	8	18	2	1	0	4	3	31	0	2	0-1	.184	.208	.224	.432	4	.976
1992—	Cant./Akr. (Eastern)	SS	130	404	56	103	16	4	3	46	37	108	1	5	7-2	.255	.315	.337	.652	40	.932
—Cleveland (A.L.)		SS	3	4	0	0	0	0	0	0	0	1	0	0	0-0	.000	.000	.000	.000	1	.857
1993—	Cant./Akr. (Eastern)	SS-3B	45	150	19	30	6	0	2	17	10	39	0	3	9-2	.200	.250	.280	.530	7	.968
—Orlando (South.)		SS	71	263	42	80	8	3	8	33	20	60	0	5	8-4	.304	.352	.449	.801	14	.961
—Iowa (Am. Assoc.)		SS	6	24	3	6	1	0	0	3	0	2	1	1	0-0	.250	.280	.292	.572	1	.976
1994—	Chicago (N.L.)	3-S-2-OF	56	132	18	32	2	3	1	9	8	29	1	4	2-2	.242	.291	.326	.617	4	.971
1995—	Chicago (N.L.) SS-2B-3B		93	245	37	60	11	4	13	40	13	69	0	8	1-0	.245	.281	.482	.762	9	.971
1996—	Chicago (N.L.)	S-3-2-OF	131	331	52	80	14	1	10	41	24	97	1	10	4-0	.242	.293	.381	.674	20	.952
1997—	Chicago (N.L.) 3-S-2-O-DH-1		121	183	33	50	8	5	7	26	14	42	0	5	2-5	.273	.323	.486	.810	8	.955
1998—	Chicago (N.L.)	3-O-S-1-2	149	488	76	124	23	7	23	75	40	140	1	12	4-6	.254	.311	.471	.782	13	.970
1999—	Chicago (N.L.)	SS-OF-1B	99	342	57	93	12	2	15	43	40	101	5	5	7-2	.272	.357	.450	.807	11	.973
—Atlanta (N.L.)		SS-1B-OF	48	166	22	42	8	0	4	19	12	44	0	5	4-1	.253	.302	.373	.675	6	.966
2000—	Milwaukee (N.L.) 3B-SS-OF		124	446	51	109	22	1	11	59	41	125	6	12	3-7	.244	.315	.372	.687	19	.955
—Indianapolis (Int'l)		3B	2	9	2	3	0	0	2	3	1	3	0	0	0-0	.333	.400	1.000	1.400	0	1.000
2001—	Milwaukee (N.L.)	SS-OF	152	542	67	135	26	2	25	78	39 *	185	2	9	5-4	.249	.300	.443	.743	18	.972
2002—	Milwaukee (N.L.)	SS	152	525	72	151	24	2	24	73	52 *	188	4	19	3-5	.288	.356	.478	.834	19	.973
2003—	Colorado (N.L.)	SS-1B	69	257	33	61	6	1	8	27	27	95	0	6	1-1	.237	.308	.362	.670	5	.984
—Chicago (N.L.)		3-S-OF-2	23	69	6	13	3	1	2	9	3	26	0	1	0-0	.188	.222	.348	.570	1	.977
—Pittsburgh (N.L.)		3B	58	193	19	43	9	1	3	21	16	56	1	1	1-0	.223	.282	.326	.608	8	.955
2004—	Los Angeles (N.L.) 2-S-3-OF-1		95	211	32	61	12	1	13	29	26	61	1	3	3-1	.289	.370	.540	.910	5	.981
American League totals (2 years)			48	102	8	18	2	1	0	4	3	33	0	2	0-1	.176	.200	.216	.416	5	.971
National League totals (11 years)			1370	4130	575	1054	180	31	159	549	355	1258	22	108	40-34	.255	.316	.429	.745	146	.968
Major League totals (13 years)			1418	4232	583	1072	182	32	159	553	358	1291	22	110	40-35	.253	.313	.424	.738	151	.969

DIVISION SERIES RECORD

Year	Team (League)	Pos.	G	AB	R	H	2B	3B	HR	RBI	BB	SO	HBP	GDP	SB-CS	Avg.	OBP	SLG	OPS	E	Avg.
1998—	Chicago (N.L.)	SS	2	7	1	2	0	0	0	0	0	2	0	0	0-0	.286	.286	.286	.571	2	.750
1999—	Atlanta (N.L.)	SS	4	11	1	1	0	0	0	0	1	3	0	1	1-0	.091	.167	.091	.258	1	.938
2004—	Los Angeles (N.L.)		1	0	0	0	0	0	0	0	1	0	0	0	0-0	...	1.000	...	1.000	0	...
Division series totals (3 years)			7	18	2	3	0	0	0	0	2	5	0	1	1-0	.167	.250	.167	.417	3	.875

CHAMPIONSHIP SERIES RECORD

Year	Team (League)	Pos.	G	AB	R	H	2B	3B	HR	RBI	BB	SO	HBP	GDP	SB-CS	Avg.	OBP	SLG	OPS	E	Avg.
1999—	Atlanta (N.L.)		2	2	0	1	0	0	0	2	0	1	0	0	0-0	.500	.500	.500	1.000	...	...

WORLD SERIES RECORD

Year	Team (League)	Pos.	G	AB	R	H	2B	3B	HR	RBI	BB	SO	HBP	GDP	SB-CS	Avg.	OBP	SLG	OPS	E	Avg.
1999—	Atlanta (N.L.)	SS-DH	2	5	0	1	1	0	0	2	0	2	0	0	1-0	.200	.200	.400	.600	0	1.000

ALL-STAR GAME RECORD

			G	AB	R	H	2B	3B	HR	RBI	BB	SO	HBP	GDP	SB-CS	Avg.	OBP	SLG	OPS	E	Avg.
All-Star Game totals (1 year)			1	3	0	0	0	0	0	0	0	2	0	0	0-0	.000	.000	.000	.000	0	1.000

HERNANDEZ, LIVAN — P

PERSONAL: Born February 20, 1975, in Villa Clara, Cuba. ... 6-2/245. ... Throws right, bats right. ... Full name: Eisler Livan Hernandez. ... Name pronounced: lee-VAHN her-NAN-dezz. ... Half-brother of Orlando Hernandez, pitcher with New York Yankees in 2004.

TRANSACTIONS/CAREER NOTES: Signed as a non-drafted free agent by Florida Marlins orgaization (January 13, 1996). ... Traded by Marlins to San Francisco Giants for Ps Jason Grilli and P Nate Bump (July 24, 1999). ... Traded by Giants with 3B/C Edwards Guzman and cash to Montreal Expos for P Jim Brower and a player to be named (March 24, 2003); Giants acquired P Matt Blank to complete deal (April 30, 2003).

H

CAREER HITTING: 133-for-564 (.236), 35 R, 26 2B, 1 3B, 5 HR, 55 RBI.

Year	Team (League)	W	L	Pct.	ERA	WHIP	G	GS	CG	ShO	Hld.	Sv.-Opp.	IP	H	R	ER	HR	BB-IBB	SO	Avg.
1996—	Charlotte (Int'l)	2	4	.333	5.14	1.94	10	10	0	0	...	0-...	49.0	61	32	28	3	34-1	45	.308
	—Portland (East.)	9	2	.818	4.34	1.23	15	15	0	0	...	0-...	93.1	81	48	45	14	34-1	95	.238
	—Florida (N.L.)	0	0	...	0.00	1.67	1	0	0	0	0	0-0	3.0	3	0	0	0	2-0	2	.273
1997—	Charlotte (Int'l)	5	3	.625	3.98	1.40	14	14	0	0	...	0-...	81.1	76	39	36	5	38-2	58	.247
	—Florida (N.L.)	9	3	.750	3.18	1.24	17	17	0	0	0	0-0	96.1	81	39	34	5	38-1	72	.229
	—Portland (East.)	0	0	...	2.25	2.25	1	1	0	0	...	0-...	4.0	2	1	1	0	7-0	2	.154
1998—	Florida (N.L.)	10	12	.455	4.72	1.57	33	33	9	0	0	0-0	234.1	* 265	133	123	37	104-8	162	.289
1999—	Florida (N.L.)	5	9	.357	4.76	1.59	20	20	2	0	0	0-0	136.0	161	78	72	17	55-3	97	.294
	—San Francisco (N.L.)	3	3	.500	4.38	1.37	10	10	0	0	0	0-0	63.2	66	32	31	6	21-2	47	.267
2000—	San Francisco (N.L.)	17	11	.607	3.75	1.36	33	33	5	2	0	0-0	240.0	254	114	100	22	73-3	165	.273
2001—	San Francisco (N.L.)	13	15	.464	5.24	1.55	34	34	2	0	0	0-0	226.2	266	143	132	24	85-7	138	.297
2002—	San Francisco (N.L.)	12	16	.429	4.38	1.41	33	33	5	3	0	0-0	216.0	233	113	105	19	71-5	134	.283
2003—	Montreal (N.L.)	15	10	.600	3.20	1.21	33	33	* 8	0	0	0-0	* 233.1	225	92	83	27	57-3	178	.253
2004—	Montreal (N.L.)	11	15	.423	3.60	1.24	35	• 35	* 9	2	0	0-0	* 255.0	234	105	102	26	83-9	186	.248
Major League totals (9 years)		95	94	.503	4.13	1.39	249	248	40	7	0	0-0	1704.1	1788	849	782	183	589-41	1181	.272

DIVISION SERIES RECORD

Year	Team (League)	W	L	Pct.	ERA	WHIP	G	GS	CG	ShO	Hld.	Sv.-Opp.	IP	H	R	ER	HR	BB-IBB	SO	Avg.
1997—	Florida (N.L.)	0	0	...	2.25	0.75	1	0	0	0	0	0-0	4.0	3	1	1	0	0-0	3	.200
2000—	San Francisco (N.L.)	1	0	1.000	1.17	1.30	1	1	0	0	0	0-0	7.2	5	1	1	0	5-0	5	.185
2002—	San Francisco (N.L.)	1	0	1.000	3.24	1.20	1	1	0	0	0	0-0	8.1	8	3	3	0	2-0	6	.250
Division series totals (3 years)		2	0	1.000	2.25	1.15	3	2	0	0	0	0-0	20.0	16	5	5	0	7-0	14	.216

CHAMPIONSHIP SERIES RECORD

Year	Team (League)	W	L	Pct.	ERA	WHIP	G	GS	CG	ShO	Hld.	Sv.-Opp.	IP	H	R	ER	HR	BB-IBB	SO	Avg.
1997—	Florida (N.L.)	2	0	1.000	0.84	0.66	2	1	1	0	0	0-0	10.2	5	1	1	1	2-0	16	.143
2002—	San Francisco (N.L.)	0	0	...	2.84	1.58	1	1	0	0	0	0-0	6.1	9	2	2	0	1-0	0	.360
Champ. series totals (2 years)		2	0	1.000	1.59	1.00	3	2	1	0	0	0-0	17.0	14	3	3	1	3-0	16	.233

WORLD SERIES RECORD

Year	Team (League)	W	L	Pct.	ERA	WHIP	G	GS	CG	ShO	Hld.	Sv.-Opp.	IP	H	R	ER	HR	BB-IBB	SO	Avg.
1997—	Florida (N.L.)	2	0	1.000	5.27	1.83	2	2	0	0	0	0-0	13.2	15	9	8	3	10-0	7	.283
2002—	San Francisco (N.L.)	0	2	.000	14.29	3.18	2	2	0	0	0	0-0	5.2	9	10	9	0	9-3	4	.360
World series totals (2 years)		2	2	.500	7.91	2.22	4	4	0	0	0	0-0	19.1	24	19	17	3	19-3	11	.308

HERNANDEZ, ORLANDO   P

PERSONAL: Born October 11, 1969, in Havana, Cuba. ... 6-2/220. ... Throws right, bats right. ... Full name: Orlando P. Hernandez. ... Name pronounced: her-NAN-dezz. ... Half-brother of Livan Hernandez, pitcher, Montreal Expos.

TRANSACTIONS/CAREER NOTES: Signed as a free agent by New York Yankees (March 23, 1998). ... On disabled list (July 18-August 6, 2000); included rehabilitation assignment to Tampa. ... On disabled list (June 1-August 21, 2001); included rehabilitation assignments to Tampa and Staten Island. ... On disabled list (May 16-June 27, 2002); included rehabilitation assignment to Columbus. ... On suspended list (July 21-28, 2002). ... Traded by Yankees to Chicago White Sox for Ps Antonio Osuna and Delvis Lantigua (January 15, 2003). ... Traded by White Sox with P Rocky Biddle, 3B/OF Jeff Liefer and cash to Montreal Expos for P Bartolo Colon and 2B/SS Jorge Nunez (January 15, 2003). ... On disabled list (March 21, 2003-entire season); included rehabilitation assignment to Brevard County. ... Signed as a free agent by Yankees (March 12, 2004). ... On disabled list (March 19-July 11, 2004); included rehabilitation assignments to Tampa and Columbus.

CAREER HITTING: 1-for-19 (.053), 1 R, 0 2B, 0 3B, 0 HR, 0 RBI.

Year	Team (League)	W	L	Pct.	ERA	WHIP	G	GS	CG	ShO	Hld.	Sv.-Opp.	IP	H	R	ER	HR	BB-IBB	SO	Avg.
1998—	Tampa (FSL)	1	1	.500	1.00	0.67	2	2	0	0	...	0-...	9.0	3	2	1	0	3-0	15	.100
	—Columbus (Int'l)	6	0	1.000	3.83	1.37	7	7	0	0	...	0-...	42.1	41	19	18	2	17-0	59	.261
	—New York (A.L.)	12	4	.750	3.13	1.17	21	21	3	1	0	0-0	141.0	113	53	49	11	52-1	131	.222
1999—	New York (A.L.)	17	9	.654	4.12	1.28	33	33	2	1	0	0-0	214.1	187	108	98	24	87-2	157	.233
2000—	New York (A.L.)	12	13	.480	4.51	1.21	29	29	3	0	0	0-0	195.2	186	104	98	34	51-2	141	.247
	—Tampa (FSL)	0	0	...	0.00	0.50	1	0	0	0	0	0-...	4.0	1	0	0	0	1-0	5	.077
2001—	New York (A.L.)	4	7	.364	4.85	1.39	17	16	0	0	0	0-0	94.2	90	51	51	19	42-1	77	.248
	—Tampa (FSL)	0	0	...	0.00	1.00	2	2	0	0	0	0-...	7.0	6	2	0	0	1-0	8	.214
	—Staten Island (NY-P)	1	0	1.000	0.00	0.50	1	1	0	0	0	0-...	6.0	2	0	0	0	1-0	11	.100
2002—	New York (A.L.)	8	5	.615	3.64	1.14	24	22	0	0	1	1-1	146.0	131	63	59	17	36-2	113	.236
	—Columbus (Int'l)	1	0	1.000	1.59	1.41	1	1	0	0	0	0-...	5.2	7	2	1	0	1-0	5	.280
2003—	Brevard County (FSL)	0	1	.000	10.80	1.80	2	2	0	0	0	0-...	5.0	5	6	6	0	4-0	7	.250
2004—	Tampa (FSL)	1	0	1.000	1.50	0.83	3	3	0	0	0	0-...	12.0	3	4	2	0	7-0	11	.079
	—Columbus (Int'l)	2	1	.667	5.60	1.13	3	3	0	0	0	0-...	17.2	17	11	11	3	3-0	16	.243
	—New York (A.L.)	8	2	.800	3.30	1.29	15	15	0	0	0	0-0	84.2	73	31	31	9	36-0	84	.230
Major League totals (6 years)		61	40	.604	3.96	1.24	139	136	8	2	1	1-1	876.1	780	410	386	114	304-8	703	.236

DIVISION SERIES RECORD

Year	Team (League)	W	L	Pct.	ERA	WHIP	G	GS	CG	ShO	Hld.	Sv.-Opp.	IP	H	R	ER	HR	BB-IBB	SO	Avg.
1998—	New York (A.L.)			Did not play.																
1999—	New York (A.L.)	1	0	1.000	0.00	1.00	1	1	0	0	0	0-0	8.0	2	0	0	0	6-0	4	.083
2000—	New York (A.L.)	1	0	1.000	2.45	1.36	1	1	0	0	1	0-0	7.1	5	2	2	1	5-0	5	.200
2001—	New York (A.L.)	1	0	1.000	3.18	1.76	1	1	0	0	0	0-0	5.2	8	2	2	0	2-0	5	.333
2002—	New York (A.L.)	0	1	.000	2.84	0.79	2	0	0	0	0	0-0	6.1	5	2	2	2	0-0	7	.208
Division series totals (4 years)		3	1	.750	1.98	1.21	6	3	0	0	1	0-0	27.1	20	6	6	3	13-0	21	.206

CHAMPIONSHIP SERIES RECORD

Year	Team (League)	W	L	Pct.	ERA	WHIP	G	GS	CG	ShO	Hld.	Sv.-Opp.	IP	H	R	ER	HR	BB-IBB	SO	Avg.
1998—	New York (A.L.)	1	0	1.000	0.00	0.71	1	1	0	0	0	0-0	7.0	3	0	0	0	2-0	6	.125
1999—	New York (A.L.)	1	0	1.000	1.80	1.20	2	2	0	0	0	0-0	15.0	12	4	3	1	6-0	13	.207
2000—	New York (A.L.)	2	0	1.000	4.20	1.40	2	2	0	0	0	0-0	15.0	13	7	7	2	8-2	14	.241
2001—	New York (A.L.)	0	1	.000	7.20	2.00	1	1	0	0	0	0-0	5.0	5	5	4	1	5-0	7	.250
2004—	New York (A.L.)	0	0	...	5.40	1.60	1	1	0	0	0	0-0	5.0	3	3	3	0	5-0	6	.167
Champ. series totals (5 years)		4	1	.800	3.26	1.32	7	7	0	0	0	0-0	47.0	36	19	17	4	26-2	46	.207

H

WORLD SERIES RECORD

Year Team (League)	W	L	Pct.	ERA	WHIP	G	GS	CG	ShO	Hld.	Sv.-Opp.	IP	H	R	ER	HR	BB-IBB	SO	Avg.
1998— New York (A.L.)	1	0	1.000	1.29	1.29	1	1	0	0	0	0-0	7.0	6	1	1	0	3-0	7	.222
1999— New York (A.L.)	1	0	1.000	1.29	0.43	1	1	0	0	0	0-0	7.0	1	1	1	1	2-0	10	.048
2000— New York (A.L.)	0	1	.000	4.91	1.64	1	1	0	0	0	0-0	7.1	9	4	4	1	3-0	12	.300
2001— New York (A.L.)	0	0	...	1.42	1.26	1	1	0	0	0	0-0	6.1	4	1	1	1	4-0	5	.222
World series totals (4 years)	**2**	**1**	**.667**	**2.28**	**1.16**	**4**	**4**	**0**	**0**	**0**	**0-0**	**27.2**	**20**	**7**	**7**	**3**	**12-0**	**34**	**.208**

HERNANDEZ, RAMON   C

PERSONAL: Born May 20, 1976, in Caracas, Venezuela. ... 6-0/210. ... Bats right, throws right. ... Full name: Ramon Jose Hernandez. ... Name pronounced: ruh-MOWN.

TRANSACTIONS/CAREER NOTES: Signed as a non-drafted free agent by Oakland Athletics organization (February 18, 1994). ... On disabled list (July 26-August 27, 1999); included rehabilitation assignment to Vancouver. ... Traded by Athletics with OF Terrence Long to San Diego Padres for OF Mark Kotsay (November 26, 2003). ... On disabled list (June 21-July 26, 2004); included rehabilitation assignment to Portland.

2004 GAMES PLAYED BY POSITION (MLB): C—108.

Year Team (League)	Pos.	G	AB	R	H	2B	3B	HR	RBI	BB	SO	HBP	GDP	SB-CS	Avg.	OBP	SLG	OPS	E (FIELDING)	Avg. (FIELDING)
1994— Dom. Athletics (DSL)	C	42	134	24	33	2	0	2	18	18	10	...	...	1-5	.246	...	.306	...	2	.991
1995— Ariz. A's (Ariz.)	3B-C-1B	48	143	37	52	9	6	4	37	39	16	8	3	6-2	.364	.510	.594	1.105	12	.972
1996— W. Mich. (Mid.)	C-DH-1B	123	447	62	114	26	2	12	68	69	62	4	22	2-3	.255	.355	.403	.758	20	.980
1997— Visalia (Calif.)	C-DH-1B	86	332	57	120	21	2	15	85	35	47	9	5	2-4	.361	.427	.572	.999	16	.976
— Huntsville (Sou.)	C-DH-1B-3	44	161	27	31	3	0	4	24	18	23	3	8	0-0	.193	.281	.286	.567	1	.997
1998— Huntsville (Sou.)	DH-C-1B	127	479	83	142	24	1	15	98	57	61	19	15	4-5	.296	.389	.445	.833	11	.981
1999— Vancouver (PCL)	C-3B-1B	77	291	38	76	11	3	13	55	23	37	7	13	1-2	.261	.326	.454	.780	5	.987
— Oakland (A.L.)	C	40	136	13	38	7	0	3	21	18	11	1	5	1-0	.279	.363	.397	.760	6	.980
2000— Oakland (A.L.)	C	143	419	52	101	19	0	14	62	38	64	7	14	1-0	.241	.311	.387	.698	* 13	.984
2001— Oakland (A.L.)	C-1B	136	453	55	115	25	0	15	60	37	68	6	10	1-1	.254	.316	.408	.724	12	.988
2002— Oakland (A.L.)	C	136	403	51	94	20	0	7	42	43	64	5	11	0-0	.233	.313	.335	.648	7	.992
2003— Oakland (A.L.)	C	140	483	70	132	24	1	21	78	33	79	12	14	0-0	.273	.331	.458	.789	8	.991
2004— Portland (PCL)	C	7	19	2	6	1	0	0	6	2	3	0	1	0-0	.316	.381	.368	.749	2	.938
— San Diego (N.L.)	C	111	384	45	106	23	0	18	63	35	45	5	16	1-0	.276	.341	.477	.818	6	.992
American League totals (5 years)		595	1894	241	480	95	1	60	263	169	286	31	54	3-1	.253	.322	.400	.721	46	.988
National League totals (1 year)		111	384	45	106	23	0	18	63	35	45	5	16	1-0	.276	.341	.477	.818	6	.992
Major League totals (6 years)		706	2278	286	586	118	1	78	326	204	331	36	70	4-1	.257	.325	.413	.738	52	.989

DIVISION SERIES RECORD

Year Team (League)	Pos.	G	AB	R	H	2B	3B	HR	RBI	BB	SO	HBP	GDP	SB-CS	Avg.	OBP	SLG	OPS	E	Avg.
2000— Oakland (A.L.)	C	5	16	3	6	2	0	0	3	0	3	1	0	0-0	.375	.412	.500	.912	1	.974
2001— Oakland (A.L.)	C	5	10	0	0	0	0	0	0	1	4	1	0	0-0	.000	.167	.000	.167	0	1.000
2002— Oakland (A.L.)	C	5	17	0	1	0	0	0	0	0	4	0	1	0-0	.059	.059	.059	.118	0	1.000
2003— Oakland (A.L.)	C	4	15	1	3	0	0	0	2	2	1	1	0	0-0	.200	.333	.200	.533	1	.974
Division series totals (4 years)		19	58	4	10	2	0	0	5	3	12	3	1	0-0	.172	.250	.207	.457	2	.985

ALL-STAR GAME RECORD

	G	AB	R	H	2B	3B	HR	RBI	BB	SO	HBP	GDP	SB-CS	Avg.	OBP	SLG	OPS	E	Avg.
All-Star Game totals (1 year)	1	1	0	0	0	0	0	0	0	0	0	0	0-0	.000	.000	.000	.000	0	1.000

HERNANDEZ, ROBERTO   P

PERSONAL: Born November 11, 1964, in Santurce, Puerto Rico. ... 6-4/250. ... Throws right, bats right. ... Full name: Roberto Manuel Hernandez. ... Name pronounced: her-NAN-dezz. ... High school: New Hampton (N.H.) Prep. ... College: South Carolina-Aiken.

TRANSACTIONS/CAREER NOTES: Selected by California Angels organization in first round (16th pick overall) of June 1986 free-agent draft; pick received as compensation for Baltimore Orioles signing Type A free-agent OF/IF Juan Beniquez. ... Traded by Angels with OF Mark Doran to Chicago White Sox for OF Mark Davis (August 2, 1989). ... Traded by White Sox with Ps Wilson Alvarez and Danny Darwin to San Francisco Giants for SS Mike Caruso, OF Brian Manning and Ps Lorenzo Barcelo, Keith Foulke, Bob Howry and Ken Vining (July 31, 1997). ... Signed as a free agent by Tampa Bay Devil Rays (November 18, 1997). ... Traded by Devil Rays to Kansas City Royals as part of three-team deal in which Devil Rays acquired OF Ben Grieve and cash from Oakland Athletics, A's acquired P Cory Lidle from Devil Rays and OF Johnny Damon, IF Mark Ellis and cash from Royals and Royals acquired C A.J. Hinch, IF Angel Berroa and cash from A's (January 8, 2001). ... On disabled list (March 22-May 2, 2002); included rehabilitation assignment to Omaha. ... Signed as a free agent by Atlanta Braves (January 22, 2003). ... On disabled list (June 12-27 and August 13-September 2, 2003); included rehabilitation assignment to Richmond. ... Signed as a free agent by Philadelphia Phillies (December 18, 2003). ... On disabled list (May 5-20, 2004).

CAREER HITTING: 1-for-2 (.500), 0 R, 0 2B, 0 3B, 0 HR, 0 RBI.

Year Team (League)	W	L	Pct.	ERA	WHIP	G	GS	CG	ShO	Hld.	Sv.-Opp.	IP	H	R	ER	HR	BB-IBB	SO	Avg.
1986— Salem (N'west)	2	2	.500	4.58	1.80	10	10	0	0	...	0-...	55.0	57	37	28	3	42-1	38	...
1987— Quad City (Midw.)	2	3	.400	6.86	1.71	7	6	0	0	...	1-...	21.0	24	21	16	2	12-0	21	.273
1988— Quad City (Midw.)	9	10	.474	3.17	1.24	24	24	6	1	...	0-...	164.2	157	70	58	8	48-0	114	.248
— Midland (Texas)	0	2	.000	6.57	1.95	3	3	0	0	...	0-...	12.1	16	13	9	0	8-0	7	.320
1989— Midland (Texas)	2	7	.222	6.89	1.94	12	12	0	0	...	0-...	64.0	94	57	49	4	30-0	42	.352
— Palm Springs (Calif.)	1	4	.200	4.64	1.52	7	7	0	0	...	0-...	42.2	49	27	22	2	16-0	33	.295
— South Bend (Mid.)	1	1	.500	3.33	1.07	4	4	0	0	...	0-...	24.1	19	9	9	1	7-0	17	.221
1990— Birmingham (Southern)	8	5	.615	3.67	1.35	17	17	1	0	...	0-...	108.0	103	57	44	6	43-2	62	.251
— Vancouver (PCL)	3	5	.375	2.84	1.25	11	11	3	1	...	0-...	79.1	70	33	25	4	26-0	49	.247
1991— Vancouver (PCL)	4	1	.800	3.22	1.43	7	7	0	0	...	0-...	44.2	41	17	16	2	23-0	40	.241
— GC White Sox (GCL)	0	0	...	0.00	0.33	1	1	0	0	...	0-...	6.0	2	0	0	0	0-0	7	.111
— Birmingham (Southern)	2	1	.667	1.99	0.75	4	4	0	0	...	0-...	22.2	11	5	5	2	6-0	25	.145
— Chicago (A.L.)	1	0	1.000	7.80	1.67	9	3	0	0	0	0-0	15.0	18	15	13	1	7-0	6	.290
1992— Chicago (A.L.)	7	3	.700	1.65	0.92	43	0	0	0	6	12-16	71.0	45	15	13	4	20-1	68	.180
— Vancouver (PCL)	3	3	.500	2.61	1.16	9	0	0	0	...	2-...	20.2	13	9	6	0	11-1	23	.176
1993— Chicago (A.L.)	3	4	.429	2.29	1.09	70	0	0	0	0	38-44	78.2	66	21	20	6	20-1	71	.228
1994— Chicago (A.L.)	4	4	.500	4.91	1.32	45	0	0	0	0	14-20	47.2	44	29	26	5	19-1	50	.243
1995— Chicago (A.L.)	3	7	.300	3.92	1.53	60	0	0	0	0	32-42	59.2	63	30	26	9	28-4	84	.266
1996— Chicago (A.L.)	6	5	.545	1.91	1.22	72	0	0	0	0	38-46	84.2	65	21	18	2	38-5	85	.208
1997— Chicago (A.L.)	5	1	.833	2.44	1.29	46	0	0	0	0	27-31	48.0	38	15	13	2	24-4	47	.216
— San Francisco (N.L.)	5	2	.714	2.48	1.32	28	0	0	0	9	4-8	32.2	29	9	9	2	14-1	35	.238
1998— Tampa Bay (A.L.)	2	6	.250	4.04	1.35	67	0	0	0	0	26-35	71.1	55	33	32	5	41-4	55	.212
1999— Tampa Bay (A.L.)	2	3	.400	3.07	1.38	72	0	0	0	0	43-47	73.1	68	27	25	1	33-1	69	.245

H

Year Team (League)	W	L	Pct.	ERA	WHIP	G	GS	CG	ShO	Hld.	Sv.-Opp.	IP	H	R	ER	HR	BB-IBB	SO	Avg.
2000—Tampa Bay (A.L.)	4	7	.364	3.19	1.35	68	0	0	0	1	32-40	73.1	76	33	26	9	23-1	61	.272
2001—Kansas City (A.L.)	5	6	.455	4.12	1.40	63	0	0	0	0	28-34	67.2	69	34	31	7	26-3	46	.266
2002—Omaha (PCL)	0	0	...	0.00	1.50	2	0	0	0	...	0-...	2.0	0	1	0	0	3-0	3	.000
—Kansas City (A.L.)	1	3	.250	4.33	1.42	53	0	0	0	0	26-33	52.0	62	29	25	6	12-2	39	.300
2003—Richmond (Int'l)	1	1	.500	9.45	2.20	6	0	0	0	0	0-...	6.2	11	9	7	0	4-0	10	.333
—Atlanta (N.L.)	5	3	.625	4.35	1.73	66	0	0	0	19	0-4	60.0	61	36	29	10	43-7	45	.263
2004—Philadelphia (N.L.)	3	5	.375	4.76	1.68	63	0	0	0	9	0-4	56.2	66	39	30	9	23-4	34	.297
American League totals (12 years)	43	49	.467	3.25	1.29	668	3	0	0	7	316-388	742.1	669	302	268	60	291-27	681	.239
National League totals (3 years)	13	10	.565	4.10	1.62	157	0	0	0	37	4-16	149.1	156	84	68	21	86-11	124	.271
Major League totals (14 years)	56	59	.487	3.39	1.35	825	3	0	0	44	320-404	891.2	825	386	336	81	377-38	805	.245

DIVISION SERIES RECORD

Year Team (League)	W	L	Pct.	ERA	WHIP	G	GS	CG	ShO	Hld.	Sv.-Opp.	IP	H	R	ER	HR	BB-IBB	SO	Avg.
1997—San Francisco (N.L.)	0	1	.000	20.25	6.00	3	0	0	0	0	0-0	1.1	5	3	3	0	3-1	1	.625
2003—Atlanta (N.L.)	0	0	...	0.00	1.00	1	0	0	0	0	0-0	1.0	1	0	0	0	0-0	0	.333
Division series totals (2 years)	0	1	.000	11.57	3.86	4	0	0	0	0	0-0	2.1	6	3	3	0	3-1	1	.545

CHAMPIONSHIP SERIES RECORD

Year Team (League)	W	L	Pct.	ERA	WHIP	G	GS	CG	ShO	Hld.	Sv.-Opp.	IP	H	R	ER	HR	BB-IBB	SO	Avg.
1993—Chicago (A.L.)	0	0	...	0.00	1.00	4	0	0	0	0	1-1	4.0	4	0	0	0	0-0	1	.267

ALL-STAR GAME RECORD

	W	L	Pct.	ERA	WHIP	G	GS	CG	ShO	Hld.	Sv.-Opp.	IP	H	R	ER	HR	BB-IBB	SO	Avg.
All-Star Game totals (2 years)	0	0	...	0.00	0.50	2	0	0	0	1	0-0	2.0	1	0	0	0	0-0	0	.143

HESSMAN, MIKE — 1B/3B

PERSONAL: Born March 5, 1978, in Fountain Valley, Calif. ... 6-5/215. ... Bats right, throws right. ... Full name: Michael Steven Hessman. ... High school: Mater Dei (Santa Ana, Calif.).

TRANSACTIONS/CAREER NOTES: Selected by Atlanta Braves organization in 15th round of 1996 free-agent draft.

2004 GAMES PLAYED BY POSITION (MLB): 1B—16, 3B—7, OF—3.

Year Team (League)	Pos.	G	AB	R	H	2B	3B	HR	RBI	BB	SO	HBP	GDP	SB-CS	Avg.	OBP	SLG	OPS	E	Avg.
1996—GC Braves (GCL)	3B-1B-OF	53	190	13	41	10	1	1	15	12	41	4	0	1-1	.216	.277	.295	.571	11	.949
1997—Macon (S. Atl.)	3B	122	459	69	108	25	0	21	74	41	167	6	6	0-2	.235	.305	.427	.732	29	.899
1998—Danville (Caro.)	3B	118	445	47	89	21	0	20	63	30	172	6	6	3-3	.200	.259	.382	.641	18	.934
1999—Myrtle Beach (Caro.)	3B-SS	103	365	62	90	25	0	23	54	47	135	11	3	0-3	.247	.347	.504	.852	13	.946
2000—Greenville (Sou.)	3B	127	437	52	80	23	1	19	50	37	178	8	9	3-1	.183	.258	.371	.629	23	.926
2001—Greenville (Sou.)	3-OF-1-P	129	478	66	110	23	2	26	80	39	124	7	5	2-4	.230	.298	.450	.748	27	.927
2002—Richmond (Int'l)	3B-1B	134	484	67	127	28	1	26	77	34	107	10	13	1-5	.262	.321	.486	.807	18	.955
2003—Danville (Appal.)	OF-DH	5	15	1	1	0	0	0	2	2	2	1	0	0-0	.067	.200	.067	.267	0	1.000
—Richmond (Int'l)	1-OF-3-DH	96	359	47	89	15	3	16	52	24	87	4	6	3-1	.248	.296	.440	.736	5	.990
—Atlanta (N.L.)	OF-1B-3B	19	21	2	6	2	0	2	3	5	6	0	2	0-0	.286	.423	.667	1.090	1	.974
2004—Atlanta (N.L.)	1B-3B-OF	29	69	8	9	3	0	2	5	1	24	1	0	0-0	.130	.155	.261	.416	6	.952
—Richmond (Int'l)	3-1-O-2-DH	78	265	48	76	14	1	19	54	28	65	7	6	4-0	.287	.365	.562	.927	4	.986
Major League totals (2 years)		48	90	10	15	5	0	4	8	6	30	1	2	0-0	.167	.227	.356	.582	7	.958

HIDALGO, RICHARD — OF

PERSONAL: Born June 28, 1975, in Caracas, Venezuela. ... 6-3/220. ... Bats right, throws right. ... Full name: Richard Jose Hidalgo. ... Name pronounced: HUH-dahl-go.

TRANSACTIONS/CAREER NOTES: Signed as a non-drafted free agent by Houston Astros organization (July 2, 1991). ... On disabled list (May 30-July 21, 1998); included rehabilitation assignment to New Orleans. ... On disabled list (August 9, 1999-remainder of season). ... On disabled list (August 23-September 9, 2002). ... On disabled list (May 23-June 8, 2003). ... Traded by Astros to New York Mets for Ps David Weathers and Jeremy Griffiths (June 17, 2004).

RECORDS: Shares major league single-game record for most times hit by pitch—3 (April 19, 2000).

2004 GAMES PLAYED BY POSITION (MLB): OF—142.

Year Team (League)	Pos.	G	AB	R	H	2B	3B	HR	RBI	BB	SO	HBP	GDP	SB-CS	Avg.	OBP	SLG	OPS	E	Avg.
1992—GC Astros (GCL)	OF	51	184	20	57	7	3	1	27	13	27	3	1	14-5	.310	.360	.397	.756	0	1.000
1993—Asheville (S. Atl.)	OF	111	403	49	109	23	3	10	55	30	76	4	3	21-13	.270	.324	.417	.740	6	.974
1994—Quad City (Midw.)	OF	124	476	68	139	47	6	12	76	23	80	7	6	12-12	.292	.331	.492	.823	11	.953
1995—Jackson (Texas)	OF	133	489	59	130	28	6	14	59	32	76	2	11	8-9	.266	.309	.434	.743	5	.981
1996—Jackson (Texas)	OF-DH	130	513	66	151	34	2	14	78	29	55	11	24	11-7	.294	.341	.450	.791	6	.981
1997—New Orleans (A.A.)	OF-DH	134	526	74	147	37	5	11	78	35	57	8	16	6-10	.279	.330	.432	.761	9	.968
—Houston (N.L.)	OF	19	62	8	19	5	0	2	6	4	18	1	0	1-0	.306	.358	.484	.842	0	1.000
1998—Houston (N.L.)	OF	74	211	31	64	15	0	7	35	17	37	2	5	3-3	.303	.355	.474	.829	3	.978
—New Orleans (PCL)	OF	10	24	0	4	2	0	0	1	3	2	0	3	0-0	.167	.259	.250	.509	0	1.000
1999—Houston (N.L.)	OF	108	383	49	87	25	2	15	56	56	73	4	5	8-5	.227	.328	.420	.748	2	.991
2000—Houston (N.L.)	OF	153	558	118	175	42	3	44	122	56	110	21	13	13-6	.314	.391	.636	1.028	7	.984
2001—Houston (N.L.)	OF	146	512	70	141	29	3	19	80	54	107	16	15	3-5	.275	.356	.455	.811	3	.991
2002—Houston (N.L.)	OF	114	388	54	91	17	4	15	48	43	85	6	13	6-2	.235	.319	.415	.734	1	.995
2003—Houston (N.L.)	OF-DH	141	514	91	159	43	4	28	88	58	104	8	10	9-7	.309	.385	.572	.957	4	.987
2004—Houston (N.L.)	OF	58	199	21	51	15	2	4	30	17	53	0	7	1-2	.256	.309	.412	.721	2	.982
—New York (N.L.)	OF	86	324	46	74	11	1	21	52	27	76	5	12	3-2	.228	.296	.463	.759	4	.977
Major League totals (8 years)		899	3151	488	861	202	19	155	517	332	663	63	80	47-32	.273	.350	.497	.847	26	.987

DIVISION SERIES RECORD

Year Team (League)	Pos.	G	AB	R	H	2B	3B	HR	RBI	BB	SO	HBP	GDP	SB-CS	Avg.	OBP	SLG	OPS	E	Avg.
1997—Houston (N.L.)	OF	2	5	1	0	0	0	0	0	1	2	0	0	0-0	.000	.167	.000	.167	0	1.000
1998—Houston (N.L.)	OF	1	4	0	1	0	0	0	0	0	1	0	0	0-0	.250	.250	.250	.500	0	1.000
1999—Houston (N.L.)		Did not play.																		
2001—Houston (N.L.)	OF	3	8	1	1	0	0	0	0	3	2	0	0	0-0	.125	.364	.125	.489	0	1.000
Division series totals (3 years)		6	17	2	2	0	0	0	0	4	5	0	0	0-0	.118	.286	.118	.403	0	1.000

HIETPAS, JOE   C

PERSONAL: Born May 1, 1979, in Appleton, Wis. ... 6-3/220. ... Bats right, throws right. ... Full name: Joseph Carl Hietpas. ... High school: Appleton North (Wis.). ... College: Northwestern.
TRANSACTIONS/CAREER NOTES: Selected by New York Mets organization in 16th round of 2001 free-agent draft.
2004 GAMES PLAYED BY POSITION (MLB): C—1.

										BATTING								FIELDING	
Year Team (League)	Pos.	G	AB	R	H	2B	3B	HR	RBI	BB	SO	HBP	GDP	SB-CS	Avg.	OBP	SLG	OPS	E	Avg.
2001—Kingsport (Appalachian)	C	11	27	3	5	1	0	0	1	6	11	1	0	0-0	.185	.353	.222	.575	0	1.000
—Binghamton (East.)	C	2	3	0	0	0	0	0	0	0	1	0	0	0-0	.000	.000	.000	.000	0	1.000
2002—Capital City (SAL)	C	33	105	9	26	8	0	1	16	14	23	0	1	0-2	.248	.336	.352	.689	0	1.000
—Brooklyn New York-Penn. (NY-P)	C	32	117	11	30	5	0	1	13	8	31	2	4	0-1	.256	.313	.325	.637	3	.985
2003—Binghamton (East.)	C	5	10	1	1	1	0	0	0	0	2	0	0	0-0	.100	.100	.200	.300	0	1.000
—St. Lucie (Fla. St.)	C	63	195	12	31	8	1	1	19	14	60	2	6	3-1	.159	.220	.226	.445	10	.981
2004—St. Lucie (Fla. St.)	C	55	191	23	48	15	1	2	27	18	51	4	3	1-1	.251	.329	.372	.700	7	.983
—Binghamton (East.)	C	43	139	13	32	10	0	3	19	19	41	3	4	0-2	.230	.335	.367	.702	6	.982
—New York (N.L.)	C	1	0	0	0	0	0	0	0	0	0	0	0	0-0	...	...	...	...	0	1.000
Major League totals (1 year)		1	0	0	0	0	0	0	0	0	0	0	0	0-0	...	...	...	...	0	1.000

HIGGINSON, BOBBY   OF

PERSONAL: Born August 18, 1970, in Philadelphia, Pa. ... 5-11/195. ... Bats left, throws right. ... Full name: Robert Leigh Higginson. ... High school: Frankford (Philadelphia). ... College: Temple.
TRANSACTIONS/CAREER NOTES: Selected by Philadelphia Phillies organization in 18th round of 1991 free-agent draft; did not sign. ... Selected by Detroit Tigers organization in 12th round of 1992 free-agent draft. ... On Detroit disabled list (May 11-June 7, 1996); included rehabilitation assignment to Toledo. ... On disabled list (June 11-26, 1997). ... On suspended list (September 26, 1997). ... On disabled list (July 24-August 24, 1999). ... On suspended list (May 10-16, 2000). ... On disabled list (May 20-June 5, 2001; June 9-July 11, 2002; and June 29-July 25, 2003). ... On suspended list (September 2-4 and September 23-25, 2003).
2004 GAMES PLAYED BY POSITION (MLB): OF—115, DH—10.

										BATTING								FIELDING	
Year Team (League)	Pos.	G	AB	R	H	2B	3B	HR	RBI	BB	SO	HBP	GDP	SB-CS	Avg.	OBP	SLG	OPS	E	Avg.
1992—Niagara Falls (N.Y.-Penn.) .	OF	70	232	35	68	17	4	2	37	33	47	1	4	12-8	.293	.383	.427	.810	2	.983
1993—Lakeland (Fla. St.)	OF	61	223	42	67	11	7	3	25	40	31	1	6	8-3	.300	.406	.453	.859	2	.979
—London (East.)	OF	63	224	25	69	15	4	4	35	19	37	0	6	3-4	.308	.358	.464	.822	2	.982
1994—Toledo (Int'l)	OF	137	476	81	131	28	3	23	67	46	99	5	9	16-8	.275	.343	.492	.835	8	.973
1995—Detroit (A.L.)	OF-DH	131	410	61	92	17	5	14	43	62	107	5	5	6-4	.224	.329	.393	.721	4	.985
1996—Detroit (A.L.)	OF-DH	130	440	75	141	35	0	26	81	65	66	1	7	6-3	.320	.404	.577	.982	9	.963
—Toledo (Int'l)	OF	3	13	4	4	0	1	0	1	3	0	0	0	0-0	.308	.438	.462	.899	0	1.000
1997—Detroit (A.L.)	OF-DH	146	546	94	163	30	5	27	101	70	85	3	10	12-7	.299	.379	.520	.899	9	.972
1998—Detroit (A.L.)	OF-DH	157	612	92	174	37	4	25	85	63	101	6	16	3-3	.284	.355	.480	.835	6	.982
1999—Detroit (A.L.)	OF-DH	107	377	51	90	18	0	12	46	64	66	2	2	4-6	.239	.351	.382	.733	3	.983
2000—Detroit (A.L.)	OF-DH	154	597	104	179	44	4	30	102	74	99	2	5	15-3	.300	.377	.538	.915	7	.979
2001—Detroit (A.L.)	OF-DH	147	541	84	150	28	6	17	71	80	65	2	8	20-12	.277	.367	.445	.813	8	.976
2002—Detroit (A.L.)	OF-DH	119	444	50	125	24	3	10	63	41	45	6	8	12-5	.282	.345	.417	.762	7	.973
2003—Detroit (A.L.)	OF-DH	130	469	61	110	13	4	14	52	59	73	3	12	8-8	.235	.320	.369	.689	5	.981
2004—Detroit (A.L.)	OF-DH	131	448	63	110	24	2	12	64	70	84	7	10	5-2	.246	.354	.388	.742	6	.975
Major League totals (10 years)		1352	4884	735	1334	270	33	187	708	648	791	37	83	91-53	.273	.359	.457	.816	64	.977

HILL, BOBBY   2B/3B

PERSONAL: Born April 3, 1978, in San Jose, Calif. ... 5-9/180. ... Bats both, throws right. ... Full name: William Robert Hill. ... High school: Leland (Calif.). ... College: Miami (Fla.).
TRANSACTIONS/CAREER NOTES: Selected by California Angels organization in fifth round of 1996 free-agent draft; did not sign. ... Selected by Chicago White Sox organization in second round of 1999 free-agent draft; did not sign. ... Selected by Chicago Cubs organization in second round of 2000 free-agent draft. ... Traded by Cubs to Pittsburgh Pirates (August 15, 2003) to complete deal in which Cubs traded IF Jose Hernandez, P Matt Bruback and a player to be named to Pirates for 3B Aramis Ramirez, OF Kenny Lofton and cash (July 23, 2003).
2004 GAMES PLAYED BY POSITION (MLB): 2B—40, 3B—25.

										BATTING								FIELDING	
Year Team (League)	Pos.	G	AB	R	H	2B	3B	HR	RBI	BB	SO	HBP	GDP	SB-CS	Avg.	OBP	SLG	OPS	E	Avg.
2000—Newark (Atl.)	SS	132	481	109	157	22	9	13	82	101	57	4	...	81-15	.326	.442	.491	.932	38	...
2001—West Tenn. (Sou.)	2B-SS	57	209	30	63	8	1	3	21	32	39	2	7	20-8	.301	.394	.392	.788	6	.973
—Ariz. Cubs (Ariz.)	2B	3	9	1	2	0	0	0	1	2	3	0	0	1-0	.222	.364	.222	.586	0	1.000
2002—Iowa (PCL)	2B	92	354	80	99	23	3	8	39	49	66	11	7	29-5	.280	.382	.429	.812	6	.986
—Chicago (N.L.)	2B-SS	59	190	26	48	7	2	4	20	17	42	4	0	6-1	.253	.327	.374	.701	3	.986
2003—Chicago (N.L.)	2B	5	4	0	1	0	0	0	0	1	2	0	1	0-0	.250	.400	.250	.650	0	1.000
—Iowa (PCL)	2B-3B	92	361	53	104	23	4	6	40	37	65	8	5	8-7	.288	.365	.424	.789	11	.973
—Nashville (PCL)	2B-DH	17	66	5	11	2	1	1	4	8	8	0	2	1-2	.167	.257	.273	.529	0	1.000
—Pittsburgh (N.L.)	2B	1	3	1	1	0	0	0	0	1	0	0	0	0-0	.333	.500	.333	.833	0	1.000
2004—Pittsburgh (N.L.)	2B-3B	126	233	28	62	7	2	2	27	20	39	12	12	0-3	.266	.353	.339	.692	2	.990
Major League totals (3 years)		191	430	55	112	14	4	6	47	39	83	16	13	6-4	.260	.344	.353	.697	5	.988

HILL, KOYIE   C

PERSONAL: Born March 9, 1979, in Tulsa, Okla. ... 6-0/190. ... Bats both, throws right. ... Full name: Koyie Dolan Hill. ... Name pronounced: koy. ... High school: Eisenhower High (Lawton, Okla.). ... College: Wichita State.
TRANSACTIONS/CAREER NOTES: Selected by Los Angeles Dodgers organization in fourth round of 2000 free-agent draft. ... Traded with P Bill Murphy and OF Reggie Abercrombie to Arizona Diamondbacks for OF Steve Finley and C Brent Mayne (July 31, 2004). ... On disabled list (August 18, 2004-remainder of season).
2004 GAMES PLAYED BY POSITION (MLB): C—11.

H

Year	Team (League)	Pos.	G	AB	R	H	2B	3B	HR	RBI	BB	SO	HBP	GDP	SB-CS	Avg.	OBP	SLG	OPS	E	Avg.
2000— Yakima (N'west)	3B-C-2B	64	251	26	65	13	1	2	29	25	47	0	7	0-7	.259	.324	.343	.666	8	.941
2001— Wilmington (S.Atl.)	C	134	498	65	150	20	2	8	79	49	82	7	7	21-12	.301	.368	.398	.765	18	.977
2002— Jacksonville (Sou.)	C	130	468	67	127	25	1	11	64	76	88	0	14	5-3	.271	.368	.400	.768	17	.981
2003— Jacksonville (Sou.)	C-DH	25	101	9	23	7	0	0	7	6	19	0	3	2-1	.228	.271	.297	.568	2	.989
— Las Vegas (PCL)	C-DH-1B	85	312	48	98	18	0	3	36	15	39	1	7	5-0	.314	.345	.401	.746	9	.982
— Los Angeles (N.L.)		3	3	0	1	1	0	0	0	0	2	0	0	0-0	.333	.333	.667	1.000	0	...
2004— Las Vegas (PCL)	C-DH-1B-3B	91	350	57	100	26	0	13	54	28	69	2	9	0-1	.286	.339	.471	.811	5	.992
— Arizona (N.L.)	C	13	36	3	9	1	0	1	6	2	6	0	1	1-0	.250	.289	.361	.651	1	.984
Major League totals (2 years)		16	39	3	10	2	0	1	6	2	8	0	1	1-0	.256	.293	.385	.677	1	.984

HILL, SHAWN — P

PERSONAL: Born April 28, 1981, in Mississauga, Ontario. ... 6-2/185. ... Throws right, bats right. ... Full name: Shawn Richard Hill. ... High school: Bishop Reding (Milton, Ontario).

TRANSACTIONS/CAREER NOTES: Selected by San Diego Padres organization in 33rd round of 1999 free-agent draft; did not sign. ... Selected by Montreal Expos organization in sixth round of 2000 free-agent draft.

CAREER HITTING: 0-for-2 (.000), 0 R, 0 2B, 0 3B, 0 HR, 0 RBI.

Year	Team (League)	W	L	Pct.	ERA	WHIP	G	GS	CG	ShO	Hld.	Sv.-Opp.	IP	H	R	ER	HR	BB-IBB	SO	Avg.
2000— GC Expos (GCL)		1	3	.250	4.81	1.44	7	7	0	0	...	0-...	24.1	25	17	13	0	10-0	20	.250
2001— Vermont (NY-P)		2	2	.500	2.27	0.84	7	7	0	0	...	0-...	35.2	22	12	9	0	8-0	23	.172
2002— Clinton (Midw.)		12	7	.632	3.44	1.25	25	25	0	0	...	0-...	146.2	149	75	56	7	35-2	99	.261
2003— Brevard County (FSL)		9	4	.692	2.56	1.14	22	21	2	1	...	0-...	126.2	118	47	36	3	26-0	66	.248
— Harrisburg (Eastern)		3	1	.750	3.54	1.67	4	4	0	0	...	0-...	20.1	23	12	8	0	11-1	12	.280
2004— Montreal (N.L.)		1	2	.333	16.00	2.67	3	3	0	0	0	0-0	9.0	17	16	16	1	7-0	10	.415
— Harrisburg (Eastern)		5	7	.417	3.39	1.25	17	17	2	0	...	0-...	87.2	90	39	33	4	20-0	53	.272
Major League totals (1 year)		1	2	.333	16.00	2.67	3	3	0	0	0	0-0	9.0	17	16	16	1	7-0	10	.415

HILLENBRAND, SHEA — 1B/3B

PERSONAL: Born July 27, 1975, in Mesa, Ariz. ... 6-1/211. ... Bats right, throws right. ... Full name: Shea Matthew Hillenbrand. ... Name pronounced: SHAY. ... High school: Mountain View (Mesa, Ariz.). ... Junior college: Mesa (Ariz.) Community College.

TRANSACTIONS/CAREER NOTES: Selected by Boston Red Sox organization in 10th round of 1996 free-agent draft. ... On disabled list (August 31, 1999-remainder of season). ... Traded by Red Sox to Arizona Diamondbacks for P Byung-Hyun Kim (May 29, 2003). ... On disabled list (June 9-29, 2003); included rehabilitation assignment to Tucson.

2004 GAMES PLAYED BY POSITION (MLB): 1B—131, 3B—17.

Year	Team (League)	Pos.	G	AB	R	H	2B	3B	HR	RBI	BB	SO	HBP	GDP	SB-CS	Avg.	OBP	SLG	OPS	E	Avg.
1996— Lowell (NY-Penn)	3B-SS-1B	72	279	33	88	18	2	2	38	18	32	8	6	4-3	.315	.371	.416	.787	33	.938
1997— Michigan (Midw.)	3B-1B	64	224	28	65	13	3	3	39	9	20	1	2	1-3	.290	.315	.415	.730	8	.950
— Sarasota (Fla. St.)	3B-1B	57	220	25	65	12	0	2	28	7	29	2	4	9-8	.295	.320	.377	.698	20	.926
1998— Michigan (Midw.)	3B-C-1B	129	498	80	174	33	4	19	93	19	49	10	11	13-7	.349	.383	.546	.929	14	.982
1999— Trenton (East.)	C	69	282	41	73	15	0	7	36	14	27	3	6	6-5	.259	.298	.387	.685	5	.987
2000— Trenton (East.)	1B-3B	135	529	77	171	35	3	11	79	19	39	8	15	3-3	.323	.355	.463	.818	15	.979
2001— Boston (A.L.)	3B-1B-DH	139	468	52	123	20	2	12	49	13	61	7	12	3-4	.263	.291	.391	.682	18	.950
2002— Boston (A.L.)	3B	156	634	94	186	43	4	18	83	25	95	12	18	4-2	.293	.330	.459	.789	* 23	.943
2003— Boston (A.L.)	3B-1B-DH	49	185	20	56	17	0	3	38	7	26	4	9	1-0	.303	.335	.443	.778	3	.989
— Tucson (PCL)	3B-1B	3	10	0	3	1	0	0	1	0	1	0	0	0-0	.300	.300	.400	.700	0	1.000
— Arizona (N.L.)	1B-3B	85	330	40	88	18	1	17	59	17	44	2	13	0-0	.267	.302	.482	.784	12	.978
2004— Arizona (N.L.)	1B-3B	148	562	68	174	36	3	15	80	24	49	12	18	2-0	.310	.348	.464	.812	16	.987
American League totals (3 years)		344	1287	166	365	80	6	33	170	45	182	23	39	8-6	.284	.317	.432	.749	44	.958
National League totals (2 years)		233	892	108	262	54	4	32	139	41	93	14	31	2-0	.294	.331	.471	.802	28	.984
Major League totals (4 years)		577	2179	274	627	134	10	65	309	86	275	37	70	10-6	.288	.322	.448	.770	72	.975

ALL-STAR GAME RECORD

	G	AB	R	H	2B	3B	HR	RBI	BB	SO	HBP	GDP	SB-CS	Avg.	OBP	SLG	OPS	E	Avg.
All-Star Game totals (1 year)	1	2	0	0	0	0	0	0	0	1	0	0	0-0	.000	.000	.000	.000	0	1.000

HINCH, A.J. — C

PERSONAL: Born May 15, 1974, in Waverly, Iowa. ... 6-1/200. ... Bats right, throws right. ... Full name: Andrew Jay Hinch. ... High school: Midwest City (Okla.). ... College: Stanford.

TRANSACTIONS/CAREER NOTES: Selected by Chicago White Sox organization in second round of 1992 free-agent draft; did not sign. ... Selected by Minnesota Twins organization in third round of 1995 free-agent draft; did not sign. ... Selected by Oakland Athletics organization in third round of 1996 free-agent draft. ... Traded by A's with IF Angel Berroa and cash to Kansas City Royals as part of three-team deal in which Royals acquired P Roberto Hernandez from Tampa Bay Devil Rays, A's acquired P Cory Lidle from Devil Rays and OF Johnny Damon, IF Mark Ellis and cash from Royals and Devil Rays received OF Ben Grieve and cash from A's (January 8, 2001). ... Released by Royals (October 15, 2002). ... Signed by Cleveland Indians organization (December 23, 2002). ... Traded by Indians to Detroit Tigers for a player to be named (March 30, 2003). ... On disabled list (July 18-August 3 and August 6-September 1, 2003); included rehabilitation assignment to Toledo. ... Refused minor league assignment and became a free agent (October 1, 2003). ... Signed by Philadelphia Phillies organization (January 7, 2004). ... Refused minor league assignment and became a free agent (October 9, 2004).

2004 GAMES PLAYED BY POSITION (MLB): C—4.

Year	Team (League)	Pos.	G	AB	R	H	2B	3B	HR	RBI	BB	SO	HBP	GDP	SB-CS	Avg.	OBP	SLG	OPS	E	Avg.
1997— Modesto (California)	C-DH-1B	95	333	70	103	25	3	20	73	42	68	11	9	8-3	.309	.400	.583	.983	3	.996
— Edmonton (PCL)	C-DH-OF	39	125	23	47	7	0	4	24	20	13	3	7	2-0	.376	.473	.528	1.001	3	.986
1998— Oakland (A.L.)	C	120	337	34	78	10	0	9	35	30	89	4	6	3-0	.231	.296	.341	.638	* 9	.986
1999— Oakland (A.L.)	C	76	205	26	44	4	1	7	24	11	41	2	4	6-2	.215	.260	.346	.607	5	.987
— Vancouver (PCL)	C	15	61	9	23	3	0	2	7	3	12	1	0	1-1	.377	.415	.525	.940	1	.989
2000— Sacramento (PCL)	C-1B	109	417	65	111	23	2	6	47	45	67	9	7	5-5	.266	.344	.374	.718	4	.994
— Oakland (A.L.)	C-DH	6	8	1	2	0	0	0	0	1	1	0	0	0-0	.250	.333	.250	.583	1	.900
2001— Kansas City (A.L.)	C-DH	45	121	10	19	3	0	6	15	8	26	3	5	1-1	.157	.226	.331	.556	7	.984
— Omaha (PCL)	C-OF	45	168	28	54	14	0	10	33	11	33	1	5	1-0	.321	.365	.583	.948	1	.995

H

Year	Team (League)	Pos.	G	AB	R	H	2B	3B	HR	RBI	BB	SO	HBP	GDP	SB-CS	Avg.	OBP	SLG	OPS	E	Avg.
2002— Kansas City (A.L.)	C	72	197	25	49	7	1	7	27	18	35	3	2	3-3	.249	.321	.401	.722	4	.989
2003— Toledo (Int'l)	C-DH-1-3	55	185	20	48	15	1	4	23	13	38	4	2	0-1	.259	.320	.416	.736	3	.991
— Detroit (A.L.)	C	27	74	7	15	3	1	3	11	3	18	2	3	0-0	.203	.247	.392	.639	2	.983
2004— Scran./W.B. (I.L.)	C-DH	77	265	21	62	9	1	2	32	24	48	8	5	0-0	.234	.313	.298	.611	4	.992
— Philadelphia (N.L.)	C	4	11	1	2	1	0	0	0	0	4	0	0	0-0	.182	.182	.273	.455	0	1.000
American League totals (6 years)		346	942	103	207	27	3	32	112	71	210	14	20	13-6	.220	.281	.357	.638	24	.987
National League totals (1 year)		4	11	1	2	1	0	0	0	0	4	0	0	0-0	.182	.182	.273	.455	0	1.000
Major League totals (7 years)		350	953	104	209	28	3	32	112	71	214	14	20	13-6	.219	.280	.356	.636	24	.987

HINSKE, ERIC — 3B

PERSONAL: Born August 5, 1977, in Menasha, Wis. ... 6-2/235. ... Bats left, throws right. ... Full name: Eric Scott Hinske. ... Name pronounced: hin-SKEE. ... High school: Menasha (Wis.). ... College: Arkansas.

TRANSACTIONS/CAREER NOTES: Selected by Chicago Cubs organization in 17th round of 1998 free-agent draft. ... Traded by Cubs to Oakland Athletics for 2B Miguel Cairo (March 28, 2001). ... Traded by Athletics with P Justin Miller to Toronto Blue Jays for P Billy Koch (December 7, 2001). ... On disabled list (May 24-June 26, 2003); included rehabilitation assignment to Syracuse.

HONORS: Named A.L. Rookie Player of the Year by THE SPORTING NEWS (2002). ... Named A.L. Rookie of the Year by Baseball Writers' Association of America (2002).

2004 GAMES PLAYED BY POSITION (MLB): 3B—153, DH—1.

										BATTING									FIELDING	
Year	Team (League)	Pos.	G	AB	R	H	2B	3B	HR	RBI	BB	SO	HBP	GDP	SB-CS	Avg.	OBP	SLG	OPS	E	Avg.
1998— Williamsport (N.Y.-Penn.) .	1B	68	248	46	74	20	0	9	57	35	61	2	2	19-3	.298	.384	.488	.872	2	.997
— Rockford (Midwest)	1B	6	20	8	9	4	0	1	4	5	6	0	0	1-0	.450	.538	.800	1.338	0	1.000
1999— Daytona (Fla. St.)	3B-1B-OF	130	445	76	132	28	6	19	79	62	90	5	5	16-10	.297	.385	.515	.900	22	.965
— Iowa (PCL)	3B-1B	4	15	3	4	0	1	1	2	1	4	0	0	0-0	.267	.313	.600	.913	1	.952
2000— West Tenn. (Sou.)	3B-1B-OF	131	436	76	113	21	9	20	73	78	133	3	7	14-5	.259	.373	.486	.859	28	.916
2001— Sacramento (PCL)	3B-2B	121	436	71	123	27	1	25	79	54	113	10	6	20-7	.282	.373	.521	.893	17	.941
2002— Toronto (A.L.)	3B	151	566	99	158	38	2	24	84	77	138	2	12	13-1	.279	.365	.481	.845	20	.946
2003— Syracuse (Int'l)	3B	2	8	2	4	1	0	1	2	0	0	0	0	0-0	.500	.500	1.000	1.500	0	1.000
— Toronto (A.L.)	3B	124	449	74	109	45	3	12	63	59	104	1	11	12-2	.243	.329	.437	.765	22	.930
2004— Toronto (A.L.)	3B-DH	155	570	66	140	23	3	15	69	54	109	4	14	12-8	.246	.312	.375	.688	8	.978
Major League totals (3 years)		430	1585	239	407	106	8	51	216	190	351	7	37	37-11	.257	.336	.430	.766	50	.952

HITCHCOCK, STERLING — P

PERSONAL: Born April 29, 1971, in Fayetteville, N.C. ... 6-0/205. ... Throws left, bats left. ... Full name: Sterling Alex Hitchcock. ... High school: Armwood (Seffner, Fla.).

TRANSACTIONS/CAREER NOTES: Selected by New York Yankees organization in ninth round of 1989 free-agent draft. ... Traded by Yankees with 3B Russ Davis to Seattle Mariners for 1B Tino Martinez and Ps Jeff Nelson and Jim Mecir (December 7, 1995). ... Traded by Mariners to San Diego Padres for P Scott Sanders (December 6, 1996). ... On disabled list (June 6-July 3, 1997; and May 27, 2000-remainder of season). ... On disabled list (March 27-July 4, 2001); included rehabilitation assignments to Lake Elsinore and Portland. ... Traded by Padres to Yankees for P Brett Jodie and OF Darren Blakely (July 30, 2001). ... On disabled list (March 22-May 8 and June 28-July 28, 2002); included rehabilitation assignments to Tampa, Columbus and GCL Yankees. ... Traded by Yankees to St. Louis Cardinals for Ps Justin Pope, and Ben Julianel (August 22, 2003). ... Signed as a free agent by Padres (December 19, 2003). ... On disabled list (April 15-August 4 and August 23-September 3, 2004); included rehabilitation assignments to Portland and Lake Elsinore. ... Placed on voluntarily retired list (September 3, 2004).

CAREER HITTING: 19-for-210 (.090), 14 R, 0 2B, 0 3B, 0 HR, 5 RBI.

Year	Team (League)	W	L	Pct.	ERA	WHIP	G	GS	CG	ShO	Hld.	Sv.-Opp.	IP	H	R	ER	HR	BB-IBB	SO	Avg.
1989— GC Yankees (GCL)	9	1	.900	1.64	0.98	13	13	0	0	...	0-...	76.2	48	16	14	1	27-0	98	.182
1990— Greensboro (S. Atl.)	12	12	.500	2.91	1.05	27	27	6	5	...	0-...	173.1	122	68	56	7	60-1	171	.197
1991— Prince William (Caro.)	7	7	.500	2.64	1.15	19	19	2	0	...	0-...	119.1	111	49	35	2	26-0	101	.239
1992— Alb./Colon. (East.)	6	9	.400	2.58	1.08	24	24	2	0	...	0-...	146.2	116	51	42	6	42-0	155	.213
— New York (A.L.)	0	2	.000	8.31	2.23	3	3	0	0	0	0-0	13.0	23	12	12	2	6-0	6	.377
1993— Columbus (Int'l)	3	5	.375	4.81	1.41	16	16	0	0	...	0-...	76.2	80	43	41	8	28-0	85	.267
— Oneonta (N.Y.-Penn)	0	0	...	0.00	0.00	1	0	0	0	...	0-...	1.0	0	0	0	0	0-0	0	.000
— New York (A.L.)	1	2	.333	4.65	1.48	6	6	0	0	0	0-0	31.0	32	18	16	4	14-1	26	.271
1994— New York (A.L.)	4	1	.800	4.20	1.56	23	5	1	0	3	2-2	49.1	48	24	23	3	29-1	37	.265
— Columbus (Int'l)	3	4	.429	4.32	1.42	10	9	1	0	...	0-...	50.0	53	30	24	4	18-0	47	.265
— Alb./Colon. (East.)	1	0	1.000	1.80	0.80	1	1	0	0	...	0-...	5.0	4	1	1	0	0-0	7	.235
1995— New York (A.L.)	11	10	.524	4.70	1.32	27	27	4	1	0	0-0	168.1	155	91	88	22	68-1	121	.245
1996— Seattle (A.L.)	13	9	.591	5.35	1.62	35	35	0	0	0	0-0	196.2	245	131	117	27	73-4	132	.309
1997— San Diego (N.L.)	10	11	.476	5.20	1.41	32	28	1	0	0	0-0	161.0	172	102	93	24	55-2	106	.276
1998— San Diego (N.L.)	9	7	.563	3.93	1.23	39	27	2	1	3	1-2	176.1	169	83	77	29	48-2	158	.251
1999— San Diego (N.L.)	12	14	.462	4.11	1.35	33	33	1	0	0	0-0	205.2	202	99	94	29	76-6	194	.254
2000— San Diego (N.L.)	1	6	.143	4.93	1.45	11	11	0	0	0	0-0	65.2	69	38	36	12	26-1	61	.267
2001— Lake Elsinore (Calif.)	0	2	.000	4.10	1.29	6	6	0	0	...	0-...	26.1	33	18	12	3	1-0	31	.292
— Portland (PCL)	2	0	1.000	3.71	1.29	3	3	0	0	...	0-...	17.0	20	7	7	1	2-0	11	.308
— San Diego (N.L.)	2	1	.667	3.32	1.32	3	3	0	0	0	0-...	19.0	22	9	7	1	3-0	15	.275
— New York (A.L.)	4	4	.500	6.49	1.66	10	9	1	0	0	0-0	51.1	67	37	37	5	18-0	28	.315
2002— Tampa (FSL)	0	0	...	1.50	0.50	1	1	0	0	...	0-...	6.0	3	1	1	0	0-0	3	.150
— Columbus (Int'l)	0	0	...	13.50	3.00	2	2	0	0	...	0-...	7.1	19	11	11	2	3-0	3	.487
— New York (A.L.)	1	2	.333	5.49	1.83	20	2	0	0	0	0-0	39.1	57	29	24	4	15-3	31	.326
— GC Yankees (GCL)	0	0	...	0.00	0.00	2	2	0	0	...	0-...	3.0	0	0	0	0	0-0	6	.000
2003— New York (A.L.)	1	3	.250	5.44	1.51	27	1	0	0	2	0-0	49.2	57	33	30	6	18-3	36	.285
— St. Louis (N.L.)	5	1	.833	3.79	1.26	8	6	0	0	0	0-0	38.0	34	17	16	8	14-1	32	.238
2004— Portland (PCL)	1	1	.500	6.35	1.59	3	3	0	0	...	0-...	11.1	17	9	8	1	1-0	6	.327
— Lake Elsinore (Calif.)	1	0	1.000	1.00	0.89	2	2	0	0	...	0-...	9.0	8	1	1	0	0-0	13	.229
— San Diego (N.L.)	0	3	.000	6.33	1.41	4	4	0	0	0	0-0	21.1	22	15	15	5	8-0	14	.265
American League totals (8 years)	35	33	.515	5.22	1.55	151	88	6	1	5	2-2	598.2	684	375	347	73	241-13	417	.288
National League totals (7 years)	39	43	.476	4.43	1.34	130	112	4	1	3	1-2	687.0	690	363	338	108	230-12	580	.260
Major League totals (13 years)	74	76	.493	4.80	1.44	281	200	10	2	8	3-4	1285.2	1374	738	685	181	471-25	997	.273

DIVISION SERIES RECORD

Year	Team (League)	W	L	Pct.	ERA	WHIP	G	GS	CG	ShO	Hld.	Sv.-Opp.	IP	H	R	ER	HR	BB-IBB	SO	Avg.
1995— New York (A.L.)	0	0	...	5.40	2.40	2	0	0	0	0	0-0	1.2	2	2	1	1	2-1	1	.333
1998— San Diego (N.L.)	1	0	1.000	1.50	0.50	1	1	0	0	0	0-0	6.0	3	1	1	0	0-0	11	.150
2001— New York (A.L.)	0	0	...	6.00	1.67	1	0	0	0	0	0-0	3.0	5	2	2	2	0-0	2	.385
Division series totals (3 years)	1	0	1.000	3.38	1.13	4	1	0	0	0	0-0	10.2	10	5	4	3	2-1	14	.256

H

Year	Team (League)	W	L	Pct.	ERA	WHIP	G	GS	CG	ShO	Hld.	Sv.-Opp.	IP	H	R	ER	HR	BB-IBB	SO	Avg.
1998— San Diego (N.L.)		2	0	1.000	0.90	1.30	2	2	0	0	0	0-0	10.0	5	1	1	0	8-1	14	.152
2001— New York (A.L.)		Did not play.																		

WORLD SERIES RECORD

Year	Team (League)	W	L	Pct.	ERA	WHIP	G	GS	CG	ShO	Hld.	Sv.-Opp.	IP	H	R	ER	HR	BB-IBB	SO	Avg.
1998— San Diego (N.L.)		0	0	...	1.50	1.33	1	1	0	0	0	0-0	6.0	7	2	1	1	1-0	7	.292
2001— New York (A.L.)		1	0	1.000	0.00	0.25	2	0	0	0	0	0-0	4.0	1	0	0	0	0-0	6	.077
World series totals (2 years)		**1**	**0**	**1.000**	**0.90**	**0.90**	**3**	**1**	**0**	**0**	**0**	**0-0**	**10.0**	**8**	**2**	**1**	**1**	**1-0**	**13**	**.216**

HOCKING, DENNY — OF/SS

PERSONAL: Born April 2, 1970, in Torrance, Calif. ... 5-10/187. ... Bats both, throws right. ... Full name: Dennis Lee Hocking. ... Name pronounced: HAWK-ing. ... High school: West Torrance (Calif.). ... Junior college: El Camino (Calif.).

TRANSACTIONS/CAREER NOTES: Selected by Minnesota Twins organization in 52nd round of 1989 free-agent draft. ... On Minnesota disabled list (March 22-April 30, May 30-June 29 and July 31-September 8, 1996); included rehabilitation assignments to Salt Lake (April 4-30, June 21-29 and August 24-September 8). ... On disabled list (April 22-May 9, 2003). ... Signed as a free agent by Colorado Rockies organization (January 9, 2004). ... Released by Rockies (July 8, 2004). ... Signed by Chicago Cubs organization (July 23, 2004).

2004 GAMES PLAYED BY POSITION (MLB): OF—30, SS—13, 2B—8, 3B—2.

Year	Team (League)	Pos.	G	AB	R	H	2B	3B	HR	RBI	BB	SO	HBP	GDP	SB-CS	Avg.	OBP	SLG	OPS	E	Avg.
1990— Elizabethton (App.) 2B-3B-SS			54	201	45	59	6	2	6	30	40	26	6	6	14-4	.294	.422	.433	.855	20	.928
1991— Kenosha (Midw.)		SS	125	432	72	110	17	8	2	36	77	69	6	6	22-10	.255	.372	.345	.717	42	.923
1992— Visalia (Calif.)		SS	135	550	117	182	34	9	7	81	72	77	8	7	38-18	.331	.415	.464	.878	38	.947
1993— Nashville (Southern)		SS	107	409	54	109	9	4	8	50	34	66	4	12	15-5	.267	.327	.367	.694	30	.937
— Minnesota (A.L.)		SS-2B	15	36	7	5	1	0	0	0	6	8	0	1	1-0	.139	.262	.167	.429	1	.977
1994— Salt Lake (PCL)		SS	112	394	61	110	14	6	5	57	28	57	2	6	13-7	.279	.327	.383	.710	26	.949
— Minnesota (A.L.)		SS	11	31	3	10	3	0	0	2	0	4	0	1	2-0	.323	.323	.419	.742	0	1.000
1995— Salt Lake (PCL) SS-2B-DH			117	397	51	112	24	2	8	75	25	41	2	10	12-8	.282	.324	.413	.737	20	.966
— Minnesota (A.L.)		SS	9	25	4	5	0	2	0	3	2	2	0	1	1-0	.200	.259	.360	.619	1	.971
1996— Salt Lake (PCL) S-O-DH-2-3-1			37	130	18	36	6	2	3	22	10	17	2	4	2-2	.277	.333	.423	.756	3	.976
— Minnesota (A.L.) O-S-2-DH-1			49	127	16	25	6	0	1	10	8	24	0	3	3-3	.197	.243	.268	.510	1	.987
1997— Minnesota (A.L.) S-3-O-2-DH-1			115	253	28	65	12	4	2	25	18	51	1	6	3-5	.257	.308	.360	.667	4	.985
1998— Minnesota (A.L.) 2-S-O-3-DH-1			110	198	32	40	6	1	3	15	16	44	0	2	2-1	.202	.259	.288	.547	4	.982
1999— Minnesota (A.L.) S-2-O-3-1			136	386	47	103	18	2	7	41	22	54	3	10	11-7	.267	.307	.378	.685	3	.992
2000— Minnesota (A.L.) O-2-3-S-1-DH			134	373	52	111	24	4	4	47	48	77	0	2	7-5	.298	.373	.416	.789	5	.985
2001— Minnesota (A.L.) S-2-O-1-DH-3			112	327	34	82	16	2	3	25	29	67	2	7	6-1	.251	.315	.339	.654	5	.984
2002— Minnesota (A.L.) 2-S-3-1-OF			102	260	28	65	13	0	2	25	24	44	1	3	0-2	.250	.310	.323	.633	10	.968
2003— Minnesota (A.L.) 2-3-S-1-O-DH			83	188	22	45	10	2	3	22	15	37	0	3	0-1	.239	.291	.362	.653	3	.988
2004— Colorado (N.L.)		O-S-2-3B	55	94	7	19	2	0	0	4	7	20	0	3	0-1	.202	.257	.223	.481	4	.964
— Iowa (PCL)		3-S-2-OF	39	104	20	30	12	0	3	22	11	20	1	1	0-2	.288	.359	.490	.849	3	.975
American League totals (11 years)			**876**	**2204**	**273**	**556**	**109**	**17**	**25**	**215**	**188**	**412**	**7**	**39**	**36-25**	**.252**	**.310**	**.351**	**.661**	**37**	**.984**
National League totals (1 year)			**55**	**94**	**7**	**19**	**2**	**0**	**0**	**4**	**7**	**20**	**0**	**3**	**0-1**	**.202**	**.257**	**.223**	**.481**	**4**	**.964**
Major League totals (12 years)			**931**	**2298**	**280**	**575**	**111**	**17**	**25**	**219**	**195**	**432**	**7**	**42**	**36-26**	**.250**	**.308**	**.346**	**.654**	**41**	**.983**

DIVISION SERIES RECORD

Year	Team (League)	Pos.	G	AB	R	H	2B	3B	HR	RBI	BB	SO	HBP	GDP	SB-CS	Avg.	OBP	SLG	OPS	E	Avg.
2002— Minnesota (A.L.)		2B-OF	3	6	0	3	1	0	0	1	0	1	0	0	0-0	.500	.500	.667	1.167	0	1.000
2003— Minnesota (A.L.)		2B	1	0	0	0	0	0	0	0	0	0	0	0	0-0	...	...	...		0	
Division series totals (2 years)			**4**	**6**	**0**	**3**	**1**	**0**	**0**	**1**	**0**	**1**	**0**	**0**	**0-0**	**.500**	**.500**	**.667**	**1.167**	**0**	**1.000**

HOFFMAN, TREVOR — P

PERSONAL: Born October 13, 1967, in Bellflower, Calif. ... 6-0/215. ... Throws right, bats right. ... Full name: Trevor William Hoffman. ... High school: Savanna (Anaheim). ... College: Arizona. ... Brother of Glenn Hoffman, coach, Los Angeles Dodgers; and infielder with three major league teams (1980-87 and 1989).

TRANSACTIONS/CAREER NOTES: Selected by Cincinnati Reds organization in 11th round of 1989 free-agent draft. ... Selected by Florida Marlins in first round (eighth pick overall) of expansion draft (November 17, 1992). ... Traded by Marlins with Ps Jose Martinez and Andres Berumen to San Diego Padres for 3B Gary Sheffield and P Rich Rodriguez (June 24, 1993). ... On disabled list (March 25-September 2, 2003); included rehabilitation assignment to Lake Elsinore.

HONORS: Named N.L. Fireman of the Year by THE SPORTING NEWS (1996 and 1998).

CAREER HITTING: 4-for-33 (.121), 1 R, 2 2B, 0 3B, 0 HR, 5 RBI.

Year	Team (League)	W	L	Pct.	ERA	WHIP	G	GS	CG	ShO	Hld.	Sv.-Opp.	IP	H	R	ER	HR	BB-IBB	SO	Avg.
1991— Cedar Rapids (Midw.)		1	1	.500	1.87	1.04	27	0	0	0	...	12-...	33.2	22	8	7	0	13-0	52	.188
— Chattanooga (Southern)		1	0	1.000	1.93	1.21	14	0	0	0	...	8-...	14.0	10	4	3	0	7-0	23	.192
1992— Chattanooga (Southern)		3	0	1.000	1.52	1.11	6	6	0	0	...	0-...	29.2	22	6	5	1	11-1	31	.212
— Nashville (A.A.)		4	6	.400	4.27	1.36	42	5	0	0	...	6-...	65.1	57	32	31	6	32-3	63	.234
1993— Florida (N.L.)		2	2	.500	3.28	1.21	28	0	0	0	8	2-3	35.2	24	13	13	5	19-7	26	.185
— San Diego (N.L.)		2	4	.333	4.31	1.40	39	0	0	0	7	3-5	54.1	56	30	26	5	20-6	53	.264
1994— San Diego (N.L.)		4	4	.500	2.57	1.05	47	0	0	0	1	20-23	56.0	39	16	16	4	20-6	68	.193
1995— San Diego (N.L.)		7	4	.636	3.88	1.16	55	0	0	0	0	31-38	53.1	48	25	23	10	14-3	52	.235
1996— San Diego (N.L.)		9	5	.643	2.25	0.92	70	0	0	0	0	42-49	88.0	50	23	22	6	31-5	111	.161
1997— San Diego (N.L.)		6	4	.600	2.66	1.02	70	0	0	0	0	37-44	81.1	59	25	24	9	24-4	111	.200
1998— San Diego (N.L.)		4	2	.667	1.48	0.85	66	0	0	0	0	* 53-54	73.0	41	12	12	2	21-2	86	.165
1999— San Diego (N.L.)		2	3	.400	2.14	0.94	64	0	0	0	0	40-43	67.1	48	23	16	5	15-2	73	.197
2000— San Diego (N.L.)		4	7	.364	2.99	0.90	70	0	0	0	0	43-50	72.1	61	29	24	7	11-4	85	.224
2001— San Diego (N.L.)		3	4	.429	3.43	1.14	62	0	0	0	0	43-46	60.1	48	25	23	10	21-2	63	.216
2002— San Diego (N.L.)		2	5	.286	2.73	1.18	61	0	0	0	0	38-41	59.1	52	20	18	2	18-2	69	.234
2003— Lake Elsinore (Calif.)		0	0	...	0.00	0.70	3	0	0	0	0	0-...	3.0	2	0	0	0	0-0	4	.182
— San Diego (N.L.)		0	0	...	2.00	1.11	9	0	0	0	0	2-2	9.0	7	2	2	1	3-0	11	.212
2004— San Diego (N.L.)		3	3	.500	2.30	0.91	55	0	0	0	0	41-45	54.2	42	14	14	5	8-1	53	.211
Major League totals (12 years)		**48**	**47**	**.505**	**2.74**	**1.05**	**696**	**0**	**0**	**0**	**16**	**393-441**	**764.2**	**575**	**257**	**233**	**71**	**225-44**	**861**	**.206**

DIVISION SERIES RECORD

Year	Team (League)	W	L	Pct.	ERA	WHIP	G	GS	CG	ShO	Hld.	Sv.-Opp.	IP	H	R	ER	HR	BB-IBB	SO	Avg.
1996— San Diego (N.L.)		0	1	.000	10.80	2.40	2	0	0	0	0	0-0	1.2	3	2	2	1	1-0	2	.375
1998— San Diego (N.L.)		0	0	...	0.00	1.33	4	0	0	0	0	2-2	3.0	3	1	0	0	1-1	4	.250
Division series totals (2 years)		**0**	**1**	**.000**	**3.86**	**1.71**	**6**	**0**	**0**	**0**	**0**	**2-2**	**4.2**	**6**	**3**	**2**	**1**	**2-1**	**6**	**.300**

H

Year	Team (League)	W	L	Pct.	ERA	WHIP	G	GS	CG	ShO	Hld.	Sv.-Opp.	IP	H	R	ER	HR	BB-IBB	SO	Avg.
1998— San Diego (N.L.)		1	0	1.000	2.08	0.92	3	0	0	0	0	1-2	4.1	2	1	1	0	2-0	7	.143

WORLD SERIES RECORD

Year	Team (League)	W	L	Pct.	ERA	WHIP	G	GS	CG	ShO	Hld.	Sv.-Opp.	IP	H	R	ER	HR	BB-IBB	SO	Avg.
1998— San Diego (N.L.)		0	1	.000	9.00	1.50	1	0	0	0	0	0-1	2.0	2	2	2	1	1-0	0	.250

ALL-STAR GAME RECORD

	W	L	Pct.	ERA	WHIP	G	GS	CG	ShO	Hld.	Sv.-Opp.	IP	H	R	ER	HR	BB-IBB	SO	Avg.
All-Star Game totals (4 years)	0	0	...	10.80	1.50	4	0	0	0	0	1	0-0	3.1	5	4	4	1	0-0	5	.333

HOLLANDSWORTH, TODD — OF

PERSONAL: Born April 20, 1973, in Dayton, Ohio. ... 6-2/215. ... Bats left, throws left. ... Full name: Todd Mathew Hollandsworth. ... Name pronounced: HAHL-enz-worth. ... High school: Newport (Bellevue, Wash.).

TRANSACTIONS/CAREER NOTES: Selected by Los Angeles Dodgers organization in third round of 1991 free-agent draft; pick received as part of compensation for Kansas City Royals signing Type B free-agent OF/DH Kirk Gibson. ... On disabled list (May 3-July 7 and August 9-September 12, 1995); included rehabilitation assignments to San Bernardino and Albuquerque. ... On disabled list (August 2-16 and August 17-September 6, 1997); included rehabilitation assignment to San Bernardino. ... On disabled list (June 5, 1998-remainder of season). ... On disabled list (April 3-23 and June 4-19, 1999); included rehabilitation assignments to San Bernardino. ... Traded by Dodgers with OF Kevin Gibbs and P Randey Dorame to Colorado Rockies for OF Tom Goodwin and cash (July 31, 2000). ... On disabled list (May 12, 2001-remainder of season). ... Traded by Rockies with P Dennys Reyes to Texas Rangers for OF Gabe Kapler and 2B Jason Romano (July 31, 2002). ... On disabled list (August 4-20, 2002). ... Signed as a free agent by Florida Marlins (January 8, 2003). ... On disabled list (August 14-September 1, 2003). ... Signed as a free agent by Chicago Cubs (December 18, 2003). ... On disabled list (June 28, 2004-remainder of season).

HONORS: Named N.L. Rookie of the Year by Baseball Writers' Association of America (1996).

2004 GAMES PLAYED BY POSITION (MLB): OF—36, DH—3, 1B—3.

									BATTING										FIELDING	
Year	Team (League)	Pos.	G	AB	R	H	2B	3B	HR	RBI	BB	SO	HBP	GDP	SB-CS	Avg.	OBP	SLG	OPS	E	Avg.
1991— GC Dodgers (GCL)		OF	6	16	1	5	0	0	0	0	0	6	0	1	0-0	.313	.313	.313	.625	0	1.000
—Yakima (N'west)		OF	56	203	34	48	5	1	8	33	27	57	4	2	11-1	.236	.338	.389	.727	7	.939
1992— Bakersfield (Calif.)		OF	119	430	70	111	23	5	13	58	50	113	3	6	27-13	.258	.338	.426	.764	6	.975
1993— San Antonio (Texas)		OF	126	474	57	119	24	9	17	63	29	101	5	7	24-12	.251	.298	.447	.746	12	.956
1994— Albuquerque (PCL)		OF	132	505	80	144	31	5	19	91	46	96	0	15	15-9	.285	.343	.479	.822	13	.949
1995— Los Angeles (N.L.)		OF	41	103	16	24	2	0	5	13	10	29	1	1	2-1	.233	.304	.398	.702	4	.938
—San Bern. (Calif.)		OF	1	2	0	1	0	0	0	0	0	1	0	0	0-1	.500	.500	.500	1.000	0	...
—Albuquerque (PCL)		OF	10	38	9	9	2	0	2	4	6	8	1	1	1-0	.237	.356	.447	.803	0	1.000
1996— Los Angeles (N.L.)		OF	149	478	64	139	26	4	12	59	41	93	2	2	21-6	.291	.348	.437	.785	5	.978
1997— Los Angeles (N.L.)		OF	106	296	39	73	20	2	4	31	17	60	0	8	5-5	.247	.286	.368	.654	3	.984
—Albuquerque (PCL)		OF	13	56	13	24	4	3	1	14	4	4	0	2	0-3	.429	.467	.661	1.127	0	1.000
—San Bern. (Calif.)		OF	2	8	1	2	0	1	0	2	1	2	0	0	0-0	.250	.333	.500	.833	0	1.000
1998— Los Angeles (N.L.)		OF	55	175	23	47	6	4	3	20	9	42	1	2	4-3	.269	.308	.400	.708	4	.957
1999— San Bern. (Calif.)		OF	4	13	3	5	2	0	0	3	2	4	1	1	0-1	.385	.500	.538	1.038	0	1.000
—Los Angeles (N.L.)		OF-1B	92	261	39	74	12	2	9	32	24	61	1	2	5-2	.284	.345	.448	.793	3	.987
2000— Los Angeles (N.L.)		OF	81	261	42	61	12	0	8	24	30	61	1	4	11-4	.234	.314	.372	.686	2	.987
—Colorado (N.L.)		OF	56	167	39	54	8	0	11	23	11	38	0	4	7-3	.323	.365	.569	.934	1	.988
2001— Colorado (N.L.)		OF	33	117	21	43	15	1	6	19	8	20	0	1	5-0	.368	.408	.667	1.075	1	.981
2002— Colorado (N.L.)		OF	95	298	39	88	21	1	11	48	26	71	1	8	7-8	.295	.352	.483	.835	4	.973
—Texas (A.L.)		OF	39	132	16	34	6	0	5	19	14	27	0	0	1-0	.258	.327	.417	.743	0	1.000
2003— Florida (N.L.)		OF-DH	93	228	32	58	23	3	3	20	22	55	0	2	2-3	.254	.317	.421	.739	2	.983
2004— Chicago (N.L.) OF-DH-1B			57	148	28	47	6	2	8	22	17	26	1	2	1-1	.318	.392	.547	.939	1	.988
American League totals (1 year)			39	132	16	34	6	0	5	19	14	27	0	0	1-0	.258	.327	.417	.743	0	1.000
National League totals (10 years)			858	2532	382	708	151	19	80	311	215	556	8	36	70-36	.280	.337	.449	.786	30	.979
Major League totals (10 years)			897	2664	398	742	157	19	85	330	229	583	8	36	71-36	.279	.336	.447	.784	30	.980

DIVISION SERIES RECORD

									BATTING										FIELDING	
Year	Team (League)	Pos.	G	AB	R	H	2B	3B	HR	RBI	BB	SO	HBP	GDP	SB-CS	Avg.	OBP	SLG	OPS	E	Avg.
1995— Los Angeles (N.L.)		OF	2	2	0	0	0	0	0	0	0	0	0	0	0-0	.000	.000	.000	.000	0	...
1996— Los Angeles (N.L.)		OF	3	12	1	4	3	0	0	1	0	3	0	0	0-0	.333	.333	.583	.917	0	1.000
2003— Florida (N.L.)			3	3	1	1	0	0	0	0	0	2	0	0	0-0	.333	.333	.333	.667	0	...
Division series totals (3 years)			8	17	2	5	3	0	0	1	0	5	0	0	0-0	.294	.294	.471	.765	0	1.000

CHAMPIONSHIP SERIES RECORD

Year	Team (League)	Pos.	G	AB	R	H	2B	3B	HR	RBI	BB	SO	HBP	GDP	SB-CS	Avg.	OBP	SLG	OPS	E	Avg.
2003— Florida (N.L.)			4	3	2	3	1	0	0	2	1	0	0	0	0-0	1.000	1.000	1.333	2.333	0	...

WORLD SERIES RECORD

Year	Team (League)	Pos.	G	AB	R	H	2B	3B	HR	RBI	BB	SO	HBP	GDP	SB-CS	Avg.	OBP	SLG	OPS	E	Avg.
2003— Florida (N.L.)			2	2	0	0	0	0	0	0	0	1	0	0	0-0	.000	.000	.000	.000	0	...

HOLLIDAY, MATT — OF

PERSONAL: Born January 15, 1980, in Stillwater, Okla. ... 6-4/235. ... Bats right, throws right. ... Full name: Matthew Thomas Holliday. ... High school: Stillwater (Okla.).

TRANSACTIONS/CAREER NOTES: Selected by Colorado Rockies organization in seventh round of 1998 free-agent draft.

2004 GAMES PLAYED BY POSITION (MLB): OF—115.

									BATTING										FIELDING	
Year	Team (League)	Pos.	G	AB	R	H	2B	3B	HR	RBI	BB	SO	HBP	GDP	SB-CS	Avg.	OBP	SLG	OPS	E	Avg.
1998— Ariz. Rockies (Ariz.)		3B	32	117	20	40	4	1	5	23	15	21	2	0	2-1	.342	.413	.521	.934	10	.851
1999— Asheville (S. Atl.)		3B	121	444	76	117	28	0	16	64	53	116	9	8	10-3	.264	.350	.435	.785	37	.871
2000— Salem (Caro.)		3B	123	460	64	126	28	2	7	72	43	74	2	12	11-5	.274	.335	.389	.724	32	.893
2001— Salem (Caro.)		OF	72	255	36	70	16	1	11	52	33	42	3	10	11-3	.275	.358	.475	.833	0	1.000
2002— Carolina (Southern)		OF	130	463	79	128	19	2	10	64	67	102	7	14	16-2	.276	.375	.391	.766	7	.961
2003— Tulsa (Texas)		OF	135	522	65	132	28	5	12	72	43	74	6	9	15-9	.253	.313	.395	.708	2	.991
2004— Colo. Springs (PCL)		OF	6	22	8	8	5	0	2	4	5	6	0	1	2-0	.364	.481	.864	1.345	0	1.000
—Colorado (N.L.)		OF	121	400	65	116	31	3	14	57	31	86	6	9	3-3	.290	.349	.488	.837	7	.963
Major League totals (1 year)			121	400	65	116	31	3	14	57	31	86	6	9	3-3	.290	.349	.488	.837	7	.963

H

HOLLINS, DAMON — OF

PERSONAL: Born June 12, 1974, in Fairfield, Calif. ... 5-11/180. ... Bats right, throws left. ... Full name: Damon Jamall Hollins. ... High school: Vallejo (Calif.).
TRANSACTIONS/CAREER NOTES: Selected by Atlanta Braves organization in fourth round of 1992 free-agent draft. ... Traded by Braves to Los Angeles Dodgers for 2B Jose Pimentel (September 9, 1998). ... Released by Dodgers (November 22, 1998). ... Signed by Cincinnati Reds organization (December 15, 1998). ... Signed as a free agent by Milwaukee Brewers organization (December 1, 1999). ... Signed as a free agent by Minnesota Twins organization (February 23, 2001). ... Traded by Twins to Braves for future considerations (July 22, 2001). ... On disabled list (August 31, 2003-remainder of season).
2004 GAMES PLAYED BY POSITION (MLB): OF—6.

Year Team (League)	Pos.	G	AB	R	H	2B	3B	HR	RBI	BB	SO	HBP	GDP	SB-CS	Avg.	OBP	SLG	OPS	E	Avg.
1992— GC Braves (GCL)	OF	49	179	35	41	12	1	1	15	30	22	2	3	15-2	.229	.346	.324	.670	1	.989
1993— Danville (Appal.)	OF	62	240	37	77	15	2	7	51	19	30	1	5	10-2	.321	.369	.488	.856	6	.946
1994— Durham (Caro.)	OF	131	485	76	131	28	0	23	88	45	115	4	9	12-7	.270	.335	.470	.805	13	.957
1995— Greenville (Sou.)	OF	129	466	64	115	26	2	18	77	44	120	4	7	6-6	.247	.313	.427	.741	8	.978
1996— Richmond (Int'l)	OF	42	146	16	29	9	0	0	8	16	37	0	2	2-3	.199	.278	.260	.538	3	.976
1997— Richmond (Int'l)	OF-DH	134	498	73	132	31	3	20	63	45	84	3	18	7-2	.265	.329	.460	.789	8	.977
1998— Richmond (Int'l)	OF-DH	119	436	61	115	26	3	13	48	45	85	0	16	10-2	.264	.330	.427	.757	5	.980
— Atlanta (N.L.)	OF	3	6	0	1	0	0	0	0	0	1	0	0	0-0	.167	.167	.167	.333	0	1.000
— Los Angeles (N.L.)	OF	5	9	1	2	0	0	0	2	0	2	0	0	0-1	.222	.222	.222	.444	0	1.000
1999— Indianapolis (Int'l)	OF	106	328	58	86	19	0	9	43	31	44	1	13	11-2	.262	.328	.402	.730	4	.983
2000— Indianapolis (Int'l)	OF	87	287	33	82	16	3	2	32	21	35	1	5	5-3	.286	.334	.383	.718	0	1.000
2001— Edmonton (PCL)	OF	69	232	29	64	8	2	6	30	22	44	2	8	3-3	.276	.342	.405	.748	5	.954
	OF	43	160	27	42	10	2	5	24	14	34	0	7	2-2	.263	.318	.444	.762	2	.981
2002— Richmond (Int'l)	OF	128	498	66	139	34	1	12	59	35	77	1	13	10-2	.279	.326	.424	.750	4	.988
2003— Richmond (Int'l)	OF	91	307	39	84	23	4	11	45	22	62	2	10	7-2	.274	.324	.482	.806	4	.981
2004— Atlanta (N.L.)	OF	7	22	3	8	2	0	0	5	0	4	0	0	0-0	.364	.364	.455	.818	0	1.000
— Richmond (Int'l)	OF-DH	109	356	50	107	26	2	20	67	24	57	0	9	5-3	.301	.341	.553	.895	7	.967
Major League totals (2 years)		15	37	4	11	2	0	0	7	0	7	0	0	0-1	.297	.297	.351	.649	0	1.000

HORGAN, JOE — P

PERSONAL: Born June 7, 1977, in Sacramento, Calif. ... 6-1/200. ... Throws left, bats left. ... Full name: Joseph Paul Horgan. ... High school: Cordova Senior (Rancho Cordova, Calif.). ... Junior college: Sacramento (Calif.) City College.
TRANSACTIONS/CAREER NOTES: Selected by New York Yankees organization in 42nd round of 1995 free-agent draft; did not sign. ... Selected by Cleveland Indians organization in 11th round of 1996 free-agent draft. ... Released by Indians (March 23, 1999). ... Signed as a free agent by San Francisco Giants organization (April 11, 1999). ... Signed as a free agent by St. Louis Cardinals organization (November 6, 2003). ... Traded by Cardinals to Montreal Expos for P Benji DeQuin (May 7, 2004).
CAREER HITTING: 1-for-4 (.250), 0 R, 0 2B, 0 3B, 0 HR, 1 RBI.

Year Team (League)	W	L	Pct.	ERA	WHIP	G	GS	CG	ShO	Hld.	Sv.-Opp.	IP	H	R	ER	HR	BB-IBB	SO	Avg.
1996— Burlington (Appalachian)	1	2	.333	4.19	1.34	23	0	0	0	...	7-...	34.1	37	25	16	1	9-0	48	.257
1997— Watertown (N.Y.-Penn.)	0	1	.000	6.10	1.72	15	4	0	0	...	0-...	38.1	48	31	26	4	18-1	31	.308
— Kinston (Caro.)	1	2	.333	7.27	1.85	4	2	0	0	...	0-...	17.1	23	15	14	1	9-0	9	.319
1998— Columbus (S. Atl.)	2	1	.667	2.38	1.18	22	1	0	0	...	0-...	34.0	19	9	9	3	21-0	27	.168
1999— Bakersfield (California)	6	10	.375	5.22	1.47	25	19	1	0	...	0-...	117.1	129	76	68	18	43-0	101	.279
2000— San Jose (California)	14	10	.583	4.60	1.54	27	27	1	0	...	0-...	166.1	190	104	85	15	66-0	92	.293
— Shreveport (Texas)	0	0	...	3.38	0.75	1	0	0	0	...	0-...	5.1	2	2	2	0	2-1	3	.111
2001— Shreveport (Texas)	3	5	.375	3.65	1.20	31	14	0	0	...	1-...	103.2	97	51	42	10	27-1	61	.246
— Fresno (PCL)	0	0	...	5.87	1.83	3	1	0	0	...	0-...	7.2	11	5	5	1	3-0	5	.333
2002— Fresno (PCL)	2	2	.500	5.93	1.49	27	4	0	0	...	0-...	57.2	65	38	38	8	21-0	37	.286
— Shreveport (Texas)	4	3	.571	4.34	1.59	10	10	1	0	...	0-...	56.0	69	35	27	5	20-1	35	.305
2003— Fresno (PCL)	7	7	.500	5.67	1.47	55	0	0	0	...	3-...	74.2	80	51	47	9	30-1	65	.276
2004— Memphis (PCL)	0	1	.000	6.52	1.76	10	0	0	0	...	0-...	9.2	14	7	7	3	3-0	8	.350
— Edmonton (PCL)	1	0	1.000	3.18	1.12	13	0	0	0	...	0-...	17.0	15	6	6	2	4-0	11	.234
— Montreal (N.L.)	4	1	.800	3.15	1.43	47	0	0	0	12	2-3	40.0	35	18	14	5	22-3	30	.230
Major League totals (1 year)	4	1	.800	3.15	1.43	47	0	0	0	12	2-3	40.0	35	18	14	5	22-3	30	.230

HOUSE, J.R. — C/1B

PERSONAL: Born November 11, 1979, in Charleston, W.Va. ... 6-0/215. ... Bats right, throws right. ... Full name: James Rodger House. ... High school: Seabreeze (Daytona Beach, Fla.).
TRANSACTIONS/CAREER NOTES: Selected by Pittsburgh Pirates organization in fifth round of 1999 free-agent draft (June 2, 1999).
2004 GAMES PLAYED BY POSITION (MLB): C—3.

Year Team (League)	Pos.	G	AB	R	H	2B	3B	HR	RBI	BB	SO	HBP	GDP	SB-CS	Avg.	OBP	SLG	OPS	E	Avg.
1999— GC Pirates (GCL)	1B-C-3B	0	33	113	13	67	9	3	5	2	0	1	0	23-1	...	.593	1.000	3.687	3	.987
— Williamsport (N.Y.-Penn.)	C-1B	26	100	11	30	6	0	1	13	9	21	0	2	0-1	.300	.358	.390	.748	3	.985
— Hickory (S. Atl.)	3B	4	11	1	3	0	0	0	0	0	3	0	0	0-0	.273	.273	.273	.545	0	...
2000— Hickory (S. Atl.)	C-1B	110	420	78	146	29	1	23	90	46	91	6	7	1-2	.348	.414	.586	.000	8	.990
2001— Altoona (East.)	C-1B	112	426	51	110	25	1	11	56	37	103	5	12	1-1	.258	.323	.399	.722	7	.991
2002— GC Pirates (GCL)	C-1B	5	16	3	5	2	0	1	2	3	1	0	0	0-0	.313	.421	.625	1.046	0	1.000
— Altoona (East.)	C	30	91	9	24	6	0	2	11	13	21	1	4	0-0	.264	.349	.396	.745	1	.994
2003— GC Pirates (GCL)	DH-C	20	65	16	47	9	0	4	1	1	4	0	0	5-0	.400	.723	1.000	4.890	1	.984
— Altoona (East.)	C-DH	20	63	12	21	6	0	2	11	5	11	0	4	0-0	.333	.382	.524	.906	1	.983
— Pittsburgh (N.L.)		1	1	0	1	0	0	0	0	0	0	0	0	0-0	1.000	1.000	1.000	2.000	0	...
2004— Nashville (PCL)	C-1B-OF-DH	92	309	38	89	21	1	15	49	23	72	4	6	1-1	.288	.344	.508	.852	4	.993
— Pittsburgh (N.L.)	C	5	9	1	1	1	0	0	0	0	2	0	1	0-0	.111	.111	.222	.333	1	1.000
Major League totals (2 years)		6	10	1	2	1	0	0	0	0	2	0	1	0-0	.200	.200	.300	.500	0	1.000

HOWARD, BEN — P

PERSONAL: Born January 15, 1979, in Danville, Ill. ... 6-0/221. ... Throws right, bats right. ... Full name: Benjamin Richard Howard. ... High school: Jackson-Central Merry (Jackson, Tenn.).
TRANSACTIONS/CAREER NOTES: Selected by San Diego Padres organization in second round of 1997 free-agent draft. ... Traded by Padres to Florida Marlins for P Blaine Neal (April 3, 2004).

CAREER HITTING: 1-for-18 (.056), 1 R, 0 2B, 0 3B, 0 HR, 0 RBI.

Year	Team (League)	W	L	Pct.	ERA	WHIP	G	GS	CG	ShO	Hld.	Sv.-Opp.	IP	H	R	ER	HR	BB-IBB	SO	Avg.
1997— Ariz. Padres (Ariz.)		1	4	.200	7.45	2.15	13	12	0	0	...	0-...	54.1	54	53	45	3	63-0	59	.255
1998— Idaho Falls (Pioneer)		4	5	.444	6.03	2.24	15	15	0	0	...	0-...	68.2	67	61	46	2	87-0	79	.260
1999— Fort Wayne (Midw.)		6	10	.375	4.73	1.61	28	28	0	0	...	0-...	144.2	123	100	76	17	110-0	131	.226
2000— Rancho Cuca. (Calif.)		5	11	.313	6.37	1.85	32	19	0	0	...	0-...	107.1	88	87	76	8	111-1	150	.227
2001— Lake Elsinore (Calif.)		8	2	.800	2.83	1.16	18	18	0	0	...	0-...	101.2	86	37	32	4	32-0	107	.229
— Mobile (Sou.)		2	0	1.000	2.40	1.07	7	5	0	0	...	0-...	30.0	17	9	8	3	15-0	29	.167
2002— Mobile (Sou.)		3	1	.750	2.18	1.27	6	6	0	0	...	0-...	33.0	26	10	8	2	16-0	30	.222
— San Diego (N.L.)		0	1	.000	9.28	2.53	3	2	0	0	0	0-0	10.2	13	11	11	4	14-1	10	.302
— Portland (PCL)		0	4	.000	6.20	1.38	11	7	0	0	...	0-...	45.0	47	34	31	10	15-0	25	.266
2003— Portland (PCL)		7	9	.438	4.55	1.30	22	22	0	0	...	0-...	130.2	118	69	66	17	49-0	68	.243
— San Diego (N.L.)		1	3	.250	3.63	1.33	6	6	0	0	0	0-0	34.2	31	17	14	10	15-1	24	.235
2004— Albuquerque (PCL)		3	0	1.000	3.67	1.49	23	0	0	0	...	1-...	34.1	29	16	14	3	22-2	28	.228
— Florida (N.L.)		1	1	.500	5.50	1.54	31	0	0	0	3	0-0	37.2	37	23	23	6	21-3	33	.261
Major League totals (3 years)		**2**	**5**	**.286**	**5.20**	**1.58**	**40**	**8**	**0**	**0**	**3**	**0-0**	**83.0**	**81**	**51**	**48**	**20**	**50-5**	**67**	**.256**

HOWARD, RYAN   1B

PERSONAL: Born November 19, 1979, in St. Louis, Mo. ... 6-4/230. ... Bats left, throws left. ... Full name: Ryan James Howard. ... High school: Lafayette (St. Louis). ... College: Southwest Missouri State.

TRANSACTIONS/CAREER NOTES: Selected by Philadelphia Phillies in fifth round of 2001 free-agent draft.

2004 GAMES PLAYED BY POSITION (MLB): 1B—8.

Year	Team (League)	Pos.	G	AB	R	H	2B	3B	HR	RBI	BB	SO	HBP	GDP	SB-CS	Avg.	OBP	SLG	OPS	E	Avg.
2001— Batavia (NY-Penn)		1B	48	169	26	46	7	3	6	35	30	55	2	1	0-0	.272	.384	.456	.840	5	.987
2002— Lakewood (S.Atl.)		1B	135	493	56	138	20	6	19	87	66	145	5	9	5-4	.280	.367	.460	.828	17	.985
2003— Clearwater (FSL)		1B	130	490	67	149	32	1	23	82	50	151	8	12	0-0	.304	.374	.514	.889	10	.991
2004— Reading (East.)		1B-DH	102	374	73	111	18	1	37	102	46	129	10	2	1-2	.297	.386	.647	1.033	7	.992
— Scran./W.B. (I.L.)		1B	29	111	21	30	10	0	9	29	14	37	2	4	0-0	.270	.362	.604	.966	6	.977
— Philadelphia (N.L.)		1B	19	39	5	11	5	0	2	5	2	13	1	2	0-0	.282	.333	.564	.897	0	1.000
Major League totals (1 year)			**19**	**39**	**5**	**11**	**5**	**0**	**2**	**5**	**2**	**13**	**1**	**2**	**0-0**	**.282**	**.333**	**.564**	**.897**	**0**	**1.000**

HOWRY, BOB   P

PERSONAL: Born August 4, 1973, in Phoenix, Ariz. ... 6-5/220. ... Throws right, bats left. ... Full name: Bobby Dean Howry. ... Name pronounced: HOW-ree. ... High school: Deer Valley (Phoenix). ... College: McNeese State.

TRANSACTIONS/CAREER NOTES: Selected by San Francisco Giants organization in fifth round of 1994 free-agent draft. ... Traded by Giants with SS Mike Caruso, OF Brian Manning and Ps Keith Foulke, Lorenzo Barcelo and Ken Vining to Chicago White Sox for Ps Wilson Alvarez, Danny Darwin and Roberto Hernandez (July 31, 1997). ... On suspended list (April 28-May 30, 2000). ... Traded by White Sox to Boston Red Sox for Ps Frank Francisco and Byeong An (July 31, 2002). ... On disabled list (August 22, 2003-remainder of season). ... Released by Red Sox (October 24, 2003). ... Signed by Cleveland Indians organization (December 17, 2003).

CAREER HITTING: 0-for-0 (.000), 0 R, 0 2B, 0 3B, 0 HR, 0 RBI.

Year	Team (League)	W	L	Pct.	ERA	WHIP	G	GS	CG	ShO	Hld.	Sv.-Opp.	IP	H	R	ER	HR	BB-IBB	SO	Avg.
1994— Everett (Northwest)		0	4	.000	4.74	2.05	5	5	0	0	...	0-...	19.0	29	15	10	3	10-2	16	.341
— Clinton (Midw.)		1	3	.250	4.20	1.56	9	8	0	0	...	0-...	49.1	61	29	23	1	16-0	22	.316
1995— San Jose (California)		12	10	.545	3.54	1.36	27	25	1	0	...	0-...	165.1	171	79	65	6	54-0	107	.277
1996— Shreveport (Texas)		12	10	.545	4.65	1.40	27	27	0	0	...	0-...	156.2	163	90	81	17	56-3	57	.269
1997— Shreveport (Texas)		6	3	.667	4.91	1.44	48	0	0	0	...	22-...	55.0	58	35	30	6	21-0	43	.270
— Birmingham (Southern)		0	0		2.84	1.50	12	0	0	0	...	0-...	12.2	16	4	4	1	3-0	3	.314
1998— Calgary (PCL)		1	2	.333	3.41	1.11	23	0	0	0	...	5-...	31.2	25	12	12	2	10-3	22	.216
— Chicago (A.L.)		0	3	.000	3.15	1.03	44	0	0	0	19	9-11	54.1	37	20	19	7	19-2	51	.194
1999— Chicago (A.L.)		5	3	.625	3.59	1.42	69	0	0	0	1	28-34	67.2	58	34	27	8	38-3	80	.229
2000— Chicago (A.L.)		2	4	.333	3.17	1.17	65	0	0	0	14	7-12	71.0	54	26	25	6	29-2	60	.216
2001— Chicago (A.L.)		4	5	.444	4.69	1.46	69	0	0	0	21	5-11	78.2	85	41	41	11	30-9	64	.279
2002— Chicago (A.L.)		2	2	.500	3.91	1.22	47	0	0	0	10	0-0	50.2	45	22	22	7	17-2	31	.245
— Boston (A.L.)		1	3	.250	5.00	1.44	20	0	0	0	5	0-1	18.0	22	15	10	2	4-2	14	.306
2003— Boston (A.L.)		0	0		12.46	3.23	4	0	0	0	0	0-1	4.1	11	6	6	1	3-1	4	.478
— Pawtucket (Int'l)		2	0	1.000	1.06	0.90	13	0	0	0	...	0-...	17.0	14	2	2	1	1-0	10	.215
2004— Buffalo (Int'l)		1	1	.500	5.19	1.08	18	0	0	0	...	0-...	26.0	22	15	15	3	6-0	24	.222
— Cleveland (A.L.)		4	2	.667	2.74	1.15	37	0	0	0	8	0-2	42.2	37	14	13	5	12-0	39	.228
Major League totals (7 years)		**18**	**22**	**.450**	**3.79**	**1.29**	**355**	**0**	**0**	**0**	**78**	**49-72**	**387.1**	**349**	**178**	**163**	**47**	**152-21**	**343**	**.242**

DIVISION SERIES RECORD

Year	Team (League)	W	L	Pct.	ERA	WHIP	G	GS	CG	ShO	Hld.	Sv.-Opp.	IP	H	R	ER	HR	BB-IBB	SO	Avg.
2000— Chicago (A.L.)		0	0	...	3.38	1.50	2	0	0	0	1	0-0	2.2	2	1	1	0	2-0	4	.222

HUCKABY, KEN   C

PERSONAL: Born January 27, 1971, in San Leandro, Calif. ... 6-1/210. ... Bats right, throws right. ... Full name: Kenneth Paul Huckaby. ... Name pronounced: HUCK-a-be. ... High school: Manteca (Calif.). ... Junior college: San Joaquin Delta (Calif.).

TRANSACTIONS/CAREER NOTES: Selected by Los Angeles Dodgers organization in 22nd round of 1991 free-agent draft. ... Signed as a free agent by Seattle Mariners organization (December 3, 1997). ... Released by Mariners (June 13, 1998). ... Signed by New York Yankees organization (June 28, 1998). ... Signed as a free agent by Arizona Diamondbacks organization (January 22, 1999). ... Released by Diamondbacks (October 29, 2001). ... Signed by Toronto Blue Jays organization (February 10, 2002). ... Refused minor league assignment and became a free agent (September 29, 2003). ... Signed by Texas Rangers organization (November 13, 2003). ... Claimed on waivers by Baltimore Orioles (July 6, 2004). ... Refused minor league assignment and became a free agent (August 16, 2004). ... Signed by Rangers organization (August 17, 2004). ... Refused minor league assignment and became a free agent (October 8, 2004).

2004 GAMES PLAYED BY POSITION (MLB): C—24.

Year	Team (League)	Pos.	G	AB	R	H	2B	3B	HR	RBI	BB	SO	HBP	GDP	SB-CS	Avg.	OBP	SLG	OPS	E	Avg.
1991— Great Falls (Pio.)		C	57	213	39	55	16	0	3	37	17	38	4	4	3-2	.258	.321	.376	.696	12	.977
1992— Vero Beach (FSL)		C	73	261	14	63	9	0	0	21	7	42	1	5	1-1	.241	.262	.276	.538	9	.982
1993— Vero Beach (FSL)		C	79	281	22	75	14	1	4	41	11	35	2	3	2-1	.267	.297	.367	.664	12	.980
— San Antonio (Texas)		C	28	82	4	18	1	0	0	5	2	7	2	0	0-0	.220	.253	.232	.485	4	.978

H

Year	Team (League)	Pos.	G	AB	R	H	2B	3B	HR	RBI	BB	SO	HBP	GDP	SB-CS	Avg.	OBP	SLG	OPS	E	Avg.
1994—	San Antonio (Texas)	C	11	41	3	11	1	0	1	9	1	1	0	1	1-0	.268	.286	.366	.652	6	.931
	—Bakersfield (Calif.)	C	77	270	29	81	18	1	2	30	10	37	2	7	2-3	.300	.329	.396	.725	10	.986
1995—	Albuquerque (PCL)	C-1B	89	278	30	90	16	2	1	40	12	26	4	16	3-1	.324	.359	.406	.766	16	.973
1996—	Albuquerque (PCL)	C	103	287	37	79	16	2	3	41	17	35	2	10	0-0	.275	.319	.376	.696	6	.990
1997—	Albuquerque (PCL)	C-DH	69	201	14	40	5	1	0	18	9	36	0	5	1-0	.199	.231	.234	.465	10	.975
1998—	Tacoma (PCL)	C-1B	16	49	4	11	2	0	0	1	5	6	0	2	0-0	.224	.296	.265	.562	0	1.000
	—Columbus (Int'l)	C	36	101	13	21	3	1	1	10	11	14	0	3	0-2	.208	.286	.287	.573	5	.978
1999—	Tucson (PCL)	C-3B-DH-1B	107	355	44	107	20	1	2	42	13	33	2	11	0-0	.301	.325	.380	.706	10	.987
2000—	Tucson (PCL)	C-3B-OF-1B	76	243	31	67	11	1	4	33	10	30	2	10	2-2	.276	.306	.379	.685	8	.982
2001—	El Paso (Texas)	1B-C	30	104	14	36	4	0	2	14	3	16	3	3	0-0	.346	.368	.442	.811	4	.983
	—Tucson (PCL)	C-1B-3B-2B	78	262	31	76	15	1	2	34	7	62	2	3	1-3	.290	.313	.378	.690	14	.972
	—Arizona (N.L.)	C	1	1	0	0	0	0	0	0	0	1	0	0	0-0	.000	.000	.000	.000	0	1.000
2002—	Syracuse (Int'l)	C-1B	21	81	7	22	2	0	0	9	2	15	0	6	0-2	.272	.286	.296	.582	3	.981
	—Toronto (A.L.)	C	88	273	29	67	6	1	3	22	9	44	0	10	0-0	.245	.270	.308	.577	6	.989
2003—	Toronto (A.L.)	C	5	11	1	2	1	0	0	2	0	2	0	0	0-0	.182	.182	.273	.455	0	1.000
	—Syracuse (Int'l)	C-1B-DH-3B	75	267	24	78	14	0	3	25	15	30	0	11	1-1	.292	.326	.378	.705	7	.987
2004—	Baltimore (A.L.)	C	8	12	1	2	1	0	0	0	0	0	0	0	0-0	.167	.167	.250	.417	0	1.000
	—Oklahoma (PCL)	C-1B	35	127	18	35	8	1	2	20	9	18	0	6	0-0	.276	.317	.402	.718	3	.988
	—Texas (A.L.)	C	16	38	3	5	2	0	0	0	5	12	0	1	0-0	.132	.233	.184	.417	2	.978
	American League totals (3 years)		117	334	34	76	10	1	3	24	14	58	0	11	0-0	.228	.259	.290	.549	8	.988
	National League totals (1 year)		1	1	0	0	0	0	0	0	0	1	0	0	0-0	.000	.000	.000	.000	0	1.000
	Major League totals (4 years)		118	335	34	76	10	1	3	24	14	59	0	11	0-0	.227	.258	.290	.547	8	.988

HUDSON, LUKE — P

PERSONAL: Born May 2, 1977, in Fountain Valley, Calif. ... 6-3/195. ... Throws right, bats right. ... Full name: Luke Stephen Hudson. ... High school: Fountain Valley (Calif.). ... College: Tennessee.

TRANSACTIONS/CAREER NOTES: Selected by Baltimore Orioles organization in fifth round of 1995 draft; did not sign. ... Selected by Colorado Rockies organization in fourth round of 1998 free-agent draft. ... Traded by Rockies with P Gabe White to Cincinnati Reds for 2B Pokey Reese and P Dennys Reyes (December 18, 2001).

CAREER HITTING: 2-for-16 (.125), 1 R, 0 2B, 0 3B, 0 HR, 2 RBI.

Year	Team (League)	W	L	Pct.	ERA	WHIP	G	GS	CG	ShO	Hld.	Sv.-Opp.	IP	H	R	ER	HR	BB-IBB	SO	Avg.
1998—	Portland (N'west)	3	6	.333	4.74	1.49	15	15	0	0	...	0-...	79.2	68	46	42	8	51-0	82	.226
1999—	Asheville (S. Atl.)	6	5	.545	4.30	1.28	21	20	1	0	...	0-...	88.0	89	47	42	10	24-0	96	.265
2000—	Salem (Caro.)	5	8	.385	3.27	1.23	19	19	2	2	...	0-...	110.0	101	47	40	9	34-0	80	.246
2001—	Carolina (Southern)	7	12	.368	4.20	1.38	29	28	1	0	...	0-...	165.0	159	90	77	19	68-0	145	.250
2002—	Louisville (Int'l)	5	9	.357	4.51	1.35	30	17	0	0	...	3-...	117.2	102	64	59	6	57-1	129	.233
	—Cincinnati (N.L.)	0	0	...	4.50	1.83	3	0	0	0	1	0-0	6.0	5	5	3	1	6-0	7	.227
2004—	Chattanooga (Southern)	7	7	.500	3.32	1.11	16	16	0	0	...	0-...	86.2	71	35	32	9	25-1	91	.225
	—Louisville (Int'l)	2	1	.667	2.84	1.05	3	3	0	0	...	0-...	19.0	15	8	6	2	5-0	17	.214
	—Cincinnati (N.L.)	4	2	.667	2.42	1.26	9	9	0	0	0	0-0	48.1	36	16	13	3	25-1	38	.208
	Major League totals (2 years)	4	2	.667	2.65	1.33	12	9	0	0	1	0-0	54.1	41	21	16	4	31-1	45	.210

HUDSON, ORLANDO — 2B

PERSONAL: Born December 12, 1977, in Darlington, S.C. ... 6-0/185. ... Bats both, throws right. ... Full name: Orlando Thill Hudson. ... High school: Darlington (S.C.). ... Junior college: Spartanburg Methodist (S.C.). ... College: Spartanburg Methodist (S.C.).

TRANSACTIONS/CAREER NOTES: Selected by Toronto Blue Jays organization in 33rd round of 1996 free-agent draft; did not sign. ... Selected by Toronto Blue Jays organization in 43rd round of 1997 free-agent draft. ... On disabled list (May 24-June 16, 2004).

2004 GAMES PLAYED BY POSITION (MLB): 2B—133.

Year	Team (League)	Pos.	G	AB	R	H	2B	3B	HR	RBI	BB	SO	HBP	GDP	SB-CS	Avg.	OBP	SLG	OPS	E	Avg.
1998—	Medicine Hat (Pio.)	2B	65	242	50	71	18	1	8	42	22	36	7	3	6-5	.293	.366	.475	.842	13	.959
1999—	Hagerstown (SAL)	2B-3B-OF	132	513	66	137	36	6	7	74	42	85	2	10	8-6	.267	.322	.402	.724	21	.946
2000—	Dunedin (Fla. St.)	2B-3B-SS	96	358	54	102	16	2	7	48	37	42	2	15	9-5	.285	.354	.399	.754	19	.941
	—Tennessee (Sou.)	3B	39	134	17	32	4	3	2	15	15	18	2	3	3-2	.239	.320	.358	.678	11	.921
2001—	Tennessee (Sou.)	2B-3B	84	306	51	94	22	8	4	52	37	42	3	12	8-3	.307	.385	.471	.856	8	.979
	—Syracuse (Int'l)	2B-3B	55	194	31	59	14	3	4	27	23	34	2	1	11-3	.304	.378	.469	.847	4	.986
2002—	Syracuse (Int'l)	2B	100	417	63	127	27	3	10	37	35	54	4	14	8-5	.305	.363	.456	.819	10	.982
	—Toronto (A.L.)	2B	54	192	20	53	10	5	4	23	11	27	2	6	0-1	.276	.319	.443	.762	4	.986
2003—	Toronto (A.L.)	2B	142	474	54	127	21	6	9	57	39	87	5	13	5-4	.268	.328	.395	.723	12	.984
2004—	Toronto (A.L.)	2B	135	489	73	132	32	7	12	58	51	98	4	12	7-3	.270	.341	.438	.779	12	.984
	Major League totals (3 years)		331	1155	147	312	63	18	25	138	101	212	11	31	12-8	.270	.332	.421	.753	28	.984

HUDSON, TIM — P

PERSONAL: Born July 14, 1975, in Columbus, Ga. ... 6-1/164. ... Throws right, bats right. ... Full name: Timothy Adam Hudson. ... High school: Glenwood (Phenix City, Ala.). ... College: Auburn.

TRANSACTIONS/CAREER NOTES: Selected by Oakland Athletics organization in 35th round of 1994 free-agent draft; did not sign. ... Selected by Athletics organization in sixth round of 1997 free-agent draft. ... On disabled list (June 23-August 7, 2004); included rehabilitation assignment to Sacramento.

HONORS: Named A.L. Rookie Pitcher of the Year by THE SPORTING NEWS (1999).

CAREER HITTING: 3-for-26 (.115), 2 R, 1 2B, 0 3B, 0 HR, 1 RBI.

Year	Team (League)	W	L	Pct.	ERA	WHIP	G	GS	CG	ShO	Hld.	Sv.-Opp.	IP	H	R	ER	HR	BB-IBB	SO	Avg.
1997—	S. Oregon (N'west)	3	1	.750	2.51	0.94	8	4	0	0	...	0-...	28.2	12	8	8	0	15-2	37	.128
1998—	Modesto (Calif.)	4	0	1.000	1.67	0.98	8	5	0	0	...	0-...	37.2	19	10	7	0	18-0	48	.148
	—Huntsville (Southern)	10	9	.526	4.54	1.54	22	22	2	0	...	0-...	134.2	136	84	68	13	71-2	104	.270
1999—	Midland (Texas)	3	0	1.000	0.50	0.67	3	3	0	0	...	0-...	18.0	9	1	1	0	3-0	18	.153
	—Vancouver (PCL)	4	0	1.000	2.20	1.20	8	8	0	0	...	0-...	49.0	38	16	12	2	21-0	61	.212
	—Oakland (A.L.)	11	2	.846	3.23	1.34	21	21	1	0	0	0-0	136.1	121	56	49	8	62-2	132	.237
2000—	Oakland (A.L.)	•20	6	.769	4.14	1.24	32	32	2	2	0	0-0	202.1	169	100	93	24	82-5	169	.227
2001—	Oakland (A.L.)	18	9	.667	3.37	1.22	35	•35	3	0	0	0-0	235.0	216	100	88	20	71-5	181	.245
2002—	Oakland (A.L.)	15	9	.625	2.98	1.25	34	34	4	2	0	0-0	238.1	237	87	79	19	62-9	152	.263
2003—	Oakland (A.L.)	16	7	.696	2.70	1.08	34	34	3	•2	0	0-0	240.0	197	84	72	15	61-9	162	.223
2004—	Sacramento (PCL)	0	0	...	6.00	1.33	1	1	0	0	...	0-...	3.0	2	2	2	0	1-0	3	.167
	—Oakland (A.L.)	12	6	.667	3.53	1.26	27	27	3	•2	0	0-0	188.2	194	82	74	8	44-3	103	.267
	Major League totals (6 years)	92	39	.702	3.30	1.22	183	183	16	8	0	0-0	1240.2	1134	509	455	94	382-33	899	.244

H

Year Team (League)	W	L	Pct.	ERA	WHIP	G	GS	CG	ShO	Hld.	Sv.-Opp.	IP	H	R	ER	HR	BB-IBB	SO	Avg.
2000—Oakland (A.L.)	0	1	.000	3.38	1.25	1	1	0	0	0	0-0	8.0	6	4	3	0	4-0	5	.194
2001—Oakland (A.L.)	1	0	1.000	0.93	0.93	2	1	0	0	0	0-0	9.2	8	1	1	1	1-0	5	.222
2002—Oakland (A.L.)	0	1	.000	6.23	1.96	2	2	0	0	0	0-0	8.2	13	11	6	2	4-0	8	.333
2003—Oakland (A.L.)	0	0	...	3.52	1.43	2	2	0	0	0	0-0	7.2	10	3	3	2	1-0	6	.323
Division series totals (4 years)	1	2	.333	3.44	1.38	7	6	0	0	0	0-0	34.0	37	19	13	5	10-0	24	.270

	W	L	Pct.	ERA	WHIP	G	GS	CG	ShO	Hld.	Sv.-Opp.	IP	H	R	ER	HR	BB-IBB	SO	Avg.
All-Star Game totals (1 year)	0	0	...	0.00	0.00	1	0	0	0	0	0-0	1.0	0	0	0	0	0-0	1	.000

HUFF, AUBREY 3B

PERSONAL: Born December 20, 1976, in Marion, Ohio. ... 6-4/231. ... Bats left, throws right. ... Full name: Aubrey Lewis Huff. ... High school: Brewer (Fort Worth, Texas). ... College: Miami (Fla.).
TRANSACTIONS/CAREER NOTES: Selected by Tampa Bay Devil Rays organization in fifth round of 1998 free-agent draft.
2004 GAMES PLAYED BY POSITION (MLB): 3B—87, 1B—38, DH—34, OF—9.

								BATTING									FIELDING	
Year Team (League)	Pos.	G	AB	R	H	2B	3B	HR	RBI	BB	SO	HBP	GDP	SB-CS	Avg.	OBP	SLG	OPS	E	Avg.
1998—Char., S.C. (SAL)	3B	69	265	38	85	19	1	13	54	24	40	0	5	3-1	.321	.371	.547	.918	8	.957
1999—Orlando (South.)	3B	133	491	85	148	40	3	22	78	64	77	4	14	2-3	.301	.385	.530	.915	29	.927
2000—Durham (Int'l)	3B-1B	108	408	73	129	36	3	20	76	51	72	5	15	2-3	.316	.394	.566	.960	21	.915
—Tampa Bay (A.L.)	3B	39	122	12	35	7	0	4	14	5	18	1	6	0-0	.287	.318	.443	.760	5	.939
2001—Durham (Int'l)	3B	17	66	14	19	6	0	3	10	5	7	0	3	0-0	.288	.338	.515	.853	4	.929
—Tampa Bay (A.L.)	3B-DH-1B	111	411	42	102	25	1	8	45	23	72	0	18	1-3	.248	.288	.372	.660	20	.940
2002—Durham (Int'l)	1B	32	126	18	41	9	0	3	20	12	13	1	4	0-0	.325	.386	.468	.854	1	1.000
—Tampa Bay (A.L.)	DH-1B-3B	113	454	67	142	25	0	23	59	37	55	1	17	4-1	.313	.364	.520	.884	8	.981
2003—Tampa Bay (A.L.)	O-DH-1-3	162	636	91	198	47	3	34	107	53	80	8	19	2-3	.311	.367	.555	.922	9	.977
2004—Tampa Bay (A.L.)	3-1-DH-O	157	600	92	178	27	2	29	104	56	74	6	9	5-1	.297	.360	.493	.853	13	.975
Major League totals (5 years)		582	2223	304	655	131	6	98	329	174	299	16	69	12-8	.295	.348	.491	.839	55	.969

HUGHES, TRAVIS P

PERSONAL: Born May 25, 1978, in Newton, Kan. ... 6-5/240. ... Throws right, bats right. ... Full name: Travis Wade Hughes. ... High school: Elwood (Kan.). ... Junior college: Cowley County (Kan.) Community College.
TRANSACTIONS/CAREER NOTES: Selected by Texas Rangers organization in 19th round of 1997 free-agent draft.
CAREER HITTING: 0-for-0 (.000), 0 R, 0 2B, 0 3B, 0 HR, 0 RBI.

Year Team (League)	W	L	Pct.	ERA	WHIP	G	GS	CG	ShO	Hld.	Sv.-Opp.	IP	H	R	ER	HR	BB-IBB	SO	Avg.
1998—Pulaski (Appalachian)	2	6	.250	3.89	1.32	22	3	0	0	...	2-...	41.2	30	25	18	2	25-1	48	.189
1999—Savannah (S. Atl.)	11	7	.611	2.81	1.15	30	23	1	0	...	2-...	157.0	127	60	49	9	54-0	150	.221
2000—Charlotte (Fla. St.)	9	9	.500	4.42	1.39	39	14	1	0	...	9-...	126.1	122	76	62	9	54-3	96	.254
2001—Tulsa (Texas)	5	7	.417	4.64	1.56	47	5	0	0	...	8-...	87.1	91	52	45	8	45-2	86	.270
2002—Tulsa (Texas)	9	7	.563	3.52	1.54	26	26	1	1	...	0-...	143.1	139	68	56	11	82-0	137	.255
2003—Oklahoma (PCL)	1	3	.250	5.46	1.84	11	11	1	0	...	0-...	57.2	79	41	35	4	27-0	36	.329
—Frisco (Texas)	4	8	.333	4.99	1.45	24	10	1	1	...	0-...	74.0	81	47	41	6	26-1	58	.277
2004—Frisco (Texas)	3	6	.333	3.70	1.52	40	0	0	0	...	7-...	63.1	63	34	26	4	33-7	68	.256
—Oklahoma (PCL)	1	2	.333	5.26	1.17	13	0	0	0	...	0-...	25.2	21	15	15	2	9-0	24	.221
—Texas (A.L.)	0	0	...	13.50	4.50	2	0	0	0	0	0-0	1.1	4	2	2	0	2-0	4	.500
Major League totals (1 year)	0	0	...	13.50	4.50	2	0	0	0	0	0-0	1.1	4	2	2	0	2-0	4	.500

HUISMAN, JUSTIN P

PERSONAL: Born April 16, 1979, in Harvey, Ill. ... 6-1/195. ... Throws right, bats right. ... Full name: Justin Ray Huisman. ... High school: Thornwood (Ill.). ... College: Mississippi.
TRANSACTIONS/CAREER NOTES: Selected by Colorado Rockies organization in 15th round of 2000 free-agent draft. ... Traded by Rockies to Kansas City Royals for 1B Chris Fallon, P Zach McClellan and cash (April 8, 2004).
CAREER HITTING: 0-for-0 (.000), 0 R, 0 2B, 0 3B, 0 HR, 0 RBI.

Year Team (League)	W	L	Pct.	ERA	WHIP	G	GS	CG	ShO	Hld.	Sv.-Opp.	IP	H	R	ER	HR	BB-IBB	SO	Avg.
2000—Portland (N'west)	3	6	.333	1.85	1.10	16	3	0	0	...	1-...	43.2	31	16	9	1	17-1	32	.196
2001—Asheville (S. Atl.)	0	3	.000	1.70	0.84	55	0	0	0	...	30-...	58.1	35	20	11	1	14-2	53	.167
2002—Carolina (Southern)	0	3	.000	6.66	1.73	18	0	0	0	...	2-...	24.1	30	22	18	4	12-3	10	.291
—Salem (Caro.)	3	4	.429	1.57	1.18	41	0	0	0	...	20-...	51.2	47	11	9	0	14-3	24	.250
2003—Tulsa (Texas)	7	2	.778	1.75	1.01	57	0	0	0	...	26-...	61.2	55	22	12	1	7-1	46	.234
2004—Kansas City (A.L.)	0	0	...	6.84	1.76	14	0	0	0	1	1-1	25.0	36	20	19	3	8-3	13	.336
—Omaha (PCL)	4	2	.667	3.61	1.61	32	0	0	0	...	6-...	42.1	50	23	17	3	18-2	37	.286
Major League totals (1 year)	0	0	...	6.84	1.76	14	0	0	0	1	1-1	25.0	36	20	19	3	8-3	13	.336

HUMMEL, TIM 3B

PERSONAL: Born November 18, 1978, in Goshen, N.Y. ... 6-2/205. ... Bats right, throws right. ... Full name: Timothy Robert Hummel. ... High school: Burke (Montgomery, N.Y.). ... College: Old Dominion.
TRANSACTIONS/CAREER NOTES: Selected by San Diego Padres organization in fifth round of 1997 free-agent draft; did not sign. ... Selected by Chicago White Sox organization in second round of 2000 free-agent draft. ... Claimed on waivers by Cincinnati Reds (August 26, 2003). ... Claimed on waivers by Boston Red Sox (September 3, 2004).
2004 GAMES PLAYED BY POSITION (MLB): 3B—32, 1B—13, 2B—1, SS—1, DH—1.

								BATTING									FIELDING	
Year Team (League)	Pos.	G	AB	R	H	2B	3B	HR	RBI	BB	SO	HBP	GDP	SB-CS	Avg.	OBP	SLG	OPS	E	Avg.
2000—Burlington (Midw.)	SS	39	144	22	47	9	1	1	21	21	20	1	2	8-3	.326	.411	.424	.834	5	.964
—Win.-Salem (Car.)	SS	27	98	15	32	7	0	1	9	13	12	2	4	1-1	.327	.416	.429	.845	8	.912
2001—Birmingham (Sou.)	2B-SS-3B	134	524	83	152	33	6	7	63	62	69	5	12	14-3	.290	.364	.416	.780	26	.958
2002—Charlotte (Int'l)	S-2-3-1	142	523	55	136	33	0	4	41	51	95	10	7	6-5	.260	.332	.346	.678	12	.981
2003—Charlotte (Int'l)	3-S-2-DH	128	476	72	135	25	3	15	80	46	83	5	10	9-3	.284	.350	.443	.794	13	.960
—Cincinnati (N.L.)	3B-SS-2B	26	84	9	19	5	0	2	10	8	13	0	1	0-0	.226	.290	.357	.647	5	.912
2004—Cincinnati (N.L.)	3-1-2-S-DH	56	110	10	24	4	0	1	7	8	17	2	1	1-0	.218	.281	.282	.563	4	.967
—Louisville (Int'l)	3-1-2-DH	42	152	18	44	13	0	2	20	12	27	2	4	2-0	.289	.345	.414	.760	3	.981
Major League totals (2 years)		82	194	19	43	9	0	3	17	16	30	2	2	1-0	.222	.285	.314	.599	9	.949

H

HUNTER, TORII   OF

PERSONAL: Born July 18, 1975, in Pine Bluff, Ark. ... 6-2/211. ... Bats right, throws right. ... Full name: Torii Kedar Hunter. ... High school: Pine Bluff (Ark.).

TRANSACTIONS/CAREER NOTES: Selected by Minnesota Twins organization in first round (20th pick overall) of 1993 free-agent draft; pick recieved as part of compensation for Cincinnati Reds signing Type A free-agent P John Smiley. ... On disabled list (April 6-21, 2001). ... On suspended list (July 20-23, 2002). ... On disabled list (April 7-25, 2004).

HONORS: Won A.L. Gold Glove as outfielder (2001-04).

2004 GAMES PLAYED BY POSITION (MLB): OF—126, DH—10.

Year	Team (League)	Pos.	G	AB	R	H	2B	3B	HR	RBI	BB	SO	HBP	GDP	SB-CS	Avg.	OBP	SLG	OPS	E	Avg.
1993— GC Twins (GCL)		OF	28	100	6	19	3	0	0	8	4	23	9	1	4-2	.190	.283	.220	.503	6	.895
1994— Fort Wayne (Midw.)		OF	91	335	57	98	17	1	10	50	25	80	10	5	8-10	.293	.358	.439	.796	7	.971
1995— Fort Myers (FSL)		OF	113	391	64	96	15	2	7	36	38	77	12	8	7-4	.246	.330	.348	.678	7	.973
1996— Fort Myers (FSL)		OF	4	16	1	3	0	0	0	1	2	5	0	0	1-1	.188	.278	.188	.465	0	1.000
— New Britain (East.)		OF	99	342	49	90	20	3	7	33	28	60	7	7	7-7	.263	.331	.401	.731	4	.982
1997— New Britain (East.)		OF-DH	127	471	57	109	22	2	8	56	47	94	3	6	8-8	.231	.305	.338	.642	7	.974
— Minnesota (A.L.)			1	0	0	0	0	0	0	0	0	0	0	0	0-0	...	.000	...	...	...	...
1998— New Britain (East.)		OF	82	308	42	87	24	3	6	32	19	64	4	2	11-9	.282	.329	.438	.768	2	.989
— Minnesota (A.L.)		OF	6	17	0	4	1	0	0	2	2	6	0	1	0-1	.235	.316	.294	.610	0	1.000
— Salt Lake (PCL)		OF-DH	26	92	15	31	7	0	4	20	1	13	1	3	2-2	.337	.347	.543	.891	2	.966
1999— Minnesota (A.L.)		OF	135	384	52	98	17	2	9	35	26	72	6	9	10-6	.255	.309	.380	.689	1	.997
2000— Minnesota (A.L.)		OF	99	336	44	94	14	7	5	44	18	68	2	13	4-3	.280	.318	.408	.726	3	.989
— Salt Lake (PCL)			55	209	58	77	17	2	18	61	11	28	3	4	11-3	.368	.403	.727	1.130	3	.973
2001— Minnesota (A.L.)		OF	148	564	82	147	32	5	27	92	29	125	8	12	9-6	.261	.306	.479	.784	4	.992
2002— Minnesota (A.L.)		OF-DH	148	561	89	162	37	4	29	94	35	118	5	17	23-8	.289	.334	.524	.859	3	.992
2003— Minnesota (A.L.)		OF-DH	154	581	83	145	31	4	26	102	50	106	5	15	6-7	.250	.312	.451	.762	4	.991
2004— Minnesota (A.L.)		OF-DH	138	520	79	141	37	0	23	81	40	101	7	23	21-7	.271	.330	.475	.805	4	.988
Major League totals (8 years)			829	2963	429	791	169	22	119	450	200	596	33	90	73-38	.267	.319	.459	.778	19	.991

DIVISION SERIES RECORD

Year	Team (League)	Pos.	G	AB	R	H	2B	3B	HR	RBI	BB	SO	HBP	GDP	SB-CS	Avg.	OBP	SLG	OPS	E	Avg.
2002— Minnesota (A.L.)		OF	5	20	4	6	4	0	0	2	1	4	0	0	0-0	.300	.333	.500	.833	0	1.000
2003— Minnesota (A.L.)		OF	4	14	3	6	0	1	1	2	2	2	0	0	0-0	.429	.500	.786	1.286	0	1.000
2004— Minnesota (A.L.)		OF	4	17	5	6	1	0	1	2	1	1	0	0	2-0	.353	.368	.588	.957	0	1.000
Division series totals (3 years)			13	51	12	18	5	1	2	6	4	7	0	0	2-0	.353	.393	.608	1.001	0	1.000

CHAMPIONSHIP SERIES RECORD

Year	Team (League)	Pos.	G	AB	R	H	2B	3B	HR	RBI	BB	SO	HBP	GDP	SB-CS	Avg.	OBP	SLG	OPS	E	Avg.
2002— Minnesota (A.L.)		OF	5	18	2	3	0	0	0	1	0	3	0	2	0-0	.167	.211	.278	.488	0	1.000

ALL-STAR GAME RECORD

			G	AB	R	H	2B	3B	HR	RBI	BB	SO	HBP	GDP	SB-CS	Avg.	OBP	SLG	OPS	E	Avg.
All-Star Game totals (1 year)			1	2	0	0	0	0	0	0	0	0	0	0	0-0	.000	.000	.000	.000	0	1.000

HYZDU, ADAM   OF

PERSONAL: Born December 6, 1971, in San Jose, Calif. ... 6-2/220. ... Bats right, throws right. ... Full name: Adam David Hyzdu. ... Name pronounced: HIGHS-doo. ... High school: Moeller (Cincinnati).

TRANSACTIONS/CAREER NOTES: Selected by San Francisco Giants organization in first round (15th pick overall) of 1990 free-agent draft; pick received as compensation for Houston Astros signing Type B free-agent IF Ken Oberkfell. ... Selected by Cincinnati Reds from Giants organization in Rule 5 major league draft (December 13, 1993). ... Released by Reds (March 23, 1996). ... Signed by Boston Red Sox organization (April 26, 1996). ... Signed by Arizona Diamondbacks organization (January 2, 1998). ... Loaned by Diamondbacks organization to Monterrey of the Mexican League (April 7-May 17, 1998). ... On disabled list (June 30-August 23, 1998). ... Signed as a free agent by Red Sox organization (January 5, 1999). ... Released by Red Sox (May 5, 1999). ... Signed by Pittsburgh Pirates organization (May 10, 1999). ... Refused minor league assignment and became a free agent (September 29, 2003). ... Signed by Red Sox organization (November 10, 2003).

2004 GAMES PLAYED BY POSITION (MLB): OF—14, DH—2.

Year	Team (League)	Pos.	G	AB	R	H	2B	3B	HR	RBI	BB	SO	HBP	GDP	SB-CS	Avg.	OBP	SLG	OPS	E	Avg.
1990— Everett (N'west)		OF	69	253	31	62	16	1	6	34	28	78	2	4	2-4	.245	.319	.387	.707	5	.963
1991— Clinton (Midw.)		OF	124	410	47	96	13	5	5	50	64	131	3	10	4-5	.234	.340	.327	.667	9	.955
1992— San Jose (Calif.)		OF	128	457	60	127	25	5	9	60	55	134	1	6	10-5	.278	.351	.414	.765	5	.976
1993— San Jose (Calif.)		OF	44	165	35	48	11	3	13	38	29	53	0	3	1-1	.291	.393	.630	1.023	3	.963
— Shreveport (Texas)		OF	86	302	30	61	17	0	6	25	20	82	1	5	0-5	.202	.253	.318	.571	4	.973
1994— Chattanooga (Sou.)		OF-DH-1B	38	133	17	35	10	0	3	9	8	21	1	1	0-2	.263	.310	.406	.716	4	.949
— Win.-Salem (Car.)		OF-DH	55	210	30	58	11	1	15	39	18	33	2	3	1-5	.276	.336	.552	.889	4	.945
— Indianapolis (A.A.)		OF	12	25	3	3	2	0	0	3	1	5	0	0	0-0	.120	.143	.200	.343	1	.917
1995— Chattanooga (Sou.)		OF	102	312	55	82	14	1	13	48	45	56	4	4	3-2	.263	.362	.439	.801	1	.995
1996— Trenton (East.)		OF-DH-C	109	374	71	126	24	3	25	80	56	75	2	7	1-8	.337	.424	.618	1.042	3	.980
1997— Pawtucket (Int'l)		OF-DH	119	413	77	114	21	1	23	84	72	113	4	6	10-6	.276	.387	.499	.886	4	.978
1998— Monterrey (Mex.)		OF	29	110	20	36	3	0	5	22	14	17	...	...	7-1	.327		.491		0	1.000
— Tucson (PCL)		OF-DH-P	34	100	21	34	7	1	4	14	15	23	0	2	0-1	.340	.419	.550	.969	1	.974
1999— Pawtucket (Int'l)		OF-DH	12	35	4	8	0	0	1	6	4	13	0	0	0-0	.229	.308	.314	.622	0	1.000
— Altoona (East.)		O-1-3-DH	91	345	64	109	26	2	24	78	40	62	3	2	8-4	.316	.392	.612	1.003	11	.965
— Nashville (PCL)		OF	14	44	6	11	1	0	5	13	4	11	0	2	0-0	.250	.313	.614	.926	0	1.000
2000— Altoona (East.)		OF-1B	142	514	96	149	39	2	31	106	94	102	8	6	3-7	.290	.405	.554	.960	1	.996
— Pittsburgh (N.L.)		OF	12	18	2	7	2	0	1	4	0	4	0	0	0-0	.389	.389	.667	1.056	0	1.000
2001— Nashville (PCL)		OF-1B-3B	69	261	38	76	17	2	11	39	17	68	0	3	1-3	.291	.332	.498	.830	1	.994
— Pittsburgh (N.L.)		OF-1B	51	72	7	15	1	0	5	9	4	18	1	1	0-1	.208	.260	.431	.690	0	1.000
2002— Nashville (PCL)		OF-1B	65	243	33	59	17	0	10	50	29	59	0	4	1-2	.243	.318	.436	.754	2	.980
— Pittsburgh (N.L.)		OF-1B	59	155	24	36	6	0	11	34	21	44	1	1	0-0	.232	.324	.484	.808	0	1.000
2003— Pittsburgh (N.L.)		OF	51	63	16	13	5	0	1	8	10	21	1	2	0-0	.206	.320	.333	.653	0	1.000
— Nashville (PCL)		OF-1B	40	135	22	38	10	1	6	18	18	28	1	2	2-2	.281	.365	.504	.869	2	.981
2004— Pawtucket (Int'l)		OF-DH	129	465	92	140	33	2	29	79	84	106	7	12	8-4	.301	.413	.568	.980	6	.976
— Boston (A.L.)		OF-DH	17	10	3	3	2	0	1	2	1	2	0	0	0-0	.300	.364	.800	1.164	0	1.000
American League totals (1 year)			17	10	3	3	2	0	1	2	1	2	0	0	0-0	.300	.364	.800	1.164	0	1.000
National League totals (4 years)			173	308	49	71	14	0	18	55	35	87	3	4	0-1	.231	.312	.451	.764	0	1.000
Major League totals (5 years)			190	318	52	74	16	0	19	57	36	89	3	4	0-1	.233	.314	.462	.776	0	1.000

H

IBANEZ, RAUL   OF

PERSONAL: Born June 2, 1972, in Manhattan, N.Y. ... 6-2/200. ... Bats left, throws right. ... Full name: Raul Javier Ibanez. ... Name pronounced: ee-BON-yez. ... High school: Sunset (Miami). ... Junior college: Miami-Dade Community College South.

TRANSACTIONS/CAREER NOTES: Selected by Seattle Mariners organization in 36th round of 1992 free-agent draft. ... On disabled list (March 30-June 29, 1998); included rehabilitation assignment to Tacoma. ... On disabled list (May 18-June 3, 1999); included rehabilitation assignment to Tacoma. ... On disabled list (August 7-22, 2000); included rehabilitation assignment to Tacoma. ... Signed as a free agent by Kansas City Royals organization (January 22, 2001). ... Signed as a free agent by Seattle Mariners (November 19, 2003). ... On disabled list (June 3-July 10, 2004); included rehabilitation assignment to Tacoma.

2004 GAMES PLAYED BY POSITION (MLB): OF—112, 1B—10, DH—2.

Year	Team (League)	Pos.	G	AB	R	H	2B	3B	HR	RBI	BB	SO	HBP	GDP	SB-CS	Avg.	OBP	SLG	OPS	E	Avg.
1992—Ariz. Mariners (Ariz.)		C-1B-OF	33	120	25	37	8	2	1	16	9	18	2	3	1-2	.308	.366	.433	.800	4	.931
1993—Appleton (Midwest)		C-1B-OF	52	157	26	43	9	0	5	21	24	31	1	2	0-2	.274	.370	.427	.796	2	.980
—Bellingham (N'west)		C	43	134	16	38	5	2	0	15	21	23	0	0	0-3	.284	.378	.351	.729	1	.993
1994—Appleton (Midwest)		C-1B-OF	91	327	55	102	30	3	7	59	32	37	2	3	10-5	.312	.375	.486	.861	10	.971
1995—Riverside (Calif.)		C-1B	95	361	59	120	23	9	20	108	41	49	2	7	4-3	.332	.395	.612	1.007	12	.977
1996—Tacoma (PCL)		OF-1B-DH	111	405	59	115	20	3	11	47	44	56	2	4	7-7	.284	.353	.430	.783	11	.951
—Port City (Sou.)		OF-DH-C-1B	19	76	12	28	8	1	1	13	8	7	0	1	3-2	.368	.424	.539	.963	4	.905
—Seattle (A.L.)		DH	4	5	0	0	0	0	0	0	0	1	1	0	0-0	.000	.167	.000	.167	0	...
1997—Tacoma (PCL)		OF	111	438	84	133	30	5	15	84	32	75	1	12	7-5	.304	.349	.498	.847	5	.976
—Seattle (A.L.)		OF-DH	11	26	3	4	0	1	1	4	0	6	0	0	0-0	.154	.154	.346	.500	0	1.000
1998—Tacoma (PCL)		OF-DH	52	190	24	41	8	1	6	25	24	47	0	3	1-1	.216	.301	.363	.664	1	.988
—Seattle (A.L.)		OF-1B-DH	37	98	12	25	7	1	2	12	5	22	0	4	0-0	.255	.291	.408	.699	1	.991
1999—Tacoma (PCL)		OF-1B-DH-C	87	209	23	54	1	0	9	27	17	32	0	4	5-1	.258	.313	.421	.734	3	.988
—Tacoma (PCL)		OF-DH-1B	8	31	6	11	1	0	3	5	1	7	0	0	1-0	.355	.375	.677	1.052	0	1.000
2000—Seattle (A.L.)		OF-DH-1B	92	140	21	32	8	0	2	15	14	25	1	1	2-0	.229	.301	.329	.630	2	.980
—Tacoma (PCL)		OF	10	40	3	10	4	0	0	6	1	3	0	0	0-0	.250	.268	.350	.618	0	1.000
2001—Kansas City (A.L.)		O-DH-1-3	104	279	44	78	11	5	13	54	32	51	0	6	0-2	.280	.353	.495	.847	5	.962
—Omaha (PCL)		OF-SS	8	27	3	4	1	0	2	5	1	10	0	0	0-0	.148	.179	.407	.586	1	.857
2002—Kansas City (A.L.)		OF-1B-DH	137	497	70	146	37	6	24	103	40	76	2	11	5-3	.294	.346	.537	.883	3	.994
2003—Kansas City (A.L.)		OF-1B-DH	157	608	95	179	33	5	18	90	49	81	3	10	8-4	.294	.345	.454	.799	4	.991
2004—Tacoma (PCL)		DH-OF	4	17	2	4	1	0	0	1	0	6	0	0	0-0	.235	.235	.294	.529	0	1.000
—Seattle (A.L.)		OF-1B-DH	123	481	67	146	31	1	16	62	36	72	1	10	1-2	.304	.353	.472	.825	5	.984
Major League totals (9 years)			752	2343	335	664	134	19	85	367	193	366	10	46	21-12	.283	.338	.466	.803	23	.987

DIVISION SERIES RECORD

Year	Team (League)	Pos.	G	AB	R	H	2B	3B	HR	RBI	BB	SO	HBP	GDP	SB-CS	Avg.	OBP	SLG	OPS	E	Avg.
2000—Seattle (A.L.)		OF	3	8	2	3	0	0	0	0	0	0	0	0	0-0	.375	.375	.375	.750	0	1.000

CHAMPIONSHIP SERIES RECORD

Year	Team (League)	Pos.	G	AB	R	H	2B	3B	HR	RBI	BB	SO	HBP	GDP	SB-CS	Avg.	OBP	SLG	OPS	E	Avg.
2000—Seattle (A.L.)		OF	6	9	0	0	0	0	0	0	0	2	0	0	0-0	.000	.000	.000	.000	0	1.000

INFANTE, OMAR   2B

PERSONAL: Born December 26, 1981, in Puerto la Cruz, Venezuela. ... 6-0/176. ... Bats right, throws right. ... Full name: Omar Rafael Infante. ... Name pronounced: in-fahn-TAY.

TRANSACTIONS/CAREER NOTES: Signed as a non-drafted free agent by Detroit Tigers organization (April 28, 1999).

2004 GAMES PLAYED BY POSITION (MLB): 2B—105, SS—23, 3B—10, OF—5.

Year	Team (League)	Pos.	G	AB	R	H	2B	3B	HR	RBI	BB	SO	HBP	GDP	SB-CS	Avg.	OBP	SLG	OPS	E	Avg.
1999—GC Tigers (GCL)		SS	25	97	11	26	4	0	0	7	4	11	0	1	4-0	.268	.294	.309	.603	8	.932
2000—W. Mich. (Mid.)		SS	12	48	7	11	0	0	0	5	5	7	2	2	1-0	.229	.327	.229	.556	1	.983
—Lakeland (Fla. St.)		SS	79	259	35	71	11	0	2	24	20	29	1	4	11-5	.274	.324	.340	.664	19	.951
2001—Erie (East.)		SS	132	540	86	163	21	4	4	62	46	87	2	9	27-12	.302	.355	.367	.721	27	.955
2002—Toledo (Int'l)		SS	120	436	49	117	16	8	4	51	28	49	0	5	19-15	.268	.309	.369	.678	26	.959
—Detroit (A.L.)		SS-2B	18	72	4	24	3	0	1	6	3	10	0	0	0-1	.333	.360	.417	.777	5	.945
2003—Toledo (Int'l)		SS	64	224	28	50	10	0	2	18	22	32	3	3	22-4	.223	.299	.295	.593	18	.942
—Detroit (A.L.)		SS-3B-2B	69	221	24	49	6	1	0	8	18	37	0	1	6-3	.222	.278	.258	.536	14	.961
2004—Detroit (A.L.)		2B-SS-3B-OF	142	503	69	133	27	9	16	55	40	112	1	4	13-7	.264	.317	.449	.766	16	.974
Major League totals (3 years)			229	796	97	206	36	10	17	69	61	159	1	5	19-11	.259	.310	.393	.703	35	.967

INGE, BRANDON   3B/C

PERSONAL: Born May 19, 1977, in Lynchburg, Va. ... 5-11/195. ... Bats right, throws right. ... Full name: Charles Brandon Inge. ... Name pronounced: inj. ... High school: Brookville (Lynchburg, Va.). ... College: Virginia Commonwealth.

TRANSACTIONS/CAREER NOTES: Selected by Detroit Tigers organization in second round of 1998 free-agent draft. ... On disabled list (June 25-August 6, 2001); included rehabilitation assignments to GCL Tigers, West Michigan and Toledo. ... On disabled list (May 12-May 27, 2002); included rehabilitation assignment to Toledo. ... On disabled list (June 26-July 15, 2004).

2004 GAMES PLAYED BY POSITION (MLB): 3B—73, C—39, OF—26.

Year	Team (League)	Pos.	G	AB	R	H	2B	3B	HR	RBI	BB	SO	HBP	GDP	SB-CS	Avg.	OBP	SLG	OPS	E	Avg.
1998—Jamestown (N.Y.-Penn.)		C	51	191	24	44	10	1	8	29	17	53	6	4	8-8	.230	.312	.419	.730	6	.981
1999—W. Mich. (Mid.)		C	100	352	54	86	25	2	9	46	39	87	3	7	15-3	.244	.320	.403	.723	8	.990
2000—Jacksonville (Sou.)		C-OF	78	298	39	77	25	1	6	50	26	73	0	10	10-3	.258	.313	.409	.722	5	.990
—Toledo (Int'l)		C	55	190	24	42	9	3	5	20	15	51	1	5	2-1	.221	.280	.379	.659	3	.991
2001—Detroit (A.L.)		C	79	189	13	34	11	0	0	15	9	41	0	2	1-4	.180	.215	.238	.453	4	.989
—GC Tigers (GCL)		C	3	10	1	1	0	0	1	2	2	2	0	0	0-0	.100	.250	.400	.650	0	1.000
—W. Mich. (Mid.)		C	4	16	3	3	1	0	0	2	2	5	1	0	0-0	.188	.316	.250	.566	0	1.000
—Toledo (Int'l)		C	27	90	11	26	11	1	2	15	7	24	1	2	1-0	.289	.337	.500	.837	2	.989
2002—Toledo (Int'l)		C	21	65	10	17	2	4	3	13	11	16	2	2	1-3	.262	.380	.554	.934	4	.978
—Detroit (A.L.)		C-DH	95	321	27	65	15	3	7	24	24	101	4	7	1-3	.202	.266	.333	.599	1	.998
2003—Toledo (Int'l)		C-DH	39	142	15	39	9	0	5	15	11	23	0	6	3-1	.275	.327	.444	.770	1	1.000
—Detroit (A.L.)		C	104	330	32	67	15	3	8	30	24	79	5	8	4-4	.203	.265	.339	.605	2	.996
2004—Detroit (A.L.)		3B-C-OF	131	408	43	117	15	7	13	64	32	72	4	4	5-4	.287	.340	.453	.793	16	.966
Major League totals (4 years)			409	1248	115	283	56	13	28	133	89	293	13	21	11-15	.227	.283	.360	.642	23	.988

ISHII, KAZUHISA   **P**

PERSONAL: Born September 9, 1973, in Chiba, Japan. ... 6-0/200. ... Throws left, bats left. ... Name pronounced: kaz-u-heesa ee-shee-ee.

TRANSACTIONS/CAREER NOTES: Signed as a free agent by Los Angeles Dodgers (February 8, 2002). ... On disabled list (September 9, 2002-remainder of season; and July 30-August 30, 2003).

CAREER HITTING: 13-for-139 (.094), 9 R, 0 2B, 1 3B, 1 HR, 8 RBI.

Year Team (League)	W	L	Pct.	ERA	WHIP	G	GS	CG	ShO	Hld.	Sv.-Opp.	IP	H	R	ER	HR	BB-IBB	SO	Avg.
1992— Yakult (Jp. Cen.)	0	0	...	4.18	1.43	12	...	0	0	...	0-...	28.0	23	13	13	4	17-...	22	...
1993— Yakult (Jp. Cen.)	3	1	.750	4.70	1.45	19	...	1	0	...	0-...	59.1	48	33	31	8	38-...	66	...
1994— Yakult (Jp. Cen.)	7	5	.583	4.08	1.56	54	...	2	2	...	0-...	108.0	92	56	49	11	77-...	98	...
1995— Yakult (Jp. Cen.)	13	4	.765	2.76	1.24	26	...	3	0	...	1-...	153.0	112	49	47	14	77-...	159	...
1996— Yakult (Jp. Cen.)	1	5	.167	5.23	1.61	8	...	0	0	...	0-...	31.0	28	19	18	6	22-...	26	...
1997— Yakult (Jp. Cen.)	10	4	.714	1.91	1.05	18	...	2	2	...	0-...	117.2	73	28	25	5	50-...	120	...
1998— Yakult (Jp. Cen.)	14	6	.700	3.30	1.29	28	...	6	0	...	0-...	196.1	149	78	72	12	105-...	241	...
1999— Yakult (Jp. Cen.)	8	6	.571	4.80	1.46	23	...	2	0	...	0-...	133.0	123	75	71	16	71-...	162	...
2000— Yakult (Jp. Cen.)	10	9	.526	2.61	1.15	29	...	3	1	...	0-...	183.0	137	54	53	15	73-...	210	...
2001— Yakult (Jp. Cen.)	12	6	.667	3.39	1.19	27	...	0	0	...	0-...	175.0	135	74	66	18	73-...	173	...
2002— Los Angeles (N.L.)	14	10	.583	4.27	1.58	28	28	0	0	0	0-0	154.0	137	82	73	20	* 106-3	143	.240
2003— Los Angeles (N.L.)	9	7	.563	3.86	1.56	27	27	0	0	0	0-0	147.0	129	72	63	16	101-4	140	.238
2004— Los Angeles (N.L.)	13	8	.619	4.71	1.47	31	31	2	2	0	0-0	172.0	155	97	90	21	98-2	99	.246
Major League totals (3 years)	36	25	.590	4.30	1.53	86	86	2	2	0	0-0	473.0	421	251	226	57	305-9	382	.242

ISRINGHAUSEN, JASON   **P**

PERSONAL: Born September 7, 1972, in Brighton, Ill. ... 6-3/230. ... Throws right, bats right. ... Full name: Jason Derek Isringhausen. ... Name pronounced: IS-ring-how-zin. ... High school: Southwestern (Brighton, Ill.). ... Junior college: Lewis & Clark (Ill.) Community College.

TRANSACTIONS/CAREER NOTES: Selected by New York Mets organization in 44th round of 1991 free-agent draft. ... On disabled list (August 13-September 1, 1996). ... On disabled list (March 24-August 27, 1997); included rehabilitation assignments to Norfolk, GCL Mets and St. Lucie. ... On disabled list (March 21, 1998-entire season). ... Traded by Mets with P Greg McMichael to Oakland Athletics for P Billy Taylor (July 31, 1999). ... Signed as a free agent by St. Louis Cardinals (December 11, 2001). ... On disabled list (March 21-June 10, 2003); included rehabilitation assignment to Tennessee.

CAREER HITTING: 21-for-102 (.206), 11 R, 4 2B, 1 3B, 2 HR, 16 RBI.

Year Team (League)	W	L	Pct.	ERA	WHIP	G	GS	CG	ShO	Hld.	Sv.-Opp.	IP	H	R	ER	HR	BB-IBB	SO	Avg.
1992— GC Mets (GCL)	2	4	.333	4.34	1.48	6	6	0	0	...	0-...	29.0	26	19	14	0	17-1	25	.230
— Kingsport (Appalachian)	4	1	.800	3.25	1.22	7	6	1	1	...	0-...	36.0	32	22	13	2	12-1	24	.222
1993— Pittsfield (N.Y.-Penn.)	7	4	.636	3.29	1.06	15	15	2	0	...	0-...	90.1	68	45	33	7	28-0	104	.204
1994— St. Lucie (Fla. St.)	6	4	.600	2.23	1.02	14	14	6	3	...	0-...	101.0	76	31	25	2	27-2	59	.211
— Binghamton (Eastern)	5	4	.556	3.02	1.09	14	14	2	0	...	0-...	92.1	78	35	31	6	23-0	69	.234
1995— Binghamton (Eastern)	2	1	.667	2.85	0.93	6	6	1	0	...	0-...	41.0	26	15	13	1	12-0	59	.174
— Norfolk (Int'l)	9	1	.900	1.55	1.01	12	12	3	3	...	0-...	87.0	64	17	15	2	24-0	75	.203
— New York (N.L.)	9	2	.818	2.81	1.28	14	14	1	0	0	0-0	93.0	88	29	29	6	31-2	55	.254
1996— New York (N.L.)	6	14	.300	4.77	1.53	27	27	2	1	0	0-0	171.2	190	103	91	13	73-5	114	.284
1997— Norfolk (Int'l)	0	2	.000	4.05	1.40	3	3	0	0	...	0-...	20.0	20	10	9	4	8-0	17	.267
— GC Mets (GCL)	1	0	1.000	1.93	0.64	1	1	0	0	...	0-...	4.2	2	1	1	0	1-0	7	.125
— St. Lucie (Fla. St.)	1	0	1.000	0.00	1.08	2	2	0	0	...	0-...	12.0	8	1	0	0	5-0	15	.190
— New York (N.L.)	2	2	.500	7.58	2.09	6	6	0	0	0	0-0	29.2	40	27	25	3	22-0	25	.336
1998— New York (N.L.)				Did not play.															
1999— Norfolk (Int'l)	3	1	.750	2.29	1.04	12	8	0	0	...	0-...	51.0	33	18	13	4	20-0	51	.182
— New York (N.L.)	1	3	.250	6.41	1.65	13	5	0	0	0	1-1	39.1	43	29	28	7	22-2	31	.279
— Oakland (A.L.)	0	1	.000	2.13	1.30	20	0	0	0	0	8-8	25.1	21	6	6	2	12-2	20	.223
2000— Oakland (A.L.)	6	4	.600	3.78	1.43	66	0	0	0	0	33-40	69.0	67	34	29	6	32-5	57	.252
2001— Oakland (A.L.)	4	3	.571	2.65	1.08	65	0	0	0	0	34-43	71.1	54	24	21	5	23-5	74	.203
2002— St. Louis (N.L.)	3	2	.600	2.48	0.98	60	0	0	0	0	32-37	65.1	46	22	18	0	18-1	68	.199
2003— Tennessee (Sou.)	0	0	...	0.00	0.50	2	2	0	0	...	0-...	2.0	1	0	0	0	0-0	3	.143
— St. Louis (N.L.)	0	1	.000	2.36	1.17	40	0	0	0	1	22-25	42.0	31	14	11	2	18-1	41	.200
2004— St. Louis (N.L.)	4	2	.667	2.87	1.04	74	0	0	0	0	* 47-54	75.1	55	27	24	5	23-4	71	.199
American League totals (3 years)	10	8	.556	3.04	1.26	151	0	0	0	0	75-91	165.2	142	64	56	13	67-12	151	.227
National League totals (7 years)	25	26	.490	3.94	1.36	234	52	3	1	1	102-117	516.1	493	251	226	36	207-15	405	.253
Major League totals (9 years)	35	34	.507	3.72	1.33	385	52	3	1	1	177-208	682.0	635	315	282	49	274-27	556	.247

DIVISION SERIES RECORD

Year Team (League)	W	L	Pct.	ERA	WHIP	G	GS	CG	ShO	Hld.	Sv.-Opp.	IP	H	R	ER	HR	BB-IBB	SO	Avg.
2000— Oakland (A.L.)	0	0	...	0.00	0.50	2	0	0	0	0	1-1	2.0	1	0	0	0	0-0	3	.143
2001— Oakland (A.L.)	0	0	...	0.00	1.00	2	0	0	0	0	2-2	2.0	1	0	0	0	1-0	3	.143
2002— St. Louis (N.L.)	0	0	...	0.00	0.00	2	0	0	0	0	2-2	2.0	0	0	0	0	0-0	1	.000
2004— St. Louis (N.L.)	0	0	...	4.50	1.50	2	0	0	0	0	0-0	2.0	1	1	1	1	2-0	2	.143
Division series totals (4 years)	0	0	...	1.13	0.75	8	0	0	0	0	5-5	8.0	3	1	1	1	3-0	9	.111

CHAMPIONSHIP SERIES RECORD

Year Team (League)	W	L	Pct.	ERA	WHIP	G	GS	CG	ShO	Hld.	Sv.-Opp.	IP	H	R	ER	HR	BB-IBB	SO	Avg.
2002— St. Louis (N.L.)	0	0	...	4.50	2.00	2	0	0	0	0	1-1	2.0	1	1	1	0	3-2	3	.167
2004— St. Louis (N.L.)	0	1	.000	4.70	1.04	6	0	0	0	0	3-4	7.2	4	4	4	1	4-2	3	.154
Champ. series totals (2 years)	0	1	.000	4.66	1.24	8	0	0	0	0	4-5	9.2	5	5	5	1	7-4	6	.156

WORLD SERIES RECORD

Year Team (League)	W	L	Pct.	ERA	WHIP	G	GS	CG	ShO	Hld.	Sv.-Opp.	IP	H	R	ER	HR	BB-IBB	SO	Avg.
2004— St. Louis (N.L.)	0	0	...	0.00	1.00	2	0	0	0	0	0-0	2.0	1	0	0	0	1-0	2	.143

ALL-STAR GAME RECORD

Year Team (League)	W	L	Pct.	ERA	WHIP	G	GS	CG	ShO	Hld.	Sv.-Opp.	IP	H	R	ER	HR	BB-IBB	SO	Avg.
All-Star Game totals (1 year)	0	0	...	9.00	3.00	1	0	0	0	0	0-0	1.0	2	1	1	0	1-0	0	.400

IZTURIS, CESAR   **SS**

PERSONAL: Born February 10, 1980, in Barquisimeto, Venezuela. ... 5-9/175. ... Bats both, throws right. ... Full name: Cesar D. Izturis. ... Name pronounced: IS-tur-is.

TRANSACTIONS/CAREER NOTES: Signed as a non-drafted free agent by Toronto Blue Jays organization (July 11, 1996). ... Traded by Blue Jays with P Paul Quantrill to Los Angeles Dodgers for Ps Luke Prokopec and Chad Ricketts (December 13, 2001).

HONORS: Won N.L. Gold Glove at shortstop (2004).

2004 GAMES PLAYED BY POSITION (MLB): SS—159.

Year	Team (League)	Pos.	G	AB	R	H	2B	3B	HR	RBI	BB	SO	HBP	GDP	SB-CS	Avg.	OBP	SLG	OPS	E	Avg.
1997— St. Catharines (NY-Penn.) .		2B-SS	70	231	32	44	3	0	1	11	15	27	1	3	6-3	.190	.241	.216	.457	16	.951
1998— Hagerstown (SAL)		2B-3B-SS	130	413	56	108	13	1	1	38	20	43	2	5	20-9	.262	.297	.305	.603	29	.952
1999— Dunedin (Fla. St.)		2B-3B-SS	131	536	77	165	28	12	3	77	22	58	6	9	32-16	.308	.337	.422	.758	21	.969
2000— Syracuse (Int'l)		SS	132	435	54	95	16	5	0	27	20	44	1	5	21-11	.218	.253	.278	.531	12	.981
2001— Syracuse (Int'l)		SS-2B	87	342	32	100	16	3	2	35	10	22	1	4	24-9	.292	.310	.374	.684	16	.962
— Toronto (A.L.)		2B-SS	46	134	19	36	6	2	2	9	2	15	0	0	8-1	.269	.279	.388	.667	3	.985
2002— Los Angeles (N.L.)		SS-2B-DH	135	439	43	102	24	2	1	31	14	39	0	12	7-7	.232	.253	.303	.556	10	.979
2003— Los Angeles (N.L.)		SS	158	558	47	140	21	6	1	40	25	70	0	8	10-5	.251	.282	.315	.597	16	.977
2004— Los Angeles (N.L.)		SS	159	670	90	193	32	9	4	62	43	70	0	6	25-9	.288	.330	.381	.710	10	.985
American League totals (1 year)			46	134	19	36	6	2	2	9	2	15	0	0	8-1	.269	.279	.388	.667	3	.985
National League totals (3 years)			452	1667	180	435	77	17	6	133	82	179	0	26	42-21	.261	.294	.338	.632	36	.980
Major League totals (4 years)			498	1801	199	471	83	19	8	142	84	194	0	26	50-22	.262	.293	.342	.635	39	.981

DIVISION SERIES RECORD

Year	Team (League)	Pos.	G	AB	R	H	2B	3B	HR	RBI	BB	SO	HBP	GDP	SB-CS	Avg.	OBP	SLG	OPS	E	Avg.
2004— Los Angeles (N.L.)		SS	4	17	1	3	1	0	0	0	1	2	0	0	0-0	.176	.222	.235	.458	0	1.000

IZTURIS, MAICER — SS/2B

PERSONAL: Born September 12, 1980, in Barquisimeto, Venezuela. ... 5-8/155. ... Bats both, throws right. ... Full name: Maicer E. Izturis.
TRANSACTIONS/CAREER NOTES: Signed as a non-drafted free agent by Cleveland Indians organization (April 1, 1998). ... Traded by Indians with OF Ryan Church to Montreal Expos for P Scott Stewart (January 5, 2004). ... Expos franchise transferred to Washington, D.C., for 2005 season.
2004 GAMES PLAYED BY POSITION (MLB): SS—23, 2B—10.

Year	Team (League)	Pos.	G	AB	R	H	2B	3B	HR	RBI	BB	SO	HBP	GDP	SB-CS	Avg.	OBP	SLG	OPS	E	Avg.
1998— Burlington (Appal.)		SS	55	217	33	63	8	2	2	33	17	32	0	4	16-6	.290	.342	.373	.715	20	.929
1999— Columbus (S. Atl.)		SS	57	220	46	66	5	3	4	23	20	28	1	2	14-2	.300	.357	.405	.761	12	.939
2000— Columbus (S. Atl.)		SS	10	29	4	8	1	0	0	1	3	3	0	1	0-0	.276	.344	.310	.654	2	.846
2001— Kinston (Caro.)		2B	114	433	47	104	16	6	1	39	31	81	8	8	32-9	.240	.300	.312	.612	17	.959
2002— Kinston (Caro.)		2B	58	233	28	61	13	1	1	30	24	26	1	2	24-6	.262	.332	.339	.671	8	.967
— Akron (East.)		2B	67	253	34	70	12	7	0	32	17	28	3	10	8-4	.277	.326	.379	.706	11	.961
2003— Akron (East.)		2B-SS	53	218	31	61	11	5	1	20	24	23	1	4	14-6	.280	.351	.390	.741	12	.946
— Buffalo (Int'l)		SS-2B	85	301	43	79	16	4	2	29	24	28	1	14	14-6	.262	.317	.362	.679	13	.967
2004— Edmonton (PCL)		SS-2B-DH	99	376	65	127	19	2	3	36	57	30	4	12	14-12	.338	.428	.423	.846	12	.969
— Montreal (N.L.)		SS-2B	32	107	10	22	5	2	1	4	10	20	2	1	4-0	.206	.286	.318	.603	8	.948
Major League totals (1 year)			32	107	10	22	5	2	1	4	10	20	2	1	4-0	.206	.286	.318	.603	8	.948

JACKSON, DAMIAN — 2B/OF

PERSONAL: Born August 16, 1973, in Los Angeles, Calif. ... 5-11/185. ... Bats right, throws right. ... Full name: Damian Jacques Jackson. ... High school: Ygnacio Valley (Concord, Calif.). ... Junior college: Laney (Calif.).
TRANSACTIONS/CAREER NOTES: Selected by Cleveland Indians organization in 44th round of 1991 free-agent draft. ... Traded by Indians with Ps Danny Graves, Jim Crowell and Scott Winchester to Cincinnati Reds for P John Smiley and IF Jeff Branson (July 31, 1997). ... Traded by Reds with OF Reggie Sanders and P Josh Harris to San Diego Padres for OF Greg Vaughn and OF/1B Mark Sweeney (February 2, 1999). ... On disabled list (May 13-June 22, 2001); included rehabilitation assignment to Portland. ... Traded by Padres with C Matt Walbeck to Detroit Tigers for C Javier Cardona and OF Rich Gomez (March 24, 2002). ... On disabled list (April 7-22, 2002). ... Released by Tigers (November 20, 2002). ... Signed by Boston Red Sox (December 18, 2002). ... Signed as a free agent by Colorado Rockies organization (January 5, 2004). ... Released by Rockies (March 28, 2004). ... Signed by Chicago Cubs organization (April 1, 2004). ... Traded by Cubs to Kansas City Royals for IF Gookie Dawkins (May 31, 2004).
2004 GAMES PLAYED BY POSITION (MLB): 2B—6, OF—5, DH—2, SS—1.

Year	Team (League)	Pos.	G	AB	R	H	2B	3B	HR	RBI	BB	SO	HBP	GDP	SB-CS	Avg.	OBP	SLG	OPS	E	Avg.
1992— Burlington (Appal.)		SS	62	226	32	56	12	1	0	23	32	31	6	1	29-5	.248	.352	.310	.662	23	.933
1993— Columbus (S. Atl.)		SS	108	350	70	94	19	3	6	45	41	61	5	1	26-7	.269	.353	.391	.744	52	.908
1994— Cant./Akr. (Eastern)		SS-OF	138	531	85	143	29	5	5	60	60	121	5	8	37-16	.269	.346	.371	.717	54	.927
1995— Cant./Akr. (Eastern)		SS	131	484	67	120	20	2	3	34	65	103	9	6	40-22	.248	.348	.316	.664	36	.939
1996— Buffalo (A.A.)		SS	133	452	77	116	15	1	12	49	48	78	7	7	24-7	.257	.333	.374	.707	29	.954
— Cleveland (A.L.)		SS	5	10	2	3	2	0	0	1	1	4	0	0	0-0	.300	.364	.500	.864	0	1.000
1997— Buffalo (A.A.)		SS-2B-OF	73	266	51	78	12	0	4	13	37	45	3		20-8	.293	.383	.383	.767	23	.942
— Cleveland (A.L.)		SS-2B	8	9	2	1	0	0	0	0	0	1	1	0	1-0	.111	.200	.111	.311	0	1.000
— Indianapolis (A.A.)		2B-SS	19	71	12	19	6	1	0	7	10	17	1	...	4-1	.268	.361	.380	.742	5	.948
— Cincinnati (N.L.)		SS-2B	12	27	6	6	2	1	1	2	4	7	0	0	1-1	.222	.323	.481	.804	1	.971
1998— Cincinnati (N.L.)		SS-OF	13	38	4	12	5	0	0	7	6	4	0	1	2-0	.316	.400	.447	.847	1	.976
— Indianapolis (Int'l)		SS-OF	131	517	102	135	36	10	6	49	62	125	10	2	25-10	.261	.349	.404	.753	44	.938
1999— San Diego (N.L.)		SS-2B-OF	133	388	56	87	20	2	9	39	53	105	3	2	34-10	.224	.320	.356	.676	26	.948
2000— San Diego (N.L.)		SS-2B-OF	138	470	68	120	27	6	6	37	42	108	3	7	28-6	.255	.345	.343	.721	25	.960
2001— San Diego (N.L.)		2B-SS-OF	122	440	67	106	21	6	4	38	44	128	6	6	23-6	.241	.316	.343	.660	8	.986
— Portland (PCL)		SS	3	10	4	3	3	0	0	0	3	1	0	0	0-1	.300	.462	.600	1.062	0	1.000
2002— Detroit (A.L.)		2-S-O-DH-3	81	245	31	63	20	1	1	25	21	36	3	3	12-3	.257	.320	.359	.679	8	.972
2003— Boston (A.L.)		2-O-S-DH-3-1-B	109	161	34	42	7	0	1	13	8	28	0	4	16-8	.261	.294	.323	.617	9	.951
2004— Iowa (PCL)		SS-OF-2B	28	97	18	27	6	5	3	13	11	20	0	0	3-1	.278	.352	.536	.888	1	.990
— Chicago (N.L.)		2B	7	15	1	1	0	0	1	1	3	6	0	0	0-0	.067	.222	.267	.489	1	.957
— Kansas City (A.L.)		OF-DH-2-S	14	15	1	2	2	0	0	2	1	6	0	0	0-0	.133	.188	.267	.454	0	1.000
— Omaha (PCL)		SS-2B	48	169	46	52	13	1	8	27	30	36	6	3	12-2	.308	.425	.538	.964	9	.961
American League totals (5 years)			217	440	70	111	31	1	2	41	31	75	4	7	29-11	.252	.305	.341	.646	17	.966
National League totals (6 years)			425	1378	202	332	75	15	21	124	172	358	12	16	88-23	.241	.328	.363	.691	62	.966
Major League totals (9 years)			642	1818	272	443	106	16	23	165	203	433	16	23	117-34	.244	.323	.358	.680	79	.966

DIVISION SERIES RECORD

Year	Team (League)	Pos.	G	AB	R	H	2B	3B	HR	RBI	BB	SO	HBP	GDP	SB-CS	Avg.	OBP	SLG	OPS	E	Avg.
2003— Boston (A.L.)		2B	4	5	0	0	0	0	0	0	0	2	0	0	0-0	.000	.000	.000	.000	0	1.000

CHAMPIONSHIP SERIES RECORD

Year	Team (League)	Pos.	G	AB	R	H	2B	3B	HR	RBI	BB	SO	HBP	GDP	SB-CS	Avg.	OBP	SLG	OPS	E	Avg.
2003— Boston (A.L.)		2B	5	3	0	1	0	0	0	1	0	1	0	0	0-1	.333	.333	.333	.667	1	.857

JACKSON, EDWIN   P

PERSONAL: Born September 9, 1983, in Neu-Ulm, West Germany. ... 6-3/190. ... Throws right, bats right. ... High school: Shaw (Columbus, Ga.).

TRANSACTIONS/CAREER NOTES: Selected by Los Angeles Dodgers organization in sixth round of 2001 free-agent draft. ... On disabled list (July 9-September 7, 2004); included rehabilitation assignment to Las Vegas.

CAREER HITTING: 1-for-10 (.100), 0 R, 0 2B, 0 3B, 0 HR, 1 RBI.

Year Team (League)	W	L	Pct.	ERA	WHIP	G	GS	CG	ShO	Hld.	Sv.-Opp.	IP	H	R	ER	HR	BB-IBB	SO	Avg.
2001— GC Dodgers (GCL)	2	1	.667	2.45	1.50	12	2	0	0	...	0-...	22.0	14	12	6	1	19-0	23	.173
2002— South Georgia (S.Atl.)	5	2	.714	1.98	1.07	19	19	0	0	...	0-...	104.2	79	34	23	2	33-0	85	.206
2003— Jacksonville (Southern)	7	7	.500	3.70	1.17	27	27	0	0	...	0-...	148.1	121	68	61	9	53-0	157	.220
— Los Angeles (N.L.)	2	1	.667	2.45	1.27	4	3	0	0	0	0-0	22.0	17	6	6	2	11-1	19	.221
2004— Las Vegas (PCL)	6	4	.600	5.86	1.60	19	19	0	0	...	0-...	90.2	90	65	59	4	55-1	70	.265
— Los Angeles (N.L.)	2	1	.667	7.30	1.70	8	5	0	0	0	0-0	24.2	31	20	20	7	11-1	16	.307
Major League totals (2 years)	**4**	**2**	**.667**	**5.01**	**1.50**	**12**	**8**	**0**	**0**	**0**	**0-0**	**46.2**	**48**	**26**	**26**	**9**	**22-2**	**35**	**.270**

JACKSON, MIKE   P

PERSONAL: Born December 22, 1964, in Houston, Texas. ... 6-0/219. ... Throws right, bats right. ... Full name: Michael Ray Jackson. ... High school: Forest Brook (Houston). ... Junior college: Hill (Texas).

TRANSACTIONS/CAREER NOTES: Selected by Philadelphia Phillies organization in 29th round of June 1983 free-agent draft; did not sign. ... Selected by Phillies organization in secondary phase of January 1984 free-agent draft. ... On disabled list (August 6-21, 1987). ... Traded by Phillies with OFs Glenn Wilson and Dave Brundage to Seattle Mariners for OF Phil Bradley and P Tim Fortugno (December 9, 1987). ... Traded by Mariners with Ps Bill Swift and Dave Burba to San Francisco Giants for OF Kevin Mitchell and P Mike Remlinger (December 11, 1991). ... On disabled list (July 24-August 9, 1993; June 17-July 2 and July 7, 1994-remainder of season). ... Signed as a free agent by Cincinnati Reds (April 8, 1995). ... On disabled list (April 20-June 5, 1995); included rehabilitation assignments to Chattanooga and Indianapolis. ... Signed as a free agent by Mariners (February 2, 1996). ... Signed as a free agent by Cleveland Indians (December 12, 1996). ... Signed as a free agent by Phillies (December 7, 1999). ... On disabled list (March 31, 2000-entire season). ... Signed as a free agent by Houston Astros (December 14, 2000). ... Signed as a free agent by Minnesota Twins organization (January 23, 2002). ... On disabled list (July 23-August 15, 2002). ... Signed as a free agent by Arizona Diamondbacks organization (January 29, 2003). ... Released by Diamondbacks (March 29, 2003). ... Signed as a free agent by Chicago White Sox organization (December 22, 2003). ... Released by White Sox (August 30, 2004).

CAREER HITTING: 5-for-28 (.179), 3 R, 2 2B, 0 3B, 0 HR, 1 RBI.

Year Team (League)	W	L	Pct.	ERA	WHIP	G	GS	CG	ShO	Hld.	Sv.-Opp.	IP	H	R	ER	HR	BB-IBB	SO	Avg.
1984— Spartanburg (SAL)	7	2	.778	2.68	1.28	14	0	0	0	...	0-...	80.2	53	35	24	8	50-0	77	.182
1985— Peninsula (Caro.)	7	9	.438	4.60	1.44	31	18	0	0	...	1-...	125.1	127	71	64	11	53-1	96	.259
1986— Reading (East.)	2	3	.400	1.66	1.08	30	0	0	0	...	6-...	43.1	25	9	8	1	22-2	42	.168
— Portland (PCL)	3	1	.750	3.18	1.37	17	0	0	0	...	3-...	22.2	18	8	8	2	13-4	23	.217
— Philadelphia (N.L.)	0	0	...	3.38	1.20	9	0	0	0	0	0-1	13.1	12	5	5	2	4-1	3	.250
1987— Philadelphia (N.L.)	3	10	.231	4.20	1.32	55	7	0	0	6	1-2	109.1	88	55	51	16	56-6	93	.219
— Maine (International)	1	0	1.000	0.82	1.27	2	2	0	0	...	0-...	11.0	9	2	1	0	5-1	13	.225
1988— Seattle (A.L.)	6	5	.545	2.63	1.18	62	0	0	0	10	4-11	99.1	74	37	29	10	43-10	76	.209
1989— Seattle (A.L.)	4	6	.400	3.17	1.36	65	0	0	0	9	7-10	99.1	81	43	35	8	54-6	94	.223
1990— Seattle (A.L.)	5	7	.417	4.54	1.40	63	0	0	0	13	3-12	77.1	64	42	39	8	44-12	69	.229
1991— Seattle (A.L.)	7	7	.500	3.25	1.11	72	0	0	0	9	14-22	88.2	64	35	32	5	34-11	74	.201
1992— San Francisco (N.L.)	6	6	.500	3.73	1.33	67	0	0	0	9	2-3	82.0	76	35	34	7	33-10	80	.252
1993— San Francisco (N.L.)	6	6	.500	3.03	1.06	81	0	0	0	34	1-6	77.1	58	28	26	7	24-6	70	.204
1994— San Francisco (N.L.)	3	2	.600	1.49	0.80	36	0	0	0	9	4-6	42.1	23	8	7	4	11-0	51	.164
1995— Chattanooga (Southern)	0	0	...	0.00	0.67	3	2	0	0	...	0-...	3.0	2	0	0	0	0-0	2	.182
— Indianapolis (A.A.)	0	0	...	0.00	0.00	2	1	0	0	...	0-...	2.0	0	0	0	0	0-0	1	.000
— Cincinnati (N.L.)	6	1	.857	2.39	1.16	40	0	0	0	9	2-4	49.0	38	13	13	5	19-1	41	.213
1996— Seattle (A.L.)	1	1	.500	3.63	1.18	73	0	0	0	15	6-9	72.0	61	32	29	11	24-3	70	.225
1997— Cleveland (A.L.)	2	5	.286	3.24	1.17	71	0	0	0	14	15-17	75.0	59	33	27	3	29-5	74	.215
1998— Cleveland (A.L.)	1	1	.500	1.55	0.88	69	0	0	0	1	40-45	64.0	43	11	11	4	13-0	55	.195
1999— Cleveland (A.L.)	3	4	.429	4.06	1.25	72	0	0	0	1	39-43	68.2	60	32	31	11	26-1	55	.232
2000— Philadelphia (N.L.)	Did not play.																		
2001— Houston (N.L.)	5	3	.625	4.70	1.30	67	0	0	0	19	4-9	69.0	68	36	36	14	22-3	46	.260
2002— Minnesota (A.L.)	2	3	.400	3.27	1.31	58	0	0	0	20	0-2	55.0	59	20	20	5	13-3	29	.284
2004— Chicago (A.L.)	2	0	1.000	5.01	1.50	45	0	0	0	3	0-0	46.2	55	27	26	7	15-2	26	.294
American League totals (10 years)	**33**	**39**	**.458**	**3.37**	**1.23**	**650**	**0**	**0**	**0**	**94**	**128-170**	**746.0**	**620**	**312**	**279**	**72**	**295-53**	**622**	**.227**
National League totals (7 years)	**29**	**28**	**.509**	**3.50**	**1.20**	**355**	**7**	**0**	**0**	**86**	**14-31**	**442.1**	**363**	**180**	**172**	**55**	**169-27**	**384**	**.225**
Major League totals (17 years)	**62**	**67**	**.481**	**3.42**	**1.22**	**1005**	**7**	**0**	**0**	**180**	**142-201**	**1188.1**	**983**	**492**	**451**	**127**	**464-80**	**1006**	**.226**

DIVISION SERIES RECORD

Year Team (League)	W	L	Pct.	ERA	WHIP	G	GS	CG	ShO	Hld.	Sv.-Opp.	IP	H	R	ER	HR	BB-IBB	SO	Avg.
1995— Cincinnati (N.L.)	0	0	...	0.00	1.09	3	0	0	0	1	0-0	3.2	4	0	0	0	0-0	1	.267
1997— Cleveland (A.L.)	1	0	1.000	0.00	0.92	4	0	0	0	1	0-0	4.1	3	0	0	0	1-0	5	.214
1998— Cleveland (A.L.)	0	0	...	4.50	1.00	3	0	0	0	1	3-3	4.0	3	2	2	1	1-0	1	.214
1999— Cleveland (A.L.)	0	0	...	4.50	1.50	2	0	0	0	0	0-0	2.0	2	1	1	0	1-1	1	.250
2001— Houston (N.L.)	0	1	.000	27.00	4.50	2	0	0	0	0	0-1	.2	3	3	2	0	0-0	1	.500
2002— Minnesota (A.L.)	0	0	...	0.00	1.50	1	0	0	0	0	0-0	.2	1	0	0	0	0-0	0	.500
Division series totals (6 years)	**1**	**1**	**.500**	**2.93**	**1.24**	**15**	**0**	**0**	**0**	**2**	**3-4**	**15.1**	**16**	**6**	**5**	**1**	**3-1**	**9**	**.271**

CHAMPIONSHIP SERIES RECORD

Year Team (League)	W	L	Pct.	ERA	WHIP	G	GS	CG	ShO	Hld.	Sv.-Opp.	IP	H	R	ER	HR	BB-IBB	SO	Avg.
1995— Cincinnati (N.L.)	0	1	.000	23.14	3.86	3	0	0	0	0	0-0	2.1	5	6	6	1	4-2	1	.455
1997— Cleveland (A.L.)	0	0	...	0.00	0.46	5	0	0	0	3	0-0	4.1	1	0	0	0	1-0	7	.077
1998— Cleveland (A.L.)	0	0	...	0.00	1.00	1	0	0	0	0	1-1	1.0	0	0	0	0	0-0	2	.000
2002— Minnesota (A.L.)	0	0	...	27.00	7.00	3	0	0	0	0	0-0	1.0	5	3	3	0	2-1	2	.625
Champ. series totals (4 years)	**0**	**1**	**.000**	**9.35**	**2.08**	**12**	**0**	**0**	**0**	**3**	**1-1**	**8.2**	**11**	**9**	**9**	**1**	**7-3**	**12**	**.306**

WORLD SERIES RECORD

Year Team (League)	W	L	Pct.	ERA	WHIP	G	GS	CG	ShO	Hld.	Sv.-Opp.	IP	H	R	ER	HR	BB-IBB	SO	Avg.
1997— Cleveland (A.L.)	0	0	...	1.93	1.71	4	0	0	0	2	0-1	4.2	5	1	1	0	3-1	4	.263

JACOBSEN, BUCKY — 1B

PERSONAL: Born August 30, 1975, in Riverton, Wyo. ... 6-4/220. ... Bats right, throws right. ... Full name: Larry William Jacobsen. ... High school: Hermiston. ... College: Lewis-Clark (Idaho) State.

TRANSACTIONS/CAREER NOTES: Selected by Milwaukee Brewers organization in seventh round of 1997 free-agent draft. ... Released by Brewers (June 15, 2002). ... Signed as a free agent by St. Louis Cardinals organization (June 24, 2002). ... Signed as a free agent by Seattle Mariners organization (November 10, 2003). ... On disabled list (September 17, 2004-remainder of season).

2004 GAMES PLAYED BY POSITION (MLB): 1B—21, DH—20.

Year Team (League)	Pos.	G	AB	R	H	2B	3B	HR	RBI	BB	SO	HBP	GDP	SB-CS	Avg.	OBP	SLG	OPS	E	Avg.
1997—Ogden (Pio.)	OF	67	238	57	78	17	2	8	52	41	44	3	4	6-6	.328	.427	.517	.943	7	.925
1998—Beloit (Midw.)	OF-1B	135	499	96	146	31	1	27	100	83	133	8	10	5-2	.293	.399	.521	.920	8	.968
1999—Huntsville (Sou.)	OF-1B	47	150	20	29	6	1	3	19	20	32	3	4	4-1	.193	.292	.307	.599	10	.941
—Stockton (Calif.)	OF-1B	46	156	22	39	8	0	5	22	21	40	4	4	3-3	.250	.352	.397	.749	1	.971
2000—Huntsville (Sou.)	1B	81	268	44	74	14	0	18	50	51	69	4	8	4-2	.276	.394	.530	.924	8	.989
2001—Huntsville (Sou.)	1B	27	93	21	41	9	0	10	28	15	14	1	3	1-2	.441	.518	.860	1.378	3	.984
—Indianapolis (Int'l)	1B	86	300	42	74	18	1	12	53	26	78	4	13	0-0	.247	.312	.433	.746	10	.986
2002—Huntsville (Sou.)	1B-OF	61	198	31	50	9	2	11	39	22	41	4	6	2-2	.253	.336	.485	.821	6	.986
—New Haven (East.)	1B-OF	34	102	13	30	11	0	4	21	9	25	2	0	0-0	.294	.360	.520	.879	2	.984
2003—Tennessee (Sou.)	1B	131	447	84	133	24	1	31	84	56	91	13	7	3-1	.298	.388	.564	.951	16	.985
2004—Tacoma (PCL)	DH-1B	81	292	59	91	22	1	26	86	50	88	8	8	1-1	.312	.422	.661	1.070	1	.976
—Seattle (A.L.)	1B-DH	42	160	17	44	9	0	9	28	14	47	1	3	0-0	.275	.335	.500	.835	3	.984
Major League totals (1 year)		42	160	17	44	9	0	9	28	14	47	1	3	0-0	.275	.335	.500	.835	3	.984

JARVIS, KEVIN — P

PERSONAL: Born August 1, 1969, in Lexington, Ky. ... 6-2/200. ... Throws right, bats left. ... Full name: Kevin Thomas Jarvis. ... High school: Tates Creek (Lexington, Ky.). ... College: Wake Forest.

TRANSACTIONS/CAREER NOTES: Selected by Cincinnati Reds organization in 21st round of 1991 free-agent draft. ... Claimed on waivers by Detroit Tigers (May 2, 1997). ... Claimed on waivers by Minnesota Twins (May 9, 1997). ... Claimed on waivers by Tigers (June 17, 1997). ... On disabled list (June 25-July 14, 1997); included rehabilitation assignment to Toledo. ... Released by Tigers (December 12, 1997). ... Signed by Chunichi Dragons of the Japan Central League (January 23, 1998). ... Signed as a free agent by Reds organization (August 27, 1998). ... Released by Reds (September 9, 1998). ... Signed by Oakland Athletics organization (January 4, 1999). ... On disabled list (April 19-June 4, 1999); included rehabilitation assignment to Modesto. ... Signed as a free agent by Colorado Rockies organization (December 1, 1999). ... On disabled list (July 28-September 1, 2000); included rehabilitation assignment to Colorado Springs. ... Signed as a free agent by San Diego Padres (January 5, 2001). ... On disabled list (April 18-May 5, May 10-June 27 and July 12, 2002-remainder of season); included rehabilitation assignments to Mobile and Lake Elsinore. ... On disabled list (March 26, 2003-June 13, 2003); included rehabilitation assignment to Lake Elsinore. ... Traded by Padres with IF Dave Hansen, C Wiki Gonzalez and OF Vince Faison to Seattle Mariners for IF Jeff Cirillo and RHP Brian Sweeney (January 6, 2004). ... Released by Mariners (May 4, 2004). ... Signed by Colorado Rockies organization (May 10, 2004). ... Released by Rockies (July 2, 2004). ... Signed by Pittsburgh Pirates organization (July 8, 2004).

CAREER HITTING: 30-for-188 (.160), 19 R, 6 2B, 0 3B, 1 HR, 14 RBI.

Year Team (League)	W	L	Pct.	ERA	WHIP	G	GS	CG	ShO	Hld.	Sv.-Opp.	IP	H	R	ER	HR	BB-IBB	SO	Avg.
1991—Princeton (Appalachian)	5	6	.455	2.42	1.19	13	13	4	1	...	0-...	85.2	73	34	23	6	29-3	79	.220
1992—Cedar Rapids (Midw.)	0	0		0.00	1.00	1	0	0	0	...	0-...	1.0	1	0	0	0	0-0	0	.333
—Char., W.Va. (SAL)	6	8	.429	3.11	1.20	28	18	2	1	...	0-...	133.0	123	59	46	3	37-1	131	.244
1993—Winston-Salem (Caro.)	8	7	.533	3.41	1.25	21	20	2	1	...	0-...	145.0	133	68	55	13	48-2	101	.241
—Chattanooga (Southern)	3	1	.750	1.69	0.99	7	3	2	0	...	0-...	37.1	26	7	7	4	11-0	18	.203
1994—Cincinnati (N.L.)	1	1	.500	7.13	1.53	6	3	0	0	0	0-0	17.2	22	14	14	4	5-0	10	.301
—Indianapolis (A.A.)	10	2	.833	3.54	1.28	21	20	2	0	...	0-...	132.1	136	55	52	13	34-2	90	.261
1995—Indianapolis (A.A.)	4	2	.667	4.45	1.32	10	10	1	0	...	0-...	60.2	62	33	30	2	18-1	37	.256
—Cincinnati (N.L.)	3	4	.429	5.70	1.56	19	11	1	0	0	0-0	79.0	91	56	50	13	32-2	33	.292
1996—Indianapolis (A.A.)	4	3	.571	5.06	1.34	8	8	0	0	...	0-...	42.2	45	27	24	3	12-0	32	.263
—Cincinnati (N.L.)	8	9	.471	5.98	1.62	24	20	2	1	0	0-0	120.1	152	93	80	17	43-5	63	.305
1997—Cincinnati (N.L.)	0	1	.000	10.13	2.10	9	0	0	0	0	1-1	13.1	21	16	15	4	7-0	12	.344
—Minnesota (A.L.)	0	0		12.46	2.38	6	2	0	0	0	0-0	13.0	23	18	18	4	8-0	9	.371
—Detroit (A.L.)	0	3	.000	5.40	1.66	17	3	0	0	0	0-0	41.2	55	28	25	9	14-0	27	.318
—Toledo (International)	0	1	.000	6.75	1.38	2	2	0	0	...	0-...	8.0	7	6	6	0	4-0	5	.226
1998—Chunichi (Jp. Cn.)	1	2	.333	4.41	1.41	4	3	0	0	...	0-...	16.1	18	8	8	...	5-...	7	...
—Indianapolis (Int'l)	1	0	1.000	9.00	1.57	2	2	0	0	0	0-0	7.0	10	7	7	3	1-0	5	.323
1999—Oakland (A.L.)	0	1	.000	11.57	2.43	4	1	0	0	0	0-0	14.0	28	19	18	6	6-0	11	.418
—Modesto (Calif.)	0	0		1.29	0.71	2	2	0	0	...	0-...	7.0	4	1	1	0	1-0	5	.167
—Vancouver (PCL)	10	2	.833	3.41	1.32	17	16	2	1	...	0-...	103.0	110	47	39	14	26-0	64	.270
2000—Colo. Springs (PCL)	3	2	.600	0.69	0.79	7	7	0	0	...	0-...	39.0	18	6	3	1	13-0	18	.138
—Colorado (N.L.)	3	4	.429	5.95	1.49	24	19	0	0	0	0-0	115.0	138	83	76	26	33-3	60	.300
2001—San Diego (N.L.)	12	11	.522	4.79	1.23	32	32	1	1	0	0-0	193.1	189	107	103	37	49-4	133	.254
2002—San Diego (N.L.)	2	4	.333	4.37	1.31	7	7	0	0	0	0-0	35.0	36	19	17	5	10-1	24	.269
—Mobile (Sou.)	0	0		0.00	0.67	1	1	0	0	0	0-...	3.0	2	0	0	0	0-0	3	.182
—Lake Elsinore (Calif.)	1	0	1.000	0.00	0.60	1	1	0	0	0	0-...	5.0	3	0	0	0	1-0	1	.133
2003—Lake Elsinore (Calif.)	2	1	.667	4.09	1.00	3	3	0	0	...	0-...	22.0	18	11	10	1	4-0	19	.222
—San Diego (N.L.)	4	8	.333	5.87	1.58	16	16	0	0	0	0-0	92.0	113	65	60	15	32-5	49	.304
2004—Seattle (A.L.)	1	0	1.000	8.31	1.92	8	0	0	0	0	0-0	13.0	20	12	12	4	5-0	7	.345
—Colo. Springs (PCL)	0	4	.000	5.79	1.45	6	6	1	0	...	0-...	37.1	44	34	24	12	10-0	25	.293
—Colorado (N.L.)	0	0		27.00	5.00	2	0	0	0	0	0-0	2.0	6	6	6	1	4-2	0	.600
—Nashville (PCL)	2	5	.286	4.11	1.60	11	11	1	0	...	0-...	65.2	93	31	30	3	12-1	46	.338
American League totals (3 years)	1	4	.200	8.04	1.95	35	6	0	0	0	0-0	81.2	126	77	73	23	33-0	54	.350
National League totals (9 years)	33	42	.440	5.67	1.47	139	108	4	3	0	1-1	667.2	768	459	421	122	215-22	384	.288
Major League totals (10 years)	34	46	.425	5.93	1.52	174	114	4	3	0	1-1	749.1	894	536	494	145	248-22	438	.296

JENKINS, GEOFF — OF

PERSONAL: Born July 21, 1974, in Olympia, Wash. ... 6-1/212. ... Bats left, throws right. ... Full name: Geoff Scott Jenkins. ... High school: Cordova Senior (Rancho Cordova, Calif.). ... College: USC.

TRANSACTIONS/CAREER NOTES: Selected by Milwaukee Brewers organization in first round (ninth pick overall) of 1995 free-agent draft. ... On disabled list (May 7-29, 2000). ... On disabled list (May 2-19 and July 29-August 28, 2001); included rehabilitation assignment to Beloit. ... On disabled list (June 18, 2002-remainder of season). ... On disabled list (March 21-April 9 and August 29, 2003-remainder of season); included rehabilitation assignment to Huntsville.

J

RECORDS: Shares major league record for most strikeouts, extra-inning game (6, June 8, 2004).
2004 GAMES PLAYED BY POSITION (MLB): OF—156.

Year Team (League)	Pos.	G	AB	R	H	2B	3B	HR	RBI	BB	SO	HBP	GDP	SB-CS	Avg.	OBP	SLG	OPS	E	Avg.
1995—Helena (Pio.)	OF	7	28	2	9	0	1	0	9	3	11	0	0	0-2	.321	.375	.393	.768	0	1.000
—Stockton (Calif.)	OF	13	47	13	12	2	0	3	12	10	12	0	0	2-0	.255	.373	.489	.862	2	.895
—El Paso (Texas)	OF	22	79	12	22	4	2	1	13	8	23	0	1	3-1	.278	.341	.418	.759	7	.857
1996—El Paso (Texas)	DH	22	77	17	22	5	4	1	11	12	21	2	2	1-2	.286	.391	.494	.885	...	...
—Stockton (Calif.)	DH-OF	37	138	27	48	8	4	3	25	20	32	3	3	3-3	.348	.433	.529	.962	0	1.000
1997—Tucson (PCL)	SS-OF	93	347	44	82	24	3	10	56	33	87	3	7	0-2	.236	.308	.409	.717	5	.961
1998—Louisville (Int'l)	OF	55	215	38	71	10	4	7	52	14	39	5	6	1-1	.330	.381	.512	.893	2	.979
—Milwaukee (N.L.)	OF	84	262	33	60	12	1	9	28	20	61	2	7	1-3	.229	.288	.386	.673	4	.968
1999—Milwaukee (N.L.)	OF	135	447	70	140	43	3	21	82	35	87	7	10	5-1	.313	.371	.564	.935	7	.974
2000—Milwaukee (N.L.)	OF	135	512	100	155	36	4	34	94	33	135	15	9	11-1	.303	.360	.588	.948	7	.975
2001—Milwaukee (N.L.)	OF	105	397	60	105	21	1	20	63	36	120	8	11	4-2	.264	.334	.474	.808	3	.986
—Beloit (Midw.)	OF	1	3	1	1	1	0	0	1	1	1	0	0	0-0	.333	.500	.667	1.167	0	...
2002—Milwaukee (N.L.)	OF	67	243	35	59	17	1	10	29	22	60	6	8	1-2	.243	.320	.444	.764	1	.992
2003—Huntsville (Sou.)	OF	6	20	6	5	0	0	2	3	1	7	0	0	1-0	.250	.286	.550	.836	0	1.000
—Milwaukee (N.L.)	OF-DH	124	487	81	144	30	2	28	95	58	120	6	12	0-0	.296	.375	.538	.913	0	1.000
2004—Milwaukee (N.L.)	OF	157	617	88	163	36	6	27	93	46	152	12	19	3-1	.264	.325	.473	.798	1	.996
Major League totals (7 years)		807	2965	467	826	195	18	149	484	250	735	56	76	25-10	.279	.344	.507	.851	23	.985

JENNINGS, JASON   P

PERSONAL: Born July 17, 1978, in Dallas, Texas. ... 6-2/245. ... Throws right, bats left. ... Full name: Jason Ryan Jennings. ... High school: Dr. Ralph H. Poteet (Mesquite, Texas). ... College: Baylor. ... Son of Jim Jennings, member of Texas Rangers organization.
TRANSACTIONS/CAREER NOTES: Selected by Arizona Diamondbacks organization in 54th round of 1996 free-agent draft; did not sign. ... Selected by Colorado Rockies organization in first round (16th pick overall) of 1999 free-agent draft.
HONORS: Named N.L. Rookie Pitcher of the Year by THE SPORTING NEWS (2002). ... Named N.L. Rookie of the Year by Baseball Writers' Association of America (2002).
CAREER HITTING: 52-for-202 (.257), 14 R, 12 2B, 0 3B, 2 HR, 22 RBI.

Year Team (League)	W	L	Pct.	ERA	WHIP	G	GS	CG	ShO	Hld.	Sv.-Opp.	IP	H	R	ER	HR	BB-IBB	SO	Avg.
1999—Portland (N'west)	1	0	1.000	1.00	0.78	2	2	0	0	...	0-...	9.0	5	1	1	0	2-0	11	.161
—Asheville (S. Atl.)	2	2	.500	3.70	1.08	12	12	0	0	...	0-...	58.1	55	27	24	3	8-0	69	.247
2000—Salem (Caro.)	7	10	.412	3.47	1.18	22	22	3	1	...	0-...	150.1	136	66	58	6	42-0	133	.234
—Carolina (Southern)	1	3	.250	3.44	1.17	6	6	0	0	...	0-...	36.2	32	19	14	4	11-0	33	.234
2001—Carolina (Southern)	2	0	1.000	2.88	1.32	4	4	0	0	...	0-...	25.0	25	9	8	1	8-0	24	.258
—Colo. Springs (PCL)	7	8	.467	4.72	1.41	22	22	4	0	...	0-...	131.2	145	80	69	9	41-0	110	.281
—Colorado (N.L.)	4	1	.800	4.58	1.55	7	7	1	1	0	0-0	39.1	42	21	20	2	19-0	26	.276
2002—Colorado (N.L.)	16	8	.667	4.52	1.46	32	32	0	0	0	0-0	185.1	201	102	93	26	70-2	127	.280
2003—Colorado (N.L.)	12	13	.480	5.11	1.65	32	32	1	0	0	0-0	181.1	212	115	103	20	88-7	119	.299
2004—Colorado (N.L.)	11	12	.478	5.51	1.70	33	33	0	0	0	0-0	201.0	* 241	125	123	27	101-14	133	.299
Major League totals (4 years)	43	34	.558	5.03	1.60	104	104	2	1	0	0-0	607.0	696	363	339	75	278-23	405	.292

JETER, DEREK   SS

PERSONAL: Born June 26, 1974, in Pequannock, N.J. ... 6-3/195. ... Bats right, throws right. ... Full name: Derek Sanderson Jeter. ... Name pronounced: JEE-ter. ... High school: Central (Kalamazoo, Mich.).
TRANSACTIONS/CAREER NOTES: Selected by New York Yankees organization in first round (sixth pick overall) of 1992 free-agent draft. ... On disabled list (June 3-19, 1998); included rehabilitation assignment to Columbus. ... On disabled list (May 12-27, 2000); included rehabilitation assignment to Tampa. ... On disabled list (March 23-April 7, 2001). ... On disabled list (April 1-May 13, 2003); included rehabilitation assignment to Trenton.
HONORS: Named Minor League Player of the Year by THE SPORTING NEWS (1994). ... Named A.L. Rookie Player of the Year by THE SPORTING NEWS (1996). ... Named A.L. Rookie of the Year by Baseball Writers' Association of America (1996). ... Won A.L. Gold Glove at shortstop (2004).
2004 GAMES PLAYED BY POSITION (MLB): SS—154.

Year Team (League)	Pos.	G	AB	R	H	2B	3B	HR	RBI	BB	SO	HBP	GDP	SB-CS	Avg.	OBP	SLG	OPS	E	Avg.
1992—GC Yankees (GCL)	SS	47	173	19	35	10	0	3	25	19	36	5	4	2-2	.202	.296	.312	.609	12	.943
—Greensboro (S. Atl.)	SS	11	37	4	9	0	0	1	4	7	16	1	0	0-1	.243	.378	.324	.702	9	.813
1993—Greensboro (S. Atl.)	SS	128	515	85	152	14	11	5	71	56	95	11	9	18-9	.295	.374	.394	.768	56	.889
1994—Tampa (Fla. St.)	SS	69	292	61	96	13	8	0	39	23	30	3	4	28-2	.329	.380	.428	.808	12	.961
—Alb./Colon. (East.)	SS	34	122	17	46	7	2	2	13	15	16	1	3	12-2	.377	.446	.516	.962	6	.961
—Columbus (Int'l)	SS	35	126	25	44	7	1	3	16	20	15	1	6	10-4	.349	.439	.492	.931	7	.955
1995—Columbus (Int'l)	SS	123	486	96	154	27	9	2	45	61	56	4	9	20-12	.317	.394	.422	.816	29	.953
—New York (A.L.)	SS	15	48	5	12	4	1	0	7	3	11	0	0	0-0	.250	.294	.375	.669	2	.962
1996—New York (A.L.)	SS	157	582	104	183	25	6	10	78	48	102	9	13	14-7	.314	.370	.430	.800	22	.969
1997—New York (A.L.)	SS	159	654	116	190	31	7	10	70	74	125	10	14	23-12	.291	.370	.405	.775	18	.975
1998—New York (A.L.)	SS	149	626	* 127	203	25	8	19	84	57	119	5	13	30-6	.324	.384	.481	.864	9	.986
—Columbus (Int'l)	SS	1	5	2	2	0	0	0	0	0	2	0	0	0-0	.400	.400	.800	1.200	1	.875
1999—New York (A.L.)	SS	158	627	134	* 219	37	9	24	102	91	116	12	12	19-8	.349	.438	.552	.989	14	.978
2000—New York (A.L.)	SS	148	593	119	201	31	4	15	73	68	99	12	14	22-4	.339	.416	.481	.896	24	.961
—Tampa (Fla. St.)	SS	1	3	2	2	1	0	0	0	0	0	0	0	0-0	.667	.667	1.000	1.667	0	1.000
2001—New York (A.L.)	SS	150	614	110	191	35	3	21	74	56	99	10	13	27-3	.311	.377	.480	.858	15	.974
2002—New York (A.L.)	SS-DH	157	644	124	191	26	0	18	75	73	114	7	14	32-3	.297	.373	.421	.794	14	.977
2003—Trenton (East.)	SS	5	18	2	8	1	1	0	5	3	0	1	0	0-0	.444	.545	.611	1.157	1	.957
—New York (A.L.)	SS	119	482	87	156	25	3	10	52	43	88	13	10	11-5	.324	.393	.450	.844	14	.968
2004—New York (A.L.)	SS	154	643	111	188	44	1	23	78	46	99	14	19	23-4	.292	.352	.471	.823	13	.981
Major League totals (10 years)		1366	5513	1037	1734	283	42	150	693	559	972	92	122	201-52	.315	.385	.463	.848	145	.974

DIVISION SERIES RECORD

Year Team (League)	Pos.	G	AB	R	H	2B	3B	HR	RBI	BB	SO	HBP	GDP	SB-CS	Avg.	OBP	SLG	OPS	E	Avg.
1996—New York (A.L.)	SS	4	17	2	7	1	0	0	1	0	2	0	0	0-0	.412	.412	.471	.882	1	.947
1997—New York (A.L.)	SS	5	21	6	7	1	0	2	3	5	5	0	0	1-0	.333	.417	.667	1.083	0	1.000
1998—New York (A.L.)	SS	3	9	0	1	0	0	0	0	2	2	0	0	0-0	.111	.273	.111	.384	0	1.000
1999—New York (A.L.)	SS	3	11	3	5	1	1	0	0	2	3	0	0	0-0	.455	.538	.727	1.266	0	1.000
2000—New York (A.L.)	SS	5	19	1	4	0	0	0	2	2	3	1	0	0-1	.211	.318	.211	.529	0	1.000

Year Team (League)	Pos.	G	AB	R	H	2B	3B	HR	RBI	BB	SO	HBP	GDP	SB-CS	Avg.	OBP	SLG	OPS	E	Avg.
2001— New York (A.L.)	SS	5	18	2	8	1	0	0	1	1	0	1	0	0-1	.444	.476	.500	.976	0	1.000
2002— New York (A.L.)	SS	4	16	6	8	0	0	2	3	2	3	0	0	0-0	.500	.526	.875	1.401	1	.944
2003— New York (A.L.)	SS	4	14	2	6	0	0	1	1	4	2	0	0	1-0	.429	.556	.643	1.198	1	.923
2004— New York (A.L.)	SS	4	19	3	6	1	0	1	4	1	4	1	0	1-0	.316	.350	.526	.876	1	.960
Division series totals (9 years)		37	144	25	52	5	1	6	14	17	24	2	1	3-2	.361	.430	.535	.965	4	.976

CHAMPIONSHIP SERIES RECORD

Year Team (League)	Pos.	G	AB	R	H	2B	3B	HR	RBI	BB	SO	HBP	GDP	SB-CS	Avg.	OBP	SLG	OPS	E	Avg.
1996— New York (A.L.)	SS	5	24	5	10	2	0	1	1	0	5	0	0	2-0	.417	.417	.625	1.042	0	1.000
1998— New York (A.L.)	SS	6	25	3	5	1	1	0	2	2	5	0	1	3-0	.200	.259	.320	.579	0	1.000
1999— New York (A.L.)	SS	5	20	3	7	1	0	1	3	2	3	0	0	0-0	.350	.409	.550	.959	2	.909
2000— New York (A.L.)	SS	6	22	6	7	0	0	2	5	6	7	0	0	1-0	.318	.464	.591	1.055	0	1.000
2001— New York (A.L.)	SS	5	17	0	2	0	0	0	2	2	2	0	0	0-0	.118	.200	.118	.318	0	1.000
2003— New York (A.L.)	SS	7	30	3	7	2	0	1	2	2	4	0	0	1-0	.233	.281	.400	.681	0	1.000
2004— New York (A.L.)	SS	7	30	5	6	1	0	0	5	6	2	0	0	1-0	.200	.333	.233	.567	2	.956
Champ. series totals (7 years)		41	168	25	44	7	1	5	20	20	28	0	1	8-0	.262	.339	.405	.743	4	.979

WORLD SERIES RECORD

Year Team (League)	Pos.	G	AB	R	H	2B	3B	HR	RBI	BB	SO	HBP	GDP	SB-CS	Avg.	OBP	SLG	OPS	E	Avg.
1996— New York (A.L.)	SS	6	20	5	5	0	0	0	1	4	6	1	1	1-0	.250	.400	.250	.650	2	.949
1998— New York (A.L.)	SS	4	17	4	6	0	0	0	1	3	3	0	1	0-0	.353	.450	.353	.803	0	1.000
1999— New York (A.L.)	SS	4	17	4	6	1	0	0	1	1	3	0	0	3-1	.353	.389	.412	.801	0	1.000
2000— New York (A.L.)	SS	5	22	6	9	2	1	2	2	3	8	0	0	0-0	.409	.480	.864	1.344	0	1.000
2001— New York (A.L.)	SS	7	27	3	4	0	0	1	1	0	6	1	0	0-0	.148	.179	.259	.438	0	1.000
2003— New York (A.L.)	SS	6	26	5	9	3	0	0	2	1	7	1	2	0-0	.346	.393	.462	.854	1	.969
World series totals (6 years)		32	129	27	39	6	1	3	8	12	33	3	4	4-1	.302	.375	.434	.809	3	.980

ALL-STAR GAME RECORD

		G	AB	R	H	2B	3B	HR	RBI	BB	SO	HBP	GDP	SB-CS	Avg.	OBP	SLG	OPS	E	Avg.
All-Star Game totals (6 years)		6	10	3	7	1	0	1	3	0	3	0	0	0-0	.700	.700	1.100	1.800	0	1.000

JIMENEZ, D'ANGELO — 2B

PERSONAL: Born December 21, 1977, in Santo Domingo, Dominican Republic. ... 6-0/195. ... Bats both, throws right. ... Name pronounced: he-MEN-ez.

TRANSACTIONS/CAREER NOTES: Signed as a non-drafted free agent by New York Yankees organization (August 1, 1994). ... On disabled list (March 23-August 24, 2000); included rehabilitation assignments to GCL Yankees, Tampa and Columbus. ... Traded by Yankees to San Diego Padres for P Jay Witasick (June 23, 2001). ... Traded by Padres to Chicago White Sox for OF Alex Fernandez and C Humberto Quintero (July 12, 2002). ... Traded by White Sox to Cincinnati Reds for P Scott Dunn (July 6, 2003). ... Career major league pitching: 0-0, 0.00 ERA, 1 G, 1.1 IP, 0 H, 0 R, 0 ER, 0 BB, 0 SO.

2004 GAMES PLAYED BY POSITION (MLB): 2B—146, SS—5.

Year Team (League)	Pos.	BATTING																	FIELDING	
		G	AB	R	H	2B	3B	HR	RBI	BB	SO	HBP	GDP	SB-CS	Avg.	OBP	SLG	OPS	E	Avg.
1995— GC Yankees (GCL)	SS	57	214	41	60	14	8	2	28	23	31	1	4	6-3	.280	.347	.449	.796	21	.927
1996— Greensboro (S. Atl.)	SS	138	537	68	131	25	5	6	48	56	113	3	7	15-17	.244	.317	.343	.660	50	.922
1997— Tampa (Fla. St.)	SS	94	352	52	99	14	6	6	48	50	50	2	3	8-14	.281	.368	.406	.775	21	.953
— Columbus (Int'l)	SS	2	7	1	1	0	0	0	1	0	1	0	1	0-0	.143	.125	.143	.268	2	.833
1998— Norwich (East.)	SS	40	152	21	41	6	2	2	21	25	26	2	3	5-5	.270	.378	.375	.753	12	.938
— Columbus (Int'l)	2B-SS	91	344	55	88	19	4	8	51	46	67	1	6	6-6	.256	.341	.404	.745	26	.946
1999— Columbus (Int'l) SS-3B-2B		126	526	97	172	32	5	15	88	59	75	1	8	26-14	.327	.392	.492	.884	26	.957
— New York (A.L.)	3B-2B	7	20	3	8	2	0	0	4	3	4	0	0	0-0	.400	.478	.500	.978	0	1.000
2000— GC Yankees (GCL)	2B-SS	4	10	2	1	0	0	0	0	5	1	0	0	0-0	.100	.400	.100	.500	2	.900
— Tampa (Fla. St.)	SS-2B	12	41	8	8	1	1	1	2	8	7	0	1	0-0	.195	.320	.341	.661	7	.875
— Columbus (Int'l)	2B-3B-SS	21	73	11	17	3	1	1	5	7	12	1	2	2-0	.233	.309	.342	.651	4	.944
2001— Columbus (Int'l) 2B-SS-3B		56	214	33	56	11	1	5	19	24	31	1	2	5-6	.262	.333	.393	.726	7	.965
— San Diego (N.L.)	SS	86	308	45	85	19	0	3	33	39	68	0	9	22-3	.276	.355	.367	.722	21	.948
2002— San Diego (N.L.)	2B-3B	87	321	39	77	11	4	3	33	34	63	0	10	4-2	.240	.311	.327	.638	12	.968
— Charlotte (Int'l)	SS	42	157	24	44	11	1	6	18	24	14	0	2	6-2	.280	.372	.478	.849	6	.966
— Chicago (A.L.) 2B-SS-3B		27	108	22	31	4	3	1	11	16	10	1	1	2-1	.287	.384	.407	.791	2	.985
2003— Chicago (A.L.)	2B-3B	73	271	35	69	11	5	7	26	32	46	0	3	4-3	.255	.332	.410	.742	9	.970
— Cincinnati (N.L.)	2B-3B	73	290	34	84	13	2	7	31	34	43	2	4	7-4	.290	.365	.421	.785	4	.990
2004— Cincinnati (N.L.)	2B-SS	152	563	76	152	28	3	12	67	82	99	2	15	13-7	.270	.364	.394	.758	7	.990
American League totals (3 years)		107	399	60	108	17	8	8	41	51	60	1	4	6-4	.271	.354	.414	.768	11	.976
National League totals (4 years)		398	1482	194	398	71	9	25	164	189	273	4	38	26-16	.269	.351	.379	.730	44	.976
Major League totals (5 years)		505	1881	254	506	88	17	33	205	240	333	5	42	32-20	.269	.352	.386	.738	55	.976

JIMENEZ, JOSE — P

PERSONAL: Born July 7, 1973, in San Pedro de Macoris, Dominican Republic. ... 6-3/230. ... Throws right, bats right. ... Full name: Jose Antena Jimenez. ... Name pronounced: he-MEN-ez.

TRANSACTIONS/CAREER NOTES: Signed as a non-drafted free agent by St. Louis Cardinals organization (October 21, 1991). ... Traded by Cardinals with Ps Manny Aybar and Rick Croushore and SS Brent Butler to Colorado Rockies for Ps Darryl Kile, Dave Veres and Luther Hackman (November 16, 1999). ... On disabled list (July 8-23 and August 20-September 17, 2001). ... Refused minor league assignment and became a free agent (September 30, 2003). ... Signed by Cleveland Indians (January 8, 2004). ... On disabled list (April 12-May 7, 2004); included rehabilitation assignment to Buffalo.

CAREER HITTING: 10-for-81 (.123), 8 R, 0 2B, 1 3B, 0 HR, 4 RBI.

Year Team (League)	W	L	Pct.	ERA	WHIP	G	GS	CG	ShO	Hld.	Sv.-Opp.	IP	H	R	ER	HR	BB-IBB	SO	Avg.
1992— Dom. Cardinals (DSL)	3	2	.600	6.10	1.87	18	2	0	0	...	0-...	48.2	68	43	33	...	23-...	21	...
1993— Dom. Cardinals (DSL)	3	5	.375	3.51	1.70	12	12	0	0	...	0-...	56.1	61	47	22	...	35-...	30	...
1994— Dom. Cardinals (DSL)	3	9	.250	2.77	1.23	19	9	0	0	...	3-...	68.1	54	43	21	...	30-...	54	...
1995— Johnson City (App.)	5	7	.417	3.49	1.17	14	14	1	1	...	0-...	90.1	81	48	35	3	25-0	85	.234
1996— Peoria (Midw.)	12	9	.571	2.92	1.22	28	27	3	1	...	0-...	172.1	158	75	56	6	53-0	129	.245
1997— Prince William (Caro.)	9	7	.563	3.09	1.17	24	24	2	0	...	0-...	145.2	128	73	50	12	42-2	81	.231
1998— Arkansas (Texas)	15	6	.714	3.11	1.25	26	26	1	1	...	0-...	179.2	156	71	62	9	68-1	88	.239
— St. Louis (N.L.)	3	0	1.000	2.95	1.41	4	3	0	0	0-0	0-0	21.1	22	8	7	0	8-0	12	.262
1999— St. Louis (N.L.)	5	14	.263	5.85	1.50	29	28	2	1	0-1	0-1	163.0	173	114	106	16	71-2	113	.275

Year Team (League)	W	L	Pct.	ERA	WHIP	G	GS	CG	ShO	Hld.	Sv.-Opp.	IP	H	R	ER	HR	BB-IBB	SO	Avg.
—Memphis (PCL)	2	2	.500	3.04	1.46	4	4	0	0	...	0-...	26.2	30	10	9	0	9-0	18	.303
2000—Colorado (N.L.)	5	2	.714	3.18	1.29	72	0	0	0	2	24-30	70.2	63	27	25	4	28-6	44	.239
2001—Colorado (N.L.)	6	1	.857	4.09	1.42	56	0	0	0	0	17-22	55.0	56	27	25	6	22-4	37	.264
2002—Colorado (N.L.)	2	10	.167	3.56	1.19	74	0	0	0	0	41-47	73.1	76	34	29	7	11-4	47	.265
2003—Colorado (N.L.)	2	10	.167	5.22	1.66	63	7	0	0	2	20-23	101.2	137	62	59	7	32-5	45	.322
2004—Buffalo (Int'l)	0	0	...	0.00	1.33	2	0	0	0	...	0-...	3.0	3	0	0	0	1-0	3	.300
—Cleveland (A.L.)	1	7	.125	8.42	1.62	31	0	0	0	1	8-11	36.1	45	37	34	6	14-2	21	.296
American League totals (1 year)	1	7	.125	8.42	1.62	31	0	0	0	1	8-11	36.1	45	37	34	6	14-2	21	.296
National League totals (6 years)	23	37	.383	4.66	1.44	298	38	2	2	4	102-123	485.0	527	272	251	40	172-21	298	.277
Major League totals (7 years)	24	44	.353	4.92	1.45	329	38	2	2	5	110-134	521.1	572	309	285	46	186-23	319	.278

JOHNSON, CHARLES — C

PERSONAL: Born July 20, 1971, in Fort Pierce, Fla. ... 6-3/225. ... Bats right, throws right. ... Full name: Charles Edward Johnson. ... High school: Westwood (Fort Pierce, Fla.). ... College: Miami (Fla.). ... Nephew of Fred McGriff, first baseman with six major league teams (1986-2004).

TRANSACTIONS/CAREER NOTES: Selected by Montreal Expos organization in first round (10th pick overall) of 1989 free-agent draft; did not sign. ... Selected by Florida Marlins organization in first round (28th pick overall) of 1992 free-agent draft. ... On disabled list (August 9-September 1, 1995); included rehabilitation assignment to Portland. ... On disabled list (July 28-September 1, 1996). ... Traded by Marlins with OFs Gary Sheffield and Jim Eisenreich, 3B Bobby Bonilla and P Manuel Barrios to Los Angeles Dodgers for C Mike Piazza and 3B Todd Zeile (May 15, 1998). ... Traded by Dodgers with OF Roger Cedeno to New York Mets for C Todd Hundley and P Arnold Gooch (December 1, 1998). ... Traded by Mets to Baltimore Orioles for P Armando Benitez (December 1, 1998). ... Traded by Orioles with DH Harold Baines to Chicago White Sox for C Brook Fordyce and Ps Miguel Felix, Juan Figueroa and Jason Lakman (July 29, 2000). ... Signed as a free agent by Marlins (December 18, 2000). ... On disabled list (March 22-April 8 and July 28-August 16, 2002); included rehabilitation assignment to Jupiter. ... Traded by Marlins with P Vic Darensbourg, OF Preston Wilson and 2B Pablo Ozuna to Colorado Rockies for P Mike Hampton, OF Juan Pierre and cash (November 16, 2002).

HONORS: Won N.L. Gold Glove at catcher (1995-98).

2004 GAMES PLAYED BY POSITION (MLB): C—91.

Year Team (League)	Pos.	G	AB	R	H	2B	3B	HR	RBI	BB	SO	HBP	GDP	SB-CS	Avg.	OBP	SLG	OPS	E	Avg.
1993—Kane Co. (Midw.)	C	135	488	74	134	29	5	19	94	62	111	2	12	9-1	.275	.356	.471	.827	12	.988
1994—Portland (East.)	C-DH	132	443	64	117	29	4	28	80	74	97	3	14	4-5	.264	.371	.524	.895	7	.991
—Florida (N.L.)	C	4	11	5	5	1	0	1	4	1	4	0	1	0-0	.455	.462	.818	1.280	0	1.000
1995—Florida (N.L.)	C	97	315	40	79	15	1	11	39	46	71	4	11	0-2	.251	.352	.410	.761	6	.992
—Portland (East.)	C	2	7	0	0	0	0	0	0	0	1	3	0	0-0	.000	.125	.000	.125	1	.958
1996—Florida (N.L.)	C	120	386	34	84	13	1	13	37	40	91	2	20	1-0	.218	.292	.358	.649	4	.995
1997—Florida (N.L.)	C	124	416	43	104	26	1	19	63	60	109	3	13	0-2	.250	.347	.454	.802	0	1.000
1998—Florida (N.L.)	C	31	113	13	25	5	0	7	23	16	30	0	3	0-1	.221	.315	.451	.767	2	.990
—Los Angeles (N.L.)	C	102	346	31	75	13	0	12	35	29	99	1	9	0-1	.217	.279	.358	.638	6	.992
1999—Baltimore (A.L.)	C	135	426	58	107	19	1	16	54	55	107	4	13	0-0	.251	.340	.413	.753	5	.994
2000—Baltimore (A.L.)	C-DH	84	286	52	84	16	0	21	55	32	69	0	8	0-0	.294	.364	.570	.934	3	.994
—Chicago (A.L.)	C	44	135	24	44	8	0	10	36	20	37	1	0	0-0	.326	.411	.607	1.019	3	.987
2001—Florida (N.L.)	C	128	451	51	117	32	0	18	75	38	133	4	8	0-0	.259	.321	.450	.771	4	.996
2002—Florida (N.L.)	C	83	244	18	53	19	0	6	36	31	61	0	10	0-0	.217	.301	.369	.670	3	.994
—Jupiter (FSL)	C	5	16	5	7	0	0	3	9	2	4	0	0	0-0	.438	.500	1.000	1.500	0	1.000
2003—Colorado (N.L.)	C	108	356	49	82	20	0	20	61	49	84	1	8	1-3	.230	.320	.455	.775	4	.993
2004—Colorado (N.L.)	C	109	305	42	72	20	0	13	47	49	91	5	6	2-1	.236	.350	.430	.780	7	.988
American League totals (2 years)		263	847	134	235	43	1	47	145	107	213	5	21	2-0	.277	.360	.497	.857	11	.993
National League totals (9 years)		906	2943	326	696	164	3	120	420	359	773	20	89	4-10	.236	.321	.417	.738	36	.994
Major League totals (11 years)		1169	3790	460	931	207	4	167	565	466	986	25	110	6-10	.246	.330	.435	.764	47	.994

DIVISION SERIES RECORD

Year Team (League)	Pos.	G	AB	R	H	2B	3B	HR	RBI	BB	SO	HBP	GDP	SB-CS	Avg.	OBP	SLG	OPS	E	Avg.
1997—Florida (N.L.)	C	3	8	5	2	1	0	1	2	3	2	1	0	0-0	.250	.500	.750	1.250	0	1.000
2000—Chicago (A.L.)	C	3	9	0	3	0	0	0	0	1	1	1	0	0-0	.333	.455	.333	.788	0	1.000
Division series totals (2 years)		6	17	5	5	1	0	1	2	4	3	2	0	0-0	.294	.478	.529	1.008	0	1.000

CHAMPIONSHIP SERIES RECORD

Year Team (League)	Pos.	G	AB	R	H	2B	3B	HR	RBI	BB	SO	HBP	GDP	SB-CS	Avg.	OBP	SLG	OPS	E	Avg.
1997—Florida (N.L.)	C	6	17	1	2	2	0	0	5	3	8	1	0	0-1	.118	.286	.235	.521	2	.965

WORLD SERIES RECORD

Year Team (League)	Pos.	G	AB	R	H	2B	3B	HR	RBI	BB	SO	HBP	GDP	SB-CS	Avg.	OBP	SLG	OPS	E	Avg.
1997—Florida (N.L.)	C	7	28	4	10	1	0	1	3	1	6	0	0	0-0	.357	.379	.464	.844	0	1.000

ALL-STAR GAME RECORD

	G	AB	R	H	2B	3B	HR	RBI	BB	SO	HBP	GDP	SB-CS	Avg.	OBP	SLG	OPS	E	Avg.
All-Star Game totals (2 years)	2	2	0	0	0	0	0	0	0	1	0	0	0-0	.000	.000	.000	.000	0	1.000

JOHNSON, JASON — P

PERSONAL: Born October 27, 1973, in Santa Barbara, Calif. ... 6-6/217. ... Throws right, bats right. ... Full name: Jason Michael Johnson. ... High school: Conner (Hebron, Ky.).

TRANSACTIONS/CAREER NOTES: Signed as a non-drafted free agent by Pittsburgh Pirates organization (July 21, 1992). ... Selected by Tampa Bay Devil Rays in first round (14th pick overall) of expansion draft (November 18, 1997). ... On disabled list (July 4, 1998-remainder of season). ... Traded by Devil Rays to Baltimore Orioles for OF Danny Clyburn and a player to be named (March 29, 1999); Devil Rays acquired SS Bolivar Voquez to complete deal (April 22, 1999). ... On disabled list (April 25-June 7 and July 23-August 9, 2002); included rehabilitation assignment to Bowie. ... Signed as a free agent by Detroit Tigers (December 30, 2003).

CAREER HITTING: 2-for-22 (.091), 1 R, 0 2B, 0 3B, 0 HR, 0 RBI.

Year Team (League)	W	L	Pct.	ERA	WHIP	G	GS	CG	ShO	Hld.	Sv.-Opp.	IP	H	R	ER	HR	BB-IBB	SO	Avg.
1992—GC Pirates (GCL)	2	0	1.000	3.68	1.64	5	0	0	0	...	0-...	7.1	6	3	3	0	6-0	3	.240
1993—GC Pirates (GCL)	1	4	.200	2.33	1.15	9	9	0	0	...	0-...	54.0	48	22	14	0	14-0	39	.239
—Welland (N.Y.-Penn)	1	5	.167	4.63	1.20	6	6	1	0	...	0-...	35.0	33	24	18	0	9-0	19	.243
1994—Augusta (S. Atl.)	2	12	.143	4.03	1.47	20	19	1	0	...	0-...	102.2	119	67	46	5	32-0	69	.285
1995—Augusta (S. Atl.)	3	5	.375	4.36	1.38	11	11	1	0	...	0-...	53.2	57	32	26	2	17-0	42	.271
—Lynchburg (Carolina)	1	2	.333	2.05	1.27	5	4	0	0	...	0-...	22.0	23	6	5	0	5-0	9	.109

Year	Team (League)	W	L	Pct.	ERA	WHIP	G	GS	CG	ShO	Hld.	Sv.-Opp.	IP	H	R	ER	HR	BB-IBB	SO	Avg.
1996—	Lynchburg (Carolina)	1	4	.200	6.50	1.53	15	5	0	0	...	0-...	44.1	56	37	32	6	12-0	27	.303
	— Augusta (S. Atl.)	4	4	.500	3.11	1.27	14	14	1	1	...	0-...	84.0	82	40	29	2	25-0	83	.256
1997—	Lynchburg (Carolina)	8	4	.667	3.71	1.29	17	17	0	0	...	0-...	99.1	98	43	41	4	30-1	92	.266
	— Carolina (Southern)	3	3	.500	4.08	1.26	9	9	1	0	...	0-...	57.1	56	31	26	6	16-0	63	.249
	— Pittsburgh (N.L.)	0	0	...	6.00	1.83	3	0	0	0	0	0-0	6.0	10	4	4	2	1-0	3	.400
1998—	Durham (Int'l)	1	0	1.000	2.92	0.65	2	2	0	0	...	0-...	12.1	6	4	4	2	2-0	14	.143
	— Tampa Bay (A.L.)	2	5	.286	5.70	1.68	13	13	0	0	0	0-0	60.0	74	38	38	9	27-0	36	.306
1999—	Rochester (Int'l)	4	2	.667	3.65	1.40	8	8	0	0	0	0-...	44.1	35	19	18	6	27-0	47	.212
	— Baltimore (A.L.)	8	7	.533	5.46	1.52	22	21	0	0	0	0-...	115.1	120	74	70	16	55-0	71	.267
2000—	Rochester (Int'l)	3	1	.750	1.47	0.96	8	8	1	1	...	0-...	55.0	32	12	9	2	21-0	56	.170
	— Baltimore (A.L.)	1	10	.091	7.02	1.67	25	13	0	0	2	0-0	107.2	119	95	84	21	61-2	79	.278
2001—	Baltimore (A.L.)	10	12	.455	4.09	1.38	32	32	2	0	0	0-0	196.0	194	109	89	28	77-3	114	.257
2002—	Baltimore (A.L.)	5	14	.263	4.59	1.39	22	22	1	0	0	0-0	131.1	141	68	67	19	41-2	97	.276
	— Bowie (East.)	1	0	1.000	0.00	1.00	1	1	0	0	...	0-...	5.0	4	0	0	0	1-0	6	.211
2003—	Baltimore (A.L.)	10	10	.500	4.18	1.56	32	32	0	0	0	0-0	189.2	216	100	88	22	80-8	118	.283
2004—	Detroit (A.L.)	8	15	.348	5.13	1.43	33	33	2	1	0	0-0	196.2	222	121	112	22	60-3	125	.284
	American League totals (7 years)	44	73	.376	4.95	1.49	179	166	5	1	2	0-0	996.2	1086	605	548	137	401-18	640	.276
	National League totals (1 year)	0	0	...	6.00	1.83	3	0	0	0	0	0-0	6.0	10	4	4	2	1-0	3	.400
	Major League totals (8 years)	44	73	.376	4.95	1.49	182	166	5	1	2	0-0	1002.2	1096	609	552	139	402-18	643	.277

JOHNSON, MARK — C

PERSONAL: Born September 12, 1975, in Wheatridge, Colo. ... 6-0/200. ... Bats left, throws right. ... Full name: Mark Landon Johnson. ... High school: Warner Robins (Ga.).

TRANSACTIONS/CAREER NOTES: Selected by Chicago White Sox organization in first round (26th pick overall) of 1994 free-agent draft. ... Traded by White Sox with Ps Keith Foulke and Joe Valentine and cash to Oakland Athletics for P Billy Koch and two players to be named (December 3, 2002); White Sox acquired P Neal Cotts and OF Daylon Holt to complete deal (December 16, 2002). ... Signed as a free agent by Milwaukee Brewers organization (November 24, 2003). ... Refused minor league assignment and became a free agent (October 7, 2004).

2004 GAMES PLAYED BY POSITION (MLB): C—5.

Year	Team (League)	Pos.	G	AB	R	H	2B	3B	HR	RBI	BB	SO	HBP	GDP	SB-CS	Avg.	OBP	SLG	OPS	E	Avg.
1994—	GC Whi. Sox (GCL)	C	32	87	10	21	5	0	0	14	14	15	3	0	1-1	.241	.365	.299	.664	3	.986
1995—	Hickory (S. Atl.)	C	107	319	31	58	9	0	2	17	59	52	3	4	3-5	.182	.313	.229	.542	11	.986
1996—	South Bend (Mid.)	C	67	214	29	55	14	3	2	27	39	25	1	8	3-3	.257	.368	.379	.747	9	.980
	— Prince Will. (Car.)	C	18	58	9	14	3	0	0	3	13	6	1	0	0-0	.241	.389	.293	.682	1	.992
1997—	Win.-Salem (Car.)	C	120	375	59	95	27	4	4	46	106	85	5	7	4-2	.253	.420	.379	.798	11	.989
1998—	Birmingham (Sou.)	C-1B	117	382	68	108	17	3	9	59	105	72	6	5	0-1	.283	.443	.414	.857	8	.990
	— Chicago (A.L.)	C	7	23	2	2	0	2	0	1	1	8	0	0	0-0	.087	.125	.261	.386	0	1.000
1999—	Chicago (A.L.)	C-DH	73	207	27	47	11	0	4	16	36	58	2	2	3-1	.227	.344	.338	.682	3	.993
2000—	Chicago (A.L.)	C-DH	75	213	29	48	11	0	3	23	27	40	1	3	3-2	.225	.315	.319	.635	4	.992
2001—	Chicago (A.L.)	C-1B	55	196	24	53	5	2	4	24	29	34	0	4	2-1	.270	.363	.378	.740	4	.991
	— Charlotte (Int'l)	C	61	173	21	43	6	1	5	18	23	31	2	5	2-1	.249	.338	.382	.720	3	.992
2002—	Chicago (A.L.)	C	86	263	31	55	8	1	4	18	30	52	3	4	0-0	.209	.297	.293	.590	3	.994
2003—	Sacramento (PCL)	C-DH	51	162	28	37	11	1	3	30	35	23	3	2	0-1	.228	.369	.364	.734	3	.992
	— Oakland (A.L.)	C	13	27	3	3	1	0	0	3	3	4	1	0	0-0	.111	.219	.148	.367	0	1.000
2004—	Indianapolis (Int'l) C-DH-1-3-O		88	281	39	72	18	0	5	38	43	44	1	4	3-2	.256	.355	.374	.728	4	.992
	— Milwaukee (N.L.)	C	7	11	1	1	0	0	0	2	3	2	0	0	0-0	.091	.267	.091	.358	1	.952
	American League totals (6 years)		315	906	113	198	37	4	16	79	120	193	9	14	8-4	.219	.314	.321	.635	13	.993
	National League totals (1 year)		7	11	1	1	0	0	0	2	3	2	0	0	0-0	.091	.267	.091	.358	1	.952
	Major League totals (7 years)		322	917	114	199	37	4	16	81	123	195	9	14	8-4	.217	.313	.318	.632	14	.993

JOHNSON, NICK — 1B

PERSONAL: Born September 19, 1978, in Sacramento, Calif. ... 6-3/224. ... Bats left, throws left. ... Full name: Nicholas Robert Johnson. ... High school: McClatchy (Sacramento). ... Nephew of Larry Bowa, shortstop with three major league teams (1970-85); and manager of San Diego Padres (1987-88) and Philadelphia Phillies (2001-04).

TRANSACTIONS/CAREER NOTES: Selected by New York Yankees organization in third round of 1996 free-agent draft. ... On disabled list (March 25, 2000-entire season). ... On disabled list (August 8-September 3, 2002); included rehabilitation assignment to Columbus. ... On disabled list (May 16-July 25, 2003); included rehabilitation assignment to Columbus. ... Traded by Yankees with OF Juan Rivera and P Randy Choate to Montreal Expos for P Javier Vazquez (December 16, 2003). ... On disabled list (March 31-May 28 and August 21, 2004-remainder of season); included rehabilitation assignments to Brevard County and Edmonton.

2004 GAMES PLAYED BY POSITION (MLB): 1B—73.

Year	Team (League)	Pos.	G	AB	R	H	2B	3B	HR	RBI	BB	SO	HBP	GDP	SB-CS	Avg.	OBP	SLG	OPS	E	Avg.
1996—	GC Yankees (GCL)	1B	47	157	31	45	11	1	2	33	30	35	9	5	0-0	.287	.422	.408	.830	3	.991
1997—	Greensboro (S. Atl.)	1B	127	433	77	118	23	1	16	75	76	99	18	5	16-3	.273	.398	.441	.839	16	.987
1998—	Tampa (Fla. St.)	1B	92	303	69	96	14	1	17	58	68	76	19	5	1-4	.317	.466	.538	1.004	12	.986
1999—	Norwich (East.)	1B	132	420	114	145	33	5	14	87	123	88	37	9	8-6	.345	.525	.548	1.073	20	.983
2000—	New York (A.L.)					Did not play.														
2001—	Columbus (Int'l)	1B	110	359	68	92	20	0	18	49	81	105	14	6	9-2	.256	.407	.462	.870	10	.989
	— New York (A.L.)	1B-DH	23	67	6	13	2	0	2	8	7	15	4	3	0-0	.194	.308	.313	.621	0	1.000
2002—	New York (A.L.) 1B-DH-OF		129	378	56	92	15	0	15	58	48	98	12	11	1-3	.243	.347	.402	.749	7	.988
	— Columbus (Int'l)	1B	3	11	1	1	0	0	0	0	1	4	0	1	0-0	.091	.167	.091	.258	0	1.000
2003—	Columbus (Int'l)	1B-DH	3	10	1	5	2	0	1	3	2	2	0	0	0-0	.500	.583	.800	1.583	1	.952
	— Trenton (East.)	1B	4	12	3	5	1	0	0	1	5	0	1	1	0-0	.417	.611	.500	1.111	0	1.000
	— New York (A.L.)	1B-DH	96	324	60	92	19	0	14	47	70	57	8	8	5-2	.284	.422	.472	.894	5	.991
2004—	Brevard County (FSL)	1B	6	21	3	4	0	0	1	5	4	6	0	1	0-0	.190	.320	.333	.653	0	1.000
	— Edmonton (PCL)	1B	3	9	2	2	1	0	0	0	4	3	0	1	0-0	.222	.462	.333	.795	0	1.000
	— Montreal (N.L.)	1B	73	251	35	63	16	0	7	33	40	58	3	5	6-3	.251	.359	.398	.758	4	.994
	American League totals (3 years)		248	769	122	197	36	0	31	113	125	170	24	23	6-5	.256	.376	.424	.800	12	.990
	National League totals (1 year)		73	251	35	63	16	0	7	33	40	58	3	5	6-3	.251	.359	.398	.758	4	.994
	Major League totals (4 years)		321	1020	157	260	52	0	38	146	165	228	27	28	12-8	.255	.372	.418	.790	16	.992

DIVISION SERIES RECORD

Year Team (League)	Pos.	G	AB	R	H	2B	3B	HR	RBI	BB	SO	HBP	GDP	SB-CS	Avg.	OBP	SLG	OPS	E	Avg.
2002— New York (A.L.)	DH-1B	3	11	1	2	0	0	0	1	1	5	0	0	0-0	.182	.250	.182	.432	0	1.000
2003— New York (A.L.)	1B	4	13	2	1	1	0	0	2	3	2	1	0	0-0	.077	.294	.154	.448	0	1.000
Division series totals (2 years)		7	24	3	3	1	0	0	3	4	7	1	0	0-0	.125	.276	.167	.443	0	1.000

CHAMPIONSHIP SERIES RECORD

Year Team (League)	Pos.	G	AB	R	H	2B	3B	HR	RBI	BB	SO	HBP	GDP	SB-CS	Avg.	OBP	SLG	OPS	E	Avg.
2003— New York (A.L.)	1B	7	26	4	6	1	0	1	3	2	4	0	1	0-0	.231	.286	.385	.670	0	1.000

WORLD SERIES RECORD

Year Team (League)	Pos.	G	AB	R	H	2B	3B	HR	RBI	BB	SO	HBP	GDP	SB-CS	Avg.	OBP	SLG	OPS	E	Avg.
2003— New York (A.L.)	1B	6	17	3	5	1	0	0	0	2	3	0	1	0-0	.294	.368	.353	.721	0	1.000

J JOHNSON, RANDY   P

PERSONAL: Born September 10, 1963, in Walnut Creek, Calif. ... 6-10/231. ... Throws left, bats right. ... Full name: Randall David Johnson. ... High school: Livermore (Calif.). ... College: USC.

TRANSACTIONS/CAREER NOTES: Selected by Atlanta Braves organization in third round of June 1982 free-agent draft; did not sign. ... Selected by Montreal Expos organization in second round of June 1985 free-agent draft. ... Traded by Expos with Ps Brian Holman and Gene Harris to Seattle Mariners for P Mark Langston and a player to be named (May 25, 1989); Expos acquired P Mike Campbell to complete deal (July 31, 1989). ... On disabled list (June 11-27, 1992). ... On disabled list (May 15-August 6 and August 27, 1996-remainder of season); included rehabilitation assignment to Everett. ... On suspended list (April 24-27, 1998). ... Traded by Mariners to Houston Astros for SS Carlos Guillen, P Freddy Garcia and a player to be named (July 31, 1998); Mariners acquired P John Halama to complete deal (October 1, 1998). ... Signed as a free agent by Arizona Diamondbacks (December 10, 1998). ... On disabled list (April 12-27 and April 28-July 20, 2003); included rehabilitation assignment to Lancaster.

HONORS: Named A.L. Pitcher of the Year by THE SPORTING NEWS (1995). ... Named A.L. Cy Young Award winner by Baseball Writers' Association of America (1995). ... Named N.L. Cy Young Award winner by Baseball Writers' Association of America (1999, 2000, 2001 and 2002).

CAREER HITTING: 67-for-520 (.129), 17 R, 13 2B, 0 3B, 1 HR, 35 RBI.

Year Team (League)	W	L	Pct.	ERA	WHIP	G	GS	CG	ShO	Hld.	Sv.-Opp.	IP	H	R	ER	HR	BB-IBB	SO	Avg.
1985— Jamestown (N.Y.-Penn.)	0	3	.000	5.93	1.94	8	8	0	0	...	0-...	27.1	29	22	18	2	24-0	21	.287
1986— W.P. Beach (FSL)	8	7	.533	3.16	1.53	26	26	2	1	...	0-...	119.2	89	49	42	3	94-0	133	.211
1987— Jacksonville (Southern)	11	8	.579	3.73	1.63	25	24	0	0	...	0-...	140.0	100	63	58	10	128-0	163	.204
1988— Indianapolis (A.A.)	8	7	.533	3.26	1.39	20	19	0	0	...	0-...	113.1	85	52	41	6	72-0	111	.209
— Montreal (N.L.)	3	0	1.000	2.42	1.15	4	4	1	0	0	0-0	26.0	23	8	7	3	7-0	25	.225
1989— Montreal (N.L.)	0	4	.000	6.67	1.85	7	6	0	0	0	0-0	29.2	29	25	22	2	26-1	26	.264
— Indianapolis (A.A.)	1	1	.500	2.00	1.22	3	3	0	0	...	0-...	18.0	13	5	4	0	9-0	17	.194
— Seattle (A.L.)	7	9	.438	4.40	1.44	22	22	2	0	0	0-0	131.0	118	75	64	11	70-1	104	.244
1990— Seattle (A.L.)	14	11	.560	3.65	1.34	33	33	5	2	0	0-0	219.2	174	103	89	26	* 120-2	194	.216
1991— Seattle (A.L.)	13	10	.565	3.98	1.50	33	33	2	1	0	0-0	201.1	151	96	89	15	* 152-0	228	.213
1992— Seattle (A.L.)	12	14	.462	3.77	1.42	31	31	6	2	0	0-0	210.1	154	104	88	13	* 144-1	* 241	* .206
1993— Seattle (A.L.)	19	8	.704	3.24	1.11	35	34	10	3	0	1-1	255.1	185	97	92	22	99-1	* 308	.203
1994— Seattle (A.L.)	13	6	.684	3.19	1.19	23	23	* 9	* 4	0	0-0	172.0	132	65	61	14	72-2	* 204	.216
1995— Seattle (A.L.)	18	2	.900	* 2.48	1.05	30	30	6	3	0	0-0	214.1	159	65	59	12	65-1	* 294	.201
1996— Seattle (A.L.)	5	0	1.000	3.67	1.19	14	8	0	0	0	1-2	61.1	48	27	25	8	25-0	85	.211
— Everett (Northwest)	0	0	...	0.00	0.00	1	1	0	0	...	0-...	2.0	0	0	0	0	0-0	5	.000
1997— Seattle (A.L.)	20	4	.833	2.28	1.05	30	29	5	2	0	0-0	213.0	147	60	54	20	77-2	291	.194
1998— Seattle (A.L.)	9	10	.474	4.33	1.29	23	23	6	2	0	0-0	160.0	146	90	77	19	60-0	213	.240
— Houston (N.L.)	10	1	.909	1.28	0.98	11	11	4	4	0	0-0	84.1	57	12	12	4	26-1	116	.191
1999— Arizona (N.L.)	17	9	.654	* 2.48	1.02	35	* 35	* 12	2	0	0-0	* 271.2	207	86	75	30	70-3	* 364	.208
2000— Arizona (N.L.)	19	7	.731	2.64	1.12	35	* 35	* 8	* 3	0	0-0	248.2	202	89	73	23	76-1	* 347	.224
2001— Arizona (N.L.)	21	6	.778	* 2.49	1.01	35	34	3	2	0	0-0	249.2	181	74	69	19	71-2	* 372	.203
2002— Arizona (N.L.)	* 24	5	.828	* 2.32	1.03	35	35	* 8	4	0	0-0	* 260.0	197	78	67	26	71-1	* 334	* .208
2003— Tucson (PCL)	0	0	...	0.00	0.00	1	1	0	0	0	0-...	4.0	0	0	0	0	0-0	4	.000
— El Paso (Texas)	0	0	...	0.00	1.00	1	1	0	0	0	0-...	4.0	3	2	0	0	1-0	5	.231
— Lancaster (Calif.)	0	1	.000	6.00	1.80	1	1	0	0	...	0-...	6.0	11	5	4	1	0-0	6	.367
— Arizona (N.L.)	6	8	.429	4.26	1.33	18	18	1	1	0	0-0	114.0	125	61	54	16	27-3	125	.280
2004— Arizona (N.L.)	16	14	.533	2.60	0.90	35	* 35	4	2	0	0-0	245.2	177	88	71	18	44-1	* 290	.197
American League totals (10 years)	130	74	.637	3.42	1.25	274	266	51	19	0	2-3	1838.1	1414	782	698	160	884-10	2162	.212
National League totals (9 years)	116	54	.682	2.65	1.06	215	213	41	18	0	0-0	1529.2	1198	521	450	141	418-13	1999	.215
Major League totals (17 years)	246	128	.658	3.07	1.16	489	479	92	37	0	2-3	3368.0	2612	1303	1148	301	1302-23	4161	.213

DIVISION SERIES RECORD

Year Team (League)	W	L	Pct.	ERA	WHIP	G	GS	CG	ShO	Hld.	Sv.-Opp.	IP	H	R	ER	HR	BB-IBB	SO	Avg.
1995— Seattle (A.L.)	2	0	1.000	2.70	1.10	2	1	0	0	0	0-0	10.0	5	3	3	1	6-1	16	.156
1997— Seattle (A.L.)	0	2	.000	5.54	1.54	2	2	1	0	0	0-0	13.0	14	8	8	3	6-0	16	.286
1998— Houston (N.L.)	0	2	.000	1.93	1.00	2	2	0	0	0	0-0	14.0	12	4	3	2	2-0	17	.226
1999— Arizona (N.L.)	0	1	.000	7.56	1.32	1	1	0	0	0	0-0	8.1	8	7	7	2	3-0	11	.250
2001— Arizona (N.L.)	0	1	.000	3.38	1.00	1	1	0	0	0	0-0	8.0	6	3	3	1	2-0	9	.222
2002— Arizona (N.L.)	0	1	.000	7.50	2.00	1	1	0	0	0	0-0	6.0	10	6	5	2	2-1	4	.370
Division series totals (6 years)	2	7	.222	4.40	1.28	9	8	1	0	0	0-0	59.1	55	31	29	11	21-2	73	.250

CHAMPIONSHIP SERIES RECORD

Year Team (League)	W	L	Pct.	ERA	WHIP	G	GS	CG	ShO	Hld.	Sv.-Opp.	IP	H	R	ER	HR	BB-IBB	SO	Avg.
1995— Seattle (A.L.)	0	1	.000	2.35	0.91	2	2	0	0	0	0-0	15.1	12	6	4	1	2-0	13	.211
2001— Arizona (N.L.)	2	0	1.000	1.13	0.81	2	2	1	1	0	0-0	16.0	10	2	2	1	3-0	19	.169
Champ. series totals (2 years)	2	1	.667	1.72	0.86	4	4	1	1	0	0-0	31.1	22	8	6	2	5-0	32	.190

WORLD SERIES RECORD

Year Team (League)	W	L	Pct.	ERA	WHIP	G	GS	CG	ShO	Hld.	Sv.-Opp.	IP	H	R	ER	HR	BB-IBB	SO	Avg.
2001— Arizona (N.L.)	3	0	1.000	1.04	0.69	3	2	1	1	0	0-0	17.1	9	2	2	0	3-0	19	.150

ALL-STAR GAME RECORD

	W	L	Pct.	ERA	WHIP	G	GS	CG	ShO	Hld.	Sv.-Opp.	IP	H	R	ER	HR	BB-IBB	SO	Avg.
All-Star Game totals (8 years)	0	0	...	0.75	0.75	8	4	0	0	0	0-0	12.0	7	1	1	1	2-0	12	.171

JOHNSON, REED — OF

PERSONAL: Born December 8, 1976, in Riverside, Calif. ... 5-10/180. ... Bats right, throws right. ... Full name: Reed Cameron Johnson. ... High school: Temecula Valley (Temecula, Calif.). ... College: Cal State Fullerton.
TRANSACTIONS/CAREER NOTES: Selected by Toronto Blue Jays organization in 17th round of 1999 free-agent draft.
2004 GAMES PLAYED BY POSITION (MLB): OF—137, DH—4.

Year	Team (League)	Pos.	G	AB	R	H	2B	3B	HR	RBI	BB	SO	HBP	GDP	SB-CS	Avg.	OBP	SLG	OPS	E	Avg.
1999—	St. Catharines (NY-Penn.)	OF	60	191	24	46	8	2	2	23	24	31	2	4	5-5	.241	.326	.335	.661	3	.976
2000—	Hagerstown (SAL)	OF	95	324	66	94	24	5	8	70	62	49	14	9	14-2	.290	.422	.469	.891	1	.995
—	Dunedin (Fla. St.)	OF	36	133	26	42	9	2	4	28	14	27	11	1	3-2	.316	.416	.504	.920	2	.975
2001—	Tennessee (Sou.)	OF	136	554	104	174	29	4	13	74	45	79	18	11	42-12	.314	.383	.451	.834	4	.983
2002—	Dunedin (Fla. St.)	OF	8	33	7	9	3	0	0	6	3	3	2	0	0-1	.273	.368	.364	.732	0	1.000
—	Syracuse (Int'l)	OF	44	159	27	37	8	3	2	10	12	23	8	1	1-4	.233	.317	.358	.675	1	.991
2003—	Syracuse (Int'l)	OF	26	101	14	33	4	1	2	16	3	13	5	2	3-1	.327	.369	.446	.815	0	1.000
—	Toronto (A.L.)	OF-DH	114	412	79	121	21	2	10	52	20	67	20	10	5-3	.294	.353	.427	.780	4	.977
2004—	Toronto (A.L.)	OF-DH	141	537	68	145	25	2	10	61	28	98	12	17	6-3	.270	.320	.380	.699	3	.989
	Major League totals (2 years)		255	949	147	266	46	4	20	113	48	165	32	27	11-6	.280	.334	.400	.735	7	.984

JOHNSTON, MIKE — P

PERSONAL: Born March 30, 1979, in Philadelphia, Pa. ... 6-2/215. ... Throws left, bats left. ... Full name: Michael Charles Johnston. ... High school: None. ... Junior college: Garrett (Md.).
TRANSACTIONS/CAREER NOTES: Selected by Pittsburgh Pirates organization in 20th round of 1998 free-agent draft. ... On disabled list (June 22-August 2, 2004); included rehabilitation assignments to GCL Pirates and Nashville.
CAREER HITTING: 0-for-0 (.000), 0 R, 0 2B, 0 3B, 0 HR, 0 RBI.

Year	Team (League)	W	L	Pct.	ERA	WHIP	G	GS	CG	ShO	Hld.	Sv.-Opp.	IP	H	R	ER	HR	BB-IBB	SO	Avg.
1998—	GC Pirates (GCL)	1	1	.333	3.34	1.28	13	3	0	0	...	0-...	29.2	28	17	11	1	10-0	17	.248
—	Erie (N.Y.-Penn)	0	0	...	4.50	2.50	2	0	0	0	...	0-...	2.0	4	4	1	0	1-0	2	.364
1999—	Williamsport (N.Y.-Penn.)	3	2	.600	4.25	1.51	14	2	0	0	...	2-...	42.1	46	26	20	5	18-0	30	.267
2000—	Hickory (S. Atl.)	4	2	.667	6.22	1.89	26	0	0	0	...	3-...	50.2	66	42	35	2	30-0	52	.320
2001—	Hickory (S. Atl.)	4	5	.444	3.38	1.39	16	16	0	0	...	0-...	93.1	88	47	35	5	42-1	80	.249
—	Lynchburg (Carolina)	4	4	.500	3.34	1.45	11	10	1	0	...	0-...	62.0	66	27	23	2	24-0	44	.272
2002—	Lynchburg (Carolina)	4	2	.667	3.63	1.33	15	10	0	0	...	0-...	57.0	50	29	23	2	26-0	50	.230
2003—	Altoona (East.)	6	2	.750	2.12	1.05	46	0	0	0	...	7-...	72.1	49	17	17	4	27-3	65	.199
2004—	Pittsburgh (N.L.)	0	3	.000	4.37	1.94	24	0	0	0	4	0-1	22.2	29	16	11	2	15-1	18	.315
—	Nashville (PCL)	0	0	...	8.40	2.13	19	0	0	0	...	0-...	15.0	19	14	14	3	13-1	6	.306
	Major League totals (1 year)	0	3	.000	4.37	1.94	24	0	0	0	4	0-1	22.2	29	16	11	2	15-1	18	.315

JONES, ANDRUW — OF

PERSONAL: Born April 23, 1977, in Willemstad, Curacao. ... 6-1/210. ... Bats right, throws right. ... Full name: Andruw Rudolf Jones. ... High school: St. Paulus (Willemstad, Curacao).
TRANSACTIONS/CAREER NOTES: Signed as a non-drafted free agent by Atlanta Braves organization (July 1, 1993).
HONORS: Won N.L. Gold Glove as outfielder (1998-2004).
2004 GAMES PLAYED BY POSITION (MLB): OF—154.

Year	Team (League)	Pos.	G	AB	R	H	2B	3B	HR	RBI	BB	SO	HBP	GDP	SB-CS	Avg.	OBP	SLG	OPS	E	Avg.
1994—	GC Braves (GCL)	OF	27	95	22	21	5	1	2	10	16	19	2	3	5-2	.221	.345	.358	.703	3	.968
—	Danville (Appal.)	OF	36	143	20	48	9	2	1	16	9	25	3	0	16-9	.336	.385	.448	.832	2	.977
1995—	Macon (S. Atl.)	OF	139	537	104	149	41	5	25	100	70	122	16	16	56-11	.277	.372	.512	.884	4	.988
1996—	Durham (Caro.)	OF	66	243	65	76	14	3	17	43	42	54	3	5	16-4	.313	.419	.605	1.024	7	.963
—	Greenville (Sou.)	OF	38	157	39	58	10	1	12	37	17	34	1	3	12-4	.369	.432	.675	1.107	1	.993
—	Richmond (Int'l)	OF	12	45	11	17	3	1	5	12	1	9	0	0	2-2	.378	.391	.822	1.214	1	.972
—	Atlanta (N.L.)	OF	31	106	11	23	7	1	5	13	7	29	0	1	3-0	.217	.265	.443	.709	2	.975
1997—	Atlanta (N.L.)	OF	153	399	60	92	18	1	18	70	56	107	4	11	20-11	.231	.329	.416	.745	7	.977
1998—	Atlanta (N.L.)	OF	159	582	89	158	33	8	31	90	40	129	4	10	27-4	.271	.321	.515	.836	2	.995
1999—	Atlanta (N.L.)	OF	•162	592	97	163	35	5	26	84	76	103	9	12	24-12	.275	.365	.483	.848	10	.981
2000—	Atlanta (N.L.)	OF	161	*656	122	199	36	6	36	104	59	100	9	12	21-6	.303	.366	.541	.907	2	.996
2001—	Atlanta (N.L.)	OF	161	625	104	157	25	2	34	104	56	142	3	10	11-4	.251	.312	.461	.772	6	.987
2002—	Atlanta (N.L.)	OF-DH	154	560	91	148	34	0	35	94	83	135	10	14	8-3	.264	.366	.513	.878	3	.993
2003—	Atlanta (N.L.)	OF	156	595	101	165	28	2	36	116	53	125	5	18	4-3	.277	.338	.513	.851	3	.993
2004—	Atlanta (N.L.)	OF	154	570	85	149	24	4	29	91	71	147	3	24	6-6	.261	.345	.488	.833	3	.993
	Major League totals (9 years)		1291	4685	760	1254	250	29	250	766	501	1017	47	112	124-49	.268	.342	.493	.835	38	.989

DIVISION SERIES RECORD

Year	Team (League)	Pos.	G	AB	R	H	2B	3B	HR	RBI	BB	SO	HBP	GDP	SB-CS	Avg.	OBP	SLG	OPS	E	Avg.
1996—	Atlanta (N.L.)	OF	3	0	0	0	0	0	0	0	1	0	0	0	0-0	...	1.000	...	1.000	0	1.000
1997—	Atlanta (N.L.)	OF	3	5	1	0	0	0	0	1	1	1	0	0	0-0	.000	.167	.000	.167	0	1.000
1998—	Atlanta (N.L.)	OF	3	9	2	0	0	0	0	1	3	2	0	0	2-0	.000	.231	.000	.231	0	1.000
1999—	Atlanta (N.L.)	OF	4	18	1	4	1	0	0	2	1	3	0	0	0-0	.222	.263	.278	.541	0	1.000
2000—	Atlanta (N.L.)	OF	3	9	3	1	0	0	1	1	4	1	0	1	0-1	.111	.385	.444	.829	0	1.000
2001—	Atlanta (N.L.)	OF	3	12	2	6	0	0	1	1	0	3	0	0	0-0	.500	.500	.750	1.250	0	1.000
2002—	Atlanta (N.L.)	OF	5	19	4	6	1	0	0	2	2	3	0	0	0-0	.316	.381	.368	.749	0	1.000
2003—	Atlanta (N.L.)	OF	5	17	1	1	0	0	0	1	4	7	0	0	0-0	.059	.238	.059	.297	1	.900
2004—	Atlanta (N.L.)	OF	5	19	4	10	2	0	2	5	2	3	0	1	1-0	.526	.571	.947	1.519	0	1.000
	Division series totals (9 years)		34	108	18	28	4	0	4	14	18	23	0	2	3-1	.259	.362	.407	.770	1	.988

CHAMPIONSHIP SERIES RECORD

Year	Team (League)	Pos.	G	AB	R	H	2B	3B	HR	RBI	BB	SO	HBP	GDP	SB-CS	Avg.	OBP	SLG	OPS	E	Avg.
1996—	Atlanta (N.L.)	OF	5	9	3	2	0	0	1	3	3	2	0	0	0-0	.222	.417	.556	.972	0	1.000
1997—	Atlanta (N.L.)	OF	5	9	0	4	0	0	0	1	1	1	0	0	0-0	.444	.500	.444	.944	0	1.000
1998—	Atlanta (N.L.)	OF	6	22	3	6	0	0	1	2	1	4	0	0	1-1	.273	.292	.409	.701	0	1.000
1999—	Atlanta (N.L.)	OF	6	23	5	5	0	0	1	1	4	3	0	1	0-1	.217	.333	.217	.551	0	1.000
2001—	Atlanta (N.L.)	OF	5	17	4	3	0	0	1	1	1	5	0	0	0-0	.176	.222	.353	.575	0	1.000
	Champ. series totals (5 years)		27	80	15	20	0	0	4	8	10	15	0	1	1-2	.250	.330	.363	.692	0	1.000

WORLD SERIES RECORD

Year Team (League)	Pos.	G	AB	R	H	2B	3B	HR	RBI	BB	SO	HBP	GDP	SB-CS	Avg.	OBP	SLG	OPS	E	Avg.
1996— Atlanta (N.L.)	OF	6	20	4	8	1	0	2	6	3	6	1	0	1-2	.400	.500	.750	1.250	0	1.000
1999— Atlanta (N.L.)	OF	4	13	1	1	0	0	0	0	1	3	0	1	0-0	.077	.143	.077	.220	0	1.000
World series totals (2 years)		10	33	5	9	1	0	2	6	4	9	1	1	1-2	.273	.368	.485	.853	0	1.000

ALL-STAR GAME RECORD

		G	AB	R	H	2B	3B	HR	RBI	BB	SO	HBP	GDP	SB-CS	Avg.	OBP	SLG	OPS	E	Avg.
All-Star Game totals (3 years)		3	7	2	3	1	0	1	4	0	3	0		0-0	.429	.429	1.000	1.429	0	1.000

JONES, BOBBY M.   P

PERSONAL: Born April 11, 1972, in Orange, N.J. ... 6-0/178. ... Throws left, bats right. ... Full name: Robert Mitchell Jones. ... High school: Rutherford (N.J.). ... Junior college: Chipola (Fla.).

TRANSACTIONS/CAREER NOTES: Selected by Milwaukee Brewers organization in 44th round of 1991 free-agent draft. ... Selected by Colorado Rockies organization from Brewers organization in Rule 5 minor league draft (December 5, 1994). ... Traded by Rockies with P Lariel Gonzalez to New York Mets for P Masato Yoshii (January 14, 2000). ... On disabled list (March 20, 2001-entire season); included rehabilitation assignments to St. Lucie, Binghamton and Norfolk. ... Traded by Mets with P Josh Reynolds and OF Jay Bay to San Diego Padres for Ps Steve Reed and Jason Middlebrook (July 31, 2002). ... Released by Padres (September 3, 2002). ... Signed by Atlanta Braves organization (January 21, 2003). ... Released by Braves (July 3, 2003). ... Signed by Kansas City Royals organization (July 9, 2003). ... Signed as a free agent by Boston Red Sox organization (November 10, 2003).

CAREER HITTING: 14-for-81 (.173), 7 R, 2 2B, 0 3B, 0 HR, 8 RBI.

Year Team (League)	W	L	Pct.	ERA	WHIP	G	GS	CG	ShO	Hld.	Sv.-Opp.	IP	H	R	ER	HR	BB-IBB	SO	Avg.
1992— Helena (Pio.)	5	4	.556	4.36	1.52	14	13	1	0	...	0-...	76.1	93	51	37	7	23-0	53	.299
1993— Beloit (Midw.)	10	10	.500	4.11	1.55	25	25	4	0	...	0-...	144.2	159	82	66	9	65-1	115	.274
1994— Stockton (Calif.)	6	12	.333	4.21	1.32	26	26	2	0	...	0-...	147.2	131	90	69	12	64-0	147	.233
1995— New Haven (East.)	5	2	.714	2.58	1.32	27	8	0	0	...	3-...	73.1	61	27	21	4	36-2	70	.230
— Colo. Springs (PCL)	1	2	.333	7.30	2.04	11	8	0	0	...	0-...	40.2	50	38	33	5	33-1	48	.305
1996— Colo. Springs (PCL)	2	8	.200	4.97	1.70	57	0	0	0	...	3-...	88.2	88	54	49	8	63-4	78	.262
1997— Colo. Springs (PCL)	7	11	.389	5.14	1.55	25	21	0	0	...	0-...	133.0	135	89	76	16	71-2	104	.268
— Colorado (N.L.)	1	1	.500	8.38	2.17	4	4	0	0	0	0-0	19.1	30	18	18	2	12-0	5	.380
1998— Colorado (N.L.)	7	8	.467	5.22	1.55	35	20	1	0	1	0-0	141.1	153	87	82	12	66-0	109	.282
1999— Colorado (N.L.)	6	10	.375	6.33	1.86	30	20	0	0	0	0-0	112.1	132	91	79	24	77-0	74	.292
— Colo. Springs (PCL)	2	1	.667	5.40	1.92	3	3	0	0	...	0-...	16.2	17	13	10	1	15-0	14	.266
2000— Norfolk (Int'l)	10	8	.556	4.32	1.35	22	21	4	1	...	0-...	133.1	122	66	64	13	58-4	100	.241
— New York (N.L.)	0	1	.000	4.15	1.48	11	1	0	0	0	0-0	21.2	18	11	10	2	14-1	20	.222
2001— St. Lucie (Fla. St.)	0	1	.000	0.93	1.03	4	4	0	0	...	0-...	9.2	6	2	1	0	4-0	9	.171
— Binghamton (Eastern)	0	0	...	0.00	0.00	2	1	0	0	...	0-...	5.0	0	0	0	0	0-0	6	.000
— Norfolk (Int'l)	0	0	...	0.00	0.00	1	1	0	0	...	0-...	2.0	0	0	0	0	0-0	0	.000
2002— Norfolk (Int'l)	1	4	.200	4.02	1.41	13	6	0	0	...	0-...	40.1	42	25	18	4	15-0	35	.255
— New York (N.L.)	0	0	...	5.29	1.82	12	0	0	0	0	0-0	17.0	20	11	10	3	11-2	11	.299
— San Diego (N.L.)	0	0	...	6.52	1.76	4	2	0	0	0	0-0	9.2	10	7	7	1	7-0	7	.270
2003— Richmond (Int'l)	1	3	.250	3.12	1.40	37	0	0	0	...	5-...	34.2	29	12	12	3	18-1	39	.232
— Omaha (PCL)	1	2	.333	3.65	1.30	20	1	0	0	...	1-...	37.0	28	15	15	4	20-1	27	.211
2004— Boston (A.L.)	0	1	.000	5.40	3.30	3	0	0	0	0	0-0	3.1	3	2	2	1	8-1	3	.273
American League totals (1 year)	0	1	.000	5.40	3.30	3	0	0	0	0	0-0	3.1	3	2	2	1	8-1	3	.273
National League totals (5 years)	14	20	.412	5.77	1.71	96	47	1	0	2	0-0	321.1	363	225	206	44	187-3	226	.289
Major League totals (6 years)	14	21	.400	5.77	1.73	99	47	1	0	2	0-0	324.2	366	227	208	45	195-4	229	.288

JONES, CHIPPER   3B/OF

PERSONAL: Born April 24, 1972, in DeLand, Fla. ... 6-4/210. ... Bats both, throws right. ... Full name: Larry Wayne Jones. ... High school: The Bolles School (Jacksonville).

TRANSACTIONS/CAREER NOTES: Selected by Atlanta Braves organization in first round (first pick overall) of 1990 free-agent draft. ... On disabled list (March 20, 1994-entire season; and March 22-April 16, 1996). ... On disabled list (April 19-May 8, 2004); included rehabilitation assignment to Rome.

HONORS: Named N.L. Rookie Player of the Year by THE SPORTING NEWS (1995). ... Named N.L. Most Valuable Player by Baseball Writers' Association of America (1999).

2004 GAMES PLAYED BY POSITION (MLB): 3B—96, OF—29, DH—7.

Year Team (League)	Pos.	G	AB	R	H	2B	3B	HR	RBI	BB	SO	HBP	GDP	SB-CS	Avg.	OBP	SLG	OPS	E	Avg.
1990— GC Braves (GCL)	SS	44	140	20	32	1	1	1	18	14	25	6	3	5-3	.229	.321	.271	.592	18	.919
1991— Macon (S. Atl.)	SS	136	473	104	154	24	11	15	98	69	70	3	6	40-11	.326	.407	.518	.925	56	.919
1992— Durham (Caro.)	SS	70	264	43	73	22	1	4	31	31	34	2	5	10-8	.277	.353	.413	.766	14	.956
— Greenville (Sou.)	SS	67	266	43	92	17	11	9	42	11	32	0	5	14-1	.346	.367	.594	.961	18	.945
1993— Richmond (Int'l)	SS	139	536	97	174	31	12	13	89	57	70	1	8	23-7	.325	.387	.500	.887	43	.931
— Atlanta (N.L.)	SS	8	3	2	2	1	0	0	0	1	1	0	0	0-0	.667	.750	1.000	1.750	0	1.000
1994— Atlanta (N.L.)				Did not play.																
1995— Atlanta (N.L.)	3B-OF	140	524	87	139	22	3	23	86	73	99	0	10	8-4	.265	.353	.450	.803	25	.935
1996— Atlanta (N.L.) 3B-SS-OF		157	598	114	185	32	5	30	110	87	88	0	14	14-1	.309	.393	.530	.923	17	.958
1997— Atlanta (N.L.)	3B-OF	157	597	100	176	41	3	21	111	76	88	0	19	20-5	.295	.371	.479	.850	15	.956
1998— Atlanta (N.L.)	3B	160	601	123	188	29	5	34	107	96	93	1	17	16-6	.313	.404	.547	.951	12	.971
1999— Atlanta (N.L.)	3B-SS	157	567	116	181	41	1	45	110	126	94	2	20	25-3	.319	.441	.633	1.074	17	.951
2000— Atlanta (N.L.)	3B-SS	156	579	118	180	38	1	36	111	95	64	2	14	14-7	.311	.404	.566	.970	25	.941
2001— Atlanta (N.L.) 3B-OF-DH		159	572	113	189	33	5	38	102	98	82	2	13	9-10	.330	.427	.605	1.032	18	.947
2002— Atlanta (N.L.)	OF	158	548	90	179	35	1	26	100	107	89	2	18	8-2	.327	.435	.537	.972	7	.975
2003— Atlanta (N.L.)	OF-DH	153	555	103	169	33	2	27	106	94	83	1	10	2-2	.305	.402	.517	.920	7	.968
2004— Rome (S. Atl.)	OF	1	4	0	0	0	0	0	0	0	0	0	0	0-0	.000	.000	.000	.000	0	1.000
— Atlanta (N.L.) 3B-OF-DH		137	472	69	117	20	1	30	96	84	96	4	14	2-0	.248	.362	.485	.847	6	.978
Major League totals (11 years)		1542	5616	1035	1705	325	27	310	1039	937	877	14	149	118-40	.304	.401	.537	.937	149	.957

DIVISION SERIES RECORD

Year Team (League)	Pos.	G	AB	R	H	2B	3B	HR	RBI	BB	SO	HBP	GDP	SB-CS	Avg.	OBP	SLG	OPS	E	Avg.
1995— Atlanta (N.L.)	3B	4	18	4	7	2	0	2	4	2	2	0	2	0-0	.389	.450	.833	1.283	0	1.000
1996— Atlanta (N.L.)	3B	3	9	2	2	0	0	1	2	3	4	0	0	1-1	.222	.417	.556	.972	1	1.000
1997— Atlanta (N.L.)	3B	3	8	3	4	0	0	1	2	3	2	0	0	1-0	.500	.583	.875	1.458	1	.833
1998— Atlanta (N.L.)	3B	3	10	2	2	1	0	0	1	4	3	0	0	0-0	.200	.429	.200	.629	0	1.000
1999— Atlanta (N.L.)	3B	4	13	2	3	0	0	0	1	5	2	0	1	0-0	.231	.421	.231	.652	1	.875

Year Team (League)	Pos.	G	AB	R	H	2B	3B	HR	RBI	BB	SO	HBP	GDP	SB-CS	Avg.	OBP	SLG	OPS	E	Avg.
2000— Atlanta (N.L.)	3B	3	12	2	4	1	0	0	1	1	4	0	0	0-0	.333	.385	.417	.801	2	.800
2001— Atlanta (N.L.)	3B	3	9	2	4	0	0	2	5	3	1	0	0	0-1	.444	.583	1.111	1.694	0	1.000
2002— Atlanta (N.L.)	OF	5	17	3	5	0	0	0	2	5	2	0	1	0-0	.294	.455	.294	.749	0	1.000
2003— Atlanta (N.L.)	OF	5	18	3	3	0	0	2	6	3	4	0	1	0-0	.167	.286	.500	.786	0	1.000
2004— Atlanta (N.L.)	3B	5	20	4	4	0	0	0	0	3	2	0	1	0-0	.200	.304	.200	.504	0	1.000
Division series totals (10 years)		38	134	27	38	3	0	8	24	32	26	0	6	2-2	.284	.417	.485	.902	4	.944

CHAMPIONSHIP SERIES RECORD

Year Team (League)	Pos.	G	AB	R	H	2B	3B	HR	RBI	BB	SO	HBP	GDP	SB-CS	Avg.	OBP	SLG	OPS	E	Avg.
1995— Atlanta (N.L.)	3B	4	16	3	7	0	0	1	3	3	1	0	0	1-0	.438	.526	.625	1.151	0	1.000
1996— Atlanta (N.L.)	3B	7	25	6	11	2	0	0	4	3	1	0	0	1-0	.440	.483	.520	1.003	1	.923
1997— Atlanta (N.L.)	3B	6	24	5	7	1	0	2	4	2	3	0	0	0-0	.292	.346	.583	.929	0	1.000
1998— Atlanta (N.L.)	3B	6	24	2	5	1	0	0	1	4	5	0	2	0-0	.208	.321	.250	.571	1	1.000
1999— Atlanta (N.L.)	3B	6	19	3	5	2	0	0	1	9	7	1	0	3-0	.263	.517	.368	.886	2	.867
2001— Atlanta (N.L.)	3B	5	19	1	5	1	0	0	2	3	6	0	0	0-0	.263	.364	.316	.679	1	.923
Champ. series totals (6 years)		34	127	20	40	7	0	3	15	24	23	1	2	5-0	.315	.425	.441	.866	4	.950

WORLD SERIES RECORD

Year Team (League)	Pos.	G	AB	R	H	2B	3B	HR	RBI	BB	SO	HBP	GDP	SB-CS	Avg.	OBP	SLG	OPS	E	Avg.
1995— Atlanta (N.L.)	3B	6	21	3	6	3	0	0	1	4	3	0	0	0-0	.286	.385	.429	.813	1	.947
1996— Atlanta (N.L.)	3B-SS	6	21	3	6	0	0	0	3	4	2	0	1	1-0	.286	.385	.429	.813	0	1.000
1999— Atlanta (N.L.)	3B	4	13	2	3	0	0	1	2	4	2	0	0	0-1	.231	.412	.462	.873	0	1.000
World series totals (3 years)		16	55	8	15	6	0	1	6	12	7	0	1	1-1	.273	.391	.436	.828	1	.972

ALL-STAR GAME RECORD

	G	AB	R	H	2B	3B	HR	RBI	BB	SO	HBP	GDP	SB-CS	Avg.	OBP	SLG	OPS	E	Avg.
All-Star Game totals (5 years)	5	10	3	4	0	0	1	1	1	0	0	1	0-0	.400	.455	.700	1.155	0	1.000

JONES, JACQUE — OF

PERSONAL: Born April 25, 1975, in San Diego, Calif. ... 5-10/195. ... Bats left, throws left. ... Full name: Jacque Dewayne Jones. ... High school: San Diego High. ... College: USC.

TRANSACTIONS/CAREER NOTES: Selected by Kansas City Royals organization in 31st round of 1993 free-agent draft; did not sign. ... Selected by Minnesota Twins organization in second round of 1996 free-agent draft. ... On disabled list (July 1-17, 2003).

2004 GAMES PLAYED BY POSITION (MLB): OF—142, DH—3.

Year Team (League)	Pos.	G	AB	R	H	2B	3B	HR	RBI	BB	SO	HBP	GDP	SB-CS	Avg.	OBP	SLG	OPS	E	Avg.
1996— Fort Myers (FSL)	OF	1	3	0	2	1	0	0	1	0	0	0	0	0-0	.667	.667	1.000	1.667	0	—
1997— Fort Myers (FSL)	OF	131	539	84	160	33	6	15	82	33	110	3	9	24-12	.297	.340	.464	.804	7	.979
1998— New Britain (East.)	OF-DH	134	518	78	155	39	3	21	85	37	134	4	4	18-11	.299	.349	.508	.856	10	.968
1999— Salt Lake (PCL)	OF	52	198	32	59	13	2	4	26	9	36	0	5	9-2	.298	.325	.444	.770	2	.987
— Minnesota (A.L.)	OF	95	322	54	93	24	2	9	44	17	63	4	7	3-4	.289	.329	.460	.789	5	.980
2000— Minnesota (A.L.)	OF	154	523	66	149	26	5	19	76	26	111	0	17	7-5	.285	.319	.463	.781	2	.994
2001— Minnesota (A.L.)	OF-DH	149	475	57	131	25	0	14	49	39	92	3	10	12-9	.276	.335	.417	.751	5	.983
2002— Minnesota (A.L.)	OF-DH	149	577	96	173	37	2	27	85	37	129	2	8	6-7	.300	.341	.511	.852	5	.986
2003— Minnesota (A.L.)	OF-DH	136	517	76	157	33	1	16	69	21	105	4	10	13-1	.304	.333	.464	.797	5	.977
2004— Minnesota (A.L.)	OF-DH	151	555	69	141	22	1	24	80	40	117	10	12	13-10	.254	.315	.427	.742	2	.994
Major League totals (6 years)		834	2969	418	844	167	11	109	403	180	617	23	64	54-36	.284	.329	.458	.787	24	.986

DIVISION SERIES RECORD

Year Team (League)	Pos.	G	AB	R	H	2B	3B	HR	RBI	BB	SO	HBP	GDP	SB-CS	Avg.	OBP	SLG	OPS	E	Avg.
2002— Minnesota (A.L.)	OF	5	20	3	5	3	0	0	1	1	8	1	1	0-0	.250	.318	.400	.718	1	.952
2003— Minnesota (A.L.)	OF	4	16	0	2	0	0	0	0	0	5	0	0	0-0	.125	.125	.125	.250	0	1.000
2004— Minnesota (A.L.)	OF	4	20	3	6	1	0	2	2	0	6	0	2	0-1	.300	.300	.650	.950	0	1.000
Division series totals (3 years)		13	56	6	13	4	0	2	3	1	19	1	3	0-1	.232	.259	.411	.669	1	.972

CHAMPIONSHIP SERIES RECORD

Year Team (League)	Pos.	G	AB	R	H	2B	3B	HR	RBI	BB	SO	HBP	GDP	SB-CS	Avg.	OBP	SLG	OPS	E	Avg.
2002— Minnesota (A.L.)	OF	5	20	0	2	1	0	0	0	0	4	0	0	0-0	.100	.095	.150	.245	0	1.000

JONES, TODD — P

PERSONAL: Born April 24, 1968, in Marietta, Ga. ... 6-3/230. ... Throws right, bats left. ... Full name: Todd Barton Jones. ... High school: Osborne (Ga.). ... College: Jacksonville State.

TRANSACTIONS/CAREER NOTES: Selected by New York Mets organization in 41st round of June 1986 free-agent draft; did not sign. ... Selected by Houston Astros organization in supplemental round ("sandwich pick" between first and second rounds, 27th pick overall) of 1989 free-agent draft; pick received as part of compensation for Texas Rangers signing Type A free-agent P Nolan Ryan. ... On suspended list (July 19-August 12 and August 18-September 12, 1996); included rehabilitation assignment to Tucson. ... Traded by Astros with OF Brian Hunter, IF Orlando Miller, P Doug Brocail and cash to Detroit Tigers for C Brad Ausmus, Ps Jose Lima, C.J. Nitkowski and Trever Miller and 1B Daryle Ward (December 10, 1996). ... Traded by Tigers to Minnesota Twins for P Mark Redman (July 28, 2001). ... Signed as a free agent by Colorado Rockies (January 15, 2002). ... Released by Rockies (June 30, 2003). ... Signed by Boston Red Sox (July 2, 2003). ... Signed as a free agent by Tampa Bay Devil Rays organization (January 11, 2004). ... Released by Devil Rays (March 24, 2004). ... Signed by Cincinnati Reds organization (March 25, 2004). ... Traded by Reds with OF Brad Correll to Philadelphia Phillies for P Josh Hancock and SS Anderson Machado (July 30, 2004).

HONORS: Named A.L. Fireman of the Year by THE SPORTING NEWS (2000).

CAREER HITTING: 3-for-16 (.188), 1 R, 1 2B, 0 3B, 0 HR, 0 RBI.

Year Team (League)	W	L	Pct.	ERA	WHIP	G	GS	CG	ShO	Hld.	Sv.-Opp.	IP	H	R	ER	HR	BB-IBB	SO	Avg.
1989— Auburn (N.Y.-Penn)	2	3	.400	5.44	1.79	11	9	1	0	...	0-...	49.2	47	39	30	2	42-1	71	.240
1990— Osceola (Florida St.)	12	10	.545	3.51	1.54	27	27	1	0	...	0-...	151.1	124	81	59	2	109-1	106	.223
1991— Osceola (Florida St.)	4	4	.500	4.35	1.44	14	14	0	0	...	0-...	72.1	69	38	35	2	35-0	51	.256
— Jackson (Texas)	4	3	.571	4.88	1.63	10	10	0	0	...	0-...	55.1	51	37	30	2	39-1	37	.241
1992— Jackson (Texas)	3	7	.300	3.14	1.45	61	0	0	0	...	25-...	66.0	52	28	23	3	44-3	60	.213
— Tucson (PCL)	0	1	.000	4.50	2.75	3	0	0	0	...	0-...	4.0	1	2	2	0	10-1	4	.077
1993— Tucson (PCL)	4	2	.667	4.44	1.64	41	0	0	0	...	12-...	48.2	49	26	24	5	31-2	45	.265
— Houston (N.L.)	1	2	.333	3.13	1.15	27	0	0	0	6	2-3	37.1	28	14	13	4	15-2	25	.214
1994— Houston (N.L.)	5	2	.714	2.72	1.07	48	0	0	0	8	5-9	72.2	52	23	22	3	26-4	63	.202

Year— Team (League)	W	L	Pct.	ERA	WHIP	G	GS	CG	ShO	Hld.	Sv.-Opp.	IP	H	R	ER	HR	BB-IBB	SO	Avg.
1995— Houston (N.L.)	6	5	.545	3.07	1.41	68	0	0	0	8	15-20	99.2	89	38	34	8	52-17	96	.237
1996— Houston (N.L.)	6	3	.667	4.40	1.62	51	0	0	0	1	17-23	57.1	61	30	28	5	32-6	44	.274
—Tucson (PCL)	0	0	...	0.00	1.50	1	0	0	0	...	0-...	2.0	1	1	0	0	2-0	0	.200
1997— Detroit (A.L.)	5	4	.556	3.09	1.36	68	0	0	0	5	31-36	70.0	60	29	24	3	35-2	70	.231
1998— Detroit (A.L.)	1	4	.200	4.97	1.48	65	0	0	0	0	28-32	63.1	58	38	35	7	36-4	57	.249
1999— Detroit (A.L.)	4	4	.500	3.80	1.49	65	0	0	0	0	30-35	66.1	64	30	28	7	35-1	64	.259
2000— Detroit (A.L.)	2	4	.333	3.52	1.44	67	0	0	0	0	• 42-46	64.0	67	28	25	6	25-1	67	.276
2001— Detroit (A.L.)	4	5	.444	4.62	1.68	45	0	0	0	3	11-17	48.2	60	31	25	6	22-1	39	.303
—Minnesota (A.L.)	1	0	1.000	3.26	1.78	24	0	0	0	7	2-4	19.1	27	8	7	3	7-0	15	.333
2002— Colorado (N.L.)	1	4	.200	4.70	1.36	79	0	0	0	30	1-3	82.1	84	43	43	10	28-3	73	.269
2003— Colorado (N.L.)	1	4	.200	8.24	2.01	33	1	0	0	3	0-5	39.1	61	39	36	8	18-0	28	.361
—Boston (A.L.)	2	1	.667	5.52	1.53	26	0	0	0	1	0-0	29.1	32	19	18	2	13-2	31	.269
2004— Cincinnati (N.L.)	8	2	.800	3.79	1.30	51	0	0	0	22	1-6	57.0	49	25	24	4	25-2	37	.243
—Philadelphia (N.L.)	3	3	.500	4.97	1.70	27	0	0	0	5	1-2	25.1	35	14	14	3	8-3	22	.330
American League totals (6 years)	19	22	.463	4.04	1.50	360	0	0	0	16	144-170	361.0	368	183	162	34	173-11	343	.266
National League totals (7 years)	31	25	.554	4.09	1.41	384	1	0	0	83	42-71	471.0	459	226	214	45	204-37	388	.259
Major League totals (12 years)	50	47	.515	4.07	1.45	744	1	0	0	99	186-241	832.0	827	409	376	79	377-48	731	.262

CHAMPIONSHIP SERIES RECORD

Year— Team (League)	W	L	Pct.	ERA	WHIP	G	GS	CG	ShO	Hld.	Sv.-Opp.	IP	H	R	ER	HR	BB-IBB	SO	Avg.
2003— Boston (A.L.)	0	0	...	0.00	6.00	1	0	0	0	0	0-0	.1	1	0	0	0	1-0	1	.500

ALL-STAR GAME RECORD

	W	L	Pct.	ERA	WHIP	G	GS	CG	ShO	Hld.	Sv.-Opp.	IP	H	R	ER	HR	BB-IBB	SO	Avg.
All-Star Game totals (1 year)	0	0	...	0.00	0.00	1	0	0	0	1	0-0	1.0	0	0	0	0	0-0	1	.000

JORDAN, BRIAN — OF

PERSONAL: Born March 29, 1967, in Baltimore, Md. ... 6-1/225. ... Bats right, throws right. ... Full name: Brian O'Neal Jordan. ... High school: Milford (Baltimore). ... College: Richmond.

TRANSACTIONS/CAREER NOTES: Selected by Cleveland Indians organization in 20th round of June 1985 free-agent draft; did not sign. ... Selected by St. Louis Cardinals organization in supplemental round ("sandwich pick" between first and second rounds, 30th pick overall) of 1988 free-agent draft; pick received as part of compensation for New York Yankees signing Type A free-agent 1B/OF Jack Clark. ... On temporarily inactive list (July 3, 1991-remainder of season). ... On disabled list (May 23-June 22, 1992); included rehabilitation assignment to Louisville. ... On disabled list (July 10, 1994-remainder of season; and March 31-April 15, 1996). ... On disabled list (May 6-June 13, June 26-August 10 and August 25, 1997-remainder of season); Included rehabilitation assignment to Louisville. ... Signed as a free agent by Atlanta Braves (November 23, 1998). ... On disabled list (April 4-19, 2000). ... Traded by Braves with Ps Odalis Perez and Andrew Brown to Los Angeles Dodgers for OF Gary Sheffield (January 15, 2002). ... On disabled list (August 17-September 1, 2002; and June 25, 2003-remainder of season). ... Signed as a free agent by Texas Rangers (January 8, 2004). ... On disabled list (March 27-April 27 and May 24-July 23, 2004); included rehabilitation assignments to Frisco and Oklahoma.

2004 GAMES PLAYED BY POSITION (MLB): OF—44, DH—17.

Year— Team (League)	Pos.	G	AB	R	H	2B	3B	HR	RBI	BB	SO	HBP	GDP	SB-CS	Avg.	OBP	SLG	OPS	E	Avg.
1988— Hamilton (N.Y.-Penn.)	OF	19	71	12	22	3	1	4	12	6	15	3	0	3-3	.310	.388	.549	.937	1	.971
1989— St. Pete. (FSL)	OF	11	43	7	15	4	1	2	11	0	8	2	1	0-2	.349	.378	.628	1.006	0	1.000
1990— Arkansas (Texas)	OF	16	50	4	8	1	0	0	0	0	11	1	1	0-0	.160	.176	.180	.356	2	.933
—St. Pete. (FSL)	OF	9	30	3	5	0	1	0	1	2	11	0	0	0-2	.167	.219	.233	.452	0	1.000
1991— Louisville (A.A.)	OF	61	212	35	56	11	4	4	24	17	41	8	5	10-4	.264	.342	.410	.752	2	.987
1992— St. Louis (N.L.)	OF	55	193	17	40	9	4	5	22	10	48	1	6	7-2	.207	.250	.373	.623	1	.991
—Louisville (A.A.)	OF	43	155	23	45	3	1	4	16	8	21	4	1	13-2	.290	.337	.400	.737	1	.989
1993— St. Louis (N.L.)	OF	67	223	33	69	10	6	10	44	12	35	4	6	6-6	.309	.351	.543	.894	4	.973
—Louisville (A.A.)	OF	38	144	24	54	13	2	5	35	16	17	3	3	9-4	.375	.442	.597	1.040	0	1.000
1994— St. Louis (N.L.)	OF-1B	53	178	14	46	8	2	5	15	16	40	1	6	4-3	.258	.320	.427	.730	1	.991
1995— St. Louis (N.L.)	OF	131	490	83	145	20	4	22	81	22	79	11	5	24-9	.296	.339	.488	.827	1	.996
1996— St. Louis (N.L.)	OF-1B	140	513	82	159	36	1	17	104	29	84	7	6	22-5	.310	.349	.483	.833	2	.994
1997— St. Louis (N.L.)	OF	47	145	17	34	5	0	0	10	10	21	6	4	6-1	.234	.311	.269	.580	0	1.000
—Louisville (A.A.)	OF-DH	6	20	1	3	0	0	0	2	1	2	1	0	0-1	.150	.227	.150	.377	0	1.000
1998— St. Louis (N.L.)	OF-DH-3B	150	564	100	178	34	7	25	91	40	66	9	18	17-5	.316	.368	.534	.902	9	.970
1999— Atlanta (N.L.)	OF	153	576	100	163	28	4	23	115	51	81	9	9	13-8	.283	.346	.465	.811	3	.990
2000— Atlanta (N.L.)	OF	133	489	71	129	26	0	17	77	38	80	5	12	10-2	.264	.320	.421	.742	3	.990
2001— Atlanta (N.L.)	OF-DH	148	560	82	165	32	3	25	97	31	88	6	18	3-2	.295	.334	.496	.830	3	.991
2002— Los Angeles (N.L.)	OF-DH	128	471	65	134	27	3	18	80	34	86	6	10	2-2	.285	.338	.469	.807	4	.982
2003— Los Angeles (N.L.)	OF-DH	66	224	28	67	9	0	6	28	23	30	4	3	1-1	.299	.372	.420	.791	1	.990
2004— Frisco (Texas)	OF-DH	6	19	1	3	1	0	0	0	0	6	0	0	0-0	.158	.158	.211	.368	0	1.000
—Oklahoma (PCL)	OF-DH	7	26	3	10	2	0	0	8	3	3	1	0	1-0	.385	.467	.462	.928	0	1.000
—Texas (A.L.)	OF-DH	61	212	27	47	13	1	5	23	16	35	1	7	2-2	.222	.275	.363	.638	1	.990
American League totals (1 year)		61	212	27	47	13	1	5	23	16	35	1	7	2-2	.222	.275	.363	.638	1	.990
National League totals (12 years)		1271	4626	692	1329	244	34	173	764	316	738	69	103	115-46	.287	.339	.467	.806	32	.988
Major League totals (13 years)		1332	4838	719	1376	257	35	178	787	332	773	70	110	117-48	.284	.336	.462	.798	33	.988

DIVISION SERIES RECORD

Year— Team (League)	Pos.	G	AB	R	H	2B	3B	HR	RBI	BB	SO	HBP	GDP	SB-CS	Avg.	OBP	SLG	OPS	E	Avg.
1996— St. Louis (N.L.)	OF	3	12	4	4	0	0	1	3	1	3	0	0	1-0	.333	.385	.583	.968	0	1.000
1999— Atlanta (N.L.)	OF	4	17	2	8	1	0	1	7	1	2	0	0	0-1	.471	.474	.706	1.180	0	1.000
2000— Atlanta (N.L.)	OF	3	11	1	4	1	0	0	4	1	1	0	0	0-0	.364	.417	.455	.871	0	1.000
2001— Atlanta (N.L.)	OF	3	11	1	2	0	0	1	2	0	5	0	0	0-1	.182	.167	.455	.621	0	1.000
Division series totals (4 years)		13	51	8	18	2	0	3	16	3	11	0	0	1-2	.353	.375	.569	.944	0	1.000

CHAMPIONSHIP SERIES RECORD

Year— Team (League)	Pos.	G	AB	R	H	2B	3B	HR	RBI	BB	SO	HBP	GDP	SB-CS	Avg.	OBP	SLG	OPS	E	Avg.
1996— St. Louis (N.L.)	OF	7	25	3	6	1	1	1	2	1	3	0	1	0-0	.240	.269	.480	.749	0	1.000
1999— Atlanta (N.L.)	OF	6	25	3	5	0	0	2	5	3	5	1	0	0-0	.200	.310	.440	.750	0	1.000
2001— Atlanta (N.L.)	OF	5	21	1	4	2	0	0	3	0	6	0	1	0-0	.190	.190	.286	.476	0	1.000
Champ. series totals (3 years)		18	71	7	15	3	1	3	10	4	14	1	2	0-0	.211	.263	.408	.672	0	1.000

WORLD SERIES RECORD

Year— Team (League)	Pos.	G	AB	R	H	2B	3B	HR	RBI	BB	SO	HBP	GDP	SB-CS	Avg.	OBP	SLG	OPS	E	Avg.
1999— Atlanta (N.L.)	OF	4	13	1	1	0	0	0	1	4	2	0	1	0-0	.077	.294	.077	.371	1	.889

ALL-STAR GAME RECORD

	G	AB	R	H	2B	3B	HR	RBI	BB	SO	HBP	GDP	SB-CS	Avg.	OBP	SLG	OPS	E	Avg.
All-Star Game totals (1 year)	1	1	0	1	0	0	0	0	0	0	0	0	0-1	1.000	1.000	1.000	2.000	0	...

JULIO, JORGE — P

PERSONAL: Born March 3, 1979, in Caracas, Venezuela. ... 6-1/232. ... Throws right, bats right. ... Full name: Jorge Dandys Julio. ... High school: Fundacion Bolivariana (Caracas, Venezuela).

TRANSACTIONS/CAREER NOTES: Signed as a non-drafted free agent by Montreal Expos organization (February 14, 1996). ... Traded by Expos to Baltimore Orioles for 3B Ryan Minor (December 22, 2000). ... On suspended list (September 24-28, 2004).

CAREER HITTING: 0-for-0 (.000), 0 R, 0 2B, 0 3B, 0 HR, 0 RBI.

Year Team (League)	W	L	Pct.	ERA	WHIP	G	GS	CG	ShO	Hld.	Sv.-Opp.	IP	H	R	ER	HR	BB-IBB	SO	Avg.
1996— DSL Expos (DSL)	1	1	.500	6.06	1.47	10	0	0	0	...	0-...	16.1	13	12	11	0	11-...	21	
1997— GC Expos (GCL)	5	6	.455	3.58	1.41	15	0	0	0	...	1-...	55.1	57	25	22	0	21-0	42	.256
—W.P. Beach (FSL)	0	0	...	...	...	1	0	0	0	...	0-...	.0	2	1	1	0	0-0	0	1.000
1998— Vermont (NY-P)	3	1	.750	2.57	1.07	7	7	0	0	...	0-...	42.0	30	12	12	1	15-0	52	.196
—Cape Fear (S. Atl.)	2	2	.500	5.68	1.42	6	6	0	0	...	0-...	31.2	33	20	20	4	12-0	20	.275
1999— Jupiter (FSL)	4	8	.333	3.92	1.31	23	22	0	0	...	0-...	114.2	116	62	50	6	34-0	80	.260
2000— Jupiter (FSL)	2	10	.167	5.90	1.61	21	15	0	0	...	1-...	79.1	93	60	52	4	35-0	67	.292
2001— Bowie (East.)	0	0	...	0.73	0.57	12	0	0	0	...	7-...	12.1	5	1	1	0	2-1	14	.125
—Baltimore (A.L.)	1	1	.500	3.80	1.59	18	0	0	0	3	0-1	21.1	25	13	9	2	9-0	22	.287
—Rochester (Int'l)	1	2	.333	3.74	1.34	34	0	0	0	...	12-...	43.1	39	27	18	4	19-3	48	.232
2002— Baltimore (A.L.)	5	6	.455	1.99	1.21	67	0	0	0	1	25-31	68.0	55	22	15	5	27-3	55	.213
2003— Baltimore (A.L.)	0	7	.000	4.38	1.52	64	0	0	0	2	36-44	61.2	60	36	30	10	34-4	52	.256
2004— Baltimore (A.L.)	2	5	.286	4.57	1.42	65	0	0	0	2	22-26	69.0	59	35	35	11	39-4	70	.228
Major League totals (4 years)	8	19	.296	3.64	1.40	214	0	0	0	8	83-102	220.0	199	106	89	28	109-11	199	.237

KAPLER, GABE — OF

PERSONAL: Born August 31, 1975, in Hollywood, Calif. ... 6-2/200. ... Bats right, throws right. ... Full name: Gabriel Stefan Kapler. ... Name pronounced: CAP-ler. ... High school: Taft (Woodland Hills, Calif.). ... Junior college: Moorpark (Calif.).

TRANSACTIONS/CAREER NOTES: Selected by Detroit Tigers organization in 57th round of 1995 free-agent draft. ... Traded by Tigers with Ps Justin Thompson, Francisco Cordero and Alan Webb, C Bill Haselman and 2B Frank Catalanotto to Texas Rangers for OF Juan Gonzalez, P Danny Patterson and C Gregg Zaun (November 2, 1999). ... On disabled list (May 4-June 9, 2000); included rehabilitation assignments to Oklahoma and Tulsa. ... On disabled list (March 23-April 22, 2001); included rehabilitation assignment to Tulsa. ... On disabled list (June 24-July 16, 2002); included rehabilitation assignment to Oklahoma. ... Traded by Rangers with 2B Jason Romano to Colorado Rockies for OF Todd Hollandsworth and P Dennys Reyes (July 31, 2002). ... Released by Rockies (June 20, 2003). ... Signed by Boston Red Sox organization (June 24, 2004).

HONORS: Named Minor League Player of the Year by The Sporting News (1998).

2004 GAMES PLAYED BY POSITION (MLB): OF—127, DH—2.

Year Team (League)	Pos.	G	AB	R	H	2B	3B	HR	RBI	BB	SO	HBP	GDP	SB-CS	Avg.	OBP	SLG	OPS	E	Avg.
1995— Jamestown (N.Y.-Penn.) ...	OF	63	236	38	68	19	4	4	34	23	37	2	4	1-2	.288	.351	.453	.804	9	.926
1996— Fayetteville (SAL)	3B-OF	138	524	81	157	45	0	26	99	62	73	7	6	14-4	.300	.378	.534	.912	7	.968
1997— Lakeland (Fla. St.)	OF	137	519	87	153	40	6	19	87	54	68	5	8	8-6	.295	.361	.505	.865	5	.978
1998— Jacksonville (Sou.)	1B-OF	139	547	113	176	47	6	28	146	66	93	5	6	6-4	.322	.393	.583	.976	5	.984
—Detroit (A.L.)	OF-DH	7	25	3	5	0	1	0	0	1	4	0	0	2-0	.200	.231	.280	.511	0	1.000
1999— Detroit (A.L.)	OF-DH	130	416	60	102	22	4	18	49	42	74	2	7	11-5	.245	.315	.447	.762	6	.981
—Toledo (Int'l)	OF	14	54	11	17	6	2	3	14	9	10	0	0	0-1	.315	.400	.667	1.067	0	1.000
2000— Texas (A.L.)	OF	116	444	59	134	32	1	14	66	42	57	0	12	8-4	.302	.360	.473	.833	• 10	.969
—Oklahoma (PCL)	OF	3	9	3	3	0	0	0	0	3	2	0	0	0-0	.333	.500	.333	.833	0	1.000
—Tulsa (Texas)	OF	3	12	3	7	0	0	1	4	1	2	0	0	0-0	.583	.615	.833	1.449	0	1.000
2001— Tulsa (Texas)	OF	5	15	2	5	1	0	0	0	6	1	0	0	0-1	.333	.524	.400	.924	0	1.000
—Texas (A.L.)	OF-DH	134	483	77	129	29	1	17	72	61	70	3	10	23-6	.267	.348	.437	.785	1	.997
2002— Texas (A.L.)	OF-DH-1B	72	196	25	51	12	1	0	17	8	30	0	3	5-2	.260	.285	.332	.617	3	.977
—Oklahoma (PCL)	OF	5	17	6	8	2	0	1	5	3	2	0	...	1-0	.471	.550	.765	1.315	0	1.000
—Colorado (N.L.)	OF	40	119	12	37	4	3	2	17	8	23	1	2	6-2	.311	.359	.445	.805	0	.970
2003— Colorado (N.L.)	OF	39	67	10	15	2	0	0	4	8	18	0	3	2-0	.224	.307	.254	.560	1	.955
—Colo. Springs (PCL)	OF	13	35	5	6	2	1	0	2	8	10	1	0	4-0	.171	.333	.286	.619	1	.955
—Lowell (NY-Penn)	OF	1	3	2	2	0	0	0	0	1	0	0	1	1-0	.667	.750	.667	1.417	0	.000
—Portland (East.)	1B-OF	1	3	1	1	1	0	0	0	0	1	0	0	0-0	.333	.333	.667	1.000	0	1.000
—Boston (A.L.)	OF-DH-1B	68	158	29	46	11	1	4	23	14	23	0	5	4-2	.291	.349	.449	.798	6	.934
2004— Boston (A.L.)	OF-DH	136	290	51	79	14	1	6	33	15	49	2	5	5-4	.272	.311	.390	.700	4	.978
American League totals (7 years)		663	2012	304	546	120	10	59	260	183	307	7	42	58-23	.271	.331	.429	.760	30	.979
National League totals (2 years)		79	186	22	52	6	3	2	21	16	41	1	5	8-2	.280	.340	.376	.716	1	.990
Major League totals (7 years)		742	2198	326	598	126	13	61	281	199	348	8	47	66-25	.272	.332	.424	.757	31	.979

DIVISION SERIES RECORD

Year Team (League)	Pos.	G	AB	R	H	2B	3B	HR	RBI	BB	SO	HBP	GDP	SB-CS	Avg.	OBP	SLG	OPS	E	Avg.
2003— Boston (A.L.)	OF-DH	4	9	0	0	0	0	0	0	0	3	0	1	0-0	.000	.000	.000	.000	0	1.000
2004— Boston (A.L.)	OF	2	5	2	1	0	0	0	0	0	0	0	0	0-0	.200	.200	.200	.400	0	1.000
Division series totals (2 years)		6	14	2	1	0	0	0	0	0	3	0	1	0-0	.071	.071	.071	.143	0	1.000

CHAMPIONSHIP SERIES RECORD

Year Team (League)	Pos.	G	AB	R	H	2B	3B	HR	RBI	BB	SO	HBP	GDP	SB-CS	Avg.	OBP	SLG	OPS	E	Avg.
2003— Boston (A.L.)	OF-DH	3	8	0	1	0	0	0	0	0	3	0	1	0-1	.125	.125	.125	.250	0	1.000
2004— Boston (A.L.)	OF	2	3	0	1	0	0	0	0	0	0	0	0	0-0	.333	.333	.333	.667	0	1.000
Champ. series totals (2 years)		5	11	0	2	0	0	0	0	0	3	0	1	0-1	.182	.182	.182	.364	0	1.000

WORLD SERIES RECORD

Year Team (League)	Pos.	G	AB	R	H	2B	3B	HR	RBI	BB	SO	HBP	GDP	SB-CS	Avg.	OBP	SLG	OPS	E	Avg.
2004— Boston (A.L.)	OF	4	2	0	0	0	0	0	0	0	1	0	0	0-0	.000	.000	.000	.000	0	1.000

KARROS, ERIC — 1B

PERSONAL: Born November 4, 1967, in Hackensack, N.J. ... 6-4/225. ... Bats right, throws right. ... Full name: Eric Peter Karros. ... Name pronounced: CARE-ose. ... High school: Patrick Henry (San Diego). ... College: UCLA.

TRANSACTIONS/CAREER NOTES: Selected by Los Angeles Dodgers organization in sixth round of 1988 free-agent draft. ... On disabled list (March 29-April 24, 1998); included rehabilitation assignment to San Bernardino. ... On disabled list (May 22-June 15, 2001). ... Traded by Dodgers with 2B Mark Grudzielanek and cash to Chicago Cubs for C Todd Hundley and OF Chad Hermansen (December 4, 2002). ... Signed as a free agent by Oakland Athletics (February 6, 2004). ... Released by A's (July 29, 2004).

HONORS: Named N.L. Rookie Player of the Year by THE SPORTING NEWS (1992). ... Named N.L. Rookie of the Year by Baseball Writers' Association of America (1992).
2004 GAMES PLAYED BY POSITION (MLB): 1B—22, DH—10.

Year Team (League)	Pos.	G	AB	R	H	2B	3B	HR	RBI	BB	SO	HBP	GDP	SB-CS	Avg.	OBP	SLG	OPS	E	Avg.
1988— Great Falls (Pio.)	3B-1B	66	268	68	98	12	1	12	55	32	35	3	7	8-2	.366	.433	.552	.985	19	.966
1989— Bakersfield (Calif.)	3B-1B	142	545	86	165	40	1	15	86	63	99	2	15	18-7	.303	.375	.462	.837	19	.986
1990— San Antonio (Texas)	1B	131	509	91	179	45	2	18	78	57	79	6	18	8-10	.352	.419	.554	.973	8	.994
1991— Albuquerque (PCL)	3B-1B	132	488	88	154	33	8	22	101	58	80	6	6	3-2	.316	.391	.551	.943	11	.991
— Los Angeles (N.L.)	1B	14	14	0	1	1	0	0	1	1	6	0	0	0-0	.071	.133	.143	.276	0	1.000
1992— Los Angeles (N.L.)	1B	149	545	63	140	30	1	20	88	37	103	2	15	2-4	.257	.304	.426	.730	9	.993
1993— Los Angeles (N.L.)	1B	158	619	74	153	27	2	23	80	34	82	2	17	0-1	.247	.287	.409	.696	12	.992
1994— Los Angeles (N.L.)	1B	111	406	51	108	21	1	14	46	29	53	2	13	2-0	.266	.310	.426	.736	• 9	.991
1995— Los Angeles (N.L.)	1B	143	551	83	164	29	3	32	105	61	115	4	14	4-4	.298	.369	.535	.905	7	.995
1996— Los Angeles (SAL)	1B	154	608	84	158	29	1	34	111	53	121	1	27	8-0	.260	.316	.479	.795	15	.990
1997— Los Angeles (N.L.)	1B •	162	628	86	167	28	0	31	104	61	116	2	10	15-7	.266	.329	.459	.787	11	.992
1998— San Bern. (Calif.)	1B	4	15	3	4	1	0	0	1	0	2	0	1	0-0	.267	.267	.333	.600	0	1.000
— Los Angeles (N.L.)	1B-DH	139	507	59	150	20	1	23	87	47	93	3	7	7-2	.296	.355	.475	.830	12	.991
1999— Los Angeles (N.L.)	1B	153	578	74	176	40	0	34	112	53	119	2	18	8-5	.305	.362	.550	.912	13	.991
2000— Los Angeles (N.L.)	1B-DH	155	584	84	146	29	0	31	106	63	122	4	18	4-3	.250	.321	.459	.780	7	.995
2001— Los Angeles (N.L.)	1B	121	438	42	103	22	0	15	63	41	101	3	15	3-1	.235	.303	.388	.691	4	.996
2002— Los Angeles (N.L.)	1B	142	524	52	142	26	1	13	73	37	74	6	11	4-2	.271	.323	.389	.722	4	.997
2003— Chicago (N.L.)	1B	114	336	37	96	16	1	12	40	28	46	0	14	1-1	.286	.340	.446	.786	6	.992
2004— Oakland (A.L.)	1B-DH	40	103	8	20	6	0	2	11	7	16	0	2	1-0	.194	.243	.311	.554	2	.989
American League totals (1 year)		40	103	8	20	6	0	2	11	7	16	0	2	1-0	.194	.243	.311	.554	2	.989
National League totals (13 years)		1715	6338	789	1704	318	11	282	1016	545	1151	31	179	58-30	.269	.326	.456	.782	109	.993
Major League totals (14 years)		1755	6441	797	1724	324	11	284	1027	552	1167	31	181	59-30	.268	.325	.454	.779	111	.993

DIVISION SERIES RECORD

Year Team (League)	Pos.	G	AB	R	H	2B	3B	HR	RBI	BB	SO	HBP	GDP	SB-CS	Avg.	OBP	SLG	OPS	E	Avg.
1995— Los Angeles (N.L.)	1B	3	12	3	6	1	0	2	4	1	0	0	0	0-0	.500	.538	1.083	1.622	0	1.000
1996— Los Angeles (N.L.)	1B	3	9	0	0	0	0	0	0	2	3	0	1	0-0	.000	.182	.000	.182	0	1.000
2003— Chicago (N.L.)	1B	4	16	4	6	0	0	2	2	0	3	0	1	0-0	.375	.375	.750	1.125	0	1.000
Division series totals (3 years)		10	37	7	12	1	0	4	6	3	6	0	2	0-0	.324	.375	.676	1.051	0	1.000

CHAMPIONSHIP SERIES RECORD

Year Team (League)	Pos.	G	AB	R	H	2B	3B	HR	RBI	BB	SO	HBP	GDP	SB-CS	Avg.	OBP	SLG	OPS	E	Avg.
2003— Chicago (N.L.)	1B	5	13	2	3	0	0	0	0	2	3	0	0	0-0	.231	.333	.231	.564	0	1.000

KARSAY, STEVE — P

PERSONAL: Born March 24, 1972, in Flushing, N.Y. ... 6-3/210. ... Throws right, bats right. ... Full name: Stefan Andrew Karsay. ... Name pronounced: CAR-say. ... High school: Christ the King (Queens, N.Y.).

TRANSACTIONS/CAREER NOTES: Selected by Toronto Blue Jays organization in first round (22nd pick overall) of 1990 free-agent draft. ... Traded by Blue Jays with a player to be named to Oakland Athletics for OF Rickey Henderson (July 31, 1993); A's acquired OF Jose Herrera to complete deal (August 6, 1993). ... On disabled list (April 26, 1994-remainder of season; April 24, 1995-entire season; and August 6, 1997-remainder of season). ... Traded by A's to Cleveland Indians for P Mike Fetters (December 8, 1997). ... On disabled list (July 2-26 and August 25-September 22, 1999). ... Traded by Indians with P Steve Reed to Atlanta Braves for P John Rocker and 3B Troy Cameron (June 22, 2001). ... Signed as a free agent by New York Yankees (December 7, 2001). ... On disabled list (March 21, 2003-entire season). ... On disabled list (March 12-September 1, 2004); included rehabilitation assignments to Staten Island, Trenton and Columbus.

CAREER HITTING: 0-for-4 (.000), 1 R, 0 2B, 0 3B, 0 HR, 0 RBI.

Year Team (League)	W	L	Pct.	ERA	WHIP	G	GS	CG	ShO	Hld.	Sv.-Opp.	IP	H	R	ER	HR	BB-IBB	SO	Avg.
1990— St. Catharines (NY-Penn.) .	1	1	.500	0.79	1.01	5	5	0	0	...	0-...	22.2	11	4	2	0	12-0	25	.141
1991— Myrtle Beach (SAL)	4	9	.308	3.58	1.30	20	20	1	0	...	0-...	110.2	96	58	44	7	48-0	100	.240
1992— Dunedin (Fla. St.)	6	3	.667	2.73	0.99	16	16	3	2	...	0-...	85.2	56	32	26	6	29-0	87	.187
1993— Knoxville (Southern)	8	4	.667	3.38	1.25	19	18	1	0	...	0-...	104.0	98	42	39	4	32-1	100	.251
— Huntsville (Southern)	0	0	...	5.14	1.14	2	2	0	0	...	0-...	14.0	13	8	8	2	3-0	22	.255
— Oakland (A.L.)	3	3	.500	4.04	1.33	8	8	0	0	0	0-0	49.0	49	23	22	4	16-1	33	.258
1994— Oakland (A.L.)	1	1	.500	2.57	1.21	4	4	1	0	0	0-0	28.0	26	8	8	1	8-0	15	.252
1995— Oakland (A.L.)			Did not play.																
1996— Modesto (Calif.)	0	1	.000	2.65	1.06	14	14	0	0	...	0-...	34.0	35	16	10	2	1-0	31	.255
1997— Oakland (A.L.)	3	12	.200	5.77	1.61	24	24	0	0	0	0-0	132.2	166	92	85	20	47-3	92	.304
1998— Buffalo (Int'l)	6	4	.600	3.76	1.32	16	14	0	0	...	0-...	79.0	89	39	33	5	15-0	63	.276
— Cleveland (A.L.)	0	2	.000	5.92	1.52	11	1	0	0	2	0-0	24.1	31	16	16	3	6-1	13	.310
1999— Cleveland (A.L.)	10	2	.833	2.97	1.28	50	3	0	0	9	1-3	78.2	71	29	26	6	30-3	68	.247
2000— Cleveland (A.L.)	5	9	.357	3.76	1.36	72	0	0	0	11	20-29	76.2	79	33	32	5	25-4	66	.266
2001— Cleveland (A.L.)	0	1	.000	1.25	0.85	31	0	0	0	8	1-1	43.1	29	6	6	1	8-2	44	.188
— Atlanta (N.L.)	3	4	.429	3.43	1.37	43	0	0	0	4	7-11	44.2	44	21	17	4	17-8	39	.265
2002— New York (A.L.)	6	4	.600	3.26	1.32	78	0	0	0	14	12-16	88.1	87	33	32	7	30-14	65	.258
2004— Trenton (East.)	1	0	1.000	7.50	1.67	4	0	0	0	...	0-...	6.0	6	5	5	0	4-0	7	.273
— Staten Island (NY-P)	0	0	...	0.00	0.67	3	0	0	0	...	0-...	3.0	1	0	0	0	1-0	1	.100
— Columbus (Int'l)	0	0	...	5.56	1.59	11	0	0	0	...	0-...	11.1	12	10	7	0	6-0	8	.255
— New York (A.L.)	0	0	...	2.70	1.05	7	0	0	0	0	0-0	6.2	5	3	2	2	2-0	4	.217
American League totals (9 years)	28	34	.452	3.91	1.36	285	40	1	0	44	34-49	527.2	543	243	229	49	172-28	400	.267
National League totals (1 year)	3	4	.429	3.43	1.37	43	0	0	0	4	7-11	44.2	44	21	17	4	17-8	39	.265
Major League totals (9 years)	31	38	.449	3.87	1.36	328	40	1	0	48	41-60	572.1	587	264	246	53	189-36	439	.266

DIVISION SERIES RECORD

Year Team (League)	W	L	Pct.	ERA	WHIP	G	GS	CG	ShO	Hld.	Sv.-Opp.	IP	H	R	ER	HR	BB-IBB	SO	Avg.
1999— Cleveland (A.L.)	0	0	...	9.00	2.00	2	0	0	0	0	0-0	3.0	5	3	3	1	1-0	3	.357
2001— Atlanta (N.L.)	0	0	...	0.00	0.00	1	0	0	0	1	0-0	1.0	0	0	0	0	0-0	1	.000
2002— New York (A.L.)	1	0	1.000	6.75	1.13	4	0	0	0	0	0-0	2.2	3	2	2	1	0-0	1	.273
Division series totals (3 years)	1	0	1.000	6.75	1.35	7	0	0	0	1	0-0	6.2	8	5	5	2	1-0	5	.286

CHAMPIONSHIP SERIES RECORD

Year Team (League)	W	L	Pct.	ERA	WHIP	G	GS	CG	ShO	Hld.	Sv.-Opp.	IP	H	R	ER	HR	BB-IBB	SO	Avg.
2001— Atlanta (N.L.)	0	0	...	2.08	0.92	4	0	0	0	0	0-0	4.1	3	1	1	0	1-1	6	.176

K

KATA, MATT — 2B

PERSONAL: Born March 14, 1978, in Fairview Park, Ohio. ... 6-1/185. ... Bats both, throws right. ... Full name: Matthew John Kata. ... Name pronounced: KATE-a. ... High school: St. Ignatius (Cleveland). ... College: Vanderbilt.

TRANSACTIONS/CAREER NOTES: Selected by Minnesota Twins organization in 20th round of 1996 free-agent draft; did not sign. ... Selected by Arizona Diamondbacks organization in ninth round of 1999 free-agent draft. ... On disabled list (May 30, 2004-remainder of season).

2004 GAMES PLAYED BY POSITION (MLB): 2B—38, 3B—3, SS—1.

										BATTING									FIELDING	
Year	Team (League)	Pos.	G	AB	R	H	2B	3B	HR	RBI	BB	SO	HBP	GDP	SB-CS	Avg.	OBP	SLG	OPS	E	Avg.
1999—South Bend (Mid.)		SS	78	318	40	83	14	5	3	33	28	46	4	5	5-6	.261	.328	.365	.692	22	.937
2000—South Bend (Mid.)		SS-2B-P-OF	133	521	82	133	22	9	6	59	52	58	6	10	38-12	.255	.327	.367	.694	39	.937
2001—Lancaster (Calif.)		2B-SS	119	494	80	146	19	6	10	54	41	79	5	4	30-8	.296	.355	.419	.774	29	.952
—El Paso (Texas)		2B	4	16	4	7	2	0	0	4	2	2	0	0	0-1	.438	.500	.563	1.063	0	1.000
2002—El Paso (Texas)		2B-SS-3B	136	578	95	172	33	9	11	57	37	79	4	6	12-7	.298	.341	.443	.784	18	.972
2003—Tucson (PCL)		2B-SS	48	201	31	58	13	5	3	25	9	29	3	1	2-3	.289	.327	.448	.775	10	.958
—Arizona (N.L.)		2B-3B-SS	78	288	42	74	16	5	7	29	25	53	1	4	3-2	.257	.315	.420	.736	4	.987
2004—Arizona (N.L.)		2B-3B-SS	42	162	17	40	9	2	2	13	13	29	0	1	4-1	.247	.301	.364	.665	2	.990
Major League totals (2 years)			120	450	59	114	25	7	9	42	38	82	1	5	7-3	.253	.310	.400	.710	6	.988

KAZMIR, SCOTT — P

PERSONAL: Born January 24, 1984, in Houston, Texas. ... 6-0/170. ... Throws left, bats left. ... Full name: Scott E. Kazmir. ... High school: Cypress Falls (Houston).

TRANSACTIONS/CAREER NOTES: Selected by New York Mets organization in first round (15th pick overall) of 2002 free-agent draft. ... Traded by Mets with P Jose Diaz to Tampa Bay Devil Rays for Ps Victor Zambrano and Bartolome Fortunato (July 30, 2004).

CAREER HITTING: 0-for-0 (.000), 0 R, 0 2B, 0 3B, 0 HR, 0 RBI.

Year	Team (League)	W	L	Pct.	ERA	WHIP	G	GS	CG	ShO	Hld.	Sv.-Opp.	IP	H	R	ER	HR	BB-IBB	SO	Avg.
2002—Brooklyn (NY-P)		0	1	.000	0.50	0.67	5	5	0	0	...	0-...	18.0	5	2	1	0	7-0	34	.089
2003—Capital City (S. Atl.)		4	4	.500	2.36	1.02	18	18	0	0	...	0-...	76.1	50	26	20	6	28-0	105	.185
—St. Lucie (Fla. St.)		1	2	.333	3.27	1.36	7	7	0	0	...	0-...	33.0	29	15	12	0	16-0	40	.240
2004—St. Lucie (Fla. St.)		1	2	.333	3.42	1.42	11	11	0	0	...	0-...	50.0	49	20	19	3	22-0	51	.257
—Binghamton (Eastern)		2	1	.667	1.73	0.96	4	4	0	0	...	0-...	26.0	16	6	5	0	9-0	29	.188
—Montgomery (Sou.)		1	2	.333	1.44	1.00	4	4	0	0	...	0-...	25.0	14	7	4	0	11-0	24	.171
—Tampa Bay (A.L.)		2	3	.400	5.67	1.62	8	7	0	0	0	0-0	33.1	33	22	21	4	21-0	41	.256
Major League totals (1 year)		2	3	.400	5.67	1.62	8	7	0	0	0	0-0	33.1	33	22	21	4	21-0	41	.256

KEARNS, AUSTIN — OF

PERSONAL: Born May 20, 1980, in Lexington, Ky. ... 6-3/220. ... Bats right, throws right. ... Full name: Austin Ryan Kearns. ... High school: Lafayette (Lexington, Ky.).

TRANSACTIONS/CAREER NOTES: Selected by Cincinnati Reds organization in first round (seventh pick overall) of 1998 free-agent draft. ... On disabled list (August 27, 2002-remainder of season). ... On disabled list (July 9, 2003-remainder of season); included rehabilitation assignment to Chattanooga. ... On disabled list (April 27-May 19 and June 2-August 24, 2004); included rehabilitation assignments to Louisville.

2004 GAMES PLAYED BY POSITION (MLB): OF—60.

										BATTING									FIELDING	
Year	Team (League)	Pos.	G	AB	R	H	2B	3B	HR	RBI	BB	SO	HBP	GDP	SB-CS	Avg.	OBP	SLG	OPS	E	Avg.
1998—Billings (Pio.)		OF	30	108	17	34	9	0	1	14	23	22	1	4	1-1	.315	.433	.426	.859	4	.905
1999—Rockford (Midwest)		OF	124	426	72	110	36	5	13	48	50	120	9	9	24-8	.258	.346	.458	.804	13	.939
2000—Dayton (Midw.)		OF	136	484	110	148	37	2	27	104	90	93	7	14	18-5	.306	.415	.558	.973	12	.955
2001—Chattanooga (Sou.)		OF	59	205	30	55	11	2	6	36	26	43	6	4	7-5	.268	.364	.429	.793	2	.979
—GC Reds (GCL)		OF	6	17	2	3	2	0	0	4	2	7	0	0	0-0	.176	.227	.294	.521	0	1.000
2002—Chattanooga (Sou.)		OF	12	41	10	11	2	0	5	13	9	9	3	0	1-0	.268	.434	.683	1.117	0	1.000
—Cincinnati (N.L.)		OF	107	372	66	117	24	3	13	56	54	81	6	11	6-3	.315	.407	.500	.907	4	.983
—Louisville (Int'l)		OF	1	4	3	3	2	0	0	2	1	0	0	0	0-0	.750	.800	1.250	2.050	0	1.000
2003—Cincinnati (N.L.)		OF	82	292	39	77	11	0	15	58	41	68	5	7	5-2	.264	.364	.455	.819	2	.990
—Chattanooga (Sou.)		OF	3	5	2	1	0	0	0	1	2	2	1	0	0-0	.200	.200	.200	.700	0	1.000
2004—Louisville (Int'l)		OF-DH	25	83	19	28	7	1	2	15	19	16	2	3	3-1	.337	.471	.518	.989	3	.949
—Cincinnati (N.L.)		OF	64	217	28	50	10	2	9	32	28	71	1	8	2-1	.230	.321	.419	.740	3	.975
Major League totals (3 years)			253	881	133	244	45	5	37	146	123	220	12	26	13-6	.277	.372	.465	.837	9	.984

KELTON, DAVID — OF/3B

PERSONAL: Born December 17, 1979, in Dothan, Ala. ... 6-3/205. ... Bats right, throws right. ... Full name: David Wayne Kelton. ... High school: LaGrange High (La Grange, Ga.).

TRANSACTIONS/CAREER NOTES: Selected by Chicago Cubs organization in second round of 1998 free-agent draft.

2004 GAMES PLAYED BY POSITION (MLB): OF—3.

										BATTING									FIELDING	
Year	Team (League)	Pos.	G	AB	R	H	2B	3B	HR	RBI	BB	SO	HBP	GDP	SB-CS	Avg.	OBP	SLG	OPS	E	Avg.
1998—Ariz. Cubs (Ariz.)		3B	50	181	39	48	7	5	6	29	23	58	2	2	16-3	.265	.353	.459	.811	15	.891
1999—Lansing (Midw.)		3B-SS	124	509	75	137	17	4	13	68	39	121	2	11	22-9	.269	.322	.395	.717	32	.893
2000—Daytona (Fla. St.)		3B	132	523	75	140	30	7	18	84	38	120	2	9	7-8	.268	.317	.455	.772	26	.896
2001—West Tenn (Sou.)		3B	58	224	33	70	9	4	12	45	24	55	1	1	1-3	.313	.378	.549	.928	15	.883
2002—West Tenn (Sou.)		1B-3B-OF	129	498	68	130	28	6	20	79	52	129	2	10	12-6	.261	.332	.462	.793	13	.988
2003—Iowa (PCL)		O-3-DH-1	121	442	62	119	24	3	16	67	46	115	2	7	8-2	.269	.338	.446	.784	15	.936
—Chicago (N.L.)		OF	10	12	1	2	1	0	0	1	0	5	0	0	0-0	.167	.167	.250	.417	0	1.000
2004—Chicago (N.L.)		OF	8	10	1	1	1	0	0	0	0	3	0	0	0-0	.100	.100	.200	.300	0	1.000
—Iowa (PCL)		OF-DH-1B	121	420	57	104	26	1	19	68	33	92	4	10	7-2	.248	.305	.450	.755	3	.984
Major League totals (2 years)			18	22	2	3	2	0	0	1	0	8	0	0	0-0	.136	.136	.227	.364	0	1.000

KENDALL, JASON — C

PERSONAL: Born June 26, 1974, in San Diego, Calif. ... 6-0/195. ... Bats right, throws right. ... Full name: Jason Daniel Kendall. ... High school: Torrance (Calif.). ... Son of Fred Kendall, catcher/first baseman with three major league teams (1969-80) and coach with Detroit Tigers (1996-98) and Colorado Rockies (2001-02).

TRANSACTIONS/CAREER NOTES: Selected by Pittsburgh Pirates organization in first round (23rd pick overall) of 1992 free-agent draft. ... On suspended list (July 21-23, 1998). ... On disabled list (July 5, 1999-remainder of season). ... On suspended list (September 19-20, 2001; July 29-August 1, 2003; and September 17-20, 2004).

HONORS: Named N.L. Rookie Player of the Year by THE SPORTING NEWS (1996).
2004 GAMES PLAYED BY POSITION (MLB): C—146.

Year Team (League)	Pos.	G	AB	R	H	2B	3B	HR	RBI	BB	SO	HBP	GDP	SB-CS	Avg.	OBP	SLG	OPS	E	Avg.
1992— GC Pirates (GCL)	C	33	111	7	29	2	0	0	10	8	9	2	3	2-2	.261	.317	.279	.596	5	.978
1993— Augusta (S. Atl.)	C	102	366	43	101	17	4	1	40	22	30	7	17	8-5	.276	.325	.352	.677	20	.964
1994— Salem (Caro.)	C	101	371	68	118	19	2	7	66	47	21	13	15	14-3	.318	.406	.437	.843	9	.980
— Carolina (Southern)	C	13	47	6	11	2	0	0	6	2	3	2	0	0-0	.234	.294	.277	.571	2	.969
1995— Carolina (Southern)	C	117	429	87	140	26	1	8	71	56	22	14	10	10-7	.326	.414	.448	.862	8	.989
1996— Pittsburgh (N.L.)	C	130	414	54	124	23	5	3	42	35	30	15	7	5-2	.300	.372	.401	.773	* 18	.980
1997— Pittsburgh (N.L.)	C	144	486	71	143	36	4	8	49	49	53	31	11	8-8	.294	.391	.434	.825	11	.990
1998— Pittsburgh (N.L.)	C	149	535	95	175	36	3	12	75	51	51	31	6	26-5	.327	.411	.473	.884	9	.992
1999— Pittsburgh (N.L.)	C	78	280	61	93	20	3	8	41	38	32	12	8	22-3	.332	.428	.511	.939	7	.988
2000— Pittsburgh (N.L.)	C	152	579	112	185	33	6	14	58	79	79	15	13	22-7	.320	.412	.470	.882	10	.991
2001— Pittsburgh (N.L.)	C-OF	157	606	84	161	22	2	10	53	44	48	20	18	13-14	.266	.335	.358	.693	17	.980
2002— Pittsburgh (N.L.)	C	145	545	59	154	25	3	3	44	49	29	9	11	15-8	.283	.350	.356	.706	9	.990
2003— Pittsburgh (N.L.)	C	150	587	84	191	29	3	6	58	49	40	25	9	8-7	.325	.399	.416	.815	10	.989
2004— Pittsburgh (N.L.)	C	147	574	86	183	32	0	3	51	60	41	19	12	11-8	.319	.399	.390	.789	10	.991
Major League totals (9 years)		1252	4606	706	1409	256	29	67	471	454	403	177	95	140-65	.306	.387	.418	.805	101	.988

ALL-STAR GAME RECORD

	G	AB	R	H	2B	3B	HR	RBI	BB	SO	HBP	GDP	SB-CS	Avg.	OBP	SLG	OPS	E	Avg.
All-Star Game totals (3 years)	3	3	0	1	0	0	0	0	0	1	0	0	0-0	.333	.333	.333	.667	0	1.000

KENNEDY, ADAM — 2B

K

PERSONAL: Born January 10, 1976, in Riverside, Calif. ... 6-1/185. ... Bats left, throws right. ... Full name: Adam Thomas Kennedy. ... High school: J.W. North (Riverside, Calif.). ... College: Cal State Northridge.
TRANSACTIONS/CAREER NOTES: Selected by St. Louis Cardinals organization in first round (20th pick overall) of 1997 free-agent draft. ... Traded by Cardinals with P Kent Bottenfield to Anaheim Angels for OF Jim Edmonds (March 23, 2000). ... On disabled list (March 23-April 13, 2001); included rehabilitation assignment to Rancho Cucamonga. ... On disabled list (April 7-22, 2003); included rehabilitation assignment to Rancho Cucamonga.
2004 GAMES PLAYED BY POSITION (MLB): 2B—144.

Year Team (League)	Pos.	G	AB	R	H	2B	3B	HR	RBI	BB	SO	HBP	GDP	SB-CS	Avg.	OBP	SLG	OPS	E	Avg.
1997— New Jersey (N.Y.-Penn.)	SS	29	114	20	39	6	3	0	19	13	10	2	3	9-1	.342	.412	.447	.860	7	.951
— Prince Will. (Car.)	SS	35	154	24	48	9	3	1	27	6	17	2	3	4-3	.312	.346	.429	.774	10	.939
1998— Prince Will. (Car.)	2B-SS	17	69	9	18	6	0	0	7	5	12	0	1	5-2	.261	.307	.348	.654	5	.938
— Arkansas (Texas)	2B-SS	52	205	35	57	11	2	6	24	8	21	2	4	6-2	.278	.307	.439	.746	15	.940
— Memphis (PCL)	2B-SS	74	305	36	93	22	7	4	41	12	42	1	3	15-4	.305	.331	.462	.794	10	.972
1999— Memphis (PCL)	2-S-O-3-DH	91	367	69	120	22	4	10	63	29	36	4	7	20-6	.327	.378	.490	.868	18	.953
— St. Louis (N.L.)	2B	33	102	12	26	10	1	1	16	3	8	2	1	0-1	.255	.284	.402	.686	4	.971
2000— Anaheim (A.L.)	2B	156	598	82	159	33	11	9	72	28	73	3	10	22-8	.266	.300	.403	.703	* 19	.976
2001— Rancho Cuca. (Calif.)	2B	3	8	3	3	2	0	0	1	2	1	1	0	3-0	.375	.545	.625	1.170	0	1.000
— Anaheim (A.L.)	2B-DH	137	478	48	129	25	3	6	40	27	71	11	7	12-7	.270	.318	.372	.690	10	.984
2002— Anaheim (A.L.)	2B-DH-OF	144	474	65	148	32	6	7	52	19	80	7	5	17-4	.312	.345	.449	.795	11	.983
2003— Rancho Cuca. (Calif.)	2B	3	11	3	3	1	0	1	1	0	2	1	0	0-0	.273	.333	.636	.970	1	.923
— Anaheim (A.L.)	2B-DH	143	449	71	121	17	1	13	49	45	73	9	7	22-9	.269	.344	.399	.743	6	.990
2004— Anaheim (A.L.)	2B	144	468	70	130	20	5	10	48	41	92	13	10	15-5	.278	.351	.406	.757	12	.982
American League totals (5 years)		724	2467	336	687	127	26	45	261	160	389	43	39	88-33	.278	.330	.406	.736	58	.983
National League totals (1 year)		33	102	12	26	10	1	1	16	3	8	2	1	0-1	.255	.284	.402	.686	4	.971
Major League totals (6 years)		757	2569	348	713	137	27	46	277	163	397	45	40	88-34	.278	.329	.406	.734	62	.982

DIVISION SERIES RECORD

Year Team (League)	Pos.	G	AB	R	H	2B	3B	HR	RBI	BB	SO	HBP	GDP	SB-CS	Avg.	OBP	SLG	OPS	E	Avg.
2002— Anaheim (A.L.)	2B	4	8	4	4	1	0	1	3	1	2	0	0	1-0	.500	.455	1.000	1.455	0	1.000

CHAMPIONSHIP SERIES RECORD

Year Team (League)	Pos.	G	AB	R	H	2B	3B	HR	RBI	BB	SO	HBP	GDP	SB-CS	Avg.	OBP	SLG	OPS	E	Avg.
2002— Anaheim (A.L.)	2B	4	14	5	5	0	0	3	5	0	2	0	0	1-0	.357	.357	1.000	1.357	0	1.000

WORLD SERIES RECORD

Year Team (League)	Pos.	G	AB	R	H	2B	3B	HR	RBI	BB	SO	HBP	GDP	SB-CS	Avg.	OBP	SLG	OPS	E	Avg.
2002— Anaheim (A.L.)	2B	7	25	1	7	2	0	0	2	0	7	1	0	0-0	.280	.308	.360	.668	0	1.000

KENNEDY, JOE — P

PERSONAL: Born May 24, 1979, in La Mesa, Calif. ... 6-4/237. ... Throws left, bats right. ... Full name: Joseph Darley Kennedy. ... High school: El Cajon Valley (El Cajon, Calif.). ... Junior college: Grossmont (Calif.).
TRANSACTIONS/CAREER NOTES: Selected by Tampa Bay Devil Rays organization in eighth round of 1998 free-agent draft. ... On suspended list (July 12-19, 2002). ... On disabled list (June 1-July 9, 2003); included rehabilitation assignments to Orlando and Durham. ... Traded by Devil Rays to Colorado Rockies as part of three-team deal in which Devil Rays acquired P Mark Hendrickson from Blue Jays, Blue Jays acquired P Justin Speier from Rockies and Rockies acquired a player to be named from Blue Jays (December 14, 2003). ... Rockies acquired P Sandy Nin to complete deal (December 15, 2003). ... On disabled list (July 3-August 10, 2004); included rehabilitation assignment to Colorado Springs. ... On suspended list (September 19-25, 2004).
CAREER HITTING: 10-for-59 (.169), 4 R, 1 2B, 1 3B, 0 HR, 5 RBI.

Year Team (League)	W	L	Pct.	ERA	WHIP	G	GS	CG	ShO	Hld.	Sv.-Opp.	IP	H	R	ER	HR	BB-IBB	SO	Avg.
1998— Princeton (Appalachian)	6	4	.600	3.74	1.37	13	13	0	0	...	0-...	67.1	66	37	28	5	26-0	44	.264
1999— Hudson Valley (NY-Penn.)	6	5	.545	2.65	1.09	16	16	1	1	...	0-...	95.0	78	33	28	2	26-0	101	.227
2000— Char., S.C. (SAL)	11	6	.647	3.30	1.11	22	22	3	2	...	0-...	136.1	122	59	50	6	29-1	142	.242
2001— Orlando (Sou.)	4	0	1.000	0.19	0.68	7	7	0	0	...	0-...	47.0	29	3	1	0	3-0	52	.178
— Durham (Int'l)	2	0	1.000	2.42	1.19	4	4	0	0	...	0-...	26.0	22	8	7	2	9-0	23	.227
— Tampa Bay (A.L.)	7	8	.467	4.44	1.33	20	20	0	0	0	0-0	117.2	122	63	58	16	34-0	78	.269
2002— Tampa Bay (A.L.)	8	11	.421	4.53	1.32	30	30	5	1	0	0-0	196.2	204	114	99	23	55-0	109	.269
2003— Orlando (Sou.)	0	0	...	8.10	2.10	1	1	0	0	...	0-...	3.1	6	3	3	0	1-0	3	.400
— Durham (Int'l)	1	0	1.000	1.42	0.90	1	1	0	0	...	0-...	6.1	6	1	1	0	0-0	4	.250
— Tampa Bay (A.L.)	3	12	.200	6.13	1.60	32	22	1	1	1	1-2	133.2	167	101	91	19	47-1	77	.303

Year Team (League)	W	L	Pct.	ERA	WHIP	G	GS	CG	ShO	Hld.	Sv.-Opp.	IP	H	R	ER	HR	BB-IBB	SO	Avg.
2004—Colo. Springs (PCL)	1	1	.500	7.11	1.50	3	2	0	0	...	0-...	12.2	17	11	10	1	2-0	12	.321
—Colorado (N.L.)	9	7	.563	3.66	1.42	27	27	1	0	0	0-0	162.1	163	68	66	17	67-12	117	.265
American League totals (3 years)	18	31	.367	4.98	1.40	82	72	6	2	1	1-2	448.0	493	278	248	58	136-1	264	.279
National League totals (1 year)	9	7	.563	3.66	1.42	27	27	1	0	0	0-0	162.1	163	68	66	17	67-12	117	.265
Major League totals (4 years)	27	38	.415	4.63	1.41	109	99	7	2	1	1-2	610.1	656	346	314	75	203-13	381	.276

KENSING, LOGAN — P

PERSONAL: Born July 3, 1982, in San Antonio, Texas. ... 6-1/185. ... Throws right, bats right. ... Full name: Logan French Kensing. ... High school: Boerne (Texas). ... College: Texas A&M.

TRANSACTIONS/CAREER NOTES: Selected by Florida Marlins organization in second round of 2003 free-agent draft.

CAREER HITTING: 0-for-2 (.000), 0 R, 0 2B, 0 3B, 0 HR, 0 RBI.

Year Team (League)	W	L	Pct.	ERA	WHIP	G	GS	CG	ShO	Hld.	Sv.-Opp.	IP	H	R	ER	HR	BB-IBB	SO	Avg.
2003—Jamestown (N.Y.-Penn.) ...	2	4	.333	5.73	1.64	8	6	0	0	...	0-...	33.0	48	23	21	1	6-0	20	.333
—Greensboro (S. Atl.)	0	2	.000	4.50	1.15	4	4	0	0	...	0-...	20.0	18	10	10	2	5-0	11	.243
2004—Jupiter (FSL)	6	7	.462	2.96	1.21	23	23	1	0	...	0-...	127.2	120	53	42	5	35-1	100	.251
—Florida (N.L.)	0	3	.000	9.88	2.05	5	3	0	0	0	0-0	13.2	19	15	15	5	9-0	7	.345
Major League totals (1 year)	0	3	.000	9.88	2.05	5	3	0	0	0	0-0	13.2	19	15	15	5	9-0	7	.345

KENT, JEFF — 2B

PERSONAL: Born March 7, 1968, in Bellflower, Calif. ... 6-1/210. ... Bats right, throws right. ... Full name: Jeffrey Frank Kent. ... High school: Edison (Huntington Beach, Calif.). ... College: California.

TRANSACTIONS/CAREER NOTES: Selected by Toronto Blue Jays organization in 20th round of 1989 free-agent draft. ... Traded by Blue Jays with a player to be named to New York Mets for P David Cone (August 27, 1992); Mets acquired OF Ryan Thompson to complete deal (September 1, 1992). ... On disabled list (July 6-21, 1995). ... Traded by New York Mets with IF Jose Vizcaino to Cleveland Indians for 2B Carlos Baerga and IF Alvaro Espinoza (July 29, 1996). ... Traded by Indians with IF Jose Vizcaino, P Julian Tavarez and a player to be named to San Francisco Giants for 3B Matt Williams and a player to be named (November 13, 1996); Indians traded P Joe Roa to Giants for OF Trinidad Hubbard to complete deal (December 16, 1996). ... On suspended list (August 22-25, 1997). ... On disabled list (June 10-July 10, 1998; August 3-21, 1999; and March 21-April 6, 2002). ... Signed as a free agent by Houston Astros (December 18, 2002). ... Placed on 15-day disabled list (June 19-July 16, 2003); included rehabilitation assignment to Round Rock. ... On suspended list (August 6-9, 2003; and September 24-26, 2004).

HONORS: Named N.L. Most Valuable Player by Baseball Writers' Association of America (2000).

2004 GAMES PLAYED BY POSITION (MLB): 2B—139, DH—2.

Year Team (League)	Pos.	G	AB	R	H	2B	3B	HR	RBI	BB	SO	HBP	GDP	SB-CS	Avg.	OBP	SLG	OPS	E	Avg.
1989—St. Catharines (NY-Penn.) .	3B-SS	73	268	34	60	14	1	13	37	33	81	6	2	5-1	.224	.318	.429	.747	29	.906
1990—Dunedin (Fla. St.)	2B	132	447	72	124	32	2	16	60	53	98	6	4	17-7	.277	.360	.465	.825	15	.978
1991—Knoxville (Southern)	2B	139	445	68	134	34	1	2	61	80	104	10	3	25-6	.256	.379	.351	.730	29	.957
1992—Toronto (A.L.)	3B-2B-1B	65	192	36	46	13	1	8	35	20	47	6	3	2-1	.240	.324	.443	.767	11	.941
—New York (N.L.)	2B-3B-SS	37	113	16	27	8	1	3	15	7	29	1	2	0-2	.239	.284	.407	.696	3	.981
1993—New York (N.L.)	2B-3B-SS	140	496	65	134	24	0	21	80	30	88	8	11	4-4	.270	.320	.446	.765	‡22	.965
1994—New York (N.L.)	2B	107	415	53	121	24	5	14	68	23	84	10	7	1-4	.292	.341	.475	.816	•14	.976
1995—New York (N.L.)	2B	125	472	65	131	22	3	20	65	29	89	8	9	3-3	.278	.327	.464	.791	10	.984
1996—New York (N.L.)	3B	89	335	45	97	20	1	9	39	21	56	1	7	4-3	.290	.331	.436	.766	21	.925
—Cleveland (A.L.)	1-2-3-DH	39	102	16	27	7	0	3	16	10	22	1	1	2-1	.265	.328	.422	.749	1	.994
1997—San Francisco (N.L.)	2B-1B	155	580	90	145	38	2	29	121	48	133	13	14	11-3	.250	.316	.472	.789	16	.981
1998—San Francisco (N.L.)	2B-1B	137	526	94	156	37	3	31	128	48	110	9	16	9-4	.297	.359	.555	.914	20	.972
1999—San Francisco (N.L.)	2B-1B	138	511	86	148	40	2	23	101	61	112	5	12	13-6	.290	.366	.511	.877	10	.984
2000—San Francisco (N.L.)	2B-1B	159	587	114	196	41	7	33	125	90	107	9	17	12-9	.334	.424	.596	1.021	12	.985
2001—San Francisco (N.L.)	2B-1B	159	607	84	181	49	6	22	106	65	96	11	11	7-6	.298	.369	.507	.877	11	.987
2002—San Francisco (N.L.)	2B-1B	152	623	102	195	42	2	37	108	52	101	4	20	5-1	.313	.368	.565	.933	16	.979
2003—Round Rock (Texas)	2B-DH	3	10	1	3	0	0	1	6	1	1	0	1	0-1	.300	.333	.600	.933	1	.875
—Houston (N.L.)	2B	130	505	77	150	39	1	22	93	39	85	5	13	6-2	.297	.351	.509	.860	11	.983
2004—Houston (N.L.)	2B-DH	145	540	96	156	34	8	27	107	49	96	6	23	7-3	.289	.348	.531	.880	7	.989
American League totals (2 years)		104	294	52	73	20	1	11	51	30	69	7	4	4-2	.248	.325	.435	.761	12	.966
National League totals (13 years)		1673	6310	987	1837	418	41	291	1156	562	1186	90	162	82-50	.291	.353	.509	.862	173	.979
Major League totals (13 years)		1777	6604	1039	1910	438	42	302	1207	592	1255	97	166	86-52	.289	.352	.505	.858	185	.978

DIVISION SERIES RECORD

Year Team (League)	Pos.	G	AB	R	H	2B	3B	HR	RBI	BB	SO	HBP	GDP	SB-CS	Avg.	OBP	SLG	OPS	E	Avg.
1996—Cleveland (A.L.)	2B-3B-1B	4	8	2	1	0	0	0	0	0	0	0	0	0-0	.125	.125	.250	.375	0	1.000
1997—San Francisco (N.L.)	2B-1B	3	10	2	3	0	0	2	2	2	1	0	0	0-0	.300	.417	.900	1.317	0	1.000
2000—San Francisco (N.L.)	2B-1B	4	16	3	6	1	0	0	1	1	3	0	0	1-0	.375	.412	.438	.849	0	1.000
2002—San Francisco (N.L.)	2B	5	19	1	5	2	0	0	1	2	7	1	0	0-0	.263	.364	.368	.732	1	.960
2004—Houston (N.L.)	2B	5	22	3	5	3	0	0	3	2	5	0	2	0-0	.227	.292	.364	.655	0	1.000
Division series totals (5 years)		21	75	11	20	7	0	2	7	7	16	1	2	1-0	.267	.337	.440	.777	1	.991

CHAMPIONSHIP SERIES RECORD

Year Team (League)	Pos.	G	AB	R	H	2B	3B	HR	RBI	BB	SO	HBP	GDP	SB-CS	Avg.	OBP	SLG	OPS	E	Avg.
2002—San Francisco (N.L.)	2B	5	19	3	5	0	0	0	0	2	4	1	1	0-0	.263	.364	.263	.627	0	1.000
2004—Houston (N.L.)	2B	7	25	3	6	2	0	3	7	3	5	2	0	0-0	.240	.367	.680	1.047	0	1.000
Champ. series totals (2 years)		12	44	6	11	2	0	3	7	5	9	3	1	0-0	.250	.365	.500	.865	0	1.000

WORLD SERIES RECORD

Year Team (League)	Pos.	G	AB	R	H	2B	3B	HR	RBI	BB	SO	HBP	GDP	SB-CS	Avg.	OBP	SLG	OPS	E	Avg.
2002—San Francisco (N.L.)	2B	7	29	6	8	1	0	3	7	1	7	0	0	0-0	.276	.290	.621	.911	0	1.000

ALL-STAR GAME RECORD

		G	AB	R	H	2B	3B	HR	RBI	BB	SO	HBP	GDP	SB-CS	Avg.	OBP	SLG	OPS	E	Avg.
All-Star Game totals (4 years)		4	7	2	2	1	0	0	0	0	1	0	0	0-0	.286	.375	.429	.804	2	.867

KEPPINGER, JEFF — 2B

PERSONAL: Born April 21, 1980, in Miami, Fla. ... 6-0/180. ... Bats right, throws right. ... Full name: Jeffrey Scott Keppinger. ... High school: Parkview (Lilburn, Ga.). ... College: Georgia.

TRANSACTIONS/CAREER NOTES: Selected by Pittsburgh Pirates organization in fourth round of 2001 free-agent draft. ... Traded by Pirates with P Kris Benson to New York Mets for 3B Ty Wigginton, IF Jose Bautista and P Matt Peterson (July 30, 2004).

Year Team (League)	Pos.	G	AB	R	H	2B	3B	HR	RBI	BATTING BB	SO	HBP	GDP	SB-CS	Avg.	OBP	SLG	OPS	FIELDING E	Avg.
2002— Hickory (S. Atl.)	2B	126	478	75	132	23	4	10	73	47	33	6	13	6-2	.276	.344	.404	.748	10	.981
2003— Lynchburg (Caro.)	2B-3B-1B	92	342	55	111	21	2	3	51	23	28	1	10	3-2	.325	.365	.424	.789	11	.972
2004— Altoona (East.)	2B-DH	81	315	44	106	17	2	1	33	27	15	0	11	10-5	.337	.387	.413	.792	6	.982
— Binghamton (East.)	2B-3B-DH	14	47	14	17	3	1	0	5	6	2	0	2	2-1	.362	.426	.468	.894	1	.981
— Norfolk (Int'l)	2B-DH	6	19	1	6	1	0	0	2	4	2	1	2	0-0	.316	.458	.368	.803	0	1.000
— New York (N.L.)	2B	33	116	9	33	2	0	3	9	6	7	0	6	2-1	.284	.317	.379	.696	2	.987
Major League totals (1 year)		33	116	9	33	2	0	3	9	6	7	0	6	2-1	.284	.317	.379	.696	2	.987

KERSHNER, JASON — P

PERSONAL: Born December 19, 1976, in Scottsdale, Ariz. ... 6-2/165. ... Throws left, bats left. ... Full name: Jason Ashley Kershner. ... High school: Saguaro (Scottsdale, Ariz.).

TRANSACTIONS/CAREER NOTES: Selected by Philadelphia Philles organization in 12th round of 1995 free-agent draft. ... Signed as a free agent by San Diego Padres organization (November 20, 2001). ... Claimed on waivers by Toronto Blue Jays (August 30, 2002).

CAREER HITTING: 0-for-0 (.000), 0 R, 0 2B, 0 3B, 0 HR, 0 RBI.

Year Team (League)	W	L	Pct.	ERA	WHIP	G	GS	CG	ShO	Hld.	Sv.-Opp.	IP	H	R	ER	HR	BB-IBB	SO	Avg.
1995— Martinsville (App.)	4	2	.667	5.14	1.52	13	13	0	0	...	0-...	63.0	67	42	36	10	29-0	64	.277
1996— Piedmont (S. Atl.)	11	9	.550	3.75	1.27	28	28	2	1	...	0-...	168.0	154	81	70	12	59-0	156	.244
1997— Clearwater (Fla. St.)	5	10	.333	3.90	1.35	22	16	0	0	...	1-...	99.1	113	49	43	9	21-0	51	.293
1998— Clearwater (Fla. St.)	3	3	.500	4.01	1.41	41	8	0	0	...	3-...	94.1	108	57	42	8	25-0	65	.292
1999— Reading (East.)	4	4	.500	5.73	1.50	57	2	0	0	...	8-...	92.2	99	67	59	14	40-3	86	.277
2000— Reading (East.)	9	2	.818	3.63	1.26	27	19	0	0	...	1-...	119.0	125	49	48	15	25-0	80	.269
— Clearwater (Fla. St.)	1	0	1.000	0.64	0.86	2	2	0	0	...	0-...	14.0	7	1	1	1	5-0	15	.149
2001— Reading (East.)	5	9	.357	4.80	1.40	26	19	0	0	...	0-...	123.2	147	75	66	18	26-1	70	.302
— Scran./W.B. (I.L.)	1	1	.500	3.60	1.00	6	1	0	0	...	0-...	15.0	12	8	6	3	3-0	7	.207
2002— Portland (PCL)	7	2	.778	3.03	1.06	31	12	0	0	...	0-...	86.0	65	30	29	8	26-0	83	.215
— San Diego (N.L.)	0	1	.000	5.79	1.34	15	0	0	0	0	0-0	18.2	15	14	12	2	10-0	11	.217
— Toronto (A.L.)	0	0	...	1.69	1.69	10	0	0	0	1	1-2	5.1	5	2	1	1	4-1	7	.227
2003— Syracuse (Int'l)	6	1	.857	2.36	1.10	24	0	0	0	...	0-...	45.2	42	15	12	1	14-1	30	.255
— Toronto (A.L.)	3	3	.500	3.17	1.07	40	0	0	0	7	0-1	54.0	43	21	19	5	15-2	32	.217
2004— Toronto (A.L.)	0	1	.000	6.04	1.70	24	2	0	0	2	0-0	22.1	30	16	15	3	8-0	15	.316
— Syracuse (Int'l)	3	2	.600	5.20	1.51	28	0	0	0	...	4-...	36.1	45	23	21	6	10-3	31	.313
American League totals (3 years)	3	4	.429	3.86	1.29	74	2	0	0	10	1-3	81.2	78	39	35	9	27-3	54	.248
National League totals (1 year)	0	1	.000	5.79	1.34	15	0	0	0	0	0-0	18.2	15	14	12	2	10-0	11	.217
Major League totals (3 years)	3	5	.375	4.22	1.30	89	2	0	0	10	1-3	100.1	93	53	47	11	37-3	65	.242

KIDA, MASAO — P

PERSONAL: Born September 12, 1968, in Tokyo, Japan. ... 6-3/210. ... Throws right, bats right. ... Name pronounced: muh-SOW KEY-duh.

TRANSACTIONS/CAREER NOTES: Signed as a free agent by Detroit Tigers (December 16, 1998). ... On disabled list (June 30-July 28, 1999); included rehabilitation assignment to Toledo. ... Released by Tigers (June 6, 2000). ... Signed by Orix Blue Wave of Japan Pacific League (June 8, 2000). ... Signed as a free agent by Los Angeles Dodgers (February 5, 2003). ... Claimed on waivers by Seattle Mariners (September 1, 2004).

CAREER HITTING: 1-for-4 (.250), 0 R, 0 2B, 0 3B, 0 HR, 0 RBI.

Year Team (League)	W	L	Pct.	ERA	WHIP	G	GS	CG	ShO	Hld.	Sv.-Opp.	IP	H	R	ER	HR	BB-IBB	SO	Avg.
1988— Miami (Florida St.)	7	17	.292	3.99	1.30	27	27	9	1	...	0-...	162.1	149	88	72	9	62-3	100	
1989— Yomiuri (Jp. Cen.)	2	1	.667	4.62	1.49	8	4	1	0	...	0-...	37.0	41	19	19	...	14-...	26	
1990— Yomiuri (Jp. Cen.)	12	8	.600	2.71	0.99	32	17	13	1	...	0-...	182.2	130	56	55	...	51-...	182	
1991— Yomiuri (Jp. Cen.)	4	7	.364	6.44	1.63	19	5	2	0	...	1-...	50.1	51	41	36	...	31-...	44	
1992— Yomiuri (Jp. Cen.)	3	6	.333	4.53	1.48	29	11	2	1	...	0-...	93.1	103	48	47	...	35-...	87	
1993— Yomiuri (Jp. Cen.)	7	7	.500	3.35	1.28	35	17	1	1	...	2-...	131.2	129	50	49	...	40-...	97	
1994— Yomiuri (Jp. Cen.)	6	8	.429	4.93	1.40	28	13	1	0	...	1-...	87.2	86	52	48	...	37-...	61	
1995— Yomiuri (Jp. Cen.)	7	9	.438	3.40	1.22	40	12	2	0	...	0-...	121.2	117	49	46	...	31-...	97	
1996— Yomiuri (Jp. Cen.)	7	9	.438	3.78	1.25	33	16	3	2	...	2-...	123.2	121	53	52	...	34-...	99	
1997— Yomiuri (Jp. Cen.)	2	2	.500	1.99	1.39	39	0	0	0	...	7-...	49.2	47	13	11	...	22-...	53	
1998— Orix (Jp. Pac.)	4	7	.364	4.62	1.37	36	13	1	0	...	0-...	97.1	97	54	50	...	36-...	74	
1999— Detroit (A.L.)	1	0	1.000	6.26	1.59	49	0	0	0	4	1-1	64.2	73	48	45	6	30-3	50	.289
— Toledo (International)	0	0	...	3.18	1.24	3	0	0	0	...	0-...	5.2	6	2	2	2	1-0	4	.273
2000— Toledo (International)	2	1	.667	2.16	1.00	21	0	0	0	...	7-...	25.0	21	6	6	3	4-1	26	.233
— Detroit (A.L.)	0	0	...	10.13	1.88	2	0	0	0	0	0-0	2.2	5	3	3	1	0-0	0	.455
2003— Las Vegas (PCL)	2	4	.333	5.02	1.30	21	12	0	0	...	1-...	84.1	89	53	47	9	23-1	57	.271
— Los Angeles (N.L.)	0	1	.000	3.00	1.50	3	2	0	0	...	0-0	12.0	15	5	4	0	3-0	8	.300
2004— GC Dodgers (GCL)	0	0	...	0.00	0.50	2	2	0	0	...	0-...	4.0	2	0	0	0	0-0	0	.143
— Las Vegas (PCL)	3	1	.750	5.97	1.49	9	5	0	0	...	0-...	37.2	40	25	25	10	16-0	32	.274
— Los Angeles (N.L.)	0	0	...	0.00	1.07	3	0	0	0	0	0-0	4.2	4	0	0	0	1-0	5	.235
— Seattle (A.L.)	0	0	...	8.38	2.07	7	0	0	0	0	0-0	9.2	15	9	9	1	5-0	5	.366
American League totals (3 years)	1	0	1.000	6.66	1.66	58	0	0	0	4	1-1	77.0	93	60	57	8	35-3	55	.303
National League totals (2 years)	0	1	.000	2.16	1.38	6	2	0	0	0	0-0	16.2	19	5	4	0	4-0	13	.284
Major League totals (4 years)	1	1	.500	5.86	1.61	64	2	0	0	4	1-1	93.2	112	65	61	8	39-3	68	.299

KIELTY, BOBBY — OF

PERSONAL: Born August 5, 1976, in Fontana, Calif. ... 6-1/225. ... Bats both, throws right. ... Full name: Robert Michael Kielty. ... Name pronounced: kell-tee. ... High school: Canyon Springs (Moreno Valley, Calif.). ... College: Mississippi.

TRANSACTIONS/CAREER NOTES: Signed as a non-drafted free agent by Minnesota Twins organization (February 16, 1999). ... Traded to Toronto Blue Jays by Minnesota Twins for OF Shannon Stewart and a player to be named (July 16, 2003); Twins acquired P Dave Gassner to complete deal (December 16, 2003). ... Traded by Blue Jays with a player to be named or cash to Oakland Athletics for P Ted Lilly (November 18, 2003).

2004 GAMES PLAYED BY POSITION (MLB): OF—67, DH—11.

K

Year Team (League)	Pos.	G	AB	R	H	2B	3B	HR	RBI	BB	SO	HBP	GDP	SB-CS	Avg.	OBP	SLG	OPS	E	Avg.
																BATTING			FIELDING	
1999— Quad City (Midw.)	OF	69	245	52	72	13	1	13	43	43	56	3	7	12-3	.294	.401	.514	.916	3	.977
2000— New Britain (East.)	OF	129	451	79	118	30	3	14	65	98	109	5	16	6-4	.262	.396	.435	.831	3	.988
— Salt Lake (PCL)	OF	9	33	8	8	4	0	0	2	7	10	0	0	0-0	.242	.375	.364	.739	1	.957
2001— Edmonton (PCL)	OF	94	341	58	98	25	2	12	50	53	76	6	11	5-0	.287	.391	.478	.869	2	.991
— Minnesota (A.L.)	OF-DH	37	104	8	26	8	0	2	14	8	25	1	2	3-0	.250	.297	.385	.681	3	.956
2002— Edmonton (PCL)	OF	2	7	0	3	1	0	0	0	1	1	0	1	0-0	.429	.500	.571	1.071	0	1.000
— Minnesota (A.L.)	OF-DH-1B	112	289	49	84	14	3	12	46	52	66	5	4	4-1	.291	.405	.484	.890	0	1.000
2003— Minnesota (A.L.)	OF-DH	75	238	40	60	13	0	9	32	42	56	3	5	6-2	.252	.370	.420	.790	2	.972
— Toronto (A.L.)	OF-1B	62	189	31	44	13	1	4	25	29	36	4	6	2-1	.233	.342	.376	.718	1	.991
2004— Oakland (A.L.)	OF-DH	83	238	29	51	14	1	7	31	35	47	3	5	1-0	.214	.321	.370	.691	1	.990
Major League totals (4 years)		369	1058	157	265	62	5	34	148	166	230	16	22	16-4	.250	.357	.415	.772	7	.987

DIVISION SERIES RECORD

Year Team (League)	Pos.	G	AB	R	H	2B	3B	HR	RBI	BB	SO	HBP	GDP	SB-CS	Avg.	OBP	SLG	OPS	E	Avg.
2002— Minnesota (A.L.)	OF-DH	3	4	0	0	0	0	0	0	0	1	0	0	0-0	.000	.000	.000	.000	0	1.000

CHAMPIONSHIP SERIES RECORD

Year Team (League)	Pos.	G	AB	R	H	2B	3B	HR	RBI	BB	SO	HBP	GDP	SB-CS	Avg.	OBP	SLG	OPS	E	Avg.
2002— Minnesota (A.L.)	DH-OF	4	3	0	0	0	0	0	1	1	2	0	0	0-0	.000	.250	.000	.250	0	...

KIESCHNICK, BROOKS — P

PERSONAL: Born June 6, 1972, in Robstown, Texas. ... 6-4/251. ... Throws right, bats left. ... Full name: Michael Brooks Kieschnick. ... High school: Mary Carroll (Corpus Christi, Texas). ... College: Texas.

TRANSACTIONS/CAREER NOTES: Selected by Chicago Cubs organization in first round (10th pick overall) of 1993 free-agent draft. ... Selected by Tampa Bay Devil Rays in third round (64th pick overall) of expansion draft (November 18, 1997). ... Loaned by Devil Rays organization to Anaheim Angels organization (May 24-September 20, 1999). ... Signed as a free agent by Cincinnati Reds organization (November 16, 1999). ... Signed as a free agent by Colorado Rockies organization (December 1, 2000). ... On disabled list (May 13-28, 2001); included rehabilitation assignment to Colorado Springs. ... Signed as a free agent by Cleveland Indians organization (February 1, 2002). ... Released by Indians (March 25, 2002). ... Signed by Chicago White Sox organization (May 16, 2002). ... Signed as a free agent by Milwaukee Brewers organization (November 8, 2002). ... On disabled list (August 9-September 3, 2004); included rehabilitation assignment to Indianapolis. Played 10 seasons as an infielder-outfielder for six organizations. (1993-2002).

CAREER HITTING: 76-for-306 (.248), 34 R, 10 2B, 1 3B, 16 HR, 46 RBI.

Year Team (League)	W	L	Pct.	ERA	WHIP	G	GS	CG	ShO	Hld.	Sv.-Opp.	IP	H	R	ER	HR	BB-IBB	SO	Avg.
1999— Durham (Int'l)	0	0	...	0.00	1.00	23	0	0	0	...	0-...	2.0	1	0	0	0	1-0	1	.125
2003— Indianapolis (Int'l)	1	0	1.000	8.56	2.00	8	0	0	0	...	0-...	13.2	17	15	13	3	10-2	14	.304
— Milwaukee (N.L.)	1	1	.500	5.26	1.49	42	0	0	0	2	0-0	53.0	66	32	31	5	13-4	39	.299
2004— Indianapolis (Int'l)	0	0	...	0.00	0.50	2	2	0	0	...	0-...	2.0	1	0	0	0	0-0	3	.143
— Milwaukee (N.L.)	1	1	.500	3.77	1.33	32	0	0	0	5	0-1	43.0	44	19	18	6	13-3	28	.262
Major League totals (2 years)	2	2	.500	4.59	1.42	74	0	0	0	7	0-1	96.0	110	51	49	11	26-7	67	.283

KIM, BYUNG-HYUN — P

PERSONAL: Born January 19, 1979, in Gwangju, South Korea. ... 5-9/180. ... Throws right, bats right. ... Name pronounced: bee-yung hee-yun. ... High school: Kwang-ju (Korea). ... College: Sungkyunkwan (South Korea).

TRANSACTIONS/CAREER NOTES: Signed as a non-drafted free agent by Arizona Diamondbacks organization (February 19, 1999). ... On disabled list (July 28-September 7, 2000). ... On disabled list (April 30-May 27, 2003); included rehabilitation assignment to Tucson. ... Traded by Diamondbacks to Boston Red Sox for IF Shea Hillenbrand (May 30, 2003). ... On disabled list (March 26-April 29, 2004); included rehabilitation assignment to Sarasota.

CAREER HITTING: 6-for-32 (.188), 0 R, 1 2B, 0 3B, 0 HR, 3 RBI.

Year Team (League)	W	L	Pct.	ERA	WHIP	G	GS	CG	ShO	Hld.	Sv.-Opp.	IP	H	R	ER	HR	BB-IBB	SO	Avg.
1999— El Paso (Texas)	2	0	1.000	2.11	0.70	10	0	0	0	...	0-...	21.1	6	5	5	0	9-0	32	.092
— Tucson (PCL)	4	0	1.000	2.40	1.20	11	3	0	0	...	1-...	30.0	21	9	8	2	15-1	40	.196
— Arizona (N.L.)	1	2	.333	4.61	1.46	25	0	0	0	3	1-4	27.1	20	15	14	2	20-2	31	.211
— Ariz. D'backs (Ariz.)	0	0	...	0.00	1.00	1	1	0	0	...	0-...	2.0	1	0	0	0	1-0	2	.167
2000— Arizona (N.L.)	6	6	.500	4.46	1.39	61	1	0	0	5	14-20	70.2	52	39	35	9	46-5	111	.200
— Tucson (PCL)	0	0	...	0.00	0.60	2	2	0	0	...	0-...	8.1	1	0	0	0	4-0	13	.042
2001— Arizona (N.L.)	5	6	.455	2.94	1.04	78	0	0	0	11	19-23	98.0	58	32	32	10	44-3	113	.173
2002— Arizona (N.L.)	8	3	.727	2.04	1.07	72	0	0	0	0	36-42	84.0	64	20	19	5	26-2	92	.208
2003— Tucson (PCL)	1	1	.500	2.55	1.00	3	3	0	0	...	0-...	17.2	17	5	5	2	1-0	8	.270
— Arizona (N.L.)	1	5	.167	3.56	1.14	7	7	0	0	0	0-0	43.0	34	17	17	6	15-0	33	.214
— Boston (A.L.)	8	5	.615	3.18	1.11	49	5	0	0	1	16-19	79.1	70	38	28	6	18-3	69	.230
2004— Sarasota (Florida State)	0	0	...	0.00	...	1	1	0	0	...	0-...	2.0	0	0	0	0	0-0	2	.000
— Pawtucket (Int'l)	2	6	.250	5.34	1.37	22	19	0	0	...	0-...	60.2	71	43	36	6	12-0	39	.289
— Boston (A.L.)	2	1	.667	6.23	1.38	7	3	0	0	0	0-0	17.1	17	15	12	1	7-1	6	.258
American League totals (2 years)	10	6	.625	3.72	1.16	56	8	0	0	1	16-19	96.2	87	53	40	7	25-4	75	.235
National League totals (5 years)	21	22	.488	3.26	1.17	243	8	0	0	19	70-89	323.0	228	123	117	32	151-12	380	.197
Major League totals (6 years)	31	28	.525	3.37	1.17	299	16	0	0	20	86-108	419.2	315	176	157	39	176-16	455	.206

DIVISION SERIES RECORD

Year Team (League)	W	L	Pct.	ERA	WHIP	G	GS	CG	ShO	Hld.	Sv.-Opp.	IP	H	R	ER	HR	BB-IBB	SO	Avg.
2001— Arizona (N.L.)	0	0	...	2.25	1	1	0	0	0	0	1-1	1.1	1	0	0	0	2-0	1	.250
2002— Arizona (N.L.)	0	0	...	18.00	5.00	1	0	0	0	0	0-0	1.0	2	2	2	0	3-1	0	.400
2003— Boston (A.L.)	0	0	...	13.50	1.50	1	0	0	0	1	0-0	.2	0	1	1	0	1-0	1	.000
Division series totals (3 years)	0	0	...	9.00	3.00	3	0	0	0	1	1-1	3.0	3	3	3	0	6-1	2	.273

CHAMPIONSHIP SERIES RECORD

Year Team (League)	W	L	Pct.	ERA	WHIP	G	GS	CG	ShO	Hld.	Sv.-Opp.	IP	H	R	ER	HR	BB-IBB	SO	Avg.
2001— Arizona (N.L.)	0	0	...	0.00	0.20	3	0	0	0	0	2-2	5.0	0	0	0	0	1-0	3	.000

WORLD SERIES RECORD

Year Team (League)	W	L	Pct.	ERA	WHIP	G	GS	CG	ShO	Hld.	Sv.-Opp.	IP	H	R	ER	HR	BB-IBB	SO	Avg.
2001— Arizona (N.L.)	0	1	.000	13.50	2.10	2	0	0	0	0	0-2	3.1	6	5	5	3	1-0	6	.375

ALL-STAR GAME RECORD

Year Team (League)	W	L	Pct.	ERA	WHIP	G	GS	CG	ShO	Hld.	Sv.-Opp.	IP	H	R	ER	HR	BB-IBB	SO	Avg.
All-Star Game totals (1 year)	0	0	...	54.00	9.00	1	0	0	0	0	0-0	.1	3	2	2	0	1-0	0	.750

KIM, SUN-WOO   P

PERSONAL: Born September 4, 1977, in Inchon, South Korea. ... 6-1/185. ... Throws right, bats right. ... College: Korea University.

TRANSACTIONS/CAREER NOTES: Signed as a non-drafted free agent by Boston Red Sox organization (November 21, 1997). ... Traded by Red Sox with P Seung Song and a player to be named to Montreal Expos for OF Cliff Floyd (July 30, 2002).

CAREER HITTING: 8-for-39 (.205), 3 R, 2 2B, 0 3B, 0 HR, 5 RBI.

Year Team (League)	W	L	Pct.	ERA	WHIP	G	GS	CG	ShO	Hld.	Sv.-Opp.	IP	H	R	ER	HR	BB-IBB	SO	Avg.
1998— Sarasota (Florida State)	12	8	.600	4.82	1.30	26	24	5	0	...	0-...	153.0	159	88	82	18	40-1	132	.264
1999— Trenton (East.)	9	8	.529	4.89	1.37	26	26	1	1	...	0-...	149.0	160	86	81	16	44-2	130	.275
2000— Pawtucket (Int'l)	11	7	.611	6.03	1.58	26	25	0	0	...	0-...	134.1	170	98	90	17	42-1	116	.309
2001— Pawtucket (Int'l)	6	7	.462	5.36	1.35	19	14	0	0	...	0-...	89.0	93	55	53	10	27-1	79	.272
— Boston (A.L.)	0	2	.000	5.83	1.80	20	2	0	0	1	0-0	41.2	54	27	27	1	21-5	27	.312
2002— Pawtucket (Int'l)	4	2	.667	3.18	1.10	8	8	1	0	...	0-...	45.1	34	18	16	4	16-0	37	.206
— Boston (A.L.)	2	0	1.000	7.45	1.41	15	2	0	0	2	0-0	29.0	34	24	24	5	7-0	18	.288
— Ottawa (Int'l)	3	0	1.000	1.24	1.03	7	7	1	1	...	0-...	43.2	29	11	6	2	16-0	28	.195
— Montreal (N.L.)	1	0	1.000	0.89	1.23	4	3	0	0	0	0-0	20.1	18	2	2	0	7-2	11	.250
2003— Montreal (N.L.)	0	1	.000	8.36	2.29	4	3	0	0	0	0-0	14.0	24	13	13	6	8-0	5	.407
— Edmonton (PCL)	10	8	.556	5.03	1.50	22	22	3	2	...	0-...	132.1	147	83	74	18	53-1	83	.281
2004— Montreal (N.L.)	4	6	.400	4.58	1.47	43	17	0	0	2	0-0	135.2	145	80	69	17	55-11	87	.275
American League totals (2 years)	2	2	.500	6.50	1.64	35	4	0	0	3	0-0	70.2	88	51	51	6	28-5	45	.302
National League totals (3 years)	5	7	.417	4.45	1.51	51	23	0	0	2	0-0	170.0	187	95	84	23	70-13	103	.284
Major League totals (4 years)	7	9	.438	5.05	1.55	86	27	0	0	5	0-0	240.2	275	146	135	29	98-18	148	.290

KING, RAY   P

PERSONAL: Born January 15, 1974, in Chicago, Ill. ... 6-1/242. ... Throws left, bats left. ... Full name: Raymond Keith King. ... High school: Ripley (Tenn.). ... College: Lambuth (Tenn.).

TRANSACTIONS/CAREER NOTES: Selected by Cincinnati Reds organization in eighth round of 1995 free-agent draft. ... Loaned by Reds organization to Atlanta Braves organization (March 22-June 11, 1996). ... Traded by Reds to Braves (June 11, 1996), completing deal in which Braves traded OF Mike Kelly to Reds for P Chad Fox and a player to be named (January 9, 1996). ... Traded by Braves to Chicago Cubs for P Jon Ratliff (January 20, 1998). ... Traded by Cubs to Milwaukee Brewers for P Doug Johnston (April 14, 2000). ... On disabled list (April 5-19, 2002); included rehabilitation assignment to Indianapolis. ... Traded by Brewers to Atlanta Braves for 3B Wes Helms and P John Foster (December 16, 2002). ... Traded by Braves with Ps Jason Marquis and Adam Wainwright to St. Louis Cardinals for OF J.D. Drew and C/OF Eli Marrero (December 14, 2003).

CAREER HITTING: 0-for-5 (.000), 0 R, 0 2B, 0 3B, 0 HR, 0 RBI.

Year Team (League)	W	L	Pct.	ERA	WHIP	G	GS	CG	ShO	Hld.	Sv.-Opp.	IP	H	R	ER	HR	BB-IBB	SO	Avg.
1995— Billings (Pio.)	3	0	1.000	1.67	1.07	28	0	0	0	...	5-...	43.0	31	11	8	1	15-3	43	.204
1996— Macon (S. Atl.)	3	5	.375	2.80	1.17	18	10	1	0	...	0-...	70.2	63	34	22	4	20-0	63	.237
— Durham (Caro.)	3	6	.333	4.46	1.44	14	14	2	0	...	0-...	82.2	104	54	41	3	15-2	52	.308
1997— Greenville (Sou.)	5	5	.500	6.85	1.66	12	9	0	0	...	0-...	65.2	85	53	50	9	24-2	42	.304
— Durham (Caro.)	6	9	.400	5.40	1.60	24	14	0	0	...	3-...	71.2	89	54	43	6	26-4	60	.300
1998— West Tenn (Sou.)	1	2	.333	2.43	1.11	25	0	0	0	...	0-...	29.2	23	9	8	1	10-0	26	.213
— Iowa (PCL)	1	3	.250	5.01	1.58	37	0	0	0	...	2-...	32.1	36	20	18	4	15-1	26	.283
1999— Iowa (PCL)	4	4	.500	1.88	1.23	37	0	0	0	...	2-...	43.0	31	11	9	1	22-3	41	.200
— Chicago (N.L.)	0	0	...	5.91	1.97	10	0	0	0	2	0-0	10.2	11	8	7	2	10-0	5	.289
2000— Iowa (PCL)	1	0	1.000	0.00	0.75	1	0	0	0	...	0-0	1.1	1	0	0	0	0-0	1	.200
— Indianapolis (Int'l)	0	3	.000	3.51	1.48	29	0	0	0	...	1-...	25.2	26	15	10	1	12-0	20	.271
— Milwaukee (N.L.)	3	2	.600	1.26	0.98	36	0	0	0	5	0-1	28.2	18	7	4	1	10-1	19	.180
2001— Milwaukee (N.L.)	0	4	.000	3.60	1.35	82	0	0	0	18	1-4	55.0	49	22	22	5	25-7	49	.241
2002— Milwaukee (N.L.)	3	2	.600	3.05	1.31	76	0	0	0	15	0-1	65.0	61	24	22	8	24-6	50	.255
— Indianapolis (Int'l)	0	0	...	0.00	2.00	1	1	0	0	...	0-...	1.0	1	0	0	0	1-0	1	.333
2003— Atlanta (N.L.)	3	4	.429	3.51	1.24	80	0	0	0	18	0-0	59.0	46	30	23	3	27-2	43	.213
2004— St. Louis (N.L.)	5	2	.714	2.61	1.08	86	0	0	0	31	0-1	62.0	43	19	18	1	24-0	40	.197
Major League totals (6 years)	14	14	.500	3.08	1.24	370	0	0	0	89	1-8	280.1	228	110	96	17	120-16	206	.225

DIVISION SERIES RECORD

Year Team (League)	W	L	Pct.	ERA	WHIP	G	GS	CG	ShO	Hld.	Sv.-Opp.	IP	H	R	ER	HR	BB-IBB	SO	Avg.
2003— Atlanta (N.L.)	0	0	...	0.00	2.00	4	0	0	0	1	0-0	1.0	1	0	0	0	1-0	0	.500
2004— St. Louis (N.L.)	0	0	...	0.00	0.00	3	0	0	0	1	0-0	2.1	0	0	0	0	0-0	1	.000
Division series totals (2 years)	0	0	...	0.00	0.60	7	0	0	0	2	0-0	3.1	1	0	0	0	1-0	1	.111

CHAMPIONSHIP SERIES RECORD

Year Team (League)	W	L	Pct.	ERA	WHIP	G	GS	CG	ShO	Hld.	Sv.-Opp.	IP	H	R	ER	HR	BB-IBB	SO	Avg.
2004— St. Louis (N.L.)	0	0	...	10.80	2.40	4	0	0	0	1	0-0	1.2	4	2	2	2	0-0	1	.500

WORLD SERIES RECORD

Year Team (League)	W	L	Pct.	ERA	WHIP	G	GS	CG	ShO	Hld.	Sv.-Opp.	IP	H	R	ER	HR	BB-IBB	SO	Avg.
2004— St. Louis (N.L.)	0	0	...	0.00	0.75	3	0	0	0	0	0-0	2.2	1	0	0	0	1-0	1	.125

KINNEY, MATT   P

PERSONAL: Born December 16, 1976, in Bangor, Maine. ... 6-5/228. ... Throws right, bats right. ... Full name: Matthew John Kinney. ... High school: Bangor (Maine).

TRANSACTIONS/CAREER NOTES: Selected by Boston Red Sox organization in sixth round of 1995 free-agent draft. ... Traded by Red Sox with P Joe Thomas and OF John Barnes to Minnesota Twins for P Greg Swindell and 1B Orlando Merced (July 31, 1998). ... On disabled list (June 30-August 19, 2002); included rehabilitation assignments to GCL Twins, Fort Myers and New Britain. ... Traded by Twins with C Javier Valentin to Milwaukee Brewers for Ps Matt Yeatman and Gerard Oakes (November 15, 2002). ... Claimed on waivers by Kansas City Royals (August 13, 2004). ... Refused minor league assignment and became a free agent (October 6, 2004).

CAREER HITTING: 4-for-66 (.061), 3 R, 1 2B, 0 3B, 0 HR, 1 RBI.

Year Team (League)	W	L	Pct.	ERA	WHIP	G	GS	CG	ShO	Hld.	Sv.-Opp.	IP	H	R	ER	HR	BB-IBB	SO	Avg.
1995— GC Red Sox (GCL)	1	3	.250	2.93	1.41	8	2	0	0	...	2-...	27.2	29	13	9	0	10-0	11	.279
1996— Lowell (NY-Penn)	3	9	.250	2.68	1.28	15	15	0	0	...	0-...	87.1	68	51	26	0	44-2	72	.207
1997— Michigan (Midw.)	8	5	.615	3.53	1.46	22	22	2	1	...	0-...	117.1	93	59	46	4	78-2	123	.217
1998— Sarasota (Florida State)	9	6	.600	4.01	1.52	22	20	2	1	...	1-...	121.1	109	70	54	5	75-3	96	.241
— Fort Myers (Fla. St.)	3	2	.600	3.13	1.31	7	7	0	0	...	0-...	37.1	31	18	13	0	18-0	39	.220
1999— New Britain (East.)	4	7	.364	7.12	1.73	14	13	0	0	...	0-...	60.2	69	54	48	8	36-0	50	.289
— GC Twins (GCL)	0	1	.000	4.76	1.59	3	3	0	0	...	0-...	5.2	6	4	3	0	3-0	8	.286

Year	Team (League)	W	L	Pct.	ERA	WHIP	G	GS	CG	ShO	Hld.	Sv.-Opp.	IP	H	R	ER	HR	BB-IBB	SO	Avg.
2000— New Britain (East.)		6	1	.857	2.71	1.26	15	15	0	0	...	0-...	86.1	74	31	26	7	35-0	93	.231
— Salt Lake (PCL)		5	2	.714	4.25	1.24	9	9	0	0	...	0-...	55.0	42	26	26	5	26-0	59	.211
— Minnesota (A.L.)		2	2	.500	5.10	1.56	8	8	0	0	0	0-0	42.1	41	26	24	7	25-1	24	.261
2001— Edmonton (PCL)		6	11	.353	5.07	1.56	29	29	2	0	...	0-...	161.2	178	101	91	25	74-0	146	.280
2002— Edmonton (PCL)		2	1	.667	8.89	1.68	5	5	0	0	...	0-...	27.1	42	27	27	9	4-0	21	.350
— Minnesota (A.L.)		2	7	.222	4.64	1.68	14	12	0	0	0	0-0	66.0	78	39	34	13	33-0	45	.295
— GC Twins (GCL)		0	0	...	3.00	1.00	2	2	0	0	...	0-...	6.0	2	2	2	1	4-0	7	.100
— Fort Myers (Fla. St.)		0	0	...	0.00	1.40	1	1	0	0	...	0-...	5.0	4	2	0	0	3-0	5	.222
— New Britain (East.)		0	0	...	6.75	1.25	1	1	0	0	...	0-...	4.0	4	4	3	1	1-0	3	.250
2003— Milwaukee (N.L.)		10	13	.435	5.19	1.47	33	31	1	0	0	0-0	190.2	201	121	110	27	80-4	135	.272
2004— Milwaukee (N.L.)		3	4	.429	5.78	1.60	32	6	0	0	3	0-0	62.1	77	41	40	8	23-1	52	.301
— Kansas City (A.L.)		0	1	.000	7.16	2.08	11	0	0	0	0	0-0	16.1	27	14	13	3	7-1	21	.365
American League totals (3 years)		4	10	.286	5.13	1.69	33	20	0	0	0	0-0	124.2	146	79	71	23	65-2	90	.295
National League totals (2 years)		13	17	.433	5.34	1.51	65	37	1	0	3	0-0	253.0	278	162	150	35	103-5	204	.279
Major League totals (4 years)		17	27	.386	5.27	1.57	98	57	1	0	3	0-0	377.2	424	241	221	58	168-7	294	.284

KLESKO, RYAN — OF/1B

PERSONAL: Born June 12, 1971, in Westminster, Calif. ... 6-3/220. ... Bats left, throws left. ... Full name: Ryan Anthony Klesko. ... High school: Westminster (Calif.).

TRANSACTIONS/CAREER NOTES: Selected by Atlanta Braves organization in fifth round of 1989 free-agent draft. ... On disabled list (May 3-18, 1995); included rehabilitation assignment to Greenville. ... Traded by Braves with 2B Bret Boone and P Jason Shiell to San Diego Padres for 2B Quilvio Veras, 1B Wally Joyner and OF Reggie Sanders (December 22, 1999). ... On diisabled list (September 1, 2003-remainder of season; and May 27-June 16, 2004).

2004 GAMES PLAYED BY POSITION (MLB): OF—104, 1B—18, DH—3.

Year	Team (League)	Pos.	G	AB	R	H	2B	3B	HR	RBI	BB	SO	HBP	GDP	SB-CS	Avg.	OBP	SLG	OPS	E	Avg.
1989— GC Braves (GCL)		DH	17	57	14	23	5	4	1	16	6	6	0	2	4-3	.404	.453	.684	1.137	...	...
— Sumter (S. Atl.)		1B	25	90	17	26	6	0	1	12	11	14	0	5	1-0	.289	.363	.389	.752	4	.979
1990— Sumter (S. Atl.)		1B	63	231	41	85	15	1	10	38	31	30	1	6	13-1	.368	.437	.571	1.008	14	.978
— Durham (Caro.)		1B	77	292	40	80	16	1	7	47	32	53	2	8	10-5	.274	.343	.408	.751	13	.976
1991— Greenville (Sou.)		1B	126	419	64	122	22	3	14	67	75	60	6	5	14-17	.291	.404	.458	.862	17	.985
1992— Richmond (Int'l)		1B	123	418	63	105	22	2	17	59	41	72	4	14	3-5	.251	.323	.435	.758	11	.989
— Atlanta (N.L.)		1B	13	14	0	0	0	0	0	1	0	5	1	0	0-0	.000	.067	.000	.067	0	1.000
1993— Richmond (Int'l)		1B-OF	98	343	59	94	14	2	22	74	47	69	2	8	4-3	.274	.361	.519	.880	12	.981
— Atlanta (N.L.)		1B-OF	22	17	3	6	1	0	2	5	3	4	0	0	0-0	.353	.450	.765	1.215	0	1.000
1994— Atlanta (N.L.)		OF-1B	92	245	42	68	13	3	17	47	26	48	1	8	1-0	.278	.344	.563	.907	7	.929
1995— Atlanta (N.L.)		OF-1B	107	329	48	102	25	2	23	70	47	72	2	8	5-4	.310	.396	.608	1.004	8	.944
— Greenville (Sou.)		DH-OF	4	13	1	3	0	0	1	4	2	1	0	1	0-0	.231	.333	.462	.795	0	1.000
1996— Atlanta (N.L.)		OF-1B	153	528	90	149	21	4	34	93	68	129	2	16	6-3	.282	.364	.530	.894	5	.977
1997— Atlanta (N.L.)		OF-1B	143	467	67	122	23	6	24	84	48	130	4	12	4-4	.261	.334	.490	.824	6	.977
1998— Atlanta (N.L.)		OF-1B	129	427	69	117	29	1	18	70	56	66	3	9	5-3	.274	.359	.473	.832	2	.990
1999— Atlanta (N.L.) 1B-OF-DH			133	404	55	120	28	2	21	80	53	69	2	6	5-2	.297	.376	.532	.908	6	.990
2000— San Diego (N.L.)		1B-OF	145	494	88	140	33	2	26	92	91	81	1	10	23-7	.283	.393	.516	.909	9	.992
2001— San Diego (N.L.)		1B	146	538	105	154	34	6	30	113	88	89	3	16	23-4	.286	.384	.539	.923	11	.991
2002— San Diego (N.L.) 1B-OF-DH			146	540	90	162	39	1	29	95	76	86	4	7	6-2	.300	.388	.537	.925	7	.993
2003— San Diego (N.L.)		1B-DH	121	397	40	100	18	0	21	67	65	83	3	11	2-5	.252	.354	.456	.810	6	.994
2004— San Diego (N.L.) OF-1B-DH			127	402	58	117	32	2	9	66	73	67	1	8	3-2	.291	.399	.448	.847	4	.986
Major League totals (13 years)			1477	4802	762	1357	296	29	254	883	694	929	27	105	83-36	.283	.373	.515	.888	71	.989

DIVISION SERIES RECORD

Year	Team (League)	Pos.	G	AB	R	H	2B	3B	HR	RBI	BB	SO	HBP	GDP	SB-CS	Avg.	OBP	SLG	OPS	E	Avg.
1995— Atlanta (N.L.)		OF	4	15	5	7	1	0	0	1	0	3	0	1	0-0	.467	.467	.533	1.000	0	1.000
1996— Atlanta (N.L.)		OF	3	8	1	1	0	0	1	1	3	4	0	0	1-0	.125	.364	.500	.864	1	.667
1997— Atlanta (N.L.)		OF	3	8	2	2	1	0	1	1	0	2	0	1	0-0	.250	.250	.750	1.000	1	.750
1998— Atlanta (N.L.)		OF	3	11	1	3	0	0	1	4	0	3	0	0	0-0	.273	.273	.545	.818	0	1.000
1999— Atlanta (N.L.)		1B	4	12	3	4	0	0	0	1	1	4	0	0	0-0	.333	.385	.333	.718	0	1.000
Division series totals (5 years)			17	54	12	17	2	0	3	8	4	16	0	2	1-0	.315	.362	.519	.881	2	.949

CHAMPIONSHIP SERIES RECORD

Year	Team (League)	Pos.	G	AB	R	H	2B	3B	HR	RBI	BB	SO	HBP	GDP	SB-CS	Avg.	OBP	SLG	OPS	E	Avg.
1995— Atlanta (N.L.)		OF	4	7	0	0	0	0	0	0	3	4	0	0	0-1	.000	.300	.000	.300	0	1.000
1996— Atlanta (N.L.)		OF	6	16	1	4	0	0	1	3	2	6	0	1	0-0	.250	.333	.438	.771	0	1.000
1997— Atlanta (N.L.)		OF	5	17	2	4	0	0	2	4	2	3	0	0	0-0	.235	.316	.588	.904	0	1.000
1998— Atlanta (N.L.)		OF	5	12	2	1	0	0	0	1	6	3	0	0	0-0	.083	.389	.083	.472	1	.750
1999— Atlanta (N.L.)		1B	4	8	1	1	0	0	1	1	2	1	0	0	0-0	.125	.300	.500	.800	2	.935
Champ. series totals (5 years)			24	60	6	10	0	0	4	9	15	17	0	1	0-1	.167	.333	.367	.700	3	.944

WORLD SERIES RECORD

Year	Team (League)	Pos.	G	AB	R	H	2B	3B	HR	RBI	BB	SO	HBP	GDP	SB-CS	Avg.	OBP	SLG	OPS	E	Avg.
1995— Atlanta (N.L.)		DH-OF	6	16	4	5	0	0	3	4	3	4	0	0	0-0	.313	.421	.875	1.296	0	1.000
1996— Atlanta (N.L.) DH-1B-OF			5	10	2	1	0	0	0	1	2	4	0	0	0-0	.100	.250	.100	.350	1	.500
1999— Atlanta (N.L.)		1B	4	12	0	2	0	0	0	0	0	1	0	0	0-0	.167	.167	.167	.333	0	1.000
World series totals (3 years)			15	38	6	8	0	0	3	5	5	9	0	0	0-0	.211	.302	.447	.750	1	.958

ALL-STAR GAME RECORD

	G	AB	R	H	2B	3B	HR	RBI	BB	SO	HBP	GDP	SB-CS	Avg.	OBP	SLG	OPS	E	Avg.
All-Star Game totals (1 year)	1	1	0	0	0	0	0	0	0	1	0	0	0-0	.000	.000	.000	.000	0	1.000

KLINE, STEVE — P

PERSONAL: Born August 22, 1972, in Sunbury, Pa. ... 6-1/215. ... Throws left, bats both. ... Full name: Steven James Kline. ... High school: Lewisburg (Pa.). ... College: West Virginia.

TRANSACTIONS/CAREER NOTES: Selected by Cleveland Indians organization in eighth round of 1993 free-agent draft. ... Traded by Indians to Montreal Expos for P Jeff Juden (July 31, 1997). ... On disabled list (April 11-27, 1999). ... Traded by Expos with P Dustin Hermanson to St. Louis Cardinals for 3B Fernando Tatis and P Britt Reames (December 14, 2000). ... On disabled list (April 29-May 31, 2002); included rehabilitation assignments to Peoria and New Haven. ... On disabled list (August 28-September 29, 2004).

K

CAREER HITTING: 2-for-13 (.154), 1 R, 1 2B, 0 3B, 0 HR, 2 RBI.

Year— Team (League)	W	L	Pct.	ERA	WHIP	G	GS	CG	ShO	Hld.	Sv.-Opp.	IP	H	R	ER	HR	BB-IBB	SO	Avg.
1993— Burlington (Appalachian) ..	1	1	.500	4.91	1.77	2	1	0	0	...	0-...	7.1	11	4	4	0	2-1	4	.355
— Watertown (N.Y.-Penn.)	5	4	.556	3.19	1.13	13	13	2	1	...	0-...	79.0	77	36	28	3	12-0	45	.248
1994— Columbus (S. Atl.)	18	5	.783	3.01	1.14	28	28	2	1	...	0-...	185.2	175	67	62	14	36-0	174	.251
1995— Cant./Akr. (Eastern)	2	3	.400	2.42	1.30	14	14	0	0	...	0-...	89.1	86	34	24	6	30-3	45	.252
1996— Cant./Akr. (Eastern)	8	12	.400	5.46	1.52	25	24	0	0	...	0-...	146.2	168	98	89	16	55-2	107	.288
1997— Cleveland (A.L.)	3	1	.750	5.81	2.09	20	1	0	0	4	0-2	26.1	42	19	17	6	13-1	17	.365
— Buffalo (A.A.)	3	3	.500	4.03	1.29	20	4	0	0	...	1-...	51.1	53	26	23	4	13-1	41	.265
— Montreal (N.L.)	1	3	.250	6.15	1.56	26	0	0	0	1	0-1	26.1	31	18	18	4	10-3	20	.307
1998— Ottawa (Int'l)	0	0	...	0.00	0.38	2	0	0	0	...	0-...	2.2	1	0	0	0	0-0	1	.125
— Montreal (N.L.)	3	6	.333	2.76	1.44	78	0	0	0	18	1-2	71.2	62	25	22	4	41-7	76	.228
1999— Montreal (N.L.)	7	4	.636	3.75	1.28	82	0	0	0	16	0-2	69.2	56	32	29	8	33-6	69	.218
2000— Montreal (N.L.)	1	5	.167	3.50	1.40	83	0	0	0	12	14-18	82.1	88	36	32	8	27-2	64	.278
2001— St. Louis (N.L.)	3	3	.500	1.80	1.09	89	0	0	0	17	9-10	75.0	53	16	15	3	29-7	54	.203
2002— St. Louis (N.L.)	2	1	.667	3.39	1.29	66	0	0	0	21	6-8	58.1	54	23	22	3	21-2	41	.251
— Peoria (Midw.)	0	0	...	0.00	0.86	2	1	0	0	...	0-...	2.1	1	0	0	0	1-0	5	.111
— New Haven (East.)	0	0	...	0.00	0.50	1	1	0	0	...	0-...	2.0	0	0	0	0	1-0	2	.000
2003— St. Louis (N.L.)	5	5	.500	3.82	1.35	78	0	0	0	18	3-7	63.2	56	29	27	5	30-5	31	.237
2004— St. Louis (N.L.)	2	2	.500	1.79	1.07	67	0	0	0	15	3-4	50.1	37	12	10	3	17-4	35	.209
American League totals (1 year)	3	1	.750	5.81	2.09	20	1	0	0	4	0-2	26.1	42	19	17	6	13-1	17	.365
National League totals (8 years)	24	29	.453	3.17	1.30	569	0	0	0	118	36-52	497.1	437	191	175	38	208-36	390	.238
Major League totals (8 years)	27	30	.474	3.30	1.34	589	1	0	0	122	36-54	523.2	479	210	192	44	221-37	407	.246

DIVISION SERIES RECORD

Year— Team (League)	W	L	Pct.	ERA	WHIP	G	GS	CG	ShO	Hld.	Sv.-Opp.	IP	H	R	ER	HR	BB-IBB	SO	Avg.
2001— St. Louis (N.L.)	0	1	.000	2.08	1.38	4	0	0	0	0	2-2	4.1	4	1	1	0	2-1	0	.308
2002— St. Louis (N.L.)	0	0	...	0.00	1.50	2	0	0	0	2	0-0	1.1	1	0	0	0	1-0	0	.200
2004— St. Louis (N.L.)	0	0	...	0.00	0.00	2	0	0	0	0	0-0	1.1	0	0	0	0	0-0	0	.000
Division series totals (3 years)	0	1	.000	1.29	1.14	8	0	0	0	2	2-2	7.0	5	1	1	0	3-1	0	.227

CHAMPIONSHIP SERIES RECORD

Year— Team (League)	W	L	Pct.	ERA	WHIP	G	GS	CG	ShO	Hld.	Sv.-Opp.	IP	H	R	ER	HR	BB-IBB	SO	Avg.
2002— St. Louis (N.L.)	0	0	...	0.00	0.86	4	0	0	0	1	0-0	2.1	2	0	0	0	0-0	1	.250
2004— St. Louis (N.L.)	0	0	...	...	...	1	0	0	0	0	0-0	.0	2	0	0	0	0-0	0	1.000
Champ. series totals (2 years)	0	0	...	0.00	1.71	5	0	0	0	1	0-0	2.1	4	0	0	0	0-0	1	.400

KNOEDLER, JUSTIN   C

PERSONAL: Born July 17, 1980, in Springfield, Ill. ... 6-2/210. ... Bats right, throws right. ... Full name: Justin Joseph Knoedler. ... High school: Springfield (Ill.). ... College: Miami (Ohio).

TRANSACTIONS/CAREER NOTES: Selected by St. Louis Cardinals organization in 41st round of 1998 free-agent draft; did not sign. ... Selected by San Francisco Giants organization in 13th round of 2000 free-agent draft; did not sign. ... Selected by San Francisco Giants organization in fifth round of 2001 free-agent draft.

2004 GAMES PLAYED BY POSITION (MLB): C—1.

Year— Team (League)	Pos.	G	AB	R	H	2B	3B	HR	RBI	BB	SO	HBP	GDP	SB-CS	Avg.	OBP	SLG	OPS	E	Avg.
2002— Hagerstown (SAL)	C	86	280	32	72	16	2	5	33	37	56	4	8	6-5	.257	.349	.382	.731	15	.977
2003— San Jose (Calif.)	C	101	354	48	91	25	2	10	43	35	78	3	5	13-3	.257	.326	.424	.749	9	.989
2004— Norwich (East.)	C-DH-OF	115	409	64	112	28	3	9	47	32	98	8	7	5-3	.274	.335	.423	.758	7	.991
— San Francisco (N.L.)	C	1	1	0	0	0	0	0	0	0	0	0	0	0-0	.000	.000	.000	.000	0	1.000
Major League totals (1 year)		1	1	0	0	0	0	0	0	0	0	0	0	0-0	.000	.000	.000	.000	0	1.000

KNOTT, JON   OF

PERSONAL: Born August 4, 1978, in Manassas, Va. ... 6-3/220. ... Bats right, throws right. ... Full name: Jonathan David Knott. ... High school: Venice (Fla.). ... College: Mississippi State.

TRANSACTIONS/CAREER NOTES: Signed as a non-drafted free agent by San Diego Padres organization (September 21, 2001).

2004 GAMES PLAYED BY POSITION (MLB): OF—5.

Year— Team (League)	Pos.	G	AB	R	H	2B	3B	HR	RBI	BB	SO	HBP	GDP	SB-CS	Avg.	OBP	SLG	OPS	E	Avg.
2002— Fort Wayne (Midw.)	OF-1B	37	126	19	42	12	3	3	18	17	33	1	1	2-1	.333	.411	.548	.959	3	.959
— Lake Elsinore (Calif.)	1B-OF-3B	93	367	55	125	33	8	8	73	46	68	3	7	5-4	.341	.414	.540	.954	9	.981
2003— Mobile (Sou.)	OF-1B	127	432	83	109	32	0	27	82	82	117	17	1	5-3	.252	.387	.514	.901	11	.980
— Portland (PCL)	1B	7	26	5	9	1	0	1	5	4	3	0	1	0-0	.346	.433	.500	.933	0	1.000
2004— San Diego (N.L.)	OF	9	14	1	3	2	0	0	1	1	5	0	0	0-0	.214	.267	.357	.624	0	1.000
— Portland (PCL)	OF-DH-1B	113	435	79	126	22	3	26	85	58	110	7	12	5-3	.290	.376	.533	.901	2	.989
Major League totals (1 year)		9	14	1	3	2	0	0	1	1	5	0	0	0-0	.214	.267	.357	.624	0	1.000

KNOTTS, GARY   P

PERSONAL: Born February 12, 1977, in Decatur, Ala. ... 6-4/230. ... Throws right, bats right. ... Full name: Gary Everett Knotts. ... High school: Brewer (Somerville, Ala.). ... Junior college: Northwest Shoals (Ala.) Communtiy College.

TRANSACTIONS/CAREER NOTES: Selected by Florida Marlins organization in 11th round of 1995 free agent draft. ... Traded by Marlins with Ps Nate Robertson and Rob Henkel to Detroit Tigers for Ps Mark Redman and Jerrod Fuell (January 11, 2003). ... On disabled list (July 28-August 13, 2004).

CAREER HITTING: 2-for-7 (.286), 2 R, 0 2B, 0 3B, 0 HR, 0 RBI.

Year— Team (League)	W	L	Pct.	ERA	WHIP	G	GS	CG	ShO	Hld.	Sv.-Opp.	IP	H	R	ER	HR	BB-IBB	SO	Avg.
1996— GC Marlins (GCL)	4	2	.667	2.04	0.91	12	9	1	1	...	0-...	57.1	35	16	13	0	17-0	48	.175
1997— Kane County (Midwest)	1	5	.167	13.05	2.50	7	7	0	0	...	0-...	20.0	33	34	29	2	17-0	19	.363
— Utica (N.Y.-Penn)	3	5	.375	3.62	1.39	12	12	1	0	...	0-...	69.2	70	34	28	3	27-1	65	.263
1998— Kane County (Midwest)	8	8	.500	3.87	1.33	27	27	3	0	...	0-...	158.1	144	84	68	11	66-1	148	.240
1999— Brevard County (FSL)	9	6	.600	4.60	1.38	16	16	3	2	...	0-...	94.0	101	52	48	7	29-0	65	.280
— Portland (East.)	6	3	.667	3.75	1.37	12	12	1	1	...	0-...	81.2	79	39	34	12	33-0	63	.255
2000— Portland (East.)	9	8	.529	4.66	1.43	27	27	2	0	...	0-...	156.1	161	102	81	15	63-1	113	.264

Year	Team (League)	W	L	Pct.	ERA	WHIP	G	GS	CG	ShO	Hld.	Sv.-Opp.	IP	H	R	ER	HR	BB-IBB	SO	Avg.
2001—	Calgary (PCL)	6	7	.462	5.46	1.51	21	21	1	1	...	0-...	118.2	136	77	72	16	43-0	104	.285
—	Florida (N.L.)	0	1	.000	6.00	1.33	2	1	0	0	0	0-0	6.0	7	4	4	1	1-0	9	.280
2002—	Florida (N.L.)	3	1	.750	4.40	1.21	28	0	0	0	5	0-1	30.2	21	15	15	6	16-0	21	.193
—	Calgary (PCL)	5	3	.625	4.25	1.60	42	0	0	0	...	3-...	53.0	53	29	25	4	32-2	44	.269
2003—	Toledo (International)	4	6	.400	5.13	1.60	13	13	0	0	...	0-...	79.0	98	54	45	15	28-3	63	.304
—	Detroit (A.L.)	3	8	.273	6.04	1.66	20	18	0	0	0	0-0	95.1	111	70	64	14	47-0	51	.288
2004—	Detroit (A.L.)	7	6	.538	5.25	1.48	36	19	0	0	2	2-2	135.1	142	83	79	20	58-3	81	.267
American League totals (2 years)		10	14	.417	5.58	1.55	56	37	0	0	2	2-2	230.2	253	153	143	34	105-3	132	.276
National League totals (2 years)		3	2	.600	4.66	1.23	30	1	0	0	5	0-1	36.2	28	19	19	7	17-0	30	.209
Major League totals (4 years)		13	16	.448	5.45	1.51	86	38	0	0	7	2-3	267.1	281	172	162	41	122-3	162	.267

KOCH, BILLY   P

PERSONAL: Born December 14, 1974, in Rockville Center, N.Y. ... 6-3/220. ... Throws right, bats right. ... Full name: William Christopher Koch. ... Name pronounced: COTCH. ... High school: West Babylon (N.Y.). ... College: Clemson.

TRANSACTIONS/CAREER NOTES: Selected by Toronto Blue Jays organization in first round (fourth pick overall) of 1996 free-agent draft. ... On disabled list (April 14, 1997-remainder of season). ... Traded by Blue Jays to Oakland Athletics for P Justin Miller and 3B Eric Hinske (December 7, 2001). ... Traded by A's with two players to be named to Chicago White Sox for Ps Keith Foulke and Joe Valentine, C Mark Johnson and cash (December 3, 2002); White Sox acquired P Neal Cotts and OF Daylon Holt to complete deal (December 16, 2002). ... On disabled list (August 12-September 2, 2003); included rehabilitation assignment to Charlotte. ... Traded by White Sox with cash to Florida Marlins for SS Wilson Valdez (June 17, 2004). ... On suspended list (September 19, 2004-remainder of season). ... Released by Marlins (October 6, 2004).

HONORS: Named A.L. Relief Pitcher of the Year by THE SPORTING NEWS (2002).

CAREER HITTING: 0-for-2 (.000), 0 R, 0 2B, 0 3B, 0 HR, 0 RBI.

Year	Team (League)	W	L	Pct.	ERA	WHIP	G	GS	CG	ShO	Hld.	Sv.-Opp.	IP	H	R	ER	HR	BB-IBB	SO	Avg.
1997—	Dunedin (Fla. St.)	0	1	.000	2.49	1.38	3	3	0	0	...	0-...	21.2	27	10	6	1	3-0	20	.325
1998—	Dunedin (Fla. St.)	14	7	.667	3.75	1.29	25	25	0	0	...	0-...	124.2	120	65	52	8	41-0	108	.252
—	Syracuse (Int'l)	0	1	.000	14.29	2.47	2	2	0	0	...	0-...	5.2	9	9	9	1	5-0	9	.360
1999—	Syracuse (Int'l)	3	0	1.000	3.86	1.44	5	5	0	0	...	0-...	25.2	27	11	11	3	10-0	22	.276
—	Toronto (A.L.)	0	5	.000	3.39	1.34	56	0	0	0	0	31-35	63.2	55	26	24	5	30-5	57	.235
2000—	Toronto (A.L.)	9	3	.750	2.63	1.22	68	0	0	0	0	33-38	78.2	78	28	23	6	18-4	60	.258
2001—	Toronto (A.L.)	2	5	.286	4.80	1.47	69	0	0	0	0	36-44	69.1	69	39	37	7	33-7	55	.265
2002—	Oakland (A.L.)	11	4	.733	3.27	1.27	84	0	0	0	0	44-50	93.2	73	38	34	7	46-6	93	.214
2003—	Charlotte (Int'l)	0	1	.000	4.91	2.20	4	0	0	0	...	0-...	3.2	5	2	2	0	3-0	2	.313
—	Chicago (A.L.)	5	5	.500	5.77	1.64	55	0	0	0	1	11-15	53.0	59	36	34	10	28-1	42	.281
2004—	Chicago (A.L.)	1	1	.500	5.40	1.71	24	0	0	0	1	8-11	23.1	24	15	14	3	16-4	25	.255
—	Florida (N.L.)	1	2	.333	3.51	1.60	23	0	0	0	3	0-0	25.2	21	10	10	3	20-0	25	.226
American League totals (6 years)		28	23	.549	3.91	1.39	356	0	0	0	2	163-193	381.2	358	182	166	38	171-27	332	.248
National League totals (1 year)		1	2	.333	3.51	1.60	23	0	0	0	3	0-0	25.2	21	10	10	3	20-0	25	.226
Major League totals (6 years)		29	25	.537	3.89	1.40	379	0	0	0	5	163-193	407.1	379	192	176	41	191-27	357	.247

DIVISION SERIES RECORD

Year	Team (League)	W	L	Pct.	ERA	WHIP	G	GS	CG	ShO	Hld.	Sv.-Opp.	IP	H	R	ER	HR	BB-IBB	SO	Avg.
2002—	Oakland (A.L.)	0	0	...	9.00	2.33	3	0	0	0	0	1-1	3.0	5	3	3	1	2-0	3	.357

KOLB, DAN   P

PERSONAL: Born March 29, 1975, in Sterling, Ill. ... 6-4/240. ... Throws right, bats right. ... Full name: Daniel Lee Kolb. ... High school: Walnut (Ill.). ... College: Illinois State.

TRANSACTIONS/CAREER NOTES: Selected by Minnesota Twins organization in 17th round of 1993 free-agent draft; did not sign. ... Selected by Texas Rangers organization in sixth round of 1995 free-agent draft. ... On Texas disabled list (October 3, 1999-remainder of season; and May 29, 2000-remainder of season). ... On disabled list (March 23-July 11, 2001); included rehabilitation assignments to Charlotte and Tulsa. ... On Texas disabled list (March 28-July 16, 2002); included rehabilitation assignments to Charlotte and Tulsa. ... Released by Rangers (March 26, 2003). ... Signed by Milwaukee Brewers organization (April 2, 2003).

CAREER HITTING: 0-for-0 (.000), 0 R, 0 2B, 0 3B, 0 HR, 0 RBI.

Year	Team (League)	W	L	Pct.	ERA	WHIP	G	GS	CG	ShO	Hld.	Sv.-Opp.	IP	H	R	ER	HR	BB-IBB	SO	Avg.
1995—	GC Rangers (GCL)	1	7	.125	2.21	1.25	12	11	0	0	...	0-...	53.0	38	22	13	0	28-0	46	.204
1996—	Char., S.C. (SAL)	8	6	.571	2.57	1.11	20	20	4	2	...	0-...	126.0	80	50	36	5	60-2	127	.181
—	Charlotte (Fla. St.)	2	2	.500	4.26	1.37	6	6	0	0	...	0-...	38.0	38	18	18	1	14-0	28	.260
—	Tulsa (Texas)	1	0	1.000	0.77	1.11	2	2	0	0	...	0-...	11.2	5	1	1	0	8-0	7	.139
1997—	Charlotte (Fla. St.)	4	10	.286	4.87	1.56	24	23	3	0	...	0-...	133.0	146	91	72	10	62-1	83	.282
—	Tulsa (Texas)	0	2	.000	4.76	1.59	2	2	0	0	...	0-...	11.1	7	7	6	1	11-0	6	.179
1998—	Tulsa (Texas)	12	11	.522	4.82	1.62	28	28	2	0	...	0-...	162.1	187	104	87	11	76-1	83	.293
—	Oklahoma (PCL)	0	0	...	0.00	2.00	1	0	0	0	...	0-...	1.0	1	0	0	0	1-0	0	.250
1999—	Tulsa (Texas)	1	2	.333	2.79	1.45	7	7	1	1	...	0-...	38.2	38	16	12	0	18-0	32	.260
—	Oklahoma (PCL)	5	3	.625	5.10	1.68	11	8	0	0	...	0-...	60.0	74	35	34	4	27-0	21	.320
—	Texas (A.L.)	2	1	.667	4.65	1.55	16	0	0	0	0	0-0	31.0	33	18	16	2	15-0	15	.268
2000—	Oklahoma (PCL)	4	1	.800	0.98	1.04	13	0	0	0	0	4-...	18.1	11	6	2	0	8-1	18	.175
—	Texas (A.L.)	0	0	...	67.50	10.50	1	0	0	0	0	0-0	.2	5	5	5	0	2-0	0	.833
2001—	Charlotte (Fla. St.)	1	2	.333	3.86	1.23	7	3	0	0	...	0-...	18.2	21	8	8	1	2-0	16	.276
—	Tulsa (Texas)	1	0	1.000	0.00	0.50	1	0	0	0	...	0-...	2.0	0	0	0	0	1-0	0	.000
—	Oklahoma (PCL)	0	1	.000	1.42	0.89	12	0	0	0	...	3-...	19.0	13	3	3	1	6-0	21	.188
—	Texas (A.L.)	0	0	...	4.70	1.63	17	0	0	0	7	0-0	15.1	15	8	8	2	10-1	15	.259
2002—	Charlotte (Fla. St.)	1	0	1.000	1.50	1.50	4	0	0	0	...	0-...	6.0	5	1	1	0	4-0	2	.227
—	Tulsa (Texas)	0	1	.000	2.16	1.44	5	1	0	0	...	0-...	8.1	9	2	2	0	3-0	4	.290
—	Texas (A.L.)	3	6	.333	4.22	1.53	34	0	0	0	2	1-4	32.0	27	17	15	1	22-2	20	.227
2003—	Indianapolis (Int'l)	0	1	.000	1.37	1.00	26	0	0	0	...	4-...	39.1	26	10	6	1	13-0	46	.183
—	Milwaukee (N.L.)	1	2	.333	1.96	1.28	37	0	0	0	4	21-23	41.1	34	10	9	2	19-3	39	.221
2004—	Milwaukee (N.L.)	0	4	.000	2.98	1.13	64	0	0	0	1	39-44	57.1	50	22	19	3	15-1	21	.234
American League totals (4 years)		5	7	.417	5.01	1.63	68	0	0	0	9	1-4	79.0	80	48	44	5	49-3	50	.261
National League totals (2 years)		1	6	.143	2.55	1.20	101	0	0	0	5	60-67	98.2	84	32	28	5	34-4	60	.228
Major League totals (6 years)		6	13	.316	3.65	1.39	169	0	0	0	14	61-71	177.2	164	80	72	10	83-7	110	.243

ALL-STAR GAME RECORD

	W	L	Pct.	ERA	WHIP	G	GS	CG	ShO	Hld.	Sv.-Opp.	IP	H	R	ER	HR	BB-IBB	SO	Avg.
All-Star Game totals (1 year)	0	0	...	0.00	1.00	1	0	0	0	0	0-0	1.0	1	0	0	0	0-0	0	.250

KONERKO, PAUL — 1B

PERSONAL: Born March 5, 1976, in Providence, R.I. ... 6-2/215. ... Bats right, throws right. ... Full name: Paul Henry Konerko. ... Name pronounced: kone-err-coe. ... High school: Chaparral (Scottsdale, Ariz.).

TRANSACTIONS/CAREER NOTES: Selected by Los Angeles Dodgers organization in first round (13th pick overall) of 1994 free-agent draft. ... Traded by Dodgers with P Dennys Reyes to Cincinnati Reds for P Jeff Shaw (July 4, 1998). ... Traded by Reds to Chicago White Sox for OF Mike Cameron (November 11, 1998).

HONORS: Named A.L. Comeback Player of the Year by THE SPORTING NEWS (2004).

2004 GAMES PLAYED BY POSITION (MLB): 1B—139, DH—16.

										BATTING										FIELDING	
Year Team (League)	Pos.	G	AB	R	H	2B	3B	HR	RBI	BB	SO	HBP	GDP	SB-CS	Avg.	OBP	SLG	OPS	E	Avg.
1994— Yakima (N'west)	DH-C	67	257	25	74	15	2	6	58	36	52	6	6	1-0	.288	.379	.432	.811	5	.984
1995— San Bern. (Calif.)	DH-C	118	448	7	124	21	1	19	77	59	88	4	12	3-1	.277	.362	.455	.817	11	.985
1996— San Antonio (Texas)	1B-DH	133	470	78	141	23	2	29	86	72	85	8	7	1-3	.300	.397	.543	.939	14	.989
— Albuquerque (PCL)	1B	4	14	2	6	0	0	1	2	1	2	0	0	0-1	.429	.467	.643	1.110	0	1.000
1997— Albuquerque (PCL)	3-1-DH-2	130	483	97	156	31	1	37	127	64	61	8	16	2-3	.323	.407	.621	1.028	24	.952
— Los Angeles (N.L.)	3B-1B	6	7	0	1	0	0	0	0	1	2	0	1	0-0	.143	.250	.143	.393	0	1.000
1998— Los Angeles (N.L.)	1-3-O-DH	49	144	14	31	1	0	4	16	10	30	2	5	0-1	.215	.272	.306	.578	2	.991
— Albuquerque (PCL)	OF-1B-3B	24	87	16	33	10	0	6	26	11	12	0	3	0-0	.379	.436	.701	1.137	3	.955
— Cincinnati (N.L.)	3B-1B-OF	26	73	7	16	3	0	3	13	6	10	1	5	0-0	.219	.284	.384	.668	0	1.000
— Indianapolis (Int'l)	3B	39	150	25	49	8	0	8	39	19	18	2	8	1-0	.327	.402	.540	.942	4	.957
1999— Chicago (A.L.)	1B-DH-3B	142	513	71	151	31	4	24	81	45	68	2	19	1-0	.294	.352	.511	.862	4	.995
2000— Chicago (A.L.)	1B-3B-DH	143	524	84	156	31	1	21	97	47	72	10	22	1-0	.298	.363	.481	.844	11	.990
2001— Chicago (A.L.)	1B-DH	156	582	92	164	35	0	32	99	54	89	9	17	1-0	.282	.349	.507	.856	8	.994
2002— Chicago (A.L.)	1B-DH	151	570	81	173	30	0	27	104	44	72	9	17	0-0	.304	.359	.498	.857	8	.993
2003— Chicago (A.L.)	1B-DH	137	444	49	104	19	0	18	65	43	50	4	28	0-0	.234	.305	.399	.704	2	.998
2004— Chicago (A.L.)	1B-DH	155	563	84	156	22	0	41	117	69	107	6	23	1-0	.277	.359	.535	.894	6	.995
American League totals (6 years)		884	3196	461	904	168	5	163	563	302	458	40	126	4-0	.283	.349	.492	.841	39	.994
National League totals (2 years)		81	224	21	48	4	0	7	29	17	42	3	11	0-1	.214	.275	.326	.601	2	.993
Major League totals (8 years)		965	3420	482	952	172	5	170	592	319	500	43	137	4-1	.278	.345	.481	.825	41	.994

DIVISION SERIES RECORD

Year Team (League)	Pos.	G	AB	R	H	2B	3B	HR	RBI	BB	SO	HBP	GDP	SB-CS	Avg.	OBP	SLG	OPS	E	Avg.
2000— Chicago (A.L.)	1B	3	9	1	0	0	0	0	0	1	1	0	1	0-0	.000	.100	.000	.100	0	1.000

ALL-STAR GAME RECORD

	G	AB	R	H	2B	3B	HR	RBI	BB	SO	HBP	GDP	SB-CS	Avg.	OBP	SLG	OPS	E	Avg.
All-Star Game totals (1 year)	1	2	0	2	2	0	0	2	0	0	0	0	0-0	1.000	1.000	2.000	3.000	0	1.000

KOPLOVE, MIKE — P

PERSONAL: Born August 30, 1976, in Philadelphia, Pa. ... 5-10/178. ... Throws right, bats right. ... Full name: Michael Paul Koplove. ... Name pronounced: COP-luv. ... High school: Chestnut Hill Academy (Philadelphia). ... College: Delaware.

TRANSACTIONS/CAREER NOTES: Selected by Arizona Diamondbacks organization in 29th round of 1998 free-agent draft. ... On disabled list (May 28-June 13 and June 19, 2003-remainder of season); included rehabilitation assignment to Tucson.

CAREER HITTING: 0-for-2 (.000), 0 R, 0 2B, 0 3B, 0 HR, 0 RBI.

Year Team (League)	W	L	Pct.	ERA	WHIP	G	GS	CG	ShO	Hld.	Sv.-Opp.	IP	H	R	ER	HR	BB-IBB	SO	Avg.
1998— Ariz. D'backs (Ariz.)	0	0	...	9.00	1.50	2	0	0	0	...	0-...	4.0	4	4	4	0	2-0	5	.250
— Lethbridge (Pio.)	1	2	.333	3.54	0.93	12	1	0	0	...	2-...	28.0	23	12	11	2	3-0	22	.217
1999— South Bend (Mid.)	5	2	.714	2.04	1.18	45	45	0	0	...	7-...	84.0	70	23	19	5	29-0	98	.227
2000— High Desert (Calif.)	2	0	1.000	1.42	0.95	20	0	0	0	...	8-...	25.1	14	4	4	0	10-0	31	.163
— El Paso (Texas)	4	3	.571	4.46	1.41	35	0	0	0	...	6-...	40.1	38	28	20	2	19-1	47	.225
2001— El Paso (Texas)	3	2	.600	2.66	1.43	34	0	0	0	...	4-...	44.0	44	18	13	3	19-3	43	.263
— Tucson (PCL)	4	1	.800	2.82	1.21	17	0	0	0	...	9-...	22.1	17	7	7	1	10-1	22	.207
— Arizona (N.L.)	0	1	.000	3.60	1.70	9	0	0	0	1	0-0	10.0	8	7	4	1	9-1	14	.211
2002— Tucson (PCL)	1	2	.333	1.17	0.82	23	0	0	0	...	3-...	30.2	21	5	4	1	4-0	31	.196
— Arizona (N.L.)	6	1	.857	3.36	1.14	55	0	0	0	10	0-0	61.2	47	24	23	2	23-4	46	.213
2003— Arizona (N.L.)	3	0	1.000	2.15	1.09	31	0	0	0	5	0-1	37.2	31	11	9	3	10-1	27	.225
— Tucson (PCL)	0	1	.000	13.50	2.60	3	0	0	0	...	1-...	2.2	4	4	4	1	3-0	2	.333
2004— Arizona (N.L.)	4	4	.500	4.05	1.42	76	0	0	0	19	2-8	86.2	86	42	39	7	37-10	55	.269
Major League totals (4 years)	13	6	.684	3.44	1.28	171	0	0	0	35	2-9	196.0	172	84	75	13	79-16	142	.240

DIVISION SERIES RECORD

Year Team (League)	W	L	Pct.	ERA	WHIP	G	GS	CG	ShO	Hld.	Sv.-Opp.	IP	H	R	ER	HR	BB-IBB	SO	Avg.
2002— Arizona (N.L.)	0	1	.000	6.75	1.50	1	0	0	0	0	0-0	1.1	2	1	1	0	0-0	1	.400

KOSKIE, COREY — 3B

PERSONAL: Born June 28, 1973, in Anola, Manitoba. ... 6-3/219. ... Bats left, throws right. ... Full name: Cordel Leonard Koskie. ... Name pronounced: KOSS-key. ... High school: Springfield Collegiate (Oakbank, Man.). ... College: University of Manitoba.

TRANSACTIONS/CAREER NOTES: Selected by Minnesota Twins organization in 26th round of 1994 free-agent draft. ... On disabled list (May 8-24, 2002; July 12-August 4, 2003; and May 12-27, 2004).

RECORDS: Shares major league record for times hit by pitch, game (3, July 27, 2004).

2004 GAMES PLAYED BY POSITION (MLB): 3B—115, DH—1.

										BATTING										FIELDING	
Year Team (League)	Pos.	G	AB	R	H	2B	3B	HR	RBI	BB	SO	HBP	GDP	SB-CS	Avg.	OBP	SLG	OPS	E	Avg.
1994— Elizabethton (App.)	3B	34	107	13	25	2	1	3	10	18	27	2	3	0-0	.234	.354	.355	.709	8	.930
1995— Fort Wayne (Midw.)	3B	123	462	64	143	37	5	16	78	38	79	9	10	2-4	.310	.370	.515	.885	36	.900
1996— Fort Myers (Fla.)	3B	95	338	43	88	19	4	9	55	40	76	1	4	1-1	.260	.338	.420	.758	19	.926
1997— New Britain (East.)	3B-DH	131	437	88	125	26	6	23	79	90	106	7	13	9-5	.286	.414	.531	.945	22	.933
1998— Salt Lake (PCL)	3B-DH	135	505	91	152	32	5	26	105	51	104	8	17	15-7	.301	.368	.539	.906	23	.935
— Minnesota (A.L.)	3B	11	29	2	4	0	0	1	2	2	10	0	0	0-0	.138	.194	.241	.435	1	.941
1999— Minnesota (A.L.)	3B-OF-DH	117	342	42	106	21	0	11	58	40	72	5	6	4-4	.310	.387	.468	.855	6	.962
2000— Minnesota (A.L.)	3B-DH	146	474	79	142	32	4	9	65	77	104	4	11	5-4	.300	.400	.441	.841	12	.966
2001— Minnesota (A.L.)	3B-DH	153	562	100	155	37	2	26	103	68	118	12	16	27-6	.276	.362	.488	.850	15	.964

Year	Team (League)	Pos.	G	AB	R	H	2B	3B	HR	RBI	BB	SO	HBP	GDP	SB-CS	Avg.	OBP	SLG	OPS	E	Avg.
2002— Minnesota (A.L.)	3B-DH	140	490	71	131	37	3	15	69	72	127	9	14	10-11	.267	.368	.447	.815	12	.969
2003— Minnesota (A.L.)	3B	131	469	76	137	29	2	14	69	77	113	7	5	11-5	.292	.393	.452	.845	9	.973
2004— Minnesota (A.L.)	3B-DH	118	422	68	106	24	2	25	71	49	103	12	6	9-3	.251	.342	.495	.837	11	.963
Major League totals (7 years)		816	2788	438	781	180	13	101	437	385	647	49	58	66-33	.280	.373	.463	.836	68	.966

					DIVISION SERIES RECORD																
Year	Team (League)	Pos.	G	AB	R	H	2B	3B	HR	RBI	BB	SO	HBP	GDP	SB-CS	Avg.	OBP	SLG	OPS	E	Avg.
2002— Minnesota (A.L.)	3B	5	21	3	3	0	1	1	5	2	6	1	0	0-0	.143	.250	.381	.631	1	.923
2003— Minnesota (A.L.)	3B	4	15	0	3	1	0	0	0	0	5	0	0	0-1	.200	.200	.267	.467	0	1.000
2004— Minnesota (A.L.)	3B	4	13	2	4	1	0	0	2	3	2	2	0	0-0	.308	.474	.385	.858	0	1.000
Division series totals (3 years)		13	49	5	10	2	1	1	7	5	13	3	0	0-1	.204	.310	.347	.657	1	.963

					CHAMPIONSHIP SERIES RECORD																
Year	Team (League)	Pos.	G	AB	R	H	2B	3B	HR	RBI	BB	SO	HBP	GDP	SB-CS	Avg.	OBP	SLG	OPS	E	Avg.
2002— Minnesota (A.L.)	3B	5	18	3	5	2	0	0	2	2	8	0	0	0-0	.278	.350	.389	.739	0	1.000

KOTCHMAN, CASEY   1B

PERSONAL: Born February 22, 1983, in St. Petersburg, Fla. ... 6-3/210. ... Bats left, throws left. ... Full name: Casey John Kotchman. ... High school: Seminole (Fla.).
TRANSACTIONS/CAREER NOTES: Selected by Anaheim Angels organization in first round (13th pick overall) of 2001 free-agent draft.
2004 GAMES PLAYED BY POSITION (MLB): 1B—34, DH—2.

											BATTING									FIELDING	
Year	Team (League)	Pos.	G	AB	R	H	2B	3B	HR	RBI	BB	SO	HBP	GDP	SB-CS	Avg.	OBP	SLG	OPS	E	Avg.
2001— Ariz. Angels (Ariz.)	1B	4	15	5	9	1	0	1	5	3	2	0	0	0-0	.600	.632	.867	1.498	1	.974
— Provo (Pio.)	1B	7	22	6	11	3	0	0	7	2	0	0	0	0-0	.500	.542	.636	1.178	0	1.000
2002— Cedar Rap. (Midw.)	1B	81	288	42	81	30	1	5	50	48	37	6	7	2-1	.281	.390	.444	.835	5	.992
2003— Ariz. Angels (Ariz.)	1B	7	27	5	9	1	0	2	6	2	3	0	1	0-0	.333	.379	.593	.972	0	1.000
— Rancho Cuca. (Calif.)	1B	57	206	42	72	12	0	8	28	30	16	6	4	2-0	.350	.441	.524	.965	5	.988
2004— Arkansas (Texas)	1B-DH	28	114	19	42	11	0	3	18	10	7	5	6	0-0	.368	.438	.544	.960	0	1.000
— Salt Lake (PCL)	1B-DH	49	199	32	74	22	0	5	38	14	25	5	9	0-0	.372	.423	.558	.967	3	.992
— Anaheim (A.L.)	1B-DH	38	116	7	26	6	0	0	15	7	11	4	3	3-0	.224	.289	.276	.565	3	.988
Major League totals (1 year)		38	116	7	26	6	0	0	15	7	11	4	3	3-0	.224	.289	.276	.565	3	.988

					DIVISION SERIES RECORD																
Year	Team (League)	Pos.	G	AB	R	H	2B	3B	HR	RBI	BB	SO	HBP	GDP	SB-CS	Avg.	OBP	SLG	OPS	E	Avg.
2004— Anaheim (A.L.)		2	1	0	0	0	0	0	0	0	0	0	0	0-0	.000	.000	.000	.000	0	...

KOTSAY, MARK   OF

PERSONAL: Born December 2, 1975, in Whittier, Calif. ... 6-0/201. ... Bats left, throws left. ... Full name: Mark Steven Kotsay. ... Name pronounced: KAH-tsay. ... High school: Santa Fe Springs (Calif.). ... College: Cal State Fullerton.
TRANSACTIONS/CAREER NOTES: Selected by Florida Marlins organization in first round (ninth pick overall) of 1996 free-agent draft. ... Traded by Marlins with OF Cesar Crespo to San Diego Padres for OF Eric Owens and Ps Matt Clement and Omar Ortiz (March 28, 2001). ... On disabled list (April 16-May 1, 2001; and May 19-June 5, 2003). ... Traded by Padres to Oakland Athletics for C Ramon Hernandez and OF Terrence Long (November 26, 2003).
2004 GAMES PLAYED BY POSITION (MLB): OF—145, DH—1.

											BATTING									FIELDING	
Year	Team (League)	Pos.	G	AB	R	H	2B	3B	HR	RBI	BB	SO	HBP	GDP	SB-CS	Avg.	OBP	SLG	OPS	E	Avg.
1996— Kane Co. (Midw.)	OF	17	60	16	17	5	0	2	8	16	8	1	3	3-0	.283	.436	.467	.903	0	1.000
1997— Portland (East.)	OF-DH	114	438	103	134	27	2	20	77	75	65	0	16	17-5	.306	.405	.514	.919	2	.992
— Florida (N.L.)	OF	14	52	5	10	1	1	0	4	4	7	0	1	3-0	.192	.250	.250	.500	1	1.000
1998— Florida (N.L.)	OF-1B	154	578	72	161	25	7	11	68	34	61	1	17	10-5	.279	.318	.403	.721	6	.984
1999— Florida (N.L.)	OF-1B	148	495	57	134	23	9	8	50	29	50	0	11	7-6	.271	.306	.402	.708	5	.987
2000— Florida (N.L.)	OF-1B	152	530	87	158	31	5	12	57	42	46	0	17	19-9	.298	.347	.443	.791	3	.990
2001— San Diego (N.L.)	OF	119	406	67	118	29	1	10	58	48	58	2	11	13-5	.291	.366	.441	.807	4	.986
2002— San Diego (N.L.)	OF	153	578	82	169	27	7	17	61	59	89	3	10	11-9	.292	.359	.452	.810	4	.989
2003— San Diego (N.L.)	OF	128	482	64	128	28	4	7	38	56	82	1	8	6-3	.266	.343	.384	.726	3	.991
2004— Oakland (A.L.)	OF-DH	148	606	78	190	37	3	15	63	55	70	2	6	8-5	.314	.370	.459	.829	6	.984
American League totals (1 year)		148	606	78	190	37	3	15	63	55	70	2	6	8-5	.314	.370	.459	.829	6	.984
National League totals (7 years)		868	3121	434	878	164	34	65	336	272	393	7	75	69-37	.281	.338	.418	.756	25	.988
Major League totals (8 years)		1016	3727	512	1068	201	37	80	399	327	463	9	81	77-42	.287	.343	.425	.768	31	.987

KROEGER, JOSH   OF

PERSONAL: Born August 31, 1982, in Davenport, Iowa. ... 6-2/200. ... Bats left, throws left. ... Full name: Joshua J. Kroeger. ... High school: Scripps Ranch (San Diego).
TRANSACTIONS/CAREER NOTES: Selected by Arizona Diamondbacks organization in fourth round of 2000 free-agent draft.
2004 GAMES PLAYED BY POSITION (MLB): OF—19.

											BATTING									FIELDING	
Year	Team (League)	Pos.	G	AB	R	H	2B	3B	HR	RBI	BB	SO	HBP	GDP	SB-CS	Avg.	OBP	SLG	OPS	E	Avg.
2000— Ariz. D'backs (Ariz.)	OF	54	222	40	66	9	3	4	28	21	41	1	3	5-4	.297	.359	.419	.778	9	.905
2001— South Bend (Mid.)	OF	79	292	36	80	15	1	3	37	18	49	4	10	4-4	.274	.324	.363	.687	9	.926
2002— Lancaster (Calif.)	OF	133	497	63	117	20	7	7	58	23	136	4	10	2-4	.235	.274	.346	.620	5	.978
2003— Lancaster (Calif.)	OF	78	305	50	104	30	6	5	55	35	58	2	9	6-6	.341	.409	.528	.937	6	.953
— El Paso (Texas)	OF	54	208	26	57	9	2	3	22	10	54	3	7	3-5	.274	.315	.380	.695	2	.984
2004— El Paso (Texas)	OF	65	245	44	81	28	4	9	46	21	48	5	7	2-1	.331	.393	.588	.970	7	.943
— Tucson (PCL)	OF-DH	59	208	30	69	23	0	10	41	15	47	2	8	2-1	.332	.376	.587	.957	5	.964
— Arizona (N.L.)	OF	22	54	5	9	3	0	0	2	1	21	0	2	0-1	.167	.182	.222	.404	0	1.000
Major League totals (1 year)		22	54	5	9	3	0	0	2	1	21	0	2	0-1	.167	.182	.222	.404	0	1.000

KROON, MARC   P

PERSONAL: Born April 2, 1973, in Bronx, N.Y. ... 6-2/190. ... Throws right, bats right. ... Full name: Marc Jason Kroon. ... High school: Shadow Mountain (Phoenix).
TRANSACTIONS/CAREER NOTES: Selected by New York Mets organization in supplemental round ("sandwich pick" between second and third rounds) of free-agent draft (June 3, 1991); pick received as part of compensation for Toronto Blue Jays signing Type C free-agent 1B/DH Pat Tabler. ... Traded by Mets to San Diego Padres (December 13, 1993), completing deal in which Mets traded OF Randy Curtis and a player to named to Padres for P Frank Seminara, OF Tracy Jones and SS Pablo Martinez (December

10, 1993). ... Traded by Padres to Cincinnati Reds for P Buddy Carlyle (April 8, 1998). ... On disabled list (May 7-June 12, 1998); included rehabilitation assignment to Indianapolis. ... Signed as a free agent by Seattle Mariners organization (December 21, 1998). ... Released by Mariners (March 22, 2000). ... Signed by Los Angeles Dodgers organization (March 27, 2000). ... Released by Dodgers (May 8, 2000). ... Re-signed by Dodgers organization (May 17, 2000). ... Released by Dodgers (March 28, 2001). ... Signed as a free agent by Anaheim Angels organization (January 30, 2003). ... Signed as a free agent by Colorado Rockies organization (December 4, 2003).
CAREER HITTING: 0-for-0 (.000), 0 R, 0 2B, 0 3B, 0 HR, 0 RBI.

Year— Team (League)	W	L	Pct.	ERA	WHIP	G	GS	CG	ShO	Hld.	Sv.-Opp.	IP	H	R	ER	HR	BB-IBB	SO	Avg.
1991— GC Mets (GCL)	2	3	.400	4.53	1.28	12	10	1	0	...	0-...	47.2	39	33	24	1	22-0	39	.215
1992— Kingsport (Appalachian)	3	5	.375	4.10	1.60	12	12	0	0	...	0-...	68.0	52	41	31	3	57-0	60	.211
1993— Capital City (S. Atl.)	2	11	.154	3.47	1.55	29	19	0	0	...	2-...	124.1	123	65	48	6	70-0	122	.269
1994— Rancho Cuca. (Calif.)	11	6	.647	4.83	1.56	26	26	0	0	...	0-...	143.1	143	86	77	14	81-1	153	.260
1995— Memphis (Sou.)	7	5	.583	3.51	1.31	22	19	0	0	...	2-...	115.1	90	49	45	12	61-1	123	.211
— San Diego (N.L.)	0	1	.000	10.80	1.80	2	0	0	0	...	0-0	1.2	1	2	2	0	2-0	2	.200
1996— Memphis (Sou.)	2	4	.333	2.89	1.31	44	0	0	0	...	22-...	46.2	33	19	15	4	28-1	56	.192
1997— Las Vegas (PCL)	1	3	.250	4.54	1.34	46	0	0	0	...	15-...	41.2	34	22	21	5	22-0	53	.233
— San Diego (N.L.)	0	0	...	7.15	1.68	12	0	0	0	1	0-0	11.1	14	9	9	2	5-0	12	.280
1998— San Diego (N.L.)	0	0	...	0.00	0.43	2	0	0	0	0	0-0	2.1	0	0	0	0	1-0	2	.000
— Cincinnati (N.L.)	0	0	...	13.50	2.81	4	0	0	0	0	0-0	5.1	7	8	8	0	8-0	4	.333
— Indianapolis (Int'l)	3	2	.600	5.63	1.86	39	0	0	0	...	1-...	46.1	39	29	29	6	47-0	36	.238
1999— Tacoma (PCL)	3	2	.600	6.11	1.47	13	5	0	0	...	0-...	35.1	31	24	24	5	21-0	38	.230
— Ariz. Mariners (Ariz.)	0	0	...	3.86	0.71	4	4	0	0	...	0-...	7.0	5	3	3	2	0-0	12	.185
2000— Albuquerque (PCL)	0	1	.000	7.36	3.55	4	1	0	0	...	1-...	3.2	6	4	3	0	7-0	1	.375
2003— Salt Lake (PCL)	2	1	.667	3.86	0.90	9	0	0	0	...	2-...	14.0	10	6	6	2	3-0	10	.192
— Arkansas (Texas)	3	3	.500	3.00	1.30	37	1	0	0	...	4-...	45.0	28	20	15	1	31-0	60	.175
2004— Colorado (N.L.)	0	0	...	6.00	2.83	6	0	0	0	0	0-0	6.0	7	4	4	1	10-0	3	.350
— Colo. Springs (PCL)	2	3	.400	2.72	1.41	50	0	0	0	...	20-...	49.2	44	23	15	3	26-0	72	.232
Major League totals (4 years)	0	2	.000	7.76	2.06	26	0	0	0	1	0-0	26.2	29	23	23	3	26-0	23	.282

KRYNZEL, DAVE — OF

PERSONAL: Born November 7, 1981, in Dayton, Ohio. ... 6-1/180. ... Bats left, throws left. ... Full name: David Benjamin Krynzel. ... High school: Green Valley (Henderson, Nev.).
TRANSACTIONS/CAREER NOTES: Selected by Milwaukee Brewers organization in first round (11th pick overall) of 2000 free-agent draft.
2004 GAMES PLAYED BY POSITION (MLB): OF—10.

Year— Team (League)	Pos.	G	AB	R	H	2B	3B	HR	RBI	BB	SO	HBP	GDP	SB-CS	Avg.	OBP	SLG	OPS	E	Avg.
2000— Ogden (Pio.)	OF	34	131	25	47	8	3	1	29	16	23	5	0	8-4	.359	.442	.489	.930	3	.955
2001— Beloit (Midw.)	OF	35	141	22	43	1	1	1	19	9	28	4	1	11-5	.305	.364	.348	.711	2	.970
— High Desert (Calif.)	OF	89	383	65	106	19	5	5	33	27	122	4	0	34-17	.277	.329	.392	.721	5	.977
2002— High Desert (Calif.)	OF	97	365	76	98	13	12	11	45	64	100	11	2	29-17	.268	.391	.460	.851	7	.971
— Huntsville (Sou.)	OF	31	129	13	31	2	3	2	13	4	30	1	0	13-5	.240	.269	.349	.617	2	.971
2003— Huntsville (Sou.)	OF	124	457	72	122	13	11	2	34	60	119	6	3	43-21	.267	.357	.357	.714	11	.963
2004— Ariz. Brewers (Ariz.)	DH	5	16	8	8	1	1	0	3	3	2	0	0	2-0	.500	.600	.688	1.266	0	1.000
— Indianapolis (Int'l)	OF-DH	69	258	36	70	10	4	6	26	20	63	3	0	10-8	.271	.327	.411	.741	1	.993
— Milwaukee (N.L.)	OF	16	41	6	9	1	0	0	3	3	15	3	0	0-0	.220	.319	.244	.563	1	.968
Major League totals (1 year)		16	41	6	9	1	0	0	3	3	15	3	0	0-0	.220	.319	.244	.563	1	.968

KUBEL, JASON — OF

PERSONAL: Born May 25, 1982, in Belle Fourche, S.D. ... 5-11/200. ... Bats left, throws right. ... Full name: Jason James Kubel. ... High school: Highland (Calif.).
TRANSACTIONS/CAREER NOTES: Selected by Minnesota Twins organization in 12th round of 2000 free-agent draft.
2004 GAMES PLAYED BY POSITION (MLB): OF—10, DH—9.

Year— Team (League)	Pos.	G	AB	R	H	2B	3B	HR	RBI	BB	SO	HBP	GDP	SB-CS	Avg.	OBP	SLG	OPS	E	Avg.
2000— GC Twins (GCL)	OF	23	78	17	22	3	2	0	13	10	9	1	1	0-0	.282	.367	.372	.738	0	1.000
2001— GC Twins (GCL)	OF	37	124	14	41	10	4	1	30	19	14	2	3	3-2	.331	.422	.500	.922	1	.980
2002— Quad City (Midw.)	OF	115	424	60	136	26	4	17	69	41	48	1	11	3-5	.321	.380	.521	.901	3	.982
2003— Fort Myers (FSL)	OF	116	420	56	125	20	4	5	82	48	54	1	11	4-6	.298	.361	.400	.761	2	.991
2004— New Britain (East.)	OF-DH	37	138	25	52	14	4	6	29	19	19	1	3	0-2	.377	.453	.667	1.116	3	.961
— Rochester (Int'l)	OF-DH	90	350	71	120	28	0	16	71	34	40	1	2	16-3	.343	.398	.560	.957	2	.990
— Minnesota (A.L.)	OF-DH	23	60	10	18	2	0	2	7	6	9	0	0	1-1	.300	.358	.433	.792	0	1.000
Major League totals (1 year)		23	60	10	18	2	0	2	7	6	9	0	0	1-1	.300	.358	.433	.792	0	1.000

DIVISION SERIES RECORD

Year— Team (League)	Pos.	G	AB	R	H	2B	3B	HR	RBI	BB	SO	HBP	GDP	SB-CS	Avg.	OBP	SLG	OPS	E	Avg.
2004— Minnesota (A.L.)	DH	2	7	0	1	1	0	0	0	0	2	0	0	0-0	.143	.143	.286	.429	0	...

LABANDEIRA, JOSH — SS

PERSONAL: Born February 25, 1979, in Tulare, Calif. ... 5-7/180. ... Bats right, throws right. ... Full name: John Joshua Labandeira. ... High school: Monache High (Porterville, Calif.). ... College: Fresno State.
TRANSACTIONS/CAREER NOTES: Selected by Montreal Expos organization in sixth round of 2001 free-agent draft. ... Expos franchise transferred to Washington, D.C., for 2005 season.
2004 GAMES PLAYED BY POSITION (MLB): SS—3, 2B—2.

Year— Team (League)	Pos.	G	AB	R	H	2B	3B	HR	RBI	BB	SO	HBP	GDP	SB-CS	Avg.	OBP	SLG	OPS	E	Avg.
2001— Vermont (N.Y.-Penn.)	SS	1	3	2	1	0	0	0	0	0	0	0	0	0-0	.333	.333	.333	.667	0	1.000
2002— Clinton (Midw.)	SS	129	493	60	141	27	3	8	67	45	73	10	16	15-12	.286	.350	.402	.752	34	.942
2003— Brevard County (FSL)	SS	62	238	41	77	13	4	0	25	24	35	1	6	6-5	.324	.386	.412	.798	12	.949
— Harrisburg (East.)	SS	60	238	25	57	18	2	2	26	20	38	1	7	0-2	.240	.298	.357	.655	13	.953
2004— Harrisburg (East.) ....SS-DH-OF		133	510	71	138	21	4	9	32	52	90	16	10	9-5	.271	.356	.380	.737	31	.952
— Montreal (N.L.)	SS-2B	7	14	0	0	0	0	0	0	0	4	0	1	0-0	.000	.000	.000	.000	1	.833
Major League totals (1 year)		7	14	0	0	0	0	0	0	0	4	0	1	0-0	.000	.000	.000	.000	1	.833

LACKEY, JOHN — P

PERSONAL: Born October 23, 1978, in Abilene, Texas. ... 6-6/235. ... Throws right, bats right. ... Full name: John Derran Lackey. ... High school: Abilene (Texas). ... Junior college: Grayson County (Texas).

TRANSACTIONS/CAREER NOTES: Selected by Anaheim Angels organization in second round of free-agent draft (June 2, 1999). ... On suspended list (June 22-27, 2004).

CAREER HITTING: 0-for-5 (.000), 0 R, 0 2B, 0 3B, 0 HR, 0 RBI.

Year — Team (League)	W	L	Pct.	ERA	WHIP	G	GS	CG	ShO	Hld.	Sv.-Opp.	IP	H	R	ER	HR	BB-IBB	SO	Avg.
1999— Boise (N'west)	6	2	.750	4.98	1.61	15	15	1	0	...	0-...	81.1	81	59	45	7	50-1	77	.264
2000— Cedar Rapids (Midw.)	3	2	.600	2.08	0.82	5	5	0	0	...	0-...	30.1	20	7	7	1	5-0	21	.185
— Lake Elsinore (Calif.)	6	6	.500	3.40	1.35	15	15	2	1	...	0-...	100.2	94	56	38	9	42-0	74	.249
— Erie (East.)	6	1	.857	3.30	1.17	8	8	2	0	...	0-...	57.1	58	23	21	6	9-0	43	.260
2001— Arkansas (Texas)	9	7	.563	3.46	1.06	18	18	3	2	...	0-...	127.1	106	55	49	11	29-0	94	.227
— Salt Lake (PCL)	3	4	.429	6.71	1.58	10	10	1	0	...	0-...	57.2	75	44	43	5	16-0	42	.322
2002— Salt Lake (PCL)	8	2	.800	2.57	1.15	16	16	2	1	...	0-...	101.2	89	35	29	8	28-0	82	.235
— Anaheim (A.L.)	9	4	.692	3.66	1.35	18	18	1	0	0	0-0	108.1	113	52	44	10	33-0	69	.267
2003— Anaheim (A.L.)	10	16	.385	4.63	1.42	33	33	2	•2	0	0-0	204.0	223	117	105	31	66-4	151	.278
2004— Anaheim (A.L.)	14	13	.519	4.67	1.39	33	32	1	1	0	0-0	198.1	215	108	103	22	60-4	144	.278
Major League totals (3 years)	33	33	.500	4.44	1.39	84	83	4	3	0	0-0	510.2	551	277	252	63	159-8	364	.276

DIVISION SERIES RECORD

Year — Team (League)	W	L	Pct.	ERA	WHIP	G	GS	CG	ShO	Hld.	Sv.-Opp.	IP	H	R	ER	HR	BB-IBB	SO	Avg.
2002— Anaheim (A.L.)	0	0	...	0.00	1.33	1	0	0	0	0	0-0	3.0	3	0	0	0	1-0	3	.250

CHAMPIONSHIP SERIES RECORD

Year — Team (League)	W	L	Pct.	ERA	WHIP	G	GS	CG	ShO	Hld.	Sv.-Opp.	IP	H	R	ER	HR	BB-IBB	SO	Avg.
2002— Anaheim (A.L.)	1	0	1.000	0.00	0.43	1	1	0	0	0	0-0	7.0	3	0	0	0	0-0	7	.130

WORLD SERIES RECORD

Year — Team (League)	W	L	Pct.	ERA	WHIP	G	GS	CG	ShO	Hld.	Sv.-Opp.	IP	H	R	ER	HR	BB-IBB	SO	Avg.
2002— Anaheim (A.L.)	1	0	1.000	4.38	1.62	3	2	0	0	0	0-0	12.1	15	6	6	0	5-4	7	.319

LAIRD, GERALD — C

PERSONAL: Born November 13, 1979, in Westminster, Calif. ... 6-2/220. ... Bats right, throws right. ... Full name: Gerald Lee Laird. ... High school: La Quinta High (Westminster,Calif.). ... Junior college: Cypress (Calif.).

TRANSACTIONS/CAREER NOTES: Selected by Oakland Athletics organization in second round of 1998 free-agent draft. ... Traded by A's with P Mario Ramos, 1B Jason Hart and OF Ryan Ludwick to Texas Rangers for P Mike Venafro and 1B Carlos Pena (January 14, 2002). ... On disabled list (May 21-July 23, 2004); included rehabilitation assignment to Oklahoma.

2004 GAMES PLAYED BY POSITION (MLB): C—49.

Year — Team (League)	Pos.	G	AB	R	H	2B	3B	HR	RBI	BB	SO	HBP	GDP	SB-CS	Avg.	OBP	SLG	OPS	E	Avg.
1999— S. Oregon (N'west)	C	60	228	45	65	7	2	2	39	28	43	2	4	10-5	.285	.361	.360	.721	11	.972
2000— Ariz. A's (Ariz.)	C	14	50	10	15	2	1	0	9	6	7	1	3	2-0	.300	.379	.380	.759	0	1.000
— Visalia (Calif.)	C	33	103	14	25	3	0	0	13	14	27	1	3	7-2	.243	.333	.272	.605	8	.969
2001— Modesto (California)	C-O-1-2-3-S	119	443	71	113	13	5	5	46	48	101	10	9	10-9	.255	.337	.341	.678	18	.976
2002— Tulsa (Texas)	C-OF	123	442	70	122	21	4	11	67	45	95	5	14	8-6	.276	.343	.416	.759	8	.988
2003— Oklahoma (PCL)	C-DH	99	338	50	88	20	5	9	42	37	61	7	7	9-3	.260	.344	.429	.773	11	.983
— Texas (A.L.)	C	19	44	9	12	2	1	1	4	5	11	1	2	0-0	.273	.360	.432	.792	1	.986
2004— Oklahoma (PCL)	C-DH	6	22	2	4	2	0	0	2	2	8	0	1	1-0	.182	.250	.273	.523	1	.955
— Texas (A.L.)	C	49	147	20	33	6	0	1	16	12	35	2	5	0-1	.224	.287	.286	.572	5	.983
Major League totals (2 years)		68	191	29	45	8	1	2	20	17	46	3	7	0-1	.236	.304	.319	.623	6	.984

LAKER, TIM — C

PERSONAL: Born November 27, 1969, in Encino, Calif. ... 6-3/225. ... Bats right, throws right. ... Full name: Timothy John Laker. ... High school: Simi Valley (Calif.). ... Junior college: Oxnard (Calif.).

TRANSACTIONS/CAREER NOTES: Selected by Kansas City Royals organization in 49th round of 1987 free-agent draft; did not sign. ... Selected by Montreal Expos organization in sixth round of 1988 free-agent draft. ... On disabled list (March 29, 1996-entire season). ... Claimed on waivers by Baltimore Orioles (March 25, 1997). ... Signed as a free agent by Tampa Bay Devil Rays (December 19, 1997). ... Released by Devil Rays (June 26, 1998). ... Signed by Pittsburgh Pirates organization (July 9, 1998). ... Released by Pirates (December 18, 1998). ... Signed by Los Angeles Dodgers organization (January 11, 1999). ... Traded by Dodgers to Pirates for a player to be named (March 26, 1999). ... Signed as a free agent by Cleveland Indians organization (December 20, 2000). ... Released by Indians (March 1, 2002). ... Re-signed by Indians organization (March 5, 2002). ... Refused minor league assignment and became a free agent (October 7, 2004). ... Career major league pitching: 0-0, 0.00 ERA, 2 G, 2.0 IP, 2 H, 0 R, 0 ER, 2 BB, 1 SO.

2004 GAMES PLAYED BY POSITION (MLB): C—41, P—1.

Year — Team (League)	Pos.	G	AB	R	H	2B	3B	HR	RBI	BB	SO	HBP	GDP	SB-CS	Avg.	OBP	SLG	OPS	E	Avg.
1988— Jamestown (N.Y.-Penn.)	C-OF	47	152	14	34	9	0	0	17	8	30	0	4	2-1	.224	.261	.283	.544	4	.992
1989— Rockford (Midwest)	C	14	48	4	11	1	1	0	4	3	6	0	1	1-0	.229	.275	.292	.566	4	.960
— Jamestown (NYP)	C	58	216	25	48	9	1	2	24	16	40	2	4	8-4	.222	.278	.301	.579	8	.984
1990— Rockford (Midwest)	C-OF	120	425	46	94	18	3	7	57	32	83	1	9	7-2	.221	.273	.327	.600	18	.981
— W.P. Beach (FSL)	C	2	3	0	0	0	0	0	0	0	1	0	0	0-0	.000	.000	.000	.000	0	1.000
1991— W.P. Beach (FSL)	C	100	333	35	77	15	2	5	33	22	51	2	9	10-1	.231	.280	.333	.613	14	.979
— Harrisburg (East.)	C	11	35	4	10	1	0	1	5	2	5	1	1	0-1	.286	.342	.400	.742	3	.959
1992— Harrisburg (East.)	C	117	409	55	99	19	3	15	68	39	89	5	10	3-1	.242	.312	.413	.725	14	.980
— Montreal (N.L.)	C	28	46	8	10	3	0	0	4	2	14	0	1	1-1	.217	.250	.283	.533	1	.991
1993— Montreal (N.L.)	C	43	86	3	17	2	1	0	7	2	16	1	2	2-0	.198	.222	.244	.466	2	.987
— Ottawa (Int'l)	C-1B	56	204	26	47	10	0	4	23	21	41	1	10	3-2	.230	.304	.338	.642	11	.972
1994— Ottawa (Int'l)	C-DH	118	424	68	131	32	2	12	71	47	96	3	10	11-6	.309	.381	.479	.860	11	.985
1995— Montreal (N.L.)	C	64	141	17	33	8	1	3	20	14	38	1	5	0-1	.234	.306	.369	.675	1	.977
1996— Montreal (N.L.)	C		Did not play.																	
1997— Rochester (Int'l)	DH-C	79	290	45	75	11	1	11	37	34	49	5	4	1-2	.259	.342	.417	.760	6	.980
— Baltimore (A.L.)	C	7	14	0	0	0	0	0	1	2	9	0	0	0-0	.000	.118	.000	.118	1	.966
1998— Durham (Int'l)	C-DH	40	134	36	32	7	0	11	26	28	32	1	4	1-1	.239	.372	.537	.909	2	.991
— Tampa Bay (A.L.)	C-DH	3	5	1	1	0	0	0	1	1	1	0	0	0-1	.200	.333	.200	.533	0	1.000

Year—Team (League)	Pos.	G	AB	R	H	2B	3B	HR	RBI	BB	SO	HBP	GDP	SB-CS	Avg.	OBP	SLG	OPS	E	Avg.
— Nashville (PCL)	C-1B-DH	44	152	30	54	16	1	11	34	21	26	3	6	1-0	.355	.441	.691	1.131	4	.987
— Pittsburgh (N.L.)	1B-C	14	24	2	9	1	0	1	2	1	3	0	1	0-0	.375	.385	.542	.926	0	1.000
1999— Nashville (PCL)	C-1-DH-3	112	405	48	109	29	3	12	65	29	68	4	10	3-0	.269	.322	.444	.766	15	.981
— Pittsburgh (N.L.)	C	6	9	0	3	0	0	0	0	0	2	0	0	0-0	.333	.333	.333	.667	0	1.000
2000— Nashville (PCL)	C-1B-3B	121	421	70	104	28	4	19	75	54	73	1	9	5-0	.247	.329	.468	.796	12	.984
2001— Buffalo (Int'l)	C-1B	86	320	45	79	13	0	20	57	28	53	4	10	2-1	.247	.314	.475	.789	6	.990
— Cleveland (A.L.)	C	16	33	5	6	0	0	1	5	6	8	0	1	0-0	.182	.308	.273	.580	1	.988
2002— Columbus (S. Atl.)	C	11	38	5	11	1	0	2	13	10	6	1	0	0-0	.289	.440	.474	.914	0	1.000
— Buffalo (Int'l)	C-1B	62	216	23	49	10	0	4	28	21	52	3	9	2-0	.227	.303	.329	.632	3	.992
2003— Cleveland (A.L.)	C-DH	52	162	17	39	11	0	3	21	9	38	0	4	2-2	.241	.281	.364	.645	5	.983
2004— Cleveland (A.L.)	C-P	44	117	12	25	2	0	3	17	7	28	1	5	0-0	.214	.262	.308	.570	4	.985
American League totals (5 years)		122	331	35	71	13	0	7	44	25	84	1	10	2-3	.215	.270	.317	.587	11	.983
National League totals (5 years)		155	306	30	72	14	2	4	33	19	73	2	9	3-2	.235	.282	.333	.615	10	.984
Major League totals (9 years)		277	637	65	143	27	2	11	77	44	157	3	19	5-5	.224	.276	.325	.601	21	.984

LAMB, MIKE   3B

PERSONAL: Born August 9, 1975, in West Covina, Calif. ... 6-1/190. ... Bats left, throws right. ... Full name: Michael Robert Lamb. ... High school: Bishop Amat (La Puente, Calif.). ... College: Cal State Fullerton.

TRANSACTIONS/CAREER NOTES: Selected by Minnesota Twins organization in 31st round of 1996 free-agent draft; did not sign. ... Selected by Texas Rangers organization in seventh round of 1997 free-agent draft. ... Traded by Rangers to New York Yankees for P Jose Garcia (February 5, 2004). ... Traded by Yankees to Houston Astros for P Juan DeLeon (March 25, 2004).

2004 GAMES PLAYED BY POSITION (MLB): 3B—57, 1B—10, 2B—7, DH—1.

Year Team (League)	Pos.	G	AB	R	H	2B	3B	HR	RBI	BB	SO	HBP	GDP	SB-CS	Avg.	OBP	SLG	OPS	E	Avg.
1997— Pulaski (Appalachian)	3B	60	233	59	78	19	3	9	47	31	18	4	5	7-2	.335	.412	.558	.970	25	.862
1998— Charlotte (Fla. St.)	3B-1B	135	536	83	162	35	3	9	93	45	63	4	10	18-7	.302	.356	.429	.785	31	.933
1999— Tulsa (Texas)	3B-C	137	544	98	176	51	5	21	100	53	65	7	11	4-3	.324	.386	.551	.937	28	.930
— Oklahoma (PCL)	3B	2	2	0	1	0	0	0	0	1	0	1	0	0-1	.500	.750	.500	1.250	0	...
2000— Oklahoma (PCL)	3B	14	55	8	14	5	1	2	5	5	6	0	5	2-1	.255	.317	.491	.808	7	.806
— Texas (A.L.)	3B-DH	138	493	65	137	25	2	6	47	34	60	4	10	0-2	.278	.328	.373	.702	•33	.913
2001— Oklahoma (PCL)	3B	69	273	35	81	19	3	8	40	13	31	3	8	0-2	.297	.331	.476	.807	15	.908
— Texas (A.L.)	3B	76	284	42	87	18	0	4	35	14	27	5	6	2-1	.306	.348	.412	.760	18	.914
2002— Oklahoma (PCL)	C-3B	6	28	3	11	1	0	0	4	1	4	0	1	0-0	.393	.414	.429	.842	3	.893
— Texas (A.L.)	1-DH-O-3-C-2	115	314	54	89	13	0	9	33	33	48	3	7	0-0	.283	.354	.411	.765	9	.980
2003— Texas (A.L.)	DH-1-O-3	28	38	3	5	0	0	0	2	2	7	1	1	1-0	.132	.190	.132	.322	0	1.000
— Oklahoma (PCL)	3B-1B-DH	73	274	45	79	19	4	9	46	42	45	2	4	1-1	.288	.383	.485	.869	11	.953
2004— Houston (N.L.)	3-1-2-DH	112	278	38	80	14	3	14	58	31	63	0	4	1-1	.288	.356	.511	.867	14	.947
American League totals (4 years)		357	1129	164	318	56	2	19	117	83	142	13	24	3-3	.282	.336	.385	.721	60	.943
National League totals (1 year)		112	278	38	80	14	3	14	58	31	63	0	4	1-1	.288	.356	.511	.867	14	.947
Major League totals (5 years)		469	1407	202	398	70	5	33	175	114	205	13	28	4-4	.283	.340	.410	.750	74	.944

DIVISION SERIES RECORD

Year Team (League)	Pos.	G	AB	R	H	2B	3B	HR	RBI	BB	SO	HBP	GDP	SB-CS	Avg.	OBP	SLG	OPS	E	Avg.
2004— Houston (N.L.)		4	3	0	0	0	0	0	1	0	0	0	0	0-0	.000	.000	.000	.000	0	...

CHAMPIONSHIP SERIES RECORD

Year Team (League)	Pos.	G	AB	R	H	2B	3B	HR	RBI	BB	SO	HBP	GDP	SB-CS	Avg.	OBP	SLG	OPS	E	Avg.
2004— Houston (N.L.)	3B	2	5	2	2	0	0	2	2	1	1	0	1	0-0	.400	.500	1.600	2.100	0	1.000

LANE, JASON   OF

PERSONAL: Born December 22, 1976, in Santa Rosa, Calif. ... 6-2/220. ... Bats right, throws left. ... Full name: Jason Dean Lane. ... High school: Santa Rosa (Calif.). ... College: USC.

TRANSACTIONS/CAREER NOTES: Selected by Houston Astros organization in sixth round of 1999 free-agent draft.

2004 GAMES PLAYED BY POSITION (MLB): OF—76, 1B—3.

Year Team (League)	Pos.	G	AB	R	H	2B	3B	HR	RBI	BB	SO	HBP	GDP	SB-CS	Avg.	OBP	SLG	OPS	E	Avg.
1999— Auburn (NY-Penn)	P-1B	74	283	46	79	18	5	13	59	38	46	3	2	6-4	.279	.366	.516	.882	9	.986
2000— Michigan (Midw.)	1B-OF	133	511	98	153	38	0	23	104	62	91	8	9	20-7	.299	.375	.509	.884	5	.986
2001— Round Rock (Texas)	OF	137	526	103	166	36	2	38	124	61	98	21	6	14-2	.316	.407	.608	1.016	2	.992
2002— New Orleans (PCL)	OF-1B	111	426	65	116	36	2	15	83	31	90	7	6	13-3	.272	.328	.472	.799	2	.993
— Houston (N.L.)	OF	44	69	12	20	3	1	4	10	10	12	0	0	1-1	.290	.375	.536	.911	1	.980
2003— New Orleans (PCL)	OF-DH-1B	71	248	37	74	17	0	7	39	30	26	3	6	2-1	.298	.374	.452	.826	4	.976
— Houston (N.L.)	OF	18	27	5	8	2	0	4	10	0	2	0	0	0-0	.296	.296	.815	1.111	0	1.000
2004— Houston (N.L.)	OF-1B	107	136	21	37	10	2	4	19	16	33	1	2	1-0	.272	.348	.463	.812	2	.974
Major League totals (3 years)		169	232	38	65	15	3	12	39	26	47	1	2	2-1	.280	.351	.526	.877	3	.978

DIVISION SERIES RECORD

Year Team (League)	Pos.	G	AB	R	H	2B	3B	HR	RBI	BB	SO	HBP	GDP	SB-CS	Avg.	OBP	SLG	OPS	E	Avg.
2004— Houston (N.L.)	OF	5	5	2	3	0	0	1	2	0	1	0	0	0-0	.600	.600	1.200	1.800	0	1.000

CHAMPIONSHIP SERIES RECORD

Year Team (League)	Pos.	G	AB	R	H	2B	3B	HR	RBI	BB	SO	HBP	GDP	SB-CS	Avg.	OBP	SLG	OPS	E	Avg.
2004— Houston (N.L.)	OF	2	1	0	0	0	0	0	0	0	0	0	0	0-0	.000	.000	.000	.000	0	1.000

LANKFORD, RAY   OF

PERSONAL: Born June 5, 1967, in Los Angeles, Calif. ... 5-11/200. ... Bats left, throws left. ... Full name: Raymond Lewis Lankford. ... High school: Grace Davis (Modesto, Calif.). ... Junior college: Modesto (Calif.). ... Nephew of Carl Nichols, catcher with Baltimore Orioles (1986-88) and Houston Astros (1989-91).

TRANSACTIONS/CAREER NOTES: Selected by Chicago Cubs organization in third round of January 1986 free-agent draft; did not sign. ... Selected by St. Louis Cardinals organization in third round of 1987 free-agent draft. ... On disabled list (June 24-July 9, 1993). ... On disabled list (March 27-April 22, 1997); included rehabilitation assignment to Prince William. ... On disabled list (March 26-April 24, 1999). ... Traded by Cardinals with cash to San Diego Padres for P Woody Williams (August 2, 2001). ... On disabled list (July 4-September 10, 2002). ... Signed as a free agent by Cardinals organization (January 9, 2004). ... On disabled list (July 22-September 1, 2004); included rehabilitation assignment to Memphis.

2004 GAMES PLAYED BY POSITION (MLB): OF—70.

Year Team (League)	Pos.	G	AB	R	H	2B	3B	HR	RBI	BB	SO	HBP	GDP	SB-CS	Avg.	OBP	SLG	OPS	E	Avg.
1987—Johnson City (App.)	OF	66	253	45	78	17	4	3	32	19	43	5	5	14-11	.308	.367	.443	.810	5	.968
1988—Springfield (Midw.)	OF	135	532	90	151	26	16	11	66	60	92	10	4	33-17	.284	.366	.455	.821	7	.976
1989—Arkansas (Texas)	OF	134	498	98	158	28	12	11	98	65	57	4	7	38-10	.317	.395	.488	.883	11	.972
1990—Louisville (A.A.)	OF	132	473	61	123	25	8	10	72	72	81	5	8	30-7	.260	.362	.410	.772	11	.969
— St. Louis (N.L.)	OF	39	126	12	36	10	1	3	12	13	27	0	1	8-2	.286	.353	.452	.805	1	.989
1991—St. Louis (N.L.)	OF	151	566	83	142	23 *	15	9	69	41	114	1	4	44-20	.251	.301	.392	.693	6	.984
1992—St. Louis (N.L.)	OF	153	598	87	175	40	6	20	86	72	147	5	5	42-24	.293	.371	.480	.851	2	.996
1993—St. Louis (N.L.)	OF	127	407	64	97	17	3	7	45	81	111	3	5	14-14	.238	.366	.346	.713	7	.978
1994—St. Louis (N.L.)	OF	109	416	89	111	25	5	19	57	58	113	4	0	11-10	.267	.359	.488	.847	6	.978
1995—St. Louis (N.L.)	OF	132	483	81	134	35	2	25	82	63	110	2	10	24-8	.277	.360	.513	.873	3	.990
1996—St. Louis (N.L.)	OF	149	545	100	150	36	8	21	86	79	133	3	12	35-7	.275	.366	.486	.852	1	.997
1997—Prince Will. (Car.)	DH-OF	4	13	3	4	1	0	0	4	4	5	0	0	1-1	.308	.444	.385	.829	0	1.000
— St. Louis (N.L.)	OF	133	465	94	137	36	3	31	98	95	125	0	9	21-11	.295	.411	.585	.996	9	.971
1998—St. Louis (N.L.)	OF-DH	154	533	94	156	37	1	31	105	86	151	3	4	26-5	.293	.391	.540	.932	5	.986
1999—St. Louis (N.L.)	OF-DH	122	422	77	129	32	1	15	63	49	110	3	6	14-4	.306	.380	.493	.873	3	.987
2000—St. Louis (N.L.)	OF-DH	128	392	73	99	16	3	26	65	70	148	4	6	5-6	.253	.367	.508	.874	5	.973
2001—St. Louis (N.L.)	OF	91	264	38	62	18	3	15	39	44	105	2	4	4-2	.235	.345	.496	.841	5	.966
— San Diego (N.L.)	OF	40	125	20	36	10	1	4	19	18	40	2	2	6-0	.288	.386	.480	.866	1	.985
2002—San Diego (N.L.)	OF-DH	81	205	20	46	7	1	6	26	30	61	2	3	2-2	.224	.326	.356	.682	5	.985
2004—Memphis (PCL)	DH-OF	9	33	5	7	0	0	3	5	3	10	1	1	0-0	.212	.297	.485	.782	0	1.000
— St. Louis (N.L.)	OF	92	200	36	51	14	1	6	22	29	55	2	6	2-2	.255	.349	.425	.774	4	.956
Major League totals (14 years)		1701	5747	968	1561	356	54	238	874	828	1550	36	77	258-117	.272	.364	.477	.840	63	.983

DIVISION SERIES RECORD

Year Team (League)	Pos.	G	AB	R	H	2B	3B	HR	RBI	BB	SO	HBP	GDP	SB-CS	Avg.	OBP	SLG	OPS	E	Avg.
1996—St. Louis (N.L.)	OF	1	2	1	1	0	0	0	0	1	0	0	0	0-0	.500	.667	.500	1.167	0	1.000
2000—St. Louis (N.L.)	OF	3	10	2	2	1	0	0	3	2	5	0	0	0-0	.200	.333	.300	.633	0	1.000
Division series totals (2 years)		4	12	3	3	1	0	0	3	3	5	0	0	0-0	.250	.400	.333	.733	0	1.000

CHAMPIONSHIP SERIES RECORD

Year Team (League)	Pos.	G	AB	R	H	2B	3B	HR	RBI	BB	SO	HBP	GDP	SB-CS	Avg.	OBP	SLG	OPS	E	Avg.
1996—St. Louis (N.L.)	OF	5	13	1	0	0	0	0	1	1	4	0	0	0-0	.000	.067	.000	.067	0	1.000
2000—St. Louis (N.L.)	OF	5	12	1	4	1	0	0	1	1	5	0	0	0-0	.333	.385	.417	.801	0	1.000
Champ. series totals (2 years)		10	25	2	4	1	0	0	2	2	9	0	0	0-0	.160	.214	.200	.414	0	1.000

ALL-STAR GAME RECORD

	G	AB	R	H	2B	3B	HR	RBI	BB	SO	HBP	GDP	SB-CS	Avg.	OBP	SLG	OPS	E	Avg.
All-Star Game totals (1 year)	1	2	0	0	0	0	0	0	1	1	0	0	0-0	.000	.333	.000	.333	0	...

LARKIN, BARRY — SS

PERSONAL: Born April 28, 1964, in Cincinnati, Ohio. ... 6-0/185. ... Bats right, throws right. ... Full name: Barry Louis Larkin. ... High school: Moeller (Cincinnati). ... College: Michigan. ... Brother of Stephen Larkin, outfielder/first baseman with Cincinnati Reds (1998).

TRANSACTIONS/CAREER NOTES: Selected by Cincinnati Reds organization in second round of June 1982 free-agent draft; did not sign. ... Selected by Reds organization in first round (fourth pick overall) of June 1985 free-agent draft. ... On disabled list (April 13-May 2, 1987). ... On disabled list (July 11-September 1, 1989); included rehabilitation assignment to Nashville. ... On disabled list (May 18-June 4, 1991; April 19-May 8, 1992; August 5, 1993-remainder of season; June 17-August 2 and September 1, 1997-remainder of season; March 12-April 7, 1998; April 22-May 16, 2000; May 17-June 15 and June 29, 2001-remainder of season; April 11-May 6, May 22-June 13 and August 23, 2003-remainder of season).

HONORS: Named N.L. Most Valuable Player by Baseball Writers' Association of America (1995). ... Won N.L. Gold Glove at shortstop (1994-96).

2004 GAMES PLAYED BY POSITION (MLB): SS—85.

Year Team (League)	Pos.	G	AB	R	H	2B	3B	HR	RBI	BB	SO	HBP	GDP	SB-CS	Avg.	OBP	SLG	OPS	E	Avg.
1985—Vermont (East.)	SS	72	255	42	68	13	2	1	31	23	21	3	13	12-1	.267	.331	.345	.676	17	.942
1986—Denver (A.A.)	2B-SS	103	413	67	136	31	10	10	51	31	43	2	1	19-6	.329	.373	.525	.898	18	.942
— Cincinnati (N.L.)	2B-SS	41	159	27	45	4	3	3	19	9	21	0	2	8-0	.283	.320	.403	.722	4	.978
1987—Cincinnati (N.L.)	SS	125	439	64	107	16	2	12	43	36	52	5	8	21-6	.244	.306	.371	.678	19	.965
1988—Cincinnati (N.L.)	SS	151	588	91	174	32	5	12	56	41	24	8	7	40-7	.296	.347	.429	.776	• 29	.960
1989—Cincinnati (N.L.)	SS	97	325	47	111	14	4	4	36	20	23	2	7	10-5	.342	.375	.446	.821	10	.976
— Nashville (A.A.)	SS	2	5	2	5	1	0	0	0	0	0	0	0	0-0	1.000	1.000	1.200	2.200	0	1.000
1990—Cincinnati (N.L.)	SS	158	614	85	185	25	6	7	67	49	49	7	14	30-5	.301	.358	.396	.753	17	.977
1991—Cincinnati (N.L.)	SS	123	464	88	140	27	4	20	69	55	64	3	7	24-6	.302	.378	.506	.884	15	.976
1992—Cincinnati (N.L.)	SS	140	533	76	162	32	6	12	78	63	58	4	13	15-4	.304	.377	.454	.831	11	.983
1993—Cincinnati (N.L.)	SS	100	384	57	121	20	3	8	51	51	33	1	13	14-1	.315	.394	.445	.839	16	.965
1994—Cincinnati (N.L.)	SS	110	427	78	119	23	5	9	52	64	58	0	6	26-2	.279	.369	.419	.788	10	.980
1995—Cincinnati (N.L.)	SS	131	496	98	158	29	6	15	66	61	49	3	6	51-5	.319	.394	.492	.886	11	.980
1996—Cincinnati (N.L.)	SS	152	517	117	154	32	4	33	89	96	52	7	20	36-10	.298	.410	.567	.977	17	.975
1997—Cincinnati (N.L.)	SS-DH	73	224	34	71	17	3	4	20	47	24	3	3	14-3	.317	.440	.473	.913	5	.980
1998—Cincinnati (N.L.)	SS	145	538	93	166	34	10	17	72	79	69	2	12	26-3	.309	.397	.504	.901	12	.979
1999—Cincinnati (N.L.)	SS	161	583	108	171	30	4	12	75	93	57	2	12	30-8	.293	.390	.420	.810	14	.978
2000—Cincinnati (N.L.)	SS-DH	102	396	71	124	26	5	11	41	48	31	1	10	14-6	.313	.390	.487	.876	11	.973
2001—Cincinnati (N.L.)	SS	45	156	29	40	12	0	2	17	27	25	2	2	3-2	.256	.373	.372	.745	9	.951
2002—Cincinnati (N.L.)	SS	145	507	72	124	37	2	7	47	44	57	3	13	13-4	.245	.305	.367	.672	12	.979
2003—Cincinnati (N.L.)	SS	70	241	39	68	16	1	2	18	22	32	1	7	2-0	.282	.345	.382	.726	9	.942
2004—Cincinnati (N.L.)	SS	111	346	55	100	15	3	8	44	34	39	1	16	2-0	.289	.352	.419	.771	4	.988
Major League totals (19 years)		2180	7937	1329	2340	441	76	198	960	939	817	55	178	379-77	.295	.371	.444	.815	235	.975

DIVISION SERIES RECORD

Year Team (League)	Pos.	G	AB	R	H	2B	3B	HR	RBI	BB	SO	HBP	GDP	SB-CS	Avg.	OBP	SLG	OPS	E	Avg.
1995—Cincinnati (N.L.)	SS	3	13	2	5	0	0	0	1	1	2	0	0	4-0	.385	.429	.385	.813	0	1.000

CHAMPIONSHIP SERIES RECORD

Year Team (League)	Pos.	G	AB	R	H	2B	3B	HR	RBI	BB	SO	HBP	GDP	SB-CS	Avg.	OBP	SLG	OPS	E	Avg.
1990— Cincinnati (N.L.)	SS	6	23	5	6	2	0	0	1	3	1	0	1	3-0	.261	.346	.348	.694	1	.973
1995— Cincinnati (N.L.)	SS	4	18	1	7	2	1	0	0	1	1	0	0	1-1	.389	.421	.611	1.032	1	.962
Champ. series totals (2 years)		10	41	6	13	4	1	0	1	4	2	0	1	4-1	.317	.378	.463	.841	2	.968

WORLD SERIES RECORD

Year Team (League)	Pos.	G	AB	R	H	2B	3B	HR	RBI	BB	SO	HBP	GDP	SB-CS	Avg.	OBP	SLG	OPS	E	Avg.
1990— Cincinnati (N.L.)	SS	4	17	3	6	1	1	0	1	2	0	0	1	0-0	.353	.421	.529	.950	0	1.000

ALL-STAR GAME RECORD

	G	AB	R	H	2B	3B	HR	RBI	BB	SO	HBP	GDP	SB-CS	Avg.	OBP	SLG	OPS	E	Avg.
All-Star Game totals (9 years)	9	18	1	2	0	0	0	2	0	3	0	0	1-0	.111	.105	.111	.216	1	.952

LAROCHE, ADAM — 1B

PERSONAL: Born November 6, 1979, in Orange County, Calif. ... 6-3/180. ... Bats left, throws left. ... Full name: David Adam LaRoche. ... High school: Fort Scott (Kan.). ... Junior college: Seminole (Okla.). ... Son of Dave LaRoche, pitcher for five major league clubs (1970-83).

TRANSACTIONS/CAREER NOTES: Selected by Florida Marlins organization in 18th round of 1998 free-agent draft; did not sign. ... Selected by Marlins organization in 42nd round of 1999 free-agent draft; did not sign. ... Selected by Atlanta Braves organization in 29th round of 2000 free-agent draft. ... On disabled list (May 29-July 2, 2004); included rehabilitation assignment to Richmond.

RECORDS: Shares major league record for most doubles, game (4, May 15, 2004).

2004 GAMES PLAYED BY POSITION (MLB): 1B—98.

Year Team (League)	Pos.	G	AB	R	H	BATTING 2B	3B	HR	RBI	BB	SO	HBP	GDP	SB-CS	Avg.	OBP	SLG	OPS	FIELDING E	Avg.
2000— Danville (Appal.)	1B	56	201	38	62	13	3	7	45	24	46	2	2	4-1	.308	.381	.507	.888	2	.994
2001— Myrtle Beach (Caro.)	1B-OF-P	126	471	49	118	31	0	7	47	30	108	9	13	10-8	.251	.305	.361	.666	8	.993
2002— Myrtle Beach (Caro.)	1B	69	250	30	84	17	0	9	53	27	37	4	3	0-2	.336	.406	.512	.918	5	.991
—Greenville (Sou.)	1B	45	173	17	50	9	0	4	19	19	38	1	6	1-1	.289	.363	.410	.773	1	.998
2003— Greenville (Sou.)	1B-P	61	219	42	62	12	1	12	37	34	53	3	6	1-2	.283	.381	.511	.892	2	.996
—Richmond (Int'l)	1B	72	264	33	78	21	0	8	35	27	58	3	6	1-2	.295	.360	.466	.826	4	.993
2004— Richmond (Int'l)	1B	4	11	1	2	0	0	1	2	1	0	0	2	0-0	.182	.250	.455	.705	0	1.000
—Atlanta (N.L.)	1B	110	324	45	90	27	1	13	45	27	78	1	10	0-0	.278	.333	.488	.821	5	.994
Major League totals (1 year)		110	324	45	90	27	1	13	45	27	78	1	10	0-0	.278	.333	.488	.821	5	.994

DIVISION SERIES RECORD

Year Team (League)	Pos.	G	AB	R	H	2B	3B	HR	RBI	BB	SO	HBP	GDP	SB-CS	Avg.	OBP	SLG	OPS	E	Avg.
2004— Atlanta (N.L.)	1B	5	17	1	4	1	0	1	4	2	5	0	1	0-0	.235	.316	.471	.786	0	1.000

LARSON, BRANDON — 3B

PERSONAL: Born May 24, 1976, in San Angelo, Texas. ... 6-0/210. ... Bats right, throws right. ... Full name: Brandon John Larson. ... High school: Holmes (San Antonio, Texas). ... College: LSU.

TRANSACTIONS/CAREER NOTES: Selected by Pittsburgh Pirates organization in 46th round of 1994 free-agent draft; did not sign. ... Selected by Pittsburgh Pirates organization in 38th round of 1995 free-agent draft; did not sign. ... Selected by San Francisco Giants organization in 44th round of 1996 free-agent draft; did not sign. ... Selected by Cincinnati Reds organization in first round (14th pick overall) of 1997 free-agent draft. ... On disabled list (August 16-31 and September 4, 2002-remainder of season); included rehabilitation assignment to Louisville. ... On disabled list (August 18, 2003-remainder of season). ... On disabled list (March 26-April 26, May 8-June 4 and July 18-September 1, 2004); included rehabilitation assignments to Louisville and Chattanooga.

2004 GAMES PLAYED BY POSITION (MLB): 3B—35.

Year Team (League)	Pos.	G	AB	R	H	BATTING 2B	3B	HR	RBI	BB	SO	HBP	GDP	SB-CS	Avg.	OBP	SLG	OPS	FIELDING E	Avg.
1997— Chattanooga (Sou.)	SS	11	41	4	11	5	1	0	6	1	10	0	1	0-0	.268	.279	.439	.718	5	.891
1998— Burlington (Midw.)	3B	18	68	5	15	3	0	2	9	4	16	0	1	2-1	.221	.264	.353	.617	0	1.000
1999— Rockford (Midwest)	3B	69	250	38	75	18	1	13	52	25	67	3	7	12-2	.300	.367	.536	.903	18	.912
—Chattanooga (Sou.)	3B	43	172	28	49	10	0	12	42	10	51	3	3	4-5	.285	.332	.552	.884	15	.885
2000— Chattanooga (Sou.)	3B	111	427	61	116	26	0	20	64	31	122	8	8	15-5	.272	.330	.473	.804	24	.917
—Louisville (Int'l)	3B	17	63	11	18	7	1	2	4	4	16	0	1	0-0	.286	.328	.524	.852	4	.929
2001— Louisville (Int'l)	3B-SS-1B	115	424	61	108	23	4	14	55	24	123	12	15	5-6	.255	.312	.415	.727	20	.949
—Cincinnati (N.L.)	3B	14	33	2	4	2	0	0	1	2	10	0	1	0-0	.121	.171	.182	.353	2	.939
2002— Louisville (Int'l)	3B-OF	80	297	47	101	20	1	25	69	24	70	3	5	1-1	.340	.393	.667	1.059	17	.917
—Cincinnati (N.L.)	OF-3B-1B	23	51	4	14	2	0	4	13	6	10	1	1	1-0	.275	.362	.549	.911	0	1.000
2003— Louisville (Int'l)	3B-1B-OF	72	282	51	91	19	2	20	74	28	70	2	7	3-0	.323	.384	.617	1.001	16	.936
—Cincinnati (N.L.)	3B-OF	32	89	6	9	1	0	1	9	13	31	0	2	2-2	.101	.212	.146	.358	4	.950
2004— Chattanooga (Sou.)	DH	2	7	1	2	1	0	1	1	0	4	0	0	0-0	.286	.286	.857	1.143	0	...
—Cincinnati (N.L.)	3B	40	118	13	25	6	0	3	14	14	35	2	2	1-0	.212	.304	.339	.643	5	.937
—Louisville (Int'l)	3B-DH	32	117	14	33	5	0	9	25	5	39	1	4	0-0	.282	.315	.556	.870	7	.910
Major League totals (4 years)		109	291	29	52	11	0	8	37	35	86	3	6	4-2	.179	.271	.299	.570	11	.950

LARUE, JASON — C

PERSONAL: Born March 19, 1974, in Houston, Texas. ... 5-11/200. ... Bats right, throws right. ... Full name: Michael Jason LaRue. ... Name pronounced: la-ROO. ... High school: Spring Valley (Spring Branch, Texas). ... College: Dallas Baptist (Texas).

TRANSACTIONS/CAREER NOTES: Selected by Cincinnati Reds organization in fifth round of 1995 free-agent draft. ... On disabled list (September 23, 2002-remainder of season). ... On disabled list (April 29-May 14, 2004); included rehabilitation assignment to Louisville.

2004 GAMES PLAYED BY POSITION (MLB): C—111, DH—1, OF—1.

Year Team (League)	Pos.	G	AB	R	H	BATTING 2B	3B	HR	RBI	BB	SO	HBP	GDP	SB-CS	Avg.	OBP	SLG	OPS	FIELDING E	Avg.
1995— Billings (Pio.)	C	58	183	35	50	8	1	5	31	16	28	12	2	3-5	.273	.366	.410	.776	8	.980
1996— Char., W.Va. (SAL)	C-1B	37	123	17	26	8	0	2	14	11	28	2	2	3-0	.211	.287	.325	.612	6	.979
1997— Char., W.Va. (SAL)	3-C-1-OF	132	473	78	149	50	3	8	81	47	90	5	8	14-4	.315	.377	.484	.861	19	.977
1998— Chattanooga (Sou.)	3B-C-1B	105	386	71	141	39	8	14	82	40	60	10	13	4-3	.365	.429	.617	1.046	10	.985
—Indianapolis (Int'l)	C	15	51	5	12	4	0	0	5	4	8	0	2	0-1	.235	.286	.314	.599	0	1.000
1999— Indianapolis (Int'l)	C-DH	70	263	42	66	12	2	12	37	15	52	4	13	0-3	.251	.299	.449	.748	7	.990
—Cincinnati (N.L.)	C	36	90	12	19	7	0	3	10	11	32	2	4	4-1	.211	.311	.389	.700	2	.990
2000— Louisville (Int'l)	C	82	307	54	78	22	1	14	48	22	52	8	4	3-2	.254	.320	.469	.790	8	.984

Year Team (League)	Pos.	G	AB	R	H	2B	3B	HR	RBI	BB	SO	HBP	GDP	SB-CS	Avg.	OBP	SLG	OPS	E	Avg.
—Cincinnati (N.L.)	C	31	98	12	23	3	0	5	12	5	19	4	1	0-0	.235	.299	.418	.717	2	.991
2001—Cincinnati (N.L.)	C-3-OF-1	121	364	39	86	21	2	12	43	27	106	9	11	3-3	.236	.303	.404	.707	7	.990
2002—Cincinnati (N.L.)	C	113	353	42	88	17	1	12	52	27	117	13	13	1-2	.249	.324	.405	.729	4	.994
2003—Cincinnati (N.L.)	C-1B-OF	118	379	52	87	23	1	16	50	33	111	20	9	3-3	.230	.321	.422	.743	11	.985
2004—Louisville (Int'l)	C	3	10	3	1	0	0	1	4	1	3	1	0	0-0	.100	.214	.400	.614	1	.917
—Cincinnati (N.L.)	C-DH-OF	114	390	46	98	24	2	14	55	26	108	24	7	0-2	.251	.334	.431	.765	8	.989
Major League totals (6 years)		533	1674	203	401	95	6	62	222	129	493	72	45	11-11	.240	.319	.415	.734	34	.989

LAWRENCE, BRIAN — P

PERSONAL: Born May 14, 1976, in Fort Collins, Colo. ... 6-0/197. ... Throws right, bats right. ... Full name: Brian Michael Lawrence. ... High school: Carthage (Texas). ... College: Northwestern State (La.).

TRANSACTIONS/CAREER NOTES: Selected by San Diego Padres organization in 17th round of 1998 free-agent draft.

CAREER HITTING: 30-for-218 (.138), 13 R, 7 2B, 0 3B, 1 HR, 16 RBI.

Year Team (League)	W	L	Pct.	ERA	WHIP	G	GS	CG	ShO	Hld.	Sv.-Opp.	IP	H	R	ER	HR	BB-IBB	SO	Avg.
1998—Idaho Falls (Pioneer)	3	0	1.000	2.45	1.23	4	4	2	1	...	0-...	22.0	22	7	6	1	5-0	21	.262
—Clinton (Midw.)	5	3	.625	2.80	0.00	12	12	2	0	...	0-...	80.1	67	34	25	5	13-0	79	.221
1999—Rancho Cuca. (Calif.)	12	8	.600	3.39	1.19	27	27	4	3	...	0-...	175.1	178	72	66	6	30-1	166	.265
2000—Mobile (Sou.)	7	6	.538	2.42	1.00	21	21	0	0	...	0-...	126.2	99	40	34	6	28-0	119	.217
—Las Vegas (PCL)	4	0	1.000	1.93	1.18	8	8	0	0	...	0-...	46.2	48	13	10	6	7-0	46	.264
2001—Portland (PCL)	1	3	.250	3.80	1.31	9	8	0	0	...	1-...	45.0	42	22	19	3	17-2	42	.239
—San Diego (N.L.)	5	5	.500	3.45	1.23	27	15	1	0	0	0-0	114.2	107	53	44	10	34-5	84	.244
2002—San Diego (N.L.)	12	12	.500	3.69	1.34	35	31	2	1	0	0-0	210.0	230	97	86	16	52-6	149	.281
2003—San Diego (N.L.)	10	15	.400	4.19	1.25	33	33	1	0	0	0-0	210.2	206	106	98	27	57-8	116	.258
2004—San Diego (N.L.)	15	14	.517	4.12	1.38	34	34	2	1	0	0-0	203.0	226	101	93	26	55-7	121	.287
Major League totals (4 years)	42	46	.477	3.91	1.31	129	113	6	3	1	0-0	738.1	769	357	321	79	198-26	470	.270

LAWTON, MATT — OF

PERSONAL: Born November 3, 1971, in Gulfport, Miss. ... 5-10/195. ... Bats left, throws right. ... Full name: Matthew Lawton III. ... Name pronounced: LAW-ton. ... High school: Harrison Central (Gulfport, Miss.). ... Junior college: Mississippi Gulf Coast Community College. ... Brother of Marcus Lawton, outfielder with New York Yankees (1989).

TRANSACTIONS/CAREER NOTES: Selected by Minnesota Twins organization in 13th round of 1991 free-agent draft. ... On disabled list (June 9-July 18, 1999); included rehabilitation assignments to Fort Myers and GCL Twins. ... Traded by Twins to New York Mets for P Rick Reed (July 30, 2001). ... Traded by Mets with OF Alex Escobar, P Jerrod Riggan and two players to be named to Cleveland Indians for 2B Roberto Alomar, P Mike Bacsik and OF Danny Peoples (December 11, 2001); Indians acquired P Billy Traber and 1B Earl Snyder to complete deal (December 13, 2001). ... On disabled list (July 12-July 27 and September 4, 2002-remainder of season); included rehabilitation assignment to Akron. ... On disabled list (July 12-August 18 and September 6, 2003-remainder of season); included rehabilitation assignments to Akron.

2004 GAMES PLAYED BY POSITION (MLB): OF—142, DH—3.

Year Team (League)	Pos.	G	AB	R	H	2B	3B	HR	RBI	BB	SO	HBP	GDP	SB-CS	Avg.	OBP	SLG	OPS	E	Avg.
1992—GC Twins (GCL)	2B	53	173	39	45	8	3	2	26	27	27	9	2	20-1	.260	.375	.376	.751	12	.958
1993—Fort Wayne (Midw.)	OF	111	340	50	97	21	3	9	38	65	42	8	8	23-15	.285	.410	.444	.854	3	.959
1994—Fort Myers (FSL)	OF	122	446	79	134	30	1	7	51	80	64	2	7	42-19	.300	.407	.419	.826	6	.971
1995—New Britain (East.)	OF-DH	114	412	75	111	19	5	13	54	56	70	12	8	26-9	.269	.371	.434	.805	2	.991
—Minnesota (A.L.)	OF-DH	21	60	11	19	4	1	1	12	7	11	3	1	1-1	.317	.414	.467	.881	1	.972
1996—Minnesota (A.L.)	OF-DH	79	252	34	65	7	1	6	42	28	28	4	6	4-4	.258	.339	.365	.704	3	.985
—Salt Lake (PCL)	OF-DH	53	212	40	63	16	1	7	33	26	34	3	2	2-4	.297	.379	.481	.860	6	.936
1997—Minnesota (A.L.)	OF	142	460	74	114	29	3	14	60	76	81	10	7	7-4	.248	.366	.415	.781	7	.976
1998—Minnesota (A.L.)	OF	152	557	91	155	36	6	21	77	86	64	15	10	16-8	.278	.387	.478	.864	4	.990
1999—Minnesota (A.L.)	OF-DH	118	406	58	105	18	0	7	54	57	42	6	11	26-4	.259	.353	.355	.708	4	.982
—Fort Myers (FSL)	OF	4	14	3	8	1	0	0	2	3	1	0	0	1-0	.571	.647	.643	1.290	0	1.000
—GC Twins (GCL)	OF	1	4	0	1	0	0	0	1	0	2	0	0	0-0	.250	.250	.250	.500	0	1.000
2000—Minnesota (A.L.)	OF-DH	156	561	84	171	44	2	13	88	91	63	7	10	23-7	.305	.405	.460	.865	5	.983
2001—Minnesota (A.L.)	OF-DH	103	376	71	110	25	0	10	51	63	46	3	14	19-6	.293	.396	.439	.835	4	.980
—New York (N.L.)	OF	48	183	24	45	11	1	3	13	22	34	8	2	10-2	.246	.352	.366	.718	0	1.000
2002—Cleveland (A.L.)	OF-DH	114	416	71	98	19	2	15	57	59	34	8	13	8-9	.236	.342	.399	.741	6	.975
—Akron (East.)	OF	3	10	1	0	0	0	0	0	3	1	0	0	0-0	.000	.231	.000	.231	0	1.000
2003—Akron (East.)	DH	5	19	1	1	0	0	0	1	2	6	0	1	0-0	.053	.143	.053	.195	0	.000
—Cleveland (A.L.)	OF-DH	99	374	57	93	19	0	15	53	47	47	7	8	10-3	.249	.343	.420	.762	1	.993
2004—Cleveland (A.L.)	OF-DH	150	591	109	164	25	0	20	70	74	84	11	21	23-9	.278	.366	.421	.788	4	.986
American League totals (10 years)		1134	4053	660	1094	226	15	122	564	588	500	74	101	137-55	.270	.370	.423	.794	39	.983
National League totals (1 year)		48	183	24	45	11	1	3	13	22	34	8	2	10-2	.246	.352	.366	.718	0	1.000
Major League totals (10 years)		1182	4236	684	1139	237	16	125	577	610	534	82	103	147-57	.269	.370	.421	.791	39	.984

ALL-STAR GAME RECORD

	G	AB	R	H	2B	3B	HR	RBI	BB	SO	HBP	GDP	SB-CS	Avg.	OBP	SLG	OPS	E	Avg.
All-Star Game totals (2 years)	2	4	1	2	0	0	0	1	0	1	0	0	1-0	.500	.500	.500	1.000	0	...

LEAGUE, BRANDON — P

PERSONAL: Born March 16, 1983, in Honolulu, Hawaii. ... 6-3/192. ... Throws right, bats right. ... Full name: Brandon Paul League. ... High school: Saint Louis High (Honolulu).

TRANSACTIONS/CAREER NOTES: Selected by Toronto Blue Jays organization in second round of 2001 free-agent draft.

CAREER HITTING: 0-for-0 (.000), 0 R, 0 2B, 0 3B, 0 HR, 0 RBI.

Year Team (League)	W	L	Pct.	ERA	WHIP	G	GS	CG	ShO	Hld.	Sv.-Opp.	IP	H	R	ER	HR	BB-IBB	SO	Avg.
2001—Medicine Hat (Pio.)	2	2	.500	4.66	1.22	9	9	0	0	...	0-...	38.2	36	23	20	3	11-1	38	.245
2002—Auburn (N.Y.-Penn)	7	2	.778	3.15	1.20	16	16	0	0	...	0-...	85.2	80	42	30	2	23-0	72	.248
2003—Char., W.Va. (SAL)	2	3	.400	1.91	1.08	12	12	0	0	...	0-...	70.2	58	15	15	1	18-0	61	.230
—Dunedin (Fla. St.)	4	3	.571	4.75	1.45	13	12	0	0	...	0-...	66.1	76	40	35	3	20-0	34	.288
2004—New Hampshire (East.)	6	4	.600	3.38	1.28	41	10	0	0	...	2-...	104.0	92	44	39	3	41-1	90	.240
—Toronto (A.L.)	1	0	1.000	0.00	0.86	3	0	0	0	...	0-0	4.2	3	0	0	0	1-0	2	.176
Major League totals (1 year)	1	0	1.000	0.00	0.86	3	0	0	0	1	0-0	4.2	3	0	0	0	1-0	2	.176

L

LECROY, MATTHEW   C

PERSONAL: Born December 13, 1975, in Belton, S.C. ... 6-2/225. ... Bats right, throws right. ... Full name: Matthew Hanks LeCroy. ... Name pronounced: LEE-croy. ... High school: Belton-Honea Path (S.C.). ... College: Clemson.

TRANSACTIONS/CAREER NOTES: Selected by New York Mets organization in supplemental round ("sandwich" pick between second and third rounds, 63rd pick overall) of 1994 free-agent draft; did not sign; pick received as compensation for Atlanta Braves signing Type C free-agent C Charlie O'Brien. ... Selected by Minnesota Twins organization in supplemental round ("sandwich" pick between first and second rounds, 50th pick overall) of 1997 free-agent draft; pick received as compensation for failure to sign 1996 first-round pick Travis Lee. ... On disabled list (April 8-May 11, 2004).

2004 GAMES PLAYED BY POSITION (MLB): DH—30, C—26, 1B—23.

Year	Team (League)	Pos.	G	AB	R	H	2B	3B	HR	RBI	BB	SO	HBP	GDP	SB-CS	Avg.	OBP	SLG	OPS	E	Avg.
1998—Fort Wayne (Midw.)		C	64	225	33	62	17	1	9	40	34	45	8	9	0-0	.276	.387	.480	.867	1	.997
—Fort Myers (FSL)		C	51	200	32	61	9	1	12	51	21	35	4	6	2-1	.305	.372	.540	.912	3	.991
—Salt Lake (PCL)		C	3	13	2	4	1	0	2	4	0	7	0	0	0-0	.308	.308	.846	1.154	0	1.000
1999—Fort Myers (FSL)		C	89	333	54	93	20	1	20	69	42	51	3	10	0-0	.279	.364	.526	.890	8	.983
—Salt Lake (PCL)		C	29	119	23	36	4	1	10	30	5	22	1	8	0-1	.303	.331	.605	.936	0	1.000
2000—Minnesota (A.L.)	C-DH-1B		56	167	18	29	10	0	5	17	17	38	2	6	0-0	.174	.254	.323	.577	4	.989
—New Britain (East.)		C	54	195	33	55	12	1	10	38	29	34	6	8	0-0	.282	.391	.508	.899	10	.970
—Salt Lake (PCL)	C-1B		16	65	15	20	5	0	5	15	4	11	0	4	0-0	.308	.348	.615	.963	0	1.000
2001—Edmonton (PCL)	C-1B		101	396	53	130	17	0	20	80	36	55	6	8	0-2	.328	.390	.523	.913	5	.980
—Minnesota (A.L.)	DH-C-1B		15	40	6	17	5	0	3	12	0	8	1	0	0-1	.425	.429	.775	1.204	0	1.000
2002—Edmonton (PCL)	C-1B		46	174	36	61	7	1	12	50	17	34	4	1	2-0	.351	.412	.609	1.021	1	.993
—Minnesota (A.L.)	DH-1B-C		63	181	19	47	11	1	7	27	13	38	0	5	0-2	.260	.306	.448	.754	1	.984
2003—Minnesota (A.L.)	DH-C-1B		107	345	39	99	19	0	17	64	25	82	4	8	0-1	.287	.342	.490	.832	3	.985
2004—Minnesota (A.L.)	DH-C-1B		88	264	25	71	14	0	9	39	16	60	5	7	0-0	.269	.321	.424	.745	5	.983
Major League totals (5 years)			329	997	107	263	59	1	41	159	71	226	12	26	0-4	.264	.318	.448	.766	13	.986

DIVISION SERIES RECORD

Year	Team (League)	Pos.	G	AB	R	H	2B	3B	HR	RBI	BB	SO	HBP	GDP	SB-CS	Avg.	OBP	SLG	OPS	E	Avg.
2002—Minnesota (A.L.)	DH		3	9	1	4	0	0	0	1	0	3	0	1	0-0	.444	.444	.444	.889	0	...
2003—Minnesota (A.L.)	DH		3	11	1	1	0	0	0	0	1	4	0	0	0-0	.091	.167	.091	.258	0	...
2004—Minnesota (A.L.)	C-1B		3	3	0	1	0	0	0	0	1	1	0	0	0-0	.333	.500	.333	.833	0	1.000
Division series totals (3 years)			9	23	2	6	0	0	0	1	2	8	0	1	0-0	.261	.320	.261	.581	0	1.000

CHAMPIONSHIP SERIES RECORD

Year	Team (League)	Pos.	G	AB	R	H	2B	3B	HR	RBI	BB	SO	HBP	GDP	SB-CS	Avg.	OBP	SLG	OPS	E	Avg.
2002—Minnesota (A.L.)	DH		1	3	0	1	0	0	0	0	0	1	0	0	0-0	.333	.333	.333	.667	0	...

LEDEE, RICKY   OF

PERSONAL: Born November 22, 1973, in Ponce, Puerto Rico. ... 6-1/216. ... Bats left, throws left. ... Full name: Ricardo Alberto Ledee. ... Name pronounced: la-DAY. ... High school: Colonel Nuestra Sonora de Valvanera (Coano, Puerto Rico).

TRANSACTIONS/CAREER NOTES: Selected by New York Yankees organization in 16th round of 1990 free-agent draft. ... Traded by Yankees with two players to be named to Cleveland Indians for OF David Justice (June 29, 2000); Indians acquired P Jake Westbrook and P Zach Day to complete deal (July 24, 2000). ... Traded by Indians to Texas Rangers for 1B/DH David Segui (July 28, 2000). ... On disabled list (March 23-June 13, 2001); included rehabilitation assignment to Oklahoma. ... Signed as a free agent by Philadelphia Phillies (January 29, 2002). ... On disabled list (June 23-July 8, 2004). ... Traded by Phillies with P Alfredo Simon to San Francisco Giants for P Felix Rodriguez (July 30, 2004).

2004 GAMES PLAYED BY POSITION (MLB): OF—37, DH—2.

Year	Team (League)	Pos.	G	AB	R	H	2B	3B	HR	RBI	BB	SO	HBP	GDP	SB-CS	Avg.	OBP	SLG	OPS	E	Avg.
1990—GC Yankees (GCL)		OF	19	37	5	4	2	0	0	1	6	18	0	1	2-0	.108	.233	.162	.395	0	1.000
1991—GC Yankees (GCL)		OF	47	165	22	44	6	2	0	18	22	40	0	3	3-1	.267	.351	.327	.678	6	.934
1992—GC Yankees (GCL)		OF	52	179	25	41	9	2	2	23	24	47	1	2	1-4	.229	.322	.335	.657	2	.971
1993—Oneonta (N.Y.-Penn.)		OF	52	192	32	49	7	6	8	20	25	46	2	2	7-5	.255	.347	.479	.826	3	.970
1994—Greensboro (S. Atl.)		OF	134	484	87	121	23	9	22	71	91	126	4	7	10-11	.250	.369	.471	.840	5	.973
1995—Greensboro (S. Atl.)		OF	89	335	65	90	16	6	14	49	51	66	2	3	10-4	.269	.368	.478	.845	3	.982
1996—Norwich (East.)		OF	39	137	27	50	11	1	8	37	16	25	1	4	2-2	.365	.421	.635	1.056	1	.980
—Columbus (Int'l)		OF	96	358	79	101	22	6	21	64	44	95	1	4	6-3	.282	.360	.553	.914	5	.952
1997—Columbus (Int'l)	OF-DH		43	170	38	52	12	1	10	39	21	49	1	5	4-0	.306	.385	.565	.950	2	.966
—GC Yankees (GCL)	DH-OF		7	21	3	7	1	0	0	2	2	4	1	1	0-0	.333	.417	.381	.798	0	1.000
1998—Columbus (Int'l)	OF-DH		96	360	70	102	21	1	19	41	54	108	4	7	7-2	.283	.378	.506	.884	4	.971
—New York (A.L.)		OF	42	79	13	19	5	2	1	12	7	29	0	1	3-1	.241	.299	.392	.691	1	.981
1999—New York (A.L.)	OF-DH		88	250	45	69	13	5	9	40	28	73	0	2	4-3	.276	.346	.476	.822	9	.942
—Columbus (Int'l)		OF	30	115	18	29	7	1	4	15	17	29	0	1	4-2	.252	.346	.435	.781	3	.953
2000—New York (A.L.)	OF-DH		62	191	23	46	11	1	7	31	26	39	1	7	7-3	.241	.332	.419	.751	2	.979
—Cleveland (A.L.)		OF	17	63	13	14	2	1	2	8	8	9	0	3	0-0	.222	.310	.381	.691	0	1.000
—Texas (A.L.)		OF	58	213	23	50	6	3	4	38	25	50	1	7	6-3	.235	.317	.347	.664	3	.977
2001—Oklahoma (PCL)		OF	4	16	4	8	1	0	1	3	1	1	0	1	0-0	.500	.529	.750	1.279	0	1.000
—Texas (A.L.)		OF	78	242	33	56	21	1	2	36	23	58	3	3	3-3	.231	.303	.351	.654	3	.979
2002—Philadelphia (N.L.)		OF	96	203	33	46	13	1	8	23	35	50	1	3	1-2	.227	.342	.419	.760	0	1.000
2003—Philadelphia (N.L.)	OF-DH		121	255	37	63	15	2	13	46	34	59	0	4	0-0	.247	.334	.475	.809	0	1.000
2004—Philadelphia (N.L.)	OF-DH		73	123	19	35	7	0	7	26	22	27	0	5	2-0	.285	.393	.512	.905	0	1.000
—San Francisco (N.L.)		OF	31	53	6	6	2	0	0	4	5	20	1	1	1-0	.113	.200	.151	.351	1	.960
American League totals (4 years)			345	1038	150	254	58	13	25	165	117	258	5	23	23-13	.245	.322	.398	.720	18	.971
National League totals (3 years)			321	634	95	150	37	3	28	99	96	156	2	13	4-2	.237	.337	.437	.774	1	.996
Major League totals (7 years)			666	1672	245	404	95	16	53	264	213	414	7	36	27-15	.242	.328	.413	.740	19	.979

DIVISION SERIES RECORD

Year	Team (League)	Pos.	G	AB	R	H	2B	3B	HR	RBI	BB	SO	HBP	GDP	SB-CS	Avg.	OBP	SLG	OPS	E	Avg.
1998—New York (A.L.)				Did not play.																	
1999—New York (A.L.)		OF	3	11	1	3	2	0	0	2	1	5	0	0	0-0	.273	.333	.455	.788	0	1.000

CHAMPIONSHIP SERIES RECORD

Year Team (League)	Pos.	G	AB	R	H	2B	3B	HR	RBI	BB	SO	HBP	GDP	SB-CS	Avg.	OBP	SLG	OPS	E	Avg.
1998— New York (A.L.)	DH-OF	3	5	0	0	0	0	0	0	0	0	0	0	0-0	.000	.000	.000	.000	0	1.000
1999— New York (A.L.)	DH-OF	3	8	2	2	0	0	1	4	1	4	0	0	0-1	.250	.333	.625	.958	1	.750
Champ. series totals (2 years)		6	13	2	2	0	0	1	4	1	4	0	0	0-1	.154	.214	.385	.599	1	.857

WORLD SERIES RECORD

Year Team (League)	Pos.	G	AB	R	H	2B	3B	HR	RBI	BB	SO	HBP	GDP	SB-CS	Avg.	OBP	SLG	OPS	E	Avg.
1998— New York (A.L.)	OF	4	10	1	6	3	0	0	4	2	1	0	0	0-1	.600	.615	.900	1.515	0	1.000
1999— New York (A.L.)	OF	3	10	0	2	1	0	0	1	1	4	0	0	0-0	.200	.273	.300	.573	0	1.000
World series totals (2 years)		7	20	1	8	4	0	0	5	3	5	0	0	0-1	.400	.458	.600	1.058	0	1.000

LEDEZMA, WILFREDO — P

PERSONAL: Born January 21, 1981, in Guarico, Venezuela. ... 6-4/212. ... Throws left, bats left. ... Full name: Wilfredo J. Ledezma. ... College: Cuidad Jardin University.

TRANSACTIONS/CAREER NOTES: Signed as a non-drafted free agent by Boston Red Sox organization (April 3, 1998). ... Selected by Detroit Tigers from Red Sox organization in Rule 5 major league draft (December 16, 2002).

CAREER HITTING: 0-for-0 (.000), 0 R, 0 2B, 0 3B, 0 HR, 0 RBI.

Year Team (League)	W	L	Pct.	ERA	WHIP	G	GS	CG	ShO	Hld.	Sv.-Opp.	IP	H	R	ER	HR	BB-IBB	SO	Avg.
1999— GC Red Sox (GCL)	5	1	.833	3.30	1.24	13	6	0	0	...	1-...	57.1	51	28	21	2	20-0	52	.233
2000— Augusta (S. Atl.)	2	4	.333	5.13	1.65	14	14	0	0	...	0-...	52.2	51	33	30	3	36-0	60	.256
2002— Augusta (S. Atl.)	2	2	.500	3.80	1.31	5	5	0	0	...	0-...	23.2	23	10	10	0	8-0	38	.250
— GC Red Sox (GCL)	0	0	...	6.00	1.33	1	0	0	0	...	0-...	3.0	4	2	2	0	0-0	3	.308
2003— Detroit (A.L.)	3	7	.300	5.79	1.60	34	8	0	0	1	0-1	84.0	99	55	54	12	35-3	49	.297
2004— Erie (East.)	10	3	.769	2.42	1.07	17	16	2	1	...	0-...	111.2	95	36	30	8	24-0	98	.228
— Detroit (A.L.)	4	3	.571	4.39	1.37	15	8	0	0	...	0-1	53.1	55	28	26	3	18-0	29	.272
Major League totals (2 years)	7	10	.412	5.24	1.51	49	16	0	0	1	0-2	137.1	154	83	80	15	53-3	78	.288

LEE, CARLOS — OF

PERSONAL: Born June 20, 1976, in Aguadulce, Panama. ... 6-2/240. ... Bats right, throws right. ... Full name: Carlos Noriel Lee.

TRANSACTIONS/CAREER NOTES: Signed as a non-drafted free agent by Chicago White Sox organization (February 8, 1994). ... On suspended list (April 28-May 1, 2000).

2004 GAMES PLAYED BY POSITION (MLB): OF—148, DH—5.

Year Team (League)	Pos.	G	AB	R	H	2B	3B	HR	RBI	BB	SO	HBP	GDP	SB-CS	Avg.	OBP	SLG	OPS	E	Avg.
1994— GC Whi. Sox (GCL)	3B	29	56	6	7	1	0	0	1	4	8	0	1	0-1	.125	.183	.143	.326	2	.959
1995— Hickory (S. Atl.)	3B	63	218	18	54	9	1	4	30	8	34	1	7	1-5	.248	.278	.353	.631	19	.848
— Bristol (Appal.)	3B-1B	67	269	43	93	17	1	7	45	8	34	2	6	17-7	.346	.365	.494	.860	18	.914
1996— Hickory (S. Atl.)	3B-1B	119	480	65	150	23	6	8	70	23	50	0	15	18-13	.313	.337	.435	.772	32	.923
1997— Win.-Salem (Car.)	3B-DH	139	546	81	173	50	4	17	82	36	65	2	12	11-5	.317	.357	.516	.874	34	.906
1998— Birmingham (Sou.)	3B-DH	138	549	77	166	33	2	21	106	39	55	2	32	11-5	.302	.350	.485	.834	35	.902
1999— Charlotte (Int'l)	3B-OF-1B	25	94	16	33	5	0	4	20	8	14	1	3	2-1	.351	.396	.532	.928	4	.951
— Chicago (A.L.)	OF-DH-1B	127	492	66	144	32	2	16	84	13	72	4	11	4-2	.293	.312	.463	.775	5	.979
2000— Chicago (A.L.)	OF-DH	152	572	107	172	29	2	24	92	38	94	3	17	13-4	.301	.345	.484	.829	3	.990
2001— Chicago (A.L.)	OF-DH	150	558	75	150	33	3	24	84	38	85	6	15	17-7	.269	.321	.468	.789	8	.969
2002— Chicago (A.L.)	OF-DH	140	492	82	130	26	2	26	80	75	73	2	5	1-4	.264	.359	.484	.843	1	.996
2003— Chicago (A.L.)	OF-DH	158	623	100	181	35	1	31	113	37	91	4	20	18-4	.291	.331	.499	.830	7	.978
2004— Chicago (A.L.)	OF-DH	153	591	103	180	37	0	31	99	54	86	7	10	11-5	.305	.366	.525	.891	0	1.000
Major League totals (6 years)		880	3328	533	957	192	10	152	552	255	501	26	78	64-26	.288	.340	.488	.828	24	.985

DIVISION SERIES RECORD

Year Team (League)	Pos.	G	AB	R	H	2B	3B	HR	RBI	BB	SO	HBP	GDP	SB-CS	Avg.	OBP	SLG	OPS	E	Avg.
2000— Chicago (A.L.)	OF	3	11	0	1	1	0	0	1	0	2	0	0	0-0	.091	.083	.182	.265	0	1.000

LEE, CLIFF — P

PERSONAL: Born August 30, 1978, in Benton, Ark. ... 6-3/190. ... Throws left, bats left. ... Full name: Clifton Phifer Lee. ... High school: Benton (Ark.). ... College: Arkansas.

TRANSACTIONS/CAREER NOTES: Selected by Montreal Expos organization in fourth round of 2000 free-agent draft. ... Traded by Expos with 1B Lee Stevens, SS Brandon Phillips and OF Grady Sizemore to Cleveland Indians for P Bartolo Colon and future considerations (June 27, 2002); Expos acquired P Tim Drew to complete deal (June 28, 2002). ... On disabled list (March 29-May 30, 2003); included rehabilitation assignment to Kinston. ... On suspended list (June 24-July 1, 2004).

CAREER HITTING: 1-for-3 (.333), 0 R, 0 2B, 0 3B, 0 HR, 0 RBI.

Year Team (League)	W	L	Pct.	ERA	WHIP	G	GS	CG	ShO	Hld.	Sv.-Opp.	IP	H	R	ER	HR	BB-IBB	SO	Avg.
2000— Cape Fear (S. Atl.)	1	4	.200	5.24	1.93	11	11	0	0	...	0-...	44.2	50	39	26	1	36-0	63	.281
2001— Jupiter (FSL)	6	7	.462	2.79	1.13	21	20	0	0	...	0-...	109.2	78	43	34	13	46-0	129	.199
2002— Harrisburg (Eastern)	7	2	.778	3.23	0.97	15	15	0	0	...	0-...	86.1	61	31	31	12	23-0	105	.197
— Akron (East.)	2	1	.667	5.40	1.26	3	3	0	0	...	0-...	16.2	11	11	10	1	10-0	18	.180
— Buffalo (Int'l)	3	2	.600	3.77	1.35	8	8	0	0	...	0-...	43.0	36	18	18	7	22-0	30	.229
— Cleveland (A.L.)	0	1	.000	1.74	1.35	2	2	0	0	0	0-0	10.1	6	2	2	1	8-1	6	.171
2003— Kinston (Caro.)	0	0	...	0.00	0.70	1	1	0	0	...	0-...	4.1	0	1	0	0	3-0	4	.000
— Akron (East.)	1	0	1.000	1.50	0.90	2	2	0	0	...	0-...	12.0	7	2	2	1	4-0	13	.167
— Buffalo (Int'l)	6	1	.857	3.27	1.50	11	11	0	0	...	0-...	63.1	62	24	23	4	31-0	61	.261
— Cleveland (A.L.)	3	3	.500	3.61	1.17	9	9	0	0	0	0-0	52.1	41	28	21	7	20-1	44	.220
2004— Cleveland (A.L.)	14	8	.636	5.43	1.50	33	33	0	0	0	0-0	179.0	188	113	108	30	81-1	161	.268
Major League totals (3 years)	17	12	.586	4.88	1.42	44	44	0	0	0	0-0	241.2	235	143	131	37	109-3	211	.255

LEE, DAVE — P

PERSONAL: Born March 12, 1973, in Pittsburgh, Pa. ... 6-1/200. ... Throws right, bats right. ... Full name: David Emmer Lee. ... High school: Langley (Pittsburgh). ... College: Mercyhurst (Pa.).

TRANSACTIONS/CAREER NOTES: Selected by Colorado Rockies organization in 23rd round of 1995 free-agent draft. ... Released by Rockies (July 17, 1995). ... Re-signed by Rockies organization (Feburary 2, 1996). ... Traded by Rockies to New York Yankees for P Jay Tessmer and IF Seth Taylor (January 3, 2001). ... Traded by Yankees to San Diego Padres for P Carlos Almanzar (March 25, 2001). ... On disabled list (July 25-August 31, 2001); included rehabilitation assignment to Mobile. ... Released by Padres (November 16, 2001). ... Signed by Minnesota Twins organization (January 29, 2002). ... Signed as a free agent by Los Angeles Dodgers organization (December 17, 2002). ... Traded by Dodgers to Cleveland Indians for OF Alex Requena (September 4, 2003). ... Refused minor league assignment and became a free agent (October 4, 2004).

CAREER HITTING: 1-for-6 (.167), 1 R, 0 2B, 0 3B, 0 HR, 0 RBI.

Year Team (League)	W	L	Pct.	ERA	WHIP	G	GS	CG	ShO	Hld.	Sv.-Opp.	IP	H	R	ER	HR	BB-IBB	SO	Avg.
1996— Portland (N'west)	5	1	.833	0.78	1.26	17	0	0	0	...	7-...	23.0	13	3	2	0	16-3	24	.171
—Salem (Caro.)	0	2	.000	2.25	1.67	8	0	0	0	...	1-...	12.0	14	6	3	1	6-0	10	.292
1997—Asheville (S. Atl.)	4	8	.333	4.08	1.58	51	0	0	0	...	22-...	53.0	61	30	24	5	23-0	59	.289
1998—Salem (Caro.)	3	5	.375	3.77	1.26	54	0	0	0	...	25-...	57.1	57	26	24	2	15-1	54	.261
1999—Carolina (Southern)	0	0	...	1.04	0.63	16	0	0	0	...	10-...	17.1	8	3	2	1	3-0	16	.136
—Colorado (N.L.)	3	2	.600	3.67	1.47	36	0	0	0	2	0-0	49.0	43	21	20	4	29-1	38	.247
—Colo. Springs (PCL)	0	0	...	0.00	0.18	6	0	0	0	...	3-...	5.2	0	0	0	0	1-0	7	.000
2000—Colorado (N.L.)	0	0	...	11.12	2.82	7	0	0	0	1	1-1	5.2	10	9	7	3	6-0	6	.357
—Colo. Springs (PCL)	2	3	.400	5.96	1.61	47	0	0	0	...	12-...	48.1	50	38	32	9	28-1	44	.265
2001—Portland (PCL)	1	0	1.000	0.75	0.83	9	0	0	0	...	1-...	12.0	5	1	1	0	5-1	14	.132
—San Diego (N.L.)	1	0	1.000	3.70	1.62	41	0	0	0	4	0-0	48.2	52	20	20	6	27-1	42	.278
—Mobile (Sou.)	0	0	...	0.00	1.00	2	0	0	0	...	0-...	2.0	2	0	0	0	0-0	3	.286
2002—Edmonton (PCL)	9	1	.900	4.59	1.72	51	0	0	0	...	5-...	64.2	80	44	33	5	31-3	70	.296
2003—Las Vegas (PCL)	3	2	.600	3.13	1.40	56	0	0	0	...	9-...	60.1	47	22	21	4	36-3	61	.212
—Cleveland (A.L.)	1	0	1.000	4.70	1.30	8	0	0	0	1	0-0	7.2	4	4	4	1	6-1	7	.143
2004—Cleveland (A.L.)	0	0	...	10.38	2.77	4	0	0	0	0	0-0	4.1	8	7	5	0	4-0	4	.348
—Buffalo (Int'l)	2	4	.333	4.88	1.48	51	0	0	0	...	9-...	66.1	63	37	36	6	35-3	55	.256
American League totals (2 years)	1	0	1.000	6.75	1.83	12	0	0	0	1	0-0	12.0	12	11	9	1	10-1	11	.235
National League totals (3 years)	4	2	.667	4.09	1.62	84	0	0	0	7	1-1	103.1	105	50	47	13	62-2	86	.270
Major League totals (5 years)	5	2	.714	4.37	1.64	96	0	0	0	8	1-1	115.1	117	61	56	14	72-3	97	.266

LEE, DERREK   1B

PERSONAL: Born September 6, 1975, in Sacramento, Calif. ... 6-5/245. ... Bats right, throws right. ... Full name: Derrek Leon Lee. ... High school: El Camino (Sacramento). ... Nephew of Leron Lee, outfielder with four major league teams (1969-76) and Lotte Orions (1977-87) of Japan League.

TRANSACTIONS/CAREER NOTES: Selected by San Diego Padres in first round (14th pick overall) of 1993 free-agent draft. ... Traded by Padres with Ps Rafael Medina and Steve Hoff to Florida Marlins for P Kevin Brown (December 15, 1997). ... Traded by Marlins to Chicago Cubs for 1B Hee Seop Choi and P Mike Nannini (November 25, 2003).

HONORS: Won N.L. Gold Glove at first base (2003).

2004 GAMES PLAYED BY POSITION (MLB): 1B—161.

Year Team (League)	Pos.	G	AB	R	H	2B	3B	HR	RBI	BB	SO	HBP	GDP	SB-CS	Avg.	OBP	SLG	OPS	E	Avg.
1993— Ariz. Padres (Ariz.)	1B	15	52	11	17	1	1	2	5	6	7	0	1	4-0	.327	.397	.500	.897	2	.985
—Rancho Cuca. (Calif.)	DH-1B	20	73	13	20	5	1	1	10	10	20	1	0	0-2	.274	.369	.411	.780	5	.960
1994—Rancho Cuca. (Calif.)	DH-1B	126	442	66	118	19	2	8	53	42	95	7	11	18-14	.267	.336	.373	.709	4	.988
1995—Rancho Cuca. (Calif.)	1B	128	502	82	151	25	2	23	95	49	130	7	8	14-7	.301	.366	.496	.862	18	.983
—Memphis (Sou.)	1B	2	9	0	1	0	0	0	1	0	2	0	0	0-0	.111	.111	.111	.222	0	1.000
1996—Memphis (Sou.)	1B-3B-DH	134	500	98	140	39	2	34	104	65	170	2	8	13-6	.280	.360	.570	.930	11	.991
1997—Las Vegas (PCL)	1B	125	472	86	153	29	2	13	64	60	116	0	9	17-3	.324	.399	.477	.876	9	.992
—San Diego (N.L.)	1B	22	54	9	14	3	0	1	4	9	24	0	1	0-0	.259	.365	.370	.735	0	1.000
1998—Florida (N.L.)	1B	141	454	62	106	29	1	17	74	47	120	10	12	5-2	.233	.318	.414	.732	8	.993
1999—Florida (N.L.)	1B	70	218	21	45	9	1	5	20	17	70	0	3	2-1	.206	.263	.326	.588	3	.994
—Calgary (PCL)	1B-DH	89	339	60	96	20	1	19	73	30	90	4	7	3-4	.283	.345	.516	.861	14	.983
2000—Florida (N.L.)	1B	158	477	70	134	18	3	28	70	63	123	4	14	0-3	.281	.368	.507	.875	8	.993
2001—Florida (N.L.)	1B	158	561	83	158	37	4	21	75	50	126	6	18	4-2	.282	.346	.474	.820	8	.994
2002—Florida (N.L.)	1B	•162	581	95	157	35	7	27	86	98	164	5	14	19-9	.270	.378	.494	.872	12	.992
2003—Florida (N.L.)	1B	155	539	91	146	31	2	31	92	88	131	10	9	21-8	.271	.379	.508	.888	5	.996
2004—Chicago (N.L.)	1B	161	605	90	168	39	1	32	98	68	128	8	14	12-5	.278	.356	.504	.860	6	.996
Major League totals (8 years)		1027	3489	521	928	201	19	162	519	440	886	45	85	63-30	.266	.353	.474	.827	50	.994

DIVISION SERIES RECORD

Year Team (League)	Pos.	G	AB	R	H	2B	3B	HR	RBI	BB	SO	HBP	GDP	SB-CS	Avg.	OBP	SLG	OPS	E	Avg.
2003— Florida (N.L.)	1B	4	16	2	4	1	0	0	2	1	2	2	0	1-0	.250	.368	.313	.681	0	1.000

CHAMPIONSHIP SERIES RECORD

Year Team (League)	Pos.	G	AB	R	H	2B	3B	HR	RBI	BB	SO	HBP	GDP	SB-CS	Avg.	OBP	SLG	OPS	E	Avg.
2003— Florida (N.L.)	1B	7	32	2	6	2	0	1	4	1	8	1	2	1-0	.188	.235	.344	.579	0	1.000

WORLD SERIES RECORD

Year Team (League)	Pos.	G	AB	R	H	2B	3B	HR	RBI	BB	SO	HBP	GDP	SB-CS	Avg.	OBP	SLG	OPS	E	Avg.
2003— Florida (N.L.)	1B	6	24	2	5	0	0	0	2	1	7	0	1	0-0	.208	.240	.208	.448	1	.977

LEE, TRAVIS   1B

PERSONAL: Born May 26, 1975, in San Diego, Calif. ... 6-3/225. ... Bats left, throws left. ... Full name: Travis Reynolds Lee. ... High school: Olympia (Wash.). ... College: San Diego State.

TRANSACTIONS/CAREER NOTES: Selected by Minnesota Twins organization in first round (second pick overall) of 1996 free-agent draft. ... Granted free agency (June 19, 1996). ... Signed by Arizona Diamondbacks organization (October 15, 1996). ... Loaned by Diamondbacks organization to Milwaukee Brewers organization (June 5, 1997-remainder of season). ... On disabled list (July 25-August 9, 1998; and August 16-September 9, 1999). ... On disabled list (May 25-June 9, 2000); included rehabilitation assignment to El Paso. ... Traded by Diamondbacks with Ps Vicente Padilla, Omar Daal and Nelson Figueroa to Philadelphia Phillies for P Curt Schilling (July 26, 2000). ... Signed as a free agent by Tampa Bay Devil Rays (February 6, 2003). ... On disabled list (April 14-29, 2003). ... Signed as a free agent by New York Yankees (March 2, 2004). ... On disabled list (March 29-April 17 and May 1, 2004-remainder of season); included rehabilitation assignment to Tampa.

2004 GAMES PLAYED BY POSITION (MLB): 1B—6.

Year Team (League)	Pos.	G	AB	R	H	2B	3B	HR	RBI	BB	SO	HBP	GDP	SB-CS	Avg.	OBP	SLG	OPS	E	Avg.
1997— High Desert (Calif.)	1B-DH	61	226	63	82	18	1	18	63	47	36	3	8	5-1	.363	.473	.690	1.163	1	.998
—Tucson (PCL)	1B-DH-OF	59	227	42	68	16	2	14	46	31	46	2	10	2-0	.300	.387	.573	.960	3	.993
1998—Arizona (N.L.)	1B	146	562	71	151	20	2	22	72	67	123	0	13	8-1	.269	.346	.429	.775	3	.998
1999—Arizona (N.L.)	1B-OF	120	375	57	89	16	2	9	50	58	50	0	10	17-3	.237	.337	.363	.700	3	.997
2000—Arizona (N.L.)	OF-1B	72	224	34	52	13	0	8	40	25	46	0	6	5-1	.232	.308	.397	.705	4	.983
—El Paso (Texas)	1B-OF	3	10	0	2	0	0	0	0	2	1	0	1	0-0	.200	.333	.200	.533	0	1.000
—Tucson (PCL)	1B-OF	7	30	4	11	4	0	0	3	1	6	0	1	1-0	.367	.387	.500	.887	0	1.000
—Philadelphia (N.L.)	1B-OF	56	180	19	43	11	1	1	14	40	33	2	6	3-0	.239	.381	.328	.709	0	1.000

Year Team (League)	Pos.	G	AB	R	H	2B	3B	HR	RBI	BB	SO	HBP	GDP	SB-CS	Avg.	OBP	SLG	OPS	E	Avg.
2001— Philadelphia (N.L.)	1B	157	555	75	143	34	2	20	90	71	109	4	15	3-4	.258	.341	.434	.775	6	.996
2002— Philadelphia (N.L.)	1B	153	536	55	142	26	2	13	70	54	104	0	12	5-3	.265	.331	.394	.725	6	.996
2003— Tampa Bay (A.L.)	1B-DH	145	542	75	149	37	3	19	70	64	97	0	13	6-2	.275	.348	.459	.807	3	.998
2004— Tampa (Fla. St.)	1B	3	12	2	3	1	0	0	3	1	4	0	1	0-0	.250	.308	.333	.641	0	1.000
— New York (A.L.)	1B	7	19	1	2	1	0	0	2	1	3	0	2	0-0	.105	.150	.158	.308	0	1.000
American League totals (2 years)		152	561	76	151	38	3	19	72	65	100	0	15	6-2	.269	.342	.449	.791	3	.998
National League totals (5 years)		704	2432	311	620	120	9	73	336	315	465	6	62	41-12	.255	.340	.402	.741	22	.996
Major League totals (7 years)		856	2993	387	771	158	12	92	408	380	565	6	77	47-14	.258	.340	.411	.751	25	.996

LEHR, JUSTIN   P

PERSONAL: Born August 3, 1977, in Orange, Calif. ... 6-1/200. ... Throws right, bats right. ... Full name: Charles Larry Lehr. ... High school: West Covina (Calif.). ... College: USC.

TRANSACTIONS/CAREER NOTES: Selected by Detroit Tigers organization in 15th round of 1995 free-agent draft; did not sign. ... Selected by Anaheim Angels organization in 10th round of 1998 free-agent draft; did not sign. ... Selected by Oakland Athletics organization in eighth round of 1999 free-agent draft.

CAREER HITTING: 0-for-0 (.000), 0 R, 0 2B, 0 3B, 0 HR, 0 RBI.

Year Team (League)	W	L	Pct.	ERA	WHIP	G	GS	CG	ShO	Hld.	Sv.-Opp.	IP	H	R	ER	HR	BB-IBB	SO	Avg.
1999— S. Oregon (N'west)	2	6	.250	5.95	1.87	14	4	0	0	...	0-...	42.1	62	36	28	3	17-3	40	.341
2000— Sacramento (PCL)	0	0	...	11.25	2.50	1	1	0	0	...	0-...	4.0	7	5	5	1	3-0	3	.389
— Modesto (Calif.)	13	6	.684	3.19	1.18	29	25	0	0	...	0-...	175.0	161	71	62	10	46-1	138	.249
2001— Midland (Texas)	11	12	.478	5.45	1.60	29	27	0	0	...	0-...	155.1	206	107	94	20	43-1	103	.318
2002— Midland (Texas)	8	3	.727	4.05	1.49	58	0	0	0	...	4-...	80.0	88	39	36	7	31-10	59	.290
2003— Sacramento (PCL)	3	2	.600	3.72	1.35	53	0	0	0	...	4-...	75.0	74	34	31	3	27-3	64	.259
2004— Sacramento (PCL)	4	2	.667	2.65	1.26	32	0	0	0	...	13-...	37.1	37	14	11	1	10-0	40	.250
— Oakland (A.L.)	1	1	.500	5.23	1.50	27	0	0	0	5	0-1	32.2	35	19	19	3	14-2	16	.280
Major League totals (1 year)	1	1	.500	5.23	1.50	27	0	0	0	5	0-1	32.2	35	19	19	3	14-2	16	.280

LEICESTER, JON   P

PERSONAL: Born February 7, 1979, in Mariposa, Calif. ... 6-2/220. ... Throws right, bats right. ... Full name: Jonathan David Leicester. ... Name pronounced: lester. ... High school: Palisades Charter (Pacific Palisades, Calif.). ... College: Memphis.

TRANSACTIONS/CAREER NOTES: Selected by Chicago Cubs organization in 11th round of 2000 free-agent draft.

CAREER HITTING: 0-for-1 (.000), 0 R, 0 2B, 0 3B, 0 HR, 0 RBI.

Year Team (League)	W	L	Pct.	ERA	WHIP	G	GS	CG	ShO	Hld.	Sv.-Opp.	IP	H	R	ER	HR	BB-IBB	SO	Avg.
2000— Eugene (N'west)	1	5	.167	5.44	1.39	17	7	0	0	...	0-...	49.2	47	36	30	4	22-1	31	.247
2001— Lansing (Midw.)	9	10	.474	5.29	1.57	28	27	1	0	...	0-...	153.0	182	117	90	16	58-0	109	.297
2002— Daytona (Fla. St.)	2	3	.400	3.97	1.53	20	14	0	0	...	0-...	81.2	77	43	36	2	48-1	57	.248
— West Tenn (Sou.)	2	2	.500	4.61	1.35	5	4	0	0	...	0-...	27.1	24	16	14	1	13-0	18	.231
2003— West Tenn (Sou.)	6	7	.462	3.89	1.34	45	9	1	1	...	6-...	106.1	89	54	46	7	53-0	106	.227
— Iowa (PCL)	0	0	...	7.20	1.60	1	1	0	0	...	0-...	5.0	6	4	4	0	2-0	4	.316
2004— Iowa (PCL)	6	2	.750	3.70	1.48	12	12	0	0	...	0-...	65.2	61	31	27	3	36-0	60	.244
— Chicago (N.L.)	5	1	.833	3.89	1.32	32	0	0	0	5	0-2	41.2	40	20	18	7	15-0	35	.256
Major League totals (1 year)	5	1	.833	3.89	1.32	32	0	0	0	5	0-2	41.2	40	20	18	7	15-0	35	.256

LEITER, AL   P

PERSONAL: Born October 23, 1965, in Toms River, N.J. ... 6-3/220. ... Throws left, bats left. ... Full name: Alois Terry Leiter. ... Name pronounced: LIGH-ter. ... High school: Central Regional (Bayville, N.J.). ... Brother of Mark Leiter, pitcher with eight major league teams (1990-99 and 2001).

TRANSACTIONS/CAREER NOTES: Selected by New York Yankees organization in second round of June 1984 free-agent draft. ... On disabled list (June 22-July 26, 1988); included rehabilitation assignment to Columbus. ... Traded by Yankees to Toronto Blue Jays for OF Jesse Barfield (April 30, 1989). ... On disabled list (May 11, 1989-remainder of season); included rehabilitation assignment to Dunedin. ... On disabled list (April 27, 1991-remainder of season); included rehabilitation assignments to Dunedin. ... On disabled list (April 24-May 9, 1993; and June 9-24, 1994). ... Signed as a free agent by Florida Marlins (December 14, 1995). ... On disabled list (May 1-20 and August 13-29, 1997). ... Traded by Marlins with 2B Ralph Milliard to New York Mets for Ps Jesus Sanchez and P A.J. Burnett and OF Robert Stratton (February 6, 1998). ... On disabled list (June 27-July 18, 1998; April 21-May 18, 2001; June 30-July 20, 2003; and May 12-June 1, 2004).

CAREER HITTING: 45-for-512 (.088), 15 R, 7 2B, 1 3B, 0 HR, 16 RBI.

Year Team (League)	W	L	Pct.	ERA	WHIP	G	GS	CG	ShO	Hld.	Sv.-Opp.	IP	H	R	ER	HR	BB-IBB	SO	Avg.
1984— Oneonta (N.Y.-Penn)	3	2	.600	3.63	1.37	10	10	0	0	...	0-...	57.0	52	32	23	1	26-0	48	.241
1985— Fort Lauderdale (FSL)	1	6	.143	6.48	1.76	17	17	1	0	...	0-...	82.0	87	70	59	3	57-1	44	.270
— Oneonta (N.Y.-Penn)	3	2	.600	2.37	1.37	6	6	2	0	...	0-...	38.0	27	14	10	0	25-0	34	.213
1986— Fort Lauderdale (FSL)	4	8	.333	4.05	1.58	22	21	1	1	...	0-...	117.2	96	64	53	2	90-1	101	.226
1987— Columbus (Int'l)	1	4	.200	6.17	1.54	5	5	0	0	...	0-...	23.1	21	18	16	1	15-0	23	.250
— Alb./Colon. (East.)	3	3	.500	3.35	1.29	15	14	2	0	...	0-...	78.0	64	34	29	4	37-0	71	.227
— New York (A.L.)	2	2	.500	6.35	1.72	4	4	0	0	0	0-0	22.2	24	16	16	2	15-0	28	.273
1988— New York (A.L.)	4	4	.500	3.92	1.43	14	14	0	0	0	0-0	57.1	49	27	25	7	33-0	60	.231
— Columbus (Int'l)	0	2	.000	3.46	1.46	4	4	0	0	...	0-...	13.0	5	7	5	0	14-0	12	.122
1989— New York (A.L.)	1	2	.333	6.08	1.65	4	4	0	0	0	0-0	26.2	23	20	18	1	21-0	22	.235
— Toronto (A.L.)	0	0	...	4.05	1.65	1	1	0	0	0	0-0	6.2	9	3	3	1	2-0	4	.310
— Dunedin (Fla. St.)	0	2	.000	5.63	2.00	3	3	0	0	...	0-...	8.0	11	5	5	0	5-0	4	.324
1990— Dunedin (Fla. St.)	0	0	...	2.63	1.25	6	6	0	0	...	0-...	24.0	18	8	7	1	12-0	14	.209
— Syracuse (Int'l)	3	8	.273	4.62	1.63	15	14	1	1	...	0-...	78.0	59	43	40	4	68-0	69	.215
— Toronto (A.L.)	0	0	...	0.00	0.47	4	0	0	0	0	0-0	6.1	1	0	0	0	2-0	5	.050
1991— Toronto (A.L.)	0	0	...	27.00	4.80	3	0	0	0	0	0-0	1.2	3	5	5	0	5-0	1	.429
— Dunedin (Fla. St.)	0	0	...	1.86	1.24	4	3	0	0	...	0-...	9.2	5	2	2	0	7-0	5	.161
1992— Syracuse (Int'l)	8	9	.471	3.86	1.37	27	27	3	1	...	0-...	163.1	159	82	70	7	64-0	108	.256
— Toronto (A.L.)	0	0	...	9.00	3.00	1	0	0	0	0	0-0	1.0	1	1	1	0	2-0	0	.200
1993— Toronto (A.L.)	9	6	.600	4.11	1.42	34	12	1	1	3	2-3	105.0	93	52	48	8	56-2	66	.240
1994— Toronto (A.L.)	6	7	.462	5.08	1.70	20	20	1	0	0	0-0	111.2	125	68	63	6	65-3	100	.285
1995— Toronto (A.L.)	11	11	.500	3.64	1.48	28	28	2	1	0	0-0	183.0	162	80	74	15	* 108-1	153	.238
1996— Florida (N.L.)	16	12	.571	2.93	1.26	33	33	2	1	0	0-0	215.1	153	74	70	14	* 119-3	200	.202
1997— Florida (N.L.)	11	9	.550	4.34	1.48	27	27	0	0	0	0-0	151.1	133	78	73	13	91-4	132	.241
1998— New York (N.L.)	17	6	.739	2.47	1.15	28	28	4	2	0	0-0	193.0	151	55	53	8	71-2	174	.216
1999— New York (N.L.)	13	12	.520	4.23	1.42	32	32	1	1	0	0-0	213.0	209	107	100	19	93-8	162	.262

Year Team (League)	W	L	Pct.	ERA	WHIP	G	GS	CG	ShO	Hld.	Sv.-Opp.	IP	H	R	ER	HR	BB-IBB	SO	Avg.
2000— New York (N.L.)	16	8	.667	3.20	1.21	31	31	2	1	0	0-0	208.0	176	84	74	19	76-1	200	.228
2001— New York (N.L.)	11	11	.500	3.31	1.20	29	29	0	0	0	0-0	187.1	178	81	69	18	46-3	142	.252
2002— New York (N.L.)	13	13	.500	3.48	1.29	33	33	2	2	0	0-0	204.1	194	99	79	23	69-5	172	.250
2003— New York (N.L.)	15	9	.625	3.99	1.49	30	30	1	1	0	0-0	180.2	176	83	80	15	94-11	139	.260
2004— New York (N.L.)	10	8	.556	3.21	1.35	30	30	0	0	0	0-0	173.2	138	65	62	16	97-8	117	.218
American League totals (9 years)	33	32	.508	4.36	1.53	113	83	4	2	3	2-3	522.0	490	272	253	40	309-6	439	.249
National League totals (9 years)	122	88	.581	3.44	1.31	273	273	12	8	0	0-0	1726.2	1508	726	660	145	756-45	1438	.237
Major League totals (18 years)	155	120	.564	3.65	1.36	386	356	16	10	3	2-3	2248.2	1998	998	913	185	1065-51	1877	.240

DIVISION SERIES RECORD

Year Team (League)	W	L	Pct.	ERA	WHIP	G	GS	CG	ShO	Hld.	Sv.-Opp.	IP	H	R	ER	HR	BB-IBB	SO	Avg.
1997— Florida (N.L.)	0	0	...	9.00	2.50	1	1	0	0	0	0-0	4.0	7	4	4	1	3-0	3	.500
1999— New York (N.L.)	0	0	...	3.52	0.78	1	1	0	0	0	0-0	7.2	3	3	3	1	3-0	4	.125
2000— New York (N.L.)	0	0	...	2.25	1.00	1	1	0	0	0	0-0	8.0	5	2	2	0	3-0	6	.185
Division series totals (3 years)	0	0	...	4.12	1.22	3	3	0	0	0	0-0	19.2	15	9	9	2	9-0	13	.231

CHAMPIONSHIP SERIES RECORD

Year Team (League)	W	L	Pct.	ERA	WHIP	G	GS	CG	ShO	Hld.	Sv.-Opp.	IP	H	R	ER	HR	BB-IBB	SO	Avg.
1993— Toronto (A.L.)	0	0	...	3.38	2.25	2	0	0	0	1	0-0	2.2	4	1	1	0	2-1	2	.364
1997— Florida (N.L.)	0	1	.000	4.32	1.80	2	1	0	0	0	0-0	8.1	13	4	4	1	2-0	6	.382
1999— New York (N.L.)	0	1	.000	6.43	1.29	2	2	0	0	0	0-0	7.0	5	6	5	0	4-0	5	.200
2000— New York (N.L.)	0	0	...	3.86	1.14	1	1	0	0	0	0-0	7.0	8	3	3	0	0-0	9	.286
Champ. series totals (4 years)	0	2	.000	4.68	1.52	7	4	0	0	1	0-0	25.0	30	14	13	1	8-1	22	.306

WORLD SERIES RECORD

Year Team (League)	W	L	Pct.	ERA	WHIP	G	GS	CG	ShO	Hld.	Sv.-Opp.	IP	H	R	ER	HR	BB-IBB	SO	Avg.
1993— Toronto (A.L.)	1	0	1.000	7.71	2.00	3	0	0	0	0	0-0	7.0	12	6	6	2	2-0	5	.375
1997— Florida (N.L.)	0	0	...	5.06	1.88	2	2	0	0	0	0-0	10.2	10	9	6	1	10-1	10	.244
2000— New York (N.L.)	0	1	.000	2.87	1.15	2	2	0	0	0	0-0	15.2	12	6	5	2	6-1	16	.207
World series totals (3 years)	1	1	.500	4.59	1.56	7	4	0	0	0	0-0	33.1	34	21	17	5	18-2	31	.260

ALL-STAR GAME RECORD

	W	L	Pct.	ERA	WHIP	G	GS	CG	ShO	Hld.	Sv.-Opp.	IP	H	R	ER	HR	BB-IBB	SO	Avg.
All-Star Game totals (2 years)	0	1	.000	6.75	2.25	2	0	0	0	0	0-0	1.1	2	2	1	0	1-0	1	.286

L

LEON, JOSE — 1B/3B

PERSONAL: Born December 8, 1976, in Caguas, Puerto Rico. ... 6-0/222. ... Bats right, throws right. ... Full name: Jose Geraldo Leon. ... Name pronounced: lee-OWN. ... High school: Tecnico de Portiro (Cayey, Puerto Rico).

TRANSACTIONS/CAREER NOTES: Selected by St. Louis Cardinals organization in 22nd round of 1994 free-agent draft. ... Traded by Cardinals to Baltimore Orioles for 1B Will Clark and cash (July 31, 2000). ... Refused minor league assignment and became a free agent (October 9, 2004).

2004 GAMES PLAYED BY POSITION (MLB): 1B—16, 3B—6, DH—5.

Year Team (League)	Pos.	G	AB	R	H	2B	3B	HR	RBI	BB	SO	HBP	GDP	SB-CS	Avg.	OBP	SLG	OPS	E	Avg.
1994— Ariz. Cardinals (Ariz.)	3B-2B	46	161	16	37	3	2	0	17	11	51	3	4	1-4	.230	.285	.273	.558	11	.922
1995— Savannah (S. Atl.)	3B-OF	41	133	15	22	4	1	0	11	10	46	1	6	0-1	.165	.229	.211	.440	8	.814
1996— Johnson City (App.)	3B-1B	59	222	29	55	9	3	10	36	17	92	2	1	5-3	.248	.306	.450	.756	11	.960
— New Jersey (N.Y.-Penn.)	3B	7	28	4	8	3	1	1	3	0	7	2	0	0-0	.286	.333	.571	.905	3	.833
1997— Peoria (Midw.) 3B-OF-1B	118	399	50	92	21	2	20	54	32	122	9	10	6-5	.231	.301	.444	.745	25	.903
1998— Prince Will. (Car.)	3B-1B	124	436	77	127	31	3	21	74	53	137	9	6	5-3	.291	.376	.521	.897	25	.935
1999— Arkansas (Texas)	3B-OF	112	335	37	78	17	0	18	54	25	114	6	5	3-3	.233	.297	.445	.742	22	.900
2000— Arkansas (Texas) 3B-1B-OF	90	297	41	80	16	3	14	41	16	66	5	7	2-1	.269	.318	.485	.802	14	.951
— Bowie (East.)	3B	18	68	7	17	1	0	1	6	4	13	2	2	5-2	.250	.311	.309	.620	2	.955
2001— Bowie (East.)	3B	26	95	18	34	9	1	4	20	8	21	1	2	1-1	.358	.413	.600	1.013	7	.879
— Rochester (Int'l)	3B	109	416	54	116	20	4	12	53	25	96	4	14	7-3	.279	.325	.433	.758	21	.933
2002— Rochester (Int'l)	3B	83	312	39	87	16	1	8	40	18	54	2	9	0-0	.279	.319	.413	.733	10	.957
— Baltimore (A.L.) 1-3-DH-OF	36	89	8	22	2	0	3	10	3	20	1	2	1-0	.247	.280	.371	.650	1	.994
2003— Baltimore (A.L.) 3B-1B-DH	21	54	6	13	1	0	0	0	3	18	2	1	0-0	.241	.305	.259	.564	2	.973
— Ottawa (Int'l) 3B-DH-1B	79	309	33	82	19	2	4	39	15	47	4	12	1-1	.265	.305	.379	.684	13	.944
2004— Ottawa (Int'l) 3B-SS-1B	83	283	45	91	21	1	17	54	24	68	7	11	1-1	.322	.382	.583	.965	18	.922
— Baltimore (A.L.) 1B-3B-DH	31	66	4	12	2	0	2	8	2	19	0	6	0-0	.182	.203	.303	.506	1	.990
Major League totals (3 years)		88	209	18	47	5	0	5	18	8	57	3	9	1-0	.225	.262	.321	.583	4	.989

LEONE, JUSTIN — 3B

PERSONAL: Born July 9, 1977, in Las Vegas, Nev. ... 6-1/190. ... Bats right, throws right. ... Full name: Justin Paul Leone. ... High school: Bonanza (Las Vegas). ... College: St. Martin's.

TRANSACTIONS/CAREER NOTES: Selected by Seattle Mariners organization in 13th round of 1999 free-agent draft. ... On disabled list (August 18, 2004-remainder of season).

2004 GAMES PLAYED BY POSITION (MLB): 3B—28, SS—2, DH—1.

Year Team (League)	Pos.	G	AB	R	H	2B	3B	HR	RBI	BB	SO	HBP	GDP	SB-CS	Avg.	OBP	SLG	OPS	E	Avg.
1999— Everett (N'west)	3B-SS	62	205	34	54	14	2	6	35	32	49	2	5	5-3	.263	.361	.439	.800	18	.911
2000— Wisconsin (Midw.) 3-S-OF-2	115	374	77	100	32	3	18	63	79	107	11	3	9-2	.267	.407	.513	.920	26	.912
2001— San Bern. (Calif.)	3B-OF	130	485	70	113	27	4	22	69	57	158	5	8	4-3	.233	.318	.441	.759	27	.927
2002— San Bern. (Calif.)	3B-SS	98	358	64	89	20	5	18	58	57	98	5	9	6-0	.249	.358	.483	.841	24	.919
2003— San Antonio (Texas)	3-S-1-2	135	455	103	131	38	7	21	92	92	104	3	7	20-6	.288	.405	.541	.946	21	.947
2004— Tacoma (PCL) 3-O-S-DH	68	253	56	68	10	5	21	51	26	82	4	5	5-6	.269	.344	.597	.931	15	.924
— Seattle (A.L.) 3B-SS-DH	31	102	15	22	5	0	6	13	9	32	3	0	1-0	.216	.298	.441	.739	9	.895
Major League totals (1 year)		31	102	15	22	5	0	6	13	9	32	3	0	1-0	.216	.298	.441	.739	9	.895

LESKANIC, CURTIS · P

PERSONAL: Born April 2, 1968, in Homestead, Pa. ... 6-0/185. ... Throws right, bats right. ... Full name: Curtis John Leskanic. ... Name pronounced: les-CAN-ik. ... High school: Steel Valley (Munhall, Pa.). ... College: LSU.

TRANSACTIONS/CAREER NOTES: Selected by Cleveland Indians organization in eighth round of 1989 free-agent draft. ... Traded by Indians with P Oscar Munoz to Minnesota Twins for 1B Paul Sorrento (March 28, 1992). ... Selected by Colorado Rockies in third round (66th pick overall) of expansion draft (November 17, 1992). ... Loaned by Rockies organization to San Diego Padres organization (April 7-May 20, 1993). ... On disabled list (May 30-June 28, 1996); included rehabilitation assignment to Colorado Springs. ... On disabled list (March 23-April 12, 1997); included rehabilitation assignment to Salem. ... Traded by Rockies to Milwaukee Brewers for P Mike Myers (November 17, 1999). ... On disabled list (May 12-30, 2000). ... On disabled list (March 30, 2002-entire season); included rehabilitation assignments to Indianapolis and Huntsville. ... Traded to Kansas City Royals by Milwaukee Brewers for P Wes Obermueller, 2B Alejandro Machado and cash (July 2, 2003). ... Released by Royals (June 15, 2004). ... Signed by Boston Red Sox (June 22, 2004). ... On disabled list (July 25-August 17, 2004); included rehabilitation assignment to Pawtucket.

CAREER HITTING: 7-for-39 (.179), 4 R, 3 2B, 0 3B, 1 HR, 7 RBI.

Year — Team (League)	W	L	Pct.	ERA	WHIP	G	GS	CG	ShO	Hld.	Sv.-Opp.	IP	H	R	ER	HR	BB-IBB	SO	Avg.
1990— Kinston (Caro.)	6	5	.545	3.68	1.24	14	14	2	0	...	0-...	73.1	61	34	30	6	30-1	71	.228
1991— Kinston (Caro.)	15	8	.652	2.79	1.34	28	28	0	0	...	0-...	174.1	143	63	54	10	91-0	163	.226
1992— Orlando (Sou.)	9	11	.450	4.30	1.45	26	23	3	0	...	0-...	152.2	158	84	73	15	64-0	126	.270
— Portland (PCL)	1	2	.333	9.98	1.57	5	3	0	0	...	0-...	15.1	16	17	17	1	8-0	14	.271
1993— Wichita (Texas)	3	2	.600	3.45	1.22	7	7	0	0	...	0-...	44.1	37	20	17	3	17-0	42	.230
— Colo. Springs (PCL)	4	3	.571	4.47	1.47	9	7	1	1	...	0-...	44.1	39	24	22	3	26-0	38	.239
— Colorado (N.L.)	1	5	.167	5.37	1.51	18	8	0	0	0	0-0	57.0	59	40	34	7	27-1	30	.266
1994— Colo. Springs (PCL)	5	7	.417	3.31	1.40	21	21	2	0	...	0-...	130.1	129	60	48	7	54-2	98	.263
— Colorado (N.L.)	1	1	.500	5.64	1.66	8	3	0	0	0	0-0	22.1	27	14	14	2	10-0	17	.314
1995— Colorado (N.L.)	6	3	.667	3.40	1.18	* 76	0	0	0	19	10-16	98.0	83	38	37	7	33-1	107	.226
1996— Colorado (N.L.)	7	5	.583	6.23	1.63	70	0	0	0	9	6-10	73.2	82	51	51	12	38-1	76	.285
— Colo. Springs (PCL)	0	0	...	3.00	2.00	3	0	0	0	...	0-...	3.0	5	1	1	0	1-0	2	.385
1997— Salem (Caro.)	0	0	...	3.86	2.57	2	1	0	0	...	0-...	2.1	5	2	1	0	1-0	3	.455
— Colorado (N.L.)	4	0	1.000	5.55	1.42	55	0	0	0	6	2-4	58.1	59	36	36	8	24-0	53	.271
— Colo. Springs (PCL)	0	0	...	3.79	1.53	10	3	0	0	...	2-...	19.0	11	9	8	1	18-0	20	.175
1998— Colorado (N.L.)	6	4	.600	4.40	1.52	66	0	0	0	12	2-5	75.2	75	37	37	9	40-2	55	.259
1999— Colorado (N.L.)	6	2	.750	5.08	1.60	63	0	0	0	8	0-3	85.0	87	54	48	7	49-4	77	.272
2000— Milwaukee (N.L.)	9	3	.750	2.56	1.41	73	0	0	0	11	12-13	77.1	58	23	22	7	51-5	75	.212
2001— Milwaukee (N.L.)	2	6	.250	3.63	1.36	70	0	0	0	2	17-24	69.1	63	30	28	11	31-5	64	.241
2002— Indianapolis (Int'l)	0	0	...	1.35	0.90	5	1	0	0	...	0-...	6.2	5	1	1	0	1-0	7	.192
— Huntsville (Southern)	0	0	...	3.00	2.00	3	0	0	0	...	0-...	3.0	4	2	1	0	2-0	2	.333
2003— Milwaukee (N.L.)	4	0	1.000	2.70	1.50	26	0	0	0	4	0-0	26.2	22	8	8	1	18-0	28	.227
— Kansas City (A.L.)	1	0	1.000	1.73	1.04	27	0	0	0	7	2-3	26.0	16	7	5	1	11-1	21	.180
2004— Kansas City (A.L.)	0	3	.000	8.04	2.36	19	0	0	0	4	2-5	15.2	23	16	14	5	14-0	15	.324
— Pawtucket (Int'l)	0	0	...	0.00	...	1	0	0	0	...	0-...	1.0	0	0	0	0	0-0	0	.000
— Boston (A.L.)	3	2	.600	3.58	1.45	32	0	0	0	2	2-3	27.2	24	11	11	3	16-3	22	.247
American League totals (2 years)	4	5	.444	3.89	1.50	78	0	0	0	13	6-11	69.1	63	34	30	9	41-4	59	.245
National League totals (10 years)	46	29	.613	4.41	1.45	525	11	0	0	71	49-75	643.1	615	331	315	71	321-19	582	.254
Major League totals (11 years)	50	34	.595	4.36	1.46	603	11	0	0	84	55-86	712.2	678	365	345	80	362-23	641	.253

DIVISION SERIES RECORD

Year — Team (League)	W	L	Pct.	ERA	WHIP	G	GS	CG	ShO	Hld.	Sv.-Opp.	IP	H	R	ER	HR	BB-IBB	SO	Avg.
1995— Colorado (N.L.)	0	1	.000	6.00	1.00	3	0	0	0	1	0-0	3.0	3	2	2	1	0-0	4	.250

CHAMPIONSHIP SERIES RECORD

Year — Team (League)	W	L	Pct.	ERA	WHIP	G	GS	CG	ShO	Hld.	Sv.-Opp.	IP	H	R	ER	HR	BB-IBB	SO	Avg.
2004— Boston (A.L.)	1	0	1.000	10.13	2.25	3	0	0	0	0	0-0	2.2	3	3	3	1	3-0	2	.300

LEVINE, AL · P

PERSONAL: Born May 22, 1968, in Park Ridge, Ill. ... 6-3/190. ... Throws right, bats left. ... Full name: Alan Brian Levine. ... Name pronounced: le-VINE. ... High school: Hoffman Estates (Ill.). ... College: Southern Illinois.

TRANSACTIONS/CAREER NOTES: Selected by Chicago White Sox in 11th round of 1991 free-agent draft. ... Traded by White Sox with P Larry Thomas to Texas Rangers for SS Benji Gil (December 19, 1997). ... Claimed on waivers by Anaheim Angels (April 2, 1999). ... On disabled list (July 31-August 19, 2000); included rehabilitation assignment to Erie. ... On disabled list (June 27-July 20, 2002); included rehabilitation assignment to Salt Lake. ... Signed as a free agent by St. Louis Cardinals (January 6, 2003). ... Released by Cardinals (March 26, 2003). ... Signed by Tampa Bay Devil Rays organization (April 2, 2003). ... Traded by Devil Rays to Kansas City for cash (July, 31, 2003). ... Signed as a free agent by Detroit Tigers (December 18, 2003).

CAREER HITTING: 0-for-0 (.000), 0 R, 0 2B, 0 3B, 0 HR, 0 RBI.

Year — Team (League)	W	L	Pct.	ERA	WHIP	G	GS	CG	ShO	Hld.	Sv.-Opp.	IP	H	R	ER	HR	BB-IBB	SO	Avg.
1991— Utica (N.Y.-Penn)	6	4	.600	3.18	1.19	16	12	2	1	...	1-...	85.0	75	45	30	2	26-0	83	.231
1992— South Bend (Mid.)	9	5	.643	2.81	1.19	23	23	2	0	...	0-...	156.2	151	67	49	6	36-1	131	.253
— Sarasota (Florida State)	0	2	.000	4.02	1.40	3	2	0	0	...	0-...	15.2	17	11	7	1	5-1	11	.293
1993— Sarasota (Florida State)	11	8	.579	3.68	1.36	27	26	5	1	...	0-...	161.1	169	87	66	6	50-3	129	.271
1994— Birmingham (Southern)	5	9	.357	3.31	1.41	18	18	1	0	...	0-...	114.1	117	50	42	7	44-1	94	.267
— Nashville (A.A.)	0	2	.000	7.88	1.88	8	4	0	0	...	0-...	24.0	34	23	21	2	11-0	24	.343
1995— Nashville (A.A.)	0	2	.000	5.14	1.93	3	3	0	0	...	0-...	14.0	20	10	8	1	7-0	14	.323
— Birmingham (Southern)	4	3	.571	2.34	1.18	43	1	0	0	...	7-...	73.0	61	22	19	2	25-5	68	.223
1996— Nashville (A.A.)	4	5	.444	3.65	1.33	43	0	0	0	...	12-...	61.2	58	27	25	4	24-6	45	.246
— Chicago (A.L.)	0	1	.000	5.40	1.58	16	0	0	0	0	0-1	18.1	22	14	11	1	7-1	12	.289
1997— Chicago (A.L.)	2	2	.500	6.91	1.87	25	0	0	0	3	0-1	27.1	35	22	21	4	16-1	22	.313
— Nashville (A.A.)	1	1	.500	7.13	1.95	26	0	0	0	...	2-...	35.1	58	32	28	3	11-1	29	.372
1998— Oklahoma (PCL)	1	3	.250	4.73	1.28	12	7	0	0	...	1-...	58.0	51	33	28	7	17-0	30	.252
— Texas (A.L.)	0	1	.000	4.50	1.45	30	0	0	0	0	0-0	58.0	68	30	29	6	16-1	19	.294
1999— Anaheim (A.L.)	1	1	.500	3.39	1.24	50	1	0	0	3	0-1	85.0	76	36	32	13	29-2	37	.247
2000— Anaheim (A.L.)	3	4	.429	3.87	1.54	51	5	0	0	5	2-2	95.1	98	44	41	10	49-5	42	.266
— Erie (East.)	0	0	...	0.00	1.50	1	1	0	0	...	0-...	2.0	3	2	0	0	0-0	0	.333
2001— Anaheim (A.L.)	8	10	.444	2.38	1.31	64	1	0	0	17	2-6	75.2	71	25	20	7	28-4	40	.257
2002— Anaheim (A.L.)	4	4	.500	4.24	1.49	52	0	0	0	10	5-7	63.2	61	35	30	8	34-3	40	.253
— Salt Lake (PCL)	0	0	...	3.00	1.67	2	0	0	0	...	0-...	3.0	5	1	1	0	0-0	0	.385
2003— Tampa Bay (A.L.)	3	5	.375	2.92	1.20	36	0	0	0	8	0-2	49.2	45	23	16	7	18-0	25	.243
— Kansas City (A.L.)	0	1	.000	2.53	1.55	18	0	0	0	2	1-2	21.1	22	6	6	2	11-1	5	.268
2004— Detroit (A.L.)	3	4	.429	4.58	1.51	65	0	0	0	16	0-1	70.2	83	37	36	10	24-1	32	.295
Major League totals (9 years)	24	33	.421	3.85	1.44	407	7	0	0	64	10-23	565.0	581	276	242	68	232-19	274	.269

L

LEWIS, COLBY — P

PERSONAL: Born August 2, 1979, in Bakersfield, Calif. ... 6-4/230. ... Throws right, bats right. ... Full name: Colby Preston Lewis. ... High school: North (Bakersfield, Calif.). ... Junior college: Bakersfield (Calif.).

TRANSACTIONS/CAREER NOTES: Selected by Texas Rangers organization in supplemental round ("sandwich pick" between first and second rounds, 38th pick overall) of 1999 free-agent draft; pick received as part of compensation for Arizona Diamondbacks signing Type A free-agent P Todd Stottlemyre. ... On disabled list (April 18, 2004-remainder of season). ... Claimed on waivers by Detroit Tigers (October 8, 2004).

CAREER HITTING: 0-for-1 (.000), 0 R, 0 2B, 0 3B, 0 HR, 0 RBI.

Year	Team (League)	W	L	Pct.	ERA	WHIP	G	GS	CG	ShO	Hld.	Sv.-Opp.	IP	H	R	ER	HR	BB-IBB	SO	Avg.
1999—	Pulaski (Appalachian)	7	3	.700	1.95	1.13	14	11	1	1	...	0-...	64.2	46	24	14	3	27-0	84	.189
2000—	Charlotte (Fla. St.)	11	10	.524	4.07	1.31	28	27	3	1	...	0-...	163.2	169	83	74	11	45-0	153	.270
2001—	Charlotte (Fla. St.)	1	0	1.000	0.00	0.00	1	0	0	0	...	0-...	4.1	0	0	0	0	0-0	8	.000
	— Tulsa (Texas)	10	10	.500	4.50	1.36	25	25	1	0	...	0-...	156.0	150	85	78	15	62-2	162	.253
2002—	Texas (A.L.)	1	3	.250	6.29	1.98	15	4	0	0	1	0-2	34.1	42	26	24	4	26-2	28	.304
	— Oklahoma (PCL)	5	6	.455	3.63	1.20	20	20	0	0	...	0-...	106.2	100	49	43	4	28-0	99	.245
2003—	Oklahoma (PCL)	5	1	.833	3.02	1.20	7	7	0	0	...	0-...	47.2	36	16	16	6	19-0	43	.208
	— Texas (A.L.)	10	9	.526	7.30	1.83	26	26	0	0	0	0-0	127.0	163	104	103	23	70-1	88	.317
2004—	Texas (A.L.)	1	1	.500	4.11	1.70	3	3	0	0	0	0-0	15.1	13	7	7	1	13-0	11	.228
	Major League totals (3 years)	12	13	.480	6.83	1.85	44	33	0	0	1	0-2	176.2	218	137	134	28	109-3	127	.307

LIDGE, BRAD — P

PERSONAL: Born December 23, 1976, in Sacramento, Calif. ... 6-5/210. ... Throws right, bats right. ... Full name: Bradley Thomas Lidge. ... College: Notre Dame.

TRANSACTIONS/CAREER NOTES: Selected by San Francisco Giants organization in 42nd round of 1995 free-agent draft; did not sign. ... Selected by Houston Astros organization in first round (17th pick overall) of 1998 free-agent draft; pick received as part of compensation for Colorado Rockies signing Type A free-agent P Darryl Kile.

CAREER HITTING: 2-for-7 (.286), 0 R, 1 2B, 0 3B, 0 HR, 2 RBI.

Year	Team (League)	W	L	Pct.	ERA	WHIP	G	GS	CG	ShO	Hld.	Sv.-Opp.	IP	H	R	ER	HR	BB-IBB	SO	Avg.
1998—	Quad City (Midw.)	0	1	.000	3.27	1.36	4	4	0	0	...	0-...	11.0	10	5	4	0	5-0	6	.227
1999—	Kissimmee (Fla. St.)	0	2	.000	3.38	1.13	6	6	0	0	...	0-...	21.1	13	8	8	0	11-0	19	.183
2000—	Kissimmee (Fla. St.)	2	1	.667	2.81	1.03	8	8	0	0	...	0-...	41.2	28	14	13	3	15-0	46	.190
2001—	Round Rock (Texas)	2	0	1.000	1.73	1.08	5	5	0	0	...	0-...	26.0	21	5	5	1	7-0	42	.219
2002—	Round Rock (Texas)	1	1	.500	2.45	1.09	5	0	0	0	...	0-...	11.0	9	4	3	0	3-0	18	.220
	— Houston (N.L.)	1	0	1.000	6.23	2.42	6	1	0	0	0	0-0	8.2	12	6	6	0	9-1	12	.333
	— New Orleans (PCL)	5	5	.500	3.39	1.16	24	19	0	0	...	0-...	111.2	83	47	42	9	42-7	110	.206
2003—	Houston (N.L.)	6	3	.667	3.60	1.20	78	0	0	0	28	1-6	85.0	60	36	34	6	42-7	97	.202
2004—	Houston (N.L.)	6	5	.545	1.90	0.92	80	0	0	0	17	29-33	94.2	57	21	20	8	30-5	157	.174
	Major League totals (3 years)	13	8	.619	2.87	1.12	164	1	0	0	45	30-39	188.1	129	63	60	14	81-13	266	.195

DIVISION SERIES RECORD

Year	Team (League)	W	L	Pct.	ERA	WHIP	G	GS	CG	ShO	Hld.	Sv.-Opp.	IP	H	R	ER	HR	BB-IBB	SO	Avg.
2004—	Houston (N.L.)	0	0	...	2.08	1.15	3	0	0	0	0	1-2	4.1	4	1	1	0	1-0	6	.286

CHAMPIONSHIP SERIES RECORD

Year	Team (League)	W	L	Pct.	ERA	WHIP	G	GS	CG	ShO	Hld.	Sv.-Opp.	IP	H	R	ER	HR	BB-IBB	SO	Avg.
2004—	Houston (N.L.)	1	0	1.000	0.00	0.38	4	0	0	0	0	2-2	8.0	1	0	0	0	2-0	14	.040

LIDLE, CORY — P

PERSONAL: Born March 22, 1972, in Hollywood, Calif. ... 5-11/192. ... Throws right, bats right. ... Full name: Cory Fulton Lidle. ... Name pronounced: LIE-dell. ... High school: South Hills (Covina, Calif.). ... Twin brother of Kevin Lidle, catcher, California Angels organization.

TRANSACTIONS/CAREER NOTES: Signed as a non-drafted free agent by Minnesota Twins organization (August 25, 1990). ... Released by Twins (April 1, 1993). ... Signed by Pocatello of the Pioneer League (May 28, 1993). ... Contract sold by Pocatello to Milwaukee Brewers organization (September 17, 1993). ... Traded by Brewers to New York Mets for C Kelly Stinnett (January 17, 1996). ... Selected by Arizona Diamondbacks in first round (13th pick overall) of 1998 expansion draft (November 18, 1997). ... On disabled list (March 31, 1998-entire season); included rehabilitation assignments to High Desert and Tucson. ... Claimed on waivers by Tampa Bay Devil Rays (October 7, 1998). ... On disabled list (March 23-September 18, 1999); included rehabilitation assignments to St. Petersburg and Durham. ... On suspended list (September 5-8, 2000). ... Traded by Devil Rays to Oakland Athletics as part of three-team deal in which Devil Rays acquired OF Ben Grieve and cash from A's, Royals acquired P Roberto Hernandez from Devil Rays and C A.J. Hinch, IF Angel Berroa and cash from A's and A's received OF Johnny Damon, IF Mark Ellis and cash from Royals (January 8, 2001). ... On disabled list (May 13-30, 2002); included rehabilitation assignment to Sacramento. ... Traded by A's to Toronto Blue Jays for IF Michael Rouse and P Christopher Mowday (November 16, 2002). ... On disabled list (August 5-25, 2003); included rehabilitation assignment to Syracuse. ... Signed as a free agent by Cincinnati Reds (January 6, 2004). ... Traded by Reds to Philadelphia Phillies for OF Javon Moran, P Joe Wilson and a player to be named or cash (August 9, 2004); Reds acquired P Elizardo Ramirez to complete deal (August 11, 2004).

CAREER HITTING: 11-for-78 (.141), 5 R, 4 2B, 0 3B, 1 HR, 6 RBI.

Year	Team (League)	W	L	Pct.	ERA	WHIP	G	GS	CG	ShO	Hld.	Sv.-Opp.	IP	H	R	ER	HR	BB-IBB	SO	Avg.
1991—	GC Twins (GCL)	1	1	.500	5.79	1.07	4	0	0	0	...	0-...	4.2	5	3	3	0	0-0	5	.263
1992—	Elizabethton (Appal.)	2	1	.667	3.71	1.40	19	2	0	0	...	6-...	43.2	40	29	18	2	21-0	32	.240
1993—	Pocatello (Pio.)	8	4	.667	4.13	1.48	17	16	3	0	...	1-...	106.2	104	59	49	6	54-0	91	.261
1994—	Stockton (Calif.)	1	2	.333	4.43	1.71	25	1	0	0	...	4-...	42.2	60	32	21	2	13-1	38	.323
	— Beloit (Midw.)	3	4	.429	2.61	1.10	13	9	1	1	...	0-...	69.0	65	24	20	4	11-0	62	.245
1995—	El Paso (Texas)	5	4	.556	3.36	1.48	45	9	0	0	...	2-...	109.2	126	52	41	6	36-3	78	.292
1996—	Binghamton (Eastern)	14	10	.583	3.31	1.23	27	27	6	1	...	0-...	190.1	186	78	70	13	49-4	141	.259
1997—	Norfolk (Int'l)	4	2	.667	3.64	1.33	7	7	1	0	...	0-...	42.0	46	20	17	1	10-0	34	.279
	— New York (N.L.)	7	2	.778	3.53	1.30	54	2	0	0	9	2-3	81.2	86	38	32	7	20-4	54	.274
1998—	High Desert (Calif.)	0	0	...	0.00	1.50	1	1	0	0	...	0-...	2.2	2	1	0	0	2-0	6	.182
	— Tucson (PCL)	0	0	...	0.00	0.86	1	1	0	0	...	0-...	4.2	2	0	0	0	2-0	2	.125
1999—	St. Pete. (FSL)	0	0	...	0.00	0.80	2	2	0	0	...	0-...	5.0	2	0	0	0	2-0	1	.118
	— Durham (Int'l)	0	0	...	4.76	1.76	3	2	0	0	...	0-...	5.2	9	3	3	0	1-0	6	.360
	— Tampa Bay (A.L.)	1	0	1.000	7.20	2.00	5	1	0	0	0	0-0	5.0	8	4	4	0	2-0	4	.364
2000—	Durham (Int'l)	6	2	.750	2.52	1.20	9	9	0	0	...	0-...	50.0	52	15	14	3	8-0	44	.267
	— Tampa Bay (A.L.)	4	6	.400	5.03	1.48	31	11	0	0	2	0-0	96.2	114	61	54	13	29-3	62	.294
2001—	Sacramento (PCL)	1	0	1.000	3.00	1.50	1	1	0	0	...	0-...	6.0	6	2	2	0	3-0	2	.261
	— Oakland (A.L.)	13	6	.684	3.59	1.15	29	29	1	0	0	0-0	188.0	170	84	75	23	47-7	118	.242
2002—	Oakland (A.L.)	8	10	.444	3.89	1.20	31	30	2	2	0	0-0	192.0	191	90	83	17	39-3	111	.258
	— Sacramento (PCL)	0	0	...	2.25	1.25	1	1	0	0	...	0-...	4.0	2	1	1	0	3-0	3	.125
2003—	Syracuse (Int'l)	0	0	...	0.00	1.20	1	1	0	0	...	0-...	4.0	5	0	0	0	0-0	3	.313
	— Toronto (A.L.)	12	15	.444	5.75	1.43	31	31	2	0	...	0-0	192.2	216	* 133	• 123	24	60-3	112	.282

Year Team (League)	W	L	Pct.	ERA	WHIP	G	GS	CG	ShO	Hld.	Sv.-Opp.	IP	H	R	ER	HR	BB-IBB	SO	Avg.
2004— Cincinnati (N.L.)	7	10	.412	5.32	1.44	24	24	3	1		0-0	149.0	170	95	88	24	44-4	93	.288
— Philadelphia (N.L.)	5	2	.714	3.90	1.14	10	10	2	§2		0-0	62.1	54	28	27	3	17-1	33	.236
American League totals (5 years)	38	37	.507	4.52	1.30	127	102	9	5	2	0-0	674.1	699	372	339	77	177-16	407	.267
National League totals (2 years)	19	14	.576	4.52	1.33	88	36	5	3	9	2-3	293.0	310	161	147	34	81-9	180	.273
Major League totals (7 years)	57	51	.528	4.52	1.31	215	138	10	5	11	2-3	967.1	1009	533	486	111	258-25	587	.269

DIVISION SERIES RECORD

Year Team (League)	W	L	Pct.	ERA	WHIP	G	GS	CG	ShO	Hld.	Sv.-Opp.	IP	H	R	ER	HR	BB-IBB	SO	Avg.
2001— Oakland (A.L.)	0	1	.000	10.80	2.40	1	1	0	0	0	0-0	3.1	5	6	4	0	3-0	0	.357
2002— Oakland (A.L.)	0	0	...	9.00	2.00	1	0	0	0	0	0-0	1.0	2	1	1	0	0-0	0	.400
Division series totals (2 years)	0	1	.000	10.38	2.31	2	1	0	0	0	0-0	4.1	7	7	5	0	3-0	0	.368

LIEBER, JON   P

PERSONAL: Born April 2, 1970, in Council Bluffs, Iowa. ... 6-2/230. ... Throws right, bats left. ... Full name: Jonathan Ray Lieber. ... Name pronounced: LEE-ber. ... High school: Abraham Lincoln (Council Bluffs, Iowa.). ... College: South Alabama.

TRANSACTIONS/CAREER NOTES: Selected by Chicago Cubs organization in ninth round of 1991 free-agent draft; did not sign. ... Selected by Kansas City Royals organization in second round of 1992 free-agent draft; pick received as part of compensation for New York Yankees signing Type A free-agent OF Danny Tartabull. ... Traded by Royals with P Dan Miceli to Pittsburgh Pirates for P Stan Belinda (July 31, 1993). ... On disabled list (August 21-September 15, 1998). ... Traded by Pirates to Chicago Cubs for OF Brant Brown (December 14, 1998). ... On disabled list (April 21-May 8, 1999; and August 2, 2002-remainder of season). ... Signed as a free agent by New York Yankees (February 4, 2003). ... On disabled list (March 21, 2003-entire season); included rehabilitation assignments to Tampa and GCL Yankees. ... On disabled list (March 19-May 1, 2004); included rehabilitation assignment to Tampa.

CAREER HITTING: 72-for-464 (.155), 27 R, 15 2B, 0 3B, 0 HR, 20 RBI.

Year Team (League)	W	L	Pct.	ERA	WHIP	G	GS	CG	ShO	Hld.	Sv.-Opp.	IP	H	R	ER	HR	BB-IBB	SO	Avg.
1992— Eugene (N'west)	3	0	1.000	1.16	0.90	5	5	0	0	...	0-...	31.0	26	6	4	1	2-0	23	.226
— Baseball City (FSL)	3	3	.500	4.65	1.71	7	6	0	0	...	0-...	31.0	45	20	16	2	8-0	19	.344
1993— Wilmington (Caro.)	9	3	.750	2.67	1.17	17	16	2	0	...	0-...	114.2	125	47	34	4	9-1	89	.272
— Memphis (Sou.)	2	1	.667	6.86	1.81	4	4	0	0	...	0-...	21.0	32	16	16	4	6-0	17	.340
— Carolina (Southern)	4	2	.667	3.97	1.44	6	6	0	0	...	0-...	34.0	39	15	15	3	10-0	28	.298
1994— Carolina (Southern)	2	0	1.000	1.29	0.71	3	3	1	1	...	0-...	21.0	13	4	3	0	2-0	21	.171
— Buffalo (A.A.)	1	1	.500	1.69	0.80	3	3	0	0	...	0-...	21.1	16	4	4	1	1-0	21	.208
— Pittsburgh (N.L.)	6	7	.462	3.73	1.30	17	17	1	0	0	0-...	108.2	116	62	45	12	25-3	71	.271
1995— Pittsburgh (N.L.)	4	7	.364	6.32	1.61	21	12	0	0	3	0-1	72.2	103	56	51	7	14-0	45	.346
— Calgary (PCL)	1	5	.167	7.01	1.83	14	14	0	0	...	0-...	77.0	122	69	60	6	19-0	34	.354
1996— Pittsburgh (N.L.)	9	5	.643	3.99	1.30	51	15	0	0	9	1-4	142.0	156	70	63	19	28-2	94	.279
1997— Pittsburgh (N.L.)	11	14	.440	4.49	1.30	33	32	1	0	0	0-0	188.1	193	102	94	23	51-8	160	.263
1998— Pittsburgh (N.L.)	8	14	.364	4.11	1.30	29	28	2	0	1	1-1	171.0	182	93	78	23	40-4	138	.269
1999— Chicago (N.L.)	10	11	.476	4.07	1.34	31	31	3	1	0	0-0	203.1	226	107	92	28	46-6	186	.279
2000— Chicago (N.L.)	12	11	.522	4.41	1.20	35	•35	6	1	0	0-0	*251.0	248	130	123	36	54-3	192	.257
2001— Chicago (N.L.)	20	6	.769	3.80	1.15	34	34	5	1	0	0-0	232.1	226	104	98	25	41-4	148	.255
2002— Chicago (N.L.)	6	8	.429	3.70	1.17	21	21	3	0	0	0-0	141.0	153	64	58	15	12-2	87	.277
2003— GC Yankees (GCL)	0	0	...	4.50	1.30	2	2	0	0	...	0-...	6.0	8	3	3	0	0-0	6	.308
— Tampa (FSL)	0	0	...	13.50	2.50	1	1	0	0	...	0-...	2.0	5	3	3	0	0-0	4	.455
2004— Tampa (FSL)	1	0	1.000	0.00	0.29	1	1	0	0	...	0-...	7.0	2	0	0	0	0-0	6	.083
— New York (A.L.)	14	8	.636	4.33	1.32	27	27	0	0	0	0-0	176.2	216	95	85	20	18-2	102	.301
American League totals (1 year)	14	8	.636	4.33	1.32	27	27	0	0	0	0-0	176.2	216	95	85	20	18-2	102	.301
National League totals (9 years)	86	83	.509	4.18	1.27	272	225	21	3	12	2-6	1510.1	1603	788	702	188	311-32	1121	.271
Major League totals (10 years)	100	91	.524	4.20	1.27	299	252	21	3	12	2-6	1687.0	1819	883	787	208	329-34	1223	.274

DIVISION SERIES RECORD

Year Team (League)	W	L	Pct.	ERA	WHIP	G	GS	CG	ShO	Hld.	Sv.-Opp.	IP	H	R	ER	HR	BB-IBB	SO	Avg.
2004— New York (A.L.)	0	0	...	4.05	1.20	1	1	0	0	0	0-0	6.2	7	3	3	0	1-0	4	.292

CHAMPIONSHIP SERIES RECORD

Year Team (League)	W	L	Pct.	ERA	WHIP	G	GS	CG	ShO	Hld.	Sv.-Opp.	IP	H	R	ER	HR	BB-IBB	SO	Avg.
2004— New York (A.L.)	1	1	.500	3.14	0.91	2	2	0	0	0	0-0	14.1	12	5	5	1	1-0	5	.231

ALL-STAR GAME RECORD

Year Team (League)	W	L	Pct.	ERA	WHIP	G	GS	CG	ShO	Hld.	Sv.-Opp.	IP	H	R	ER	HR	BB-IBB	SO	Avg.
All-Star Game totals (1 year)	0	0	...	18.00	3.00	1	0	0	0	0	0-0	1.0	3	2	2	2	0-0	1	.500

LIEBERTHAL, MIKE   C

PERSONAL: Born January 18, 1972, in Glendale, Calif. ... 6-0/190. ... Bats right, throws right. ... Full name: Michael Scott Lieberthal. ... Name pronounced: LEE-ber-thal. ... High school: Westlake (Westlake Village, Calif.).

TRANSACTIONS/CAREER NOTES: Selected by Philadelphia Phillies organization in first round (third pick overall) of 1990 free-agent draft. ... On disabled list (August 22, 1996-remainder of season; July 24-September 2, 1998; July 18-August 4 and September 11, 2000-remainder of season; and May 13, 2001-remainder of season).

HONORS: Won N.L. Gold Glove at catcher (1999). ... Named N.L. Comeback Player of the Year by THE SPORTING NEWS (2002).

2004 GAMES PLAYED BY POSITION (MLB): C—129.

Year Team (League)	Pos.	G	AB	R	H	2B	3B	HR	RBI	BB	SO	HBP	GDP	SB-CS	Avg.	OBP	SLG	OPS	E	Avg.
1990— Martinsville (App.)	C	49	184	26	42	9	0	4	22	11	40	2	3	2-0	.228	.279	.342	.622	5	.990
1991— Spartanburg (SAL)	C	72	243	34	74	17	0	0	31	23	25	5	4	1-2	.305	.372	.374	.747	10	.984
— Clearwater (FSL)	C	16	52	7	15	2	0	0	7	3	12	1	2	0-0	.288	.333	.327	.660	1	.993
1992— Reading (East.)	C	86	309	30	88	16	1	2	37	19	26	10	15	4-1	.285	.342	.705	.705	7	.988
— Scran./W.B. (I.L.)	C	16	45	4	9	1	0	0	4	2	5	1	2	0-0	.200	.245	.222	.467	1	.989
1993— Scran./W.B. (I.L.)	C	112	382	35	100	17	0	7	40	24	32	6	15	2-0	.262	.313	.361	.674	11	.985
1994— Scran./W.B. (I.L.)	C-DH	84	296	23	69	16	0	1	32	21	29	2	7	1-1	.233	.286	.297	.583	9	.983
— Philadelphia (N.L.)	C	24	79	6	21	3	1	1	5	3	5	1	4	0-0	.266	.301	.367	.668	4	.969
1995— Philadelphia (N.L.)	C	16	47	1	12	2	0	0	4	5	5	0	1	0-0	.255	.327	.298	.625	1	.991
— Scran./W.B. (I.L.)	C-DH-3B	85	278	44	78	20	2	6	42	44	26	9	14	1-4	.281	.388	.432	.819	5	.991
1996— Philadelphia (N.L.)	C	50	166	21	42	8	0	7	23	10	30	2	4	0-0	.253	.297	.428	.724	3	.990
1997— Philadelphia (N.L.)	C-DH	134	455	59	112	27	1	20	77	44	76	4	10	3-4	.246	.314	.442	.755	12	.988
1998— Philadelphia (N.L.)	C	86	313	39	80	15	3	8	45	17	44	7	4	2-1	.256	.304	.399	.703	8	.988

Year Team (League)	Pos.	G	AB	R	H	2B	3B	HR	RBI	BB	SO	HBP	GDP	SB-CS	Avg.	OBP	SLG	OPS	E	Avg.
1999— Philadelphia (N.L.)	C	145	510	84	153	33	1	31	96	44	86	11	15	0-0	.300	.363	.551	.914	3	.997
2000— Philadelphia (N.L.)	C	108	389	55	108	30	0	15	71	40	53	6	12	2-0	.278	.352	.470	.822	5	.994
2001— Philadelphia (N.L.)	C	34	121	21	28	8	0	2	11	12	21	3	2	0-0	.231	.316	.347	.663	2	.992
2002— Philadelphia (N.L.)	C	130	476	46	133	29	2	15	52	38	58	14	16	0-1	.279	.349	.443	.792	6	.993
2003— Philadelphia (N.L.)	C	131	508	68	159	30	1	13	81	38	59	12	14	0-0	.313	.373	.453	.825	9	.990
2004— Philadelphia (N.L.)	C	131	476	58	129	31	1	17	61	37	69	11	19	1-1	.271	.335	.447	.783	6	.993
Major League totals (11 years)		989	3540	458	977	216	10	129	526	288	506	71	101	8-7	.276	.340	.452	.791	59	.991

ALL-STAR GAME RECORD

	G	AB	R	H	2B	3B	HR	RBI	BB	SO	HBP	GDP	SB-CS	Avg.	OBP	SLG	OPS	E	Avg.
All-Star Game totals (2 years)	2	3	1	1	0	0	0	0	0	0	0	1	0-0	.333	.333	.333	.667	0	1.000

LIEFER, JEFF   OF/3B

PERSONAL: Born August 17, 1974, in Fontana, Calif. ... 6-3/210. ... Bats left, throws right. ... Full name: Jeffrey David Liefer. ... Name pronounced: LEAF-er. ... High school: Upland (Calif.). ... College: Long Beach State.

TRANSACTIONS/CAREER NOTES: Selected by Cleveland Indians organization in sixth round of 1992 free-agent draft; did not sign. ... Selected by Chicago White Sox organization in first round (25th pick overall) of 1995 free-agent draft. ... On disabled list (March 25-April 17, 2000). ... Traded by White Sox with Ps Orlando Hernandez and Rocky Biddle and cash to Montreal Expos for P Bartolo Colon and 2B/SS Jorge Nunez (January 15, 2003). ... Claimed on waivers by Tampa Bay Devil Rays (June 6, 2003). ... Signed as a free agent by Milwaukee Brewers organization (January 5, 2004). ... Refused minor league assignment and became a free agent (October 4, 2004).

2004 GAMES PLAYED BY POSITION (MLB): DH—3, OF—3.

								BATTING												FIELDING	
Year Team (League)	Pos.	G	AB	R	H	2B	3B	HR	RBI	BB	SO	HBP	GDP	SB-CS	Avg.	OBP	SLG	OPS	E	Avg.
1996— South Bend (Mid.)	3B-DH	74	277	60	90	14	0	15	58	30	62	5	3	6-5	.325	.396	.538	.933	23	.802
— Prince Will. (Car.)	DH	37	147	17	33	6	0	1	13	11	27	0	6	0-0	.224	.277	.286	.562	0	...
1997— Birmingham (Sou.)	OF-DH	119	474	67	113	24	9	15	71	38	115	7	10	2-0	.238	.302	.422	.724	8	.955
1998— Birmingham (Sou.)	1B-DH-OF	127	471	84	137	33	6	21	89	60	125	9	9	1-2	.291	.381	.520	.901	11	.987
— Calgary (PCL)	OF-DH-1B	8	31	3	8	3	0	1	10	2	12	0	1	0-0	.258	.303	.452	.755	0	1.000
1999— Chicago (A.L.)	OF-1B-DH	45	113	8	28	7	1	0	14	8	28	0	3	2-0	.248	.295	.327	.623	0	1.000
— Charlotte (Int'l)	1B-OF-3B	46	171	36	58	17	1	9	34	21	26	1	3	2-1	.339	.412	.608	1.021	3	.988
2000— Charlotte (Int'l)	1B-OF-3B	120	445	75	125	29	1	32	91	53	107	2	17	2-3	.281	.356	.566	.923	9	.987
— Chicago (A.L.)	OF-1B	5	11	0	2	0	0	0	0	0	4	0	0	0-0	.182	.182	.182	.364	1	.900
2001— Charlotte (Int'l)	1B-3B	32	119	23	34	7	0	6	21	15	41	4	1	3-1	.286	.381	.496	.877	3	.989
— Chicago (A.L.)	OF-3-1-DH	83	254	36	65	13	0	18	39	20	69	2	6	0-1	.256	.313	.520	.833	7	.964
2002— Chicago (A.L.)	OF-1B-DH	76	204	28	47	8	0	7	26	19	60	0	3	0-1	.230	.295	.373	.667	2	.992
2003— Montreal (N.L.)	1B	35	88	6	17	3	0	3	18	3	26	0	2	0-1	.193	.217	.330	.547	3	.980
— Tampa Bay (A.L.)	3B-DH-OF	9	25	4	3	1	0	1	3	3	13	0	0	0-0	.120	.214	.280	.494	1	.938
— Durham (Int'l)	OF-DH-1-3	44	157	20	41	10	3	7	24	14	49	1	2	0-0	.261	.326	.497	.822	1	.988
2004— Milwaukee (N.L.)	OF	16	28	2	6	2	0	1	5	2	8	0	2	0-0	.214	.258	.393	.651	0	1.000
— Indianapolis (Int'l)	1-OF-3-DH	107	370	60	104	25	1	20	83	47	63	4	9	1-0	.281	.364	.516	.880	4	.995
American League totals (5 years)		218	607	76	145	29	1	26	82	50	174	2	12	2-1	.239	.297	.418	.716	11	.982
National League totals (2 years)		51	116	8	23	5	0	4	23	5	34	0	4	0-1	.198	.228	.345	.572	3	.981
Major League totals (6 years)		269	723	84	168	34	1	30	105	55	208	2	16	2-2	.232	.286	.407	.693	14	.982

LIGTENBERG, KERRY   P

PERSONAL: Born May 11, 1971, in Rapid City, S.D. ... 6-2/222. ... Throws right, bats right. ... Full name: Kerry Dale Ligtenberg. ... Name pronounced: lite-en-berg. ... High school: Park (Cottage Grove, Minn.). ... College: Minnesota.

TRANSACTIONS/CAREER NOTES: Contract sold by Minneapolis of the independent North Central League to Seattle Mariners organization (March 28, 1995). ... Released by Mariners (April 2, 1995). ... Contract sold by Minneapolis of the independent Prairie League to Atlanta Braves organization (January 27, 1996). ... On disabled list (April 3, 1999-entire season). ... Signed as a free agent by Baltimore Orioles (January 16, 2003). ... Signed as a free agent by Toronto Blue Jays (December 9, 2003). ... On disabled list (June 11-26, 2004).

CAREER HITTING: 0-for-0 (.000), 0 R, 0 2B, 0 3B, 0 HR, 0 RBI.

Year Team (League)	W	L	Pct.	ERA	WHIP	G	GS	CG	ShO	Hld.	Sv.-Opp.	IP	H	R	ER	HR	BB-IBB	SO	Avg.
1994— Minneapolis (NCL)	5	5	.500	3.31	1.29	19	19	2	...	...	0-...	114.1	103	47	42	11	44-4	94	.239
1995— Minneapolis (PRA)	11	2	.846	2.73	1.17	17	15	4	...	...	0-...	108.2	101	41	33	...	26-...	100	...
1996— Durham (Caro.)	7	4	.636	2.41	1.24	49	0	0	0	...	20-...	59.2	58	20	16	3	16-3	76	.251
1997— Greenville (Sou.)	3	1	.750	2.04	0.96	31	0	0	0	...	16-...	35.1	20	8	8	3	14-1	43	.160
— Richmond (Int'l)	0	3	.000	4.32	0.92	14	0	0	0	...	1-...	25.0	21	13	12	3	2-0	35	.236
— Atlanta (N.L.)	1	0	1.000	3.00	1.07	15	0	0	0	0	1-1	15.0	12	5	5	4	4-2	19	.211
1998— Atlanta (N.L.)	3	2	.600	2.71	1.03	75	0	0	0	11	30-34	73.0	51	24	22	6	24-1	79	.193
1999— Atlanta (N.L.)			Did not play.																
2000— Atlanta (N.L.)	2	3	.400	3.61	1.28	59	0	0	0	12	12-14	52.1	43	21	21	7	24-5	51	.226
— Richmond (Int'l)	0	0	...	0.00	0.71	5	0	0	0	...	1-...	5.2	0	0	0	0	4-0	7	.000
2001— Atlanta (N.L.)	3	3	.500	3.02	1.34	53	0	0	0	...	1-2	59.2	50	22	20	4	30-8	56	.226
— Richmond (Int'l)	0	0	...	0.00	1.00	1	0	0	0	...	0-...	1.0	0	0	0	0	1-0	2	.000
2002— Atlanta (N.L.)	3	4	.429	2.97	1.28	52	0	0	0	2	0-0	66.2	52	23	22	6	33-3	51	.213
2003— Baltimore (A.L.)	4	2	.667	3.34	1.25	68	0	0	0	14	1-4	59.1	60	23	22	9	14-3	47	.263
2004— Toronto (A.L.)	1	6	.143	6.38	1.78	57	0	0	0	4	3-5	55.0	73	40	39	6	25-7	49	.313
American League totals (2 years)	5	8	.385	4.80	1.50	125	0	0	0	18	4-9	114.1	133	63	61	15	39-10	96	.289
National League totals (5 years)	12	12	.500	3.04	1.21	254	0	0	0	25	44-51	266.2	208	95	90	27	115-19	256	.213
Major League totals (7 years)	17	20	.459	3.57	1.30	379	0	0	0	43	48-60	381.0	341	158	151	42	154-29	352	.237

DIVISION SERIES RECORD

Year Team (League)	W	L	Pct.	ERA	WHIP	G	GS	CG	ShO	Hld.	Sv.-Opp.	IP	H	R	ER	HR	BB-IBB	SO	Avg.
1998— Atlanta (N.L.)	0	0	...	0.00	1.50	3	0	0	0	0	0-0	3.1	1	0	0	0	4-1	3	.111
2000— Atlanta (N.L.)	0	0	...	5.40	0.60	3	0	0	0	0	0-0	1.2	0	1	1	0	1-1	3	.000
2001— Atlanta (N.L.)			Did not play.																
2002— Atlanta (N.L.)	0	0	...	0.00	0.00	1	0	0	0	0	0-0	2.0	0	0	0	0	0-0	1	.000
Division series totals (3 years)	0	0	...	1.29	0.86	7	0	0	0	0	0-0	7.0	1	1	1	0	5-2	7	.048

Year Team (League)	W	L	Pct.	ERA	WHIP	G	GS	CG	ShO	Hld.	Sv.-Opp.	IP	H	R	ER	HR	BB-IBB	SO	Avg.
1997— Atlanta (N.L.)	0	0	...	0.00	0.33	2	0	0	0	0	0-0	3.0	1	0	0	0	0-0	4	.111
1998— Atlanta (N.L.)	0	1	.000	7.36	1.36	4	0	0	0	0	0-0	3.2	3	3	3	2	2-0	5	.214
2001— Atlanta (N.L.)	0	0	...	0.00	0.33	2	0	0	0	0	0-0	3.0	0	0	0	0	1-0	2	.000
Champ. series totals (3 years)	0	1	.000	2.79	0.72	8	0	0	0	0	0-0	9.2	4	3	3	2	3-0	11	.129

LILLY, TED   P

PERSONAL: Born January 4, 1976, in Lomita, Calif. ... 6-1/190. ... Throws left, bats left. ... Full name: Theodore Roosevelt Lilly. ... Name pronounced: LILL-ee. ... High school: Yosemite (Oakhurst, Calif.). ... Junior college: Fresno City (Calif.).

TRANSACTIONS/CAREER NOTES: Selected by Los Angeles Dodgers in 23rd round of 1996 free-agent draft. ... Traded by Dodgers with 2B Wilton Guerrero, OF Peter Bergeron and 1B Jonathan Tucker to Montreal Expos for P Carlos Perez, SS Mark Grudzielanek and IF Hiram Bocachica (July 31, 1998). ... Traded by Expos to New York Yankees (March 17, 2000), as part of deal in which Yankees traded P Hideki Irabu to Expos for P Jake Westbrook and two players to be named (December 29, 1999); Yankees acquired P Christian Parker to complete deal (March 22, 2000). ... On disabled list (April 2-May 23, 2000); included rehabilitation assignments to Tampa and Columbus. ... On suspended list (August 11-17, 2001). ... Traded by Yankees with OF John-Ford Griffin and P Jason Arnold to Oakland Athletics as part of three-team deal in which Tigers acquired 1B Carlos Pena, P Franklyn German and a player to be named from A's and Yankees acquired P Jeff Weaver from Tigers (July 5, 2002); Tigers acquired P Jeremy Bonderman to complete deal (August 22, 2002). ... On disabled list (July 23-September 10, 2002). ... Traded by Athletics to Toronto Blue Jays for OF Bobby Kielty and a player to be named (November 18, 2003).

CAREER HITTING: 1-for-17 (.059), 0 R, 0 2B, 0 3B, 0 HR, 0 RBI.

Year Team (League)	W	L	Pct.	ERA	WHIP	G	GS	CG	ShO	Hld.	Sv.-Opp.	IP	H	R	ER	HR	BB-IBB	SO	Avg.
1996— Yakima (N'west)	4	0	1.000	0.84	0.73	13	8	0	0	...	0-...	53.2	25	9	5	0	14-1	75	.135
1997— San Bernardino (Calif.)	7	8	.467	2.81	1.10	23	21	2	1	...	0-...	134.2	116	52	42	9	32-0	158	.234
1998— San Antonio (Texas)	8	4	.667	3.30	1.35	17	17	0	0	...	0-...	111.2	114	50	41	8	37-0	96	.266
— Albuquerque (PCL)	1	3	.250	4.94	1.55	5	5	0	0	...	0-...	31.0	39	20	17	3	9-0	25	.310
— Ottawa (Int'l)	2	2	.500	4.85	1.64	7	7	0	0	...	0-...	39.0	45	28	21	8	19-0	49	.280
1999— Ottawa (Int'l)	8	5	.615	3.84	1.17	16	16	0	0	...	0-...	89.0	81	40	38	12	23-0	78	.241
— Montreal (N.L.)	0	1	.000	7.61	1.65	9	3	0	0	0	0-0	23.2	30	20	20	7	9-0	28	.309
2000— Tampa (FSL)	0	0	...	1.35	0.90	1	1	0	0	...	0-...	6.2	5	3	1	0	1-0	6	.192
— Columbus (Int'l)	8	11	.421	4.19	1.49	22	22	3	1	...	0-...	137.1	157	77	64	14	48-0	127	.287
— New York (A.L.)	0	0	...	5.63	1.63	7	0	0	0	0	0-0	8.0	8	6	5	1	5-0	11	.235
2001— Columbus (Int'l)	0	0	...	2.84	0.95	5	5	0	0	...	0-...	25.1	16	10	8	2	8-0	30	.176
— New York (A.L.)	5	6	.455	5.37	1.47	26	21	0	0	0	0-0	120.2	126	81	72	20	51-1	112	.267
2002— New York (A.L.)	3	6	.333	3.40	1.06	16	11	2	1	0	0-0	76.2	57	31	29	10	24-3	59	.202
— Oakland (A.L.)	2	1	.667	4.63	1.29	6	5	0	0	0	0-0	23.1	23	12	12	5	7-0	18	.253
2003— Oakland (A.L.)	12	10	.545	4.34	1.33	32	31	0	0	0	0-0	178.1	179	92	86	24	58-3	147	.255
2004— Toronto (A.L.)	12	10	.545	4.06	1.32	32	32	2	1	0	0-0	197.1	171	92	89	26	89-2	168	.230
American League totals (5 years)	34	33	.507	4.36	1.32	119	100	4	2	0	0-0	604.1	564	314	293	86	234-9	515	.242
National League totals (1 year)	0	1	.000	7.61	1.65	9	3	0	0	0	0-0	23.2	30	20	20	7	9-0	28	.309
Major League totals (6 years)	34	34	.500	4.49	1.33	128	103	4	2	0	0-0	628.0	594	334	313	93	243-9	543	.245

Year Team (League)	W	L	Pct.	ERA	WHIP	G	GS	CG	ShO	Hld.	Sv.-Opp.	IP	H	R	ER	HR	BB-IBB	SO	Avg.
2002— Oakland (A.L.)	0	1	.000	13.50	2.75	2	0	0	0	0	0-1	4.0	10	6	6	1	1-0	3	.476
2003— Oakland (A.L.)	0	0	...	0.00	0.44	2	1	0	0	0	0-0	9.0	2	1	0	0	2-0	7	.065
Division series totals (2 years)	0	1	.000	4.15	1.15	4	1	0	0	0	0-1	13.0	12	7	6	1	3-0	10	.231

Year Team (League)	W	L	Pct.	ERA	WHIP	G	GS	CG	ShO	Hld.	Sv.-Opp.	IP	H	R	ER	HR	BB-IBB	SO	Avg.
All-Star Game totals (1 year)	0	0	...	0.00	2.00	1	0	0	0	0	0-0	1.0	2	0	0	0	0-0	1	.400

LIMA, JOSE   P

PERSONAL: Born September 30, 1972, in Santiago, Dominican Republic. ... 6-2/205. ... Throws right, bats right. ... Full name: Jose Desiderio Lima. ... Name pronounced: LEE-mah. ... High school: Escuela Primaria Las Charcas (Santiago, Dominican Republic).

TRANSACTIONS/CAREER NOTES: Signed as a non-drafted free agent by Detroit Tigers organization (July 5, 1989). ... Traded by Tigers with C Brad Ausmus, Ps C.J. Nitkowski and Trever Miller and 1B Daryle Ward to Houston Astros for OF Brian Hunter, IF Orlando Miller, Ps Doug Brocail and Todd Jones and cash (December 10, 1996). ... On suspended list (May 9-15, 2001). ... Traded by Astros to Detroit Tigers for P Dave Mlicki (June 23, 2001). ... Released by Tigers (September 7, 2002). ... Contract purchased by Kansas City Royals from Newark of the independent Atlantic League (June 4, 2003). ... On disabled list (August 2-18 and August 24-September 18, 2003). ... Signed as a free agent by Los Angeles Dodgers organization (January 27, 2004).

CAREER HITTING: 37-for-284 (.130), 18 R, 4 2B, 0 3B, 0 HR, 10 RBI.

Year Team (League)	W	L	Pct.	ERA	WHIP	G	GS	CG	ShO	Hld.	Sv.-Opp.	IP	H	R	ER	HR	BB-IBB	SO	Avg.
1990— Bristol (Appalachian)	3	8	.273	5.02	1.47	14	12	1	0	...	1-...	75.1	89	49	42	9	22-3	64	.299
1991— Lakeland (Fla. St.)	0	1	.000	10.38	2.08	4	1	0	0	...	0-...	8.2	16	10	10	1	2-0	5	.421
— Fayetteville (S. Atl.)	1	3	.250	4.97	1.34	18	7	0	0	...	0-...	58.0	53	38	32	4	25-0	60	.241
1992— Lakeland (Fla. St.)	5	11	.313	3.16	1.01	25	25	5	2	...	0-...	151.0	132	57	53	14	21-2	137	.237
1993— London (East.)	8	13	.381	4.07	1.24	27	27	2	0	...	0-...	177.0	160	96	80	19	59-4	138	.238
1994— Toledo (International)	7	9	.438	3.60	1.21	23	22	3	2	...	0-...	142.1	124	70	57	16	48-1	117	.235
— Detroit (A.L.)	0	1	.000	13.50	2.10	3	1	0	0	0	0-0	6.2	11	10	10	2	3-1	7	.355
1995— Lakeland (Fla. St.)	3	1	.750	2.57	1.10	4	4	0	0	...	0-...	21.0	23	11	6	2	0-0	20	.271
— Toledo (International)	5	3	.625	3.01	1.11	11	11	1	0	...	0-...	74.2	69	26	25	9	14-2	40	.247
— Detroit (A.L.)	3	9	.250	6.11	1.40	15	15	0	0	0	0-0	73.2	85	52	50	10	18-4	37	.288
1996— Toledo (International)	5	4	.556	6.78	1.52	12	12	0	0	...	0-...	69.0	93	53	52	11	12-0	57	.322
— Detroit (A.L.)	5	6	.455	5.70	1.50	39	4	0	0	6	3-7	72.2	87	48	46	13	22-4	59	.296
1997— Houston (N.L.)	1	6	.143	5.28	1.27	52	1	0	0	3	2-2	75.0	79	45	44	9	16-2	63	.271
1998— Houston (N.L.)	16	8	.667	3.70	1.12	33	33	3	1	0	0-0	233.1	229	100	96	34	32-1	169	.256
1999— Houston (N.L.)	21	10	.677	3.58	1.22	35	•35	3	0	0	0-0	246.1	256	108	98	30	44-2	187	.265
2000— Houston (N.L.)	7	16	.304	6.65	1.62	33	33	0	0	0	0-0	196.1	251	* 152	* 145	* 48	68-3	124	.313
2001— Houston (N.L.)	1	2	.333	7.30	1.75	14	9	0	0	0	0-0	53.0	77	48	43	12	16-1	41	.350
— Detroit (A.L.)	5	10	.333	4.71	1.26	18	18	2	0	0	0-0	112.2	120	66	59	23	22-2	43	.274
2002— Detroit (A.L.)	4	6	.400	7.77	1.57	20	12	0	0	0	0-0	68.1	86	60	59	12	21-0	33	.314
2003— Kansas City (A.L.)	8	3	.727	4.91	1.45	14	14	0	0	0	0-0	73.1	80	40	40	7	26-0	32	.280

Year Team (League)	W	L	Pct.	ERA	WHIP	G	GS	CG	ShO	Hld.	Sv.-Opp.	IP	H	R	ER	HR	BB-IBB	SO	Avg.
2004— Los Angeles (N.L.)	13	5	.722	4.07	1.24	36	24	0	0	1	0-0	170.1	178	81	77	33	34-6	93	.271
American League totals (6 years)	25	35	.417	5.83	1.43	109	64	2	0	6	3-7	407.1	469	276	264	67	112-11	211	.290
National League totals (6 years)	59	47	.557	4.65	1.31	203	135	6	1	4	2-2	974.1	1070	534	503	166	210-15	677	.279
Major League totals (11 years)	84	82	.506	5.00	1.35	312	199	8	1	10	5-9	1381.2	1539	810	767	233	322-26	888	.282

DIVISION SERIES RECORD

Year Team (League)	W	L	Pct.	ERA	WHIP	G	GS	CG	ShO	Hld.	Sv.-Opp.	IP	H	R	ER	HR	BB-IBB	SO	Avg.
1997— Houston (N.L.)	0	0	...	0.00	1.00	1	0	0	0	0	0-0	1.0	0	0	0	0	1-0	1	.000
1998— Houston (N.L.)		Did not play.																	
1999— Houston (N.L.)	0	1	.000	5.40	1.65	1	1	0	0	0	0-0	6.2	9	4	4	0	2-2	4	.333
2004— Los Angeles (N.L.)	1	0	1.000	0.00	0.67	1	1	1	1	0	0-0	9.0	5	0	0	0	1-0	4	.161
Division series totals (3 years)	1	1	.500	2.16	1.08	3	2	1	1	0	0-0	16.2	14	4	4	0	4-2	9	.233

ALL-STAR GAME RECORD

Year Team (League)	W	L	Pct.	ERA	WHIP	G	GS	CG	ShO	Hld.	Sv.-Opp.	IP	H	R	ER	HR	BB-IBB	SO	Avg.
All-Star Game totals (1 year)	0	0	...	0.00	1.00	0	0	0	0	0	0-0	1.0	0	0	0	0	0-0	0	.250

LINCOLN, MIKE   P

PERSONAL: Born April 10, 1975, in Carmichael, Calif. ... 6-2/213. ... Throws right, bats right. ... Full name: Michael George Lincoln. ... High school: Casa Roble (Orangevale, Calif.). ... College: Tennessee.

TRANSACTIONS/CAREER NOTES: Selected by Montreal Expos organization in 51st round of 1993 free-agent draft; did not sign. ... Selected by San Francisco Giants organization in 37th round of 1994 free-agent draft; did not sign. ... Selected by San Francisco Giants organization in 40th round of 1995 free-agent draft; did not sign. ... Selected by Minnesota Twins organization in 13th round of 1996 free-agent draft. ... On disabled list (July 23, 2000-remainder of season). ... Released by Twins (January 15, 2001). ... Signed by Pittsburgh Pirates organization (February 17, 2001). ... On disabled list (August 13-28, 2001). ... On disabled list (March 24-July 1, 2003); included rehabilitation assignment to Nashville. ... Signed as a free agent by St. Louis Cardinals (January 9, 2004). ... On disabled list (May 4, 2004-remainder of season).

CAREER HITTING: 1-for-10 (.100), 0 R, 0 2B, 0 3B, 0 HR, 0 RBI.

Year Team (League)	W	L	Pct.	ERA	WHIP	G	GS	CG	ShO	Hld.	Sv.-Opp.	IP	H	R	ER	HR	BB-IBB	SO	Avg.
1996— Fort Myers (Fla. St.)	5	2	.714	4.07	1.49	12	11	0	0	...	0-...	59.2	64	31	27	5	25-0	24	.279
1997— Fort Myers (Fla. St.)	13	4	.765	2.28	1.16	20	20	1	1	...	0-...	134.0	130	41	34	4	25-0	75	.252
1998— New Britain (East.)	15	7	.682	3.22	1.24	26	26	1	0	...	0-...	173.1	180	80	62	13	35-0	109	.270
1999— Minnesota (A.L.)	3	10	.231	6.84	1.68	18	15	0	0	1	0-...	76.1	102	59	58	11	26-0	27	.321
— Salt Lake (PCL)	5	2	.714	7.78	1.75	9	9	0	0	...	0-...	59.0	82	52	51	12	21-0	39	.335
2000— Salt Lake (PCL)	4	1	.800	3.87	1.18	12	12	2	1	...	0-...	74.1	72	35	32	4	16-1	37	.252
— Minnesota (A.L.)	0	3	.000	10.89	2.37	8	4	0	0	0	0-...	20.2	36	25	25	10	13-0	15	.383
2001— Nashville (PCL)	5	4	.556	3.44	1.25	18	13	1	0	...	0-...	91.2	90	39	35	10	25-0	71	.251
— Pittsburgh (N.L.)	2	1	.667	2.68	1.12	31	0	0	0	7	0-2	40.1	34	16	12	3	11-0	24	.225
2002— Pittsburgh (N.L.)	2	4	.333	3.11	1.48	55	0	0	0	11	0-3	72.1	80	28	25	7	27-8	50	.290
— Nashville (PCL)	0	0	...	1.23	1.09	10	0	0	0	...	2-...	14.2	14	2	2	0	2-0	15	.237
2003— Nashville (PCL)	1	1	.500	0.71	0.90	8	0	0	0	...	0-...	12.2	8	2	1	1	4-0	9	.186
— Pittsburgh (N.L.)	3	4	.429	5.20	1.40	36	0	0	0	5	5-8	36.1	38	22	21	5	13-0	28	.277
2004— St. Louis (N.L.)	3	2	.600	5.19	0.92	13	0	0	0	1	0-2	17.1	10	12	10	1	6-0	14	.164
American League totals (2 years)	3	13	.188	7.70	1.82	26	19	0	0	1	0-0	97.0	138	84	83	21	39-0	42	.335
National League totals (4 years)	10	11	.476	3.68	1.32	135	0	0	0	24	5-15	166.1	162	78	68	16	57-8	116	.259
Major League totals (6 years)	13	24	.351	5.16	1.50	161	19	0	0	25	5-15	263.1	300	162	151	37	96-8	158	.289

LINDEN, TODD   OF

PERSONAL: Born June 30, 1980, in Edmonds, Wash. ... 6-3/210. ... Bats both, throws right. ... Full name: Todd A. Linden. ... High school: Central Kitsap (Silverdale, Wash.). ... College: LSU.

TRANSACTIONS/CAREER NOTES: Selected by San Francisco Giants in supplemental round ("sandwich pick" between first and second rounds, 41st pick overall) of 2001 free-agent draft; pick received as part of compensation for Cleveland Indians signing Type A free-agent OF Ellis Burks.

2004 GAMES PLAYED BY POSITION (MLB): OF—11.

Year Team (League)	Pos.	G	AB	R	H	2B	3B	HR	RBI	BB	SO	HBP	GDP	SB-CS	Avg.	OBP	SLG	OPS	E	Avg.
2002— Shreveport (Texas)	OF	111	392	64	123	26	2	12	52	61	101	12	12	9-5	.314	.419	.482	.901	3	.987
— Fresno (PCL)	OF	29	100	18	25	2	1	3	10	20	35	1	2	2-0	.250	.380	.380	.760	0	1.000
2003— Fresno (PCL)	OF-DH	125	471	75	131	24	3	11	56	40	105	17	9	14-4	.278	.356	.412	.768	4	.985
— San Francisco (N.L.)	OF	18	38	2	8	1	0	1	6	1	8	0	2	0-0	.211	.231	.316	.547	1	.929
2004— Fresno (PCL)	OF-DH	130	489	93	127	28	2	23	75	63	149	1	9	8-6	.260	.349	.466	.816	7	.976
— San Francisco (N.L.)	OF	16	32	6	5	1	0	0	1	5	7	1	0	0-0	.156	.289	.188	.477	0	1.000
Major League totals (2 years)		34	70	8	13	2	0	1	7	6	15	1	2	0-0	.186	.260	.257	.517	1	.957

LINEBRINK, SCOTT   P

PERSONAL: Born August 4, 1976, in Austin, Texas. ... 6-3/208. ... Throws right, bats right. ... Full name: Scott Cameron Linebrink. ... High school: McNeil (Austin, Texas). ... College: Texas State.

TRANSACTIONS/CAREER NOTES: Selected by San Francisco Giants organization in second round of 1997 free-agent draft. ... Traded by Giants to Houston Astros for P Doug Henry (July 30, 2000). ... On disabled list (May 20-June 17, 2002); included rehabilitation assignment to New Orleans and Round Rock. ... Claimed on waivers by San Diego Padres (May 29, 2003).

CAREER HITTING: 3-for-15 (.200), 0 R, 1 2B, 0 3B, 0 HR, 0 RBI.

Year Team (League)	W	L	Pct.	ERA	WHIP	G	GS	CG	ShO	Hld.	Sv.-Opp.	IP	H	R	ER	HR	BB-IBB	SO	Avg.
1997— Salem-Keizer (N'west)	0	0	...	4.50	1.30	3	3	0	0	...	0-...	10.0	7	5	5	1	6-0	6	.194
— San Jose (California)	2	1	.667	3.18	1.38	6	6	0	0	...	0-...	28.1	29	11	10	2	10-0	40	.264
1998— Shreveport (Texas)	10	8	.556	5.02	1.41	21	21	0	0	...	0-...	113.0	101	66	63	12	58-1	128	.243
1999— Shreveport (Texas)	1	8	.111	6.44	1.43	10	10	0	0	...	0-...	43.1	48	31	31	7	14-0	33	.279
2000— Fresno (PCL)	1	4	.200	5.23	1.06	28	7	0	0	...	4-...	62.0	54	42	36	10	12-0	49	.225
— San Francisco (N.L.)	0	0	...	11.57	3.86	3	0	0	0	0	0-0	2.1	7	3	3	1	2-0	0	.500
— Houston (N.L.)	0	0	...	4.66	1.76	8	0	0	0	0	0-0	9.2	11	5	5	3	6-0	6	.289
— New Orleans (PCL)	2	0	1.000	1.80	1.47	11	0	0	0	...	1-...	15.0	15	4	3	0	7-0	22	.259
2001— Houston (N.L.)	0	0	...	2.61	1.16	9	0	0	0	0	0-0	10.1	6	4	3	0	6-0	9	.176
— New Orleans (PCL)	7	6	.538	3.50	1.06	50	0	0	0	...	8-...	72.0	52	28	28	4	24-6	72	.204

Year Team (League)	W	L	Pct.	ERA	WHIP	G	GS	CG	ShO	Hld.	Sv.-Opp.	IP	H	R	ER	HR	BB-IBB	SO	Avg.
2002—Houston (N.L.)	0	0	...	7.03	1.81	22	0	0	0	1	0-0	24.1	31	21	19	2	13-4	24	.298
—New Orleans (PCL)	1	1	.500	6.00	1.87	13	0	0	0	...	0-...	15.0	17	11	10	1	11-3	16	.293
—Round Rock (Texas)	0	0	...	0.00	2.00	2	2	0	0	...	0-...	2.0	2	0	0	0	2-0	1	.286
2003—New Orleans (PCL)	0	2	.000	2.70	1.30	2	2	0	0	...	0-...	10.0	8	3	3	1	5-0	6	.222
—Houston (N.L.)	1	1	.500	4.26	1.64	9	6	0	0	0	0-0	31.2	38	15	15	4	14-1	17	.317
—San Diego (N.L.)	2	1	.667	2.82	1.27	43	0	0	0	6	0-0	60.2	55	22	19	5	22-3	51	.244
2004—San Diego (N.L.)	7	3	.700	2.14	1.04	73	0	0	0	28	0-5	84.0	61	22	20	8	26-2	83	.209
Major League totals (5 years)	10	5	.667	3.39	1.34	167	6	0	0	35	0-5	223.0	209	92	84	23	89-10	190	.253

LIRIANO, PEDRO   P

PERSONAL: Born October 23, 1980, in Fantino, Dominican Republic. ... 6-2/170. ... Throws right, bats right. ... Full name: Pedro Antonio Liriano. ... High school: Fourth Bachillerato (D.R.). ... Cousin of Ramon Ortiz, pitcher, Anaheim Angels.

TRANSACTIONS/CAREER NOTES: Signed as a non-drafted free agent by Anaheim Angels organization (November 10, 1998). ... Traded by Angels to Milwaukee Brewers (September 20, 2002), completing deal in which Angels acquired OF Alex Ochoa and C Sal Fasano from Brewers for C Jorge Fabregas and two players to be named (July 31, 2002); Brewers acquired 2B Johnny Raburn as part of deal (August 14, 2002).

CAREER HITTING: 0-for-1 (.000), 0 R, 0 2B, 0 3B, 0 HR, 0 RBI.

Year Team (League)	W	L	Pct.	ERA	WHIP	G	GS	CG	ShO	Hld.	Sv.-Opp.	IP	H	R	ER	HR	BB-IBB	SO	Avg.
2001—Provo (Pio.)	11	2	.846	2.78	1.43	15	14	0	0	...	0-...	77.2	80	39	24	3	31-0	76	.265
2002—Rancho Cuca. (Calif.)	10	14	.417	3.60	1.21	28	28	1	1	...	0-...	167.1	129	86	67	14	74-1	176	.212
2003—Huntsville (Southern)	9	13	.409	3.79	1.40	27	26	0	0	...	0-...	142.2	138	77	60	12	62-2	116	.256
2004—Indianapolis (Int'l)	3	10	.231	5.20	1.58	29	21	1	0	...	1-...	126.1	149	81	73	21	50-1	97	.300
—Milwaukee (N.L.)	0	0	...	4.02	1.15	11	0	0	0	1	0-0	15.2	15	10	7	3	3-0	10	.238
Major League totals (1 year)	0	0	...	4.02	1.15	11	0	0	0	1	0-0	15.2	15	10	7	3	3-0	10	.238

LITTLE, MARK   OF

PERSONAL: Born July 11, 1972, in Edwardsville, Ill. ... 6-0/205. ... Bats right, throws right. ... Full name: Mark Travis Little. ... High school: Edwardsville (Ill.). ... College: Memphis.

TRANSACTIONS/CAREER NOTES: Selected by Texas Rangers organization in eighth round of 1994 free-agent draft. ... Traded by Rangers to St. Louis Cardinals (August 9, 1998), completing deal in which Cardinals traded P Todd Stottlemyre and SS Royce Clayton to Rangers for P Darren Oliver, 3B Fernando Tatis and a player to be named (July 31, 1998). ... Signed as a free agent by Colorado Rockies organization (November 21, 2000). ... On disabled list (May 29-August 5 and August 25, 2001-remainder of season); included rehabilitation assignment to Colorado Springs. ... Traded by Rockies with P John Thomson to New York Mets for OFs Jay Payton and Robert Stratton and P Mark Corey (July 31, 2002). ... Traded by Mets to Arizona Diamondbacks for a player to be named (August 16, 2002); Mets acquired P P.J. Bevis to complete deal (August 20, 2002). ... Released by Diamondbacks (May 30, 2003). ... Signed by Cleveland Indians organization (June 2, 2003). ... Released by Indians (July 28, 2004).

2004 GAMES PLAYED BY POSITION (MLB): OF—11.

Year Team (League)	Pos.	G	AB	R	H	2B	3B	HR	RBI	BB	SO	HBP	GDP	SB-CS	Avg.	OBP	SLG	OPS	E	Avg.
1994—Hudson Valley (NY-Penn.)	OF	54	208	33	61	15	5	3	27	22	38	1	4	14-5	.293	.357	.457	.814	6	.959
1995—Charlotte (Fla. St.)	OF	115	438	75	112	31	8	9	50	51	108	14	4	20-14	.256	.350	.425	.775	10	.966
1996—Tulsa (Texas)	OF	101	409	69	119	24	2	13	50	48	88	10	5	22-10	.291	.377	.455	.831	9	.968
1997—Okla. City (A.A.)	OF-DH-1B	121	415	72	109	23	4	15	45	39	100	8	8	21-9	.263	.338	.446	.783	8	.973
1998—Oklahoma (PCL)	OF-DH	69	274	58	81	20	4	8	46	16	60	10	4	9-6	.296	.351	.485	.836	1	.994
—Memphis (PCL)	OF	19	63	9	17	3	3	0	6	6	10	2	0	0-3	.270	.342	.413	.755	1	.971
—St. Louis (N.L.)	OF	7	12	0	1	0	0	0	0	2	5	0	0	0-0	.083	.214	.083	.298	0	1.000
1999—Memphis (PCL)	OF	51	196	40	58	11	5	3	22	10	48	6	3	12-4	.296	.347	.449	.796	5	.960
2000—Memphis (PCL)	OF	107	424	70	120	29	7	15	64	51	98	11	2	22-11	.283	.373	.491	.864	7	.974
2001—Colorado (N.L.)	OF	51	85	18	29	6	0	3	13	1	20	4	0	5-2	.341	.378	.518	.895	0	1.000
—Colo. Springs (PCL)	OF	9	40	6	15	2	0	0	4	3	9	1	1	0-2	.375	.432	.425	.857	0	1.000
2002—Colorado (N.L.)	OF	61	105	20	21	5	2	0	5	13	28	4	1	2-1	.200	.311	.286	.597	2	.970
—New York (N.L.)	OF	3	3	0	0	0	0	0	0	0	1	0	0	0-1	.000	.000	.000	.000	0	...
—Norfolk (Int'l)	OF	2	10	1	5	0	0	0	2	1	3	0	0	0-0	.500	.545	.500	1.045	0	1.000
—Tucson (PCL)	OF	13	54	6	17	3	1	2	8	0	11	0	2	2-1	.315	.304	.519	.822	1	.976
—Arizona (N.L.)	OF	15	22	8	6	0	1	0	2	2	5	4	0	0-0	.273	.429	.364	.792	0	1.000
2003—Tucson (PCL)	OF-DH	31	95	13	30	5	4	5	13	3	18	5	0	3-1	.316	.369	.611	.980	2	.951
—Buffalo (Int'l)	OF-DH	45	146	20	41	5	1	2	16	5	45	6	1	4-2	.281	.329	.370	.699	2	.982
2004—Cleveland (A.L.)	OF	11	20	0	4	0	0	0	2	0	7	2	0	0-0	.200	.261	.200	.461	0	1.000
—Buffalo (Int'l)	OF	68	239	37	75	17	4	11	39	9	40	7	3	4-6	.314	.349	.556	.905	2	.984
American League totals (1 year)		11	20	0	4	0	0	0	2	0	7	2	0	0-0	.200	.261	.200	.461	0	1.000
National League totals (3 years)		137	227	46	57	11	3	3	20	18	59	12	1	8-4	.251	.339	.366	.704	2	.985
Major League totals (4 years)		148	247	46	61	11	3	3	22	18	66	14	1	8-4	.247	.332	.352	.684	2	.986

DIVISION SERIES RECORD

Year Team (League)	Pos.	G	AB	R	H	2B	3B	HR	RBI	BB	SO	HBP	GDP	SB-CS	Avg.	OBP	SLG	OPS	E	Avg.
2002—Arizona (N.L.)	OF	2	4	0	0	0	0	0	0	0	2	0	0	0-0	.000	.000	.000	.000	0	1.000

LOAIZA, ESTEBAN   P

PERSONAL: Born December 31, 1971, in Tijuana, Mexico. ... 6-3/215. ... Throws right, bats right. ... Full name: Esteban Antonio Veyna Loaiza. ... Name pronounced: s-TAY-bahn low-EYE-zah. ... High school: Mar Vista (Imperial Beach, Calif.).

TRANSACTIONS/CAREER NOTES: Signed as a non-drafted free agent by Pittsburgh Pirates organization (March 21, 1991). ... Loaned by Pirates organization to Mexico City Red Devils of the Mexican League (May 7-28, 1993; and June 19-August 14, 1996). ... Traded by Pirates to Texas Rangers for P Todd Van Poppel and 2B Warren Morris (July 17, 1998). ... On disabled list (May 12-July 5, 1999; included rehabilitation assignment to Oklahoma City. ... Traded by Rangers to Toronto Blue Jays for P Darwin Cubillan and 2B/SS Michael Young (July 19, 2000). ... On disabled list (March 22-May 14, 2002; included rehabilitation assignments to Dunedin, Syracuse and Tennessee. ... Signed as a free agent by Chicago White Sox organization (January 27, 2003). ... Traded by White Sox to New York Yankees for P Jose Contreras and cash (July 31, 2004).

CAREER HITTING: 31-for-179 (.173), 12 R, 2 2B, 1 3B, 0 HR, 11 RBI.

Year Team (League)	W	L	Pct.	ERA	WHIP	G	GS	CG	ShO	Hld.	Sv.-Opp.	IP	H	R	ER	HR	BB-IBB	SO	Avg.
1991—GC Pirates (GCL)	5	1	.833	2.26	1.20	11	11	1	1	...	0-...	51.2	48	17	13	0	14-0	41	.241
1992—Augusta (S. Atl.)	10	8	.556	3.89	1.35	26	25	3	0	...	0-...	143.1	134	72	62	7	60-0	123	.249
1993—Salem (Caro.)	6	7	.462	3.39	1.31	17	17	3	0	...	0-...	109.0	113	53	41	7	30-0	61	.268
—M.C. Red Devils (Mex.)	1	1	.500	5.18	1.48	4	3	0	0	...	0-...	24.1	32	18	14	...	4-...	15	...
—Carolina (Southern)	2	1	.667	3.77	1.19	7	7	1	0	...	0-...	43.0	39	18	18	5	12-1	40	.241

Year	Team (League)	W	L	Pct.	ERA	WHIP	G	GS	CG	ShO	Hld.	Sv.-Opp.	IP	H	R	ER	HR	BB-IBB	SO	Avg.
1994—	Carolina (Southern)	10	5	.667	3.79	1.29	24	24	3	0	...	0-...	154.1	169	69	65	15	30-0	115	.280
1995—	Pittsburgh (N.L.)	8	9	.471	5.16	1.51	32	•31	1	0	0	0-0	172.2	205	*115	*99	21	55-3	85	.300
1996—	Calgary (PCL)	3	4	.429	4.02	1.24	12	11	1	1	...	0-0	69.1	61	34	31	5	25-2	38	.243
—	Pittsburgh (N.L.)	2	3	.400	4.96	1.59	10	10	1	1	0	0-0	52.2	65	32	29	11	19-2	32	.308
—	M.C. Red Devils (Mex.)	2	0	1.000	2.43	1.26	5	5	0	0	...	0-...	33.1	28	12	9	...	14-...	16	...
1997—	Pittsburgh (N.L.)	11	11	.500	4.13	1.38	33	32	1	0	0	0-0	196.1	214	99	90	17	56-9	122	.279
1998—	Pittsburgh (N.L.)	6	5	.545	4.52	1.37	21	14	0	0	0	0-1	91.2	96	50	46	13	30-1	53	.275
—	Texas (A.L.)	3	6	.333	5.90	1.58	14	14	1	0	0	0-0	79.1	103	57	52	15	22-3	55	.316
1999—	Texas (A.L.)	9	5	.643	4.56	1.40	30	15	0	0	0	0-0	120.1	128	65	61	10	40-2	77	.275
—	Oklahoma (PCL)	0	0	...	0.00	1.38	2	2	0	0	0	0-...	4.1	3	0	0	0	3-0	6	.188
2000—	Texas (A.L.)	5	6	.455	5.37	1.53	20	17	0	0	0	1-1	107.1	133	67	64	21	31-1	75	.302
—	Toronto (A.L.)	5	7	.417	3.62	1.32	14	14	1	1	0	0-0	92.0	95	45	37	8	26-0	62	.270
2001—	Toronto (A.L.)	11	11	.500	5.02	1.47	36	30	1	1	0	0-0	190.0	239	113	106	27	40-1	110	.307
2002—	Dunedin (Fla. St.)	0	0	...	0.00	0.80	2	2	0	0	0	0-...	5.0	2	0	0	0	2-0	2	.125
—	Toronto (A.L.)	9	10	.474	5.71	1.52	25	25	3	1	0	0-0	151.1	192	102	96	18	38-3	87	.309
—	Syracuse (Int'l)	0	0	...	2.08	0.92	1	1	0	0	0	0-0	4.1	4	1	1	0	0-0	4	.222
—	Tennessee (Sou.)	2	0	1.000	1.88	0.77	2	2	0	0	0	0-...	14.1	10	3	3	0	1-0	13	.208
2003—	Chicago (A.L.)	21	9	.700	2.90	1.11	34	34	1	0	0	0-0	226.1	196	75	73	17	56-2	*207	.233
2004—	Chicago (A.L.)	9	5	.643	4.86	1.43	21	21	2	1	0	0-0	140.2	156	81	76	23	45-3	83	.283
—	New York (A.L.)	1	2	.333	8.50	2.06	10	6	0	0	0	0-0	42.1	61	43	40	9	26-2	34	.337
American League totals (7 years)		73	61	.545	4.74	1.42	204	176	9	4	0	1-1	1149.2	1303	648	605	148	324-17	790	.286
National League totals (4 years)		27	28	.491	4.63	1.44	96	87	3	1	0	0-1	513.1	580	296	264	62	160-15	292	.289
Major League totals (10 years)		100	89	.529	4.70	1.42	300	263	12	5	0	1-2	1663.0	1883	944	869	210	484-32	1082	.287

DIVISION SERIES RECORD

Year	Team (League)	W	L	Pct.	ERA	WHIP	G	GS	CG	ShO	Hld.	Sv.-Opp.	IP	H	R	ER	HR	BB-IBB	SO	Avg.
1998—	Texas (A.L.)	Did not play.																		
1999—	Texas (A.L.)	0	1	.000	3.86	0.86	1	1	0	0	0	0-0	7.0	5	3	3	1	1-0	4	.192
2004—	New York (A.L.)	0	0	...	0.00	2.00	1	0	0	0	0	0-0	2.0	4	0	0	0	0-0	0	.500
Division series totals (2 years)		0	1	.000	3.00	1.11	2	1	0	0	0	0-0	9.0	9	3	3	1	1-0	4	.265

CHAMPIONSHIP SERIES RECORD

Year	Team (League)	W	L	Pct.	ERA	WHIP	G	GS	CG	ShO	Hld.	Sv.-Opp.	IP	H	R	ER	HR	BB-IBB	SO	Avg.
2004—	New York (A.L.)	0	1	.000	1.42	1.26	2	0	0	0	0	0-0	6.1	5	1	1	0	3-0	5	.217

ALL-STAR GAME RECORD

	W	L	Pct.	ERA	WHIP	G	GS	CG	ShO	Hld.	Sv.-Opp.	IP	H	R	ER	HR	BB-IBB	SO	Avg.
All-Star Game totals (2 years)	0	0	...	0.00	1.00	2	1	0	0	0	0-0	3.0	2	0	0	0	1-0	1	.182

LO DUCA, PAUL — C

PERSONAL: Born April 12, 1972, in Brooklyn, N.Y. ... 5-10/185. ... Bats right, throws right. ... Full name: Paul Anthony Lo Duca. ... Name pronounced: lah-duke-uh. ... High school: Apollo (Phoenix). ... College: Arizona State.

TRANSACTIONS/CAREER NOTES: Selected by Los Angeles Dodgers organization in 25th round of 1993 free-agent draft. ... On disabled list (April 29-May 21, 2001); included rehabilitation assignment to Las Vegas. ... Traded by Dodgers with P Guillermo Mota and OF Juan Encarnacion to Florida Marlins for Ps Brad Penny and Bill Murphy and 1B Hee Seop Choi (July 30, 2004).

2004 GAMES PLAYED BY POSITION (MLB): C—130, OF—9, 1B—3.

Year	Team (League)	Pos.	G	AB	R	H	2B	3B	HR	RBI	BB	SO	HBP	GDP	SB-CS	Avg.	OBP	SLG	OPS	E	Avg.
1993—	Vero Beach (FSL)	C	39	134	17	42	6	0	0	13	13	22	2	2	0-0	.313	.380	.358	.738	2	.992
1994—	Bakersfield (Calif.)	C-1B	123	455	65	144	32	1	6	68	52	49	3	5	16-9	.316	.387	.431	.818	5	.993
1995—	San Antonio (Texas)	3B-C-1B	61	199	27	49	8	0	1	8	26	25	2	12	5-5	.246	.339	.302	.641	11	.973
1996—	Vero Beach (FSL)	3B-C-1B	124	439	54	134	22	0	3	66	70	38	2	14	8-2	.305	.400	.376	.776	18	.980
1997—	San Antonio (Texas)	C-1B	105	385	63	126	28	2	7	69	46	27	3	17	16-8	.327	.399	.465	.864	7	.990
1998—	Albuquerque (PCL)	3B-C-1B	126	451	69	144	30	3	8	58	59	40	5	20	19-7	.319	.399	.452	.852	17	.980
—	Los Angeles (N.L.)	C	6	14	2	4	1	0	1	0	1	0	0	0	0-0	.286	.286	.357	.643	0	1.000
1999—	Los Angeles (N.L.)	C	36	95	11	22	1	0	3	11	10	9	2	3	1-2	.232	.312	.337	.649	2	.990
—	Albuquerque (PCL)	C	26	76	17	28	9	0	1	8	10	1	6	0	1-1	.368	.478	.526	1.005	4	.978
2000—	Albuquerque (PCL)	C-0-1-3-2	78	279	47	98	27	3	4	54	33	14	2	13	8-5	.351	.421	.513	.933	9	.979
—	Los Angeles (N.L.)	C-OF-3B	34	65	6	16	2	0	2	8	6	8	0	2	0-2	.246	.301	.369	.671	1	.993
2001—	Los Angeles (N.L.)	C-1-O-DH	125	460	71	147	28	0	25	90	39	30	6	11	2-4	.320	.374	.543	.917	9	.990
—	Las Vegas (PCL)	C-1B	3	9	3	3	2	0	0	3	1	0	0	0	0-0	.333	.400	.556	.956	1	.950
2002—	Los Angeles (N.L.)	C-1B-OF	149	580	74	163	38	1	10	64	34	31	10	20	3-1	.281	.330	.402	.731	9	.992
2003—	Los Angeles (N.L.)	C-1B-OF	147	568	64	155	34	2	7	52	44	54	10	21	0-2	.273	.335	.377	.712	16	.988
2004—	Los Angeles (N.L.)	C-OF-1B	91	349	41	105	18	1	10	49	22	27	6	15	2-4	.301	.351	.444	.795	3	.995
—	Florida (N.L.)	C	52	186	27	48	11	1	3	31	14	22	3	7	2-1	.258	.314	.376	.690	1	.997
Major League totals (7 years)			640	2317	296	660	133	5	60	306	169	182	37	79	10-16	.285	.340	.424	.764	41	.991

ALL-STAR GAME RECORD

	G	AB	R	H	2B	3B	HR	RBI	BB	SO	HBP	GDP	SB-CS	Avg.	OBP	SLG	OPS	E	Avg.
All-Star Game totals (2 years)	2	2	0	1	0	0	0	0	0	0	0	0	0-0	.500	.500	.500	1.000	0	1.000

LOE, KAMERON — P

PERSONAL: Born September 10, 1981, in Simi Valley, Calif. ... 6-8/225. ... Throws right, bats right. ... Full name: Kameron D. Loe. ... High school: Granada Hills (Chatworth, Calif.). ... College: Cal State Northridge.

TRANSACTIONS/CAREER NOTES: Selected by Philadelphia Phillies organization in 39th round of 1999 free-agent draft; did not sign. ... Selected by Texas Rangers organization in 20th round of 2002 free-agent draft.

CAREER HITTING: 0-for-0 (.000), 0 R, 0 2B, 0 3B, 0 HR, 0 RBI.

Year	Team (League)	W	L	Pct.	ERA	WHIP	G	GS	CG	ShO	Hld.	Sv.-Opp.	IP	H	R	ER	HR	BB-IBB	SO	Avg.
2002—	Pulaski (Appalachian)	4	4	.500	4.47	1.39	14	11	0	0	...	1-...	58.1	64	34	29	3	17-0	55	.271
2003—	Clinton (Midw.)	4	3	.571	1.95	1.00	23	11	0	0	...	2-...	97.0	78	34	21	3	19-0	94	.217
—	Stockton (Calif.)	3	0	1.000	0.96	0.85	9	4	0	0	...	1-...	37.2	26	7	4	1	6-0	31	.183
2004—	Frisco (Texas)	7	7	.500	3.10	1.33	19	19	0	0	...	0-...	113.1	122	42	39	5	29-3	97	.280
—	Oklahoma (PCL)	5	2	.714	3.27	1.24	8	8	0	0	...	0-...	52.1	52	20	19	6	13-0	42	.265
—	Texas (A.L.)	0	0	...	5.40	1.80	2	1	0	0	0	0-0	6.2	6	5	4	0	6-0	3	.273
Major League totals (1 year)		0	0	...	5.40	1.80	2	1	0	0	0	0-0	6.2	6	5	4	0	6-0	3	.273

LOFTON, KENNY — OF

PERSONAL: Born May 31, 1967, in East Chicago, Ind. ... 6-0/180. ... Bats left, throws left. ... Full name: Kenneth Lofton. ... High school: Washington (East Chicago, Ind.). ... College: Arizona.

TRANSACTIONS/CAREER NOTES: Selected by Houston Astros organization in 17th round of 1988 free-agent draft. ... Traded by Astros with IF Dave Rohde to Cleveland Indians for P Willie Blair and C Eddie Taubensee (December 10, 1991). ... On disabled list (July 17-August 1, 1995). ... Traded by Indians with P Alan Embree to Atlanta Braves for OFs Marquis Grissom and David Justice (March 25, 1997). ... On disabled list (June 18-July 5 and July 6-28, 1997). ... Signed as a free agent by Indians (December 8, 1997). ... On disabled list (July 28-August 14 and August 17-September 1, 1999; April 30-May 12, 2000; and May 16-June 1, 2001). ... Signed as a free agent by Chicago White Sox (February 1, 2002). ... Traded by White Sox to San Francisco Giants for Ps Felix Diaz and Ryan Meaux (July 28, 2002). ... Signed as a free agent by Pittsburgh Pirates (March 14, 2003). ... Traded by Pirates with 3B Aramis Ramirez to Chicago Cubs for IF Jose Hernandez, P Matt Bruback and a player to be named (July 23, 2003); Pirates acquired IF Bobby Hill to complete deal (August 15, 2003). ... Signed as a free agent by New York Yankees (January 6, 2004). ... On disabled list (April 17-May 2 and May 28-June 12, 2004); included rehabilitation assignments to Tampa and Trenton.

HONORS: Won A.L. Gold Glove as outfielder (1993-96).

2004 GAMES PLAYED BY POSITION (MLB): OF—74, DH—4.

Year Team (League)	Pos.	G	AB	R	H	2B	3B	HR	RBI	BB	SO	HBP	GDP	SB-CS	Avg.	OBP	SLG	OPS	E	Avg.
1988— Auburn (NY-Penn)	OF	48	187	23	40	6	1	1	14	19	51	0	3	26-4	.214	.286	.273	.559	4	.961
1989— Auburn (NY-Penn)	OF	34	110	21	29	3	1	0	8	14	30	0	1	26-5	.264	.336	.309	.645	8	.837
— Asheville (S. Atl.)	OF	22	82	14	27	2	0	1	9	12	10	1	1	14-6	.329	.421	.390	.811	2	.951
1990— Osceola (Fla. St.)	OF	124	481	98	159	15	5	2	35	61	77	3	4	62-16	.331	.407	.395	.802	7	.974
1991— Tucson (PCL)	OF	130	545	93	168	19	17	2	50	52	95	0	2	40-23	.308	.367	.417	.784	9	.974
— Houston (N.L.)	OF	20	74	9	15	1	0	0	0	5	19	0	0	2-1	.203	.253	.216	.469	1	.977
1992— Cleveland (A.L.)	OF	148	576	96	164	15	8	5	42	68	54	2	7	* 66-12	.285	.362	.365	.726	8	.982
1993— Cleveland (A.L.)	OF	148	569	116	185	28	8	1	42	81	83	1	8	* 70-14	.325	.408	.408	.815	• 9	.979
1994— Cleveland (A.L.)	OF	112	459	105	* 160	32	9	12	57	52	56	2	5	* 60-12	.349	.412	.536	.948	2	.993
1995— Cleveland (A.L.)	OF-DH	118	481	93	149	22	* 13	7	53	40	49	1	6	* 54-15	.310	.362	.453	.815	• 8	.970
1996— Cleveland (A.L.)	OF	154	* 662	132	210	35	4	14	67	61	82	0	7	* 75-17	.317	.372	.446	.817	10	.975
1997— Atlanta (N.L.)	OF	122	493	90	164	20	6	5	48	64	83	2	10	27-20	.333	.409	.428	.837	5	.983
1998— Cleveland (A.L.)	OF	154	600	101	169	31	6	12	64	87	80	2	7	54-10	.282	.371	.413	.785	• 8	.978
1999— Cleveland (A.L.)	OF-DH	120	465	110	140	28	6	7	39	79	84	6	6	25-6	.301	.405	.432	.838	3	.989
2000— Cleveland (A.L.)	OF-DH	137	543	107	151	23	5	15	73	79	72	4	11	30-7	.278	.369	.422	.791	4	.989
2001— Cleveland (A.L.)	OF	133	517	91	135	21	4	14	66	47	69	2	8	16-8	.261	.322	.398	.721	6	.981
2002— Chicago (A.L.)	OF	93	352	68	91	20	6	8	42	49	51	0	0	22-8	.259	.348	.418	.766	0	1.000
— San Francisco (N.L.)	OF	46	180	30	48	10	3	3	9	23	22	1	1	7-3	.267	.353	.406	.759	0	1.000
2003— Pittsburgh (N.L.)	OF	84	339	58	94	19	4	9	26	28	29	2	2	18-5	.277	.333	.437	.770	0	1.000
— Chicago (N.L.)	OF	56	208	39	68	13	4	3	20	18	22	2	4	12-4	.327	.381	.471	.852	3	.974
2004— Trenton (East.)	OF	4	14	0	3	1	0	0	2	1	3	0	0	0-0	.214	.267	.286	.552	0	1.000
— New York (A.L.)	OF-DH	83	276	51	76	10	7	3	18	31	27	1	4	7-3	.275	.346	.395	.741	2	.989
American League totals (11 years)		1400	5500	1070	1630	265	76	98	563	674	707	21	69	479-112	.296	.372	.426	.798	60	.983
National League totals (4 years)		328	1294	226	389	63	17	20	103	138	175	7	17	66-33	.301	.369	.422	.791	9	.989
Major League totals (14 years)		1728	6794	1296	2019	328	93	118	666	812	882	28	86	545-145	.297	.372	.425	.797	69	.984

DIVISION SERIES RECORD

Year Team (League)	Pos.	G	AB	R	H	2B	3B	HR	RBI	BB	SO	HBP	GDP	SB-CS	Avg.	OBP	SLG	OPS	E	Avg.
1995— Cleveland (A.L.)	OF	3	13	1	2	0	0	0	0	1	3	1	0	0-0	.154	.267	.154	.421	2	.818
1996— Cleveland (A.L.)	OF	4	18	3	3	0	0	0	1	2	3	0	0	5-0	.167	.250	.167	.417	0	1.000
1997— Atlanta (N.L.)	OF	3	13	2	2	1	0	0	0	1	2	0	1	0-1	.154	.214	.231	.445	0	1.000
1998— Cleveland (A.L.)	OF	4	16	5	6	1	0	2	4	1	1	0	0	2-0	.375	.412	.813	1.224	0	1.000
1999— Cleveland (A.L.)	OF	5	16	5	2	1	0	0	1	5	6	0	0	2-0	.125	.333	.188	.521	1	.933
2001— Cleveland (A.L.)	OF	5	19	2	2	0	0	1	3	3	5	0	1	0-0	.105	.217	.263	.481	0	1.000
2002— San Francisco (N.L.)	OF	5	20	5	7	1	0	0	2	2	3	0	0	1-0	.350	.391	.400	.791	0	1.000
2003— Chicago (N.L.)	OF	5	21	3	6	1	0	0	1	2	2	0	1	3-1	.286	.348	.333	.681	0	1.000
2004— New York (A.L.)	DH	1	4	0	1	0	0	0	1	0	1	0	0	0-0	.250	.250	.250	.500	0	...
Division series totals (9 years)		35	140	26	31	5	0	3	13	17	26	1	3	13-2	.221	.306	.321	.628	3	.963

CHAMPIONSHIP SERIES RECORD

Year Team (League)	Pos.	G	AB	R	H	2B	3B	HR	RBI	BB	SO	HBP	GDP	SB-CS	Avg.	OBP	SLG	OPS	E	Avg.
1995— Cleveland (A.L.)	OF	6	24	4	11	0	2	0	3	4	6	0	0	5-0	.458	.517	.625	1.142	0	1.000
1997— Atlanta (N.L.)	OF	6	27	3	5	0	1	0	1	1	7	0	1	1-1	.185	.214	.259	.474	2	.833
1998— Cleveland (A.L.)	OF	6	27	2	5	1	0	1	3	1	7	0	0	1-0	.185	.214	.333	.548	1	.889
2002— San Francisco (N.L.)	OF	5	21	4	5	0	0	1	2	2	4	1	0	1-0	.238	.333	.381	.714	0	1.000
2003— Chicago (N.L.)	OF	7	31	8	10	1	0	0	2	3	4	0	0	1-0	.323	.382	.355	.737	0	1.000
2004— New York (A.L.)	DH	3	10	1	3	0	0	1	2	2	3	0	0	1-0	.300	.417	.600	1.017	0	...
Champ. series totals (6 years)		33	140	22	39	2	3	3	13	13	31	1	1	10-1	.279	.342	.400	.742	3	.962

WORLD SERIES RECORD

Year Team (League)	Pos.	G	AB	R	H	2B	3B	HR	RBI	BB	SO	HBP	GDP	SB-CS	Avg.	OBP	SLG	OPS	E	Avg.
1995— Cleveland (A.L.)	OF	6	25	6	5	1	0	0	0	3	1	0	0	6-1	.200	.286	.240	.526	0	1.000
2002— San Francisco (N.L.)	OF	7	31	7	9	1	1	0	2	2	2	0	0	3-0	.290	.333	.387	.720	1	.962
World series totals (2 years)		13	56	13	14	2	1	0	2	5	3	0	0	9-1	.250	.311	.321	.633	1	.974

ALL-STAR GAME RECORD

	G	AB	R	H	2B	3B	HR	RBI	BB	SO	HBP	GDP	SB-CS	Avg.	OBP	SLG	OPS	E	Avg.
All-Star Game totals (5 years)	5	14	1	5	0	0	0	2	1	3	0	0	5-0	.357	.400	.357	.757	0	1.000

LOGAN, NOOK — OF

PERSONAL: Born November 28, 1979, in Natchez, Miss. ... 6-2/180. ... Bats both, throws right. ... Full name: Exavier Prente Logan. ... High school: Natchez (Miss.). ... Junior college: Copiah-Lincoln.

TRANSACTIONS/CAREER NOTES: Selected by New York Yankees organization in 40th round of 1998 free-agent draft; did not sign. ... Selected by Detroit Tigers organization in third round of 2000 free-agent draft.

2004 GAMES PLAYED BY POSITION (MLB): OF—46.

Year	Team (League)	Pos.	G	AB	R	H	2B	3B	HR	RBI	BB	SO	HBP	GDP	SB-CS	Avg.	OBP	SLG	OPS	E	Avg.
2000— GC Tigers (GCL)		SS	43	136	29	38	2	2	0	14	31	36	1	1	20-3	.279	.412	.324	.735	21	.887
— Lakeland (Fla. St.)		SS	11	42	4	14	1	0	0	3	2	13	0	0	2-1	.333	.364	.357	.721	7	.860
2001— W. Mich. (Mid.)		OF	128	522	82	137	19	8	1	27	53	129	2	3	67-19	.262	.330	.335	.666	9	.968
2002— Lakeland (Fla. St.)		OF	124	506	75	136	14	7	2	26	40	111	0	2	55-16	.269	.321	.336	.657	10	.970
2003— Erie (East.)		OF	136	514	71	129	16	7	4	38	51	103	1	5	37-13	.251	.316	.333	.649	3	.991
2004— Toledo (Int'l.)		OF	105	426	67	112	14	9	2	27	23	95	3	3	38-11	.263	.303	.352	.650	5	.979
— Detroit (A.L.)		OF	47	133	12	37	5	2	0	10	13	24	1	1	8-2	.278	.340	.346	.686	2	.984
Major League totals (1 year)			47	133	12	37	5	2	0	10	13	24	1	1	8-2	.278	.340	.346	.686	2	.984

LOHSE, KYLE — P

PERSONAL: Born October 4, 1978, in Chico, Calif. ... 6-2/201. ... Throws right, bats right. ... Full name: Kyle Matthew Lohse. ... Name pronounced: lowshe. ... High school: Hamilton Union (Hamilton City, Calif.). ... Junior college: Butte (Calif.).

TRANSACTIONS/CAREER NOTES: Selected by Chicago Cubs organization in 29th round of 1996 free-agent draft. ... Traded with P Jason Ryan by Cubs to Minnesota Twins for Ps Rick Aguilera and Scott Downs (May 21, 1999).

CAREER HITTING: 4-for-15 (.267), 0 R, 1 2B, 0 3B, 0 HR, 1 RBI.

Year	Team (League)	W	L	Pct.	ERA	WHIP	G	GS	CG	ShO	Hld.	Sv.-Opp.	IP	H	R	ER	HR	BB-IBB	SO	Avg.
1997— Ariz. Cubs (Ariz.)		2	2	.500	3.02	1.43	12	11	0	0	...	0-...	47.2	46	22	16	0	22-0	49	.249
1998— Rockford (Midwest)		13	8	.619	3.22	1.19	28	26	3	1	...	0-...	170.2	158	76	61	8	45-1	121	.246
1999— Daytona (Fla. St.)		5	3	.625	2.89	1.21	9	9	1	1	...	0-...	53.0	48	21	17	4	16-0	41	.242
— Fort Myers (Fla. St.)		2	3	.400	5.18	1.34	7	7	0	0	...	0-...	41.2	47	28	24	5	9-0	33	.292
— New Britain (East.)		3	4	.429	5.89	1.56	11	11	1	0	...	0-...	70.1	87	49	46	9	23-0	41	.315
2000— New Britain (East.)		3	18	.143	6.04	1.50	28	28	0	0	...	0-...	167.0	196	123	112	23	55-0	124	.291
2001— New Britain (East.)		3	1	.750	2.37	0.95	6	6	0	0	...	0-...	38.0	32	10	10	5	4-0	32	.230
— Edmonton (PCL)		4	2	.667	3.12	1.29	8	8	1	1	...	0-...	49.0	50	21	17	3	13-0	48	.262
— Minnesota (A.L.)		4	7	.364	5.68	1.45	19	16	0	0	0	0-0	90.1	102	60	57	16	29-0	64	.284
2002— Minnesota (A.L.)		13	8	.619	4.23	1.39	32	31	1	1	0	0-1	180.2	181	92	85	26	70-2	124	.259
2003— Minnesota (A.L.)		14	11	.560	4.61	1.27	33	33	2	1	0	0-0	201.0	211	107	103	28	45-1	130	.268
2004— Minnesota (A.L.)		9	13	.409	5.34	1.63	35	34	1	1	0	0-0	194.0	240	128	115	28	76-5	131	.305
Major League totals (4 years)		40	39	.506	4.86	1.43	119	114	4	3	0	0-1	666.0	734	387	360	98	220-8	429	.279

DIVISION SERIES RECORD

Year	Team (League)	W	L	Pct.	ERA	WHIP	G	GS	CG	ShO	Hld.	Sv.-Opp.	IP	H	R	ER	HR	BB-IBB	SO	Avg.
2002— Minnesota (A.L.)		0	0	...	0.00	0.50	2	0	0	0	0	0-0	4.0	2	0	0	0	0-0	5	.143
2003— Minnesota (A.L.)		0	1	.000	5.40	1.60	1	1	0	0	0	0-0	5.0	6	3	3	1	2-0	5	.286
2004— Minnesota (A.L.)		0	1	.000	4.50	0.50	1	0	0	0	0	0-0	2.0	1	1	1	0	0-0	3	.143
Division series totals (3 years)		0	2	.000	3.27	1.00	4	1	0	0	0	0-0	11.0	9	4	4	1	2-0	13	.214

CHAMPIONSHIP SERIES RECORD

Year	Team (League)	W	L	Pct.	ERA	WHIP	G	GS	CG	ShO	Hld.	Sv.-Opp.	IP	H	R	ER	HR	BB-IBB	SO	Avg.
2002— Minnesota (A.L.)		0	0	...	0.00	0.00	1	0	0	0	0	0-0	1.0	0	0	0	0	0-0	1	.000

LONG, TERRENCE — OF

PERSONAL: Born February 29, 1976, in Montgomery, Ala. ... 6-1/200. ... Bats left, throws left. ... Full name: Terrence Deon Long. ... High school: Stanhope Elmore (Millbrook, Ala.).

TRANSACTIONS/CAREER NOTES: Selected by New York Mets organization in first round (20th pick overall) of 1994 free-agent draft; pick received as compensation for Baltimore Orioles signing Type A free-agent P Sid Fernandez. ... Traded by Mets with P Leo Vasquez to Oakland Athletics for P Kenny Rogers (July 23, 1999). ... On suspended list (September 9-12, 2003). ... Traded by A's with C Ramon Hernandez to San Diego Padres for OF Mark Kotsay (November 26, 2003). ... Traded by Padres with P Dennis Tankersley and cash to Kansas City Royals for Ps Darrell May and Ryan Bukvich (November 8, 2004).

2004 GAMES PLAYED BY POSITION (MLB): OF—87, DH—1.

Year	Team (League)	Pos.	G	AB	R	H	2B	3B	HR	RBI	BB	SO	HBP	GDP	SB-CS	Avg.	OBP	SLG	OPS	E	Avg.
1994— Kingsport (Appalachian)		1B-OF	60	215	39	50	9	2	12	39	32	52	4	2	9-3	.233	.340	.460	.800	5	.980
1995— Capital City (SAL)		OF	55	178	27	35	1	2	2	13	28	43	1	3	8-5	.197	.309	.258	.568	5	.937
— Pittsfield (N.Y.-Penn.)		OF	51	187	24	48	9	4	4	31	18	36	1	2	11-4	.257	.324	.412	.735	1	.991
1996— Capital City (SAL)		DH-OF	123	473	66	136	26	9	12	66	36	120	5	9	32-7	.288	.342	.457	.798	5	.981
1997— St. Lucie (Fla. St.)		OF-DH	126	470	52	118	29	7	8	61	40	102	2	6	24-8	.251	.310	.394	.704	7	.972
1998— Binghamton (East.)		OF-DH	130	455	69	135	20	10	16	58	62	105	2	8	23-11	.297	.380	.490	.871	10	.958
1999— Norfolk (Int'l)		OF	78	304	41	99	20	4	7	47	23	41	1	6	14-6	.326	.374	.487	.861	4	.980
— New York (N.L.)			3	3	0	0	0	0	0	0	0	2	0	1	0-0	.000	.000	.000	.000	...	...
— Vancouver (PCL)		OF	40	154	16	38	6	2	2	21	10	29	1	4	7-5	.247	.297	.351	.648	4	.961
2000— Sacramento (PCL)		OF	15	60	11	24	6	0	3	15	4	4	0	2	0-3	.400	.431	.650	1.081	3	.903
— Oakland (A.L.)		OF	138	584	104	168	34	4	18	80	43	77	1	5	5-0	.288	.336	.452	.788	• 10	.971
2001— Oakland (A.L.)		OF	• 162	629	90	178	37	4	12	85	52	103	0	17	9-3	.283	.335	.412	.747	7	.980
2002— Oakland (A.L.)		OF	• 162	587	71	141	32	4	16	67	48	96	2	17	3-6	.240	.298	.390	.689	8	.980
2003— Oakland (A.L.)		OF-DH	140	486	64	119	22	2	14	61	31	67	3	9	4-1	.245	.293	.385	.678	4	.984
2004— San Diego (N.L.)		OF-DH	136	288	31	85	19	4	3	28	19	51	1	13	3-2	.295	.335	.420	.756	2	.986
American League totals (4 years)			602	2286	329	606	125	14	60	293	174	343	6	61	21-10	.265	.317	.411	.728	29	.978
National League totals (2 years)			139	291	31	85	19	4	3	28	19	53	1	14	3-2	.292	.332	.416	.748	2	.986
Major League totals (6 years)			741	2577	360	691	144	18	63	321	193	396	7	75	24-12	.268	.319	.411	.730	31	.979

DIVISION SERIES RECORD

Year	Team (League)	Pos.	G	AB	R	H	2B	3B	HR	RBI	BB	SO	HBP	GDP	SB-CS	Avg.	OBP	SLG	OPS	E	Avg.
2000— Oakland (A.L.)		OF	5	19	2	3	0	0	1	1	3	2	0	2	0-0	.158	.273	.316	.589	1	.923
2001— Oakland (A.L.)		OF	5	18	3	7	3	0	2	3	1	2	0	0	0-0	.389	.421	.889	1.310	0	1.000
2002— Oakland (A.L.)		OF	5	18	1	3	0	0	1	1	1	2	0	0	0-0	.167	.211	.333	.544	0	1.000
2003— Oakland (A.L.)		OF	4	8	0	2	0	0	0	1	1	3	0	0	0-0	.250	.333	.250	.583	0	1.000
Division series totals (4 years)			19	63	6	15	3	0	4	5	6	9	0	2	0-0	.238	.304	.476	.781	1	.974

LOOPER, BRADEN — P

PERSONAL: Born October 28, 1974, in Weatherford, Okla. ... 6-3/220. ... Throws right, bats right. ... Full name: Braden LaVern Looper. ... High school: Mangum (Okla.). ... College: Wichita State.

TRANSACTIONS/CAREER NOTES: Selected by St. Louis Cardinals organization in first round (third pick overall) of 1996 free-agent draft. ... Traded by Cardinals with P Armando Almanza and SS Pablo Ozuna to Florida Marlins for SS Edgar Renteria (December 14, 1998). ... Signed as a free agent by New York Mets (January 8, 2004).

CAREER HITTING: 1-for-8 (.125), 1 R, 0 2B, 0 3B, 0 HR, 0 RBI.

Year	Team (League)	W	L	Pct.	ERA	WHIP	G	GS	CG	ShO	Hld.	Sv.-Opp.	IP	H	R	ER	HR	BB-IBB	SO	Avg.
1997—	Prince William (Caro.)	3	6	.333	4.48	1.49	12	12	0	0	...	0-...	64.1	71	38	32	6	25-0	58	.276
—	Arkansas (Texas)	1	4	.200	5.91	1.45	19	0	0	0	...	5-...	21.1	24	14	14	2	7-2	20	.286
1998—	St. Louis (N.L.)	0	1	.000	5.40	1.80	4	0	0	0	0	0-2	3.1	5	4	2	1	1-0	4	.357
—	Memphis (PCL)	2	3	.400	3.10	1.38	40	0	0	0	...	20-...	40.2	43	16	14	3	13-1	43	.270
1999—	Florida (N.L.)	3	3	.500	3.80	1.53	72	0	0	0	8	0-4	83.0	96	43	35	7	31-6	50	.293
2000—	Florida (N.L.)	5	1	.833	4.41	1.59	73	0	0	0	18	2-5	67.1	71	41	33	4	36-6	29	.268
2001—	Florida (N.L.)	3	3	.500	3.55	1.31	71	0	0	0	16	3-6	71.0	63	28	28	8	30-3	52	.242
2002—	Florida (N.L.)	2	5	.286	3.14	1.17	78	0	0	0	16	13-16	86.0	73	31	30	8	28-3	55	.230
2003—	Florida (N.L.)	6	4	.600	3.68	1.38	74	0	0	0	...	28-34	80.2	82	34	33	4	29-1	51	.264
2004—	New York (N.L.)	2	5	.286	2.70	1.22	71	0	0	0	0	29-34	83.1	86	28	25	5	16-3	60	.266
	Major League totals (7 years)	21	22	.488	3.53	1.36	443	0	0	0	58	75-101	474.2	476	209	186	36	171-22	306	.262

DIVISION SERIES RECORD

Year	Team (League)	W	L	Pct.	ERA	WHIP	G	GS	CG	ShO	Hld.	Sv.-Opp.	IP	H	R	ER	HR	BB-IBB	SO	Avg.
2003—	Florida (N.L.)	1	0	1.000	0.00	1.80	2	0	0	0	1	0-0	1.2	1	1	0	0	2-1	0	.167

CHAMPIONSHIP SERIES RECORD

Year	Team (League)	W	L	Pct.	ERA	WHIP	G	GS	CG	ShO	Hld.	Sv.-Opp.	IP	H	R	ER	HR	BB-IBB	SO	Avg.
2003—	Florida (N.L.)	0	0	...	0.00	1.20	2	0	0	0	1	1-1	1.2	1	0	0	0	1-1	1	.167

WORLD SERIES RECORD

Year	Team (League)	W	L	Pct.	ERA	WHIP	G	GS	CG	ShO	Hld.	Sv.-Opp.	IP	H	R	ER	HR	BB-IBB	SO	Avg.
2003—	Florida (N.L.)	1	0	1.000	9.82	1.64	4	0	0	0	0	0-0	3.2	6	4	4	2	0-0	4	.353

LOPEZ, AQUILINO — P

PERSONAL: Born April 21, 1975, in Villa Altagracia, Dominican Republic. ... 6-3/165. ... Throws right, bats right. ... Name pronounced: aquil-LEENO.

TRANSACTIONS/CAREER NOTES: Signed as a non-drafted free agent by Seattle Mariners organization (July 3, 1997). ... Selected by Toronto Blue Jays from Mariners organization in Rule 5 major league draft (December 16, 2002).

CAREER HITTING: 0-for-0 (.000), 0 R, 0 2B, 0 3B, 0 HR, 0 RBI.

Year	Team (League)	W	L	Pct.	ERA	WHIP	G	GS	CG	ShO	Hld.	Sv.-Opp.	IP	H	R	ER	HR	BB-IBB	SO	Avg.
1999—	Everett (Northwest)	7	6	.538	3.80	1.21	15	15	1	0	...	0-...	87.2	76	44	37	8	30-2	93	.230
2000—	Wisconsin (Midw.)	6	1	.857	1.85	0.99	39	5	1	1	...	17-...	68.0	47	16	14	1	20-4	67	.193
2001—	San Antonio (Texas)	4	3	.571	3.02	1.16	42	0	0	0	...	2-...	62.2	48	24	21	4	25-2	79	.209
2002—	Tacoma (PCL)	4	4	.500	2.39	1.06	34	11	0	0	...	5-...	109.1	89	33	29	6	27-2	103	.221
2003—	Toronto (A.L.)	1	3	.250	3.42	1.25	72	0	0	0	16	14-16	73.2	58	31	28	5	34-5	64	.212
2004—	Toronto (A.L.)	1	1	.500	6.00	1.62	18	0	0	0	3	0-0	21.0	21	15	14	5	13-3	13	.266
—	Syracuse (Int'l)	1	6	.143	7.17	1.59	32	0	0	0	...	5-...	42.2	58	36	34	8	10-0	32	.326
	Major League totals (2 years)	2	4	.333	3.99	1.33	90	0	0	0	19	14-16	94.2	79	46	42	10	47-8	77	.224

LOPEZ, FELIPE — SS/3B

PERSONAL: Born May 12, 1980, in Bayamon, Puerto Rico. ... 6-1/185. ... Bats both, throws right. ... Full name: Felipe Lopez Jr.. ... High school: Lake Brantley (Altamonte Springs, Fla.).

TRANSACTIONS/CAREER NOTES: Selected by Toronto Blue Jays organization in first round (eighth pick overall) of 1998 free-agent draft. ... Traded by Blue Jays to Cincinnati Reds as part of four-team deal in which Blue Jays acquired a player to be named from Oakland Athletics, A's acquired 1B Erubiel Durazo from Arizona Diamondbacks and Diamondbacks acquired P Elmer Dessens and cash from Reds (December 15, 2002); Blue Jays acquired P Jason Arnold to complete deal (December 16, 2002).

2004 GAMES PLAYED BY POSITION (MLB): SS—51, 3B—24, 2B—2.

Year	Team (League)	Pos.	G	AB	R	H	2B	3B	HR	RBI	BB	SO	HBP	GDP	SB-CS	Avg.	OBP	SLG	OPS	E	Avg.
1998—	St. Catharines (NY-Penn.) .	SS	19	83	14	31	5	2	1	11	3	14	0	1	4-2	.373	.395	.518	.913	9	.895
—	Dunedin (Fla. St.)	SS	4	13	3	5	0	1	1	1	0	3	0	1	0-0	.385	.385	.769	1.154	4	.692
1999—	Hagerstown (SAL)	SS	134	537	87	149	27	4	14	80	61	157	3	7	21-14	.277	.351	.421	.772	22	.960
2000—	Tennessee (Sou.)	SS	127	463	52	119	18	4	9	41	31	110	1	6	12-11	.257	.303	.371	.675	44	.923
2001—	Tennessee (Sou.)	SS-2B	19	72	12	16	2	1	2	4	9	23	0	1	4-4	.222	.309	.361	.670	8	.904
—	Syracuse (Int'l)	SS-2B-3B	89	358	65	100	19	7	16	44	30	94	3	5	13-5	.279	.337	.506	.842	19	.950
—	Toronto (A.L.)	3B-SS	49	177	21	46	5	4	5	23	12	39	0	2	4-3	.260	.304	.418	.722	9	.938
2002—	Toronto (A.L.)	SS-3B-DH	85	282	35	64	15	3	8	34	23	90	1	4	5-4	.227	.287	.387	.673	8	.975
—	Syracuse (Int'l)	SS	43	173	35	55	11	2	3	16	29	37	1	3	13-0	.318	.419	.457	.875	16	.934
2003—	Cincinnati (N.L.)	SS-3B-2B	59	197	28	42	7	2	2	13	28	59	1	2	8-5	.213	.313	.299	.612	16	.928
—	Louisville (Int'l)	SS-2B	35	143	22	40	11	0	2	18	12	38	0	0	2-5	.280	.333	.399	.732	9	.940
2004—	Louisville (Int'l)	SS-2B-3B	75	293	50	80	11	3	9	43	25	71	2	2	2-2	.273	.329	.423	.752	13	.956
—	Cincinnati (N.L.)	SS-3B-2B	79	264	35	64	18	2	7	31	25	81	3	1	1-1	.242	.314	.405	.719	15	.949
	American League totals (2 years)		134	459	56	110	20	7	13	57	35	129	1	6	9-7	.240	.293	.399	.692	17	.964
	National League totals (2 years)		138	461	63	106	25	4	9	44	53	140	4	3	9-6	.230	.313	.360	.674	31	.940
	Major League totals (4 years)		272	920	119	216	45	11	22	101	88	269	5	9	18-13	.235	.304	.379	.683	48	.951

LOPEZ, JAVIER — P

PERSONAL: Born July 11, 1977, in San Juan, Puerto Rico. ... 6-4/200. ... Throws left, bats left. ... Full name: Javier Alfonso Lopez. ... College: Virginia.

TRANSACTIONS/CAREER NOTES: Selected by Arizona Diamondbacks organization in fourth round of 1998 free-agent draft. ... Selected by Boston Red Sox from Diamondbacks organization in Rule 5 major league draft (December 16, 2002). ... Traded by Red Sox to Colorado Rockies for future considerations (March 18, 2003); Red Sox acquired P Ryan Cameron to complete deal (March 29, 2003).

CAREER HITTING: 1-for-7 (.143), 1 R, 0 2B, 0 3B, 0 HR, 1 RBI.

Year— Team (League)	W	L	Pct.	ERA	WHIP	G	GS	CG	ShO	Hld.	Sv.-Opp.	IP	H	R	ER	HR	BB-IBB	SO	Avg.
1998— South Bend (Mid.)	2	4	.333	6.55	2.05	16	9	0	0	...	0-...	44.0	60	36	32	2	30-0	31	.328
1999— South Bend (Mid.)	4	6	.400	6.00	1.67	20	20	0	0	...	0-...	99.0	122	74	66	9	43-0	70	.300
2000— High Desert (Calif.)	4	8	.333	5.22	1.53	30	21	0	0	...	2-...	136.1	152	87	79	14	57-0	98	.288
2001— Lancaster (Calif.)	1	3	.250	2.63	1.46	17	0	0	0	...	1-...	24.0	30	9	7	2	5-0	18	.313
— El Paso (Texas)	1	0	1.000	7.43	1.95	22	1	0	0	...	0-...	40.0	64	39	33	6	14-2	21	.370
2002— El Paso (Texas)	2	2	.500	2.72	1.08	61	0	0	0	...	6-...	46.1	34	16	14	3	16-1	47	.204
2003— Colorado (N.L.)	4	1	.800	3.70	1.20	75	0	0	0	15	1-2	58.1	58	25	24	5	12-2	40	.258
2004— Colo. Springs (PCL)	0	1	.000	4.00	1.33	8	0	0	0	...	0-...	9.0	10	4	4	2	2-0	9	.294
— Colorado (N.L.)	1	2	.333	7.52	1.75	64	0	0	0	12	0-1	40.2	45	34	34	1	26-4	20	.287
Major League totals (2 years)	5	3	.625	5.27	1.42	139	0	0	0	27	1-3	99.0	103	59	58	6	38-6	60	.270

LOPEZ, JAVY — C

PERSONAL: Born November 5, 1970, in Ponce, Puerto Rico. ... 6-3/224. ... Bats right, throws right. ... Full name: Javier Torres Lopez. ... Name pronounced: HAH-vee LOE-pezz. ... High school: Academia Cristo Rey (Urb la Ramble Ponce, Puerto Rico).

TRANSACTIONS/CAREER NOTES: Signed as a non-drafted free agent by Atlanta Braves organization (November 6, 1987). ... On disabled list (July 6-22, 1997; June 21-July 15 and July 25, 1999-remainder of season; and August 1-16, 2002). ... Signed as a free agent by Baltimore Orioles (January 6, 2004).

HONORS: Named Comeback Player of the Year by THE SPORTING NEWS (2003).

2004 GAMES PLAYED BY POSITION (MLB): C—132, DH—21.

Year— Team (League)	Pos.	G	AB	R	H	2B	3B	HR	RBI	BB	SO	HBP	GDP	SB-CS	Avg.	OBP	SLG	OPS	E	Avg.
1988— GC Braves (GCL)	C	31	94	8	18	4	0	1	9	3	19	0	0	1-0	.191	.214	.266	.480	7	.958
1989— Pulaski (Appalachian)	C	51	153	27	40	8	1	3	27	5	35	1	8	3-2	.261	.284	.386	.670	5	.983
1990— Burlington (Midw.)	C	116	422	48	112	17	3	11	55	14	84	5	10	0-2	.265	.297	.398	.695	11	.986
1991— Durham (Caro.)	C	113	384	43	94	14	2	11	51	25	88	3	10	10-3	.245	.294	.378	.672	6	.991
1992— Greenville (Sou.)	C	115	442	63	142	28	3	16	60	24	47	5	8	7-3	.321	.362	.507	.868	8	.990
— Atlanta (N.L.)	C	9	16	3	6	2	0	0	2	0	1	0	0	0-0	.375	.375	.500	.875	0	1.000
1993— Richmond (Int'l)	C	100	380	56	116	23	2	17	74	12	53	6	8	1-6	.305	.334	.511	.845	10	.987
— Atlanta (N.L.)	C	8	16	1	6	1	1	1	2	0	2	1	0	0-0	.375	.412	.750	1.162	1	.975
1994— Atlanta (N.L.)	C	80	277	27	68	9	0	13	35	17	61	5	12	0-2	.245	.299	.419	.718	3	.995
1995— Atlanta (N.L.)	C	100	333	37	105	11	4	14	51	14	57	2	13	0-1	.315	.344	.499	.842	8	.988
1996— Atlanta (N.L.)	C	138	489	56	138	19	1	23	69	28	84	3	17	1-6	.282	.322	.466	.788	6	.994
1997— Atlanta (N.L.)	C	123	414	52	122	28	1	23	68	40	82	5	9	1-1	.295	.361	.534	.895	6	.993
1998— Atlanta (N.L.)	C-DH	133	489	73	139	21	1	34	106	30	85	6	22	5-3	.284	.328	.540	.868	5	.995
1999— Atlanta (N.L.)	C-DH	65	246	34	78	18	1	11	45	20	41	3	6	0-3	.317	.375	.533	.908	4	.991
2000— Atlanta (N.L.)	C	134	481	60	138	21	1	24	89	35	80	4	20	0-0	.287	.337	.484	.822	6	.993
2001— Atlanta (N.L.)	C	128	438	45	117	16	1	17	66	28	82	10	12	1-0	.267	.322	.425	.747	10	.989
2002— Atlanta (N.L.)	C	109	347	31	81	15	0	11	52	26	63	8	15	0-1	.233	.299	.372	.670	10	.986
2003— Atlanta (N.L.)	C-DH	129	457	89	150	29	3	43	109	33	90	4	10	0-1	.328	.378	.687	1.065	5	.994
2004— Baltimore (A.L.)	C-DH	150	579	83	183	33	3	23	86	47	97	6	16	0-0	.316	.370	.503	.873	5	.994
American League totals (1 year)		150	579	83	183	33	3	23	86	47	97	6	16	0-0	.316	.370	.503	.872	5	.994
National League totals (12 years)		1156	4003	508	1148	190	14	214	694	271	728	51	136	8-18	.287	.337	.502	.839	64	.992
Major League totals (13 years)		1306	4582	591	1331	223	17	237	780	318	825	57	152	8-18	.290	.341	.502	.843	69	.992

DIVISION SERIES RECORD

Year— Team (League)	Pos.	G	AB	R	H	2B	3B	HR	RBI	BB	SO	HBP	GDP	SB-CS	Avg.	OBP	SLG	OPS	E	Avg.
1995— Atlanta (N.L.)	C	3	9	0	4	0	0	0	3	0	3	0	0	0-1	.444	.400	.444	.844	0	1.000
1996— Atlanta (N.L.)	C	2	7	1	2	0	0	1	1	1	0	0	0	1-0	.286	.375	.714	1.089	1	.958
1997— Atlanta (N.L.)	C	2	7	3	2	2	0	1	2	1	0	0	0	0-0	.286	.444	1.016	1.016	0	1.000
1998— Atlanta (N.L.)	C	2	7	1	2	0	0	1	1	1	0	0	0	0-0	.286	.375	.714	1.089	0	1.000
2000— Atlanta (N.L.)	C	3	11	0	1	0	0	0	0	0	1	0	0	0-1	.091	.091	.091	.182	0	1.000
2002— Atlanta (N.L.)	C	4	15	4	5	1	0	2	4	1	3	0	1	0-0	.333	.375	.800	1.175	0	1.000
2003— Atlanta (N.L.)	C	5	21	1	7	2	0	0	0	0	6	0	0	0-0	.333	.333	.429	.762	1	.977
Division series totals (7 years)		21	77	10	23	5	0	4	10	5	15	0	1	1-2	.299	.337	.519	.857	2	.989

CHAMPIONSHIP SERIES RECORD

Year— Team (League)	Pos.	G	AB	R	H	2B	3B	HR	RBI	BB	SO	HBP	GDP	SB-CS	Avg.	OBP	SLG	OPS	E	Avg.
1992— Atlanta (N.L.)	C	1	1	0	0	0	0	0	0	0	0	0	0	0-0	.000	.000	.000	.000	0	1.000
1995— Atlanta (N.L.)	C	3	14	2	5	1	0	1	3	0	1	0	0	0-0	.357	.357	.643	1.000	0	1.000
1996— Atlanta (N.L.)	C	7	24	8	13	5	0	2	6	3	1	1	1	1-0	.542	.607	1.000	1.607	0	1.000
1997— Atlanta (N.L.)	C	5	17	0	1	1	0	0	2	1	7	0	0	0-0	.059	.100	.118	.218	0	1.000
1998— Atlanta (N.L.)	C	6	20	2	6	0	0	1	1	0	7	0	1	0-0	.300	.300	.450	.750	1	.978
2001— Atlanta (N.L.)	C	5	14	1	2	0	0	1	2	1	4	0	0	0-0	.143	.200	.357	.557	1	.957
Champ. series totals (6 years)		27	90	13	27	7	0	5	14	5	20	1	2	1-0	.300	.337	.544	.881	2	.990

WORLD SERIES RECORD

Year— Team (League)	Pos.	G	AB	R	H	2B	3B	HR	RBI	BB	SO	HBP	GDP	SB-CS	Avg.	OBP	SLG	OPS	E	Avg.
1992— Atlanta (N.L.)		Did not play.																		
1995— Atlanta (N.L.)	C	6	17	1	3	2	0	1	3	1	1	1	1	0-0	.176	.263	.471	.734	0	1.000
1996— Atlanta (N.L.)	C	6	21	3	4	0	0	0	1	3	4	0	2	0-0	.190	.280	.190	.470	0	1.000
World series totals (2 years)		12	38	4	7	2	0	1	4	4	5	1	3	0-0	.184	.273	.316	.589	0	1.000

ALL-STAR GAME RECORD

	G	AB	R	H	2B	3B	HR	RBI	BB	SO	HBP	GDP	SB-CS	Avg.	OBP	SLG	OPS	E	Avg.
All-Star Game totals (3 years)	3	4	1	1	0	0	1	1	0	1	0	0	0-0	.250	.250	1.000	1.250	0	1.000

LOPEZ, JOSE — SS

PERSONAL: Born November 24, 1983, in Anzoategui, Venezuela. ... 6-2/170. ... Bats right, throws right. ... Full name: Jose Celestino Lopez. ... High school: Unidad Educativa Cas Puerta Barcelona (Venezuela).

TRANSACTIONS/CAREER NOTES: Signed as a non-drafted free agent by Seattle Mariners organization (July 2, 2000).

2004 GAMES PLAYED BY POSITION (MLB): SS—57, 3B—1.

Year	Team (League)	Pos.	G	AB	R	H	2B	3B	HR	RBI	BB	SO	HBP	GDP	SB-CS	Avg.	OBP	SLG	OPS	E	Avg.
2001— Everett (N'west)	SS-2B		70	289	42	74	15	0	2	20	13	44	10	3	13-6	.256	.309	.329	.638	17	.950
2002— San Bern. (Calif.)	SS-2B		123	522	82	169	39	5	8	60	27	45	5	8	31-13	.324	.360	.464	.824	31	.939
2003— San Antonio (Texas)	SS-2B-3B		132	538	82	139	35	2	13	69	27	56	10	12	18-8	.258	.303	.403	.706	28	.954
2004— Ariz. Mariners (Ariz.)	3B-SS-2B		4	12	3	2	1	0	0	1	2	1	0	1	1-0	.167	.267	.250	.517	1	.933
— Tacoma (PCL)	S-3-2-DH		74	275	40	81	19	0	13	39	16	30	6	2	6-2	.295	.342	.505	.834	20	.934
— Seattle (A.L.)	SS-3B		57	207	28	48	13	0	5	22	8	31	1	1	0-1	.232	.263	.367	.630	10	.956
Major League totals (1 year)			57	207	28	48	13	0	5	22	8	31	1	1	0-1	.232	.263	.367	.630	10	.956

LOPEZ, LUIS — 3B/SS

PERSONAL: Born September 4, 1970, in Cirda, Puerto Rico. ... 5-11/175. ... Bats both, throws right. ... Full name: Luis Manuel Lopez. ... Name pronounced: LOE-pezz. ... High school: San Jose (Caguas, Puerto Rico).

TRANSACTIONS/CAREER NOTES: Signed as a non-drafted free agent by San Diego Padres organization (September 9, 1987). ... On disabled list (April 24, 1995-entire season). ... On disabled list (March 29-April 18 and July 31-September 1, 1996); included rehabilitation assignments to Las Vegas. ... Traded by Padres to Houston Astros for P Sean Runyan (March 15, 1997). ... Traded by Astros to New York Mets for IF Tim Bogar (March 31, 1997). ... Traded by Mets to Milwaukee Brewers for P Bill Pulsipher (January 21, 2000). ... On disabled list (March 30-May 19, 2002); included rehabilitation assignment to Indianapolis. ... Released by Brewers (June 6, 2002). ... Signed by Baltimore Orioles organization (June 18, 2002). ... Released by Orioles (October 1, 2002). ... Signed by Colorado Rockies organization (December 27, 2002). ... Traded by Rockies to Baltimore Orioles for cash considerations (July 1, 2003). ... Refused minor league assignment and became a free agent (October 8, 2004).

2004 GAMES PLAYED BY POSITION (MLB): SS—14, 3B—11, DH—8, 2B—6, 1B—6.

Year	Team (League)	Pos.	G	AB	R	H	2B	3B	HR	RBI	BB	SO	HBP	GDP	SB-CS	Avg.	OBP	SLG	OPS	E	Avg.
1988— Spokane (N'west)	SS	70	312	50	95	13	1	0	35	18	59	4	7	14-5	.304	.348	.353	.701	47	.877
1989— Char., S.C. (SAL)	SS	127	460	50	102	15	1	1	29	17	85	2	9	12-9	.222	.251	.265	.516	74	.895
1990— Riverside (Calif.)	SS	14	46	5	17	3	1	1	4	3	3	0	1	4-2	.370	.408	.543	.952	6	.903
1991— Wichita (Texas)	2B-SS	125	452	43	121	17	1	1	41	18	70	8	8	6-7	.268	.305	.316	.621	26	.959
1992— Las Vegas (PCL)	SS-OF	120	395	44	92	8	8	1	31	19	65	3	12	6-4	.233	.271	.301	.573	30	.949
1993— Las Vegas (PCL)	SS-2B	131	491	52	150	36	6	6	58	27	62	5	7	8-0	.306	.346	.440	.786	29	.955
— San Diego (N.L.)	2B	17	43	1	5	1	0	0	1	0	8	0	0	0-0	.116	.114	.140	.253	1	.983
1994— Las Vegas (PCL)	2B	12	49	2	10	2	2	0	6	1	5	0	0	0-0	.204	.216	.327	.542	2	.973
— San Diego (N.L.)	SS-2B-3B	77	235	29	65	16	1	2	20	15	39	3	7	3-2	.277	.325	.379	.704	14	.952
1995— San Diego (N.L.)					Did not play.															
1996— Las Vegas (PCL)	2B-SS	18	68	4	14	3	0	1	12	2	15	0	0	0-0	.206	.229	.294	.523	2	.976
— San Diego (N.L.)	SS-2B-3B	63	139	10	25	3	0	2	11	9	35	1	7	0-0	.180	.233	.245	.478	4	.975
1997— Norfolk (Int'l)	SS-2B-3B	48	203	32	67	12	1	4	19	9	29	1	1	2-6	.330	.358	.458	.816	14	.935
— New York (N.L.)	SS-2B-3B	78	178	19	48	12	1	1	19	12	42	4	2	2-4	.270	.330	.365	.695	9	.963
1998— New York (N.L.)	2-S-3-OF	117	266	37	67	13	2	2	22	20	60	4	10	2-2	.252	.312	.338	.650	11	.961
1999— New York (N.L.)	SS-2B-3B	68	104	11	22	4	0	2	13	12	33	3	1	1-1	.212	.308	.308	.616	4	.962
2000— Milwaukee (N.L.)	SS-2B-3B	78	201	24	53	14	0	6	27	9	35	5	2	1-2	.264	.309	.423	.732	8	.969
2001— Milwaukee (N.L.)	3B-SS-2B	92	222	22	60	8	3	4	18	14	44	5	6	0-1	.270	.326	.387	.714	8	.959
2002— Indianapolis (Int'l)	2B-SS-3B	6	22	2	5	0	0	0	0	0	4	1	0	0-0	.227	.261	.227	.488	0	1.000
— Milwaukee (N.L.)	SS	6	8	1	0	0	0	0	1	2	1	0	0	0-0	.000	.200	.000	.200	0	1.000
— Rochester (Int'l)	2B-SS	17	68	12	22	6	0	3	8	3	11	1	1	0-0	.324	.361	.544	.905	1	.988
— Baltimore (A.L.)	S-2-DH-1	52	109	10	23	6	0	2	9	3	20	0	1	1-0	.211	.232	.321	.553	3	.969
2003— Colo. Springs (PCL)	2-SS-1-3	47	140	14	29	10	0	3	18	9	29	2	2	0-1	.207	.265	.343	.608	7	.961
— Ottawa (Int'l)	2-S-DH-3	52	186	23	49	6	0	5	32	6	24	5	3	1-1	.263	.299	.376	.675	7	.969
2004— Baltimore (A.L.)	S-3-DH-2-1	56	88	7	16	5	0	1	8	3	20	1	1	0-0	.182	.211	.273	.483	6	.923
American League totals (2 years)		108	197	17	39	11	0	3	17	6	40	1	4	1-0	.198	.222	.299	.522	9	.949
National League totals (9 years)		596	1396	154	345	71	7	19	132	93	297	25	35	9-12	.247	.304	.349	.653	59	.963
Major League totals (10 years)		704	1593	171	384	82	7	22	149	99	337	26	39	10-12	.241	.294	.343	.637	68	.961

DIVISION SERIES RECORD

Year	Team (League)	Pos.	G	AB	R	H	2B	3B	HR	RBI	BB	SO	HBP	GDP	SB-CS	Avg.	OBP	SLG	OPS	E	Avg.
1996— San Diego (N.L.)		1	0	0	0	0	0	0	0	0	0	0	0	0-0	.000	.000	.000	.000	0	.000
1999— New York (N.L.)					Did not play.																

CHAMPIONSHIP SERIES RECORD

Year	Team (League)	Pos.	G	AB	R	H	2B	3B	HR	RBI	BB	SO	HBP	GDP	SB-CS	Avg.	OBP	SLG	OPS	E	Avg.
1999— New York (N.L.)					Did not play.																

LOPEZ, LUIS — 1B

PERSONAL: Born October 5, 1973, in Brooklyn, N.Y. ... 6-0/205. ... Bats right, throws right. ... Full name: Luis Lopez Jr..

TRANSACTIONS/CAREER NOTES: Signed by Ogden of the Pioneer League (July 8, 1995). ... Signed as a free agent by Toronto Blue Jays organization (June 15, 1996). ... Claimed on waivers by Oakland Athletics (December 22, 2001). ... Signed as a free agent by Montreal Expos organization (January 22, 2004). ... Released by Expos (June 2004). ... Signed by Atlanta Braves organization (June 15, 2004).

2004 GAMES PLAYED BY POSITION (MLB): 1B—8.

Year	Team (League)	Pos.	G	AB	R	H	2B	3B	HR	RBI	BB	SO	HBP	GDP	SB-CS	Avg.	OBP	SLG	OPS	E	Avg.
1995— St. Paul (Northern)		13	27	4	3	0	0	0	0	7	3	...	...	0-...	.111	...	.111	...	1	.963
— Ogden (Pioneer)	3B	46	182	36	65	15	0	7	39	16	20	...	...	1-...	.357	...	.555	...	11	.930
1996— St. Catharines (NY-Penn.)	3B-1B-OF	74	260	36	74	17	2	7	40	27	31	7	4	2-3	.285	.364	.446	.810	3	.995
1997— Hagerstown (S. Atl.)	3B-1B	136	503	96	180	47	4	11	99	60	45	8	14	5-8	.358	.430	.533	.963	3	.996
1998— Knoxville (Southern)	3B-1B	119	450	70	141	27	1	15	85	58	55	3	18	0-2	.313	.389	.478	.867	3	.995
— Syracuse (Int'l)	3B-1B	11	41	6	9	0	0	1	3	6	6	0	2	0-0	.220	.313	.293	.605	1	.967
1999— Syracuse (Int'l)	3B-1B	136	531	76	171	35	2	4	69	40	58	1	22	1-0	.322	.366	.418	.784	6	.992
2000— Syracuse (Int'l)	3B-1B	130	491	64	161	27	1	7	79	48	33	2	10	3-1	.328	.384	.430	.814	7	.983
2001— Syracuse (Int'l)	1B-3B	87	339	57	110	26	2	10	73	39	31	2	9	1-1	.324	.391	.501	.893	0	1.000
— Toronto (A.L.)	3B-1B-DH	41	119	10	29	4	0	3	10	8	16	0	10	0-0	.244	.291	.353	.644	5	.944
2002— Sacramento (PCL)	3B	131	516	66	146	28	0	9	72	64	63	1	17	2-3	.283	.361	.390	.750	14	.957
2003— Sacramento (PCL)	3B-DH-1B	131	498	67	122	28	0	18	72	40	68	4	17	0-1	.245	.303	.410	.713	12	.961
2004— Montreal (N.L.)	1B	11	26	0	4	0	0	0	0	0	9	1	1	0-0	.154	.185	.154	.339	0	1.000
— Edmonton (PCL)	3B	23	68	9	14	1	0	1	9	9	11	0	2	0-0	.206	.295	.265	.560	0	1.000
— Richmond (Int'l)	DH-1B-3B	69	232	37	77	18	0	9	51	30	27	3	11	0-0	.332	.412	.526	.938	4	.979
American League totals (1 year)		41	119	10	29	4	0	3	10	8	16	0	10	0-0	.244	.291	.353	.644	5	.944
National League totals (1 year)		11	26	0	4	0	0	0	0	0	9	1	1	0-0	.154	.185	.154	.339	0	1.000
Major League totals (2 years)		52	145	10	33	4	0	3	10	8	25	1	11	0-0	.228	.273	.317	.590	5	.965

L

LOPEZ, MENDY — 2B/3B

PERSONAL: Born October 15, 1973, in Pimentel, Dominican Republic. ... 6-2/200. ... Bats right, throws right. ... Full name: Mendy Aupe Lopez. ... High school: Liceo Los Trinitanos (Santo Domingo, Dominican Republic).

TRANSACTIONS/CAREER NOTES: Signed as a non-drafted free agent by Kansas City Royals organization (February 26, 1992). ... Released by Royals (December 13, 1999). ... Signed by Florida Marlins organization (January 12, 2000). ... Signed as a free agent by Houston Astros organization (January 8, 2001). ... Claimed on waivers by Pittsburgh Pirates (August 13, 2001). ... Released by Pirates (October 11, 2002). ... Signed as a free agent by Royals orgaqnization (November 30, 2002). ... On disabled list (July 5-August 12, 2003); included rehabilitation assignment to AZL Royals. ... Released by Royals (July 10, 2004).

2004 GAMES PLAYED BY POSITION (MLB): 2B—6, 3B—4, SS—4, OF—4, 1B—2.

Year Team (League)	Pos.	G	AB	R	H	2B	3B	HR	RBI	BB	SO	HBP	GDP	SB-CS	Avg.	OBP	SLG	OPS	E	Avg.
1992— Dom. Royals (DSL)	SS	49	145	22	40	1	0	1	23	22	15	...	...	7-...	.276	...	.303	...	26	.901
1993— Dom. Royals (DSL)	IF	28	98	15	27	5	2	0	20	11	5	...	...	2-...	.276	...	.367	...	15	.894
1994— GC Royals (GCL)	2B-3B-SS	59	235	56	85	19	3	5	50	22	27	3	5	10-2	.362	.415	.532	.947	12	.959
1995— Wilmington (Caro.)	3B-SS	130	428	42	116	29	3	2	36	28	73	5	12	18-10	.271	.322	.367	.689	25	.944
1996— Wichita (Texas)	3B-SS	93	327	47	92	20	5	6	32	26	67	4	6	14-4	.281	.341	.428	.769	24	.935
1997— Omaha (A.A.)	3B	17	52	6	12	2	0	1	6	8	21	0	0	0-0	.231	.333	.327	.660	6	.898
— Wichita (Texas)	SS	101	357	56	83	16	3	5	42	36	70	3	8	7-5	.232	.304	.336	.640	20	.961
1998— Omaha (PCL)	SS-3B	60	195	18	35	6	1	3	14	18	44	1	0	2-3	.179	.252	.267	.519	10	.960
— Kansas City (A.L.)	SS-3B	74	206	18	50	10	2	1	15	12	40	1	6	5-2	.243	.286	.325	.612	15	.956
1999— Omaha (PCL)	SS-2B-3B	61	222	41	69	8	0	12	40	18	41	0	5	2-2	.311	.361	.509	.870	8	.971
— GC Royals (GCL)	SS	3	5	0	1	1	0	0	2	3	1	1	0	0-0	.200	.500	.400	.900	0	1.000
— Kansas City (A.L.)	2B-SS	7	20	2	8	0	1	0	3	0	5	1	0	0-0	.400	.429	.500	.929	0	1.000
2000— Calgary (PCL)	SS-2B-3B	56	225	34	73	20	1	7	29	13	38	0	2	1-1	.324	.361	.516	.877	12	.955
— Florida (N.L.)		4	3	0	0	0	0	0	0	1	1	0	0	0-0	.000	.250	.000	.250	...	...
2001— New Orleans (PCL)	2-S-1-O-3	63	208	37	58	11	1	14	36	18	49	3	5	2-2	.279	.343	.543	.887	3	.990
— Houston (N.L.)	2B-3B	10	15	3	4	0	0	1	3	2	4	1	0	0-0	.267	.389	.467	.856	0	1.000
— Pittsburgh (N.L.)	2B-SS-OF	22	43	5	10	3	1	0	4	4	16	0	0	0-0	.233	.292	.349	.641	1	.983
2002— Nashville (PCL)	SS-3B-2B	101	385	60	97	26	0	11	72	34	99	2	10	4-1	.252	.309	.405	.714	9	.977
— Pittsburgh (N.L.)		3	3	0	0	0	0	0	0	0	3	0	0	0-0	.000	.000	.000	.000	0	...
2003— Royals-1 (Ariz.)	2B-3B-SS	7	20	9	5	1	0	3	6	4	5	1	0	0-0	.250	.400	.750	1.150	0	1.000
— Kansas City (A.L.)	1-3-2-S-O	52	94	13	26	5	1	3	11	4	28	0	3	2-0	.277	.306	.447	.753	1	.993
2004— Kansas City (A.L.)	2-3-S-O-1	18	38	4	4	0	0	1	4	4	9	1	3	0-0	.105	.209	.184	.394	3	.921
— Omaha (PCL)	SS-2B	31	123	20	36	6	1	13	26	9	31	0	0	1-2	.293	.341	.675	1.016	4	.970
American League totals (4 years)		**151**	**358**	**37**	**88**	**15**	**4**	**5**	**33**	**20**	**82**	**3**	**12**	**7-2**	**.246**	**.291**	**.352**	**.643**	**19**	**.965**
National League totals (3 years)		**39**	**64**	**8**	**14**	**3**	**1**	**1**	**7**	**7**	**24**	**1**	**0**	**0-0**	**.219**	**.301**	**.344**	**.645**	**1**	**.985**
Major League totals (7 years)		**190**	**422**	**45**	**102**	**18**	**5**	**6**	**40**	**27**	**106**	**4**	**12**	**7-2**	**.242**	**.292**	**.351**	**.643**	**20**	**.967**

LOPEZ, MICKEY — 2B

PERSONAL: Born November 17, 1973, in Miami, Fla. ... 5-9/170. ... Bats both, throws right. ... Full name: Raymond Michael Lopez. ... High school: Westminster Christian (Miami). ... College: Florida State.

TRANSACTIONS/CAREER NOTES: Selected by Milwaukee Brewers organization in 13th round of 1995 free-agent draft. ... Traded by Brewers to Philadelphia Phillies for a player to be named (March 31, 2001); Brewers acquired P Bobby Sismondo to complete deal (August 2, 2001). ... Signed as a free agent by Chicago Cubs organization (November 27, 2001). ... Released by Cubs (March 30, 2003). ... Signed by Seattle Mariners organization (April 10, 2003).

2004 GAMES PLAYED BY POSITION (MLB): 2B—3, DH—3.

Year Team (League)	Pos.	G	AB	R	H	2B	3B	HR	RBI	BB	SO	HBP	GDP	SB-CS	Avg.	OBP	SLG	OPS	E	Avg.
1995— Helena (Pio.)	SS-2B	57	225	66	73	19	2	1	41	38	20	5	1	12-8	.324	.426	.440	.866	20	.930
1996— Beloit (Midw.)	2B-SS	61	236	35	64	10	2	0	14	28	36	1	8	12-8	.271	.351	.331	.681	12	.962
— Stockton (Calif.)	2B-SS	64	217	30	61	10	1	0	25	23	36	4	0	6-4	.281	.359	.336	.696	10	.969
1997— El Paso (Texas)	2B	134	483	79	145	21	10	3	58	48	60	5	10	20-10	.300	.366	.404	.770	17	.976
1998— El Paso (Texas)	2B-SS	120	459	81	127	24	9	2	64	46	61	2	11	12-10	.277	.342	.381	.723	34	.952
— Louisville (Int'l)	2B-3B	3	4	1	1	0	0	0	0	2	0	0	0	0-0	.250	.500	.250	.750	0	1.000
1999— Huntsville (Sou.)	2B-SS	83	315	58	94	16	5	5	40	46	46	5	9	31-4	.298	.392	.429	.820	12	.973
— Louisville (Int'l)	2B	49	181	43	58	17	2	5	31	37	25	2	1	11-7	.320	.439	.519	.958	6	.976
2000— Indianapolis (Int'l)	2B-SS	67	208	38	54	14	1	2	22	37	26	4	5	14-7	.260	.375	.365	.741	13	.949
— Huntsville (Sou.)	2B-3B	53	212	42	71	22	4	4	26	30	32	0	5	16-7	.335	.416	.533	.949	6	.975
2001— Reading (East.)	2B-SS-OF	107	382	71	104	18	6	11	47	63	58	7	6	21-6	.272	.383	.437	.820	15	.963
2002— West Tenn (Sou.)	SS-OF-2B	17	62	11	17	2	0	0	7	5	9	1	0	5-2	.274	.324	.306	.630	9	.868
— Iowa (PCL)	2-S-O-3-P	107	338	48	89	25	1	5	39	39	45	4	5	8-5	.263	.340	.388	.728	10	.972
2003— Tacoma (PCL)	2B-SS-OF	129	455	68	125	23	4	7	41	47	50	6	12	20-12	.275	.346	.389	.735	9	.985
2004— Tacoma (PCL)	2-S-3-DH-O	109	391	70	112	20	5	10	41	45	59	7	6	13-10	.286	.369	.440	.798	14	.985
— Seattle (A.L.)	2B-DH	6	4	1	1	0	0	0	0	1	0	1	0	0-0	.250	.500	.250	.750	0	1.000
Major League totals (1 year)		**6**	**4**	**1**	**1**	**0**	**0**	**0**	**0**	**1**	**0**	**1**	**0**	**0-0**	**.250**	**.500**	**.250**	**.750**	**0**	**1.000**

LOPEZ, RODRIGO — P

PERSONAL: Born December 14, 1975, in Tlalnepantla, Mexico. ... 6-1/190. ... Throws right, bats right. ... Full name: Rodrigo Munoz Lopez. ... Name pronounced: rod-REE-go.

TRANSACTIONS/CAREER NOTES: Contract sold by Aguila of the Mexican League to San Diego Padres organization (March 21, 1995). ... Loaned by Padres to Mexico City Red Devils of the Mexican League (March 13-August 19, 1998). ... Signed as a free agent by Baltimore Orioles organization (February 4, 2002). ... On disabled list (May 2-June 15, 2003); included rehabilitation assignment to Bowie.

HONORS: Named A.L. Rookie Pitcher of the Year by THE SPORTING NEWS (2002).

CAREER HITTING: 1-for-14 (.071), 1 R, 0 2B, 0 3B, 0 HR, 0 RBI.

Year Team (League)	W	L	Pct.	ERA	WHIP	G	GS	CG	ShO	Hld.	Sv.-Opp.	IP	H	R	ER	HR	BB-IBB	SO	Avg.
1993— Aguila (Mex.)	0	0	...	36.00	6.00	2	0	0	0	...	0-...	1.0	3	4	4	0	3-...	0	...
1994— Aguila (Mex.)	0	0	...	4.97	1.42	10	0	0	0	...	0-...	12.2	15	7	7	2	3-...	5	...
1995— Ariz. Padres (Ariz.)	1	1	.500	5.45	1.59	11	7	0	0	...	1-...	34.2	41	29	21	0	14-0	33	.287
1996— Poza Rica (Mex.)	1	1	.500	3.54	1.52	7	3	0	0	...	1-...	20.1	15	8	8	2	16-...	22	...
— Idaho Falls (Pioneer)	4	4	.500	5.70	1.55	15	14	0	0	...	1-...	71.0	76	52	45	3	34-0	72	.283
1997— Clinton (Midw.)	6	8	.429	3.18	1.19	37	14	2	0	...	9-...	121.2	103	49	43	6	42-1	123	.228

Year	Team (League)	W	L	Pct.	ERA	WHIP	G	GS	CG	ShO	Hld.	Sv.-Opp.	IP	H	R	ER	HR	BB-IBB	SO	Avg.
1998—M.C. Red Devils (Mex.)		10	6	.625	3.35	1.49	26	26	1	0	...	0-...	163.2	165	73	61	9	79-...	95	...
—Mobile (Sou.)		3	0	1.000	1.40	0.97	4	4	2	1	...	0-...	25.2	21	11	4	1	4-0	20	.219
1999—Mobile (Sou.)		10	8	.556	4.41	1.45	28	28	1	1	...	0-...	169.1	187	91	83	14	58-3	138	.286
2000—Las Vegas (PCL)		8	7	.533	4.69	1.54	20	20	1	0	...	0-...	109.1	123	66	57	9	45-1	100	.289
—San Diego (N.L.)		0	3	.000	8.76	2.15	6	6	0	0	0	0-0	24.2	40	24	24	5	13-0	17	.377
2001—Lake Elsinore (Calif.)		0	1	.000	0.69	1.46	9	0	0	0	0	0-...	13.0	15	7	1	1	4-0	9	.278
—Portland (PCL)		2	2	.500	3.44	1.15	11	8	0	0	0	0-...	52.1	45	22	20	7	15-0	37	.230
2002—Baltimore (A.L.)		15	9	.625	3.57	1.19	33	28	1	0	0	0-...	196.2	172	83	78	23	62-4	136	.234
2003—Bowie (East.)		1	0	1.000	0.00	0.50	1	1	0	0	...	0-...	6.1	3	0	0	0	0-0	13	.143
—Baltimore (A.L.)		7	10	.412	5.82	1.57	26	26	3	1	0	0-...	147.0	188	101	95	24	43-6	103	.313
2004—Baltimore (A.L.)		14	9	.609	3.59	1.28	37	23	1	1	4	0-1	170.2	164	71	68	21	54-2	121	.252
American League totals (3 years)		36	28	.563	4.22	1.33	96	77	5	2	4	0-1	514.1	524	255	241	68	159-12	360	.264
National League totals (1 year)		0	3	.000	8.76	2.15	6	6	0	0	0	0-0	24.2	40	24	24	5	13-0	17	.377
Major League totals (4 years)		36	31	.537	4.42	1.37	102	83	5	2	4	0-1	539.0	564	279	265	73	172-12	377	.270

LORETTA, MARK   2B

PERSONAL: Born August 14, 1971, in Santa Monica, Calif. ... 6-0/186. ... Bats right, throws right. ... Full name: Mark David Loretta. ... High school: St. Francis (La Canada, Calif.). ... College: Northwestern.

TRANSACTIONS/CAREER NOTES: Selected by Milwaukee Brewers organization in seventh round of 1993 free-agent draft. ... On disabled list (June 3-August 16, 2000); included rehabilitation assignment to Indianapolis. ... On disabled list (March 27-May 19, 2001); included rehabilitation assignment to Indianapolis. ... Traded by Brewers to Houston Astros from two players to be named (August 31, 2002); Brewers acquired P Wayne Franklin (September 3, 2002) and 2B Keith Ginter (September 5, 2002) to complete deal. ... Signed as a free agent by San Diego Padres (December 16, 2002). ... Career major league pitching: 0-0, 0.00 ERA, 1 G, 1.0 IP, 1 H, 0 R, 0 ER, 1 BB, 2 SO.

2004 GAMES PLAYED BY POSITION (MLB): 2B—154.

Year	Team (League)	Pos.	G	AB	R	H	2B	3B	HR	RBI	BB	SO	HBP	GDP	SB-CS	Avg.	OBP	SLG	OPS	E	Avg.
1993—Helena (Pio.)		SS	6	28	5	9	1	0	1	8	1	4	1	1	0-0	.321	.367	.464	.831	0	1.000
—Stockton (Calif.)		3B-SS	53	201	36	73	4	1	4	31	22	17	2	6	8-2	.363	.427	.453	.880	15	.943
1994—El Paso (Texas)		IF	77	302	50	95	13	6	0	38	27	33	2	12	8-5	.315	.369	.397	.766	11	.973
—New Orleans (A.A.)		2B-SS	43	138	16	29	7	0	1	14	12	13	3	2	2-1	.210	.282	.283	.565	11	.945
1995—New Orleans (A.A.)		S-3-2-DH	127	479	48	137	22	5	7	79	34	47	9	12	8-9	.286	.340	.397	.737	25	.959
—Milwaukee (A.L.)		SS-2B-DH	19	50	13	13	3	0	1	3	4	7	1	1	1-1	.260	.327	.380	.707	1	.984
1996—New Orleans (A.A.)		SS	19	71	10	18	5	1	0	11	9	8	2	1	1-1	.254	.345	.352	.697	5	.948
—Milwaukee (A.L.)		2B-3B-SS	73	154	20	43	3	0	1	13	14	15	0	7	2-1	.279	.339	.318	.657	2	.989
1997—Milwaukee (A.L.)		2-S-1-3	132	418	56	120	17	5	5	47	47	60	2	15	5-5	.287	.354	.388	.742	15	.976
1998—Milwaukee (N.L.)		1-S-3-2-0	140	434	55	137	29	6	6	54	42	47	7	14	9-6	.316	.382	.424	.806	6	.991
1999—Milwaukee (N.L.)		S-1-2-3	153	587	93	170	34	5	5	67	52	59	10	14	4-1	.290	.354	.390	.744	13	.986
2000—Milwaukee (N.L.)		SS-2B	91	352	49	99	21	1	7	40	37	38	1	9	0-3	.281	.350	.406	.757	2	.995
—Indianapolis (Int'l)		SS	10	25	6	6	1	0	0	5	2	4	1	1	0-0	.240	.310	.280	.590	0	1.000
2001—Indianapolis (Int'l)		SS-2B-3B	8	31	4	3	0	0	1	2	2	4	0	1	0-0	.097	.152	.097	.248	3	.850
—Milwaukee (N.L.)		2-3-S-DH	102	384	40	111	14	2	2	29	28	46	7	6	1-2	.289	.346	.352	.698	8	.978
2002—Milwaukee (N.L.)		3-S-1-2-DH	86	217	23	58	14	0	2	19	23	32	5	6	0-0	.267	.350	.359	.709	3	.982
—Houston (N.L.)		3B-SS-2B	21	66	10	28	4	0	2	8	9	5	0	1	1-1	.424	.481	.576	1.056	2	.964
2003—San Diego (N.L.)		2B-SS	154	589	74	185	28	4	13	72	54	62	3	17	5-4	.314	.372	.441	.814	7	.990
2004—San Diego (N.L.)		2B	154	620	108	208	47	2	16	76	58	45	9	10	5-3	.335	.391	.495	.886	10	.987
American League totals (3 years)			224	622	89	176	23	5	7	63	65	82	3	23	8-7	.283	.349	.370	.718	18	.979
National League totals (7 years)			901	3249	452	996	191	14	53	365	303	334	42	77	25-20	.307	.369	.423	.792	51	.987
Major League totals (10 years)			1125	3871	541	1172	214	19	60	428	368	416	45	100	33-27	.303	.366	.414	.780	69	.986

ALL-STAR GAME RECORD

	G	AB	R	H	2B	3B	HR	RBI	BB	SO	HBP	GDP	SB-CS	Avg.	OBP	SLG	OPS	E	Avg.
All-Star Game totals (1 year)	1	2	0	1	0	0	0	0	0	0	0	0	0-0	.500	.500	.500	1.000	0	1.000

LOWE, DEREK   P

PERSONAL: Born June 1, 1973, in Dearborn, Mich. ... 6-6/210. ... Throws right, bats right. ... Full name: Derek Christopher Lowe. ... High school: Edsel Ford (Dearborn, Mich.).

TRANSACTIONS/CAREER NOTES: Selected by Seattle Mariners organization in eighth round of 1991 free-agent draft. ... Traded by Mariners with C Jason Varitek to Boston Red Sox for P Heathcliff Slocumb (July 31, 1997). ... On suspended list (September 15-20, 2002).

CAREER HITTING: 2-for-20 (.100), 0 R, 1 2B, 0 3B, 0 HR, 1 RBI.

Year	Team (League)	W	L	Pct.	ERA	WHIP	G	GS	CG	ShO	Hld.	Sv.-Opp.	IP	H	R	ER	HR	BB-IBB	SO	Avg.
1991—Ariz. Mariners (Ariz.)		5	3	.625	2.41	1.11	12	12	0	0	...	0-...	71.0	58	26	19	2	21-0	60	.217
1992—Bellingham (N'west)		7	3	.700	2.42	1.06	14	13	2	1	...	0-...	85.2	69	34	23	2	22-0	66	.216
1993—Riverside (California)		12	9	.571	5.26	1.62	27	26	3	2	...	0-...	154.0	189	104	90	9	60-0	80	.304
1994—Jacksonville (Southern)		7	10	.412	4.94	1.50	26	26	2	0	...	0-...	151.1	177	92	83	7	50-1	75	.291
1995—Ariz. Mariners (Ariz.)		1	0	1.000	0.93	0.72	2	2	0	0	...	0-...	9.2	5	1	1	0	2-0	11	.152
—Port City (Sou.)		1	6	.143	6.08	1.73	10	10	1	0	...	0-...	53.1	70	41	36	8	22-1	30	.327
1996—Port City (Sou.)		5	3	.625	3.05	1.12	10	10	0	0	...	0-...	65.0	56	27	22	7	17-0	33	.235
—Tacoma (PCL)		6	9	.400	4.54	1.48	17	16	1	1	...	0-...	105.0	118	64	53	7	37-1	54	.285
1997—Tacoma (PCL)		3	4	.429	3.45	1.27	10	9	1	0	...	0-...	57.1	53	26	22	3	20-0	49	.242
—Seattle (A.L.)		2	4	.333	6.96	1.49	12	9	0	0	0	0-0	53.0	59	43	41	11	20-2	39	.282
—Pawtucket (Int'l)		4	0	1.000	2.37	1.12	6	5	0	0	...	0-...	30.1	23	8	8	3	11-0	21	.213
—Boston (A.L.)		0	2	.000	3.38	1.13	8	0	0	0	1	0-2	16.0	15	6	6	0	3-1	13	.268
1998—Boston (A.L.)		3	9	.250	4.02	1.37	63	10	0	0	12	4-9	123.0	126	65	55	5	42-5	77	.267
1999—Boston (A.L.)		6	3	.667	2.63	0.00	74	0	0	0	22	15-20	109.1	84	35	32	7	25-1	80	.208
2000—Boston (A.L.)		4	4	.500	2.56	1.23	74	0	0	0	0	• 42-47	91.1	90	27	26	6	22-5	79	.257
2001—Boston (A.L.)		5	10	.333	3.53	1.44	67	3	0	0	4	24-30	91.2	103	39	36	7	29-9	82	.283
2002—Boston (A.L.)		21	8	.724	2.58	0.97	32	32	1	1	0	0-0	219.2	166	65	63	12	48-0	127	.211
2003—Boston (A.L.)		17	7	.708	4.47	1.42	33	33	1	0	0	0-0	203.1	216	113	101	17	72-4	110	.272
2004—Boston (A.L.)		14	12	.538	5.42	1.61	33	33	0	0	0	0-0	182.2	224	* 138	110	15	71-2	105	.299
Major League totals (8 years)		72	59	.550	3.88	1.30	396	120	2	1	39	85-108	1090.0	1083	531	470	80	332-29	712	.259

DIVISION SERIES RECORD

Year Team (League)	W	L	Pct.	ERA	WHIP	G	GS	CG	ShO	Hld.	Sv.-Opp.	IP	H	R	ER	HR	BB-IBB	SO	Avg.
1998— Boston (A.L.)	0	0	...	2.08	0.92	2	0	0	0	1	0-0	4.1	3	1	1	0	1-1	2	.200
1999— Boston (A.L.)	1	1	.500	4.32	0.84	3	0	0	0	0	0-0	8.1	6	7	4	2	1-0	7	.188
2003— Boston (A.L.)	0	1	.000	0.93	1.45	3	1	0	0	0	1-1	9.2	7	2	1	0	7-2	6	.200
2004— Boston (A.L.)	1	0	1.000	0.00	2.00	1	0	0	0	0	0-0	1.0	1	0	0	0	1-0	0	.333
Division series totals (4 years)	**2**	**2**	**.500**	**2.31**	**1.16**	**9**	**1**	**0**	**0**	**1**	**1-1**	**23.1**	**17**	**10**	**6**	**2**	**10-3**	**15**	**.200**

CHAMPIONSHIP SERIES RECORD

Year Team (League)	W	L	Pct.	ERA	WHIP	G	GS	CG	ShO	Hld.	Sv.-Opp.	IP	H	R	ER	HR	BB-IBB	SO	Avg.
1999— Boston (A.L.)	0	0	...	1.42	1.26	3	0	0	0	0	0-1	6.1	6	3	1	0	2-0	7	.231
2003— Boston (A.L.)	0	2	.000	6.43	1.50	2	2	0	0	0	0-0	14.0	14	10	10	1	7-1	5	.255
2004— Boston (A.L.)	1	0	1.000	3.18	0.71	2	2	0	0	0	0-0	11.1	7	4	4	1	1-0	6	.175
Champ. series totals (3 years)	**1**	**2**	**.333**	**4.26**	**1.17**	**7**	**4**	**0**	**0**	**0**	**0-1**	**31.2**	**27**	**17**	**15**	**2**	**10-1**	**18**	**.223**

WORLD SERIES RECORD

Year Team (League)	W	L	Pct.	ERA	WHIP	G	GS	CG	ShO	Hld.	Sv.-Opp.	IP	H	R	ER	HR	BB-IBB	SO	Avg.
2004— Boston (A.L.)	1	0	1.000	0.00	0.57	1	1	0	0	0	0-0	7.0	3	0	0	0	1-0	4	.130

ALL-STAR GAME RECORD

Year Team (League)	W	L	Pct.	ERA	WHIP	G	GS	CG	ShO	Hld.	Sv.-Opp.	IP	H	R	ER	HR	BB-IBB	SO	Avg.
All-Star Game totals (2 years)	**0**	**0**	**...**	**3.00**	**0.67**	**2**	**1**	**0**	**0**	**1**	**0-0**	**3.0**	**2**	**1**	**1**	**0**	**0-0**	**0**	**.182**

LOWELL, MIKE — 3B

PERSONAL: Born February 24, 1974, in San Juan, Puerto Rico. ... 6-3/210. ... Bats right, throws right. ... Full name: Michael Averett Lowell. ... High school: Coral Gables (Fla.). ... College: Florida International.

TRANSACTIONS/CAREER NOTES: Selected by New York Yankees organization in 20th round of 1995 free-agent draft. ... Traded by Yankees to Florida Marlins for Ps Ed Yarnall, Mark Johnson and Todd Noel (February 1, 1999). ... On disabled list (March 26-May 29, 1999); included rehabilitation assignments to Calgary. ... On disabled list (May 13-29, 2000). ... On disabled list (August 31-September 28, 2003).

2004 GAMES PLAYED BY POSITION (MLB): 3B—154, DH—3.

Year Team (League)	Pos.	G	AB	R	H	2B	3B	HR	RBI	BB	SO	HBP	GDP	SB-CS	Avg.	OBP	SLG	OPS	E	Avg.
1995— Oneonta (N.Y.-Penn.)	3B	72	281	36	73	18	0	1	27	23	34	3	5	3-1	.260	.316	.335	.651	24	.911
1996— Greensboro (S. Atl.)	3B-SS	113	433	58	122	33	0	8	64	46	43	4	7	10-3	.282	.355	.413	.768	32	.925
— Tampa (Fla. St.)	3B	24	78	8	22	5	0	0	11	3	13	0	2	1-1	.282	.298	.346	.644	3	.954
1997— Norwich (East.)	3B-SS	78	285	60	98	17	0	15	47	48	30	4	11	2-1	.344	.439	.561	1.000	15	.927
— Columbus (Int'l)	3B-SS	57	210	36	58	13	1	15	45	23	34	3	6	2-4	.276	.347	.562	.909	5	.954
1998— Columbus (Int'l) 3B-SS-1B		126	510	79	155	34	3	26	99	37	85	6	10	4-0	.304	.355	.535	.890	21	.950
— New York (A.L.)	3B-DH	8	15	1	4	0	0	0	0	0	1	0	0	0-0	.267	.267	.267	.533	0	1.000
1999— Calgary (PCL)	3B	24	83	11	26	3	0	2	9	8	19	0	0	0-0	.313	.374	.422	.795	4	.939
— Florida (N.L.)	3B	97	308	32	78	15	0	12	47	26	69	5	8	0-0	.253	.317	.419	.736	4	.981
2000— Florida (N.L.)	3B	140	508	73	137	38	0	22	91	54	75	9	4	4-0	.270	.344	.474	.818	12	.968
2001— Florida (N.L.)	3B	146	551	65	156	37	0	18	100	43	79	10	9	1-2	.283	.340	.448	.789	9	.976
2002— Florida (N.L.)	3B	160	597	88	165	44	0	24	92	65	92	4	16	4-3	.276	.346	.471	.816	14	.969
2003— Florida (N.L.)	3B-DH	130	492	76	136	27	1	32	105	56	78	3	14	3-1	.276	.350	.530	.881	9	.973
2004— Florida (N.L.)	3B-DH	158	598	87	175	44	1	27	85	64	77	6	17	5-1	.293	.365	.505	.870	7	.982
American League totals (1 year)		8	15	1	4	0	0	0	0	0	1	0	0	0-0	.267	.267	.267	.533	0	1.000
National League totals (6 years)		831	3054	421	847	205	2	135	520	308	470	37	68	17-7	.277	.346	.478	.824	55	.974
Major League totals (7 years)		839	3069	422	851	205	2	135	520	308	471	37	68	17-7	.277	.346	.477	.823	55	.974

DIVISION SERIES RECORD

Year Team (League)	Pos.	G	AB	R	H	2B	3B	HR	RBI	BB	SO	HBP	GDP	SB-CS	Avg.	OBP	SLG	OPS	E	Avg.
2003— Florida (N.L.)	3B	2	3	0	0	0	0	0	0	0	1	0	0	0-0	.000	.000	.000	.000	0	1.000

CHAMPIONSHIP SERIES RECORD

Year Team (League)	Pos.	G	AB	R	H	2B	3B	HR	RBI	BB	SO	HBP	GDP	SB-CS	Avg.	OBP	SLG	OPS	E	Avg.
2003— Florida (N.L.)	3B	7	20	5	4	0	0	2	3	3	4	0	0	0-0	.200	.304	.500	.804	0	1.000

WORLD SERIES RECORD

Year Team (League)	Pos.	G	AB	R	H	2B	3B	HR	RBI	BB	SO	HBP	GDP	SB-CS	Avg.	OBP	SLG	OPS	E	Avg.
2003— Florida (N.L.)	3B	6	23	1	5	1	0	0	2	2	3	0	0	0-0	.217	.280	.261	.541	0	1.000

ALL-STAR GAME RECORD

Year Team (League)		G	AB	R	H	2B	3B	HR	RBI	BB	SO	HBP	GDP	SB-CS	Avg.	OBP	SLG	OPS	E	Avg.
All-Star Game totals (3 years)		3	6	1	3	1	0	0	0	0	1	0	0	0-0	.500	.500	.667	1.167	0	1.000

LOWRY, NOAH — P

PERSONAL: Born October 10, 1980, in Ventura, Calif. ... 6-2/210. ... Throws left, bats right. ... Full name: Noah Ryan Lowry. ... High school: Nordhoff (Ojai, Calif.). ... College: Pepperdine.

TRANSACTIONS/CAREER NOTES: Selected by Texas Rangers organization in 19th round of 1999 free-agent draft; did not sign. ... Selected by San Francisco Giants organization in first round (30th pick overall) of 2001 free-agent draft.

CAREER HITTING: 7-for-35 (.200), 3 R, 2 2B, 0 3B, 0 HR, 0 RBI.

Year Team (League)	W	L	Pct.	ERA	WHIP	G	GS	CG	ShO	Hld.	Sv.-Opp.	IP	H	R	ER	HR	BB-IBB	SO	Avg.
2001— Salem-Keizer (N'west)	1	1	.500	3.60	1.36	8	7	0	0	...	0-...	25.0	26	15	10	2	8-0	28	.265
2002— San Jose (California)	6	5	.545	2.15	0.99	15	12	0	0	...	0-...	58.2	38	21	14	4	20-0	62	.186
2003— Norwich (East.)	9	6	.600	4.72	1.47	23	23	2	0	...	0-...	118.1	127	66	62	7	47-0	97	.285
— Fresno (PCL)	1	0	1.000	2.37	1.11	4	4	0	0	...	0-...	19.0	15	5	5	0	6-0	13	.227
— San Francisco (N.L.)	0	0	...	0.00	0.47	4	0	0	0	0	0-0	6.1	1	0	0	0	2-0	5	.048
2004— Fresno (PCL)	7	5	.583	4.13	1.41	17	17	1	1	...	0-...	89.1	98	53	41	9	28-0	73	.278
— San Francisco (N.L.)	6	0	1.000	3.82	1.29	16	14	2	1	0	0-0	92.0	91	41	39	10	28-1	72	.259
Major League totals (2 years)	6	0	1.000	3.57	1.24	20	14	2	1	0	0-0	98.1	92	41	39	10	30-1	77	.247

LUDWICK, RYAN — OF

PERSONAL: Born July 13, 1978, in Satellite Beach, Fla. ... 6-3/203. ... Bats right, throws left. ... Full name: Ryan Andrew Ludwick. ... High school: Durango (Las Vegas, Nev.). ... College: UNLV. ... Brother of Eric Ludwick, pitcher for four major league teams (1996-99).

TRANSACTIONS/CAREER NOTES: Selected by Oakland Athletics organization in second round of 1999 free-agent draft. ... Traded by A's with 1B Jason Hart, P Mario Ramos and C Gerald Laird to Texas Rangers for 1B Carlos Pena and P Mike Venafro (January 14, 2002). ... Traded by Rangers to Cleveland Indians for P Ricardo Rodriguez (July 18, 2003). ... On disabled list (April 2-July 5, 2004); included rehabilitation assignment to Akron.

2004 GAMES PLAYED BY POSITION (MLB): OF—15.

Year Team (League)	Pos.	G	AB	R	H	2B	3B	HR	RBI	BB	SO	HBP	GDP	SB-CS	Avg.	OBP	SLG	OPS	E	Avg.
1999— Modesto (California)	OF	43	171	28	47	11	3	4	34	19	45	3	0	2-1	.275	.348	.444	.793	0	1.000
2000— Modesto (California)	OF	129	493	86	130	26	3	29	102	68	128	6	9	10-6	.264	.359	.505	.864	5	.983
2001— Midland (Texas)	OF	119	443	82	119	23	3	25	96	53	113	7	6	9-10	.269	.352	.503	.856	6	.977
— Sacramento (PCL)	OF	17	57	10	13	3	0	1	7	2	16	0	0	2-0	.228	.246	.333	.579	1	.981
2002— Oklahoma (PCL)	OF	78	305	62	87	27	4	15	52	38	76	5	6	2-2	.285	.370	.548	.918	5	.973
— Texas (A.L.)	OF	23	81	10	19	6	0	1	9	7	24	0	4	2-1	.235	.295	.346	.641	0	1.000
2003— Oklahoma (PCL)	OF-DH	81	317	51	96	24	3	17	63	33	71	5	9	1-1	.303	.372	.558	.931	3	.975
— Texas (A.L.)	OF	8	26	3	4	1	0	0	0	4	9	0	0	0-0	.154	.267	.192	.459	0	1.000
— Cleveland (A.L.)	OF-DH	39	136	14	36	7	1	7	26	8	39	0	1	2-0	.265	.306	.485	.791	0	1.000
2004— Akron (East.)	OF-DH	8	26	4	7	2	0	1	5	1	5	0	0	0-0	.269	.286	.462	.747	0	1.000
— Buffalo (Int'l)	OF-DH	44	166	25	45	15	0	8	30	16	52	4	4	0-0	.271	.346	.506	.852	1	.980
— Cleveland (A.L.)	OF	15	50	3	11	2	0	2	4	2	14	2	0	0-0	.220	.278	.380	.658	1	.970
Major League totals (3 years)		85	293	30	70	16	1	10	39	21	86	2	5	4-1	.239	.294	.403	.697	1	.994

LUGO, JULIO — SS

PERSONAL: Born November 16, 1975, in Barahona, Dominican Republic. ... 6-1/170. ... Bats right, throws right. ... Full name: Julio Cesar Lugo. ... Name pronounced: lou-GO. ... Junior college: Connors State (Okla.).

TRANSACTIONS/CAREER NOTES: Selected by Houston Astros organization in 43rd round of 1994 free-agent draft. ... On disabled list (August 13, 2002-remainder of season). ... Released by Astros (May 9, 2003). ... Signed by Tampa Bay Devil Rays (May 15, 2003).

2004 GAMES PLAYED BY POSITION (MLB): SS—143, 2B—8, DH—5.

Year Team (League)	Pos.	G	AB	R	H	2B	3B	HR	RBI	BB	SO	HBP	GDP	SB-CS	Avg.	OBP	SLG	OPS	E	Avg.
1995— Auburn (NY-Penn)	2B-SS-OF	59	230	36	67	6	3	1	16	26	31	2	7	17-7	.291	.368	.357	.725	12	.944
1996— Quad City (Midw.)	2B-3B-SS	101	393	60	116	18	2	10	50	32	75	3	7	24-11	.295	.350	.427	.777	29	.934
1997— Kissimmee (Fla. St.)	2B-3B-SS	125	505	89	135	22	14	7	61	46	99	2	8	35-8	.267	.329	.408	.736	41	.938
1998— Kissimmee (Fla. St.)	SS	128	509	81	154	20	14	7	62	49	72	4	13	51-18	.303	.367	.438	.805	42	.921
1999— Jackson (Texas)	SS-2B	116	445	77	142	24	5	10	42	44	53	3	6	25-11	.319	.381	.463	.844	29	.946
2000— New Orleans (PCL)	2B-SS	24	101	22	33	4	1	3	12	11	20	0	2	12-7	.327	.393	.475	.868	4	.964
— Houston (N.L.)	SS-2B-OF	116	420	78	119	22	5	10	40	37	93	4	9	22-9	.283	.346	.431	.777	17	.963
2001— Houston (N.L.)	SS-OF-2B	140	513	93	135	20	3	10	37	46	116	5	7	12-11	.263	.326	.372	.698	22	.964
2002— Houston (N.L.)	SS	88	322	45	84	15	1	8	35	28	74	2	6	9-3	.261	.322	.388	.710	8	.976
2003— Houston (N.L.)	SS	22	65	6	16	3	0	0	2	9	12	0	2	2-1	.246	.338	.292	.630	3	.966
— Tampa Bay (A.L.)	SS	117	433	58	119	13	4	15	53	35	88	4	5	10-3	.275	.333	.427	.760	17	.970
2004— Tampa Bay (A.L.)	SS-2B-DH	157	581	83	160	41	4	7	75	54	106	5	8	21-5	.275	.338	.396	.734	26	.964
American League totals (2 years)		274	1014	141	279	54	8	22	128	89	194	9	13	31-8	.275	.336	.409	.745	43	.966
National League totals (4 years)		366	1320	222	354	60	9	28	114	120	295	11	24	45-24	.268	.333	.391	.723	50	.966
Major League totals (5 years)		640	2334	363	633	114	17	50	242	209	489	20	37	76-32	.271	.334	.399	.732	93	.966

DIVISION SERIES RECORD

Year Team (League)	Pos.	G	AB	R	H	2B	3B	HR	RBI	BB	SO	HBP	GDP	SB-CS	Avg.	OBP	SLG	OPS	E	Avg.
2001— Houston (N.L.)	SS	3	8	1	0	0	0	0	0	0	2	0	1	0-0	.000	.000	.000	.000	3	.786

LUNA, HECTOR — SS/2B

PERSONAL: Born February 1, 1980, in Montecristi, Dominican Republic. ... 6-1/170. ... Bats right, throws right. ... Full name: Hector R. Luna.

TRANSACTIONS/CAREER NOTES: Signed as a non-drafted free agent by Cleveland Indians organization (February 2, 1999). ... Selected by Tampa Bay Devil Rays from Indians organization in Rule 5 major league draft (December 16, 2002); returned to Indians organization (April 2, 2003). ... Selected by St. Louis Cardinals from Indians organization in Rule 5 major league draft (December 15, 2003).

2004 GAMES PLAYED BY POSITION (MLB): SS—24, 2B—19, 3B—16, OF—10.

Year Team (League)	Pos.	G	AB	R	H	2B	3B	HR	RBI	BB	SO	HBP	GDP	SB-CS	Avg.	OBP	SLG	OPS	E	Avg.
2000— Burlington (Appal.)	SS	55	201	25	41	5	0	1	15	27	35	3	4	19-4	.204	.306	.244	.550	26	.900
— Mahoning Valley (NY-P)	SS	5	19	2	6	2	0	0	4	1	3	0	0	0-0	.316	.350	.421	.771	2	.875
2001— Columbus (S. Atl.)	SS	66	241	36	64	8	3	3	23	23	48	5	2	15-4	.266	.339	.361	.700	22	.933
2002— Kinston (Caro.)	SS	128	468	67	129	15	6	11	51	39	79	3	7	32-11	.276	.334	.404	.738	32	.947
2003— Akron (East.)	SS-2B	127	462	87	137	19	2	2	38	48	64	5	10	17-5	.297	.368	.359	.727	35	.936
2004— St. Louis (N.L.)	S-2-3-OF	83	173	25	43	7	2	3	22	13	37	2	2	6-3	.249	.304	.364	.668	7	.962
Major League totals (1 year)		83	173	25	43	7	2	3	22	13	37	2	2	6-3	.249	.304	.364	.668	7	.962

CHAMPIONSHIP SERIES RECORD

Year Team (League)	Pos.	G	AB	R	H	2B	3B	HR	RBI	BB	SO	HBP	GDP	SB-CS	Avg.	OBP	SLG	OPS	E	Avg.
2004— St. Louis (N.L.)	2B-SS	2	4	0	0	0	0	0	0	0	2	0	0	0-0	.000	.000	.000	.000	0	1.000

WORLD SERIES RECORD

Year Team (League)	Pos.	G	AB	R	H	2B	3B	HR	RBI	BB	SO	HBP	GDP	SB-CS	Avg.	OBP	SLG	OPS	E	Avg.
2004— St. Louis (N.L.)	2B	1	1	0	0	0	0	0	0	0	1	0	0	0-0	.000	.000	.000	.000	0	...

L

MABRY, JOHN OF

PERSONAL: Born October 17, 1970, in Wilmington, Del. ... 6-4/210. ... Bats left, throws right. ... Full name: John Steven Mabry. ... Name pronounced: MAY-bree. ... High school: Bohemia Manor (Chesapeake City, Md.). ... College: West Chester (Pa.).

TRANSACTIONS/CAREER NOTES: Selected by St. Louis Cardinals organization in sixth round of 1991 free-agent draft. ... On disabled list (August 20-September 24, 1997). ... Signed as a free agent by Seattle Mariners (December 30, 1998). ... On disabled list (August 14, 1999-remainder of season). ... On disabled list (April 22-May 12, 2000); included rehabilitation assignment to Tacoma. ... Traded by Mariners with P Tom Davey to San Diego Padres for OF Al Martin (July 31, 2000). ... Signed as a free agent by Cardinals organization (January 5, 2001). ... Traded by Cardinals to Florida Marlins for cash (April 9, 2001). ... On disabled list (April 16-May 20, 2001); included rehabilitation assignment to Brevard County. ... Signed as a free agent by Philadelphia Phillies organization (January 28, 2002). ... Traded by Phillies to Oakland Athletics for 1B/OF Jeremy Giambi (May 22, 2002). ... Signed as a free agent by Seattle Mariners (January 15, 2003). ... On disabled list (May 28-June 20, 2003); included rehabilitation assignment to Tacoma. ... Career major league pitching: 0-0, 63.00 ERA, 2 G, 1.0 IP, 6 H, 7 R, 7 ER, 4 BB, 0 SO.

2004 GAMES PLAYED BY POSITION (MLB): OF—57, 3B—20, 1B—14.

Year Team (League)	Pos.	G	AB	R	H	2B	3B	HR	RBI	BB	SO	HBP	GDP	SB-CS	Avg.	OBP	SLG	OPS	E	Avg.
1991—Hamilton (N.Y.-Penn.)	OF	49	187	25	58	11	0	1	31	17	18	2	6	9-3	.310	.370	.385	.755	5	.943
—Savannah (S. Atl.)	OF	22	86	10	20	6	1	0	8	7	12	0	2	1-0	.233	.284	.326	.610	1	.974
1992—Springfield (Midw.)	OF	115	438	63	115	13	6	11	57	24	39	0	12	2-8	.263	.300	.395	.695	6	.969
1993—Arkansas (Texas)	OF	136	528	68	153	32	2	16	72	27	68	4	17	7-15	.290	.326	.449	.775	3	.989
—Louisville (A.A.)	OF	4	7	0	1	0	0	0	1	0	1	0	1	0-0	.143	.143	.143	.286	0	1.000
1994—Louisville (A.A.)	OF	122	477	76	125	30	1	15	68	32	67	3	14	2-6	.262	.311	.423	.735	2	.992
—St. Louis (N.L.)	OF	6	23	2	7	3	0	0	3	2	4	0	0	0-0	.304	.360	.435	.795	0	1.000
1995—St. Louis (N.L.)	1B-OF	129	388	35	119	21	1	5	41	24	45	2	6	0-3	.307	.347	.405	.752	4	.994
—Louisville (A.A.)	OF	4	12	0	1	0	0	0	0	0	0	0	0	0-0	.083	.083	.083	.167	1	.889
1996—St. Louis (N.L.)	1B-OF	151	543	63	161	30	2	13	74	37	84	3	21	3-2	.297	.342	.431	.773	8	.994
1997—St. Louis (N.L.)	OF-1B-3B	116	388	40	110	19	0	5	36	39	77	3	11	0-1	.284	.352	.371	.723	1	.998
1998—St. Louis (N.L.)	OF-3B-1B	142	377	41	94	22	0	9	46	30	76	1	6	0-2	.249	.305	.379	.684	9	.968
1999—Seattle (A.L.)	OF-3-1-DH	87	262	34	64	14	0	9	33	20	60	1	6	2-1	.244	.297	.401	.698	10	.964
2000—Seattle (A.L.)	3-OF-DH-1	48	103	18	25	5	0	1	7	10	31	2	1	0-1	.243	.322	.320	.642	4	.934
—Tacoma (PCL)	OF	4	14	1	3	1	0	0	1	0	4	0	0	0-0	.214	.214	.286	.500	1	.800
—San Diego (N.L.)	OF-1B-P	48	123	17	28	8	0	7	25	5	38	0	3	0-0	.228	.256	.463	.719	1	.983
2001—St. Louis (N.L.)	1B-OF	5	7	0	0	0	0	0	0	0	2	0	0	0-0	.000	.000	.000	.000	0	1.000
—Florida (N.L.)	OF-DH-1B	82	147	14	32	7	0	6	20	13	44	5	6	1-0	.218	.299	.388	.687	2	.964
—Brevard County (FSL)	OF	4	13	0	2	0	0	0	4	2	1	0	0	0-0	.154	.250	.154	.404	0	1.000
2002—Philadelphia (N.L.)	1B-OF	21	21	1	6	0	0	0	3	1	5	0	0	0-0	.286	.304	.286	.590	0	1.000
—Oakland (A.L.)	OF-1B	89	193	27	53	13	1	11	40	14	37	1	7	1-1	.275	.322	.523	.846	2	.992
2003—Tacoma (PCL)	DH	3	11	1	4	0	0	0	0	2	1	0	0	0-0	.364	.462	.364	.825	0	.000
—Seattle (A.L.)	OF-DH-1B	64	104	12	22	6	0	3	16	15	21	3	3	0-0	.212	.328	.356	.684	1	.987
2004—Memphis (PCL)	1B-OF-3B	39	136	27	46	7	0	12	35	17	29	2	3	0-0	.338	.406	.654	1.061	2	.991
—St. Louis (N.L.)	OF-3B-1B	87	240	32	71	11	0	13	40	26	63	1	6	0-1	.296	.363	.504	.867	6	.972
American League totals (4 years)		288	662	91	164	38	1	24	96	59	149	6	17	3-3	.248	.313	.417	.730	17	.974
National League totals (9 years)		787	2257	245	628	121	3	58	288	177	438	15	59	4-9	.278	.332	.412	.744	31	.990
Major League totals (11 years)		1075	2919	336	792	159	4	82	384	236	587	21	76	7-12	.271	.328	.413	.741	48	.987

DIVISION SERIES RECORD

Year Team (League)	Pos.	G	AB	R	H	2B	3B	HR	RBI	BB	SO	HBP	GDP	SB-CS	Avg.	OBP	SLG	OPS	E	Avg.
1996—St. Louis (N.L.)	1B	3	10	1	3	0	1	0	1	1	1	0	0	0-0	.300	.364	.500	.864	0	1.000
2002—Oakland (A.L.)	1B-OF	2	2	0	0	0	0	0	0	0	1	0	0	0-0	.000	.000	.000	.000	0	1.000
2004—St. Louis (N.L.)		1	1	0	0	0	0	0	0	0	1	0	0	0-0	.000	.000	.000	.000	0	...
Division series totals (3 years)		6	13	1	3	0	1	0	1	1	3	0	0	0-0	.231	.286	.385	.670	0	1.000

CHAMPIONSHIP SERIES RECORD

Year Team (League)	Pos.	G	AB	R	H	2B	3B	HR	RBI	BB	SO	HBP	GDP	SB-CS	Avg.	OBP	SLG	OPS	E	Avg.
1996—St. Louis (N.L.)	1B-OF	7	23	1	6	0	0	0	0	0	6	1	0	0-0	.261	.292	.261	.553	0	1.000
2004—St. Louis (N.L.)	OF	4	6	0	1	0	0	0	1	0	3	0	0	0-0	.167	.167	.167	.333	0	1.000
Champ. series totals (2 years)		11	29	1	7	0	0	0	1	0	9	1	0	0-0	.241	.267	.241	.508	0	1.000

WORLD SERIES RECORD

Year Team (League)	Pos.	G	AB	R	H	2B	3B	HR	RBI	BB	SO	HBP	GDP	SB-CS	Avg.	OBP	SLG	OPS	E	Avg.
2004—St. Louis (N.L.)	OF	2	4	0	0	0	0	0	0	0	2	0	0	0-0	.000	.000	.000	.000	0	1.000

MACDOUGAL, MIKE P

PERSONAL: Born March 5, 1977, in Las Vegas, Nev. ... 6-4/195. ... Throws right, bats both. ... Full name: Robert Meiklejohn MacDougal. ... High school: Mesa (Ariz.). ... College: Wake Forest.

TRANSACTIONS/CAREER NOTES: Selected by Baltimore Orioles organization in 22nd round of 1996 free-agent draft; did not sign. ... Selected by Baltimore Orioles organization in 17th round of 1998 free-agent draft; did not sign. ... Selected by Kansas City Royals organization in first round (25th pick overall) of 1999 free-agent draft; pick received as part of compensation for Boston Red Sox signing Type A free-agent 2B Jose Offerman. ... On disabled list (March 26-April 24, 2004); included rehabilitation assignment to Wichita.

CAREER HITTING: 0-for-0 (.000), 0 R, 0 2B, 0 3B, 0 HR, 0 RBI.

Year Team (League)	W	L	Pct.	ERA	WHIP	G	GS	CG	ShO	Hld.	Sv.-Opp.	IP	H	R	ER	HR	BB-IBB	SO	Avg.
1999—Spokane (N'west)	2	2	.500	4.47	1.29	11	11	0	0	...	0-...	46.1	43	25	23	3	17-0	57	.251
2000—Wilmington (Caro.)	9	7	.563	3.92	1.32	26	25	0	0	...	1-...	144.2	115	79	63	5	76-0	129	.219
—Wichita (Texas)	0	1	.000	7.71	1.97	2	2	0	0	...	0-...	11.2	16	10	10	0	7-0	9	.356
2001—Omaha (PCL)	8	8	.500	4.68	1.52	28	27	1	0	...	0-...	144.1	144	90	75	13	76-0	110	.259
—Kansas City (A.L.)	1	1	.500	4.70	1.43	3	3	0	0	0	0-0	15.1	18	10	8	2	4-0	7	.290
2002—Omaha (PCL)	3	5	.375	5.60	2.02	12	10	0	0	...	0-...	53.0	52	42	33	4	55-0	30	.265
—Wichita (Texas)	1	1	.500	3.06	1.98	4	4	1	0	...	0-...	17.2	11	12	6	1	24-0	14	.193
—GC Royals (GCL)	0	0	...	3.00	1.00	1	1	0	0	...	0-...	3.0	3	1	1	0	0-0	3	.273
—Wilmington (Caro.)	0	1	.000	1.08	0.96	5	0	0	0	...	2-...	8.1	3	4	1	1	5-0	10	.107
—Kansas City (A.L.)	0	1	.000	5.00	1.33	6	0	0	0	0	0-0	9.0	5	5	5	0	7-1	10	.161
2003—Kansas City (A.L.)	3	5	.375	4.08	1.50	68	0	0	0	1	27-35	64.0	64	36	29	4	32-0	57	.267
2004—Omaha (PCL)	0	1	.000	5.65	1.60	14	0	0	0	...	2-...	14.1	12	9	9	1	11-0	8	.222
—Wichita (Texas)	1	0	1.000	1.47	1.53	17	2	0	0	...	1-...	18.1	14	7	3	0	14-0	13	.209
—Kansas City (A.L.)	1	1	.500	5.56	2.21	13	0	0	0	...	1-3	11.1	16	8	7	2	9-0	14	.314
Major League totals (4 years)	5	8	.385	4.42	1.56	90	3	0	0	1	28-38	99.2	103	59	49	8	52-1	88	.268

M

MACHADO, ANDERSON   SS

PERSONAL: Born January 25, 1981, in Caracas, Venezuela. ... 5-11/170. ... Bats both, throws right. ... Full name: Anderson Javier Machado. ... Name pronounced: ma-CHAH-do. ... High school: Liceo De Aplicacion (Caracas, Venezuela).
TRANSACTIONS/CAREER NOTES: Signed as a non-drafted free agent by Philadelphia Phillies organization (January 14, 1998). ... On disabled list (March 26-April 29, 2004). ... Traded by Phillies with P Josh Hancock to Cincinnati Reds for P Todd Jones and OF Brad Correll (July 30, 2004).
2004 GAMES PLAYED BY POSITION (MLB): SS—17.

Year	Team (League)	Pos.	G	AB	R	H	2B	3B	HR	RBI	BB	SO	HBP	GDP	SB-CS	Avg.	OBP	SLG	OPS	E	Avg.
1998—Dom. Phillies (DSL)		68	219	26	44	7	0	0	17	30	44	...	...	4-...	.201	...	.233	...	...	...
1999—Clearwater (FSL)	SS	1	2	0	0	0	0	0	0	0	1	0	0	0-0	.000	.000	.000	.000	0	...
—GC Phillies (GCL)	2B-SS-3B	43	143	26	37	6	3	2	12	15	38	2	5	6-3	.259	.335	.385	.720	8	.958
—Piedmont (S. Atl.)	SS	20	60	7	14	4	2	0	7	7	20	1	0	2-1	.233	.324	.367	.690	8	.910
2000—Clearwater (FSL)	SS	117	417	55	102	19	7	1	35	54	103	0	7	32-18	.245	.330	.331	.661	43	.934
—Reading (East.)	SS	3	11	2	4	1	0	1	2	0	4	0	0	0-0	.364	.364	.727	1.091	4	.929
2001—Clearwater (FSL)	SS	82	272	49	71	5	8	5	36	31	66	4	3	23-9	.261	.342	.393	.735	16	.962
—Reading (East.)	SS	31	101	13	15	2	0	1	8	12	25	0	1	5-2	.149	.237	.198	.435	9	.941
2002—Reading (East.)	SS	126	450	71	113	24	3	12	77	72	118	2	5	40-11	.251	.353	.398	.751	28	.954
2003—Reading (East.)	SS	123	423	80	83	19	4	5	20	108	120	1	2	49-15	.196	.360	.296	.656	26	.951
—Philadelphia (N.L.)		1	0	0	0	0	0	0	0	0	0	0	0	1-0	...	...	...	...	0	...
2004—Clearwater (FSL)	SS	7	22	0	5	0	0	0	1	4	2	0	0	0-0	.227	.346	.227	.573	4	.852
—Scran./W.B. (I.L.)	SS	78	295	51	67	12	5	6	26	50	73	1	1	11-6	.227	.337	.363	.700	20	.943
—Louisville (Int'l)	SS	31	109	14	25	5	2	0	12	10	26	1	1	3-2	.229	.295	.312	.607	9	.932
—Cincinnati (N.L.)	SS	17	56	6	15	5	1	0	4	10	26	0	0	3-1	.268	.379	.393	.772	4	.937
Major League totals (2 years)		18	56	6	15	5	1	0	4	10	26	0	0	4-1	.268	.379	.393	.772	4	.937

MACHADO, ROBERT   C

PERSONAL: Born June 3, 1973, in Puerto Cabello, Venezuela. ... 6-0/219. ... Bats right, throws right. ... Full name: Robert Alexis Machado. ... Name pronounced: muh-CHA-doh.
TRANSACTIONS/CAREER NOTES: Signed as a non-drafted free agent by Chicago White Sox organization (August 10, 1989). ... Released by White Sox (May 19, 1999). ... Signed by Montreal Expos organization (May 21, 1999). ... Signed as a free agent by Seattle Mariners organization (November 17, 1999). ... Signed as a free agent by Chicago Cubs organization (December 13, 2000). ... Traded by Cubs to Milwaukee Brewers for OF Jackson Melian (June 8, 2002). ... Released by Brewers (March 26, 2003). ... Signed by Baltimore Orioles organization (May 8, 2003). ... Refused minor league assignment and became a free agent (October 8, 2004).
2004 GAMES PLAYED BY POSITION (MLB): C—35.

Year	Team (League)	Pos.	G	AB	R	H	2B	3B	HR	RBI	BB	SO	HBP	GDP	SB-CS	Avg.	OBP	SLG	OPS	E	Avg.
1990—Dominican Orioles/W.S. (DSL)		55	191	28	53	9	0	5	20	14	32	...	...	2-...	.277	...	.403	...	...	...
1991—GC Whi. Sox (GCL)	C	38	126	11	31	4	1	0	15	6	21	6	2	2-1	.246	.309	.294	.603	8	.977
1992—Utica (N.Y.-Penn)	C	45	161	16	44	13	1	2	20	5	26	0	3	1-5	.273	.293	.404	.697	12	.963
1993—South Bend (Mid.)	C	75	281	34	86	14	3	4	33	19	59	4	6	1-2	.306	.354	.399	.752	12	.979
1994—Prince Will. (Car.)	C	93	312	45	81	17	1	11	44	27	68	4	10	0-1	.260	.326	.426	.752	16	.979
1995—Nashville (A.A.)	C	16	49	7	7	3	0	1	5	7	12	0	1	0-1	.143	.250	.265	.515	3	.972
—Prince Will. (Car.)	C	83	272	37	69	14	0	6	31	40	47	7	6	0-0	.254	.363	.371	.734	5	.992
1996—Birmingham (Sou.)	C-DH	87	309	35	74	16	0	6	28	20	56	3	9	1-4	.239	.291	.350	.641	5	.991
—Chicago (A.L.)	C	4	6	1	4	1	0	0	2	0	0	0	1	0-0	.667	.667	.833	1.500	0	1.000
1997—Nashville (A.A.)	C-DH	84	308	43	83	18	0	8	30	12	61	1	6	5-0	.269	.297	.406	.703	6	.988
—Chicago (A.L.)	C	10	15	1	3	0	1	0	2	1	6	0	0	0-0	.200	.250	.333	.583	0	1.000
1998—Calgary (PCL)	C-DH	66	239	31	63	19	0	4	27	20	33	3	9	2-2	.264	.326	.393	.719	6	.987
—Chicago (A.L.)	C	34	111	14	23	6	0	3	15	7	22	0	3	0-0	.207	.254	.342	.597	4	.981
1999—Charlotte (Int'l)	C	16	54	4	11	3	0	2	7	4	13	2	...	0-0	.204	.283	.370	.654	3	.976
—Ottawa (Int'l)	C-DH	21	75	6	17	5	0	0	3	0	13	4	...	0-1	.227	.266	.293	.559	3	.981
—Montreal (N.L.)	C	17	22	3	4	1	0	0	0	2	6	0	0	0-0	.182	.250	.227	.477	0	1.000
2000—Tacoma (PCL)	C	92	330	41	99	20	0	9	58	28	43	3	10	1-5	.300	.357	.442	.800	11	.989
—Seattle (A.L.)	C	8	14	2	3	0	0	1	1	1	4	0	0	0-0	.214	.267	.429	.695	0	1.000
2001—Iowa (PCL)	C	53	180	20	51	11	0	8	30	11	36	2	5	0-0	.283	.332	.478	.809	5	.988
—Chicago (N.L.)	C	52	135	13	30	10	0	2	13	7	26	1	4	0-0	.222	.266	.341	.606	1	.997
2002—Chicago (N.L.)	C-1B	22	58	5	16	4	0	1	5	5	11	0	2	0-0	.276	.333	.397	.730	2	.985
—Milwaukee (N.L.)	C-1B	51	153	14	39	10	1	2	17	12	30	1	5	0-0	.255	.310	.373	.682	4	.988
2003—Ottawa (Int'l)	C-DH	59	221	30	74	17	0	8	38	17	36	3	6	0-0	.335	.390	.520	.910	2	.994
—Baltimore (A.L.)	C	18	49	8	13	1	0	1	3	6	12	0	0	0-0	.265	.345	.347	.692	1	.990
2004—Ottawa (Int'l)	C-DH	34	126	22	40	12	0	3	20	10	20	0	5	0-1	.317	.368	.484	.852	2	.991
—Baltimore (A.L.)	C	37	73	5	11	3	0	1	3	4	18	0	2	0-0	.151	.195	.233	.428	1	.994
American League totals (6 years)		111	268	31	57	11	1	6	26	19	62	0	6	0-0	.213	.265	.328	.593	6	.989
National League totals (3 years)		142	368	35	89	25	1	5	35	26	73	2	11	0-0	.242	.294	.356	.650	7	.992
Major League totals (9 years)		253	636	66	146	36	2	11	61	45	135	2	17	0-0	.230	.282	.344	.626	13	.991

MACIAS, JOSE   2B/OF

PERSONAL: Born January 25, 1972, in Panama City, Panama. ... 5-8/190. ... Bats both, throws right. ... Full name: Jose Prade Macias. ... Name pronounced: muh-SEE-us. ... High school: Instituto Technologico (Panama City, Panama).
TRANSACTIONS/CAREER NOTES: Signed as a non-drafted free agent by Montreal Expos organization (February 14, 1992). ... Selected by Detroit Tigers organization from Expos organization in Rule 5 minor league draft (December 9, 1996). ... Traded by Tigers to Expos for 3B Chris Truby (May 16, 2002). ... On disabled list (September 10, 2002-remainder of season). ... On suspended list (April 6-9, 2003). ... Traded by Expos to Chicago Cubs for P Wilton Chavez (December 19, 2003). ... On disabled list (March 26-April 14, 2004).
2004 GAMES PLAYED BY POSITION (MLB): OF—28, 3B—18, 2B—16.

Year	Team (League)	Pos.	G	AB	R	H	2B	3B	HR	RBI	BB	SO	HBP	GDP	SB-CS	Avg.	OBP	SLG	OPS	E	Avg.
1992—Dom. Expos (DSL)	OF	61	198	58	58	5	1	2	23	60	11	...	...	41-...	.293	...	.359	...	7	.942
1993—Dom. Expos (DSL)	OF	64	211	60	66	12	1	4	26	59	26	...	...	38-...	.313	...	.436	...	7	.954
1994—GC Expos (GCL)	2B-3B-OF	31	104	23	28	8	2	1	6	14	15	0	3	4-1	.269	.356	.413	.769	4	.937

M

Year	Team (League)	Pos.	G	AB	R	H	2B	3B	HR	RBI	BB	SO	HBP	GDP	SB-CS	Avg.	OBP	SLG	OPS	E	Avg.
1995— Vermont (N.Y.-Penn.)	2B-3B-OF	53	176	24	42	4	2	0	9	19	19	2	3	11-7	.239	.320	.284	.604	9	.949
1996— Delmarva (S. Atl.)	2B-3B-OF	116	369	64	91	13	4	1	33	56	48	6	2	38-15	.247	.353	.312	.665	8	.970
1997— Lakeland (Fla. St.)	2B-OF	122	424	54	113	18	2	2	52	52	33	2	10	10-14	.267	.348	.333	.680	7	.989
1998— Jacksonville (Sou.)	2B	128	511	82	156	28	10	12	71	52	46	4	4	6-9	.305	.372	.470	.842	14	.977
1999— Toledo (Int'l)	2B-OF-SS	112	438	44	107	18	8	2	36	36	60	4	8	10-5	.244	.306	.336	.642	18	.969
— Detroit (A.L.)	2B	5	4	2	1	0	0	1	2	0	1	0	0	0-0	.250	.250	1.000	1.250	0	1.000
2000— Toledo (Int'l)	OF-SS-2B	33	130	19	30	5	0	0	8	17	17	1	3	2-3	.231	.322	.269	.591	6	.940
— Detroit (A.L.)	2-3-OF-S-DH	73	173	25	44	3	5	2	24	18	24	1	3	2-0	.254	.328	.364	.692	4	.977
2001— Detroit (A.L.)	3-OF-2-DH	137	488	62	131	24	6	8	51	32	54	3	7	21-6	.268	.316	.391	.707	12	.970
2002— Detroit (A.L.)	2B-OF-3B	33	107	10	25	4	0	0	6	8	13	1	4	3-2	.234	.291	.271	.562	5	.959
— Montreal (N.L.)	OF-3-2-S	90	231	33	59	17	1	7	33	13	44	1	2	5-6	.255	.294	.429	.723	6	.968
2003— Montreal (N.L.)	OF-3-2-DH	111	272	31	65	15	2	4	22	11	45	2	5	4-3	.239	.273	.353	.626	5	.964
2004— Chicago (N.L.)	OF-3B-2B	98	194	23	52	6	3	3	22	5	38	2	2	4-1	.268	.292	.376	.668	1	.989
American League totals (4 years)		248	772	99	201	31	11	11	83	58	92	5	14	26-8	.260	.315	.372	.686	21	.970
National League totals (3 years)		299	697	87	176	38	6	14	77	29	127	5	9	13-10	.253	.285	.385	.670	12	.971
Major League totals (6 years)		547	1469	186	377	69	17	25	160	87	219	10	23	39-18	.257	.301	.378	.679	33	.970

MACKOWIAK, ROB   3B/OF

PERSONAL: Born June 20, 1976, in Oak Lawn, Ill. ... 5-10/195. ... Bats left, throws right. ... Full name: Robert William Mackowiak. ... Name pronounced: mah-KOH-vee-ak. ... High school: Oak Lawn (Ill.), then Lake Central (Schererville, Ind.) ... Junior college: South Suburban (Ill.).

TRANSACTIONS/CAREER NOTES: Selected by Cincinnati Reds organization in 30th round of 1995 free-agent draft; did not sign. ... Selected by Pittsburgh Pirates organization in 53rd round of 1996 free-agent draft. ... On disabled list (July 20-August 18, 2001); included rehabilitation assignment to Nashville.

2004 GAMES PLAYED BY POSITION (MLB): OF—118, 3B—55, 1B—1.

Year	Team (League)	Pos.	G	AB	R	H	2B	3B	HR	RBI	BB	SO	HBP	GDP	SB-CS	Avg.	OBP	SLG	OPS	E	Avg.
1996— GC Pirates (GCL)	SS-OF	27	86	8	23	6	1	0	14	13	11	1	3	3-1	.267	.366	.360	.727	10	.796
1997— Erie (N.Y.-Penn)	3-P-C-1-OF	61	203	26	58	14	2	1	25	21	47	7	5	1-7	.286	.371	.389	.760	6	.949
1998— Augusta (S. Atl.)	1B-OF	25	70	16	17	4	0	1	8	13	19	1	2	4-2	.243	.369	.343	.712	2	.941
— Lynchburg (Caro.)	2B-3B-OF	86	292	30	80	24	6	3	31	17	65	4	4	6-3	.274	.321	.428	.749	18	.916
1999— Lynchburg (Caro.)	2B-OF	74	263	51	80	7	4	7	30	18	57	6	5	9-3	.304	.362	.441	.803	1	.996
— Altoona (East.)	1B-OF	53	195	21	51	15	3	3	27	8	34	7	6	0-2	.262	.308	.415	.724	8	.971
2000— Altoona (East.)	2-3-S-OF	134	526	82	156	33	4	13	87	22	96	9	8	18-5	.297	.332	.449	.780	17	.965
2001— Nashville (PCL)	OF-2B-3B	32	118	14	31	5	0	4	14	7	39	0	0	1-1	.263	.302	.407	.708	7	.940
— Pittsburgh (N.L.)	OF-2-3-1	83	214	30	57	15	2	4	21	15	52	3	3	4-3	.266	.319	.411	.730	6	.965
2002— Pittsburgh (N.L.)	OF-3B-2B	136	385	57	94	22	0	16	48	42	120	7	0	9-3	.244	.328	.426	.754	6	.974
2003— Nashville (PCL)	1-3-2-OF	59	217	21	50	11	1	2	23	18	51	0	3	7-3	.230	.286	.318	.604	9	.978
— Pittsburgh (N.L.)	OF-3B-2B	77	174	20	47	4	4	6	19	15	53	4	1	6-0	.270	.342	.443	.785	2	.983
2004— Pittsburgh (N.L.)	OF-3B-1B	155	491	65	121	22	6	17	75	50	114	6	3	13-4	.246	.319	.420	.739	9	.968
Major League totals (4 years)		451	1264	172	319	63	14	43	163	122	339	20	7	32-10	.252	.325	.423	.748	23	.971

MADDUX, GREG   P

PERSONAL: Born April 14, 1966, in San Angelo, Texas. ... 6-0/185. ... Throws right, bats right. ... Full name: Gregory Alan Maddux. ... Name pronounced: MADD-ucks. ... High school: Valley (Las Vegas). ... Brother of Mike Maddux, coach, Milwaukee Brewers, and pitcher with nine major league teams (1986-2000).

TRANSACTIONS/CAREER NOTES: Selected by Chicago Cubs organization in second round of June 1984 free-agent draft. ... Signed as a free agent by Atlanta Braves (December 9, 1992). ... On disabled list (March 23-April 12, 2002). ... Signed as a free agent by Cubs (March 23, 2004).

HONORS: Named N.L. Pitcher of the Year by THE SPORTING NEWS (1993-95). ... Named N.L. Cy Young Award winner by Baseball Writers' Association of America (1992-95). ... Won N.L. Gold Glove at pitcher (1990-2002 and 2004).

CAREER HITTING: 235-for-1330 (.177), 93 R, 31 2B, 2 3B, 4 HR, 69 RBI.

Year	Team (League)	W	L	Pct.	ERA	WHIP	G	GS	CG	ShO	Hld.	Sv.-Opp.	IP	H	R	ER	HR	BB-IBB	SO	Avg.
1984— Pikeville (Appal.)		6	2	.750	2.63	1.21	14	12	2	2	...	0-...	85.2	63	35	25	2	41-2	62	.205
1985— Peoria (Midw.)		13	9	.591	3.19	1.23	27	27	6	0	...	0-...	186.0	176	86	66	9	52-0	125	.245
1986— Pittsfield (East.)		4	3	.571	2.73	1.02	8	8	4	2	...	0-...	62.2	49	22	19	1	15-0	35	.214
— Iowa (Am. Assoc.)		10	1	.909	3.02	1.22	18	18	5	2	...	0-...	128.1	127	49	43	3	30-3	65	.259
— Chicago (N.L.)		2	4	.333	5.52	1.77	6	5	1	0	0	0-0	31.0	44	20	19	3	11-2	20	.336
1987— Chicago (N.L.)		6	14	.300	5.61	1.64	30	27	1	1	0	0-0	155.2	181	111	97	17	74-13	101	.294
— Iowa (Am. Assoc.)		3	0	1.000	0.98	1.05	4	4	2	2	...	0-...	27.2	17	3	3	1	12-0	22	.179
1988— Chicago (N.L.)		18	8	.692	3.18	1.25	34	34	9	3	0	0-0	249.0	230	97	88	13	81-16	140	.244
1989— Chicago (N.L.)		19	12	.613	2.95	1.28	35	35	7	1	0	0-0	238.1	222	90	78	13	82-13	135	.249
1990— Chicago (N.L.)		15	15	.500	3.46	1.32	35	• 35	8	2	0	0-0	237.0	* 242	* 116	91	11	71-10	144	.265
1991— Chicago (N.L.)		15	11	.577	3.35	1.13	37	* 37	7	2	0	0-0	* 263.0	232	113	98	18	66-9	198	.237
1992— Chicago (N.L.)		• 20	11	.645	2.18	1.01	35	• 35	9	4	0	0-0	* 268.0	201	68	65	7	70-7	199	.210
1993— Atlanta (N.L.)		20	10	.667	* 2.36	1.05	36	• 36	* 8	1	0	0-0	* 267.0	228	85	70	14	52-7	197	.232
1994— Atlanta (N.L.)		• 16	6	.727	* 1.56	0.90	25	25	* 10	• 3	0	0-0	* 202.0	150	44	35	4	31-3	156	.207
1995— Atlanta (N.L.)		* 19	2	.905	* 1.63	0.81	28	28	* 10	• 3	0	0-0	• 209.2	147	39	38	8	23-3	181	.197
1996— Atlanta (N.L.)		15	11	.577	2.72	1.03	35	35	5	1	0	0-0	245.0	225	85	74	11	28-11	172	.241
1997— Atlanta (N.L.)		19	4	.826	2.20	0.95	33	33	5	2	0	0-0	232.2	200	58	57	9	20-6	177	.236
1998— Atlanta (N.L.)		18	9	.667	* 2.22	0.98	34	34	9	* 5	0	0-0	251.0	201	75	62	13	45-10	204	.220
1999— Atlanta (N.L.)		19	9	.679	3.57	1.34	33	33	4	0	0	0-0	219.1	258	103	87	16	37-8	136	.294
2000— Atlanta (N.L.)		19	9	.679	3.00	1.07	35	• 35	6	• 3	0	0-0	249.1	225	91	83	19	42-12	190	.238
2001— Atlanta (N.L.)		17	11	.607	3.05	1.06	34	34	3	• 3	0	0-0	233.0	220	86	79	20	27-10	173	.253
2002— Atlanta (N.L.)		16	6	.727	2.62	1.20	34	34	0	0	0	0-0	199.1	194	67	58	14	45-7	118	.257
2003— Atlanta (N.L.)		16	11	.593	3.96	1.18	36	* 36	1	0	0	0-0	218.1	225	112	96	24	33-7	124	.268
2004— Chicago (N.L.)		16	11	.593	4.02	1.18	33	33	2	1	0	0-0	212.2	218	103	95	35	33-4	151	.269
Major League totals (19 years)		305	174	.637	2.95	1.13	608	604	105	35	0	0-0	4181.1	3843	1583	1370	269	871-158	2916	.245

DIVISION SERIES RECORD

Year	Team (League)	W	L	Pct.	ERA	WHIP	G	GS	CG	ShO	Hld.	Sv.-Opp.	IP	H	R	ER	HR	BB-IBB	SO	Avg.
1995— Atlanta (N.L.)		1	0	1.000	4.50	1.50	2	2	1	0	0	0-0	14.0	19	7	7	3	2-1	7	.365
1996— Atlanta (N.L.)		1	0	1.000	0.00	0.43	1	1	0	0	0	0-0	7.0	3	2	0	0	0-0	7	.125
1997— Atlanta (N.L.)		1	0	1.000	1.00	0.89	1	1	1	0	0	0-0	9.0	7	1	1	0	1-0	6	.219
1998— Atlanta (N.L.)		1	0	1.000	2.57	1.00	1	1	0	0	0	0-0	7.0	7	2	2	0	0-0	4	.250

Year — Team (League)	W	L	Pct.	ERA	WHIP	G	GS	CG	ShO	Hld.	Sv.-Opp.	IP	H	R	ER	HR	BB-IBB	SO	Avg.
1999— Atlanta (N.L.)	0	1	.000	2.57	2.14	2	1	0	0	0	0-0	7.0	10	2	2	1	5-2	5	.370
2000— Atlanta (N.L.)	0	1	.000	11.25	3.00	1	1	0	0	0	0-0	4.0	9	7	5	1	3-2	2	.429
2001— Atlanta (N.L.)	0	0	...	3.00	1.17	1	1	0	0	0	0-0	6.0	4	3	2	1	3-0	5	.190
2002— Atlanta (N.L.)	1	0	1.000	3.00	1.00	1	1	0	0	0	0-0	6.0	5	2	2	1	1-1	3	.238
2003— Atlanta (N.L.)	0	1	.000	3.00	1.17	1	1	0	0	0	0-0	6.0	6	2	2	0	1-0	1	.240
Division series totals (9 years)	**5**	**3**	**.625**	**3.14**	**1.30**	**11**	**10**	**1**	**0**	**0**	**0-0**	**66.0**	**70**	**28**	**23**	**7**	**16-6**	**40**	**.279**

CHAMPIONSHIP SERIES RECORD

Year — Team (League)	W	L	Pct.	ERA	WHIP	G	GS	CG	ShO	Hld.	Sv.-Opp.	IP	H	R	ER	HR	BB-IBB	SO	Avg.
1989— Chicago (N.L.)	0	1	.000	13.50	2.32	2	2	0	0	0	0-0	7.1	13	12	11	2	4-2	5	.382
1993— Atlanta (N.L.)	1	1	.500	4.97	1.42	2	2	0	0	0	0-0	12.2	11	8	7	2	7-1	11	.224
1995— Atlanta (N.L.)	1	0	1.000	1.13	1.13	1	1	0	0	0	0-0	8.0	7	1	1	0	2-0	4	.226
1996— Atlanta (N.L.)	1	1	.500	2.51	1.19	2	2	0	0	0	0-0	14.1	15	9	4	1	2-1	10	.263
1997— Atlanta (N.L.)	0	2	.000	1.38	1.00	2	2	0	0	0	0-0	13.0	9	7	2	0	4-1	16	.191
1998— Atlanta (N.L.)	0	1	.000	3.00	1.33	2	2	0	0	0	1-1	6.0	5	2	2	0	3-1	4	.217
1999— Atlanta (N.L.)	1	0	1.000	1.93	0.93	2	2	0	0	0	0-0	14.0	12	3	3	1	1-0	7	.222
2001— Atlanta (N.L.)	0	2	.000	5.40	1.60	2	2	0	0	0	0-0	10.0	14	8	6	0	2-1	7	.311
Champ. series totals (8 years)	**4**	**8**	**.333**	**3.80**	**1.30**	**15**	**14**	**0**	**0**	**0**	**1-1**	**85.1**	**86**	**50**	**36**	**6**	**25-7**	**64**	**.253**

WORLD SERIES RECORD

Year — Team (League)	W	L	Pct.	ERA	WHIP	G	GS	CG	ShO	Hld.	Sv.-Opp.	IP	H	R	ER	HR	BB-IBB	SO	Avg.
1995— Atlanta (N.L.)	1	1	.500	2.25	0.75	2	2	1	0	0	0-0	16.0	9	6	4	1	3-1	8	.158
1996— Atlanta (N.L.)	1	1	.500	1.72	0.96	2	2	0	0	0	0-0	15.2	14	3	3	0	1-0	5	.246
1999— Atlanta (N.L.)	0	1	.000	2.57	1.14	1	1	0	0	0	0-0	7.0	5	4	2	0	3-0	5	.208
World series totals (3 years)	**2**	**3**	**.400**	**2.09**	**0.91**	**5**	**5**	**1**	**0**	**0**	**0-0**	**38.2**	**28**	**13**	**9**	**1**	**7-1**	**18**	**.203**

ALL-STAR GAME RECORD

	W	L	Pct.	ERA	WHIP	G	GS	CG	ShO	Hld.	Sv.-Opp.	IP	H	R	ER	HR	BB-IBB	SO	Avg.
All-Star Game totals (4 years)	0	0	...	3.24	1.20	4	3	0	0	0	0-0	8.1	9	3	3	2	1-0	3	.281

MADRITSCH, BOBBY — P

PERSONAL: Born February 28, 1976, in Oak Lawn, Ill. ... 6-2/190. ... Throws left, bats left. ... Full name: Robert A. Madritsch. ... High school: Reavis (Burbank, Ill.). ... College: Point Park (Pa.).

TRANSACTIONS/CAREER NOTES: Selected by Cincinnati Reds organization in sixth round of 1998 free-agent draft. ... Released by Reds (March 24, 2001). ... Contract purchased by Seattle Mariners organization from Winnipeg of the independent Northern League (September 25, 2002).

CAREER HITTING: 0-for-0 (.000), 0 R, 0 2B, 0 3B, 0 HR, 0 RBI.

Year — Team (League)	W	L	Pct.	ERA	WHIP	G	GS	CG	ShO	Hld.	Sv.-Opp.	IP	H	R	ER	HR	BB-IBB	SO	Avg.
1998— Billings (Pio.)	7	3	.700	2.80	1.33	14	13	0	0	...	0-...	80.1	72	30	25	3	35-1	87	.240
2000— GC Reds (GCL)	1	1	.500	2.01	1.07	6	4	0	0	...	0-...	22.1	15	5	5	0	9-0	27	.192
— Dayton (Midw.)	0	0	...	0.90	1.50	2	2	0	0	...	0-...	10.0	8	1	1	0	7-0	7	.222
2002— Winnipeg (North.)	11	4	.733	2.30	1.04	19	18	2	0	...	0-...	125.1	94	35	32	6	36-...	153	—
2003— San Antonio (Texas)	13	7	.650	3.63	1.26	27	27	2	1	...	0-...	158.2	133	75	64	11	67-0	154	.226
2004— Tacoma (PCL)	5	2	.714	3.75	1.40	12	12	0	0	...	0-...	62.1	61	33	26	3	26-0	53	.251
— Seattle (A.L.)	6	3	.667	3.27	1.22	15	11	1	0	0	0-0	88.0	74	33	32	3	33-2	60	.232
Major League totals (1 year)	**6**	**3**	**.667**	**3.27**	**1.22**	**15**	**11**	**1**	**0**	**0**	**0-0**	**88.0**	**74**	**33**	**32**	**3**	**33-2**	**60**	**.232**

MADSON, RYAN — P

PERSONAL: Born August 28, 1980, in Long Beach, Calif. ... 6-6/190. ... Throws right, bats left. ... Full name: Ryan Michael Madson. ... High school: Valley View High (Moreno County, Calif.).

TRANSACTIONS/CAREER NOTES: Selected by Philadelphia Phillies organization in ninth round of 1998 free-agent draft. ... On suspended list (April 16-19, 2004). ... On disabled list (July 26-September 3, 2004); included rehabilitation assignment to Reading.

CAREER HITTING: 0-for-3 (.000), 0 R, 0 2B, 0 3B, 0 HR, 0 RBI.

Year — Team (League)	W	L	Pct.	ERA	WHIP	G	GS	CG	ShO	Hld.	Sv.-Opp.	IP	H	R	ER	HR	BB-IBB	SO	Avg.
1998— Martinsville (App.)	3	3	.500	4.83	1.43	12	10	0	0	...	0-...	54.0	57	38	29	5	20-0	52	.265
1999— Batavia (N.Y.-Penn)	5	5	.500	4.72	1.40	15	15	0	0	...	0-...	87.2	80	51	46	5	43-0	75	.247
2000— Piedmont (S. Atl.)	14	5	.737	2.59	1.16	21	21	2	1	...	0-...	135.2	113	50	39	5	45-0	123	.225
2001— Clearwater (Fla. St.)	9	9	.500	3.90	1.58	22	21	1	0	...	0-...	117.2	137	68	51	4	49-1	101	.291
2002— Reading (East.)	16	4	.800	3.20	1.18	26	26	2	0	...	0-...	171.1	150	68	61	11	53-0	132	.242
2003— Clearwater (Fla. St.)	0	0	...	5.63	1.63	2	2	0	0	...	0-...	8.0	11	5	5	0	2-0	9	.324
— Scran./W.B. (I.L.)	12	8	.600	3.50	1.27	26	26	0	0	...	0-...	157.0	157	70	61	9	42-2	138	.262
— Philadelphia (N.L.)	0	0	...	0.00	0.00	1	0	0	0	0	0-0	2.0	0	0	0	0	0-0	0	.000
2004— Reading (East.)	0	0	...	4.50	2.50	2	1	0	0	...	0-...	2.0	3	2	1	1	2-0	1	.375
— Philadelphia (N.L.)	9	3	.750	2.34	1.13	52	1	0	0	7	1-2	77.0	68	23	20	6	19-4	55	.238
Major League totals (2 years)	**9**	**3**	**.750**	**2.28**	**1.10**	**53**	**1**	**0**	**0**	**7**	**1-2**	**79.0**	**68**	**23**	**20**	**6**	**19-4**	**55**	**.233**

MAGRUDER, CHRIS — OF

PERSONAL: Born April 26, 1977, in Tacoma, Wash. ... 5-11/200. ... Bats both, throws right. ... Full name: Christopher James Magruder. ... High school: West Valley (Yakima, Wash.). ... College: Washington.

TRANSACTIONS/CAREER NOTES: Selected by San Francisco Giants in second round of 1998 free-agent draft; pick received as part of compensation for Tampa Bay Devil Rays signing Type A free-agent P Wilson Alvarez. ... Traded with Ps Todd Ozias and Erasmo Ramirez to Texas Rangers for 1B Andres Galarraga (July 24, 2001). ... Traded by Rangers to Cleveland Indians for OF Rashad Eldridge (April 4, 2002). ... Signed as a free agent by Milwaukee Brewers organization (November 11, 2003).

2004 GAMES PLAYED BY POSITION (MLB): OF—24.

									BATTING								FIELDING	
Year — Team (League)	Pos.	G	AB	R	H	2B	3B	HR	RBI	BB	SO	HBP	GDP	SB-CS	Avg.	OBP	SLG	OPS	E	Avg.
1998— Salem-Keizer (N'west)	OF	47	177	43	59	8	5	3	18	37	21	8	2	14-7	.333	.464	.486	.950	2	.976
— Bakersfield (Calif.)	OF	22	92	21	28	7	0	1	4	13	16	0	2	3-0	.304	.390	.413	.804	0	1.000
1999— Shreveport (Texas)	OF	133	476	78	122	21	4	6	60	69	85	8	15	17-12	.256	.358	.355	.713	3	.988
2000— Shreveport (Texas)	OF	134	496	85	140	33	3	6	39	67	75	8	11	18-10	.282	.375	.385	.760	5	.983
2001— Fresno (PCL)	OF	54	214	37	60	7	1	10	30	18	45	7		3-1	.280	.354	.463	.817	1	.992
— Shreveport (Texas)	OF	40	149	22	38	6	3	2	11	15	27	3	2	5-3	.255	.335	.376	.711	2	.979

M

Year	Team (League)	Pos.	G	AB	R	H	2B	3B	HR	RBI	BB	SO	HBP	GDP	SB-CS	Avg.	OBP	SLG	OPS	E	Avg.
	—Oklahoma (PCL)	OF	33	127	28	46	14	4	5	21	21	19	4	...	1-2	.362	.464	.654	1.118	1	.986
	—Texas (A.L.)	OF	17	29	3	5	0	0	0	1	1	5	1	1	0-0	.172	.226	.172	.398	0	1.000
2002—	Cleveland (A.L.)	OF	87	258	34	56	15	1	6	29	15	55	1	7	2-0	.217	.261	.353	.614	2	.987
	—Buffalo (Int'l)	OF	54	191	28	51	10	2	5	16	26	34	3	2	3-2	.267	.364	.419	.782	1	.991
2003—	Mahoning Valley (NY-P)	OF-DH	3	11	5	2	2	0	0	0	2	1	1	0	2-0	.182	.357	.364	.721	0	1.000
	—Akron (East.)	DH-OF	3	13	0	6	0	0	0	3	1	2	0	0	1-0	.462	.500	.462	.962	0	1.000
	—Buffalo (Int'l)	OF	41	137	20	45	7	2	3	15	15	27	1	3	5-1	.328	.391	.474	.865	0	1.000
	—Cleveland (A.L.)	OF	9	26	3	9	2	1	1	3	3	6	1	0	0-1	.346	.433	.615	1.049	0	1.000
2004—	Indianapolis (Int'l)	OF-DH	79	305	37	83	17	4	6	39	21	55	10	4	7-4	.272	.337	.413	.750	0	1.000
	—Milwaukee (N.L.)	OF	56	89	11	21	6	1	2	10	8	21	2	3	0-1	.236	.310	.393	.703	0	1.000
	American League totals (3 years)		113	313	40	70	17	2	7	33	19	66	3	8	2-1	.224	.273	.358	.631	2	.989
	National League totals (1 year)		56	89	11	21	6	1	2	10	8	21	2	3	0-1	.236	.310	.393	.703	0	1.000
	Major League totals (4 years)		169	402	51	91	23	3	9	43	27	87	5	11	2-2	.226	.281	.366	.647	2	.991

MAHAY, RON — P

PERSONAL: Born June 28, 1971, in Crestwood, Ill. ... 6-2/185. ... Throws left, bats left. ... Full name: Ronald Matthew Mahay. ... High school: Alan B. Shepard (Palos Heights, Ill.). ... Junior college: South Suburban (Ill.).

TRANSACTIONS/CAREER NOTES: Selected by Boston Red Sox organization in 18th round of 1991 free-agent draft. ... Played outfield in Red Sox organization (1991-95); played five games as an outfielder with Red Sox in 1995; major league batting totals: .250 (4-for-20), 2 2B, 0 3B, 1 HR, 3 RBI. ... Claimed on waivers by Oakland Athletics (March 30, 1999). ... Traded by A's to Florida Marlins for cash (May 11, 2000). ... Signed as a free agent by San Diego Padres organization (November 20, 2000). ... Released by Padres (May 15, 2001). ... Signed by Chicago Cubs organization (May 19, 2001). ... On disabled list (May 24-June 13, 2002); included rehabilitation assignment to Iowa. ... Released by Cubs (September 30, 2002). ... Signed by Texas Rangers (November 13, 2002).

CAREER HITTING: 6-for-27 (.222), 3 R, 3 2B, 0 3B, 1 HR, 3 RBI.

Year	Team (League)	W	L	Pct.	ERA	WHIP	G	GS	CG	ShO	Hld.	Sv.-Opp.	IP	H	R	ER	HR	BB-IBB	SO	Avg.
1996—	Sarasota (Florida State)	2	2	.500	3.82	1.36	31	4	0	0	...	2-...	70.2	61	33	30	5	35-0	68	.236
	—Trenton (East.)	0	1	.000	29.45	4.91	1	1	0	0	...	0-...	3.2	12	13	12	1	6-0	0	.522
1997—	Trenton (East.)	3	3	.500	3.10	1.03	17	4	0	0	...	5-...	40.2	29	16	14	0	13-0	47	.193
	—Pawtucket (Int'l)	1	0	1.000	0.00	0.86	2	0	0	0	...	0-...	4.2	3	0	0	0	1-0	6	.176
	—Boston (A.L.)	3	0	1.000	2.52	1.20	28	0	0	0	6	0-2	25.0	19	7	7	3	11-0	22	.204
1998—	Pawtucket (Int'l)	3	1	.750	4.17	1.37	23	1	0	0	...	3-...	41.0	37	20	19	8	19-2	41	.234
	—Boston (A.L.)	1	1	.500	3.46	1.58	29	0	0	0	7	1-2	26.0	26	16	10	2	15-1	14	.263
1999—	Vancouver (PCL)	7	2	.778	4.29	1.50	32	15	0	0	...	0-...	107.0	116	57	51	12	45-0	73	.280
	—Oakland (A.L.)	2	0	1.000	1.86	0.57	6	1	0	0	0	1-1	19.1	8	4	4	2	3-0	15	.123
2000—	Oakland (A.L.)	0	1	.000	9.00	2.19	5	2	0	0	0	0-0	16.0	26	18	16	4	9-0	5	.366
	—Florida (N.L.)	1	0	1.000	6.04	1.86	18	0	0	0	2	0-0	25.1	31	17	17	6	16-1	27	.310
	—Calgary (PCL)	0	1	.000	4.85	1.08	8	0	0	0	...	0-...	13.0	7	7	7	1	7-1	15	.175
2001—	Portland (PCL)	1	2	.333	3.78	1.08	14	0	0	0	...	0-...	16.2	13	9	7	2	5-0	18	.210
	—Iowa (PCL)	3	1	.750	2.31	0.84	36	0	0	0	...	14-...	46.2	29	12	12	5	10-1	52	.182
	—Chicago (N.L.)	0	0	...	2.61	1.40	17	0	0	0	2	0-0	20.2	14	6	6	4	15-1	24	.197
2002—	Iowa (PCL)	0	0	...	1.93	1.01	39	0	0	0	...	2-...	46.2	32	11	10	3	15-1	50	.189
	—Chicago (N.L.)	2	0	1.000	8.59	1.43	11	0	0	0	0	0-0	14.2	13	14	14	6	8-0	14	.228
2003—	Oklahoma (PCL)	4	2	.667	4.22	1.10	26	0	0	0	...	3-...	42.2	36	21	20	5	10-0	51	.224
	—Texas (A.L.)	3	3	.500	3.18	1.17	35	0	0	0	9	0-3	45.1	33	19	16	3	20-7	38	.195
2004—	Texas (A.L.)	3	0	1.000	2.55	1.30	60	0	0	0	14	0-2	67.0	60	23	19	5	29-5	54	.235
	American League totals (6 years)	12	5	.706	3.26	1.30	163	3	0	0	36	2-10	198.2	172	87	72	19	87-13	148	.229
	National League totals (3 years)	3	0	1.000	5.49	1.60	46	0	0	0	4	2-0	60.2	58	37	37	16	39-2	65	.254
	Major League totals (8 years)	15	5	.750	3.78	1.37	209	3	0	0	40	2-10	259.1	230	124	109	35	126-15	213	.235

MAINE, JOHN — P

PERSONAL: Born May 8, 1981, in Fredericksburg, Va. ... 6-4/193. ... Throws right, bats right. ... Full name: John K. Maine. ... College: Charlotte.

TRANSACTIONS/CAREER NOTES: Selected by Baltimore Orioles organization in sixth round of 2002 free-agent draft.

CAREER HITTING: 0-for-0 (.000), 0 R, 0 2B, 0 3B, 0 HR, 0 RBI.

Year	Team (League)	W	L	Pct.	ERA	WHIP	G	GS	CG	ShO	Hld.	Sv.-Opp.	IP	H	R	ER	HR	BB-IBB	SO	Avg.
2002—	Aberdeen (NY-P)	1	1	.500	1.74	0.87	4	2	0	0	...	0-...	10.1	6	2	2	0	3-0	21	.154
	—Delmarva (S.Atl.)	1	1	.500	1.36	0.76	6	5	0	0	...	0-...	33.0	21	8	5	0	4-0	39	.178
2003—	Delmarva (S.Atl.)	7	3	.700	1.53	0.80	14	14	1	0	...	0-...	76.1	43	16	13	1	18-0	108	.165
	—Frederick (Caro.)	6	1	.857	3.07	0.97	12	12	1	1	...	0-...	70.1	48	27	24	5	20-0	77	.190
2004—	Bowie (East.)	4	0	1.000	2.25	0.82	5	5	0	0	...	0-...	28.0	16	8	7	1	7-0	34	.160
	—Baltimore (A.L.)	0	1	.000	9.82	2.73	1	1	0	0	0	0-0	3.2	7	4	4	1	3-0	1	.438
	—Ottawa (Int'l)	5	7	.417	3.91	1.46	22	22	0	0	...	0-...	119.2	123	59	52	12	52-0	105	.266
	Major League totals (1 year)	0	1	.000	9.82	2.73	1	1	0	0	0	0-0	3.2	7	4	4	1	3-0	1	.438

MAJEWSKI, GARY — P

PERSONAL: Born February 26, 1980, in Houston, Texas. ... 6-1/215. ... Throws right, bats right. ... Full name: Gary Wayne Majewski. ... High school: St. Pius X (Houston).

TRANSACTIONS/CAREER NOTES: Selected by Chicago White Sox organization in second round of 1998 free-agent draft. ... Traded by White Sox with Ps Andre Simpson and Orlando Rodriguez to Los Angeles Dodgers for Ps Antonio Osuna and Carlos Ortega (March 22, 2001). ... Traded by Dodgers with P Onan Masaoka and OF Jeff Barry to White Sox for P James Baldwin (July 26, 2001). ... Selected by Toronto Blue Jays from White Sox organization in Rule 5 major league draft (December 16, 2002). ... Returned to White Sox (March 17, 2003). ... Traded by White Sox with P Jon Rauch to Montreal Expos for OF Carl Everett (July 18, 2004).

CAREER HITTING: 0-for-2 (.000), 0 R, 0 2B, 0 3B, 0 HR, 0 RBI.

Year	Team (League)	W	L	Pct.	ERA	WHIP	G	GS	CG	ShO	Hld.	Sv.-Opp.	IP	H	R	ER	HR	BB-IBB	SO	Avg.
1999—	Bristol (Appalachian)	7	1	.875	3.05	1.36	13	13	1	1	...	0-...	76.2	67	34	26	4	37-0	91	.243
	—Burlington (Midw.)	0	0	...	37.80	4.50	2	0	0	0	...	0-...	3.1	11	14	14	3	4-0	1	.524
2000—	Burlington (Midw.)	6	7	.462	3.07	1.12	22	22	3	3	...	0-...	134.2	83	53	46	8	68-0	137	.182
	—Winston-Salem (Caro.)	2	4	.333	5.11	1.32	6	6	0	0	...	0-...	37.0	32	21	21	1	17-0	24	.239
2001—	Vero Beach (FSL)	4	5	.444	6.24	1.85	23	13	0	0	...	1-...	75.0	103	57	52	9	36-0	41	.340
	—Winston-Salem (Caro.)	4	2	.667	2.93	1.21	9	6	1	0	...	0-...	43.0	42	15	14	3	10-0	31	.266
2002—	Birmingham (Southern)	5	3	.625	2.65	1.27	57	1	0	0	...	4-...	74.2	61	31	22	3	34-2	75	.221
2003—	Charlotte (Int'l)	6	4	.600	3.96	1.25	42	1	0	0	...	4-...	72.2	62	33	32	3	29-2	72	.231
2004—	Charlotte (Int'l)	3	3	.500	3.19	1.09	35	0	0	0	...	14-...	42.1	30	16	15	2	16-0	41	.208
	—Edmonton (PCL)	1	2	.333	3.86	1.59	15	0	0	0	...	1-...	16.1	18	8	7	0	8-1	17	.295
	—Montreal (N.L.)	0	1	.000	3.86	1.57	16	0	0	0	...	1-2	21.0	28	15	9	2	5-1	12	.326
	Major League totals (1 year)	0	1	.000	3.86	1.57	16	0	0	0	...	1-2	21.0	28	15	9	2	5-1	12	.326

M

MAJEWSKI, VAL — OF

PERSONAL: Born June 19, 1981, in New Brunswick, N.J. ... 6-2/200. ... Bats left, throws left. ... Full name: Walter V. Majewski. ... High school: Freehold Township (Freehold, N.J.). ... College: Rutgers.

TRANSACTIONS/CAREER NOTES: Selected by Baltimore Orioles organization in third round of 2002 free-agent draft.

2004 GAMES PLAYED BY POSITION (MLB): OF—4, DH—3.

											BATTING									FIELDING	
Year Team (League)	Pos.	G	AB	R	H	2B	3B	HR	RBI	BB	SO	HBP	GDP	SB-CS	Avg.	OBP	SLG	OPS		E	Avg.
2002— Aberdeen (NY-P)	OF	31	110	22	33	7	4	1	15	13	14	1	3	8-4	.300	.376	.464	.840		1	.988
— Delmarva (S. Atl.)	OF	7	17	2	2	0	0	1	3	1	1	0	1	0-0	.118	.158	.294	.452		0	1.000
2003— Delmarva (S. Atl.)	OF	56	208	38	63	15	8	7	48	28	20	1	3	10-1	.303	.383	.553	.936		2	.980
— GC Orioles (GCL)	OF	1	3	0	1	0	0	0	0	1	0	0	0	0-0	.333	.500	.333	.833		0	1.000
— Aberdeen (NY-P)	OF	4	16	2	6	2	2	0	3	1	2	0	1	1-0	.375	.412	.750	1.162		0	1.000
— Frederick (Carolina)	OF	41	159	15	46	18	1	5	20	7	23	1	2	0-0	.289	.321	.509	.831		4	.938
2004— Bowie (East.)	OF-DH	112	433	71	133	24	5	15	80	33	68	5	7	14-4	.307	.359	.490	.842		5	.978
— Baltimore (A.L.)	OF-DH	9	13	3	2	1	0	0	1	0	1	0	0	0-0	.154	.154	.231	.385		0	1.000
Major League totals (1 year)		9	13	3	2	1	0	0	1	0	1	0	0	0-0	.154	.154	.231	.385		0	1.000

MALASKA, MARK — P

PERSONAL: Born January 17, 1978, in Youngstown, Ohio. ... 6-3/208. ... Throws left, bats left. ... Full name: Dennis Mark Malaska. ... High school: Cardinal Mooney (Youngstown, Ohio). ... College: Akron.

TRANSACTIONS/CAREER NOTES: Selected by Tampa Bay Devil Rays organization in eighth round of 2000 free-agent draft. ... Claimed on waivers by Boston Red Sox (December 8, 2003).

CAREER HITTING: 0-for-0 (.000), 0 R, 0 2B, 0 3B, 0 HR, 0 RBI.

Year Team (League)	W	L	Pct.	ERA	WHIP	G	GS	CG	ShO	Hld.	Sv.-Opp.	IP	H	R	ER	HR	BB-IBB	SO	Avg.
2000— Char., S.C. (SAL)	0	0	...	9.00	1.50	2	0	0	0	...	0-...	2.0	3	2	2	1	0-0	3	.375
— Hudson Valley (NY-Penn.)	0	2	.000	4.91	1.44	10	5	0	0	...	0-...	40.1	44	27	22	1	14-2	36	.273
2001— Char., S.C. (SAL)	7	12	.368	2.92	1.20	25	25	1	0	...	0-...	157.0	153	71	51	11	35-0	152	.249
— Bakersfield (California)	2	1	.667	4.08	1.08	3	3	0	0	...	0-...	17.2	14	8	8	1	5-0	13	.219
2002— Bakersfield (California)	7	4	.636	2.96	1.20	15	15	2	2	...	0-...	91.1	98	48	30	5	12-0	94	.263
— Orlando (Sou.)	4	5	.444	3.69	1.56	12	11	1	0	...	1-...	70.2	82	37	29	4	28-2	49	.292
2003— Orlando (Sou.)	1	1	.500	2.16	1.00	19	0	0	0	...	1-...	25.0	21	6	6	2	4-1	22	.236
— Durham (Int'l)	1	1	.500	4.30	1.39	15	0	0	0	...	0-...	23.0	24	12	11	1	8-0	22	.270
— Tampa Bay (A.L.)	2	1	.667	2.81	1.56	22	0	0	0	7	0-3	16.0	13	7	5	0	12-3	17	.232
2004— Boston (A.L.)	1	1	.500	4.50	1.65	19	0	0	0	1	0-0	20.0	21	11	10	2	12-1	12	.266
— Pawtucket (Int'l)	1	1	.500	4.21	1.46	33	0	0	0	...	1-...	36.1	42	17	17	7	11-2	31	.292
Major League totals (2 years)	3	2	.600	3.75	1.61	41	0	0	0	8	0-3	36.0	34	18	15	2	24-4	29	.252

MANTEI, MATT — P

PERSONAL: Born July 7, 1973, in Tampa, Fla. ... 6-1/198. ... Throws right, bats right. ... Full name: Matthews Bruce Mantei. ... Name pronounced: MAN-tie. ... High school: River Valley (Three Oaks, Mich.).

TRANSACTIONS/CAREER NOTES: Selected by Seattle Mariners organization in 25th round of 1991 free-agent draft. ... Selected by Florida Marlins from Mariners organization in Rule 5 major league draft (December 5, 1994). ... On disabled list (April 20-June 18 and July 29-September 1, 1995); included rehabilitation assignments to Portland and Charlotte. ... On disabled list (June 19, 1996-remainder of season; March 31, 1997-entire season; and August 19-September 4, 1998). ... Traded by Marlins to Arizona Diamondbacks for Ps Vladimir Nunez and Brad Penny and a player to be named (July 9, 1999); Marlins acquired OF Abraham Nunez to complete deal (December 13, 1999). ... On disabled list (April 2-21 and May 5-21, 2000); included rehabilitation assignment to Tucson. ... On disabled list (April 25, 2001-remainder of season). ... On disabled list (March 22-June 27, 2002); included rehabilitation assignments to El Paso and Tucson. ... On disabled list (May 28-June 30, 2003); included rehabilitation assignment to Tucson. ... On disabled list (May 9, 2004-remainder of season).

CAREER HITTING: 1-for-5 (.200), 0 R, 0 2B, 0 3B, 0 HR, 0 RBI.

Year Team (League)	W	L	Pct.	ERA	WHIP	G	GS	CG	ShO	Hld.	Sv.-Opp.	IP	H	R	ER	HR	BB-IBB	SO	Avg.
1991— Ariz. Mariners (Ariz.)	1	4	.200	6.69	2.03	17	5	0	0	...	0-...	40.1	54	40	30	0	28-2	29	.321
1992— Ariz. Mariners (Ariz.)	1	1	.500	5.63	1.44	3	3	0	0	...	0-...	16.0	18	10	10	1	5-0	19	.286
1993— Bellingham (N'west)	1	1	.500	5.96	1.60	26	0	0	0	...	12-...	25.2	26	19	17	2	15-0	34	.260
1994— Appleton (Midw.)	5	1	.833	2.06	1.31	48	0	0	0	...	26-...	48.0	42	14	11	2	21-3	70	.240
1995— Portland (East.)	1	0	1.000	2.38	1.32	8	0	0	0	...	1-...	11.1	10	3	3	0	5-0	15	.244
— Charlotte (Int'l)	0	0	.000	2.57	0.86	6	0	0	0	...	0-...	7.0	1	3	2	1	5-0	10	.050
— Florida (N.L.)	0	1	.000	4.73	1.88	12	0	0	0	0	0-0	13.1	12	8	7	1	13-0	15	.245
1996— Florida (N.L.)	1	0	1.000	6.38	1.85	14	0	0	0	0	0-1	18.1	13	13	13	2	21-1	25	.197
— Charlotte (Int'l)	0	2	.000	4.70	1.70	7	0	0	0	...	2-...	7.2	6	4	4	1	7-0	8	.214
1997— Brevard County (FSL)	0	0	...	6.00	1.67	4	0	0	0	...	0-...	6.0	4	4	4	1	6-0	11	.190
— Portland (East.)	1	0	1.000	6.75	2.25	5	0	0	0	...	0-...	4.0	1	3	3	0	8-0	7	.083
1998— Charlotte (Int'l)	1	2	.333	5.51	1.78	16	0	0	0	...	3-...	16.1	11	10	10	2	18-1	25	.196
— Florida (N.L.)	3	4	.429	2.96	1.12	42	0	0	0	2	9-12	54.2	38	19	18	1	23-3	63	.203
1999— Florida (N.L.)	1	2	.333	2.72	1.35	35	0	0	0	0	10-12	36.1	24	11	11	4	25-1	50	.186
— Arizona (N.L.)	0	1	.000	2.79	1.34	30	0	0	0	0	22-25	29.0	20	10	9	1	19-0	49	.192
2000— Tucson (PCL)	0	0	...	2.45	1.09	4	2	0	0	...	0-...	3.2	1	1	1	0	0-0	2	.100
— Arizona (N.L.)	1	0	.500	4.57	1.46	47	0	0	0	0	17-20	45.1	31	24	23	4	35-1	53	.193
2001— Arizona (N.L.)	0	0	...	2.57	1.43	8	0	0	0	1	2-2	7.0	6	2	2	2	4-0	12	.222
2002— El Paso (Texas)	0	1	.000	2.25	1.00	4	3	0	0	...	0-...	4.0	3	3	1	0	1-0	5	.200
— Tucson (PCL)	1	0	1.000	0.00	1.20	9	1	0	0	...	0-...	10.0	8	1	0	0	4-0	9	.211
— Arizona (N.L.)	2	2	.500	4.73	1.50	31	0	0	0	2	0-1	26.2	28	15	14	3	12-0	26	.257
2003— Tucson (PCL)	0	0	...	2.25	0.50	3	0	0	0	...	0-...	4.0	2	1	1	1	0-0	4	.154
— Arizona (N.L.)	5	4	.556	2.62	1.00	50	0	0	0	0	29-32	55.0	37	17	16	6	18-1	68	.191
2004— Arizona (N.L.)	0	3	.000	11.81	2.16	12	0	0	0	0	4-7	10.2	17	15	14	5	6-1	13	.354
Major League totals (9 years)	13	18	.419	3.86	1.36	281	0	0	0	5	93-112	296.1	226	134	127	29	176-8	374	.210

DIVISION SERIES RECORD

Year Team (League)	W	L	Pct.	ERA	WHIP	G	GS	CG	ShO	Hld.	Sv.-Opp.	IP	H	R	ER	HR	BB-IBB	SO	Avg.
1999— Arizona (N.L.)	0	1	.000	4.50	2.00	1	0	0	0	0	0-0	2.0	1	1	1	1	3-1	1	.167
2002— Arizona (N.L.)	0	0	...	54.00	6.00	1	0	0	0	0	0-0	.1	1	2	2	0	1-0	0	.500
Division series totals (2 years)	0	1	.000	11.57	2.57	2	0	0	0	0	0-0	2.1	2	3	3	1	4-1	1	.250

M

MANZANILLO, JOSIAS   P

PERSONAL: Born October 16, 1967, in San Pedro de Macoris, Dominican Republic. ... 6-0/200. ... Throws right, bats right. ... Name pronounced: hose-EYE-ess man-zah-NEE-oh. ... Brother of Ravelo Manzanillo, pitcher with two major league teams (1988 and 1994-95).

TRANSACTIONS/CAREER NOTES: Signed as a non-drafted free agent by Boston Red Sox organization (January 10, 1983). ... Granted free agency (March 24, 1992). ... Signed as a free agent by Kansas City Royals organization (April 3, 1992). ... Signed as a free agent by Milwaukee Brewers organization (November 20, 1992). ... Traded by Brewers to New York Mets for OF Wayne Housie (June 12, 1993). ... On disabled list (July 27, 1994-remainder of season). ... Claimed on waivers by New York Yankees (June 5, 1995). ... On disabled list (July 6, 1995-remainder of season). ... Signed as a free agent by Seattle Mariners organization (December 21, 1996). ... On disabled list (April 9-May 6 and May 25-July 1, 1997); included rehabilitation assignments to Memphis and Tacoma. ... Released by Mariners (July 17, 1997). ... Signed by Houston Astros organization (July 27, 1997). ... Signed as a free agent by Tampa Bay Devil Rays organization (December 18, 1997). ... Released by Devil Rays (July 1, 1998). ... Signed by Mets organization (July 3, 1998). ... Signed as a free agent by Pittsburgh Pirates organization (February 9, 2000). ... On disabled list (May 4-July 13, 2002); included rehabilitation assignments to Nashville and Hickory. ... Released by Pirates (August 15, 2002). ... Signed by Cincinnati Reds organization (January 22, 2003). ... Signed as a free agent by Florida Marlins organization (May 20, 2004).

CAREER HITTING: 1-for-12 (.083), 0 R, 0 2B, 0 3B, 0 HR, 0 RBI.

Year	Team (League)	W	L	Pct.	ERA	WHIP	G	GS	CG	ShO	Hld.	Sv.-Opp.	IP	H	R	ER	HR	BB-IBB	SO	Avg.
1983—Elmira (N.Y.-Penn)		1	5	.167	7.98	1.88	12	4	0	0	...	0-...	38.1	52	44	34	7	20-1	19	...
1984—Elmira (N.Y.-Penn)		2	3	.400	5.26	2.06	14	0	0	0	...	1-...	25.2	27	24	15	1	26-1	15	.273
1985—Greensboro (S. Atl.)		1	1	.500	9.75	2.50	7	0	0	0	...	1-...	12.0	12	13	13	1	18-0	10	.273
— Elmira (N.Y.-Penn)		2	4	.333	3.86	1.82	19	4	0	0	...	1-...	39.2	36	19	17	1	36-4	43	.254
1986—Winter Haven (FSL)		13	5	.722	2.27	1.34	23	21	3	2	...	0-...	142.2	110	51	36	3	81-0	102	.217
1987—New Britain (East.)		2	0	1.000	4.50	1.60	2	2	0	0	...	0-...	10.0	8	5	5	1	8-0	12	.216
1988—New Britain (East.)	Did not play.																			
1989—New Britain (East.)		9	10	.474	3.66	1.45	26	26	3	1	...	0-...	147.2	129	78	60	11	85-7	93	.232
1990—New Britain (East.)		4	4	.500	3.41	1.39	12	12	2	1	...	0-...	74.0	66	34	28	3	37-1	51	.238
— Pawtucket (Int'l)		4	7	.364	5.55	1.45	15	15	0	0	...	0-...	82.2	75	57	51	9	45-0	77	.236
1991—Pawtucket (Int'l)		5	5	.500	5.61	1.58	20	16	0	0	...	0-...	102.2	109	69	64	12	53-0	65	.275
— New Britain (East.)		2	2	.500	2.90	1.31	7	7	0	0	...	0-...	49.2	37	25	16	0	28-1	35	.208
— Boston (A.L.)		0	0	...	18.00	5.00	1	0	0	0	0	0-0	1.0	2	2	2	0	3-0	1	.400
1992—Omaha (Am. Assoc.)		7	10	.412	4.36	1.53	26	21	0	0	...	0-...	136.1	138	76	66	12	71-0	114	.271
— Memphis (Sou.)		0	2	.000	7.36	1.64	2	0	0	0	...	0-...	7.1	6	6	6	0	6-0	8	.231
1993—Milwaukee (A.L.)		1	1	.500	9.53	1.88	10	1	0	0	0	1-2	17.0	22	20	18	1	10-3	10	.314
— New Orleans (A.A.)		0	1	.000	9.00	1.00	1	0	0	0	...	0-...	1.0	1	1	1	1	0-0	3	.250
— Norfolk (Int'l)		1	5	.167	3.11	1.27	14	12	2	1	...	0-...	84.0	82	40	29	3	25-1	79	.258
— New York (N.L.)		0	0	...	3.00	1.42	6	0	0	0	0	0-0	12.0	8	7	4	1	9-0	11	.186
1994—Norfolk (Int'l)		0	1	.000	4.38	1.46	8	0	0	0	...	3-...	12.1	12	6	6	1	6-1	10	.255
— New York (N.L.)		3	2	.600	2.66	0.99	37	0	0	0	11	2-5	47.1	34	15	14	4	13-2	48	.200
1995—New York (N.L.)		1	2	.333	7.88	1.50	12	0	0	0	0	0-0	16.0	18	15	14	3	6-2	14	.273
— New York (A.L.)		0	0	...	2.08	1.62	11	0	0	0	0	0-0	17.1	19	4	4	1	9-2	11	.279
1996—	Did not play.																			
1997—Seattle (A.L.)		0	1	.000	5.40	1.96	16	0	0	0	1	0-1	18.1	19	13	11	3	17-1	18	.275
— Memphis (Sou.)		0	0	...	3.00	0.33	2	0	0	0	...	0-...	3.0	1	1	1	1	0-0	6	.100
— Tacoma (PCL)		0	0	...	6.43	1.71	11	0	0	0	...	1-...	14.0	16	10	10	4	8-0	15	.286
— New Orleans (A.A.)		0	0	...	4.40	1.60	11	0	0	0	...	0-...	14.1	17	7	7	3	6-0	11	.304
1998—Durham (Int'l)		7	6	.538	4.64	1.44	19	14	0	0	...	1-...	85.1	93	57	44	12	30-0	61	.272
— Norfolk (Int'l)		4	4	.500	3.24	1.39	13	12	1	0	...	1-...	77.2	77	35	28	5	31-0	72	.263
1999—New York (N.L.)		0	0	...	5.79	1.23	12	0	0	0	1	0-0	18.2	19	12	12	5	4-1	25	.264
2000—Nashville (PCL)		0	2	.000	2.70	1.07	15	0	0	0	...	3-...	23.1	19	8	7	0	6-1	23	.226
— Pittsburgh (N.L.)		2	2	.500	3.38	1.40	43	0	0	0	5	0-2	58.2	50	23	22	6	32-4	39	.240
2001—Pittsburgh (N.L.)		3	2	.600	3.39	1.08	71	0	0	0	9	2-7	79.2	60	32	30	4	26-3	80	.211
2002—Nashville (PCL)		1	0	1.000	2.66	0.98	15	1	0	0	...	1-...	20.1	18	6	6	3	2-1	14	.234
— Pittsburgh (N.L.)		0	0	...	7.62	1.92	13	0	0	0	0	0-1	13.0	20	11	11	5	5-0	4	.364
— Hickory (S. Atl.)		0	0	...	9.00	2.50	1	0	0	0	...	0-...	2.0	5	3	2	1	0-0	1	.417
2003—Cincinnati (N.L.)		0	2	.000	12.66	2.34	9	0	0	0	0	0-1	10.2	21	20	15	7	4-0	12	.389
— Louisville (Int'l)		1	1	.500	4.18	1.30	22	0	0	0	...	0-...	28.0	25	17	13	0	11-1	16	.250
2004—Albuquerque (PCL)		0	1	.000	5.25	1.33	11	0	0	0	...	5-...	12.0	15	8	7	3	1-0	9	.300
— Florida (N.L.)		3	3	.500	6.12	1.64	26	0	0	0	2	1-4	32.1	38	24	22	6	15-2	27	.292
American League totals (4 years)		1	2	.333	5.87	1.88	38	1	0	0	1	1-3	53.2	62	39	35	5	39-6	40	.292
National League totals (9 years)		12	13	.480	4.49	1.32	229	0	0	0	28	5-20	288.1	268	159	144	41	114-14	260	.247
Major League totals (11 years)		13	15	.464	4.71	1.41	267	1	0	0	29	6-23	342.0	330	198	179	46	153-20	300	.255

MAROTH, MIKE   P

PERSONAL: Born August 17, 1977, in Orlando, Fla. ... 6-0/190. ... Throws left, bats left. ... Full name: Michael Warren Maroth. ... Name pronounced: mah-ROTH. ... High school: William R. Boone (Orlando, Fla.). ... College: Central Florida.

TRANSACTIONS/CAREER NOTES: Selected by Boston Red Sox organization in third round of 1998 free-agent draft. ... Traded by Red Sox to Detroit Tigers for P Bryce Florie (July 31, 1999).

CAREER HITTING: 2-for-12 (.167), 1 R, 0 2B, 0 3B, 0 HR, 1 RBI.

Year	Team (League)	W	L	Pct.	ERA	WHIP	G	GS	CG	ShO	Hld.	Sv.-Opp.	IP	H	R	ER	HR	BB-IBB	SO	Avg.
1998—GC Red Sox (GCL)		1	1	.500	0.00	0.87	4	2	0	0	...	0-...	12.2	9	3	0	0	2-0	14	.191
— Lowell (NY-Penn)		2	3	.400	2.90	1.13	6	6	0	0	...	0-...	31.0	22	13	10	1	13-0	34	.200
1999—Sarasota (Florida State)		11	6	.647	4.04	1.43	20	19	0	0	...	0-...	111.1	124	65	50	3	35-1	64	.289
— Lakeland (Fla. St.)		2	1	.667	3.24	1.50	3	3	0	0	...	0-...	16.2	18	7	6	1	7-0	11	...
— Jacksonville (Southern)		1	2	.333	4.79	1.65	4	4	0	0	...	0-...	20.2	27	15	11	2	7-0	10	.310
2000—Jacksonville (Southern)		9	14	.391	3.94	1.42	27	26	2	1	...	0-...	164.1	176	79	72	14	58-0	85	.289
2001—Toledo (International)		7	10	.412	4.65	1.58	24	23	0	0	...	0-...	131.2	158	80	68	11	50-1	63	.302
2002—Toledo (International)		8	1	.889	2.82	1.02	11	11	1	0	...	0-...	73.1	53	25	23	7	22-0	51	.201
— Detroit (A.L.)		6	10	.375	4.48	1.34	21	21	0	0	0	0-0	128.2	136	68	64	7	36-1	58	.276
2003—Detroit (A.L.)		9	* 21	.300	5.73	1.45	33	33	1	0	0	0-0	193.1	231	131	•123	34	50-2	87	.299
2004—Detroit (A.L.)		11	13	.458	4.31	1.40	33	33	2	1	0	0-0	217.0	244	112	104	25	59-1	108	.288
Major League totals (3 years)		26	44	.371	4.86	1.40	87	87	3	1	0	0-0	539.0	611	311	291	66	145-4	253	.289

M

MARQUIS, JASON — P

PERSONAL: Born August 21, 1978, in Manhasset, N.Y. ... 6-1/210. ... Throws right, bats left. ... Full name: Jason Scott Marquis. ... Name pronounced: mar-KEE. ... High school: Tottenville (Staten Island, N.Y.).

TRANSACTIONS/CAREER NOTES: Selected by Atlanta Braves organization in supplemental round ("sandwich" pick between first and second rounds, 35th pick overall) of 1996 free-agent draft; pick received as compensation for Braves' failure to sign 1995 first-round pick Chad Hutchinson. ... On disabled list (April 22-May 12, 2002). ... Traded with Ps Ray King and Adam Wainwright to St. Louis Cardinals for OF J.D. Drew and C/OF Eli Marrero (December 14, 2003).

CAREER HITTING: 28-for-145 (.193), 15 R, 7 2B, 0 3B, 1 HR, 11 RBI.

Year Team (League)	W	L	Pct.	ERA	WHIP	G	GS	CG	ShO	Hld.	Sv.-Opp.	IP	H	R	ER	HR	BB-IBB	SO	Avg.
1996— Danville (Appalachian)	1	1	.500	4.63	1.59	7	4	0	0	...	0-...	23.1	30	18	12	0	7-0	24	.286
1997— Macon (S. Atl.)	14	10	.583	4.38	1.49	28	28	0	0	...	0-...	141.2	156	78	69	10	55-1	121	.278
1998— Danville (Caro.)	2	12	.143	4.87	1.40	22	22	1	0	...	0-...	114.2	120	65	62	3	41-0	135	.269
1999— Myrtle Beach (Caro.)	3	0	1.000	0.28	1.22	6	6	0	0	...	0-...	32.0	22	2	1	0	17-0	41	.191
— Greenville (Sou.)	3	4	.429	4.58	1.47	12	12	1	0	...	0-...	55.0	52	33	28	7	29-0	35	.241
2000— Greenville (Sou.)	4	2	.667	3.57	1.34	11	11	0	0	...	0-...	68.0	68	35	27	10	23-0	49	.262
— Atlanta (N.L.)	1	0	1.000	5.01	1.50	15	0	0	0	1	0-1	23.1	23	16	13	4	12-1	17	.261
— Richmond (Int'l)	0	3	.000	9.00	1.95	6	6	0	0	...	0-...	20.0	26	21	20	2	13-0	18	.321
2001— Atlanta (N.L.)	5	6	.455	3.48	1.33	38	16	0	0	2	0-2	129.1	113	62	50	14	59-4	98	.234
2002— Atlanta (Int'l)	0	1	.000	3.60	1.20	1	1	0	0	...	0-...	5.0	5	2	2	0	1-0	6	.263
— Atlanta (N.L.)	8	9	.471	5.04	1.54	22	22	0	0	0	0-0	114.1	127	66	64	19	49-3	84	.283
2003— Richmond (Int'l)	8	4	.667	3.35	1.40	15	15	3	1	...	0-...	94.0	93	40	35	5	34-0	75	.256
— Atlanta (N.L.)	0	0	...	5.53	1.56	21	2	0	0	0	1-1	40.2	43	27	25	3	18-2	19	.270
2004— St. Louis (N.L.)	15	7	.682	3.71	1.42	32	32	0	0	0	0-0	201.1	215	90	83	26	70-1	138	.275
Major League totals (5 years)	**29**	**22**	**.569**	**4.16**	**1.43**	**128**	**72**	**0**	**0**	**3**	**1-4**	**509.0**	**521**	**261**	**235**	**66**	**208-11**	**356**	**.266**

DIVISION SERIES RECORD

Year Team (League)	W	L	Pct.	ERA	WHIP	G	GS	CG	ShO	Hld.	Sv.-Opp.	IP	H	R	ER	HR	BB-IBB	SO	Avg.
2001— Atlanta (N.L.)				Did not play.															
2004— St. Louis (N.L.)	0	0	...	8.10	2.40	1	1	0	0	0	0-0	3.1	4	3	3	3	4-0	0	.308

CHAMPIONSHIP SERIES RECORD

Year Team (League)	W	L	Pct.	ERA	WHIP	G	GS	CG	ShO	Hld.	Sv.-Opp.	IP	H	R	ER	HR	BB-IBB	SO	Avg.
2001— Atlanta (N.L.)	0	0	...	0.00	2.00	2	0	0	0	0	0-0	2.0	2	4	0	1	2-0	3	.222
2004— St. Louis (N.L.)	0	0	...	6.75	1.75	1	1	0	0	0	0-0	4.0	5	3	3	0	2-0	2	.294
Champ. series totals (2 years)	**0**	**0**	**...**	**4.50**	**1.83**	**3**	**1**	**0**	**0**	**0**	**0-0**	**6.0**	**7**	**7**	**3**	**1**	**4-0**	**5**	**.269**

WORLD SERIES RECORD

Year Team (League)	W	L	Pct.	ERA	WHIP	G	GS	CG	ShO	Hld.	Sv.-Opp.	IP	H	R	ER	HR	BB-IBB	SO	Avg.
2004— St. Louis (N.L.)	0	1	.000	3.86	1.86	2	1	0	0	0	0-0	7.0	6	3	3	1	7-1	4	.231

MARRERO, ELI — OF

PERSONAL: Born November 17, 1973, in Havana, Cuba. ... 6-1/180. ... Bats right, throws right. ... Full name: Elieser Marrero. ... Name pronounced: muh-RARE-ro. ... High school: Coral Gables (Fla.).

TRANSACTIONS/CAREER NOTES: Selected by St. Louis Cardinals organization in third round of 1993 free-agent draft. ... On disabled list (March 22-April 13, 1998). ... On disabled list (July 2-September 1, 2000); included rehabilitation assignment to Memphis. ... On disabled list (May 12-September 1, 2003); included rehabilitation assignment to Memphis. ... Traded with OF J.D. Drew to Atlanta Braves for Ps Jason Marquis, Ray King and Adam Wainwright (December 14, 2003). ... On disabled list (March 29-April 14 and April 25-May 29, 2004); included rehabilitation assignments to Greenville and Richmond.

2004 GAMES PLAYED BY POSITION (MLB): OF—73.

Year Team (League)	Pos.	G	AB	R	H	2B	3B	HR	RBI	BB	SO	HBP	GDP	SB-CS	Avg.	OBP	SLG	OPS	E	Avg.
1993— Johnson City (App.)	C	18	61	10	22	8	0	2	14	12	9	1	0	2-2	.361	.467	.590	1.057	1	.994
1994— Savannah (S. Atl.)	C	116	421	71	110	16	3	21	79	39	92	5	6	5-4	.261	.328	.463	.791	15	.984
1995— St. Pete. (FSL)	C	107	383	43	81	16	1	10	55	23	55	1	10	9-4	.211	.254	.337	.590	10	.984
1996— Arkansas (Texas)	C-DH	116	374	65	101	17	3	19	65	32	55	6	7	9-6	.270	.336	.484	.820	3	.996
1997— Louisville (A.A.)	C-DH	112	395	60	108	21	7	20	68	25	53	3	8	4-4	.273	.318	.514	.832	7	.991
— St. Louis (N.L.)	C	17	45	4	11	2	0	2	7	2	13	0	1	4-0	.244	.271	.422	.693	3	.969
1998— St. Louis (N.L.)	C-1B	83	254	28	62	18	1	4	20	28	42	0	5	6-2	.244	.318	.370	.688	4	.991
— Memphis (PCL)	C-DH	32	130	22	31	5	0	7	21	13	23	0	3	5-4	.238	.306	.438	.744	2	.991
1999— St. Louis (N.L.)	C-1B	114	317	32	61	13	1	6	34	18	56	1	14	11-2	.192	.236	.297	.533	7	.988
2000— St. Louis (N.L.)	C-1B	53	102	21	23	3	1	5	17	9	16	3	3	5-0	.225	.302	.422	.723	0	1.000
— Memphis (PCL)	C	6	15	1	1	0	0	0	0	0	2	0	1	0-0	.067	.067	.067	.133	0	1.000
2001— St. Louis (N.L.)	C-OF-1B	86	203	37	54	11	3	6	23	15	39	0	4	6-3	.266	.312	.438	.751	7	.983
2002— St. Louis (N.L.)	OF-C-1B	131	397	63	104	19	1	18	66	40	72	0	5	14-2	.262	.327	.451	.777	7	.981
2003— Memphis (PCL)	OF-DH	5	12	2	3	1	0	1	1	1	0	1	1	0-0	.250	.357	.583	.940	0	1.000
— St. Louis (N.L.)	OF-C-1B	41	107	10	24	4	2	2	20	7	17	0	0	0-1	.224	.267	.355	.622	1	.989
2004— Greenville (Sou.)	OF	3	12	3	5	1	0	2	5	2	6	0	1	0-0	.417	.500	1.500	1.500	0	1.000
— Richmond (Int'l)	OF	6	24	1	5	2	0	0	3	1	3	0	0	0-0	.208	.240	.292	.532	0	1.000
— Atlanta (N.L.)	OF	90	250	37	80	18	1	10	40	23	50	1	4	4-1	.320	.374	.520	.894	1	.992
Major League totals (8 years)		**615**	**1675**	**232**	**419**	**88**	**10**	**53**	**227**	**142**	**303**	**5**	**36**	**50-11**	**.250**	**.307**	**.410**	**.717**	**30**	**.987**

DIVISION SERIES RECORD

Year Team (League)	Pos.	G	AB	R	H	2B	3B	HR	RBI	BB	SO	HBP	GDP	SB-CS	Avg.	OBP	SLG	OPS	E	Avg.
2000— St. Louis (N.L.)				Did not play.																
2001— St. Louis (N.L.)	C	3	7	0	0	0	0	0	0	0	0	0	0	0-0	.000	.000	.000	.000	0	1.000
2002— St. Louis (N.L.)	OF	2	6	0	0	0	0	0	1	0	1	0	0	0-0	.000	.000	.000	.000	0	1.000
2004— Atlanta (N.L.)	OF	3	5	0	1	0	0	0	0	0	2	0	0	0-0	.200	.200	.200	.400	0	...
Division series totals (3 years)		**8**	**18**	**0**	**1**	**0**	**0**	**0**	**1**	**0**	**3**	**0**	**0**	**0-0**	**.056**	**.053**	**.056**	**.108**	**0**	**1.000**

CHAMPIONSHIP SERIES RECORD

Year Team (League)	Pos.	G	AB	R	H	2B	3B	HR	RBI	BB	SO	HBP	GDP	SB-CS	Avg.	OBP	SLG	OPS	E	Avg.
2000— St. Louis (N.L.)	C	4	4	0	0	0	0	0	0	1	0	0	0	0-0	.000	.000	.000	.000	0	1.000
2002— St. Louis (N.L.)	OF	4	16	1	3	1	0	1	1	1	1	0	0	0-0	.188	.235	.438	.673	0	1.000
Champ. series totals (2 years)		**8**	**20**	**1**	**3**	**1**	**0**	**1**	**1**	**2**	**1**	**0**	**0**	**0-0**	**.150**	**.190**	**.350**	**.540**	**0**	**1.000**

M

MARSONEK, SAM   P

PERSONAL: Born July 10, 1978, in Tampa, Fla. ... 6-6/225. ... Throws right, bats right. ... Full name: Samuel R. Marsonek. ... High school: Jesuit (Tampa, Fla.).

TRANSACTIONS/CAREER NOTES: Selected by Texas Rangers organization in first round (24th pick overall) of 1996 free-agent draft. ... Traded by Rangers with P Brandon Knight to New York Yankees for OF Chad Curtis (December 14, 1999). ... On disabled list (July 15, 2004-remainder of season); included rehabilitation assignments to GCL Yankees, Tampa and Columbus.

CAREER HITTING: 0-for-0 (.000), 0 R, 0 2B, 0 3B, 0 HR, 0 RBI.

Year Team (League)	W	L	Pct.	ERA	WHIP	G	GS	CG	ShO	Hld.	Sv.-Opp.	IP	H	R	ER	HR	BB-IBB	SO	Avg.
1997— Charlotte (Fla. St.)	0	2	.000	7.56	1.92	2	2	0	0	...	0-...	8.1	14	10	7	3	2-0	7	.368
— Pulaski (Appalachian)	7	3	.700	5.02	1.53	12	11	0	0	...	0-...	71.2	90	57	40	4	20-0	65	.297
1998— Savannah (S. Atl.)	0	0	...	3.86	1.43	2	2	0	0	...	0-...	7.0	7	7	3	0	3-0	4	.241
— GC Rangers (GCL)	0	0	...	0.00	0.43	2	2	0	0	...	0-...	4.2	2	1	0	0	0-0	2	.118
1999— Charlotte (Fla. St.)	3	9	.250	5.54	1.52	15	15	2	0	...	0-...	91.0	111	69	56	8	27-0	61	.299
2000— Greensboro (S. Atl.)	6	7	.462	4.25	1.44	18	18	1	0	...	0-...	114.1	114	64	54	8	51-0	78	.264
2001— Tampa (FSL)	8	8	.500	3.51	1.21	24	23	5	2	...	0-...	138.1	128	67	54	6	39-2	120	.245
2002— Norwich (East.)	5	8	.385	5.01	1.44	19	13	1	0	...	0-...	100.2	111	68	56	6	34-1	75	.276
2003— Columbus (Int'l)	4	4	.500	4.84	1.37	54	2	0	0	...	18-...	83.2	84	52	45	9	31-0	57	.258
2004— Columbus (Int'l)	1	5	.167	3.15	1.20	35	0	0	0	...	17-...	40.0	36	20	14	5	12-2	28	.240
— New York (A.L.)	0	0	...	0.00	1.50	1	0	0	0	0	0-0	1.1	2	0	0	0	0-0	0	.333
— GC Yankees (GCL)	0	0	...	3.00	0.70	2	1	0	0	...	1-...	3.0	2	1	1	1	0-0	3	.182
— Tampa (FSL)	0	0	...	0.00	0.75	3	0	0	0	...	0-...	4.0	3	0	0	0	0-0	3	.214
Major League totals (1 year)	**0**	**0**	**...**	**0.00**	**1.50**	**1**	**0**	**0**	**0**	**0**	**0-0**	**1.1**	**2**	**0**	**0**	**0**	**0-0**	**0**	**.333**

MARTE, DAMASO   P

PERSONAL: Born February 14, 1975, in Santo Domingo, Dominican Republic. ... 6-2/200. ... Throws left, bats left. ... Full name: Damaso Savinon Marte. ... Name pronounced: da-muh-so mar-TAY.

TRANSACTIONS/CAREER NOTES: Signed as a non-drafted free agent by Seattle Mariners organization (October 28, 1992). ... Signed as a free agent by New York Yankees organization (November 16, 2000). ... Traded by Yankees to Pittsburgh Pirates for IF Enrique Wilson (June 13, 2001). ... Traded by Pirates with IF Edwin Yan to Chicago White Sox for P Matt Guerrier (March 27, 2002).

CAREER HITTING: 0-for-5 (.000), 0 R, 0 2B, 0 3B, 0 HR, 0 RBI.

Year Team (League)	W	L	Pct.	ERA	WHIP	G	GS	CG	ShO	Hld.	Sv.-Opp.	IP	H	R	ER	HR	BB-IBB	SO	Avg.
1993— Dom. Mariners (DSL)	2	5	.286	6.55	1.99	17	15	2	0	...	0-...	56.1	62	48	41	...	50-...	29	...
1994— Dom. Mariners (DSL)	7	0	1.000	3.86	1.55	17	13	0	0	...	0-...	65.1	53	41	28	...	48-...	80	...
1995— Everett (Northwest)	2	2	.500	2.21	0.95	11	11	5	0	...	0-...	36.2	25	11	9	2	10-0	39	.195
1996— Wisconsin (Midw.)	8	6	.571	4.49	1.47	26	26	2	1	...	0-...	142.1	134	82	71	8	75-5	115	.248
1997— Lancaster (Calif.)	8	8	.500	4.13	1.48	25	25	2	1	...	0-...	139.1	144	75	64	15	62-1	127	.272
1998— Orlando (Sou.)	7	6	.538	5.27	1.51	22	20	0	0	...	0-...	121.1	136	82	71	14	47-0	99	.281
1999— Tacoma (PCL)	3	3	.500	5.13	1.62	31	11	0	0	...	0-...	73.2	79	43	42	13	40-1	59	.271
— Seattle (A.L.)	0	1	.000	9.35	2.54	5	0	0	0	0	0-0	8.2	16	9	9	3	6-0	3	.390
2000— Ariz. Mariners (Ariz.)	0	0	...	0.00	0.20	2	2	0	0	...	0-...	5.0	1	0	0	0	0-0	6	.063
— New Haven (East.)	0	0	...	1.59	1.41	4	0	0	0	...	0-...	5.2	6	1	1	1	2-0	4	.286
2001— Norwich (East.)	3	1	.750	3.50	1.00	23	0	0	0	...	1-...	36.0	29	16	14	3	7-0	36	.215
— Nashville (PCL)	0	0	...	3.38	0.56	4	0	0	0	...	0-...	5.1	3	2	2	2	0-0	4	.167
— Pittsburgh (N.L.)	0	1	.000	4.71	1.27	23	0	0	0	0	0-0	36.1	34	21	19	5	12-3	39	.250
2002— Chicago (A.L.)	1	1	.500	2.83	1.03	68	0	0	0	14	10-12	60.1	44	19	19	5	18-2	72	.204
2003— Chicago (A.L.)	4	2	.667	1.58	1.05	71	0	0	0	14	11-18	79.2	50	16	14	3	34-6	87	.185
2004— Chicago (A.L.)	6	5	.545	3.42	1.22	74	0	0	0	21	6-12	73.2	56	28	28	10	34-4	68	.217
American League totals (4 years)	**11**	**9**	**.550**	**2.83**	**1.16**	**218**	**0**	**0**	**0**	**49**	**27-42**	**222.1**	**166**	**72**	**70**	**21**	**92-12**	**230**	**.211**
National League totals (1 year)	**0**	**1**	**.000**	**4.71**	**1.27**	**23**	**0**	**0**	**0**	**0**	**0-0**	**36.1**	**34**	**21**	**19**	**5**	**12-3**	**39**	**.250**
Major League totals (5 years)	**11**	**10**	**.524**	**3.10**	**1.18**	**241**	**0**	**0**	**0**	**49**	**27-42**	**258.2**	**200**	**93**	**89**	**26**	**104-15**	**269**	**.217**

MARTIN, TOM   P

PERSONAL: Born May 21, 1970, in Charleston, S.C. ... 6-1/206. ... Throws left, bats left. ... Full name: Thomas Edgar Martin. ... High school: Bay (Panama City, Fla.).

TRANSACTIONS/CAREER NOTES: Selected by Baltimore Orioles organization in sixth round of 1988 free-agent draft. ... Traded by Orioles with 3B Craig Worthington to San Diego Padres for P Jim Lewis and OF Steve Martin (February 17, 1992). ... Selected by Atlanta Braves organization from Padres organization in Rule 5 minor league draft (December 13, 1993). ... Loaned by Braves organization to Mexico City Tigers of the Mexican League (May 1-7, 1995). ... Released by Braves (January 25, 1996). ... Signed by Houston Astros organization (February 21, 1996). ... On disabled list (May 30-June 15, 1997). ... Selected by Arizona Diamondbacks in second round (29th pick overall) of expansion draft (November 18, 1997). ... Traded by Diamondbacks with 3B Travis Fryman and cash to Cleveland Indians for 3B Matt Williams (December 1, 1997). ... On disabled list (April 30-May 18 and August 31-September 19, 1998); included rehabilitation assignments to Buffalo. ... On disabled list (April 4-August 9, 1999); included rehabilitation assignment to Akron. ... On disabled list (June 13-August 4, 2000); included rehabilitation assignment to Buffalo. ... Traded by Indians to New York Mets for C Javier Ochoa (January 11, 2001). ... On disabled list (May 13-August 16, 2001); included rehabilitation assignments to Brooklyn and Norfolk. ... Released by Mets (October 11, 2001). ... Signed by Tampa Bay Devil Rays organization (January 28, 2002). ... On disabled list (April 23-September 30, 2002). ... Released by Devil Rays (September 30, 2002). ... Signed by Los Angeles Dodgers organization (February 26, 2003). ... Traded by Dodgers to Braves for P Matt Merricks (July 31, 2004).

CAREER HITTING: 0-for-7 (.000), 0 R, 0 2B, 0 3B, 0 HR, 0 RBI.

Year Team (League)	W	L	Pct.	ERA	WHIP	G	GS	CG	ShO	Hld.	Sv.-Opp.	IP	H	R	ER	HR	BB-IBB	SO	Avg.
1989— Bluefield (Appalachian)	3	3	.500	4.62	1.56	8	8	0	0	...	0-...	39.0	36	28	20	3	25-0	31	.242
— Erie (N.Y.-Penn)	0	5	.000	6.64	1.65	7	7	0	0	...	0-...	40.2	42	39	30	2	25-0	44	.259
1990— Wausau (Midw.)	2	3	.400	2.48	1.45	9	9	0	0	...	0-...	40.0	31	25	11	1	27-0	45	.209
1991— Kane County (Midwest)	4	10	.286	3.64	1.49	38	10	0	0	...	6-...	99.0	92	50	40	4	56-3	106	.247
1992— High Desert (Calif.)	0	2	.000	9.37	2.39	11	0	0	0	...	0-...	16.1	23	19	17	4	16-0	10	.333
— Waterloo (Midw.)	2	6	.250	4.25	1.53	39	2	0	0	...	3-...	55.0	62	38	26	3	22-4	57	.287
1993— Rancho Cuca. (Calif.)	1	4	.200	5.61	1.87	47	1	0	0	...	0-...	59.1	72	41	37	4	39-2	53	.305
1994— Greenville (Sou.)	5	6	.455	4.62	1.47	36	6	0	0	...	0-...	74.0	82	40	38	6	27-3	51	.288
1995— Richmond (Int'l)	0	0	...	9.00	2.22	7	0	0	0	...	0-...	9.0	10	9	9	4	10-2	3	.286
— M.C. Tigers (Mex.)	0	1	.000	27.00	4.50	1	1	0	0	...	0-...	1.1	5	5	4	0	1-...	0	...
1996— Tucson (PCL)	0	0	...	0.00	1.33	5	0	0	0	...	0-...	6.0	6	0	0	0	2-2	1	.261
— Jackson (Texas)	6	2	.750	3.24	1.51	57	0	0	0	...	3-...	75.0	71	35	27	8	42-4	58	.250
1997— Houston (N.L.)	5	3	.625	2.09	1.34	55	0	0	0	7	2-3	56.0	52	13	13	2	23-2	36	.254
1998— Cleveland (A.L.)	1	1	.500	12.89	2.80	14	0	0	0	3	0-0	14.2	29	21	21	3	12-0	9	.408
— Buffalo (Int'l)	3	1	.750	6.00	1.64	41	0	0	0	...	0-...	36.0	46	25	24	4	13-0	35	.309
1999— Akron (East.)	0	0	...	1.00	0.78	3	3	0	0	...	0-...	9.0	4	1	1	0	3-0	9	.138

M

Year	Team (League)	W	L	Pct.	ERA	WHIP	G	GS	CG	ShO	Hld.	Sv.-Opp.	IP	H	R	ER	HR	BB-IBB	SO	Avg.
	— Cleveland (A.L.)	0	1	.000	8.68	1.71	6	0	0	0	0	0-0	9.1	13	9	9	2	3-1	8	.325
	— Buffalo (Int'l)	1	0	1.000	3.00	1.00	5	0	0	0	...	0-...	6.0	5	2	2	1	1-0	6	.208
2000—	Cleveland (A.L.)	1	0	1.000	4.05	1.41	31	0	0	0	0	0-0	33.1	32	16	15	3	15-2	21	.254
	— Buffalo (Int'l)	0	1	.000	3.60	1.30	9	3	0	0	...	0-...	10.0	12	4	4	1	1-0	4	.300
2001—	Norfolk (Int'l)	2	1	.667	6.26	1.78	23	0	0	0	...	1-...	23.0	31	17	16	4	10-0	24	.330
	— New York (N.L.)	1	0	1.000	10.06	1.94	14	0	0	0	1	0-0	17.0	23	22	19	4	10-2	12	.319
	— Brooklyn (NY-P)	0	0	...	0.00	2.00	1	1	0	0	...	0-...	1.0	2	0	0	0	0-0	0	.500
2002—	Durham (Int'l)	0	0	...	0.00	1.20	4	0	0	0	...	2-...	3.1	3	0	0	0	1-0	6	.231
	— Tampa Bay (A.L.)	0	0	...	16.20	3.60	2	0	0	0	0	0-0	1.2	5	3	3	0	1-0	1	.500
2003—	Los Angeles (N.L.)	1	2	.333	3.53	1.18	80	0	0	0	28	0-1	51.0	36	21	20	6	24-4	51	.198
2004—	Los Angeles (N.L.)	0	1	.000	4.13	1.62	47	0	0	0	5	1-1	28.1	32	13	13	3	14-1	18	.291
	— Atlanta (N.L.)	0	1	.000	3.71	1.29	29	0	0	0	7	0-3	17.0	17	7	7	4	5-2	12	.270
American League totals (4 years)		2	2	.500	7.32	1.86	53	0	0	0	3	0-0	59.0	79	49	48	8	31-3	39	.320
National League totals (4 years)		7	7	.500	3.83	1.39	225	0	0	0	48	3-8	169.1	160	76	72	19	76-11	129	.253
Major League totals (8 years)		9	9	.500	4.73	1.52	278	0	0	0	51	3-8	228.1	239	125	120	27	107-14	168	.272

DIVISION SERIES RECORD

Year	Team (League)	W	L	Pct.	ERA	WHIP	G	GS	CG	ShO	Hld.	Sv.-Opp.	IP	H	R	ER	HR	BB-IBB	SO	Avg.
1997—	Houston (N.L.)	0	0	...	0.00	3.00	2	0	0	0	0	0-0	.2	1	1	0	0	1-0	0	.333
2004—	Atlanta (N.L.)	0	0	...	54.00	15.00	2	0	0	0	0	0-0	.1	4	2	2	0	1-0	0	1.000
Division series totals (2 years)		0	0	...	18.00	7.00	4	0	0	0	0	0-0	1.0	5	3	2	0	2-0	0	.714

MARTINEZ, ANASTACIO — P

PERSONAL: Born November 3, 1978, in Villa Mella, Dominican Republic. ... 6-2/180. ... Throws right, bats right. ... Full name: Anastacio Euclides Martinez. ... High school: Liceo Santa Cruz (Dominican Republic).

CAREER HITTING: 0-for-0 (.000), 0 R, 0 2B, 0 3B, 0 HR, 0 RBI.

Year	Team (League)	W	L	Pct.	ERA	WHIP	G	GS	CG	ShO	Hld.	Sv.-Opp.	IP	H	R	ER	HR	BB-IBB	SO	Avg.
1998—	GC Red Sox (GCL)	2	3	.400	3.18	1.12	12	10	0	0	...	0-...	51.0	45	28	18	2	12-0	50	.232
1999—	Augusta (S. Atl.)	2	4	.333	6.30	1.55	10	10	0	0	...	0-...	40.0	44	37	28	7	18-0	36	.262
	— Lowell (NY-Penn)	0	3	.000	3.68	1.54	11	11	0	0	...	0-...	51.1	61	36	21	4	18-0	43	.289
2000—	GC Red Sox (GCL)	0	1	.000	9.45	2.70	2	1	0	0	...	0-...	6.2	15	9	7	0	3-0	1	.441
	— Augusta (S. Atl.)	9	6	.600	4.64	1.50	23	23	0	0	...	0-...	120.1	130	69	62	8	50-0	107	.279
2001—	Sarasota (Florida State)	9	12	.429	3.35	1.17	25	24	1	0	...	0-...	145.0	130	69	54	12	39-0	123	.236
2002—	Trenton (East.)	5	12	.294	5.31	1.63	27	27	0	0	...	0-...	139.0	152	98	82	12	75-0	127	.276
2003—	Portland (East.)	3	1	.750	2.25	1.38	34	0	0	0	...	14-...	40.0	31	13	10	3	24-0	37	.212
	— Altoona (East.)	0	0	...	2.25	1.75	3	0	0	0	...	0-...	4.0	6	1	1	1	1-0	1	.400
	— Pawtucket (Int'l)	2	1	.667	1.93	1.07	8	0	0	0	...	0-...	14.0	12	3	3	2	3-0	15	.226
2004—	Boston (A.L.)	2	1	.667	8.44	1.78	11	0	0	0	0	0-0	10.2	13	10	10	2	6-0	5	.289
	— Pawtucket (Int'l)	3	3	.500	3.74	1.54	38	0	0	0	...	1-...	67.1	73	37	28	5	31-2	57	.277
Major League totals (1 year)		2	1	.667	8.44	1.78	11	0	0	0	0	0-0	10.2	13	10	10	2	6-0	5	.289

MARTINEZ, EDGAR — DH

PERSONAL: Born January 2, 1963, in New York, N.Y. ... 5-11/205. ... Bats right, throws right. ... High school: Dorado (Puerto Rico). ... College: American College (P.R.). ... Cousin of Carmelo Martinez, first baseman/outfielder with six major league teams (1983-91).

TRANSACTIONS/CAREER NOTES: Signed as a non-drafted free agent by Seattle Mariners organization (December 19, 1982). ... On Seattle disabled list (April 4-May 17, June 15-July 21 and August 17, 1993-remainder of season); included rehabilitation assignment to Jacksonville. ... On disabled list (April 16-May 6, 1994; July 21-August 12, 1996; and July 17-August 3, 2001). ... On suspended list (October 3-5, 2001). ... On disabled list (April 12-June 14, 2002).

2004 GAMES PLAYED BY POSITION (MLB): DH—122, 3B—1.

										BATTING									FIELDING	
Year	Team (League)	Pos.	G	AB	R	H	2B	3B	HR	RBI	BB	SO	HBP	GDP	SB-CS	Avg.	OBP	SLG	OPS	E	Avg.
1983—	Bellingham (N'west)	3B	32	104	14	18	1	1	0	5	18	24	2	...	1-3	.173	.304	.202	.506	6	.930
1984—	Wausau (Midw.)	3B	126	433	72	131	32	2	15	66	84	57	3	7	11-9	.303	.414	.490	.904	25	.930
1985—	Chattanooga (Sou.)	3B	111	357	43	92	15	5	3	47	71	30	5	16	1-3	.258	.378	.353	.730	19	.947
	— Calgary (PCL)	2B-3B	20	68	8	24	7	1	0	14	12	7	0	2	1-0	.353	.450	.485	.935	4	.937
1986—	Chattanooga (Sou.)	2B-3B	132	451	71	119	29	5	6	74	89	35	2	8	2-5	.264	.383	.390	.773	15	.960
1987—	Calgary (PCL)	3B	129	438	75	144	31	1	10	66	82	47	2	10	3-5	.329	.434	.473	.907	20	.949
	— Seattle (A.L.)	3B-DH	13	43	6	16	5	2	0	5	2	5	1	0	0-0	.372	.413	.581	.994	0	1.000
1988—	Calgary (PCL)	2B-3B	95	331	63	120	19	4	8	64	66	40	3	9	9-1	.363	.467	.517	.983	20	.921
	— Seattle (A.L.)	3B	14	32	0	9	4	0	0	5	4	7	0	0	0-0	.281	.351	.406	.758	1	.929
1989—	Seattle (A.L.)	3B	65	171	20	41	5	0	2	20	17	26	3	3	2-1	.240	.314	.304	.619	6	.949
	— Calgary (PCL)	2B-3B	32	113	30	39	11	0	3	23	22	13	3	1	2-2	.345	.457	.522	.979	12	.867
1990—	Seattle (A.L.)	3B-DH	144	487	71	147	27	2	11	49	74	62	5	13	1-4	.302	.397	.433	.830	* 27	.928
1991—	Seattle (A.L.)	3B-DH	150	544	98	167	35	1	14	52	84	72	8	19	0-3	.307	.405	.452	.857	15	.962
1992—	Seattle (A.L.) 3B-DH-1B	135	528	100	181	• 46	3	18	73	54	61	4	15	14-4	* .343	.404	.544	.948	17	.946
1993—	Seattle (A.L.)	DH-3B	42	135	20	32	7	0	4	13	28	19	0	4	0-0	.237	.366	.378	.744	2	.889
	— Jacksonville (Sou.)	DH	4	14	2	5	0	0	1	3	2	0	0	1	0-0	.357	.438	.571	1.009	...	...
1994—	Seattle (A.L.)	3B-DH	89	326	47	93	23	1	13	51	53	42	3	2	6-2	.285	.387	.482	.869	9	.950
1995—	Seattle (A.L.)	DH-3B-1B	• 145	511	• 121	182	• 52	0	29	113	116	87	8	11	4-3	* .356	* .479	.628	1.107	2	.944
1996—	Seattle (A.L.)	DH-1B-3B	139	499	121	163	52	2	26	103	123	84	8	15	3-3	.327	.464	.595	1.059	1	.968
1997—	Seattle (A.L.) DH-1B-3B	155	542	104	179	35	1	28	108	119	86	11	21	2-4	.330	.456	.554	1.009	1	.986
1998—	Seattle (A.L.)	DH-1B	154	556	86	179	46	1	29	102	106	96	3	13	1-1	.322	* .429	.565	.993	0	1.000
1999—	Seattle (A.L.)	DH-1B	142	502	86	169	35	1	24	86	97	99	6	12	7-2	.337	* .447	.554	1.001	0	1.000
2000—	Seattle (A.L.)	DH-1B	153	556	100	180	31	0	37	* 145	96	95	6	13	3-0	.324	.423	.579	1.002	0	1.000
2001—	Seattle (A.L.)	DH-1B	132	470	80	144	40	1	23	116	93	90	9	11	4-1	.306	.423	.543	.966	0	1.000
2002—	Seattle (A.L.)	DH	97	328	42	91	23	0	15	59	67	69	6	6	1-1	.277	.403	.485	.888	0	...
2003—	Seattle (A.L.)	DH	145	497	72	146	25	0	24	98	92	95	7	17	0-1	.294	.406	.489	.895	0	...
2004—	Seattle (A.L.)	DH-3B	141	486	45	128	23	0	12	63	58	107	4	15	1-0	.263	.342	.385	.727	0	...
Major League totals (18 years)			2055	7213	1219	2247	514	15	309	1261	1283	1202	89	190	49-30	.312	.418	.515	.933	81	.952

DIVISION SERIES RECORD

Year — Team (League)	Pos.	G	AB	R	H	2B	3B	HR	RBI	BB	SO	HBP	GDP	SB-CS	Avg.	OBP	SLG	OPS	E	Avg.
1995— Seattle (A.L.)	DH	5	21	6	12	3	0	2	10	6	2	0	0	0-0	.571	.667	1.000	1.667	...	
1997— Seattle (A.L.)	DH	4	16	2	3	0	0	2	3	0	3	0	0	0-0	.188	.188	.563	.750	...	
2000— Seattle (A.L.)	DH	3	11	2	4	1	0	1	2	2	1	0	1	0-0	.364	.462	.727	1.189	...	
2001— Seattle (A.L.)	DH	5	16	3	5	1	0	2	5	5	2	0	0	1-0	.313	.476	.750	1.226	...	
Division series totals (4 years)		17	64	13	24	5	0	7	20	13	8	0	1	1-0	.375	.481	.781	1.262	...	

CHAMPIONSHIP SERIES RECORD

Year — Team (League)	Pos.	G	AB	R	H	2B	3B	HR	RBI	BB	SO	HBP	GDP	SB-CS	Avg.	OBP	SLG	OPS	E	Avg.
1995— Seattle (A.L.)	DH	6	23	0	2	0	0	0	0	2	5	1	1	1-1	.087	.192	.087	.279	...	
2000— Seattle (A.L.)	DH	6	21	2	5	1	0	1	4	3	5	0	0	0-0	.238	.333	.429	.762	...	
2001— Seattle (A.L.)	DH	5	20	1	3	1	0	0	0	1	6	0	1	0-0	.150	.190	.200	.390	...	
Champ. series totals (3 years)		17	64	3	10	2	0	1	4	6	16	1	2	1-1	.156	.239	.234	.474	...	

ALL-STAR GAME RECORD

	G	AB	R	H	2B	3B	HR	RBI	BB	SO	HBP	GDP	SB-CS	Avg.	OBP	SLG	OPS	E	Avg.
All-Star Game totals (7 years)	7	12	1	2	0	0	1	1	0	4	1	0	0-1	.167	.231	.417	.647	0	

MARTINEZ, PEDRO — P

PERSONAL: Born October 25, 1971, in Manoguayabo, Dominican Republic. ... 5-11/180. ... Throws right, bats right. ... Full name: Pedro Jaime Martinez. ... College: Ohio Dominican. ... Brother of Ramon J. Martinez, pitcher with three major league teams (1988-2001).

TRANSACTIONS/CAREER NOTES: Signed as a non-drafted free agent by Los Angeles Dodgers organization (June 18, 1988). ... Traded by Dodgers to Montreal Expos for 2B Delino DeShields (November 19, 1993). ... On suspended list (April 1-9, 1997). ... Traded by Expos to Boston Red Sox for P Carl Pavano and a player to be named (November 18, 1997); Expos acquired P Tony Armas Jr. to complete deal (December 18, 1997). ... On disabled list (July 19-August 3, 1999; June 29-July 13, 2000; June 27-August 26 and September 8, 2001-remainder of season; and May 16-June 11, 2003).

HONORS: Named Minor League Player of the Year by THE SPORTING NEWS (1991). ... Named N.L. Pitcher of the Year by THE SPORTING NEWS (1997). ... Named A.L. Pitcher of the Year by THE SPORTING NEWS (1999 and 2000). ... Named N.L. Cy Young Award winner by Baseball Writers' Association of America (1997). ... Named A.L. Cy Young Award winner by Baseball Writers' Association of America (1999 and 2000).

CAREER HITTING: 25-for-265 (.094), 14 R, 3 2B, 2 3B, 0 HR, 11 RBI.

Year — Team (League)	W	L	Pct.	ERA	WHIP	G	GS	CG	ShO	Hld.	Sv.-Opp.	IP	H	R	ER	HR	BB-IBB	SO	Avg.
1988— Dom. Dodgers (DSL)	5	1	.833	3.10	1.24	8	7	1	0	...	0-...	49.1	45	25	17	...	16-...	28	...
1989— Dom. Dodgers (DSL)	7	2	.778	2.73	0.98	13	7	2	3	...	1-...	85.2	59	30	26	...	25-...	63	...
1990— Great Falls (Pio.)	8	3	.727	3.62	1.48	14	14	0	0	...	0-...	77.0	74	39	31	5	40-1	82	.253
1991— Bakersfield (California)	8	0	1.000	2.05	0.98	10	10	0	0	...	0-...	61.1	41	17	14	3	19-0	83	.189
— San Antonio (Texas)	7	5	.583	1.76	1.15	12	12	4	3	...	0-...	76.2	57	21	15	1	31-1	74	.210
— Albuquerque (PCL)	3	3	.500	3.66	1.12	6	6	0	0	...	0-...	39.1	28	17	16	3	16-0	35	.201
1992— Albuquerque (PCL)	7	6	.538	3.81	1.28	20	20	3	1	...	0-...	125.1	104	57	53	10	57-0	124	.229
— Los Angeles (N.L.)	0	1	.000	2.25	0.88	2	1	0	0	0	0-0	8.0	6	2	2	0	1-0	8	.200
1993— Albuquerque (PCL)	0	0	...	3.00	0.67	1	1	0	0	...	0-...	3.0	1	1	1	0	1-0	4	.100
— Los Angeles (N.L.)	10	5	.667	2.61	1.24	65	2	0	0	14	2-3	107.0	76	34	31	5	57-4	119	.201
1994— Montreal (N.L.)	11	5	.688	3.42	1.11	24	23	1	1	0	1-1	144.2	115	58	55	11	45-3	142	.220
1995— Montreal (N.L.)	14	10	.583	3.51	1.15	30	30	2	2	0	0-0	194.2	158	79	76	21	66-1	174	.227
1996— Montreal (N.L.)	13	10	.565	3.70	1.20	33	33	4	1	0	0-0	216.2	189	100	89	19	70-3	222	.232
1997— Montreal (N.L.)	17	8	.680	* 1.90	0.93	31	31	* 13	4	0	0-0	241.1	158	65	51	16	67-5	305	.184
1998— Boston (A.L.)	19	7	.731	2.89	1.09	33	33	3	2	0	0-0	233.2	188	82	75	26	67-3	251	.217
1999— Boston (A.L.)	* 23	4	.852	* 2.07	0.92	31	29	5	1	0	0-0	213.1	160	56	49	9	37-1	* 313	.205
2000— Boston (A.L.)	18	6	.750	* 1.74	0.74	29	29	7	* 4	0	0-0	217.0	128	44	42	17	32-0	* 284	.167
2001— Boston (A.L.)	7	3	.700	2.39	0.93	18	18	1	0	0	0-0	116.2	84	33	31	5	25-0	163	.199
2002— Boston (A.L.)	20	4	.833	* 2.26	0.92	30	30	2	0	0	0-0	199.1	144	62	50	13	40-1	* 239	.198
2003— Boston (A.L.)	14	4	.778	* 2.22	1.04	29	29	3	0	0	0-0	186.2	147	52	46	7	47-0	206	.215
2004— Boston (A.L.)	16	9	.640	3.90	1.17	33	33	1	1	0	0-0	217.0	193	99	94	26	61-0	227	.238
American League totals (7 years)	117	37	.760	2.52	0.98	203	201	22	8	0	0-0	1383.2	1044	428	387	103	309-5	1683	.206
National League totals (6 years)	65	39	.625	3.00	1.10	185	120	20	8	14	3-4	912.1	702	338	304	72	306-16	970	.213
Major League totals (13 years)	182	76	.705	2.71	1.03	388	321	42	16	14	3-4	2296.0	1746	766	691	175	615-21	2653	.209

DIVISION SERIES RECORD

Year — Team (League)	W	L	Pct.	ERA	WHIP	G	GS	CG	ShO	Hld.	Sv.-Opp.	IP	H	R	ER	HR	BB-IBB	SO	Avg.
1998— Boston (A.L.)	1	0	1.000	3.86	0.86	1	1	0	0	0	0-0	7.0	6	3	3	2	0-0	8	.222
1999— Boston (A.L.)	1	0	1.000	0.00	0.70	2	1	0	0	0	0-0	10.0	3	0	0	0	4-0	11	.091
2003— Boston (A.L.)	1	0	1.000	3.86	1.29	2	2	0	0	0	0-0	14.0	13	6	6	0	5-0	9	.250
2004— Boston (A.L.)	1	0	1.000	3.86	1.14	1	1	0	0	0	0-0	7.0	6	3	3	0	2-0	6	.240
Division series totals (4 years)	4	0	1.000	2.84	1.03	6	5	0	0	0	0-0	38.0	28	12	12	2	11-0	34	.204

CHAMPIONSHIP SERIES RECORD

Year — Team (League)	W	L	Pct.	ERA	WHIP	G	GS	CG	ShO	Hld.	Sv.-Opp.	IP	H	R	ER	HR	BB-IBB	SO	Avg.
1999— Boston (A.L.)	1	0	1.000	0.00	0.57	1	1	0	0	0	0-0	7.0	2	0	0	0	2-0	12	.087
2003— Boston (A.L.)	0	1	.000	5.65	1.26	2	2	0	0	0	0-0	14.1	16	9	9	3	2-0	14	.276
2004— Boston (A.L.)	0	1	.000	6.23	1.77	3	2	0	0	0	0-0	13.0	14	9	9	2	9-0	14	.269
Champ. series totals (3 years)	1	2	.333	4.72	1.31	6	5	0	0	0	0-0	34.1	32	18	18	5	13-0	40	.241

WORLD SERIES RECORD

Year — Team (League)	W	L	Pct.	ERA	WHIP	G	GS	CG	ShO	Hld.	Sv.-Opp.	IP	H	R	ER	HR	BB-IBB	SO	Avg.
2004— Boston (A.L.)	1	0	1.000	0.00	0.71	1	1	0	0	0	0-0	7.0	3	0	0	0	2-0	6	.136

ALL-STAR GAME RECORD

	W	L	Pct.	ERA	WHIP	G	GS	CG	ShO	Hld.	Sv.-Opp.	IP	H	R	ER	HR	BB-IBB	SO	Avg.
All-Star Game totals (3 years)	1	0	1.000	0.00	0.50	3	1	0	0	0	0-0	4.0	2	0	0	0	0-0	8	.143

MARTINEZ, RAMON — SS

PERSONAL: Born October 10, 1972, in Philadelphia, Pa. ... 6-1/190. ... Bats right, throws right. ... Full name: Ramon E. Martinez. ... High school: Escuela Superior Catholica (Bayamon, Puerto Rico). ... Junior college: Vernon (Texas).

TRANSACTIONS/CAREER NOTES: Signed as a non-drafted free agent by Kansas City Royals organization (January 15, 1993). ... Traded by Royals to San Francisco Giants (December 9, 1996), completing deal in which Giants traded P Jamie Brewington to Royals for a player to be named (November 26, 1996). ... On disabled list (August 21-September 5, 1999; and June 1-16, 2002). ... Signed as a free agent by Chicago Cubs (January 2, 2003). ... On disabled list (September 16, 2004-remainder of season).

2004 GAMES PLAYED BY POSITION (MLB): SS—73, 3B—24, 2B—6.

							BATTING												FIELDING	
Year	Team (League)	Pos.	G	AB	R	H	2B	3B	HR	RBI	BB	SO	HBP	GDP	SB-CS	Avg.	OBP	SLG	OPS	E	Avg.
1993— GC Royals (GCL)		2B	37	97	16	23	5	0	0	9	8	6	2	5	3-0	.237	.303	.289	.591	5	.973
— Wilmington (Caro.)		2B-SS	24	75	8	19	4	0	0	6	11	9	1	2	1-4	.253	.352	.307	.659	6	.954
1994— Wilmington (Caro.)		2B	90	325	40	87	13	2	2	35	35	25	4	14	6-3	.268	.341	.338	.680	16	.964
— Rockford (Midwest)		2B	6	18	3	5	0	0	0	3	4	2	0	1	1-0	.278	.409	.278	.687	1	.955
1995— Wichita (Texas)		2B-SS	103	393	58	108	20	2	3	51	42	50	4	11	11-8	.275	.344	.359	.703	9	.982
1996— Omaha (A.A.)		2B	85	320	35	81	12	3	6	41	21	34	3	6	3-2	.253	.305	.366	.671	12	.969
— Wichita (Texas)		2B	26	93	16	32	4	1	1	8	7	8	0	4	4-1	.344	.390	.441	.831	6	.956
1997— Shreveport (Texas)		SS	105	404	72	129	32	4	5	54	40	48	3	6	4-5	.319	.382	.455	.838	18	.968
— Phoenix (PCL)		2B-SS	18	57	6	16	2	0	1	7	5	9	0	1	1-0	.281	.333	.368	.702	3	.959
1998— Fresno (PCL)		2B-SS	98	364	58	114	21	2	14	59	38	42	2	11	0-3	.313	.375	.497	.872	10	.980
— San Francisco (N.L.)		2B	19	19	4	6	1	0	0	0	4	2	0	0	0-0	.316	.435	.368	.803	0	1.000
1999— San Francisco (N.L.)		2-S-3-DH	61	144	21	38	6	0	5	19	14	17	0	2	1-2	.264	.327	.410	.737	6	.966
— Fresno (PCL)		SS-DH-3B	29	114	13	37	7	1	2	17	10	17	0	2	2-0	.325	.376	.456	.832	5	.951
2000— San Francisco (N.L.)		S-2-3-1	88	189	30	57	13	2	6	25	15	22	1	6	3-2	.302	.354	.487	.841	1	.995
2001— San Francisco (N.L.)		3B-2B-SS	128	391	48	99	18	3	5	37	38	52	5	11	1-2	.253	.323	.353	.676	8	.980
2002— San Francisco (N.L.)		S-2-1-0-3	72	181	26	49	10	2	4	25	14	26	4	1	2-0	.271	.335	.414	.749	8	.965
2003— Chicago (N.L.)		2-3-S-1	108	293	30	83	16	1	3	34	24	50	2	8	0-1	.283	.333	.375	.709	10	.966
2004— Chicago (N.L.)		SS-3B-2B	102	260	22	64	15	1	3	30	26	40	1	5	1-0	.246	.313	.346	.659	9	.970
Major League totals (7 years)			578	1477	181	396	79	9	26	170	135	209	13	33	8-7	.268	.330	.387	.717	42	.974

DIVISION SERIES RECORD

Year	Team (League)	Pos.	G	AB	R	H	2B	3B	HR	RBI	BB	SO	HBP	GDP	SB-CS	Avg.	OBP	SLG	OPS	E	Avg.
2000— San Francisco (N.L.)		2B-SS	2	6	0	2	0	0	0	0	0	2	0	0	0-0	.333	.333	.333	.667	0	1.000
2002— San Francisco (N.L.)			1	0	0	0	0	0	0	0	1	0	0	0	0-0	....	1.000	....	1.000	0	....
2003— Chicago (N.L.)		SS	2	4	0	0	0	0	0	0	0	2	0	0	0-0	.000	.000	.000	.000	0	1.000
Division series totals (3 years)			5	10	0	2	0	0	0	0	1	4	0	0	0-0	.200	.273	.200	.473	0	1.000

CHAMPIONSHIP SERIES RECORD

Year	Team (League)	Pos.	G	AB	R	H	2B	3B	HR	RBI	BB	SO	HBP	GDP	SB-CS	Avg.	OBP	SLG	OPS	E	Avg.
2002— San Francisco (N.L.)		SS	2	1	0	0	0	0	0	1	0	0	0	0	0-0	.000	.000	.000	.000	0	1.000
2003— Chicago (N.L.)		SS-2B	4	4	0	0	0	0	0	0	1	0	0	0	0-0	.000	.000	.000	.000	0	1.000
Champ. series totals (2 years)			6	5	0	0	0	0	0	1	1	0	0	0	0-0	.000	.000	.000	.000	0	1.000

WORLD SERIES RECORD

Year	Team (League)	Pos.	G	AB	R	H	2B	3B	HR	RBI	BB	SO	HBP	GDP	SB-CS	Avg.	OBP	SLG	OPS	E	Avg.
2002— San Francisco (N.L.)			2	2	0	0	0	0	0	0	0	2	0	0	0-0	.000	.000	.000	.000	0	....

MARTINEZ, SANDY   C

PERSONAL: Born October 8, 1970, in Villa Mella, Dominican Republic. ... 6-2/215. ... Bats left, throws right. ... Full name: Angel Sandy Martinez. ... High school: Villa Mella (Dominican Republic).

TRANSACTIONS/CAREER NOTES: Signed as a non-drafted free agent by Toronto Blue Jays organization (January 10, 1990). ... On disabled list (August 17-September 1, 1996); included rehabilitation assignment to Knoxville. ... Traded by Blue Jays to Chicago Cubs for a player to be named (December 11, 1997); Blue Jays acquired P Trevor Schaffer to complete deal (December 19, 1997). ... On suspended list (July 1-3, 1998). ... On disabled list (May 13-June 10, 1999); included rehabilitation assignment to Iowa. ... Signed as a free agent by Florida Marlins organization (December 6, 1999). ... Signed as a free agent by Montreal Expos organization (November 17, 2000). ... On disabled list (April 4, 2001-remainder of season). ... Signed as a free agent by Tampa Bay Devil Rays organization (November 21, 2002). ... Released by Devil Rays (March 30, 2003). ... Signed by Kansas City Royals organization (April 12, 2003). ... Released by Royals (June 8, 2003). ... Signed by Pittsburgh Pirates organization (January 27, 2004). ... Traded by Pirates to Cleveland Indians for a player to be named (April 8, 2004). ... Traded by Indians to Boston Red Sox for cash (August 31, 2004).

2004 GAMES PLAYED BY POSITION (MLB): C—4.

							BATTING												FIELDING	
Year	Team (League)	Pos.	G	AB	R	H	2B	3B	HR	RBI	BB	SO	HBP	GDP	SB-CS	Avg.	OBP	SLG	OPS	E	Avg.
1990— Dom. B. Jays (DSL)		C	44	145	21	35	2	0	0	10	18	15	...	...	1-...	.241	...	.255	...	...	...
1991— Dunedin (Fla. St.)		C	12	38	3	7	1	0	0	3	7	7	1	0	0-0	.184	.326	.211	.537	2	.978
— Medicine Hat (Pio.)		C	34	98	8	17	1	0	2	16	12	29	2	2	0-1	.173	.272	.245	.517	3	.982
1992— Dunedin (Fla. St.)		C	4	15	4	3	1	0	2	4	0	3	1	1	0-0	.200	.250	.667	.917	1	.929
— Medicine Hat (Pio.)		SS-C-1B	57	206	27	52	15	0	4	39	14	62	1	6	0-0	.252	.300	.384	.684	5	.985
1993— Hagerstown (SAL)		C	94	338	41	89	16	1	9	46	19	71	6	8	1-1	.263	.313	.396	.710	14	.976
1994— Dunedin (Fla. St.)		C-DH-1B	122	450	50	117	14	6	7	52	22	79	11	15	1-3	.260	.310	.364	.674	14	.980
1995— Knoxville (Southern)		C-DH	41	144	14	33	8	1	2	22	6	34	0	2	0-1	.229	.257	.340	.597	5	.980
— Toronto (A.L.)		C	62	191	12	46	12	0	2	25	7	45	1	1	0-0	.241	.268	.335	.603	5	.986
1996— Toronto (A.L.)		C	76	229	17	52	9	3	3	18	16	58	4	4	0-0	.227	.278	.332	.609	3	.993
— Knoxville (Southern)		C-DH	4	16	2	3	0	0	0	0	0	5	0	0	0-0	.188	.188	.188	.375	1	.950
1997— Syracuse (Int'l)		C-DH	96	322	28	72	12	1	4	29	27	76	5	9	7-2	.224	.292	.304	.596	9	.986
— Toronto (A.L.)		C	3	2	1	0	0	0	0	0	1	1	0	0	0-0	.000	.333	.000	.333	1	.933
1998— Chicago (N.L.)		C	45	87	7	23	9	1	0	7	13	21	1	3	1-0	.264	.360	.391	.751	3	.985
1999— Chicago (N.L.)		C	17	30	1	5	0	0	1	1	0	11	0	0	0-0	.167	.167	.267	.433	2	.959
— Iowa (PCL)		C	36	125	8	29	6	0	2	18	5	29	0	2	1-0	.232	.258	.328	.586	1	.996
2000— Florida (N.L.)		C	10	18	1	4	2	0	0	0	0	8	0	0	0-0	.222	.222	.333	.556	0	1.000
— Calgary (PCL)		C	86	277	45	83	20	0	15	48	16	57	2	5	2-1	.300	.338	.534	.872	4	.990
2001— Montreal (N.L.)		C	1	1	0	0	0	0	0	0	0	0	0	1	0-0	.000	.000	.000	.000	0	1.000
2002— Ottawa (Int'l)		C	39	133	12	30	3	1	3	18	10	41	2	3	2-0	.226	.288	.331	.618	1	.996
2003— Omaha (PCL)		C-DH	24	73	12	18	1	0	3	13	5	15	3	1	0-1	.247	.313	.384	.697	0	1.000
2004— Cleveland (A.L.)		C	1	2	0	0	0	0	0	0	0	1	0	0	0-0	.000	.000	.000	.000	0	1.000
— Buffalo (Int'l)		C-DH	62	197	29	54	8	1	17	47	12	44	0	7	2-0	.274	.316	.584	.900	3	.992
— Boston (A.L.)		C	3	4	0	0	0	0	0	1	0	0	0	0	0-0	.000	.000	.000	.000	0	1.000
American League totals (4 years)			145	428	30	98	21	3	5	43	24	107	5	5	0-0	.229	.277	.327	.604	9	.989
National League totals (4 years)			73	136	9	32	11	1	1	8	13	40	1	4	1-0	.235	.305	.353	.658	5	.983
Major League totals (8 years)			218	564	39	130	32	4	6	51	37	147	6	9	1-0	.230	.284	.333	.617	14	.988

DIVISION SERIES RECORD

Year	Team (League)	Pos.	G	AB	R	H	2B	3B	HR	RBI	BB	SO	HBP	GDP	SB-CS	Avg.	OBP	SLG	OPS	E	Avg.
1998— Chicago (N.L.)		C	1	1	1	1	0	0	0	0	0	0	0	0	0-0	1.000	1.000	1.000	2.000	0	1.000

M

MARTINEZ, TINO — 1B

PERSONAL: Born December 7, 1967, in Tampa, Fla. ... 6-2/230. ... Bats left, throws right. ... Full name: Constantino Martinez. ... High school: Tampa Catholic. ... College: Tampa.

TRANSACTIONS/CAREER NOTES: Selected by Boston Red Sox organization in third round of June 1985 free-agent draft; did not sign. ... Selected by Seattle Mariners organization in first round (14th pick overall) of 1988 free-agent draft. ... On disabled list (August 10, 1993-remainder of season). ... Traded by Mariners with Ps Jeff Nelson and Jim Mecir to New York Yankees for P Sterling Hitchcock and 3B Russ Davis (December 7, 1995). ... Signed as a free agent by St. Louis Cardinals (December 19, 2001). ... Traded by Cardinals to Tampa Bay Devil Rays for P Evan Rust and 1B J.P. Davis (November 21, 2003).

2004 GAMES PLAYED BY POSITION (MLB): 1B—114, DH—19.

Year Team (League)	Pos.	G	AB	R	H	2B	3B	HR	RBI	BB	SO	HBP	GDP	SB-CS	Avg.	OBP	SLG	OPS	E	Avg.
1989— Williamsport (East.)	1B	137	509	51	131	29	2	13	64	59	54	0	11	7-1	.257	.330	.399	.729	7	.995
1990— Calgary (PCL)	3B-1B	128	453	83	145	28	1	17	93	74	37	3	9	8-5	.320	.413	.499	.912	10	.991
— Seattle (A.L.)	1B	24	68	4	15	4	0	0	5	9	9	0	0	0-0	.221	.308	.279	.587	0	1.000
1991— Calgary (PCL)	3B-1B	122	442	94	144	34	5	18	86	82	44	3	5	3-3	.326	.428	.548	.976	9	.992
— Seattle (A.L.)	DH-1B	36	112	11	23	2	0	4	9	11	24	0	2	0-0	.205	.272	.330	.602	2	.993
1992— Seattle (A.L.)	1B-DH	136	460	53	118	19	2	16	66	42	77	2	24	2-1	.257	.316	.411	.727	4	.995
1993— Seattle (A.L.)	1B-DH	109	408	48	108	25	1	17	60	45	56	5	7	0-3	.265	.343	.456	.799	3	.997
1994— Seattle (A.L.)	1B-DH	97	329	42	86	21	0	20	61	29	52	1	9	1-2	.261	.320	.508	.828	2	.997
1995— Seattle (A.L.)	1B-DH	141	519	92	152	35	3	31	111	62	91	4	10	0-0	.293	.369	.551	.920	8	.993
1996— New York (A.L.)	1B-DH	155	595	82	174	28	0	25	117	68	85	2	18	2-1	.292	.364	.466	.830	5	.996
1997— New York (A.L.)	1B-DH	158	594	96	176	31	2	44	141	75	75	3	15	3-1	.296	.371	.577	.948	8	.994
1998— New York (A.L.)	1B	142	531	92	149	33	1	28	123	61	83	6	18	2-1	.281	.355	.505	.860	10	.992
1999— New York (A.L.)	1B	159	589	95	155	27	2	28	105	69	86	3	14	3-4	.263	.341	.458	.800	7	.995
2000— New York (A.L.)	1B	155	569	69	147	37	4	16	91	52	74	8	16	4-1	.258	.328	.422	.749	7	.994
2001— New York (A.L.)	1B-DH	154	589	89	165	24	2	34	113	42	89	2	12	1-2	.280	.329	.501	.830	5	.996
2002— St. Louis (N.L.)	1B	150	511	63	134	25	1	21	75	58	71	2	12	3-2	.262	.337	.438	.776	5	.996
2003— St. Louis (N.L.)	1B-DH	138	476	66	130	25	2	15	69	53	71	9	14	1-1	.273	.352	.429	.781	3	.997
2004— Tampa Bay (A.L.)	1B-DH	138	458	63	120	20	1	23	76	66	72	9	10	3-1	.262	.362	.461	.823	3	.997
American League totals (13 years)		1604	5821	836	1588	306	18	286	1078	631	873	45	155	21-17	.273	.345	.479	.824	64	.995
National League totals (2 years)		288	987	129	264	50	3	36	144	111	142	11	26	4-3	.267	.345	.434	.778	8	.997
Major League totals (15 years)		1892	6808	965	1852	356	21	322	1222	742	1015	56	181	25-20	.272	.345	.472	.817	72	.995

DIVISION SERIES RECORD

Year Team (League)	Pos.	G	AB	R	H	2B	3B	HR	RBI	BB	SO	HBP	GDP	SB-CS	Avg.	OBP	SLG	OPS	E	Avg.
1995— Seattle (A.L.)	1B	5	22	4	9	1	0	1	5	3	4	0	0	0-1	.409	.480	.591	1.071	0	1.000
1996— New York (A.L.)	1B	4	15	3	4	2	0	0	0	3	1	0	0	0-0	.267	.389	.400	.789	0	1.000
1997— New York (A.L.)	1B	5	18	1	4	1	0	1	4	2	4	1	0	0-0	.222	.333	.444	.778	0	1.000
1998— New York (A.L.)	1B	3	11	1	3	2	0	0	0	0	2	0	0	0-0	.273	.273	.455	.727	0	1.000
1999— New York (A.L.)	1B	3	11	2	2	0	0	0	0	2	5	0	0	0-0	.182	.308	.182	.490	1	.968
2000— New York (A.L.)	1B	5	19	2	8	2	0	0	4	1	3	0	0	0-0	.421	.429	.526	.955	1	.980
2001— New York (A.L.)	1B	5	18	1	2	0	0	1	2	1	6	2	0	0-0	.111	.238	.278	.516	0	1.000
2002— St. Louis (N.L.)	1B	3	11	2	0	0	0	0	0	2	1	0	0	0-0	.000	.154	.000	.154	0	1.000
Division series totals (8 years)		33	125	16	32	8	0	3	15	14	23	3	0	0-1	.256	.343	.392	.735	2	.994

CHAMPIONSHIP SERIES RECORD

Year Team (League)	Pos.	G	AB	R	H	2B	3B	HR	RBI	BB	SO	HBP	GDP	SB-CS	Avg.	OBP	SLG	OPS	E	Avg.
1995— Seattle (A.L.)	1B	6	22	1	3	0	0	0	0	3	7	0	0	0-0	.136	.240	.136	.376	1	.980
1996— New York (A.L.)	1B	5	22	3	4	1	0	0	0	0	2	1	0	0-0	.182	.217	.227	.445	1	1.000
1998— New York (A.L.)	1B	6	19	1	2	1	0	0	1	6	8	1	0	2-0	.105	.333	.158	.491	1	.981
1999— New York (A.L.)	1B	5	19	3	5	1	0	1	3	2	4	1	0	0-0	.263	.364	.474	.837	0	1.000
2000— New York (A.L.)	1B	6	25	5	8	2	0	1	1	2	4	0	1	0-0	.320	.370	.520	.890	0	1.000
2001— New York (A.L.)	1B	5	20	3	5	1	0	1	3	0	4	0	0	0-1	.250	.250	.450	.700	0	1.000
2002— St. Louis (N.L.)	1B	4	14	1	2	0	0	0	1	2	1	0	0	1-0	.143	.250	.143	.393	0	1.000
Champ. series totals (7 years)		37	141	17	29	6	0	3	9	15	30	3	1	3-1	.206	.294	.312	.606	2	.994

WORLD SERIES RECORD

Year Team (League)	Pos.	G	AB	R	H	2B	3B	HR	RBI	BB	SO	HBP	GDP	SB-CS	Avg.	OBP	SLG	OPS	E	Avg.
1996— New York (A.L.)	1B	6	11	0	1	0	0	0	0	2	5	0	0	0-0	.091	.231	.091	.322	0	1.000
1998— New York (A.L.)	1B	4	13	4	5	0	0	1	4	4	2	0	0	0-0	.385	.529	.615	1.145	0	1.000
1999— New York (A.L.)	1B	4	15	3	4	0	0	1	5	2	4	0	0	0-0	.267	.353	.467	.820	0	1.000
2000— New York (A.L.)	1B	5	22	3	8	1	0	0	2	1	4	0	0	0-0	.364	.391	.409	.800	0	1.000
2001— New York (A.L.)	1B	6	21	1	4	0	0	1	3	2	2	0	0	0-0	.190	.261	.333	.594	0	1.000
World series totals (5 years)		25	82	11	22	1	0	3	14	11	17	0	0	0-0	.268	.355	.390	.745	0	1.000

ALL-STAR GAME RECORD

	G	AB	R	H	2B	3B	HR	RBI	BB	SO	HBP	GDP	SB-CS	Avg.	OBP	SLG	OPS	E	Avg.
All-Star Game totals (2 years)	2	3	0	1	0	0	0	0	0	0	0	0	0-0	.333	.333	.333	.667	0	1.000

MARTINEZ, VICTOR — C

PERSONAL: Born December 23, 1978, in Ciudad Bolivar, Venezuela. ... 6-2/190. ... Bats both, throws right. ... Full name: Victor Jesus Martinez.

TRANSACTIONS/CAREER NOTES: Signed as a non-drafted free agent by Cleveland Indians organization (July 15, 1996). ... On disabled list (August 9-September 2, 2003); included rehabilitation assignment to Akron.

2004 GAMES PLAYED BY POSITION (MLB): C—132, DH—8.

Year Team (League)	Pos.	G	AB	R	H	2B	3B	HR	RBI	BB	SO	HBP	GDP	SB-CS	Avg.	OBP	SLG	OPS	E	Avg.
1997— Maracay 1 (VSL)		53	122	21	42	12	0	0	26	32	11	...	...	6-...	.344	...	.443	...	...	...
1998— Guacara 2 (VSL)		55	160	28	43	13	0	1	27	32	14	...	...	8-...	.269	...	.369	...	...	...
1999— Mahoning Valley (NY-P)	C	64	235	37	65	9	0	4	36	27	31	1	4	0-1	.277	.346	.366	.712	8	.984
2000— Kinston (Caro.)	C	26	83	9	18	7	0	0	8	11	5	1	3	1-1	.217	.313	.301	.614	5	.980
— Columbus (S. Atl.)	C	21	70	11	26	9	1	2	12	11	6	1	1	0-0	.371	.452	.614	1.067	2	.988
2001— Kinston (Caro.)	C	114	420	59	138	33	2	10	57	39	60	8	12	3-3	.329	.394	.488	.882	16	.985
2002— Akron (East.)	C	121	443	84	149	40	0	22	85	58	62	8	10	3-3	.336	.417	.576	.993	10	.988

M

Year	Team (League)	Pos.	G	AB	R	H	2B	3B	HR	RBI	BB	SO	HBP	GDP	SB-CS	Avg.	OBP	SLG	OPS	E	Avg.
— Cleveland (A.L.)	C-DH	12	32	2	9	1	0	1	5	3	2	0	1	0-0	.281	.333	.406	.740	1	.983
2003— Buffalo (Int'l)	C-1B-DH	73	274	42	90	19	0	7	45	26	32	8	14	3-5	.328	.395	.474	.869	4	.993
— Akron (East.)	DH-C	3	12	1	4	2	0	0	2	0	1	0	1	0-0	.333	.333	.500	.833	0	1.000
— Cleveland (A.L.)	C-DH	49	159	15	46	4	0	1	16	13	21	1	8	1-1	.289	.345	.333	.678	1	.996
2004— Cleveland (A.L.)	C-DH	141	520	77	147	38	1	23	108	60	69	5	16	0-1	.283	.359	.492	.851	6	.994
Major League totals (3 years)		202	711	94	202	43	1	25	129	76	92	6	25	1-2	.284	.355	.453	.807	8	.994

ALL-STAR GAME RECORD

	G	AB	R	H	2B	3B	HR	RBI	BB	SO	HBP	GDP	SB-CS	Avg.	OBP	SLG	OPS	E	Avg.
All-Star Game totals (1 year)	1	1	0	0	0	0	0	0	0	0	0	0	0-0	.000	.000	.000	.000	0	1.000

MATEO, HENRY — 2B

PERSONAL: Born October 14, 1976, in Santo Domingo, Dominican Republic. ... 6-0/176. ... Bats both, throws right. ... Full name: Henry Antonio Valera Mateo. ... Name pronounced: MAH-ta-yo. ... High school: Centro Estudios Libres (Santurce, Puerto Rico).

TRANSACTIONS/CAREER NOTES: Selected by Montreal Expos organization in second round of 1995 free-agent draft. ... Expos franchise transferred to Washington, D.C., for 2005 season.

2004 GAMES PLAYED BY POSITION (MLB): 2B—9, OF—1.

								BATTING												FIELDING	
Year	Team (League)	Pos.	G	AB	R	H	2B	3B	HR	RBI	BB	SO	HBP	GDP	SB-CS	Avg.	OBP	SLG	OPS	E	Avg.
1995— GC Expos (GCL)	2B-SS	38	122	11	18	0	0	0	6	14	47	5	2	2-7	.148	.261	.148	.408	9	.951
1996— GC Expos (GCL)	2B	14	44	8	11	3	0	0	3	5	11	3	0	5-1	.250	.365	.318	.684	7	.901
1997— Vermont (N.Y.-Penn.)	2B	67	228	32	56	9	3	1	31	30	44	7	4	21-11	.246	.348	.325	.673	14	.956
1998— Cape Fear (S. Atl.)	2B	114	416	72	115	20	5	4	41	40	111	13	5	22-16	.276	.355	.377	.733	15	.971
— Jupiter (FSL)	2B	12	43	11	12	3	1	0	6	2	6	2	0	3-0	.279	.333	.395	.729	0	1.000
1999— Jupiter (FSL)	2B	118	447	69	116	27	7	4	58	44	112	10	4	32-16	.260	.335	.378	.713	17	.962
2000— Harrisburg (East.)	2B	140	530	91	152	25	11	5	63	58	97	6	4	48-16	.287	.362	.404	.766	24	.962
2001— Ottawa (Int'l)	2B	118	500	71	134	14	12	5	43	33	89	7	2	47-14	.268	.322	.374	.696	22	.963
— Montreal (N.L.)	2B	5	9	1	3	1	0	0	0	0	1	0	0	0-0	.333	.333	.444	.778	2	.818
2002— Ottawa (Int'l)	2B-SS	74	285	35	73	10	6	5	25	18	53	3	6	15-6	.256	.306	.386	.692	12	.970
— Montreal (N.L.)	2B-SS	22	23	1	4	0	1	0	0	2	6	0	0	2-0	.174	.240	.217	.501	1	.950
2003— Montreal (N.L.)	2B-OF-DH-SS	100	154	29	37	3	1	0	7	11	38	3	0	11-1	.240	.304	.273	.576	4	.973
2004— GC Expos (GCL)	2B	5	14	7	4	2	0	0	2	6	2	2	0	4-0	.286	.545	.429	.974	0	1.000
— Edmonton (PCL)	2B-DH	30	119	23	36	8	3	0	9	8	16	2	5	10-1	.303	.354	.420	.774	8	.937
— Montreal (N.L.)	2B-OF	40	44	3	12	2	0	0	0	1	9	0	1	2-3	.273	.289	.318	.607	4	.882
Major League totals (4 years)		167	230	34	56	6	2	0	7	14	54	3	1	15-4	.243	.296	.287	.583	11	.948

MATEO, JULIO — P

PERSONAL: Born August 2, 1977, in Bani, Dominican Republic. ... 6-0/177. ... Throws right, bats right. ... Full name: Julio Cesar Mateo.

TRANSACTIONS/CAREER NOTES: Signed as a non-drafted free agent by Seattle Mariners organization (May 15, 1996). ... On disabled list (July 29-September 16, 2004).

CAREER HITTING: 0-for-0 (.000), 0 R, 0 2B, 0 3B, 0 HR, 0 RBI.

Year	Team (League)	W	L	Pct.	ERA	WHIP	G	GS	CG	ShO	Hld.	Sv.-Opp.	IP	H	R	ER	HR	BB-IBB	SO	Avg.
1996— Dom. Mariners (DSL)	4	2	.667	1.74	1.18	14	5	2	1	...	1-...	51.2	42	14	10	...	19-...	23	...
1997— Ariz. Mariners (Ariz.)	3	1	.750	3.30	1.13	13	6	0	0	...	1-...	60.0	45	32	22	1	23-0	54	.205
1998— Lancaster (Calif.)	0	0	...	6.75	1.50	1	0	0	0	...	0-...	1.1	1	1	1	1	1-0	1	.250
— Everett (Northwest)	3	3	.500	4.70	1.49	28	0	0	0	...	4-...	38.1	40	25	20	6	17-1	37	.274
1999— Wisconsin (Midw.)	1	3	.250	4.34	1.34	20	0	0	0	...	4-...	29.0	31	18	14	2	8-2	27	.261
2000— Wisconsin (Midw.)	4	8	.333	4.19	1.25	36	1	0	0	...	4-...	68.2	63	38	32	12	23-1	73	.241
2001— San Bernardino (Calif.)	5	4	.556	2.86	1.12	56	0	0	0	...	26-...	66.0	58	28	21	5	16-5	79	.230
2002— San Antonio (Texas)	1	0	1.000	0.52	0.58	12	0	0	0	...	0-...	17.1	7	3	1	2	3-0	18	.121
— Tacoma (PCL)	4	2	.667	4.06	1.48	20	0	0	0	...	6-...	31.0	39	15	14	2	7-1	23	.317
— Seattle (A.L.)	0	0	...	4.29	1.52	12	0	0	0	2	0-0	21.0	20	10	10	2	12-0	15	.247
2003— Seattle (A.L.)	4	0	1.000	3.15	0.96	50	0	0	0	10	1-1	85.2	69	32	30	14	13-1	71	.220
2004— Seattle (A.L.)	1	2	.333	4.68	1.25	45	0	0	0	6	1-4	57.2	56	30	30	11	16-3	43	.251
Major League totals (3 years)	5	2	.714	3.83	1.13	107	0	0	0	10	2-5	164.1	145	72	70	27	41-4	129	.235

MATEO, RUBEN — OF

PERSONAL: Born February 10, 1978, in San Cristobal, Dominican Republic. ... 6-0/210. ... Bats right, throws right. ... Full name: Ruben Amaurys Mateo. ... Name pronounced: ma-TAY-oh. ... High school: Liceo Jose Manuel Maria Balance (San Cristobal, Dominican Republic).

TRANSACTIONS/CAREER NOTES: Signed as a non-drafted free agent by Texas Rangers organization (October 24, 1994). ... On disabled list (June 23-July 9 and August 5, 1999-remainder of season); included rehabilitation assignment to Oklahoma. ... On disabled list (June 3, 2000-remainder of season). ... Traded by Rangers with 3B Edwin Encarnacion to Cincinnati Reds for P Rob Bell (June 15, 2001). ... Signed as a free agent by Pittsburgh Pirates organization (February 7, 2004). ... Traded by Pirates to Kansas City Royals for cash (July 2, 2004). ... Refused minor league assignment and became a free agent (August 30, 2004).

2004 GAMES PLAYED BY POSITION (MLB): OF—40, DH—1.

								BATTING												FIELDING	
Year	Team (League)	Pos.	G	AB	R	H	2B	3B	HR	RBI	BB	SO	HBP	GDP	SB-CS	Avg.	OBP	SLG	OPS	E	Avg.
1995— Dom. Rangers (DSL)	OF	48	176	30	53	9	3	4	42	20	23	...	...	1-2	.301	...	.455	...	1	.982
1996— Char., S.C. (SAL)	OF-DH	134	496	65	129	30	8	8	58	26	78	12	8	30-9	.260	.309	.401	.710	7	.970
1997— Charlotte (Fla. St.)	OF-DH	99	385	63	121	23	8	12	67	22	55	6	16	20-5	.314	.359	.509	.868	8	.958
1998— Tulsa (Texas)	OF	107	433	79	134	32	3	18	75	30	56	15	7	18-8	.309	.371	.522	.893	7	.970
— Charlotte (Fla. St.)	OF	1	4	0	0	0	0	0	1	0	1	0	0	0-0	.000	.000	.000	.000	0	1.000
1999— Texas (A.L.)	OF-DH	32	122	16	29	9	1	5	18	4	28	1	2	3-0	.238	.268	.451	.719	1	1.000
— Oklahoma (PCL)	OF	63	253	53	85	12	0	18	62	14	36	8	5	6-3	.336	.385	.597	.982	5	.963
2000— Texas (A.L.)	OF	52	206	32	60	11	0	7	19	10	34	5	5	0-0	.291	.339	.447	.786	3	.980
2001— Texas (A.L.)	OF	40	129	18	32	5	2	1	13	9	28	6	4	1-0	.248	.322	.341	.663	1	.986
— Oklahoma (PCL)	OF	14	51	3	11	3	1	1	8	2	8	0	1	1-2	.216	.241	.333	.574	1	.957
— Louisville (Int'l)	OF	65	251	35	63	16	4	2	25	13	45	8	7	2-0	.251	.307	.371	.677	5	.954
2002— Louisville (Int'l)	OF	52	209	37	63	14	0	9	23	11	40	3	2	6-2	.301	.342	.498	.840	3	.967
— Cincinnati (N.L.)	OF	46	86	11	22	6	0	2	7	6	20	2	1	0-0	.256	.319	.395	.715	0	1.000
2003— Louisville (Int'l)	OF	57	217	36	71	15	1	9	50	26	34	5	3	3-1	.327	.408	.530	.938	2	.984

Year	Team (League)	Pos.	G	AB	R	H	2B	3B	HR	RBI	BB	SO	HBP	GDP	SB-CS	Avg.	OBP	SLG	OPS	E	Avg.
— Cincinnati (N.L.)	OF	74	207	16	50	9	0	3	18	12	53	3	4	0-0	.242	.290	.329	.619	2	.982
2004— Nashville (PCL)	OF-DH	35	114	21	36	12	0	11	25	12	33	2	0	2-2	.316	.391	.711	1.101	1	.981
— Pittsburgh (N.L.)	OF-DH	19	33	4	8	0	0	3	7	5	6	1	1	0-0	.242	.359	.515	.874	1	.933
— Kansas City (A.L.)	OF	32	93	9	18	4	3	0	7	3	20	2	2	1-1	.194	.235	.301	.536	0	1.000
American League totals (4 years)		156	550	75	139	29	6	13	57	26	110	14	13	11-1	.253	.302	.398	.701	4	.988
National League totals (3 years)		139	326	31	80	15	0	8	32	23	79	6	6	0-0	.245	.305	.365	.670	3	.981
Major League totals (6 years)		295	876	106	219	44	6	21	89	49	189	20	19	11-1	.250	.303	.386	.689	7	.986

MATHENY, MIKE   C

PERSONAL: Born September 22, 1970, in Reynoldsburg, Ohio. ... 6-3/220. ... Bats right, throws right. ... Full name: Michael Scott Matheny. ... Name pronounced: ma-THEE-nee. ... High school: Reynoldsburg (Ohio). ... College: Michigan.

TRANSACTIONS/CAREER NOTES: Selected by Toronto Blue Jays organization in 31st round of 1988 free-agent draft; did not sign. ... Selected by Milwaukee Brewers organization in eighth round of 1991 free-agent draft. ... On disabled list (June 15-July 12, 1998); included rehabilitation assignment to Beloit. ... Signed as a free agent by Blue Jays (December 23, 1998). ... Released by Blue Jays (November 16, 1999). ... Signed by St. Louis Cardinals (December 15, 1999). ... On suspended list (September 26-28, 2003). ... On disabled list (June 3-18, 2004).

HONORS: Won N.L. Gold Glove at catcher (2000, 2003 and 2004).

2004 GAMES PLAYED BY POSITION (MLB): C—122, 1B—1.

Year	Team (League)	Pos.	G	AB	R	H	2B	3B	HR	RBI	BB	SO	HBP	GDP	SB-CS	Avg.	OBP	SLG	OPS	E	Avg.
1991— Helena (Pio.)	C	64	253	35	72	14	0	2	34	19	52	6	10	2-4	.285	.348	.364	.711	5	.991
1992— Stockton (Calif.)	C	106	333	42	73	13	2	6	46	35	81	3	11	2-2	.219	.297	.324	.621	8	.989
1993— El Paso (Texas)	C	107	339	39	86	21	2	2	28	17	73	2	6	1-4	.254	.292	.345	.638	9	.986
1994— Milwaukee (A.L.)	C	28	53	3	12	3	0	1	2	3	13	2	1	0-1	.226	.293	.340	.633	1	.989
— New Orleans (A.A.)	C-DH-1B	57	177	20	39	10	1	4	21	16	39	4	5	1-1	.220	.299	.356	.655	5	.987
1995— Milwaukee (A.L.)	C	80	166	13	41	9	1	0	21	12	28	2	3	2-1	.247	.306	.313	.619	4	.986
— New Orleans (A.A.)	C	6	17	3	6	2	0	3	4	0	5	3	0	0-0	.353	.450	1.000	1.450	0	1.000
1996— Milwaukee (A.L.)	C-DH	106	313	31	64	15	2	8	46	14	80	3	9	3-2	.204	.243	.342	.584	8	.985
— New Orleans (A.A.)	C-DH	20	66	3	15	4	0	1	6	2	17	0	1	1-0	.227	.246	.333	.580	0	1.000
1997— Milwaukee (A.L.)	C-1B	123	320	29	78	16	1	4	32	17	68	7	9	0-1	.244	.294	.338	.631	5	.993
1998— Milwaukee (N.L.)	C-1B	108	320	24	76	13	0	6	27	11	63	7	6	1-0	.238	.278	.334	.612	8	.987
— Beloit (Midw.)	DH-C	2	8	1	2	1	0	0	2	1	3	0	0	0-0	.250	.333	.375	.708	0	1.000
1999— Toronto (A.L.)	C	57	163	16	35	6	0	3	17	12	37	1	3	0-0	.215	.271	.307	.578	2	.995
2000— St. Louis (N.L.)	C-1B	128	417	43	109	22	1	6	47	32	96	4	11	0-0	.261	.317	.362	.679	5	.994
2001— St. Louis (N.L.)	C-1B	121	381	40	83	12	0	7	42	28	76	4	11	0-1	.218	.276	.304	.581	4	.995
2002— St. Louis (N.L.)	C-1B	110	315	31	77	12	1	3	35	32	49	2	3	1-3	.244	.313	.317	.630	4	.994
2003— St. Louis (N.L.)	C-1B	141	441	43	111	18	4	8	47	44	81	2	11	1-1	.252	.320	.356	.676	1	1.000
2004— St. Louis (N.L.)	C-1B	122	385	28	95	22	1	5	50	23	83	3	12	0-2	.247	.292	.348	.640	1	.999
American League totals (5 years)		394	1015	92	230	49	4	16	118	58	226	15	25	5-5	.227	.276	.330	.606	20	.990
National League totals (6 years)		730	2259	209	551	99	5	35	248	170	448	22	54	3-7	.244	.301	.339	.639	22	.995
Major League totals (11 years)		1124	3274	301	781	148	9	51	366	228	674	37	79	8-12	.239	.293	.336	.629	42	.994

DIVISION SERIES RECORD

Year	Team (League)	Pos.	G	AB	R	H	2B	3B	HR	RBI	BB	SO	HBP	GDP	SB-CS	Avg.	OBP	SLG	OPS	E	Avg.
2000— St. Louis (N.L.)		Did not play.																			
2001— St. Louis (N.L.)	C	4	10	0	2	0	0	0	0	0	3	0	0	0-0	.200	.200	.200	.400	0	1.000
2002— St. Louis (N.L.)	C	3	9	3	4	1	0	0	2	2	1	0	0	0-0	.444	.545	.556	1.101	0	1.000
2004— St. Louis (N.L.)	C	4	14	1	4	0	0	1	5	0	2	0	0	0-0	.286	.286	.500	.786	0	1.000
Division series totals (3 years)		11	33	4	10	1	0	1	7	2	6	0	0	0-0	.303	.343	.424	.767	0	1.000

CHAMPIONSHIP SERIES RECORD

Year	Team (League)	Pos.	G	AB	R	H	2B	3B	HR	RBI	BB	SO	HBP	GDP	SB-CS	Avg.	OBP	SLG	OPS	E	Avg.
2000— St. Louis (N.L.)		Did not play.																			
2002— St. Louis (N.L.)	C	5	19	2	6	2	0	1	1	0	2	0	0	0-0	.316	.316	.579	.895	0	1.000
2004— St. Louis (N.L.)	C	7	19	0	2	0	0	0	1	1	8	0	0	0-0	.105	.150	.105	.255	0	1.000
Champ. series totals (2 years)		12	38	2	8	2	0	1	1	1	10	0	0	0-0	.211	.231	.342	.573	0	1.000

WORLD SERIES RECORD

Year	Team (League)	Pos.	G	AB	R	H	2B	3B	HR	RBI	BB	SO	HBP	GDP	SB-CS	Avg.	OBP	SLG	OPS	E	Avg.
2004— St. Louis (N.L.)	C	4	8	0	2	0	0	0	2	0	3	0	0	0-0	.250	.200	.250	.450	0	1.000

MATOS, LUIS   OF

PERSONAL: Born October 30, 1978, in Bayamon, Puerto Rico. ... 6-0/208. ... Bats right, throws right. ... Full name: Luis David Matos. ... Name pronounced: MAH-tose. ... High school: Disciple of Christ Academy (Bayamon, Puerto Rico).

TRANSACTIONS/CAREER NOTES: Selected by Baltimore Orioles organization in 10th round of 1996 free-agent draft. ... On disabled list (March 30-August 24, 2001); included rehabilitation assignments to GCL Orioles, Frederick and Bowie. ... On Baltimore disabled list (March 29-June 6, 2002); included rehabilitation assignment to Frederick. ... On disabled list (July 22, 2004-remainder of season).

2004 GAMES PLAYED BY POSITION (MLB): OF—89.

Year	Team (League)	Pos.	G	AB	R	H	2B	3B	HR	RBI	BB	SO	HBP	GDP	SB-CS	Avg.	OBP	SLG	OPS	E	Avg.
1996— GC Orioles (GCL)	OF	43	130	21	38	2	0	0	13	15	18	2	3	12-7	.292	.374	.308	.682	1	.983
1997— Delmarva (S. Atl.)	OF	36	119	10	25	1	2	0	13	9	21	2	2	8-5	.210	.275	.252	.527	2	.972
— Bluefield (Appal.)	OF	61	240	37	66	7	3	2	35	20	36	4	5	26-4	.275	.340	.354	.694	3	.977
1998— Delmarva (S. Atl.)	OF	133	503	73	137	26	6	7	32	38	90	7	9	42-14	.272	.328	.390	.718	10	.964
— Bowie (East.)	OF	5	19	2	5	0	0	1	3	1	1	0	0	1-1	.263	.300	.421	.721	1	.833
1999— Frederick (Carolina)	OF	68	273	40	81	15	1	7	41	20	35	2	6	27-6	.297	.343	.436	.779	2	.987
— Bowie (East.)	OF	66	283	41	67	11	1	9	36	15	39	1	6	14-4	.237	.272	.378	.650	3	.982
2000— Rochester (Int'l)		11	35	2	6	1	0	0	0	3	8	1	0	2-0	.171	.256	.200	.456	0	1.000
— Bowie (East.)	OF	50	181	26	49	7	5	2	33	17	23	5	3	8-8	.271	.345	.398	.742	1	.984
— Baltimore (A.L.)	OF-DH	72	182	21	41	6	3	1	17	12	30	3	7	13-4	.225	.281	.308	.589	2	.988
2001— GC Orioles (GCL)	DH	3	14	1	4	0	0	2	2	0	3	0	0	0-0	.286	.286	.429	.714	...	
— Frederick (Carolina)	DH	2	7	3	3	0	1	0	2	1	3	0	0	0-0	.429	.500	.857	1.357	...	

M

Year Team (League)	Pos.	G	AB	R	H	2B	3B	HR	RBI	BB	SO	HBP	GDP	SB-CS	Avg.	OBP	SLG	OPS	E	Avg.
— Bowie (East.)	OF	13	46	6	14	5	0	1	8	5	7	1	0	0-1	.304	.385	.478	.863	1	.955
— Baltimore (A.L.)	OF	31	98	16	21	7	0	4	12	11	30	1	1	7-0	.214	.300	.408	.708	1	.985
2002— Frederick (Carolina)	OF	3	12	2	4	1	0	0	1	2	3	0	0	0-0	.333	.429	.417	.845	0	1.000
— Bowie (East.)	OF	62	218	34	60	14	2	9	40	32	45	2	6	14-4	.275	.370	.482	.852	1	.992
— Baltimore (A.L.)	OF-DH	17	31	0	4	1	0	0	1	1	6	0	1	1-0	.129	.156	.161	.318	0	1.000
2003— Ottawa (Int'l)	OF	45	175	28	53	16	4	1	25	13	34	1	8	6-1	.303	.347	.457	.804	1	.990
— Baltimore (A.L.)	OF-DH	109	439	70	133	23	3	13	36	28	90	7	9	15-7	.303	.353	.458	.811	4	.987
2004— Baltimore (A.L.)	OF	89	330	36	74	18	0	6	28	19	60	5	7	12-4	.224	.275	.333	.609	1	.996
Major League totals (5 years)		318	1080	143	273	55	6	24	103	71	216	16	25	48-15	.253	.307	.381	.688	8	.990

MATSUI, HIDEKI — OF

PERSONAL: Born June 12, 1974, in Kanazawa, Japan. ... 6-2/230. ... Bats left, throws right. ... Name pronounced: mat-SOO-ee.

TRANSACTIONS/CAREER NOTES: Signed as a free agent by New York Yankees (December 19, 2002).

2004 GAMES PLAYED BY POSITION (MLB): OF—160.

Year Team (League)	Pos.	G	AB	R	H	2B	3B	HR	RBI	BB	SO	HBP	GDP	SB-CS	Avg.	OBP	SLG	OPS	E	Avg.
1993— Yomiuri (Jp. Cen.)		57	184	27	41	9	0	11	27				...	1-0	.223	.296	.451	.747	1	...
1994— Yomiuri (Jp. Cen.)		130	503	70	148	23	4	20	66	57	101	4	...	6-3	.294	.368	.475	.843	5	...
1995— Yomiuri (Jp. Cen.)		131	501	76	142	31	1	22	80	62	93	2	...	9-7	.283	.363	.481	.844	3	...
1996— Yomiuri (Jp. Cen.)		130	487	97	153	34	1	38	99	71	98	4	...	7-2	.314	.401	.622	1.023	6	...
1997— Yomiuri (Jp. Cen.)		135	484	93	144	18	0	37	103	100	84	6	...	9-3	.298	.419	.564	.984	7	...
1998— Yomiuri (Jp. Cen.)		135	487	103	142	24	3	34	100	104	101	8	...	3-5	.292	.421	.563	.984	4	...
1999— Yomiuri (Jp. Cen.)		135	471	100	143	24	2	42	95	93	99	2	...	0-4	.304	.416	.631	1.047	1	...
2000— Yomiuri (Jp. Cen.)		135	474	116	150	32	1	42	108	106	108	2	...	5-2	.316	.438	.654	1.092	2	...
2001— Yomiuri (Jp. Cen.)		140	481	107	160	23	3	36	104	120	96	3	...	3-3	.333	.463	.617	1.081	6	...
2002— Yomiuri (Jp. Cen.)		140	500	112	167	27	1	50	107	114	104	6	...	3-4	.334	.461	.692	1.153	2	...
2003— New York (A.L.)	OF-DH	163	623	82	179	42	1	16	106	63	86	3	25	2-2	.287	.353	.435	.788	8	.977
2004— New York (A.L.)	OF	162	584	109	174	34	2	31	108	88	103	3	11	3-0	.298	.390	.522	.912	7	.978
Major League totals (2 years)		325	1207	191	353	76	3	47	214	151	189	6	36	5-2	.292	.371	.477	.848	15	.977

DIVISION SERIES RECORD

Year Team (League)	Pos.	G	AB	R	H	2B	3B	HR	RBI	BB	SO	HBP	GDP	SB-CS	Avg.	OBP	SLG	OPS	E	Avg.
2003— New York (A.L.)	OF	4	15	2	4	1	0	1	3	2	3	0	1	0-0	.267	.353	.533	.886	0	1.000
2004— New York (A.L.)	OF	4	17	3	7	1	0	1	3	3	4	0	0	0-0	.412	.476	.647	1.123	0	1.000
Division series totals (2 years)		8	32	5	11	2	0	2	6	5	7	0	1	0-0	.344	.421	.594	1.015	0	1.000

CHAMPIONSHIP SERIES RECORD

Year Team (League)	Pos.	G	AB	R	H	2B	3B	HR	RBI	BB	SO	HBP	GDP	SB-CS	Avg.	OBP	SLG	OPS	E	Avg.
2003— New York (A.L.)	OF	7	26	3	8	3	0	0	4	1	3	0	1	0-0	.308	.321	.423	.745	1	.889
2004— New York (A.L.)	OF	7	34	9	14	6	1	2	10	2	4	0	0	0-0	.412	.444	.824	1.268	0	1.000
Champ. series totals (2 years)		14	60	12	22	9	1	2	14	3	7	0	1	0-0	.367	.391	.650	1.041	1	.960

WORLD SERIES RECORD

Year Team (League)	Pos.	G	AB	R	H	2B	3B	HR	RBI	BB	SO	HBP	GDP	SB-CS	Avg.	OBP	SLG	OPS	E	Avg.
2003— New York (A.L.)	OF	6	23	1	6	0	0	1	4	3	2	1	0	0-0	.261	.370	.391	.762	0	1.000

ALL-STAR GAME RECORD

	G	AB	R	H	2B	3B	HR	RBI	BB	SO	HBP	GDP	SB-CS	Avg.	OBP	SLG	OPS	E	Avg.
All-Star Game totals (2 years)	2	3	0	1	0	0	0	0	1	0	0		0-0	.333	.333	.333	.667	0	1.000

MATSUI, KAZUO — SS

PERSONAL: Born October 23, 1975, in Osaka, Japan. ... 5-10/185. ... Bats both, throws right. ... High school: PL Gakeun (Osaka, Japan).

TRANSACTIONS/CAREER NOTES: Signed as a free agent by New York Mets (December 10, 2003). ... On disabled list (August 9-September 24, 2004).

2004 GAMES PLAYED BY POSITION (MLB): SS—110, 2B—3.

Year Team (League)	Pos.	G	AB	R	H	2B	3B	HR	RBI	BB	SO	HBP	GDP	SB-CS	Avg.	OBP	SLG	OPS	E	Avg.
1995— Seibu (Jp. Pac.)		69	204	25	45	9	1	2	62	7	26	0	4	21-1	.221	.245	.304	.549	...	...
1996— Seibu (Jp. Pac.)		130	473	51	134	22	5	1	29	14	93	3	2	50-9	.283	.307	.357	.664	...	...
1997— Seibu (Jp. Pac.)		135	576	91	178	23	13	7	63	44	89	5	4	62-15	.309	.362	.431	.793	...	...
1998— Seibu (Jp. Pac.)		135	575	92	179	38	5	9	58	55	89	1	10	43-14	.311	.370	.442	.812	...	...
1999— Seibu (Jp. Pac.)		135	539	87	178	29	4	15	67	56	75	0	7	32-7	.330	.389	.482	.872	...	...
2000— Seibu (Jp. Pac.)		135	550	99	177	40	11	23	90	46	60	2	8	26-3	.322	.372	.560	.932	...	...
2001— Seibu (Jp. Pac.)		140	552	94	170	28	2	24	76	46	83	6	13	26-0	.308	.365	.496	.861	...	...
2002— Seibu (Jp. Pac.)		140	582	119	193	46	6	36	87	53	112	4	4	33-11	.332	.389	.617	1.006	...	...
2003— Seibu (Jp. Pac.)		140	587	104	179	36	4	33	84	55	124	4	4	13-10	.305	.365	.549	.914	...	...
2004— New York (N.L.)	SS-2B	114	460	65	125	32	2	7	44	40	97	2	3	14-3	.272	.331	.396	.727	24	.955
Major League totals (1 year)		114	460	65	125	32	2	7	44	40	97	2	3	14-3	.272	.331	.396	.727	24	.955

MATTHEWS, MIKE — P

PERSONAL: Born October 24, 1973, in Fredericksburg, Va. ... 6-2/205. ... Throws left, bats left. ... Full name: Michael Scott Matthews. ... High school: Woodbridge Senior (Va.). ... Junior college: Montgomery (Md.).

TRANSACTIONS/CAREER NOTES: Selected by Cleveland Indians organization in second round of 1992 free-agent draft. ... Traded by Indians to Boston Red Sox for IF Jose Olmeda (August 4, 1999). ... Traded by Red Sox with C David Menham to St. Louis Cardinals for P Kent Mercker (August 24, 1999). ... On disabled list (July 16, 2000-remainder of season; and August 21-September 11, 2001). ... Traded by Cardinals to Milwaukee Brewers (September 11, 2002), completing deal in which Brewers traded P Jamey Wright and cash to Cardinals for OF Chris Morris and a player to be named (August 29, 2002). ... Claimed on waivers by San Diego Padres (March 26, 2003). ... Signed as a free agent by Cincinnati Reds organization (January 16, 2004). ... On disabled list (July 3-September 3, 2004); included rehabilitation assignment to Louisville. ... Refused minor league assignment and became a free agent (October 10, 2004).

CAREER HITTING: 3-for-25 (.120), 2 R, 0 2B, 0 3B, 1 HR, 1 RBI.

Year Team (League)	W	L	Pct.	ERA	WHIP	G	GS	CG	ShO	Hld.	Sv.-Opp.	IP	H	R	ER	HR	BB-IBB	SO	Avg.
1992— Burlington (Appalachian) ..	7	0	1.000	1.01	0.96	10	10	0	0	...	0-...	62.1	33	13	7	1	27-0	55	.156
— Watertown (N.Y.-Penn.)	1	0	1.000	3.27	1.64	2	2	2	0	...	0-...	11.0	10	4	4	0	8-0	5	.263

Year—Team (League)	W	L	Pct.	ERA	WHIP	G	GS	CG	ShO	Hld	Sv.-Opp.	IP	H	R	ER	HR	BB-IBB	SO	Avg.
1993—									Did not play.										
1994—Columbus (S. Atl.)	6	8	.429	3.08	1.37	23	23	0	0	...	0-...	119.2	120	53	41	8	44-1	99	.270
1995—Cant./Akr. (Eastern)	5	8	.385	5.93	1.68	15	15	1	0	...	0-...	74.1	82	62	49	6	43-1	37	.283
1996—Cant./Akr. (Eastern)	9	11	.450	4.66	1.55	27	27	3	0	...	0-...	162.1	178	96	84	13	74-3	112	.287
1997—Buffalo (A.A.)	0	2	.000	7.71	2.00	5	5	0	0	...	0-...	21.0	32	19	18	7	10-0	17	.344
—Akron (East.)	6	8	.429	3.82	1.53	19	19	3	1	...	0-...	113.0	116	62	48	13	57-0	69	.273
1998—Buffalo (Int'l)	9	6	.600	4.63	1.57	24	23	0	0	...	0-...	130.1	137	79	67	19	68-1	86	.275
1999—Buffalo (Int'l)	1	2	.333	7.59	1.92	25	0	0	0	...	0-...	21.1	23	18	18	3	18-0	16	.303
—Akron (East.)	0	5	.000	8.77	1.99	6	6	0	0	...	0-...	25.2	36	30	25	7	15-0	10	.336
—Trenton (East.)	0	0	...	4.63	1.71	3	3	0	0	...	0-...	11.2	11	7	6	1	9-0	8	.268
—Arkansas (Texas)	2	0	1.000	0.00	0.33	2	2	1	1	...	0-...	12.0	3	0	0	0	1-0	10	.079
2000—Memphis (PCL)	3	1	.750	3.12	1.25	9	9	0	0	...	0-0	52.0	33	19	18	4	32-1	50	.182
—St. Louis (N.L.)	0	0	...	11.57	2.68	14	0	0	0	2	0-0	9.1	15	12	12	2	10-2	8	.349
2001—St. Louis (N.L.)	3	4	.429	3.24	1.20	51	10	0	0	3	1-3	89.0	74	32	32	11	33-4	72	.227
2002—St. Louis (N.L.)	2	1	.667	3.89	1.49	43	0	0	0	4	0-2	41.2	40	21	18	5	22-2	32	.260
—Milwaukee (N.L.)	0	0	...	4.50	2.50	4	0	0	0	0	0-0	4.0	3	2	2	0	7-1	2	.214
2003—San Diego (N.L.)	6	4	.600	4.45	1.45	77	0	0	0	16	0-3	64.2	65	34	32	4	29-5	44	.271
2004—Louisville (Int'l)	1	0	1.000	1.53	0.96	15	0	0	0	...	1-...	17.2	12	3	3	1	5-0	16	.188
—Cincinnati (N.L.)	2	1	.667	6.30	1.57	35	0	0	0	5	0-0	30.0	31	22	21	7	16-1	15	.265
Major League totals (5 years)	13	10	.565	4.41	1.45	224	10	0	0	30	1-8	238.2	228	123	117	29	117-15	173	.255

DIVISION SERIES RECORD

Year Team (League)	W	L	Pct.	ERA	WHIP	G	GS	CG	ShO	Hld.	Sv.-Opp.	IP	H	R	ER	HR	BB-IBB	SO	Avg.
2001—St. Louis (N.L.)	0	1	.000	40.50	6.00	1	0	0	0	0	0-1	.2	4	3	3	1	0-0	0	.667

MATTHEWS JR., GARY — OF

PERSONAL: Born August 25, 1974, in San Francisco, Calif. ... 6-3/225. ... Bats both, throws right. ... Full name: Gary Nathaniel Matthews Jr. ... High school: Granada Hills (Calif.). ... Junior college: Mission (Calif.). ... Son of Gary Matthews, coach, Chicago Cubs, and outfielder with five major league teams (1972-87).

TRANSACTIONS/CAREER NOTES: Selected by San Diego Padres organization in 13th round of 1993 free-agent draft. ... Traded by Padres to Chicago Cubs for P Rodney Myers (March 23, 2000). ... Claimed on waivers by Pittsburgh Pirates (August 10, 2001). ... Traded by Pirates to New York Mets for cash (December 28, 2001). ... Traded by Mets to Baltimore Orioles for P John Bale (April 3, 2002). ... On disabled list (August 25-September 11, 2002). ... Claimed on waivers by Padres (May 23, 2003). ... Claimed on waivers by Atlanta Braves (November 24, 2003). ... Released by Braves (March 31, 2004). ... Signed by Texas Rangers organization (April 7, 2004).

2004 GAMES PLAYED BY POSITION (MLB): OF—85, DH—1.

Year—Team (League)	Pos.	G	AB	R	H	2B	3B	HR	RBI	BB	SO	HBP	GDP	SB-CS	Avg.	OBP	SLG	OPS	E	Avg.
1994—Spokane (N'west)	2B-OF	52	191	23	40	6	1	0	18	19	58	2	4	3-5	.209	.286	.251	.538	4	.961
1995—Clinton (Midw.)	OF	128	421	57	100	18	4	2	40	68	109	6	8	28-8	.238	.349	.314	.663	9	.966
1996—Rancho Cuca. (Calif.)	OF	123	435	65	118	21	11	7	54	60	102	6	11	7-8	.271	.366	.418	.784	16	.934
1997—Rancho Cuca. (Calif.)	OF	69	268	66	81	15	4	8	40	49	57	3	4	10-4	.302	.416	.478	.893	5	.959
—Mobile (Sou.)	OF	28	90	14	22	4	1	2	12	15	29	1	1	3-1	.244	.352	.378	.730	2	.960
1998—Mobile (Sou.)	OF	72	254	62	78	15	4	7	51	55	50	1	6	11-1	.307	.428	.480	.908	1	.995
1999—Las Vegas (PCL)	OF	121	422	57	108	23	3	9	52	58	104	7	13	17-6	.256	.352	.386	.739	7	.976
—San Diego (N.L.)	OF	23	36	4	8	0	0	0	7	9	9	0	1	2-0	.222	.378	.222	.600	0	1.000
2000—Iowa (PCL)	OF	60	211	27	51	11	3	5	22	18	41	0	4	6-1	.242	.300	.393	.693	4	.970
—Chicago (N.L.)	OF	80	158	24	30	1	2	4	14	15	28	1	2	3-0	.190	.264	.297	.562	2	.978
2001—Chicago (N.L.)	OF	106	258	41	56	9	1	9	30	38	55	1	4	5-3	.217	.320	.364	.684	4	.976
—Pittsburgh (N.L.)	OF	46	147	22	36	6	1	5	14	22	45	0	4	3-2	.245	.341	.347	.743	3	.971
2002—New York (N.L.)		2	1	0	0	0	0	0	0	0	0	0	0	0-0	.000	.000	.000	.000	...	...
—Baltimore (A.L.)	OF-DH	109	344	54	95	25	3	7	38	43	69	1	4	15-5	.276	.355	.427	.782	6	.969
2003—Baltimore (A.L.)	OF-DH	41	162	21	33	12	1	2	20	9	29	1	4	0-3	.204	.250	.327	.577	0	1.000
—San Diego (N.L.)	OF	103	306	50	83	19	1	4	22	34	66	1	4	12-5	.271	.346	.379	.725	1	.993
2004—Oklahoma (PCL)	OF-DH	38	145	33	47	9	4	9	36	23	29	0	2	4-1	.324	.409	.628	1.037	2	.971
—Texas (A.L.)	OF-DH	87	280	37	77	17	1	11	36	33	64	1	1	5-1	.275	.360	.461	.811	2	.990
American League totals (3 years)		237	786	112	205	54	5	20	94	85	162	3	9	20-9	.261	.333	.419	.751	8	.984
National League totals (5 years)		360	906	141	213	35	5	22	87	118	203	3	15	25-10	.235	.325	.358	.683	10	.981
Major League totals (6 years)		597	1692	253	418	89	10	42	181	203	365	6	24	45-19	.247	.328	.386	.714	18	.983

MAUER, JOE — C

PERSONAL: Born April 19, 1983, in St. Paul, Minn. ... 6-4/220. ... Bats left, throws right. ... Full name: Joseph Patrick Mauer. ... High school: Cretin-Durham Hall (St. Paul). ... Brother of Jake Mauer, infielder in the Twins organization.

TRANSACTIONS/CAREER NOTES: Selected by Minnesota Twins organization in first round (first pick overall) of 2001 free-agent draft ... On disabled list (April 7-June 2 and July 16, 2004-remainder of season); included rehabilitation assignments to Fort Myers and Rochester.

2004 GAMES PLAYED BY POSITION (MLB): C—32, DH—1.

Year—Team (League)	Pos.	G	AB	R	H	2B	3B	HR	RBI	BB	SO	HBP	GDP	SB-CS	Avg.	OBP	SLG	OPS	E	Avg.
2001—Elizabethton (App.)	C	32	110	14	44	6	2	0	14	19	10	1	5	4-0	.400	.492	.491	.983	4	.980
2002—Quad City (Midw.)	C-1B	110	411	58	124	23	1	4	62	61	42	2	16	0-0	.302	.393	.392	.785	6	.993
2003—Fort Myers (FSL)	C-1B	62	233	25	78	13	1	4	44	24	24	1	11	3-0	.335	.395	.412	.807	0	1.000
—New Britain (East.)	C	73	276	48	94	17	1	4	41	25	25	5	10	0-0	.341	.400	.453	.853	3	.992
2004—Fort Myers (FSL)	DH-C	2	6	0	4	0	0	0	2	2	2	0	0	0-0	.667	.750	.667	1.417	0	1.000
—Rochester (Int'l)	DH-C	5	19	1	6	3	0	0	2	1	4	0	1	0-0	.316	.333	.474	.807	0	1.000
—Minnesota (A.L.)	C-DH	35	107	18	33	8	1	6	17	11	14	1	1	1-0	.308	.369	.570	.939	2	.991
Major League totals (1 year)		35	107	18	33	8	1	6	17	11	14	1	1	1-0	.308	.369	.570	.939	2	.991

MAURER, DAVE — P

PERSONAL: Born February 23, 1975, in Minneapolis, Minn. ... 6-2/205. ... Throws left, bats right. ... Full name: David Charles Maurer. ... Name pronounced: MOW-er. ... High school: Apple Valley (Minn.). ... College: Oklahoma State. ... Brother of Mike Maurer, pitcher, Oakland Athletics organization; son of Thomas Maurer, pitcher in Minnesota Twins organization.

TRANSACTIONS/CAREER NOTES: Selected by Boston Red Sox organization in 34th round of 1994 free-agent draft; did not sign. ... Selected by San Diego Padres organization in 11th round of 1997 free-agent draft. ... Selected by San Francisco Giants from Padres organization in Rule 5 major league draft (December 13, 1999). ... Returned to Padres (March 20, 2000). ... Released by Padres (June 1, 2001). ... Signed by Cincinnati Reds organization (June 1, 2001). ... Released by Reds (July 26, 2001). ... Signed

M

by Oakland Athletics organization (July 29, 2001). ... Signed as a free agent by Cleveland Indians organization (December 18, 2001). ... Signed as a free agent by Toronto Blue Jays organization (November 20, 2003).

CAREER HITTING: 0-for-1 (.000), 0 R, 0 2B, 0 3B, 0 HR, 0 RBI.

Year Team (League)	W	L	Pct.	ERA	WHIP	G	GS	CG	ShO	Hld.	Sv.-Opp.	IP	H	R	ER	HR	BB-IBB	SO	Avg.
1997— Clinton (Midw.)	0	4	.000	2.88	1.14	25	0	0	0	...	3-...	34.1	24	15	11	1	15-0	43	.194
1998— Rancho Cuca. (Calif.)	5	2	.714	2.70	1.22	48	0	0	0	...	5-...	83.1	56	27	25	1	46-1	93	.190
1999— Mobile (Sou.)	4	4	.500	3.63	1.18	54	0	0	0	...	3-...	72.0	59	30	29	7	26-5	59	.221
2000— Mobile (Sou.)	1	2	.333	2.70	0.68	24	0	0	0	...	0-...	26.2	15	8	8	2	3-1	28	.165
— Las Vegas (PCL)	4	1	.800	3.25	1.40	35	0	0	0	...	0-...	44.1	47	19	16	5	15-1	44	.264
— San Diego (N.L.)	1	0	1.000	3.68	1.36	14	0	0	0	2	0-1	14.2	15	8	6	2	5-1	13	.263
2001— San Diego (N.L.)	0	0	...	10.80	2.40	3	0	0	0	0	0-0	5.0	8	6	6	1	4-0	4	.348
— Portland (PCL)	0	0	...	4.34	1.07	17	0	0	0	...	1-...	18.2	11	9	9	4	9-2	21	.172
— Louisville (Int'l)	0	1	.000	4.15	1.15	18	0	0	0	...	1-...	21.2	18	11	10	4	7-0	23	.225
— Sacramento (PCL)	0	0	...	5.54	1.69	11	0	0	0	...	0-...	13.0	14	9	8	2	8-0	21	.269
2002— Buffalo (Int'l)	5	1	.833	2.90	1.08	36	3	0	0	...	5-...	68.1	50	27	22	6	24-0	73	.204
— Cleveland (A.L.)	0	1	.000	13.50	2.25	2	0	0	0	0	0-0	1.1	3	2	2	1	0-0	0	.429
2004— Toronto (A.L.)	0	0	...	54.00	8.25	3	0	0	0	0	0-0	1.1	6	8	8	1	5-0	1	.600
— Syracuse (Int'l)	0	0	...	3.56	1.28	43	4	0	0	...	2-...	65.2	58	27	26	7	26-0	64	.242
American League totals (2 years)	0	1	.000	33.75	5.25	5	0	0	0	0	0-0	2.2	9	10	10	2	5-0	1	.529
National League totals (2 years)	1	0	1.000	5.49	1.63	17	0	0	0	2	0-1	19.2	23	14	12	3	9-1	17	.288
Major League totals (4 years)	1	1	.500	8.87	2.06	22	0	0	0	2	0-1	22.1	32	24	22	5	14-1	18	.330

MAY, DARRELL — P

PERSONAL: Born June 13, 1972, in San Bernardino, Calif. ... 6-2/185. ... Throws left, bats left. ... Full name: Darrell Kevin May. ... High school: Rogue River (Ore.). ... Junior college: Sacramento (Calif.) City College.

TRANSACTIONS/CAREER NOTES: Selected by Atlanta Braves organization in 46th round of 1992 free-agent draft. ... Claimed on waivers by Pittsburgh Pirates (April 4, 1996). ... Claimed on waivers by California Angels (September 6, 1996). ... Angels franchise renamed Anaheim Angels for 1997 season. ... Released by Angels (March 27, 1998). ... Signed as a free agent by Kansas City Royals organization (December 17, 2001). ... On disabled list (March 27-April 13 and April 14-May 18, 2002) included rehabilitation assignments to Omaha and Wichita. ... Traded by Royals with P Ryan Bukvich to San Diego Padres for OF Terrence Long, P Dennis Tankersley and cash (November 8, 2004).

CAREER HITTING: 1-for-17 (.059), 1 R, 0 2B, 0 3B, 0 HR, 0 RBI.

Year Team (League)	W	L	Pct.	ERA	WHIP	G	GS	CG	ShO	Hld.	Sv.-Opp.	IP	H	R	ER	HR	BB-IBB	SO	Avg.
1992— GC Braves (GCL)	4	3	.571	1.36	0.89	12	7	0	0	...	1-...	53.0	34	13	8	0	13-0	61	.182
1993— Macon (S. Atl.)	10	4	.714	2.24	0.99	17	17	0	0	...	0-...	104.1	81	29	26	6	22-1	111	.213
— Durham (Caro.)	5	2	.714	2.09	1.16	9	9	0	0	...	0-...	51.2	44	18	12	4	16-0	47	.232
1994— Durham (Caro.)	8	2	.800	3.01	1.22	12	12	1	0	...	0-...	74.2	74	29	25	6	17-1	73	.259
— Greenville (Sou.)	5	3	.625	3.11	1.23	11	11	1	0	...	0-...	63.2	61	25	22	4	17-0	42	.251
1995— Greenville (Sou.)	2	8	.200	3.55	1.11	15	15	0	0	...	0-...	91.1	81	44	36	18	20-0	79	.233
— Richmond (Int'l)	4	2	.667	3.71	1.35	9	9	0	0	...	0-...	51.0	53	21	21	1	16-1	42	.270
— Atlanta (N.L.)	0	0	...	11.25	2.50	2	0	0	0	0	0-0	4.0	10	5	5	0	0-0	1	.500
1996— Calgary (PCL)	7	6	.538	4.10	1.38	23	22	1	1	...	0-...	131.2	146	64	60	17	36-6	75	.284
— Pittsburgh (N.L.)	0	1	.000	9.35	2.19	5	2	0	0	1	0-0	8.2	15	10	9	5	4-0	5	.357
— California (A.L.)	0	0	...	10.13	1.88	5	0	0	0	0	0-0	2.2	3	3	3	1	2-0	1	.333
1997— Vancouver (PCL)	7	5	.583	3.26	1.20	13	12	2	2	...	0-...	80.0	65	31	29	10	31-0	62	.223
— Anaheim (A.L.)	2	1	.667	5.23	1.57	29	2	0	0	...	0-1	51.2	56	31	30	6	25-2	42	.277
1998— Hanshin (Jp. Cn.)	4	9	.308	3.47	1.37	21	21	1	1	...	0-...	129.2	122	55	50	...	55-...	94	...
— Hanshin (Jp. West.)	1	2	.333	5.82	1.24	5	3	0	0	...	0-...	17.0	19	11	11	...	2-...	11	...
1999— Hanshin (Jp. Cn.)	6	7	.462	4.25	1.24	18	18	0	0	...	0-...	112.1	101	56	53	...	38-...	113	...
— Hanshin (Jp. West.)	1	0	1.000	0.00	0.60	2	2	0	0	...	0-...	10.0	4	1	0	...	2-...	12	...
2000— Yomiuri (Jp. Cen.)	12	7	.632	2.95	1.05	24	24	3	3	...	0-...	155.1	123	52	51	...	40-...	165	...
— Yomiuri (Jp. East.)	0	0	...	0.00	0.75	1	0	0	0	...	0-...	4.0	2	0	0	...	1-...	4	...
2001— Yomiuri (Jp. Cen.)	10	8	.556	4.13	1.29	26	26	1	0	...	0-...	159.0	160	74	73	...	45-...	168	...
2002— Omaha (PCL)	1	0	1.000	0.75	0.67	2	2	0	0	...	0-...	12.0	8	1	1	0	0-0	9	.471
— Kansas City (A.L.)	4	10	.286	5.35	1.48	30	21	2	1	0	0-1	131.1	144	83	78	28	50-3	95	.277
— Wichita (Texas)	0	0	...	2.08	1.15	1	1	0	0	...	0-...	4.1	4	1	1	0	1-0	5	.235
2003— Kansas City (A.L.)	10	8	.556	3.77	1.19	35	32	2	1	0	0-1	210.0	197	98	88	31	53-1	115	.246
2004— Kansas City (A.L.)	9	* 19	.321	5.61	1.55	31	31	3	1	0	0-0	186.0	234	130	116	38	55-4	120	.306
American League totals (5 years)	25	38	.397	4.87	1.41	130	86	7	3	0	0-3	581.2	634	345	315	104	185-10	373	.276
National League totals (2 years)	0	1	.000	9.95	2.29	7	2	0	0	1	0-0	12.2	25	15	14	5	4-0	6	.403
Major League totals (6 years)	25	39	.391	4.98	1.43	137	88	7	3	1	0-3	594.1	659	360	329	109	189-10	379	.279

MAYNE, BRENT — C

PERSONAL: Born April 19, 1968, in Loma Linda, Calif. ... 6-1/190. ... Bats left, throws right. ... Full name: Brent Danem Mayne. ... High school: Costa Mesa (Calif.). ... College: Cal State Fullerton.

TRANSACTIONS/CAREER NOTES: Selected by Kansas City Royals organization in first round (13th pick overall) of 1989 free-agent draft. ... Traded by Royals to New York Mets for OF Al Shirley (December 19, 1995). ... Signed as a free agent by Seattle Mariners organization (January 10, 1997). ... Released by Mariners (March 28, 1997). ... Signed by Oakland Athletics organization (April 8, 1997). ... Signed as a free agent by San Francisco Giants (November 21, 1997). ... Signed as a free agent by Colorado Rockies (December 9, 1999). ... Traded by Rockies to Royals for P Mac Suzuki and C Sal Fasano (June 24, 2001). ... On disabled list (April 30-May 28, 2002); included rehabilitation assignment to Wichita. ... On suspended list (September 25-27, 2002). ... Signed as a free agent by Arizona Diamondbacks (December 18, 2003). ... On disabled list (June 6-July 15, 2004); included rehabilitation assignment to Tucson. ... Traded by Diamondbacks with OF Steve Finley for C Koyie Hill, P Bill Murphy and OF Reggie Abercrombie (July 31, 2004). ... Career major league pitching: 1-0, 0.00 ERA, 1 G, 1.0 IP, 0 H, 0 R, 0 ER, 1 BB, 0 SO.

2004 GAMES PLAYED BY POSITION (MLB): C—77, 1B—1.

Year Team (League)	Pos.	G	AB	R	H	2B	3B	HR	RBI	BB	SO	HBP	GDP	SB-CS	Avg.	OBP	SLG	OPS	E	Avg.
1989— Baseball City (FSL)	C	7	24	5	13	3	1	0	8	6	3	0	0	0-1	.542	.542	.750	1.292	0	1.000
1990— Memphis (Sou.)	C	115	412	48	110	16	3	2	61	52	51	2	13	5-2	.267	.346	.335	.681	11	.983
— Kansas City (A.L.)	C	5	13	2	3	0	0	0	1	3	3	0	0	0-1	.231	.375	.231	.606	1	.970
1991— Kansas City (A.L.)	DH-C	85	231	22	58	8	0	3	31	23	42	0	6	2-4	.251	.315	.325	.640	6	.987
1992— Kansas City (A.L.)	C-3B	82	213	16	48	10	0	0	18	11	26	0	5	0-4	.225	.260	.272	.532	3	.991
1993— Kansas City (A.L.)	C-DH	71	205	22	52	9	1	2	22	18	31	1	6	3-2	.254	.317	.337	.654	2	.995
1994— Kansas City (A.L.)	C-DH	46	144	19	37	5	1	2	20	14	27	0	1	1-0	.257	.323	.347	.670	1	.996

Year	Team (League)	Pos.	G	AB	R	H	2B	3B	HR	RBI	BB	SO	HBP	GDP	SB-CS	Avg.	OBP	SLG	OPS	E	Avg.
1995— Kansas City (A.L.)	C	110	307	23	77	18	1	1	27	25	41	3	16	0-1	.251	.313	.326	.638	3	.995
1996— New York (N.L.)	C	70	99	9	26	6	0	1	6	12	22	0	4	0-1	.263	.342	.354	.696	0	1.000
1997— Edmonton (PCL)	C	2	3	0	0	0	0	0	0	0	1	0	0	0-0	.000	.000	.000	.000	0	1.000
— Oakland (A.L.)	C	85	256	29	74	12	0	6	22	18	33	4	6	1-0	.289	.343	.406	.749	2	.996
1998— San Francisco (N.L.)	C	94	275	26	75	15	0	3	32	37	47	1	8	2-1	.273	.359	.360	.719	5	.991
1999— San Francisco (N.L.)	C	117	322	39	97	32	0	2	39	43	65	5	16	2-2	.301	.389	.419	.808	3	.995
2000— Colorado (N.L.)	C-P	117	335	36	101	21	0	6	64	47	48	1	12	1-3	.301	.381	.418	.799	6	.990
2001— Colorado (N.L.)	C-1B	49	160	15	53	7	0	0	20	16	24	0	4	0-0	.331	.385	.375	.760	1	.997
— Kansas City (A.L.)	C	51	166	13	40	4	1	2	20	10	17	1	8	1-2	.241	.283	.313	.597	2	.993
2002— Kansas City (A.L.)	C	101	326	35	77	8	2	4	30	34	54	2	8	4-4	.236	.309	.310	.619	4	.993
— Wichita (Texas)	C	2	4	0	2	0	0	0	1	1	0	0	1	0-0	.500	.600	.500	1.100	0	1.000
2003— Kansas City (A.L.)	C	113	372	39	91	17	1	6	36	32	59	3	10	0-2	.245	.307	.344	.651	4	.994
2004— Tucson (PCL)	C	5	11	1	1	0	0	0	0	1	4	0	0	0-0	.091	.167	.091	.258	0	1.000
— Arizona (N.L.)	C-1B	36	94	9	24	6	1	0	10	13	17	0	5	0-0	.255	.343	.340	.683	2	.990
— Los Angeles (N.L.)	C	47	96	5	18	0	0	0	5	14	24	0	2	0-0	.188	.286	.188	.473	0	1.000
American League totals (10 years)		749	2233	220	557	91	7	26	227	188	333	14	68	12-20	.249	.309	.331	.641	28	.993
National League totals (6 years)		530	1381	139	394	87	1	12	176	182	247	7	51	6-7	.285	.367	.376	.743	17	.994
Major League totals (15 years)		1279	3614	359	951	178	8	38	403	370	580	21	119	18-27	.263	.332	.348	.680	45	.993

DIVISION SERIES RECORD

Year	Team (League)	Pos.	G	AB	R	H	2B	3B	HR	RBI	BB	SO	HBP	GDP	SB-CS	Avg.	OBP	SLG	OPS	E	Avg.
2004— Los Angeles (N.L.)	C	4	6	1	2	0	0	0	0	2	0	0	0	0-0	.333	.500	.333	.833	0	1.000

MCCARTY, DAVE   1B

PERSONAL: Born November 23, 1969, in Houston, Texas. ... 6-5/215. ... Bats right, throws left. ... Full name: David Andrew McCarty. ... High school: Sharpstown (Houston). ... College: Stanford.

TRANSACTIONS/CAREER NOTES: Selected by Minnesota Twins organization in first round (third pick overall) of 1991 free-agent draft. ... Traded by Twins to Cincinnati Reds for P John Courtright (June 8, 1995). ... Traded by Reds with OF Deion Sanders and Ps Ricky Pickett, Scott Service and John Roper to San Francisco Giants for OF Darren Lewis and Ps Mark Portugal and Dave Burba (July 21, 1995). ... On disabled list (June 6-27, 1996); included rehabilitation assignment to Phoenix. ... Traded by Giants to Seattle Mariners for OFs Jay Leach and Scott Smith (January 30, 1998). ... Signed as a free agent by Detroit Tigers organization (December 18, 1998). ... Signed as a free agent by Oakland Athletics organization (November 23, 1999). ... Traded by A's to Kansas City Royals for cash (March 24, 2000). ... Released by Royals (May 15, 2002). ... Signed by Tampa Bay Devil Rays organization (May 21, 2002). ... Released by Devil Rays (August 7, 2002). ... Signed by A's organization (November 18, 2002). ... Claimed on waivers by Boston Red Sox (August 4, 2003). ... On disabled list (August 13-September 1, 2004); included rehabilitation assignments to Lowell and Pawtucket. ... Career major league pitching: 0-0, 2.45 ERA, 3 G, 3.2 IP, 2 H, 1 R, 1 ER, 1 BB, 4 SO.

2004 GAMES PLAYED BY POSITION (MLB): 1B—67, OF—17, P—3, DH—3.

Year	Team (League)	Pos.	G	AB	R	H	2B	3B	HR	RBI	BB	SO	HBP	GDP	SB-CS	Avg.	OBP	SLG	OPS	E	Avg.
1991— Visalia (Calif.)	OF	15	50	16	19	3	0	3	8	13	7	3	0	3-1	.380	.530	.620	1.150	0	1.000
— Orlando (South.)	OF	28	88	18	23	4	0	3	11	10	20	2	1	0-1	.261	.350	.409	.759	1	.977
1992— Orlando (South.)	1B-OF	129	456	75	124	16	2	18	79	55	89	8	8	6-6	.272	.356	.434	.790	9	.977
— Portland (PCL)	1B-OF	7	26	7	13	2	0	1	8	5	3	1	1	1-0	.500	.594	.692	1.286	1	.977
1993— Portland (PCL)	OF-1B	40	143	42	55	11	0	8	31	27	25	1	3	5-2	.385	.477	.629	1.106	2	.990
— Minnesota (A.L.)	OF-1B-DH	98	350	36	75	15	2	2	21	19	80	1	13	2-6	.214	.257	.286	.542	8	.983
1994— Minnesota (A.L.)	1B-OF	44	131	21	34	8	2	1	12	7	32	5	3	2-1	.260	.322	.374	.696	5	.982
— Salt Lake (PCL)	OF-1B	55	186	32	47	9	3	3	19	35	34	4	9	1-3	.253	.379	.382	.761	5	.976
1995— Minnesota (A.L.)	1B-OF	25	55	10	12	3	1	0	4	4	18	1	1	0-1	.218	.279	.309	.588	1	.993
— Indianapolis (A.A.)	1B	37	140	31	47	10	1	8	32	15	30	1	5	0-0	.336	.401	.593	.994	2	.994
— Phoenix (PCL)	1B-OF-DH	37	151	31	53	19	2	4	19	17	27	6	6	1-1	.351	.434	.583	1.017	2	.995
— San Francisco (N.L.)	OF-1B	12	20	1	5	1	0	0	2	2	4	0	0	1-0	.250	.318	.300	.618	1	.950
1996— San Francisco (N.L.)	1B-OF	91	175	16	38	3	0	6	24	18	43	2	5	2-1	.217	.294	.337	.632	3	.990
— Phoenix (PCL)	OF-1B	6	25	4	10	1	1	1	7	2	4	0	0	0-0	.400	.429	.640	1.069	0	1.000
1997— Phoenix (PCL)	1B-DH-OF	121	434	85	153	27	5	22	92	49	75	2	18	9-4	.353	.419	.590	1.009	3	.995
1998— Tacoma (PCL)	OF-1B-DH	108	398	73	126	30	2	11	52	59	85	6	15	9-6	.317	.411	.485	.896	2	.996
— Seattle (A.L.)	OF-1B	8	18	1	5	0	0	1	2	5	4	0	0	1-0	.278	.435	.444	.879	0	1.000
1999— Toledo (Int'l)	1B-OF-DH	132	466	85	125	24	3	31	77	70	110	4	9	6-6	.268	.366	.532	.899	2	.998
2000— Kansas City (A.L.)	1B-OF-DH	103	270	34	75	14	2	12	53	22	68	0	6	0-0	.278	.329	.478	.807	5	.991
2001— Kansas City (A.L.)	1B-OF-DH	98	200	26	50	10	0	7	26	24	45	1	8	0-0	.250	.328	.405	.733	8	.984
2002— Kansas City (A.L.)	1B-DH	13	32	3	3	1	0	1	2	2	10	0	1	0-0	.094	.147	.219	.366	0	1.000
— Durham (Int'l)	1B-OF	29	114	25	37	7	1	8	22	14	33	0	1	0-1	.325	.398	.614	1.012	2	.992
— Tampa Bay (A.L.)	OF	12	34	2	6	0	0	1	2	4	9	2	0	0-0	.176	.300	.265	.565	0	1.000
2003— Sacramento (PCL)	1B-DH-OF	91	352	69	95	23	2	15	72	44	71	3	12	4-1	.270	.351	.474	.826	4	.993
— Oakland (A.L.)	1B	8	26	2	7	2	0	0	2	1	7	0	0	0-0	.269	.286	.346	.632	1	.970
— Boston (A.L.)	OF-1B-DH	16	27	4	11	3	0	1	6	2	7	0	0	0-0	.407	.448	.630	1.078	1	.970
2004— Pawtucket (Int'l)	1B-DH	3	7	2	2	0	0	0	1	4	2	1	0	0-0	.286	.583	.286	.869	0	1.000
— Lowell (NY-Penn)	1B	1	3	1	2	1	0	0	1	1	0	0	0	0-0	.667	.750	1.000	1.750	0	1.000
— Boston (A.L.)	1-OF-P-DH	91	151	24	39	8	1	4	17	14	40	2	5	1-0	.258	.327	.404	.731	3	.991
American League totals (9 years)		516	1294	163	317	64	8	30	147	104	320	12	37	6-8	.245	.305	.376	.681	32	.987
National League totals (2 years)		103	195	17	43	4	0	6	26	20	47	2	5	3-1	.221	.297	.333	.630	4	.988
Major League totals (10 years)		619	1489	180	360	68	8	36	173	124	367	14	42	9-9	.242	.304	.371	.675	36	.987

DIVISION SERIES RECORD

Year	Team (League)	Pos.	G	AB	R	H	2B	3B	HR	RBI	BB	SO	HBP	GDP	SB-CS	Avg.	OBP	SLG	OPS	E	Avg.
2003— Boston (A.L.)		1	0	0	0	0	0	0	0	0	0	0	0	0-0	...	...	...	...	0	...

CHAMPIONSHIP SERIES RECORD

Year	Team (League)	Pos.	G	AB	R	H	2B	3B	HR	RBI	BB	SO	HBP	GDP	SB-CS	Avg.	OBP	SLG	OPS	E	Avg.
2003— Boston (A.L.)		1	1	0	0	0	0	0	0	0	1	0	0	0-0	.000	.000	.000	.000	0	...

MCCONNELL, SAM   P

PERSONAL: Born December 31, 1975, in Middletown, Ohio. ... 6-5/204. ... Throws left, bats left. ... Full name: John Samuel McConnell. ... College: Ball State.

TRANSACTIONS/CAREER NOTES: Selected by Pittsburgh Pirates in 11th round of 1997 free-agent draft. ... Released by Pirates (March 28, 2002). ... Signed as a free agent by Philadelphia Phillies organization (March 29, 2002). ... Signed as a free agent by Atlanta Braves organization (November 12, 2002).

M

CAREER HITTING: 0-for-1 (.000), 0 R, 0 2B, 0 3B, 0 HR, 0 RBI.

Year — Team (League)	W	L	Pct.	ERA	WHIP	G	GS	CG	ShO	Hld.	Sv.-Opp.	IP	H	R	ER	HR	BB-IBB	SO	Avg.
1997— Erie (N.Y.-Penn)	2	2	.500	5.06	1.36	17	10	0	0	...	0-...	58.2	56	38	33	7	24-0	45	.243
1998— Augusta (S. Atl.)	4	3	.571	3.20	1.09	8	8	1	0	...	0-...	45.0	36	22	16	2	13-1	35	.216
— Lynchburg (Carolina)	8	5	.615	2.90	1.14	19	19	3	1	...	0-...	121.0	118	48	39	4	20-0	80	.257
— Carolina (Southern)	0	1	.000	4.50	1.50	2	1	0	0	...	0-...	12.0	15	7	6	2	3-0	5	.313
1999— Lynchburg (Carolina)	7	3	.700	3.19	1.09	15	15	4	2	...	0-...	101.2	84	41	36	8	27-1	70	.232
— Altoona (East.)	1	7	.125	6.64	1.84	13	12	1	0	...	0-...	62.1	82	52	46	7	33-1	40	.324
2000— Altoona (East.)	9	2	.818	1.61	1.03	20	13	3	1	...	0-...	106.0	83	24	19	3	26-0	61	.213
— Nashville (PCL)	1	4	.200	6.43	1.51	8	8	0	0	...	0-...	49.0	58	36	35	8	16-0	22	.301
2001— Nashville (PCL)	7	10	.412	6.03	1.49	26	23	1	0	...	0-...	134.1	159	103	90	20	41-2	98	.291
2002— Reading (East.)	2	4	.333	3.65	1.41	29	7	0	0	...	3-...	69.0	78	31	28	7	19-3	43	.290
— Scran./W.B. (I.L.)	0	3	.000	3.53	1.60	7	7	0	0	...	0-...	35.2	41	17	14	6	16-0	23	.291
2003— Greenville (Sou.)	1	0	1.000	4.11	1.43	16	0	0	0	...	0-...	15.1	18	7	7	0	4-0	8	.300
— Richmond (Int'l)	8	4	.667	2.70	1.19	22	13	0	0	...	0-...	93.1	94	31	28	5	17-2	64	.265
2004— Atlanta (N.L.)	1	0	1.000	3.86	1.61	10	0	0	0	0	0-0	9.1	11	4	4	0	4-1	4	.289
— Richmond (Int'l)	7	7	.500	3.91	1.25	22	18	0	0	...	0-...	103.2	102	51	45	8	28-0	56	.259
Major League totals (1 year)	1	0	1.000	3.86	1.61	10	0	0	0	0	0-0	9.1	11	4	4	0	4-1	4	.289

MCCRACKEN, QUINTON — OF

PERSONAL: Born August 16, 1970, in Wilmington, N.C. ... 5-7/188. ... Bats both, throws right. ... Full name: Quinton Antoine McCracken. ... High school: South Brunswick (Southport, N.C.). ... College: Duke.

TRANSACTIONS/CAREER NOTES: Selected by Colorado Rockies organization in 25th round of 1992 free-agent draft. ... Selected by Tampa Bay Devil Rays in first round (fourth pick overall) of expansion draft (November 18, 1997). ... On disabled list (May 25, 1999-remainder of season). ... Released by Devil Rays (November 27, 2000). ... Signed by St. Louis Cardinals (December 22, 2000). ... Released by Cardinals (March 28, 2001). ... Signed by Minnesota Twins organization (April 13, 2001). ... Signed as a free agent by Arizona Diamondbacks (January 9, 2002). ... Traded by Diamondbacks to Seattle Mariners for 1B Greg Colbrunn and cash (December 15, 2003). ... Released by Mariners (June 7, 2004). ... Signed by Diamondbacks organization (June 11, 2004).

2004 GAMES PLAYED BY POSITION (MLB): OF—45, DH—6.

Year — Team (League)	Pos.	G	AB	R	H	2B	3B	HR	RBI	BB	SO	HBP	GDP	SB-CS	Avg.	OBP	SLG	OPS	E	Avg.
1992— Bend (N'west)	2B-OF	67	232	37	65	13	2	0	27	25	39	0	6	18-6	.280	.347	.353	.701	17	.930
1993— Central Valley (Cal.)	2B-OF	127	483	94	141	17	7	2	58	78	90	2	15	60-19	.292	.390	.369	.758	13	.946
1994— New Haven (East.)	OF	136	544	94	151	27	4	5	39	48	72	4	6	36-19	.278	.338	.369	.708	8	.972
1995— New Haven (East.)	OF-DH	55	221	33	79	11	4	1	26	21	32	3	2	26-8	.357	.419	.457	.876	3	.971
— Colo. Springs (PCL)	OF-DH	61	244	55	88	14	6	3	28	23	30	1	4	17-6	.361	.418	.504	.922	1	.991
— Colorado (N.L.)	OF	3	1	0	0	0	0	0	0	0	1	0	0	0-0	.000	.000	.000	.000	0	...
1996— Colorado (N.L.)	OF	124	283	50	82	13	6	3	40	32	62	1	5	17-6	.290	.363	.410	.773	6	.957
1997— Colorado (N.L.)	OF	147	325	69	95	11	1	3	36	42	62	1	6	28-11	.292	.374	.360	.734	4	.980
1998— Tampa Bay (A.L.)	OF	155	614	77	179	38	7	7	59	41	107	3	12	19-10	.292	.335	.410	.745	3	.980
1999— Tampa Bay (A.L.)	OF	40	148	20	37	6	1	1	18	14	23	1	7	6-5	.250	.317	.324	.641	1	.988
2000— Tampa Bay (A.L.)	OF	15	31	5	4	0	0	0	2	6	4	0	3	0-1	.129	.270	.129	.399	0	1.000
— Durham (Int'l)	OF	85	334	54	87	18	2	2	28	34	57	2	10	13-7	.260	.332	.344	.676	4	.977
2001— Edmonton (PCL)	OF	81	361	53	122	27	4	4	45	21	54	1	5	8-10	.338	.374	.468	.842	5	.971
— Minnesota (A.L.)	OF-DH	24	64	7	14	2	2	0	3	5	13	0	4	0-1	.219	.275	.313	.588	0	1.000
2002— Arizona (N.L.)	OF	123	349	60	108	27	8	3	40	32	68	2	3	5-4	.309	.367	.458	.825	1	.995
2003— Arizona (N.L.)	OF-DH	115	203	17	46	5	2	0	18	15	34	0	4	5-1	.227	.276	.271	.547	1	.983
2004— Seattle (A.L.)	OF-DH	19	20	6	3	0	0	0	0	2	4	0	1	1-1	.150	.227	.150	.377	0	1.000
— Tucson (PCL)	OF	15	58	7	19	5	1	1	8	3	5	0	1	2-2	.328	.361	.500	.861	0	1.000
— Arizona (N.L.)	OF	55	156	20	45	11	1	2	13	13	23	0	2	2-4	.288	.341	.410	.751	1	.979
American League totals (5 years)		253	877	115	237	46	10	8	82	68	151	4	25	26-18	.270	.323	.373	.695	4	.992
National League totals (6 years)		567	1317	216	376	67	18	11	147	134	250	4	20	57-26	.285	.351	.389	.740	13	.980
Major League totals (10 years)		820	2194	331	613	113	28	19	229	202	401	8	45	83-44	.279	.340	.382	.722	17	.985

DIVISION SERIES RECORD

Year — Team (League)	Pos.	G	AB	R	H	2B	3B	HR	RBI	BB	SO	HBP	GDP	SB-CS	Avg.	OBP	SLG	OPS	E	Avg.
2002— Arizona (N.L.)	OF	3	11	1	4	1	0	0	2	1	2	0	0	0-0	.364	.417	.455	.871	0	1.000

MCDONALD, DARNELL — OF

PERSONAL: Born November 17, 1978, in Fort Collins, Colo. ... 5-11/210. ... Bats right, throws right. ... Full name: Darnell T. McDonald. ... High school: Cherry Creek (Englewood, Colo.).

TRANSACTIONS/CAREER NOTES: Selected by Baltimore Orioles in first round (26th pick overall) of 1997 free-agent draft. ... Refused minor league assignment and became a free agent (October 15, 2004).

2004 GAMES PLAYED BY POSITION (MLB): OF—13, DH—1.

Year — Team (League)	Pos.	G	AB	R	H	2B	3B	HR	RBI	BB	SO	HBP	GDP	SB-CS	Avg.	OBP	SLG	OPS	E	Avg.
1998— Delmarva (S. Atl.)	OF	134	528	87	138	24	5	6	44	33	117	5	5	35-11	.261	.308	.360	.668	11	.940
— Frederick (Carolina)	OF	4	18	3	4	2	0	1	2	3	6	0	1	2-0	.222	.333	.500	.833	0	1.000
1999— Frederick (Carolina)	OF	130	507	81	135	23	5	6	73	61	92	5	13	26-9	.266	.347	.367	.713	10	.956
2000— Bowie (East.)	OF	116	459	59	111	13	5	6	43	29	87	4	7	11-4	.242	.290	.331	.621	9	.960
2001— Bowie (East.)	OF	30	117	16	33	7	1	3	21	9	28	1	1	3-3	.282	.336	.436	.772	2	.968
— Rochester (Int'l)	OF	104	391	37	93	19	2	2	35	29	75	1	8	13-9	.238	.291	.312	.603	12	.957
2002— Bowie (East.)	OF	37	144	21	42	9	1	4	15	22	27	2	1	9-3	.292	.393	.451	.844	1	.984
— Rochester (Int'l)	OF	91	332	43	96	21	6	4	35	32	78	2	8	11-3	.289	.353	.443	.796	5	.983
2003— Ottawa (Int'l)	OF	40	152	19	45	7	1	0	20	18	27	1	3	5-7	.296	.374	.355	.730	3	.968
2004— Ottawa (Int'l)	OF-DH	107	410	44	96	32	1	7	44	34	100	3	12	12-6	.234	.294	.368	.658	7	.973
— Baltimore (A.L.)	OF-DH	17	32	3	5	1	0	0	1	2	6	0	0	1-0	.156	.206	.188	.393	0	1.000
Major League totals (1 year)		17	32	3	5	1	0	0	1	2	6	0	0	1-0	.156	.206	.188	.393	0	1.000

MCDONALD, JOHN — SS

PERSONAL: Born September 24, 1974, in New London, Conn. ... 5-11/175. ... Bats right, throws right. ... Full name: John Joseph McDonald. ... High school: East Lyme (Conn.). ... College: Providence.

TRANSACTIONS/CAREER NOTES: Selected by Cleveland Indians organization in 12th round of 1996 free-agent draft. ... On disabled list (June 30-July 17 and August 27, 2003-remainder of season); included rehabilitation assignments to Mahoning Valley and Lake County.

2004 GAMES PLAYED BY POSITION (MLB): SS—30, 2B—12, 3B—9, DH—8.

Year Team (League)	Pos.	G	AB	R	H	2B	3B	HR	RBI	BB	SO	HBP	GDP	SB-CS	Avg.	OBP	SLG	OPS	E	Avg.
1996— Watertown (N.Y.-Penn.)	SS	75	278	48	75	11	0	2	26	32	49	5	3	11-1	.270	.354	.331	.685	18	.946
1997— Kinston (Caro.)	SS	130	541	77	140	27	3	5	53	51	75	2	12	6-5	.259	.324	.348	.671	25	.961
1998— Akron (East.)	SS	132	514	68	118	18	2	2	43	43	61	6	7	17-6	.230	.293	.284	.578	23	.966
1999— Akron (East.)	SS-2B	55	226	31	67	12	0	1	26	19	26	2	5	7-3	.296	.351	.363	.713	8	.970
— Buffalo (Int'l)	SS-3B-2B	66	237	30	75	12	1	0	25	11	23	2	5	6-3	.316	.349	.376	.725	13	.956
— Cleveland (A.L.)	2B-SS	18	21	2	7	0	0	0	0	0	3	0	2	0-1	.333	.333	.333	.667	1	.967
2000— Buffalo (Int'l)	SS-2B	75	286	37	77	17	2	1	36	21	29	1	7	4-3	.269	.315	.353	.668	8	.975
— Mahoning Valley (NY-P) ...	SS	5	17	0	2	1	0	0	1	2	3	0	0	0-0	.118	.211	.176	.387	0	1.000
— Cleveland (A.L.)	SS-2B	9	9	0	4	0	0	0	0	0	1	0	0	0-0	.444	.444	.444	.889	0	1.000
— Kinston (Caro.)	SS	1	3	0	1	0	0	0	0	0	0	0	0	0-0	.333	.333	.333	.667	0	1.000
2001— Cleveland (A.L.)	SS-2B	17	22	1	2	1	0	0	0	1	7	1	0	0-0	.091	.167	.136	.303	1	.964
— Buffalo (Int'l)	SS-2B-3B	116	410	52	100	17	1	2	33	33	72	6	11	17-10	.244	.305	.305	.610	23	.957
2002— Cleveland (A.L.)	2-S-3-DH	93	264	35	66	11	3	1	12	10	50	5	4	3-0	.250	.288	.326	.614	8	.979
2003— Mahoning Valley (NY-P)	SS	1	2	1	0	0	0	0	0	0	1	0	0	0-0	.000	.333	.000	.333	0	1.000
— Lake County (S.Atl.) ...	SS	1	3	0	0	0	0	0	0	0	0	0	0	0-0	.000	.000	.000	.000	0	1.000
— Cleveland (A.L.)	2B-SS-3B	82	214	21	46	9	1	1	14	11	31	2	4	3-3	.215	.258	.280	.538	10	.964
2004— Cleveland (A.L.)	SS-2B-3B-DH	66	93	17	19	5	1	2	7	4	11	0	2	0-0	.204	.237	.344	.581	5	.965
Major League totals (6 years)		285	623	76	144	26	5	4	33	26	103	8	12	6-4	.231	.269	.308	.577	25	.971

MCEWING, JOE — 2B/SS

PERSONAL: Born October 19, 1972, in Bristol, Pa. ... 5-11/210. ... Bats right, throws right. ... Full name: Joseph Earl McEwing. ... High school: Bishop Egan (Fairless Hills, Pa.). ... Junior college: Morris (N.J.) County College.

TRANSACTIONS/CAREER NOTES: Selected by St. Louis Cardinals organization in 28th round of 1992 free-agent draft. ... Traded by Cardinals to New York Mets for P Jesse Orosco (March 18, 2000). ... On disabled list (July 14-31, 2002); included rehabilitation assignments to Brooklyn and Binghamton. ... On disabled list (August 20, 2004-remainder of season).

2004 GAMES PLAYED BY POSITION (MLB): 2B—34, OF—15, SS—13, 1B—11, 3B—1.

Year Team (League)	Pos.	G	AB	R	H	2B	3B	HR	RBI	BB	SO	HBP	GDP	SB-CS	Avg.	OBP	SLG	OPS	E	Avg.
1992— Ariz. Cardinals (Ariz.)	SS-OF	55	211	55	71	4	2	0	13	24	18	5	1	23-7	.336	.415	.374	.789	1	.991
1993— Savannah (S. Atl.)	OF	138	511	94	127	35	1	0	43	89	73	4	7	22-9	.249	.362	.321	.683	5	.982
1994— Madison (Midw.)	OF	90	346	58	112	24	2	4	47	32	53	1	5	18-15	.324	.380	.439	.819	5	.974
— St. Pete. (FSL)	2B-OF	50	197	22	49	7	0	1	20	19	32	1	4	8-4	.249	.314	.299	.613	2	.985
1995— St. Pete. (FSL)	2B-OF	75	281	33	64	13	0	1	23	25	49	1	5	2-3	.228	.289	.285	.574	15	.955
— Arkansas (Texas)	2B-OF	42	121	16	30	4	0	2	12	9	13	1	4	3-2	.248	.305	.331	.636	0	1.000
1996— Arkansas (Texas)	2B-OF	106	216	27	45	7	3	2	14	13	32	0	8	2-4	.208	.252	.296	.548	2	.987
1997— Arkansas (Texas)	P	103	263	33	68	6	3	4	35	19	39	1	6	2-4	.259	.309	.350	.659	2	.988
1998— Arkansas (Texas)	P	60	223	45	79	21	4	9	46	21	18	1	2	4-2	.354	.409	.605	1.014	1	.994
— Memphis (PCL)	2-3-S-O	78	329	52	110	30	7	6	46	21	39	3	4	11-10	.334	.379	.523	.901	3	.982
— St. Louis (N.L.)	2B-OF	10	20	5	4	1	0	0	1	1	3	1	0	0-1	.200	.273	.250	.523	0	1.000
1999— St. Louis (N.L.)	2-0-3-1-S	152	513	65	141	28	4	9	44	41	87	6	3	7-4	.275	.333	.398	.730	11	.981
2000— Norfolk (Int'l)	0-2-3-S	43	171	28	44	10	2	5	18	16	34	0	3	7-3	.257	.319	.427	.746	4	.973
— New York (N.L.)	0-3-2-S	87	153	20	34	14	1	2	19	5	29	1	2	3-1	.222	.248	.366	.614	5	.957
2001— New York (N.L.)	0-3-S-2-1-DH	116	283	41	80	17	3	8	30	17	57	10	2	8-5	.283	.342	.449	.791	3	.981
2002— New York (N.L.)	0-S-1-2-3	105	196	22	39	8	1	3	26	9	50	3	0	4-4	.199	.242	.296	.538	7	.967
— Brooklyn (NY-P)	DH	1	4	0	1	0	0	0	1	0	0	0	0	0-0	.250	.250	.250	.500	...	...
— Binghamton (East.)	2B-3B	1	5	0	0	0	0	0	0	0	1	0	0	0-0	.000	.000	.000	.000	0	1.000
2003— Norfolk (Int'l)	OF-2B-3B-1B	5	19	3	6	0	0	1	3	2	2	2	0	3-0	.316	.435	.474	.908	0	1.000
— New York (N.L.)	2-S-O-1-3	119	278	31	67	11	0	1	16	25	57	3	6	3-0	.241	.309	.291	.601	6	.984
2004— New York (N.L.)	2-O-S-1-3	75	138	17	35	3	1	1	16	9	32	0	1	4-1	.254	.297	.312	.609	3	.986
Major League totals (7 years)		664	1581	201	400	82	10	24	152	107	315	24	13	29-16	.253	.307	.363	.671	35	.979

DIVISION SERIES RECORD

Year Team (League)	Pos.	G	AB	R	H	2B	3B	HR	RBI	BB	SO	HBP	GDP	SB-CS	Avg.	OBP	SLG	OPS	E	Avg.
2000— New York (N.L.)	3B-OF	4	1	0	1	0	0	0	0	0	0	0	0	0-0	1.000	1.000	1.000	2.000	0	...

CHAMPIONSHIP SERIES RECORD

Year Team (League)	Pos.	G	AB	R	H	2B	3B	HR	RBI	BB	SO	HBP	GDP	SB-CS	Avg.	OBP	SLG	OPS	E	Avg.
2000— New York (N.L.)	3B-OF	4	0	2	0	0	0	0	0	0	0	0	0	0-0	...	...	...	...	0	1.000

WORLD SERIES RECORD

Year Team (League)	Pos.	G	AB	R	H	2B	3B	HR	RBI	BB	SO	HBP	GDP	SB-CS	Avg.	OBP	SLG	OPS	E	Avg.
2000— New York (N.L.)	OF	3	1	1	0	0	0	0	0	0	0	0	0	0-0	.000	.000	.000	.000	0	1.000

MCGRIFF, FRED — 1B

PERSONAL: Born October 31, 1963, in Tampa, Fla. ... 6-3/225. ... Bats left, throws left. ... Full name: Frederick Stanley McGriff. ... High school: Jefferson (Tampa). ... Cousin of Terry McGriff, catcher with four major league teams (1987-90, 1993 and 1994); and uncle of Charles Johnson, catcher, Colorado Rockies.

TRANSACTIONS/CAREER NOTES: Selected by New York Yankees organization in ninth round of June 1981 free-agent draft. ... Traded by Yankees with OF Dave Collins, P Mike Morgan and cash to Toronto Blue Jays for OF/C Tom Dodd and P Dale Murray (December 9, 1982). ... Traded by Blue Jays with SS Tony Fernandez to San Diego Padres for OF Joe Carter and 2B Roberto Alomar (December 5, 1990). ... On suspended list (June 23-26, 1992). ... Traded by Padres to Atlanta Braves for OFs Melvin Nieves, Vince Moore and P Donnie Elliott (July 18, 1993). ... Traded by Braves to Tampa Bay Devil Rays for cash considerations (November 18, 1997). ... Traded by Devil Rays to Chicago Cubs for P Manny Aybar and a player to be named (July 27, 2001); Devil Rays acquired SS Jason Smith to complete deal (August 5, 2001). ... Signed as a free agent by Los Angeles Dodgers (December 20, 2002). ... On disabled list (June 14-August 22, 2003); included rehabilitation assignments to Vero Beach and GCL Dodgers. ... Signed by Devil Rays organization (February 10, 2004). ... Released by Devil Rays (July 26, 2004).

2004 GAMES PLAYED BY POSITION (MLB): DH—14, 1B—6.

Year Team (League)	Pos.	G	AB	R	H	2B	3B	HR	RBI	BB	SO	HBP	GDP	SB-CS	Avg.	OBP	SLG	OPS	E	Avg.
													BATTING						FIELDING	
1981—GC Yankees (GCL)	1B	29	81	6	12	2	0	0	9	11	20	1	...	0-0	.148	.255	.173	.428	7	.963
1982—GC Yankees (GCL)	1B	62	217	38	59	11	1	9	41	48	63	5	...	6-6	.272	.413	.456	.870	8	.986
1983—Florence (S. Atl.)	1B	33	119	26	37	3	1	7	26	20	35	1	...	3-0	.311	.414	.529	.944	6	.978
—Kinston (Caro.)	1B	94	350	53	85	14	1	21	57	55	112	6	...	3-2	.243	.354	.469	.822	10	.988
1984—Knoxville (Southern)	1B	56	189	29	47	13	2	9	25	29	55	1	2	0-2	.249	.347	.481	.828	10	.981
—Syracuse (Int'l)	1B	70	238	28	56	10	1	13	28	26	89	0	3	0-1	.235	.309	.450	.759	3	.996
1985—Syracuse (Int'l)	1B	51	176	19	40	8	2	5	20	23	53	4	2	0-0	.227	.330	.381	.711	5	.989
1986—Syracuse (Int'l)	1B-OF	133	468	69	121	23	4	19	74	83	119	4	16	0-3	.259	.369	.447	.816	10	.992
—Toronto (A.L.)	DH-1B	3	5	1	1	0	0	0	0	0	2	0	0	0-0	.200	.200	.200	.400	0	1.000
1987—Toronto (A.L.)	DH-1B	107	295	58	73	16	0	20	43	60	104	1	3	3-2	.247	.376	.505	.881	2	.983
1988—Toronto (A.L.)	1B	154	536	100	151	35	4	34	82	79	149	4	15	6-1	.282	.376	.552	.928	5 *	.997
1989—Toronto (A.L.)	DH-1B	161	551	98	148	27	3	* 36	92	119	132	4	14	7-4	.269	.399	.525	.924	* 17	.989
1990—Toronto (A.L.)	DH-1B	153	557	91	167	21	1	35	88	94	108	2	7	5-3	.300	.400	.530	.930	6	.996
1991—San Diego (N.L.)	1B	153	528	84	147	19	1	31	106	105	135	2	14	4-1	.278	.396	.494	.890	14	.990
1992—San Diego (N.L.)	1B	152	531	79	152	30	4	* 35	104	96	108	1	14	8-6	.286	.394	.556	.950	• 12	.991
1993—San Diego (N.L.)	1B	83	302	52	83	11	1	18	46	42	55	1	9	4-3	.275	.361	.497	.858	12	.983
—Atlanta (N.L.)	1B	68	255	59	79	18	1	19	55	34	51	1	5	1-0	.310	.392	.612	1.004	5	.992
1994—Atlanta (N.L.)	1B	113	424	81	135	25	1	34	94	50	76	1	8	7-3	.318	.389	.623	1.012	7	.994
1995—Atlanta (N.L.)	1B	• 144	528	85	148	27	1	27	93	65	99	5	19	3-6	.280	.361	.489	.850	5	.996
1996—Atlanta (N.L.)	1B	159	617	81	182	37	1	28	107	68	116	2	20	7-3	.295	.365	.494	.859	12	.992
1997—Atlanta (N.L.)	1B	152	564	77	156	25	1	22	97	68	112	4	22	5-0	.277	.356	.441	.797	13	.990
1998—Tampa Bay (A.L.)	1B-DH	151	564	73	160	33	0	19	81	79	118	2	14	7-2	.284	.371	.443	.815	6	.995
1999—Tampa Bay (A.L.)	1B-DH	144	529	75	164	30	1	32	104	86	107	1	12	1-0	.310	.405	.552	.957	13	.989
2000—Tampa Bay (A.L.)	1B-DH	158	566	82	157	18	0	27	106	91	120	0	16	2-0	.277	.373	.452	.826	10	.993
2001—Tampa Bay (A.L.)	1B-DH	97	343	40	109	18	0	19	61	40	69	0	7	1-1	.318	.387	.536	.923	9	.986
—Chicago (N.L.)	1B	49	170	27	48	7	2	12	41	26	37	3	6	0-1	.282	.383	.559	.942	4	.990
2002—Chicago (N.L.)	1B-DH	146	523	67	143	27	2	30	103	63	99	4	13	1-2	.273	.353	.505	.858	7	.993
2003—Vero Beach (FSL)	DH-1B	2	6	0	1	0	0	0	0	1	2	0	0	0-0	.167	.286	.167	.452	0	1.000
—GC Dodgers (GCL)	1B	1	3	1	2	1	0	0	0	0	0	0	0	0-0	.667	.667	1.000	1.667	0	1.000
—Los Angeles	1B	86	297	32	74	14	0	13	40	31	66	1	7	0-0	.249	.322	.428	.750	8	.989
2004—Durham (Int'l)	DH-1B	7	21	4	5	0	0	1	4	5	6	0	0	0-0	.238	.385	.286	.766	1	.909
—Tampa Bay (A.L.)	DH-1B	27	72	7	13	3	0	2	7	9	19	0	1	0-0	.181	.272	.306	.577	0	1.000
American League totals (10 years)		1155	4018	625	1143	201	9	224	664	657	928	14	89	32-13	.284	.384	.506	.891	68	.992
National League totals (10 years)		1305	4739	724	1347	240	15	269	886	648	954	25	137	40-25	.284	.370	.512	.882	99	.991
Major League totals (19 years)		2460	8757	1349	2490	441	24	493	1550	1305	1882	39	226	72-38	.284	.377	.509	.886	167	.992

DIVISION SERIES RECORD

Year Team (League)	Pos.	G	AB	R	H	2B	3B	HR	RBI	BB	SO	HBP	GDP	SB-CS	Avg.	OBP	SLG	OPS	E	Avg.
1995—Atlanta (N.L.)	1B	4	18	4	6	0	0	2	6	2	3	0	1	0-0	.333	.400	.667	1.067	0	1.000
1996—Atlanta (N.L.)	1B	3	9	1	3	1	0	1	3	2	1	0	0	0-1	.333	.417	.778	1.194	0	1.000
1997—Atlanta (N.L.)	1B	3	9	4	2	0	0	0	1	3	2	0	0	0-0	.222	.417	.222	.639	0	1.000
Division series totals (3 years)		10	36	9	11	1	0	3	10	7	6	0	1	0-1	.306	.409	.583	.992	0	1.000

CHAMPIONSHIP SERIES RECORD

Year Team (League)	Pos.	G	AB	R	H	2B	3B	HR	RBI	BB	SO	HBP	GDP	SB-CS	Avg.	OBP	SLG	OPS	E	Avg.
1989—Toronto (A.L.)	1B	5	21	1	3	0	0	0	3	0	4	0	0	0-0	.143	.143	.143	.286	1	.974
1993—Atlanta (N.L.)	1B	6	23	6	10	2	0	1	4	4	7	0	0	0-0	.435	.519	.652	1.171	0	1.000
1995—Atlanta (N.L.)	1B	4	16	5	7	4	0	0	0	3	0	0	0	0-0	.438	.526	.688	1.214	0	1.000
1996—Atlanta (N.L.)	1B	7	28	6	7	0	1	2	7	3	5	0	1	0-0	.250	.323	.536	.858	1	.982
1997—Atlanta (N.L.)	1B	6	21	0	7	1	0	0	4	2	7	0	0	0-0	.333	.375	.381	.756	1	.977
Champ. series totals (5 years)		28	109	18	34	7	1	3	18	12	23	0	1	0-0	.312	.377	.477	.854	3	.987

WORLD SERIES RECORD

Year Team (League)	Pos.	G	AB	R	H	2B	3B	HR	RBI	BB	SO	HBP	GDP	SB-CS	Avg.	OBP	SLG	OPS	E	Avg.
1995—Atlanta (N.L.)	1B	6	23	5	6	2	0	2	3	3	7	0	1	1-0	.261	.346	.609	.955	1	.986
1996—Atlanta (N.L.)	1B	6	20	4	6	0	0	2	6	5	4	0	1	0-0	.300	.423	.600	1.023	0	1.000
World series totals (2 years)		12	43	9	12	2	0	4	9	8	11	0	2	1-0	.279	.385	.605	.989	1	.993

ALL-STAR GAME RECORD

	G	AB	R	H	2B	3B	HR	RBI	BB	SO	HBP	GDP	SB-CS	Avg.	OBP	SLG	OPS	E	Avg.
All-Star Game totals (5 years)	5	11	1	3	0	0	1	3	0	5	0	0	0-0	.273	.273	.545	.818	0	1.000

MCKAY, CODY C

PERSONAL: Born January 11, 1974, in Vancouver, British Columbia. ... 6-0/208. ... Bats left, throws right. ... Full name: Cody Dean McKay. ... High school: Horizon (Scottsdale, Ariz.). ... College: Arizona State. ... Son of Dave McKay, coach, St. Louis Cardinals, and infielder with three major league teams (1975-82).

TRANSACTIONS/CAREER NOTES: Selected by St. Louis Cardinals organization in fifth round of 1995 free-agent draft; did not sign. ... Selected by Oakland Athletics organization in ninth round of 1996 free-agent draft. ... Signed as a free agent by Milwaukee Brewers organization (November 7, 2002). ... Signed as a free agent by Cardinals organization (November 5, 2003). ... Career major league pitching: 0-0, 0.00 ERA, 1 G, 2.0 IP, 0 H, 0 R, 0 ER, 1 BB, 0 SO.

2004 GAMES PLAYED BY POSITION (MLB): C—18, 3B—7, P—1, 1B—1.

Year Team (League)	Pos.	G	AB	R	H	2B	3B	HR	RBI	BB	SO	HBP	GDP	SB-CS	Avg.	OBP	SLG	OPS	E	Avg.
1996—S. Oregon (N'west)	C-3B	69	254	33	68	13	0	3	30	25	42	6	7	0-5	.268	.344	.354	.698	12	.971
1997—Modesto (California)	3B-C	125	390	47	97	20	1	7	50	46	69	16	9	4-2	.249	.349	.359	.708	20	.966
1998—Modesto (California)	C-3B-1B	107	402	59	114	25	1	6	58	40	62	17	12	2-4	.284	.370	.396	.766	13	.986
—Huntsville (Sou.)	1-3-S-C-O	9	21	5	6	0	0	1	1	6	5	2	0	0-0	.286	.483	.429	.911	0	1.000
—Edmonton (PCL)	C-3B	19	57	6	13	3	0	0	5	7	5	3	2	1-0	.228	.343	.281	.624	0	1.000
1999—Midland (Texas)	C-3B-1B	94	333	59	98	21	1	6	43	38	40	8	11	1-2	.294	.375	.417	.792	14	.975
2000—Midland (Texas)	C-3B-1B	115	427	70	136	35	2	5	89	67	54	10	15	1-5	.319	.414	.445	.859	14	.980
—Sacramento (PCL)	C-1B	16	58	8	13	4	0	1	7	5	14	1	0	0-0	.224	.297	.345	.642	1	.989
2001—Sacramento (PCL)	C-3B-OF	99	350	36	92	19	0	6	57	41	64	5	12	1-0	.263	.324	.369	.692	6	.991
2002—Sacramento (PCL)	C-3B-1B-OF	108	378	55	109	16	1	13	57	21	59	10	4	2-1	.288	.337	.439	.777	5	.991
—Oakland (A.L.)	C	2	3	0	2	0	0	0	2	0	1	0	0	0-0	.667	.500	.667	1.167	0	1.000

Year Team (League)	Pos.	G	AB	R	H	2B	3B	HR	RBI	BB	SO	HBP	GDP	SB-CS	Avg.	OBP	SLG	OPS	E	Avg.
2003— Indianapolis (Int'l)	C-1-DH-3	109	371	32	86	15	1	6	43	26	50	9	13	2-2	.232	.294	.326	.620	10	.987
2004— Memphis (PCL)	C-3B	27	90	9	25	4	1	3	15	4	15	3	1	0-0	.278	.323	.444	.768	2	.985
— St. Louis (N.L.)	C-3B-P-1B	35	74	7	17	2	0	0	6	2	14	2	3	0-0	.230	.269	.257	.526	1	.989
American League totals (1 year)		2	3	0	2	0	0	0	2	0	1	0	0	0-0	.667	.500	.667	1.167	0	1.000
National League totals (1 year)		35	74	7	17	2	0	0	6	2	14	2	3	0-0	.230	.269	.257	.526	1	.989
Major League totals (2 years)		37	77	7	19	2	0	0	8	2	15	2	3	0-0	.247	.280	.273	.553	1	.990

MCLEARY, MARTY — P

PERSONAL: Born October 26, 1974, in Kettering, Ohio. ... 6-5/230. ... Throws right, bats right. ... Full name: Marty Lee McLeary. ... High school: Mansfield (Ohio) Christian. ... College: Mt. Vernon Nazarene (Ohio).

TRANSACTIONS/CAREER NOTES: Selected by Boston Red Sox organization in 10th round of 1997 free-agent draft. ... Selected by Montreal Expos from Red Sox organization in Rule 5 major league draft (December 13, 1999). ... Returned to Red Sox organization (March 17, 2000). ... Released by Red Sox (April 15, 2003). ... Signed by Florida Marlins organization (April 29, 2003). ... Traded by Marlins to San Diego Padres for P Bryan Gaal (April 8, 2004).

CAREER HITTING: 0-for-0 (.000), 0 R, 0 2B, 0 3B, 0 HR, 0 RBI.

Year Team (League)	W	L	Pct.	ERA	WHIP	G	GS	CG	ShO	Hld.	Sv.-Opp.	IP	H	R	ER	HR	BB-IBB	SO	Avg.
1997— Lowell (NY-Penn)	3	6	.333	3.75	1.43	13	13	0	0	...	0-...	62.1	53	38	26	2	36-1	43	.232
1998— Michigan (Midw.)	5	7	.417	4.16	1.51	37	7	0	0	...	0-...	88.2	99	58	41	4	35-2	54	.281
1999— Sarasota (Florida State)	1	0	1.000	12.08	2.84	8	0	0	0	...	0-...	12.2	29	20	17	1	7-0	11	.468
— Augusta (S. Atl.)	5	6	.455	3.12	1.21	35	9	0	0	...	3-...	80.2	73	34	28	8	25-1	90	.240
2000— Trenton (East.)	2	9	.182	4.56	1.73	43	8	0	0	...	5-...	96.2	114	66	49	5	53-3	53	.295
2001— Trenton (East.)	9	6	.600	3.46	1.61	35	0	0	0	...	2-...	54.2	58	30	21	2	30-5	42	.274
— Pawtucket (Int'l)	1	2	.333	3.00	1.43	18	0	0	0	...	0-...	30.0	28	13	10	4	15-1	20	.259
2002— Pawtucket (Int'l)	1	1	.500	7.32	1.88	18	1	0	0	...	0-...	35.2	44	30	29	6	23-0	19	.312
— Trenton (East.)	0	2	.000	4.86	1.68	11	0	0	0	...	0-...	16.2	20	12	9	0	8-2	10	.313
2003— Carolina (Southern)	1	1	.500	1.80	1.23	11	2	0	0	...	0-...	30.0	22	8	6	1	15-0	22	.208
— Albuquerque (PCL)	1	1	.500	4.32	1.74	20	1	0	0	...	0-...	33.1	40	22	16	3	18-1	17	.294
2004— Albuquerque (PCL)	0	1	.000	16.20	2.40	1	0	0	0	...	0-...	1.2	4	3	3	2	0-0	2	.500
— San Diego (N.L.)	0	0	...	14.73	2.45	3	0	0	0	0	0-0	3.2	7	6	6	2	2-0	4	.438
— Portland (PCL)	5	4	.556	2.99	1.27	44	7	0	0	...	13-...	84.1	65	30	28	4	42-1	81	.215
Major League totals (1 year)	0	0	...	14.73	2.45	3	0	0	0	0	0-0	3.2	7	6	6	2	2-0	4	.438

MCLEMORE, MARK — 3B/2B

PERSONAL: Born October 4, 1964, in San Diego, Calif. ... 5-11/217. ... Bats both, throws right. ... Full name: Mark Tremell McLemore. ... High school: Samuel F.B. Morse (San Diego).

TRANSACTIONS/CAREER NOTES: Selected by California Angels organization in ninth round of June 1982 free-agent draft. ... On disabled list (May 24-August 2, 1988); included rehabilitation assignments to Palm Springs and Edmonton. ... On disabled list (May 17-August 17, 1990); included rehabilitation assignments to Edmonton and Palm Springs. ... Traded by Angels to Cleveland Indians (August 17, 1990), completing deal in which Indians traded C Ron Tingley to Angels for a player to be named (September 6, 1989). ... Released by Indians (December 13, 1990). ... Signed by Houston Astros organization (March 6, 1991). ... On disabled list (May 9-June 25, 1991); included rehabilitation assignments to Tucson and Jackson. ... Released by Astros (June 25, 1991). ... Signed by Baltimore Orioles organization (July 5, 1991). ... Re-signed by Orioles organization (January 6, 1993). ... Signed as a free agent by Texas Rangers (December 13, 1994). ... On disabled list (May 15-June 12 and August 19-September 28, 1997); included rehabilitation assignments to Charlotte and Oklahoma City. ... On disabled list (June 7-22, 1998). ... Signed as a free agent by Seattle Mariners (December 20, 1999). ... On suspended list (June 20-24, 2000). ... Signed as a free agent by Baltimore Orioles organization (February 4, 2004). ... Released by Orioles (April 3, 2004). ... Signed by Oakland Athletics (April 5, 2004). ... On disabled list (April 5-May 11, 2004); included rehabilitation assignment to Sacramento.

2004 GAMES PLAYED BY POSITION (MLB): 2B—47, 3B—27, OF—1.

Year Team (League)	Pos.	G	AB	R	H	2B	3B	HR	RBI	BB	SO	HBP	GDP	SB-CS	Avg.	OBP	SLG	OPS	E	Avg.
1982— Salem (N'west)	2B-SS	55	165	42	49	6	2	0	25	39	38	2	...	14-6	.297	.431	.358	.788	11	.949
1983— Peoria (Midw.)	2B-SS	95	329	42	79	7	3	0	18	53	64	2	...	15-11	.240	.346	.286	.626	24	.946
1984— Redwood (Calif.)	2B-SS	134	482	102	142	8	3	0	45	106	75	1	2	59-15	.295	.421	.324	.744	25	.966
1985— Midland (Texas)	2B-SS	117	458	80	124	17	6	2	46	66	59	1	4	31-16	.271	.362	.347	.709	19	.971
1986— Midland (Texas)	2B	63	237	54	75	9	1	1	29	48	18	1	5	38-8	.316	.428	.384	.803	13	.964
— Edmonton (PCL)	2B	73	286	41	79	13	1	0	23	39	30	0	0	29-9	.276	.359	.329	.687	7	.982
— California (A.L.)	2B	5	4	0	0	0	0	0	0	1	2	0	0	0-1	.000	.200	.000	.200	0	1.000
1987— California (A.L.)	2B-SS-DH	138	433	61	102	13	3	3	41	48	72	0	7	25-8	.236	.310	.300	.610	17	.975
1988— California (A.L.)	2B-3B-DH	77	233	38	56	11	2	2	16	25	28	0	4	13-7	.240	.312	.330	.642	6	.979
— Palm Springs (Calif.)	2B	11	44	9	15	3	1	0	6	11	7	1	1	7-3	.341	.474	.455	.928	1	.977
— Edmonton (PCL)	2B	12	45	7	12	3	0	0	6	4	4	0	1	7-1	.267	.327	.333	.660	1	.986
1989— Edmonton (PCL)	2B	114	430	60	105	13	2	2	34	49	67	1	14	26-11	.244	.321	.298	.619	10	.983
— California (A.L.)	2B-DH	32	103	12	25	3	1	0	14	7	19	1	2	6-1	.243	.295	.291	.586	5	.966
1990— California (A.L.)	2B	20	48	4	7	2	0	0	2	4	9	0	1	1-0	.146	.212	.188	.399	0	1.000
— Edmonton (PCL)	2B-SS	9	39	4	10	2	0	0	3	6	10	0	0	0-3	.256	.356	.308	.663	4	.933
— Palm Springs (Calif.)	2B	6	22	3	6	0	0	0	2	3	7	0	0	0-2	.273	.360	.273	.633	0	1.000
— Colo. Springs (PCL)	2B-SS-DH	14	54	11	15	2	0	1	7	11	8	0	...	5-0	.278	.400	.370	.770	3	.969
— Cleveland (A.L.)	2B-3B-SS	8	12	2	2	0	0	0	0	0	6	0	0	0-0	.167	.167	.167	.333	4	.922
1991— Houston (N.L.)	2B	21	61	6	9	1	0	0	2	6	13	0	1	0-1	.148	.221	.164	.385	2	.975
— Tucson (PCL)	2B	4	14	2	5	1	0	0	0	2	1	0	2	0-0	.357	.438	.429	.866	0	1.000
— Jackson (Texas)	2B	7	22	6	5	3	0	0	4	6	3	0	0	1-0	.227	.393	.500	.893	0	1.000
— Rochester (Int'l)	2B	57	228	32	64	11	4	1	28	27	29	0	5	12-5	.281	.354	.377	.731	5	.984
1992— Baltimore (A.L.)	2B-DH	101	228	40	56	7	2	0	27	21	26	0	6	11-5	.246	.308	.294	.602	7	.978
1993— Baltimore (A.L.)	OF-2-3-DH	148	581	81	165	27	5	4	72	64	92	1	21	21-15	.284	.353	.368	.721	6	.986
1994— Baltimore (A.L.)	2B-OF-DH	104	343	44	88	11	1	3	29	51	50	1	7	20-5	.257	.354	.321	.674	9	.982
1995— Texas (A.L.)	OF-2B-DH	129	467	73	122	20	5	5	41	69	71	3	10	21-11	.261	.346	.358	.703	4	.991
1996— Texas (A.L.)	2B-OF	147	517	84	150	23	4	5	46	87	69	0	16	27-10	.290	.389	.378	.768	12	.985
1997— Texas (A.L.)	2B-OF	89	349	47	91	17	2	1	25	40	54	2	5	7-5	.261	.338	.330	.668	8	.980
— Charlotte (Fla. St.)	2B	2	7	1	4	1	0	0	3	2	1	0	0	1-1	.571	.667	.714	1.381	0	1.000
— Okla. City (A.A.)	2B-DH	3	10	0	1	0	0	0	1	1	1	0	0	1-0	.100	.167	.100	.267	0	1.000
1998— Texas (A.L.)	2B-DH	126	461	79	114	15	1	5	53	89	64	2	15	12-4	.247	.369	.317	.686	15	.975
1999— Texas (A.L.)	2B-OF-DH	144	566	105	155	20	7	6	45	83	79	0	8	16-8	.274	.363	.366	.729	12	.983
2000— Seattle (A.L.)	2B-OF	138	481	72	118	23	1	3	46	81	78	1	12	30-14	.245	.353	.316	.669	8	.988
2001— Seattle (A.L.)	O-3-S-2-DH	125	409	78	117	16	9	5	57	69	84	0	12	39-7	.286	.384	.406	.790	12	.963

Year	Team (League)	Pos.	G	AB	R	H	2B	3B	HR	RBI	BB	SO	HBP	GDP	SB-CS	Avg.	OBP	SLG	OPS	E	Avg.
2002— Seattle (A.L.)	O-3-DH-2-S	104	337	54	91	17	2	7	41	61	63	1	3	18-10	.270	.380	.395	.774	7	.966
2003— Seattle (A.L.)	S-3-O-DH-2	99	309	34	72	15	2	2	37	38	71	2	4	5-5	.233	.318	.314	.632	7	.973
2004— Sacramento (PCL)	2B-DH-SS	6	19	2	10	1	0	0	5	5	2	0	0	0-0	.526	.625	.579	1.204	1	.941
— Oakland (A.L.)	2B-3B-OF	77	250	29	62	14	0	2	21	41	33	1	4	0-2	.248	.355	.328	.683	7	.977
American League totals (18 years)		1811	6131	937	1593	254	47	53	613	869	970	15	133	272-118	.260	.351	.343	.693	146	.980
National League totals (1 year)		21	61	6	9	1	0	0	2	6	13	0	1	0-1	.148	.221	.164	.385	2	.975
Major League totals (19 years)		1832	6192	943	1602	255	47	53	615	875	983	15	134	272-119	.259	.349	.341	.690	148	.980

DIVISION SERIES RECORD

Year	Team (League)	Pos.	G	AB	R	H	2B	3B	HR	RBI	BB	SO	HBP	GDP	SB-CS	Avg.	OBP	SLG	OPS	E	Avg.
1996— Texas (A.L.)	2B	4	15	1	2	0	0	0	2	0	4	0	0	0-1	.133	.133	.133	.267	0	1.000
1998— Texas (A.L.)	2B	3	10	0	1	1	0	0	0	2	3	0	0	0-0	.100	.250	.200	.450	0	1.000
1999— Texas (A.L.)	2B	3	10	0	1	0	0	0	0	1	3	0	0	0-0	.100	.182	.100	.282	0	1.000
2000— Seattle (A.L.)	2B	3	9	1	1	0	0	0	0	2	1	0	0	0-0	.111	.273	.111	.384	1	.957
2001— Seattle (A.L.)	SS-OF	5	18	0	3	0	0	0	3	1	8	0	1	0-0	.167	.211	.167	.377	0	1.000
Division series totals (5 years)		18	62	2	8	1	0	0	5	6	19	0	1	0-1	.129	.206	.145	.351	1	.989

CHAMPIONSHIP SERIES RECORD

Year	Team (League)	Pos.	G	AB	R	H	2B	3B	HR	RBI	BB	SO	HBP	GDP	SB-CS	Avg.	OBP	SLG	OPS	E	Avg.
2000— Seattle (A.L.)	2B	5	16	2	4	3	0	0	2	1	2	1	0	0-0	.250	.333	.438	.771	2	.923
2001— Seattle (A.L.)	2B-SS-OF	5	14	1	2	0	1	0	3	2	2	0	0	0-0	.143	.250	.286	.536	0	1.000
Champ. series totals (2 years)		10	30	3	6	3	1	0	5	3	4	1	0	0-0	.200	.294	.367	.661	2	.939

MCMILLON, BILLY   OF

PERSONAL: Born November 17, 1971, in Otero, N.M. ... 5-11/195. ... Bats left, throws left. ... Full name: William Edward McMillon. ... High school: Bishopville (S.C.). ... College: Clemson.

TRANSACTIONS/CAREER NOTES: Selected by Florida Marlins organization in eighth round of 1993 free-agent draft. ... Traded by Marlins to Philadelphia Phillies for OF/1B Darren Daulton (July 21, 1997). ... Signed as a free agent by Detroit Tigers organization (January 10, 2000). ... Claimed on waivers by Oakland Athletics (June 13, 2001). ... On disabled list (July 23, 2001-remainder of season). ... Released by A's (November 12, 2001). ... Signed by Marlins organization (December 29, 2001). ... Released by Marlins (March 30, 2002). ... Signed by New York Yankees organization (April 8, 2002). ... Signed as a free agent by A's organization (November 18, 2002). ... On disabled list (June 10-August 11, 2004); included rehabilitation assignment to Sacramento.

2004 GAMES PLAYED BY POSITION (MLB): OF—21, DH—6, 1B—3.

Year	Team (League)	Pos.	G	AB	R	H	2B	3B	HR	RBI	BB	SO	HBP	GDP	SB-CS	Avg.	OBP	SLG	OPS	E	Avg.
1993— Elmira (N.Y.-Penn)	OF	57	226	38	69	14	2	6	35	31	43	4	3	5-4	.305	.398	.465	.863	5	.931
1994— Kane Co. (Midw.)	OF	137	496	88	125	25	3	17	101	84	99	10	13	7-3	.252	.366	.417	.783	7	.966
1995— Portland (East.)	OF	141	518	92	162	29	3	14	93	96	90	7	10	15-9	.313	.423	.461	.885	4	.982
1996— Charlotte (Int'l)	OF-DH	97	347	72	122	32	2	17	70	36	76	5	8	5-3	.352	.418	.602	1.020	4	.973
— Florida (N.L.)	OF	28	51	4	11	0	0	0	4	5	14	0	1	0-0	.216	.286	.216	.501	0	1.000
1997— Charlotte (Int'l)	OF	57	204	34	57	18	0	8	26	32	51	...	0	8-0	.279	...	.485	...	2	.978
— Florida (N.L.)	OF	13	18	0	2	1	0	0	1	0	7	0	0	0-0	.111	.111	.167	.278	0	1.000
— Philadelphia (N.L.)	OF	24	72	10	21	4	1	2	13	6	17	0	1	2-1	.292	.333	.458	.792	1	.957
— Scran./W.B. (I.L.)	OF	26	92	18	27	8	1	4	21	12	24	...		2-0	.293	...	.533	...	0	1.000
1998— Scran./W.B. (I.L.)	OF-DH	77	267	42	69	16	1	13	38	34	59	3	6	6-3	.258	.345	.472	.817	2	.986
1999— Scran./W.B. (I.L.)	OF-DH	132	464	97	141	38	4	16	85	65	79	6	10	11-2	.304	.389	.506	.895	5	.979
2000— Toledo (Int'l)	OF	105	380	61	131	30	1	13	50	71	65	2	18	3-1	.345	.446	.532	.978	6	.973
— Detroit (A.L.)	DH-OF	46	123	20	37	7	1	4	24	19	19	1	2	1-0	.301	.388	.472	.859	1	.964
2001— Detroit (A.L.)	OF-DH	20	34	1	3	1	0	1	4	2	12	1	1	0-0	.088	.162	.206	.368	0	1.000
— Oakland (A.L.)	OF-DH	20	58	6	17	7	1	0	10	5	13	1	0	1-0	.293	.354	.448	.802	1	.950
2002— Columbus (Int'l)	OF-1B	115	442	72	133	32	3	8	46	59	71	6	6	2-5	.301	.388	.441	.829	1	.993
2003— Sacramento (PCL)	OF-DH	38	153	31	51	10	0	8	35	17	30	1	3	1-1	.333	.401	.556	.957	2	.966
— Oakland (A.L.)	OF-DH-1B	66	153	15	41	11	0	6	26	19	36	2	3	0-0	.268	.354	.458	.812	1	.981
2004— Sacramento (PCL)	DH-OF	10	32	7	14	4	0	3	10	7	3	1	0	0-0	.438	.550	.844	1.394	0	1.000
— Oakland (A.L.)	OF-DH-1B	52	92	10	17	4	0	3	11	4	22	1	2	0-1	.185	.255	.326	.581	0	1.000
American League totals (4 years)		204	460	52	115	30	2	14	75	53	102	6	8	2-1	.250	.331	.415	.746	3	.978
National League totals (2 years)		65	141	14	34	5	1	2	18	11	38	0	2	2-1	.241	.290	.333	.624	2	.970
Major League totals (6 years)		269	601	66	149	35	3	16	93	64	140	6	10	4-2	.248	.322	.396	.718	5	.976

DIVISION SERIES RECORD

Year	Team (League)	Pos.	G	AB	R	H	2B	3B	HR	RBI	BB	SO	HBP	GDP	SB-CS	Avg.	OBP	SLG	OPS	E	Avg.
2003— Oakland (A.L.)	OF	3	6	0	1	0	0	0	1	1	1	0	0	0-0	.167	.286	.167	.452	0	1.000

MCPHERSON, DALLAS   3B

PERSONAL: Born July 23, 1980, in Greensboro, N.C. ... 6-4/230. ... Bats left, throws right. ... Full name: Dallas Lyle McPherson. ... High school: Randleman (N.C.). ... College: Citadel.

TRANSACTIONS/CAREER NOTES: Selected by Atlanta Braves organization in 44th round of 1998 free-agent draft; did not sign. ... Selected by Anaheim Angels organization in second round of 2001 free-agent draft.

2004 GAMES PLAYED BY POSITION (MLB): 3B—14.

Year	Team (League)	Pos.	G	AB	R	H	2B	3B	HR	RBI	BB	SO	HBP	GDP	SB-CS	Avg.	OBP	SLG	OPS	E	Avg.
2001— Provo (Pio.)	3B-1B	31	124	30	49	11	0	5	29	12	22	0	2	1-0	.395	.449	.605	1.053	11	.901
2002— Cedar Rap. (Midw.)	3B	132	499	71	138	24	3	15	88	78	128	7	9	30-6	.277	.381	.427	.807	31	.898
2003— Rancho Cuca. (Calif.)	3B	77	292	65	90	21	6	18	59	41	79	6	4	12-6	.308	.404	.606	1.010	14	.926
— Arkansas (Texas)	3B	28	102	22	32	9	1	5	27	19	25	1	4	4-0	.314	.426	.569	.995	2	.955
2004— Arkansas (Texas)	3B-DH	68	262	53	84	17	6	20	69	34	74	4	2	6-5	.321	.404	.660	1.056	12	.929
— Salt Lake (PCL)	3B-DH-OF	67	259	54	81	19	8	20	57	23	95	1	5	6-3	.313	.370	.680	1.047	17	.887
— Anaheim (A.L.)	3B	16	40	5	9	1	0	3	6	3	17	0	0	1-0	.225	.279	.475	.754	0	1.000
Major League totals (1 year)		16	40	5	9	1	0	3	6	3	17	0	0	1-0	.225	.279	.475	.754	0	1.000

DIVISION SERIES RECORD

Year	Team (League)	Pos.	G	AB	R	H	2B	3B	HR	RBI	BB	SO	HBP	GDP	SB-CS	Avg.	OBP	SLG	OPS	E	Avg.
2004— Anaheim (A.L.)	3B	3	9	0	1	0	0	0	1	0	4	0	0	0-0	.111	.111	.111	.222	0	1.000

MEADOWS, BRIAN   P

PERSONAL: Born November 21, 1975, in Montgomery, Ala. ... 6-4/230. ... Throws right, bats right. ... Full name: Matthew Brian Meadows. ... High school: Charles Henderson (Troy, Ala.).

TRANSACTIONS/CAREER NOTES: Selected by Florida Marlins organization in third round of 1994 free-agent draft; pick received as compensation for Colorado Rockies signing Type B free-agent SS Walt Weiss. ... On disabled list (July 28-August 13, 1998). ... Traded by Marlins to San Diego Padres for P Dan Miceli (November 15, 1999). ... Traded by Padres to Kansas City Royals for P Jay Witasick (July 31, 2000). ... Signed as a free agent by Minnesota Twins organization (January 15, 2002). ... Released by Twins (March 30, 2002). ... Signed by Pittsburgh Pirates organization (April 5, 2002).

CAREER HITTING: 21-for-179 (.117), 12 R, 3 2B, 0 3B, 0 HR, 8 RBI.

Year Team (League)	W	L	Pct.	ERA	WHIP	G	GS	CG	ShO	Hld.	Sv.-Opp.	IP	H	R	ER	HR	BB-IBB	SO	Avg.
1994— GC Marlins (GCL)	3	0	1.000	1.95	1.08	8	7	0	0	...	0-...	37.0	34	9	8	1	6-0	33	.236
1995— Kane County (Midwest)	9	9	.500	4.22	1.39	26	26	1	1	...	0-...	147.0	163	90	69	11	41-0	103	.281
1996— Brevard County (FSL)	8	7	.533	3.58	1.05	24	23	3	1	...	0-...	146.0	129	73	58	13	25-1	69	.231
— Portland (East.)	0	1	.000	4.33	1.11	4	4	1	0	...	0-...	27.0	26	15	13	1	4-0	13	.263
1997— Portland (East.)	9	7	.563	4.61	1.43	29	29	4	0	...	0-...	175.2	204	99	90	23	48-4	115	.292
1998— Florida (N.L.)	11	13	.458	5.21	1.54	31	31	1	0	0	0-0	174.1	222	106	101	20	46-3	88	.315
1999— Florida (N.L.)	11	15	.423	5.60	1.52	31	31	0	0	0	0-0	178.1	214	117	111	31	57-5	72	.302
2000— San Diego (N.L.)	7	8	.467	5.34	1.60	22	22	0	0	0	0-0	124.2	150	80	74	24	50-6	53	.301
— Kansas City (A.L.)	6	2	.750	4.77	1.37	11	10	2	0	0	0-0	71.2	84	39	38	8	14-0	26	.293
2001— Kansas City (A.L.)	1	6	.143	6.97	1.60	19	10	0	0	0	0-0	50.1	73	41	39	12	12-2	21	.351
— Omaha (PCL)	6	5	.545	6.17	1.55	18	18	0	0	...	0-...	105.0	143	73	72	21	20-1	74	.332
2002— Nashville (PCL)	9	8	.529	4.27	1.25	23	22	1	1	...	0-...	126.1	132	69	60	15	26-1	98	.267
— Pittsburgh (N.L.)	1	6	.143	3.88	1.21	11	11	0	0	0	0-0	62.2	62	29	27	7	14-8	31	.256
2003— Nashville (PCL)	7	0	1.000	1.41	0.60	9	8	1	1	...	0-...	51.0	32	11	8	2	4-0	40	.178
— Pittsburgh (N.L.)	2	1	.667	4.72	1.34	34	7	0	0	5	1-1	76.1	91	45	40	8	11-2	38	.290
2004— Pittsburgh (N.L.)	2	4	.333	3.58	1.22	68	0	0	0	13	1-2	78.0	76	40	31	7	19-7	46	.259
American League totals (2 years)	**7**	**8**	**.467**	**5.68**	**1.50**	**21**	**20**	**2**	**0**	**0**	**0-0**	**122.0**	**157**	**80**	**77**	**20**	**26-2**	**47**	**.317**
National League totals (6 years)	**34**	**47**	**.420**	**4.98**	**1.46**	**197**	**102**	**1**	**0**	**18**	**2-3**	**694.1**	**815**	**417**	**384**	**97**	**197-31**	**328**	**.295**
Major League totals (7 years)	**41**	**55**	**.427**	**5.08**	**1.46**	**218**	**122**	**3**	**0**	**18**	**2-3**	**816.1**	**972**	**497**	**461**	**117**	**223-33**	**375**	**.299**

MECHE, GIL   P

PERSONAL: Born September 8, 1978, in Lafayette, La. ... 6-3/200. ... Throws right, bats right. ... Full name: Gilbert Allen Meche. ... Name pronounced: MESH. ... High school: Acadiana (Lafayette, La.).

TRANSACTIONS/CAREER NOTES: Selected by Seattle Mariners organization in first round (22nd pick overall) of 1996 free-agent draft. ... On disabled list (May 29-June 13 and July 31, 2000-remainder of season); included rehabilitation assignments to Tacoma, Wisconsin and Everett. ... On disabled list (March 31, 2001-entire season).

CAREER HITTING: 1-for-5 (.200), 0 R, 0 2B, 0 3B, 0 HR, 0 RBI.

Year Team (League)	W	L	Pct.	ERA	WHIP	G	GS	CG	ShO	Hld.	Sv.-Opp.	IP	H	R	ER	HR	BB-IBB	SO	Avg.
1996— Ariz. Mariners (Ariz.)	0	1	.000	6.00	1.67	2	0	0	0	...	0-...	3.0	4	2	2	0	1-0	4	.333
1997— Everett (Northwest)	3	4	.429	3.98	1.33	12	12	1	0	...	0-...	74.2	75	40	33	7	24-0	62	.264
— Wisconsin (Midw.)	0	2	.000	3.00	1.33	2	2	0	0	...	0-...	12.0	12	5	4	1	4-0	14	.261
1998— Wisconsin (Midw.)	8	7	.533	3.44	1.34	26	0	0	0	...	0-...	149.0	136	77	57	9	63-0	168	.238
1999— New Haven (East.)	3	4	.429	3.05	1.31	10	10	0	0	...	0-...	59.0	51	24	20	3	26-0	56	.231
— Tacoma (PCL)	2	2	.500	3.19	1.42	6	6	0	0	...	0-...	31.0	31	12	11	3	13-0	24	.261
— Seattle (A.L.)	8	4	.667	4.73	1.52	16	15	0	0	0	0-0	85.2	73	48	45	9	57-1	47	.237
2000— Seattle (A.L.)	4	4	.500	3.78	1.34	15	15	1	1	0	0-0	85.2	75	37	36	7	40-0	60	.240
— Tacoma (PCL)	1	1	.500	3.86	1.43	3	3	0	0	...	0-...	14.0	10	7	6	1	10-0	15	.200
— Wisconsin (Midw.)	0	0	...	0.00	0.60	1	1	0	0	...	0-...	5.0	1	0	0	0	2-0	6	.067
— Everett (Northwest)	0	1	.000	9.00	3.00	1	1	0	0	...	0-...	1.0	3	1	1	0	0-0	1	.600
2001— Seattle (A.L.)			Did not play.																
2002— San Antonio (Texas)	4	6	.400	6.51	1.54	25	13	0	0	...	0-...	65.0	68	49	47	8	32-0	56	.271
2003— Seattle (A.L.)	15	13	.536	4.59	1.34	32	32	1	0	0	0-0	186.1	187	97	95	30	63-2	130	.263
2004— Tacoma (PCL)	1	3	.250	5.05	1.44	10	10	0	0	...	0-...	57.0	55	37	32	8	27-1	45	.249
— Seattle (A.L.)	7	7	.500	5.01	1.46	23	23	1	1	0	0-0	127.2	139	73	71	21	47-0	99	.273
Major League totals (4 years)	**34**	**28**	**.548**	**4.58**	**1.40**	**86**	**85**	**3**	**2**	**0**	**0-0**	**485.1**	**474**	**255**	**247**	**67**	**207-3**	**336**	**.257**

MECIR, JIM   P

PERSONAL: Born May 16, 1970, in Queens, N.Y. ... 6-1/230. ... Throws right, bats both. ... Full name: James Jason Mecir. ... Name pronounced: mah-SEAR. ... High school: Smithtown East (St. James, N.Y.). ... College: Eckerd (Fla.).

TRANSACTIONS/CAREER NOTES: Selected by Seattle Mariners organization in third round of 1991 free-agent draft. ... Traded by Mariners with 1B Tino Martinez and P Jeff Nelson to New York Yankees for P Sterling Hitchcock and 3B Russ Davis (December 7, 1995). ... Traded by Yankees to Boston Red Sox (September 29, 1997), completing deal in which Yankees traded P Tony Armas Jr. and a player to be named to Red Sox for C Mike Stanley and IF Randy Brown (August 13, 1997). ... Selected by Tampa Bay Devil Rays in second round (36th pick overall) of expansion draft (November 18, 1997). ... On disabled list (May 12, 1999-remainder of season; and April 27-May 23, 2000). ... Traded by Devil Rays with P Todd Belitz to Oakland Athletics for P Jesus Colome and a player to be named (July 28, 2000). ... On disabled list (August 2-September 5, 2001); included rehabilitation assignment to Sacramento. ... On suspended list (September 2-7, 2002). ... On disabled list (March 21-April 23 and July 24-August 13, 2003); included rehabilitation assignment to Sacramento.

CAREER HITTING: 0-for-1 (.000), 0 R, 0 2B, 0 3B, 0 HR, 0 RBI.

Year Team (League)	W	L	Pct.	ERA	WHIP	G	GS	CG	ShO	Hld.	Sv.-Opp.	IP	H	R	ER	HR	BB-IBB	SO	Avg.
1991— San Bernardino (Calif.)	3	5	.375	4.22	1.55	14	12	0	0	...	1-...	70.1	72	40	33	3	37-0	48	.268
1992— San Bernardino (Calif.)	4	5	.444	4.67	1.59	14	11	0	0	...	0-...	61.2	72	40	32	8	26-0	53	.289
1993— Riverside (California)	9	11	.450	4.33	1.50	26	26	1	0	...	0-...	145.1	160	89	70	3	58-2	85	.281
1994— Jacksonville (Southern)	6	5	.545	2.69	1.34	46	0	0	0	...	13-...	80.1	73	28	24	5	35-3	53	.245
1995— Tacoma (PCL)	1	4	.200	3.10	1.31	40	0	0	0	...	8-...	69.2	63	29	24	3	28-7	46	.238
— Seattle (A.L.)	0	0	...	0.00	1.50	2	0	0	0	0	0-0	4.2	5	1	0	0	2-0	3	.263
1996— Columbus (Int'l)	3	3	.500	2.27	1.09	33	0	0	0	...	7-...	47.2	37	14	12	2	15-2	51	.214
— New York (A.L.)	1	1	.500	5.13	1.61	26	0	0	0	0	0-0	40.1	42	24	23	6	23-4	38	.275
1997— Columbus (Int'l)	1	1	.500	1.00	0.74	24	0	0	0	...	11-...	27.0	14	4	3	0	6-0	34	.157
— New York (A.L.)	0	4	.000	5.88	1.37	25	0	0	0	1	0-1	33.2	36	23	22	5	10-1	25	.279
1998— Tampa Bay (A.L.)	7	2	.778	3.11	1.20	68	0	0	0	14	0-3	84.0	68	30	29	6	33-5	77	.225
1999— Tampa Bay (A.L.)	0	1	.000	2.61	1.40	17	0	0	0	6	0-2	20.2	15	7	6	0	14-0	15	.205
2000— Tampa Bay (A.L.)	7	2	.778	3.08	1.15	38	0	0	0	11	1-4	49.2	35	17	17	2	22-0	33	.201
— Oakland (A.L.)	3	1	.750	2.80	1.39	25	0	0	0	10	4-9	35.1	35	14	11	2	14-2	37	.255

M

Year Team (League)	W	L	Pct.	ERA	WHIP	G	GS	CG	ShO	Hld.	Sv.-Opp.	IP	H	R	ER	HR	BB-IBB	SO	Avg.
2001— Oakland (A.L.)	2	8	.200	3.43	1.27	54	0	0	0	17	3-8	63.0	54	25	24	4	26-7	61	.231
—Sacramento (PCL)	0	0	...	0.00	1.00	1	1	0	0	...	0-...	1.0	1	0	0	0	0-0	0	.250
2002— Oakland (A.L.)	6	4	.600	4.26	1.43	61	0	0	0	20	1-6	67.2	68	36	32	5	29-4	53	.259
2003—Sacramento (PCL)	0	0	...	5.40	2.10	3	2	0	0	...	0-...	3.1	5	4	2	0	2-0	3	.313
—Oakland (A.L.)	2	3	.400	5.59	1.51	41	0	0	0	12	1-2	37.0	40	25	23	4	16-1	25	.280
2004—Oakland (A.L.)	0	5	.000	3.59	1.34	65	0	0	0	21	2-7	47.2	45	21	19	5	19-2	49	.239
Major League totals (10 years)	28	31	.475	3.83	1.35	422	0	0	0	112	12-42	483.2	443	223	206	39	208-26	416	.244

DIVISION SERIES RECORD

Year Team (League)	W	L	Pct.	ERA	WHIP	G	GS	CG	ShO	Hld.	Sv.-Opp.	IP	H	R	ER	HR	BB-IBB	SO	Avg.
2000— Oakland (A.L.)	0	0	...	0.00	0.19	3	0	0	0	1	0-0	5.1	1	0	0	0	0-0	2	.059
2001— Oakland (A.L.)	0	0	...	5.40	1.20	2	0	0	0	1	0-0	3.1	4	2	2	1	0-0	4	.286
2002— Oakland (A.L.)	0	0	...	0.00	0.00	1	0	0	0	0	0-0	1.0	0	0	0	0	0-0	2	.000
2003— Oakland (A.L.)	0	0	...	0.00	3.00	1	0	0	0	0	0-0	.2	1	0	0	0	1-1	0	.333
Division series totals (4 years)	0	0	...	1.74	0.68	7	0	0	0	2	0-0	10.1	6	2	2	1	1-1	8	.162

MELHUSE, ADAM — C

PERSONAL: Born March 27, 1972, in Santa Clara, Calif. ... 6-2/200. ... Bats both, throws right. ... Full name: Adam Michael Melhuse. ... High school: Lincoln (Stockton, Calif.). ... College: UCLA.

TRANSACTIONS/CAREER NOTES: Selected by Toronto Blue Jays organization in 13th round of 1993 free-agent draft. ... Released by Blue Jays (April 2, 1999). ... Re-signed by Blue Jays organization (April 6, 1999). ... Signed as a free agent by Los Angeles Dodgers organization (December 15, 1999). ... Traded by Dodgers to Colorado Rockies for cash (June 17, 2000). ... Signed as a free agent by Chicago Cubs organization (November 8, 2001). ... Released by Cubs (July 17, 2002). ... Signed by Rockies organization (July 18, 2002). ... Signed as a free agent by Oakland Athletics organization (November 6, 2002).

2004 GAMES PLAYED BY POSITION (MLB): C—64, 3B—3, 1B—1.

Year Team (League)	Pos.	G	AB	R	H	2B	3B	HR	RBI	BB	SO	HBP	GDP	SB-CS	Avg.	OBP	SLG	OPS	E	Avg.
1993— St. Catharines (NY-Penn.) .	3B	73	266	40	68	14	2	5	32	45	61	0	4	4-0	.256	.360	.380	.740	14	.927
1994— Hagerstown (SAL)	C-1B	118	422	61	109	16	3	11	58	53	77	1	13	6-8	.258	.338	.389	.727	13	.983
1995— Dunedin (Fla. St.)	C-1B-OF	123	428	43	92	20	0	4	41	61	87	1	7	6-1	.215	.312	.290	.601	13	.980
1996— Dunedin (Fla. St.)	3-C-1-OF	97	315	50	78	23	2	13	51	69	68	3	5	3-1	.248	.384	.457	.841	15	.978
—Knoxville (Southern)	C	32	94	13	20	3	0	1	6	14	29	0	3	0-1	.213	.312	.277	.589	2	.989
1997— Knoxville (Southern)	C-1B-OF	31	87	14	20	3	0	3	10	19	19	0	1	0-0	.230	.364	.368	.732	2	.990
—Syracuse (Int'l)	2B-C-OF	118	118	7	28	5	1	2	9	12	18	1	2	1-1	.237	.311	.347	.658	1	.992
1998— Knoxville (Southern)	C-1B-OF	76	240	56	72	22	0	15	43	70	39	0	6	4-4	.300	.458	.579	1.037	11	.977
—Syracuse (Int'l)	3B-C	12	38	4	11	3	0	1	7	7	4	0	0	0-0	.289	.391	.447	.839	2	.965
1999— Knoxville (Southern)	3B-C-1B	107	374	79	110	25	0	19	69	108	76	4	10	5-6	.294	.454	.513	.967	4	.986
—Syracuse (Int'l)	C	21	71	15	20	5	0	2	16	10	20	0	1	1-1	.282	.370	.437	.807	0	1.000
2000— San Antonio (Texas)	C-OF-3-1	16	58	17	23	7	0	2	9	11	9	2	2	3-0	.397	.500	.621	1.121	2	.973
—Albuquerque (PCL)	C-1-3-OF	36	108	21	37	9	0	1	19	22	21	...	...	4-2	.343	...	.454	...	0	1.000
—Los Angeles (N.L.)		1	1	0	0	0	0	0	0	0	0	0	0	0-0	.000	.000	.000	.000	...	...
—Colorado (N.L.)	1B-C-OF	23	23	3	4	0	1	0	4	3	5	0	1	0-0	.174	.269	.261	.530	0	1.000
—Colo. Springs (PCL)	OF-C-1B	42	140	23	39	5	1	3	18	21	35	...	...	2-3	.279	...	.393	...	2	.987
2001— Colo. Springs (PCL)	C-1B-OF	54	184	26	49	10	1	7	32	31	42	2	8	0-1	.266	.378	.446	.824	5	.986
—Colorado (N.L.)	C-1B	40	71	5	13	2	0	1	8	6	18	0	3	1-0	.183	.241	.254	.494	1	.991
2002— Iowa (PCL) C-3-1-OF-S		72	226	33	66	19	0	7	39	28	47	0	...	2-3	.292	.370	.469	.839	7	.983
—Colo. Springs (PCL)	C-1B	34	115	25	40	10	1	6	20	16	23	0	...	2-1	.348	.424	.609	1.033	4	.982
2003— Sacramento (PCL)	C-OF-3-DH	45	147	26	42	9	0	3	17	26	32	1	5	0-1	.286	.394	.408	.802	2	.992
—Oakland (A.L.)	C-3B-1B	40	77	13	23	7	0	5	14	9	19	0	2	0-0	.299	.372	.584	.957	2	.986
2004— Oakland (A.L.)	C-3B-1B	69	214	23	55	11	0	11	31	16	47	0	4	0-1	.257	.309	.463	.771	3	.992
American League totals (2 years)		109	291	36	78	18	0	16	45	25	66	0	6	0-1	.268	.326	.495	.821	5	.991
National League totals (2 years)		64	95	8	17	2	1	1	12	9	24	0	4	1-0	.179	.245	.253	.498	1	.992
Major League totals (4 years)		173	386	44	95	20	1	17	57	34	90	0	10	1-1	.246	.306	.435	.741	6	.991

DIVISION SERIES RECORD

Year Team (League)	Pos.	G	AB	R	H	2B	3B	HR	RBI	BB	SO	HBP	GDP	SB-CS	Avg.	OBP	SLG	OPS	E	Avg.
2003— Oakland (A.L.)	C	2	5	1	3	0	1	0	1	0	1	0	0	0-0	.600	.600	1.000	1.600	0	1.000

MENCH, KEVIN — OF

PERSONAL: Born January 7, 1978, in Wilmington, Del. ... 6-0/225. ... Bats right, throws right. ... Full name: Kevin Ford Mench. ... High school: St. Mark's (Wilmington, Del.). ... College: Delaware.

TRANSACTIONS/CAREER NOTES: Selected by Texas Rangers organization in fourth round of 1999 free-agent draft; pick received as part of compensation for Arizona Diamondbacks signing Type A free-agent P Todd Stottlemyre. ... On disabled list (March 21-April 17 and July 9, 2003-remainder of season); included rehabilitation assignment to Frisco. ... On disabled list (May 24-June 12, 2004); included rehabilitation assignment to Frisco.

2004 GAMES PLAYED BY POSITION (MLB): OF—109, DH—14.

Year Team (League)	Pos.	G	AB	R	H	2B	3B	HR	RBI	BB	SO	HBP	GDP	SB-CS	Avg.	OBP	SLG	OPS	E	Avg.
1999— Pulaski (Appalachian)	OF	65	260	36	94	22	1	16	60	28	48	2	2	12-2	.362	.420	.638	1.059	1	.989
—Savannah (S. Atl.)	OF	6	23	4	7	1	1	2	8	2	4	0	1	0-0	.304	.360	.696	1.056	2	.900
2000— Charlotte (Fla. St.)	OF	132	491	118	164	39	9	27	121	78	72	7	9	19-7	.334	.427	.615	1.042	1	.996
2001— Tulsa (Texas)	OF	120	475	78	126	34	2	26	83	34	76	6	7	4-6	.265	.319	.509	.828	4	.983
2002— Oklahoma (PCL)	OF	26	98	17	21	8	0	6	15	17	33	2	7	0-0	.214	.342	.480	.821	2	.965
—Texas (A.L.)	OF-DH	110	366	52	95	20	2	15	60	31	83	8	4	1-1	.260	.327	.448	.775	2	.990
2003— Frisco (Texas)	OF	3	11	1	1	0	0	0	0	1	2	0	0	0-0	.091	.167	.091	.258	0	1.000
—Oklahoma (PCL)	OF	29	105	16	28	8	0	4	21	19	15	1	1	2-0	.267	.366	.457	.824	0	1.000
—Texas (A.L.)	OF	38	125	15	40	12	0	2	11	10	17	3	2	1-1	.320	.381	.464	.845	1	.984
2004— Frisco (Texas)	DH-OF	4	16	3	5	0	0	1	1	1	0	0	0	0-0	.313	.353	.500	.853	0	1.000
—Texas (A.L.)	OF-DH	125	438	69	122	30	3	26	71	33	63	6	6	0-0	.279	.335	.539	.874	1	.995
Major League totals (3 years)		273	929	136	257	62	5	43	142	74	163	17	12	2-2	.277	.338	.493	.831	4	.992

PERSONAL: Born June 15, 1972, in Los Santos, Panama. ... 6-2/190. ... Throws right, bats right.

TRANSACTIONS/CAREER NOTES: Signed as a non-drafted free agent by New York Yankees organization (November 13, 1991). ... On disabled list (June 28-July 28 and August 4, 2000-remainder of season); included rehabilitation assignment to Tampa. ... On disabled list (March 26-April 10, 2001; and March 24-April 7, 2002). ... Signed as a free agent by Boston Red Sox (December 31, 2002). ... On disabled list (June 13-July 5 and August 3-September 3, 2003); included rehabilitation assignments to GCL Red Sox, Sarasota and Pawtucket. ... On disabled list (April 8-July 15, 2004); included rehabilitation assignments to Sarasota and Pawtucket.

CAREER HITTING: 0-for-3 (.000), 0 R, 0 2B, 0 3B, 0 HR, 0 RBI.

Year Team (League)	W	L	Pct.	ERA	WHIP	G	GS	CG	ShO	Hld.	Sv.-Opp.	IP	H	R	ER	HR	BB-IBB	SO	Avg.
1992— Dom. Yankees (DSL)	10	2	.833	2.13	1.10	15	15	5	0	...	0-...	109.2	93	37	26	...	28-...	79	...
1993— GC Yankees (GCL)	4	5	.444	2.79	0.98	15	9	0	0	...	1-...	67.2	59	26	21	3	7-0	61	.224
— Greensboro (S. Atl.)	0	1	.000	2.45	2.18	2	0	0	0	...	0-...	3.2	3	1	1	0	5-0	3	.231
1994— Tampa (FSL)	12	6	.667	3.01	1.25	22	21	1	0	...	0-...	134.1	133	54	45	7	35-1	110	.258
1995— Norwich (East.)	5	6	.455	3.21	1.34	19	19	2	1	...	0-...	89.2	87	39	32	4	33-0	68	.254
— Columbus (Int'l)	1	0	1.000	2.57	0.86	2	2	0	0	...	0-...	14.0	10	4	4	0	2-0	13	.208
1996— Columbus (Int'l)	6	2	.750	2.51	1.19	15	15	0	0	...	0-...	97.0	96	30	27	2	19-0	61	.266
— New York (A.L.)	4	5	.444	6.79	1.70	12	11	0	0	0	0-0	53.0	80	43	40	5	10-1	34	.343
1997— Columbus (Int'l)	0	0	...	5.68	1.26	1	1	0	0	...	0-...	6.1	7	6	4	1	1-0	4	.233
— New York (A.L.)	8	6	.571	4.24	1.38	39	15	0	0	4	2-4	133.2	157	67	63	15	28-2	82	.292
1998— New York (A.L.)	10	2	.833	3.25	1.24	41	14	1	1	5	1-4	130.1	131	50	47	9	30-6	56	.264
1999— New York (A.L.)	9	9	.500	4.29	1.36	53	6	0	0	4	3-6	123.2	141	68	59	13	27-3	80	.284
2000— New York (A.L.)	7	4	.636	4.25	1.31	14	9	1	1	0	0-1	65.2	66	32	31	9	20-1	30	.260
— Tampa (FSL)	0	2	.000	7.20	1.80	2	2	0	0	...	0-...	5.0	9	4	4	0	0-0	7	.409
2001— New York (A.L.)	8	4	.667	3.75	1.11	56	2	0	0	13	6-8	100.2	89	44	42	9	23-3	70	.241
2002— New York (A.L.)	8	4	.667	3.44	1.29	62	0	0	0	12	4-8	91.2	102	43	35	8	16-2	61	.275
2003— GC Red Sox (GCL)	0	0	...	0.00	0.40	2	2	0	0	...	0-...	7.0	3	0	0	0	0-0	4	.130
— Sarasota (Florida State)	1	0	1.000	0.00	0.60	1	1	0	0	...	0-...	5.0	2	0	0	0	1-0	4	.133
— Pawtucket (Int'l)	0	0	...	2.00	0.90	4	0	0	0	...	1-...	9.0	8	2	2	1	0-0	8	.242
— Boston (A.L.)	3	5	.375	6.75	1.77	37	5	0	0	3	0-1	66.2	98	51	50	10	20-4	36	.349
2004— Sarasota (Florida State)	0	1	.000	4.50	1.50	2	2	0	0	...	0-...	4.0	6	2	2	0	0-0	3	.353
— Pawtucket (Int'l)	0	1	.000	4.15	1.50	6	0	0	0	...	0-...	8.2	13	5	4	2	0-0	3	.351
— Boston (A.L.)	2	1	.667	3.52	1.04	27	0	0	0	3	0-0	30.2	25	12	12	3	7-1	13	.225
Major League totals (9 years)	59	40	.596	4.29	1.34	341	62	2	2	44	16-32	796.0	889	410	379	81	181-23	462	.282

DIVISION SERIES RECORD

Year Team (League)	W	L	Pct.	ERA	WHIP	G	GS	CG	ShO	Hld.	Sv.-Opp.	IP	H	R	ER	HR	BB-IBB	SO	Avg.
1997— New York (A.L.)	1	1	.500	2.45	0.82	2	0	0	0	0	0-0	3.2	3	1	1	0	0-0	2	.250
1998— New York (A.L.)				Did not play.															
1999— New York (A.L.)				Did not play.															
2001— New York (A.L.)	0	0	...	0.00	0.69	3	0	0	0	1	0-0	4.1	2	0	0	0	1-1	5	.133
2002— New York (A.L.)	0	0	...	13.50	3.75	2	0	0	0	0	0-0	1.1	5	2	2	1	0-0	0	.625
Division series totals (3 years)	1	1	.500	2.89	1.18	7	0	0	0	1	0-0	9.1	10	3	3	1	1-1	7	.286

CHAMPIONSHIP SERIES RECORD

Year Team (League)	W	L	Pct.	ERA	WHIP	G	GS	CG	ShO	Hld.	Sv.-Opp.	IP	H	R	ER	HR	BB-IBB	SO	Avg.
1998— New York (A.L.)	0	0	...	0.00	0.92	2	0	0	0	1	0-0	4.1	4	0	0	0	0-0	1	.235
1999— New York (A.L.)	0	0	...	0.00	0.00	2	0	0	0	1	1-1	2.1	0	0	0	0	0-0	2	.000
2001— New York (A.L.)	0	0	...	1.69	0.94	3	0	0	0	1	0-0	5.1	3	1	1	1	2-1	4	.158
2004— Boston (A.L.)	0	1	.000	4.50	1.00	2	0	0	0	0	0-0	2.0	2	1	1	0	0-0	1	.250
Champ. series totals (4 years)	0	1	.000	1.29	0.79	9	0	0	0	3	1-1	14.0	9	2	2	1	2-1	8	.176

WORLD SERIES RECORD

Year Team (League)	W	L	Pct.	ERA	WHIP	G	GS	CG	ShO	Hld.	Sv.-Opp.	IP	H	R	ER	HR	BB-IBB	SO	Avg.
1998— New York (A.L.)	1	0	1.000	9.00	2.00	1	0	0	0	0	0-0	1.0	2	1	1	0	0-0	1	.500
1999— New York (A.L.)	0	0	...	10.80	2.40	1	0	0	0	0	0-0	1.2	3	2	2	0	1-0	0	.429
2001— New York (A.L.)	0	0	...	0.00	0.38	2	0	0	0	0	0-0	2.2	1	0	0	0	0-0	1	.111
World series totals (3 years)	1	0	1.000	5.06	1.31	4	0	0	0	0	0-0	5.1	6	3	3	0	1-0	2	.300

PERSONAL: Born January 7, 1971, in Staten Island, N.Y. ... 5-8/198. ... Bats right, throws right. ... Name pronounced: men-a-keen-o. ... High school: Susan E. Wagner (Staten Island, N.Y.). ... College: Alabama.

TRANSACTIONS/CAREER NOTES: Selected by Chicago White Sox organization in 45th round of 1993 free-agent draft. ... Selected by Oakland Athletics organization from White Sox organization in Rule 5 minor league draft (December 15, 1997). ... On disabled list (March 26-April 22, 2004); included rehabilitation assignment to Midland. ... Traded by Athletics to Toronto Blue Jays for future considerations (May 12, 2004). ... Career major league pitching: 0-0, 27.00 ERA, 2 G, 1.1 IP, 8 H, 4 R, 4 ER, 0 BB, 0 SO.

2004 GAMES PLAYED BY POSITION (MLB): 2B—42, DH—19, SS—14, 3B—7, P—1.

Year Team (League)	Pos.	G	AB	R	H	2B	3B	HR	RBI	BB	SO	HBP	GDP	SB-CS	Avg.	OBP	SLG	OPS	E	Avg.
1993— GC Whi. Sox (GCL)	2B	17	45	10	11	4	1	1	9	12	4	4	1	3-1	.244	.443	.444	.887	1	.979
— Hickory (S. Atl.)	2B	50	178	35	50	6	3	4	19	33	28	4	4	11-2	.281	.403	.416	.819	6	.977
1994— South Bend (Mid.)	2B	106	379	77	113	21	5	5	48	78	70	9	8	15-8	.298	.427	.420	.847	10	.979
1995— Prince Will. (Car.)	2B	137	476	65	124	31	3	6	58	96	75	11	17	6-2	.261	.391	.376	.767	15	.975
1996— Birmingham (Sou.)	2B	125	415	77	121	25	3	12	62	64	84	8	5	7-9	.292	.391	.453	.844	13	.978
1997— Nashville (A.A.)	2B-3B-OF	37	113	20	26	4	0	4	11	26	31	6	2	3-2	.230	.397	.372	.769	9	.948
— Birmingham (Sou.)	2B-3B	90	318	78	95	28	4	12	60	79	77	11	7	7-3	.299	.447	.525	.972	11	.974
1998— Edmonton (PCL)	2B	106	378	72	105	11	7	10	40	70	75	10	11	9-10	.278	.403	.423	.826	7	.979
1999— Vancouver (PCL)	3-S-2-DH	130	501	103	155	31	9	15	88	73	97	9	12	4-5	.309	.403	.497	.900	10	.980
— Oakland (A.L.) SS-DH-3B		9	9	0	2	0	0	0	0	0	4	0	0	0-0	.222	.222	.222	.444	0	1.000
2000— Oakland (A.L.) 2-S-3-DH		66	145	31	37	9	1	6	26	20	45	1	1	1-4	.255	.345	.455	.800	6	.974
— Sacramento (PCL)	SS-3B	38	38	8	12	0	2	2	5	4	0	0	1	1-0	.316	.395	.526	.922	0	1.000
2001— Oakland (A.L.) 2-S-3-DH		139	471	82	114	22	2	12	60	79	97	19	13	2-3	.242	.369	.374	.742	16	.976
2002— Oakland (A.L.) 2-3-S-DH		38	132	22	27	7	0	3	15	20	32	1	4	0-0	.205	.312	.326	.637	2	.986
— Sacramento (PCL)	SS-2B-3B	84	314	50	78	12	0	6	50	46	58	8	10	10-3	.248	.356	.344	.700	22	.941
2003— Oakland (A.L.) 2-3-S-DH		43	83	10	16	0	0	2	9	19	16	4	2	0-0	.193	.364	.265	.630	4	.962

M

Year Team (League)	Pos.	G	AB	R	H	2B	3B	HR	RBI	BB	SO	HBP	GDP	SB-CS	Avg.	OBP	SLG	OPS	E	Avg.
2004— Midland (Texas)	2B-DH	4	13	1	4	0	0	0	0	2	1	0	0	0-0	.308	.400	.308	.708	1	.750
— Sacramento (PCL)	2B-DH	4	15	2	4	0	0	0	1	1	0	1	0	0-0	.267	.353	.267	.620	0	1.000
— Oakland (A.L.)	2B	13	33	0	3	0	0	0	1	1	8	1	2	0-0	.091	.143	.091	.234	1	.978
— Toronto (A.L.)	2-DH-S-3-P	72	236	40	71	13	4	9	25	36	44	3	3	0-2	.301	.400	.504	.904	1	.995
Major League totals (6 years)		380	1109	185	270	51	7	32	136	175	246	29	25	3-9	.243	.358	.389	.747	30	.979

DIVISION SERIES RECORD

Year Team (League)	Pos.	G	AB	R	H	2B	3B	HR	RBI	BB	SO	HBP	GDP	SB-CS	Avg.	OBP	SLG	OPS	E	Avg.
2000— Oakland (A.L.)	P	1	0	0	0	0	0	0	0	0	0	0	0	0-0	...	...	...	...	0	1.000
2001— Oakland (A.L.)	2B	4	12	2	1	0	0	0	0	1	4	0	0	0-0	.083	.154	.083	.237	1	.957
2003— Oakland (A.L.)	2B	1	0	0	0	0	0	0	0	0	0	0	0	0-0	...	...	...	...	0	...
Division series totals (3 years)		6	12	2	1	0	0	0	0	1	4	0	0	0-0	.083	.154	.083	.237	1	.960

MERCKER, KENT   P

PERSONAL: Born February 1, 1968, in Indianapolis, Ind. ... 6-2/205. ... Throws left, bats left. ... Full name: Kent Franklin Mercker. ... High school: Dublin (Ohio).

TRANSACTIONS/CAREER NOTES: Selected by Atlanta Braves organization in first round (fifth pick overall) of June 1986 free-agent draft. ... On disabled list (August 9-24, 1991). ... Traded by Braves to Baltimore Orioles for Ps Joe Borowski and Rachaad Stewart (December 17, 1995). ... Traded by Orioles to Cleveland Indians for 1B Eddie Murray (July 21, 1996). ... Signed as a free agent by Cincinnati Reds (December 10, 1996). ... On disabled list (August 17-September 2, 1997). ... Signed as a free agent by St. Louis Cardinals (December 16, 1997). ... On disabled list (June 14-July 1, 1998). ... Traded by Cardinals to Boston Red Sox for P Mike Matthews and C David Benham (August 24, 1999). ... On disabled list (September 7-23, 1999). ... Signed as a free agent by Anaheim Angels organization (January 26, 2000). ... On disabled list (May 12-August 12, 2000); included rehabilitation assignment to Lake Elsinore. ... Signed as a free agent by Red Sox organization (January 5, 2001). ... Released by Red Sox (March 29, 2001). ... Signed by Colorado Rockies organization (January 31, 2002). ... On disabled list (June 6-July 30, 2002); included rehabilitation assignment to Colorado Springs. ... On suspended list (September 20-23, 2002). ... Signed as a free agent by Cincinnati Reds organization (January 7, 2003). ... On disabled list (June 25-July 10, 2003). ... Claimed on waivers by Atlanta Braves (August 12, 2003). ... Signed as a free agent by Chicago Cubs (December 19, 2003). ... On disabled list (May 16-June 4, 2004). ... On suspended list (September 13-15, 2004).

CAREER HITTING: 28-for-248 (.113), 12 R, 5 2B, 2 3B, 1 HR, 18 RBI.

Year Team (League)	W	L	Pct.	ERA	WHIP	G	GS	CG	ShO	Hld.	Sv.-Opp.	IP	H	R	ER	HR	BB-IBB	SO	Avg.
1986— GC Braves (GCL)	4	3	.571	2.47	1.12	9	8	0	0	...	0-...	47.1	37	21	13	1	16-1	42	.200
1987— Durham (Caro.)	0	1	.000	5.40	1.46	3	3	0	0	...	0-...	11.2	11	8	7	1	6-0	14	.256
1988— Durham (Caro.)	11	4	.733	2.75	1.17	19	19	5	0	...	0-...	127.2	102	44	39	5	47-0	159	.214
— Greenville (Sou.)	3	1	.750	3.35	1.28	9	9	0	0	...	0-...	48.1	36	20	18	2	26-1	60	.201
1989— Richmond (Int'l)	9	12	.429	3.20	1.20	27	27	4	0	...	0-...	168.2	107	66	60	17	95-4	144	.183
— Atlanta (N.L.)	0	0	...	12.46	3.23	2	1	0	0	0	0-0	4.1	8	6	6	0	6-0	4	.400
1990— Richmond (Int'l)	5	4	.556	3.55	1.49	12	10	0	0	...	1-...	58.1	60	30	23	1	27-1	69	.260
— Atlanta (N.L.)	4	7	.364	3.17	1.39	36	0	0	0	0	7-10	48.1	43	22	17	6	24-3	39	.236
1991— Atlanta (N.L.)	5	3	.625	2.58	1.24	50	4	0	0	3	6-8	73.1	56	23	21	5	35-3	62	.211
1992— Atlanta (N.L.)	3	2	.600	3.42	1.26	53	0	0	0	6	6-9	68.1	51	27	26	4	35-1	49	.207
1993— Atlanta (N.L.)	3	1	.750	2.86	1.33	43	6	0	0	4	0-3	66.0	52	24	21	2	36-3	59	.214
1994— Atlanta (N.L.)	9	4	.692	3.45	1.20	20	17	2	1	0	0-0	112.1	90	46	43	16	45-3	111	.220
1995— Atlanta (N.L.)	7	8	.467	4.15	1.41	29	26	0	0	0	0-0	143.0	140	73	66	16	61-2	102	.258
1996— Baltimore (A.L.)	3	6	.333	7.76	1.86	14	12	0	0	0	0-0	58.0	73	56	50	12	35-1	22	.307
— Buffalo (A.A.)	0	2	.000	3.94	1.25	3	3	0	0	...	0-...	16.0	11	7	7	3	9-0	11	.193
— Cleveland (A.L.)	1	0	1.000	3.09	1.11	10	0	0	0	2	0-0	11.2	10	4	4	1	3-1	7	.244
1997— Cincinnati (N.L.)	8	11	.421	3.92	1.36	28	25	0	0	0	0-0	144.2	135	65	63	16	62-6	75	.250
1998— St. Louis (N.L.)	11	11	.500	5.07	1.56	30	29	0	0	0	0-0	161.2	199	99	91	11	53-4	72	.310
1999— St. Louis (N.L.)	6	5	.545	5.12	1.70	25	18	0	0	0	0-0	103.2	125	73	59	16	51-3	64	.303
— Boston (A.L.)	2	0	1.000	3.51	1.40	5	5	0	0	0	0-0	25.2	23	12	10	0	13-0	17	.235
2000— Anaheim (A.L.)	1	3	.250	6.52	1.78	21	7	0	0	1	0-0	48.1	57	35	35	12	29-3	30	.300
— Lake Elsinore (Calif.)	0	0	...	0.00	0.00	1	1	0	0	...	0-...	4.0	0	0	0	0	0-0	3	.000
2001—			Did not play.																
2002— Colorado (N.L.)	3	1	.750	6.14	1.75	58	0	0	0	9	0-3	44.0	55	33	30	12	22-2	37	.299
— Colo. Springs (PCL)	0	0	...	21.60	3.00	2	0	0	0	...	0-...	1.2	3	4	4	2	2-0	0	.429
2003— Cincinnati (N.L.)	0	2	.000	2.35	1.46	49	0	0	0	10	0-3	38.1	31	13	10	5	25-2	41	.225
— Atlanta (N.L.)	0	0	...	1.06	1.29	18	0	0	0	1	1-2	17.0	15	3	2	1	7-2	7	.231
2004— Chicago (N.L.)	3	1	.750	2.55	1.25	71	0	0	0	16	0-3	53.0	39	15	15	4	27-2	51	.205
American League totals (3 years)	7	9	.438	6.20	1.69	50	24	0	0	3	0-0	143.2	163	107	99	25	80-5	76	.287
National League totals (13 years)	62	56	.525	3.92	1.42	512	126	2	1	49	20-41	1078.0	1039	522	470	114	489-36	773	.255
Major League totals (15 years)	69	65	.515	4.19	1.45	562	150	2	1	52	20-41	1221.2	1202	629	569	139	569-41	849	.259

DIVISION SERIES RECORD

Year Team (League)	W	L	Pct.	ERA	WHIP	G	GS	CG	ShO	Hld.	Sv.-Opp.	IP	H	R	ER	HR	BB-IBB	SO	Avg.
1995— Atlanta (N.L.)	0	0	...	0.00	0.00	1	0	0	0	0	0-0	.1	0	0	0	0	0-0	0	.000
1999— Boston (A.L.)	0	0	...	10.80	3.60	1	1	0	0	0	0-0	1.2	3	2	2	0	3-0	1	.500
2003— Atlanta (N.L.)	0	0	...	0.00	1.00	1	0	0	0	0	0-0	1.0	0	0	0	0	1-0	1	.000
Division series totals (3 years)	0	0	...	6.00	2.33	3	1	0	0	0	0-0	3.0	3	2	2	0	4-0	2	.333

CHAMPIONSHIP SERIES RECORD

Year Team (League)	W	L	Pct.	ERA	WHIP	G	GS	CG	ShO	Hld.	Sv.-Opp.	IP	H	R	ER	HR	BB-IBB	SO	Avg.
1991— Atlanta (N.L.)	0	1	.000	13.50	3.00	1	0	0	0	0	0-0	.2	0	1	1	0	2-0	0	.000
1992— Atlanta (N.L.)	0	0	...	0.00	0.67	2	0	0	0	0	0-0	3.0	1	0	0	0	1-0	1	.100
1993— Atlanta (N.L.)	0	0	...	1.80	1.00	5	0	0	0	0	0-0	5.0	3	1	1	0	2-0	4	.176
1999— Boston (A.L.)	0	1	.000	4.70	2.09	2	2	0	0	0	0-0	7.2	12	4	4	2	4-0	5	.353
Champ. series totals (4 years)	0	2	.000	3.31	1.53	10	2	0	0	0	0-0	16.1	16	6	6	2	9-0	10	.254

WORLD SERIES RECORD

Year Team (League)	W	L	Pct.	ERA	WHIP	G	GS	CG	ShO	Hld.	Sv.-Opp.	IP	H	R	ER	HR	BB-IBB	SO	Avg.
1991— Atlanta (N.L.)	0	0	...	0.00	0.00	2	0	0	0	0	0-0	1.0	0	0	0	0	0-0	1	.000
1995— Atlanta (N.L.)	0	0	...	4.50	1.50	1	0	0	0	1	0-0	2.0	1	1	1	0	2-0	2	.143
World series totals (2 years)	0	0	...	3.00	1.00	3	0	0	0	1	0-0	3.0	1	1	1	0	2-0	3	.100

MERLONI, LOU — 1B/3B

PERSONAL: Born April 6, 1971, in Framingham, Mass. ... 5-10/200. ... Bats right, throws right. ... Full name: Louis William Merloni. ... Name pronounced: mer-LONE-ee. ... High school: Framingham (Mass.) South. ... College: Providence.

TRANSACTIONS/CAREER NOTES: Selected by Boston Red Sox organization in 10th round of 1993 free-agent draft. ... On disabled list (June 29-September 12, 1998); included rehabilitation assignment to GCL Red Sox. ... Contract sold by Red Sox to Yokohama of the Japan Central League (November 22, 1999). ... Re-signed by Red Sox organization (July 28, 2000). ... On disabled list (June 6-21, 2001); included rehabilitation assignment to Pawtucket. ... Claimed on waivers by San Diego Padres (March 25, 2003). ... On disabled list (June 9-July 4, 2003); included rehabilitation assignment to Lake Elsinore. ... Traded by Padres to Red Sox for P Rene Miniel (August 28, 2003). ... Signed as a free agent by Cleveland Indians organization (January 12, 2004). ... On disabled list (August 9-September 1, 2004); included rehabilitation assignment to Mahoning Valley. ... Refused minor league assignment and became a free agent (October 14, 2004).

2004 GAMES PLAYED BY POSITION (MLB): 1B—42, 3B—10, 2B—7, OF—4, DH—3.

Year Team (League)	Pos.	G	AB	R	H	2B	3B	HR	RBI	BB	SO	HBP	GDP	SB-CS	Avg.	OBP	SLG	OPS	E	Avg.
1993— GC Red Sox (GCL)	SS	4	14	4	5	1	0	0	1	1	1	1	0	1-1	.357	.438	.429	.866	1	.952
— Fort Laud. (FSL)	3B-SS	44	156	14	38	1	1	2	21	13	26	1	6	1-1	.244	.299	.301	.600	8	.951
1994— Sarasota (Fla. St.)	2B-3B-SS	113	419	59	120	16	2	1	63	36	57	7	11	5-2	.286	.345	.341	.687	18	.965
1995— Trenton (East.)	2B-3B-SS	93	318	42	88	16	1	1	30	39	50	11	1	7-7	.277	.373	.343	.716	20	.951
1996— Trenton (East.)	2-3-SS-1	28	95	11	22	6	1	3	16	9	18	5	2	0-2	.232	.330	.411	.741	8	.930
— GC Red Sox (GCL)	2B	1	4	1	1	0	0	0	1	0	0	0	0	0-0	.250	.200	.250	.450	0	1.000
— Pawtucket (Int'l)	2B-3B-SS	38	115	19	29	6	0	1	12	10	20	3	1	0-1	.252	.328	.330	.659	8	.945
1997— Trenton (East.)	2B-3B-SS	69	255	49	79	17	4	5	37	30	43	12	2	3-2	.310	.402	.467	.869	9	.957
— Pawtucket (Int'l)	2B-3B-SS	49	165	24	49	10	0	5	24	15	20	4	4	0-2	.297	.368	.448	.816	4	.979
1998— Pawtucket (Int'l)	2B-3B-SS	27	88	17	34	3	1	8	22	16	13	8	2	2-2	.386	.518	.716	1.234	2	.976
— Boston (A.L.)	2B-3B-SS	39	96	10	27	6	0	1	15	7	20	2	1	1-0	.281	.343	.375	.718	5	.962
— GC Red Sox (GCL)	2B	1	1	0	0	0	0	0	0	0	0	0	0	0-0	.000	.000	.000	.000	0	...
1999— Boston (A.L.)	S-3-2-DH-1-O	43	126	18	32	7	0	1	13	8	16	2	6	0-0	.254	.307	.333	.640	10	.940
— Pawtucket (Int'l)	S-3-DH-1-2	66	229	45	64	14	1	7	36	30	38	9	4	1-1	.279	.383	.441	.824	12	.945
2000— Yo. Bay. (Jp. Cn.)		42	94	10	20	4	0	1	3	7	15	...	...	0-...	.213	...	.287	...	...	...
— Pawtucket (Int'l)	SS-2-3-1	11	39	6	16	2	0	1	5	3	3	0	2	0-1	.410	.452	.538	.991	4	.897
— Boston (A.L.)	3B	40	128	10	41	11	2	0	18	4	22	1	8	1-0	.320	.341	.438	.778	7	.928
2001— Pawtucket (Int'l)	SS-2-3-1	52	195	30	51	12	0	4	20	15	37	5	6	2-0	.262	.330	.385	.715	10	.954
— Boston (A.L.)	SS-2B-3B	52	146	21	39	10	0	3	13	6	31	3	6	2-1	.267	.306	.397	.703	3	.983
2002— Boston (A.L.)	2-3-S-1-O	84	194	28	48	12	2	4	18	20	35	5	4	1-2	.247	.332	.392	.724	5	.982
— Pawtucket (Int'l)	3B-SS-OF	8	25	1	5	2	0	0	2	1	3	1	2	0-0	.200	.250	.280	.530	0	1.000
2003— Lake Elsinore (Calif.)	2B-3B-SS	5	19	3	9	3	0	1	7	1	0	0	0	0-0	.474	.476	.789	1.266	0	1.000
— San Diego (N.L.)	3-S-2-1-O	65	151	20	41	7	2	1	17	22	33	1	3	2-3	.272	.362	.364	.726	6	.962
— Portland (P.C.L.)	3B-SS-OF	15	30	4	7	1	0	1	4	4	8	0	0	0-0	.233	.324	.267	.590	0	1.000
2004— Mahoning Valley (NY-P)	DH	2	8	1	2	0	0	1	4	0	3	0	0	0-0	.250	.250	.625	.875	0	...
— Cleveland (A.L.)	1-3-2-O-DH	71	190	25	55	12	1	4	28	14	41	3	9	1-2	.289	.343	.426	.769	4	.989
American League totals (7 years)		344	910	116	249	59	5	13	106	63	173	16	34	6-5	.274	.329	.392	.721	34	.972
National League totals (1 year)		65	151	20	41	7	2	1	17	22	33	1	3	2-3	.272	.362	.364	.726	6	.962
Major League totals (7 years)		409	1061	136	290	66	7	14	123	85	206	17	37	8-8	.273	.334	.388	.722	40	.971

DIVISION SERIES RECORD

Year Team (League)	Pos.	G	AB	R	H	2B	3B	HR	RBI	BB	SO	HBP	GDP	SB-CS	Avg.	OBP	SLG	OPS	E	Avg.
1999— Boston (A.L.)	SS	3	6	1	2	0	0	0	1	1	1	0	0	0-0	.333	.429	.333	.762	1	.833

CHAMPIONSHIP SERIES RECORD

Year Team (League)	Pos.	G	AB	R	H	2B	3B	HR	RBI	BB	SO	HBP	GDP	SB-CS	Avg.	OBP	SLG	OPS	E	Avg.
1999— Boston (A.L.)		1	0	0	0	0	0	0	0	1	0	0	0	0-0	...	1.000	...	1.000		

MESA, JOSE — P

PERSONAL: Born May 22, 1966, in Azua, Dominican Republic. ... 6-3/232. ... Throws right, bats right. ... Full name: Jose Ramon Mesa. ... Name pronounced: MAY-sa. ... High school: Santa School (Azua, Dominican Republic).

TRANSACTIONS/CAREER NOTES: Signed as a non-drafted free agent by Toronto Blue Jays organization (October 31, 1981). ... Traded by Blue Jays to Baltimore Orioles (September 4, 1987), completing deal in which Orioles traded P Mike Flanagan to Blue Jays for P Oswald Peraza and a player to be named (August 31, 1987). ... Traded by Orioles to Cleveland Indians for OF Kyle Washington (July 14, 1992). ... On suspended list (April 5-8, 1993). ... Traded by Indians with IF Shawon Dunston and P Alvin Morman to San Francisco Giants for P Steve Reed and OF Jacob Cruz (July 23, 1998). ... Signed as a free agent by Seattle Mariners (November 13, 1998). ... Signed as a free agent by Philadelphia Phillies (November 17, 2000). ... On suspended list (August 28-30, 2001). ... Signed as a free agent by Pittsburgh Pirates organization (January 29, 2004).

HONORS: Named A.L. Fireman of the Year by THE SPORTING NEWS (1995).

CAREER HITTING: 0-for-0 (.000), 1 R, 0 2B, 0 3B, 0 HR, 0 RBI.

Year Team (League)	W	L	Pct.	ERA	WHIP	G	GS	CG	ShO	Hld.	Sv.-Opp.	IP	H	R	ER	HR	BB-IBB	SO	Avg.
1982— GC Blue Jays (GCL)	6	4	.600	2.70	0.94	13	12	6	3	...	1-...	83.1	58	34	25	1	20-0	40	...
1983— Florence (S. Atl.)	6	12	.333	5.48	1.74	28	27	1	0	...	0-...	141.1	153	116	86	14	93-0	91	...
1984— Florence (S. Atl.)	4	3	.571	3.76	1.64	7	7	0	0	...	0-...	38.1	38	24	16	3	25-0	35	.255
— Kinston (Caro.)	5	2	.714	3.91	1.56	10	9	0	0	...	0-...	50.2	51	23	22	2	28-0	24	.267
1985— Kinston (Caro.)	5	10	.333	6.16	1.77	30	20	0	0	...	1-...	106.2	110	89	73	11	79-2	71	.269
1986— Vent. County (Cal.)	10	6	.625	3.86	1.40	24	24	2	1	...	0-...	142.1	141	71	61	6	58-0	113	.256
— Knoxville (Southern)	2	2	.500	4.35	1.52	9	8	2	1	...	0-...	41.1	40	32	20	6	23-0	30	.242
1987— Knoxville (Southern)	10	13	.435	5.21	1.60	35	35	4	2	...	0-...	193.1	206	131	112	19	104-0	115	.273
— Baltimore (A.L.)	1	3	.250	6.03	1.69	6	5	0	0	1	0-0	31.1	38	23	21	7	15-0	17	.297
1988— Rochester (Int'l)	0	3	.000	8.62	2.23	11	2	0	0	...	0-...	15.2	21	20	15	2	14-0	15	.328
1989— Rochester (Int'l)	0	0	...	5.40	1.60	7	1	0	0	...	0-...	10.0	10	6	6	2	6-0	3	.263
— Hagerstown (Eastern)	0	0	...	1.38	1.00	3	3	0	0	...	0-...	13.0	9	2	2	0	4-0	12	.191
1990— Hagerstown (Eastern)	5	5	.500	3.42	1.35	15	15	3	1	...	0-...	79.0	77	35	30	4	30-0	72	.258
— Rochester (Int'l)	1	2	.333	2.42	1.27	4	4	0	0	...	0-...	26.0	21	11	7	2	12-0	23	.223
— Baltimore (A.L.)	3	2	.600	3.86	1.37	7	7	0	0	...	0-0	46.2	37	20	20	2	27-2	24	.218
1991— Baltimore (A.L.)	6	11	.353	5.97	1.72	23	23	1	0	...	0-0	123.2	151	86	82	11	62-2	64	.307
— Rochester (Int'l)	3	3	.500	3.86	1.31	8	8	1	0	...	0-...	51.1	37	25	22	4	30-0	48	.203
1992— Baltimore (A.L.)	3	8	.273	5.19	1.54	13	12	0	0	...	0-0	67.2	77	41	39	9	27-1	22	.287

Year	Team (League)	W	L	Pct.	ERA	WHIP	G	GS	CG	ShO	Hld.	Sv.-Opp.	IP	H	R	ER	HR	BB-IBB	SO	Avg.
	—Cleveland (A.L.)	4	4	.500	4.16	1.45	15	15	1	1	0	0-0	93.0	92	45	43	5	43-0	40	.262
1993—	Cleveland (A.L.)	10	12	.455	4.92	1.41	34	33	3	0	0	0-0	208.2	232	122	114	21	62-2	118	.286
1994—	Cleveland (A.L.)	7	5	.583	3.82	1.33	51	0	0	0	8	2-6	73.0	71	33	31	3	26-7	63	.254
1995—	Cleveland (A.L.)	3	0	1.000	1.13	1.03	62	0	0	0	0	* 46-48	64.0	49	9	8	3	17-2	58	.216
1996—	Cleveland (A.L.)	2	7	.222	3.73	1.34	69	0	0	0	0	39-44	72.1	69	32	30	6	28-4	64	.257
1997—	Cleveland (A.L.)	4	4	.500	2.40	1.35	66	0	0	0	9	16-21	82.1	83	28	22	7	28-3	69	.259
1998—	Cleveland (A.L.)	3	4	.429	5.17	1.50	44	0	0	0	7	1-3	54.0	61	36	31	7	20-3	35	.282
	—San Francisco (N.L.)	5	3	.625	3.52	1.57	32	0	0	0	6	0-1	30.2	30	14	12	1	18-2	28	.256
1999—	Seattle (A.L.)	3	6	.333	4.98	1.81	68	0	0	0	1	33-38	68.2	84	42	38	11	40-4	42	.305
2000—	Seattle (A.L.)	4	6	.400	5.36	1.61	66	0	0	0	11	1-3	80.2	89	48	48	11	41-0	84	.280
2001—	Philadelphia (N.L.)	3	3	.500	2.34	1.23	71	0	0	0	1	42-46	69.1	65	26	18	4	20-2	59	.246
2002—	Philadelphia (N.L.)	4	6	.400	2.97	1.37	74	0	0	0	0	45-54	75.2	65	26	25	5	39-7	64	.231
2003—	Philadelphia (N.L.)	5	7	.417	6.52	1.76	61	0	0	0	2	24-28	58.0	71	44	42	7	31-2	45	.296
2004—	Pittsburgh (N.L.)	5	2	.714	3.25	1.41	70	0	0	0	0	43-48	69.1	78	26	25	6	20-3	37	.291
	American League totals (12 years)	53	72	.424	4.45	1.47	524	95	6	2	37	138-163	1066.0	1133	565	527	103	436-30	700	.275
	National League totals (5 years)	22	21	.512	3.62	1.44	308	0	0	0	9	154-177	303.0	309	136	122	23	128-16	233	.264
	Major League totals (16 years)	75	93	.446	4.27	1.47	832	95	6	2	46	292-340	1369.0	1442	701	649	126	564-46	933	.272

DIVISION SERIES RECORD

Year	Team (League)	W	L	Pct.	ERA	WHIP	G	GS	CG	ShO	Hld.	Sv.-Opp.	IP	H	R	ER	HR	BB-IBB	SO	Avg.
1995—	Cleveland (A.L.)	0	0		0.00	1.00	2	0	0	0	0	0-0	2.0	0	0	0	0	2-0	0	.000
1996—	Cleveland (A.L.)	0	1	.000	3.86	1.71	2	0	0	0	0	0-1	4.2	8	2	2	1	0-0	7	.381
1997—	Cleveland (A.L.)	0	0		2.70	1.80	2	0	0	0	0	1-1	3.1	5	1	1	1	1-0	2	.333
2000—	Seattle (A.L.)	1	0	1.000	0.00	0.50	2	0	0	0	0	0-0	2.0	0	0	0	0	1-1	2	.000
	Division series totals (4 years)	1	1	.500	2.25	1.42	8	0	0	0	1	1-2	12.0	13	3	3	2	4-1	11	.277

CHAMPIONSHIP SERIES RECORD

Year	Team (League)	W	L	Pct.	ERA	WHIP	G	GS	CG	ShO	Hld.	Sv.-Opp.	IP	H	R	ER	HR	BB-IBB	SO	Avg.
1995—	Cleveland (A.L.)	0	0		2.25	1.00	4	0	0	0	0	1-1	4.0	3	1	1	1	1-0	1	.214
1997—	Cleveland (A.L.)	1	0	1.000	3.38	1.50	4	0	0	0	0	2-4	5.1	5	2	2	0	3-1	5	.238
2000—	Seattle (A.L.)	0	0		12.46	1.85	3	0	0	0	0	0-0	4.1	5	6	6	2	3-0	3	.313
	Champ. series totals (3 years)	1	0	1.000	5.93	1.46	11	0	0	0	0	3-5	13.2	13	9	9	3	7-1	9	.255

WORLD SERIES RECORD

Year	Team (League)	W	L	Pct.	ERA	WHIP	G	GS	CG	ShO	Hld.	Sv.-Opp.	IP	H	R	ER	HR	BB-IBB	SO	Avg.
1995—	Cleveland (A.L.)	1	0	1.000	4.50	1.50	2	0	0	0	0	1-1	4.0	5	2	2	1	1-0	4	.333
1997—	Cleveland (A.L.)	0	0		5.40	2.20	5	0	0	0	0	1-2	5.0	10	3	3	0	1-0	5	.417
	World series totals (2 years)	1	0	1.000	5.00	1.89	7	0	0	0	0	2-3	9.0	15	5	5	1	2-0	9	.385

ALL-STAR GAME RECORD

		W	L	Pct.	ERA	WHIP	G	GS	CG	ShO	Hld.	Sv.-Opp.	IP	H	R	ER	HR	BB-IBB	SO	Avg.
	All-Star Game totals (1 year)	0	0		0.00	0.00	1	0	0	0	0	0-0	1.0	0	0	0	0	0-0	1	.000

MEYER, DAN   P

PERSONAL: Born July 3, 1981, in Woodbury, N.J. ... 6-3/210. ... Throws left, bats right. ... Full name: Daniel L. Meyer. ... High school: Kingsway (N.J.). ... College: James Madison (Va.).

TRANSACTIONS/CAREER NOTES: Selected by Atlanta Braves organization in supplemental round ("sandwich pick" between first and second rounds, 34 pick overall) of 2002 free-agent draft; pick received as compensation for New York Yankees signing Type A free-agent P Steve Karsay.

CAREER HITTING: 0-for-0 (.000), 0 R, 0 2B, 0 3B, 0 HR, 0 RBI.

Year	Team (League)	W	L	Pct.	ERA	WHIP	G	GS	CG	ShO	Hld.	Sv.-Opp.	IP	H	R	ER	HR	BB-IBB	SO	Avg.
2002—	Danville (Appalachian)	3	3	.500	2.74	0.99	13	13	1	0	...	0-...	65.2	47	22	20	4	18-0	77	.198
2003—	Rome (S. Atl.)	4	4	.500	2.87	1.11	15	15	0	0	...	0-...	81.2	76	35	26	6	15-1	95	.248
	—Myrtle Beach (Caro.)	3	6	.333	2.87	1.10	13	13	0	0	...	0-...	78.1	69	29	25	7	17-1	63	.236
2004—	Greenville (Sou.)	6	3	.667	2.22	0.95	14	13	0	0	...	0-...	65.0	50	17	16	1	12-0	86	.209
	—Richmond (Int'l)	3	3	.500	2.79	1.42	12	11	0	0	...	0-...	61.1	62	23	19	6	25-1	60	.264
	—Atlanta (N.L.)	0	0		0.00	1.50	2	0	0	0	0	0-0	2.0	2	0	0	0	1-1	1	.286
	Major League totals (1 year)	0	0		0.00	1.50	2	0	0	0	0	0-0	2.0	2	0	0	0	1-1	1	.286

MICELI, DAN   P

PERSONAL: Born September 9, 1970, in Newark, N.J. ... 6-0/215. ... Throws right, bats right. ... Full name: Daniel Miceli. ... Name pronounced: muh-SELL-ee. ... High school: Dr. Phillips (Orlando).

TRANSACTIONS/CAREER NOTES: Signed as a non-drafted free agent by Kansas City Royals organization (March 7, 1990). ... Traded by Royals with P Jon Lieber to Pittsburgh Pirates for P Stan Belinda (July 31, 1993). ... Traded by Pirates to Detroit Tigers for P Clint Sodowsky (November 1, 1996). ... Traded by Tigers with P Donne Wall and 3B Ryan Balfe to San Diego Padres for P Tim Worrell and OF Trey Beamon (November 19, 1997). ... Traded by Padres to Florida Marlins for P Brian Meadows (November 15, 1999). ... On disabled list (May 30-July 19, 2000); included rehabilitation assignments to GCL Marlins and Brevard County. ... Released by Marlins (June 25, 2001). ... Signed by Colorado Rockies organization (July 2, 2001). ... Signed as a free agent by Texas Rangers organization (January 29, 2002). ... Released by Rangers (May 6, 2002). ... Signed by Rockies organization (December 19, 2002). ... Refused minor league assignment and became a free agent (May 13, 2003). ... Signed by Cleveland Indians organization (May 15, 2003). ... Traded by Indians with OF Karim Garcia to New York Yankees for a player to be named (June 25, 2003). ... Traded by Yankees to Houston Astros for a player to be named or cash (July 29, 2003). ... On disabled list (August 22-September 9, 2004).

CAREER HITTING: 2-for-22 (.091), 0 R, 0 2B, 0 3B, 0 HR, 0 RBI.

Year	Team (League)	W	L	Pct.	ERA	WHIP	G	GS	CG	ShO	Hld.	Sv.-Opp.	IP	H	R	ER	HR	BB-IBB	SO	Avg.
1990—	GC Royals (GCL)	3	4	.429	3.91	1.40	27	0	0	0	...	4-...	53.0	45	27	23	0	29-5	48	.234
1991—	Eugene (N'west)	0	1	.000	2.14	1.07	25	0	0	0	...	10-...	33.2	18	8	8	1	18-0	43	.158
1992—	Appleton (Midw.)	1	1	.500	1.93	0.69	23	0	0	0	...	9-...	23.1	12	6	5	0	4-1	44	.145
	—Memphis (Sou.)	3	0	1.000	1.91	0.88	32	0	0	0	...	4-...	37.2	20	10	8	5	13-0	46	.160
1993—	Memphis (Sou.)	6	4	.600	4.60	1.59	40	0	0	0	...	7-...	58.2	54	30	30	7	39-3	68	.242
	—Carolina (Southern)	0	2	.000	5.11	1.22	13	0	0	0	...	10-...	12.1	11	8	7	2	4-1	19	.234
	—Pittsburgh (N.L.)	0	0		5.06	1.69	9	0	0	0	0	0-0	5.1	6	3	3	0	3-0	4	.273
1994—	Buffalo (A.A.)	1	1	.500	1.88	0.88	19	0	0	0	...	2-...	24.0	15	5	5	2	6-0	31	.185
	—Pittsburgh (N.L.)	2	1	.667	5.93	1.43	28	0	0	0	4	2-3	27.1	28	19	18	5	11-2	27	.267
1995—	Pittsburgh (N.L.)	4	4	.500	4.66	1.53	58	0	0	0	2	21-27	58.0	61	30	30	7	28-5	56	.270
1996—	Pittsburgh (N.L.)	2	10	.167	5.78	1.68	44	9	0	0	4	1-1	85.2	99	65	55	15	45-5	66	.291
	—Carolina (Southern)	1	0	1.000	1.00	0.56	9	0	0	0	...	1-...	9.0	4	1	1	0	1-0	17	.125

M

Year Team (League)	W	L	Pct.	ERA	WHIP	G	GS	CG	ShO	Hld.	Sv.-Opp.	IP	H	R	ER	HR	BB-IBB	SO	Avg.
1997—Detroit (A.L.)	3	2	.600	5.01	1.39	71	0	0	0	11	3-8	82.2	77	49	46	13	38-4	79	.248
1998—San Diego (N.L.)	10	5	.667	3.22	1.25	67	0	0	0	20	2-8	72.2	64	28	26	6	27-4	70	.238
1999—San Diego (N.L.)	4	5	.444	4.46	1.50	66	0	0	0	9	2-4	68.2	67	39	34	7	36-5	59	.266
2000—Florida (N.L.)	6	4	.600	4.25	1.29	45	0	0	0	11	0-3	48.2	45	23	23	4	18-2	40	.242
—GC Marlins (GCL)	0	0	...	0.00	0.33	2	2	0	0	...	0-...	3.0	0	0	0	0	1-0	3	.000
—Brevard County (FSL)	1	0	1.000	0.00	0.50	5	4	0	0	...	0-...	6.0	3	2	2	1	0-0	7	.143
2001—Florida (N.L.)	0	5	.000	6.93	1.62	29	0	0	0	8	0-3	24.2	29	21	19	5	11-2	31	.287
—Colo. Springs (PCL)	0	2	.000	6.00	1.00	4	0	0	0	...	0-...	3.0	2	2	2	0	1-1	4	.200
—Colorado (N.L.)	2	0	1.000	2.21	1.13	22	0	0	0	0	1-1	20.1	18	8	5	2	5-0	17	.231
2002—Texas (A.L.)	0	2	.000	8.64	1.92	9	0	0	0	0	0-1	8.1	13	8	8	1	3-0	5	.333
2003—Colorado (N.L.)	0	2	.000	5.66	1.60	14	0	0	0	1	0-0	20.2	24	13	13	7	9-1	18	.286
—Buffalo (Int'l)	0	1	.000	3.00	1.30	5	0	0	0	...	0-...	6.0	7	2	2	1	1-1	6	.280
—Cleveland (A.L.)	1	1	.500	1.20	1.00	13	0	0	0	0	0-1	15.0	9	4	2	1	6-1	19	.164
—New York (A.L.)	0	0	...	5.79	1.50	7	0	0	0	1	1-1	4.2	4	3	3	2	3-0	1	.211
—Houston (N.L.)	1	1	.500	2.10	0.97	23	0	0	0	3	0-0	30.0	22	7	7	3	7-1	20	.208
2004—Houston (N.L.)	6	6	.500	3.59	1.30	74	0	0	0	24	2-8	77.2	74	34	31	10	27-12	83	.247
American League totals (3 years)	4	5	.444	4.80	1.38	100	0	0	0	12	4-11	110.2	103	64	59	17	50-5	104	.243
National League totals (10 years)	37	43	.463	4.40	1.42	479	9	0	0	86	31-58	539.2	537	290	264	71	227-39	491	.260
Major League totals (12 years)	41	48	.461	4.47	1.41	579	9	0	0	98	35-69	650.1	640	354	323	88	277-44	595	.257

DIVISION SERIES RECORD

Year Team (League)	W	L	Pct.	ERA	WHIP	G	GS	CG	ShO	Hld.	Sv.-Opp.	IP	H	R	ER	HR	BB-IBB	SO	Avg.
1998—San Diego (N.L.)	1	1	.500	2.70	0.60	3	0	0	0	1	0-0	3.1	2	1	1	0	0-0	4	.200
2004—Houston (N.L.)	0	1	.000	5.40	0.90	3	0	0	0	1	0-0	3.1	2	2	2	1	1-0	2	.167
Division series totals (2 years)	1	2	.333	4.05	0.75	6	0	0	0	2	0-0	6.2	4	3	3	1	1-0	6	.182

CHAMPIONSHIP SERIES RECORD

Year Team (League)	W	L	Pct.	ERA	WHIP	G	GS	CG	ShO	Hld.	Sv.-Opp.	IP	H	R	ER	HR	BB-IBB	SO	Avg.
1998—San Diego (N.L.)	0	0	...	13.50	6.00	3	0	0	0	1	0-0	.2	4	1	1	1	0-0	1	.667
2004—Houston (N.L.)	0	2	.000	27.00	3.00	2	0	0	0	0	0-0	1.1	3	4	4	3	1-0	0	.429
Champ. series totals (2 years)	0	2	.000	22.50	4.00	5	0	0	0	1	0-0	2.0	7	5	5	4	1-0	1	.538

WORLD SERIES RECORD

Year Team (League)	W	L	Pct.	ERA	WHIP	G	GS	CG	ShO	Hld.	Sv.-Opp.	IP	H	R	ER	HR	BB-IBB	SO	Avg.
1998—San Diego (N.L.)	0	0	...	0.00	2.40	0	0	0	0	0	0-0	1.2	2	0	0	0	2-0	1	.286

MICHAELS, JASON   OF

PERSONAL: Born May 4, 1976, in Tampa, Fla. ... 6-0/204. ... Bats right, throws right. ... Full name: Jason Drew Michaels. ... High school: Jesuit (Tampa, Fla.). ... College: Miami (Fla.). ... Grandson of John Michaels, pitcher with Boston Red Sox (1932).

TRANSACTIONS/CAREER NOTES: Selected by San Diego Padres organization in 49th round of 1994 free-agent draft; did not sign. ... Selected by Tampa Bay Devil Rays organization in 44th round of 1996 free-agent draft; did not sign. ... Selected by St. Louis Cardinals organization in 15th round of 1997 free-agent draft; did not sign. ... Selected by Philadelphia Phillies organization in fourth round of 1998 free-agent draft. ... On disabled list (March 21-April 14, 2003); included rehabilitation assignment to Clearwater.

2004 GAMES PLAYED BY POSITION (MLB): OF—78, DH—1.

Year Team (League)	Pos.	G	AB	R	H	2B	3B	HR	RBI	BB	SO	HBP	GDP	SB-CS	Avg.	OBP	SLG	OPS	E	Avg.
1998—Batavia (NY-Penn)	OF	67	235	45	63	14	3	11	49	40	69	4	5	4-2	.268	.381	.494	.874	5	.949
1999—Clearwater (FSL)	OF	122	451	91	138	31	6	14	65	68	103	3	7	10-7	.306	.396	.494	.890	1	.996
2000—Reading (East.)	OF	113	437	71	129	30	4	10	74	28	87	3	9	7-4	.295	.337	.451	.788	6	.977
2001—Scran./W.B. (I.L.)	OF	109	418	58	109	19	3	17	69	37	126	8	7	11-3	.261	.332	.443	.774	0	1.000
—Philadelphia (N.L.)	OF	6	6	0	1	0	0	0	1	0	2	0	0	0-0	.167	.167	.167	.333	0	...
2002—Scran./W.B. (I.L.)	OF	9	32	3	9	2	0	0	7	5	5	0	1	1-3	.281	.359	.344	.703	0	1.000
—Philadelphia (N.L.)	OF-DH-3B	81	105	16	28	10	3	2	11	13	33	1	1	1-1	.267	.347	.476	.823	2	.923
2003—Clearwater (FSL)	OF	4	14	1	0	0	0	0	0	2	4	0	0	0-0	.000	.125	.000	.125	0	1.000
—Philadelphia (N.L.)	OF	76	109	20	36	11	0	5	17	15	22	1	3	0-0	.330	.416	.569	.985	1	.976
2004—Philadelphia (N.L.)	OF-DH	115	299	44	82	12	0	10	40	42	80	2	3	2-2	.274	.364	.415	.779	3	.983
Major League totals (4 years)		278	519	80	147	33	3	17	69	70	137	4	7	3-3	.283	.370	.457	.826	6	.975

MIENTKIEWICZ, DOUG   1B

PERSONAL: Born June 19, 1974, in Toledo, Ohio. ... 6-2/206. ... Bats left, throws right. ... Full name: Douglas Andrew Mientkiewicz. ... Name pronounced: mint-KAY-vich. ... High school: Westminster Christian (Miami). ... College: Florida State.

TRANSACTIONS/CAREER NOTES: Selected by Minnesota Twins organization in fifth round of 1995 free-agent draft. ... On disabled list (July 7-23, 2004). ... Traded by Twins to Boston Red Sox as part of four-team deal in which Twins acquired P Justin Jones from Cubs, Red Sox acquired SS Orlando Cabrera from Expos, Expos acquired SS Alex S. Gonzalez, P Francis Beltran and IF Brendan Harris from Cubs, and Cubs acquired SS Nomar Garciaparra and Matt Murton from Red Sox (July 31, 2004).

HONORS: Won A.L. Gold Glove at first base (2001).

2004 GAMES PLAYED BY POSITION (MLB): 1B—124, 2B—1.

Year Team (League)	Pos.	G	AB	R	H	2B	3B	HR	RBI	BB	SO	HBP	GDP	SB-CS	Avg.	OBP	SLG	OPS	E	Avg.
1995—Fort Myers (FSL)	1B	38	110	9	27	6	1	1	15	18	19	1	1	2-2	.245	.357	.345	.702	1	.994
1996—Fort Myers (FSL)	1B	133	492	69	143	36	4	5	79	66	47	3	10	12-2	.291	.374	.411	.784	3	.998
1997—New Britain (East.)	1B-OF	132	467	87	119	28	2	15	61	98	67	7	8	21-8	.255	.390	.420	.810	5	.995
1998—New Britain (East.)	1B-OF	139	502	96	162	45	0	16	88	96	58	6	6	11-4	.323	.432	.508	.940	12	.995
—Minnesota (A.L.)	1B	8	25	1	5	1	0	0	2	4	3	0	0	1-1	.200	.310	.240	.550	0	1.000
1999—Minnesota (A.L.)	1B	118	327	34	75	21	3	2	32	43	51	4	13	1-1	.229	.324	.330	.655	3	.997
2000—Salt Lake (PCL)	1-3-2-0	130	485	96	162	32	3	18	96	61	68	3	17	9-5	.334	.406	.524	.929	10	.989
—Minnesota (A.L.)	1B	3	14	0	6	0	0	0	4	0	0	0	1	0-0	.429	.400	.429	.829	0	1.000
2001—Minnesota (A.L.)	1B-DH	151	543	77	166	39	1	15	74	67	92	9	10	2-6	.306	.387	.464	.851	4	.997
2002—Minnesota (A.L.)	1B	143	467	60	122	29	1	10	64	74	69	6	7	1-2	.261	.365	.392	.756	5	.996
2003—Minnesota (A.L.)	1-0-2-3-DH	142	487	67	146	38	1	11	65	74	55	5	9	4-1	.300	.393	.450	.843	4	.997
2004—Minnesota (A.L.)	1B	84	284	34	70	18	0	5	25	38	38	3	9	2-2	.246	.340	.363	.703	4	.994
—Boston (A.L.)	1B-2B	49	107	13	23	6	1	1	10	10	18	1	3	0-1	.215	.286	.318	.603	1	.996
Major League totals (7 years)		692	2254	286	613	152	7	44	276	310	326	28	52	11-14	.272	.363	.404	.768	21	.996

Year	Team (League)	Pos.	G	AB	R	H	2B	3B	HR	RBI	BB	SO	HBP	GDP	SB-CS	Avg.	OBP	SLG	OPS	E	Avg.
2002— Minnesota (A.L.)	1B	5	20	3	5	0	0	2	4	1	1	0	0	0-0	.250	.286	.550	.836	0	1.000
2003— Minnesota (A.L.)	1B	4	15	0	2	0	0	0	1	2	0	0	0	0-0	.133	.188	.133	.321	0	1.000
2004— Boston (A.L.)	1B	3	4	0	2	0	0	0	1	0	0	0	0	0-0	.500	.500	.500	1.000	0	1.000
Division series totals (3 years)		12	39	3	9	0	0	2	5	3	2	0	0	0-0	.231	.268	.385	.653	0	1.000

CHAMPIONSHIP SERIES RECORD

Year	Team (League)	Pos.	G	AB	R	H	2B	3B	HR	RBI	BB	SO	HBP	GDP	SB-CS	Avg.	OBP	SLG	OPS	E	Avg.
2002— Minnesota (A.L.)	1B	5	18	1	5	1	0	0	2	1	2	0	0	0-0	.278	.316	.333	.649	0	1.000
2004— Boston (A.L.)	1B	4	4	0	2	1	0	0	0	0	1	0	0	0-0	.500	.500	.750	1.250	0	1.000
Champ. series totals (2 years)		9	22	1	7	2	0	0	2	1	3	0	0	0-0	.318	.348	.409	.757	0	1.000

WORLD SERIES RECORD

Year	Team (League)	Pos.	G	AB	R	H	2B	3B	HR	RBI	BB	SO	HBP	GDP	SB-CS	Avg.	OBP	SLG	OPS	E	Avg.
2004— Boston (A.L.)	1B	4	1	0	0	0	0	0	0	0	0	0	0	0-0	.000	.000	.000	.000	0	1.000

MILES, AARON   2B

PERSONAL: Born December 15, 1976, in Pittsburg, Calif. ... 5-7/180. ... Bats both, throws right. ... Full name: Aaron Wade Miles. ... High school: Antioch High (California).
TRANSACTIONS/CAREER NOTES: Selected by Houston Astros organization in 19th round of 1995 free-agent draft. ... Selected by Chicago White Sox organization from Astros organization in Rule 5 minor league draft (December 11, 2000). ... Traded by White Sox to Colorado Rockies for IF Juan Uribe (December 2, 2003).
2004 GAMES PLAYED BY POSITION (MLB): 2B—128.

Year	Team (League)	Pos.	G	AB	R	H	2B	3B	HR	RBI	BB	SO	HBP	GDP	SB-CS	Avg.	OBP	SLG	OPS	E	Avg.
1995— GC Astros (GCL)	SS-2B	47	171	32	44	9	3	0	18	14	14	0	3	9-6	.257	.312	.345	.657	14	.916
1996— GC Astros (GCL)	2B	55	214	48	63	3	2	0	15	20	18	1	3	14-7	.294	.357	.327	.685	10	.947
1997— Quad City (Midw.)	2B	97	370	55	97	13	2	1	35	30	45	2	8	18-11	.262	.318	.316	.634	14	.961
1998— Quad City (Midw.)	2B-3B-OF	108	369	42	90	22	6	2	37	25	52	1	7	28-13	.244	.293	.352	.645	28	.945
1999— Michigan (Midw.)	2B	112	470	72	149	28	8	10	71	28	33	2	8	17-12	.317	.353	.474	.828	11	.964
2000— Kissimmee (Fla. St.)	2B	75	295	40	86	20	1	2	36	28	29	0	7	11-6	.292	.352	.386	.738	17	.950
2001— Birmingham (Sou.)	3B-2B	84	343	53	89	16	3	8	42	26	35	2	10	13-5	.259	.313	.394	.706	6	.943
2002— Birmingham (Sou.)	2B-3B	138	531	67	171	39	1	9	68	40	45	2	4	25-16	.322	.369	.450	.819	26	.956
2003— Charlotte (Int'l)	2B-DH-3B	133	546	80	166	34	5	11	50	40	52	1	9	8-9	.304	.351	.445	.796	15	.973
— Chicago (A.L.)	2B-DH	8	12	3	4	3	0	0	2	0	0	0	0	0-0	.333	.333	.583	.917	0	1.000
2004— Colo. Springs (PCL)	2B	12	54	8	18	3	0	0	8	2	4	0	1	2-2	.333	.345	.389	.734	2	.968
— Colorado (N.L.)	2B	134	522	75	153	15	3	6	47	29	53	2	12	12-7	.293	.329	.368	.697	10	.984
American League totals (1 year)		8	12	3	4	3	0	0	2	0	0	0	0	0-0	.333	.333	.583	.917	0	1.000
National League totals (1 year)		134	522	75	153	15	3	6	47	29	53	2	12	12-7	.293	.329	.368	.697	10	.984
Major League totals (2 years)		142	534	78	157	18	3	6	49	29	53	2	12	12-7	.294	.329	.373	.702	10	.984

MILLAR, KEVIN   OF/1B

PERSONAL: Born September 24, 1971, in Los Angeles, Calif. ... 6-0/210. ... Bats right, throws right. ... Full name: Kevin Charles Millar. ... Name pronounced: mi-LAR. ... High school: University (Los Angeles). ... College: Lamar. ... Nephew of Wayne Nordhagen, outfielder with four major league teams (1976-83).
TRANSACTIONS/CAREER NOTES: Contract purchased by Florida Marlins organization from Saint Paul of the independent Northern League (September 20, 1993). ... On Florida disabled list (April 19, 1998-remainder of season); included rehabilitation assignment to Charlotte. ... On Florida disabled list (May 4-28, 2002); included rehabilitation assignment to Portland. ... Claimed on waivers by Boston Red Sox (January 14, 2003); rejected claim. ... Traded by Marlins to Red Sox for cash considerations (February 15, 2003).
2004 GAMES PLAYED BY POSITION (MLB): OF—74, 1B—69, DH—8.

Year	Team (League)	Pos.	G	AB	R	H	2B	3B	HR	RBI	BB	SO	HBP	GDP	SB-CS	Avg.	OBP	SLG	OPS	E	Avg.
1993— St. Paul (Nor.)		63	227	33	59	11	1	5	30	24	27	...	...	2-...	.260	...	.383	...	18	.911
1994— Kane Co. (Midw.)	1B	135	477	75	144	35	2	19	93	74	88	13	12	3-3	.302	.405	.503	.908	11	.990
1995— Brevard County (FSL)	1B	129	459	53	132	32	2	13	68	70	66	12	8	4-4	.288	.388	.451	.839	12	.991
1996— Portland (East.)	3B-1B	130	472	69	150	32	0	18	86	37	53	9	13	6-5	.318	.375	.500	.875	15	.983
1997— Portland (East.)	3B-1B	135	511	94	175	34	2	32	131	66	53	10	11	2-3	.342	.423	.605	1.027	17	.987
1998— Florida (N.L.)	3B	2	2	1	1	0	0	0	0	1	0	0	0	0-0	.500	.667	.500	1.167	1	.833
— Charlotte (Int'l)	3B-1B	14	46	14	15	3	0	4	15	9	7	2	3	1-0	.326	.448	.652	1.100	4	.930
1999— Calgary (PCL)	OF-3B-1B	36	143	24	43	11	1	7	26	11	19	0	5	2-0	.301	.348	.538	.887	2	.973
— Florida (N.L.)	1B-3B-OF	105	351	48	100	17	4	9	67	40	64	7	7	1-0	.285	.362	.433	.795	4	.995
2000— Florida (N.L.)	1-OF-3-DH	123	259	36	67	14	3	14	42	36	47	8	5	0-0	.259	.364	.498	.862	5	.985
2001— Florida (N.L.)	O-1-3-DH	144	449	62	141	39	5	20	85	39	70	5	8	0-0	.314	.374	.557	.931	2	.993
2002— Florida (N.L.)	O-DH-3-1	126	438	58	134	41	0	16	57	40	74	5	15	0-2	.306	.366	.509	.875	4	.981
— Portland (East.)		3	12	1	1	0	0	1	3	0	5	0	0	0-0	.083	.077	.333	.410	0	1.000
2003— Boston (A.L.)	1B-OF-DH	148	544	83	150	30	1	25	96	60	108	5	14	3-2	.276	.348	.472	.820	5	.995
2004— Boston (A.L.)	OF-1B-DH	150	508	74	151	36	0	18	74	57	91	17	16	1-1	.297	.383	.474	.857	9	.986
American League totals (2 years)		298	1052	157	301	66	1	43	170	117	199	22	30	4-3	.286	.365	.473	.838	14	.992
National League totals (5 years)		500	1499	205	443	111	12	59	251	156	255	25	35	1-2	.296	.367	.504	.871	16	.990
Major League totals (7 years)		798	2551	362	744	177	13	102	421	273	454	47	65	5-5	.292	.366	.491	.858	30	.991

DIVISION SERIES RECORD

Year	Team (League)	Pos.	G	AB	R	H	2B	3B	HR	RBI	BB	SO	HBP	GDP	SB-CS	Avg.	OBP	SLG	OPS	E	Avg.
2003— Boston (A.L.)	1B	5	21	0	5	0	0	0	0	2	4	0	0	0-0	.238	.304	.238	.542	0	1.000
2004— Boston (A.L.)	1B	3	10	2	3	0	0	1	4	1	1	0	0	0-0	.300	.364	.600	.964	0	1.000
Division series totals (2 years)		8	31	2	8	0	0	1	4	3	5	0	0	0-0	.258	.324	.355	.678	0	1.000

CHAMPIONSHIP SERIES RECORD

Year	Team (League)	Pos.	G	AB	R	H	2B	3B	HR	RBI	BB	SO	HBP	GDP	SB-CS	Avg.	OBP	SLG	OPS	E	Avg.
2003— Boston (A.L.)	1B	7	29	3	7	0	0	1	3	1	9	0	0	0-0	.241	.267	.345	.611	1	.986
2004— Boston (A.L.)	1B	7	24	4	6	3	0	0	2	5	4	0	0	0-0	.250	.379	.375	.754	0	1.000
Champ. series totals (2 years)		14	53	7	13	3	0	1	5	6	13	0	0	0-0	.245	.322	.358	.681	1	.992

WORLD SERIES RECORD

Year	Team (League)	Pos.	G	AB	R	H	2B	3B	HR	RBI	BB	SO	HBP	GDP	SB-CS	Avg.	OBP	SLG	OPS	E	Avg.
2004— Boston (A.L.)	1B	4	8	2	1	1	0	0	0	2	2	1	0	0-0	.125	.364	.250	.614	1	.900

M

MILLER, CORKY   C

PERSONAL: Born March 18, 1976, in Yucaipa, Calif. ... 6-1/225. ... Bats right, throws right. ... Full name: Corky Abraham Philip Miller. ... High school: Yucaipa (Calif.). ... College: Nevada-Reno.

TRANSACTIONS/CAREER NOTES: Selected by California Angels organization in 23rd round of 1994 free-agent draft; did not sign. ... Signed as a non-drafted free agent by Cincinnati Reds organization (June 5, 1998). ... Claimed on waivers by Minnesota Twins (October 4, 2004).

2004 GAMES PLAYED BY POSITION (MLB): C—12.

										BATTING									FIELDING	
Year Team (League)	Pos.	G	AB	R	H	2B	3B	HR	RBI	BB	SO	HBP	GDP	SB-CS	Avg.	OBP	SLG	OPS	E	Avg.
1998— Billings (Pio.)	C	45	129	28	35	8	0	5	24	24	24	21	2	1-4	.271	.455	.450	.904	14	.963
1999— Rockford (Midwest)	C	66	195	43	56	10	1	10	40	33	42	20	5	3-6	.287	.438	.503	.940	14	.975
— Chattanooga (Sou.)	C	33	104	20	23	10	0	4	16	11	30	11	3	0-0	.221	.354	.433	.787	3	.989
2000— Chattanooga (Sou.)	C	103	317	40	74	18	0	9	44	41	51	30	12	5-8	.233	.373	.375	.748	16	.981
2001— Chattanooga (Sou.)	C	59	170	25	47	12	0	9	42	25	32	19	1	1-2	.276	.425	.506	.931	7	.985
— Louisville (Int'l)	C	44	144	30	50	11	0	7	28	10	19	12	2	2-0	.347	.431	.569	1.001	2	.994
— Cincinnati (N.L.)	C	17	49	5	9	2	0	3	7	4	16	2	1	1-0	.184	.263	.408	.671	1	.991
2002— Louisville (Int'l)	C	43	134	14	31	5	0	6	21	16	21	6	6	1-2	.231	.340	.403	.743	2	.993
— Cincinnati (N.L.)	C	39	114	9	29	10	0	3	15	9	20	4	7	0-0	.254	.328	.421	.749	2	.992
2003— Louisville (Int'l)	C-DH	103	354	49	88	28	0	11	43	35	58	7	12	0-0	.249	.326	.421	.747	7	.989
— Cincinnati (N.L.)	C	14	30	4	8	0	0	1	5	7	7	2	1	0-0	.267	.395	.267	.661	0	1.000
2004— Louisville (Int'l)	C-DH	74	227	31	50	14	0	6	37	25	44	9	4	0-0	.220	.316	.361	.677	4	.990
— Cincinnati (N.L.)	C	13	39	2	1	0	0	0	3	6	12	3	3	0-0	.026	.204	.026	.230	1	.989
Major League totals (4 years)		83	232	20	47	12	0	6	26	24	55	11	12	1-0	.203	.301	.332	.633	4	.992

MILLER, DAMIAN   C

PERSONAL: Born October 13, 1969, in La Crosse, Wis. ... 6-3/220. ... Bats right, throws right. ... Full name: Damian Donald Miller. ... High school: West Salem (Wis.). ... College: Viterbo (Wis.).

TRANSACTIONS/CAREER NOTES: Selected by Minnesota Twins organization in 20th round of 1990 free-agent draft. ... Selected by Arizona Diamondbacks in second round (47th pick overall) of expansion draft (November 18, 1997). ... On disabled list (July 24-August 14, 2002); included rehabilitation assignment to Tucson. ... Traded by Diamondbacks to Chicago Cubs for P David Noyce and OF Gary Johnson (November 13, 2002). ... Traded by Cubs to Oakland Athletics for C Michael Barrett (December 21, 2003).

2004 GAMES PLAYED BY POSITION (MLB): C—109.

										BATTING									FIELDING	
Year Team (League)	Pos.	G	AB	R	H	2B	3B	HR	RBI	BB	SO	HBP	GDP	SB-CS	Avg.	OBP	SLG	OPS	E	Avg.
1990— Elizabethton (App.)	C	14	45	7	10	1	0	1	6	9	3	0	2	1-0	.222	.352	.311	.663	2	.982
1991— Kenosha (Midw.)	C-1B-OF	80	267	28	62	11	1	3	34	24	53	2	4	3-2	.232	.297	.315	.612	4	.990
1992— Kenosha (Midw.)	C	115	377	53	110	27	2	5	56	53	66	7	13	6-1	.292	.385	.414	.799	9	.989
1993— Fort Myers (FSL)	C	87	325	31	69	12	1	1	26	31	44	0	5	6-3	.212	.281	.265	.546	8	.985
— Nashville (Southern)	C	4	13	0	3	0	0	0	0	2	4	0	0	0-0	.231	.333	.231	.564	0	1.000
1994— Nashville (Southern)	C	103	328	36	88	10	0	8	35	35	51	1	11	4-6	.268	.336	.372	.708	8	.989
1995— Salt Lake (PCL)	C-OF	83	295	39	84	23	1	3	41	15	39	3	11	2-4	.285	.324	.400	.724	5	.998
1996— Salt Lake (PCL)	C-1B	104	385	54	110	27	1	7	55	25	58	6	13	1-4	.286	.336	.416	.751	6	.992
1997— Salt Lake (PCL)	C-DH	85	314	48	106	19	3	11	82	29	62	3	7	6-1	.338	.395	.522	.918	6	.988
— Minnesota (A.L.)	C-DH	25	66	5	18	1	0	2	13	2	12	0	2	0-0	.273	.282	.379	.660	0	1.000
1998— Tucson (PCL)	C	18	63	14	22	7	1	0	11	9	9	2	2	0-0	.349	.434	.492	.926	3	.973
— Arizona (N.L.)	C-DH-OF-1	57	168	17	48	14	2	3	14	11	43	2	2	1-0	.286	.337	.446	.783	4	.986
1999— Arizona (N.L.)	C	86	296	35	80	19	0	11	47	19	78	2	6	0-0	.270	.316	.446	.762	6	.991
2000— Arizona (N.L.)	C-1B	100	324	43	89	24	0	10	44	36	74	1	6	2-2	.275	.347	.441	.788	7	.991
2001— Arizona (N.L.)	C	123	380	45	103	19	0	13	47	35	80	4	9	0-1	.271	.337	.424	.761	7	.993
2002— Arizona (N.L.)	C	101	297	40	74	22	0	11	42	38	88	3	14	0-0	.249	.340	.434	.775	2	.997
— Tucson (PCL)	C	3	9	1	3	1	0	0	0	0	1	0	1	0-0	.333	.333	.444	.778	0	1.000
2003— Chicago (N.L.)	C	114	352	34	82	19	1	9	36	39	91	1	15	1-0	.233	.310	.369	.680	3	.997
2004— Oakland (A.L.)	C	110	397	39	108	25	0	9	58	39	87	2	19	0-1	.272	.339	.403	.742	1	.999
American League totals (2 years)		135	463	44	126	26	0	11	71	41	99	2	21	0-1	.272	.331	.400	.730	1	.999
National League totals (6 years)		581	1817	214	476	117	3	57	230	178	454	13	52	4-3	.262	.331	.424	.755	29	.994
Major League totals (8 years)		716	2280	258	602	143	3	68	301	219	553	15	73	4-4	.264	.331	.419	.750	30	.994

DIVISION SERIES RECORD

										BATTING									FIELDING	
Year Team (League)	Pos.	G	AB	R	H	2B	3B	HR	RBI	BB	SO	HBP	GDP	SB-CS	Avg.	OBP	SLG	OPS	E	Avg.
2001— Arizona (N.L.)	C	5	15	1	4	0	0	0	0	1	3	1	0	0-0	.267	.353	.267	.620	0	1.000
2002— Arizona (N.L.)	C	1	2	0	1	1	0	0	0	2	0	0	0	0-0	.500	.750	1.000	1.750	0	1.000
2003— Chicago (N.L.)	C	4	11	0	1	1	0	0	1	2	5	0	0	0-0	.091	.231	.182	.413	0	1.000
Division series totals (3 years)		10	28	1	6	2	0	0	1	5	8	1	0	0-0	.214	.353	.286	.639	0	1.000

CHAMPIONSHIP SERIES RECORD

										BATTING									FIELDING	
Year Team (League)	Pos.	G	AB	R	H	2B	3B	HR	RBI	BB	SO	HBP	GDP	SB-CS	Avg.	OBP	SLG	OPS	E	Avg.
2001— Arizona (N.L.)	C	5	17	0	3	0	0	0	0	2	5	0	2	0-0	.176	.263	.176	.440	0	1.000
2003— Chicago (N.L.)	C	4	10	0	2	1	0	0	1	2	2	0	0	0-0	.200	.333	.300	.633	0	1.000
Champ. series totals (2 years)		9	27	0	5	1	0	0	1	4	7	0	2	0-0	.185	.290	.222	.513	0	1.000

WORLD SERIES RECORD

										BATTING									FIELDING	
Year Team (League)	Pos.	G	AB	R	H	2B	3B	HR	RBI	BB	SO	HBP	GDP	SB-CS	Avg.	OBP	SLG	OPS	E	Avg.
2001— Arizona (N.L.)	C	6	20	3	4	2	0	0	2	1	11	1	1	0-0	.200	.273	.300	.573	1	.982

ALL-STAR GAME RECORD

									BATTING									FIELDING	
	G	AB	R	H	2B	3B	HR	RBI	BB	SO	HBP	GDP	SB-CS	Avg.	OBP	SLG	OPS	E	Avg.
All-Star Game totals (1 year)	1	3	1	2	2	0	0	1	0	0	0	0	0-0	.667	.667	1.333	2.000	0	1.000

MILLER, JUSTIN   P

PERSONAL: Born August 27, 1977, in Torrance, Calif. ... 6-2/209. ... Throws right, bats right. ... Full name: Justin Mark Miller. ... High school: Torrance (Calif.). ... Junior college: Los Angeles Harbor.

TRANSACTIONS/CAREER NOTES: Selected by San Francisco Giants organization in 34th round of 1995 free-agent draft; did not sign. ... Selected by Colorado Rockies organization in fifth round of 1997 free-agent draft. ... Traded by Rockies with cash to Oakland Athletics as part of three-team deal in which Brewers acquired P Jimmy Haynes from A's, Rockies acquired 3B Jeff Cirillo, P Scott Karl and cash from Brewers and Brewers acquired P Jamey Wright and C Henry Blanco from Rockies (December 13, 1999). ... Traded by A's with 3B Eric Hinske to Toronto Blue Jays for P Billy Koch (December 7, 2001). ... On disabled list (May 31-August 4, 2004).

M

CAREER HITTING: 0-for-2 (.000), 0 R, 0 2B, 0 3B, 0 HR, 0 RBI.

Year	Team (League)	W	L	Pct.	ERA	WHIP	G	GS	CG	ShO	Hld.	Sv.-Opp.	IP	H	R	ER	HR	BB-IBB	SO	Avg.
1997—Portland (N'west)		4	2	.667	2.14	1.31	14	11	0	0	...	0-...	67.1	68	26	16	3	20-0	54	.262
1998—Asheville (S. Atl.)		13	8	.619	3.69	1.33	27	27	3	1	...	0-...	163.1	177	89	67	14	40-0	142	.275
1999—Salem (Caro.)		1	2	.333	4.14	1.24	8	8	0	0	...	0-...	37.0	35	18	17	3	11-0	35	.245
2000—Midland (Texas)		5	4	.556	4.55	1.32	18	18	0	0	...	0-...	87.0	74	49	44	8	41-1	82	.230
—Sacramento (PCL)		4	1	.800	2.47	1.01	9	9	0	0	...	0-...	54.2	42	18	15	3	13-0	34	.210
2001—Sacramento (PCL)		7	10	.412	4.75	1.44	29	28	1	0	...	0-...	165.0	174	94	87	26	64-1	134	.276
2002—Syracuse (Int'l)		3	2	.600	1.61	1.12	8	8	0	0	...	0-...	44.2	34	11	8	0	16-0	29	.207
—Toronto (A.L.)		9	5	.643	5.54	1.65	25	18	0	0	1	0-0	102.1	103	70	63	12	66-2	68	.268
2003—Dunedin (Fla. St.)		0	1	.000	4.50	0.80	1	1	0	0	...	0-...	6.0	3	3	3	0	2-0	5	.167
2004—Syracuse (Int'l)		1	1	.500	2.16	1.20	3	3	0	0	...	0-...	16.2	16	6	4	2	4-0	21	.242
—Toronto (A.L.)		3	4	.429	6.06	1.75	19	15	0	0	0	0-0	81.2	101	58	55	14	42-3	47	.316
Major League totals (2 years)		12	9	.571	5.77	1.70	44	33	0	0	1	0-0	184.0	204	128	118	26	108-5	115	.289

MILLER, MATT — P

PERSONAL: Born November 23, 1971, in Greenwood, Miss. ... 6-3/215. ... Throws right, bats right. ... Full name: Matt Jacob Miller. ... High school: Monterey (Lubbock, Texas). ... College: Delta State.

TRANSACTIONS/CAREER NOTES: Signed as a free agent by Texas Rangers organization (December 1, 1997). ... Released by Rangers (March 29, 1998). ... Contract purchased by Rangers organization from Greenville of the independent Big South League (June 27, 1998). ... Signed as a free agent by San Diego Padres organization (November 5, 2000). ... Signed as a free agent by Oakland Athletics organization (November 19, 2001). ... Signed as a free agent by Colorado Rockies organization (November 20, 2002). ... Signed as a free agent by Cleveland Indians organization (January 5, 2004).

CAREER HITTING: 0-for-0 (.000), 0 R, 0 2B, 0 3B, 0 HR, 0 RBI.

Year	Team (League)	W	L	Pct.	ERA	WHIP	G	GS	CG	ShO	Hld.	Sv.-Opp.	IP	H	R	ER	HR	BB-IBB	SO	Avg.
1996—Greenville (Big South)		5	2	.714	6.07	1.82	19	6	0	0	...	1-...	69.2	77	51	47	2	50-0	54	.286
1997—Greenville (Big South)		12	3	.800	2.26	1.16	15	15	5	3	...	0-...	107.1	76	34	27	0	49-0	129	.203
1998—Greenville (Big South)		1	7	.125	2.85	1.21	8	8	4	0	...	0-...	53.2	46	26	17	1	19-1	49	.230
—Savannah (S. Atl.)		3	1	.750	2.29	0.99	17	0	0	0	...	3-...	35.1	25	9	9	0	10-0	46	.203
1999—Charlotte (Fla. St.)		1	2	.333	3.03	1.35	22	0	0	0	...	8-...	29.2	27	12	10	0	13-1	39	.231
—Tulsa (Texas)		6	4	.600	3.38	1.25	34	0	0	0	...	7-...	56.0	42	24	21	2	28-2	83	.213
2000—GC Rangers (GCL)		0	0	...	4.50	1.00	1	0	0	0	...	0-...	2.0	2	1	1	0	0-0	3	.250
—Tulsa (Texas)		0	0	...	14.73	3.00	3	0	0	0	...	0-...	3.2	7	7	6	0	4-0	4	.412
—Oklahoma (PCL)		3	3	.500	3.58	1.57	39	0	0	0	...	4-...	60.1	61	29	24	2	34-4	69	.264
2001—Portland (PCL)		1	7	.125	3.63	1.30	44	0	0	0	...	17-...	44.2	44	22	18	1	14-2	43	.254
2002—Sacramento (PCL)		3	7	.300	4.31	1.54	54	0	0	0	...	6-...	71.0	81	42	34	5	28-8	63	.286
2003—Colorado (N.L.)		0	0	...	2.08	1.62	4	0	0	0	0	0-0	4.1	5	1	1	0	2-0	5	.313
—Colo. Springs (PCL)		5	0	1.000	2.13	1.09	61	0	0	0	...	3-...	63.1	46	17	15	0	23-1	83	.204
2004—Buffalo (Int'l)		1	2	.333	1.93	1.14	13	0	0	0	...	2-...	14.0	10	4	3	0	6-1	17	.196
—Cleveland (A.L.)		4	1	.800	3.09	1.17	57	0	0	0	7	1-2	55.1	42	22	19	1	23-8	55	.216
American League totals (1 year)		4	1	.800	3.09	1.17	57	0	0	0	7	1-2	55.1	42	22	19	1	23-8	55	.216
National League totals (1 year)		0	0	...	2.08	1.62	4	0	0	0	0	0-0	4.1	5	1	1	0	2-0	5	.313
Major League totals (2 years)		4	1	.800	3.02	1.21	61	0	0	0	7	1-2	59.2	47	23	20	1	25-8	60	.224

MILLER, TREVER — P

PERSONAL: Born May 29, 1973, in Louisville, Ky. ... 6-3/200. ... Throws left, bats right. ... Full name: Trever Douglas Miller. ... High school: Trinity (Louisville, Ky.).

TRANSACTIONS/CAREER NOTES: Selected by Detroit Tigers organization in supplemental round ("sandwich pick" between first and second rounds, 41st pick overall) of 1991 free-agent draft; pick received as part of compensation for Atlanta Braves signing Type A free-agent C Mike Heath. ... Traded by Tigers with C Brad Ausmus, Ps Jose Lima and C.J. Nitkowski and 1B Daryle Ward to Houston Astros for OF Brian Hunter, IF Orlando Miller, Ps Doug Brocail and Todd Jones and cash (December 10, 1996). ... On disabled list (August 23-September 7, 1998). ... Traded by Astros to Philadelphia Phillies for P Yorkis Perez (March 29, 2000). ... Claimed on waivers by Los Angeles Dodgers (May 19, 2000). ... Signed as a free agent by Boston Red Sox organization (January 22, 2001). ... Signed as a free agent by Cincinnati Reds organization (December 21, 2001). ... Released by Reds (September 4, 2002). ... Signed by Toronto Blue Jays organization (October 30, 2002). ... Signed as a free agent by Tampa Bay Devil Rays (January 7, 2004).

CAREER HITTING: 1-for-6 (.167), 1 R, 1 2B, 0 3B, 0 HR, 0 RBI.

Year	Team (League)	W	L	Pct.	ERA	WHIP	G	GS	CG	ShO	Hld.	Sv.-Opp.	IP	H	R	ER	HR	BB-IBB	SO	Avg.
1991—Bristol (Appalachian)		2	7	.222	5.67	1.65	13	13	0	0	...	0-...	54.0	60	44	34	7	29-0	46	.278
1992—Bristol (Appalachian)		3	8	.273	4.93	1.47	12	12	1	0	...	0-...	69.1	75	45	38	4	27-0	64	.271
1993—Fayetteville (S. Atl.)		8	13	.381	4.19	1.35	28	28	2	0	...	0-...	161.0	151	99	75	7	67-0	116	.245
1994—Trenton (East.)		7	16	.304	4.39	1.43	26	26	6	0	...	0-...	174.1	198	95	85	9	51-0	73	.290
1995—Jacksonville (Southern)		8	2	.800	2.72	1.28	31	16	3	2	...	0-...	122.1	122	46	37	5	34-0	77	.261
1996—Toledo (International)		13	6	.684	4.90	1.40	27	27	0	0	...	0-...	165.1	167	98	90	19	65-1	115	.260
—Detroit (A.L.)		0	4	.000	9.18	2.22	5	4	0	0	0	0-0	16.2	28	17	17	3	9-0	8	.384
1997—New Orleans (A.A.)		6	7	.462	3.30	1.41	29	27	2	0	...	0-...	163.2	177	71	60	15	54-1	99	.283
1998—Houston (N.L.)		2	0	1.000	3.04	1.44	37	1	0	0	...	1-2	53.1	57	21	18	4	20-1	30	.266
1999—Houston (N.L.)		3	2	.600	5.07	1.75	47	0	0	0	4	1-1	49.2	58	29	28	6	29-1	37	.299
2000—Philadelphia (N.L.)		0	0	...	8.36	2.00	14	0	0	0	0	0-0	14.0	19	16	13	3	9-1	10	.317
—Los Angeles (N.L.)		0	0	...	23.14	4.71	2	0	0	0	0	0-0	2.1	8	6	6	0	3-0	1	.571
—Albuquerque (PCL)		4	2	.667	3.41	1.38	12	9	1	1	...	0-...	58.0	60	29	22	5	20-0	39	.268
2001—Sarasota (Florida State)		0	0	...	2.25	0.50	3	2	0	0	...	0-...	8.0	3	2	2	0	1-0	6	.115
—Pawtucket (Int'l)		3	11	.214	5.20	1.52	33	15	0	0	...	0-...	116.0	142	79	67	16	34-2	93	.307
2002—Louisville (Int'l)		9	5	.643	3.18	1.21	65	0	0	0	...	0-...	82.0	76	30	29	6	23-4	80	.242
2003—Toronto (A.L.)		2	2	.500	4.61	1.41	*79	0	0	0	16	3-4	52.2	46	30	27	7	28-3	44	.231
2004—Tampa Bay (A.L.)		1	1	.500	3.12	1.29	60	0	0	0	9	1-3	49.0	48	21	17	3	15-4	43	.257
American League totals (3 years)		3	7	.300	4.64	1.47	144	4	0	0	25	4-7	118.1	122	68	61	13	52-7	95	.266
National League totals (3 years)		5	2	.714	4.90	1.70	100	1	0	0	5	2-3	119.1	142	72	65	13	61-3	78	.295
Major League totals (6 years)		8	9	.471	4.77	1.59	244	5	0	0	30	6-10	237.2	264	140	126	26	113-10	173	.281

DIVISION SERIES RECORD

Year	Team (League)	W	L	Pct.	ERA	WHIP	G	GS	CG	ShO	Hld.	Sv.-Opp.	IP	H	R	ER	HR	BB-IBB	SO	Avg.
1998—Houston (N.L.)		0	0	...	...	...	1	0	0	0	...	0-0	.0	0	0	0	0	1-0	0	...
1999—Houston (N.L.)		0	0	...	0.00	0.75	2	0	0	0	1	0-0	1.1	1	0	0	0	2-0	2	.200
Division series totals (2 years)		0	0	...	0.00	1.50	3	0	0	0	1	0-0	1.1	1	0	0	0	1-0	2	.200

M

MILLER, WADE   P

PERSONAL: Born September 13, 1976, in Reading, Pa. ... 6-2/220. ... Throws right, bats right. ... Full name: Wade T. Miller. ... High school: Brandywine Heights (Pa.). ... College: Alvernia (Pa.).

TRANSACTIONS/CAREER NOTES: Selected by Houston Astros organization in 20th round of 1996 free-agent draft. ... On disabled list (April 15-May 29, 2002); included rehabilitation assignment to New Orleans. ... On disabled list (June 26, 2004-remainder of season).

CAREER HITTING: 43-for-259 (.166), 20 R, 9 2B, 0 3B, 0 HR, 17 RBI.

Year Team (League)	W	L	Pct.	ERA	WHIP	G	GS	CG	ShO	Hld.	Sv.-Opp.	IP	H	R	ER	HR	BB-IBB	SO	Avg.
1996— GC Astros (GCL)	3	4	.429	3.79	1.07	11	10	0	0	...	0-...	57.0	49	26	24	1	12-0	53	.233
— Auburn (N.Y.-Penn)	1	1	.500	5.00	1.33	2	2	0	0	...	0-...	9.0	8	9	5	0	4-0	11	.216
1997— Quad City (Midw.)	5	3	.625	3.36	0.93	10	8	2	0	...	0-...	59.0	45	27	22	7	10-0	50	.201
— Kissimmee (Fla. St.)	10	2	.833	1.80	0.93	14	14	4	1	...	0-...	100.0	79	28	20	3	14-1	76	.214
1998— Jackson (Texas)	5	0	1.000	2.32	1.23	10	10	0	0	...	0-...	62.0	49	23	16	7	27-2	48	.213
1999— New Orleans (PCL)	11	9	.550	4.38	1.36	26	26	2	0	...	0-...	162.1	156	85	79	16	64-0	135	.248
— Houston (N.L.)	0	1	.000	9.58	2.13	5	1	0	0	...	0-0	10.1	17	11	11	4	5-0	8	.362
2000— New Orleans (PCL)	4	5	.444	3.67	1.26	16	15	0	0	...	0-...	105.1	95	46	43	6	38-1	81	.245
— Houston (N.L.)	6	6	.500	5.14	1.39	16	16	2	0	...	0-0	105.0	104	66	60	14	42-1	89	.257
2001— Houston (N.L.)	16	8	.667	3.40	1.22	32	32	1	0	...	0-0	212.0	183	91	80	31	76-3	183	.234
2002— Houston (N.L.)	15	4	.789	3.28	1.29	26	26	1	1	...	0-0	164.2	151	63	60	14	62-9	144	.249
— New Orleans (PCL)	0	0	...	2.25	1.38	2	2	0	0	...	0-...	8.0	10	4	2	0	1-0	9	.323
2003— Houston (N.L.)	14	13	.519	4.13	1.31	33	33	0	0	...	0-0	187.1	168	96	86	17	77-1	161	.242
2004— Houston (N.L.)	7	7	.500	3.35	1.35	15	15	0	0	...	0-0	88.2	76	35	33	11	44-0	74	.228
Major League totals (6 years)	**58**	**39**	**.598**	**3.87**	**1.31**	**127**	**123**	**5**	**1**	**0**	**0-0**	**768.0**	**699**	**362**	**330**	**91**	**306-14**	**659**	**.244**

DIVISION SERIES RECORD

Year Team (League)	W	L	Pct.	ERA	WHIP	G	GS	CG	ShO	Hld.	Sv.-Opp.	IP	H	R	ER	HR	BB-IBB	SO	Avg.
2001— Houston (N.L.)	0	0	...	2.57	1.00	1	1	0	0	0	0-0	7.0	7	2	2	0	0-0	6	.292

MILLWOOD, KEVIN   P

PERSONAL: Born December 24, 1974, in Gastonia, N.C. ... 6-4/235. ... Throws right, bats right. ... Full name: Kevin Austin Millwood. ... High school: Bessemer City (N.C.).

TRANSACTIONS/CAREER NOTES: Selected by Atlanta Braves organization in 11th round of 1993 free-agent draft. ... On disabled list (May 7-July 20, 2001); included rehabilitation assignments to Macon and Greenville. ... Traded by Braves to Philadelphia Phillies for C Johnny Estrada (December 20, 2002). ... On disabled list (August 6-September 12, 2004).

CAREER HITTING: 53-for-426 (.124), 18 R, 14 2B, 0 3B, 2 HR, 24 RBI.

Year Team (League)	W	L	Pct.	ERA	WHIP	G	GS	CG	ShO	Hld.	Sv.-Opp.	IP	H	R	ER	HR	BB-IBB	SO	Avg.
1993— GC Braves (GCL)	3	3	.500	3.06	1.28	12	9	0	0	...	0-...	50.0	36	27	17	3	28-0	49	.196
1994— Danville (Appalachian)	3	3	.500	3.72	1.65	13	5	0	0	...	1-...	46.0	42	25	19	4	34-2	56	.247
— Macon (S. Atl.)	0	5	.000	5.79	1.93	12	4	0	0	...	1-...	32.2	31	31	21	4	32-1	24	.242
1995— Macon (S. Atl.)	5	6	.455	4.63	1.39	29	12	0	0	...	0-...	103.0	86	65	53	10	57-0	89	.219
1996— Durham (Caro.)	6	9	.400	4.28	1.31	33	20	1	0	...	1-...	149.1	138	77	71	17	58-0	139	.248
1997— Greenville (Sou.)	3	5	.375	4.11	1.35	11	11	0	0	...	0-...	61.1	59	37	28	8	24-0	61	.250
— Richmond (Int'l)	7	0	1.000	1.93	0.89	9	9	1	0	...	0-...	60.2	38	13	13	2	16-0	46	.178
— Atlanta (N.L.)	5	3	.625	4.03	1.48	12	8	0	0	...	0-0	51.1	55	26	23	1	21-1	42	.282
1998— Atlanta (N.L.)	17	8	.680	4.08	1.33	31	29	3	1	1	0-0	174.1	175	86	79	18	56-3	163	.258
1999— Atlanta (N.L.)	18	7	.720	2.68	0.99	33	33	2	0	0	0-0	228.0	168	80	68	24	59-2	205	.202
2000— Atlanta (N.L.)	10	13	.435	4.66	1.29	36	•35	0	0	0	0-0	212.2	213	115	110	26	62-2	168	.258
2001— Atlanta (N.L.)	7	7	.500	4.31	1.33	21	21	0	0	0	0-0	121.0	121	66	58	20	40-6	84	.260
— Macon (S. Atl.)	0	0	...	0.00	0.00	1	1	0	0	0	0-...	3.0	0	0	0	0	0-0	5	.000
— Greenville (Sou.)	0	1	.000	4.50	1.20	2	2	0	0	0	0-...	10.0	9	6	5	2	3-0	10	.243
2002— Atlanta (N.L.)	18	8	.692	3.24	1.16	35	34	1	1	0	0-0	217.0	186	83	78	16	65-7	178	.230
2003— Philadelphia (N.L.)	14	12	.538	4.01	1.25	35	35	5	•3	0	0-0	222.0	210	103	99	19	68-6	169	.250
2004— Philadelphia (N.L.)	9	6	.600	4.85	1.46	25	25	0	0	0	0-0	141.0	155	81	76	14	51-5	125	.278
Major League totals (8 years)	**98**	**64**	**.605**	**3.89**	**1.25**	**228**	**220**	**11**	**5**	**1**	**0-0**	**1367.1**	**1283**	**640**	**591**	**138**	**422-32**	**1134**	**.247**

DIVISION SERIES RECORD

Year Team (League)	W	L	Pct.	ERA	WHIP	G	GS	CG	ShO	Hld.	Sv.-Opp.	IP	H	R	ER	HR	BB-IBB	SO	Avg.
1999— Atlanta (N.L.)	1	0	1.000	0.90	0.10	2	1	0	0	0	1-1	10.0	1	1	1	1	0-0	9	.031
2000— Atlanta (N.L.)	0	1	.000	7.71	1.50	1	1	0	0	0	0-0	4.2	4	4	4	2	3-0	3	.222
2001— Atlanta (N.L.)	Did not play.																		
2002— Atlanta (N.L.)	1	1	.500	3.27	0.64	2	2	0	0	0	0-0	11.0	7	4	4	3	0-0	14	.175
Division series totals (3 years)	**2**	**2**	**.500**	**3.16**	**0.58**	**5**	**4**	**0**	**0**	**0**	**1-1**	**25.2**	**12**	**9**	**9**	**6**	**3-0**	**26**	**.133**

CHAMPIONSHIP SERIES RECORD

Year Team (League)	W	L	Pct.	ERA	WHIP	G	GS	CG	ShO	Hld.	Sv.-Opp.	IP	H	R	ER	HR	BB-IBB	SO	Avg.
1999— Atlanta (N.L.)	1	0	1.000	3.55	1.11	2	2	0	0	0	0-0	12.2	13	6	5	1	1-0	9	.260
2001— Atlanta (N.L.)	0	0	...	0.00	0.00	1	0	0	0	0	0-0	1.0	0	0	0	0	0-0	1	.000
Champ. series totals (2 years)	**1**	**0**	**1.000**	**3.29**	**1.02**	**3**	**2**	**0**	**0**	**0**	**0-0**	**13.2**	**13**	**6**	**5**	**1**	**1-0**	**10**	**.245**

WORLD SERIES RECORD

Year Team (League)	W	L	Pct.	ERA	WHIP	G	GS	CG	ShO	Hld.	Sv.-Opp.	IP	H	R	ER	HR	BB-IBB	SO	Avg.
1999— Atlanta (N.L.)	0	1	.000	18.00	5.00	1	1	0	0	0	0-0	2.0	8	5	4	0	2-0	2	.615

ALL-STAR GAME RECORD

Year Team (League)	W	L	Pct.	ERA	WHIP	G	GS	CG	ShO	Hld.	Sv.-Opp.	IP	H	R	ER	HR	BB-IBB	SO	Avg.
All-Star Game totals (1 year)	**0**	**0**	**...**	**0.00**	**1.00**	**1**	**0**	**0**	**0**	**0**	**0-0**	**1.0**	**1**	**0**	**0**	**0**	**0-0**	**1**	**.250**

MILTON, ERIC   P

PERSONAL: Born August 4, 1975, in State College, Pa. ... 6-3/208. ... Throws left, bats left. ... Full name: Eric Robert Milton. ... High school: Bellefonte (Pa.). ... College: Maryland.

TRANSACTIONS/CAREER NOTES: Selected by New York Yankees organization in first round (20th pick overall) of 1996 free-agent draft. ... Traded by Yankees with P Danny Mota, OF Brian Buchanan, SS Cristian Guzman and cash to Minnesota Twins for 2B Chuck Knoblauch (February 6, 1998). ... On disabled list (August 7-September 2, 2002). ... On disabled list (March 13-September 14, 2003); included rehabilitation assignments to Fort Myers and New Britain. ... Traded by Twins to Philadelphia Phillies for P Carlos Silva, IF Nick Punto and a player to be named (December 3, 2003); Twins acquired P Bobby Korecky to complete deal (December 16, 2003).

M

CAREER HITTING: 16-for-85 (.188), 5 R, 1 2B, 0 3B, 0 HR, 7 RBI.

Year	Team (League)	W	L	Pct.	ERA	WHIP	G	GS	CG	ShO	Hld.	Sv.-Opp.	IP	H	R	ER	HR	BB-IBB	SO	Avg.
1997—	Tampa (FSL)	8	3	.727	3.09	0.99	14	14	1	0	...	0-...	93.1	78	35	32	8	14-0	95	.223
—	Norwich (East.)	6	3	.667	3.13	1.22	14	14	1	0	...	0-...	77.2	59	29	27	2	36-0	67	.210
1998—	Minnesota (A.L.)	8	14	.364	5.64	1.54	32	32	1	0	0	0-0	172.1	195	113	108	25	70-0	107	.282
1999—	Minnesota (A.L.)	7	11	.389	4.49	1.23	34	34	5	2	0	0-0	206.1	190	111	103	28	63-2	163	.243
2000—	Minnesota (A.L.)	13	10	.565	4.86	1.25	33	33	0	0	0	0-0	200.0	205	123	108	35	44-0	160	.260
2001—	Minnesota (A.L.)	15	7	.682	4.32	1.28	35	34	2	1	0	0-0	220.2	222	109	106	35	61-0	157	.257
2002—	Minnesota (A.L.)	13	9	.591	4.84	1.19	29	29	2	1	0	0-0	171.0	173	96	92	24	30-0	121	.258
2003—	Fort Myers (Fla. St.)	0	0	...	0.00	1.50	1	1	0	0	...	0-...	2.0	1	0	0	0	2-0	2	.143
—	Minnesota (A.L.)	1	0	1.000	2.65	0.94	3	3	0	0	0	0-0	17.0	15	5	5	2	1-0	7	.234
2004—	Philadelphia (N.L.)	14	6	.700	4.75	1.35	34	34	0	0	0	0-0	201.0	196	110	106	43	75-6	161	.255
American League totals (6 years)		57	51	.528	4.76	1.29	166	165	10	4	0	0-0	987.1	1000	557	522	149	269-2	715	.259
National League totals (1 year)		14	6	.700	4.75	1.35	34	34	0	0	0	0-0	201.0	196	110	106	43	75-6	161	.255
Major League totals (7 years)		71	57	.555	4.76	1.30	200	199	10	4	0	0-0	1188.1	1196	667	628	192	344-8	876	.258

DIVISION SERIES RECORD

Year	Team (League)	W	L	Pct.	ERA	WHIP	G	GS	CG	ShO	Hld.	Sv.-Opp.	IP	H	R	ER	HR	BB-IBB	SO	Avg.
2002—	Minnesota (A.L.)	1	0	1.000	2.57	1.00	1	1	0	0	0	0-0	7.0	6	2	2	1	1-0	3	.222
2003—	Minnesota (A.L.)	0	0	...	0.00	0.60	1	0	0	0	0	0-0	3.1	2	0	0	0	0-0	2	.167
Division series totals (2 years)		1	0	1.000	1.74	0.87	2	1	0	0	0	0-0	10.1	8	2	2	1	1-0	5	.205

CHAMPIONSHIP SERIES RECORD

Year	Team (League)	W	L	Pct.	ERA	WHIP	G	GS	CG	ShO	Hld.	Sv.-Opp.	IP	H	R	ER	HR	BB-IBB	SO	Avg.
2002—	Minnesota (A.L.)	0	0		1.50	1.17	1	1	0	0	0	0-0	6.0	5	1	1	1	2-0	4	.217

MINOR, DAMON — 1B

PERSONAL: Born January 5, 1974, in Canton, Ohio. ... 6-7/230. ... Bats left, throws left. ... Full name: Damon Reed Minor. ... High school: Hammon (Okla.). ... College: Oklahoma. ... Brother of Ryan Minor, third baseman with two major league teams (1998-2001).
TRANSACTIONS/CAREER NOTES: Selected by New York Mets organization in 19th round of 1995 free-agent draft; did not sign. ... Selected by San Francisco Giants organization in 12th round of 1996 free-agent draft. ... On disabled list (March 23-April 10, 2001). ... On disabled list (April 7-23, 2002); included rehabiliation assignment to Fresno. ... Traded by Giants to Philadelphia Phillies for P Mike Wilson (May 19, 2003). ... Signed as a free agent by Giants organization (February 6, 2004).
2004 GAMES PLAYED BY POSITION (MLB): 1B—17, DH—1.

Year	Team (League)	Pos.	G	AB	R	H	2B	3B	HR	RBI	BB	SO	HBP	GDP	SB-CS	Avg.	OBP	SLG	OPS	E	Avg.
1996—	Bellingham (N'west)	1B	75	269	44	65	11	1	12	55	47	86	5	5	0-2	.242	.363	.424	.787	5	.993
1997—	Bakersfield (Calif.)	1B	140	532	98	154	34	1	31	99	87	143	5	6	2-1	.289	.391	.532	.923	22	.984
1998—	Shreveport (Texas)	1B	81	289	39	69	11	1	14	52	30	51	6	3	1-0	.239	.321	.429	.750	8	.988
—	San Jose (Calif.)	1B	48	176	26	50	10	1	7	36	28	40	2	1	0-1	.284	.386	.472	.858	6	.987
1999—	Shreveport (Texas)	1B	136	473	76	129	33	4	20	82	80	115	8	10	1-0	.273	.385	.486	.871	9	.993
2000—	Fresno (PCL)	1B	133	482	84	140	27	1	30	106	87	97	1	11	0-0	.290	.394	.537	.931	11	.991
—	San Francisco (N.L.)	2B-1B	10	9	3	4	0	0	3	6	2	1	0	0	0-0	.444	.545	1.444	1.990	0	1.000
2001—	Fresno (PCL)	1B-OF	112	406	74	125	22	3	24	71	44	83	5	5	1-1	.308	.380	.554	.934	11	.988
—	San Francisco (N.L.)	1B	19	45	3	7	1	0	0	3	3	8	0	1	0-0	.156	.208	.178	.386	1	.989
2002—	San Francisco (N.L.)	1B-DH	83	173	21	41	6	0	10	24	24	34	2	8	0-0	.237	.333	.445	.778	1	.997
—	Fresno (PCL)	1B	9	29	8	15	6	1	0	5	5	5	0	0	0-0	.517	.588	.793	1.381	2	.972
2003—	Fresno (PCL)	1B-DH	37	141	16	33	2	1	8	21	6	29	3	3	0-0	.234	.278	.433	.711	1	.995
—	Scran./W.B. (I.L.)	DH-1B	91	328	45	76	17	1	16	65	27	60	9	10	1-2	.232	.305	.436	.741	3	.991
2004—	San Francisco (N.L.)	1B-DH	24	58	14	14	2	0	6	12	18	4	2	0-0	.241	.405	.276	.681	0	1.000
—	Fresno (PCL)	1B-DH	97	338	48	102	23	3	17	56	50	78	6	7	0-0	.302	.399	.538	.937	3	.994
Major League totals (4 years)			136	285	35	66	9	0	13	39	41	61	6	11	0-0	.232	.338	.400	.738	2	.996

MIRABELLI, DOUG — C

PERSONAL: Born October 18, 1970, in Kingman, Ariz. ... 6-1/220. ... Bats right, throws right. ... Full name: Douglas Anthony Mirabelli. ... Name pronounced: mirr-uh-BEL-ee. ... High school: Valley (Las Vegas). ... College: Wichita State.
TRANSACTIONS/CAREER NOTES: Selected by Detroit Tigers organization in sixth round of 1989 free-agent draft; did not sign. ... Selected by San Francisco Giants organization in fifth round of 1992 free-agent draft. ... Traded by Giants to Texas Rangers for cash (March 27, 2001). ... Traded by Rangers to Boston Red Sox for P Justin Duchscherer (June 12, 2001).
2004 GAMES PLAYED BY POSITION (MLB): C—53, DH—4.

Year	Team (League)	Pos.	G	AB	R	H	2B	3B	HR	RBI	BB	SO	HBP	GDP	SB-CS	Avg.	OBP	SLG	OPS	E	Avg.
1992—	San Jose (Calif.)	C	53	177	30	41	11	1	0	21	24	18	4	7	1-3	.232	.333	.305	.638	10	.973
1993—	San Jose (Calif.)	C	113	371	58	100	19	2	1	48	72	55	4	7	0-4	.270	.390	.340	.730	9	.989
1994—	Shreveport (Texas)	C-1B	85	255	23	56	8	0	4	24	36	48	0	6	3-1	.220	.316	.298	.614	3	.993
1995—	Phoenix (PCL)	C	23	66	3	11	0	1	0	7	12	10	1	5	1-0	.167	.296	.197	.493	2	.985
—	Shreveport (Texas)	C-1B	40	126	14	38	13	0	0	16	20	14	0	3	1-0	.302	.397	.405	.802	3	.986
1996—	Shreveport (Texas)	C-DH-1B	115	380	60	112	23	0	21	70	76	49	6	9	0-1	.295	.419	.521	.940	7	.989
—	Phoenix (PCL)	C	14	47	10	14	7	0	0	7	4	7	1	1	0-0	.298	.365	.447	.812	2	.982
—	San Francisco (N.L.)	C	9	18	2	4	1	0	0	1	3	4	0	0	0-0	.222	.333	.278	.611	0	1.000
1997—	Phoenix (PCL)	C-DH	100	332	49	88	23	2	8	48	58	69	7	9	1-2	.265	.384	.419	.803	4	.994
—	San Francisco (N.L.)	C	6	7	0	1	0	0	0	0	1	3	0	0	0-0	.143	.250	.143	.393	0	1.000
1998—	Fresno (PCL)	C-DH	85	265	45	69	12	2	13	52	52	55	3	9	2-0	.260	.386	.468	.854	3	.995
—	San Francisco (N.L.)	C	10	17	2	4	2	0	1	4	2	6	1	0	0-0	.235	.316	.529	.845	1	.974
1999—	Fresno (PCL)	C-1B-DH	86	320	63	100	24	1	14	51	48	56	1	6	8-2	.313	.398	.525	.923	5	.993
—	San Francisco (N.L.)	C	33	87	10	22	6	0	1	10	9	25	1	1	0-0	.253	.327	.356	.683	0	1.000
2000—	San Francisco (N.L.)	C	82	230	23	53	10	2	6	28	36	57	2	6	1-0	.230	.337	.370	.707	7	.985
2001—	Texas (A.L.)	C-DH	23	49	4	5	2	0	3	13	10	21	0	1	0-0	.102	.254	.265	.520	1	.990
—	Boston (A.L.)	C-DH	54	141	16	38	8	0	9	26	17	36	4	2	0-0	.270	.360	.518	.877	2	.995
2002—	Boston (A.L.)	C-DH	57	151	17	34	7	0	7	25	17	33	3	6	0-0	.225	.312	.411	.723	0	1.000
2003—	Boston (A.L.)	C-DH-1B	62	163	23	42	13	0	6	18	11	36	1	3	0-0	.258	.307	.448	.755	5	.986
2004—	Boston (A.L.)	C-DH	59	160	27	45	12	0	9	32	19	46	3	5	0-0	.281	.368	.525	.893	2	.993
American League totals (4 years)			255	664	87	164	42	0	33	104	74	172	11	17	0-0	.247	.330	.459	.790	10	.993
National League totals (5 years)			140	359	37	84	19	2	8	43	51	95	3	7	1-0	.234	.332	.365	.697	8	.989
Major League totals (9 years)			395	1023	124	248	61	2	41	147	125	267	14	24	1-0	.242	.331	.426	.757	18	.992

M

DIVISION SERIES RECORD

Year— Team (League)	Pos.	G	AB	R	H	2B	3B	HR	RBI	BB	SO	HBP	GDP	SB-CS	Avg.	OBP	SLG	OPS	E	Avg.
2000— San Francisco (N.L.)	C	2	2	0	0	0	0	0	0	1	1	0	0	0-0	.000	.333	.000	.333	0	1.000
2003— Boston (A.L.)	C	2	4	2	2	1	0	0	0	0	2	0	0	0-0	.500	.500	.750	1.250	0	1.000
Division series totals (2 years)		4	6	2	2	1	0	0	0	1	3	0	0	0-0	.333	.429	.500	.929	0	1.000

CHAMPIONSHIP SERIES RECORD

Year— Team (League)	Pos.	G	AB	R	H	2B	3B	HR	RBI	BB	SO	HBP	GDP	SB-CS	Avg.	OBP	SLG	OPS	E	Avg.
2003— Boston (A.L.)	C	3	7	0	2	0	0	0	0	0	2	0	0	0-0	.286	.286	.286	.571	0	1.000
2004— Boston (A.L.)	C	1	1	0	0	0	0	0	0	0	0	0	0	0-0	.000	.000	.000	.000	0	1.000
Champ. series totals (2 years)		4	8	0	2	0	0	0	0	0	2	0	0	0-0	.250	.250	.250	.500	0	1.000

WORLD SERIES RECORD

Year— Team (League)	Pos.	G	AB	R	H	2B	3B	HR	RBI	BB	SO	HBP	GDP	SB-CS	Avg.	OBP	SLG	OPS	E	Avg.
2004— Boston (A.L.)	C	1	3	1	1	0	0	0	0	0	0	0	0	0-0	.333	.333	.333	.667	0	1.000

MITRE, SERGIO   P

PERSONAL: Born February 16, 1981, in Los Angeles, Calif. ... 6-4/210. ... Throws right, bats right. ... Full name: Sergio Armando Mitre. ... High school: Montgomery (Chula Vista, Calif.). ... Junior college: San Diego City College.

TRANSACTIONS/CAREER NOTES: Selected by Chicago Cubs organization in seventh round of 2001 free-agent draft.

CAREER HITTING: 2-for-17 (.118), 1 R, 1 2B, 0 3B, 0 HR, 0 RBI.

Year— Team (League)	W	L	Pct.	ERA	WHIP	G	GS	CG	ShO	Hld.	Sv.-Opp.	IP	H	R	ER	HR	BB-IBB	SO	Avg.
2001— Boise (N'west)	8	4	.667	3.07	1.13	15	15	1	1	...	0-...	91.0	85	37	31	2	18-1	71	.243
2002— Lansing (Midw.)	8	10	.444	2.83	1.14	27	27	2	0	...	0-...	168.2	166	72	53	7	27-1	96	.261
2003— West Tenn (Sou.)	7	9	.438	3.34	1.39	25	24	0	0	...	0-...	145.2	162	75	54	6	41-0	128	.282
—Chicago (N.L.)	0	1	.000	8.31	2.19	3	2	0	0	0	0-0	8.2	15	8	8	1	4-1	3	.395
2004— Iowa (PCL)	6	4	.600	2.98	1.32	18	15	1	1	...	1-...	102.2	97	38	34	9	39-1	95	.255
—Chicago (N.L.)	2	4	.333	6.62	1.76	12	9	0	0	0	0-0	51.2	71	38	38	6	20-1	37	.327
Major League totals (2 years)	2	5	.286	6.86	1.82	15	11	0	0	0	0-0	60.1	86	46	46	7	24-2	40	.337

MOELLER, CHAD   C

PERSONAL: Born February 18, 1975, in Upland, Calif. ... 6-3/210. ... Bats right, throws right. ... Full name: Chad Edward Moeller. ... Name pronounced: MOE-ler. ... High school: Upland (Calif.). ... College: USC.

TRANSACTIONS/CAREER NOTES: Selected by New York Yankees organization in 25th round of 1993 free-agent draft; did not sign. ... Selected by Minnesota Twins organization in seventh round of 1996 free-agent draft. ... On disabled list (August 12-30, 2000). ... Traded by Twins to Arizona Diamondbacks for SS Hanley Frias (March 28, 2001). ... Traded by Diamondbacks with SS Craig Counsell, 2B Junior Spivey, 1B Lyle Overbay and Ps Chris Capuano and Jorge de la Rosa to Milwaukee Brewers for 1B Richie Sexson, P Shane Nance and a player to be named (December 1, 2003); Diamondbacks acquired OF Noochie Varner to complete deal (December 15, 2003).

2004 GAMES PLAYED BY POSITION (MLB): C—100.

Year— Team (League)	Pos.	G	AB	R	H	2B	3B	HR	RBI	BB	SO	HBP	GDP	SB-CS	Avg.	OBP	SLG	OPS	E	Avg.
1996— Elizabethton (App.)	C	17	59	17	21	4	0	4	13	18	9	2	3	1-2	.356	.519	.627	1.146	1	.991
1997— Fort Wayne (Midw.)	C	108	384	58	111	18	3	9	39	48	76	13	8	11-8	.289	.386	.422	.808	15	.984
1998— Fort Myers (FSL)	C	66	254	37	83	24	1	6	39	31	37	3	8	2-3	.327	.406	.500	.906	9	.980
— New Britain (East.)	C	58	187	21	44	10	0	6	23	24	41	3	4	2-1	.235	.332	.385	.717	6	.987
1999— New Britain (East.)	C	89	250	29	62	11	3	4	24	21	44	6	7	0-0	.248	.317	.364	.681	10	.984
2000— Salt Lake (PCL)	C	47	167	30	48	13	1	5	20	9	45	0	6	0-1	.287	.322	.467	.789	2	.993
— Minnesota (A.L.)	C	48	128	13	27	3	1	1	9	9	33	0	4	1-0	.211	.261	.273	.534	6	.979
2001— Tucson (PCL)	C	78	274	41	75	20	0	8	36	25	54	2	8	1-4	.274	.337	.434	.771	5	.989
— Arizona (N.L.)	C	25	56	8	13	0	1	1	2	6	12	0	2	0-0	.232	.306	.321	.628	0	1.000
2002— Tucson (PCL)	C	60	211	37	67	8	2	10	48	29	46	3	4	1-0	.318	.401	.517	.917	3	.994
— Arizona (N.L.)	C	37	105	10	30	11	1	2	16	17	23	0	6	0-1	.286	.385	.467	.852	1	.997
2003— Arizona (N.L.)	C	78	239	29	64	17	1	5	29	23	59	2	7	1-2	.268	.335	.435	.770	7	.987
2004— Milwaukee (N.L.)	C	101	317	25	66	13	1	5	27	21	74	4	12	0-1	.208	.265	.303	.568	1	.999
American League totals (1 year)		48	128	13	27	3	1	1	9	9	33	0	4	1-0	.211	.261	.273	.534	6	.979
National League totals (4 years)		241	717	72	173	41	4	15	74	67	168	6	27	1-4	.241	.310	.372	.683	9	.995
Major League totals (5 years)		289	845	85	200	44	5	16	83	76	201	6	31	2-4	.237	.303	.357	.660	15	.993

DIVISION SERIES RECORD

Year— Team (League)	Pos.	G	AB	R	H	2B	3B	HR	RBI	BB	SO	HBP	GDP	SB-CS	Avg.	OBP	SLG	OPS	E	Avg.
2002— Arizona (N.L.)	C	3	5	0	2	0	0	0	0	0	1	0	0	0-0	.400	.400	.400	.800	0	1.000

MOHR, DUSTAN   OF

PERSONAL: Born June 19, 1976, in Hattiesburg, Miss. ... 6-1/214. ... Bats right, throws right. ... Full name: Dustan Kyle Mohr. ... High school: Oak Grove (Miss.). ... College: Alabama.

TRANSACTIONS/CAREER NOTES: Selected by California Angels organization in 20th round of 1994 free-agent draft; did not sign. ... Selected by Cleveland Indians organization in ninth round of 1997 free-agent draft. ... Released by Indians (March 31, 2000). ... Signed by Minnesota Twins organization (April 1, 2000). ... Traded by Twins to San Francisco Giants for P J.T. Thomas (December 15, 2003).

2004 GAMES PLAYED BY POSITION (MLB): OF—95, DH—2.

Year— Team (League)	Pos.	G	AB	R	H	2B	3B	HR	RBI	BB	SO	HBP	GDP	SB-CS	Avg.	OBP	SLG	OPS	E	Avg.
1997— Watertown (N.Y.-Penn.)	OF	74	275	52	80	20	2	7	53	31	76	4	1	3-6	.291	.366	.455	.821	1	.993
1998— Kinston (Caro.)	OF	134	491	60	119	23	9	19	65	39	146	9	7	8-4	.242	.309	.442	.751	7	.968
1999— Akron (East.)	OF	12	42	3	7	2	1	0	2	5	7	0	1	0-1	.167	.255	.262	.517	0	1.000
— Kinston (Caro.)	OF	112	429	46	120	29	3	8	60	26	104	1	13	6-6	.280	.322	.417	.739	6	.973
2000— Fort Myers (FSL)	OF	101	370	58	98	19	2	11	75	35	65	8	11	7-4	.265	.338	.416	.754	4	.978
2001— New Britain (East.)	OF	135	518	90	174	41	3	24	91	49	111	4	6	9-9	.336	.395	.566	.961	6	.978
— Minnesota (A.L.)	OF-DH	20	51	6	12	2	0	0	4	5	17	0	0	1-1	.235	.298	.275	.573	0	1.000
2002— Minnesota (A.L.)	OF-DH	120	383	55	103	23	2	12	45	31	86	1	5	6-3	.269	.325	.433	.759	2	.992
2003— Minnesota (A.L.)	OF-DH	121	348	50	87	22	0	10	36	33	106	1	10	5-2	.250	.314	.399	.714	6	.976
2004— San Francisco (N.L.)	OF-DH	117	263	52	72	20	1	7	28	46	64	8	5	0-3	.274	.394	.437	.831	3	.981
American League totals (3 years)		261	782	111	202	47	2	22	85	69	209	2	15	12-6	.258	.319	.408	.726	8	.985
National League totals (1 year)		117	263	52	72	20	1	7	28	46	64	8	5	0-3	.274	.394	.437	.831	3	.981
Major League totals (4 years)		378	1045	163	274	67	3	29	113	115	273	10	20	12-9	.262	.339	.415	.754	11	.984

M

Year	Team (League)	Pos.	G	AB	R	H	2B	3B	HR	RBI	BB	SO	HBP	GDP	SB-CS	Avg.	OBP	SLG	OPS	E	Avg.
2002— Minnesota (A.L.)		OF	4	2	1	2	1	0	0	0	1	0	0	0	0-0	1.000	1.000	1.500	2.500	0	1.000

CHAMPIONSHIP SERIES RECORD

Year	Team (League)	Pos.	G	AB	R	H	2B	3B	HR	RBI	BB	SO	HBP	GDP	SB-CS	Avg.	OBP	SLG	OPS	E	Avg.
2002— Minnesota (A.L.)		OF	5	12	3	5	1	0	0	0	0	4	0	0	1-0	.417	.417	.500	.917	0	1.000

MOLINA, BENGIE — C

PERSONAL: Born July 20, 1974, in Rio Piedras, Puerto Rico. ... 5-11/220. ... Bats right, throws right. ... Full name: Benjamin Jose Molina. ... High school: Maestra Ladi (Puerto Rico). ... Junior college: Arizona Western. ... Brother of Jose Molina, catcher, Anaheim Angels; brother of Yadier Molina, catcher, St. Louis Cardinals.

TRANSACTIONS/CAREER NOTES: Signed as a non-drafted free agent by California Angels organization (May 23, 1993). ... Angels franchise renamed Anaheim Angels for 1997 season. ... On disabled list (May 5-June 27, 2001); included rehabilitation assignments to Rancho Cucamonga and Salt Lake. ... On Anaheim disabled list (July 17-August 1, 2002); included rehabilitation assignment to Rancho Cucamonga. ... On disabled list (September 5, 2003-remainder of season; and June 4-19 and August 1-17, 2004).

HONORS: Won A.L. Gold Glove at catcher (2002 and 2003).

2004 GAMES PLAYED BY POSITION (MLB): C—89, DH—5.

Year	Team (League)	Pos.	G	AB	R	H	2B	3B	HR	RBI	BB	SO	HBP	GDP	SB-CS	Avg.	OBP	SLG	OPS	E	Avg.
1993— Ariz. Angels (Ariz.)		C	27	80	9	21	6	2	0	10	10	4	1	1	0-2	.263	.348	.388	.735	0	1.000
1994— Cedar Rap. (Midw.)		C	48	171	14	48	8	0	3	16	8	12	3	1	1-2	.281	.324	.380	.704	10	.975
1995— Vancouver (PCL)			2	2	0	0	0	0	0	0	0	1	0	0	0-0	.000	.000	.000	.000	0	1.000
—Cedar Rap. (Midw.)		C	39	133	15	39	9	0	4	17	15	11	1	4	1-1	.293	.367	.451	.818	7	.978
—Lake Elsinore (Calif.)		C	27	96	21	37	7	2	2	12	8	7	4	2	0-0	.385	.450	.563	1.012	1	.995
1996— Midland (Texas)		C	108	365	45	100	21	2	8	54	25	25	6	16	0-1	.274	.327	.408	.735	7	.990
1997— Lake Elsinore (Calif.)		C	36	149	18	42	10	2	4	33	7	9	0	5	0-1	.282	.308	.456	.765	1	.996
—Midland (Texas)		C	29	106	18	35	8	0	6	30	10	7	0	2	0-0	.330	.381	.575	.957	2	.978
1998— Vancouver (PCL)		C	49	184	13	54	9	1	1	22	5	14	0	6	1-1	.293	.311	.370	.680	5	.986
—Midland (Texas)		C	41	154	28	55	8	0	9	39	14	7	3	7	0-1	.357	.419	.584	1.003	3	.988
—Anaheim (A.L.)		C	2	1	0	0	0	0	0	0	0	0	0	0	0-0	.000	.000	.000	.000	0	1.000
1999— Edmonton (PCL)		C-DH	65	241	28	69	16	0	7	41	15	17	6	7	1-2	.286	.338	.440	.778	3	.993
—Anaheim (A.L.)		C	31	101	8	26	5	0	1	10	6	6	2	5	0-1	.257	.312	.337	.649	2	.991
2000— Anaheim (A.L.)		C-DH	130	473	59	133	20	2	14	71	23	33	6	17	1-0	.281	.318	.421	.739	7	.991
2001— Anaheim (A.L.)		C-DH	96	325	31	85	11	0	6	40	16	51	8	8	0-1	.262	.309	.351	.660	5	.991
—Rancho Cuca. (Calif.)		C	3	11	1	6	1	0	0	2	0	1	0	0	0-0	.545	.545	.636	1.182	0	1.000
—Salt Lake (PCL)		C	5	18	2	5	1	0	0	3	2	3	0	2	0-0	.278	.350	.333	.683	0	1.000
2002— Anaheim (A.L.)		C	122	428	34	105	18	0	5	47	15	34	4	15	0-0	.245	.274	.322	.596	1	.999
—Rancho Cuca. (Calif.)		C	1	2	0	1	0	0	0	0	0	1	0	1	0-0	.500	.750	.500	1.250	0	1.000
2003— Anaheim (A.L.)		C	119	409	37	115	24	0	14	71	13	31	2	17	1-1	.281	.304	.443	.746	5	.993
2004— Anaheim (A.L.)		C-DH	97	337	36	93	13	0	10	54	18	35	2	18	0-1	.276	.313	.404	.717	3	.995
Major League totals (7 years)			597	2074	205	557	91	2	50	293	91	190	24	80	2-4	.269	.304	.387	.690	23	.994

DIVISION SERIES RECORD

Year	Team (League)	Pos.	G	AB	R	H	2B	3B	HR	RBI	BB	SO	HBP	GDP	SB-CS	Avg.	OBP	SLG	OPS	E	Avg.
2002— Anaheim (A.L.)		C	4	15	0	4	2	0	0	2	0	1	0	1	0-0	.267	.267	.400	.667	0	1.000
2004— Anaheim (A.L.)		C	3	6	0	1	0	0	0	0	0	2	0	0	0-0	.167	.167	.167	.333	0	1.000
Division series totals (2 years)			7	21	0	5	2	0	0	2	0	3	0	1	0-0	.238	.238	.333	.571	0	1.000

CHAMPIONSHIP SERIES RECORD

Year	Team (League)	Pos.	G	AB	R	H	2B	3B	HR	RBI	BB	SO	HBP	GDP	SB-CS	Avg.	OBP	SLG	OPS	E	Avg.
2002— Anaheim (A.L.)		C	5	14	0	3	0	1	0	2	1	2	1	0	0-0	.214	.313	.357	.670	0	1.000

WORLD SERIES RECORD

Year	Team (League)	Pos.	G	AB	R	H	2B	3B	HR	RBI	BB	SO	HBP	GDP	SB-CS	Avg.	OBP	SLG	OPS	E	Avg.
2002— Anaheim (A.L.)		C	7	21	2	6	2	0	0	2	3	1	0	2	0-0	.286	.375	.381	.756	1	.979

M

MOLINA, JOSE — C

PERSONAL: Born June 3, 1975, in Bayamon, Puerto Rico. ... 6-2/220. ... Bats right, throws right. ... Full name: Jose Benjamin Molina. ... Name pronounced: mo-LEE-nah. ... High school: Maestro Ladi (Vega Alta, Puerto Rico). ... Brother of Bengie Molina, catcher, Anaheim Angels; brother of Yadier Molina, catcher, St. Louis Cardinals.

TRANSACTIONS/CAREER NOTES: Selected by Chicago Cubs organization in 14th round of 1993 free-agent draft. ... Released by Cubs (November 27, 2000). ... Signed by Anaheim Angels organization (May 17, 2001). ... On disabled list (May 21-July 1, 2001); included rehabilitation assignment to Salt Lake.

2004 GAMES PLAYED BY POSITION (MLB): C—70, 1B—2, DH—1.

Year	Team (League)	Pos.	G	AB	R	H	2B	3B	HR	RBI	BB	SO	HBP	GDP	SB-CS	Avg.	OBP	SLG	OPS	E	Avg.
1993— GC Cubs (GCL)		C-1B	33	78	5	17	2	0	0	4	12	12	0	2	3-2	.218	.322	.244	.566	7	.960
—Daytona (Fla. St.)		C	3	7	0	1	0	0	0	1	2	0	0	0	0-1	.143	.333	.143	.476	0	1.000
1994— Peoria (Midw.)		C	78	253	31	58	13	1	1	33	24	61	4	5	4-3	.229	.302	.300	.602	13	.980
1995— Daytona (Fla. St.)		C	82	233	27	55	9	1	1	19	29	53	7	7	1-0	.236	.336	.296	.632	8	.987
1996— Rockford (Midwest)		C	96	305	35	69	10	1	2	27	36	71	3	8	2-4	.226	.310	.285	.596	11	.985
1997— Daytona (Fla. St.)		C	55	179	17	45	9	1	0	23	14	25	1	5	4-0	.251	.306	.313	.619	8	.981
—Iowa (Am. Assoc.)		C	1	3	0	1	0	0	0	0	1	0	1	0	0-0	.333	.500	.333	.833	0	1.000
—Orlando (South.)		C	37	99	10	17	3	0	1	15	12	28	2	4	0-1	.172	.267	.232	.500	2	.993
1998— West Tenn (Sou.)		C-1B	109	320	33	71	10	1	2	28	32	74	3	10	1-5	.222	.296	.278	.574	8	.991
1999— West Tenn (Sou.)		C	14	35	2	6	3	0	0	5	2	14	0	1	0-0	.171	.211	.257	.468	2	.982
—Iowa (PCL)		C	74	240	24	63	11	1	4	26	20	54	4	3	0-1	.263	.327	.367	.694	7	.987
—Chicago (N.L.)		C	10	19	3	5	1	0	0	1	2	4	0	0	0-0	.263	.333	.316	.649	0	1.000
2000— Iowa (PCL)		C-1B	76	248	22	58	9	0	1	17	23	61	0	6	1-4	.234	.296	.282	.578	11	.981
2001— Salt Lake (PCL)		C	61	213	29	64	11	1	5	31	14	49	2	7	1-2	.300	.349	.432	.781	2	.996
—Anaheim (A.L.)		C	15	37	8	10	3	0	2	4	3	8	0	2	0-0	.270	.325	.514	.839	0	1.000
2002— Salt Lake (PCL)		C	79	290	30	89	14	2	4	43	12	60	4	4	0-3	.307	.341	.410	.751	4	.994

Year	Team (League)	Pos.	G	AB	R	H	2B	3B	HR	RBI	BB	SO	HBP	GDP	SB-CS	Avg.	OBP	SLG	OPS	E	Avg.
—Anaheim (A.L.)	C	29	70	5	19	3	0	0	5	5	15	0	2	0-2	.271	.312	.314	.626	3	.983
2003—Anaheim (A.L.)	C	53	114	12	21	4	0	0	6	1	26	3	1	0-0	.184	.210	.219	.429	1	.996
2004—Anaheim (A.L.)	C-1B-DH	73	203	26	53	10	2	3	25	10	52	0	6	4-1	.261	.296	.374	.670	3	.994
American League totals (4 years)		170	424	51	103	20	2	5	40	19	101	3	11	4-3	.243	.278	.335	.613	7	.993
National League totals (1 year)		10	19	3	5	1	0	0	1	2	4	0	0	0-0	.263	.333	.316	.649	0	1.000
Major League totals (5 years)		180	443	54	108	21	2	5	41	21	105	3	11	4-3	.244	.281	.334	.615	7	.993

DIVISION SERIES RECORD

Year	Team (League)	Pos.	G	AB	R	H	2B	3B	HR	RBI	BB	SO	HBP	GDP	SB-CS	Avg.	OBP	SLG	OPS	E	Avg.
2004—Anaheim (A.L.)	C	2	3	2	1	0	0	0	0	2	0	0	0	0-0	.333	.600	.333	.933	0	1.000

CHAMPIONSHIP SERIES RECORD

Year	Team (League)	Pos.	G	AB	R	H	2B	3B	HR	RBI	BB	SO	HBP	GDP	SB-CS	Avg.	OBP	SLG	OPS	E	Avg.
2002—Anaheim (A.L.)	C	3	1	0	0	0	0	0	0	0	0	0	0	0-0	.000	.000	.000	.000	0	1.000

WORLD SERIES RECORD

Year	Team (League)	Pos.	G	AB	R	H	2B	3B	HR	RBI	BB	SO	HBP	GDP	SB-CS	Avg.	OBP	SLG	OPS	E	Avg.
2002—Anaheim (A.L.)	C	3	0	0	0	0	0	0	0	0	0	0	0	0-0	...	...	...	...	0	1.000

MOLINA, YADIER   C

PERSONAL: Born July 13, 1982, in Bayamon, Puerto Rico. ... 5-11/225. ... Bats right, throws right. ... Full name: Yadier B. Molina. ... High school: Escuela Superior Maestro Ladi (Vega Alta, P.R.). ... Brother of Bengie Molina, catcher, Anaheim Angels; brother of Jose Molina, catcher, Angels.

TRANSACTIONS/CAREER NOTES: Selected by St. Louis Cardinals organization in fourth round of 2000 free-agent draft.

2004 GAMES PLAYED BY POSITION (MLB): C—51.

Year	Team (League)	Pos.	G	AB	R	H	2B	3B	HR	RBI	BB	SO	HBP	GDP	SB-CS	Avg.	OBP	SLG	OPS	E	Avg.
											BATTING										**FIELDING**	
2001—Johnson City (App.)	C	44	158	18	41	11	0	4	18	12	23	3	4	1-1	.259	.320	.405	.725	7	.986
2002—Peoria (Midw.)	C	112	393	39	110	20	0	7	50	21	36	10	14	2-7	.280	.331	.384	.715	14	.985
2003—Tennessee (Sou.)	C	104	364	32	100	13	1	2	51	25	45	5	11	0-1	.275	.327	.332	.660	8	.991
2004—Memphis (PCL)	C	37	129	19	39	6	0	1	14	17	14	2	2	0-0	.302	.387	.372	.750	1	1.000
—St. Louis (N.L.)	C	51	135	12	36	6	0	2	15	13	20	0	4	0-1	.267	.329	.356	.684	2	.993
Major League totals (1 year)		51	135	12	36	6	0	2	15	13	20	0	4	0-1	.267	.329	.356	.684	2	.993

CHAMPIONSHIP SERIES RECORD

Year	Team (League)	Pos.	G	AB	R	H	2B	3B	HR	RBI	BB	SO	HBP	GDP	SB-CS	Avg.	OBP	SLG	OPS	E	Avg.
2004—St. Louis (N.L.)	C	1	4	0	1	0	0	0	0	0	0	0	0	0-0	.250	.250	.250	.500	0	1.000

WORLD SERIES RECORD

Year	Team (League)	Pos.	G	AB	R	H	2B	3B	HR	RBI	BB	SO	HBP	GDP	SB-CS	Avg.	OBP	SLG	OPS	E	Avg.
2004—St. Louis (N.L.)	C	3	3	0	0	0	0	0	0	0	1	0	0	0-0	.000	.000	.000	.000	0	1.000

MONDESI, RAUL   OF

PERSONAL: Born March 12, 1971, in San Cristobal, Dominican Republic. ... 5-11/230. ... Bats right, throws right. ... Full name: Raul Ramon Mondesi. ... Name pronounced: MON-de-see. ... High school: Liceo Manuel Maria Valencia (Dominican Republic).

TRANSACTIONS/CAREER NOTES: Signed as a non-drafted free agent by Los Angeles Dodgers organization (June 6, 1988). ... Traded by Dodgers with P Pedro Borbon to Toronto Blue Jays for OF Shawn Green and 2B Jorge Nunez (November 8, 1999). ... On disabled list (July 22-September 20, 2000). ... Traded by Blue Jays to New York Yankees for P Scott Wiggins (July 1, 2002). ... Traded by Yankees with cash to Arizona Diamondbacks for OF David Delluci, P Bret Prinz and C Jon-Mark Sprowl (July 29, 2003). ... Signed as a free agent by Pittsburgh Pirates (February 24, 2004). ... On restricted list (May 11-19, 2004). ... Released by Pirates (May 19, 2004). ... Signed by Anaheim Angels (May 30, 2004). ... On disabled list (June 9-July 30, 2004); included rehabilitation assignment to Rancho Cucamonga. ... Released by Angels (July 30, 2004).

HONORS: Named N.L. Rookie Player of the Year by THE SPORTING NEWS (1994). ... Named N.L. Rookie of the Year by Baseball Writers' Association of America (1994). ... Won N.L. Gold Glove as outfielder (1995 and 1997).

2004 GAMES PLAYED BY POSITION (MLB): OF—33, DH—1.

Year	Team (League)	Pos.	G	AB	R	H	2B	3B	HR	RBI	BB	SO	HBP	GDP	SB-CS	Avg.	OBP	SLG	OPS	E	Avg.
											BATTING										**FIELDING**	
1988—Dom. Dodgers (DSL)	OF	36	117	21	26	10	1	2	44	23	36	...	...	4-0	.222	...	.376	...	...	...
1989—Dom. Dodgers (DSL)	OF	46	156	32	43	15	3	2	27	16	26	...	...	8-0	.276	...	.449	...	...	...
1990—Great Falls (Pio.)	OF	44	175	35	53	10	4	8	31	11	30	2	0	30-6	.303	.349	.543	.892	1	.986
1991—Bakersfield (Calif.)	OF	28	106	23	30	7	2	3	13	5	21	3	1	9-4	.283	.330	.472	.802	3	.940
—San Antonio (Texas)	OF	53	213	32	58	11	5	5	26	8	47	4	1	8-3	.272	.307	.441	.748	4	.964
—Albuquerque (PCL)	OF	2	9	3	3	0	1	0	0	0	1	0	0	1-0	.333	.333	.556	.889	1	...
1992—Albuquerque (PCL)	OF	35	138	23	43	4	7	4	15	9	35	1	0	2-3	.312	.358	.529	.887	7	.933
—San Antonio (Texas)	OF	18	68	8	18	2	2	2	14	1	24	0	1	3-2	.265	.264	.441	.705	1	.974
1993—Albuquerque (PCL)	OF	110	425	65	119	22	7	12	65	18	85	2	4	13-10	.280	.309	.449	.758	10	.957
—Los Angeles (N.L.)	OF	42	86	13	25	3	1	4	10	4	16	0	1	4-1	.291	.322	.488	.811	3	.951
1994—Los Angeles (N.L.)	OF	112	434	63	133	27	8	16	56	16	78	2	9	11-8	.306	.333	.516	.849	8	.965
1995—Los Angeles (N.L.)	OF	139	536	91	153	23	6	26	88	33	96	4	7	27-4	.285	.328	.496	.824	6	.980
1996—Los Angeles (N.L.)	OF	157	634	98	188	40	7	24	88	32	122	6	5	14-7	.297	.334	.495	.830	•12	.967
1997—Los Angeles (N.L.)	OF	159	616	95	191	42	5	30	87	44	105	6	11	32-15	.310	.360	.541	.901	4	.989
1998—Los Angeles (N.L.)	OF	148	580	85	162	26	5	30	90	30	112	3	8	16-10	.279	.316	.497	.813	6	.980
1999—Los Angeles (N.L.)	OF	159	601	98	152	29	5	33	99	71	134	3	3	36-9	.253	.332	.483	.815	6	.982
2000—Toronto (A.L.)	OF	96	388	78	105	22	2	24	67	32	73	3	8	22-6	.271	.329	.523	.852	7	.967
2001—Toronto (A.L.)	OF	149	572	88	144	26	4	27	84	73	128	6	13	30-11	.252	.342	.453	.794	8	.972
2002—Toronto (A.L.)	OF-DH	75	299	51	67	16	1	15	45	31	57	3	8	9-2	.224	.301	.435	.736	2	.984
—New York (A.L.)	OF-DH	71	270	39	65	18	0	11	43	28	46	2	3	6-4	.241	.315	.430	.744	4	.969
2003—New York (A.L.)	OF-DH	98	361	56	93	23	3	16	49	38	66	2	6	17-7	.258	.330	.471	.801	3	.986
—Arizona (N.L.)	OF	45	162	27	49	8	1	8	22	18	31	1	3	5-4	.302	.372	.512	.884	3	.965
2004—Pittsburgh (N.L.)	OF	26	99	8	28	8	0	2	14	11	27	0	1	0-2	.283	.355	.424	.779	3	.939
—Anaheim (A.L.)	OF-DH	8	34	2	4	1	0	1	1	2	4	1	1	0-1	.118	.189	.235	.424	0	1.000
—Rancho Cuca. (Calif.)	DH-OF	2	8	2	1	0	0	0	1	0	2	0	1	0-0	.125	.222	.125	.347	0	1.000
—Salt Lake (PCL)	OF	2	6	1	2	0	0	1	2	1	2	0	0	0-0	.333	.429	.833	1.262	1	.800
American League totals (5 years)		497	1924	314	478	106	10	94	289	204	374	17	39	84-31	.248	.324	.460	.785	24	.976
National League totals (9 years)		987	3748	578	1081	206	38	173	554	259	721	24	49	145-60	.288	.336	.502	.838	51	.975
Major League totals (12 years)		1484	5672	892	1559	312	48	267	843	463	1095	41	88	229-91	.275	.332	.488	.820	75	.975

M

DIVISION SERIES RECORD

Year	Team (League)	Pos.	G	AB	R	H	2B	3B	HR	RBI	BB	SO	HBP	GDP	SB-CS	Avg.	OBP	SLG	OPS	E	Avg.
1995— Los Angeles (N.L.)		OF	3	9	0	2	0	0	0	1	0	2	1	0	0-0	.222	.300	.222	.522	0	1.000
1996— Los Angeles (N.L.)		OF	3	11	0	2	2	0	0	1	0	4	0	0	0-0	.182	.182	.364	.545	0	1.000
2002— New York (A.L.)		OF	4	12	1	3	0	0	0	1	3	1	2	0	0-0	.250	.471	.250	.721	0	1.000
Division series totals (3 years)			10	32	1	7	2	0	0	3	3	7	3	0	0-0	.219	.342	.281	.623	0	1.000

ALL-STAR GAME RECORD

			G	AB	R	H	2B	3B	HR	RBI	BB	SO	HBP	GDP	SB-CS	Avg.	OBP	SLG	OPS	E	Avg.
All-Star Game totals (1 year)			1	1	0	0	0	0	0	0	0	0	0	0	0-0	.000	.000	.000	.000	0	1.000

MONROE, CRAIG — OF

PERSONAL: Born February 27, 1977, in Texarkana, Texas. ... 6-1/220. ... Bats right, throws right. ... Full name: Craig Keystone Monroe. ... High school: Texas (Texarkana, Texas).

TRANSACTIONS/CAREER NOTES: Selected by Texas Rangers organization in eighth round of 1995 free-agent draft. ... Claimed on waivers by Detroit Tigers (February 1, 2002). ... On disabled list (July 21-August 7, 2004); included rehabilitation assignment to Toledo.

2004 GAMES PLAYED BY POSITION (MLB): OF—125, DH—2.

Year	Team (League)	Pos.	BATTING																	FIELDING	
			G	AB	R	H	2B	3B	HR	RBI	BB	SO	HBP	GDP	SB-CS	Avg.	OBP	SLG	OPS	E	Avg.
1995— GC Rangers (GCL)		OF	54	193	22	48	6	2	0	33	18	25	2	1	13-2	.249	.316	.301	.617	4	.962
1996— Char., S.C. (SAL)		OF	49	153	11	23	11	1	0	9	18	48	3	3	2-2	.150	.253	.235	.488	4	.954
— Hudson Valley (NY-Penn.) .		OF	67	268	53	74	16	6	5	29	23	63	2	4	21-7	.276	.336	.437	.772	6	.938
1997— Charlotte (Fla. St.)		OF	92	328	54	77	23	1	7	41	44	80	0	5	24-1	.235	.320	.375	.695	7	.959
1998— Charlotte (Fla. St.)		OF	132	472	73	114	26	4	17	76	66	102	3	15	50-13	.242	.334	.434	.768	11	.951
1999— Charlotte (Fla. St.)		OF	130	480	77	125	21	1	17	81	42	102	4	8	40-15	.260	.321	.415	.735	7	.980
— Oklahoma (PCL)		OF	6	16	2	4	1	0	0	1	1	4	4	0	0-0	.250	.429	.313	.741	0	1.000
2000— Tulsa (Texas)		OF	120	464	89	131	34	5	20	89	64	91	2	12	12-13	.282	.366	.506	.873	12	.948
2001— Oklahoma (PCL)		OF	114	410	60	115	25	5	20	75	46	85	5	11	10-8	.280	.358	.512	.870	5	.975
— Texas (A.L.)		OF-DH	27	52	8	11	1	0	2	5	6	18	0	1	2-0	.212	.293	.346	.639	0	1.000
2002— Toledo (Int'l)		OF	99	358	61	115	30	4	10	49	35	57	2	8	7-3	.321	.379	.511	.890	3	.983
— Detroit (A.L.)		OF-DH	13	25	3	3	1	0	1	1	0	5	1	1	0-2	.120	.154	.280	.434	1	.950
2003— Toledo (Int'l)		OF-DH	14	47	14	19	4	1	2	6	4	10	0	0	1-0	.404	.451	.660	1.111	0	1.000
— Detroit (A.L.)		OF-DH	128	425	51	102	18	1	23	70	27	89	2	10	4-2	.240	.287	.449	.736	7	.970
2004— Toledo (Int'l)		OF-DH	6	25	4	8	4	0	2	6	0	6	0	0	0-0	.320	.308	.720	1.028	0	1.000
— Detroit (A.L.)		OF-DH	128	447	65	131	27	3	18	72	29	79	2	8	3-4	.293	.337	.488	.824	11	.960
Major League totals (4 years)			296	949	127	247	47	4	44	148	62	191	5	20	9-8	.260	.307	.457	.765	19	.967

MORA, MELVIN — 3B

PERSONAL: Born February 2, 1972, in Agua Negra, Venezuela. ... 5-11/200. ... Bats right, throws right. ... Name pronounced: MORE-a. ... High school: Libertador (Venezuela).

TRANSACTIONS/CAREER NOTES: Signed as a non-drafted free agent by Houston Astros organization (March 30, 1991). ... Signed as a free agent by New York Mets organization (July 24, 1998). ... On disabled list (May 13-30, 2000); included rehabilitation assignment to Norfolk. ... Traded by Mets with 3B Mike Kinkade and Ps Leslie Brea and Pat Gorman to Baltimore Orioles for SS Mike Bordick (July 28, 2000). ... On suspended list (September 13-16, 2002). ... On disabled list (August 1-September 2, 2003); included rehabilitation assignment to Bowie. ... On disabled list (July 3-18, 2004).

RECORDS: Shares major league record for most times hit by pitch, game (3, July 18, 2002).

2004 GAMES PLAYED BY POSITION (MLB): 3B—137, SS—1, DH—1.

Year	Team (League)	Pos.	BATTING																	FIELDING	
			G	AB	R	H	2B	3B	HR	RBI	BB	SO	HBP	GDP	SB-CS	Avg.	OBP	SLG	OPS	E	Avg.
1991— Dom. Astros (DSL).			58	211	38	63	18	1	0	20	19	22	...	...	21-	.299		.393		...	...
1992— GC Astros (GCL)		2B-3B-OF	49	144	28	32	3	0	0	8	18	16	5	2	16-3	.222	.327	.243	.570	4	.961
1993— Asheville (S. Atl.)			108	365	66	104	22	2	2	31	36	46	9	7	20-13	.285	.356	.373	.729	17	.936
1994— Osceola (Fla. St.)		3B-OF	118	425	57	120	29	4	8	46	37	60	10	8	24-16	.282	.352	.424	.777	15	.947
1995— Jackson (Texas)		2B-3B-OF	123	467	63	139	32	0	3	45	32	57	9	11	22-11	.298	.350	.385	.735	6	.977
— Tucson (PCL)		OF	2	5	3	3	0	1	0	1	2	0	0	0	1-0	.600	.714	1.000	1.714	0	1.000
1996— Jackson (Texas)		2B-3-S-OF	70	255	36	73	6	1	5	23	14	23	6	4	4-7	.286	.336	.376	.712	7	.959
— Tucson (PCL)		2B-3B-OF	62	228	35	64	11	2	3	26	17	27	1	7	3-5	.281	.328	.386	.714	14	.912
1997— New Orleans (A.A.)			119	370	55	95	15	3	2	38	47	52	11	7	7-7	.257	.356	.330	.686	11	.956
1998— Mercury (Taiwan)			...	164	34	55	11	2	3	11	...	...	...	...	...-...	.335		.482		...	...
— St. Lucie (Fla. St.)		2B-3B-OF	17	55	5	15	0	0	0	8	5	9	0	1	1-1	.273	.328	.273	.601	1	.985
— Norfolk (Int'l)		2B-3B-OF	11	28	5	5	1	0	0	2	5	7	0	0	0-0	.179	.303	.214	.517	2	.875
1999— Norfolk (Int'l)		SS-OF-2-3	82	304	55	92	17	2	8	36	41	54	7	8	18-8	.303	.393	.451	.844	16	.942
— New York (N.L.)		OF-2B-3-S	66	31	6	5	0	0	0	1	4	7	1	0	2-1	.161	.278	.161	.439	0	1.000
2000— New York (N.L.)		SS-OF-2-3	79	215	35	56	13	2	6	30	18	48	2	3	7-3	.260	.317	.423	.740	8	.962
— Norfolk (Int'l)		OF-2B-SS	8	27	7	9	2	0	0	7	7	3	0	0	2-0	.333	.471	.407	.878	0	1.000
— Baltimore (A.L.)		SS-2B	53	199	25	58	9	3	2	17	17	32	4	2	5-8	.291	.353	.397	.756	12	.953
2001— Baltimore (A.L.)		OF-SS-2B	128	436	49	109	28	0	7	48	41	91	14	6	11-4	.250	.329	.362	.692	11	.974
2002— Baltimore (A.L.)		OF-S-2-DH	149	557	86	130	30	4	19	64	70	108	20	7	16-10	.233	.338	.404	.742	12	.976
2003— Bowie (East.)		OF	6	21	3	6	0	0	2	5	2	4	0	0	0-0	.286	.348	.571	.919	0	1.000
— Baltimore (A.L.) OF-SS-2B-1B			96	344	68	109	17	1	15	48	49	71	12	3	6-3	.317	.418	.503	.921	2	.992
2004— Baltimore (A.L.)		3B-SS-DH	140	550	111	187	41	0	27	104	66	95	11	10	11-6	.340 *	.419	.562	.981	21	.948
American League totals (5 years)			566	2086	339	593	125	8	70	281	243	397	61	28	49-31	.284	.373	.453	.825	58	.968
National League totals (2 years)			145	246	41	61	13	2	6	31	22	55	3	3	9-4	.248	.312	.390	.702	8	.967
Major League totals (6 years)			711	2332	380	654	138	10	76	312	265	452	64	31	58-35	.280	.367	.446	.812	66	.968

DIVISION SERIES RECORD

Year	Team (League)	Pos.	G	AB	R	H	2B	3B	HR	RBI	BB	SO	HBP	GDP	SB-CS	Avg.	OBP	SLG	OPS	E	Avg.
1999— New York (N.L.)		OF	3	1	1	0	0	0	0	0	1	0	0	0	0-0	.000	.500	.000	.500	0	1.000

CHAMPIONSHIP SERIES RECORD

Year	Team (League)	Pos.	G	AB	R	H	2B	3B	HR	RBI	BB	SO	HBP	GDP	SB-CS	Avg.	OBP	SLG	OPS	E	Avg.
1999— New York (N.L.)		OF	6	14	3	6	0	0	1	2	2	2	0	0	2-0	.429	.500	.643	1.143	0	1.000

ALL-STAR GAME RECORD

			G	AB	R	H	2B	3B	HR	RBI	BB	SO	HBP	GDP	SB-CS	Avg.	OBP	SLG	OPS	E	Avg.
All-Star Game totals (1 year)			1	0	0	0	0	0	0	0	0	0	0	0	0-0	...	...	...	...	0	...

M

MORDECAI, MIKE — 3B/SS

PERSONAL: Born December 13, 1967, in Birmingham, Ala. ... 5-10/182. ... Bats right, throws right. ... Full name: Michael Howard Mordecai. ... Name pronounced: more-duh-KYE. ... High school: Hewitt Trussville (Ala.). ... College: South Alabama.

TRANSACTIONS/CAREER NOTES: Selected by Pittsburgh Pirates organization in 33rd round of June 1986 free-agent draft; did not sign. ... Selected by Atlanta Braves organization in sixth round of 1989 free-agent draft. ... On disabled list (April 19-May 11, 1996); included rehabilitation assignment to Richmond. ... Signed as a free agent by Montreal Expos organization (March 27, 1998). ... On disabled list (June 24-July 24, 1998); included rehabilitation assignments to Jupiter and Ottawa. ... Traded by Expos with Ps Carl Pavano, Graeme Lloyd and Justin Wayne to Florida Marlins for OF Cliff Floyd, P Claudio Vargas, 2B/OF Wilton Guerrero, cash and a player to be named (July 11, 2002); Expos acquired P Don Levinski to complete deal (August 6, 2002).

2004 GAMES PLAYED BY POSITION (MLB): 3B—19, 2B—4, SS—3, C—1.

Year	Team (League)	Pos.	G	AB	R	H	2B	3B	HR	RBI	BB	SO	HBP	GDP	SB-CS	Avg.	OBP	SLG	OPS	E	Avg.
1989—	Burlington (Midw.)	3B-SS	65	241	39	61	11	1	1	22	33	43	5	2	12-5	.253	.352	.320	.672	21	.920
—	Greenville (Sou.)	2B-3B	4	8	0	3	0	0	0	1	1	1	0	0	0-0	.375	.444	.375	.819	0	1.000
1990—	Durham (Caro.)	SS	72	271	42	76	11	7	3	36	42	45	2	9	10-6	.280	.379	.406	.784	29	.920
1991—	Durham (Caro.)	SS	109	397	52	104	15	2	4	42	40	58	2	7	30-16	.262	.330	.340	.670	27	.945
1992—	Greenville (Sou.)	SS	65	222	31	58	13	1	4	31	29	31	0	6	9-6	.261	.344	.383	.727	11	.964
—	Richmond (Int'l)	2B-3B-SS	36	118	12	29	3	0	1	6	5	19	0	1	0-4	.246	.272	.297	.569	10	.937
1993—	Richmond (Int'l)	C	72	205	29	55	8	1	2	14	14	33	1	4	10-2	.268	.318	.346	.665	9	.964
1994—	Richmond (Int'l)	S-1-3-DH	99	382	67	107	25	1	14	57	35	50	2	5	14-7	.280	.340	.461	.800	22	.947
—	Atlanta (N.L.)	SS	4	4	1	1	0	0	1	3	1	0	0	0	0-0	.250	.400	1.000	1.400	0	1.000
1995—	Atlanta (N.L.)	2-1-3-S-O	69	75	10	21	6	0	3	11	9	16	0	0	0-0	.280	.353	.480	.833	0	1.000
1996—	Atlanta (N.L.)	2-3-S-1	66	108	12	26	5	0	2	8	9	24	0	1	1-0	.241	.297	.343	.639	2	.977
—	Richmond (Int'l)	SS	3	11	2	2	0	0	1	2	0	3	0	0	0-0	.182	.167	.455	.621	0	1.000
1997—	Atlanta (N.L.)	3-2-S-1-DH-O	61	81	8	14	2	1	0	3	6	16	0	4	0-1	.173	.227	.222	.449	0	1.000
—	Richmond (Int'l)	2-3-DH-S	31	122	23	38	10	0	3	15	9	17	1	0	0-1	.311	.361	.467	.828	1	.989
1998—	Montreal (N.L.)	S-2-3-1	73	119	12	24	4	2	3	10	9	20	0	2	1-0	.202	.258	.345	.602	5	.960
—	Jupiter (FSL)	2B-SS	2	8	0	0	0	0	0	0	1	3	0	1	0-0	.000	.111	.000	.111	0	1.000
—	Ottawa (Int'l)	SS-2B	6	22	2	5	2	0	0	1	3	3	0	1	0-0	.227	.320	.318	.638	1	.969
1999—	Montreal (N.L.)	2-S-3-1	109	226	29	53	10	2	5	25	20	31	1	1	2-5	.235	.297	.363	.660	7	.970
2000—	Montreal (N.L.)	3-S-2-1	86	169	20	48	16	0	4	16	12	34	1	1	2-2	.284	.335	.450	.785	8	.942
2001—	Montreal (N.L.)	3-2-S-DH-C-1-O	96	254	28	71	17	2	3	32	19	53	1	6	2-2	.280	.330	.398	.727	3	.985
2002—	Montreal (N.L.)	3-2-S-1-O	55	74	9	15	4	0	0	4	8	14	1	2	1-1	.203	.289	.257	.546	4	.948
—	Florida (N.L.)	SS-3B-1B	38	77	10	22	4	0	0	7	5	13	1	1	1-1	.286	.337	.338	.675	1	.989
2003—	Florida (N.L.)	SS-2-3-1	65	89	11	19	4	0	2	8	8	21	0	0	3-0	.213	.276	.326	.601	3	.961
2004—	Florida (N.L.)	3-2-S-C	69	84	7	19	3	0	1	5	6	18	0	1	0-1	.226	.278	.298	.575	3	.945
	Major League totals (11 years)		791	1360	157	333	75	7	24	132	112	260	5	19	13-13	.245	.303	.363	.666	36	.970

DIVISION SERIES RECORD

Year	Team (League)	Pos.	G	AB	R	H	2B	3B	HR	RBI	BB	SO	HBP	GDP	SB-CS	Avg.	OBP	SLG	OPS	E	Avg.
1995—	Atlanta (N.L.)	SS	2	3	1	2	1	0	0	2	0	0	0	0	0-0	.667	.667	1.000	1.667	0	1.000
1996—	Atlanta (N.L.)			Did not play.																	

CHAMPIONSHIP SERIES RECORD

Year	Team (League)	Pos.	G	AB	R	H	2B	3B	HR	RBI	BB	SO	HBP	GDP	SB-CS	Avg.	OBP	SLG	OPS	E	Avg.
1995—	Atlanta (N.L.)	SS	2	2	0	0	0	0	0	0	0	1	0	0	0-0	.000	.000	.000	.000	0	...
1996—	Atlanta (N.L.)	2B-3B	4	4	1	1	0	0	0	0	0	0	0	0	0-0	.250	.250	.250	.500	0	1.000
2003—	Florida (N.L.)	SS-2B	3	5	1	1	1	0	0	3	0	0	0	0	0-0	.200	.200	.400	.600	0	...
	Champ. series totals (3 years)		9	11	2	2	1	0	0	3	0	2	0	0	0-0	.182	.182	.273	.455	0	1.000

WORLD SERIES RECORD

Year	Team (League)	Pos.	G	AB	R	H	2B	3B	HR	RBI	BB	SO	HBP	GDP	SB-CS	Avg.	OBP	SLG	OPS	E	Avg.
1995—	Atlanta (N.L.)	SS-DH	3	3	0	1	0	0	0	0	0	1	0	0	0-0	.333	.333	.333	.667	0	1.000
1996—	Atlanta (N.L.)		1	1	0	0	0	0	0	0	0	0	0	0	0-0	.000	.000	.000	.000		...
	World series totals (2 years)		4	4	0	1	0	0	0	0	0	1	0	0	0-0	.250	.250	.250	.500	0	1.000

MORENO, ORBER — P

PERSONAL: Born April 27, 1977, in Caracas, Venezuela. ... 6-3/200. ... Throws right, bats right. ... Full name: Orber Aquiles Moreno. ... Name pronounced: MORE-a-no. ... High school: Luisa Caceres (Venezuela).

TRANSACTIONS/CAREER NOTES: Signed as a non-drafted free agent by Kansas City Royals organization (November 10, 1993). ... On disabled list (June 10, 1999-remainder of season); included rehabilitation assignment to GCL Royals. ... On disabled list (March 24, 2000-entire season; and March 31-May 28, 2001). ... Released by Royals (October 3, 2002). ... Signed by New York Mets organization (March 6, 2003). ... On disabled list (June 5-24 and July 23, 2004-remainder of season); included rehabilitation assignments to GCL Mets and St. Lucie.

CAREER HITTING: 0-for-2 (.000), 0 R, 0 2B, 0 3B, 0 HR, 0 RBI.

Year	Team (League)	W	L	Pct.	ERA	WHIP	G	GS	CG	ShO	Hld.	Sv.-Opp.	IP	H	R	ER	HR	BB-IBB	SO	Avg.
1994—	Dom. Royals (DSL)	3	3	.500	3.19	1.15	16	11	0	0	...	1-...	67.2	51	33	24	0	27-...	44	...
1995—	GC Royals (GCL)	1	1	.500	2.45	1.00	8	3	0	0	...	0-...	22.0	15	9	6	0	7-0	21	.188
1996—	GC Royals (GCL)	5	1	.833	1.36	1.01	12	7	0	0	...	1-...	46.1	37	15	7	2	10-0	50	.214
1997—	Lansing (Midw.)	4	8	.333	4.81	1.41	27	25	0	0	...	0-...	138.1	150	83	74	15	45-0	128	.278
1998—	Wilmington (Caro.)	3	2	.600	0.82	0.55	23	0	0	0	...	7-...	33.0	8	3	3	1	10-1	50	.077
—	Wichita (Texas)	0	1	.000	2.88	1.17	24	0	0	0	...	7-...	34.1	28	13	11	1	12-3	40	.215
1999—	Omaha (PCL)	3	1	.750	2.10	0.82	16	0	0	0	...	4-...	25.2	17	6	6	2	4-0	30	.183
—	Kansas City (A.L.)	0	0	...	5.63	1.25	7	0	0	0	1	0-1	8.0	4	5	5	1	6-0	7	.143
—	GC Royals (GCL)	0	0	...	0.00	0.00	1	1	0	0	...	0-...	1.0	0	0	0	0	0-0	1	.000
2000—	Kansas City (A.L.)			Did not play.																
2001—	Wilmington (Caro.)	1	1	.500	2.53	1.00	8	1	0	0	...	1-...	10.2	12	5	3	1	1-0	16	.261
—	Wichita (Texas)	0	0	...	0.00	0.58	5	0	0	0	...	1-...	8.2	3	0	0	0	2-0	10	.107
—	Omaha (PCL)	1	1	.500	4.71	1.29	17	0	0	0	...	3-...	21.0	19	11	11	4	8-0	25	.232
2002—	GC Royals (GCL)	0	0	...	0.00	0.50	2	2	0	0	...	0-...	2.0	1	0	0	0	0-0	3	.143
2003—	Binghamton (Eastern)	2	0	1.000	1.69	0.90	4	0	0	0	...	1-...	5.1	4	1	1	1	1-0	7	.200
—	Norfolk (Int'l)	5	1	.833	1.90	1.00	38	0	0	0	...	12-...	52.0	36	11	11	1	17-0	58	.191
—	New York (N.L.)	0	0	...	7.88	1.63	7	0	0	0	0	0-0	8.0	10	7	7	1	3-0	5	.313
2004—	GC Mets (GCL)	0	1	.000	40.50	7.50	1	1	0	0	...	0-...	.2	4	3	3	0	1-0	1	.667
—	St. Lucie (Fla. St.)	0	0	...	27.00	4.00	1	0	0	0	...	0-...	1.0	4	3	3	0	0-0	1	.571
—	New York (N.L.)	3	1	.750	3.38	1.15	33	0	0	0	1	1-3	34.2	29	17	13	0	11-0	29	.221
	American League totals (1 year)	0	0	...	5.63	1.25	7	0	0	0	1	0-1	8.0	4	5	5	1	6-0	7	.143
	National League totals (2 years)	3	1	.750	4.22	1.24	40	0	0	0	1	1-3	42.2	39	24	20	1	14-0	34	.239
	Major League totals (3 years)	3	1	.750	4.44	1.24	47	0	0	0	2	1-4	50.2	43	29	25	2	20-0	41	.225

M

MORNEAU, JUSTIN — 1B

PERSONAL: Born May 15, 1981, in New Westminster, British Columbia. ... 6-4/228. ... Bats left, throws right. ... Full name: Justin Ernest Morneau. ... Name pronounced: more-no. ... High school: New Westminster Academy (B.C.).

TRANSACTIONS/CAREER NOTES: Selected by Minnesota Twins organization in third round of 1999 free-agent draft.

2004 GAMES PLAYED BY POSITION (MLB): 1B—61, DH—11.

Year Team (League)	Pos.	G	AB	R	H	2B	3B	HR	RBI	BB	SO	HBP	GDP	SB-CS	Avg.	OBP	SLG	OPS	E	Avg.
1999— GC Twins (GCL)		17	53	3	16	5	0	0	9	2	6	1	2	0-1	.302	.333	.396	.730	...	...
2000— GC Twins (GCL)	1B-C-OF	52	194	47	78	21	0	10	58	30	18	0	5	3-1	.402	.478	.665	1.143	3	.992
— Elizabethton (App.)	C	6	23	4	5	0	0	1	3	1	6	0	0	0-0	.217	.250	.348	.598	0	1.000
2001— Quad City (Midw.)	1B	64	236	50	84	17	2	12	53	26	38	3	4	0-0	.356	.420	.597	1.018	8	.985
— Fort Myers (FSL)	1B	53	197	25	58	10	3	4	40	24	41	8	4	0-0	.294	.385	.437	.821	3	.994
— New Britain (East.)	1B	10	38	3	6	1	0	0	4	3	8	0	1	0-0	.158	.214	.184	.399	0	1.000
2002— New Britain (East.)	1B	126	494	72	147	31	4	16	80	42	88	6	8	7-0	.298	.356	.474	.830	13	.989
2003— New Britain (East.)	1B	20	79	14	26	3	1	6	13	7	14	0	0	0-0	.329	.384	.620	1.004	0	1.000
— Rochester (Int'l)	1B-DH	71	265	39	71	11	1	16	42	28	56	4	2	0-2	.268	.344	.498	.843	4	.993
— Minnesota (A.L.)	DH-1B	40	106	14	24	4	0	4	16	9	30	0	4	0-0	.226	.287	.377	.664	1	.971
2004— Rochester (Int'l)	1B-DH	72	288	51	88	23	0	22	63	32	47	3	7	1-1	.306	.377	.615	.992	4	.994
— Minnesota (A.L.)	1B-DH	74	280	39	76	17	0	19	58	28	54	2	4	0-0	.271	.340	.536	.875	3	.995
Major League totals (2 years)		114	386	53	100	21	0	23	74	37	84	2	8	0-0	.259	.326	.492	.818	4	.993

DIVISION SERIES RECORD

Year Team (League)	Pos.	G	AB	R	H	2B	3B	HR	RBI	BB	SO	HBP	GDP	SB-CS	Avg.	OBP	SLG	OPS	E	Avg.
2004— Minnesota (A.L.)	1B	4	17	1	4	2	0	0	2	0	3	0	0	0-0	.235	.235	.353	.588	0	1.000

MORRIS, MATT — P

PERSONAL: Born August 9, 1974, in Middletown, N.Y. ... 6-5/220. ... Throws right, bats right. ... Full name: Matthew Christian Morris. ... High school: Valley Central (Montgomery, N.Y.). ... College: Seton Hall.

TRANSACTIONS/CAREER NOTES: Selected by Milwaukee Brewers organization in 25th round of 1992 free-agent draft; did not sign. ... Selected by St. Louis Cardinals organization in first round (12th pick overall) of 1995 free-agent draft. ... On disabled list (March 24-April 11 and April 12-July 10, 1998); included rehabilitation assignments to Arkansas and Memphis. ... On disabled list (March 26, 1999-entire season). ... On disabled list (April 2-May 28, 2000); included rehabilitation assignments to Arkansas and Memphis. ... On disabled list (August 24-September 10, 2002; and July 22-August 23, 2003).

HONORS: Named N.L. Rookie Pitcher of the Year by THE SPORTING NEWS (1997). ... Named N.L. Comeback Player of the Year by THE SPORTING NEWS (2001).

CAREER HITTING: 60-for-362 (.166), 23 R, 11 2B, 0 3B, 1 HR, 26 RBI.

Year Team (League)	W	L	Pct.	ERA	WHIP	G	GS	CG	ShO	Hld.	Sv.-Opp.	IP	H	R	ER	HR	BB-IBB	SO	Avg.
1995— New Jersey (N.Y.-Penn.)	2	0	1.000	1.64	1.36	2	2	0	0	...	0-...	11.0	12	3	2	1	3-0	13	.286
— St. Pete. (FSL)	3	2	.600	2.38	0.97	6	6	1	1	...	0-...	34.0	22	16	9	1	11-0	31	.182
1996— Arkansas (Texas)	12	12	.500	3.88	1.35	27	27	4	4	...	0-...	167.0	178	79	72	14	48-1	120	.274
— Louisville (A.A.)	0	1	.000	3.38	1.13	1	1	0	0	...	0-...	8.0	8	3	3	0	1-0	9	.258
1997— St. Louis (N.L.)	12	9	.571	3.19	1.28	33	33	3	0	0	0-0	217.0	208	88	77	12	69-2	149	.258
1998— Arkansas (Texas)	0	0	...	0.00	1.00	1	0	0	0	0	1-...	4.0	4	0	0	0	0-0	2	.235
— St. Louis (N.L.)	7	5	.583	2.53	1.26	17	17	2	1	0	0-0	113.2	101	37	32	8	42-6	79	.243
— Memphis (PCL)	1	0	1.000	4.50	1.43	4	4	0	0	0	0-...	14.0	16	8	7	1	4-0	21	.286
1999— St. Louis (N.L.)			Did not play.																
2000— Arkansas (Texas)	0	0	...	6.43	1.71	2	2	0	0	...	0-...	7.0	8	5	5	0	4-0	7	.296
— Memphis (PCL)	1	2	.333	7.98	1.77	3	3	0	0	...	0-...	14.2	20	13	13	2	6-1	8	.351
— St. Louis (N.L.)	3	3	.500	3.57	1.32	31	0	0	0	7	4-7	53.0	53	22	21	3	17-1	34	.261
2001— St. Louis (N.L.)	• 22	8	.733	3.16	1.26	34	34	2	1	0	0-0	216.1	218	86	76	13	54-3	185	.265
2002— St. Louis (N.L.)	17	9	.654	3.42	1.30	32	32	1	1	0	0-0	210.1	210	86	80	14	64-3	171	.261
2003— St. Louis (N.L.)	11	8	.579	3.76	1.18	27	27	5	• 3	0	0-0	172.1	164	76	72	20	39-1	120	.252
2004— St. Louis (N.L.)	15	10	.600	4.72	1.29	32	32	3	2	0	0-0	202.0	205	116	106	25	56-3	131	.266
Major League totals (7 years)	87	52	.626	3.53	1.27	206	175	16	8	7	4-7	1184.2	1159	511	464	107	341-19	869	.259

DIVISION SERIES RECORD

Year Team (League)	W	L	Pct.	ERA	WHIP	G	GS	CG	ShO	Hld.	Sv.-Opp.	IP	H	R	ER	HR	BB-IBB	SO	Avg.
2000— St. Louis (N.L.)	0	0	...	0.00	0.50	2	0	0	0	0	0-0	2.0	0	0	0	0	1-0	0	.000
2001— St. Louis (N.L.)	0	1	.000	1.20	1.20	2	2	0	0	0	0-0	15.0	13	2	2	1	5-0	12	.236
2002— St. Louis (N.L.)	1	0	1.000	1.29	1.29	1	1	0	0	0	0-0	7.0	7	2	1	0	2-0	3	.259
2004— St. Louis (N.L.)	0	1	.000	5.14	1.14	1	1	0	0	0	0-0	7.0	6	4	4	2	2-1	5	.231
Division series totals (4 years)	1	2	.333	2.03	1.16	6	4	0	0	0	0-0	31.0	26	8	7	3	10-1	20	.228

CHAMPIONSHIP SERIES RECORD

Year Team (League)	W	L	Pct.	ERA	WHIP	G	GS	CG	ShO	Hld.	Sv.-Opp.	IP	H	R	ER	HR	BB-IBB	SO	Avg.
2000— St. Louis (N.L.)	0	0	...	4.91	1.36	2	0	0	0	0	0-0	3.2	3	2	2	0	2-1	2	.214
2002— St. Louis (N.L.)	0	2	.000	6.23	1.69	2	2	0	0	0	0-0	13.0	16	9	9	2	6-1	6	.320
2004— St. Louis (N.L.)	0	0	...	5.40	1.90	2	2	0	0	0	0-0	10.0	11	6	6	3	8-1	6	.297
Champ. series totals (3 years)	0	2	.000	5.74	1.73	6	4	0	0	0	0-0	26.2	30	17	17	5	16-3	14	.297

WORLD SERIES RECORD

Year Team (League)	W	L	Pct.	ERA	WHIP	G	GS	CG	ShO	Hld.	Sv.-Opp.	IP	H	R	ER	HR	BB-IBB	SO	Avg.
2004— St. Louis (N.L.)	0	1	.000	8.31	1.85	1	1	0	0	0	0-0	4.1	4	4	4	0	4-0	3	.250

ALL-STAR GAME RECORD

Year Team (League)	W	L	Pct.	ERA	WHIP	G	GS	CG	ShO	Hld.	Sv.-Opp.	IP	H	R	ER	HR	BB-IBB	SO	Avg.
All-Star Game totals (1 year)	0	0	...	0.00	1.00	1	0	0	0	0	0-0	1.0	1	0	0	0	0-0	1	.250

MOSS, DAMIAN — P

PERSONAL: Born November 24, 1976, in Darlinghurst, Australia. ... 6-0/187. ... Throws left, bats right. ... Full name: Damian Joseph Moss. ... High school: Liverpool Boys (Australia).

TRANSACTIONS/CAREER NOTES: Signed as a non-drafted free agent by Atlanta Braves organization (July 1, 1993). ... On disabled list (March 27, 1998-entire season; and April 3-June 1, 1999). ... On disabled list (May 11-June 18, 2001); included rehabilitation assignment to Greenville. ... Traded by Braves with P Merkin Valdez to San Francisco Giants for P Russ Ortiz (December 17, 2002). ... Traded by Giants with Ps Kiurt Ainsworth and Ryan Hannaman to Baltimore Orioles for P Sidney Ponson (July 31, 2003). ...

M

Signed as a free agent by Tampa Bay Devil Rays (January 22, 2004). ... Released by Devil Rays (August 13, 2004). ... Signed by Cincinnati Reds organization (August 15, 2004).

CAREER HITTING: 12-for-80 (.150), 3 R, 1 2B, 0 3B, 0 HR, 3 RBI.

Year	Team (League)	W	L	Pct.	ERA	WHIP	G	GS	CG	ShO	Hld.	Sv.-Opp.	IP	H	R	ER	HR	BB-IBB	SO	Avg.
1994— Danville (Appalachian)	2	5	.286	3.58	1.41	12	12	1	1	...	0-...	60.1	30	28	24	1	55-0	77	.154
1995— Macon (S. Atl.)	9	10	.474	3.56	1.37	27	27	0	0	...	0-...	149.1	134	73	59	13	70-0	177	.236
1996— Durham (Caro.)	9	1	.900	2.25	1.10	14	14	0	0	...	0-...	84.0	52	25	21	9	40-0	89	.182
— Greenville (Sou.)	2	5	.286	4.97	1.59	11	10	0	0	...	0-...	58.0	57	41	32	5	35-0	48	.258
1997— Greenville (Sou.)	6	8	.429	5.35	1.50	21	19	1	0	...	0-...	112.2	111	73	67	13	58-0	116	.263
1998— Greenville (Sou.)	Did not play.																		
1999— Macon (S. Atl.)	0	3	.000	4.32	1.15	12	12	0	0	...	0-...	41.2	33	20	20	8	15-0	49	.217
— Greenville (Sou.)	1	3	.250	8.54	2.17	7	7	0	0	...	0-...	32.2	50	33	31	6	21-0	22	.345
2000— Richmond (Int'l)	9	6	.600	3.14	1.47	29	28	0	0	...	0-...	160.2	130	67	56	14	106-0	123	.222
2001— Richmond (Int'l)	5	4	.556	3.15	1.27	17	16	0	0	...	0-...	88.2	75	34	31	10	38-1	94	.231
— Atlanta (N.L.)	0	0	...	3.00	1.33	5	1	0	0	0	0-0	9.0	3	3	3	1	9-0	8	.097
— Greenville (Sou.)	0	1	.000	3.00	0.78	3	2	0	0	...	0-...	9.0	7	3	3	0	0-0	10	.206
2002— Atlanta (N.L.)	12	6	.667	3.42	1.28	33	29	0	0	0	0-0	179.0	140	80	68	20	89-5	111	.221
2003— San Francisco (N.L.)	9	7	.563	4.70	1.60	21	20	0	0	0	0-0	115.0	121	62	60	12	63-3	57	.273
— Baltimore (A.L.)	1	5	.167	6.22	1.82	10	9	0	0	0	0-0	50.2	63	40	35	12	29-2	22	.307
2004— Tampa Bay (A.L.)	0	1	.000	16.88	2.25	5	2	0	0	0	0-0	8.0	13	15	15	2	5-0	6	.351
— Durham (Int'l)	5	9	.357	5.87	1.96	20	17	0	0	...	0-...	89.0	109	68	58	7	65-0	67	.311
— Louisville (Int'l)	0	3	.000	10.13	2.36	4	3	0	0	...	0-...	18.2	29	23	21	4	15-0	12	.363
American League totals (2 years)	1	6	.143	7.67	1.88	15	11	0	0	0	0-0	58.2	76	55	50	14	34-2	28	.314
National League totals (3 years)	21	13	.618	3.89	1.40	59	50	0	0	0	0-0	303.0	264	145	131	33	161-8	176	.238
Major League totals (4 years)	22	19	.537	4.50	1.48	74	61	0	0	0	0-0	361.2	340	200	181	47	195-10	204	.252

DIVISION SERIES RECORD

Year	Team (League)	W	L	Pct.	ERA	WHIP	G	GS	CG	ShO	Hld.	Sv.-Opp.	IP	H	R	ER	HR	BB-IBB	SO	Avg.
2002— Atlanta (N.L.)	0	0	...	3.00	1.00	2	0	0	0	0	0-0	3.0	2	1	1	0	1-0	3	.182

MOTA, GUILLERMO — P

PERSONAL: Born July 25, 1973, in San Pedro de Macoris, Dominican Republic. ... 6-4/205. ... Throws right, bats right. ... Full name: Guillermo Reynoso Mota. ... Name pronounced: mo-TAH. ... High school: Jose Joaquin Perez (San Pedro de Macoris, Dominican Republic).

TRANSACTIONS/CAREER NOTES: Signed as a non-drafted free agent by New York Mets organization (September 7, 1990). ... Played infield in Mets organization (1991-96). ... Selected by Montreal Expos organization from Mets organization in Rule 5 minor league draft (December 9, 1996). ... On disabled list (July 13-September 1, 2001); included rehabilitation assignment to Ottawa. ... Traded by Expos with OF Wilkin Ruan to Los Angeles Dodgers for P Matt Herges and IF Jorge Nunez (March 24, 2002). ... On suspended list (March 30-April 4, 2003). ... Traded by Dodgers with C Paul Lo Duca and OF Juan Encarnacion to Florida Marlins for Ps Brad Penny and Bill Murphy and 1B Hee Seop Choi (July 30, 2004).

CAREER HITTING: 7-for-30 (.233), 4 R, 1 2B, 0 3B, 2 HR, 6 RBI.

Year	Team (League)	W	L	Pct.	ERA	WHIP	G	GS	CG	ShO	Hld.	Sv.-Opp.	IP	H	R	ER	HR	BB-IBB	SO	Avg.
1997— Cape Fear (S. Atl.)	5	10	.333	4.36	1.33	25	23	0	0	...	0-...	126.0	135	65	61	8	33-0	112	.278
1998— Jupiter (FSL)	3	2	.600	0.66	0.59	20	0	0	0	...	2-...	41.0	18	6	3	0	6-0	27	.130
— Harrisburg (Eastern)	2	0	1.000	1.06	0.71	12	0	0	0	...	4-...	17.0	10	2	2	0	2-0	19	.172
1999— Ottawa (Int'l)	2	0	1.000	1.89	1.11	14	0	0	0	...	5-...	19.0	16	6	4	0	5-0	17	.235
— Montreal (N.L.)	2	4	.333	2.93	1.43	51	0	0	0	3	0-1	55.1	54	24	18	5	25-3	27	.257
2000— Ottawa (Int'l)	4	5	.444	2.29	1.27	35	0	0	0	...	7-...	63.0	49	16	16	4	31-3	35	.220
— Montreal (N.L.)	1	1	.500	6.00	1.30	29	0	0	0	5	0-0	30.0	27	21	20	3	12-0	24	.245
2001— Montreal (N.L.)	1	3	.250	5.26	1.39	53	0	0	0	12	0-3	49.2	51	30	29	9	18-1	31	.271
— Ottawa (Int'l)	0	0	...	2.25	0.25	4	0	0	0	...	0-...	4.0	1	1	1	1	0-0	4	.077
2002— Las Vegas (PCL)	1	3	.250	2.95	1.15	20	0	0	0	...	1-...	36.2	34	13	12	1	8-1	38	.260
— Los Angeles (N.L.)	1	3	.250	4.15	1.19	43	0	0	0	4	0-1	60.2	45	30	28	4	27-6	49	.202
2003— Los Angeles (N.L.)	6	3	.667	1.97	0.99	76	0	0	0	13	1-3	105.0	78	23	23	7	26-4	99	.206
2004— Los Angeles (N.L.)	8	4	.667	2.14	1.24	52	0	0	0	17	1-1	63.0	51	15	15	4	27-5	52	.228
— Florida (N.L.)	1	4	.200	4.81	1.01	26	0	0	0	13	3-7	33.2	24	18	18	4	10-1	33	.200
Major League totals (6 years)	20	22	.476	3.42	1.20	330	0	0	0	67	5-16	397.1	330	161	151	36	145-20	315	.227

MOTTOLA, CHAD — OF

PERSONAL: Born October 15, 1971, in Augusta, Ga. ... 6-3/220. ... Bats right, throws right. ... Full name: Charles Edward Mottola. ... Name pronounced: muh-TOE-lah. ... High school: St. Thomas Aquinas (Fort Lauderdale, Fla.). ... College: Central Florida.

TRANSACTIONS/CAREER NOTES: Selected by Baltimore Orioles organization in 10th round of 1989 free-agent draft; did not sign. ... Selected by Cincinnati Reds organization in first round (fifth pick overall) of 1992 free-agent draft. ... Traded by Reds to Texas Rangers for a player to be named (April 18, 1998); Reds acquired OF Andrew Vessel to complete deal (November 4, 1998). ... Signed as a free agent by Chicago White Sox organization (December 17, 1998). ... Signed as a free agent by Toronto Blue Jays organization (November 17, 1999). ... Traded by Blue Jays to Florida Marlins for cash (January 16, 2001). ... Signed as a free agent by Blue Jays organization (December 18, 2001). ... Signed as a free agent by Tampa Bay Devil Rays organization (November 1, 2002). ... Released by Devil Rays (June 8, 2003). ... Signed by Boston Red Sox organization (June 12, 2003). ... Signed as a free agent by Baltimore Orioles organization (December 19, 2003).

2004 GAMES PLAYED BY POSITION (MLB): OF—5.

Year	Team (League)	Pos.	G	AB	R	H	2B	3B	HR	RBI	BB	SO	HBP	GDP	SB-CS	Avg.	OBP	SLG	OPS	E	Avg.
1992— Billings (Pio.)	OF	57	213	53	61	8	3	12	37	25	43	0	4	12-3	.286	.361	.521	.882	3	.970
1993— Win.-Salem (Car.)	OF	137	493	76	138	25	3	21	91	62	109	2	9	13-7	.280	.361	.471	.831	15	.940
1994— Chattanooga (Sou.)	OF	118	402	44	97	19	1	7	41	30	68	1	12	9-12	.241	.294	.346	.640	1	.996
1995— Chattanooga (Sou.)	OF	51	181	32	53	13	1	10	39	13	32	1	2	1-2	.293	.342	.541	.883	3	.974
— Indianapolis (A.A.)	OF	69	239	40	62	11	1	8	37	20	50	0	6	8-1	.259	.315	.414	.730	4	.976
1996— Indianapolis (A.A.)	OF-DH	103	362	45	95	24	3	9	47	21	93	4	10	9-6	.262	.307	.420	.727	6	.968
— Cincinnati (N.L.)	OF	35	79	10	17	3	0	3	6	6	16	0	0	2-2	.215	.271	.367	.638	0	1.000
1997— Indianapolis (A.A.)	OF-DH	83	284	33	82	10	6	7	45	16	43	4	12	12-4	.289	.333	.440	.773	8	.947
— Chattanooga (Sou.)	OF-DH	46	174	35	63	9	3	5	32	16	23	1	3	7-1	.362	.408	.534	.943	3	.963
1998— Indianapolis (Int'l)	OF	5	12	2	5	0	0	1	2	4	0	0	0	0-2	.417	.563	.667	1.229	0	1.000
— Tulsa (Texas)	DH-OF	8	26	9	13	1	0	1	7	10	1	0	0	3-0	.500	.639	.654	1.293	0	1.000
— Oklahoma (PCL)	OF-DH	74	257	29	68	13	1	2	22	18	49	1	7	8-3	.265	.313	.346	.659	6	.953
1999— Charlotte (Int'l)	OF-DH	140	511	95	164	32	4	20	94	60	83	3	7	18-6	.321	.391	.517	.907	6	.981

M

Year Team (League)	Pos.	G	AB	R	H	2B	3B	HR	RBI	BB	SO	HBP	GDP	SB-CS	Avg.	OBP	SLG	OPS	E	Avg.
2000—Syracuse (Int'l)	OF	134	505	85	156	25	3	33	102	37	99	5	11	30-15	.309	.359	.566	.925	10	.964
—Toronto (A.L.)	OF	3	9	1	2	0	0	0	2	0	4	1	0	0-0	.222	.300	.222	.522	0	1.000
2001—Calgary (PCL)	OF	119	457	66	135	23	2	15	66	30	85	4	5	11-5	.295	.343	.453	.796	8	.968
—Florida (N.L.)	OF	5	7	1	0	0	0	0	1	2	2	0	0	0-0	.000	.200	.000	.200	0	1.000
2002—Syracuse (Int'l)	OF	122	476	77	124	35	1	13	67	51	87	4	9	12-2	.261	.333	.420	.753	12	.946
2003—Durham (Int'l)	OF-DH	56	213	24	55	7	1	6	28	19	37	1	4	6-3	.258	.319	.385	.704	1	.988
—Pawtucket (Int'l)	OF-DH	21	72	11	23	3	2	3	18	6	10	1	1	0-1	.319	.380	.542	.922	1	.966
2004—Baltimore (A.L.-DH)	OF	6	14	2	2	1	0	1	3	2	3	0	1	0-0	.143	.250	.429	.679	0	1.000
—Ottawa (Int'l)	OF-1B-DH	117	457	60	121	22	0	22	69	22	90	9	13	8-0	.265	.308	.457	.766	7	.979
American League totals (2 years)		9	23	3	4	1	0	1	5	2	7	1	1	0-0	.174	.269	.348	.617	0	1.000
National League totals (2 years)		40	86	11	17	3	0	3	7	8	18	0	0	2-2	.198	.263	.337	.600	0	1.000
Major League totals (4 years)		49	109	14	21	4	0	4	12	10	25	1	1	2-2	.193	.264	.339	.604	0	1.000

MOYER, JAMIE P

PERSONAL: Born November 18, 1962, in Sellersville, Pa. ... 6-0/175. ... Throws left, bats left. ... High school: Souderton (Pa.) Area. ... College: St. Joseph's (Pa.). ... Son-in-law of Digger Phelps, ESPN college basketball analyst, and Notre Dame basketball coach (1971-72 through 1990-91).

TRANSACTIONS/CAREER NOTES: Selected by Chicago Cubs organization in sixth round of June 1984 free-agent draft. ... Traded by Cubs with OF Rafael Palmeiro and P Drew Hall to Texas Rangers for Ps Mitch Williams, Paul Kilgus and Steve Wilson, IFs Curtis Wilkerson and Luis Benitez and OF Pablo Delgado (December 5, 1988). ... On disabled list (May 31-September 1, 1989); included rehabilitation assignments to GCL Rangers and Tulsa. ... Released by Rangers (November 13, 1990). ... Signed by St. Louis Cardinals organization (January 9, 1991). ... Released by Cardinals (October 14, 1991). ... Signed by Cubs organization (January 8, 1992). ... Released by Cubs (March 30, 1992). ... Signed by Detroit Tigers organization (May 24, 1992). ... Signed as a free agent by Baltimore Orioles organization (December 14, 1992). ... Signed as a free agent by Boston Red Sox (January 2, 1996). ... Traded by Red Sox to Seattle Mariners for OF Darren Bragg (July 30, 1996). ... On disabled list (March 23-April 29, 1997); included rehabilitation assignment to Tacoma. ... On disabled list (April 15-June 2, 2000).

CAREER HITTING: 27-for-173 (.156), 11 R, 2 2B, 0 3B, 0 HR, 6 RBI.

Year Team (League)	W	L	Pct.	ERA	WHIP	G	GS	CG	ShO	Hld.	Sv.-Opp.	IP	H	R	ER	HR	BB-IBB	SO	Avg.
1984—Geneva (N.Y.-Penn)	9	3	.750	1.89	0.86	14	14	5	2	...	0-...	104.2	59	27	22	1	31-0	120	.160
1985—Winston-Salem (Caro.)	8	2	.800	2.30	1.11	12	12	6	2	...	0-...	94.0	82	36	24	1	22-3	94	.232
—Pittsfield (East.)	7	6	.538	3.72	1.36	15	15	3	0	...	0-...	96.2	99	49	40	4	32-1	51	.265
1986—Pittsfield (East.)	3	1	.750	0.88	1.05	6	6	0	0	...	0-...	41.0	27	10	4	2	16-0	42	.186
—Iowa (Am. Assoc.)	3	2	.600	2.55	0.85	6	6	0	0	...	0-...	42.1	25	14	12	2	11-0	25	.162
—Chicago (N.L.)	7	4	.636	5.05	1.71	16	16	1	1	0	0-0	87.1	107	52	49	10	42-1	45	.311
1987—Chicago (N.L.)	12	15	.444	5.10	1.53	35	33	1	0	0	0-0	201.0	210	127	* 114	28	97-9	147	.271
1988—Chicago (N.L.)	9	15	.375	3.48	1.32	34	30	3	1	0	0-2	202.0	212	84	78	20	55-7	121	.272
1989—Texas (A.L.)	4	9	.308	4.86	1.54	15	15	1	0	0	0-0	76.0	84	51	41	10	33-0	44	.283
—GC Rangers (GCL)	1	0	1.000	1.64	0.82	3	3	0	0	...	0-...	11.0	8	4	2	0	1-0	15	.195
—Tulsa (Texas)	1	1	.500	5.11	1.54	2	2	1	1	...	0-...	12.1	16	8	7	1	3-0	9	.320
1990—Texas (A.L.)	2	6	.250	4.66	1.50	33	10	1	0	1	0-0	102.1	115	59	53	6	39-4	58	.290
1991—St. Louis (N.L.)	0	5	.000	5.74	1.72	8	7	0	0	0	0-0	31.1	38	21	20	5	16-0	20	.319
—Louisville (A.A.)	5	10	.333	3.80	1.34	20	20	1	0	...	0-...	125.2	125	64	53	16	43-4	69	.260
1992—Toledo (International)	10	8	.556	2.86	1.19	21	20	5	0	...	0-...	138.2	128	48	44	8	37-3	80	.246
1993—Rochester (Int'l)	6	0	1.000	1.67	1.02	8	8	1	1	...	0-...	54.0	42	13	10	2	13-0	41	.211
—Baltimore (A.L.)	12	9	.571	3.43	1.26	25	25	3	1	0	0-0	152.0	154	63	58	11	38-2	90	.265
1994—Baltimore (A.L.)	5	7	.417	4.77	1.32	23	23	0	0	0	0-0	149.0	158	81	79	23	38-3	87	.271
1995—Baltimore (A.L.)	8	6	.571	5.21	1.27	27	18	0	0	0	0-0	115.2	117	70	67	18	30-0	65	.265
1996—Boston (A.L.)	7	1	.875	4.50	1.53	23	10	0	0	1	0-0	90.0	111	50	45	14	27-2	50	.300
—Seattle (A.L.)	6	2	.750	3.31	1.20	11	11	0	0	0	0-0	70.2	66	36	26	9	19-3	29	.243
1997—Tacoma (PCL)	1	0	1.000	0.00	0.20	1	1	0	0	...	0-...	5.0	1	0	0	0	0-0	6	.063
—Seattle (A.L.)	17	5	.773	3.86	1.22	30	30	2	0	0	0-0	188.2	187	82	81	21	43-2	113	.256
1998—Seattle (A.L.)	15	9	.625	3.53	1.18	34	34	4	3	0	0-0	234.1	234	99	92	23	42-2	158	.256
1999—Seattle (A.L.)	14	8	.636	3.87	1.24	32	32	4	0	0	0-0	228.0	235	108	98	23	48-1	137	.267
2000—Seattle (A.L.)	13	10	.565	5.49	1.47	26	26	0	0	0	0-0	154.0	173	103	94	22	53-2	98	.281
2001—Seattle (A.L.)	20	6	.769	3.43	1.10	33	33	1	0	0	0-0	209.2	187	84	80	24	44-4	119	.239
2002—Seattle (A.L.)	13	8	.619	3.32	1.08	34	34	4	2	0	0-0	230.2	198	89	85	28	50-4	147	.230
2003—Seattle (A.L.)	21	7	.750	3.27	1.23	33	33	1	0	0	0-0	215.0	199	83	78	19	66-3	129	.246
2004—Seattle (A.L.)	7	13	.350	5.21	1.39	34	33	1	0	0	0-0	202.0	217	127	117	44	63-3	125	.272
American League totals (14 years)	164	106	.607	4.07	1.27	413	367	22	6	2	0-0	2418.0	2435	1185	1094	295	633-35	1449	.261
National League totals (4 years)	28	39	.418	4.50	1.49	93	86	5	2	0	0-2	521.2	567	284	261	63	210-17	333	.281
Major League totals (18 years)	192	145	.570	4.15	1.31	506	453	27	8	2	0-2	2939.2	3002	1469	1355	358	843-52	1782	.264

DIVISION SERIES RECORD

Year Team (League)	W	L	Pct.	ERA	WHIP	G	GS	CG	ShO	Hld.	Sv.-Opp.	IP	H	R	ER	HR	BB-IBB	SO	Avg.
1997—Seattle (A.L.)	0	1	.000	5.79	1.29	1	1	0	0	0	0-0	4.2	5	3	3	1	1-0	2	.278
2001—Seattle (A.L.)	2	0	1.000	1.50	0.83	2	2	0	0	0	0-0	12.0	8	2	2	0	2-0	10	.186
Division series totals (2 years)	2	1	.667	2.70	0.96	3	3	0	0	0	0-0	16.2	13	5	5	1	3-0	12	.213

CHAMPIONSHIP SERIES RECORD

Year Team (League)	W	L	Pct.	ERA	WHIP	G	GS	CG	ShO	Hld.	Sv.-Opp.	IP	H	R	ER	HR	BB-IBB	SO	Avg.
2001—Seattle (A.L.)	1	0	1.000	2.57	0.71	1	1	0	0	0	0-0	7.0	4	2	2	1	1-0	5	.167

ALL-STAR GAME RECORD

	W	L	Pct.	ERA	WHIP	G	GS	CG	ShO	Hld.	Sv.-Opp.	IP	H	R	ER	HR	BB-IBB	SO	Avg.
All-Star Game totals (1 year)	0	0	...	0.00	0.00	1	0	0	0	0	0-0	1.0	0	0	0	0	0-0	1	.000

MUELLER, BILL 3B

PERSONAL: Born March 17, 1971, in Maryland Heights, Mo. ... 5-10/180. ... Bats both, throws right. ... Full name: William Richard Mueller. ... Name pronounced: MILL-er. ... High school: DeSmet (Creve Coeur, Mo.). ... College: Southwest Missouri State.

TRANSACTIONS/CAREER NOTES: Selected by San Francisco Giants organization in 15th round of 1993 free-agent draft. ... On disabled list (July 1-16, 1997). ... On disabled list (April 6-May 17, 1999); included rehabilitation assignment to Fresno. ... Traded by Giants to Chicago Cubs for P Tim Worrell (November 19, 2000). ... On disabled list (May 14-August 13, 2001); included rehabilitation assignment to Iowa. ... On disabled list (March 28-May 6, 2002); included rehabilitation assignment to Iowa. ... Traded by Cubs with cash to Giants for P Jeff Verplancke (September 3, 2002). ... Signed as a free agent by Boston Red Sox (January 14, 2003). ... On disabled list (May 20-July 2, 2004); included rehabilitation assignment to Pawtucket.

2004 GAMES PLAYED BY POSITION (MLB): 3B—96, 2B—14.

Year Team (League)	Pos.	G	AB	R	H	2B	3B	HR	RBI	BB	SO	HBP	GDP	SB-CS	Avg.	OBP	SLG	OPS	E	Avg.
1993—Everett (N'west)	2B	58	200	31	60	8	2	1	24	42	17	3	3	13-6	.300	.425	.375	.800	8	.966
1994—San Jose (Calif.)	2B-3B-SS	120	431	79	130	20	9	· 5	72	103	47	3	15	4-8	.302	.435	.425	.859	29	.925
1995—Shreveport (Texas)	2B-3B	88	330	56	102	16	2	1	39	53	36	4	9	6-5	.309	.406	.379	.784	5	.978
—Phoenix (PCL)	2B-3B	41	172	23	51	13	6	2	19	19	31	0	7	0-0	.297	.365	.477	.841	7	.941
1996—Phoenix (PCL)	3-S-2-DH	106	440	73	133	14	6	4	36	44	40	1	11	2-5	.302	.365	.389	.753	11	.969
—San Francisco (N.L.)	3B-2B	55	200	31	66	15	1	0	19	24	26	1	1	0-0	.330	.401	.415	.816	6	.962
1997—San Francisco (N.L.)	3B	128	390	51	114	26	3	7	44	48	71	3	10	4-3	.292	.369	.428	.797	14	.956
1998—San Francisco (N.L.)	3B-2B	145	534	93	157	27	0	9	59	79	83	1	12	3-3	.294	.383	.395	.778	19	.953
1999—San Francisco (N.L.)	3B-2B	116	414	61	120	24	0	2	36	65	52	3	11	4-2	.290	.388	.362	.751	12	.959
—Fresno (PCL)	3B	3	12	3	5	0	1	0	6	0	0	0	0	0-0	.417	.385	.583	.968	3	.800
2000—San Francisco (N.L.)	3B-2B	153	560	97	150	29	4	10	55	52	62	6	16	4-2	.268	.333	.388	.721	9	.975
2001—Chicago (N.L.)	3B-2B	70	210	38	62	12	1	6	23	37	19	3	4	1-1	.295	.403	.448	.851	8	.942
—Iowa (PCL)	3B	8	26	3	11	3	0	0	4	1	2	0	0	0-0	.423	.444	.538	.983	0	1.000
2002—Iowa (PCL)	3B	6	16	2	6	1	0	1	5	2	0	0	0	0-1	.375	.474	.625	1.099	1	.909
—Chicago (N.L.)	3B	103	353	51	94	19	4	7	37	51	41	0	8	0-0	.266	.355	.402	.757	6	.973
—San Francisco (N.L.)	3B	8	13	0	2	0	0	0	1	1	1	0	1	0-0	.154	.214	.154	.368	0	1.000
2003—Boston (A.L.)	3-2-DH-S	146	524	85	171	45	5	19	85	59	77	7	11	1-4	* .326	.398	.540	.938	16	.956
2004—Pawtucket (Int'l)	3B	4	13	1	4	2	0	0	2	2	0	0	0	0-0	.308	.400	.462	.862	1	.857
—Boston (A.L.)	3B-2B	110	399	75	113	27	1	12	57	51	56	4	8	2-2	.283	.365	.446	.811	17	.944
American League totals (2 years)		256	923	160	284	72	6	31	142	110	133	11	19	3-6	.308	.384	.499	.883	33	.951
National League totals (7 years)		778	2674	422	765	152	13	41	274	357	355	17	63	16-11	.286	.370	.399	.769	74	.961
Major League totals (9 years)		1034	3597	582	1049	224	19	72	416	467	488	28	82	19-17	.292	.374	.425	.798	107	.958

DIVISION SERIES RECORD

Year Team (League)	Pos.	G	AB	R	H	2B	3B	HR	RBI	BB	SO	HBP	GDP	SB-CS	Avg.	OBP	SLG	OPS	E	Avg.
1997—San Francisco (N.L.)	3B	3	12	1	3	0	0	1	1	0	0	0	1	0-1	.250	.250	.500	.750	0	1.000
2000—San Francisco (N.L.)	3B	4	20	2	5	2	0	0	0	4	4	0	1	0-0	.250	.250	.350	.600	0	1.000
2003—Boston (A.L.)	3B	5	19	0	2	1	0	0	0	3	4	0	1	0-0	.105	.227	.158	.385	0	1.000
2004—Boston (A.L.)	3B	3	12	3	4	0	0	0	0	0	1	0	0	0-0	.333	.385	.333	.718	0	1.000
Division series totals (4 years)		15	63	6	14	3	0	1	1	4	9	0	3	0-1	.222	.269	.317	.586	0	1.000

CHAMPIONSHIP SERIES RECORD

Year Team (League)	Pos.	G	AB	R	H	2B	3B	HR	RBI	BB	SO	HBP	GDP	SB-CS	Avg.	OBP	SLG	OPS	E	Avg.
2003—Boston (A.L.)	3B	7	27	1	6	2	0	0	0	2	7	0	1	0-0	.222	.276	.296	.572	0	1.000
2004—Boston (A.L.)	3B	7	30	4	8	1	0	0	1	2	1	1	3	0-0	.267	.333	.300	.633	0	1.000
Champ. series totals (2 years)		14	57	5	14	3	0	0	1	4	8	1	4	0-0	.246	.306	.298	.605	0	1.000

WORLD SERIES RECORD

Year Team (League)	Pos.	G	AB	R	H	2B	3B	HR	RBI	BB	SO	HBP	GDP	SB-CS	Avg.	OBP	SLG	OPS	E	Avg.
2004—Boston (A.L.)	2B	4	14	3	6	2	0	0	2	4	0	0	1	0-0	.429	.556	.571	1.127	3	.850

MULDER, MARK   P

PERSONAL: Born August 5, 1977, in South Holland, Ill. ... 6-6/208. ... Throws left, bats left. ... Full name: Mark Alan Mulder. ... High school: Thornwood (South Holland, Ill.). ... College: Michigan State.

TRANSACTIONS/CAREER NOTES: Selected by Detroit Tigers organization in 55th round of 1995 free-agent draft; did not sign. ... Selected by Oakland Athletics organization in first round (second pick overall) of 1998 free-agent draft. ... On disabled list (April 12-May 10, 2002; and August 20, 2003-remainder of season).

CAREER HITTING: 1-for-22 (.045), 2 R, 0 2B, 0 3B, 0 HR, 1 RBI.

Year Team (League)	W	L	Pct.	ERA	WHIP	G	GS	CG	ShO	Hld.	Sv.-Opp.	IP	H	R	ER	HR	BB-IBB	SO	Avg.
1999—Vancouver (PCL)	6	7	.462	4.06	1.42	22	22	1	0	...	0-...	128.2	152	69	58	13	31-0	81	.300
2000—Sacramento (PCL)	1	1	.500	5.40	2.28	2	2	0	0	...	0-...	8.1	15	11	5	1	4-0	6	.375
—Oakland (A.L.)	9	10	.474	5.44	1.69	27	27	0	0	0	0-...	154.0	191	106	93	22	69-3	88	.308
2001—Oakland (A.L.)	* 21	8	.724	3.45	1.16	34	34	6	* 4	0	0-0	229.1	214	92	88	16	51-4	153	.249
2002—Oakland (A.L.)	19	7	.731	3.47	1.14	30	30	2	1	0	0-0	207.1	182	88	80	21	55-3	159	.232
2003—Oakland (A.L.)	15	9	.625	3.13	1.18	26	26	•9	•2	0	0-0	186.2	180	66	65	15	40-2	128	.259
2004—Oakland (A.L.)	17	8	.680	4.43	1.36	33	33	• 5	1	0	0-0	225.2	223	119	111	25	83-1	140	.264
Major League totals (5 years)	81	42	.659	3.92	1.28	150	150	22	8	0	0-0	1003.0	990	471	437	99	298-13	668	.260

DIVISION SERIES RECORD

Year Team (League)	W	L	Pct.	ERA	WHIP	G	GS	CG	ShO	Hld.	Sv.-Opp.	IP	H	R	ER	HR	BB-IBB	SO	Avg.
2000—Oakland (A.L.)	Did not play.																		
2001—Oakland (A.L.)	1	1	.500	2.45	1.45	2	2	0	0	0	0-0	11.0	14	5	3	0	2-0	7	.318
2002—Oakland (A.L.)	1	1	.500	2.08	1.31	2	2	0	0	0	0-0	13.0	14	3	3	1	3-1	12	.280
Division series totals (2 years)	2	2	.500	2.25	1.38	4	4	0	0	0	0-0	24.0	28	8	6	1	5-1	19	.298

ALL-STAR GAME RECORD

	W	L	Pct.	ERA	WHIP	G	GS	CG	ShO	Hld.	Sv.-Opp.	IP	H	R	ER	HR	BB-IBB	SO	Avg.
All-Star Game totals (2 years)	1	0	1.000	4.50	1.75	2	1	0	0		0-0	4.0	7	2	2	1	0-0	2	.412

MULHOLLAND, TERRY   P

PERSONAL: Born March 9, 1963, in Uniontown, Pa. ... 6-3/220. ... Throws left, bats right. ... Full name: Terence John Mulholland. ... Name pronounced: mul-HOLLAND. ... High school: Laurel Highlands (Uniontown, Pa.). ... College: Marietta (Ohio).

TRANSACTIONS/CAREER NOTES: Selected by San Francisco Giants organization in first round (24th pick overall) of June 1984 free-agent draft; pick received as compensation for Detroit Tigers signing free-agent IF Darrell Evans. ... On disabled list (August 1, 1988-remainder of season). ... Traded by Giants with P Dennis Cook and 3B Charlie Hayes to Philadelphia Phillies for P Steve Bedrosian and a player to be named (June 18, 1989); Giants acquired IF Rick Parker to complete deal (August 7, 1989). ... On disabled list (June 12-28, 1990); included rehabilitation assignment to Scranton/Wilkes-Barre. ... Traded by Phillies with a player to be named to New York Yankees for Ps Bobby Munoz and Ryan Karp and 2B Kevin Jordan (February 9, 1994); Yankees acquired P Jeff Patterson to complete deal (November 8, 1994). ... Signed as a free agent by Giants (April 8, 1995). ... On disabled list (June 6-July 4, 1995); included rehabilitation assignment to Phoenix. ... Signed as a free agent by Phillies organization (February 17, 1996). ... Traded by Phillies to Seattle Mariners for IF Desi Relaford (July 31, 1996). ... Signed as a free agent by Chicago Cubs (December 10, 1996). ... Claimed on waivers by Giants (August 8, 1997). ... Signed as a free agent by Cubs (February 2, 1998). ... Traded by Cubs with IF Jose Hernandez to Atlanta Braves for Ps Micah Bowie and Ruben Quevedo and a player to be named (July 31, 1999); Cubs acquired P Joey Nation to complete deal (August 24, 1999). ... Signed as a free agent by Pittsburgh Pirates (December 10, 2000). ... On disabled list (April 5-20 and June 12-August 1, 2001); included rehabilitation assignment to Altoona. ... Traded by Pirates to Los Angeles Dodgers for Ps Mike Fetters and Adrian Burnside (July 31, 2001). ... On disabled list (May 3-June 4, 2002). ... Traded by Dodgers with Ps Ricardo Rodriguez and Francisco Cruceta to Cleveland

Indians for P Paul Shuey (July 28, 2002). ... Signed as a free agent by Seattle Mariners organization (February 10, 2004). ... Released by Mariners (April 1, 2004). ... Signed by Minnesota Twins organization (April 5, 2004).

CAREER HITTING: 69-for-619 (.111), 26 R, 13 2B, 1 3B, 2 HR, 23 RBI.

Year Team (League)	W	L	Pct.	ERA	WHIP	G	GS	CG	ShO	Hld.	Sv.-Opp.	IP	H	R	ER	HR	BB-IBB	SO	Avg.
1984— Everett (Northwest)	1	0	1.000	0.00	0.74	3	3	0	0	...	0-...	19.0	10	2	0	0	4-0	15	...
— Fresno (Calif.)	5	2	.714	2.95	1.59	9	9	0	0	...	0-...	42.2	32	17	14	1	36-0	39	...
1985— Shreveport (Texas)	9	8	.529	2.90	1.43	26	26	8	3	...	0-...	176.2	166	79	57	9	87-2	122	.250
1986— Phoenix (PCL)	8	5	.615	4.46	1.51	17	17	3	0	...	0-...	111.0	112	60	55	6	56-4	77	.269
— San Francisco (N.L.)	1	7	.125	4.94	1.57	15	10	0	0	0	0-0	54.2	51	33	30	3	35-2	27	.251
1987— Phoenix (PCL)	7	12	.368	5.07	1.68	37	29	3	1	...	1-...	172.1	200	124	97	7	90-0	94	.289
1988— Phoenix (PCL)	7	3	.700	3.58	1.59	19	14	3	2	...	0-...	100.2	116	45	40	2	44-0	57	.291
— San Francisco (N.L.)	2	1	.667	3.72	1.24	9	6	2	1	1	0-0	46.0	50	20	19	3	7-0	18	.281
1989— Phoenix (PCL)	4	5	.444	2.99	1.19	13	10	3	0	...	0-...	78.1	67	30	26	3	26-2	61	.242
— San Francisco (N.L.)	0	0	...	4.09	1.73	5	1	0	0	1	0-0	11.0	15	5	5	0	4-0	6	.319
— Philadelphia (N.L.)	4	7	.364	5.00	1.48	20	17	2	1	0	0-0	104.1	122	61	58	8	32-3	60	.292
1990— Philadelphia (N.L.)	9	10	.474	3.34	1.18	33	26	6	1	0	0-1	180.2	172	78	67	15	42-7	75	.252
— Scran./W.B. (I.L.)	0	1	.000	3.00	1.83	1	1	0	0	...	0-...	6.0	9	4	2	0	2-0	2	.360
1991— Philadelphia (N.L.)	16	13	.552	3.61	1.21	34	34	8	3	0	0-0	232.0	231	100	93	15	49-2	142	.260
1992— Philadelphia (N.L.)	13	11	.542	3.81	1.19	32	32	*12	2	0	0-0	229.0	227	101	97	14	46-3	125	.261
1993— Philadelphia (N.L.)	12	9	.571	3.25	1.14	29	28	7	2	0	0-0	191.0	177	80	69	20	40-2	116	.241
1994— New York (A.L.)	6	7	.462	6.49	1.55	24	19	2	0	0	0-0	120.2	150	94	87	24	37-1	72	.303
1995— San Francisco (N.L.)	5	13	.278	5.80	1.53	29	24	2	0	0	0-0	149.0	190	112	96	25	38-1	65	.313
— Phoenix (PCL)	0	0	...	2.25	1.25	1	1	0	0	...	0-...	4.0	4	3	1	0	1-0	4	.235
1996— Philadelphia (N.L.)	8	7	.533	4.66	1.34	21	21	3	0	0	0-0	133.1	157	74	69	17	21-1	52	.293
— Seattle (A.L.)	5	4	.556	4.67	1.49	12	12	0	0	0	0-0	69.1	75	38	36	5	28-3	34	.286
1997— Chicago (N.L.)	6	12	.333	4.07	1.32	25	25	1	0	0	0-0	157.0	162	79	71	20	45-2	74	.271
— San Francisco (N.L.)	0	1	.000	5.16	1.15	15	2	0	0	1	0-0	29.2	28	21	17	4	6-1	25	.248
1998— Chicago (N.L.)	6	5	.545	2.89	1.24	70	6	0	0	19	3-5	112.0	100	49	36	7	39-7	72	.235
1999— Chicago (N.L.)	6	6	.500	5.15	1.54	26	16	0	0	1	0-0	110.0	137	71	63	16	32-4	44	.309
— Atlanta (N.L.)	4	2	.667	2.98	1.28	16	8	0	0	3	1-1	60.1	64	24	20	5	13-2	39	.274
2000— Atlanta (N.L.)	9	9	.500	5.11	1.53	54	20	1	0	2	1-3	156.2	198	96	89	24	41-7	78	.308
2001— Pittsburgh (N.L.)	0	0	...	3.72	1.32	22	1	0	0	3	0-0	36.1	38	15	15	5	10-1	17	.277
— Altoona (East.)	0	2	.000	3.86	2.57	2	2	0	0	...	0-...	2.1	5	3	1	0	1-0	3	.417
— Los Angeles (N.L.)	1	1	.500	5.83	1.60	19	3	0	0	4	0-0	29.1	40	20	19	7	7-0	25	.315
2002— Los Angeles (N.L.)	0	0	...	7.31	1.63	21	0	0	0	0	0-0	32.0	45	29	26	10	7-0	17	.331
— Cleveland (A.L.)	3	2	.600	4.60	1.49	16	3	0	0	2	0-0	47.0	56	27	24	5	14-3	21	.301
2003— Cleveland (A.L.)	3	4	.429	4.91	1.56	45	3	0	0	2	0-2	99.0	117	60	54	17	37-6	42	.295
2004— Minnesota (A.L.)	5	9	.357	5.18	1.59	39	15	0	0	2	0-0	123.1	163	76	71	17	33-3	60	.327
American League totals (5 years)	22	26	.458	5.33	1.55	136	52	2	0	6	0-2	459.1	561	295	272	68	149-16	229	.305
National League totals (15 years)	102	114	.472	4.20	1.32	495	280	44	10	35	5-10	2054.1	2204	1068	959	218	514-45	1077	.275
Major League totals (18 years)	124	140	.470	4.41	1.36	631	332	46	10	41	5-12	2513.2	2765	1363	1231	286	663-61	1306	.281

DIVISION SERIES RECORD

Year Team (League)	W	L	Pct.	ERA	WHIP	G	GS	CG	ShO	Hld.	Sv.-Opp.	IP	H	R	ER	HR	BB-IBB	SO	Avg.
1998— Chicago (N.L.)	0	1	.000	11.57	1.71	2	0	0	0	0	0-0	2.1	2	3	3	0	2-0	2	.222
1999— Atlanta (N.L.)	0	0	...	27.00	4.50	2	0	0	0	2	0-0	.2	3	2	2	0	0-0	0	.600
2000— Atlanta (N.L.)	0	0	...	5.40	0.90	3	0	0	0	0	0-0	3.1	1	2	2	0	2-0	1	.100
2004— Minnesota (A.L.)	0	0	...	3.00	1.00	1	0	0	0	0	0-0	3.0	3	1	1	1	0-0	0	.250
Division series totals (4 years)	0	1	.000	7.71	1.39	8	0	0	0	2	0-0	9.1	9	8	8	1	4-0	3	.250

CHAMPIONSHIP SERIES RECORD

Year Team (League)	W	L	Pct.	ERA	WHIP	G	GS	CG	ShO	Hld.	Sv.-Opp.	IP	H	R	ER	HR	BB-IBB	SO	Avg.
1993— Philadelphia (N.L.)	0	1	.000	7.20	2.00	1	1	0	0	0	0-0	5.0	9	5	4	0	1-0	2	.391
1999— Atlanta (N.L.)	0	0	...	0.00	0.75	2	0	0	0	1	0-0	2.2	1	0	0	0	1-0	2	.143
Champ. series totals (2 years)	0	1	.000	4.70	1.57	3	1	0	0	1	0-0	7.2	10	5	4	0	2-0	4	.333

WORLD SERIES RECORD

Year Team (League)	W	L	Pct.	ERA	WHIP	G	GS	CG	ShO	Hld.	Sv.-Opp.	IP	H	R	ER	HR	BB-IBB	SO	Avg.
1993— Philadelphia (N.L.)	1	0	1.000	6.75	1.59	2	2	0	0	0	0-0	10.2	14	8	8	2	3-0	5	.326
1999— Atlanta (N.L.)	0	0	...	7.36	1.64	2	0	0	0	0	0-0	3.2	5	3	3	1	1-1	3	.313
World series totals (2 years)	1	0	1.000	6.91	1.60	4	2	0	0	0	0-0	14.1	19	11	11	3	4-1	8	.322

ALL-STAR GAME RECORD

Year Team (League)	W	L	Pct.	ERA	WHIP	G	GS	CG	ShO	Hld.	Sv.-Opp.	IP	H	R	ER	HR	BB-IBB	SO	Avg.
All-Star Game totals (1 year)	0	0	...	4.50	1.50	1	1	0	0	0	0-0	2.0	1	1	1	1	2-0	0	.143

MUNOZ, ARNIE   P

PERSONAL: Born June 21, 1982, in Mao, Dominican Republic. ... 5-9/170. ... Throws left, bats left. ... Full name: Arnaldo Rafael Munoz. ... High school: Instituto Platon (Navarette, D.R.).

TRANSACTIONS/CAREER NOTES: Signed as a non-drafted free agent by Chicago White Sox organization (December 20, 1998).

CAREER HITTING: 0-for-1 (.000), 0 R, 0 2B, 0 3B, 0 HR, 0 RBI.

Year Team (League)	W	L	Pct.	ERA	WHIP	G	GS	CG	ShO	Hld.	Sv.-Opp.	IP	H	R	ER	HR	BB-IBB	SO	Avg.
1999— Ariz. White Sox (Ariz.)	0	2	.000	5.25	1.75	14	0	0	0	...	1-...	12.0	13	10	7	1	8-0	12	.255
2000— Burlington (Midw.)	2	3	.400	6.81	1.83	22	0	0	0	...	0-...	38.1	45	34	29	2	25-0	44	.294
2001— Kannapolis (S.Atl.)	6	3	.667	2.49	1.04	60	0	0	0	...	12-...	79.2	41	24	22	2	42-2	115	.161
2002— Birmingham (Southern)	6	1	1.000	2.61	1.26	51	0	0	0	...	6-...	72.1	62	29	21	6	29-0	78	.231
2003— Charlotte (Int'l)	4	3	.571	4.75	1.44	49	0	0	0	...	6-...	55.0	52	35	29	7	27-2	63	.254
2004— Birmingham (Southern)	7	2	.778	2.05	0.99	13	13	0	0	...	0-...	74.2	52	24	17	1	22-3	68	.195
— Charlotte (Int'l)	2	6	.250	5.68	1.58	13	13	0	0	...	0-...	69.2	81	48	44	11	29-0	60	.288
— Chicago (A.L.)	0	1	.000	10.05	2.23	11	1	0	0	0	0-0	14.1	20	16	16	4	12-1	11	.339
Major League totals (1 year)	0	1	.000	10.05	2.23	11	1	0	0	0	0-0	14.1	20	16	16	4	12-1	11	.339

MUNRO, PETE P

PERSONAL: Born June 14, 1975, in Flushing, N.Y. ... 6-3/210. ... Throws right, bats right. ... Full name: Peter Daniel Munro. ... Name pronounced: mun-ROW. ... High school: Benjamin Cardozo (Bayside, N.Y.). ... Junior college: Okaloosa-Walton (Fla.) Community College.

TRANSACTIONS/CAREER NOTES: Selected by Boston Red Sox organization in sixth round of 1993 free-agent draft. ... Traded by Red Sox with P Jay Yennaco to Toronto Blue Jays for 1B/DH Mike Stanley (July 30, 1998). ... On disabled list (June 4-July 3, 2000); included rehabilitation assignments to Dunedin and Syracuse. ... Traded by Blue Jays to Texas Rangers (August 8, 2000); completing deal in which Rangers traded OF Dave Martinez to Blue Jays for a player to be named (August 4, 2000). ... Signed as a free agent by Houston Astros organization (January 17, 2002). ... Signed as a free agent by Minnesota Twins organization (December 18, 2003). ... Released by Twins (June 1, 2004). ... Signed by Astros (June 4, 2004).

CAREER HITTING: 5-for-53 (.094), 5 R, 0 2B, 0 3B, 0 HR, 3 RBI.

Year	Team (League)	W	L	Pct.	ERA	WHIP	G	GS	CG	ShO	Hld.	Sv.-Opp.	IP	H	R	ER	HR	BB-IBB	SO	Avg.
1994—	....			Did not play.																
1995—	Utica (N.Y.-Penn)	5	4	.556	2.60	1.24	14	14	0	0	...	0-...	90.0	79	38	26	3	33-1	74	.230
1996—	Sarasota (Florida State)	11	6	.647	3.60	1.39	27	25	2	2	...	1-...	155.0	153	76	62	4	62-1	115	.258
1997—	Trenton (East.)	7	10	.412	4.95	1.38	22	22	1	0	...	0-...	116.1	113	76	64	12	47-0	109	.260
1998—	Pawtucket (Int'l)	5	4	.556	4.05	1.37	18	17	0	0	...	0-...	106.2	111	49	48	10	35-2	75	.275
—	Syracuse (Int'l)	2	5	.286	7.46	1.81	8	8	0	0	...	0-...	44.2	58	42	37	7	23-2	42	.312
1999—	Toronto (A.L.)	0	2	.000	6.02	1.68	31	2	0	0	4	0-1	55.1	70	38	37	6	23-0	38	.318
—	Syracuse (Int'l)	6	1	.857	3.10	1.48	18	11	0	0	...	0-...	69.2	70	29	24	4	33-1	68	.257
2000—	Syracuse (Int'l)	4	3	.571	2.48	1.25	10	10	2	0	...	0-...	61.2	52	20	17	1	25-0	45	.235
—	Dunedin (Fla. St.)	0	1	.000	5.56	1.32	3	3	0	0	...	0-...	11.1	11	7	7	0	4-0	12	.256
—	Toronto (A.L.)	1	1	.500	5.96	2.10	9	3	0	0	0	0-0	25.2	38	22	17	1	16-0	16	.355
—	Oklahoma (PCL)	1	2	.333	4.65	1.32	5	5	1	1	...	0-...	31.0	27	17	16	3	14-0	15	.229
2001—	Oklahoma (PCL)	8	6	.571	4.67	1.49	33	8	0	0	...	0-...	88.2	89	50	46	12	43-1	73	.264
2002—	New Orleans (PCL)	7	1	.875	2.39	0.88	19	13	1	1	...	0-...	94.1	68	30	25	3	15-1	73	.200
—	Houston (N.L.)	5	5	.500	3.57	1.39	19	14	0	0	1	0-0	80.2	89	37	32	5	23-3	45	.283
2003—	Houston (N.L.)	3	4	.429	4.67	1.65	40	0	0	0	3	0-1	54.0	63	30	28	7	26-2	27	.294
—	New Orleans (PCL)	0	4	.000	6.04	1.80	5	4	0	0	...	0-...	22.1	28	16	15	1	12-1	12	.308
2004—	Rochester (Int'l)	6	3	.667	3.88	1.22	10	10	0	0	...	0-...	51.0	51	30	22	6	11-0	34	.258
—	Houston (N.L.)	4	7	.364	5.15	1.46	21	19	0	0	0	0-0	99.2	120	59	57	12	26-2	63	.302
	American League totals (2 years)	1	3	.250	6.00	1.81	40	5	0	0	4	0-1	81.0	108	60	54	7	39-0	54	.330
	National League totals (3 years)	12	16	.429	4.49	1.48	80	35	0	0	4	0-1	234.1	272	126	117	24	75-7	135	.294
	Major League totals (5 years)	13	19	.406	4.88	1.57	120	40	0	0	8	0-2	315.1	380	186	171	31	114-7	189	.304

CHAMPIONSHIP SERIES RECORD

Year	Team (League)	W	L	Pct.	ERA	WHIP	G	GS	CG	ShO	Hld.	Sv.-Opp.	IP	H	R	ER	HR	BB-IBB	SO	Avg.
2004—	Houston (N.L.)	0	0	...	9.00	2.14	2	2	0	0	0	0-0	7.0	14	7	7	2	1-0	5	.412

MUNSON, ERIC 3B

PERSONAL: Born October 3, 1977, in San Diego, Calif. ... 6-3/225. ... Bats left, throws right. ... Full name: Eric Walter Munson. ... High school: Mount Carmel (San Diego). ... College: USC.

TRANSACTIONS/CAREER NOTES: Selected by Atlanta Braves organization in second round of 1996 free-agent draft; did not sign. ... Selected by Detroit Tigers organization in first round (third pick overall) of 1999 free-agent draft. ... On disabled list (August 12, 2003-remainder of season).

2004 GAMES PLAYED BY POSITION (MLB): 3B—94, DH—7, C—1.

Year	Team (League)	Pos.	G	AB	R	H	2B	3B	HR	RBI	BB	SO	HBP	GDP	SB-CS	Avg.	OBP	SLG	OPS	E	Avg.
1999—	Lakeland (Fla. St.)	DH	2	6	0	2	0	0	0	1	1	1	0	0	0-0	.333	.429	.333	.762	...	...
—	W. Mich. (Mid.)	1B-C	67	252	42	67	16	1	14	44	37	47	9	4	3-1	.266	.378	.504	.882	3	.991
2000—	Jacksonville (Sou.)	1B	98	365	52	92	21	4	15	68	39	96	18	8	5-2	.252	.348	.455	.803	8	.989
—	Detroit (A.L.)	1B	3	5	0	0	0	0	0	1	0	1	0	0	0-0	.000	.000	.000	.000	1	.941
2001—	Erie (East.)	1B	142	519	88	135	35	1	26	102	84	141	11	6	0-3	.260	.371	.482	.853	17	.985
—	Detroit (A.L.)	1B	17	66	4	10	3	1	1	6	3	21	0	2	0-1	.152	.188	.273	.461	1	.994
2002—	Toledo (Int'l)	1B	136	477	77	125	30	4	24	84	77	114	7	9	1-3	.262	.367	.493	.860	12	.990
—	Detroit (A.L.)	DH-1B	18	59	3	11	0	0	2	5	6	11	1	1	0-0	.186	.269	.288	.557	1	.970
2003—	Detroit (A.L.)	3B-DH	99	313	28	75	9	0	18	50	35	61	1	4	3-0	.240	.312	.441	.753	19	.920
2004—	Detroit (A.L.)	3B-DH-C	109	321	36	68	14	2	19	49	29	90	6	1	1-1	.212	.289	.445	.735	16	.934
	Major League totals (5 years)		246	764	71	164	26	3	40	111	73	184	8	8	4-2	.215	.287	.414	.701	38	.945

MURPHY, DONNIE 2B

PERSONAL: Born March 10, 1983, in Lakewood, Calif. ... 5-10/180. ... Bats right, throws right. ... Full name: Donald Rex Murphy. ... High school: Poly High (Riverside, Calif.). ... Junior college: Orange Coast.

TRANSACTIONS/CAREER NOTES: Selected by Kansas City Royals organization in fifth round of 2002 free-agent draft.

2004 GAMES PLAYED BY POSITION (MLB): 2B—7.

Year	Team (League)	Pos.	G	AB	R	H	2B	3B	HR	RBI	BB	SO	HBP	GDP	SB-CS	Avg.	OBP	SLG	OPS	E	Avg.
2002—	Spokane (N'west)	SS	28	109	20	33	10	2	0	15	6	17	3	2	0-0	.303	.356	.431	.787	8	.931
—	Burlington (Midw.)	SS	33	120	12	27	6	3	0	15	11	31	4	1	0-2	.225	.300	.325	.625	10	.934
2003—	Burlington (Midw.)	2B-SS	132	504	77	158	29	6	5	98	65	78	9	8	15-6	.313	.397	.425	.821	14	.977
2004—	Wilmington (Caro.)	2B-SS-DH	129	485	67	123	32	4	10	73	52	96	4	16	1-1	.254	.326	.398	.724	20	.969
—	Kansas City (A.L.)	2B	7	27	1	5	3	0	0	3	0	7	0	1	1-0	.185	.185	.296	.481	0	1.000
	Major League totals (1 year)		7	27	1	5	3	0	0	3	0	7	0	1	1-0	.185	.185	.296	.481	0	1.000

MURRAY, CALVIN OF

PERSONAL: Born July 30, 1971, in Dallas, Texas. ... 5-11/180. ... Bats right, throws right. ... Full name: Calvin Duane Murray. ... Name pronounced: MUR-ee. ... High school: Warren Travis White (Dallas). ... College: Texas.

TRANSACTIONS/CAREER NOTES: Selected by Cleveland Indians organization in first round (11th pick overall) of 1989 free-agent draft; did not sign. ... Selected by San Francisco Giants organization in first round (seventh pick overall) of 1992 free-agent draft. ... Traded by Giants to Texas Rangers for cash (April 22, 2002). ... Signed as a free agent by Los Angeles Dodgers organization (December 26, 2002). ... Released by Dodgers (August 14, 2003). ... Signed by Chicago Cubs organization (January 12, 2004). ... Refused minor league assignment and became a free agent (October 9, 2004).

M

Year Team (League)	Pos.	G	AB	R	H	2B	3B	HR	RBI	BB	SO	HBP	GDP	SB-CS	Avg.	OBP	SLG	OPS	E	Avg.
										BATTING									FIELDING	
1993—Shreveport (Texas)	OF	37	138	15	26	6	0	0	6	14	29	2	0	12-6	.188	.271	.232	.503	2	.976
—San Jose (Calif.)	OF	85	345	61	97	24	1	9	42	40	63	4	4	42-10	.281	.362	.435	.797	2	.991
—Phoenix (PCL)	OF	5	19	4	6	1	1	0	0	2	5	0	0	1-1	.316	.381	.474	.855	2	.867
1994—Shreveport (Texas)	OF	108	480	67	111	19	5	2	35	47	81	5	4	33-13	.231	.304	.304	.608	3	.989
1995—Phoenix (PCL)	OF	13	50	8	9	1	0	4	10	4	6	0	2	2-2	.180	.236	.440	.676	0	1.000
—Shreveport (Texas)	OF	110	441	77	104	17	3	2	29	59	70	3	5	26-10	.236	.329	.302	.631	2	.993
1996—Shreveport (Texas)	OF	50	169	32	44	7	0	7	24	25	33	1	5	6-5	.260	.352	.426	.778	3	.969
—Phoenix (PCL)	OF	83	311	50	76	16	6	3	28	43	60	3	1	12-6	.244	.341	.363	.704	2	.991
1997—Shreveport (Texas)	OF	122	419	83	114	25	3	10	56	66	73	4	7	52-6	.272	.375	.418	.792	5	.978
1998—Fresno (PCL)	OF	33	90	16	21	3	1	3	5	12	18	0	2	3-1	.233	.324	.389	.712	0	1.000
—Shreveport (Texas)	OF	88	337	63	104	22	5	8	39	58	45	5	8	34-15	.309	.418	.475	.892	7	.966
1999—Fresno (PCL)	OF-DH	130	548	122	183	31	7	23	73	49	88	3	6	42-14	.334	.389	.542	.931	6	.980
—San Francisco (N.L.)	OF	15	19	1	5	2	0	0	5	2	4	0	0	1-0	.263	.333	.368	.702	0	1.000
2000—San Francisco (N.L.)	OF	108	194	35	47	12	1	2	22	29	33	3	0	9-3	.242	.348	.345	.693	3	.980
2001—San Francisco (N.L.)	OF	106	326	54	80	14	2	6	25	32	57	3	5	8-8	.245	.319	.356	.674	5	.979
—Fresno (PCL)	OF	35	138	17	36	6	1	4	12	12	33	1	2	3-3	.261	.322	.406	.728	2	.978
2002—San Francisco (N.L.)	OF	11	12	0	0	0	0	0	0	1	2	0	0	0-0	.000	.077	.000	.077	1	.917
—Texas (A.L.)	OF-DH	37	77	16	13	5	1	0	1	6	15	1	0	4-0	.169	.238	.260	.498	0	1.000
—Oklahoma (PCL)	OF	33	139	23	37	7	1	2	14	11	20	0	3	4-0	.266	.318	.374	.692	0	1.000
2003—Las Vegas (PCL)	OF-DH	102	312	45	81	18	6	3	40	27	50	3	5	13-4	.260	.322	.385	.707	1	.995
2004—Iowa (PCL)	OF	130	457	84	142	24	7	7	54	43	65	2	10	25-4	.311	.368	.440	.808	2	.992
—Chicago (N.L.)	OF	11	5	2	1	0	0	0	0	1	1	0	0	0-0	.200	.333	.200	.533	0	1.000
American League totals (1 year)		37	77	16	13	5	1	0	1	6	15	1	0	4-0	.169	.238	.260	.498	0	1.000
National League totals (5 years)		251	556	92	133	28	3	8	53	65	96	6	5	18-11	.239	.325	.344	.668	9	.978
Major League totals (5 years)		288	633	108	146	33	4	8	54	71	111	7	5	22-11	.231	.315	.333	.648	9	.981

DIVISION SERIES RECORD

Year Team (League)	Pos.	G	AB	R	H	2B	3B	HR	RBI	BB	SO	HBP	GDP	SB-CS	Avg.	OBP	SLG	OPS	E	Avg.
2000—San Francisco (N.L.)	OF	3	5	0	1	0	0	0	0	0	3	0	0	0-0	.200	.200	.200	.400	0	1.000

MUSSINA, MIKE — P

PERSONAL: Born December 8, 1968, in Williamsport, Pa. ... 6-2/185. ... Throws right, bats left. ... Full name: Michael Cole Mussina. ... Name pronounced: myoo-SEE-nuh. ... High school: Montoursville (Pa.). ... College: Stanford.

TRANSACTIONS/CAREER NOTES: Selected by Baltimore Orioles organization in 11th round of 1987 free-agent draft; did not sign. ... Selected by Orioles organization in first round (20th pick overall) of 1990 free-agent draft. ... On disabled list (July 22-August 20, 1993); included rehabilitation assignment to Bowie. ... On disabled list (April 17-May 3 and May 15-June 6, 1998). ... Signed as a free agent by New York Yankees (November 30, 2000). ... On disabled list (July 7-August 18, 2004); included rehabilitation assignment to Columbus.

HONORS: Won A.L. Gold Glove at pitcher (1996-99, 2001 and 2003).

CAREER HITTING: 8-for-38 (.211), 3 R, 1 2B, 0 3B, 0 HR, 5 RBI.

Year Team (League)	W	L	Pct.	ERA	WHIP	G	GS	CG	ShO	Hld.	Sv.-Opp.	IP	H	R	ER	HR	BB-IBB	SO	Avg.
1990—Hagerstown (Eastern)	3	0	1.000	1.49	0.97	7	7	1	1	...	0-...	42.1	34	10	7	1	7-0	40	.214
—Rochester (Int'l)	0	0	...	1.35	0.90	2	2	0	0	...	0-...	13.1	8	2	2	2	4-0	15	.174
1991—Rochester (Int'l)	10	4	.714	2.87	1.14	19	19	3	1	...	0-...	122.1	108	42	39	9	31-0	107	.235
—Baltimore (A.L.)	4	5	.444	2.87	1.12	12	12	2	0	0	0-0	87.2	77	31	28	7	21-0	52	.239
1992—Baltimore (A.L.)	18	5	.783	2.54	1.08	32	32	8	4	0	0-0	241.0	212	70	68	16	48-2	130	.239
1993—Baltimore (A.L.)	14	6	.700	4.46	1.23	25	25	3	2	0	0-0	167.2	163	84	83	20	44-2	117	.256
—Bowie (East.)	1	0	1.000	2.25	0.75	2	2	0	0	...	0-...	8.0	5	2	2	0	1-0	10	.172
1994—Baltimore (A.L.)	16	5	.762	3.06	1.16	24	24	3	0	0	0-0	176.1	163	63	60	19	42-1	99	.248
1995—Baltimore (A.L.)	* 19	9	.679	3.29	1.07	32	32	7	* 4	0	0-0	221.2	187	86	81	24	50-4	158	.226
1996—Baltimore (A.L.)	19	11	.633	4.81	1.37	36	* 36	4	1	0	0-0	243.1	264	137	130	31	69-0	204	.275
1997—Baltimore (A.L.)	15	8	.652	3.20	1.12	33	33	4	1	0	0-0	224.2	197	87	80	27	54-3	218	.234
1998—Baltimore (A.L.)	13	10	.565	3.49	1.11	29	29	4	2	0	0-0	206.1	189	85	80	22	41-3	175	.242
1999—Baltimore (A.L.)	18	7	.720	3.50	1.27	31	31	4	0	0	0-0	203.1	207	88	79	16	52-0	172	.268
2000—Baltimore (A.L.)	11	15	.423	3.79	1.19	34	34	6	1	0	0-0	* 237.2	236	105	100	28	46-0	210	.255
2001—New York (A.L.)	17	11	.607	3.15	1.07	34	34	4	3	0	0-0	228.2	202	87	80	20	42-2	214	.237
2002—New York (A.L.)	18	10	.643	4.05	1.19	33	33	2	0	0	0-0	215.2	208	103	97	27	48-1	182	.253
2003—New York (A.L.)	17	8	.680	3.40	1.08	31	31	2	1	0	0-0	214.2	192	86	81	21	40-4	195	.238
2004—Columbus (Int'l)	0	0	...	0.00	0.67	1	1	0	0	0	0-...	3.0	2	0	0	0	0-0	5	.182
—New York (A.L.)	12	9	.571	4.59	1.32	27	27	1	0	0	0-0	164.2	178	91	84	22	40-1	132	.276
Major League totals (14 years)	211	119	.639	3.59	1.17	413	413	54	21	0	0-0	2833.1	2675	1203	1131	300	637-23	2258	.249

DIVISION SERIES RECORD

Year Team (League)	W	L	Pct.	ERA	WHIP	G	GS	CG	ShO	Hld.	Sv.-Opp.	IP	H	R	ER	HR	BB-IBB	SO	Avg.
1996—Baltimore (A.L.)	0	0	...	4.50	1.50	1	1	0	0	0	0-0	6.0	7	4	3	1	2-0	6	.280
1997—Baltimore (A.L.)	2	0	1.000	1.93	0.71	2	2	0	0	0	0-0	14.0	7	3	3	3	3-0	16	.143
2001—New York (A.L.)	1	0	1.000	0.00	0.71	1	1	0	0	0	0-0	7.0	4	0	0	0	1-0	4	.167
2002—New York (A.L.)	0	0	...	9.00	1.50	1	1	0	0	0	0-0	7.0	6	4	4	1	0-0	2	.333
2003—New York (A.L.)	0	1	.000	3.86	1.43	1	1	0	0	0	0-0	7.0	7	3	3	0	3-1	6	.280
2004—New York (A.L.)	0	1	.000	2.57	1.14	1	1	0	0	0	0-0	7.0	7	2	2	1	1-0	7	.280
Division series totals (6 years)	3	2	.600	3.00	1.07	7	7	0	0	0	0-0	45.0	38	16	15	6	10-1	41	.229

CHAMPIONSHIP SERIES RECORD

Year Team (League)	W	L	Pct.	ERA	WHIP	G	GS	CG	ShO	Hld.	Sv.-Opp.	IP	H	R	ER	HR	BB-IBB	SO	Avg.
1996—Baltimore (A.L.)	0	1	.000	5.87	1.30	1	1	0	0	0	0-0	7.2	8	5	5	1	2-0	6	.267
1997—Baltimore (A.L.)	0	0	...	0.60	0.53	2	2	0	0	0	0-0	15.0	4	1	1	0	4-0	25	.082
2001—New York (A.L.)	1	0	1.000	0.83	0.83	1	1	0	0	0	0-0	6.0	4	2	2	1	1-0	3	.182
2003—New York (A.L.)	0	2	.000	4.11	1.30	3	2	0	0	0	0-0	15.1	16	7	7	5	4-1	17	.267
2004—New York (A.L.)	1	0	1.000	4.26	0.95	2	2	0	0	0	0-0	12.2	10	6	6	0	2-0	15	.204
Champ. series totals (5 years)	2	3	.400	3.34	0.97	9	8	0	0	0	0-0	56.2	42	21	21	7	13-1	66	.200

M

WORLD SERIES RECORD

Year Team (League)	W	L	Pct.	ERA	WHIP	G	GS	CG	ShO	Hld.	Sv.-Opp.	IP	H	R	ER	HR	BB-IBB	SO	Avg.
2001— New York (A.L.)	0	1	.000	4.09	1.36	2	2	0	0	0	0-0	11.0	11	7	5	4	4-3	14	.256
2003— New York (A.L.)	1	0	1.000	1.29	1.14	1	1	0	0	0	0-0	7.0	7	1	1	0	1-1	9	.259
World series totals (2 years)	1	1	.500	3.00	1.28	3	3	0	0	0	0-0	18.0	18	8	6	4	5-4	23	.257

ALL-STAR GAME RECORD

Year	W	L	Pct.	ERA	WHIP	G	GS	CG	ShO	Hld.	Sv.-Opp.	IP	H	R	ER	HR	BB-IBB	SO	Avg.
All-Star Game totals (3 years)	0	0	...	0.00	1.00	3	0	0	0	0	0-0	3.0	2	0	0	0	1-0	3	.182

MYERS, BRETT   P

PERSONAL: Born August 17, 1980, in Jacksonville, Fla. ... 6-4/223. ... Throws right, bats right. ... Full name: Brett Allen Myers. ... High school: Englewood (Jacksonville, Fla.).
TRANSACTIONS/CAREER NOTES: Selected by Philadelphia Phillies organization in first round (12th pick overall) of 1999 free-agent draft.
CAREER HITTING: 22-for-136 (.162), 9 R, 6 2B, 0 3B, 0 HR, 3 RBI.

Year Team (League)	W	L	Pct.	ERA	WHIP	G	GS	CG	ShO	Hld.	Sv.-Opp.	IP	H	R	ER	HR	BB-IBB	SO	Avg.
1999— GC Phillies (GCL)	2	1	.667	2.33	0.89	7	5	0	0	...	0-...	27.0	17	8	7	0	7-0	30	.177
2000— Piedmont (S. Atl.)	13	7	.650	3.18	1.33	27	27	2	1	...	0-...	175.1	165	78	62	7	69-0	140	.252
2001— Reading (East.)	13	4	.765	3.87	1.28	26	23	1	1	...	0-...	156.0	156	71	67	21	43-1	130	.258
2002— Scran./W.B. (I.L.)	9	6	.600	3.59	1.10	19	19	4	1	...	0-...	128.0	121	54	51	9	20-0	97	.252
— Philadelphia (N.L.)	4	5	.444	4.25	1.42	12	12	1	0	0	0-0	72.0	73	38	34	11	29-1	34	.277
2003— Philadelphia (N.L.)	14	9	.609	4.43	1.46	32	32	1	1	0	0-0	193.0	205	99	95	20	76-8	143	.272
2004— Philadelphia (N.L.)	11	11	.500	5.52	1.47	32	31	1	0	0	0-0	176.0	196	113	108	31	62-4	116	.281
Major League totals (3 years)	29	25	.537	4.84	1.45	76	75	3	2	0	0-0	441.0	474	250	237	62	167-13	293	.276

MYERS, GREG   C

PERSONAL: Born April 14, 1966, in Riverside, Calif. ... 6-2/225. ... Bats left, throws right. ... Full name: Gregory Richard Myers. ... High school: Riverside (Calif.) Polytechnical.
TRANSACTIONS/CAREER NOTES: Selected by Toronto Blue Jays organization in third round of June 1984 free-agent draft. ... On disabled list (March 26-June 5, 1989); included rehabilitation assignment to Knoxville. ... On disabled list (May 5-25, 1990); included rehabilitation assignment to Syracuse. ... Traded by Blue Jays with OF Rob Ducey to California Angels for P Mark Eichhorn (July 30, 1992). ... On disabled list (August 27, 1992-remainder of season). ... On disabled list (April 24-June 21, 1994); included rehabilitation assignments to Lake Elsinore. ... On disabled list (April 21-May 6, June 1-21 and September 30, 1995-remainder of season). ... Signed as a free agent by Minnesota Twins (December 8, 1995). ... On disabled list (July 14-August 2, 1996; and August 9-24, 1997). ... Traded by Twins to Atlanta Braves for a player to be named (September 5, 1997); Twins acquired 1B Steve Hacker to complete deal (December 18, 1997). ... Signed as a free agent by San Diego Padres (November 25, 1997). ... On disabled list (June 4-July 24, 1998); included rehabilitation assignments to Rancho Cucamonga and Las Vegas. ... On disabled list (June 29-July 26, 1999); included rehabilitation assignment to Rancho Cucamonga. ... Traded by Padres to Braves for P Doug Dent (July 26, 1999). ... Signed as a free agent by Baltimore Orioles (December 17, 1999). ... On disabled list (April 2-17, 2000). ... Released by Orioles (June 14, 2001). ... Signed by Oakland Athletics (June 23, 2001). ... Signed as a free agent by Blue Jays (December 11, 2002). ... On disabled list (April 24, 2004-remainder of season).
2004 GAMES PLAYED BY POSITION (MLB): C—4, DH—1.

Year Team (League)	Pos.	G	AB	R	H	2B	3B	HR	RBI	BB	SO	HBP	GDP	SB-CS	Avg.	OBP	SLG	OPS	E	Avg.
1984— Medicine Hat (Pio.)	C	38	133	20	42	9	0	2	20	16	6	0	4	0-0	.316	.387	.429	.815	4	.984
1985— Florence (S. Atl.)	C	134	489	52	109	19	2	5	62	39	54	2	12	0-0	.223	.279	.301	.580	7	.989
1986— Ventura (Calif.)	C	124	451	65	133	23	4	20	79	43	46	2	10	9-4	.295	.355	.497	.852	19	.980
1987— Syracuse (Int'l)	C	107	342	35	84	19	1	10	47	22	46	1	5	3-3	.246	.292	.395	.686	11	.984
— Toronto (A.L.)	C	7	9	1	1	0	0	0	0	0	3	0	0	0-0	.111	.111	.111	.222	0	1.000
1988— Syracuse (Int'l)	C	34	120	18	34	7	1	7	21	8	24	0	1	1-0	.283	.328	.533	.861	1	.986
1989— Knoxville (Southern)	C	29	90	11	30	10	0	5	19	3	16	0	2	1-0	.333	.351	.611	.962	1	.993
— Toronto (A.L.)	DH-C	17	44	0	5	2	0	0	1	2	9	0	2	0-1	.114	.152	.159	.311	0	1.000
— Syracuse (Int'l)	C	24	89	8	24	6	0	1	11	4	9	0	3	0-0	.270	.301	.371	.672	1	.985
1990— Toronto (A.L.)	C	87	250	33	59	7	1	5	22	22	33	0	12	0-1	.236	.293	.332	.625	3	.993
— Syracuse (Int'l)	C	3	11	0	2	1	0	0	2	1	1	0	0	0-0	.182	.231	.273	.503	0	1.000
1991— Toronto (A.L.)	C	107	309	25	81	22	0	8	36	21	45	0	13	0-0	.262	.306	.411	.717	11	.979
1992— Toronto (A.L.)	C	22	61	4	14	6	0	1	13	5	5	0	2	0-0	.230	.279	.377	.656	1	.991
— California (A.L.)	C-DH	8	17	0	4	1	0	0	0	0	6	0	0	0-0	.235	.235	.294	.529	0	1.000
1993— California (A.L.)	C-DH	108	290	27	74	10	0	7	40	17	47	2	8	3-3	.255	.298	.362	.660	6	.986
1994— California (A.L.)	C-DH	45	126	10	31	6	0	2	8	10	27	0	3	0-2	.246	.299	.341	.641	2	.991
— Lake Elsinore (Calif.)	C-DH	10	32	4	8	2	0	0	5	2	6	0	2	0-0	.250	.286	.313	.598	0	1.000
1995— California (A.L.)	C-DH	85	273	35	71	12	2	9	38	17	49	1	4	0-1	.260	.304	.418	.721	8	.989
1996— Minnesota (A.L.)	C	97	329	37	94	22	3	6	47	19	52	0	11	0-0	.286	.320	.426	.746	8	.985
1997— Minnesota (A.L.)	C-DH	62	165	24	44	11	1	5	28	16	29	0	4	0-0	.267	.328	.436	.764	3	.986
— Atlanta (N.L.)	C	9	9	0	1	0	0	0	1	1	3	0	0	0-0	.111	.200	.111	.311	0	1.000
1998— San Diego (N.L.)	C	69	171	19	42	10	0	4	20	17	36	0	6	0-0	.246	.312	.374	.686	4	.987
— Rancho Cuca. (Calif.)	C-DH	3	9	1	0	0	0	0	0	0	2	0	1	0-0	.000	.182	.000	.182	0	1.000
— Las Vegas (PCL)	C	3	9	0	5	0	0	0	1	0	0	0	0	0-0	.556	.556	.556	1.111	0	1.000
1999— San Diego (N.L.)	C	50	128	9	37	4	0	3	15	13	14	0	5	0-0	.289	.355	.391	.745	3	.986
— Rancho Cuca. (Calif.)	C-DH	3	3	0	0	0	0	0	0	1	1	0	0	0-0	.000	.250	.000	.250	0	1.000
— Atlanta (N.L.)	C	34	72	10	16	2	0	2	9	13	16	0	1	0-0	.222	.337	.333	.671	1	.994
2000— Baltimore (A.L.)	C-DH	43	125	9	28	6	0	3	12	8	29	0	7	0-0	.224	.271	.344	.615	0	1.000
2001— Baltimore (A.L.)	DH-C	25	74	11	20	2	0	4	18	8	17	0	3	0-0	.270	.341	.459	.801	0	1.000
— Sacramento (PCL)	C	2	5	0	0	0	0	0	1	3	2	0	1	0-0	.000	.375	.000	.375	0	1.000
— Oakland (A.L.)	C-DH	33	87	13	16	1	0	7	13	13	21	0	2	0-0	.184	.290	.437	.727	0	1.000
2002— Oakland (A.L.)	C-DH	65	144	15	32	5	0	6	21	26	36	0	4	0-0	.222	.341	.382	.723	1	.997
2003— Toronto (A.L.)	C-DH	121	329	51	101	19	0	15	52	37	57	0	14	0-3	.307	.374	.502	.876	8	.982
2004— Toronto (A.L.)	C-DH	8	18	0	4	2	0	1	2	4	4	0	1	0-0	.222	.300	.333	.633	0	1.000
American League totals (15 years)		940	2650	295	679	134	7	78	350	223	469	3	92	3-11	.256	.312	.400	.712	47	.988
National League totals (3 years)		162	380	38	96	16	0	9	45	44	69	0	12	0-1	.253	.329	.366	.694	8	.989
Major League totals (17 years)		1102	3030	333	775	150	7	87	395	267	538	3	104	3-12	.256	.314	.396	.710	55	.989

DIVISION SERIES RECORD

Year Team (League)	Pos.	G	AB	R	H	2B	3B	HR	RBI	BB	SO	HBP	GDP	SB-CS	Avg.	OBP	SLG	OPS	E	Avg.
1998— San Diego (N.L.)	C	1	0	0	0	0	0	0	0	0	0	0	0	0-0	...	...	...	...	0	...
1999— Atlanta (N.L.)			Did not play.																	
2001— Oakland (A.L.)	C	3	7	0	1	0	0	0	0	0	3	0	1	0-0	.143	.143	.143	.286	1	.929
2002— Oakland (A.L.)	C	2	1	0	0	0	0	0	0	0	1	0	0	0-0	.000	.000	.000	.000	0	1.000
Division series totals (3 years)		6	8	0	1	0	0	0	0	0	4	0	1	0-0	.125	.125	.125	.250	1	.944

CHAMPIONSHIP SERIES RECORD

Year Team (League)	Pos.	G	AB	R	H	2B	3B	HR	RBI	BB	SO	HBP	GDP	SB-CS	Avg.	OBP	SLG	OPS	E	Avg.
1991— Toronto (A.L.)		Did not play.																		
1998— San Diego (N.L.)		2	1	1	1	0	0	1	2	1	0	0	0	0-0	1.000	1.000	4.000	5.000	...	...
1999— Atlanta (N.L.)	C	2	2	0	0	0	0	0	0	1	1	0	0	0-0	.000	.333	.000	.333	0	1.000
Champ. series totals (2 years)		4	3	1	1	0	0	1	2	2	1	0	0	0-0	.333	.600	1.333	1.933	0	1.000

WORLD SERIES RECORD

Year Team (League)	Pos.	G	AB	R	H	2B	3B	HR	RBI	BB	SO	HBP	GDP	SB-CS	Avg.	OBP	SLG	OPS	E	Avg.
1998— San Diego (N.L.)	C	2	4	0	0	0	0	0	0	2	0	0	0	0-0	.000	.000	.000	.000	0	1.000
1999— Atlanta (N.L.)	C	4	6	0	2	0	0	0	1	0	1	0	0	0-0	.333	.429	.333	.762	0	1.000
World series totals (2 years)		6	10	0	2	0	0	0	1	2	1	0	0	0-0	.200	.273	.200	.473	0	1.000

MYERS, MIKE   P

PERSONAL: Born June 26, 1969, in Arlington Heights, Ill. ... 6-3/219. ... Throws left, bats left. ... Full name: Michael Stanley Myers. ... High school: Crystal Lake (Ill.) Central. ... College: Iowa State.

TRANSACTIONS/CAREER NOTES: Selected by San Francisco Giants organization in fourth round of 1990 free-agent draft. ... Selected by Florida Marlins from Giants organization in Rule 5 major league draft (December 7, 1992). ... On disabled list (June 7-August 5, 1994); included rehabilitation assignment to Brevard County. ... Traded by Marlins to Detroit Tigers (August 9, 1995), completing deal in which Tigers traded P Buddy Groom to Marlins for a player to be named (August 7, 1995). ... Traded by Tigers with P Rick Greene and SS Santiago Perez to Milwaukee Brewers for P Bryce Florie and a player to be named (November 20, 1997). ... Traded by Brewers to Colorado Rockies for P Curtis Leskanic (November 17, 1999). ... Traded by Rockies to Arizona Diamondbacks for OF Jack Cust and C J.D. Closser (January 7, 2002). ... Signed as a free agent by Seattle Mariners organization (January 16, 2004). ... Traded by Mariners to Boston Red Sox for a player to be named (August 6, 2004).

CAREER HITTING: 0-for-1 (.000), 0 R, 0 2B, 0 3B, 0 HR, 0 RBI.

Year Team (League)	W	L	Pct.	ERA	WHIP	G	GS	CG	ShO	Hld.	Sv.-Opp.	IP	H	R	ER	HR	BB-IBB	SO	Avg.
1990— Everett (Northwest)	4	5	.444	3.90	1.42	15	14	1	0	...	0-...	85.1	91	43	37	9	30-0	73	.269
1991— Clinton (Midw.)	5	3	.625	2.62	1.21	11	11	1	0	...	0-...	65.1	61	23	19	3	18-0	59	.253
— Ariz. Giants (Ariz.)	0	1	.000	12.00	2.33	1	0	0	0	...	0-...	3.0	5	5	4	0	2-0	2	.357
1992— San Jose (California)	5	1	.833	2.30	1.10	8	8	0	0	...	0-...	54.2	43	20	14	1	17-0	40	.221
— Clinton (Midw.)	1	2	.333	1.19	0.96	7	7	0	0	...	0-...	37.2	28	11	5	0	8-0	32	.207
1993— Edmonton (PCL)	7	14	.333	5.18	1.53	27	27	3	0	...	0-...	161.2	195	109	93	20	52-1	112	.296
1994— Edmonton (PCL)	1	5	.167	5.55	1.65	12	11	0	0	...	0-...	60.0	78	42	37	9	21-0	55	.307
— Brevard County (FSL)	0	0	...	0.79	0.97	3	2	0	0	...	0-...	11.1	7	1	1	1	4-0	15	.184
1995— Florida (N.L.)	0	0	...	0.00	2.00	2	0	0	0	0	0-0	2.0	1	0	0	0	3-0	0	.167
— Charlotte (Int'l)	0	5	.000	5.65	1.53	37	0	0	0	...	0-...	36.2	41	25	23	6	15-1	24	.283
— Toledo (International)	0	0	...	4.32	1.08	6	0	0	0	...	0-...	8.1	6	4	4	1	3-0	8	.194
— Detroit (A.L.)	1	0	1.000	9.95	2.21	11	0	0	0	1	0-1	6.1	10	7	7	1	4-0	4	.385
1996— Detroit (A.L.)	1	5	.167	5.01	1.61	83	0	0	0	17	6-8	64.2	70	41	36	6	34-8	69	.272
1997— Detroit (A.L.)	0	4	.000	5.70	1.55	88	0	0	0	18	2-5	53.2	58	36	34	12	25-2	50	.274
1998— Milwaukee (N.L.)	2	2	.500	2.70	1.32	70	0	0	0	23	1-3	50.0	46	19	15	5	22-1	40	.249
1999— Milwaukee (N.L.)	2	1	.667	5.23	1.43	71	0	0	0	14	0-3	41.1	46	24	24	7	13-1	35	.291
2000— Colorado (N.L.)	0	1	.000	1.99	1.06	78	0	0	0	15	1-2	45.1	24	10	10	2	24-3	41	.160
2001— Colorado (N.L.)	2	3	.400	3.60	1.40	73	0	0	0	10	0-2	40.0	32	17	16	2	24-7	36	.225
2002— Arizona (N.L.)	4	3	.571	4.38	1.51	69	0	0	0	17	4-9	37.0	39	19	18	2	17-0	31	.275
2003— Arizona (N.L.)	0	0	...	5.70	1.62	64	0	0	0	6	0-3	36.1	38	23	23	4	21-1	21	.262
2004— Seattle (A.L.)	4	1	.800	4.88	1.66	50	0	0	0	8	0-0	27.2	29	15	15	3	17-4	23	.279
— Boston (A.L.)	1	0	1.000	4.20	1.47	25	0	0	0	2	0-0	15.0	16	7	7	2	6-1	9	.267
American League totals (4 years)	7	10	.412	5.32	1.61	257	0	0	0	46	8-14	167.1	183	106	99	24	86-15	155	.278
National League totals (7 years)	10	11	.476	3.79	1.38	427	0	0	0	85	6-22	252.0	224	111	106	22	124-13	204	.243
Major League totals (10 years)	17	21	.447	4.40	1.47	684	0	0	0	131	14-36	419.1	407	217	205	46	210-28	359	.258

DIVISION SERIES RECORD

Year Team (League)	W	L	Pct.	ERA	WHIP	G	GS	CG	ShO	Hld.	Sv.-Opp.	IP	H	R	ER	HR	BB-IBB	SO	Avg.
2002— Arizona (N.L.)	0	0	...	0.00	1.20	2	0	0	0	0	0-0	1.2	2	0	0	0	0-0	1	.333
2004— Boston (A.L.)	0	0	...	27.00	3.00	2	0	0	0	1	0-0	.1	0	1	1	0	1-0	1	.000
Division series totals (2 years)	0	0	...	4.50	1.50	4	0	0	0	1	0-0	2.0	2	1	1	0	1-0	2	.286

CHAMPIONSHIP SERIES RECORD

Year Team (League)	W	L	Pct.	ERA	WHIP	G	GS	CG	ShO	Hld.	Sv.-Opp.	IP	H	R	ER	HR	BB-IBB	SO	Avg.
2004— Boston (A.L.)	0	0	...	7.71	2.57	3	0	0	0	0	0-0	2.1	5	2	2	1	1-0	4	.455

MYERS, RODNEY   P

PERSONAL: Born June 26, 1969, in Rockford, Ill. ... 6-1/200. ... Throws right, bats right. ... Full name: Rodney Luther Myers. ... High school: Rockford (Ill.) East. ... College: Wisconsin.

TRANSACTIONS/CAREER NOTES: Selected by Kansas City Royals organization in 12th round of 1990 free-agent draft. ... Loaned by Royals organization to Lethbridge (June 10-September 16, 1992). ... Selected by Chicago Cubs from Royals organization in Rule 5 major league draft (December 4, 1995). ... Traded by Cubs to San Diego Padres for OF Gary Matthews Jr. (March 23, 2000). ... On disabled list (March 29-May 5 and May 12, 2000-remainder of season); included rehabilitation assignment to Rancho Cucamonga. ... On disabled list (May 20-June 19, 2001); included rehabilitation assignment to Portland. ... Signed as a free agent by Los Angeles Dodgers (December 24, 2002). ... Released by Dodgers (November 20, 2003). ... Re-signed by Dodgers organization (March 1, 2004). ... Released by Dodgers (July 2004). ... Signed by New York Mets organization (July 5, 2004).

CAREER HITTING: 3-for-18 (.167), 2 R, 1 2B, 0 3B, 0 HR, 1 RBI.

Year Team (League)	W	L	Pct.	ERA	WHIP	G	GS	CG	ShO	Hld.	Sv.-Opp.	IP	H	R	ER	HR	BB-IBB	SO	Avg.
1990— Eugene (N'west)	0	2	.000	1.19	1.41	6	4	0	0	...	0-...	22.2	19	9	3	2	13-0	17	.226
1991— Appleton (Midw.)	1	1	.500	2.60	1.73	9	4	0	0	...	0-...	27.2	22	9	8	0	26-0	29	.224
1992— Lethbridge (Pio.)	5	8	.385	4.01	1.49	15	15	5	0	...	0-...	103.1	93	57	46	3	61-1	76	.245
1993— Rockford (Midwest)	7	3	.700	1.79	0.97	12	12	5	2	...	0-...	85.1	65	22	17	3	18-0	65	.217
— Memphis (Sou.)	3	6	.333	5.62	1.60	12	12	1	1	...	0-...	65.2	73	46	41	8	32-0	42	.294
1994— Wilmington (Caro.)	1	1	.500	4.82	1.07	4	0	0	0	...	1-...	9.1	9	6	5	1	1-0	9	.250
— Memphis (Sou.)	5	1	.833	1.03	1.06	42	0	0	0	...	9-...	69.2	45	20	8	3	29-2	53	.184
1995— Omaha (Am. Assoc.)	4	5	.444	4.10	1.47	38	0	0	0	...	2-...	48.1	52	26	22	5	19-1	38	.277
1996— Chicago (N.L.)	2	1	.667	4.68	1.47	45	0	0	0	1	0-0	67.1	61	38	35	6	38-3	50	.243
1997— Iowa (Am. Assoc.)	7	8	.467	4.09	1.27	24	23	1	0	...	0-...	140.2	140	76	64	18	38-1	79	.261
— Chicago (N.L.)	0	0	...	6.00	2.11	5	1	0	0	...	0-0	9.0	12	6	6	1	7-1	6	.333
1998— Iowa (PCL)	7	5	.583	3.91	1.27	33	13	2	0	...	11-...	101.1	84	47	44	10	45-1	86	.226

Year	Team (League)	W	L	Pct.	ERA	WHIP	G	GS	CG	ShO	Hld.	Sv.-Opp.	IP	H	R	ER	HR	BB-IBB	SO	Avg.
	—Chicago (N.L.)	0	0	...	7.00	1.78	12	0	0	0	0	0-1	18.0	26	14	14	3	6-0	15	.342
1999—	Iowa (PCL)	2	4	.333	4.06	1.29	20	1	0	0	...	2-...	31.0	29	18	14	3	11-3	24	.248
	—Chicago (N.L.)	3	1	.750	4.38	1.51	46	0	0	0	8	0-1	63.2	71	34	31	10	25-2	41	.289
2000—	Rancho Cuca. (Calif.)	0	0	...	0.00	0.50	3	2	0	0	...	0-...	4.0	2	0	0	0	0-0	4	.154
	—San Diego (N.L.)	0	0	...	4.50	1.00	3	0	0	0	0	0-0	2.0	2	1	1	0	0-0	3	.250
2001—	San Diego (N.L.)	1	2	.333	5.32	1.54	37	0	0	0	3	1-2	47.1	53	31	28	6	20-0	29	.291
	—Portland (PCL)	1	1	.500	3.00	1.20	8	1	0	0	...	0-...	15.0	13	5	5	1	5-0	14	.245
2002—	Portland (PCL)	5	2	.714	3.70	1.25	42	0	0	0	...	4-...	48.2	48	23	20	2	13-1	35	.259
	—San Diego (N.L.)	1	1	.500	5.91	1.83	14	0	0	0	2	0-0	21.1	29	20	14	1	10-0	11	.333
2003—	Las Vegas (PCL)	9	1	.900	3.30	1.20	46	1	0	0	...	1-...	71.0	66	32	26	4	22-1	48	.246
	—Los Angeles (N.L.)	0	0	...	6.00	1.56	4	0	0	0	0	0-0	9.0	10	7	6	1	4-0	5	.270
2004—	Los Angeles (N.L.)	0	0	...	0.00	0.50	1	0	0	0	0	0-0	2.0	1	0	0	0	0-0	1	.167
	—Las Vegas (PCL)	4	1	.800	4.74	1.39	24	0	0	0	0	0-...	38.0	42	22	20	3	11-2	25	.278
	—Kingsport (Appalachian)	0	2	.000	23.14	3.86	2	1	0	0	...	0-...	2.1	5	7	6	1	4-0	3	.417
Major League totals (9 years)		7	5	.583	5.07	1.56	167	1	0	0	14	1-4	239.2	265	151	135	28	110-6	161	.285

MYETTE, AARON   P

PERSONAL: Born September 26, 1977, in New Westminster, British Columbia. ... 6-4/210. ... Throws right, bats right. ... Full name: Aaron Kenneth Myette. ... Name pronounced: MY-ett. ... High school: Johnston Heights Sectional (Surrey, B.C.). ... Junior college: Central Arizona. ... Son of Kenneth Myette, pitcher with Cincinnati Reds organization (1969).

TRANSACTIONS/CAREER NOTES: Selected by Seattle Mariners organization in 17th round of 1995 free-agent draft; did not sign. ... Selected by Chicago White Sox organization in supplemental round ("sandwich pick" between first and second rounds, 43rd pick overall) of 1997 free-agent draft; pick received as part of compensation for Florida Marlins signing free-agent P Alex Fernandez. ... On disabled list (March 25-May 9, 2000). ... Traded by White Sox with P Brian Schmack to Texas Rangers for SS Royce Clayton (December 14, 2000). ... Traded by Rangers with 1B Travis Hafner to Cleveland Indians for C Einar Diaz and P Ryan Drese (December 6, 2002). ... On disabled list (March 26-April 20, 2003); included rehabilitation assignment to Buffalo. ... Traded by Indians to Philadelphia Phillies for OF Lyle Mouton (July 9, 2003). ... Signed as a free agent by Cincinnati Reds organization (December 24, 2003). ... Refused minor league assignment and became a free agent (October 11, 2004).

CAREER HITTING: 0-for-0 (.000), 0 R, 0 2B, 0 3B, 0 HR, 0 RBI.

Year	Team (League)	W	L	Pct.	ERA	WHIP	G	GS	CG	ShO	Hld.	Sv.-Opp.	IP	H	R	ER	HR	BB-IBB	SO	Avg.
1997—	Bristol (Appalachian)	4	3	.571	3.61	1.25	9	8	1	0	...	0-...	47.1	39	28	19	9	20-0	50	.207
	—Hickory (S. Atl.)	3	1	.750	1.14	0.95	5	5	0	0	...	0-...	31.2	19	6	4	1	11-0	27	.178
1998—	Hickory (S. Atl.)	9	4	.692	2.47	1.12	17	17	0	0	...	0-...	102.0	84	43	28	4	30-0	103	.223
	—Winston-Salem (Caro.)	4	2	.667	2.01	1.03	6	6	1	1	...	0-...	44.2	32	14	10	4	14-0	54	.198
1999—	Birmingham (Southern)	12	7	.632	3.66	1.31	28	28	0	0	...	0-...	164.2	138	76	67	19	77-0	135	.225
	—Chicago (A.L.)	0	2	.000	6.32	1.98	4	3	0	0	0	0-0	15.2	17	11	11	2	14-1	11	.266
2000—	Birmingham (Southern)	2	0	1.000	3.52	1.24	3	3	0	0	...	0-0	15.1	11	7	6	1	8-0	21	.190
	—Charlotte (Int'l)	5	5	.500	4.35	1.42	19	18	0	0	...	0-0	111.2	103	58	54	18	56-0	85	.245
	—Chicago (A.L.)	0	0	...	0.00	1.50	2	0	0	0	0	0-0	2.2	0	0	0	0	4-0	1	.000
2001—	Oklahoma (PCL)	4	3	.571	3.73	1.34	12	12	2	0	...	0-...	70.0	64	32	29	5	30-0	76	.241
	—Texas (A.L.)	4	5	.444	7.14	1.62	19	15	0	0	0	0-0	80.2	94	65	64	12	37-0	67	.293
	—Tulsa (Texas)	1	0	1.000	3.00	0.67	1	1	0	0	...	0-...	6.0	3	0	0	0	1-0	2	.143
2002—	Oklahoma (PCL)	7	4	.636	3.14	1.23	16	16	2	1	...	0-...	106.0	86	41	37	5	44-0	106	.222
	—Texas (A.L.)	2	5	.286	10.06	2.17	15	12	0	0	0	0-0	48.1	64	57	54	11	41-0	48	.325
2003—	Akron (East.)	0	0	...	0.40	0.40	2	0	0	0	0	0-...	5.0	0	0	0	0	2-0	7	.000
	—Cleveland (A.L.)	0	0	...	23.63	3.38	2	0	0	0	0	0-0	2.2	7	7	7	1	2-0	1	.467
	—Buffalo (Int'l)	0	0	...	4.59	1.70	23	1	0	0	...	1-...	33.1	33	21	17	4	23-1	25	.262
	—Scran./W.B. (I.L.)	5	4	.556	4.27	1.20	11	10	0	0	...	0-...	59.0	50	28	28	4	20-0	54	.229
2004—	Louisville (Int'l)	3	3	.500	2.89	1.30	41	1	0	0	...	19-...	62.1	45	27	20	2	36-4	58	.193
	—Cincinnati (N.L.)	0	0	...	8.31	2.54	5	0	0	0	0	0-0	4.1	3	4	4	0	8-0	6	.188
American League totals (5 years)		6	12	.333	8.16	1.87	42	30	0	0	0	0-0	150.0	182	140	136	26	98-1	128	.301
National League totals (1 year)		0	0	...	8.31	2.54	5	0	0	0	0	0-0	4.1	3	4	4	0	8-0	6	.188
Major League totals (6 years)		6	12	.333	8.16	1.89	47	30	0	0	0	0-0	154.1	185	144	140	26	106-1	134	.298

NADY, XAVIER   OF

PERSONAL: Born November 14, 1978, in Carmel, Calif. ... 6-2/205. ... Bats right, throws right. ... Full name: Xavier C. Nady. ... Name pronounced: ZAV-yer NAY-dee. ... High school: Salinas (Calif.). ... College: California.

TRANSACTIONS/CAREER NOTES: Selected by St. Louis Cardinals organization in fourth round of 1997 free-agent draft; did not sign. ... Selected by San Diego Padres organization in second round of 2000 free-agent draft.

2004 GAMES PLAYED BY POSITION (MLB): OF—22, DH—2.

Year	Team (League)	Pos.	G	AB	R	H	2B	3B	HR	RBI	BB	SO	HBP	GDP	SB-CS	Avg.	OBP	SLG	OPS	E	Avg.
2000—	San Diego (N.L.)		1	1	1	1	0	0	0	0	0	0	0	0	0-0	1.000	1.000	1.000	2.000	...	...
2001—	Lake Elsinore (Calif.)	1B	137	524	96	158	38	1	26	100	62	109	10	14	6-0	.302	.381	.527	.908	10	.989
2002—	Lake Elsinore (Calif.)	OF	45	169	41	47	6	3	13	37	28	40	1	2	2-0	.278	.382	.580	.962	0	1.000
	—Portland (PCL)	OF	85	315	46	89	12	1	10	43	20	60	3	11	0-1	.283	.329	.422	.752	2	.981
2003—	Portland (PCL)	OF-DH	37	136	19	36	7	0	7	23	12	28	2	2	0-0	.265	.329	.471	.800	3	.954
	—San Diego (N.L.)	OF	110	371	50	99	17	1	9	39	24	74	4	14	6-2	.267	.321	.391	.712	6	.968
2004—	Portland (PCL)	OF-1B-DH	74	291	52	97	19	1	22	70	22	42	7	7	3-0	.333	.394	.632	1.026	4	.981
	—San Diego (N.L.)	OF-DH	34	77	7	19	4	0	3	9	5	13	1	4	0-0	.247	.301	.416	.717	2	.923
Major League totals (3 years)			145	449	58	119	21	1	12	48	29	87	7	18	6-2	.265	.319	.396	.715	8	.963

NAGEOTTE, CLINT   P

PERSONAL: Born October 25, 1980, in Parma, Ohio. ... 6-3/200. ... Throws right, bats right. ... Full name: Clinton Scott Nageotte. ... High school: Brooklyn (Ohio).

TRANSACTIONS/CAREER NOTES: Selected by Seattle Mariners organization in fifth round of 1999 free-agent draft. ... On disabled list (August 28, 2004-remainder of season).

CAREER HITTING: 0-for-2 (.000), 0 R, 0 2B, 0 3B, 0 HR, 0 RBI.

Year	Team (League)	W	L	Pct.	ERA	WHIP	G	GS	CG	ShO	Hld.	Sv.-Opp.	IP	H	R	ER	HR	BB-IBB	SO	Avg.
2000—	Ariz. Mariners (Ariz.)	4	1	.800	2.16	1.14	12	7	0	0	...	1-...	50.0	29	15	12	0	28-0	59	.167
2001—	Wisconsin (Midw.)	11	8	.579	3.13	1.25	28	26	0	0	...	0-...	152.1	141	65	53	10	50-1	187	.246
2002—	San Bernardino (Calif.)	9	6	.600	4.54	1.34	29	29	1	0	...	0-...	164.2	153	101	83	10	68-0	214	.241
2003—	San Antonio (Texas)	11	7	.611	3.10	1.26	27	27	2	1	...	0-...	154.0	127	60	53	6	67-1	157	.224
2004—	Tacoma (PCL)	6	6	.500	4.46	1.40	14	14	0	0	...	0-...	80.2	78	42	40	9	35-0	63	.256
	—Seattle (A.L.)	1	6	.143	7.36	2.05	12	5	0	0	0	0-0	36.2	48	31	30	3	27-1	24	.324
Major League totals (1 year)		1	6	.143	7.36	2.05	12	5	0	0	0	0-0	36.2	48	31	30	3	27-1	24	.324

NAKAMURA, MIKE   P

PERSONAL: Born September 6, 1976, in Nara, Japan. ... 5-10/170. ... Throws right, bats right. ... Full name: Micheal Yoshihide Nakamura. ... College: South Alabama.
CAREER HITTING: 0-for-0 (.000), 0 R, 0 2B, 0 3B, 0 HR, 0 RBI.

Year	Team (League)	W	L	Pct.	ERA	WHIP	G	GS	CG	ShO	Hld.	Sv.-Opp.	IP	H	R	ER	HR	BB-IBB	SO	Avg.
1998—	Fort Wayne (Midw.)	2	5	.286	3.26	1.39	29	9	0	0	...	1-...	80.0	82	41	29	8	29-0	70	.266
—	Fort Myers (Fla. St.)	1	3	.250	3.45	1.33	8	6	1	0	...	0-...	28.2	28	15	11	3	10-0	21	.257
1999—	Fort Myers (Fla. St.)	2	0	1.000	1.83	0.71	14	0	0	0	...	2-...	19.2	9	5	4	1	5-0	18	.138
2000—	Fort Myers (Fla. St.)	1	0	1.000	1.52	1.06	32	0	0	0	...	12-...	41.1	33	9	7	0	11-1	46	.228
2001—	New Britain (East.)	5	1	.833	1.77	1.15	48	0	0	0	...	5-...	86.1	75	20	17	3	24-5	109	.229
2002—	Edmonton (PCL)	4	3	.571	4.74	1.23	46	4	0	0	...	2-...	87.1	85	51	46	7	22-0	80	.254
2003—	Minnesota (A.L.)	0	0	...	7.82	1.74	12	0	0	0	1	1-1	12.2	20	11	11	4	2-0	14	.339
—	Rochester (Int'l)	6	6	.500	2.99	1.26	43	0	0	0	...	2-...	78.1	71	28	26	4	28-1	95	.244
2004—	Toronto (A.L.)	0	3	.000	7.36	1.32	19	0	0	0	2	0-...	25.2	27	23	21	7	7-0	24	.262
—	Syracuse (Int'l)	3	2	.600	7.36	1.07	31	1	0	0	...	4-...	55.0	42	20	19	3	17-2	76	.213
Major League totals (2 years)		0	3	.000	7.51	1.46	31	0	0	0	3	1-1	38.1	47	34	32	11	9-0	38	.290

NANCE, SHANE   P

PERSONAL: Born September 7, 1977, in Pasadena, Texas. ... 5-8/191. ... Throws left, bats left. ... Full name: Joseph Shane Nance. ... High school: Dobie (Texas). ... College: Houston.
TRANSACTIONS/CAREER NOTES: Selected by Los Angeles Dodgers organization in 24th round of 1999 free-agent draft; did not sign. ... Selected by Los Angeles Dodgers organization in 11th round of 2000 free-agent draft. ... Traded by Dodgers with P Ben Diggins to Milwaukee Brewers for 3B Tyler Houston and a player to be named (July 23, 2002); Dodgers acquired P Brian Mallette to complete deal (October 16, 2002). ... On disabled list (September 1, 2002-remainder of season). ... Traded with 1B Richie Sexson and a player to be named to Milwaukee Brewers for SS Craig Counsell, 2B Junior Spivey, 1B Lyle Overbay, C Chad Moeller and Ps Chris Capuano and Jorge de la Rosa (December 1, 2003); Diamondbacks acquired OF Noochie Varner to complete deal (December 15, 2003). ... On disabled list (March 26-May 7, 2004); included rehabilitation assignment to Tucson.
CAREER HITTING: 1-for-3 (.333), 0 R, 0 2B, 0 3B, 0 HR, 1 RBI.

Year	Team (League)	W	L	Pct.	ERA	WHIP	G	GS	CG	ShO	Hld.	Sv.-Opp.	IP	H	R	ER	HR	BB-IBB	SO	Avg.
2000—	Yakima (N'west)	2	4	.333	2.48	1.09	12	9	0	0	...	0-...	58.0	41	19	16	1	22-0	66	.203
2001—	Jacksonville (Southern)	7	0	1.000	1.59	1.06	28	0	0	0	...	1-...	45.1	31	11	8	4	17-1	44	.195
—	Vero Beach (FSL)	6	3	.667	2.63	1.02	21	0	0	0	...	4-...	48.0	28	15	14	3	21-1	63	.164
2002—	Las Vegas (PCL)	11	3	.786	4.17	1.44	37	0	0	0	...	1-...	58.1	58	32	27	5	26-1	53	.260
—	Indianapolis (Int'l)	3	0	1.000	0.00	1.08	9	0	0	0	...	0-...	16.2	12	0	0	0	6-0	10	.207
—	Milwaukee (N.L.)	0	0	...	4.26	1.26	4	0	0	0	0	0-0	6.1	4	3	3	1	4-0	5	.174
2003—	Indianapolis (Int'l)	2	4	.333	1.38	0.90	35	1	0	0	...	3-...	52.1	34	10	8	4	13-1	53	.185
—	Milwaukee (N.L.)	0	2	.000	4.81	1.81	26	0	0	0	0	0-1	24.1	34	16	13	5	10-1	25	.327
2004—	Tucson (PCL)	2	4	.333	6.35	1.83	46	2	0	0	...	2-...	45.1	61	38	32	5	22-3	48	.314
—	Arizona (N.L.)	1	1	.500	5.84	2.51	19	0	0	0	3	0-1	12.1	19	11	8	2	12-4	9	.352
Major League totals (3 years)		1	3	.250	5.02	1.93	49	0	0	0	4	0-2	43.0	57	30	24	8	26-5	39	.315

NARRON, SAM   P

PERSONAL: Born July 12, 1981, in Goldsboro, N.C. ... 6-7/200. ... Throws left, bats left. ... Full name: Samuel Franklin Narron. ... High school: Eastern Wayne (Goldsboro, N.C.). ... College: East Carolina. ... Nephew of Jerry Narron, coach, Cincinnati Reds, and catcher with three major league teams (1979-81, 1983-87); minor league manager in Baltimore Orioles organization (1989-92); coach with Orioles (1993-94); and coach and manager with Texas Rangers (1995-2002).
TRANSACTIONS/CAREER NOTES: Selected by Texas Rangers in 15th round of 2002 free-agent draft. ... Claimed on waivers by Milwaukee Brewers (September 24, 2004).
CAREER HITTING: 0-for-0 (.000), 0 R, 0 2B, 0 3B, 0 HR, 0 RBI.

Year	Team (League)	W	L	Pct.	ERA	WHIP	G	GS	CG	ShO	Hld.	Sv.-Opp.	IP	H	R	ER	HR	BB-IBB	SO	Avg.
2002—	Pulaski (Appalachian)	6	1	.857	3.88	1.23	14	9	0	0	...	3-...	69.2	78	34	30	10	8-0	50	.292
2003—	Stockton (Calif.)	10	4	.714	3.48	1.22	26	14	0	0	...	0-...	103.1	107	48	40	8	19-0	75	.276
2004—	Frisco (Texas)	6	0	1.000	2.36	1.24	13	8	0	0	...	0-...	53.1	56	23	14	6	10-0	27	.264
—	Texas (A.L.)	0	0	...	13.50	3.38	1	1	0	0	0	0-0	2.2	5	4	4	3	4-0	1	.385
—	Oklahoma (PCL)	8	2	.800	4.43	1.45	17	16	1	1	...	0-...	101.2	123	55	50	14	24-0	31	.308
Major League totals (1 year)		0	0	...	13.50	3.38	1	1	0	0	0	0-0	2.2	5	4	4	3	4-0	1	.385

NATHAN, JOE   P

PERSONAL: Born November 22, 1974, in Houston, Texas. ... 6-4/205. ... Throws right, bats right. ... Full name: Joseph Michael Nathan. ... High school: Pine Bush (N.Y.). ... College: SUNY-Stony Brook.
TRANSACTIONS/CAREER NOTES: Selected by San Francisco Giants organization in sixth round of 1995 free-agent draft. ... Played shortstop in Giants' minor league organization (1995). ... On disabled list (May 13-June 6 and July 14-August 19, 2000); included rehabilitation assignments to San Jose, Bakersfield and Fresno. ... Traded by Giants with Ps Boof Bonser and Francisco Liriano to Minnesota Twins for C A.J. Pierzynski and a player to be named or cash (November 14, 2003).
CAREER HITTING: 10-for-62 (.161), 4 R, 3 2B, 0 3B, 2 HR, 4 RBI.

Year	Team (League)	W	L	Pct.	ERA	WHIP	G	GS	CG	ShO	Hld.	Sv.-Opp.	IP	H	R	ER	HR	BB-IBB	SO	Avg.
1996—						Did not play.														
1997—	Salem-Keizer (N'west)	2	1	.667	2.47	1.27	18	5	0	0	...	2-...	62.0	53	22	17	7	26-0	44	.243
1998—	San Jose (California)	8	6	.571	3.32	1.21	22	22	0	0	...	0-...	122.0	100	51	45	13	48-0	118	.224
—	Shreveport (Texas)	1	3	.250	8.80	1.89	4	4	0	0	...	0-...	15.1	20	15	15	4	9-0	10	.317
1999—	Shreveport (Texas)	0	1	.000	3.12	1.38	2	2	0	0	...	0-...	8.2	5	4	3	0	7-0	7	.179
—	San Francisco (N.L.)	7	4	.636	4.18	1.44	19	14	0	0	0	1-1	90.1	84	45	42	17	46-0	54	.243
—	Fresno (PCL)	6	4	.600	4.46	1.39	13	13	1	0	...	0-...	74.2	68	44	37	11	36-0	82	.244
2000—	San Francisco (N.L.)	5	2	.714	5.21	1.63	20	15	0	0	0	0-1	93.1	89	63	54	12	63-4	61	.255
—	San Jose (California)	0	1	.000	3.60	1.00	1	1	0	0	...	0-...	5.0	4	2	2	1	0-0	2	.235
—	Bakersfield (California)	1	0	1.000	5.06	1.69	1	1	0	0	...	0-...	5.1	2	3	3	0	7-0	6	.118
—	Fresno (PCL)	0	2	.000	4.40	1.53	3	3	0	0	...	0-...	14.1	15	8	7	4	7-0	9	.268
2001—	Fresno (PCL)	0	5	.000	7.77	2.07	10	10	0	0	...	0-...	46.1	63	47	40	13	33-0	21	.333
—	Shreveport (Texas)	3	6	.333	6.93	1.76	21	7	0	0	...	0-...	62.1	73	49	48	11	37-5	33	.299
2002—	Fresno (PCL)	6	12	.333	5.60	1.65	31	25	1	0	...	0-...	146.1	167	97	91	20	74-0	117	.283
—	San Francisco (N.L.)	0	0	...	0.00	0.27	4	0	0	0	0	0-0	3.2	1	0	0	0	0-0	2	.083
2003—	San Francisco (N.L.)	12	4	.750	2.96	1.06	78	0	0	0	20	0-3	79.0	51	26	26	7	33-3	83	.186
2004—	Minnesota (A.L.)	1	2	.333	1.62	0.98	73	0	0	0	0	44-47	72.1	48	14	13	3	23-3	89	.187
American League totals (1 year)		1	2	.333	1.62	0.98	73	0	0	0	0	44-47	72.1	48	14	13	3	23-3	89	.187
National League totals (4 years)		24	10	.706	4.12	1.38	121	29	0	0	20	1-5	266.1	225	134	122	36	142-7	200	.229
Major League totals (5 years)		25	12	.676	3.59	1.29	194	29	0	0	20	45-52	338.2	273	148	135	39	165-10	289	.221

DIVISION SERIES RECORD

Year — Team (League)	W	L	Pct.	ERA	WHIP	G	GS	CG	ShO	Hld.	Sv.-Opp.	IP	H	R	ER	HR	BB-IBB	SO	Avg.
2003— San Francisco (N.L.)	0	1	.000	81.00	15.00	2	0	0	0	0	0-1	.1	4	3	3	1	1-0	1	.800
2004— Minnesota (A.L.)	0	1	.000	3.60	1.40	3	0	0	0	0	1-1	5.0	2	2	2	0	5-2	6	.118
Division series totals (2 years)	0	2	.000	8.44	2.25	5	0	0	0	0	1-2	5.1	6	5	5	1	6-2	7	.273

ALL-STAR GAME RECORD

Year — Team (League)	W	L	Pct.	ERA	WHIP	G	GS	CG	ShO	Hld.	Sv.-Opp.	IP	H	R	ER	HR	BB-IBB	SO	Avg.
All-Star Game totals (1 year)	0	0	...	0.00	0.00	1	0	0	0	0	0-0	1.0	0	0	0	0	0-0	2	.000

NAVARRO, DIONER   C

PERSONAL: Born February 9, 1984, in Caracas, Venezuela. ... 5-10/190. ... Bats both, throws right. ... Full name: Dioner Faviau Navarro.
TRANSACTIONS/CAREER NOTES: Signed as a non-drafted free agent by New York Yankees organization (August 21, 2000).
2004 GAMES PLAYED BY POSITION (MLB): C—4.

Year — Team (League)	Pos.	G	AB	R	H	2B	3B	HR	RBI	BB	SO	HBP	GDP	SB-CS	Avg.	OBP	SLG	OPS	E	Avg.
2001— GC Yankees (GCL)	C	43	143	27	40	10	1	2	22	17	23	0	4	6-0	.280	.345	.406	.751	3	.991
2002— Greensboro (S. Atl.)	C	92	328	41	78	12	2	8	36	39	61	5	9	1-2	.238	.326	.360	.686	8	.987
— Tampa (Fla. St.)	C	1	1	2	1	1	0	0	0	0	0	0	0	0-0	.500	.000	3.000	3.000	0	1.000
2003— Tampa (Fla. St.)	C	52	197	28	59	16	4	3	28	17	27	4	4	1-0	.299	.364	.467	.831	3	.992
— Trenton (East.)	C	58	208	28	71	15	0	4	37	18	26	1	6	2-3	.341	.388	.471	.859	4	.986
2004— Trenton (East.)	C-DH	70	255	32	69	14	1	3	29	33	44	1	6	1-0	.271	.354	.369	.720	7	.984
— Columbus (Int'l)	C-DH	40	136	18	34	8	2	1	16	14	17	1	1	1-0	.250	.316	.360	.672	2	.994
— New York (A.L.)	C	5	7	2	3	0	0	0	1	0	0	0	1	0-0	.429	.429	.429	.857	0	1.000
Major League totals (1 year)		5	7	2	3	0	0	0	1	0	0	0	1	0-0	.429	.429	.429	.857	0	1.000

NEAGLE, DENNY   P

PERSONAL: Born September 13, 1968, in Annapolis, Md. ... 6-3/225. ... Throws left, bats left. ... Full name: Dennis Edward Neagle. ... Name pronounced: NAY-gul. ... High school: Arundel (Gambrills, Md.). ... College: Minnesota.
TRANSACTIONS/CAREER NOTES: Selected by Minnesota Twins organization in third round of 1989 free-agent draft. ... On disabled list (July 28-August 12, 1991). ... Traded by Twins with OF Midre Cummings to Pittsburgh Pirates for P John Smiley (March 17, 1992). ... Traded by Pirates to Atlanta Braves for 1B Ron Wright and a player to be named (August 28, 1996); Pirates acquired P Jason Schmidt to complete deal (August 30, 1996). ... Traded by Braves with OF Michael Tucker and P Rob Bell to Cincinnati Reds for 2B Bret Boone and P Mike Remlinger (November 10, 1998). ... On disabled list (March 24-April 21 and May 24-July 29, 1999); included rehabilitation assignment to Indianapolis. ... Traded by Reds with OF Mike Frank to New York Yankees for 3B Drew Henson, OF Jackson Melian and Ps Brian Reith and Ed Yarnall (July 12, 2000). ... Signed as a free agent by Colorado Rockies (December 4, 2000). ... On disabled list (June 9-24, 2001). ... On disabled list (March 27-June 17 and July 21, 2003-remainder of season); included rehabilitation assignments to Visalia and Colorado Springs. ... On disabled list (April 3, 2004-entire season).
CAREER HITTING: 87-for-531 (.164), 31 R, 17 2B, 0 3B, 5 HR, 44 RBI.

Year — Team (League)	W	L	Pct.	ERA	WHIP	G	GS	CG	ShO	Hld.	Sv.-Opp.	IP	H	R	ER	HR	BB-IBB	SO	Avg.
1989— Elizabethton (Appal.)	1	2	.333	4.50	1.27	6	3	0	0	...	1-...	22.0	20	11	11	1	8-0	32	.250
— Kenosha (Midw.)	2	1	.667	1.65	0.94	6	6	1	1	...	0-...	43.2	25	9	8	3	16-0	40	.175
1990— Visalia (Calif.)	8	0	1.000	1.43	0.87	10	10	0	0	...	0-...	63.0	39	13	10	2	16-0	92	.175
— Orlando (Sou.)	12	3	.800	2.45	1.03	17	17	4	1	...	0-...	121.1	94	40	33	11	31-0	94	.212
1991— Portland (PCL)	9	4	.692	3.27	1.27	19	17	1	1	...	0-...	104.2	101	41	38	6	32-1	94	.254
— Minnesota (A.L.)	0	1	.000	4.05	1.75	7	3	0	0	0	0-0	20.0	28	9	9	3	7-2	14	.329
1992— Pittsburgh (N.L.)	4	6	.400	4.48	1.44	55	6	0	0	5	2-4	86.1	81	46	43	9	43-8	77	.247
1993— Pittsburgh (N.L.)	3	5	.375	5.31	1.46	50	7	0	0	6	1-1	81.1	82	49	48	10	37-3	73	.258
— Buffalo (A.A.)	0	0	...	0.00	1.50	3	0	0	0	...	0-...	3.1	3	0	0	0	2-0	6	.250
1994— Pittsburgh (N.L.)	9	10	.474	5.12	1.34	24	24	2	0	0	0-0	137.0	135	80	78	18	49-3	122	.259
1995— Pittsburgh (N.L.)	13	8	.619	3.43	1.27	31	★ 31	5	1	0	0-0	• 209.2	★ 221	91	80	20	45-3	150	.273
1996— Pittsburgh (N.L.)	14	6	.700	3.05	1.20	27	27	1	0	0	0-0	182.2	186	67	62	21	34-2	131	.267
— Atlanta (N.L.)	2	3	.400	5.59	1.40	6	6	1	0	0	0-0	38.2	40	26	24	5	14-0	18	.268
1997— Atlanta (N.L.)	★ 20	5	.800	2.97	1.08	34	34	4	4	0	0-0	233.1	204	87	77	18	49-5	172	.233
1998— Atlanta (N.L.)	16	11	.593	3.55	1.22	32	31	5	2	0	0-0	210.1	196	91	83	25	60-3	165	.250
1999— Indianapolis (Int'l)	2	0	1.000	4.67	0.75	3	3	0	0	...	0-...	17.1	11	9	9	2	2-0	9	.177
— Cincinnati (N.L.)	9	5	.643	4.27	1.21	20	19	0	0	0	0-0	111.2	95	54	53	23	40-3	76	.229
2000— Cincinnati (N.L.)	8	2	.800	3.52	1.37	18	18	0	0	0	0-0	117.2	111	48	46	15	50-3	88	.247
— New York (A.L.)	7	7	.500	5.81	1.42	16	15	1	0	0	0-0	91.1	99	61	59	16	31-1	58	.278
2001— Colorado (N.L.)	9	8	.529	5.38	1.48	30	30	0	0	0	0-0	170.2	192	107	102	29	60-3	139	.284
2002— Colorado (N.L.)	8	11	.421	5.26	1.42	35	28	1	0	2	0-0	164.1	170	101	96	26	63-5	111	.266
2003— Visalia (Calif.)	1	0	1.000	0.00	0.60	2	2	0	0	0	0-...	10.0	4	0	0	0	2-0	13	.118
— Colo. Springs (PCL)	3	0	1.000	3.38	1.30	4	4	0	0	...	0-...	24.0	28	10	9	2	4-0	16	.292
— Colorado (N.L.)	2	4	.333	7.90	1.67	7	7	0	0	0	0-0	35.1	47	31	31	12	12-0	21	.320
2004— Colorado (N.L.)			Did not play.																
American League totals (2 years)	7	8	.467	5.14	1.48	23	18	1	0	0	0-0	111.1	127	70	68	19	38-3	72	.288
National League totals (12 years)	117	84	.582	4.16	1.30	369	268	19	7	13	3-5	1779.0	1760	878	823	231	556-41	1343	.258
Major League totals (13 years)	124	92	.574	4.24	1.31	392	286	20	7	13	3-5	1890.1	1887	948	891	250	594-44	1415	.260

DIVISION SERIES RECORD

Year — Team (League)	W	L	Pct.	ERA	WHIP	G	GS	CG	ShO	Hld.	Sv.-Opp.	IP	H	R	ER	HR	BB-IBB	SO	Avg.
1998— Atlanta (N.L.)			Did not play.																
2000— New York (A.L.)			Did not play.																

CHAMPIONSHIP SERIES RECORD

Year — Team (League)	W	L	Pct.	ERA	WHIP	G	GS	CG	ShO	Hld.	Sv.-Opp.	IP	H	R	ER	HR	BB-IBB	SO	Avg.
1992— Pittsburgh (N.L.)	0	0	...	27.00	4.20	2	0	0	0	0	0-0	1.2	4	5	5	0	3-1	0	.444
1996— Atlanta (N.L.)	0	0	...	2.35	0.65	2	1	0	0	0	0-0	7.2	2	2	2	0	3-0	8	.080
1997— Atlanta (N.L.)	1	0	1.000	0.00	0.50	2	1	1	1	0	0-0	12.0	5	0	0	0	1-0	9	.125
1998— Atlanta (N.L.)	0	0	...	3.52	1.30	2	1	0	0	0	0-0	7.2	8	3	3	1	2-0	9	.258
2000— New York (A.L.)	0	2	.000	4.50	1.30	2	2	0	0	0	0-0	10.0	6	5	5	1	7-0	7	.176
Champ. series totals (5 years)	1	2	.333	3.46	1.05	10	5	1	1	0	0-0	39.0	25	15	15	2	16-1	33	.180

WORLD SERIES RECORD

Year — Team (League)	W	L	Pct.	ERA	WHIP	G	GS	CG	ShO	Hld.	Sv.-Opp.	IP	H	R	ER	HR	BB-IBB	SO	Avg.
1996— Atlanta (N.L.)	0	0	...	3.00	1.50	2	1	0	0	0	0-0	6.0	5	3	2	0	4-0	3	.227
2000— New York (A.L.)	0	0	...	3.86	1.29	1	1	0	0	0	0-0	4.2	4	2	2	1	2-0	3	.222
World series totals (2 years)	0	0	...	3.38	1.41	3	2	0	0	0	0-0	10.2	9	5	4	1	6-0	6	.225

NEAL, BLAINE   P

PERSONAL: Born April 6, 1978, in Marlton, N.J. ... 6-5/248. ... Throws right, bats left. ... High school: Bishop Eustace Prep (Pennsauken, N.J.).

TRANSACTIONS/CAREER NOTES: Selected by Florida Marlins organization in fourth round of 1996 free-agent draft. ... Traded by Marlins to San Diego Padres for P Ben Howard (April 3, 2004).

CAREER HITTING: 0-for-0 (.000), 0 R, 0 2B, 0 3B, 0 HR, 0 RBI.

Year Team (League)	W	L	Pct.	ERA	WHIP	G	GS	CG	ShO	Hld.	Sv.-Opp.	IP	H	R	ER	HR	BB-IBB	SO	Avg.
1996— GC Marlins (GCL)	1	1	.500	4.60	1.30	7	5	0	0	...	1-...	29.1	32	18	15	1	6-0	15	.274
1997— GC Marlins (GCL)	4	1	.800	3.63	1.57	10	0	0	0	...	1-...	22.1	24	11	9	1	11-0	19	.267
1999— Kane County (Midwest)	4	2	.667	2.32	1.00	26	0	0	0	...	6-...	31.0	21	8	8	2	10-0	31	.200
2000— Brevard County (FSL)	2	2	.500	2.15	1.18	41	0	0	0	...	11-...	54.1	40	27	13	1	24-3	65	.200
2001— Portland (East.)	2	3	.400	2.36	1.20	54	0	0	0	...	21-...	53.1	43	17	14	1	21-3	45	.218
— Florida (N.L.)	0	0	...	6.75	2.25	4	0	0	0	0	0-0	5.1	7	4	4	0	5-0	3	.304
2002— Calgary (PCL)	3	1	.750	2.90	1.35	29	0	0	0	...	11-...	31.0	27	11	10	2	15-1	26	.233
— Florida (N.L.)	3	0	1.000	2.73	1.39	32	0	0	0	2	0-0	33.0	32	12	10	1	14-2	33	.248
2003— Albuquerque (PCL)	3	2	.600	2.33	1.50	40	0	0	0	...	21-...	46.1	55	22	12	1	16-2	32	.304
— Florida (N.L.)	0	0	...	8.14	2.24	18	0	0	0	2	0-0	21.0	38	20	19	2	9-1	10	.413
2004— Portland (PCL)	4	2	.667	1.86	1.14	27	0	0	0	...	1-...	38.2	32	10	8	0	12-2	38	.225
— San Diego (N.L.)	1	1	.500	4.07	1.43	40	0	0	0	3	0-2	42.0	49	19	19	6	11-3	36	.295
Major League totals (4 years)	**4**	**1**	**.800**	**4.62**	**1.63**	**94**	**0**	**0**	**0**	**7**	**0-2**	**101.1**	**126**	**55**	**52**	**9**	**39-6**	**82**	**.307**

NELSON, JEFF   P

PERSONAL: Born November 17, 1966, in Baltimore, Md. ... 6-8/225. ... Throws right, bats right. ... Full name: Jeffrey Allan Nelson. ... High school: Catonsville (Md.). ... Junior college: Catonsville (Md.) Community College.

TRANSACTIONS/CAREER NOTES: Selected by Los Angeles Dodgers organization in 22nd round of June 1984 free-agent draft. ... Selected by Seattle Mariners organization from Dodgers organization in Rule 5 minor league draft (December 9, 1986). ... On disabled list (July 16, 1989-remainder of season). ... Traded by Mariners with 1B Tino Martinez and P Jim Mecir to New York Yankees for P Sterling Hitchcock and 3B Russ Davis (December 7, 1995). ... On suspended list (September 3-5, 1996; and May 28-29, 1998). ... On disabled list (June 26-September 4, 1998); included rehabilitation assignment to Tampa. ... On disabled list (May 3-20 and June 3-August 11, 1999); included rehabilitation assignments to GCL Yankees and Tampa. ... Signed as a free agent by Mariners (December 4, 2000). ... On disabled list (May 8-June 27, 2002); included rehabilitation assignment to Everett. ... Traded by Mariners to Yankees for P Armando Benitez (August 6, 2003). ... Signed as a free agent by Texas Rangers (January 14, 2004). ... On disabled list (May 13-July 26 and August 1-September 1, 2004); included rehabilitation assignments to Frisco and Oklahoma.

CAREER HITTING: 0-for-2 (.000), 0 R, 0 2B, 0 3B, 0 HR, 0 RBI.

Year Team (League)	W	L	Pct.	ERA	WHIP	G	GS	CG	ShO	Hld.	Sv.-Opp.	IP	H	R	ER	HR	BB-IBB	SO	Avg.
1984— Great Falls (Pio.)	0	0	...	54.00	9.00	1	0	0	0	...	0-...	.2	3	4	4	1	3-0	1	...
— GC Dodgers (GCL)	0	0	...	1.35	0.90	9	0	0	0	...	0-...	13.1	6	3	2	0	6-0	7	.122
1985— GC Dodgers (GCL)	0	5	.000	5.51	2.20	14	7	0	0	...	0-...	47.1	72	50	29	1	32-0	31	.344
1986— Bakersfield (California)	0	7	.000	6.69	2.29	24	11	0	0	...	0-...	71.1	79	83	53	9	84-1	37	.252
— Great Falls (Pio.)	0	0	...	13.50	4.00	3	0	0	0	...	0-...	2.0	5	3	3	0	3-2	1	...
1987— Salinas (Calif.)	3	7	.300	5.74	1.89	17	16	1	0	...	0-...	80.0	80	61	51	2	71-0	43	.261
1988— San Bernardino (Calif.)	8	9	.471	5.54	1.70	27	27	1	1	...	0-...	149.1	163	115	92	9	91-2	94	.287
1989— Williamsport (Eastern)	7	5	.583	3.31	1.35	15	15	2	0	...	0-...	92.1	72	41	34	2	53-1	61	.217
1990— Williamsport (Eastern)	1	4	.200	6.44	1.92	10	10	0	0	...	0-...	43.1	65	35	31	2	18-1	14	.359
— Peninsula (Caro.)	2	2	.500	3.15	1.20	18	7	1	1	...	6-...	60.0	47	21	21	5	25-1	49	.214
1991— Jacksonville (Southern)	4	0	1.000	1.27	1.13	21	0	0	0	...	12-...	28.1	23	5	4	0	9-0	34	.225
— Calgary (PCL)	3	4	.429	3.90	1.67	28	0	0	0	...	21-...	32.1	39	19	14	1	15-3	26	.310
1992— Calgary (PCL)	1	0	1.000	0.00	0.27	2	0	0	0	...	0-...	3.2	0	0	0	0	1-0	0	.000
— Seattle (A.L.)	1	7	.125	3.44	1.42	66	0	0	0	6	6-14	81.0	71	34	31	7	44-12	46	.245
1993— Calgary (PCL)	1	0	1.000	1.17	1.04	5	0	0	0	...	1-...	7.2	6	1	1	0	2-0	6	.222
— Seattle (A.L.)	5	3	.625	4.35	1.52	71	0	0	0	17	1-11	60.0	57	30	29	5	34-10	61	.258
1994— Seattle (A.L.)	0	0	...	2.76	1.30	28	0	0	0	2	0-0	42.1	35	18	13	3	20-4	44	.226
— Calgary (PCL)	1	4	.200	2.84	1.11	18	0	0	0	...	8-...	25.1	21	9	8	1	7-1	30	.236
1995— Seattle (A.L.)	7	3	.700	2.17	1.08	62	0	0	0	14	2-4	78.2	58	21	19	4	27-5	96	.209
1996— New York (A.L.)	4	4	.500	4.36	1.49	73	0	0	0	10	2-4	74.1	75	38	36	6	36-1	91	.262
1997— New York (A.L.)	3	7	.300	2.86	1.14	77	0	0	0	22	2-8	78.2	53	32	25	7	37-12	81	.191
1998— New York (A.L.)	5	3	.625	3.79	1.64	45	0	0	0	10	3-6	40.1	44	18	17	1	22-4	35	.278
— Tampa (FSL)	0	0	...	0.00	1.00	2	0	0	0	...	0-...	2.0	1	1	0	0	1-0	4	.143
1999— New York (A.L.)	2	1	.667	4.15	1.62	39	0	0	0	10	1-2	30.1	27	14	14	2	22-2	35	.245
— GC Yankees (GCL)	0	0	...	0.00	1.00	2	2	0	0	...	0-...	2.0	1	0	0	0	1-0	3	.143
— Tampa (FSL)	0	0	...	0.00	1.00	3	3	0	0	...	0-...	3.0	1	0	0	0	2-0	5	.100
2000— New York (A.L.)	8	4	.667	2.45	1.28	73	0	0	0	15	0-4	69.2	44	24	19	2	45-1	71	.183
2001— Seattle (A.L.)	4	3	.571	2.76	1.13	69	0	0	0	26	4-5	65.1	30	21	20	3	44-1	88	.136
2002— Seattle (A.L.)	3	2	.600	3.94	1.38	41	0	0	0	12	2-4	45.2	36	20	20	4	27-3	55	.221
— Everett (Northwest)	0	1	.000	0.00	0.75	1	1	0	0	...	0-...	1.1	1	0	0	0	0-0	4	.200
2003— Seattle (A.L.)	3	2	.600	3.35	1.27	46	0	0	0	6	7-11	37.2	34	16	14	3	14-1	47	.248
— New York (A.L.)	1	0	1.000	4.58	1.53	24	0	0	0	8	1-3	17.2	17	9	9	1	10-2	21	.246
2004— Oklahoma (PCL)	0	1	.000	16.20	1.80	2	2	0	0	...	0-...	1.2	3	3	3	0	0-0	3	.375
— Frisco (Texas)	0	0	...	2.46	0.82	3	3	0	0	...	0-...	3.2	2	1	1	0	1-0	3	.154
— Texas (A.L.)	1	2	.333	5.32	1.52	29	0	0	0	9	1-1	23.2	17	16	14	3	19-0	22	.207
Major League totals (13 years)	**47**	**41**	**.534**	**3.38**	**1.34**	**743**	**0**	**0**	**0**	**167**	**32-77**	**745.1**	**598**	**311**	**280**	**51**	**401-58**	**793**	**.223**

DIVISION SERIES RECORD

Year Team (League)	W	L	Pct.	ERA	WHIP	G	GS	CG	ShO	Hld.	Sv.-Opp.	IP	H	R	ER	HR	BB-IBB	SO	Avg.
1995— Seattle (A.L.)	0	1	.000	3.18	1.76	3	0	0	0	...	0-0	5.2	7	2	2	0	3-0	7	.304
1996— New York (A.L.)	1	0	1.000	0.00	1.09	2	0	0	0	...	0-0	3.2	2	0	0	0	2-1	5	.154
1997— New York (A.L.)	0	0	...	0.00	1.50	4	0	0	0	2	0-0	4.0	4	0	0	0	2-0	5	.267
1998— New York (A.L.)	0	0	...	0.00	1.13	2	0	0	0	1	0-0	2.2	2	0	0	0	1-0	3	.222
1999— New York (A.L.)	0	0	...	0.00	1.20	3	0	0	0	1	0-0	1.2	1	0	0	0	1-0	2	.167
2000— New York (A.L.)	0	0	...	0.00	0.00	2	0	0	0	1	0-0	2.0	0	0	0	0	0-0	2	.000
2001— Seattle (A.L.)	0	0	...	0.00	0.67	3	0	0	0	2	0-0	3.0	1	0	0	0	1-0	5	.100
2003— New York (A.L.)	0	0	...	...	...	1	0	0	0	0	0-0	.0	0	0	0	0	1-0	0	...
Division series totals (8 years)	**1**	**1**	**.500**	**0.79**	**1.24**	**20**	**0**	**0**	**0**	**7**	**0-0**	**22.2**	**17**	**2**	**2**	**0**	**11-1**	**24**	**.207**

CHAMPIONSHIP SERIES RECORD

Year Team (League)	W	L	Pct.	ERA	WHIP	G	GS	CG	ShO	Hld.	Sv.-Opp.	IP	H	R	ER	HR	BB-IBB	SO	Avg.
1995— Seattle (A.L.)	0	0	...	0.00	2.67	3	0	0	0	1	0-0	3.0	3	0	0	0	5-1	3	.333
1996— New York (A.L.)	0	1	.000	11.57	2.14	2	0	0	0	0	0-0	2.1	5	3	3	1	0-0	2	.385
1998— New York (A.L.)	0	1	.000	20.25	3.00	3	0	0	0	0	0-0	1.1	3	3	3	0	1-0	3	.429
1999— New York (A.L.)	0	0	...	0.00	0.00	2	0	0	0	2	0-0	.2	0	0	0	0	0-0	0	.000
2000— New York (A.L.)	0	0	...	9.00	1.67	3	0	0	0	1	0-0	3.0	5	3	3	2	0-0	6	.357
2001— Seattle (A.L.)	0	0	...	0.00	0.86	2	0	0	0	0	0-0	2.1	1	0	0	0	1-0	5	.143
2003— New York (A.L.)	0	0	...	6.00	1.33	4	0	0	0	0	0-0	3.0	4	2	2	0	0-0	3	.364
Champ. series totals (7 years)	**0**	**2**	**.000**	**6.32**	**1.79**	**19**	**0**	**0**	**0**	**4**	**0-0**	**15.2**	**21**	**11**	**11**	**3**	**7-1**	**20**	**.339**

WORLD SERIES RECORD

Year Team (League)	W	L	Pct.	ERA	WHIP	G	GS	CG	ShO	Hld.	Sv.-Opp.	IP	H	R	ER	HR	BB-IBB	SO	Avg.
1996— New York (A.L.)	0	0	...	0.00	0.46	3	0	0	0	0	0-0	4.1	1	0	0	0	1-0	5	.071
1998— New York (A.L.)	0	0	...	0.00	1.29	3	0	0	0	1	0-0	2.1	2	1	0	0	1-0	4	.222
1999— New York (A.L.)	0	0	...	0.00	1.13	4	0	0	0	1	0-0	2.2	2	0	0	0	1-0	3	.200
2000— New York (A.L.)	1	0	1.000	10.13	2.25	3	0	0	0	1	0-0	2.2	5	3	3	1	1-0	1	.417
2003— New York (A.L.)	0	0	...	0.00	1.50	3	0	0	0	0	0-0	4.0	4	0	0	0	2-0	5	.267
World series totals (5 years)	**1**	**0**	**1.000**	**1.69**	**1.25**	**16**	**0**	**0**	**0**	**3**	**0-0**	**16.0**	**14**	**4**	**3**	**1**	**6-0**	**18**	**.233**

ALL-STAR GAME RECORD

	W	L	Pct.	ERA	WHIP	G	GS	CG	ShO	Hld.	Sv.-Opp.	IP	H	R	ER	HR	BB-IBB	SO	Avg.
All-Star Game totals (1 year)	0	0	...	0.00	1.00	1	0	0	0	1	0-0	1.0	0	0	0	0	1-0	1	.000

NELSON, JOE — P

PERSONAL: Born October 25, 1974, in Alameda, Calif. ... 6-2/185. ... Throws right, bats right. ... Full name: Joseph Georrge Nelson. ... College: San Francisco.
TRANSACTIONS/CAREER NOTES: Selected by Atlanta Braves organization in fourth round of 1996 free-agent draft. ... On disabled list (June 19, 2001-remainder of season). ... Signed by Boston Red Sox organization (August 11, 2002).
CAREER HITTING: 0-for-0 (.000), 0 R, 0 2B, 0 3B, 0 HR, 0 RBI.

Year Team (League)	W	L	Pct.	ERA	WHIP	G	GS	CG	ShO	Hld.	Sv.-Opp.	IP	H	R	ER	HR	BB-IBB	SO	Avg.
1996— Eugene (N'west)	5	3	.625	4.37	1.40	14	13	0	0	...	0-...	70.0	69	43	34	5	29-1	67	.255
1997— Durham (Caro.)	10	6	.625	4.76	1.40	25	24	0	0	...	0-...	124.2	114	74	66	17	61-1	99	.247
1998— Greenville (Sou.)	6	9	.400	4.98	1.78	45	12	1	1	...	2-...	108.1	124	76	60	9	69-2	74	.295
1999— Greenville (Sou.)	1	1	.500	2.37	1.09	25	0	0	0	...	8-...	30.1	19	15	8	2	14-2	37	.173
— Richmond (Int'l)	2	3	.400	4.54	1.43	12	3	0	0	...	1-...	33.2	33	18	17	2	15-0	31	.254
2000— GC Braves (GCL)	1	0	1.000	2.25	1.50	4	0	0	0	...	1-...	4.0	3	1	1	0	3-0	7	.088
— Jamestown (N.Y.-Penn.)	0	0	...	2.25	1.00	3	0	0	0	...	0-...	4.0	3	3	1	0	1-0	7	.200
2001— Richmond (Int'l)	1	2	.333	1.13	0.93	29	0	0	0	...	8-...	39.2	23	5	5	1	14-2	40	.172
— Atlanta (N.L.)	0	0	...	36.00	4.50	2	0	0	0	0	0-0	2.0	7	9	8	1	2-0	0	.583
2002— Trenton (East.)	0	0	...	14.54	2.54	4	0	0	0	...	0-...	4.1	9	8	7	1	2-0	3	.409
2004— Portland (East.)	3	2	.600	1.78	1.02	25	0	0	0	...	13-...	30.1	16	8	6	1	15-0	49	.152
— Boston (A.L.)	0	0	...	16.88	2.63	3	0	0	0	0	0-0	2.2	4	5	5	0	3-0	5	.364
— Pawtucket (Int'l)	0	0	...	4.64	1.69	16	0	0	0	...	0-...	21.1	27	14	11	1	9-0	31	.307
American League totals (1 year)	0	0	...	16.88	2.63	3	0	0	0	0	0-0	2.2	4	5	5	0	3-0	5	.364
National League totals (1 year)	0	0	...	36.00	4.50	2	0	0	0	0	0-0	2.0	7	9	8	1	2-0	0	.583
Major League totals (2 years)	0	0	...	25.07	3.43	5	0	0	0	0	0-0	4.2	11	14	13	1	5-0	5	.478

NEU, MIKE — P

PERSONAL: Born March 9, 1978, in Napa, Calif. ... 5-10/175. ... Throws right, bats both. ... Full name: Michael Neu. ... Name pronounced: new. ... College: Miami (Fla.).
TRANSACTIONS/CAREER NOTES: Selected by Cincinnati Reds organization in 29th round of 1999 free-agent draft. ... Selected by Oakland Athletics fromReds organization in Rule 5 major league draft (December 16, 2002). ... Traded by A's with P Bill Murphy to Florida Marlins for P Mark Redman (December 16, 2003).
CAREER HITTING: 0-for-0 (.000), 0 R, 0 2B, 0 3B, 0 HR, 0 RBI.

Year Team (League)	W	L	Pct.	ERA	WHIP	G	GS	CG	ShO	Hld.	Sv.-Opp.	IP	H	R	ER	HR	BB-IBB	SO	Avg.
1999— Rockford (Midwest)	0	1	.000	4.50	1.61	9	0	0	0	...	1-...	18.0	17	10	9	1	12-1	23	.246
2000— Clinton (Midw.)	7	7	.500	3.13	1.43	58	0	0	0	...	24-...	69.0	47	27	24	5	52-8	95	.191
2001— Mudville (Calif.)	3	2	.600	2.37	1.24	53	0	0	0	...	21-...	64.2	50	21	17	3	30-4	102	.209
2002— Chattanooga (Southern)	1	0	1.000	1.33	1.15	21	0	0	0	...	7-...	27.0	22	4	4	0	9-1	38	.218
— Louisville (Int'l)	2	3	.400	4.02	1.31	40	0	0	0	...	16-...	40.1	35	19	18	4	18-0	47	.232
2003— Oakland (A.L.)	0	0	...	3.64	1.64	32	0	0	0	0	1-1	42.0	43	18	17	2	26-2	20	.261
2004— Florida (N.L.)	0	0	...	4.50	1.75	1	0	0	0	0	0-0	4.0	5	2	2	1	2-0	5	.313
— Albuquerque (PCL)	1	2	.333	6.34	1.85	35	0	0	0	...	6-...	38.1	47	33	27	2	24-1	28	.303
American League totals (1 year)	0	0	...	3.64	1.64	32	0	0	0	0	1-1	42.0	43	18	17	2	26-2	20	.261
National League totals (1 year)	0	0	...	4.50	1.75	1	0	0	0	0	0-0	4.0	5	2	2	1	2-0	5	.313
Major League totals (2 years)	0	0	...	3.72	1.65	33	0	0	0	0	1-1	46.0	48	20	19	3	28-2	22	.265

NEVIN, PHIL — 1B

PERSONAL: Born January 19, 1971, in Fullerton, Calif. ... 6-2/231. ... Bats right, throws right. ... Full name: Phillip Joseph Nevin. ... High school: El Dorado (Placentia, Calif.). ... College: Cal State Fullerton.
TRANSACTIONS/CAREER NOTES: Selected by Los Angeles Dodgers organization in third round of 1989 free-agent draft; did not sign. ... Selected by Houston Astros organization in first round (first pick overall) of 1992 free-agent draft. ... Traded by Astros to Detroit Tigers (August 15, 1995), completing deal in which Tigers traded P Mike Henneman to Astros for a player to be named (August 10, 1995). ... On disabled list (March 21-April 16, 1997); included rehabilitation assignment to Lakeland. ... Traded by Tigers with C Matt Walbeck to Anaheim Angels for P Nick Skuse (November 20, 1997). ... On suspended list (June 12-15, 1998). ... Traded by Angels with P Keith Volkman to San Diego Padres for IF Andy Sheets and OF Gus Kennedy (March 29, 1999). ... On disabled list (April 1-16, 1999); included rehabilitaion assignment to Las Vegas. ... On disabled list (May 12-27 and May 30-July 12, 2002); included rehabilitation assignment to Lake Elsinore. ... On disabled list (March 25-July 23, 2003); included rehabilitation assignments to Lake Elsinore and Portland. ... On disabled list (July 5-21, 2004).
2004 GAMES PLAYED BY POSITION (MLB): 1B—144, DH—2, C—1.

Year Team (League)	Pos.	G	AB	R	H	2B	3B	HR	RBI	BB	SO	HBP	GDP	SB-CS	Avg.	OBP	SLG	OPS	E	Avg.
1993— Tucson (PCL)	3B-OF	123	448	67	128	21	3	10	93	52	99	3	12	8-1	.286	.359	.413	.772	29	.898
1994— Tucson (PCL)	3B-OF	118	445	67	117	20	1	12	79	55	101	4	21	3-2	.263	.343	.393	.736	32	.907
1995— Tucson (PCL)	3B-DH	62	223	31	65	16	0	7	41	27	39	1	9	2-3	.291	.371	.457	.828	14	.923
— Houston (N.L.)	3B	18	60	4	7	1	0	0	1	7	13	1	2	1-0	.117	.221	.133	.354	3	.933

Year	Team (League)	Pos.	G	AB	R	H	2B	3B	HR	RBI	BB	SO	HBP	GDP	SB-CS	Avg.	OBP	SLG	OPS	E	Avg.
	— Toledo (Int'l)	OF-DH	7	23	3	7	2	0	1	3	1	5	0	2	0-0	.304	.333	.522	.855	0	1.000
	— Detroit (A.L.)	OF-DH	29	96	9	21	3	1	2	12	11	27	3	3	0-0	.219	.318	.333	.652	2	.963
1996—	Jacksonville (Sou.)	C-DH-3-O-1	98	344	77	101	18	1	24	69	60	83	3	9	6-2	.294	.397	.561	.958	11	.977
	— Detroit (A.L.)	3B-OF-C-DH	38	120	15	35	5	0	8	19	8	39	1	1	1-0	.292	.338	.533	.872	5	.951
1997—	Lakeland (Fla. St.)	3B-DH-1B	3	9	3	5	1	0	1	4	3	2	0	0	0-0	.556	.667	1.000	1.667	1	.929
	— Lakeland (Fla. St.)	3B-DH-1B	3	19	1	3	1	0	1	3	2	1	0	1	0-0	.158	.238	.316	.554	0	1.000
	— Toledo (Int'l)	1B-3B-DH	5	19	1	3	1	0	1	3	2	1	0	1	0-0	.158	.238	.316	.554	0	1.000
	— Detroit (A.L.)	O-DH-3-1-C	93	251	32	59	16	1	9	35	25	68	1	5	0-1	.235	.306	.414	.720	2	.982
1998—	Anaheim (A.L.)	C-DH-1B	75	237	27	54	8	1	8	27	17	67	5	6	0-0	.228	.291	.371	.663	5	.989
1999—	Las Vegas (PCL)	C-3B-1B	3	10	2	2	0	0	2	2	0	2	1	1	0-0	.200	.200	1.000	1.000	0	1.000
	— San Diego (N.L.)	3-C-O-1-DH	128	383	52	103	27	0	24	85	51	82	1	7	1-0	.269	.352	.527	.880	5	.989
2000—	San Diego (N.L.)	3B	143	538	87	163	34	1	31	107	59	121	4	17	2-0	.303	.374	.543	.916	* 26	.929
2001—	San Diego (N.L.)	3B-DH	149	546	97	167	31	0	41	126	71	147	4	13	4-4	.306	.388	.588	.976	27	.930
2002—	San Diego (N.L.)	3B-1B	107	407	53	116	16	0	12	57	38	87	1	12	4-0	.285	.344	.413	.757	18	.963
	— Lake Elsinore (Calif.)	3B	2	6	2	2	1	0	1	6	1	2	0	0	0-0	.333	.375	1.000	1.375	2	.000
2003—	Lake Elsinore (Calif.)	DH	5	15	1	4	1	0	0	5	2	2	0	1	0-0	.267	.300	.333	.633	0	.000
	— Portland (PCL) DH-1B-OF		6	18	0	2	0	0	0	1	1	1	0	2	0-0	.111	.158	.111	.269	0	1.000
	— San Diego (N.L.)	1B-OF	59	226	30	63	8	0	13	46	21	44	0	9	2-0	.279	.339	.487	.825	2	.994
2004—	San Diego (N.L.)	1B-DH-C	147	547	78	158	31	1	26	105	66	121	5	16	0-0	.289	.368	.492	.859	13	.990
	American League totals (4 years)		235	704	83	169	32	3	27	93	61	201	10	15	1-1	.240	.308	.409	.717	14	.980
	National League totals (7 years)		751	2707	401	777	148	2	147	527	313	615	16	76	14-4	.287	.362	.506	.868	94	.971
	Major League totals (10 years)		986	3411	484	946	180	5	174	620	374	816	26	91	15-5	.277	.351	.486	.837	108	.973

ALL-STAR GAME RECORD

	G	AB	R	H	2B	3B	HR	RBI	BB	SO	HBP	GDP	SB-CS	Avg.	OBP	SLG	OPS	E	Avg.
All-Star Game totals (1 year)	1	1	0	0	0	0	0	0	0	0	0	0	0-0	.000	.000	.000	.000	0	...

NEWHAN, DAVID   3B

PERSONAL: Born September 7, 1973, in Fullerton, Calif. ... 5-10/180. ... Bats left, throws right. ... Full name: David Matthew Newhan. ... High school: Esperanza (Calif.). ... College: Pepperdine.

TRANSACTIONS/CAREER NOTES: Selected by Oakland Athletics organization in 17th round of 1995 free-agent draft. ... Traded by A's with P Don Wengert to San Diego Padres for P Doug Bochtler and SS Jorge Velandia (December 15, 1997). ... Traded by Padres to Philadelphia Phillies (August 7, 2000), completing deal in which Phillies traded SS Desi Relaford to Padres for a player to be named (August 4, 2000). ... On disabled list (April 15, 2001-remainder of season); included rehabilitation assignments to Scranton/Wilkes-Barre. ... Signed as a free agent by Los Angeles Dodgers organization (February 5, 2002). ... Signed as a free agent by Colorado Rockies organization (May 8, 2003). ... Signed as a free agent by Texas Rangers organization (November 10, 2003). ... Released by Rangers (June 17, 2004) ... Signed by Baltimore Orioles (June 18, 2004).

2004 GAMES PLAYED BY POSITION (MLB): OF—42, DH—32, 3B—17, 1B—2.

								BATTING											FIELDING	
Year	Team (League)	Pos.	G	AB	R	H	2B	3B	HR	RBI	BB	SO	HBP	GDP	SB-CS	Avg.	OBP	SLG	OPS	E	Avg.
1995—	S. Oregon (N'west)	OF	42	145	25	39	8	1	6	21	29	30	1	2	10-5	.269	.388	.462	.850	2	.964
	— W. Mich. (Mid.)	OF	25	96	9	21	5	0	3	8	13	26	1	2	3-2	.219	.315	.365	.680	1	.976
1996—	Modesto (California)	OF	117	455	96	137	27	3	25	75	62	106	2	8	17-8	.301	.386	.538	.924	5	.964
1997—	Visalia (Calif.)	2B	67	241	52	67	15	2	7	48	44	58	3	5	9-3	.278	.389	.444	.833	10	.966
	— Huntsville (Sou.)	2B	57	212	40	67	13	2	5	35	28	59	2	4	5-5	.316	.398	.467	.865	14	.934
1998—	Mobile (Sou.)	2B-3B-SS	121	491	89	128	26	3	12	45	68	110	2	8	27-8	.261	.352	.399	.751	14	.975
1999—	Las Vegas (PCL)	2B-SS	98	374	49	107	25	1	14	49	30	84	2	8	22-4	.286	.342	.471	.812	20	.952
	— San Diego (N.L.)	2B-3B-1B	32	43	7	6	1	0	2	6	1	11	0	0	0-0	.140	.159	.302	.461	2	.970
2000—	San Diego (N.L.)	OF-2B-3B	14	20	5	3	1	0	1	2	6	7	0	0	0-0	.150	.350	.350	.696	0	1.000
	— Las Vegas (PCL)	2B-OF	66	244	41	62	5	2	5	35	37	61	0	4	9-3	.254	.351	.352	.704	7	.975
	— Scran./W.B. (I.L.)	2B	25	83	10	21	3	0	3	8	11	15	0	0	3-1	.253	.337	.398	.734	1	.991
	— Philadelphia (N.L.)	2B	10	17	3	3	0	0	2	6	2	2	0	2	0-0	.176	.263	.176	.440	0	1.000
2001—	Philadelphia (N.L.)	2B	7	6	2	2	1	0	0	1	1	0	0	0	0-0	.333	.375	.500	.875	0	.000
	— Scran./W.B. (I.L.)	2B	13	55	4	6	1	0	0	2	4	11	1	1	0-0	.109	.183	.127	.311	1	.969
2003—	Colo. Springs (PCL)	2-1-O-DH	72	244	43	85	17	2	3	28	16	36	2	6	6-4	.348	.392	.471	.863	14	.959
2004—	Oklahoma (PCL)	2-DH-3-1	61	262	57	86	21	6	9	38	26	55	1	3	10-0	.328	.387	.557	.944	10	.967
	— Baltimore (A.L.)	O-DH-3-1	95	373	66	116	15	7	8	54	27	72	4	4	11-1	.311	.361	.453	.814	5	.960
	American League totals (1 year)		95	373	66	116	15	7	8	54	27	72	4	4	11-1	.311	.361	.453	.814	5	.960
	National League totals (3 years)		63	86	17	14	3	0	3	9	10	24	0	2	2-1	.163	.247	.302	.550	2	.981
	Major League totals (4 years)		158	459	83	130	18	7	11	63	37	96	4	6	13-2	.283	.339	.425	.764	7	.970

NITKOWSKI, C.J.   P

PERSONAL: Born March 9, 1973, in Suffern, N.Y. ... 6-3/200. ... Throws left, bats left. ... Full name: Christopher John Nitkowski. ... Name pronounced: nit-COW-ski. ... High school: Don Bosco (N.J.). ... College: St. John's.

TRANSACTIONS/CAREER NOTES: Selected by Cincinnati Reds organization in first round (ninth pick overall) of 1994 free-agent draft. ... Traded by Reds with P David Tuttle and a player to be named to Detroit Tigers for P David Wells (July 31, 1995); Tigers acquired IF Mark Lewis to complete deal (November 16, 1995). ... On disabled list (August 11-29, 1996). ... Traded by Tigers with C Brad Ausmus, Ps Jose Lima and Trever Miller and 1B Daryle Ward to Houston Astros for OF Brian Hunter, IF Orlando Miller, Ps Doug Brocail and P Todd Jones and cash (December 10, 1996). ... Traded by Astros with C Brad Ausmus to Tigers for C Paul Bako, Ps Dean Crow, Mark Persails and Brian Powell and 3B Carlos Villalobos (January 14, 1999). ... On suspended list (May 28-30, 1999). ... Traded by Tigers with cash to New York Mets for a player to be named (September 1, 2001); Tigers acquired P Kyle Kessel to complete deal (December 13, 2001). ... Released by Astros (March 25, 2002). ... Re-signed by Astros organization (March 28, 2002). ... Released by Astros (June 6, 2002). ... Signed by St. Louis Cardinals organization (June 6, 2002). ... Released by Cardinals (July 21, 2002). ... Signed by Texas Rangers organization (July 29, 2002). ... Released by Rangers (September 30, 2002). ... Re-signed by Rangers organization (November 15, 2002). ... Signed as a free agent by Atlanta Braves organization (December 6, 2003). ... Released by Braves (June 22, 2004). ... Signed by New York Yankees organization (June 29, 2004).

CAREER HITTING: 2-for-15 (.133), 1 R, 0 2B, 0 3B, 0 HR, 1 RBI.

Year	Team (League)	W	L	Pct.	ERA	WHIP	G	GS	CG	ShO	Hld.	Sv.-Opp.	IP	H	R	ER	HR	BB-IBB	SO	Avg.
1994—	Chattanooga (Southern)	6	3	.667	3.50	1.35	14	14	0	0	...	0-...	74.2	61	30	29	4	40-0	60	.227
1995—	Chattanooga (Southern)	4	2	.667	2.50	1.17	8	8	0	0	...	0-...	50.1	39	20	14	1	20-0	52	.217
	— Indianapolis (A.A.)	0	2	.000	5.20	1.37	6	6	0	0	...	0-...	27.2	28	16	16	3	10-0	21	.262
	— Cincinnati (N.L.)	1	3	.250	6.12	1.73	9	7	0	0	0	0-1	32.1	41	25	22	4	15-1	18	.306
	— Detroit (A.L.)	1	4	.200	7.09	1.86	11	11	0	0	0	0-0	39.1	53	32	31	7	20-2	13	.335
1996—	Toledo (International)	4	6	.400	4.46	1.41	19	19	1	0	...	0-...	111.0	104	60	55	13	53-1	103	.254
	— Detroit (A.L.)	2	3	.400	8.08	2.19	11	8	0	0	0	0-0	45.2	62	44	41	7	38-1	36	.332

Year	Team (League)	W	L	Pct.	ERA	WHIP	G	GS	CG	ShO	Hld.	Sv.-Opp.	IP	H	R	ER	HR	BB-IBB	SO	Avg.
1997— New Orleans (A.A.)		8	10	.444	3.98	1.37	28	28	1	0	...	0-...	174.1	183	82	77	10	56-2	141	.276
1998— Houston (N.L.)		3	3	.500	3.77	1.21	43	0	0	0	8	3-5	59.2	49	27	25	4	23-2	44	.228
— New Orleans (PCL)		0	1	.000	6.00	1.93	5	3	0	0	...	1-...	15.0	22	12	10	1	7-0	18	.338
1999— Detroit (A.L.)		4	5	.444	4.30	1.32	68	7	0	0	11	0-0	81.2	63	44	39	11	45-3	66	.213
2000— Detroit (A.L.)		4	9	.308	5.25	1.58	67	11	0	0	15	0-2	109.2	124	79	64	13	49-3	81	.286
2001— Detroit (A.L.)		0	3	.000	5.56	1.81	56	0	0	0	6	0-6	45.1	51	30	28	7	31-7	38	.285
— Toledo (International)		0	0	...	0.00	1.00	1	0	0	0	...	0-...	1.0	1	0	0	0	0-0	1	.250
— New York (N.L.)		1	0	1.000	0.00	1.06	5	0	0	0	0	0-...	5.2	3	0	0	0	3-1	4	.167
2002— New Orleans (PCL)		1	2	.333	2.78	1.24	24	0	0	0	...	2-...	22.2	21	7	7	1	7-1	20	.244
— Memphis (PCL)		1	2	.333	9.82	2.25	12	0	0	0	...	0-...	14.2	24	18	16	3	9-0	12	.348
— Oklahoma (PCL)		1	1	.500	1.80	1.20	9	0	0	0	...	0-...	10.0	8	3	2	0	4-0	11	.211
— Texas (A.L.)		0	1	.000	2.63	1.76	12	0	0	0	1	0-0	13.2	11	4	4	0	13-0	14	.224
2003— Texas (A.L.)		0	0	...	7.45	2.59	6	0	0	0	1	0-0	9.2	17	8	8	0	8-1	5	.415
— Oklahoma (PCL)		5	4	.556	4.09	1.50	33	6	0	0	...	2-...	81.1	88	40	37	6	31-2	53	.281
2004— Atlanta (N.L.)		1	0	1.000	4.50	1.60	22	0	0	0	...	0-0	20.0	22	11	10	3	6-0	16	.275
— Columbus (Int'l)		0	0	...	1.42	0.87	16	0	0	0	...	0-...	12.2	8	3	2	0	3-0	11	.182
— New York (A.L.)		1	1	.500	7.62	1.85	19	0	0	0	...	0-0	13.0	18	11	11	1	6-0	10	.327
American League totals (8 years)		12	26	.316	5.68	1.70	250	37	0	0	34	0-8	358.0	399	252	226	46	210-17	263	.285
National League totals (4 years)		6	6	.500	4.36	1.41	79	7	0	0	8	3-6	117.2	115	63	57	11	51-4	82	.257
Major League totals (9 years)		18	32	.360	5.35	1.63	329	44	0	0	42	3-14	475.2	514	315	283	57	261-21	345	.279

NIVAR, RAMON   OF

PERSONAL: Born February 22, 1980, in San Cristobal, Dominican Republic. ... 5-10/185. ... Bats right, throws right. ... Full name: Ramon A. Nivar.

TRANSACTIONS/CAREER NOTES: Signed as a non-drafted free agent by Texas Rangers organization (January 25, 1998).

2004 GAMES PLAYED BY POSITION (MLB): OF—6.

Year	Team (League)	Pos.	G	AB	R	H	2B	3B	HR	RBI	BB	SO	HBP	GDP	SB-CS	Avg.	OBP	SLG	OPS	E	Avg.
2000— Charlotte (Fla. St.)		SS-3B	42	152	12	44	7	1	1	20	5	28	0	2	8-3	.289	.310	.368	.679	11	.947
— Savannah (S. Atl.)		SS	39	164	19	51	9	0	1	17	2	29	3	3	6-5	.311	.331	.384	.716	15	.917
2001— Charlotte (Fla. St.)		2B-SS	128	515	69	124	20	1	2	32	28	65	5	7	28-18	.241	.286	.295	.581	29	.955
2002— Charlotte (Fla. St.)		2B-SS	114	472	98	144	21	8	3	41	32	44	6	15	39-15	.305	.353	.403	.755	10	.983
2003— Frisco (Texas)		2B-SS-OF	79	317	53	110	17	4	4	37	20	23	2	5	9-9	.347	.387	.464	.851	12	.970
— Oklahoma (PCL)		OF-2B	23	89	11	30	2	2	2	12	5	5	0	4	6-1	.337	.368	.472	.840	1	.987
— Texas (A.L.)		OF-2B	28	90	9	19	1	2	0	7	4	10	1	1	4-2	.211	.253	.267	.519	3	.961
2004— Texas (A.L.)		OF	7	18	3	4	0	0	0	4	0	7	0	0	1-1	.222	.211	.222	.433	0	1.000
— Oklahoma (PCL)		OF-2B-DH	113	462	62	122	21	0	10	52	14	43	4	10	15-15	.264	.290	.374	.665	5	.987
Major League totals (2 years)			35	108	12	23	1	2	0	11	4	17	1	1	5-3	.213	.246	.259	.505	3	.966

NIX, LAYNCE   OF

PERSONAL: Born October 30, 1980, in Houston, Texas. ... 6-0/200. ... Bats left, throws left. ... Full name: Layne Michael Nix. ... Name pronounced: nicks. ... High school: Midland High (Texas).

TRANSACTIONS/CAREER NOTES: Selected by Texas Rangers organization in fourth round of 2000 free-agent draft. ... On disabled list (June 14-July 10, 2004); included rehabilitation assignment to Frisco.

2004 GAMES PLAYED BY POSITION (MLB): OF—114.

Year	Team (League)	Pos.	G	AB	R	H	2B	3B	HR	RBI	BB	SO	HBP	GDP	SB-CS	Avg.	OBP	SLG	OPS	E	Avg.
2000— GC Rangers (GCL)		OF	51	199	34	45	7	1	2	25	23	37	2	3	4-2	.226	.307	.302	.609	1	.991
2001— Savannah (S. Atl.)		OF	104	407	50	113	26	8	8	59	37	94	2	7	9-6	.278	.337	.440	.777	5	.976
— Charlotte (Fla. St.)		OF	9	37	4	11	3	1	0	4	2	13	0	2	0-0	.297	.316	.432	.748	0	1.000
2002— Charlotte (Fla. St.)		OF	137	512	86	146	27	3	21	110	72	105	6	9	17-1	.285	.374	.473	.847	3	.988
2003— Frisco (Texas)		OF-DH	87	335	52	95	23	0	15	63	34	68	0	4	9-2	.284	.344	.487	.831	3	.984
— Texas (A.L.)		OF-DH	53	184	25	47	10	0	8	30	9	53	0	1	3-0	.255	.289	.440	.729	5	.963
2004— Frisco (Texas)		OF	7	26	2	7	1	0	0	2	1	10	0	1	0-1	.269	.296	.308	.604	0	1.000
— Texas (A.L.)		OF	115	371	58	92	20	4	14	46	23	113	2	6	1-1	.248	.293	.437	.730	1	.996
Major League totals (2 years)			168	555	83	139	30	4	22	76	32	166	2	7	4-1	.250	.292	.438	.730	6	.984

NIXON, TROT   OF

PERSONAL: Born April 11, 1974, in Durham, N.C. ... 6-2/211. ... Bats left, throws left. ... Full name: Christopher Trotman Nixon. ... High school: New Hanover (Wilmington, N.C.).

TRANSACTIONS/CAREER NOTES: Selected by Boston Red Sox organization in first round (seventh pick overall) of 1993 free-agent draft. ... On disabled list (June 27-July 25, 2000); included rehabilitation assignment to GCL Red Sox. ... On disabled list (March 26-June 16 and July 25-September 7, 2004); included rehabilitation assignments to Pawtucket.

2004 GAMES PLAYED BY POSITION (MLB): OF—40, DH—3.

Year	Team (League)	Pos.	G	AB	R	H	2B	3B	HR	RBI	BB	SO	HBP	GDP	SB-CS	Avg.	OBP	SLG	OPS	E	Avg.
1994— Lynchburg (Caro.)		OF	71	264	33	65	12	0	12	43	44	53	3	5	10-3	.246	.357	.428	.785	4	.974
1995— Sarasota (Fla. St.)		OF	73	264	43	80	11	4	5	39	45	46	1	5	7-5	.303	.404	.432	.836	2	.986
— Trenton (East.)		OF	25	94	9	15	3	1	2	8	7	20	0	0	2-1	.160	.214	.277	.490	0	1.000
1996— Trenton (East.)		OF-DH	123	438	55	110	11	4	11	63	50	65	3	6	7-9	.251	.329	.370	.698	5	.979
— Boston (A.L.)		OF	2	4	2	2	1	0	0	0	0	1	0	0	1-0	.500	.500	.750	1.250	0	1.000
1997— Pawtucket (Int'l)		OF	130	475	80	116	18	3	20	61	63	86	1	11	11-4	.244	.331	.421	.753	4	.986
1998— Pawtucket (Int'l)		OF-DH-1B	135	509	97	158	26	4	23	74	76	81	5	10	26-13	.310	.400	.513	.913	11	.957
— Boston (A.L.)		OF	13	27	3	7	1	0	0	1	1	3	0	0	0-0	.259	.286	.296	.582	0	1.000
1999— Boston (A.L.)		OF	124	381	67	103	22	5	15	52	53	75	3	7	3-1	.270	.357	.472	.830	1	.968
2000— Boston (A.L.)		OF-DH	123	427	66	118	27	8	12	60	63	85	2	11	8-1	.276	.368	.461	.830	2	.991
— GC Red Sox (GCL)		OF	3	10	3	4	0	0	1	5	2	0	1	0	0-0	.400	.500	.700	1.238	0	1.000
2001— Boston (A.L.)		OF-DH	148	535	100	150	31	4	27	88	79	113	7	8	7-4	.280	.376	.505	.881	3	.973
2002— Boston (A.L.)		OF	152	532	81	136	36	3	24	94	65	109	5	7	4-2	.256	.338	.470	.808	5	.984

N

Year Team (League)	Pos.	G	AB	R	H	2B	3B	HR	RBI	BB	SO	HBP	GDP	SB-CS	Avg.	OBP	SLG	OPS	E	Avg.
2003— Boston (A.L.)	OF	134	441	81	135	24	6	28	87	65	96	3	3	4-2	.306	.396	.578	.975	4	.983
2004— Sarasota (Fla. St.)	OF	1	3	1	2	1	0	0	1	0	0	0	0	0-0	.667	.667	1.000	1.667	0	—
— Pawtucket (Int'l)	OF-DH	6	21	2	7	1	0	0	2	2	3	0	0	0-0	.333	.391	.381	.772	1	.750
— Boston (A.L.)	OF-DH	48	149	24	47	9	1	6	23	15	24	1	3	0-0	.315	.377	.510	.887	1	.985
Major League totals (8 years)		744	2496	424	698	151	27	112	404	341	506	21	39	27-10	.280	.367	.496	.863	27	.980

DIVISION SERIES RECORD

Year Team (League)	Pos.	G	AB	R	H	2B	3B	HR	RBI	BB	SO	HBP	GDP	SB-CS	Avg.	OBP	SLG	OPS	E	Avg.
1998— Boston (A.L.)	OF	2	3	0	1	0	0	0	0	1	0	0	0	0-0	.333	.500	.333	.833	0	1.000
1999— Boston (A.L.)	OF	5	14	5	3	3	0	0	6	4	5	0	0	0-0	.214	.350	.429	.779	0	1.000
2003— Boston (A.L.)	OF	4	10	1	2	0	0	1	2	1	3	0	0	0-0	.200	.273	.500	.773	0	1.000
2004— Boston (A.L.)	OF	2	8	0	2	0	0	0	2	1	1	0	1	0-0	.250	.400	.250	.650	0	1.000
Division series totals (4 years)		13	35	6	8	3	0	1	10	8	9	0	1	0-0	.229	.356	.400	.756	0	1.000

CHAMPIONSHIP SERIES RECORD

Year Team (League)	Pos.	G	AB	R	H	2B	3B	HR	RBI	BB	SO	HBP	GDP	SB-CS	Avg.	OBP	SLG	OPS	E	Avg.
1999— Boston (A.L.)	OF	4	14	2	4	2	0	0	0	1	5	0	0	0-0	.286	.333	.429	.762	0	1.000
2003— Boston (A.L.)	OF	7	24	3	8	1	0	3	5	3	7	1	1	1-2	.333	.429	.750	1.179	0	1.000
2004— Boston (A.L.)	OF	7	29	4	6	1	0	1	3	0	5	0	0	0-0	.207	.207	.345	.552	0	1.000
Champ. series totals (3 years)		18	67	9	18	4	0	4	8	4	17	1	1	1-2	.269	.319	.507	.827	0	1.000

WORLD SERIES RECORD

Year Team (League)	Pos.	G	AB	R	H	2B	3B	HR	RBI	BB	SO	HBP	GDP	SB-CS	Avg.	OBP	SLG	OPS	E	Avg.
2004— Boston (A.L.)	OF	4	14	1	5	3	0	1	3	1	1	0	0	0-0	.357	.400	.571	.971	0	1.000

NOMO, HIDEO — P

PERSONAL: Born August 31, 1968, in Osaka, Japan. ... 6-2/210. ... Throws right, bats right. ... Name pronounced: hih-DAY-oh NO-mo. ... High school: Seijyo Kogyo (Japan).

TRANSACTIONS/CAREER NOTES: Signed as free agent by Los Angeles Dodgers organization (February 8, 1995). ... Loaned by Dodgers organization to Bakersfield (April 27-May 1, 1995). ... Traded by Dodgers with P Brad Clontz to New York Mets for Ps Dave Mlicki and Greg McMichael (June 4, 1998). ... Released by Mets (March 26, 1999). ... Signed by Chicago Cubs organization (April 2, 1999). ... Released by Cubs (April 23, 1999). ... Signed by Milwaukee Brewers organization (April 29, 1999). ... Claimed on waivers by Philadelphia Phillies (October 28, 1999). ... Signed as a free agent by Detroit Tigers organization (January 21, 2000). ... On disabled list (July 30-August 18, 2000). ... Released by Tigers (November 2, 2000). ... Signed by Boston Red Sox (December 15, 2000). ... Signed as a free agent by Dodgers (December 21, 2001). ... On disabled list (May 20-June 8 and July 1-September 1, 2004); included rehabilitation assignments to Las Vegas.

HONORS: Named N.L. Rookie Pitcher of the Year by THE SPORTING NEWS (1995). ... Named N.L. Rookie of the Year by Baseball Writers' Association of America (1995).

CAREER HITTING: 65-for-481 (.135), 22 R, 14 2B, 1 3B, 4 HR, 26 RBI.

Year Team (League)	W	L	Pct.	ERA	WHIP	G	GS	CG	ShO	Hld.	Sv.-Opp.	IP	H	R	ER	HR	BB-IBB	SO	Avg.
1990— Kintetsu (Jap. Pac.)	18	8	.692	2.91	1.17	29	27	21	2	...	0-...	235.0	167	...	76	...	109-...	287	...
1991— Kintetsu (Jap. Pac.)	17	11	.607	3.05	1.28	31	29	22	4	...	1-...	242.1	183	...	82	...	128-...	287	...
1992— Kintetsu (Jap. Pac.)	18	8	.692	2.66	1.23	30	29	17	5	...	0-...	216.2	150	...	64	...	117-...	228	...
1993— Kintetsu (Jap. Pac.)	17	12	.586	3.70	1.43	32	32	14	2	...	0-...	243.1	201	...	100	...	148-...	276	...
1994— Kintetsu (Jap. Pac.)	8	7	.533	3.63	0.75	17	17	6	0	...	0-...	114.0	...	...	46	...	86-...	126	...
1995— Bakersfield (California)	0	1	.000	3.38	1.31	1	1	0	0	...	0-...	5.1	6	2	2	0	1-0	6	.273
— Los Angeles (N.L.)	13	6	.684	2.54	1.06	28	28	4	•3	0	0-0	191.1	124	63	54	14	78-2	* 236	.182
1996— Los Angeles (N.L.)	16	11	.593	3.19	1.16	33	33	3	2	0	0-0	228.1	180	93	81	23	85-6	234	.218
1997— Los Angeles (N.L.)	14	12	.538	4.25	1.37	33	33	1	0	0	0-0	207.1	193	104	98	23	92-2	233	.243
1998— Los Angeles (N.L.)	2	7	.222	5.05	1.40	12	12	0	0	0	0-0	67.2	57	39	38	8	38-0	73	.228
— New York (N.L.)	4	5	.444	4.82	1.44	17	16	1	0	0	0-0	89.2	73	49	48	11	56-2	94	.224
1999— Iowa (PCL)	1	1	.500	3.71	1.41	3	3	0	0	...	0-...	17.0	12	7	7	1	12-0	18	.200
— Huntsville (Southern)	1	0	1.000	0.00	0.86	1	1	0	0	...	0-...	7.0	5	0	0	0	1-0	7	.217
— Milwaukee (N.L.)	12	8	.600	4.54	1.42	28	28	0	0	0	0-0	176.1	173	96	89	27	78-2	161	.250
2000— Detroit (A.L.)	8	12	.400	4.74	1.47	32	31	0	0	0	0-0	190.0	191	102	100	31	89-1	181	.263
2001— Boston (A.L.)	13	10	.565	4.50	1.35	33	33	2	2	0	0-0	198.0	171	105	99	26	* 96-2	* 220	.231
2002— Los Angeles (N.L.)	16	6	.727	3.39	1.32	34	34	0	0	0	0-0	220.1	189	92	83	26	101-5	193	.236
2003— Los Angeles (N.L.)	16	13	.552	3.09	1.25	33	33	2	2	0	0-0	218.1	175	82	75	24	98-6	177	.223
2004— Las Vegas (PCL)	1	1	.500	5.71	1.73	4	4	0	0	...	0-...	17.1	22	11	11	4	8-0	25	.324
— Los Angeles (N.L.)	4	11	.267	8.25	1.75	18	18	0	0	0	0-0	84.0	105	77	77	19	42-1	54	.312
American League totals (2 years)	21	22	.488	4.62	1.41	65	64	3	2	0	0-0	388.0	362	207	199	57	185-3	401	.247
National League totals (8 years)	97	79	.551	3.90	1.31	236	235	13	7	0	0-0	1483.1	1269	695	643	175	668-26	1455	.232
Major League totals (10 years)	118	101	.539	4.05	1.33	301	299	16	9	0	0-0	1871.1	1631	902	842	232	853-29	1856	.235

DIVISION SERIES RECORD

Year Team (League)	W	L	Pct.	ERA	WHIP	G	GS	CG	ShO	Hld.	Sv.-Opp.	IP	H	R	ER	HR	BB-IBB	SO	Avg.
1995— Los Angeles (N.L.)	0	1	.000	9.00	1.80	1	1	0	0	0	0-0	5.0	7	5	5	2	2-1	6	.318
1996— Los Angeles (N.L.)	0	1	.000	12.27	2.73	1	1	0	0	0	0-0	3.2	5	5	5	1	5-0	3	.333
Division series totals (2 years)	0	2	.000	10.38	2.19	2	2	0	0	0	0-0	8.2	12	10	10	3	7-1	9	.324

ALL-STAR GAME RECORD

Year Team (League)	W	L	Pct.	ERA	WHIP	G	GS	CG	ShO	Hld.	Sv.-Opp.	IP	H	R	ER	HR	BB-IBB	SO	Avg.
All-Star Game totals (1 year)	0	0	...	0.00	0.50	1	1	0	0	0	0-0	2.0	1	0	0	0	0-0	3	.167

NORTON, GREG — 3B/1B

PERSONAL: Born July 6, 1972, in San Leandro, Calif. ... 6-1/200. ... Bats both, throws right. ... Full name: Gregory Blakemoor Norton. ... High school: Bishop O'Dowd (Oakland). ... College: Oklahoma. ... Son of Jerry Norton, outfielder with Pittsburgh Pirates organization.

TRANSACTIONS/CAREER NOTES: Selected by San Francisco Giants organization in seventh round of 1990 free-agent draft; did not sign. ... Selected by Chicago White Sox organization in second round of 1993 free-agent draft. ... Signed as a free agent by Colorado Rockies (January 5, 2001). ... On disabled list (June 30-July 18, 2002); included rehabilitation assignment to Colorado Springs. ... Signed by Detroit Tigers organization (January 14, 2004). ... On disabled list (June 18-July 25, 2004); included rehabilitation assignment to Toledo. ... Refused minor league assignment and became a free agent (October 4, 2004).

2004 GAMES PLAYED BY POSITION (MLB): 3B—18, DH—7, 1B—7, OF—6.

Year Team (League)	Pos.	G	AB	R	H	2B	3B	HR	RBI	BB	SO	HBP	GDP	SB-CS	Avg.	OBP	SLG	OPS	E	Avg.
1993— GC Whi. Sox (GCL)	3B	3	9	1	2	0	0	0	2	1	1	0	0	0-0	.222	.300	.222	.522	0	1.000
— Hickory (S. Atl.)	3B-SS	71	254	36	62	12	2	4	36	41	44	1	6	0-2	.244	.347	.354	.701	17	.928

Year	Team (League)	Pos.	G	AB	R	H	2B	3B	HR	RBI	BB	SO	HBP	GDP	SB-CS	Avg.	OBP	SLG	OPS	E	Avg.
1994—South Bend (Mid.)	3B	127	477	73	137	22	2	6	64	62	71	2	7	5-3	.287	.369	.379	.749	30	.922
1995—Birmingham (Sou.)	3B	133	469	65	117	23	2	6	60	64	90	5	10	19-12	.249	.339	.345	.685	25	.938
1996—Birmingham (Sou.)	SS	76	287	40	81	14	3	8	44	33	55	1	5	5-5	.282	.357	.436	.793	17	.949
—Nashville (A.A.) SS-3B-DH	43	164	28	47	14	2	7	26	17	42	0	1	2-3	.287	.350	.524	.874	13	.914	
—Chicago (A.L.) SS-3B-DH	11	23	4	5	0	0	2	3	4	6	0	0	0-1	.217	.333	.478	.812	2	.867	
1997—Nashville (A.A.) 3-S-2-DH	114	414	82	114	27	1	26	76	57	101	4	9	3-5	.275	.366	.534	.900	38	.897	
—Chicago (A.L.)	18	34	5	9	2	2	0	1	2	8	0	0	0-0	.265	.306	.441	.747	3	.864	
1998—Chicago (A.L.) 1-3-DH-2	105	299	38	71	17	2	9	36	26	77	2	11	3-3	.237	.301	.398	.699	6	.991	
1999—Chicago (A.L.) 3B-1B-DH	132	436	62	111	26	0	16	50	69	93	2	11	4-4	.255	.358	.424	.782	§ 27	.931	
2000—Chicago (A.L.) 3B-1B-DH	71	201	25	49	6	1	6	28	26	47	2	2	1-0	.244	.333	.373	.706	8	.960	
—Charlotte (Int'l) 3B-1B-SS	29	97	18	28	4	0	5	17	24	23	2	0	1-0	.289	.435	.485	.920	1	.991	
2001—Colorado (N.L.) 0-3-1-DH	117	225	30	60	13	2	13	40	19	65	0	6	1-0	.267	.321	.516	.837	4	.968	
2002—Colorado (N.L.) 3-1-O-DH	113	168	19	37	8	1	7	37	24	52	0	4	2-3	.220	.314	.405	.719	5	.955	
—Colo. Springs (PCL)	1B-3B	3	12	2	1	0	0	0	0	3	5	0	0	0-0	.083	.267	.083	.350	0	1.000
2003—Colorado (N.L.) 3B-1B-OF	114	179	19	47	15	0	6	31	16	47	1	4	2-1	.263	.325	.447	.772	6	.941	
2004—Detroit (A.L.) 3-DH-1-O	41	86	9	15	1	0	2	2	12	21	0	3	0-0	.174	.276	.256	.531	1	.985	
—Toledo (Int'l)	3B-1B	53	184	26	38	6	1	4	16	24	48	0	4	1-1	.207	.297	.315	.612	4	.978
American League totals (6 years)		378	1079	143	260	52	5	35	120	139	252	6	27	8-8	.241	.329	.396	.725	47	.966
National League totals (3 years)		344	572	68	144	36	3	26	108	59	164	1	14	5-4	.252	.320	.462	.782	15	.955
Major League totals (9 years)		722	1651	211	404	88	8	61	228	198	416	7	41	13-12	.245	.326	.419	.745	62	.964

NORTON, PHIL   P

PERSONAL: Born February 1, 1976, in Texarkana, Texas. ... 6-0/215. ... Throws left, bats right. ... Full name: Phillip Douglas Norton. ... High school: Pleasant Grove (Texarkana, Texas). ... Junior college: Texarkana (Texas). ... College: Texarkana (Texas).

TRANSACTIONS/CAREER NOTES: Selected by Chicago Cubs organization in 10th round of 1996 free-agent draft. ... Released by Cubs (January 14, 2002). ... Re-signed by Cubs organization (March 21, 2002). ... Traded by Chicago Cubs to Cincinnati Reds for P John Koronka (August 25, 2003).

CAREER HITTING: 2-for-4 (.500), 1 R, 0 2B, 0 3B, 0 HR, 0 RBI.

Year	Team (League)	W	L	Pct.	ERA	WHIP	G	GS	CG	ShO	Hld.	Sv.-Opp.	IP	H	R	ER	HR	BB-IBB	SO	Avg.
1996—GC Cubs (GCL)	0	0	...	0.00	0.33	1	0	0	0	...	0-...	3.0	1	0	0	0	0-0	6	.100
—Williamsport (N.Y.-Penn.) .	7	4	.636	2.54	1.19	15	13	2	1	...	0-...	85.0	68	33	24	1	33-2	77	.211
1997—Rockford (Midwest)	9	3	.750	3.22	1.25	18	18	3	0	...	0-...	109.0	92	51	39	4	44-1	114	.225
—Daytona (Fla. St.)	3	2	.600	2.34	1.23	7	6	3	0	...	0-...	42.1	40	11	11	5	12-0	44	.253
—Orlando (Sou.)	1	0	1.000	2.57	1.43	2	1	0	0	...	0-...	7.0	8	2	2	0	2-1	7	.308
1998—Daytona (Fla. St.)	4	3	.571	3.27	1.26	10	10	0	0	...	0-...	66.0	57	30	24	4	26-1	54	.233
—West Tenn (Sou.)	6	6	.500	3.52	1.40	19	19	1	1	...	0-...	120.1	118	60	47	11	50-1	119	.261
1999—West Tenn (Sou.)	7	4	.636	2.39	1.32	14	13	0	0	...	0-...	86.2	72	30	23	5	42-4	81	.230
—Iowa (PCL)	5	6	.455	6.67	1.64	14	14	0	0	...	0-...	79.2	98	63	59	20	33-0	61	.305
2000—Iowa (PCL)	8	13	.381	4.96	1.69	28	26	2	1	...	0-...	159.2	166	100	88	16	104-4	126	.271
—Chicago (N.L.)	0	1	.000	9.35	2.42	2	2	0	0	...	0-0	8.2	14	10	9	5	7-0	6	.350
2001—Iowa (PCL)	6	3	.667	2.69	1.44	46	3	0	0	...	2-...	73.2	65	27	22	3	41-7	75	.251
2003—Chicago (N.L.)	0	0	...	5.40	1.50	4	0	0	0	0	0-0	3.1	2	2	2	0	3-0	0	.182
—Iowa (PCL)	4	2	.667	3.78	1.40	48	1	0	0	...	1-...	47.2	44	26	20	4	24-3	43	.242
—Cincinnati (N.L.)	0	0	...	2.45	0.89	17	0	0	0	5	0-0	14.2	7	4	4	0	6-0	7	.149
2004—Cincinnati (N.L.)	2	5	.286	5.07	1.66	69	0	0	0	9	0-2	65.2	71	41	37	5	38-7	48	.284
Major League totals (3 years)	2	6	.250	5.07	1.60	92	2	0	0	14	0-2	92.1	94	57	52	10	54-7	61	.270

NOVOA, ROBERTO   P

PERSONAL: Born August 15, 1979, in Las Matas de Farfan, Dominican Republic. ... 6-5/200. ... Throws right, bats right.

TRANSACTIONS/CAREER NOTES: Signed as a non-drafted free agent by Pittsburgh Pirates organization (July 3, 1999). ... Traded by Pirates to Detroit Tigers (December 17, 2002), as part of deal in which Pirates acquired 1B Randall Simon for P Adrian Burnside and two players to be named (November 25, 2002); Tigers acquired 3B Kody Kirkland to complete deal (May 24, 2003).

CAREER HITTING: 0-for-0 (.000), 0 R, 0 2B, 0 3B, 0 HR, 0 RBI.

Year	Team (League)	W	L	Pct.	ERA	WHIP	G	GS	CG	ShO	Hld.	Sv.-Opp.	IP	H	R	ER	HR	BB-IBB	SO	Avg.
2001—Williamsport (N.Y.-Penn.) .	5	5	.500	3.39	1.21	14	13	1	0	...	0-...	79.2	76	40	30	4	20-0	55	.255
2002—Hickory (S. Atl.)	1	5	.167	5.48	1.78	10	10	0	0	...	0-...	42.2	61	30	26	2	15-0	29	.335
—Williamsport (N.Y.-Penn.) .	8	3	.727	3.65	1.05	12	12	0	0	...	0-...	66.2	62	32	27	4	8-0	56	.240
2003—Lakeland (Fla. St.)	4	5	.444	3.73	1.19	19	15	2	0	...	0-...	99.0	93	45	41	8	25-0	71	.243
2004—Erie (East.)	7	0	1.000	2.96	1.03	41	0	0	0	...	4-...	79.0	63	32	26	7	18-1	59	.216
—Detroit (A.L.)	1	1	.500	5.57	1.48	16	0	0	0	3	0-1	21.0	25	15	13	4	6-0	15	.309
Major League totals (1 year)	1	1	.500	5.57	1.48	16	0	0	0	3	0-1	21.0	25	15	13	4	6-0	15	.309

NUNEZ, ABRAHAM   OF

PERSONAL: Born February 5, 1977, in Haina, Dominican Republic. ... 6-3/210. ... Bats both, throws right.

TRANSACTIONS/CAREER NOTES: Signed as a non-drafted free agent by Arizona Diamondbacks organization (September 17, 1996). ... Traded by Diamondbacks to Florida Marlins (December 13, 1999), completing deal in which Diamondbacks traded Ps Vladimir Nunez and Brad Penny and a player to be named to Marlins for P Matt Mantei (July 9, 1999). ... On disabled list (March 21-June 23, 2003); included rehabilitation assignment to Jupiter. ... Traded by Marlins to Kansas City Royals for P Rudy Seanez (July 31, 2004).

2004 GAMES PLAYED BY POSITION (MLB): OF—105, DH—2.

Year	Team (League)	Pos.	G	AB	R	H	2B	3B	HR	RBI	BB	SO	HBP	GDP	SB-CS	Avg.	OBP	SLG	OPS	E	Avg.
1997—Ariz. D'backs (Ariz.)	OF	54	213	52	65	17	4	6	21	26	40	2	4	3-3	.305	.384	.423	.807	1	.990
—Lethbridge (Pio.)	OF	2	6	2	1	0	0	0	1	1	0	0	0	0-0	.167	.286	.167	.452	0	1.000
1998—South Bend (Mid.)	OF	110	364	44	93	14	2	9	47	67	81	3	4	12-14	.255	.371	.379	.750	14	.944
1999—High Desert (Calif.)	OF	130	488	106	133	29	6	22	93	86	122	0	10	40-13	.273	.378	.492	.870	14	.951
2000—Portland (East.)	OF	74	221	39	61	17	3	6	42	44	64	0	3	8-6	.276	.392	.462	.853	0	1.000
—Brevard County (FSL)	DH	31	103	17	20	4	0	1	9	28	34	2	3	11-3	.194	.376	.262	.638	...	...
2001—Portland (East.)	OF	136	467	75	112	14	9	17	53	88	155	3	4	26-19	.240	.357	.418	.774	8	.976
2002—Calgary (PCL)	OF	129	428	68	107	24	5	21	60	51	112	1	4	31-6	.250	.329	.477	.805	7	.978
—Florida (N.L.)	OF	19	17	2	2	0	0	0	1	0	1	0	0	0-1	.118	.118	.118	.235	0	1.000

Year Team (League)	Pos.	G	AB	R	H	2B	3B	HR	RBI	BB	SO	HBP	GDP	SB-CS	Avg.	OBP	SLG	OPS	E	Avg.
2003— Jupiter (FSL)	OF-DH	8	29	6	8	3	0	0	2	4	9	0	1	1-0	.276	.364	.379	.743	0	1.000
— Albuquerque (PCL)	OF	59	212	35	66	13	2	1	38	32	56	0	1	9-4	.311	.398	.547	.945	3	.979
2004— Florida (N.L.)	OF	58	64	9	11	1	1	1	5	9	21	0	3	1-2	.172	.274	.266	.540	0	1.000
— Kansas City (A.L.)	OF-DH	59	221	31	50	9	0	5	29	25	48	0	4	0-1	.226	.304	.335	.638	1	.993
American League totals (1 year)		59	221	31	50	9	0	5	29	25	48	0	4	0-1	.226	.304	.335	.638	1	.993
National League totals (2 years)		77	81	11	13	1	1	1	6	9	26	0	4	1-3	.160	.244	.235	.479	0	1.000
Major League totals (2 years)		136	302	42	63	10	1	6	35	34	74	0	8	1-4	.209	.288	.308	.596	1	.995

NUNEZ, ABRAHAM O.   2B/SS

PERSONAL: Born March 16, 1976, in Santo Domingo, Dominican Republic. ... 5-11/190. ... Bats both, throws right. ... Full name: Abraham Orlando Nunez. ... Name pronounced: NOON-yez. ... High school: Emmanuel (Santo Domingo, Dominican Republic).

TRANSACTIONS/CAREER NOTES: Signed as a non-drafted free agent by Toronto Blue Jays organization (May 5, 1994). ... Traded by Blue Jays with P Mike Halperin and C/OF Craig Wilson to Pittsburgh Pirates (December 11, 1996), completing deal in which Blue Jays traded Ps Jose Silva and Jose Pett, IF Brandon Cromer and three players to be named to Pirates for OF/1B Orlando Merced, IF Carlos Garcia and P Dan Plesac (November 14, 1996). ... Career major league pitching: 0-0, 0.00 ERA, 1 G, 0.1 IP, 0 H, 0 R, 0 ER, 0 BB, 0 SO.

2004 GAMES PLAYED BY POSITION (MLB): 2B—32, SS—13, 3B—6, P—1, DH—1.

Year Team (League)	Pos.	G	AB	R	H	2B	3B	HR	RBI	BB	SO	HBP	GDP	SB-CS	Avg.	OBP	SLG	OPS	E	Avg.
1994— Dom. B. Jays (DSL)	2B	59	188	31	47	5	0	0	15	42	37	...	...	22-...	.250	...	.277	...	12	.938
1995— Dom. B. Jays (DSL)	2B	54	186	49	56	10	3	4	25	30	27	...	...	24-...	.301	...	.452	...	7	.962
1996— St. Catharines (NY-Penn.) .	2B-SS	75	297	43	83	6	4	3	26	31	43	4	2	37-14	.279	.353	.357	.710	15	.962
1997— Lynchburg (Caro.)	SS	78	304	45	79	9	4	3	32	23	47	1	5	29-14	.260	.313	.345	.658	15	.955
— Carolina (Southern)	SS	47	198	31	65	6	1	1	14	20	28	0	2	10-5	.328	.385	.384	.768	11	.949
— Pittsburgh (N.L.)	SS-2B	19	40	3	9	2	2	0	6	3	10	1	1	1-0	.225	.289	.375	.664	0	1.000
1998— Nashville (PCL)	SS	94	366	50	91	12	3	3	32	39	73	5	9	16-8	.249	.328	.322	.651	21	.953
— Lynchburg (Caro.)	SS-2B	5	18	2	4	1	0	0	2	3	1	0	2	1-0	.222	.333	.278	.611	1	.960
— Pittsburgh (N.L.)	SS-2B	24	52	6	10	2	0	1	2	12	14	0	1	4-2	.192	.344	.288	.632	7	.930
1999— Pittsburgh (N.L.)	SS-2B	90	259	25	57	8	0	0	17	28	54	1	2	9-1	.220	.299	.251	.550	14	.959
— Nashville (PCL)	SS	15	58	12	18	0	0	0	3	5	8	0	2	1-0	.310	.365	.310	.675	2	.971
2000— Nashville (PCL)	SS-2B	90	351	49	97	11	1	3	29	36	46	1	7	20-6	.276	.344	.339	.683	13	.970
— Pittsburgh (N.L.)	SS-2B	40	91	10	20	1	0	1	8	8	14	0	3	0-0	.220	.283	.264	.547	2	.982
2001— Pittsburgh (N.L.)	2-S-3-O	115	301	30	79	11	4	1	21	28	53	1	0	8-2	.262	.326	.336	.662	4	.990
2002— Pittsburgh (N.L.)	2B-SS-DH	112	253	28	59	14	1	2	15	27	44	2	2	3-4	.233	.311	.320	.631	7	.977
— Nashville (PCL)	SS-2B-OF	5	18	3	4	0	0	0	0	2	7	0	0	4-1	.222	.300	.222	.522	0	1.000
2003— Pittsburgh (N.L.)	2B-SS-3B	118	311	37	77	8	7	4	35	26	53	3	8	9-3	.248	.310	.357	.667	8	.980
2004— Pittsburgh (N.L.)	2-S-3-P-DH	112	182	17	43	9	0	2	13	10	36	0	8	1-3	.236	.275	.319	.593	3	.982
Major League totals (8 years)		630	1489	156	354	55	14	11	117	142	278	8	25	35-15	.238	.306	.316	.622	45	.976

NUNEZ, FRANKLIN   P

PERSONAL: Born January 18, 1977, in Nagua, Dominican Republic. ... 6-0/175. ... Throws right, bats right. ... High school: Escuela Cano Abajo (Dominican Republic).

TRANSACTIONS/CAREER NOTES: Signed as non-drafted free agent by Los Angeles Dodgers organization (September 1, 1994). ... Released by Dodgers (January 12, 1996). ... Signed by Philadelphia Phillies organization (June 20, 1998). ... On disabled list (July 13, 1999-remainder of season). ... Claimed on waivers by New York Mets (October 10, 2002). ... Signed as a free agent by Tampa Bay Devil Rays organization (February 13, 2004).

CAREER HITTING: 0-for-0 (.000), 0 R, 0 2B, 0 3B, 0 HR, 0 RBI.

Year Team (League)	W	L	Pct.	ERA	WHIP	G	GS	CG	ShO	Hld.	Sv.-Opp.	IP	H	R	ER	HR	BB-IBB	SO	Avg.
1995— Dom. Dodgers (DSL)	1	0	1.000	7.36	2.14	12	1	0	0	...	0-...	22.0	27	25	18	...	20-...	17	...
1996—			Did not play.																
1997—			Did not play.																
1998— Dom. Phillies (DSL)	0	2	.000	2.18	1.12	5	5	1	0	...	0-...	33.0	23	14	8	...	14-...	37	...
— Martinsville (App.)	2	2	.500	2.49	1.22	6	4	0	0	...	0-...	25.1	23	10	7	0	8-0	19	.232
1999— Piedmont (S. Atl.)	4	8	.333	3.39	1.22	13	13	0	0	...	0-...	77.0	69	39	29	4	25-0	88	.238
2000— Clearwater (Fla. St.)	10	4	.714	3.62	1.51	23	14	1	0	...	2-...	112.0	112	54	45	4	57-0	81	.264
2001— Reading (East.)	8	7	.533	4.42	1.44	39	14	0	0	...	3-...	110.0	107	68	54	9	51-3	112	.252
2002— Scran./W.B. (I.L.)	2	1	.667	3.18	1.24	4	4	0	0	...	0-...	17.0	9	6	6	2	12-0	16	.158
— GC Phillies (GCL)	0	0	...	0.00	1.50	1	1	0	0	...	0-...	2.0	2	0	0	0	1-0	4	.250
2003— Brooklyn (NY-P)	0	0	...	5.06	1.69	7	0	0	0	...	0-...	5.1	5	4	3	0	4-0	8	.250
2004— Montgomery (Sou.)	0	1	.000	0.84	0.66	6	0	0	0	...	0-...	10.2	4	3	1	0	3-0	19	.114
— Durham (Int'l)	4	2	.667	2.81	1.36	40	0	0	0	...	9-...	51.1	36	21	16	1	34-0	70	.193
— Tampa Bay (A.L.)	0	3	.000	5.91	1.69	8	0	0	0	0	0-1	10.2	11	8	7	1	7-0	14	.268
Major League totals (1 year)	0	3	.000	5.91	1.69	8	0	0	0	0	0-1	10.2	11	8	7	1	7-0	14	.268

NUNEZ, VLADIMIR   P

PERSONAL: Born March 15, 1975, in Havana, Cuba. ... 6-4/240. ... Throws right, bats right. ... Full name: Vladimir Nunez Zarabaza. ... Name pronounced: NOON-yez.

TRANSACTIONS/CAREER NOTES: Signed as a non-drafted free agent by Arizona Diamondbacks organization (February 1, 1996). ... Traded by Diamondbacks with P Brad Penny and a player to be named to Florida Marlins for P Matt Mantei (July 9, 1999); Marlins acquired OF Abraham Nunez to complete deal (December 13, 1999). ... On disabled list (July 19-August 3, 2001); included rehabilitation assignment to Kane County. ... Signed as a free agent by Colorado Rockies organization (January 13, 2004).

CAREER HITTING: 8-for-59 (.136), 3 R, 0 2B, 0 3B, 1 HR, 5 RBI.

Year Team (League)	W	L	Pct.	ERA	WHIP	G	GS	CG	ShO	Hld.	Sv.-Opp.	IP	H	R	ER	HR	BB-IBB	SO	Avg.
1996— Visalia (Calif.)	1	6	.143	5.43	1.53	12	10	0	0	...	0-...	53.0	64	45	32	10	17-0	37	.306
— Lethbridge (Pio.)	10	0	1.000	2.22	1.04	14	13	0	0	...	0-...	85.0	78	25	21	4	10-0	93	.243
1997— High Desert (Calif.)	8	5	.615	5.17	1.32	28	28	1	1	...	0-...	158.1	169	102	91	36	40-1	142	.271
1998— Tucson (PCL)	4	4	.500	4.91	1.47	31	13	1	0	...	2-...	95.1	103	58	52	12	37-0	78	.277
— Arizona (N.L.)	0	0	...	10.13	1.69	4	0	0	0	0	0-0	5.1	7	6	6	0	2-0	2	.318
1999— Tucson (PCL)	1	0	1.000	6.75	1.88	3	0	0	0	...	0-...	2.2	5	2	2	0	0-0	3	.455
— Arizona (N.L.)	3	2	.600	2.91	1.44	27	0	0	0	3	1-2	34.0	29	15	11	2	20-5	28	.242
— Florida (N.L.)	4	8	.333	4.58	1.34	17	12	0	0	1	0-1	74.2	66	48	38	9	34-1	58	.243
2000— Florida (N.L.)	0	6	.000	7.90	1.79	17	12	0	0	1	0-0	68.1	88	63	60	12	34-2	45	.319
— Calgary (PCL)	6	7	.462	4.12	1.45	15	15	1	0	...	0-...	89.2	92	43	41	9	38-1	95	.272
2001— Florida (N.L.)	4	5	.444	2.74	1.18	52	3	0	0	4	0-1	92.0	79	33	28	7	30-5	64	.234

Year Team (League)	W	L	Pct.	ERA	WHIP	G	GS	CG	ShO	Hld.	Sv.-Opp.	IP	H	R	ER	HR	BB-IBB	SO	Avg.
—Kane County (Midwest)	0	0	...	9.00	3.00	1	1	0	0	...	0-...	1.0	3	1	1	0	0-0	0	.600
2002— Florida (N.L.)	6	5	.545	3.41	1.20	77	0	0	0	11	20-28	97.2	80	38	37	8	37-1	73	.224
2003— Florida (N.L.)	0	3	.000	16.03	2.63	14	0	0	0	2	0-3	10.2	21	21	19	7	7-0	10	.396
—Albuquerque (PCL)	4	1	.800	4.76	1.30	46	3	0	0	...	5-...	68.0	67	36	36	13	20-0	54	.259
2004— Colorado (N.L.)	3	3	.500	7.01	1.56	22	0	0	0	3	0-3	25.2	26	22	20	6	14-0	22	.280
—Colo. Springs (PCL)	2	5	.286	5.68	1.55	23	8	0	0	...	3-...	63.1	76	44	40	7	22-0	60	.299
Major League totals (7 years)	20	32	.385	4.83	1.41	230	27	0	0	25	21-38	408.1	396	246	219	53	178-14	302	.259

OBERMUELLER, WES — P

PERSONAL: Born December 22, 1976, in Cedar Rapids, Iowa. ... 6-2/209. ... Throws right, bats right. ... Full name: Wesley Mitchell Obermueller. ... High school: Washington (Vinton, Iowa). ... College: Iowa.

TRANSACTIONS/CAREER NOTES: Selected by Kansas City Royals organization in second round of 1999 free-agent draft. ... Traded by Royals to Milwaukee Brewers for P Curtis Leskanic (July 2, 2003).

CAREER HITTING: 18-for-62 (.290), 3 R, 3 2B, 0 3B, 0 HR, 6 RBI.

Year Team (League)	W	L	Pct.	ERA	WHIP	G	GS	CG	ShO	Hld.	Sv.-Opp.	IP	H	R	ER	HR	BB-IBB	SO	Avg.
1999— GC Royals (GCL)	2	1	.667	2.58	1.17	11	7	0	0	...	0-...	38.1	33	16	11	2	12-1	39	.228
2000— Char., W.Va. (SAL)	3	0	1.000	1.14	0.76	8	7	0	0	...	0-...	31.2	19	6	4	0	5-0	29	.174
2001— Wilmington (Caro.)	0	2	.000	3.08	1.42	20	6	0	0	...	0-...	38.0	38	15	13	3	16-1	28	.266
2002— Wilmington (Caro.)	5	0	1.000	2.76	1.14	8	4	0	0	...	0-...	45.2	38	14	14	1	14-0	44	.228
—Wichita (Texas)	9	5	.643	2.90	1.31	17	17	0	0	...	0-...	105.2	98	39	34	6	40-3	65	.250
—Kansas City (A.L.)	0	2	.000	11.74	2.09	2	2	0	0	...	0-0	7.2	14	10	10	3	2-0	5	.378
2003— Omaha (PCL)	10	5	.667	4.40	1.40	17	17	2	0	...	0-...	106.1	108	61	52	11	42-1	62	.262
—Indianapolis (Int'l)	0	2	.000	4.70	1.60	3	3	0	0	...	0-...	15.1	18	9	8	1	6-0	11	.300
—Milwaukee (N.L.)	2	5	.286	5.07	1.61	12	11	0	0	...	0-0	65.2	81	40	37	10	25-2	34	.301
2004— Indianapolis (Int'l)	0	3	.000	5.19	1.42	4	4	1	0	...	0-...	26.0	30	16	15	3	7-0	17	.294
—Milwaukee (N.L.)	6	8	.429	5.80	1.53	25	20	1	1	...	0-0	118.0	138	80	76	15	42-0	59	.291
American League totals (1 year)	0	2	.000	11.74	2.09	2	2	0	0	...	0-0	7.2	14	10	10	3	2-0	5	.378
National League totals (2 years)	8	13	.381	5.54	1.56	37	31	1	1	0	0-0	183.2	219	120	113	25	67-2	93	.294
Major League totals (3 years)	8	15	.348	5.79	1.58	39	33	1	1	0	0-0	191.1	233	130	123	28	69-2	98	.298

OFFERMAN, JOSE — DH

PERSONAL: Born November 11, 1968, in San Pedro de Macoris, Dominican Republic. ... 6-0/192. ... Bats both, throws right. ... Full name: Jose Antonio Offerman. ... High school: Colegio Biblico Cristiano (Dominican Republic). ... College: Biblico Cristiano (D.R.).

TRANSACTIONS/CAREER NOTES: Signed as a non-drafted free agent by Los Angeles Dodgers organization (July 24, 1986). ... Traded by Dodgers to Kansas City Royals for P Billy Brewer (December 17, 1995). ... On disabled list (April 6-29, July 7-22 and August 14-September 6, 1997). ... Signed as a free agent by Boston Red Sox (November 16, 1998). ... On disabled list (May 27-June 10 and July 30-August 16, 2000). ... Traded by Red Sox to Seattle Mariners for cash considerations (August 8, 2002). ... Signed as a free agent by Montreal Expos organization (February 25, 2003). ... Released by Expos (March 28, 2003). ... Signed as a free agent by Minnesota Twins organization (February 10, 2004). ... Refused minor league assignment and became a free agent (October 15, 2004).

HONORS: Named Minor League Player of the Year by THE SPORTING NEWS (1990).

2004 GAMES PLAYED BY POSITION (MLB): DH—39, 1B—7, 2B—3.

Year Team (League)	Pos.	G	AB	R	H	2B	3B	HR	RBI	BB	SO	HBP	GDP	SB-CS	Avg.	OBP	SLG	OPS	E	Avg.
1987—			Did not play.																	
1988— Vero Beach (FSL)	SS	4	14	4	4	2	0	0	2	2	0	0	0	0-0	.286	.375	.429	.804	5	.643
—Great Falls (Pio.)	SS	60	251	75	83	11	5	2	28	38	42	2	3	57-10	.331	.421	.438	.859	18	.926
1989— Bakersfield (Calif.)	SS	62	245	53	75	9	4	2	22	35	48	2	5	37-13	.306	.396	.400	.796	30	.901
—San Antonio (Texas)	SS	68	278	47	80	6	3	2	22	40	39	1	1	32-13	.288	.379	.353	.732	20	.932
1990— Albuquerque (PCL)	2B-SS	117	454	104	148	16	11	0	56	71	81	2	7	60-19	.326	.416	.410	.826	36	.937
—Los Angeles (N.L.)	SS	29	58	7	9	0	0	1	7	4	14	0	0	1-0	.155	.210	.207	.417	4	.946
1991— Albuquerque (PCL)	SS	79	289	58	86	8	4	0	29	47	58	0	5	32-15	.298	.396	.353	.749	11	.956
—Los Angeles (N.L.)	SS	52	113	10	22	2	0	0	3	25	32	1	5	3-2	.195	.345	.212	.558	10	.945
1992— Los Angeles (N.L.)	SS	149	534	67	139	20	8	1	30	57	98	0	5	23-16	.260	.331	.333	.664	* 42	.935
1993— Los Angeles (N.L.)	SS	158	590	77	159	21	6	1	62	71	75	2	12	30-13	.269	.346	.331	.676	* 37	.950
1994— Los Angeles (N.L.)	SS	72	243	27	51	8	4	1	25	38	38	0	6	2-1	.210	.314	.288	.603	11	.967
—Albuquerque (PCL)	SS	56	224	43	74	7	5	1	31	37	48	0	4	9-4	.330	.419	.420	.839	13	.957
1995— Los Angeles (N.L.)	SS	119	429	69	123	14	6	4	33	69	67	3	5	2-7	.287	.389	.375	.765	* 35	.932
1996— Kansas City (A.L.)	1-2-SS-OF	151	561	85	170	33	8	5	47	74	98	1	9	24-10	.303	.384	.417	.801	16	.986
1997— Kansas City (A.L.)	2B-DH	106	424	59	126	23	6	2	39	41	64	0	9	9-10	.297	.359	.394	.753	9	.981
1998— Kansas City (A.L.)	2B	158	607	102	191	28	* 13	7	66	89	96	5	7	45-12	.315	.403	.438	.841	19	.974
1999— Boston (A.L.)	2B-DH-1B	149	586	107	172	37	* 11	8	69	96	79	2	11	18-12	.294	.391	.435	.826	14	.977
2000— Boston (A.L.)	2B-1B-DH	116	451	73	115	14	3	9	41	70	70	1	9	0-8	.255	.354	.359	.713	11	.983
2001— Boston (A.L.)	2B	128	524	76	140	23	3	9	49	61	97	1	9	5-2	.267	.342	.374	.716	14	.982
2002— Boston (A.L.)	1B-DH-OF	72	237	39	55	10	4	4	27	33	29	1	9	8-5	.232	.325	.325	.650	3	.991
—Seattle (A.L.)	1-0-DH-2	29	47	9	11	2	1	0	4	4	9	0	1	1-1	.234	.294	.383	.677	0	1.000
2004— Minnesota (A.L.)	DH-1B-2B	77	172	22	44	4	2	2	22	29	31	0	1	1-1	.256	.363	.395	.759	3	.955
American League totals (8 years)		986	3609	572	1024	184	47	47	364	497	573	11	63	111-61	.284	.370	.400	.770	89	.982
National League totals (6 years)		579	1967	257	503	65	24	8	160	264	324	6	33	61-39	.256	.344	.325	.669	139	.944
Major League totals (14 years)		1565	5576	829	1527	249	71	55	524	761	897	17	96	172-100	.274	.361	.374	.734	228	.969

DIVISION SERIES RECORD

Year Team (League)	Pos.	G	AB	R	H	2B	3B	HR	RBI	BB	SO	HBP	GDP	SB-CS	Avg.	OBP	SLG	OPS	E	Avg.
1995— Los Angeles (N.L.)		1	0	0	0	0	0	0	0	0	0	0	0	0-0	...	...	...	...	...	...
1999— Boston (A.L.)	2B	5	18	4	7	1	0	1	6	7	0	0	0	0-1	.389	.560	.611	1.171	0	1.000
2004— Minnesota (A.L.)		3	3	0	0	0	0	0	1	0	0	0	0	0-0	.000	.000	.000	.000	0	...
Division series totals (3 years)		9	21	4	7	1	0	1	7	7	0	0	0	0-1	.333	.500	.524	1.024	0	1.000

CHAMPIONSHIP SERIES RECORD

Year Team (League)	Pos.	G	AB	R	H	2B	3B	HR	RBI	BB	SO	HBP	GDP	SB-CS	Avg.	OBP	SLG	OPS	E	Avg.
1999— Boston (A.L.)	2B	5	24	4	11	0	1	0	2	1	3	0	1	1-0	.458	.480	.542	1.022	2	.917

ALL-STAR GAME RECORD

	G	AB	R	H	2B	3B	HR	RBI	BB	SO	HBP	GDP	SB-CS	Avg.	OBP	SLG	OPS	E	Avg.
All-Star Game totals (2 years)	2	1	0	0	0	0	0	0	0	0	0	0	0-0	.000	.000	.000	.000	1	.750

OHKA, TOMO — P

PERSONAL: Born March 18, 1976, in Kyoto, Japan. ... 6-1/200. ... Throws right, bats right. ... Full name: Tomokazu Ohka. ... Name pronounced: TOE-mo-KAH-zoo OH-kah. ... High school: Kyoto Siesio (Kyoto, Japan).
TRANSACTIONS/CAREER NOTES: Contract purchased by Boston Red Sox from Yokohama of the Japan Central League (November 20, 1998). ... Traded by Red Sox with P Rich Rundles to Montreal Expos for P Ugueth Urbina (July 31, 2001). ... On suspended list (September 24-30, 2002). ... On disabled list (June 11-September 14, 2004).
CAREER HITTING: 22-for-153 (.144), 6 R, 1 2B, 0 3B, 0 HR, 6 RBI.

Year — Team (League)	W	L	Pct.	ERA	WHIP	G	GS	CG	ShO	Hld.	Sv.-Opp.	IP	H	R	ER	HR	BB-IBB	SO	Avg.
1994— Yoko. Bay. (Jp. Cn.)	1	1	.500	4.18	1.68	15	2	0	0	...	0-...	28.0	29	13	13	...	18-...	18	...
1995— Yoko. Bay. (Jp. Cn.)	0	0		1.93	1.71	3	1	0	0	...	0-...	9.1	3	2	2	...	13-...	6	...
1996— Yoko. Bay. (Jp. Cn.)	0	1	.000	9.50	2.28	14	1	0	0	...	0-...	18.0	27	19	19	...	14-...	11	...
1997—				Did not play.															
1998— Yoko. Bay. (Jp. Cn.)	0	0		9.00	2.00	2	0	0	0	...	0-...	2.0	2	2	2	...	2-...	1	...
1999— Trenton (East.)	8	0	1.000	3.00	1.22	12	12	0	0	...	0-...	72.0	63	26	24	9	25-0	53	.233
— Pawtucket (Int'l)	7	0	1.000	1.58	1.04	12	12	1	1	...	0-...	68.1	60	17	12	5	11-0	63	.230
— Boston (A.L.)	1	2	.333	6.23	2.08	8	2	0	0	0	0-0	13.0	21	12	9	2	6-0	8	.362
2000— Pawtucket (Int'l)	9	6	.600	2.96	1.03	19	19	3	2	...	0-...	130.2	111	52	43	15	23-1	78	.232
— Boston (A.L.)	3	6	.333	3.12	1.38	13	12	0	0	0	0-0	69.1	70	25	24	7	26-0	40	.263
2001— Boston (A.L.)	2	5	.286	6.19	1.68	12	11	0	0	0	0-...	52.1	69	40	36	7	19-0	37	.317
— Pawtucket (Int'l)	2	5	.286	5.57	1.52	8	8	1	0	...	0-...	42.0	55	35	26	5	9-0	33	.322
— Montreal (N.L.)	1	4	.200	4.77	1.37	10	10	0	0	0	0-0	54.2	65	30	29	8	10-0	31	.302
2002— Montreal (N.L.)	13	8	.619	3.18	1.24	32	31	2	0	0	0-0	192.2	194	83	68	19	45-11	118	.264
2003— Montreal (N.L.)	10	12	.455	4.16	1.40	34	34	2	0	0	0-0	199.0	233	106	92	24	45-11	118	.292
2004— Montreal (N.L.)	3	7	.300	3.40	1.39	15	15	0	0	0	0-0	84.2	98	40	32	11	20-1	38	.288
American League totals (3 years)	6	13	.316	4.61	1.57	33	25	0	0	0	0-0	134.2	160	77	69	16	51-0	85	.295
National League totals (4 years)	27	31	.466	3.75	1.34	91	90	4	0	0	0-0	531.0	590	259	221	62	120-19	305	.282
Major League totals (6 years)	33	44	.429	3.92	1.38	124	115	4	0	0	0-0	665.2	750	336	290	78	171-19	390	.285

OJEDA, AUGIE — SS/2B

PERSONAL: Born December 20, 1974, in Los Angeles, Calif. ... 5-8/175. ... Bats both, throws right. ... Full name: Octavio Augie Ojeda. ... Name pronounced: oh-HAY-dah. ... High school: Pius X (Downey, Calif.). ... College: Tennessee.
TRANSACTIONS/CAREER NOTES: Selected by Baltimore Orioles organization in 13th round of 1996 free-agent draft. ... Traded by Orioles to Chicago Cubs for P Richard Negrette (December 13, 1999). ... Claimed on waivers by Minnesota Twins (November 24, 2003).
2004 GAMES PLAYED BY POSITION (MLB): 2B—20, SS—7, 3B—4.

Year — Team (League)	Pos.	G	AB	R	H	2B	3B	HR	RBI	BB	SO	HBP	GDP	SB-CS	Avg.	OBP	SLG	OPS	E	Avg.
1997— Bowie (East.)	SS	58	204	33	60	9	1	2	23	31	17	3	6	7-0	.294	.390	.377	.767	9	.967
— Frederick (Carolina)	SS	34	128	25	44	11	1	1	20	18	18	1	1	2-5	.344	.429	.469	.897	5	.966
— Rochester (Int'l)	SS	15	47	5	11	3	1	0	6	8	4	0	2	1-2	.234	.345	.340	.686	5	.922
1998— GC Orioles (GCL)	SS	4	15	6	6	2	0	0	2	3	1	2	0	3-0	.400	.550	.533	1.083	0	1.000
— Bowie (East.)	3B-SS	73	254	36	65	18	2	1	19	36	30	3	5	0-3	.256	.354	.323	.677	11	.964
1999— Rochester (Int'l)	SS	1	1	0	0	0	0	0	0	0	0	0	0	0-0	.000	.000	.000	.000	0	...
— Bowie (East.)	3B-SS	134	460	73	123	18	4	10	60	57	47	11	7	6-2	.267	.359	.389	.748	19	.969
2000— Iowa (PCL)	SS-2B	113	396	56	111	23	2	8	43	33	27	7	10	16-6	.280	.343	.409	.752	11	.976
— Chicago (N.L.)	SS-2B	28	77	10	17	3	1	2	8	10	9	0	1	0-1	.221	.307	.364	.670	1	.990
2001— Chicago (N.L.)	3B-SS-2B	78	144	16	29	5	1	1	12	12	20	2	2	1-0	.201	.269	.271	.540	6	.962
2002— Chicago (N.L.)	SS-2B-3B	30	70	4	13	4	0	0	4	5	5	1	2	1-0	.186	.247	.243	.490	3	.969
— Iowa (PCL)	SS-3B	73	291	54	67	20	4	1	27	31	30	9	2	5-3	.230	.318	.337	.655	5	.984
2003— Iowa (PCL)	SS-2B-3B	106	283	42	71	10	3	2	23	34	25	10	6	4-0	.251	.351	.329	.679	9	.978
— Chicago (N.L.)	SS-2B-3B	12	25	2	3	0	0	0	0	1	5	1	1	0-0	.120	.185	.120	.305	0	1.000
2004— Rochester (Int'l)	S-3-2-DH	90	331	49	80	19	0	2	21	39	33	6	11	7-5	.242	.331	.317	.648	7	.980
— Minnesota (A.L.)	2B-SS-3B	30	59	16	20	1	0	2	7	10	3	0	1	1-1	.339	.429	.458	.886	2	.978
American League totals (1 year)		30	59	16	20	1	0	2	7	10	3	0	1	1-1	.339	.429	.458	.886	2	.978
National League totals (4 years)		148	316	32	62	12	2	3	24	28	39	4	6	2-1	.196	.267	.275	.542	10	.974
Major League totals (5 years)		178	375	48	82	13	2	5	31	38	42	4	6	3-2	.219	.294	.304	.598	12	.975

OJEDA, MIGUEL — C

PERSONAL: Born January 29, 1975, in Sonora, Mexico. ... 6-2/190. ... Bats right, throws right. ... Full name: Miguel Arturo Ojeda.
TRANSACTIONS/CAREER NOTES: Signed as a non-drafted free agent by Pittsburgh Pirates organization (May 28, 1993). ... Loaned by Pirates organization to Mexico City Reds of the Mexican League for the entire 1995, 1996 and 1997 seasons and part of the 1998 season. ... Traded by Pirates to Red Devils for future considerations (December 14, 1998). ... Signed as a free agent by San Diego Padres organization (January 12, 2003). ... Released by Padres (March 24, 2003). ... Contract purchased by Padres from Red Devils (May 17, 2003). ... On disabled list (August 16-September 1, 2004); included rehabilitation assignment to Portland.
2004 GAMES PLAYED BY POSITION (MLB): C—50.

Year — Team (League)	Pos.	G	AB	R	H	2B	3B	HR	RBI	BB	SO	HBP	GDP	SB-CS	Avg.	OBP	SLG	OPS	E	Avg.
1993— GC Pirates (GCL)	C	27	97	9	27	3	1	3	11	10	18	0	1	2-0	.278	.339	.423	.762	3	.983
1994— Welland (N.Y.-Penn.)	C-1B-P	48	142	11	27	6	0	2	8	5	30	2	0	1-0	.190	.228	.275	.503	0	1.000
1998— Carolina (Southern)	C	18	58	4	9	2	0	1	4	3	12	1	0	0-0	.155	.210	.241	.451	1	.991
2003— San Diego (N.L.)	C-1B	61	141	13	33	6	0	4	22	18	26	3	2	1-1	.234	.331	.362	.693	6	.982
2004— Portland (PCL)	C	5	19	4	5	0	0	2	3	2	3	0	0	0-0	.263	.333	.579	.912	1	.974
— San Diego (N.L.)	C	62	156	23	40	3	0	8	26	15	34	1	1	0-0	.256	.322	.429	.751	1	.996
Major League totals (2 years)		123	297	36	73	9	0	12	48	33	60	4	3	1-1	.246	.326	.397	.724	7	.988

OLERUD, JOHN — 1B

PERSONAL: Born August 5, 1968, in Seattle, Wash. ... 6-5/225. ... Bats left, throws left. ... Full name: John Garrett Olerud. ... Name pronounced: OLE-le-RUDE. ... High school: Interlake (Bellevue, Wash.). ... College: Washington State. ... Son of John E. Olerud, minor league catcher (1965-70); and cousin of Dale Sveum, infielder with seven major league teams (1986-99).
TRANSACTIONS/CAREER NOTES: Selected by New York Mets organization in 27th round of 1986 free-agent draft; did not sign. ... Selected by Toronto Blue Jays organization in third round of 1989 free-agent draft. ... Traded by Blue Jays with cash to Mets for P Robert Person (December 20, 1996). ... Signed as a free agent by Seattle Mariners (December 15, 1999). ... Released by Mariners (July 23, 2004). ... Signed by New York Yankees (August 3, 2004).

HONORS: Won A.L. Gold Glove at first base (2000, 2002 and 2003).
2004 GAMES PLAYED BY POSITION (MLB): 1B—124.

Year — Team (League)	Pos.	G	AB	R	H	2B	3B	HR	RBI	BB	SO	HBP	GDP	SB-CS	Avg.	OBP	SLG	OPS	E	Avg.
1989— Toronto (A.L.)	DH-1B	6	8	2	3	0	0	0	0	0	1	0	0	0-0	.375	.375	.375	.750	0	1.000
1990— Toronto (A.L.)	DH-1B	111	358	43	95	15	1	14	48	57	75	1	5	0-2	.265	.364	.430	.794	2	.986
1991— Toronto (A.L.)	DH-1B	139	454	64	116	30	1	17	68	68	84	6	12	0-2	.256	.353	.438	.791	5	.996
1992— Toronto (A.L.)	1B-DH	138	458	68	130	28	0	16	66	70	61	1	15	1-0	.284	.375	.450	.825	7	.994
1993— Toronto (A.L.)	1B-DH	158	551	109	200	* 54	2	24	107	114	65	7	12	0-2	* .363	* .473	.599	1.072	10	.992
1994— Toronto (A.L.)	1B-DH	108	384	47	114	29	2	12	67	61	53	3	11	1-2	.297	.393	.477	.870	6	.993
1995— Toronto (A.L.)	1B	135	492	72	143	32	0	8	54	84	54	4	17	0-0	.291	.398	.404	.802	4	.997
1996— Toronto (A.L.)	1B-DH	125	398	59	109	25	0	18	61	60	37	10	10	1-0	.274	.382	.472	.854	2	.998
1997— New York (N.L.)	1B	154	524	90	154	34	1	22	102	85	67	13	19	0-0	.294	.400	.489	.889	7	.995
1998— New York (N.L.)	1B	160	557	91	197	36	4	22	93	96	73	4	15	2-2	.354	.447	.551	.998	5	.996
1999— New York (N.L.)	1B	• 162	581	107	173	39	0	19	96	125	66	11	22	3-0	.298	.427	.463	.890	9	.994
2000— Seattle (A.L.)	1B	159	565	84	161	45	0	14	103	102	96	4	17	0-0	.285	.392	.439	.831	5	.996
2001— Seattle (A.L.)	1B	159	572	91	173	32	1	21	95	94	70	5	21	3-1	.302	.401	.472	.873	4	.993
2002— Seattle (A.L.)	1B-DH	154	553	85	166	39	0	22	102	98	96	6	19	0-0	.300	.403	.490	.893	5	.996
2003— Seattle (A.L.)	1B	152	539	64	145	35	0	10	83	84	67	6	20	0-1	.269	.372	.390	.761	3	.998
2004— Seattle (A.L.)	1B	78	261	29	64	13	1	5	22	40	41	6	6	0-0	.245	.354	.360	.714	1	.998
— New York (A.L.)	1B	49	164	16	46	7	0	4	26	21	20	2	5	0-0	.280	.367	.396	.763	1	.997
American League totals (13 years)		1671	5757	833	1665	384	8	185	902	953	790	60	170	6-12	.289	.391	.455	.847	60	.995
National League totals (3 years)		476	1662	288	524	109	5	63	291	306	206	28	56	5-2	.315	.425	.501	.926	21	.995
Major League totals (16 years)		2147	7419	1121	2189	493	13	248	1193	1259	996	88	226	11-14	.295	.399	.465	.864	81	.995

DIVISION SERIES RECORD

Year — Team (League)	Pos.	G	AB	R	H	2B	3B	HR	RBI	BB	SO	HBP	GDP	SB-CS	Avg.	OBP	SLG	OPS	E	Avg.
1999— New York (N.L.)	1B	4	16	3	7	0	0	1	6	3	2	0	0	0-0	.438	.526	.625	1.151	0	1.000
2000— Seattle (A.L.)	1B	3	10	2	3	0	0	1	2	2	1	1	1	0-0	.300	.462	.600	1.062	0	1.000
2001— Seattle (A.L.)	1B	5	17	1	3	0	0	0	1	3	5	0	1	0-0	.176	.300	.176	.476	0	1.000
2004— New York (A.L.)	1B	4	14	2	3	2	0	0	0	1	2	1	0	0-0	.214	.313	.357	.670	0	1.000
Division series totals (4 years)		16	57	8	16	2	0	2	9	9	10	2	2	0-0	.281	.397	.421	.818	0	1.000

CHAMPIONSHIP SERIES RECORD

Year — Team (League)	Pos.	G	AB	R	H	2B	3B	HR	RBI	BB	SO	HBP	GDP	SB-CS	Avg.	OBP	SLG	OPS	E	Avg.
1991— Toronto (A.L.)	1B	5	19	1	3	0	0	0	3	3	1	0	0	0-0	.158	.273	.158	.431	0	1.000
1992— Toronto (A.L.)	1B	6	23	4	8	2	0	1	4	2	5	0	0	0-0	.348	.400	.565	.965	0	1.000
1993— Toronto (A.L.)	1B	6	23	5	8	1	0	0	3	4	1	1	1	0-0	.348	.464	.391	.856	1	.983
1999— New York (N.L.)	1B	6	27	4	8	0	0	2	6	2	3	0	1	0-0	.296	.345	.519	.863	2	.969
2000— Seattle (A.L.)	1B	6	20	3	7	3	0	1	2	2	2	0	1	1-0	.350	.391	.650	1.041	0	1.000
2001— Seattle (A.L.)	1B	5	19	2	4	0	0	1	3	2	4	0	1	0-0	.211	.286	.368	.654	0	1.000
2004— New York (A.L.)	1B	4	12	1	2	0	0	1	2	1	1	0	0	0-0	.167	.231	.417	.647	0	1.000
Champ. series totals (7 years)		38	143	20	40	6	0	6	23	16	17	1	4	1-0	.280	.354	.448	.802	3	.991

WORLD SERIES RECORD

Year — Team (League)	Pos.	G	AB	R	H	2B	3B	HR	RBI	BB	SO	HBP	GDP	SB-CS	Avg.	OBP	SLG	OPS	E	Avg.
1992— Toronto (A.L.)	1B	4	13	2	4	0	0	0	0	4	0	0	0	0-0	.308	.308	.308	.615	0	1.000
1993— Toronto (A.L.)	1B	5	17	5	4	1	0	1	2	4	1	0	0	0-0	.235	.364	.471	.834	0	1.000
World series totals (2 years)		9	30	7	8	1	0	1	2	4	5	0	0	0-0	.267	.343	.400	.743	0	1.000

ALL-STAR GAME RECORD

	G	AB	R	H	2B	3B	HR	RBI	BB	SO	HBP	GDP	SB-CS	Avg.	OBP	SLG	OPS	E	Avg.
All-Star Game totals (2 years)	2	4	0	0	0	0	0	0	0	0	0	0	0-0	.000	.000	.000	.000	0	1.000

OLIVER, DARREN — P

PERSONAL: Born October 6, 1970, in Kansas City, Mo. ... 6-2/220. ... Throws left, bats right. ... Full name: Darren Christopher Oliver. ... High school: Rio Linda (Calif.) Senior. ... Son of Bob Oliver, first baseman/outfielder with five major league teams (1965 and 1969-1975).

TRANSACTIONS/CAREER NOTES: Selected by Texas Rangers organization in third round of 1988 free-agent draft. ... On disabled list (June 27, 1995-remainder of season). ... On disabled list (June 11-26, 1998); included rehabilitation assignment to Oklahoma City. ... Traded by Rangers with 3B Fernando Tatis and a player to be named to St. Louis Cardinals for P Todd Stottlemyre and SS Royce Clayton (July 31, 1998); Cardinals acquired OF Mark Little to complete deal (August 9, 1998). ... Signed as a free agent by Rangers (January 27, 2000). ... On disabled list (June 21-July 20 and August 1-September 1, 2000); included rehabilitation assignments to Oklahoma and Tulsa. ... On disabled list (May 8-June 6, 2001); included rehabilitation assignments to Oklahoma and Tulsa. ... Traded by Rangers to Boston Red Sox for OF Carl Everett (December 13, 2001). ... Released by Red Sox (July 2, 2002). ... Signed by Cardinals organization (July 19, 2002). ... Released by Cardinals (August 13, 2002). ... Signed by Colorado Rockies organization (January 29, 2003). ... Signed as a free agent by Florida Marlins (February 6, 2004). ... Traded by Marlins to Houston Astros for future considerations (July 22, 2004). ... On disabled list (August 6-September 6, 2004).

CAREER HITTING: 46-for-202 (.228), 15 R, 10 2B, 0 3B, 1 HR, 18 RBI.

Year — Team (League)	W	L	Pct.	ERA	WHIP	G	GS	CG	ShO	Hld.	Sv.-Opp.	IP	H	R	ER	HR	BB-IBB	SO	Avg.
1988— GC Rangers (GCL)	5	1	.833	2.15	1.05	12	9	0	0	...	0-...	54.1	39	16	13	0	18-0	59	.203
1989— Gastonia (S. Atl.)	8	7	.533	3.16	1.37	24	23	2	1	...	0-...	122.1	86	54	43	4	82-1	108	.199
1990— GC Rangers (GCL)	0	0	...	0.00	0.33	3	3	0	0	...	0-...	6.0	1	1	0	0	1-0	7	.053
— Gastonia (S. Atl.)	0	0	...	13.50	2.50	1	1	0	0	...	0-...	2.0	1	3	3	0	4-0	2	.143
1991— Charlotte (Fla. St.)	0	1	.000	4.50	1.13	2	2	0	0	...	0-...	8.0	6	4	4	1	3-0	12	.200
1992— Charlotte (Fla. St.)	1	0	1.000	0.72	0.84	8	2	1	1	...	2-...	25.0	11	2	2	0	10-2	33	.133
— Tulsa (Texas)	0	1	.000	3.14	1.33	3	3	0	0	...	0-...	14.1	15	9	5	1	4-0	14	.246
1993— Tulsa (Texas)	7	5	.583	1.96	1.25	46	0	0	0	...	6-...	73.1	51	18	16	1	41-5	77	.197
— Texas (A.L.)	0	0	...	2.70	0.90	2	0	0	0	0	0-0	3.1	2	1	1	1	1-1	4	.154
1994— Texas (A.L.)	4	0	1.000	3.42	1.50	43	0	0	0	9	2-3	50.0	40	24	19	4	35-4	50	.223
— Oklahoma City (A.A.)	0	0	...	0.00	0.55	6	0	0	0	...	1-...	7.1	1	0	0	0	3-2	6	.045
1995— Texas (A.L.)	4	2	.667	4.22	1.61	17	7	0	0	0	0-...	49.0	47	25	23	3	32-1	39	.257
1996— Charlotte (Fla. St.)	0	1	.000	3.00	0.92	2	1	0	0	...	0-...	12.0	8	4	4	1	3-0	9	.190
— Texas (A.L.)	14	6	.700	4.66	1.53	30	30	1	1	0	0-0	173.2	190	97	90	20	76-3	112	.279
1997— Texas (A.L.)	13	12	.520	4.20	1.47	32	32	3	1	0	0-0	201.1	213	111	94	29	82-3	104	.271
1998— Texas (A.L.)	6	7	.462	6.53	1.77	19	19	2	0	0	0-0	103.1	140	84	75	11	43-1	65	.325
— Oklahoma (PCL)	0	0	...	0.00	0.60	1	1	0	0	...	0-...	5.0	2	0	0	0	1-0	1	.118

O

Year	Team (League)	W	L	Pct.	ERA	WHIP	G	GS	CG	ShO	Hld.	Sv.-Opp.	IP	H	R	ER	HR	BB-IBB	SO	Avg.
	— St. Louis (N.L.)	4	4	.500	4.26	1.53	10	10	0	0	0	0-0	57.0	64	31	27	7	23-1	29	.283
1999—	St. Louis (N.L.)	9	9	.500	4.26	1.38	30	30	2	1	0	0-0	196.1	197	96	93	16	74-4	119	.266
2000—	Texas (A.L.)	2	9	.182	7.42	1.79	21	21	0	0	0	0-0	108.0	151	95	89	16	42-3	49	.339
	— Oklahoma (PCL)	2	1	.667	1.97	1.13	7	7	1	1	...	0-...	32.0	22	11	7	2	14-0	28	.196
	— Tulsa (Texas)	0	1	.000	11.57	2.57	1	1	0	0	...	0-...	4.2	10	7	6	0	2-0	5	.417
2001—	Texas (A.L.)	11	11	.500	6.02	1.65	28	28	1	0	0	0-0	154.0	189	109	103	23	65-0	104	.306
	— Oklahoma (PCL)	0	0	...	0.00	1.00	1	1	0	0	...	0-...	3.0	3	0	0	0	0-0	3	.250
	— Tulsa (Texas)	0	1	.000	5.40	1.20	1	1	0	0	...	0-...	5.0	4	3	3	1	2-0	5	.235
2002—	Boston (A.L.)	4	5	.444	4.66	1.67	14	9	1	1	0	0-0	58.0	70	30	30	7	27-0	32	.317
	— Memphis (PCL)	0	2	.000	7.88	2.13	5	5	0	0	...	0-...	16.0	17	16	14	1	17-0	9	.298
2003—	Colorado (N.L.)	13	11	.542	5.04	1.45	33	32	1	0	0	0-0	180.1	201	108	101	21	61-3	88	.284
2004—	Florida (N.L.)	2	3	.400	6.44	1.57	18	8	0	0	0	0-0	58.2	75	44	42	13	17-1	33	.319
	— Houston (N.L.)	1	0	1.000	3.86	1.14	9	2	0	0	0	0-0	14.0	12	6	6	1	4-0	13	.240
American League totals (9 years)		58	52	.527	5.24	1.60	206	146	8	3	9	2-3	900.2	1042	576	524	114	403-16	552	.293
National League totals (4 years)		29	27	.518	4.78	1.44	100	82	3	1	0	0-0	506.1	549	285	269	58	179-9	282	.280
Major League totals (12 years)		87	79	.524	5.07	1.54	306	228	11	4	9	2-3	1407.0	1591	861	793	172	582-25	834	.288

DIVISION SERIES RECORD

Year	Team (League)	W	L	Pct.	ERA	WHIP	G	GS	CG	ShO	Hld.	Sv.-Opp.	IP	H	R	ER	HR	BB-IBB	SO	Avg.
1996—	Texas (A.L.)	0	1	.000	3.38	1.00	1	1	0	0	0	0-0	8.0	6	3	3	1	2-0	3	.231

OLIVO, MIGUEL — C

PERSONAL: Born July 15, 1978, in Villa Vasquez, Dominican Republic. ... 6-0/215. ... Bats right, throws right. ... Full name: Miguel Eduardo Olivo.

TRANSACTIONS/CAREER NOTES: Signed as a non-drafted free agent by Oakland Athletics organization (September 30, 1996). ... Traded by A's to Chicago White Sox (December 12, 2000); completing deal in which White Sox traded P Chad Bradford to A's for player to be named (December 7, 2000). ... Traded by White Sox with OF Jeremy Reed and SS Michael Morse to Seattle Mariners for RHP Freddy Garcia and C Ben Davis (June 27, 2004). ... On disabled list (June 30-July 15, 2004); included rehabilitation assignment to Everett. ... On suspended list (October 2-3, 2004).

2004 GAMES PLAYED BY POSITION (MLB): C—95.

											BATTING									FIELDING	
Year	Team (League)	Pos.	G	AB	R	H	2B	3B	HR	RBI	BB	SO	HBP	GDP	SB-CS	Avg.	OBP	SLG	OPS	E	Avg.
1997—	Dom. Athletics (DSL)		63	221	37	60	11	4	6	57	34	36	...		6-...	.271		.439		...	...
1998—	Ariz. A's (Ariz.)	C-OF	46	164	30	51	11	3	2	23	8	43	4	5	2-2	.311	.356	.451	.807	8	.977
1999—	Modesto (California)	C	73	243	46	74	13	6	9	42	21	60	2	6	4-5	.305	.363	.519	.882	15	.974
2000—	Modesto (California)	C	58	227	40	64	11	5	5	35	16	53	2	8	5-2	.282	.332	.441	.773	19	.959
	— Midland (Texas)	C	19	59	8	14	2	0	1	9	5	15	0	3	0-0	.237	.297	.322	.619	2	.980
2001—	Birmingham (Sou.)	C	93	316	45	82	23	1	14	55	37	62	7	4	6-3	.259	.347	.472	.819	9	.988
2002—	Birmingham (Sou.)	C	106	359	51	110	24	10	6	49	40	66	5	11	29-13	.306	.381	.479	.860	13	.983
	— Chicago (A.L.)	C	6	19	2	4	1	0	1	5	2	5	0	1	0-0	.211	.286	.421	.707	0	1.000
2003—	Chicago (A.L.)	C	114	317	37	75	19	1	6	27	19	80	4	3	6-4	.237	.287	.360	.646	9	.988
2004—	Chicago (A.L.)	C	46	141	21	38	7	2	7	26	10	29	0	2	5-4	.270	.316	.496	.812	4	.984
	— Everett (N'west)	C	2	6	0	0	0	0	0	0	0	2	0	0	0-0	...	.000	.000	.000	1	.909
	— Seattle (A.L.)	C	50	160	25	32	8	2	6	14	10	55	3	2	2-2	.200	.260	.388	.648	1	.997
Major League totals (3 years)			216	637	85	149	35	5	20	72	41	169	7	8	13-10	.234	.286	.399	.685	14	.989

OLMEDO, RAY — SS/2B

PERSONAL: Born May 31, 1981, in Maracay, Venezuela. ... 5-11/155. ... Bats both, throws right. ... Full name: Rainer Gustavo Olmedo. ... Name pronounced: ray-NEAR oh-MAY-doe.

2004 GAMES PLAYED BY POSITION (MLB): SS—7.

											BATTING									FIELDING	
Year	Team (League)	Pos.	G	AB	R	H	2B	3B	HR	RBI	BB	SO	HBP	GDP	SB-CS	Avg.	OBP	SLG	OPS	E	Avg.
1999—	GC Reds (GCL)	2B-SS-3B	54	195	30	46	12	1	1	19	12	28	1	1	13-7	.236	.281	.323	.604	16	.936
2000—	Dayton (Midw.)	SS-2B	111	369	50	94	19	1	4	41	30	70	1	11	17-11	.255	.309	.344	.654	29	.946
2001—	Mudville California (Calif.)	SS	129	536	57	131	23	4	0	28	24	121	8	15	38-17	.244	.285	.302	.587	40	.930
2002—	Chattanooga (Sou.)	SS-2B	132	478	62	118	21	1	3	30	53	86	7	4	15-16	.247	.331	.314	.645	25	.961
2003—	Chattanooga (Sou.)	SS-2B	49	160	23	47	11	0	2	15	14	29	0	3	3-3	.294	.349	.400	.749	10	.951
	— Louisville (Int'l)	SS-2B	9	25	4	6	1	0	1	4	2	6	0	0	0-0	.240	.296	.400	.696	1	.983
	— Cincinnati (N.L.)	SS-2B	79	230	24	55	6	1	0	17	13	46	0	4	1-1	.239	.280	.274	.554	14	.948
2004—	Cincinnati (N.L.)	SS	8	1	0	0	0	0	0	0	1	0	0	0	0-0	.000	.500	.000	.500	0	1.000
	— Louisville (Int'l)	2B-SS	82	294	33	84	13	7	2	26	23	40	2	8	2-3	.286	.342	.398	.740	13	.968
Major League totals (2 years)			87	231	24	55	6	1	0	17	14	46	0	4	1-1	.238	.282	.273	.554	14	.949

OLSON, TIM — 3B/SS

O

PERSONAL: Born August 1, 1978, in Grand Forks, N.D. ... 6-2/200. ... Bats right, throws right. ... Full name: Timothy Lane Olson. ... High school: St. Mary's Central (Bismarck, N.D.). ... College: Florida.

TRANSACTIONS/CAREER NOTES: Selected by Tampa Bay Devil Rays organization in 36th round of 1998 free-agent draft; did not sign. ... Selected by Arizona Diamondbacks organization in seventh round of 2000 free-agent draft.

2004 GAMES PLAYED BY POSITION (MLB): 3B—19, SS—17, OF—4.

											BATTING									FIELDING	
Year	Team (League)	Pos.	G	AB	R	H	2B	3B	HR	RBI	BB	SO	HBP	GDP	SB-CS	Avg.	OBP	SLG	OPS	E	Avg.
2000—	South Bend (Mid.)	OF-3B	68	261	37	57	14	2	2	26	15	49	4	5	15-3	.218	.281	.310	.591	9	.947
2001—	Lancaster (Calif.)	SS-3B-OF	61	239	36	69	12	4	6	32	14	49	3	4	13-9	.289	.336	.448	.784	24	.906
	— El Paso (Texas)	SS	46	167	29	53	13	0	2	24	11	36	6	4	4-4	.317	.378	.431	.810	20	.914
2002—	El Paso (Texas)	SS-OF-2B	126	433	61	118	24	2	10	64	27	91	19	13	9-11	.273	.337	.406	.744	31	.942
2003—	El Paso (Texas)	SS-OF	14	56	5	11	2	0	2	8	5	19	0	1	0-2	.196	.258	.339	.597	4	.940
	— Tucson (PCL)	SS-OF-2B	115	397	59	104	22	0	6	40	31	77	6	14	11-2	.262	.323	.363	.686	29	.943
2004—	Arizona (N.L.)	3B-SS-OF	48	97	8	18	7	0	2	5	16	18	0	4	1-0	.186	.301	.320	.620	6	.946
	— Tucson (PCL)	SS-OF-3B-2B	37	147	32	44	11	0	7	25	16	28	2	2	5-1	.299	.373	.517	.883	5	.961
Major League totals (1 year)			48	97	8	18	7	0	2	5	16	18	0	4	1-0	.186	.301	.320	.620	6	.946

ORDONEZ, MAGGLIO — OF

PERSONAL: Born January 28, 1974, in Caracas, Venezuela. ... 6-0/215. ... Bats right, throws right. ... Name pronounced: or-DOAN-yez.
TRANSACTIONS/CAREER NOTES: Signed as a non-drafted free agent by Chicago White Sox organization (May 18, 1991). ... On suspended list (May 1-6, 2000). ... On disabled list (May 26-July 8 and July 22, 2004-remainder of season).
2004 GAMES PLAYED BY POSITION (MLB): OF—43, DH—7.

									BATTING										FIELDING	
Year Team (League)	Pos.	G	AB	R	H	2B	3B	HR	RBI	BB	SO	HBP	GDP	SB-CS	Avg.	OBP	SLG	OPS	E	Avg.
1991— Dominican Orioles/W.S. (DSL)		25	94	17	28	3	1	0	8	6	12	...	...	4-...	.298	...	.351	...	...	...
1992— GC Whi. Sox (GCL)	OF	38	111	17	20	10	2	1	14	13	26	2	2	6-4	.180	.276	.333	.609	0	1.000
1993— Hickory (S. Atl.)	OF	84	273	32	59	14	4	3	20	26	66	0	6	5-5	.216	.284	.330	.614	6	.959
1994— Hickory (S. Atl.)	OF	132	490	86	144	24	5	11	69	45	57	1	11	16-7	.294	.353	.431	.783	6	.980
1995— Prince Will. (Car.)	OF	131	487	61	116	24	2	12	65	41	71	3	16	11-5	.238	.299	.370	.669	6	.978
1996— Birmingham (Sou.)	OF	130	479	66	126	41	0	18	67	39	74	9	16	9-10	.263	.330	.461	.792	6	.976
1997— Nashville (A.A.)	OF-DH	135	523	65	172	29	3	14	90	32	61	2	18	14-10	.329	.364	.476	.840	5	.983
—Chicago (A.L.)	OF	21	69	12	22	6	0	4	11	2	8	0	1	1-2	.319	.338	.580	.918	0	1.000
1998— Chicago (A.L.)	OF	145	535	70	151	25	2	14	65	28	53	9	19	7-9	.282	.326	.415	.741	5	.985
1999— Chicago (A.L.)	OF-DH	157	624	100	188	34	3	30	117	47	64	1	24	13-6	.301	.349	.510	.858	3	.991
2000— Chicago (A.L.)	OF	153	588	102	185	34	3	32	126	60	64	2	28	18-4	.315	.371	.546	.917	5	.983
2001— Chicago (A.L.)	OF-DH	160	593	97	181	40	1	31	113	70	70	5	14	25-7	.305	.382	.533	.914	5	.983
2002— Chicago (A.L.)	OF-DH	153	590	116	189	47	1	38	135	53	77	7	21	7-5	.320	.381	.597	.978	4	.986
2003— Chicago (A.L.)	OF-DH	160	606	95	192	46	3	29	99	57	73	7	20	9-5	.317	.380	.546	.926	2	.994
2004— Chicago (A.L.)	OF-DH	52	202	32	59	8	2	9	37	16	22	3	4	0-2	.292	.351	.485	.837	1	.990
Major League totals (8 years)		1001	3807	624	1167	240	15	187	703	333	431	34	131	82-38	.307	.364	.525	.889	25	.988

DIVISION SERIES RECORD

									BATTING											
Year Team (League)	Pos.	G	AB	R	H	2B	3B	HR	RBI	BB	SO	HBP	GDP	SB-CS	Avg.	OBP	SLG	OPS	E	Avg.
2000— Chicago (A.L.)	OF	3	11	0	2	0	1	0	1	2	2	0	1	1-0	.182	.308	.364	.671	0	1.000

ALL-STAR GAME RECORD

	G	AB	R	H	2B	3B	HR	RBI	BB	SO	HBP	GDP	SB-CS	Avg.	OBP	SLG	OPS	E	Avg.
All-Star Game totals (4 years)	4	6	1	3	1	0	1	2	0	0	0	0	0-0	.500	.429	1.167	1.595	0	1.000

ORDONEZ, REY — SS

PERSONAL: Born January 11, 1971, in Havana, Cuba. ... 5-9/159. ... Bats right, throws right. ... Full name: Reynaldo Ordonez. ... Name pronounced: RAY or-DOAN-yez. ... High school: Espa (Havana, Cuba). ... College: Fajardo (Cuba).
TRANSACTIONS/CAREER NOTES: Signed by New York Mets organization (February 8, 1994) after Mets won negotiating rights in a lottery of Cuban defectors (October 29, 1993). ... On disabled list (June 2-July 11, 1997; and May 30, 2000-remainder of season). ... Traded by Mets to Tampa Bay Devil Rays for two players to be named (December 15, 2002); Mets acquired IFs Russ Johnson and Josh Pressley to complete deal (December 19, 2002). ... On disabled list (May 9, 2003-remainder of season). ... Signed as a free agent by San Diego Padres organization (January 16, 2004). ... Released by Padres (May 12, 2004). ... Signed by Chicago Cubs organization (May 20, 2004). ... Refused minor league assignment and became a free agent (July 23, 2004).
HONORS: Won N.L. Gold Glove at shortstop (1997-99).
2004 GAMES PLAYED BY POSITION (MLB): SS—22.

									BATTING										FIELDING	
Year Team (League)	Pos.	G	AB	R	H	2B	3B	HR	RBI	BB	SO	HBP	GDP	SB-CS	Avg.	OBP	SLG	OPS	E	Avg.
1993— St. Paul (Nor.)		15	60	10	17	4	0	0	7	3	9	...	...	3-...	.283	...	.350	...	2	.971
1994— St. Lucie (Fla. St.)	SS	79	314	47	97	21	2	2	40	14	28	0	8	11-6	.309	.336	.408	.744	15	.966
—Binghamton (East.)	SS	48	191	22	50	10	2	1	20	4	18	1	2	4-3	.262	.279	.351	.630	8	.961
1995— Norfolk (Int'l)	SS	125	439	49	94	21	4	2	50	27	50	3	12	11-13	.214	.261	.294	.554	21	.967
1996— New York (N.L.)	SS	151	502	51	129	12	4	1	30	22	53	1	12	1-3	.257	.289	.303	.592	27	.962
1997— New York (N.L.)	SS	120	356	35	77	5	3	1	33	18	36	1	10	11-5	.216	.255	.256	.510	9	.983
1998— New York (N.L.)	SS	153	505	46	124	20	2	1	42	23	60	1	11	3-6	.246	.278	.299	.577	17	.975
1999— New York (N.L.)	SS	154	520	49	134	24	2	1	60	49	59	1	16	8-4	.258	.319	.317	.636	4	.994
2000— New York (N.L.)	SS	45	133	10	25	5	0	0	9	17	16	0	4	0-0	.188	.278	.226	.504	6	.965
2001— New York (N.L.)	SS	149	461	31	114	24	4	3	44	34	43	1	17	3-2	.247	.299	.336	.635	12	.980
2002— New York (N.L.)	SS	144	460	53	117	25	2	1	42	24	46	2	19	2-2	.254	.292	.324	.616	19	.969
2003— Tampa Bay (A.L.)	SS	34	117	14	37	11	0	3	22	2	12	1	3	0-2	.316	.328	.487	.815	5	.970
2004— Daytona (Fla. St.)	SS	3	8	0	1	1	0	0	1	0	1	0	0	0-0	.125	.111	.250	.361	0	1.000
—Iowa (PCL)	SS-2B	6	24	3	7	2	0	0	3	1	1	0	0	0-0	.292	.320	.375	.695	1	.971
—Chicago (N.L.)	SS	23	61	2	10	3	0	1	5	2	14	0	1	0-0	.164	.190	.262	.453	3	.959
American League totals (1 year)		34	117	14	37	11	0	3	22	2	12	1	3	0-2	.316	.328	.487	.815	5	.970
National League totals (8 years)		939	2998	277	730	118	17	9	265	189	327	7	90	28-22	.243	.288	.303	.591	97	.976
Major League totals (9 years)		973	3115	291	767	129	17	12	287	191	339	8	93	28-24	.246	.289	.310	.600	102	.976

DIVISION SERIES RECORD

									BATTING											
Year Team (League)	Pos.	G	AB	R	H	2B	3B	HR	RBI	BB	SO	HBP	GDP	SB-CS	Avg.	OBP	SLG	OPS	E	Avg.
1999— New York (N.L.)	SS	4	14	1	4	1	0	0	2	0	5	0	1	1-0	.286	.286	.357	.643	0	1.000

CHAMPIONSHIP SERIES RECORD

									BATTING											
Year Team (League)	Pos.	G	AB	R	H	2B	3B	HR	RBI	BB	SO	HBP	GDP	SB-CS	Avg.	OBP	SLG	OPS	E	Avg.
1999— New York (N.L.)	SS	6	24	0	1	0	0	0	0	0	2	0	1	0-0	.042	.042	.042	.083	0	1.000

OROPESA, EDDIE — P

PERSONAL: Born November 23, 1971, in Colen Matanzas, Cuba. ... 6-1/204. ... Throws left, bats left. ... Full name: Edilberto Oropesa. ... College: Matanzas (Cuba).
TRANSACTIONS/CAREER NOTES: Selected by Los Angeles Dodgers organization in 14th round of 1994 free-agent draft. ... Selected by San Francisco Giants organization from Dodgers organization in Rule 5 minor league draft (December 9, 1996). ... Loaned by Giants organization to Reynosa of the Mexican League (July 8-August 5, 1999). ... Signed as a free agent by Philadelphia Phillies organization (November 15, 2000). ... On disabled list (June 13-July 5, 2001); included rehabilitation assignment to Scranton/Wilkes-Barre. ... Signed as a free agent by Arizona Diamondbacks organization (November 20, 2001). ... Signed as a free agent by San Diego Padres organization (December 23, 2003). ... Released by Padres (September 15, 2003).
CAREER HITTING: 0-for-0 (.000), 0 R, 0 2B, 0 3B, 0 HR, 0 RBI.

Year Team (League)	W	L	Pct.	ERA	WHIP	G	GS	CG	ShO	Hld.	Sv.-Opp.	IP	H	R	ER	HR	BB-IBB	SO	Avg.
1993—St. Paul (Nor.)	3	1	.750	1.93	0.80	4	3	0	0	...	0-...	18.2	6	4	4		9-...	19	
1994—Vero Beach (FSL)	4	3	.571	2.13	1.10	19	10	1	1	...	0-...	72.0	54	24	17	2	25-2	67	.215
1995—San Antonio (Texas)	1	1	.500	3.12	1.96	16	0	0	0	...	1-...	17.1	22	8	6	2	12-1	16	.319
—Vero Beach (FSL)	3	1	.750	3.81	1.24	19	1	0	0	...	1-...	28.1	25	12	12	0	10-0	23	.240
—San Bernardino (Calif.)	0	0	...	0.00	0.00	1	0	0	0	...	1-...	1.0	0	0	0	0	0-0	0	.000
1996—San Bernardino (Calif.)	11	6	.647	3.34	1.34	33	19	0	0	...	1-...	156.1	133	74	58	8	77-1	133	.229
1997—Shreveport (Texas)	7	7	.500	3.92	1.50	43	9	1	0	...	0-...	124.0	122	58	54	7	64-0	65	.270
1998—Shreveport (Texas)	7	11	.389	3.78	1.47	32	20	2	0	...	1-...	143.0	143	71	60	6	67-3	104	.266
—Pres. Lions (Taiw.)	0	2	.000	6.43	0.79	8	0	0	0	...	1-...	14.0	...		10		11-...	6	
1999—Fresno (PCL)	6	5	.545	4.85	1.59	21	18	1	0	...	0-...	102.0	113	69	55	15	49-0	61	.280
—Bakersfield (California)	2	0	1.000	3.60	1.40	2	1	0	0	...	0-...	10.0	13	5	4	2	1-0	10	.325
—Reynosa (Mex.)	0	4	.000	7.06	2.22	7	3	0	0	...	0-...	21.2	32	19	17	3	16-...	8	
2000—Shreveport (Texas)	2	4	.333	3.07	1.44	59	2	0	0	...	4-...	76.1	70	38	26	6	40-6	76	.238
2001—Philadelphia (N.L.)	1	0	1.000	4.74	1.74	30	0	0	0	...	6	0-1	19.0	16	10	10	1	17-6	15	.232
—Scran./W.B. (I.L.)	1	0	1.000	2.35	1.17	14	1	0	0	...	0-...	15.1	14	5	4	1	4-1	11	.246
—Clearwater (Fla. St.)	0	0	...	0.00	1.50	2	0	0	0	...	0-...	2.0	2	0	0	0	1-0	3	.250
2002—Arizona (N.L.)	2	0	1.000	10.30	2.13	32	0	0	0	...	7	0-1	25.1	39	30	29	6	15-0	18	.348
—Tucson (PCL)	1	0	1.000	3.86	1.40	29	0	0	0	...	0-...	25.2	23	11	11	2	13-2	26	.242
2003—Tucson (PCL)	0	1	.000	2.35	1.20	15	0	0	0	...	0-...	15.1	14	4	4	0	4-1	9	.246
—Arizona (N.L.)	3	3	.500	5.82	1.68	47	0	0	0	...	10	0-0	38.2	38	27	25	3	27-2	39	.257
2004—San Diego (N.L.)	2	1	.667	11.00	2.11	16	0	0	0	...	1	0-0	9.0	6	12	11	1	13-3	6	.188
—Portland (PCL)	3	3	.500	2.31	1.05	37	0	0	0	...	1-...	46.2	30	15	12	2	19-1	55	.185
Major League totals (4 years)	8	4	.667	7.34	1.86	125	0	0	0	24	0-2	92.0	99	79	75	11	72-11	78	.274

ORTIZ, DAVID — 1B/DH

PERSONAL: Born November 18, 1975, in Santo Domingo, Dominican Republic. ... 6-4/230. ... Bats left, throws left. ... Full name: David Americo Ortiz. ... Name pronounced: or-TEEZ. ... High school: Estudia Espallat (Dominican Republic). ... Formerly known as David Arias.

TRANSACTIONS/CAREER NOTES: Signed as a non-drafted free agent by Seattle Mariners organization (November 28, 1992). ... Traded by Mariners to Minnesota Twins (September 13, 1996), completing deal in which Twins traded 3B Dave Hollins to Mariners for a player to be named (August 29, 1996). ... On disabled list (May 10-July 9, 1998); included rehabilitation assignment to Salt Lake. ... On disabled list (May 5-July 21, 2001); included rehabilitation assignments to GCL Twins, Fort Myers and New Britain. ... On disabled list (April 19-May 12, 2002). ... Released by Twins (December 16, 2002). ... Signed by Boston Red Sox (January 22, 2003). ... On suspended list (August 1-7, 2004).

2004 GAMES PLAYED BY POSITION (MLB): DH—115, 1B—34.

										BATTING										FIELDING	
Year Team (League)	Pos.	G	AB	R	H	2B	3B	HR	RBI	BB	SO	HBP	GDP	SB-CS	Avg.	OBP	SLG	OPS		E	Avg.
1993—Dom. Mariners (DSL)		61	201	61	53	17	1	7	31	34	44	...		1-...	.264	...	.463				
1994—Ariz. Mariners (Ariz.)	1B	53	167	14	41	10	1	2	20	14	46	2	2	1-4	.246	.305	.353	.658		6	.985
1995—Ariz. Mariners (Ariz.)	1B	48	184	30	61	18	4	4	37	23	52	1	2	2-0	.332	.403	.538	.941		5	.989
1996—Wisconsin (Midw.)	1B-DH-3B	129	485	89	156	34	2	18	93	52	108	5	5	3-4	.322	.390	.511	.901		13	.989
1997—Fort Myers (FSL)	1B-DH	61	239	45	79	15	0	13	58	22	53	1	3	2-1	.331	.385	.556	.941		9	.984
—New Britain (East.)	DH-1B	69	258	40	83	22	2	14	56	21	78	4	6	2-6	.322	.379	.585	.964		3	.990
—Salt Lake (PCL)	1B-DH	10	42	5	9	1	0	4	10	2	11	0	4	0-1	.214	.250	.524	.774		0	1.000
—Minnesota (A.L.)	1B	15	49	10	16	3	0	1	6	2	19	0	1	0-0	.327	.353	.449	.802		1	.989
1998—Minnesota (A.L.)	1B-DH	86	278	47	77	20	0	9	46	39	72	5	8	1-0	.277	.371	.446	.817		6	.989
—Salt Lake (PCL)	1B-DH	11	37	5	9	3	0	2	6	3	9	0	0	0-0	.243	.300	.486	.786		3	.966
1999—Salt Lake (PCL)	1B-DH	130	476	85	150	35	3	30	110	79	105	3	8	2-2	.315	.412	.590	1.002		20	.980
—Minnesota (A.L.)	DH-1B-OF	10	20	1	0	0	0	0	0	5	12	0	0	0-0	.000	.200	.000	.200		0	1.000
2000—Minnesota (A.L.)	DH-1B	130	415	59	117	36	1	10	63	57	81	0	13	1-0	.282	.364	.446	.810		1	.996
2001—Minnesota (A.L.)	DH-1B	89	303	46	71	17	1	18	48	40	68	1	6	1-0	.234	.324	.475	.799		0	1.000
—GC Twins (GCL)	DH	4	10	3	4	0	0	0	1	3	1	0	0	1-0	.400	.538	.400	.938		...	...
—Fort Myers (FSL)	1B	1	3	0	0	0	0	0	0	1	0	0	0	0-0	.000	.250	.000	.250		0	1.000
—New Britain (East.)	1B	9	37	3	9	4	0	0	1	3	9	0	0	0-0	.243	.293	.351	.644		0	1.000
2002—Minnesota (A.L.)	DH-1B	125	412	52	112	32	1	20	75	43	87	3	5	1-2	.272	.339	.500	.839		1	.990
2003—Boston (A.L.)	DH-1B	128	448	79	129	39	2	31	101	58	83	1	9	0-0	.288	.369	.592	.961		3	.992
2004—Boston (A.L.)	DH-1B	150	582	94	175	47	3	41	139	75	133	4	12	0-0	.301	.380	.603	.983		4	.986
Major League totals (8 years)		733	2507	388	697	194	8	130	478	319	555	14	56	4-2	.278	.359	.517	.876		16	.991

DIVISION SERIES RECORD

Year Team (League)	Pos.	G	AB	R	H	2B	3B	HR	RBI	BB	SO	HBP	GDP	SB-CS	Avg.	OBP	SLG	OPS	E	Avg.
2002—Minnesota (A.L.)	DH	4	13	0	3	0	0	0	2	0	5	0	0	0-0	.231	.231	.385	.615	...	...
2003—Boston (A.L.)	DH	5	21	0	2	1	0	0	2	2	7	0	0	0-0	.095	.174	.143	.317	0	...
2004—Boston (A.L.)	DH	3	11	4	6	2	0	1	4	5	2	0	0	0-0	.545	.688	1.000	1.688	0	...
Division series totals (3 years)		12	45	4	11	5	0	1	8	7	14	0	0	0-0	.244	.346	.422	.768	0	

CHAMPIONSHIP SERIES RECORD

Year Team (League)	Pos.	G	AB	R	H	2B	3B	HR	RBI	BB	SO	HBP	GDP	SB-CS	Avg.	OBP	SLG	OPS	E	Avg.
2002—Minnesota (A.L.)	DH	5	16	0	5	1	0	0	2	0	5	0	0	0-0	.313	.313	.375	.688	...	...
2003—Boston (A.L.)	DH	7	26	4	7	1	0	2	6	3	8	1	1	0-0	.269	.367	.538	.905	0	...
2004—Boston (A.L.)	DH	7	31	6	12	0	1	3	11	4	7	0	0	0-1	.387	.457	.742	1.199	0	...
Champ. series totals (3 years)		19	73	10	24	2	1	5	19	7	20	1	1	0-1	.329	.395	.589	.984	0	

WORLD SERIES RECORD

Year Team (League)	Pos.	G	AB	R	H	2B	3B	HR	RBI	BB	SO	HBP	GDP	SB-CS	Avg.	OBP	SLG	OPS	E	Avg.
2004—Boston (A.L.)	DH-1B	4	13	3	4	1	0	1	4	1	0	0	0	0-0	.308	.471	.615	1.086	0	1.000

ALL-STAR GAME RECORD

	G	AB	R	H	2B	3B	HR	RBI	BB	SO	HBP	GDP	SB-CS	Avg.	OBP	SLG	OPS	E	Avg.
All-Star Game totals (1 year)	1	1	2	1	0	0	1	2	2	0	0	0	0-0	1.000	1.000	4.000	5.000	0	1.000

ORTIZ, RAMON — P

PERSONAL: Born May 23, 1973, in Cotui, Dominican Republic. ... 6-0/175. ... Throws right, bats right. ... Full name: Ramon Diogenes Ortiz. ... Name pronounced: or-TEEZ. ... High school: 8th Intermedian (Dominican Republic). ... Cousin of Pedro Liriano, pitcher, Milwaukee Brewers.

TRANSACTIONS/CAREER NOTES: Signed as a non-drafted free agent by California Angels organization (June 20, 1995). ... Angels franchise renamed Anaheim Angels for 1997 season. ... On disabled list (March 20-April 11, 2000); included rehabilitation assignment to Lake Elsinore.

CAREER HITTING: 0-for-22 (.000), 1 R, 0 2B, 0 3B, 0 HR, 0 RBI.

Year Team (League)	W	L	Pct.	ERA	WHIP	G	GS	CG	ShO	Hld.	Sv.-Opp.	IP	H	R	ER	HR	BB-IBB	SO	Avg.
1995—Dom. Angels (DSL).	8	6	.571	2.23	1.37	16	16	7	0	...	0-...	97.0	79	44	24		54-...	100	...
1996—Ariz. Angels (Ariz.)	5	4	.556	2.12	1.21	16	8	2	2	...	1-...	68.0	55	28	16	5	27-0	78	.216
—Boise (N'west)	1	1	.500	3.66	1.37	3	3	0	0	...	0-...	19.2	21	10	8	3	6-0	18	.263
1997—Cedar Rapids (Midw.)	11	10	.524	3.58	1.15	27	27	8	4	...	0-...	181.0	156	78	72	22	53-0	225	.230
1998—Midland (Texas)	2	1	.667	5.55	1.40	7	7	0	0	...	0-...	47.0	50	31	29	10	16-0	53	.275
1999—Erie (East.)	9	4	.692	2.82	1.25	15	15	2	2	...	0-...	102.0	88	38	32	12	40-0	86	.237
—Edmonton (PCL)	5	3	.625	4.05	1.22	9	9	0	0	...	0-...	53.1	46	26	24	7	19-0	64	.227
—Anaheim (A.L.)	2	3	.400	6.52	1.55	9	9	0	0	0	0-0	48.1	50	35	35	7	25-0	44	.265
2000—Lake Elsinore (Calif.)	1	0	1.000	3.00	1.67	1	1	0	0	0	0-0	6.0	8	2	2	0	2-0	7	.333
—Anaheim (A.L.)	8	6	.571	5.09	1.36	18	18	2	0	0	0-0	111.1	96	69	63	18	55-0	73	.236
—Edmonton (PCL)	6	6	.500	4.55	1.25	15	15	1	0	...	0-...	89.0	74	49	45	7	37-0	76	.223
2001—Anaheim (A.L.)	13	11	.542	4.36	1.43	32	32	2	0	0	0-0	208.2	223	114	101	25	76-6	135	.274
2002—Anaheim (A.L.)	15	9	.625	3.77	1.18	32	32	4	1	0	0-0	217.1	188	97	91	* 40	68-0	162	.230
2003—Anaheim (A.L.)	16	13	.552	5.20	1.51	32	32	1	0	0	0-0	180.0	209	121	104	28	63-0	94	.287
2004—Anaheim (A.L.)	5	7	.417	4.43	1.38	34	14	0	0	0	0-0	128.0	139	64	63	18	38-4	82	.280
Major League totals (6 years)	59	49	.546	4.60	1.38	157	137	9	1	0	0-0	893.2	905	500	457	136	325-10	590	.262

DIVISION SERIES RECORD

Year Team (League)	W	L	Pct.	ERA	WHIP	G	GS	CG	ShO	Hld.	Sv.-Opp.	IP	H	R	ER	HR	BB-IBB	SO	Avg.
2002—Anaheim (A.L.)	0	0	...	20.25	2.63	1	1	0	0	0	0-0	2.2	3	6	6	0	4-0	1	.333
2004—Anaheim (A.L.)	0	0	...	4.50	1.50	1	0	0	0	0	0-0	2.0	2	1	1	0	1-1	0	.250
Division series totals (2 years)	0	0	...	13.50	2.14	2	1	0	0	0	0-0	4.2	5	7	7	0	5-1	1	.294

CHAMPIONSHIP SERIES RECORD

Year Team (League)	W	L	Pct.	ERA	WHIP	G	GS	CG	ShO	Hld.	Sv.-Opp.	IP	H	R	ER	HR	BB-IBB	SO	Avg.
2002—Anaheim (A.L.)	1	0	1.000	5.06	2.06	1	1	0	0	0	0-0	5.1	10	3	3	0	1-0	3	.435

WORLD SERIES RECORD

Year Team (League)	W	L	Pct.	ERA	WHIP	G	GS	CG	ShO	Hld.	Sv.-Opp.	IP	H	R	ER	HR	BB-IBB	SO	Avg.
2002—Anaheim (A.L.)	1	0	1.000	7.20	1.80	1	1	0	0	0	0-0	5.0	5	4	4	2	4-1	3	.263

ORTIZ, RUSS — P

PERSONAL: Born June 5, 1974, in Encino, Calif. ... 6-1/208. ... Throws right, bats right. ... Full name: Russell Reid Ortiz. ... Name pronounced: OR-teez. ... High school: Montclair Prep (Van Nuys, Calif.). ... College: Oklahoma.

TRANSACTIONS/CAREER NOTES: Selected by San Francisco Giants organization in fourth round of 1995 free-agent draft. ... Traded by Giants to Atlanta Braves for Ps Damian Moss and P Merkin Valdez (December 17, 2002).

CAREER HITTING: 87-for-422 (.206), 41 R, 21 2B, 0 3B, 6 HR, 41 RBI.

Year Team (League)	W	L	Pct.	ERA	WHIP	G	GS	CG	ShO	Hld.	Sv.-Opp.	IP	H	R	ER	HR	BB-IBB	SO	Avg.
1995—Bellingham (N'west)	2	0	1.000	0.52	0.93	25	0	0	0	...	11-...	34.1	19	4	2	1	13-0	55	.162
—San Jose (California)	0	1	.000	1.50	1.00	5	0	0	0	...	0-...	6.0	4	1	1	0	2-0	7	.190
1996—San Jose (California)	0	0	...	0.25	0.98	34	0	0	0	...	23-...	36.2	16	2	1	0	20-0	63	.131
—Shreveport (Texas)	1	2	.333	4.05	1.61	26	0	0	0	...	13-...	26.2	22	14	12	0	21-3	29	.220
1997—Shreveport (Texas)	2	3	.400	4.13	1.57	12	12	0	0	...	0-...	56.2	52	28	26	3	37-0	50	.252
—Phoenix (PCL)	4	3	.571	5.51	1.53	14	14	0	0	...	0-...	85.0	96	57	52	11	34-0	70	.287
1998—San Francisco (N.L.)	4	4	.500	4.99	1.54	22	13	0	0	1	0-0	88.1	90	51	49	11	46-1	75	.269
—Fresno (PCL)	3	1	.750	1.60	1.13	10	10	0	0	...	0-...	50.2	35	10	9	3	22-0	59	.198
1999—San Francisco (N.L.)	18	9	.667	3.81	1.51	33	33	3	0	0	0-0	207.2	189	109	88	24	125-5	164	.244
2000—San Francisco (N.L.)	14	12	.538	5.01	1.55	33	32	0	0	0	0-0	195.2	192	117	109	28	112-7	167	.261
2001—San Francisco (N.L.)	17	9	.654	3.29	1.27	33	33	1	1	0	0-0	218.2	187	90	80	13	91-3	169	.232
2002—San Francisco (N.L.)	14	10	.583	3.61	1.33	33	33	2	0	0	0-0	214.1	191	89	86	15	94-5	137	.241
2003—Atlanta (N.L.)	* 21	7	.750	3.81	1.31	34	34	1	1	0	0-0	212.1	177	101	90	17	* 102-7	149	.223
2004—Atlanta (N.L.)	15	9	.625	4.13	1.51	34	34	2	1	0	0-0	204.2	197	98	94	23	112-7	143	.258
Major League totals (7 years)	103	60	.632	4.00	1.42	222	212	9	3	1	0-0	1341.2	1223	655	596	131	682-29	1004	.245

DIVISION SERIES RECORD

Year Team (League)	W	L	Pct.	ERA	WHIP	G	GS	CG	ShO	Hld.	Sv.-Opp.	IP	H	R	ER	HR	BB-IBB	SO	Avg.
2000—San Francisco (N.L.)	0	0	...	1.69	1.13	1	1	0	0	0	0-0	5.1	2	1	1	0	4-1	4	.118
2002—San Francisco (N.L.)	2	0	1.000	2.19	1.38	2	2	0	0	0	0-0	12.1	9	3	3	0	8-1	8	.200
2003—Atlanta (N.L.)	1	1	.500	5.06	2.06	2	2	0	0	0	0-0	10.2	15	6	6	1	7-1	9	.333
2004—Atlanta (N.L.)	0	0	...	15.00	2.67	1	1	0	0	0	0-0	3.0	7	5	5	1	1-0	1	.467
Division series totals (4 years)	3	1	.750	4.31	1.69	6	6	0	0	0	0-0	31.1	33	15	15	2	20-3	22	.270

CHAMPIONSHIP SERIES RECORD

Year Team (League)	W	L	Pct.	ERA	WHIP	G	GS	CG	ShO	Hld.	Sv.-Opp.	IP	H	R	ER	HR	BB-IBB	SO	Avg.
2002—San Francisco (N.L.)	0	0	...	7.71	1.71	1	1	0	0	0	0-0	4.2	5	4	4	2	3-0	3	.263

WORLD SERIES RECORD

Year Team (League)	W	L	Pct.	ERA	WHIP	G	GS	CG	ShO	Hld.	Sv.-Opp.	IP	H	R	ER	HR	BB-IBB	SO	Avg.
2002—San Francisco (N.L.)	0	0	...	10.13	1.88	2	2	0	0	0	0-0	8.0	13	9	9	1	2-0	2	.361

ALL-STAR GAME RECORD

	W	L	Pct.	ERA	WHIP	G	GS	CG	ShO	Hld.	Sv.-Opp.	IP	H	R	ER	HR	BB-IBB	SO	Avg.
All-Star Game totals (1 year)	0	0	...	0.00	1.00	1	0	0	0	0	0-0	1.0	0	0	0	0	1-0	2	.000

OSBORNE, DONOVAN — P

PERSONAL: Born June 21, 1969, in Roseville, Calif. ... 6-2/210. ... Throws left, bats left. ... Full name: Donovan Alan Osborne. ... High school: Carson City (Nev.). ... College: UNLV.

TRANSACTIONS/CAREER NOTES: Selected by Montreal Expos organization in ninth round of 1987 free-agent draft; did not sign. ... Selected by St. Louis Cardinals organization in first round (13th pick overall) of 1990 free-agent draft. ... On disabled list (April 2, 1994-entire season). ... On disabled list (May 15-July 14, 1995); included rehabilitation assignments to Arkansas and Louisville. ... On disabled list (March 25-April 17, 1996); included rehabilitation assignments to St. Petersburg and Louisville. ... On disabled list (May 3-July 29, 1997). ... On disabled list (March 22-April 16 and May 8-August 8, 1998); included rehabilitation assignments to Arkansas and Memphis. ... On disabled list (May 7, 1999-remainder of season). ... Signed as a free agent by Chicago Cubs organization (February 5, 2002). ... On disabled list (May 8-September 2, 2002).

... Released by Cubs (September 2, 2002). ... Signed by New York Mets organization (February 23, 2003). ... Released by Mets (March 25, 2003). ... Signed by New York Yankees organization (February 4, 2004). ... Released by Yankees (May 25, 2004). ... Signed by San Diego Padres organization (June 11, 2004). ... Released by Padres (July 5, 2004).

CAREER HITTING: 42-for-259 (.162), 18 R, 10 2B, 1 3B, 1 HR, 19 RBI.

Year	Team (League)	W	L	Pct.	ERA	WHIP	G	GS	CG	ShO	Hld.	Sv.-Opp.	IP	H	R	ER	HR	BB-IBB	SO	Avg.
1990—	Hamilton (N.Y.-Penn.)	0	2	.000	3.60	1.30	4	4	0	0	...	0-...	20.0	21	8	8	0	5-1	14	.266
—	Savannah (S. Atl.)	2	2	.500	2.61	1.14	6	6	1	0	...	0-...	41.1	40	20	12	2	7-0	28	.255
1991—	Arkansas (Texas)	8	12	.400	3.63	1.33	26	26	3	0	...	0-...	166.0	178	82	67	6	43-3	130	.280
1992—	St. Louis (N.L.)	11	9	.550	3.77	1.29	34	29	0	0	1	0-0	179.0	193	91	75	14	38-2	104	.275
1993—	St. Louis (N.L.)	10	7	.588	3.76	1.28	26	26	1	0	0	0-0	155.2	153	73	65	18	47-4	83	.257
1994—	St. Louis (N.L.)			Did not play.																
1995—	St. Louis (N.L.)	4	6	.400	3.81	1.29	19	19	0	0	0	0-0	113.1	112	58	48	17	34-2	82	.260
—	Arkansas (Texas)	0	1	.000	2.45	1.27	2	2	0	0	...	0-...	11.0	12	4	3	0	2-0	6	.279
—	Louisville (A.A.)	0	1	.000	3.86	1.14	1	1	0	0	...	0-...	7.0	8	3	3	0	0-0	3	.276
1996—	St. Pete. (FSL)	1	0	1.000	0.00	0.33	1	1	0	0	...	0-...	6.0	2	0	0	0	0-0	2	.105
—	Louisville (A.A.)	1	0	1.000	2.57	1.14	1	1	0	0	...	0-...	7.0	6	2	2	1	2-0	3	.273
—	St. Louis (N.L.)	13	9	.591	3.53	1.25	30	30	2	1	0	0-0	198.2	191	87	78	22	57-5	134	.254
1997—	St. Louis (N.L.)	3	7	.300	4.93	1.33	14	14	0	0	0	0-0	80.1	84	46	44	10	23-2	51	.274
—	Louisville (A.A.)	0	1	.000	4.73	1.35	3	3	0	0	...	0-...	13.1	13	7	7	2	5-1	13	.255
1998—	Arkansas (Texas)	2	0	1.000	4.26	1.00	5	5	0	0	...	0-...	19.0	16	9	9	2	3-0	21	.219
—	Memphis (PCL)	0	0	...	6.23	1.15	1	1	0	0	...	0-...	4.1	5	4	3	2	0-0	6	.263
—	St. Louis (N.L.)	5	4	.556	4.09	1.27	14	14	1	1	0	0-0	83.2	84	42	38	11	22-2	60	.256
1999—	St. Louis (N.L.)	1	3	.250	5.52	1.50	6	6	0	0	0	0-0	29.1	34	18	18	4	10-0	21	.298
2000—	....			Did not play.																
2001—	....			Did not play.																
2002—	Chicago (N.L.)	0	1	.000	6.19	1.81	11	0	0	0	0	0-0	16.0	19	11	11	1	10-2	13	.297
2004—	New York (A.L.)	2	0	1.000	7.13	1.70	9	2	0	0	0	0-0	17.2	25	16	14	3	5-0	10	.347
—	Portland (PCL)	2	2	.500	8.56	2.27	7	2	0	0	...	0-...	13.2	26	14	13	4	5-0	12	.426
American League totals (1 year)		2	0	1.000	7.13	1.70	9	2	0	0	0	0-0	17.2	25	16	14	3	5-0	10	.347
National League totals (8 years)		47	46	.505	3.96	1.30	154	138	4	2	1	0-0	856.0	870	426	377	97	241-19	548	.264
Major League totals (9 years)		49	46	.516	4.03	1.31	163	140	4	2	1	0-0	873.2	895	442	391	100	246-19	558	.266

DIVISION SERIES RECORD

Year	Team (League)	W	L	Pct.	ERA	WHIP	G	GS	CG	ShO	Hld.	Sv.-Opp.	IP	H	R	ER	HR	BB-IBB	SO	Avg.
1996—	St. Louis (N.L.)	0	0	...	9.00	1.75	1	1	0	0	0	0-0	4.0	7	4	4	1	0-0	5	.368

CHAMPIONSHIP SERIES RECORD

Year	Team (League)	W	L	Pct.	ERA	WHIP	G	GS	CG	ShO	Hld.	Sv.-Opp.	IP	H	R	ER	HR	BB-IBB	SO	Avg.
1996—	St. Louis (N.L.)	1	1	.500	9.39	2.09	2	2	0	0	0	0-0	7.2	12	8	8	0	4-0	6	.353

OSIK, KEITH   C

PERSONAL: Born October 22, 1968, in Port Jefferson, N.Y. ... 6-0/213. ... Bats right, throws right. ... Full name: Keith Richard Osik. ... Name pronounced: OH-sick. ... High school: Shoreham (N.Y.)-Wading River. ... College: LSU.

TRANSACTIONS/CAREER NOTES: Selected by Texas Rangers organization in 47th round of 1987 free-agent draft; did not sign. ... Selected by Pittsburgh Pirates organization in 24th round of 1990 free-agent draft. ... On disabled list (July 16-August 13, 1996); included rehabilitation assignment to Erie. ... On disabled list (July 21-August 13, 1999); included rehabilitation assignment to Nashville. ... On disabled list (April 30-May 15, 2001). ... Signed as a free agent by Milwaukee Brewers organization (January 10, 2003). ... Signed as a free agent by Baltimore Orioles organization (January 14, 2004). ... Released by Orioles (June 1, 2004). ... Signed by Florida Marlins organization (June 10, 2004). ... Released by Marlins (July 15, 2004). ... Signed by Tampa Bay Devil Rays organization (July 28, 2004). ... Career major league pitching: 0-0, 40.50 ERA, 2 G, 2.0 IP, 7 H, 9 R, 9 ER, 2 BB, 2 SO.

2004 GAMES PLAYED BY POSITION (MLB): C—11.

Year	Team (League)	Pos.	G	AB	R	H	2B	3B	HR	RBI	BB	SO	HBP	GDP	SB-CS	Avg.	OBP	SLG	OPS	E	Avg.
1990—	Welland (N.Y.-Penn.)	C	29	97	13	27	4	0	1	20	11	12	2	1	2-6	.278	.354	.351	.704	2	.978
1991—	Salem (Caro.)	2B-3B-C	87	300	31	81	12	1	6	35	38	48	3	13	2-3	.270	.356	.377	.732	12	.970
—	Carolina (Southern)	3B-C	17	43	9	13	3	1	0	5	5	5	0	1	0-0	.302	.375	.419	.794	2	.980
1992—	Carolina (Southern)	C	129	425	41	110	17	1	5	45	52	69	15	12	2-9	.259	.354	.339	.696	19	.956
1993—	Carolina (Southern)	C	103	371	40	104	21	2	10	47	30	46	9	13	0-2	.280	.348	.429	.777	6	.992
1994—	Buffalo (A.A.)	C-O-1-DH-2-P	83	260	27	55	16	0	5	33	28	41	3	5	0-1	.212	.294	.331	.624	8	.983
1995—	Calgary (PCL)	C-1-O-P-3	90	301	40	101	25	1	10	59	21	42	5	5	2-2	.336	.384	.525	.909	4	.992
1996—	Pittsburgh (N.L.)	C-3B-OF	48	140	18	41	14	1	1	14	14	22	1	3	1-0	.293	.361	.429	.790	6	.978
—	Erie (N.Y.-Penn)	C	3	10	1	3	1	0	0	2	1	2	1	0	0-0	.300	.417	.400	.817	0	1.000
1997—	Pittsburgh (N.L.)	C-2-3-1	49	105	10	27	9	1	0	7	9	21	1	1	0-1	.257	.322	.362	.684	2	.989
1998—	Pittsburgh (N.L.)	C-3B	39	98	8	21	4	0	0	7	13	16	2	4	1-2	.214	.316	.255	.571	1	.995
1999—	Pittsburgh (N.L.)	C-P	66	167	12	31	3	1	2	13	11	30	1	8	0-0	.186	.239	.252	.490	1	.997
—	Nashville (PCL)	C	4	11	0	1	0	0	0	0	1	1	1	0	0-0	.091	.167	.091	.258	0	1.000
2000—	Pittsburgh (N.L.)	C-3-1-P-DH	46	123	11	36	6	1	4	22	14	11	5	2	3-0	.293	.387	.455	.843	2	.989
2001—	Pittsburgh (N.L.)	C-1-3-2-O	56	120	9	25	4	0	2	13	13	24	3	1	1-0	.208	.299	.292	.591	1	.996
2002—	Pittsburgh (N.L.)	C-3-1-2-O	55	100	6	16	3	0	2	11	6	25	1	2	0-0	.160	.211	.250	.461	1	.994
2003—	Milwaukee (N.L.)	C	80	241	22	60	12	0	2	21	31	44	3	7	0-1	.249	.342	.324	.665	5	.991
2004—	Baltimore (A.L.)	C	11	25	0	2	0	0	0	0	0	7	0	1	0-0	.080	.080	.080	.160	0	1.000
—	Albuquerque (PCL)	C	19	56	5	10	3	1	1	5	5	7	1	6	0-0	.179	.254	.321	.575	0	1.000
—	Durham (Int'l)	C	26	82	6	20	0	0	1	8	6	10	1	1	0-0	.244	.300	.280	.580	0	1.000
American League totals (1 year)			11	25	0	2	0	0	0	0	0	7	0	1	0-0	.080	.080	.080	.160	0	1.000
National League totals (8 years)			439	1094	96	257	55	4	13	108	111	193	17	28	6-4	.235	.314	.328	.642	19	.991
Major League totals (9 years)			450	1119	96	259	55	4	13	108	111	200	17	29	6-4	.231	.309	.323	.632	19	.991

OSUNA, ANTONIO   P

PERSONAL: Born April 12, 1973, in Sinaloa, Mexico. ... 5-11/227. ... Throws right, bats right. ... Full name: Antonio Pedro Osuna. ... Name pronounced: oh-SOON-a. ... High school: Secondaria Federal (Mexico).

TRANSACTIONS/CAREER NOTES: Signed as a non-drafted free agent by Los Angeles Dodgers organization (June 12, 1991). ... Loaned by Dodgers to Mexico City Tigres of the Mexican League (March 6-September 25, 1992). ... On disabled list (May 19-June 16, 1995); included rehabilitation assignment to San Bernardino. ... On disabled list (September 9, 1998-remainder of season). ... On disabled list (March 25-April 16, April 18-May 3 and May 19, 1999-remainder of season); included rehabilitation assignments to San Bernardino. ... On disabled list (March 31-May 5, 2000); included rehabilitation assignment to San Bernardino. ... Traded by Dodgers with P Carlos Ortega to Chicago White Sox for Ps Gary Majewski, Andre Simpson and Orlando Rodriguez (March 17, 2001). ... On disabled list (April 12, 2001-remainder of season). ... Traded by White Sox with P Delvis Lantigua to New York Yankees for P Orlando Hernandez and cash (January 15, 2003). ... On disabled list (April 23-May 14 and June 14-July 13, 2003); included rehabilitation assignments to Tampa and GCL Yankees. ... Signed as a free agent by San Diego Padres organization (February 5, 2004). ... On disabled list (May 12-31 and June 11-September 1, 2004); included rehabilitation assignment to Lake Elsinore.

CAREER HITTING: 1-for-9 (.111), 0 R, 0 2B, 0 3B, 0 HR, 1 RBI.

Year Team (League)	W	L	Pct.	ERA	WHIP	G	GS	CG	ShO	Hld.	Sv.-Opp.	IP	H	R	ER	HR	BB-IBB	SO	Avg.
1991— GC Dodgers (GCL)	0	0	...	0.82	0.73	8	0	0	0	...	4-...	11.0	8	5	1	0	0-0	13	.186
— Yakima (N'west)	0	0	...	3.20	1.03	13	0	0	0	...	5-...	25.1	18	10	9	1	8-0	39	.205
1992— M.C. Tigers (Mex.)	13	7	.650	4.05	1.53	28	26	3	1	...	0-...	166.2	181	80	75	16	74-...	129	...
1993— Bakersfield (California)	0	2	.000	4.91	1.31	14	2	0	0	...	2-...	18.1	19	10	10	2	5-0	20	.268
1994— San Antonio (Texas)	1	2	.333	0.98	0.80	35	0	0	0	...	19-...	46.0	19	6	5	0	18-1	53	.127
— Albuquerque (PCL)	0	0	...	0.00	1.00	6	0	0	0	...	4-...	6.0	5	1	0	0	1-0	8	.227
1995— Los Angeles (N.L.)	2	4	.333	4.43	1.32	39	0	0	0	11	0-2	44.2	39	22	22	5	20-2	46	.241
— San Bernardino (Calif.)	0	0	...	1.29	1.14	5	0	0	0	...	0-...	7.0	3	1	1	1	5-0	11	.130
— Albuquerque (PCL)	0	1	.000	4.42	1.31	19	0	0	0	...	11-...	18.1	-15	9	9	2	9-0	19	.227
1996— Albuquerque (PCL)	0	0	...	0.00	2.00	1	0	0	0	...	0-...	1.0	2	0	0	0	0-0	1	.500
— Los Angeles (N.L.)	9	6	.600	3.00	1.15	73	0	0	0	16	4-9	84.0	65	33	28	6	32-12	85	.220
1997— Albuquerque (PCL)	1	1	.500	1.93	0.93	13	0	0	0	...	6-...	14.0	9	3	3	0	4-0	26	.176
— Los Angeles (N.L.)	3	4	.429	2.19	1.05	48	0	0	0	10	0-0	61.2	46	15	15	6	19-2	68	.209
1998— Los Angeles (N.L.)	7	1	.875	3.06	1.27	54	0	0	0	12	6-11	64.2	50	26	22	8	32-0	72	.214
1999— San Bernardino (Calif.)	0	0	...	2.33	1.29	13	4	0	0	...	0-...	19.1	19	6	5	0	6-0	27	.260
— Los Angeles (N.L.)	0	0	...	7.71	1.50	5	0	0	0	2	0-0	4.2	4	5	4	0	3-0	5	.222
2000— San Bernardino (Calif.)	0	2	.000	4.91	0.95	3	3	0	0	...	0-...	7.1	4	4	4	2	3-0	11	.167
— Albuquerque (PCL)	0	0	...	0.00	1.24	3	1	0	0	...	0-...	5.2	2	0	0	0	5-0	7	.095
— Los Angeles (N.L.)	3	6	.333	3.74	1.37	46	0	0	0	4	0-3	67.1	57	30	28	7	35-2	70	.229
2001— Chicago (A.L.)	0	0	...	20.77	2.31	4	0	0	0	...	0-1	4.1	8	10	10	3	2-1	6	.421
2002— Chicago (A.L.)	8	2	.800	3.86	1.36	59	0	0	0	9	11-14	67.2	64	32	29	1	28-4	66	.250
2003— GC Yankees (GCL)	0	0	...	0.00	1.00	1	1	0	0	...	0-...	1.0	1	0	0	0	0-0	2	.250
— Tampa (FSL)	0	0	...	0.00	0.50	2	2	0	0	...	0-...	4.0	1	0	0	0	1-0	5	.083
— New York (A.L.)	2	5	.286	3.73	1.54	48	0	0	0	9	0-1	50.2	58	22	21	3	20-3	47	.282
2004— Lake Elsinore (Calif.)	0	0	...	2.46	0.55	7	2	0	0	...	0-...	7.1	2	2	2	0	2-0	12	.083
— San Diego (N.L.)	1	2	.667	2.45	1.17	31	0	0	0	2	0-2	36.2	32	11	10	3	11-0	36	.232
American League totals (3 years)	10	7	.588	4.40	1.47	111	0	0	0	18	11-16	122.2	130	64	60	7	50-8	119	.270
National League totals (7 years)	26	22	.542	3.19	1.22	296	0	0	0	57	10-27	363.2	293	142	129	35	152-18	382	.222
Major League totals (10 years)	36	29	.554	3.50	1.29	407	0	0	0	75	21-43	486.1	423	206	189	42	202-26	501	.235

DIVISION SERIES RECORD

Year Team (League)	W	L	Pct.	ERA	WHIP	G	GS	CG	ShO	Hld.	Sv.-Opp.	IP	H	R	ER	HR	BB-IBB	SO	Avg.
1995— Los Angeles (N.L.)	0	1	.000	2.70	1.20	3	0	0	0	...	0-0	3.1	3	1	1	0	1-1	3	.231
1996— Los Angeles (N.L.)	0	1	.000	4.50	2.00	2	0	0	0	...	0-0	2.0	3	1	1	1	1-0	4	.429
Division series totals (2 years)	0	2	.000	3.38	1.50	5	0	0	0	...	0-0	5.1	6	2	2	1	2-1	7	.300

OSWALT, ROY   P

PERSONAL: Born August 29, 1977, in Weir, Miss. ... 6-0/185. ... Throws right, bats right. ... Full name: Roy Edward Oswalt. ... Name pronounced: OWES-walt. ... High school: Weir (Miss.). ... Junior college: Holmes (Miss.) Community College.

TRANSACTIONS/CAREER NOTES: Selected by Houston Astros organization in 23rd round of 1996 free-agent draft. ... On suspended list (August 29-September 3, 2002). ... On disabled list (May 16-31, June 12-July 7 and July 30-September 8, 2003); included rehabilitation assignment to New Orleans.

HONORS: Named N.L. Rookie Pitcher of the Year by THE SPORTING NEWS (2001).

CAREER HITTING: 36-for-234 (.154), 13 R, 5 2B, 0 3B, 0 HR, 13 RBI.

Year Team (League)	W	L	Pct.	ERA	WHIP	G	GS	CG	ShO	Hld.	Sv.-Opp.	IP	H	R	ER	HR	BB-IBB	SO	Avg.
1997— GC Astros (GCL)	1	1	.500	0.64	1.13	5	5	0	0	...	0-...	28.1	25	7	2	2	7-0	28	.227
— Auburn (N.Y.-Penn)	2	4	.333	4.53	1.26	9	9	1	1	...	0-...	51.2	50	29	26	1	15-1	44	.253
1998— GC Astros (GCL)	1	1	.500	2.25	0.69	4	4	0	0	...	0-...	16.0	10	6	4	2	1-0	27	.182
— Auburn (N.Y.-Penn)	4	5	.444	2.18	1.14	11	11	0	0	...	0-...	70.1	49	24	17	3	31-0	67	.194
1999— Michigan (Midw.)	13	4	.765	4.46	1.31	22	22	2	0	...	0-...	151.1	144	78	75	8	54-0	143	.250
2000— Kissimmee (Fla. St.)	4	3	.571	2.98	1.39	8	8	0	0	...	0-...	45.1	52	15	15	1	11-0	47	.294
— Round Rock (Texas)	11	4	.733	1.94	0.99	19	18	2	2	...	0-...	129.2	106	37	28	5	22-1	141	.216
2001— New Orleans (PCL)	2	3	.400	4.35	1.23	5	5	0	0	...	0-...	31.0	32	16	15	4	6-0	34	.267
— Houston (N.L.)	14	3	.824	2.73	1.06	28	20	3	1	0	0-0	141.2	126	48	43	13	24-2	144	.235
2002— Houston (N.L.)	19	9	.679	3.01	1.19	35	34	0	0	0	0-0	233.0	215	86	78	17	62-4	208	.247
2003— New Orleans (PCL)	0	0	...	3.00	1.00	1	1	0	0	...	0-...	3.0	3	1	1	0	0-0	2	.250
— Houston (N.L.)	10	5	.667	2.97	1.14	21	21	0	0	0	0-0	127.1	116	48	42	15	29-0	108	.246
2004— Houston (N.L.)	* 20	10	.667	3.49	1.24	36	• 35	2	2	0	0-0	237.0	233	100	92	17	62-5	206	.260
Major League totals (4 years)	63	27	.700	3.11	1.17	120	110	5	3	0	0-0	739.0	690	282	255	62	177-11	666	.249

DIVISION SERIES RECORD

Year Team (League)	W	L	Pct.	ERA	WHIP	G	GS	CG	ShO	Hld.	Sv.-Opp.	IP	H	R	ER	HR	BB-IBB	SO	Avg.
2004— Houston (N.L.)	1	0	1.000	2.38	1.68	2	2	0	0	0	0-0	11.1	15	3	3	2	4-0	8	.313

CHAMPIONSHIP SERIES RECORD

Year Team (League)	W	L	Pct.	ERA	WHIP	G	GS	CG	ShO	Hld.	Sv.-Opp.	IP	H	R	ER	HR	BB-IBB	SO	Avg.
2004— Houston (N.L.)	0	0	...	6.75	1.88	2	1	0	0	0	0-0	8.0	11	6	6	1	4-0	2	.367

OTSUKA, AKINORI   P

PERSONAL: Born January 13, 1972, in Chiba, Japan. ... 6-0/200. ... Throws right, bats right. ... High school: Yokoshiba.

TRANSACTIONS/CAREER NOTES: Signed as a free agent by San Diego Padres (December 9, 2003).

CAREER HITTING: 0-for-1 (.000), 0 R, 0 2B, 0 3B, 0 HR, 0 RBI.

Year Team (League)	W	L	Pct.	ERA	WHIP	G	GS	CG	ShO	Hld.	Sv.-Opp.	IP	H	R	ER	HR	BB-IBB	SO	Avg.
1997— Kintetsu (Jap. Pac.)	4	5	.444	2.07	1.09	52	0	0	0	...	7-...	82.2	44	22	19	2	46-0	127	...
1998— Kintetsu (Jap. Pac.)	3	2	.600	2.11	1.23	49	0	0	0	...	35-...	55.1	43	19	13	5	25-0	74	...
1999— Kintetsu (Jap. Pac.)	1	4	.200	2.73	1.15	25	0	0	0	...	6-...	29.2	24	12	9	1	10-0	32	...

O

Year Team (League)	W	L	Pct.	ERA	WHIP	G	GS	CG	ShO	Hld.	Sv.-Opp.	IP	H	R	ER	HR	BB-IBB	SO	Avg.
2000— Kinetsu (Jap. Pac.)	1	3	.250	2.38	1.06	39	0	0	0	...	24-...	41.2	31	11	11	3	13-0	49	...
2001— Kinetsu (Jap. Pac.)	2	5	.286	4.02	1.02	48	0	0	0	...	26-...	56.0	42	25	25	7	15-0	82	...
2002— Kinetsu (Jap. Pac.)	2	1	.667	1.28	0.59	41	0	0	0	...	22-...	42.1	22	7	6	4	3-0	54	...
2003— Chunichi (Jp. Cn.)	1	3	.250	2.09	0.84	51	0	0	0	...	17-...	43.0	31	10	10	4	5-0	56	...
2004— San Diego (N.L.)	7	2	.778	1.75	1.06	73	0	0	0	34	2-7	77.1	56	16	15	6	26-6	87	.199
Major League totals (1 year)	7	2	.778	1.75	1.06	73	0	0	0	34	2-7	77.1	56	16	15	6	26-6	87	.199

OVERBAY, LYLE — 1B

PERSONAL: Born January 28, 1977, in Centralia, Wash. ... 6-2/227. ... Bats left, throws left. ... Full name: Lyle Stefan Overbay. ... College: Nevada.
TRANSACTIONS/CAREER NOTES: Selected by Arizona Diamondbacks organization in 18th round of 1999 free-agent draft. ... Traded with SS Craig Counsell, 2B Junior Spivey, C Chad Moeller and Ps Chris Capuano and Jorge de la Rosa to Milwaukee Brewers for 1B Richie Sexson, P Shane Nance and a player to be named (December 1, 2003); Diamondbacks acquired OF Noochie Varner to complete deal (December 15, 2003).
2004 GAMES PLAYED BY POSITION (MLB): 1B—158.

Year Team (League)	Pos.	G	AB	R	H	2B	3B	HR	RBI	BB	SO	HBP	GDP	SB-CS	Avg.	OBP	SLG	OPS	FIELDING E	Avg.
1999— Missoula (Pio.)	1B-OF	75	306	66	105	25	7	12	101	40	53	2	14	10-3	.343	.418	.588	1.006	10	.986
2000— South Bend (Mid.)	1B	71	259	47	86	19	3	6	47	27	36	2	2	9-2	.332	.397	.498	.895	11	.983
— El Paso (Texas)	1B	62	244	43	86	16	2	8	49	28	39	2	6	3-2	.352	.420	.533	.953	12	.979
2001— El Paso (Texas)	1B-OF	138	532	82	187	49	3	13	100	67	92	5	6	5-4	.352	.423	.528	.951	13	.987
— Arizona (N.L.)		2	2	0	1	0	0	0	0	0	1	0	0	0-0	.500	.500	.500	1.000	...	...
2002— Tucson (PCL)	1B	134	525	83	180	40	0	19	109	42	86	7	12	0-0	.343	.396	.528	.923	10	.991
— Arizona (N.L.)		10	10	0	1	0	0	0	1	0	5	0	0	0-0	.100	.100	.100	.200	1	.947
2003— Tucson (PCL)	1B-DH	35	119	24	34	11	0	4	16	28	19	0	2	0-0	.286	.419	.479	.898	5	.985
— Arizona (N.L.)	1B	86	254	23	70	20	0	4	28	35	67	2	8	1-0	.276	.365	.402	.767	2	.997
2004— Milwaukee (N.L.)	1B	159	579	83	174	* 53	1	16	87	81	128	2	11	2-1	.301	.385	.478	.863	11	.992
Major League totals (4 years)		257	845	106	246	73	1	20	116	116	201	4	19	3-1	.291	.376	.451	.827	13	.994

PADILLA, JUAN — P

PERSONAL: Born February 17, 1977, in Rio Piedras, Puerto Rico. ... 6-0/200. ... Throws right, bats right. ... Full name: Juan Miguel Padilla. ... College: Jacksonville.
TRANSACTIONS/CAREER NOTES: Selected by Minnesota Twins in 24th round of 1998 free-agent draft. ... Traded by Twins to New York Yankees (September 2, 2003), completing deal in which Twins acquired P Jesse Orosco for a player to be named (August 31, 2003). ... Claimed on waivers by Cincinnati Reds (September 3, 2004). ... Refused minor league assignment and became a free agent (October 4, 2004).
CAREER HITTING: 0-for-0 (.000), 0 R, 0 2B, 0 3B, 0 HR, 0 RBI.

Year Team (League)	W	L	Pct.	ERA	WHIP	G	GS	CG	ShO	Hld.	Sv.-Opp.	IP	H	R	ER	HR	BB-IBB	SO	Avg.
1998— GC Twins (GCL)	1	1	.500	1.40	0.78	17	0	0	0	...	10-...	25.2	19	4	4	1	1-0	27	.202
1999— Quad City (Midw.)	0	2	.000	2.40	1.60	12	0	0	0	...	0-...	15.0	18	8	4	0	6-2	16	.290
— New Britain (East.)	1	1	.500	6.63	2.00	11	0	0	0	...	2-...	19.0	31	15	14	3	7-0	12	.383
— Fort Myers (Fla. St.)	2	2	.500	3.48	1.46	22	0	0	0	...	0-...	33.2	32	14	13	1	17-2	28	.260
2000— Quad City (Midw.)	2	2	.500	1.91	1.00	32	0	0	0	...	16-...	33.0	24	7	7	0	9-2	40	.200
— New Britain (East.)	0	1	.000	3.74	1.37	23	0	0	0	...	0-...	33.2	35	15	14	1	11-0	24	.269
2001— Fort Myers (Fla. St.)	6	4	.600	2.99	1.40	56	0	0	0	...	23-...	69.1	72	35	23	2	25-6	77	.261
2002— New Britain (East.)	3	5	.375	3.31	1.33	54	0	0	0	...	29-...	65.1	69	30	24	2	18-6	52	.267
2003— Rochester (Int'l)	7	4	.636	3.36	1.22	57	0	0	0	...	6-...	91.0	94	40	34	7	17-3	68	.266
2004— Trenton (East.)	0	0	...	9.00	1.75	3	0	0	0	...	0-...	4.0	4	4	4	1	3-0	4	.267
— New York (A.L.)	0	0	...	3.97	1.76	6	0	0	0	0	0-0	11.1	16	5	5	1	4-0	5	.348
— Columbus (Int'l)	2	1	.667	2.03	0.95	44	0	0	0	...	2-...	57.2	49	20	13	1	6-2	52	.232
— Cincinnati (N.L.)	1	0	1.000	10.67	2.16	12	0	0	0	0	0-0	14.1	23	17	17	6	8-0	12	.359
American League totals (1 year)	0	0	...	3.97	1.76	6	0	0	0	0	0-0	11.1	16	5	5	1	4-0	5	.348
National League totals (1 year)	1	0	1.000	10.67	2.16	12	0	0	0	0	0-0	14.1	23	17	17	6	8-0	12	.359
Major League totals (1 year)	1	0	1.000	7.71	1.99	18	0	0	0	0	0-0	25.2	39	22	22	7	12-0	17	.355

PADILLA, VICENTE — P

PERSONAL: Born September 27, 1977, in Chinandega, Nicaragua. ... 6-2/219. ... Throws right, bats right. ... Full name: Vicente D. Padilla. ... Name pronounced: pa-DEE-ya. ... High school: Ruben Dario (Nicaragua).
TRANSACTIONS/CAREER NOTES: Signed as a non-drafted free agent by Arizona Diamondbacks organization (August 31, 1998). ... Traded by Diamondbacks with 1B/OF Travis Lee and Ps Omar Daal and Nelson Figueroa to Philadelphia Phillies for P Curt Schilling (July 26, 2000). ... On disabled list (May 4-30, 2001); included rehabilitation assignment to Scranton/Wilkes-Barre. ... On disabled list (May 30-August 10, 2004); included rehabilitation assignments to Scranton/Wilkes-Barre and Clearwater.
CAREER HITTING: 13-for-164 (.079), 5 R, 2 2B, 0 3B, 0 HR, 9 RBI.

Year Team (League)	W	L	Pct.	ERA	WHIP	G	GS	CG	ShO	Hld.	Sv.-Opp.	IP	H	R	ER	HR	BB-IBB	SO	Avg.
1999— High Desert (Calif.)	4	1	.800	3.73	1.32	9	9	0	0	...	0-...	50.2	50	27	21	3	17-0	55	.253
— Tucson (PCL)	7	4	.636	3.75	1.40	18	14	0	0	...	0-...	93.2	107	47	39	6	24-7	58	.292
— Arizona (N.L.)	0	1	.000	16.88	3.75	5	0	0	0	1	0-1	2.2	7	5	5	1	3-0	0	.467
2000— Tucson (PCL)	0	1	.000	4.42	1.64	12	3	0	0	...	1-...	18.1	22	9	9	2	8-0	22	.306
— Arizona (N.L.)	2	1	.667	2.31	1.20	27	0	0	0	7	0-1	35.0	32	10	9	0	10-2	30	.242
— Philadelphia (N.L.)	2	6	.250	5.34	1.91	28	0	0	0	8	2-6	30.1	40	23	18	3	18-5	21	.328
2001— Philadelphia (N.L.)	3	1	.750	4.24	1.41	23	0	0	0	1	0-3	34.0	36	18	16	1	12-0	29	.273
— Scran./W.B. (I.L.)	7	0	1.000	2.42	0.92	16	16	0	0	...	0-...	81.2	64	24	22	8	11-0	75	.217
2002— Philadelphia (N.L.)	14	11	.560	3.28	1.22	32	32	1	1	0	0-0	206.0	198	83	75	16	53-5	128	.254
2003— Philadelphia (N.L.)	14	12	.538	3.62	1.24	32	32	1	1	0	0-0	208.2	196	94	84	22	62-4	133	.251
2004— Clearwater (Fla. St.)	0	1	.000	9.00	2.00	1	1	0	0	...	0-...	2.0	3	2	2	0	1-0	1	.333
— Scran./W.B. (I.L.)	0	0	...	13.50	2.36	2	2	0	0	...	0-...	4.2	6	7	7	1	5-0	6	.286
— Philadelphia (N.L.)	7	7	.500	4.53	1.34	20	20	0	0	0	0-0	115.1	119	63	58	16	36-6	82	.267
Major League totals (6 years)	42	39	.519	3.77	1.30	167	84	2	2	17	2-11	632.0	628	296	265	59	194-22	423	.261

ALL-STAR GAME RECORD																			
Year	W	L	Pct.	ERA	WHIP	G	GS	CG	ShO	Hld.	Sv.-Opp.	IP	H	R	ER	HR	BB-IBB	SO	Avg.
All-Star Game totals (1 year)	0	0	...	0.00	0.50	1	0	0	0	0	0-0	2.0	0	0	0	0	1-0	0	.000

P

PERSONAL: Born January 19, 1969, in Hoboken, N.J. ... 5-11/180. ... Bats left, throws left. ... Name pronounced: pal-MAIR-oh. ... High school: Southridge (Miami). ... College: Miami (Fla.). ... Cousin of Rafael Palmeiro, first baseman, Baltimore Orioles.

TRANSACTIONS/CAREER NOTES: Selected by California Angels organization in 33rd round of 1991 free-agent draft. ... On disabled list (September 1-26, 1994). ... Angels franchise renamed Anaheim Angels for 1997 season. ... On disabled list (August 23-September 7, 1997). ... Signed as a free agent by St. Louis Cardinals (February 2, 2003). ... Signed as a free agent by Houston Astros (January 19, 2004).

2004 GAMES PLAYED BY POSITION (MLB): OF—37.

										BATTING									FIELDING	
Year	Team (League)	Pos.	G	AB	R	H	2B	3B	HR	RBI	BB	SO	HBP	GDP	SB-CS	Avg.	OBP	SLG	OPS	E	Avg.
1991— Boise (N'west)	OF	70	277	56	77	11	2	1	24	33	22	3	8	8-8	.278	.358	.343	.701	2	.986
1992— Quad City (Midw.)	OF	127	451	83	143	22	4	0	41	56	41	5	5	31-13	.317	.393	.384	.777	6	.973
1993— Midland (Texas)	OF	131	535	85	163	19	5	0	64	42	35	2	13	18-14	.305	.356	.359	.715	9	.973
1994— Vancouver (PCL)	OF	117	458	79	150	28	4	1	47	58	46	1	7	21-16	.328	.402	.413	.815	1	.996
1995— Vancouver (PCL)	OF-DH	107	398	66	122	21	4	0	47	41	34	3	11	16-7	.307	.371	.379	.751	1	.995
—California (A.L.)	OF-DH	15	20	3	7	0	0	0	1	1	1	0	0	0-0	.350	.381	.350	.731	0	1.000
1996— Vancouver (PCL)	OF	62	245	40	75	13	4	0	33	30	19	4	4	7-3	.306	.384	.392	.776	5	.959
—California (A.L.)	OF-DH	50	87	6	25	6	1	0	6	8	13	2	1	0-1	.287	.361	.379	.740	1	1.000
1997— Anaheim (A.L.)	OF-DH	74	134	19	29	2	2	0	8	17	11	1	4	2-2	.216	.307	.261	.568	2	.975
1998— Vancouver (PCL)	OF	43	140	21	42	13	3	1	29	16	10	0	2	3-1	.300	.363	.457	.820	0	1.000
—California (A.L.)	OF-DH	75	165	28	53	7	2	0	21	20	11	0	2	5-4	.321	.395	.388	.782	0	1.000
1999— Anaheim (A.L.)	OF-DH	109	317	46	88	12	1	1	23	39	30	6	4	5-5	.278	.364	.331	.696	1	.994
2000— Anaheim (A.L.)	OF-DH	108	243	38	73	20	2	0	25	38	20	2	4	4-1	.300	.395	.399	.794	2	.984
2001— Anaheim (A.L.)	OF-DH	104	230	29	56	10	1	2	23	25	24	3	3	6-6	.243	.319	.322	.641	1	.989
2002— Anaheim (A.L.)	OF-DH	110	263	35	79	12	1	0	31	30	22	0	7	7-2	.300	.368	.354	.722	1	.993
2003— St. Louis (N.L.)	OF	141	317	37	86	13	1	3	33	32	31	2	1	3-3	.271	.336	.347	.683	0	1.000
2004— Houston (N.L.)	OF	102	133	19	32	5	0	3	12	18	19	3	1	2-1	.241	.344	.346	.690	0	1.000
American League totals (8 years)		645	1459	204	410	69	10	3	138	178	132	14	25	29-21	.281	.361	.348	.710	7	.991
National League totals (2 years)		243	450	56	118	18	1	6	45	50	50	5	2	5-4	.262	.339	.347	.685	0	1.000
Major League totals (10 years)		888	1909	260	528	87	11	9	183	228	182	19	27	34-25	.277	.356	.348	.704	7	.993

DIVISION SERIES RECORD

										BATTING									FIELDING	
Year	Team (League)	Pos.	G	AB	R	H	2B	3B	HR	RBI	BB	SO	HBP	GDP	SB-CS	Avg.	OBP	SLG	OPS	E	Avg.
2004— Houston (N.L.)	OF	5	4	0	1	0	0	0	0	0	0	0	0	0-0	.250	.250	.250	.500	0	...

CHAMPIONSHIP SERIES RECORD

										BATTING									FIELDING	
Year	Team (League)	Pos.	G	AB	R	H	2B	3B	HR	RBI	BB	SO	HBP	GDP	SB-CS	Avg.	OBP	SLG	OPS	E	Avg.
2002— Anaheim (A.L.)	OF	2	2	0	0	0	0	0	0	0	1	0	0	0-0	.000	.000	.000	.000	0	...
2004— Houston (N.L.)	OF	7	6	0	2	1	0	0	0	0	1	0	0	0-0	.333	.429	.500	.929	0	...
Champ. series totals (2 years)		9	8	0	2	1	0	0	0	0	1	1	0	0-0	.250	.333	.375	.708	0	...

WORLD SERIES RECORD

										BATTING									FIELDING	
Year	Team (League)	Pos.	G	AB	R	H	2B	3B	HR	RBI	BB	SO	HBP	GDP	SB-CS	Avg.	OBP	SLG	OPS	E	Avg.
2002— Anaheim (A.L.)	OF	4	4	1	1	1	0	0	0	0	2	0	0	0-0	.250	.250	.500	.750	0	...

PERSONAL: Born September 24, 1964, in Havana, Cuba. ... 6-0/214. ... Bats left, throws left. ... Full name: Rafael Corrales Palmeiro. ... Name pronounced: pahl-MARE-oh. ... High school: Jackson (Miami). ... College: Mississippi State. ... Cousin of Orlando Palmeiro, outfielder with Houston Astros in 2004.

TRANSACTIONS/CAREER NOTES: Selected by New York Mets organization in eighth round of June 1982 free-agent draft; did not sign. ... Selected by Chicago Cubs organization in first round (22nd pick overall) of June 1985 free-agent draft; pick received as compensation for San Diego Padres signing Type A free-agent P Tim Stoddard. ... Traded by Cubs with Ps Jamie Moyer and Drew Hall to Texas Rangers for Ps Mitch Williams, Paul Kilgus and Steve Wilson, IFs Curtis Wilkerson and Luis Benitez and OF Pablo Delgado (December 5, 1988). ... Signed as a free agent by Baltimore Orioles (December 12, 1993). ... Signed as a free agent by Rangers (December 4, 1998). ... Signed as a free agent by Orioles (January 14, 2004).

RECORDS: Shares A.L. record for most seasons leading league in assists by first baseman—6.

HONORS: Won A.L. Gold Glove at first base (1997-99). ... Named Major League Player of the Year by THE SPORTING NEWS (1999).

2004 GAMES PLAYED BY POSITION (MLB): 1B—130, DH—20.

										BATTING									FIELDING	
Year	Team (League)	Pos.	G	AB	R	H	2B	3B	HR	RBI	BB	SO	HBP	GDP	SB-CS	Avg.	OBP	SLG	OPS	E	Avg.
1985— Peoria (Midw.)	OF	73	279	34	83	22	4	5	51	31	34	2	4	9-3	.297	.369	.459	.828	1	.992
1986— Pittsfield (East.)	OF	140	509	66	156	29	2	12	95	54	32	2	8	15-7	.306	.367	.442	.809	3	.988
—Chicago (N.L.)	OF	22	73	9	18	4	0	3	12	4	6	1	1	1-1	.247	.295	.425	.720	4	.900
1987— Iowa (Am. Assoc.)	1B-OF	57	214	36	64	14	3	11	41	22	22	3	2	4-3	.299	.366	.547	.913	2	.988
—Chicago (N.L.)	1B-OF	84	221	32	61	15	1	14	30	20	26	1	4	2-2	.276	.336	.543	.879	1	.995
1988— Chicago (N.L.)	1B-OF	152	580	75	178	41	5	8	53	38	34	3	11	12-2	.307	.349	.436	.785	5	.985
1989— Texas (A.L.)	DH-1B	156	559	76	154	23	4	8	64	63	48	6	18	4-3	.275	.354	.374	.728	12	.991
1990— Texas (A.L.)	DH-1B	154	598	72	*191	35	6	14	89	40	59	3	24	3-3	.319	.361	.468	.829	7	.995
1991— Texas (A.L.)	DH-1B	159	631	115	203	*49	3	26	88	68	72	6	17	4-3	.322	.389	.532	.922	*12	.992
1992— Texas (A.L.)	1B-DH	159	608	84	163	27	4	22	85	72	83	10	10	2-3	.268	.352	.434	.786	7	.995
1993— Texas (A.L.)	1B	160	597	*124	176	40	2	37	105	73	85	5	8	22-3	.295	.371	.554	.926	5	.997
1994— Baltimore (A.L.)	1B	111	436	82	139	32	0	23	76	54	63	2	11	7-3	.319	.392	.550	.942	4	.996
1995— Baltimore (A.L.)	1B	143	554	89	172	30	2	39	104	62	65	3	12	3-1	.310	.380	.583	.963	4	.997
1996— Baltimore (A.L.)	1B-DH	162	626	110	181	40	2	39	142	95	96	3	9	8-0	.289	.381	.546	.927	8	.995
1997— Baltimore (A.L.)	1B-DH	158	614	95	156	24	2	38	110	67	109	6	14	5-2	.254	.329	.485	.815	10	.993
1998— Baltimore (A.L.)	1B-DH	162	619	98	183	36	1	43	121	79	91	7	14	11-7	.296	.379	.565	.945	9	.994
1999— Texas (A.L.)	DH-1B	158	565	96	183	30	1	47	148	97	69	3	13	2-4	.324	.420	.630	1.050	1	.996
2000— Texas (A.L.)	1B-DH	158	565	102	163	29	3	39	120	103	77	3	14	2-1	.289	.397	.558	.954	4	.995
2001— Texas (A.L.)	1B-DH	160	600	98	164	33	0	47	123	101	90	7	8	1-1	.273	.381	.563	.944	8	.992
2002— Texas (A.L.)	1B-DH	155	546	99	149	34	0	43	105	104	94	6	10	2-0	.273	.391	.571	.962	5	.994
2003— Texas (A.L.)	DH-1B	154	561	92	146	21	2	38	112	84	77	5	7	2-0	.260	.359	.508	.867	2	.996
2004— Baltimore (A.L.)	1B	154	550	68	142	29	0	23	88	86	61	6	15	2-1	.258	.359	.436	.796	8	.993
American League totals (16 years)		2463	9229	1500	2665	512	32	526	1680	1248	1239	80	204	80-35	.289	.375	.522	.897	106	.994
National League totals (3 years)		258	874	116	257	60	6	25	95	62	66	5	19	15-5	.294	.341	.462	.804	10	.982
Major League totals (19 years)		2721	10103	1616	2922	572	38	551	1775	1310	1305	85	223	95-40	.289	.372	.517	.889	116	.994

P

DIVISION SERIES RECORD

Year Team (League)	Pos.	G	AB	R	H	2B	3B	HR	RBI	BB	SO	HBP	GDP	SB-CS	Avg.	OBP	SLG	OPS	E	Avg.
1996— Baltimore (A.L.)	1B	4	17	4	3	1	0	1	2	1	6	1	0	0-0	.176	.263	.412	.675	1	.973
1997— Baltimore (A.L.)	1B	4	12	2	3	2	0	0	0	0	2	0	0	0-0	.250	.250	.417	.667	0	1.000
1999— Texas (A.L.)	DH	3	11	0	3	0	0	0	0	1	1	0	0	0-0	.273	.333	.273	.606	...	...
Division series totals (3 years)		11	40	6	9	3	0	1	2	2	9	1	0	0-0	.225	.279	.375	.654	1	.985

CHAMPIONSHIP SERIES RECORD

Year Team (League)	Pos.	G	AB	R	H	2B	3B	HR	RBI	BB	SO	HBP	GDP	SB-CS	Avg.	OBP	SLG	OPS	E	Avg.
1996— Baltimore (A.L.)	1B	5	17	4	4	0	0	2	4	4	4	0	0	0-0	.235	.364	.588	.952	0	1.000
1997— Baltimore (A.L.)	1B	6	25	3	7	2	0	1	2	0	10	1	1	0-0	.280	.308	.480	.788	0	1.000
Champ. series totals (2 years)		11	42	7	11	2	0	3	6	4	14	1	1	0-0	.262	.333	.524	.857	0	1.000

ALL-STAR GAME RECORD

	G	AB	R	H	2B	3B	HR	RBI	BB	SO	HBP	GDP	SB-CS	Avg.	OBP	SLG	OPS	E	Avg.
All-Star Game totals (4 years)	4	4	1	3	0	0	0	2	2	0	0	0	0-0	.750	.833	.750	1.583	0	1.000

PARK, CHAN HO — P

PERSONAL: Born June 30, 1973, in Kong Ju City, South Korea. ... 6-2/210. ... Throws right, bats right. ... Full name: Chan Ho Park. ... High school: Kong Ju (Kong Ju City, Korea). ... College: Hanyang Univ. (South Korea).

TRANSACTIONS/CAREER NOTES: Signed as a non-drafted free agent by Los Angeles Dodgers organization (January 14, 1994). ... On suspended list (June 8-17, 1999). ... Signed as a free agent by Texas Rangers (December 23, 2001). ... On Texas disabled list (April 2-May 12 and August 7-23, 2002); included rehabilitation assignment to Oklahoma (August 18-23). ... On disabled list (April 28-June 7 and June 8, 2003-remainder of season); included rehabilitation assignments to Frisco and Oklahoma. ... On disabled list (May 20-August 26, 2004); included rehabilitation assignments to AZL Rangers, Frisco and Oklahoma.

CAREER HITTING: 58-for-345 (.168), 24 R, 15 2B, 1 3B, 2 HR, 23 RBI.

Year Team (League)	W	L	Pct.	ERA	WHIP	G	GS	CG	ShO	Hld.	Sv.-Opp.	IP	H	R	ER	HR	BB-IBB	SO	Avg.
1994— Los Angeles (N.L.)	0	0	...	11.25	2.50	2	0	0	0	0	0-0	4.0	5	5	5	1	5-0	6	.294
— San Antonio (Texas)	5	7	.417	3.55	1.46	20	20	0	0	...	0-...	101.1	91	52	40	4	57-0	100	.241
1995— Albuquerque (PCL)	6	7	.462	4.91	1.54	23	22	0	0	...	0-...	110.0	93	64	60	10	76-2	101	.233
— Los Angeles (N.L.)	0	0	...	4.50	1.00	2	1	0	0	0	0-0	4.0	2	2	2	1	2-0	7	.143
1996— Los Angeles (N.L.)	5	5	.500	3.64	1.41	48	10	0	0	4	0-0	108.2	82	48	44	7	71-3	119	.209
1997— Los Angeles (N.L.)	14	8	.636	3.38	1.14	32	29	2	0	0	0-0	192.0	149	80	72	24	70-1	166	.213
1998— Los Angeles (N.L.)	15	9	.625	3.71	1.34	34	34	2	0	0	0-0	220.2	199	101	91	16	97-1	191	.244
1999— Los Angeles (N.L.)	13	11	.542	5.23	1.58	33	33	0	0	0	0-0	194.1	208	120	113	31	100-4	174	.276
2000— Los Angeles (N.L.)	18	10	.643	3.27	1.31	34	34	3	1	0	0-0	226.0	173	92	82	21	124-4	217	.214
2001— Los Angeles (N.L.)	15	11	.577	3.50	1.17	36	•35	2	1	0	0-0	234.0	183	98	91	23	91-1	218	.216
2002— Texas (A.L.)	9	8	.529	5.75	1.59	25	25	0	0	0	0-0	145.2	154	95	93	20	78-2	121	.273
— Oklahoma (PCL)	0	1	.000	27.00	4.00	1	1	0	0	...	0-...	3.0	9	9	9	0	3-0	3	.500
2003— Frisco (Texas)	1	0	1.000	2.45	1.30	2	2	0	0	...	0-...	11.0	10	5	3	0	4-0	6	.238
— Oklahoma (PCL)	1	0	1.000	5.89	1.90	3	3	0	0	...	0-...	18.1	27	12	12	4	8-0	12	.346
— Texas (A.L.)	1	3	.250	7.58	1.99	7	7	0	0	0	0-0	29.2	34	26	25	5	25-0	16	.306
2004— Rangers (Ariz.)	1	1	.500	1.71	1.00	4	4	0	0	...	0-...	21.0	15	6	4	0	6-0	20	.197
— Frisco (Texas)	0	2	.000	8.74	1.85	2	2	0	0	...	0-...	11.1	16	11	11	1	5-0	5	.356
— Oklahoma (PCL)	0	2	.000	3.72	1.24	4	4	0	0	...	0-...	19.1	21	8	8	4	3-0	19	.273
— Texas (A.L.)	4	7	.364	5.46	1.44	16	16	0	0	0	0-0	95.2	105	63	58	22	33-0	63	.281
American League totals (3 years)	14	18	.438	5.85	1.58	48	48	0	0	0	0-0	271.0	293	184	176	47	136-2	200	.279
National League totals (8 years)	80	54	.597	3.80	1.32	221	176	9	2	4	0-0	1183.2	1001	546	500	124	560-14	1098	.230
Major League totals (11 years)	94	72	.566	4.18	1.37	269	224	9	2	4	0-0	1454.2	1294	730	676	171	696-16	1298	.240

ALL-STAR GAME RECORD

	W	L	Pct.	ERA	WHIP	G	GS	CG	ShO	Hld.	Sv.-Opp.	IP	H	R	ER	HR	BB-IBB	SO	Avg.
All-Star Game totals (1 year)	0	1	.000	9.00	1.00	1	0	0	0	0	0-0	1.0	1	1	1	1	0-0	1	.250

PARRA, JOSE — P

PERSONAL: Born November 28, 1972, in Jacagua, Dominican Republic. ... 5-11/175. ... Throws right, bats right. ... Full name: Jose Miguel Parra. ... Name pronounced: PAHR-uh. ... High school: Liceo Evangelico Jacagua (Dominican Republic).

TRANSACTIONS/CAREER NOTES: Signed as a non-drafted free agent by Los Angeles Dodgers organization (December 7, 1989). ... On disabled list (May 15-June 17 and August 13, 1993-remainder of season). ... Traded by Dodgers with 3B/1B Ron Coomer, P Greg Hansell and a player to be named to Minnesota Twins for Ps Kevin Tapani and Mark Guthrie (July 31, 1995); Twins acquired OF Chris Latham to complete deal (October 30, 1995). ... Granted free agency (November 1997). ... Signed by Yomiuri of the Japan Central League (January 13, 1999). ... Signed as a free agent by Pittsburgh Pirates organization (January 14, 2000). ... Loaned by Pirates to Mexico City Red Devils of the Mexican League (March 12-July 31, 2001). ... Released by Pirates (July 31, 2001). ... Signed by Arizona Diamondbacks organization (November 20, 2001). ... Released by Diamondbacks (June 5, 2002). ... Signed by New York Mets organization (January 31, 2004). ... On disabled list (July 18, 2004-remainder of season); included rehabilitation assignment to Binghamton.

CAREER HITTING: 0-for-0 (.000), 0 R, 0 2B, 0 3B, 0 HR, 0 RBI.

Year Team (League)	W	L	Pct.	ERA	WHIP	G	GS	CG	ShO	Hld.	Sv.-Opp.	IP	H	R	ER	HR	BB-IBB	SO	Avg.
1989— Dom. Dodgers (DSL)	8	1	.889	1.87	1.19	13	11	4	3	...	2-...	67.1	60	21	14	...	20-...	51	...
1990— GC Dodgers (GCL)	5	3	.625	2.67	1.19	10	10	1	0	...	0-...	57.1	50	22	17	1	18-0	50	.243
1991— Great Falls (Pio.)	4	6	.400	6.16	1.62	14	14	1	1	...	0-...	64.1	86	58	44	5	18-0	55	.320
1992— Bakersfield (California)	7	8	.467	3.59	1.38	24	23	3	0	...	0-...	143.0	151	73	57	7	47-4	107	.270
— San Antonio (Texas)	2	0	1.000	6.14	1.98	3	3	0	0	...	0-...	14.2	22	12	10	0	7-0	7	.349
1993— San Antonio (Texas)	1	8	.111	3.15	1.03	17	17	0	0	...	0-...	111.1	103	46	39	10	12-2	87	.244
1994— Albuquerque (PCL)	10	10	.500	4.78	1.57	27	27	1	0	...	0-...	145.0	190	92	77	10	38-2	90	.325
1995— Albuquerque (PCL)	3	2	.600	5.13	1.50	12	10	1	1	...	1-...	52.2	62	33	30	7	17-3	33	.298
— Los Angeles (N.L.)	0	0	...	4.35	1.55	8	0	0	0	2	0-0	10.1	10	8	5	2	6-1	7	.256
— Minnesota (A.L.)	1	5	.167	7.59	1.70	12	12	0	0	0	0-0	61.2	83	59	52	11	22-0	29	.313
1996— Salt Lake (PCL)	5	3	.625	5.11	1.45	23	1	0	0	...	8-...	44.0	51	25	25	2	13-2	26	.295
— Minnesota (A.L.)	5	5	.500	6.04	1.64	27	5	0	0	0	0-1	70.0	88	48	47	15	27-0	50	.308
1997— Salt Lake (PCL)	2	8	.200	6.03	1.66	50	4	0	0	...	8-...	94.0	126	73	63	8	30-7	61	.320
1998— Samsung (Korean)	7	8	.467	3.67	1.24	60	4	0	0	...	19-...	95.2	79	45	39	...	40-...	55	...
1999— Yomiuri (Jp. East.)	4	3	.571	2.75	1.34	13	11	0	0	...	0-...	59.0	63	26	18	...	16-...	48	...
— Yomiuri (Jp. Cen.)	2	3	.400	5.32	1.39	12	9	0	0	...	0-...	47.1	43	29	28	5	23-...	25	...
2000— Nashville (PCL)	6	5	.545	5.22	1.68	23	21	0	0	...	1-...	101.2	106	66	59	7	65-0	68	.274
— Pittsburgh (N.L.)	0	1	.000	6.94	2.06	6	2	0	0	0	0-0	11.2	17	9	9	1	7-0	9	.354

P

Year Team (League)	W	L	Pct.	ERA	WHIP	G	GS	CG	ShO	Hld.	Sv.-Opp.	IP	H	R	ER	HR	BB-IBB	SO	Avg.
2001—M.C. Red Devils (Mex.)	4	5	.444	3.20	1.32	45	0	0	0	...	24-...	50.2	44	20	18	3	23-...	47	...
—Oaxaca (Mex.)	1	0	1.000	0.71	1.03	12	0	0	0	...	9-...	12.2	6	4	1	0	7-...	16	...
—Pres. Lions (Taiw.)	0	2	.000	0.00	0.93	10				...	0-...	14.0	9				4-...	10	...
2002—Tucson (PCL)	0	0	...	0.00	0.54	7	0	0	0	...	1-...	9.1	3	0	0	0	2-0	10	.094
—Arizona (N.L.)	0	1	.000	3.21	1.71	16	0	0	0	4	0-0	14.0	13	5	5	0	11-2	8	.255
2004—Norfolk (Int'l)	2	1	.667	1.63	1.05	24	0	0	0	...	16-...	27.2	19	6	5	1	10-1	35	.192
—New York (N.L.)	1	0	1.000	3.21	1.43	13	0	0	0	1	0-0	14.0	14	6	5	2	6-1	14	.255
—Binghamton (Eastern)	0	0	...			1	0	0	0		0-...	1.0	0	0	0	0	0-0	0	...
American League totals (2 years)	**6**	**10**	**.375**	**6.77**	**1.67**	**39**	**17**	**0**	**0**	**0**	**0-1**	**131.2**	**171**	**107**	**99**	**26**	**49-0**	**79**	**.310**
National League totals (4 years)	**1**	**2**	**.333**	**4.32**	**1.68**	**43**	**2**	**0**	**0**	**5**	**0-0**	**50.0**	**54**	**28**	**24**	**7**	**30-4**	**38**	**.280**
Major League totals (5 years)	**7**	**12**	**.368**	**6.09**	**1.67**	**82**	**19**	**0**	**0**	**5**	**0-1**	**181.2**	**225**	**135**	**123**	**33**	**79-4**	**117**	**.302**

PARRISH, JOHN   P

PERSONAL: Born November 26, 1977, in Lancaster, Pa. ... 5-11/192. ... Throws left, bats left. ... Full name: John Henry Parrish Jr.. ... High school: J.P. McCaskey (Lancaster, Pa.).

TRANSACTIONS/CAREER NOTES: Selected by Baltimore Orioles organization in 25th round of 1996 free-agent draft. ... On disabled list (March 30, 2002-entire season).

CAREER HITTING: 0-for-1 (.000), 0 R, 0 2B, 0 3B, 0 HR, 0 RBI.

Year Team (League)	W	L	Pct.	ERA	WHIP	G	GS	CG	ShO	Hld.	Sv.-Opp.	IP	H	R	ER	HR	BB-IBB	SO	Avg.
1996—GC Orioles (GCL)	2	0	1.000	1.86	1.24	11	0	0	0	...	2-...	19.1	13	5	4	0	11-0	33	.181
—Bluefield (Appalachian)	2	1	.667	2.70	1.50	8	0	0	0	...	1-...	13.1	11	6	4	0	9-1	18	.229
1997—Delmarva (S.Atl.)	3	3	.500	3.84	1.39	23	10	0	0	...	1-...	72.2	69	39	31	7	32-3	76	.250
—Bowie (East.)	1	0	1.000	1.80	1.00	1	1	0	0	...	0-...	5.0	3	1	1	0	2-0	3	.167
—Frederick (Caro.)	1	3	.250	6.04	1.75	5	5	0	0	...	0-...	22.1	23	18	15	3	16-0	17	.274
1998—Frederick (Caro.)	4	4	.500	3.27	1.26	16	16	1	0	...	0-...	82.2	77	39	30	5	27-1	81	.246
1999—Delmarva (S.Atl.)	0	1	.000	7.20	1.50	4	0	0	0	...	0-...	10.0	9	8	8	1	6-1	10	.225
—Frederick (Caro.)	2	2	.500	4.17	1.25	6	6	0	0	...	0-...	36.2	34	17	17	4	12-0	44	.250
—Bowie (East.)	0	2	.000	4.04	1.65	12	10	0	0	...	0-...	55.2	49	28	25	4	43-1	42	.258
2000—Bowie (East.)	2	0	1.000	1.69	1.19	3	3	0	0	...	0-...	16.0	12	3	3	0	7-0	16	.214
—Rochester (Int'l)	6	7	.462	4.24	1.36	18	18	0	0	...	0-...	104.0	85	54	49	10	56-1	87	.235
—Baltimore (A.L.)	2	4	.333	7.18	2.06	8	8	0	0	0	0-0	36.1	40	32	29	6	35-0	28	.288
2001—Rochester (Int'l)	7	7	.500	3.52	1.25	26	19	1	0	...	0-...	133.0	115	68	52	11	51-4	126	.231
—Baltimore (A.L.)	1	2	.333	6.14	1.77	16	1	0	0	2	0-0	22.0	22	17	15	5	17-1	20	.256
2002—Baltimore (A.L.)				Did not play.															
2003—Bowie (East.)	3	3	.500	2.00	1.20	49	0	0	0	...	6-...	76.1	58	22	17	5	33-0	85	.214
—Baltimore (A.L.)	0	1	.000	1.90	1.06	14	0	0	0	1	0-2	23.2	17	7	5	2	8-2	15	.205
2004—Baltimore (A.L.)	6	3	.667	3.46	1.58	56	1	0	0	2	1-1	78.0	68	39	30	4	55-6	71	.238
Major League totals (4 years)	**9**	**10**	**.474**	**4.44**	**1.64**	**94**	**10**	**0**	**0**	**5**	**1-3**	**160.0**	**147**	**95**	**79**	**17**	**115-9**	**134**	**.247**

PASCUCCI, VAL   OF

PERSONAL: Born November 17, 1978, in Bellflower, Calif. ... 6-6/235. ... Bats right, throws right. ... Full name: Valentino Martin Pascucci. ... Name pronounced: pas-KOO-chee. ... High school: Richard Gahr (Cerritos, Calif.). ... College: Oklahoma.

TRANSACTIONS/CAREER NOTES: Selected by Milwaukee Brewers organization in 11th round of 1996 free-agent draft; did not sign. ... Selected by Montreal Expos organization in 15th round of 1999 free-agent draft.

2004 GAMES PLAYED BY POSITION (MLB): OF—17, 1B—5.

Year Team (League)	Pos.	G	AB	R	H	2B	3B	HR	RBI	BB	SO	HBP	GDP	SB-CS	Avg.	OBP	SLG	OPS	E	Avg.
1999—Vermont (N.Y.-Penn.)	OF	72	259	62	91	26	1	7	48	53	46	14	5	17-2	.351	.482	.541	1.022	6	.956
2000—Cape Fear (S. Atl.)	OF	20	69	17	22	4	0	3	10	16	15	0	2	5-0	.319	.442	.507	.949	1	.975
—Jupiter (FSL)	OF-1B	113	405	70	115	30	2	14	66	66	98	11	9	14-6	.284	.394	.472	.866	7	.975
2001—Harrisburg (East.)	OF-1B	138	476	79	116	17	1	21	67	65	114	11	8	8-8	.244	.344	.416	.760	6	.983
2002—Harrisburg (East.)	OF-1B-3B	137	459	73	108	14	1	27	82	93	115	13	13	2-0	.235	.374	.447	.821	9	.976
2003—Edmonton (PCL)	OF-1B	138	459	80	129	29	1	15	85	101	132	9	11	3-2	.281	.419	.447	.865	9	.981
2004—Edmonton (PCL)	1-O-DH-3	109	393	83	117	32	1	25	92	78	96	8	11	9-2	.298	.422	.575	.990	9	.988
—Montreal (N.L.)	OF-1B	32	62	6	11	1	0	2	6	10	22	1	3	1-0	.177	.297	.290	.588	1	.977
Major League totals (1 year)		**32**	**62**	**6**	**11**	**1**	**0**	**2**	**6**	**10**	**22**	**1**	**3**	**1-0**	**.177**	**.297**	**.290**	**.588**	**1**	**.977**

PATTERSON, COREY   OF

PERSONAL: Born August 13, 1979, in Atlanta, Ga. ... 5-9/180. ... Bats left, throws right. ... Full name: Donald Corey Patterson. ... High school: Harrison (Kennesaw, Ga.). ... Son of Don Patterson, defensive back with Detroit Lions (1979) and New York Giants (1980).

TRANSACTIONS/CAREER NOTES: Selected by Chicago Cubs organization in first round (third pick overall) of 1998 free-agent draft. ... On disabled list (July 7, 2003-remainder of season).

2004 GAMES PLAYED BY POSITION (MLB): OF—157.

Year Team (League)	Pos.	G	AB	R	H	2B	3B	HR	RBI	BB	SO	HBP	GDP	SB-CS	Avg.	OBP	SLG	OPS	E	Avg.
1999—Lansing (Midw.)	OF	112	475	94	152	35	17	20	79	25	85	5	5	33-9	.320	.358	.592	.949	9	.965
2000—West Tenn (Sou.)	OF	118	444	73	116	26	5	22	82	45	115	10	7	27-15	.261	.338	.491	.829	3	.990
—Chicago (N.L.)	OF	11	42	9	7	1	0	2	2	3	14	1	0	1-1	.167	.239	.333	.572	1	.963
2001—Iowa (PCL)	OF	89	367	63	93	22	3	7	32	29	65	1	2	19-8	.253	.308	.387	.694	6	.968
—Chicago (N.L.)	OF	59	131	26	29	3	0	4	14	6	33	3	1	4-0	.221	.266	.336	.602	2	.976
2002—Chicago (N.L.)	OF	153	592	71	150	30	5	14	54	19	142	8	8	18-3	.253	.284	.392	.676	3	.990
2003—Chicago (N.L.)	OF	83	329	49	98	17	7	13	55	15	77	1	5	16-5	.298	.329	.511	.839	4	.975
2004—Chicago (N.L.)	OF	157	631	91	168	33	6	24	72	45	168	5	7	32-9	.266	.320	.452	.771	1	.997
Major League totals (5 years)		**463**	**1725**	**246**	**452**	**84**	**18**	**57**	**197**	**88**	**434**	**18**	**21**	**71-18**	**.262**	**.303**	**.431**	**.734**	**11**	**.988**

PATTERSON, DANNY   P

PERSONAL: Born February 17, 1971, in San Gabriel, Calif. ... 6-0/190. ... Throws right, bats right. ... Full name: Danny Shane Patterson. ... High school: San Gabriel (Calif.). ... Junior college: Cerritos (Calif.).

TRANSACTIONS/CAREER NOTES: Selected by Texas Rangers organization in 47th round of 1989 free-agent draft. ... On disabled list (May 22-June 14, 1997); included rehabilitation assignment to Tulsa. ... On Texas disabled list (March 22-April 17, 1998); included rehabilitation assignments to Tulsa and Oklahoma. ... Traded by Rangers with OF Juan Gonzalez and C Gregg Zaun to Detroit Tigers for Ps Justin Thompson, Francisco Cordero and Alan Webb, OF Gabe Kapler, C Bill Haselman and 2B Frank Catalanotto

(November 2, 1999). ... On disabled list (July 22-August 7, 2000). ... On disabled list (April 4-May 31 and June 9, 2002-remainder of season) included rehabilitation assignment to Toledo. ... On disabled list (March 29-July 17, 2003); included rehabilitation assignment to Toledo. ... On disabled list (June 28-July 22, 2004); included rehabilitation assignment to Toledo. ... Released by Tigers (August 11, 2004). ... Signed by St. Louis Cardinals organization (August 15, 2004).

CAREER HITTING: 0-for-1 (.000), 0 R, 0 2B, 0 3B, 0 HR, 0 RBI.

Year	Team (League)	W	L	Pct.	ERA	WHIP	G	GS	CG	ShO	Hld.	Sv.-Opp.	IP	H	R	ER	HR	BB-IBB	SO	Avg.
1990—	Butte (Pio.)	0	3	.000	6.35	1.76	13	3	0	0	...	1-...	28.1	36	23	20	3	14-1	18	.308
1991—	GC Rangers (GCL)	5	3	.625	3.24	1.10	11	9	0	0	...	0-...	50.0	43	21	18	1	12-0	46	.232
1992—	Gastonia (S. Atl.)	4	6	.400	3.59	1.32	23	21	3	1	...	0-...	105.1	106	47	42	9	33-3	84	.261
1993—	Charlotte (Fla. St.)	5	6	.455	2.51	1.22	47	0	0	0	...	7-...	68.0	55	22	19	2	28-4	41	.219
1994—	Charlotte (Fla. St.)	1	0	1.000	4.61	1.32	7	0	0	0	...	0-...	13.2	13	7	7	1	5-0	9	.255
—	Tulsa (Texas)	1	4	.200	1.64	1.18	30	1	0	0	...	6-...	44.0	35	13	8	2	17-1	33	.223
1995—	Tulsa (Texas)	2	2	.500	6.19	1.60	26	0	0	0	...	5-...	36.1	45	27	25	2	13-2	24	.306
—	Oklahoma City (A.A.)	1	0	1.000	1.65	1.17	14	0	0	0	...	2-...	27.1	23	8	5	0	9-2	9	.240
1996—	Oklahoma City (A.A.)	6	2	.750	1.68	1.17	44	0	0	0	...	10-...	80.1	79	22	15	5	15-3	53	.256
—	Texas (A.L.)	0	0	...	0.00	1.50	7	0	0	0	0	0-0	8.2	10	4	0	0	3-1	5	.286
1997—	Texas (A.L.)	10	6	.625	3.42	1.31	54	0	0	0	9	1-8	71.0	70	29	27	3	23-4	69	.263
—	Tulsa (Texas)	0	0	...	4.50	2.50	2	2	0	0	...	0-...	2.0	5	4	1	0	0-0	1	.417
1998—	Tulsa (Texas)	0	0	...	4.50	0.75	2	1	0	0	...	0-...	4.0	3	2	2	1	0-0	4	.214
—	Oklahoma (PCL)	0	0	...	4.50	2.50	1	0	0	0	...	0-...	2.0	4	1	1	0	1-0	2	.400
—	Texas (A.L.)	2	5	.286	4.45	1.37	56	0	0	0	19	2-2	60.2	64	31	30	11	19-2	33	.274
1999—	Texas (A.L.)	2	0	1.000	5.67	1.59	53	0	0	0	4	0-1	60.1	77	38	38	5	19-3	43	.304
—	Oklahoma (PCL)	1	0	1.000	0.00	0.67	2	0	0	0	...	0-...	3.0	1	0	0	0	1-0	4	.100
2000—	Detroit (A.L.)	5	1	.833	3.97	1.46	58	0	0	0	12	0-2	56.2	69	26	25	4	14-2	29	.309
2001—	Detroit (A.L.)	5	4	.556	3.06	1.18	60	0	0	0	16	1-5	64.2	64	24	22	4	12-5	27	.274
2002—	Detroit (A.L.)	0	2	.000	15.00	2.33	6	0	0	0	0	0-1	3.0	5	5	5	0	2-0	1	.357
—	Toledo (International)	0	0	...	0.00	0.20	5	1	0	0	...	0-...	5.0	1	0	0	0	0-0	3	.067
2003—	Toledo (International)	1	0	1.000	2.45	1.20	10	0	0	0	...	0-...	11.0	8	3	3	0	5-1	6	.211
—	Detroit (A.L.)	0	0	...	4.08	1.08	19	0	0	0	1	3-3	17.2	15	8	8	1	4-0	19	.227
2004—	Toledo (International)	1	0	1.000	4.15	1.15	3	0	0	0	...	0-...	4.1	3	2	2	0	2-1	3	.188
—	Detroit (A.L.)	0	4	.000	4.75	1.44	37	0	0	0	3	2-4	41.2	44	24	22	7	16-2	24	.282
—	Memphis (PCL)	0	0	...	6.75	2.25	9	0	0	0	...	0-...	6.2	8	5	5	0	7-0	7	.296
Major League totals (9 years)		**24**	**22**	**.522**	**4.14**	**1.38**	**350**	**0**	**0**	**0**	**64**	**9-26**	**384.1**	**418**	**189**	**177**	**35**	**112-19**	**250**	**.282**

DIVISION SERIES RECORD

Year	Team (League)	W	L	Pct.	ERA	WHIP	G	GS	CG	ShO	Hld.	Sv.-Opp.	IP	H	R	ER	HR	BB-IBB	SO	Avg.
1996—	Texas (A.L.)	0	0	...	0.00	3.00	1	0	0	0	0	0-0	.1	1	0	0	0	0-0	0	.500
1999—	Texas (A.L.)	0	0	...	0.00	1.00	1	0	0	0	0	0-0	1.0	1	0	0	0	0-0	0	.250
Division series totals (2 years)		**0**	**0**	**...**	**0.00**	**1.50**	**2**	**0**	**0**	**0**	**0**	**0-0**	**1.1**	**2**	**0**	**0**	**0**	**0-0**	**0**	**.333**

PATTERSON, JOHN — P

PERSONAL: Born January 30, 1978, in Orange, Texas. ... 6-5/208. ... Throws right, bats right. ... Full name: John Hollis Patterson. ... High school: West Orange-Stark (Orange, Texas).

TRANSACTIONS/CAREER NOTES: Signed as a non-drafted free agent by Arizona Diamondbacks organization (November 7, 1996). ... On disabled list (April 6-24 and May 6-September 8, 2000). ... Traded by Diamondbacks to Montreal Expos for P Randy Choate (March 27, 2004). ... On disabled list (April 28-July 15, 2004); included rehabilitation assignments to Brevard County and Harrisburg. ... Expos franchise relocated to Washington, D.C., for 2005 season.

CAREER HITTING: 6-for-56 (.107), 2 R, 0 2B, 0 3B, 0 HR, 2 RBI.

Year	Team (League)	W	L	Pct.	ERA	WHIP	G	GS	CG	ShO	Hld.	Sv.-Opp.	IP	H	R	ER	HR	BB-IBB	SO	Avg.
1997—	South Bend (Mid.)	1	9	.100	3.23	1.24	18	18	0	0	...	0-...	78.0	63	32	28	3	34-0	95	.221
1998—	High Desert (Calif.)	8	7	.533	2.83	1.13	25	25	0	0	...	0-...	127.0	102	54	40	12	42-0	148	.217
1999—	El Paso (Texas)	8	6	.571	4.40	1.40	18	18	2	0	...	0-...	100.0	98	61	53	16	42-0	117	.256
—	Tucson (PCL)	1	5	.167	7.04	1.99	7	6	0	0	...	0-...	30.2	43	26	24	3	18-0	29	.331
2000—	Tucson (PCL)	0	2	.000	7.80	2.00	3	2	0	0	...	0-...	15.0	21	14	13	1	9-0	10	.323
2001—	Lancaster (Calif.)	0	0	...	5.79	1.29	2	2	0	0	...	0-...	9.1	9	6	6	3	3-0	9	.243
—	El Paso (Texas)	1	2	.333	4.26	1.54	5	5	0	0	...	0-...	25.1	30	15	12	2	9-0	19	.297
—	Tucson (PCL)	2	7	.222	5.85	1.67	13	12	0	0	...	0-...	67.2	82	50	44	9	31-3	40	.301
2002—	Tucson (PCL)	10	5	.667	4.23	1.44	19	18	0	0	...	0-...	112.2	117	59	53	14	45-1	104	.265
—	Arizona (N.L.)	2	0	1.000	3.23	1.11	7	5	0	0	0	0-0	30.2	27	11	11	7	7-0	31	.235
2003—	Tucson (PCL)	10	5	.667	2.63	1.30	18	18	2	2	...	0-...	109.1	100	48	32	6	43-0	74	.241
—	Arizona (N.L.)	1	4	.200	6.05	1.65	16	8	0	0	1	1-1	55.0	61	39	37	7	30-5	43	.287
2004—	Harrisburg (Eastern)	0	0	...	0.00	0.50	1	1	0	0	...	0-...	4.0	0	0	0	0	2-0	9	.000
—	Brevard County (FSL)	0	0	...	0.00	0.52	2	2	0	0	...	0-...	7.2	3	0	0	0	1-0	7	.111
—	Montreal (N.L.)	4	7	.364	5.03	1.48	19	19	0	0	...	0-...	98.1	100	58	55	18	46-4	99	.260
Major League totals (3 years)		**7**	**11**	**.389**	**5.04**	**1.47**	**42**	**32**	**0**	**0**	**1**	**1-1**	**184.0**	**188**	**108**	**103**	**32**	**83-9**	**173**	**.262**

PAUL, JOSH — C

PERSONAL: Born May 19, 1975, in Evanston, Ill. ... 6-1/200. ... Bats right, throws right. ... Full name: Joshua William Paul. ... High school: Buffalo Grove (Ill.). ... College: Vanderbilt.

TRANSACTIONS/CAREER NOTES: Selected by Chicago White Sox organization in second round of 1996 free-agent draft. ... Refused minor league assignment and became a free agent (June 25, 2003). ... Signed by Chicago Cubs organization (July 4, 2003). ... Released by Cubs (October 31, 2003). ... Signed by Anaheim Angels organization (January 15, 2004).

2004 GAMES PLAYED BY POSITION (MLB): C—37, OF—4, DH—2.

Year	Team (League)	Pos.	G	AB	R	H	2B	3B	HR	RBI	BB	SO	HBP	GDP	SB-CS	Avg.	OBP	SLG	OPS	E	Avg.
1996—	GC Whi. Sox (GCL)		1	0	0	0	0	0	0	0	1	0	0	0	0-0	...	1.000	...	1.000	...	...
—	Hickory (S. Atl.)	C	59	226	41	74	16	0	8	37	21	53	1	2	13-4	.327	.386	.504	.890	2	.991
1997—	Birmingham (Sou.)	C	34	115	18	34	5	0	1	16	12	25	1	4	6-2	.296	.367	.365	.732	3	.988
—	GC Whi. Sox (GCL)	C	5	14	3	6	0	1	0	0	1	3	0	1	1-0	.429	.467	.571	1.038	3	.900
1998—	Win.-Salem (Car.)	C	123	444	66	113	20	7	11	63	38	91	5	11	20-8	.255	.319	.405	.724	3	.997
1999—	Birmingham (Sou.)	C-DH	93	319	47	89	19	3	4	42	29	68	5	6	6-6	.279	.345	.395	.740	5	.992
—	Chicago (A.L.)	C	6	18	2	4	1	0	0	1	0	4	0	0	0-0	.222	.222	.278	.500	0	1.000
2000—	Chicago (A.L.)	C-OF	36	71	15	20	3	2	1	8	5	17	1	3	1-0	.282	.338	.423	.760	4	.974

P

Year	Team (League)	Pos.	G	AB	R	H	2B	3B	HR	RBI	BB	SO	HBP	GDP	SB-CS	Avg.	OBP	SLG	OPS	E	Avg.
—Charlotte (Int'l)	C-OF	51	168	28	40	5	1	4	19	13	38	2	3	6-2	.238	.299	.351	.650	2	.994
2001—Chicago (A.L.)	C	57	139	20	37	11	0	3	18	13	25	0	3	6-2	.266	.327	.410	.737	6	.980
—Charlotte (Int'l)	C	22	75	11	21	4	0	4	14	7	18	0	0		.280	.337	.493	.831	0	1.000
2002—Charlotte (Int'l)	C-1B-OF	65	231	18	63	15	2	0	17	17	45	1	7	10-4	.273	.323	.355	.678	3	.993
—Chicago (A.L.)	C-OF	33	104	11	25	4	0	0	11	9	22	1	1	2-0	.240	.302	.279	.581	2	.991
2003—Charlotte (Int'l)	C-2B-DH	19	64	6	12	0	1	2	5	5	14	0	1	1-1	.188	.243	.313	.555	2	.982
—Chicago (A.L.)	C-DH	13	17	6	6	0	0	0	4	3	3	0	0	0-0	.353	.450	.353	.803	0	1.000
—Iowa (PCL)	C-OF-DH-1B	47	146	12	37	4	0	2	15	8	30	1	5	0-2	.253	.297	.322	.619	1	.995
—Chicago (N.L.)	C	3	6	0	0	0	0	0	0	0	3	0	0	0-0	.000	.000	.000	.000	0	1.000
2004—Anaheim (A.L.)	C-OF-DH	46	70	11	17	3	0	2	10	7	17	0	2	2-1	.243	.308	.371	.679	1	.993
American League totals (6 years)		191	419	65	109	22	2	6	52	37	88	2	9	11-3	.260	.320	.365	.686	13	.985
National League totals (1 year)		3	6	0	0	0	0	0	0	0	3	0	0	0-0	.000	.000	.000	.000	0	1.000
Major League totals (6 years)		194	425	65	109	22	2	6	52	37	91	2	9	11-3	.256	.316	.360	.676	13	.986

DIVISION SERIES RECORD

Year	Team (League)	Pos.	G	AB	R	H	2B	3B	HR	RBI	BB	SO	HBP	GDP	SB-CS	Avg.	OBP	SLG	OPS	E	Avg.
2000—Chicago (A.L.)	C	1	0	0	0	0	0	0	0	0	0	0	0	0-0	...	...	...	...	0	1.000

PAVANO, CARL — P

PERSONAL: Born January 8, 1976, in New Britain, Conn. ... 6-5/241. ... Throws right, bats right. ... Full name: Carl Anthony Pavano. ... Name pronounced: pa-VAH-no. ... High school: Southington (Conn.).

TRANSACTIONS/CAREER NOTES: Selected by Boston Red Sox organization in 13th round of 1994 free-agent draft. ... Traded by Red Sox with a player to be named to Montreal Expos for P Pedro Martinez (November 18, 1997); Expos acquired P Tony Armas to complete deal (December 18, 1997). ... On disabled list (July 12-September 11, 1999); included rehabilitation assignments to Ottawa. ... On disabled list (June 25, 2000-remainder of season). ... On disabled list (March 23-August 15, 2001); included rehabilitation assignments to Jupiter and Ottawa. ... Traded by Expos with Ps Graeme Lloyd and Justin Wayne and IF Mike Mordecai to Florida Marlins for OF Cliff Floyd, P Claudio Vargas, 2B/OF Wilton Guerrero, cash and a player to be named (July 11, 2002); Expos acquired P Don Levinski to complete deal (August 6, 2002).

CAREER HITTING: 41-for-288 (.142), 14 R, 8 2B, 2 3B, 2 HR, 14 RBI.

Year	Team (League)	W	L	Pct.	ERA	WHIP	G	GS	CG	ShO	Hld.	Sv.-Opp.	IP	H	R	ER	HR	BB-IBB	SO	Avg.
1994—GC Red Sox (GCL)	4	3	.571	1.84	0.86	9	7	0	0	...	0-...	44.0	31	14	9	1	7-0	47	.186
1995—Michigan (Midw.)	6	6	.500	3.45	1.21	22	22	1	0	...	0-...	141.0	118	63	54	7	52-0	138	.227
1996—Trenton (East.)	16	5	.762	2.63	1.09	27	26	6	2	...	0-...	185.0	154	66	54	16	47-2	146	.230
1997—Pawtucket (Int'l)	11	6	.647	3.12	1.13	23	23	3	0	...	0-...	161.2	148	62	56	13	34-2	147	.239
1998—Jupiter (FSL)	0	0	...	6.60	1.53	4	4	0	0	...	0-...	15.0	20	11	11	1	3-0	14	.333
—Ottawa (Int'l)	1	0	1.000	2.41	1.02	3	3	0	0	...	0-...	18.2	12	5	5	1	7-0	14	.190
—Montreal (N.L.)	6	9	.400	4.21	1.28	24	23	0	0	0	0-0	134.2	130	70	63	18	43-1	83	.251
1999—Montreal (N.L.)	6	8	.429	5.63	1.46	19	18	1	1	0	0-0	104.0	117	66	65	18	35-1	70	.285
—Ottawa (Int'l)	0	1	.000	9.00	1.40	2	2	0	0	...	0-...	5.0	7	5	5	1	0-0	3	.318
2000—Montreal (N.L.)	8	4	.667	3.06	1.27	15	15	0	0	0	0-0	97.0	89	40	33	8	34-1	64	.248
2001—Jupiter (FSL)	1	1	.500	2.19	0.97	3	3	0	0	...	0-...	12.1	10	7	3	1	2-0	11	.213
—Ottawa (Int'l)	2	1	.667	3.58	1.16	4	4	0	0	...	0-...	27.2	27	13	11	4	5-0	19	.248
—Montreal (N.L.)	1	6	.143	6.33	1.76	8	8	0	0	0	0-0	42.2	59	33	30	7	16-1	36	.331
2002—Montreal (N.L.)	3	8	.273	6.30	1.74	15	14	0	0	0	0-0	74.1	98	55	52	14	31-5	51	.318
—Ottawa (Int'l)	3	0	1.000	3.10	1.23	3	3	0	0	...	0-...	20.1	23	8	7	2	2-0	9	.295
—Florida (N.L.)	3	2	.600	3.79	1.46	22	8	0	0	3	0-0	61.2	76	33	26	5	14-3	41	.306
2003—Florida (N.L.)	12	13	.480	4.30	1.26	33	32	2	0	0	0-0	201.0	204	99	96	19	49-10	133	.265
2004—Florida (N.L.)	18	8	.692	3.00	1.17	31	31	2	2	0	0-0	222.1	212	80	74	16	49-13	139	.253
Major League totals (7 years)	57	58	.496	4.21	1.34	167	149	5	3	3	0-0	937.2	985	476	439	95	271-35	617	.271

DIVISION SERIES RECORD

Year	Team (League)	W	L	Pct.	ERA	WHIP	G	GS	CG	ShO	Hld.	Sv.-Opp.	IP	H	R	ER	HR	BB-IBB	SO	Avg.
2003—Florida (N.L.)	2	0	1.000	0.00	0.75							2.2	1	0	0	0	1-1	1	.111

CHAMPIONSHIP SERIES RECORD

Year	Team (League)	W	L	Pct.	ERA	WHIP	G	GS	CG	ShO	Hld.	Sv.-Opp.	IP	H	R	ER	HR	BB-IBB	SO	Avg.
2003—Florida (N.L.)	0	0	...	2.35	1.17	3	1	0	0		0-0	7.2	8	2	2	0	1-0	8	.286

WORLD SERIES RECORD

Year	Team (League)	W	L	Pct.	ERA	WHIP	G	GS	CG	ShO	Hld.	Sv.-Opp.	IP	H	R	ER	HR	BB-IBB	SO	Avg.
2003—Florida (N.L.)	0	0		1.00	1.00	2	1	0	0		0-0	9.0	8	1	1	0	1-0	6	.250

ALL-STAR GAME RECORD

	W	L	Pct.	ERA	WHIP	G	GS	CG	ShO	Hld.	Sv.-Opp.	IP	H	R	ER	HR	BB-IBB	SO	Avg.
All-Star Game totals (1 year)	0	0	...	9.00	1.50	1	0	0	0		0-0	2.0	3	2	2	1	0-0	1	.333

PAYTON, JAY — OF

PERSONAL: Born November 22, 1972, in Zanesville, Ohio. ... 5-10/185. ... Bats right, throws right. ... Full name: Jason Lee Payton. ... High school: Zanesville (Ohio). ... College: Georgia Tech.

TRANSACTIONS/CAREER NOTES: Selected by New York Mets organization in supplemental round ("sandwich pick" between first and second rounds, 29th pick overall) of 1994 free-agent draft; pick received as part of compensation for Baltimore Orioles signing Type A free-agent P Sid Fernandez. ... On disabled list (April 3, 1997-entire season). ... On disabled list (March 21-June 8, 1999); included rehabilitation assignment to St. Lucie. ... On disabled list (May 8-June 26, 2001); included rehabilitation assignment to St. Lucie. ... Traded by Mets with P Mark Corey and OF Robert Stratton to Colorado Rockies for P John Thomson and OF Mark Little (July 31, 2002). ... Signed as a free agent by San Diego Padres (January 13, 2004).

2004 GAMES PLAYED BY POSITION (MLB): OF—137, DH—1.

Year	Team (League)	Pos.	G	AB	R	H	2B	3B	HR	RBI	BB	SO	HBP	GDP	SB-CS	Avg.	OBP	SLG	OPS	E	Avg.
1994—Pittsfield (N.Y.-Penn.)	OF	58	219	47	80	16	2	3	37	23	18	9	1	10-2	.365	.439	.498	.937	5	.964
—Binghamton (East.)	OF	8	25	3	7	1	0	0	1	2	3	1	1	1-1	.280	.357	.320	.677	1	.917
1995—Binghamton (East.)	OF	85	357	59	123	20	3	14	54	29	32	2	11	16-7	.345	.395	.535	.930	3	.988
—Norfolk (Int'l)	OF	50	196	33	47	11	4	4	30	11	22	2	5	11-3	.240	.284	.398	.682	2	.982
1996—Norfolk (Int'l)	DH-OF	55	153	30	47	6	3	6	26	11	26	3	3	10-1	.307	.363	.503	.866	0	1.000
—GC Mets (GCL)	DH	3	13	3	5	1	0	1	2	0	1	0	0	1-0	.385	.385	.692	1.077	...	...
—St. Lucie (Fla. St.)	DH	9	26	4	8	2	0	0	1	4	5	0	1	2-1	.308	.400	.385	.785	...	...

P

Year	Team (League)	Pos.	G	AB	R	H	2B	3B	HR	RBI	BB	SO	HBP	GDP	SB-CS	Avg.	OBP	SLG	OPS	E	Avg.
—	—Binghamton (East.)	DH	4	10	0	2	0	0	0	2	2	2	0	0	0-1	.200	.286	.200	.486	...	...
1997—	....				Did not play.																
1998—	Norfolk (Int'l) OF-1B-DH		82	322	45	84	14	4	8	30	26	50	1	5	12-7	.261	.318	.404	.722	7	.980
	— St. Lucie (Fla. St.)	OF	3	7	0	1	0	0	0	0	3	1	0	0	0-0	.143	.400	.143	.543	0	1.000
	— New York (N.L.)	OF	15	22	2	7	1	0	0	0	1	4	0	0	0-0	.318	.348	.364	.711	0	1.000
1999—	St. Lucie (Fla. St.)	OF	7	26	3	9	1	1	0	3	4	5	0	1	0-1	.346	.433	.462	.895	1	.955
	— Norfolk (Int'l)	OF-DH	38	144	27	56	13	2	8	35	12	13	1	2	2-2	.389	.437	.674	1.110	1	.984
	— New York (N.L.)	OF	13	8	1	2	1	0	0	1	0	2	1	0	1-2	.250	.333	.375	.708	0	1.000
2000—	New York (N.L.)	OF	149	488	63	142	23	1	17	62	30	60	3	9	5-11	.291	.331	.447	.778	6	.981
2001—	New York (N.L.)	OF	104	361	44	92	16	1	8	34	18	52	5	11	4-3	.255	.298	.371	.669	4	.984
	— St. Lucie (Fla. St.)	OF	4	16	7	6	3	0	0	0	4	1	0	0	0-0	.375	.500	.563	1.063	0	1.000
2002—	New York (N.L.)	OF	87	275	33	78	6	3	8	31	21	34	1	8	4-1	.284	.336	.415	.750	1	.994
	— Colorado (N.L.)	OF	47	170	36	57	14	4	8	28	8	20	3	3	3-3	.335	.376	.606	.982	0	1.000
2003—	Colorado (N.L.)	OF	157	600	93	181	32	5	28	89	43	77	7	27	6-4	.302	.354	.512	.865	4	.987
2004—	San Diego (N.L.)	OF-DH	143	458	57	119	17	4	8	55	43	56	4	12	2-0	.260	.326	.367	.693	4	.989
	Major League totals (7 years)		715	2382	329	678	110	18	77	300	164	305	24	70	25-24	.285	.335	.443	.778	19	.987

Year	Team (League)	Pos.	G	AB	R	H	2B	3B	HR	RBI	BB	SO	HBP	GDP	SB-CS	Avg.	OBP	SLG	OPS	E	Avg.
	DIVISION SERIES RECORD																				
2000—	New York (N.L.)	OF	4	17	1	3	0	0	0	2	0	4	0	1	1-1	.176	.167	.176	.343	0	1.000

Year	Team (League)	Pos.	G	AB	R	H	2B	3B	HR	RBI	BB	SO	HBP	GDP	SB-CS	Avg.	OBP	SLG	OPS	E	Avg.
	CHAMPIONSHIP SERIES RECORD																				
2000—	New York (N.L.)	OF	5	19	1	3	0	0	1	3	2	5	1	1	0-0	.158	.273	.316	.589	0	1.000

Year	Team (League)	Pos.	G	AB	R	H	2B	3B	HR	RBI	BB	SO	HBP	GDP	SB-CS	Avg.	OBP	SLG	OPS	E	Avg.
	WORLD SERIES RECORD																				
2000—	New York (N.L.)	OF	5	21	3	7	0	0	1	3	0	5	0	0	0-0	.333	.333	.476	.810	2	.895

PEARCE, JOSH · P

PERSONAL: Born August 20, 1977, in Yakima, Wash. ... 6-3/220. ... Throws right, bats right. ... Full name: Joshua Ray Pearce. ... High school: West Valley (Yakima, Wash.). ... College: Arizona.

TRANSACTIONS/CAREER NOTES: Selected by New York Mets organization in 40th round of 1996 free-agent draft; did not sign. ... Selected by Anaheim Angels organization in 41st round of 1997 free-agent draft; did not sign. ... Selected by St. Louis Cardinals organization in supplemental round ("sandwich pick" between second and third rounds) of 1999 free-agent draft; pick received as compensation for Seattle Mariners signing Type C free-agent C Tom Lampkin. ... On disabled list (August 30, 2002-remainder of season).

CAREER HITTING: 1-for-4 (.250), 0 R, 0 2B, 0 3B, 0 HR, 1 RBI.

Year	Team (League)	W	L	Pct.	ERA	WHIP	G	GS	CG	ShO	Hld.	Sv.-Opp.	IP	H	R	ER	HR	BB-IBB	SO	Avg.
1999—	New Jersey (N.Y.-Penn.) ...	3	7	.300	4.98	1.26	14	14	1	1	...	0-...	77.2	78	45	43	8	20-0	78	.257
2000—	Potomac (Caro.)	5	3	.625	3.45	1.28	10	10	1	0	...	0-...	62.2	70	25	24	5	10-0	42	.283
	— Arkansas (Texas)	5	6	.455	5.46	1.56	17	17	0	0	...	0-...	97.1	117	68	59	13	35-2	63	.298
2001—	New Haven (East.)	6	8	.429	2.34	0.78	18	18	0	0	...	0-...	185.0	111	55	48	11	34-1	96	.253
	— Memphis (PCL)	4	4	.500	2.58	0.73	10	10	0	0	...	0-...	115.1	72	43	33	11	12-1	36	.266
2002—	Memphis (PCL)	0	4	.000	7.65	1.55	4	4	0	0	...	0-...	20.0	28	18	17	8	3-0	17	.322
	— St. Louis (N.L.)	0	0	...	7.62	2.15	3	3	0	0	0	0-0	13.0	20	13	11	1	8-0	1	.377
2003—	Palm Beach (FSL)	1	4	.200	3.21	1.10	6	5	0	0	...	0-...	28.0	28	10	10	2	2-0	15	.275
	— Tennessee (Sou.)	2	1	.667	4.09	1.10	5	5	0	0	...	0-...	33.0	34	15	15	3	3-0	20	.270
	— Memphis (PCL)	3	3	.500	4.08	1.30	10	9	0	0	...	0-...	46.1	51	22	21	8	8-1	27	.280
	— St. Louis (N.L.)	0	0	...	3.00	1.44	7	0	0	0	1	0-0	9.0	11	3	3	0	2-0	4	.306
2004—	St. Louis (N.L.)	0	0	...	3.86	1.29	3	0	0	0	0	0-0	2.1	3	1	1	0	0-0	0	.375
	— Memphis (PCL)	3	2	.600	3.26	1.35	26	0	0	0	...	1-...	30.1	35	12	11	1	6-1	31	.297
	Major League totals (3 years)	0	0	...	5.55	1.81	13	3	0	0	1	0-0	24.1	34	17	15	1	10-0	5	.351

PEAVY, JAKE · P

PERSONAL: Born May 31, 1981, in Mobile, Ala. ... 6-1/180. ... Throws right, bats right. ... Full name: Jacob Edward Peavy. ... Name pronounced: PEE-vee. ... High school: St. Paul (Mobile, Ala.).

TRANSACTIONS/CAREER NOTES: Selected by San Diego Padres organization in 15th round of 1999 free-agent draft. ... On disabled list (May 20-July 2, 2004); included rehabilitation assignment to Mobile.

CAREER HITTING: 21-for-147 (.143), 13 R, 4 2B, 0 3B, 0 HR, 6 RBI.

Year	Team (League)	W	L	Pct.	ERA	WHIP	G	GS	CG	ShO	Hld.	Sv.-Opp.	IP	H	R	ER	HR	BB-IBB	SO	Avg.
1999—	Ariz. Padres (Ariz.)	7	1	.875	1.34	1.02	13	11	1	0	...	0-...	73.2	52	16	11	4	23-0	90	.202
	— Idaho Falls (Pioneer)	2	0	1.000	0.00	0.55	2	2	0	0	...	0-...	11.0	5	0	0	0	1-0	13	.135
2000—	Fort Wayne (Midw.)	13	8	.619	2.90	1.20	26	25	0	0	...	0-...	133.2	107	61	43	6	53-0	164	.216
2001—	Mobile (Sou.)	2	1	.667	2.57	1.11	5	5	0	0	...	0-...	28.0	19	8	8	3	12-1	44	.192
	— Lake Elsinore (Calif.)	7	5	.583	3.08	1.03	19	19	0	0	...	0-...	105.1	76	41	36	6	33-1	144	.200
2002—	Mobile (Sou.)	4	5	.444	2.80	1.18	14	14	0	0	...	0-...	80.1	65	26	25	4	30-0	89	.220
	— San Diego (N.L.)	6	7	.462	4.52	1.42	17	17	0	0	0	0-0	97.2	106	54	49	11	33-4	90	.274
2003—	San Diego (N.L.)	12	11	.522	4.11	1.31	32	32	0	0	0	0-0	194.2	173	94	89	33	82-3	156	.238
2004—	Mobile (Sou.)	0	1	.000	5.79	1.93	1	1	0	0	...	0-...	4.2	7	4	3	1	2-0	4	.318
	— San Diego (N.L.)	15	6	.714	* 2.27	1.20	27	27	0	0	0	0-0	166.1	146	49	42	13	53-4	173	.236
	Major League totals (3 years)	33	24	.579	3.53	1.29	76	76	0	0	0	0-0	458.2	425	197	180	57	168-11	419	.245

PELLOW, KIT · OF

PERSONAL: Born August 28, 1973, in Kansas City, Mo. ... 6-1/205. ... Bats right, throws right. ... Full name: Kit Donovan Pellow. ... High school: Olathe North (Kan.). ... College: Arkansas.

TRANSACTIONS/CAREER NOTES: Selected by Kansas City Royals organization in 60th round of 1994 free-agent draft; did not sign. ... Selected by Royals organization in 22nd round of 1996 free-agent draft. ... Signed as a free agent by Colorado Rockies organization (November 11, 2002).

2004 GAMES PLAYED BY POSITION (MLB): OF—36, 1B—5, 3B—4, C—4.

P

Year — Team (League)	Pos.	G	AB	R	H	2B	3B	HR	RBI	BB	SO	HBP	GDP	SB-CS	Avg.	OBP	SLG	OPS	E	Avg.
1996—Spokane (N'west) 1B-OF-3B-C		71	279	48	80	18	2	18	66	20	52	8	5	8-3	.287	.344	.559	.903	14	.971
1997—Lansing (Midw.)	3B-1B	65	256	39	76	17	2	11	52	24	74	6	5	2-0	.297	.366	.508	.873	33	.890
—Wichita (Texas)	3B	68	241	40	60	12	1	10	41	21	72	2	5	5-2	.249	.311	.432	.742	24	.898
1998—Wichita (Texas)	3B	103	374	70	100	24	3	29	73	27	107	6	2	4-3	.267	.324	.580	.905	26	.904
—Omaha (PCL)	3B	14	54	8	10	3	0	2	6	2	19	0	1	2-0	.185	.207	.352	.559	3	.919
1999—Omaha (PCL)	3B-1B	131	475	88	136	28	4	35	99	20	117	18	11	6-5	.286	.335	.583	.918	33	.906
2000—Omaha (PCL)	1B	117	421	61	105	17	3	22	75	38	89	16	5	6-4	.249	.331	.461	.792	6	.992
2001—Omaha (PCL)	1B	129	484	81	141	15	0	20	81	37	101	13	3	4-3	.291	.353	.446	.799	8	.993
2002—Omaha (PCL)	3B-1B	105	402	65	116	25	2	27	76	21	82	19	7	4-2	.289	.350	.562	.912	19	.950
—Kansas City (A.L.) 3B-1B-DH		29	63	6	15	1	0	1	5	9	21	1	2	1-1	.238	.342	.302	.644	5	.929
2003—Asheville (S. Atl.) 1B-3B-DH		6	20	3	9	2	0	1	8	5	5	2	0	0-0	.450	.571	.700	1.271	1	.967
—Colo. Springs (PCL) 1-C-3-O-DH		89	320	48	93	15	1	19	57	25	75	12	5	2-1	.291	.363	.522	.885	7	.989
—Colorado (N.L.) C-1B-OF		11	18	6	8	3	1	1	4	0	4	2	0	0-0	.444	.476	.889	1.365	0	1.000
2004—Colorado (N.L.) OF-1B-3B-C		59	121	15	29	5	1	2	10	8	43	4	3	1-0	.240	.308	.347	.655	1	.987
—Colo. Springs (PCL) OF-C-3B-1B		13	42	10	15	4	0	3	14	4	7	1	0	0-0	.357	.417	.667	1.083	3	.943
American League totals (1 year)		29	63	6	15	1	0	1	5	9	21	1	2	1-1	.238	.342	.302	.644	5	.929
National League totals (2 years)		70	139	21	37	8	2	3	14	8	47	6	3	1-0	.266	.331	.417	.748	1	.990
Major League totals (3 years)		99	202	27	52	9	2	4	19	17	68	7	5	2-1	.257	.335	.381	.716	6	.964

PENA, CARLOS   1B

PERSONAL: Born May 17, 1978, in Santo Domingo, Dominican Republic. ... 6-2/215. ... Bats left, throws left. ... Full name: Carlos Felipe Pena. ... Name pronounced: PAIN-yuh. ... High school: Haverhill (Mass.). ... College: Northeastern (Mass.).

TRANSACTIONS/CAREER NOTES: Selected by Texas Rangers organization in first round (10th pick overall) of 1998 free-agent draft. ... Traded by Rangers with P Mike Venafro to Oakland Athletics for 1B Jason Hart, P Marion Ramos, C Gerald Laird and OF Ryan Ludwick (January 14, 2002). ... Traded by A's to Detroit Tigers with P Franklyn German and a player to be named as part of three-team deal in which New York Yankees acquired P Jeff Weaver from Tigers and A's acquired P Ted Lilly, OF John-Ford Griffin and P Jason Arnold from Yankees (July 5, 2002); Tigers acquired P Jeremy Bonderman to complete deal (August 22, 2002). ... On disabled list (June 2-27, 2003); included rehabilitation assignment to Toledo.

2004 GAMES PLAYED BY POSITION (MLB): 1B—135, DH—5.

Year — Team (League)	Pos.	G	AB	R	H	2B	3B	HR	RBI	BB	SO	HBP	GDP	SB-CS	Avg.	OBP	SLG	OPS	E	Avg.
1998—GC Rangers (GCL)	1B	2	5	1	2	0	0	0	0	3	1	0	0	1-1	.400	.625	.400	1.025	0	1.000
—Savannah (S. Atl.)	1B-OF	30	117	22	38	14	0	6	20	8	26	4	0	3-2	.325	.385	.598	.983	3	.986
—Charlotte (Fla. St.)	1B	7	22	1	6	1	0	0	3	2	8	1	0	0-1	.273	.360	.318	.678	1	.977
1999—Charlotte (Fla. St.)	1B	136	501	85	128	31	8	18	103	74	135	16	7	2-5	.255	.365	.457	.822	16	.986
2000—Tulsa (Texas)	1B	138	529	117	158	36	2	28	105	101	108	9	7	12-0	.299	.414	.533	.947	22	.982
2001—Oklahoma (PCL)	1B	119	431	71	124	38	3	23	74	80	127	8	6	11-3	.288	.408	.550	.958	11	.989
—Texas (A.L.)	1B-DH	22	62	6	16	4	1	3	12	10	17	0	1	0-0	.258	.361	.500	.861	2	.987
2002—Oakland (A.L.)	1B	40	124	12	27	4	0	7	16	15	38	1	2	0-0	.218	.305	.419	.724	1	.997
—Sacramento (PCL)	1B	44	175	30	42	10	1	10	33	24	49	4	3	3-0	.240	.340	.480	.820	3	.992
—Detroit (A.L.)	1B-DH	75	273	31	69	13	4	12	36	26	73	2	5	2-2	.253	.321	.462	.783	3	.996
2003—Toledo (Int'l)	1B-DH	8	30	4	10	4	1	0	5	4	7	1	0	0-0	.333	.429	.533	.962	1	.986
—Detroit (A.L.)	1B-DH	131	452	51	112	21	6	18	50	53	123	6	6	4-5	.248	.332	.440	.772	13	.990
2004—Detroit (A.L.)	1B-DH	142	481	89	116	22	4	27	82	70	146	3	11	7-1	.241	.338	.472	.810	6	.995
Major League totals (4 years)		410	1392	189	340	64	15	67	196	174	397	12	25	13-8	.244	.331	.456	.787	25	.993

PENA, WILY MO   OF

PERSONAL: Born January 23, 1982, in Laguna Salada, Dominican Republic. ... 6-3/215. ... Bats right, throws right. ... Full name: Wily Modesto Pena. ... Name pronounced: will-ee moe PAIN-ya.

TRANSACTIONS/CAREER NOTES: Signed as a non-drafted free agent by New York Mets organization (1998); contract nullified by commissioner's office; was declared a free agent (March 7, 1999). ... Signed by New York Yankees organization (April 1, 1999). ... On disabled list (July 13, 2000-remainder of season). ... Traded by Yankees to Cincinnati Reds for 3B Drew Henson and OF Michael Coleman (March 21, 2001). ... On disabled list (July 5-30, 2003); included rehabilitation assignment to Louisville.

2004 GAMES PLAYED BY POSITION (MLB): OF—91.

Year — Team (League)	Pos.	G	AB	R	H	2B	3B	HR	RBI	BB	SO	HBP	GDP	SB-CS	Avg.	OBP	SLG	OPS	E	Avg.
1999—GC Yankees (GCL)	OF	45	166	21	41	10	1	7	26	12	54	7	2	3-2	.247	.323	.446	.768	2	.947
2000—Greensboro (S. Atl.)	OF	67	249	41	51	7	1	10	28	18	91	5	9	6-5	.205	.268	.361	.630	4	.964
—Staten Island N.Y.-Penn. (NY-P)	OF	20	73	7	22	1	2	0	10	2	23	4	1	2-0	.301	.354	.370	.724	0	1.000
2001—Dayton (Midw.)	OF	135	511	87	135	25	5	26	113	33	177	17	6	26-10	.264	.327	.485	.813	9	.972
2002—Chattanooga (Sou.)	OF	105	388	47	99	23	1	11	47	36	126	9	9	8-0	.255	.330	.405	.735	4	.979
—Cincinnati (N.L.)	OF	13	18	1	4	0	0	1	1	0	11	0	0	0-0	.222	.222	.389	.611	0	1.000
2003—Louisville (Int'l)	OF	14	51	16	19	3	0	4	14	5	13	3	0	0-0	.373	.450	.667	1.117	2	.933
—Cincinnati (N.L.)	OF-3B	80	165	20	36	6	1	5	16	12	53	3	2	3-2	.218	.281	.358	.641	2	.978
2004—Cincinnati (N.L.)	OF	110	336	45	87	10	1	26	66	22	108	6	7	5-2	.259	.316	.527	.843	7	.969
Major League totals (3 years)		203	519	66	127	16	2	32	83	34	172	9	9	8-4	.245	.302	.468	.771	9	.972

PENNY, BRAD   P

PERSONAL: Born May 24, 1978, in Broken Arrow, Okla. ... 6-4/250. ... Throws right, bats right. ... Full name: Bradley Wayne Penny. ... High school: Broken Arrow (Okla.).

TRANSACTIONS/CAREER NOTES: Selected by Arizona Diamondbacks organization in fifth round of 1996 free-agent draft. ... Traded by Diamondbacks with P Vladimir Nunez and a player to be named to Florida Marlins for P Matt Mantei (July 9, 1999); Marlins acquired OF Abraham Nunez to complete deal (December 13, 1999). ... On disabled list (July 20-September 2, 2000); included rehabilitation assignments to Brevard County and Calgary. ... On disabled list (May 19-July 2, 2002); included rehabilitation assignment to Jupiter. ... On suspended list (March 30-April 6, 2003). ... Traded with 1B Hee Seop Choi and P Bill Murphy to Los Angeles Dodgers for C Paul Lo Duca, P Guillermo Mota and OF Juan Encarnacion (July 30, 2004). ... On disabled list (August 9-September 22, 2004).

CAREER HITTING: 35-for-274 (.128), 12 R, 4 2B, 2 3B, 2 HR, 13 RBI.

Year — Team (League)	W	L	Pct.	ERA	WHIP	G	GS	CG	ShO	Hld.	Sv.-Opp.	IP	H	R	ER	HR	BB-IBB	SO	Avg.
1996—Ariz. D'backs (Ariz.)	2	2	.500	2.36	1.01	11	8	0	0	...	0-...	49.2	36	18	13	1	14-0	52	.197
1997—South Bend (Mid.)	10	5	.667	2.73	1.13	25	25	0	0	...	0-...	118.2	91	44	36	4	43-2	116	.208
1998—High Desert (Calif.)	14	5	.737	2.96	1.05	28	28	1	0	...	0-...	164.0	138	65	54	15	35-0	207	.225
1999—El Paso (Texas)	2	7	.222	4.80	1.49	17	17	0	0	...	0-...	90.0	109	56	48	9	25-0	100	.303

P

Year	Team (League)	W	L	Pct.	ERA	WHIP	G	GS	CG	ShO	Hld.	Sv.-Opp.	IP	H	R	ER	HR	BB-IBB	SO	Avg.
— Portland (East.)		1	0	1.000	3.90	1.30	6	6	0	0	...	0-...	32.1	28	15	14	3	14-0	35	.231
2000—	Florida (N.L.)	8	7	.533	4.81	1.50	23	22	0	0	0	0-0	119.2	120	70	64	13	60-4	80	.263
— Brevard County (FSL)		0	1	.000	1.13	1.13	2	2	0	0	...	0-...	8.0	5	2	1	0	4-0	11	.172
— Calgary (PCL)		2	0	1.000	1.80	1.20	3	3	0	0	...	0-...	15.0	8	8	3	1	10-0	16	.157
2001—	Florida (N.L.)	10	10	.500	3.69	1.16	31	31	1	1	0	0-0	205.0	183	92	84	15	54-3	154	.240
2002—	Florida (N.L.)	8	7	.533	4.66	1.53	24	24	1	1	0	0-0	129.1	148	76	67	18	50-7	93	.289
— Jupiter (FSL)		0	0	...	0.00	0.65	2	2	0	0	0	0-...	7.2	5	0	0	0	0-0	9	.179
2003—	Florida (N.L.)	14	10	.583	4.13	1.28	32	32	0	0	0	0-0	196.1	195	96	90	21	56-6	138	.264
2004—	Florida (N.L.)	8	8	.500	3.15	1.24	21	21	0	0	0	0-0	131.1	124	50	46	10	39-6	105	.250
— Los Angeles (N.L.)		1	2	.333	3.09	1.03	3	3	0	0	0	0-0	11.2	6	5	4	2	6-0	6	.154
Major League totals (5 years)		49	44	.527	4.03	1.31	134	133	2	2	0	0-0	793.1	776	389	355	79	265-26	576	.258

DIVISION SERIES RECORD

Year	Team (League)	W	L	Pct.	ERA	WHIP	G	GS	CG	ShO	Hld.	Sv.-Opp.	IP	H	R	ER	HR	BB-IBB	SO	Avg.
2003—	Florida (N.L.)	0	0	...	6.35	1.06	2	1	0	0	0	0-1	5.2	5	4	4	0	1-0	6	.250

CHAMPIONSHIP SERIES RECORD

Year	Team (League)	W	L	Pct.	ERA	WHIP	G	GS	CG	ShO	Hld.	Sv.-Opp.	IP	H	R	ER	HR	BB-IBB	SO	Avg.
2003—	Florida (N.L.)	1	1	.500	15.75	3.00	3	1	0	0	0	0-0	4.0	9	7	7	2	3-1	0	.450

WORLD SERIES RECORD

Year	Team (League)	W	L	Pct.	ERA	WHIP	G	GS	CG	ShO	Hld.	Sv.-Opp.	IP	H	R	ER	HR	BB-IBB	SO	Avg.
2003—	Florida (N.L.)	2	0	1.000	2.19	1.62	2	1	0	0	0	0-0	12.1	15	4	3	1	5-0	7	.319

PERALTA, JHONNY   SS

PERSONAL: Born May 28, 1982, in Santiago, Dominican Republic. ... 6-1/185. ... Bats right, throws right. ... Full name: Jhonny Antonio Peralta. ... Name pronounced: pah-RALL-tah.

TRANSACTIONS/CAREER NOTES: Signed as a non-drafted free agent by Cleveland Indians organization (April 14, 1999).

2004 GAMES PLAYED BY POSITION (MLB): SS—7, 3B—2.

Year	Team (League)	Pos.	G	AB	R	H	2B	3B	HR	RBI	BB	SO	HBP	GDP	SB-CS	Avg.	OBP	SLG	OPS	E	Avg.
2000—	Columbus (S. Atl.)	SS-3B	106	349	52	84	13	1	3	34	59	102	2	13	7-6	.241	.352	.309	.661	26	.948
2001—	Kinston (Caro.)	SS	125	441	57	106	24	2	7	47	58	148	1	9	4-8	.240	.328	.351	.680	27	.952
2002—	Akron (East.)	SS	130	470	62	132	28	5	15	62	45	97	5	6	4-2	.281	.343	.457	.800	21	.965
2003—	Buffalo (Int'l)	SS-3B	63	237	25	61	12	1	1	21	15	45	3	6	1-3	.257	.310	.329	.639	10	.969
	— Cleveland (A.L.)	SS-3B	77	242	24	55	10	1	4	21	20	65	4	5	1-3	.227	.295	.326	.621	8	.977
2004—	Buffalo (Int'l) SS-3B-DH	138	556	109	181	44	2	15	86	54	126	4	16	8-4	.326	.384	.493	.876	27	.948
	— Cleveland (A.L.)	SS-3B	8	25	2	6	1	0	0	2	3	6	0	0	0-1	.240	.321	.280	.601	3	.900
Major League totals (2 years)			85	267	26	61	11	1	4	23	23	71	4	5	1-4	.228	.297	.322	.619	11	.970

PERCIVAL, TROY   P

PERSONAL: Born August 9, 1969, in Fontana, Calif. ... 6-3/235. ... Throws right, bats right. ... Full name: Troy Eugene Percival. ... Name pronounced: PURR-si-vul. ... High school: Moreno Valley (Calif.). ... College: UC-Riverside.

TRANSACTIONS/CAREER NOTES: Selected by California Angels organization in sixth round of 1990 free-agent draft. ... Played catcher in Angels organization (1990). ... Angels franchise renamed Anaheim Angels for 1997 season. ... On disabled list (April 7-May 16, 1997); included rehabilitation assignment to Lake Elsinore. ... On disabled list (August 5-26, 2000); included rehabilitation assignment to Lake Elsinore. ... On disabled list (April 3-18 and July 12-27, 2002; May 23-June 7, 2003; and June 2-27, 2004).

CAREER HITTING: 0-for-1 (.000), 0 R, 0 2B, 0 3B, 0 HR, 0 RBI.

Year	Team (League)	W	L	Pct.	ERA	WHIP	G	GS	CG	ShO	Hld.	Sv.-Opp.	IP	H	R	ER	HR	BB-IBB	SO	Avg.
1991—	Boise (N'west)	2	0	1.000	1.41	1.07	28	0	0	0	...	12-...	38.1	23	7	6	0	18-1	63	.172
1992—	Palm Springs (Calif.)	1	1	.500	5.06	1.31	11	0	0	0	...	2-...	10.2	6	7	6	0	8-1	16	.188
	— Midland (Texas)	3	0	1.000	2.37	1.53	20	0	0	0	...	5-...	19.0	18	5	5	1	11-1	21	.254
1993—	Vancouver (PCL)	0	1	.000	6.27	1.98	18	0	0	0	...	4-...	18.2	24	14	13	0	13-1	19	.320
1994—	Vancouver (PCL)	2	6	.250	4.13	1.51	49	0	0	0	...	15-...	61.0	63	31	28	4	29-5	73	.285
1995—	California (A.L.)	3	2	.600	1.95	0.85	62	0	0	0	29	3-6	74.0	37	19	16	6	26-2	94	.147
1996—	California (A.L.)	0	2	.000	2.31	0.93	62	0	0	0	2	36-39	74.0	38	20	19	8	31-4	100	.149
1997—	Anaheim (A.L.)	5	5	.500	3.46	1.19	55	0	0	0	0	27-31	52.0	40	20	20	6	22-2	72	.205
	— Lake Elsinore (Calif.)	0	0	...	0.00	0.50	2	1	0	0	0	0-...	2.0	1	0	0	0	0-0	3	.143
1998—	Anaheim (A.L.)	2	7	.222	3.65	1.23	67	0	0	0	0	42-48	66.2	45	31	27	5	37-4	87	.186
1999—	Anaheim (A.L.)	4	6	.400	3.79	1.05	60	0	0	0	0	31-39	57.0	38	24	24	9	22-0	58	.186
2000—	Anaheim (A.L.)	5	5	.500	4.50	1.44	54	0	0	0	0	32-42	50.0	42	27	25	7	30-4	49	.228
	— Lake Elsinore (Calif.)	0	0	...	4.50	1.00	2	2	0	0	0	0-...	2.0	1	1	1	0	1-0	1	.143
2001—	Anaheim (A.L.)	4	2	.667	2.65	0.99	57	0	0	0	0	39-42	57.2	39	19	17	3	18-1	71	.187
2002—	Anaheim (A.L.)	4	1	.800	1.92	1.12	58	0	0	0	0	40-44	56.1	38	12	12	5	25-1	68	.188
2003—	Anaheim (A.L.)	0	5	.000	3.47	1.14	52	0	0	0	0	33-37	49.1	33	22	19	7	23-1	48	.184
2004—	Anaheim (A.L.)	2	3	.400	2.90	1.25	52	0	0	0	0	33-38	49.2	43	19	16	7	19-3	33	.230
Major League totals (10 years)		29	38	.433	2.99	1.10	579	0	0	0	31	316-366	586.2	393	213	195	63	253-22	680	.186

DIVISION SERIES RECORD

Year	Team (League)	W	L	Pct.	ERA	WHIP	G	GS	CG	ShO	Hld.	Sv.-Opp.	IP	H	R	ER	HR	BB-IBB	SO	Avg.
2002—	Anaheim (A.L.)	0	0	...	5.40	1.80	3	0	0	0	0	2-2	3.1	6	2	2	0	0-0	4	.375

CHAMPIONSHIP SERIES RECORD

Year	Team (League)	W	L	Pct.	ERA	WHIP	G	GS	CG	ShO	Hld.	Sv.-Opp.	IP	H	R	ER	HR	BB-IBB	SO	Avg.
2002—	Anaheim (A.L.)	0	0	...	0.00	0.00	3	0	0	0	0	2-2	3.1	0	0	0	0	0-0	3	.000

WORLD SERIES RECORD

Year	Team (League)	W	L	Pct.	ERA	WHIP	G	GS	CG	ShO	Hld.	Sv.-Opp.	IP	H	R	ER	HR	BB-IBB	SO	Avg.
2002—	Anaheim (A.L.)	0	0	...	3.00	1.00	3	0	0	0	0	3-3	3.0	2	1	1	1	1-0	3	.182

ALL-STAR GAME RECORD

		W	L	Pct.	ERA	WHIP	G	GS	CG	ShO	Hld.	Sv.-Opp.	IP	H	R	ER	HR	BB-IBB	SO	Avg.
All-Star Game totals (3 years)		0	0	...	0.00	1.00	3	0	0	0	1	0-0	3.0	2	0	0	0	1-0	4	.182

P

PEREZ, ANTONIO — 2B

PERSONAL: Born January 26, 1980, in Bani, Dominican Republic. ... 5-11/170. ... Bats right, throws right. ... Full name: Antonio Miguel Perez.

TRANSACTIONS/CAREER NOTES: Signed as a non-drafted free agent by Cincinnati Reds organization (March 21, 1998). ... Traded by Reds with OF Mike Cameron and Ps Brett Tomko and Jake Meyer to Seattle Mariners for OF Ken Griffey (February 10, 2000). ... Traded by Mariners to Tampa Bay Devil Rays for OF Randy Winn (October 28, 2002). ... Traded by Devil Rays to Los Angeles Dodgers for OF/IF Jason Romano (April 3, 2004).

2004 GAMES PLAYED BY POSITION (MLB): 2B—2, SS—1.

											BATTING									FIELDING	
Year	Team (League)	Pos.	G	AB	R	H	2B	3B	HR	RBI	BB	SO	HBP	GDP	SB-CS	Avg.	OBP	SLG	OPS	E	Avg.
1999—Rockford (Midwest)		SS-2B	119	385	69	111	20	3	7	41	43	80	13	3	35-24	.288	.376	.410	.787	36	.929
2000—Lancaster (Calif.)		SS	98	395	90	109	36	6	17	63	58	99	8	3	28-16	.276	.376	.527	.903	27	.939
2001—San Antonio (Texas)		SS	5	21	3	3	0	0	0	0	0	7	0	0	0-0	.143	.143	.143	.286	6	.818
2002—Ariz. Mariners (Ariz.)		2B-SS	6	15	3	5	1	0	1	3	4	2	1	0	4-0	.333	.476	.600	1.076	0	1.000
—San Antonio (Texas)		2B-SS	72	240	30	62	8	2	2	24	11	64	10	3	15-9	.258	.312	.333	.645	13	.955
2003—Orlando (South.)		2B-DH	24	81	16	22	5	1	2	10	18	18	4	0	3-1	.272	.423	.432	.855	3	.967
—Durham (Int'l)		2B-DH	34	134	27	38	12	2	6	20	10	38	3	2	3-1	.284	.345	.537	.882	8	.958
—Tampa Bay (A.L.)		2-3-S-DH	48	125	19	31	6	1	2	12	18	34	1	1	4-1	.248	.345	.360	.705	2	.985
2004—Las Vegas (PCL)		SS-2B-DH	125	476	92	141	24	6	22	88	61	87	7	1	23-12	.296	.379	.511	.890	20	.963
—Los Angeles (N.L.)		2B-SS	13	13	5	3	1	0	0	0	0	5	1	0	1-0	.231	.286	.308	.593	1	.857
American League totals (1 year)			48	125	19	31	6	1	2	12	18	34	1	1	4-1	.248	.345	.360	.705	2	.985
National League totals (1 year)			13	13	5	3	1	0	0	0	0	5	1	0	1-0	.231	.286	.308	.593	1	.857
Major League totals (2 years)			61	138	24	34	7	1	2	12	18	39	2	1	5-1	.246	.340	.355	.695	3	.979

PEREZ, EDDIE — C

PERSONAL: Born May 4, 1968, in Ciudad Ojeda, Venezuela. ... 6-1/220. ... Bats right, throws right. ... Full name: Eduardo Rafael Perez. ... High school: Doctor Raul Cuenca (Cuidad Ojeda, Venezuela).

TRANSACTIONS/CAREER NOTES: Signed as a non-drafted free agent by Atlanta Braves organization (September 27, 1986). ... On disabled list (August 30-September 14, 1996; included rehabilitation assignment to Greenville. ... Traded by Braves to Cleveland Indians for a player to be named (March 21, 2002); Braves acquired OF Jason Fitzgerald to complete deal (September 18, 2002). ... Signed as a free agent by Milwaukee Brewers organization (January 24, 2003). ... Signed as a free agent by Braves (December 19, 2003).

2004 GAMES PLAYED BY POSITION (MLB): C—66, 1B—1.

											BATTING									FIELDING	
Year	Team (League)	Pos.	G	AB	R	H	2B	3B	HR	RBI	BB	SO	HBP	GDP	SB-CS	Avg.	OBP	SLG	OPS	E	Avg.
1987—GC Braves (GCL)		C	31	89	8	18	1	0	1	5	8	14	1	4	0-0	.202	.273	.247	.520	4	.980
1988—Burlington (Midw.)		C-1B	64	186	14	43	8	0	4	19	10	33	0	6	1-0	.231	.269	.339	.608	11	.963
1989—Sumter (S. Atl.)		C-1B	114	401	39	93	21	0	5	44	44	68	5	10	2-6	.232	.312	.322	.634	13	.985
1990—Sumter (S. Atl.)		C-1B	41	123	11	22	7	1	3	17	14	18	2	7	0-0	.179	.271	.325	.597	3	.991
—Durham (Caro.)		C-1B	31	93	9	22	1	0	3	10	1	12	1	3	0-0	.237	.250	.344	.594	3	.986
1991—Durham (Caro.)		C-1B	92	277	38	75	10	1	9	41	17	33	3	7	0-3	.271	.317	.412	.728	8	.986
—Greenville (Sou.)		1B	1	4	0	1	0	0	0	0	0	1	0	1	0-0	.250	.250	.250	.500	1	1.000
1992—Greenville (Sou.)		C-1B	91	275	28	63	16	0	6	41	24	41	2	11	3-3	.229	.292	.353	.645	14	.980
1993—Greenville (Sou.)		C-1B	28	84	15	28	6	0	6	17	2	8	0	4	1-0	.333	.341	.619	.960	3	.982
1994—Richmond (Int'l)		C-1B	113	388	37	101	16	2	9	49	18	47	3	4	1-1	.260	.294	.381	.675	12	.985
1995—Richmond (Int'l)		C-DH-1B	92	324	31	86	19	0	5	40	12	58	2	12	1-2	.265	.294	.370	.664	7	.989
—Atlanta (N.L.)		C-1B	7	13	1	4	1	0	1	4	0	2	0	0	0-0	.308	.308	.615	.923	0	1.000
1996—Atlanta (N.L.)		C-1B	68	156	19	40	9	1	4	17	8	19	1	6	0-0	.256	.293	.404	.697	3	.990
1997—Atlanta (N.L.)		C-1B	73	191	20	41	5	0	6	18	10	35	2	8	0-1	.215	.259	.335	.594	5	.989
1998—Atlanta (N.L.)		C-1B-DH	61	149	18	50	12	0	6	32	15	28	2	3	1-1	.336	.404	.537	.941	2	.994
1999—Atlanta (N.L.)		C	104	309	30	77	17	0	7	30	17	40	6	9	0-1	.249	.299	.372	.671	5	.993
2000—Atlanta (N.L.)		C	7	22	0	4	1	0	0	3	0	2	0	0	0-0	.182	.182	.227	.409	1	.976
2001—Greenville (Sou.)		C-1B	10	38	7	13	2	0	4	5	0	9	1	0	0-0	.342	.359	.711	1.070	1	.984
—Atlanta (N.L.)		C	5	10	0	3	0	0	0	0	0	2	0	0	0-0	.300	.300	.300	.600	0	1.000
2002—Cleveland (A.L.)		C	42	117	6	25	9	0	4	5	5	25	1	6	0-0	.214	.252	.291	.543	3	.988
2003—Milwaukee (N.L.)		C	107	350	26	95	17	1	11	45	17	47	0	16	0-1	.271	.304	.420	.724	6	.991
2004—Atlanta (N.L.)		C-1B	74	170	14	39	12	0	3	13	11	29	3	5	0-0	.229	.286	.353	.639	3	.991
American League totals (1 year)			42	117	6	25	9	0	4	5	5	25	1	6	0-0	.214	.252	.291	.543	3	.988
National League totals (9 years)			506	1370	128	353	74	2	38	162	78	204	14	47	1-4	.258	.302	.398	.700	25	.991
Major League totals (10 years)			548	1487	134	378	83	2	38	166	83	229	15	53	1-4	.254	.298	.389	.688	28	.991

DIVISION SERIES RECORD

Year	Team (League)	Pos.	G	AB	R	H	2B	3B	HR	RBI	BB	SO	HBP	GDP	SB-CS	Avg.	OBP	SLG	OPS	E	Avg.
1995—Atlanta (N.L.)			Did not play.																		
1996—Atlanta (N.L.)		C	1	3	0	1	0	0	0	0	0	0	0	0	0-0	.333	.333	.333	.667	0	1.000
1997—Atlanta (N.L.)		C	1	3	0	0	0	0	0	0	0	1	0	0	0-0	.000	.000	.000	.000	0	1.000
1998—Atlanta (N.L.)		C	1	5	1	1	0	0	1	4	0	2	0	0	0-0	.200	.200	.800	1.000	0	1.000
1999—Atlanta (N.L.)		C	4	16	1	4	0	0	0	3	0	3	0	1	0-0	.250	.235	.250	.485	0	1.000
2001—Atlanta (N.L.)			Did not play.																		
2004—Atlanta (N.L.)		C	3	3	0	0	0	0	0	0	0	1	0	0	0-0	.000	.000	.000	.000	0	1.000
Division series totals (5 years)			10	30	2	6	0	0	1	7	0	7	0	1	0-0	.200	.194	.300	.494	0	1.000

CHAMPIONSHIP SERIES RECORD

Year	Team (League)	Pos.	G	AB	R	H	2B	3B	HR	RBI	BB	SO	HBP	GDP	SB-CS	Avg.	OBP	SLG	OPS	E	Avg.
1995—Atlanta (N.L.)			Did not play.																		
1996—Atlanta (N.L.)		C-1B	4	1	0	0	0	0	0	0	1	0	0	0	0-0	.000	.500	.000	.500	0	1.000
1997—Atlanta (N.L.)		C	2	3	0	0	0	0	0	0	0	0	0	0	0-0	.000	.000	.000	.000	0	1.000
1998—Atlanta (N.L.)		C	3	4	0	3	0	0	0	0	0	0	0	0	0-0	.750	.750	.750	1.500	0	1.000
1999—Atlanta (N.L.)		C	6	20	2	10	2	0	2	5	1	3	0	0	0-0	.500	.524	.900	1.424	0	1.000
2001—Atlanta (N.L.)			Did not play.																		
Champ. series totals (4 years)			15	28	2	13	2	0	2	5	2	3	0	0	0-0	.464	.500	.760	1.250	0	1.000

WORLD SERIES RECORD

Year	Team (League)	Pos.	G	AB	R	H	2B	3B	HR	RBI	BB	SO	HBP	GDP	SB-CS	Avg.	OBP	SLG	OPS	E	Avg.
1995—Atlanta (N.L.)			Did not play.																		
1996—Atlanta (N.L.)		C	2	1	0	0	0	0	0	0	0	0	0	0	0-0	.000	.000	.000	.000	0	1.000
1999—Atlanta (N.L.)		C	3	8	0	1	0	0	0	0	1	3	0	1	0-0	.125	.222	.125	.347	0	1.000
World series totals (2 years)			5	9	0	1	0	0	0	0	1	3	0	1	0-0	.111	.200	.111	.311	0	1.000

PEREZ, EDUARDO — 1B

PERSONAL: Born September 11, 1969, in Cincinnati, Ohio. ... 6-4/240. ... Bats right, throws right. ... Full name: Eduardo Atanasio Perez. ... High school: Robinson (Santurce, Puerto Rico). ... College: Florida State. ... Son of Tony Perez, special assistant to general manager, Florida Marlins; infielder with four major league teams (1964-86) and manager of Cincinnati Reds (1993).

TRANSACTIONS/CAREER NOTES: Selected by California Angels organization in first round (17th pick overall) of 1991 free-agent draft. ... Traded by Angels to Cincinnati Reds for OF Will Pennyfeather (April 5, 1996). ... Released by Reds (December 14, 1998). ... Signed by St. Louis Cardinals organization (February 16, 1999). ... On disabled list (June 25-July 13 and August 13-September 1, 2000); included rehabilitation assignment to Memphis. ... Contract sold by Cardinals to Hanshin of the Japan Central League (December 20, 2000). ... Signed as a free agent by Cardinals organization (February 8, 2002). ... Signed as a free agent by Tampa Bay Devil Rays (December 11, 2003). ... On disabled list (May 10, 2004-remainder of season).

2004 GAMES PLAYED BY POSITION (MLB): 1B—5, DH—3, OF—3, 3B—1.

Year	Team (League)	Pos.	G	AB	R	H	2B	3B	HR	RBI	BB	SO	HBP	GDP	SB-CS	Avg.	OBP	SLG	OPS	E	Avg.
1991—	Boise (N'west)	1B-OF	46	160	35	46	13	0	1	22	19	39	4	4	12-3	.288	.375	.388	.763	3	.969
1992—	Palm Springs (Calif.)	3B-SS-OF	54	204	37	64	8	4	3	35	23	33	3	5	14-3	.314	.386	.436	.823	16	.882
—	Midland (Texas)	3B-1B-OF	62	235	27	54	8	1	3	23	22	49	1	7	19-7	.230	.295	.311	.606	13	.920
1993—	Vancouver (PCL)	3B-1B-OF	96	363	66	111	23	6	12	70	28	83	3	5	21-7	.306	.360	.501	.862	23	.922
—	California (A.L.)	3B-DH	52	180	16	45	6	2	4	30	9	39	2	4	5-4	.250	.292	.372	.664	5	.962
1994—	California (A.L.)	1B	38	129	10	27	7	0	5	16	12	29	0	5	3-0	.209	.275	.380	.654	1	.997
—	Vancouver (PCL)	3B-DH	61	219	37	65	14	3	7	38	34	53	3	7	9-4	.297	.394	.484	.878	12	.926
—	Ariz. Angels (Ariz.)	3B	1	3	0	0	0	0	0	0	1	1	0	0	0-0	.000	.250	.000	.250	0	1.000
1995—	California (A.L.)	3B-DH	29	71	9	12	4	1	1	7	12	9	2	3	0-2	.169	.302	.296	.598	7	.883
—	Vancouver (PCL)	3B-DH-1B	69	246	39	80	12	7	6	37	25	34	2	5	6-2	.325	.386	.504	.890	6	.968
1996—	Indianapolis (A.A.)	3B-1B-DH	122	451	84	132	29	5	21	84	51	69	6	11	11-0	.293	.371	.519	.890	21	.939
—	Cincinnati (N.L.)	1B-3B	18	36	8	8	0	0	3	5	5	9	0	2	0-0	.222	.317	.472	.789	0	1.000
1997—	Cincinnati (N.L.)	1-O-3-DH	106	297	44	75	18	0	16	52	29	76	2	6	5-1	.253	.321	.475	.796	2	.996
1998—	Cincinnati (N.L.)	1B-3B-OF	84	172	20	41	4	0	4	30	21	45	2	2	0-1	.238	.325	.331	.656	5	.985
1999—	Memphis (PCL)	1B-3B-DH	119	416	67	133	31	0	18	82	45	92	6	11	7-8	.320	.393	.524	.917	9	.989
—	St. Louis (N.L.)	OF-1B	21	32	6	11	2	0	1	9	7	6	0	0	0-0	.344	.462	.500	.962	1	.970
2000—	St. Louis (N.L.)	1B-OF-3B	35	91	9	27	4	0	3	10	5	19	3	2	1-0	.297	.350	.440	.790	0	1.000
—	Memphis (PCL)	1B-3B-OF	77	277	57	80	12	3	19	66	43	48	1	9	10-4	.289	.383	.560	.942	8	.980
2001—	Hanshin (Jp. Cn.)		52	167	20	37	11	0	3	19	21	48	...	...	3-...	.222		.341		2	.982
2002—	St. Louis (N.L.)	OF-1-3-DH	96	154	22	31	9	0	10	26	17	36	3	7	0-0	.201	.290	.455	.744	2	.982
2003—	St. Louis (N.L.)	OF-3-1-DH	105	253	47	72	16	0	11	41	29	53	4	7	5-2	.285	.365	.478	.843	7	.951
2004—	Tampa Bay (A.L.)	1-DH-OF-3	13	38	2	8	2	0	1	7	4	9	0	1	0-0	.211	.286	.342	.628	0	1.000
American League totals (4 years)			132	418	37	92	19	3	11	60	37	86	4	13	8-6	.220	.288	.359	.647	13	.977
National League totals (7 years)			465	1035	156	265	53	0	48	173	113	244	14	26	11-4	.256	.335	.446	.781	17	.988
Major League totals (11 years)			597	1453	193	357	72	3	59	233	150	330	18	39	19-10	.246	.321	.421	.743	30	.985

DIVISION SERIES RECORD

Year	Team (League)	Pos.	G	AB	R	H	2B	3B	HR	RBI	BB	SO	HBP	GDP	SB-CS	Avg.	OBP	SLG	OPS	E	Avg.
2002—	St. Louis (N.L.)		1	1	0	0	0	0	0	0	0	0	0	0	0-0	.000	.000	.000	.000	0	...

CHAMPIONSHIP SERIES RECORD

Year	Team (League)	Pos.	G	AB	R	H	2B	3B	HR	RBI	BB	SO	HBP	GDP	SB-CS	Avg.	OBP	SLG	OPS	E	Avg.
2002—	St. Louis (N.L.)	OF	3	4	1	1	0	0	1	1	1	0	0	0	0-0	.250	.400	1.000	1.400	0	1.000

PEREZ, NEIFI — SS/2B

PERSONAL: Born June 2, 1973, in Villa Mella, Dominican Republic. ... 6-0/197. ... Bats both, throws right. ... Full name: Neifi Neftali Perez. ... Name pronounced: NAY-fee.

TRANSACTIONS/CAREER NOTES: Signed as a non-drafted free agent by Colorado Rockies organization (November 9, 1992). ... On disabled list (April 8-23, 2001). ... Traded by Rockies to Kansas City Royals for OF Jermaine Dye (July 25, 2001). ... Claimed on waivers by San Francisco Giants (November 20, 2002). ... Released by Giants (August 13, 2004). ... Signed by Chicago Cubs organization (August 19, 2004).

HONORS: Won N.L. Gold Glove as shortstop (2000).

2004 GAMES PLAYED BY POSITION (MLB): SS—76, 2B—41, 3B—2.

Year	Team (League)	Pos.	G	AB	R	H	2B	3B	HR	RBI	BB	SO	HBP	GDP	SB-CS	Avg.	OBP	SLG	OPS	E	Avg.
1993—	Bend (N'west)	2B-SS	75	296	35	77	11	4	3	32	19	43	2	3	19-14	.260	.306	.355	.661	25	.937
1994—	Central Valley (Cal.)	SS	134	506	64	121	16	7	1	35	32	79	2	6	9-7	.239	.284	.304	.589	39	.940
1995—	Colo. Springs (PCL)	SS	11	36	4	10	4	0	0	2	0	5	0	0	1-1	.278	.278	.389	.667	3	.936
—	New Haven (East.)	SS	116	427	59	108	28	3	5	43	24	52	2	6	5-2	.253	.295	.368	.663	18	.967
1996—	Colo. Springs (PCL)	SS	133	570	77	180	28	12	7	72	21	48	2	13	16-13	.316	.337	.444	.781	25	.963
—	Colorado (N.L.)	SS-2B	17	45	4	7	2	0	0	3	0	8	0	2	2-2	.156	.156	.200	.356	2	.961
1997—	Colo. Springs (PCL)	SS	68	303	68	110	24	3	8	46	17	27	0	3	8-2	.363	.393	.541	.934	8	.975
—	Colorado (N.L.)	SS-2B-3B	83	313	46	91	13	10	5	31	21	43	1	3	4-3	.291	.333	.444	.777	9	.981
1998—	Colorado (N.L.)	SS-C	•162	647	80	177	25	9	9	59	38	70	1	7	5-6	.274	.313	.382	.695	20	.975
1999—	Colorado (N.L.)	SS	157	*690	108	193	27	•11	12	70	28	54	1	4	13-5	.280	.307	.403	.710	14	.981
2000—	Colorado (N.L.)	SS	•162	651	92	187	39	11	10	71	30	63	0	9	3-6	.287	.314	.427	.741	18	.978
2001—	Colorado (N.L.)	SS	87	382	65	114	19	8	7	47	16	49	0	8	6-2	.298	.326	.445	.771	10	.976
—	Kansas City (A.L.)	SS-2B	49	199	18	48	7	1	1	12	10	19	1	2	3-4	.241	.277	.302	.579	5	.980
2002—	Kansas City (A.L.)	SS-2B	145	554	65	131	20	4	3	37	20	53	0	11	8-9	.236	.260	.303	.564	20	.971
2003—	San Francisco (N.L.)	2B-SS-3B	120	328	27	84	19	4	1	31	14	23	0	9	3-2	.256	.285	.348	.632	5	.989
2004—	San Francisco (N.L.)	SS-2B-3B	103	319	28	74	12	1	2	33	21	35	0	7	0-1	.232	.276	.295	.571	6	.986
—	Iowa (PCL)	SS	10	34	1	7	1	0	0	3	0	5	0	0	0-0	.206	.206	.235	.441	0	1.000
—	Chicago (N.L.)	SS-2B	23	62	12	23	5	0	2	6	3	6	0	1	1-0	.371	.400	.548	.948	2	.972
American League totals (2 years)			194	753	83	179	27	5	4	49	30	72	1	13	11-13	.238	.265	.303	.568	25	.974
National League totals (8 years)			914	3437	462	950	161	54	48	351	171	351	3	51	37-27	.276	.309	.397	.705	86	.980
Major League totals (9 years)			1108	4190	545	1129	188	59	52	400	201	423	4	64	48-40	.269	.301	.380	.681	111	.979

DIVISION SERIES RECORD

Year	Team (League)	Pos.	G	AB	R	H	2B	3B	HR	RBI	BB	SO	HBP	GDP	SB-CS	Avg.	OBP	SLG	OPS	E	Avg.
2003—	San Francisco (N.L.)	2B	3	3	1	1	1	0	0	0	1	0	0	0	0-0	.333	.500	.667	1.167	0	1.000

P

PEREZ, ODALIS   P

PERSONAL: Born June 7, 1977, in Las Matas de Farfan, Dominican Republic. ... 6-0/150. ... Throws left, bats left. ... Full name: Odalis Amadol Perez. ... Name pronounced: oh-DALL-iss. ... High school: Damian Davis Ortiz (Las Matas de Farfan, Dominican Republic).

TRANSACTIONS/CAREER NOTES: Signed as a non-drafted free agent by Atlanta Braves organization (July 2, 1994). ... On disabled list (July 23, 1999-remainder of season; and April 2, 2000-entire season). ... On disabled list (July 22-September 1, 2001); included rehabilitation assignment to Richmond. ... Traded by Braves with OF Brian Jordan and P Andrew Brown to Los Angeles Dodgers for OF Gary Sheffield (January 15, 2002). ... On disabled list (June 27-July 17, 2004).

CAREER HITTING: 31-for-234 (.132), 15 R, 8 2B, 0 3B, 1 HR, 10 RBI.

Year Team (League)	W	L	Pct.	ERA	WHIP	G	GS	CG	ShO	Hld.	Sv.-Opp.	IP	H	R	ER	HR	BB-IBB	SO	Avg.
1995— GC Braves (GCL)	3	5	.375	2.22	1.02	12	12	1	1	...	0-...	65.0	48	22	16	0	18-0	62	.200
1996— Eugene (N'west)	2	1	.667	3.80	1.56	10	6	0	0	...	0-...	23.2	26	16	10	2	11-0	38	.268
1997— Macon (S. Atl.)	4	5	.444	1.65	1.08	36	0	0	0	...	5-...	87.1	67	31	16	4	27-1	100	.209
1998— Greenville (Sou.)	6	5	.545	4.02	1.36	23	21	0	0	...	0-...	132.0	127	67	59	15	53-2	143	.256
— Richmond (Int'l)	1	2	.333	2.96	1.36	13	0	0	0	...	3-...	24.1	26	10	8	4	7-1	22	.283
— Atlanta (N.L.)	0	1	.000	4.22	1.31	10	0	0	0	5	0-1	10.2	10	5	5	1	4-0	5	.244
1999— Atlanta (N.L.)	4	6	.400	6.00	1.65	18	17	0	0	0	0-0	93.0	100	65	62	12	53-2	82	.275
2000— Atlanta (N.L.)					Did not play.														
2001— Atlanta (N.L.)	7	8	.467	4.91	1.54	24	16	0	0	0	0-0	95.1	108	55	52	7	39-0	71	.290
— Richmond (Int'l)	1	0	1.000	2.74	1.09	5	5	0	0	...	0-...	23.0	23	7	7	1	2-0	22	.256
2002— Los Angeles (N.L.)	15	10	.600	3.00	0.99	32	32	4	2	0	0-0	222.1	182	76	74	21	38-5	155	.226
2003— Los Angeles (N.L.)	12	12	.500	4.52	1.28	30	30	0	0	0	0-0	185.1	191	98	93	28	46-4	141	.267
2004— Los Angeles (N.L.)	7	6	.538	3.25	1.14	31	31	0	0	0	0-0	196.1	180	76	71	26	44-4	128	.250
Major League totals (6 years)	**45**	**43**	**.511**	**4.00**	**1.24**	**145**	**126**	**4**	**2**	**5**	**0-1**	**803.0**	**771**	**375**	**357**	**95**	**224-15**	**582**	**.255**

DIVISION SERIES RECORD

Year Team (League)	W	L	Pct.	ERA	WHIP	G	GS	CG	ShO	Hld.	Sv.-Opp.	IP	H	R	ER	HR	BB-IBB	SO	Avg.
1998— Atlanta (N.L.)	1	0	1.000	0.00	0.00	1	0	0	0	0	0-0	.2	0	0	0	0	0-0	1	.000
2004— Los Angeles (N.L.)	0	1	.000	14.40	3.00	2	2	0	0	0	0-0	5.0	8	8	8	4	7-0	3	.364
Division series totals (2 years)	**1**	**1**	**.500**	**12.71**	**2.65**	**3**	**2**	**0**	**0**	**0**	**0-0**	**5.2**	**8**	**8**	**8**	**4**	**7-0**	**4**	**.348**

CHAMPIONSHIP SERIES RECORD

Year Team (League)	W	L	Pct.	ERA	WHIP	G	GS	CG	ShO	Hld.	Sv.-Opp.	IP	H	R	ER	HR	BB-IBB	SO	Avg.
1998— Atlanta (N.L.)	0	0	...	54.00	21.00	2	0	0	0	0	0-0	.1	5	2	2	0	2-1	0	1.000

ALL-STAR GAME RECORD

	W	L	Pct.	ERA	WHIP	G	GS	CG	ShO	Hld.	Sv.-Opp.	IP	H	R	ER	HR	BB-IBB	SO	Avg.
All-Star Game totals (1 year)	0	0	...	0.00	2.00	1	0	0	0	0	0-0	1.0	2	1	0	0	0-0	2	.400

PEREZ, OLIVER   P

PERSONAL: Born August 15, 1981, in Culiacan, Mexico. ... 6-0/190. ... Throws left, bats left.

TRANSACTIONS/CAREER NOTES: Signed as a non-drafted free agent by San Diego Padres organization (March 4, 1999). ... Loaned by Padres organization to Yucatan of the Mexican League (June 2-22 and July 18, 2000-remainder of season). ... On disabled list (August 7-September 2, 2002). ... Traded by Padres with OF Jason Bay and a player to be named to Pittsburgh Pirates for OF Brian Giles (August 26, 2003); Pirates acquired P Cory Stewart to complete deal (October 2, 2003).

CAREER HITTING: 22-for-127 (.173), 3 R, 0 2B, 0 3B, 0 HR, 4 RBI.

Year Team (League)	W	L	Pct.	ERA	WHIP	G	GS	CG	ShO	Hld.	Sv.-Opp.	IP	H	R	ER	HR	BB-IBB	SO	Avg.
1999— Ariz. Padres (Ariz.)	1	2	.333	5.08	1.55	15	2	0	0	...	3-...	28.1	28	20	16	1	16-0	37	.243
2000— Yucatan (Mex.)	3	2	.600	4.40	1.30	11	6	0	0	...	1-...	43.0	39	24	21	...	17-...	37	...
— Idaho Falls (Pioneer)	3	1	.750	4.07	1.36	5	5	0	0	...	0-...	24.1	24	14	11	1	9-0	27	.270
2001— Fort Wayne (Midw.)	8	5	.615	3.46	1.25	19	19	0	0	...	0-...	101.1	84	46	39	9	43-0	98	.230
— Lake Elsinore (Calif.)	2	4	.333	2.72	1.32	9	9	0	0	...	0-...	53.0	45	22	16	4	25-0	62	.225
2002— Lake Elsinore (Calif.)	3	3	.500	1.85	1.23	9	8	0	0	...	0-...	48.2	36	13	10	0	24-0	66	.209
— Mobile (Sou.)	1	0	1.000	1.17	1.17	4	4	0	0	...	0-...	23.0	11	3	3	1	16-0	34	.147
— San Diego (N.L.)	4	5	.444	3.50	1.32	16	15	0	0	0	0-0	90.0	71	37	35	13	48-1	94	.218
2003— Portland (PCL)	3	3	.500	3.02	1.20	8	8	0	0	0	0-...	47.2	44	20	16	6	12-0	48	.246
— San Diego (N.L.)	4	7	.364	5.38	1.62	19	19	0	0	0	0-0	103.2	103	65	62	20	65-2	117	.258
— Pittsburgh (N.L.)	0	3	.000	5.87	1.65	5	5	0	0	0	0-0	23.0	26	15	15	2	12-1	24	.283
2004— Pittsburgh (N.L.)	12	10	.545	2.98	1.15	30	30	2	1	0	0-0	196.0	145	71	65	22	81-2	239	.207
Major League totals (3 years)	**20**	**25**	**.444**	**3.86**	**1.34**	**70**	**69**	**2**	**1**	**0**	**0-0**	**412.2**	**345**	**188**	**177**	**57**	**206-6**	**474**	**.227**

PEREZ, TIMO   OF

PERSONAL: Born April 8, 1975, in Bani, Dominican Republic. ... 5-9/167. ... Bats left, throws left. ... Full name: Timoniel Perez.

TRANSACTIONS/CAREER NOTES: Signed as a free agent by New York Mets organization (March 17, 2000). ... On disabled list (April 9-27, 2001); included rehabilitation assignment to Norfolk. ... On disabled list (May 26-June 10, 2003); included rehabilitation assignment to Norfolk. ... Traded by Mets to Chicago White Sox for P Matt Ginter (March 27, 2004).

2004 GAMES PLAYED BY POSITION (MLB): OF—80, DH—6.

Year Team (League)	Pos.	G	AB	R	H	2B	3B	HR	RBI	BB	SO	HBP	GDP	SB-CS	Avg.	OBP	SLG	OPS	E	Avg.
1994— Hiroshima (DSL)		51	206	40	70	9	8	0	21	31	7	...	...	8-...	.340	...	.461	...	...	...
1995—			Did not play.																	
1996— Hiroshima (Jp. Cn.)		31	54	8	15	1	0	1	7	2	7	...	...	3-...	.278	...	.352	...	...	...
1997— Hiroshima (Jap. West.)		19	69	9	21	3	1	2	12	10	3	...	...	9-...	.304	...	.464	...	...	...
— Hiroshima (Jp. Cn.)		86	139	17	34	4	2	3	15	10	16	...	...	4-...	.245	...	.367	...	...	...
1998— Hiroshima (Jap. West.)		2	7	0	2	0	0	0	0	0	0	...	...	0-...	.286	...	.286	...	...	...
— Hiroshima (Jp. Cn.)		98	230	22	68	8	1	5	35	20	21	...	...	2-...	.296	...	.404	...	...	...
1999— Hiroshima (Jap. West.)		60	160	19	58	13	4	1	24	34	13	...	...	6-...	.363	...	.513	...	...	...
— Hiroshima (Jp. Cn.)		12	23	2	4	0	0	0	2	3	3	...	...	0-...	.174	...	.174	...	...	...
2000— St. Lucie (Fla. St.)	OF	8	31	3	11	4	0	1	8	2	1	1	...	3-3	.355	.400	.581	.981	0	1.000
— Norfolk (Int'l)	OF	72	291	45	104	17	5	6	37	16	25	3	4	13-7	.357	.392	.904	.904	5	.990
— New York (N.L.)	OF	24	49	11	14	4	1	1	3	3	5	1	0	1-1	.286	.333	.469	.803	1	.970
2001— New York (N.L.)	OF	85	239	26	59	9	1	5	22	12	25	2	4	1-6	.247	.287	.356	.643	0	1.000
— Norfolk (Int'l)	OF	48	192	37	69	10	2	6	19	12	18	2	1	15-2	.359	.399	.526	.925	5	.951
2002— Norfolk (Int'l)	OF	5	21	5	12	2	1	1	5	2	2	...	1	3-1	.571	.609	.905	1.513	0	1.000

P

Year—Team (League)	Pos.	G	AB	R	H	2B	3B	HR	RBI	BB	SO	HBP	GDP	SB-CS	Avg.	OBP	SLG	OPS	E	Avg.
— New York (N.L.)	OF	136	444	52	131	27	6	8	47	23	36	2	10	10-6	.295	.331	.437	.768	6	.979
2003— Norfolk (Int'l)	OF	3	9	2	2	0	0	1	1	1	0	0	0	0-0	.222	.300	.556	.856	0	1.000
— New York (N.L.)	OF	127	346	32	93	21	0	4	42	18	29	2	5	5-6	.269	.301	.364	.666	2	.989
2004— Chicago (A.L.)	OF-DH	103	293	38	72	12	0	5	40	15	29	2	9	3-1	.246	.285	.338	.623	2	.986
American League totals (1 year)		103	293	38	72	12	0	5	40	15	29	2	9	3-1	.246	.285	.338	.623	2	.986
National League totals (4 years)		372	1078	121	297	61	6	18	114	56	95	7	16	17-19	.276	.312	.397	.709	9	.986
Major League totals (5 years)		475	1371	159	369	73	8	23	154	71	124	9	25	20-20	.269	.306	.384	.691	11	.986

DIVISION SERIES RECORD

Year Team (League)	Pos.	G	AB	R	H	2B	3B	HR	RBI	BB	SO	HBP	GDP	SB-CS	Avg.	OBP	SLG	OPS	E	Avg.
2000— New York (N.L.)		4	17	2	5	1	0	0	3	0	2	0	0	1-0	.294	.294	.353	.647	0	1.000

CHAMPIONSHIP SERIES RECORD

Year Team (League)	Pos.	G	AB	R	H	2B	3B	HR	RBI	BB	SO	HBP	GDP	SB-CS	Avg.	OBP	SLG	OPS	E	Avg.
2000— New York (N.L.)	OF	5	23	8	7	1	0	0	0	1	3	0	0	2-1	.304	.333	.391	.725	1	.947

WORLD SERIES RECORD

Year Team (League)	Pos.	G	AB	R	H	2B	3B	HR	RBI	BB	SO	HBP	GDP	SB-CS	Avg.	OBP	SLG	OPS	E	Avg.
2000— New York (N.L.)	OF	5	16	1	2	0	0	0	0	1	4	0	0	0-0	.125	.176	.125	.301	1	.900

PEREZ, TOMAS — 2B/3B

PERSONAL: Born December 29, 1973, in Barquisimeto, Venezuela. ... 5-11/192. ... Bats both, throws right. ... Full name: Tomas Orlando Perez.

TRANSACTIONS/CAREER NOTES: Signed as a non-drafted free agent by Montreal Expos organization (July 11, 1991). ... Selected by California Angels from Expos organization in Rule 5 major league draft (December 5, 1994). ... Traded by Angels to Toronto Blue Jays for cash December 5, 1994). ... On disabled list (June 25-July 25, 1997); included rehabilitation assignment to Syracuse. ... Traded by Blue Jays to Angels for IF Dave Hollins and cash (March 30, 1999). ... Signed as a free agent by Philadelphia Phillies organization (December 15, 1999). ... On disabled list (March 26-April 16, 2002); included rehabilitation assignment to Reading. ... Career major league pitching: 0-0, 0.00 ERA, 1 G, 0.1 IP, 0 H, 0 R, 0 ER, 0 BB, 0 SO.

2004 GAMES PLAYED BY POSITION (MLB): 3B—22, 2B—17, SS—10, 1B—10.

										BATTING									FIELDING	
Year—Team (League)	Pos.	G	AB	R	H	2B	3B	HR	RBI	BB	SO	HBP	GDP	SB-CS	Avg.	OBP	SLG	OPS	E	Avg.
1992— Dom. Expos (DSL)	IF	44	151	35	46	7	0	1	19	27	20	...		12-...	.305	...	.371	...	12	.954
1993— GC Expos (GCL)	SS	52	189	27	46	3	1	2	21	23	25	0	5	8-3	.243	.322	.302	.624	12	.965
1994— Burlington (Midw.)	2B-SS	119	465	76	122	22	1	8	47	48	78	1	2	8-10	.262	.329	.366	.695	34	.944
1995— Toronto (A.L.)	SS-2B-3B	41	98	12	24	3	1	1	8	7	18	0	6	0-1	.245	.292	.327	.619	5	.962
1996— Syracuse (Int'l)	SS-2B	40	123	15	34	10	1	1	13	7	19	0	2	8-1	.276	.313	.398	.711	7	.962
— Toronto (A.L.)	2B-3B-SS	91	295	24	74	13	4	1	19	25	29	1	10	1-2	.251	.311	.332	.643	15	.964
1997— Syracuse (Int'l)	SS	89	303	32	68	13	0	1	20	37	67	0	9	3-4	.224	.308	.277	.585	12	.973
— Toronto (A.L.)	SS-2B	40	123	9	24	3	2	0	9	11	28	1	2	1-1	.195	.267	.252	.519	3	.984
1998— Syracuse (Int'l)	SS-2B	116	404	40	102	15	4	3	37	18	67	1	10	4-7	.252	.284	.332	.616	15	.977
— Toronto (A.L.)	SS-2B	6	9	1	1	0	0	0	0	1	3	0	1	0-0	.111	.200	.111	.311	0	1.000
1999— Edmonton (PCL)	SS-2B	83	296	31	77	17	1	4	40	19	43	2	1	2-2	.260	.306	.365	.671	4	.976
2000— Philadelphia (N.L.)	SS	45	140	17	31	7	1	1	13	11	30	1	3	1-1	.221	.278	.307	.585	4	.976
— Scran./W.B. (I.L.)	3B-SS-2B	77	279	44	82	16	2	10	56	16	48	2	5	4-1	.294	.334	.473	.808	9	.962
2001— Philadelphia (N.L.)	2-3-S-OF	62	135	11	41	7	1	3	19	7	22	2	2	0-1	.304	.347	.437	.784	1	.993
2002— Reading (East.)	2B-SS	2	9	2	4	0	0	0	1	0	1	0	0	0-0	.444	.444	.444	.889	0	1.000
— Philadelphia (N.L.)	2B-3-S-1	92	212	22	53	13	1	5	20	21	40	1	5	1-0	.250	.319	.392	.711	4	.985
2003— Philadelphia (N.L.)	3-2-1-S	125	298	39	79	18	1	5	33	23	54	0	7	0-1	.265	.316	.383	.698	9	.969
2004— Philadelphia (N.L.)	3-2-S-1	86	176	22	38	13	2	6	24	9	44	1	2	0-0	.216	.257	.415	.671	6	.969
American League totals (4 years)		178	525	46	123	19	7	2	36	44	78	2	19	2-4	.234	.295	.309	.604	23	.969
National League totals (5 years)		410	961	111	242	58	6	20	106	71	190	4	19	2-3	.252	.305	.387	.692	24	.977
Major League totals (9 years)		588	1486	157	365	77	13	22	142	115	268	6	38	4-7	.246	.301	.359	.661	47	.974

PERISHO, MATT — P

PERSONAL: Born June 8, 1975, in Burlington, Iowa. ... 6-0/200. ... Throws left, bats left. ... Full name: Matthew Alan Perisho. ... Name pronounced: PAIR-ih-show. ... High school: McClintock (Tempe, Ariz.).

TRANSACTIONS/CAREER NOTES: Selected by California Angels organization in third round of 1993 free-agent draft. ... Angels franchise renamed Anaheim Angels for 1997 season. ... Traded by Angels to Texas Rangers for IF Mike Bell (October 31, 1997). ... Traded by Rangers to Detroit Tigers for Ps Kevin Mobley and Brandon Villafuerte (December 15, 2000). ... On disabled list (May 5-25, 2001); included rehabilitation assignment to Toledo. ... Released by Tigers (October 1, 2002). ... Signed by Tampa Bay Devil Rays organization (November 6, 2002). ... Released by Devil Rays (July 1, 2003). ... Signed by Arizona Diamondbacks organization (July 14, 2003). ... Released by Diamondbacks (July 27, 2003). ... Signed by Colorado Rockies organization (July 29, 2003). ... Signed as a free agent by Florida Marlins organization (December 19, 2003).

CAREER HITTING: 0-for-5 (.000), 0 R, 0 2B, 0 3B, 0 HR, 0 RBI.

Year—Team (League)	W	L	Pct.	ERA	WHIP	G	GS	CG	ShO	Hld.	Sv.-Opp.	IP	H	R	ER	HR	BB-IBB	SO	Avg.
1993— Ariz. Angels (Ariz.)	7	3	.700	3.66	1.27	11	11	1	1	...	0-...	64.0	58	32	26	1	23-0	65	.245
1994— Cedar Rapids (Midw.)	12	9	.571	4.33	1.71	27	27	0	0	...	0-...	147.2	165	90	71	11	88-0	107	.283
1995— Lake Elsinore (Calif.)	8	9	.471	6.32	1.71	24	22	0	0	...	0-...	115.1	137	91	81	10	60-0	68	.294
1996— Lake Elsinore (Calif.)	7	5	.583	4.20	1.47	21	18	1	1	...	0-...	128.2	131	72	60	9	58-0	97	.271
— Midland (Texas)	3	2	.600	3.21	1.28	8	8	0	0	...	0-...	53.1	48	22	19	4	20-0	50	.246
1997— Midland (Texas)	5	2	.714	2.96	1.18	10	10	3	1	...	0-...	73.0	60	26	24	5	26-1	62	.221
— Anaheim (A.L.)	0	2	.000	6.00	1.93	11	8	0	0	0	0-0	45.0	59	34	30	6	28-0	35	.324
— Vancouver (PCL)	4	4	.500	5.33	1.85	9	9	1	0	...	0-...	52.1	68	42	31	3	29-1	47	.313
1998— Tulsa (Texas)	0	0	...	6.00	2.00	1	1	0	0	...	0-...	3.0	3	3	2	0	3-0	1	.231
— Oklahoma (PCL)	8	5	.615	3.89	1.47	15	15	1	0	...	0-...	90.1	91	41	39	6	42-0	60	.267
— Texas (A.L.)	0	2	.000	4.60	2.22	3	2	0	0	0	0-0	15.0	15	17	15	2	9-0	5	.500
1999— Oklahoma (PCL)	15	7	.682	4.61	1.52	27	27	2	0	...	0-...	156.1	160	86	80	14	78-1	150	.270
— Texas (A.L.)	0	0	...	2.61	0.97	4	1	0	0	0	0-0	10.1	8	3	3	0	2-1	17	.211
2000— Detroit (A.L.)	2	7	.222	7.37	1.93	34	13	0	0	0	0-1	105.0	136	99	86	20	67-3	74	.316
2001— Detroit (A.L.)	2	3	.400	5.72	1.73	30	4	0	0	4	0-2	39.1	54	29	25	5	14-1	19	.327
— Toledo (International)	2	3	.400	1.71	1.26	25	0	0	0	...	9-...	42.0	42	10	8	3	11-0	28	.261
2002— Toledo (International)	4	4	.500	2.45	1.23	51	2	0	0	...	1-...	66.0	62	20	18	4	19-4	44	.246
— Detroit (A.L.)	0	0	...	8.71	2.13	7	0	0	0	0	0-0	10.1	16	11	10	2	6-0	13	.372
2003— Durham (Int'l)	7	4	.636	6.52	1.40	34	0	0	0	...	1-...	38.2	43	29	28	5	12-2	41	.276
— Tucson (PCL)	0	0	...	9.82	1.60	4	0	0	0	...	0-...	3.2	4	4	4	1	2-0	2	.286
— Colo. Springs (PCL)	1	1	.500	3.42	1.60	20	0	0	0	...	0-...	23.2	25	16	9	1	14-2	15	.260

P

Year Team (League)	W	L	Pct.	ERA	WHIP	G	GS	CG	ShO	Hld.	Sv.-Opp.	IP	H	R	ER	HR	BB-IBB	SO	Avg.
2004—Florida (N.L.)	5	3	.625	4.40	1.51	66	0	0	0	10	0-2	47.0	45	23	23	6	26-2	42	.247
American League totals (6 years)	4	14	.222	7.07	1.92	86	28	0	0	4	0-3	215.0	288	193	169	35	125-5	150	.324
National League totals (1 year)	5	3	.625	4.40	1.51	66	0	0	0	10	0-2	47.0	45	23	23	6	26-2	42	.247
Major League totals (7 years)	9	17	.346	6.60	1.85	152	28	0	0	14	0-5	262.0	333	216	192	41	151-7	192	.311

PERRY, HERBERT — 1B

PERSONAL: Born September 15, 1969, in Live Oak, Fla. ... 6-2/230. ... Bats right, throws right. ... Full name: Herbert Edward Perry. ... High school: Lafayette (Mayo, Fla.). ... College: Florida. ... Brother of Chan Perry, outfielder/first baseman with two major league teams (2000 and 2002).

TRANSACTIONS/CAREER NOTES: Selected by Cleveland Indians organization in second round of 1991 free-agent draft. ... On disabled list (September 11, 1996-remainder of season; and March 26, 1997-entire season). ... Selected by Tampa Bay Devil Rays in third round (68th pick overall) of expansion draft (November 18, 1997). ... On disabled list (March 25, 1998-entire season); included rehabilitation assignments to Durham, GCL Devil Rays and St. Petersburg. ... On disabled list (July 22-September 1, 1999); included rehabilitation assignment to Durham. ... Claimed on waivers by Chicago White Sox (April 21, 2000). ... On disabled list (June 8-22, 2001). ... Traded by White Sox to Texas Rangers for a player to be named (November 27, 2001); White Sox acquired P Corey Lee to complete deal (December 17, 2001). ... On disabled list (March 21-May 10 and May 29, 2003-remainder of season); included rehabilitation assignment to Frisco. ... On disabled list (July 5-26 and August 15-September 1 and September 11, 2004, remainder of season); included rehabilitation assignment to Frisco.

2004 GAMES PLAYED BY POSITION (MLB): DH—21, 1B—15, 3B—6.

Year Team (League)	Pos.	G	AB	R	H	2B	3B	HR	RBI	BB	SO	HBP	GDP	SB-CS	Avg.	OBP	SLG	OPS	E	Avg.
1991— Watertown (N.Y.-Penn.)	DH	14	52	3	11	2	0	0	5	8	7	2	3	0-0	.212	.339	.250	.589	...	...
1992— Kinston (Caro.)	3B-1B-OF	121	449	74	125	16	1	19	77	46	89	12	9	12-0	.278	.358	.445	.804	5	.985
1993— Cant./Akr. (Eastern)	1B-3B	89	327	52	88	21	1	9	55	37	47	15	5	7-4	.269	.364	.422	.786	10	.979
1994— Charlotte (Int'l)	1-3-DH-O	102	376	67	123	20	4	13	70	41	55	5	10	9-4	.327	.397	.505	.902	6	.993
— Cleveland (A.L.)	3B-1B	4	9	1	1	0	0	0	1	3	1	1	0	0-0	.111	.357	.111	.468	1	.968
1995— Buffalo (A.A.)	1B-DH	49	180	27	57	14	1	2	17	15	18	3	4	1-0	.317	.375	.439	.814	3	.994
— Cleveland (A.L.)	1B-DH-3B	52	162	23	51	13	1	3	23	13	28	4	5	1-3	.315	.376	.463	.839	0	1.000
1996— Buffalo (A.A.)	1-3-DH-O	40	151	21	51	7	1	5	30	7	19	2	0	4-0	.338	.375	.497	.872	4	.984
— Cleveland (A.L.)	1B-3B	7	12	1	1	1	0	0	0	1	2	0	0	1-0	.083	.154	.167	.321	0	1.000
1997— Cleveland (A.L.)			Did not play.																	
1998— Durham (Int'l)	1B-DH	5	17	1	5	4	0	0	1	0	2	1	2	0-0	.294	.333	.529	.863	0	1.000
— GC Devil Rays (GCL)	3B-DH	8	26	1	3	0	0	0	3	5	1	0	0	0-0	.115	.233	.115	.349	1	.900
— St. Pete. (FSL)	3B	2	8	1	1	0	0	0	2	2	2	0	0	0-0	.125	.300	.125	.425	1	.875
1999— Durham (Int'l)	DH-1B-3B	27	103	21	32	8	0	5	20	6	21	2	3	0-0	.311	.360	.534	.894	2	.971
— Tampa Bay (A.L.)	3-1-O-DH	66	209	29	53	10	1	6	32	16	42	10	13	0-0	.254	.331	.397	.728	5	.975
2000— Tampa Bay (A.L.)	3B-1B	9	28	2	6	1	0	0	1	2	7	0	0	0-0	.214	.267	.250	.517	1	.944
— Chicago (A.L.)	3B-DH-O	109	383	69	118	29	1	12	61	22	68	9	13	4-1	.308	.356	.483	.839	9	.970
2001— Chicago (A.L.)	3B-1B-DH	92	285	38	73	21	1	7	32	23	55	7	11	2-2	.256	.326	.411	.736	10	.957
2002— Texas (A.L.)	3-1-DH-O	132	450	64	124	24	1	22	77	34	66	6	17	4-2	.276	.333	.480	.813	14	.960
2003— Frisco (Texas)	DH-1B	9	34	5	11	2	0	1	6	3	3	2	2	0-0	.324	.410	.471	.881	1	1.000
— Texas (A.L.)	1B-3B	11	24	1	4	1	0	0	2	3	0	0	0	0-0	.167	.167	.208	.375	0	1.000
2004— Frisco (Texas)	DH-1B	8	29	4	12	3	0	0	4	3	7	0	0	0-0	.414	.455	.517	.972	0	1.000
— Texas (A.L.)	DH-1B-3B	49	134	13	30	2	1	5	17	14	19	3	3	0-0	.224	.307	.366	.673	2	.984
Major League totals (9 years)		529	1696	241	461	102	6	55	246	128	291	40	62	12-8	.272	.335	.436	.771	42	.976

DIVISION SERIES RECORD

Year Team (League)	Pos.	G	AB	R	H	2B	3B	HR	RBI	BB	SO	HBP	GDP	SB-CS	Avg.	OBP	SLG	OPS	E	Avg.
1995— Cleveland (A.L.)		1	1	0	0	0	0	0	0	0	0	0	0	0-0	.000	.000	.000	.000	...	...
2000— Chicago (A.L.)	3B	3	9	0	4	1	0	0	1	2	2	0	0	0-0	.444	.500	.556	1.056	0	1.000
Division series totals (2 years)		4	10	0	4	1	0	0	1	2	2	0	0	0-0	.400	.462	.500	.962	0	1.000

CHAMPIONSHIP SERIES RECORD

Year Team (League)	Pos.	G	AB	R	H	2B	3B	HR	RBI	BB	SO	HBP	GDP	SB-CS	Avg.	OBP	SLG	OPS	E	Avg.
1995— Cleveland (A.L.)	1B	3	8	0	0	0	0	0	0	1	3	0	0	0-1	.000	.111	.000	.111	0	1.000

WORLD SERIES RECORD

Year Team (League)	Pos.	G	AB	R	H	2B	3B	HR	RBI	BB	SO	HBP	GDP	SB-CS	Avg.	OBP	SLG	OPS	E	Avg.
1995— Cleveland (A.L.)	1B	3	5	0	0	0	0	0	0	0	2	0	0	0-0	.000	.000	.000	.000	0	1.000

PETERSON, ADAM — P

PERSONAL: Born May 18, 1979, in Savannah, Ga. ... 6-3/220. ... Throws right, bats right. ... Full name: Adam L. Peterson. ... High school: Oconto Falls (Abrams, Wis.). ... College: Wichita State.

TRANSACTIONS/CAREER NOTES: Selected by Philadelphia Phillies organization in 13th round of 1998 free-agent draft; did not sign. ... Selected by Kansas City Royals organization in 15th round of 2000 free-agent draft; did not sign. ... Selected by New York Yankees organization in eighth round of 2001 free-agent draft; did not sign. ... Selected by Toronto Blue Jays organization in fourth round of 2002 free-agent draft.

CAREER HITTING: 0-for-0 (.000), 0 R, 0 2B, 0 3B, 0 HR, 0 RBI.

Year Team (League)	W	L	Pct.	ERA	WHIP	G	GS	CG	ShO	Hld.	Sv.-Opp.	IP	H	R	ER	HR	BB-IBB	SO	Avg.
2002— Auburn (N.Y.-Penn)	2	0	1.000	2.30	1.21	18	0	0	0	...	5-...	31.1	29	10	8	2	9-1	19	.246
2003— Char., W.Va. (SAL)	2	4	.333	2.19	1.14	10	0	0	0	...	1-...	24.2	15	8	6	1	13-2	19	.190
— Dunedin (Fla. St.)	1	0	1.000	0.71	0.39	9	0	0	0	...	1-...	12.2	5	1	1	0	0-0	13	.116
— New Haven (East.)	2	0	.500	4.88	1.29	24	0	0	0	...	9-...	24.0	24	13	13	1	7-1	24	.261
2004— New Hampshire (East.)	2	2	.500	2.54	1.06	27	0	0	0	...	15-...	28.1	20	8	8	1	10-0	38	.198
— Toronto (A.L.)	0	0	...	16.88	3.75	3	0	0	0	0	0-0	2.2	7	5	5	1	3-0	2	.467
— Syracuse (Int'l)	2	2	.500	12.86	2.57	19	0	0	0	...	0-...	21.0	38	30	30	6	16-1	19	.404
Major League totals (1 year)	0	0	...	16.88	3.75	3	0	0	0	0	0-0	2.2	7	5	5	1	3-0	2	.467

PETTITTE, ANDY — P

PERSONAL: Born June 15, 1972, in Baton Rouge, La. ... 6-5/225. ... Throws left, bats left. ... Full name: Andrew Eugene Pettitte. ... Name pronounced: pet-it. ... High school: Deer Park (Texas). ... Junior college: San Jacinto (Texas).

TRANSACTIONS/CAREER NOTES: Selected by New York Yankees organization in 22nd round of 1990 free-agent draft; did not sign. ... Signed as a non-drafted free agent by Yankees organization (May 25, 1991). ... On disabled list (March 26-April 17, 1999); included rehabilitation assignment to Tampa. ... On disabled list (April 13-26, 2000; and June 15-July 1, 2001). ... On disabled list (April 16-June 14, 2002); included rehabilitation assignments to Tampa and Norwich. ... Signed as a free agent by Houston Astros (December 16, 2003). ... On disabled list (April 7-29, May 27-June 29 and August 18, 2004-remainder of season); included rehabilitation assignment to Round Rock.

P

CAREER HITTING: 7-for-51 (.137), 0 R, 2 2B, 0 3B, 0 HR, 4 RBI.

Year — Team (League)	W	L	Pct.	ERA	WHIP	G	GS	CG	ShO	Hld.	Sv.-Opp.	IP	H	R	ER	HR	BB-IBB	SO	Avg.
1991— GC Yankees (GCL)	4	1	.800	0.98	0.65	6	6	0	0	...	0-...	36.2	16	6	4	0	8-0	51	.127
— Oneonta (N.Y.-Penn)	2	2	.500	2.18	1.48	6	6	1	0	...	0-...	33.0	33	18	8	1	16-0	32	.252
1992— Greensboro (S. Atl.)	10	4	.714	2.20	1.17	27	27	2	1	...	0-...	168.0	141	53	41	4	55-0	130	.232
1993— Prince William (Caro.)	11	9	.550	3.04	1.21	26	26	2	1	...	0-...	159.2	146	68	54	7	47-0	129	.248
— Albany (East.)	1	0	1.000	3.60	1.40	1	1	0	0	...	0-...	5.0	5	4	2	0	2-0	6	.250
1994— Alb./Colon. (East.)	7	2	.778	2.71	1.07	11	11	0	0	...	0-...	73.0	60	32	22	5	18-1	50	.220
— Columbus (Int'l)	7	2	.778	2.98	1.26	16	16	3	0	...	0-...	96.2	101	40	32	3	21-0	61	.272
1995— New York (A.L.)	12	9	.571	4.17	1.41	31	26	0	0	0	0-0	175.0	183	86	81	15	63-3	114	.272
— Columbus (Int'l)	0	0	...	0.00	0.60	2	2	0	0	0	0-...	11.2	7	0	0	0	0-0	8	.184
1996— New York (A.L.)	* 21	8	.724	3.87	1.36	35	34	2	0	0	0-0	221.0	229	105	95	23	72-2	162	.271
1997— New York (A.L.)	18	7	.720	2.88	1.24	35	•35	4	1	0	0-0	240.1	233	86	77	7	65-0	166	.256
1998— New York (A.L.)	16	11	.593	4.24	1.45	33	32	5	0	0	0-0	216.1	226	110	102	20	87-1	146	.274
1999— Tampa (FSL)	1	0	1.000	0.00	1.20	1	1	0	0	0	0-...	5.0	4	0	0	0	2-0	8	.222
1999— New York (A.L.)	14	11	.560	4.70	1.59	31	31	0	0	0	0-0	191.2	216	105	100	20	89-3	121	.289
2000— New York (A.L.)	19	9	.679	4.35	1.46	32	32	3	1	0	0-0	204.2	219	111	99	17	80-4	125	.271
2001— New York (A.L.)	15	10	.600	3.99	1.32	31	31	2	0	0	0-0	200.2	224	103	89	14	41-3	164	.281
2002— New York (A.L.)	13	5	.722	3.27	1.31	22	22	3	1	0	0-0	134.2	144	58	49	6	32-2	97	.272
— Tampa (FSL)	0	0	...	0.00	0.60	2	2	0	0	0	0-...	5.0	3	0	0	0	0-0	4	.167
— Norwich (East.)	0	0	...	1.42	0.32	1	1	0	0	0	0-...	6.1	2	1	1	0	0-0	5	.095
2003— New York (A.L.)	21	8	.724	4.02	1.33	33	33	1	0	0	0-0	208.1	227	109	93	21	50-3	180	.272
2004— Round Rock (Texas)	0	0	...	2.25	0.75	2	2	0	0	...	0-...	8.0	4	2	2	1	2-0	9	.143
— Houston (N.L.)	6	4	.600	3.90	1.23	15	15	0	0	0	0-0	83.0	71	37	36	8	31-2	79	.226
American League totals (9 years)	149	78	.656	3.94	1.38	283	276	23	3	0	0-0	1792.2	1901	873	785	143	579-21	1275	.273
National League totals (1 year)	6	4	.600	3.90	1.23	15	15	0	0	0	0-0	83.0	71	37	36	8	31-2	79	.226
Major League totals (10 years)	155	82	.654	3.94	1.38	298	291	23	3	0	0-0	1875.2	1972	910	821	151	610-23	1354	.271

DIVISION SERIES RECORD

Year — Team (League)	W	L	Pct.	ERA	WHIP	G	GS	CG	ShO	Hld.	Sv.-Opp.	IP	H	R	ER	HR	BB-IBB	SO	Avg.
1995— New York (A.L.)	0	0	...	5.14	1.71	1	1	0	0	0	0-0	7.0	9	4	4	1	3-0	0	.346
1996— New York (A.L.)	0	0	...	5.68	1.58	1	1	0	0	0	0-0	6.1	4	4	4	2	6-0	3	.190
1997— New York (A.L.)	0	2	.000	8.49	1.37	2	2	0	0	0	0-0	11.2	15	11	11	1	1-0	5	.333
1998— New York (A.L.)	1	0	1.000	1.29	0.43	1	1	0	0	0	0-0	7.0	3	1	1	0	0-0	9	.125
1999— New York (A.L.)	1	0	1.000	1.23	0.95	1	1	0	0	0	0-0	7.1	7	1	1	1	0-0	5	.241
2000— New York (A.L.)	1	0	1.000	3.97	1.59	2	2	0	0	0	0-0	11.1	15	5	5	0	3-0	7	.326
2001— New York (A.L.)	0	1	.000	1.42	1.42	1	1	0	0	0	0-0	6.1	7	1	1	1	2-0	4	.269
2002— New York (A.L.)	0	0	...	12.00	2.67	1	1	0	0	0	0-0	3.0	8	4	4	2	0-0	1	.471
2003— New York (A.L.)	1	0	1.000	1.29	1.00	1	1	0	0	0	0-0	7.0	4	1	1	1	3-0	10	.154
Division series totals (9 years)	4	3	.571	4.30	1.34	11	11	0	0	0	0-0	67.0	72	32	32	9	18-0	43	.277

CHAMPIONSHIP SERIES RECORD

Year — Team (League)	W	L	Pct.	ERA	WHIP	G	GS	CG	ShO	Hld.	Sv.-Opp.	IP	H	R	ER	HR	BB-IBB	SO	Avg.
1996— New York (A.L.)	1	0	1.000	3.60	1.00	2	2	0	0	0	0-0	15.0	10	6	6	4	5-0	7	.185
1998— New York (A.L.)	0	1	.000	11.57	2.36	1	1	0	0	0	0-0	4.2	8	6	6	4	3-0	1	.364
1999— New York (A.L.)	1	0	1.000	2.45	1.23	1	1	0	0	0	0-0	7.1	8	2	2	0	1-0	5	.296
2000— New York (A.L.)	1	0	1.000	2.70	1.50	1	1	0	0	0	0-0	6.2	9	2	2	0	1-0	2	.346
2001— New York (A.L.)	2	0	1.000	2.51	0.91	2	2	0	0	0	0-0	14.1	11	4	4	0	2-0	8	.216
2003— New York (A.L.)	1	0	1.000	4.63	1.80	2	2	0	0	0	0-0	11.2	17	6	6	2	4-0	10	.340
Champ. series totals (6 years)	6	1	.857	3.92	1.32	9	9	0	0	0	0-0	59.2	63	26	26	10	16-0	33	.274

WORLD SERIES RECORD

Year — Team (League)	W	L	Pct.	ERA	WHIP	G	GS	CG	ShO	Hld.	Sv.-Opp.	IP	H	R	ER	HR	BB-IBB	SO	Avg.
1996— New York (A.L.)	1	1	.500	5.91	1.41	2	2	0	0	0	0-0	10.2	11	7	7	1	4-0	5	.275
1998— New York (A.L.)	1	0	1.000	0.00	1.09	1	1	0	0	0	0-0	7.1	5	0	0	0	3-0	4	.192
1999— New York (A.L.)	0	0	...	12.27	3.00	1	1	0	0	0	0-0	3.2	10	5	5	0	1-0	1	.500
2000— New York (A.L.)	0	0	...	1.98	1.46	2	2	0	0	0	0-0	13.2	16	5	3	0	4-1	9	.302
2001— New York (A.L.)	0	2	.000	10.00	1.56	2	2	0	0	0	0-0	9.0	12	10	10	1	2-1	9	.324
2003— New York (A.L.)	1	1	.500	0.57	1.02	2	2	0	0	0	0-0	15.2	12	3	1	0	4-1	14	.207
World series totals (6 years)	3	4	.429	3.90	1.40	10	10	0	0	0	0-0	60.0	66	30	26	2	18-3	42	.282

ALL-STAR GAME RECORD

Year — Team (League)	W	L	Pct.	ERA	WHIP	G	GS	CG	ShO	Hld.	Sv.-Opp.	IP	H	R	ER	HR	BB-IBB	SO	Avg.
All-Star Game totals (1 year)	0	0	...	0.00	1.00	1	0	0	0	0	0-0	1.0	1	0	0	0	0-0	1	.250

PHELPS, JOSH — DH

PERSONAL: Born May 12, 1978, in Anchorage, Alaska. ... 6-3/220. ... Bats right, throws right. ... Full name: Joshua Lee Phelps. ... High school: Lakeland (Rathdrum, Idaho).

TRANSACTIONS/CAREER NOTES: Selected by Toronto Blue Jays organization in 10th round of 1996 free-agent draft. ... On disabled list (July 7-25, 2003); included rehabilitation assignment to Syracuse. ... Traded by Blue Jays to Cleveland Indians for 1B Eric Crozier (August 6, 2004).

2004 GAMES PLAYED BY POSITION (MLB): DH—81, 1B—20.

Year — Team (League)	Pos.	G	AB	R	H	2B	3B	HR	RBI	BB	SO	HBP	GDP	SB-CS	Avg.	OBP	SLG	OPS	E	Avg.
1996— Medicine Hat (Pio.)	C-OF	59	191	26	46	3	0	5	29	27	65	6	5	5-3	.241	.351	.335	.686	9	.964
1997— Hagerstown (SAL)	C	68	233	26	49	9	1	7	24	15	72	8	6	3-2	.210	.279	.348	.627	21	.965
1998— Hagerstown (SAL)	3B-C-OF	117	385	48	102	24	1	8	44	40	80	8	12	2-0	.265	.342	.395	.737	19	.975
1999— Dunedin (Fla. St.)	C	110	406	72	133	27	4	20	88	28	104	8	13	6-3	.328	.379	.562	.941	1	.994
2000— Tennessee (Sou.)	C	56	184	23	42	9	1	9	28	15	66	7	6	1-0	.228	.308	.435	.742	5	.983
— Toronto (A.L.)	C	1	1	0	0	0	0	0	0	0	1	0	0	0-0	.000	.000	.000	.000	0	1.000
— Dunedin (Fla. St.)	C	30	113	26	36	7	0	12	34	12	34	1	2	0-0	.319	.386	.699	1.085	1	.992
2001— Tennessee (Sou.)	C	136	486	95	142	36	1	31	97	80	127	17	5	3-3	.292	.406	.562	.968	2	.996
— Toronto (A.L.)	C	8	12	3	0	0	0	0	1	2	5	0	1	1-0	.000	.143	.000	.143	0	1.000
2002— Syracuse (Int'l)	C-1B	70	257	50	75	20	1	24	64	32	83	5	6	0-0	.292	.380	.658	1.037	4	.985
— Toronto (A.L.)	DH-1B	74	265	41	82	20	1	15	58	19	82	3	7	0-0	.309	.362	.562	.925	0	1.000
2003— Syracuse (Int'l)	DH	11	11	2	5	0	0	2	4	1	3	0	0	0-0	.455	.500	1.000	1.500	0	.000
— Toronto (A.L.)	DH-1B	119	396	57	106	18	1	20	66	39	115	17	12	1-2	.268	.358	.470	.827	2	.967
2004— Toronto (A.L.)	DH-1B	79	295	38	70	13	2	12	51	18	73	7	9	0-0	.237	.296	.417	.713	2	.981
— Cleveland (A.L.)	DH-1B	24	76	13	23	6	0	5	10	4	20	0	0	0-0	.303	.338	.579	.916	1	.978
Major League totals (5 years)		305	1045	152	281	57	4	52	186	82	296	27	33	2-2	.269	.337	.480	.818	5	.980

P

PHELPS, TOMMY P

PERSONAL: Born March 4, 1974, in Seoul, South Korea. ... 6-3/215. ... Throws left, bats left. ... Full name: Thomas Allen Phelps. ... High school: Robinson (Tampa, Fla.).
TRANSACTIONS/CAREER NOTES: Selected by Montreal Expos organization in eighth round of 1992 free-agent draft. ... Released by Expos (June 20, 1999). ... Signed by Detroit Tigers organization (November 23, 2000). ... Signed as a free agent by Florida Marlins organization (March 6, 2002). ... On disabled list (August 2-September 1, 2003); included rehabilitation assignment to Jupiter.
CAREER HITTING: 1-for-17 (.059), 1 R, 0 2B, 0 3B, 0 HR, 0 RBI.

Year Team (League)	W	L	Pct.	ERA	WHIP	G	GS	CG	ShO	Hld.	Sv.-Opp.	IP	H	R	ER	HR	BB-IBB	SO	Avg.
1993— Burlington (Midw.)	2	4	.333	3.73	1.20	8	8	0	0	...	0-...	41.0	36	18	17	4	13-0	33	.229
— Jamestown (N.Y.-Penn.)	3	8	.273	4.58	1.51	16	15	1	0	...	0-...	92.1	102	62	47	4	37-1	74	.278
1994— Burlington (Midw.)	8	8	.500	5.55	1.61	23	23	1	1	...	0-...	118.1	143	91	73	9	48-1	82	.307
1995— W.P. Beach (FSL)	0	2	.000	16.20	4.20	2	2	0	0	...	0-...	5.0	10	10	9	0	11-0	5	.455
— Albany (S. Atl.)	10	9	.526	3.33	1.38	24	24	1	0	...	0-...	135.1	142	76	50	6	45-0	119	.262
1996— W.P. Beach (FSL)	10	2	.833	2.89	1.25	18	18	1	1	...	0-...	112.0	105	42	36	5	35-0	71	.246
— Harrisburg (Eastern)	2	2	.500	2.47	1.31	8	8	2	2	...	0-...	47.1	43	16	13	3	19-2	23	.249
1997— Harrisburg (Eastern)	10	6	.625	4.71	1.52	18	18	0	0	...	0-...	101.1	115	68	53	14	39-1	86	.285
1998— Jupiter (FSL)	2	2	.500	4.39	1.39	7	7	0	0	...	0-...	41.0	42	21	20	3	15-0	21	.259
— Harrisburg (Eastern)	5	4	.556	3.62	1.39	12	10	0	0	...	0-...	59.2	57	29	24	5	26-0	26	.266
1999— Harrisburg (Eastern)	3	6	.333	5.71	1.58	13	13	1	0	...	0-...	64.2	76	53	41	13	26-0	36	.288
2000— Jacksonville (Southern)	6	6	.500	4.94	1.34	38	11	0	0	...	0-...	102.0	111	59	56	17	26-2	62	.277
2001— Toledo (International)	3	2	.600	3.62	1.56	29	0	0	0	...	1-...	59.2	74	30	24	4	19-3	53	.298
— Erie (East.)	1	1	.500	3.58	1.26	15	2	0	0	...	2-...	32.2	33	14	13	1	8-2	31	.268
2002— Calgary (PCL)	4	2	.667	3.15	1.36	51	0	0	0	...	2-...	74.1	76	27	26	8	21-3	62	.266
2003— Albuquerque (PCL)	0	0	...	1.17	1.04	5	0	0	0	...	0-...	7.2	5	1	1	1	3-0	13	.217
— Florida (N.L.)	3	2	.600	4.00	1.48	27	7	0	0	1	0-0	63.0	70	32	28	3	23-1	43	.282
— Jupiter (FSL)	0	0	...	6.00	1.67	2	1	0	0	...	0-...	3.0	5	2	2	0	0-0	3	.357
2004— Florida (N.L.)	1	1	.500	4.76	1.35	19	4	0	0	4	0-0	34.0	34	20	18	6	12-0	28	.268
— GC Marlins (GCL)	0	0	...	0.00	0.00	1	1	0	0	...	0-...	1.0	0	0	0	0	0-0	1	.000
— Jupiter (FSL)	0	0	...	0.00	1.50	1	0	0	0	...	0-...	1.1	2	3	0	0	0-0	1	.333
Major League totals (2 years)	**4**	**3**	**.571**	**4.27**	**1.43**	**46**	**11**	**0**	**0**	**5**	**0-0**	**97.0**	**104**	**52**	**46**	**9**	**35-1**	**71**	**.277**

PHELPS, TRAVIS P

PERSONAL: Born July 25, 1977, in Neosho, Mo. ... 6-2/170. ... Throws right, bats right. ... Full name: Travis Howard Phelps. ... High school: Wheaton (Mo.). ... Junior college: Crowder (Mo.).
TRANSACTIONS/CAREER NOTES: Selected by Tampa Bay Devil Rays organization in 89th round of 1996 free-agent draft. ... Released by Devil Rays (March 26, 2003). ... Signed by Milwaukee Brewers organization (October 27, 2003). ... Refused minor league assignment and became a free agent (October 15, 2004).
CAREER HITTING: 0-for-1 (.000), 0 R, 0 2B, 0 3B, 0 HR, 0 RBI.

Year Team (League)	W	L	Pct.	ERA	WHIP	G	GS	CG	ShO	Hld.	Sv.-Opp.	IP	H	R	ER	HR	BB-IBB	SO	Avg.
1997— Princeton (Appalachian)	4	3	.571	4.88	1.53	14	13	1	0	...	0-...	62.2	73	42	34	4	23-0	60	.292
1998— Char., S.C. (SAL)	5	8	.385	4.85	1.48	18	18	0	0	...	0-...	91.0	100	54	49	4	35-0	96	.277
1999— St. Pete. (FSL)	10	8	.556	4.24	1.40	24	23	1	1	...	0-...	133.2	148	70	63	6	39-0	101	.287
2000— Orlando (Sou.)	7	8	.467	3.00	1.21	21	21	2	0	...	0-...	108.0	85	44	36	5	46-0	106	.220
— Durham (Int'l)	3	1	.750	4.85	1.52	6	6	0	0	...	0-...	29.2	29	17	16	0	16-0	21	.257
2001— Durham (Int'l)	2	0	1.000	0.00	0.77	9	0	0	0	...	0-...	15.2	11	0	0	0	1-0	12	.204
— Tampa Bay (A.L.)	2	2	.500	3.48	1.24	49	0	0	0	13	5-6	62.0	53	30	24	6	24-1	54	.226
2002— Tampa Bay (A.L.)	1	2	.333	4.78	1.51	26	0	0	0	3	0-0	37.2	30	20	20	7	27-0	36	.222
— Durham (Int'l)	3	2	.600	4.35	1.39	27	0	0	0	...	8-...	31.0	29	15	15	2	14-1	34	.248
2003— Richmond (Int'l)	9	5	.643	3.47	1.20	47	8	0	0	...	4-...	93.1	77	44	36	11	38-1	91	.223
2004— Indianapolis (Int'l)	8	5	.615	4.37	1.30	28	14	0	0	...	0-...	107.0	114	58	52	11	25-1	84	.273
— Milwaukee (N.L.)	0	1	.000	10.50	1.83	4	0	0	0	0	0-0	6.0	8	7	7	2	3-0	3	.286
American League totals (2 years)	**3**	**4**	**.429**	**3.97**	**1.34**	**75**	**0**	**0**	**0**	**16**	**5-6**	**99.2**	**83**	**50**	**44**	**13**	**51-1**	**90**	**.224**
National League totals (1 year)	**0**	**1**	**.000**	**10.50**	**1.83**	**4**	**0**	**0**	**0**	**0**	**0-0**	**6.0**	**8**	**7**	**7**	**2**	**3-0**	**3**	**.286**
Major League totals (3 years)	**3**	**5**	**.375**	**4.34**	**1.37**	**79**	**0**	**0**	**0**	**16**	**5-6**	**105.2**	**91**	**57**	**51**	**15**	**54-1**	**93**	**.229**

PHILLIPS, ANDY 2B

PERSONAL: Born April 6, 1977, in Tuscaloosa, Ala. ... 6-0/205. ... Bats right, throws right. ... Full name: George Andrew Phillips. ... High school: Demopolis Academy (Demopolis, Ala.).
TRANSACTIONS/CAREER NOTES: Selected by New York Yankees in seventh round of 1999 free-agent draft.
2004 GAMES PLAYED BY POSITION (MLB): 3B—4, DH—1.

Year Team (League)	Pos.	G	AB	R	H	2B	3B	HR	RBI	BB	SO	HBP	GDP	SB-CS	Avg.	OBP	SLG	OPS	E	Avg.
1999— Staten Island New York-Pennsyl (NY-P)	3B	64	233	35	75	11	7	7	48	37	40	3	4	3-3	.322	.417	.519	.936	16	.904
2000— Tampa (Fla. St.)	3B	127	478	66	137	33	2	13	58	46	98	2	9	2-0	.287	.346	.446	.792	30	.912
— Norwich (East.)	3B	7	28	5	7	2	1	0	3	3	11	0	1	1-0	.250	.393	.715	2	.913		
2001— Norwich (East.)	2B	51	183	23	49	9	2	6	25	21	54	0	6	1-0	.268	.340	.437	.777	17	.915
— Tampa (Fla. St.)	2B	75	288	43	87	17	4	11	50	25	55	3	6	3-3	.302	.353	.503	.856	10	.968
2002— Norwich (East.)	2B	73	272	58	83	24	2	19	51	33	56	3	6	4-3	.305	.381	.618	.999	7	.979
— Columbus (Int'l)	2B-1B	51	205	32	54	11	1	9	36	10	46	0	8	0-1	.263	.296	.459	.755	3	.985
2003— Columbus (Int'l)	1B	67	7	14	4	0	2	5	5	17	0	4	0-0	.209	.264	.358	.622	2	.955	
2004— Trenton (East.)	3B-1B	10	42	8	15	2	1	4	16	3	1	0	0	3-0	.357	.383	.738	1.121	1	.982
— Columbus (Int'l)	1-DH-2-3	115	434	82	137	19	6	25	84	51	61	2	19	2-1	.316	.386	.560	.955	13	.984
— New York (A.L.)	3B-DH	5	8	1	2	0	0	1	2	0	1	0	1	0-0	.250	.250	.625	.875	0	1.000
Major League totals (1 year)		**5**	**8**	**1**	**2**	**0**	**0**	**1**	**2**	**0**	**1**	**0**	**1**	**0-0**	**.250**	**.250**	**.625**	**.875**	**0**	**1.000**

PHILLIPS, BRANDON 2B

PERSONAL: Born June 28, 1981, in Raleigh, N.C. ... 5-11/185. ... Bats right, throws right. ... Full name: Brandon Emil Phillips. ... High school: Redan (Stone Mountain, Ga.).
TRANSACTIONS/CAREER NOTES: Selected by Montreal Expos organization in second round of 1999 free-agent draft. ... Traded by Expos with 1B Lee Stevens, P Cliff Lee and OF Grady Sizemore to Cleveland Indians for P Bartolo Colon and future considerations (June 27, 2002); Expos acquired P Tim Drew to complete deal (June 28, 2002).
2004 GAMES PLAYED BY POSITION (MLB): 2B—6.

P

Year Team (League)	Pos.	G	AB	R	H	2B	3B	HR	RBI	BB	SO	HBP	GDP	SB-CS	Avg.	OBP	SLG	OPS	E	Avg.
1999— GC Expos (GCL)	SS	47	169	23	49	11	3	1	21	15	35	3	6	12-3	.290	.358	.408	.767	17	.915
2000— Cape Fear (S. Atl.)	SS-2B	126	484	74	117	17	8	11	72	38	97	9	11	23-8	.242	.306	.378	.684	36	.941
2001— Jupiter (FSL)	SS	55	194	36	55	12	2	4	23	38	45	6	3	17-3	.284	.414	.428	.842	18	.930
— Harrisburg (East.) SS-2B-3B		67	265	35	79	19	0	7	36	12	42	4	9	13-6	.298	.337	.449	.786	12	.958
2002— Harrisburg (East.)	SS	60	245	40	80	13	2	9	35	16	33	5	7	6-3	.327	.380	.506	.886	14	.936
— Ottawa (Int'l)	SS	10	35	1	9	4	0	1	5	2	6	0	...	0-0	.257	.297	.457	.754	0	1.000
— Buffalo (Int'l)	SS-2B	55	223	30	63	14	0	8	27	14	39	1	...	8-2	.283	.321	.453	.774	15	.952
— Cleveland (A.L.)	2B	11	31	5	8	3	1	0	4	3	6	1	0	0-0	.258	.247	.279	.526	2	.957
2003— Buffalo (Int'l)	2B	43	154	14	27	7	0	3	13	12	22	3	3	7-3	.175	.247	.279	.526	3	.985
— Cleveland (A.L.)	2B	112	370	36	77	18	1	6	33	14	77	3	12	4-5	.208	.242	.311	.553	11	.981
2004— Buffalo (Int'l)	2B-SS	135	521	83	158	34	4	8	50	44	56	8	12	14-11	.303	.363	.430	.793	28	.955
— Cleveland (A.L.)	2B	6	22	1	4	2	0	0	1	2	5	0	1	0-2	.182	.250	.273	.523	1	.973
Major League totals (3 years)		129	423	42	89	23	2	6	38	19	88	4	13	4-7	.210	.251	.317	.567	14	.979

PHILLIPS, JASON — 1B/C

PERSONAL: Born September 27, 1976, in La Mesa, Calif. ... 6-1/177. ... Bats right, throws right. ... Full name: Jason Lloyd Phillips. ... High school: El Capitan (Lakeside, Calif.). ... College: San Diego State.

TRANSACTIONS/CAREER NOTES: Selected by New York Mets organization in 24th round of 1997 free-agent draft.

2004 GAMES PLAYED BY POSITION (MLB): C—87, 1B—38.

Year Team (League)	Pos.	G	AB	R	H	2B	3B	HR	RBI	BB	SO	HBP	GDP	SB-CS	Avg.	OBP	SLG	OPS	E	Avg.
1997— Pittsfield (N.Y.-Penn.)	C	48	155	15	32	9	0	2	17	13	24	4	2	4-0	.206	.282	.303	.585	4	.990
1998— Capital City (SAL)	C	69	251	36	68	15	1	5	37	23	35	5	3	5-2	.271	.343	.398	.741	4	.994
— St. Lucie (Fla. St.)	C	8	28	4	13	2	0	0	2	2	1	0	1	0-0	.464	.500	.536	1.036	0	1.000
1999— St. Lucie (Fla. St.)	C	81	283	36	73	12	1	9	48	43	28	8	10	0-1	.258	.367	.403	.770	4	.992
— Binghamton (East.)	C	39	141	19	32	5	0	7	23	13	20	3	4	0-0	.227	.304	.411	.715	5	.984
2000— St. Lucie (Fla. St.)	C	80	297	53	82	21	0	6	41	23	19	8	12	1-1	.276	.343	.407	.751	6	.989
— Binghamton (East.)	C	27	98	16	38	4	0	0	13	7	9	2	3	0-0	.388	.435	.429	.864	3	.983
2001— Binghamton (East.)	C	93	317	42	93	21	0	11	55	31	25	5	9	0-1	.293	.362	.464	.826	3	.995
— New York (N.L.)	C	6	7	2	1	1	0	0	0	0	1	0	0	0-0	.143	.143	.286	.429	0	1.000
— Norfolk (Int'l)	C	19	66	8	20	2	0	2	14	7	8	0	2	0-0	.303	.365	.424	.789	0	1.000
2002— Norfolk (Int'l)	C	88	323	35	91	22	1	13	65	24	29	2	10	1-0	.282	.327	.477	.804	4	.993
— New York (N.L.)	C	11	19	4	7	0	0	1	3	1	1	1	1	0-0	.368	.409	.526	.935	0	1.000
2003— Norfolk (Int'l)	C-1B-DH	22	78	13	27	5	0	4	20	11	9	2	4	0-1	.346	.435	.564	.999	8	.991
— New York (N.L.)	1B-C	119	403	45	120	25	0	11	58	39	50	10	21	0-1	.298	.373	.442	.815	1	.999
2004— New York (N.L.)	C-1B	128	362	34	79	18	0	7	34	35	42	8	11	0-1	.218	.298	.326	.624	1	.999
Major League totals (4 years)		264	791	85	207	44	0	19	95	75	94	19	33	0-2	.262	.337	.389	.727	9	.995

PHILLIPS, PAUL — C

PERSONAL: Born April 15, 1977, in Demopolis, Ala. ... 5-11/185. ... Bats right, throws right. ... Full name: Paul Anthony Phillips. ... High school: West Lauderdale (Collinsville, Miss.). ... College: Alabama.

TRANSACTIONS/CAREER NOTES: Selected by Kansas City Royals organization in 59th round of 1995 free-agent draft; did not sign. ... Selected by Houston Astros organization in 25th round of 1996 free-agent draft; did not sign. ... Selected by Kansas City Royals organization in ninth round of 1998 free-agent draft. ... On disabled list (April 5, 2001-entire season).

2004 GAMES PLAYED BY POSITION (MLB): C—4.

Year Team (League)	Pos.	G	AB	R	H	2B	3B	HR	RBI	BB	SO	HBP	GDP	SB-CS	Avg.	OBP	SLG	OPS	E	Avg.
1998— Spokane (N'west)	C-OF-1B	59	234	55	72	12	2	4	25	18	19	4	2	12-1	.308	.366	.427	.793	10	.978
— Wilmington (Caro.)	C	2	5	0	2	0	0	0	2	0	1	0	0	0-0	.400	.333	.400	.733	0	1.000
1999— Wichita (Texas)	C-OF-3B	108	393	58	105	20	2	3	56	26	38	2	8	8-9	.267	.314	.351	.665	10	.984
2000— Wichita (Texas)	C-OF	82	291	49	85	11	5	4	30	21	22	1	11	4-5	.292	.338	.405	.743	9	.983
2003— Royals-1 (Ariz.)	C	4	13	3	6	2	0	1	2	1	0	0	0	0-0	.462	.500	.846	1.346	1	.967
— Wilmington (Caro.)	C	13	46	1	11	1	0	0	6	1	6	1	3	0-1	.239	.271	.261	.532	1	.988
2004— Omaha (PCL)	C-DH-OF	86	311	40	97	17	1	6	41	20	36	3	10	4-3	.312	.358	.431	.783	3	.995
— Kansas City (A.L.)	C	4	5	2	1	0	0	0	0	0	1	1	0	0-0	.200	.333	.200	.533	0	1.000
Major League totals (1 year)		4	5	2	1	0	0	0	0	0	1	1	0	0-0	.200	.333	.200	.533	0	1.000

PIAZZA, MIKE — C/1B

PERSONAL: Born September 4, 1968, in Norristown, Pa. ... 6-3/215. ... Bats right, throws right. ... Full name: Michael Joseph Piazza. ... Name pronounced: pee-AH-zuh. ... High school: Phoenixville (Pa.) Area. ... Junior college: Miami-Dade Community College North.

TRANSACTIONS/CAREER NOTES: Selected by Los Angeles Dodgers organization in 62nd round of 1988 free-agent draft. ... On disabled list (May 11-June 4, 1995). ... Traded by Dodgers with 3B Todd Zeile to Florida Marlins for OFs Gary Sheffield and Jim Eisenreich, 3B Bobby Bonilla, C Charles Johnson and P Manuel Barrios (May 15, 1998). ... Traded by Marlins to New York Mets for OF Preston Wilson and Ps Ed Yarnall and Geoff Goetz (May 22, 1998). ... On disabled list (April 10-25, 1999). ... On suspended list (April 2-6, 2003). ... On disabled list (May 17-August 13, 2003); included rehabilitation assignment to Norfolk. ... On disabled list (August 7-30, 2004); included rehabilitation assignment to St. Lucie.

HONORS: Named N.L. Rookie Player of the Year by THE SPORTING NEWS (1993). ... Named N.L. Rookie of the Year by Baseball Writers' Association of America (1993).

2004 GAMES PLAYED BY POSITION (MLB): 1B—68, C—50, DH—8.

Year Team (League)	Pos.	G	AB	R	H	2B	3B	HR	RBI	BB	SO	HBP	GDP	SB-CS	Avg.	OBP	SLG	OPS	E	Avg.
1989— Salem (N'west)	C	57	198	22	53	11	0	8	25	13	51	2	11	0-0	.268	.318	.444	.762	6	.977
1990— Vero Beach (FSL)	C-1B	88	272	27	68	20	0	6	45	11	68	1	6	0-1	.250	.281	.390	.670	16	.967
1991— Bakersfield (Calif.)	C-1B	117	448	71	124	27	2	29	80	47	83	3	19	0-3	.277	.344	.540	.884	15	.981
1992— San Antonio (Texas)	C	31	114	18	43	11	0	7	21	13	18	0	2	0-0	.377	.441	.658	1.099	4	.981
— Albuquerque (PCL)	C-1B	94	358	54	122	22	5	16	69	37	57	2	9	1-3	.341	.405	.564	.969	9	.985
— Los Angeles (N.L.)	C	21	69	5	16	3	0	1	7	4	12	1	1	0-0	.232	.284	.319	.603	1	.990
1993— Los Angeles (N.L.)	C-1B	149	547	81	174	24	2	35	112	46	86	3	10	3-4	.318	.370	.561	.932	§ 11	.989

P

Year Team (League)	Pos.	G	AB	R	H	2B	3B	HR	RBI	BB	SO	HBP	GDP	SB-CS	Avg.	OBP	SLG	OPS	E	Avg.
1994— Los Angeles (N.L.)	C	107	405	64	129	18	0	24	92	33	65	1	11	1-3	.319	.370	.541	.910	*10	.985
1995— Los Angeles (N.L.)	C	112	434	82	150	17	0	32	93	39	80	1	10	1-0	.346	.400	.606	1.006	9	.990
1996— Los Angeles (N.L.)	C	148	547	87	184	16	0	36	105	81	93	1	21	0-3	.336	.422	.563	.985	9	.992
1997— Los Angeles (N.L.)	C-DH	152	556	104	201	32	1	40	124	69	77	3	19	5-1	.362	.431	.638	1.070	*16	.986
1998— Los Angeles (N.L.)	C	37	149	20	42	5	0	9	30	11	27	0	3	0-0	.282	.329	.497	.826	2	.993
—Florida (N.L.)	C	5	18	1	5	0	1	0	5	0	0	0	0	0-0	.278	.263	.389	.652	1	.968
—New York (N.L.)	C-DH	109	394	67	137	33	0	23	76	47	53	2	12	1-0	.348	.417	.607	1.024	8	.989
1999— New York (N.L.)	C-DH	141	534	100	162	25	0	40	124	51	70	1	27	2-2	.303	.361	.575	.936	11	.989
2000— New York (N.L.)	C-DH	136	482	90	156	26	0	38	113	58	69	3	15	4-2	.324	.398	.614	1.012	3	.997
2001— New York (N.L.)	C-DH	141	503	81	151	29	0	36	94	67	87	2	20	0-2	.300	.384	.573	.957	9	.991
2002— New York (N.L.)	C-DH	135	478	69	134	23	2	33	98	57	82	3	26	0-3	.280	.359	.544	.903	*12	.986
2003— Norfolk (Int'l)	C-DH-1B	5	17	2	3	0	0	1	2	1	3	0	0	0-0	.176	.222	.353	.575	0	1.000
—New York (N.L.)	C-1B	68	234	37	67	13	0	11	34	35	40	1	11	0-0	.286	.377	.483	.860	7	.982
2004— St. Lucie (Fla. St.)	DH-1B	2	6	0	3	1	0	0	2	1	0	0	0	0-0	.500	.500	.667	1.167	0	1.000
—New York (N.L.)	1B-C-DH	129	455	47	121	21	0	20	54	68	78	2	14	0-0	.266	.362	.444	.806	13	.984
Major League totals (13 years)		1590	5805	935	1829	285	6	378	1161	666	919	24	200	17-20	.315	.385	.562	.947	122	.989

DIVISION SERIES RECORD

Year Team (League)	Pos.	G	AB	R	H	2B	3B	HR	RBI	BB	SO	HBP	GDP	SB-CS	Avg.	OBP	SLG	OPS	E	Avg.
1995— Los Angeles (N.L.)	C	3	14	1	3	1	0	1	1	0	2	0	0	0-0	.214	.214	.500	.714	0	1.000
1996— Los Angeles (N.L.)	C	3	10	1	3	0	0	0	2	1	2	0	0	0-0	.300	.333	.300	.633	0	1.000
1999— New York (N.L.)	C	2	9	0	2	0	0	0	0	0	4	0	0	0-0	.222	.222	.222	.444	0	1.000
2000— New York (N.L.)	C	4	14	1	3	1	0	0	0	4	3	0	0	0-0	.214	.389	.286	.675	0	1.000
Division series totals (4 years)		12	47	3	11	2	0	1	3	5	11	0	0	0-0	.234	.302	.340	.642	0	1.000

CHAMPIONSHIP SERIES RECORD

Year Team (League)	Pos.	G	AB	R	H	2B	3B	HR	RBI	BB	SO	HBP	GDP	SB-CS	Avg.	OBP	SLG	OPS	E	Avg.
1999— New York (N.L.)	C	6	24	1	4	0	0	1	4	1	6	0	0	0-0	.167	.192	.292	.484	3	.940
2000— New York (N.L.)	C	5	17	7	7	3	0	2	4	5	0	0	1	0-0	.412	.545	.941	1.487	0	1.000
Champ. series totals (2 years)		11	41	8	11	3	0	3	8	6	6	0	1	0-0	.268	.354	.561	.915	3	.967

WORLD SERIES RECORD

Year Team (League)	Pos.	G	AB	R	H	2B	3B	HR	RBI	BB	SO	HBP	GDP	SB-CS	Avg.	OBP	SLG	OPS	E	Avg.
2000— New York (N.L.)	DH-C	5	22	3	6	2	0	2	4	0	4	0	0	0-1	.273	.273	.636	.909	0	1.000

ALL-STAR GAME RECORD

		G	AB	R	H	2B	3B	HR	RBI	BB	SO	HBP	GDP	SB-CS	Avg.	OBP	SLG	OPS	E	Avg.
All-Star Game totals (10 years)		10	23	2	6	1	0	2	5	1	4	0	0	0-0	.261	.292	.565	.857	0	1.000

PICKERING, CALVIN — 1B

PERSONAL: Born September 29, 1976, in St. Thomas, Virgin Islands. ... 6-5/267. ... Bats left, throws left. ... Full name: Calvin Elroy Pickering. ... High school: King (Tampa).
TRANSACTIONS/CAREER NOTES: Selected by Baltimore Orioles organization in 35th round of 1995 free-agent draft. ... On disabled list (June 20-August 6, 2000). ... Traded by Orioles to Cincinnati Reds for future considerations (August 30, 2001). ... Claimed on waivers by Boston Red Sox (September 6, 2001). ... On disabled list (March 22, 2002-entire season). ... Refused minor league assignment and became a free agent (October 14, 2002). ... Signed by Seattle Mariners organization (January 16, 2003). ... Released by Mariners (March 18, 2003). ... Contract purchased by Cincinnati Reds organization from Vaqueros of the Mexican League (August 4, 2003). ... Signed as a free agent by Kansas City Royals organization (November 11, 2003).
2004 GAMES PLAYED BY POSITION (MLB): DH—27, 1B—8.

					BATTING														FIELDING	
Year Team (League)	Pos.	G	AB	R	H	2B	3B	HR	RBI	BB	SO	HBP	GDP	SB-CS	Avg.	OBP	SLG	OPS	E	Avg.
1995— GC Orioles (GCL)	DH-1B	15	60	8	30	10	0	1	22	2	6	0	3	0-0	.500	.508	.717	1.225	3	.968
1996— Bluefield (Appal.)	1B-DH	60	200	45	65	14	1	18	66	28	64	2	4	8-2	.325	.411	.675	1.086	9	.979
1997— Delmarva (S. Atl.)	1B-DH	122	444	88	138	31	1	25	79	53	139	9	14	6-3	.311	.394	.554	.949	27	.974
1998— Bowie (East.)	1B-OF-DH	139	488	93	151	28	2	31	114	98	119	11	20	4-6	.309	.434	.566	1.000	22	.981
—Baltimore (A.L.)	1B-DH	9	21	4	5	0	0	2	3	3	4	0	2	0-0	.238	.333	.524	.857	1	.969
1999— Rochester (Int'l)	1B-OF	103	372	63	106	20	0	16	63	60	99	11	10	1-3	.285	.396	.468	.864	13	.985
—Baltimore (A.L.)	1B-DH	23	40	4	5	1	0	1	5	11	16	0	1	0-0	.125	.314	.225	.539	2	.960
2000— Rochester (Int'l)	1B	60	197	20	43	10	0	6	30	36	70	1	4	2-2	.218	.339	.360	.699	12	.978
2001— Rochester (Int'l)	1B	131	461	62	130	25	0	21	98	64	149	10	16	0-1	.282	.379	.473	.852	8	.986
—Louisville (Int'l)	1B	4	4	1	1	0	0	1	1	1	2	0	0	0-0	.250	.400	1.000	1.400	0	1.000
—Cincinnati (N.L.)	DH	4	4	0	1	0	0	0	1	0	2	0	0	0-0	.250	.250	.250	.500		
—Boston (A.L.)	1B-DH	17	50	4	14	1	0	3	7	8	13	0	4	0-0	.280	.379	.480	.859	0	1.000
2002— Boston (A.L.)								Did not play.												
2003— Louisville (Int'l)	1B-DH	26	81	10	23	3	0	4	18	17	31	3	2	0-0	.284	.422	.469	.891	1	.991
2004— Omaha (PCL)	1B-DH	89	299	65	94	12	1	35	79	70	85	7	8	0-1	.314	.451	.712	1.164	12	.975
—Kansas City (A.L.)	DH-1B	35	122	21	30	8	1	7	26	18	42	0	6	0-0	.246	.338	.500	.838	0	1.000
American League totals (4 years)		84	233	33	54	10	1	13	41	40	75	0	13	1-0	.232	.342	.451	.792	3	.988
National League totals (1 year)		4	4	0	1	0	0	0	1	0	2	0	0	0-0	.250	.250	.250	.500	...	...
Major League totals (4 years)		88	237	33	55	10	1	13	42	40	77	0	13	1-0	.232	.341	.447	.788	3	.988

PIEDRA, JORGE — OF

PERSONAL: Born April 17, 1979, in Sun Valley, Calif. ... 6-0/190. ... Bats left, throws left. ... Full name: Jorge Moises Piedra. ... High school: Notre Dame (Van Nuys, Calif.).
TRANSACTIONS/CAREER NOTES: Signed as a non-drafted free agent by Los Angeles Dodgers organization (August 14, 1997). ... Traded by Dodgers with P Jamie Arnold to Chicago Cubs for P Ismael Valdez (July 26, 2000). ... Traded by Cubs to Colorado Rockies for a player to be named (May 3, 2002).
2004 GAMES PLAYED BY POSITION (MLB): OF—34.

					BATTING														FIELDING	
Year Team (League)	Pos.	G	AB	R	H	2B	3B	HR	RBI	BB	SO	HBP	GDP	SB-CS	Avg.	OBP	SLG	OPS	E	Avg.
1998— Great Falls (Pio.)	OF	72	282	72	108	22	7	2	33	39	29	1	4	16-7	.383	.460	.532	.992	7	.949
1999— San Bern. (Calif.)	OF	8	30	6	9	2	0	0	3	3	3	0	0	1-0	.300	.343	.367	.710	0	1.000
—Vero Beach (FSL)	OF	15	59	13	17	3	1	1	6	7	9	0	0	2-2	.288	.358	.424	.782	2	.933
2000— Vero Beach (FSL)	OF	92	360	59	102	11	6	6	52	29	57	5	6	21-5	.283	.339	.397	.736	6	.974
—Daytona (Fla. St.)	OF	34	139	24	48	11	1	1	17	6	15	0	0	8-4	.345	.367	.460	.828	4	.974
2001— West Tenn. (Sou.)	OF	124	441	55	108	26	6	8	54	37	80	8	8	12-5	.245	.310	.385	.696	5	.980

Year Team (League)	Pos.	G	AB	R	H	2B	3B	HR	RBI	BB	SO	HBP	GDP	SB-CS	Avg.	OBP	SLG	OPS	E	Avg.
2002— West Tenn (Sou.)	OF	23	60	5	10	3	1	0	4	3	11	1	1	2-0	.167	.219	.250	.469	1	.971
— Salem (Caro.)	OF	104	392	64	118	37	12	13	64	37	55	8	4	10-2	.301	.366	.556	.922	5	.975
2003—Tulsa (Texas)	OF	96	357	56	98	17	7	18	53	31	50	8	6	5-2	.275	.342	.513	.854	5	.973
2004— Colo. Springs (PCL)	OF-DH	99	377	71	126	29	5	15	55	23	56	3	7	4-3	.334	.372	.557	.924	4	.978
— Colorado (N.L.)	OF	38	91	15	27	8	0	3	10	5	19	1	1	0-1	.297	.340	.484	.824	0	1.000
Major League totals (1 year)		38	91	15	27	8	0	3	10	5	19	1	1	0-1	.297	.340	.484	.824	0	1.000

PIERRE, JUAN — OF

PERSONAL: Born August 14, 1977, in Mobile, Ala. ... 6-0/180. ... Bats left, throws left. ... Full name: Juan D'Vaughn Pierre. ... Name pronounced: pee-AIR. ... High school: Alexandria (La.). ... College: South Alabama.

TRANSACTIONS/CAREER NOTES: Selected by Seattle Mariners organization in 30th round of 1995 free-agent draft; did not sign. ... Selected by Mariners organization in 48th round of 1996 free-agent draft; did not sign. ... Selected by Colorado Rockies organization in 13th round of 1998 free-agent draft. ... Traded by Rockies with P Mike Hampton and cash to Florida Marlins for C Charles Johnson, P Vic Darensbourg, OF Preston Wilson and 2B Pablo Ozuna (November 16, 2002).

2004 GAMES PLAYED BY POSITION (MLB): OF—162.

								BATTING											FIELDING	
Year Team (League)	Pos.	G	AB	R	H	2B	3B	HR	RBI	BB	SO	HBP	GDP	SB-CS	Avg.	OBP	SLG	OPS	E	Avg.
1998— Portland (N'west)	OF	64	264	55	93	9	2	0	30	19	11	2	3	38-9	.352	.399	.402	.800	5	.955
1999—Asheville (S. Atl.)	OF	140	585	93	187	28	5	1	55	38	37	8	12	66-19	.320	.366	.390	.756	4	.981
2000—Carolina (Southern)	OF	107	439	63	143	16	4	0	32	33	26	5	4	46-12	.326	.376	.380	.757	2	.992
— Colo. Springs (PCL)	OF	4	17	3	8	0	1	0	1	0	0	0	0	1-1	.471	.471	.588	1.059	0	1.000
— Colorado (N.L.)	OF	51	200	26	62	2	0	0	20	13	15	1	2	7-6	.310	.353	.320	.673	3	.975
2001— Colorado (N.L.)	OF	156	617	108	202	26	11	2	55	41	29	10	6	• 46-17	.327	.378	.415	.793	8	.979
2002— Colorado (N.L.)	OF	152	592	90	170	20	5	1	35	31	52	9	7	47-12	.287	.332	.343	.675	2	.995
2003— Florida (N.L.)	OF	162	* 668	100	204	28	7	1	41	55	35	5	9	* 65-20	.305	.361	.373	.734	3	.993
2004— Florida (N.L.)	OF	162	* 678	100	* 221	22	• 12	3	49	45	35	8	9	45-24	.326	.374	.407	.781	2	.995
Major League totals (5 years)		683	2755	424	859	98	35	7	200	185	166	33	33	210-79	.312	.361	.380	.742	18	.989

DIVISION SERIES RECORD

Year Team (League)	Pos.	G	AB	R	H	2B	3B	HR	RBI	BB	SO	HBP	GDP	SB-CS	Avg.	OBP	SLG	OPS	E	Avg.
2003— Florida (N.L.)	OF	4	19	5	5	1	0	0	3	1	1	0	0	1-0	.263	.300	.316	.616	0	1.000

CHAMPIONSHIP SERIES RECORD

Year Team (League)	Pos.	G	AB	R	H	2B	3B	HR	RBI	BB	SO	HBP	GDP	SB-CS	Avg.	OBP	SLG	OPS	E	Avg.
2003— Florida (N.L.)	OF	7	33	5	10	1	2	0	1	2	1	0	0	1-3	.303	.343	.455	.797	0	1.000

WORLD SERIES RECORD

Year Team (League)	Pos.	G	AB	R	H	2B	3B	HR	RBI	BB	SO	HBP	GDP	SB-CS	Avg.	OBP	SLG	OPS	E	Avg.
2003— Florida (N.L.)	OF	6	21	2	7	2	0	0	3	5	2	1	0	1-1	.333	.481	.429	.910	0	1.000

PIERZYNSKI, A.J. — C

PERSONAL: Born December 30, 1976, in Bridgehampton, N.Y. ... 6-3/245. ... Bats left, throws right. ... Full name: Anthony John Pierzynski. ... Name pronounced: PEER-zin-skee. ... High school: Dr. Phillips (Orlando).

TRANSACTIONS/CAREER NOTES: Selected by Minnesota Twins organization in third round of 1994 free-agent draft. ... Traded by Twins with a player to be named or cash to San Francisco Giants for Ps Joe Nathan, Boof Bonser and Francisco Liriano (November 14, 2003).

2004 GAMES PLAYED BY POSITION (MLB): C—118.

								BATTING											FIELDING	
Year Team (League)	Pos.	G	AB	R	H	2B	3B	HR	RBI	BB	SO	HBP	GDP	SB-CS	Avg.	OBP	SLG	OPS	E	Avg.
1994—GC Twins (GCL)	DH-C	43	152	21	44	8	1	1	19	12	19	0	3	0-2	.289	.337	.375	.712	8	.966
1995— Fort Wayne (Midw.)	C	22	84	10	26	5	1	2	14	2	10	1	1	0-0	.310	.322	.464	.786	10	.939
— Elizabethton (App.)	C-1B	56	205	29	68	13	1	7	45	14	23	0	6	0-2	.332	.373	.507	.880	12	.974
1996— Fort Wayne (Midw.)	C-DH-OF	114	431	48	118	30	3	7	70	22	53	2	10	0-4	.274	.308	.406	.714	21	.972
1997— Fort Myers (FSL)	C-DH-1B	118	412	49	115	23	1	9	64	16	59	6	9	2-1	.279	.313	.405	.718	10	.987
1998— New Britain (East.)	C-DH	59	212	30	63	11	0	3	17	10	25	2	4	0-2	.297	.333	.392	.725	2	.996
— Salt Lake (PCL)	C	59	208	29	53	7	2	7	30	9	24	0	4	3-1	.255	.284	.409	.693	7	.983
— Minnesota (A.L.)	C	9	10	1	3	0	0	0	1	1	2	1	0	0-0	.300	.385	.300	.685	0	1.000
1999— Salt Lake (PCL)	C	67	228	29	59	10	0	1	25	16	29	0	11	0-0	.259	.307	.316	.623	7	.984
— Minnesota (A.L.)	C	9	22	3	6	2	0	0	3	1	4	1	0	0-0	.273	.333	.364	.697	0	1.000
2000— New Britain (East.)	C	62	228	36	68	17	2	4	34	8	22	9	13	0-0	.298	.341	.443	.784	6	.982
— Salt Lake (PCL)	C	41	155	22	52	14	1	4	25	5	22	1	3	1-1	.335	.354	.516	.870	3	.990
— Minnesota (A.L.)	C	33	88	12	27	5	1	2	11	5	14	2	1	1-0	.307	.354	.455	.809	0	1.000
2001— Minnesota (A.L.)	C-DH	114	381	51	110	33	2	7	55	16	57	4	7	1-7	.289	.322	.441	.763	10	.985
2002— Minnesota (A.L.)	C	130	440	54	132	31	6	6	49	13	61	11	14	1-2	.300	.334	.439	.773	6	.996
2003— Minnesota (A.L.)	C	137	487	63	152	35	3	11	74	24	55	15	13	3-1	.312	.360	.464	.824	6	.993
2004— San Francisco (N.L.)	C	131	471	45	128	28	2	11	77	19	27	15	27	0-1	.272	.319	.410	.729	1	.999
American League totals (6 years)		430	1428	184	430	106	12	26	193	60	193	34	35	6-10	.301	.341	.447	.788	19	.993
National League totals (1 year)		131	471	45	128	28	2	11	77	19	27	15	27	0-1	.272	.319	.410	.729	1	.999
Major League totals (7 years)		561	1899	229	558	134	14	37	270	79	220	49	62	6-11	.294	.336	.438	.773	20	.994

DIVISION SERIES RECORD

Year Team (League)	Pos.	G	AB	R	H	2B	3B	HR	RBI	BB	SO	HBP	GDP	SB-CS	Avg.	OBP	SLG	OPS	E	Avg.
2002— Minnesota (A.L.)	C	5	16	4	7	0	1	1	4	2	2	0	0	0-0	.438	.500	.750	1.250	1	.969
2003— Minnesota (A.L.)	C	4	13	1	3	0	1	1	2	2	0	0	1	0-0	.231	.333	.462	.795	0	1.000
Division series totals (2 years)		9	29	5	10	0	1	2	5	4	2	0	1	0-0	.345	.424	.621	1.045	1	.984

CHAMPIONSHIP SERIES RECORD

Year Team (League)	Pos.	G	AB	R	H	2B	3B	HR	RBI	BB	SO	HBP	GDP	SB-CS	Avg.	OBP	SLG	OPS	E	Avg.
2002— Minnesota (A.L.)	C	5	16	1	4	0	0	0	2	2	0	0	0	0-1	.250	.235	.250	.485	2	.938

ALL-STAR GAME RECORD

	Pos.	G	AB	R	H	2B	3B	HR	RBI	BB	SO	HBP	GDP	SB-CS	Avg.	OBP	SLG	OPS	E	Avg.
All-Star Game totals (1 year)		1	3	0	0	0	0	0	0	0	0	0	0	0-0	.000	.000	.000	.000	0	1.000

P

PINEIRO, JOEL　　　　　　　　　　P

PERSONAL: Born September 25, 1978, in Rio Padres, Puerto Rico. ... 6-1/200. ... Throws right, bats right. ... Full name: Joel Alberto Pineiro. ... High school: Colonial (Orlando). ... Junior college: Edison (Fla.) Community College.

TRANSACTIONS/CAREER NOTES: Selected by Seattle Mariners organization in 12th round of 1997 free-agent draft. ... On suspended list (October 3-6, 2001). ... On disabled list (July 26, 2004-remainder of season).

CAREER HITTING: 2-for-16 (.125), 1 R, 1 2B, 0 3B, 0 HR, 2 RBI.

Year Team (League)	W	L	Pct.	ERA	WHIP	G	GS	CG	ShO	Hld.	Sv.-Opp.	IP	H	R	ER	HR	BB-IBB	SO	Avg.
1997— Ariz. Mariners (Ariz.)	1	0	1.000	0.00	0.33	1	0	0	0	...	0-...	3.0	1	0	0	0	0-0	4	.100
— Everett (Northwest)	4	2	.667	5.33	1.47	18	6	0	0	...	2-...	49.0	54	33	29	2	18-1	59	.267
1998— Wisconsin (Midw.)	8	4	.667	3.19	1.25	16	16	1	0	...	0-...	96.0	92	40	34	8	28-1	84	.252
— Lancaster (Calif.)	2	0	1.000	7.80	1.78	9	9	1	1	...	0-...	45.0	58	40	39	6	22-0	48	.307
— Orlando (Sou.)	1	0	1.000	5.40	1.80	1	1	0	0	...	0-...	5.0	7	4	3	0	2-0	2	.368
1999— New Haven (East.)	10	15	.400	4.72	1.46	28	25	0	0	...	0-...	166.0	190	105	87	18	52-0	116	.290
2000— New Haven (East.)	2	1	.667	4.13	1.03	9	9	0	0	...	0-...	52.1	42	25	24	6	12-0	43	.218
— Tacoma (PCL)	7	1	.875	2.80	1.23	10	9	2	2	...	0-...	61.0	53	20	19	3	22-1	41	.232
— Seattle (A.L.)	1	0	1.000	5.59	1.97	8	1	0	0	0	0-0	19.1	25	13	12	3	13-0	10	.316
2001— Tacoma (PCL)	6	3	.667	3.62	1.31	18	10	0	0	...	0-...	77.0	68	31	31	8	33-0	64	.242
— Seattle (A.L.)	6	2	.750	2.03	0.94	17	11	0	0	2	0-0	75.1	50	24	17	2	21-0	56	.191
2002— Seattle (A.L.)	14	7	.667	3.24	1.25	37	28	2	1	3	0-0	194.1	189	75	70	24	54-1	136	.256
2003— Seattle (A.L.)	16	11	.593	3.78	1.27	32	32	3	•2	0	0-0	211.2	192	94	89	19	76-3	151	.241
2004— Seattle (A.L.)	6	11	.353	4.67	1.33	21	21	1	0	0	0-0	140.2	144	77	73	21	43-1	111	.265
Major League totals (5 years)	**43**	**31**	**.581**	**3.66**	**1.26**	**115**	**93**	**6**	**3**	**5**	**0-0**	**641.1**	**600**	**283**	**261**	**69**	**207-5**	**464**	**.248**

DIVISION SERIES RECORD

Year Team (League)	W	L	Pct.	ERA	WHIP	G	GS	CG	ShO	Hld.	Sv.-Opp.	IP	H	R	ER	HR	BB-IBB	SO	Avg.
2001— Seattle (A.L.)		Did not play.																	

CHAMPIONSHIP SERIES RECORD

Year Team (League)	W	L	Pct.	ERA	WHIP	G	GS	CG	ShO	Hld.	Sv.-Opp.	IP	H	R	ER	HR	BB-IBB	SO	Avg.
2001— Seattle (A.L.)	0	0	...	4.50	3.00	1	0	0	0	0	0-0	2.0	4	1	1	0	2-0	5	.400

PODSEDNIK, SCOTT　　　　　　　　　　OF

PERSONAL: Born March 18, 1976, in West, Texas. ... 6-0/188. ... Bats left, throws left. ... Full name: Scott Eric Podsednik. ... Name pronounced: puh-SED-nik. ... High school: West (Texas).

TRANSACTIONS/CAREER NOTES: Selected by Texas Rangers organization in third round of 1994 free-agent draft. ... Traded by Rangers to Florida Marlins (October 8, 1995), completing deal in which Marlins traded P Bobby Witt to Texas Rangers for two players to be named (August 8, 1995); Rangers also traded P Wilson Heredia to Marlins (August 11, 1995). ... Selected by Rangers organization from Marlins organization in Rule 5 minor league draft (December 15, 1997). ... Signed as a free agent by Seattle Mariners organization (November 1, 2000). ... Claimed on waivers by Milwaukee Brewers (October 13, 2002).

HONORS: Named N.L. Rookie Player of the Year by THE SPORTING NEWS (2003).

2004 GAMES PLAYED BY POSITION (MLB): OF—153.

Year Team (League)	Pos.	G	AB	R	H	2B	3B	HR	RBI	BB	SO	HBP	GDP	SB-CS	Avg.	OBP	SLG	OPS	E	Avg.
1994— GC Rangers (GCL)	OF	60	211	34	48	7	1	1	17	41	34	3	1	18-5	.227	.357	.284	.641	0	1.000
1995— Hudson Valley (NY-Penn.)	OF	65	252	42	67	3	0	0	20	35	31	1	9	20-6	.266	.355	.278	.633	3	.978
1996— Brevard County (FSL)	OF	108	383	39	100	9	2	0	30	45	65	3	8	20-10	.261	.343	.295	.638	4	.984
1997— Kane Co. (Midw.)	OF	135	531	80	147	23	4	3	49	60	72	3	5	28-11	.277	.352	.352	.704	5	.977
1998— Charlotte (Fla. St.)	OF	81	302	55	86	12	4	4	39	44	32	0	2	26-8	.285	.369	.391	.760	2	.986
— Tulsa (Texas)	OF	17	75	9	18	4	1	0	4	6	11	0	3	5-2	.240	.296	.320	.616	0	1.000
1999— GC Rangers (GCL)	OF	5	17	6	7	2	0	0	5	2	3	0	1	1-0	.412	.474	.529	1.003	0	1.000
— Tulsa (Texas)	OF	37	116	10	18	4	0	0	1	5	13	0	3	6-2	.155	.190	.190	.380	1	.987
2000— Tulsa (Texas)	OF	49	169	20	42	7	2	2	13	30	33	1	4	19-4	.249	.361	.349	.710	3	.968
2001— Tacoma (PCL)	OF	66	269	46	78	15	4	3	30	13	46	2	0	12-5	.290	.327	.409	.736	5	.967
— Seattle (A.L.)	OF	5	6	1	1	0	1	0	3	0	1	0	1	0-0	.167	.167	.500	.667	0	1.000
2002— Tacoma (PCL)	OF	125	438	63	122	25	6	9	61	43	70	9	18	35-13	.279	.347	.425	.772	5	.985
— Seattle (A.L.)	OF-DH	14	20	2	4	0	0	1	5	4	6	0	1	0-0	.200	.320	.350	.670	1	.938
2003— Milwaukee (N.L.)	OF	154	558	100	175	29	8	9	58	56	91	4	11	43-10	.314	.379	.443	.822	3	.992
2004— Milwaukee (N.L.)	OF	154	640	85	156	27	7	12	39	58	105	7	7	* 70-13	.244	.313	.364	.677	4	.990
American League totals (2 years)		**19**	**26**	**3**	**5**	**0**	**1**	**1**	**8**	**4**	**7**	**0**	**2**	**0-0**	**.192**	**.290**	**.385**	**.675**	**1**	**.947**
National League totals (2 years)		**308**	**1198**	**185**	**331**	**56**	**15**	**21**	**97**	**114**	**196**	**11**	**18**	**113-23**	**.276**	**.344**	**.401**	**.745**	**7**	**.991**
Major League totals (4 years)		**327**	**1224**	**188**	**336**	**56**	**16**	**22**	**105**	**118**	**203**	**11**	**20**	**113-23**	**.275**	**.343**	**.400**	**.743**	**8**	**.990**

POLANCO, PLACIDO　　　　　　　　　　2B/3B

PERSONAL: Born October 10, 1975, in Santo Domingo, Dominican Republic. ... 5-10/190. ... Bats right, throws right. ... Full name: Placido Enrique Polanco. ... Name pronounced: PLAH-si-doh poh-LAHN-co. ... High school: Santo Clara (Santo Domingo, Dominican Republic). ... Junior college: Miami-Dade Community College Wolfson.

TRANSACTIONS/CAREER NOTES: Selected by St. Louis Cardinals in 19th round of 1994 free-agent draft. ... On disabled list (July 1-16, 2000). ... Traded by Cardinals with Ps Bud Smith and Mike Timlin to Philadelphia Phillies for 3B Scott Rolen and P Doug Nickle (July 29, 2002). ... On disabled list (April 16-May 1, 2003). ... On disabled list (May 8-June 7, 2004); included rehabilitation assignment to Reading and Scranton/Wilkes-Barre.

2004 GAMES PLAYED BY POSITION (MLB): 2B—109, 3B—13.

Year Team (League)	Pos.	G	AB	R	H	2B	3B	HR	RBI	BB	SO	HBP	GDP	SB-CS	Avg.	OBP	SLG	OPS	E	Avg.
1994— Ariz. Cardinals (Ariz.)	2B-SS	32	127	17	27	4	0	1	10	2	15	1	2	4-2	.213	.259	.268	.527	10	.932
1995— Peoria (Midw.)	2B-SS	103	361	43	96	7	4	2	41	18	30	2	8	7-6	.266	.303	.324	.627	21	.950
1996— St. Pete. (FSL)	2B	137	540	65	157	29	5	0	51	24	34	5	31	4-4	.291	.323	.363	.686	4	.993
1997— Arkansas (Texas)	2B	129	508	71	148	16	3	2	51	29	51	3	11	19-5	.291	.331	.346	.678	14	.979
1998— Memphis (PCL)	2B-SS	70	246	36	69	19	1	1	21	16	15	3	8	6-3	.280	.331	.378	.709	5	.984
— St. Louis (N.L.)	SS-2B	45	114	10	29	3	2	1	11	5	9	1	1	2-0	.254	.292	.342	.634	7	.961
1999— St. Louis (N.L.)	2B-3B-SS	88	220	24	61	9	3	1	19	15	24	0	7	1-3	.277	.321	.359	.680	8	.972
— Memphis (PCL)	2B-SS-3B	29	120	18	33	4	1	0	10	3	11	1	7	2-0	.275	.296	.325	.621	2	.985
2000— St. Louis (N.L.)	2-3-S-1	118	323	50	102	12	3	5	39	16	26	1	8	4-4	.316	.347	.418	.765	3	.991
2001— St. Louis (N.L.)	3-S-2-DH	144	564	87	173	26	4	3	38	25	43	6	22	12-3	.307	.342	.383	.725	4	.992

Year	Team (League)	Pos.	G	AB	R	H	2B	3B	HR	RBI	BB	SO	HBP	GDP	SB-CS	Avg.	OBP	SLG	OPS	E	Avg.
2002— St. Louis (N.L.)	3B-SS-2B		94	342	47	97	19	1	5	27	12	27	4	12	3-1	.284	.316	.389	.705	6	.978
— Philadelphia (N.L.)	3B		53	206	28	61	13	1	4	22	14	14	4	3	2-2	.296	.353	.427	.780	3	.983
2003— Philadelphia (N.L.)	2B-3B		122	492	87	142	30	3	14	63	42	38	8	16	14-2	.289	.352	.447	.799	6	.989
2004— Reading (East.)	2B		1	3	0	2	0	0	0	0	0	0	0	0	0-0	.667	.667	.667	1.333	0	1.000
— Scran./W.B. (I.L.)	2B		1	3	1	0	0	0	0	0	1	0	0	0	0-0	...	.250	...	.250	0	1.000
— Philadelphia (N.L.)	2B-3B		126	503	74	150	21	0	17	55	27	39	12	13	7-4	.298	.345	.441	.786	3	.995
Major League totals (7 years)			790	2764	407	815	133	17	50	274	156	220	36	82	45-19	.295	.339	.410	.748	40	.986

DIVISION SERIES RECORD

Year	Team (League)	Pos.	G	AB	R	H	2B	3B	HR	RBI	BB	SO	HBP	GDP	SB-CS	Avg.	OBP	SLG	OPS	E	Avg.
2000— St. Louis (N.L.)	3B		3	10	1	3	0	0	0	3	1	0	0	0	1-0	.300	.364	.300	.664	0	1.000
2001— St. Louis (N.L.)	3B		5	15	1	4	0	0	0	1	1	1	0	1	1-0	.267	.294	.267	.561	1	.941
Division series totals (2 years)			8	25	2	7	0	0	0	4	2	1	0	1	2-0	.280	.321	.280	.601	1	.957

CHAMPIONSHIP SERIES RECORD

Year	Team (League)	Pos.	G	AB	R	H	2B	3B	HR	RBI	BB	SO	HBP	GDP	SB-CS	Avg.	OBP	SLG	OPS	E	Avg.
2000— St. Louis (N.L.)	3B		4	5	0	1	0	0	0	0	2	1	0	0	0-0	.200	.429	.200	.629	0	1.000

POLITTE, CLIFF   P

PERSONAL: Born February 27, 1974, in St. Louis, Mo. ... 5-11/200. ... Throws right, bats right. ... Full name: Cliff Anthony Politte. ... Name pronounced: po-LEET. ... High school: Vianney (Kirkwood, Mo.). ... Junior college: Jefferson (Mo.). ... Son of Clifford Politte, pitcher in St. Louis Cardinals organization (1959-65).

TRANSACTIONS/CAREER NOTES: Selected by St. Louis Cardinals organization in 54th round of 1995 free-agent draft. ... Traded by Cardinals with OF Ron Gant and P Jeff Brantley to Philadelphia Phillies for Ps Ricky Bottalico and Garrett Stephenson (November 19, 1998). ... On disabled list (March 31-July 6, 2001); included rehabilitation assignment to Clearwater. ... Traded by Phillies to Toronto Blue Jays for P Dan Plesac (May 26, 2002). ... On disabled list (June 29-July 25, 2003); included rehabilitation assignment to Syracuse. ... Signed as a free agent by Chicago White Sox (January 7, 2004).

CAREER HITTING: 3-for-32 (.094), 2 R, 1 2B, 0 3B, 0 HR, 2 RBI.

Year	Team (League)	W	L	Pct.	ERA	WHIP	G	GS	CG	ShO	Hld.	Sv.-Opp.	IP	H	R	ER	HR	BB-IBB	SO	Avg.
1996— Peoria (Midw.)	14	6	.700	2.59	1.04	25	25	0	0	...	0-...	149.2	108	50	43	8	47-0	151	.199
1997— Prince William (Caro.)	11	1	.917	2.24	0.00	19	19	0	0	...	0-...	120.1	89	37	30	11	31-0	118	.203
— Arkansas (Texas)	4	1	.800	2.15	1.17	6	6	0	0	...	0-...	37.2	35	15	9	3	9-1	26	.257
1998— St. Louis (N.L.)	2	3	.400	6.32	1.70	8	8	0	0	0	0-0	37.0	45	32	26	6	18-0	22	.304
— Memphis (PCL)	1	4	.200	7.64	1.88	10	10	0	0	0	0-0	50.2	71	46	43	10	24-0	42	.332
— Arkansas (Texas)	5	3	.625	2.96	1.07	10	10	1	1	...	0-...	67.0	56	25	22	6	16-0	61	.230
1999— Reading (East.)	9	8	.529	3.63	1.33	37	13	1	0	...	5-...	109.0	112	45	44	12	33-3	97	.270
— Philadelphia (N.L.)	1	0	1.000	7.13	1.92	13	0	0	0	1	0-0	17.2	19	14	14	2	15-0	15	.275
2000— Scran./W.B. (I.L.)	8	4	.667	3.12	1.20	21	20	1	0	...	0-...	112.2	94	45	39	8	41-2	106	.227
— Philadelphia (N.L.)	4	3	.571	3.66	1.39	12	8	0	0	0	0-...	59.0	55	24	24	8	27-1	50	.248
2001— Clearwater (Fla. St.)	0	1	.000	2.45	1.00	7	7	0	0	...	0-...	11.0	8	4	3	0	3-0	15	.200
— Philadelphia (N.L.)	2	3	.400	2.42	1.23	23	0	0	0	1	0-0	26.0	24	8	7	2	8-3	23	.250
2002— Philadelphia (N.L.)	2	0	1.000	3.86	1.71	13	0	0	0	0	0-1	16.1	19	10	7	0	9-1	15	.288
— Toronto (A.L.)	1	3	.250	3.61	0.99	55	0	0	0	25	1-3	57.1	38	23	23	5	19-1	57	.186
2003— Syracuse (Int'l)	0	0	...	0.00	0.00	1	0	0	0	...	0-...	1.0	0	0	0	0	0	1	.000
— Toronto (A.L.)	1	5	.167	5.66	1.40	54	0	0	0	8	12-18	49.1	52	32	31	11	17-4	40	.269
2004— Chicago (A.L.)	0	3	.000	4.38	1.44	54	0	0	0	19	1-1	51.1	52	26	25	6	22-5	48	.261
American League totals (3 years)	2	11	.154	4.50	1.27	163	0	0	0	52	14-22	158.0	142	81	79	22	58-10	145	.238
National League totals (5 years)	11	9	.550	4.50	1.53	69	16	0	0	2	0-2	156.0	162	88	78	18	77-5	125	.270
Major League totals (7 years)	13	20	.394	4.50	1.40	232	16	0	0	54	14-23	314.0	304	169	157	40	135-15	270	.254

POND, SIMON   OF

PERSONAL: Born October 27, 1976, in North Vancouver, British Columbia. ... 6-1/205. ... Bats left, throws right. ... Full name: Simon Emilio Pond. ... High school: North Shore (North Vancouver).

TRANSACTIONS/CAREER NOTES: Selected by Montreal Expos organization in eighth round of 1994 free-agent draft. ... Traded by Expos to Cleveland Indians for future considerations (May 1, 2000). ... Released by Indians (March 29, 2002). ... Signed by Toronto Blue Jays organization (March 30, 2002).

2004 GAMES PLAYED BY POSITION (MLB): OF—9, DH—6.

Year	Team (League)	Pos.	G	AB	R	H	2B	3B	HR	RBI	BB	SO	HBP	GDP	SB-CS	Avg.	OBP	SLG	OPS	E	Avg.
1994— GC Expos (GCL)	3B-SS		40	147	18	38	7	0	0	15	16	25	1	4	1-1	.259	.329	.306	.635	9	.885
1995— Albany (S. Atl.)	3B		23	80	4	17	5	0	0	7	4	25	2	3	1-0	.213	.267	.275	.542	16	.789
— GC Expos (GCL)	3B-2B-OF		45	133	13	20	6	1	0	12	22	34	1	3	2-3	.150	.276	.211	.486	12	.918
1996— Vermont (N.Y.-Penn.)	3B		69	253	37	76	16	1	3	40	26	26	3	7	9-3	.300	.368	.407	.776	21	.877
1997— Cape Fear (S. Atl.)	3B-1B		118	444	48	120	11	0	3	47	37	46	2	22	12-8	.270	.326	.315	.642	22	.948
1998— Jupiter (FSL)	3-1-2-O		105	344	40	82	15	1	1	32	24	58	6	7	1-4	.238	.296	.297	.593	32	.907
— Harrisburg (East.)	1B		2	3	0	0	0	0	0	0	1	1	0	0	0-0	.000	.250	.000	.250	0	1.000
1999— Jupiter (FSL)	1B-3B-2B		127	434	47	111	25	1	10	77	48	83	14	10	4-8	.256	.341	.387	.728	5	.991
2000— Jupiter (FSL)	1B-3B		19	63	7	13	1	0	3	8	9	13	1	0	1-0	.206	.315	.365	.680	1	.991
— Kinston (Caro.)	3B-1B-OF		64	237	40	76	18	0	6	37	22	49	3	9	14-3	.321	.383	.473	.855	9	.932
2001— Kinston (Caro.)	1B		25	97	13	33	8	1	4	24	10	12	1	0	1-1	.340	.400	.567	.967	2	.989
— Akron (East.)	1B-OF-3B		114	388	46	104	29	3	11	46	30	70	2	9	2-3	.268	.320	.443	.763	5	.993
2002— Dunedin (Fla. St.)	3B-1B		103	401	58	114	25	7	13	68	46	73	3	9	2-3	.284	.357	.479	.836	12	.972
2003— New Haven (East.)	3B-1B		61	228	44	77	17	1	7	49	39	33	4	6	1-1	.338	.440	.513	.953	20	.913
— Syracuse (Int'l)	3B-1B		63	248	33	76	21	1	5	36	16	42	2	5	1-1	.306	.353	.460	.813	3	.988
2004— Toronto (A.L.)	OF-DH		16	49	4	8	2	0	1	6	5	12	1	3	0-0	.163	.250	.265	.515	0	1.000
— Syracuse (Int'l)	OF-3-DH-1		78	302	36	84	24	1	7	36	19	72	3	7	1-0	.278	.325	.434	.753	6	.963
Major League totals (1 year)			16	49	4	8	2	0	1	6	5	12	1	3	0-0	.163	.250	.265	.515	0	1.000

PONSON, SIDNEY   P

PERSONAL: Born November 2, 1976, in Noord, Aruba. ... 6-1/266. ... Throws right, bats right. ... Full name: Sidney Alton Ponson. ... Name pronounced: pon-SONE. ... College: Maria College (Aruba).

TRANSACTIONS/CAREER NOTES: Signed as a non-drafted free agent by Baltimore Orioles organization (August 17, 1993). ... On disabled list (April 16-May 9, 2001); included rehabilitation assignment to Bowie. ... On disabled list (August 7-September 1, 2002). ... Traded by Orioles to San Francisco Giants for Ps Kurt Ainsworth, Damian Moss and Ryan Hannaman (July 31, 2003). ... Signed as a free agent by Orioles (January 26, 2004).

P

CAREER HITTING: 5-for-46 (.109), 3 R, 2 2B, 0 3B, 0 HR, 0 RBI.

Year Team (League)	W	L	Pct.	ERA	WHIP	G	GS	CG	ShO	Hld.	Sv.-Opp.	IP	H	R	ER	HR	BB-IBB	SO	Avg.
1994— GC Orioles (GCL)	4	3	.571	2.96	1.16	12	10	1	0	...	0-...	73.0	68	30	24	5	17-0	53	.245
1995— Bluefield (Appalachian)	6	3	.667	4.17	1.22	13	13	0	0	...	0-...	77.2	79	44	36	7	16-0	56	.260
1996— Frederick (Caro.)	7	6	.538	3.45	1.18	18	16	3	0	...	0-...	107.0	98	56	41	6	28-0	110	.244
1997— Bowie (East.)	2	7	.222	5.42	1.46	13	13	1	1	...	0-...	74.2	77	51	45	11	32-2	56	.269
— GC Orioles (GCL)	1	0	1.000	0.00	0.00	1	0	0	0	...	0-...	2.0	0	0	0	0	0-0	1	.000
1998— Rochester (Int'l)	1	0	1.000	0.00	1.00	1	1	0	0	...	0-...	5.0	4	0	0	1	1-0	3	.211
— Baltimore (A.L.)	8	9	.471	5.27	1.47	31	20	0	0	0	1-2	135.0	157	82	79	19	42-2	85	.293
1999— Baltimore (A.L.)	12	12	.500	4.71	1.46	32	32	6	0	0	0-0	210.0	227	118	110	35	80-2	112	.282
2000— Baltimore (A.L.)	9	13	.409	4.82	1.38	32	32	6	1	0	0-0	222.0	223	125	119	30	83-0	152	.258
2001— Baltimore (A.L.)	5	10	.333	4.94	1.43	23	23	3	1	0	0-0	138.1	161	83	76	21	37-0	84	.289
— Bowie (East.)	0	0	...	0.00	1.00	1	1	0	0	0	0-...	4.0	3	0	0	0	1-0	2	.231
2002— Baltimore (A.L.)	7	9	.438	4.09	1.34	28	28	3	0	0	0-0	176.0	172	84	80	26	63-1	120	.258
2003— Baltimore (A.L.)	14	6	.700	3.77	1.28	21	21	4	0	0	0-0	148.0	147	65	62	10	43-2	100	.258
— San Francisco (N.L.)	3	6	.333	3.71	1.21	10	10	0	0	0	0-0	68.0	64	29	28	6	18-3	34	.255
2004— Baltimore (A.L.)	11	15	.423	5.30	1.55	33	33	•5	•2	0	0-0	215.2	* 265	136	* 127	23	69-3	115	.305
American League totals (7 years)	66	74	.471	4.72	1.42	200	189	27	4	0	1-2	1245.0	1352	693	653	164	417-10	768	.278
National League totals (1 year)	3	6	.333	3.71	1.21	10	10	0	0	0	0-0	68.0	64	29	28	6	18-3	34	.255
Major League totals (7 years)	69	80	.463	4.67	1.41	210	199	27	4	0	1-2	1313.0	1416	722	681	170	435-13	802	.277

DIVISION SERIES RECORD

Year Team (League)	W	L	Pct.	ERA	WHIP	G	GS	CG	ShO	Hld.	Sv.-Opp.	IP	H	R	ER	HR	BB-IBB	SO	Avg.
2003— San Francisco (N.L.)	0	0	...	7.20	1.40	1	1	0	0	0	0-0	5.0	7	4	4	0	0-0	3	.318

PORTER, COLIN — OF

PERSONAL: Born November 23, 1975, in Tucson, Ariz. ... 6-2/210. ... Bats left, throws left. ... Full name: Colin Frederick Porter. ... College: Arizona.

TRANSACTIONS/CAREER NOTES: Selected by Houston Astros organization in 17th round of 1998 free-agent draft. ... Claimed on waivers by St. Louis Cardinals (January 22, 2004).

2004 GAMES PLAYED BY POSITION (MLB): OF—14.

Year Team (League)	Pos.	G	AB	R	H	2B	3B	HR	RBI	BB	SO	HBP	GDP	SB-CS	Avg.	OBP	SLG	OPS	E	Avg.
1998— Auburn (NY-Penn)	OF	67	240	40	68	18	4	4	30	19	61	5	3	14-11	.283	.347	.442	.789	2	.976
1999— Michigan (Midw.)	OF	127	453	91	132	28	9	18	68	53	123	7	4	23-13	.291	.369	.512	.881	4	.987
2000— Round Rock (Texas)	OF	124	435	76	119	25	5	14	57	56	130	6	6	17-9	.274	.363	.451	.814	4	.985
2001— Round Rock (Texas)	OF	25	100	14	32	5	5	2	12	5	25	1	0	1-3	.320	.358	.530	.888	1	.983
— New Orleans (PCL)	OF	101	312	48	74	14	1	7	33	34	105	3	2	11-6	.237	.314	.356	.670	0	1.000
2002— New Orleans (PCL)	OF	134	461	59	122	30	5	6	38	46	127	0	5	28-7	.265	.331	.390	.721	8	.965
2003— New Orleans (PCL)	OF-DH	102	356	52	114	23	6	11	50	22	80	3	3	22-6	.320	.361	.511	.872	3	.989
— Houston (N.L.)	OF	24	32	5	6	0	0	0	0	1	17	0	1	1-0	.188	.212	.188	.400	0	1.000
2004— St. Louis (N.L.)	OF	23	35	3	11	1	0	1	2	0	13	0	2	0-0	.314	.314	.429	.743	0	1.000
— Memphis (PCL)	OF	101	330	46	86	20	2	10	34	25	75	2	5	13-5	.261	.316	.424	.740	1	.995
Major League totals (2 years)		47	67	8	17	1	0	1	2	1	30	0	3	1-0	.254	.265	.313	.578	0	1.000

POSADA, JORGE — C

PERSONAL: Born August 17, 1971, in Santurce, Puerto Rico. ... 6-2/205. ... Bats both, throws right. ... Full name: Jorge Rafael Posada. ... Name pronounced: hor-hay po-sa-da. ... High school: Colegio Alejandrino (Puerto Rico). ... Junior college: Calhoun (Ala.) Community College.

TRANSACTIONS/CAREER NOTES: Selected by New York Yankees organization in 24th round of 1990 free-agent draft. ... On suspended list (July 17-18, 2000; and September 26-October 2, 2001).

2004 GAMES PLAYED BY POSITION (MLB): C—134.

Year Team (League)	Pos.	G	AB	R	H	2B	3B	HR	RBI	BB	SO	HBP	GDP	SB-CS	Avg.	OBP	SLG	OPS	E	Avg.
1991— Oneonta (N.Y.-Penn.)	2B-C	71	217	34	51	5	5	4	33	51	51	4	3	6-4	.235	.388	.359	.748	21	.947
1992— Greensboro (S. Atl.)	3B-C	101	339	60	94	22	4	12	58	58	87	6	8	11-6	.277	.389	.472	.861	11	.965
1993— Prince Will. (Car.)	3B-C	118	410	71	106	27	2	17	61	67	90	6	7	17-5	.259	.366	.459	.825	15	.981
— Albany (East.)	C	7	25	3	7	0	0	0	0	2	7	0	1	0-0	.280	.333	.280	.613	2	.958
1994— Columbus (Int'l)	C-OF	92	313	46	75	13	3	11	48	32	81	1	3	5-5	.240	.308	.406	.713	11	.977
1995— Columbus (Int'l)	C-DH	108	368	60	94	32	5	8	51	54	101	1	14	4-4	.255	.350	.435	.785	4	.993
— New York (A.L.)	C	1	0	0	0	0	0	0	0	0	0	0	0	0-0	...	.000	...	...	0	1.000
1996— Columbus (Int'l)	C-DH-OF	106	354	76	96	22	6	11	62	79	86	3	13	3-3	.271	.405	.460	.866	10	.985
— New York (A.L.)	C-DH	8	14	1	1	0	0	0	0	1	6	0	1	0-0	.071	.133	.071	.205	0	1.000
1997— New York (A.L.)	C	60	188	29	47	12	0	6	25	30	33	3	2	1-2	.250	.359	.410	.768	3	.992
1998— New York (A.L.)	C-DH-1B	111	358	56	96	23	0	17	63	47	92	0	14	0-1	.268	.350	.475	.824	4	.994
1999— New York (A.L.)	C-DH-1B	112	379	50	93	19	2	12	57	53	91	3	9	1-0	.245	.341	.401	.742	5	.993
2000— New York (A.L.)	C-1B-DH	151	505	92	145	35	1	28	86	107	151	8	11	2-2	.287	.417	.527	.943	8	.992
2001— New York (A.L.)	C-DH-1B	138	484	59	134	28	1	22	95	62	132	6	10	2-6	.277	.363	.475	.838	11	.990
2002— New York (A.L.)	C-DH	143	511	79	137	40	1	20	99	81	143	3	23	1-0	.268	.370	.468	.837	12	.988
2003— New York (A.L.)	C-DH	142	481	83	135	24	0	30	101	93	110	10	13	2-4	.281	.405	.518	.922	6	.994
2004— New York (A.L.)	C	137	449	72	122	31	0	21	81	88	92	9	24	1-3	.272	.400	.481	.881	9	.990
Major League totals (10 years)		1003	3369	521	910	212	5	156	607	562	850	42	107	10-18	.270	.379	.475	.854	58	.992

DIVISION SERIES RECORD

Year Team (League)	Pos.	G	AB	R	H	2B	3B	HR	RBI	BB	SO	HBP	GDP	SB-CS	Avg.	OBP	SLG	OPS	E	Avg.
1995— New York (A.L.)		1	0	1	0	0	0	0	0	0	0	0	0	0-0	...	...	...	...	0	...
1997— New York (A.L.)	C	2	2	0	0	0	0	0	0	0	1	0	0	0-0	.000	.000	.000	.000	0	1.000
1998— New York (A.L.)	C	1	2	1	0	0	0	0	0	1	2	0	0	0-0	.000	.333	.000	.333	0	1.000
1999— New York (A.L.)	C	1	4	0	1	1	0	0	0	0	1	0	0	0-0	.250	.250	.500	.750	0	1.000
2000— New York (A.L.)	C	5	17	2	4	2	0	0	1	3	5	0	0	0-0	.235	.350	.353	.703	0	1.000
2001— New York (A.L.)	C	5	18	3	8	1	0	1	2	2	2	0	1	1-0	.444	.500	.667	1.167	0	1.000
2002— New York (A.L.)	C	4	17	2	4	0	0	1	3	0	3	0	1	0-0	.235	.222	.412	.634	1	.955
2003— New York (A.L.)	C	4	17	1	3	1	0	0	0	0	6	0	0	0-0	.176	.176	.235	.412	0	1.000
2004— New York (A.L.)	C	4	18	2	4	0	0	0	0	0	6	0	1	0-0	.222	.222	.222	.444	0	1.000
Division series totals (9 years)		27	95	12	24	5	0	2	6	6	25	0	3	1-0	.253	.294	.368	.663	1	.994

P

CHAMPIONSHIP SERIES RECORD

Year Team (League)	Pos.	G	AB	R	H	2B	3B	HR	RBI	BB	SO	HBP	GDP	SB-CS	Avg.	OBP	SLG	OPS	E	Avg.
1998— New York (A.L.)	C	5	11	1	2	0	0	1	2	4	2	0	1	0-1	.182	.400	.455	.855	0	1.000
1999— New York (A.L.)	C	3	10	1	1	0	0	1	2	1	2	0	0	0-0	.100	.182	.400	.582	1	.955
2000— New York (A.L.)	C	6	19	2	3	1	0	0	3	5	5	1	0	0-1	.158	.360	.211	.571	0	1.000
2001— New York (A.L.)	C	5	14	4	3	1	0	0	0	6	7	0	0	0-0	.214	.450	.286	.736	0	1.000
2003— New York (A.L.)	C	7	27	5	8	4	0	1	6	3	4	0	1	0-0	.296	.367	.556	.922	0	1.000
2004— New York (A.L.)	C	7	27	4	7	1	0	0	2	7	1	1	1	0-0	.259	.417	.296	.713	0	1.000
Champ. series totals (6 years)		33	108	17	24	7	0	3	15	26	21	2	3	0-2	.222	.380	.370	.750	1	.996

WORLD SERIES RECORD

Year Team (League)	Pos.	G	AB	R	H	2B	3B	HR	RBI	BB	SO	HBP	GDP	SB-CS	Avg.	OBP	SLG	OPS	E	Avg.
1998— New York (A.L.)	C	3	9	2	3	0	0	1	2	2	2	0	1	0-0	.333	.455	.667	1.121	0	1.000
1999— New York (A.L.)	C	2	8	0	2	1	0	0	1	0	3	0	1	0-0	.250	.250	.375	.625	0	1.000
2000— New York (A.L.)	C	5	18	2	4	1	0	0	1	5	4	0	1	0-0	.222	.391	.278	.669	0	1.000
2001— New York (A.L.)	C	7	23	2	4	1	0	1	1	3	8	0	2	0-0	.174	.269	.348	.617	1	.986
2003— New York (A.L.)	C	6	19	0	3	1	0	0	1	5	7	0	0	1-1	.158	.333	.211	.544	0	1.000
World series totals (5 years)		23	77	6	16	4	0	2	6	15	24	0	5	1-1	.208	.337	.338	.675	1	.995

ALL-STAR GAME RECORD

	G	AB	R	H	2B	3B	HR	RBI	BB	SO	HBP	GDP	SB-CS	Avg.	OBP	SLG	OPS	E	Avg.
All-Star Game totals (4 years)	4	8	0	1	1	0	0	0	0	5	0	0	0-0	.125	.125	.250	.375	0	1.000

POTE, LOU — P

PERSONAL: Born August 21, 1971, in Evergreen Park, Ill. ... 6-3/208. ... Throws right, bats right. ... Full name: Louis William Pote. ... High school: De La Salle Institute (Chicago). ... Junior college: Kishwaukee (Ill.).

TRANSACTIONS/CAREER NOTES: Selected by San Francisco Giants organization in 29th round of 1990 free-agent draft. ... Traded by Giants to Montreal Expos for P Luis Aquino (July 24, 1995). ... Released by Expos (March 28, 1997). ... Signed by St. Louis Cardinals organization (August 7, 1997). ... Signed by Anaheim Angels organization (December 15, 1997). ... Released by Angels (January 21, 2003). ... Signed as a free agent by Oakland Athletics organization (January 8, 2004). ... Traded to Cleveland Indians for cash (May 26, 2004). ... Refused minor league assignment and became a free agent (June 15, 2004). ... Signed by San Diego Padres organization (June 19, 2004).

CAREER HITTING: 0-for-0 (.000), 0 R, 0 2B, 0 3B, 0 HR, 0 RBI.

Year Team (League)	W	L	Pct.	ERA	WHIP	G	GS	CG	ShO	Hld.	Sv.-Opp.	IP	H	R	ER	HR	BB-IBB	SO	Avg.
1991— Ariz. Giants (Ariz.)	2	3	.400	2.55	1.35	8	8	0	0	...	0-...	42.1	38	23	12	0	19-0	41	.232
— Everett (Northwest)	2	0	1.000	2.51	1.08	5	4	0	0	...	0-...	28.2	24	8	8	2	7-0	26	.224
1992— Shreveport (Texas)	4	2	.667	0.96	0.93	20	3	0	0	...	0-...	37.2	20	7	4	1	15-2	26	.159
— San Jose (California)	0	1	.000	4.66	1.86	4	3	0	0	...	0-...	9.2	11	5	5	0	7-0	8	.297
1993— Shreveport (Texas)	8	7	.533	4.07	1.44	19	19	0	0	...	0-...	108.1	111	53	49	10	45-1	81	.271
1994— Ariz. Giants (Ariz.)	1	0	1.000	0.00	0.76	4	4	0	0	...	0-...	19.2	9	0	0	0	6-0	30	.136
— Shreveport (Texas)	2	2	.500	2.83	1.33	5	5	0	0	...	0-...	28.2	31	11	9	2	7-0	15	.279
1995— Shreveport (Texas)	2	2	.500	5.33	1.76	28	0	0	0	...	3-...	50.2	63	41	30	8	26-1	30	.323
— Harrisburg (Eastern)	0	1	.000	5.40	1.38	9	4	0	0	...	0-...	28.1	32	17	17	3	7-0	24	.283
1996— Harrisburg (Eastern)	1	7	.125	5.07	1.55	25	18	0	0	...	1-...	104.2	114	66	59	15	48-2	61	.277
1997— Arkansas (Texas)	0	0	...	1.54	0.99	7	3	0	0	...	0-...	23.1	15	10	4	1	8-0	21	.176
1998— Midland (Texas)	8	10	.444	5.31	1.61	32	19	6	1	...	0-...	154.1	194	110	91	18	54-1	117	.309
1999— Edmonton (PCL)	7	9	.438	4.50	1.41	24	23	3	0	...	0-...	150.0	171	80	75	19	41-0	118	.290
— Anaheim (A.L.)	1	1	.500	2.15	1.19	20	0	0	0	3	3-3	29.1	23	9	7	1	12-1	20	.219
2000— Anaheim (A.L.)	1	1	.500	3.40	1.37	32	1	0	0	1	1-1	50.1	52	23	19	4	17-1	44	.267
— Edmonton (PCL)	2	1	.667	3.52	1.34	24	0	0	0	...	12-...	30.2	27	14	12	2	14-0	28	.231
2001— Anaheim (A.L.)	2	0	1.000	4.15	1.38	44	1	0	0	0	2-3	86.2	88	41	40	11	32-5	66	.258
2002— Anaheim (A.L.)	0	2	.000	3.22	1.17	31	0	0	0	1	0-1	50.1	33	20	18	7	26-2	32	.194
— Salt Lake (PCL)	2	1	.667	6.00	1.33	7	7	0	0	...	0-...	39.0	42	29	26	3	10-0	43	.268
2004— Sacramento (PCL)	1	2	.333	3.38	1.31	19	0	0	0	...	2-...	26.2	23	10	10	1	12-1	20	.242
— Cleveland (A.L.)	0	0	...	9.00	1.33	2	0	0	0	0	0-0	3.0	3	3	3	0	1-0	5	.250
— Portland (PCL)	1	0	1.000	7.20	1.60	4	0	0	0	...	1-...	5.0	5	4	4	1	3-0	6	.250
Major League totals (5 years)	4	4	.500	3.56	1.31	129	2	0	0	6	6-8	219.2	199	96	87	23	88-9	167	.242

POWELL, BRIAN — P

PERSONAL: Born October 10, 1973, in Bainbridge, Ga. ... 6-2/215. ... Throws right, bats right. ... Full name: William Brian Powell. ... High school: Bainbridge (Ga.). ... College: Georgia.

TRANSACTIONS/CAREER NOTES: Selected by Detroit Tigers organization in second round of 1995 free-agent draft. ... Traded by Tigers with C Paul Bako, Ps Dean Crow and Mark Persails and 3B Carlos Villalobos to Houston Astros for C Brad Ausmus and P C.J. Nitkowski (January 14, 1999). ... On disabled list (May 25, 1999-remainder of season). ... Signed as a free agent by Tigers organization (December 19, 2001). ... Released by Tigers (October 2, 2002). ... Signed by San Francisco Giants organization (December 28, 2002). ... Traded by Giants to Philadelphia Phillies for cash (July 24, 2003). ... On disabled list (May 16-June 15 and August 19-September 3, 2004); included rehabilitation assignment to Scranton/Wilkes-Barre. ... Refused minor league assignment and became a free agent (October 9, 2004).

CAREER HITTING: 3-for-21 (.143), 2 R, 1 2B, 0 3B, 0 HR, 0 RBI.

Year Team (League)	W	L	Pct.	ERA	WHIP	G	GS	CG	ShO	Hld.	Sv.-Opp.	IP	H	R	ER	HR	BB-IBB	SO	Avg.
1995— Jamestown (N.Y.-Penn.)	2	1	.667	3.08	1.03	5	5	0	0	...	0-...	26.1	19	12	9	1	8-0	15	.202
— Fayetteville (S. Atl.)	4	0	1.000	1.61	0.93	5	5	0	0	...	0-...	28.0	15	5	5	0	11-0	37	.156
1996— Lakeland (Fla. St.)	8	13	.381	4.90	1.39	29	27	5	0	...	0-...	174.1	195	106	95	12	47-0	84	.286
1997— Lakeland (Fla. St.)	13	9	.591	2.50	1.03	27	27	8	2	...	0-...	183.1	153	70	51	9	35-2	122	.224
1998— Jacksonville (Southern)	10	2	.833	3.07	1.15	14	14	2	1	...	0-...	93.2	84	37	32	6	24-0	51	.242
— Toledo (International)	0	0	...	0.00	0.71	1	1	0	0	...	0-...	7.0	5	0	0	0	0-0	7	.185
— Detroit (A.L.)	3	8	.273	6.35	1.64	18	16	0	0	0	0-0	83.2	101	67	59	17	36-2	46	.294
1999— New Orleans (PCL)	4	4	.500	6.19	1.56	9	9	0	0	...	0-...	48.0	54	39	33	5	21-0	36	.284
2000— New Orleans (PCL)	9	4	.692	4.95	1.39	18	18	1	0	...	0-...	102.3	103	63	57	9	41-1	57	.263
— Houston (N.L.)	2	1	.667	5.74	1.50	9	5	0	0	0	0-0	31.1	34	21	20	8	13-0	14	.279
2001— New Orleans (PCL)	9	8	.529	3.17	1.25	24	23	3	2	...	0-...	144.2	142	65	51	13	39-1	96	.260
— Houston (N.L.)	0	1	.000	18.00	2.67	1	1	0	0	0	0-0	3.0	5	6	6	1	1-0	3	.357
2002— Toledo (International)	10	3	.769	3.92	1.28	20	20	0	0	...	0-...	119.1	127	54	52	8	26-0	82	.270
— Detroit (A.L.)	1	5	.167	4.84	1.47	13	9	0	0	0	0-0	57.2	64	34	31	11	21-0	30	.278
2003— San Francisco (N.L.)	0	1	.000	13.50	1.93	1	1	0	0	0	0-0	4.2	8	7	7	3	1-0	3	.381
— Fresno (PCL)	7	8	.467	4.19	1.50	23	15	0	0	...	0-...	101.0	118	57	47	10	32-2	59	.291

P

Year Team (League)	W	L	Pct.	ERA	WHIP	G	GS	CG	ShO	Hld.	Sv.-Opp.	IP	H	R	ER	HR	BB-IBB	SO	Avg.
—Scran./W.B. (I.L.)	2	4	.333	4.61	1.30	8	7	2	1	...	0-...	52.2	57	33	27	1	12-2	36	.275
2004—Scran./W.B. (I.L.)	3	1	.750	1.62	0.74	8	8	2	1	...	0-...	44.1	27	11	8	2	6-0	29	.168
—Philadelphia (N.L.)	1	2	.333	5.03	1.40	17	2	0	0	0	0-0	39.1	39	23	22	5	16-4	24	.275
American League totals (2 years)	4	13	.235	5.73	1.57	31	25	0	0	0	0-0	141.1	165	101	90	28	57-2	76	.288
National League totals (4 years)	3	5	.375	6.32	1.52	28	9	0	0	0	0-0	78.1	86	57	55	17	33-4	44	.288
Major League totals (6 years)	7	18	.280	5.94	1.55	59	34	0	0	0	0-0	219.2	251	158	145	45	90-6	120	.288

POWELL, JAY — P

PERSONAL: Born January 9, 1972, in Meridian, Miss. ... 6-4/230. ... Throws right, bats right. ... Full name: James Willard Powell. ... High school: West Lauderdale (Collinsville, Miss.). ... College: Mississippi State. ... Brother-in-law of Bud Brown, defensive back with Miami Dolphins (1984-88).

TRANSACTIONS/CAREER NOTES: Selected by San Diego Padres organization in 11th round of 1990 free-agent draft; did not sign. ... Selected by Baltimore Orioles organization in first round (19th pick overall) of 1993 free-agent draft. ... Traded by Orioles to Florida Marlins for IF Bret Barberie (December 6, 1994). ... On disabled list (April 20-May 10, 1996); included rehabilitation assignment to Brevard County. ... Traded by Marlins with C Scott Makarewicz to Houston Astros for C Ramon Castro (July 6, 1998). ... On disabled list (May 17-June 3, June 19-August 6 and August 18, 2000-remainder of season); included rehabilitation assignments to New Orleans and Round Rock. ... Traded by Astros to Colorado Rockies for P Ron Villone (June 27, 2001). ... Signed as a free agent by Texas Rangers (December 13, 2001). ... On disabled list (March 31-June 10, 2002); included rehabilitation assignment to Tulsa and Oklahoma. ... On disabled list (April 13-May 3, 2003); included rehabilitation assignment to Frisco. ... On disabled list (June 5, 2004-remainder of season).

CAREER HITTING: 2-for-12 (.167), 0 R, 0 2B, 0 3B, 0 HR, 1 RBI.

Year Team (League)	W	L	Pct.	ERA	WHIP	G	GS	CG	ShO	Hld.	Sv.-Opp.	IP	H	R	ER	HR	BB-IBB	SO	Avg.
1993—Albany (S. Atl.)	0	2	.000	4.55	1.52	6	6	0	0	...	0-...	27.2	29	19	14	0	13-0	29	.274
1994—Frederick (Caro.)	7	7	.500	4.96	1.51	26	20	0	0	...	1-...	123.1	132	79	68	13	54-0	87	.269
1995—Portland (East.)	5	4	.556	1.87	1.08	50	0	0	0	...	24-...	53.0	42	12	11	2	15-1	53	.219
—Florida (N.L.)	0	0	...	1.08	1.56	9	0	0	0	2	0-0	8.1	7	2	1	0	6-1	4	.241
1996—Florida (N.L.)	4	3	.571	4.54	1.50	67	0	0	0	10	2-5	71.1	71	41	36	5	36-1	52	.255
—Brevard County (FSL)	0	0	...	0.00	1.00	1	1	0	0	...	0-...	2.0	0	0	0	0	0-0	4	.000
1997—Florida (N.L.)	7	2	.778	3.28	1.27	74	0	0	0	24	2-4	79.2	71	35	29	3	30-3	65	.242
1998—Florida (N.L.)	4	4	.500	4.21	1.60	33	0	0	0	0	3-6	36.1	36	19	17	5	22-6	24	.263
—Houston (N.L.)	3	3	.500	2.38	1.09	29	0	0	0	3	4-5	34.0	22	9	9	1	15-3	38	.182
1999—Houston (N.L.)	5	4	.556	4.32	1.63	67	0	0	0	16	4-7	75.0	82	38	36	5	40-4	77	.282
2000—Houston (N.L.)	1	1	.500	5.67	1.78	29	0	0	0	5	0-0	27.0	29	18	17	1	19-1	16	.271
—New Orleans (PCL)	0	0	...	4.50	2.00	2	1	0	0	...	0-...	2.0	2	1	1	0	2-0	2	.286
—Round Rock (Texas)	0	0	...	0.00	0.50	1	1	0	0	...	0-...	2.0	0	0	0	0	1-0	1	.000
2001—Texas (A.L.)	2	2	.500	3.72	1.65	35	0	0	0	5	0-5	36.1	41	18	15	4	19-0	28	.275
—Colorado (N.L.)	3	1	.750	2.79	1.19	39	0	0	0	3	7-8	38.2	34	18	12	5	12-3	26	.245
2002—Tulsa (Texas)	0	0	...	0.00	0.50	2	0	0	0	...	0-...	2.0	0	0	0	0	1-0	0	.000
—Oklahoma (PCL)	2	0	1.000	12.38	2.13	8	0	0	0	...	0-...	8.0	14	11	11	2	3-1	8	.359
—Texas (A.L.)	3	2	.600	3.44	1.49	51	0	0	0	12	0-4	49.2	50	28	19	5	24-4	35	.253
2003—Frisco (Texas)	0	0	...	2.70	1.50	4	0	0	0	...	1-...	6.2	5	2	2	0	5-0	8	.208
—Texas (A.L.)	3	0	1.000	7.82	1.86	51	0	0	0	2	0-0	50.2	75	58	51	7	34-3	40	.319
2004—Texas (A.L.)	1	1	.500	3.38	1.46	23	0	0	0	4	0-0	24.0	24	11	9	3	11-1	17	.267
American League totals (3 years)	7	3	.700	5.37	1.65	125	0	0	0	18	0-4	132.1	149	97	79	15	69-8	92	.285
National League totals (7 years)	29	20	.592	3.81	1.46	382	0	0	0	68	22-40	406.2	393	198	172	27	199-22	330	.255
Major League totals (10 years)	36	23	.610	4.19	1.50	507	0	0	0	86	22-44	539.0	542	295	251	42	268-30	422	.262

DIVISION SERIES RECORD

Year Team (League)	W	L	Pct.	ERA	WHIP	G	GS	CG	ShO	Hld.	Sv.-Opp.	IP	H	R	ER	HR	BB-IBB	SO	Avg.
1997—Florida (N.L.)				Did not play.															
1998—Houston (N.L.)	0	0	...	11.57	2.14	3	0	0	0	1	0-0	2.1	2	3	3	1	3-1	3	.222
1999—Houston (N.L.)	0	1	.000	6.00	1.33	3	0	0	0	0	0-0	3.0	3	2	2	0	1-1	3	.250
Division series totals (2 years)	0	1	.000	8.44	1.69	6	0	0	0	1	0-0	5.1	5	5	5	1	4-2	6	.238

CHAMPIONSHIP SERIES RECORD

Year Team (League)	W	L	Pct.	ERA	WHIP	G	GS	CG	ShO	Hld.	Sv.-Opp.	IP	H	R	ER	HR	BB-IBB	SO	Avg.
1997—Florida (N.L.)	0	0	...	0.00	0.00	1	0	0	0	1	0-0	.2	0	0	0	0	0-0	1	.000

WORLD SERIES RECORD

Year Team (League)	W	L	Pct.	ERA	WHIP	G	GS	CG	ShO	Hld.	Sv.-Opp.	IP	H	R	ER	HR	BB-IBB	SO	Avg.
1997—Florida (N.L.)	1	0	1.000	7.36	2.45	4	0	0	0	0	0-0	3.2	5	3	3	1	4-0	2	.333

PRATT, ANDY — P

PERSONAL: Born August 27, 1979, in Mesa, Ariz. ... 6-0/185. ... Throws left, bats left. ... Full name: Andrew Elias Pratt. ... High school: Chino Valley (Ariz.).

TRANSACTIONS/CAREER NOTES: Selected by Texas Rangers organization in ninth round of 1998 free-agent draft. ... Traded by Rangers to Atlanta Braves for P Ben Kozlowski (April 9, 2002). ... Traded by Braves with IF Richard Lewis to Chicago Cubs for Ps Juan Cruz and Steve Smyth (March 25, 2004). ... Traded by Cubs to Milwaukee Brewers (September 3, 2004), completing deal in which Brewers traded OF Ben Grieve to Cubs for a player to be named (August 31, 2004).

CAREER HITTING: 0-for-0 (.000), 0 R, 0 2B, 0 3B, 0 HR, 0 RBI.

Year Team (League)	W	L	Pct.	ERA	WHIP	G	GS	CG	ShO	Hld.	Sv.-Opp.	IP	H	R	ER	HR	BB-IBB	SO	Avg.
1998—GC Rangers (GCL)	4	3	.571	3.86	1.13	12	8	0	0	...	0-...	56.0	49	25	24	4	14-0	49	.238
1999—Savannah (S. Atl.)	4	4	.500	2.89	1.14	13	13	1	1	...	0-...	71.2	66	30	23	4	16-0	100	.242
2000—Charlotte (Fla. St.)	7	4	.636	2.72	1.01	16	16	2	1	...	0-...	92.2	68	37	28	8	26-0	95	.203
—Tulsa (Texas)	1	6	.143	7.22	1.89	11	11	0	0	...	0-...	52.1	66	48	42	7	33-0	42	.303
2001—Tulsa (Texas)	8	10	.444	4.61	1.38	27	26	3	1	...	0-...	168.0	175	99	86	18	57-0	132	.268
2002—Greenville (Sou.)	4	9	.308	4.26	1.46	20	18	1	1	...	0-...	93.0	92	54	44	5	44-0	67	.262
—Richmond (Int'l)	4	2	.667	3.10	1.08	6	6	1	1	...	0-...	40.2	35	15	14	2	9-0	36	.232
—Atlanta (N.L.)	0	0	...	6.75	3.75	1	0	0	0	0	0-0	1.1	1	1	1	0	4-0	1	.200
2003—Richmond (Int'l)	7	10	.412	3.40	1.40	28	27	1	0	...	0-...	156.0	146	77	59	10	77-0	161	.250
2004—Chicago (N.L.)	0	1	.000	21.60	4.20	4	0	0	0	0	0-0	1.2	6	4	4	0	7-1	1	.000
—Iowa (PCL)	0	4	.000	19.00	3.22	4	4	0	0	...	0-...	9.0	14	19	19	2	15-0	8	.400
—Ariz. Cubs (Ariz.)	1	0	1.000	6.75	1.10	4	3	0	0	...	0-...	8.0	5	6	6	0	4-0	10	.167
—Lansing (Midw.)	0	0	...	8.68	1.82	5	2	0	0	...	0-...	9.1	13	10	9	2	4-0	6	.325
—West Tenn (Sou.)	0	5	.000	9.28	2.11	6	5	0	0	...	0-...	21.1	24	27	22	6	21-0	26	.282
—Huntsville (Southern)	1	0	1.000	1.80	1.00	1	1	0	0	...	0-...	5.0	5	1	1	0	0-0	6	.250
Major League totals (2 years)	0	1	.000	15.00	4.00	5	0	0	0	0	0-0	3.0	7	5	5	0	11-1	2	.100

P

PERSONAL: Born February 9, 1967, in Bellevue, Neb. ... 6-3/236. ... Bats right, throws right. ... Full name: Todd Alan Pratt. ... High school: Hilltop (Chula Vista, Calif.).

TRANSACTIONS/CAREER NOTES: Selected by Boston Red Sox organization in sixth round of June 1985 free-agent draft. ... Selected by Cleveland Indians organization from Red Sox organization in Rule 5 minor league draft (December 7, 1987). ... Returned to Red Sox organization (March 28, 1988). ... Signed as a free agent by Baltimore Orioles organization (November 13, 1991). ... Selected by Philadelphia Phillies from Orioles organization in Rule 5 major league draft (December 9, 1991). ... On disabled list (April 28-May 27, 1993); included rehabilitation assignment to Scranton/Wilkes-Barre. ... Signed as a free agent by Chicago Cubs organization (April 8, 1995). ... Signed as a free agent by Seattle Mariners organization (January 25, 1996). ... Released by Mariners (March 27, 1996). ... Signed by New York Mets organization (December 23, 1996). ... On disabled list (May 7-June 23, 1998); included rehabilitation assignments to St. Lucie, GCL Mets and Norfolk. ... Traded by Mets to Phillies for C Gary Bennett (July 23, 2001). ... On suspended list (May 17-20, 2004).

2004 GAMES PLAYED BY POSITION (MLB): C—43.

Year Team (League)	Pos.	G	AB	R	H	2B	3B	HR	RBI	BB	SO	HBP	GDP	SB-CS	Avg.	OBP	SLG	OPS	E	Avg.
1985— Elmira (N.Y.-Penn)	C	39	119	7	16	1	1	0	5	10	27	1	6	0-1	.134	.206	.160	.366	6	.979
1986— Greensboro (S. Atl.)	C-1B	107	348	63	84	16	0	12	56	75	114	5	10	0-1	.241	.380	.391	.770	15	.983
1987— Winter Haven (FSL)	C-1B-OF	118	407	57	105	22	0	12	65	70	94	1	10	0-1	.258	.364	.400	.764	15	.980
1988— New Britain (East.)	C-1B	124	395	41	89	15	2	8	49	41	110	3	7	1-4	.225	.299	.334	.633	15	.975
1989— New Britain (East.)	C-1B	109	338	30	77	17	1	2	35	44	66	7	10	1-2	.228	.325	.302	.637	11	.977
1990— New Britain (East.)	C-1B	70	195	15	45	14	1	2	22	18	56	0	7	0-1	.231	.293	.344	.637	4	.978
1991— Pawtucket (Int'l)	C-1B	68	219	68	64	16	0	11	41	23	42	3	9	0-3	.292	.367	.516	.883	4	.985
1992— Reading (East.)	C	41	132	20	44	6	1	6	26	24	28	0	1	2-0	.333	.436	.530	.966	3	.970
— Scran./W.B. (I.L.)	C-1B	41	125	20	40	9	1	7	28	30	14	0	5	1-0	.320	.446	.576	1.022	4	.977
— Philadelphia (N.L.)	C	16	46	6	13	1	0	2	10	4	12	0	2	0-0	.283	.340	.435	.775	2	.972
1993— Philadelphia (N.L.)	C	33	87	8	25	6	0	5	13	5	19	1	2	0-0	.287	.330	.529	.859	2	.989
— Scran./W.B. (I.L.)	C	3	9	1	2	1	0	0	1	3	1	0	0	0-0	.222	.417	.333	.750	0	1.000
1994— Philadelphia (N.L.)	C	28	102	10	20	6	1	2	9	12	29	0	1	0-1	.196	.281	.333	.614	0	1.000
1995— Chicago (N.L.)	C	25	60	3	8	2	0	0	4	6	21	0	1	0-0	.133	.209	.167	.376	3	.981
— Iowa (Am. Assoc.)	C-1B-DH	23	58	3	19	1	0	0	5	4	17	0	0	0-0	.328	.371	.345	.716	2	.978
1996—	Did not play.																			
1997— Norfolk (Int'l)	C-DH	59	206	42	62	8	3	9	34	26	48	2	8	1-2	.301	.383	.500	.883	4	.988
— New York (N.L.)	C	39	106	12	30	6	0	2	19	13	32	2	1	0-1	.283	.372	.396	.768	2	.990
1998— Norfolk (Int'l)	DH-C-OF-1	35	118	16	42	6	0	7	30	15	19	4	4	2-0	.356	.442	.585	1.027	2	.984
— New York (N.L.)	C-1B	41	69	9	19	9	1	2	18	2	20	0	0	0-0	.275	.296	.522	.818	2	.976
— St. Lucie (Fla. St.)	C-1B-OF	5	20	2	9	1	0	1	3	1	5	2	0	1-0	.450	.522	.650	1.172	0	1.000
— GC Mets (GCL)	C-OF	2	4	1	1	0	0	0	0	4	1	0	0	0-0	.250	.625	.250	.875	0	1.000
1999— New York (N.L.)	C-1B-OF	71	140	18	41	4	0	3	21	15	32	3	1	2-0	.293	.369	.386	.754	1	.996
2000— New York (N.L.)	C-DH	80	160	33	44	6	0	8	25	22	31	5	5	0-0	.275	.378	.463	.840	1	.997
2001— New York (N.L.)	C	45	80	6	13	5	0	2	4	15	36	2	4	1-0	.163	.306	.300	.606	1	.994
— Philadelphia (N.L.)	C-1B	35	93	12	19	3	0	2	7	19	25	1	2	0-0	.204	.345	.301	.646	3	.986
2002— Philadelphia (N.L.)	C-1B	39	106	14	33	11	0	3	16	24	28	4	3	2-0	.311	.449	.500	.949	0	1.000
2003— Philadelphia (N.L.)	C-1B	43	125	16	34	10	1	4	20	22	38	6	3	0-0	.272	.400	.464	.864	1	.997
2004— Philadelphia (N.L.)	C	45	128	16	33	5	0	3	16	18	38	1	5	0-0	.258	.351	.367	.719	0	1.000
Major League totals (12 years)		540	1302	163	332	74	3	38	182	177	361	25	32	5-2	.255	.352	.404	.756	18	.993

DIVISION SERIES RECORD

Year Team (League)	Pos.	G	AB	R	H	2B	3B	HR	RBI	BB	SO	HBP	GDP	SB-CS	Avg.	OBP	SLG	OPS	E	Avg.
1999— New York (N.L.)	C	3	8	2	1	0	0	1	1	2	1	0	0	0-0	.125	.300	.500	.800	0	1.000
2000— New York (N.L.)	C	1	1	0	0	0	0	0	0	0	0	0	0	0-0	.000	.000	.000	.000	0	1.000
Division series totals (2 years)		4	9	2	1	0	0	1	1	2	1	0	0	0-0	.111	.273	.444	.717	0	1.000

CHAMPIONSHIP SERIES RECORD

Year Team (League)	Pos.	G	AB	R	H	2B	3B	HR	RBI	BB	SO	HBP	GDP	SB-CS	Avg.	OBP	SLG	OPS	E	Avg.
1993— Philadelphia (N.L.)	C	1	1	0	0	0	0	0	0	0	0	1	0	0-0	.000	.000	.000	.000	0	1.000
1999— New York (N.L.)	C	4	2	0	1	0	0	0	3	1	1	0	0	0-0	.500	.500	.500	1.000	0	1.000
Champ. series totals (2 years)		5	3	0	1	0	0	0	3	1	2	1	0	0-0	.333	.400	.333	.733	0	1.000

WORLD SERIES RECORD

Year Team (League)	Pos.	G	AB	R	H	2B	3B	HR	RBI	BB	SO	HBP	GDP	SB-CS	Avg.	OBP	SLG	OPS	E	Avg.
1993— Philadelphia (N.L.)	Did not play.																			
2000— New York (N.L.)	C	1	2	1	0	0	0	0	0	0	1	2	2	0-0	.000	.600	.000	.600	0	1.000

PERSONAL: Born December 17, 1968, in Washington, District of Columbia. ... 6-0/210. ... Bats left, throws right. ... Full name: Curtis John Pride. ... High school: John F. Kennedy (Silver Spring, Md.). ... College: William & Mary (Va.).

TRANSACTIONS/CAREER NOTES: Selected by New York Mets organization in 10th round of June 1986 free-agent draft. ... Signed as a free agent by Montreal Expos organization (December 8, 1992). ... Signed as a free agent by Detroit Tigers organization (March 31, 1996). ... On disabled list (April 13-May 10, 1996); included rehabilitation assignment to Toledo. ... Signed as a free agent by Boston Red Sox organization (August 30, 1997). ... Signed as a free agent by Atlanta Braves organization (February 6, 1998). ... On suspended list (May 27-28, 1998). ... On disabled list (June 28-July 14, 1998); included rehabilitation assignment to Richmond. ... Released by Braves (December 1, 1998). ... Signed by Kansas City Royals organization (February 24, 1999). ... Released by Royals (March 4, 1999). ... Signed by Mets organization (January 20, 2000). ... Traded by Mets to Red Sox for a player to be named (April 26, 2000); Mets acquired SS Gavin Jackson to complete deal (July 9, 2000). ... Released by Red Sox (July 8, 2000). ... Signed by Los Angeles Dodgers organization (July 18, 2000). ... Signed as a free agent by Expos organization (December 21, 2000). ... On disabled list (June 18-August 21, 2001); included rehabilitation assignments to Jupiter and Ottawa. ... Signed as a free agent by Pittsburgh Pirates organization (March 5, 2002). ... Contract purchased by New York Yankees organization from Nashua of the independent Atlantic League (May 23, 2003). ... Signed as a free agent by Anaheim Angels organization (May 31, 2004).

2004 GAMES PLAYED BY POSITION (MLB): OF—24, DH—2.

Year Team (League)	Pos.	G	AB	R	H	2B	3B	HR	RBI	BB	SO	HBP	GDP	SB-CS	Avg.	OBP	SLG	OPS	E	Avg.
1986— Kingsport (Appalachian)	OF	27	46	5	5	0	0	1	4	6	24	1	0	5-0	.109	.226	.174	.400	0	1.000
1987— Kingsport (Appalachian)	OF	31	104	22	25	4	0	1	9	16	34	1	0	14-5	.240	.347	.308	.655	5	.894
1988— Kingsport (Appalachian)	OF	70	268	59	76	13	1	8	27	50	48	1	2	23-7	.284	.397	.429	.826	5	.961
1989— Pittsfield (N.Y.-Penn.)	OF	55	212	35	55	7	3	6	23	25	47	2	1	9-2	.259	.342	.406	.747	4	.964
1990— Columbia (S. Atl.)	OF	53	191	38	51	4	4	6	25	21	45	0	3	11-8	.267	.338	.424	.762	11	.874
1991— St. Lucie (Fla. St.)	OF	116	392	57	102	21	7	9	37	43	94	2	8	24-5	.260	.336	.418	.755	4	.981
1992— Binghamton (East.)	OF	118	388	54	88	15	3	10	42	47	110	4	5	14-11	.227	.316	.358	.674	8	.964

P

Year — Team (League)	Pos.	G	AB	R	H	2B	3B	HR	RBI	BB	SO	HBP	GDP	SB-CS	Avg.	OBP	SLG	OPS	E	Avg.
1993— Harrisburg (East.)	OF	50	180	51	64	6	3	15	39	12	36	4	2	21-6	.356	.404	.672	1.076	2	.972
— Ottawa (Int'l)	OF	69	262	55	79	11	4	6	22	34	61	3	3	29-12	.302	.388	.443	.831	2	.986
— Montreal (N.L.)	OF	10	9	3	4	1	1	1	5	0	3	0	0	1-0	.444	.444	1.111	1.556	0	1.000
1994— W.P. Beach (FSL)	OF	3	8	5	6	1	0	1	3	4	2	0	0	2-2	.750	.833	1.250	2.083	0	1.000
— Ottawa (Int'l)	OF-DH	82	300	56	77	16	4	9	32	39	81	2	3	22-6	.257	.345	.427	.772	3	.982
1995— Ottawa (Int'l)	OF-DH	42	154	25	43	8	3	4	24	12	35	2	2	8-4	.279	.339	.448	.787	2	.974
— Montreal (N.L.)	OF	48	63	10	11	1	0	0	2	5	16	0	2	3-2	.175	.235	.190	.426	2	.920
1996— Detroit (A.L.)	OF-DH	95	267	52	80	17	5	10	31	31	63	0	2	11-6	.300	.372	.513	.886	3	.967
— Toledo (Int'l)	DH-OF	9	26	4	6	1	0	1	2	9	7	1	1	4-1	.231	.444	.385	.829	0	1.000
1997— Detroit (A.L.)	OF-DH	79	162	21	34	4	4	2	19	24	45	1	4	6-4	.210	.314	.321	.635	1	.980
— Pawtucket (Int'l)	OF	1	3	0	0	0	0	0	0	0	2	0	0	0-0	.000	.000	.000	.000	0	1.000
— Boston (A.L.)		2	2	1	1	0	0	1	1	0	1	0	0	0-0	.500	.500	2.500	2.500	...	...
1998— Atlanta (N.L.)	OF-DH	70	107	19	27	6	1	3	9	9	29	3	2	4-0	.252	.325	.411	.736	0	1.000
— Richmond (Int'l)	OF-DH	21	78	11	19	2	1	2	6	15	17	0	3	8-0	.244	.366	.372	.737	0	1.000
1999— Nashua (Atl.)	DH	14	32	0	2	0	0	0	2	7	11	...	...	0-0	.063		.063		...	...
2000— Norfolk (Int'l)	OF	15	31	9	9	2	2	1	4	11	7	...	...	3-2	.290		.581		1	.929
— Pawtucket (Int'l)	OF	48	154	44	47	10	2	9	31	38	31	...	...	12-1	.305		.571		1	.990
— Boston (A.L.)	OF-DH	9	20	4	5	1	0	0	0	1	7	0	0	0-0	.250	.286	.300	.586	0	1.000
— Albuquerque (PCL)	OF	38	133	30	39	7	3	6	17	20	37	0	2	7-5	.293	.383	.526	.909	3	.959
2001— Ottawa (Int'l)	OF	22	81	14	27	4	1	5	15	12	26	2	2	6-1	.333	.432	.593	1.024	1	.963
— Montreal (N.L.)	OF-DH	36	76	8	19	3	1	1	9	9	22	2	4	3-2	.250	.345	.345	.700	0	1.000
— Jupiter (FSL)	OF	6	21	3	4	1	0	0	3	3	3	0	0	0-1	.190	.292	.238	.530	0	1.000
2002— Nashville (PCL)	OF	110	385	71	114	22	1	10	46	33	75	7	7	22-8	.296	.362	.436	.798	6	.968
2003— New York (A.L.)	OF	4	12	1	1	0	0	1	1	0	2	0	1	0-0	.083	.083	.333	.417	0	1.000
— Columbus (Int'l)	OF-DH	55	225	44	65	11	4	7	34	20	48	4	7	7-7	.289	.357	.467	.824	1	.991
2004— Ariz. Angels (Ariz.)	DH	4	14	1	3	1	0	0	3	1	6	0	0	1-0	.214	.250	.286	.536	0	1.000
— Salt Lake (PCL)	OF	19	65	13	28	8	1	2	10	4	12	1	0	2-0	.431	.465	.677	1.142	0	1.000
— Anaheim (A.L.)	OF-DH	35	40	5	10	3	0	0	3	0	11	1	1	1-0	.250	.268	.325	.593	0	1.000
American League totals (5 years)		224	503	84	131	25	9	14	55	56	129	2	8	18-10	.260	.336	.429	.766	4	.979
National League totals (4 years)		164	255	40	61	11	3	5	25	23	70	5	8	11-4	.239	.313	.365	.678	2	.980
Major League totals (9 years)		388	758	124	192	36	12	19	80	79	199	7	16	29-14	.253	.329	.408	.736	6	.979

DIVISION SERIES RECORD

Year — Team (League)	Pos.	G	AB	R	H	2B	3B	HR	RBI	BB	SO	HBP	GDP	SB-CS	Avg.	OBP	SLG	OPS	E	Avg.
2004— Anaheim (A.L.)		2	2	0	0	0	0	0	0	0	1	0	0	0-0	.000	.000	.000	.000	0	...

PRIETO, ALEX   2B/SS

PERSONAL: Born June 19, 1976, in Caracas, Venezuela. ... 5-11/205. ... Bats right, throws right. ... Full name: Alejandro Antonio Prieto. ... High school: Juan Pablos II (Caracas, Venezuela).

TRANSACTIONS/CAREER NOTES: Signed as a non-drafted free agent by Kansas City Royals organization (November 12, 1992). ... Signed as a free agent by Minnesota Twins organization (November 8, 2002). ... Refused minor league assignment and became a free agent (October 6, 2004).

2004 GAMES PLAYED BY POSITION (MLB): 2B—8, 3B—5, SS—3, DH—1.

| | | | | | | | | | | BATTING | | | | | | | | | FIELDING | |
Year — Team (League)	Pos.	G	AB	R	H	2B	3B	HR	RBI	BB	SO	HBP	GDP	SB-CS	Avg.	OBP	SLG	OPS	E	Avg.
1993— GC Royals (GCL)	SS-2B-OF	43	114	14	28	3	0	0	6	9	13	0	1	4-2	.246	.301	.272	.573	18	.885
1994— GC Royals (GCL)	SS-2B-3B	18	60	15	18	5	0	2	17	2	5	4	0	1-0	.300	.358	.483	.842	9	.885
1995— Springfield (Midw.)	SS	124	431	61	108	9	3	2	44	40	69	6	10	11-7	.251	.322	.299	.621	38	.936
1996— Wilmington (Caro.)	SS	119	447	65	127	19	6	1	40	31	66	3	7	26-15	.284	.331	.360	.691	40	.929
1997— Wilmington (Caro.)	SS	129	437	52	94	13	3	3	38	41	59	2	6	20-8	.215	.282	.279	.561	37	.940
1998— Wichita (Texas)	SS-2B-OF	113	384	61	101	18	7	2	35	31	54	2	13	4-8	.263	.321	.362	.683	35	.934
1999— Wichita (Texas)	S-2-3-O	114	360	56	106	23	4	6	41	35	47	1	10	12-6	.294	.356	.431	.786	25	.949
2000— Omaha (PCL)	S-2-3-O	118	384	54	101	19	0	7	37	26	40	6	12	14-6	.263	.318	.367	.685	15	.970
2001— Omaha (PCL)	3-2-S-O	105	376	45	106	21	3	8	44	36	59	1	12	9-2	.282	.344	.418	.761	7	.982
2002— Edmonton (PCL)	2B-SS-3B	80	276	38	73	14	1	7	29	19	47	2	5	4-4	.264	.315	.399	.714	12	.963
2003— Rochester (Int'l)	S-3-2-1-DH	69	234	27	62	9	1	5	21	12	49	0	6	6-3	.265	.298	.376	.674	8	.974
— Minnesota (A.L.)	2B-SS	8	11	1	1	0	0	0	0	0	4	0	0	0-0	.091	.091	.091	.182	0	1.000
2004— Minnesota (A.L.)	2-3-S-DH	16	32	4	8	1	0	1	4	3	9	0	1	0-1	.250	.306	.375	.681	0	1.000
— Rochester (Int'l)	3-S-1-2-DH	84	289	39	72	13	0	6	22	29	52	1	5	2-3	.249	.316	.356	.672	11	.971
Major League totals (2 years)		24	43	5	9	1	0	1	4	3	13	0	1	0-1	.209	.255	.302	.558	0	1.000

PRINZ, BRET   P

PERSONAL: Born June 15, 1977, in Chicago Heights, Ill. ... 6-2/216. ... Throws right, bats right. ... Full name: Bret Randolph Prinz. ... High school: Centennial (Peoria, Ariz.). ... Junior college: Phoenix (Ariz.).

TRANSACTIONS/CAREER NOTES: Selected by Boston Red Sox organization in 30th round of 1997 free-agent draft; did not sign. ... Selected by Arizona Diamondbacks organization in 18th round of 1998 free-agent draft. ... On disabled list (April 1-July 24, 2003); included rehabilitation assignment to Tucson. ... Traded by Diamondbacks with OF David Dellucci and C Jon-Mark Sprowl to New York Yankees for OF Raul Mondesi and cash (July 29, 2003).

CAREER HITTING: 0-for-0 (.000), 0 R, 0 2B, 0 3B, 0 HR, 0 RBI.

Year — Team (League)	W	L	Pct.	ERA	WHIP	G	GS	CG	ShO	Hld.	Sv.-Opp.	IP	H	R	ER	HR	BB-IBB	SO	Avg.
1998— Ariz. D'backs (Ariz.)	0	0	...	3.38	1.31	4	0	0	0	...	0-...	5.1	7	3	2	0	0-0	3	.304
— Lethbridge (Pio.)	4	2	.667	3.09	1.33	11	10	0	0	...	0-...	46.2	49	26	16	2	13-0	30	.262
1999— South Bend (Mid.)	6	10	.375	4.48	1.31	30	23	0	0	...	0-...	138.2	129	82	69	16	52-0	98	.247
2000— South Bend (Mid.)	1	0	1.000	0.00	0.41	6	0	0	0	...	1-...	7.1	2	2	0	0	1-0	10	.083
— El Paso (Texas)	9	1	.900	3.56	1.43	53	0	0	0	...	26-...	60.2	71	24	24	6	16-3	69	.293
2001— Tucson (PCL)	0	0	...	0.00	0.18	5	0	0	0	...	3-...	5.2	1	0	0	0	0-0	6	.056
— Arizona (N.L.)	4	1	.800	2.63	1.27	46	0	0	0	6	9-12	41.0	33	13	12	4	19-1	27	.220
2002— Arizona (N.L.)	0	0	.000	9.45	2.48	20	0	0	0	5	0-2	13.1	23	14	14	1	10-1	10	.404
— Tucson (PCL)	1	0	1.000	2.97	1.30	37	0	0	0	...	18-...	39.1	42	14	13	4	9-1	34	.269
— Lancaster (Calif.)	1	0	1.000	0.00	0.43	5	0	0	0	...	0-...	7.0	2	0	0	0	1-0	6	.071
2003— Arizona (N.L.)	0	0	...	0.00	2.00	1	0	0	0	0	0-...	1.0	1	0	0	0	1-1	1	.250
— Lancaster (Calif.)	0	0	...	0.00	0.00	1	1	0	0	...	0-...	1.0	0	0	0	0	0-0	2	.000
— El Paso (Texas)	0	0	...	4.50	2.00	2	0	0	0	...	0-...	2.0	3	1	1	0	1-0	2	.333

P

Year	Team (League)	W	L	Pct.	ERA	WHIP	G	GS	CG	ShO	Hld.	Sv.-Opp.	IP	H	R	ER	HR	BB-IBB	SO	Avg.
	— Tucson (PCL)	0	1	.000	6.00	1.80	10	0	0	0	...	0-...	12.0	19	9	8	1	3-0	7	.345
	— New York (A.L.)	0	0	...	18.00	4.50	2	0	0	0	0	0-0	2.0	6	4	4	1	3-1	2	.500
	— Columbus (Int'l)	0	1	.000	8.03	1.70	10	0	0	0	...	0-...	12.1	20	11	11	2	1-0	13	.364
2004—	Columbus (Int'l)	3	1	.750	3.52	1.17	29	0	0	0	...	11-...	30.2	27	12	12	3	9-0	33	.241
	— New York (A.L.)	1	0	1.000	5.08	1.48	26	0	0	0	1	0-0	28.1	28	17	16	5	14-0	22	.259
American League totals (2 years)		1	0	1.000	5.93	1.68	28	0	0	0	1	0-0	30.1	34	21	20	6	17-1	24	.283
National League totals (3 years)		4	3	.571	4.23	1.57	67	0	0	0	11	9-14	55.1	57	27	26	5	30-3	38	.270
Major League totals (4 years)		5	3	.625	4.83	1.61	95	0	0	0	12	9-14	85.2	91	48	46	11	47-4	62	.275

PRIOR, MARK — P

PERSONAL: Born September 7, 1980, in San Diego, Calif. ... 6-5/230. ... Throws right, bats right. ... Full name: Mark William Prior. ... High school: University of San Diego High (Calif.). ... College: USC.

TRANSACTIONS/CAREER NOTES: Selected by New York Yankees organization in supplemental round ("sandwich" pick between first and second rounds, 43rd pick overall) of 1998 free-agent draft; did not sign; pick received as compensation for Yankees' failing to sign 1997 first-round pick Tyrell Godwin. ... Selected by Chicago Cubs organization in first round (second pick overall) of 2001 free-agent draft. ... On disabled list (September 2-17, 2002; and July 12-August 4, 2003). ... On disabled list (March 26-June 4, 2004); included rehabilitation assignments to Lansing and Iowa.

CAREER HITTING: 29-for-143 (.203), 14 R, 8 2B, 0 3B, 1 HR, 10 RBI.

Year	Team (League)	W	L	Pct.	ERA	WHIP	G	GS	CG	ShO	Hld.	Sv.-Opp.	IP	H	R	ER	HR	BB-IBB	SO	Avg.
2002—	West Tenn (Sou.)	4	1	.800	2.60	1.04	6	6	0	0	...	0-...	34.2	26	16	10	0	10-0	55	.198
	— Iowa (PCL)	1	1	.500	1.65	1.29	3	3	0	0	...	0-...	16.1	13	10	3	1	8-0	24	.203
	— Chicago (N.L.)	6	6	.500	3.32	1.17	19	19	1	0	0	0-0	116.2	98	45	43	14	38-0	147	.226
2003—	Chicago (N.L.)	18	6	.750	2.43	1.10	30	30	3	1	0	0-0	211.1	183	67	57	15	50-4	245	.231
2004—	Lansing (Midw.)	0	0	...	1.23	0.41	2	2	0	0	...	0-...	7.1	2	1	1	0	1-0	13	.087
	— Iowa (PCL)	1	0	1.000	3.38	0.75	1	1	0	0	...	0-...	5.1	3	2	2	2	1-0	10	.158
	— Chicago (N.L.)	6	4	.600	4.02	1.35	21	21	0	0	0	0-0	118.2	112	53	53	14	48-2	139	.251
Major League totals (3 years)		30	16	.652	3.08	1.18	70	70	4	1	0	0-0	446.2	393	165	153	43	136-6	531	.235

DIVISION SERIES RECORD

Year	Team (League)	W	L	Pct.	ERA	WHIP	G	GS	CG	ShO	Hld.	Sv.-Opp.	IP	H	R	ER	HR	BB-IBB	SO	Avg.
2003—	Chicago (N.L.)	1	0	1.000	1.00	0.67	1	1	1	0	0	0-0	9.0	2	1	1	0	4-0	7	.071

CHAMPIONSHIP SERIES RECORD

Year	Team (League)	W	L	Pct.	ERA	WHIP	G	GS	CG	ShO	Hld.	Sv.-Opp.	IP	H	R	ER	HR	BB-IBB	SO	Avg.
2003—	Chicago (N.L.)	1	1	.500	3.14	1.33	2	2	0	0	0	0-0	14.1	14	8	5	2	5-0	11	.241

PROCTOR, SCOTT — P

PERSONAL: Born January 2, 1977, in Stuart, Fla. ... 6-1/198. ... Throws right, bats right. ... Full name: Scott Christopher Proctor. ... High school: Martin County (Stuart, Fla.). ... College: Florida State.

TRANSACTIONS/CAREER NOTES: Selected by New York Mets organization in 17th round of 1995 free-agent draft; did not sign. ... Selected by Los Angeles Dodgers organization in fifth round of 1998 free-agent draft. ... Traded by Dodgers with OF Bubba Crosby to New York Yankees for IF Robin Ventura (July 31, 2003).

CAREER HITTING: 0-for-0 (.000), 0 R, 0 2B, 0 3B, 0 HR, 0 RBI.

Year	Team (League)	W	L	Pct.	ERA	WHIP	G	GS	CG	ShO	Hld.	Sv.-Opp.	IP	H	R	ER	HR	BB-IBB	SO	Avg.
1998—	Yakima (N'west)	0	1	.000	10.80	2.00	3	1	0	0	...	2-...	5.0	9	8	6	1	1-0	4	.391
1999—	Yakima (N'west)	4	2	.667	7.20	1.66	16	6	0	0	...	1-...	50.0	57	45	40	4	26-0	41	.286
2000—	Vero Beach (FSL)	3	7	.300	5.16	1.65	35	5	0	0	...	1-...	89.0	93	65	51	13	54-1	70	.268
2001—	Vero Beach (FSL)	6	4	.600	2.48	1.14	15	15	0	0	...	0-...	90.2	73	30	25	8	30-1	79	.226
	— Jacksonville (Southern) ..	4	3	.571	4.17	1.41	10	9	0	0	...	0-...	49.2	39	26	23	6	31-1	48	.220
2002—	Jacksonville (Southern) ..	7	9	.438	3.51	1.47	26	25	0	0	...	0-...	133.1	111	63	52	10	85-1	131	.227
2003—	Jacksonville (Southern) ..	1	2	.333	1.00	1.00	17	0	0	0	...	0-...	27.0	20	6	3	0	7-3	24	.208
	— Las Vegas (PCL)	4	2	.667	3.66	1.22	24	0	0	0	...	1-...	39.1	35	17	16	2	13-3	35	.246
	— Columbus (Int'l)	2	0	1.000	1.42	0.84	10	0	0	0	...	0-...	19.0	13	3	3	2	3-0	26	.197
2004—	Columbus (Int'l)	2	3	.400	2.86	1.25	35	0	0	0	...	4-...	44.0	37	15	14	4	18-2	42	.233
	— New York (A.L.)	2	1	.667	5.40	1.72	26	0	0	0	2	0-0	25.0	29	18	15	5	14-0	21	.284
Major League totals (1 year)		2	1	.667	5.40	1.72	26	0	0	0	2	0-0	25.0	29	18	15	5	14-0	21	.284

PUFFER, BRANDON — P

PERSONAL: Born October 5, 1975, in Downey, Calif. ... 6-3/190. ... Throws right, bats right. ... Full name: Brandon Duane Puffer. ... High school: Capistrano Valley (Mission Viejo, Calif.).

TRANSACTIONS/CAREER NOTES: Selected by Minnesota Twins organization in 27th round of 1994 free-agent draft. ... Released by Twins (May 6, 1996). ... Signed by California Angels organization (May 28, 1996). ... Franchise renamed Anaheim Angels for 1997 season. ... Released by Angels (December 15, 1997). ... Signed as a free agent by Cincinnati Reds organization (January 14, 1998). ... Signed as a free agent by Colorado Rockies organization (November 18, 1999). ... Released by Rockies (May 18, 2000). ... Contract purchased by Houston Astros organization from Somerset of the independent Atlantic League (July 17, 2000). ... Released by Astros (November 19, 2003). ... Signed by San Diego Padres organization (January 7, 2004). ... Traded by Padres to Boston Red Sox for future considerations (July 2, 2004).

CAREER HITTING: 0-for-9 (.000), 0 R, 0 2B, 0 3B, 0 HR, 0 RBI.

Year	Team (League)	W	L	Pct.	ERA	WHIP	G	GS	CG	ShO	Hld.	Sv.-Opp.	IP	H	R	ER	HR	BB-IBB	SO	Avg.
1994—	GC Twins (GCL)	2	2	.500	3.06	1.47	18	0	0	0	...	2-...	35.1	33	18	12	1	19-0	40	.248
1995—	GC Twins (GCL)	0	3	.000	2.88	1.23	14	5	0	0	...	1-...	40.2	29	21	13	0	21-0	35	.191
1996—	Ariz. Angels (Ariz.)	0	1	.000	3.60	1.60	1	1	0	0	...	0-...	5.0	7	2	2	0	1-0	3	.318
	— Boise (N'west)	2	0	1.000	4.45	1.25	16	0	0	0	...	1-...	30.1	27	19	15	3	11-0	22	.239
1997—	Boise (N'west)	0	0	...	2.35	0.78	6	0	0	0	...	1-...	15.1	10	5	4	0	2-0	15	.169
	— Cedar Rapids (Midw.)	0	0	...	2.60	1.04	10	0	0	0	...	0-...	17.1	8	6	5	0	10-0	11	.143
1998—	Char., W.Va. (SAL)	2	7	.222	6.93	1.80	29	0	0	0	...	1-...	50.2	68	45	39	4	23-4	36	.325
	— Chattanooga (Southern)	0	0	...	3.12	0.58	7	0	0	0	...	0-...	8.2	3	3	3	2	3-0	6	.071
1999—	Clinton (Midw.)	1	2	.333	1.99	1.22	59	0	0	0	...	34-...	63.1	53	20	14	2	24-3	60	.223
2000—	Asheville (S. Atl.)	0	0	...	8.16	2.09	14	0	0	0	...	5-...	14.1	19	16	13	3	11-3	15	.322
	— Somerset (Atl.)	2	2	.500	3.52	1.48	15	0	0	0	...	1-...	23.0	25	12	9	...	9-...	21	...
	— Kissimmee (Fla. St.)	2	3	.400	1.27	1.36	18	0	0	0	...	9-...	21.1	18	6	3	0	11-4	26	.225
2001—	Round Rock (Texas)	6	1	.857	2.07	1.05	56	0	0	0	...	8-...	82.2	52	19	19	4	35-2	91	.181
2002—	New Orleans (PCL)	2	1	.667	1.80	0.80	11	0	0	0	...	0-...	15.0	8	3	3	1	4-0	13	.157
	— Houston (N.L.)	3	3	.500	4.43	1.52	55	0	0	0	2	0-0	69.0	67	37	34	8	38-8	48	.258

Year—Team (League)	W	L	Pct.	ERA	WHIP	G	GS	CG	ShO	Hld.	Sv.-Opp.	IP	H	R	ER	HR	BB-IBB	SO	Avg.
2003—Houston (N.L.)	0	0	...	5.14	1.90	13	0	0	0	1	0-1	21.0	24	13	12	2	16-3	10	.300
— New Orleans (PCL)	7	3	.700	2.91	1.30	44	0	0	0	...	5-...	52.2	50	23	17	1	16-1	41	.253
2004—Portland (PCL)	1	1	.500	3.34	1.30	22	0	0	0	...	2-...	32.1	32	15	12	1	10-2	19	.254
— San Diego (N.L.)	0	1	.000	5.50	1.94	14	0	0	0	0	0-0	18.0	24	13	11	3	11-1	12	.320
— Pawtucket (Int'l)	3	2	.600	3.26	1.38	24	0	0	0	...	10-...	30.1	31	11	11	1	11-6	21	.263
Major League totals (3 years)	3	4	.429	4.75	1.67	82	0	0	0	3	0-1	108.0	115	63	57	8	65-12	70	.277

PUJOLS, ALBERT — 1B

PERSONAL: Born January 16, 1980, in Santo Domingo, Dominican Republic. ... 6-3/225. ... Bats right, throws right. ... Full name: Jose Albert Pujols. ... Name pronounced: POO-holes. ... High school: Fort Osage (Independence, Mo.). ... Junior college: Maple Woods (Mo.) Community College.

TRANSACTIONS/CAREER NOTES: Selected by St. Louis Cardinals organization in 13th round of 1999 free-agent draft. ... On suspended list (August 19-21, 2003).

HONORS: Named N.L. Rookie Player of the Year by THE SPORTING NEWS (2001). ... Named N.L. Rookie of the Year by Baseball Writers' Association of America (2001). ... Named Major League Player of the Year by the SPORTING NEWS (2003).

2004 GAMES PLAYED BY POSITION (MLB): 1B—150, DH—3.

Year—Team (League)	Pos.	G	AB	R	H	2B	3B	HR	RBI	BB	SO	HBP	GDP	SB-CS	Avg.	OBP	SLG	OPS	E	Avg.
2000— Peoria (Midw.)	3B	109	395	62	128	32	6	17	84	38	37	5	10	2-4	.324	.389	.565	.953	19	.948
— Potomac (Caro.)	3B	21	81	11	23	8	1	2	10	7	8	0	3	1-1	.284	.341	.481	.822	3	.957
— Memphis (PCL)	3B	3	14	1	3	1	0	0	2	1	2	0	0	1-0	.214	.267	.286	.552	0	1.000
2001—St. Louis (N.L.)	OF-3-1-DH	161	590	112	194	47	4	37	130	69	93	9	21	1-3	.329	.403	.610	1.013	20	.967
2002—St. Louis (N.L.)	O-3-1-DH-S	157	590	118	185	40	2	34	127	72	69	9	20	2-4	.314	.394	.561	.955	11	.975
2003—St. Louis (N.L.)	OF-1B-DH	157	591	* 137	* 212	* 51	1	43	124	79	65	10	13	5-1	* .359	.439	.667	1.106	4	.993
2004—St. Louis (N.L.)	1B-DH	154	592	* 133	196	51	2	46	123	84	52	7	21	5-5	.331	.415	.657	1.072	10	.994
Major League totals (4 years)		629	2363	500	787	189	9	160	504	304	279	35	75	13-13	.333	.413	.624	1.037	45	.986

DIVISION SERIES RECORD

Year—Team (League)	Pos.	G	AB	R	H	2B	3B	HR	RBI	BB	SO	HBP	GDP	SB-CS	Avg.	OBP	SLG	OPS	E	Avg.
2001—St. Louis (N.L.)	1B-OF	5	18	1	2	0	1	0	2	2	2	0	1	0-0	.111	.200	.278	.478	1	.964
2002—St. Louis (N.L.)	OF-3B-1B	3	10	3	3	0	0	1	3	3	1	0	0	0-0	.300	.462	.500	.962	1	.833
2004—St. Louis (N.L.)	1B	4	15	4	5	0	0	2	5	3	0	0	1	0-0	.333	.444	.733	1.178	0	1.000
Division series totals (3 years)		12	43	8	10	0	1	3	10	8	3	0	2	0-0	.233	.353	.488	.841	2	.974

CHAMPIONSHIP SERIES RECORD

Year—Team (League)	Pos.	G	AB	R	H	2B	3B	HR	RBI	BB	SO	HBP	GDP	SB-CS	Avg.	OBP	SLG	OPS	E	Avg.
2002—St. Louis (N.L.)	OF	5	19	2	5	1	0	1	2	2	5	1	0	0-0	.263	.364	.474	.837	0	1.000
2004—St. Louis (N.L.)	1B	7	28	10	14	2	0	4	9	4	3	0	0	0-0	.500	.563	1.000	1.563	0	1.000
Champ. series totals (2 years)		12	47	12	19	3	0	5	11	6	8	1	0	0-0	.404	.481	.787	1.269	0	1.000

WORLD SERIES RECORD

Year—Team (League)	Pos.	G	AB	R	H	2B	3B	HR	RBI	BB	SO	HBP	GDP	SB-CS	Avg.	OBP	SLG	OPS	E	Avg.
2004—St. Louis (N.L.)	1B	4	15	1	5	2	0	0	0	3	1	0	0	0-0	.333	.412	.467	.878	0	1.000

ALL-STAR GAME RECORD

		G	AB	R	H	2B	3B	HR	RBI	BB	SO	HBP	GDP	SB-CS	Avg.	OBP	SLG	OPS	E	Avg.
All-Star Game totals (3 years)			3	6	1	3	2	0	0	3	1	0	0	0-0	.500	.571	.833	1.405	0	1.000

PULIDO, CARLOS — P

PERSONAL: Born August 5, 1971, in Caracas, Venezuela. ... 6-0/205. ... Throws left, bats left. ... Full name: Juan Carlos Pulido. ... Name pronounced: puh-LEE-doe. ... High school: Liceo Andres Bello (Caracas, Venezuela).

TRANSACTIONS/CAREER NOTES: Signed as a non-drafted free agent by Minnesota Twins organization (February 28, 1989). ... Signed as a free agent by Chicago Cubs organization (February 19, 1996). ... Signed as a free agent by Montreal Expos organization (December 26, 1996). ... Contract purchased by New York Mets organization from Somerset of the independent Atlantic League (September 1, 1998). ... Signed as a free agent by Twins organization (November 22. 2002).

CAREER HITTING: 0-for-0 (.000), 0 R, 0 2B, 0 3B, 0 HR, 0 RBI.

Year—Team (League)	W	L	Pct.	ERA	WHIP	G	GS	CG	ShO	Hld.	Sv.-Opp.	IP	H	R	ER	HR	BB-IBB	SO	Avg.
1989—GC Twins (GCL)	3	0	1.000	2.25	1.00	22	0	0	0	...	2-...	36.0	22	9	9	0	14-0	46	.177
1990—Kenosha (Midw.)	5	5	.500	2.34	1.48	56	0	0	0	...	6-...	61.2	55	21	16	2	36-3	70	.242
1991—Visalia (Calif.)	1	5	.167	2.01	1.24	57	0	0	0	...	17-...	80.2	77	34	18	2	23-2	102	.253
— Portland (PCL)	0	0	...	16.20	3.00	2	0	0	0	...	0-...	1.2	4	3	3	1	1-0	2	.444
1992—Orlando (Sou.)	6	2	.750	4.40	1.36	52	5	0	0	...	1-...	100.1	99	52	49	7	37-0	87	.257
1993—Portland (PCL)	10	6	.625	4.19	1.47	33	22	1	0	...	0-...	146.0	169	74	68	8	45-1	79	.296
1994—Minnesota (A.L.)	3	7	.300	5.98	1.51	19	14	0	0	0	0-...	84.1	87	57	56	17	40-1	32	.273
1995—Salt Lake (PCL)	8	1	.889	4.67	1.50	43	3	0	0	...	3-...	71.1	87	42	37	10	20-4	38	.292
1996—Iowa (Am. Assoc.)	2	8	.200	5.31	1.66	28	17	0	0	...	0-...	101.2	133	64	60	17	36-3	48	.322
— Orlando (Sou.)	2	2	.500	7.45	2.07	6	0	0	0	...	0-...	9.2	17	9	8	0	3-0	12	.362
1997—Ottawa (Int'l)	5	2	.714	5.42	1.43	44	5	0	0	...	0-...	76.1	84	47	46	10	25-2	44	.276
1998—Somerset (Atl.)	2	2	.500	3.31	1.19	12	2	1	0	...	0-...	35.1	30	14	13	3	12-1	33	.234
— Norfolk (Int'l)	0	0	...	1.69	1.13	3	0	0	0	...	0-...	5.1	6	1	1	1	0-0	6	.300
1999—Somerset (Atl.)	9	4	.692	4.42	1.16	22	22	0	0	...	0-...	148.2	137	77	73	20	36-...	105	...
2003—Rochester (Int'l)	12	5	.706	3.56	1.20	25	25	1	0	...	0-...	149.1	145	65	59	13	40-0	87	.262
— Minnesota (A.L.)	0	1	.000	4.02	1.15	7	1	0	0	1	0-0	15.2	15	9	7	0	3-0	6	.254
2004—Minnesota (A.L.)	0	0	...	8.74	1.76	6	0	0	0	1	0-0	11.1	16	13	11	2	4-1	9	.333
— Rochester (Int'l)	1	3	.250	11.72	2.04	5	5	0	0	...	0-...	17.2	29	24	23	7	7-0	12	.367
Major League totals (3 years)	3	8	.273	5.98	1.48	32	15	0	0	2	0-0	111.1	118	79	74	19	47-2	47	.277

PUNTO, NICK — 2B/SS

PERSONAL: Born November 8, 1977, in San Diego, Calif. ... 5-9/176. ... Bats both, throws right. ... Full name: Nicholas Paul Punto. ... Name pronounced: POON-toh. ... High school: Trabuco Hills (Mission Vieh Vijo, Calif.). ... Junior college: Saddleback (Calif.) Community College.

TRANSACTIONS/CAREER NOTES: Selected by Minnesota Twins organization in 33rd round of 1997 free-agent draft; did not sign. ... Selected by Philadelphia Phillies organization in 21st round of 1998 free-agent draft. ... Traded by Phillies with RHP Carlos Silva and a player to be named to Minnesota Twins for LHP Eric Milton (December 3, 2003); Twins acquired P Bobby Korecky to complete deal (December 16, 2003). ... On disabled list (May 9-June 30 and July 27, 2004-remainder of season); included rehabilitation assignment to Quad City.

P

2004 GAMES PLAYED BY POSITION (MLB): 2B—19, SS—11, DH—3, 3B—2, OF—2.

Year	Team (League)	Pos.	G	AB	R	H	2B	3B	HR	RBI	BB	SO	HBP	GDP	SB-CS	Avg.	OBP	SLG	OPS	E	Avg.
1998—Batavia (NY-Penn)		2B-SS	72	279	51	69	9	4	1	20	42	48	1	4	19-7	.247	.347	.319	.666	27	.924
1999—Clearwater (FSL)		SS	106	400	65	122	18	6	1	48	67	53	3	13	16-6	.305	.404	.388	.792	24	.958
2000—Reading (East.)		SS	121	456	77	116	15	4	5	47	69	71	2	5	33-10	.254	.351	.338	.689	20	.963
2001—Scran./W.B. (I.L.)		SS	123	463	57	106	19	5	1	39	68	114	0	15	33-9	.229	.327	.298	.625	21	.964
—Philadelphia (N.L.)		SS	4	5	0	2	0	0	0	0	0	0	0	0	0-0	.400	.400	.400	.800	0	1.000
2002—Philadelphia (N.L.)		2B-SS	9	6	0	1	0	0	0	0	0	3	0	0	0-0	.167	.167	.167	.333	1	.750
—Scran./W.B. (I.L.)		SS	115	443	74	120	12	5	1	29	76	84	2	5	42-8	.271	.378	.327	.705	19	.967
2003—Scran./W.B. (I.L.)		SS	25	111	19	35	7	1	0	9	7	13	0	0	7-1	.315	.353	.396	.749	4	.969
—Philadelphia (N.L.)		SS	64	92	14	20	2	0	1	4	7	22	0	0	2-1	.217	.273	.272	.544	2	.980
2004—Quad Cities (Mid.)		SS-2B-3B	4	16	4	7	1	0	1	6	2	2	0	0	1-0	.438	.500	.688	1.188	0	1.000
—Minnesota (A.L.)		2-S-DH-3-O	38	91	17	23	0	0	2	12	12	19	0	2	6-0	.253	.340	.319	.658	1	.991
American League totals (1 year)			38	91	17	23	0	0	2	12	12	19	0	2	6-0	.253	.340	.319	.658	1	.991
National League totals (3 years)			77	103	14	23	2	0	1	4	7	25	0	0	2-1	.223	.273	.272	.545	3	.972
Major League totals (4 years)			115	194	31	46	2	0	3	16	19	44	0	2	8-1	.237	.305	.294	.599	4	.981

PUTZ, J.J.   P

PERSONAL: Born February 22, 1977, in Trenton, Mich. ... 6-5/220. ... Throws right, bats right. ... Full name: Joseph Jason Putz. ... High school: Trenton (Mich.). ... College: Michigan.

TRANSACTIONS/CAREER NOTES: Selected by Chicago White Sox organization in third round of 1995 free-agent draft; did not sign. ... Selected by Minnesota Twins organization in 17th round of 1998 free-agent draft; did not sign. ... Selected by Seattle Mariners organization in sixth round of 1999 free-agent draft.

CAREER HITTING: 0-for-0 (.000), 0 R, 0 2B, 0 3B, 0 HR, 0 RBI.

Year	Team (League)	W	L	Pct.	ERA	WHIP	G	GS	CG	ShO	Hld.	Sv.-Opp.	IP	H	R	ER	HR	BB-IBB	SO	Avg.
1999—Everett (Northwest)	0	0	...	4.84	1.52	10	0	0	0		2-...	22.1	23	13	12	2	11-1	17	.288
2000—Wisconsin (Midw.)	12	6	.667	3.15	1.35	26	25	3	2		0-...	142.2	130	71	50	4	63-2	105	.247
2001—San Antonio (Texas)	7	9	.438	3.83	1.38	27	26	0	0		0-...	148.0	145	80	63	11	59-2	135	.259
2002—San Antonio (Texas)	3	10	.231	3.64	1.33	15	15	1	1		0-...	84.0	84	41	34	7	28-0	60	.264
—Tacoma (PCL)	2	4	.333	3.83	1.33	9	9	0	0		0-...	54.0	51	23	23	4	21-0	39	.258
2003—Tacoma (PCL)	0	3	.000	2.51	1.20	41	0	0	0		11-...	86.0	69	30	24	4	34-0	60	.225
—Seattle (A.L.)	0	0	...	4.91	1.91	3	0	0	0	0	0-0	3.2	4	2	2	0	3-0	3	.267
2004—Tacoma (PCL)	0	0	...	4.32	1.56	7	0	0	0		3-...	8.1	10	5	4	2	3-0	13	.278
—Seattle (A.L.)	0	3	.000	4.71	1.43	54	0	0	0	3	9-13	63.0	66	35	33	10	24-4	47	.274
Major League totals (2 years)	0	3	.000	4.73	1.46	57	0	0	0 /	3	9-13	66.2	70	37	35	10	27-4	50	.273

QUALLS, CHAD   P

PERSONAL: Born August 17, 1978, in Lomita, Calif. ... 6-5/220. ... Throws right, bats right. ... Full name: Chad Michael Qualls. ... High school: Narbonne (Harbor City, Calif.). ... College: Nevada.

TRANSACTIONS/CAREER NOTES: Selected by Toronto Blue Jays organization in 52nd round of 1997 free-agent draft; did not sign. ... Selected by Houston Astros organization in second round of 2000 free-agent draft.

CAREER HITTING: 0-for-1 (.000), 0 R, 0 2B, 0 3B, 0 HR, 0 RBI.

Year	Team (League)	W	L	Pct.	ERA	WHIP	G	GS	CG	ShO	Hld.	Sv.-Opp.	IP	H	R	ER	HR	BB-IBB	SO	Avg.
2001—Michigan (Midw.)	15	6	.714	3.72	1.11	26	26	3	2	...	0-...	162.0	149	77	67	8	31-0	125	.239
2002—Round Rock (Texas)	6	13	.316	4.36	1.48	29	29	0	0	...	0-...	163.0	174	92	79	8	67-3	142	.273
2003—Round Rock (Texas)	8	11	.421	3.85	1.34	28	28	3	2	...	0-...	175.1	174	85	75	12	61-0	132	.264
2004—New Orleans (PCL)	3	6	.333	5.57	1.54	32	14	1	0	...	1-...	106.2	134	69	66	8	30-3	72	.312
—Houston (N.L.)	4	0	1.000	3.55	1.27	25	0	0	0	9	1-2	33.0	34	13	13	3	8-1	24	.266
Major League totals (1 year)	4	0	1.000	3.55	1.27	25	0	0	0	9	1-2	33.0	34	13	13	3	8-1	24	.266

DIVISION SERIES RECORD

Year	Team (League)	W	L	Pct.	ERA	WHIP	G	GS	CG	ShO	Hld.	Sv.-Opp.	IP	H	R	ER	HR	BB-IBB	SO	Avg.
2004—Houston (N.L.)	0	0	...	6.75	1.25	4	0	0	0	1	0-1	4.0	4	3	3	1	1-0	3	.250

CHAMPIONSHIP SERIES RECORD

Year	Team (League)	W	L	Pct.	ERA	WHIP	G	GS	CG	ShO	Hld.	Sv.-Opp.	IP	H	R	ER	HR	BB-IBB	SO	Avg.
2004—Houston (N.L.)	0	1	.000	11.25	2.50	2	0	0	0		0-0	4.0	8	5	5	0	2-1	4	.444

QUANTRILL, PAUL   P

PERSONAL: Born November 3, 1968, in London, Ontario. ... 6-1/198. ... Throws right, bats left. ... Full name: Paul John Quantrill. ... Name pronounced: KWAN-trill. ... High school: Okemos (Mich.). ... College: Wisconsin.

TRANSACTIONS/CAREER NOTES: Selected by Los Angeles Dodgers organization in 26th round of June 1986 free-agent draft; did not sign. ... Selected by Boston Red Sox organization in sixth round of 1989 free-agent draft. ... Traded by Red Sox with OF Billy Hatcher to Philadelphia Phillies for OF Wes Chamberlain and P Mike Sullivan (May 31, 1994). ... Traded by Phillies to Toronto Blue Jays for 3B Howard Battle and P Ricardo Jordan (December 6, 1995). ... On disabled list (March 27-June 15, 1999); included rehabilitation assignments to Dunedin and Syracuse. ... Traded by Blue Jays with 2B/SS Cesar Izturis to Los Angeles Dodgers for Ps Luke Prokopec and Chad Ricketts (December 13, 2001). ... Signed as a free agent by New York Yankees (December 17, 2003).

CAREER HITTING: 7-for-66 (.106), 5 R, 0 2B, 0 3B, 0 HR, 0 RBI.

Year	Team (League)	W	L	Pct.	ERA	WHIP	G	GS	CG	ShO	Hld.	Sv.-Opp.	IP	H	R	ER	HR	BB-IBB	SO	Avg.
1989—GC Red Sox (GCL)	0	0	...	0.00	0.40	2	0	0	0	...	2-...	5.0	2	0	0	0	0-0	5	.111
—Elmira (N.Y.-Penn)	5	4	.556	3.43	1.34	20	7	5	0	...	2-...	76.0	90	37	29	5	12-2	57	.299
1990—Winter Haven (FSL)	2	5	.286	4.14	1.14	7	7	1	0	...	0-...	45.2	46	24	21	3	6-0	14	.264
—New Britain (East.)	7	11	.389	3.53	1.29	22	22	1	1	...	0-...	132.2	148	65	52	3	23-2	53	.290
1991—New Britain (East.)	2	1	.667	2.06	1.14	5	5	1	0	...	0-...	35.0	32	14	8	2	8-0	18	.248
—Pawtucket (Int'l)	10	7	.588	4.45	1.28	25	23	6	2	...	0-...	155.2	169	81	77	14	30-1	75	.282
1992—Pawtucket (Int'l)	6	8	.429	4.46	1.33	19	18	4	1	...	0-...	119.0	143	63	59	16	20-1	56	.300
—Boston (A.L.)	2	3	.400	2.19	1.42	27	0	0	0	3	1-5	49.1	55	18	12	1	15-5	24	.288
1993—Boston (A.L.)	6	12	.333	3.91	1.41	49	14	1	1	3	1-2	138.0	151	73	60	13	44-14	66	.279
1994—Boston (A.L.)	1	1	.500	3.52	1.30	17	0	0	0	2	0-2	23.0	25	10	9	4	5-1	15	.278
—Philadelphia (N.L.)	2	2	.500	6.00	1.63	18	1	0	0	1	1-2	30.0	39	21	20	3	10-3	13	.331
—Scran./W.B. (I.L.)	3	3	.500	3.47	1.07	8	8	1	1	...	0-...	57.0	55	25	22	5	6-0	36	.253
1995—Philadelphia (N.L.)	11	12	.478	4.67	1.43	33	29	0	0		0-0	179.1	212	102	93	20	44-3	103	.295

Year Team (League)	W	L	Pct.	ERA	WHIP	G	GS	CG	ShO	Hld.	Sv.-Opp.	IP	H	R	ER	HR	BB-IBB	SO	Avg.
1996— Toronto (A.L.)	5	14	.263	5.43	1.66	38	20	0	0	1	0-2	134.1	172	90	81	27	51-3	86	.317
1997— Toronto (A.L.)	6	7	.462	1.94	1.36	77	0	0	0	16	5-10	88.0	103	25	19	5	17-3	56	.297
1998— Toronto (A.L.)	3	4	.429	2.59	1.38	82	0	0	0	27	7-14	80.0	88	26	23	5	22-6	59	.285
1999— Dunedin (Fla. St.)	0	1	.000	4.50	1.00	5	4	0	0	...	0-...	6.0	5	3	3	1	1-0	2	.238
— Syracuse (Int'l)	0	0	...	0.00	0.50	2	0	0	0	...	0-...	2.0	1	0	0	0	0-0	1	.167
— Toronto (A.L.)	3	2	.600	3.33	1.44	41	0	0	0	8	0-4	48.2	53	19	18	5	17-1	28	.282
2000— Toronto (A.L.)	2	5	.286	4.52	1.49	68	0	0	0	13	1-3	83.2	100	45	42	7	25-1	47	.298
2001— Toronto (A.L.)	11	2	.846	3.04	1.18	80	0	0	0	21	2-9	83.0	86	29	28	6	12-7	58	.274
2002— Los Angeles (N.L.)	5	4	.556	2.70	1.37	86	0	0	0	33	1-3	76.2	80	27	23	1	25-7	53	.267
2003— Los Angeles (N.L.)	2	5	.286	1.75	0.98	* 89	0	0	0	28	1-5	77.1	61	18	15	2	15-2	44	.227
2004— New York (A.L.)	7	3	.700	4.72	1.51	* 86	0	0	0	22	1-5	95.1	124	54	50	5	20-9	37	.316
American League totals (10 years)	46	53	.465	3.74	1.44	565	34	1	1	116	18-56	823.1	957	389	342	78	228-50	476	.294
National League totals (4 years)	20	23	.465	3.74	1.34	226	30	0	0	62	3-10	363.1	392	168	151	26	94-15	213	.279
Major League totals (13 years)	66	76	.465	3.74	1.41	791	64	1	1	178	21-66	1186.2	1349	557	493	104	322-65	689	.290

DIVISION SERIES RECORD

Year Team (League)	W	L	Pct.	ERA	WHIP	G	GS	CG	ShO	Hld.	Sv.-Opp.	IP	H	R	ER	HR	BB-IBB	SO	Avg.
2004— New York (A.L.)	1	0	1.000	0.00	1.00	2	0	0	0	0	0-0	2.0	2	0	0	0	0-0	1	.250

CHAMPIONSHIP SERIES RECORD

Year Team (League)	W	L	Pct.	ERA	WHIP	G	GS	CG	ShO	Hld.	Sv.-Opp.	IP	H	R	ER	HR	BB-IBB	SO	Avg.
2004— New York (A.L.)	0	1	.000	5.40	2.40	4	0	0	0	0	0-0	3.1	8	2	2	1	0-0	2	.444

ALL-STAR GAME RECORD

	W	L	Pct.	ERA	WHIP	G	GS	CG	ShO	Hld.	Sv.-Opp.	IP	H	R	ER	HR	BB-IBB	SO	Avg.
All-Star Game totals (1 year)	0	0	...	27.00	6.00	1	0	0	0	1	0-0	.1	2	1	1	0	0-0	0	.667

QUINLAN, ROBB — 3B/1B

PERSONAL: Born March 17, 1977, in St. Paul, Minn. ... 6-1/200. ... Bats right, throws right. ... Full name: Robb William Quinlan. ... High school: Hill-Murray (Maplewood, Minnesota). ... Brother of Tom Quinlan, infielder with three major league teams (1990, 1992, 1994 and 1996).

TRANSACTIONS/CAREER NOTES: Selected by California Angels organization in 33rd round of 1995 free-agent draft; did not sign. ... Selected by Anaheim Angels organization in 10th round of 1999 free-agent draft. ... On disabled list (August 16, 2004-remainder of season).

2004 GAMES PLAYED BY POSITION (MLB): 3B—32, 1B—13, OF—9, DH—4.

Year Team (League)	Pos.	G	AB	R	H	2B	3B	HR	RBI	BB	SO	HBP	GDP	SB-CS	Avg.	OBP	SLG	OPS	E	Avg.
1999— Boise (N'west)	3B-2B-1B	73	295	51	95	20	1	9	77	35	52	4	5	5-3	.322	.400	.488	.888	27	.892
2000— Lake Elsinore (Calif.)	1B-OF	127	482	79	153	35	5	5	85	67	82	2	7	6-4	.317	.396	.442	.838	16	.986
2001— Arkansas (Texas)	1B-OF	129	492	82	145	33	7	14	79	53	84	6	12	0-4	.295	.366	.476	.841	8	.993
2002— Salt Lake (PCL)	OF-1B	136	528	95	176	31	13	20	112	41	93	4	16	8-2	.333	.376	.555	.931	3	.988
2003— Salt Lake (PCL)	1B-OF-DH	95	393	55	122	18	4	9	68	25	59	1	9	10-3	.310	.352	.445	.797	0	1.000
— Anaheim (A.L.)	1B-DH-OF	38	94	13	27	4	2	0	4	6	16	0	3	1-2	.287	.330	.372	.702	2	.988
2004— Salt Lake (PCL)	1B-3B-OF	27	108	15	32	9	1	2	17	14	14	0	2	1-1	.296	.377	.454	.831	3	.987
— Anaheim (A.L.)	3-1-O-DH	56	160	23	55	14	0	5	23	14	26	2	1	3-1	.344	.401	.525	.926	1	.994
Major League totals (2 years)		94	254	36	82	18	2	5	27	20	42	2	4	4-3	.323	.375	.469	.844	3	.991

QUINTERO, HUMBERTO — C

PERSONAL: Born August 8, 1979, in Maracaibo, Venezuela. ... 6-1/190. ... Bats right, throws right. ... High school: Andres Bello (Maracaibo, Venezuela).

TRANSACTIONS/CAREER NOTES: Signed as a non-drafted free agent by Chicago White Sox organization (January 16, 1997). ... Traded by White Sox with OF Alex Fernandez to San Diego Padres for IF D'Angelo Jimenez (July 12, 2002).

2004 GAMES PLAYED BY POSITION (MLB): C—21.

Year Team (League)	Pos.	G	AB	R	H	2B	3B	HR	RBI	BB	SO	HBP	GDP	SB-CS	Avg.	OBP	SLG	OPS	E	Avg.
1999— Bristol (Appal.)	C	48	155	30	43	5	2	0	15	9	11	6	8	11-1	.277	.341	.335	.677	6	.987
2000— Burlington (Midw.)	C	75	248	23	59	12	2	0	24	15	31	3	8	10-6	.238	.287	.302	.590	8	.986
— Ariz. White Sox (Ariz.)	C-OF	15	56	13	22	2	2	0	8	0	3	2	2	1-0	.393	.414	.500	.914	3	.976
2001— Kannapolis (S.Atl.)	C	60	197	32	53	7	1	1	20	8	20	7	5	7-3	.269	.321	.330	.651	7	.989
— Win.-Salem (Car.)	C	43	154	15	37	6	0	0	12	5	19	2	3	9-3	.240	.268	.279	.548	3	.992
— Birmingham (Sou.)	C	5	19	0	4	0	0	0	2	0	2	1	0	0-0	.211	.250	.211	.461	1	.971
2002— Birmingham (Sou.)	C	4	12	1	6	0	0	0	3	0	1	1	0	1-0	.500	.538	.500	1.038	0	1.000
— Charlotte (Int'l)	C	15	41	2	9	1	0	0	5	3	8	0	3	0-0	.220	.273	.244	.517	3	.964
— Win.-Salem (Car.)	C	52	160	15	31	1	1	0	12	8	23	4	4	2-3	.194	.247	.213	.460	4	.990
— Mobile (Sou.)	C	37	125	11	30	8	0	1	14	5	12	3	3	0-3	.240	.286	.328	.614	5	.983
2003— Mobile (Sou.)	C-DH	110	386	37	115	26	0	3	52	19	41	9	17	0-0	.298	.343	.389	.732	5	.995
— San Diego (N.L.)	C	12	23	1	5	0	0	0	2	1	6	0	0	0-0	.217	.250	.217	.467	1	.982
2004— Portland (PCL)	C-DH	68	259	36	82	25	0	5	30	8	18	5	7	0-0	.317	.348	.471	.819	6	.989
— San Diego (N.L.)	C	23	72	7	18	3	0	2	10	5	16	0	5	0-2	.250	.295	.375	.670	0	1.000
Major League totals (2 years)		35	95	8	23	3	0	2	12	6	22	0	5	0-2	.242	.284	.337	.621	1	.995

QUIROZ, GUILLERMO — C

PERSONAL: Born November 29, 1981, in Maracaibo, Venezuela. ... 6-1/202. ... Bats right, throws right. ... Full name: Guillermo Antonio Quiroz.

TRANSACTIONS/CAREER NOTES: Signed as non-drafted free agent by Toronto Blue Jays organization (September 25, 1998). ... Recalled by Toronto from New Haven (September 15, 2003).

2004 GAMES PLAYED BY POSITION (MLB): C—15, DH—2.

Year Team (League)	Pos.	G	AB	R	H	2B	3B	HR	RBI	BB	SO	HBP	GDP	SB-CS	Avg.	OBP	SLG	OPS	E	Avg.
1999— Medicine Hat (Pio.)	C	63	208	25	46	7	0	9	28	18	55	4	4	0-2	.221	.296	.385	.680	10	.981
2000— Hagerstown (SAL)	C	43	136	14	22	4	0	1	12	16	44	4	3	0-1	.162	.269	.213	.482	2	.994
— Queens (NY-P)	C	55	196	27	44	9	0	5	29	27	48	4	4	1-2	.224	.329	.347	.676	7	.987
2001— Char., W.Va. (SAL)	C	82	261	25	52	12	0	7	25	29	67	6	5	5-1	.199	.294	.326	.620	9	.986

Year Team (League)	Pos.	G	AB	R	H	2B	3B	HR	RBI	BB	SO	HBP	GDP	SB-CS	Avg.	OBP	SLG	OPS	E	Avg.
2002— Dunedin (Fla. St.)	C	111	411	50	107	28	1	12	68	35	91	9	18	1-0	.260	.330	.421	.751	11	.984
— Syracuse (Int'l)	C	13	45	7	10	4	0	1	6	3	14	0	1	0-0	.222	.271	.378	.649	2	.956
2003— New Haven (East.)	C	108	369	63	104	27	0	20	79	45	83	12	13	0-0	.282	.372	.518	.889	4	.994
2004— Syracuse (Int'l)	C-DH	76	255	32	58	19	1	8	32	28	54	3	8	0-0	.227	.309	.404	.706	3	.994
— Toronto (A.L.)	C-DH	17	52	2	11	2	0	0	6	2	8	2	1	1-0	.212	.263	.250	.513	2	.976
Major League totals (1 year)		17	52	2	11	2	0	0	6	2	8	2	1	1-0	.212	.263	.250	.513	2	.976

RABURN, RYAN   3B

PERSONAL: Born April 17, 1981, in Tampa, Fla. ... 6-0/185. ... Bats right, throws right. ... Full name: Ryan N. Raburn. ... High school: Durant (Plant City, Fla.). ... Junior college: South Florida Community College.

TRANSACTIONS/CAREER NOTES: Selected by Tampa Bay Devil Rays organization in 18th round of 1999 free-agent draft; did not sign. ... Selected by Detroit Tigers organization in fifth round of 2001 free-agent draft.

2004 GAMES PLAYED BY POSITION (MLB): 2B—11.

Year Team (League)	Pos.	G	AB	R	H	2B	3B	HR	RBI	BB	SO	HBP	GDP	SB-CS	Avg.	OBP	SLG	OPS	E	Avg.
2001— GC Tigers (GCL)	3B	19	58	4	9	2	0	1	5	9	19	3	0	2-1	.155	.300	.241	.541	1	.960
— Oneonta (N.Y.-Penn.)	3B-2B	44	171	25	62	17	8	8	42	17	42	0	7	1-3	.363	.418	.696	1.114	23	.798
2002— GC Tigers (GCL)	3B	8	30	4	9	3	1	1	5	3	7	0	2	0-0	.300	.364	.567	.930	3	.833
— W. Mich. (Mid.)	3B	40	150	27	33	10	1	6	28	16	46	4	2	0-2	.220	.306	.420	.726	12	.786
2003— W. Mich. (Mid.)	3B	16	57	14	20	7	0	3	12	6	14	2	0	1-1	.351	.431	.632	1.062	2	.889
— Lakeland (Fla. St.)	3B	95	325	52	72	14	3	12	56	45	89	10	5	2-1	.222	.332	.394	.726	21	.911
2004— Lakeland (Fla. St.)	2B	3	11	1	3	1	0	1	3	1	6	0	0	0-0	.273	.333	.636	.970	4	.810
— Erie (East.)	2B-DH	98	366	66	110	29	4	16	63	47	96	7	9	3-0	.301	.390	.533	.912	26	.950
— Detroit (A.L.)	2B	12	29	4	4	1	0	0	1	2	15	0	0	1-0	.138	.194	.172	.366	1	.969
Major League totals (1 year)		12	29	4	4	1	0	0	1	2	15	0	0	1-0	.138	.194	.172	.366	1	.969

RADKE, BRAD   P

PERSONAL: Born October 27, 1972, in Eau Claire, Wis. ... 6-2/184. ... Throws right, bats right. ... Full name: Brad William Radke. ... Name pronounced: RAD-key. ... High school: Jesuit (Tampa).

TRANSACTIONS/CAREER NOTES: Selected by Minnesota Twins organization in eighth round of 1991 free-agent draft. ... On disabled list (August 4-21, 2001). ... On disabled list (May 14-30 and May 31-August 3, 2002); included rehabilitation assignments to GCL Twins and Fort Myers. ... On suspended list (May 17-23, 2003).

CAREER HITTING: 3-for-23 (.130), 0 R, 0 2B, 0 3B, 0 HR, 0 RBI.

Year Team (League)	W	L	Pct.	ERA	WHIP	G	GS	CG	ShO	Hld.	Sv.-Opp.	IP	H	R	ER	HR	BB-IBB	SO	Avg.
1991— GC Twins (GCL)	3	4	.429	3.08	1.11	10	9	1	0	...	1-...	49.2	41	21	17	0	14-0	46	.220
1992— Kenosha (Midw.)	10	10	.500	2.93	1.18	26	25	4	1	...	0-...	165.2	149	70	54	8	47-1	127	.243
1993— Fort Myers (Fla. St.)	3	5	.375	3.82	1.15	14	14	0	0	...	0-...	92.0	85	42	39	3	21-1	69	.243
— Nashville (Sou.)	2	6	.250	4.62	1.28	13	13	1	0	...	0-...	76.0	81	42	39	6	16-0	76	.267
1994— Nashville (Sou.)	12	9	.571	2.66	1.08	29	28	5	1	...	0-...	186.1	167	66	55	9	34-0	123	.240
1995— Minnesota (A.L.)	11	14	.440	5.32	1.34	29	28	2	1	0	0-0	181.0	195	112	107	* 32	47-0	75	.275
1996— Minnesota (A.L.)	11	16	.407	4.46	1.24	35	35	3	0	0	0-0	232.0	231	125	115	40	57-2	148	.256
1997— Minnesota (A.L.)	20	10	.667	3.87	1.19	35	* 35	4	1	0	0-0	239.2	238	114	103	28	48-1	174	.257
1998— Minnesota (A.L.)	12	14	.462	4.30	1.32	32	32	5	1	0	0-0	213.2	238	109	102	23	43-1	146	.283
1999— Minnesota (A.L.)	12	14	.462	3.75	1.29	33	33	4	0	0	0-0	218.2	239	97	91	28	44-0	121	.280
2000— Minnesota (A.L.)	12	* 16	.429	4.45	1.38	34	34	3	1	0	0-0	226.2	261	119	112	27	51-1	141	.287
2001— Minnesota (A.L.)	15	11	.577	3.94	1.15	33	33	6	2	0	0-0	226.0	235	105	99	24	26-0	137	.271
2002— Minnesota (A.L.)	9	5	.643	4.72	1.22	21	21	2	1	0	0-0	118.1	124	64	62	12	20-0	62	.272
— GC Twins (GCL)	0	0	...	0.00	0.67	1	1	0	0	...	0-...	3.0	2	0	0	0	0-0	4	.182
— Fort Myers (Fla. St.)	0	1	.000	3.12	1.27	2	2	0	0	...	0-...	8.2	11	6	3	1	0-0	6	.289
2003— Minnesota (A.L.)	14	10	.583	4.49	1.27	33	33	3	1	0	0-0	212.1	242	111	106	32	28-2	120	.288
2004— Minnesota (A.L.)	11	8	.579	3.48	1.16	34	34	1	1	0	0-0	219.2	229	92	85	23	26-1	143	.267
Major League totals (10 years)	127	118	.518	4.23	1.26	319	318	34	9	0	0-0	2088.0	2232	1048	982	269	390-8	1267	.273

DIVISION SERIES RECORD

Year Team (League)	W	L	Pct.	ERA	WHIP	G	GS	CG	ShO	Hld.	Sv.-Opp.	IP	H	R	ER	HR	BB-IBB	SO	Avg.
2002— Minnesota (A.L.)	2	0	1.000	1.54	1.29	2	2	0	0	0	0-0	11.2	14	6	2	1	1-0	7	.280
2003— Minnesota (A.L.)	0	1	.000	2.84	1.11	1	1	0	0	0	0-0	6.1	5	2	2	0	2-0	4	.227
2004— Minnesota (A.L.)	0	0	...	7.11	1.74	1	1	0	0	0	0-0	6.1	8	5	5	3	3-0	0	.320
Division series totals (3 years)	2	1	.667	3.33	1.36	4	4	0	0	0	0-0	24.1	27	13	9	4	6-0	11	.278

CHAMPIONSHIP SERIES RECORD

Year Team (League)	W	L	Pct.	ERA	WHIP	G	GS	CG	ShO	Hld.	Sv.-Opp.	IP	H	R	ER	HR	BB-IBB	SO	Avg.
2002— Minnesota (A.L.)	0	1	.000	2.70	0.90	1	1	0	0	0	0-0	6.2	5	2	2	0	1-0	4	.217

ALL-STAR GAME RECORD

	W	L	Pct.	ERA	WHIP	G	GS	CG	ShO	Hld.	Sv.-Opp.	IP	H	R	ER	HR	BB-IBB	SO	Avg.
All-Star Game totals (1 year)	0	0	...	9.00	3.00	1	0	0	0	...	0-0	1.0	2	1	1	0	1-0	1	.400

RAINES JR., TIM   OF

PERSONAL: Born August 31, 1979, in Memphis, Tenn. ... 5-10/190. ... Bats right, throws right. ... Full name: Timothy Raines Jr.. ... High school: Seminole (Sanford, Fla.). ... Son of Tim Raines, coach, Chicago White Sox, and outfielder with five major league teams (1979-99 and 2001).

TRANSACTIONS/CAREER NOTES: Selected by Baltimore Orioles organization in sixth round of 1998 free-agent draft.

2004 GAMES PLAYED BY POSITION (MLB): OF—38, DH—4.

Year Team (League)	Pos.	G	AB	R	H	2B	3B	HR	RBI	BB	SO	HBP	GDP	SB-CS	Avg.	OBP	SLG	OPS	E	Avg.
1998— GC Orioles (GCL)	OF	56	197	40	48	7	4	1	13	30	53	12	0	37-4	.244	.377	.335	.712	3	.978
1999— Delmarva (S. Atl.)	OF	117	415	80	103	24	8	2	49	71	130	13	1	49-16	.248	.359	.359	.718	10	.961
2000— Frederick (Carolina)	OF	127	457	89	108	21	3	2	36	67	106	13	8	81-19	.236	.348	.309	.657	9	.972
2001— Frederick (Carolina)	OF	23	84	15	21	3	1	3	13	13	23	0	4	14-4	.250	.351	.417	.767	1	.976
— Bowie (East.)	OF	65	254	46	74	14	1	4	30	34	60	3	3	29-10	.291	.380	.402	.782	4	.976
— Rochester (Int'l)	OF	40	133	19	34	5	1	2	12	11	30	0	2	11-3	.256	.313	.353	.666	1	.986

Year	Team (League)	Pos.	G	AB	R	H	2B	3B	HR	RBI	BB	SO	HBP	GDP	SB-CS	Avg.	OBP	SLG	OPS	E	Avg.
—Baltimore (A.L.)	OF	7	23	6	4	2	0	0	0	3	8	0	0	3-0	.174	.269	.261	.530	0	1.000
2002—Bowie (East.)	OF	123	491	66	128	17	4	5	25	34	101	2	8	33-15	.261	.310	.342	.652	6	.978
2003—Bowie (East.)	OF-DH	66	247	44	76	15	4	4	26	21	40	5	3	28-6	.308	.371	.449	.820	3	.976
—Ottawa (Int'l)	OF	52	214	37	64	11	5	3	23	19	37	1	3	23-9	.299	.357	.439	.797	1	.993
—Baltimore (A.L.)	OF-DH	20	43	4	6	1	1	0	2	2	12	1	2	0-0	.140	.196	.209	.405	1	.974
2004—Ottawa (Int'l)	OF	72	267	32	70	13	1	1	23	18	69	5	4	24-7	.262	.314	.330	.644	3	.982
—Baltimore (A.L.)	OF-DH	48	94	14	24	6	0	0	5	4	16	1	2	7-3	.255	.293	.319	.612	0	1.000
Major League totals (3 years)		75	160	24	34	9	1	0	7	9	36	2	4	10-3	.213	.263	.281	.544	1	.991

RAKERS, AARON   P

PERSONAL: Born January 22, 1977, in Highland, Ill. ... 6-3/205. ... Throws right, bats right. ... Full name: Aaron James Rakers. ... Name pronounced: Rockers. ... High school: Wesclin (Trenton, Ill.). ... College: SIU-Edwardsville.

TRANSACTIONS/CAREER NOTES: Selected by Baltimore Orioles organzation in 23rd round of 1999 free-agent draft.

CAREER HITTING: 0-for-0 (.000), 0 R, 0 2B, 0 3B, 0 HR, 0 RBI.

Year	Team (League)	W	L	Pct.	ERA	WHIP	G	GS	CG	ShO	Hld.	Sv.-Opp.	IP	H	R	ER	HR	BB-IBB	SO	Avg.
1999—Bluefield (Appalachian)	0	0	...	2.57	1.14	3	0	0	0	...	0-...	7.0	5	2	2	1	3-0	12	.200
—Delmarva (S.Atl.)	4	1	.800	1.42	0.87	18	0	0	0	...	8-...	25.1	9	6	4	0	13-0	38	.108
2000—Frederick (Caro.)	1	1	.500	1.55	0.86	26	0	0	0	...	8-...	40.2	23	8	7	2	12-1	57	.163
—Bowie (East.)	3	2	.600	2.79	1.03	24	0	0	0	...	8-...	29.0	20	11	9	5	10-0	21	.194
2001—Bowie (East.)	4	4	.500	2.39	1.21	51	0	0	0	...	14-...	60.1	53	21	16	8	20-1	74	.227
2002—Bowie (East.)	5	1	.833	2.06	1.06	36	0	0	0	...	10-...	48.0	39	12	11	3	12-2	45	.232
2003—Bowie (East.)	5	0	1.000	2.75	1.17	31	0	0	0	...	8-...	39.1	27	12	12	7	19-1	42	.196
—Ottawa (Int'l)	2	4	.333	5.13	1.14	21	0	0	0	...	1-...	26.1	19	18	15	1	11-2	26	.202
2004—Ottawa (Int'l)	4	5	.444	2.75	1.14	54	1	0	0	...	1-...	78.2	65	27	24	8	25-4	80	.229
—Baltimore (A.L.)	0	0	...	4.15	1.38	3	0	0	0	0	0-0	4.1	5	2	2	0	1-0	3	.278
Major League totals (1 year)	0	0	...	4.15	1.38	3	0	0	0	0	0-0	4.1	5	2	2	0	1-0	3	.278

RAMIREZ, ARAMIS   3B

PERSONAL: Born June 25, 1978, in Santo Domingo, Dominican Republic. ... 6-1/215. ... Bats right, throws right. ... Full name: Aramis Nin Ramirez. ... Name pronounced: ah-RAH-mis.

TRANSACTIONS/CAREER NOTES: Signed as a non-drafted free agent by Pittsburgh Pirates organization (November 7, 1994). ... On suspended list (July 24-29, 1998). ... On disabled list (August 10-September 4, 1998); included rehabilitation assignment to Nashville. ... On disabled list (August 29, 2000-remainder of season). ... Traded by Pirates with OF Kenny Lofton to Chicago Cubs for IF Jose Hernandez, P Matt Bruback and a player to be named (July 23, 2003); Pirates acquired IF Bobby Hill to complete deal (August 15, 2003).

2004 GAMES PLAYED BY POSITION (MLB): 3B—144.

Year	Team (League)	Pos.	G	AB	R	H	2B	3B	HR	RBI	BB	SO	HBP	GDP	SB-CS	Avg.	OBP	SLG	OPS	E	Avg.
																	BATTING			FIELDING	
1995—Dom. Pirates (DSL)	3B	64	214	41	63	13	0	11	54	42	26	...	...	2-...	.294	...	.509	...	19	.886
1996—Erie (N.Y.-Penn)	3B	61	223	37	68	14	4	9	42	31	41	7	7	0-0	.305	.403	.525	.928	17	.896
—Augusta (S. Atl.)	3B	6	20	3	4	1	0	1	2	1	7	2	0	0-2	.200	.304	.400	.704	2	.833
1997—Lynchburg (Caro.)	3B	137	482	85	134	24	2	29	114	80	103	12	12	5-3	.278	.390	.517	.907	39	.897
1998—Nashville (PCL) 3B-SS-DH	47	168	19	46	10	0	5	18	24	28	4	3	0-2	.274	.374	.423	.796	8	.932
—Pittsburgh (N.L.)	3B	72	251	23	59	9	1	6	24	18	72	4	3	0-1	.235	.296	.351	.646	9	.941
1999—Nashville (PCL)	3B	131	460	92	151	35	1	21	74	73	56	9	11	5-3	.328	.425	.546	.971	42	.884
—Pittsburgh (N.L.)	3B	18	56	2	10	2	1	0	7	6	9	0	0	0-0	.179	.254	.250	.504	3	.930
2000—Pittsburgh (N.L.)	3B	73	254	19	65	15	2	6	35	10	36	5	9	0-0	.256	.293	.402	.695	14	.917
—Nashville (PCL)	3B	44	167	28	59	12	2	4	26	11	26	4	5	2-1	.353	.407	.521	.928	9	.930
2001—Pittsburgh (N.L.)	3B	158	603	83	181	40	4	34	112	40	100	8	9	5-4	.300	.350	.536	.885	25	.945
2002—Pittsburgh (N.L.) 3B-DH	142	522	51	122	26	0	18	71	29	95	8	17	2-0	.234	.279	.387	.666	19	.946
2003—Pittsburgh (N.L.)	3B	96	375	44	105	25	1	12	67	25	68	7	17	1-1	.280	.330	.448	.778	23	.924
—Chicago (N.L.)	3B	63	232	31	60	7	1	15	39	17	31	3	4	1-1	.259	.314	.491	.805	10	.939
2004—Chicago (N.L.)	3B	145	547	99	174	32	1	36	103	49	62	3	25	0-2	.318	.373	.578	.951	10	.969
Major League totals (7 years)		767	2840	352	776	156	7	127	458	194	473	38	84	9-9	.273	.324	.467	.791	113	.942

DIVISION SERIES RECORD

Year	Team (League)	Pos.	G	AB	R	H	2B	3B	HR	RBI	BB	SO	HBP	GDP	SB-CS	Avg.	OBP	SLG	OPS	E	Avg.
2003—Chicago (N.L.)	3B	5	18	2	5	1	0	1	3	2	2	0	1	0-0	.278	.350	.500	.850	0	1.000

CHAMPIONSHIP SERIES RECORD

Year	Team (League)	Pos.	G	AB	R	H	2B	3B	HR	RBI	BB	SO	HBP	GDP	SB-CS	Avg.	OBP	SLG	OPS	E	Avg.
2003—Chicago (N.L.)	3B	7	26	4	6	0	1	3	7	5	6	1	1	0-0	.231	.375	.654	1.029	0	1.000

RAMIREZ, ELIZARDO   P

PERSONAL: Born January 28, 1983, in Villa Mella, Dominican Republic. ... 6-0/180. ... Throws right, bats both. ... High school: Liceo Pedregal (D.R.).

TRANSACTIONS/CAREER NOTES: Signed as a non-drafted free agent by Philadelphia Phillies organization (July 2, 1999). ... Traded by Phillies to Cincinnati Reds (August 11, 2004) to complete deal in which Phillies acquired P Cory Lidle from Reds for OF Javon Moran, P Joe Wilson and a player to be named (August 9, 2004).

CAREER HITTING: 0-for-0 (.000), 0 R, 0 2B, 0 3B, 0 HR, 0 RBI.

Year	Team (League)	W	L	Pct.	ERA	WHIP	G	GS	CG	ShO	Hld.	Sv.-Opp.	IP	H	R	ER	HR	BB-IBB	SO	Avg.
2002—GC Phillies (GCL)	7	1	.875	1.10	0.63	11	11	2	1	...	0-...	73.1	44	18	9	3	2-0	73	.165
2003—Clearwater (Fla. St.)	13	9	.591	3.78	1.36	27	25	1	0	...	0-...	157.1	181	85	66	4	33-0	101	.290
2004—Clearwater (Fla. St.)	5	1	.833	2.44	1.07	9	9	1	0	...	0-...	59.0	55	17	16	3	8-0	33	.249
—Philadelphia (N.L.)	0	0	...	4.80	1.47	7	0	0	0	0	0-0	15.0	17	8	8	3	5-1	9	.283
—Reading (East.)	2	5	.286	6.68	1.93	8	8	1	0	...	0-...	33.2	51	34	25	4	14-1	20	.345
—Chattanooga (Southern)	1	0	1.000	3.19	1.26	5	5	1	1	...	0-...	31.0	35	11	11	6	4-1	23	.282
Major League totals (1 year)	0	0	...	4.80	1.47	7	0	0	0	0	0-0	15.0	17	8	8	3	5-1	9	.283

RAMIREZ, ERASMO   P

PERSONAL: Born April 29, 1976, in Santa Ana, Calif. ... 6-0/190. ... Throws left, bats left. ... High school: Saddleback (Calif.). ... College: Cal State Fullerton.

TRANSACTIONS/CAREER NOTES: Selected by San Francisco Giants organization in 11th round of 1998 free-agent draft. ... Traded by Giants with P Todd Ozias and OF Chris Magruder to Texas Rangers for 1B Andres Galarraga (July 24, 2001). ... On disabled list (August 17-September 1, 2004).

CAREER HITTING: 0-for-0 (.000), 0 R, 0 2B, 0 3B, 0 HR, 0 RBI.

Year Team (League)	W	L	Pct.	ERA	WHIP	G	GS	CG	ShO	Hld.	Sv.-Opp.	IP	H	R	ER	HR	BB-IBB	SO	Avg.
1998—Bakersfield (California)	1	1	.500	3.38	0.75	14	0	0	0	...	3-...	21.1	10	8	8	0	6-0	17	.143
—Salem-Keizer (N'west)	0	1	.000	3.72	1.09	9	2	0	0	...	0-...	19.1	19	11	8	3	2-0	23	.247
1999—San Jose (California)	2	0	1.000	2.67	0.87	31	0	0	0	...	5-...	57.1	42	18	17	2	8-0	52	.206
2000—Shreveport (Texas)	0	5	.000	6.44	1.72	39	2	0	0	...	1-...	58.2	80	45	42	7	21-5	46	.340
2001—San Jose (California)	3	2	.600	3.41	0.88	17	0	0	0	...	1-...	31.2	23	14	12	2	5-0	33	.193
—Shreveport (Texas)	2	0	1.000	2.16	0.90	22	1	0	0	...	1-...	33.1	25	10	8	1	5-0	39	.205
—Tulsa (Texas)	2	1	.667	4.41	1.35	12	0	0	0	...	0-...	16.1	17	8	8	3	5-0	18	.270
2002—Tulsa (Texas)	4	2	.667	3.00	1.09	34	0	0	0	...	2-...	54.0	51	23	18	1	8-0	34	.254
—Oklahoma (PCL)	4	1	.800	1.29	0.90	25	0	0	0	...	1-...	21.0	15	5	3	0	4-1	17	.195
2003—Frisco (Texas)	1	0	1.000	6.00	1.67	3	0	0	0	...	0-...	3.0	4	2	2	1	1-0	4	.286
—Oklahoma (PCL)	2	1	.667	1.53	1.08	22	0	0	0	...	4-...	35.1	36	8	6	0	2-0	20	.257
—Texas (A.L.)	3	1	.750	3.86	1.12	34	0	0	0	2	0-1	49.0	46	21	21	4	9-0	28	.251
2004—Oklahoma (PCL)	1	0	1.000	6.16	1.42	14	0	0	0	...	0-...	19.0	23	15	13	2	4-1	9	.299
—Texas (A.L.)	5	3	.625	4.29	1.15	34	0	0	0	3	0-2	35.2	34	19	17	5	7-1	21	.252
Major League totals (2 years)	8	4	.667	4.04	1.13	68	0	0	0	5	0-3	84.2	80	40	38	9	16-1	49	.252

RAMIREZ, HORACIO — P

PERSONAL: Born November 24, 1979, in Carson, Calif. ... 6-1/219. ... Throws left, bats left. ... High school: Inglewood (Calif.).
TRANSACTIONS/CAREER NOTES: Selected by Atlanta Braves organization in fifth round of 1997 free-agent draft. ... On disabled list (March 22-June 18, 2002); included rehabilitation assignment to Macon and Greenville. ... On disabled list (May 26-September 25, 2004); included rehabilitation assignment to Greenville.
CAREER HITTING: 8-for-82 (.098), 3 R, 0 2B, 1 3B, 0 HR, 3 RBI.

Year Team (League)	W	L	Pct.	ERA	WHIP	G	GS	CG	ShO	Hld.	Sv.-Opp.	IP	H	R	ER	HR	BB-IBB	SO	Avg.
1997—GC Braves (GCL)	3	3	.500	2.25	1.09	11	8	0	0	...	0-...	44.0	30	13	11	1	18-0	61	.192
1998—Macon (S. Atl.)	1	7	.125	5.86	1.55	12	12	0	0	...	0-...	55.1	70	50	36	8	16-0	38	.310
—Eugene (N'west)	2	7	.222	6.31	1.81	16	8	0	0	...	0-...	55.2	84	51	39	4	17-0	39	.346
1999—Macon (S. Atl.)	6	3	.667	2.67	1.22	17	14	1	1	...	0-...	77.2	70	30	23	6	25-0	43	.248
2000—Myrtle Beach (Caro.)	15	8	.652	3.22	1.20	27	26	3	2	...	0-...	148.1	136	57	53	14	42-0	125	.242
2001—Greenville (Sou.)	1	1	.500	4.91	1.70	3	3	0	0	...	0-...	14.2	17	8	8	2	8-0	17	.309
2002—Macon (S. Atl.)	0	2	.000	6.00	2.17	2	1	0	0	...	0-...	6.0	11	10	4	0	2-0	5	.355
—Greenville (Sou.)	9	5	.643	3.03	1.27	16	16	0	0	...	0-...	92.0	85	41	31	5	32-0	64	.253
2003—Atlanta (N.L.)	12	4	.750	4.00	1.39	29	29	1	0	0	0-0	182.1	181	91	81	21	72-10	100	.263
2004—Greenville (Sou.)	2	0	1.000	3.09	1.54	3	2	0	0	...	0-...	11.2	15	4	4	0	3-0	2	.349
—Richmond (Int'l)	0	0	...	8.00	1.78	2	2	0	0	...	0-...	9.0	15	8	8	1	1-0	3	.385
—Atlanta (N.L.)	2	4	.333	2.39	1.34	10	9	1	0	0	0-0	60.1	51	24	16	7	30-5	31	.226
Major League totals (2 years)	14	8	.636	3.60	1.38	39	38	2	0	0	0-0	242.2	232	115	97	28	102-15	131	.254

RAMIREZ, MANNY — OF

PERSONAL: Born May 30, 1972, in Santo Domingo, Dominican Republic. ... 6-0/213. ... Bats right, throws right. ... Full name: Manuel Aristides Ramirez. ... Name pronounced: ruh-MEER-ez. ... High school: George Washington (New York).
TRANSACTIONS/CAREER NOTES: Selected by Cleveland Indians organization in first round (13th pick overall) of 1991 free-agent draft. ... On suspended list (June 8-11, 1999). ... On disabled list (May 30-July 13, 2000); included rehabilitation assignments to Akron and Buffalo. ... Signed as a free agent by Boston Red Sox (December 13, 2000). ... On disabled list (May 14-June 25, 2002); included rehabilitation assignment to Pawtucket.
2004 GAMES PLAYED BY POSITION (MLB): OF—132, DH—19.

Year Team (League)	Pos.	G	AB	R	H	2B	3B	HR	RBI	BB	SO	HBP	GDP	SB-CS	Avg.	OBP	SLG	OPS	E	Avg.
1991—Burlington (Appal.)	OF	59	215	44	70	11	4	19	63	34	41	6	4	7-8	.326	.426	.679	1.105	3	.966
1992—Kinston (Caro.)	OF	81	291	52	81	18	4	13	63	45	74	4	9	1-3	.278	.379	.502	.881	6	.967
1993—Cant./Akr. (Eastern)	OF	89	344	67	117	32	0	17	79	45	68	2	11	2-2	.340	.414	.581	.996	5	.967
—Charlotte (Int'l)	OF	40	145	38	46	12	0	14	36	27	35	2	1	1-1	.317	.424	.690	1.113	3	.961
—Cleveland (A.L.)	DH-OF	22	53	5	9	1	0	2	5	2	8	0	3	0-0	.170	.200	.302	.502	0	1.000
1994—Cleveland (A.L.)	OF-DH	91	290	51	78	22	0	17	60	42	72	0	6	4-2	.269	.357	.521	.878	1	.994
1995—Cleveland (A.L.)	OF-DH	137	484	85	149	26	1	31	107	75	112	5	13	6-6	.308	.402	.558	.960	5	.978
1996—Cleveland (A.L.)	OF-DH	152	550	94	170	45	3	33	112	85	104	3	18	8-5	.309	.399	.582	.981	9	.970
1997—Cleveland (A.L.)	OF-DH	150	561	99	184	40	0	26	88	79	115	7	19	2-3	.328	.415	.538	.953	7	.975
1998—Cleveland (A.L.)	OF-DH	150	571	108	168	35	2	45	145	76	121	6	18	5-3	.294	.377	.599	.976	7	.977
1999—Cleveland (A.L.)	OF-DH	147	522	131	174	34	3	44	*165	96	131	13	12	2-4	.333	.442	*.663	1.105	7	.975
2000—Cleveland (A.L.)	OF-DH	118	439	92	154	34	2	38	122	86	117	3	9	1-1	.351	.457	*.697	1.154	2	.986
—Akron (East.)	DH	1	2	1	1	0	0	1	2	1	0	0	0	0-0	.500	.750	2.000	2.750	...	...
—Buffalo (Int'l)	DH	5	11	5	5	1	0	3	7	6	1	0	1	0-0	.455	.647	1.364	2.011	...	...
2001—Boston (A.L.)	DH-OF	142	529	93	162	33	2	41	125	81	147	8	9	0-1	*.306	.405	.609	1.014	0	1.000
2002—Boston (A.L.)	OF-DH	120	436	84	152	31	0	33	107	73	85	8	13	0-0	*.349	*.450	.647	1.097	5	.959
—Pawtucket (Int'l)	OF	11	30	2	3	1	0	1	2	8	9	1	1	0-0	.100	.308	.233	.541	0	1.000
2003—Boston (A.L.)	OF-DH	154	569	117	185	36	1	37	104	97	94	6	22	3-1	.325	*.427	.587	1.014	4	.982
2004—Boston (A.L.)	OF-DH	152	568	108	175	44	0	*43	130	82	124	6	17	2-4	.308	.397	*.613	1.009	7	.967
Major League totals (12 years)		1535	5572	1067	1760	381	14	390	1270	874	1230	67	159	33-30	.316	.411	.599	1.010	54	.977

DIVISION SERIES RECORD

Year Team (League)	Pos.	G	AB	R	H	2B	3B	HR	RBI	BB	SO	HBP	GDP	SB-CS	Avg.	OBP	SLG	OPS	E	Avg.
1995—Cleveland (A.L.)	OF	3	12	1	0	0	0	0	0	1	2	1	0	0-0	.000	.143	.000	.143	0	1.000
1996—Cleveland (A.L.)	OF	4	16	4	6	2	0	2	2	1	4	0	1	0-0	.375	.412	.875	1.287	0	1.000
1997—Cleveland (A.L.)	OF	5	21	2	3	1	0	0	3	0	3	0	2	0-0	.143	.143	.190	.333	1	.750
1998—Cleveland (A.L.)	OF	4	14	2	5	2	0	2	4	1	4	2	0	0-0	.357	.471	.929	1.399	0	1.000
1999—Cleveland (A.L.)	OF	5	18	5	1	1	0	0	1	4	8	1	0	0-0	.056	.261	.111	.372	0	1.000
2003—Boston (A.L.)	OF	5	20	2	4	0	0	1	3	3	7	0	0	0-0	.200	.304	.350	.654	0	1.000
2004—Boston (A.L.)	OF	3	13	3	5	2	0	1	7	1	4	0	0	0-0	.385	.385	.769	1.144	0	1.000
Division series totals (7 years)		29	114	19	24	8	0	6	19	11	32	4	3	0-0	.211	.298	.439	.736	1	.977

CHAMPIONSHIP SERIES RECORD

Year Team (League)	Pos.	G	AB	R	H	2B	3B	HR	RBI	BB	SO	HBP	GDP	SB-CS	Avg.	OBP	SLG	OPS	E	Avg.
1995—Cleveland (A.L.)	OF	6	21	2	6	0	0	2	2	2	5	0	1	0-0	.286	.348	.571	.919	0	1.000
1997—Cleveland (A.L.)	OF	6	21	3	6	1	0	2	3	5	5	1	1	0-0	.286	.444	.619	1.063	1	.933

R

Year Team (League)	Pos.	G	AB	R	H	2B	3B	HR	RBI	BB	SO	HBP	GDP	SB-CS	Avg.	OBP	SLG	OPS	E	Avg.
1998— Cleveland (A.L.)	OF	6	21	2	7	1	0	2	4	4	9	0	1	0-0	.333	.423	.667	1.090	0	1.000
2003— Boston (A.L.)	OF	7	29	6	9	1	0	2	4	1	4	0	2	0-1	.310	.333	.552	.885	0	1.000
2004— Boston (A.L.)	OF	7	30	3	9	1	0	0	0	5	4	0	1	0-0	.300	.400	.333	.733	1	.947
Champ. series totals (5 years)		32	122	16	37	4	0	8	13	17	27	1	6	0-1	.303	.390	.533	.923	2	.971

WORLD SERIES RECORD

Year Team (League)	Pos.	G	AB	R	H	2B	3B	HR	RBI	BB	SO	HBP	GDP	SB-CS	Avg.	OBP	SLG	OPS	E	Avg.
1995— Cleveland (A.L.)	OF	6	18	2	4	0	0	1	2	4	5	0	1	1-0	.222	.364	.389	.753	0	1.000
1997— Cleveland (A.L.)	OF	7	26	3	4	0	0	2	6	6	5	0	2	0-0	.154	.294	.385	.679	1	.944
2004— Boston (A.L.)	OF	4	17	2	7	0	0	1	4	3	3	0	0	0-0	.412	.500	.588	1.088	2	.750
World series totals (3 years)		17	61	7	15	0	0	4	12	13	13	0	3	1-0	.246	.368	.443	.811	3	.912

ALL-STAR GAME RECORD

		G	AB	R	H	2B	3B	HR	RBI	BB	SO	HBP	GDP	SB-CS	Avg.	OBP	SLG	OPS	E	Avg.
All-Star Game totals (6 years)		6	7	2	3	0	1	4	3	2	0	0	0	0-0	.429	.545	.857	1.403	0	1.000

R

RANDA, JOE   3B

PERSONAL: Born December 18, 1969, in Milwaukee, Wis. ... 5-11/190. ... Bats right, throws right. ... Full name: Joseph Gregory Randa. ... High school: Kettle-Moraine (Wales, Wis.). ... College: Tennessee.

TRANSACTIONS/CAREER NOTES: Selected by California Angels organization in 30th round of 1989 free-agent draft; did not sign. ... Selected by Kansas City Royals organization in 11th round of 1991 free-agent draft. ... On disabled list (May 5-27, 1996); included rehabilitation assignment to Omaha. ... Traded by Royals with Ps Jeff Granger, Jeff Martin and Jeff Wallace to Pittsburgh Pirates for SS Jay Bell and 1B Jeff King (December 13, 1996). ... On disabled list (June 28-July 27, 1997); included rehabilitation assignment to Calgary. ... Selected by Arizona Diamondbacks in third round (57th pick overall) of expansion draft (November 18, 1997). ... Traded by Diamondbacks with P Matt Drews and 3B Gabe Alvarez to Detroit Tigers for 3B Travis Fryman (November 18, 1997). ... Traded by Tigers to New York Mets for P Willie Blair (December 4, 1998). ... Traded by Mets to Royals for OF Juan LeBron (December 10, 1998). ... On disabled list (July 8-23, 2003; and June 28-July 24, 2004).

2004 GAMES PLAYED BY POSITION (MLB): 3B—119, DH—6, 1B—3.

								BATTING												FIELDING	
Year Team (League)	Pos.	G	AB	R	H	2B	3B	HR	RBI	BB	SO	HBP	GDP	SB-CS	Avg.	OBP	SLG	OPS	E	Avg.
1991— Eugene (Northwest)	3B	72	275	53	93	20	2	11	59	46	29	6	8	6-1	.338	.438	.545	.984	14	.923
1992— Appleton (Midwest)	3B	72	266	55	80	13	0	5	43	34	37	6	6	6-2	.301	.385	.406	.791	12	.941
— Baseball City (FSL)	3B-SS	51	189	22	52	7	0	1	12	12	21	2	4	4-3	.275	.324	.328	.652	6	.961
1993— Memphis (Sou.)	3B	131	505	74	149	31	5	11	72	39	64	3	10	8-7	.295	.343	.442	.784	25	.942
1994— Omaha (A.A.)	3B	127	455	65	125	27	2	10	51	30	49	8	18	5-2	.275	.327	.409	.736	24	.945
1995— Kansas City (A.L.)	3B-2B-DH	34	70	6	12	2	0	1	5	6	17	0	2	0-1	.171	.237	.243	.480	3	.952
— Omaha (A.A.)	3B	64	233	33	64	10	2	8	33	22	33	2	9	2-2	.275	.341	.438	.779	6	.958
1996— Kansas City (A.L.)	3-2-1-DH	110	337	36	102	24	1	6	47	26	47	1	10	13-4	.303	.351	.433	.784	10	.960
— Omaha (A.A.)	3B	3	9	1	1	0	1	0	0	1	1	0	1	0-0	.111	.200	.333	.533	0	1.000
1997— Pittsburgh (N.L.)	3B-2B	126	443	58	134	27	9	7	60	41	64	6	10	4-2	.302	.366	.451	.817	21	.948
— Calgary (PCL)	3B	3	11	4	4	1	0	1	4	3	4	0	1	0-0	.364	.500	.727	1.227	1	.900
1998— Detroit (A.L.)	3-2-DH-1	138	460	56	117	21	2	9	50	41	70	7	9	8-7	.254	.323	.367	.690	7	.981
1999— Kansas City (A.L.)	3B	156	628	92	197	36	8	16	84	50	80	3	15	5-4	.314	.363	.473	.836	22	.952
2000— Kansas City (A.L.)	3B-DH	158	612	88	186	29	4	15	106	36	66	6	19	6-3	.304	.343	.438	.781	19	.957
2001— Kansas City (A.L.)	3B-DH-2B	151	581	59	147	34	2	13	83	42	80	6	15	3-2	.253	.307	.386	.693	13	.966
2002— Kansas City (A.L.)	3B-DH	151	549	63	155	36	5	11	80	46	69	9	13	2-1	.282	.341	.426	.768	10	.972
2003— Kansas City (A.L.)	3B-DH	131	502	80	146	31	1	16	72	41	61	7	12	1-0	.291	.348	.452	.800	7	.980
2004— Kansas City (A.L.)	3B-DH-1B	128	485	65	139	31	2	8	56	40	77	6	11	0-1	.287	.343	.408	.751	11	.969
American League totals (9 years)		1157	4224	545	1201	244	25	95	583	328	567	45	106	38-23	.284	.338	.421	.760	102	.966
National League totals (1 year)		126	443	58	134	27	9	7	60	41	64	6	10	4-2	.302	.366	.451	.817	21	.948
Major League totals (10 years)		1283	4667	603	1335	271	34	102	643	369	631	51	116	42-25	.286	.341	.424	.765	123	.964

RANDOLPH, STEPHEN   P

PERSONAL: Born May 1, 1974, in Okinawa, Japan. ... 6-3/202. ... Throws left, bats left. ... Full name: Stephen LeCharles Randolph. ... High school: James Bowie (Simms, Texas). ... College: Texas.

TRANSACTIONS/CAREER NOTES: Selected by Oakland Athletics organization in 10th round of 1994 free-agent draft; did not sign. ... Selected by New York Yankees organization in 18th round of 1995 free-agent draft. ... Selected by Arizona Diamondbacks from Yankees organization in Rule 5 major league draft (December 15, 1997). ... On disabled list (May 4-30, 2003); included rehabilitation assignment to Tucson.

CAREER HITTING: 5-for-15 (.333), 4 R, 3 2B, 0 3B, 0 HR, 3 RBI.

Year Team (League)	W	L	Pct.	ERA	WHIP	G	GS	CG	ShO	Hld.	Sv.-Opp.	IP	H	R	ER	HR	BB-IBB	SO	Avg.
1995— GC Yankees (GCL)	4	0	1.000	2.22	1.11	8	3	0	0	...	0-...	24.1	11	7	6	1	16-0	34	.145
— Oneonta (N.Y.-Penn)	0	3	.000	7.48	1.94	6	6	0	0	...	0-...	21.2	19	22	18	0	23-0	31	.229
1996— Greensboro (S. Atl.)	4	7	.364	3.77	1.59	32	17	0	0	...	0-...	100.1	64	46	42	8	96-1	111	.188
1997— Tampa (FSL)	4	7	.364	3.87	1.44	34	13	1	0	...	1-...	95.1	74	55	41	8	63-5	108	.217
1998— High Desert (Calif.)	4	4	.500	3.59	1.32	17	17	0	0	...	0-...	85.1	71	44	34	6	42-0	104	.231
— Tucson (PCL)	1	3	.250	3.18	1.54	17	1	0	0	...	0-...	22.2	16	11	8	1	19-2	23	.205
1999— El Paso (Texas)	2	2	.500	2.64	1.40	8	8	0	0	...	0-...	44.1	39	14	13	1	23-0	38	.244
— Ariz. D'backs (Ariz.)	0	0	...	4.50	1.17	2	2	0	0	...	0-...	6.0	5	3	3	0	2-0	7	.217
— Tucson (PCL)	0	7	.000	6.91	1.90	11	10	1	0	...	0-...	41.2	47	37	32	7	32-1	26	.281
2000— Tucson (PCL)	0	0	...	8.78	2.25	5	3	0	0	...	0-...	13.1	11	13	13	3	19-0	6	.229
2001— Tucson (PCL)	2	0	1.000	6.33	2.02	18	0	0	0	...	0-...	21.1	24	15	15	2	19-1	16	.282
— El Paso (Texas)	5	6	.455	5.16	1.63	18	14	1	1	...	0-...	75.0	69	50	43	11	53-1	66	.244
2002— Tucson (PCL)	15	7	.682	3.47	1.42	28	27	1	1	...	0-...	163.1	151	70	63	15	81-2	129	.250
2003— Tucson (PCL)	1	0	1.000	3.86	1.18	7	0	0	0	...	0-...	9.1	8	5	4	1	3-0	6	.229
— Arizona (N.L.)	8	1	.889	4.05	1.55	50	0	0	0	2	0-0	60.0	50	28	27	7	43-3	50	.226
2004— Arizona (N.L.)	2	5	.286	5.51	1.82	45	6	0	0	2	0-0	81.2	73	56	50	11	76-2	62	.235
Major League totals (2 years)	10	6	.625	4.89	1.71	95	6	0	0	4	0-0	141.2	123	84	77	18	119-5	112	.232

RANSOM, CODY   SS/2B

PERSONAL: Born February 17, 1976, in Mesa, Ariz. ... 6-2/211. ... Bats right, throws right. ... Full name: Bryan Cody Ransom. ... High school: Chandler (Ariz.). ... College: Grand Canyon (Ariz.).

TRANSACTIONS/CAREER NOTES: Selected by San Francisco Giants organization in ninth round of 1998 free-agent draft.

2004 GAMES PLAYED BY POSITION (MLB): SS—45, 2B—16, 3B—1, OF—1.

Year	Team (League)	Pos.	G	AB	R	H	2B	3B	HR	RBI	BB	SO	HBP	GDP	SB-CS	Avg.	OBP	SLG	OPS	E	Avg.
1998—Salem-Keizer (N'west)	SS	71	236	52	55	12	7	6	27	43	56	2	4	19-6	.233	.351	.419	.770	24	.928
1999—Bakersfield (Calif.)	SS	99	356	69	98	12	6	11	47	54	108	8	2	15-8	.275	.382	.435	.817	30	.938
—Shreveport (Texas)	SS	14	41	6	5	0	0	2	4	4	22	1	0	0-0	.122	.208	.268	.477	3	.953
2000—Shreveport (Texas)	SS	130	459	58	92	21	3	7	47	40	141	0	9	9-3	.200	.263	.305	.568	25	.958
2001—Fresno (PCL)	SS	134	469	77	113	21	6	23	78	44	137	0	10	17-2	.241	.303	.458	.762	12	.980
—San Francisco (N.L.)	SS	9	7	1	0	0	0	0	0	0	5	0	0	0-0	.000	.000	.000	.000	0	1.000
2002—Fresno (PCL)	SS	135	449	53	93	18	4	13	46	47	151	3	5	6-4	.207	.283	.352	.635	15	.974
—San Francisco (N.L.)	SS	7	3	2	2	0	0	0	1	1	1	0	0	0-0	.667	.750	.667	1.417	0	1.000
2003—Fresno (PCL)	SS	112	396	56	100	16	4	12	50	45	91	3	14	14-4	.253	.331	.404	.735	20	.959
—San Francisco (N.L.)	SS	20	27	7	6	1	0	1	1	1	11	0	0	0-0	.222	.250	.370	.620	1	.963
2004—Fresno (PCL)	2-S-3-DH	36	136	29	42	6	2	10	21	19	30	1	1	8-0	.309	.397	.603	1.000	4	.975
—San Francisco (N.L.)	S-2-3-OF	78	68	13	17	6	0	1	11	6	20	1	2	2-2	.250	.320	.382	.702	5	.954
Major League totals (4 years)		114	105	23	25	7	0	2	13	8	37	1	2	2-2	.238	.298	.362	.660	6	.959

RAUCH, JON — P

PERSONAL: Born September 27, 1978, in Louisville, Ky. ... 6-11/260. ... Throws right, bats right. ... Full name: Jon Erich Rauch. ... Name pronounced: ROUSH. ... High school: Oldham County (Buckner, Ky.). ... College: Morehead State.

TRANSACTIONS/CAREER NOTES: Selected by Chicago White Sox organization in third round of 1999 free-agent draft. ... Traded by White Sox with RHP Gary Majewski to Montreal Expos for OF Carl Everett (July 18, 2004). ... On disabled list (August 14-September 14, 2004).

HONORS: Named Minor League Player of the Year by THE SPORTING NEWS (2000).

CAREER HITTING: 1-for-6 (.167), 1 R, 0 2B, 0 3B, 1 HR, 2 RBI.

Year	Team (League)	W	L	Pct.	ERA	WHIP	G	GS	CG	ShO	Hld.	Sv.-Opp.	IP	H	R	ER	HR	BB-IBB	SO	Avg.
1999—Bristol (Appalachian)	4	4	.500	4.45	1.43	14	9	0	0	...	2-...	56.2	65	44	28	4	16-1	66	.269
—Winston-Salem (Caro.)	0	0	...	3.00	1.17	1	1	0	0	...	0-...	6.0	4	3	2	1	3-0	7	.174
2000—Winston-Salem (Caro.)	11	3	.786	2.86	1.23	18	18	1	0	...	0-...	110.0	102	49	35	10	33-0	124	.249
—Birmingham (Southern)	5	1	.833	2.25	0.93	8	8	2	2	...	0-...	56.0	36	18	14	4	16-0	63	.179
2001—Charlotte (Int'l)	1	3	.250	5.79	1.25	6	6	0	0	...	0-...	28.0	28	20	18	8	7-0	27	.248
2002—Chicago (A.L.)	2	1	.667	6.59	1.47	8	6	0	0	0	0-...	28.2	28	26	21	7	14-2	19	.248
—Charlotte (Int'l)	7	8	.467	4.28	1.22	19	19	1	0	...	0-...	109.1	91	60	52	14	42-2	97	.226
2003—Charlotte (Int'l)	7	1	.875	4.11	1.30	24	23	1	0	...	0-...	124.2	121	60	57	16	35-1	94	.258
2004—Chicago (A.L.)	1	1	.500	6.23	2.31	2	2	0	0	0	0-...	8.2	16	6	6	0	4-0	4	.432
—Charlotte (Int'l)	6	3	.667	3.11	1.13	14	13	0	0	...	0-...	72.1	57	27	25	9	25-0	61	.218
—Edmonton (PCL)	1	1	.500	4.50	1.06	3	3	0	0	...	0-...	18.0	17	9	9	3	2-0	13	.246
—Montreal (N.L.)	3	0	1.000	1.54	0.90	9	2	0	0	0	0-...	23.1	14	4	4	1	7-2	18	.175
American League totals (2 years)	3	2	.600	6.51	1.66	10	8	0	0	0	0-0	37.1	44	32	27	7	18-2	23	.293
National League totals (1 year)	3	0	1.000	1.54	0.90	9	2	0	0	0	0-0	23.1	14	4	4	1	7-2	18	.175
Major League totals (2 years)	6	2	.750	4.60	1.37	19	10	0	0	0	0-0	60.2	58	36	31	8	25-4	41	.252

REDDING, TIM — P

PERSONAL: Born February 12, 1978, in Rochester, N.Y. ... 6-0/200. ... Throws right, bats right. ... Full name: Timothy James Redding. ... Junior college: Monroe (N.Y.) Community College.

TRANSACTIONS/CAREER NOTES: Selected by Houston Astros organization in 20th round of 1997 free-agent draft.

CAREER HITTING: 19-for-113 (.168), 5 R, 3 2B, 0 3B, 0 HR, 5 RBI.

Year	Team (League)	W	L	Pct.	ERA	WHIP	G	GS	CG	ShO	Hld.	Sv.-Opp.	IP	H	R	ER	HR	BB-IBB	SO	Avg.
1998—Auburn (N.Y.-Penn)	7	3	.700	4.52	1.34	16	15	0	0	...	1-...	73.2	49	44	37	2	50-0	98	.188
1999—Michigan (Midw.)	8	6	.571	4.97	1.52	43	11	0	0	...	14-...	105.0	84	69	58	4	76-1	144	.221
2000—Kissimmee (Fla. St.)	12	5	.706	2.68	1.18	24	24	0	0	...	0-...	154.2	125	62	46	4	57-1	170	.219
—Round Rock (Texas)	2	0	1.000	3.46	1.38	5	5	0	0	...	0-...	26.0	14	12	10	4	22-0	22	.167
2001—Round Rock (Texas)	10	2	.833	2.18	0.98	14	14	1	1	...	0-...	90.2	64	26	22	4	25-0	113	.192
—New Orleans (PCL)	4	1	.800	4.54	1.09	6	6	0	0	...	0-...	37.2	22	21	19	4	19-0	42	.172
—Houston (N.L.)	3	1	.750	5.50	1.54	13	9	0	0	0	0-0	55.2	62	38	34	11	24-0	55	.286
2002—New Orleans (PCL)	3	3	.500	5.21	1.18	11	7	0	0	...	0-...	38.0	32	22	22	6	13-1	50	.232
—Houston (N.L.)	3	6	.333	5.40	1.54	18	14	0	0	0	0-0	73.1	78	49	44	10	35-3	63	.276
2003—Houston (N.L.)	10	14	.417	3.68	1.39	33	32	0	0	0	0-0	176.0	179	85	72	16	65-4	116	.261
2004—New Orleans (PCL)	1	3	.250	6.04	1.48	5	5	0	0	...	0-...	28.1	30	21	19	2	12-0	26	.268
—Houston (N.L.)	5	7	.417	5.72	1.67	27	17	0	0	0	0-0	100.2	125	73	64	15	43-3	56	.309
Major League totals (4 years)	21	28	.429	4.75	1.51	91	72	0	0	0	0-0	405.2	444	245	214	52	167-10	290	.279

REDMAN, MARK — P

PERSONAL: Born January 5, 1974, in San Diego, Calif. ... 6-5/245. ... Throws left, bats left. ... Full name: Mark Allen Redman. ... High school: Escondido (Calif.). ... College: Oklahoma.

TRANSACTIONS/CAREER NOTES: Selected by Detroit Tigers organization in 41st round of 1992 free-agent draft; did not sign. ... Selected by Minnesota Twins organization in first round (13th pick overall) of 1995 free-agent draft. ... On disabled list (July 25-August 10, 1999). ... On disabled list (May 21-July 28, 2001); included rehabilitation assignment to Edmonton. ... Traded by Twins to Tigers for P Todd Jones (July 28, 2001). ... On disabled list (July 28-August 22, 2001); included rehabilitation assignment to Toledo. ... Traded by Tigers with P Jerrod Fuell to Florida Marlins for Ps Gary Knotts, Nate Robertson and Rob Henkel (January 11, 2003). ... On disabled list (April 30-May 30, 2003). ... Traded by Marlins to Oakland Athletics for Ps Mike Neu and Bill Murphy (December 16, 2003).

CAREER HITTING: 2-for-75 (.027), 1 R, 0 2B, 0 3B, 0 HR, 1 RBI.

Year	Team (League)	W	L	Pct.	ERA	WHIP	G	GS	CG	ShO	Hld.	Sv.-Opp.	IP	H	R	ER	HR	BB-IBB	SO	Avg.
1995—Fort Myers (Fla. St.)	2	1	.667	2.76	1.26	8	5	0	0	...	0-...	32.2	28	13	10	4	13-0	26	.239
1996—Fort Myers (Fla. St.)	3	4	.429	1.85	1.17	13	13	0	0	...	0-...	82.2	63	24	17	1	34-0	75	.220
—New Britain (East.)	7	7	.500	3.81	1.42	16	16	3	0	...	0-...	106.1	101	51	45	5	50-1	96	.251
—Salt Lake (PCL)	0	0	...	9.00	2.25	1	1	0	0	...	0-...	4.0	7	4	4	1	2-0	4	.389
1997—Salt Lake (PCL)	8	15	.348	6.31	1.79	29	28	0	0	...	1-...	158.1	204	123	111	19	80-3	125	.316
1998—New Britain (East.)	4	2	.667	1.52	1.20	8	8	0	0	...	0-...	47.1	40	11	8	3	17-0	51	.237
—Salt Lake (PCL)	6	7	.462	5.53	1.53	19	18	0	0	...	0-...	99.1	111	75	61	13	41-1	88	.282
1999—Salt Lake (PCL)	9	9	.500	5.05	1.44	24	24	1	0	...	0-...	133.2	141	87	75	12	51-1	114	.272
—Minnesota (A.L.)	1	0	1.000	8.53	1.89	5	1	0	0	0	0-0	12.2	17	13	12	3	7-0	11	.298
2000—Minnesota (A.L.)	12	9	.571	4.76	1.41	32	24	0	0	0	0-0	151.1	168	81	80	22	45-0	117	.281

Year Team (League)	W	L	Pct.	ERA	WHIP	G	GS	CG	ShO	Hld.	Sv.-Opp.	IP	H	R	ER	HR	BB-IBB	SO	Avg.
2001— Minnesota (A.L.)	2	4	.333	4.22	1.55	9	9	0	0	0	0-0	49.0	57	26	23	6	19-0	29	.286
— Edmonton (PCL)	0	0	...	13.50	3.00	1	1	0	0	...	0-...	1.1	3	2	2	0	1-0	0	.500
— Toledo (International)	0	1	.000	5.27	1.10	3	3	0	0	...	0-...	13.2	14	10	8	3	1-0	12	.259
— Detroit (A.L.)	0	2	.000	6.00	1.67	2	2	0	0	0	0-0	9.0	11	6	6	1	4-0	4	.306
2002— Detroit (A.L.)	8	15	.348	4.21	1.29	30	30	3	0	0	0-0	203.0	211	107	95	15	51-2	109	.268
2003— Florida (N.L.)	14	9	.609	3.59	1.22	29	29	3	0	0	0-0	190.2	172	82	76	16	61-3	151	.239
2004— Oakland (A.L.)	11	12	.478	4.71	1.50	32	32	2	0	0	0-0	191.0	218	110	100	28	68-6	102	.292
American League totals (5 years)	34	42	.447	4.62	1.42	110	98	5	0	0		616.0	682	343	316	75	194-8	372	.281
National League totals (1 year)	14	9	.609	3.59	1.22	29	29	3	0	0		190.2	172	82	76	16	61-3	151	.239
Major League totals (6 years)	48	51	.485	4.37	1.37	139	127	8	0	0	0-0	806.2	854	425	392	91	255-11	523	.272

DIVISION SERIES RECORD

Year Team (League)	W	L	Pct.	ERA	WHIP	G	GS	CG	ShO	Hld.	Sv.-Opp.	IP	H	R	ER	HR	BB-IBB	SO	Avg.
2003— Florida (N.L.)	0	0	...	3.00	1.67	1	1	0	0	0	0-0	6.0	7	2	2	0	3-1	4	.280

CHAMPIONSHIP SERIES RECORD

Year Team (League)	W	L	Pct.	ERA	WHIP	G	GS	CG	ShO	Hld.	Sv.-Opp.	IP	H	R	ER	HR	BB-IBB	SO	Avg.
2003— Florida (N.L.)	0	0	...	6.52	1.76	2	2	0	0	0	0-0	9.2	13	7	7	2	4-0	4	.342

WORLD SERIES RECORD

Year Team (League)	W	L	Pct.	ERA	WHIP	G	GS	CG	ShO	Hld.	Sv.-Opp.	IP	H	R	ER	HR	BB-IBB	SO	Avg.
2003— Florida (N.L.)	0	1	.000	15.43	3.00	1	1	0	0	0	0-0	2.1	5	4	4	1	2-0	2	.500

REDMAN, TIKE — OF

PERSONAL: Born March 10, 1977, in Tuscaloosa, Ala. ... 5-11/172. ... Bats left, throws left. ... Full name: Julian Jawonn Redman. ... High school: Tuscaloosa (Ala.) Academy.
TRANSACTIONS/CAREER NOTES: Selected by Pittsburgh Pirates organization in fifth round of 1996 free-agent draft. ... Released by Pirates (December 18, 2002). ... Re-signed by Pirates organization (January 17, 2003).
2004 GAMES PLAYED BY POSITION (MLB): OF—147.

Year Team (League)	Pos.	G	AB	R	H	2B	3B	HR	RBI	BB	SO	HBP	GDP	SB-CS	Avg.	OBP	SLG	OPS	E	Avg.
1996— GC Pirates (GCL)	OF	26	104	20	31	4	1	1	16	12	12	0	0	15-3	.298	.368	.385	.752	1	.978
— Erie (N.Y.-Penn)	OF	43	170	31	50	4	6	2	21	17	30	0	2	7-3	.294	.353	.424	.776	7	.920
1997— Lynchburg (Caro.)	1B-OF	125	415	55	104	18	5	4	45	45	82	7	8	21-8	.251	.333	.347	.680	6	.975
1998— Lynchburg (Caro.)	OF	131	525	70	135	26	10	6	46	32	73	1	5	36-16	.257	.298	.379	.677	8	.971
1999— Altoona (East.)	OF	136	532	84	143	20	12	3	60	52	52	1	9	29-16	.269	.332	.368	.700	9	.972
2000— Nashville (PCL)	OF	121	506	62	132	24	11	4	51	32	73	3	4	24-18	.261	.306	.375	.682	5	.981
— Pittsburgh (N.L.)	OF	9	18	2	6	1	0	1	1	1	7	0	0	1-0	.333	.368	.556	.924	0	1.000
2001— Nashville (PCL)	OF	95	398	53	121	18	10	3	42	24	37	4	6	21-7	.304	.347	.422	.769	7	.970
— Pittsburgh (N.L.)	OF	37	125	8	28	4	1	1	4	4	25	0	2	3-5	.224	.246	.296	.542	2	.980
2002— Nashville (PCL)	OF	76	311	40	84	9	4	2	20	21	24	1	3	16-7	.270	.315	.344	.660	3	.982
2003— Nashville (PCL)	OF-DH	100	360	60	106	12	7	4	29	36	32	0	5	42-9	.294	.357	.400	.757	3	.987
— Pittsburgh (N.L.)	OF	56	230	36	76	16	5	3	19	14	18	2	1	7-3	.330	.374	.483	.857	2	.985
2004— Pittsburgh (N.L.)	OF	155	546	65	153	19	4	8	51	23	52	3	6	18-6	.280	.310	.374	.684	5	.986
Major League totals (4 years)		257	919	111	263	40	10	13	75	42	102	5	9	29-14	.286	.319	.394	.713	9	.985

REDMOND, MIKE — C

PERSONAL: Born May 5, 1971, in Seattle, Wash. ... 5-11/200. ... Bats right, throws right. ... Full name: Michael Patrick Redmond. ... High school: Gonzaga Prep (Spokane, Wash.). ... College: Gonzaga.
TRANSACTIONS/CAREER NOTES: Signed as a non-drafted free agent by Florida Marlins organization (August 18, 1992). ... On disabled list (August 24-September 8, 1998).
2004 GAMES PLAYED BY POSITION (MLB): C—79.

Year Team (League)	Pos.	G	AB	R	H	2B	3B	HR	RBI	BB	SO	HBP	GDP	SB-CS	Avg.	OBP	SLG	OPS	E	Avg.
1993— Kane Co. (Midw.)	C	43	100	10	20	2	0	0	10	6	17	4	1	2-0	.200	.273	.220	.493	1	.996
1994— Kane Co. (Midw.)	C	92	306	39	83	10	0	1	24	26	31	9	10	3-4	.271	.344	.314	.658	6	.992
— Brevard County (FSL)	C	12	42	4	11	4	0	0	2	3	4	1	1	0-0	.262	.326	.357	.683	0	1.000
1995— Portland (East.)	3B-C	105	333	37	85	11	1	3	39	22	27	3	9	2-2	.255	.305	.321	.626	6	.992
1996— Portland (East.)	C	120	394	43	113	22	0	4	44	26	45	5	12	3-4	.287	.335	.373	.708	4	.996
1997— Charlotte (Int'l)	C	22	61	8	13	5	1	1	2	1	10	3	1	0-1	.213	.262	.377	.639	2	.985
— GC Marlins (GCL)	DH	16	55	7	19	3	0	0	5	9	5	3	1	2-0	.345	.463	.400	.863	...	...
— Brevard County (FSL)	1B	5	17	2	0	0	0	0	0	2	2	0	2	0-0	.000	.105	.000	.105	0	1.000
1998— Portland (East.)	C	8	28	7	9	4	0	1	7	2	2	2	3	0-0	.321	.406	.571	.978	1	.983
— Charlotte (Int'l)	C	18	58	4	14	2	0	2	7	0	3	1	3	0-0	.241	.246	.379	.625	0	1.000
— Florida (N.L.)	C	37	118	10	39	9	0	2	12	5	16	2	6	0-0	.331	.368	.458	.826	2	.992
1999— Florida (N.L.)	C	84	242	22	73	9	0	1	27	26	34	5	8	0-0	.302	.381	.351	.732	4	.992
2000— Florida (N.L.)	C	87	210	17	53	8	1	0	15	13	19	8	5	0-0	.252	.316	.300	.616	2	.996
2001— Florida (N.L.)	C	43	141	19	44	4	0	4	14	13	13	2	6	0-0	.312	.376	.426	.801	2	.994
2002— Florida (N.L.)	C-1B	89	256	19	78	15	0	2	28	21	34	8	4	0-2	.305	.372	.387	.758	4	.993
2003— Florida (N.L.)	C-3B-1B	59	125	12	30	7	1	0	11	7	16	5	2	0-0	.240	.302	.312	.614	1	.995
2004— Florida (N.L.)	C	81	246	19	63	15	0	2	25	14	28	8	10	1-0	.256	.315	.341	.656	1	.996
Major League totals (7 years)		485	1338	118	380	67	2	11	132	99	160	38	41	1-2	.284	.348	.362	.710	17	.994

CHAMPIONSHIP SERIES RECORD

Year Team (League)	Pos.	G	AB	R	H	2B	3B	HR	RBI	BB	SO	HBP	GDP	SB-CS	Avg.	OBP	SLG	OPS	E	Avg.
2003— Florida (N.L.)	C	1	0	1	0	0	0	0	0	1	0	0	0	0-0	...	1.000	...	1.000	0	1.000

WORLD SERIES RECORD

Year Team (League)	Pos.	G	AB	R	H	2B	3B	HR	RBI	BB	SO	HBP	GDP	SB-CS	Avg.	OBP	SLG	OPS	E	Avg.
2003— Florida (N.L.)	C	1	1	0	0	0	0	0	0	0	0	0	0	0-0	.000	.000	.000	.000	0	1.000

R

REED, JEREMY   OF

PERSONAL: Born June 15, 1981, in San Dimas, Calif. ... 6-0/185. ... Bats left, throws left. ... Full name: Jeremy T. Reed. ... High school: Bonita (LaVerne, Calif.). ... College: Long Beach State.

TRANSACTIONS/CAREER NOTES: Selected by Chicago White Sox organization in second round of 2002 free-agent draft. ... Traded by White Sox with C Miguel Olivo and SS Michael Morse to Seattle Mariners for P Freddy Garcia and C Ben Davis (June 27, 2004).

2004 GAMES PLAYED BY POSITION (MLB): OF—16.

Year	Team (League)	Pos.	G	AB	R	H	2B	3B	HR	RBI	BB	SO	HBP	GDP	SB-CS	Avg.	OBP	SLG	OPS	E	Avg.
2002—	Kannapolis (S.Atl.)	OF	57	210	37	67	15	0	4	32	11	24	11	7	17-5	.319	.377	.448	.825	0	1.000
2003—	Win.-Salem (Car.)	OF	65	222	37	74	18	1	4	52	41	17	1	5	27-6	.333	.431	.477	.909	3	.979
—	Birmingham (Sou.)	OF	66	242	51	99	17	3	7	43	29	19	2	7	18-13	.409	.474	.591	1.065	0	1.000
2004—	Charlotte (Int'l)	OF-DH	73	276	44	76	14	1	8	37	36	34	3	7	12-7	.275	.357	.420	.771	1	.995
—	Tacoma (PCL)	OF	61	233	40	71	10	5	5	36	23	22	0	6	14-2	.305	.366	.455	.821	3	.982
—	Seattle (A.L.)	OF	18	58	11	23	4	0	0	5	7	4	1	2	3-1	.397	.470	.466	.935	1	.981
Major League totals (1 year)			18	58	11	23	4	0	0	5	7	4	1	2	3-1	.397	.470	.466	.935	1	.981

REED, STEVE   P

PERSONAL: Born March 11, 1965, in Los Angeles, Calif. ... 6-2/212. ... Throws right, bats right. ... Full name: Steven Vincent Reed. ... High school: Chatsworth (Calif.). ... College: Lewis-Clark (Idaho) State.

TRANSACTIONS/CAREER NOTES: Signed as a non-drafted free agent by San Francisco Giants organization (June 24, 1988). ... Selected by Colorado Rockies in third round (60th pick overall) of expansion draft (November 17, 1992). ... Signed as a free agent by Giants (December 24, 1997). ... Traded by Giants with OF Jacob Cruz to Cleveland Indians for Ps Jose Mesa and Alvin Morman and IF Shawon Dunston (July 23, 1998). ... Traded by Indians with P Steve Karsay to Atlanta Braves for P John Rocker and 3B Troy Cameron (June 22, 2001). ... Signed as a free agent by San Diego Padres organization (January 23, 2002). ... Traded by Padres with P Jason Middlebrook to New York Mets for Ps Bobby M. Jones and Josh Reynolds and OF Jason Bay (July 31, 2002). ... Signed as a free agent by Rockies (January 24, 2003). ... On suspended list (September 25-27, 2004).

CAREER HITTING: 4-for-25 (.160), 0 R, 0 2B, 0 3B, 0 HR, 1 RBI.

Year	Team (League)	W	L	Pct.	ERA	WHIP	G	GS	CG	ShO	Hld.	Sv.-Opp.	IP	H	R	ER	HR	BB-IBB	SO	Avg.
1988—	Pocatello (Pio.)	4	1	.800	2.54	1.09	31	0	0	0	...	13-...	46.0	42	20	13	3	8-1	49	.237
1989—	Clinton (Midw.)	5	3	.625	1.05	0.97	60	0	0	0	...	26-...	94.2	54	16	11	1	38-10	104	.171
—	San Jose (California)	0	0	...	0.00	0.50	2	0	0	0	...	0-...	2.0	0	0	0	0	1-0	3	.000
1990—	Shreveport (Texas)	3	1	.750	1.64	1.21	45	1	0	0	...	8-...	60.1	53	20	11	2	20-6	59	.230
1991—	Shreveport (Texas)	2	0	1.000	0.83	0.92	15	0	0	0	...	7-...	21.2	17	2	2	1	3-0	26	.218
—	Phoenix (PCL)	2	3	.400	4.31	1.31	41	0	0	0	...	6-...	56.1	62	33	27	5	12-0	46	.279
1992—	Shreveport (Texas)	1	0	1.000	0.62	0.62	27	0	0	0	...	23-...	29.0	18	3	2	1	0-0	33	.175
—	Phoenix (PCL)	0	1	.000	3.48	1.19	29	0	0	0	...	20-...	31.0	27	13	12	2	10-3	30	.237
—	San Francisco (N.L.)	1	0	1.000	2.30	1.02	18	0	0	0	1	0-0	15.2	13	5	4	2	3-0	11	.220
1993—	Colorado (N.L.)	9	5	.643	4.48	1.30	64	0	0	0	9	3-6	84.1	80	47	42	13	30-5	51	.259
—	Colo. Springs (PCL)	0	0	...	0.00	0.89	11	0	0	0	...	7-...	12.1	8	1	0	0	3-1	10	.182
1994—	Colorado (N.L.)	3	2	.600	3.94	1.64	61	0	0	0	14	3-10	64.0	79	33	28	9	26-3	51	.306
1995—	Colorado (N.L.)	5	2	.714	2.14	0.98	71	0	0	0	11	3-6	84.0	61	24	20	8	21-3	79	.203
1996—	Colorado (N.L.)	4	3	.571	3.96	1.13	70	0	0	0	22	0-6	75.0	66	38	33	11	19-0	51	.239
1997—	Colorado (N.L.)	4	6	.400	4.04	1.22	63	0	0	0	10	6-13	62.1	49	28	28	10	27-1	43	.219
1998—	San Francisco (N.L.)	2	1	.667	1.48	0.90	50	0	0	0	13	1-5	54.2	30	10	9	4	19-5	50	.160
—	Cleveland (A.L.)	2	2	.500	6.66	1.32	20	0	0	0	8	0-1	25.2	26	19	19	4	8-0	23	.260
1999—	Cleveland (A.L.)	3	2	.600	4.23	1.44	63	0	0	0	8	0-3	61.2	69	33	29	10	20-5	44	.285
2000—	Cleveland (A.L.)	2	0	1.000	4.34	1.41	57	0	0	0	9	0-1	56.0	58	30	27	7	21-4	39	.269
2001—	Cleveland (A.L.)	1	1	.500	3.62	1.17	31	0	0	0	6	0-1	27.1	22	11	11	3	10-2	21	.212
—	Atlanta (N.L.)	2	2	.500	3.48	1.39	39	0	0	0	5	1-1	31.0	30	14	12	3	13-3	25	.259
2002—	San Diego (N.L.)	2	4	.333	1.98	1.05	40	0	0	0	11	1-3	41.0	33	9	9	2	10-2	36	.228
—	New York (N.L.)	0	1	.000	2.08	1.04	24	0	0	0	6	0-1	26.0	23	6	6	0	4-1	14	.240
2003—	Colorado (N.L.)	5	3	.625	3.27	1.34	67	0	0	0	14	0-2	63.1	59	24	23	9	26-3	39	.254
2004—	Colorado (N.L.)	3	8	.273	3.68	1.35	65	0	0	0	15	0-4	66.0	72	29	27	7	17-7	38	.281
American League totals (4 years)		8	5	.615	4.54	1.37	171	0	0	0	31	0-6	170.2	175	93	86	24	59-11	127	.264
National League totals (11 years)		40	37	.519	3.25	1.21	632	0	0	0	131	18-57	667.1	595	267	241	78	215-33	488	.242
Major League totals (13 years)		48	42	.533	3.51	1.25	803	0	0	0	162	18-63	838.0	770	360	327	102	274-44	615	.247

DIVISION SERIES RECORD

Year	Team (League)	W	L	Pct.	ERA	WHIP	G	GS	CG	ShO	Hld.	Sv.-Opp.	IP	H	R	ER	HR	BB-IBB	SO	Avg.
1995—	Colorado (N.L.)	0	0	...	0.00	1.13	3	0	0	0	1	0-1	2.2	2	0	0	0	1-1	3	.200
1998—	Cleveland (A.L.)	1	0	1.000	40.50	3.00	2	0	0	0	0	0-0	.2	1	3	3	0	1-0	1	.333
1999—	Cleveland (A.L.)	0	0	...	30.86	4.29	2	0	0	0	0	0-0	2.1	9	8	8	1	1-0	1	.600
2001—	Atlanta (N.L.)	0	0	...	0.00	0.00	1	0	0	0	1	0-0	.1	0	0	0	0	0-0	0	.000
Division series totals (4 years)		1	0	1.000	16.50	2.50	8	0	0	0	2	0-1	6.0	12	11	11	1	3-1	5	.414

CHAMPIONSHIP SERIES RECORD

Year	Team (League)	W	L	Pct.	ERA	WHIP	G	GS	CG	ShO	Hld.	Sv.-Opp.	IP	H	R	ER	HR	BB-IBB	SO	Avg.
1998—	Cleveland (A.L.)	0	0	...	0.00	0.60	3	0	0	0	0	0-0	1.2	0	0	0	0	1-0	0	.000
2001—	Atlanta (N.L.)	0	0	...	...	...	1	0	0	0	0	0-...	.0	0	0	0	0	0-0	0	...
Champ. series totals (2 years)		0	0	...	0.00	0.60	4	0	0	0	0	0-0	1.2	0	0	0	0	1-0	0	.000

REESE, POKEY   SS

PERSONAL: Born June 10, 1973, in Columbia, S.C. ... 5-11/180. ... Bats right, throws right. ... Full name: Calvin Reese Jr.. ... High school: Lower Richland (Hopkins, S.C.).

TRANSACTIONS/CAREER NOTES: Selected by Cincinnati Reds organization in first round (20th pick overall) of 1991 free-agent draft. ... Traded by Reds with P Dennys Reyes to Colorado Rockies for Ps Gabe White and Luke Hudson (December 18, 2001). ... Traded by Rockies to Boston Red Sox for C Scott Hatteberg (December 19, 2001). ... Signed as a free agent by Pittsburgh Pirates organization (January 30, 2002). ... On disabled list (April 20-May 5, 2002). ... On disabled list (May 14, 2003-remainder of season). ... Signed as a free agent by Boston Red Sox (December 23, 2003). ... On disabled list (July 20-September 7, 2004).

HONORS: Won N.L. Gold Glove at second base (1999 and 2000).

2004 GAMES PLAYED BY POSITION (MLB): SS—71, 2B—30.

Year—Team (League)	Pos.	G	AB	R	H	2B	3B	HR	RBI	BB	SO	HBP	GDP	SB-CS	Avg.	OBP	SLG	OPS	E	Avg.
1991—Princeton (Appal.)	SS	62	231	30	55	8	3	3	27	23	44	0	4	10-8	.238	.305	.338	.642	31	.885
1992—Char., W.Va. (SAL)	SS	106	380	50	102	19	3	6	53	24	75	5	2	19-8	.268	.315	.382	.696	34	.932
1993—Chattanooga (Sou.)	SS	102	345	35	73	17	4	3	37	23	77	1	2	8-5	.212	.258	.310	.568	25	.951
1994—Chattanooga (Sou.)	SS	134	484	77	130	23	4	12	49	43	75	7	6	21-4	.269	.336	.407	.743	38	.939
1995—Indianapolis (A.A.)	SS	89	343	51	82	21	1	10	46	36	81	4	3	8-5	.239	.316	.394	.710	27	.935
1996—Indianapolis (A.A.)	SS-3B	79	280	26	65	16	0	1	23	21	46	5	10	5-2	.232	.294	.300	.594	22	.944
1997—Cincinnati (N.L.)	SS-2B-3B	128	397	48	87	15	0	4	26	31	82	5	1	25-7	.219	.284	.287	.571	15	.969
—Indianapolis (A.A.)	SS	17	72	12	17	2	0	4	11	9	12	0	2	4-0	.236	.321	.431	.752	3	.966
1998—Cincinnati (N.L.)	3B-SS-2B	59	133	20	34	2	2	1	16	14	28	0	3	3-2	.256	.322	.323	.645	8	.941
1999—Cincinnati (N.L.)	2B-SS	149	585	85	167	37	5	10	52	35	81	6	9	38-7	.285	.330	.417	.747	7	.991
2000—Cincinnati (N.L.)	2B	135	518	76	132	20	6	12	46	45	86	6	8	29-3	.255	.319	.386	.705	14	.980
2001—Cincinnati (N.L.)	SS-2B	133	428	50	96	20	2	9	40	34	82	3	7	25-4	.224	.284	.343	.627	15	.975
2002—Pittsburgh (N.L.)	2B	119	421	46	111	25	0	4	50	41	81	3	4	12-1	.264	.330	.352	.681	8	.988
2003—Pittsburgh (N.L.)	2B	37	107	9	23	2	0	1	12	9	31	0	2	6-0	.215	.271	.262	.533	6	.969
2004—Boston (A.L.)	SS-2B	96	244	32	54	7	2	3	29	17	60	0	5	6-2	.221	.271	.303	.574	7	.982
American League totals (1 year)		96	244	32	54	7	2	3	29	17	60	0	5	6-2	.221	.271	.303	.574	7	.982
National League totals (7 years)		760	2589	334	650	121	15	41	242	209	471	23	34	138-24	.251	.310	.357	.667	73	.979
Major League totals (8 years)		856	2833	366	704	128	17	44	271	226	531	23	39	144-26	.248	.307	.352	.659	80	.980

DIVISION SERIES RECORD

Year—Team (League)	Pos.	G	AB	R	H	2B	3B	HR	RBI	BB	SO	HBP	GDP	SB-CS	Avg.	OBP	SLG	OPS	E	Avg.
2004—Boston (A.L.)	2B	3	0	1	0	0	0	0	0	0	0	0	0	0-0	...	...	...	...	0	1.000

CHAMPIONSHIP SERIES RECORD

Year—Team (League)	Pos.	G	AB	R	H	2B	3B	HR	RBI	BB	SO	HBP	GDP	SB-CS	Avg.	OBP	SLG	OPS	E	Avg.
2004—Boston (A.L.)	2B	3	1	0	0	0	0	0	0	0	1	0	0	0-0	.000	.000	.000	.000	0	1.000

WORLD SERIES RECORD

Year—Team (League)	Pos.	G	AB	R	H	2B	3B	HR	RBI	BB	SO	HBP	GDP	SB-CS	Avg.	OBP	SLG	OPS	E	Avg.
2004—Boston (A.L.)	2B	4	1	0	0	0	0	0	0	0	0	0	0	0-0	.000	.000	.000	.000	0	1.000

REGILIO, NICK   P

PERSONAL: Born September 4, 1978, in Miami, Fla. ... 6-2/205. ... Throws right, bats right. ... Full name: Nicholas D. Regilio. ... College: Jacksonville.
TRANSACTIONS/CAREER NOTES: Selected by Texas Rangers organization in second round of 1999 free-agent draft.
CAREER HITTING: 0-for-0 (.000), 0 R, 0 2B, 0 3B, 0 RBI.

Year—Team (League)	W	L	Pct.	ERA	WHIP	G	GS	CG	ShO	Hld.	Sv.-Opp.	IP	H	R	ER	HR	BB-IBB	SO	Avg.
1999—Pulaski (Appalachian)	4	2	.667	1.63	0.93	11	8	1	1	...	0-...	49.2	30	12	9	2	16-0	58	.172
2000—Charlotte (Fla. St.)	4	3	.571	4.52	1.44	20	20	0	0	...	0-...	85.2	94	54	43	8	29-0	63	.286
2001—Charlotte (Fla. St.)	6	2	.750	1.55	0.98	11	11	1	1	...	0-...	64.0	47	16	11	5	16-0	60	.200
—Tulsa (Texas)	1	3	.250	5.54	1.58	10	10	0	0	...	0-...	52.0	62	34	32	2	20-0	40	.297
2002—Oklahoma (PCL)	1	0	1.000	10.80	2.80	1	1	0	0	...	0-...	5.0	9	6	6	1	5-0	4	.391
—Tulsa (Texas)	6	8	.429	3.44	1.38	19	19	2	1	...	0-...	104.2	97	46	40	8	47-2	59	.245
2003—Rangers (Ariz.)	0	0	...	0.00	1.00	2	2	0	0	...	0-...	5.0	4	2	0	0	1-0	7	.235
—Frisco (Texas)	0	1	.000	21.60	3.60	1	0	0	0	...	0-...	1.2	5	4	4	0	1-0	2	.556
2004—Texas (A.L.)	0	4	.000	6.05	1.81	6	4	0	0	0	0-0	19.1	20	16	13	3	15-1	12	.278
—Oklahoma (PCL)	6	5	.545	4.71	1.57	17	17	0	0	...	0-...	91.2	98	49	48	6	46-0	72	.282
Major League totals (1 year)	0	4	.000	6.05	1.81	6	4	0	0	0	0-0	19.1	20	16	13	3	15-1	12	.278

REITH, BRIAN   P

PERSONAL: Born February 28, 1978, in Fort Wayne, Ind. ... 6-5/220. ... Throws right, bats right. ... Full name: Brian Eric Reith. ... Name pronounced: REETH. ... High school: Concordia Lutheran (Fort Wayne, Ind.).
TRANSACTIONS/CAREER NOTES: Selected by New York Yankees organization in sixth round of 1996 free-agent draft. ... Traded by Yankees with 3B Drew Henson, OF Jackson Melian and P Ed Yarnall to Cincinnati Reds for P Denny Neagle and OF Mike Frank (July 12, 2000). ... Claimed on waivers by Philadelphia Phillies (July 11, 2002). ... Claimed on waivers by Reds (August 6, 2002).
CAREER HITTING: 3-for-19 (.158), 0 R, 0 2B, 0 3B, 0 HR, 2 RBI.

Year—Team (League)	W	L	Pct.	ERA	WHIP	G	GS	CG	ShO	Hld.	Sv.-Opp.	IP	H	R	ER	HR	BB-IBB	SO	Avg.
1996—GC Yankees (GCL)	2	3	.400	4.13	1.44	10	4	0	0	...	0-...	32.2	31	16	15	1	16-0	21	.254
1997—GC Yankees (GCL)	4	2	.667	2.86	1.33	12	11	1	0	...	0-...	63.0	70	28	20	1	14-0	40	.281
1998—Greensboro (S. Atl.)	6	7	.462	2.28	0.00	20	20	3	1	...	0-...	118.1	86	42	30	7	32-0	116	.196
1999—Tampa (FSL)	9	9	.500	4.70	1.50	26	23	0	0	...	0-...	139.2	174	87	73	12	35-1	101	.307
2000—Tampa (FSL)	9	4	.692	2.18	1.12	18	18	1	1	...	0-...	119.2	101	39	29	4	33-0	100	.227
—Dayton (Midw.)	2	1	.667	2.88	1.19	5	5	0	0	...	0-...	34.1	33	12	11	2	8-0	30	.252
—Chattanooga (Southern)	1	3	.250	3.90	1.40	5	5	0	0	...	0-...	30.0	31	14	13	3	11-0	29	.277
2001—Chattanooga (Southern)	6	4	.600	3.97	1.39	18	18	1	1	...	0-...	104.1	103	63	46	10	42-1	89	.259
—Cincinnati (N.L.)	0	7	.000	7.81	1.79	9	8	0	0	0	0-0	40.1	56	37	35	13	16-0	22	.333
—Louisville (Int'l)	0	0	...	3.60	1.60	1	1	0	0	...	0-...	5.0	7	2	2	0	1-0	6	.368
2002—Scran./W.B. (I.L.)	0	4	.000	7.00	2.06	4	4	0	0	...	0-...	18.0	26	18	14	1	11-0	13	.329
—Louisville (Int'l)	8	9	.471	4.75	1.38	23	22	0	0	...	0-...	132.2	137	76	70	15	46-3	99	.267
2003—Louisville (Int'l)	3	1	.750	1.96	0.90	16	0	0	0	...	1-...	23.0	12	9	5	1	9-2	28	.152
—Cincinnati (N.L.)	2	3	.400	4.11	1.58	42	1	0	0	4	1-1	61.1	61	32	28	8	36-6	39	.263
2004—Cincinnati (N.L.)	2	2	.500	7.27	1.88	22	0	0	0	4	0-1	26.0	30	21	21	5	19-1	24	.288
—Louisville (Int'l)	2	3	.400	3.72	1.76	26	1	0	0	...	0-...	36.1	51	17	15	1	13-0	32	.342
Major League totals (3 years)	4	12	.250	5.92	1.71	73	9	0	0	8	1-2	127.2	147	90	84	26	71-7	85	.292

REITSMA, CHRIS   P

PERSONAL: Born December 31, 1977, in Minneapolis, Minn. ... 6-5/235. ... Throws right, bats right. ... Full name: Christopher Michael Reitsma. ... Name pronounced: REETS-muh. ... High school: Calgary (Alta.) Christian.
TRANSACTIONS/CAREER NOTES: Selected by Boston Red Sox organization in supplemental round ("sandwich pick" between first and second rounds, 34th pick overall) of 1996 free-agent draft; pick received as compensation for Toronto Blue Jays signing free-agent P Erik Hanson. ... Selected by Tampa Bay Devil Rays from Red Sox organiza-

tion in Rule 5 major league draft (December 13, 1999). ... Returned to Red Sox (March 28, 2000). ... Traded by Red Sox with P John Curtice to Cincinnati Reds for OF Dante Bichette (August 31, 2000). ... Traded by Reds to Atlanta Braves for Ps Jung Bong and Bubba Nelson (March 26, 2004).

CAREER HITTING: 9-for-86 (.105), 3 R, 1 2B, 0 3B, 0 HR, 5 RBI.

Year	Team (League)	W	L	Pct.	ERA	WHIP	G	GS	CG	ShO	Hld.	Sv.-Opp.	IP	H	R	ER	HR	BB-IBB	SO	Avg.
1996— GC Red Sox (GCL)		3	1	.750	1.35	0.94	7	6	0	0	...	0-...	26.2	24	7	4	0	1-0	32	.229
1997— Michigan (Midw.)		4	1	.800	2.90	1.41	9	9	0	0	...	0-...	49.2	57	23	16	4	13-0	41	.285
1998— Sarasota (Florida State)		0	0	...	2.84	1.34	8	8	0	0	...	0-...	12.2	12	6	4	0	5-0	9	.245
1999— Sarasota (Florida State)		4	10	.286	5.61	1.53	19	19	0	0	...	0-...	96.1	116	71	60	11	31-1	79	.294
2000— Sarasota (Florida State)		3	4	.429	3.66	1.16	11	11	0	0	...	0-...	64.0	57	29	26	3	17-0	47	.238
— Trenton (East.)		7	2	.778	2.58	1.09	14	14	1	0	...	0-...	90.2	78	28	26	7	21-1	58	.232
2001— Cincinnati (N.L.)		7	15	.318	5.29	1.42	36	29	0	0	1	0-0	182.0	209	121	107	23	49-6	96	.288
2002— Cincinnati (N.L.)		6	12	.333	3.64	1.37	32	21	1	1	0	0-0	138.1	144	73	56	17	45-5	84	.267
— Louisville (Int'l)		2	0	1.000	3.86	1.19	3	3	1	0	...	0-...	21.0	17	10	9	2	8-1	13	.224
2003— Louisville (Int'l)		1	2	.333	4.00	1.50	4	4	0	0	...	0-...	18.0	22	10	8	1	5-0	11	.293
— Cincinnati (N.L.)		9	5	.643	4.29	1.32	57	3	0	0	3	12-18	84.0	92	41	40	14	19-6	53	.281
2004— Atlanta (N.L.)		6	4	.600	4.07	1.37	84	0	0	0	31	2-9	79.2	89	38	36	9	20-3	60	.284
Major League totals (4 years)		28	36	.438	4.44	1.38	209	53	1	1	35	14-27	484.0	534	273	239	63	133-20	293	.280

DIVISION SERIES RECORD

Year	Team (League)	W	L	Pct.	ERA	WHIP	G	GS	CG	ShO	Hld.	Sv.-Opp.	IP	H	R	ER	HR	BB-IBB	SO	Avg.
2004— Atlanta (N.L.)		0	0	...	18.00	2.00	3	0	0	0	...	0-0	3.0	5	6	6	2	1-0	2	.417

RELAFORD, DESI — 2B/3B

PERSONAL: Born September 16, 1973, in Valdosta, Ga. ... 5-9/180. ... Bats both, throws right. ... Full name: Desmond Lamont Relaford. ... High school: Sandalwood (Jacksonville).

TRANSACTIONS/CAREER NOTES: Selected by Seattle Mariners organization in fourth round of 1991 free-agent draft. ... Traded by Mariners to Philadelphia Phillies for P Terry Mulholland (July 31, 1996). ... On disabled list (June 17-September 13, 1999); included rehabilitation assignment to Clearwater. ... Traded by Phillies to San Diego Padres for a player to be named later (August 4, 2000); Phillies acquired IF David Newhan to complete deal (August 7, 2000). ... Claimed on waivers by New York Mets (October 12, 2000). ... Traded by Mets with OF Tsuyoshi Shinjo to San Francisco Giants for P Shawn Estes (December 16, 2001). ... Traded by Giants with cash to Mariners for 3B David Bell (January 25, 2002). ... Signed as a free agent by Kansas City Royals (January 10, 2003). ... On disabled list (April 6-29, 2004); included rehabilitation assignment to Omaha. ... Career major league pitching: 0-0, 0.00 ERA, 1 G, 1.0 IP, 0 H, 0 R, 0 ER, 0 BB, 1 SO.

2004 GAMES PLAYED BY POSITION (MLB): 3B—42, 2B—36, OF—32, SS—12.

Year	Team (League)	Pos.	G	AB	R	H	2B	3B	HR	RBI	BB	SO	HBP	GDP	SB-CS	Avg.	OBP	SLG	OPS	E	Avg.
1991— Ariz. Mariners (Ariz.)	2B-SS	46	163	36	44	7	3	0	18	22	24	1	0	17-3	.270	.351	.350	.700	24	.885
1992— Peninsula (Caro.)	SS	130	445	53	96	18	1	3	34	39	88	1	7	27-7	.216	.277	.281	.558	52	.913
1993— Jacksonville (Sou.)	2B-3B-SS	133	472	49	115	16	4	8	47	50	103	7	4	16-12	.244	.323	.345	.668	38	.935
1994— Jacksonville (Sou.)	SS	37	143	24	29	7	3	3	11	22	28	0	2	10-1	.203	.305	.357	.662	4	.979
— Riverside (Calif.)	SS	99	374	95	116	27	5	5	59	78	78	4	1	27-6	.310	.429	.449	.878	36	.921
1995— Port City (Sou.)	SS-2B-DH	90	352	51	101	11	2	7	27	41	58	2	4	25-9	.287	.365	.389	.754	31	.930
— Tacoma (PCL)	2B-SS	30	113	20	27	5	1	2	7	13	24	0	2	6-0	.239	.313	.354	.666	6	.960
1996— Tacoma (PCL)	2B-SS-DH	93	317	27	65	12	0	4	32	23	58	1	7	10-6	.205	.259	.281	.539	20	.960
— Philadelphia (N.L.)	SS-2B	15	40	2	7	2	0	0	1	3	9	0	1	1-0	.175	.233	.225	.458	2	.959
— Scran./W.B. (I.L.)	SS	21	85	12	20	4	1	1	11	8	19	1	0	7-1	.235	.305	.341	.646	6	.938
1997— Scran./W.B. (I.L.)	SS	131	517	82	138	34	4	5	53	43	77	7	12	29-8	.267	.329	.400	.729	34	.942
— Philadelphia (N.L.)	SS	15	38	3	7	1	2	0	6	5	6	0	0	3-0	.184	.279	.316	.595	1	.977
1998— Philadelphia (N.L.)	SS	142	494	45	121	25	3	5	41	33	87	3	9	9-5	.245	.293	.338	.631	24	.960
1999— Philadelphia (N.L.)	SS	65	211	31	51	11	2	1	26	19	34	6	5	4-3	.242	.322	.327	.649	14	.952
— Clearwater (FSL)	SS	2	7	1	2	0	0	0	1	1	1	0	0	0-0	.286	.375	.286	.661	1	.800
2000— Philadelphia (N.L.)	SS	83	253	29	56	12	3	3	30	48	45	9	7	5-0	.221	.363	.328	.691	24	.930
— San Diego (N.L.)	SS	45	157	26	32	2	0	2	16	27	26	3	3	8-0	.204	.330	.255	.585	† 7	.965
2001— New York (N.L.)	2B-SS-3B	120	301	43	91	27	0	8	36	27	65	5	4	13-5	.302	.364	.472	.836	11	.963
2002— Seattle (A.L.)	S-3-0-2-DH	112	329	55	88	13	2	6	43	33	51	6	6	10-3	.267	.339	.374	.713	10	.965
2003— Kansas City (A.L.)	2-3-0-S-DH	141	500	70	127	27	5	8	59	40	70	6	10	20-4	.254	.315	.376	.691	16	.971
2004— Omaha (PCL)	DH-2B-SS	4	15	1	4	1	0	0	3	2	1	0	0	0-0	.267	.353	.333	.686	0	1.000
— Kansas City (A.L.)	3-2-0-S	114	380	45	84	14	0	6	34	34	56	8	10	5-4	.221	.296	.305	.601	12	.968
American League totals (3 years)		367	1209	170	299	54	7	20	136	107	177	20	26	35-11	.247	.316	.353	.669	38	.969
National League totals (6 years)		485	1494	179	365	80	10	19	156	162	272	26	29	43-13	.244	.326	.349	.676	83	.954
Major League totals (9 years)		852	2703	349	664	134	17	39	292	269	449	46	55	78-24	.246	.322	.351	.673	121	.960

REMLINGER, MIKE — P

PERSONAL: Born March 23, 1966, in Middletown, N.Y. ... 6-1/215. ... Throws left, bats left. ... Full name: Michael John Remlinger. ... Name pronounced: REM-lin-jurr. ... High school: Carver (Plymouth, Mass.). ... College: Dartmouth.

TRANSACTIONS/CAREER NOTES: Selected by San Francisco Giants organization in first round (16th pick overall) of 1987 free-agent draft. ... Traded by Giants with OF Kevin Mitchell to Seattle Mariners for Ps Bill Swift, Mike Jackson and Dave Burba (December 11, 1991). ... Signed as a free agent by New York Mets organization (November 22, 1993). ... Traded by Mets to Cincinnati Reds for OF Cobi Cradle (May 11, 1995). ... Traded by Reds to Kansas City Royals as part of three-team deal in which Reds acquired OF Andre King from St. Louis Cardinals and Cardinals acquired SS Luis Ordaz from Reds and OF Miguel Mejia from Royals (December 4, 1995). ... Claimed on waivers by Reds (April 4, 1996). ... Traded by Reds with 2B Bret Boone to Atlanta Braves for Ps Denny Neagle and Rob Bell and OF Michael Tucker (November 10, 1998). ... On disabled list (April 3-18, 1999; June 23-July 13, 2000; and August 8-24, 2002). ... Signed as a free agent by Chicago Cubs (December 3, 2002). ... On disabled list (March 26-May 22 and June 24-July 11, 2004); included rehabilitation assignment to Iowa.

CAREER HITTING: 8-for-110 (.073), 5 R, 3 2B, 0 3B, 0 HR, 8 RBI.

Year	Team (League)	W	L	Pct.	ERA	WHIP	G	GS	CG	ShO	Hld.	Sv.-Opp.	IP	H	R	ER	HR	BB-IBB	SO	Avg.
1987— Everett (Northwest)		0	0	...	3.60	1.20	2	1	0	0	...	0-...	5.0	1	2	2	0	5-0	11	.071
— Clinton (Midw.)		2	1	.667	3.30	1.17	6	5	0	0	...	0-...	30.0	21	12	11	2	14-0	43	.196
— Shreveport (Texas)		4	2	.667	2.36	1.05	6	6	0	0	...	0-...	34.1	14	11	9	2	22-0	51	.120
1988— Shreveport (Texas)		1	0	1.000	0.69	0.85	3	3	0	0	...	0-...	13.0	7	4	1	0	4-0	18	.163
1989— Shreveport (Texas)		4	6	.400	2.98	1.34	16	16	0	0	...	0-...	90.2	68	43	30	2	73-0	92	.212
— Phoenix (PCL)		1	6	.143	9.21	2.40	11	10	0	0	...	0-...	43.0	51	47	44	8	52-0	28	.290
1990— Shreveport (Texas)		9	11	.450	3.90	1.50	25	25	2	1	...	0-...	147.2	149	82	64	9	72-1	75	.270
1991— Phoenix (PCL)		5	5	.500	6.38	1.78	19	19	1	1	...	0-...	108.2	134	86	77	15	59-0	68	.305
— San Francisco (N.L.)		2	1	.667	4.37	1.60	8	6	1	1	0	0-0	35.0	36	17	17	5	20-1	19	.271

Year Team (League)	W	L	Pct.	ERA	WHIP	G	GS	CG	ShO	Hld.	Sv.-Opp.	IP	H	R	ER	HR	BB-IBB	SO	Avg.
1992— Calgary (PCL)	1	7	.125	6.65	2.06	21	11	0	0	...	0-...	70.1	97	65	52	7	48-1	24	.342
— Jacksonville (Southern)	1	1	.500	3.46	1.38	5	5	0	0	...	0-...	26.0	25	15	10	1	11-0	21	.250
1993— Calgary (PCL)	4	3	.571	5.53	1.80	19	18	0	0	...	0-...	84.2	100	57	52	8	52-0	51	.300
— Jacksonville (Southern)	1	3	.250	6.58	1.49	7	7	0	0	...	0-...	39.2	40	30	29	7	19-0	23	.261
1994— Norfolk (Int'l)	2	4	.333	3.14	1.30	12	9	0	0	...	0-...	63.0	57	29	22	5	25-0	45	.242
— New York (N.L.)	1	5	.167	4.61	1.65	10	9	0	0	1	0-0	54.2	55	30	28	9	35-4	33	.261
1995— New York (N.L.)	0	1	.000	6.35	1.59	5	0	0	0	0	0-1	5.2	7	5	4	1	2-0	6	.292
— Cincinnati (N.L.)	0	0	...	9.00	5.00	2	0	0	0	0	0-0	1.0	2	1	1	0	3-0	1	.500
— Indianapolis (A.A.)	5	3	.625	4.05	1.54	41	1	0	0	...	0-...	46.2	40	24	21	4	32-4	58	.231
1996— Indianapolis (A.A.)	4	3	.571	2.52	1.21	28	13	0	0	...	0-...	89.1	64	29	25	4	44-0	97	.203
— Cincinnati (N.L.)	0	1	.000	5.60	1.57	19	4	0	0	1	0-0	27.1	24	17	17	4	19-2	19	.245
1997— Cincinnati (N.L.)	8	8	.500	4.14	1.29	69	12	2	0	14	2-2	124.0	100	61	57	11	60-6	145	.223
1998— Cincinnati (N.L.)	8	15	.348	4.82	1.53	35	28	1	1	0	0-0	164.1	164	96	88	23	87-1	144	.266
1999— Atlanta (N.L.)	10	1	.909	2.37	1.21	73	0	0	0	21	1-3	83.2	66	24	22	9	35-5	81	.215
2000— Atlanta (N.L.)	5	3	.625	3.47	1.27	71	0	0	0	23	12-16	72.2	55	29	28	6	37-1	72	.207
2001— Atlanta (N.L.)	3	3	.500	2.76	1.20	74	0	0	0	31	1-5	75.0	67	25	23	9	23-4	93	.234
2002— Atlanta (N.L.)	7	3	.700	1.99	1.12	73	0	0	0	30	0-5	68.0	48	17	15	3	28-3	69	.198
2003— Chicago (N.L.)	6	5	.545	3.65	1.35	73	0	0	0	17	0-1	69.0	54	30	28	11	39-4	83	.211
2004— Iowa (PCL)	0	0	...	16.20	1.80	2	0	0	0	...	0-...	1.2	3	3	3	1	0-0	1	.375
— Chicago (N.L.)	1	2	.333	3.44	1.34	48	0	0	0	13	2-6	36.2	33	16	14	3	16-3	35	.246
Major League totals (12 years)	51	48	.515	3.77	1.36	560	59	4	2	151	18-39	817.0	711	368	342	94	404-34	800	.235

DIVISION SERIES RECORD

Year Team (League)	W	L	Pct.	ERA	WHIP	G	GS	CG	ShO	Hld.	Sv.-Opp.	IP	H	R	ER	HR	BB-IBB	SO	Avg.
1999— Atlanta (N.L.)	0	0	...	9.82	1.91	2	0	0	0	0	0-1	3.2	4	4	4	1	3-2	4	.308
2000— Atlanta (N.L.)	0	0	...	2.70	1.80	3	0	0	0	0	0-0	3.1	6	1	1	1	0-0	3	.375
2001— Atlanta (N.L.)	0	0	...	0.00	0.00	1	0	0	0	1	0-0	.1	0	0	0	0	0-0	0	.000
2002— Atlanta (N.L.)	0	0	...	4.50	2.50	3	0	0	0	1	0-0	2.0	3	1	1	0	2-0	3	.333
2003— Chicago (N.L.)	0	0	...	0.00	1.50	2	0	0	0	0	0-0	.2	0	0	0	0	1-0	1	.000
Division series totals (5 years)	0	0	...	5.40	1.90	11	0	0	0	2	0-1	10.0	13	6	6	2	6-2	11	.317

CHAMPIONSHIP SERIES RECORD

Year Team (League)	W	L	Pct.	ERA	WHIP	G	GS	CG	ShO	Hld.	Sv.-Opp.	IP	H	R	ER	HR	BB-IBB	SO	Avg.
1999— Atlanta (N.L.)	0	1	.000	3.18	1.06	5	0	0	0	3	0-0	5.2	3	2	2	0	3-0	4	.158
2001— Atlanta (N.L.)	0	0	...	0.00	2.14	3	0	0	0	0	0-0	2.1	3	0	0	0	2-0	2	.333
2003— Chicago (N.L.)	0	0	...	2.70	1.20	5	0	0	0	0	1-1	3.1	3	1	1	1	1-0	2	.214
Champ. series totals (3 years)	0	1	.000	2.38	1.32	13	0	0	0	3	1-1	11.1	9	3	3	1	6-0	8	.214

WORLD SERIES RECORD

Year Team (League)	W	L	Pct.	ERA	WHIP	G	GS	CG	ShO	Hld.	Sv.-Opp.	IP	H	R	ER	HR	BB-IBB	SO	Avg.
1999— Atlanta (N.L.)	0	1	.000	9.00	2.00	2	0	0	0	1	0-0	1.0	1	1	1	1	1-0	0	.333

ALL-STAR GAME RECORD

	W	L	Pct.	ERA	WHIP	G	GS	CG	ShO	Hld.	Sv.-Opp.	IP	H	R	ER	HR	BB-IBB	SO	Avg.
All-Star Game totals (1 year)	0	0	...	27.00	3.00	1	0	0	0	1	0-0	.2	1	2	2	0	1-0	0	.333

RENTERIA, EDGAR — SS

PERSONAL: Born August 7, 1975, in Barranquilla, Colombia. ... 6-1/200. ... Bats right, throws right. ... Full name: Edgar Enrique Renteria. ... Name pronounced: ren-ter-ee-AH. ... High school: Instituto Los Alpes (Barranquilla, Colombia).

TRANSACTIONS/CAREER NOTES: Signed as a non-drafted free agent by Florida Marlins organization (February 14, 1992). ... On disabled list (June 24-July 11, 1996); included rehabilitation assignment to Charlotte. ... On disabled list (August 25-September 9, 1998). ... Traded by Marlins to St. Louis Cardinals for Ps Braden Looper and Armando Almanza and SS Pablo Ozuna (December 14, 1998).

HONORS: Won N.L. Gold Glove at shortstop (2002 and 2003).

2004 GAMES PLAYED BY POSITION (MLB): SS—149.

Year Team (League)	Pos.	G	AB	R	H	2B	3B	HR	RBI	BB	SO	HBP	GDP	SB-CS	Avg.	OBP	SLG	OPS	E	Avg.
1992— GC Marlins (GCL)	SS	43	163	25	47	8	1	0	9	8	29	2	1	10-6	.288	.329	.350	.679	24	.897
1993— Kane Co. (Midw.)	SS	116	384	40	78	8	0	1	35	35	94	0	3	7-8	.203	.268	.232	.500	34	.934
1994— Brevard County (FSL)	SS	128	439	46	111	15	1	0	36	35	56	0	14	6-11	.253	.307	.292	.598	23	.959
1995— Portland (East.)	SS	135	508	70	147	15	7	7	68	32	85	2	10	30-11	.289	.329	.388	.717	33	.944
1996— Charlotte (Int'l)	SS	35	132	17	37	8	0	2	16	9	17	0	5	10-4	.280	.326	.386	.713	7	.959
— Florida (N.L.)	SS	106	431	68	133	18	3	5	31	33	68	2	12	16-2	.309	.358	.399	.757	11	.979
1997— Florida (N.L.)	SS	154	617	90	171	21	3	4	52	45	108	4	17	32-15	.277	.327	.340	.668	17	.975
1998— Florida (N.L.)	SS	133	517	79	146	18	2	3	31	48	78	4	13	41-22	.282	.347	.342	.689	20	.966
1999— St. Louis (N.L.)	SS	154	585	92	161	36	2	11	63	53	82	2	16	37-8	.275	.334	.400	.734	26	.959
2000— St. Louis (N.L.)	SS	150	562	94	156	32	1	16	76	63	77	1	19	21-13	.278	.346	.423	.770	27	.958
2001— St. Louis (N.L.)	SS-DH-1B	141	493	54	128	19	3	10	57	39	73	3	15	17-4	.260	.314	.371	.685	24	.961
2002— St. Louis (N.L.)	SS	152	544	77	166	36	2	11	83	49	57	4	17	22-7	.305	.364	.439	.803	19	.970
2003— St. Louis (N.L.)	SS	157	587	96	194	47	1	13	100	65	54	1	21	34-7	.330	.394	.480	.874	16	.975
2004— St. Louis (N.L.)	SS	149	586	84	168	37	0	10	72	39	78	1	14	17-11	.287	.327	.401	.728	11	.983
Major League totals (9 years)		1296	4922	734	1423	264	17	83	565	434	675	22	144	237-89	.289	.346	.400	.746	171	.969

DIVISION SERIES RECORD

Year Team (League)	Pos.	G	AB	R	H	2B	3B	HR	RBI	BB	SO	HBP	GDP	SB-CS	Avg.	OBP	SLG	OPS	E	Avg.
1997— Florida (N.L.)	SS	3	13	1	2	0	0	0	1	2	4	0	1	0-0	.154	.267	.154	.421	2	.909
2000— St. Louis (N.L.)	SS	3	10	5	2	0	0	0	4	1	0	0	0	2-0	.200	.429	.200	.629	1	.909
2001— St. Louis (N.L.)	SS	5	17	2	4	1	0	1	1	2	4	0	1	0-0	.235	.316	.471	.786	1	.955
2002— St. Louis (N.L.)	SS	3	12	3	3	0	0	0	0	1	1	0	1	2-0	.250	.308	.250	.558	1	.909
2004— St. Louis (N.L.)	SS	4	11	4	5	2	0	0	4	3	1	1	0	1-1	.455	.600	.636	1.236	0	1.000
Division series totals (5 years)		18	63	15	16	3	0	1	6	12	11	1	3	5-1	.254	.382	.349	.731	5	.943

CHAMPIONSHIP SERIES RECORD

Year Team (League)	Pos.	G	AB	R	H	2B	3B	HR	RBI	BB	SO	HBP	GDP	SB-CS	Avg.	OBP	SLG	OPS	E	Avg.
1997— Florida (N.L.)	SS	6	22	4	5	1	0	0	3	3	6	1	1	1-0	.227	.346	.273	.619	0	1.000
2000— St. Louis (N.L.)	SS	5	20	4	6	1	0	0	4	0	2	0	0	3-0	.300	.286	.350	.636	0	1.000
2002— St. Louis (N.L.)	SS	5	19	0	3	0	0	0	0	0	2	1	0	0-0	.158	.190	.158	.348	1	.900
2004— St. Louis (N.L.)	SS	7	24	1	4	0	0	0	2	2	5	0	0	0-0	.167	.231	.167	.397	0	1.000
Champ. series totals (4 years)		23	85	9	18	2	0	0	7	5	15	2	2	4-0	.212	.266	.235	.501	1	.989

Year	Team (League)	Pos.	G	AB	R	H	2B	3B	HR	RBI	BB	SO	HBP	GDP	SB-CS	Avg.	OBP	SLG	OPS	E	Avg.
1997— Florida (N.L.)		SS	7	31	3	9	2	0	0	3	3	5	0	0	0-0	.290	.353	.355	.708	1	.974
2004— St. Louis (N.L.)		SS	4	15	2	5	3	0	0	1	2	2	0	1	0-0	.333	.412	.533	.945	1	.941
World series totals (2 years)			11	46	5	14	5	0	0	4	5	7	0	1	0-0	.304	.373	.413	.786	2	.964

ALL-STAR GAME RECORD

			G	AB	R	H	2B	3B	HR	RBI	BB	SO	HBP	GDP	SB-CS	Avg.	OBP	SLG	OPS	E	Avg.
All-Star Game totals (4 years)			4	8	2	1	1	0	0	1	0	1	0	1	0-0	.125	.125	.250	.375	0	1.000

RESTOVICH, MICHAEL — OF

PERSONAL: Born January 3, 1979, in Rochester, Minn. ... 6-4/257. ... Bats right, throws right. ... Full name: Michael Jerome Restovich. ... High school: Mayo (Rochester, Minn.).

TRANSACTIONS/CAREER NOTES: Selected by Minnesota Twins organization in second round of 1997 free-agent draft.

2004 GAMES PLAYED BY POSITION (MLB): OF—19, DH—5.

								BATTING												**FIELDING**	
Year	Team (League)	Pos.	G	AB	R	H	2B	3B	HR	RBI	BB	SO	HBP	GDP	SB-CS	Avg.	OBP	SLG	OPS	E	Avg.
1998— Elizabethton (App.)		OF	65	242	68	86	20	1	13	64	54	58	9	10	5-2	.355	.489	.607	1.096	9	.912
— Fort Wayne (Midw.)		OF	11	45	9	20	5	2	0	6	4	12	0	1	0-0	.444	.490	.644	1.134	0	1.000
1999— Quad City (Midw.)		3B-OF	131	493	91	154	30	6	19	107	74	100	13	9	7-9	.312	.412	.513	.925	6	.958
2000— Fort Myers (FSL)		OF	135	475	73	125	27	9	8	64	61	100	4	11	19-7	.263	.350	.408	.758	6	.975
2001— New Britain (East.)		1B-OF	140	501	69	135	33	4	23	84	54	125	6	8	15-7	.269	.345	.489	.834	3	.989
2002— Edmonton (PCL)		OF	138	518	95	148	32	7	29	98	53	151	4	10	11-7	.286	.353	.542	.896	6	.976
— Minnesota (A.L.)		OF-DH	8	13	3	4	0	0	1	1	1	4	0	2	1-0	.308	.357	.538	.896	0	1.000
2003— Rochester (Int'l)		OF-DH	119	454	75	125	34	2	16	72	47	117	4	10	10-3	.275	.346	.465	.811	3	.989
— Minnesota (A.L.)		OF-DH	24	53	10	15	3	2	0	4	10	12	1	3	0-0	.283	.406	.415	.821	0	1.000
2004— Rochester (Int'l)		OF-DH	106	425	65	105	20	3	20	63	25	104	2	13	4-3	.247	.291	.449	.740	5	.975
— Minnesota (A.L.)		OF-DH	29	47	9	12	3	0	2	6	4	10	0	0	0-0	.255	.314	.447	.761	0	1.000
Major League totals (3 years)			61	113	22	31	6	2	3	11	15	26	1	5	1-0	.274	.364	.442	.807	0	1.000

REYES, AL — P

PERSONAL: Born April 10, 1970, in San Cristobal, Dominican Republic. ... 6-1/212. ... Throws right, bats right. ... Full name: Rafael Alberto Reyes. ... Name pronounced: RAY-ess. ... High school: Francisco del Rosario Sanche (Santo Domingo, Dominican Republic).

TRANSACTIONS/CAREER NOTES: Signed as a non-drafted free agent by Montreal Expos organization (February 17, 1988). ... Selected by Milwaukee Brewers from Expos organization in Rule 5 major league draft (December 5, 1994). ... On disabled list (July 19, 1995-remainder of season). ... On disabled list (July 25-September 8, 1998); included rehabilitation assignment to Louisville. ... Traded by Brewers to Baltimore Orioles (July 21, 1999), completing deal in which Orioles traded P Rocky Coppinger to Brewers for a player to be named (July 16, 1999). ... Traded by Orioles to Los Angeles Dodgers for P Alan Mills and cash (June 13, 2000). ... Released by Dodgers (January 22, 2001). ... Re-signed by Dodgers (February 1, 2001). ... Signed as a free agent by Pittsburgh Pirates organization (January 25, 2002). ... Released by Pirates (March 10, 2003). ... Signed by New York Yankees organization (March 19, 2003). ... Released by Yankees (July 25, 2003). ... Signed by Tampa Bay Devil Rays organization (January 12, 2004). ... Released by Devil Rays (June 1, 2004). ... Signed by St. Louis Cardinals organization (June 3, 2004).

CAREER HITTING: 3-for-11 (.273), 2 R, 0 2B, 0 3B, 0 HR, 0 RBI.

Year	Team (League)	W	L	Pct.	ERA	WHIP	G	GS	CG	ShO	Hld.	Sv.-Opp.	IP	H	R	ER	HR	BB-IBB	SO	Avg.
1989— DSL Expos (DSL)		3	4	.429	2.79	1.42	12	10	1	0	...	0-...	71.0	68	36	22	4	33-...	49	...
1990— W.P. Beach (FSL)		5	4	.556	4.74	1.58	16	10	0	0	...	1-...	57.0	58	32	30	4	32-2	47	.272
1991— Rockford (Midwest)		0	1	.000	5.56	1.41	3	3	0	0	...	0-...	11.1	14	8	7	1	2-0	10	.304
1992— Albany (S. Atl.)		0	2	.000	3.95	1.35	27	0	0	0	...	4-...	27.1	24	14	12	0	13-0	29	.226
1993— Burlington (Midw.)		7	6	.538	2.68	1.05	53	0	0	0	...	11-...	74.0	52	33	22	7	26-3	80	.193
1994— Harrisburg (Eastern)		2	2	.500	3.25	1.17	60	0	0	0	...	35-...	69.1	68	26	25	4	13-0	60	.257
1995— Milwaukee (A.L.)		1	1	.500	2.43	1.11	27	0	0	0	4	1-1	33.1	19	9	9	3	18-2	29	.167
1996— Beloit (Midw.)		1	0	1.000	1.83	1.17	13	0	0	0	...	0-...	19.2	17	7	4	1	6-0	22	.227
— Milwaukee (A.L.)		1	0	1.000	7.94	1.76	5	0	0	0	0	0-0	5.2	8	5	5	1	2-0	2	.320
1997— Tucson (PCL)		2	4	.333	5.02	1.50	38	0	0	0	...	7-...	57.1	52	39	32	12	34-2	70	.243
— Milwaukee (A.L.)		1	2	.333	5.46	1.38	19	0	0	0	1	1-1	29.2	32	19	18	4	9-0	28	.274
1998— Milwaukee (N.L.)		5	1	.833	3.95	1.51	50	0	0	0	10	0-1	57.0	55	26	25	9	31-1	58	.255
— Louisville (Int'l)		0	1	.000	8.31	1.62	3	2	0	0	...	0-...	4.1	5	5	4	1	2-0	5	.294
1999— Louisville (Int'l)		0	0	.000	8.38	1.97	6	0	0	0	...	0-...	9.2	12	9	9	0	7-2	8	.343
— Milwaukee (N.L.)		2	0	1.000	4.25	1.44	26	0	0	0	2	0-1	36.0	27	17	17	5	25-1	39	.206
— Baltimore (A.L.)		2	3	.400	4.85	1.31	27	0	0	0	4	0-3	29.2	23	16	16	4	16-2	28	.225
2000— Rochester (Int'l)		0	1	.000	7.71	1.89	9	0	0	0	...	2-...	11.2	13	11	10	2	9-1	17	.271
— Baltimore (A.L.)		1	0	1.000	6.92	1.85	13	0	0	0	2	0-1	13.0	13	10	10	2	11-1	10	.271
— Albuquerque (PCL)		3	2	.600	3.72	1.40	30	0	0	0	...	8-...	38.2	33	20	16	5	21-0	39	.226
— Los Angeles (N.L.)		0	0	...	0.00	0.45	6	0	0	0	1	0-0	6.2	2	0	0	0	1-0	8	.087
2001— Las Vegas (PCL)		0	1	.000	3.38	1.16	19	0	0	0	...	0-...	29.1	24	11	11	3	10-1	37	.218
— Los Angeles (N.L.)		2	1	.667	3.86	1.60	19	0	0	0	0	1-2	25.2	28	13	11	3	13-1	23	.269
2002— Nashville (PCL)		7	3	.700	2.70	0.93	43	0	0	0	...	1-...	66.2	40	21	20	5	22-2	90	.167
— Pittsburgh (N.L.)		0	0	...	2.65	0.94	15	0	0	0	3	0-1	17.0	9	5	5	1	7-0	21	.161
2003— Columbus (Int'l)		1	1	.500	3.71	1.20	15	0	0	0	...	2-...	17.0	16	7	7	1	5-0	21	.239
— New York (A.L.)		0	0	...	3.18	1.29	13	0	0	0	0	0-1	17.0	13	7	6	1	9-1	9	.203
2004— Durham (Int'l)		2	1	.667	2.46	1.23	20	0	0	0	...	10-...	22.0	22	6	6	0	5-1	22	.265
— Memphis (PCL)		2	2	.500	2.95	1.16	37	0	0	0	...	23-...	39.2	32	13	13	7	14-3	47	.219
— St. Louis (N.L.)		0	0	...	0.75	0.42	12	0	0	0	0	0-0	12.0	3	1	1	0	2-0	11	.081
American League totals (6 years)		6	6	.500	4.49	1.35	104	0	0	0	11	2-7	128.1	108	66	64	15	65-6	106	.230
National League totals (6 years)		9	2	.818	3.44	1.32	128	0	0	0	16	1-5	154.1	124	62	59	18	79-3	160	.219
Major League totals (10 years)		15	8	.652	3.92	1.33	232	0	0	0	27	3-12	282.2	232	128	123	33	144-9	266	.224

WORLD SERIES RECORD

Year	Team (League)	W	L	Pct.	ERA	WHIP	G	GS	CG	ShO	Hld.	Sv.-Opp.	IP	H	R	ER	HR	BB-IBB	SO	Avg.
2004— St. Louis (N.L.)		0	0	...	0.00	0.00	2	0	0	0	0	0-0	1.1	0	0	0	0	0-0	0	.000

REYES, DENNYS   P

PERSONAL: Born April 19, 1977, in Higuera de Zaragoza, Mexico. ... 6-3/245. ... Throws left, bats right. ... Name pronounced: RAY-us. ... High school: Ignacio Zaragoza (Higuera de Zaragoza, Mexico).

TRANSACTIONS/CAREER NOTES: Signed as a non-drafted free agent by Los Angeles Dodgers organization (July 5, 1993). ... Loaned by Dodgers organization to Mexico City Red Devils of the Mexican League (March 28-August 22, 1995). ... Traded by Dodgers with 1B/3B Paul Konerko to Cincinnati Reds for P Jeff Shaw (July 4, 1998). ... On disabled list (May 30-July 2, 2001). ... Traded by Reds with 2B Pokey Reese to Colorado Rockies for Ps Gabe White and Luke Hudson (December 18, 2001). ... Traded by Rockies with OF Todd Hollandsworth to Texas Rangers for OF Gabe Kapler and 2B Jason Romano (July 31, 2002). ... Signed as a free agent by Pittsburgh Pirates organization (January 24, 2003). ... Refused minor league assignment and became a free agent (May 19, 2003). ... Signed by Arizona Diamondbacks organization (June 11, 2003). ... Refused minor league assignment and became a free agent (October 3, 2003). ... Signed by Kansas City Royals organization (October 30, 2003).

CAREER HITTING: 3-for-49 (.061), 2 R, 1 2B, 0 3B, 0 HR, 0 RBI.

Year Team (League)	W	L	Pct.	ERA	WHIP	G	GS	CG	ShO	Hld.	Sv.-Opp.	IP	H	R	ER	HR	BB-IBB	SO	Avg.
1993— M.C. Red Devils (Mex.)	0	1	.000	5.06	2.44	1	1	0	0	...	0-...	5.1	4	4	3	1	9-...	5	...
1994— Vero Beach (FSL)	2	4	.333	6.70	1.82	9	9	0	0	...	0-...	41.2	58	37	31	6	18-0	25	.324
— Great Falls (Pio.)	7	1	.875	3.78	1.44	14	9	0	0	...	0-...	66.2	71	37	28	0	25-0	70	.267
1995— M.C. Red Devils (Mex.)	5	5	.500	6.60	1.99	17	15	1	0	...	0-...	58.2	76	49	43	4	41-...	44	...
— Vero Beach (FSL)	1	0	1.000	1.80	1.40	3	2	0	0	...	0-...	10.0	8	2	2	0	6-0	9	.222
1996— San Bernardino (Calif.)	11	12	.478	4.17	1.46	29	28	0	0	...	0-...	166.0	166	106	77	11	77-0	176	.259
1997— San Antonio (Texas)	8	1	.889	3.02	1.33	12	12	1	0	...	0-...	80.1	79	33	27	6	28-1	66	.262
— Albuquerque (PCL)	6	3	.667	5.65	1.80	10	10	1	0	...	0-...	57.1	70	40	36	4	33-0	45	.303
— Los Angeles (N.L.)	2	3	.400	3.83	1.47	14	5	0	0	0	0-0	47.0	51	21	20	4	18-3	36	.280
1998— Albuquerque (PCL)	1	4	.200	1.44	1.12	7	7	1	1	...	0-...	43.2	31	13	7	5	18-0	58	.197
— Los Angeles (N.L.)	0	4	.000	4.71	1.64	11	3	0	0	0	0-0	28.2	27	17	15	1	20-4	33	.255
— Indianapolis (Int'l)	2	0	1.000	3.00	1.42	4	4	0	0	...	0-...	24.0	20	10	8	1	14-0	27	.233
— Cincinnati (N.L.)	3	1	.750	4.42	1.60	8	7	0	0	0	0-...	38.2	35	19	19	2	27-1	44	.255
1999— Cincinnati (N.L.)	2	2	.500	3.79	1.49	65	1	0	0	14	2-3	61.2	53	30	26	5	39-1	72	.232
2000— Cincinnati (N.L.)	2	1	.667	4.53	1.65	62	0	0	0	10	0-1	43.2	43	31	22	5	29-0	36	.262
2001— Cincinnati (N.L.)	2	6	.250	4.92	1.62	35	6	0	0	6	0-0	53.0	51	35	29	5	35-1	52	.248
— Louisville (Int'l)	4	2	.667	3.67	1.46	7	6	0	0	...	0-...	34.1	34	15	14	3	16-0	34	.260
2002— Colorado (N.L.)	0	1	.000	4.24	1.66	43	0	0	0	4	0-0	40.1	43	19	19	1	24-3	30	.279
— Texas (A.L.)	4	3	.571	6.38	1.80	15	5	0	0	0	0-0	42.1	55	33	30	9	21-1	29	.316
2003— Pittsburgh (N.L.)	0	0	...	10.45	1.84	12	0	0	0	2	0-0	10.1	10	13	12	1	9-1	11	.263
— Tucson (PCL)	2	1	.667	2.84	1.50	33	0	0	0	...	2-...	31.2	24	16	10	0	22-2	30	.207
— Arizona (N.L.)	0	0	...	11.57	2.57	3	0	0	0	0	0-0	2.1	5	3	3	1	1-0	5	.417
2004— Kansas City (A.L.)	4	8	.333	4.75	1.52	40	12	0	0	5	0-1	108.0	114	64	57	12	50-3	91	.273
American League totals (2 years)	8	11	.421	5.21	1.60	55	17	0	0	5	0-1	150.1	169	97	87	21	71-4	120	.286
National League totals (7 years)	11	18	.379	4.56	1.60	253	22	0	0	36	2-4	325.2	318	188	165	25	202-14	319	.259
Major League totals (8 years)	19	29	.396	4.76	1.60	308	39	0	0	41	2-5	476.0	487	285	252	46	273-18	439	.268

REYES, JOSE   2B

PERSONAL: Born June 11, 1983, in Villa Gonzalez, Dominican Republic. ... 6-0/160. ... Bats both, throws right. ... Full name: Jose Bernabe Reyes.

TRANSACTIONS/CAREER NOTES: Signed as a non-drafted free agent by New York Mets organization (August 16, 1999). ... On disabled list (September 1, 2003-remainder of season). ... On disabled list (March 26-June 19 and August 13-September 24, 2004); included rehabilitation assignments to St. Lucie and Binghamton.

2004 GAMES PLAYED BY POSITION (MLB): 2B—43, SS—10.

Year Team (League)	Pos.	G	AB	R	H	2B	3B	HR	RBI	BB	SO	HBP	GDP	SB-CS	Avg.	OBP	SLG	OPS	E	Avg.
2000— Kingsport (Appalachian) ...SS-3B-2B-OF	49	132	22	33	3	3	0	8	20	37	3	1	10-4	.250	.359	.318	.677	11	.942
2001— Capital City (SAL)	SS	108	407	71	125	22	15	5	48	18	71	2	4	30-10	.307	.337	.472	.809	18	.964
2002— St. Lucie (Fla. St.)	SS	69	288	58	83	10	11	6	38	30	35	1	5	31-13	.288	.353	.462	.815	12	.967
— Binghamton (East.)	SS	65	275	46	79	16	8	2	24	16	42	2	2	27-11	.287	.331	.425	.757	17	.940
2003— Norfolk (Int'l)	SS-DH	42	160	28	43	6	4	0	13	15	25	1	2	26-5	.269	.333	.356	.690	5	.969
— New York (N.L.)	SS	69	274	47	84	12	4	5	32	13	36	0	1	13-3	.307	.334	.434	.769	9	.973
2004— St. Lucie (Fla. St.)	2B	6	23	3	6	2	0	0	1	0	3	0	1	2-0	.261	.261	.348	.609	2	.917
— Binghamton (East.)	2B	4	18	2	2	0	0	0	3	2	4	0	0	3-1	.111	.190	.111	.302	0	1.000
— New York (N.L.)	2B-SS	53	220	33	56	16	2	2	14	5	31	0	1	19-2	.255	.271	.373	.644	6	.975
Major League totals (2 years)		122	494	80	140	28	6	7	46	18	67	0	2	32-5	.283	.307	.407	.714	15	.974

REYES, RENE   OF

PERSONAL: Born February 21, 1978, in Margarita, Venezuela. ... 5-11/213. ... Bats both, throws right. ... Name pronounced: RAY-es. ... High school: Nueva Esparata (Margarita, Venezuela).

TRANSACTIONS/CAREER NOTES: Signed as a non-drafted free agent by Colorado Rockies organization (August 29, 1996).

2004 GAMES PLAYED BY POSITION (MLB): OF—21.

Year Team (League)	Pos.	G	AB	R	H	2B	3B	HR	RBI	BB	SO	HBP	GDP	SB-CS	Avg.	OBP	SLG	OPS	E	Avg.
1998— Ariz. Rockies (Ariz.)	1B-C	0	49	177	40	108	9	4	5	15	1	1	7	15-16	...	.610	5.000	4.494	17	.961
1999— Ariz. Rockies (Ariz.)	1B	22	97	21	35	4	4	1	20	4	14	2	2	6-1	.361	.398	.515	.914	2	.989
— Asheville (S. Atl.)	1B	40	160	26	56	6	1	3	19	6	22	1	1	1-0	.350	.377	.456	.834	0	1.000
2001— Asheville (S. Atl.)	OF-1B	128	484	71	156	27	2	11	61	28	80	12	9	53-12	.322	.371	.455	.826	11	.983
2002— Carolina (Southern)	OF-1B	123	455	64	133	33	4	14	54	29	69	5	10	10-11	.292	.339	.475	.813	11	.979
2003— Colo. Springs (PCL)	OF-DH	98	370	60	127	23	3	6	50	22	56	2	11	12-8	.343	.380	.470	.851	5	.970
— Colorado (N.L.)	OF	53	116	13	30	7	1	2	7	5	19	0	3	2-1	.259	.287	.388	.675	2	.964
2004— Colorado (N.L.)	OF	28	61	5	9	2	0	0	1	5	17	0	0	0-0	.148	.212	.180	.392	0	1.000
— Colo. Springs (PCL)	OF-DH	87	313	44	96	23	1	6	47	18	60	2	7	10-5	.307	.348	.444	.792	6	.957
Major League totals (2 years)		81	177	18	39	9	1	2	8	10	36	0	3	2-1	.220	.261	.316	.577	2	.977

REYNOLDS, SHANE   P

PERSONAL: Born March 26, 1968, in Bastrop, La. ... 6-3/215. ... Throws right, bats right. ... Full name: Richard Shane Reynolds. ... High school: Ouachita Christian (Monroe, La.). ... College: Texas.

TRANSACTIONS/CAREER NOTES: Selected by Houston Astros organization in third round of 1989 free-agent draft. ... On disabled list (June 10-July 14, 1997); included rehabilitation assignment to New Orleans. ... On disabled list (August 2, 2000-remainder of season). ... On disabled list (March 31-April 18 and August 14-September 1, 2001); included rehabilitation assignments to Round Rock and New Orleans. ... On disabled list (June 14, 2002-remainder of season). ... Released by Astros (March 27, 2003). ...

Signed by Atlanta Braves (April 10, 2003). ... Signed as a free agent by Arizona Diamondbacks (December 23, 2003). ... On disabled list (April 4-June 28 and June 29, 2004-remainder of season); included rehabilitation assignments to El Paso and Tucson.

CAREER HITTING: 77-for-546 (.141), 34 R, 15 2B, 0 3B, 5 HR, 43 RBI.

Year	Team (League)	W	L	Pct.	ERA	WHIP	G	GS	CG	ShO	Hld.	Sv.-Opp.	IP	H	R	ER	HR	BB-IBB	SO	Avg.
1989—	Auburn (N.Y.-Penn)	3	2	.600	2.31	1.43	6	6	1	0	...	0-...	35.0	36	16	9	1	14-0	23	.275
—	Asheville (S. Atl.)	5	3	.625	3.68	1.44	8	8	2	1	...	0-...	51.1	53	25	21	2	21-0	33	.268
1990—	Columbus (Sou.)	9	10	.474	4.81	1.62	29	27	2	1	...	0-...	155.1	181	104	83	14	70-1	92	.293
1991—	Jackson (Texas)	8	9	.471	4.47	1.50	27	27	2	0	...	0-...	151.0	165	93	75	8	62-1	116	.278
1992—	Tucson (PCL)	9	8	.529	3.68	1.34	25	22	2	0	...	1-...	142.0	156	73	58	4	34-2	106	.279
—	Houston (N.L.)	1	3	.250	7.11	1.89	8	5	0	0	0	0-0	25.1	42	22	20	2	6-1	10	.385
1993—	Tucson (PCL)	10	6	.625	3.62	1.21	25	20	2	0	...	1-...	139.1	147	74	56	4	21-0	106	.268
—	Houston (N.L.)	0	0	...	0.82	1.55	5	1	0	0	0	0-0	11.0	11	4	1	0	6-1	10	.256
1994—	Houston (N.L.)	8	5	.615	3.05	1.20	33	14	1	1	5	0-0	124.0	128	46	42	10	21-3	110	.263
1995—	Houston (N.L.)	10	11	.476	3.47	1.23	30	30	3	2	0	0-0	189.1	196	87	73	15	37-6	175	.263
1996—	Houston (N.L.)	16	10	.615	3.65	1.13	35	35	4	1	0	0-0	239.0	227	103	97	20	44-3	204	.249
1997—	Houston (N.L.)	9	10	.474	4.23	1.30	30	30	2	0	0	0-0	181.0	189	92	85	19	47-5	152	.267
—	New Orleans (A.A.)	1	0	1.000	0.00	0.80	1	1	0	0	...	0-...	5.0	3	0	0	0	1-0	6	.176
1998—	Houston (N.L.)	19	8	.704	3.51	1.33	35	•35	3	1	0	0-0	233.1	257	99	91	25	53-2	209	.280
1999—	Houston (N.L.)	16	14	.533	3.85	1.24	35	•35	4	2	0	0-0	231.2	250	108	99	23	37-0	197	.275
2000—	Houston (N.L.)	7	8	.467	5.22	1.40	22	22	0	0	0	0-0	131.0	150	86	76	20	45-2	93	.287
2001—	Round Rock (Texas)	1	0	1.000	1.29	1.00	1	1	0	0	...	0-...	7.0	5	1	1	0	2-0	5	.200
—	New Orleans (PCL)	1	0	1.000	0.00	1.14	1	1	0	0	...	0-...	7.0	8	0	0	0	1-0	7	.276
—	Houston (N.L.)	14	11	.560	4.34	1.34	28	28	3	0	0	0-0	182.2	208	95	88	24	36-2	102	.290
2002—	Houston (N.L.)	3	6	.333	4.86	1.43	13	13	0	0	0	0-0	74.0	80	43	40	13	26-2	47	.274
2003—	Atlanta (N.L.)	11	9	.550	5.43	1.49	30	29	0	0	0	0-0	167.1	191	104	101	20	59-6	94	.293
2004—	El Paso (Texas)	0	1	.000	5.79	1.93	2	2	0	0	...	0-...	4.2	7	3	3	0	2-0	3	.350
—	Tucson (PCL)	2	1	.667	5.27	1.21	5	5	1	1	...	0-...	27.1	30	16	16	5	3-0	28	.268
—	Arizona (N.L.)	0	1	.000	4.50	4.00	1	0	0	0	0	0-0	2.0	6	6	1	0	2-0	0	.500
Major League totals (13 years)		**114**	**96**	**.543**	**4.09**	**1.31**	**305**	**278**	**20**	**7**	**5**		**1791.2**	**1935**	**895**	**814**	**191**	**419-33**	**1403**	**.275**

DIVISION SERIES RECORD

Year	Team (League)	W	L	Pct.	ERA	WHIP	G	GS	CG	ShO	Hld.	Sv.-Opp.	IP	H	R	ER	HR	BB-IBB	SO	Avg.
1997—	Houston (N.L.)	0	1	.000	3.00	1.00	1	1	0	0	0	0-0	6.0	5	2	2	1	1-0	5	.227
1998—	Houston (N.L.)	0	0	...	2.57	0.71	1	1	0	0	0	0-0	7.0	4	2	2	0	1-0	5	.160
1999—	Houston (N.L.)	1	1	.500	4.09	1.73	2	2	0	0	0	0-0	11.0	16	5	5	0	3-0	5	.372
2001—	Houston (N.L.)	0	1	.000	9.00	1.75	1	1	0	0	0	0-0	4.0	6	4	4	2	1-0	1	.375
Division series totals (4 years)		**1**	**3**	**.250**	**4.18**	**1.32**	**5**	**5**	**0**	**0**	**0**	**0-0**	**28.0**	**31**	**13**	**13**	**3**	**6-0**	**16**	**.292**

RHODES, ARTHUR   P

PERSONAL: Born October 24, 1969, in Waco, Texas. ... 6-2/212. ... Throws left, bats left. ... Full name: Arthur Lee Rhodes. ... High school: LaVega (Waco, Texas).

TRANSACTIONS/CAREER NOTES: Selected by Baltimore Orioles organization in second round of 1988 free-agent draft. ... On disabled list (May 16-August 2, 1993); included rehabilitation assignment to Rochester. ... On disabled list (May 2-20, 1994); included rehabilitation assignment to Frederick. ... On disabled list (August 25, 1995-remainder of season; and July 14-August 2 and August 6-September 27, 1996). ... On Baltimore disabled list (July 5-August 17, 1998); included rehabilitation assignment to Rochester. ... Signed as a free agent by Seattle Mariners (December 21, 1999). ... Signed as a free agent by Oakland Athletics (December 23, 2003). ... On disabled list (June 28-August 18, 2004); included rehabilitation assignment to Sacramento.

CAREER HITTING: 1-for-4 (.250), 0 R, 0 2B, 0 3B, 0 HR, 0 RBI.

Year	Team (League)	W	L	Pct.	ERA	WHIP	G	GS	CG	ShO	Hld.	Sv.-Opp.	IP	H	R	ER	HR	BB-IBB	SO	Avg.
1988—	Bluefield (Appalachian)	3	4	.429	3.31	1.25	11	7	0	0	...	0-...	35.1	29	17	13	1	15-0	44	.210
1989—	Erie (N.Y.-Penn)	2	0	1.000	1.16	0.74	5	5	1	0	...	0-...	31.0	13	7	4	1	10-0	45	.124
—	Frederick (Caro.)	2	2	.500	5.18	1.56	7	6	0	0	...	0-...	24.1	19	16	14	2	19-0	28	.213
1990—	Frederick (Caro.)	4	6	.400	2.12	1.03	13	13	3	0	...	0-...	80.2	62	25	19	6	21-0	103	.207
—	Hagerstown (Eastern)	3	4	.429	3.73	1.40	12	12	0	0	...	0-...	72.1	62	32	30	3	39-0	60	.238
1991—	Hagerstown (Eastern)	7	4	.636	2.70	1.13	19	19	2	2	...	0-...	106.2	73	37	32	2	47-1	115	.194
—	Baltimore (A.L.)	0	3	.000	8.00	1.94	8	8	0	0	0	0-0	36.0	47	35	32	4	23-0	23	.320
1992—	Rochester (Int'l)	6	6	.500	3.72	1.28	17	17	1	0	...	0-...	101.2	84	48	42	7	46-0	115	.220
—	Baltimore (A.L.)	7	5	.583	3.63	1.33	15	15	2	1	0	0-0	94.1	87	39	38	6	38-2	77	.250
1993—	Baltimore (A.L.)	5	6	.455	6.51	1.63	17	17	0	0	0	0-0	85.2	91	62	62	16	49-1	49	.274
—	Rochester (Int'l)	1	1	.500	4.05	1.54	6	6	0	0	...	0-...	26.2	26	12	12	5	15-0	33	.260
1994—	Baltimore (A.L.)	3	5	.375	5.81	1.54	10	10	3	2	0	0-0	52.2	51	34	34	8	30-1	47	.254
—	Frederick (Caro.)	0	0	...	0.00	0.60	1	1	0	0	...	0-...	5.0	3	0	0	0	0-0	7	.176
—	Rochester (Int'l)	7	5	.583	2.79	1.15	15	15	3	0	...	0-...	90.1	70	41	28	7	34-1	86	.208
1995—	Baltimore (A.L.)	2	5	.286	6.21	1.54	19	9	0	0	0	0-1	75.1	68	53	52	13	48-1	77	.239
—	Rochester (Int'l)	2	1	.667	2.70	1.17	4	4	1	0	...	0-...	30.0	27	12	9	2	8-0	33	.239
1996—	Baltimore (A.L.)	9	1	.900	4.08	1.34	28	2	0	0	2	1-1	53.0	48	28	24	6	23-3	62	.241
1997—	Baltimore (A.L.)	10	3	.769	3.02	1.06	53	0	0	0	9	1-2	95.1	75	32	32	9	26-5	102	.218
1998—	Baltimore (A.L.)	4	4	.500	3.51	1.29	45	0	0	0	10	4-8	77.0	65	30	30	8	34-2	83	.233
—	Rochester (Int'l)	0	0	...	4.50	2.00	1	1	0	0	0	0-...	2.0	3	1	1	0	1-0	1	.333
1999—	Baltimore (A.L.)	3	4	.429	5.43	1.66	43	0	0	0	5	3-5	53.0	43	37	32	9	45-6	59	.221
2000—	Seattle (A.L.)	5	8	.385	4.28	1.15	72	0	0	0	24	0-7	69.1	51	34	33	6	29-3	77	.205
2001—	Seattle (A.L.)	8	0	1.000	1.72	0.85	71	0	0	0	32	3-7	68.0	46	14	13	5	12-0	83	.189
2002—	Seattle (A.L.)	10	4	.714	2.33	0.83	66	0	0	0	27	2-7	69.2	45	18	18	4	13-1	81	.187
2003—	Seattle (A.L.)	3	3	.500	4.17	1.31	67	0	0	0	18	3-6	54.0	53	25	25	4	18-2	48	.256
2004—	Sacramento (PCL)	0	0	...	0.00	0.50	2	2	0	0	...	0-...	2.0	0	0	0	0	1-0	3	.000
—	Oakland (A.L.)	3	3	.500	5.12	1.73	37	0	0	0	3	9-14	38.2	46	23	22	9	21-4	34	.293
Major League totals (14 years)		**72**	**54**	**.571**	**4.36**	**1.33**	**551**	**61**	**5**	**3**	**130**	**26-58**	**922.0**	**816**	**464**	**447**	**107**	**409-31**	**902**	**.238**

DIVISION SERIES RECORD

Year	Team (League)	W	L	Pct.	ERA	WHIP	G	GS	CG	ShO	Hld.	Sv.-Opp.	IP	H	R	ER	HR	BB-IBB	SO	Avg.
1996—	Baltimore (A.L.)	0	0	...	9.00	2.00	2	0	0	0	0	0-0	1.0	1	1	1	0	1-0	1	.250
1997—	Baltimore (A.L.)	0	0	...	0.00	0.00	1	0	0	0	0	0-0	2.1	0	0	0	0	0-0	4	.000
2000—	Seattle (A.L.)	0	0	...	0.00	0.75	3	0	0	0	1	0-0	2.2	0	0	0	0	2-0	2	.000
2001—	Seattle (A.L.)	0	0	...	0.00	0.38	3	0	0	0	2	0-0	2.2	1	0	0	0	0-0	1	.111
Division series totals (4 years)		**0**	**0**	**...**	**1.04**	**0.58**	**9**	**0**	**0**	**0**	**3**	**0-0**	**8.2**	**2**	**1**	**1**	**0**	**3-0**	**8**	**.077**

CHAMPIONSHIP SERIES RECORD

Year Team (League)	W	L	Pct.	ERA	WHIP	G	GS	CG	ShO	Hld.	Sv.-Opp.	IP	H	R	ER	HR	BB-IBB	SO	Avg.
1996— Baltimore (A.L.)	0	0	...	0.00	1.00	3	0	0	0	...	0-0	2.0	2	0	0	0	0-0	2	.286
1997— Baltimore (A.L.)	0	0	...	0.00	2.14	2	0	0	0	...	0-0	2.1	2	0	0	0	3-1	2	.250
2000— Seattle (A.L.)	0	1	.000	31.50	6.00	4	0	0	0	1	0-2	2.0	8	7	7	1	4-1	5	.615
2001— Seattle (A.L.)	0	0	...	4.50	1.00	2	0	0	0	0	0-1	2.0	2	1	1	1	0-0	2	.250
Champ. series totals (4 years)	0	1	.000	8.64	2.52	11	0	0	0	1	0-3	8.1	14	8	8	2	7-2	11	.389

RIEDLING, JOHN P

PERSONAL: Born August 29, 1975, in Fort Lauderdale, Fla. ... 5-11/190. ... Throws right, bats right. ... Full name: John Richard Riedling. ... Name pronounced: READ-ling. ... High school: Ely (Pompano Beach, Fla.).

TRANSACTIONS/CAREER NOTES: Selected by Cincinnati Reds organization in 22nd round of 1994 free-agent draft. ... Released by Reds (December 14, 1998). ... Re-signed by Reds organization (January 5, 1999). ... On disabled list (May 27-August 12 and August 31, 2001-remainder of season); included rehabilitation assignment to Louisville. ... On disabled list (March 26-May 1 and August 20-September 4, 2002; and June 12-27, 2003).

CAREER HITTING: 4-for-25 (.160), 2 R, 0 2B, 0 3B, 0 HR, 2 RBI.

Year Team (League)	W	L	Pct.	ERA	WHIP	G	GS	CG	ShO	Hld.	Sv.-Opp.	IP	H	R	ER	HR	BB-IBB	SO	Avg.
1994— Billings (Pio.)	4	1	.800	5.48	2.03	15	15	0	0	...	0-...	44.1	62	36	27	0	28-0	27	.333
1995— Billings (Pio.)	2	2	.500	7.04	1.88	13	7	0	0	...	1-...	38.1	51	38	30	4	21-2	28	.305
1996— Char., W.Va. (SAL)	6	10	.375	3.99	1.44	26	26	0	0	...	0-...	140.0	135	85	62	2	66-6	90	.258
1997— Burlington (Midw.)	4	6	.400	5.26	1.44	35	16	0	0	...	0-...	102.2	101	70	60	8	47-0	104	.253
1998— Chattanooga (Southern)	3	10	.231	5.00	1.68	24	20	0	0	...	0-...	102.2	112	70	57	10	60-5	86	.277
1999— Chattanooga (Southern)	9	5	.643	3.43	1.45	40	0	0	0	...	5-...	42.0	41	23	16	2	20-3	38	.253
— Indianapolis (Int'l)	1	0	1.000	1.54	1.06	24	0	0	0	...	1-...	35.0	19	9	6	1	18-2	26	.160
2000— Louisville (Int'l)	6	3	.667	2.52	1.24	53	0	0	0	...	5-...	75.0	63	24	21	7	30-3	75	.226
— Cincinnati (N.L.)	3	1	.750	2.35	1.24	13	0	0	0	2	1-2	15.1	11	7	4	1	8-0	18	.208
2001— Cincinnati (N.L.)	1	1	.500	2.41	1.07	29	0	0	0	5	1-3	33.2	22	9	9	1	14-0	23	.186
— Louisville (Int'l)	0	0	...	0.00	1.00	1	0	0	0	...	0-...	1.0	0	0	0	0	1-0	1	.000
2002— Chattanooga (Southern) ...	1	1	.500	11.05	2.45	6	0	0	0	...	0-...	7.1	13	11	9	0	5-2	5	.382
— Louisville (Int'l)	1	0	1.000	4.66	1.45	7	0	0	0	...	0-...	9.2	10	6	5	0	4-0	10	.256
— Cincinnati (N.L.)	2	4	.333	2.70	1.39	33	0	0	0	8	0-0	46.2	39	16	14	2	26-6	30	.234
2003— Cincinnati (N.L.)	2	3	.400	4.90	1.52	55	8	0	0	6	1-4	101.0	107	61	55	7	47-0	65	.270
2004— Cincinnati (N.L.)	5	3	.625	5.10	1.67	70	0	0	0	14	0-7	77.2	90	54	44	10	40-5	46	.286
Major League totals (5 years)	13	12	.520	4.13	1.47	200	8	0	0	35	3-16	274.1	269	147	126	21	135-11	182	.256

RIGGS, ADAM 1B/OF

PERSONAL: Born October 4, 1972, in Steubenville, Ohio. ... 6-0/190. ... Bats right, throws right. ... Full name: Adam David Riggs. ... High school: Lenape Valley (Stanhope, N.J.). ... College: South Carolina-Aiken.

TRANSACTIONS/CAREER NOTES: Selected by Los Angeles Dodgers organization in 22nd round of 1994 free-agent draft. ... On disabled list (June 5, 1998-remainder of season). ... Signed as a free agent by San Diego Padres organization (January 9, 2001). ... Signed as a free agent by Detroit Tigers organization (November 13, 2001). ... Released by Tigers (March 28, 2002). ... Contract purchased by St. Louis Cardinals organization from Saltillo of the Mexican League (July 4, 2002). ... Signed as a free agent by Anaheim Angels organization (January 22, 2003). ... Released by Angels (October 18, 2004).

2004 GAMES PLAYED BY POSITION (MLB): OF—8, DH—4, 2B—1, 1B—1.

Year Team (League)	Pos.	G	AB	R	H	2B	3B	HR	RBI	BB	SO	HBP	GDP	SB-CS	Avg.	OBP	SLG	OPS	E	Avg.
1994— Great Falls (Pio.)	2B	62	234	55	73	20	3	5	44	31	38	4	2	19-8	.312	.399	.487	.886	23	.908
— Yakima (N'west)	2B	4	7	1	2	1	0	0	0	0	1	0	0	0-0	.286	.286	.429	.714	...	...
1995— San Bern. (Calif.)	2B	134	542	111	196	39	5	24	106	59	91	10	9	31-10	.362	.431	.585	1.016	41	.928
1996— San Antonio (Texas)	2B	134	506	68	143	31	6	14	66	37	82	9	13	16-6	.283	.339	.451	.790	27	.962
1997— Albuquerque (PCL) 2B-3B-OF		57	227	59	69	8	3	13	28	29	39	3	2	12-2	.304	.390	.537	.927	8	.973
— Los Angeles (N.L.)	2B	9	20	3	4	1	0	0	1	4	3	0	0	1-0	.200	.333	.250	.583	0	1.000
1998— Albuquerque (PCL)	2B	44	170	30	63	13	3	4	25	21	29	3	1	12-6	.371	.446	.553	.999	10	.954
1999— Albuquerque (PCL) 2B-3B-DH		133	513	87	150	29	7	13	81	54	114	10	8	25-17	.292	.368	.452	.820	23	.963
2000— Albuquerque (PCL) 3B-2B-OF		124	348	71	109	24	4	12	57	35	67	2	11	11-7	.313	.376	.509	.885	19	.939
2001— Portland (PCL) 2B-3B-OF		110	394	42	103	18	2	21	65	12	78	0	9	8-3	.261	.282	.477	.759	16	.961
— San Diego (N.L.)	2B-3B	12	36	2	7	1	0	0	1	2	8	0	1	1-1	.194	.237	.222	.459	0	1.000
2002— Memphis (PCL)	OF-3-2-1	43	122	26	28	9	0	2	11	23	27	0	3	5-1	.230	.347	.352	.699	7	.929
2003— Salt Lake (PCL)	DH-O-1-2	103	394	59	116	35	4	14	82	37	67	5	13	8-2	.294	.354	.490	.844	7	.974
— Anaheim (A.L.)	1-OF-2-DH	24	61	11	15	4	1	3	5	9	9	0	2	3-1	.246	.343	.492	.835	2	.981
2004— Salt Lake (PCL)	O-DH-1-3-2	112	450	104	149	33	8	29	90	30	80	4	5	8-3	.331	.373	.633	1.006	6	.976
— Anaheim (A.L.)	O-DH-2-1	16	36	2	7	3	0	0	3	1	10	0	2	1-0	.194	.216	.278	.494	0	1.000
American League totals (2 years)		40	97	13	22	7	1	3	8	10	19	0	4	4-1	.227	.299	.412	.711	2	.983
National League totals (2 years)		21	56	5	11	2	0	0	2	6	11	0	1	2-1	.196	.274	.232	.506	0	1.000
Major League totals (4 years)		61	153	18	33	9	1	3	10	16	30	0	5	6-2	.216	.290	.346	.636	2	.989

DIVISION SERIES RECORD

Year Team (League)	Pos.	G	AB	R	H	2B	3B	HR	RBI	BB	SO	HBP	GDP	SB-CS	Avg.	OBP	SLG	OPS	E	Avg.
2004— Anaheim (A.L.)	OF	2	1	0	0	0	0	0	0	0	0	0	0	0-0	.000	.000	.000	.000	0	...

RILEY, MATT P

PERSONAL: Born August 2, 1979, in Antioch, Calif. ... 6-1/221. ... Throws left, bats left. ... Full name: Matthew Paul Riley. ... High school: Liberty Union (Oakley, Calif.). ... Junior college: Sacramento (Calif.) City College.

TRANSACTIONS/CAREER NOTES: Selected by Baltimore Orioles organization in third round of 1997 free-agent draft. ... On disabled list (September 29, 2000-remainder of season; April 1, 2001-entire season; and May 10-25, 2004).

CAREER HITTING: 0-for-2 (.000), 0 R, 0 2B, 0 3B, 0 HR, 0 RBI.

Year Team (League)	W	L	Pct.	ERA	WHIP	G	GS	CG	ShO	Hld.	Sv.-Opp.	IP	H	R	ER	HR	BB-IBB	SO	Avg.
1998— Delmarva (S.Atl.)	5	4	.556	1.19	1.04	16	14	0	0	...	0-...	83.0	42	19	11	0	44-0	136	.152
1999— Frederick (Caro.)	3	2	.600	2.61	0.93	8	8	0	0	...	0-...	51.2	34	19	15	5	14-0	58	.188
— Bowie (East.)	10	6	.625	3.22	1.23	20	20	3	0	...	0-...	125.2	113	53	45	13	42-0	131	.241
— Baltimore (A.L.)	0	0	...	7.36	2.73	3	3	0	0	...	0-0	11.0	17	9	9	4	13-0	6	.378

Year Team (League)	W	L	Pct.	ERA	WHIP	G	GS	CG	ShO	Hld.	Sv.-Opp.	IP	H	R	ER	HR	BB-IBB	SO	Avg.
2000— Rochester (Int'l)	0	2	.000	14.14	2.71	2	2	0	0	...	0-...	7.0	15	12	11	3	4-0	8	.417
— Bowie (East.)	5	7	.417	6.08	1.66	19	14	2	0	...	1-...	74.0	74	56	50	9	49-0	66	.262
2001— Baltimore (A.L.)			Did not play.																
2002— Bowie (East.)	4	10	.286	6.34	1.68	22	22	0	0	...	0-...	109.1	136	84	77	12	48-1	105	.306
2003— Bowie (East.)	5	2	.714	3.11	1.10	14	14	1	1	...	0-...	72.1	56	27	25	4	23-1	73	.210
— Ottawa (Int'l)	4	2	.667	3.58	1.40	13	13	0	0	...	0-...	70.1	70	30	28	4	28-1	77	.261
— Baltimore (A.L.)	1	0	1.000	1.80	1.20	2	2	0	0	0	0-0	10.0	7	2	2	1	5-0	8	.194
2004— Ottawa (Int'l)	1	2	.333	1.71	1.17	10	10	0	0	0	0-...	42.0	26	9	8	3	23-0	51	.181
— Baltimore (A.L.)	3	4	.429	5.63	1.63	14	13	0	0	0	0-0	64.0	60	43	40	11	44-0	60	.244
Major League totals (3 years)	4	4	.500	5.40	1.72	19	18	0	0	0	0-0	85.0	84	54	51	16	62-0	74	.257

RINCON, JUAN — P

PERSONAL: Born January 23, 1979, in Maracaibo, Venezuela. ... 5-11/201. ... Throws right, bats right. ... Full name: Juan Manuel Rincon. ... Name pronounced: rin-CONE. ... High school: Instituto Cervantes (Maracaibo, Venezuela).

TRANSACTIONS/CAREER NOTES: Signed as a non-drafted free agent by Minnesota Twins organization (November 15, 1996).

CAREER HITTING: 1-for-2 (.500), 0 R, 0 2B, 0 3B, 0 HR, 0 RBI.

Year Team (League)	W	L	Pct.	ERA	WHIP	G	GS	CG	ShO	Hld.	Sv.-Opp.	IP	H	R	ER	HR	BB-IBB	SO	Avg.
1997— GC Twins (GCL)	3	3	.500	2.95	1.36	11	10	1	0	...	0-...	58.0	55	21	19	0	24-0	46	.259
— Elizabethton (Appal.)	0	1	.000	3.86	1.50	2	1	0	0	...	0-...	9.1	11	4	4	0	3-0	7	.289
1998— Fort Wayne (Midw.)	6	4	.600	3.83	1.43	37	13	0	0	...	6-...	96.1	84	51	41	6	54-1	74	.232
1999— Quad City (Midw.)	14	8	.636	2.92	1.30	28	28	0	0	...	0-...	163.1	146	67	53	8	66-3	153	.239
2000— Fort Myers (Fla. St.)	5	3	.625	2.13	1.18	13	13	0	0	...	0-...	76.0	67	26	18	3	23-2	55	.238
— New Britain (East.)	3	9	.250	4.65	1.52	15	15	2	0	...	0-...	89.0	96	55	46	9	39-0	79	.267
2001— New Britain (East.)	14	6	.700	2.88	1.22	29	23	2	1	...	0-...	153.1	130	60	49	9	57-5	133	.226
— Minnesota (A.L.)	0	0	...	6.35	2.12	4	0	0	0	0	0-0	5.2	7	5	4	1	5-0	4	.318
2002— Edmonton (PCL)	7	4	.636	4.78	1.44	19	16	3	0	...	0-...	101.2	111	56	54	12	35-0	75	.278
— Minnesota (A.L.)	0	2	.000	6.28	1.85	10	3	0	0	0	0-1	28.2	44	23	20	5	9-0	21	.352
2003— Rochester (Int'l)	0	2	.000	7.56	2.00	2	2	0	0	...	0-...	8.1	12	7	7	0	5-0	8	.364
— Minnesota (A.L.)	5	6	.455	3.68	1.31	58	0	0	0	5	0-1	85.2	74	38	35	5	38-7	63	.231
2004— Minnesota (A.L.)	11	6	.647	2.63	1.02	77	0	0	0	16	2-6	82.0	52	27	24	5	32-1	106	.181
Major League totals (4 years)	16	14	.533	3.70	1.29	149	3	0	0	21	2-8	202.0	177	93	83	16	84-8	194	.234

DIVISION SERIES RECORD

Year Team (League)	W	L	Pct.	ERA	WHIP	G	GS	CG	ShO	Hld.	Sv.-Opp.	IP	H	R	ER	HR	BB-IBB	SO	Avg.
2003— Minnesota (A.L.)	0	0	...	0.00	2.14	3	0	0	0	0	0-0	2.1	1	0	0	0	4-0	1	.143
2004— Minnesota (A.L.)	0	0	...	10.80	1.80	3	0	0	0	1	0-0	3.1	4	4	4	1	2-0	5	.308
Division series totals (2 years)	0	0	...	6.35	1.94	6	0	0	0	1	0-0	5.2	5	4	4	1	6-0	6	.250

RINCON, RICARDO — P

PERSONAL: Born April 13, 1970, in Veracruz, Mexico. ... 5-9/190. ... Throws left, bats left. ... Full name: Ricardo Rincon Rincon Espinoza. ... Name pronounced: rin-CONE.

TRANSACTIONS/CAREER NOTES: Contract purchased by Pittsburgh Pirates organization from Mexico City Red Devils of the Mexican League (March 30, 1997). ... On disabled list (March 22-April 14, 1998); included rehabilitation assignments to Carolina and Nashville. ... Traded by Pirates to Cleveland Indians for OF Brian Giles (November 18, 1998). ... On disabled list (April 12-May 14, 1999); included rehabilitation assignment to Akron. ... On disabled list (May 17-August 23, 2000); included rehabilitation assignment to Buffalo. ... Traded by Indians to Oakland Athletics for IF Marshall McDougall (July 30, 2002).

CAREER HITTING: 0-for-4 (.000), 0 R, 0 2B, 0 3B, 0 HR, 0 RBI.

Year Team (League)	W	L	Pct.	ERA	WHIP	G	GS	CG	ShO	Hld.	Sv.-Opp.	IP	H	R	ER	HR	BB-IBB	SO	Avg.
1990— Union Laguna (Mex.)	3	0	1.000	3.78	1.78	19	4	0	0	...	0-...	47.2	53	22	20	6	32-...	29	...
1991— Union Laguna (Mex.)	2	8	.200	6.54	1.98	32	9	0	0	...	1-...	74.1	99	60	54	12	48-...	66	...
1992— Union Laguna (Mex.)	6	5	.545	3.91	1.48	49	9	0	0	...	4-...	89.2	87	45	39	4	46-...	91	...
1993— Torreon (Mex.)	7	3	.700	3.17	1.41	57	4	0	0	...	8-...	82.1	80	33	29	8	36-...	81	...
1994— M.C. Red Devils (Mex.)	2	4	.333	3.21	1.44	20	9	0	0	...	1-...	53.1	57	23	19	4	20-...	38	...
1995— M.C. Red Devils (Mex.)	6	6	.500	5.16	1.69	27	11	0	0	...	3-...	75.0	86	45	43	7	41-...	41	...
1996— M.C. Red Devils (Mex.)	5	3	.625	2.97	1.08	78	0	0	0	...	10-...	78.2	58	28	26	2	27-...	60	...
1997— Pittsburgh (N.L.)	4	8	.333	3.45	1.25	62	0	0	0	18	4-6	60.0	51	26	23	5	24-6	71	.230
1998— Carolina (Southern)	0	0	...	6.00	2.33	2	0	0	0	...	0-...	3.0	5	2	2	1	2-0	1	.385
— Nashville (PCL)	0	0	...	0.00	0.00	1	0	0	0	...	0-...	1.0	0	0	0	0	0-0	1	.000
— Pittsburgh (N.L.)	0	2	.000	2.91	1.22	60	0	0	0	11	14-17	65.0	50	31	21	6	29-2	64	.208
1999— Cleveland (A.L.)	2	3	.400	4.43	1.46	59	0	0	0	11	0-2	44.2	41	22	22	6	24-5	30	.248
— Akron (East.)	0	0	...	5.40	1.20	2	0	0	0	...	0-...	1.2	2	1	1	1	0-0	2	.250
2000— Cleveland (A.L.)	2	0	1.000	2.70	1.50	35	0	0	0	10	0-...	20.0	17	7	6	1	13-1	20	.224
— Buffalo (Int'l)	0	0	...	0.00	0.50	2	0	0	0	...	0-...	2.0	1	1	0	0	0-0	2	.111
2001— Cleveland (A.L.)	2	1	.667	2.83	1.20	67	0	0	0	12	2-4	54.0	44	18	17	3	21-5	50	.223
2002— Cleveland (A.L.)	1	4	.200	4.79	1.23	46	0	0	0	11	0-3	35.2	36	21	19	3	8-1	30	.263
— Oakland (A.L.)	0	0	...	3.10	0.69	25	0	0	0	16	1-2	20.1	11	7	7	1	3-0	19	.164
2003— Oakland (A.L.)	8	4	.667	3.25	1.39	64	0	0	0	13	0-3	55.1	45	21	20	4	32-4	40	.230
2004— Oakland (A.L.)	1	1	.500	3.68	1.52	67	0	0	0	18	0-4	44.0	45	22	18	3	22-4	40	.256
American League totals (6 years)	16	13	.552	3.58	1.32	363	0	0	0	91	3-18	274.0	239	118	109	21	123-20	229	.236
National League totals (2 years)	4	10	.286	3.17	1.23	122	0	0	0	29	18-23	125.0	101	57	44	11	53-8	135	.219
Major League totals (8 years)	20	23	.465	3.45	1.29	485	0	0	0	120	21-41	399.0	340	175	153	32	176-28	364	.230

DIVISION SERIES RECORD

Year Team (League)	W	L	Pct.	ERA	WHIP	G	GS	CG	ShO	Hld.	Sv.-Opp.	IP	H	R	ER	HR	BB-IBB	SO	Avg.
1999— Cleveland (A.L.)	0	0	...	40.50	4.50	1	0	0	0	0	0-0	.2	2	3	3	1	1-0	1	.500
2001— Cleveland (A.L.)	0	0	...	9.00	1.00	3	0	0	0	0	0-0	2.0	2	2	2	0	0-0	3	.286
2002— Oakland (A.L.)	0	0	...	0.00	0.67	2	0	0	0	1	0-0	3.0	2	0	0	0	0-0	2	.182
2003— Oakland (A.L.)	0	0	...	4.50	1.25	4	0	0	0	1	0-1	4.0	4	2	2	2	1-0	3	.267
Division series totals (4 years)	0	0	...	6.52	1.24	10	0	0	0	2	0-1	9.2	10	7	7	3	2-0	9	.270

RIOS, ALEXIS — OF

PERSONAL: Born February 18, 1981, in Coffee, Ala. ... 6-5/194. ... Bats right, throws right. ... Full name: Alexis Israel Rios. ... High school: San Pedro Martin (Guaynabo, P.R.).

TRANSACTIONS/CAREER NOTES: Selected by Toronto Blue Jays organization in first round (19th pick overall) of 1999 free-agent draft.

2004 GAMES PLAYED BY POSITION (MLB): OF—111.

Year Team (League)	Pos.	G	AB	R	H	2B	3B	HR	RBI	BB	SO	HBP	GDP	SB-CS	Avg.	OBP	SLG	OPS	E	Avg.
1999—Medicine Hat (Pio.)	OF	67	234	35	63	7	3	0	13	17	31	1	6	8-4	.269	.321	.325	.646	6	.955
2000—Hagerstown (SAL)		22	74	5	17	3	1	0	5	2	14	1	0	2-3	.230	.256	.297	.554	...	...
—Queens (NY-P)	OF	50	206	22	55	9	2	1	25	11	22	4	5	5-5	.267	.314	.345	.659	3	.957
2001—Char., W.Va. (SAL)	OF	130	480	40	126	20	9	2	58	25	59	4	16	22-14	.263	.296	.354	.651	13	.944
2002—Dunedin (Fla. St.)	OF	111	456	60	139	22	8	3	61	27	55	3	19	14-8	.305	.344	.408	.752	8	.967
2003—New Haven (East.)	OF	127	514	86	181	32	11	11	82	39	85	6	22	11-3	.352	.402	.521	.924	3	.990
2004—Syracuse (Int'l)	OF	46	185	14	48	10	1	3	23	9	30	0	10	2-1	.259	.292	.373	.665	4	.964
—Toronto (A.L.)	OF	111	426	55	122	24	7	1	28	31	84	2	14	15-3	.286	.338	.383	.720	2	.991
Major League totals (1 year)		111	426	55	122	24	7	1	28	31	84	2	14	15-3	.286	.338	.383	.720	2	.991

RISKE, DAVID — P

PERSONAL: Born October 23, 1976, in Renton, Wash. ... 6-2/190. ... Throws right, bats right. ... Full name: David R. Riske. ... Name pronounced: RISK-ee. ... High school: Lindbergh (Renton, Wash.). ... Junior college: Green River (Wash.) Community College.

TRANSACTIONS/CAREER NOTES: Selected by Cleveland Indians organization in 56th round of 1996 free-agent draft. ... On disabled list (March 25-April 28, May 29-September 4 and September 14, 2000-remainder of season); included rehabilitation assignment to Akron. ... On disabled list (June 19-July 17, 2002); included rehabilitation assignment to Akron.

CAREER HITTING: 0-for-0 (.000), 0 R, 0 2B, 0 3B, 0 HR, 0 RBI.

Year Team (League)	W	L	Pct.	ERA	WHIP	G	GS	CG	ShO	Hld.	Sv.-Opp.	IP	H	R	ER	HR	BB-IBB	SO	Avg.
1997—Kinston (Caro.)	4	4	.500	2.25	1.26	39	0	0	0	...	2-...	72.0	58	22	18	3	33-4	90	.227
1998—Kinston (Caro.)	1	1	.500	2.33	1.17	53	0	0	0	...	33-...	54.0	48	15	14	4	15-0	67	.241
—Akron (East.)	0	0	...	0.00	0.67	2	0	0	0	...	1-...	3.0	1	0	0	0	1-0	5	.100
1999—Akron (East.)	0	0	...	1.90	0.76	23	0	0	0	...	12-...	23.2	5	6	5	1	13-0	33	.067
—Buffalo (Int'l)	3	0	1.000	0.65	0.76	23	0	0	0	...	6-...	27.2	14	3	2	0	7-0	22	.151
—Cleveland (A.L.)	1	1	.500	8.36	1.86	12	0	0	0	0	0-1	14.0	20	15	13	2	6-0	16	.333
2000—Akron (East.)	0	0	...	0.00	0.50	3	1	0	0	...	1-...	4.0	2	0	0	0	0-0	4	.143
—Buffalo (Int'l)	0	0	...	3.00	1.33	2	0	0	0	...	1-...	3.0	2	1	1	0	2-0	2	.182
2001—Buffalo (Int'l)	1	2	.333	2.36	1.16	38	0	0	0	...	15-...	53.1	45	16	14	2	17-0	72	.232
—Cleveland (A.L.)	2	0	1.000	1.98	1.39	26	0	0	0	3	1-1	27.1	20	7	6	3	18-3	29	.206
2002—Cleveland (A.L.)	2	2	.500	5.26	1.64	51	0	0	0	5	1-1	51.1	49	32	30	8	35-4	65	.257
—Akron (East.)	0	0	...	3.00	1.00	4	2	0	0	...	0-...	6.0	5	2	2	1	1-0	10	.217
—Buffalo (Int'l)	0	1	.000	3.72	1.03	9	0	0	0	...	3-...	9.2	6	4	4	2	4-0	17	.182
2003—Cleveland (A.L.)	2	2	.500	2.29	0.96	68	0	0	0	17	8-13	74.2	52	21	19	9	20-3	82	.196
2004—Cleveland (A.L.)	7	3	.700	3.72	1.42	72	0	0	0	9	5-12	77.1	69	32	32	11	41-4	78	.240
Major League totals (5 years)	14	8	.636	3.68	1.35	229	0	0	0	34	15-28	244.2	210	107	100	33	120-14	270	.233

DIVISION SERIES RECORD

Year Team (League)	W	L	Pct.	ERA	WHIP	G	GS	CG	ShO	Hld.	Sv.-Opp.	IP	H	R	ER	HR	BB-IBB	SO	Avg.
2001—Cleveland (A.L.)	0	0	...	0.00	0.82	3	0	0	0	...	0-0	3.2	2	0	0	0	1-0	5	.154

RITCHIE, TODD — P

PERSONAL: Born November 7, 1971, in Portsmouth, Va. ... 6-3/205. ... Throws right, bats right. ... Full name: Todd Everett Ritchie. ... High school: Duncanville (Texas).

TRANSACTIONS/CAREER NOTES: Selected by Minnesota Twins organization in first round (12th pick overall) of 1990 free-agent draft. ... Released by Twins (October 3, 1998). ... Signed by Pittsburgh Pirates organization (December 22, 1998). ... On disabled list (August 21-September 6, 1999; and July 24-August 11, 2000). ... Traded by Pirates with C Lee Evans to Chicago White Sox for Ps Kip Wells and Sean Lowe and Josh Fogg (December 13, 2001). ... On disabled list (August 4-September 10, 2002). ... Signed as a free agent by Milwaukee Brewers (January 14, 2003). ... On disabled list (April 25, 2003-remainder of season). ... Signed as a free agent by Tampa Bay Devil Rays organization (January 23, 2004).

CAREER HITTING: 33-for-187 (.176), 9 R, 5 2B, 0 3B, 0 HR, 6 RBI.

Year Team (League)	W	L	Pct.	ERA	WHIP	G	GS	CG	ShO	Hld.	Sv.-Opp.	IP	H	R	ER	HR	BB-IBB	SO	Avg.
1990—Elizabethton (Appal.)	5	2	.714	1.94	1.06	11	11	1	0	...	0-...	65.0	45	22	14	5	24-0	49	.198
1991—Kenosha (Midw.)	7	6	.538	3.55	1.40	21	21	0	0	...	0-...	116.2	113	53	46	3	50-0	101	.259
1992—Visalia (Calif.)	11	9	.550	5.06	1.49	28	28	3	1	...	0-...	172.2	193	113	97	13	65-2	129	.284
1993—Nashville (Sou.)	3	2	.600	3.66	1.31	12	10	0	0	...	0-...	46.2	46	21	19	2	15-0	41	.260
1994—Nashville (Sou.)	0	2	.000	4.24	1.82	4	4	0	0	...	0-...	17.0	24	10	8	1	7-0	9	.364
1995—New Britain (East.)	4	9	.308	5.73	1.67	24	21	0	0	...	0-...	113.0	135	78	72	12	54-0	60	.303
1996—New Britain (East.)	3	7	.300	5.44	1.58	29	10	0	0	...	4-...	82.2	101	55	50	6	30-1	53	.302
—Salt Lake (PCL)	0	4	.000	5.47	1.54	16	0	0	0	...	0-...	24.2	27	15	15	5	11-0	19	.276
1997—Minnesota (A.L.)	2	3	.400	4.58	1.54	42	0	0	0	3	0-2	74.2	87	41	38	11	28-0	44	.290
1998—Minnesota (A.L.)	0	0	...	5.63	1.63	15	0	0	0	0	0-...	24.0	30	17	15	1	9-0	21	.288
—Salt Lake (PCL)	1	3	.250	4.15	1.42	36	0	0	0	...	4-...	60.2	55	38	28	5	31-3	62	.239
1999—Nashville (PCL)	0	0	...	1.80	1.40	1	1	0	0	...	0-...	5.0	6	1	1	0	1-0	2	.300
—Pittsburgh (N.L.)	15	9	.625	3.50	1.29	28	26	2	0	1	0-0	172.1	169	79	67	17	54-3	107	.259
2000—Pittsburgh (N.L.)	9	8	.529	4.81	1.39	31	31	1	1	0	0-0	187.0	208	111	100	26	51-1	124	.282
2001—Pittsburgh (N.L.)	11	15	.423	4.47	1.27	33	33	4	2	0	0-0	207.1	211	118	103	23	52-7	124	.259
2002—Chicago (A.L.)	5	15	.250	6.06	1.71	26	23	0	0	0	0-0	133.2	176	104	90	18	52-2	77	.318
2003—Milwaukee (N.L.)	1	2	.333	5.08	1.62	5	5	0	0	0	0-0	28.1	36	17	16	4	10-0	15	.319
2004—Char., S.C. (SAL)	1	1	.500	4.09	1.45	2	2	0	0	...	0-...	11.0	13	6	5	0	3-0	13	.295
—Montgomery (Sou.)	1	0	1.000	2.46	1.00	2	2	0	0	...	0-...	11.0	8	4	3	1	3-0	4	.216
—Durham (Int'l)	4	6	.400	6.29	1.52	16	16	0	0	...	0-...	88.2	112	71	62	19	23-0	41	.303
—Tampa Bay (A.L.)	0	2	.000	9.00	2.25	4	2	0	0	0	0-0	8.0	12	9	8	4	6-0	4	.343
American League totals (4 years)	7	20	.259	5.65	1.66	87	25	0	0	3	0-2	240.1	305	171	151	34	95-2	146	.307
National League totals (4 years)	36	34	.514	4.33	1.33	97	95	7	3	1	0-0	595.0	624	325	286	70	167-11	370	.269
Major League totals (8 years)	43	54	.443	4.71	1.43	184	120	7	3	4	0-2	835.1	929	496	437	104	262-13	516	.281

RIVAS, LUIS — 2B

PERSONAL: Born August 30, 1979, in La Guaira, Venezuela. ... 5-11/186. ... Bats right, throws right. ... Full name: Luis Wilfredo Rivas. ... Name pronounced: REE-vas. ... High school: Riceniado Le Guaria (La Guaria, Venezuela).

TRANSACTIONS/CAREER NOTES: Signed as a non-drafted free agent by Minnesota Twins organization (October 9, 1995). ... On disabled list (April 7-June 4, 2002); included rehabilitation assignment to Fort Myers. ... On disabled list (May 19-June 8, 2004); included rehabilitation assignment to Rochester.

2004 GAMES PLAYED BY POSITION (MLB): 2B—109.

									BATTING										FIELDING	
Year Team (League)	Pos.	G	AB	R	H	2B	3B	HR	RBI	BB	SO	HBP	GDP	SB-CS	Avg.	OBP	SLG	OPS	E	Avg.
1996— GC Twins (GCL)	SS	53	201	29	52	12	1	1	13	18	37	0	2	35-10	.259	.320	.343	.663	21	.922
1997— Fort Wayne (Midw.)	SS	121	419	61	100	20	6	1	30	33	90	5	5	28-18	.239	.301	.322	.623	58	.907
1998— Fort Myers (FSL)	SS	126	463	58	130	21	5	4	51	14	75	3	11	34-8	.281	.302	.374	.676	55	.913
1999— New Britain (East.)	SS-2B	132	527	78	134	30	7	7	49	41	92	2	16	31-14	.254	.309	.378	.687	39	.934
2000— New Britain (East.)	2B-SS	82	328	56	82	23	6	3	40	36	41	4	3	11-4	.250	.329	.384	.713	11	.971
— Salt Lake (PCL)	2B-SS	41	157	33	50	14	1	3	25	13	21	2	3	7-4	.318	.376	.478	.853	2	.989
— Minnesota (A.L.)	2B-SS	16	58	8	18	4	1	0	6	2	4	0	2	2-0	.310	.323	.414	.736	1	.984
2001— Minnesota (A.L.)	2B	153	563	70	150	21	6	7	47	40	99	6	15	31-11	.266	.319	.362	.682	15	.974
2002— Minnesota (A.L.)	2B	93	316	46	81	23	4	4	35	19	51	3	12	9-4	.256	.305	.392	.697	5	.986
— Fort Myers (FSL)	2B	6	22	1	2	0	1	0	3	2	2	0	0	1-0	.091	.167	.182	.348	2	.900
2003— Minnesota (A.L.)	2B-DH	135	475	69	123	16	9	8	43	30	65	5	20	17-7	.259	.308	.381	.689	10	.982
2004— Rochester (Int'l)	2B	3	14	2	3	0	0	0	1	0	2	1	0	1-0	.214	.267	.214	.481	0	1.000
— Minnesota (A.L.)	2B	109	336	44	86	19	5	10	34	13	53	1	8	15-1	.256	.283	.432	.715	3	.994
Major League totals (5 years)		506	1748	237	458	83	25	29	165	104	272	15	57	74-23	.262	.307	.388	.695	34	.983

DIVISION SERIES RECORD

									BATTING										FIELDING	
Year Team (League)	Pos.	G	AB	R	H	2B	3B	HR	RBI	BB	SO	HBP	GDP	SB-CS	Avg.	OBP	SLG	OPS	E	Avg.
2002— Minnesota (A.L.)	2B	4	12	2	3	1	0	0	0	1	2	0	2	0-0	.250	.308	.333	.641	0	1.000
2003— Minnesota (A.L.)	2B	4	13	0	0	0	0	0	1	0	4	0	1	0-0	.000	.000	.000	.000	0	1.000
2004— Minnesota (A.L.)	2B	3	1	0	0	0	0	0	0	0	0	0	0	0-0	.000	.000	.000	.000	0	1.000
Division series totals (3 years)		11	26	2	3	1	0	0	1	1	6	0	3	0-0	.115	.143	.154	.297	0	1.000

CHAMPIONSHIP SERIES RECORD

									BATTING										FIELDING	
Year Team (League)	Pos.	G	AB	R	H	2B	3B	HR	RBI	BB	SO	HBP	GDP	SB-CS	Avg.	OBP	SLG	OPS	E	Avg.
2002— Minnesota (A.L.)	2B	5	12	1	3	0	0	0	1	1	3	0	2	0-0	.250	.308	.250	.558	0	1.000

RIVERA, CARLOS — 1B

PERSONAL: Born June 10, 1978, in Fajardo, Puerto Rico. ... 6-1/235. ... Bats left, throws left. ... Full name: Carlos Alberto Rivera. ... High school: Rio Grande (Puerto Rico).

TRANSACTIONS/CAREER NOTES: Selected by Pittsburgh Pirates organization in 10th round of 1996 free-agent draft.

2004 GAMES PLAYED BY POSITION (MLB): 1B—7.

									BATTING										FIELDING	
Year Team (League)	Pos.	G	AB	R	H	2B	3B	HR	RBI	BB	SO	HBP	GDP	SB-CS	Avg.	OBP	SLG	OPS	E	Avg.
1996— GC Pirates (GCL)	1B	48	183	24	52	8	3	3	26	15	22	1	8	1-1	.284	.338	.410	.748	6	.982
1997— Augusta (S. Atl.)	1B-OF	120	415	52	113	16	5	9	65	19	82	10	9	4-1	.272	.316	.400	.716	6	.993
1998— Lynchburg (Caro.)	1B	29	113	11	26	4	0	4	16	0	19	1	3	0-1	.230	.235	.372	.606	2	.989
— Augusta (S. Atl.)	1B-OF	87	316	38	90	17	1	5	53	11	46	6	9	3-5	.285	.318	.392	.711	6	.989
1999— Hickory (S. Atl.)	1B-P	119	457	63	147	30	1	13	86	15	45	11	13	2-1	.322	.355	.477	.832	15	.985
2000— GC Pirates (GCL)	1B	6	24	2	7	0	0	0	0	1	2	0	1	0-0	.292	.320	.292	.612	0	1.000
— Lynchburg (Caro.)	1B	64	233	20	63	17	0	5	47	6	34	2	7	0-1	.270	.284	.408	.692	1	.998
2001— Altoona (East.)	1B-OF	111	389	44	91	30	0	10	50	13	71	1	11	0-2	.234	.258	.388	.646	10	.989
2002— Altoona (East.)	1B	128	494	67	149	28	2	22	84	27	75	8	18	1-1	.302	.345	.500	.845	7	.993
2003— Nashville (PCL)	1B-DH	72	262	28	69	18	0	9	31	13	38	1	2	3-1	.263	.300	.435	.735	2	.997
— Pittsburgh (N.L.)	1B	78	95	12	21	5	0	3	10	8	28	1	2	0-0	.221	.283	.368	.651	4	.984
2004— Pittsburgh (N.L.)	1B	7	15	1	3	0	0	0	1	1	3	0	0	0-0	.200	.250	.200	.450	0	1.000
— Nashville (PCL)	1B-OF-DH	93	312	46	91	19	0	17	50	24	54	3	13	6-7	.292	.348	.516	.864	6	.990
Major League totals (2 years)		85	110	13	24	5	0	3	11	9	31	1	2	0-0	.218	.279	.345	.624	4	.986

RIVERA, JUAN — OF

PERSONAL: Born July 3, 1978, in Guarenas, Venezuela. ... 6-2/205. ... Bats right, throws right. ... Full name: Juan Luis Rivera.

TRANSACTIONS/CAREER NOTES: Signed as a non-drafted free agent by New York Yankees organization (April 12, 1996). ... On disabled list (June 9-August 19, 2002); included rehabilitation assignments to GCL Yankees and Columbus. ... Traded by Yankees with 1B Nick Johnson and P Randy Choate to Montreal Expos for Javier Vazquez (December 16, 2003).

2004 GAMES PLAYED BY POSITION (MLB): OF—121, DH—1.

									BATTING										FIELDING	
Year Team (League)	Pos.	G	AB	R	H	2B	3B	HR	RBI	BB	SO	HBP	GDP	SB-CS	Avg.	OBP	SLG	OPS	E	Avg.
1996— Dom. Yankees (DSL)	OF	10	18	0	3	0	0	0	2	0	1	...	...	0-...	.167	...	.167	...	0	1.000
1997— Maracay 1 (VSL)		52	142	25	40	9	0	0	14	12	16	...	...	12-...	.282	...	.345	...	...	...
1998— GC Yankees (GCL)	OF	57	210	43	70	9	1	12	45	26	27	1	10	8-5	.333	.408	.557	.965	2	.979
— Oneonta (N.Y.-Penn.)	OF	6	18	2	5	0	0	1	3	1	4	0	0	1-1	.278	.316	.444	.760	0	1.000
1999— Tampa (Fla. St.)	OF	109	426	50	112	20	2	14	77	26	67	5	13	5-3	.263	.308	.418	.725	4	.979
— GC Yankees (GCL)	OF	5	18	7	6	0	0	1	4	4	1	0	1	0-0	.333	.455	.500	.955	1	1.000
2000— Norwich (East.)	OF	17	62	9	14	5	0	2	12	6	15	0	2	0-0	.226	.294	.403	.697	1	.955
— Tampa (Fla. St.)	1B-OF	115	409	62	113	26	1	14	69	33	56	6	9	11-7	.276	.336	.447	.783	5	.978
2001— Norwich (East.)	OF	77	316	50	101	18	3	14	58	15	50	3	10	5-7	.320	.353	.528	.882	6	.963
— Columbus (Int'l)	OF	55	199	39	65	11	1	14	40	15	31	1	7	4-5	.327	.372	.603	.975	4	.970
— New York (A.L.)	OF	3	4	0	0	0	0	0	0	0	0	0	0	0-0	.000	.000	.000	.000	0	1.000
2002— Columbus (Int'l)	OF	65	265	40	86	21	1	8	47	13	39	1	4	5-1	.325	.355	.502	.856	6	.955
— New York (A.L.)	OF	28	83	9	22	5	0	1	6	6	10	0	4	1-1	.265	.311	.361	.673	2	.966
— GC Yankees (GCL)	OF	4	13	1	4	2	0	0	4	2	3	1	1	0-0	.308	.438	.462	.899	0	1.000
2003— Columbus (Int'l)	OF	79	308	47	100	21	0	7	37	26	37	0	8	1-3	.325	.374	.461	.835	3	.982
— New York (A.L.)	OF	57	173	22	46	14	0	7	26	10	27	0	8	0-0	.266	.304	.468	.773	2	.979
2004— Montreal (N.L.)	OF-DH	134	391	48	120	24	1	12	49	34	45	1	11	6-2	.307	.364	.465	.829	3	.986
American League totals (3 years)		88	260	31	68	19	0	8	32	16	37	0	12	1-1	.262	.302	.427	.729	4	.974
National League totals (1 year)		134	391	48	120	24	1	12	49	34	45	1	11	6-2	.307	.364	.465	.829	3	.986
Major League totals (4 years)		222	651	79	188	43	1	20	81	50	82	1	23	7-3	.289	.339	.450	.790	7	.981

Year Team (League)	Pos.	G	AB	R	H	2B	3B	HR	RBI	BB	SO	HBP	GDP	SB-CS	Avg.	OBP	SLG	OPS	E	Avg.
						DIVISION SERIES RECORD														
2002— New York (A.L.)	OF	4	12	2	3	0	0	0	3	1	3	0	0	0-0	.250	.308	.250	.558	0	1.000
2003— New York (A.L.)	OF	4	12	2	4	0	0	0	1	0	1	0	1	0-0	.333	.385	.333	.718	0	1.000
Division series totals (2 years)		8	24	4	7	0	0	0	3	2	3	0	1	0-0	.292	.346	.292	.638	0	1.000

Year Team (League)	Pos.	G	AB	R	H	2B	3B	HR	RBI	BB	SO	HBP	GDP	SB-CS	Avg.	OBP	SLG	OPS	E	Avg.
						CHAMPIONSHIP SERIES RECORD														
2003— New York (A.L.)	OF	2	2	0	0	0	0	0	0	0	0	1	0	0-0	.000	.000	.000	.000	0	1.000

Year Team (League)	Pos.	G	AB	R	H	2B	3B	HR	RBI	BB	SO	HBP	GDP	SB-CS	Avg.	OBP	SLG	OPS	E	Avg.
						WORLD SERIES RECORD														
2003— New York (A.L.)	OF	4	6	0	1	1	0	0	1	1	1	0		0-0	.167	.286	.333	.619	0	1.000

R RIVERA, MARIANO   P

PERSONAL: Born November 29, 1969, in Panama City, Panama. ... 6-2/170. ... Throws right, bats right.

TRANSACTIONS/CAREER NOTES: Signed as a non-drafted free agent by New York Yankees organization (February 17, 1990). ... On disabled list (April 6-24, 1998). ... On disabled list (June 10-25, July 21-August 8 and August 18-September 21, 2002); included rehabilitation assignment to GCL Yankees (August 6-8). ... On disabled list (March 25-April 29, 2003).

HONORS: Named A.L. Fireman of the Year by THE SPORTING NEWS (1997 and 1999). ... Named A.L. Reliever of the Year by THE SPORTING NEWS (2001 and 2004).

CAREER HITTING: 0-for-0 (.000), 0 R, 0 2B, 0 3B, 0 HR, 0 RBI.

Year Team (League)	W	L	Pct.	ERA	WHIP	G	GS	CG	ShO	Hld.	Sv.-Opp.	IP	H	R	ER	HR	BB-IBB	SO	Avg.
1990— GC Yankees (GCL)	5	1	.833	0.17	0.46	22	1	1	1	...	1-...	52.0	17	3	1	0	7-0	58	.102
1991— Greensboro (S. Atl.)	4	9	.308	2.75	1.21	29	15	1	0	...	0-...	114.2	103	48	35	2	36-0	123	.237
1992— Fort Lauderdale (FSL)	5	3	.625	2.28	0.76	10	10	3	1	...	0-...	59.1	40	17	15	5	5-0	42	.191
1993— Greensboro (S. Atl.)	1	0	1.000	2.06	1.17	10	10	0	0	...	0-...	39.1	31	12	9	0	15-0	32	.214
— GC Yankees (GCL)	0	1	.000	2.25	0.75	2	2	0	0	...	0-...	4.0	2	1	1	0	1-0	6	.143
1994— Tampa (FSL)	3	0	1.000	2.21	1.25	7	7	0	0	...	0-...	36.2	34	12	9	2	12-0	27	.258
— Alb./Colon. (East.)	3	0	1.000	2.27	1.04	9	9	0	0	...	0-...	63.1	58	20	16	5	8-0	39	.242
— Columbus (Int'l)	4	2	.667	5.81	1.42	6	6	1	0	...	0-...	31.0	34	22	20	5	10-0	23	.268
1995— Columbus (Int'l)	2	2	.500	2.10	0.93	7	7	1	1	...	0-...	30.0	25	10	7	2	3-0	30	.227
— New York (A.L.)	5	3	.625	5.51	1.51	19	10	0	0	0	0-1	67.0	71	43	41	11	30-0	51	.266
1996— New York (A.L.)	8	3	.727	2.09	0.99	61	0	0	0	27	5-8	107.2	73	25	25	1	34-3	130	.189
1997— New York (A.L.)	6	4	.600	1.88	1.19	66	0	0	0	0	43-52	71.2	65	17	15	5	20-6	68	.237
1998— New York (A.L.)	3	0	1.000	1.91	1.06	54	0	0	0	0	36-41	61.1	48	13	13	3	17-1	36	.215
1999— New York (A.L.)	4	3	.571	1.83	0.88	66	0	0	0	0	* 45-49	69.0	43	15	14	2	18-3	52	.176
2000— New York (A.L.)	7	4	.636	2.85	1.10	66	0	0	0	0	36-41	75.2	58	26	24	4	25-3	58	.208
2001— New York (A.L.)	4	6	.400	2.34	0.90	71	0	0	0	0	* 50-57	80.2	61	24	21	5	12-2	83	.209
2002— New York (A.L.)	1	4	.200	2.74	1.00	45	0	0	0	2	28-32	46.0	35	16	14	3	11-2	41	.203
— GC Yankees (GCL)	0	0	...	0.00	1.50	1	1	0	0	0	0-...	2.0	2	0	0	0	1-0	2	.286
2003— New York (A.L.)	5	2	.714	1.66	1.00	64	0	0	0	0	40-46	70.2	61	15	13	3	10-1	63	.235
2004— New York (A.L.)	4	2	.667	1.94	1.08	74	0	0	0	0	* 53-57	78.2	65	17	17	3	20-3	66	.225
Major League totals (10 years)	47	31	.603	2.43	1.07	586	10	0	0	29	336-384	728.1	580	211	197	40	197-24	648	.216

Year Team (League)	W	L	Pct.	ERA	WHIP	G	GS	CG	ShO	Hld.	Sv.-Opp.	IP	H	R	ER	HR	BB-IBB	SO	Avg.
							DIVISION SERIES RECORD												
1995— New York (A.L.)	1	0	1.000	0.00	0.75	3	0	0	0	0	0-0	5.1	3	0	0	0	1-1	8	.167
1996— New York (A.L.)	0	0	...	0.00	0.21	2	0	0	0	1	0-0	4.2	0	0	0	0	1-0	1	.000
1997— New York (A.L.)	0	0	...	4.50	1.00	2	0	0	0	0	1-2	2.0	2	1	1	1	0-0	1	.250
1998— New York (A.L.)	0	0	...	0.00	0.60	3	0	0	0	0	2-2	3.1	1	0	0	0	1-0	2	.091
1999— New York (A.L.)	0	0	...	0.00	0.33	2	0	0	0	0	2-2	3.0	1	0	0	0	0-0	3	.111
2000— New York (A.L.)	0	0	...	0.00	0.40	3	0	0	0	0	3-3	5.0	2	0	0	0	0-0	2	.111
2001— New York (A.L.)	0	0	...	0.00	0.80	3	0	0	0	0	2-2	5.0	4	1	0	0	0-0	4	.211
2002— New York (A.L.)	0	0	...	0.00	1.00	1	0	0	0	0	1-1	1.0	1	0	0	0	0-0	0	.250
2003— New York (A.L.)	0	0	...	0.00	0.00	2	0	0	0	0	2-2	4.0	0	0	0	0	0-0	4	.000
2004— New York (A.L.)	1	0	1.000	0.00	0.35	4	0	0	0	0	0-1	5.2	2	0	0	0	0-0	2	.111
Division series totals (10 years)	2	0	1.000	0.23	0.49	25	0	0	0	1	13-15	39.0	16	2	1	1	3-1	27	.122

Year Team (League)	W	L	Pct.	ERA	WHIP	G	GS	CG	ShO	Hld.	Sv.-Opp.	IP	H	R	ER	HR	BB-IBB	SO	Avg.
							CHAMPIONSHIP SERIES RECORD												
1996— New York (A.L.)	1	0	1.000	0.00	1.75	2	0	0	0	1	0-0	4.0	6	0	0	0	1-0	5	.333
1998— New York (A.L.)	0	0	...	0.00	0.18	4	0	0	0	0	1-1	5.2	0	0	0	0	1-0	5	.000
1999— New York (A.L.)	1	0	1.000	0.00	1.07	3	0	0	0	0	2-2	4.2	5	0	0	0	0-0	3	.294
2000— New York (A.L.)	0	0	...	1.93	0.86	3	0	0	0	0	1-1	4.2	4	1	1	0	0-0	1	.222
2001— New York (A.L.)	1	0	1.000	1.93	0.64	4	0	0	0	0	2-2	4.2	2	1	1	0	1-0	3	.125
2003— New York (A.L.)	1	0	1.000	1.13	0.63	4	0	0	0	0	2-2	8.0	5	1	1	0	0-0	6	.172
2004— New York (A.L.)	0	0	...	1.29	1.14	5	0	0	0	0	2-4	7.0	6	1	1	0	2-0	6	.250
Champ. series totals (7 years)	4	0	1.000	0.93	0.85	25	0	0	0	1	10-12	38.2	28	4	4	0	5-0	29	.203

Year Team (League)	W	L	Pct.	ERA	WHIP	G	GS	CG	ShO	Hld.	Sv.-Opp.	IP	H	R	ER	HR	BB-IBB	SO	Avg.
							WORLD SERIES RECORD												
1996— New York (A.L.)	0	0	...	1.59	1.24	4	0	0	0	2	0-0	5.2	4	1	1	0	3-0	4	.211
1998— New York (A.L.)	0	0	...	0.00	1.15	3	0	0	0	0	3-3	4.1	5	0	0	0	0-0	4	.294
1999— New York (A.L.)	1	0	1.000	0.00	0.86	3	0	0	0	0	2-2	4.2	3	0	0	0	1-0	3	.188
2000— New York (A.L.)	0	0	...	3.00	0.83	4	0	0	0	0	2-2	6.0	4	2	2	1	1-0	7	.182
2001— New York (A.L.)	1	1	.500	1.42	1.11	4	0	0	0	0	1-2	6.1	6	2	1	0	1-1	7	.250
2003— New York (A.L.)	0	0	...	0.00	0.50	2	0	0	0	0	1-1	4.0	2	0	0	0	0-0	4	.143
World series totals (6 years)	2	1	.667	1.16	0.97	20	0	0	0	2	9-10	31.0	24	5	4	1	6-1	29	.214

	W	L	Pct.	ERA	WHIP	G	GS	CG	ShO	Hld.	Sv.-Opp.	IP	H	R	ER	HR	BB-IBB	SO	Avg.
							ALL-STAR GAME RECORD												
All-Star Game totals (4 years)	0	0	...	0.00	0.75	4	0	0	0	0	1-1	4.0	3	1	0	0	0-0	1	.214

RIVERA, RENE   C

PERSONAL: Born July 31, 1983, in Bayamon, Puerto Rico. ... 5-10/190. ... Bats right, throws right. ... High school: Papa Juan XXIII (Bayamon, P.R.).
TRANSACTIONS/CAREER NOTES: Selected by Seattle Mariners organization in second round of 2001 free-agent draft.
2004 GAMES PLAYED BY POSITION (MLB): C—2.

Year Team (League)	Pos.	G	AB	R	H	2B	3B	HR	RBI	BB	SO	HBP	GDP	SB-CS	Avg.	OBP	SLG	OPS	E	Avg.
2001— Everett (N'west)	C	15	45	3	4	1	0	2	3	1	19	0	1	0-0	.089	.106	.244	.351	1	.992
— Ariz. Mariners (Ariz.)	C	21	71	13	24	4	0	2	12	2	11	1	0	0-0	.338	.360	.479	.839	4	.977
2002— Everett (N'west)	C	62	227	29	55	18	1	1	26	16	38	9	3	5-2	.242	.314	.344	.657	7	.987
2003— Wisconsin (Midw.)	C	116	407	39	112	19	0	9	54	38	81	7	6	2-2	.275	.344	.388	.732	11	.987
2004— Tacoma (PCL)	C	4	15	3	6	1	0	1	1	0	3	0	0	0-0	.400	.400	.667	1.067	0	1.000
— Inland Empire (Calif.)	C-DH	107	379	41	89	22	1	6	53	28	70	9	17	0-1	.235	.300	.346	.646	7	.993
— Seattle (A.L.)	C	2	3	0	0	0	0	0	0	0	1	0	0	0-0	.000	.000	.000	.000	0	1.000
Major League totals (1 year)		2	3	0	0	0	0	0	0	0	1	0	0	0-0	.000	.000	.000	.000	0	1.000

ROA, JOE   P

PERSONAL: Born October 11, 1971, in Southfield, Mich. ... 6-2/200. ... Throws right, bats right. ... Full name: Joseph Rodger Roa. ... Name pronounced: ROH-ah. ... High school: Hazel Park (Mich.).
TRANSACTIONS/CAREER NOTES: Selected by Atlanta Braves organization in 18th round of 1989 free-agent draft. ... Traded by Braves to New York Mets organization (August 29, 1991), completing deal in which Mets traded P Alejandro Pena to Braves for P Tony Castillo and a player to be named (August 28, 1991). ... Traded by Mets organization with OF Jeromy Burnitz to Cleveland Indians for Ps Dave Mlicki, Paul Byrd and Jerry DiPoto and a player to be named (November 18, 1994); Mets acquired 2B Jesus Azuaje to complete deal (December 6, 1994). ... Traded by Indians to San Francisco Giants for OF Trenidad Hubbard (December 16, 1996), completing deal in which Giants traded 3B Matt Williams and a player to be named to Indians for IFs Jeff Kent and Jose Vizcaino, P Julian Tavarez and a player to be named (November 13, 1996). ... Signed as a free agent by Kansas City Royals organization (December 17, 1998). ... Released by Royals (March 29, 1999). ... Signed by Indians organization (March 28, 2000). ... Signed as a free agent by Florida Marlins organization (December 28, 2000). ... Released by Marlins (March 19, 2002). ... Signed by Pittsburgh Pirates organization (March 22, 2002). ... Traded by Pirates to Philadelphia Phillies for future considerations (March 28, 2002). ... Refused minor league assignment and became a free agent (June 3, 2003). ... Signed by Milwaukee Brewers organization (June 12, 2003). ... Released by Brewers (July 3, 2003). ... Signed by Colorado Rockies organization (July 4, 2003). ... Claimed on waivers by San Diego Padres (July 23, 2003). ... Refused minor league assignment and became a free agent (September 30, 2003). ... Signed by Minnesota Twins organization (December 2, 2003). ... Refused minor league assignment and became a free agent (October 8, 2004).
CAREER HITTING: 10-for-47 (.213), 1 R, 1 2B, 0 3B, 0 HR, 3 RBI.

Year Team (League)	W	L	Pct.	ERA	WHIP	G	GS	CG	ShO	Hld.	Sv.-Opp.	IP	H	R	ER	HR	BB-IBB	SO	Avg.
1989— GC Braves (GCL)	2	2	.500	2.89	1.34	13	4	0	0	...	0-...	37.1	40	18	12	2	10-1	21	.276
1990— Pulaski (Appalachian)	4	2	.667	2.97	1.07	14	11	3	1	...	0-...	75.2	55	29	25	3	26-0	49	.195
1991— Macon (S. Atl.)	13	3	.813	2.17	0.99	30	18	4	2	...	1-...	141.0	106	46	34	6	33-4	96	.206
1992— St. Lucie (Fla. St.)	9	7	.563	3.63	1.22	26	24	2	1	...	0-...	156.1	176	80	63	9	15-1	61	.287
1993— Binghamton (Eastern)	12	7	.632	3.87	1.28	32	23	2	1	...	0-...	167.1	190	80	72	9	24-0	73	.291
1994— Binghamton (Eastern)	2	1	.667	1.80	0.95	3	3	0	0	...	0-...	20.0	18	6	4	0	1-0	11	.240
— Norfolk (Int'l)	8	8	.500	3.49	1.30	25	25	5	0	...	0-...	167.2	184	82	65	16	34-1	74	.283
1995— Buffalo (A.A.)	17	3	.850	3.50	1.19	25	24	3	0	...	0-...	164.2	168	71	64	9	28-1	93	.264
— Cleveland (A.L.)	0	1	.000	6.00	1.83	1	1	0	0	0	0-0	6.0	9	4	4	1	2-0	0	.360
1996— Buffalo (A.A.)	11	8	.579	3.27	1.19	26	24	5	0	...	0-...	165.1	161	66	60	19	36-0	82	.257
— Cleveland (A.L.)	0	0	...	10.80	4.20	1	0	0	0	0	0-0	1.2	4	2	2	0	3-0	0	.500
1997— San Francisco (N.L.)	2	5	.286	5.21	1.61	28	3	0	0	2	0-0	65.2	86	40	38	8	20-5	34	.333
— Phoenix (PCL)	3	1	.750	4.75	1.50	6	5	0	0	...	0-...	36.0	43	21	19	4	11-0	16	.297
1998— Fresno (PCL)	12	9	.571	5.17	1.38	27	27	2	1	...	0-...	162.0	192	102	93	26	32-0	97	.293
1999—			Did not play.																
2000— Akron (East.)	6	5	.545	3.41	1.25	19	14	1	0	...	0-...	103.0	91	48	39	7	38-0	59	.235
2001— Portland (East.)	0	2	.000	3.00	1.08	7	7	0	0	...	0-...	36.0	36	15	12	2	3-1	26	.267
— Calgary (PCL)	6	6	.500	3.92	1.18	19	19	1	0	...	0-...	124.0	134	58	54	16	12-2	81	.276
2002— Scran./W.B. (I.L.)	14	0	1.000	1.86	0.89	17	17	1	0	...	0-...	111.0	83	24	23	4	16-2	74	.209
— Philadelphia (N.L.)	4	4	.500	4.04	1.28	14	11	0	0	0	0-0	71.1	78	33	32	11	13-2	35	.279
2003— Philadelphia (N.L.)	0	2	.000	6.05	1.66	6	3	0	0	0	0-0	19.1	28	13	13	3	4-0	16	.341
— Indianapolis (Int'l)	2	2	.500	4.74	1.40	5	4	0	0	...	0-...	24.2	32	15	13	3	3-0	18	.323
— Colorado (N.L.)	0	0	...	4.05	1.05	4	0	0	0	0	0-0	6.2	7	3	3	2	0-0	4	.269
— San Diego (N.L.)	1	1	.500	6.75	1.58	18	1	0	0	0	0-0	25.1	34	20	19	5	6-0	18	.315
2004— Minnesota (A.L.)	2	3	.400	4.50	1.54	48	0	0	0	2	0-1	70.0	84	38	35	9	24-0	47	.297
American League totals (3 years)	2	4	.333	4.75	1.62	50	1	0	0	2	0-1	77.2	97	44	41	10	29-0	47	.307
National League totals (3 years)	7	12	.368	5.02	1.47	70	18	0	0	2	0-0	188.1	233	109	105	29	43-7	107	.309
Major League totals (6 years)	9	16	.360	4.94	1.51	120	19	0	0	4	0-1	266.0	330	153	146	39	72-7	154	.308

ROBBINS, JAKE   P

PERSONAL: Born May 23, 1976, in Charlotte, N.C. ... 6-5/190. ... Throws right, bats right. ... Full name: Phillip Jacob Robbins. ... High school: Myers Park (Charlotte, N.C.).
TRANSACTIONS/CAREER NOTES: Selected by New York Yankees organization in 11th round of 1994 free-agent draft. ... Signed as a free agent by Atlanta Braves organization (November 17, 2000). ... Released by Braves (July 31, 2002). ... Signed by Colorado Rockies organization (August 5, 2002). ... Signed as a free agent by Milwaukee Brewers organization (January 17, 2003). ... Released by Brewers (April 3, 2003). ... Signed by Cleveland Indians organization (April 8, 2003).
CAREER HITTING: 0-for-0 (.000), 0 R, 0 2B, 0 3B, 0 HR, 0 RBI.

Year Team (League)	W	L	Pct.	ERA	WHIP	G	GS	CG	ShO	Hld.	Sv.-Opp.	IP	H	R	ER	HR	BB-IBB	SO	Avg.
1994— GC Yankees (GCL)	0	2	.000	5.09	1.57	8	3	0	0	...	0-...	23.0	21	16	13	2	15-0	14	.256
1995— GC Yankees (GCL)	2	3	.400	5.54	1.34	14	3	0	0	...	0-...	37.1	32	26	23	2	18-1	17	.234
— Oneonta (N.Y.-Penn)	0	0	...	0.00	0.00	1	0	0	0	...	0-...	1.0	0	0	0	0	0-0	1	.000
1996— Greensboro (S. Atl.)	1	8	.111	6.45	1.74	18	12	0	0	...	0-...	74.0	80	59	53	5	49-0	50	.282
— Oneonta (N.Y.-Penn)	3	4	.429	4.50	1.50	11	11	0	0	...	0-...	66.0	64	42	33	3	35-1	47	.251
1997— Greensboro (S. Atl.)	6	4	.600	5.77	1.67	20	19	0	0	...	0-...	101.1	114	81	65	6	55-1	72	.285
— Tampa (FSL)	1	1	.500	5.06	1.75	3	3	0	0	...	0-...	16.0	18	14	9	2	10-1	5	.295
1998— Tampa (FSL)	11	6	.647	3.84	1.57	26	25	2	2	...	0-...	152.1	167	83	65	5	72-2	87	.283
1999— Norwich (East.)	3	12	.200	5.43	1.60	20	19	2	1	...	0-...	111.0	118	80	67	7	60-3	63	.273
— Tampa (FSL)	3	3	.500	4.75	1.51	7	7	0	0	...	0-...	41.2	44	30	22	3	19-2	31	.270
2000— Norwich (East.)	3	5	.375	2.78	1.51	48	4	0	0	...	0-...	71.1	68	45	22	4	40-1	53	.247
— Columbus (Int'l)	0	0	...	9.00	4.00	1	0	0	0	...	0-...	1.0	3	1	1	0	1-0	0	.500

Year Team (League)	W	L	Pct.	ERA	WHIP	G	GS	CG	ShO	Hld.	Sv.-Opp.	IP	H	R	ER	HR	BB-IBB	SO	Avg.
2001— Richmond (Int'l)	5	3	.625	5.51	1.58	57	0	0	0	...	1-...	78.1	73	51	48	1	51-3	53	.252
2002— Richmond (Int'l)	1	4	.200	4.76	1.80	47	0	0	0	...	3-...	56.2	59	36	30	3	43-6	37	.269
— Colo. Springs (PCL)	1	2	.333	12.00	2.50	11	0	0	0	...	0-...	12.0	17	18	16	3	13-0	15	.327
2003— Akron (East.)	6	3	.667	2.16	1.17	34	0	0	0	...	8-...	58.1	44	18	14	1	24-0	38	.218
2004— Akron (East.)	2	1	.667	3.28	0.93	12	0	0	0	...	1-...	24.2	16	10	9	4	7-0	21	.182
— Buffalo (Int'l)	6	1	.857	3.20	1.24	32	2	0	0	...	4-...	64.2	51	24	23	4	29-1	40	.214
— Cleveland (A.L.)	0	0	...	5.40	1.80	2	0	0	0	...	0-0	1.2	3	1	1	1	0-0	0	.375
Major League totals (1 year)	0	0	...	5.40	1.80	2	0	0	0	0	0-0	1.2	3	1	1	1	0-0	0	.375

ROBERTS, BRIAN — 2B

PERSONAL: Born October 9, 1977, in Durham, N.C. ... 5-9/176. ... Bats both, throws right. ... Full name: Brian Michael Roberts. ... High school: Chapel Hill (N.C.). ... College: South Carolina.

TRANSACTIONS/CAREER NOTES: Selected by Baltimore Orioles organization in supplemental round ("sandwich pick" between first and second rounds, 50th pick overall) of 1999 free-agent draft; pick received as part of compensation for Texas Rangers signing Type A free-agent 1B Rafael Palmeiro.

2004 GAMES PLAYED BY POSITION (MLB): 2B—150, DH—6.

Year Team (League)	Pos.	G	AB	R	H	2B	3B	HR	RBI	BB	SO	HBP	GDP	SB-CS	Avg.	OBP	SLG	OPS	E	Avg.
1999—Delmarva (S. Atl.)	SS	47	167	22	40	12	1	0	21	27	42	1	0	17-5	.240	.347	.323	.670	8	.964
2000—Frederick (Carolina)	SS	48	163	27	49	6	3	0	16	27	24	1	4	13-10	.301	.403	.374	.777	8	.952
—GC Orioles (GCL)	SS	9	29	8	9	1	2	1	3	7	4	0	0	7-1	.310	.432	.586	1.019	2	.905
2001—Bowie (East.)	2B-SS	22	81	12	24	7	0	1	7	9	12	1	2	10-0	.296	.366	.420	.785	3	.968
—Rochester (Int'l)	SS	44	161	16	43	4	1	1	12	28	22	0	0	23-3	.267	.376	.323	.699	13	.927
—Baltimore (A.L.) SS-2B-DH	75	273	42	69	12	3	2	17	13	36	0	3	12-3	.253	.284	.341	.624	16	.941
2002—Rochester (Int'l)	2B	78	313	49	86	9	7	3	30	40	46	3	3	22-4	.275	.361	.374	.735	7	.978
—Baltimore (A.L.)	2B-DH	38	128	18	29	6	0	1	11	15	21	1	3	9-2	.227	.308	.297	.605	3	.977
2003—Ottawa (Int'l)	2B-SS	44	178	36	56	13	1	0	15	27	12	0	3	19-6	.315	.401	.399	.800	4	.979
—Baltimore (A.L.) 2B-DH-SS	112	460	65	124	22	4	5	41	46	58	1	9	23-6	.270	.337	.367	.704	9	.983
2004—Baltimore (A.L.)	2B-DH	159	641	107	175	* 50	2	4	53	71	95	1	3	29-12	.273	.344	.376	.720	8	.988
Major League totals (4 years)		384	1502	232	397	90	9	12	122	145	210	3	18	73-23	.264	.328	.360	.688	36	.978

ROBERTS, DAVE — OF

PERSONAL: Born May 31, 1972, in Okinawa, Japan. ... 5-10/180. ... Bats left, throws left. ... Full name: David Ray Roberts. ... High school: Rancho Buena Vista (Oceanside, Calif.). ... College: UCLA.

TRANSACTIONS/CAREER NOTES: Selected by Cleveland Indians organization in 47th round of 1993 free-agent draft; did not sign. ... Selected by Detroit Tigers organization in 28th round of 1994 free-agent draft. ... Loaned by Tigers organization to Oakland Athletics organization (March 30-August 30, 1996). ... Traded by Tigers with P Tim Worrell to Cleveland Indians for OF Geronimo Berroa (June 24, 1998). ... On disabled list (March 31-June 24, 2001); included rehabilitation assignment to Akron. ... Traded by Indians to Los Angeles Dodgers for Ps Christian Bridenbaugh and Nial Hughes (December 21, 2001). ... On disabled list (May 17-June 1 and July 2-26, 2003); included rehabilitation assignments to Las Vegas and Ogden. ... On disabled list (May 5-28, 2004); included rehabilitation assignment to Vero Beach. ... Traded by Dodgers to Boston Red Sox for OF Henri Stanley (July 31, 2004).

2004 GAMES PLAYED BY POSITION (MLB): OF—100, DH—1.

Year Team (League)	Pos.	G	AB	R	H	2B	3B	HR	RBI	BB	SO	HBP	GDP	SB-CS	Avg.	OBP	SLG	OPS	E	Avg.
1994—Jamestown (N.Y.-Penn.) ...	OF	54	178	33	52	7	2	0	12	29	27	1	0	12-8	.292	.392	.354	.746	0	1.000
1995—Lakeland (Fla. St.)	OF	92	357	67	108	10	5	3	30	39	43	1	7	30-8	.303	.371	.384	.755	1	.985
1996—Visalia (Calif.)	OF	126	482	112	131	24	7	5	37	98	105	1	6	65-21	.272	.391	.382	.773	5	.977
—Jacksonville (Sou.)	OF	3	9	0	2	0	0	0	0	1	0	0	0	0-1	.222	.300	.222	.522	0	1.000
1997—Jacksonville (Sou.)	OF	105	415	76	123	24	2	4	41	45	62	2	5	23-5	.296	.366	.393	.759	4	.954
1998—Jacksonville (Sou.)	OF	69	279	71	91	14	5	5	42	53	59	3	4	21-9	.326	.434	.466	.900	1	1.000
—Akron (East.)	OF	56	227	49	82	10	5	7	33	35	30	1	3	28-6	.361	.447	.542	.989	1	.992
—Buffalo (Int'l)	OF	5	15	2	2	0	0	0	0	3	0	0	0	2-0	.133	.125	.133	.258	0	1.000
1999—Buffalo (Int'l)	OF-DH	89	350	65	95	17	10	0	38	43	52	2	1	39-3	.271	.351	.377	.728	1	.996
—Cleveland (A.L.)	OF	41	143	26	34	4	0	2	12	9	16	0	0	11-3	.238	.281	.308	.589	0	1.000
2000—Buffalo (Int'l)	OF	120	462	93	135	16	3	13	55	59	68	2	3	39-11	.292	.373	.424	.798	1	.997
—Cleveland (A.L.)	OF	19	10	1	2	0	0	0	0	2	2	0	0	1-1	.200	.333	.200	.533	0	1.000
2001—Akron (East.)	OF	17	64	9	13	5	0	0	2	9	8	1	1	4-0	.203	.307	.281	.588	1	.969
—Buffalo (Int'l)	OF	62	241	34	73	12	4	0	22	18	44	2	2	17-6	.303	.352	.386	.738	3	.978
—Cleveland (A.L.)	OF-DH	15	12	3	4	1	0	0	1	2	0	0	0	0-1	.333	.385	.417	.801	0	1.000
2002—Los Angeles (N.L.)	OF	127	422	63	117	14	7	3	34	48	51	2	4	45-10	.277	.353	.365	.718	0	1.000
2003—Las Vegas (PCL)	OF	2	5	2	0	0	0	0	0	1	0	0	0	0-0	.000	.167	.000	.167	0	.000
—Ogden (Pio.)	OF	3	10	4	4	0	0	0	0	1	0	0	0	1-0	.400	.455	.400	.855	0	1.000
—Los Angeles (N.L.)	OF	107	388	56	97	6	5	2	16	43	39	4	0	40-14	.250	.331	.307	.638	5	.976
2004—Vero Beach (FSL)	OF	2	8	0	0	0	0	0	0	0	0	0	0	0-0	...	.000	...	.000	0	1.000
—Los Angeles (N.L.)	OF	68	233	45	59	4	7	2	21	28	31	4	2	33-1	.253	.340	.356	.696	3	.976
—Boston (A.L.)	OF-DH	45	86	19	22	10	0	2	14	10	17	1	2	5-2	.256	.330	.442	.772	1	.982
American League totals (4 years)		120	251	49	62	15	0	4	28	22	37	1	2	17-7	.247	.306	.355	.660	1	.994
National League totals (3 years)		302	1043	164	273	24	19	7	71	119	121	10	3	118-25	.262	.342	.341	.683	8	.986
Major League totals (6 years)		422	1294	213	335	39	19	11	99	141	158	11	5	135-32	.259	.335	.344	.679	9	.988

DIVISION SERIES RECORD

Year Team (League)	Pos.	G	AB	R	H	2B	3B	HR	RBI	BB	SO	HBP	GDP	SB-CS	Avg.	OBP	SLG	OPS	E	Avg.
1999—Cleveland (A.L.)	OF	2	3	0	0	0	0	0	0	2	0	0	0	0-0	.000	.000	.000	.000	0	1.000
2004— Boston (A.L.)		1	0	0	0	0	0	0	0	0	0	0	0	0-0	...	...	...	...	0	...
Division series totals (2 years)		3	3	0	0	0	0	0	0	2	0	0	0	0-0	.000	.000	.000	.000	0	1.000

CHAMPIONSHIP SERIES RECORD

Year Team (League)	Pos.	G	AB	R	H	2B	3B	HR	RBI	BB	SO	HBP	GDP	SB-CS	Avg.	OBP	SLG	OPS	E	Avg.
2004—Boston (A.L.)		2	0	2	0	0	0	0	0	0	0	0	0	1-0	...	...	...	...	0	...

WORLD SERIES RECORD

Year Team (League)	Pos.	G	AB	R	H	2B	3B	HR	RBI	BB	SO	HBP	GDP	SB-CS	Avg.	OBP	SLG	OPS	E	Avg.
2004—Boston (A.L.)	Did not play.																			

ROBERTS, GRANT — P

PERSONAL: Born September 13, 1977, in El Cajon, Calif. ... 6-3/205. ... Throws right, bats right. ... Full name: Grant William Roberts. ... High school: Grossmont (La Mesa, Calif.).

TRANSACTIONS/CAREER NOTES: Selected by New York Mets organization in 11th round of 1995 free-agent draft. ... On disabled list (June 9-30 and July 13-September 10, 2002); included rehabilitation assignment to Binghamton. ... On disabled list (March 28-August 7, 2003); included rehabilitation assignments to St. Lucie and Norfolk. ... On disabled list (May 25, 2004-remainder of season).

CAREER HITTING: 1-for-4 (.250), 1 R, 0 2B, 0 3B, 0 HR, 0 RBI.

Year	Team (League)	W	L	Pct.	ERA	WHIP	G	GS	CG	ShO	Hld.	Sv.-Opp.	IP	H	R	ER	HR	BB-IBB	SO	Avg.
1995—	GC Mets (GCL)	2	1	.667	2.15	1.13	11	3	0	0	...	0-...	29.1	19	13	7	1	14-1	24	.186
1996—	Kingsport (Appalachian)	9	1	.900	2.10	1.17	13	13	2	2	...	0-...	68.2	43	18	16	3	37-1	92	.179
1997—	Capital City (S. Atl.)	11	3	.786	2.36	1.10	22	22	2	1	...	0-...	129.2	98	37	34	4	44-0	122	.208
1998—	St. Lucie (Fla. St.)	4	5	.444	4.23	1.51	17	17	0	0	...	0-...	72.1	72	37	34	11	37-0	70	.258
1999—	Binghamton (Eastern)	7	6	.538	4.87	1.40	23	23	0	0	...	0-...	131.1	135	81	71	9	49-0	94	.267
	—Norfolk (Int'l)	2	1	.667	4.50	1.54	5	5	0	0	...	0-...	28.0	32	15	14	1	11-2	30	.291
2000—	Norfolk (Int'l)	7	8	.467	3.38	1.38	25	25	5	0	...	0-...	157.1	154	67	59	6	63-5	115	.254
	—New York (N.L.)	0	0	...	11.57	2.14	4	1	0	0	0	0-...	7.0	11	10	9	0	4-1	6	.344
2001—	Norfolk (Int'l)	3	5	.375	4.52	1.46	30	6	0	0	...	2-...	67.2	80	38	34	4	19-1	54	.297
	—New York (N.L.)	1	0	1.000	3.81	1.23	16	0	0	0	1	0-1	26.0	24	11	11	2	8-1	29	.240
2002—	New York (N.L.)	3	1	.750	2.20	1.31	34	0	0	0	0	0-...	45.0	43	12	11	3	16-7	31	.253
	—Binghamton (Eastern)	0	0	...	0.00	0.00	1	1	0	0	...	0-...	1.0	0	0	0	0	0-0	1	.000
2003—	St. Lucie (Fla. St.)	1	0	1.000	...	0.90	5	2	0	0	...	0-...	9.0	5	4	0	0	3-0	5	.156
	—Norfolk (Int'l)	0	0	...	3.52	1.60	8	0	0	0	...	0-...	7.2	7	3	3	0	5-0	6	.233
	—New York (N.L.)	0	3	.000	3.79	1.16	18	0	0	0	4	1-1	19.0	19	9	8	0	3-1	10	.257
2004—	New York (N.L.)	0	0	...	17.36	3.21	4	0	0	0	0	0-...	4.2	9	9	9	2	6-1	1	.429
Major League totals (5 years)		4	4	.500	4.25	1.41	76	1	0	0	5	1-2	101.2	106	51	48	7	37-11	77	.267

ROBERTS, WILLIS — P

PERSONAL: Born June 19, 1975, in San Cristobal, Dominican Republic. ... 6-3/240. ... Throws right, bats right. ... Full name: Willis Augusto Roberts.

TRANSACTIONS/CAREER NOTES: Signed as a non-drafted free agent by Detroit Tigers organization (February 18, 1992). ... Released by Tigers (February 1, 2000). ... Signed by Cincinnati Reds organization (February 1, 2000). ... Signed as a free agent by Baltimore Orioles organization (November 16, 2000). ... On suspended list (September 13-18, 2002). ... On disabled list (June 29, 2003-remainder of season). ... Signed as a free agent by Pittsburgh Pirates organization (January 21, 2004). ... Refused minor league assignment and became a free agent (August 21, 2004).

CAREER HITTING: 1-for-5 (.200), 0 R, 0 2B, 0 3B, 0 HR, 0 RBI.

Year	Team (League)	W	L	Pct.	ERA	WHIP	G	GS	CG	ShO	Hld.	Sv.-Opp.	IP	H	R	ER	HR	BB-IBB	SO	Avg.
1992—	Dominican Tigers (DSL)	0	6	.000	8.23	2.54	12	7	1	0	...	0-...	35.0	43	49	32	...	46-...	17	...
1993—	Bristol (Appalachian)	2	3	.400	1.38	1.35	10	2	0	0	...	1-...	26.0	24	16	4	0	11-0	23	.235
1994—	Bristol (Appalachian)	1	2	.333	3.92	0.82	4	4	0	0	...	0-...	20.2	9	9	9	1	8-0	17	.129
1995—	Fayetteville (S. Atl.)	6	3	.667	2.70	1.40	17	15	0	0	...	0-...	80.0	72	33	24	2	40-0	52	.248
1996—	Lakeland (Fla. St.)	9	7	.563	2.89	1.35	23	22	2	0	...	0-...	149.1	133	60	48	5	69-0	105	.246
1997—	Jacksonville (Southern)	6	15	.286	6.28	1.64	26	26	2	0	...	0-...	149.0	181	120	104	18	64-0	86	.301
1998—	Jacksonville (Southern)	3	1	.750	2.19	1.26	12	2	0	0	...	0-...	24.2	21	10	6	0	10-1	15	.233
	—Toledo (International)	3	3	.500	4.61	1.66	39	0	0	0	...	2-...	54.2	63	33	28	4	28-2	40	.294
1999—	Toledo (International)	5	8	.385	6.26	1.86	31	9	0	0	...	0-...	92.0	112	68	64	10	59-3	52	.307
	—Detroit (A.L.)	0	0	...	13.50	2.25	1	0	0	0	0	0-0	3.1	3	4	2	0	0-0	5	.500
2000—	Chattanooga (Southern)	4	0	1.000	3.06	1.42	5	5	0	0	...	0-...	32.1	33	12	11	0	13-1	28	.280
	—Louisville (Int'l)	7	8	.467	5.66	1.56	25	20	2	1	...	0-...	124.0	138	80	78	19	55-0	66	.288
2001—	Baltimore (A.L.)	9	10	.474	4.91	1.49	46	18	1	0	1	6-10	132.0	142	75	72	15	55-1	95	.274
2002—	Baltimore (A.L.)	5	4	.556	3.36	1.48	66	0	0	0	13	1-3	75.0	79	34	28	5	32-3	51	.270
2003—	Baltimore (A.L.)	3	1	.750	5.72	1.45	26	0	0	0	1	0-0	39.1	41	26	25	7	16-2	26	.273
2004—	Nashville (PCL)	6	3	.667	5.87	1.51	35	0	0	0	...	5-...	38.1	45	26	25	5	13-2	32	.298
	—Pittsburgh (N.L.)	0	0	...	5.25	1.75	9	0	0	0	2	0-0	12.0	12	7	7	0	9-0	7	.279
American League totals (4 years)		17	15	.531	4.62	1.49	139	18	1	0	15	7-13	247.2	265	139	127	27	103-6	172	.274
National League totals (1 year)		0	0	...	5.25	1.75	9	0	0	0	2	0-0	12.0	12	7	7	0	9-0	7	.279
Major League totals (5 years)		17	15	.531	4.64	1.50	148	18	1	0	17	7-13	259.2	277	146	134	27	112-6	179	.274

ROBERTSON, JERIOME — P

PERSONAL: Born March 30, 1977, in San Jose, Calif. ... 6-1/200. ... Throws left, bats left. ... Full name: Jeriome Paul Robertson. ... Name pronounced: JER-oh-mee. ... High school: Exeter (Calif.) Union. ... College: Washington.

TRANSACTIONS/CAREER NOTES: Selected by Houston Astros organization in 24th round of 1995 free-agent draft. ... Traded by Astros to Cleveland Indians for OFs Luke Scott and Willy Tavares (March 31, 2004). ... Traded by Indians to Montreal Expos for P Pierre-Luc Marceau (August 3, 2004).

HONORS: Named Pacific Coast League Pitcher of the Year (2002).

CAREER HITTING: 8-for-52 (.154), 4 R, 0 2B, 1 3B, 0 HR, 3 RBI.

Year	Team (League)	W	L	Pct.	ERA	WHIP	G	GS	CG	ShO	Hld.	Sv.-Opp.	IP	H	R	ER	HR	BB-IBB	SO	Avg.
1996—	GC Astros (GCL)	5	3	.625	1.72	0.84	13	13	1	1	...	0-...	78.1	51	20	15	2	15-0	98	.181
	—Kissimmee (Fla. St.)	0	0	...	2.57	0.71	1	1	0	0	...	0-...	7.0	4	4	2	0	1-0	2	.154
1997—	Quad City (Midw.)	11	8	.579	4.07	1.42	26	25	2	1	...	1-...	146.0	151	86	66	12	56-1	135	.261
1998—	Kissimmee (Fla. St.)	10	10	.500	3.70	1.36	28	28	2	0	...	0-...	175.0	185	83	72	13	53-3	131	.276
1999—	Jackson (Texas)	15	7	.682	3.06	1.20	28	28	1	0	...	0-...	191.0	184	81	65	22	45-2	133	.253
2000—	Kissimmee (Fla. St.)	2	1	.667	4.66	1.14	5	5	1	1	...	0-...	29.0	28	19	15	1	5-0	13	.248
	—Round Rock (Texas)	2	2	.500	4.13	1.31	11	10	0	0	...	0-...	61.0	62	36	28	8	18-1	30	.257
	—New Orleans (PCL)	1	7	.125	7.07	1.75	9	9	0	0	...	0-...	49.2	64	42	39	10	23-1	27	.323
2001—	Round Rock (Texas)	5	1	.833	3.91	1.49	57	0	0	0	...	3-...	73.2	89	33	32	10	21-0	72	.296
2002—	New Orleans (PCL)	12	8	.600	2.55	1.14	27	27	2	1	...	0-...	180.0	160	59	51	13	45-0	114	.238
	—Houston (N.L.)	0	2	.000	6.52	1.86	11	1	0	0	0	0-0	9.2	13	8	7	4	5-3	6	.394
2003—	New Orleans (PCL)	1	0	1.000	6.75	1.30	1	1	0	0	...	0-...	6.2	7	5	5	2	2-0	6	.269
	—Houston (N.L.)	15	9	.625	5.10	1.52	32	31	0	0	0	0-0	160.2	180	98	91	23	64-8	99	.287
2004—	Buffalo (Int'l)	4	5	.444	7.28	1.76	14	12	0	0	...	0-...	64.1	91	58	52	10	22-1	28	.331
	—Cleveland (A.L.)	1	1	.500	12.21	2.21	8	0	0	0	2	0-0	14.0	22	22	19	5	9-2	6	.349
	—Edmonton (PCL)	1	3	.250	5.73	1.64	7	7	0	0	...	0-...	33.0	44	21	21	6	10-0	22	.331
American League totals (1 year)		1	1	.500	12.21	2.21	8	0	0	0	2	0-0	14.0	22	22	19	5	9-2	6	.349
National League totals (2 years)		15	11	.577	5.18	1.54	43	32	0	0	0	0-0	170.1	193	106	98	27	69-11	105	.292
Major League totals (3 years)		16	12	.571	5.71	1.59	51	32	0	0	2	0-1	184.1	215	128	117	32	78-13	111	.297

R

ROBERTSON, NATE   P

PERSONAL: Born September 3, 1977, in Wichita, Kan. ... 6-2/215. ... Throws left, bats right. ... Full name: Nathan D. Robertson. ... High school: Maize (Kan.). ... College: Wichita State.

TRANSACTIONS/CAREER NOTES: Selected by Chicago White Sox organization in 35th round of 1995 free-agent draft; did not sign. ... Selected by White Sox organization in 15th round of 1998 free-agent draft; did not sign. ... Selected by Florida Marlins organization in fifth round of 1999 free-agent draft. ... Traded by Marlins with Ps Gary Knotts and Rob Henkel to Detroit Tigers for Ps Mark Redman and Jerrod Fuell (January 11, 2003).

CAREER HITTING: 0-for-5 (.000), 0 R, 0 2B, 0 3B, 0 HR, 0 RBI.

Year Team (League)	W	L	Pct.	ERA	WHIP	G	GS	CG	ShO	Hld.	Sv.-Opp.	IP	H	R	ER	HR	BB-IBB	SO	Avg.
1999— Kane County (Midwest)	6	1	.857	2.29	1.06	8	8	1	1	...	0-...	51.0	42	14	13	1	12-0	33	.230
— Utica (N.Y.-Penn)	2	0	1.000	2.77	1.15	5	5	0	0	...	0-...	26.0	22	9	8	0	8-0	26	.244
2000— Kane County (Midwest)	0	2	.000	5.09	1.70	6	6	0	0	...	0-...	17.2	24	13	10	0	6-0	15	.324
2001— Brevard County (FSL)	11	4	.733	2.88	1.30	19	19	2	0	...	0-...	106.1	95	44	34	3	43-1	67	.244
2002— Portland (East.)	10	9	.526	3.42	1.26	27	27	3	0	...	0-...	163.0	156	77	62	12	50-2	109	.260
— Florida (N.L.)	0	1	.000	11.88	2.28	6	1	0	0	0	0-0	8.1	15	11	11	3	4-1	3	.375
2003— Toledo (International)	9	7	.563	3.14	1.20	24	23	3	1	...	0-...	155.0	145	62	54	14	47-2	102	.250
— Detroit (A.L.)	1	2	.333	5.44	1.75	8	8	0	0	0	0-0	44.2	55	27	27	6	23-2	33	.306
2004— Detroit (A.L.)	12	10	.545	4.90	1.40	34	32	1	0	0	1-1	196.2	210	116	107	30	66-1	155	.274
American League totals (2 years)	13	12	.520	5.00	1.47	42	40	1	0	0	1-1	241.1	265	143	134	36	89-3	188	.280
National League totals (1 year)	0	1	.000	11.88	2.28	6	1	0	0	0	0-0	8.1	15	11	11	3	4-1	3	.375
Major League totals (3 years)	13	13	.500	5.23	1.49	48	41	1	0	0	1-1	249.2	280	154	145	39	93-4	191	.284

ROBINSON, KERRY   OF

PERSONAL: Born October 3, 1973, in St. Louis, Mo. ... 6-0/175. ... Bats left, throws left. ... Full name: Kerry Keith Robinson. ... High school: Hazelwood East (St. Louis). ... College: Southeast Missouri State.

TRANSACTIONS/CAREER NOTES: Selected by St. Louis Cardinals organization in 34th round of 1995 free-agent draft. ... Selected by Tampa Bay Devil Rays in second round (44th pick overall) of expansion draft (November 18, 1997). ... Claimed on waivers by Seattle Mariners (November 19, 1998). ... Traded by Mariners to Cincinnati Reds for P Todd Williams (July 22, 1999). ... Released by Reds (March 30, 2000). ... Signed by New York Yankees organization (April 9, 2000). ... Signed as a free agent by Cardinals organization (December 7, 2000). ... Traded by Cardinals to San Diego Padres for OF Brian L. Hunter (March 29, 2004). ... Refused minor league assignment and became a free agent (October 9, 2004).

2004 GAMES PLAYED BY POSITION (MLB): OF—49, DH—2.

Year Team (League)	Pos.	G	AB	R	H	2B	3B	HR	RBI	BB	SO	HBP	GDP	SB-CS	Avg.	OBP	SLG	OPS	E	Avg.
1995— Johnson City (App.)	OF	60	250	44	74	12	8	1	26	16	30	0	3	14-10	.296	.336	.420	.756	6	.938
1996— Peoria (Midw.)	OF	123	440	98	158	17	4	2	47	51	51	3	2	50-26	.359	.422	.430	.852	7	.962
1997— Arkansas (Texas)	OF	135	523	80	168	16	3	2	62	54	64	2	7	40-23	.321	.386	.375	.760	7	.966
— Louisville (A.A.)	OF	2	9	0	1	0	0	0	0	0	1	0	0	0-0	.111	.111	.111	.222	0	1.000
1998— Orlando (South.)	OF	72	309	45	83	7	5	2	26	27	28	0	6	28-9	.269	.325	.343	.668	0	1.000
— Durham (Int'l)	OF	58	242	28	73	7	4	1	28	23	30	0	1	18-11	.302	.361	.376	.737	2	.987
— Tampa Bay (A.L.)	OF	2	3	0	0	0	0	0	0	0	1	0	0	0-0	.000	.000	.000	.000	0	1.000
1999— Tacoma (PCL)	OF-DH	79	335	53	108	16	9	0	34	14	44	0	4	30-7	.322	.348	.424	.771	4	.974
— Indianapolis (Int'l)	OF	34	129	24	34	3	2	1	14	4	12	1	2	14-4	.264	.285	.341	.626	2	.977
— Cincinnati (N.L.)	OF	9	1	4	0	0	0	0	0	0	1	0	0	0-1	.000	.000	.000	.000	0	...
2000— Columbus (Int'l)	OF	119	437	71	139	17	9	0	32	41	40	2	5	37-18	.318	.378	.398	.777	3	.988
2001— Memphis (PCL)	OF	10	40	4	13	1	0	0	3	4	10	0	1	4-2	.325	.386	.350	.736	0	1.000
— St. Louis (N.L.)	OF	114	186	34	53	6	1	1	15	12	20	2	1	11-2	.285	.330	.344	.674	2	.981
2002— St. Louis (N.L.)	OF-DH	124	181	27	47	7	4	1	15	11	29	0	1	7-4	.260	.301	.359	.660	2	.977
2003— Memphis (PCL)	OF	16	61	14	21	2	1	0	3	1	7	0	0	5-0	.344	.355	.410	.765	1	.979
— St. Louis (N.L.)	OF	116	208	19	52	6	3	1	16	8	27	1	3	6-1	.250	.281	.322	.603	0	1.000
2004— Portland (PCL)	OF-DH	42	170	31	52	6	3	2	20	19	15	3	4	25-1	.306	.383	.412	.795	1	.986
— San Diego (N.L.)	OF-DH	80	92	20	27	4	0	0	5	5	8	1	0	11-4	.293	.330	.337	.667	0	1.000
American League totals (1 year)		2	3	0	0	0	0	0	0	0	1	0	0	0-0	.000	.000	.000	.000	0	1.000
National League totals (5 years)		443	668	104	179	23	8	3	51	36	85	4	5	35-12	.268	.307	.340	.647	4	.988
Major League totals (6 years)		445	671	104	179	23	8	3	51	36	86	4	5	35-12	.267	.305	.338	.644	4	.988

DIVISION SERIES RECORD

Year Team (League)	Pos.	G	AB	R	H	2B	3B	HR	RBI	BB	SO	HBP	GDP	SB-CS	Avg.	OBP	SLG	OPS	E	Avg.
2001— St. Louis (N.L.)	OF	4	2	0	1	0	0	0	1	0	0	0	0	0-0	.500	.500	.500	1.000	0	...
2002— St. Louis (N.L.)		2	2	0	1	0	0	0	1	0	0	0	0	0-0	.500	.500	.500	1.000	0	...
Division series totals (2 years)		6	4	0	2	0	0	0	2	0	0	0	0	0-0	.500	.500	.500	1.000	0	...

CHAMPIONSHIP SERIES RECORD

Year Team (League)	Pos.	G	AB	R	H	2B	3B	HR	RBI	BB	SO	HBP	GDP	SB-CS	Avg.	OBP	SLG	OPS	E	Avg.
2002— St. Louis (N.L.)	OF	3	2	1	0	0	0	0	0	1	1	0	0	0-1	.000	.333	.000	.333	0	...

RODRIGUEZ, ALEX   3B

PERSONAL: Born July 27, 1975, in New York, N.Y. ... 6-3/210. ... Bats right, throws right. ... Full name: Alexander Emmanuel Rodriguez. ... Name pronounced: rod-RI-guez. ... High school: Westminster Christian (Miami).

TRANSACTIONS/CAREER NOTES: Selected by Seattle Mariners organization in first round (first pick overall) of 1993 free-agent draft. ... On disabled list (April 22-May 7, 1996); included rehabilitation assignment to Tacoma. ... On disabled list (June 12-27, 1997; April 7-May 14, 1999; and July 8-24, 2000). ... Signed as a free agent by Texas Rangers (December 11, 2000). ... Traded by Rangers to New York Yankees for 2B Alfonso Soriano and a player to be named (Feburary 16, 2004). ... On suspended list (August 14-19, 2004).

HONORS: Named Major League Player of the Year by THE SPORTING NEWS (1996 and 2002). ... Named A.L. Most Valuable Player by Baseball Writers' Association of America (2003). ... Won A.L. Gold Glove at shortstop (2002 and 2003).

2004 GAMES PLAYED BY POSITION (MLB): 3B—155, SS—2.

Year Team (League)	Pos.	G	AB	R	H	2B	3B	HR	RBI	BB	SO	HBP	GDP	SB-CS	Avg.	OBP	SLG	OPS	E	Avg.
1994— Appleton (Midwest)	SS-DH	65	248	49	79	17	6	14	55	24	44	2	7	16-5	.319	.379	.605	.984	19	.934
— Jacksonville (Sou.)	SS	17	59	7	17	4	1	1	8	10	13	0	1	2-1	.288	.391	.441	.832	3	.964
— Seattle (A.L.)	SS	17	54	4	11	0	0	0	2	3	20	0	0	3-0	.204	.241	.204	.445	6	.915
— Calgary (PCL)	SS	32	119	22	37	7	4	6	21	8	25	1	1	2-4	.311	.359	.588	.948	3	.980

Year Team (League)	Pos.	G	AB	R	H	2B	3B	HR	RBI	BB	SO	HBP	GDP	SB-CS	Avg.	OBP	SLG	OPS	E	Avg.
1995—Tacoma (PCL)	SS-DH	54	214	37	77	12	3	15	45	18	44	2	2	2-4	.360	.411	.654	1.065	10	.961
—Seattle (A.L.)	SS-DH	48	142	15	33	6	2	5	19	6	42	0	0	4-2	.232	.264	.408	.672	8	.953
1996—Seattle (A.L.)	SS	146	601	*141	215	*54	1	36	123	59	104	4	15	15-4	*.358	.414	.631	1.045	15	.977
—Tacoma (PCL)	SS	2	5	0	1	0	0	0	0	2	1	0	0	0-0	.200	.429	.200	.629	1	.833
1997—Seattle (A.L.)	SS-DH	141	587	100	176	40	3	23	84	41	99	5	14	29-6	.300	.350	.496	.846	*24	.962
1998—Seattle (A.L.)	SS-DH	161	*686	123	*213	35	5	42	124	45	121	10	12	46-13	.311	.360	.560	.920	18	.975
1999—Seattle (A.L.)	SS	129	502	110	143	25	0	42	111	56	109	5	12	21-7	.285	.357	.586	.943	14	.977
2000—Seattle (A.L.)	SS	148	554	134	175	34	2	41	132	100	121	7	10	15-4	.316	.420	.607	1.026	10	.986
2001—Texas (A.L.)	SS-DH	•162	632	*133	201	34	1	*52	135	75	131	16	17	18-3	.318	.399	.622	1.021	18	.985
2002—Texas (A.L.)		•162	624	125	187	27	2	*57	*142	87	122	10	14	9-4	.300	.392	.623	1.015	10	.987
2003—Texas (A.L.)	SS-DH	161	607	*124	181	30	6	*47	118	87	126	15	16	17-3	.298	.396	*.600	.995	8	.989
2004—New York (A.L.)	3B-SS	155	601	112	172	24	2	36	106	80	131	10	18	28-4	.286	.375	.512	.888	13	.966
Major League totals (11 years)		1430	5590	1121	1707	309	24	381	1096	639	1126	82	128	205-50	.305	.381	.574	.955	144	.976

DIVISION SERIES RECORD

Year Team (League)	Pos.	G	AB	R	H	2B	3B	HR	RBI	BB	SO	HBP	GDP	SB-CS	Avg.	OBP	SLG	OPS	E	Avg.
1995—Seattle (A.L.)	SS	1	1	1	0	0	0	0	0	0	0	0	0	0-0	.000	.000	.000	.000	0	...
1997—Seattle (A.L.)	SS	4	16	1	5	1	0	1	1	0	5	0	0	0-0	.313	.313	.563	.875	0	1.000
2000—Seattle (A.L.)	SS	3	13	0	4	0	0	0	2	0	2	0	1	0-1	.308	.308	.308	.615	0	1.000
2004—New York (A.L.)	3B	4	19	3	8	3	0	1	3	2	1	0	0	2-1	.421	.476	.737	1.213	0	1.000
Division series totals (4 years)		12	49	5	17	4	0	2	6	2	8	0	1	2-2	.347	.373	.551	.924	0	1.000

CHAMPIONSHIP SERIES RECORD

Year Team (League)	Pos.	G	AB	R	H	2B	3B	HR	RBI	BB	SO	HBP	GDP	SB-CS	Avg.	OBP	SLG	OPS	E	Avg.
1995—Seattle (A.L.)		1	1	0	0	0	0	0	0	0	1	0	0	0-0	.000	.000	.000	.000	...	...
2000—Seattle (A.L.)	SS	6	22	4	9	2	0	2	5	3	8	0	0	1-0	.409	.480	.773	1.253	0	1.000
2004—New York (A.L.)	3B	7	31	8	8	2	0	2	5	4	6	2	1	0-0	.258	.378	.516	.895	0	1.000
Champ. series totals (3 years)		14	54	12	17	4	0	4	10	7	15	2	1	1-0	.315	.413	.611	1.024	0	1.000

ALL-STAR GAME RECORD

	G	AB	R	H	2B	3B	HR	RBI	BB	SO	HBP	GDP	SB-CS	Avg.	OBP	SLG	OPS	E	Avg.
All-Star Game totals (7 years)	7	17	3	5	0	1	1	2	0	9	0	0	0-0	.294	.294	.588	.882	0	1.000

RODRIGUEZ, EDDY   P

PERSONAL: Born August 8, 1981, in San Pedro de Macoris, Dominican Republic. ... 6-1/194. ... Throws right, bats right.
TRANSACTIONS/CAREER NOTES: Signed as a non-drafted free agent by Baltimore Orioles organization (March 15, 1999).
CAREER HITTING: 0-for-1 (.000), 0 R, 0 2B, 0 3B, 0 HR, 0 RBI.

Year Team (League)	W	L	Pct.	ERA	WHIP	G	GS	CG	ShO	Hld.	Sv.-Opp.	IP	H	R	ER	HR	BB-IBB	SO	Avg.
2000—GC Orioles (GCL)	2	1	.667	2.00	1.33	18	0	0	0	...	6-...	27.0	17	8	6	0	19-1	31	.185
—Delmarva (S.Atl.)	0	0	...	1.80	1.40	4	0	0	0	...	0-...	5.0	5	1	1	1	2-0	3	.263
2001—Delmarva (S.Atl.)	5	3	.625	3.39	1.33	41	0	0	0	...	1-...	61.0	58	27	23	4	23-0	64	.247
—Bowie (East.)	1	1	.500	2.08	1.50	5	0	0	0	...	2-...	8.2	7	2	2	0	6-1	10	.241
2002—Frederick (Caro.)	0	3	.000	2.23	0.99	38	0	0	0	...	11-...	48.1	28	14	12	3	20-3	58	.169
—Bowie (East.)	0	0	...	5.63	1.63	6	0	0	0	...	1-...	8.0	6	6	5	1	7-0	7	.200
2003—Bowie (East.)	3	4	.429	2.34	1.15	56	0	0	0	...	13-...	73.0	49	26	19	3	35-2	66	.188
2004—Ottawa (Int'l)	1	0	1.000	5.12	1.64	28	0	0	0	...	3-...	31.2	34	19	18	4	18-0	31	.266
—Baltimore (A.L.)	1	0	1.000	4.78	1.52	29	0	0	0	...	0-0	43.1	36	23	23	5	30-5	37	.231
Major League totals (1 year)	1	0	1.000	4.78	1.52	29	0	0	0	0	0-0	43.1	36	23	23	5	30-5	37	.231

RODRIGUEZ, FELIX   P

PERSONAL: Born December 5, 1972, in Montecristi, Dominican Republic. ... 6-1/198. ... Throws right, bats right. ... Full name: Felix Antonio Rodriguez. ... High school: Liceo Bijiador (Monte Cristi, Dominican Republic).
TRANSACTIONS/CAREER NOTES: Signed as a non-drafted free agent by Los Angeles Dodgers organization (October 17, 1989). ... Played catcher in Dodgers organization (1990-92). ... Claimed on waivers by Cincinnati Reds (December 18, 1996). ... Traded by Reds to Arizona Diamondbacks for a player to be named (November 11, 1997); Reds acquired P Scott Winchester to complete deal (November 18, 1997). ... On disabled list (June 21-July 30, 1998); included rehabilitation assignments to AZL Diamondbacks and Tucson. ... Traded by Diamondbacks to San Francisco Giants for future considerations (December 8, 1998); Diamondbacks acquired P Troy Brohawn and OF Chris Van Rossum to complete deal (December 21, 1998). ... On disabled list (August 3-18, 2003). ... Traded by Giants to Philadelphia Phillies for OF Ricky Ledee and P Alfredo Simon (July 30, 2004).
CAREER HITTING: 4-for-16 (.250), 4 R, 1 2B, 0 3B, 1 HR, 3 RBI.

Year Team (League)	W	L	Pct.	ERA	WHIP	G	GS	CG	ShO	Hld.	Sv.-Opp.	IP	H	R	ER	HR	BB-IBB	SO	Avg.
1993—Vero Beach (FSL)	8	8	.500	3.75	1.36	32	20	2	1	...	0-...	132.0	109	71	55	15	71-1	80	.225
1994—San Antonio (Texas)	6	8	.429	4.03	1.42	26	26	0	0	...	0-...	136.1	106	70	61	8	88-3	126	.219
1995—Albuquerque (PCL)	3	2	.600	4.24	1.53	14	11	0	0	...	0-...	51.0	52	29	24	5	26-0	46	.269
—Los Angeles (N.L.)	1	1	.500	2.53	1.50	11	0	0	0	0	0-1	10.2	11	3	3	2	5-0	5	.275
1996—Albuquerque (PCL)	3	9	.250	5.53	1.59	27	19	0	0	...	0-...	107.1	111	70	66	17	60-1	65	.280
1997—Indianapolis (A.A.)	3	3	.500	1.01	1.43	23	0	0	0	...	1-...	26.2	22	10	3	0	16-1	26	.212
—Cincinnati (N.L.)	0	0	...	4.30	1.65	26	1	0	0	...	0-0	46.0	48	23	22	2	28-2	34	.271
1998—Arizona (N.L.)	0	2	.000	6.14	1.66	43	0	0	0	...	5-8	44.0	44	31	30	5	29-1	36	.259
—Ariz. D'backs (Ariz.)	0	0	...	4.15	1.15	3	2	0	0	...	0-...	4.1	3	4	2	0	2-0	5	.200
—Tucson (PCL)	0	0	...	9.00	3.00	1	0	0	0	...	0-...	1.0	1	1	1	0	2-0	0	.250
1999—San Francisco (N.L.)	2	3	.400	3.80	1.45	47	0	0	0	3	0-1	66.1	67	32	28	6	29-2	55	.262
2000—San Francisco (N.L.)	4	2	.667	2.64	1.31	76	0	0	0	30	3-8	81.2	65	29	24	5	42-2	95	.220
2001—San Francisco (N.L.)	9	1	.900	1.68	1.00	71	0	0	0	32	0-3	80.1	53	16	15	5	27-2	91	.188
2002—San Francisco (N.L.)	8	6	.571	4.17	1.19	71	0	0	0	24	0-6	69.0	53	33	32	5	29-1	58	.212
2003—San Francisco (N.L.)	8	2	.800	3.10	1.44	68	0	0	0	19	2-3	61.0	59	21	21	5	29-2	46	.259
2004—San Francisco (N.L.)	3	5	.375	3.43	1.39	53	0	0	0	13	0-3	44.2	43	18	17	7	19-2	31	.250
—Philadelphia (N.L.)	2	3	.400	3.00	1.33	23	0	0	0	7	1-1	21.0	18	7	7	1	10-2	28	.231
Major League totals (9 years)	37	25	.597	3.41	1.35	498	1	0	0	128	11-34	524.2	461	213	199	43	247-16	479	.237

DIVISION SERIES RECORD

Year Team (League)	W	L	Pct.	ERA	WHIP	G	GS	CG	ShO	Hld.	Sv.-Opp.	IP	H	R	ER	HR	BB-IBB	SO	Avg.
2000—San Francisco (N.L.)	0	1	.000	6.23	1.62	3	0	0	0	0	0-0	4.1	6	3	3	1	1-0	6	.316
2002—San Francisco (N.L.)	0	0	...	0.00	1.00	3	0	0	0	1	0-0	3.0	1	0	0	0	2-0	2	.111
2003—San Francisco (N.L.)	0	1	.000	2.25	1.25	3	0	0	0	0	0-0	4.0	4	3	1	0	1-1	5	.235
Division series totals (3 years)	0	2	.000	3.18	1.32	9	0	0	0	2	0-0	11.1	11	6	4	1	4-1	13	.244

R

R

CHAMPIONSHIP SERIES RECORD

Year Team (League)	W	L	Pct.	ERA	WHIP	G	GS	CG	ShO	Hld.	Sv.-Opp.	IP	H	R	ER	HR	BB-IBB	SO	Avg.
2002— San Francisco (N.L.)	0	0	...	1.93	1.07	4	0	0	0	...	0-0	4.2	3	1	1	0	2-0	2	.200

WORLD SERIES RECORD

Year Team (League)	W	L	Pct.	ERA	WHIP	G	GS	CG	ShO	Hld.	Sv.-Opp.	IP	H	R	ER	HR	BB-IBB	SO	Avg.
2002— San Francisco (N.L.)	0	1	.000	4.76	0.88	6	0	0	0	...	0-0	5.2	4	3	3	2	1-0	3	.190

RODRIGUEZ, FRANCISCO   P

PERSONAL: Born January 7, 1982, in Caracas, Venezuela. ... 6-0/185. ... Throws right, bats right. ... Full name: Francisco Jose Rodriguez.
TRANSACTIONS/CAREER NOTES: Signed as a non-drafted free agent by Anaheim Angels organization (September 24, 1998).
CAREER HITTING: 0-for-0 (.000), 0 R, 0 2B, 0 3B, 0 HR, 0 RBI.

Year Team (League)	W	L	Pct.	ERA	WHIP	G	GS	CG	ShO	Hld.	Sv.-Opp.	IP	H	R	ER	HR	BB-IBB	SO	Avg.
1999— Butte (Pio.)	1	1	.500	3.31	1.05	12	9	1	0	...	0-...	51.2	33	21	19	1	21-1	69	.179
— Boise (N'west)	1	0	1.000	5.40	0.80	1	1	0	0	...	0-...	5.0	3	4	3	0	1-0	6	.150
2000— Lake Elsinore (Calif.)	4	4	.500	2.81	1.17	13	12	0	0	...	0-...	64.0	43	29	20	2	32-0	79	.189
2001— Rancho Cuca. (Calif.)	5	7	.417	5.38	1.60	20	20	1	1	...	0-...	113.2	127	72	68	13	55-1	147	.277
2002— Arkansas (Texas)	3	3	.500	1.96	1.14	23	0	0	0	...	9-...	41.1	32	13	9	2	15-0	61	.206
— Salt Lake (PCL)	2	3	.400	2.57	1.02	27	0	0	0	...	6-...	42.0	30	13	12	1	13-0	59	.204
— Anaheim (A.L.)	0	0	...	0.00	0.88	5	0	0	0	0	0-0	5.2	3	0	0	0	2-1	13	.167
2003— Anaheim (A.L.)	8	3	.727	3.03	0.99	59	0	0	0	7	2-6	86.0	50	30	29	12	35-5	95	.172
2004— Anaheim (A.L.)	4	1	.800	1.82	1.00	69	0	0	0	27	12-19	84.0	51	21	17	2	33-1	123	.172
Major League totals (3 years)	**12**	**4**	**.750**	**2.36**	**0.99**	**133**	**0**	**0**	**0**	**34**	**14-25**	**175.2**	**104**	**51**	**46**	**14**	**70-7**	**231**	**.172**

DIVISION SERIES RECORD

Year Team (League)	W	L	Pct.	ERA	WHIP	G	GS	CG	ShO	Hld.	Sv.-Opp.	IP	H	R	ER	HR	BB-IBB	SO	Avg.
2002— Anaheim (A.L.)	2	0	1.000	3.18	0.71	3	0	0	0	0	0-1	5.2	2	2	2	1	2-0	8	.105
2004— Anaheim (A.L.)	0	2	.000	3.86	1.50	2	0	0	0	0	0-0	4.2	4	2	2	0	3-1	5	.235
Division series totals (2 years)	**2**	**2**	**.500**	**3.48**	**1.06**	**5**	**0**	**0**	**0**	**0**	**0-1**	**10.1**	**6**	**4**	**4**	**1**	**5-1**	**13**	**.167**

CHAMPIONSHIP SERIES RECORD

Year Team (League)	W	L	Pct.	ERA	WHIP	G	GS	CG	ShO	Hld.	Sv.-Opp.	IP	H	R	ER	HR	BB-IBB	SO	Avg.
2002— Anaheim (A.L.)	2	0	1.000	0.00	0.92	4	0	0	0	2	0-1	4.1	2	0	0	0	2-0	7	.143

WORLD SERIES RECORD

Year Team (League)	W	L	Pct.	ERA	WHIP	G	GS	CG	ShO	Hld.	Sv.-Opp.	IP	H	R	ER	HR	BB-IBB	SO	Avg.
2002— Anaheim (A.L.)	1	1	.500	2.08	0.81	4	0	0	0	1	0-0	8.2	6	3	2	1	1-0	13	.194

ALL-STAR GAME RECORD

	W	L	Pct.	ERA	WHIP	G	GS	CG	ShO	Hld.	Sv.-Opp.	IP	H	R	ER	HR	BB-IBB	SO	Avg.
All-Star Game totals (1 year)	0	0	...	0.00	0.00	1	0	0	0	0	0-0	.2	0	0	0	0	0-0	0	.000

RODRIGUEZ, IVAN   C

PERSONAL: Born November 30, 1971, in Vega Baja, Puerto Rico. ... 5-9/218. ... Bats right, throws right. ... Name pronounced: rod-RI-gez. ... High school: Lina Padron Rivera (Vega Baja, Puerto Rico).
TRANSACTIONS/CAREER NOTES: Signed as a non-drafted free agent by Texas Rangers organization (July 27, 1988). ... On disabled list (June 6-27, 1992; July 25, 2000-remainder of season; May 2-17 and August 31, 2001-remainder of season). ... On disabled list (April 15-June 7, 2002; included rehabilitation assignment to Charlotte. ... On suspended list (September 28-29, 2002). ... Signed as a free agent by Florida Marlins (January 22, 2003). ... Signed as a free agent by Detroit Tigers (February 6, 2004).
HONORS: Named A.L. Most Valuable Player by Baseball Writers' Association of America (1999). ... Won A.L. Gold Glove at catcher (1992-2001 and 2004).
2004 GAMES PLAYED BY POSITION (MLB): C—124, DH—8.

Year Team (League)	Pos.	G	AB	R	H	2B	3B	HR	RBI	BB	SO	HBP	GDP	SB-CS	Avg.	OBP	SLG	OPS	E	Avg.
1989— Gastonia (S. Atl.)	C	112	386	38	92	22	1	7	42	21	58	2	6	2-5	.238	.278	.355	.633	11	.986
1990— Charlotte (Fla. St.)	C	109	408	48	117	17	7	2	55	12	50	7	6	1-0	.287	.316	.377	.693	14	.983
1991— Tulsa (Texas)	C	50	175	16	48	7	2	3	28	6	27	1	5	1-2	.274	.294	.389	.683	3	.988
— Texas (A.L.)	C	88	280	24	74	16	0	3	27	5	42	0	10	0-1	.264	.276	.354	.630	10	.983
1992— Texas (A.L.)	C-DH	123	420	39	109	16	1	8	37	24	73	1	15	0-0	.260	.300	.360	.659	* 15	.983
1993— Texas (A.L.)	C-DH	137	473	56	129	28	4	10	66	29	70	4	16	8-7	.273	.315	.412	.727	8	.991
1994— Texas (A.L.)	C	99	363	56	108	19	1	16	57	31	42	7	10	6-3	.298	.360	.488	.848	5	.992
1995— Texas (A.L.)	C-DH	130	492	56	149	32	2	12	67	16	48	4	11	0-2	.303	.327	.449	.776	8	.990
1996— Texas (A.L.)	C-DH	153	639	116	192	47	3	19	86	38	55	4	15	5-0	.300	.342	.473	.814	• 10	.989
1997— Texas (A.L.)	C-DH	150	597	98	187	34	4	20	77	38	89	8	18	7-3	.313	.360	.484	.844	7	.992
1998— Texas (A.L.)	C-DH	145	579	88	186	40	4	21	91	32	88	3	18	9-0	.321	.358	.513	.871	6	.994
1999— Texas (A.L.)	C-DH	144	600	116	199	29	1	35	113	24	64	1	31	25-12	.332	.356	.558	.914	7	.993
2000— Texas (A.L.)	C-DH	91	363	66	126	27	4	27	83	19	48	1	17	5-5	.347	.375	.667	1.042	2	.996
2001— Texas (A.L.)	C-DH	111	442	70	136	24	2	25	65	23	73	4	13	10-3	.308	.347	.541	.888	7	.990
2002— Texas (A.L.)	C-DH	108	408	67	128	32	2	19	60	25	71	2	13	5-4	.314	.353	.542	.895	7	.990
— Charlotte (Fla. St.)	C	3	9	1	3	0	0	0	0	0	3	0	0	0-0	.333	.333	.333	.667	0	1.000
2003— Florida (N.L.)	C-DH	144	511	90	152	36	3	16	85	55	92	6	18	10-6	.297	.369	.474	.843	8	.992
2004— Detroit (A.L.)	C-DH	135	527	72	176	32	2	19	86	41	91	3	15	7-4	.334	.383	.510	.893	11	.987
American League totals (13 years)		**1614**	**6183**	**924**	**1899**	**376**	**30**	**234**	**915**	**345**	**854**	**42**	**202**	**87-44**	**.307**	**.345**	**.491**	**.836**	**103**	**.990**
National League totals (1 year)		**144**	**511**	**90**	**152**	**36**	**3**	**16**	**85**	**55**	**92**	**6**	**18**	**10-6**	**.297**	**.369**	**.474**	**.843**	**8**	**.992**
Major League totals (14 years)		**1758**	**6694**	**1014**	**2051**	**412**	**33**	**250**	**1000**	**400**	**946**	**48**	**220**	**97-50**	**.306**	**.347**	**.490**	**.837**	**111**	**.990**

DIVISION SERIES RECORD

Year Team (League)	Pos.	G	AB	R	H	2B	3B	HR	RBI	BB	SO	HBP	GDP	SB-CS	Avg.	OBP	SLG	OPS	E	Avg.
1996— Texas (A.L.)	C	4	16	1	6	1	0	0	2	2	3	0	0	0-0	.375	.444	.438	.882	0	1.000
1998— Texas (A.L.)	C	3	10	0	1	0	0	0	1	0	5	0	0	0-0	.100	.100	.100	.200	0	1.000
1999— Texas (A.L.)	C	3	12	0	3	1	0	0	0	0	2	0	1	1-0	.250	.250	.333	.583	0	1.000
2003— Florida (N.L.)	C	4	17	3	6	1	0	1	6	3	1	0	0	0-0	.353	.450	.588	1.038	0	1.000
Division series totals (4 years)		**14**	**55**	**4**	**16**	**3**	**0**	**1**	**9**	**5**	**11**	**0**	**1**	**1-0**	**.291**	**.350**	**.400**	**.750**	**0**	**1.000**

CHAMPIONSHIP SERIES RECORD

Year Team (League)	Pos.	G	AB	R	H	2B	3B	HR	RBI	BB	SO	HBP	GDP	SB-CS	Avg.	OBP	SLG	OPS	E	Avg.
2003— Florida (N.L.)	C	7	28	5	9	2	0	2	10	5	7	0	0	0-0	.321	.424	.607	1.031	1	.983

WORLD SERIES RECORD

Year Team (League)	Pos.	G	AB	R	H	2B	3B	HR	RBI	BB	SO	HBP	GDP	SB-CS	Avg.	OBP	SLG	OPS	E	Avg.
2003— Florida (N.L.)	C	6	22	2	6	2	0	0	1	1	4	0	1	0-0	.273	.292	.364	.655	0	1.000

ALL-STAR GAME RECORD

	G	AB	R	H	2B	3B	HR	RBI	BB	SO	HBP	GDP	SB-CS	Avg.	OBP	SLG	OPS	E	Avg.
All-Star Game totals (11 years)	11	31	4	10	1	1	0	3	0	5	0	0	1-0	.323	.323	.419	.742	0	1.000

RODRIGUEZ, RICARDO   P

PERSONAL: Born May 21, 1978, in Manga, Dominican Republic. ... 6-3/190. ... Throws right, bats right. ... Full name: Ricardo Antonio Rodriguez.

TRANSACTIONS/CAREER NOTES: Signed as a non-drafted free agent by Los Angeles Dodgers organization (September 2, 1996). ... Traded by Dodgers with Ps Terry Mulholland and Francisco Cruceta to Cleveland Indians for P Paul Shuey (July 28, 2002). ... On disabled list (June 9-26 and July 2, 2003-remainder of season); included rehabilitation assignment to Buffalo. ... Traded by Indians with OF Shane Spencer to Texas Rangers for OF Ryan Ludwick (July 18, 2003). ... On disabled list (July 23, 2004-remainder of season).

CAREER HITTING: 0-for-5 (.000), 0 R, 0 2B, 0 3B, 0 HR, 0 RBI.

Year Team (League)	W	L	Pct.	ERA	WHIP	G	GS	CG	ShO	Hld.	Sv.-Opp.	IP	H	R	ER	HR	BB-IBB	SO	Avg.
1997— San. Dom. (In.-Am.)	1	2	.333	6.40	2.10	12	10	0	0	...	0-...	32.1	42	39	23	6	26-...	20	...
1998— Dom. Dodgers (DSL)	1	1	.500	3.55	1.88	13	9	1	1	...	0-...	33.0	28	19	13	1	34-...	36	...
1999— San. Dom. (In.-Am.)	3	2	.600	3.43	1.24	9	9	0	0	...	0-...	42.0	34	22	16	2	18-...	51	...
2000— Great Falls (Pio.)	10	3	.769	1.88	0.93	15	15	2	0	...	0-...	95.2	66	32	20	2	23-0	129	.192
2001— Vero Beach (FSL)	14	6	.700	3.21	1.25	26	26	2	0	...	0-...	154.1	133	67	55	13	60-0	154	.232
2002— Jacksonville (Southern)	5	4	.556	1.99	1.01	11	11	2	0	...	0-...	68.0	56	21	15	4	13-0	44	.224
— Las Vegas (PCL)	1	0	1.000	3.86	1.54	2	2	0	0	...	0-...	11.2	13	5	5	1	5-0	7	.295
— Buffalo (Int'l)	3	1	.750	3.60	1.32	4	4	0	0	...	0-...	25.0	26	10	10	1	7-0	14	.271
— Cleveland (A.L.)	2	2	.500	5.66	1.40	7	7	0	0	0	0-0	41.1	40	27	26	5	18-3	24	.255
2003— Cleveland (A.L.)	3	9	.250	5.73	1.43	15	15	0	0	0	0-0	81.2	89	57	52	16	28-1	41	.275
— Buffalo (Int'l)	0	1	.000	4.32	1.10	2	2	0	0	...	0-...	8.1	6	4	4	2	3-0	7	.200
2004— Oklahoma (PCL)	2	2	.500	5.11	1.46	6	6	1	0	...	0-...	37.0	42	23	21	5	12-0	18	.296
— Texas (A.L.)	3	1	.750	2.03	1.50	5	4	1	1	0	0-0	26.2	28	10	6	1	12-0	15	.262
Major League totals (3 years)	8	12	.400	5.05	1.44	27	26	1	1	0	0-0	149.2	157	94	84	22	58-4	80	.267

ROGERS, KENNY   P

PERSONAL: Born November 10, 1964, in Savannah, Ga. ... 6-1/211. ... Throws left, bats left. ... Full name: Kenneth Scott Rogers. ... High school: Plant City (Fla.).

TRANSACTIONS/CAREER NOTES: Selected by Texas Rangers organization in 39th round of June 1982 free-agent draft. ... Signed as a free agent by New York Yankees (December 30, 1995). ... Traded by Yankees with IF Mariano Duncan and P Kevin Henthorne to San Diego Padres for OF Greg Vaughn and Ps Kerry Taylor and Chris Clark (July 4, 1997); trade later voided because Vaughn failed physical (July 6). ... Traded by Yankees with cash to Oakland Athletics for a player to be named (November 7, 1997); Yankees acquired 3B Scott Brosius to complete deal (November 18, 1997). ... Traded by A's to New York Mets for OF Terrence Long and P Leo Vasquez (July 23, 1999). ... Signed as a free agent by Rangers (December 29, 1999). ... On disabled list (July 24, 2001-remainder of season). ... Signed as a free agent by Minnesota Twins (March 17, 2003). ... On suspended list (July 11-19, 2003). ... Signed as a free agent by Rangers (January 14, 2004).

HONORS: Won A.L. Gold Glove as pitcher (2000, 2002 and 2004).

CAREER HITTING: 7-for-53 (.132), 5 R, 0 2B, 0 3B, 0 HR, 3 RBI.

Year Team (League)	W	L	Pct.	ERA	WHIP	G	GS	CG	ShO	Hld.	Sv.-Opp.	IP	H	R	ER	HR	BB-IBB	SO	Avg.
1982— GC Rangers (GCL)	0	0	...	0.00	0.00	2	0	0	0	...	0-...	3.0	0	0	0	0	0-0	4	...
1983— GC Rangers (GCL)	4	1	.800	2.36	1.13	15	6	0	0	...	1-...	53.1	40	21	14	0	20-0	36	.246
1984— Burlington (Midw.)	4	7	.364	3.98	1.29	39	4	1	0	...	3-...	92.2	87	52	41	9	33-3	93	.246
1985— Daytona Beach (FSL)	0	1	.000	7.20	2.30	6	0	0	0	...	0-...	10.0	12	9	8	0	11-1	9	.300
— Burlington (Midw.)	2	5	.286	2.84	1.36	33	4	2	1	...	4-...	95.0	67	34	30	3	62-9	96	.202
1986— Tulsa (Texas)	0	3	.000	9.91	2.16	10	4	0	0	...	0-...	26.1	39	30	29	4	18-1	23	.333
— Salem (Caro.)	2	7	.222	6.27	1.53	12	12	0	0	...	0-...	66.0	75	54	46	9	26-0	46	.282
1987— Charlotte (Fla. St.)	0	3	.000	4.76	1.47	5	3	0	0	...	0-...	17.0	17	13	9	1	8-0	14	.258
— Tulsa (Texas)	1	5	.167	5.35	1.67	28	6	0	0	...	2-...	69.0	80	51	41	5	35-3	59	.291
1988— Charlotte (Fla. St.)	2	0	1.000	1.27	0.93	8	6	0	0	...	1-...	35.1	22	8	5	1	11-0	26	.179
— Tulsa (Texas)	4	6	.400	4.00	1.28	13	13	2	0	...	0-...	83.1	73	43	37	6	34-0	76	.233
1989— Texas (A.L.)	3	4	.429	2.93	1.38	73	0	0	0	15	2-5	73.2	60	28	24	2	42-9	63	.232
1990— Texas (A.L.)	10	6	.625	3.13	1.38	69	3	0	0	6	15-23	97.2	93	40	34	6	42-5	74	.249
1991— Texas (A.L.)	10	10	.500	5.42	1.66	63	9	0	0	11	5-6	109.2	121	80	66	14	61-7	73	.281
1992— Texas (A.L.)	3	6	.333	3.09	1.35	81	0	0	0	16	6-10	78.2	80	32	27	7	26-8	70	.261
1993— Texas (A.L.)	16	10	.615	4.10	1.35	35	33	5	0	1	0-0	208.1	210	108	95	18	71-2	140	.263
1994— Texas (A.L.)	11	8	.579	4.46	1.32	24	24	6	2	0	0-0	167.1	169	93	83	24	52-1	120	.260
1995— Texas (A.L.)	17	7	.708	3.38	1.29	31	31	3	1	0	0-0	208.0	192	87	78	26	76-1	140	.243
1996— New York (A.L.)	12	8	.600	4.68	1.46	30	30	2	1	0	0-0	179.0	179	97	93	16	83-2	92	.261
1997— New York (A.L.)	6	7	.462	5.65	1.54	31	22	1	0	1	0-0	145.0	161	100	91	18	62-1	78	.280
1998— Oakland (A.L.)	16	8	.667	3.17	1.18	34	34	7	1	0	0-0	238.2	215	96	84	19	67-0	138	.242
1999— Oakland (A.L.)	5	3	.625	4.30	1.47	19	19	3	0	0	0-0	119.1	135	66	57	8	41-0	68	.288
— New York (N.L.)	5	1	.833	4.03	1.30	12	12	2	1	0	0-0	76.0	71	35	34	8	28-1	58	.253
2000— Texas (A.L.)	13	13	.500	4.55	1.47	34	34	2	0	0	0-0	227.1	257	126	115	20	78-2	127	.285
2001— Texas (A.L.)	5	7	.417	6.19	1.65	20	20	0	0	0	0-0	120.2	150	88	83	18	49-2	74	.307
2002— Texas (A.L.)	13	8	.619	3.84	1.34	33	33	2	1	0	0-0	210.2	212	101	90	21	70-1	107	.261
2003— Minnesota (A.L.)	13	8	.619	4.57	1.42	33	31	0	0	0	0-0	195.0	227	108	99	22	50-5	116	.292
2004— Texas (A.L.)	18	9	.667	4.76	1.48	35	•35	2	1	0	0-0	211.2	248	117	112	24	66-0	126	.292
American League totals (16 years)	171	122	.584	4.28	1.41	645	358	33	7	50	28-44	2590.2	2709	1367	1231	263	936-46	1606	.269
National League totals (1 year)	5	1	.833	4.03	1.30	12	12	2	1	0	0-0	76.0	71	35	34	8	28-1	58	.253
Major League totals (16 years)	176	123	.589	4.27	1.40	657	370	35	8	50	28-44	2666.2	2780	1402	1265	271	964-47	1664	.269

DIVISION SERIES RECORD

Year Team (League)	W	L	Pct.	ERA	WHIP	G	GS	CG	ShO	Hld.	Sv.-Opp.	IP	H	R	ER	HR	BB-IBB	SO	Avg.
1996— New York (A.L.)	0	0	...	9.00	3.50	2	1	0	0	0	0-0	2.0	5	2	2	0	2-0	1	.455
1999— New York (N.L.)	0	1	.000	8.31	1.62	1	1	0	0	0	0-0	4.1	5	4	4	0	2-0	6	.278
2003— Minnesota (A.L.)	0	0	...	0.00	1.50	1	0	0	0	0	0-0	1.1	1	0	0	0	1-1	3	.200
Division series totals (3 years)	0	1	.000	7.04	2.09	4	2	0	0	0	0-0	7.2	11	6	6	0	5-1	10	.324

CHAMPIONSHIP SERIES RECORD

Year Team (League)	W	L	Pct.	ERA	WHIP	G	GS	CG	ShO	Hld.	Sv.-Opp.	IP	H	R	ER	HR	BB-IBB	SO	Avg.
1996— New York (A.L.)	0	0	...	12.00	2.33	1	1	0	0	0	0-0	3.0	5	4	4	1	2-0	3	.385
1999— New York (N.L.)	0	2	.000	5.87	2.35	3	1	0	0	0	0-0	7.2	11	5	5	2	7-2	2	.393
Champ. series totals (2 years)	0	2	.000	7.59	2.34	4	2	0	0	0	0-0	10.2	16	9	9	3	9-2	5	.390

WORLD SERIES RECORD

Year Team (League)	W	L	Pct.	ERA	WHIP	G	GS	CG	ShO	Hld.	Sv.-Opp.	IP	H	R	ER	HR	BB-IBB	SO	Avg.
1996— New York (A.L.)	0	0	...	22.50	3.50	1	1	0	0	0	0-0	2.0	5	5	5	1	2-0	0	.500

ALL-STAR GAME RECORD

	W	L	Pct.	ERA	WHIP	G	GS	CG	ShO	Hld.	Sv.-Opp.	IP	H	R	ER	HR	BB-IBB	SO	Avg.
All-Star Game totals (1 year)	0	0	...	9.00	1.00	1	0	0	0	0	0-1	1.0	1	1	1	1	0-0	2	.250

R ROLEN, SCOTT   3B

PERSONAL: Born April 4, 1975, in Jasper, Ind. ... 6-4/240. ... Bats right, throws right. ... Full name: Scott Bruce Rolen. ... Name pronounced: ROH-len. ... High school: Jasper (Ind.).

TRANSACTIONS/CAREER NOTES: Selected by Philadelphia Phillies organization in second round of 1993 free-agent draft. ... On disabled list (May 24-June 8, 2000). ... Traded by Phillies with P Doug Nickle to St. Louis Cardinals for IF/OF Placido Polanco and Ps Bud Smith and Mike Timlin (July 29, 2002).

RECORDS: Shares major league record for most strikeouts, nine-inning game—5 (August 23, 1999).

HONORS: Named N.L. Rookie Player of the Year by THE SPORTING NEWS (1997). ... Named N.L. Rookie of the Year by Baseball Writers' Association of America (1997). ... Won N.L. Gold Glove at third base (1998 and 2000-04).

2004 GAMES PLAYED BY POSITION (MLB): 3B—141.

Year Team (League)	Pos.	G	AB	R	H	2B	3B	HR	RBI	BB	SO	HBP	GDP	SB-CS	Avg.	OBP	SLG	OPS	E	Avg.
1993— Martinsville (App.)	3B	25	80	8	25	5	0	0	12	10	15	7	3	3-4	.313	.429	.375	.804	10	.889
1994— Spartanburg (SAL)	3B	138	513	83	151	34	5	14	72	55	90	4	8	6-8	.294	.363	.462	.825	38	.917
1995— Clearwater (FSL)	3B	66	238	45	69	13	2	10	39	37	46	5	4	4-0	.290	.392	.487	.880	20	.899
— Reading (East.)	3B	20	76	16	22	3	0	3	15	7	14	1	2	1-0	.289	.353	.447	.800	4	.934
1996— Reading (East.)	3B	61	230	44	83	22	2	9	42	34	32	5	5	8-3	.361	.445	.591	1.037	9	.949
— Scran./W.B. (I.L.)	3B	45	168	23	46	17	0	2	19	28	28	0	9	4-5	.274	.376	.411	.786	6	.952
— Philadelphia (N.L.)	3B	37	130	10	33	7	0	4	18	13	27	1	4	0-2	.254	.322	.400	.722	4	.954
1997— Philadelphia (N.L.)	3B	156	561	93	159	35	3	21	92	76	138	13	6	16-6	.283	.377	.469	.846	24	.948
1998— Philadelphia (N.L.)	3B	160	601	120	174	45	4	31	110	93	141	11	10	14-7	.290	.391	.532	.923	14	.970
1999— Philadelphia (N.L.)	3B	112	421	74	113	28	1	26	77	67	114	3	8	12-2	.268	.368	.525	.893	14	.960
2000— Philadelphia (N.L.)	3B	128	483	88	144	32	6	26	89	51	99	5	4	8-1	.298	.370	.551	.920	10	.971
2001— Philadelphia (N.L.)	3B	151	554	96	160	39	1	25	107	74	127	13	6	16-5	.289	.378	.498	.876	12	.973
2002— Philadelphia (N.L.)	3B	100	375	52	97	21	4	17	66	52	68	8	12	5-2	.259	.358	.472	.830	8	.973
— St. Louis (N.L.)	3B	55	205	37	57	8	4	14	44	20	34	4	9	3-2	.278	.354	.561	.915	8	.958
2003— St. Louis (N.L.)	3B	154	559	98	160	44	1	28	104	82	104	9	19	13-3	.286	.382	.528	.910	13	.969
2004— St. Louis (N.L.)	3B	142	500	109	157	32	4	34	124	72	92	13	8	4-3	.314	.409	.598	1.007	10	.977
Major League totals (9 years)		1195	4389	777	1254	296	28	226	831	600	944	80	87	91-33	.286	.378	.520	.898	117	.966

DIVISION SERIES RECORD

Year Team (League)	Pos.	G	AB	R	H	2B	3B	HR	RBI	BB	SO	HBP	GDP	SB-CS	Avg.	OBP	SLG	OPS	E	Avg.
2002— St. Louis (N.L.)	3B	2	7	1	3	0	0	1	2	0	2	1	0	0-0	.429	.500	.857	1.357	0	1.000
2004— St. Louis (N.L.)	3B	4	12	1	0	0	0	0	0	6	3	0	0	0-0	.000	.333	.000	.333	0	1.000
Division series totals (2 years)		6	19	2	3	0	0	1	2	6	5	1	0	0-0	.158	.385	.316	.700	0	1.000

CHAMPIONSHIP SERIES RECORD

Year Team (League)	Pos.	G	AB	R	H	2B	3B	HR	RBI	BB	SO	HBP	GDP	SB-CS	Avg.	OBP	SLG	OPS	E	Avg.
2004— St. Louis (N.L.)	3B	7	29	6	9	2	0	3	6	2	9	0	1	0-0	.310	.355	.690	1.044	0	1.000

WORLD SERIES RECORD

Year Team (League)	Pos.	G	AB	R	H	2B	3B	HR	RBI	BB	SO	HBP	GDP	SB-CS	Avg.	OBP	SLG	OPS	E	Avg.
2004— St. Louis (N.L.)	3B	4	15	0	0	0	0	0	1	1	1	0	1	0-0	.000	.059	.000	.059	0	1.000

ALL-STAR GAME RECORD

	G	AB	R	H	2B	3B	HR	RBI	BB	SO	HBP	GDP	SB-CS	Avg.	OBP	SLG	OPS	E	Avg.
All-Star Game totals (3 years)	3	6	1	2	0	0	0	0	0	1	1	0	0-0	.333	.429	.333	.762	0	1.000

ROLLINS, JIMMY   SS

PERSONAL: Born November 27, 1978, in Oakland, Calif. ... 5-8/167. ... Bats both, throws right. ... Full name: James Calvin Rollins. ... High school: Encinal (Alameda, Calif.). ... Cousin of Tony Tarasco, outfielder with six major league teams (1988-99).

TRANSACTIONS/CAREER NOTES: Selected by Philadelphia Phillies organization in second round of 1996 free-agent draft.

2004 GAMES PLAYED BY POSITION (MLB): SS—154.

Year Team (League)	Pos.	G	AB	R	H	2B	3B	HR	RBI	BB	SO	HBP	GDP	SB-CS	Avg.	OBP	SLG	OPS	E	Avg.
1996— Martinsville (App.)	SS	49	172	22	41	3	1	1	16	28	20	2	2	11-5	.238	.351	.285	.636	20	.906
1997— Piedmont (S. Atl.)	SS	139	560	94	151	22	8	6	59	52	80	0	4	46-6	.270	.330	.370	.700	26	.960
1998— Clearwater (FSL)	SS	119	495	72	121	18	9	6	35	41	62	4	9	23-9	.244	.306	.354	.659	29	.952
1999— Reading (East.)	SS	133	532	81	145	21	8	11	56	51	47	1	8	24-12	.273	.336	.404	.740	22	.965
— Scran./W.B. (I.L.)	SS	4	13	0	1	1	0	0	0	1	1	0	0	1-0	.077	.143	.154	.297	1	.960
2000— Scran./W.B. (I.L.)	SS	133	470	67	129	28	11	12	69	49	55	2	4	24-7	.274	.341	.457	.798	26	.958
— Philadelphia (N.L.)	SS	14	53	5	17	1	1	0	5	2	7	0	0	3-0	.321	.345	.377	.723	1	.978
2001— Philadelphia (N.L.)	SS	158	656	97	180	29	*12	14	54	48	108	2	5	•46-8	.274	.323	.419	.743	14	.979
2002— Philadelphia (N.L.)	SS-2B	154	*637	82	156	33	*10	11	60	54	103	4	14	31-13	.245	.306	.380	.686	14	.980
2003— Philadelphia (N.L.)	SS	156	628	85	165	42	6	8	62	54	113	0	9	20-12	.263	.320	.380	.707	14	.979
2004— Philadelphia (N.L.)	SS	154	657	119	190	43	•12	14	73	57	73	3	4	30-12	.289	.348	.455	.803	9	.986
Major League totals (5 years)		636	2631	388	708	148	41	47	254	215	404	9	32	130-42	.269	.325	.410	.735	52	.981

ALL-STAR GAME RECORD

	G	AB	R	H	2B	3B	HR	RBI	BB	SO	HBP	GDP	SB-CS	Avg.	OBP	SLG	OPS	E	Avg.
All-Star Game totals (2 years)	2	2	2	2	0	0	0	0	1	0	0	0	1-0	1.000	1.000	1.000	2.000	0	1.000

ROLLS, DAMIAN — 3B

PERSONAL: Born September 15, 1977, in Manhattan, Kan. ... 6-2/215. ... Bats right, throws right. ... Full name: Damian Michael Rolls. ... High school: F.L. Schlagle (Kansas City, Kan.).

TRANSACTIONS/CAREER NOTES: Selected by Los Angeles Dodgers organization in first round (23rd pick overall) of 1996 free-agent draft. ... Selected by Kansas City Royals from Dodgers organization in Rule 5 major league draft (December 13, 1999). ... Traded by Royals to Tampa Bay Devil Rays for cash (December 13, 1999). ... On disabled list (March 25-September 1, 2000); included rehabilitation assignments to St. Petersburg and Orlando. ... On disabled list (April 23-May 27, 2003); included rehabilitation assignment to Durham. ... On disabled list (May 24-July 2, 2004); included rehabilitation assignment to Durham.

2004 GAMES PLAYED BY POSITION (MLB): OF—24, 3B—19, DH—5, 2B—2, 1B—1.

Year	Team (League)	Pos.	G	AB	R	H	2B	3B	HR	RBI	BB	SO	HBP	GDP	SB-CS	Avg.	OBP	SLG	OPS	E	Avg.
1996— Yakima (N'west)		3B	66	257	31	68	11	1	4	27	7	46	3	5	8-3	.265	.291	.362	.653	23	.893
1997— Savannah (S. Atl.)		3B	130	475	57	100	17	5	5	47	38	83	5	9	11-3	.211	.274	.299	.573	31	.920
1998— Vero Beach (FSL)		3B	73	266	28	65	9	0	0	30	23	43	2	6	13-3	.244	.307	.278	.585	13	.951
— San Antonio (Texas)		3B	50	160	18	35	6	0	1	9	6	28	0	9	2-0	.219	.246	.275	.521	9	.947
1999— Vero Beach (FSL)		3B-2B	127	474	68	141	26	2	9	54	36	66	14	6	24-13	.297	.361	.418	.779	25	.924
2000— St. Pete. (FSL)		3B	5	16	2	3	2	0	0	0	2	3	1	0	1-0	.188	.316	.313	.628	0	1.000
— Orlando (South.)		3B	14	51	6	13	5	0	0	7	7	6	1	0	1-1	.255	.350	.353	.703	3	.906
— Tampa Bay (A.L.)		3B-DH	4	3	0	1	0	0	0	0	0	1	0	0	0-0	.333	.333	.333	.667	0	—
2001— Tampa Bay (A.L.)		2-0-DH-3	81	237	33	62	11	1	2	12	10	47	0	5	12-4	.262	.292	.342	.633	6	.974
2002— Orlando (South.)		OF	2	7	1	3	0	1	0	0	1	0	0	0	0-1	.429	.500	.714	1.214	0	1.000
— Durham (Int'l)		OF-3B	67	244	41	65	6	4	6	35	21	43	5	4	15-0	.266	.332	.398	.730	6	.962
— Tampa Bay (A.L.)		OF	21	89	15	26	6	1	0	6	3	16	2	1	2-5	.292	.330	.382	.712	3	.947
2003— Durham (Int'l)		OF	18	77	11	19	4	1	0	9	4	15	0	0	4-2	.247	.284	.325	.609	2	.913
— Tampa Bay (A.L.)		3B-OF-2B	107	373	43	95	20	0	7	46	19	84	7	5	11-3	.255	.301	.365	.666	7	.975
2004— Durham (Int'l)		OF-3B-2B	23	97	23	27	7	0	3	14	7	17	3	2	2-1	.278	.346	.443	.789	0	1.000
— Tampa Bay (A.L.)		0-3-DH-2-1	53	117	12	19	5	0	0	9	10	36	1	4	2-1	.162	.231	.205	.436	2	.976
Major League totals (5 years)			266	819	103	203	42	2	9	73	42	184	10	15	27-13	.248	.291	.337	.628	18	.972

ROMANO, JASON — OF

PERSONAL: Born June 24, 1979, in Tampa, Fla. ... 6-0/185. ... Bats right, throws right. ... Full name: Jason Anthony Romano. ... Name pronounced: ROW-maun-oh. ... High school: Hillsborough (Tampa, Fla.).

TRANSACTIONS/CAREER NOTES: Selected by Texas Rangers organization in supplemental round ("sandwich pick" between first and second rounds, 39th pick overall) of 1997 free-agent draft; pick received as part of compensation for New York Yankees signing Type A free-agent P Mike Stanton. ... Traded by Rangers with OF Gabe Kapler to Colorado Rockies for OF Todd Hollandsworth and P Dennys Reyes (July 31, 2002). ... Traded by Rockies to Los Angeles Dodgers for OF Luke Allen (January 27, 2003). ... Traded by Dodgers to Tampa Bay Devil Rays for IF Antonio Perez (April 4, 2004). ... Claimed on waivers by Cincinnati Reds (April 22, 2004). ... On disabled list (July 26, 2004-remainder of season).

2004 GAMES PLAYED BY POSITION (MLB): OF—12, 2B—1.

Year	Team (League)	Pos.	G	AB	R	H	2B	3B	HR	RBI	BB	SO	HBP	GDP	SB-CS	Avg.	OBP	SLG	OPS	E	Avg.
1997— GC Rangers (GCL)		3B	34	109	27	28	5	3	2	11	13	19	3	1	13-4	.257	.349	.413	.762	15	.810
1998— Savannah (S. Atl.)		2B	134	524	72	142	19	4	7	52	46	94	8	6	40-17	.271	.336	.363	.699	32	.952
— Charlotte (Fla. St.)		2B	7	24	3	5	1	0	0	1	2	2	0	0	1-2	.208	.259	.250	.509	1	.978
1999— Charlotte (Fla. St.)		2B	120	459	84	143	27	14	13	71	39	72	13	4	34-15	.312	.376	.516	.893	23	.957
2000— Tulsa (Texas)		2B	131	535	87	145	35	2	8	70	56	84	6	13	25-10	.271	.343	.389	.732	24	.963
2001— Tulsa (Texas)		2B	46	186	19	45	9	1	1	19	16	31	1	8	8-3	.242	.304	.317	.621	8	.962
— Oklahoma (PCL)		2B-OF	41	149	32	47	6	1	4	13	20	28	0	4	3-4	.315	.394	.450	.844	2	.981
— GC Rangers (GCL)		2B-OF	5	21	2	3	0	0	0	0	1	8	0	0	1-0	.143	.182	.143	.325	5	.808
— Charlotte (Fla. St.)		OF	3	10	3	4	2	0	0	1	4	1	0	0	1-0	.400	.571	.600	1.171	0	1.000
2002— Oklahoma (PCL)		OF-2B-SS	48	196	28	53	8	1	4	28	19	41	0	...	10-3	.270	.329	.383	.711	5	.972
— Texas (A.L.)		0-2-DH-3	29	54	8	11	4	0	0	4	4	13	0	0	2-0	.204	.254	.278	.532	1	.981
— Colo. Springs (PCL)		OF-2B-SS	31	129	20	40	7	2	0	9	6	27	0	0	8-3	.310	.338	.395	.734	3	.973
— Colorado (N.L.)		2-S-0-3	18	37	9	12	0	1	0	1	3	11	0	0	4-1	.324	.375	.378	.753	4	.907
2003— Las Vegas (PCL)		OF-2-3-S	57	216	45	66	18	4	4	23	11	32	0	3	10-6	.306	.336	.481	.818	4	.977
— Los Angeles (N.L.)		OF-2B-DH	37	36	3	3	0	0	0	1	1	8	0	2	2-0	.083	.108	.083	.191	0	1.000
2004— Tampa Bay (A.L.)		2B-OF	4	8	0	1	0	0	0	1	0	2	0	0	0-0	.125	.125	.125	.250	1	.800
— Louisville (Int'l)		OF	40	163	22	55	12	4	2	16	3	24	0	0	3-1	.337	.347	.497	.844	1	.989
— Cincinnati (N.L.)		OF	22	26	3	4	0	0	1	3	2	10	0	0	0-0	.154	.214	.269	.484	0	1.000
American League totals (2 years)			33	62	8	12	4	0	0	5	4	15	0	0	2-0	.194	.239	.258	.497	2	.965
National League totals (3 years)			77	99	15	19	0	1	1	4	6	29	0	2	6-1	.192	.238	.242	.481	4	.944
Major League totals (3 years)			110	161	23	31	4	1	1	9	10	44	0	2	8-1	.193	.238	.248	.487	6	.953

ROMERO, J.C. — P

PERSONAL: Born June 4, 1976, in Rio Piedras, Puerto Rico. ... 5-11/198. ... Throws left, bats both. ... Full name: Juan Carlos Romero. ... High school: Berwing (San Juan, Puerto Rico). ... College: Mobile (Ala.).

TRANSACTIONS/CAREER NOTES: Selected by Minnesota Twins organization in 21st round of 1997 free-agent draft. ... On disabled list (March 25-May 10, 2000); included rehabilitation assignment to Fort Myers.

CAREER HITTING: 1-for-3 (.333), 1 R, 1 2B, 0 3B, 0 HR, 0 RBI.

Year	Team (League)	W	L	Pct.	ERA	WHIP	G	GS	CG	ShO	Hld.	Sv.-Opp.	IP	H	R	ER	HR	BB-IBB	SO	Avg.
1997— Elizabethton (Appal.)	3	2	.600	4.88	1.42	18	0	0	0	...	3-...	24.0	27	16	13	4	7-0	29	.276
— Fort Myers (Fla. St.)	1	1	.500	4.38	1.22	7	1	0	0	...	0-...	12.1	11	6	6	1	4-0	9	.244
1998— New Britain (East.)	6	3	.667	2.19	1.17	51	1	0	0	...	2-...	78.0	48	28	19	3	43-3	79	.178
1999— New Britain (East.)	4	4	.500	3.40	1.60	36	1	0	0	...	7-...	53.0	51	25	20	6	34-0	53	.254
— Salt Lake (PCL)	4	1	.800	3.20	1.63	15	0	0	0	...	1-...	19.2	18	11	7	1	14-0	20	.250
— Minnesota (A.L.)	0	0	...	3.72	1.34	5	0	0	0	0	0-0	9.2	13	4	4	0	6-0	4	.333
2000— Fort Myers (Fla. St.)	0	0	...	1.93	1.07	2	0	0	0	...	0-...	4.2	4	1	1	0	1-0	3	.222
— Salt Lake (PCL)	4	2	.667	3.44	1.30	17	11	1	0	...	4-...	65.1	60	40	25	6	25-0	38	.244
— Minnesota (A.L.)	2	7	.222	7.02	1.77	12	11	0	0	0	0-0	57.2	72	51	45	8	30-0	50	.312
2001— Minnesota (A.L.)	1	4	.200	6.23	1.46	14	11	0	0	0	0-0	65.0	71	48	45	10	24-1	39	.277
— Edmonton (PCL)	3	3	.500	3.68	1.43	12	10	0	0	...	0-...	63.2	67	33	26	4	24-0	55	.276

- 407 -

Year Team (League)	W	L	Pct.	ERA	WHIP	G	GS	CG	ShO	Hld.	Sv.-Opp.	IP	H	R	ER	HR	BB-IBB	SO	Avg.
2002—Minnesota (A.L.)	9	2	.818	1.89	1.21	81	0	0	0	33	1-5	81.0	62	17	17	3	36-4	76	.213
2003—Minnesota (A.L.)	2	0	1.000	5.00	1.71	73	0	0	0	22	0-4	63.0	66	37	35	7	42-7	50	.272
2004—Rochester (Int'l)	0	0	...	2.25	1.13	3	3	0	0	...	0-...	8.0	4	2	2	1	5-0	11	.143
—Minnesota (A.L.)	7	4	.636	3.51	1.33	74	0	0	0	16	1-8	74.1	61	32	29	4	38-6	69	.224
Major League totals (6 years)	21	17	.553	4.49	1.47	259	22	0	0	71	2-17	350.2	345	189	175	32	170-18	288	.259

DIVISION SERIES RECORD

Year Team (League)	W	L	Pct.	ERA	WHIP	G	GS	CG	ShO	Hld.	Sv.-Opp.	IP	H	R	ER	HR	BB-IBB	SO	Avg.
2002—Minnesota (A.L.)	0	0	...	0.00	1.20	3	0	0	0	2	0-0	3.1	3	0	0	0	1-0	2	.231
2003—Minnesota (A.L.)	0	0	...	0.00	1.50	3	0	0	0	0	0-0	3.1	3	0	0	0	2-1	1	.250
2004—Minnesota (A.L.)	0	0	...	9.00	1.00	2	0	0	0	0	0-0	1.0	0	1	1	0	1-0	1	.000
Division series totals (3 years)	0	0	...	1.17	1.30	8	0	0	0	2	0-0	7.2	6	1	1	0	4-1	4	.231

CHAMPIONSHIP SERIES RECORD

Year Team (League)	W	L	Pct.	ERA	WHIP	G	GS	CG	ShO	Hld.	Sv.-Opp.	IP	H	R	ER	HR	BB-IBB	SO	Avg.
2002—Minnesota (A.L.)	0	1	.000	22.50	3.00	4	0	0	0	0	0-0	2.0	4	5	5	1	2-0	3	.400

ROSE, MIKE — C

PERSONAL: Born August 25, 1976, in Sacramento, Calif. ... 6-1/185. ... Bats both, throws right. ... Full name: Michael John-Ferrero Rose. ... High school: Jesuit High (Sacramento).

TRANSACTIONS/CAREER NOTES: Selected by Houston Astros organization in fifth round of 1995 free-agent draft. ... Released by Astros (March 16, 2000). ... Signed by Arizona Diamondbacks organization (March 21, 2000). ... Traded by Diamondbacks to Boston Red Sox for cash (August 18, 2001). ... Released by Red Sox (April 26, 2002). ... Signed by Kansas City Royals organization (May 1, 2002). ... Signed as a free agent by Oakland Athletics organization (November 6, 2002).

2004 GAMES PLAYED BY POSITION (MLB): C—2.

									BATTING										FIELDING	
Year Team (League)	Pos.	G	AB	R	H	2B	3B	HR	RBI	BB	SO	HBP	GDP	SB-CS	Avg.	OBP	SLG	OPS	E	Avg.
1995—GC Astros (GCL)	C-1B	35	89	13	23	2	1	1	9	11	18	3	1	2-1	.258	.359	.337	.696	1	.996
1996—Kissimmee (Fla. St.)	C	2	1	0	0	0	0	0	0	0	1	0	0	0-0	.000	.000	.000	.000	0	1.000
—Auburn (NY-Penn)	C	61	180	20	45	5	1	2	11	30	41	1	5	9-3	.250	.360	.322	.682	7	.984
1997—Quad City (Midw.)	C	79	234	22	60	6	1	3	27	28	62	4	1	3-1	.256	.342	.329	.671	10	.983
1998—Kissimmee (Fla. St.)	C	18	62	9	14	4	0	3	9	8	14	0	2	1-0	.226	.314	.435	.750	3	.973
—Quad City (Midw.)	C-OF	88	267	48	81	13	2	7	40	52	56	1	5	10-8	.303	.417	.446	.863	8	.988
1999—Kissimmee (Fla. St.)	C	95	303	61	84	16	2	11	32	59	64	3	7	12-6	.277	.398	.452	.850	13	.981
—Jackson (Texas)	C	45	45	8	11	0	0	3	8	13	10	0	1	0-2	.244	.414	.444	.858	2	.983
2000—El Paso (Texas)	C-OF	117	352	58	100	22	1	10	62	68	70	1	16	8-11	.284	.398	.438	.835	16	.980
2001—Tucson (PCL)	C	20	55	9	10	1	2	0	8	12	16	0	3	0-0	.182	.324	.273	.596	0	1.000
—El Paso (Texas)	C-OF-3B	62	205	28	53	13	1	3	23	37	40	0	8	4-4	.259	.370	.376	.746	4	.984
—Trenton (East.)	C	9	24	3	4	0	0	1	2	6	10	0	0	0-1	.167	.333	.292	.625	0	1.000
2002—Trenton (East.)	C	10	29	1	3	1	1	0	0	5	7	0	2	0-0	.103	.235	.207	.442	0	1.000
—Omaha (PCL)	C	52	177	22	46	12	2	3	17	28	40	1	7	2-3	.260	.364	.401	.765	6	.981
—Wichita (Texas)	C-OF	14	59	13	18	5	0	2	14	7	11	0	3	0-1	.305	.379	.492	.870	1	.977
2003—Sacramento (PCL)	C-OF	70	221	44	58	10	1	8	30	44	50	4	6	2-1	.262	.390	.425	.815	8	.982
2004—Sacramento (PCL)	C-DH	107	349	56	98	20	2	6	49	76	80	3	14	0-0	.281	.407	.401	.808	8	.988
—Oakland (A.L.)	C	2	2	1	0	0	0	0	0	0	2	0	0	0-0	.000	.000	.000	.000	0	1.000
Major League totals (1 year)		2	2	1	0	0	0	0	0	0	2	0	0	0-0	.000	.000	.000	.000	0	1.000

ROSS, DAVID — C

PERSONAL: Born March 19, 1977, in Bainbridge, Ga. ... 6-2/205. ... Bats right, throws right. ... Full name: David Wade Ross. ... High school: Florida (Tallahassee, Fla.). ... College: Florida.

TRANSACTIONS/CAREER NOTES: Selected by Los Angeles Dodgers organization in 19th round of 1995 free-agent draft; did not sign. ... Selected by Dodgers organization in seventh round of 1998 free-agent draft.

2004 GAMES PLAYED BY POSITION (MLB): C—67.

									BATTING										FIELDING	
Year Team (League)	Pos.	G	AB	R	H	2B	3B	HR	RBI	BB	SO	HBP	GDP	SB-CS	Avg.	OBP	SLG	OPS	E	Avg.
1998—Yakima (N'west)	C	59	191	31	59	14	1	6	25	34	49	1	5	2-2	.309	.412	.487	.899	10	.979
1999—Vero Beach (FSL)	C-1B-OF	114	375	47	85	19	1	7	39	46	111	7	10	5-9	.227	.318	.339	.657	16	.979
2000—San Bern. (Calif.)	C	51	191	27	49	11	1	7	21	17	43	1	3	3-2	.257	.319	.435	.754	3	.992
—San Antonio (Texas)	C	24	67	11	14	2	1	3	12	9	17	1	0	1-0	.209	.308	.403	.711	1	.994
2001—Jacksonville (Sou.)	C	74	246	35	65	13	1	11	45	34	72	10	5	1-1	.264	.372	.459	.831	9	.985
2002—Las Vegas (PCL)	C	92	293	48	87	16	2	15	68	35	86	9	4	1-1	.297	.384	.519	.903	7	.989
—Los Angeles (N.L.)	C	8	10	2	2	1	0	1	2	2	4	1	0	0-0	.200	.385	.600	.985	0	1.000
2003—Las Vegas (PCL)	C	24	86	12	19	4	0	5	16	11	27	1	0	0-2	.221	.313	.442	.755	2	.989
—Los Angeles (N.L.)	C	40	124	19	32	7	0	10	18	13	42	2	4	0-0	.258	.336	.556	.892	4	.986
2004—Los Angeles (N.L.)	C	70	165	13	28	3	1	5	15	15	62	5	3	0-0	.170	.253	.291	.544	3	.992
Major League totals (3 years)		118	299	34	62	11	1	16	35	30	108	8	7	0-0	.207	.292	.411	.703	7	.990

DIVISION SERIES RECORD

									BATTING										FIELDING	
Year Team (League)	Pos.	G	AB	R	H	2B	3B	HR	RBI	BB	SO	HBP	GDP	SB-CS	Avg.	OBP	SLG	OPS	E	Avg.
2004—Los Angeles (N.L.)	C	2	3	0	0	0	0	0	0	1	0	0	0	0-0	.000	.250	.000	.250	1	.923

ROWAND, AARON — OF

PERSONAL: Born August 29, 1977, in Portland, Ore. ... 6-0/205. ... Bats right, throws right. ... Full name: Aaron Ryan Rowand. ... High school: Glendora (Calif.). ... College: Cal State Fullerton.

TRANSACTIONS/CAREER NOTES: Selected by New York Mets organization in 40th round of 1995 free-agent draft; did not sign. ... Selected by Chicago White Sox organization in supplemental round ("sandwich pick" between first and second rounds, 35th pick overall) of 1998 free-agent draft; pick received as part of compensation for Tampa Bay Devil Rays signing Type A free-agent OF Dave Martinez.

2004 GAMES PLAYED BY POSITION (MLB): OF—137.

									BATTING										FIELDING	
Year Team (League)	Pos.	G	AB	R	H	2B	3B	HR	RBI	BB	SO	HBP	GDP	SB-CS	Avg.	OBP	SLG	OPS	E	Avg.
1998—Hickory (S. Atl.)	OF	61	222	42	76	13	3	5	32	21	36	6	5	7-3	.342	.410	.496	.906	3	.966
1999—Win.-Salem (Car.)	OF	133	512	96	143	37	3	24	88	33	94	13	13	15-9	.279	.336	.504	.840	5	.973

Year Team (League)	Pos.	G	AB	R	H	2B	3B	HR	RBI	BB	SO	HBP	GDP	SB-CS	Avg.	OBP	SLG	OPS	E	Avg.
2000— Birmingham (Sou.)	OF	139	532	80	137	26	5	20	98	38	117	14	12	22-7	.258	.321	.438	.759	8	.975
2001— Charlotte (Int'l)	OF	82	329	54	97	28	0	16	48	21	47	9	9	8-2	.295	.353	.526	.879	6	.966
— Chicago (A.L.)	OF	63	123	21	36	5	0	4	20	15	28	4	2	5-1	.293	.385	.431	.816	1	.991
2002— Chicago (A.L.)	OF	126	302	41	78	16	2	7	29	12	54	6	8	0-1	.258	.298	.394	.692	4	.983
2003— Charlotte (Int'l)	OF	32	120	15	29	9	0	3	13	11	12	2	3	0-0	.242	.316	.392	.707	5	.950
— Chicago (A.L.)	OF-DH	93	157	22	45	8	0	6	24	7	21	3	1	0-0	.287	.327	.452	.780	0	1.000
2004— Chicago (A.L.)	OF	140	487	94	151	38	2	24	69	30	91	10	5	17-5	.310	.361	.544	.905	8	.975
Major League totals (4 years)		422	1069	178	310	67	4	41	142	64	194	23	16	22-7	.290	.342	.475	.817	13	.983

RUETER, KIRK   P

PERSONAL: Born December 1, 1970, in Centralia, Ill. ... 6-2/212. ... Throws left, bats left. ... Full name: Kirk Wesley Rueter. ... Name pronounced: REE-ter. ... High school: Nashville (Ill.) Community. ... College: Murray State.

TRANSACTIONS/CAREER NOTES: Selected by Montreal Expos organization in 18th round of 1991 free-agent draft. ... On disabled list (May 10-26, 1996); included rehabilitation assignment to Ottawa. ... Traded by Expos with P Tim Scott to San Francisco Giants for P Mark Leiter (July 30, 1996). ... On disabled list (July 9-25 and July 26-August 24, 2003); included rehabilitation assignment to Fresno.

HONORS: Named N.L. Rookie Pitcher of the Year by THE SPORTING NEWS (1993).

CAREER HITTING: 90-for-592 (.152), 43 R, 8 2B, 0 3B, 0 HR, 39 RBI.

Year Team (League)	W	L	Pct.	ERA	WHIP	G	GS	CG	ShO	Hld.	Sv.-Opp.	IP	H	R	ER	HR	BB-IBB	SO	Avg.
1991— GC Expos (GCL)	1	1	.500	0.95	1.05	5	4	0	0		0-...	19.0	16	5	2	0	4-0	19	.232
— Sumter (S. Atl.)	3	1	.750	1.33	1.03	8	5	0	0		0-...	40.2	32	8	6	3	10-0	27	.215
1992— Rockford (Midwest)	11	9	.550	2.58	1.07	26	26	6	2		0-...	174.1	150	68	50	5	36-2	153	.232
1993— Harrisburg (Eastern)	5	0	1.000	1.36	0.91	9	8	1	1		0-...	59.2	47	10	9	4	7-0	36	.218
— Ottawa (Int'l)	4	2	.667	2.70	1.13	7	7	1	0		0-...	43.1	46	20	13	7	3-0	27	.277
— Montreal (N.L.)	8	0	1.000	2.73	1.20	14	14	1	0	0	0-0	85.2	85	33	26	5	18-1	31	.264
1994— Montreal (N.L.)	7	3	.700	5.17	1.40	20	20	0	0	0	0-0	92.1	106	60	53	11	23-1	50	.294
— Ottawa (Int'l)	0	0	...	4.50	0.50	1	1	0	0		0-...	2.0	1	1	1	1	0-0	1	.143
1995— Montreal (N.L.)	5	3	.625	3.23	0.99	9	9	1	1	0	0-0	47.1	38	17	17	3	9-0	28	.224
— Ottawa (Int'l)	9	7	.563	3.06	1.20	20	20	3	1		0-...	120.2	120	50	41	7	25-0	67	.260
1996— Ottawa (Int'l)	1	2	.333	4.20	1.60	3	3	1	0		0-...	15.0	21	7	7	3	3-0	3	.333
— Montreal (N.L.)	5	6	.455	4.58	1.44	16	16	0	0	0	0-0	78.2	91	44	40	12	22-0	30	.295
— San Francisco (N.L.)	1	2	.333	1.93	0.99	4	3	0	0	0	0-0	23.1	18	6	5	0	5-0	16	.207
— Phoenix (PCL)	1	2	.333	3.51	1.44	5	5	0	0		0-...	25.2	25	12	10	2	12-0	15	.253
1997— San Francisco (N.L.)	13	6	.684	3.45	1.28	32	32	0	0	0	0-0	190.2	194	83	73	17	51-8	115	.264
1998— San Francisco (N.L.)	16	9	.640	4.36	1.33	33	33	1	0	0	0-0	187.2	193	100	91	27	57-3	102	.265
1999— San Francisco (N.L.)	15	10	.600	5.41	1.48	33	33	1	0	0	0-0	184.2	219	118	111	28	55-2	94	.297
2000— San Francisco (N.L.)	11	9	.550	3.96	1.45	32	31	0	0	0	0-0	184.0	205	92	81	18	62-5	71	.290
2001— San Francisco (N.L.)	14	12	.538	4.42	1.43	34	34	0	0	0	0-0	195.1	213	105	96	25	66-4	83	.283
2002— San Francisco (N.L.)	14	8	.636	3.23	1.27	33	33	0	0	0	0-0	203.2	204	83	73	22	54-7	76	.262
2003— Fresno (PCL)	0	0	...	0.00	0.60	1	1	0	0		0-...	4.2	1	0	0	0	2-0	6	.071
— San Francisco (N.L.)	10	5	.667	4.53	1.48	27	27	0	0	0	0-0	147.0	170	77	74	14	47-2	41	.297
2004— San Francisco (N.L.)	9	12	.429	4.73	1.53	33	33	0	0	0	0-0	190.1	225	108	100	21	66-5	56	.296
Major League totals (12 years)	128	85	.601	4.18	1.38	320	318	4	1	0	0-0	1810.2	1961	926	840	208	535-38	793	.279

DIVISION SERIES RECORD

Year Team (League)	W	L	Pct.	ERA	WHIP	G	GS	CG	ShO	Hld.	Sv.-Opp.	IP	H	R	ER	HR	BB-IBB	SO	Avg.
1997— San Francisco (N.L.)	0	0	...	1.29	1.00	1	1	0	0	0	0-0	7.0	4	1	1	1	3-0	5	.160
2000— San Francisco (N.L.)	0	0	...	0.00	0.92	1	1	0	0	0	0-0	4.1	3	0	0	0	1-0	1	.200
2002— San Francisco (N.L.)	0	1	.000	18.00	3.00	1	1	0	0	0	0-0	3.0	7	7	6	2	2-0	1	.500
2003— San Francisco (N.L.)	0	0	...	3.60	1.00	1	1	0	0	0	0-0	5.0	3	2	2	1	2-0	2	.167
Division series totals (4 years)	0	1	.000	4.19	1.29	4	3	0	0	0	0-0	19.1	17	10	9	4	8-0	9	.236

CHAMPIONSHIP SERIES RECORD

Year Team (League)	W	L	Pct.	ERA	WHIP	G	GS	CG	ShO	Hld.	Sv.-Opp.	IP	H	R	ER	HR	BB-IBB	SO	Avg.
2002— San Francisco (N.L.)	1	0	1.000	4.09	1.55	2	2	0	0	0	0-0	11.0	15	5	5	2	2-0	3	.326

WORLD SERIES RECORD

Year Team (League)	W	L	Pct.	ERA	WHIP	G	GS	CG	ShO	Hld.	Sv.-Opp.	IP	H	R	ER	HR	BB-IBB	SO	Avg.
2002— San Francisco (N.L.)	0	0	...	2.70	1.10	2	1	0	0	0	0-0	10.0	10	3	3	1	1-0	5	.263

RUSCH, GLENDON   P

PERSONAL: Born November 7, 1974, in Seattle, Wash. ... 6-1/220. ... Throws left, bats left. ... Full name: Glendon James Rusch. ... Name pronounced: RUSH. ... High school: Shorecrest (Seattle).

TRANSACTIONS/CAREER NOTES: Selected by Kansas City Royals organization in 17th round of 1993 free-agent draft. ... On disabled list (June 16-July 1, 1997); included rehabilitation assignment to Omaha. ... On disabled list (August 9-September 4, 1998); included rehabilitation assignment to Omaha. ... Traded by Royals to New York Mets for P Dan Murray (September 14, 1999). ... Traded by Mets with IF Lenny Harris to Milwaukee Brewers as part of three-team deal in which Brewers also acquired OF Alex Ochoa from Colorado Rockies, Mets acquired P Jeff D'Amico, OF Jeromy Burnitz, IF Lou Collier, OF/1B Mark Sweeney from Brewers and 1B/OF Ross Gload and P Craig House from Rockies and Rockies acquired 1B/3B Todd Zeile, OF Benny Agbayani and cash from Mets (January 21, 2002). ... Signed as a free agent by Texas Rangers organization (January 21, 2004). ... Released by Rangers. ... Signed by Chicago Cubs organization (April 1, 2004).

CAREER HITTING: 38-for-249 (.153), 13 R, 1 2B, 0 3B, 3 HR, 19 RBI.

Year Team (League)	W	L	Pct.	ERA	WHIP	G	GS	CG	ShO	Hld.	Sv.-Opp.	IP	H	R	ER	HR	BB-IBB	SO	Avg.
1993— GC Royals (GCL)	4	2	.667	1.60	0.87	11	10	0	0	...	0-...	62.0	43	14	11	0	11-0	48	.197
— Rockford (Midwest)	0	1	.000	3.38	2.13	2	2	0	0	...	0-...	8.0	10	6	3	0	7-0	8	.313
1994— Rockford (Midwest)	8	5	.615	4.66	1.27	28	17	1	1	...	1-...	114.0	111	61	59	5	34-2	122	.256
1995— Wilmington (Caro.)	14	6	.700	1.74	0.87	26	26	1	1	...	0-...	165.2	110	41	32	5	34-3	147	.188
1996— Omaha (Am. Assoc.)	11	9	.550	3.98	1.28	28	28	1	0	...	0-...	169.2	177	88	75	15	40-3	117	.267
1997— Kansas City (A.L.)	6	9	.400	5.50	1.51	30	27	1	0	0	0-0	170.1	206	111	104	28	52-0	116	.301
— Omaha (Am. Assoc.)	0	1	.000	4.50	1.33	1	1	0	0	...	0-...	6.0	7	3	3	1	1-0	2	.292
1998— Kansas City (A.L.)	6	15	.286	5.88	1.56	29	24	1	1	0	1-1	154.2	191	104	101	22	50-0	94	.304
— Omaha (PCL)	1	1	.500	7.98	1.77	3	3	0	0	...	0-...	14.2	20	18	13	4	6-0	14	.317
1999— Omaha (PCL)	4	7	.364	4.42	1.54	20	20	1	0	...	0-...	114.0	143	68	56	10	33-0	102	.307
— GC Royals (GCL)	0	0	...	1.50	1.00	2	2	0	0	...	0-...	6.0	3	1	1	0	3-0	9	.136
— Kansas City (A.L.)	0	1	.000	15.75	2.50	3	0	0	0	...	0-0	4.0	7	7	7	1	3-0	4	.368

Year Team (League)	W	L	Pct.	ERA	WHIP	G	GS	CG	ShO	Hld.	Sv.-Opp.	IP	H	R	ER	HR	BB-IBB	SO	Avg.
—New York (N.L.)	0	0	...	0.00	1.00	1	0	0	0	0	0-0	1.0	1	0	0	0	0-0	0	.333
2000—New York (N.L.)	11	11	.500	4.01	1.26	31	30	2	0	0	0-0	190.2	196	91	85	18	44-2	157	.267
2001—New York (N.L.)	8	12	.400	4.63	1.45	33	33	1	0	0	0-0	179.0	216	101	92	23	43-2	156	.301
2002—Milwaukee (N.L.)	10	•16	.385	4.70	1.44	34	34	4	1	0	0-0	210.2	227	118	110	30	76-1	140	.279
2003—Indianapolis (Int'l)	1	1	.500	3.86	1.00	4	3	1	0	...	0-...	21.0	17	9	9	4	4-0	20	.218
—Milwaukee (N.L.)	1	12	.077	6.42	1.75	32	19	1	0	7	1-1	123.1	171	93	88	11	45-3	93	.331
2004—Iowa (PCL)	2	0	1.000	1.90	1.00	4	4	0	0	...	0-...	19.0	18	6	4	0	1-0	16	.257
—Chicago (N.L.)	6	2	.750	3.47	1.23	32	16	0	0	3	2-2	129.2	127	54	50	10	33-1	90	.256
American League totals (3 years)	12	25	.324	5.80	1.55	62	51	2	1	0	1-1	329.0	404	222	212	51	105-0	214	.303
National League totals (6 years)	36	53	.404	4.58	1.41	163	132	8	1	10	3-3	834.1	938	457	425	92	241-9	636	.286
Major League totals (8 years)	48	78	.381	4.93	1.45	225	183	10	2	10	4-4	1163.1	1342	679	637	143	346-9	850	.291

DIVISION SERIES RECORD

Year Team (League)	W	L	Pct.	ERA	WHIP	G	GS	CG	ShO	Hld.	Sv.-Opp.	IP	H	R	ER	HR	BB-IBB	SO	Avg.
2000—New York (N.L.)	0	0	...	0.00	0.00	1	0	0	0	0	0-0	.2	0	0	0	0	0-0	2	.000

CHAMPIONSHIP SERIES RECORD

Year Team (League)	W	L	Pct.	ERA	WHIP	G	GS	CG	ShO	Hld.	Sv.-Opp.	IP	H	R	ER	HR	BB-IBB	SO	Avg.
2000—New York (N.L.)	1	0	1.000	0.00	0.82	2	0	0	0	0	0-0	3.2	3	0	0	0	0-0	3	.250

WORLD SERIES RECORD

Year Team (League)	W	L	Pct.	ERA	WHIP	G	GS	CG	ShO	Hld.	Sv.-Opp.	IP	H	R	ER	HR	BB-IBB	SO	Avg.
2000—New York (N.L.)	0	0	...	2.25	2.00	3	0	0	0	0	0-0	4.0	6	1	1	0	2-1	2	.353

RYAN, B.J.   P

PERSONAL: Born December 28, 1975, in Bossier City, La. ... 6-6/249. ... Throws left, bats left. ... Full name: Robert Victor Ryan. ... High school: Airline (Bossier City, La.). ... College: Southwestern Louisiana.

TRANSACTIONS/CAREER NOTES: Selected by Cincinnati Reds organization in 17th round of 1998 free-agent draft. ... Traded by Reds with P Jacobo Sequea to Baltimore Orioles for P Juan Guzman (July 31, 1999).

CAREER HITTING: 0-for-2 (.000), 0 R, 0 2B, 0 3B, 0 HR, 0 RBI.

Year Team (League)	W	L	Pct.	ERA	WHIP	G	GS	CG	ShO	Hld.	Sv.-Opp.	IP	H	R	ER	HR	BB-IBB	SO	Avg.
1998—Billings (Pio.)	2	1	.667	1.93	1.07	14	0	0	0	...	4-...	18.2	15	4	4	0	5-0	25	.211
—Char., W.Va. (SAL)	0	0	...	2.08	0.46	3	0	0	0	...	2-...	4.1	1	1	1	0	1-0	5	.077
—Chattanooga (Southern)	1	0	1.000	2.20	1.16	16	0	0	0	...	4-...	16.1	13	4	4	0	6-0	21	.220
1999—Chattanooga (Southern)	2	1	.667	2.59	1.20	35	0	0	0	...	6-...	41.2	33	13	12	1	17-0	46	.217
—Indianapolis (Int'l)	1	0	1.000	4.00	1.33	11	0	0	0	...	0-...	9.0	9	4	4	0	3-1	12	.265
—Cincinnati (N.L.)	0	0	...	4.50	2.50	1	0	0	0	0	0-0	2.0	4	1	1	0	1-0	1	.500
—Rochester (Int'l)	0	0	...	2.51	0.84	11	0	0	0	...	1-...	14.1	8	4	4	2	4-1	20	.160
—Baltimore (A.L.)	1	0	1.000	2.95	1.15	13	0	0	0	0	0-0	18.1	9	6	6	0	12-1	28	.150
2000—Baltimore (A.L.)	2	3	.400	5.91	1.57	42	0	0	0	7	0-3	42.2	36	29	28	7	31-1	41	.225
—Rochester (Int'l)	0	1	.000	4.74	1.30	14	4	0	0	...	0-...	24.2	23	13	13	4	9-0	28	.247
2001—Baltimore (A.L.)	2	4	.333	4.25	1.45	61	0	0	0	14	2-4	53.0	47	31	25	6	30-4	54	.233
2002—Baltimore (A.L.)	2	1	.667	4.68	1.46	67	0	0	0	12	1-2	57.2	51	31	30	7	33-4	56	.241
2003—Baltimore (A.L.)	4	1	.800	3.40	1.37	76	0	0	0	19	0-2	50.1	42	19	19	1	27-0	63	.227
2004—Baltimore (A.L.)	4	6	.400	2.28	1.14	76	0	0	0	21	3-7	87.0	64	24	22	4	35-9	122	.200
American League totals (6 years)	15	15	.500	3.79	1.35	335	0	0	0	73	6-18	309.0	249	140	130	25	168-19	364	.219
National League totals (1 year)	0	0	...	4.50	2.50	1	0	0	0	0	0-0	2.0	4	1	1	0	1-0	1	.500
Major League totals (6 years)	15	15	.500	3.79	1.36	336	0	0	0	73	6-18	311.0	253	141	131	25	169-19	365	.221

RYAN, MICHAEL   OF

PERSONAL: Born July 6, 1977, in Indiana, Pa. ... 6-0/193. ... Bats left, throws right. ... Full name: Michael Sean Ryan. ... High school: Indiana (Pa.).

TRANSACTIONS/CAREER NOTES: Selected by Minnesota Twins organization in fifth round of 1996 free-agent draft. ... On disabled list (June 14-July 20, 2004); included rehabilitation assignment to Rochester.

2004 GAMES PLAYED BY POSITION (MLB): OF—15, DH—11.

Year Team (League)	Pos.	G	AB	R	H	2B	3B	HR	RBI	BB	SO	HBP	GDP	SB-CS	Avg.	OBP	SLG	OPS	E	Avg.
1996—GC Twins (GCL)	3B	43	157	12	31	8	2	0	13	13	20	1	3	3-0	.197	.260	.274	.534	10	.910
1997—Elizabethton (App.)	3B	62	220	44	66	10	4	3	29	38	39	3	8	2-2	.300	.404	.386	.790	28	.825
1998—Fort Wayne (Midw.)	3B-1B	113	412	68	131	24	6	9	72	44	92	2	8	7-3	.318	.382	.471	.853	33	.906
1999—Fort Myers (FSL)	2B	131	507	85	139	26	5	8	71	63	60	5	11	3-4	.274	.356	.393	.749	35	.949
2000—New Britain (East.)	OF-2B	122	481	64	133	23	8	11	69	34	79	2	13	4-3	.277	.323	.426	.749	9	.965
—Salt Lake (PCL)	OF	3	9	1	2	0	0	0	2	3	2	0	1	0-0	.222	.417	.222	.639	0	1.000
2001—Edmonton (PCL)	OF-2B	135	527	89	152	36	7	18	73	52	121	2	17	1-6	.288	.353	.486	.839	11	.966
2002—Edmonton (PCL)	OF	131	540	92	141	36	6	31	101	55	124	2	9	4-5	.261	.330	.522	.852	3	.987
—Minnesota (A.L.)	OF-DH	7	11	3	1	0	0	0	0	0	2	0	0	0-0	.091	.091	.091	.182	0	1.000
2003—Rochester (Int'l)	OF-DH	115	408	56	92	20	4	15	60	38	89	1	8	6-1	.225	.289	.404	.694	2	.988
—Minnesota (A.L.)	OF-DH	27	61	13	24	7	0	5	13	6	12	0	4	2-1	.393	.441	.754	1.195	0	1.000
2004—Minnesota (A.L.)	OF-DH	36	71	9	17	2	1	0	7	4	16	0	2	1-1	.239	.280	.296	.576	1	.947
—Rochester (Int'l)	OF-DH	50	175	29	37	7	1	6	16	16	38	1	3	3-4	.211	.281	.366	.647	1	.987
Major League totals (3 years)		70	143	25	42	9	1	5	20	10	30	0	6	3-2	.294	.338	.476	.813	1	.982

DIVISION SERIES RECORD

Year Team (League)	Pos.	G	AB	R	H	2B	3B	HR	RBI	BB	SO	HBP	GDP	SB-CS	Avg.	OBP	SLG	OPS	E	Avg.
2003—Minnesota (A.L.)		1	1	0	0	0	0	0	0	0	1	0	0	0-0	.000	.000	.000	.000	0	...

SAARLOOS, KIRK   P

PERSONAL: Born May 23, 1979, in Long Beach, Calif. ... 6-0/180. ... Throws right, bats right. ... Full name: Kirk Craig Saarloos. ... Name pronounced: sar-LOHS. ... College: Cal State Fullerton.

TRANSACTIONS/CAREER NOTES: Selected by Houston Astros organization in third round of 2001 free-agent draft. ... Traded by Astros to Oakland Athletics for RHP Chad Harville (April 17, 2004). ... On disabled list (July 30, 2004-remainder of season).

CAREER HITTING: 2-for-35 (.057), 0 R, 1 2B, 0 3B, 0 HR, 3 RBI.

S

Year Team (League)	W	L	Pct.	ERA	WHIP	G	GS	CG	ShO	Hld.	Sv.-Opp.	IP	H	R	ER	HR	BB-IBB	SO	Avg.
2001—Lexington (S.Atl.)	1	1	.500	1.17	0.82	22	0	0	0	...	11-...	30.2	18	5	4	1	7-0	40	.165
2002—Round Rock (Texas)	10	1	.909	1.40	0.83	13	13	1	1	...	0-...	83.1	48	17	13	1	21-0	82	.168
—New Orleans (PCL)	2	0	1.000	2.25	0.88	4	2	0	0	...	0-...	16.0	12	4	4	1	2-0	19	.211
—Houston (N.L.)	6	7	.462	6.01	1.49	17	17	1	1	0	0-0	85.1	100	59	57	12	27-5	54	.301
2003—New Orleans (PCL)	5	0	1.000	3.08	1.10	13	7	2	1	...	0-0	61.1	54	22	21	4	11-1	34	.242
—Houston (N.L.)	2	1	.667	4.93	1.46	36	4	0	0	4	0-0	49.1	55	31	27	4	17-3	43	.281
2004—New Orleans (PCL)	0	2	.000	15.43	2.57	2	2	0	0	...	0-...	7.0	17	15	12	4	1-0	6	.447
—Oakland (A.L.)	2	1	.667	4.44	1.60	6	5	0	0	0	0-...	24.1	27	13	12	4	12-0	10	.284
—Sacramento (PCL)	2	0	1.000	3.54	1.38	5	5	0	0	...	0-...	20.1	19	8	8	1	9-0	17	.250
American League totals (1 year)	2	1	.667	4.44	1.60	6	5	0	0	0	0-0	24.1	27	13	12	4	12-0	10	.284
National League totals (2 years)	8	8	.500	5.61	1.48	53	21	1	1	4	0-0	134.2	155	90	84	16	44-8	97	.294
Major League totals (3 years)	10	9	.526	5.43	1.50	59	26	1	1	4	0-0	159.0	182	103	96	20	56-8	107	.292

SABATHIA, C.C. — P

PERSONAL: Born July 21, 1980, in Vallejo, Calif. ... 6-7/290. ... Throws left, bats left. ... Full name: Carsten Charles Sabathia. ... Name pronounced: sa-BATH-ee-a. ... High school: Vallejo (Calif.).

TRANSACTIONS/CAREER NOTES: Selected by Cleveland Indians organization in first round (20th pick overall) of 1998 free-agent draft.

HONORS: Named A.L. Rookie Pitcher of the Year by THE SPORTING NEWS (2001).

CAREER HITTING: 5-for-19 (.263), 1 R, 0 2B, 0 3B, 0 HR, 0 RBI.

Year Team (League)	W	L	Pct.	ERA	WHIP	G	GS	CG	ShO	Hld.	Sv.-Opp.	IP	H	R	ER	HR	BB-IBB	SO	Avg.
1998—Burlington (Appalachian)	1	0	1.000	4.50	1.56	5	5	0	0	...	0-...	18.0	20	14	9	1	8-0	35	.274
1999—Mahoning Valley (NY-P)	0	0	...	1.83	1.07	6	6	0	0	...	0-...	19.2	9	5	4	0	12-0	27	.143
—Columbus (S. Atl.)	2	0	1.000	1.08	0.78	3	3	0	0	...	0-...	16.2	8	2	2	1	5-0	20	.140
—Kinston (Caro.)	3	3	.500	5.34	1.53	7	7	0	0	...	0-...	32.0	30	22	19	3	19-0	29	.256
2000—Kinston (Caro.)	3	2	.600	3.54	1.29	10	10	2	2	...	0-...	56.0	48	23	22	4	24-0	69	.234
—Akron (East.)	3	7	.300	3.59	1.36	17	17	0	0	...	0-...	90.1	75	41	36	6	48-0	90	.223
2001—Cleveland (A.L.)	17	5	.773	4.39	1.35	33	33	0	0	0	0-0	180.1	149	93	88	19	95-1	171	.228
2002—Cleveland (A.L.)	13	11	.542	4.37	1.36	33	33	2	0	0	0-0	210.0	198	109	102	17	88-2	149	.252
2003—Cleveland (A.L.)	13	9	.591	3.60	1.30	30	30	2	1	0	0-0	197.2	190	85	79	19	66-3	141	.255
2004—Cleveland (A.L.)	11	10	.524	4.12	1.32	30	30	1	1	0	0-0	188.0	176	90	86	20	72-3	139	.252
Major League totals (4 years)	54	35	.607	4.12	1.33	126	126	5	2	0	0-0	776.0	713	377	355	75	321-9	600	.247

DIVISION SERIES RECORD

Year Team (League)	W	L	Pct.	ERA	WHIP	G	GS	CG	ShO	Hld.	Sv.-Opp.	IP	H	R	ER	HR	BB-IBB	SO	Avg.
2001—Cleveland (A.L.)	1	0	1.000	3.00	1.83	1	1	0	0	0	0-0	6.0	6	2	2	0	5-1	5	.261

ALL-STAR GAME RECORD

	W	L	Pct.	ERA	WHIP	G	GS	CG	ShO	Hld.	Sv.-Opp.	IP	H	R	ER	HR	BB-IBB	SO	Avg.
All-Star Game totals (1 year)	0	0	...	27.00	4.00	1	0	0	0	0	0-0	1.0	4	3	3	0	0-0	0	.571

SADLER, DONNIE — SS/OF

PERSONAL: Born June 17, 1975, in Gohlson, Texas. ... 5-6/175. ... Bats right, throws right. ... Full name: Donnie Lamont Sadler. ... High school: Valley Mills (Texas).

TRANSACTIONS/CAREER NOTES: Selected by Boston Red Sox organization in 11th round of 1994 free-agent draft. ... Traded by Red Sox with OF Michael Coleman to Cincinnati Reds for IF Chris Stynes (November 16, 2000). ... Traded by Reds to Kansas City Royals for P Cary Ammons (June 20, 2001). ... On disabled list (June 14-July 8, 2002); included rehabilitation assignment to Omaha. ... Claimed on waivers by Texas Rangers (July 8, 2002). ... Released by Rangers (September 30, 2002). ... Re-signed by Rangers (November 13, 2002). ... Signed as a free agent by Arizona Diamondbacks organization (November 20, 2004). ... Refused minor league assignment and became a free agent (June 9, 2004). ... Signed by Chicago White Sox organization (June 16, 2004). ... Released by White Sox (July 20, 2004).

2004 GAMES PLAYED BY POSITION (MLB): OF—6, SS—3, 2B—2, 3B—2.

Year Team (League)	Pos.	G	AB	R	H	2B	3B	HR	RBI	BB	SO	HBP	GDP	SB-CS	Avg.	OBP	SLG	OPS	E	Avg.
1994—GC Red Sox (GCL)	2B-3B-SS	53	206	52	56	8	6	1	16	23	27	3	1	32-8	.272	.349	.384	.732	18	.928
1995—Michigan (Midw.)	SS	118	438	103	124	25	8	9	55	79	85	6	5	41-13	.283	.397	.438	.836	28	.944
1996—Trenton (East.)	SS-OF	115	454	68	121	20	8	6	46	38	75	6	4	34-8	.267	.329	.385	.715	27	.940
1997—Pawtucket (Int'l)	2B-SS-OF	125	481	74	102	18	2	11	36	57	121	2	11	20-14	.212	.295	.326	.621	15	.976
1998—Boston (A.L.)	2B-SS-OF	58	124	21	28	4	4	3	15	6	28	3	1	4-0	.226	.276	.395	.671	5	.973
—Pawtucket (Int'l)	2B-SS	36	131	25	29	5	1	2	10	26	23	0	1	11-1	.221	.348	.321	.669	4	.978
1999—Boston (A.L.)	S-2-3-O-DH	49	107	18	30	1	1	0	4	5	20	0	1	2-1	.280	.313	.346	.658	9	.916
—Pawtucket (Int'l)	SS-DH	43	172	23	50	12	4	1	17	16	36	3	3	4-2	.291	.361	.424	.786	10	.944
—GC Red Sox (GCL)	SS	4	13	2	5	2	0	0	1	2	1	0	0	0-0	.385	.467	.538	1.005	1	.950
2000—Pawtucket (Int'l)	OF-SS-2B	91	313	45	63	6	5	5	23	45	60	4	8	10-1	.201	.306	.300	.606	7	.979
—Boston (A.L.)	S-O-2-3-DH	49	99	14	22	5	0	1	10	5	18	1	1	3-1	.222	.262	.303	.565	3	.976
2001—Cincinnati (N.L.)	2-S-O-DH	39	84	9	17	3	0	1	3	9	20	0	3	3-3	.202	.280	.274	.553	3	.965
—Kansas City (A.L.)	O-3-2-S-DH	54	101	19	13	3	0	1	10	9	17	2	0	4-1	.129	.212	.158	.371	2	.987
2002—Kansas City (A.L.)	F-3-2-S-DH	35	68	10	13	1	1	0	5	4	12	0	0	3-1	.191	.233	.235	.468	3	.943
—Omaha (PCL)	3B-SS-2B	5	21	6	7	0	0	0	0	2	3	1	...	0-2	.333	.417	.333	.750	0	1.000
—Texas (A.L.)	O-S-3-2-DH	38	30	6	3	1	0	0	2	3	7	2	1	2-2	.100	.229	.133	.362	0	1.000
—Oklahoma (PCL)	OF-2B	12	43	7	10	3	1	0	4	6	7	1	...	2-1	.233	.340	.349	.689	1	.978
2003—Oklahoma (PCL)	S-2-DH-O	19	66	14	20	4	1	1	6	10	9	2	1	6-1	.303	.405	.439	.844	4	.956
—Texas (A.L.)	OF-3-S-2	77	131	27	26	5	2	1	5	13	34	2	1	4-3	.198	.277	.290	.567	4	.966
2004—Arizona (N.L.)	OF-S-2-3	18	23	1	3	2	0	0	1	1	7	0	0	0-0	.130	.167	.217	.384	0	1.000
—Charlotte (Int'l)	DH	3	7	0	1	0	0	0	0	1	3	0	0	0-0	.143	.250	.143	.393	0	...
American League totals (6 years)		360	660	115	135	24	8	5	43	45	136	10	5	22-9	.205	.263	.288	.551	26	.967
National League totals (2 years)		57	107	10	20	5	0	1	3	10	27	0	3	3-3	.187	.256	.262	.518	3	.969
Major League totals (7 years)		417	767	125	155	29	8	6	46	55	163	10	8	25-12	.202	.262	.284	.546	29	.967

DIVISION SERIES RECORD

Year Team (League)	Pos.	G	AB	R	H	2B	3B	HR	RBI	BB	SO	HBP	GDP	SB-CS	Avg.	OBP	SLG	OPS	E	Avg.
1998—Boston (A.L.)	2B	3	0	0	0	0	0	0	0	0	0	0	0	0-0	...	...	...	...	0	1.000
1999—Boston (A.L.)	3B-DH	2	2	1	1	1	0	0	0	0	1	0	0	0-0	.500	.500	1.000	1.500	0	1.000
Division series totals (2 years)		5	2	1	1	1	0	0	0	0	1	0	0	0-0	.500	.500	1.000	1.500	0	1.000

Year Team (League)	Pos.	G	AB	R	H	2B	3B	HR	RBI	BB	SO	HBP	GDP	SB-CS	Avg.	OBP	SLG	OPS	E	Avg.

Year Team (League)	Pos.	G	AB	R	H	2B	3B	HR	RBI	BB	SO	HBP	GDP	SB-CS	Avg.	OBP	SLG	OPS	E	Avg.
1999— Boston (A.L.)	DH-OF	2	0	0	0	0	0	0	0	0	0	0	0	0-0	...	...	...	...	0	...

SAENZ, CHRIS — P

PERSONAL: Born August 14, 1981, in Tuscon, Ariz. ... 6-3/200. ... Throws right, bats right. ... Full name: Christopher Andrew Saenz. ... High school: Tucson (Ariz.). ... Junior college: Pima (Ariz.) Community College.

TRANSACTIONS/CAREER NOTES: Selected by Milwaukee Brewers in 28th round of 2001 free-agent draft.

CAREER HITTING: 0-for-2 (.000), 0 R, 0 2B, 0 3B, 0 HR, 0 RBI.

Year Team (League)	W	L	Pct.	ERA	WHIP	G	GS	CG	ShO	Hld.	Sv.-Opp.	IP	H	R	ER	HR	BB-IBB	SO	Avg.
2001— Ogden (Pio.)	3	1	.750	4.24	1.22	21	4	0	0	...	0-...	46.2	43	25	22	5	14-2	48	.251
2002— Beloit (Midw.)	3	5	.375	3.51	1.22	37	0	0	0	...	8-...	74.1	59	31	29	5	32-1	99	.217
2003— High Desert (Calif.)	9	9	.500	5.20	1.38	26	26	1	0	...	0-...	128.0	121	80	74	20	56-0	136	.251
— Huntsville (Southern)	0	0	...	1.50	1.17	1	0	0	0	...	0-...	6.0	4	2	1	0	3-0	6	.200
2004— Milwaukee (N.L.)	1	0	1.000	0.00	0.83	1	1	0	0	0	0-0	6.0	2	0	0	0	3-0	7	.100
— Huntsville (Southern)	5	5	.500	4.15	1.11	14	14	0	0	...	0-...	84.2	76	41	39	10	18-1	84	.238
Major League totals (1 year)	1	0	1.000	0.00	0.83	1	1	0	0	0	0-0	6.0	2	0	0	0	3-0	7	.100

SAENZ, OLMEDO — 1B

PERSONAL: Born October 8, 1970, in Chitre Herrera, Panama. ... 5-11/221. ... Bats right, throws right. ... Full name: Olmedo Sanchez Saenz. ... Name pronounced: SIGNS.

TRANSACTIONS/CAREER NOTES: Signed as a non-drafted free agent by Chicago White Sox organization (May 11, 1990). ... Signed as a free agent by Oakland Athletics (November 13, 1998). ... On disabled list (July 26-August 16, 1999); included rehabilitation assignment to Vancouver. ... On Oakland disabled list (August 1-September 19, 2000); included rehabilitation assignment to Sacramento. ... Signed as a free agent by Los Angeles Dodgers organization (December 19, 2003).

2004 GAMES PLAYED BY POSITION (MLB): 1B—25, DH—4, 3B—2.

Year Team (League)	Pos.	G	AB	R	H	2B	3B	HR	RBI	BB	SO	HBP	GDP	SB-CS	Avg.	OBP	SLG	OPS	E	Avg.
1991— South Bend (Mid.)	3B	56	192	23	47	10	1	2	22	21	48	5	3	5-3	.245	.332	.339	.670	12	.890
— Sarasota (Fla. St.)	3B	5	19	1	2	0	1	0	2	2	0	0	1	0-1	.105	.190	.211	.401	3	.842
1992— South Bend (Mid.)	3B-1B	132	493	66	121	26	4	7	59	36	52	11	16	16-13	.245	.309	.357	.666	48	.895
1993— Sarasota (Fla. St.)	3B	33	121	13	31	9	4	0	27	9	18	2	1	3-1	.256	.316	.397	.712	5	.933
— South Bend (Mid.)	3B	13	50	3	18	4	1	0	7	7	7	0	1	1-1	.360	.439	.480	.919	4	.913
— Birmingham (Sou.)	3B	49	173	30	60	17	2	6	29	20	21	5	7	2-1	.347	.427	.572	.999	14	.899
1994— Nashville (A.A.)	3B-DH	107	383	48	100	27	2	12	59	30	57	9	5	3-2	.261	.326	.436	.762	22	.917
— Chicago (A.L.)	3B	5	14	2	2	0	1	0	0	0	5	0	1	0-0	.143	.143	.286	.429	0	1.000
1995— Nashville (A.A.)	3B	111	415	60	126	26	1	13	74	45	60	12	11	0-2	.304	.385	.465	.850	24	.939
1996— Nashville (A.A.)	3B-DH	134	476	86	124	29	1	18	63	53	80	13	5	4-2	.261	.350	.439	.789	22	.939
1997— GC Whi. Sox (GCL)	DH	2	2	0	1	1	0	0	0	0	0	1	0	0-0	1.000	1.000	2.000	3.000	...	...
1998— Calgary (PCL)	3B-DH	124	466	89	146	29	0	29	102	45	49	22	16	3-3	.313	.394	.562	.957	21	.937
1999— Oakland (A.L.)	3B-1B-DH	97	255	41	70	18	0	11	41	22	47	15	6	1-1	.275	.363	.475	.837	8	.971
— Vancouver (PCL)	3B	2	5	1	3	1	0	0	2	0	1	0	0	0-0	.600	.571	.800	1.371	0	1.000
2000— Oakland (A.L.)	DH-3B-1B	76	214	40	67	12	2	9	33	25	40	7	6	1-0	.313	.401	.514	.915	4	.977
— Sacramento (PCL)	DH	1	4	1	2	0	0	0	1	0	0	0	0	0-0	.500	.500	.500	1.000	...	...
2001— Oakland (A.L.)	DH-1B-3B	106	305	33	67	21	1	9	32	19	64	13	9	0-1	.220	.291	.384	.675	5	.979
2002— Oakland (A.L.)	1B-3B-DH	68	156	15	43	10	1	6	18	13	31	7	2	1-1	.276	.354	.468	.822	5	.980
2003— Ariz. A's (Ariz.)	1B-3B-DH	13	45	13	15	2	0	2	8	8	6	2	1	0-0	.333	.455	.511	.966	1	.974
— Modesto (California)	1B	1	4	0	0	0	0	0	1	0	1	0	0	0-0	.000	.200	.000	.200	0	.000
2004— Los Angeles (N.L.)	1B-DH-3B	77	111	17	31	1	0	8	22	12	33	2	4	0-0	.279	.352	.505	.856	2	.986
American League totals (5 years)		352	944	131	249	61	5	35	124	79	187	42	24	3-3	.264	.345	.450	.795	22	.977
National League totals (1 year)		77	111	17	31	1	0	8	22	12	33	2	4	0-0	.279	.352	.505	.856	2	.986
Major League totals (6 years)		429	1055	148	280	62	5	43	146	91	220	44	28	3-3	.265	.345	.456	.801	24	.978

Year Team (League)	Pos.	G	AB	R	H	2B	3B	HR	RBI	BB	SO	HBP	GDP	SB-CS	Avg.	OBP	SLG	OPS	E	Avg.
2000— Oakland (A.L.)	DH	4	13	1	3	0	0	1	4	0	2	1	1	0-0	.231	.267	.462	.728	...	...
2001— Oakland (A.L.)	DH	3	4	0	0	0	0	0	0	0	1	0	0	0-0	.000	.000	.000	.000	...	...
2002— Oakland (A.L.)	1B	1	0	0	0	0	0	0	0	1	0	0	0	0-0	...	1.000	...	1.000	0	1.000
Division series totals (3 years)		8	17	1	3	0	0	1	4	1	3	1	1	0-0	.176	.250	.353	.603	0	1.000

SALMON, TIM — DH/OF

PERSONAL: Born August 24, 1968, in Long Beach, Calif. ... 6-3/235. ... Bats right, throws right. ... Full name: Timothy James Salmon. ... Name pronounced: SAM-en. ... High school: Greenway (Phoenix). ... College: Grand Canyon (Ariz.). ... Brother of Mike Salmon, safety with San Francisco 49ers (1997).

TRANSACTIONS/CAREER NOTES: Selected by Atlanta Braves organization in 18th round of June 1986 free-agent draft; did not sign. ... Selected by California Angels organization in third round of 1989 free-agent draft. ... On disabled list (July 18-August 3, 1994). ... Angels franchise renamed Anaheim Angels for 1997 season. ... On disabled list (April 23-May 9, 1998). ... On disabled list (May 4-July 17, 1999); included rehabilitation assignment to Lake Elsinore. ... On disabled list (July 1-19, 2001); included rehabilitation assignment to Rancho Cucamonga. ... On disabled list (August 14-September 1, 2002). ... On disabled list (April 30-June 9 and August 24, 2004-remainder of season); included rehabilitation assignments to Rancho Cucamonga.

HONORS: Named Minor League Player of the Year by THE SPORTING NEWS (1992). ... Named A.L. Rookie Player of the Year by THE SPORTING NEWS (1993). ... Named A.L. Rookie of the Year by Baseball Writers' Association of America (1993).

2004 GAMES PLAYED BY POSITION (MLB): DH—39, OF—8.

Year Team (League)	Pos.	G	AB	R	H	2B	3B	HR	RBI	BB	SO	HBP	GDP	SB-CS	Avg.	OBP	SLG	OPS	E	Avg.
1989— Bend (N'west)	OF	55	196	37	48	6	5	6	31	33	60	6	2	2-4	.245	.367	.418	.785	4	.958
1990— Palm Springs (Calif.)	OF	36	118	19	34	6	0	2	21	21	44	4	1	11-1	.288	.413	.390	.802	1	.985
— Midland (Texas)	OF	27	97	17	26	3	1	3	16	18	38	1	1	1-0	.268	.385	.412	.797	3	.950
1991— Midland (Texas)	OF	131	465	100	114	26	4	23	94	89	166	6	6	12-6	.245	.372	.467	.839	10	.966
1992— Edmonton (PCL)	OF	118	409	101	142	38	4	29	105	91	103	6	9	9-7	.347	.469	.672	1.141	3	.988
— California (A.L.)	OF	23	79	8	14	1	0	2	6	11	23	1	1	1-1	.177	.283	.266	.548	2	.953
1993— California (A.L.)	OF-DH	142	515	93	146	35	1	31	95	82	135	5	6	5-6	.284	.382	.536	.918	7	.980
1994— California (A.L.)	OF	100	373	67	107	18	2	23	70	54	102	5	3	1-3	.287	.382	.531	.912	8	.966
1995— California (A.L.)	OF-DH	143	537	111	177	34	3	34	105	91	111	6	9	5-5	.330	.429	.594	1.024	4	.988

Year	Team (League)	Pos.	G	AB	R	H	2B	3B	HR	RBI	BB	SO	HBP	GDP	SB-CS	Avg.	OBP	SLG	OPS	E	Avg.
1996— California (A.L.)		OF-DH	156	581	90	166	27	4	30	98	93	125	4	8	4-2	.286	.386	.501	.887	8	.975
1997— Anaheim (A.L.)		OF-DH	157	582	95	172	28	1	33	129	95	142	7	7	9-12	.296	.394	.517	.911	11	.971
1998— Anaheim (A.L.)		DH-OF	136	463	84	139	28	1	26	88	90	100	3	4	0-1	.300	.410	.533	.943	2	.959
1999— Anaheim (A.L.)		OF-DH	98	353	60	94	24	2	17	69	63	82	0	7	4-1	.266	.372	.490	.862	4	.981
— Lake Elsinore (Calif.)		DH	1	5	0	3	2	0	0	2	0	1	0	0	0-0	.600	.600	1.000	1.600	0	...
2000— Anaheim (A.L.)		OF-DH	158	568	108	165	36	2	34	97	104	139	6	14	0-2	.290	.394	.540	.945	6	.979
2001— Anaheim (A.L.)		OF-DH	137	475	63	108	21	1	17	49	96	121	8	11	9-3	.227	.365	.383	.748	3	.989
— Rancho Cuca. (Calif.)		OF	2	7	1	1	1	0	0	0	1	4	0	0	0-0	.143	.250	.286	.536	1	.667
2002— Anaheim (A.L.)		OF-DH	138	483	84	138	37	1	22	88	71	102	7	6	6-3	.286	.380	.503	.883	3	.986
2003— Anaheim (A.L.)		OF-DH	148	528	78	145	35	4	19	72	77	93	10	12	3-1	.275	.374	.464	.838	6	.958
2004— Rancho Cuca. (Calif.)		DH	7	23	5	8	1	1	2	6	4	6	0	0	0-0	.348	.444	.739	1.184	0	...
— Anaheim (A.L.)		DH-OF	60	186	15	47	7	0	2	23	14	41	2	2	1-0	.253	.306	.323	.628	0	1.000
Major League totals (13 years)			1596	5723	956	1618	331	22	290	989	941	1316	64	90	48-40	.283	.386	.500	.886	64	.978

DIVISION SERIES RECORD

Year	Team (League)	Pos.	G	AB	R	H	2B	3B	HR	RBI	BB	SO	HBP	GDP	SB-CS	Avg.	OBP	SLG	OPS	E	Avg.
2002— Anaheim (A.L.)		OF	4	19	3	5	1	0	2	7	1	5	0	0	0-0	.263	.300	.632	.932	0	1.000

CHAMPIONSHIP SERIES RECORD

Year	Team (League)	Pos.	G	AB	R	H	2B	3B	HR	RBI	BB	SO	HBP	GDP	SB-CS	Avg.	OBP	SLG	OPS	E	Avg.
2002— Anaheim (A.L.)		OF	5	14	0	3	0	0	0	3	1	0	1	1	0-0	.214	.353	.214	.567	0	1.000

WORLD SERIES RECORD

Year	Team (League)	Pos.	G	AB	R	H	2B	3B	HR	RBI	BB	SO	HBP	GDP	SB-CS	Avg.	OBP	SLG	OPS	E	Avg.
2002— Anaheim (A.L.)		OF	7	26	7	9	1	0	2	5	4	7	1	0	1-0	.346	.452	.615	1.067	1	.917

S

SANCHEZ, ALEX   OF

PERSONAL: Born August 26, 1976, in Havana, Cuba. ... 5-10/180. ... Bats left, throws left. ... Full name: Alexis Sanchez. ... Junior college: Miami-Dade Community College Wolfson.

TRANSACTIONS/CAREER NOTES: Selected by Tampa Bay Devil Rays organization in fifth round of 1996 free-agent draft. ... Claimed on waivers by Milwaukee Brewers (April 6, 2001). ... On disabled list (July 16-31, 2001; and September 2, 2002-remainder of season). ... Traded by Brewers to Detroit Tigers for P Chad Petty and OF Noochie Varner (May 27, 2003). ... On disabled list (July 8-29 and August 9, 2004-remainder of season); included rehabilitation assignment to Toledo.

2004 GAMES PLAYED BY POSITION (MLB): OF—78, DH—1.

Year	Team (League)	Pos.	G	AB	R	H	2B	3B	HR	RBI	BB	SO	HBP	GDP	SB-CS	Avg.	OBP	SLG	OPS	E	Avg.
													BATTING							FIELDING	
1996— GC Devil Rays (GCL)		OF	56	227	36	64	7	6	1	22	10	35	6	2	20-12	.282	.328	.379	.707	3	.968
1997— Char., S.C. (SAL)		OF	131	537	73	155	15	6	0	34	37	72	3	7	92-40	.289	.336	.339	.675	11	.963
1998— St. Pete. (FSL)		OF	128	545	77	180	17	9	1	50	31	70	1	5	66-33	.330	.360	.400	.760	12	.965
1999— Orlando (South.)		OF	121	500	68	127	12	4	2	29	26	88	0	8	48-26	.254	.290	.306	.596	14	.958
— Durham (Int'l)		OF	3	10	2	2	1	0	0	0	1	0	0	0	0-0	.200	.273	.300	.573	0	1.000
2000— Durham (Int'l)		OF	107	446	76	130	18	3	2	33	30	66	5	6	52-20	.291	.342	.359	.700	6	.977
— Orlando (South.)		OF	20	86	12	25	2	1	0	4	5	13	1	1	2-6	.291	.337	.337	.644	1	.972
2001— Indianapolis (Int'l)		OF	83	335	52	105	14	5	1	26	22	44	2	2	27-8	.313	.359	.394	.753	6	.968
— Milwaukee (N.L.)		OF	30	68	7	14	3	2	0	4	5	13	0	0	6-2	.206	.260	.309	.569	1	.963
2002— Milwaukee (N.L.)		OF	112	394	55	114	10	7	1	33	31	62	2	4	37-14	.289	.343	.358	.701	5	.982
2003— Milwaukee (N.L.)		OF	43	163	15	46	10	3	0	10	7	28	2	1	8-6	.282	.316	.380	.696	1	.990
— Detroit (A.L.)		OF	101	394	43	114	13	5	1	22	18	46	1	4	44-18	.289	.320	.355	.675	6	.979
2004— Toledo (Int'l)		OF	2	10	0	0	0	0	0	0	0	6	0	0	0-0	.000	...	.000	.000	0	1.000
— Detroit (A.L.)		OF-DH	79	332	41	107	9	3	2	26	7	50	0	5	19-13	.322	.335	.386	.721	9	.952
American League totals (2 years)			180	726	84	221	22	8	3	48	25	96	1	9	63-31	.304	.327	.369	.696	15	.968
National League totals (3 years)			185	625	77	174	23	12	1	47	43	103	4	5	51-22	.278	.327	.358	.685	7	.983
Major League totals (4 years)			365	1351	161	395	45	20	4	95	68	199	5	14	114-53	.292	.327	.364	.691	22	.975

SANCHEZ, DUANER   P

PERSONAL: Born October 14, 1979, in Cotui, Dominican Republic. ... 6-0/190. ... Throws right, bats right. ... High school: Francisco H. Carvajal (Cotui, Dominican Repblic).

TRANSACTIONS/CAREER NOTES: Signed as a non-drafted free agent by Arizona Diamondbacks organization (October 16, 1996). ... Traded by Diamondbacks to Pittsburgh Pirates for P Mike Fetters (July 6, 2002). ... Claimed on waivers by Los Angeles Dodgers (November 20, 2003).

CAREER HITTING: 1-for-4 (.250), 1 R, 1 2B, 0 3B, 0 HR, 2 RBI.

Year	Team (League)	W	L	Pct.	ERA	WHIP	G	GS	CG	ShO	Hld.	Sv.-Opp.	IP	H	R	ER	HR	BB-IBB	SO	Avg.
1997—Dominican Diamondbacks (DSL)		4	4	.500	5.13	1.76	21	6	0	0	...	1-...	59.2	57	50	34	...	48-...	44	...
1998—Dominican Diamondbacks (DSL)		2	3	.400	1.79	1.19	14	8	1	0	...	1-...	50.1	36	19	10	...	24-...	44	...
1999—High Desert (Calif.)		0	0	...	7.53	1.67	3	3	0	0	...	0-...	14.1	15	13	12	2	9-0	9	.288
— Missoula (Pio.)		5	3	.625	3.13	1.22	13	11	0	0	...	0-...	63.1	54	34	22	3	23-0	51	.224
2000—South Bend (Mid.)		8	9	.471	3.65	1.25	28	28	4	0	...	0-...	165.1	152	80	67	6	54-1	121	.243
2001—El Paso (Texas)		3	7	.300	6.78	1.66	13	13	0	0	...	0-...	70.1	92	56	53	5	25-1	41	.324
— Lancaster (Calif.)		2	4	.333	4.58	1.41	10	10	1	0	...	0-...	59.0	65	44	30	7	18-0	49	.274
2002—El Paso (Texas)		4	3	.571	3.03	1.23	31	0	0	0	...	13-...	35.2	31	16	12	1	13-1	37	.223
— Arizona (N.L.)		0	0	...	4.91	2.18	6	0	0	0	1	0-1	3.2	3	2	2	1	5-0	4	.214
— Tucson (PCL)		1	1	.500	6.75	1.31	4	0	0	0	...	1-...	5.1	6	4	4	1	1-0	9	.261
— Nashville (PCL)		0	3	.000	4.76	1.50	20	0	0	0	...	6-...	22.2	23	12	12	2	11-2	20	.274
— Pittsburgh (N.L.)		0	0	...	15.43	2.14	3	0	0	0	0	0-0	2.1	3	4	4	1	2-0	2	.300
2003—Nashville (PCL)		4	4	.500	3.69	1.50	41	1	0	0	...	1-...	61.0	63	28	25	3	27-5	34	.265
— Pittsburgh (N.L.)		1	0	1.000	16.50	2.67	6	0	0	0	0	0-0	6.0	15	11	11	2	1-0	3	.500
2004—Los Angeles (N.L.)		3	1	.750	3.38	1.35	67	0	0	0	4	0-1	80.0	81	34	30	9	27-2	44	.266
Major League totals (3 years)		4	1	.800	4.60	1.49	82	0	0	0	5	0-2	92.0	102	51	47	13	35-2	53	.285

DIVISION SERIES RECORD

Year	Team (League)	W	L	Pct.	ERA	WHIP	G	GS	CG	ShO	Hld.	Sv.-Opp.	IP	H	R	ER	HR	BB-IBB	SO	Avg.
2004— Los Angeles (N.L.)		0	0	...	0.00	1.00	2	0	0	0	0	0-0	2.0	1	0	0	0	1-0	3	.143

SANCHEZ, FREDDY   2B/3B

PERSONAL: Born December 21, 1977, in Hollywood, Calif. ... 5-10/192. ... Bats right, throws right. ... Full name: Frederick Philip Sanchez. ... Junior college: Oklahoma City Community College. ... College: Oklahoma City.

TRANSACTIONS/CAREER NOTES: Selected by Boston Red Sox organization in 11th round of 2000 free-agent draft. ... Traded by Red Sox with P Mike Gonzalez and cash to Pittsburgh Pirates for Ps Jeff Suppan, Brandon Lyon and Anastacio Martinez (July 31, 2003). ... On disabled list (March 26-July 9, 2004); included rehabilitation assignment to Nashville.

2004 GAMES PLAYED BY POSITION (MLB): SS—4, 2B—3, 3B—1.

										BATTING									FIELDING	
Year	Team (League)	Pos.	G	AB	R	H	2B	3B	HR	RBI	BB	SO	HBP	GDP	SB-CS	Avg.	OBP	SLG	OPS	E	Avg.
2000—Lowell (NY-Penn)	SS	34	132	24	38	13	2	1	14	9	16	3	1	2-4	.288	.347	.439	.787	4	.974
—Augusta (S. Atl.)	SS	30	109	17	33	7	0	0	15	11	19	1	1	4-0	.303	.372	.367	.739	3	.976
2001—Sarasota (Fla. St.)	SS	69	280	40	95	19	4	1	24	22	30	2	3	5-3	.339	.388	.446	.834	17	.944
—Trenton (East.)	SS	44	178	25	58	20	0	2	19	9	21	2	6	3-1	.326	.363	.472	.835	9	.948
2002—Trenton (East.)	SS-2B	80	311	60	102	23	1	3	38	37	45	5	9	19-3	.328	.403	.437	.841	16	.955
—Pawtucket (Int'l)	SS-2B	45	183	25	55	10	1	4	28	12	21	3	3	5-3	.301	.350	.432	.782	13	.942
—Boston (A.L.)	2B-SS-DH	12	16	3	3	0	0	0	2	2	3	0	0	0-0	.188	.278	.188	.465	0	1.000
2003—Boston (A.L.)	3B-SS-2B	20	34	6	8	2	0	0	2	0	8	0	0	0-0	.235	.235	.294	.529	0	1.000
—Pawtucket (Int'l)	S-2-3-DH	58	211	46	72	17	0	5	25	31	36	2	7	8-0	.341	.430	.493	.923	4	.983
—Nashville (PCL)	2B	1	5	1	2	1	0	0	0	0	1	0	0	0-0	.400	.400	.600	1.000	0	1.000
2004—Nashville (PCL)	SS-2B-3B	44	125	10	33	7	1	1	11	11	17	1	3	4-1	.264	.326	.360	.686	2	.983
—Pittsburgh (N.L.)	SS-2B-3B	9	19	2	3	0	0	0	2	0	3	0	0	0-0	.158	.158	.158	.316	1	.917
American League totals (2 years)		32	50	9	11	2	0	0	4	2	11	0	0	0-0	.220	.250	.260	.510	0	1.000
National League totals (1 year)		9	19	2	3	0	0	0	2	0	3	0	0	0-0	.158	.158	.158	.316	1	.917
Major League totals (3 years)		41	69	11	14	2	0	0	6	2	14	0	0	0-0	.203	.225	.232	.457	1	.986

SANCHEZ, JESUS   P

PERSONAL: Born October 11, 1974, in Nizao Bani, Dominican Republic. ... 5-10/165. ... Throws left, bats left. ... Full name: Jesus Paulino Sanchez. ... Name pronounced: HAY-soos.

TRANSACTIONS/CAREER NOTES: Signed as a non-drafted free agent by New York Mets organization (June 7, 1992). ... Traded by Mets with P A.J. Burnett and OF Robert Stratton to Florida Marlins for P Al Leiter and 2B Ralph Milliard (February 6, 1998). ... Traded by Marlins to Chicago Cubs for P Nate Teut (December 11, 2001). ... Released by Cubs (October 1, 2002). ... Signed by Houston Astros organization (December 10, 2002). ... Released by Astros (March 30, 2003). ... Signed by Colorado Rockies (August 24, 2003). ... Refused minor league assignment and became a free agent (September 30, 2003). ... Signed by Cincinnati Reds organization (January 23, 2004). ... Refused minor league assignment and became a free agent (July 21, 2004). ... Signed by Toronto Blue Jays organization (July 28, 2004).

CAREER HITTING: 25-for-142 (.176), 10 R, 0 2B, 1 3B, 0 HR, 6 RBI.

Year	Team (League)	W	L	Pct.	ERA	WHIP	G	GS	CG	ShO	Hld.	Sv.-Opp.	IP	H	R	ER	HR	BB-IBB	SO	Avg.
1992—Dom. Mets (DSL)	5	5	.500	4.19	1.52	15	15	1	0	...	0-...	81.2	86	52	38	...	38-...	72	...
1993—Dom. Mets (DSL)	7	3	.700	2.40	1.20	16	13	2	2	...	0-...	82.1	63	30	22	...	36-...	94	...
1994—Kingsport (Appalachian)	7	4	.636	1.96	1.01	13	12	3	0	...	0-...	87.1	61	27	19	2	27-0	71	.193
1995—Capital City (S. Atl.)	9	7	.563	3.13	1.25	27	27	4	0	...	0-...	169.2	154	76	59	9	58-0	177	.243
1996—St. Lucie (Fla. St.)	9	3	.750	1.96	0.84	16	16	2	1	...	0-...	92.0	53	22	20	6	24-0	81	.168
1997—Binghamton (Eastern)	13	10	.565	4.30	1.25	26	26	3	0	...	0-...	165.1	146	87	79	25	61-2	176	.237
1998—Florida (N.L.)	7	9	.438	4.47	1.55	35	29	0	0	0	0-1	173.0	178	98	86	18	91-2	137	.272
1999—Florida (N.L.)	5	7	.417	6.01	1.89	59	10	0	0	11	0-2	76.1	84	53	51	16	60-11	62	.291
—Calgary (PCL)	0	0	...	5.79	1.39	4	1	0	0	...	1-...	9.1	9	6	6	0	5-0	14	.242
2000—Florida (N.L.)	9	12	.429	5.34	1.50	32	32	2	2	0	0-0	182.0	197	118	108	32	76-4	123	.280
2001—Calgary (PCL)	6	1	.857	3.21	1.24	16	11	0	0	...	0-...	75.2	61	32	27	4	33-0	58	.216
—Florida (N.L.)	2	4	.333	4.74	1.47	16	9	0	0	0	0-0	62.2	61	33	33	7	31-2	46	.256
2002—Chicago (N.L.)	0	0	...	12.96	3.00	8	0	0	0	0	0-0	8.1	15	12	12	4	10-1	6	.395
—Iowa (PCL)	8	9	.471	5.90	1.67	26	24	0	0	...	0-...	125.0	144	90	82	27	65-3	94	.294
2003—Colo. Springs (PCL)	2	0	1.000	3.98	1.40	46	3	0	0	...	2-...	63.1	61	28	28	4	26-1	52	.257
—Colorado (N.L.)	0	0	...	9.00	1.88	9	0	0	0	1	0-0	8.0	11	8	8	1	4-2	2	.324
2004—Louisville (Int'l)	3	2	.600	3.00	1.28	22	5	0	0	...	1-...	60.0	49	22	20	6	28-2	51	.225
—Cincinnati (N.L.)	0	2	.000	7.53	1.88	3	3	0	0	0	0-0	14.1	18	12	12	4	10-1	8	.305
—Syracuse (Int'l)	1	4	.200	6.84	1.64	7	4	0	0	...	0-...	25.0	28	21	19	5	13-1	20	.283
Major League totals (7 years)	23	34	.404	5.32	1.61	162	83	2	2	12	0-3	524.2	564	334	310	82	281-22	384	.280

SANCHEZ, REY   2B

PERSONAL: Born October 5, 1967, in Rio Piedras, Puerto Rico. ... 5-9/170. ... Bats right, throws right. ... Full name: Rey Francisco Sanchez. ... Name pronounced: RAY SAN-chezz. ... High school: Live Oak (Morgan Hill, Calif.).

TRANSACTIONS/CAREER NOTES: Selected by Texas Rangers organization in 13th round of June 1986 free-agent draft. ... Traded by Rangers to Chicago Cubs for IF Bryan House (January 3, 1990). ... On disabled list (April 6, 1990-entire season). ... On disabled list (May 6-21, 1992); included rehabilitation assignment to Iowa. ... On disabled list (July 24-August 9, 1995). ... On disabled list (June 5-July 20 and August 11-September 1, 1996); included rehabilitation assignment to Iowa. ... Traded by Cubs to New York Yankees for P Frisco Parotte (August 16, 1997). ... Signed as a free agent by San Francisco Giants (January 22, 1998). ... Signed as a free agent by Kansas City Royals (December 11, 1998). ... Traded by Royals to Atlanta Braves for P Brad Voyles and 2B Alejandro Machado (July 31, 2001). ... Signed as a free agent by Boston Red Sox organization (February 27, 2002). ... On disabled list (June 13-July 11, 2002). ... On suspended list (September 15-16, 2002). ... Signed as a free agent by New York Mets (December 27, 2002). ... On disabled list (May 10-27 and June 6-July 1, 2003); included rehabilitation assignment to Binghamton. ... Traded by Mets with cash to Seattle Mariners for OF Kenny Kelly (July 29, 2003). ... Signed as a free agent by Tampa Bay Devil Rays (December 19, 2003).

2004 GAMES PLAYED BY POSITION (MLB): 2B—87, SS—4.

										BATTING									FIELDING	
Year	Team (League)	Pos.	G	AB	R	H	2B	3B	HR	RBI	BB	SO	HBP	GDP	SB-CS	Avg.	OBP	SLG	OPS	E	Avg.
1986—GC Rangers (GCL)	2B-SS	52	169	27	49	3	1	0	23	41	18	3	3	10-10	.290	.435	.320	.754	15	.938
1987—Gastonia (S. Atl.)	SS	50	160	19	35	1	2	1	10	22	17	2	9	6-3	.219	.321	.269	.589	18	.933
—Butte (Pio.)	SS	49	189	36	69	10	6	0	25	21	12	2	6	22-6	.365	.430	.481	.911	12	.953
1988—Charlotte (Fla. St.)	SS	128	418	60	128	6	5	0	38	35	24	5	14	29-11	.306	.364	.345	.709	35	.948
1989—Okla. City (A.A.)	SS	134	464	38	104	10	4	1	39	21	50	2	14	4-4	.224	.259	.269	.529	29	.958
1990—Iowa (Am. Assoc.)		Did not play.																		
1991—Iowa (Am. Assoc.)	SS	126	417	60	121	16	5	2	46	37	27	7	11	13-7	.290	.356	.367	.723	17	.971
—Chicago (N.L.)	2B-SS	13	23	1	6	0	0	0	2	4	3	0	0	0-0	.261	.370	.261	.631	0	1.000
1992—Iowa (Am. Assoc.)	SS-2B	20	76	12	26	3	0	0	3	4	1	0	3	6-3	.342	.375	.382	.757	5	.956

Year	Team (League)	Pos.	G	AB	R	H	2B	3B	HR	RBI	BB	SO	HBP	GDP	SB-CS	Avg.	OBP	SLG	OPS	E	Avg.
—	Chicago (N.L.)	SS-2B	74	255	24	64	14	3	1	19	10	17	3	7	2-1	.251	.285	.341	.626	9	.975
1993—	Chicago (N.L.)	SS	105	344	35	97	11	2	0	28	15	22	3	8	1-1	.282	.316	.326	.642	15	.969
1994—	Chicago (N.L.)	2B-SS-3B	96	291	26	83	13	1	0	24	20	29	7	9	2-5	.285	.345	.337	.682	9	.980
1995—	Chicago (N.L.)	2B-SS	114	428	57	119	22	2	3	27	14	48	1	9	6-4	.278	.301	.360	.661	7	.987
1996—	Chicago (N.L.)	SS	95	289	28	61	9	0	1	12	22	42	3	6	7-1	.211	.272	.253	.525	11	.977
—	Iowa (Am. Assoc.)	SS	3	12	2	2	0	0	0	1	1	2	0	0	2-0	.167	.231	.167	.397	1	.933
1997—	Chicago (N.L.)	SS-2B-3B	97	205	14	51	9	0	1	12	11	26	0	7	4-2	.249	.287	.307	.594	6	.977
—	New York (A.L.)	2B-SS	38	138	21	43	12	0	1	15	5	21	1	1	0-4	.312	.338	.420	.758	4	.978
1998—	San Francisco (N.L.)	SS-2B	109	316	44	90	14	2	2	30	16	47	4	11	0-0	.285	.325	.361	.686	8	.981
1999—	Kansas City (A.L.)	SS	134	479	66	141	18	6	2	56	22	48	4	14	11-5	.294	.329	.370	.698	13	.982
2000—	Kansas City (A.L.)	SS	143	509	68	139	18	2	1	38	28	55	4	17	7-3	.273	.314	.322	.637	4	.994
2001—	Kansas City (A.L.)	SS	100	390	46	118	14	5	0	28	11	34	2	11	9-1	.303	.322	.364	.686	3	.994
—	Atlanta (N.L.)	SS	49	154	10	35	4	1	0	9	4	15	0	9	2-0	.227	.245	.266	.512	3	.986
2002—	Boston (A.L.)	2B-SS	107	357	46	102	12	3	1	38	17	31	2	9	2-2	.286	.318	.345	.662	5	.989
2003—	Binghamton (East.)	SS	3	9	1	1	0	0	0	0	1	1	0	3	0-0	.111	.200	.111	.311	1	.900
—	New York (N.L.)	SS-2B	56	174	11	36	3	1	0	12	8	18	0	7	1-1	.207	.240	.236	.476	4	.981
—	Seattle (A.L.)	SS	46	170	22	50	5	1	0	11	8	21	2	3	1-0	.294	.330	.335	.665	4	.979
2004—	Tampa Bay (A.L.)	2B-SS	91	285	23	70	14	3	2	26	12	28	3	6	0-1	.246	.281	.337	.617	5	.988
American League totals (7 years)			659	2328	292	663	93	20	7	212	103	238	18	61	30-16	.285	.317	.351	.668	38	.988
National League totals (10 years)			808	2479	250	642	99	12	8	175	124	267	21	73	25-15	.259	.298	.318	.617	72	.979
Major League totals (14 years)			1467	4807	542	1305	192	32	15	387	227	505	39	134	55-31	.271	.308	.334	.642	110	.983

DIVISION SERIES RECORD

Year	Team (League)	Pos.	G	AB	R	H	2B	3B	HR	RBI	BB	SO	HBP	GDP	SB-CS	Avg.	OBP	SLG	OPS	E	Avg.
1997—	New York (A.L.)	2B	5	15	1	3	1	0	0	1	1	2	0	0	0-0	.200	.250	.267	.517	0	1.000
2001—	Atlanta (N.L.)	SS	3	9	1	2	1	0	0	0	0	2	0	1	0-0	.222	.222	.333	.556	1	.944
Division series totals (2 years)			8	24	2	5	2	0	0	1	1	4	0	1	0-0	.208	.240	.292	.532	1	.979

CHAMPIONSHIP SERIES RECORD

Year	Team (League)	Pos.	G	AB	R	H	2B	3B	HR	RBI	BB	SO	HBP	GDP	SB-CS	Avg.	OBP	SLG	OPS	E	Avg.
2001—	Atlanta (N.L.)	SS	5	17	1	5	1	0	0	0	0	4	0	0	0-0	.294	.294	.353	.647	2	.900

SANDERS, REGGIE   OF

PERSONAL: Born December 1, 1967, in Florence, S.C. ... 6-1/205. ... Bats right, throws right. ... Full name: Reginald Laverne Sanders. ... High school: Wilson (Florence, S.C.). ... Junior college: Spartanburg Methodist (S.C.). ... College: Spartanburg Methodist (S.C.).

TRANSACTIONS/CAREER NOTES: Selected by Cincinnati Reds organization in seventh round of 1987 free-agent draft. ... On disabled list (August 24-September 20, 1991; and May 13-29 and July 17-August 2, 1992). ... On suspended list (June 3-9, 1994). ... On disabled list (April 20-May 22, May 31-June 15 and September 17, 1996-remainder of season); included rehabilitation assignment to Indianapolis. ... On disabled list (April 19-May 6 and May 24-July 31, 1997); included rehabilitation assignments to Chattanooga and Indianapolis. ... Traded by Reds with SS Damian Jackson and P Josh Harris to San Diego Padres for OF Greg Vaughn and OF/1B Mark Sweeney (February 2, 1999). ... On disabled list (June 3-18, 1999). ... Traded by Padres with 2B Quilvio Veras and 1B Wally Joyner to Atlanta Braves for OF/1B Ryan Klesko, 2B Bret Boone and P Jason Shiell (December 22, 1999). ... On disabled list (April 30-May 23 and July 28-August 15, 2000). ... Signed as a free agent by Arizona Diamondbacks (January 5, 2001). ... On disabled list (March 23-April 8, 2001); included rehabilitation assignment to Tucson. ... Signed as a free agent by San Francisco Giants (January 8, 2002). ... Signed as a free agent by Pittsburgh Pirates (February 25, 2003). ... Signed as a free agent by St. Louis Cardinals (December 19, 2003).

2004 GAMES PLAYED BY POSITION (MLB): OF—119, DH—1.

Year	Team (League)	Pos.	G	AB	R	H	2B	3B	HR	RBI	BB	SO	HBP	GDP	SB-CS	Avg.	OBP	SLG	OPS	E	Avg.
1988—	Billings (Pio.)	SS	17	64	11	15	1	1	0	3	6	4	0	1	10-2	.234	.296	.281	.577	3	.944
1989—	Greensboro (S. Atl.)	SS	81	315	53	91	18	5	9	53	29	63	3	3	21-7	.289	.353	.463	.817	42	.875
1990—	Cedar Rap. (Midw.)	OF	127	466	89	133	21	4	17	63	59	97	4	8	40-15	.285	.370	.457	.827	10	.962
1991—	Chattanooga (Sou.)	OF	86	302	50	95	15	8	8	49	41	67	1	5	15-2	.315	.394	.497	.890	3	.982
—	Cincinnati (N.L.)	OF	9	40	6	8	0	1	1	3	0	9	0	1	1-1	.200	.200	.275	.475	0	1.000
1992—	Cincinnati (N.L.)	OF	116	385	62	104	26	6	12	36	48	98	4	6	16-7	.270	.356	.462	.819	6	.978
1993—	Cincinnati (N.L.)	OF	138	496	90	136	16	4	20	83	51	118	5	10	27-10	.274	.343	.444	.786	8	.975
1994—	Cincinnati (N.L.)	OF	107	400	66	105	20	8	17	62	41 *	114	2	2	21-9	.263	.332	.480	.812	6	.975
1995—	Cincinnati (N.L.)	OF	133	484	91	148	36	6	28	99	69	122	8	9	36-12	.306	.397	.579	.975	5	.982
1996—	Cincinnati (N.L.)	OF	81	287	49	72	17	1	14	33	44	86	2	8	24-8	.251	.353	.463	.817	2	.988
—	Indianapolis (A.A.)	OF-DH	4	12	3	5	2	0	0	1	1	4	1	0	0-1	.417	.500	.583	1.083	0	1.000
1997—	Cincinnati (N.L.)	OF	86	312	52	79	19	2	19	56	42	93	3	9	13-7	.253	.347	.510	.857	5	.974
—	Chattanooga (Sou.)	OF	3	11	3	6	1	1	1	3	1	2	1	0	0-0	.545	.615	1.091	1.706	0	1.000
—	Indianapolis (A.A.)	OF	5	19	1	4	0	0	1	1	6	6	0	0	0-0	.211	.250	.211	.461	2	.750
1998—	Cincinnati (N.L.)	OF	135	481	83	129	18	6	14	59	51	137	7	10	20-9	.268	.346	.418	.764	5	.978
1999—	San Diego (N.L.)	OF-DH	133	478	92	136	24	7	26	72	65	108	6	10	36-13	.285	.376	.527	.904	5	.975
2000—	Atlanta (N.L.)	OF	103	340	43	79	23	4	11	37	32	78	2	9	21-4	.232	.302	.403	.705	6	.964
2001—	Tucson (PCL)	OF	2	6	0	2	1	0	0	1	2	0	0	2	1-0	.333	.500	.500	1.000	0	1.000
—	Arizona (N.L.)	OF	126	441	84	116	21	3	33	90	46	126	5	2	14-10	.263	.337	.549	.886	1	.996
2002—	San Francisco (N.L.)	OF	140	505	75	126	23	4	23	85	47	121	12	10	18-6	.250	.324	.455	.779	5	.984
2003—	Pittsburgh (N.L.)	OF-DH	130	453	74	129	27	4	31	87	38	110	5	10	15-5	.285	.345	.567	.913	4	.983
2004—	St. Louis (N.L.)	OF-DH	135	446	64	116	27	3	22	67	33	118	4	5	21-5	.260	.315	.482	.797	4	.981
Major League totals (14 years)			1572	5548	931	1483	297	57	271	869	607	1438	65	101	283-106	.267	.344	.488	.832	64	.980

DIVISION SERIES RECORD

Year	Team (League)	Pos.	G	AB	R	H	2B	3B	HR	RBI	BB	SO	HBP	GDP	SB-CS	Avg.	OBP	SLG	OPS	E	Avg.
1995—	Cincinnati (N.L.)	OF	3	13	3	2	1	0	1	2	1	9	0	0	2-0	.154	.214	.462	.676	1	.875
2000—	Atlanta (N.L.)	OF	3	9	0	0	0	0	0	0	2	5	0	0	0-0	.000	.182	.000	.182	0	1.000
2001—	Arizona (N.L.)	OF	5	14	2	5	1	0	1	1	3	3	0	0	1-0	.357	.471	.643	1.113	0	1.000
2002—	San Francisco (N.L.)	OF	5	18	1	4	1	0	0	1	3	5	0	1	0-0	.222	.333	.278	.611	0	1.000
2004—	St. Louis (N.L.)	OF	4	14	3	4	0	0	1	1	0	2	1	2	1-0	.286	.333	.500	.833	0	1.000
Division series totals (5 years)			20	68	9	15	3	0	3	5	9	24	1	3	4-0	.221	.321	.397	.718	1	.980

CHAMPIONSHIP SERIES RECORD

Year	Team (League)	Pos.	G	AB	R	H	2B	3B	HR	RBI	BB	SO	HBP	GDP	SB-CS	Avg.	OBP	SLG	OPS	E	Avg.
1995—	Cincinnati (N.L.)	OF	4	16	0	2	0	0	0	0	2	10	0	2	0-1	.125	.222	.125	.347	1	.875
2001—	Arizona (N.L.)	OF	5	17	2	2	0	0	1	5	5	5	0	0	1-0	.118	.318	.118	.436	0	1.000
2002—	San Francisco (N.L.)	OF	4	16	0	1	0	0	0	0	0	4	0	0	0-0	.063	.063	.063	.125	0	1.000
2004—	St. Louis (N.L.)	OF	6	21	1	4	2	0	0	0	1	5	0	1	0-0	.190	.227	.286	.513	0	1.000
Champ. series totals (4 years)			19	70	3	9	2	0	1	5	8	24	0	3	1-1	.129	.218	.157	.375	1	.980

Year Team (League)	Pos.	G	AB	R	H	2B	3B	HR	RBI	BB	SO	HBP	GDP	SB-CS	Avg.	OBP	SLG	OPS	E	Avg.
2001— Arizona (N.L.)	OF	6	23	6	7	1	0	0	1	1	7	1	1	1-0	.304	.360	.348	.708	0	1.000
2002— San Francisco (N.L.)	OF	7	21	3	5	0	0	2	6	2	9	0	0	1-0	.238	.280	.524	.804	0	1.000
2004— St. Louis (N.L.)	OF-DH	4	9	1	0	0	0	0	0	4	5	0	0	1-0	.000	.308	.000	.308	0	1.000
World series totals (3 years)		17	53	10	12	1	0	2	7	7	21	1	1	3-0	.226	.317	.358	.676	0	1.000

ALL-STAR GAME RECORD

	G	AB	R	H	2B	3B	HR	RBI	BB	SO	HBP	GDP	SB-CS	Avg.	OBP	SLG	OPS	E	Avg.
All-Star Game totals (1 year)	1	1	0	0	0	0	0	0	0	1	0	0	0-0	.000	.000	.000	.000	0	...

SANTANA, JOHAN   P

PERSONAL: Born March 13, 1979, in Tovar Merida, Venezuela. ... 6-0/206. ... Throws left, bats left. ... Full name: Johan Alexander Santana. ... High school: Liceo Nucete Sardi (Venezuela).

TRANSACTIONS/CAREER NOTES: Signed as a non-drafted free agent by Houston Astros organization (July 2, 1995). ... Selected by Florida Marlins from Astros organization in Rule 5 major league draft (December 13, 1999). ... Traded by Marlins with cash to Minnesota Twins for P Jared Camp (December 13, 1999). ... On disabled list (July 7-September 21, 2001).

HONORS: Named A.L. Pitcher of the Year by THE SPORTING NEWS (2004). Named A.L. Cy Young Award winner. (2004)

CAREER HITTING: 5-for-16 (.313), 0 R, 0 2B, 0 3B, 0 HR, 2 RBI.

Year Team (League)	W	L	Pct.	ERA	WHIP	G	GS	CG	ShO	Hld.	Sv.-Opp.	IP	H	R	ER	HR	BB-IBB	SO	Avg.
1996— Dom. Astros (DSL).	4	3	.571	2.70	1.20	23	1	0	0	...	3-...	40.0	26	16	12	...	22-...	51	...
1997— GC Astros (GCL)	0	4	.000	7.93	1.84	9	5	1	0	...	0-...	36.1	49	36	32	2	18-0	25	.322
— Auburn (N.Y.-Penn)	0	0	...	2.25	1.75	1	1	0	0	...	0-...	4.0	1	1	1	0	6-0	5	.083
1998— Quad City (Midw.)	0	1	.000	9.45	2.55	2	1	0	0	...	0-...	6.2	14	7	7	1	3-0	6	.452
— Auburn (N.Y.-Penn)	7	5	.583	4.36	1.18	15	15	1	1	...	0-...	86.2	81	52	42	9	21-0	88	.243
1999— Michigan (Midw.)	8	8	.500	4.66	1.35	27	26	1	0	...	0-...	160.1	162	94	83	14	55-0	150	.263
2000— Minnesota (A.L.)	2	3	.400	6.49	1.81	30	5	0	0	0	0-0	86.0	102	64	62	11	54-0	64	.302
2001— Minnesota (A.L.)	1	0	1.000	4.74	1.51	15	4	0	0	0	0-0	43.2	50	25	23	6	16-0	28	.292
2002— Edmonton (PCL)	5	2	.714	3.14	1.32	11	9	0	0	...	0-...	48.2	37	24	17	7	27-0	75	.202
— Minnesota (A.L.)	8	6	.571	2.99	1.23	27	14	0	0	3	1-1	108.1	84	41	36	7	49-0	137	.212
2003— Minnesota (A.L.)	12	3	.800	3.07	1.10	45	18	0	0	5	0-0	158.1	127	56	54	17	47-1	169	.216
2004— Minnesota (A.L.)	20	6	.769	* 2.61	0.92	34	34	1	1	0	0-0	228.0	156	70	66	24	54-0	* 265	.192
Major League totals (5 years)	43	18	.705	3.47	1.18	151	75	1	1	8	1-1	624.1	519	258	241	65	220-1	663	.225

DIVISION SERIES RECORD

Year Team (League)	W	L	Pct.	ERA	WHIP	G	GS	CG	ShO	Hld.	Sv.-Opp.	IP	H	R	ER	HR	BB-IBB	SO	Avg.
2002— Minnesota (A.L.)	0	0	...	6.00	1.67	2	0	0	0	1	0-0	3.0	3	2	2	0	2-0	2	.250
2003— Minnesota (A.L.)	0	1	.000	7.04	1.57	2	2	0	0	0	0-0	7.2	9	6	6	0	3-1	6	.290
2004— Minnesota (A.L.)	1	0	1.000	0.75	1.50	2	2	0	0	0	0-0	12.0	14	1	1	0	4-0	12	.304
Division series totals (3 years)	1	1	.500	3.57	1.54	6	4	0	0	1	0-0	22.2	26	9	9	0	9-1	20	.292

CHAMPIONSHIP SERIES RECORD

Year Team (League)	W	L	Pct.	ERA	WHIP	G	GS	CG	ShO	Hld.	Sv.-Opp.	IP	H	R	ER	HR	BB-IBB	SO	Avg.
2002— Minnesota (A.L.)	0	1	.000	10.80	1.20	4	0	0	0	0	0-0	3.1	4	4	4	1	0-0	4	.286

SANTIAGO, BENITO   C

PERSONAL: Born March 9, 1965, in Ponce, Puerto Rico. ... 6-1/200. ... Bats right, throws right. ... Full name: Benito Rivera Santiago. ... Name pronounced: sahn-tee-AH-go. ... High school: John F. Kennedy (Ponce, Puerto Rico).

TRANSACTIONS/CAREER NOTES: Signed as a non-drafted free agent by San Diego Padres organization (September 1, 1982). ... On disabled list (June 15-August 10, 1990); included rehabilitation assignment to Las Vegas. ... On disabled list (May 31-July 11, 1992); included rehabilitation assignment to Las Vegas. ... Signed as a free agent by Florida Marlins (December 16, 1992). ... On suspended list (May 5-9, 1994). ... Signed as a free agent by Cincinnati Reds (April 17, 1995). ... On disabled list (May 8-July 4, 1995). ... Signed as a free agent by Philadelphia Phillies (January 30, 1996). ... Signed as a free agent by Toronto Blue Jays (December 9, 1996). ... On disabled list (April 14-29, 1997). ... On disabled list (March 18-September 3, 1998); included rehabilitation assignments to Dunedin and Syracuse. ... Signed as a free agent by Chicago Cubs (December 10, 1998). ... Signed as a free agent by Reds organization (February 24, 2000). ... Signed as a free agent by San Francisco Giants organization (March 17, 2001). ... On suspended list (September 20-22, 2002). ... On disabled list (July 14-29, 2003). ... Signed as a free agent by Kansas City Royals (December 11, 2003). ... On disabled list (June 19, 2004-remainder of season).

HONORS: Named N.L. Rookie Player of the Year by THE SPORTING NEWS (1987). ... Named N.L. Rookie of the Year by Baseball Writers' Association of America (1987). ... Won N.L. Gold Glove at catcher (1988-90).

2004 GAMES PLAYED BY POSITION (MLB): C—49.

Year Team (League)	Pos.	G	AB	R	H	2B	3B	HR	RBI	BB	SO	HBP	GDP	SB-CS	Avg.	OBP	SLG	OPS	E	Avg.
1983— Miami (Fla. St.)	C	122	429	34	106	25	3	5	56	11	79	7	...	3-7	.247	.276	.354	.630	21	.963
1984— Reno (Calif.)	C	114	416	64	116	20	6	16	83	36	75	4	11	5-2	.279	.338	.471	.809	25	.969
1985— Beaumont (Texas)	3B-C-1B	101	372	55	111	16	6	5	52	16	59	2	6	12-2	.298	.328	.414	.742	15	.976
1986— Las Vegas (PCL)	C	117	437	55	125	26	3	17	71	17	81	1	12	19-7	.286	.312	.476	.788	21	.968
— San Diego (N.L.)	C	17	62	10	18	2	0	3	6	2	12	0	0	0-1	.290	.308	.468	.775	5	.946
1987— San Diego (N.L.)	C	146	546	64	164	33	2	18	79	16	112	5	12	21-12	.300	.324	.467	.791	* 22	.976
1988— San Diego (N.L.)	C	139	492	49	122	22	2	10	46	24	82	1	18	15-7	.248	.282	.362	.643	* 12	.985
1989— San Diego (N.L.)	C	129	462	50	109	16	3	16	62	26	89	1	9	11-6	.236	.277	.387	.664	* 20	.975
1990— San Diego (N.L.)	C	100	344	42	93	8	5	11	53	27	55	3	4	5-5	.270	.323	.419	.741	12	.980
— Las Vegas (PCL)	C	6	20	5	6	2	0	1	8	3	1	0	1	1-0	.300	.375	.550	.925	0	1.000
1991— San Diego (N.L.)	C-OF	152	580	60	155	22	3	17	87	23	114	4	21	8-10	.267	.296	.403	.700	‡ 14	.985
1992— San Diego (N.L.)	C	106	386	37	97	21	0	10	42	21	52	0	14	2-5	.251	.287	.383	.671	* 12	.982
— Las Vegas (PCL)	C	4	13	3	4	0	0	1	2	1	1	0	0	0-0	.308	.357	.538	.896	1	1.000
1993— Florida (N.L.)	C-OF	139	469	49	108	19	6	13	50	37	88	5	9	10-7	.230	.291	.380	.671	• 11	.987
1994— Florida (N.L.)	C	101	337	35	92	14	2	11	41	25	57	1	11	1-2	.273	.322	.424	.746	5	.991
1995— Cincinnati (N.L.)	C-1B	81	266	40	76	20	4	11	44	24	48	4	7	2-2	.286	.351	.485	.836	2	.996
1996— Philadelphia (N.L.)	C-1B	136	481	71	127	21	2	30	85	49	104	1	8	2-0	.264	.332	.503	.835	11	.988
1997— Toronto (A.L.)	C-DH	97	341	31	83	10	0	13	42	17	80	2	10	1-0	.243	.279	.387	.667	2	.997
1998— Dunedin (Fla. St.)	DH-C	11	37	4	6	1	0	1	5	3	9	0	1	3-0	.162	.225	.270	.495	0	1.000
— Syracuse (Int'l)	C-DH	5	22	0	5	2	0	0	2	1	3	0	0	0-0	.227	.261	.318	.579	0	1.000
— Toronto (A.L.)	C	15	29	3	9	5	0	0	4	1	6	0	0	0-0	.310	.333	.483	.816	0	1.000

Year Team (League)	Pos.	G	AB	R	H	2B	3B	HR	RBI	BB	SO	HBP	GDP	SB-CS	Avg.	OBP	SLG	OPS	E	Avg.
1999— Chicago (N.L.)	C-1B	109	350	28	87	18	3	7	36	32	71	2	12	1-1	.249	.313	.377	.691	6	.990
2000— Cincinnati (N.L.)	C	89	252	22	66	11	1	8	45	19	45	1	7	2-2	.262	.310	.409	.719	3	.994
2001— San Francisco (N.L.)	C-1B	133	477	39	125	25	4	6	45	23	78	2	19	5-4	.262	.295	.369	.664	5	.994
2002— San Francisco (N.L.)	C	126	478	56	133	24	5	16	74	27	73	2	19	4-2	.278	.315	.450	.765	4	.995
2003— San Francisco (N.L.)	C	108	401	53	112	21	2	11	56	29	69	2	13	0-1	.279	.329	.424	.753	5	.993
2004— Kansas City (A.L.)	C	49	175	15	48	10	0	6	23	8	32	2	9	1-2	.274	.312	.434	.746	1	.996
American League totals (3 years)		161	545	49	140	25	0	19	69	26	118	4	20	2-2	.257	.293	.407	.700	3	.997
National League totals (16 years)		1811	6383	705	1684	297	40	198	851	404	1149	34	183	89-67	.264	.308	.416	.724	149	.987
Major League totals (19 years)		1972	6928	754	1824	322	40	217	920	430	1267	38	203	91-69	.263	.307	.415	.722	152	.987

DIVISION SERIES RECORD

Year Team (League)	Pos.	G	AB	R	H	2B	3B	HR	RBI	BB	SO	HBP	GDP	SB-CS	Avg.	OBP	SLG	OPS	E	Avg.
1995— Cincinnati (N.L.)	C	3	9	2	3	0	0	1	3	3	3	0	0	0-0	.333	.462	.667	1.128	0	1.000
2002— San Francisco (N.L.)	C	5	21	1	5	2	0	0	5	1	5	0	1	0-0	.238	.273	.333	.606	1	.971
2003— San Francisco (N.L.)	C	4	11	0	2	0	0	0	0	1	2	0	0	0-0	.182	.250	.182	.432	0	1.000
Division series totals (3 years)		12	41	3	10	2	0	1	8	5	10	0	1	0-0	.244	.319	.366	.685	1	.986

CHAMPIONSHIP SERIES RECORD

Year Team (League)	Pos.	G	AB	R	H	2B	3B	HR	RBI	BB	SO	HBP	GDP	SB-CS	Avg.	OBP	SLG	OPS	E	Avg.
1995— Cincinnati (N.L.)	C	4	13	0	3	0	0	0	0	2	3	0	1	0-0	.231	.333	.231	.564	0	1.000
2002— San Francisco (N.L.)	C	5	20	2	6	0	0	2	6	2	4	0	1	0-0	.300	.364	.600	.964	0	1.000
Champ. series totals (2 years)		9	33	2	9	0	0	2	6	4	7	0	2	0-0	.273	.351	.455	.806	0	1.000

WORLD SERIES RECORD

Year Team (League)	Pos.	G	AB	R	H	2B	3B	HR	RBI	BB	SO	HBP	GDP	SB-CS	Avg.	OBP	SLG	OPS	E	Avg.
2002— San Francisco (N.L.)	C	7	26	2	6	0	0	0	5	3	4	0	3	0-0	.231	.300	.231	.531	1	.976

ALL-STAR GAME RECORD

	G	AB	R	H	2B	3B	HR	RBI	BB	SO	HBP	GDP	SB-CS	Avg.	OBP	SLG	OPS	E	Avg.
All-Star Game totals (4 years)	4	7	0	1	0	0	0	0	0	4	0	0	0-0	.143	.143	.143	.286	1	.875

SANTIAGO, RAMON — SS/2B

PERSONAL: Born August 31, 1979, in Las Matas de Farfan, Dominican Republic. ... 5-11/167. ... Bats both, throws right. ... Full name: Ramon D. Santiago.
TRANSACTIONS/CAREER NOTES: Signed as a non-drafted free agent by Detroit Tigers organization (July 29, 1998). ... On disabled list (July 24-September 1, 2002). ... Traded by Tigers with SS Juan Gonzalez to Seattle Mariners for SS Carlos Guillen (January 8, 2004).
2004 GAMES PLAYED BY POSITION (MLB): SS—16, DH—2.

Year Team (League)	Pos.	G	AB	R	H	2B	3B	HR	RBI	BB	SO	HBP	GDP	SB-CS	Avg.	OBP	SLG	OPS	E	Avg.
1999— GC Tigers (GCL)	SS	35	134	25	43	9	2	0	11	9	17	1	3	20-7	.321	.361	.418	.778	4	.974
— Oneonta (N.Y.-Penn.)	SS	12	50	9	17	1	2	1	8	2	12	1	0	5-0	.340	.377	.500	.877	1	.979
2000— W. Mich. (Mid.)	SS	98	379	69	103	15	1	1	42	34	60	12	10	39-12	.272	.346	.325	.670	8	.976
2001— Lakeland (Fla. St.)	DH	120	429	64	115	15	3	2	46	54	60	11	7	34-8	.268	.361	.331	.692	...	...
2002— Erie (East.)	SS	22	75	9	21	0	2	1	7	3	12	3	2	6-0	.280	.329	.373	.703	3	.966
— Toledo (Int'l)	SS	9	28	8	12	1	0	2	6	3	4	2	0	0-2	.429	.515	.679	1.194	2	.956
— Detroit (A.L.)	SS-DH	65	222	33	54	5	5	4	20	13	48	8	2	8-5	.243	.306	.365	.671	7	.977
2003— Detroit (A.L.)	SS-2B	141	444	41	100	18	1	2	29	33	66	10	9	10-4	.225	.292	.284	.576	20	.970
2004— Tacoma (PCL)	SS-2B	71	243	35	47	7	2	1	24	24	31	10	3	9-6	.193	.288	.251	.539	6	.981
— Seattle (A.L.)	SS-DH	19	39	8	7	1	0	0	2	3	3	1	1	0-0	.179	.256	.205	.461	3	.946
Major League totals (3 years)		225	705	82	161	24	6	6	51	49	117	19	12	18-9	.228	.295	.305	.600	30	.971

SANTOS, VICTOR — P

PERSONAL: Born October 2, 1976, in San Pedro de Macoris, Dominican Republic. ... 6-3/190. ... Throws right, bats right. ... Full name: Victor Irving Santos. ... High school: Passaic (N.J.).
TRANSACTIONS/CAREER NOTES: Signed as a non-drafted free agent by Detroit Tigers organization (June 11, 1995). ... Traded by Tigers with IF Ronnie Merrill to Colorado Rockies for P Jose Paniagua (March 25, 2002). ... Released by Rockies (October 9, 2002). ... Signed by Texas Rangers organization (November 13, 2002). ... Signed as a free agent by Milwaukee Brewers organization (December 3, 2003).
CAREER HITTING: 3-for-43 (.070), 0 R, 1 2B, 0 3B, 0 HR, 1 RBI.

Year Team (League)	W	L	Pct.	ERA	WHIP	G	GS	CG	ShO	Hld.	Sv.-Opp.	IP	H	R	ER	HR	BB-IBB	SO	Avg.
1995— Dominican Tigers (DSL)	7	5	.583	3.72	1.37	15	12	3	2	...	0-...	77.1	88	46	32	...	18-...	75	
1996— Lakeland (Fla. St.)	2	2	.500	2.22	0.99	5	4	0	0	...	0-...	28.1	19	11	7	2	9-0	25	.194
— GC Tigers (GCL)	3	2	.600	1.98	1.14	9	9	0	0	...	0-...	50.0	44	12	11	1	13-0	39	.251
1997— Lakeland (Fla. St.)	10	5	.667	3.23	1.34	26	26	4	2	...	0-...	145.0	136	74	52	10	59-1	108	.248
1998— Lakeland (Fla. St.)	5	2	.714	2.51	1.12	16	15	0	0	...	1-...	100.1	88	38	28	9	24-1	74	.235
— Toledo (International)	1	2	.333	11.05	2.32	5	3	0	0	...	0-...	14.2	24	22	18	5	10-0	12	.353
— Jacksonville (Southern)	4	2	.667	4.17	1.50	6	6	0	0	...	0-...	36.2	40	20	17	2	15-1	37	.288
1999— Jacksonville (Southern)	12	6	.667	3.49	1.20	28	28	2	1	...	0-...	173.0	150	86	67	16	58-2	146	.230
2000— GC Tigers (GCL)	0	0	...	0.00	1.33	1	1	0	0	...	0-...	3.0	2	1	0	0	2-0	5	.182
— Lakeland (Fla. St.)	1	0	1.000	0.00	1.20	1	1	0	0	...	0-...	5.0	5	0	0	0	1-0	4	.263
— Toledo (International)	0	1	.000	11.37	2.05	2	2	0	0	...	0-...	6.1	7	8	8	4	6-0	2	.280
2001— Detroit (A.L.)	2	2	.500	3.30	1.45	33	7	0	0	2	0-0	76.1	62	33	28	9	49-4	52	.222
— Toledo (International)	2	1	.667	6.37	1.75	6	6	0	0	...	0-...	35.1	50	27	25	6	12-0	22	.340
2002— Colo. Springs (PCL)	4	9	.308	5.72	1.61	21	21	1	1	...	0-...	118.0	147	81	75	17	43-0	134	.307
— Colorado (N.L.)	0	4	.000	10.38	2.42	24	2	0	0	1	0-0	26.0	41	30	30	3	22-3	25	.360
2003— Texas (A.L.)	0	2	.000	7.01	1.75	8	4	0	0	0	0-0	25.2	29	21	20	5	16-1	15	.299
— Oklahoma (PCL)	5	4	.556	3.41	1.40	20	16	1	1	...	1-...	108.1	112	54	41	6	35-0	65	.264
2004— Indianapolis (Int'l)	0	0	...	3.48	1.55	3	3	0	0	...	0-...	10.1	12	4	4	1	4-0	11	.308
— Milwaukee	11	12	.478	4.97	1.47	31	28	0	0	0	0-0	154.0	169	95	85	18	57-5	115	.278
American League totals (2 years)	2	4	.333	4.24	1.53	41	11	0	0	2	0-0	102.0	91	54	48	14	65-5	67	.242
National League totals (2 years)	11	16	.407	5.75	1.61	55	30	0	0	1	0-0	180.0	210	125	115	21	79-8	140	.291
Major League totals (4 years)	13	20	.394	5.20	1.58	96	41	0	0	3	0-0	282.0	301	179	163	35	144-13	207	.274

SAUERBECK, SCOTT — P

PERSONAL: Born November 9, 1971, in Cincinnati, Ohio. ... 6-3/200. ... Throws left, bats right. ... Full name: Scott William Sauerbeck. ... Name pronounced: SOW-er-beck. ... High school: Northwest (Cincinnati). ... College: Miami (Ohio).

TRANSACTIONS/CAREER NOTES: Selected by New York Mets organization in 23rd round of 1994 free-agent draft. ... Selected by Pittsburgh Pirates from Mets organization in Rule 5 major league draft (December 14, 1998). ... On Pittsburgh disabled list (June 14-July 3, 2000); included rehabilitation assignment to Nashville (June 29-July 3). ... Traded by Pirates with P Jeff Suppan to Boston Red Sox for 2B Freddy Sanchez (July 31, 2003). ... Signed as a free agent by Cleveland Indians organization (March 20, 2004).

CAREER HITTING: 0-for-7 (.000), 0 R, 0 2B, 0 3B, 0 HR, 0 RBI.

Year Team (League)	W	L	Pct.	ERA	WHIP	G	GS	CG	ShO	Hld.	Sv.-Opp.	IP	H	R	ER	HR	BB-IBB	SO	Avg.
1994— Pittsfield (N.Y.-Penn.)	3	1	.750	2.05	1.20	21	0	0	0	...	1-...	48.1	39	16	11	0	19-2	39	.222
1995— St. Lucie (Fla. St.)	0	1	.000	2.03	1.50	20	1	0	0	...	0-...	26.2	26	10	6	0	14-1	25	.260
— Capital City (S. Atl.)	5	4	.556	3.27	1.27	19	0	0	0	...	2-...	33.0	28	14	12	2	14-1	33	.230
1996— St. Lucie (Fla. St.)	6	6	.500	2.27	1.29	17	16	2	2	...	0-...	99.1	101	37	25	1	27-0	62	.269
— Binghamton (Eastern)	3	3	.500	3.47	1.29	8	8	2	0	...	0-...	46.2	48	24	18	4	12-0	30	.274
1997— Binghamton (Eastern)	8	9	.471	4.93	1.48	27	20	2	0	...	0-...	131.1	144	89	72	15	50-0	88	.280
— Norfolk (Int'l)	1	0	1.000	3.60	1.40	1	1	0	0	...	0-...	5.0	3	2	2	0	4-0	4	.200
1998— Norfolk (Int'l)	7	13	.350	3.93	1.54	27	27	2	0	...	0-...	160.1	178	82	70	8	69-1	119	.287
1999— Pittsburgh (N.L.)	4	1	.800	2.00	1.34	65	0	0	0	10	2-5	67.2	53	19	15	6	38-5	55	.220
2000— Pittsburgh (N.L.)	5	4	.556	4.04	1.81	75	0	0	0	13	1-4	75.2	76	36	34	4	61-8	83	.270
— Nashville (PCL)	0	0	...	0.00	0.50	2	0	0	0	...	0-...	2.0	1	0	0	0	0-0	0	.167
2001— Pittsburgh (N.L.)	2	2	.500	5.60	1.61	70	0	0	0	19	2-4	62.2	61	41	39	4	40-6	79	.257
2002— Pittsburgh (N.L.)	5	4	.556	2.30	1.23	78	0	0	0	28	0-0	62.2	50	18	16	4	27-4	70	.220
2003— Pittsburgh (N.L.)	3	4	.429	4.05	1.38	53	0	0	0	16	0-4	40.0	30	20	18	5	25-2	32	.207
— Boston (A.L.)	0	1	.000	6.48	2.10	26	0	0	0	2	0-1	16.2	17	14	12	1	18-3	18	.266
2004— Cleveland (A.L.)	Did not play.																		
American League totals (1 year)	0	1	.000	6.48	2.10	26	0	0	0	2	0-1	16.2	17	14	12	1	18-3	18	.266
National League totals (5 years)	19	15	.559	3.56	1.49	341	0	0	0	86	5-17	308.2	270	134	122	23	191-25	319	.239
Major League totals (5 years)	19	16	.543	3.71	1.52	367	0	0	0	88	5-18	325.1	287	148	134	24	209-28	337	.240

CHAMPIONSHIP SERIES RECORD

Year Team (League)	W	L	Pct.	ERA	WHIP	G	GS	CG	ShO	Hld.	Sv.-Opp.	IP	H	R	ER	HR	BB-IBB	SO	Avg.
2003— Boston (A.L.)	0	0	...	0.00	6.00	1	0	0	0	0	0-0	.1	1	0	0	0	1-0	0	.500

SCHILLING, CURT — P

PERSONAL: Born November 14, 1966, in Anchorage, Alaska. ... 6-5/235. ... Throws right, bats right. ... Full name: Curtis Montague Schilling. ... Name pronounced: SHILL-ing. ... High school: Shadow Mountain (Phoenix). ... Junior college: Yavapai (Ariz.).

TRANSACTIONS/CAREER NOTES: Selected by Boston Red Sox organization in second round of January 1986 free-agent draft. ... Traded by Red Sox with OF Brady Anderson to Baltimore Orioles for P Mike Boddicker (July 29, 1988). ... Traded by Orioles with P Pete Harnisch and OF Steve Finley to Houston Astros for 1B Glenn Davis (January 10, 1991). ... Traded by Astros to Philadelphia Phillies for P Jason Grimsley (April 2, 1992). ... On disabled list (May 17-July 25, 1994); included rehabilitation assignments to Scranton/Wilkes-Barre and Reading. ... On disabled list (July 19, 1995-remainder of season). ... On disabled list (March 23-May 14, 1996); included rehabilitation assignments to Clearwater and Scranton/Wilkes-Barre. ... On disabled list (August 8-September 3, 1999). ... On disabled list (March 25-April 30, 2000); included rehabilitation assignments to Clearwater and Scranton/Wilkes-Barre. ... Traded by Phillies to Arizona Diamondbacks for 1B/OF Travis Lee and Ps Omar Daal, Vicente Padilla and Nelson Figueroa (July 26, 2000). ... On disabled list (April 18-May 3 and May 31-July 12, 2003); included rehabilitation assignment to Tucson. ... Traded by Diamondbacks to Boston Red Sox for Ps Casey Fossum, Brandon Lyon and Jorge de la Rosa and a player to be named (November 28, 2003); Diamondbacks acquired OF Michael Goss to complete deal (December 15, 2003).

HONORS: Named N.L. Pitcher of the Year by THE SPORTING NEWS (2001 and 2002).

CAREER HITTING: 115-for-769 (.150), 39 R, 13 2B, 1 3B, 0 HR, 29 RBI.

Year Team (League)	W	L	Pct.	ERA	WHIP	G	GS	CG	ShO	Hld.	Sv.-Opp.	IP	H	R	ER	HR	BB-IBB	SO	Avg.
1986— Elmira (N.Y.-Penn)	7	3	.700	2.59	1.30	16	15	2	1	...	0-...	93.2	92	34	27	3	30-1	75	.254
1987— Greensboro (S. Atl.)	8	15	.348	3.82	1.33	29	28	7	3	...	0-...	184.0	179	96	78	10	65-8	189	.255
1988— New Britain (East.)	8	5	.615	2.97	1.24	21	17	4	1	...	0-...	106.0	91	44	35	4	40-0	62	.232
— Charlotte (Sou.)	5	2	.714	3.18	1.30	7	7	2	1	...	0-...	45.1	36	19	16	3	23-0	32	.217
— Baltimore (A.L.)	0	3	.000	9.82	2.18	4	4	0	0	...	0-0	14.2	22	19	16	3	10-1	4	.355
1989— Rochester (Int'l)	13	11	.542	3.21	1.27	27	27	9	3	...	0-...	185.1	176	76	66	11	59-0	109	.254
— Baltimore (A.L.)	0	1	.000	6.23	1.50	5	1	0	0	0	0-0	8.2	10	6	6	2	3-0	6	.286
1990— Rochester (Int'l)	4	4	.500	3.92	1.37	15	14	1	0	...	0-...	87.1	95	46	38	10	25-1	83	.277
— Baltimore (A.L.)	1	2	.333	2.54	1.24	35	0	0	0	5	3-9	46.0	38	13	13	1	19-0	32	.229
1991— Houston (N.L.)	3	5	.375	3.81	1.56	56	0	0	0	5	8-11	75.2	79	35	32	2	39-7	71	.271
— Tucson (PCL)	0	1	.000	3.42	1.18	13	0	0	0	...	3-...	23.2	16	9	9	0	12-1	21	.186
1992— Philadelphia (N.L.)	14	11	.560	2.35	0.99	42	26	10	4	0	2-3	226.1	165	67	59	11	59-4	147	* .201
1993— Philadelphia (N.L.)	16	7	.696	4.02	1.24	34	34	7	2	0	0-0	235.1	234	114	105	23	57-6	186	.259
1994— Philadelphia (N.L.)	2	8	.200	4.48	1.40	13	13	1	0	0	0-0	82.1	87	42	41	10	28-3	58	.270
— Scran./W.B. (I.L.)	0	0	...	1.80	1.10	2	2	0	0	...	0-...	10.0	6	2	2	0	5-0	6	.171
— Reading (East.)	0	0	...	0.00	1.75	1	1	0	0	...	0-...	4.0	6	0	0	0	1-0	4	.375
1995— Philadelphia (N.L.)	7	5	.583	3.57	1.05	17	17	1	0	0	0-0	116.0	96	52	46	12	26-2	114	.220
1996— Clearwater (Fla. St.)	2	0	1.000	1.29	0.71	2	2	0	0	...	0-...	14.0	9	2	2	0	1-0	17	.173
— Scran./W.B. (I.L.)	1	0	1.000	1.38	1.08	2	2	0	0	...	0-...	13.0	9	2	2	0	5-0	10	.200
— Philadelphia (N.L.)	9	10	.474	3.19	1.09	26	26	* 8	2	0	0-0	183.1	149	69	65	16	50-5	182	.223
1997— Philadelphia (N.L.)	17	11	.607	2.97	1.05	35	* 35	7	2	0	0-0	254.1	208	96	84	25	58-3	* 319	.224
1998— Philadelphia (N.L.)	15	14	.517	3.25	1.11	35	* 35	* 15	2	0	0-0	* 268.2	236	101	97	23	61-3	* 300	.236
1999— Philadelphia (N.L.)	15	6	.714	3.54	1.13	24	24	8	1	0	0-0	180.1	159	74	71	25	44-0	152	.237
2000— Clearwater (Fla. St.)	1	0	1.000	1.31	0.58	4	4	0	0	...	0-...	20.2	10	3	3	0	2-0	23	.137
— Scran./W.B. (I.L.)	0	0	...	3.60	2.00	1	1	0	0	...	0-...	5.0	9	2	2	0	1-0	7	.375
— Philadelphia (N.L.)	6	6	.500	3.91	1.26	16	16	4	1	0	0-0	112.2	110	49	49	17	32-4	96	.253
— Arizona (N.L.)	5	6	.455	3.69	1.10	13	13	† 4	1	0	0-0	97.2	94	41	40	10	13-0	72	.257
2001— Arizona (N.L.)	* 22	6	.786	2.98	1.08	35	* 35	* 6	1	0	0-0	* 256.2	237	86	85	* 37	39-0	293	.245
2002— Arizona (N.L.)	23	7	.767	3.23	0.97	36	35	5	1	0	0-0	259.1	218	95	93	29	33-1	316	.224
2003— Tucson (PCL)	1	0	1.000	4.50	1.30	2	2	0	0	...	0-...	10.0	10	5	5	3	3-0	15	.256
— Arizona (N.L.)	8	9	.471	2.95	1.05	24	24	3	2	0	0-0	168.0	144	58	55	17	32-2	194	.230
2004— Boston (A.L.)	* 21	6	.778	3.26	1.06	32	32	3	0	0	0-0	226.2	206	84	82	23	35-0	203	.239
American League totals (4 years)	22	12	.647	3.56	1.16	76	37	3	0	5	3-9	296.0	276	122	117	29	67-1	245	.246
National League totals (13 years)	162	111	.593	3.30	1.11	406	333	79	19	5	10-14	2516.2	2216	979	922	257	571-40	2500	.235
Major League totals (17 years)	184	123	.599	3.32	1.11	482	370	82	19	10	13-23	2812.2	2492	1101	1039	286	638-41	2745	.236

DIVISION SERIES RECORD

Year — Team (League)	W	L	Pct.	ERA	WHIP	G	GS	CG	ShO	Hld.	Sv.-Opp.	IP	H	R	ER	HR	BB-IBB	SO	Avg.
2001— Arizona (N.L.)	2	0	1.000	0.50	0.61	2	2	2	1	0	0-0	18.0	9	1	1	1	2-0	18	.143
2002— Arizona (N.L.)	0	0	...	1.29	1.14	1	1	0	0	0	0-0	7.0	7	1	1	1	1-0	7	.250
2004— Boston (A.L.)	1	0	1.000	2.70	1.65	1	1	0	0	0	0-0	6.2	9	3	2	2	2-0	4	.300
Division series totals (3 years)	3	0	1.000	1.14	0.95	4	4	2	1	0	0-0	31.2	25	5	4	4	5-0	29	.207

CHAMPIONSHIP SERIES RECORD

Year — Team (League)	W	L	Pct.	ERA	WHIP	G	GS	CG	ShO	Hld.	Sv.-Opp.	IP	H	R	ER	HR	BB-IBB	SO	Avg.
1993— Philadelphia (N.L.)	0	0	...	1.69	1.00	2	2	0	0	0	0-0	16.0	11	4	3	0	5-0	19	.193
2001— Arizona (N.L.)	1	0	1.000	0.67	0.67	1	1	1	0	0	0-0	9.0	4	1	1	0	2-0	12	.133
2004— Boston (A.L.)	1	1	.500	6.30	1.20	2	2	0	0	0	0-0	10.0	10	7	7	1	2-0	5	.256
Champ. series totals (3 years)	2	1	.667	2.83	0.97	5	5	1	0	0	0-0	35.0	25	12	11	1	9-0	36	.198

WORLD SERIES RECORD

Year — Team (League)	W	L	Pct.	ERA	WHIP	G	GS	CG	ShO	Hld.	Sv.-Opp.	IP	H	R	ER	HR	BB-IBB	SO	Avg.
1993— Philadelphia (N.L.)	1	1	.500	3.52	1.17	2	2	1	1	0	0-0	15.1	13	7	6	2	5-0	9	.236
2001— Arizona (N.L.)	1	0	1.000	1.69	0.66	3	3	0	0	0	0-0	21.1	12	4	4	2	2-0	26	.162
2004— Boston (A.L.)	1	0	1.000	0.00	0.83	1	1	0	0	0	0-0	6.0	4	1	0	0	1-0	4	.174
World series totals (3 years)	3	1	.750	2.11	0.87	6	6	1	1	0	0-0	42.2	29	12	10	4	8-0	39	.191

ALL-STAR GAME RECORD

	W	L	Pct.	ERA	WHIP	G	GS	CG	ShO	Hld.	Sv.-Opp.	IP	H	R	ER	HR	BB-IBB	SO	Avg.
All-Star Game totals (3 years)	0	1	.000	3.00	1.17	3	2	0	0	0	0-0	6.0	6	2	2	0	1-0	9	.261

SCHMIDT, JASON — P

PERSONAL: Born January 29, 1973, in Lewiston, Idaho. ... 6-5/205. ... Throws right, bats right. ... Full name: Jason David Schmidt. ... High school: Kelso (Wash.).

TRANSACTIONS/CAREER NOTES: Selected by Atlanta Braves organization in eighth round of 1991 free-agent draft. ... On disabled list (July 15-August 30, 1996); included rehabilitation assignment to Greenville. ... Traded by Braves to Pittsburgh Pirates (August 30, 1996), completing deal in which Pirates traded P Denny Neagle to Braves for a player to be named (August 28, 1996). ... On disabled list (April 15-May 1 and June 10, 2000-remainder of season); included rehabilitation assignment to GCL Pirates. ... On disabled list (March 31-May 10, 2001); included rehabilitation assignments to Altoona and Nashville. ... Traded by Pirates with OF John Vander Wal to San Francisco Giants for OF Armando Rios and P Ryan Vogelsong (July 30, 2001). ... On disabled list (March 21-April 24, 2002); included rehabilitation assignment to Fresno. ... On disabled list (March 26-April 16, 2004); included rehabilitation assignment to San Jose.

HONORS: Named N.L. Pitcher of the Year by THE SPORTING NEWS (2004).

CAREER HITTING: 47-for-465 (.101), 21 R, 6 2B, 0 3B, 4 HR, 17 RBI.

Year — Team (League)	W	L	Pct.	ERA	WHIP	G	GS	CG	ShO	Hld.	Sv.-Opp.	IP	H	R	ER	HR	BB-IBB	SO	Avg.
1991— GC Braves (GCL)	3	4	.429	2.38	1.21	11	11	0	0	...	0-...	45.1	32	21	12	0	23-0	44	.189
1992— Pulaski (Appalachian)	3	4	.429	4.01	1.18	11	11	0	0	...	0-...	58.1	38	36	26	4	31-0	56	.170
— Macon (S. Atl.)	0	3	.000	4.01	2.03	7	7	0	0	...	0-...	24.2	31	18	11	2	19-0	33	.316
1993— Durham (Caro.)	7	11	.389	4.94	1.50	22	22	0	0	...	0-...	116.2	128	69	64	12	47-3	110	.286
1994— Greenville (Sou.)	8	7	.533	3.65	1.34	24	24	1	0	...	0-...	140.2	135	64	57	9	54-1	131	.255
1995— Atlanta (N.L.)	2	2	.500	5.76	1.80	9	2	0	0	0	0-1	25.0	27	17	16	2	18-3	19	.287
— Richmond (Int'l)	8	6	.571	2.25	1.25	19	19	0	0	...	0-...	116.0	97	40	29	2	48-3	95	.233
1996— Atlanta (N.L.)	3	4	.429	6.75	1.72	13	11	0	0	0	0-0	58.2	69	48	44	8	32-0	48	.296
— Richmond (Int'l)	3	0	1.000	2.56	1.20	7	7	0	0	...	0-...	45.2	36	17	13	2	19-1	41	.220
— Greenville (Sou.)	0	0	...	9.00	2.00	1	1	0	0	...	0-...	2.0	4	2	2	0	0-0	2	.444
— Pittsburgh (N.L.)	2	2	.500	4.06	1.59	6	6	1	0	0	0-0	37.2	39	19	17	2	21-0	26	.271
1997— Pittsburgh (N.L.)	10	9	.526	4.60	1.43	32	32	2	0	0	0-0	187.2	193	106	96	16	76-2	136	.265
1998— Pittsburgh (N.L.)	11	14	.440	4.07	1.40	33	33	0	0	0	0-0	214.1	228	106	97	24	71-3	158	.275
1999— Pittsburgh (N.L.)	13	11	.542	4.19	1.43	33	33	0	0	0	0-0	212.2	219	110	99	24	85-4	148	.262
2000— Pittsburgh (N.L.)	2	5	.286	5.40	1.77	11	11	0	0	0	0-0	63.1	71	43	38	6	41-2	51	.284
— GC Pirates (GCL)	0	0	...	2.25	1.25	1	1	0	0	...	0-...	4.0	4	2	1	0	1-0	1	.267
2001— Altoona (East.)	0	1	.000	0.96	0.86	3	3	0	0	...	0-...	9.1	7	1	1	0	1-0	17	.200
— Nashville (PCL)	1	0	1.000	0.00	0.57	1	1	0	0	...	0-...	7.0	4	0	0	0	0-0	6	.160
— Pittsburgh (N.L.)	6	6	.500	4.61	1.30	14	14	1	0	0	0-0	84.0	81	46	43	11	28-2	77	.256
— San Francisco (N.L.)	7	1	.875	3.39	1.36	11	11	0	0	0	0-0	66.1	57	29	25	2	33-1	65	.230
2002— Fresno (PCL)	2	0	1.000	3.00	1.08	2	2	0	0	...	0-...	12.0	11	4	4	0	2-0	12	.262
— San Francisco (N.L.)	13	8	.619	3.45	1.19	29	29	2	2	0	0-0	185.1	148	78	71	15	73-1	196	.218
2003— San Francisco (N.L.)	17	5	.773	* 2.34	0.95	29	29	5	•3	0	0-...	207.2	152	56	54	14	46-1	208	.200
2004— San Jose (California)	1	0	1.000	0.00	0.60	1	1	0	0	...	0-...	5.0	2	0	0	0	1-0	7	.118
— San Francisco (N.L.)	18	7	.720	3.20	1.08	32	32	4	•3	0	0-0	225.0	165	84	80	18	77-3	251	.202
Major League totals (10 years)	104	74	.584	3.90	1.31	252	243	17	8	0	0-1	1567.2	1449	742	680	142	601-22	1383	.244

DIVISION SERIES RECORD

Year — Team (League)	W	L	Pct.	ERA	WHIP	G	GS	CG	ShO	Hld.	Sv.-Opp.	IP	H	R	ER	HR	BB-IBB	SO	Avg.
2002— San Francisco (N.L.)	0	1	.000	6.75	1.31	1	1	0	0	0	0-0	5.1	3	4	4	0	4-1	5	.158
2003— San Francisco (N.L.)	1	0	1.000	0.00	0.33	1	1	1	1	0	0-0	9.0	3	0	0	0	0-0	5	.100
Division series totals (2 years)	1	1	.500	2.51	0.70	2	2	1	1	0	0-0	14.1	6	4	4	0	4-1	10	.122

CHAMPIONSHIP SERIES RECORD

Year — Team (League)	W	L	Pct.	ERA	WHIP	G	GS	CG	ShO	Hld.	Sv.-Opp.	IP	H	R	ER	HR	BB-IBB	SO	Avg.
2002— San Francisco (N.L.)	1	0	1.000	1.17	0.65	1	1	0	0	0	0-0	7.2	4	1	1	0	1-0	8	.160

WORLD SERIES RECORD

Year — Team (League)	W	L	Pct.	ERA	WHIP	G	GS	CG	ShO	Hld.	Sv.-Opp.	IP	H	R	ER	HR	BB-IBB	SO	Avg.
2002— San Francisco (N.L.)	1	0	1.000	5.23	1.94	2	2	0	0	0	0-0	10.1	16	6	6	2	4-0	14	.348

ALL-STAR GAME RECORD

	W	L	Pct.	ERA	WHIP	G	GS	CG	ShO	Hld.	Sv.-Opp.	IP	H	R	ER	HR	BB-IBB	SO	Avg.
All-Star Game totals (1 year)	0	0	...	0.00	0.50	1	1	0	0	0	0-0	2.0	1	0	0	0	0-0	3	.143

SCHNEIDER, BRIAN — C

PERSONAL: Born November 26, 1976, in Jacksonville, Fla. ... 6-1/196. ... Bats left, throws right. ... Full name: Brian Duncan Schneider. ... High school: Northampton (Pa.).

TRANSACTIONS/CAREER NOTES: Selected by Montreal Expos organization in fifth round of 1995 free-agent draft.

2004 GAMES PLAYED BY POSITION (MLB): C—133.

Year Team (League)	Pos.	G	AB	R	H	2B	3B	HR	RBI	BB	SO	HBP	GDP	SB-CS	Avg.	OBP	SLG	OPS	E	Avg.
1995— GC Expos (GCL)	C	30	97	7	22	3	0	0	4	14	23	1	1	2-4	.227	.330	.258	.588	3	.982
1996— GC Expos (GCL)	C	52	144	26	44	5	2	0	23	24	15	3	3	2-3	.306	.415	.368	.783	3	.988
—Delmarva (S. Atl.)	C	5	9	0	3	0	0	0	1	1	1	1	1	0-0	.333	.455	.333	.788	0	1.000
1997— Cape Fear (S. Atl.)	C	113	381	46	96	20	1	4	49	53	45	4	9	3-6	.252	.345	.341	.687	10	.988
1998— Cape Fear (S. Atl.)	C	38	134	33	40	7	2	7	30	16	9	3	3	6-3	.299	.381	.537	.918	6	.980
—Jupiter (FSL)	C	82	302	32	82	12	1	3	30	22	38	1	9	4-4	.272	.321	.348	.669	11	.981
1999— Harrisburg (East.)	C-1B	121	421	48	111	19	1	17	66	32	56	2	6	2-2	.264	.318	.435	.753	6	.992
2000— Ottawa (Int'l)	C-1B	67	238	22	59	22	3	4	31	16	42	0	5	1-0	.248	.285	.416	.701	8	.982
—Montreal (N.L.)	C	45	115	6	27	6	0	0	11	7	24	0	1	0-1	.235	.276	.287	.563	6	.974
2001— Ottawa (Int'l)	C	97	338	33	93	27	1	6	43	27	55	4	5	2-0	.275	.336	.414	.750	4	.994
—Montreal (N.L.)	C	27	41	4	13	3	0	1	6	6	3	0	0	0-0	.317	.396	.463	.859	0	1.000
2002— Montreal (N.L.)	C-OF	73	207	21	57	19	2	5	30	21	41	0	7	1-2	.275	.339	.459	.798	3	.993
2003— Montreal (N.L.)	C-DH	108	335	34	77	26	1	9	46	37	75	2	12	0-2	.230	.309	.394	.703	3	.996
2004— Montreal (N.L.)	C	135	436	40	112	20	3	12	49	42	63	3	8	0-1	.257	.325	.399	.724	2	.998
Major League totals (5 years)		388	1134	105	286	74	6	27	141	113	206	5	28	1-6	.252	.321	.399	.720	14	.994

SCHOENEWEIS, SCOTT — P

PERSONAL: Born October 2, 1973, in Long Branch, N.J. ... 6-0/195. ... Throws left, bats left. ... Full name: Scott David Schoeneweis. ... Name pronounced: show-en-weiss. ... High school: Lenape (Medford, N.J.). ... College: Duke.

TRANSACTIONS/CAREER NOTES: Selected by California Angels organization in third round of 1996 free-agent draft. ... Angels franchise renamed Anaheim Angels for 1997 season. ... On disabled list (June 17-July 26, 2000); included rehabilitation assignments to Lake Elsinore and Edmonton. ... Traded by Anaheim Angels with P Doug Nickle to Chicago White Sox for Ps Gary Glover, Scott Dunn, and Tim Bittner (July 29, 2003). ... On disabled list (June 22-July 7 and August 5-September 30, 2004).

CAREER HITTING: 2-for-7 (.286), 0 R, 1 2B, 0 3B, 0 HR, 1 RBI.

Year Team (League)	W	L	Pct.	ERA	WHIP	G	GS	CG	ShO	Hld.	Sv.-Opp.	IP	H	R	ER	HR	BB-IBB	SO	Avg.
1996— Lake Elsinore (Calif.)	8	3	.727	3.94	1.21	14	12	0	0	...	0-...	93.2	86	47	41	6	27-0	83	.244
1997— Midland (Texas)	7	5	.583	5.96	1.62	20	20	3	0	...	0-...	113.1	145	84	75	7	39-0	84	.313
1998— Vancouver (PCL)	11	8	.579	4.50	1.37	27	27	2	0	...	0-...	180.0	188	102	90	18	59-0	133	.266
1999— Anaheim (A.L.)	1	1	.500	5.49	1.55	31	0	0	0	3	0-0	39.1	47	27	24	4	14-1	22	.294
—Edmonton (PCL)	2	4	.333	7.64	1.98	9	7	0	0	...	0-...	35.1	58	35	30	6	12-0	29	.360
2000— Anaheim (A.L.)	7	10	.412	5.45	1.47	27	27	1	1	0	0-0	170.0	183	112	103	21	67-2	78	.276
—Lake Elsinore (Calif.)	0	0	...	1.93	1.29	1	1	0	0	...	0-...	4.2	3	1	1	0	3-0	3	.200
—Edmonton (PCL)	0	0	...	0.00	0.43	1	1	0	0	...	0-...	7.0	2	1	0	0	1-0	6	.083
2001— Anaheim (A.L.)	10	11	.476	5.08	1.48	32	32	1	0	0	0-0	205.1	227	122	116	21	77-2	104	.281
2002— Anaheim (A.L.)	9	8	.529	4.88	1.42	54	15	0	0	11	1-4	118.0	119	68	64	17	49-4	65	.264
2003— Anaheim (A.L.)	1	1	.500	3.96	1.22	39	0	0	0	4	0-1	38.2	37	19	17	2	10-3	29	.250
—Chicago (A.L.)	2	1	.667	4.50	1.35	20	0	0	0	0	0-1	26.0	26	16	13	1	9-2	27	.255
2004— Chicago (A.L.)	6	9	.400	5.59	1.58	20	19	0	0	0	0-0	112.2	129	74	70	17	49-0	69	.291
Major League totals (6 years)	36	41	.468	5.16	1.47	223	93	2	1	18	1-6	710.0	768	438	407	83	275-14	394	.277

DIVISION SERIES RECORD

Year Team (League)	W	L	Pct.	ERA	WHIP	G	GS	CG	ShO	Hld.	Sv.-Opp.	IP	H	R	ER	HR	BB-IBB	SO	Avg.
2002— Anaheim (A.L.)	0	0	...	27.00	6.00	3	0	0	0	0	0-1	.1	2	1	1	0	0-0	0	.667

CHAMPIONSHIP SERIES RECORD

Year Team (League)	W	L	Pct.	ERA	WHIP	G	GS	CG	ShO	Hld.	Sv.-Opp.	IP	H	R	ER	HR	BB-IBB	SO	Avg.
2002— Anaheim (A.L.)	0	0	...	0.00	0.00	1	0	0	0	0	0-0	.2	0	0	0	0	0-0	0	.000

WORLD SERIES RECORD

Year Team (League)	W	L	Pct.	ERA	WHIP	G	GS	CG	ShO	Hld.	Sv.-Opp.	IP	H	R	ER	HR	BB-IBB	SO	Avg.
2002— Anaheim (A.L.)	0	0	...	0.00	1.00	2	0	0	0	0	0-0	2.0	1	0	0	0	1-0	2	.167

SCUTARO, MARCO — 2B

PERSONAL: Born October 30, 1975, in San Felipe, Venezuela. ... 5-10/170. ... Bats right, throws right. ... Full name: Marcos Scutaro. ... Name pronounced: scoo-TAHR-oh.

TRANSACTIONS/CAREER NOTES: Signed as a non-drafted free agent by Cleveland Indians organization (July 26, 1994). ... Traded by Indians to Milwaukee Brewers (August 30, 2000); completing deal in which Indians traded 1B Richie Sexson, Ps Paul Rigdon and Kane Davis and a player to be named to Brewers for Ps Bob Wickman, Jason Bere and Steve Woodard (July 28, 2000). ... Claimed on waivers by New York Mets (April 5, 2002). ... Claimed on waivers by Oakland Athletics (October 9, 2003).

2004 GAMES PLAYED BY POSITION (MLB): 2B—123, SS—16, 3B—1.

Year Team (League)	Pos.	G	AB	R	H	2B	3B	HR	RBI	BB	SO	HBP	GDP	SB-CS	Avg.	OBP	SLG	OPS	E	Avg.
1995— Dom. Inds. (DSL)	3B	66	262	71	103	18	6	0	38	20	11	...	...	32-...	.393	...	.508	...	17	.931
1996— Columbus (S. Atl.)	2B-3B-SS	85	315	66	79	12	3	10	45	38	86	4	6	6-3	.251	.334	.403	.737	17	.959
1997— Kinston (Caro.)	2B-3B	97	378	58	103	17	6	10	59	35	72	9	3	23-7	.272	.346	.429	.774	11	.972
—Buffalo (A.A.)	2B-3B-SS	21	57	8	15	3	0	1	6	6	8	0	4	0-1	.263	.328	.368	.697	3	.959
1998— Akron (East.)	2B-SS	124	462	68	146	27	6	11	62	47	71	10	8	33-16	.316	.387	.472	.859	15	.976
—Buffalo (Int'l)	2B-3B	8	26	3	6	3	0	0	4	0	2	0	0	0-0	.231	.231	.346	.577	2	.939
1999— Buffalo (Int'l)	2B-SS	129	462	76	126	24	2	8	51	61	69	6	5	21-6	.273	.362	.385	.747	16	.974
2000— Buffalo (Int'l)	2B-SS	124	425	67	117	20	5	5	54	61	53	9	...	9-6	.275	.373	.381	.754	15	.976
—Indianapolis (Int'l)	2B-SS	4	13	5	7	1	1	1	3	1	2	0	1	1-0	.538	.571	1.000	1.571	0	1.000
2001— Indianapolis (Int'l)	2B-3B-SS	132	495	87	146	29	3	11	50	62	83	10	9	11-11	.295	.382	.432	.815	19	.968
2002— Norfolk (Int'l)	2-S-3-0	97	354	48	113	22	6	7	28	30	61	2	7	7-8	.319	.375	.475	.849	10	.974
—New York (N.L.)	2-S-3-0	27	36	2	8	0	1	1	6	0	11	0	1	0-1	.222	.216	.361	.577	1	.968
2003— Norfolk (Int'l)	3-2-S-0-DH	70	244	42	76	18	3	9	32	33	34	6	6	11-6	.311	.401	.520	.921	7	.970
—New York (N.L.)	2B-SS	48	75	10	16	4	0	2	6	13	14	1	1	2-0	.213	.333	.347	.680	2	.981
2004— Oakland (A.L.)	2B-SS-3B	137	455	50	124	32	1	7	43	16	58	0	9	0-0	.273	.297	.393	.690	5	.992
American League totals (1 year)		137	455	50	124	32	1	7	43	16	58	0	9	0-0	.273	.297	.393	.690	5	.992
National League totals (2 years)		75	111	12	24	4	1	3	12	13	25	1	2	2-1	.216	.299	.351	.651	3	.978
Major League totals (3 years)		212	566	62	148	36	2	10	55	29	83	1	11	2-1	.261	.297	.385	.682	8	.989

SEANEZ, RUDY — P

PERSONAL: Born October 20, 1968, in Brawley, Calif. ... 5-11/200. ... Throws right, bats right. ... Full name: Rudy Caballero Seanez. ... Name pronounced: see-AHN-ez. ... High school: Brawley (Calif.) Union.

TRANSACTIONS/CAREER NOTES: Selected by Cleveland Indians organization in fourth round of June 1986 free-agent draft. ... On disabled list (April 1-16 and July 30-September 2, 1991); included rehabilitation assignment to Colorado Springs. ... Traded by Indians to Los Angeles Dodgers for Ps Dennis Cook and Mike Christopher (December 10, 1991). ... On disabled list (March 29, 1992-entire season). ... Traded by Dodgers to Colorado Rockies for 2B Jody Reed (November 17, 1992). ... On disabled list (April 4-July 16, 1993); included rehabilitation assignments to Central Valley and Colorado Springs. ... Signed as a free agent by San Diego Padres organization (July 22, 1993). ... Released by Padres (November 18, 1993). ... Signed by Dodgers organization (January 12, 1994). ... On disabled list (May 28-June 16, 1995); included rehabilitation assignment to San Bernardino. ... Signed as a free agent by New York Mets organization (January 15, 1997). ... Traded by Mets to Kansas City Royals for future considerations (May 30, 1997). ... Signed as a free agent by Atlanta Braves organization (December 9, 1997). ... On disabled list (August 21, 1999-remainder of season). ... On Atlanta disabled list (March 23-April 27, 2000 and June 14-remainder of season); included rehabilitation assignment to Greenville. ... Signed as a free agent by Padres organization (February 14, 2001). ... On disabled list (June 6-21, 2001). ... Traded by Padres to Braves for a player to be named (August 31, 2001); Padres acquired P Winston Abreu to complete deal (September 6, 2001). ... Signed as a free agent by Texas Rangers (January 28, 2002). ... On disabled list (May 30-September 2, 2002); included rehabilitation assignments to Oklahoma. ... Released by Rangers (May 3, 2003). ... Signed by Boston Red Sox organization (May 6, 2003). ... Released by Red Sox (July 30, 2003). ... Signed by Chicago Cubs organization (August 1, 2003). ... Signed by Kansas City Royals organization (February 12, 2004). ... Traded by Royals to Florida Marlins for OF Abraham Nunez (July 31, 2004).

CAREER HITTING: 0-for-4 (.000), 1 R, 0 2B, 0 3B, 0 HR, 0 RBI.

Year Team (League)	W	L	Pct.	ERA	WHIP	G	GS	CG	ShO	Hld.	Sv.-Opp.	IP	H	R	ER	HR	BB-IBB	SO	Avg.
1986— Burlington (Appalachian) ..	5	2	.714	3.20	1.20	13	12	1	1	...	0-...	76.0	59	37	27	5	32-0	56	.212
1987— Waterloo (Midw.)	0	4	.000	6.75	1.67	10	10	0	0	...	0-...	34.2	35	29	26	6	23-0	23	.263
1988— Waterloo (Midw.)	6	6	.500	4.69	1.46	22	22	1	1	...	0-...	113.1	98	69	59	10	68-0	93	.230
1989— Kinston (Caro.)	8	10	.444	4.14	1.81	25	25	1	0	...	0-...	113.0	94	66	52	0	111-1	149	.223
— Colo. Springs (PCL)	0	0	...	0.00	1.00	1	0	0	0	...	0-...	1.0	1	0	0	0	0-0	0	.250
— Cleveland (A.L.)	0	0	...	3.60	1.00	5	0	0	0	0	0-0	5.0	1	2	2	0	4-1	7	.071
1990— Cant./Akr. (Eastern)	1	0	1.000	2.16	1.26	15	0	0	0	...	5-...	16.2	9	4	4	0	12-0	27	.170
— Cleveland (A.L.)	2	1	.667	5.60	1.72	24	0	0	0	3	0-0	27.1	22	17	17	2	25-1	24	.220
— Colo. Springs (PCL)	1	4	.200	6.75	2.08	12	0	0	0	...	1-...	12.0	15	10	9	2	10-0	7	.313
1991— Cleveland (A.L.)	0	0	...	7.27	2.25	16	0	0	0	...	0-...	17.1	17	14	14	2	12-0	19	.274
— Cant./Akr. (Eastern)	4	2	.667	2.58	1.23	25	0	0	0	...	7-...	38.1	17	12	11	2	30-1	73	.132
— Cleveland (A.L.)	0	0	...	16.20	3.40	5	0	0	0	0	0-1	5.0	10	12	9	2	7-0	7	.385
1992— Los Angeles (N.L.)					Did not play.														
1993— Central Valley (Cal.)	0	2	.000	9.72	2.40	5	1	0	0	...	0-...	8.1	9	9	9	0	11-0	7	.265
— Colo. Springs (PCL)	0	0	...	9.00	1.33	3	0	0	0	...	0-...	3.0	3	3	3	1	1-0	5	.250
— Las Vegas (PCL)	0	1	.000	6.41	1.78	14	0	0	0	...	0-...	19.2	24	15	14	2	11-0	14	.308
— San Diego (N.L.)	0	0	...	13.50	3.00	3	0	0	0	0	0-0	3.1	8	6	5	1	2-0	1	.471
1994— Albuquerque (PCL)	2	1	.667	5.32	1.86	20	0	0	0	...	9-...	22.0	28	14	13	3	13-1	26	.308
— Los Angeles (N.L.)	1	1	.500	2.66	1.39	17	0	0	0	1	0-1	23.2	24	7	7	2	9-1	18	.273
1995— Los Angeles (N.L.)	1	3	.250	6.75	1.64	37	0	0	0	6	3-4	34.2	39	27	26	5	18-3	29	.285
— San Bernardino (Calif.)	2	0	1.000	0.00	0.83	4	0	0	0	...	1-...	6.0	2	0	0	0	3-0	5	.100
1996— Albuquerque (PCL)	0	2	.000	6.52	1.97	21	0	0	0	...	6-...	19.1	27	18	14	0	11-1	20	.325
1997— Norfolk (Int'l)	1	0	1.000	4.05	1.73	9	0	0	0	...	0-...	13.1	12	8	6	1	11-0	17	.231
— Omaha (Am. Assoc.)	2	5	.286	6.51	1.66	28	3	0	0	...	0-...	47.0	53	42	34	13	25-0	46	.270
1998— Richmond (Int'l)	2	0	1.000	1.29	0.95	16	0	0	0	...	7-...	21.0	13	9	3	1	7-1	33	.169
— Atlanta (N.L.)	4	1	.800	2.75	1.14	34	0	0	0	8	2-4	36.0	25	13	11	2	16-0	50	.195
1999— Atlanta (N.L.)	6	1	.857	3.35	1.27	56	0	0	0	18	3-8	53.2	47	21	20	3	21-1	41	.234
2000— Greenville (Sou.)	0	0	...	0.00	1.00	2	1	0	0	...	0-...	2.0	2	0	0	0	0-0	3	.250
— Atlanta (N.L.)	2	4	.333	4.29	1.14	23	0	0	0	6	2-3	21.0	15	11	10	3	9-1	20	.192
2001— Lake Elsinore (Calif.)	2	0	1.000	2.08	1.04	7	0	0	0	...	0-...	8.2	7	3	2	1	2-0	8	.219
— San Diego (N.L.)	0	2	.000	2.63	1.25	26	0	0	0	5	1-3	24.0	15	8	7	3	15-0	24	.175
— Atlanta (N.L.)	0	0	...	3.00	1.00	12	0	0	0	4	0-0	12.0	8	4	4	1	4-0	17	.182
2002— Texas (A.L.)	1	3	.250	5.73	1.58	33	0	0	0	10	0-4	33.0	28	25	21	5	24-1	40	.230
— Oklahoma (PCL)	0	0	...	4.50	1.00	4	0	0	0	...	0-...	4.0	4	2	2	0	0-0	3	.267
2003— Oklahoma (PCL)	0	1	.000	2.08	1.80	5	0	0	0	...	0-...	4.1	3	4	1	0	5-0	7	.176
— Boston (A.L.)	0	1	.000	6.23	1.96	9	0	0	0	...	0-1	8.2	11	7	6	2	6-1	9	.297
— Pawtucket (Int'l)	2	2	.500	6.10	1.50	17	0	0	0	...	3-...	20.2	20	14	14	5	10-1	24	.253
— Iowa (PCL)	1	2	.333	3.46	1.60	13	0	0	0	...	2-...	13.0	12	10	5	1	9-2	13	.235
2004— Omaha (PCL)	2	1	.667	1.57	0.90	24	0	0	0	...	3-...	34.1	19	8	6	3	12-0	41	.152
— Kansas City (A.L.)	0	0	.000	3.91	1.39	16	0	0	0	1	0-1	23.0	21	10	10	0	11-2	21	.244
— Florida (N.L.)	3	1	.750	2.74	1.13	23	0	0	0	3	0-1	23.0	18	7	7	3	8-1	25	.212
American League totals (6 years)	3	6	.333	5.74	1.67	92	0	0	0	14	0-7	102.0	93	73	65	11	77-6	108	.242
National League totals (8 years)	17	13	.567	3.77	1.30	231	0	0	0	51	11-24	231.1	199	104	97	23	102-7	225	.231
Major League totals (13 years)	20	19	.513	4.37	1.41	323	0	0	0	65	11-31	333.1	292	177	162	34	179-13	333	.234

DIVISION SERIES RECORD

Year Team (League)	W	L	Pct.	ERA	WHIP	G	GS	CG	ShO	Hld.	Sv.-Opp.	IP	H	R	ER	HR	BB-IBB	SO	Avg.
1998— Atlanta (N.L.)	0	0	...	0.00	0.00	1	0	0	0	0	0-0	1.0	0	0	0	0	0-0	0	.000
2001— Atlanta (N.L.)	1	0	1.000	0.00	1.00	1	0	0	0	0	0-0	1.0	0	0	0	0	1-0	0	.000
Division series totals (2 years)	1	0	1.000	0.00	0.50	2	0	0	0	0	0-0	2.0	0	0	0	0	1-0	0	.000

CHAMPIONSHIP SERIES RECORD

Year Team (League)	W	L	Pct.	ERA	WHIP	G	GS	CG	ShO	Hld.	Sv.-Opp.	IP	H	R	ER	HR	BB-IBB	SO	Avg.
1998— Atlanta (N.L.)	0	0	...	6.00	1.00	4	0	0	0	1	0-0	3.0	2	2	2	0	1-0	4	.200
2001— Atlanta (N.L.)	0	0	...	0.00	2.00	2	0	0	0	0	0-0	2.0	1	0	0	0	3-2	3	.143
Champ. series totals (2 years)	0	0	...	3.60	1.40	6	0	0	0	1	0-0	5.0	3	2	2	0	4-2	7	.176

SEAY, BOBBY — P

PERSONAL: Born June 20, 1978, in Sarasota, Fla. ... 6-2/235. ... Throws left, bats left. ... Full name: Robert Michael Seay. ... Name pronounced: see. ... High school: Sarasota (Fla.).

TRANSACTIONS/CAREER NOTES: Selected by Chicago White Sox organization in first round (12th pick overall) of 1996 free-agent draft. ... Rights relinquished by White Sox (August 15, 1996). ... Signed by Tampa Bay Devil Rays organization (November 8, 1996). ... On disabled list (March 22-June 3, 2002); included rehabilitation assignment to Orlando. ... On disabled list (April 24-June 3, 2003).

CAREER HITTING: 0-for-0 (.000), 0 R, 0 2B, 0 3B, 0 HR, 0 RBI.

Year—Team (League)	W	L	Pct.	ERA	WHIP	G	GS	CG	ShO	Hld.	Sv.-Opp.	IP	H	R	ER	HR	BB-IBB	SO	Avg.
1997—Char., S.C. (SAL)	3	4	.429	4.55	1.52	13	13	0	0	...	0-...	61.1	56	35	31	2	37-0	64	.249
1998—Char., S.C. (SAL)	1	7	.125	4.30	1.28	15	15	0	0	...	0-...	69.0	59	40	33	10	29-0	74	.236
1999—St. Pete. (FSL)	2	6	.250	3.00	1.39	12	11	0	0	...	0-...	57.0	56	25	19	0	23-0	45	.271
— Orlando (Sou.)	1	2	.333	7.94	2.18	6	6	0	0	...	0-...	17.0	22	15	15	2	15-0	16	.319
2000—Orlando (Sou.)	8	7	.533	3.88	1.40	24	24	0	0	...	0-...	132.1	132	64	57	13	53-1	106	.265
2001—Orlando (Sou.)	2	5	.286	5.98	1.65	15	13	0	0	...	0-...	64.2	81	48	43	9	26-0	49	.310
— Tampa Bay (A.L.)	1	1	.500	6.23	1.38	12	0	0	0	0	0-0	13.0	13	11	9	3	5-1	12	.260
2002—Orlando (Sou.)	2	0	1.000	3.28	1.29	15	3	0	0	...	0-...	35.2	31	16	13	2	15-0	24	.237
— Durham (Int'l)	0	0	...	6.00	1.13	10	0	0	0	...	0-...	15.0	15	10	10	1	2-0	14	.254
2003—Tampa Bay (A.L.)	0	0	...	3.00	1.44	12	0	0	0	0	0-1	9.0	7	3	3	0	6-0	5	.226
— Durham (Int'l)	3	0	1.000	2.10	1.30	25	0	0	0	...	0-...	30.0	23	10	7	1	15-0	29	.205
2004—Durham (Int'l)	2	1	.667	1.72	0.95	29	0	0	0	...	1-...	36.2	26	9	7	3	9-0	35	.195
— Tampa Bay (A.L.)	0	0	...	2.38	1.15	21	0	0	0	0	0-0	22.2	21	6	6	2	5-1	17	.239
Major League totals (3 years)	1	1	.500	3.63	1.28	45	0	0	0	0	0-1	44.2	41	20	18	5	16-2	34	.243

SEGUI, DAVID — DH

PERSONAL: Born July 19, 1966, in Kansas City, Kan. ... 6-1/218. ... Bats both, throws left. ... Full name: David Vincent Segui. ... Name pronounced: seh-GHEE. ... High school: Bishop Ward (Kansas City, Kan.). ... College: Louisiana Tech. ... Son of Diego Segui, pitcher with five major league teams (1962-75 and 1977).

TRANSACTIONS/CAREER NOTES: Selected by Baltimore Orioles organization in 18th round of 1987 free-agent draft. ... On suspended list (August 16-19, 1993). ... Traded by Orioles to New York Mets for SS Kevin Baez and P Tom Wegmann (March 27, 1994). ... On disabled list (June 20-July 5, 1994). ... Traded by Mets to Montreal Expos for P Reid Cornelius (June 8, 1995). ... On disabled list (July 4-August 16, 1996; and June 4-21, 1997). ... On suspended list (July 26, 1997). ... Signed as a free agent by Seattle Mariners (December 12, 1997). ... Traded by Mariners to Toronto Blue Jays for Ps Tom Davey and Steve Sinclair (July 28, 1999). ... On suspended list (July 30-31, 1999). ... On disabled list (August 8-September 2, 1999). ... Traded by Blue Jays with cash to Texas Rangers as part of three-team deal in which Blue Jays acquired 1B Brad Fullmer from Montreal Expos and Expos acquired 1B Lee Stevens from Rangers (March 16, 2000). ... Traded by Rangers to Cleveland Indians for OF Ricky Ledee (July 28, 2000). ... Signed as a free agent by Orioles (December 21, 2000). ... On disabled list (April 28-May 15 and July 16-August 4, 2001; and May 18, 2002-remainder of season). ... On disabled list (March 21-April 5, April 18-May 3 and July 26, 2003-remainder of season); included rehabilitation assignment to Frederick. ... On disabled list (April 25-September 1 and September 9, 2004-remainder of season); included rehabilitation assignments to Frederick and Bowie.

2004 GAMES PLAYED BY POSITION (MLB): DH—15, 1B—2.

Year—Team (League)	Pos.	G	AB	R	H	2B	3B	HR	RBI	BB	SO	HBP	GDP	SB-CS	Avg.	OBP	SLG	OPS	E	Avg.
1988—Hagerstown (Car.)	1B-OF	60	190	35	51	12	4	3	31	22	23	3	7	0-0	.268	.347	.421	.768	9	.976
1989—Frederick (Carolina)	1B	83	284	43	90	19	0	10	50	41	32	4	4	2-1	.317	.407	.489	.896	4	.995
— Hagerstown (East.)	1B	44	173	22	56	14	1	1	27	16	16	2	6	0-0	.324	.383	.434	.817	1	.998
1990—Rochester (Int'l)	1B-OF	86	307	55	103	28	0	2	51	45	28	0	15	5-4	.336	.415	.446	.861	3	.996
— Baltimore (A.L.)	DH-1B	40	123	14	30	7	0	2	15	11	15	1	12	0-0	.244	.311	.350	.661	3	.990
1991—Rochester (Int'l)	1B-OF	28	96	9	26	2	0	1	10	15	6	1	6	1-1	.271	.365	.323	.688	0	1.000
— Baltimore (A.L.)	DH-1B-OF	86	212	15	59	7	0	2	22	12	19	0	7	1-1	.278	.316	.340	.655	3	.990
1992—Baltimore (A.L.)	1B-OF	115	189	21	44	9	0	1	17	20	23	0	4	1-0	.233	.306	.296	.603	1	.998
1993—Baltimore (A.L.)	1B-DH	146	450	54	123	27	0	10	60	58	53	0	18	2-1	.273	.351	.400	.751	5	.996
1994—New York (N.L.)	1B-OF	92	336	46	81	17	0	10	43	33	43	1	6	0-0	.241	.308	.387	.695	5	.993
1995—New York (N.L.)	OF-1B	33	73	9	24	3	1	2	11	12	9	1	2	1-3	.329	.420	.479	.900	0	1.000
— Montreal (N.L.)	1B-OF	97	383	59	117	22	3	10	57	28	38	2	8	1-4	.305	.355	.457	.812	3	.997
1996—Montreal (N.L.)	1B	115	416	69	119	30	1	11	58	60	54	0	8	4-4	.286	.375	.442	.818	7	.993
1997—Montreal (N.L.)	1B	125	459	75	141	22	3	21	68	57	66	1	9	1-0	.307	.381	.505	.886	6	.995
1998—Seattle (A.L.)	1B-OF	143	522	79	159	36	1	19	84	49	80	0	12	3-1	.305	.359	.487	.845	1	.999
1999—Seattle (A.L.)	1B	90	345	43	101	22	3	9	39	32	43	1	9	1-2	.293	.352	.452	.804	3	.996
— Toronto (A.L.)	DH-1B	31	95	14	30	5	0	5	13	8	17	0	1	0-0	.316	.365	.526	.892	1	.955
2000—Texas (A.L.)	DH-1B	93	351	52	118	29	1	11	57	34	51	0	12	0-1	.336	.391	.519	.909	0	1.000
— Cleveland (A.L.)	1B-DH-OF	57	223	41	74	13	0	8	46	19	33	1	8	0-0	.332	.384	.498	.881	0	1.000
2001—Baltimore (A.L.)	1B-DH	82	292	48	88	18	1	6	46	49	61	4	4	1-1	.301	.406	.473	.879	9	.983
2002—Baltimore (A.L.)	DH-1B	26	95	10	25	4	0	2	16	11	22	0	0	0-0	.263	.336	.368	.705	0	1.000
2003—Frederick (Carolina)	DH	1	4	0	1	0	0	0	0	0	0	1	0	0-0	.250	.250	.250	.500	0	.000
— Baltimore (A.L.)	DH-1B	67	224	26	59	10	1	5	25	26	47	1	8	1-0	.263	.341	.384	.725	0	1.000
2004—Bowie (East.)	DH	3	11	2	4	1	0	0	1	0	3	1	1	0-0	.364	.417	.455	.871	0	...
— Frederick (Carolina)	DH-1B	3	10	1	1	0	0	1	2	1	2	0	0	0-0	.100	.167	.400	.567	0	1.000
— Baltimore (A.L.)	DH-1B	18	59	8	20	3	0	1	7	5	13	1	3	0-1	.339	.400	.441	.841	0	1.000
American League totals (11 years)		994	3180	425	930	190	7	85	447	334	477	9	98	10-8	.292	.358	.437	.795	26	.995
National League totals (4 years)		462	1667	258	482	94	9	54	237	190	210	5	33	7-11	.289	.361	.454	.815	21	.995
Major League totals (15 years)		1456	4847	683	1412	284	16	139	684	524	687	14	131	17-19	.291	.359	.443	.802	47	.995

SEIBEL, PHIL — P

PERSONAL: Born January 28, 1979, in Louisville, Ky. ... 6-1/195. ... Throws left, bats left. ... Full name: Phillip Matthew Seibel. ... High school: Cypress (Calif.). ... College: Texas.

TRANSACTIONS/CAREER NOTES: Selected by Montreal Expos organization in eighth round of 2000 free-agent draft. ... Traded by Expos with P Scott Strickland and OF Matt Watson to New York Mets for Ps Bruce Chen and Dicky Gonzalez, SS Luis Figueroa and a player to be named (April 5, 2002); Expos acquired P Saul Rivera to complete trade (July 14, 2002). ... Claimed on waivers by Boston Red Sox (November 20, 2003). ... Released by Red Sox (September 22, 2004).

CAREER HITTING: 0-for-0 (.000), 0 R, 0 2B, 0 3B, 0 HR, 0 RBI.

Year—Team (League)	W	L	Pct.	ERA	WHIP	G	GS	CG	ShO	Hld.	Sv.-Opp.	IP	H	R	ER	HR	BB-IBB	SO	Avg.
2001—Jupiter (FSL)	10	7	.588	3.95	1.28	29	21	0	0	...	0-...	134.1	144	70	59	12	28-0	88	.273
2002—Binghamton (Eastern)	10	8	.556	3.97	1.31	28	25	2	0	...	0-...	149.2	147	78	66	17	49-2	114	.263
2003—Norfolk (Int'l)	2	3	.400	6.03	1.60	11	5	0	0	...	0-...	34.1	38	25	23	5	17-0	25	.281
— Binghamton (Eastern)	5	5	.500	3.59	1.34	17	17	0	0	...	0-...	82.2	79	48	33	6	32-0	71	.253
2004—Boston (A.L.)	0	0	...	0.00	1.36	2	0	0	0	0	0-...	3.2	0	0	0	0	5-0	1	.000
— Pawtucket (Int'l)	1	2	.333	3.02	1.21	8	7	0	0	...	0-...	44.2	42	16	15	7	12-0	31	.255
— GC Red Sox (GCL)	0	0	...	2.25	0.80	3	3	0	0	...	0-...	4.0	2	1	1	1	1-0	6	.143
— Portland (East.)	0	1	.000	7.50	1.67	3	1	0	0	...	0-...	6.0	8	5	5	3	2-0	6	.320
Major League totals (1 year)	0	0	...	0.00	1.36	2	0	0	0	0	0-0	3.2	0	0	0	0	5-0	1	.000

SELE, AARON   P

PERSONAL: Born June 25, 1970, in Golden Valley, Minn. ... 6-5/230. ... Throws right, bats right. ... Full name: Aaron Helmer Sele. ... Name pronounced: SEE-lee. ... High school: North Kitsap (Poulsbo, Wash.). ... College: Washington State.

TRANSACTIONS/CAREER NOTES: Selected by Minnesota Twins organization in 37th round of 1988 free-agent draft; did not sign. ... Selected by Boston Red Sox organization in first round (23rd pick overall) of 1991 free-agent draft. ... On disabled list (May 24, 1995-remainder of season); included rehabilitation assignments to Trenton, Sarasota and Pawtucket. ... On disabled list (August 14-September 1, 1996); included rehabilitation assignment to Pawtucket. ... Traded by Red Sox with P Mark Brandenburg and C Bill Haselman to Texas Rangers for C Jim Leyritz and OF Damon Buford (November 6, 1997). ... Signed as a free agent by Seattle Mariners (January 10, 2000). ... Signed as a free agent by Anaheim Angels (January 4, 2002). ... On disabled list (August 21-September 29, 2002). ... On disabled list (March 21-May 9, 2003); included rehabilitation assignments to Rancho Cucamonga and Salt Lake. ... On disabled list (June 11-26, 2004).

HONORS: Named A.L. Rookie Pitcher of the Year by THE SPORTING NEWS (1993).

CAREER HITTING: 4-for-25 (.160), 2 R, 1 2B, 0 3B, 0 HR, 1 RBI.

Year — Team (League)	W	L	Pct.	ERA	WHIP	G	GS	CG	ShO	Hld.	Sv.-Opp.	IP	H	R	ER	HR	BB-IBB	SO	Avg.
1991— Winter Haven (FSL)	3	6	.333	4.96	1.41	13	11	4	0	...	1-...	69.0	65	42	38	2	32-2	51	.247
1992— Lynchburg (Carolina)	13	5	.722	2.91	1.18	20	19	2	1	...	0-...	127.0	104	51	41	5	46-0	112	.222
— New Britain (East.)	2	1	.667	6.27	1.76	7	6	1	0	...	0-...	33.0	43	29	23	2	15-0	29	.305
1993— Pawtucket (Int'l)	8	2	.800	2.19	1.03	14	14	2	1	...	0-...	94.1	74	30	23	8	23-0	87	.216
— Boston (A.L.)	7	2	.778	2.74	1.33	18	18	0	0	0	0-0	111.2	100	42	34	5	48-2	93	.237
1994— Boston (A.L.)	8	7	.533	3.83	1.40	22	22	2	0	0	0-0	143.1	140	68	61	13	60-2	105	.261
1995— Boston (A.L.)	3	1	.750	3.06	1.42	6	6	0	0	0	0-0	32.1	32	14	11	3	14-0	21	.252
— Trenton (East.)	0	1	.000	3.38	1.25	2	2	0	0	...	0-...	8.0	8	3	3	0	2-0	9	.286
— Sarasota (Florida State)	0	0	...	0.00	1.00	2	2	0	0	...	0-...	7.0	6	0	0	0	1-0	8	.231
— Pawtucket (Int'l)	0	0	...	9.00	2.20	2	2	0	0	...	0-...	5.0	9	5	5	3	2-0	1	.409
1996— Boston (A.L.)	7	11	.389	5.32	1.65	29	29	1	0	0	0-0	157.1	192	110	93	14	67-2	137	.303
— Pawtucket (Int'l)	0	0	...	6.00	1.33	1	1	0	0	...	0-...	3.0	3	2	2	0	1-0	4	.250
1997— Boston (A.L.)	13	12	.520	5.38	1.56	33	33	1	0	0	0-0	177.1	196	115	106	25	80-4	122	.279
1998— Texas (A.L.)	19	11	.633	4.23	1.52	33	33	3	2	0	0-0	212.2	239	116	100	14	84-6	167	.283
1999— Texas (A.L.)	18	9	.667	4.79	1.53	33	33	2	2	0	0-0	205.0	244	115	109	21	70-3	186	.293
2000— Seattle (A.L.)	17	10	.630	4.51	1.39	34	34	2	2	0	0-0	211.2	221	110	106	17	74-7	137	.271
2001— Seattle (A.L.)	15	5	.750	3.60	1.24	34	33	2	1	0	0-0	215.0	216	93	86	25	51-2	114	.261
2002— Anaheim (A.L.)	8	9	.471	4.89	1.49	26	26	1	1	0	0-0	160.0	190	92	87	21	49-2	82	.299
2003— Rancho Cuca. (Calif.)	0	0	...	4.50	1.90	3	2	0	0	...	0-...	8.0	12	4	4	0	3-0	7	.375
— Salt Lake (PCL)	1	2	.333	6.43	1.80	3	3	0	0	...	0-...	14.0	16	10	10	2	9-0	8	.296
— Anaheim (A.L.)	7	11	.389	5.77	1.59	25	25	0	0	0	0-0	121.2	135	82	78	17	58-1	53	.284
2004— Anaheim (A.L.)	9	4	.692	5.05	1.62	28	24	0	0	0	0-0	132.0	163	84	74	16	51-2	51	.310
Major League totals (12 years)	**131**	**92**	**.587**	**4.52**	**1.48**	**321**	**316**	**14**	**8**	**0**	**0-0**	**1880.0**	**2068**	**1041**	**945**	**191**	**706-33**	**1268**	**.280**

DIVISION SERIES RECORD

Year — Team (League)	W	L	Pct.	ERA	WHIP	G	GS	CG	ShO	Hld.	Sv.-Opp.	IP	H	R	ER	HR	BB-IBB	SO	Avg.
1998— Texas (A.L.)	0	1	.000	6.00	1.50	1	1	0	0	0	0-0	6.0	8	4	4	2	1-0	4	.320
1999— Texas (A.L.)	0	1	.000	5.40	2.20	1	1	0	0	0	0-0	5.0	6	4	3	0	5-2	3	.286
2000— Seattle (A.L.)	0	0	...	1.23	0.82	1	1	0	0	0	0-0	7.1	3	1	1	0	3-0	1	.143
2001— Seattle (A.L.)	0	1	.000	9.00	2.50	1	1	0	0	0	0-0	2.0	5	4	2	0	0-0	0	.417
Division series totals (4 years)	**0**	**3**	**.000**	**4.43**	**1.52**	**4**	**4**	**0**	**0**	**0**	**0-0**	**20.1**	**22**	**13**	**10**	**2**	**9-2**	**8**	**.278**

CHAMPIONSHIP SERIES RECORD

Year — Team (League)	W	L	Pct.	ERA	WHIP	G	GS	CG	ShO	Hld.	Sv.-Opp.	IP	H	R	ER	HR	BB-IBB	SO	Avg.
2000— Seattle (A.L.)	0	1	.000	6.00	1.50	1	1	0	0	0	0-0	6.0	9	4	4	2	0-0	4	.333
2001— Seattle (A.L.)	0	2	.000	3.60	1.50	2	2	0	0	0	0-0	10.0	11	8	4	3	4-0	5	.282
Champ. series totals (2 years)	**0**	**3**	**.000**	**4.50**	**1.50**	**3**	**3**	**0**	**0**	**0**	**0-0**	**16.0**	**20**	**12**	**8**	**5**	**4-0**	**9**	**.303**

ALL-STAR GAME RECORD

	W	L	Pct.	ERA	WHIP	G	GS	CG	ShO	Hld.	Sv.-Opp.	IP	H	R	ER	HR	BB-IBB	SO	Avg.
All-Star Game totals (1 year)	0	0	...	0.00	1.00	1	0	0	0	0	0-0	1.0	1	0	0	0	0-0	0	.250

SEO, JAE WEONG   P

PERSONAL: Born May 24, 1977, in Kwanju, South Korea. ... 6-1/215. ... Throws right, bats right. ... Full name: Jae Weong Seo. ... Name pronounced: jay wong sew. ... High school: First (Kwanju, South Korea). ... College: Inha (South Korea).

TRANSACTIONS/CAREER NOTES: Signed as a non-drafted free agent by New York Mets organization (December 17, 1997). ... On disabled list (April 6, 2000-entire season).

CAREER HITTING: 10-for-83 (.120), 5 R, 2 2B, 0 3B, 0 HR, 1 RBI.

Year — Team (League)	W	L	Pct.	ERA	WHIP	G	GS	CG	ShO	Hld.	Sv.-Opp.	IP	H	R	ER	HR	BB-IBB	SO	Avg.
1998— St. Lucie (Fla. St.)	3	1	.750	2.27	1.01	8	7	0	0	...	0-...	35.2	26	13	9	2	10-0	37	.206
— GC Mets (GCL)	0	0	...	0.00	0.80	2	0	0	0	...	0-...	5.0	4	0	0	0	0-0	0	.235
1999— St. Lucie (Fla. St.)	2	0	1.000	1.84	0.68	3	3	0	0	...	0-...	14.2	8	3	3	0	2-0	14	.154
2000— St. Lucie (Fla. St.)				Did not play.															
2001— St. Lucie (Fla. St.)	2	3	.400	3.55	1.07	6	5	0	0	...	0-...	25.1	21	11	10	2	6-0	19	.221
— Binghamton (Eastern)	5	1	.833	1.94	0.91	12	10	0	0	...	0-...	60.1	44	14	13	3	11-1	47	.206
— Norfolk (Int'l)	2	2	.500	3.42	1.25	9	9	0	0	...	0-...	47.1	53	18	18	4	6-1	25	.296
2002— Binghamton (Eastern)	0	0	...	5.40	1.20	1	0	0	0	...	0-...	5.0	5	3	3	1	1-0	6	.250
— Norfolk (Int'l)	6	9	.400	3.99	1.30	26	24	1	0	...	0-...	128.2	145	66	57	14	22-1	87	.284
— New York (N.L.)	0	0	...	0.00	0.00	1	0	0	0	0	0-0	1.0	0	0	0	0	0-0	1	.000
2003— New York (N.L.)	9	12	.429	3.82	1.27	32	31	0	0	0	0-0	188.1	193	94	80	18	46-11	110	.260
2004— Norfolk (Int'l)	0	2	.000	2.82	1.34	4	4	0	0	...	0-...	22.1	22	7	7	1	8-0	20	.272
— New York (N.L.)	5	10	.333	4.90	1.56	24	21	0	0	0	0-0	117.2	133	67	64	17	50-7	54	.299
Major League totals (3 years)	**14**	**22**	**.389**	**4.22**	**1.37**	**57**	**52**	**0**	**0**	**0**	**0-0**	**307.0**	**326**	**161**	**144**	**35**	**96-18**	**165**	**.274**

SERRANO, JIMMY   P

PERSONAL: Born May 9, 1976, in Grand Junction, Colo. ... 5-10/170. ... Throws right, bats right. ... Full name: James Serrano. ... High school: Central (Grand Junction). ... College: New Mexico.

TRANSACTIONS/CAREER NOTES: Selected by Montreal Expos in 18th round of 1998 free-agent draft. ... Traded by Expos with OF Jason Bay to New York Mets for IF Lou Collier (March 27, 2002). ... Traded by Mets to Kansas City Royals for cash (July 5, 2003).

CAREER HITTING: 0-for-0 (.000), 0 R, 0 2B, 0 3B, 0 HR, 0 RBI.

Year Team (League)	W	L	Pct.	ERA	WHIP	G	GS	CG	ShO	Hld.	Sv.-Opp.	IP	H	R	ER	HR	BB-IBB	SO	Avg.
1998— Vermont (NY-P)	0	0	...	1.17	0.52	7	0	0	0	...	5-...	7.2	3	1	1	0	1-0	12	.111
—Cape Fear (S. Atl.)	2	0	1.000	3.65	1.50	15	0	0	0	...	3-...	24.2	22	11	10	2	15-0	29	.227
1999— Jupiter (FSL)	8	5	.615	2.13	0.92	44	1	0	0	...	8-...	93.0	59	25	22	4	27-4	118	.183
2000— Harrisburg (Eastern)	4	5	.444	4.20	1.43	55	0	0	0	...	16-...	75.0	64	39	35	6	43-2	80	.234
2001— Harrisburg (Eastern)	6	3	.667	2.18	1.01	47	0	0	0	...	20-...	53.2	30	20	13	4	24-4	73	.160
—Ottawa (Int'l)	0	1	.000	4.50	2.13	9	0	0	0	...	0-...	8.0	11	5	4	0	6-0	11	.314
2002— Norfolk (Int'l)	8	6	.571	4.01	1.61	53	0	0	0	...	3-...	74.0	88	40	33	3	31-5	76	.293
2003— Norfolk (Int'l)	1	2	.333	2.39	1.16	27	0	0	0	...	3-...	49.0	38	13	13	2	19-3	47	.224
—Omaha (PCL)	3	2	.600	3.21	1.29	19	0	0	0	...	3-...	28.0	25	12	10	2	11-0	28	.245
2004— Omaha (PCL)	1	1	.500	5.01	1.64	16	1	0	0	...	0-...	32.1	32	23	18	4	21-0	41	.256
—Wichita (Texas)	3	1	.750	1.96	0.93	11	11	1	1	...	0-...	64.1	42	18	14	6	18-0	74	.181
—Kansas City (A.L.)	1	2	.333	4.68	1.44	10	5	0	0	0	0-0	32.2	35	17	17	5	12-0	25	.280
Major League totals (1 year)	1	2	.333	4.68	1.44	10	5	0	0	0	0-0	32.2	35	17	17	5	12-0	25	.280

SERVICE, SCOTT   P

PERSONAL: Born February 26, 1967, in Cincinnati, Ohio. ... 6-6/240. ... Throws right, bats right. ... Full name: Scott David Service. ... High school: Aiken (Cincinnati).

TRANSACTIONS/CAREER NOTES: Signed as a non-drafted free agent by Philadelphia Phillies organization (August 24, 1985). ... Signed as a free agent by Montreal Expos organization (November 15, 1990). ... Contract sold by Expos to Chunichi of the Japan Central League (July 23, 1991). ... Signed as a free agent by Expos organization (January 10, 1992). ... Signed as a free agent by Cincinnati Reds organization (June 9, 1992). ... Claimed on waivers by Colorado Rockies (June 28, 1993). ... Claimed on waivers by Reds (July 7, 1993). ... Released by Reds (November 17, 1994). ... Re-signed by Reds organization (February 24, 1995). ... Traded by Reds with OF Deion Sanders, Ps John Roper and Ricky Pickett and IF Dave McCarty to San Francisco Giants for OF Darren Lewis and Ps Mark Portugal and Dave Burba (July 21, 1995). ... Released by Giants (March 26, 1996). ... Signed by Reds organization (April 2, 1996). ... Claimed on waivers by Oakland Athletics (March 27, 1997). ... Claimed on waivers by Reds (April 4, 1997). ... Traded by Reds with P Hector Carrasco to Kansas City Royals for OF Jon Nunnally and IF/OF Chris Stynes (July 15, 1997). ... On suspended list (June 15-16, 1998). ... Released by Royals (December 17, 1999). ... Signed by Oakland Athletics (December 30, 1999). ... Signed as a free agent by Los Angeles Dodgers organization (December 5, 2000). ... Released by Dodgers (March 13, 2001). ... Signed by Reds organization (June 23, 2001). ... Signed as a free agent by Pittsburgh Pirates organization (January 5, 2002). ... Signed as a free agent by Arizona Diamondbacks organization (February 12, 2003). ... Claimed on waivers by Toronto Blue Jays (June 16, 2003). ... Released by Blue Jays (August 10, 2003). ... Signed by Reds organization (August 26, 2003). ... Signed as a free agent by Diamondbacks organization (April 1, 2004). ... On disabled list (July 9-September 7, 2004); included rehabilitation assignment to Tucson.

CAREER HITTING: 1-for-17 (.059), 0 R, 0 2B, 0 3B, 0 HR, 1 RBI.

Year Team (League)	W	L	Pct.	ERA	WHIP	G	GS	CG	ShO	Hld.	Sv.-Opp.	IP	H	R	ER	HR	BB-IBB	SO	Avg.
1986— Spartanburg (SAL)	1	6	.143	5.83	1.74	14	9	1	0	...	0-...	58.2	68	44	38	3	34-0	49	.287
—Utica (N.Y.-Penn)	5	4	.556	2.67	1.17	10	10	2	0	...	0-...	70.2	65	30	21	1	18-0	43	.240
—Clearwater (Fla. St.)	1	2	.333	3.20	1.38	4	4	1	1	...	0-...	25.1	20	10	9	2	15-0	19	.225
1987— Reading (East.)	0	3	.000	7.78	1.93	5	4	0	0	...	0-...	19.2	22	19	17	5	16-1	12	.278
—Clearwater (Fla. St.)	13	4	.765	2.48	1.15	21	21	5	2	...	0-...	137.2	127	46	38	8	32-0	73	.247
1988— Reading (East.)	3	4	.429	2.86	1.31	10	9	1	1	...	0-...	56.2	52	25	18	4	22-2	39	.241
—Maine (International)	8	8	.500	3.67	1.27	19	18	1	0	...	0-...	110.1	109	51	45	10	31-3	87	.256
—Philadelphia (N.L.)	0	0	...	1.69	1.50	5	0	0	0	0	0-0	5.1	7	1	1	0	1-0	6	.333
1989— Scran./W.B. (I.L.)	3	1	.750	2.16	1.50	23	0	0	0	...	6-...	33.1	27	8	8	2	23-6	23	.227
—Reading (East.)	6	6	.500	3.26	1.10	23	10	1	1	...	1-...	85.2	71	36	31	8	23-0	82	.226
1990— Scran./W.B. (I.L.)	5	4	.556	4.76	1.45	45	9	0	0	...	2-...	96.1	96	56	51	10	44-1	94	.258
1991— Indianapolis (A.A.)	6	7	.462	2.97	1.01	18	17	3	1	...	0-...	121.1	83	42	40	7	39-0	91	.194
—Chunichi (Jp. Cn.)	0	0	...	9.00	0.00	1	...	...	...	...	0-...	1.0	0	1	1	0	0-...	0	...
1992— Indianapolis (A.A.)	2	0	1.000	0.74	0.86	13	0	0	0	...	2-...	24.1	12	3	2	0	9-0	25	.148
—Montreal (N.L.)	0	0	...	14.14	2.86	5	0	0	0	1	0-...	7.0	15	11	11	1	5-0	11	.417
—Nashville (A.A.)	6	2	.750	2.29	1.26	39	2	0	0	...	4-...	70.2	54	22	18	2	35-3	87	.209
1993— Indianapolis (A.A.)	4	2	.667	4.45	1.38	21	1	0	0	...	2-...	30.1	25	16	15	5	17-3	28	.223
—Colorado (N.L.)	0	0	...	9.64	1.93	3	0	0	0	0	0-0	4.2	8	5	5	1	1-0	3	.400
—Cincinnati (N.L.)	2	2	.500	3.70	1.23	26	0	0	0	3	2-2	41.1	36	19	17	5	15-4	40	.235
1994— Indianapolis (A.A.)	5	5	.500	2.31	1.06	40	0	0	0	...	13-...	58.1	35	16	15	1	27-9	67	.172
—Cincinnati (N.L.)	1	2	.333	7.36	1.50	6	0	0	0	0	0-0	7.1	8	9	6	2	3-0	5	.267
1995— Indianapolis (A.A.)	4	1	.800	2.18	1.16	36	0	0	0	...	18-...	41.1	33	13	10	4	15-2	48	.214
—San Francisco (N.L.)	3	1	.750	3.19	1.23	28	0	0	0	7	0-0	31.0	18	11	11	4	20-4	30	.176
1996— Indianapolis (A.A.)	1	4	.200	3.00	0.92	35	1	0	0	...	15-...	48.0	34	18	16	5	10-2	58	.190
—Cincinnati (N.L.)	1	0	1.000	3.94	1.44	34	1	0	0	3	0-0	48.0	51	21	21	7	18-4	46	.277
1997— Cincinnati (N.L.)	0	0	...	11.81	2.25	4	0	0	0	1	0-0	5.1	11	7	7	1	1-0	3	.458
—Indianapolis (A.A.)	3	2	.600	3.71	1.24	33	0	0	0	...	15-...	34.0	30	15	14	5	12-1	53	.231
—Omaha (Am. Assoc.)	0	0	...	0.00	0.89	16	0	0	0	...	9-...	14.2	9	0	0	0	4-0	16	.170
—Kansas City (A.L.)	0	3	.000	4.76	1.29	12	0	0	0	2	0-1	17.0	17	9	9	1	5-0	19	.274
1998— Kansas City (A.L.)	6	4	.600	3.48	1.26	73	0	0	0	18	4-8	82.2	70	35	32	7	34-4	95	.231
1999— Kansas City (A.L.)	5	5	.500	6.09	1.71	68	0	0	0	8	8-15	75.1	87	51	51	13	42-8	68	.294
2000— Oakland (A.L.)	1	2	.333	6.38	1.75	20	0	0	0	1	1-1	36.2	45	31	26	5	19-1	35	.302
—Sacramento (PCL)	6	2	.750	1.30	0.91	33	0	0	0	...	13-...	41.2	27	8	6	1	11-4	50	.175
2001— Dayton (Midw.)	0	0	...	0.00	0.35	4	0	0	0	...	2-...	5.2	2	0	0	0	0-0	6	.095
—Louisville (Int'l)	2	0	1.000	4.74	1.30	20	0	0	0	...	5-...	24.2	22	13	13	6	10-1	27	.242
2002— Nashville (PCL)	4	4	.500	3.36	1.15	47	0	0	0	...	6-...	61.2	47	25	23	8	24-3	70	.209
2003— Tucson (PCL)	0	0	...	0.00	0.00	9	0	0	0	...	5-...	12.1	6	2	0	0	2-0	13	.133
—Arizona (N.L.)	0	2	.000	4.91	1.25	18	0	0	0	0	1-1	18.1	21	10	10	1	2-1	18	.288
—Toronto (A.L.)	0	0	...	4.50	1.44	15	0	0	0	3	0-1	16.0	17	8	8	3	6-0	17	.274
—Louisville (Int'l)	0	0	...	2.45	0.80	4	0	0	0	...	0-...	3.2	3	1	1	0	0-0	7	.214
2004— Tucson (PCL)	5	0	1.000	3.24	1.36	24	0	0	0	...	9-...	25.0	28	9	9	2	6-0	28	.283
—Arizona (N.L.)	1	1	.500	7.08	1.67	21	0	0	0	1	0-2	20.1	24	17	16	5	10-2	17	.286
American League totals (5 years)	12	14	.462	4.98	1.50	188	0	0	0	32	13-26	227.2	236	134	126	29	105-13	234	.271
National League totals (9 years)	8	8	.500	5.01	1.46	150	1	0	0	16	3-5	188.2	199	111	105	27	76-15	179	.274
Major League totals (12 years)	20	22	.476	4.99	1.48	338	1	0	0	48	16-31	416.1	435	245	231	56	182-28	413	.272

SEXSON, RICHIE   1B

PERSONAL: Born December 29, 1974, in Portland, Ore. ... 6-8/237. ... Bats right, throws right. ... Full name: Richmond Lockwood Sexson. ... Name pronounced: SECKS-un. ... High school: Prairie (Brush Prairie, Wash.).

TRANSACTIONS/CAREER NOTES: Selected by Cleveland Indians organization in 24th round of 1993 free-agent draft. ... Traded by Indians with Ps Paul Rigdon and Kane Davis and a player to be named to Milwaukee Brewers for Ps Bob Wickman, Steve Woodard and Jason Bere (July 28, 2000); Brewers acquired 2B Marco Scutaro to complete deal (August 30). ... Traded by Brewers with P Shane Nance and a player to be named to Arizona Diamondbacks for SS Craig Counsell, 2B Junior Spivey, 1B Lyle Overbay, C Chad Moeller and Ps Chris Capuano and Jorge de la Rosa (December 1, 2003); Diamondbacks acquired OF Noochie Varner to complete deal (December 15, 2003). ... On disabled list (April 29-May 21 and May 23, 2004-remainder of season).

RECORDS: Shares major league record for most strikeouts, nine-inning game (5, May 29, 2001).

2004 GAMES PLAYED BY POSITION (MLB): 1B—23.

Year Team (League)	Pos.	G	AB	R	H	2B	3B	HR	RBI	BB	SO	HBP	GDP	SB-CS	Avg.	OBP	SLG	OPS	E	Avg.
																		BATTING		FIELDING
1993— Burlington (Appal.)	1B	40	97	11	18	3	0	1	5	18	21	1	1	1-1	.186	.316	.247	.564	4	.988
1994— Columbus (S. Atl.)	1B	130	488	88	133	25	2	14	77	37	87	14	5	7-3	.273	.338	.418	.756	10	.990
1995— Kinston (Caro.)	1B	131	494	80	151	34	0	22	85	43	115	10	8	4-6	.306	.368	.508	.876	12	.990
1996— Cant./Akr. (Eastern)	1B	133	518	85	143	33	3	16	76	39	118	6	13	2-1	.276	.331	.444	.775	11	.989
1997— Buffalo (A.A.)	1B-DH	115	434	57	113	20	2	31	88	27	87	4	11	5-1	.260	.307	.530	.837	4	.996
— Cleveland (A.L.)	1B-DH	5	11	1	3	0	0	0	0	0	2	0	2	0-0	.273	.273	.273	.545	0	1.000
1998— Buffalo (Int'l)	OF-1B-DH	89	344	58	102	20	1	21	74	50	68	3	11	1-2	.297	.386	.544	.929	3	.990
— Cleveland (A.L.)	1B-DH	49	174	28	54	14	1	11	35	6	42	3	3	1-1	.310	.344	.592	.936	6	.984
1999— Cleveland (A.L.)	1B-OF-DH	134	479	72	122	17	7	31	116	34	117	4	19	3-3	.255	.305	.514	.818	7	.989
2000— Cleveland (A.L.)	OF-1B-DH	91	324	45	83	16	1	16	44	25	96	4	8	1-0	.256	.315	.460	.774	1	.997
— Milwaukee (N.L.)	1B	57	213	44	63	14	0	14	47	34	63	3	3	1-0	.296	.398	.559	.957	5	.991
2001— Milwaukee (N.L.)	1B	158	598	94	162	24	3	45	125	60	178	6	20	2-4	.271	.342	.547	.889	8	.995
2002— Milwaukee (N.L.)	1B-DH	157	570	86	159	37	2	29	102	70	136	8	17	0-0	.279	.364	.504	.867	7	.995
2003— Milwaukee (N.L.)	1B	162	606	97	165	28	2	45	124	98	151	9	18	2-3	.272	.379	.548	.927	11	.993
2004— Arizona (N.L.)	1B	23	90	20	21	4	0	9	23	14	21	0	2	0-0	.233	.337	.578	.914	1	.996
American League totals (4 years)		279	988	146	262	47	9	58	195	65	257	11	32	5-4	.265	.314	.507	.822	14	.989
National League totals (5 years)		557	2077	341	570	107	7	142	421	276	549	26	60	5-7	.274	.365	.538	.902	32	.994
Major League totals (8 years)		836	3065	487	832	154	16	200	616	341	806	37	92	10-11	.271	.349	.528	.877	46	.993

DIVISION SERIES RECORD

Year Team (League)	Pos.	G	AB	R	H	2B	3B	HR	RBI	BB	SO	HBP	GDP	SB-CS	Avg.	OBP	SLG	OPS	E	Avg.
1998— Cleveland (A.L.)	1B	3	2	0	0	0	0	0	0	2	1	0	0	0-0	.000	.500	.000	.500	0	1.000
1999— Cleveland (A.L.)	1B-OF	3	6	1	1	0	0	0	1	1	3	0	0	0-0	.167	.286	.167	.452	0	1.000
Division series totals (2 years)		6	8	1	1	0	0	0	1	3	4	0	0	0-0	.125	.364	.125	.489	0	1.000

CHAMPIONSHIP SERIES RECORD

Year Team (League)	Pos.	G	AB	R	H	2B	3B	HR	RBI	BB	SO	HBP	GDP	SB-CS	Avg.	OBP	SLG	OPS	E	Avg.
1998— Cleveland (A.L.)	1B	3	6	0	0	0	0	0	0	3	0	1	0-0	.000	.000	.000	.000	0	1.000

ALL-STAR GAME RECORD

	G	AB	R	H	2B	3B	HR	RBI	BB	SO	HBP	GDP	SB-CS	Avg.	OBP	SLG	OPS	E	Avg.
All-Star Game totals (2 years)	2	3	0	0	0	0	0	0	0	1	0	0	0-0	.000	.000	.000	0	1.000

SHEETS, BEN — P

PERSONAL: Born July 18, 1978, in Baton Rouge, La. ... 6-1/218. ... Throws right, bats right. ... Full name: Ben M. Sheets. ... High school: St. Amant (La.). ... College: Northeast Louisiana.

TRANSACTIONS/CAREER NOTES: Selected by Milwaukee Brewers organization in first round (10th pick overall) of 1999 free-agent draft. ... On disabled list (August 6-September 21, 2001).

CAREER HITTING: 23-for-243 (.095), 8 R, 1 2B, 0 3B, 0 HR, 7 RBI.

Year Team (League)	W	L	Pct.	ERA	WHIP	G	GS	CG	ShO	Hld.	Sv.-Opp.	IP	H	R	ER	HR	BB-IBB	SO	Avg.
1999— Ogden (Pio.)	0	1	.000	5.63	1.25	2	2	0	0	...	0-...	8.0	8	5	5	2	2-0	12	.267
— Stockton (Calif.)	1	0	1.000	3.58	1.34	5	5	0	0	...	0-...	27.2	23	11	11	1	14-0	28	.232
2000— Huntsville (Southern)	5	3	.625	1.88	1.11	13	13	0	0	...	0-...	72.0	55	17	15	4	25-0	60	.215
— Indianapolis (Int'l)	3	5	.375	2.87	1.32	14	13	1	0	...	0-...	81.2	77	31	26	4	31-0	59	.251
2001— Milwaukee (N.L.)	11	10	.524	4.76	1.41	25	25	1	1	0	0-0	151.1	166	89	80	23	48-6	94	.283
— Indianapolis (Int'l)	1	1	.500	3.38	1.59	2	2	0	0	...	0-...	10.2	14	5	4	0	3-0	6	.318
2002— Milwaukee (N.L.)	11	•16	.407	4.15	1.42	34	34	1	0	0	0-0	216.2	237	105	100	21	70-10	170	.281
2003— Milwaukee (N.L.)	11	13	.458	4.45	1.25	34	34	1	0	0	0-0	220.2	232	122	109	29	43-2	157	.268
2004— Milwaukee (N.L.)	12	14	.462	2.70	0.98	34	34	5	0	0	0-0	237.0	201	85	71	25	32-1	264	.226
Major League totals (4 years)	45	53	.459	3.92	1.25	127	127	8	1	0	0-0	825.2	836	401	360	98	193-19	685	.262

ALL-STAR GAME RECORD

	W	L	Pct.	ERA	WHIP	G	GS	CG	ShO	Hld.	Sv.-Opp.	IP	H	R	ER	HR	BB-IBB	SO	Avg.
All-Star Game totals (2 years)	0	0	...	0.00	0.00	2	0	0	0	...	0-...	1.1	0	0	0	0	0-0	1	.000

SHEFFIELD, GARY — OF

PERSONAL: Born November 18, 1968, in Tampa, Fla. ... 6-0/205. ... Bats right, throws right. ... Full name: Gary Antonian Sheffield. ... High school: Hillsborough (Tampa). ... Nephew of Dwight Gooden, pitcher with five major league teams (1984-2000).

TRANSACTIONS/CAREER NOTES: Selected by Milwaukee Brewers organization in first round (sixth pick overall) of June 1986 free-agent draft. ... On disabled list (July 14-September 9, 1989). ... On suspended list (August 31-September 3, 1990). ....On disabled list (June 15-July 3 and July 25, 1991-remainder of season). ... Traded by Brewers with P Geoff Kellogg to San Diego Padres for P Ricky Bones, SS Jose Valentin and OF Matt Mieske (March 27, 1992). ... Traded by Padres with P Rich Rodriguez to Florida Marlins for Ps Trevor Hoffman, Jose Martinez and Andres Berumen (June 24, 1993). ... On suspended list (July 9-12, 1993). ... On disabled list (May 10-25 and May 28-June 12, 1994); included rehabilitation assignment to Portland. ... On disabled list (June 11-September 1, 1995; and May 14-29, 1997). ... Traded by Marlins with 3B Bobby Bonilla, C Charles Johnson, OF Jim Eisenreich and P Manuel Barrios to Los Angeles Dodgers for C Mike Piazza and 3B Todd Zeile (May 15, 1998). ... On suspended list (August 4-6, 1998; and August 23-27, 2000). ... On disabled list (May 24-June 8, 2001). ... Traded by Dodgers to Atlanta Braves for OF Brian Jordan and Ps Odalis Perez and Andrew Brown (January 15, 2002). ... Signed as a free agent by New York Yankees (December 19, 2003).

HONORS: Named Minor League co-Player of the Year by THE SPORTING NEWS (1988). ... Named Major League Player of the Year by THE SPORTING NEWS (1992). ... Named N.L. Comeback Player of the Year by THE SPORTING NEWS (1992).

2004 GAMES PLAYED BY POSITION (MLB): OF—136, DH—18, 3B—2.

Year Team (League)	Pos.	G	AB	R	H	2B	3B	HR	RBI	BB	SO	HBP	GDP	SB-CS	Avg.	OBP	SLG	OPS	E	Avg.
																		BATTING		FIELDING
1986— Helena (Pio.)	SS	57	222	53	81	12	2	15	71	20	14	3	3	14-4	.365	.413	.640	1.052	24	.911
1987— Stockton (Calif.)	SS	129	469	84	130	23	3	17	103	81	49	8	7	25-15	.277	.388	.448	.836	39	.937
1988— El Paso (Texas)	3B-SS-OF	77	296	70	93	19	3	19	65	35	41	3	9	5-4	.314	.386	.591	.978	23	.936
— Denver (A.A.)	3B-SS	57	212	42	73	9	5	9	54	21	22	5	3	8-4	.344	.407	.561	.969	8	.950

Year	Team (League)	Pos.	G	AB	R	H	2B	3B	HR	RBI	BB	SO	HBP	GDP	SB-CS	Avg.	OBP	SLG	OPS	E	Avg.
—Milwaukee (A.L.)		SS	24	80	12	19	1	0	4	12	7	0	0	5	3-1	.238	.295	.400	.695	3	.967
1989—Milwaukee (A.L.)		3B-SS-DH	95	368	34	91	18	0	5	32	27	33	4	4	10-6	.247	.303	.337	.640	16	.955
—Denver (A.A.)		SS	7	29	3	4	1	1	0	0	2	0	0	1	0-0	.138	.194	.241	.435	0	1.000
1990—Milwaukee (A.L.)		3B	125	487	67	143	30	1	10	67	44	41	3	11	25-10	.294	.350	.421	.771	25	.934
1991—Milwaukee (A.L.)		3B-DH	50	175	25	34	12	2	2	22	19	15	3	3	5-5	.194	.277	.320	.597	8	.922
1992—San Diego (N.L.)		3B	146	557	87	184	34	3	33	100	48	40	6	19	5-6	* .330	.385	.580	.965	16	.961
1993—San Diego (N.L.)		3B	68	258	34	76	12	2	10	36	18	30	3	9	5-1	.295	.344	.473	.817	15	.905
—Florida (N.L.)		3B	72	236	33	69	8	3	10	37	29	34	6	2	12-4	.292	.378	.479	.857	19	.894
1994—Florida (N.L.)		OF	87	322	61	89	16	1	27	78	51	50	6	10	12-6	.276	.380	.584	.964	5	.970
—Portland (East.)		OF	2	7	1	2	1	0	0	0	1	3	0	0	0-0	.286	.375	.429	.804	0	1.000
1995—Florida (N.L.)		OF	63	213	46	69	8	0	16	46	55	45	4	3	19-4	.324	.467	.587	1.054	7	.942
1996—Florida (N.L.)		OF	161	519	118	163	33	1	42	120	142	66	10	16	16-9	.314	* .465	.624	1.090	6	.976
1997—Florida (N.L.)		OF-DH	135	444	86	111	22	1	21	71	121	79	15	7	11-7	.250	.424	.446	.870	5	.980
1998—Florida (N.L.)		OF	40	136	21	37	11	1	6	28	26	16	2	1	4-2	.272	.392	.500	.892	1	.986
—Los Angeles (N.L.)		OF	90	301	52	95	16	1	16	57	69	30	6	4	11-8	.316	.444	.535	.979	1	.994
1999—Los Angeles (N.L.)		OF-DH	152	549	103	165	20	0	34	101	101	64	4	10	11-5	.301	.407	.523	.930	7	.972
2000—Los Angeles (N.L.)		OF-DH	141	501	105	163	24	3	43	109	101	71	4	16	4-6	.325	.438	.643	1.081	• 10	.954
2001—Los Angeles (N.L.)		OF-DH	143	515	98	160	28	2	36	100	94	67	4	12	10-4	.311	.417	.583	1.000	6	.972
2002—Atlanta (N.L.)		OF-DH	135	492	82	151	26	0	25	84	72	53	11	16	12-2	.307	.404	.512	.916	4	.984
2003—Atlanta (N.L.)		OF	155	576	126	190	37	2	39	132	86	55	8	16	18-4	.330	.419	.604	1.023	4	.986
2004—New York (A.L.)		OF-DH-3B	154	573	117	166	30	1	36	121	92	83	11	16	5-6	.290	.393	.534	.927	6	.979
American League totals (5 years)			448	1683	255	453	91	4	57	254	189	179	21	39	48-28	.269	.345	.430	.775	58	.952
National League totals (12 years)			1588	5619	1052	1722	295	20	358	1099	1013	700	89	140	157-65	.306	.416	.557	.973	106	.965
Major League totals (17 years)			2036	7302	1307	2175	386	24	415	1353	1202	879	110	179	205-93	.298	.400	.528	.928	164	.961

DIVISION SERIES RECORD

Year	Team (League)	Pos.	G	AB	R	H	2B	3B	HR	RBI	BB	SO	HBP	GDP	SB-CS	Avg.	OBP	SLG	OPS	E	Avg.
1997—Florida (N.L.)		OF	3	9	3	5	1	0	1	1	5	0	0	0	1-0	.556	.714	1.000	1.714	0	1.000
2002—Atlanta (N.L.)		OF	5	16	3	1	0	0	1	1	7	3	0	1	0-0	.063	.348	.250	.598	0	1.000
2003—Atlanta (N.L.)		OF	4	14	0	2	0	0	1	1	2	0	1	0	0-0	.143	.294	.143	.437	0	1.000
2004—New York (A.L.)		OF	4	18	2	4	1	0	1	2	3	1	0	1	0-1	.222	.333	.444	.778	0	1.000
Division series totals (4 years)			16	57	8	12	2	0	4	4	17	4	1	2	1-1	.211	.400	.404	.804	0	1.000

CHAMPIONSHIP SERIES RECORD

Year	Team (League)	Pos.	G	AB	R	H	2B	3B	HR	RBI	BB	SO	HBP	GDP	SB-CS	Avg.	OBP	SLG	OPS	E	Avg.
1997—Florida (N.L.)		OF	6	17	6	4	0	0	1	1	7	3	0	0	0-0	.235	.458	.412	.870	0	1.000
2004—New York (A.L.)		OF	7	30	7	10	3	0	1	5	6	8	0	1	0-0	.333	.444	.533	.978	0	1.000
Champ. series totals (2 years)			13	47	13	14	3	0	2	6	13	11	0	1	0-0	.298	.450	.489	.939	0	1.000

WORLD SERIES RECORD

Year	Team (League)	Pos.	G	AB	R	H	2B	3B	HR	RBI	BB	SO	HBP	GDP	SB-CS	Avg.	OBP	SLG	OPS	E	Avg.
1997—Florida (N.L.)		OF	7	24	4	7	1	0	1	5	5	8	5	1	0-0	.292	.485	.458	.943	1	.941

ALL-STAR GAME RECORD

			G	AB	R	H	2B	3B	HR	RBI	BB	SO	HBP	GDP	SB-CS	Avg.	OBP	SLG	OPS	E	Avg.
All-Star Game totals (8 years)			8	11	3	2	0	0	1	2	2	0	0	1	0-0	.182	.308	.455	.762	0	1.000

SHELTON, CHRIS   C/1B

PERSONAL: Born June 26, 1980, in Salt Lake City, Utah. ... 6-0/220. ... Bats right, throws right. ... Full name: Christopher Bob Shelton. ... High school: Cottonwood (Salt Lake City). ... College: Utah.

TRANSACTIONS/CAREER NOTES: Selected by Pittsburgh Pirates organization in 33rd round of 2001 free-agent draft. ... Selected by Detroit Tigers from Pirates organization in Rule 5 major league draft (December 15, 2003). ... On disabled list (May 31-July 10, 2004); included rehabilitation assignment to Toledo.

2004 GAMES PLAYED BY POSITION (MLB): DH—11, 1B—8, C—6, OF—1.

Year	Team (League)	Pos.	G	AB	R	H	2B	3B	HR	RBI	BB	SO	HBP	GDP	SB-CS	Avg.	OBP	SLG	OPS	E	Avg.
2001—Williamsport (N.Y.-Penn.)		C-1B	50	174	22	53	11	0	2	33	33	31	2	1	4-1	.305	.415	.402	.817	7	.985
2002—Hickory (S. Atl.)		1B-C-OF	93	332	72	113	27	2	17	65	47	74	5	1	0-0	.340	.425	.587	1.013	1	.998
2003—Lynchburg (Caro.)		1B-C	95	315	71	113	24	1	21	69	68	67	5	6	1-4	.359	.478	.641	1.119	4	.993
—Altoona (East.)		1B-C	35	122	17	34	10	1	0	14	8	23	2	1	0-1	.279	.331	.377	.708	2	.993
2004—Toledo (Int'l)		DH-1B	18	62	5	21	2	0	0	7	10	13	0	0	0-0	.339	.425	.371	.796	2	.973
—Detroit (A.L.)		DH-1B-C-OF	27	46	6	9	1	0	1	3	9	14	0	2	0-0	.196	.321	.283	.604	0	1.000
Major League totals (1 year)			27	46	6	9	1	0	1	3	9	14	0	2	0-0	.196	.321	.283	.604	0	1.000

SHERRILL, GEORGE   P

PERSONAL: Born April 19, 1977, in Memphis, Tenn. ... 6-0/210. ... Throws left, bats left. ... Full name: George Friederich Sherrill. ... College: Austin Peay.

TRANSACTIONS/CAREER NOTES: Signed as a free agent by Seattle Mariners organization (July 2, 2003). ... On disabled list (September 17, 2004-remainder of season).

CAREER HITTING: 0-for-0 (.000), 0 R, 0 2B, 0 3B, 0 HR, 0 RBI.

Year	Team (League)	W	L	Pct.	ERA	WHIP	G	GS	CG	ShO	Hld.	Sv.-Opp.	IP	H	R	ER	HR	BB-IBB	SO	Avg.
2003—San Antonio (Texas)		3	0	1.000	0.33	1.13	16	0	0	0	...	0-...	27.1	19	2	1	1	12-1	31	.198
2004—Tacoma (PCL)		4	2	.667	2.33	1.01	36	0	0	0	...	13-...	50.1	42	13	13	4	9-1	62	.223
—Seattle (A.L.)		2	1	.667	3.80	1.39	21	0	0	0	3	0-0	23.2	24	12	10	3	9-1	16	.258
Major League totals (1 year)		2	1	.667	3.80	1.39	21	0	0	0	3	0-0	23.2	24	12	10	3	9-1	16	.258

SHIELDS, SCOT   P

PERSONAL: Born July 22, 1975, in Fort Lauderdale, Fla. ... 6-1/170. ... Throws right, bats right. ... Full name: Robert Scot Shields. ... High school: Fort Lauderdale (Fla.). ... College: Lincoln Memorial (Tenn.).

TRANSACTIONS/CAREER NOTES: Selected by Anaheim Angels organization in 38th round of 1997 free-agent draft.

CAREER HITTING: 0-for-1 (.000), 0 R, 0 2B, 0 3B, 0 HR, 0 RBI.

Year	Team (League)	W	L	Pct.	ERA	WHIP	G	GS	CG	ShO	Hld.	Sv.-Opp.	IP	H	R	ER	HR	BB-IBB	SO	Avg.
1997—Boise (N'west)		7	2	.778	2.94	1.33	30	0	0	0	...	2-...	52.0	45	20	17	1	24-4	61	.233
1998—Cedar Rapids (Midw.)		6	5	.545	3.65	1.23	58	0	0	0	...	7-...	74.0	62	33	30	5	29-0	81	.232

Year Team (League)	W	L	Pct.	ERA	WHIP	G	GS	CG	ShO	Hld.	Sv.-Opp.	IP	H	R	ER	HR	BB-IBB	SO	Avg.
1999—Lake Elsinore (Calif.)	10	3	.769	2.52	1.21	24	9	2	1	...	1-...	107.1	91	37	30	1	39-4	113	.233
—Erie (East.)	4	4	.500	2.89	1.11	10	10	1	1	...	0-...	74.2	57	26	24	10	26-0	81	.216
2000—Edmonton (PCL)	7	13	.350	5.41	1.47	27	27	4	1	...	0-...	163.0	158	114	98	16	82-0	156	.250
2001—Salt Lake (PCL)	6	11	.353	4.97	1.25	21	21	4	0	...	0-...	137.2	141	84	76	24	31-0	104	.267
—Anaheim (A.L.)	0	0	...	0.00	1.36	8	0	0	0	0	0-0	11.0	8	1	0	0	7-0	7	.200
2002—Salt Lake (PCL)	2	2	.500	3.06	0.96	28	1	0	0	...	1-...	47.0	39	18	16	5	6-0	50	.223
—Anaheim (A.L.)	5	3	.625	2.20	1.06	29	1	0	0	3	0-0	49.0	31	13	12	4	21-1	30	.188
2003—Anaheim (A.L.)	5	6	.455	2.85	1.19	44	13	0	0	3	1-1	148.1	138	56	47	12	38-6	111	.247
2004—Anaheim (A.L.)	8	2	.800	3.33	1.30	60	0	0	0	17	4-7	105.1	97	42	39	6	40-5	109	.238
Major League totals (4 years)	18	11	.621	2.81	1.21	141	14	0	0	23	5-8	313.2	274	112	98	22	106-12	257	.234

DIVISION SERIES RECORD

Year Team (League)	W	L	Pct.	ERA	WHIP	G	GS	CG	ShO	Hld.	Sv.-Opp.	IP	H	R	ER	HR	BB-IBB	SO	Avg.
2004—Anaheim (A.L.)	0	0	...	6.00	2.33	2	0	0	0	0	0-0	3.0	5	2	2	1	2-1	3	.357

WORLD SERIES RECORD

Year Team (League)	W	L	Pct.	ERA	WHIP	G	GS	CG	ShO	Hld.	Sv.-Opp.	IP	H	R	ER	HR	BB-IBB	SO	Avg.
2002—Anaheim (A.L.)	0	0	...	5.40	3.00	1	0	0	0	0	0-0	1.2	5	5	1	2	0-0	1	.455

SHOUSE, BRIAN   P

PERSONAL: Born September 26, 1968, in Effingham, Ill. ... 5-11/190. ... Throws left, bats left. ... Full name: Brian Douglas Shouse. ... High school: Effingham (Ill.). ... College: Bradley.

TRANSACTIONS/CAREER NOTES: Selected by Pittsburgh Pirates organization in 13th round of 1990 free-agent draft. ... Released by Pirates (May 16, 1996). ... Signed by Baltimore Orioles organization (May 22, 1996). ... Signed as a free agent by Boston Red Sox organization (October 28, 1997). ... Contract sold by Red Sox to Kintetsu of the Japan Pacific League (June 25, 1998). ... Signed as a free agent by Arizona Diamondbacks organization (November 19, 1998). ... On disabled list (September 18, 1999-remainder of season). ... Signed as a free agent by New York Mets organization (December 2, 1999). ... Released by Mets (April 14, 2000). ... Signed by Orioles organization (May 13, 2000). ... Signed as a free agent by Houston Astros organization (December 22, 2000). ... Signed as a free agent by Kansas City Royals organization (December 7, 2001). ... On disabled list (April 28-May 13, 2002). ... Released by Royals (June 27, 2002). ... Signed by Astros organization (July 22, 2002). ... Signed as a free agent by Texas Rangers organization (November 13, 2002). ... On disabled list (March 27-May 13, 2004); included rehabilitation assignment to Oklahoma.

CAREER HITTING: 0-for-0 (.000), 0 R, 0 2B, 0 3B, 0 HR, 0 RBI.

Year Team (League)	W	L	Pct.	ERA	WHIP	G	GS	CG	ShO	Hld.	Sv.-Opp.	IP	H	R	ER	HR	BB-IBB	SO	Avg.
1990—Welland (N.Y.-Penn)	4	3	.571	5.22	1.44	17	1	0	0	...	2-...	39.2	50	27	23	2	7-0	39	.309
1991—Augusta (S. Atl.)	2	3	.400	3.19	1.00	26	0	0	0	...	8-...	31.0	22	13	11	1	9-1	32	.200
—Salem (Caro.)	2	1	.667	2.94	1.49	17	0	0	0	...	3-...	33.2	35	12	11	2	15-2	25	.269
1992—Carolina (Southern)	5	6	.455	2.44	1.28	59	0	0	0	...	4-...	77.1	71	31	21	3	28-4	79	.252
1993—Buffalo (A.A.)	1	0	1.000	3.83	1.37	48	0	0	0	...	2-...	51.2	54	24	22	7	17-2	25	.276
—Pittsburgh (N.L.)	0	0	...	9.00	2.25	6	0	0	0	0	0-0	4.0	7	4	4	1	2-0	3	.368
1994—Buffalo (A.A.)	3	4	.429	3.63	1.13	43	0	0	0	...	0-...	52.0	44	22	21	6	15-4	31	.232
1995—Carolina (Southern)	7	6	.538	4.47	1.26	21	20	0	0	...	0-...	114.2	126	64	57	14	19-2	76	.281
—Calgary (PCL)	4	4	.500	6.18	1.75	8	8	1	0	...	0-...	39.1	62	35	27	2	7-0	17	.354
1996—Calgary (PCL)	1	0	1.000	10.66	2.05	12	1	0	0	...	0-...	12.2	22	15	15	4	4-1	12	.367
—Rochester (Int'l)	1	2	.333	4.50	1.38	32	0	0	0	...	0-...	50.0	53	27	25	6	16-1	45	.270
1997—Rochester (Int'l)	6	2	.750	2.27	0.97	54	0	0	0	...	9-...	71.1	48	21	18	6	21-4	81	.191
1998—Pawtucket (Int'l)	2	0	1.000	2.90	0.90	22	1	0	0	...	6-...	31.0	21	11	10	7	7-0	25	.188
—Boston (A.L.)	0	1	.000	5.63	1.63	7	0	0	0	1	0-0	8.0	9	5	5	2	4-0	5	.281
—Kintetsu (Jap. Pac.)	0	2	.000	6.58	2.04	13	3	0	0	...	0-...	26.0	40	20	19	...	13-...	20	...
—Kintetsu (Jp. West.)	1	0	1.000	1.38	1.23	5	2	0	0	...	0-...	13.0	9	2	2	0	7-...	9	...
1999—Tucson (PCL)	3	4	.429	6.25	1.81	30	0	0	0	...	0-...	44.2	63	35	31	4	18-3	32	.339
2000—Norfolk (Int'l)	0	1	.000	15.00	2.67	4	0	0	0	...	0-...	3.0	6	5	5	2	2-0	1	.429
—Rochester (Int'l)	4	4	.500	2.79	1.33	43	0	0	0	...	0-...	58.0	63	20	18	4	14-1	52	.279
2001—New Orleans (PCL)	2	2	.500	2.89	1.25	56	1	0	0	...	1-...	53.0	51	21	17	4	15-0	56	.249
2002—Kansas City (A.L.)	0	0	...	6.14	1.64	23	0	0	0	2	0-0	14.2	15	10	10	3	9-1	11	.259
—Omaha (PCL)	0	0	...	11.57	3.43	5	0	0	0	...	0-...	2.1	7	3	3	0	1-0	2	.538
—New Orleans (PCL)	1	0	1.000	3.43	0.95	19	0	0	0	...	0-...	21.0	17	10	8	2	3-0	20	.215
2003—Oklahoma (PCL)	0	1	.000	3.68	1.50	6	0	0	0	...	1-...	7.1	8	3	3	0	3-0	2	.286
—Texas (A.L.)	0	1	.000	3.10	1.25	62	0	0	0	10	1-1	61.0	62	24	21	4	14-6	40	.267
2004—Oklahoma (PCL)	0	0	...	6.14	2.18	9	0	0	0	...	0-...	7.1	12	5	5	1	4-1	3	.375
—Texas (A.L.)	2	1	1.000	2.23	1.22	53	0	0	0	12	0-0	44.1	36	12	11	3	18-3	34	.224
American League totals (4 years)	2	2	.500	3.30	1.30	145	0	0	0	25	1-1	128.0	122	51	47	9	45-10	90	.253
National League totals (1 year)	0	0	...	9.00	2.25	6	0	0	0	0	0-0	4.0	7	4	4	1	2-0	3	.368
Major League totals (5 years)	2	2	.500	3.48	1.33	151	0	0	0	25	1-1	132.0	129	55	51	10	47-10	93	.257

SHUEY, PAUL   P

PERSONAL: Born September 16, 1970, in Lima, Ohio. ... 6-3/215. ... Throws right, bats right. ... Full name: Paul Kenneth Shuey. ... Name pronounced: SHOE-ee. ... High school: Millbrook (Raleigh, N.C.). ... College: North Carolina.

TRANSACTIONS/CAREER NOTES: Selected by Cleveland Indians organization in first round (second pick overall) of 1992 free-agent draft. ... On disabled list (June 27-July 21, 1994); included rehabilitation assignment to Charlotte. ... On disabled list (May 4-22, 1995). ... On disabled list (April 25-May 18, June 19-July 4 and July 11-August 1, 1997); included rehabilitation assignments to Buffalo and Akron. ... On disabled list (April 11-June 15, 1998); included rehabilitation assignments to Akron and Buffalo. ... On disabled list (April 26-May 11, 1999); included rehabilitation assignment to Buffalo. ... On disabled list (May 21-June 27, 2000); included rehabilitation assignment to Akron. ... On disabled list (June 13-29 and July 22-September 18, 2001); included rehabilitation assignment to Akron. ... On disabled list (June 10-25, 2002); included rehabilitation assignment to Akron. ... Traded by Indians to Los Angeles Dodgers for Ps Terry Mulholland, Ricardo Rodriguez and Francisco Cruceta (July 28, 2002). ... On disabled list (April 25-May 17, 2003); included rehabilitation assignment to Las Vegas. ... On disabled list (April 3, 2004-entire season); included rehabilitation assignments to Ogden and Las Vegas.

CAREER HITTING: 1-for-7 (.143), 0 R, 0 2B, 0 3B, 0 HR, 0 RBI.

Year Team (League)	W	L	Pct.	ERA	WHIP	G	GS	CG	ShO	Hld.	Sv.-Opp.	IP	H	R	ER	HR	BB-IBB	SO	Avg.
1992—Columbus (S. Atl.)	5	5	.500	3.35	1.40	14	14	0	0	...	0-...	78.0	62	35	29	2	47-2	73	.221
1993—Cant./Akr. (Eastern)	4	8	.333	7.30	1.82	27	7	0	0	...	0-...	61.2	76	50	50	13	36-3	41	.308
—Kinston (Caro.)	1	0	1.000	4.84	1.66	15	0	0	0	...	0-...	22.1	29	12	12	1	8-0	27	.326
1994—Kinston (Caro.)	1	0	1.000	3.75	1.08	13	0	0	0	...	8-...	12.0	10	5	5	1	3-0	16	.227
—Cleveland (A.L.)	0	1	.000	8.49	2.23	14	0	0	0	1	5-5	11.2	14	11	11	1	12-1	16	.280
—Charlotte (Int'l)	2	1	.667	1.93	1.07	20	0	0	0	...	10-...	23.1	15	9	5	1	10-0	25	.181

Year Team (League)	W	L	Pct.	ERA	WHIP	G	GS	CG	ShO	Hld.	Sv.-Opp.	IP	H	R	ER	HR	BB-IBB	SO	Avg.
1995— Cleveland (A.L.)	0	2	.000	4.26	1.58	7	0	0	0	0	0-0	6.1	5	4	3	0	5-0	5	.238
— Buffalo (A.A.)	1	2	.333	2.63	1.02	25	0	0	0	...	11-...	27.1	21	9	8	2	7-0	27	.214
1996— Buffalo (A.A.)	3	2	.600	0.81	0.69	19	0	0	0	...	4-...	33.1	14	4	3	1	9-2	57	.126
— Cleveland (A.L.)	5	2	.714	2.85	1.32	42	0	0	0	7	4-7	53.2	45	19	17	6	26-3	44	.231
1997— Cleveland (A.L.)	4	2	.667	6.20	1.78	40	0	0	0	4	2-3	45.0	52	31	31	5	28-3	46	.294
— Buffalo (A.A.)	0	0	...	3.60	1.60	2	0	0	0	...	0-...	5.0	4	2	2	0	4-0	6	.222
— Akron (East.)	0	0	...	3.38	1.25	3	0	0	0	...	0-...	8.0	10	3	3	1	0-0	9	.313
1998— Cleveland (A.L.)	5	4	.556	3.00	1.35	43	0	0	0	12	2-5	51.0	44	19	17	6	25-5	58	.229
— Akron (East.)	0	0	...	54.00	12.00	1	0	0	0	...	0-...	.1	3	2	2	0	1-0	0	.750
— Buffalo (Int'l)	0	0	...	2.51	1.19	11	0	0	0	...	0-...	14.1	11	4	4	0	6-0	22	.204
1999— Cleveland (A.L.)	8	5	.615	3.53	1.32	72	0	0	0	19	6-12	81.2	68	37	32	8	40-7	103	.223
— Buffalo (Int'l)	0	0	...	0.00	1.00	1	0	0	0	...	0-...	1.0	0	0	0	0	1-0	1	.000
2000— Cleveland (A.L.)	4	2	.667	3.39	1.27	57	0	0	0	28	0-5	63.2	51	25	24	4	30-3	69	.219
— Akron (East.)	0	0	...	4.50	1.00	2	1	0	0	...	0-...	2.0	1	1	1	0	1-0	1	.143
2001— Cleveland (A.L.)	5	3	.625	2.82	1.45	47	0	0	0	9	2-5	54.1	53	25	17	1	26-5	70	.251
— Akron (East.)	0	0	...	0.00	1.00	1	0	0	0	...	0-...	1.0	0	0	0	0	1-0	2	.000
2002— Cleveland (A.L.)	3	0	1.000	2.41	1.10	39	0	0	0	12	0-2	37.1	31	11	10	1	10-1	39	.225
— Akron (East.)	0	0	...	4.50	1.00	2	0	0	0	...	0-...	2.0	2	1	1	0	0-0	3	.250
— Los Angeles (N.L.)	5	2	.714	4.40	1.50	28	0	0	0	7	1-3	30.2	25	18	15	2	21-1	24	.217
2003— Las Vegas (PCL)	0	1	.000	27.00	3.00	1	1	0	0	...	0-...	1.0	2	3	3	1	1-0	1	.400
— Los Angeles (N.L.)	6	4	.600	3.00	1.20	62	0	0	0	10	0-1	69.0	50	24	23	6	33-3	60	.207
2004— Las Vegas (PCL)	0	1	.000	18.00	3.67	3	0	0	0	...	0-...	3.0	9	6	6	2	2-0	2	.500
— Ogden (Pio.)	0	0	...	3.38	2.25	2	2	0	0	...	0-...	2.2	2	2	1	0	4-0	4	.222
American League totals (9 years)	34	21	.618	3.60	1.40	361	0	0	0	92	21-44	404.2	363	182	162	32	202-28	450	.239
National League totals (2 years)	11	6	.647	3.43	1.29	90	0	0	0	17	1-4	99.2	75	42	38	8	54-4	84	.210
Major League totals (10 years)	45	27	.625	3.57	1.38	451	0	0	0	109	22-48	504.1	438	224	200	40	256-32	534	.233

DIVISION SERIES RECORD

Year Team (League)	W	L	Pct.	ERA	WHIP	G	GS	CG	ShO	Hld.	Sv.-Opp.	IP	H	R	ER	HR	BB-IBB	SO	Avg.
1996— Cleveland (A.L.)	0	0	...	9.00	3.50	3	0	0	0	0	0-0	2.0	5	2	2	2	2-0	2	.500
1998— Cleveland (A.L.)	0	0	...	0.00	1.33	3	0	0	0	2	0-0	3.0	3	0	0	0	1-0	4	.273
1999— Cleveland (A.L.)	1	1	.500	11.25	2.00	3	0	0	0	0	0-0	4.0	4	5	5	1	4-1	5	.250
2001— Cleveland (A.L.)	0	0	...	6.75	2.25	2	0	0	0	0	0-0	1.1	3	1	1	1	0-0	2	.429
Division series totals (4 years)	1	1	.500	6.97	2.13	11	0	0	0	2	0-0	10.1	15	8	8	4	7-1	13	.341

CHAMPIONSHIP SERIES RECORD

Year Team (League)	W	L	Pct.	ERA	WHIP	G	GS	CG	ShO	Hld.	Sv.-Opp.	IP	H	R	ER	HR	BB-IBB	SO	Avg.
1998— Cleveland (A.L.)	0	0	...	0.00	1.74	5	0	0	0	0	0-0	6.1	4	0	0	0	7-2	7	.200

SIERRA, RUBEN — DH/OF

PERSONAL: Born October 6, 1965, in Rio Piedras, Puerto Rico. ... 6-1/215. ... Bats both, throws right. ... Full name: Ruben Angel Sierra. ... High school: Dr. Secario Rosario (Rio Piedras, Puerto Rico).

TRANSACTIONS/CAREER NOTES: Signed as a non-drafted free agent by Texas Rangers organization (November 21, 1982). ... Traded by Rangers with Ps Jeff Russell and Bobby Witt and cash to Oakland Athletics for OF Jose Canseco (August 31, 1992). ... On disabled list (July 7-22, 1995). ... Traded by A's with P Jason Beverlin to New York Yankees for OF/DH Danny Tartabull (July 28, 1995). ... Traded by Yankees with P Matt Drews to Detroit Tigers for 1B/DH Cecil Fielder (July 31, 1996). ... Traded by Tigers to Cincinnati Reds for OF Decomba Conner and P Ben Bailey (October 28, 1996). ... Released by Reds (May 9, 1997). ... Signed by Toronto Blue Jays organization (May 11, 1997). ... Released by Blue Jays (June 16, 1997). ... Signed by Chicago White Sox organization (January 9, 1998). ... Released by White Sox (May 29, 1998). ... Signed by New York Mets organization (June 20, 1998). ... Signed as a free agent by Cleveland Indians organization (December 23, 1999). ... Released by Indians (March 20, 2000). ... Signed by Rangers organization (May 1, 2000). ... Re-signed by Rangers organization (December 13, 2000). ... On disabled list (July 27-August 11, 2001). ... Signed as a free agent by Seattle Mariners (January 3, 2002). ... Signed as a free agent by Rangers organization (January 27, 2003). ... Traded by Rangers to Yankees for OF Marcus Thames (June 6, 2003).

HONORS: Named A.L. Player of the Year by THE SPORTING NEWS (1989). ... Named A.L. Comeback Player of the Year by THE SPORTING NEWS (2001).

2004 GAMES PLAYED BY POSITION (MLB): DH—56, OF—29.

Year Team (League)	Pos.	G	AB	R	H	2B	3B	HR	RBI	BB	SO	HBP	GDP	SB-CS	Avg.	OBP	SLG	OPS	E	Avg.
1983— GC Rangers (GCL)	OF	48	182	26	44	7	3	1	26	16	38	1	...	3-4	.242	.300	.330	.630	4	.948
1984— Burlington (Midw.)	OF	138	482	55	127	33	5	6	75	49	97	1	9	13-9	.263	.331	.390	.721	20	.928
1985— Tulsa (Texas)	OF	137	545	63	138	34	8	13	74	35	111	1	8	22-7	.253	.297	.417	.713	15	.943
1986— Okla. City (A.A.)	OF	46	189	31	56	11	2	9	41	15	27	0	5	8-2	.296	.341	.519	.860	2	.983
— Texas (A.L.)	DH-OF	113	382	50	101	13	10	16	55	22	65	1	8	7-8	.264	.302	.476	.779	6	.972
1987— Texas (A.L.)	OF	158	* 643	97	169	35	4	30	109	39	114	2	18	16-11	.263	.302	.470	.771	11	.963
1988— Texas (A.L.)	DH-OF	156	615	77	156	32	2	23	91	44	91	1	15	18-4	.254	.301	.424	.725	7	.979
1989— Texas (A.L.)	OF	• 162	634	101	194	35	* 14	29	* 119	43	82	2	7	8-2	.306	.347	* .543	.889	9	.973
1990— Texas (A.L.)	DH-OF	159	608	70	170	37	2	16	96	49	86	1	15	9-0	.280	.330	.426	.756	10	.967
1991— Texas (A.L.)	OF	161	661	110	203	44	5	25	116	56	91	0	17	16-4	.307	.357	.502	.859	7	.979
1992— Texas (A.L.)	OF-DH	124	500	66	139	30	6	14	70	31	59	0	9	12-4	.278	.315	.446	.761	7	.970
— Oakland (A.L.)	OF-DH	27	101	17	28	4	1	3	17	14	9	0	2	2-0	.277	.359	.426	.785	0	1.000
1993— Oakland (A.L.)	OF-DH	158	630	77	147	23	5	22	101	52	97	0	17	25-5	.233	.288	.390	.678	7	.977
1994— Oakland (A.L.)	OF-DH	110	426	71	114	21	1	23	92	23	64	0	15	8-5	.268	.298	.484	.781	* 9	.948
1995— Oakland (A.L.)	OF-DH	70	264	40	70	17	0	12	42	24	42	0	4	4-4	.265	.323	.466	.789	4	.957
— New York (A.L.)	DH-OF	56	215	33	56	15	0	7	44	22	34	0	6	1-0	.260	.322	.428	.750	1	.950
1996— Campeche (Mex.)	DH	1	1	1	0	0	0	0	0	0	0	...	...	0-0	.000	...	.000	...	...	...
— New York (A.L.)	DH-OF	96	360	39	93	17	1	11	52	40	58	0	10	1-3	.258	.327	.403	.730	1	.984
— Detroit (A.L.)	OF-DH	46	158	22	35	9	1	1	20	20	25	0	2	3-1	.222	.306	.310	.616	5	.914
1997— Cincinnati (N.L.)	OF	25	90	6	22	5	1	2	7	6	21	0	1	0-0	.244	.292	.389	.681	0	1.000
— Syracuse (Int'l)	OF	8	32	5	7	2	0	1	5	2	6	0	0	0-0	.219	.265	.375	.640	1	.923
— Toronto (A.L.)	OF-DH	14	48	4	10	0	2	1	5	3	13	0	0	0-0	.208	.250	.354	.604	1	1.000
1998— Chicago (A.L.)	OF-DH	27	74	7	16	4	1	4	11	3	11	0	2	2-0	.216	.247	.459	.706	0	1.000
— Norfolk (Int'l)	OF-DH	28	108	16	28	5	0	3	19	13	18	0	4	3-0	.259	.331	.389	.720	0	1.000
1999— Atlantic City (Atl.)	DH-OF	112	422	76	124	22	2	28	82	59	63	...	...	3-2	.294	...	.555	...	3	.960
2000— Cancun (Mex.)	OF	16	62	8	22	2	1	3	12	10	10	...	...	0-1	.355	...	.565	...	0	1.000

Year Team (League)	Pos.	G	AB	R	H	2B	3B	HR	RBI	BB	SO	HBP	GDP	SB-CS	Avg.	OBP	SLG	OPS	E	Avg.
—Oklahoma (PCL)	OF	112	439	70	143	26	3	18	82	55	63	0	24	5-2	.326	.398	.522	.919	6	.962
—Texas (A.L.)	DH	20	60	5	14	0	0	1	7	4	9	0	1	1-0	.233	.281	.283	.565	...	...
2001—Oklahoma (PCL)	OF	24	94	14	25	2	1	3	12	10	14	0	5	2-0	.266	.337	.404	.741	0	1.000
—Texas (A.L.)	DH-OF	94	344	55	100	22	1	23	67	19	52	0	13	2-0	.291	.322	.561	.884	4	.937
2002—Seattle (A.L.)	OF-DH	122	419	47	113	23	0	13	60	31	66	0	17	4-0	.270	.319	.418	.736	2	.979
2003—Texas (A.L.)	OF-DH	43	133	14	35	9	0	3	12	14	27	0	2	1-1	.263	.333	.399	.732	1	.962
—New York (A.L.)	DH-OF	63	174	19	48	8	1	6	31	13	20	0	7	1-0	.276	.323	.437	.760	0	1.000
2004—New York (A.L.)	DH-OF	107	307	40	75	12	1	17	65	25	55	0	5	1-0	.244	.296	.456	.752	1	.977
American League totals (18 years)		2086	7756	1061	2086	410	58	300	1282	591	1170	7	190	142-52	.269	.317	.453	.770	93	.970
National League totals (1 year)		25	90	6	22	5	1	2	7	6	21	0	1	0-0	.244	.292	.389	.681	0	1.000
Major League totals (18 years)		2111	7846	1067	2108	415	59	302	1289	597	1191	7	191	142-52	.269	.317	.452	.769	93	.970

DIVISION SERIES RECORD

Year Team (League)	Pos.	G	AB	R	H	2B	3B	HR	RBI	BB	SO	HBP	GDP	SB-CS	Avg.	OBP	SLG	OPS	E	Avg.
1995—New York (A.L.)	DH	5	23	2	4	2	0	2	5	2	7	0	0	0-0	.174	.231	.522	.753	...	...
2003—New York (A.L.)	OF	1	2	0	0	0	0	0	0	0	0	0	0	0-0	.000	.000	.000	.000	0	...
2004—New York (A.L.)	DH	3	12	1	2	0	0	1	3	2	3	0	0	1-0	.167	.286	.417	.702	0	...
Division series totals (3 years)		9	37	3	6	2	0	3	8	4	10	0	0	1-0	.162	.238	.459	.698	0	...

CHAMPIONSHIP SERIES RECORD

Year Team (League)	Pos.	G	AB	R	H	2B	3B	HR	RBI	BB	SO	HBP	GDP	SB-CS	Avg.	OBP	SLG	OPS	E	Avg.
1992—Oakland (A.L.)	OF	6	24	4	8	2	1	1	7	2	1	0	1	1-2	.333	.357	.625	.982	0	1.000
2003—New York (A.L.)	OF	3	2	1	1	0	0	1	1	1	0	0	0	0-0	.500	.667	2.000	2.667	0	...
2004—New York (A.L.)	DH	5	21	1	7	1	1	0	2	3	8	0	0	0-0	.333	.417	.476	.893	0	...
Champ. series totals (3 years)		14	47	6	16	3	2	2	10	6	9	0	1	1-2	.340	.400	.617	1.017	0	1.000

WORLD SERIES RECORD

Year Team (League)	Pos.	G	AB	R	H	2B	3B	HR	RBI	BB	SO	HBP	GDP	SB-CS	Avg.	OBP	SLG	OPS	E	Avg.
2003—New York (A.L.)	OF	5	4	0	1	0	1	0	2	1	3	0	0	0-0	.250	.400	.750	1.150	0	...

ALL-STAR GAME RECORD

		G	AB	R	H	2B	3B	HR	RBI	BB	SO	HBP	GDP	SB-CS	Avg.	OBP	SLG	OPS	E	Avg.
All-Star Game totals (4 years)		4	9	3	4	0	0	1	3	0	2	0	0	0-0	.444	.444	.778	1.222	0	1.000

SILVA, CARLOS — P

PERSONAL: Born April 23, 1979, in Bolivar, Venezuela. ... 6-4/240. ... Throws right, bats right. ... High school: U.E. General Ezequiel Zamora Bolivar.

TRANSACTIONS/CAREER NOTES: Signed as a non-drafted free agent by Philadelphia Phillies organization (March 22, 1996). ... On disabled list (May 27-June 14, 2002); included rehabilitation assignment to Reading. ... On suspended list (July 17-22, 2003). ... Traded by Phillies with IF Nick Punto and a player to be named to Minnesota Twins for P Eric Milton (December 3, 2003); Twins acquired P Bobby Korecky to complete deal (December 16, 2003).

CAREER HITTING: 2-for-14 (.143), 0 R, 1 2B, 0 3B, 0 HR, 1 RBI.

Year Team (League)	W	L	Pct.	ERA	WHIP	G	GS	CG	ShO	Hld.	Sv.-Opp.	IP	H	R	ER	HR	BB-IBB	SO	Avg.
1996—Martinsville (App.)	0	0	...	4.00	1.39	7	1	0	0	...	0-...	18.0	20	11	8	1	5-0	16	.299
1997—Martinsville (App.)	2	2	.500	5.15	1.39	11	11	0	0	...	0-...	57.2	66	46	33	9	14-0	31	.284
1998—Martinsville (App.)	1	4	.200	5.05	1.27	7	7	1	0	...	0-...	41.0	48	24	23	2	4-0	21	.284
—Batavia (N.Y.-Penn)	2	3	.400	6.35	1.54	9	7	0	0	...	0-...	45.1	61	37	32	4	9-0	27	.314
1999—Piedmont (S. Atl.)	11	8	.579	3.12	1.32	26	26	3	1	...	0-...	164.1	176	79	57	6	41-2	99	.273
2000—Clearwater (Fla. St.)	8	13	.381	3.57	1.45	26	24	4	0	...	0-...	176.1	229	99	70	7	26-1	82	.314
2001—Reading (East.)	15	8	.652	3.90	1.24	28	28	4	1	...	0-...	180.0	197	85	78	20	27-0	100	.284
2002—Philadelphia (N.L.)	5	0	1.000	3.21	1.31	68	0	0	0	8	1-5	84.0	88	34	30	4	22-6	41	.282
—Reading (East.)	0	0	...	0.00	0.00	2	0	0	0	...	1-...	3.0	0	0	0	0	0-0	1	.000
2003—Philadelphia (N.L.)	3	1	.750	4.43	1.48	62	1	0	0	4	1-3	87.1	92	43	43	7	37-5	48	.280
2004—Minnesota (A.L.)	14	8	.636	4.21	1.43	33	33	1	1	0	0-0	203.0	255	100	95	23	35-2	76	.310
American League totals (1 year)	14	8	.636	4.21	1.43	33	33	1	1	0	0-0	203.0	255	100	95	23	35-2	76	.310
National League totals (2 years)	8	1	.889	3.83	1.39	130	1	0	0	12	2-8	171.1	180	77	73	11	59-11	89	.281
Major League totals (3 years)	22	9	.710	4.04	1.41	163	34	1	1	12	2-8	374.1	435	177	168	34	94-13	165	.297

DIVISION SERIES RECORD

Year Team (League)	W	L	Pct.	ERA	WHIP	G	GS	CG	ShO	Hld.	Sv.-Opp.	IP	H	R	ER	HR	BB-IBB	SO	Avg.
2004—Minnesota (A.L.)	0	1	.000	10.80	2.00	1	1	0	0	0	0-0	5.0	10	6	6	1	0-0	1	.417

SIMON, RANDALL — 1B

PERSONAL: Born May 25, 1975, in Willemstad, Curacao. ... 6-0/240. ... Bats left, throws left. ... Full name: Randall Carlito Simon. ... High school: Juan Pablo Duarte Tech (Willemstad, Curacao).

TRANSACTIONS/CAREER NOTES: Signed as a non-drafted free agent by Atlanta Braves organization (July 17, 1992). ... Released by Braves (March 31, 2000). ... Signed by Florida Marlins organization (April 5, 2000). ... Released by Marlins (May 8, 2000). ... Signed by New York Yankees organization (May 14, 2000). ... Signed as a free agent by Detroit Tigers organization (January 18, 2001). ... Traded by Tigers to Pittsburgh Pirates for P Adrian Burnside and two players to be named (November 25, 2002); Tigers acquired P Roberto Novoa (December 16, 2002) and IF Kody Kirkland (May 24, 2003) to complete deal. ... On disabled list (June 21-July 7, 2003); included rehabilitation assignment to Nashville. ... On suspended list (July 10-13, 2003). ... Traded by Pirates to Chicago Cubs for OF Ray Sadler (August 17, 2003). ... Signed as a free agent by Pirates (February 19, 2004). ... On disabled list (April 25-May 28, 2004); included rehabilitation assignment to Nashville. ... Released by Pirates (August 14, 2004). ... Signed by Tampa Bay Devil Rays (August 19, 2004). ... Released by Devil Rays (September 8, 2004).

2004 GAMES PLAYED BY POSITION (MLB): 1B—47, DH—10.

Year Team (League)	Pos.	G	AB	R	H	2B	3B	HR	RBI	BB	SO	HBP	GDP	SB-CS	Avg.	OBP	SLG	OPS	E	Avg.
1992—Dominican Braves (DSL) ...	C	11	43	7	12	4	2	0	7	5	6	...	...	1-...	.279	...	.465	...	4	.979
1993—Danville (Appal.)	1B	61	232	28	59	17	1	3	31	10	34	2	4	1-1	.254	.289	.375	.664	10	.980
1994—Macon (S. Atl.)	1B	106	358	48	105	23	1	10	54	6	56	1	7	7-6	.293	.305	.447	.752	9	.986
1995—Durham (Caro.)	1B	122	420	56	111	18	1	18	79	36	63	5	15	6-5	.264	.326	.440	.767	10	.989
1996—Greenville (Sou.)	1B-OF	134	498	74	139	26	2	18	77	37	61	4	13	4-9	.279	.331	.448	.779	16	.980
1997—Richmond (Int'l)	1B-DH	133	519	62	160	45	1	14	102	17	76	4	18	1-6	.308	.335	.480	.814	14	.988
—Atlanta (N.L.)	1B	13	14	2	6	1	0	0	1	1	2	0	1	0-0	.429	.467	.500	.967	0	1.000
1998—Richmond (Int'l)	1B-DH	126	484	52	124	20	1	13	70	24	62	2	22	4-4	.256	.292	.382	.674	11	.989
—Atlanta (N.L.)	1B	7	16	2	3	0	0	0	4	0	1	0	0	0-0	.188	.176	.188	.364	0	1.000
1999—Atlanta (N.L.)	1B	90	218	26	69	16	0	5	25	17	25	1	10	2-2	.317	.367	.459	.826	3	.994

Year	Team (League)	Pos.	G	AB	R	H	2B	3B	HR	RBI	BB	SO	HBP	GDP	SB-CS	Avg.	OBP	SLG	OPS	E	Avg.
— Richmond (Int'l)		1B-DH	15	59	7	16	4	0	1	8	3	10	0	0	0-1	.271	.302	.390	.691	0	1.000
2000— Calgary (PCL)		1B	22	68	5	20	3	0	1	11	0	3	0	1	0-0	.294	.290	.382	.672	4	.966
— Columbus (Int'l)		1B-OF	94	364	52	97	20	4	17	74	35	42	0	17	6-5	.266	.325	.484	.809	9	.987
2001— Toledo (Int'l)		1B	59	222	27	75	13	0	10	31	21	21	2	8	0-3	.338	.400	.532	.932	7	.986
— Detroit (A.L.)		1B-DH	81	256	28	78	14	2	6	37	15	28	0	9	0-1	.305	.341	.445	.786	5	.992
2002— Detroit (A.L.)		DH-1B	130	482	51	145	17	1	19	82	13	30	4	13	0-1	.301	.320	.459	.779	7	.988
2003— Nashville (PCL)		1B	2	8	3	3	1	0	1	2	0	0	0	1	0-0	.375	.375	1.250		0	1.000
— Pittsburgh (N.L.)		1B	91	307	34	84	14	0	10	51	12	30	2	6	0-0	.274	.305	.417	.722	4	.994
— Chicago (N.L.)		1B	33	103	13	29	3	0	6	21	4	7	2	1	0-0	.282	.318	.485	.804	2	.991
2004— Nashville (PCL)		1B-DH	17	64	5	17	4	0	1	6	2	8	1	4	1-0	.266	.294	.375	.669	0	1.000
— Pittsburgh (N.L.)		1B-DH	61	175	14	34	6	0	3	14	15	17	2	8	0-0	.194	.264	.280	.544	5	.992
— Tampa Bay (A.L.)		DH-1B	8	17	2	2	0	0	0	0	3	2	1	0	0-0	.118	.286	.118	.403	0	...
American League totals (3 years)			219	755	81	225	31	3	25	119	31	60	5	22	0-2	.298	.326	.446	.773	10	.990
National League totals (5 years)			295	833	91	225	40	0	24	116	49	82	7	26	2-2	.270	.315	.405	.719	12	.994
Major League totals (7 years)			514	1588	172	450	71	3	49	235	80	142	12	48	2-4	.283	.320	.424	.745	22	.992

DIVISION SERIES RECORD

Year	Team (League)	Pos.	G	AB	R	H	2B	3B	HR	RBI	BB	SO	HBP	GDP	SB-CS	Avg.	OBP	SLG	OPS	E	Avg.
1999— Atlanta (N.L.)		Did not play.																			
2003— Chicago (N.L.)		1B	4	7	1	3	1	0	0	2	0	2	0	0	0-0	.429	.429	.571	1.000	0	1.000

CHAMPIONSHIP SERIES RECORD

Year	Team (League)	Pos.	G	AB	R	H	2B	3B	HR	RBI	BB	SO	HBP	GDP	SB-CS	Avg.	OBP	SLG	OPS	E	Avg.
1999— Atlanta (N.L.)		Did not play.																			
2003— Chicago (N.L.)		1B	6	17	3	5	2	0	1	4	0	3	0	1	0-0	.294	.294	.588	.882	1	.970

WORLD SERIES RECORD

Year	Team (League)	Pos.	G	AB	R	H	2B	3B	HR	RBI	BB	SO	HBP	GDP	SB-CS	Avg.	OBP	SLG	OPS	E	Avg.
1999— Atlanta (N.L.)		Did not play.																			

SIMONTACCHI, JASON   P

PERSONAL: Born November 13, 1973, in Mountain View, Calif. ... 6-2/190. ... Throws right, bats right. ... Full name: Jason William Simontacchi. ... Name pronounced: cy-mun-TACH-ee. ... College: Albertson (Idaho).

TRANSACTIONS/CAREER NOTES: Selected by Kansas City Royals organization in 21st round of 1996 free-agent draft. ... Released by Royals (July 30, 1997). ... Signed as a free agent by Pittsburgh Pirates organization (January 6, 1999). ... Released by Pirates (September 29, 1999). ... Signed as a free agent by Minnesota Twins organization (September 27, 2000). ... Signed as a free agent by St. Louis Cardinals organization (December 21, 2001).

CAREER HITTING: 18-for-90 (.200), 9 R, 1 2B, 0 3B, 0 HR, 2 RBI.

Year	Team (League)	W	L	Pct.	ERA	WHIP	G	GS	CG	ShO	Hld.	Sv.-Opp.	IP	H	R	ER	HR	BB-IBB	SO	Avg.
1996— Spokane (N'west)	2	5	.286	5.17	1.57	14	6	0	0	...	2-...	47.0	59	37	27	8	15-0	43	.312
1997— Lansing (Midw.)	3	7	.300	6.97	1.78	29	1	0	0	...	2-...	60.2	93	56	47	7	15-1	38	.346
1998— Springfield (Fron.)	10	2	.833	2.95	1.13	16	16	3	...	...	0-...	110.0	103	43	36	14	21-3	92	.247
1999— Hickory (S. Atl.)	4	6	.400	4.02	1.30	23	7	0	0	...	1-...	69.1	71	34	31	8	19-1	66	.264
2000—				Played in Italy.															
2001— Edmonton (PCL)	7	13	.350	5.34	1.50	32	18	2	0	...	0-...	143.1	192	97	85	21	23-1	83	.327
2002— Memphis (PCL)	5	1	.833	2.34	1.16	6	6	0	0	...	0-...	42.1	44	12	11	2	5-1	28	.273
— St. Louis (N.L.)	11	5	.688	4.02	1.31	24	24	0	0	0	0-0	143.1	134	64	64	18	54-4	72	.253
2003— St. Louis (N.L.)	9	5	.643	5.56	1.54	46	16	1	0	7	1-3	126.1	153	82	78	21	41-0	74	.299
2004— Memphis (PCL)	7	4	.636	4.33	1.40	33	8	0	0	...	2-...	81.0	101	44	39	8	12-2	55	.308
— St. Louis (N.L.)	0	0	...	5.28	1.57	13	0	0	0		0-0	15.1	17	10	9	5	7-0	3	.304
Major League totals (3 years)	20	10	.667	4.77	1.42	83	40	1	0	7	1-3	285.0	304	160	151	44	102-4	149	.277

SIMPSON, ALLAN   P

PERSONAL: Born August 26, 1977, in Springfield, Ill. ... 6-4/185. ... Throws right, bats right. ... Full name: Larry Allan Simpson. ... High school: Cheyenne (North Las Vegas, Nev.). ... Junior college: Taft (Calif.).

TRANSACTIONS/CAREER NOTES: Selected by Seattle Mariners organization in eighth round of 1997 free-agent draft. ... Traded by Mariners to Colorado Rockies for P Chris Buglovsky (December 15, 2003).

CAREER HITTING: 0-for-1 (.000), 0 R, 0 2B, 0 3B, 0 HR, 0 RBI.

Year	Team (League)	W	L	Pct.	ERA	WHIP	G	GS	CG	ShO	Hld.	Sv.-Opp.	IP	H	R	ER	HR	BB-IBB	SO	Avg.
1997— Everett (Northwest)	0	3	.000	6.84	1.90	16	0	0	0	...	0-...	26.1	26	23	20	1	24-1	26	.263
1998— Wisconsin (Midw.)	3	5	.375	4.44	1.61	19	19	0	0	...	0-...	93.1	89	52	46	5	61-0	86	.257
— Ariz. Mariners (Ariz.)	1	0	1.000	0.96	1.18	3	0	0	0	...	1-...	9.1	8	2	1	1	3-0	12	.235
1999— Wisconsin (Midw.)	2	9	.182	4.38	1.45	24	13	1	0	...	0-...	90.1	83	56	44	4	48-0	88	.245
— Lancaster (Calif.)	0	0	...	6.33	1.45	9	0	0	0	...	0-...	21.1	17	16	15	4	14-0	25	.218
2000— Lancaster (Calif.)	3	2	.600	3.29	1.17	46	0	0	0	...	6-...	52.0	34	17	12	1	27-1	67	.184
2001— San Bernardino (Calif.)	1	0	1.000	1.80	1.03	16	0	0	0	...	1-...	30.0	19	7	6	1	12-1	40	.178
— San Antonio (Texas)	2	1	.667	1.86	1.03	22	0	0	0	...	1-...	38.2	25	8	8	1	15-1	37	.184
2002— San Antonio (Texas)	10	5	.667	3.06	1.25	56	0	0	0	...	7-...	82.1	53	33	28	4	50-5	99	.189
2003— Tacoma (PCL)	2	5	.286	4.16	1.63	43	0	0	0	...	1-...	60.0	60	30	29	7	42-1	69	.251
2004— Colo. Springs (PCL)	2	1	.667	2.80	1.13	27	0	0	0	...	4-...	35.1	30	14	11	1	10-0	43	.236
— Colorado (N.L.)	2	1	.667	5.08	1.64	32	0	0	0	1	0-1	39.0	44	26	22	4	20-0	46	.289
Major League totals (1 year)	2	1	.667	5.08	1.64	32	0	0	0	1	0-1	39.0	44	26	22	4	20-0	46	.289

SIZEMORE, GRADY   OF

PERSONAL: Born August 2, 1982, in Seattle, Wash. ... 6-2/200. ... Bats left, throws left. ... High school: Cascade (Everett, Wash.).

TRANSACTIONS/CAREER NOTES: Selected by Montreal Expos organization in third round of 2000 free-agent draft. ... Traded by Expos with 1B Lee Stevens, IF Brandon Phillips and P Cliff Lee to Cleveland Indians for P Bartolo Colon and a player to be named (June 27, 2002); Expos acquired P Tim Drew to complete deal (June 28, 2002).

2004 GAMES PLAYED BY POSITION (MLB): OF—42.

Year	Team (League)	Pos.	G	AB	R	H	2B	3B	HR	RBI	BB	SO	HBP	GDP	SB-CS	Avg.	OBP	SLG	OPS	E	Avg.
									BATTING											FIELDING	
2000— GC Expos (GCL)		OF-1B	55	205	31	60	8	3	1	14	23	24	6	1	16-2	.293	.380	.376	.756	3	.975
2001— Clinton (Midw.)		OF	123	451	64	121	16	4	2	61	81	92	4	7	32-11	.268	.381	.335	.716	7	.972

Year	Team (League)	Pos.	G	AB	R	H	2B	3B	HR	RBI	BB	SO	HBP	GDP	SB-CS	Avg.	OBP	SLG	OPS	E	Avg.
2002— Brevard County (FSL)	OF	75	256	37	66	15	4	0	26	36	41	2	6	9-9	.258	.351	.348	.699	3	.977
— Kinston (Caro.)	OF	47	172	31	59	9	3	3	20	33	30	1	1	14-7	.343	.451	.483	.934	4	.949
2003— Akron (East.)	OF	128	496	96	151	26	11	13	78	46	73	11	5	10-9	.304	.373	.480	.853	4	.986
2004— Buffalo (Int'l)	OF-DH	101	418	73	120	23	8	8	51	42	72	8	6	15-10	.287	.360	.438	.787	1	.996
— Cleveland (A.L.)	OF	43	138	15	34	6	2	4	24	14	34	5	0	2-0	.246	.333	.406	.739	1	.991
Major League totals (1 year)		43	138	15	34	6	2	4	24	14	34	5	0	2-0	.246	.333	.406	.739	1	.991

SLEDGE, TERRMEL — OF

PERSONAL: Born March 18, 1977, in Fayetteville, N.C. ... 6-0/185. ... Bats left, throws left. ... High school: John F. Kennedy (Granada Hills, Calif.). ... College: Long Beach State.

TRANSACTIONS/CAREER NOTES: Selected by Cincinnati Reds organization in 45th round of 1998 free-agent draft; did not sign. ... Selected by Seattle Mariners organization in eighth round of 1999 free-agent draft. ... Traded by Mariners to Montreal Expos (September 27, 2000), completing deal in which Mariners acquired C Chris Widger for two players to be named (August 8, 2000); Expos acquired P Sean Spencer as part of deal (August 10, 2000). ... Expos franchise transferred to Washington, D.C., for 2005 season.

2004 GAMES PLAYED BY POSITION (MLB): OF—114, 1B—10.

Year	Team (League)	Pos.	G	AB	R	H	2B	3B	HR	RBI	BB	SO	HBP	GDP	SB-CS	Avg.	OBP	SLG	OPS	E	Avg.
									BATTING											FIELDING	
1999— Everett (N'west)	OF	62	233	43	74	8	3	5	32	27	35	9	2	9-8	.318	.406	.442	.848	4	.958
2000— Wisconsin (Midw.)	OF	7	23	5	5	2	2	0	3	3	3	1	1	1-0	.217	.333	.478	.812	0	1.000
— Lancaster (Calif.)	OF	103	384	90	130	22	7	11	75	72	49	17	4	35-11	.339	.458	.518	.976	3	.981
2001— Harrisburg (East.)	1B-OF	129	448	66	124	22	6	9	48	51	72	9	5	30-8	.277	.359	.413	.772	15	.985
2002— Harrisburg (East.)	OF-1B	102	396	74	119	18	6	8	43	55	70	12	4	11-8	.301	.401	.437	.838	1	.996
— Ottawa (Int'l)	OF-1B	24	80	12	21	5	2	1	11	11	15	1	2	1-1	.263	.359	.413	.771	2	.972
2003— Edmonton (PCL)	OF-1B	131	497	95	161	26	9	22	92	61	93	5	10	13-5	.324	.397	.545	.942	8	.972
2004— Montreal (N.L.)	OF-1B	133	398	45	107	20	6	15	62	40	66	1	2	3-3	.269	.336	.462	.799	3	.990
Major League totals (1 year)		133	398	45	107	20	6	15	62	40	66	1	2	3-3	.269	.336	.462	.799	3	.990

SMALL, AARON — P

PERSONAL: Born November 23, 1971, in Oxnard, Calif. ... 6-5/225. ... Throws right, bats right. ... Full name: Aaron James Small. ... High school: South Hills (Covina, Calif.).

TRANSACTIONS/CAREER NOTES: Selected by Toronto Blue Jays organization in 22nd round of 1989 free-agent draft. ... Traded by Blue Jays to Florida Marlins for a player to be named (April 26, 1995); Blue Jays acquired P Ernie Delgado to complete deal (September 19, 1995). ... Claimed on waivers by Seattle Mariners (January 23, 1996). ... Claimed on waivers by Oakland Athletics (January 29, 1996). ... Claimed on waivers by Arizona Diamondbacks (June 26, 1998). ... Released by Diamondbacks (March 30, 1999). ... Signed by Milwaukee Brewers organization (April 12, 1999). ... Released by Brewers (May 23, 1999). ... Signed by Tampa Bay Devil Rays organization (May 27, 1999). ... Signed as a free agent by Colorado Rockies organization (January 5, 2000). ... Signed as a free agent by Anaheim Angels organization (December 21, 2000). ... Released by Angels (May 4, 2001). ... Signed by Atlanta Braves organization (May 10, 2001). ... Released by Braves (September 30, 2002). ... Signed by Chicago Cubs organization (January 13, 2003). ... Released by Cubs (March 29, 2003). ... Signed by Marlins organization (April 30, 2003). ... Refused minor league assignment and became a free agent (October 4, 2004).

CAREER HITTING: 0-for-3 (.000), 0 R, 0 2B, 0 3B, 0 HR, 0 RBI.

Year	Team (League)	W	L	Pct.	ERA	WHIP	G	GS	CG	ShO	Hld.	Sv.-Opp.	IP	H	R	ER	HR	BB-IBB	SO	Avg.
1989— Medicine Hat (Pio.)	1	7	.125	5.86	1.57	15	14	0	0	...	0-...	70.2	80	55	46	2	31-1	40	.279
1990— Myrtle Beach (SAL)	9	9	.500	2.80	1.40	27	27	1	0	...	0-...	147.2	150	72	46	6	56-2	96	.262
1991— Dunedin (Fla. St.)	8	7	.533	2.73	1.15	24	23	1	0	...	0-...	148.1	129	51	45	5	42-1	92	.240
1992— Knoxville (Southern)	5	12	.294	5.27	1.58	27	24	2	1	...	0-...	135.0	152	94	79	13	61-0	79	.283
1993— Knoxville (Southern)	4	4	.500	3.39	1.49	48	9	0	0	...	16-...	93.0	99	44	35	5	40-4	44	.273
1994— Knoxville (Southern)	5	5	.500	2.99	1.35	29	11	1	1	...	5-...	96.1	92	37	32	4	38-0	75	.258
— Syracuse (Int'l)	3	2	.600	2.22	1.15	13	0	0	0	...	0-...	24.1	19	8	6	2	9-2	15	.218
— Toronto (A.L.)	0	0	...	9.00	3.50	1	0	0	0	...	0-0	2.0	5	2	2	1	2-0	0	.500
1995— Syracuse (Int'l)	0	0	...	5.40	2.40	1	0	0	0	...	0-...	1.2	3	1	1	1	1-0	2	.375
— Charlotte (Int'l)	2	1	.667	2.88	1.13	33	0	0	0	...	10-...	40.2	36	15	13	2	10-1	31	.229
— Florida (N.L.)	1	0	1.000	1.42	2.05	7	0	0	0	...	0-0	6.1	7	2	1	1	6-0	5	.269
1996— Oakland (A.L.)	1	3	.250	8.16	2.06	12	3	0	0	0	0-0	28.2	37	28	26	3	22-1	17	.308
— Edmonton (PCL)	8	6	.571	4.29	1.16	25	19	1	1	...	1-...	119.2	111	65	57	9	28-0	83	.244
1997— Edmonton (PCL)	1	0	1.000	0.00	0.20	1	1	0	0	...	0-...	5.0	1	0	0	0	0-0	4	.063
— Oakland (A.L.)	9	5	.643	4.28	1.54	71	0	0	0	8	4-6	96.2	109	50	46	6	40-6	57	.294
1998— Oakland (A.L.)	1	1	.500	7.25	1.81	24	0	0	0	3	0-0	36.0	51	34	29	3	14-3	19	.333
— Arizona (N.L.)	3	1	.750	3.69	1.26	23	0	0	0	1	0-2	31.2	32	14	13	5	8-1	14	.269
1999— Louisville (Int'l)	1	1	.500	9.43	2.52	11	0	0	0	...	0-...	21.0	38	24	22	3	15-1	11	.400
— Durham (Int'l)	4	6	.400	6.34	1.51	21	18	0	0	...	0-...	99.1	118	81	70	16	32-2	52	.295
2000— Colo. Springs (PCL)	11	6	.647	5.61	1.48	36	18	0	0	...	0-...	131.2	152	87	82	14	43-0	85	.285
2001— Salt Lake (PCL)	0	1	.000	1.69	1.69	3	0	0	0	...	0-...	5.1	8	1	1	1	1-0	5	.364
— Richmond (Int'l)	10	7	.588	3.83	1.33	41	11	0	0	...	0-...	96.1	97	50	41	14	31-5	61	.257
2002— Richmond (Int'l)	0	3	.000	6.39	2.00	14	4	0	0	...	0-...	31.0	48	27	22	2	14-1	19	.364
— Atlanta (N.L.)	0	0	...	27.00	12.00	1	0	0	0	0	0-0	.1	2	1	1	0	2-0	1	.667
— GC Braves (GCL)	0	0	...	6.00	1.50	5	5	0	0	...	0-...	6.0	9	4	4	0	0-0	3	.360
2003— Carolina (Southern)	3	4	.429	4.83	1.50	8	7	0	0	...	0-...	41.0	47	23	22	5	14-0	24	.290
— Albuquerque (PCL)	6	4	.600	4.63	1.30	14	14	0	0	...	0-...	89.1	95	50	46	12	18-0	56	.270
2004— Albuquerque (PCL)	9	9	.500	5.06	1.47	27	24	2	0	...	0-...	154.2	199	95	87	18	29-2	109	.315
— Florida (N.L.)	0	0	...	8.27	1.90	7	0	0	0	1	0-0	16.1	24	15	15	5	7-0	8	.343
American League totals (4 years)	11	9	.550	5.68	1.71	108	3	0	0	11	4-6	163.1	202	114	103	13	78-10	93	.309
National League totals (4 years)	4	1	.800	4.94	1.61	38	0	0	0	2	0-2	54.2	65	32	30	11	23-1	28	.298
Major League totals (7 years)	15	10	.600	5.49	1.69	146	3	0	0	13	4-8	218.0	267	146	133	24	101-11	121	.306

SMITH, JASON — 2B/SS

PERSONAL: Born July 24, 1977, in Meridian, Miss. ... 6-3/199. ... Bats left, throws right. ... Full name: Jason William Smith. ... High school: Demopolis (Ala.). ... Junior college: Meridian (Miss.) Community College.

TRANSACTIONS/CAREER NOTES: Selected by Los Angeles Dodgers organization in 42nd round of 1995 free-agent draft; did not sign. ... Selected by Chicago Cubs organization in 23rd round of 1996 free-agent draft. ... Traded by Cubs to Tampa Bay Devil Rays (August 5, 2001), completing deal in which Devil Rays traded 1B Fred McGriff to Cubs for P Manny Aybar and a player to be named (July 27, 2001). ... Refused minor league assignment and became a free agent (October 16, 2003). ... Signed by Detroit Tigers organization (December 8, 2003).

2004 GAMES PLAYED BY POSITION (MLB): 2B—34, SS—20, 3B—5, DH—2.

Year Team (League)	Pos.	G	AB	R	H	2B	3B	HR	RBI	BATTING BB	SO	HBP	GDP	SB-CS	Avg.	OBP	SLG	OPS	FIELDING E	Avg.
1997—Williamsport (N.Y.-Penn.) .	SS	51	205	25	59	5	2	0	11	10	44	0	0	9-2	.288	.321	.332	.653	19	.930
—Rockford (Midwest)	SS	9	33	4	6	0	1	0	3	2	11	0	1	1-0	.182	.229	.242	.471	5	.884
1998—Rockford (Midwest)	SS	126	464	67	111	15	9	7	60	31	122	1	2	23-6	.239	.286	.356	.642	38	.939
1999—Daytona (Fla. St.)	SS	39	142	22	37	5	2	5	26	12	29	3	2	9-3	.261	.329	.430	.759	7	.953
2000—West Tenn (Sou.)	SS	119	481	55	114	22	7	12	61	22	130	2	7	16-10	.237	.273	.387	.659	37	.927
2001—Iowa (PCL)	SS	70	240	31	56	8	6	4	15	12	71	1	4	6-3	.233	.271	.367	.637	19	.942
—Chicago (N.L.)	SS	2	1	0	0	0	0	0	0	0	1	0	0	0-0	.000	.000	.000	.000	0	1.000
—Durham (Int'l)	SS	8	31	2	6	1	0	0	3	0	11	0	0	0-0	.194	.194	.226	.419	3	.917
2002—Tampa Bay (A.L.)	3-S-2-DH	26	65	9	13	1	2	1	6	2	24	0	0	3-0	.200	.224	.323	.547	6	.905
—Durham (Int'l)	SS-3B	54	206	29	57	11	2	4	28	10	44	1	2	5-1	.277	.312	.408	.720	16	.936
2003—Tampa Bay (A.L.)	3B	1	4	0	1	0	0	0	0	0	0	0	0	0-0	.250	.250	.250	.500	2	.500
—Durham (Int'l)	S-2-3-DH	130	515	76	147	20	14	15	71	11	128	5	1	14-9	.285	.304	.466	.770	23	.959
2004—Toledo (Int'l)	3B	33	122	18	33	8	2	3	13	6	26	0	1	5-1	.270	.300	.443	.743	6	.938
—Detroit (A.L.)	2-S-3-DH	61	155	20	37	7	4	5	19	8	37	1	0	1-2	.239	.280	.432	.713	5	.977
American League totals (3 years)		88	224	29	51	8	6	6	25	10	61	1	0	4-2	.228	.264	.397	.661	13	.955
National League totals (1 year)		2	1	0	0	0	0	0	0	0	1	0	0	0-0	.000	.000	.000	.000	0	1.000
Major League totals (4 years)		90	225	29	51	8	6	6	25	10	62	1	0	4-2	.227	.263	.396	.658	13	.955

SMITH, TRAVIS   P

PERSONAL: Born November 7, 1972, in Springfield, Ore. ... 5-10/165. ... Throws right, bats right. ... Full name: Travis William Smith. ... High school: Bend (Ore.). ... College: Texas Tech.

TRANSACTIONS/CAREER NOTES: Selected by Milwaukee Brewers organization in 19th round of 1995 free-agent draft. ... On disabled list (June 23, 1998-remainder of season). ... Released by Brewers (October 5, 1998). ... Re-signed by Brewers organization (March 30, 1999). ... Released by Brewers (October 14, 1999). ... Re-signed by Brewers (December 7, 1999). ... Signed as a free agent by Houston Astros organization (November 1, 2000). ... Signed as a free agent by St. Louis Cardinals organization (November 21, 2001). ... Signed as a free agent by Atlanta Braves organization (November 10, 2003). ... Refused minor league assignment and became a free agent (October 15, 2004).

CAREER HITTING: 4-for-27 (.148), 0 R, 0 2B, 0 3B, 0 HR, 2 RBI.

Year Team (League)	W	L	Pct.	ERA	WHIP	G	GS	CG	ShO	Hld.	Sv.-Opp.	IP	H	R	ER	HR	BB-IBB	SO	Avg.
1995—Helena (Pio.)	4	2	.667	2.41	1.07	20	7	0	0	...	5-...	56.0	41	16	15	4	19-0	63	.207
1996—Stockton (Calif.)	6	1	.857	1.84	1.31	14	6	0	0	...	1-...	58.2	56	17	12	4	21-0	48	.260
—El Paso (Texas)	7	4	.636	4.18	1.47	17	17	3	1	...	0-...	107.2	119	56	50	6	39-0	68	.281
1997—El Paso (Texas)	16	3	.842	4.15	1.45	28	28	5	1	...	0-...	184.1	210	106	85	12	58-2	107	.288
1998—Louisville (Int'l)	4	6	.400	5.32	1.51	12	11	0	0	...	0-...	67.2	77	44	40	9	25-1	36	.294
—Milwaukee (N.L.)	0	0	...	0.00	0.50	1	0	0	0	0	0-0	2.0	1	0	0	0	0-0	1	.143
1999—Ogden (Pio.)	0	0	...	0.00	0.00	1	1	0	0	...	0-...	1.0	1	0	0	0	0-0	3	.000
—Stockton (Calif.)	0	2	.000	6.14	1.64	3	3	0	0	...	0-...	7.1	9	6	5	1	3-0	8	.300
—Huntsville (Southern)	3	2	.600	5.87	1.51	7	7	0	0	...	0-...	38.1	40	27	25	3	18-0	23	.268
2000—Huntsville (Southern)	12	7	.632	3.73	1.15	27	24	1	1	...	0-...	154.1	141	77	64	13	37-0	113	.242
—Indianapolis (Int'l)	1	1	.500	12.66	2.63	3	3	0	0	...	0-...	10.2	19	18	15	6	9-1	5	.413
2001—Round Rock (Texas)	15	8	.652	3.09	1.12	29	22	1	0	...	1-...	160.1	154	66	55	7	26-0	85	.251
—New Orleans (PCL)	0	0	...	0.00	2.00	1	0	0	0	...	0-...	2.0	3	0	0	0	1-0	0	.333
2002—Memphis (PCL)	4	7	.364	2.31	1.05	16	13	1	0	...	0-...	85.2	76	24	22	7	14-1	62	.238
—St. Louis (N.L.)	4	2	.667	7.17	1.65	12	10	0	0	0	0-0	54.0	69	44	43	10	20-0	32	.322
2004—Richmond (Int'l)	10	2	.833	2.59	1.15	20	19	1	0	...	0-...	107.2	98	31	31	6	26-0	93	.246
—Atlanta (N.L.)	2	3	.400	6.20	1.48	16	4	0	0	...	0-...	40.2	48	28	28	12	12-2	26	.293
Major League totals (3 years)	6	5	.545	6.61	1.55	29	14	0	0	1	0-0	96.2	118	72	71	22	32-2	59	.306

SMOLTZ, JOHN   P

PERSONAL: Born May 15, 1967, in Warren, Mich. ... 6-3/220. ... Throws right, bats right. ... Full name: John Andrew Smoltz. ... High school: Waverly (Lansing, Mich.).

TRANSACTIONS/CAREER NOTES: Selected by Detroit Tigers organization in 22nd round of June 1985 free-agent draft. ... Traded by Tigers to Atlanta Braves for P Doyle Alexander (August 12, 1987). ... On suspended list (June 20-29, 1994). ... On disabled list (March 29-April 15, and May 24-June 20, 1998); included rehabilitation assignments to Greenville and Macon. ... On disabled list (May 17-June 1 and July 5-24, 1999); included rehabilitation assignment to Greenville. ... On disabled list (April 2, 2000-entire season). ... On disabled list (March 23-May 17 and June 10-July 22, 2001); included rehabilitation assignments to Macon and Greenville. ... On disabled list (August 27-September 20, 2003).

HONORS: Named N.L. Pitcher of the Year by THE SPORTING NEWS (1996). ... Named N.L. Cy Young Award winner by Baseball Writers' Association of America (1996).

CAREER HITTING: 127-for-739 (.172), 69 R, 20 2B, 1 3B, 5 HR, 51 RBI.

Year Team (League)	W	L	Pct.	ERA	WHIP	G	GS	CG	ShO	Hld.	Sv.-Opp.	IP	H	R	ER	HR	BB-IBB	SO	Avg.
1986—Lakeland (Fla. St.)	7	8	.467	3.56	1.22	17	14	2	1	...	0-...	96.0	86	44	38	7	31-0	47	.242
1987—Glens Falls (East.)	4	10	.286	5.68	1.63	21	21	0	0	...	0-...	130.0	131	89	82	17	81-2	86	.268
—Richmond (Int'l)	0	1	.000	6.19	1.75	3	3	0	0	...	0-...	16.0	17	11	11	2	11-0	5	.266
1988—Richmond (Int'l)	10	5	.667	2.79	1.15	20	20	3	0	...	0-...	135.1	118	49	42	9	37-1	115	.233
—Atlanta (N.L.)	2	7	.222	5.48	1.67	12	12	0	0	0	0-0	64.0	74	40	39	10	33-4	37	.285
1989—Atlanta (N.L.)	12	11	.522	2.94	1.12	29	29	5	0	0	0-0	208.0	160	79	68	15	72-2	168	.212
1990—Atlanta (N.L.)	14	11	.560	3.85	1.28	34	34	6	2	0	0-0	231.1	206	109	99	20	* 90-3	170	.240
1991—Atlanta (N.L.)	14	13	.519	3.80	1.23	36	36	5	0	0	0-0	229.2	206	101	97	16	77-1	148	.243
1992—Atlanta (N.L.)	15	12	.556	2.85	1.16	35	• 35	9	3	0	0-0	246.2	206	90	78	17	80-5	* 215	.224
1993—Atlanta (N.L.)	15	11	.577	3.62	1.26	35	• 35	7	2	0	0-0	243.2	208	104	98	23	100-12	208	.232
1994—Atlanta (N.L.)	6	10	.375	4.14	1.25	21	21	1	0	0	0-0	134.2	120	69	62	15	48-4	113	.239
1995—Atlanta (N.L.)	12	7	.632	3.18	1.24	29	29	2	1	0	0-0	192.2	166	76	68	15	72-8	193	.232
1996—Atlanta (N.L.)	* 24	8	.750	2.94	1.00	35	35	6	2	0	0-0	* 253.2	199	93	83	19	55-3	* 276	.216
1997—Atlanta (N.L.)	15	12	.556	3.02	1.16	35	• 35	7	2	0	0-0	* 256.0	* 234	97	86	21	63-9	241	.242
1998—Greenville (Sou.)	0	1	.000	2.57	1.00	3	3	0	0	...	0-...	14.0	11	4	4	2	3-0	16	.216
—Macon (S. Atl.)	0	0	...	3.60	0.80	2	2	0	0	...	0-...	10.0	7	4	4	1	1-0	14	.179
—Atlanta (N.L.)	17	3	.850	2.90	1.13	26	26	2	2	0	0-0	167.2	145	58	54	10	44-2	173	.231
1999—Atlanta (N.L.)	11	8	.579	3.19	1.12	29	29	1	1	0	0-0	186.1	168	70	66	14	40-2	156	.245
—Greenville (Sou.)	0	0	...	4.50	1.50	2	1	0	0	...	0-...	4.0	5	2	2	0	1-0	7	.294
2000—Atlanta (N.L.)			Did not play.																
2001—Greenville (Sou.)	0	0	...	0.00	0.50	3	1	0	0	...	0-...	6.0	3	0	0	0	0-0	6	.150
—Macon (S. Atl.)	0	0	...	1.80	0.80	1	1	0	0	...	0-...	5.0	4	1	1	0	0-0	5	.235

Year Team (League)	W	L	Pct.	ERA	WHIP	G	GS	CG	ShO	Hld.	Sv.-Opp.	IP	H	R	ER	HR	BB-IBB	SO	Avg.
— Atlanta (N.L.)	3	3	.500	3.36	1.07	36	5	0	0	5	10-11	59.0	53	24	22	7	10-2	57	.238
2002— Atlanta (N.L.)	3	2	.600	3.25	1.03	75	0	0	0	0	* 55-59	80.1	59	30	29	4	24-1	85	.206
2003— Atlanta (N.L.)	0	2	.000	1.12	0.87	62	0	0	0	0	45-49	64.1	48	9	8	2	8-1	73	.204
2004— Atlanta (N.L.)	0	1	.000	2.76	1.08	73	0	0	0	0	44-49	81.2	75	25	25	8	13-2	85	.245
Major League totals (16 years)	**163**	**121**	**.574**	**3.27**	**1.17**	**602**	**361**	**47**	**14**	**5**	**154-168**	**2699.2**	**2327**	**1074**	**982**	**216**	**829-61**	**2398**	**.232**

DIVISION SERIES RECORD

Year Team (League)	W	L	Pct.	ERA	WHIP	G	GS	CG	ShO	Hld.	Sv.-Opp.	IP	H	R	ER	HR	BB-IBB	SO	Avg.
1995— Atlanta (N.L.)	0	0	...	7.94	1.06	1	1	0	0	0	0-0	5.2	5	5	5	2	1-0	6	.238
1996— Atlanta (N.L.)	1	0	1.000	1.00	0.67	1	1	0	0	0	0-0	9.0	4	1	1	0	2-0	7	.129
1997— Atlanta (N.L.)	1	0	1.000	1.00	0.44	1	1	1	0	0	0-0	9.0	3	1	1	1	1-0	11	.097
1998— Atlanta (N.L.)	1	0	1.000	1.17	0.65	1	1	0	0	0	0-0	7.2	5	1	1	1	0-0	6	.185
1999— Atlanta (N.L.)	1	0	1.000	5.14	1.29	1	1	0	0	0	0-0	7.0	6	4	4	2	3-0	3	.222
2001— Atlanta (N.L.)	0	0	...	2.25	0.75	3	0	0	0	0	2-2	4.0	3	1	1	1	0-0	3	.214
2002— Atlanta (N.L.)	0	0	...	2.70	1.20	2	0	0	0	0	0-0	3.1	2	1	1	1	2-0	7	.182
2003— Atlanta (N.L.)	1	0	1.000	6.00	1.33	2	0	0	0	0	1-2	3.0	4	2	2	0	0-0	1	.364
2004— Atlanta (N.L.)	1	0	1.000	0.00	1.20	2	0	0	0	0	0-0	5.0	4	0	0	0	2-0	4	.235
Division series totals (9 years)	**6**	**0**	**1.000**	**2.68**	**0.88**	**14**	**5**	**1**	**0**	**0**	**3-4**	**53.2**	**36**	**16**	**16**	**8**	**11-0**	**48**	**.189**

CHAMPIONSHIP SERIES RECORD

Year Team (League)	W	L	Pct.	ERA	WHIP	G	GS	CG	ShO	Hld.	Sv.-Opp.	IP	H	R	ER	HR	BB-IBB	SO	Avg.
1991— Atlanta (N.L.)	2	0	1.000	1.76	1.11	2	2	1	1	0	0-0	15.1	14	3	3	2	3-0	15	.230
1992— Atlanta (N.L.)	2	0	1.000	2.66	1.18	3	3	0	0	0	0-0	20.1	14	7	6	1	10-2	19	.194
1993— Atlanta (N.L.)	0	1	.000	0.00	2.05	1	1	0	0	0	0-0	6.1	8	2	0	0	5-0	10	.296
1995— Atlanta (N.L.)	0	0	...	2.57	1.29	1	1	0	0	0	0-0	7.0	7	2	2	0	2-0	2	.269
1996— Atlanta (N.L.)	2	0	1.000	1.20	1.00	2	2	0	0	0	0-0	15.0	12	2	2	0	3-0	12	.214
1997— Atlanta (N.L.)	0	1	.000	7.50	1.67	1	1	0	0	0	0-0	6.0	5	5	5	1	5-2	9	.227
1998— Atlanta (N.L.)	0	0	...	3.95	1.39	2	2	0	0	0	0-0	13.2	13	6	6	2	6-0	13	.250
1999— Atlanta (N.L.)	0	0	...	6.23	0.92	3	1	0	0	0	1-1	8.2	8	6	6	2	0-0	8	.235
2001— Atlanta (N.L.)	0	0	...	0.00	0.00	2	0	0	0	0	0-0	3.0	0	0	0	0	0-0	1	.000
Champ. series totals (9 years)	**6**	**2**	**.750**	**2.83**	**1.21**	**17**	**13**	**1**	**1**	**0**	**1-1**	**95.1**	**81**	**33**	**30**	**8**	**34-4**	**89**	**.226**

WORLD SERIES RECORD

Year Team (League)	W	L	Pct.	ERA	WHIP	G	GS	CG	ShO	Hld.	Sv.-Opp.	IP	H	R	ER	HR	BB-IBB	SO	Avg.
1991— Atlanta (N.L.)	0	0	...	1.26	0.98	2	2	0	0	0	0-0	14.1	13	2	2	1	1-0	11	.241
1992— Atlanta (N.L.)	1	0	1.000	2.70	1.50	2	2	0	0	0	0-0	13.1	13	5	4	0	7-0	12	.255
1995— Atlanta (N.L.)	0	0	...	15.43	3.43	1	1	0	0	0	0-0	2.1	6	4	4	0	2-0	4	.462
1996— Atlanta (N.L.)	1	1	.500	0.64	1.00	2	2	0	0	0	0-0	14.0	6	2	1	0	8-0	14	.125
1999— Atlanta (N.L.)	0	1	.000	3.86	1.29	1	1	0	0	0	0-0	7.0	6	3	3	0	3-1	11	.222
World series totals (5 years)	**2**	**2**	**.500**	**2.47**	**1.27**	**8**	**8**	**0**	**0**	**0**	**0-0**	**51.0**	**44**	**16**	**14**	**1**	**21-1**	**52**	**.228**

ALL-STAR GAME RECORD

	W	L	Pct.	ERA	WHIP	G	GS	CG	ShO	Hld.	Sv.-Opp.	IP	H	R	ER	HR	BB-IBB	SO	Avg.
All-Star Game totals (5 years)	1	1	.500	1.93	1.29	5	0	0	0	0	0-0	4.2	5	1	1	0	1-0	2	.278

SNARE, RYAN   P

PERSONAL: Born February 8, 1979, in Clearwater, Fla. ... 6-0/200. ... Throws left, bats left. ... Full name: Ryan Delbert Snare. ... High school: East Lake (Clearwater, Fla.). ... College: North Carolina.

TRANSACTIONS/CAREER NOTES: Selected by Atlanta Braves organization in ninth round of 1997 free-agent draft; did not sign. ... Selected by Cincinnati Reds organization in second round of 2000 free-agent draft. ... Traded by Reds with OF Juan Encarnacion and IF Wilton Guerrero to Florida Marlins for P Ryan Dempster (July 11, 2002). ... Traded by Marlins with 1B Adrian Gonzalez and OF Will Smith to Texas Rangers for P Ugueth Urbina (July 11, 2003).

CAREER HITTING: 0-for-0 (.000), 0 R, 0 2B, 0 3B, 0 HR, 0 RBI.

Year Team (League)	W	L	Pct.	ERA	WHIP	G	GS	CG	ShO	Hld.	Sv.-Opp.	IP	H	R	ER	HR	BB-IBB	SO	Avg.
2001— Dayton (Midw.)	9	5	.643	3.05	1.20	21	20	0	0	...	0-...	115.0	101	45	39	7	37-1	118	.238
2002— Stockton (Calif.)	8	2	.800	3.07	1.12	13	13	0	0	...	0-...	82.0	74	36	28	4	18-0	81	.238
— Chattanooga (Southern)	0	0	...	3.00	1.33	5	0	0	0	...	0-...	6.0	5	3	2	1	3-0	4	.263
— Portland (East.)	4	2	.667	3.44	1.18	11	9	0	0	...	0-...	55.0	46	25	21	6	19-0	52	.224
2003— Carolina (Southern)	5	4	.556	3.67	1.31	18	18	0	0	...	0-...	103.0	98	46	42	4	37-0	77	.253
— Oklahoma (PCL)	4	5	.444	3.46	1.32	9	9	0	0	...	0-...	54.2	59	26	21	7	13-0	28	.277
2004— Texas (A.L.)	0	0	...	10.80	2.10	1	0	0	0	0	0-0	3.1	5	5	4	3	2-0	0	.333
— Oklahoma (PCL)	11	6	.647	4.72	1.60	26	24	0	0	...	0-...	137.1	171	88	72	16	49-0	79	.306
Major League totals (1 year)	**0**	**0**	**...**	**10.80**	**2.10**	**1**	**0**	**0**	**0**	**0**	**0-0**	**3.1**	**5**	**5**	**4**	**3**	**2-0**	**0**	**.333**

SNEAD, ESIX   OF

PERSONAL: Born June 7, 1976, in Fort Myers, Fla. ... 5-10/170. ... Bats both, throws right. ... High school: Williston (Fla.). ... College: Central Florida.

TRANSACTIONS/CAREER NOTES: Selected by St. Louis Cardinals organization in 18th round of 1998 free-agent draft. ... Claimed on waivers by New York Mets (November 20, 2001).

2004 GAMES PLAYED BY POSITION (MLB): OF—1.

Year Team (League)	Pos.	G	AB	R	H	2B	3B	HR	RBI	BB	SO	HBP	GDP	SB-CS	Avg.	OBP	SLG	OPS	E	Avg.
1998— New Jersey (N.Y.-Penn.)	OF	58	193	38	45	4	4	1	16	33	54	7	3	42-11	.233	.365	.311	.676	3	.976
1999— Potomac (Caro.)	OF	67	249	37	45	8	5	0	14	32	57	4	2	45-12	.181	.281	.253	.534	2	.989
— Peoria (Midw.)	OF	59	181	35	35	7	1	2	18	35	42	2	3	29-9	.193	.329	.276	.605	4	.975
2000— Potomac (Caro.)	OF	132	493	82	116	14	3	1	34	72	98	7	7	109-35	.235	.340	.282	.622	7	.979
2001— New Haven (East.)	OF	133	520	71	121	21	6	1	33	44	115	12	4	64-23	.233	.307	.302	.609	6	.983
2002— Binghamton (East.)	OF	125	401	62	101	9	6	3	42	45	72	6	4	66-18	.252	.335	.327	.661	4	.985
— New York (N.L.)	OF	17	13	3	4	0	0	1	3	1	4	0	0	4-3	.308	.357	.538	.896	0	1.000
2003— Norfolk (Int'l)	OF-DH	137	472	64	104	14	6	3	31	41	83	5	8	61-7	.220	.287	.294	.581	4	.989
2004— New York (N.L.)	OF	1	0	1	0	0	0	0	0	0	0	0	0	0-0	...	...	...	...	0	...
— Norfolk (Int'l)	OF-DH	79	269	42	72	10	2	0	21	35	53	2	2	40-10	.268	.352	.320	.671	6	.970
Major League totals (2 years)		**18**	**13**	**4**	**4**	**0**	**0**	**1**	**3**	**1**	**4**	**0**	**0**	**4-3**	**.308**	**.357**	**.538**	**.896**	**0**	**1.000**

SNELL, IAN — P

PERSONAL: Born October 30, 1981, in Dover, Del. ... 5-11/170. ... Throws right, bats right. ... Full name: Ian Dante Snell. ... High school: Caesar Rodney (Camden, Del.).
TRANSACTIONS/CAREER NOTES: Selected by Pittsburgh Pirates organization in 26th round of 2000 free-agent draft.
CAREER HITTING: 0-for-2 (.000), 0 R, 0 2B, 0 3B, 0 HR, 0 RBI.

Year— Team (League)	W	L	Pct.	ERA	WHIP	G	GS	CG	ShO	Hld.	Sv.-Opp.	IP	H	R	ER	HR	BB-IBB	SO	Avg.
2000— GC Pirates (GCL)	1	0	1.000	2.35	0.78	4	0	0	0	...	0-...	7.2	5	2	2	1	1-0	8	.200
2001— GC Pirates (GCL)	3	0	1.000	0.47	0.89	3	3	0	0	...	0-...	19.0	12	2	1	0	5-0	13	.185
— Williamsport (N.Y.-Penn.)	7	0	1.000	1.39	1.01	10	9	1	0	...	0-...	64.2	55	16	10	2	10-0	56	.230
2002— Hickory (S. Atl.)	11	6	.647	2.71	1.23	24	22	0	0	...	0-...	139.2	127	49	42	8	45-0	149	.243
2003— Lynchburg (Carolina)	10	3	.769	3.33	1.19	20	20	1	1	...	0-...	116.1	105	46	43	3	33-1	122	.244
— Altoona (East.)	4	0	1.000	1.96	1.25	6	6	0	0	...	0-...	36.2	36	13	8	2	10-0	23	.252
2004— Altoona (East.)	11	7	.611	3.16	1.24	26	26	3	2	...	0-...	151.0	147	54	53	16	40-2	142	.259
— Pittsburgh (N.L.)	0	1	.000	7.50	1.92	3	1	0	0	...	0-0	12.0	14	10	10	2	9-0	9	.298
Major League totals (1 year)	0	1	.000	7.50	1.92	3	1	0	0	...	0-0	12.0	14	10	10	2	9-0	9	.298

SNOW, J.T. — 1B

PERSONAL: Born February 26, 1968, in Long Beach, Calif. ... 6-2/209. ... Bats left, throws left. ... Full name: Jack Thomas Snow. ... High school: Los Alamitos (Calif.). ... College: Arizona. ... Son of Jack Snow, wide receiver with Los Angeles Rams (1965-75).
TRANSACTIONS/CAREER NOTES: Selected by New York Yankees organization in fifth round of 1989 free-agent draft. ... Traded by Yankees with Ps Jerry Nielsen and Russ Springer to California Angels for P Jim Abbott (December 6, 1992). ... Traded by Angels to San Francisco Giants for Ps Allen Watson and Fausto Macey (November 27, 1996). ... On disabled list (May 27-June 14, June 24-July 15 and July 27-August 7, 2001); included rehabilitation assignments to Fresno. ... On disabled list (June 18-July 3 and August 17-September 1, 2003). ... On disabled list (May 22-June 25, 2004); included rehabilitation assignment to Fresno.
HONORS: Won A.L. Gold Glove at first base (1995-96). ... Won N.L. Gold Glove at first base (1997-2000).
2004 GAMES PLAYED BY POSITION (MLB): 1B—100.

Year— Team (League)	Pos.	G	AB	R	H	2B	3B	HR	RBI	BB	SO	HBP	GDP	SB-CS	Avg.	OBP	SLG	OPS	E	Avg.
1989— Oneonta (N.Y.-Penn.)	1B	73	274	41	80	18	2	8	51	29	35	2	9	4-1	.292	.359	.419	.819	6	.991
1990— Prince Will. (Car.)	1B	138	520	57	133	25	1	8	72	46	65	5	20	2-0	.256	.318	.354	.672	12	.991
1991— Alb./Colon. (East.)	1B	132	477	78	133	33	3	13	76	67	78	3	10	5-1	.279	.364	.442	.807	8	.993
1992— Columbus (Int'l)	1B-OF	135	492	81	154	26	4	15	78	70	65	1	9	3-3	.313	.395	.474	.869	8	.993
— New York (A.L.)	1B-DH	7	14	1	2	1	0	0	2	5	5	0	0	0-0	.143	.368	.214	.583	0	1.000
1993— California (A.L.)	1B	129	419	60	101	18	2	16	57	55	88	2	10	3-0	.241	.328	.408	.736	6	.995
— Vancouver (PCL)	1B	23	94	19	32	9	1	5	24	10	13	1	2	0-0	.340	.410	.617	1.027	2	.991
1994— Vancouver (PCL)	1B-DH	53	189	35	56	13	2	8	43	22	32	0	5	1-2	.296	.364	.513	.878	1	.998
— California (A.L.)	1B	61	223	22	49	4	0	8	30	19	48	3	2	0-1	.220	.289	.345	.634	2	.996
1995— California (A.L.)	1B	143	544	80	157	22	1	24	102	52	91	3	16	2-1	.289	.353	.465	.818	4	.997
1996— California (A.L.)	1B	155	575	69	148	20	1	17	67	56	96	5	19	1-6	.257	.327	.384	.711	10	.993
1997— San Francisco (N.L.)	1B	157	531	81	149	36	1	28	104	96	124	1	8	6-4	.281	.387	.510	.898	7	.995
1998— San Francisco (N.L.)	1B	138	435	65	108	29	1	15	79	58	84	0	12	1-2	.248	.332	.423	.755	1	.993
1999— San Francisco (N.L.)	1B	161	570	93	156	25	2	24	98	86	121	5	16	0-4	.274	.370	.451	.821	6	.996
2000— San Francisco (N.L.)	1B	155	536	82	152	33	2	19	96	66	129	11	20	1-3	.284	.365	.459	.824	6	.995
2001— San Francisco (N.L.)	1B	101	285	43	70	12	1	8	34	55	81	4	2	0-0	.246	.371	.379	.750	1	.995
— Fresno (PCL)	1B	4	12	1	0	0	0	0	0	2	7	0	0	0-0	.000	.143	.000	.143	0	1.000
2002— San Francisco (N.L.)	1B	143	422	47	104	26	2	6	53	59	90	7	11	0-0	.246	.344	.360	.704	7	.993
2003— San Francisco (N.L.)	1B	103	330	48	90	18	3	8	51	55	55	8	7	1-2	.273	.387	.418	.806	5	.994
2004— Fresno (PCL)	1B	2	7	1	2	0	0	1	2	0	1	0	0	0-0	.286	.286	.714	1.000	0	1.000
— San Francisco (N.L.)	1B	107	346	62	113	32	1	12	60	58	61	7	5	4-0	.327	.429	.529	.958	4	.995
American League totals (5 years)		495	1775	232	457	65	4	65	258	187	328	13	47	6-8	.257	.331	.408	.739	22	.995
National League totals (8 years)		1065	3455	521	942	211	13	120	575	533	745	43	81	13-15	.273	.372	.445	.817	37	.996
Major League totals (13 years)		1560	5230	753	1399	276	17	185	833	720	1073	56	128	19-23	.267	.358	.433	.791	59	.995

DIVISION SERIES RECORD

Year— Team (League)	Pos.	G	AB	R	H	2B	3B	HR	RBI	BB	SO	HBP	GDP	SB-CS	Avg.	OBP	SLG	OPS	E	Avg.
1997— San Francisco (N.L.)	1B	3	6	0	1	0	0	0	0	1	1	0	0	0-0	.167	.286	.167	.452	0	1.000
2000— San Francisco (N.L.)	1B	4	10	1	4	0	0	1	3	4	1	0	0	0-0	.400	.571	.700	1.271	0	1.000
2002— San Francisco (N.L.)	1B	5	19	3	6	2	0	1	3	1	5	0	0	0-0	.316	.350	.579	.929	0	1.000
2003— San Francisco (N.L.)	1B	4	16	0	5	0	0	0	3	0	3	0	0	0-0	.313	.313	.313	.625	2	.929
Division series totals (4 years)		16	51	4	16	2	0	2	9	6	10	0	0	0-0	.314	.386	.471	.857	2	.982

CHAMPIONSHIP SERIES RECORD

Year— Team (League)	Pos.	G	AB	R	H	2B	3B	HR	RBI	BB	SO	HBP	GDP	SB-CS	Avg.	OBP	SLG	OPS	E	Avg.
2002— San Francisco (N.L.)	1B	5	20	1	5	1	1	0	2	1	4	0	1	0-0	.250	.286	.400	.686	0	1.000

WORLD SERIES RECORD

Year— Team (League)	Pos.	G	AB	R	H	2B	3B	HR	RBI	BB	SO	HBP	GDP	SB-CS	Avg.	OBP	SLG	OPS	E	Avg.
2002— San Francisco (N.L.)	1B	7	27	6	11	1	0	1	4	2	1	0	0	0-0	.407	.448	.556	1.004	0	1.000

SNYDER, CHRIS — C

PERSONAL: Born February 12, 1981, in Houston, Texas. ... 6-3/220. ... Bats right, throws right. ... Full name: Christopher Ryan Snyder. ... High school: Spring Woods (Houston). ... College: Houston.
TRANSACTIONS/CAREER NOTES: Selected by Arizona Diamondbacks organization in second round of 2002 free-agent draft.
2004 GAMES PLAYED BY POSITION (MLB): C—29.

Year— Team (League)	Pos.	G	AB	R	H	2B	3B	HR	RBI	BB	SO	HBP	GDP	SB-CS	Avg.	OBP	SLG	OPS	E	Avg.
2002— Lancaster (Calif.)	C-DH	60	217	31	56	16	0	9	44	25	54	3	7	0-0	.258	.337	.456	.794	3	.992
2003— Lancaster (Calif.)	C-DH	69	245	53	77	16	2	10	53	35	43	8	4	0-1	.314	.414	.518	.932	7	.984
— El Paso (Texas)	C-DH	53	188	21	38	14	0	4	26	19	29	4	9	0-0	.202	.286	.340	.627	3	.991
2004— El Paso (Texas)	C-DH-1B	99	346	66	104	31	0	15	57	46	57	6	7	3-1	.301	.389	.520	.909	9	.987
— Arizona (N.L.)	C	29	96	10	23	6	0	5	15	13	25	0	0	0-0	.240	.327	.458	.786	0	1.000
Major League totals (1 year)		29	96	10	23	6	0	5	15	13	25	0	0	0-0	.240	.327	.458	.786	0	1.000

SNYDER, EARL — 1B/DH

PERSONAL: Born May 6, 1976, in New Britain, Conn. ... 6-0/207. ... Bats right, throws right. ... Full name: Earl Clifford Snyder. ... College: Hartford.

TRANSACTIONS/CAREER NOTES: Selected by New York Mets organization in 36th round of 1998 free-agent draft. ... Traded by Mets with P Billy Traber to Cleveland Indians (December 13, 2001), completing deal in which Mets traded OF Matt Lawton, OF Alex Escobar, P Jerrod Riggan and two players to be named to Indians for 2B Roberto Alomar, P Mike Bacsik and OF Danny Peoples (December 11, 2001). ... Claimed on waivers by Boston Red Sox (January 17, 2003).

2004 GAMES PLAYED BY POSITION (MLB): 3B—1.

Year	Team (League)	Pos.	G	AB	R	H	2B	3B	HR	RBI	BB	SO	HBP	GDP	SB-CS	Avg.	OBP	SLG	OPS	E	Avg.
1998—Pittsfield (N.Y.-Penn.)		1B-OF	71	262	39	66	8	1	11	40	23	60	2	6	0-1	.252	.316	.416	.732	5	.989
1999—Capital City (SAL)		1B-3B	136	486	73	130	25	4	28	97	55	117	2	5	2-1	.267	.339	.508	.847	13	.989
2000—St. Lucie (Fla. St.)		1B	134	514	84	145	36	0	25	93	57	127	8	8	4-4	.282	.358	.498	.856	15	.988
2001—Norfolk (Int'l)		1B	6	19	5	9	3	0	0	3	3	1	1	0	0-1	.474	.565	.632	1.197	1	.981
—Binghamton (East.)		1B-3B-OF	114	405	69	114	35	2	20	75	58	111	4	5	4-2	.281	.374	.526	.900	9	.989
2002—Buffalo (Int'l)		3B-1B-OF	110	400	69	105	29	1	19	66	43	96	6	6	0-2	.263	.341	.483	.823	19	.965
—Cleveland (A.L.)		1B-3B-DH	18	55	5	11	2	0	1	4	6	21	0	1	0-0	.200	.279	.570	.571	2	.982
2003—Pawtucket (Int'l)		3-1-0-DH	130	467	61	119	25	1	22	71	24	113	8	6	0-0	.255	.299	.454	.753	11	.971
2004—Boston (A.L.)		3B	1	4	0	1	0	0	0	0	0	1	0	0	0-0	.250	.250	.250	.500	0	1.000
—Pawtucket (Int'l)		3-1-S-O-DH	136	538	85	147	43	1	36	104	35	128	7	14	1-1	.273	.323	.558	.880	15	.974
Major League totals (2 years)			19	59	5	12	2	0	1	4	6	22	0	2	0-0	.203	.277	.288	.565	2	.983

SORIANO, ALFONSO — 2B

PERSONAL: Born January 7, 1976, in San Pedro de Macoris, Dominican Republic. ... 6-1/180. ... Bats right, throws right. ... Full name: Alfonso Guilleard Soriano. ... Name pronounced: soar-ee-ah-no. ... High school: Eugenio Maria de Osto (Dominican Republic).

TRANSACTIONS/CAREER NOTES: Signed by Hiroshima Toyo Carp of Japan Central League (November 1994). ... Retired from Japan Central League and declared free agent by Major League Baseball (1998). ... Signed by New York Yankees (September 29, 1998). ... Traded by Yankees with a player to be named to Texas Rangers for SS Alex Rodriguez (February 16, 2004).

2004 GAMES PLAYED BY POSITION (MLB): 2B—142, DH—3.

Year	Team (League)	Pos.	G	AB	R	H	2B	3B	HR	RBI	BB	SO	HBP	GDP	SB-CS	Avg.	OBP	SLG	OPS	E	Avg.
1995—Hiroshima (DSL)			63	227	52	83	12	3	4	55	30	19	...	...	8-...	.366	...	.498	...	...	...
1996—Hiroshima (Jap. West.)			57	131	11	28	...	...	0	13	...	...	...	...	...-...	.214	...	.214	...	...	...
1997—Hiroshima (Jap. West.)			68	242	28	61	13	2	8	34	13	35	...	...	14-...	.252	...	.421	...	...	...
—Hiroshima (Jp. Cn.)		OF	9	17	2	2	0	0	0	0	2	4	...	...	0-...	.118	...	.118	...	...	...
1998—				Did not play.																	
1999—Norwich (East.)		SS-DH	89	361	57	110	20	3	15	68	32	67	4	9	24-16	.305	.363	.501	.865	27	.937
—GC Yankees (GCL)		SS-DH	5	19	7	5	2	0	1	5	1	3	1	1	0-0	.263	.318	.526	.844	1	.929
—Columbus (Int'l)		SS-3B-DH	20	82	8	15	5	1	2	11	5	18	0	1	1-1	.183	.225	.341	.566	3	.955
—New York (A.L.)		DH-SS	9	8	2	1	0	0	1	1	0	3	0	0	0-1	.125	.125	.500	.625	1	.500
2000—Columbus (Int'l)		SS-2B	111	459	90	133	32	6	12	66	25	85	3	8	14-7	.290	.327	.464	.791	21	.952
—New York (A.L.)		3-S-2-DH	22	50	5	9	3	0	2	3	1	15	0	0	2-0	.180	.196	.360	.556	7	.837
2001—New York (A.L.)		2B-DH	158	574	77	154	34	3	18	73	29	125	3	7	43-14	.268	.304	.432	.736	19	.973
2002—New York (A.L.)		2B-DH	156	* 696	* 128	* 209	51	2	39	102	23	157	14	8	* 41-13	.300	.332	.547	.880	* 23	.968
2003—New York (A.L.)		2B	156	* 682	114	198	36	5	38	91	38	130	12	8	35-8	.290	.338	.525	.863	19	.975
2004—Texas (A.L.)		2B-DH	145	608	77	170	32	4	28	91	33	121	10	7	18-5	.280	.324	.484	.807	23	.969
Major League totals (6 years)			646	2618	403	741	156	14	126	361	124	551	39	30	139-41	.283	.323	.498	.820	92	.969

DIVISION SERIES RECORD

Year	Team (League)	Pos.	G	AB	R	H	2B	3B	HR	RBI	BB	SO	HBP	GDP	SB-CS	Avg.	OBP	SLG	OPS	E	Avg.
2001—New York (A.L.)		2B	5	18	2	4	0	0	0	3	1	5	0	0	2-1	.222	.263	.222	.485	0	1.000
2002—New York (A.L.)		2B	4	17	2	2	1	0	1	2	1	4	1	0	1-0	.118	.211	.353	.563	1	.958
2003—New York (A.L.)		2B	4	19	2	7	1	0	0	4	0	6	0	0	2-0	.368	.368	.421	.789	1	.938
Division series totals (3 years)			13	54	6	13	2	0	1	9	2	15	1	1	5-1	.241	.281	.333	.614	2	.964

CHAMPIONSHIP SERIES RECORD

Year	Team (League)	Pos.	G	AB	R	H	2B	3B	HR	RBI	BB	SO	HBP	GDP	SB-CS	Avg.	OBP	SLG	OPS	E	Avg.
2001—New York (A.L.)		2B	5	15	5	6	0	0	1	2	3	3	1	0	2-0	.400	.526	.600	1.126	1	.955
2003—New York (A.L.)		2B	7	30	0	4	1	0	0	3	1	11	1	1	2-0	.133	.188	.167	.354	1	.973
Champ. series totals (2 years)			12	45	5	10	1	0	1	5	4	14	2	1	4-0	.222	.314	.311	.625	2	.966

WORLD SERIES RECORD

Year	Team (League)	Pos.	G	AB	R	H	2B	3B	HR	RBI	BB	SO	HBP	GDP	SB-CS	Avg.	OBP	SLG	OPS	E	Avg.
2001—New York (A.L.)		2B	7	25	1	6	0	0	1	2	0	7	0	0	0-1	.240	.240	.360	.600	3	.927
2003—New York (A.L.)		2B-OF	6	22	2	5	0	0	1	2	2	9	0	1	1-1	.227	.292	.364	.655	0	1.000
World series totals (2 years)			13	47	3	11	0	0	2	4	2	16	0	1	1-2	.234	.265	.362	.627	3	.955

ALL-STAR GAME RECORD

			G	AB	R	H	2B	3B	HR	RBI	BB	SO	HBP	GDP	SB-CS	Avg.	OBP	SLG	OPS	E	Avg.
All-Star Game totals (3 years)			3	8	2	3	0	0	2	4	0	3	0	0	0-0	.375	.375	1.125	1.500	0	1.000

SORIANO, RAFAEL — P

PERSONAL: Born December 19, 1979, in San Jose, Dominican Republic. ... 6-1/175. ... Throws right, bats right.

TRANSACTIONS/CAREER NOTES: Signed as a non-drafted free agent by Seattle Mariners organization (August 30, 1996). ... Played first base and outfield in Mariners organization (1997-98). ... On disabled list (July 3-August 2, 2002). ... On disabled list (May 10, 2004-remainder of season); included rehabilitation assignment to Tacoma.

HONORS: Named A.L. Rookie Pitcher of the Year by THE SPORTING NEWS (2003).

CAREER HITTING: 0-for-4 (.000), 0 R, 0 2B, 0 3B, 0 HR, 0 RBI.

Year	Team (League)	W	L	Pct.	ERA	WHIP	G	GS	CG	ShO	Hld.	Sv.-Opp.	IP	H	R	ER	HR	BB-IBB	SO	Avg.
1999—Everett (Northwest)	5	4	.556	3.11	1.39	14	14	0	0	...	0-...	75.1	56	34	26	8	49-0	83	.208
2000—Wisconsin (Midw.)	8	4	.667	2.87	1.20	21	21	0	0	...	0-...	122.1	97	41	39	3	50-0	90	.225
2001—San Bernardino (Calif.)	6	3	.667	2.53	0.99	15	15	2	1	...	0-...	89.0	49	28	25	4	39-0	98	.164
—San Antonio (Texas)	2	2	.500	3.35	0.99	8	8	0	0	...	0-...	48.1	34	18	18	5	14-0	53	.192
2002—San Antonio (Texas)	2	3	.400	2.31	1.01	10	8	0	0	...	0-...	46.2	32	13	12	6	15-0	52	.190

S

Year	Team (League)	W	L	Pct.	ERA	WHIP	G	GS	CG	ShO	Hld.	Sv.-Opp.	IP	H	R	ER	HR	BB-IBB	SO	Avg.
	— Seattle (A.L.)	0	3	.000	4.56	1.29	10	8	0	0	...	1-1	47.1	45	25	24	8	16-1	32	.243
2003—	Tacoma (PCL)	4	3	.571	3.19	0.90	11	10	0	0	...	0-...	62.0	43	24	22	2	12-0	63	.192
	— Seattle (A.L.)	3	0	1.000	1.53	0.79	40	0	0	0	5	1-2	53.0	30	9	9	2	12-1	68	.162
2004—	Inland Empire (Calif.)	0	0	...	2.25	1.00	2	2	0	0	...	0-...	8.0	7	3	2	1	1-0	9	.241
	— San Antonio (Texas)	1	0	1.000	1.13	0.50	2	1	0	0	...	0-...	8.0	4	1	1	1	0-0	10	.154
	— Seattle (A.L.)	0	3	.000	13.50	3.60	6	0	0	0	0	0-1	3.1	9	6	5	0	3-0	3	.450
	— Tacoma (PCL)	0	0	...	2.46	1.09	3	3	0	0	...	0-...	3.2	2	1	1	1	2-0	5	.154
	Major League totals (3 years)	3	6	.333	3.30	1.11	56	8	0	0	5	2-4	103.2	84	40	38	10	31-2	103	.215

SOSA, JORGE — P

PERSONAL: Born April 28, 1977, in Santo Domingo, Dominican Republic. ... 6-2/170. ... Throws right, bats both. ... Full name: Jorge Bolivar Sosa. ... Name pronounced: hor-hey.

TRANSACTIONS/CAREER NOTES: Signed as a non-drafted free agent by Colorado Rockies organization (June 23, 1995). ... Played outfield in Rockies organization (1995-2000). ... Selected by Seattle Mariners from Rockies organization in Rule 5 minor league draft (December 11, 2000). ... Selected by Milwaukee Brewers from Mariners organization in Rule 5 major league draft (December 13, 2001). ... Claimed on waivers by Tampa Bay Devil Rays (March 18, 2002). ... On disabled list (May 26-June 25, 2002); included rehabilitation assignment to Orlando.

CAREER HITTING: 0-for-0 (.000), 0 R, 0 2B, 0 3B, 0 HR, 0 RBI.

Year	Team (League)	W	L	Pct.	ERA	WHIP	G	GS	CG	ShO	Hld.	Sv.-Opp.	IP	H	R	ER	HR	BB-IBB	SO	Avg.
2001—	Everett (Northwest)	3	1	.750	1.69	1.09	21	7	0	0	...	7-...	58.2	45	22	11	2	19-0	57	.204
	— Wisconsin (Midw.)	0	0	...	9.00	1.50	2	0	0	0	...	0-...	2.0	3	2	2	1	0-0	4	.333
2002—	Tampa Bay (A.L.)	2	7	.222	5.53	1.43	31	14	0	0	1	0-0	99.1	88	63	61	16	54-0	48	.236
	— Orlando (Sou.)	0	0	...	0.00	0.71	2	2	0	0	...	0-...	7.0	4	2	0	1	1-0	3	.167
2003—	Durham (Int'l)	1	1	.500	5.47	1.70	4	4	0	0	...	0-...	24.2	32	15	15	3	9-0	17	.314
	— Tampa Bay (A.L.)	5	12	.294	4.62	1.53	29	19	1	1	0	0-0	128.2	137	71	66	14	60-4	72	.278
2004—	Durham (Int'l)	1	2	.333	2.77	0.85	3	3	0	0	...	0-...	13.0	11	5	4	0	0-0	23	.224
	— Tampa Bay (A.L.)	4	7	.364	5.53	1.55	43	8	0	0	6	1-1	99.1	100	67	61	17	54-3	94	.259
	Major League totals (3 years)	11	26	.297	5.17	1.51	103	41	1	1	7	1-1	327.1	325	201	188	47	168-7	214	.260

SOSA, SAMMY — OF

PERSONAL: Born November 12, 1968, in San Pedro de Macoris, Dominican Republic. ... 6-0/220. ... Bats right, throws right. ... Full name: Samuel Peralta Sosa.

TRANSACTIONS/CAREER NOTES: Signed as a non-drafted free agent by Texas Rangers organization (July 30, 1985). ... Traded by Rangers with SS Scott Fletcher and P Wilson Alvarez to Chicago White Sox for OF Harold Baines and IF Fred Manrique (July 29, 1989). ... Traded by White Sox with P Ken Patterson to Chicago Cubs for OF George Bell (March 30, 1992). ... On disabled list (June 13-July 27, and August 7-September 16, 1992); included rehabilitation assignment to Iowa. ... On disabled list (August 21, 1996-remainder of season). ... On disabled list (May 10-30, 2003). ... On suspended list (June 11-18, 2003). ... On disabled list (May 16-June 18, 2004); included rehabilitation assignment to West Tenn.

HONORS: Named Major League Player of the Year by THE SPORTING NEWS (1998). ... Named N.L. Most Valuable Player by Baseball Writers' Association of America (1998).

2004 GAMES PLAYED BY POSITION (MLB): OF—124, DH—2.

Year	Team (League)	Pos.	G	AB	R	H	2B	3B	HR	RBI	BB	SO	HBP	GDP	SB-CS	Avg.	OBP	SLG	OPS	E	Avg.
1986—	GC Rangers (GCL)	OF	61	229	38	63	19	1	4	28	22	51	0	4	11-3	.275	.336	.419	.755	6	.944
1987—	Gastonia (S. Atl.)	OF	129	519	73	145	27	4	11	59	21	123	0	5	22-8	.279	.312	.410	.722	17	.920
1988—	Charlotte (Fla. St.)	OF	131	507	70	116	13	12	9	51	35	106	4	14	42-24	.229	.282	.355	.637	7	.971
1989—	Tulsa (Texas)	OF	66	273	45	81	15	4	7	31	15	52	3	4	16-11	.297	.338	.458	.796	4	.967
	— Texas (A.L.)	DH-OF	25	84	8	20	3	0	1	3	0	20	0	3	0-2	.238	.238	.310	.548	2	.944
	— Okla. City (A.A.)	OF	10	39	2	4	2	0	0	3	2	8	0	2	4-2	.103	.146	.154	.300	2	.917
	— Vancouver (PCL)	OF	13	49	7	18	3	0	1	5	0	20	0	1	0-1	.367	.367	.490	.857	0	1.000
	— Chicago (A.L.)	OF	33	99	19	27	5	0	3	10	11	27	2	3	7-3	.273	.351	.414	.765	2	.969
1990—	Chicago (A.L.)	OF	153	532	72	124	26	10	15	70	33	150	6	10	32-16	.233	.283	.404	.687	* 13	.962
1991—	Chicago (A.L.)	DH-OF	116	316	39	64	10	1	10	33	14	98	2	5	13-6	.203	.240	.335	.576	6	.970
	— Vancouver (PCL)	OF	32	116	19	31	7	2	3	19	17	32	1	2	9-2	.267	.358	.440	.797	3	.970
1992—	Chicago (A.L.)	OF	67	262	41	68	7	2	8	25	19	63	4	4	15-7	.260	.317	.393	.710	6	.961
	— Iowa (Am. Assoc.)	OF	5	19	3	6	2	0	0	1	1	2	0	0	3-0	.316	.350	.421	.771	0	1.000
1993—	Chicago (N.L.)	OF	159	598	92	156	25	5	33	93	38	135	4	14	36-11	.261	.309	.485	.794	9	.976
1994—	Chicago (N.L.)	OF	105	426	59	128	17	6	25	70	25	92	2	7	22-13	.300	.339	.545	.884	7	.973
1995—	Chicago (N.L.)	OF	•144	564	89	151	17	3	36	119	58	134	5	8	34-7	.268	.340	.500	.840	* 13	.962
1996—	Chicago (N.L.)	OF	124	498	84	136	21	2	40	100	34	134	5	14	18-5	.273	.323	.564	.888	10	.964
1997—	Chicago (N.L.)	OF	•162	642	90	161	31	4	36	119	45	* 174	2	16	22-12	.251	.300	.480	.779	8	.977
1998—	Chicago (N.L.)	OF	159	643	* 134	198	20	0	66	* 158	73	* 171	3	20	18-9	.308	.377	.647	1.024	9	.975
1999—	Chicago (N.L.)	OF	•162	625	114	180	24	2	63	141	78	* 171	3	17	7-8	.288	.367	.635	1.002	9	.978
2000—	Chicago (N.L.)	OF	156	604	106	193	38	1	* 50	138	91	168	2	12	7-4	.320	.406	.634	1.040	•10	.970
2001—	Chicago (N.L.)	OF	160	577	* 146	189	34	5	64	* 160	116	153	6	6	0-2	.328	.437	.737	1.174	6	.980
2002—	Chicago (N.L.)	OF	150	556	* 122	160	19	2	* 49	108	103	144	3	14	2-0	.288	.399	.594	.993	6	.980
2003—	Chicago (N.L.)	OF	137	517	99	144	22	0	40	103	62	143	5	14	0-1	.279	.358	.553	.911	5	.977
2004—	West Tenn. (Sou.)	DH	2	6	0	2	1	0	0	1	1	2	0	0	0-0	.333	.429	.500	.929	0	...
	— Chicago (N.L.)	OF-DH	126	478	69	121	21	0	35	80	56	133	2	9	0-0	.253	.332	.517	.849	4	.984
	American League totals (3 years)		327	1031	138	235	44	11	29	116	58	295	10	21	52-27	.228	.273	.376	.650	23	.966
	National League totals (13 years)		1811	6990	1245	1985	296	32	545	1414	798	1815	44	155	181-79	.284	.358	.569	.928	102	.974
	Major League totals (16 years)		2138	8021	1383	2220	340	43	574	1530	856	2110	54	176	233-106	.277	.348	.545	.892	125	.973

DIVISION SERIES RECORD

Year	Team (League)	Pos.	G	AB	R	H	2B	3B	HR	RBI	BB	SO	HBP	GDP	SB-CS	Avg.	OBP	SLG	OPS	E	Avg.
1998—	Chicago (N.L.)	OF	3	11	0	2	1	0	0	0	1	4	0	0	0-2	.182	.250	.273	.523	0	1.000
2003—	Chicago (N.L.)	OF	5	16	1	3	1	0	0	1	6	4	0	1	1-0	.188	.409	.250	.659	0	1.000
	Division series totals (2 years)		8	27	1	5	2	0	0	1	7	8	0	1	1-2	.185	.353	.259	.612	0	1.000

CHAMPIONSHIP SERIES RECORD

Year	Team (League)	Pos.	G	AB	R	H	2B	3B	HR	RBI	BB	SO	HBP	GDP	SB-CS	Avg.	OBP	SLG	OPS	E	Avg.
2003—	Chicago (N.L.)	OF	7	26	7	8	1	0	2	6	6	9	1	0	0-0	.308	.455	.577	1.031	0	1.000

ALL-STAR GAME RECORD

	G	AB	R	H	2B	3B	HR	RBI	BB	SO	HBP	GDP	SB-CS	Avg.	OBP	SLG	OPS	E	Avg.
All-Star Game totals (6 years)	6	13	0	2	0	0	0	1	0	4	0	0	0-0	.154	.154	.154	.308	0	1.000

SPARKS, STEVE   P

PERSONAL: Born July 2, 1965, in Tulsa, Okla. ... 6-0/195. ... Throws right, bats right. ... Full name: Steven William Sparks. ... High school: Holland Hall (Tulsa, Okla.). ... College: Sam Houston State.

TRANSACTIONS/CAREER NOTES: Selected by Milwaukee Brewers organization in fifth round of 1987 free-agent draft. ... On disabled list (March 24, 1997-entire season). ... Signed as a free agent by Anaheim Angels (February 23, 1998). ... Signed as a free agent by Philadelphia Phillies organization (February 1, 2000). ... Released by Phillies (February 28, 2000). ... Signed by Detroit Tigers organization (March 2, 2000). ... Released by Tigers (August 27, 2003). ... Signed by Oakland Athletics organization (August 30, 2003). ... Signed as a free agent by Arizona Diamondbacks (January 6, 2004).

CAREER HITTING: 5-for-41 (.122), 1 R, 1 2B, 0 3B, 0 HR, 3 RBI.

Year Team (League)	W	L	Pct.	ERA	WHIP	G	GS	CG	ShO	Hld.	Sv.-Opp.	IP	H	R	ER	HR	BB-IBB	SO	Avg.
1987— Helena (Pio.)	6	3	.667	4.68	1.53	10	9	2	0	...	0-...	57.2	68	44	30	8	20-1	47	.298
1988— Beloit (Midw.)	9	13	.409	3.79	1.30	25	24	5	1	...	0-...	164.0	162	80	69	8	51-2	96	.260
1989— Stockton (Calif.)	13	5	.722	2.41	1.09	23	22	3	2	...	0-...	164.0	125	55	44	6	53-0	126	.210
1990— Stockton (Calif.)	10	7	.588	3.69	1.29	19	19	5	1	...	0-...	129.1	136	63	53	4	31-0	77	.270
— El Paso (Texas)	1	2	.333	6.53	1.91	7	6	1	0	...	0-...	30.1	43	24	22	4	15-0	17	.341
1991— Stockton (Calif.)	9	10	.474	3.06	1.44	24	24	8	2	...	0-...	179.2	160	70	61	4	98-2	139	.246
— El Paso (Texas)	1	2	.333	9.53	2.29	4	4	0	0	...	0-...	17.0	30	22	18	1	9-0	10	.370
1992— El Paso (Texas)	9	8	.529	5.37	1.49	28	22	3	0	...	1-...	140.2	159	99	84	11	50-1	79	.295
1993— New Orleans (A.A.)	9	13	.409	3.84	1.41	29	28	7	1	...	0-...	180.1	174	89	77	17	80-1	104	.260
1994— New Orleans (A.A.)	10	12	.455	4.46	1.37	28	27	5	1	...	0-...	183.2	183	101	91	23	68-0	105	.261
1995— Milwaukee (A.L.)	9	11	.450	4.63	1.47	33	27	3	0	0	0-0	202.0	210	111	104	17	86-1	96	.274
1996— Milwaukee (A.L.)	4	7	.364	6.60	1.75	20	13	1	0	0	0-0	88.2	103	66	65	19	52-0	21	.297
— New Orleans (A.A.)	2	6	.250	4.99	1.72	11	10	3	2	...	0-...	57.2	64	43	32	8	35-0	27	.284
1997— Milwaukee (A.L.)				Did not play.															
1998— Midland (Texas)	0	4	.000	7.08	1.57	7	7	0	0	...	0-...	40.2	49	38	32	3	15-0	34	.295
— Vancouver (PCL)	0	4	.000	2.89	1.04	4	4	2	0	...	0-...	28.0	23	11	9	2	6-0	19	.223
— Anaheim (A.L.)	9	4	.692	4.34	1.46	22	20	0	0	0	0-0	128.2	130	66	62	14	58-0	90	.263
1999— Anaheim (A.L.)	5	11	.313	5.42	1.67	28	26	0	0	0	0-0	147.2	165	101	89	21	82-0	73	.281
2000— Toledo (International)	5	7	.417	3.77	1.40	16	14	1	0	...	0-...	90.2	86	53	38	8	41-0	44	.250
— Detroit (A.L.)	7	5	.583	4.07	1.32	20	15	1	1	0	1-1	104.0	108	55	47	7	29-0	53	.263
2001— Detroit (A.L.)	14	9	.609	3.65	1.33	35	33	* 8	1	0	0-0	232.0	244	110	94	22	64-1	116	.271
2002— Detroit (A.L.)	8	16	.333	5.52	1.61	32	30	3	0	0	0-0	189.0	238	134	116	23	67-3	98	.306
2003— Detroit (A.L.)	0	6	.000	4.72	1.44	42	0	0	0	0	2-4	89.2	95	57	47	11	34-4	49	.278
— Oakland (A.L.)	0	0	...	5.71	1.27	9	0	0	0	0	0-0	17.1	19	11	11	2	3-0	5	.271
2004— Arizona (N.L.)	3	7	.300	6.04	1.52	29	18	0	0	0	0-0	120.2	139	89	81	18	45-2	57	.287
American League totals (8 years)	56	69	.448	4.77	1.49	241	164	16	2	0	3-5	1199.0	1312	711	635	136	475-9	601	.279
National League totals (1 year)	3	7	.300	6.04	1.52	29	18	0	0	0	0-0	120.2	139	89	81	18	45-2	57	.287
Major League totals (9 years)	59	76	.437	4.88	1.49	270	182	16	2	0	3-5	1319.2	1451	800	716	154	520-11	658	.280

DIVISION SERIES RECORD

Year Team (League)	W	L	Pct.	ERA	WHIP	G	GS	CG	ShO	Hld.	Sv.-Opp.	IP	H	R	ER	HR	BB-IBB	SO	Avg.
2003— Oakland (A.L.)	0	0	...	4.50	1.25	1	0	0	0	0	0-0	4.0	2	2	2	1	3-0	1	.143

SPEIER, JUSTIN   P

PERSONAL: Born November 6, 1973, in Walnut Creek, Calif. ... 6-4/205. ... Throws right, bats right. ... Full name: Justin James Speier. ... Name pronounced: SPY-er. ... High school: Brophy College Prep (Phoenix). ... College: Nicholls State. ... Son of Chris Speier, coach, Chicago Cubs, and infielder with five major league teams (1971-89).

TRANSACTIONS/CAREER NOTES: Selected by Chicago Cubs organization in 55th round of 1995 free-agent draft. ... Traded by Cubs with 3B Kevin Orie and P Todd Noel to Florida Marlins for Ps Felix Heredia and Steve Hoff (July 31, 1998). ... Traded by Marlins to Atlanta Braves for a player to be named (April 1, 1999); Marlins acquired P Matthew Targac to complete deal (June 11, 1999). ... Claimed on waivers by Cleveland Indians (November 23, 1999). ... Traded by Indians to New York Mets for OF Brian Jenkins (May 19, 2001). ... Claimed on waivers by Colorado Rockies (May 29, 2001). ... On disabled list (March 31-May 6, 2002); included rehabilitation assignment to Colorado Springs. ... Traded by Rockies to Toronto Blue Jays as part of three-team deal in which Rockies acquired P Joe Kennedy from Devil Rays and a player to be named from Blue Jays, and Devil Rays acquired P Mark Hendrickson from Blue Jays (December 14, 2003); Rockies acquired P Sandy Nin to complete deal (December 15, 2003). ... On disabled list (May 11-June 8, 2004); included rehabilitation assignment to Dunedin.

CAREER HITTING: 3-for-17 (.176), 0 R, 0 2B, 0 3B, 0 HR, 0 RBI.

Year Team (League)	W	L	Pct.	ERA	WHIP	G	GS	CG	ShO	Hld.	Sv.-Opp.	IP	H	R	ER	HR	BB-IBB	SO	Avg.
1995— Williamsport (N.Y.-Penn.)	2	1	.667	1.49	0.85	30	0	0	0	...	12-...	36.1	27	6	6	1	4-0	39	.203
1996— Daytona (Fla. St.)	2	4	.333	3.76	1.33	33	0	0	0	...	13-...	38.1	32	19	16	3	19-3	34	.225
— Orlando (Sou.)	4	1	.800	2.05	1.06	24	0	0	0	...	6-...	26.1	23	7	6	2	5-1	14	.228
1997— Orlando (Sou.)	6	5	.545	4.48	1.28	50	0	0	0	...	6-...	78.1	77	46	39	8	23-0	63	.260
— Iowa (Am. Assoc.)	2	0	1.000	0.00	0.49	8	0	0	0	...	1-...	12.1	5	0	0	0	1-0	9	.128
1998— Iowa (PCL)	3	3	.500	5.05	1.37	45	0	0	0	...	12-...	51.2	52	31	29	10	19-1	49	.261
— Chicago (N.L.)	0	0	...	13.50	2.25	1	0	0	0	0	0-0	1.1	2	2	2	0	1-0	2	.333
— Florida (N.L.)	0	3	.000	8.38	1.91	18	0	0	0	1	0-1	19.1	25	18	18	7	12-1	15	.325
1999— Richmond (Int'l)	2	4	.333	5.62	1.75	27	0	0	0	...	3-...	41.2	51	28	26	4	22-4	39	.293
— Atlanta (N.L.)	0	0	...	5.65	1.43	19	0	0	0	0	0-0	28.2	28	18	18	8	13-1	22	.248
2000— Buffalo (Int'l)	0	0	...	4.15	1.23	13	0	0	0	...	9-...	13.0	13	6	6	0	3-0	12	.255
— Cleveland (A.L.)	5	2	.714	3.29	1.24	47	0	0	0	6	0-1	68.1	57	27	25	9	28-3	69	.226
2001— Cleveland (A.L.)	2	0	1.000	6.97	1.55	12	0	0	0	0	0-0	20.2	24	16	16	5	8-0	15	.293
— Colorado (N.L.)	4	3	.571	3.70	1.05	42	0	0	0	4	0-1	56.0	47	24	23	8	12-3	47	.229
— Colo. Springs (PCL)	1	0	1.000	1.46	1.38	11	0	0	0	...	2-...	12.1	10	2	2	0	7-0	16	.227
2002— Colo. Springs (PCL)	2	0	1.000	3.86	1.64	12	0	0	0	...	2-...	14.0	20	7	6	2	3-1	14	.333
— Colorado (N.L.)	5	1	.833	4.33	1.12	63	0	0	0	18	1-4	62.1	51	31	30	9	19-4	47	.216
2003— Colorado (N.L.)	3	1	.750	4.05	1.31	72	0	0	0	12	9-12	73.1	73	37	33	11	23-6	66	.257
2004— Dunedin (Fla. St.)	0	0	...	4.50	1.50	2	2	0	0	...	0-...	2.0	3	1	1	1	0-0	2	.333
— Toronto (A.L.)	3	8	.273	3.91	1.25	62	0	0	0	7	7-11	69.0	61	32	30	8	25-6	52	.239
American League totals (3 years)	10	10	.500	4.04	1.28	121	0	0	0	13	7-12	158.0	142	75	71	22	61-9	136	.241
National League totals (5 years)	12	8	.600	4.63	1.27	215	0	0	0	35	10-18	241.0	226	130	124	43	80-15	199	.245
Major League totals (7 years)	22	18	.550	4.40	1.28	336	0	0	0	48	17-30	399.0	368	205	195	65	141-24	335	.244

SPENCER, SHANE — OF

PERSONAL: Born February 20, 1972, in Key West, Fla. ... 6-0/225. ... Bats right, throws right. ... Full name: Michael Shane Spencer. ... High school: Granite Hills (El Cajon, Calif.).

TRANSACTIONS/CAREER NOTES: Selected by New York Yankees organization in 28th round of 1990 free-agent draft. ... On disabled list (July 3-27, 1999); included rehabilitation assignment to Columbus. ... On disabled list (July 12, 2000-remainder of season). ... On disabled list (March 31-April 29, 2001); included rehabilitation assignment to Columbus. ... Signed as a free agent by Cleveland Indians (January 14, 2003). ... Traded by Indians with P Ricardo Rodriguez to Texas Rangers for OF Ryan Ludwick (July 18, 2003). ... Refused minor league assignment and became a free agent (October 15, 2003). ... Signed by New York Mets organization (January 28, 2004). ... On disabled list (July 23-31, 2004). ... Released by Mets (August 6, 2004). ... Signed by Yankees organization (August 16, 2004).

2004 GAMES PLAYED BY POSITION (MLB): OF—62, DH—1, 1B—1.

Year Team (League)	Pos.	G	AB	R	H	2B	3B	HR	RBI	BB	SO	HBP	GDP	SB-CS	Avg.	OBP	SLG	OPS	E	Avg.
1990— GC Yankees (GCL)	OF	42	147	20	27	4	0	0	7	20	23	1	3	11-2	.184	.284	.211	.495	3	.965
1991— GC Yankees (GCL)	OF	44	160	25	49	7	0	0	30	14	19	2	6	9-2	.306	.361	.350	.711	3	.959
— Oneonta (N.Y.-Penn.)	OF	18	53	10	13	2	1	0	3	10	9	1	1	2-2	.245	.375	.321	.696	1	.917
1992— Greensboro (S. Atl.)	OF	83	258	43	74	10	2	3	27	33	37	3	12	8-2	.287	.372	.376	.748	0	1.000
1993— Greensboro (S. Atl.)	OF	122	431	89	116	35	2	12	80	52	62	3	8	14-2	.269	.346	.443	.789	5	.967
1994— Tampa (Fla. St.)	OF	90	334	44	97	22	3	8	53	30	53	1	8	5-3	.290	.350	.446	.796	4	.962
1995— Tampa (Fla. St.)	OF	134	500	87	150	31	3	16	88	61	60	7	7	14-8	.300	.382	.470	.852	6	.966
1996— Norwich (East.)	3B-1B-OF	126	450	70	114	19	0	29	89	68	99	4	6	4-2	.253	.353	.489	.842	3	.988
— Columbus (Int'l)		9	31	7	11	4	0	3	6	5	5	1	0	0-1	.355	.459	.774	1.234	1	.963
1997— Columbus (Int'l)	OF-DH-3B	125	452	78	109	34	4	30	86	71	105	4	8	0-2	.241	.346	.533	.879	4	.980
1998— New York (A.L.)	OF-DH-1B	27	67	18	25	6	0	10	27	5	12	0	0	0-1	.373	.411	.910	1.321	0	1.000
— Columbus (Int'l)	OF-DH-1B	87	342	66	110	29	1	18	67	41	59	3	8	1-3	.322	.397	.570	.967	5	.979
1999— New York (A.L.)	OF-DH	71	205	25	48	8	0	8	20	18	51	2	1	0-4	.234	.301	.390	.691	0	1.000
— Columbus (Int'l)	OF-DH	14	50	17	18	2	0	2	10	9	8	0	3	0-0	.360	.458	.520	.978	1	.958
2000— New York (A.L.)	OF-DH	73	248	33	70	11	3	9	40	19	45	2	4	1-2	.282	.330	.460	.789	1	.989
2001— Columbus (Int'l)	OF	49	173	17	40	10	1	3	14	23	21	2	9	4-1	.231	.323	.353	.676	1	.985
— New York (A.L.)	OF-DH	80	283	40	73	14	2	10	46	21	58	4	4	4-1	.258	.315	.428	.743	1	.989
2002— New York (A.L.)	OF-DH	94	288	32	71	15	2	6	34	31	62	4	5	0-3	.247	.324	.375	.699	4	.975
2003— Cleveland (A.L.)	OF-1B-DH	64	210	23	57	10	0	8	26	18	52	1	6	2-0	.271	.328	.433	.761	1	.993
— Texas (A.L.)	OF-DH	55	185	16	42	10	0	4	23	27	40	2	2	0-0	.227	.329	.346	.675	2	.982
2004— New York (N.L.)	OF-DH-1B	74	185	21	52	10	1	4	26	13	37	2	1	6-0	.281	.332	.411	.742	3	.977
— Tampa (Fla. St.)	OF-DH	3	9	0	4	0	0	0	2	1	1	0	1	0-0	.444	.500	.444	.944	0	1.000
— Columbus (Int'l)	OF-DH	15	48	6	12	3	0	0	4	7	14	2	1	1-0	.250	.368	.313	.681	0	1.000
American League totals (6 years)		464	1486	187	386	74	7	55	216	139	320	15	22	7-11	.260	.325	.430	.755	9	.989
National League totals (1 year)		74	185	21	52	10	1	4	26	13	37	2	1	6-0	.281	.332	.411	.742	3	.977
Major League totals (7 years)		538	1671	208	438	84	8	59	242	152	357	17	23	13-11	.262	.326	.428	.754	12	.987

DIVISION SERIES RECORD

Year Team (League)	Pos.	G	AB	R	H	2B	3B	HR	RBI	BB	SO	HBP	GDP	SB-CS	Avg.	OBP	SLG	OPS	E	Avg.
1998— New York (A.L.)	OF	2	6	3	3	0	0	2	4	0	1	0	0	0-0	.500	.500	1.500	2.000	0	1.000
1999— New York (A.L.)		Did not play.																		
2001— New York (A.L.)	OF	3	8	1	2	1	0	0	0	1	4	0	0	0-0	.250	.333	.375	.708	0	1.000
2002— New York (A.L.)	OF	1	0	0	0	0	0	0	0	0	0	0	0	0-0	...	...	...	...	0	...
Division series totals (3 years)		6	14	4	5	1	0	2	4	1	5	0	0	0-0	.357	.400	.857	1.257	0	1.000

CHAMPIONSHIP SERIES RECORD

Year Team (League)	Pos.	G	AB	R	H	2B	3B	HR	RBI	BB	SO	HBP	GDP	SB-CS	Avg.	OBP	SLG	OPS	E	Avg.
1998— New York (A.L.)	OF	3	10	1	1	0	0	0	0	1	3	0	1	0-0	.100	.182	.100	.282	0	1.000
1999— New York (A.L.)	OF	3	9	1	1	0	0	0	0	1	6	0	0	0-0	.111	.200	.111	.311	0	1.000
2001— New York (A.L.)	OF	5	7	1	2	1	0	0	0	1	1	0	0	1-0	.286	.375	.429	.804	0	1.000
Champ. series totals (3 years)		11	26	3	4	1	0	0	0	3	10	0	1	1-0	.154	.241	.192	.434	0	1.000

WORLD SERIES RECORD

Year Team (League)	Pos.	G	AB	R	H	2B	3B	HR	RBI	BB	SO	HBP	GDP	SB-CS	Avg.	OBP	SLG	OPS	E	Avg.
1998— New York (A.L.)	OF	1	3	1	1	0	0	0	0	0	2	0	0	0-0	.333	.333	.667	1.000	0	1.000
1999— New York (A.L.)		Did not play.																		
2001— New York (A.L.)	OF	7	20	1	4	0	0	1	2	2	6	0	0	0-0	.200	.273	.350	.623	0	1.000
World series totals (2 years)		8	23	2	5	1	0	1	2	2	8	0	0	0-0	.217	.280	.391	.671	0	1.000

SPIEZIO, SCOTT — 3B/1B

PERSONAL: Born September 21, 1972, in Joliet, Ill. ... 6-2/220. ... Bats both, throws right. ... Full name: Scott Edward Spiezio. ... Name pronounced: SPEE-zio. ... High school: Morris (Ill.). ... College: Illinois. ... Son of Ed Spiezio, third baseman with three major league teams (1964-72).

TRANSACTIONS/CAREER NOTES: Selected by Oakland Athletics organization in sixth round of 1993 free-agent draft. ... On disabled list (June 8-25, 1997); included rehabilitation assignment to Southern Oregon. ... On disabled list (June 15-July 31, 1998); included rehabilitation assignment to Edmonton. ... Signed as a free agent by Anaheim Angels (January 11, 2000). ... Signed as a free agent by Seattle Mariners (December 19, 2003). ... On disabled list (March 28-April 17, 2004); included rehabilitation assignment to Inland Empire.

2004 GAMES PLAYED BY POSITION (MLB): 3B—66, 1B—42, DH—2.

Year Team (League)	Pos.	G	AB	R	H	2B	3B	HR	RBI	BB	SO	HBP	GDP	SB-CS	Avg.	OBP	SLG	OPS	E	Avg.
1993— S. Oregon (N'west)	3B-1B	31	125	32	41	10	2	3	19	16	18	0	1	0-1	.328	.404	.512	.916	9	.928
— Modesto (California)	3B-1B	32	110	12	28	9	1	1	13	23	19	1	4	1-5	.255	.388	.382	.770	5	.949
1994— Modesto (California)	3B-SS-1B	127	453	84	127	32	5	14	68	88	72	7	15	5-0	.280	.399	.466	.864	18	.951
1995— Huntsville (Sou.)	2B-3B-1B	141	528	78	149	33	8	13	86	67	78	4	10	10-3	.282	.359	.449	.808	29	.935
1996— Edmonton (PCL)	3B-1B-DH	140	523	87	137	30	4	20	91	56	66	4	7	6-5	.262	.335	.449	.784	15	.970
— Oakland (A.L.)	3B-DH	9	29	6	9	2	0	2	8	4	4	0	0	0-1	.310	.394	.586	.980	2	.846
1997— Oakland (A.L.)	2B-3B	147	538	58	131	28	4	14	65	44	75	1	13	9-3	.243	.300	.388	.688	7	.990
— S. Oregon (N'west)	2B-DH	2	9	1	5	0	0	0	2	2	1	0	0	0-0	.556	.583	.556	1.139	1	.875
1998— Oakland (A.L.)	2B-DH	114	406	54	105	19	1	9	50	44	56	2	10	1-3	.259	.333	.377	.709	13	.975
— Edmonton (PCL)	2B-DH	5	13	3	3	1	0	1	4	3	2	0	0	0-0	.231	.375	.538	.913	1	.889
1999— Oakland (A.L.)	2-3-1-DH	89	247	31	60	24	0	8	33	29	36	2	5	0-0	.243	.324	.437	.761	7	.976
— Vancouver (PCL)	2B-3B-DH	28	105	27	41	7	1	6	27	15	16	2	3	0-0	.390	.475	.648	1.123	4	.969

Year Team (League)	Pos.	G	AB	R	H	2B	3B	HR	RBI	BB	SO	HBP	GDP	SB-CS	Avg.	OBP	SLG	OPS	E	Avg.
2000—Anaheim (A.L.)	DH-1-3-O-2	123	297	47	72	11	2	17	49	40	56	3	5	1-2	.242	.334	.465	.799	3	.984
2001—Anaheim (A.L.)	1-DH-O-3	139	457	57	124	29	4	13	54	34	65	5	6	5-2	.271	.326	.438	.764	2	.998
2002—Anaheim (A.L.)	1B-3-O-2	153	491	80	140	34	2	12	82	67	52	4	12	6-7	.285	.371	.436	.807	5	.996
2003—Anaheim (A.L.)	1B-3B-OF	158	521	69	138	36	7	16	83	46	66	5	12	6-3	.265	.326	.453	.779	11	.988
2004—Inland Empire (Calif.)	3B-DH	2	5	0	0	0	0	0	1	0	1	0	0	0-0	...	.000	.000	.000	0	1.000
—Seattle (A.L.)	3B-1B-DH	112	367	38	79	12	3	10	41	36	60	4	7	4-1	.215	.288	.346	.634	11	.977
Major League totals (9 years)		1044	3353	440	858	195	23	101	465	344	470	26	70	32-22	.256	.327	.418	.745	61	.988

DIVISION SERIES RECORD

Year Team (League)	Pos.	G	AB	R	H	2B	3B	HR	RBI	BB	SO	HBP	GDP	SB-CS	Avg.	OBP	SLG	OPS	E	Avg.
2002—Anaheim (A.L.)	1B	4	15	2	6	1	0	1	6	2	1	0	0	0-0	.400	.471	.667	1.137	0	1.000

CHAMPIONSHIP SERIES RECORD

Year Team (League)	Pos.	G	AB	R	H	2B	3B	HR	RBI	BB	SO	HBP	GDP	SB-CS	Avg.	OBP	SLG	OPS	E	Avg.
2002—Anaheim (A.L.)	1B	5	17	5	6	2	0	1	5	2	1	0	0	1-0	.353	.421	.647	1.068	0	1.000

WORLD SERIES RECORD

Year Team (League)	Pos.	G	AB	R	H	2B	3B	HR	RBI	BB	SO	HBP	GDP	SB-CS	Avg.	OBP	SLG	OPS	E	Avg.
2002—Anaheim (A.L.)	1B	7	23	3	6	1	1	1	8	6	1	0	1	1-0	.261	.400	.522	.922	0	1.000

SPIVEY, JUNIOR — 2B

PERSONAL: Born January 28, 1975, in Oklahoma City, Okla. ... 6-0/201. ... Bats right, throws right. ... Full name: Ernest Lee Spivey. ... Name pronounced: spy-VEE. ... High school: Douglass (Oklahoma City). ... Junior college: Cowley County (Kan.) Community College.

TRANSACTIONS/CAREER NOTES: Selected by St. Louis Cardinals organization in 28th round of 1995 free-agent draft; did not sign. ... Selected by Arizona Diamondbacks organization in 36th round of 1996 free-agent draft. ... Loaned by Diamondbacks organization to Texas Rangers organization (July 18-August 29, 1998). ... On disabled list (June 11-26, 2002). ... On disabled list (June 15-July 21, 2003); included rehabilitation assignments to El Paso and Tucson. ... Traded by Diamondbacks with SS Craig Counsell, 1B Lyle Overbay, C Chad Moeller and Ps Chris Capuano and Jorge de la Rosa to Milwaukee Brewers for 1B Richie Sexson, P Shane Nance and a player to be named (December 1, 2003); Diamondbacks acquired OF Noochie Varner to complete deal (December 15, 2003). ... On disabled list (July 3, 2004-remainder of season).

2004 GAMES PLAYED BY POSITION (MLB): 2B—58, SS—1.

									BATTING										FIELDING	
Year Team (League)	Pos.	G	AB	R	H	2B	3B	HR	RBI	BB	SO	HBP	GDP	SB-CS	Avg.	OBP	SLG	OPS	E	Avg.
1996—Ariz. D'backs (Ariz.)	2B-3B-SS	20	69	13	23	0	0	0	3	12	16	4	0	11-2	.333	.453	.333	.787	3	.970
—Lethbridge (Pio.)	2B-SS	31	107	30	36	3	4	2	25	23	24	3	2	8-3	.336	.459	.495	.955	10	.930
1997—High Desert (Calif.)	2B	136	491	88	134	24	6	6	53	69	115	11	9	14-9	.273	.373	.383	.756	33	.949
1998—High Desert (Calif.)	2B-3B-SS	79	285	64	80	14	5	5	35	64	61	3	4	34-12	.281	.416	.418	.834	20	.949
—Tulsa (Texas)	2B	34	119	26	37	10	1	3	16	28	25	3	1	8-4	.311	.450	.487	.938	3	.980
1999—El Paso (Texas)	2B-SS	44	164	40	48	10	4	3	19	36	27	2	5	14-10	.293	.424	.457	.881	9	.963
2000—Tucson (PCL)	2B-SS-3B	28	117	21	33	8	4	3	16	11	17	0	4	3-1	.282	.341	.496	.837	6	.958
—El Paso (Texas)	2B	6	19	5	8	5	0	1	2	0	5	0	1	0-0	.421	.421	.842	1.263	0	1.000
2001—Tucson (PCL)	2B-SS	54	194	25	45	6	0	6	27	27	32	0	4	9-6	.232	.326	.356	.681	3	.990
—Arizona (N.L.)	2B-SS	72	163	33	42	6	3	5	21	23	47	2	3	3-0	.258	.355	.423	.778	3	.985
2002—Arizona (N.L.)	2B	143	538	103	162	34	6	16	78	65	100	16	10	11-6	.301	.389	.476	.865	15	.977
2003—El Paso (Texas)	2B	4	11	2	5	1	0	0	1	2	1	1	1	2-0	.455	.533	.545	1.079	1	.909
—Tucson (PCL)	2B	4	15	3	4	2	0	0	1	1	1	0	0	0-0	.267	.313	.400	.713	0	1.000
—Arizona (N.L.)	2B-OF	106	365	52	93	22	2	13	50	33	95	7	7	4-3	.255	.326	.433	.759	8	.982
2004—Milwaukee (N.L.)	2B-SS	59	228	33	62	13	0	7	28	25	48	7	7	5-3	.272	.359	.421	.780	11	.963
Major League totals (4 years)		380	1294	221	359	75	11	41	177	146	290	32	27	23-12	.277	.362	.447	.809	37	.977

DIVISION SERIES RECORD

Year Team (League)	Pos.	G	AB	R	H	2B	3B	HR	RBI	BB	SO	HBP	GDP	SB-CS	Avg.	OBP	SLG	OPS	E	Avg.
2002—Arizona (N.L.)	2B	3	13	0	2	0	0	0	0	1	3	0	0	0-0	.154	.214	.154	.368	0	1.000

ALL-STAR GAME RECORD

	G	AB	R	H	2B	3B	HR	RBI	BB	SO	HBP	GDP	SB-CS	Avg.	OBP	SLG	OPS	E	Avg.
All-Star Game totals (1 year)	1	2	0	0	0	0	0	0	0	1	0	0	0-0	.000	.000	.000	.000	0	1.000

SPRINGER, RUSS — P

PERSONAL: Born November 7, 1968, in Alexandria, La. ... 6-4/211. ... Throws right, bats right. ... Full name: Russell Paul Springer. ... High school: Grant (Dry Prong, La.). ... College: LSU.

TRANSACTIONS/CAREER NOTES: Selected by New York Yankees organization in seventh round of 1989 free-agent draft. ... Traded by Yankees with 1B J.T. Snow and P Jerry Nielsen to California Angels for P Jim Abbott (December 6, 1992). ... On disabled list (August 2, 1993-remainder of season). ... Traded by Angels to Philadelphia Phillies (August 15, 1995), completing deal in which Phillies traded OF Dave Gallagher to Angels for 2B Kevin Flora and a player to be named (August 9, 1995). ... Released by Phillies (December 20, 1996). ... Signed by Houston Astros organization (December 30, 1996). ... On disabled list (June 17-July 10, 1997); included rehabilitation assignment to Jackson. ... Selected by Arizona Diamondbacks in third round (61st pick overall) of expansion draft (November 18, 1997). ... Traded by Diamondbacks to Atlanta Braves for P Alan Embree (June 23, 1998). ... On disabled list (August 6-21, 1998). ... On disabled list (April 3-May 17, 1999); included rehabilitation assignment to Richmond. ... Signed as a free agent by Diamondbacks (December 3, 1999). ... On disabled list (May 23, 2001-remainder of season); included rehabilitation assignment to Tucson. ... Signed as a free agent by St. Louis Cardinals organization (December 19, 2002). ... On disabled list (May 1-August 30, 2003); included rehabilitation assignment to Memphis. ... Signed as a free agent by Astros organization (June 19, 2004).

CAREER HITTING: 2-for-26 (.077), 1 R, 0 2B, 0 3B, 0 HR, 0 RBI.

Year Team (League)	W	L	Pct.	ERA	WHIP	G	GS	CG	ShO	Hld.	Sv.-Opp.	IP	H	R	ER	HR	BB-IBB	SO	Avg.
1989—GC Yankees (GCL)	3	0	1.000	1.50	1.00	6	6	0	0	...	0-...	24.0	14	8	4	0	10-0	34	.167
1990—GC Yankees (GCL)	0	2	.000	1.20	0.93	4	4	0	0	...	0-...	15.0	10	6	2	0	4-0	17	.172
—Greensboro (S. Atl.)	2	3	.400	3.67	1.46	10	10	0	0	...	0-...	56.1	51	33	23	3	31-0	51	.236
1991—Fort Lauderdale (FSL)	5	9	.357	3.49	1.18	25	25	2	0	...	0-...	152.1	118	68	59	9	62-1	139	.213
—Alb./Colon. (East.)	1	0	1.000	1.80	1.00	2	2	0	0	...	0-...	15.0	9	4	3	0	6-1	16	.167
1992—Columbus (Int'l)	8	5	.615	2.69	1.16	20	20	1	0	...	0-...	123.2	89	46	37	11	54-0	95	.204
—New York (A.L.)	0	0	...	6.19	1.75	14	0	0	0	2	0-0	16.0	18	11	11	0	10-0	12	.281
1993—Vancouver (PCL)	5	4	.556	4.27	1.54	11	9	1	0	...	0-...	59.0	58	37	28	5	33-1	40	.256
—California (A.L.)	1	6	.143	7.20	1.75	14	9	1	0	...	0-...	60.0	73	48	48	11	32-1	31	.303
1994—Vancouver (PCL)	7	4	.636	3.04	1.16	12	12	4	0	...	0-...	83.0	77	35	28	7	19-0	58	.242
—California (A.L.)	2	2	.500	5.52	1.47	18	5	0	0	1	2-3	45.2	53	28	28	9	14-0	28	.291
1995—California (A.L.)	1	2	.333	6.10	1.65	19	6	0	0	1	1-2	51.2	60	37	35	11	25-1	38	.290
—Vancouver (PCL)	2	0	1.000	3.44	1.38	6	5	0	0	...	0-...	34.0	24	16	13	2	23-0	23	.200

Year	Team (League)	W	L	Pct.	ERA	WHIP	G	GS	CG	ShO	Hld.	Sv.-Opp.	IP	H	R	ER	HR	BB-IBB	SO	Avg.
	—Philadelphia (N.L.)	0	0	...	3.71	1.20	14	0	0	0	0	0-0	26.2	22	11	11	5	10-3	32	.227
1996—	Philadelphia (N.L.)	3	10	.231	4.66	1.49	51	7	0	0	6	0-3	96.2	106	60	50	12	38-6	94	.272
1997—	Houston (N.L.)	3	3	.500	4.23	1.36	54	0	0	0	9	3-7	55.1	48	28	26	4	27-2	74	.232
	—Jackson (Texas)	0	0	...	9.00	2.00	1	0	0	0	...	0-...	1.0	2	1	1	0	0-0	2	.400
1998—	Arizona (N.L.)	4	3	.571	4.13	1.32	26	0	0	0	1	0-3	32.2	29	16	15	4	14-1	37	.232
	—Atlanta (N.L.)	1	1	.500	4.05	1.90	22	0	0	0	6	0-1	20.0	22	10	9	0	16-3	19	.301
1999—	Richmond (Int'l)	1	0	1.000	1.17	0.65	11	0	0	0	...	2-...	15.1	9	2	2	0	1-0	13	.170
	—Atlanta (N.L.)	2	1	.667	3.42	1.12	49	0	0	0	8	1-1	47.1	31	20	18	5	22-2	49	.185
2000—	Arizona (N.L.)	2	4	.333	5.08	1.56	52	0	0	0	3	0-2	62.0	63	36	35	11	34-6	59	.261
2001—	Arizona (N.L.)	0	0	...	7.13	1.36	18	0	0	0	2	1-1	17.2	20	16	14	5	4-0	12	.274
	—Tucson (PCL)	0	0	...	4.91	1.36	7	3	0	0	...	0-...	7.1	7	4	4	0	3-0	6	.250
2003—	Memphis (PCL)	0	0	...	1.42	0.90	7	0	0	0	...	0-...	6.1	2	1	1	1	4-0	5	.105
	—St. Louis (N.L.)	1	1	.500	8.31	1.44	17	0	0	0	5	0-1	17.1	19	16	16	8	6-0	11	.271
2004—	New Orleans (PCL)	1	2	.333	3.48	1.45	26	0	0	0	...	6-...	31.0	31	13	12	3	14-3	33	.263
	—Houston (N.L.)	0	1	.000	2.63	1.54	16	0	0	0	5	0-0	13.2	15	4	4	1	6-0	9	.278
	American League totals (4 years)	4	10	.286	6.33	1.64	65	20	1	0	3	3-5	173.1	204	124	122	31	81-2	109	.294
	National League totals (9 years)	16	24	.400	4.58	1.42	319	7	0	0	45	5-19	389.1	375	217	198	55	177-23	396	.250
	Major League totals (12 years)	20	34	.370	5.12	1.49	384	27	1	0	48	8-24	562.2	579	341	320	86	258-25	505	.264

DIVISION SERIES RECORD

Year	Team (League)	W	L	Pct.	ERA	WHIP	G	GS	CG	ShO	Hld.	Sv.-Opp.	IP	H	R	ER	HR	BB-IBB	SO	Avg.
1997—	Houston (N.L.)	0	0	...	5.40	1.80	2	0	0	0	0	0-0	1.2	2	1	1	0	1-0	3	.286
1998—	Atlanta (N.L.)					Did not play.														
1999—	Atlanta (N.L.)	0	0	...	0.00	3.00	1	0	0	0	0	0-0	1.0	2	0	0	0	1-0	1	.400
2004—	Houston (N.L.)	0	1	.000	18.00	2.00	2	0	0	0	0	0-0	2.0	3	4	4	1	1-0	5	.333
	Division series totals (3 years)	0	1	.000	9.64	2.14	5	0	0	0	0	0-0	4.2	7	5	5	1	3-0	9	.333

CHAMPIONSHIP SERIES RECORD

Year	Team (League)	W	L	Pct.	ERA	WHIP	G	GS	CG	ShO	Hld.	Sv.-Opp.	IP	H	R	ER	HR	BB-IBB	SO	Avg.
1998—	Atlanta (N.L.)					Did not play.														
1999—	Atlanta (N.L.)	1	0	1.000	0.00	0.50	2	0	0	0	0	0-0	2.0	0	0	0	0	1-0	1	.000

WORLD SERIES RECORD

Year	Team (League)	W	L	Pct.	ERA	WHIP	G	GS	CG	ShO	Hld.	Sv.-Opp.	IP	H	R	ER	HR	BB-IBB	SO	Avg.
1999—	Atlanta (N.L.)	0	0	...	0.00	0.43	2	0	0	0	0	0-0	2.1	1	0	0	0	0-0	1	.125

STAIRS, MATT — OF

PERSONAL: Born February 27, 1968, in Saint John, New Brunswick. ... 5-9/210. ... Bats left, throws right. ... Full name: Matthew Wade Stairs. ... High school: Fredericton (N.B.).

TRANSACTIONS/CAREER NOTES: Signed as a non-drafted free agent by Montreal Expos organization (January 17, 1989). ... Contract sold by Expos to Chunichi of the Japan Central League (June 8, 1993). ... Signed as a free agent by Expos organization (December 15, 1993). ... Traded by Expos with P Pete Young to Boston Red Sox for cash (February 18, 1994). ... Signed as a free agent by Oakland Athletics organization (December 1, 1995). ... Traded by A's to Chicago Cubs for P Eric Ireland (November 20, 2000). ... Signed as a free agent by Milwaukee Brewers (January 25, 2002). ... On disabled list (May 16-June 3, 2002). ... Signed as a free agent by Pittsburgh Pirates organization (December 18, 2002). ... On disabled list (May 19-June 10, 2003); included rehabilitation assignment to Nashville. ... Signed as a free agent by Kansas City Royals (December 9, 2003). ... On disabled list (August 7-22, 2004).

2004 GAMES PLAYED BY POSITION (MLB): OF—71, 1B—30, DH—22.

Year	Team (League)	Pos.	G	AB	R	H	2B	3B	HR	RBI	BB	SO	HBP	GDP	SB-CS	Avg.	OBP	SLG	OPS	E	Avg.
1989—	W.P. Beach (FSL)	2B-3B-SS	36	111	12	21	3	1	1	9	9	18	0	3	0-0	.189	.248	.261	.509	4	.956
	—Jamestown (N.Y.-Penn.)	2B-3B	14	43	8	11	1	0	1	5	3	5	0	0	1-2	.256	.304	.349	.653	6	.893
	—Rockford (Midwest)	3B	44	141	20	40	9	2	2	14	15	29	2	4	5-4	.284	.358	.418	.777	7	.929
1990—	W.P. Beach (FSL)	2B-3B	55	183	30	62	9	3	3	30	41	19	5	5	15-2	.339	.468	.470	.937	17	.899
	—Jacksonville (Sou.)	2-3-S-OF	79	280	26	71	17	0	3	34	22	43	3	6	5-3	.254	.310	.346	.656	22	.893
1991—	Harrisburg (East.)	2B-3B-OF	129	505	87	168	30	10	13	78	66	47	3	14	23-11	.333	.411	.509	.920	22	.958
1992—	Indianapolis (A.A.)	OF	110	401	57	107	23	4	11	56	49	61	4	10	11-11	.267	.351	.426	.777	3	.985
	—Montreal (N.L.)	OF	13	30	2	5	2	0	0	5	7	7	0	0	0-0	.167	.316	.233	.549	1	.933
1993—	Ottawa (Int'l)	OF	34	125	18	35	4	2	3	20	11	15	2	3	4-1	.280	.348	.416	.764	0	1.000
	—Montreal (N.L.)	OF	6	8	1	3	1	0	0	2	0	1	0	1	0-0	.375	.375	.500	.875	0	1.000
	—Chunichi (Jp. Cn.)		60	132	10	33	6	0	6	23	7	34			1-...	.250		.432	...	3	...
1994—	New Britain (East.)	OF-DH-1B	93	317	44	98	25	2	9	61	53	38	3	10	10-7	.309	.407	.486	.893	4	.975
1995—	Pawtucket (Int'l)	OF-DH	75	271	40	77	17	0	13	56	29	41	1	10	3-3	.284	.352	.491	.843	0	1.000
	—Boston (A.L.)	OF-DH	39	88	8	23	7	1	1	17	4	14	1	4	0-1	.261	.298	.398	.696	2	.913
1996—	Oakland (A.L.)	OF-DH-1B	61	137	21	38	5	1	10	23	19	23	1	2	1-1	.277	.367	.547	.915	1	.987
	—Edmonton (PCL)	DH-OF-1B	51	180	35	62	16	1	8	41	21	34	0	4	0-0	.344	.401	.578	.979	3	.944
1997—	Oakland (A.L.)	OF-DH-1B	133	352	62	105	19	0	27	73	50	60	3	6	3-2	.298	.386	.582	.969	4	.974
1998—	Oakland (A.L.)	DH-OF-1B	149	523	88	154	33	1	26	106	59	93	6	13	8-3	.294	.370	.511	.880	0	1.000
1999—	Oakland (A.L.)	OF-DH-1B	146	531	94	137	26	3	38	102	89	124	2	8	2-7	.258	.366	.533	.899	5	.981
2000—	Oakland (A.L.)	OF-DH-1B	143	476	74	108	26	0	21	81	78	122	1	7	5-2	.227	.333	.414	.747	4	.980
2001—	Chicago (N.L.)	1-O-DH-2	128	340	48	85	21	0	17	61	52	76	7	4	2-3	.250	.358	.462	.820	4	.993
2002—	Milwaukee (N.L.)	OF	107	270	41	66	15	0	16	41	36	50	8	7	2-0	.244	.349	.478	.827	1	.993
2003—	Nashville (PCL)	OF-1B-DH	7	18	4	3	0	0	2	3	7	2	1	0	0-0	.167	.444	.500	.944	0	1.000
	—Pittsburgh (N.L.)	OF-1B-DH	121	305	49	89	20	1	20	57	45	64	5	7	0-1	.292	.389	.561	.950	3	.990
2004—	Kansas City (A.L.)	OF-1B-DH	126	439	48	117	21	3	18	66	49	92	5	15	1-0	.267	.345	.451	.796	5	.986
	American League totals (7 years)		797	2546	395	682	137	9	141	468	348	528	19	55	20-16	.268	.358	.495	.853	21	.982
	National League totals (5 years)		375	953	141	248	59	1	53	166	140	198	20	19	4-4	.260	.364	.491	.855	9	.991
	Major League totals (12 years)		1172	3499	536	930	196	10	194	634	488	726	39	74	24-20	.266	.359	.494	.853	30	.986

DIVISION SERIES RECORD

Year	Team (League)	Pos.	G	AB	R	H	2B	3B	HR	RBI	BB	SO	HBP	GDP	SB-CS	Avg.	OBP	SLG	OPS	E	Avg.
1995—	Boston (A.L.)		1	1	0	0	0	0	0	0	0	1	0	0	0-0	.000	.000	.000	.000	...	...
2000—	Oakland (A.L.)	OF	3	9	0	1	1	0	0	0	1	1	0	0	0-0	.111	.111	.222	.333	0	1.000
	Division series totals (2 years)		4	10	0	1	1	0	0	0	1	2	0	0	0-0	.100	.100	.200	.300	0	1.000

STANDRIDGE, JASON   P

PERSONAL: Born November 9, 1978, in Birmingham, Ala. ... 6-4/230. ... Throws right, bats right. ... Full name: Jason Wayne Standridge. ... High school: Hewitt-Trussville (Ala.).
TRANSACTIONS/CAREER NOTES: Selected by Tampa Bay Devil Rays organization in first round (31st pick overall) of 1997 free-agent draft. ... On disabled list (March 24-May 19, 2004); included rehabilitation assignments to Montgomery and Durham.
CAREER HITTING: 0-for-0 (.000), 0 R, 0 2B, 0 3B, 0 HR, 0 RBI.

Year Team (League)	W	L	Pct.	ERA	WHIP	G	GS	CG	ShO	Hld.	Sv.-Opp.	IP	H	R	ER	HR	BB-IBB	SO	Avg.
1997— GC Devil Rays (GCL)	0	6	.000	3.59	1.20	13	13	0	0	...	0-...	57.2	56	30	23	3	13-1	55	.250
1998— Princeton (Appalachian)	4	4	.500	7.00	1.75	12	12	0	0	...	0-...	63.0	82	61	49	4	28-0	47	.314
1999— Char., S.C. (SAL)	9	1	.900	2.02	0.96	18	18	3	3	...	0-...	116.0	80	35	26	6	31-1	84	.197
— St. Pete. (FSL)	4	4	.500	3.91	1.43	8	8	0	0	...	0-...	48.1	49	21	21	0	20-0	26	.268
2000— St. Pete. (FSL)	2	4	.333	3.38	1.36	10	10	1	0	...	0-...	56.0	45	28	21	4	31-0	41	.214
— Orlando (Sou.)	6	8	.429	3.62	1.32	17	17	2	0	...	0-...	97.0	85	46	39	4	43-0	55	.237
2001— Durham (Int'l)	5	10	.333	5.28	1.76	20	20	0	0	...	0-...	102.1	130	73	60	13	50-0	48	.315
— Tampa Bay (A.L.)	0	0		4.66	1.71	9	1	0	0	0	0-0	19.1	19	10	10	5	14-1	9	.260
— Orlando (Sou.)	0	2	.000	5.59	1.66	2	2	0	0	...	0-...	9.2	12	6	6	0	4-0	7	.300
2002— Durham (Int'l)	10	9	.526	3.12	1.34	29	29	0	0	...	0-...	173.0	168	71	60	12	64-1	111	.259
— Tampa Bay (A.L.)	0	0		9.00	3.67	1	0	0	0	0	0-0	3.0	7	3	3	1	4-0	1	.500
2003— Tampa Bay (A.L.)	0	5	.000	6.37	1.63	8	7	1	0	0	0-0	35.1	38	25	25	7	16-0	20	.275
— Durham (Int'l)	2	4	.333	4.50	1.50	12	10	0	0	...	1-...	60.0	62	32	30	5	28-0	37	.270
2004— Montgomery (Sou.)	1	0	1.000	3.60	1.70	2	2	0	0	...	0-...	10.0	13	4	4	1	4-0	8	.361
— Tampa Bay (A.L.)	0	0		9.00	1.80	3	1	0	0	0	0-0	10.0	14	10	10	5	4-0	7	.326
— Durham (Int'l)	8	4	.667	3.85	1.37	20	20	2	0	...	0-...	119.1	120	56	51	7	44-0	76	.265
Major League totals (4 years)	**0**	**5**	**.000**	**6.38**	**1.71**	**21**	**9**	**1**	**0**	**0**	**0-0**	**67.2**	**78**	**48**	**48**	**18**	**38-1**	**37**	**.291**

STANFORD, JASON   P

PERSONAL: Born January 23, 1977, in Tucson, Ariz. ... 6-2/200. ... Throws left, bats left. ... Full name: Jason John Stanford. ... High school: Canyon Del Oro (Tucson, Ariz.). ... College: Charlotte.
TRANSACTIONS/CAREER NOTES: Signed as a non-drafted free agent by Cleveland Indians organization (November 16, 1999). ... On disabled list (April 16, 2004-remainder of season); included rehabilitation assignment to Buffalo.
CAREER HITTING: 0-for-0 (.000), 0 R, 0 2B, 0 3B, 0 HR, 0 RBI.

Year Team (League)	W	L	Pct.	ERA	WHIP	G	GS	CG	ShO	Hld.	Sv.-Opp.	IP	H	R	ER	HR	BB-IBB	SO	Avg.
2000— Columbus (S. Atl.)	7	4	.636	2.73	1.29	14	14	0	0	...	0-...	79.0	82	32	24	3	20-0	72	.265
— Kinston (Caro.)	4	3	.571	2.57	1.21	11	11	1	0	...	0-...	70.0	68	22	20	2	17-0	58	.250
— Akron (East.)	1	0	1.000	1.59	1.06	1	1	0	0	...	0-...	5.2	5	1	1	0	1-0	5	.238
2001— Akron (East.)	6	11	.353	4.07	1.30	24	24	1	0	...	0-...	141.2	152	71	64	11	32-4	108	.276
— Buffalo (Int'l)	1	0	1.000	0.00	0.33	1	1	1	1	...	0-...	9.0	3	0	0	0	0-0	10	.103
2002— Buffalo (Int'l)	3	1	.750	2.78	1.23	6	5	0	0	...	0-...	35.2	33	12	11	5	11-0	23	.244
— Akron (East.)	7	6	.538	3.43	1.38	18	18	1	1	...	0-...	102.1	108	44	39	3	33-0	86	.276
2003— Buffalo (Int'l)	10	4	.714	3.43	1.18	20	20	1	0	...	0-...	126.0	124	57	48	13	25-1	108	.261
— Cleveland (A.L.)	1	3	.250	3.60	1.28	13	8	0	0	0	0-0	50.0	48	20	20	5	16-1	30	.246
2004— Cleveland (A.L.)	0	1	.000	0.82	1.55	2	2	0	0	0	0-0	11.0	12	1	1	0	5-0	5	.279
— Buffalo (Int'l)	0	0		0.00	1.50	1	1	0	0	...	0-...	3.1	2	0	0	0	3-0	4	.167
Major League totals (2 years)	**1**	**4**	**.200**	**3.10**	**1.33**	**15**	**10**	**0**	**0**	**0**	**0-0**	**61.0**	**60**	**21**	**21**	**5**	**21-1**	**35**	**.252**

STANTON, MIKE   P

PERSONAL: Born June 2, 1967, in Houston, Texas. ... 6-1/215. ... Throws left, bats left. ... Full name: William Michael Stanton. ... High school: Midland (Texas). ... Junior college: Alvin (Texas) Community College.
TRANSACTIONS/CAREER NOTES: Selected by Atlanta Braves organization in 13th round of 1987 free-agent draft. ... On disabled list (April 27, 1990-remainder of season); included rehabilitation assignments to Greenville. ... Traded by Braves with a player to be named to Boston Red Sox for two players to be named (July 31, 1995); Red Sox acquired P Matt Murray and Braves acquired OF Marc Lewis and P Mike Jacobs to complete deal (August 31, 1995). ... Traded by Red Sox to Texas Rangers for Ps Mark Brandenburg and Kerry Lacy (July 31, 1996). ... Signed as a free agent by New York Yankees (December 11, 1996). ... On suspended list (July 3-10, 1998). ... Signed as a free agent by New York Mets (December 16, 2002). ... On disabled list (May 22-June 6 and June 11-July 13, 2003); included rehabilitation assignments to Binghamton and Brooklyn.
CAREER HITTING: 8-for-19 (.421), 2 R, 1 2B, 0 3B, 0 HR, 3 RBI.

Year Team (League)	W	L	Pct.	ERA	WHIP	G	GS	CG	ShO	Hld.	Sv.-Opp.	IP	H	R	ER	HR	BB-IBB	SO	Avg.
1987— Pulaski (Appalachian)	4	8	.333	3.24	1.27	15	13	3	2	...	0-...	83.1	64	37	30	7	42-0	82	.212
1988— Burlington (Midw.)	11	5	.688	3.62	1.45	30	23	1	1	...	0-...	154.0	154	86	62	7	69-2	160	.258
— Durham (Caro.)	1	0	1.000	1.46	1.54	2	2	1	1	...	0-...	12.1	14	3	2	0	5-0	14	.280
1989— Greenville (Sou.)	4	1	.800	1.58	1.23	47	0	0	0	...	19-...	51.1	32	10	9	1	31-3	58	.189
— Richmond (Int'l)	2	0	1.000	0.00	0.95	13	0	0	0	...	8-...	20.0	6	0	0	0	13-2	20	.097
— Atlanta (N.L.)	0	1	.000	1.50	1.04	20	0	0	0	2	7-8	24.0	17	4	4	0	8-1	27	.207
1990— Atlanta (N.L.)	0	3	.000	18.00	2.86	7	0	0	0	0	2-3	7.0	16	16	14	1	4-2	7	.444
— Greenville (Sou.)	0	1	.000	1.59	1.76	4	4	0	0	...	0-...	5.2	7	1	1	1	3-0	4	.292
1991— Atlanta (N.L.)	5	5	.500	2.88	1.06	74	0	0	0	15	7-10	78.0	62	27	25	6	21-6	54	.217
1992— Atlanta (N.L.)	5	4	.556	4.10	1.24	65	0	0	0	15	8-11	63.2	59	32	29	6	20-2	44	.247
1993— Atlanta (N.L.)	4	6	.400	4.67	1.54	63	0	0	0	5	27-33	52.0	51	35	27	4	29-7	43	.255
1994— Atlanta (N.L.)	3	1	.750	3.55	1.47	49	0	0	0	10	3-4	45.2	41	18	18	2	26-3	35	.248
1995— Atlanta (N.L.)	1	1	.500	5.59	1.91	26	0	0	0	4	1-2	19.1	31	14	12	3	6-2	13	.369
— Boston (A.L.)	1	0	1.000	3.00	1.19	22	0	0	0	4	0-1	21.0	17	9	7	3	8-0	10	.224
1996— Boston (A.L.)	4	3	.571	3.83	1.44	59	0	0	0	15	1-5	56.1	58	24	24	9	23-4	46	.275
— Texas (A.L.)	0	1	.000	3.22	1.07	22	0	0	0	7	0-1	22.1	20	8	8	2	4-1	14	.241
1997— New York (A.L.)	6	1	.857	2.57	1.26	64	0	0	0	26	3-5	66.2	50	19	19	3	34-2	70	.205
1998— New York (A.L.)	4	1	.800	5.47	1.23	67	0	0	0	18	6-10	79.0	71	51	48	13	26-1	69	.239
1999— New York (A.L.)	2	2	.500	4.33	1.43	73	1	0	0	21	0-5	62.1	71	30	30	5	18-4	59	.289
2000— New York (A.L.)	2	3	.400	4.10	1.35	69	0	0	0	15	0-4	80.1	68	32	31	5	24-2	75	.263
2001— New York (A.L.)	9	4	.692	2.58	1.36	76	0	0	0	23	0-1	80.1	80	25	23	4	29-9	78	.263
2002— New York (A.L.)	7	1	.875	3.00	1.29	79	0	0	0	17	6-9	78.0	73	29	26	4	28-3	44	.256
2003— Binghamton (Eastern)	0	1	.000	9.00	6.00	1	1	0	0	...	0-...	1.0	6	3	1	0	0-0	1	.750
— Brooklyn (NY-P)	0	0		0.00	0.50	1	1	0	0	...	0-...	2.0	1	0	0	0	0-0	1	.167
— New York (N.L.)	2	7	.222	4.57	1.24	50	0	0	0	10	5-7	45.1	37	25	23	6	19-4	34	.219
2004— New York (N.L.)	6	2	.750	3.16	1.34	83	0	0	0	25	0-6	77.0	70	32	27	6	33-6	58	.237
American League totals (8 years)	**35**	**16**	**.686**	**3.64**	**1.31**	**531**	**1**	**0**	**0**	**146**	**16-41**	**534.0**	**508**	**227**	**216**	**48**	**194-26**	**465**	**.253**
National League totals (9 years)	**22**	**34**	**.393**	**3.91**	**1.33**	**437**	**0**	**0**	**0**	**86**	**60-84**	**412.0**	**384**	**203**	**179**	**34**	**166-33**	**315**	**.247**
Major League totals (16 years)	**57**	**50**	**.533**	**3.76**	**1.32**	**968**	**1**	**0**	**0**	**232**	**76-125**	**946.0**	**892**	**430**	**395**	**82**	**360-59**	**780**	**.250**

S

DIVISION SERIES RECORD

Year	Team (League)	W	L	Pct.	ERA	WHIP	G	GS	CG	ShO	Hld.	Sv.-Opp.	IP	H	R	ER	HR	BB-IBB	SO	Avg.
1995—	Boston (A.L.)	0	0	...	0.00	0.43	1	0	0	0	0	0-0	2.1	1	0	0	0	0-0	4	.125
1996—	Texas (A.L.)	0	1	.000	2.70	1.50	3	0	0	0	0	0-0	3.1	2	2	1	1	3-0	3	.200
1997—	New York (A.L.)	0	0	...	0.00	2.00	3	0	0	0	1	0-0	1.0	1	0	0	0	1-0	3	.250
1998—	New York (A.L.)			Did not play.																
1999—	New York (A.L.)			Did not play.																
2000—	New York (A.L.)	1	0	1.000	2.08	1.38	3	0	0	0	0	0-0	4.1	5	1	1	0	1-0	3	.294
2001—	New York (A.L.)	1	0	1.000	0.00	0.64	3	0	0	0	0	0-0	4.2	3	0	0	0	0-0	1	.176
2002—	New York (A.L.)	0	1	.000	10.13	2.63	3	0	0	0	0	0-1	2.2	6	3	3	0	1-1	1	.500
	Division series totals (6 years)	**2**	**2**	**.500**	**2.45**	**1.31**	**16**	**0**	**0**	**0**	**1**	**0-1**	**18.1**	**18**	**6**	**5**	**1**	**6-1**	**15**	**.265**

CHAMPIONSHIP SERIES RECORD

Year	Team (League)	W	L	Pct.	ERA	WHIP	G	GS	CG	ShO	Hld.	Sv.-Opp.	IP	H	R	ER	HR	BB-IBB	SO	Avg.
1991—	Atlanta (N.L.)	0	0	...	2.45	1.91	3	0	0	0	1		3.2	4	1	1	0	3-1	3	.333
1992—	Atlanta (N.L.)	0	0	...	0.00	0.92	5	0	0	0	2		4.1	2	1	0	0	2-1	5	.154
1993—	Atlanta (N.L.)	0	0	...	0.00	2.00	1	0	0	0	0		1.0	1	0	0	0	1-0	0	.250
1998—	New York (A.L.)	0	0	...	0.00	0.82	3	0	0	0	1		3.2	2	0	0	0	1-1	4	.167
1999—	New York (A.L.)	0	0	...	0.00	6.00	3	0	0	0	0		.1	1	0	0	0	2-0	0	.500
2000—	New York (A.L.)			Did not play.																
2001—	New York (A.L.)	0	0	...	27.00	3.00	2	0	0	0	0		1.0	1	3	3	0	2-1	0	.200
	Champ. series totals (6 years)	**0**	**0**	**...**	**2.57**	**1.50**	**17**	**0**	**0**	**0**	**4**	**0-0**	**14.0**	**11**	**5**	**4**	**0**	**10-4**	**12**	**.229**

WORLD SERIES RECORD

Year	Team (League)	W	L	Pct.	ERA	WHIP	G	GS	CG	ShO	Hld.	Sv.-Opp.	IP	H	R	ER	HR	BB-IBB	SO	Avg.
1991—	Atlanta (N.L.)	1	0	1.000	0.00	0.95	5	0	0	0	0	0-0	7.1	5	0	0	0	2-2	7	.200
1992—	Atlanta (N.L.)	0	0	...	0.00	1.00	4	0	0	0	1	1-1	5.0	3	0	0	0	2-2	1	.188
1998—	New York (A.L.)	0	0	...	27.00	4.50	1	0	0	0	0	0-0	.2	3	2	2	0	0-0	1	.600
1999—	New York (A.L.)	0	0	...	0.00	0.00	1	0	0	0	0	0-0	.1	0	0	0	0	0-0	1	.000
2000—	New York (A.L.)	2	0	1.000	0.00	0.00	4	0	0	0	1	0-0	4.1	0	0	0	0	0-0	7	.000
2001—	New York (A.L.)	0	0	...	3.18	0.71	5	0	0	0	1	0-0	5.2	3	2	2	0	1-0	3	.167
	World series totals (6 years)	**3**	**0**	**1.000**	**1.54**	**0.81**	**20**	**0**	**0**	**0**	**3**	**1-1**	**23.1**	**14**	**4**	**4**	**0**	**5-4**	**20**	**.182**

ALL-STAR GAME RECORD

Year	Team (League)	W	L	Pct.	ERA	WHIP	G	GS	CG	ShO	Hld.	Sv.-Opp.	IP	H	R	ER	HR	BB-IBB	SO	Avg.
	All-Star Game totals (1 year)	**0**	**0**	**...**	**0.00**	**0.00**	**1**	**0**	**0**	**0**	**1**	**0-0**	**.2**	**0**	**0**	**0**	**0**	**0-0**	**0**	**.000**

STARK, DENNY — P

PERSONAL: Born October 27, 1974, in Edgerton, Ohio. ... 6-2/210. ... Throws right, bats right. ... Full name: Dennis Stark. ... High school: Edgerton (Ohio). ... College: Toledo.

TRANSACTIONS/CAREER NOTES: Selected by Seattle Mariners organization in fourth round of 1996 free-agent draft. ... On disabled list (August 31, 2000-remainder of season). ... Traded by Mariners with Ps Jose Paniagua and Brian Fuentes to Colorado Rockies for 3B Jeff Cirillo (December 15, 2001). ... On disabled list (March 21-July 1, 2003); included rehabilitation assignments to Visalia, Tulsa and Colorado Springs. ... On disabled list (July 20, 2004-remainder of season). ... Refused minor league assignment and became a free agent (October 6, 2004).

CAREER HITTING: 7-for-71 (.099), 5 R, 3 2B, 0 3B, 1 HR, 8 RBI.

Year	Team (League)	W	L	Pct.	ERA	WHIP	G	GS	CG	ShO	Hld.	Sv.-Opp.	IP	H	R	ER	HR	BB-IBB	SO	Avg.
1996—	Everett (Northwest)	1	3	.250	4.45	1.38	12	4	0	0	...	0-...	30.1	25	19	15	2	17-0	49	.225
1997—	Wisconsin (Midw.)	6	3	.667	1.97	0.93	16	15	1	0	...	0-...	91.1	52	27	20	3	33-0	105	.162
	—Lancaster (Calif.)	1	1	.500	3.24	1.38	3	3	0	0	...	0-...	16.2	13	7	6	1	10-0	17	.224
1998—	Lancaster (Calif.)	1	2	.333	4.29	1.67	5	5	0	0	...	0-...	21.0	18	12	10	1	17-0	21	.222
	—Ariz. Mariners (Ariz.)	0	0	...	2.16	1.32	3	1	0	0	...	0-...	8.1	9	2	2	0	2-0	13	.265
1999—	New Haven (East.)	9	11	.450	4.40	1.45	26	26	2	1	...	0-...	147.1	151	82	72	14	62-0	103	.268
	—Seattle (A.L.)	0	0	...	9.95	2.21	5	0	0	0	0	0-0	6.1	10	8	7	0	4-0	4	.370
2000—	New Haven (East.)	4	3	.571	2.19	0.97	8	8	1	0	...	0-...	49.1	31	13	12	1	17-0	42	.181
2001—	Tacoma (PCL)	14	2	.875	2.37	1.09	24	24	0	0	...	0-...	151.2	124	52	40	12	41-0	130	.225
	—Seattle (A.L.)	1	1	.500	9.20	1.70	4	3	0	0	0	0-0	14.2	21	15	15	5	4-0	12	.333
	—San Antonio (Texas)	1	0	1.000	0.00	0.83	1	1	0	0	...	0-...	6.0	2	0	0	0	3-0	7	.095
2002—	Colo. Springs (PCL)	1	2	.333	3.82	1.30	7	7	0	0	...	0-...	37.2	35	20	16	4	14-0	38	.246
	—Colorado (N.L.)	11	4	.733	4.00	1.34	32	20	0	0	1	0-1	128.1	108	69	57	25	64-4	64	.225
2003—	Visalia (Calif.)	0	0	...	0.00	0.80	1	1	0	0	...	0-...	4.0	2	0	0	0	1-0	5	.143
	—Tulsa (Texas)	0	1	.000	6.23	1.80	1	1	0	0	...	0-...	4.1	4	5	3	0	4-0	3	.250
	—Colo. Springs (PCL)	0	2	.000	5.95	1.60	4	4	0	0	...	0-...	19.2	22	14	13	1	9-0	10	.275
	—Colorado (N.L.)	3	3	.500	5.83	1.67	17	13	0	0	0	0-0	78.2	98	57	51	12	33-2	30	.305
2004—	Colorado (N.L.)	0	5	.000	11.42	2.73	6	6	0	0	0	0-0	26.0	53	43	33	9	18-3	10	.427
	—Colo. Springs (PCL)	8	2	.800	3.50	1.24	14	13	0	0	...	0-...	79.2	73	36	31	9	26-0	51	.244
	American League totals (2 years)	**1**	**1**	**.500**	**9.43**	**1.86**	**9**	**3**	**0**	**0**	**0**	**0-0**	**21.0**	**31**	**23**	**22**	**5**	**8-0**	**16**	**.344**
	National League totals (3 years)	**14**	**12**	**.538**	**5.45**	**1.61**	**55**	**39**	**0**	**0**	**1**	**0-1**	**233.0**	**259**	**169**	**141**	**46**	**115-9**	**104**	**.280**
	Major League totals (5 years)	**15**	**13**	**.536**	**5.78**	**1.63**	**64**	**42**	**0**	**0**	**1**	**0-1**	**254.0**	**290**	**192**	**163**	**51**	**123-9**	**120**	**.286**

STEWART, JOSH — P

PERSONAL: Born December 5, 1978, in Paducah, Ky. ... 6-3/205. ... Throws left, bats left. ... Full name: Joshua Craig Stewart. ... High school: Livingston Central (Ky.). ... College: Memphis.

TRANSACTIONS/CAREER NOTES: Selected by Boston Red Sox organization in 29th round of 1996 free-agent draft; did not sign. ... Selected by Chicago White Sox organization in fifth round of 1999 free-agent draft. ... On disabled list (August 31, 2003-remainder of season).

CAREER HITTING: 0-for-0 (.000), 0 R, 0 2B, 0 3B, 0 HR, 0 RBI.

Year	Team (League)	W	L	Pct.	ERA	WHIP	G	GS	CG	ShO	Hld.	Sv.-Opp.	IP	H	R	ER	HR	BB-IBB	SO	Avg.
1999—	Bristol (Appalachian)	1	0	1.000	1.50	1.00	5	0	0	0	...	1-...	18.0	13	5	3	0	5-0	25	.206
	—Burlington (Midw.)	2	0	1.000	7.28	1.79	16	0	0	0	...	1-...	29.2	32	25	24	6	21-0	35	.283
2000—	Burlington (Midw.)	9	9	.500	4.57	1.56	25	25	1	1	...	0-...	138.0	157	84	70	14	58-2	82	.290
2001—	Winston-Salem (Caro.)	4	6	.400	3.82	1.45	12	12	1	0	...	0-...	63.2	64	41	27	6	28-1	38	.258
	—Birmingham (Southern)	3	4	.429	6.67	1.85	16	16	0	0	...	0-...	82.1	110	68	61	7	42-0	47	.330
2002—	Birmingham (Southern)	11	7	.611	3.53	1.34	26	26	1	1	...	0-...	150.1	145	65	59	11	56-1	92	.255
2003—	Chicago (A.L.)	1	2	.333	5.96	1.76	5	5	0	0	0	0-0	25.2	28	18	17	4	16-0	13	.272
	—Bristol (Appalachian)	0	0	...	0.00	1.17	2	2	0	0	...	0-...	6.0	5	0	0	0	2-0	5	.227
	—Charlotte (Int'l)	0	3	.000	6.15	1.67	5	5	0	0	...	0-...	26.1	38	18	18	4	6-0	10	.345
2004—	Chicago (A.L.)	0	1	.000	15.26	2.48	3	2	0	0	0	0-0	7.2	16	13	13	3	3-0	5	.444
	—Charlotte (Int'l)	8	7	.533	3.94	1.34	25	25	0	0	...	0-...	148.2	155	70	65	20	44-0	82	.275
	Major League totals (2 years)	**1**	**3**	**.250**	**8.10**	**1.89**	**8**	**7**	**0**	**0**	**0**	**0-0**	**33.1**	**44**	**31**	**30**	**7**	**19-0**	**18**	**.317**

STEWART, SCOTT — P

PERSONAL: Born August 14, 1975, in Stoughton, Mass. ... 6-2/225. ... Throws left, bats right. ... Full name: Scott Edward Stewart. ... High school: East Gaston (Mount Holly, N.C.).

TRANSACTIONS/CAREER NOTES: Selected by Texas Rangers organization in 20th round of 1994 free-agent draft. ... Released by Rangers (May 30, 1995). ... Signed by Minnesota Twins organization (June 13, 1995). ... Released by Twins (July 13, 1995). ... Contract purchased by New York Mets organization from St. Paul of the independent Northern League (February 25, 1997). ... Signed as a free agent by Montreal Expos organization (November 17, 2000). ... On disabled list (May 11-June 2, 2001); included rehabilitation assignment to Ottawa. ... On disabled list (July 10-September 1, 2003); included rehabilitation assignment to Brevard County. ... Traded by Expos to Cleveland Indians for OF Ryan Church and SS Maicer Izturis (January 5, 2004). ... Traded by Indians to Los Angeles Dodgers for future considerations (August 18, 2003).

CAREER HITTING: 0-for-4 (.000), 0 R, 0 2B, 0 3B, 0 HR, 0 RBI.

Year Team (League)	W	L	Pct.	ERA	WHIP	G	GS	CG	ShO	Hld.	Sv.-Opp.	IP	H	R	ER	HR	BB-IBB	SO	Avg.
1994— GC Rangers (GCL)	4	1	.800	2.82	1.09	14	8	0	0	...	1-...	54.1	47	22	17	1	12-0	62	.228
1995— Char., S.C. (SAL)	1	7	.125	3.69	1.19	11	11	1	0	...	0-...	75.2	76	38	31	6	14-1	47	.269
— GC Twins (GCL)	0	0	...	6.35	1.94	3	1	0	0	...	0-...	5.2	7	4	4	0	4-0	9	.292
1996— St. Paul (Nor.)	6	8	.429	5.84	1.89	19	18	0	0	...	0-...	86.1	121	70	56	13	42-2	54	...
1997— St. Lucie (Fla. St.)	5	10	.333	4.01	1.07	22	18	4	0	...	0-...	123.1	114	62	55	8	18-1	64	.246
1998— Binghamton (Eastern)	8	5	.615	3.70	1.33	24	13	0	0	...	2-...	90.0	91	44	37	12	29-2	65	.263
— Norfolk (Int'l)	0	6	.000	6.66	1.60	9	9	0	0	...	0-...	51.1	60	43	38	12	22-0	32	.290
1999— Norfolk (Int'l)	6	4	.600	4.42	1.45	35	14	0	0	...	0-...	99.2	109	55	49	9	36-1	85	.275
— Binghamton (Eastern)	1	0	1.000	0.00	0.60	1	1	0	0	...	0-...	5.0	3	0	0	0	0-0	5	.167
2000— Norfolk (Int'l)	3	5	.375	3.50	1.36	53	1	0	0	...	5-...	72.0	80	32	28	3	18-2	57	.281
2001— Montreal (N.L.)	3	1	.750	3.78	1.17	62	0	0	0	8	3-4	47.2	43	20	20	5	13-0	39	.243
— Ottawa (Int'l)	0	0	...	1.80	1.20	4	0	0	0	...	0-...	5.0	5	1	1	0	1-0	4	.278
2002— Montreal (N.L.)	4	2	.667	3.09	1.11	67	0	0	0	14	17-19	64.0	49	29	22	4	22-5	67	.207
2003— Brevard County (FSL)	0	0	...	0.00	0.50	2	2	0	0	...	0-...	3.2	1	0	0	0	1-0	4	.083
— Montreal (N.L.)	3	1	.750	3.98	1.51	51	0	0	0	13	0-1	43.0	52	22	19	5	13-4	29	.306
2004— Cleveland (A.L.)	0	2	.000	7.24	2.12	23	0	0	0	4	0-2	13.2	23	14	11	2	6-2	18	.365
— Buffalo (Int'l)	3	1	.750	4.22	1.44	27	0	0	0	...	6-...	32.0	37	15	15	4	9-1	21	.285
— Las Vegas (PCL)	0	0	...	2.46	1.09	4	0	0	0	...	0-...	3.2	3	1	1	0	1-0	7	.231
— Los Angeles (N.L.)	1	0	1.000	5.84	2.11	11	0	0	0	...	0-0	12.1	20	8	8	3	6-3	8	.392
American League totals (1 year)	0	2	.000	7.24	2.12	23	0	0	0	4	0-2	13.2	23	14	11	2	6-2	18	.365
National League totals (4 years)	11	4	.733	3.72	1.31	191	0	0	0	35	20-24	167.0	164	79	69	17	54-12	143	.258
Major League totals (4 years)	11	6	.647	3.99	1.37	214	0	0	0	39	20-26	180.2	187	93	80	19	60-14	161	.268

STEWART, SHANNON — OF

PERSONAL: Born February 25, 1974, in Cincinnati, Ohio. ... 5-11/200. ... Bats right, throws right. ... Full name: Shannon Harold Stewart. ... High school: Southridge Senior (Miami).

TRANSACTIONS/CAREER NOTES: Selected by Toronto Blue Jays organization in first round (19th pick overall) of 1992 free-agent draft; pick received as part of compensation for Los Angeles Dodgers signing Type A free-agent P Tom Candiotti. ... On disabled list (April 29-May 14, 2000); included rehabilitation assignment to Dunedin. ... On disabled list (May 1-16, 2002). ... On disabled list (May 29-June 23, 2003); included rehabilitation assignment to Syracuse. ... Traded by Blue Jays to Minnesota Twins for OF Bobby Kielty (July 16, 2003). ... On disabled list (May 18-July 15, 2004); included rehabilitation assignment to Rochester.

RECORDS: Shares major league record for most doubles, game (4, July 18, 2000).

2004 GAMES PLAYED BY POSITION (MLB): OF—71, DH—21.

Year Team (League)	Pos.	G	AB	R	H	2B	3B	HR	RBI	BB	SO	HBP	GDP	SB-CS	Avg.	OBP	SLG	OPS	E	Avg.
1992— GC Jays (GCL)	OF	50	172	44	40	1	0	1	11	24	27	3	3	32-5	.233	.333	.256	.589	1	.988
1993— St. Catharines (NY-Penn.)	OF	75	301	53	84	15	2	3	29	33	43	2	7	25-10	.279	.351	.372	.723	0	1.000
1994— Hagerstown (SAL)	OF	56	225	39	73	10	5	4	25	23	39	1	3	15-11	.324	.386	.467	.853	1	.990
1995— Knoxville (Southern)	OF-DH	138	498	89	143	24	6	5	55	89	61	6	13	42-16	.287	.398	.390	.788	6	.980
— Toronto (A.L.)	OF	12	38	2	8	0	0	0	1	5	5	1	0	2-0	.211	.318	.211	.529	1	.955
1996— Syracuse (Int'l)	OF	112	420	77	125	26	8	6	42	54	61	2	6	35-8	.298	.377	.440	.818	5	.983
— Toronto (A.L.)	OF	7	17	2	3	1	0	0	2	1	4	0	1	1-0	.176	.222	.235	.458	1	.800
1997— Toronto (A.L.)	OF-DH	44	168	25	48	13	7	0	22	19	24	4	3	10-3	.286	.368	.446	.814	2	.980
— Syracuse (Int'l)	OF	58	208	41	72	13	1	5	24	36	26	4	1	9-6	.346	.452	.490	.942	2	.983
1998— Toronto (A.L.)	OF	144	516	90	144	29	3	12	55	67	77	15	5	51-18	.279	.377	.417	.794	6	.980
1999— Toronto (A.L.)	OF-DH	145	608	102	185	28	2	11	67	59	83	8	12	37-14	.304	.371	.411	.782	5	.981
2000— Toronto (A.L.)	OF	136	583	107	186	43	5	21	69	37	79	6	12	20-5	.319	.363	.518	.882	2	.993
— Dunedin (Fla. St.)	OF	1	3	2	3	1	0	0	1	0	0	0	0	0-1	1.000	1.000	1.333	2.333	0	...
2001— Toronto (A.L.)	OF-DH	155	640	103	202	44	7	12	60	46	72	11	9	27-10	.316	.371	.463	.834	5	.981
2002— Toronto (A.L.)	OF-DH	141	577	103	175	38	6	10	45	54	60	9	17	14-2	.303	.371	.442	.813	2	.990
2003— Syracuse (Int'l)	OF	1	3	0	0	0	0	0	0	0	1	0	0	0-0	.000	.250	.250	.250	0	1.000
— Toronto (A.L.)	OF-DH	71	303	47	89	22	2	7	35	27	30	2	6	1-2	.294	.347	.449	.796	4	.974
— Minnesota (A.L.)	OF-DH	65	270	43	87	22	0	6	38	25	36	4	4	3-4	.322	.384	.470	.854	1	.993
2004— Rochester (Int'l)	DH-OF	3	9	3	3	1	0	0	0	1	2	0	0	0-0	.333	.400	.444	.844	0	...
— Minnesota (A.L.)	OF-DH	92	378	46	115	17	2	11	47	47	44	1	5	6-3	.304	.380	.447	.827	3	.972
Major League totals (10 years)		1012	4098	670	1242	257	34	90	441	387	514	61	74	172-61	.303	.370	.448	.818	32	.983

DIVISION SERIES RECORD

Year Team (League)	Pos.	G	AB	R	H	2B	3B	HR	RBI	BB	SO	HBP	GDP	SB-CS	Avg.	OBP	SLG	OPS	E	Avg.
2003— Minnesota (A.L.)	OF	4	15	0	6	2	0	0	2	2	4	0	0	1-0	.400	.471	.533	1.004	0	1.000
2004— Minnesota (A.L.)	OF-DH	4	20	1	4	0	0	0	2	0	2	0	0	0-0	.200	.190	.200	.390	0	1.000
Division series totals (2 years)		8	35	1	10	2	0	0	4	2	6	0	0	1-0	.286	.316	.343	.659	0	1.000

STINNETT, KELLY — C

PERSONAL: Born February 4, 1970, in Lawton, Okla. ... 5-11/225. ... Bats right, throws right. ... Full name: Kelly Lee Stinnett. ... Name pronounced: sti-NETT. ... High school: Lawton (Okla.). ... Junior college: Seminole (Okla.).

TRANSACTIONS/CAREER NOTES: Selected by Cleveland Indians organization in 11th round of 1989 free-agent draft. ... Selected by New York Mets from Indians organization in Rule 5 major league draft (December 13, 1993). ... Traded by Mets to Milwaukee Brewers for P Cory Lidle (January 17, 1996). ... On disabled list (July 27-September 2, 1997). ... Selected by Arizona Diamondbacks in third round (65th pick overall) of expansion draft (November 18, 1997). ... Signed as a free agent by Cincinnati Reds (January 9, 2001). ... On disabled list (September 4, 2001-remainder of season). ... On disabled list (April 6-July 15, 2002); included rehabilitation assignments to Louisville. ... Traded by Reds to Philadelphia Phillies for OF Eric Valent (August 31, 2003). ... Signed as a free agent by Kansas City Royals (December 19, 2003). ... On disabled list (June 20, 2004-remainder of season).

2004 GAMES PLAYED BY POSITION (MLB): C—20.

Year	Team (League)	Pos.	G	AB	R	H	2B	3B	HR	RBI	BB	SO	HBP	GDP	SB-CS	Avg.	OBP	SLG	OPS	E	Avg.
1990—	Watertown (N.Y.-Penn.)	C-1B	60	192	29	46	10	2	2	21	40	43	4	8	3-7	.240	.378	.344	.722	18	.957
1991—	Columbus (S. Atl.)	C-1B	102	384	49	101	15	1	14	74	26	70	9	17	4-1	.263	.321	.417	.737	28	.966
1992—	Cant./Akr. (Eastern)	C	91	296	37	84	10	0	6	32	16	43	4	8	7-6	.284	.326	.378	.704	13	.979
1993—	Charlotte (Int'l)	C	98	288	42	79	10	3	6	33	17	52	2	4	0-0	.274	.318	.392	.711	8	.985
1994—	New York (N.L.)	C	47	150	20	38	6	2	2	14	11	28	5	3	2-0	.253	.323	.360	.683	5	.979
1995—	New York (N.L.)	C	77	196	23	43	8	1	4	18	29	65	6	3	2-0	.219	.338	.332	.669	7	.983
1996—	Milwaukee (A.L.)	C-DH	14	26	1	2	0	0	0	0	2	11	1	0	0-0	.077	.172	.077	.249	2	.960
	New Orleans (A.A.)	C-DH-3B	95	334	63	96	21	1	27	70	31	83	13	6	3-3	.287	.366	.599	.965	11	.980
1997—	Tucson (PCL)	C-DH-1B	64	209	50	67	15	3	10	43	42	46	6	2	1-1	.321	.444	.565	1.009	2	.993
	Milwaukee (A.L.)	C-DH	30	36	2	9	4	0	0	3	3	9	0	0	0-0	.250	.308	.361	.669	1	.989
1998—	Arizona (N.L.)	C-DH	92	274	35	71	14	1	11	34	35	74	6	9	0-1	.259	.353	.438	.791	8	.984
1999—	Arizona (N.L.)	C	88	284	36	66	13	0	14	38	24	83	5	4	2-1	.232	.302	.426	.728	6	.990
2000—	Arizona (N.L.)	C	76	240	22	52	7	0	8	33	19	56	6	5	0-1	.217	.291	.346	.636	6	.990
2001—	Cincinnati (N.L.)	C-DH	63	187	27	48	11	0	9	25	17	61	5	5	2-2	.257	.333	.460	.793	12	.966
2002—	Cincinnati (N.L.)	C	34	93	10	21	5	0	3	13	15	25	0	1	2-0	.226	.333	.376	.710	2	.990
	Louisville (Int'l)	C	30	86	6	17	6	0	0	5	3	24	0	1	0-0	.198	.225	.267	.492	2	.988
2003—	Cincinnati (N.L.)	C	60	179	14	41	13	0	3	19	13	51	4	3	0-0	.229	.294	.352	.646	2	.993
	Philadelphia (N.L.)	C	7	7	0	3	0	0	0	0	1	1	0	0	0-0	.429	.500	.429	.929	0	1.000
2004—	Kansas City (A.L.)	C	20	59	10	18	0	0	3	7	5	16	2	0	0-0	.305	.379	.458	.836	3	.971
	American League totals (3 years)		64	121	13	29	4	0	3	10	10	36	3	0	0-0	.240	.313	.347	.661	6	.975
	National League totals (8 years)		544	1610	187	383	77	4	54	194	164	444	37	33	10-5	.238	.321	.391	.713	48	.985
	Major League totals (11 years)		608	1731	200	412	81	4	57	204	174	480	40	33	10-5	.238	.321	.388	.709	54	.984

DIVISION SERIES RECORD

Year	Team (League)	Pos.	G	AB	R	H	2B	3B	HR	RBI	BB	SO	HBP	GDP	SB-CS	Avg.	OBP	SLG	OPS	E	Avg.
1999—	Arizona (N.L.)	C	4	14	1	2	1	0	0	0	1	4	0	0	0-0	.143	.200	.214	.414	0	1.000

STONE, RICKY — P

PERSONAL: Born February 28, 1975, in Hamilton, Ohio. ... 6-1/195. ... Throws right, bats right. ... Full name: Ricky L. Stone. ... High school: Hamilton (Ohio).

TRANSACTIONS/CAREER NOTES: Selected by Los Angeles Dodgers organization in fourth round of 1994 free-agent draft. ... Signed as a free agent by Houston Astros organization (January 8, 2001). ... Claimed on waivers by San Diego Padres (June 18, 2004). ... Refused minor league assignment and became a free agent (October 8, 2004). ... Signed by Cincinnati Reds organization (November 1, 2004).

CAREER HITTING: 0-for-8 (.000). 0 R, 0 2B, 0 3B, 0 HR, 0 RBI.

Year	Team (League)	W	L	Pct.	ERA	WHIP	G	GS	CG	ShO	Hld.	Sv.-Opp.	IP	H	R	ER	HR	BB-IBB	SO	Avg.
1994—	Great Falls (Pio.)	2	2	.500	4.44	1.56	13	7	0	0	...	2-...	50.2	55	40	25	5	24-0	48	.268
1995—	San Bernardino (Calif.) ..	3	5	.375	6.52	1.79	12	12	0	0	...	2-...	58.0	79	50	42	7	25-0	31	.333
	Yakima (N'west)	4	4	.500	5.25	1.54	16	6	0	0	...	2-...	48.0	54	31	28	5	20-0	28	.289
1996—	Savannah (S. Atl.)	2	1	.667	3.98	1.36	5	5	0	0	...	0-...	31.2	34	15	14	2	9-0	31	.288
	Vero Beach (FSL)	8	6	.571	3.83	1.43	21	21	1	0	...	0-...	112.2	115	58	48	9	46-0	74	.267
1997—	San Antonio (Texas)	0	3	.000	5.47	1.77	25	5	0	0	...	3-...	52.2	63	33	32	4	30-0	46	.304
	San Bernardino (Calif.) ..	3	3	.500	3.35	0.93	8	8	0	0	...	0-...	53.2	40	22	20	4	10-0	40	.209
1998—	San Antonio (Texas)	7	2	.778	3.84	1.24	13	13	1	1	...	0-...	82.0	76	40	35	7	26-0	69	.251
	Albuquerque (PCL)	5	5	.500	5.38	1.53	18	16	0	0	...	0-...	105.1	120	69	63	13	41-0	85	.287
1999—	Albuquerque (PCL)	6	10	.375	5.50	1.65	27	27	2	0	...	0-...	167.0	205	123	102	23	71-4	132	.306
2000—	Albuquerque (PCL)	9	5	.643	4.94	1.56	48	7	0	0	...	5-...	120.1	146	79	66	9	42-3	75	.309
2001—	New Orleans (PCL)	6	3	.667	3.59	1.31	51	8	0	0	...	2-...	95.1	98	42	38	8	27-4	78	.269
	Houston (N.L.)	0	0	...	2.35	1.30	6	0	0	0	...	0-0	7.2	8	3	2	1	2-1	4	.258
2002—	Houston (N.L.)	3	3	.500	3.61	1.45	78	0	0	0	12	1-2	77.1	78	36	31	9	34-3	63	.266
2003—	Houston (N.L.)	4	6	.400	3.69	1.29	65	0	0	0	7	1-1	83.0	76	36	34	11	31-4	47	.247
2004—	New Orleans (PCL)	1	0	1.000	4.50	1.00	2	0	0	0	...	0-0	2.0	2	1	1	0	0-0	0	.250
	Houston (N.L.)	1	1	.500	5.68	1.74	16	0	0	0	1	0-0	19.0	26	12	12	5	7-3	16	.317
	Portland (PCL)	0	0	...	3.38	2.06	3	0	0	0	...	0-0	5.1	9	5	2	2	2-0	2	.409
	San Diego (N.L.)	1	1	.500	6.89	1.50	27	0	0	0	...	0-0	32.2	40	27	25	6	9-0	22	.301
	Major League totals (4 years)	11	9	.550	4.26	1.42	192	0	0	0	20	2-3	219.2	228	114	104	32	83-11	152	.269

STURTZE, TANYON — P

PERSONAL: Born October 12, 1970, in Worcester, Mass. ... 6-5/200. ... Throws right, bats right. ... Full name: Tanyon James Sturtze. ... Name pronounced: sturts. ... High school: St. Peter-Marian (Worcester, Mass.). ... Junior college: Quinsigamond (Mass.) Community College.

TRANSACTIONS/CAREER NOTES: Selected by Oakland Athletics organization in 23rd round of 1990 free-agent draft. ... Selected by Chicago Cubs from A's organization in Rule 5 major league draft (December 5, 1994). ... Signed as a free agent by Texas Rangers (November 20, 1996). ... Released by Rangers (March 6, 1998). ... Re-signed by Rangers organization (March 11, 1998). ... Signed as a free agent by Chicago White Sox organization (November 23, 1998). ... On suspended list (May 1-3, 2000). ... Traded by White Sox to Tampa Bay Devil Rays for IF Tony Graffanino (May 31, 2000). ... On disabled list (August 27, 2000-remainder of season). ... Signed as a free agent by Toronto Blue Jays (December 22, 2002). ... On suspended list (September 26-28, 2003). ... Signed as a free agent by Los Angeles Dodgers organization (December 19, 2003). ... Released by Dodgers (March 29, 2004). ... Signed by Florida Marlins organization (March 30, 2004). ... Released by Marlins (April 2, 2004). ... Signed by Dodgers organization (April 14, 2004). ... Traded by Dodgers to New York Yankees for 1B Bryan Myrow (May 15, 2004). ... On suspended list (August 12-15, 2004).

CAREER HITTING: 1-for-16 (.063). 0 R, 0 2B, 0 3B, 0 HR, 0 RBI.

Year	Team (League)	W	L	Pct.	ERA	WHIP	G	GS	CG	ShO	Hld.	Sv.-Opp.	IP	H	R	ER	HR	BB-IBB	SO	Avg.
1990—	Ariz. A's (Ariz.)	2	5	.286	5.44	1.71	12	10	0	0	...	0-...	48.0	55	41	29	3	27-0	30	.276
1991—	Madison (Midw.)	10	5	.667	3.09	1.19	27	27	0	0	...	0-...	163.0	136	77	56	5	58-5	88	.223
1992—	Modesto (Calif.)	7	11	.389	3.75	1.46	25	25	1	0	...	0-...	151.0	143	72	63	6	78-1	126	.254
1993—	Huntsville (Southern)	5	12	.294	4.78	1.53	28	28	1	1	...	0-...	165.2	169	102	88	16	85-2	112	.269
1994—	Huntsville (Southern)	6	3	.667	3.22	1.35	17	17	1	0	...	0-...	103.1	100	40	37	5	39-1	63	.269
	Tacoma (PCL)	4	5	.444	4.04	1.65	11	9	0	0	...	0-...	64.2	73	36	29	5	34-2	28	.284
1995—	Chicago (N.L.)	0	0	...	9.00	1.50	2	0	0	0	0	0-0	2.0	2	2	2	1	1-0	0	.250
	Iowa (Am. Assoc.)	4	7	.364	6.80	1.74	23	17	1	1	...	0-...	86.0	108	66	65	18	42-1	48	.314
1996—	Iowa (Am. Assoc.)	6	4	.600	4.85	1.56	51	1	0	0	...	4-...	72.1	80	42	39	7	33-2	51	.290
	Chicago (N.L.)	1	0	1.000	9.00	1.91	6	0	0	0	0	0-0	11.0	16	11	11	3	5-0	7	.348
1997—	Oklahoma City (A.A.)	8	6	.571	5.10	1.57	25	19	1	0	...	0-...	114.2	133	76	65	10	47-1	79	.295
	Texas (A.L.)	1	1	.500	8.27	1.93	9	5	0	0	...	0-0	32.2	45	30	30	6	18-0	18	.338

Year	Team (League)	W	L	Pct.	ERA	WHIP	G	GS	CG	ShO	Hld.	Sv.-Opp.	IP	H	R	ER	HR	BB-IBB	SO	Avg.
1998—GC Rangers (GCL)		0	1	.000	7.71	2.29	3	3	0	0	...	0-...	7.0	12	7	6	1	4-0	10	.364
—Charlotte (Fla. St.)		0	1	.000	6.00	1.00	1	0	0	0	...	0-...	3.0	2	3	2	0	1-0	3	.200
—Tulsa (Texas)		1	0	1.000	5.40	2.40	1	0	0	0	...	0-...	1.2	2	1	1	1	2-0	3	.400
—Oklahoma (PCL)		3	1	.750	3.34	1.46	13	3	0	0	...	0-...	35.0	33	13	13	3	18-0	31	.252
1999—Charlotte (Int'l)		9	4	.692	4.05	1.19	33	14	2	1	...	3-...	104.1	83	53	47	7	41-1	107	.214
—Chicago (A.L.)		0	0	...	0.00	1.00	1	1	0	0	0	0-0	6.0	4	0	0	0	2-0	2	.200
2000—Chicago (A.L.)		1	2	.333	12.06	2.55	10	1	0	0	0	0-0	15.2	25	23	21	4	15-0	6	.379
—Tampa Bay (A.L.)		4	0	1.000	2.56	1.16	19	5	0	0	0	0-0	52.2	47	16	15	4	14-1	38	.236
2001—Tampa Bay (A.L.)		11	12	.478	4.42	1.43	39	27	0	0	3	1-3	195.1	200	98	96	23	79-0	110	.271
2002—Tampa Bay (A.L.)		4	* 18	.182	5.18	1.61	33	33	4	0	0	0-0	224.0	* 271	* 141	* 129	33	* 89-2	137	.302
2003—Toronto (A.L.)		7	6	.538	5.94	1.68	40	8	0	0	0	0-0	89.1	107	67	59	14	43-3	54	.296
2004—Las Vegas (PCL)		3	0	1.000	2.50	1.06	6	6	0	0	0	0-...	36.0	26	11	10	2	12-0	32	.203
—New York (A.L.)		6	2	.750	5.47	1.40	28	3	0	0	1	1-1	77.1	75	49	47	9	33-2	56	.254
American League totals (7 years)		34	41	.453	5.16	1.54	179	83	4	0	5	2-4	693.0	774	424	397	93	293-8	421	.286
National League totals (2 years)		1	0	1.000	9.00	1.85	8	0	0	0	0	0-0	13.0	18	13	13	4	6-0	7	.333
Major League totals (9 years)		35	41	.461	5.23	1.55	187	83	4	0	5	2-4	706.0	792	437	410	97	299-8	428	.287

DIVISION SERIES RECORD

Year	Team (League)	W	L	Pct.	ERA	WHIP	G	GS	CG	ShO	Hld.	Sv.-Opp.	IP	H	R	ER	HR	BB-IBB	SO	Avg.
2004—New York (A.L.)		0	0	...	6.75	2.63	2	0	0	0	0	0-0	2.2	4	2	2	1	3-0	4	.333

CHAMPIONSHIP SERIES RECORD

Year	Team (League)	W	L	Pct.	ERA	WHIP	G	GS	CG	ShO	Hld.	Sv.-Opp.	IP	H	R	ER	HR	BB-IBB	SO	Avg.
2004—New York (A.L.)		0	0	...	2.70	1.20	4	0	0	0	2	0-0	3.1	2	1	1	1	2-0	2	.182

STYNES, CHRIS — 3B

PERSONAL: Born January 19, 1973, in Queens, N.Y. ... 5-9/207. ... Bats right, throws right. ... Full name: Christopher Desmond Stynes. ... High school: Boca Raton (Fla.).
TRANSACTIONS/CAREER NOTES: Selected by Toronto Blue Jays in third round of 1991 free-agent draft. ... Traded by Blue Jays with P David Sinnes and IF Tony Medrano to Kansas City Royals for P David Cone (April 6, 1995). ... Traded by Royals with OF Jon Nunnally to Cincinnati Reds for Ps Hector Carrasco and Scott Service (July 15, 1997). ... Traded by Reds to Boston Red Sox for OF Michael Coleman and IF Donnie Sadler (November 16, 2000). ... On disabled list (April 6-24 and May 10-June 7, 2001); included rehabilitation assignment to Pawtucket. ... Signed as a free agent by Chicago Cubs (January 2, 2002). ... Released by Cubs (December 4, 2002). ... Signed by Colorado Rockies (January 7, 2003). ... Signed as a free agent by Pittsburgh Pirates (January 6, 2004). ... Released by Pirates (July 31, 2004).
2004 GAMES PLAYED BY POSITION (MLB): 3B—71.

Year	Team (League)	Pos.	G	AB	R	H	2B	3B	HR	RBI	BB	SO	HBP	GDP	SB-CS	Avg.	OBP	SLG	OPS	E	Avg.
1991—GC Jays (GCL)	3B	57	219	29	67	15	1	4	39	9	39	1	1	10-3	.306	.336	.438	.775	6	.957
1992—Myrtle Beach (SAL)	3B	127	489	67	139	36	0	7	46	16	43	8	8	28-14	.284	.315	.401	.716	26	.919
1993—Dunedin (Fla. St.)	3B	123	496	72	151	28	5	7	48	25	40	3	12	19-9	.304	.339	.423	.762	21	.938
1994—Knoxville (Southern)	2B	136	545	79	173	32	4	8	79	23	36	7	12	28-12	.317	.351	.435	.785	20	.968
1995—Omaha (A.A.)	2B-3B	83	306	51	84	12	5	9	42	27	24	5	7	4-5	.275	.338	.435	.773	13	.964
—Kansas City (A.L.)	2B-DH	22	35	7	6	1	0	0	2	4	3	0	3	0-0	.171	.256	.200	.456	1	.982
1996—Omaha (A.A.)	O-3-2-DH	72	284	50	101	22	2	10	40	18	17	4	7	7-3	.356	.398	.553	.951	9	.951
—Kansas City (A.L.)	O-2-DH-3	36	92	8	27	6	0	0	6	2	5	0	1	2-5	.293	.309	.359	.667	3	.939
1997—Omaha (A.A.)	2-O-DH-3	82	332	53	88	18	1	8	44	19	25	0	...	3-1	.265	.303	.398	.701	10	.948
—Indianapolis (A.A.)	2B	21	86	14	31	8	0	1	17	2	5	1	...	4-1	.360	.374	.488	.862	2	.982
—Cincinnati (N.L.)	OF-2B-3B	49	198	31	69	7	1	6	28	11	13	4	5	11-2	.348	.394	.485	.879	2	.984
1998—Cincinnati (N.L.)	O-3-2-S	123	347	52	88	10	1	6	27	32	36	4	5	15-1	.254	.323	.340	.663	6	.990
1999—Cincinnati (N.L.)	2B-3B-OF	73	113	18	27	1	0	2	14	12	13	0	2	5-2	.239	.310	.301	.610	6	.953
2000—Cincinnati (N.L.)	3B-2B-OF	119	380	71	127	24	1	12	40	32	54	2	5	5-2	.334	.386	.497	.883	7	.970
2001—Boston (A.L.)	3B-2B-OF	96	361	52	101	19	2	8	33	20	56	3	12	4-5	.280	.322	.410	.732	6	.980
—Pawtucket (Int'l)	2B-3B	4	15	1	5	1	0	0	1	1	2	1	0	0-0	.333	.412	.400	.812	0	1.000
2002—Chicago (N.L.)	3B-2B	98	195	25	47	9	1	5	26	21	29	1	5	1-1	.241	.314	.374	.688	5	.957
2003—Colorado (N.L.)	3B-2B	138	443	71	113	31	3	11	73	48	76	6	8	3-1	.255	.335	.413	.748	9	.974
2004—Pittsburgh (N.L.)	3B	74	162	16	35	10	0	1	16	9	23	2	2	0-0	.216	.266	.296	.562	1	.992
American League totals (3 years)		154	488	67	134	26	2	8	41	26	64	3	16	9-7	.275	.315	.385	.700	10	.975
National League totals (7 years)		674	1838	284	506	92	7	43	224	165	244	19	32	40-9	.275	.340	.403	.743	32	.975
Major League totals (10 years)		828	2326	351	640	118	9	51	265	191	308	22	48	49-16	.275	.335	.399	.734	42	.975

SULLIVAN, SCOTT — P

PERSONAL: Born March 13, 1971, in Carrollton, Ala. ... 6-3/210. ... Throws right, bats right. ... Full name: William Scott Sullivan. ... High school: Pickens Academy (Carrollton, Ala.). ... College: Auburn.
TRANSACTIONS/CAREER NOTES: Selected by Cincinnati Reds organization in second round of 1993 free-agent draft. ... On disabled list (August 10-25, 2002; and July 14-August 7, 2003). ... Traded by Reds to Chicago White Sox for IF Tim Hummel and cash (August 21, 2003). ... Signed by Kansas City Royals (December 9, 2003). ... On disabled list (August 26, 2004-remainder of season).
CAREER HITTING: 4-for-48 (.083), 1 R, 0 2B, 0 3B, 0 HR, 1 RBI.

Year	Team (League)	W	L	Pct.	ERA	WHIP	G	GS	CG	ShO	Hld.	Sv.-Opp.	IP	H	R	ER	HR	BB-IBB	SO	Avg.
1993—Billings (Pio.)		5	0	1.000	1.67	1.07	18	7	2	2	...	3-...	54.0	33	13	10	1	25-0	79	.174
1994—Chattanooga (Southern)		11	7	.611	3.41	1.16	34	13	2	0	...	7-...	121.1	101	60	46	8	40-1	111	.220
1995—Indianapolis (A.A.)		4	3	.571	3.53	1.28	44	0	0	0	...	1-...	58.2	51	31	23	2	24-4	54	.232
—Cincinnati (N.L.)		0	0	...	4.91	1.64	3	0	0	0	0	0-0	3.2	4	2	2	0	2-0	2	.286
1996—Indianapolis (A.A.)		5	2	.714	2.73	1.21	53	3	0	0	...	1-...	108.2	95	38	33	10	37-3	77	.233
—Cincinnati (N.L.)		0	0	...	2.25	1.50	7	0	0	0	0	0-0	8.0	7	2	2	0	5-0	3	.250
1997—Cincinnati (N.L.)		5	3	.625	3.24	1.12	59	0	0	0	13	1-2	97.1	79	36	35	12	30-8	96	.220
—Indianapolis (A.A.)		3	1	.750	1.30	0.72	19	0	0	0	...	2-...	27.2	16	4	4	0	4-1	23	.186
1998—Cincinnati (N.L.)		5	5	.500	5.21	1.31	67	0	0	0	5	1-4	102.0	98	62	59	14	36-4	86	.253
1999—Cincinnati (N.L.)		5	4	.556	3.01	1.19	79	0	0	0	13	3-5	113.2	88	41	38	10	47-4	78	.217
2000—Cincinnati (N.L.)		3	6	.333	3.47	1.18	79	0	0	0	22	3-6	106.1	87	44	41	14	38-8	96	.226
2001—Cincinnati (N.L.)		7	1	.875	3.31	1.26	79	0	0	0	20	0-3	103.1	94	44	38	10	36-8	82	.243
2002—Cincinnati (N.L.)		6	5	.545	6.06	1.58	71	0	0	0	19	1-3	78.2	93	60	53	15	31-11	78	.294
2003—Cincinnati (N.L.)		6	0	1.000	3.62	1.31	50	0	0	0	10	0-1	49.2	39	22	20	4	26-4	43	.211
—Chicago (A.L.)		0	0	...	3.77	1.05	15	0	0	0	0	0-0	14.1	9	6	6	2	6-0	13	.184
2004—Kansas City (A.L.)		3	4	.429	4.77	1.61	49	0	0	0	6	0-1	60.1	73	34	32	8	24-10	45	.308
American League totals (2 years)		3	4	.429	4.58	1.50	64	0	0	0	8	0-1	74.2	82	40	38	10	30-10	58	.287
National League totals (9 years)		37	24	.607	3.91	1.27	494	0	0	0	102	9-24	662.2	589	313	288	79	251-47	564	.239
Major League totals (10 years)		40	28	.588	3.98	1.29	558	0	0	0	110	9-25	737.1	671	353	326	89	281-57	622	.244

S

SUPPAN, JEFF — P

PERSONAL: Born January 2, 1975, in Oklahoma City, Okla. ... 6-2/220. ... Throws right, bats right. ... Full name: Jeffrey Scot Suppan. ... Name pronounced: SOO-pahn. ... High school: Crespi (Encino, Calif.).

TRANSACTIONS/CAREER NOTES: Selected by Boston Red Sox organization in second round of 1993 free-agent draft. ... On disabled list (August 25, 1996-remainder of season). ... Selected by Arizona Diamondbacks in first round (third pick overall) of expansion draft (November 18, 1997). ... Traded by Diamondbacks to Kansas City Royals for cash (September 3, 1998). ... Signed as a free agent by Pittsburgh Pirates (January 31, 2003). ... Traded by Pirates with Ps Brandon Lyon and Anastacio Martinez to Boston Red Sox for 2B Freddy Sanchez, P Mike Gonzalez and cash (July 31, 2003). ... Signed as a free agent by St. Louis Cardinals (December 18, 2003).

CAREER HITTING: 25-for-138 (.181), 7 R, 1 2B, 0 3B, 0 HR, 4 RBI.

Year	Team (League)	W	L	Pct.	ERA	WHIP	G	GS	CG	ShO	Hld.	Sv.-Opp.	IP	H	R	ER	HR	BB-IBB	SO	Avg.
1993—	GC Red Sox (GCL)	4	3	.571	2.18	1.18	10	9	2	1	...	0-...	57.2	52	20	14	0	16-0	64	.237
1994—	Sarasota (Florida State)	13	7	.650	3.26	1.17	27	27	4	2	...	0-...	174.0	153	74	63	10	50-0	173	.236
1995—	Trenton (East.)	6	2	.750	2.36	1.13	15	15	1	1	...	0-...	99.0	86	35	26	5	26-1	88	.232
—	Boston (A.L.)	1	2	.333	5.96	1.50	8	3	0	0	1	0-0	22.2	29	15	15	4	5-1	19	.312
—	Pawtucket (Int'l)	2	3	.400	5.32	1.29	7	7	0	0	...	0-...	45.2	50	29	27	9	9-0	32	.278
1996—	Boston (A.L.)	1	1	.500	7.54	1.85	8	4	0	0	0	0-0	22.2	29	19	19	3	13-0	13	.330
—	Pawtucket (Int'l)	10	6	.625	3.22	1.07	22	22	7	1	0	0-0	145.1	130	66	52	16	25-1	142	.233
1997—	Pawtucket (Int'l)	5	1	.833	3.71	1.09	9	9	2	1	0	0-...	60.2	51	26	25	7	15-0	40	.233
—	Boston (A.L.)	7	3	.700	5.69	1.57	23	22	0	0	0	0-0	112.1	140	75	71	12	36-1	67	.305
1998—	Arizona (N.L.)	1	7	.125	6.68	1.56	13	13	1	0	0	0-0	66.0	82	55	49	12	21-1	39	.301
—	Tucson (PCL)	4	3	.571	3.63	1.37	13	12	0	0	0	0-0	67.0	75	29	27	4	17-1	62	.277
—	Kansas City (A.L.)	0	0	...	0.71	0.79	4	1	0	0	0	0-0	12.2	9	1	1	1	1-0	12	.200
1999—	Kansas City (A.L.)	10	12	.455	4.53	1.36	32	32	4	1	0	0-0	208.2	222	113	105	28	62-4	103	.274
2000—	Kansas City (A.L.)	10	9	.526	4.94	1.49	35	33	3	1	0	0-0	217.0	240	120	119	36	84-3	128	.284
2001—	Kansas City (A.L.)	10	14	.417	4.37	1.38	34	34	1	0	0	0-0	218.1	227	120	106	26	74-3	120	.267
2002—	Kansas City (A.L.)	9	16	.360	5.32	1.43	33	33	3	1	0	0-0	208.0	229	134	123	32	68-3	109	.279
2003—	Pittsburgh (N.L.)	10	7	.588	3.57	1.26	21	21	3	0	0	0-0	141.0	147	57	56	11	31-5	78	.268
—	Boston (A.L.)	3	4	.429	5.57	1.43	11	11	0	0	0	0-0	63.0	70	41	39	12	20-0	32	.281
2004—	St. Louis (N.L.)	16	9	.640	4.16	1.37	31	31	0	0	0	0-0	188.0	192	98	87	25	65-1	110	.265
American League totals (9 years)		51	61	.455	4.96	1.44	188	172	11	3	1	0-0	1085.1	1195	639	598	154	363-15	603	.280
National League totals (3 years)		27	23	.540	4.37	1.36	65	65	4	2	0	0-0	395.0	421	210	192	48	117-7	227	.272
Major League totals (10 years)		78	84	.481	4.80	1.42	253	237	15	5	1	0-0	1480.1	1616	849	790	202	480-22	830	.278

DIVISION SERIES RECORD

Year	Team (League)	W	L	Pct.	ERA	WHIP	G	GS	CG	ShO	Hld.	Sv.-Opp.	IP	H	R	ER	HR	BB-IBB	SO	Avg.
2004—	St. Louis (N.L.)	1	0	1.000	2.57	0.71	1	1	0	0	0	0-0	7.0	2	2	2	1	3-0	2	.091

CHAMPIONSHIP SERIES RECORD

Year	Team (League)	W	L	Pct.	ERA	WHIP	G	GS	CG	ShO	Hld.	Sv.-Opp.	IP	H	R	ER	HR	BB-IBB	SO	Avg.
2004—	St. Louis (N.L.)	1	1	.500	3.00	1.00	2	2	0	0	0	0-0	12.0	8	5	4	2	4-0	9	.186

WORLD SERIES RECORD

Year	Team (League)	W	L	Pct.	ERA	WHIP	G	GS	CG	ShO	Hld.	Sv.-Opp.	IP	H	R	ER	HR	BB-IBB	SO	Avg.
2004—	St. Louis (N.L.)	0	1	.000	7.71	1.93	1	1	0	0	0	0-0	4.2	8	4	4	1	1-0	5	.364

SURHOFF, B.J. — OF/DH

PERSONAL: Born August 4, 1964, in Bronx, N.Y. ... 6-1/210. ... Bats left, throws right. ... Full name: William James Surhoff. ... High school: Rye (N.Y.). ... College: North Carolina. ... Son of Dick Surhoff, forward with two NBA teams (1952-53 and 1953-54); brother of Rich Surhoff, pitcher with Philadelphia Phillies and Texas Rangers (1985).

TRANSACTIONS/CAREER NOTES: Selected by New York Yankees organization in fifth round of June 1982 free-agent draft; did not sign. ... Selected by Milwaukee Brewers organization in first round (first pick overall) of June 1985 free-agent draft. ... On suspended list (August 23-25, 1990). ... On disabled list (March 25-April 16, April 20-May 23 and July 7, 1994-remainder of season); included rehabilitation assignments to El Paso and New Orleans. ... On disabled list (May 18-June 2, 1996). ... Traded by Orioles with P Gabe Molina to Atlanta Braves for OF Trenidad Hubbard, C Fernando Lunar and P Luis Rivera (July 31, 2000). ... On disabled list (April 28, 2002-remainder of season). ... Signed as a free agent by Orioles organization (February 12, 2002). ... On disabled list (May 4-28 and July 25-August 12, 2003; and June 19-July 27, 2004).

HONORS: Named College Player of the Year by THE SPORTING NEWS (1985).

2004 GAMES PLAYED BY POSITION (MLB): OF—70, DH—18, 1B—10.

Year	Team (League)	Pos.	G	AB	R	H	2B	3B	HR	RBI	BB	SO	HBP	GDP	SB-CS	Avg.	OBP	SLG	OPS	FIELDING E	FIELDING Avg.
1985—	Beloit (Midw.)	C	76	289	39	96	13	4	7	58	22	35	0	3	10-9	.332	.373	.478	.851	3	.994
1986—	Vancouver (PCL)	C	116	458	71	141	19	3	5	59	29	30	8	16	21-8	.308	.356	.395	.751	7	.989
1987—	Milwaukee (A.L.)	DH-C	115	395	50	118	22	3	7	68	36	30	0	13	11-10	.299	.350	.423	.773	11	.985
1988—	Milwaukee (A.L.)	C	139	493	47	121	21	0	5	38	31	49	3	12	21-6	.245	.292	.318	.611	8	.988
1989—	Milwaukee (A.L.)	3B-DH-C	126	436	42	108	17	4	5	55	25	29	3	8	14-12	.248	.287	.339	.626	10	.983
1990—	Milwaukee (A.L.)	3B-C	135	474	55	131	21	4	6	59	41	37	1	8	18-7	.276	.331	.376	.706	12	.983
1991—	Milwaukee (A.L.)	DH-C	143	505	57	146	19	4	5	68	26	33	0	21	5-8	.289	.319	.372	.691	4	.995
1992—	Milwaukee (A.L.)	C-1-DH-O-3	139	480	63	121	19	1	4	62	46	41	2	9	14-8	.252	.314	.321	.635	6	.992
1993—	Milwaukee (A.L.)	3-O-1-C-DH	148	552	66	151	38	3	7	79	36	47	2	9	12-9	.274	.318	.391	.709	18	.956
1994—	El Paso (Texas)	OF	3	12	2	3	1	0	0	0	0	2	0	0	0-0	.250	.250	.333	.583	0	1.000
—	Milwaukee (A.L.)	3-C-1-O-DH	40	134	20	35	11	2	5	22	16	14	0	5	0-1	.261	.336	.485	.821	4	.974
—	New Orleans (A.A.)	3B-OF-C-1B	5	19	3	6	2	0	0	1	1	2	0	0	0-0	.316	.350	.421	.771	0	1.000
1995—	Milwaukee (A.L.)	O-1-C-DH	117	415	72	133	26	3	13	73	37	43	4	7	7-3	.320	.378	.492	.870	5	.991
1996—	Baltimore (A.L.)	3-O-DH-1	143	537	74	157	27	6	21	82	47	79	3	0	0-1	.292	.352	.482	.834	15	.955
1997—	Baltimore (A.L.)	O-DH-3-1	147	528	80	150	30	4	18	88	49	60	5	7	1-1	.284	.345	.458	.803	2	.993
1998—	Baltimore (A.L.)	OF-1B	162	573	79	160	34	1	22	92	49	81	1	13	9-7	.279	.332	.457	.789	3	.989
1999—	Baltimore (East.)	OF-DH-3B	* 162	* 673	104	207	38	1	28	107	43	78	2	15	5-1	.308	.347	.492	.839	0	1.000
2000—	Baltimore (A.L.)	OF-DH	103	411	56	120	27	0	13	57	29	46	2	5	7-2	.292	.341	.453	.793	3	.987
—	Atlanta (N.L.)	OF	44	128	13	37	9	2	1	11	12	12	1	5	3-0	.289	.352	.414	.766	0	1.000
2001—	Atlanta (N.L.)	OF-DH	141	484	68	131	33	1	10	58	38	48	1	5	9-3	.271	.321	.405	.726	3	.986
2002—	Atlanta (N.L.)	1B-OF	25	75	5	22	5	0	0	9	9	5	0	1	1-3	.293	.369	.360	.729	0	1.000
2003—	Baltimore (A.L.)	DH-OF-1B	93	319	32	94	20	0	5	41	29	29	1	4	2-2	.295	.353	.404	.758	2	.991
2004—	Baltimore (A.L.)	OF-DH-1B	100	343	49	106	12	1	8	50	30	46	1	9	2-0	.309	.365	.420	.785	2	.989
American League totals (16 years)			2012	7268	946	2058	382	37	172	1041	570	742	30	152	128-78	.283	.334	.417	.751	105	.985
National League totals (3 years)			210	687	86	190	47	3	11	78	59	65	2	11	13-6	.277	.332	.402	.734	3	.992
Major League totals (18 years)			2222	7955	1032	2248	429	40	183	1119	629	807	32	163	141-84	.283	.334	.416	.749	108	.986

DIVISION SERIES RECORD

Year Team (League)	Pos.	G	AB	R	H	2B	3B	HR	RBI	BB	SO	HBP	GDP	SB-CS	Avg.	OBP	SLG	OPS	E	Avg.
1996— Baltimore (A.L.)	OF	4	13	3	5	0	0	3	5	0	1	0	0	0-0	.385	.385	1.077	1.462	0	1.000
1997— Baltimore (A.L.)	OF	3	11	0	3	1	0	0	2	0	2	0	0	0-0	.273	.273	.364	.636	0	1.000
2000— Atlanta (N.L.)		2	2	0	1	0	0	0	0	0	0	0	0	0-0	.500	.500	.500	1.000	...	...
2001— Atlanta (N.L.)	OF	3	11	1	3	1	0	0	0	0	0	1	1	1-0	.273	.333	.364	.697	0	1.000
Division series totals (4 years)		12	37	4	12	2	0	3	7	0	3	1	1	1-0	.324	.342	.622	.964	0	1.000

CHAMPIONSHIP SERIES RECORD

Year Team (League)	Pos.	G	AB	R	H	2B	3B	HR	RBI	BB	SO	HBP	GDP	SB-CS	Avg.	OBP	SLG	OPS	E	Avg.
1996— Baltimore (A.L.)	OF	5	15	0	4	0	0	0	2	1	2	0	1	0-0	.267	.294	.267	.561	0	1.000
1997— Baltimore (A.L.)	1B-OF	6	25	1	5	2	0	1	2	2	0	0	1	0-0	.200	.259	.280	.539	0	1.000
2001— Atlanta (N.L.)	OF	4	13	1	3	0	0	1	2	0	1	0	0	0-1	.231	.231	.462	.692	0	1.000
Champ. series totals (3 years)		15	53	2	12	2	0	1	5	3	5	0	2	0-1	.226	.263	.321	.584	0	1.000

ALL-STAR GAME RECORD

	G	AB	R	H	2B	3B	HR	RBI	BB	SO	HBP	GDP	SB-CS	Avg.	OBP	SLG	OPS	E	Avg.
All-Star Game totals (1 year)	1	2	0	0	0	0	0	0	0	0	0	0	0-0	.000	.000	.000	.000	0	...

SUTTON, LARRY — 1B/OF

PERSONAL: Born May 14, 1970, in West Covina, Calif. ... 6-0/185. ... Bats left, throws left. ... Full name: Larry James Sutton. ... High school: Mater Dei (Santa Ana, Calif.). ... College: Illinois.

TRANSACTIONS/CAREER NOTES: Selected by Kansas City organization in 21st round of 1992 free-agent draft. ... On disabled list (June 6-July 27, 1999); included rehabilitation assignments to GCL Royals and Omaha. ... Signed as a free agent by St. Louis Cardinals organization (December 8, 1999). ... Traded by Cardinals to Minnesota Twins for SS Hanley Frias (July 2, 2001). ... Signed as a free agent by Oakland Athletics organization (January 24, 2002). ... Released by A's (October 7, 2002). ... Signed by Boston Red Sox organization (November 22, 2002). ... Signed as a free agent by Florida Marlins organization (January 23, 2004).

2004 GAMES PLAYED BY POSITION (MLB): 1B—1.

Year Team (League)	Pos.	G	AB	R	H	2B	3B	HR	RBI	BB	SO	HBP	GDP	SB-CS	Avg.	OBP	SLG	OPS	E	Avg.
1992— Eugene (Northwest)	1B	70	238	45	74	17	3	15	58	48	33	5	3	3-6	.311	.433	.597	1.030	14	.975
— Appleton (Midwest)	DH	1	2	1	0	0	0	0	0	2	1	0	0	0-1	.000	.500	.000	.500	...	...
1993— Rockford (Midwest)	1B	113	361	67	97	24	1	7	50	95	65	8	3	3-5	.269	.424	.399	.823	11	.989
1994— Wilmington (Caro.)	1B	129	480	91	147	33	1	26	94	81	71	6	7	2-1	.306	.406	.542	.948	12	.990
1995— Wichita (Texas)	1B	53	197	31	53	11	1	5	32	26	33	2	3	1-1	.269	.357	.411	.768	7	.986
1996— Wichita (Texas)	1B-OF-DH	125	463	84	137	22	2	22	84	77	66	8	11	4-1	.296	.401	.495	.895	13	.989
1997— Omaha (A.A.)	1B-DH	106	380	61	114	27	1	19	72	61	57	0	6	0-0	.300	.395	.526	.921	5	.994
— Kansas City (A.L.)	1B-DH-OF	27	69	9	20	2	0	2	8	5	12	0	0	0-0	.290	.338	.406	.744	0	1.000
1998— Kansas City (A.L.)	OF-1B-DH	111	310	29	76	14	2	5	42	29	46	3	5	3-3	.245	.311	.352	.663	2	.989
1999— Kansas City (A.L.)	1B-DH-OF	43	102	14	23	6	0	2	15	13	17	0	4	1-0	.225	.308	.343	.651	3	.987
— GC Royals (GCL)	1B-DH-OF	9	31	7	8	2	0	1	6	7	6	1	1	0-0	.258	.410	.419	.830	1	.977
— Omaha (PCL)	1B-OF	39	148	28	41	8	1	3	12	27	24	1	4	4-1	.277	.390	.405	.795	4	.985
2000— Memphis (PCL)	1B	95	347	61	89	21	2	12	70	67	56	3	12	4-1	.256	.377	.432	.809	8	.991
— St. Louis (N.L.)	1B-OF	23	25	5	8	0	0	1	6	5	7	0	0	0-0	.320	.406	.440	.846	1	1.000
2001— St. Louis (N.L.)	1B-OF	33	42	3	5	1	0	1	3	1	10	0	1	0-0	.119	.140	.214	.354	0	1.000
— Memphis (PCL)	1B	29	99	12	26	5	0	2	13	21	16	0	3	1-1	.263	.392	.374	.765	1	.995
— Edmonton (PCL)	OF-1B	45	147	23	37	7	3	3	24	23	32	1	4	0-1	.252	.351	.401	.752	2	.984
2002— Sacramento (PCL)	1B-OF	116	431	83	126	40	2	12	81	93	108	1	9	2-0	.292	.417	.478	.895	11	.978
— Oakland (A.L.)	1B-OF	7	19	3	2	0	0	1	3	1	8	0	0	0-0	.105	.150	.263	.413	0	1.000
2004— Florida (N.L.)	1B	8	5	0	1	0	0	0	1	1	2	0	0	0-0	.200	.333	.200	.533	0	1.000
— Albuquerque (PCL)	1B-DH-OF	91	308	70	114	31	1	21	71	59	61	5	4	3-1	.370	.472	.682	1.154	7	.990
American League totals (4 years)		188	500	55	121	22	2	10	68	48	83	3	9	4-3	.242	.308	.354	.662	5	.991
National League totals (3 years)		64	72	8	14	1	0	2	10	7	19	0	1	0-0	.194	.259	.292	.551	0	1.000
Major League totals (7 years)		252	572	63	135	23	2	12	78	55	102	3	10	4-3	.236	.302	.346	.648	5	.992

SUZUKI, ICHIRO — OF

PERSONAL: Born October 22, 1973, in Kasugai, Japan. ... 5-9/172. ... Bats left, throws right. ... Name pronounced: ee-chee-row. ... High school: Aikoudai Meiden (Kasugai, Japan).

TRANSACTIONS/CAREER NOTES: Signed as a free agent by Seattle Mariners (November 18, 2000).

RECORDS: Holds major league record for most hits, season (262, 2004).

HONORS: Named A.L. Rookie of the Year by THE SPORTING NEWS (2001). ... Named A.L. Rookie of the Year by Baseball Writers' Association of America (2001). ... Named A.L. Most Valuable Player by Baseball Writers' Association of America (2001). ... Won A.L. Gold Glove as outfielder (2001-04).

2004 GAMES PLAYED BY POSITION (MLB): OF—158, DH—3.

Year Team (League)	Pos.	G	AB	R	H	2B	3B	HR	RBI	BB	SO	HBP	GDP	SB-CS	Avg.	OBP	SLG	OPS	E	Avg.
1992— Orix (Jap. Pacific)		40	95	9	24	5	0	0	5	3	11	...	...	3-2	.253	...	.305	...	...	...
1993— Orix (Jap. Pacific)		43	64	4	12	2	0	1	3	2	7	...	...	0-2	.188	...	.266	...	...	...
1994— Orix (Jap. Pacific)		130	546	111	210	41	6	13	54	51	53	...	...	29-7	.385	...	.549	...	...	...
1995— Orix (Jap. Pacific)		130	524	104	179	23	4	25	80	68	52	...	...	49-9	.342	...	.544	...	...	...
1996— Orix (Jap. Pacific)		130	542	104	193	24	4	16	84	56	52	...	...	35-3	.356	...	.504	...	...	...
1997— Orix (Jap. Pacific)		135	536	94	185	31	4	17	91	62	36	...	...	39-4	.345	...	.513	...	...	...
1998— Orix (Jap. Pacific)		135	506	79	181	36	3	13	71	43	35	...	...	11-4	.358	...	.518	...	...	...
1999— Orix (Jap. Pacific)		103	411	80	141	27	2	21	68	45	46	...	...	12-1	.343	...	.572	...	...	...
2000— Orix (Jap. Pacific)		105	395	73	153	22	1	12	74	54	36	...	...	21-...	.387	...	.539	...	...	...
2001— Seattle (A.L.)	OF-DH	157	* 692	127	* 242	34	8	8	69	30	53	8	3	56-14	* .350	.381	.457	.838	1	.997
2002— Seattle (A.L.)	OF-DH	157	647	111	208	27	8	8	51	68	62	5	8	31-15	.321	.388	.425	.813	3	.991
2003— Seattle (A.L.)	OF	159	679	111	212	29	8	13	62	36	69	6	3	34-8	.312	.352	.436	.788	2	.994
2004— Seattle (A.L.)	OF-DH	161	* 704	101	* 262	24	5	8	60	49	63	4	6	36-11	* .372	.414	.455	.869	3	.992
Major League totals (4 years)		634	2722	450	924	114	29	37	242	183	247	23	20	157-48	.339	.384	.443	.828	9	.994

DIVISION SERIES RECORD

Year Team (League)	Pos.	G	AB	R	H	2B	3B	HR	RBI	BB	SO	HBP	GDP	SB-CS	Avg.	OBP	SLG	OPS	E	Avg.
2001— Seattle (A.L.)	OF	5	20	4	12	1	0	0	2	1	0	0	0	1-2	.600	.619	.650	1.269	1	.900

CHAMPIONSHIP SERIES RECORD

Year Team (League)	Pos.	G	AB	R	H	2B	3B	HR	RBI	BB	SO	HBP	GDP	SB-CS	Avg.	OBP	SLG	OPS	E	Avg.
2001— Seattle (A.L.)	OF	5	18	3	4	1	0	1	1	4	4	0	1	2-0	.222	.364	.278	.641	0	1.000

ALL-STAR GAME RECORD

	G	AB	R	H	2B	3B	HR	RBI	BB	SO	HBP	GDP	SB-CS	Avg.	OBP	SLG	OPS	E	Avg.
All-Star Game totals (4 years)	4	10	2	2	1	0	0	0	2	0	0	0	1-0	.200	.333	.300	.633	0	1.000

SWEENEY, BRIAN — P

PERSONAL: Born June 13, 1974, in Yonkers, N.Y. ... 6-2/202. ... Throws right, bats right. ... Full name: Brian Edward Sweeney. ... High school: Yonkers (N.Y.). ... College: Mercy (N.Y.).

TRANSACTIONS/CAREER NOTES: Signed as a non-drafted free agent by Seattle Mariners organization (September 17, 1996). ... Traded by Mariners with IF Jeff Cirillo and cash to San Diego Padres for P Kevin Jarvis, IF Dave Hansen, C Wiki Gonzalez and OF Vince Faison (January 6, 2004).

CAREER HITTING: 0-for-4 (.000), 0 R, 0 2B, 0 3B, 0 HR, 0 RBI.

Year Team (League)	W	L	Pct.	ERA	WHIP	G	GS	CG	ShO	Hld.	Sv.-Opp.	IP	H	R	ER	HR	BB-IBB	SO	Avg.
1997— Lancaster (Calif.)	6	3	.667	3.80	1.22	40	0	0	0	...	1-...	85.1	83	39	36	11	21-1	73	.252
1998— Lancaster (Calif.)	6	0	1.000	3.63	1.19	17	4	0	0	...	0-...	52.0	41	26	21	6	21-1	48	.218
1999— Lancaster (Calif.)	0	0	...	6.75	1.82	5	0	0	0	...	0-...	9.1	14	7	7	4	3-0	14	.341
— Tacoma (PCL)	0	2	.000	6.75	1.75	5	1	0	0	...	0-...	16.0	26	17	12	5	2-0	10	.366
— New Haven (East.)	4	6	.400	4.69	1.40	23	18	0	0	...	1-...	111.1	125	65	58	18	31-1	83	.285
2000— Tacoma (PCL)	0	1	.000	6.00	1.67	2	1	0	0	...	0-...	6.0	9	4	4	2	1-0	1	.360
— New Haven (East.)	4	3	.571	3.40	1.43	19	7	0	0	...	1-...	47.2	49	20	18	3	19-0	27	.268
2001— San Antonio (Texas)	7	4	.636	3.80	1.34	37	9	0	0	...	1-...	104.1	117	47	44	8	23-1	96	.283
2002— Tacoma (PCL)	9	5	.643	3.80	1.30	30	23	1	1	...	2-...	142.0	157	67	60	16	28-0	113	.275
2003— Tacoma (PCL)	11	10	.524	4.28	1.40	29	21	0	0	...	0-...	141.0	165	80	67	17	32-0	115	.288
— Seattle (A.L.)	0	0	...	1.93	0.86	5	0	0	0	0	0-0	9.1	7	2	2	0	1-0	7	.212
2004— Portland (PCL)	11	4	.733	3.83	1.24	24	23	0	0	0	0-...	138.2	130	65	59	16	42-1	110	.242
— San Diego (N.L.)	1	0	1.000	5.65	1.53	7	2	0	0	0	0-0	14.1	20	9	9	1	2-0	10	.328
American League totals (1 year)	0	0	...	1.93	0.86	5	0	0	0	0	0-0	9.1	7	2	2	0	1-0	7	.212
National League totals (1 year)	1	0	1.000	5.65	1.53	7	2	0	0	0	0-0	14.1	20	9	9	1	2-0	10	.328
Major League totals (2 years)	1	0	1.000	4.18	1.27	12	2	0	0	0	0-0	23.2	27	11	11	1	3-0	17	.287

S

SWEENEY, MARK — OF

PERSONAL: Born October 26, 1969, in Framingham, Mass. ... 6-1/215. ... Bats left, throws left. ... Full name: Mark Patrick Sweeney. ... High school: Holliston (Mass.). ... College: Maine.

TRANSACTIONS/CAREER NOTES: Selected by Los Angeles Dodgers organization in 39th round of 1990 free-agent draft; did not sign. ... Selected by California Angels organization in ninth round of 1991 free-agent draft. ... Traded by Angels with a player to be named to St. Louis Cardinals for P John Habyan (July 8, 1995); Cardinals acquired IF Rod Correia to complete deal (January 31, 1996). ... Traded by Cardinals with Ps Danny Jackson and Rich Batchelor to San Diego Padres for P Fernando Valenzuela, 3B Scott Livingstone and OF Phil Plantier (June 13, 1997). ... Traded by Padres with OF Greg Vaughn to Cincinnati Reds for OF Reggie Sanders, SS Damian Jackson and P Josh Harris (February 2, 1999). ... Traded by Reds with a player to be named to Milwaukee Brewers for OF Alex Ochoa (January 14, 2000); Brewers acquired P Gene Altman to complete deal (May 15, 2000). ... On disabled list (March 31-May 7 and July 18-August 14, 2000); included rehabilitation assignments to Indianapolis. ... Traded by Brewers with P Jeff D'Amico, OF Jeromy Burnitz, IF Lou Collier and cash to New York Mets as part of three-team deal in which Mets also acquired 1B/OF Ross Gload and P Craig House from Colorado Rockies, Rockies acquired IF Todd Zeile, OF Benny Agbayani and cash from Mets and Brewers acquired P Glendon Rusch and IF/OF Lenny Harris from Mets and OF Alex Ochoa from Rockies (January 21, 2002). ... Released by Mets (March 13, 2002). ... Signed by Padres organization (March 16, 2002). ... On disabled list (June 6-26, 2002). ... Released by Padres (July 15, 2002). ... Signed as a free agent by Rockies organization (January 21, 2003).

2004 GAMES PLAYED BY POSITION (MLB): OF—28, 1B—15, DH—4.

Year Team (League)	Pos.	G	AB	R	H	2B	3B	HR	RBI	BB	SO	HBP	GDP	SB-CS	Avg.	OBP	SLG	OPS	E	Avg.
1991— Boise (N'west)	OF	70	234	45	66	10	3	4	34	51	42	5	7	9-5	.282	.416	.402	.818	4	.954
1992— Quad City (Midw.)	OF	120	424	65	115	20	5	14	76	47	85	4	6	15-11	.271	.346	.441	.787	4	.981
1993— Palm Springs (Calif.)	OF-1B	66	245	41	87	18	3	3	47	42	29	2	4	9-6	.355	.449	.490	.938	7	.955
— Midland (Texas)	OF	51	188	41	67	13	2	9	32	27	22	6	5	1-1	.356	.444	.590	1.035	1	.989
1994— Vancouver (PCL)	DH-1B-OF	103	344	59	98	12	3	8	49	59	50	5	3	3-3	.285	.394	.407	.801	2	.994
— Midland (Texas)	OF-1B-DH	14	50	13	15	3	0	3	18	10	10	0	3	1-1	.300	.403	.540	.943	2	.973
1995— Vancouver (PCL)	OF-DH-1B	69	226	48	78	14	2	7	59	43	33	2	6	3-1	.345	.452	.518	.970	2	.981
— Louisville (A.A.)	1B	22	76	15	28	8	0	2	22	14	8	2	0	2-0	.368	.468	.553	1.021	2	.990
— St. Louis (N.L.)	1B-OF	37	77	5	21	2	0	2	13	10	15	0	3	1-1	.273	.348	.377	.725	2	.988
1996— St. Louis (N.L.)	OF-1B	98	170	32	45	9	0	3	22	33	29	1	4	3-0	.265	.387	.371	.758	3	.977
1997— St. Louis (N.L.)	OF-1B	44	61	5	13	3	0	0	4	9	14	1	2	0-1	.213	.319	.262	.582	1	1.000
— San Diego (N.L.)	OF-1B	71	103	11	33	4	0	2	19	11	18	0	1	2-2	.320	.383	.417	.800	2	.957
1998— San Diego (N.L.)	OF-1B-DH	122	192	17	45	8	3	2	15	26	37	1	5	1-2	.234	.324	.339	.663	1	.994
1999— Cincinnati (N.L.)	1B-OF	37	31	6	11	3	0	2	7	4	9	0	2	0-0	.355	.429	.645	1.074	0	1.000
— Indianapolis (Int'l)	OF-DH-1B	86	311	66	100	17	1	12	51	59	40	4	7	3-2	.322	.432	.498	.931	5	.982
2000— Milwaukee (N.L.)	DH-1B-OF	71	73	9	16	6	0	1	6	12	18	1	1	0-0	.219	.337	.342	.680	0	1.000
— Indianapolis (Int'l)	1B-OF	18	55	13	28	8	0	2	14	10	8	0	3	0-0	.509	.585	.764	1.348	0	1.000
2001— Indianapolis (Int'l)	OF-1B	109	404	65	116	34	1	6	69	56	71	2	6	3-1	.287	.373	.421	.793	1	.994
— Milwaukee (N.L.)	OF-1B	48	89	9	23	3	1	3	11	12	23	0	1	2-1	.258	.347	.416	.762	1	.971
2002— San Diego (N.L.)	1B-OF-DH	48	65	3	11	3	0	1	4	4	19	0	1	0-0	.169	.217	.262	.479	2	.956
— Portland (PCL)	1B	1	1	0	1	0	0	0	0	0	0	0	0	0-0	1.000	1.000	1.000	2.000	0	...
2003— Colo. Springs (PCL)	OF-1B-DH	51	165	24	49	10	1	5	35	34	32	0	5	1-4	.297	.407	.461	.867	2	.985
— Colorado (N.L.)	OF-1B-DH	67	97	13	25	9	2	4	27	9	27	0	2	0-1	.258	.321	.412	.733	0	1.000
2004— Colorado (N.L.)	OF-1B-DH	122	177	25	47	12	2	9	40	32	51	2	2	1-0	.266	.377	.508	.885	0	1.000
Major League totals (10 years)		765	1135	135	290	62	6	27	155	162	260	6	23	10-8	.256	.349	.392	.741	11	.986

DIVISION SERIES RECORD

Year Team (League)	Pos.	G	AB	R	H	2B	3B	HR	RBI	BB	SO	HBP	GDP	SB-CS	Avg.	OBP	SLG	OPS	E	Avg.
1996— St. Louis (N.L.)		1	1	0	1	0	0	0	0	0	0	0	0	0-0	1.000	1.000	1.000	2.000	...	...
1998— San Diego (N.L.)		2	1	0	0	0	0	0	0	1	0	0	0	0-1	.000	.500	.000	.500	...	...
Division series totals (2 years)		3	2	0	1	0	0	0	0	1	0	0	0	0-1	.500	.667	.500	1.167	...	...

CHAMPIONSHIP SERIES RECORD

Year Team (League)	Pos.	G	AB	R	H	2B	3B	HR	RBI	BB	SO	HBP	GDP	SB-CS	Avg.	OBP	SLG	OPS	E	Avg.
1996— St. Louis (N.L.)	OF	5	4	1	0	0	0	0	0	0	2	0	0	0-0	.000	.000	.000	.000	0	1.000
1998— San Diego (N.L.)		3	2	1	0	0	0	0	0	1	1	0	0	0-0	.000	.333	.000	.333	...	...
Champ. series totals (2 years)		8	6	2	0	0	0	0	0	1	3	0	0	0-0	.000	.143	.000	.143	0	1.000

WORLD SERIES RECORD

Year Team (League)	Pos.	G	AB	R	H	2B	3B	HR	RBI	BB	SO	HBP	GDP	SB-CS	Avg.	OBP	SLG	OPS	E	Avg.
1998— San Diego (N.L.)		3	3	0	2	0	0	0	1	0	0	0	0	0-0	.667	.667	.667	1.333	...	...

SWEENEY, MIKE — 1B

PERSONAL: Born July 22, 1973, in Orange, Calif. ... 6-3/225. ... Bats right, throws right. ... Full name: Michael John Sweeney. ... High school: Ontario (Calif.).
TRANSACTIONS/CAREER NOTES: Selected by Kansas City Royals organization in 10th round of 1991 free-agent draft. ... On suspended list (August 17-27, 2001). ... On disabled list (July 14-August 13, 2002); included rehabilitation assignment to Omaha. ... On disabled list (June 21-August 8, 2003); included rehabilitation assignment to Omaha. ... On disabled list (August 22, 2004-remainder of season).
2004 GAMES PLAYED BY POSITION (MLB): 1B—55, DH—48.

Year Team (League)	Pos.	G	AB	R	H	2B	3B	HR	RBI	BB	SO	HBP	GDP	SB-CS	Avg.	OBP	SLG	OPS	E	Avg.
1991—GC Royals (GCL)	C-1B	38	102	8	22	3	0	1	11	11	9	0	2	1-0	.216	.287	.275	.561	4	.972
1992—Eugene (Northwest)	C	59	199	17	44	12	1	4	28	13	54	4	0	3-3	.221	.280	.352	.632	14	.967
1993—Eugene (Northwest)	C	53	175	32	42	10	2	6	29	30	41	3	2	1-0	.240	.359	.423	.782	7	.983
1994—Rockford (Midwest)	C	86	276	47	83	20	3	10	52	55	43	9	8	0-1	.301	.427	.504	.931	6	.988
1995—Wilmington (Caro.)	C-DH-3B	99	332	61	103	23	1	18	53	60	39	9	4	6-1	.310	.424	.548	.972	7	.989
—Kansas City (A.L.)	C	4	4	1	1	0	0	0	0	0	0	0	0	0-0	.250	.250	.250	.500	1	.875
1996—Wichita (Texas)	DH-C	66	235	45	75	18	1	14	51	32	29	2	5	3-2	.319	.399	.583	.982	1	.995
—Omaha (A.A.)	C-DH	25	101	14	26	9	0	3	16	6	13	3	0	0-0	.257	.318	.436	.754	0	1.000
—Kansas City (A.L.)	C-DH	50	165	23	46	10	0	4	24	18	21	4	7	1-2	.279	.358	.412	.770	1	.994
1997—Kansas City (A.L.)	C-DH	84	240	30	58	8	0	7	31	17	33	6	8	3-2	.242	.306	.363	.668	3	.993
—Omaha (A.A.)	C-DH	40	144	22	34	8	1	10	29	18	20	2	3	0-2	.236	.323	.514	.837	1	.996
1998—Kansas City (A.L.)	C	92	282	32	73	18	0	8	35	24	38	2	7	2-3	.259	.320	.408	.728	•9	.984
1999—Kansas City (A.L.)	1B-DH-C	150	575	101	185	44	2	22	102	54	48	10	21	6-1	.322	.387	.520	.907	12	.981
2000—Kansas City (A.L.)	1B-DH	159	618	105	206	30	0	29	144	71	67	15	15	8-3	.333	.407	.523	.930	9	.991
2001—Kansas City (A.L.)	1B-DH	147	559	97	170	46	0	29	99	64	64	2	13	10-3	.304	.374	.542	.916	12	.989
2002—Kansas City (A.L.)	1B-DH	126	471	81	160	31	1	24	86	61	46	6	9	9-7	.340	.417	.563	.979	9	.991
—Omaha (PCL)	1B	3	12	2	3	1	0	1	4	1	2	0	1	0-0	.250	.286	.583	.869	0	1.000
2003—Omaha (PCL)	DH	2	8	3	2	1	0	1	1	1	1	0	0	0-0	.250	.333	.750	1.083	0	.000
—Kansas City (A.L.)	DH-1B	108	392	62	115	18	1	16	83	64	56	2	13	3-2	.293	.391	.467	.858	4	.990
2004—Kansas City (A.L.)	1B-DH	106	411	56	118	23	0	22	79	33	44	6	7	3-2	.287	.347	.504	.851	4	.992
Major League totals (10 years)		1026	3717	588	1132	228	4	161	683	406	417	53	100	45-25	.305	.377	.498	.875	64	.989

ALL-STAR GAME RECORD

	G	AB	R	H	2B	3B	HR	RBI	BB	SO	HBP	GDP	SB-CS	Avg.	OBP	SLG	OPS	E	Avg.
All-Star Game totals (3 years)	3	3	0	0	0	0	0	0	0	0	0	0	0-0	.000	.000	.000	.000	0	1.000

SWISHER, NICK — OF

PERSONAL: Born November 25, 1980, in Parkersburg, W.Va. ... 6-0/194. ... Bats both, throws left. ... Full name: Nicolas Thompson Swisher. ... High school: Parkersburg (W. Va.). ... College: Ohio State. ... Son of Steve Swisher, catcher with three major league teams (1974-82).
TRANSACTIONS/CAREER NOTES: Selected by Oakland Athletics organization in first round (16th pick overall) of 2002 free-agent draft.
2004 GAMES PLAYED BY POSITION (MLB): OF—16, 1B—3, DH—2.

Year Team (League)	Pos.	G	AB	R	H	2B	3B	HR	RBI	BB	SO	HBP	GDP	SB-CS	Avg.	OBP	SLG	OPS	E	Avg.
2002—Vancouver (N'west)	OF	13	44	10	11	3	0	2	12	13	11	2	0	3-0	.250	.433	.455	.888	0	1.000
—Visalia (Calif.)	OF	49	183	22	44	13	2	4	23	26	48	2	6	3-1	.240	.340	.399	.739	4	.953
2003—Modesto (California)	OF-1B	51	189	38	56	14	2	10	43	41	49	2	4	0-2	.296	.418	.550	.968	4	.969
—Midland (Texas)	OF	76	287	36	66	24	2	5	43	37	76	6	8	0-1	.230	.324	.380	.704	5	.971
2004—Sacramento (PCL)	OF-DH-1B	125	443	109	119	28	2	29	92	103	109	3	16	3-3	.269	.406	.537	.940	7	.977
—Oakland (A.L.)	OF-1B-DH	20	60	11	15	4	0	2	8	8	11	2	2	0-0	.250	.352	.417	.769	3	.935
Major League totals (1 year)		20	60	11	15	4	0	2	8	8	11	2	2	0-0	.250	.352	.417	.769	3	.935

SZUMINSKI, JASON — P

PERSONAL: Born December 11, 1978, in San Diego, Calif. ... 6-5/221. ... Throws right, bats right. ... Full name: Jason Ernest Szuminski. ... High school: Douglas MacArthur (San Antonio). ... College: MIT.
TRANSACTIONS/CAREER NOTES: Selected by Chicago Cubs organization in 27th round of 2000 free-agent draft. ... Selected by Kansas City Royals from Cubs organization in Rule 5 major league draft (December 15, 2003). ... Traded by Royals with cash to San Diego Padres for OF Rich Thompson (December 15, 2004). ... Returned to Cubs organization (May 11, 2004).
CAREER HITTING: 0-for-1 (.000), 0 R, 0 2B, 0 3B, 0 HR, 0 RBI.

Year Team (League)	W	L	Pct.	ERA	WHIP	G	GS	CG	ShO	Hld.	Sv.-Opp.	IP	H	R	ER	HR	BB-IBB	SO	Avg.
2000—Ariz. Cubs (Ariz.)	2	1	.667	2.43	1.28	10	4	0	0	...	0-...	40.2	39	15	11	0	13-0	31	.253
—Lansing (Midw.)	3	1	.750	3.38	1.36	4	4	0	0	...	0-...	21.1	19	8	8	0	10-0	7	.247
2001—Lansing (Midw.)	4	3	.571	6.44	2.01	14	4	0	0	...	0-...	36.1	56	27	26	2	17-0	22	.359
2002—Daytona (Fla. St.)	5	2	.714	5.12	1.49	39	7	0	0	...	1-...	91.1	95	61	52	7	41-0	53	.261
2003—Daytona (Fla. St.)	2	1	.667	3.65	1.54	10	3	0	0	...	0-...	24.2	29	12	10	0	9-1	23	.296
—West Tenn (Sou.)	7	4	.636	2.26	1.17	29	3	0	0	...	2-...	59.2	51	19	15	1	19-2	45	.233
—Iowa (PCL)	0	0	...	3.55	0.95	3	2	0	0	...	0-...	12.2	11	5	5	0	1-0	5	.234
2004—San Diego (N.L.)	0	0	...	7.20	2.30	7	4	0	0	...	0-0	10.0	12	9	8	3	11-2	5	.286
—Iowa (PCL)	3	2	.600	4.94	1.80	41	2	0	0	...	8-...	51.0	57	40	28	6	35-5	31	.289
Major League totals (1 year)	0	0	...	7.20	2.30	7	4	0	0	...	0-0	10.0	12	9	8	3	11-2	5	.286

TADANO, KAZUHITO — P

PERSONAL: Born April 25, 1980, in Tokyo, Japan. ... 6-0/180. ... Throws right, bats right. ... College: Rikkyo (Japan).
TRANSACTIONS/CAREER NOTES: Signed as a non-drafted free agent by Cleveland Indians organization (March 8, 2003). ... On disabled list (September 16, 2004-remainder of season).
CAREER HITTING: 1-for-3 (.333), 1 R, 0 2B, 0 3B, 0 HR, 0 RBI.

Year Team (League)	W	L	Pct.	ERA	WHIP	G	GS	CG	ShO	Hld.	Sv.-Opp.	IP	H	R	ER	HR	BB-IBB	SO	Avg.
2003—Kinston (Caro.)	2	1	.667	1.89	0.84	7	1	0	0	...	0-...	19.0	13	5	4	0	3-0	28	.191
—Buffalo (Int'l)	0	0	...	3.86	1.43	2	0	0	0	...	0-...	7.0	6	3	3	0	4-1	6	.231
—Akron (East.)	4	1	.800	1.24	1.06	31	0	0	0	...	3-...	72.2	62	15	10	4	15-2	78	.226
2004—Buffalo (Int'l)	2	4	.333	5.44	1.41	12	8	0	0	...	0-...	44.2	49	28	27	9	14-0	39	.275
—Cleveland (A.L.)	1	1	.500	4.65	1.45	14	4	0	0	...	0-0	50.1	55	30	26	6	18-0	39	.272
Major League totals (1 year)	1	1	.500	4.65	1.45	14	4	0	0	...	0-0	50.1	55	30	26	6	18-0	39	.272

T

TAGUCHI, SO   OF

PERSONAL: Born July 2, 1969, in Hyogo Prefecture, Japan. ... 5-10/163. ... Bats right, throws right. ... Name pronounced: tah-gu-chee. ... College: Kansai Gakuin (Japan).
TRANSACTIONS/CAREER NOTES: Signed as a free agent by St. Louis Cardinals (January 9, 2002).
2004 GAMES PLAYED BY POSITION (MLB): OF—103.

										BATTING										FIELDING	
Year Team (League)	Pos.	G	AB	R	H	2B	3B	HR	RBI	BB	SO	HBP	GDP	SB-CS	Avg.	OBP	SLG	OPS	E	Avg.
1992— Orix (Jap. Pacific)	OF	47	123	...	33	...	...	1	7	...	...	...	...	5-,..	.268	...	.293	...	...	...
1993— Orix (Jap. Pacific)	OF	31	83	...	23	...	...	0	5	...	...	...	...	3-,..	.277	...	.277	...		
1994— Orix (Jap. Pacific)	OF	108	329	...	101	...	...	6	43	...	...	...	...	10-..	.307	...	.362			
1995— Orix (Jap. Pacific)	OF	130	495	...	122	...	...	9	61	...	...	...	...	14-..	.246	...	.301			
1996— Orix (Jap. Pacific)	OF	128	509	...	142	...	...	7	44	...	...	...	...	10-..	.279	...	.320			
1997— Orix (Jap. Pacific)	OF	135	572	...	168	...	...	10	56	...	...	...	...	7-..	.294	...	.346			
1998— Orix (Jap. Pacific)	OF	132	497	...	135	...	...	9	41	...	...	...	...	8-..	.272	...	.326			
1999— Orix (Jap. Pacific)	OF	133	524	...	141	...	...	9	56	...	...	...	...	11-..	.269	...	.321			
2000— Orix (Jap. Pacific)	OF	129	509	...	142	...	...	8	49	...	...	...	...	9-..	.279	...	.326			
2001— Orix (Jap. Pacific)	OF	134	453	70	127	21	6	8	42	43	88	...	...	6-..	.280	...	.406			
2002— Memphis (PCL)	OF	91	304	37	75	17	0	5	36	13	44	5	5	6-3	.247	.286	.352	.638	2	.990
—St. Louis (N.L.)	OF	19	15	4	6	0	0	0	2	2	1	0	0	1-0	.400	.471	.400	.871	1	.929
—New Haven (East.)	OF	26	107	21	33	10	0	1	15	9	15	3	1	3-1	.308	.375	.430	.805	2	.970
2003— Memphis (PCL)	OF-DH	90	258	31	66	8	2	2	24	22	36	2	5	14-5	.256	.318	.326	.644	1	.994
—St. Louis (N.L.)	OF-2B	43	54	9	14	3	1	3	13	4	11	0	2	0-0	.259	.310	.519	.829	0	1.000
2004— Memphis (PCL)	OF-DH	17	55	5	18	4	0	1	7	1	10	2	2	6-0	.327	.362	.455	.817	0	1.000
—St. Louis (N.L.)	OF	109	179	26	52	10	2	3	25	12	23	2	6	6-3	.291	.337	.419	.756	2	.980
Major League totals (3 years)		171	248	39	72	13	3	6	40	18	35	2	8	7-3	.290	.339	.440	.779	3	.980

DIVISION SERIES RECORD

Year Team (League)	Pos.	G	AB	R	H	2B	3B	HR	RBI	BB	SO	HBP	GDP	SB-CS	Avg.	OBP	SLG	OPS	E	Avg.
2004— St. Louis (N.L.)	OF	1	0	0	0	0	0	0	0	0	0	0	0	0-0	...	...	...	...	0	...

CHAMPIONSHIP SERIES RECORD

Year Team (League)	Pos.	G	AB	R	H	2B	3B	HR	RBI	BB	SO	HBP	GDP	SB-CS	Avg.	OBP	SLG	OPS	E	Avg.
2004— St. Louis (N.L.)	OF	3	2	0	0	0	0	0	0	0	1	0	0	0-0	.000	.000	.000	.000	0	1.000

WORLD SERIES RECORD

Year Team (League)	Pos.	G	AB	R	H	2B	3B	HR	RBI	BB	SO	HBP	GDP	SB-CS	Avg.	OBP	SLG	OPS	E	Avg.
2004— St. Louis (N.L.)	DH-OF	2	4	1	1	0	0	0	1	0	2	0	0	0-0	.250	.250	.250	.500	0	1.000

TAKATSU, SHINGO   P

PERSONAL: Born November 25, 1968, in Hiroshima, Japan. ... 6-0/180. ... Throws right, bats right. ... High school: Hiroshima Technical (Hiroshima, Japan). ... College: Koshien University (Japan).
TRANSACTIONS/CAREER NOTES: Signed as a free agent by Chicago White Sox (January 22, 2004).
CAREER HITTING: 0-for-0 (.000), 0 R, 0 2B, 0 3B, 0 HR, 0 RBI.

Year Team (League)	W	L	Pct.	ERA	WHIP	G	GS	CG	ShO	Hld.	Sv.-Opp.	IP	H	R	ER	HR	BB-IBB	SO	Avg.
1991— Yakult (Jp. Cen.)	1	1	.500	4.23	1.45	13	1	1	0	...	0-...	27.2	34	15	13	4	6-...	25	...
1992— Yakult (Jp. Cen.)	5	3	.625	4.68	1.45	23	8	3	0	...	0-...	82.2	84	48	43	10	36-...	63	...
1993— Yakult (Jp. Cen.)	6	4	.600	2.30	1.19	56	1	0	0	...	20-...	78.1	69	28	20	3	24-...	72	...
1994— Yakult (Jp. Cen.)	8	4	.667	2.86	1.29	47	0	0	0	...	19-...	72.1	63	25	23	7	30-...	54	...
1995— Yakult (Jp. Cen.)	1	3	.250	2.61	1.16	39	0	0	0	...	28-...	48.1	42	14	14	2	14-...	36	...
1996— Yakult (Jp. Cen.)	2	6	.250	3.24	1.44	39	0	0	0	...	21-...	50.0	56	18	18	7	16-...	35	...
1997— Yakult (Jp. Cen.)	7	4	.636	2.04	0.95	51	3	0	0	...	7-...	79.1	55	20	18	9	20-...	68	...
1998— Yakult (Jp. Cen.)	2	3	.400	5.56	1.76	42	0	0	0	...	3-...	45.1	54	29	28	6	26-...	32	...
1999— Yakult (Jp. Cen.)	1	1	.500	2.18	0.97	40	0	0	0	...	30-...	41.1	32	11	10	6	8-...	38	...
2000— Yakult (Jp. Cen.)	0	1	.000	2.08	1.15	35	0	0	0	...	29-...	34.2	32	8	8	4	8-...	29	...
2001— Yakult (Jp. Cen.)	0	4	.000	2.61	1.20	52	0	0	0	...	37-...	51.2	49	17	15	3	13-...	39	...
2002— Yakult (Jp. Cen.)	0	2	.000	3.89	1.15	44	0	0	0	...	32-...	41.2	37	19	18	6	11-...	28	...
2003— Yakult (Jp. Cen.)	2	3	.400	3.00	1.50	44	0	0	0	...	34-...	42.0	42	18	14	7	21-...	26	...
2004— Chicago (A.L.)	6	4	.600	2.31	0.98	59	0	0	0	4	19-20	62.1	40	17	16	6	21-3	50	.182
Major League totals (1 year)	6	4	.600	2.31	0.98	59	0	0	0	4	19-20	62.1	40	17	16	6	21-3	50	.182

TANKERSLEY, DENNIS   P

PERSONAL: Born February 24, 1979, in Troy, Mo. ... 6-2/185. ... Throws right, bats right. ... Full name: Dennis Lee Tankersley. ... Name pronounced: TANK-ers-lee. ... High school: St. Charles (Mo.). ... Junior college: Meramec (Mo.).
TRANSACTIONS/CAREER NOTES: Selected by Boston Red Sox organization in 38th round of 1997 free-agent draft; did not sign. ... Selected by Boston Red Sox organization in 38th round of 1998 free-agent draft. ... Traded by Red Sox with IF Cesar Saba to San Diego Padres for 3B Ed Sprague (June 30, 2000). ... Traded by Padres with OF Terrence Long and cash to Kansas City Royals for Ps Darrell May and Ryan Bukvich (November 8, 2004).
CAREER HITTING: 6-for-21 (.286), 2 R, 1 2B, 0 3B, 1 HR, 2 RBI.

Year Team (League)	W	L	Pct.	ERA	WHIP	G	GS	CG	ShO	Hld.	Sv.-Opp.	IP	H	R	ER	HR	BB-IBB	SO	Avg.
1999— GC Red Sox (GCL)	1	0	1.000	0.76	0.64	11	6	0	0	...	1-...	35.2	14	7	3	2	9-1	57	.116
2000— Augusta (S. Atl.)	5	3	.625	4.06	1.39	15	15	1	1	...	0-...	75.1	73	41	34	4	32-0	74	.252
—Fort Wayne (Midw.)	5	2	.714	2.85	1.10	12	12	0	0	...	0-...	66.1	48	25	21	5	25-0	87	.205
2001— Lake Elsinore (Calif.)	5	1	.833	0.52	0.78	9	8	0	0	...	0-...	52.1	29	5	3	1	12-0	68	.158
—Mobile (Sou.)	4	1	.800	2.07	0.98	13	13	0	0	...	0-...	69.2	44	23	16	6	24-1	89	.174
—Portland (PCL)	1	2	.333	6.91	1.67	3	3	0	0	...	0-...	14.1	16	13	11	2	8-0	16	.286
2002— Mobile (Sou.)	3	3	.500	3.02	1.34	10	10	0	0	...	0-...	50.2	47	20	17	1	21-0	56	.245
—San Diego (N.L.)	1	4	.200	8.06	1.93	17	9	0	0	...	0-0	51.1	59	46	46	10	40-3	39	.304
—Portland (PCL)	3	4	.429	3.88	1.43	9	9	0	0	...	0-...	51.0	43	29	22	6	30-0	51	.229
2003— San Diego (N.L.)	0	1	.000	...	...	1	1	0	0	...	0-0	.0	3	7	7	0	4-0	0	1.000
—Portland (PCL)	8	11	.421	4.65	1.40	27	27	0	0	...	0-...	151.0	149	82	78	15	67-0	148	.257
2004— Portland (PCL)	7	4	.636	3.15	1.26	19	19	0	0	...	0-...	120.0	114	52	42	10	37-1	86	.253
—San Diego (N.L.)	0	5	.000	5.14	1.49	9	6	0	0	1	0-0	35.0	35	25	20	3	17-3	29	.254
Major League totals (3 years)	1	10	.091	7.61	1.83	27	16	0	0	1	0-0	86.1	97	78	73	13	61-6	68	.290

TAVAREZ, JULIAN   P

PERSONAL: Born May 22, 1973, in Santiago, Dominican Republic. ... 6-2/195. ... Throws right, bats left. ... Name pronounced: JOOL-ee-en tah-VAR-rez. ... High school: Santiago (Dominican Republic) Public School.

TRANSACTIONS/CAREER NOTES: Signed as a non-drafted free agent by Cleveland Indians organization (March 16, 1990). ... On suspended list (June 18-21, 1996). ... Traded by Indians with 2B Jeff Kent, IF Jose Vizcaino and a player to be named to San Francisco Giants for 3B Matt Williams and a player to be named (November 13, 1996); Indians traded P Joe Roa to Giants for OF Trenidad Hubbard to complete deal (December 16, 1996). ... On disabled list (July 13-August 7, 1998); included rehabilitation assignment to Fresno. ... On suspended list (September 14-16, 1998). ... On disabled list (May 1-June 1, 1999); included rehabilitation assignment to Fresno. ... Claimed on waivers by Colorado Rockies (November 21, 1999). ... Signed as a free agent by Chicago Cubs (November 16, 2000). ... On suspended list (April 29-May 5, 2001). ... Traded by Cubs with Ps Jose Cueto and Dontrelle Willis and C Ryan Jorgensen to Florida Marlins for Ps Antonio Alfonseca and Matt Clement (March 27, 2002). ... On disabled list (April 17-May 12, 2002). ... Signed as a free agent by Pittsburgh Pirates organization (January 28, 2003). ... On suspended list (June 22-25, 2003). ... Signed as a free agent by St. Louis Cardinals (January 9, 2004). ... On suspended list (September 24-October 2, 2004).

HONORS: Named A.L. Rookie Pitcher of the Year by THE SPORTING NEWS (1995).

CAREER HITTING: 15-for-135 (.111), 8 R, 0 2B, 0 3B, 0 HR, 9 RBI.

Year Team (League)	W	L	Pct.	ERA	WHIP	G	GS	CG	ShO	Hld.	Sv.-Opp.	IP	H	R	ER	HR	BB-IBB	SO	Avg.
1990— DSL Indians (DSL)	5	5	.500	3.29	1.62	14	12	3	0	...	0-...	82.0	85	53	30	...	48-...	33	...
1991— DSL Indians (DSL)	8	2	.800	2.67	1.01	19	18	1	0	...	0-...	121.1	95	41	36	...	28-...	75	...
1992— Burlington (Appalachian)	6	3	.667	2.68	1.12	14	14	2	2	...	0-...	87.1	86	41	26	3	12-0	69	.250
1993— Kinston (Caro.)	11	5	.688	2.42	1.09	18	18	2	1	...	0-...	119.0	102	48	32	6	28-0	107	.228
—Cant./Akr. (Eastern)	2	1	.667	0.95	0.79	3	2	1	1	...	0-...	19.0	14	2	2	0	1-0	11	.212
—Cleveland (A.L.)	2	2	.500	6.57	1.78	8	7	0	0	0	0-0	37.0	53	29	27	7	13-2	19	.340
1994— Charlotte (Int'l.)	15	6	.714	3.48	1.19	26	26	2	2	...	0-...	176.0	167	79	68	15	43-0	102	.247
—Cleveland (A.L.)	0	1	.000	21.60	4.20	1	1	0	0	0	0-0	1.2	6	8	4	1	1-1	0	.500
1995— Cleveland (A.L.)	10	2	.833	2.44	1.14	57	0	0	0	19	0-4	85.0	76	36	23	7	21-0	68	.235
1996— Cleveland (A.L.)	4	7	.364	5.36	1.52	51	4	0	0	13	0-0	80.2	101	49	48	9	22-5	46	.315
—Buffalo (A.A.)	1	0	1.000	1.29	0.93	2	2	0	0	...	0-...	14.0	10	2	2	0	3-0	10	.200
1997— San Francisco (N.L.)	6	4	.600	3.87	1.42	* 89	0	0	0	26	0-3	88.1	91	43	38	6	34-5	38	.277
1998— San Francisco (N.L.)	5	3	.625	3.80	1.55	60	0	0	0	10	1-6	85.1	96	41	36	5	36-11	52	.298
—Fresno (PCL)	0	0	...	19.29	2.57	1	0	0	0	...	0-...	2.1	6	5	5	0	0-0	1	.500
1999— San Francisco (N.L.)	2	0	1.000	5.93	1.65	47	0	0	0	5	0-2	54.2	65	38	36	7	25-3	33	.295
—Fresno (PCL)	0	0	...	2.25	0.75	4	1	0	0	...	0-...	8.0	3	2	2	1	3-0	9	.115
—San Jose (California)	0	0	...	0.00	0.50	1	1	0	0	...	0-...	4.0	1	0	0	0	1-0	3	.091
2000— Colorado (N.L.)	11	5	.688	4.43	1.48	51	12	1	0	6	1-1	120.0	124	68	59	11	53-9	62	.268
2001— Chicago (N.L.)	10	9	.526	4.52	1.49	34	28	0	0	2	0-0	161.1	172	98	81	13	69-4	107	.277
2002— Florida (N.L.)	10	12	.455	5.39	1.70	29	27	0	0	0	0-0	153.2	188	100	92	9	74-7	67	.308
2003— Pittsburgh (N.L.)	3	3	.500	3.66	1.22	64	0	0	0	9	11-14	83.2	75	37	34	1	27-8	39	.244
2004— St. Louis (N.L.)	7	4	.636	2.38	1.18	77	0	0	0	19	4-6	64.1	57	21	17	1	19-0	48	.238
American League totals (4 years)	16	12	.571	4.49	1.43	117	12	0	0	32	0-4	204.1	236	122	100	24	57-8	133	.290
National League totals (8 years)	54	40	.574	4.36	1.49	451	67	1	0	77	17-33	811.1	868	446	393	53	337-47	446	.279
Major League totals (12 years)	70	52	.574	4.39	1.47	568	79	1	0	109	17-37	1015.2	1104	568	495	77	394-55	579	.281

DIVISION SERIES RECORD

Year Team (League)	W	L	Pct.	ERA	WHIP	G	GS	CG	ShO	Hld.	Sv.-Opp.	IP	H	R	ER	HR	BB-IBB	SO	Avg.
1995— Cleveland (A.L.)	0	0	...	6.75	1.88	3	0	0	0	1	0-1	2.2	5	2	2	1	0-0	3	.385
1996— Cleveland (A.L.)	0	0	...	0.00	2.25	2	0	0	0	0	0-0	1.1	1	0	0	0	2-0	1	.250
1997— San Francisco (N.L.)	0	1	.000	4.50	1.50	3	0	0	0	0	0-0	4.0	4	2	2	1	2-1	0	.267
2004— St. Louis (N.L.)	0	0	...	0.00	0.86	2	0	0	0	0	0-0	2.1	2	0	0	0	0-0	3	.222
Division series totals (4 years)	0	1	.000	3.48	1.55	10	0	0	0	1	0-1	10.1	12	4	4	2	4-1	7	.293

CHAMPIONSHIP SERIES RECORD

Year Team (League)	W	L	Pct.	ERA	WHIP	G	GS	CG	ShO	Hld.	Sv.-Opp.	IP	H	R	ER	HR	BB-IBB	SO	Avg.
1995— Cleveland (A.L.)	0	1	.000	2.70	1.20	4	0	0	0	1	0-0	3.1	3	1	1	0	1-1	2	.200
2004— St. Louis (N.L.)	2	1	.667	3.00	0.83	5	0	0	0	1	0-0	6.0	3	2	2	2	2-1	3	.150
Champ. series totals (2 years)	2	2	.500	2.89	0.96	9	0	0	0	2	0-0	9.1	6	3	3	2	3-2	5	.171

WORLD SERIES RECORD

Year Team (League)	W	L	Pct.	ERA	WHIP	G	GS	CG	ShO	Hld.	Sv.-Opp.	IP	H	R	ER	HR	BB-IBB	SO	Avg.
1995— Cleveland (A.L.)	0	0	...	0.00	1.15	5	0	0	0	0	0-0	4.1	3	0	0	0	2-0	1	.250
2004— St. Louis (N.L.)	0	1	.000	4.50	0.50	2	0	0	0	0	0-0	2.0	1	2	1	1	0-0	1	.125
World series totals (2 years)	0	1	.000	1.42	0.95	7	0	0	0	0	0-0	6.1	4	2	1	1	2-0	2	.200

TAVERAS, WILLY   OF

PERSONAL: Born December 25, 1981, in Tenares, Dominican Republic. ... 6-0/160. ... Bats right, throws right.

TRANSACTIONS/CAREER NOTES: Signed as a non-drafted free agent by Cleveland Indians organization (May 27, 1999). ... Selected by Houston Astros from Indians organization in Rule 5 major league draft (December 15, 2003). ... Offered back to Indians organization; Indians declined offer (April 2, 2004).

2004 GAMES PLAYED BY POSITION (MLB): OF—7.

Year Team (League)	Pos.	G	AB	R	H	2B	3B	HR	RBI	BB	SO	HBP	GDP	SB-CS	Avg.	OBP	SLG	OPS	E	Avg.
2000— Burlington (Appal.)	OF	50	190	46	50	4	3	1	16	23	44	6	0	36-9	.263	.356	.332	.687	5	.961
2001— Columbus (S. Atl.)	OF	97	395	55	107	15	7	3	32	22	73	6	7	29-9	.271	.317	.367	.684	11	.952
2002— Columbus (S. Atl.)	OF	85	313	68	83	14	1	4	27	45	68	18	3	54-12	.265	.385	.355	.740	10	.944
2003— Kinston (Caro.)	OF	113	397	64	112	9	6	2	35	52	68	12	4	57-12	.282	.381	.350	.731	6	.978
2004— Round Rock (Texas)	OF-DH	103	409	76	137	13	1	2	27	38	76	9	2	55-11	.335	.402	.386	.776	6	.974
—Houston (N.L.)	OF	10	1	2	0	0	0	0	0	0	1	0	0	1-0	.000	.000	.000	.000	0	1.000
Major League totals (1 year)		10	1	2	0	0	0	0	0	0	1	0	0	1-0	.000	.000	.000	.000	0	1.000

TAYLOR, AARON   P

PERSONAL: Born August 20, 1977, in Valdosta, Ga. ... 6-8/245. ... Throws right, bats right. ... Full name: Aaron Wade Taylor. ... High school: Lowndes (Valdosta, Ga.).

TRANSACTIONS/CAREER NOTES: Selected by Atlanta Braves organization in 11th round of 1996 free-agent draft. ... Selected by Seattle Mariners organization from Braves organization in Rule 5 minor league draft (December 13, 1999). ... On disabled list (April 1-July 2, 2004); included rehabilitation assignments to Inland Empire and San Antonio.

CAREER HITTING: 0-for-0 (.000), 0 R, 0 2B, 0 3B, 0 HR, 0 RBI.

Year	Team (League)	W	L	Pct.	ERA	WHIP	G	GS	CG	ShO	Hld.	Sv.-Opp.	IP	H	R	ER	HR	BB-IBB	SO	Avg.
1996— GC Braves (GCL)		0	9	.000	7.74	1.83	13	9	0	0	...	0-...	52.1	68	54	45	0	28-0	33	.315
1997— Danville (Appalachian)		1	8	.111	5.53	1.73	15	7	0	0	...	0-...	55.1	65	49	34	4	31-0	38	.288
1998— Danville (Appalachian)		3	6	.333	6.25	1.71	14	14	1	0	...	0-...	72.0	87	60	50	9	36-0	55	.300
1999— Macon (S. Atl.)		6	7	.462	4.88	1.42	27	8	0	0	...	1-...	79.1	86	56	43	9	27-2	78	.270
2000— Everett (Northwest)		1	4	.200	7.43	1.79	15	14	0	0	...	0-...	63.0	76	54	52	5	37-0	57	.304
2001— Wisconsin (Midw.)		3	1	.750	2.45	1.02	28	0	0	0	...	9-...	29.1	19	9	8	1	11-2	50	.184
2002— San Antonio (Texas)		4	3	.571	2.34	1.10	61	0	0	0	...	24-...	77.0	51	28	20	5	34-0	93	.184
— Seattle (A.L.)		0	0	...	9.00	1.60	5	0	0	0	0	0-1	5.0	8	5	5	2	0-0	6	.348
2003— Tacoma (PCL)		1	3	.250	2.45	1.10	33	0	0	0	...	16-...	40.1	30	11	11	3	13-1	34	.208
— Seattle (A.L.)		0	0	...	8.53	1.82	10	0	0	0	0	0-0	12.2	17	12	12	0	6-0	9	.315
2004— Inland Empire (Calif.)		0	1	.000	13.50	2.25	1	1	0	0	...	0-...	1.1	2	3	2	0	1-0	2	.400
— San Antonio (Texas)		3	1	.750	2.89	1.10	30	0	0	0	...	0-...	37.1	27	13	12	2	14-0	37	.200
— Seattle (A.L.)		0	0	...	9.82	2.18	5	0	0	0	0	0-0	3.2	5	4	4	2	3-0	4	.313
Major League totals (3 years)		0	0	...	8.86	1.83	20	0	0	0	0	0-1	21.1	30	21	21	4	9-0	19	.323

TEIXEIRA, MARK — 1B

PERSONAL: Born April 11, 1980, in Annapolis, Md. ... 6-3/220. ... Bats both, throws right. ... Full name: Mark Charles Teixeira. ... Name pronounced: tuh-SHARE-uh. ... High school: Mount St. Joseph (Baltimore). ... College: Georgia Tech.

TRANSACTIONS/CAREER NOTES: Selected by Boston Red Sox organization in ninth round of 1998 free-agent draft; did not sign. ... Selected by Texas Rangers organization in first round (fifth pick overall) of 2001 free-agent draft. ... On disabled list (April 13-29, 2004); included rehabilitation assignment to Frisco.

2004 GAMES PLAYED BY POSITION (MLB): 1B—142, OF—7, DH—2.

Year	Team (League)	Pos.	G	AB	R	H	2B	3B	HR	RBI	BB	SO	HBP	GDP	SB-CS	Avg.	OBP	SLG	OPS	E	Avg.
2001—						Did not play.															
2002— Charlotte (Fla. St.)		3B	38	150	32	48	10	2	9	41	21	24	3	4	2-0	.320	.411	.593	1.005	9	.902
— Tulsa (Texas)		3B	48	171	31	54	11	3	10	28	25	36	4	2	3-2	.316	.415	.591	1.006	12	.925
2003— Texas (A.L.)		1-0-3-DH	146	529	66	137	29	5	26	84	44	120	14	14	1-2	.259	.331	.480	.811	12	.989
2004— Frisco (Texas)		1B	1	3	0	0	0	0	0	0	0	1	1	0	0-0	...	.250	...	.250	0	1.000
— Texas (A.L.)		1B-OF-DH	145	545	101	153	34	2	38	112	68	117	10	6	4-1	.281	.370	.560	.929	10	.992
Major League totals (2 years)			291	1074	167	290	63	7	64	196	112	237	24	20	5-3	.270	.351	.520	.871	22	.991

TEJADA, MIGUEL — SS

PERSONAL: Born May 25, 1976, in Bani, Dominican Republic. ... 5-9/209. ... Bats right, throws right. ... Full name: Miguel Odalis Tejada. ... Name pronounced: mee-GHEL tay-HA-duh.

TRANSACTIONS/CAREER NOTES: Signed as a non-drafted free agent by Oakland Athletics organization (July 17, 1993). ... On disabled list (March 22-May 20, 1998); included rehabilitation assignments to Edmonton and Huntsville. ... Signed as a free agent by Baltimore Orioles (December 18, 2003).

HONORS: Named A.L. Most Valuable Player by Baseball Writers' Association of America (2002).

2004 GAMES PLAYED BY POSITION (MLB): SS—162.

Year	Team (League)	Pos.	G	AB	R	H	2B	3B	HR	RBI	BB	SO	HBP	GDP	SB-CS	Avg.	OBP	SLG	OPS	E	Avg.
1994— Dom. Athletics (DSL)		2B	74	218	51	64	9	1	18	62	37	36	...	...	13-...	.294	...	.592	...	16	.927
1995— S. Oregon (N'west)		SS	74	269	45	66	15	5	8	44	41	54	2	3	19-2	.245	.346	.428	.774	26	.930
1996— Modesto (California)		SS-DH-3B	114	458	97	128	12	5	20	72	51	93	4	9	27-16	.279	.352	.459	.810	45	.925
1997— Huntsville (Sou.)		SS	128	502	85	138	20	3	22	97	50	99	7	9	15-11	.275	.344	.458	.802	36	.948
— Oakland (A.L.)		SS	26	99	10	20	3	2	2	10	2	22	3	3	2-0	.202	.240	.333	.574	4	.969
1998— Edmonton (PCL)		SS	1	3	0	0	0	0	0	0	1	1	0	1	0-0	.000	.250	.000	.250	0	1.000
— Huntsville (Sou.)		SS-DH	15	52	9	17	6	0	2	7	4	8	0	2	1-0	.327	.362	.558	.920	5	.922
— Oakland (A.L.)		SS	105	365	53	85	20	1	11	45	28	86	7	8	5-6	.233	.298	.384	.681	26	.951
1999— Oakland (A.L.)		SS	159	593	93	149	33	4	21	84	57	94	10	11	8-7	.251	.325	.427	.751	21	.973
2000— Oakland (A.L.)		SS	160	607	105	167	32	1	30	115	66	102	4	15	6-0	.275	.349	.479	.828	21	.972
2001— Oakland (A.L.)		SS	• 162	622	107	166	31	3	31	113	43	89	13	14	11-5	.267	.326	.476	.801	20	.973
2002— Oakland (A.L.)		SS	* 162	662	108	204	30	0	34	131	38	84	11	21	7-2	.308	.354	.508	.861	19	.975
2003— Oakland (A.L.)		SS	162	636	98	177	42	0	27	106	53	65	6	12	10-0	.278	.336	.472	.807	21	.972
2004— Baltimore (A.L.)		SS	162	653	107	203	40	2	34	* 150	48	73	10	24	4-1	.311	.360	.534	.894	24	.970
Major League totals (8 years)			1098	4237	681	1171	231	13	190	754	335	615	64	108	53-21	.276	.336	.472	.807	156	.970

DIVISION SERIES RECORD

Year	Team (League)	Pos.	G	AB	R	H	2B	3B	HR	RBI	BB	SO	HBP	GDP	SB-CS	Avg.	OBP	SLG	OPS	E	Avg.
2000— Oakland (A.L.)		SS	5	20	5	7	2	0	0	1	2	2	0	0	1-0	.350	.409	.450	.859	0	1.000
2001— Oakland (A.L.)		SS	5	21	1	6	3	0	0	1	0	3	1	0	0-0	.286	.304	.429	.733	1	.958
2002— Oakland (A.L.)		SS	5	21	3	3	1	0	1	4	1	7	0	0	0-0	.143	.174	.333	.507	1	.947
2003— Oakland (A.L.)		SS	5	23	0	2	1	0	0	2	0	4	0	0	0-0	.087	.087	.130	.217	1	.957
Division series totals (4 years)			20	85	9	18	7	0	1	8	3	16	1	0	1-0	.212	.242	.329	.571	3	.966

ALL-STAR GAME RECORD

			G	AB	R	H	2B	3B	HR	RBI	BB	SO	HBP	GDP	SB-CS	Avg.	OBP	SLG	OPS	E	Avg.
All-Star Game totals (2 years)			2	3	1	1	0	0	0	0	0	0	0	0	0-0	.333	.333	.333	.667	0	1.000

TEJERA, MICHAEL — P

PERSONAL: Born October 18, 1976, in Havana, Cuba. ... 5-9/192. ... Throws left, bats left. ... Name pronounced: te-HAIR-ah. ... High school: Southwest (Miami).

TRANSACTIONS/CAREER NOTES: Selected by Florida Marlins organization in sixth round of 1995 free-agent draft. ... On disabled list (April 2, 2000-entire season). ... Claimed on waivers by Texas Rangers (September 10, 2004). ... Refused minor league assignment and became a free agent (October 14, 2004).

CAREER HITTING: 8-for-52 (.154), 5 R, 0 2B, 0 3B, 1 HR, 5 RBI.

Year	Team (League)	W	L	Pct.	ERA	WHIP	G	GS	CG	ShO	Hld.	Sv.-Opp.	IP	H	R	ER	HR	BB-IBB	SO	Avg.
1995— GC Marlins (GCL)		3	1	.750	2.65	1.29	11	3	0	0	...	2-...	34.0	28	13	10	2	16-1	28	.235
1996— GC Marlins (GCL)		1	0	1.000	3.60	1.20	2	0	0	0	...	0-...	5.0	6	2	2	0	0-0	2	.286
1997— Utica (N.Y.-Penn)		3	3	.500	3.76	1.10	12	12	0	0	...	0-...	69.1	65	36	29	8	11-0	67	.248
1998— Kane County (Midwest)		6	1	.857	2.77	1.03	10	10	0	0	...	0-...	55.1	44	20	17	3	13-0	47	.221
— Portland (East.)		9	5	.643	4.11	1.39	18	18	2	2	...	0-...	107.1	113	55	49	15	36-2	97	.268

Year Team (League)	W	L	Pct.	ERA	WHIP	G	GS	CG	ShO	Hld.	Sv.-Opp.	IP	H	R	ER	HR	BB-IBB	SO	Avg.
1999— Portland (East.)	13	4	.765	2.62	1.18	25	25	0	0	...	0-...	154.2	137	55	45	13	45-1	152	.238
— Calgary (PCL)	0	2	.000	12.00	2.56	2	2	0	0	...	0-...	9.0	19	14	12	2	4-0	5	.452
— Florida (N.L.)	0	0	...	11.37	2.37	3	1	0	0	0	0-0	6.1	10	8	8	1	5-0	7	.385
2000— Florida (N.L.)					Did not play.														
2001— Portland (East.)	9	8	.529	3.57	1.30	25	25	0	0	...	0-...	141.0	143	61	56	17	41-0	131	.266
2002— Florida (N.L.)	8	8	.500	4.45	1.46	47	18	0	0	8	1-3	139.2	144	71	69	17	60-3	95	.269
2003— Florida (N.L.)	3	4	.429	4.67	1.46	50	6	0	0	5	2-2	81.0	82	44	42	6	36-3	58	.267
2004— Florida (N.L.)	0	1	.000	18.00	3.00	2	2	0	0	0	0-0	4.0	6	8	8	0	6-0	3	.375
— Jupiter (FSL)	0	0	...	0.00	1.80	1	1	0	0	...	0-...	3.1	3	1	0	0	3-0	1	.231
— Albuquerque (PCL)	8	4	.667	3.97	1.31	22	19	0	0	...	0-...	113.1	109	56	50	17	39-0	88	.253
— Texas (A.L.)	0	0	...	10.13	2.25	6	0	0	0	0	0-0	5.1	9	6	6	1	3-0	7	.360
American League totals (1 year)	0	0	...	10.13	2.25	6	0	0	0	0	0-0	5.1	9	6	6	1	3-0	7	.360
National League totals (4 years)	11	13	.458	4.95	1.51	102	27	0	0	13	3-5	231.0	242	131	127	24	107-6	163	.273
Major League totals (4 years)	11	13	.458	5.06	1.53	108	27	0	0	13	3-5	236.1	251	137	133	25	110-6	170	.276

CHAMPIONSHIP SERIES RECORD

Year Team (League)	W	L	Pct.	ERA	WHIP	G	GS	CG	ShO	Hld.	Sv.-Opp.	IP	H	R	ER	HR	BB-IBB	SO	Avg.
2003— Florida (N.L.)	0	1	.000	6.75	1.50	2	0	0	0	0	0-0	1.1	2	1	1	0	0-0	1	.333

TELEMACO, AMAURY   P

PERSONAL: Born January 19, 1974, in Higuey, Dominican Republic. ... 6-3/234. ... Throws right, bats right. ... Full name: Amaury Regalado Telemaco. ... Name pronounced: ah-MARR-ee tel-ah-MAH-ko. ... High school: Cristo Rey (La Romana, Dominican Republic).

TRANSACTIONS/CAREER NOTES: Signed as a non-drafted free agent by Chicago Cubs organization (May 23, 1991). ... On disabled list (August 20-September 4, 1996); included rehabilitation assignment to Iowa. ... Claimed on waivers by Arizona Diamondbacks (May 15, 1998). ... On disabled list (March 26-May 8, 1999); included rehabilitation assignment to Tucson. ... Claimed on waivers by Philadelphia Phillies (June 8, 1999). ... On disabled list (June 9-July 30, 2004); included rehabilitation assignment to Scranton/Wilkes-Barre.

CAREER HITTING: 14-for-116 (.121), 6 R, 4 2B, 1 3B, 0 HR, 3 RBI.

Year Team (League)	W	L	Pct.	ERA	WHIP	G	GS	CG	ShO	Hld.	Sv.-Opp.	IP	H	R	ER	HR	BB-IBB	SO	Avg.
1991— Puerta Plata (DSL)	3	3	.500	3.55	1.71	15	13	0	0	...	0-...	66.0	81	43	26	...	32-...	43	...
1992— Huntington (Appal.)	3	5	.375	4.01	1.15	12	12	2	0	...	0-...	76.1	71	45	34	6	17-0	93	.240
— Peoria (Midw.)	0	1	.000	7.94	2.47	2	1	0	0	...	0-...	5.2	9	5	5	0	5-0	5	.360
1993— Peoria (Midw.)	8	11	.421	3.45	1.27	23	23	3	0	...	0-...	143.2	129	69	55	9	54-0	133	.241
1994— Daytona (Fla. St.)	7	3	.700	3.40	1.11	11	11	2	0	...	0-...	76.2	62	35	29	4	23-0	59	.221
— Orlando (Sou.)	3	5	.375	3.45	1.21	12	12	2	0	...	0-...	62.2	56	29	24	6	20-0	49	.239
1995— Orlando (Sou.)	8	8	.500	3.29	1.04	22	22	3	1	...	0-...	147.2	112	60	54	13	42-3	151	.211
1996— Iowa (Am. Assoc.)	3	1	.750	3.06	1.12	8	8	1	0	...	0-...	50.0	38	19	17	5	18-2	42	.210
— Chicago (N.L.)	5	7	.417	5.46	1.43	25	17	0	0	0	0-0	97.1	108	67	59	20	31-2	64	.281
1997— Iowa (Am. Assoc.)	5	9	.357	4.51	1.40	18	18	3	2	...	0-...	113.2	121	70	57	20	38-1	75	.267
— Chicago (N.L.)	0	3	.000	6.16	1.53	10	5	0	0	0	0-0	38.0	47	26	26	4	11-0	29	.303
— Orlando (Sou.)	1	0	1.000	2.25	1.38	1	1	0	0	...	0-...	8.0	9	2	2	0	2-0	6	.281
1998— Chicago (N.L.)	1	1	.500	3.90	1.30	14	0	0	0	1	0-0	27.2	23	12	12	5	13-0	18	.219
— Arizona (N.L.)	6	9	.400	3.94	1.32	27	18	0	0	0	0-0	121.0	127	63	53	13	33-2	60	.271
1999— Tucson (PCL)	0	3	.000	5.09	1.53	13	12	0	0	...	0-...	17.2	21	11	10	1	6-0	17	.304
— Arizona (N.L.)	1	0	1.000	7.50	2.17	5	0	0	0	0	0-0	6.0	7	5	5	2	6-1	2	.333
— Philadelphia (N.L.)	3	0	1.000	5.55	1.38	44	0	0	0	3	0-1	47.0	45	29	29	8	20-3	41	.250
2000— Philadelphia (N.L.)	1	3	.250	6.66	1.60	13	2	0	0	0	0-0	24.1	25	22	18	6	14-0	22	.275
— Scran./W.B. (I.L.)	8	3	.727	3.87	1.27	21	21	0	0	...	0-...	123.1	115	60	53	15	42-0	88	.248
2001— Philadelphia (N.L.)	5	5	.500	5.54	1.40	24	14	1	0	1	0-0	89.1	93	59	55	15	32-3	59	.274
— Scran./W.B. (I.L.)	1	2	.333	4.01	1.50	4	4	0	0	...	0-...	24.2	31	11	11	4	6-0	25	.307
2002— Scran./W.B. (I.L.)	1	0	1.000	1.80	1.00	1	1	0	0	...	0-...	5.0	5	3	1	0	1-0	3	.263
— GC Phillies (GCL)	1	0	1.000	1.64	0.55	2	2	0	0	...	0-...	11.0	4	2	2	0	2-0	5	.105
— Reading (East.)	0	0	...	9.00	1.00	1	1	0	0	...	0-...	1.0	1	1	1	1	0-0	1	.333
— Clearwater (Fla. St.)	0	1	.000	1.50	1.50	3	3	0	0	...	0-...	12.0	15	5	2	0	3-0	10	.300
2003— Scran./W.B. (I.L.)	10	9	.526	3.24	0.90	25	24	3	2	...	0-...	155.1	125	59	56	15	22-1	116	.222
— Philadelphia (N.L.)	1	4	.200	3.97	1.15	8	8	0	0	0	0-0	45.1	41	22	20	5	11-2	29	.238
2004— Scran./W.B. (I.L.)	0	0	...	0.00	...	1	1	0	0	...	0-...	1.0	0	0	0	0	0-0	2	.000
— Philadelphia (N.L.)	0	2	.000	4.31	1.29	42	0	0	0	5	0-0	54.1	51	27	26	12	19-2	32	.249
Major League totals (8 years)	23	34	.404	4.96	1.38	212	64	1	0	10	0-2	550.1	567	332	303	90	190-15	356	.267

TERRERO, LUIS   OF

PERSONAL: Born May 18, 1980, in Barahona, Dominican Republic. ... 6-2/206. ... Bats right, throws right. ... Full name: Luis Enrique Terrero. ... Name pronounced: LOU-eese tuh-RARE-oh. ... High school: Barney Morgan (Barahona, Dominican Republic).

TRANSACTIONS/CAREER NOTES: Signed as a non-drafted free agent by Arizona Diamondbacks organization (October 15, 1997).

2004 GAMES PLAYED BY POSITION (MLB): OF—61.

Year Team (League)	Pos.	G	AB	R	H	2B	3B	HR	RBI	BB	SO	HBP	GDP	SB-CS	Avg.	OBP	SLG	OPS	E	Avg.
1999— Missoula (Pio.)	OF	71	272	74	78	13	7	8	40	32	91	5	2	27-10	.287	.365	.474	.839	11	.928
2000— High Desert (Calif.)	OF	19	79	10	15	3	1	0	1	3	16	1	2	5-5	.190	.229	.253	.482	3	.941
— Missoula (Pio.)	OF	68	276	48	72	10	0	8	44	10	75	8	5	23-11	.261	.305	.384	.689	5	.949
2001— South Bend (Mid.)	OF	24	89	4	14	2	0	1	8	0	29	2	2	3-0	.157	.176	.213	.389	0	1.000
— Yakima (N'west)	OF	11	41	7	13	2	1	0	2	2	8	0	0	0-3	.317	.349	.415	.763	0	1.000
— Lancaster (Calif.)	OF	19	71	16	32	5	1	4	11	1	14	1	3	5-0	.451	.466	.775	1.240	1	.971
— El Paso (Texas)	OF	34	147	29	44	13	3	3	8	4	45	3	2	9-2	.299	.331	.490	.821	5	.943
2002— El Paso (Texas)	OF	104	360	49	103	20	6	8	54	23	89	8	9	18-22	.286	.342	.442	.784	7	.973
2003— Arizona (N.L.)	OF	5	4	0	1	0	0	0	0	0	1	1	0	0-0	.250	.400	.250	.650	0	1.000
— Tucson (PCL)	OF-DH	118	467	83	134	20	15	3	46	31	103	11	6	23-19	.287	.345	.413	.758	10	.968
2004— Tucson (PCL)	OF-DH	58	217	36	68	9	6	3	35	17	48	4	7	15-3	.313	.374	.535	.909	3	.978
— Arizona (N.L.)	OF	62	229	21	56	14	0	4	14	20	78	5	5	10-2	.245	.319	.358	.677	8	.938
Major League totals (2 years)		67	233	21	57	14	0	4	14	20	79	6	5	10-2	.245	.320	.356	.677	8	.939

THAMES, MARCUS — OF

PERSONAL: Born March 6, 1977, in Louisville, Miss. ... 6-2/205. ... Bats right, throws right. ... Full name: Marcus Markey Thames. ... Name pronounced: timms. ... Junior college: East Central (Miss.) Community College.

TRANSACTIONS/CAREER NOTES: Selected by New York Yankees organization in 30th round of 1996 free-agent draft. ... Traded by Yankees to Texas Rangers for OF Ruben Sierra (June 6, 2003). ... Signed as a free agent by Detroit Tigers organization (December 8, 2003)

2004 GAMES PLAYED BY POSITION (MLB): OF—52, DH—5.

Year	Team (League)	Pos.	G	AB	R	H	2B	3B	HR	RBI	BB	SO	HBP	GDP	SB-CS	Avg.	OBP	SLG	OPS	E	Avg.
1997—GC Yankees (GCL)		OF	57	195	51	67	17	4	7	36	16	26	3	3	6-4	.344	.394	.579	.974	2	.978
— Greensboro (S. Atl.)		OF	4	16	2	5	1	0	0	2	0	3	0	0	1-0	.313	.313	.375	.688	0	1.000
1998—Tampa (Fla. St.)		OF	122	457	62	130	18	3	11	59	24	78	8	5	13-6	.284	.328	.409	.737	9	.970
1999—Norwich (East.)		OF	51	182	25	41	6	2	4	26	22	40	3	2	0-1	.225	.316	.346	.662	7	.929
— Tampa (Fla. St.)		OF	69	266	47	65	12	4	11	38	33	58	3	1	3-0	.244	.332	.444	.776	3	.974
2000—Norwich (East.)		OF	131	474	72	114	30	2	15	79	50	89	4	13	1-5	.241	.313	.407	.721	9	.959
2001—Norwich (East.)		OF	139	520	114	167	43	4	31	97	73	101	7	6	10-4	.321	.410	.598	1.008	8	.973
2002—Columbus (Int'l)		OF	107	386	51	80	21	3	13	45	43	71	7	8	5-4	.207	.297	.378	.675	5	.983
— New York (A.L.)		OF	7	13	2	3	1	0	1	2	0	4	0	0	0-0	.231	.231	.538	.769	0	1.000
2003—Columbus (Int'l)		OF	52	194	26	54	15	2	8	28	17	48	1	4	3-4	.278	.332	.407	.739	3	.977
— Oklahoma (PCL)		OF-DH	18	66	9	17	4	0	2	7	8	12	0	2	1-0	.258	.338	.409	.747	1	.968
— Texas (A.L.)		OF-DH	30	73	12	15	2	0	1	4	8	18	2	2	0-1	.205	.298	.274	.572	0	1.000
2004—Toledo (Int'l)		OF-DH	64	234	57	77	21	1	24	59	33	40	2	5	4-1	.329	.410	.735	1.145	2	.979
— Detroit (A.L.)		OF-DH	61	165	24	42	12	0	10	33	16	42	2	3	0-1	.255	.326	.509	.835	0	1.000
Major League totals (3 years)			98	251	38	60	15	0	12	39	24	64	4	5	0-2	.239	.313	.442	.755	0	1.000

THOMAS, BRAD — P

PERSONAL: Born October 12, 1977, in Sydney, Australia. ... 6-4/234. ... Throws left, bats left. ... Full name: Bradley Richard Thomas. ... High school: Mitchell (Australia).

TRANSACTIONS/CAREER NOTES: Signed as a non-drafted free agent by Los Angeles Dodgers organization (July 2, 1995). ... Released by Dodgers (May 9, 1997). ... Signed by Minnesota Twins organization (May 12, 1997). ... Traded by Twins to Boston Red Sox for future considerations (April 21, 2004). ... On disabled list (April 23, 2004-remainder of season); included rehabilitation assignment to Pawtucket.

CAREER HITTING: 0-for-0 (.000), 0 R, 0 2B, 0 3B, 0 HR, 0 RBI.

Year	Team (League)	W	L	Pct.	ERA	WHIP	G	GS	CG	ShO	Hld.	Sv.-Opp.	IP	H	R	ER	HR	BB-IBB	SO	Avg.
1996—Great Falls (Pio.)		3	2	.600	6.31	1.65	11	5	0	0	...	0-...	35.2	48	27	25	2	11-0	28	.320
1997—Elizabethton (Appal.)		3	4	.429	4.48	1.41	14	13	0	0	...	0-...	70.1	78	43	35	5	21-0	53	.279
1998—Fort Wayne (Midw.)		11	8	.579	2.95	1.25	27	26	1	0	...	0-...	152.1	146	68	50	9	45-1	126	.248
1999—Fort Myers (Fla. St.)		8	11	.421	4.78	1.49	27	27	1	1	...	0-...	152.2	182	99	81	11	46-0	108	.300
2000—Fort Myers (Fla. St.)		6	2	.750	1.66	1.20	12	12	0	0	...	0-...	65.0	62	33	12	3	16-0	57	.239
— New Britain (East.)		6	6	.500	4.06	1.67	14	13	1	1	...	0-...	75.1	80	47	34	3	46-1	66	.277
2001—New Britain (East.)		10	3	.769	1.96	0.98	19	19	1	0	...	0-...	119.1	91	37	26	4	26-0	97	.206
— Minnesota (A.L.)		0	2	.000	9.37	2.08	5	5	0	0	0	0-0	16.1	20	17	17	6	14-0	6	.303
2002—Edmonton (PCL)		6	12	.333	5.74	1.51	28	27	1	0	...	0-...	152.0	175	112	97	20	54-0	97	.291
2003—GC Twins (GCL)		0	0	...	0.00	0.70	2	2	0	0	...	0-...	10.0	6	0	0	0	1-0	12	.167
— Rochester (Int'l)		0	3	.000	3.53	1.30	15	11	0	0	...	0-...	58.2	68	23	23	3	10-0	50	.292
— Minnesota (A.L.)		0	1	.000	7.71	1.93	3	0	0	0	0	0-0	4.2	6	4	4	1	3-1	2	.316
2004—Minnesota (A.L.)		0	0	...	16.88	3.00	3	0	0	0	0	0-0	2.2	7	5	5	0	1-0	0	.500
— Pawtucket (Int'l)		0	1	.000	10.39	2.77	4	1	0	0	...	0-...	4.1	6	9	5	0	6-0	1	.353
Major League totals (3 years)		0	3	.000	9.89	2.15	11	5	0	0	0	0-0	23.2	33	26	26	7	18-1	8	.333

THOMAS, CHARLES — OF

PERSONAL: Born December 26, 1978, in Fairfield, Calif. ... 6-0/190. ... Bats left, throws left. ... Full name: Charles Wesley Thomas. ... High school: Asheville (N.C.). ... College: Western Carolina.

TRANSACTIONS/CAREER NOTES: Selected by Atlanta Braves organization in 19th round of 2000 free-agent draft.

2004 GAMES PLAYED BY POSITION (MLB): OF—71.

Year	Team (League)	Pos.	G	AB	R	H	2B	3B	HR	RBI	BB	SO	HBP	GDP	SB-CS	Avg.	OBP	SLG	OPS	E	Avg.
2000—Jamestown (N.Y.-Penn.)		OF	68	264	39	80	20	8	1	25	19	58	1	7	10-2	.303	.351	.451	.802	4	.974
2001—Myrtle Beach (Caro.)		OF	12	44	4	7	1	0	0	6	3	8	0	3	1-0	.159	.208	.182	.390	0	1.000
— Macon (S. Atl.)		OF	108	408	59	102	19	5	11	59	32	87	3	6	17-7	.250	.307	.402	.709	3	.984
2002—Myrtle Beach (Caro.)		OF	2	7	0	2	0	0	0	0	0	2	0	0	0-0	.286	.286	.286	.571	0	1.000
— Greenville (Sou.)		OF	71	229	40	53	8	0	2	18	28	43	4	5	5-3	.231	.322	.293	.615	2	.987
2003—Myrtle Beach (Caro.)		OF	66	207	30	50	8	1	2	15	29	54	8	5	6-2	.242	.357	.319	.675	4	.969
— Greenville (Sou.)		OF	47	176	29	57	14	4	0	23	18	25	3	1	5-4	.324	.396	.449	.845	2	.983
2004—Richmond (Int'l)		OF-DH	61	215	31	77	18	4	4	32	16	40	6	3	7-5	.358	.416	.535	.936	3	.969
— Atlanta (N.L.)		OF	83	236	35	68	8	4	7	31	21	45	9	3	3-1	.288	.368	.445	.813	1	.993
Major League totals (1 year)			83	236	35	68	8	4	7	31	21	45	9	3	3-1	.288	.368	.445	.813	1	.993

DIVISION SERIES RECORD

Year	Team (League)	Pos.	G	AB	R	H	2B	3B	HR	RBI	BB	SO	HBP	GDP	SB-CS	Avg.	OBP	SLG	OPS	E	Avg.
2004—Atlanta (N.L.)		OF	5	16	1	4	0	0	0	0	2	5	1	0	1-0	.250	.368	.250	.618	0	1.000

THOMAS, FRANK — DH/1B

PERSONAL: Born May 27, 1968, in Columbus, Ga. ... 6-5/275. ... Bats right, throws right. ... Full name: Frank Edward Thomas. ... High school: Columbus (Ga.). ... College: Auburn.

TRANSACTIONS/CAREER NOTES: Selected by Chicago White Sox organization in first round (seventh pick overall) of 1989 free-agent draft. ... On disabled list (July 11-30, 1996; June 7-22, 1997; May 10, 2001-remainder of season; and July 7, 2004-remainder of season).

HONORS: Named Major League Player of the Year by THE SPORTING NEWS (1993). ... Named A.L. Most Valuable Player by Baseball Writers' Association of America (1993-94). ... Named A.L. Comeback Player of the Year by THE SPORTING NEWS (2000).

2004 GAMES PLAYED BY POSITION (MLB): DH—65, 1B—4.

Year	Team (League)	Pos.	G	AB	R	H	2B	3B	HR	RBI	BB	SO	HBP	GDP	SB-CS	Avg.	OBP	SLG	OPS	E	Avg.
1989—GC Whi. Sox (GCL)	1B	17	52	8	19	5	0	1	11	11	3	1	0	4-0	.365	.470	.519	.989	2	.986
—Sarasota (Fla. St.)	1B	55	188	27	52	9	1	4	30	31	33	3	6	0-1	.277	.386	.399	.785	7	.985
1990—Birmingham (Sou.)	1B	109	353	85	114	27	5	18	71	112	74	5	13	7-5	.323	.487	.581	1.068	14	.987
—Chicago (A.L.)	DH-1B	60	191	39	63	11	3	7	31	44	54	2	5	0-1	.330	.454	.529	.983	5	.989
1991—Chicago (A.L.)	DH-1B	158	559	104	178	31	2	32	109	*138	112	1	20	1-2	.318	*.453	.553	1.006	2	.996
1992—Chicago (A.L.)	1B-DH	160	573	108	185	•46	2	24	115	*122	88	5	19	6-3	.323	*.439	.536	.975	13	.992
1993—Chicago (A.L.)	1B-DH	153	549	106	174	36	0	41	128	112	54	2	10	4-2	.317	.426	.607	1.033	15	.989
1994—Chicago (A.L.)	1B-DH	113	399	*106	141	34	1	38	101	*109	61	2	15	2-3	.353	*.487	*.729	1.217	7	.991
1995—Chicago (A.L.)	1B-DH	•145	493	102	152	27	0	40	111	*136	74	6	14	3-2	.308	.454	.606	1.061	7	.991
1996—Chicago (A.L.)	1B	141	527	110	184	26	0	40	134	109	70	5	25	1-1	.349	.459	.626	1.085	9	.992
1997—Chicago (A.L.)	1B-DH	146	530	110	184	35	0	35	125	109	69	3	15	1-1	*.347	.456	.611	1.067	11	.986
1998—Chicago (A.L.)	DH-1B	160	585	109	155	35	2	29	109	110	93	6	14	7-0	.265	.381	.480	.861	2	.984
1999—Chicago (A.L.)	DH-1B	135	486	74	148	36	0	15	77	87	66	9	15	3-3	.305	.414	.471	.885	4	.990
2000—Chicago (A.L.)	DH-1B	159	582	115	191	44	0	43	143	112	94	5	13	1-3	.328	.436	.625	1.061	1	.995
2001—Chicago (A.L.)	DH-1B	20	68	8	15	3	0	4	10	10	12	0	0	0-0	.221	.316	.441	.758	0	.955
2002—Chicago (A.L.)	DH-1B	148	523	77	132	29	1	28	92	88	115	7	10	3-0	.252	.361	.472	.834	2	.955
2003—Chicago (A.L.)	DH-1B	153	546	87	146	35	0	42	105	100	115	12	11	0-0	.267	.390	.562	.952	1	.995
2004—Chicago (A.L.)	DH-1B	74	240	53	65	16	0	18	49	64	57	6	2	0-2	.271	.434	.563	.997	0	1.000
Major League totals (15 years)		1925	6851	1308	2113	444	11	436	1439	1450	1134	71	188	32-23	.308	.429	.567	.996	80	.991

DIVISION SERIES RECORD

Year	Team (League)	Pos.	G	AB	R	H	2B	3B	HR	RBI	BB	SO	HBP	GDP	SB-CS	Avg.	OBP	SLG	OPS	E	Avg.
2000—Chicago (A.L.)	DH-1B	3	9	0	0	0	0	0	0	4	0	0	0	0-0	.000	.308	.000	.308	0	1.000

CHAMPIONSHIP SERIES RECORD

Year	Team (League)	Pos.	G	AB	R	H	2B	3B	HR	RBI	BB	SO	HBP	GDP	SB-CS	Avg.	OBP	SLG	OPS	E	Avg.
1993—Chicago (A.L.)	DH-1B	6	17	2	6	0	1	0	3	10	5	0	0	0-0	.353	.593	.529	1.122	0	1.000

ALL-STAR GAME RECORD

		G	AB	R	H	2B	3B	HR	RBI	BB	SO	HBP	GDP	SB-CS	Avg.	OBP	SLG	OPS	E	Avg.
All-Star Game totals (3 years)		3	5	2	4	0	0	1	3	1	0	0	0	0-0	.800	.833	1.400	2.233	0	1.000

THOME, JIM — 1B

T

PERSONAL: Born August 27, 1970, in Peoria, Ill. ... 6-4/244. ... Bats left, throws right. ... Full name: James Howard Thome. ... Name pronounced: TOE-mee. ... High school: Limestone (Bartonville, Ill.). ... Junior college: Illinois Central. ... College: Illinois Central.

TRANSACTIONS/CAREER NOTES: Selected by Cleveland Indians organization in 13th round of 1989 free-agent draft. ... On disabled list (March 28-May 18, 1992); included rehabilitation assignment to Canton/Akron. ... On disabled list (May 20-June 15, 1992); included rehabilitation assignment to Canton/Akron. ... On disabled list (August 8-September 16, 1998). ... Signed as a free agent by Philadelphia Phillies (December 3, 2002).

RECORDS: Shares major league record for most strikeouts, nine-inning game—5 (April 9, 2000).

2004 GAMES PLAYED BY POSITION (MLB): 1B—134, DH—6.

Year	Team (League)	Pos.	G	AB	R	H	2B	3B	HR	RBI	BB	SO	HBP	GDP	SB-CS	Avg.	OBP	SLG	OPS	E	Avg.
1989—GC Indians (GCL)	3B-SS	55	186	22	44	5	3	0	22	21	33	1	5	6-4	.237	.314	.296	.610	21	.909
1990—Burlington (Appal.)	3B	34	118	31	44	7	1	12	34	27	18	4	2	6-3	.373	.503	.754	1.258	11	.907
—Kinston (Caro.)	3B	33	117	19	36	4	1	4	16	24	26	1	4	4-1	.308	.427	.462	.888	8	.905
1991—Cant./Akr. (Eastern)	3B	84	294	47	99	20	2	5	45	44	58	4	7	8-2	.337	.426	.469	.895	17	.924
—Colo. Springs (PCL)	3B	41	151	20	43	7	3	2	28	12	29	0	4	0-0	.285	.331	.411	.742	6	.949
—Cleveland (A.L.)	3B	27	98	7	25	4	2	1	9	5	16	1	4	1-1	.255	.298	.367	.665	8	.900
1992—Colo. Springs (PCL)	3B	12	48	11	15	4	1	2	14	6	16	1	0	0-0	.313	.400	.563	.963	4	.784
—Cleveland (A.L.)	3B	40	117	8	24	3	1	2	12	10	34	2	3	2-0	.205	.275	.299	.574	11	.882
—Cant./Akr. (Eastern)	3B	30	107	16	36	9	2	1	14	24	30	1	3	0-2	.336	.462	.486	.948	4	.920
1993—Charlotte (Int'l)	3B	115	410	85	136	21	4	25	102	76	94	7	9	1-3	.332	.441	.585	1.026	15	.951
—Cleveland (A.L.)	3B	47	154	28	41	11	0	7	22	29	36	4	3	2-1	.266	.385	.474	.859	6	.950
1994—Cleveland (A.L.)	3B	98	321	58	86	20	1	20	52	46	84	0	11	3-3	.268	.359	.523	.882	15	.940
1995—Cleveland (A.L.)	3B-DH	137	452	92	142	29	3	25	73	97	113	5	8	4-3	.314	.438	.558	.996	16	.948
1996—Cleveland (A.L.)	3B-DH	151	505	122	157	28	5	38	116	123	141	6	13	2-2	.311	.450	.612	1.062	17	.953
1997—Cleveland (A.L.)	1B	147	496	104	142	25	0	40	102	*120	146	3	9	1-1	.286	.423	.579	1.001	10	.993
1998—Cleveland (A.L.)	1B-DH	123	440	89	129	34	2	30	85	89	141	4	7	1-0	.293	.413	.584	.998	10	.991
1999—Cleveland (A.L.)	1B-DH	146	494	101	137	27	2	33	108	*127	*171	4	6	0-0	.277	.426	.540	.967	6	.994
2000—Cleveland (A.L.)	1B-DH	158	557	106	150	33	1	37	106	118	171	4	8	1-0	.269	.398	.531	.929	5	.995
2001—Cleveland (A.L.)	1B-DH	156	526	101	153	26	1	49	124	111	*185	4	9	0-1	.291	.416	.624	1.040	10	.992
2002—Cleveland (A.L.)	1B-DH	147	480	101	146	19	2	52	118	*122	139	5	5	1-2	.304	.445	*.677	1.122	10	.991
2003—Philadelphia (N.L.)	1B-DH	159	578	111	154	30	3	*47	131	111	*182	4	5	0-3	.266	.385	.573	.958	5	.997
2004—Philadelphia (N.L.)	1B-DH	143	508	97	139	28	1	42	105	104	144	2	10	0-2	.274	.396	.581	.977	7	.994
American League totals (12 years)		1377	4640	917	1332	259	20	334	927	997	1377	42	86	18-14	.287	.414	.567	.982	124	.985
National League totals (2 years)		302	1086	208	293	58	4	89	236	215	326	6	15	0-5	.270	.391	.576	.967	12	.995
Major League totals (14 years)		1679	5726	1125	1625	317	24	423	1163	1212	1703	48	101	18-19	.284	.410	.569	.979	136	.987

DIVISION SERIES RECORD

Year	Team (League)	Pos.	G	AB	R	H	2B	3B	HR	RBI	BB	SO	HBP	GDP	SB-CS	Avg.	OBP	SLG	OPS	E	Avg.
1995—Cleveland (A.L.)	3B	3	13	1	2	0	0	1	3	1	6	0	0	0-0	.154	.214	.385	.599	0	1.000
1996—Cleveland (A.L.)	3B	4	10	1	3	0	0	0	0	1	5	1	0	0-0	.300	.417	.300	.717	0	1.000
1997—Cleveland (A.L.)	1B	4	15	1	3	0	0	0	1	5	5	0	0	0-0	.200	.200	.200	.400	0	1.000
1998—Cleveland (A.L.)	DH-1B	4	15	2	2	0	0	2	2	2	5	0	0	0-0	.133	.235	.533	.769	0	1.000
1999—Cleveland (A.L.)	1B	5	17	7	6	0	0	4	10	4	5	0	0	0-0	.353	.476	1.059	1.535	0	1.000
2001—Cleveland (A.L.)	1B	5	19	2	3	0	0	1	1	2	8	0	0	0-0	.158	.238	.316	.554	0	1.000
Division series totals (6 years)		25	89	14	19	0	0	8	17	10	34	1	0	0-0	.213	.300	.483	.783	0	1.000

CHAMPIONSHIP SERIES RECORD

Year	Team (League)	Pos.	G	AB	R	H	2B	3B	HR	RBI	BB	SO	HBP	GDP	SB-CS	Avg.	OBP	SLG	OPS	E	Avg.
1995—Cleveland (A.L.)	3B	5	15	2	4	0	0	2	5	2	3	0	1	0-0	.267	.353	.667	1.020	1	.857
1997—Cleveland (A.L.)	1B	6	14	3	1	0	0	0	0	5	4	0	0	0-0	.071	.316	.071	.387	1	1.000
1998—Cleveland (A.L.)	DH-1B	6	23	4	7	0	0	4	8	1	8	1	0	0-0	.304	.360	.826	1.186	0	1.000
Champ. series totals (3 years)		17	52	9	12	0	0	6	13	8	15	1	1	0-0	.231	.344	.577	.921	1	.989

WORLD SERIES RECORD

Year Team (League)	Pos.	G	AB	R	H	2B	3B	HR	RBI	BB	SO	HBP	GDP	SB-CS	Avg.	OBP	SLG	OPS	E	Avg.
1995— Cleveland (A.L.)	3B	6	19	1	4	1	0	1	2	2	5	0	0	0-0	.211	.286	.421	.707	1	.889
1997— Cleveland (A.L.)	1B	7	28	8	8	0	1	2	4	5	7	0	2	0-0	.286	.394	.571	.965	1	.984
World series totals (2 years)		13	47	9	12	1	1	3	6	7	12	0	2	0-0	.255	.352	.511	.862	2	.972

ALL-STAR GAME RECORD

	G	AB	R	H	2B	3B	HR	RBI	BB	SO	HBP	GDP	SB-CS	Avg.	OBP	SLG	OPS	E	Avg.
All-Star Game totals (4 years)	4	7	2	1	0	0	1	1	3	2	0	0	0-0	.143	.400	.143	.543	0	1.000

THOMPSON, RICH — OF

PERSONAL: Born April 23, 1979, in Reading, Pa. ... 6-3/180. ... Bats left, throws right. ... Full name: Richard Charles Thompson. ... High school: Montrose (Pa.). ... College: James Madison (Va.).

TRANSACTIONS/CAREER NOTES: Selected by Toronto Blue Jays organization in sixth round of 2000 free-agent draft. ... Traded by Blue Jays to Pittsburgh Pirates for P John Wasdin (July 8, 2003). ... Selected by San Diego Padres from Pirates organization in Rule 5 major league draft (December 15, 2003). ... Traded by Padres to Kansas City Royals for P Jason Szuminski and cash (December 15, 2003).

2004 GAMES PLAYED BY POSITION (MLB): OF—3, DH—1.

									BATTING										FIELDING	
Year Team (League)	Pos.	G	AB	R	H	2B	3B	HR	RBI	BB	SO	HBP	GDP	SB-CS	Avg.	OBP	SLG	OPS	E	Avg.
2000— Queens (NY-P)	OF	68	252	42	66	9	5	1	27	45	57	6	0	28-8	.262	.386	.349	.735	6	.956
2001— Dunedin (Fla. St.)	OF	112	454	90	141	14	6	1	60	44	72	9	3	39-11	.311	.380	.374	.754	3	.989
— Syracuse (Int'l)	OF	17	53	5	13	1	0	0	3	4	12	0	1	5-1	.245	.293	.283	.576	0	1.000
2002— Tennessee (Sou.)	OF	135	554	109	155	13	4	2	44	50	86	20	1	45-13	.280	.361	.329	.689	2	.992
2003— New Haven (East.)	OF	49	182	39	57	5	1	0	9	10	24	8	1	15-3	.313	.373	.352	.725	3	.952
— Syracuse (Int'l)	OF	28	112	13	33	2	1	0	7	9	10	5	1	11-1	.295	.373	.330	.703	1	.988
— Nashville (PCL)	OF	35	109	17	28	3	2	0	11	9	21	4	0	22-3	.257	.333	.321	.654	0	1.000
2004— Kansas City (A.L.)	OF-DH	6	1	1	0	0	0	0	0	0	0	1	0	1-0	.000	.000	.000	.000	0	1.000
— Nashville (PCL)	OF	112	411	73	118	7	13	5	36	26	62	13	0	41-15	.287	.348	.404	.752	7	.974
Major League totals (1 year)		6	1	1	0	0	0	0	0	0	0	1	0	1-0	.000	.000	.000	.000	0	1.000

THOMSON, JOHN — P

PERSONAL: Born October 1, 1973, in Vicksburg, Miss. ... 6-3/220. ... Throws right, bats right. ... Full name: John Carl Thomson. ... Name pronounced: TOM-son. ... High school: Sulphur (La.). ... Junior college: Blinn (Texas).

TRANSACTIONS/CAREER NOTES: Selected by Colorado Rockies organization in seventh round of 1993 free-agent draft. ... On disabled list (June 16-July 26, 1998); included rehabilitation assignment to Asheville. ... On disabled list (May 19-July 19, 1999); included rehabilitation assignment to Salem. ... On disabled list (March 23, 2000-remainder of season); included rehabilitation assignments to AZL Rockies and Portland. ... On disabled list (March 23-May 12 and May 26-August 2, 2001); included rehabilitation assignments to Colorado Springs. ... Traded by Rockies with OF Mark Little to New York Mets for OFs Jay Payton and Robert Stratton and P Mark Corey (July 31, 2002). ... Signed as a free agent by Texas Rangers (January 3, 2003). ... Signed as a free agent by Atlanta Braves (December 10, 2003).

CAREER HITTING: 50-for-263 (.190), 17 R, 2 2B, 1 3B, 0 HR, 16 RBI.

Year Team (League)	W	L	Pct.	ERA	WHIP	G	GS	CG	ShO	Hld.	Sv.-Opp.	IP	H	R	ER	HR	BB-IBB	SO	Avg.
1993— Ariz. Rockies (Ariz.)	3	5	.375	4.62	1.46	11	11	0	0	...	0-...	50.2	43	40	26	0	31-0	36	.225
1994— Asheville (S. Atl.)	6	6	.500	2.85	1.17	19	15	1	1	...	0-...	88.1	70	34	28	3	33-1	79	.219
— Central Valley (Cal.)	3	1	.750	3.28	1.24	9	8	0	0	...	0-...	49.1	43	20	18	0	18-1	41	.239
1995— New Haven (East.)	7	8	.467	4.18	1.43	26	24	0	0	...	0-...	131.1	132	69	61	8	56-0	82	.261
1996— New Haven (East.)	9	4	.692	2.86	1.12	16	16	1	0	...	0-...	97.2	82	35	31	8	27-1	86	.230
— Colo. Springs (PCL)	4	7	.364	5.04	1.46	11	11	0	0	...	0-...	69.2	76	45	39	6	26-2	62	.280
1997— Colo. Springs (PCL)	4	2	.667	3.43	1.19	7	7	0	0	...	0-...	42.0	36	18	16	4	14-1	49	.235
— Colorado (N.L.)	7	9	.438	4.71	1.47	27	27	2	1	0	0-0	166.1	193	94	87	15	51-0	106	.296
1998— Colorado (N.L.)	8	11	.421	4.81	1.39	26	26	2	0	0	0-0	161.0	174	86	86	21	49-0	106	.282
— Asheville (S. Atl.)	1	0	1.000	0.00	0.67	2	2	0	0	...	0-...	9.0	5	1	0	0	1-0	12	.161
1999— Colorado (N.L.)	1	10	.091	8.04	1.93	14	13	1	0	0	0-0	62.2	85	62	56	11	36-1	34	.324
— Colo. Springs (PCL)	0	2	.000	9.45	2.20	5	5	1	0	...	0-...	20.0	36	25	21	3	8-0	19	.414
— Salem (Caro.)	0	1	.000	9.00	2.00	1	1	0	0	...	0-...	2.0	4	2	2	0	0-0	2	.400
2000— Ariz. Rockies (Ariz.)	0	1	.000	13.50	2.25	3	3	0	0	...	0-...	5.1	8	8	8	0	4-0	7	.333
— Portland (N'west)	0	0	...	2.25	1.25	1	1	0	0	...	0-...	4.0	4	1	1	0	1-0	3	.250
2001— Colo. Springs (PCL)	5	3	.625	3.31	1.28	12	12	0	0	...	0-...	68.0	74	29	25	6	13-0	52	.274
— Colorado (N.L.)	4	5	.444	4.04	1.16	14	14	1	1	0	0-0	93.2	84	46	42	15	25-3	68	.239
2002— Colorado (N.L.)	7	8	.467	4.88	1.28	21	21	0	0	0	0-0	127.1	136	77	69	21	27-6	76	.268
— New York (N.L.)	2	6	.250	4.31	1.51	9	9	0	0	0	0-0	54.1	65	39	26	7	17-3	31	.290
2003— Texas (A.L.)	13	14	.481	4.85	1.30	35	35	3	1	0	0-0	217.0	234	125	117	27	49-2	136	.276
2004— Atlanta (N.L.)	14	8	.636	3.72	1.32	33	33	0	0	0	0-0	198.1	210	93	82	20	52-5	133	.276
American League totals (1 year)	13	14	.481	4.85	1.30	35	35	3	1	0	0-0	217.0	234	125	117	27	49-2	136	.276
National League totals (6 years)	43	57	.430	4.67	1.39	144	143	6	2	0	0-0	863.2	947	497	448	110	257-18	554	.281
Major League totals (7 years)	56	71	.441	4.71	1.38	179	178	9	3	0	0-0	1080.2	1181	622	565	137	306-20	690	.280

DIVISION SERIES RECORD

Year Team (League)	W	L	Pct.	ERA	WHIP	G	GS	CG	ShO	Hld.	Sv.-Opp.	IP	H	R	ER	HR	BB-IBB	SO	Avg.
2004— Atlanta (N.L.)	0	0	...	0.00	6.00	1	1	0	0	...	0-0	.1	1	0	0	0	1-0	0	.500

THORNTON, MATT — P

PERSONAL: Born September 15, 1976, in Three Rivers, Mich. ... 6-6/220. ... Throws left, bats left. ... Full name: Matthew J. Thornton. ... High school: Centreville High (Allendale,Mich.). ... College: Grand Valley State.

TRANSACTIONS/CAREER NOTES: Selected by Detroit Tigers organization in 27th round of 1995 free-agent draft; did not sign. ... Selected by Seattle Mariners organization in first round (22nd pick overall) of 1998 free-agent draft. ... On disabled list (August 15, 2003-remainder of season).

CAREER HITTING: 0-for-0 (.000), 0 R, 0 2B, 0 3B, 0 HR, 0 RBI.

Year Team (League)	W	L	Pct.	ERA	WHIP	G	GS	CG	ShO	Hld.	Sv.-Opp.	IP	H	R	ER	HR	BB-IBB	SO	Avg.
1998— Everett (Northwest)	0	0	...	27.00	3.00	2	0	0	0	...	0-...	1.1	1	4	4	0	3-0	0	.200
1999— Wisconsin (Midw.)	0	0	...	4.91	2.18	25	1	0	0	...	1-...	29.1	39	19	16	1	25-0	34	.320
2000— Wisconsin (Midw.)	6	9	.400	4.01	1.61	26	17	0	0	...	0-...	103.1	94	59	46	2	72-1	88	.245
2001— San Bernardino (Calif.)	14	7	.667	2.52	1.18	27	27	0	0	...	0-...	157.0	126	56	44	9	60-0	192	.220
2002— San Antonio (Texas)	1	5	.167	3.63	1.31	12	12	0	0	...	0-...	62.0	52	31	25	3	29-0	44	.237
2003— Inland Empire (Calif.)	0	0	...	4.00	1.44	2	2	0	0	...	0-...	9.0	9	4	4	2	4-0	14	.265
— San Antonio (Texas)	3	0	1.000	0.36	0.67	4	4	0	0	...	0-...	25.1	8	3	1	0	9-0	31	.104
— Tacoma (PCL)	0	2	.000	8.00	1.89	2	2	0	0	...	0-...	9.0	14	11	8	2	3-0	5	.359
2004— Tacoma (PCL)	7	5	.583	5.42	1.80	16	15	1	0	...	0-...	83.0	86	58	50	4	63-1	74	.273
— Seattle (A.L.)	1	2	.333	4.13	1.68	19	1	0	0	...	0-0	32.2	30	15	15	2	25-1	30	.250
Major League totals (1 year)	1	2	.333	4.13	1.68	19	1	0	0	...	0-0	32.2	30	15	15	2	25-1	30	.250

THURSTON, JOE — 2B/SS

PERSONAL: Born September 29, 1979, in Fairfield, Calif. ... 5-11/175. ... Bats left, throws right. ... Full name: Joseph William Thurston. ... High school: Vallejo (Calif.). ... Junior college: Sacramento (Calif.) City College.
TRANSACTIONS/CAREER NOTES: Selected by Boston Red Sox organization in 45th round of 1997 free-agent draft; did not sign. ... Selected by Los Angeles Dodgers organization in fourth round of 1999 free-agent draft.
2004 GAMES PLAYED BY POSITION (MLB): 2B—4.

										BATTING									FIELDING	
Year Team (League)	Pos.	G	AB	R	H	2B	3B	HR	RBI	BB	SO	HBP	GDP	SB-CS	Avg.	OBP	SLG	OPS	E	Avg.
1999— Yakima (N'west)	SS-1B	71	277	48	79	10	3	0	32	27	34	21	3	27-17	.285	.387	.343	.730	29	.899
— San Bern. (Calif.)	SS	2	3	0	0	0	0	0	0	0	1	1	0	0-0	.000	.250	.000	.250	0	1.000
2000— San Bern. (Calif.)	2B-SS	138	551	97	167	31	8	4	70	56	61	17	8	43-25	.303	.380	.410	.790	34	.953
2001— Jacksonville (Sou.)	2B-SS	144	80	145	25	7	7	46	48	65	12	5	20-18	.267	.338	.377	.715	17	.973
2002— Las Vegas (PCL)	2B-SS	136	587	106	196	39	13	12	55	25	60	12	10	22-9	.334	.372	.506	.878	21	.973
— Los Angeles (N.L.)	2B	8	13	1	6	1	0	0	1	0	1	0	0	0-0	.462	.429	.538	.967	0	1.000
2003— Las Vegas (PCL)	2B-SS	132	538	77	156	27	6	7	68	31	48	18	10	1-12	.290	.345	.401	.746	15	.978
— Los Angeles (N.L.)	2B	12	10	2	2	0	0	0	0	1	1	0	0	0-0	.200	.273	.200	.473	1	.857
2004— Las Vegas (PCL)	2B-DH	101	317	38	90	17	3	4	23	20	46	17	5	7-2	.284	.356	.394	.750	10	.977
— Los Angeles (N.L.)	2B	17	17	1	3	1	1	0	1	0	5	0	0	0-0	.176	.167	.353	.520	0	1.000
Major League totals (3 years)		37	40	4	11	2	1	0	2	1	7	0	0	0-0	.275	.279	.375	.654	1	.955

TIFFEE, TERRY — 3B

PERSONAL: Born April 21, 1979, in North Little Rock, Ark. ... 6-3/210. ... Bats both, throws right. ... Full name: Terry R. Tiffee. ... High school: Sylvan Hills (Sherwood, Ark.). ... Junior college: Pratt (Kan.) Community College.
TRANSACTIONS/CAREER NOTES: Selected by Minnesota Twins organization in 26th round of 1999 free-agent draft.
2004 GAMES PLAYED BY POSITION (MLB): 3B—12, DH—1, 1B—1.

										BATTING									FIELDING	
Year Team (League)	Pos.	G	AB	R	H	2B	3B	HR	RBI	BB	SO	HBP	GDP	SB-CS	Avg.	OBP	SLG	OPS	E	Avg.
2000— Quad City (Midw.)	3B-1B	129	493	59	125	25	0	7	60	29	73	0	14	2-0	.254	.292	.347	.639	31	.872
2001— Quad City (Midw.)	3B-1B	128	495	65	153	32	1	11	86	32	48	1	13	3-1	.309	.347	.444	.791	30	.942
2002— Fort Myers (FSL)	1B-3B	126	473	47	133	31	0	8	64	25	49	2	12	0-3	.281	.316	.397	.714	14	.982
2003— New Britain (East.)	3B-1B	139	530	77	167	31	3	14	93	31	49	2	13	4-1	.315	.351	.464	.815	21	.951
2004— Rochester (Int'l)	3B-DH-1B	82	316	42	97	26	3	12	68	21	26	4	9	0-0	.307	.357	.522	.871	14	.942
— Minnesota (A.L.)	3B-DH-1B	17	44	7	12	4	0	2	8	3	3	1	2	0-0	.273	.333	.500	.833	1	.968
Major League totals (1 year)		17	44	7	12	4	0	2	8	3	3	1	2	0-0	.273	.333	.500	.833	1	.968

TIMLIN, MIKE — P

PERSONAL: Born March 10, 1966, in Midland, Texas. ... 6-4/210. ... Throws right, bats right. ... Full name: Michael August Timlin. ... Name pronounced: TIM-lin. ... High school: Midland (Texas). ... College: Southwestern (Texas).
TRANSACTIONS/CAREER NOTES: Selected by Toronto Blue Jays organization in fifth round of 1987 free-agent draft. ... On disabled list (August 2-17, 1991). ... On disabled list (March 27-June 12, 1992); included rehabilitation assignments to Dunedin and Syracuse. ... On disabled list (May 25-June 9, 1994). ... On disabled list (June 22-August 18, 1995); included rehabilitation assignment to Syracuse. ... Traded by Blue Jays with P Paul Spoljaric to Seattle Mariners for OF Jose Cruz Jr. (July 31, 1997). ... Signed as a free agent by Baltimore Orioles (November 16, 1998). ... On disabled list (April 2-17, 2000). ... Traded by Orioles with cash to St. Louis Cardinals for 1B Chris Richard and P Mark Nussbeck (July 29, 2000). ... On disabled list (July 26-August 17, 2001). ... Traded by Cardinals with IF/OF Placido Polanco and P Bud Smith to Philadelphia Phillies for 3B Scott Rolen and P Doug Nickle (July 29, 2002). ... Signed as a free agent by Boston Red Sox (December 18, 2002).
CAREER HITTING: 0-for-7 (.000), 0 R, 0 2B, 0 3B, 0 HR, 0 RBI.

Year Team (League)	W	L	Pct.	ERA	WHIP	G	GS	CG	ShO	Hld.	Sv.-Opp.	IP	H	R	ER	HR	BB-IBB	SO	Avg.
1987— Medicine Hat (Pio.)	4	8	.333	5.14	1.39	13	12	2	0	...	0-...	75.1	79	50	43	4	26-0	66	.271
1988— Myrtle Beach (SAL)	10	6	.625	2.86	1.30	35	22	0	0	...	0-...	151.0	119	68	48	4	77-2	106	.215
1989— Dunedin (Fla. St.)	5	8	.385	3.25	1.42	33	7	1	0	...	7-...	88.2	90	44	32	2	36-2	64	.262
1990— Dunedin (Fla. St.)	7	2	.778	1.43	1.03	42	0	0	0	...	22-...	50.1	36	11	8	0	16-2	46	.197
— Knoxville (Southern)	1	2	.333	1.73	1.04	17	0	0	0	...	8-...	26.0	20	6	5	0	7-1	21	.206
1991— Toronto (A.L.)	11	6	.647	3.16	1.33	63	3	0	0	9	3-8	108.1	94	43	38	6	50-11	85	.233
1992— Dunedin (Fla. St.)	0	0	...	0.90	1.10	6	1	0	0	...	1-...	10.0	9	2	1	0	2-0	7	.243
— Syracuse (Int'l)	0	1	.000	8.74	1.76	7	1	0	0	...	3-...	11.1	15	11	11	3	5-1	7	.333
— Toronto (A.L.)	0	2	.000	4.12	1.49	26	0	0	0	1	1-1	43.2	45	23	20	0	20-5	35	.271
1993— Toronto (A.L.)	4	2	.667	4.69	1.62	54	0	0	0	9	1-4	55.2	63	32	29	7	27-3	49	.284
— Dunedin (Fla. St.)	0	0	...	1.00	0.44	4	0	0	0	...	1-...	9.0	4	1	1	0	0-0	8	.133
1994— Toronto (A.L.)	0	1	.000	5.18	1.53	34	0	0	0	5	2-4	40.0	41	25	23	5	20-0	38	.261
1995— Toronto (A.L.)	4	3	.571	2.14	1.31	31	0	0	0	4	5-9	42.0	38	13	10	1	17-5	36	.242
— Syracuse (Int'l)	1	1	.500	1.04	0.98	8	0	0	0	...	0-...	17.1	13	6	2	2	4-0	13	.197
1996— Toronto (A.L.)	1	6	.143	3.65	1.15	59	0	0	0	2	31-38	56.2	47	25	23	4	18-4	52	.229
1997— Toronto (A.L.)	3	2	.600	2.87	1.19	38	0	0	0	2	9-13	47.0	41	17	15	6	15-4	36	.243
— Seattle (A.L.)	3	2	.600	3.86	1.29	26	0	0	0	7	1-5	25.2	28	13	11	2	5-1	9	.280
1998— Seattle (A.L.)	3	3	.500	2.95	1.18	70	0	0	0	6	19-24	79.1	78	26	26	5	16-2	60	.264
1999— Baltimore (A.L.)	3	9	.250	3.57	1.17	62	0	0	0	9	27-36	63.0	51	30	25	9	23-3	50	.221
2000— Baltimore (A.L.)	2	3	.400	4.89	1.49	37	0	0	0	1	11-15	35.0	37	22	19	6	15-3	26	.276
— St. Louis (N.L.)	3	1	.750	3.34	1.69	25	0	0	0	5	1-3	29.2	30	11	11	2	20-3	26	.265
2001— St. Louis (N.L.)	4	5	.444	4.09	1.33	67	0	0	0	12	3-7	72.2	78	35	33	6	19-4	47	.277
2002— St. Louis (N.L.)	1	3	.250	2.51	0.90	42	1	0	0	12	0-2	61.0	48	19	17	9	7-2	35	.215
— Philadelphia (N.L.)	3	3	.500	3.79	0.95	30	0	0	0	8	0-2	35.2	27	16	15	6	7-0	15	.206
2003— Boston (A.L.)	6	4	.600	3.55	1.03	72	0	0	0	17	2-6	83.2	77	37	33	11	9-3	65	.239
2004— Boston (A.L.)	5	4	.556	4.13	1.23	76	0	0	0	20	1-4	76.1	75	35	35	8	19-3	56	.257
American League totals (12 years)	45	47	.489	3.65	1.28	648	3	0	0	83	113-167	756.1	715	341	307	70	254-47	597	.250
National League totals (3 years)	11	12	.478	3.44	1.19	164	1	0	0	37	4-14	199.0	183	81	76	23	53-9	123	.244
Major League totals (14 years)	56	59	.487	3.61	1.26	812	4	0	0	120	117-181	955.1	898	422	383	93	307-56	720	.249

DIVISION SERIES RECORD

Year Team (League)	W	L	Pct.	ERA	WHIP	G	GS	CG	ShO	Hld.	Sv.-Opp.	IP	H	R	ER	HR	BB-IBB	SO	Avg.
1997— Seattle (A.L.)	0	0	...	54.00	6.00	1	0	0	0	0	0-0	.2	3	4	4	1	1-1	1	.600
2000— St. Louis (N.L.)	0	0	...	10.80	3.60	2	0	0	0	1	0-0	1.2	5	2	2	1	1-0	2	.500
2001— St. Louis (N.L.)	0	0	...	0.00	0.75	1	0	0	0	0	0-0	1.1	1	0	0	0	0-0	5	.200
2003— Boston (A.L.)	0	0	...	0.00	0.00	3	0	0	0	0	0-0	4.1	0	0	0	0	0-0	5	.000
2004— Boston (A.L.)	0	0	...	9.00	1.33	3	0	0	0	1	0-0	3.0	3	3	3	1	1-0	5	.250
Division series totals (5 years)	0	0	...	7.36	1.36	10	0	0	0	4	0-0	11.0	12	9	9	3	3-1	13	.267

CHAMPIONSHIP SERIES RECORD

Year Team (League)	W	L	Pct.	ERA	WHIP	G	GS	CG	ShO	Hld.	Sv.-Opp.	IP	H	R	ER	HR	BB-IBB	SO	Avg.
1991— Toronto (A.L.)	0	1	.000	3.18	1.24	4	0	0	0	0	0-1	5.2	5	4	2	1	2-1	5	.208
1992— Toronto (A.L.)	0	0	...	6.75	3.00	2	0	0	0	0	0-0	1.1	4	1	1	0	0-0	1	.500
1993— Toronto (A.L.)	0	0	...	3.86	1.29	1	0	0	0	1	0-0	2.1	3	1	1	0	0-0	2	.300
2000— St. Louis (N.L.)	0	1	.000	0.00	0.90	3	0	0	0	0	0-0	3.1	1	3	0	0	2-0	0	.091
2003— Boston (A.L.)	0	0	...	0.00	0.56	5	0	0	0	0	3	0-0	5.1	1	0	0	0	2-1	6	.059
2004— Boston (A.L.)	0	0	...	4.76	2.65	5	0	0	0	0	0-1	5.2	10	3	3	0	5-0	2	.400
Champ. series totals (6 years)	0	2	.000	2.66	1.48	20	0	0	0	4	0-2	23.2	24	12	7	1	11-2	16	.253

WORLD SERIES RECORD

Year Team (League)	W	L	Pct.	ERA	WHIP	G	GS	CG	ShO	Hld.	Sv.-Opp.	IP	H	R	ER	HR	BB-IBB	SO	Avg.
1992— Toronto (A.L.)	0	0	...	0.00	0.00	2	0	0	0	0	1-1	1.1	0	0	0	0	0-0	0	.000
1993— Toronto (A.L.)	0	0	...	0.00	0.86	2	0	0	0	1	0-0	2.1	2	0	0	0	0-0	4	.250
2004— Boston (A.L.)	0	0	...	6.00	1.00	3	0	0	0	0	0-0	3.0	2	2	2	0	1-0	0	.200
World series totals (3 years)	0	0	...	2.70	0.75	7	0	0	0	1	1-1	6.2	4	2	2	0	1-0	4	.182

TOMKO, BRETT   P

PERSONAL: Born April 7, 1973, in Euclid, Ohio. ... 6-4/215. ... Throws right, bats right. ... Full name: Brett Daniel Tomko. ... Name pronounced: TOM-koh. ... High school: El Dorado (Placentia, Calif.). ... College: Florida Southern.

TRANSACTIONS/CAREER NOTES: Selected by Los Angeles Dodgers organization in 20th round of 1994 free-agent draft; did not sign. ... Selected by Cincinnati Reds organization in second round of 1995 free-agent draft. ... Traded by Reds with OF Mike Cameron, IF Antonio Perez and P Jake Meyer to Seattle Mariners for OF Ken Griffey (February 10, 2000). ... On disabled list (June 7-24, 2000). ... Traded by Mariners with C Tom Lampkin and SS Ramon Vazquez to San Diego Padres for C Ben Davis, P Wascar Serrano and SS Alex Arias (December 11, 2001). ... Traded by Padres to St. Louis Cardinals for P Luther Hackman and a player to be named (December 15, 2002); Padres acquired P Mike Wodnicki to complete deal (December 16, 2002). ... Signed as a free agent by San Francisco Giants (January 12, 2004). ... On disabled list (June 8-24, 2004); included rehabilitation assignment to Fresno.

CAREER HITTING: 59-for-339 (.174), 18 R, 8 2B, 0 3B, 0 HR, 23 RBI.

Year Team (League)	W	L	Pct.	ERA	WHIP	G	GS	CG	ShO	Hld.	Sv.-Opp.	IP	H	R	ER	HR	BB-IBB	SO	Avg.
1995— Char., W.Va. (SAL)	4	2	.667	1.84	1.02	9	7	0	0		0-...	49.0	41	12	10	1	9-1	46	.228
1996— Chattanooga (Southern) ...	11	7	.611	3.88	1.17	27	27	0	0		0-...	157.2	131	73	68	20	54-4	164	.226
1997— Indianapolis (A.A.)	6	3	.667	2.95	1.02	10	10	0	0		0-...	61.0	53	21	20	7	9-0	60	.232
— Cincinnati (N.L.)	11	7	.611	3.43	1.21	22	19	0	0	0	0-0	126.0	106	50	48	14	47-4	95	.234
1998— Cincinnati (N.L.)	13	12	.520	4.44	1.24	34	34	1	0	0	0-0	210.2	198	111	104	22	64-3	162	.247
1999— Cincinnati (N.L.)	5	7	.417	4.92	1.37	33	26	1	0	1	0-0	172.0	175	103	94	31	60-10	132	.263
— Indianapolis (Int'l)	2	0	1.000	4.97	1.26	2	2	0	0		0-...	12.2	15	7	7	1	1-0	9	.288
2000— Tacoma (PCL)	1	0	1.000	2.84	1.42	2	2	0	0		0-...	12.2	13	4	4	1	5-1	8	.271
— Seattle (A.L.)	7	5	.583	4.68	1.43	32	8	0	0	3	1-2	92.1	92	53	48	12	40-4	59	.264
2001— Seattle (A.L.)	3	1	.750	5.19	1.64	11	4	0	0	0	0-1	34.2	42	24	20	9	15-2	22	.288
— Tacoma (PCL)	10	6	.625	4.04	1.17	19	18	3	2		0-...	127.0	124	64	57	12	25-1	117	.254
2002— San Diego (N.L.)	10	10	.500	4.49	1.33	32	32	3	0	0	0-0	204.1	212	107	102	31	60-9	126	.267
2003— St. Louis (N.L.)	13	9	.591	5.28	1.52	33	32	0	0	0	0-0	202.2	* 252	126	• 119	35	57-2	114	.305
2004— Fresno (PCL)	0	0	...	5.40	1.20	1	1	0	0		0-...	5.0	4	3	3	1	2-0	4	.211
— San Francisco (N.L.)	11	7	.611	4.04	1.34	32	31	2	1	0	0-0	194.0	196	98	87	19	64-3	108	.260
American League totals (2 years)	10	6	.625	4.82	1.49	43	12	0	0	3	1-3	127.0	134	77	68	21	55-6	81	.271
National League totals (6 years)	63	52	.548	4.49	1.34	186	174	9	1	1	0-0	1109.2	1139	595	554	152	352-31	737	.265
Major League totals (8 years)	73	58	.557	4.53	1.36	229	186	9	1	4	1-3	1236.2	1273	672	622	173	407-37	818	.266

DIVISION SERIES RECORD

Year Team (League)	W	L	Pct.	ERA	WHIP	G	GS	CG	ShO	Hld.	Sv.-Opp.	IP	H	R	ER	HR	BB-IBB	SO	Avg.
2000— Seattle (A.L.)	0	0	...	0.00	0.75	1	0	0	0	0	0-0	2.2	1	0	0	0	1-0	5	.125

CHAMPIONSHIP SERIES RECORD

Year Team (League)	W	L	Pct.	ERA	WHIP	G	GS	CG	ShO	Hld.	Sv.-Opp.	IP	H	R	ER	HR	BB-IBB	SO	Avg.
2000— Seattle (A.L.)	0	0	...	7.20	1.40	2	0	0	0	0	0-0	5.0	3	4	4	0	4-1	4	.176

TONIS, MIKE   C

PERSONAL: Born February 9, 1979, in Sacramento, Calif. ... 6-3/220. ... Bats right, throws right. ... Full name: Michael Timothy Tonis. ... High school: Elk Grove (Calif.). ... College: UC-Davis.

TRANSACTIONS/CAREER NOTES: Selected by Kansas City Royals organization in 52nd round of 1997 free-agent draft; did not sign. ... Selected by Kansas City Royals organization in second round of 2000 free-agent draft.

2004 GAMES PLAYED BY POSITION (MLB): C—2.

Year Team (League)	Pos.	G	AB	R	H	2B	3B	HR	RBI	BB	SO	HBP	GDP	SB-CS	Avg.	OBP	SLG	OPS	E	Avg.
2000— Char., W.Va. (SAL)	C	28	100	10	20	8	0	0	17	9	22	1	1	1-0	.200	.268	.280	.548	5	.973
— Omaha (PCL)	C	2	8	1	4	0	0	0	3	0	3	0	0	0-0	.500	.500	.500	1.000	0	1.000
2001— Wilmington (Caro.)	C	33	123	15	31	8	0	3	18	15	34	2	6	0-0	.252	.343	.390	.733	2	.992
— Wichita (Texas)	C	63	226	36	61	11	1	9	43	22	41	4	7	1-1	.270	.344	.447	.791	7	.985
2002— GC Royals (GCL)	DH	6	17	2	3	0	0	1	3	2	3	1	0	0-0	.176	.300	.353	.653	...	...
2003— Wichita (Texas)	C	87	307	34	73	18	0	2	24	23	52	3	14	3-1	.238	.296	.316	.611	7	.987
2004— Kansas City (A.L.)	C	2	6	0	0	0	0	0	0	1	1	0	1	0-0	.000	.143	.000	.143	0	1.000
— Wichita (Texas)	C-DH	78	263	24	60	13	0	3	29	23	53	1	10	0-0	.228	.289	.319	.606	3	.993
Major League totals (1 year)		2	6	0	0	0	0	0	0	1	1	0	1	0-0	.000	.143	.000	.143	0	1.000

TORCATO, TONY   OF

PERSONAL: Born October 25, 1979, in Woodland, Calif. ... 6-1/219. ... Bats left, throws right. ... Full name: Anthony Dale Torcato. ... Name pronounced: tor-ka-TO. ... High school: Woodland (Calif.).

TRANSACTIONS/CAREER NOTES: Selected by San Francisco Giants organization in first round (19th pick overall) of 1998 free-agent draft; pick received as part of compensation for Houston Astros signing Type B free-agent P Doug Henry.

Year Team (League)	Pos.	G	AB	R	H	2B	3B	HR	RBI	BB	SO	HBP	GDP	SB-CS	Avg.	OBP	SLG	OPS	E	Avg.
1998— Salem-Keizer (N'west)	3B	59	220	31	64	15	2	3	43	14	38	3	0	4-2	.291	.333	.418	.752	17	.886
1999— Bakersfield (Calif.)	3B	110	422	50	123	25	0	4	58	30	67	3	6	2-1	.291	.338	.379	.717	28	.886
2000— San Jose (Calif.)	3B	119	490	77	159	37	2	7	88	41	62	6	2	19-4	.324	.379	.451	.830	40	.882

Year Team (League)	Pos.	G	AB	R	H	2B	3B	HR	RBI	BB	SO	HBP	GDP	SB-CS	Avg.	OBP	SLG	OPS	E	Avg.
—Shreveport (Texas)	3B	2	8	1	4	0	0	0	2	0	1	0	0	0-0	.500	.500	.500	1.000	0	1.000
2001—San Jose (Calif.)	OF	67	258	38	88	21	2	2	47	17	40	4	5	9-3	.341	.381	.461	.842	1	.952
—Shreveport (Texas)	OF	36	147	13	43	9	1	1	23	9	15	4	6	0-1	.293	.344	.388	.731	2	.975
—Fresno (PCL)	OF	35	150	20	48	8	1	2	8	2	20	0	5	0-1	.320	.329	.427	.756	1	.985
2002—Fresno (PCL)	OF	130	490	64	142	23	3	13	64	29	65	2	6	4-6	.290	.330	.429	.758	8	.964
—San Francisco (N.L.)	OF	5	11	0	3	1	0	0	0	0	2	0	0	0-0	.273	.273	.364	.636	0	1.000
2003—Fresno (PCL) 1-0-3-DH		106	423	36	125	18	2	3	48	6	33	2	18	4-0	.296	.304	.369	.672	12	.981
—San Francisco (N.L.)	OF	14	16	0	3	1	0	0	1	0	4	1	0	0-0	.188	.235	.250	.485	1	.833
2004—Fresno (PCL) OF-1B-DH		119	395	39	114	22	0	3	57	11	35	5	8	4-1	.289	.314	.367	.681	2	.993
—San Francisco (N.L.)		13	9	1	5	0	0	0	2	1	0	1	0	0-0	.556	.583	.556	1.139	0	...
Major League totals (3 years)		32	36	1	11	2	0	0	3	1	6	2	0	0-0	.306	.350	.361	.711	1	.875

TORREALBA, YORVIT   C

PERSONAL: Born July 19, 1978, in Caracas, Venezuela. ... 5-11/190. ... Bats right, throws right. ... Full name: Yorvit Adolfo Torrealba. ... Name pronounced: yor-VEET tor-EE-all-buh. ... High school: Vincente Emilio Sojo (Venezuela).
TRANSACTIONS/CAREER NOTES: Signed as a non-drafted free agent by San Francisco Giants organization (September 14, 1994).
2004 GAMES PLAYED BY POSITION (MLB): C—59.

Year Team (League)	Pos.	G	AB	R	H	2B	3B	HR	RBI	BB	SO	HBP	GDP	SB-CS	Avg.	OBP	SLG	OPS	E	Avg.
1995—Bellingham (N'west)	C	26	71	2	11	3	0	0	8	2	14	1	1	0-1	.155	.187	.197	.384	5	.973
1996—San Jose (Calif.)	C	2	5	0	0	0	0	0	0	0	1	0	0	0-0	.000	.167	.000	.167	0	1.000
—Burlington (Midw.)	C	1	4	0	0	0	0	0	0	0	1	0	1	0-0	.000	.000	.000	.000	0	1.000
—Bellingham (N'west)	C	48	150	23	40	4	0	1	10	9	27	0	7	4-1	.267	.304	.313	.618	2	.994
1997—Bakersfield (Calif.)	C	119	446	52	122	15	3	4	40	31	58	5	8	4-2	.274	.326	.348	.673	6	.993
1998—Shreveport (Texas)	C	59	196	18	46	7	0	0	13	18	30	4	3	0-5	.235	.311	.270	.581	2	.996
—San Jose (Calif.)	C	21	70	10	20	2	0	0	10	1	6	0	2	2-2	.286	.292	.314	.606	2	.989
—Fresno (PCL)	C	4	11	1	2	1	0	0	1	1	4	0	0	0-0	.182	.250	.273	.523	0	1.000
1999—Shreveport (Texas)	C	65	217	25	53	10	1	4	19	9	34	2	6	0-2	.244	.278	.355	.633	2	.994
—Fresno (PCL)	C	17	63	9	16	2	0	2	10	4	11	2	2	0-1	.254	.319	.381	.700	2	.988
—San Jose (Calif.)	C	19	73	10	23	3	0	2	14	6	15	1	2	0-0	.315	.370	.438	.809	5	.975
2000—Shreveport (Texas)	C	108	398	50	114	21	1	4	32	34	55	6	17	2-3	.286	.350	.374	.724	8	.990
2001—Fresno (PCL)	C	115	394	56	108	23	3	8	36	19	65	4	11	2-3	.274	.313	.409	.721	9	.989
—San Francisco (N.L.)	C	3	4	0	2	0	1	0	2	0	0	0	0	0-0	.500	.500	1.000	1.500	0	1.000
2002—San Francisco (N.L.)	C	53	136	17	38	10	0	2	14	14	20	2	11	0-0	.279	.355	.397	.752	2	.993
2003—San Francisco (N.L.)	C-OF	66	200	22	52	10	2	4	29	14	39	2	3	1-0	.260	.312	.390	.702	1	.997
2004—San Francisco (N.L.)	C	64	172	19	39	7	3	6	23	17	31	2	7	2-0	.227	.302	.407	.709	2	.995
Major League totals (4 years)		186	512	58	131	27	6	12	68	45	90	6	21	3-0	.256	.322	.402	.724	5	.995

DIVISION SERIES RECORD

Year Team (League)	Pos.	G	AB	R	H	2B	3B	HR	RBI	BB	SO	HBP	GDP	SB-CS	Avg.	OBP	SLG	OPS	E	Avg.
2003—San Francisco (N.L.)	C	2	3	0	0	0	0	0	1	0	0	0	0	0-0	.000	.000	.000	.000	1	.909

TORRES, ANDRES   OF

PERSONAL: Born January 26, 1978, in Aguada, Puerto Rico. ... 5-10/190. ... Bats both, throws right. ... Full name: Andres Vungo Torres. ... Junior college: Miami-Dade Community College North.
TRANSACTIONS/CAREER NOTES: Selected by Florida Marlins organization in 23rd round of 1997 free-agent draft; did not sign. ... Selected by Detroit Tigers organization in fourth round of 1998 free-agent draft. ... Refused minor league assignment and became a free agent (April 22, 2004). ... Signed by Chicago White Sox organization (April 24, 2004).
2004 GAMES PLAYED BY POSITION (MLB): DH—2, OF—1.

Year Team (League)	Pos.	G	AB	R	H	2B	3B	HR	RBI	BB	SO	HBP	GDP	SB-CS	Avg.	OBP	SLG	OPS	E	Avg.
1998—Jamestown (N.Y.-Penn.) ...	OF	48	192	28	45	2	6	1	21	25	50	1	1	13-2	.234	.323	.323	.646	5	.944
1999—W. Mich. (Mid.)	OF	117	407	72	96	20	5	2	34	92	116	10	2	39-18	.236	.385	.324	.710	7	.972
2000—Lakeland (Fla. St.)	OF	108	398	82	118	11	11	3	33	63	82	5	10	65-16	.296	.399	.402	.801	6	.979
—Jacksonville (Sou.)	OF	14	54	3	8	0	0	0	0	5	14	0	1	2-0	.148	.220	.148	.368	1	.971
2001—Erie (East.)	OF	64	252	54	74	16	3	1	23	36	50	5	1	19-11	.294	.391	.393	.784	1	.993
2002—Toledo (Int'l)	OF	115	462	80	123	17	8	4	42	53	116	5	3	42-12	.266	.345	.364	.709	10	.967
—Detroit (A.L.)	OF	19	70	7	14	1	1	0	3	6	16	1	2	2-2	.200	.266	.243	.509	1	.981
2003—Toledo (Int'l)	OF	70	271	36	69	13	3	2	16	18	61	0	1	27-11	.255	.301	.347	.648	5	.973
—Detroit (A.L.)	OF-DH	59	168	23	37	4	3	1	9	10	35	0	5	5-5	.220	.263	.298	.560	1	.991
2004—Detroit (A.L.)	DH-OF	3	0	1	0	0	0	0	0	0	0	0	0	1-0	...	...	...	...	0	...
—Bristol (Appal.)	DH-OF	6	22	8	8	0	0	1	2	3	4	1	0	5-0	.364	.462	.500	.962	0	1.000
—Charlotte (Int'l)	OF	87	322	49	95	11	4	8	26	35	74	5	3	23-7	.295	.371	.429	.799	6	.975
Major League totals (3 years)		81	238	31	51	5	4	1	12	16	51	1	7	8-7	.214	.264	.282	.545	2	.987

TORRES, SALOMON   P

PERSONAL: Born March 11, 1972, in San Pedro de Macoris, Dominican Republic. ... 5-11/210. ... Throws right, bats right. ... Full name: Salomon Ramirez Torres. ... High school: Centro Academico Rogus (San Pedro de Macoris, Dominican Republic).
TRANSACTIONS/CAREER NOTES: Signed as a non-drafted free agent by San Francisco Giants organization (September 15, 1989). ... Traded by Giants to Seattle Mariners for P Shawn Estes and IF Wilson Delgado (May 21, 1995). ... Claimed on waivers by Montreal Expos (April 18, 1997). ... On voluntarily retired list (August 1, 1997-January 29, 2001). ... Released by Expos (January 29, 2001). ... Signed as a free agent by Pittsburgh Pirates organization (January 8, 2002). ... On disabled list (August 6-29, 2003); included rehabilitation assignment to Nashville. ... On suspended list (July 19-22, 2004).
CAREER HITTING: 12-for-93 (.129), 5 R, 1 2B, 1 3B, 0 HR, 1 RBI.

Year Team (League)	W	L	Pct.	ERA	WHIP	G	GS	CG	ShO	Hld.	Sv.-Opp.	IP	H	R	ER	HR	BB-IBB	SO	Avg.
1990—San Pedro (DSL)	11	1	.917	0.50	0.82	13	13	6	0	...	0-...	90.0	44	15	5	...	30-...	101	...
1991—Clinton (Midw.)	16	5	.762	1.41	0.93	28	28	8	3	...	0-...	210.1	148	48	33	4	47-2	214	.195
1992—Shreveport (Texas)	6	10	.375	4.21	1.24	25	25	4	2	...	0-...	162.1	167	93	76	10	34-2	151	.263
1993—Shreveport (Texas)	7	4	.636	2.70	0.95	12	12	2	1	...	0-...	83.1	67	27	25	6	12-0	67	.218
—Phoenix (PCL)	7	4	.636	3.50	1.25	14	14	4	1	...	0-...	105.1	105	43	41	5	27-0	99	.261

Year	Team (League)	W	L	Pct.	ERA	WHIP	G	GS	CG	ShO	Hld.	Sv.-Opp.	IP	H	R	ER	HR	BB-IBB	SO	Avg.
—San Francisco (N.L.)		3	5	.375	4.03	1.43	8	8	0	0		0	0-0	44.2	37	21	20	5	27-3	23	.231
1994—San Francisco (N.L.)		2	8	.200	5.44	1.53	16	14	1	0		0	0-0	84.1	95	55	51	10	34-2	42	.292
—Phoenix (PCL)		5	6	.455	4.22	1.47	13	13	0	0		...	0-...	79.0	85	49	37	7	31-0	64	.278
1995—San Francisco (N.L.)		0	1	1.000	9.00	2.50	4	1	0	0		0	0-0	8.0	13	8	8	4	7-0	2	.394
—Phoenix (PCL)		0	0	...	0.00	1.00	1	0	0	0		...	0-...	2.0	2	0	0	0	0-0	5	.286
—Tacoma (PCL)		1	1	.500	3.21	1.18	5	4	0	0		...	0-...	28.0	20	10	10	2	13-1	19	.206
—Seattle (A.L.)		3	8	.273	6.00	1.79	16	13	1	0		0	0-0	72.0	87	53	48	12	42-3	45	.291
1996—Tacoma (PCL)		7	10	.412	5.29	1.50	22	21	3	1			0-...	134.1	150	87	79	16	52-1	121	.279
—Seattle (A.L.)		3	3	.500	4.59	1.37	10	7	1	1		0	0-0	49.0	44	27	25	5	23-2	36	.242
1997—Seattle (A.L.)		0	0	...	27.00	3.00	2	0	0	0		0	0-0	3.1	7	10	10	0	3-0	0	.412
—Montreal (N.L.)		0	0	...	7.25	1.66	12	0	0	0		0	0-0	22.1	25	19	18	2	12-0	11	.284
—Ottawa (Int'l)		0	0	...	5.40	1.80	2	1	0	0		...	0-...	5.0	7	5	3	0	2-0	2	.318
1998—	Did not play.																			
1999—	Did not play.																			
2000—	Did not play.																			
2001—Samsung (Korean)		0	2	.000	0.00	2.00	2	...	...	...		...	0-...	5.0	...	...	...	...	10-...	5	...
2002—Nashville (PCL)		8	5	.615	3.83	1.28	26	24	2	1			0-...	162.1	169	78	69	12	39-2	136	.270
—Pittsburgh (N.L.)		2	1	.667	2.70	1.37	5	5	0	0		0	0-0	30.0	28	10	9	2	13-1	12	.257
2003—Nashville (PCL)		1	0	1.000	1.80	0.60	1	1	0	0		0	0-...	5.0	2	1	1	0	1-0	4	.118
—Pittsburgh (N.L.)		7	5	.583	4.76	1.40	41	16	0	0		6	2-3	121.0	128	65	64	19	42-5	84	.276
2004—Pittsburgh (N.L.)		7	7	.500	2.64	1.18	84	0	0	0		30	0-4	92.0	87	33	27	6	22-6	62	.256
American League totals (3 years)		6	11	.353	6.01	1.66	28	20	2	1		0	0-0	124.1	138	90	83	17	68-5	81	.277
National League totals (7 years)		21	27	.438	4.41	1.42	170	44	1	0		36	2-7	402.1	413	211	197	48	157-17	236	.272
Major League totals (8 years)		27	38	.415	4.78	1.47	198	64	3	1		36	2-7	526.2	551	301	280	65	225-22	317	.273

TOWERS, JOSH   P

PERSONAL: Born February 26, 1977, in Port Hueneme, Calif. ... 6-1/188. ... Throws right, bats right. ... Full name: Joshua Eric Towers. ... High school: Hueneme (Oxnard, Calif.). ... Junior college: Oxnard (Calif.).

TRANSACTIONS/CAREER NOTES: Selected by Baltimore Orioles organization in 15th round of 1996 free-agent draft. ... On disabled list (October 1, 2001-remainder of season). ... Signed as a free agent by Toronto Blue Jays organization (November 8, 2002).

CAREER HITTING: 0-for-4 (.000), 0 R, 0 2B, 0 3B, 0 HR, 0 RBI.

Year	Team (League)	W	L	Pct.	ERA	WHIP	G	GS	CG	ShO	Hld.	Sv.-Opp.	IP	H	R	ER	HR	BB-IBB	SO	Avg.
1996—Bluefield (Appalachian)		4	1	.800	5.24	1.24	14	9	0	0			0-...	55.0	63	35	32	9	5-0	61	.278
1997—Delmarva (S.Atl.)		0	0	...	3.44	1.09	9	1	0	0		...	1-...	18.1	18	8	7	1	2-0	16	.261
—Frederick (Caro.)		6	2	.750	4.86	1.71	25	3	0	0		...	1-...	53.2	74	36	29	4	18-0	64	.323
1998—Frederick (Caro.)		8	7	.533	3.34	1.00	25	20	3	0		...	1-...	145.1	137	58	54	11	9-0	122	.247
—Bowie (East.)		2	1	.667	3.50	1.33	5	2	0	0		...	0-...	18.0	20	9	7	1	4-0	7	.270
1999—Bowie (East.)		12	7	.632	3.76	1.22	29	28	5	2			0-...	189.0	204	86	79	26	26-1	106	.276
2000—Rochester (Int'l)		8	6	.571	3.47	1.20	24	24	5	1			0-...	148.0	157	63	57	17	21-0	102	.269
2001—Rochester (Int'l)		3	1	.750	3.51	1.17	6	6	1	1			0-...	41.0	40	18	16	2	8-2	27	.255
—Baltimore (A.L.)		8	10	.444	4.49	1.29	24	20	1	1		0	0-0	140.1	165	74	70	21	16-0	58	.297
2002—Baltimore (A.L.)		0	3	.000	7.90	1.72	5	3	0	0		0	0-0	27.1	42	24	24	11	5-0	13	.362
—Rochester (Int'l)		0	9	.000	7.57	1.78	15	13	1	0			0-...	69.0	109	65	58	16	14-0	43	.353
2003—Syracuse (Int'l)		5	7	.417	3.32	1.20	21	20	1	1			0-...	132.2	133	55	49	10	20-1	76	.259
—Toronto (A.L.)		8	1	.889	4.48	1.15	14	9	0	0		0	1-1	64.1	67	34	32	15	7-1	42	.266
2004—Syracuse (Int'l)		3	1	.750	2.50	1.11	6	5	0	0		0	0-...	36.0	33	11	10	5	7-0	25	.246
—Toronto (A.L.)		9	9	.500	5.11	1.50	21	21	0	0		0	0-0	116.1	148	70	66	16	26-4	51	.310
Major League totals (4 years)		25	23	.521	4.96	1.37	64	52	2	1		0	1-1	348.1	422	202	192	63	54-5	164	.301

TRACHSEL, STEVE   P

PERSONAL: Born October 31, 1970, in Oxnard, Calif. ... 6-4/205. ... Throws right, bats right. ... Full name: Stephen Christopher Trachsel. ... Name pronounced: track-s'l. ... High school: Troy (Fullerton, Calif.). ... College: Long Beach State.

TRANSACTIONS/CAREER NOTES: Selected by Chicago Cubs organization in eighth round of 1991 free-agent draft. ... On disabled list (July 20-August 4, 1994). ... Signed as a free agent by Tampa Bay Devil Rays (January 28, 2000). ... Traded by Devil Rays with P Mark Guthrie to Toronto Blue Jays for 2B Brent Abernathy and cash (July 31, 2000). ... Signed as a free agent by New York Mets (December 11, 2000). ... On disabled list (July 1-22, 2002); included rehabilitation assignment to Binghamton.

HONORS: Named N.L. Rookie Pitcher of the Year by THE SPORTING NEWS (1994).

CAREER HITTING: 97-for-574 (.169), 45 R, 16 2B, 1 3B, 2 HR, 38 RBI.

Year	Team (League)	W	L	Pct.	ERA	WHIP	G	GS	CG	ShO	Hld.	Sv.-Opp.	IP	H	R	ER	HR	BB-IBB	SO	Avg.
1991—Geneva (N.Y.-Penn)		1	0	1.000	1.26	1.12	2	2	0	0		...	0-...	14.1	10	2	2	0	6-0	7	.217
—Winston-Salem (Caro.)		4	4	.500	3.67	1.21	12	12	1	0		...	0-...	73.2	70	38	30	3	19-0	69	.245
1992—Charlotte (Sou.)		13	8	.619	3.06	1.13	29	29	5	2		...	0-...	191.0	180	76	65	19	35-3	135	.250
1993—Iowa (Am. Assoc.)		13	6	.684	3.96	1.26	27	26	1	1		...	0-...	170.2	170	78	75	20	45-0	135	.264
—Chicago (N.L.)		0	2	.000	4.58	0.97	3	3	0	0		0	0-0	19.2	16	10	10	4	3-0	14	.219
1994—Chicago (N.L.)		9	7	.563	3.21	1.28	22	22	1	0		0	0-0	146.0	133	57	52	19	54-4	108	.242
—Iowa (Am. Assoc.)		0	2	.000	10.00	2.00	2	2	0	0		0	0-...	9.0	11	10	10	1	7-0	8	.289
1995—Chicago (N.L.)		7	13	.350	5.15	1.56	30	29	2	0		0	0-0	160.2	174	104	92	25	76-8	117	.277
1996—Orlando (Sou.)		0	1	.000	2.77	0.85	2	2	0	0		0	0-...	13.0	11	6	4	0	0-0	12	.220
—Chicago (N.L.)		13	9	.591	3.03	1.19	31	31	3	2		0	0-0	205.0	181	82	69	30	62-3	132	.235
1997—Chicago (N.L.)		8	12	.400	4.51	1.46	34	34	0	0		0	0-0	201.1	225	110	101	32	69-6	160	.287
1998—Chicago (N.L.)		15	8	.652	4.46	1.38	33	33	1	0		0	0-0	208.0	204	107	103	27	84-5	149	.260
1999—Chicago (N.L.)		8	*18	.308	5.56	1.41	34	34	4	0		0	0-0	205.2	226	133	127	32	64-4	149	.280
2000—Tampa Bay (A.L.)		6	10	.375	4.58	1.52	23	23	3	1		0	0-0	137.2	160	76	70	16	49-1	78	.294
—Toronto (A.L.)		2	5	.286	5.29	1.54	11	11	0	0		0	0-0	63.0	72	40	37	10	25-1	32	.293
2001—New York (N.L.)		11	13	.458	4.46	1.24	28	28	1	1		0	0-0	173.2	168	90	86	28	47-7	144	.254
—Norfolk (Int'l)		2	0	1.000	2.79	0.98	3	3	1	1		0	0-...	19.1	13	6	6	0	6-0	12	.188
2002—New York (N.L.)		11	11	.500	3.37	1.38	30	30	1	1		0	0-0	173.2	170	80	65	16	69-4	105	.258
—Binghamton (Eastern)		1	0	1.000	0.00	1.24	1	1	0	0		0	0-...	5.2	3	1	0	0	4-0	5	.150
2003—New York (N.L.)		16	10	.615	3.78	1.31	33	33	2	2		0	0-0	204.2	204	90	86	26	65-9	111	.264
2004—New York (N.L.)		12	13	.480	4.00	1.41	33	33	0	0		0	0-0	202.2	203	104	90	25	83-9	117	.262
American League totals (1 year)		8	15	.348	4.80	1.52	34	34	3	1		0	0-0	200.2	232	116	107	26	74-2	110	.294
National League totals (11 years)		110	116	.487	4.17	1.36	311	310	15	6		0	0-0	1901.0	1904	967	881	264	676-59	1306	.262
Major League totals (12 years)		118	131	.474	4.23	1.37	345	344	18	7		0	0-0	2101.2	2136	1083	988	290	750-61	1416	.265

ALL-STAR GAME RECORD

	W	L	Pct.	ERA	WHIP	G	GS	CG	ShO	Hld.	Sv.-Opp.	IP	H	R	ER	HR	BB-IBB	SO	Avg.
All-Star Game totals (1 year)	0	0	...	0.00	0.00	1	0	0	0	0	0-0	1.0	0	0	0	0	0-0	3	.000

T

TRACY, ANDY — 3B

PERSONAL: Born December 11, 1973, in Bowling Green, Ohio. ... 6-3/225. ... Bats left, throws right. ... Full name: Andrew Michael Tracy. ... High school: Bowling Green (Ohio). ... College: Bowling Green (Ohio).

TRANSACTIONS/CAREER NOTES: Selected by Cincinnati Reds organization in 28th round of 1995 free-agent draft; did not sign. ... Selected by Montreal Expos organization in 16th round of 1996 free-agent draft. ... Claimed on waivers by New York Mets (March 27, 2002). ... Released by Mets (April 9, 2003). ... Signed by Colorado Rockies organization (April 25, 2003). ... Refused minor league assignment and became a free agent (October 6, 2004).

2004 GAMES PLAYED BY POSITION (MLB): 3B—1.

											BATTING									FIELDING	
Year	Team (League)	Pos.	G	AB	R	H	2B	3B	HR	RBI	BB	SO	HBP	GDP	SB-CS	Avg.	OBP	SLG	OPS	E	Avg.
1996—Vermont (N.Y.-Penn.)		3B-1B	57	175	26	47	11	1	4	24	32	37	2	8	1-1	.269	.384	.411	.795	6	.987
1997—Cape Fear (S. Atl.)		1B	59	210	31	63	9	2	8	43	21	47	3	4	6-1	.300	.369	.476	.845	8	.985
1998—Jupiter (FSL)		3B-1B	71	251	37	67	16	1	11	53	39	69	3	3	6-4	.267	.366	.470	.836	5	.993
—Harrisburg (East.)		1B-OF	62	211	33	48	12	3	10	33	24	62	4	5	1-2	.227	.314	.455	.769	6	.989
1999—Harrisburg (East.)		3B-1B-OF	134	493	96	135	26	2	37	128	70	139	6	10	6-1	.274	.369	.560	.929	25	.945
2000—Ottawa (Int'l)		1B-3B	55	195	28	60	18	0	10	36	34	63	2	2	2-2	.308	.410	.554	.964	6	.986
—Montreal (N.L.)		1B	83	192	29	50	8	1	11	32	22	61	2	3	1-0	.260	.339	.484	.824	6	.975
2001—Montreal (N.L.)		3B-1B-DH	38	55	4	6	1	0	2	8	6	26	0	1	0-0	.109	.190	.236	.427	0	1.000
—Ottawa (Int'l)		3B-1B	53	190	17	39	11	1	4	19	24	72	2	2	4-2	.205	.300	.337	.636	8	.959
2002—Norfolk (Int'l)		3B-1B	125	432	61	86	16	1	20	61	56	123	3	4	4-1	.199	.295	.380	.675	9	.982
2003—Tulsa (Texas)		3B-1B-DH	106	384	75	115	24	1	25	62	41	116	4	1	3-3	.299	.371	.563	.934	13	.965
2004—Colo. Springs (PCL)		1-3-DH-O	126	464	98	146	42	3	33	120	58	115	2	8	4-2	.315	.390	.631	1.022	12	.987
—Colorado (N.L.)		3B	15	16	1	3	1	0	0	1	1	8	0	0	0-0	.188	.235	.250	.485	0	1.000
Major League totals (3 years)			136	263	34	59	10	1	13	41	29	95	2	4	1-0	.224	.302	.418	.720	6	.978

TRACY, CHAD — 3B

PERSONAL: Born May 22, 1980, in Charlotte, N.C. ... 6-2/200. ... Bats left, throws right. ... Full name: Chad Austin Tracy. ... High school: West Mecklenburg (Charlotte). ... College: East Carolina.

TRANSACTIONS/CAREER NOTES: Selected by Arizona Diamondbacks organization in seventh round of 2001 free-agent draft.

2004 GAMES PLAYED BY POSITION (MLB): 3B—135, 1B—11, OF—1.

											BATTING									FIELDING	
Year	Team (League)	Pos.	G	AB	R	H	2B	3B	HR	RBI	BB	SO	HBP	GDP	SB-CS	Avg.	OBP	SLG	OPS	E	Avg.
2001—Yakima (N'west)		3B	10	36	2	10	1	0	0	5	3	5	1	1	1-0	.278	.350	.306	.656	0	1.000
—South Bend (Mid.)		3B-1B	54	215	43	73	11	0	4	36	19	19	2	4	3-0	.340	.393	.447	.840	17	.896
2002—El Paso (Texas)		3B-1B	129	514	80	177	39	5	8	74	38	51	4	10	2-3	.344	.389	.486	.875	26	.931
2003—Tucson (PCL)		3B	133	522	91	169	31	4	10	80	41	52	4	5	0-2	.324	.372	.456	.827	20	.951
2004—Tucson (PCL)		3B-OF	11	40	7	16	4	0	2	11	8	5	0	0	2-0	.400	.490	.650	1.140	3	.921
—Arizona (N.L.)		3B-1B-OF	143	481	45	137	29	3	8	53	45	60	0	11	2-3	.285	.343	.407	.750	26	.938
Major League totals (1 year)			143	481	45	137	29	3	8	53	45	60	0	11	2-3	.285	.343	.407	.750	26	.938

TREANOR, MATT — C

PERSONAL: Born March 3, 1976, in Garden Grove, Calif. ... 6-2/220. ... Bats right, throws right. ... Full name: Matthew Aaron Treanor. ... High school: Mater Dei (Calif.).

TRANSACTIONS/CAREER NOTES: Selected by Kansas City Royals organization in fourth round of 1994 free-agent draft. ... Traded by Royals to Florida Marlins for P Matt Whisenant (July 29, 1997).

2004 GAMES PLAYED BY POSITION (MLB): C—27.

											BATTING									FIELDING	
Year	Team (League)	Pos.	G	AB	R	H	2B	3B	HR	RBI	BB	SO	HBP	GDP	SB-CS	Avg.	OBP	SLG	OPS	E	Avg.
1994—GC Royals (GCL)		C-2B-OF	46	99	17	18	5	0	1	12	14	23	3	2	1-1	.182	.299	.263	.562	6	.968
1995—Springfield (Midw.)		C	75	211	17	39	6	2	3	19	21	59	4	1	1-1	.185	.269	.275	.544	11	.976
1996—Lansing (Midw.)		C-OF	119	384	56	100	18	2	6	33	35	63	13	9	5-3	.260	.342	.365	.706	16	.978
1997—Wilmington (Caro.)		C	80	257	22	51	6	1	5	25	25	59	2	4	1-6	.198	.275	.288	.563	12	.978
—Brevard County (FSL)		C	23	70	11	15	4	1	0	3	12	14	2	1	0-0	.214	.345	.300	.645	0	1.000
1998—Brevard County (FSL)		C-3B-1B	80	243	24	57	8	0	3	28	38	45	5	4	3-2	.235	.346	.305	.651	4	.989
1999—Kane Co. (Midw.)		C	86	308	56	88	21	1	10	53	36	65	15	9	4-1	.286	.385	.458	.843	8	.988
2000—Brevard County (FSL)		C-1B	109	350	51	86	17	0	3	37	48	65	14	6	3-3	.246	.357	.320	.677	12	.986
2001—GC Marlins (GCL)		C	11	34	10	14	4	0	1	4	7	7	0	0	3-0	.412	.512	.618	1.130	1	.968
—Kane Co. (Midw.)		C	1	1	2	1	0	0	0	0	3	0	0	0	0-0	1.000	1.000	1.000	2.000	0	1.000
—Portland (East.)		C-1B	35	89	7	14	2	0	2	8	13	18	9	1	1-1	.157	.324	.247	.572	1	.996
2002—Portland (East.)		C	50	156	24	39	5	1	9	28	28	33	7	5	3-0	.250	.387	.468	.855	9	.977
—Calgary (PCL)		C-1B	36	95	10	27	8	0	1	18	12	13	5	4	1-1	.284	.393	.400	.793	3	.984
2003—Albuquerque (PCL)		C	98	315	45	86	18	1	11	40	39	44	17	8	9-4	.273	.380	.441	.821	11	.984
2004—Albuquerque (PCL)		C	62	198	32	51	8	0	8	38	33	44	10	5	2-0	.258	.385	.419	.781	4	.991
—Florida (N.L.)		C	29	55	7	13	2	0	0	1	4	13	2	3	0-0	.236	.311	.273	.584	3	.976
Major League totals (1 year)			29	55	7	13	2	0	0	1	4	13	2	3	0-0	.236	.311	.273	.584	3	.976

TREMIE, CHRIS — C

PERSONAL: Born October 17, 1969, in Houston, Texas. ... 6-0/215. ... Bats right, throws right. ... Full name: Christopher James Tremie. ... High school: South Houston. ... College: Houston.

TRANSACTIONS/CAREER NOTES: Selected by Houston Astros organization in 41st round of 1988 free-agent draft; did not sign. ... Selected by Chicago White Sox organization in 39th round of 1992 free-agent draft. ... Selected by Philadelphia Phillies organization from White Sox organization in Rule 5 minor league draft (December 9, 1996). ... Traded by Phillies to Texas Rangers for cash (March 29, 1998). ... Signed as a free agent by Pittsburgh Pirates organization (December 22, 1998). ... Signed as a free agent by Florida Marlins organization (November 2, 1999). ... Contract purchased by Marlins organization from Atlantic City of the independent Atlantic League (July 24, 2000). ... Signed as a free agent by Houston Astros organization (December 18, 2000).

2004 GAMES PLAYED BY POSITION (MLB): C—1.

											BATTING									FIELDING	
Year	Team (League)	Pos.	G	AB	R	H	2B	3B	HR	RBI	BB	SO	HBP	GDP	SB-CS	Avg.	OBP	SLG	OPS	E	Avg.
1992—Utica (N.Y.-Penn)		C	6	16	1	1	0	0	0	0	0	5	0	0	0-0	.063	.063	.063	.125	1	.977
1993—Hickory (S. Atl.)		C	49	155	7	29	6	1	1	17	9	26	4	5	0-0	.187	.250	.258	.508	4	.990
—GC Whi. Sox (GCL)		C	2	4	0	0	0	0	0	0	0	0	0	...	0-...	.000	...	.000	...	0	1.000
—Sarasota (Fla. St.)		C	14	37	2	6	1	0	0	5	2	4	3	1	0-0	.162	.262	.189	.451	0	1.000

Year Team (League)	Pos.	G	AB	R	H	2B	3B	HR	RBI	BB	SO	HBP	GDP	SB-CS	Avg.	OBP	SLG	OPS	E	Avg.
1994— Birmingham (Sou.)	C	92	302	32	68	13	0	2	29	17	44	6	3	4-1	.225	.278	.288	.566	6	.991
1995— Nashville (A.A.)	C	67	190	13	38	4	0	2	16	13	37	2	6	0-0	.200	.259	.253	.511	1	.998
— Chicago (A.L.)	C-DH	10	24	0	4	0	0	0	0	1	2	0	0	0-0	.167	.200	.167	.367	1	.976
1996— Nashville (A.A.)	C	70	215	17	47	10	1	0	26	18	48	2	4	2-0	.219	.282	.274	.556	2	.996
1997— Reading (East.)	C	97	295	20	60	11	1	2	31	36	61	5	7	0-5	.203	.296	.268	.564	4	.995
1998— Oklahoma (PCL)	C	78	247	35	55	10	0	0	12	24	47	5	12	1-1	.223	.303	.263	.566	3	.995
— Texas (A.L.)	DH	2	3	2	1	1	0	0	0	1	1	0	0	0-0	.333	.500	.667	1.167	...	...
1999— Nashville (PCL)	C-3B	47	121	20	30	7	0	3	16	14	29	2	4	4-0	.248	.331	.380	.711	4	.988
— Pittsburgh (N.L.)	C	9	14	1	1	0	0	0	1	2	4	0	0	0-0	.071	.188	.071	.259	0	1.000
2000— Calgary (PCL)	C-3B	46	120	16	32	7	1	2	17	15	24	0	4	0-1	.267	.348	.392	.740	1	.995
2001— Round Rock (Texas)	C-1B	66	220	28	50	7	0	5	28	22	33	2	8	0-4	.227	.302	.327	.629	4	.993
— New Orleans (PCL)	C	8	17	0	2	1	0	0	2	4	2	0	0	0-0	.118	.273	.176	.449	0	1.000
2002— Round Rock (Texas)	C-3B-1B	50	134	16	31	3	0	2	19	13	18	0	3	0-1	.231	.295	.299	.594	2	.990
2003— Round Rock (Texas)	C-1-3-DH	93	301	33	73	11	1	9	35	26	50	5	10	0-1	.243	.309	.375	.684	8	.988
2004— New Orleans (PCL)	C	69	195	23	47	6	1	2	24	24	30	5	7	0-1	.241	.332	.313	.645	8	.982
— Houston (N.L.)	C	1	0	0	0	0	0	0	0	0	0	0	0	0-0	...	...	...	...	0	...
American League totals (2 years)		12	27	2	5	1	0	0	0	2	3	0	0	0-0	.185	.241	.222	.464	1	.976
National League totals (2 years)		10	14	1	1	0	0	0	1	2	4	0	0	0-0	.071	.188	.071	.259	0	1.000
Major League totals (4 years)		22	41	3	6	1	0	0	1	4	7	0	0	0-0	.146	.222	.171	.393	1	.986

TSAO, CHIN-HUI — P

PERSONAL: Born June 2, 1981, in Hua-Lien, Taiwan. ... 6-2/177. ... Throws right, bats right. ... Full name: Chin-Hui Tsao.

TRANSACTIONS/CAREER NOTES: Signed as a non-drafted free agent by Colorado Rockies organization (October 7, 1999). ... On disabled list (August 27-September 16, 2003).

CAREER HITTING: 2-for-13 (.154), 2 R, 1 2B, 0 3B, 0 HR, 0 RBI.

Year Team (League)	W	L	Pct.	ERA	WHIP	G	GS	CG	ShO	Hld.	Sv.-Opp.	IP	H	R	ER	HR	BB-IBB	SO	Avg.
2000— Asheville (S. Atl.)	11	8	.579	2.73	1.10	24	24	0	0	...	0-...	145.0	119	54	44	8	40-0	187	.220
2001— Salem (Caro.)	0	4	.000	4.67	1.62	4	4	0	0	...	0-...	17.1	23	11	9	1	5-0	18	.333
2002— Tri-Cities (N'west)	0	0	...	0.00	0.73	3	3	0	0	...	0-...	11.0	6	2	0	0	2-0	16	.150
— Salem (Caro.)	4	2	.667	2.09	0.97	9	9	0	0	...	0-...	47.1	34	13	11	3	12-0	45	.204
2003— Tulsa (Texas)	11	4	.733	2.46	1.01	18	18	0	0	...	0-...	113.1	88	34	31	7	26-0	125	.214
— Colorado (N.L.)	3	3	.500	6.02	1.57	9	8	0	0	0	0-0	43.1	48	30	29	11	20-1	29	.284
2004— Asheville (S. Atl.)	1	0	1.000	1.80	0.90	2	2	0	0	...	0-...	10.0	8	2	2	1	1-0	14	.211
— Tulsa (Texas)	1	1	.500	2.77	1.08	2	2	0	0	...	0-...	13.0	12	4	4	1	2-0	10	.261
— Colo. Springs (PCL)	1	1	.500	8.53	2.13	4	4	0	0	...	0-...	12.2	22	12	12	5	5-0	14	.379
— Colorado (N.L.)	0	0	...	3.86	0.86	10	0	0	0	1	1-2	9.1	7	4	4	2	1-0	11	.200
Major League totals (2 years)	3	3	.500	5.64	1.44	19	8	0	0	1	1-2	52.2	55	34	33	13	21-1	40	.270

TUCKER, MICHAEL — OF

PERSONAL: Born June 25, 1971, in South Boston, Va. ... 6-2/195. ... Bats left, throws right. ... Full name: Michael Anthony Tucker. ... High school: Bluestone (Skipwith, Va.). ... College: Longwood College (Va.).

TRANSACTIONS/CAREER NOTES: Selected by Kansas City Royals organization in first round (10th pick overall) of 1992 free-agent draft. ... On disabled list (June 4-21 and August 28, 1996-remainder of season); included rehabilitation assignment to Wichita. ... Traded by Royals with IF Keith Lockhart to Atlanta Braves for OF Jermaine Dye and P Jamie Walker (March 27, 1997). ... Traded by Braves with Ps Denny Neagle and Rob Bell to Cincinnati Reds for 2B Bret Boone and P Mike Remlinger (November 10, 1998). ... Traded by Reds to Chicago Cubs for Ps Chris Booker and Ben Shaffar (July 20, 2001). ... Traded by Cubs to Royals for a player to be named (December 19, 2001); Cubs acquired P Shawn Sonnier to complete deal (March 15, 2002). ... On disabled list (August 5-September 24, 2003). ... Signed as a free agent by San Francisco Giants (December 7, 2003).

2004 GAMES PLAYED BY POSITION (MLB): OF—124.

Year Team (League)	Pos.	G	AB	R	H	2B	3B	HR	RBI	BB	SO	HBP	GDP	SB-CS	Avg.	OBP	SLG	OPS	E	Avg.
1993— Wilmington (Caro.)	2B	61	239	42	73	14	2	6	44	34	49	2	0	12-2	.305	.391	.456	.847	10	.965
— Memphis (Sou.)	2B	72	244	38	68	7	4	9	35	42	51	6	1	12-5	.279	.392	.451	.843	13	.962
1994— Omaha (A.A.)	OF	132	485	75	134	16	7	21	77	69	111	3	6	11-3	.276	.366	.468	.834	7	.967
1995— Kansas City (A.L.)	OF-DH	62	177	23	46	10	0	4	17	18	51	1	3	2-3	.260	.332	.384	.716	1	.986
— Omaha (A.A.)	OF	71	275	37	84	18	4	4	28	24	39	4	3	11-4	.305	.367	.444	.811	2	.986
1996— Kansas City (A.L.) OF-1B-DH		108	339	55	88	18	4	12	53	40	69	7	7	10-4	.260	.346	.442	.789	2	.992
— Wichita (Texas)	OF-1B	6	20	4	9	1	3	0	7	5	4	0	0	0-2	.450	.538	.800	1.338	0	1.000
1997— Atlanta (N.L.)	OF	138	499	80	141	25	7	14	56	44	116	6	7	12-7	.283	.347	.445	.792	5	.980
1998— Atlanta (N.L.)	OF	130	414	54	101	27	3	13	46	49	112	3	4	8-3	.244	.327	.418	.745	1	.995
1999— Cincinnati (N.L.)	OF	133	296	55	75	8	5	11	44	37	81	3	5	11-4	.253	.338	.426	.764	2	.990
2000— Cincinnati (N.L.)	OF-2B	148	270	55	72	13	4	15	36	44	64	7	6	13-6	.267	.381	.511	.892	5	.969
2001— Cincinnati (N.L.)	OF	86	231	31	56	10	1	7	30	23	55	1	4	12-5	.242	.308	.385	.693	3	.978
— Chicago (N.L.)	OF-1B	63	205	31	54	9	7	5	31	23	47	1	4	4-3	.263	.339	.449	.788	3	.978
2002— Kansas City (A.L.)	O-DH-1-2	144	475	65	118	27	6	12	56	56	105	3	5	23-9	.248	.330	.406	.737	4	.985
2003— Kansas City (A.L.)	OF-DH	104	389	61	102	20	5	13	55	39	88	2	8	8-10	.262	.331	.440	.771	2	.989
2004— San Francisco (N.L.)	OF	140	464	77	119	21	6	13	62	70	106	2	5	5-2	.256	.353	.412	.765	6	.978
American League totals (4 years)		418	1380	204	354	75	15	41	181	153	313	13	23	43-26	.257	.335	.422	.756	9	.988
National League totals (6 years)		838	2379	383	618	113	33	78	305	290	581	23	35	65-30	.260	.343	.433	.777	25	.981
Major League totals (10 years)		1256	3759	587	972	188	48	119	486	443	894	36	58	108-56	.259	.340	.429	.769	34	.984

DIVISION SERIES RECORD

Year Team (League)	Pos.	G	AB	R	H	2B	3B	HR	RBI	BB	SO	HBP	GDP	SB-CS	Avg.	OBP	SLG	OPS	E	Avg.
1997— Atlanta (N.L.)	OF	2	6	0	1	0	0	0	1	0	1	0	0	0-0	.167	.167	.167	.333	0	1.000
1998— Atlanta (N.L.)	OF	3	8	1	2	0	0	1	2	2	0	0	0	1-0	.250	.400	.625	1.025	0	1.000
Division series totals (2 years)		5	14	1	3	0	0	1	3	2	1	0	0	1-0	.214	.313	.429	.741	0	1.000

CHAMPIONSHIP SERIES RECORD

Year Team (League)	Pos.	G	AB	R	H	2B	3B	HR	RBI	BB	SO	HBP	GDP	SB-CS	Avg.	OBP	SLG	OPS	E	Avg.
1997— Atlanta (N.L.)	OF	5	10	1	1	0	0	1	1	3	4	0	0	0-0	.100	.308	.400	.708	0	1.000
1998— Atlanta (N.L.)	OF	6	13	1	5	1	0	1	5	2	5	0	0	0-0	.385	.467	.692	1.159	0	1.000
Champ. series totals (2 years)		11	23	2	6	1	0	2	6	5	9	0	0	0-0	.261	.393	.565	.958	0	1.000

TUCKER, T.J. — P

PERSONAL: Born August 20, 1978, in Clearwater, Fla. ... 6-3/266. ... Throws right, bats right. ... Full name: Thomas John Tucker. ... High school: River Ridge (New Port Richey, Fla.).

TRANSACTIONS/CAREER NOTES: Selected by Montreal Expos organization in supplemental round ("sandwich pick" between first and second rounds, 47th pick overall) of 1997 free-agent draft; pick received as compensation for Chicago Cubs signing free-agent P Mel Rojas. ... On disabled list (June 10, 2000-remainder of season; and August 18-September 6, 2002). ... On disabled list (August 18-September 6, 2002).

CAREER HITTING: 10-for-36 (.278), 4 R, 1 2B, 0 3B, 0 HR, 0 RBI.

Year Team (League)	W	L	Pct.	ERA	WHIP	G	GS	CG	ShO	Hld.	Sv.-Opp.	IP	H	R	ER	HR	BB-IBB	SO	Avg.
1997— GC Expos (GCL)	1	0	1.000	1.93	1.29	3	2	0	0	...	0-...	4.2	5	1	1	0	1-0	11	.278
1998— GC Expos (GCL)	1	0	1.000	0.75	0.78	7	7	0	0	...	0-...	36.0	23	5	3	1	5-0	40	.178
— Vermont (NY-P)	3	1	.750	2.18	1.18	6	6	0	0	...	0-...	33.0	24	9	8	0	15-0	34	.205
— Jupiter (FSL)	1	1	.500	1.00	0.56	2	1	0	0	...	0-...	9.0	5	1	1	0	0-0	10	.167
1999— Jupiter (FSL)	5	1	.833	1.23	0.91	7	7	0	0	...	0-...	44.0	24	7	6	2	16-0	35	.156
— Harrisburg (Eastern)	8	5	.615	4.10	1.27	19	19	1	1	...	0-...	116.1	110	55	53	12	38-0	85	.249
2000— Harrisburg (Eastern)	2	1	.667	3.60	1.11	8	8	0	0	...	0-...	45.0	33	19	18	7	17-0	24	.208
— Montreal (N.L.)	0	1	.000	11.57	2.00	2	2	0	0	0	0-0	7.0	11	9	9	5	3-0	2	.344
2001— Harrisburg (Eastern)	5	5	.500	3.73	1.39	13	13	0	0	...	0-...	82.0	77	38	34	10	37-0	57	.255
— Ottawa (Int'l)	3	5	.375	3.11	1.20	14	14	1	0	...	0-...	84.0	68	42	29	11	33-0	63	.220
2002— Montreal (N.L.)	6	3	.667	4.11	1.63	57	0	0	0	17	4-7	61.1	69	32	28	5	31-9	42	.290
2003— Edmonton (PCL)	1	0	1.000	2.76	1.40	3	3	0	0	...	0-...	16.1	16	5	5	2	7-0	6	.262
— Montreal (N.L.)	2	3	.400	4.73	1.38	45	7	0	0	3	0-2	80.0	90	49	42	8	20-1	47	.278
2004— Edmonton (PCL)	2	0	1.000	4.86	1.86	3	3	0	0	...	0-...	16.2	26	15	9	3	5-0	3	.342
— Montreal (N.L.)	4	2	.667	3.72	1.33	54	1	0	0	3	0-2	67.2	73	28	28	5	17-6	44	.275
Major League totals (4 years)	12	9	.571	4.46	1.45	158	10	0	0	23	4-11	216.0	243	118	107	23	71-16	135	.283

TURNBOW, DERRICK — P

PERSONAL: Born January 25, 1978, in Union City, Tenn. ... 6-3/210. ... Throws right, bats right. ... Full name: Thomas Derrick Turnbow. ... High school: Franklin (Tenn.).

TRANSACTIONS/CAREER NOTES: Selected by Philadelphia Phillies organization in fifth round of 1997 free-agent draft. ... Selected by Anaheim Angels from Phillies organization in Rule 5 major league draft (December 13, 1999). ... On disabled list (April 20, 2001-remainder of season). ... Claimed on waivers by Milwaukee Brewers (October 14, 2004).

CAREER HITTING: 0-for-1 (.000), 0 R, 0 2B, 0 3B, 0 HR, 0 RBI.

Year Team (League)	W	L	Pct.	ERA	WHIP	G	GS	CG	ShO	Hld.	Sv.-Opp.	IP	H	R	ER	HR	BB-IBB	SO	Avg.
1997— Martinsville (App.)	1	3	.250	7.40	2.05	7	7	0	0	...	0-...	24.1	34	29	20	5	16-1	7	.354
1998— Martinsville (App.)	2	6	.250	5.01	1.31	13	13	1	0	...	0-...	70.0	66	44	39	7	26-1	45	.249
1999— Piedmont (S. Atl.)	12	8	.600	3.35	1.14	26	26	4	1	...	0-...	161.0	130	67	60	10	53-0	149	.221
2000— Anaheim (A.L.)	0	0	...	4.74	1.89	24	1	0	0	1	0-...	38.0	36	21	20	7	36-...	25	.254
2001— Arkansas (Texas)	0	0	...	2.57	1.21	3	3	0	0	...	0-...	14.0	12	4	4	0	5-0	11	.240
2002— Ariz. Angels (Ariz.)	0	1	.000	4.50	1.00	3	3	0	0	...	0-...	8.0	5	5	4	0	3-0	12	.161
— Rancho Cuca. (Calif.)	0	0	...	5.25	2.08	13	0	0	0	...	0-...	12.0	16	11	7	1	9-0	14	.320
2003— Arkansas (Texas)	1	0	1.000	0.00	0.60	7	0	0	0	...	3-...	14.0	4	0	0	0	5-0	19	.087
— Salt Lake (PCL)	1	2	.333	5.73	1.70	35	0	0	0	...	2-...	55.0	68	36	35	5	24-0	63	.300
— Anaheim (A.L.)	2	0	1.000	0.59	0.65	11	0	0	0	0	0-0	15.1	7	1	1	0	3-0	15	.140
2004— Anaheim (A.L.)	0	0	...	0.00	1.42	4	0	0	0	0	0-0	6.1	2	0	0	0	7-0	3	.105
— Salt Lake (PCL)	2	6	.250	5.06	1.57	46	3	0	0	...	6-...	74.2	75	46	42	8	42-0	56	.275
Major League totals (3 years)	2	0	1.000	3.17	1.53	39	1	0	0	1	0-0	59.2	45	22	21	7	46-0	43	.213

UPTON, B.J. — SS

PERSONAL: Born August 21, 1984, in Norfolk, Va. ... 6-3/180. ... Bats right, throws right. ... Full name: Melvin Emanuel Upton. ... High school: Greenbrier Christian Academy (Chesapeake, Va.).

TRANSACTIONS/CAREER NOTES: Selected by Tampa Bay Devil Rays organization in first round (second pick overall) of 2002 free-agent draft.

2004 GAMES PLAYED BY POSITION (MLB): SS—16, DH—14, 3B—13, OF—1.

			BATTING																FIELDING	
Year Team (League)	Pos.	G	AB	R	H	2B	3B	HR	RBI	BB	SO	HBP	GDP	SB-CS	Avg.	OBP	SLG	OPS	E	Avg.
2003— Char., S.C. (SAL)	SS	101	384	70	116	22	6	7	46	57	80	5	8	38-17	.302	.394	.445	.839	42	.907
— Orlando (South.)	SS	29	105	14	29	8	0	1	16	16	25	2	1	2-4	.276	.376	.381	.757	14	.879
2004— Montgom. (Sou.)	SS-DH	29	104	21	34	7	1	2	15	14	28	0	0	3-0	.327	.407	.471	.878	10	.900
— Durham (Int'l)	SS-DH	69	264	65	82	17	1	12	36	42	72	3	9	17-5	.311	.411	.519	.924	25	.916
— Tampa Bay (A.L.)	SS-DH-3B-OF	45	159	19	41	8	2	4	12	15	46	1	1	4-1	.258	.324	.409	.733	9	.905
Major League totals (1 year)		45	159	19	41	8	2	4	12	15	46	1	1	4-1	.258	.324	.409	.733	9	.905

URBINA, UGUETH — P

PERSONAL: Born February 15, 1974, in Caracas, Venezuela. ... 6-0/205. ... Throws right, bats right. ... Full name: Ugueth Urtain Urbina. ... Name pronounced: oo-get oor-bee-NAH. ... High school: Liceo Peres Bonalde de Miranda (Miranda, Venezuala).

TRANSACTIONS/CAREER NOTES: Signed as a non-drafted free agent by Montreal Expos organization (July 2, 1990). ... On disabled list (May 9, 2000-remainder of season). ... Traded by Expos to Boston Red Sox for Ps Tomo Ohka and Rich Rundles (July 31, 2001). ... Signed as a free agent by Texas Rangers (December 20, 2002). ... Traded by Rangers to Florida Marlins for 1B Adrian Gonzalez, P Ryan Snare and OF Will Smith (July 11, 2003). ... Signed as a free agent by Detroit Tigers (March 29, 2004).

HONORS: Named N.L. Fireman of the Year by THE SPORTING NEWS (1999).

CAREER HITTING: 5-for-53 (.094), 3 R, 0 2B, 0 3B, 0 HR, 1 RBI.

Year Team (League)	W	L	Pct.	ERA	WHIP	G	GS	CG	ShO	Hld.	Sv.-Opp.	IP	H	R	ER	HR	BB-IBB	SO	Avg.
1991— GC Expos (GCL)	3	3	.500	2.29	1.08	10	10	3	1	...	0-...	63.0	58	24	16	2	10-0	51	.244
1992— Albany (S. Atl.)	7	13	.350	3.22	1.16	24	24	5	2	...	0-...	142.1	111	68	51	14	54-0	100	.215
1993— Burlington (Midw.)	2	3	.400	4.50	1.37	10	8	0	0	...	0-...	46.0	41	31	23	7	22-1	30	.105
— Harrisburg (Eastern)	4	5	.444	3.99	1.40	11	11	3	1	...	0-...	70.0	66	32	31	5	32-1	45	.259
1994— Harrisburg (Eastern)	9	3	.750	3.28	1.14	21	21	0	0	...	0-...	120.2	95	49	44	11	43-0	86	.216
1995— W.P. Beach (FSL)	1	0	1.000	0.00	0.56	2	2	0	0	...	0-...	9.0	4	0	0	0	1-0	11	.143
— Ottawa (Int'l)	6	2	.750	3.04	1.06	13	11	2	1	...	0-...	68.0	46	26	23	1	26-0	55	.191
— Montreal (N.L.)	2	2	.500	6.17	1.71	7	4	0	0	0	0-0	23.1	26	17	16	6	14-1	15	.280

Year Team (League)	W	L	Pct.	ERA	WHIP	G	GS	CG	ShO	Hld.	Sv.-Opp.	IP	H	R	ER	HR	BB-IBB	SO	Avg.
1996— W.P. Beach (FSL)	1	1	.500	1.29	1.14	3	3	0	0	...	0-...	14.0	13	3	2	0	3-0	21	.255
— Ottawa (Int'l)	2	0	1.000	2.66	0.97	5	5	0	0	...	0-...	23.2	17	9	7	2	6-0	28	.195
— Montreal (N.L.)	10	5	.667	3.71	1.28	33	17	0	0	6	0-1	114.0	102	54	47	18	44-4	108	.234
1997— Montreal (N.L.)	5	8	.385	3.78	1.26	63	0	0	0	1	27-32	64.1	52	29	27	9	29-2	84	.215
1998— Montreal (N.L.)	6	3	.667	1.30	1.01	64	0	0	0	0	34-38	69.1	37	11	10	2	33-2	94	.157
1999— Montreal (N.L.)	6	6	.500	3.69	1.26	71	0	0	0	0	* 41-50	75.2	59	35	31	6	36-6	100	.208
2000— Montreal (N.L.)	0	1	.000	4.05	1.20	13	0	0	0	0	8-10	13.1	11	6	6	1	5-0	22	.224
2001— Montreal (N.L.)	2	1	.667	4.24	1.35	45	0	0	0	1	15-18	46.2	42	24	22	8	21-1	57	.236
— Boston (A.L.)	0	1	.000	2.25	0.95	19	0	0	0	2	9-10	20.0	16	5	5	1	3-0	32	.219
2002— Boston (A.L.)	1	6	.143	3.00	1.07	61	0	0	0	0	40-46	60.0	44	21	20	8	20-5	71	.202
2003— Texas (A.L.)	0	4	.000	4.19	1.32	39	0	0	0	0	26-30	38.2	33	19	18	6	18-2	41	.232
— Florida (N.L.)	3	0	1.000	1.41	0.94	33	0	0	0	11	6-8	38.1	23	6	6	2	13-0	37	.174
2004— Lakeland (Fla. St.)	0	0	...	0.00	1.50	2	0	0	0	0	0-...	2.0	3	3	0	0	0-0	1	.273
— Detroit (A.L.)	4	6	.400	4.50	1.30	54	0	0	0	0	21-24	54.0	38	28	27	7	32-3	56	.194
American League totals (4 years)	5	17	.227	3.65	1.18	173	0	0	0	2	96-110	172.2	131	73	70	22	73-10	200	.208
National League totals (8 years)	34	26	.567	3.34	1.23	329	21	0	0	19	131-157	445.0	352	182	165	52	195-16	517	.213
Major League totals (10 years)	39	43	.476	3.42	1.22	502	21	0	0	21	227-267	617.2	483	255	235	74	268-26	717	.212

DIVISION SERIES RECORD

Year Team (League)	W	L	Pct.	ERA	WHIP	G	GS	CG	ShO	Hld.	Sv.-Opp.	IP	H	R	ER	HR	BB-IBB	SO	Avg.
2003— Florida (N.L.)	0	0	...	3.00	1.67	3	0	0	0	0	1-1	3.0	4	1	1	0	1-1	2	.333

CHAMPIONSHIP SERIES RECORD

Year Team (League)	W	L	Pct.	ERA	WHIP	G	GS	CG	ShO	Hld.	Sv.-Opp.	IP	H	R	ER	HR	BB-IBB	SO	Avg.
2003— Florida (N.L.)	1	0	1.000	2.57	0.29	4	0	0	0	0	1-2	7.0	2	2	2	1	0-0	10	.087

WORLD SERIES RECORD

Year Team (League)	W	L	Pct.	ERA	WHIP	G	GS	CG	ShO	Hld.	Sv.-Opp.	IP	H	R	ER	HR	BB-IBB	SO	Avg.
2003— Florida (N.L.)	0	0	...	6.00	1.67	3	0	0	0	0	2-3	3.0	2	2	2	0	3-0	2	.182

ALL-STAR GAME RECORD

	W	L	Pct.	ERA	WHIP	G	GS	CG	ShO	Hld.	Sv.-Opp.	IP	H	R	ER	HR	BB-IBB	SO	Avg.
All-Star Game totals (2 years)	0	1	.000	13.50	2.00	2	0	0	0	0	0-1	2.0	3	3	3	0	1-0	3	.333

URDANETA, LINO — P

PERSONAL: Born November 20, 1979, in Caracas, Venezuela. ... 6-1/168. ... Throws right, bats right.

TRANSACTIONS/CAREER NOTES: Signed as a non-drafted free agent by Los Angeles Dodgers organization (August 31, 1996). ... Signed as a free agent by Cleveland Indians organization (November 10, 2003). ... Selected by Detroit Tigers from Indians organization in Rule 5 major league draft (December 15, 2003). ... On disabled list (March 29-September 1, 2004); included rehabilitation assignments to Lakeland and Toledo.

CAREER HITTING: 0-for-0 (.000), 0 R, 0 2B, 0 3B, 0 HR, 0 RBI.

Year Team (League)	W	L	Pct.	ERA	WHIP	G	GS	CG	ShO	Hld.	Sv.-Opp.	IP	H	R	ER	HR	BB-IBB	SO	Avg.
1999— Vero Beach (FSL)	5	4	.556	4.84	1.40	27	5	0	0	...	0-...	67.0	74	42	36	10	20-1	43	.286
2000— Vero Beach (FSL)	5	4	.556	5.42	1.63	27	7	0	0	...	0-...	78.0	103	60	47	7	24-1	40	.325
2001— Wilmington (S.Atl.)	1	2	.333	7.61	1.77	10	4	0	0	...	0-...	23.2	31	23	20	7	11-0	16	.330
2002— Vero Beach (FSL)	2	2	.500	2.41	1.07	52	0	0	0	...	32-...	52.1	39	15	14	3	17-3	30	.207
— Jacksonville (Southern)	0	0	...	0.00	4.00	1	0	0	0	...	0-...	1.0	3	0	0	0	1-0	1	.600
2003— Jacksonville (Southern)	0	8	.000	4.29	1.42	44	0	0	0	...	6-...	65.0	68	37	31	4	24-5	42	.280
2004— Lakeland (Fla. St.)	0	2	.000	11.57	2.14	2	2	0	0	...	0-...	2.1	5	3	3	0	0-0	0	.455
— Toledo (International)	0	2	.000	9.69	1.92	9	1	0	0	...	0-...	13.0	22	14	14	4	3-0	4	.379
— Detroit (A.L.)	0	0	...	...	...	1	0	0	0	0	0-...	.0	5	6	6	0	1-0	0	1.000
Major League totals (1 year)	0	0	...	...	...	1	0	0	0	0	0-0	.0	5	6	6	0	1-0	0	1.000

URIBE, JUAN — 2B/SS

PERSONAL: Born July 22, 1979, in Bani, Dominican Republic. ... 5-11/175. ... Bats right, throws right. ... Full name: Juan C. Uribe. ... Name pronounced: ohh-ree-bay. ... High school: Abel Uribe (Dominican Republic).

TRANSACTIONS/CAREER NOTES: Signed as a non-drafted free agent by Colorado Rockies organization (January 15, 1997). ... On disabled list (March 18-June 3, 2003); included rehabilitation assignments to Visalia and Tulsa. ... Traded by Rockies to Chicago White Sox for 2B Aaron Miles (December 2, 2003).

2004 GAMES PLAYED BY POSITION (MLB): 2B—77, SS—38, 3B—27, DH—2.

							BATTING										FIELDING	
Year Team (League)	Pos.	G	AB	R	H	2B	3B	HR	RBI	BB	SO	HBP	GDP	SB-CS	Avg.	OBP	SLG	OPS	E	Avg.
1997— DSL Rockies (DSL)		65	234	32	63	12	0	0	29	31	22	...	...	7-...	.269	...	.321	...		
1998— Ariz. Rockies (Ariz.)	SS	40	148	25	41	5	3	0	17	12	25	3	1	8-1	.277	.339	.351	.691	14	.927
1999— Asheville (S. Atl.)	SS	125	430	57	115	28	3	9	46	20	79	6	12	11-7	.267	.307	.409	.716	38	.938
2000— Salem (Caro.)	SS	134	485	64	124	22	7	13	65	38	100	4	11	22-5	.256	.314	.410	.724	26	.961
2001— Carolina (Southern)	SS	3	13	1	3	1	0	0	1	0	4	0	1	1-0	.231	.231	.308	.538	2	.833
— Colorado (N.L.)	SS	72	273	32	82	15	11	8	53	8	55	2	6	3-0	.300	.325	.524	.849	5	.983
— Colo. Springs (PCL)	SS	74	281	40	87	27	7	7	48	12	43	2	8	11-8	.310	.340	.530	.870	16	.960
2002— Colorado (N.L.)	SS	155	566	69	136	25	7	6	49	34	120	5	17	9-2	.240	.286	.341	.627	27	.966
2003— Visalia (Calif.)	2B-SS	2	9	4	5	1	0	1	1	1	0	1	0	0-0	.556	.600	.667	1.267	0	1.000
— Tulsa (Texas)	2-3-S-OF	5	20	3	5	2	0	1	4	0	2	0	0	0-0	.250	.238	.500	.738	0	1.000
— Colorado (N.L.)	SS-2B-OF	87	316	45	80	19	3	10	33	17	60	3	3	7-2	.253	.297	.427	.724	12	.974
2004— Chicago (A.L.)	2-S-3-DH	134	502	82	142	31	6	23	74	32	96	3	10	9-11	.283	.327	.506	.833	11	.982
American League totals (1 year)		134	502	82	142	31	6	23	74	32	96	3	10	9-11	.283	.327	.506	.833	11	.982
National League totals (3 years)		314	1155	146	298	59	21	24	135	59	235	10	26	19-4	.258	.298	.408	.706	44	.972
Major League totals (4 years)		448	1657	228	440	90	27	47	209	91	331	13	36	28-15	.266	.307	.438	.744	55	.974

UTLEY, CHASE — 2B

PERSONAL: Born December 17, 1978, in Pasadena, Calif. ... 6-1/183. ... Bats left, throws right. ... Full name: Chase Cameron Utley. ... High school: Long Beach Poly (California). ... College: UCLA.

TRANSACTIONS/CAREER NOTES: Selected by Los Angeles Dodgers organization in second round of 1997 free-agent draft; did not sign. ... Selected by Philadelphia Phillies organization in first round (15th pick overall) of 2000 free-agent draft.

2004 GAMES PLAYED BY POSITION (MLB): 2B—50, 1B—13.

Year Team (League)	Pos.	G	AB	R	H	2B	3B	HR	RBI	BB	SO	HBP	GDP	SB-CS	Avg.	OBP	SLG	OPS	E	Avg.
												BATTING							FIELDING	
2000— Batavia (NY-Penn)	2B	40	153	21	47	13	1	2	22	18	23	2	3	5-3	.307	.383	.444	.827	3	.983
2001— Clearwater (FSL)	2B	122	467	65	120	25	2	16	59	37	88	12	6	19-8	.257	.324	.422	.746	17	.970
2002— Scran./W.B. (I.L.)	3B	125	464	73	122	39	1	17	70	46	89	20	5	8-3	.263	.352	.461	.813	28	.918
2003— Scran./W.B. (I.L.)	2B	113	431	80	139	26	2	18	77	41	75	11	3	10-4	.323	.390	.517	.907	13	.978
— Philadelphia (N.L.)	2B	43	134	13	32	10	1	2	21	11	22	6	3	2-0	.239	.322	.373	.696	3	.983
2004— Scran./W.B. (I.L.)	2B	33	123	23	35	8	1	6	25	18	29	0	2	4-2	.285	.368	.512	.880	5	.970
— Philadelphia (N.L.)	2B-1B	94	267	36	71	11	2	13	57	15	40	2	6	4-1	.266	.308	.468	.776	4	.988
Major League totals (2 years)		137	401	49	103	21	3	15	78	26	62	8	9	6-1	.257	.313	.436	.749	7	.986

VALDEZ, ISMAEL   P

PERSONAL: Born August 21, 1973, in Ciudad Victoria, Mexico. ... 6-4/230. ... Throws right, bats right. ... Full name: Ismael Valdes. ... Name pronounced: ees-mah-ALE val-DEZ. ... High school: Mexico (Ciudad Victoria).

TRANSACTIONS/CAREER NOTES: Signed as a non-drafted free agent by Los Angeles Dodgers (June 14, 1991). ... Loaned by Dodgers organization to Mexico City Tigers of the Mexican League (April 21-June 26, 1992; and March 17-August 19, 1993). ... On disabled list (July 6-28, 1997). ... On disabled list (July 26-September 1, 1998); included rehabilitation assignments to Vero Beach and San Bernardino. ... Traded by Dodgers with 2B Eric Young to Chicago Cubs for Ps Terry Adams and Chad Ricketts and a player to be named (December 12, 1999); Dodgers acquired P Brian Stephenson to complete deal (December 16, 1999). ... On disabled list (March 20-May 4, 2000); included rehabilitation assignment to Daytona. ... Traded by Cubs to Dodgers for P Jamie Arnold, OF Jorge Piedra and cash (July 26, 2000). ... On suspended list (September 12-18, 2000). ... Signed as a free agent by Anaheim Angels (January 4, 2001). ... On disabled list (March 29-April 14 and June 15-July 4, 2001). ... Signed as a free agent by Texas Rangers (January 28, 2002). ... Traded by Rangers to Seattle Mariners for 2B Jermaine Clark and P Derrick Van Dusen (August 18, 2002). ... Signed as a free agent by Rangers (January 15, 2003). ... On disabled list (April 20-May 17 and July 24-August 18, 2003); included rehabilitation assignments to Frisco and Oklahoma. ... Signed by San Diego Padres (December 18, 2003). ... Traded by Padres to Florida Marlins for P Travis Chick (July 31, 2004).

CAREER HITTING: 50-for-386 (.130), 20 R, 9 2B, 0 3B, 1 HR, 17 RBI.

Year Team (League)	W	L	Pct.	ERA	WHIP	G	GS	CG	ShO	Hld.	Sv.-Opp.	IP	H	R	ER	HR	BB-IBB	SO	Avg.
1991— GC Dodgers (GCL)	2	2	.500	2.32	1.13	10	10	0	0	...	0-...	50.1	44	15	13	0	13-0	44	.233
1992— M.C. Tigers (Mex.)	0	0	...	19.64	4.36	5	0	0	0	...	0-...	3.2	15	9	8	1	1-...	2	...
— La Vega (DSL)	3	0	1.000	1.42	1.16	6	0	0	0	...	0-...	38.0	27	9	6	0	17-...	34	...
1993— M.C. Tigers (Mex.)	16	7	.696	3.94	1.42	26	25	11	1	...	0-...	173.2	192	87	76	16	55-...	113	...
— San Antonio (Texas)	1	0	1.000	1.38	0.92	3	2	0	0	...	0-...	13.0	12	2	2	0	0-0	11	.240
1994— San Antonio (Texas)	2	3	.400	3.38	1.18	8	8	0	0	...	0-...	53.1	54	22	20	4	9-1	55	.263
— Albuquerque (PCL)	4	1	.800	3.40	1.27	8	8	0	0	...	0-...	45.0	44	21	17	1	13-0	39	.256
— Los Angeles (N.L.)	3	1	.750	3.18	1.09	21	1	0	0	4	0-0	28.1	21	10	10	2	10-2	28	.206
1995— Los Angeles (N.L.)	13	11	.542	3.05	1.11	33	27	6	2	2	1-1	197.2	168	76	67	17	51-5	150	.228
1996— Los Angeles (N.L.)	15	7	.682	3.32	1.21	33	33	0	0	0	0-0	225.0	219	94	83	20	54-10	173	.251
1997— Los Angeles (N.L.)	10	11	.476	2.65	1.11	30	30	0	0	0	0-0	196.2	171	68	58	16	47-1	140	.234
1998— Los Angeles (N.L.)	11	10	.524	3.98	1.36	27	27	2	2	0	0-0	174.0	171	82	77	17	66-4	122	.256
— Vero Beach (FSL)	0	0	...	0.00	1.00	1	1	0	0	...	0-...	3.0	2	0	0	0	1-0	3	.200
— San Bernardino (Calif.)	1	0	1.000	2.84	1.26	1	1	0	0	...	0-...	6.1	7	2	2	0	1-0	4	.280
1999— Los Angeles (N.L.)	9	14	.391	3.98	1.33	32	32	2	1	0	0-0	203.1	213	97	90	32	58-2	143	.270
2000— Daytona (Fla. St.)	1	0	1.000	1.80	1.20	1	1	0	0	...	0-...	5.0	3	2	1	0	3-0	5	.176
— Chicago (N.L.)	2	4	.333	5.37	1.46	12	12	0	0	0	0-0	67.0	71	40	40	17	27-2	45	.273
— Los Angeles (N.L.)	0	3	.000	6.08	1.65	9	8	0	0	0	0-0	40.0	53	29	27	5	13-0	29	.327
2001— Anaheim (A.L.)	9	13	.409	4.45	1.39	27	27	1	0	0	0-0	163.2	177	82	81	20	50-3	100	.277
2002— Texas (A.L.)	6	9	.400	3.93	1.17	23	23	0	0	0	0-0	146.2	135	65	64	19	36-1	75	.242
— Seattle (A.L.)	2	3	.400	4.93	1.42	8	8	1	0	0	0-0	49.1	59	29	27	7	11-0	27	.299
2003— Frisco (Texas)	1	2	.333	2.03	1.10	3	3	0	0	0	0-...	13.1	12	5	3	0	2-0	6	.235
— Texas (A.L.)	8	8	.500	6.10	1.54	22	22	0	0	0	0-0	115.0	148	83	78	23	29-0	47	.318
2004— San Diego (N.L.)	9	6	.600	5.53	1.51	23	20	0	0	0	0-0	114.0	141	75	70	21	31-1	37	.303
— Florida (N.L.)	5	3	.625	4.50	1.41	11	11	0	0	0	0-0	56.0	61	30	28	12	18-2	30	.277
American League totals (3 years)	25	33	.431	4.74	1.36	80	80	2	0	0	0-0	474.2	519	259	250	69	126-4	249	.279
National League totals (8 years)	77	70	.524	3.80	1.28	231	201	11	6	6	1-1	1302.0	1289	601	550	159	375-29	897	.257
Major League totals (11 years)	102	103	.498	4.05	1.30	311	281	13	6	6	1-1	1776.2	1808	860	800	228	501-33	1146	.263

DIVISION SERIES RECORD

Year Team (League)	W	L	Pct.	ERA	WHIP	G	GS	CG	ShO	Hld.	Sv.-Opp.	IP	H	R	ER	HR	BB-IBB	SO	Avg.
1995— Los Angeles (N.L.)	0	0	...	0.00	0.57	1	1	0	0	0	0-0	7.0	3	2	0	1	1-0	6	.125
1996— Los Angeles (N.L.)	0	1	.000	4.26	0.79	1	1	0	0	0	0-0	6.1	5	3	3	3	0-0	5	.208
Division series totals (2 years)	0	1	.000	2.03	0.68	2	2	0	0	0	0-0	13.1	8	5	3	4	1-0	11	.167

VALDEZ, MERKIN   P

PERSONAL: Born November 10, 1981, in San Cristobal, Dominican Republic. ... 6-5/208. ... Throws right, bats right. ... Full name: Merkin R. Valdez. ... Changed name from Manuel Mateo. ... Traded by Braves with P Damian Moss to San Francisco Giants for P Russ Ortiz (December 17, 2002).

TRANSACTIONS/CAREER NOTES: Signed as a non-drafted free agent by Atlanta Braves organization (November 18, 1999). ... Changed name from Manuel Mateo. ... Traded by Braves with P Damian Moss to San Francisco Giants for P Russ Ortiz (December 17, 2002).

CAREER HITTING: 0-for-0 (.000), 0 R, 0 2B, 0 3B, 0 HR, 0 RBI.

Year Team (League)	W	L	Pct.	ERA	WHIP	G	GS	CG	ShO	Hld.	Sv.-Opp.	IP	H	R	ER	HR	BB-IBB	SO	Avg.
2002— GC Braves (GCL)	7	3	.700	1.98	0.86	12	8	1	1	...	0-...	68.1	47	18	15	0	12-0	76	.193
2003— Hagerstown (S. Atl.)	9	5	.643	2.25	1.08	26	26	2	1	...	0-...	156.0	119	42	39	11	49-0	166	.213
2004— Fresno (PCL)	0	0	...	7.20	2.00	1	1	0	0	0	0-...	5.0	6	4	4	0	4-0	5	.333
— San Jose (California)	3	1	.750	2.52	0.98	7	7	0	0	0	0-...	35.2	30	12	10	4	5-0	44	.219
— San Francisco (N.L.)	0	0	...	27.00	4.20	2	0	0	0	0	0-0	1.2	4	5	5	1	3-0	2	.444
— Norwich (East.)	1	4	.200	4.32	1.20	10	7	0	0	0	1-...	41.2	35	21	20	3	15-0	31	.224
Major League totals (1 year)	0	0	...	27.00	4.20	2	0	0	0	0	0-0	1.2	4	5	5	1	3-0	2	.444

VALDEZ, WILSON   SS

PERSONAL: Born May 20, 1978, in Nizao, Dominican Republic. ... 5-11/160. ... Bats right, throws right. ... Full name: Wilson Antonio Valdez. ... High school: Aliro Paulino (Nizao, D.R.).

TRANSACTIONS/CAREER NOTES: Signed as a non-drafted free agent by Montreal Expos organization (February 4, 1997). ... Claimed on waivers by Florida Marlins (March 29, 2002). ... Traded by Marlins to Chicago White Sox for P Billy Koch and cash (June 17, 2004).

2004 GAMES PLAYED BY POSITION (MLB): SS—12, 2B—5.

Year	Team (League)	Pos.	G	AB	R	H	2B	3B	HR	RBI	BB	SO	HBP	GDP	SB-CS	Avg.	OBP	SLG	OPS	E	Avg.
1999— GC Expos (GCL)	SS-2B	22	82	12	24	2	0	0	7	5	7	0	1	10-0	.293	.330	.317	.647	3	.972
— Vermont (N.Y.-Penn.)	SS-2B	36	130	19	32	7	0	1	10	7	21	0	3	4-3	.246	.283	.323	.606	8	.956
2000— Cape Fear (S. Atl.)	2B-SS	15	49	6	12	2	0	0	3	2	9	0	0	3-0	.245	.275	.286	.560	5	.921
— Vermont (N.Y.-Penn.)	SS	65	248	32	66	8	1	1	30	17	32	1	3	16-9	.266	.312	.319	.631	20	.944
2001— Clinton (Midw.)	SS	59	214	31	54	8	1	0	11	9	22	2	5	6-7	.252	.286	.299	.585	11	.966
— Jupiter (FSL)	SS	64	233	34	58	13	2	2	19	10	33	2	4	7-3	.249	.286	.348	.633	8	.971
2002— Portland (East.)	SS	114	375	51	98	19	5	1	30	15	47	4	12	18-6	.261	.294	.347	.641	28	.944
2003— Carolina (Southern)	2B-SS	37	144	28	45	6	2	0	14	15	17	0	2	16-5	.313	.373	.382	.755	4	.978
— Albuquerque (PCL)	SS-2B	90	338	45	97	12	4	0	18	19	37	1	10	33-9	.287	.326	.346	.672	11	.974
2004— Albuquerque (PCL)	SS	66	285	36	91	11	3	2	25	16	35	2	8	19-12	.319	.357	.400	.753	6	.982
— Charlotte (Int'l)	SS	70	281	37	85	7	2	2	15	12	41	3	6	13-5	.302	.338	.363	.694	6	.979
— Chicago (A.L.)	SS-2B	19	43	8	10	1	0	1	4	2	5	0	1	1-2	.233	.267	.326	.592	1	.980
Major League totals (1 year)		19	43	8	10	1	0	1	4	2	5	0	1	1-2	.233	.267	.326	.592	1	.980

VALENT, ERIC   1B/OF

PERSONAL: Born April 4, 1977, in La Mirada, Calif. ... 5-11/195. ... Bats left, throws left. ... Full name: Eric Christian Valent. ... Name pronounced: va-LENT. ... High school: Canyon (Anaheim, Calif.). ... College: UCLA.

TRANSACTIONS/CAREER NOTES: Selected by Detroit Tigers organization in 26th round of 1995 free-agent draft; did not sign. ... Selected by Philadelphia Phillies organization in supplemental round ('sandwich pick' between first and second rounds, 42nd pick overall) of 1998 free-agent draft; pick received as compensation for failure to sign 1997 first-round pick J.D. Drew. ... Traded by Phillies to Cincinnati Reds (September 2, 2003), completing deal in which Reds traded C Kelly Stinnett to Phillies for a player to be named (August 31, 2003). ... Selected by New York Mets organization from Reds organization in Rule 5 minor league draft (December 15, 2003).

2004 GAMES PLAYED BY POSITION (MLB): OF—46, 1B—27.

Year	Team (League)	Pos.	G	AB	R	H	2B	3B	HR	RBI	BB	SO	HBP	GDP	SB-CS	Avg.	OBP	SLG	OPS	E	Avg.
1998— Piedmont (S. Atl.)	OF	22	89	24	38	12	0	8	28	14	19	0	0	0-0	.427	.500	.831	1.331	2	.952
— Clearwater (FSL)	OF	34	125	24	33	8	1	5	25	16	29	3	4	1-2	.264	.359	.464	.823	0	1.000
1999— Clearwater (FSL)	OF	134	520	91	150	31	9	20	106	58	110	5	10	5-3	.288	.359	.498	.857	9	.969
2000— Reading (East.)	OF	128	469	81	121	22	5	22	90	70	89	5	7	2-3	.258	.356	.467	.823	4	.984
2001— Scran./W.B. (I.L.)	OF-1B	117	448	65	122	30	2	21	78	49	105	8	13	0-1	.272	.352	.489	.841	3	.992
— Philadelphia (N.L.)	OF-DH	22	41	3	4	2	0	0	1	4	11	1	0	0-0	.098	.196	.146	.342	0	1.000
2002— Scran./W.B. (I.L.)	OF-1B	140	546	69	137	34	2	9	84	49	94	1	13	0-2	.251	.311	.370	.681	10	.980
— Philadelphia (N.L.)	OF-1B	7	10	1	2	0	0	0	0	0	3	0	1	0-0	.200	.200	.200	.400	1	.750
2003— Scran./W.B. (I.L.)	OF-1B	134	450	62	98	27	2	12	51	60	102	1	5	0-0	.218	.308	.367	.675	8	.974
— Cincinnati (N.L.)	OF	18	42	3	9	0	0	1	2	2	9	0	0	0-0	.214	.250	.214	.464	0	1.000
2004— New York (N.L.)	OF-1B	130	270	39	72	15	2	13	34	28	61	1	10	0-1	.267	.337	.481	.818	1	.996
Major League totals (4 years)		177	363	46	87	17	2	13	36	34	84	2	11	0-1	.240	.308	.405	.712	2	.994

VALENTIN, JAVIER   C

PERSONAL: Born September 19, 1975, in Manati, Puerto Rico. ... 5-10/192. ... Bats both, throws right. ... Full name: Jose Javier Valentin. ... Name pronounced: val-en-TEEN. ... High school: Fernando Callejo (Manati, Puerto Rico). ... Brother of Jose Valentin, shortstop with Chicago White Sox in 2004.

TRANSACTIONS/CAREER NOTES: Selected by Minnesota Twins organization in third round of 1993 free-agent draft. ... Traded by Twins with P Matt Kinney to Milwaukee Brewers for Ps Matt Yeatman and Gerard Oakes (November 15, 2002). ... Traded by Brewers to Tampa Bay Devil Rays for OF Jason Conti (March 24, 2003). ... Refused minor league assignment and became a free agent (October 15, 2003). ... Signed by Cincinnati Reds organization (January 9, 2004).

2004 GAMES PLAYED BY POSITION (MLB): C—55, 1B—7.

Year	Team (League)	Pos.	G	AB	R	H	2B	3B	HR	RBI	BB	SO	HBP	GDP	SB-CS	Avg.	OBP	SLG	OPS	E	Avg.
1993— GC Twins (GCL)	3B-DH-C	32	103	18	27	6	1	1	19	14	19	1	1	0-2	.262	.344	.369	.713	5	.966
— Elizabethton (App.)	C	9	24	3	5	1	0	0	3	4	2	1	0	0-0	.208	.345	.250	.595	2	.977
1994— Elizabethton (App.)	3B-C	54	210	23	44	5	0	9	27	15	44	2	9	0-1	.210	.263	.362	.625	12	.966
1995— Fort Wayne (Midw.)	3B-C	112	383	59	124	26	5	19	65	47	75	2	7	0-5	.324	.400	.567	.967	23	.974
1996— Fort Myers (FSL)	C-DH-3B	87	338	34	89	26	1	7	54	32	65	4	5	1-0	.263	.330	.408	.738	4	.991
— New Britain (East.)	C-3B-DH	48	165	22	39	8	0	3	14	16	35	1	2	0-0	.236	.308	.339	.647	5	.978
1997— New Britain (East.)	C-DH-3B	102	370	41	90	17	0	8	50	30	61	1	5	2-3	.243	.297	.354	.651	6	.990
— Minnesota (A.L.)	C	4	7	1	2	0	0	0	0	0	3	0	0	0-0	.286	.286	.286	.571	0	1.000
1998— Minnesota (A.L.)	C-DH	55	162	11	32	7	1	3	18	11	30	0	7	0-0	.198	.247	.309	.556	5	.984
1999— Minnesota (A.L.)	C	78	218	22	54	12	1	5	28	22	39	1	2	0-0	.248	.313	.381	.694	1	.998
2000— Salt Lake (PCL)	C	39	140	25	50	16	2	7	35	9	27	1	1	1-0	.357	.397	.650	1.047	1	.994
2001— Edmonton (PCL)	C-3B-1B	121	431	53	121	29	2	17	71	47	108	4	14	0-1	.281	.352	.476	.827	14	.977
2002— Edmonton (PCL)	C-3B-1B	127	455	69	130	33	1	21	80	41	96	5	15	0-1	.286	.346	.501	.847	9	.984
— Minnesota (A.L.)	C	4	4	0	2	0	0	0	0	0	0	0	0	0-0	.500	.500	.500	1.000	0	1.000
2003— Tampa Bay (A.L.)	C-DH	49	135	13	30	7	1	3	15	5	31	1	7	0-0	.222	.254	.356	.609	0	1.000
2004— Cincinnati (N.L.)	C-1B	82	202	18	47	10	1	6	20	17	36	1	4	0-0	.233	.293	.381	.674	4	.989
American League totals (5 years)		190	526	47	120	26	3	11	61	38	103	2	16	0-0	.228	.279	.352	.631	6	.994
National League totals (1 year)		82	202	18	47	10	1	6	20	17	36	1	4	0-0	.233	.293	.381	.674	4	.989
Major League totals (6 years)		272	728	65	167	36	4	17	81	55	139	3	20	0-0	.229	.283	.360	.643	10	.993

VALENTIN, JOSE   SS

PERSONAL: Born October 12, 1969, in Manati, Puerto Rico. ... 5-10/195. ... Bats left, throws right. ... Full name: Jose Antonio Valentin. ... Name pronounced: val-en-TEEN. ... High school: Fernando Callejo (Manati, Puerto Rico). ... Brother of Javier Valentin, catcher, Cincinnati Reds.

TRANSACTIONS/CAREER NOTES: Signed as a non-drafted free agent by San Diego Padres organization (October 12, 1986). ... Traded by Padres with P Ricky Bones and OF Matt Mieske to Milwaukee Brewers for 3B Gary Sheffield and P Geoff Kellogg (March 27, 1992). ... On disabled list (April 14-May 5, 1997); included rehabilitation assignment to Beloit. ... On disabled list (April 13-June 16, 1999); included rehabilitation assignment to Louisville. ... Traded by Brewers with P Cal Eldred to Chicago White Sox for Ps Jaime Navarro and John Snyder (January 12, 2000). ... On disabled list (June 8-24, 2001). ... On disabled list (April 19-May 7, 2004); included rehabilitation assignment to Charlotte.

2004 GAMES PLAYED BY POSITION (MLB): SS—122, DH—2.

Year	Team (League)	Pos.	G	AB	R	H	2B	3B	HR	RBI	BB	SO	HBP	GDP	SB-CS	Avg.	OBP	SLG	OPS	E	Avg.
1987— Spokane (N'west)	SS	70	244	52	61	8	2	2	24	35	38	1	4	8-5	.250	.346	.324	.670	26	.914
1988— Char., S.C. (SAL)	SS	133	444	56	103	20	1	6	44	45	83	3	10	11-4	.232	.304	.322	.627	60	.911
1989— Riverside (Calif.)	SS	114	381	40	74	10	5	10	41	37	93	5	4	8-7	.194	.273	.325	.598	46	.924
— Wichita (Texas)	3B-SS	18	49	8	12	1	0	2	5	5	12	0	1	1-0	.245	.315	.388	.703	8	.899

Year Team (League)	Pos.	G	AB	R	H	2B	3B	HR	RBI	BB	SO	HBP	GDP	SB-CS	Avg.	OBP	SLG	OPS	E	Avg.
1990— Wichita (Texas)	SS	11	36	4	10	2	0	0	2	5	7	0	1	2-1	.278	.366	.333	.699	2	.959
1991— Wichita (Texas)	SS	129	447	73	112	22	5	17	68	55	115	4	5	8-6	.251	.335	.436	.771	40	.939
1992— Denver (A.A.)	SS	139	492	78	118	19	11	3	45	53	99	5	8	9-4	.240	.317	.341	.658	38	.941
— Milwaukee (A.L.)	2B-SS	4	3	1	0	0	0	0	1	0	0	0	0	0-0	.000	.000	.000	.000	1	.667
1993— New Orleans (A.A.)	SS-1B	97	389	56	96	22	5	9	53	47	87	8	3	9-10	.247	.337	.398	.736	29	.951
— Milwaukee (A.L.)	SS	19	53	10	13	1	2	1	7	7	16	1	1	1-0	.245	.344	.396	.740	6	.922
1994— Milwaukee (A.L.)	SS-2-3-DH	97	285	47	68	19	0	11	46	38	75	2	1	12-3	.239	.330	.421	.751	‡ 20	.961
1995— Milwaukee (A.L.)	SS-DH-3B	112	338	62	74	23	5	11	49	37	83	0	0	16-8	.219	.293	.402	.695	15	.971
1996— Milwaukee (A.L.)	SS-DH	154	552	90	143	33	7	24	95	66	145	4	4	17-4	.259	.336	.475	.811	* 37	.950
1997— Milwaukee (A.L.)	SS-DH	136	494	58	125	23	1	17	58	39	109	4	5	19-8	.253	.310	.407	.717	20	.967
— Beloit (Midw.)	SS	2	6	3	3	1	0	0	2	1	0	0	0	0-0	.500	.625	.667	1.292	0	1.000
1998— Milwaukee (N.L.)	SS-DH	151	428	65	96	24	0	16	49	63	105	1	2	10-7	.224	.323	.418	.716	21	.963
1999— Milwaukee (N.L.)	SS	89	256	45	58	9	5	10	38	48	52	2	3	3-2	.227	.347	.418	.765	22	.937
— Louisville (Int'l)	SS	6	20	6	5	0	0	3	3	4	3	0	0	0-1	.250	.375	.700	1.075	0	1.000
2000— Chicago (A.L.)	SS-OF	144	568	107	155	37	6	25	92	59	106	4	11	19-2	.273	.343	.491	.835	‡ 36	.950
2001— Chicago (A.L.)	SS-OF	124	438	74	113	22	2	28	68	50	114	3	7	9-6	.258	.336	.509	.845	22	.947
2002— Chicago (A.L.)	3B-SS-DH	135	474	70	118	26	4	25	75	43	99	2	9	3-3	.249	.311	.479	.790	19	.957
2003— Chicago (A.L.)	SS-DH	144	503	79	119	26	2	28	74	54	114	3	6	8-3	.237	.313	.463	.776	20	.969
2004— Charlotte (Int'l)	SS-DH	8	31	1	2	0	0	0	0	2	15	0	0	0-0	.065	.121	.065	.186	2	.895
— Chicago (A.L.)	SS-DH	125	450	73	97	20	3	30	70	43	139	3	5	8-6	.216	.287	.473	.760	20	.965
American League totals (11 years)		1194	4158	671	1025	230	30	200	635	436	1000	22	49	112-43	.247	.319	.461	.780	216	.959
National League totals (2 years)		240	684	110	154	33	5	26	87	111	157	3	5	13-9	.225	.333	.402	.735	43	.953
Major League totals (13 years)		1434	4842	781	1179	263	35	226	722	547	1157	25	54	125-52	.243	.321	.452	.773	259	.958

DIVISION SERIES RECORD

Year Team (League)	Pos.	G	AB	R	H	2B	3B	HR	RBI	BB	SO	HBP	GDP	SB-CS	Avg.	OBP	SLG	OPS	E	Avg.
2000— Chicago (A.L.)	SS	3	10	2	3	2	0	1	2	2	0	0	0	3-0	.300	.417	.500	.917	1	.964

VALENTINE, JOE   P

PERSONAL: Born December 24, 1979, in Las Vegas, Nev. ... 6-2/210. ... Throws right, bats right. ... Full name: Joseph John Valentine. ... Junior college: Jefferson Davis (Ala.) Community College.
TRANSACTIONS/CAREER NOTES: Selected by Chicago White Sox organization in 26th round of 1999 free-agent draft. ... Selected by Montreal Expos from White Sox organization in Rule 5 major league draft (December 13, 2001). ... Traded by Expos to Detroit Tigers for cash (December 13, 2001). ... Returned to White Sox organization (April 1, 2002). ... Traded by White Sox with P Keith Foulke, C Mark Johnson and cash to Oakland Athletics for P Billy Koch and two players to be named (December 3, 2002); White Sox acquired P Neal Cotts and OF Daylon Holt to complete deal (December 16, 2002). ... Traded by Oakland Athletics with Ps Aaron Harang and Jeff Bruksch to Cincinnati Reds for OF Jose Guillen (July 30, 2003).
CAREER HITTING: 0-for-1 (.000), 0 R, 0 2B, 0 3B, 0 HR, 0 RBI.

Year Team (League)	W	L	Pct.	ERA	WHIP	G	GS	CG	ShO	Hld.	Sv.-Opp.	IP	H	R	ER	HR	BB-IBB	SO	Avg.
1999— Ariz. White Sox (Ariz.)	0	0	...	0.00	0.69	3	0	0	0	...	0-...	4.1	2	0	0	0	1-0	2	.154
— Bristol (Appalachian)	0	0	...	7.02	2.16	11	0	0	0	...	0-...	16.2	27	17	13	2	9-0	14	.360
2000— Bristol (Appalachian)	2	1	.667	2.88	1.04	19	0	0	0	...	7-...	25.0	14	10	8	1	12-1	30	.163
2001— Kannapolis (S.Atl.)	2	2	.500	2.93	1.01	30	0	0	0	...	14-...	30.2	21	10	10	0	10-1	33	.194
— Winston-Salem (Caro.)	5	1	.833	1.01	1.01	27	0	0	0	...	8-...	44.2	18	7	5	0	27-3	50	.122
2002— Birmingham (Southern)	4	1	.800	1.97	1.11	55	0	0	0	...	36-...	59.1	36	16	13	1	30-3	63	.173
2003— Sacramento (PCL)	1	3	.250	4.82	1.55	40	0	0	0	...	4-...	52.1	44	33	28	5	37-3	53	.222
— Cincinnati (N.L.)	0	0	...	18.00	3.00	2	0	0	0	0	0-0	2.0	5	4	4	1	1-0	1	.455
— Louisville (Int'l)	1	0	1.000	0.79	0.71	9	0	0	0	...	1-...	11.1	5	1	1	0	3-0	8	.132
2004— Louisville (Int'l)	5	5	.500	5.01	1.47	30	9	0	0	...	0-...	64.2	63	41	36	8	32-0	61	.258
— Cincinnati (N.L.)	2	3	.400	5.22	1.64	24	1	0	0	5	4-4	29.1	23	18	17	4	25-1	29	.211
Major League totals (2 years)	2	3	.400	6.03	1.72	26	1	0	0	5	4-4	31.1	28	22	21	5	26-1	30	.233

VALVERDE, JOSE   P

PERSONAL: Born July 24, 1979, in San Pedro de Macoris, Dominican Republic. ... 6-4/254. ... Throws right, bats right. ... Full name: Jose Rafael Valverde. ... Name pronounced: val-VARE-day. ... High school: Wscuela San Lorenzo (El Seybo, Dominican Republic).
TRANSACTIONS/CAREER NOTES: Signed as a non-drafted free agent by Arizona Diamondbacks organization (February 6, 1997). ... On disabled list (June 14, 2004-remainder of season); included rehabilitation assignment to Tucson.
CAREER HITTING: 1-for-1 (1.000), 1 R, 1 2B, 0 3B, 0 HR, 0 RBI.

Year Team (League)	W	L	Pct.	ERA	WHIP	G	GS	CG	ShO	Hld.	Sv.-Opp.	IP	H	R	ER	HR	BB-IBB	SO	Avg.
1999— Ariz. D'backs (Ariz.)	1	2	.333	4.08	1.53	20	0	0	0	...	8-...	28.2	34	21	13	1	10-0	47	.274
— South Bend (Mid.)	0	0	...	0.00	1.50	2	0	0	0	...	0-...	2.2	2	0	0	0	2-0	3	.250
2000— South Bend (Mid.)	0	5	.000	5.40	1.77	31	0	0	0	...	14-...	31.2	31	20	19	1	25-0	39	.254
— Missoula (Pio.)	1	0	1.000	0.00	0.60	12	0	0	0	...	4-...	11.2	3	0	0	0	4-0	24	.075
2001— El Paso (Texas)	2	2	.500	3.92	1.52	39	0	0	0	...	13-...	41.1	36	19	18	1	27-0	72	.225
2002— Tucson (PCL)	4	2	.333	5.85	1.43	49	0	0	0	...	5-...	32	45	33	31	8	23-1	65	.250
2003— Tucson (PCL)	1	1	.500	3.10	1.38	22	0	0	0	...	5-...	29.0	26	11	10	1	14-1	26	.236
— Arizona (N.L.)	2	1	.667	2.15	0.99	54	0	0	0	8	10-11	50.1	24	16	12	4	26-2	71	.137
2004— Arizona (N.L.)	1	2	.333	4.25	1.35	29	0	0	0	5	8-10	29.2	23	17	14	7	17-4	38	.213
— Tucson (PCL)	1	1	.500	4.22	1.31	10	1	0	0	...	3-...	10.2	9	5	5	0	5-0	5	.225
Major League totals (2 years)	3	3	.500	2.93	1.13	83	0	0	0	13	18-21	80.0	47	33	26	11	43-6	109	.166

VAN BENSCHOTEN, JOHN   P

PERSONAL: Born April 14, 1980, in San Diego, Calif. ... 6-4/217. ... Throws right, bats right. ... Full name: John Wesley Van Benschoten. ... High school: Milford (Ohio). ... College: Kent State.
TRANSACTIONS/CAREER NOTES: Selected by Pittsburgh Pirates organization in first round (eight overall pick) of 2001 free-agent draft.
CAREER HITTING: 1-for-8 (.125), 2 R, 0 2B, 0 3B, 1 HR, 2 RBI.

Year Team (League)	W	L	Pct.	ERA	WHIP	G	GS	CG	ShO	Hld.	Sv.-Opp.	IP	H	R	ER	HR	BB-IBB	SO	Avg.
2001— Williamsport (N.Y.-Penn.)	0	2	.000	3.51	1.29	9	9	0	0	...	0-...	25.2	23	11	10	0	10-0	19	.247
2002— Hickory (S. Atl.)	11	4	.733	2.80	1.22	27	27	0	0	...	0-...	148.0	119	57	46	6	62-1	145	.219
2003— Lynchburg (Carolina)	6	0	1.000	2.22	1.05	9	9	0	0	...	0-...	48.2	33	14	12	1	18-0	49	.192
— Altoona (East.)	7	6	.538	3.69	1.43	17	17	1	0	...	0-...	90.1	95	46	37	5	34-1	78	.268
2004— Nashville (PCL)	4	11	.267	4.72	1.40	23	23	0	0	...	0-...	131.2	135	75	69	16	49-1	101	.261
— Pittsburgh (N.L.)	1	3	.250	6.91	1.81	6	5	0	0	...	0-0	28.2	33	27	22	3	19-0	18	.300
Major League totals (1 year)	1	3	.250	6.91	1.81	6	5	0	0	...	0-0	28.2	33	27	22	3	19-0	18	.300

V

VANDER WAL, JOHN — OF

PERSONAL: Born April 29, 1966, in Grand Rapids, Mich. ... 6-1/204. ... Bats left, throws left. ... Full name: John Henry Vander Wal. ... High school: Hudsonville (Mich.). ... College: Western Michigan.

TRANSACTIONS/CAREER NOTES: Selected by Houston Astros organization in eighth round of June 1984 free-agent draft; did not sign. ... Selected by Montreal Expos organization in third round of 1987 free-agent draft. ... Traded by Expos with OF Ronnie Hall to Colorado Rockies for cash (March 31, 1994). ... Traded by Rockies to San Diego Padres for two players to be named (August 31, 1998); Rockies acquired P Roberto Ramirez and OF Kevin Buford to complete deal (October 29, 1998). ... Traded by Padres with Ps Geraldo Padua and James Sak to Pittsburgh Pirates for OF Al Martin and cash (February 23, 2000). ... Traded by Pirates with P Jason Schmidt to San Francisco Giants for OF Armando Rios and P Ryan Vogelsong (July 30, 2001). ... Traded by Giants to New York Yankees for P Jay Witasick (December 13, 2001). ... Signed as a free agent by Milwaukee Brewers organization (January 28, 2003). ... Signed by Cincinnati Reds (January 14, 2004). ... Released by Reds (March 14, 2004). ... Re-signed by Reds organization (March 17, 2004). ... Refused minor league assignment and became a free agent (October 6, 2004).

2004 GAMES PLAYED BY POSITION (MLB): OF—7, 1B—4.

Year	Team (League)	Pos.	G	AB	R	H	2B	3B	HR	RBI	BB	SO	HBP	GDP	SB-CS	Avg.	OBP	SLG	OPS	E	Avg.
1987—	Jamestown (N.Y.-Penn.) ...	OF	18	69	24	33	12	3	3	15	3	14	0	2	3-2	.478	.493	.870	1.363	0	1.000
	—W.P. Beach (FSL)	OF	50	189	29	54	11	2	2	22	30	25	0	2	8-3	.286	.378	.397	.775	3	.972
1988—	W.P. Beach (FSL)	OF	62	231	50	64	15	2	10	33	32	40	3	0	11-4	.277	.368	.489	.857	1	.991
	—Jacksonville (Sou.)	OF	58	208	22	54	14	0	3	14	17	49	1	3	3-4	.260	.317	.370	.687	0	1.000
1989—	Jacksonville (Sou.)	OF	71	217	30	55	9	2	6	24	22	51	1	5	2-3	.253	.322	.396	.719	1	.987
1990—	Jacksonville (Sou.)	OF	77	277	45	84	25	3	8	40	39	46	3	7	6-3	.303	.393	.502	.894	1	.991
	—Indianapolis (A.A.)	OF	51	135	16	40	6	0	2	14	13	28	0	3	0-1	.296	.358	.385	.743	2	.963
1991—	Indianapolis (A.A.)	OF	133	478	84	140	36	8	15	71	79	118	2	10	8-1	.293	.393	.496	.888	1	.995
	—Montreal (N.L.)	OF	21	61	4	13	4	1	1	8	1	18	0	2	0-0	.213	.222	.361	.583	0	1.000
1992—	Montreal (N.L.)	OF-1B	105	213	21	51	8	2	4	20	24	36	0	2	3-0	.239	.316	.352	.669	2	.985
1993—	Montreal (N.L.)	1B-OF	106	215	34	50	7	4	5	30	27	30	1	4	6-3	.233	.320	.372	.692	4	.986
1994—	Colorado (N.L.)	1B-OF	91	110	12	27	3	1	5	15	16	31	0	4	2-1	.245	.339	.427	.766	0	1.000
1995—	Colorado (N.L.)	1B-OF	105	101	15	35	8	1	5	21	16	23	0	2	1-1	.347	.432	.594	1.026	2	.965
1996—	Colorado (N.L.)	OF-1B	104	151	20	38	6	2	5	31	19	38	1	1	2-2	.252	.335	.417	.752	1	.987
1997—	Colorado (N.L.) OF-1B-DH		76	92	7	16	2	0	1	11	10	33	0	2	1-1	.174	.255	.228	.483	1	.974
	—Colo. Springs (PCL) 1B-OF-DH		25	103	29	42	12	1	3	19	11	28	0	1	1-1	.408	.465	.631	1.096	4	.977
1998—	Colorado (N.L.) OF-DH-1B		89	104	18	30	10	1	5	20	16	29	0	1	0-0	.288	.380	.548	.928	0	1.000
	—San Diego (N.L.)	OF-1B	20	25	3	6	3	0	0	0	6	5	0	1	0-0	.240	.387	.360	.747	0	1.000
1999—	San Diego (N.L.) OF-1B-DH		132	246	26	67	18	0	6	41	37	59	2	5	2-1	.272	.368	.419	.787	1	.996
2000—	Pittsburgh (N.L.) OF-1B-DH		134	384	74	115	29	0	24	94	72	92	2	7	11-2	.299	.410	.563	.972	6	.985
2001—	Pittsburgh (N.L.) OF-1B-DH		97	313	39	87	22	3	11	50	42	84	1	7	7-4	.278	.361	.473	.834	4	.982
	—San Francisco (N.L.)	OF-1B	49	139	19	35	6	1	3	20	26	38	0	3	1-2	.252	.370	.374	.744	0	1.000
2002—	New York (A.L.) OF-DH-1B		84	219	30	57	17	1	6	20	23	58	0	7	1-1	.260	.327	.429	.756	2	.983
2003—	Milwaukee (N.L.)	OF	117	327	50	84	25	1	14	45	46	104	1	5	1-2	.257	.350	.468	.818	3	.984
2004—	Louisville (Int'l) 1B-OF-DH		16	48	5	9	3	0	2	2	5	10	0	1	2-0	.188	.264	.250	.514	0	1.000
	—Cincinnati (N.L.)	OF-1B	42	51	2	6	2	0	2	4	4	20	0	0	0-0	.118	.182	.275	.456	0	1.000
American League totals (1 year)			84	219	30	57	17	1	6	20	23	58	0	7	1-1	.260	.327	.429	.756	2	.983
National League totals (13 years)			1288	2532	344	660	153	17	91	410	362	640	8	46	37-19	.261	.353	.442	.795	24	.988
Major League totals (14 years)			1372	2751	374	717	170	18	97	430	385	698	8	53	38-20	.261	.351	.441	.792	26	.987

DIVISION SERIES RECORD

Year	Team (League)	Pos.	G	AB	R	H	2B	3B	HR	RBI	BB	SO	HBP	GDP	SB-CS	Avg.	OBP	SLG	OPS	E	Avg.
1995—	Colorado (N.L.)		4	4	0	0	0	0	0	0	0	2	0	1	0-0	.000	.000	.000	.000	...	...
1998—	San Diego (N.L.)		3	3	1	1	0	1	0	2	0	1	0	0	0-0	.333	.333	1.000	1.333	...	...
2002—	New York (A.L.)	OF	2	2	0	0	0	0	0	0	0	1	0	0	0-0	.000	.000	.000	.000	0	...
Division series totals (3 years)			9	9	1	1	0	1	0	2	0	4	0	1	0-0	.111	.111	.333	.444	0	...

CHAMPIONSHIP SERIES RECORD

Year	Team (League)	Pos.	G	AB	R	H	2B	3B	HR	RBI	BB	SO	HBP	GDP	SB-CS	Avg.	OBP	SLG	OPS	E	Avg.
1998—	San Diego (N.L.)	OF	3	7	1	3	0	0	1	2	0	2	0	0	0-0	.429	.429	.857	1.286	0	1.000

WORLD SERIES RECORD

Year	Team (League)	Pos.	G	AB	R	H	2B	3B	HR	RBI	BB	SO	HBP	GDP	SB-CS	Avg.	OBP	SLG	OPS	E	Avg.
1998—	San Diego (N.L.)	OF	4	5	0	2	1	0	0	0	0	2	0	0	0-0	.400	.400	.600	1.000	0	1.000

V

VAN POPPEL, TODD — P

PERSONAL: Born December 9, 1971, in Hinsdale, Ill. ... 6-5/235. ... Throws right, bats right. ... Full name: Todd Matthew Van Poppel. ... Name pronounced: VAN-pop-pell. ... High school: St. Martin (Arlington, Texas).

TRANSACTIONS/CAREER NOTES: Selected by Oakland Athletics organization in first round (14th pick overall) of 1990 free-agent draft; pick received as part of compensation for Milwaukee Brewers signing Type A free-agent DH Dave Parker. ... On disabled list (May 28-September 11, 1992). ... Claimed on waivers by Detroit Tigers (August 6, 1996). ... Claimed on waivers by California Angels (November 12, 1996). ... Franchise renamed Anaheim Angels for 1997 season. ... Released by Angels (March 26, 1997). ... Signed by Kansas City Royals organization (April 17, 1997). ... Released by Royals (June 6, 1997). ... Signed by Texas Rangers organization (June 20, 1997). ... Traded by Rangers with 2B Warren Morris to Pittsburgh Pirates for P Esteban Loaiza (July 17, 1998). ... Signed as a free agent by Chicago Cubs organization (November 22, 1999). ... Signed as a free agent by Texas Rangers (November 26, 2001). ... On disabled list (March 21-May 3, 2003); included rehabilitation assignment to Frisco. ... Released by Rangers (June 4, 2003). ... Signed by Cincinnati Reds organization (June 12, 2003).

CAREER HITTING: 9-for-57 (.158), 5 R, 1 2B, 0 3B, 0 HR, 2 RBI.

Year	Team (League)	W	L	Pct.	ERA	WHIP	G	GS	CG	ShO	Hld.	Sv.-Opp.	IP	H	R	ER	HR	BB-IBB	SO	Avg.
1990—	S. Oregon (N'west)	1	1	.500	1.13	0.79	5	5	0	0	...	0-...	24.0	10	5	3	1	9-0	32	.125
	—Madison (Midw.)	2	1	.667	3.95	1.32	3	3	0	0	...	0-...	13.2	8	11	6	0	10-0	17	.163
1991—	Huntsville (Southern)	6	13	.316	3.47	1.57	24	24	1	1	...	0-...	132.1	118	69	51	2	90-0	115	.236
	—Oakland (A.L.)	0	0	...	9.64	1.93	1	1	0	0	0	0-0	4.2	7	6	5	1	2-0	6	.368
1992—	Tacoma (PCL)	4	2	.667	3.97	1.74	9	9	0	0	...	0-...	45.1	44	22	20	1	35-0	29	.277
1993—	Tacoma (PCL)	4	8	.333	5.83	1.54	16	16	0	0	...	0-...	78.2	67	53	51	5	54-0	71	.230
	—Oakland (A.L.)	6	6	.500	5.04	1.64	16	16	0	0	0	0-0	84.0	76	50	47	10	62-0	47	.243
1994—	Oakland (A.L.)	7	10	.412	6.09	1.69	23	23	0	0	0	0-0	116.2	108	80	79	20	• 89-2	83	.250
1995—	Oakland (A.L.)	4	8	.333	4.88	1.31	36	14	1	0	1	0-0	138.1	125	77	75	16	56-1	122	.244
1996—	Oakland (A.L.)	1	5	.167	7.71	1.89	28	6	1	0	1	1-2	63.0	86	56	54	16	33-3	37	.333
	—Detroit (A.L.)	2	4	.333	11.39	2.26	9	9	1	1	0	0-0	36.1	53	51	46	11	29-0	16	.338
1997—	Omaha (Am. Assoc.)	1	5	.167	8.03	2.00	11	6	0	0	...	0-...	37.0	50	36	33	10	24-0	27	.321

Year	Team (League)	W	L	Pct.	ERA	WHIP	G	GS	CG	ShO	Hld.	Sv.-Opp.	IP	H	R	ER	HR	BB-IBB	SO	Avg.
	—Charlotte (Fla. St.)	0	4	.000	4.04	1.29	6	6	2	0	...	0-...	35.2	36	19	16	3	10-0	33	.263
	—Tulsa (Texas)	3	3	.500	5.06	1.59	7	7	0	0	...	0-...	42.2	53	27	24	2	15-0	26	.303
1998—	Tulsa (Texas)	0	0	...	4.50	1.50	1	1	0	0	...	0-...	4.0	2	2	2	1	4-0	2	.154
	—Oklahoma (PCL)	5	5	.500	3.72	1.30	15	13	2	0	...	0-...	87.0	88	44	36	11	25-0	69	.257
	—Texas (A.L.)	1	2	.333	8.84	1.86	4	4	0	0	0	0-0	19.1	26	20	19	5	10-0	10	.313
	—Pittsburgh (N.L.)	1	2	.333	5.36	1.51	18	7	0	0	0	0-0	47.0	53	32	28	4	18-3	32	.286
1999—	Nashville (PCL)	10	6	.625	4.95	1.44	27	27	2	0	...	0-...	163.2	173	95	90	23	62-1	157	.271
2000—	Iowa (PCL)	3	4	.429	3.10	1.16	10	6	0	0	...	0-...	40.2	37	18	14	2	10-0	52	.237
	—Chicago (N.L.)	4	5	.444	3.75	1.48	51	2	0	0	7	2-5	86.1	80	38	36	10	48-2	77	.249
2001—	Chicago (N.L.)	4	1	.800	2.52	1.35	59	0	0	0	5	0-0	75.0	63	22	21	9	38-4	90	.223
2002—	Texas (A.L.)	3	2	.600	5.45	1.50	50	0	0	0	3	1-2	72.2	80	44	44	14	29-1	85	.275
2003—	Frisco (Texas)	0	0	...	2.00	1.10	2	2	0	0	...	0-...	9.0	8	2	2	0	2-0	7	.235
	—Texas (A.L.)	1	0	1.000	8.53	2.29	7	1	0	0	0	0-...	12.2	20	14	12	1	9-2	9	.345
	—Louisville (Int'l)	4	3	.571	3.17	1.10	20	5	0	0	...	1-...	54.0	49	23	19	4	11-1	45	.247
	—Cincinnati (N.L.)	2	1	.667	4.54	1.04	9	4	0	0	1	0-...	35.2	31	18	18	7	6-0	25	.228
2004—	Cincinnati (N.L.)	4	6	.400	6.09	1.46	48	11	0	0	2	0-1	115.1	136	80	78	22	32-3	72	.298
	American League totals (8 years)	25	37	.403	6.26	1.64	174	74	2	1	4	2-4	547.2	581	397	381	91	319-9	415	.274
	National League totals (5 years)	15	15	.500	4.53	1.41	185	24	0	0	15	2-6	359.1	363	190	181	52	142-12	296	.263
	Major League totals (11 years)	40	52	.435	5.58	1.55	359	98	2	1	19	4-10	907.0	944	587	562	143	461-21	711	.269

VARGAS, CLAUDIO P

PERSONAL: Born June 19, 1978, in Valverde Mao, Dominican Republic. ... 6-3/228. ... Throws right, bats right. ... Full name: Claudio Almonte Vargas.

TRANSACTIONS/CAREER NOTES: Signed as a non-drafted free agent by Florida Marlins organization (August 25, 1995). ... Traded by Marlins with OF Cliff Floyd, OF/2B Wilton Guerrero and cash to Montreal Expos for Ps Carl Pavano, Graeme Lloyd and Justin Wayne, IF Mike Mordecai and a player to be named (July 11, 2002); Marlins acquired P Don Levinski to complete deal (August 6, 2002). ... On disabled list (August 6-September 15, 2003).

CAREER HITTING: 1-for-52 (.019), 1 R, 0 2B, 0 3B, 0 HR, 0 RBI.

Year	Team (League)	W	L	Pct.	ERA	WHIP	G	GS	CG	ShO	Hld.	Sv.-Opp.	IP	H	R	ER	HR	BB-IBB	SO	Avg.
1998—	Brevard County (FSL)	0	1	.000	4.66	1.97	2	2	0	0	...	0-...	9.2	15	5	5	1	4-0	9	.366
	—GC Marlins (GCL)	0	4	.000	4.08	1.08	5	4	0	0	...	0-...	28.2	24	15	13	1	7-0	27	.226
1999—	Kane County (Midwest)	5	5	.500	3.88	1.38	19	19	1	0	...	0-...	99.2	97	47	43	8	41-0	88	.255
2000—	Brevard County (FSL)	10	5	.667	3.28	1.17	24	23	0	0	...	0-...	145.1	126	64	53	10	44-3	143	.234
	—Portland (East.)	1	1	.500	3.60	1.47	3	2	0	0	...	0-...	15.0	16	9	6	1	6-0	13	.276
2001—	Portland (East.)	8	9	.471	4.19	1.19	27	27	0	0	...	0-...	159.0	122	77	74	25	67-1	151	.211
2002—	Calgary (PCL)	4	11	.267	6.72	1.61	17	16	1	0	...	0-...	76.1	88	63	57	18	35-0	61	.291
	—Harrisburg (Eastern)	2	2	.500	4.64	1.42	8	8	0	0	...	0-...	33.0	38	17	17	2	9-0	34	.286
2003—	Edmonton (PCL)	0	0	...	2.79	1.24	2	2	0	0	...	0-...	9.2	7	3	3	1	5-2	12	.189
	—Harrisburg (Eastern)	1	0	1.000	0.75	0.83	2	2	0	0	...	0-...	12.0	7	1	1	0	3-0	13	.171
	—Montreal (N.L.)	6	8	.429	4.34	1.33	23	20	0	0	0	0-0	114.0	111	59	55	16	41-5	62	.255
2004—	Montreal (N.L.)	5	5	.500	5.25	1.55	45	14	0	0	3	0-0	118.1	120	75	69	26	64-7	89	.266
	Major League totals (2 years)	11	13	.458	4.80	1.45	68	34	0	0	3	0-0	232.1	231	134	124	42	105-12	151	.260

VARITEK, JASON C

PERSONAL: Born April 11, 1972, in Rochester, Mich. ... 6-2/230. ... Bats both, throws right. ... Full name: Jason Andrew Varitek. ... Name pronounced: VAIR-eh-teck. ... High school: Lake Brantley (Longwood, Fla.). ... College: Georgia Tech.

TRANSACTIONS/CAREER NOTES: Selected by Minnesota Twins organization first round (21st pick overall) of 1993 free-agent draft; did not sign. ... Selected by Seattle Mariners organization in first round (14th pick overall) of 1994 free-agent draft. ... Traded by Mariners with P Derek Lowe to Boston Red Sox for P Heathcliff Slocumb (July 31, 1997). ... On disabled list (June 8, 2001-remainder of season). ... On suspended list (September 16-20, 2002).

2004 GAMES PLAYED BY POSITION (MLB): C—130, DH—1.

Year	Team (League)	Pos.	G	AB	R	H	2B	3B	HR	RBI	BB	SO	HBP	GDP	SB-CS	Avg.	OBP	SLG	OPS	E	Avg.
1995—	Port City (Sou.)	C	104	352	42	79	14	3	10	44	61	126	2	8	0-1	.224	.340	.366	.706	8	.988
1996—	Port City (Sou.)	C-DH-3B-OF	134	503	63	132	34	1	12	67	66	93	4	14	7-6	.262	.350	.406	.756	5	.993
1997—	Tacoma (PCL)	C-DH	87	307	54	78	13	0	15	48	34	71	2	13	0-1	.254	.329	.443	.772	3	.995
	—Pawtucket (Int'l)	C	20	66	6	13	5	0	1	5	8	12	0	4	0-0	.197	.284	.318	.602	1	.993
	—Boston (A.L.)	C	1	1	0	1	0	0	0	0	0	0	0	0	0-0	1.000	1.000	1.000	2.000	0	1.000
1998—	Boston (A.L.)	C-DH	86	221	31	56	13	0	7	33	17	45	2	8	2-2	.253	.309	.407	.716	5	.988
1999—	Boston (A.L.)	C-DH	144	483	70	130	39	2	20	76	46	85	2	13	1-2	.269	.330	.482	.813	* 11	.990
2000—	Boston (A.L.)	C-DH	139	448	55	111	31	1	10	65	60	84	6	16	1-1	.248	.342	.388	.730	7	.992
2001—	Boston (A.L.)	C	51	174	19	51	11	1	7	25	21	35	1	6	0-0	.293	.371	.489	.859	2	.996
2002—	Boston (A.L.)	C-DH	132	467	58	124	27	1	10	61	41	95	7	13	4-3	.266	.332	.392	.724	4	.996
2003—	Boston (A.L.)	C-DH	142	451	63	123	31	1	25	85	51	106	7	10	3-2	.273	.351	.512	.863	9	.990
2004—	Boston (A.L.)	C-DH	137	463	67	137	30	1	18	73	62	126	10	11	10-3	.296	.390	.482	.872	2	.998
	Major League totals (8 years)		832	2708	363	733	182	7	97	418	298	576	35	77	21-13	.271	.347	.451	.798	40	.993

DIVISION SERIES RECORD

Year	Team (League)	Pos.	G	AB	R	H	2B	3B	HR	RBI	BB	SO	HBP	GDP	SB-CS	Avg.	OBP	SLG	OPS	E	Avg.
1998—	Boston (A.L.)	C	1	4	0	1	0	0	0	1	0	1	0	0	0-0	.250	.250	.250	.500	0	1.000
1999—	Boston (A.L.)	C	5	21	7	5	3	0	1	3	0	4	1	0	0-0	.238	.273	.524	.797	0	1.000
2003—	Boston (A.L.)	C	5	14	4	4	0	0	2	2	2	2	0	0	0-0	.286	.375	.714	1.089	0	1.000
2004—	Boston (A.L.)	C	3	12	3	2	0	0	1	2	2	5	1	1	0-0	.167	.333	.417	.750	0	1.000
	Division series totals (4 years)		14	51	14	12	3	0	4	8	4	12	2	1	0-0	.235	.316	.529	.845	0	1.000

CHAMPIONSHIP SERIES RECORD

Year	Team (League)	Pos.	G	AB	R	H	2B	3B	HR	RBI	BB	SO	HBP	GDP	SB-CS	Avg.	OBP	SLG	OPS	E	Avg.
1999—	Boston (A.L.)	C	5	20	1	4	1	1	1	1	1	4	0	1	0-0	.200	.238	.500	.738	1	.978
2003—	Boston (A.L.)	C	6	20	4	6	2	0	2	3	1	5	0	0	0-0	.300	.333	.700	1.033	0	1.000
2004—	Boston (A.L.)	C	7	28	5	9	1	0	2	7	2	6	0	0	0-0	.321	.355	.571	.926	0	1.000
	Champ. series totals (3 years)		18	68	10	19	4	1	5	11	4	15	0	1	0-0	.279	.315	.588	.903	1	.993

WORLD SERIES RECORD

Year	Team (League)	Pos.	G	AB	R	H	2B	3B	HR	RBI	BB	SO	HBP	GDP	SB-CS	Avg.	OBP	SLG	OPS	E	Avg.
2004—	Boston (A.L.)	C	4	13	2	2	0	1	0	2	1	4	1	0	0-0	.154	.267	.308	.574	0	1.000

V

VASQUEZ, JORGE   P

PERSONAL: Born July 16, 1978, in Nagua, Dominican Republic. ... 6-1/165. ... Throws right, bats right. ... Full name: Jorge Luis Vasquez. ... High school: San Jose de Villa (Nagua, D.R.).
TRANSACTIONS/CAREER NOTES: Signed as a non-drafted free agent by Kansas City Royals organization (September 1, 1998).
CAREER HITTING: 0-for-0 (.000), 0 R, 0 2B, 0 3B, 0 HR, 0 RBI.

Year Team (League)	W	L	Pct.	ERA	WHIP	G	GS	CG	ShO	Hld.	Sv.-Opp.	IP	H	R	ER	HR	BB-IBB	SO	Avg.
2001— GC Royals (GCL)	0	1	.000	1.13	0.69	4	2	0	0	...	0-...	16.0	10	2	2	0	1-0	19	.167
— Spokane (N'west)	1	6	.143	5.01	1.25	10	8	0	0	...	0-...	50.1	50	33	28	3	13-0	67	.259
2002— Burlington (Midw.)	2	1	.667	1.57	0.80	22	0	0	0	...	6-...	46.0	22	8	8	3	15-0	55	.141
— Wilmington (Caro.)	0	0	...	4.91	1.36	10	0	0	0	...	0-...	11.0	12	6	6	1	3-0	17	.255
2003— Wilmington (Caro.)	1	2	.333	1.96	1.43	17	0	0	0	...	7-...	23.0	19	7	5	1	14-3	31	.224
— Wichita (Texas)	3	1	.750	1.92	1.10	36	0	0	0	...	22-...	51.2	39	12	11	3	18-2	52	.212
2004— Kansas City (A.L.)	0	0	...	8.10	1.50	2	0	0	0	0	0-0	3.1	4	4	3	1	1-0	4	.267
— Wichita (Texas)	4	5	.444	4.68	1.32	49	0	0	0	...	18-...	59.2	52	34	31	4	27-1	71	.227
Major League totals (1 year)	0	0	...	8.10	1.50	2	0	0	0	0	0-0	3.1	4	4	3	1	1-0	4	.267

VAZQUEZ, JAVIER   P

PERSONAL: Born July 25, 1976, in Ponce, Puerto Rico. ... 6-2/205. ... Throws right, bats right. ... Full name: Javier Carlos Vazquez. ... Name pronounced: VAS-kez. ... High school: Colegio de Ponce (Ponce, Puerto Rico).
TRANSACTIONS/CAREER NOTES: Selected by Montreal Expos organization in fifth round of 1994 free-agent draft. ... On suspended list (July 23-27, 1998). ... Traded by Expos to New York Yankees for 1B Nick Johnson, OF Juan Rivera and LHP Randy Choate (December 16, 2003).
CAREER HITTING: 76-for-363 (.209), 29 R, 9 2B, 2 3B, 0 HR, 22 RBI.

Year Team (League)	W	L	Pct.	ERA	WHIP	G	GS	CG	ShO	Hld.	Sv.-Opp.	IP	H	R	ER	HR	BB-IBB	SO	Avg.
1994— GC Expos (GCL)	5	2	.714	2.53	0.77	15	11	1	1	...	0-...	67.2	37	25	19	0	15-0	56	.155
1995— Albany (S. Atl.)	6	6	.500	5.08	1.52	21	21	1	0	...	0-...	102.2	109	67	58	8	47-0	87	.273
1996— Delmarva (S.Atl.)	14	3	.824	2.68	1.19	27	27	1	0	...	0-...	164.1	138	64	49	12	57-0	173	.229
1997— W.P. Beach (FSL)	6	3	.667	2.16	1.12	19	19	1	0	...	0-...	112.2	98	40	27	8	28-0	100	.231
— Harrisburg (Eastern)	4	0	1.000	1.07	0.64	6	6	1	0	...	0-...	42.0	15	5	5	2	12-0	47	.107
1998— Montreal (N.L.)	5	15	.250	6.06	1.53	33	32	0	0	...	0-...	172.1	196	121	116	31	68-2	139	.292
1999— Montreal (N.L.)	9	8	.529	5.00	1.33	26	26	3	1	...	0-...	154.2	154	98	86	20	52-4	113	.255
— Ottawa (Int'l)	4	2	.667	4.85	1.43	7	7	0	0	...	0-...	42.2	45	24	23	7	16-0	46	.280
2000— Montreal (N.L.)	11	9	.550	4.05	1.42	33	33	2	1	...	0-...	217.2	247	104	98	24	61-10	196	.286
2001— Montreal (N.L.)	16	11	.593	3.42	1.08	32	32	5	•3	...	0-...	223.2	197	92	85	24	44-4	208	.235
2002— Montreal (N.L.)	10	13	.435	3.91	1.27	34	34	2	0	...	0-...	230.1	*243	111	100	28	49-6	179	.271
2003— Montreal (N.L.)	13	12	.520	3.24	1.11	34	34	4	1	...	0-...	230.2	198	93	83	28	57-5	241	.229
2004— New York (A.L.)	14	10	.583	4.91	1.29	32	32	0	0	...	0-0	198.0	195	114	108	33	60-3	150	.255
American League totals (1 year)	14	10	.583	4.91	1.29	32	32	0	0		0-0	198.0	195	114	108	33	60-3	150	.255
National League totals (6 years)	64	68	.485	4.16	1.27	192	191	16	6	0	0-0	1229.1	1235	619	568	155	331-31	1076	.260
Major League totals (7 years)	78	78	.500	4.26	1.28	224	223	16	6	0	0-0	1427.1	1430	733	676	188	391-34	1226	.260

DIVISION SERIES RECORD

Year Team (League)	W	L	Pct.	ERA	WHIP	G	GS	CG	ShO	Hld.	Sv.-Opp.	IP	H	R	ER	HR	BB-IBB	SO	Avg.
2004— New York (A.L.)	0	0	...	9.00	1.80	1	1	0	0	...	0-0	5.0	7	5	5	1	2-0	6	.368

CHAMPIONSHIP SERIES RECORD

Year Team (League)	W	L	Pct.	ERA	WHIP	G	GS	CG	ShO	Hld.	Sv.-Opp.	IP	H	R	ER	HR	BB-IBB	SO	Avg.
2004— New York (A.L.)	1	0	1.000	9.95	2.53	2	0	0	0	...	0-0	6.1	9	7	7	3	7-0	6	.346

ALL-STAR GAME RECORD

Year Team (League)	W	L	Pct.	ERA	WHIP	G	GS	CG	ShO	Hld.	Sv.-Opp.	IP	H	R	ER	HR	BB-IBB	SO	Avg.
All-Star Game totals (1 year)	0	0	...	0.00	0.00	1	0	0	0	...	0-0	1.0	0	0	0	0	0-0	2	.000

VAZQUEZ, RAMON   3B/SS

PERSONAL: Born August 21, 1976, in Aibonito, Puerto Rico. ... 5-11/170. ... Bats left, throws right. ... Full name: Ramon Luis Vazquez. ... Junior college: Indian Hills (Iowa) Community College.
TRANSACTIONS/CAREER NOTES: Selected by Seattle Mariners organization in 27th round of 1995 free-agent draft. ... Traded by Mariners with P Brett Tomko and C Tom Lampkin to San Diego Padres for C Ben Davis, P Wascar Serrano and SS Alex Arias (December 11, 2001). ... On disabled list (June 1-July 7, 2003); included rehabilitation assignment to Lake Elsinore. ... On disabled list (May 20-June 20, 2004); included rehabilitation assignment to Portland.
2004 GAMES PLAYED BY POSITION (MLB): SS—22, 2B—10, 3B—9, 1B—3.

Year Team (League)	Pos.	G	AB	R	H	2B	3B	HR	RBI	BB	SO	HBP	GDP	SB-CS	Avg.	OBP	SLG	OPS	E	Avg.
1995— Ariz. Mariners (Ariz.)	2B-3B-SS	39	141	20	29	3	1	0	11	19	27	2	2	4-3	.206	.309	.241	.550	11	.941
1996— Everett (N'west)	SS	33	126	25	35	5	2	1	18	26	26	1	3	7-2	.278	.392	.373	.765	20	.873
— Tacoma (PCL)	2B-SS	18	49	7	11	2	1	0	4	4	12	1	2	0-0	.224	.296	.306	.602	1	.985
— Wisconsin (Midw.)	3B	3	10	1	3	1	0	0	4	2	2	0	1	0-0	.300	.417	.400	.817	2	.818
1997— Wisconsin (Midw.)	SS	131	479	79	129	25	5	8	49	78	93	3	8	16-10	.269	.373	.392	.765	35	.935
1998— Lancaster (Calif.)	SS	121	468	77	129	26	4	2	72	81	66	2	6	15-11	.276	.384	.361	.745	31	.944
1999— New Haven (East.)	2B-3B-SS	127	438	58	113	27	3	5	45	62	77	5	11	8-1	.258	.354	.368	.722	31	.942
2000— New Haven (East.)	SS	124	405	80	116	25	4	8	59	52	76	2	6	1-6	.286	.367	.427	.794	22	.961
2001— Tacoma (PCL)	SS	127	466	85	140	28	1	10	79	76	84	1	13	9-7	.300	.397	.429	.827	12	.979
— Seattle (A.L.)	SS-2B-3B-DH	17	35	5	8	0	0	0	4	0	3	0	0	0-0	.229	.222	.229	.451	1	.969
2002— San Diego (N.L.)	2B-SS-3B	128	423	50	116	21	5	2	32	45	79	1	6	7-2	.274	.344	.362	.706	7	.986
2003— Lake Elsinore (Calif.)	SS	5	16	3	3	0	1	0	4	3	3	1	1	0-0	.188	.350	.375	.725	1	.950
— San Diego (N.L.)	SS-3B-2B	116	422	56	110	17	4	3	30	52	88	2	4	10-3	.261	.342	.341	.684	14	.968
2004— Portland (PCL)	2B-3B-SS	53	184	36	55	21	1	8	34	33	28	0	2	2-0	.299	.402	.554	.956	2	.991
— San Diego (N.L.)	SS-2B-3B-1B	52	115	12	27	3	2	1	13	11	24	0	1	1-1	.235	.297	.322	.619	1	.991
American League totals (1 year)		17	35	5	8	0	0	0	4	0	3	0	0	0-0	.229	.222	.229	.451	1	.969
National League totals (3 years)		296	960	118	253	41	11	6	75	108	191	3	12	18-6	.264	.338	.348	.686	22	.979
Major League totals (4 years)		313	995	123	261	41	11	6	79	108	194	3	12	18-6	.262	.334	.344	.678	23	.979

DIVISION SERIES RECORD

Year Team (League)	Pos.	G	AB	R	H	2B	3B	HR	RBI	BB	SO	HBP	GDP	SB-CS	Avg.	OBP	SLG	OPS	E	Avg.
2001— Seattle (A.L.)		Did not play.																		

CHAMPIONSHIP SERIES RECORD

Year Team (League)	Pos.	G	AB	R	H	2B	3B	HR	RBI	BB	SO	HBP	GDP	SB-CS	Avg.	OBP	SLG	OPS	E	Avg.
2001— Seattle (A.L.)		Did not play.																		

VENAFRO, MIKE — P

PERSONAL: Born August 2, 1973, in Takoma Park, Md. ... 5-10/180. ... Throws left, bats left. ... Full name: Michael Robert Venafro. ... Name pronounced: VEN-a-fro. ... High school: Paul VI (Fairfax, Va.). ... College: James Madison (Va.).

TRANSACTIONS/CAREER NOTES: Selected by Texas Rangers organization in 29th round of 1995 free-agent draft. ... Traded by Rangers with 1B Carlos Pena to Oakland Athletics for 1B Jason Hart, P Mario Ramos, C Gerald Laird and OF Ryan Ludwick (January 14, 2002). ... Signed as a free agent by Atlanta Braves (January 13, 2003). ... Released by Braves (March 26, 2003). ... Signed by Tampa Bay Devil Rays (March 28, 2003). ... Released by Devil Rays (June 30, 2003). ... Signed by Houston Astros organization (July 10, 2003). ... Released by Astros (August 29, 2003). ... Signed by Kansas City Royals organization (November 21, 2003). ... Traded by Royals to Los Angeles Dodgers for P Elvin Nina (August 10, 2004).

CAREER HITTING: 0-for-0 (.000), 0 R, 0 2B, 0 3B, 0 HR, 0 RBI.

Year Team (League)	W	L	Pct.	ERA	WHIP	G	GS	CG	ShO	Hld.	Sv.-Opp.	IP	H	R	ER	HR	BB-IBB	SO	Avg.
1995— Hudson Valley (NY-Penn.) .	9	1	.900	2.13	1.14	32	0	0	0	...	2-...	50.2	37	13	12	0	21-2	32	.216
1996— Char., S.C. (SAL)	1	3	.250	3.51	1.32	50	0	0	0	...	19-...	59.0	57	27	23	0	21-3	62	.250
1997— Charlotte (Fla. St.)	4	2	.667	3.43	1.61	35	0	0	0	...	10-...	44.2	51	17	17	2	21-1	35	.305
— Tulsa (Texas)	0	1	.000	3.45	1.60	11	0	0	0	...	1-...	15.2	13	12	6	1	12-0	13	.220
1998— Tulsa (Texas)	3	4	.429	3.10	1.30	46	0	0	0	...	14-...	52.1	42	21	18	5	26-0	45	.219
— Okla. City (PCL)	0	0	...	6.35	1.71	13	0	0	0	...	0-...	17.0	19	12	12	3	10-0	15	.271
1999— Oklahoma (PCL)	0	0	...	5.40	1.37	6	0	0	0	...	1-...	11.2	16	7	7	2	0-0	7	.348
— Texas (A.L.)	3	2	.600	3.29	1.24	65	0	0	0	19	0-1	68.1	63	29	25	4	22-0	37	.251
2000— Texas (A.L.)	3	1	.750	3.83	1.51	77	0	0	0	17	1-2	56.1	64	27	24	2	21-4	32	.295
2001— Texas (A.L.)	5	5	.500	4.80	1.37	70	0	0	0	21	4-8	60.0	54	35	32	2	28-4	29	.240
2002— Oakland (A.L.)	2	2	.500	4.62	1.59	47	0	0	0	15	0-0	37.0	45	22	19	5	14-2	16	.308
— Sacramento (PCL)	0	1	.000	6.97	1.26	8	0	0	0	...	0-...	10.1	12	8	8	2	1-0	14	.293
2003— Tampa Bay (A.L.)	1	0	1.000	4.74	1.42	24	0	0	0	4	0-0	19.0	24	10	10	1	3-0	9	.308
— New Orleans (PCL)	2	1	.667	3.54	1.40	23	0	0	0	...	0-...	28.0	35	11	11	0	5-1	11	.310
2004— Omaha (PCL)	2	4	.333	4.37	1.54	35	0	0	0	...	2-...	57.2	70	30	28	8	19-2	41	.308
— Las Vegas (PCL)	0	1	.000	7.11	1.58	5	0	0	0	...	1-...	6.1	8	5	5	0	2-0	4	.320
— Los Angeles (N.L.)	0	0	...	4.00	1.56	17	0	0	0	2	0-0	9.0	11	5	4	1	3-1	6	.306
American League totals (5 years)	14	10	.583	4.11	1.40	283	0	0	0	76	5-11	240.2	250	123	110	14	88-10	123	.273
National League totals (1 year)	0	0	...	4.00	1.56	17	0	0	0	2	0-0	9.0	11	5	4	1	3-1	6	.306
Major League totals (6 years)	14	10	.583	4.11	1.41	300	0	0	0	78	5-11	249.2	261	128	114	15	91-11	129	.274

DIVISION SERIES RECORD

Year Team (League)	W	L	Pct.	ERA	WHIP	G	GS	CG	ShO	Hld.	Sv.-Opp.	IP	H	R	ER	HR	BB-IBB	SO	Avg.
1999— Texas (A.L.)	0	0	...	0.00	3.00	2	0	0	0	...	0-0	1.0	2	2	0	1	1-0	0	.333
2004— Los Angeles (N.L.)	0	0	...	0.00	0.00	2	0	0	0	...	0-0	.2	0	0	0	0	0-0	1	.000
Division series totals (2 years)	0	0	...	0.00	1.80	4	0	0	0	...	0-0	1.2	2	2	0	1	1-0	1	.250

VENTURA, ROBIN — 1B/3B

PERSONAL: Born July 14, 1967, in Santa Maria, Calif. ... 6-1/198. ... Bats left, throws right. ... Full name: Robin Mark Ventura. ... High school: Righetti (Santa Maria, Calif.). ... College: Oklahoma State.

TRANSACTIONS/CAREER NOTES: Selected by Chicago White Sox organization in first round (10th pick overall) of 1988 free-agent draft. ... On suspended list (August 23-25, 1993). ... On disabled list (March 31-July 24, 1997); included rehabilitation assignments to Nashville and Birmingham. ... Signed as a free agent by New York Mets (December 1, 1998). ... On disabled list (July 14-29, 2000). ... Traded by Mets to New York Yankees for OF David Justice (December 7, 2001). ... Traded by New York Yankees to Los Angeles Dodgers for OF Bubba Crosby and P Scott Proctor (July 31, 2003). ... Announced retirement (October 10, 2004). ... Career major league pitching: 0-0, 0.00 ERA, 1 G, 1.0 IP, 1 H, 0 R, 0 ER, 0 BB, 0 SO.

HONORS: Named College Player of the Year by THE SPORTING NEWS (1987-88). ... Won A.L. Gold Glove at third base (1991-93, 1996 and 1998). ... Won N.L. Gold Glove at third base (1999).

2004 GAMES PLAYED BY POSITION (MLB): 1B—40, 3B—11, P—1.

Year Team (League)	Pos.	G	AB	R	H	2B	3B	HR	RBI	BB	SO	HBP	GDP	SB-CS	Avg.	OBP	SLG	OPS	E	Avg.
1989— Birmingham (Sou.)	2B-3B-1B	129	454	75	126	25	2	3	67	93	51	6	9	9-7	.278	.403	.361	.764	27	.930
— Chicago (A.L.)	3B	16	45	5	8	3	0	0	7	8	6	1	1	0-0	.178	.298	.244	.543	2	.962
1990— Chicago (A.L.)	3B-1B	150	493	48	123	17	1	5	54	55	53	1	5	1-4	.249	.324	.318	.643	25	.939
1991— Chicago (A.L.)	3B-1B	157	606	92	172	25	1	23	100	80	67	4	22	2-4	.284	.367	.442	.810	‡18	.966
1992— Chicago (A.L.)	3B-1B	157	592	85	167	38	1	16	93	93	71	0	14	2-4	.282	.375	.431	.806	23	.957
1993— Chicago (A.L.)	3B-1B	157	554	85	145	27	1	22	94	105	82	3	18	1-6	.262	.379	.433	.812	14	.966
1994— Chicago (A.L.) 3B-1B-SS		109	401	57	113	15	1	18	78	61	69	2	8	3-1	.282	.373	.459	.832	20	.931
1995— Chicago (A.L.) 3B-1B-DH		135	492	79	145	22	0	26	93	75	98	1	8	4-3	.295	.384	.498	.882	19	.956
1996— Chicago (A.L.)	3B-1B	158	586	96	168	31	2	34	105	78	81	2	18	1-3	.287	.368	.520	.888	11	.975
1997— Nashville (A.A.)	3B-DH	15	15	3	6	1	0	2	5	2	1	0	0	0-1	.400	.471	.867	1.337	0	1.000
— Birmingham (Sou.)	3B	4	17	3	5	1	0	1	2	1	1	0	2	0-0	.294	.333	.529	.863	2	.714
— Chicago (A.L.)	3B	54	183	27	48	10	1	6	26	34	21	0	3	0-0	.262	.373	.426	.799	7	.956
1998— Chicago (A.L.)	3B	161	590	84	155	31	4	21	91	79	111	4	10	1-1	.263	.349	.436	.785	15	.966
1999— New York (N.L.)	3B-1B	161	588	88	177	38	0	32	120	74	109	3	14	1-1	.301	.379	.529	.908	9	.980
2000— New York (N.L.)	3B-1B	141	469	61	109	23	1	24	84	75	91	2	14	3-5	.232	.338	.439	.777	17	.955
2001— New York (N.L.)	3B	142	456	70	108	20	0	21	61	88	101	1	13	2-5	.237	.359	.419	.778	16	.957
2002— New York (A.L.)	3B	141	465	68	115	17	0	27	93	90	101	2	14	3-1	.247	.368	.458	.826	* 23	.944
2003— New York (A.L.) 3B-DH-2B		89	283	31	71	13	0	9	42	40	62	0	8	0-0	.251	.344	.392	.736	5	.975
— Los Angeles (N.L.)	1B-3B	49	109	11	24	5	1	5	13	18	25	0	3	0-0	.220	.331	.422	.753	3	.989
2004— Los Angeles (N.L.)	1B-3B-P	102	152	19	37	3	0	5	28	22	31	0	3	0-0	.243	.337	.362	.699	0	1.000
American League totals (12 years)		1484	5290	757	1430	249	12	207	876	798	822	17	129	18-27	.270	.364	.439	.803	182	.958
National League totals (5 years)		595	1774	249	455	89	2	87	306	277	357	6	47	6-11	.256	.356	.456	.812	45	.974
Major League totals (16 years)		2079	7064	1006	1885	338	14	294	1182	1075	1179	23	176	24-38	.267	.362	.444	.806	227	.963

DIVISION SERIES RECORD

Year Team (League)	Pos.	G	AB	R	H	2B	3B	HR	RBI	BB	SO	HBP	GDP	SB-CS	Avg.	OBP	SLG	OPS	E	Avg.
1999— New York (N.L.)	3B	4	14	1	3	1	0	0	1	4	2	0	0	0-0	.214	.389	.357	.746	0	1.000
2000— New York (N.L.)	3B-1B	4	14	1	2	0	0	1	2	4	1	1	1	0-0	.143	.368	.357	.726	0	1.000
2002— New York (A.L.)	3B	4	14	1	4	2	0	0	4	1	2	0	1	0-0	.286	.313	.429	.741	0	1.000
2004— Los Angeles (N.L.)		3	3	0	0	0	0	0	0	0	1	0	0	0-0	.000	.000	.000	.000	0	...
Division series totals (4 years)		15	45	3	9	4	0	1	7	9	6	1	2	0-0	.200	.339	.356	.695	0	1.000

CHAMPIONSHIP SERIES RECORD

Year Team (League)	Pos.	G	AB	R	H	2B	3B	HR	RBI	BB	SO	HBP	GDP	SB-CS	Avg.	OBP	SLG	OPS	E	Avg.
1993—Chicago (A.L.)	3B-1B	6	20	2	4	0	0	1	5	6	6	0	0	0-0	.200	.370	.350	.720	1	.938
1999—New York (N.L.)	3B	6	25	2	3	1	0	0	1	2	5	0	1	0-0	.120	.185	.160	.345	0	1.000
2000—New York (N.L.)	3B	5	14	4	3	1	0	0	5	6	0	0	0	0-0	.214	.409	.286	.695	1	.938
Champ. series totals (3 years)		17	59	8	10	2	0	1	11	14	11	0	1	0-0	.169	.316	.254	.570	2	.962

WORLD SERIES RECORD

Year Team (League)	Pos.	G	AB	R	H	2B	3B	HR	RBI	BB	SO	HBP	GDP	SB-CS	Avg.	OBP	SLG	OPS	E	Avg.
2000—New York (N.L.)	3B	5	20	1	3	1	0	1	1	1	5	0	0	0-0	.150	.190	.350	.540	0	1.000

ALL-STAR GAME RECORD

		G	AB	R	H	2B	3B	HR	RBI	BB	SO	HBP	GDP	SB-CS	Avg.	OBP	SLG	OPS	E	Avg.
All-Star Game totals (2 years)		2	3	1	2	1	0	0	1	0	1	0	0	0-0	.667	.667	1.000	1.667	0	1.000

VIDRO, JOSE — 2B

PERSONAL: Born August 27, 1974, in Mayaguez, Puerto Rico. ... 5-11/193. ... Bats both, throws right. ... Full name: Jose Angel Vidro. ... Name pronounced: VEE-droe. ... High school: Blanco Morales (Sabana Grande, Puerto Rico).

TRANSACTIONS/CAREER NOTES: Selected by Montreal Expos organization in sixth round of 1992 free-agent draft. ... On disabled list (May 20-June 12, 2001; and August 26, 2004-remainder of season). ... Expos franchise transferred to Washington, D.C., for 2005 season.

2004 GAMES PLAYED BY POSITION (MLB): 2B—105, DH—4.

Year Team (League)	Pos.	G	AB	R	H	2B	3B	HR	RBI	BB	SO	HBP	GDP	SB-CS	Avg.	OBP	SLG	OPS	E	Avg.
1992—GC Expos (GCL)	2B	54	200	29	66	6	2	4	31	16	31	0	5	10-1	.330	.376	.440	.816	4	.982
1993—Burlington (Midw.)	2B	76	287	39	69	19	0	2	34	28	54	5	7	3-2	.240	.317	.328	.644	7	.974
1994—W.P. Beach (FSL)	2B	125	465	57	124	30	2	4	49	51	56	5	5	8-2	.267	.344	.366	.709	20	.964
1995—W.P. Beach (FSL)	IF	44	163	20	53	15	2	3	24	8	21	2	5	0-1	.325	.360	.497	.857	4	.981
—Harrisburg (East.)	IF	64	246	33	64	16	2	4	38	20	37	1	5	7-7	.260	.315	.390	.705	9	.966
1996—Harrisburg (East.)	IF	126	452	57	117	25	3	18	82	29	71	2	6	3-1	.259	.300	.447	.747	15	.964
1997—Ottawa (Int'l)	3B-2B-DH	73	279	40	90	17	0	13	47	22	40	1	6	2-0	.323	.370	.523	.894	8	.967
—Montreal (N.L.)	3B-2B-DH	67	169	19	42	12	1	2	17	11	20	2	1	1-0	.249	.297	.367	.664	4	.955
1998—Montreal (N.L.)	2B-3B	83	205	24	45	12	0	0	18	27	33	4	5	2-2	.220	.318	.278	.596	6	.972
—Ottawa (Int'l)	2B-3B-DH	63	235	35	68	14	2	2	32	24	25	4	4	5-2	.289	.361	.391	.752	6	.973
1999—Montreal (N.L.)	2-1-OF-3	140	494	67	150	45	2	12	59	29	51	4	12	0-4	.304	.346	.476	.822	11	.981
2000—Montreal (N.L.)	2B	153	606	101	200	51	2	24	97	49	69	2	17	5-4	.330	.379	.540	.918	10	.986
2001—Montreal (N.L.)	2B-DH	124	486	82	155	34	1	15	59	31	49	10	18	4-1	.319	.371	.486	.856	9	.983
2002—Montreal (N.L.)	2B	152	604	103	190	43	3	19	96	60	70	3	12	2-1	.315	.378	.490	.868	11	.986
2003—Montreal (N.L.)	2B	144	509	77	158	36	0	15	65	69	50	7	16	3-2	.310	.397	.470	.866	10	.983
2004—Montreal (N.L.)	2B-DH	110	412	51	121	24	0	14	60	49	43	0	14	3-1	.294	.367	.454	.821	6	.987
Major League totals (8 years)		973	3485	524	1061	257	9	101	471	325	385	32	95	20-15	.304	.367	.470	.837	67	.983

ALL-STAR GAME RECORD

		G	AB	R	H	2B	3B	HR	RBI	BB	SO	HBP	GDP	SB-CS	Avg.	OBP	SLG	OPS	E	Avg.
All-Star Game totals (3 years)		3	5	0	0	0	0	0	0	0	2	0	0	0-0	.000	.000	.000	.000	1	.750

VILLACIS, EDUARDO — P

PERSONAL: Born August 29, 1979, in Caracas, Venezuela. ... 6-2/170. ... Throws right, bats right. ... Full name: Eduardo Enrique Villacis. ... High school: Instituto Victegui (Venezuela).

TRANSACTIONS/CAREER NOTES: Signed as a non-drafted free agent by Colorado Rockies organization (May 14, 1998). ... Traded by Rockies to Kansas City Royals for P Bryan Rekar (May 18, 2002). ... Claimed on waivers by Chicago White Sox (May 26, 2004).

CAREER HITTING: 0-for-0 (.000). 0 R, 0 2B, 0 3B, 0 HR, 0 RBI.

Year Team (League)	W	L	Pct.	ERA	WHIP	G	GS	CG	ShO	Hld.	Sv.-Opp.	IP	H	R	ER	HR	BB-IBB	SO	Avg.
2000—Portland (N'west)	0	0	...	0.00	1.62	5	0	0	0	...	1-...	4.1	4	1	0	0	3-1	4	.235
—Ariz. Rockies (Ariz.)	4	2	.667	1.86	1.20	13	9	0	0	...	1-...	48.1	39	17	10	0	19-1	37	.222
2001—Tri-Cities (N'west)	4	1	.800	4.26	1.16	11	0	0	0	...	0-...	19.0	14	9	9	2	8-1	20	.200
—Casper (Pio.)	1	0	1.000	0.00	1.17	1	1	0	0	...	0-...	6.0	5	1	0	0	2-0	3	.217
2002—Asheville (S. Atl.)	1	0	1.000	1.89	0.74	11	1	0	0	...	0-...	19.0	12	4	4	2	2-0	8	.174
—Wilmington (Caro.)	2	1	.667	2.25	1.04	17	0	0	0	...	1-...	28.0	19	8	7	2	10-1	15	.190
2003—Wilmington (Caro.)	6	2	.750	2.82	1.14	42	4	0	0	...	2-...	92.2	78	36	29	4	28-3	64	.227
2004—Kansas City (A.L.)	0	1	.000	13.50	3.00	1	1	0	0	0	0-0	3.1	6	5	5	1	4-0	0	.375
—Wichita (Texas)	2	0	1.000	2.67	0.92	8	3	0	0	...	0-...	30.1	22	11	9	3	6-0	21	.195
—Birmingham (Southern)	6	4	.600	3.28	1.32	19	18	0	0	...	0-...	96.0	93	40	35	9	34-5	71	.257
Major League totals (1 year)	0	1	.000	13.50	3.00	1	1	0	0	0	0-0	3.1	6	5	5	1	4-0	0	.375

VILLAFUERTE, BRANDON — P

PERSONAL: Born December 17, 1975, in Hilo, Hawaii. ... 5-11/195. ... Throws right, bats right. ... Full name: Brandon Paul Villafuerte. ... Name pronounced: vila-FERT-tee. ... High school: Live Oak (Morgan Hill, Calif.). ... Junior college: West Valley (Calif.). ... College: West Valley (Calif.).

TRANSACTIONS/CAREER NOTES: Selected by Florida Marlins organization in 37th round of 1993 free-agent draft; did not sign. ... Selected by New York Mets organization 66th round of 1994 free-agent draft. ... Traded by Mets with a player to be named to Marlins for OF Robert Stratton (March 20,1998); Marlins acquired 2B Cesar Crespo to complete deal (September 14, 1998). ... Traded by Marlins to Detroit Tigers for P Mike Drumright (July 31, 1999). ... Traded by Tigers with P Kevin Mobley to Texas Rangers for P Matt Perisho (December 15, 2000). ... Signed as a free agent by San Diego Padres organization (December 6, 2001). ... Released by Padres (January 13, 2004). ... Signed by Arizona Diamondbacks (February 4, 2004). ... Refused minor league assignment and became a free agent (July 25, 2004).

CAREER HITTING: 0-for-2 (.000). 0 R, 0 2B, 0 3B, 0 HR, 0 RBI.

Year Team (League)	W	L	Pct.	ERA	WHIP	G	GS	CG	ShO	Hld.	Sv.-Opp.	IP	H	R	ER	HR	BB-IBB	SO	Avg.
1995—Kingsport (Appalachian)	5	1	.833	5.63	1.69	20	0	0	0	...	0-...	32.0	28	21	20	0	26-0	42	.243
1996—Pittsfield (N.Y.-Penn.)	8	3	.727	3.02	1.28	18	7	1	0	...	1-...	62.2	53	21	21	5	27-0	59	.231
1997—Capital City (S. Atl.)	3	1	.750	2.38	1.20	47	3	0	0	...	7-...	75.2	58	23	20	6	33-0	88	.216
1998—Brevard County (FSL)	1	0	1.000	0.93	0.83	1	0	0	0	...	0-...	9.2	7	3	1	0	1-0	6	.212
—Portland (East.)	0	2	.000	4.97	1.86	30	0	0	0	...	1-...	54.1	68	35	30	3	33-2	52	.311
—Charlotte (Int'l)	1	0	1.000	6.35	2.03	10	0	0	0	...	0-...	11.1	15	8	8	2	8-0	9	.333
1999—Portland (East.)	6	8	.429	3.50	1.37	22	12	0	0	...	0-...	100.1	97	45	39	11	40-3	85	.261
—Jacksonville (Southern)	0	2	.000	1.88	1.21	15	0	0	0	...	5-...	24.0	17	6	5	0	12-0	20	.200

Year Team (League)	W	L	Pct.	ERA	WHIP	G	GS	CG	ShO	Hld.	Sv.-Opp.	IP	H	R	ER	HR	BB-IBB	SO	Avg.
2000— Toledo (International)	4	9	.308	6.67	1.84	46	6	0	0		4-...	87.2	112	70	65	7	49-1	85	.309
— Detroit (A.L.)	0	0	...	10.38	1.85	3	0	0	0	0	0-0	4.1	4	5	5	0	4-0	1	.250
2001— Oklahoma (PCL)	5	5	.500	2.83	1.40	38	0	0	0		10-...	63.2	63	21	20	4	26-1	65	.267
— Texas (A.L.)	0	0	...	14.29	2.82	6	0	0	0	0	0-0	5.2	12	9	9	3	4-0	4	.414
2002— Portland (PCL)	8	4	.667	2.02	1.12	47	0	0	0		1-...	58.0	43	17	13	2	22-1	54	.207
— San Diego (N.L.)	1	2	.333	1.41	1.28	31	0	0	0	8	1-1	32.0	29	5	5	2	12-2	25	.248
2003— Lake Elsinore (Calif.)	0	0	...	0.00	1.00	2	0	0	0		2-...	2.0	1	0	0	0	1-0	2	.143
— Portland (PCL)	3	1	.750	1.84	1.30	37	0	0	0		12-...	44.0	42	10	9	1	14-1	40	.258
— San Diego (N.L.)	0	2	.000	4.20	1.60	31	0	0	0	2	2-5	40.2	39	20	19	7	26-2	34	.252
2004— Tucson (PCL)	2	2	.500	2.64	1.21	23	0	0	0		4-...	30.2	27	10	9	3	10-2	23	.233
— Arizona (N.L.)	0	3	.000	4.05	1.95	20	0	0	0	0	0-0	20.0	25	9	9	2	14-2	13	.313
American League totals (2 years)	0	0	...	12.60	2.40	9	0	0	0	0	0-0	10.0	16	14	14	3	8-0	5	.356
National League totals (3 years)	1	7	.125	3.21	1.56	82	0	0	0	10	3-6	92.2	93	34	33	11	52-6	72	.264
Major League totals (5 years)	1	7	.125	4.12	1.65	91	0	0	0	10	3-6	102.2	109	48	47	14	60-6	77	.275

VILLARREAL, OSCAR — P

PERSONAL: Born November 22, 1981, in Nuevo Leon, Mexico. ... 6-0/205. ... Throws right, bats left. ... Full name: Oscar Eduardo Villarreal. ... Name pronounced: VEE-yuh-ray-al.

TRANSACTIONS/CAREER NOTES: Signed as a non-drafted free agent by Arizona Diamondbacks organization (November 6, 1998). ... On disabled list (May 10, 2004-remainder of season); included rehabilitation assignment to Tucson.

CAREER HITTING: 0-for-3 (.000), 0 R, 0 2B, 0 3B, 0 HR, 0 RBI.

Year Team (League)	W	L	Pct.	ERA	WHIP	G	GS	CG	ShO	Hld.	Sv.-Opp.	IP	H	R	ER	HR	BB-IBB	SO	Avg.
1999— Ariz. D'backs (Ariz.)	1	5	.167	3.78	1.38	14	11	0	0		0-...	64.1	64	39	27	1	25-0	51	.260
2000— Tucson (PCL)	1	0	1.000	2.08	1.85	2	0	0	0		0-...	4.1	6	1	1	0	2-0	4	.353
— South Bend (Mid.)	1	3	.250	4.41	1.65	13	5	0	0		0-...	32.2	37	19	16	0	17-3	30	.274
— Ariz. D'backs (Ariz.)	0	0	...	9.00	2.00	1	0	0	0		0-...	1.0	2	1	1	0	0-0	1	.400
— High Desert (Calif.)	0	2	.000	3.65	1.54	9	4	0	0		0-...	24.2	24	20	10	4	14-0	18	.253
2001— El Paso (Texas)	6	9	.400	4.41	1.54	27	27	0	0		0-...	140.2	154	96	69	10	63-1	108	.274
2002— El Paso (Texas)	6	3	.667	3.74	1.17	14	12	1	0		0-...	84.1	73	36	35	2	26-0	85	.233
— Tucson (PCL)	3	3	.500	4.36	1.41	10	10	0	0		0-...	64.0	68	33	31	8	22-0	40	.278
2003— Arizona (N.L.)	10	7	.588	2.57	1.29	86	1	0	0	10	0-4	98.0	80	40	28	6	46-10	80	.222
2004— Arizona (N.L.)	0	2	.000	7.00	1.78	17	0	0	0	2	0-0	18.0	25	14	14	3	7-1	17	.342
— Tucson (PCL)	0	2	.000	14.34	2.25	6	5	0	0		0-...	10.2	20	17	17	3	4-0	12	.385
Major League totals (2 years)	10	9	.526	3.26	1.36	103	1	0	0	12	0-4	116.0	105	54	42	9	53-11	97	.242

VILLONE, RON — P

PERSONAL: Born January 16, 1970, in Englewood, N.J. ... 6-3/230. ... Throws left, bats left. ... Full name: Ronald Thomas Villone. ... Name pronounced: vill-OWN. ... High school: South Bergenfield (Bergenfield, N.J.). ... College: Massachusetts.

TRANSACTIONS/CAREER NOTES: Selected by Seattle Mariners in first round (14th pick overall) of 1992 free-agent draft. ... Traded by Mariners with OF Marc Newfield to San Diego Padres for P Andy Benes and a player to be named (July 31, 1995); Mariners acquired P Greg Keagle to complete deal (September 16, 1995). ... Traded by Padres with P Bryce Florie and OF Marc Newfield to Milwaukee Brewers for OF Greg Vaughn and a player to be named later (July 31, 1996); Padres acquired OF Gerald Parent to complete deal (September 16, 1996). ... Traded by Brewers with Ps Ben McDonald and Mike Fetters to Cleveland Indians for OF Marquis Grissom and P Jeff Juden (December 8, 1997). ... On disabled list (August 15-September 1, 1998); included rehabilitation assignment to Buffalo. ... Released by Indians (April 2, 1999). ... Signed by Cincinnati Reds organization (April 5, 1999). ... Traded by Reds to Colorado Rockies for two players to be named (November 8, 2000); Reds acquired Ps Jeff Taglienti and Justin Carter to complete deal (December 20, 2000). ... Traded by Rockies to Houston Astros for P Jay Powell (June 27, 2001). ... Signed as a free agent by Pittsburgh Pirates organization (February 12, 2002). ... On disabled list (August 15-September 1, 2002). ... Signed as a free agent by Arizona Diamondbacks organization (January 29, 2003). ... Released by Diamondbacks (May 15, 2003). ... Signed by Astros organization (May 19, 2003). ... Signed as a free agent by Mariners (February 10, 2004).

CAREER HITTING: 22-for-168 (.131), 7 R, 3 2B, 1 3B, 1 HR, 7 RBI.

Year Team (League)	W	L	Pct.	ERA	WHIP	G	GS	CG	ShO	Hld.	Sv.-Opp.	IP	H	R	ER	HR	BB-IBB	SO	Avg.
1993— Riverside (California)	7	4	.636	4.21	1.63	16	16	0	0		0-...	83.1	74	47	39	5	62-0	82	.241
— Jacksonville (Southern)	3	4	.429	4.38	1.41	11	11	0	0		0-...	63.2	49	34	31	6	41-3	66	.219
1994— Jacksonville (Southern)	6	7	.462	3.86	1.56	41	5	0	0		8-...	79.1	56	37	34	7	68-3	94	.199
1995— Seattle (A.L.)	0	2	.000	7.91	2.22	19	0	0	0		0-3	19.1	20	19	17	6	23-0	26	.270
— Tacoma (PCL)	1	0	1.000	0.61	0.94	22	0	0	0		13-...	29.2	9	6	2	1	19-0	43	.095
— San Diego (N.L.)	2	1	.667	4.21	1.36	19	0	0	0	3	1-2	25.2	24	12	12	5	11-0	37	.242
1996— Las Vegas (PCL)	2	1	.667	1.64	1.00	23	0	0	0		3-...	22.0	13	5	4	0	9-0	29	.169
— San Diego (N.L.)	1	1	.500	2.95	1.31	21	0	0	0	4	0-1	18.1	17	6	6	2	7-0	19	.243
— Milwaukee (A.L.)	0	0	...	3.28	1.30	23	0	0	0	5	2-2	24.2	14	9	9	4	18-0	19	.175
1997— Milwaukee (A.L.)	1	0	1.000	3.42	1.71	50	0	0	0	8	0-2	52.2	54	23	20	4	36-2	40	.271
1998— Buffalo (Int'l)	2	2	.500	2.01	1.39	23	0	0	0		7-...	22.1	20	11	5	2	11-1	28	.235
— Cleveland (A.L.)	0	0	...	6.00	1.93	25	0	0	0	1	0-0	27.0	30	18	18	3	22-0	15	.297
1999— Indianapolis (Int'l)	2	0	1.000	1.42	1.16	18	0	0	0		1-...	19.0	9	3	3	1	13-1	23	.155
— Cincinnati (N.L.)	9	7	.563	4.23	1.31	29	22	0	0	0	2-2	142.2	114	70	67	8	73-2	97	.219
2000— Cincinnati (N.L.)	10	10	.500	5.43	1.65	35	23	0	0		0-0	141.0	154	95	85	22	78-3	77	.286
2001— Colorado (N.L.)	1	3	.250	6.36	1.82	22	6	0	0	2	0-0	46.2	56	35	33	6	29-4	48	.295
— Houston (N.L.)	5	7	.417	5.56	1.49	31	6	0	0	0	0-1	68.0	77	46	42	12	24-1	65	.282
2002— Pittsburgh (N.L.)	4	6	.400	5.81	1.39	45	7	0	0	0	0-0	93.0	95	63	60	8	34-3	55	.270
2003— Tucson (PCL)	1	1	.500	3.55	1.30	15	0	0	0		1-...	25.1	20	14	10	2	12-1	22	.233
— New Orleans (PCL)	3	1	.750	1.23	1.20	5	5	0	0		0-...	29.1	24	5	4	0	10-0	18	.233
— Houston (N.L.)	6	6	.500	4.13	1.30	19	19	0	0	0	0-0	106.2	91	51	49	16	48-1	91	.233
2004— Seattle (A.L.)	8	6	.571	4.08	1.42	56	10	0	0	7	0-1	117.0	102	64	53	12	64-3	86	.232
American League totals (5 years)	9	8	.529	4.38	1.59	173	10	0	0	24	2-8	240.2	220	133	117	29	163-5	186	.246
National League totals (7 years)	38	41	.481	4.96	1.45	221	83	0	0	14	3-6	642.0	628	378	354	79	304-14	489	.258
Major League totals (10 years)	47	49	.490	4.80	1.49	394	93	2	0	38	5-14	882.2	848	511	471	108	467-19	675	.255

DIVISION SERIES RECORD

Year Team (League)	W	L	Pct.	ERA	WHIP	G	GS	CG	ShO	Hld.	Sv.-Opp.	IP	H	R	ER	HR	BB-IBB	SO	Avg.
2001— Houston (N.L.)	0	0	...	0.00	0.00	1	0	0	0		0-0	.2	0	0	0	0	0-0	0	.000

V

VINA, FERNANDO — 2B

PERSONAL: Born April 16, 1969, in Sacramento, Calif. ... 5-9/180. ... Bats left, throws right. ... Name pronounced: VEEN-yah. ... High school: Valley (Sacramento). ... College: Arizona State.

TRANSACTIONS/CAREER NOTES: Selected by New York Yankees organization in 51st round of 1988 free-agent draft; did not sign. ... Selected by New York Mets organization in ninth round of 1990 free-agent draft. ... Selected by Seattle Mariners from Mets organization in Rule 5 major league draft (December 7, 1992). ... Returned to Mets organization (June 15, 1993). ... On disabled list (May 22-June 6, 1994). ... Traded by Mets to Milwaukee Brewers (December 22, 1994), completing deal in which Brewers traded P Doug Henry for two players to be named (November 30, 1994); Brewers acquired C Javier Gonzalez as partial completion of deal (December 6, 1994). ... On disabled list (April 20-July 17, 1997); included rehabilitation assignments to Stockton and Tucson. ... On suspended list (May 11-13 and May 25-27, 1999). ... On disabled list (May 10-25 and June 4, 1999-remainder of season); included rehabilitation assignment to Beloit. ... Traded by Brewers to St. Louis Cardinals for P Juan Acevedo and two players to be named (December 20, 1999); Brewers acquired P Matt Parker and C Eliezer Alfonzo to complete deal (June 13, 2000). ... On disabled list (June 20-July 4, 2000). ... On disabled list (May 26-August 30, 2003); included rehabilitation assignment to Memphis. ... Signed as a free agent by Detroit Tigers (December 19, 2003). ... On disabled list (May 12, 2004-remainder of season).

HONORS: Won N.L. Gold Glove at second base (2001 and 2002).

2004 GAMES PLAYED BY POSITION (MLB): 2B—29.

Year Team (League)	Pos.	G	AB	R	H	2B	3B	HR	RBI	BB	SO	HBP	GDP	SB-CS	Avg.	OBP	SLG	OPS	E	Avg.
1991— Columbia (S. Atl.)	2B	129	498	77	135	23	6	6	50	46	27	13	5	42-22	.271	.344	.378	.721	21	.965
1992— St. Lucie (Fla. St.)	2B	111	421	61	124	15	5	1	42	32	26	3	7	36-17	.295	.347	.361	.708	17	.971
— Tidewater (Int'l)	2B	11	30	3	6	0	0	0	2	0	2	0	1	0-0	.200	.194	.200	.394	1	.978
1993— Seattle (A.L.)	2B-SS-DH	24	45	5	10	2	0	0	2	4	3	3	0	6-0	.222	.327	.267	.594	0	1.000
— Norfolk (Int'l)	SS-2B-OF	73	287	24	66	6	4	4	27	7	17	4	12	16-11	.230	.258	.321	.578	14	.964
1994— New York (N.L.)	2-3-S-O	79	124	20	31	6	0	0	6	12	11	12	4	3-1	.250	.372	.298	.670	4	.963
— Norfolk (Int'l)	SS-2B	6	17	2	3	0	0	0	1	1	1	1	0	1-1	.176	.250	.176	.426	1	.952
1995— Milwaukee (A.L.)	2B-SS-3B	113	288	46	74	7	7	3	29	22	28	9	6	6-3	.257	.327	.361	.688	8	.982
1996— Milwaukee (A.L.)	2B	140	554	94	157	19	10	7	46	38	35	13	15	16-7	.283	.342	.392	.733	* 16	.979
1997— Milwaukee (A.L.)	2B-DH	79	324	37	89	12	2	4	28	12	23	7	4	8-7	.275	.312	.361	.673	7	.982
— Stockton (Calif.)	2B	3	9	2	4	1	0	0	3	0	0	0	0	0-2	.444	.444	.667	1.111	0	1.000
— Tucson (PCL)	2B	6	19	3	9	3	0	1	5	3	1	2	0	0-1	.474	.583	.789	1.373	2	.923
1998— Milwaukee (N.L.)	2B	159	637	101	198	39	7	7	45	54	46	25	7	22-16	.311	.386	.427	.813	12	.986
1999— Milwaukee (N.L.)	2B	37	154	17	41	7	0	1	16	14	6	4	1	5-2	.266	.339	.331	.670	1	.995
— Beloit (Midw.)	2B-DH	2	10	1	2	1	0	0	0	0	2	0	0	0-1	.200	.200	.300	.500	2	.500
2000— St. Louis (N.L.)	2B	123	487	81	146	24	6	4	31	36	36	28	5	10-8	.300	.380	.398	.779	7	.988
2001— St. Louis (N.L.)	2B	154	631	95	191	30	8	9	56	32	35	22	7	17-7	.303	.357	.418	.775	9	.987
2002— St. Louis (N.L.)	2B	150	622	75	168	29	5	1	54	44	36	18	11	17-11	.270	.333	.338	.670	13	.987
2003— Memphis (PCL)	2B-DH	5	17	1	3	0	0	1	2	2	0	1	0	0-0	.176	.250	.176	.426	0	1.000
— St. Louis (N.L.)	2B	61	259	35	65	14	4	4	23	11	24	11	5	4-4	.251	.309	.382	.691	8	.974
2004— Detroit (A.L.)	2B	29	115	21	26	5	0	0	7	9	9	5	6	2-1	.226	.308	.270	.577	5	.970
American League totals (5 years)		385	1326	203	356	45	19	14	112	85	98	37	31	38-18	.268	.328	.363	.691	36	.980
National League totals (7 years)		763	2914	424	840	149	30	26	231	203	194	120	40	78-49	.288	.358	.387	.744	54	.985
Major League totals (12 years)		1148	4240	627	1196	194	49	40	343	288	292	157	71	116-67	.282	.348	.379	.728	90	.983

DIVISION SERIES RECORD

Year Team (League)	Pos.	G	AB	R	H	2B	3B	HR	RBI	BB	SO	HBP	GDP	SB-CS	Avg.	OBP	SLG	OPS	E	Avg.
2000— St. Louis (N.L.)	2B	3	13	3	4	0	0	1	3	1	1	1	0	0-1	.308	.400	.538	.938	0	1.000
2001— St. Louis (N.L.)	2B	5	19	2	6	0	0	1	2	0	1	1	0	1-0	.316	.350	.474	.824	0	1.000
2002— St. Louis (N.L.)	2B	3	15	3	9	0	0	0	1	1	0	0	0	0-1	.600	.625	.600	1.225	0	1.000
Division series totals (3 years)		11	47	8	19	0	0	2	6	2	2	2	0	1-2	.404	.451	.532	.983	0	1.000

CHAMPIONSHIP SERIES RECORD

Year Team (League)	Pos.	G	AB	R	H	2B	3B	HR	RBI	BB	SO	HBP	GDP	SB-CS	Avg.	OBP	SLG	OPS	E	Avg.
2000— St. Louis (N.L.)	2B	5	23	3	6	1	0	0	1	4	0	0	0	0-0	.261	.292	.304	.596	1	.960
2002— St. Louis (N.L.)	2B	5	23	2	6	2	0	0	2	0	1	0	0	0-0	.261	.250	.348	.598	0	1.000
Champ. series totals (2 years)		10	46	5	12	3	0	0	3	4	1	0	0	0-0	.261	.271	.326	.597	1	.977

ALL-STAR GAME RECORD

	G	AB	R	H	2B	3B	HR	RBI	BB	SO	HBP	GDP	SB-CS	Avg.	OBP	SLG	OPS	E	Avg.
All-Star Game totals (1 year)	1	1	0	1	0	0	0	0	0	0	0	0	0-0	1.000	1.000	1.000	2.000	1	.667

V

VIZCAINO, JOSE — 2B/SS

PERSONAL: Born March 26, 1968, in San Cristobal, Dominican Republic. ... 6-1/190. ... Bats both, throws right. ... Full name: Jose Luis Vizcaino. ... Name pronounced: vis-kie-ee-no. ... High school: Americo Tolentino (Palenque de San Cristobal, Dominican Republic).

TRANSACTIONS/CAREER NOTES: Signed as a non-drafted free agent by Los Angeles Dodgers organization (February 18, 1986). ... Traded by Dodgers to Chicago Cubs for IF Greg Smith (December 14, 1990). ... On disabled list (April 20-May 6 and August 26-September 16, 1992). ... Traded by Cubs to New York Mets for Ps Anthony Young and Ottis Smith (March 30, 1994). ... Traded by Mets with 2B Jeff Kent to Cleveland Indians for 2B Carlos Baerga and IF Alvaro Espinoza (July 29, 1996). ... Traded by Indians with 2B Jeff Kent, P Julian Tavarez and a player to be named to San Francisco Giants for 3B Matt Williams and a player to be named (November 13, 1996); Indians traded P Joe Roa to Giants for OF Trenidad Hubbard to complete deal (December 16, 1996). ... Signed as a free agent by Dodgers (December 8, 1997). ... On disabled list (June 22-September 9, 1998; and May 19-June 4, 1999). ... Traded by Dodgers to New York Yankees for IF/DH Jim Leyritz (June 20, 2000). ... Signed as a free agent by Houston Astros (November 20, 2000). ... On disabled list (June 25-August 21, 2003); included rehabilitation assignment to New Orleans.

2004 GAMES PLAYED BY POSITION (MLB): SS—64, 2B—37, 3B—21, 1B—8.

Year Team (League)	Pos.	G	AB	R	H	2B	3B	HR	RBI	BB	SO	HBP	GDP	SB-CS	Avg.	OBP	SLG	OPS	E	Avg.
1987— GC Dodgers (GCL)	SS-1B	49	150	26	38	5	1	0	12	22	24	0	1	8-5	.253	.347	.300	.647	13	.933
1988— Bakersfield (Calif.)	SS	122	433	77	126	11	4	0	38	50	54	7	6	13-14	.291	.372	.335	.707	30	.946
1989— Albuquerque (PCL)	SS	129	434	60	123	10	4	1	44	33	41	1	10	16-14	.283	.333	.332	.665	30	.951
— Los Angeles (N.L.)	SS	7	10	2	2	0	0	0	0	0	1	0	0	0-0	.200	.200	.200	.400	2	.882
1990— Albuquerque (PCL)	2B-SS	81	276	46	77	10	2	2	38	30	33	0	6	13-6	.279	.346	.351	.698	14	.964
— Los Angeles (N.L.)	2B-SS	37	51	3	14	1	1	0	2	4	8	0	1	1-1	.275	.327	.333	.661	2	.962
1991— Chicago (N.L.)	2B-3B-SS	93	145	7	38	5	0	0	10	5	18	0	1	2-1	.262	.283	.297	.579	7	.960
1992— Chicago (N.L.)	SS-3B-2B	86	285	25	64	10	4	1	17	14	35	0	4	3-0	.225	.260	.298	.558	9	.970
1993— Chicago (N.L.)	SS-3B-2B	151	551	74	158	19	4	4	54	46	71	3	9	12-9	.287	.340	.358	.697	17	.974
1994— New York (N.L.)	SS	103	410	47	105	13	3	3	33	33	62	2	5	1-11	.256	.310	.324	.635	13	.970
1995— New York (N.L.)	SS-2B	135	509	66	146	21	5	3	56	35	76	1	14	8-3	.287	.332	.365	.698	10	.984

— 474 —

Year Team (League)	Pos.	G	AB	R	H	2B	3B	HR	RBI	BB	SO	HBP	GDP	SB-CS	Avg.	OBP	SLG	OPS	E	Avg.
1996— New York (N.L.)	2B	96	363	47	110	12	6	1	32	28	58	3	6	9-5	.303	.356	.377	.733	6	.986
—Cleveland (A.L.) 2B-SS-DH		48	179	23	51	5	2	0	13	7	24	0	2	6-2	.285	.310	.335	.645	4	.982
1997— San Francisco (N.L.)	SS-2B	151	568	77	151	19	7	5	50	48	87	0	13	8-8	.266	.323	.350	.673	16	.976
1998— Los Angeles (N.L.)	SS	67	237	30	62	9	0	3	29	17	35	1	4	7-3	.262	.311	.338	.649	4	.985
1999— Los Angeles (N.L.)	S-2-3-0	94	266	27	67	9	0	1	29	20	23	1	9	2-1	.252	.305	.297	.601	7	.976
2000— Los Angeles (N.L.) S-3-2-DH-1		40	93	9	19	2	1	0	4	10	15	1	3	1-0	.204	.288	.247	.536	2	.978
—New York (A.L.)	2-3-DH-S	73	174	23	48	8	1	0	10	12	28	0	3	5-7	.276	.319	.333	.652	2	.991
2001— Houston (N.L.) SS-2B-3B		107	256	38	71	8	3	1	14	15	33	2	6	3-2	.277	.322	.344	.666	14	.939
2002— Houston (N.L.)	S-3-2-1	125	406	53	123	19	2	5	37	24	40	1	5	3-5	.303	.342	.397	.738	4	.989
2003— New Orleans (PCL)	2B-SS	2	8	1	2	0	0	1	1	1	0	0	0	0-0	.250	.333	.625	.958	1	.889
—Houston (N.L.)	S-2-3-1	91	189	14	47	7	3	3	26	8	22	1	5	0-1	.249	.281	.365	.646	5	.970
2004— Houston (N.L.)	S-2-3-1B	138	358	34	98	21	3	3	33	20	39	0	8	1-1	.274	.311	.374	.685	11	.972
American League totals (2 years)		121	353	46	99	13	3	0	23	19	52	0	5	11-9	.280	.315	.334	.649	6	.986
National League totals (16 years)		1521	4697	553	1275	175	42	33	426	327	623	16	93	61-51	.271	.319	.348	.667	129	.975
Major League totals (16 years)		1642	5050	599	1374	188	45	33	449	346	675	16	98	72-60	.272	.319	.347	.665	135	.976

DIVISION SERIES RECORD

Year Team (League)	Pos.	G	AB	R	H	2B	3B	HR	RBI	BB	SO	HBP	GDP	SB-CS	Avg.	OBP	SLG	OPS	E	Avg.
1996— Cleveland (A.L.)	2B	3	12	1	4	2	0	0	1	1	1	0	0	0-0	.333	.385	.500	.885	1	.875
1997— San Francisco (N.L.)	SS	3	11	1	2	1	0	0	0	0	5	0	0	0-0	.182	.182	.273	.455	0	1.000
2000— New York (A.L.)	2B	1	0	1	0	0	0	0	0	0	0	0	0	0-0	...	...	...	...	0	1.000
2001— Houston (N.L.)	SS	3	6	0	1	0	0	0	0	1	0	0	0	0-0	.167	.167	.167	.333	0	1.000
2004— Houston (N.L.)	SS	5	19	2	2	0	0	0	1	1	2	0	1	0-0	.105	.143	.105	.248	0	1.000
Division series totals (5 years)		15	48	5	9	3	0	0	2	2	9	0	1	0-0	.188	.216	.250	.466	1	.978

CHAMPIONSHIP SERIES RECORD

Year Team (League)	Pos.	G	AB	R	H	2B	3B	HR	RBI	BB	SO	HBP	GDP	SB-CS	Avg.	OBP	SLG	OPS	E	Avg.
2000— New York (A.L.)	2B	4	2	3	2	1	0	0	2	0	0	0	0	2-0	1.000	.667	1.500	2.167	0	1.000
2004— Houston (N.L.)	SS-2B	7	28	1	7	1	0	0	0	0	1	0	0	0-1	.250	.250	.286	.536	1	.963
Champ. series totals (2 years)		11	30	4	9	2	0	0	2	0	1	0	0	2-1	.300	.290	.367	.657	1	.966

WORLD SERIES RECORD

Year Team (League)	Pos.	G	AB	R	H	2B	3B	HR	RBI	BB	SO	HBP	GDP	SB-CS	Avg.	OBP	SLG	OPS	E	Avg.
2000— New York (A.L.)	2B	4	17	0	4	0	0	0	1	0	5	0	0	0-1	.235	.235	.235	.471	0	1.000

VIZCAINO, LUIS   P

PERSONAL: Born August 6, 1974, in Bani, Dominican Republic. ... 5-11/184. ... Throws right, bats right. ... Name pronounced: vis-ki-ee-no.

TRANSACTIONS/CAREER NOTES: Signed as a non-drafted free agent by Oakland Athletics organization (December 9, 1994). ... Traded by A's to Texas Rangers for P Justin Duchscherer (March 18, 2002). ... Traded by Rangers to Milwaukee Brewers for P Jesus Pena (March 24, 2002).

CAREER HITTING: 0-for-2 (.000), 0 R, 0 2B, 0 3B, 0 HR, 0 RBI.

Year Team (League)	W	L	Pct.	ERA	WHIP	G	GS	CG	ShO	Hld.	Sv.-Opp.	IP	H	R	ER	HR	BB-IBB	SO	Avg.
1995— Dominican Athletics (DSL)	10	2	.833	2.27	1.06	16	15	5	1	...	0-...	115.0	93	41	29		29-...	89	...
1996— Ariz. A's (Ariz.)	6	3	.667	4.07	1.37	15	10	0	0	...	1-...	59.2	58	36	27	1	24-1	52	.247
1997— Modesto (Calif.)	0	3	.000	13.19	2.58	7	0	0	0	...	0-...	14.1	24	24	21	4	13-4	15	.387
—S. Oregon (N'west)	1	6	.143	7.93	1.87	22	5	0	0	...	0-...	47.2	62	51	42	5	27-0	42	.308
1998— Modesto (Calif.)	6	3	.667	2.74	1.13	23	16	0	0	...	0-...	102.0	72	39	31	5	43-1	108	.196
—Huntsville (Southern)	3	2	.600	4.66	1.68	7	7	0	0	...	0-...	38.2	43	27	20	8	22-0	26	.279
1999— Midland (Texas)	8	7	.533	5.85	1.61	25	19	0	0	...	0-...	104.2	120	74	68	18	48-2	88	.287
—Oakland (A.L.)	0	0	...	5.40	1.80	1	0	0	0	0	0-0	3.1	3	2	2	1	3-0	2	.231
—Vancouver (PCL)	0	1	.000	1.38	1.46	7	0	0	0	...	0-...	13.0	13	4	2	0	6-0	7	.260
2000— Oakland (A.L.)	0	1	.000	7.45	1.86	12	0	0	0	0	0-0	19.1	25	17	16	2	11-0	18	.305
—Sacramento (PCL)	6	2	.750	5.03	1.43	33	2	0	0	...	5-...	48.1	48	27	27	4	21-0	41	.276
2001— Sacramento (PCL)	2	2	.500	2.14	1.07	27	0	0	0	...	7-...	42.0	35	10	10	5	10-4	56	.220
—Oakland (A.L.)	2	1	.667	4.66	1.36	36	0	0	0	3	1-1	36.2	38	19	19	8	12-1	31	.266
2002— Milwaukee (N.L.)	5	3	.625	2.99	1.05	76	0	0	0	19	5-6	81.1	55	27	27	6	30-4	79	.192
2003— Milwaukee (N.L.)	4	3	.571	6.39	1.44	75	0	0	0	9	0-6	62.0	64	45	44	16	25-3	61	.263
2004— Milwaukee (N.L.)	4	4	.500	3.75	1.18	73	0	0	0	21	1-5	72.0	61	35	30	12	24-3	63	.228
American League totals (3 years)	2	2	.500	5.61	1.55	49	0	0	0	3	1-1	59.1	66	38	37	11	26-1	51	.277
National League totals (3 years)	13	10	.565	4.22	1.20	224	0	0	0	49	6-17	215.1	180	107	101	34	79-10	203	.226
Major League totals (6 years)	15	12	.556	4.52	1.28	273	0	0	0	52	7-18	274.2	246	145	138	45	105-11	254	.238

VIZQUEL, OMAR   SS

PERSONAL: Born April 24, 1967, in Caracas, Venezuela. ... 5-9/175. ... Bats both, throws right. ... Full name: Omar Enrique Vizquel. ... Name pronounced: viz-KELL. ... High school: Francisco Espejo (Caracas, Venezuela).

TRANSACTIONS/CAREER NOTES: Signed as a non-drafted free agent by Seattle Mariners organization (April 1, 1984). ... On disabled list (April 7-May 13, 1990); included rehabilitation assignments to Calgary and San Bernardino. ... On disabled list (April 13-May 11, 1992); included rehabilitation assignment to Calgary. ... Traded by Mariners to Cleveland Indians for SS Felix Fermin, 1B Reggie Jefferson and cash (December 20, 1993). ... On disabled list (April 23-June 13, 1994); included rehabilitation assignment to Charlotte. ... On suspended list (September 17-18, 1998). ... On disabled list (June 12-August 26 and September 6, 2003-remainder of season); included rehabilitation assignment to Lake County.

HONORS: Won A.L. Gold Glove at shortstop (1993-2001).

2004 GAMES PLAYED BY POSITION (MLB): SS—147.

Year Team (League)	Pos.	G	AB	R	H	2B	3B	HR	RBI	BB	SO	HBP	GDP	SB-CS	Avg.	OBP	SLG	OPS	E	Avg.
1984— Butte (Pio.)	2B-SS	15	45	7	14	2	0	0	4	3	8	0	0	2-0	.311	.347	.356	.702	5	.894
1985— Bellingham (N'west)	2B-SS	50	187	24	42	9	0	5	17	12	27	0	0	4-3	.225	.270	.353	.623	19	.932
1986— Wausau (Midw.)	2B-SS	105	352	60	75	13	2	4	28	64	56	2	6	19-6	.213	.333	.295	.629	16	.968
1987— Salinas (Calif.)	2B-SS	114	407	61	107	12	8	0	38	57	55	0	5	25-19	.263	.350	.332	.682	25	.938
1988— Vermont (East.)	SS	103	374	54	95	18	2	1	35	42	44	3	6	30-11	.254	.328	.329	.657	19	.959
—Calgary (PCL)	SS	33	107	10	24	2	3	1	12	5	14	0	1	2-4	.224	.259	.327	.586	6	.957
1989— Seattle (A.L.)	SS	143	387	45	85	7	3	1	20	28	40	1	6	1-4	.220	.273	.261	.534	18	.971
—Calgary (PCL)	SS	7	28	3	6	2	0	0	3	3	4	1	1	0-2	.214	.313	.286	.598	0	1.000

V

Year Team (League)	Pos.	G	AB	R	H	2B	3B	HR	RBI	BB	SO	HBP	GDP	SB-CS	Avg.	OBP	SLG	OPS	E	Avg.
1990—Calgary (PCL)	SS	48	150	18	35	6	2	0	8	13	10	2	3	4-3	.233	.299	.300	.599	6	.972
—San Bern. (Calif.)	SS	6	28	5	7	0	0	0	3	3	1	0	0	1-2	.250	.323	.250	.573	3	.914
—Seattle (A.L.)	SS	81	255	19	63	3	2	2	18	18	22	0	7	4-1	.247	.295	.298	.593	7	.980
1991—Seattle (A.L.)	2B-SS	142	426	42	98	16	4	1	41	45	37	0	8	7-2	.230	.302	.293	.595	13	.980
1992—Seattle (A.L.)	SS	136	483	49	142	20	4	0	21	32	38	2	14	15-13	.294	.340	.352	.692	7	.989
—Calgary (PCL)	SS	6	22	0	6	1	0	0	2	1	3	1	3	0-1	.273	.333	.318	.652	1	.972
1993—Seattle (A.L.)	SS-DH	158	560	68	143	14	2	2	31	50	71	4	7	12-14	.255	.319	.298	.618	15	.980
1994—Cleveland (A.L.)	SS	69	286	39	78	10	1	1	33	23	23	0	4	13-4	.273	.325	.325	.650	6	.981
—Charlotte (Int'l)	SS	7	26	3	7	1	0	0	1	2	1	0	0	1-0	.269	.321	.308	.629	1	.967
1995—Cleveland (A.L.)	SS	136	542	87	144	28	0	6	56	59	59	1	4	29-11	.266	.333	.351	.684	9	.986
1996—Cleveland (A.L.)	SS	151	542	98	161	36	1	9	64	56	42	4	10	35-9	.297	.362	.417	.779	20	.971
1997—Cleveland (A.L.)	SS	153	565	89	158	23	6	5	49	57	58	2	16	43-12	.280	.347	.368	.715	10	.985
1998—Cleveland (A.L.)	SS	151	576	86	166	30	6	2	50	62	64	4	10	37-12	.288	.358	.372	.730	5	.993
1999—Cleveland (A.L.)	SS-OF	144	574	112	191	36	4	5	66	65	50	1	8	42-9	.333	.397	.436	.833	15	.976
2000—Cleveland (A.L.)	SS	156	613	101	176	27	3	6	66	87	72	5	13	22-10	.287	.377	.375	.753	3	.995
2001—Cleveland (A.L.)	SS	155	611	84	156	26	8	2	50	61	72	2	14	13-9	.255	.323	.334	.657	7	.989
2002—Cleveland (A.L.)	SS	151	582	85	160	31	5	14	72	56	64	8	7	18-10	.275	.341	.418	.759	7	.990
2003—Lake County (S.Atl.)	SS	4	14	0	1	0	0	0	0	1	2	0	0	1-0	.071	.133	.071	.205	0	1.000
—Cleveland (A.L.)	SS	64	250	43	61	13	2	2	19	29	20	0	11	8-3	.244	.321	.336	.657	7	.978
2004—Cleveland (A.L.)	SS	148	567	82	165	28	3	7	59	57	62	1	12	19-6	.291	.353	.388	.741	11	.982
Major League totals (16 years)		2138	7819	1129	2147	348	54	66	715	785	794	35	151	318-129	.275	.341	.358	.699	160	.983

DIVISION SERIES RECORD

Year Team (League)	Pos.	G	AB	R	H	2B	3B	HR	RBI	BB	SO	HBP	GDP	SB-CS	Avg.	OBP	SLG	OPS	E	Avg.
1995—Cleveland (A.L.)	SS	3	12	2	2	1	0	0	4	2	2	0	0	1-0	.167	.286	.250	.536	0	1.000
1996—Cleveland (A.L.)	SS	4	14	4	6	1	0	0	2	3	4	0	0	4-2	.429	.500	.500	1.000	0	1.000
1997—Cleveland (A.L.)	SS	5	18	3	9	0	0	0	1	2	1	0	0	4-0	.500	.550	.500	1.050	0	1.000
1998—Cleveland (A.L.)	SS	4	15	1	1	0	0	0	0	1	0	0	0	0-0	.067	.125	.067	.192	0	1.000
1999—Cleveland (A.L.)	SS	5	21	3	5	1	1	0	3	2	3	0	0	0-0	.238	.304	.381	.685	0	1.000
2001—Cleveland (A.L.)	SS	5	22	2	9	1	1	0	6	1	1	0	0	1-0	.409	.435	.545	.980	1	.964
Division series totals (6 years)		26	102	15	32	4	2	0	16	11	11	0	0	10-2	.314	.377	.392	.769	1	.992

CHAMPIONSHIP SERIES RECORD

Year Team (League)	Pos.	G	AB	R	H	2B	3B	HR	RBI	BB	SO	HBP	GDP	SB-CS	Avg.	OBP	SLG	OPS	E	Avg.
1995—Cleveland (A.L.)	SS	6	23	2	2	1	0	0	2	5	2	0	0	3-0	.087	.241	.130	.372	0	1.000
1997—Cleveland (A.L.)	SS	6	25	1	1	0	0	0	0	2	10	1	0	0-0	.040	.143	.040	.183	0	1.000
1998—Cleveland (A.L.)	SS	6	25	2	11	0	1	0	0	1	3	1	0	4-1	.440	.481	.520	1.001	1	.974
Champ. series totals (3 years)		18	73	5	14	1	1	0	2	8	15	2	0	7-1	.192	.286	.233	.519	1	.990

WORLD SERIES RECORD

Year Team (League)	Pos.	G	AB	R	H	2B	3B	HR	RBI	BB	SO	HBP	GDP	SB-CS	Avg.	OBP	SLG	OPS	E	Avg.
1995—Cleveland (A.L.)	SS	6	23	4	4	0	1	0	1	3	5	0	0	1-0	.174	.269	.261	.530	0	1.000
1997—Cleveland (A.L.)	SS	7	30	5	7	2	0	0	1	3	5	0	0	5-0	.233	.303	.300	.603	0	1.000
World series totals (2 years)		13	53	8	11	2	1	0	2	6	10	0	0	6-0	.208	.288	.283	.571	0	1.000

ALL-STAR GAME RECORD

		G	AB	R	H	2B	3B	HR	RBI	BB	SO	HBP	GDP	SB-CS	Avg.	OBP	SLG	OPS	E	Avg.
All-Star Game totals (3 years)		3	5	0	2	0	0	0	1	1	0	0	0	0-0	.400	.500	.800	1.300	0	1.000

VOGELSONG, RYAN   P

PERSONAL: Born July 22, 1977, in Charlotte, N.C. ... 6-3/213. ... Throws right, bats right. ... Full name: Ryan Andrew Vogelsong. ... High school: Octorara Area (Atglen, Pa.). ... College: Kutztown State (Pa.).

TRANSACTIONS/CAREER NOTES: Selected by San Francisco Giants organization in fifth round of 1998 free-agent draft. ... Traded by Giants with OF Armando Rios to Pittsburgh Pirates for P Jason Schmidt (July 30, 2001). ... On disabled list (March 30-August 1, 2002); included rehabilitation assignments to Lynchburg and Altoona.

CAREER HITTING: 9-for-47 (.191), 2 R, 3 2B, 0 3B, 0 HR, 3 RBI.

Year Team (League)	W	L	Pct.	ERA	WHIP	G	GS	CG	ShO	Hld.	Sv.-Opp.	IP	H	R	ER	HR	BB-IBB	SO	Avg.
1998—Salem-Keizer (N'west)	6	1	.857	1.77	0.95	10	10	0	0	...	0-...	56.0	37	15	11	5	16-0	66	.186
—San Jose (California)	0	0	...	7.58	1.42	4	4	0	0	...	0-...	19.0	23	16	16	3	4-0	26	.307
1999—San Jose (California)	4	4	.500	2.45	0.92	13	13	0	0	...	0-...	69.2	37	26	19	3	27-0	86	.154
—Shreveport (Texas)	0	2	.000	7.31	1.94	6	6	0	0	...	0-...	28.1	40	25	23	7	15-0	23	.336
2000—Shreveport (Texas)	6	10	.375	4.23	1.43	27	27	1	0	...	0-...	155.1	153	82	73	15	69-2	147	.260
—San Francisco (N.L.)	0	0	...	0.00	1.00	1	0	0	0	0	0-0	6.0	4	0	0	0	2-0	6	.182
2001—Fresno (PCL)	3	3	.500	2.79	0.91	10	10	0	0	...	0-...	58.0	35	18	18	6	18-0	53	.170
—San Francisco (N.L.)	0	3	.000	5.65	1.50	13	0	0	0	1	0-0	28.2	29	21	18	5	14-0	17	.257
—Nashville (PCL)	2	3	.400	3.98	1.29	6	6	0	0	...	0-...	31.2	26	15	14	2	15-0	33	.230
—Pittsburgh (N.L.)	0	2	.000	12.00	2.67	2	2	0	0	0	0-0	6.0	10	10	8	1	6-1	7	.357
2002—Lynchburg (Carolina)	1	1	.500	8.04	1.66	4	4	0	0	...	0-...	15.2	19	14	14	0	7-0	20	.297
—Altoona (East.)	1	5	.167	5.56	1.31	8	8	0	0	...	0-...	43.2	47	27	27	5	10-0	35	.278
2003—Nashville (PCL)	12	8	.600	4.29	1.30	26	26	1	1	...	0-...	149.0	142	75	71	12	54-5	146	.250
—Pittsburgh (N.L.)	2	2	.500	6.55	1.77	6	5	0	0	0	0-0	22.0	30	19	16	1	9-3	15	.323
2004—Pittsburgh (N.L.)	6	13	.316	6.50	1.62	31	26	0	0	0	0-0	133.0	148	97	96	22	67-7	92	.285
Major League totals (4 years)	8	20	.286	6.35	1.63	56	33	0	0	1	0-0	195.2	221	147	138	29	98-11	137	.285

WAECHTER, DOUG   P

PERSONAL: Born January 28, 1981, in St. Petersburg, Fla. ... 6-4/209. ... Throws right, bats right. ... Full name: Douglas Michael Waechter. ... High school: Northeast Senior High (St. Petersburg, Florida).

TRANSACTIONS/CAREER NOTES: Selected by Tampa Bay Devil Rays organization in third round of 1999 free-agent draft. ... On disabled list (June 9-September 6, 2004); included rehabilitation assignment to Durham.

CAREER HITTING: 0-for-0 (.000), 0 R, 0 2B, 0 3B, 0 HR, 0 RBI.

Year Team (League)	W	L	Pct.	ERA	WHIP	G	GS	CG	ShO	Hld.	Sv.-Opp.	IP	H	R	ER	HR	BB-IBB	SO	Avg.
1999—Princeton (Appalachian)	0	5	.000	9.77	2.31	11	7	0	0	...	0-...	35.0	46	45	38	2	35-0	38	.317
2000—Hudson Valley (NY-Penn.) .	4	4	.500	2.35	1.24	14	14	2	2	...	0-...	72.2	53	23	19	2	37-0	58	.205

W

Year	Team (League)	W	L	Pct.	ERA	WHIP	G	GS	CG	ShO	Hld.	Sv.-Opp.	IP	H	R	ER	HR	BB-IBB	SO	Avg.
2001—	Char., S.C. (SAL)	8	11	.421	4.34	1.42	26	26	1	0	...	0-...	153.1	179	97	74	14	38-1	107	.285
2002—	Char., S.C. (SAL)	3	3	.500	3.47	1.51	7	7	0	0	...	0-...	36.1	39	20	14	2	16-3	36	.277
	— Bakersfield (California)	6	3	.667	2.66	1.32	17	17	0	0	...	0-...	108.1	114	43	32	9	29-0	101	.267
	— Orlando (Sou.)	1	3	.250	9.00	2.22	4	4	1	0	...	0-...	18.0	27	20	18	4	13-0	18	.338
2003—	Orlando (Sou.)	5	3	.625	4.13	1.22	13	12	0	0	...	0-...	76.1	74	39	35	6	19-0	45	.257
	— Durham (Int'l)	3	3	.500	3.33	1.23	10	10	0	0	...	0-...	51.1	51	25	19	9	12-0	35	.262
	— Tampa Bay (A.L.)	3	2	.600	3.31	1.25	6	5	1	1	0	0-0	35.1	29	13	13	4	15-0	29	.225
2004—	Durham (Int'l)	0	2	.000	6.75	1.70	8	8	0	0	...	0-...	29.1	33	22	22	11	17-0	22	.277
	— Tampa Bay (A.L.)	5	7	.417	6.01	1.44	14	14	0	0	0	0-0	70.1	68	54	47	20	33-1	36	.252
	Major League totals (2 years)	8	9	.471	5.11	1.37	20	19	1	1	0	0-0	105.2	97	67	60	24	48-1	65	.243

WAGNER, BILLY   P

PERSONAL: Born July 25, 1971, in Tannersville, Va. ... 5-11/195. ... Throws left, bats left. ... Full name: William Edward Wagner. ... High school: Tazewell (Va.). ... Junior college: Ferrum (Va.).

TRANSACTIONS/CAREER NOTES: Selected by Houston Astros organization in first round (12th pick overall) of 1993 free-agent draft. ... On disabled list (August 23-September 7, 1996). ... On disabled list (July 16-August 7, 1998); included rehabilitation assignment to Jackson. ... On disabled list (June 21, 2000-remainder of season). ... On disabled list (June 4-June 19, 2001); included rehabilitation assignment to Round Rock. ... Traded by Astros to Philadelphia Phillies for Ps Brandon Duckworth, Taylor Buchholz and Ezequiel Astascio (November 3, 2003). ... On disabled list (May 8-June 8 and July 22-September 4, 2004); included rehabilitation assignment to Reading. ... On suspended list (September 17-19, 2004).

CAREER HITTING: 1-for-17 (.059), 1 R, 0 2B, 0 3B, 0 HR, 1 RBI.

Year	Team (League)	W	L	Pct.	ERA	WHIP	G	GS	CG	ShO	Hld.	Sv.-Opp.	IP	H	R	ER	HR	BB-IBB	SO	Avg.
1993—	Auburn (N.Y.-Penn)	1	3	.250	4.08	1.74	7	7	0	0	...	0-...	28.2	25	19	13	2	25-0	31	.231
1994—	Quad City (Midw.)	8	9	.471	3.29	1.24	26	26	2	0	...	0-...	153.0	99	71	56	9	91-0	204	.188
1995—	Jackson (Texas)	2	2	.500	2.57	1.21	12	12	0	0	...	0-...	70.0	49	25	20	7	36-1	77	.199
	— Tucson (PCL)	5	3	.625	3.18	1.34	13	13	0	0	...	0-...	76.1	70	28	27	3	32-0	80	.245
	— Houston (N.L.)	0	0	...	0.00	0.00	1	0	0	0	0	0-0	.1	0	0	0	0	0-0	0	.000
1996—	Tucson (PCL)	6	2	.750	3.28	1.28	12	12	1	1	...	0-...	74.0	62	32	27	2	33-0	86	.225
	— Houston (N.L.)	2	2	.500	2.44	1.12	37	0	0	0	3	9-13	51.2	28	16	14	6	30-2	67	.165
1997—	Houston (N.L.)	7	8	.467	2.85	1.19	62	0	0	0	1	23-29	66.1	49	23	21	5	30-1	106	.204
1998—	Houston (N.L.)	4	3	.571	2.70	1.18	58	0	0	0	1	30-35	60.0	46	19	18	6	25-1	97	.211
	— Jackson (Texas)	0	0	...	0.00	0.33	3	1	0	0	...	0-...	3.0	1	0	0	0	0-0	7	.100
1999—	Houston (N.L.)	4	1	.800	1.57	0.78	66	0	0	0	1	39-42	74.2	35	14	13	5	23-1	124	.135
2000—	Houston (N.L.)	2	4	.333	6.18	1.66	28	0	0	0	0	6-15	27.2	28	19	19	6	18-0	28	.255
2001—	Houston (N.L.)	2	5	.286	2.73	1.02	64	0	0	0	0	39-41	62.2	44	19	19	5	20-0	79	.198
	— Round Rock (Texas)	0	0	...	0.00	0.00	1	1	0	0	...	0-...	1.0	0	0	0	0	0-0	2	.000
2002—	Houston (N.L.)	4	2	.667	2.52	0.97	70	0	0	0	0	35-41	75.0	51	21	21	7	22-5	88	.196
2003—	Houston (N.L.)	1	4	.200	1.78	0.87	78	0	0	0	0	44-47	86.0	52	18	17	8	23-5	105	.169
2004—	Reading (East.)	0	0	...	0.00	1.00	1	1	0	0	...	0-...	1.0	1	0	0	0	0-0	2	.250
	— Philadelphia (N.L.)	4	0	1.000	2.42	0.77	45	0	0	0	1	21-25	48.1	31	16	13	5	6-1	59	.181
	Major League totals (10 years)	30	29	.508	2.52	1.02	509	0	0	0	7	246-288	552.2	364	165	155	53	197-16	753	.186

DIVISION SERIES RECORD																				
Year	Team (League)	W	L	Pct.	ERA	WHIP	G	GS	CG	ShO	Hld.	Sv.-Opp.	IP	H	R	ER	HR	BB-IBB	SO	Avg.
1997—	Houston (N.L.)	0	0	...	18.00	3.00	1	0	0	0	0	0-0	1.0	3	2	2	0	0-0	2	.500
1998—	Houston (N.L.)	1	0	1.000	18.00	4.00	1	0	0	0	0	0-1	1.0	4	2	2	1	0-0	1	.571
1999—	Houston (N.L.)	0	0	...	0.00	0.00	1	0	0	0	0	0-0	1.0	0	0	0	0	0-0	1	.000
2001—	Houston (N.L.)	0	0	...	5.40	0.60	2	0	0	0	0	0-0	1.2	1	1	1	1	0-0	3	.167
	Division series totals (4 years)	1	0	1.000	9.64	1.71	5	0	0	0	0	0-1	4.2	8	5	5	2	0-0	7	.364

ALL-STAR GAME RECORD																				
		W	L	Pct.	ERA	WHIP	G	GS	CG	ShO	Hld.	Sv.-Opp.	IP	H	R	ER	HR	BB-IBB	SO	Avg.
	All-Star Game totals (3 years)	0	0	...	4.50	0.50	3	0	0	0	1	0-0	2.0	1	1	1	1	0-0	2	.143

WAGNER, RYAN   P

PERSONAL: Born July 15, 1982, in Yoakum, Texas. ... 6-4/210. ... Throws right, bats right. ... Full name: Ryan Scott Wagner. ... High school: Yoakum (Texas). ... College: Houston.

TRANSACTIONS/CAREER NOTES: Selected by Cincinnati Reds organization in first round (14th pick overall) of 2003 free-agent draft.

CAREER HITTING: 0-for-0 (.000), 0 R, 0 2B, 0 3B, 0 HR, 0 RBI.

Year	Team (League)	W	L	Pct.	ERA	WHIP	G	GS	CG	ShO	Hld.	Sv.-Opp.	IP	H	R	ER	HR	BB-IBB	SO	Avg.
2003—	Chattanooga (Southern)	1	0	1.000	0.00	0.80	5	0	0	0	...	0-...	5.0	2	1	0	0	2-0	6	.125
	— Louisville (Int'l)	0	1	.000	4.50	1.25	4	0	0	0	...	0-...	4.0	5	2	2	0	0-0	4	.313
	— Cincinnati (N.L.)	2	0	1.000	1.66	1.15	17	0	0	0	6	0-1	21.2	13	4	4	2	12-1	25	.173
2004—	Louisville (Int'l)	1	0	1.000	2.70	1.32	15	0	0	0	...	1-...	16.2	13	5	5	0	9-0	19	.210
	— Cincinnati (N.L.)	3	2	.600	4.70	1.66	49	0	0	0	8	0-3	51.2	59	31	27	7	27-2	37	.284
	Major League totals (2 years)	5	2	.714	3.80	1.51	66	0	0	0	14	0-4	73.1	72	35	31	9	39-3	62	.254

WAKEFIELD, TIM   P

PERSONAL: Born August 2, 1966, in Melbourne, Fla. ... 6-2/210. ... Throws right, bats right. ... Full name: Timothy Stephen Wakefield. ... High school: Eau Gallie (Melbourne, Fla.). ... College: Florida Tech.

TRANSACTIONS/CAREER NOTES: Selected by Pittsburgh Pirates organization in eighth round of 1988 free-agent draft. ... Played infield in Pirates organization (1988-89). ... Released by Pirates (April 20, 1995). ... Signed by Boston Red Sox organization (April 26, 1995). ... On disabled list (April 15-May 6, 1997).

HONORS: Named N.L. Rookie Pitcher of the Year by THE SPORTING NEWS (1992). ... Named A.L. Comeback Player of the Year by THE SPORTING NEWS (1995).

CAREER HITTING: 10-for-84 (.119), 3 R, 2 2B, 0 3B, 1 HR, 3 RBI.

Year	Team (League)	W	L	Pct.	ERA	WHIP	G	GS	CG	ShO	Hld.	Sv.-Opp.	IP	H	R	ER	HR	BB-IBB	SO	Avg.
1989—	Welland (N.Y.-Penn)	1	1	.500	3.40	1.29	36	1	0	0	...	2-...	39.2	30	17	15	1	21-0	42	.211
1990—	Salem (Caro.)	10	14	.417	4.73	1.43	28	28	2	0	...	0-...	190.1	187	109	100	24	85-2	127	.261
1991—	Carolina (Southern)	15	8	.652	2.90	1.13	26	25	8	1	...	0-...	183.0	155	68	59	13	51-6	120	.231
	— Buffalo (A.A.)	0	1	.000	11.57	1.93	1	1	0	0	...	0-...	4.2	8	6	6	3	1-0	4	.364
1992—	Buffalo (A.A.)	10	3	.769	3.06	1.28	20	20	6	1	...	0-...	135.1	122	52	46	10	51-1	71	.246

W

Year	Team (League)	W	L	Pct.	ERA	WHIP	G	GS	CG	ShO	Hld.	Sv.-Opp.	IP	H	R	ER	HR	BB-IBB	SO	Avg.
— Pittsburgh (N.L.)	8	1	.889	2.15	1.21	13	13	4	1	0	0-0	92.0	76	26	22	3	35-1	51	.232
1993— Pittsburgh (N.L.)	6	11	.353	5.61	1.71	24	20	3	2	0	0-0	128.1	145	83	80	14	75-2	59	.291
— Carolina (Southern)	3	5	.375	6.99	1.59	9	9	1	0	...	0-...	56.2	68	48	44	5	22-0	36	.293
1994— Buffalo (A.A.)	5	15	.250	5.84	1.68	30	29	4	1	...	0-...	175.2	197	127	114	27	98-0	83	.290
1995— Pawtucket (Int'l)	2	1	.667	2.52	1.28	4	4	0	0	...	0-...	25.0	23	10	7	1	9-0	14	.253
— Boston (A.L.)	16	8	.667	2.95	1.18	27	27	6	1	0	0-0	195.1	163	76	64	22	68-0	119	.227
1996— Boston (A.L.)	14	13	.519	5.14	1.55	32	32	6	0	0	0-0	211.2	238	* 151	121	38	90-0	140	.280
1997— Boston (A.L.)	12	• 15	.444	4.25	1.39	35	29	4	2	1	0-0	201.1	193	109	95	24	87-5	151	.256
1998— Boston (A.L.)	17	8	.680	4.58	1.34	36	33	2	0	0	0-0	216.0	211	123	110	30	79-1	146	.252
1999— Boston (A.L.)	6	11	.353	5.08	1.56	49	17	0	0	0	15-18	140.0	146	93	79	19	72-2	104	.266
2000— Boston (A.L.)	6	10	.375	5.48	1.47	51	17	0	0	3	0-1	159.1	170	107	97	31	65-3	102	.272
2001— Boston (A.L.)	9	12	.429	3.90	1.36	45	17	0	0	3	3-5	168.2	156	84	73	13	73-5	148	.248
2002— Boston (A.L.)	11	5	.688	2.81	1.05	45	15	0	0	5	3-5	163.1	121	57	51	15	51-2	134	.204
2003— Boston (A.L.)	11	7	.611	4.09	1.30	35	33	0	0	0	1-1	202.1	193	106	92	23	71-0	169	.246
2004— Boston (A.L.)	12	10	.545	4.87	1.38	32	30	0	0	1	0-0	188.1	197	121	102	29	63-3	116	.264
American League totals (10 years)	114	99	.535	4.31	1.36	387	250	18	3	13	22-30	1846.1	1788	1027	884	244	719-21	1329	.253
National League totals (2 years)	14	12	.538	4.17	1.50	37	33	7	3	0	0-0	220.1	221	109	102	17	110-3	110	.268
Major League totals (12 years)	128	111	.536	4.29	1.37	424	283	25	6	13	22-30	2066.2	2009	1136	986	261	829-24	1439	.254

DIVISION SERIES RECORD

Year	Team (League)	W	L	Pct.	ERA	WHIP	G	GS	CG	ShO	Hld.	Sv.-Opp.	IP	H	R	ER	HR	BB-IBB	SO	Avg.
1995— Boston (A.L.)	0	1	.000	11.81	1.88	1	1	0	0	0	0-0	5.1	5	7	7	1	5-0	4	.238
1998— Boston (A.L.)	0	1	.000	33.75	3.75	1	1	0	0	0	0-0	1.1	3	5	5	0	2-0	1	.500
1999— Boston (A.L.)	0	0	...	13.50	3.50	2	0	0	0	0	0-0	2.0	3	3	3	0	4-0	4	.300
2003— Boston (A.L.)	0	1	.000	3.52	1.17	2	1	0	0	0	0-0	7.2	6	5	3	0	3-0	7	.207
Division series totals (4 years)	0	3	.000	9.92	1.90	6	3	0	0	0	0-0	16.1	17	20	18	1	14-0	16	.258

CHAMPIONSHIP SERIES RECORD

Year	Team (League)	W	L	Pct.	ERA	WHIP	G	GS	CG	ShO	Hld.	Sv.-Opp.	IP	H	R	ER	HR	BB-IBB	SO	Avg.
1992— Pittsburgh (N.L.)	2	0	1.000	3.00	1.06	2	2	2	0	0	0-0	18.0	14	6	6	4	5-0	7	.206
1999— Boston (A.L.)			Did not play.																
2003— Boston (A.L.)	2	1	.667	2.57	1.00	3	2	0	0	0	0-0	14.0	8	4	4	1	6-0	10	.163
2004— Boston (A.L.)	1	0	1.000	8.59	1.64	3	0	0	0	0	0-0	7.1	9	7	7	1	3-2	6	.281
Champ. series totals (3 years)	5	1	.833	3.89	1.14	8	4	2	0	0	0-0	39.1	31	17	17	6	14-2	23	.208

WORLD SERIES RECORD

Year	Team (League)	W	L	Pct.	ERA	WHIP	G	GS	CG	ShO	Hld.	Sv.-Opp.	IP	H	R	ER	HR	BB-IBB	SO	Avg.
2004— Boston (A.L.)	0	0	...	12.27	2.18	1	1	0	0	0	0-0	3.2	3	5	5	1	5-0	2	.300

WALKER, JAMIE — P

PERSONAL: Born July 1, 1971, in McMinnville, Tenn. ... 6-2/195. ... Throws left, bats left. ... Full name: Jamie Ross Walker. ... High school: Warren County (McMinnville, Tenn.). ... College: Austin Peay.

TRANSACTIONS/CAREER NOTES: Selected by Houston Astros organization in 10th round of 1992 free-agent draft. ... Selected by Atlanta Braves organization from Astros organization in Rule 5 major league draft (December 9, 1996). ... Traded by Braves with OF Jermaine Dye to Kansas City Royals for OF Michael Tucker and IF Keith Lockhart (March 27, 1997). ... On disabled list (June 5-24, 1997); included rehabilitation assignment to Wichita. ... On disabled list (June 1, 1998-remainder of season). ... Released by Royals (July 27, 2000). ... Signed by Cleveland Indians organization (February 9, 2001). ... Signed as a free agent by Detroit Tigers organization (December 19, 2001).

CAREER HITTING: 0-for-0 (.000), 0 R, 0 2B, 0 3B, 0 HR, 0 RBI.

Year	Team (League)	W	L	Pct.	ERA	WHIP	G	GS	CG	ShO	Hld.	Sv.-Opp.	IP	H	R	ER	HR	BB-IBB	SO	Avg.
1992— Auburn (N.Y.-Penn)	4	6	.400	3.13	1.15	15	14	0	0	...	0-...	83.1	75	35	29	4	21-0	67	.243
1993— Quad City (Midw.)	3	11	.214	5.13	1.43	25	24	1	1	...	0-...	131.2	140	92	75	12	48-1	121	.271
1994— Quad City (Midw.)	8	10	.444	4.18	1.40	32	18	0	0	...	1-...	125.0	133	80	58	10	42-2	104	.269
1995— Jackson (Texas)	4	2	.667	4.50	1.43	50	0	0	0	...	2-...	58.0	59	29	29	6	24-5	38	.269
1996— Jackson (Texas)	5	1	.833	2.50	1.28	45	7	0	0	...	2-...	101.0	94	34	28	7	35-2	79	.249
1997— Kansas City (A.L.)	3	3	.500	5.44	1.53	50	0	0	0	3	0-1	43.0	46	28	26	6	20-3	24	.271
— Wichita (Texas)	0	1	.000	9.45	1.65	5	0	0	0	...	0-...	6.2	6	8	7	1	5-0	6	.261
1998— Omaha (PCL)	5	1	.833	2.70	1.46	7	7	0	0	...	0-...	46.2	57	15	14	3	11-1	21	.313
— Kansas City (A.L.)	0	1	.000	9.87	1.90	6	2	0	0	1	0-0	17.1	30	20	19	5	3-0	15	.380
1999— Omaha (PCL)	0	1	.000	4.67	1.50	4	4	0	0	...	0-...	17.1	22	12	9	1	4-0	11	.314
— GC Royals (GCL)	1	0	1.000	3.38	1.25	2	2	0	0	...	0-...	8.0	10	3	3	1	0-0	9	.286
2000— Omaha (PCL)	3	10	.231	5.22	1.60	24	15	0	0	...	0-...	101.2	138	65	59	25	25-1	52	.336
2001— Buffalo (Int'l)	7	2	.778	3.87	1.41	38	8	0	0	...	2-...	93.0	104	44	40	12	27-1	51	.282
2002— Toledo (International)	0	1	.000	1.98	0.73	10	0	0	0	...	1-...	13.2	7	3	3	2	3-0	9	.156
— Detroit (A.L.)	1	1	.500	3.71	0.94	57	0	0	0	5	1-4	43.2	32	19	18	9	9-1	40	.199
2003— Detroit (A.L.)	4	3	.571	3.32	1.20	78	0	0	0	12	1-7	65.0	61	30	24	9	17-1	45	.247
2004— Detroit (A.L.)	3	4	.429	3.20	1.25	70	0	0	0	18	1-7	64.2	69	28	23	8	12-3	53	.263
Major League totals (5 years)	11	12	.478	4.24	1.28	261	2	0	0	39	5-19	233.2	238	125	110	37	61-8	177	.259

W

WALKER, KEVIN — P

PERSONAL: Born September 20, 1976, in Irving, Texas. ... 6-4/190. ... Throws left, bats left. ... Full name: Kevin Michael Walker. ... High school: Grand Prairie (Texas).

TRANSACTIONS/CAREER NOTES: Selected by San Diego Padres organization in sixth round of 1995 free-agent draft. ... On disabled list (April 20-May 8 and May 23, 2001-remainder of season). ... On disabled list (March 27-August 8 and August 12-September 1, 2002); included rehabilitation assignments to Lake Elsinore and Portland. ... On disabled list (March 26-June 9, 2003); included rehabilitation assignment to Lake Elsinore. ... Claimed on waivers by San Francisco Giants (March 31, 2004).

CAREER HITTING: 1-for-4 (.250), 0 R, 0 2B, 0 3B, 0 HR, 0 RBI.

Year	Team (League)	W	L	Pct.	ERA	WHIP	G	GS	CG	ShO	Hld.	Sv.-Opp.	IP	H	R	ER	HR	BB-IBB	SO	Avg.
1995— Ariz. Padres (Ariz.)	5	5	.500	3.01	1.20	13	12	0	0	...	0-...	71.2	74	34	24	1	12-0	69	.267
1996— Idaho Falls (Pioneer)	1	0	1.000	3.00	1.00	1	1	0	0	...	0-...	6.0	4	3	2	1	2-0	4	.182
— Clinton (Midw.)	4	6	.400	4.74	1.49	13	13	0	0	...	0-...	76.0	80	46	40	9	33-0	43	.276
1997— Clinton (Midw.)	6	10	.375	4.88	1.54	19	19	3	1	...	0-...	110.2	133	80	60	9	37-0	80	.298
1998— Clinton (Midw.)	2	0	1.000	1.23	1.23	2	2	0	0	...	0-...	14.2	11	2	2	0	7-0	10	.216
— Rancho Cuca. (Calif.)	11	7	.611	4.15	1.40	22	22	0	0	...	0-...	121.1	122	62	56	10	48-0	94	.267
1999— Rancho Cuca. (Calif.)	1	1	.500	3.46	1.38	27	1	0	0	...	4-...	39.0	35	19	15	2	19-3	35	.243
2000— Mobile (Sou.)	0	1	.000	2.25	0.50	4	0	0	0	...	0-...	4.0	1	1	1	1	1-0	6	.077
— San Diego (N.L.)	7	1	.875	4.19	1.31	70	0	0	0	19	0-0	66.2	49	35	31	5	38-6	56	.206

Year Team (League)	W	L	Pct.	ERA	WHIP	G	GS	CG	ShO	Hld.	Sv.-Opp.	IP	H	R	ER	HR	BB-IBB	SO	Avg.
2001— San Diego (N.L.)	0	0	...	3.00	1.08	16	0	0	0	4	0-1	12.0	5	4	4	0	8-2	17	.122
2002— Lake Elsinore (Calif.)	0	0	...	0.00	0.43	5	1	0	0	...	0-...	7.0	3	0	0	0	0-0	10	.136
— Portland (PCL)	0	0	...	3.00	0.33	3	0	0	0	...	0-...	3.0	1	1	1	1	0-0	4	.100
— San Diego (N.L.)	0	1	.000	5.63	2.13	11	0	0	0	1	0-1	8.0	12	6	5	2	5-1	11	.333
2003— Lake Elsinore (Calif.)	0	0	...	13.50	2.00	4	0	0	0	...	0-...	4.0	6	6	6	1	2-0	3	.333
— Portland (PCL)	3	1	.750	4.08	1.40	34	1	0	0	...	0-...	46.1	53	24	21	5	10-1	43	.291
— San Diego (N.L.)	0	0	...	5.40	1.50	11	0	0	0	0	0-0	6.2	5	4	4	1	5-0	5	.200
2004— San Francisco (N.L.)	0	0	...	16.20	3.00	5	0	0	0	1	0-0	1.2	3	3	3	1	2-0	1	.429
— Fresno (PCL)	1	3	.250	4.26	1.64	48	1	0	0	...	1-...	69.2	79	33	33	8	35-6	63	.298
Major League totals (5 years)	7	2	.778	4.45	1.39	113	0	0	0	25	0-2	95.0	74	52	47	9	58-9	90	.213

WALKER, LARRY — OF

PERSONAL: Born December 1, 1966, in Maple Ridge, British Columbia. ... 6-3/235. ... Bats left, throws right. ... Full name: Larry Kenneth Robert Walker. ... High school: Maple Ridge (B.C.) Senior Secondary School.

TRANSACTIONS/CAREER NOTES: Signed as a non-drafted free agent by Montreal Expos organization (November 14, 1984). ... On disabled list (April 4, 1988-entire season; June 28-July 13, 1991; and May 26-June 10, 1993). ... On suspended list (June 24-28, 1994). ... Signed as a free agent by Colorado Rockies (April 8, 1995). ... On disabled list (June 10-August 15, 1996); included rehabilitation assignments to Salem and Colorado Springs. ... On disabled list (June 18-July 3, 1998; March 29-April 14, 1999; May 11-June 9 and August 20, 2000-remainder of season). ... On disabled list (March 26-June 21, 2004); included rehabilitation assignment to Tulsa. ... Traded by Rockies with cash to St. Louis Cardinals for P Matt Burch and two players to be named (August 6, 2004); Rockies acquired Ps Chris Narveson and Luis Martinez to complete deal (August 11, 2004).

HONORS: Named N.L. Most Valuable Player by Baseball Writers' Association of America (1997). ... Won N.L. Gold Glove as outfielder (1992-93, 1997-99 and 2001-02).

2004 GAMES PLAYED BY POSITION (MLB): OF—75, DH—1.

Year Team (League)	Pos.	G	AB	R	H	2B	3B	HR	RBI	BB	SO	HBP	GDP	SB-CS	Avg.	OBP	SLG	OPS	E	Avg.
1985— Utica (N.Y.-Penn)	3B-1B	62	215	24	48	8	2	2	26	18	57	5	1	12-6	.223	.297	.307	.604	8	.981
1986— Burlington (Midw.)	3B-OF	95	332	67	96	12	6	29	74	46	112	9	4	16-8	.289	.387	.623	1.011	10	.940
— W.P. Beach (FSL)	OF	38	113	20	32	7	5	4	16	26	32	2	2	2-2	.283	.423	.540	.962	0	1.000
1987— Jacksonville (Sou.)	OF	128	474	91	136	25	7	26	83	67	120	9	6	24-3	.287	.383	.534	.917	9	.968
1988— Montreal (N.L.)					Did not play.															
1989— Indianapolis (A.A.)	OF	114	385	68	104	18	2	12	59	50	87	9	8	36-6	.270	.361	.421	.782	11	.959
— Montreal (N.L.)	OF	20	47	4	8	0	0	0	4	5	13	1	0	1-1	.170	.264	.170	.434	0	1.000
1990— Montreal (N.L.)	OF	133	419	59	101	18	3	19	51	49	112	5	8	21-7	.241	.326	.434	.761	4	.985
1991— Montreal (N.L.)	1B-OF	137	487	59	141	30	2	16	64	42	102	5	7	14-9	.290	.349	.458	.807	6	.990
1992— Montreal (N.L.)	OF	143	528	85	159	31	4	23	93	41	97	6	9	18-6	.301	.353	.506	.859	2	.993
1993— Montreal (N.L.)	OF-1B	138	490	85	130	24	5	22	86	80	76	6	8	29-7	.265	.371	.469	.841	6	.982
1994— Montreal (N.L.)	OF-1B	103	395	76	127	* 44	2	19	86	47	74	4	8	15-5	.322	.394	.587	.981	9	.980
1995— Colorado (N.L.)	OF	131	494	96	151	31	5	36	101	49	72	9	13	16-3	.306	.381	.607	.988	3	.988
1996— Colorado (N.L.)	OF	83	272	58	75	18	4	18	58	20	58	9	7	18-2	.276	.342	.570	.912	1	.994
— Salem (Caro.)	DH	2	8	3	4	3	0	1	1	0	1	0	1	0-0	.500	.500	1.250	1.750	...	...
— Colo. Springs (PCL)	OF	3	11	2	4	0	0	2	8	1	4	0	0	0-0	.364	.385	.909	1.294	0	1.000
1997— Colorado (N.L.) OF-1B-DH		153	568	143	208	46	4	* 49	130	78	90	14	15	33-8	.366 *	.452 *	.720 *	1.172	2	.993
1998— Colorado (N.L.)	O-2-3-DH	130	454	113	165	46	3	23	67	64	61	4	11	14-4	.363	.445	.630	1.075	4	.984
1999— Colorado (N.L.)	OF-DH	127	438	108	166	26	4	37	115	57	52	12	12	11-4	.379 *	.458 *	.710	1.168	4	.982
2000— Colorado (N.L.)	OF-DH	87	314	64	97	21	7	9	51	46	40	9	12	5-5	.309	.409	.506	.915	1	.994
2001— Colorado (N.L.)	OF-DH	142	497	107	174	35	3	38	123	82	103	14	9	14-5	.350 *	.449	.662	1.111	4	.984
2002— Colorado (N.L.)	OF-DH	136	477	95	161	40	4	26	104	65	73	7	8	6-5	.338	.421	.602	1.023	4	.984
2003— Colorado (N.L.)	OF-DH	143	454	86	129	25	7	16	79	98	81	11	9	7-4	.284	.422	.476	.898	4	.983
2004— Tulsa (Texas)	OF	5	9	3	2	0	0	1	2	1	2	1	0	0-0	.222	.462	.556	1.017	0	1.000
— Colorado (N.L.)	OF-DH	38	108	22	35	9	3	6	20	25	23	4	2	2-0	.324	.464	.630	1.093	4	.984
— St. Louis (N.L.)	OF	44	150	29	42	11	1	11	27	24	34	4	6	4-0	.280	.393	.560	.953	1	.983
Major League totals (16 years)		1888	6592	1289	2069	451	61	368	1259	872	1167	129	144	228-75	.314	.401	.568	.969	55	.987

DIVISION SERIES RECORD

Year Team (League)	Pos.	G	AB	R	H	2B	3B	HR	RBI	BB	SO	HBP	GDP	SB-CS	Avg.	OBP	SLG	OPS	E	Avg.
1995— Colorado (N.L.)	OF	4	14	3	3	0	0	1	3	3	4	1	1	1-0	.214	.389	.429	.817	0	1.000
2004— St. Louis (N.L.)	OF	4	15	6	5	1	0	2	3	2	5	1	0	1-0	.333	.444	.800	1.244	0	1.000
Division series totals (2 years)		8	29	9	8	1	0	3	6	5	9	2	1	2-0	.276	.417	.621	1.037	0	1.000

CHAMPIONSHIP SERIES RECORD

Year Team (League)	Pos.	G	AB	R	H	2B	3B	HR	RBI	BB	SO	HBP	GDP	SB-CS	Avg.	OBP	SLG	OPS	E	Avg.
2004— St. Louis (N.L.)	OF	7	29	6	7	1	1	2	5	3	8	0	0	0-0	.241	.313	.552	.864	0	1.000

WORLD SERIES RECORD

Year Team (League)	Pos.	G	AB	R	H	2B	3B	HR	RBI	BB	SO	HBP	GDP	SB-CS	Avg.	OBP	SLG	OPS	E	Avg.
2004— St. Louis (N.L.)	OF	4	14	2	5	0	0	2	3	2	2	0	0	0-0	.357	.438	.929	1.366	0	1.000

ALL-STAR GAME RECORD

		G	AB	R	H	2B	3B	HR	RBI	BB	SO	HBP	GDP	SB-CS	Avg.	OBP	SLG	OPS	E	Avg.
All-Star Game totals (5 years)		5	7	1	1	0	0	0	2	1	0	0	0-0	.143	.333	.143	.476	0	1.000		

WALKER, TODD — 2B

PERSONAL: Born May 25, 1973, in Bakersfield, Calif. ... 6-0/185. ... Bats left, throws right. ... Full name: Todd Arthur Walker. ... High school: Airline (Bossier City, La.). ... College: LSU.

TRANSACTIONS/CAREER NOTES: Selected by Texas Rangers organization in 51st round of 1991 free-agent draft; did not sign. ... Selected by Minnesota Twins organization in first round (eighth pick overall) of 1994 free-agent draft (June 2, 1994). ... Traded by Twins with OF/1B Butch Huskey to Colorado Rockies for 2B Todd Sears and cash (July 16, 2000). ... Traded by Rockies with OF Robin Jennings to Cincinnati Reds for OF Alex Ochoa (July 19, 2001). ... Traded by Reds to Boston Red Sox for two players to be named (December 12, 2002); Reds acquired P Josh Thigpen and 3B Tony Blanco to complete deal (December 16, 2002). ... Signed as a free agent by Chicago Cubs (January 6, 2004).

2004 GAMES PLAYED BY POSITION (MLB): 2B—89, 1B—5, OF—1.

Year Team (League)	Pos.	G	AB	R	H	2B	3B	HR	RBI	BB	SO	HBP	GDP	SB-CS	Avg.	OBP	SLG	OPS	E	Avg.
1994— Fort Myers (FSL)	2B	46	171	29	52	5	2	10	34	32	15	0	4	6-3	.304	.406	.532	.938	9	.959
1995— New Britain (East.)	2B-3B	137	513	83	149	27	3	21	85	63	101	2	13	23-9	.290	.365	.478	.843	27	.955
1996— Salt Lake (PCL) 2B-2B-DH	3B-2B-DH	135	551	94	187	41	9	28	111	57	91	5	17	13-8	.339	.400	.599	.999	19	.955

W

Year	Team (League)	Pos.	G	AB	R	H	2B	3B	HR	RBI	BB	SO	HBP	GDP	SB-CS	Avg.	OBP	SLG	OPS	E	Avg.
—Minnesota (A.L.)	3B-2B-DH		25	82	8	21	6	0	0	6	4	13	0	4	2-0	.256	.281	.329	.610	2	.965
1997—Minnesota (A.L.)	3B-2B-DH		52	156	15	37	7	1	3	16	11	30	1	5	7-0	.237	.288	.353	.641	4	.968
—Salt Lake (PCL)	3B-DH		83	322	69	111	20	1	11	53	46	49	1	10	5-5	.345	.420	.516	.936	24	.901
1998—Minnesota (A.L.)	2B-DH		143	528	85	167	41	3	12	62	47	65	1	13	19-7	.316	.372	.473	.845	13	.978
1999—Minnesota (A.L.)	2B-DH		143	531	62	148	37	4	6	46	52	83	1	15	18-10	.279	.343	.397	.740	7	.984
2000—Minnesota (A.L.)	2B-DH		23	77	14	18	1	0	2	8	7	10	0	3	3-0	.234	.287	.325	.612	4	.946
—Salt Lake (PCL)	2B		63	249	51	81	14	1	2	37	32	32	0	6	8-3	.325	.398	.414	.812	11	.964
—Colorado (N.L.)	2B		57	171	28	54	10	4	7	36	20	19	1	2	4-1	.316	.385	.544	.928	5	.975
2001—Colorado (N.L.)	2B		85	290	52	86	18	2	12	43	25	40	0	8	1-3	.297	.349	.497	.846	7	.981
—Cincinnati (N.L.)	2B-SS		66	261	41	77	17	0	5	32	26	42	1	6	0-5	.295	.361	.418	.779	4	.987
2002—Cincinnati (N.L.)	2B		155	612	79	183	42	3	11	64	50	81	3	9	8-5	.299	.353	.431	.785	8	.989
2003—Boston (A.L.)	2B-DH		144	587	92	166	38	4	13	85	48	54	1	17	1-1	.283	.333	.428	.760	16	.975
2004—Chicago (N.L.)	2B-1B-OF		129	372	60	102	19	4	15	50	43	52	4	2	0-3	.274	.352	.468	.820	7	.982
American League totals (6 years)			530	1961	276	557	130	12	36	223	169	255	5	57	50-18	.284	.339	.418	.756	46	.976
National League totals (4 years)			492	1706	260	502	106	13	50	225	164	234	9	27	13-17	.294	.357	.460	.816	31	.985
Major League totals (9 years)			1022	3667	536	1059	236	25	86	448	333	489	14	84	63-35	.289	.347	.437	.784	77	.981

DIVISION SERIES RECORD

Year	Team (League)	Pos.	G	AB	R	H	2B	3B	HR	RBI	BB	SO	HBP	GDP	SB-CS	Avg.	OBP	SLG	OPS	E	Avg.
2003—Boston (A.L.)	2B		5	16	4	5	0	0	3	4	0	1	1	0	0-0	.313	.353	.875	1.228	2	.857

CHAMPIONSHIP SERIES RECORD

Year	Team (League)	Pos.	G	AB	R	H	2B	3B	HR	RBI	BB	SO	HBP	GDP	SB-CS	Avg.	OBP	SLG	OPS	E	Avg.
2003—Boston (A.L.)	2B		7	27	5	10	1	1	2	2	1	2	1	0	0-0	.370	.414	.704	1.118	0	1.000

WALKER, TYLER — P

PERSONAL: Born May 15, 1976, in San Francisco, Calif. ... 6-3/255. ... Throws right, bats right. ... Full name: Tyler Lanier Walker. ... High school: University (San Francisco). ... College: California.

TRANSACTIONS/CAREER NOTES: Selected by New York Mets organization in second round of 1997 free-agent draft. ... Claimed on waivers by Detroit Tigers (April 3, 2003). ... Signed as a free agent by San Francisco Giants organization (December 6, 2003).

CAREER HITTING: 0-for-9 (.000), 0 R, 0 2B, 0 3B, 0 HR, 0 RBI.

Year	Team (League)	W	L	Pct.	ERA	WHIP	G	GS	CG	ShO	Hld.	Sv.-Opp.	IP	H	R	ER	HR	BB-IBB	SO	Avg.
1997—GC Mets (GCL)	0	0	...	1.00	1.11	5	0	0	0	...	3-...	9.0	8	1	1	0	2-1	9	.235
—Pittsfield (N.Y.-Penn.)	0	0	...	13.50	4.50	1	0	0	0	...	0-...	2.0	2	2	1	1	1-0	1	.400
1998—Capital City (S. Atl.)	5	5	.500	4.12	1.38	34	13	0	0	...	1-...	115.2	122	63	53	9	38-0	110	.268
1999—St. Lucie (Fla. St.)	6	5	.545	2.94	1.17	13	13	2	0	...	0-...	79.2	64	31	26	6	29-2	64	.219
—Binghamton (Eastern)	6	4	.600	6.22	1.62	13	13	0	0	...	0-...	68.0	78	49	47	11	32-0	59	.292
2000—Binghamton (Eastern)	7	6	.538	2.75	1.13	22	22	0	0	...	0-...	121.0	82	43	37	3	55-1	111	.191
—Norfolk (Int'l)	1	3	.250	2.39	1.44	5	5	0	0	...	0-...	26.1	29	7	7	0	9-0	17	.290
2001—St. Lucie (Fla. St.)	0	2	.000	8.04	1.40	4	4	0	0	...	0-...	15.2	19	14	14	0	3-0	11	.288
—Binghamton (Eastern)	1	0	1.000	0.40	0.99	4	3	0	0	...	0-...	22.1	9	2	1	1	13-1	13	.127
—Norfolk (Int'l)	3	2	.600	4.02	1.04	8	8	0	0	...	0-...	40.1	34	19	18	7	8-0	35	.230
2002—Norfolk (Int'l)	10	5	.667	3.99	1.34	28	25	1	1	...	1-...	142.0	152	65	63	13	38-3	109	.275
—New York (N.L.)	1	0	1.000	5.91	1.50	5	1	0	0	0	0-0	10.2	11	7	7	3	5-1	7	.250
2003—Toledo (International)	2	9	.182	4.45	1.40	26	22	1	0	...	0-...	131.1	139	73	65	13	47-5	117	.270
2004—Fresno (PCL)	1	1	.500	1.72	1.15	9	1	0	0	...	0-...	15.2	16	5	3	1	2-0	15	.250
—San Francisco (N.L.)	5	1	.833	4.24	1.46	52	0	0	0	5	1-1	63.2	69	31	30	8	24-1	48	.288
Major League totals (2 years)	6	1	.857	4.48	1.47	57	1	0	0	5	1-1	74.1	80	38	37	11	29-2	55	.282

WARD, DARYLE — 1B/OF

PERSONAL: Born June 27, 1975, in Lynwood, Calif. ... 6-2/230. ... Bats left, throws left. ... Full name: Daryle Lamar Ward. ... High school: Brethren Christian (Riverside, Calif.). ... Junior college: Rancho Santiago (Calif.). ... College: Rancho Santiago (Calif.). ... Son of Gary Ward, outfielder with four major league teams (1979-90) and coach, Chicago White Sox (2001-03).

TRANSACTIONS/CAREER NOTES: Selected by Detroit Tigers organization in 15th round of 1994 free-agent draft. ... Traded by Tigers with C Brad Ausmus and Ps Jose Lima, C.J. Nitkowski and Trever Miller to Houston Astros for OF Brian Hunter, IF Orlando Miller, Ps Doug Brocail and Todd Jones and cash (December 10, 1996). ... Traded by Astros to Los Angeles Dodgers for P Ruddy Lugo (January 25, 2003). ... Refused minor league assignment and became a free agent (September 30, 2003). ... Signed by Pittsburgh Pirates organization (December 8, 2003). ... On disabled list (June 26-August 15, 2004); included rehabilitation assignment to Nashville.

2004 GAMES PLAYED BY POSITION (MLB): 1B—71, OF—12.

Year	Team (League)	Pos.	G	AB	R	H	2B	3B	HR	RBI	BB	SO	HBP	GDP	SB-CS	Avg.	OBP	SLG	OPS	E	Avg.
																			FIELDING		
1994—Bristol (Appal.)	1B		48	161	17	43	6	0	5	30	19	33	0	3	5-1	.267	.343	.398	.740	11	.968
1995—Fayetteville (SAL)	1B		137	524	75	149	32	0	14	106	46	111	5	13	1-2	.284	.344	.426	.769	14	.987
1996—Lakeland (Fla. St.)	1B-DH		128	464	65	135	29	4	10	68	57	77	6	9	1-1	.291	.373	.435	.808	8	.993
—Toledo (Int'l)	1B		6	23	1	4	0	0	0	1	0	3	0	2	0-0	.174	.174	.174	.348	1	.979
1997—Jackson (Texas)	1B-DH		114	422	72	139	25	4	19	90	46	68	3	11	4-2	.329	.398	.524	.922	12	.988
—New Orleans (A.A.)	1B		14	48	4	18	1	0	2	8	7	7	0	0	0-0	.375	.455	.521	.975	2	.976
1998—New Orleans (PCL)	OF-1B-DH		116	463	78	141	31	1	23	96	41	78	2	17	2-0	.305	.361	.525	.886	13	.976
—Houston (N.L.)			4	3	1	1	0	0	0	1	0	2	0	0	0-0	.333	.500	.333	.833	...	...
1999—New Orleans (PCL)	1B-OF		61	241	56	85	15	1	28	65	23	43	3	3	1-1	.353	.416	.772	1.188	5	.991
—Houston (N.L.)	OF-1B-DH		64	150	11	41	6	0	8	30	9	31	0	3	0-0	.273	.311	.473	.784	2	.973
2000—Houston (N.L.)	OF-1B-DH		119	264	36	68	10	2	20	47	15	61	0	6	0-0	.258	.295	.538	.833	1	.992
2001—Houston (N.L.)	OF-1B-DH		95	213	21	56	15	0	9	39	19	48	1	3	0-0	.263	.323	.460	.784	1	.988
2002—Houston (N.L.)	OF-DH		136	453	41	125	31	4	12	72	33	82	1	9	1-3	.276	.324	.424	.748	3	.981
2003—Jacksonville (Sou.)	1B-OF		4	16	0	2	0	0	0	1	0	3	0	0	0-0	.125	.125	.125	.250	1	.950
—Los Angeles (N.L.)	1B-OF		52	109	6	20	1	0	0	9	3	19	1	4	0-0	.183	.211	.193	.403	1	.992
—Las Vegas (PCL)	1B-DH		34	128	16	38	9	0	4	24	10	22	0	3	0-0	.297	.343	.461	.804	2	.992
2004—Nashville (PCL)	1B-DH-OF		28	96	14	27	7	0	7	17	5	16	0	3	0-0	.281	.317	.573	.890	0	1.000
—Pittsburgh (N.L.)	1B-OF		79	293	39	73	17	2	15	57	22	45	3	8	0-0	.249	.305	.474	.780	5	.992
Major League totals (7 years)			549	1485	155	384	80	4	64	254	102	288	6	33	1-3	.259	.306	.447	.753	13	.989

DIVISION SERIES RECORD

Year	Team (League)	Pos.	G	AB	R	H	2B	3B	HR	RBI	BB	SO	HBP	GDP	SB-CS	Avg.	OBP	SLG	OPS	E	Avg.
1999—Houston (N.L.)	OF		3	7	1	1	0	0	1	1	0	2	0	0	0-0	.143	.143	.571	.714	1	.750
2001—Houston (N.L.)			2	2	1	1	0	0	1	2	0	0	0	0	0-0	.500	.500	2.000	2.500	...	...
Division series totals (2 years)			5	9	2	2	0	0	2	3	0	2	0	0	0-0	.222	.222	.889	1.111	1	.750

W

WASDIN, JOHN   P

PERSONAL: Born August 5, 1972, in Fort Belvoir, Va. ... 6-2/190. ... Throws right, bats right. ... Full name: John Truman Wasdin. ... Name pronounced: WAAZ-din. ... High school: Amos P. Godby (Tallahassee, Fla.). ... College: Florida State.

TRANSACTIONS/CAREER NOTES: Selected by New York Yankees organization in 41st round of 1990 free-agent draft; did not sign. ... Selected by Oakland Athletics organization in first round (25th pick overall) of 1993 free-agent draft. ... Traded by A's with cash to Boston Red Sox for OF Jose Canseco (January 27, 1997). ... On disabled list (July 18-August 5, 1999); included rehabilitation assignment to GCL Red Sox. ... Traded by Red Sox with Ps Brian Rose and Jeff Taglienti and 2B Jeff Frye to Colorado Rockies for Ps Rolando Arrojo and Rick Croushore, 2B Mike Lansing and cash (July 27, 2000). ... On suspended list (September 8-10, 2000). ... Released by Rockies (June 7, 2001). ... Signed by Baltimore Orioles organization (July 18, 2001). ... Traded by Orioles to Philadelphia Phillies for P Chris Brock (December 13, 2001). ... Signed as a free agent by Yomiuri of the Japan Central League (January 9, 2002). ... Signed as a free agent by Pittsburgh Pirates organization (December 1, 2002). ... Traded by Pittsburgh Pirates to Toronto Blue Jays for OF Rich Thompson (July 8, 2003). ... Refused minor league assignment and became a free agent (September 29, 2003). ... Signed by Texas Rangers organization (October 21, 2003).

CAREER HITTING: 3-for-14 (.214), 2 R, 1 2B, 0 3B, 0 HR, 1 RBI.

Year Team (League)	W	L	Pct.	ERA	WHIP	G	GS	CG	ShO	Hld.	Sv.-Opp.	IP	H	R	ER	HR	BB-IBB	SO	Avg.
1993— Ariz. A's (Ariz.)	0	0	...	3.00	1.00	1	1	0	0	...	0-...	3	3	1	1	0	0-0	1	.250
— Madison (Midw.)	2	3	.400	1.86	0.85	9	9	0	0	...	0-...	48.1	32	11	10	1	9-1	40	.186
— Modesto (Calif.)	0	3	.000	3.86	1.29	3	3	0	0	...	0-...	16.1	17	9	7	0	4-0	11	.266
1994— Modesto (Calif.)	3	1	.750	1.69	0.83	6	4	0	0	...	0-...	26.2	17	6	5	2	5-0	30	.179
— Huntsville (Southern)	12	3	.800	3.43	1.09	21	21	0	0	...	0-...	141.2	126	61	54	13	29-2	108	.236
1995— Edmonton (PCL)	12	8	.600	5.52	1.33	29	28	2	1	...	0-...	174.1	193	117	107	26	38-3	111	.281
— Oakland (A.L.)	1	1	.500	4.67	0.98	5	2	0	0	0	0-0	17.1	14	9	9	4	3-0	6	.215
1996— Edmonton (PCL)	2	1	.667	4.14	1.38	9	9	0	0	...	0-...	50.0	52	23	23	6	17-2	30	.267
— Oakland (A.L.)	8	7	.533	5.96	1.48	25	21	1	0	0	0-1	131.1	145	96	87	24	50-5	75	.283
1997— Boston (A.L.)	4	6	.400	4.40	1.28	53	7	0	0	11	0-2	124.2	121	68	61	18	38-4	84	.251
1998— Boston (A.L.)	6	4	.600	5.25	1.44	47	8	0	0	4	0-1	96.0	111	57	56	14	27-8	59	.288
— Pawtucket (Int'l)	1	0	1.000	3.00	1.33	4	2	0	0	...	0-...	12.0	11	6	4	0	5-0	10	.239
1999— Pawtucket (Int'l)	1	1	.500	2.12	0.88	5	5	0	0	...	0-...	29.2	19	9	7	1	7-0	28	.184
— Boston (A.L.)	8	3	.727	4.12	1.13	45	0	0	0	2	2-5	74.1	66	38	34	14	18-0	57	.236
— GC Red Sox (GCL)	0	0	...	0.00	0.50	1	1	0	0	...	0-...	2.0	1	0	0	0	0-0	4	.143
2000— Boston (A.L.)	1	3	.250	5.04	1.49	25	1	0	0	0	1-2	44.2	48	25	25	8	15-1	36	.273
— Pawtucket (Int'l)	1	0	1.000	2.25	0.56	5	3	0	0	...	1-...	16.0	7	4	4	0	2-0	11	.130
— Colorado (N.L.)	0	3	.000	5.80	1.43	14	3	0	0	0	0-0	35.2	42	23	23	6	9-2	35	.302
2001— Colorado (N.L.)	2	1	.667	7.03	1.64	18	0	0	0	0	0-3	24.1	32	19	19	7	8-2	17	.320
— Rochester (Int'l)	2	1	.667	3.98	1.57	5	3	0	0	...	0-...	20.1	27	9	9	3	5-0	20	.321
— Baltimore (A.L.)	1	1	.500	4.17	1.41	26	0	0	0	4	0-2	49.2	54	25	23	4	16-4	47	.277
2003— Nashville (PCL)	8	4	.667	3.04	1.10	18	18	3	1	...	0-...	112.1	101	46	38	4	24-4	116	.238
— Toronto (A.L.)	0	1	.000	23.40	4.00	3	2	0	0	0	0-...	5.0	16	13	13	2	4-0	5	.533
— Syracuse (Int'l)	2	1	.667	5.23	1.40	10	1	0	0	...	0-...	20.2	28	13	12	1	1-0	21	.318
2004— Oklahoma (PCL)	7	1	.875	3.46	1.09	18	14	2	1	...	0-...	104.0	94	43	40	10	19-0	81	.242
— Texas (A.L.)	2	4	.333	6.78	1.63	15	10	0	0	0	0-...	65.0	83	52	49	18	23-2	36	.305
American League totals (9 years)	**31**	**30**	**.508**	**5.28**	**1.40**	**244**	**51**	**1**	**0**	**21**	**3-13**	**608.0**	**658**	**383**	**357**	**106**	**194-24**	**405**	**.274**
National League totals (2 years)	**2**	**4**	**.333**	**6.30**	**1.52**	**32**	**3**	**0**	**0**	**0**	**0-3**	**60.0**	**74**	**42**	**42**	**13**	**17-4**	**52**	**.310**
Major League totals (9 years)	**33**	**34**	**.493**	**5.38**	**1.41**	**276**	**54**	**1**	**0**	**21**	**3-16**	**668.0**	**732**	**425**	**399**	**119**	**211-28**	**457**	**.278**

DIVISION SERIES RECORD

Year Team (League)	W	L	Pct.	ERA	WHIP	G	GS	CG	ShO	Hld.	Sv.-Opp.	IP	H	R	ER	HR	BB-IBB	SO	Avg.
1998— Boston (A.L.)	0	0	...	10.80	1.80	1	0	0	0	0	0-0	1.2	2	2	2	1	1-0	2	.286
1999— Boston (A.L.)	0	0	...	27.00	3.60	2	0	0	0	0	0-0	1.2	2	5	5	1	4-0	1	.400
Division series totals (2 years)	**0**	**0**	**...**	**18.90**	**2.70**	**3**	**0**	**0**	**0**	**0**	**0-0**	**3.1**	**4**	**7**	**7**	**2**	**5-0**	**3**	**.333**

CHAMPIONSHIP SERIES RECORD

Year Team (League)	W	L	Pct.	ERA	WHIP	G	GS	CG	ShO	Hld.	Sv.-Opp.	IP	H	R	ER	HR	BB-IBB	SO	Avg.
1999— Boston (A.L.)					Did not play.														

WASHBURN, JARROD   P

PERSONAL: Born August 13, 1974, in La Crosse, Wis. ... 6-1/195. ... Throws left, bats left. ... Full name: Jarrod Michael Washburn. ... High school: Webster (Wis.). ... College: Wisconsin-Oshkosh.

TRANSACTIONS/CAREER NOTES: Selected by California Angels organizaiton in second round of 1995 free-agent draft. ... Angels franchise renamed Anaheim Angels for 1997 season. ... On disabled list (March 25-April 9, July 22-August 7 and August 8, 2000-remainder of season); included rehabilitation assignment to Lake Elsinore. ... On disabled list (March 23-April 16, 2001); included rehabilitation assignment to Salt Lake. ... On disabled list (July 21-September 2, 2004); included rehabilitation assignment to Rancho Cucamonga.

CAREER HITTING: 8-for-24 (.333), 1 R, 0 2B, 0 3B, 0 HR, 3 RBI.

Year Team (League)	W	L	Pct.	ERA	WHIP	G	GS	CG	ShO	Hld.	Sv.-Opp.	IP	H	R	ER	HR	BB-IBB	SO	Avg.
1995— Boise (N'west)	3	2	.600	3.33	1.07	8	8	0	0	...	0-...	46.0	35	17	17	1	14-0	54	.208
— Cedar Rapids (Midw.)	0	1	.000	3.44	1.31	3	3	0	0	...	0-...	18.1	17	7	7	1	7-0	20	.258
1996— Lake Elsinore (Calif.)	6	3	.667	3.30	1.21	14	14	3	0	...	0-...	92.2	79	38	34	5	33-0	93	.229
— Midland (Texas)	5	6	.455	4.40	1.16	13	13	1	0	...	0-...	88.0	77	44	43	11	25-0	58	.235
— Vancouver (PCL)	0	2	.000	10.80	2.88	2	2	0	0	...	0-...	8.1	12	16	10	1	12-0	5	.333
1997— Midland (Texas)	15	12	.556	4.80	1.46	29	29	5	1	...	0-...	189.1	211	115	101	23	65-0	146	.288
— Vancouver (PCL)	0	0	...	3.60	1.20	1	1	0	0	...	0-...	5.0	4	2	2	0	2-0	6	.211
1998— Vancouver (PCL)	4	5	.444	4.32	1.46	14	14	2	0	...	0-...	91.2	91	44	44	7	43-0	66	.261
— Anaheim (A.L.)	6	3	.667	4.62	1.31	15	11	0	0	1	0-0	74.0	70	40	38	11	27-1	48	.248
— Midland (Texas)	0	1	.000	6.23	1.73	1	1	0	0	...	0-...	8.2	13	8	6	2	2-0	8	.351
1999— Edmonton (PCL)	1	5	.167	4.73	1.14	11	11	1	0	...	0-...	59.0	50	31	31	6	17-0	55	.226
— Anaheim (A.L.)	4	5	.444	5.25	1.41	16	10	0	0	1	0-0	61.2	61	36	36	6	26-0	39	.261
2000— Lake Elsinore (Calif.)	0	0	...	6.00	1.67	1	1	0	0	...	0-...	3.0	3	2	2	0	2-0	7	.250
— Edmonton (PCL)	3	0	1.000	3.52	1.57	5	5	0	0	...	0-...	30.2	35	13	12	2	13-0	20	.299
— Anaheim (A.L.)	7	2	.778	3.74	1.20	14	14	0	0	0	0-0	84.1	64	38	35	16	37-0	49	.215
2001— Salt Lake (PCL)	0	1	.000	5.87	1.30	1	1	0	0	...	0-...	7.2	9	5	5	1	1-0	5	.300
— Anaheim (A.L.)	11	10	.524	3.77	1.29	30	30	1	0	0	0-0	193.1	196	89	81	25	54-4	126	.263
2002— Anaheim (A.L.)	18	6	.750	3.15	1.17	32	32	1	0	0	0-0	206.0	183	75	72	19	59-1	139	.235
2003— Anaheim (A.L.)	10	15	.400	4.43	1.25	32	32	2	0	0	0-0	207.1	205	106	102	34	54-4	118	.256
2004— Rancho Cuca. (Calif.)	0	0	...	2.25	1.75	1	1	0	0	...	0-...	4.0	4	1	1	0	3-0	5	.250
— Anaheim (A.L.)	11	8	.579	4.64	1.33	25	25	1	1	0	0-0	149.1	159	81	77	20	40-1	86	.269
Major League totals (7 years)	**67**	**49**	**.578**	**4.07**	**1.27**	**164**	**154**	**5**	**1**	**2**	**0-0**	**976.0**	**938**	**465**	**441**	**131**	**297-11**	**605**	**.252**

DIVISION SERIES RECORD

Year Team (League)	W	L	Pct.	ERA	WHIP	G	GS	CG	ShO	Hld.	Sv.-Opp.	IP	H	R	ER	HR	BB-IBB	SO	Avg.
2002— Anaheim (A.L.)	1	0	1.000	3.75	1.25	2	2	0	0	0	0-0	12.0	12	6	5	3	3-0	4	.286
2004— Anaheim (A.L.)	0	1	.000	10.80	2.70	2	1	0	0	0	0-0	3.1	6	8	4	2	3-0	3	.353
Division series totals (2 years)	1	1	.500	5.28	1.57	4	3	0	0	0	0-0	15.1	18	14	9	5	6-0	7	.305

CHAMPIONSHIP SERIES RECORD

Year Team (League)	W	L	Pct.	ERA	WHIP	G	GS	CG	ShO	Hld.	Sv.-Opp.	IP	H	R	ER	HR	BB-IBB	SO	Avg.
2002— Anaheim (A.L.)	0	0	...	1.29	0.86	1	1	0	0	0	0-0	7.0	6	1	1	0	0-0	7	.207

WORLD SERIES RECORD

Year Team (League)	W	L	Pct.	ERA	WHIP	G	GS	CG	ShO	Hld.	Sv.-Opp.	IP	H	R	ER	HR	BB-IBB	SO	Avg.
2002— Anaheim (A.L.)	0	2	.000	9.31	1.97	2	2	0	0	0	0-0	9.2	12	10	10	3	7-2	6	.324

WATKINS, STEVE — P

PERSONAL: Born July 19, 1978, in Lubbock, Texas. ... 6-4/190. ... Throws right, bats right. ... Full name: Stephen Douglas Watkins. ... High school: Lubbock (Texas) Christian.
TRANSACTIONS/CAREER NOTES: Selected by San Diego Padres organization in 16th round of 1998 free-agent draft. ... Refused minor league assignment and became a free agent (October 12, 2004).
CAREER HITTING: 0-for-0 (.000), 0 R, 0 2B, 0 3B, 0 HR, 0 RBI.

Year Team (League)	W	L	Pct.	ERA	WHIP	G	GS	CG	ShO	Hld.	Sv.-Opp.	IP	H	R	ER	HR	BB-IBB	SO	Avg.
1998— Idaho Falls (Pioneer)	0	1	.000	40.50	7.00	2	1	0	0		0-...	2.0	10	12	9	3	4-0	0	.625
— Ariz. Padres (Ariz.)	1	0	1.000	1.31	1.21	9	3	0	0		0-...	20.2	15	4	3	0	10-0	20	.203
1999— Fort Wayne (Midw.)	0	3	.000	8.47	1.94	4	4	0	0		0-...	17.0	24	17	16	3	9-0	21	.338
— Idaho Falls (Pioneer)	5	2	.714	4.40	1.39	12	11	0	0		0-...	61.1	60	39	30	5	25-0	75	.254
2000— Rancho Cuca. (Calif.)	7	6	.538	3.70	1.38	27	27	0	0		0-...	151.0	118	75	62	10	90-0	163	.216
2001— Lake Elsinore (Calif.)	2	0	1.000	1.84	1.02	5	5	1	1		0-...	29.1	23	6	6	0	7-0	23	.207
— Mobile (Sou.)	4	8	.333	5.73	1.65	23	19	0	0		0-...	97.1	108	74	62	14	53-2	55	.283
2002— Mobile (Sou.)	4	8	.333	3.78	1.48	37	15	1	0		0-...	116.2	124	65	49	8	49-3	88	.281
2003— Mobile (Sou.)	5	4	.556	4.17	1.32	18	18	0	0		0-...	101.1	100	50	47	8	34-1	75	.277
— Portland (PCL)	1	0	1.000	3.08	1.22	14	0	0	0		0-...	26.1	20	11	9	1	12-0	23	.206
2004— Mobile (Sou.)	4	3	.571	3.64	1.10	10	10	0	0		0-...	59.1	50	28	24	6	15-0	57	.231
— Portland (PCL)	5	3	.625	3.07	1.29	22	6	0	0		0-...	55.2	53	20	19	3	19-0	58	.248
— San Diego (N.L.)	0	0		6.28	1.47	11	0	0	0	0	0-0	14.1	17	10	10	3	4-0	7	.293
Major League totals (1 year)	0	0		6.28	1.47	11	0	0	0	0	0-0	14.1	17	10	10	3	4-0	7	.293

WAYNE, JUSTIN — P

PERSONAL: Born April 16, 1979, in Honolulu, Hawaii. ... 6-3/205. ... Throws right, bats right. ... Full name: Justin Morgan Wayne. ... High school: Punahou (Honolulu).
TRANSACTIONS/CAREER NOTES: Selected by Boston Red Sox organization in ninth round of 1997 free-agent draft; did not sign. ... Selected by Montreal Expos organization in first round (fifth pick overall) of 2000 free-agent draft. ... Traded by Expos with Ps Carl Pavano and Graeme Lloyd and IF Mike Mordecai to Florida Marlins for P Claudio Vargas, OF/2B Wilton Guerrero, OF Cliff Floyd, a player to be named and cash (July 11, 2002); Expos acquired P Don Levinski to complete deal (August 5, 2002). ... On disabled list (March 25-April 12, 2003); included rehabilitation assignment to Jupiter. ... On disabled list (June 4-19, 2004); included rehabilitation assignments to Jupiter and Albuquerque.
CAREER HITTING: 0-for-12 (.000), 0 R, 0 2B, 0 3B, 0 HR, 0 RBI.

Year Team (League)	W	L	Pct.	ERA	WHIP	G	GS	CG	ShO	Hld.	Sv.-Opp.	IP	H	R	ER	HR	BB-IBB	SO	Avg.
2000— Jupiter (FSL)	0	3	.000	5.81	1.41	5	5	0	0	...	0-...	26.1	26	22	17	2	11-0	24	.263
2001— Jupiter (FSL)	2	3	.400	3.02	0.96	8	7	0	0	...	0-...	41.2	31	16	14	0	9-0	35	.204
— Harrisburg (Eastern)	9	2	.818	2.62	1.31	14	14	2	0	...	0-...	92.2	87	28	27	4	34-0	70	.248
2002— Harrisburg (Eastern)	5	2	.714	2.37	1.07	17	17	0	0	...	0-...	98.2	74	41	26	7	32-0	47	.213
— Florida (N.L.)	2	3	.400	5.32	1.48	5	5	0	0	0	0-0	23.2	22	16	14	3	13-0	16	.244
— Portland (East.)	3	3	.500	4.85	1.31	7	7	1	1	...	0-...	42.2	43	26	23	3	13-0	30	.269
— Calgary (PCL)	0	1	.000	6.35	1.24	2	2	0	0	...	0-...	11.1	8	8	8	3	6-0	10	.195
2003— Jupiter (FSL)	0	0		0.00	1.00	1	1	0	0	...	0-...	6.0	6	0	0	0	0-0	4	.250
— Florida (N.L.)	0	2	.000	11.81	2.63	2	2	0	0	0	0-0	5.0	9	7	7	1	5-0	1	.375
— Albuquerque (PCL)	4	12	.250	4.24	1.30	23	23	2	0	...	0-...	136.0	138	81	64	10	40-0	82	.266
2004— Jupiter (FSL)	0	0		0.00	1.00	2	1	0	0	...	0-...	3.0	3	0	0	0	0-0	3	.250
— Florida (N.L.)	3	3	.500	5.79	1.62	19	1	0	0	1	0-2	32.2	35	24	21	6	18-1	20	.282
— Albuquerque (PCL)	1	5	.167	6.58	1.77	13	13	0	0	...	0-...	65.2	82	53	48	11	34-1	43	.307
Major League totals (3 years)	5	8	.385	6.13	1.65	26	8	0	0	1	0-2	61.2	66	47	42	10	36-1	37	.277

WEATHERS, DAVID — P

PERSONAL: Born September 25, 1969, in Lawrenceburg, Tenn. ... 6-3/230. ... Throws right, bats right. ... Full name: John David Weathers. ... High school: Loretto (Tenn.). ... Junior college: Motlow State (Tenn.) Community College.
TRANSACTIONS/CAREER NOTES: Selected by Toronto Blue Jays organization in third round of 1988 free-agent draft. ... Selected by Florida Marlins in second round (29th pick overall) of expansion draft (November 17, 1992). ... On disabled list (June 26-July 13, 1995); included rehabilitation assignments to Brevard County and Charlotte. ... Traded by Marlins to New York Yankees for P Mark Hutton (July 31, 1996). ... Traded by Yankees to Cleveland Indians for OF Chad Curtis (June 9, 1997). ... Claimed on waivers by Cincinnati Reds (December 20, 1997). ... Claimed on waivers by Milwaukee Brewers (June 24, 1998). ... On disabled list (August 2-22, 2000). ... Traded by Brewers with P Roberto Miniel to Chicago Cubs for P Ruben Quevedo and OF Pete Zoccolillo (July 30, 2001). ... Signed as a free agent by New York Mets (December 13, 2001). ... On suspended list (September 20-22, 2002). ... Traded by Mets with P Jeremy Griffiths to Houston Astros for OF Richard Hidalgo (June 17, 2004). ... Released by Astros (September 3, 2004). ... Signed by Marlins (September 8, 2004).
CAREER HITTING: 14-for-138 (.101), 7 R, 0 2B, 0 3B, 2 HR, 4 RBI.

Year Team (League)	W	L	Pct.	ERA	WHIP	G	GS	CG	ShO	Hld.	Sv.-Opp.	IP	H	R	ER	HR	BB-IBB	SO	Avg.
1988— St. Catharines (NY-Penn.) .	4	4	.500	3.02	1.34	15	12	0	0	...	0-...	62.2	58	30	21	3	26-0	36	.245
1989— Myrtle Beach (SAL)	11	13	.458	3.86	1.44	31	31	2	0	...	0-...	172.2	163	99	74	3	86-2	111	.247
1990— Dunedin (Fla. St.)	10	7	.588	3.70	1.37	27	27	2	0	...	0-...	158.0	158	82	65	2	59-0	96	.266
1991— Knoxville (Southern)	10	7	.588	2.45	1.22	24	22	5	2	...	0-...	139.1	121	51	38	3	49-1	114	.236
— Toronto (A.L.)	1	0	1.000	4.91	2.18	15	0	0	0	1	0-0	14.2	15	9	8	1	17-3	13	.263
1992— Syracuse (Int'l)	2	4	.200	4.66	1.43	12	10	0	0	...	0-...	48.1	48	29	25	3	21-2	30	.254
— Toronto (A.L.)	0	0	...	8.10	2.10	2	0	0	0	0	0-0	3.1	5	3	3	1	2-0	3	.385
1993— Edmonton (PCL)	11	4	.733	3.83	1.40	22	22	3	1	...	0-...	141.0	150	77	60	12	47-2	117	.271
— Florida (N.L.)	2	3	.400	5.12	1.53	14	6	0	0	0	0-0	45.2	57	26	26	3	13-1	34	.306
1994— Florida (N.L.)	8	12	.400	5.27	1.67	24	24	0	0	0	0-0	135.0	166	87	79	13	59-9	72	.306

Year Team (League)	W	L	Pct.	ERA	WHIP	G	GS	CG	ShO	Hld.	Sv.-Opp.	IP	H	R	ER	HR	BB-IBB	SO	Avg.
1995— Florida (N.L.)	4	5	.444	5.98	1.73	28	15	0	0	1	0-0	90.1	104	68	60	8	52-3	60	.295
— Brevard County (FSL)	0	0	...	0.00	1.25	1	1	0	0		0-...	4.0	4	0	0	0	1-0	3	.286
— Charlotte (Int'l)	0	1	.000	9.00	3.00	1	1	0	0		0-...	5.0	10	5	5	0	5-0	0	.455
1996— Florida (N.L.)	2	2	.500	4.54	1.58	31	8	0	0	3	0-0	71.1	85	41	36	7	28-4	40	.302
— Charlotte (Int'l)	0	0	...	7.71	3.43	1	0	0	0		0-...	2.1	5	2	2	0	3-0	0	.500
— New York (A.L.)	0	2	.000	9.35	2.13	11	4	0	0	0	0-0	17.1	23	19	18	1	14-1	13	.315
— Columbus (Int'l)	0	2	.000	5.40	1.50	3	3	0	0		0-...	16.2	20	13	10	1	5-0	7	.299
1997— New York (A.L.)	0	1	.000	10.00	2.44	10	0	0	0		0-1	9.0	15	10	10	1	7-0	4	.375
— Columbus (Int'l)	2	2	.500	3.19	1.15	5	5	1	0		0-...	36.2	35	18	13	3	7-0	35	.250
— Buffalo (A.A.)	4	3	.571	3.15	1.28	11	11	2	1		0-...	68.2	71	37	24	7	17-0	51	.266
— Cleveland (A.L.)	1	2	.333	7.56	1.86	9	1	0	0	0	0-0	16.2	23	14	14	2	8-0	14	.343
1998— Cincinnati (N.L.)	2	4	.333	6.21	1.81	16	9	0	0	0	0-0	62.1	86	47	43	3	27-2	51	.330
— Milwaukee (N.L.)	4	1	.800	3.21	1.22	28	0	0	0	3	0-1	47.2	44	22	17	3	14-1	43	.246
1999— Milwaukee (N.L.)	7	4	.636	4.65	1.51	63	0	0	0	9	2-6	93.0	102	49	48	14	38-3	74	.279
2000— Milwaukee (N.L.)	3	5	.375	3.07	1.38	69	0	0	0	14	1-7	76.1	73	29	26	7	32-8	50	.260
2001— Milwaukee (N.L.)	3	4	.429	2.03	1.08	52	0	0	0	10	4-7	57.2	37	14	13	3	25-7	46	.188
— Chicago (N.L.)	1	1	.500	3.18	1.31	28	0	0	0	6	0-3	28.1	28	10	10	3	9-1	20	.269
2002— New York (N.L.)	6	3	.667	2.91	1.36	71	0	0	0	18	0-5	77.1	69	30	25	6	36-7	61	.245
2003— New York (N.L.)	1	6	.143	3.08	1.45	77	0	0	0	26	7-9	87.2	87	33	30	6	40-6	75	.264
2004— New York (N.L.)	5	3	.625	4.28	1.66	32	0	0	0	6	0-1	33.2	41	19	16	5	15-0	25	.304
— Houston (N.L.)	1	4	.200	4.78	1.38	26	0	0	0	5	0-3	32.0	31	20	17	5	13-1	26	.261
— Florida (N.L.)	1	0	1.000	2.70	1.20	8	2	0	0	1	0-0	16.2	13	5	5	2	7-1	10	.232
American League totals (4 years)	2	5	.286	7.82	2.11	47	5	0	0	1	0-1	61.0	81	55	53	6	48-4	47	.324
National League totals (11 years)	50	57	.467	4.25	1.50	567	64	0	0	102	14-42	955.0	1023	500	451	88	408-54	687	.279
Major League totals (14 years)	52	62	.456	4.46	1.54	614	69	0	0	103	14-43	1016.0	1104	555	504	94	456-58	734	.282

DIVISION SERIES RECORD

Year Team (League)	W	L	Pct.	ERA	WHIP	G	GS	CG	ShO	Hld.	Sv.-Opp.	IP	H	R	ER	HR	BB-IBB	SO	Avg.
1996— New York (A.L.)	1	0	1.000	0.00	0.20	2	0	0	0	0	0-0	5.0	1	0	0	0	0-0	5	.071

CHAMPIONSHIP SERIES RECORD

Year Team (League)	W	L	Pct.	ERA	WHIP	G	GS	CG	ShO	Hld.	Sv.-Opp.	IP	H	R	ER	HR	BB-IBB	SO	Avg.
1996— New York (A.L.)	1	0	1.000	0.00	1.00	2	0	0	0	0	0-0	3.0	3	0	0	0	0-0	0	.250

WORLD SERIES RECORD

Year Team (League)	W	L	Pct.	ERA	WHIP	G	GS	CG	ShO	Hld.	Sv.-Opp.	IP	H	R	ER	HR	BB-IBB	SO	Avg.
1996— New York (A.L.)	0	0	...	3.00	1.67	3	0	0	0	1	0-0	3.0	2	1	1	0	3-1	3	.200

WEAVER, JEFF   P

PERSONAL: Born August 22, 1976, in Northridge, Calif. ... 6-5/200. ... Throws right, bats right. ... Full name: Jeffrey Charles Weaver. ... High school: Simi Valley (Calif.). ... College: Fresno State. ... Cousin of Jed Weaver, tight end, New England Patriots.

TRANSACTIONS/CAREER NOTES: Selected by Chicago White Sox organziation in second-round of 1997 free-agent draft; did not sign; pick received as part of compensation for Chicago Cubs signing Type A free-agent P Kevin Tapani. ... Selected by Detroit Tigers organization in first round (14th pick overall) of 1998 free-agent draft. ... Traded by Tigers to New York Yankees as part of three-team deal in which Oakland Athletics acquired Ps Ted Lilly and Jason Arnold and OF John-Ford Griffin from Yankees and Tigers acquired 1B Carlos Pena, P Franklyn German and a player to be named from A's (July 5, 2002); Tigers acquired P Jeremy Bonderman to complete deal (August 22, 2002). ... Traded by Yankees with Ps Yhency Brazoban and Brandon Wheedon and cash to Los Angeles Dodgers for P Kevin Brown (December 13, 2003).

CAREER HITTING: 19-for-89 (.213), 5 R, 3 2B, 1 3B, 0 HR, 3 RBI.

Year Team (League)	W	L	Pct.	ERA	WHIP	G	GS	CG	ShO	Hld.	Sv.-Opp.	IP	H	R	ER	HR	BB-IBB	SO	Avg.
1998— Jamestown (N.Y.-Penn.) ...	1	0	1.000	1.50	0.58	3	3	0	0		0-...	12.0	6	4	2	0	1-0	12	.143
— West. Mich. (Mid.)	1	0	1.000	1.38	0.62	2	2	0	0		0-...	13.0	8	3	2	1	0-0	21	.182
1999— Jacksonville (Southern)	0	0	...	3.00	0.83	1	1	0	0		0-...	6.0	5	2	2	0	0-0	6	.227
— Detroit (A.L.)	9	12	.429	5.55	1.42	30	29	0	0		0-0	163.2	176	104	101	27	56-2	114	.278
2000— Toledo (International)	0	1	.000	3.38	1.13	1	1	0	0		0-...	5.1	5	2	2	1	1-0	10	.250
— Detroit (A.L.)	11	15	.423	4.32	1.29	31	30	2	0		0-0	200.0	205	102	96	26	52-2	136	.267
2001— Detroit (A.L.)	13	16	.448	4.08	1.32	33	33	5	0		0-0	229.1	235	116	104	19	68-4	152	.266
2002— Detroit (A.L.)	6	8	.429	3.18	1.19	17	17	3	†3		0-0	121.2	112	50	43	4	33-1	75	.243
— New York (A.L.)	5	3	.625	4.04	1.23	15	8	0	†0	0	2-2	78.0	81	38	35	12	15-3	57	.260
2003— New York (A.L.)	7	9	.438	5.99	1.62	32	24	0	0	1	0-0	159.1	211	113	106	16	47-2	93	.320
2004— Los Angeles (N.L.)	13	13	.500	4.01	1.30	34	34	0	0	0	0-0	220.0	219	103	98	19	67-9	153	.260
American League totals (5 years)	51	63	.447	4.59	1.36	158	141	10	3	1	2-2	952.0	1020	523	485	104	271-14	627	.274
National League totals (1 year)	13	13	.500	4.01	1.30	34	34	0	0	0	0-0	220.0	219	103	98	19	67-9	153	.260
Major League totals (6 years)	64	76	.457	4.48	1.35	192	175	10	3	1	2-2	1172.0	1239	626	583	123	338-23	780	.272

DIVISION SERIES RECORD

Year Team (League)	W	L	Pct.	ERA	WHIP	G	GS	CG	ShO	Hld.	Sv.-Opp.	IP	H	R	ER	HR	BB-IBB	SO	Avg.
2002— New York (A.L.)	0	0	...	6.75	2.63	2	0	0	0	0	0-0	2.2	4	2	2	0	3-1	1	.444
2004— Los Angeles (N.L.)	0	1	.000	11.57	2.14	1	1	0	0	0	0-0	4.2	8	6	6	0	2-0	4	.381
Division series totals (2 years)	0	1	.000	9.82	2.32	3	1	0	0	0	0-0	7.1	12	8	8	0	5-1	5	.400

WORLD SERIES RECORD

Year Team (League)	W	L	Pct.	ERA	WHIP	G	GS	CG	ShO	Hld.	Sv.-Opp.	IP	H	R	ER	HR	BB-IBB	SO	Avg.
2003— New York (A.L.)	0	1	.000	9.00	1.00	1	0	0	0	0	0-0	1.0	1	1	1	1	0-0	0	.250

WEBB, BRANDON   P

PERSONAL: Born May 9, 1979, in Ashland, Ky. ... 6-2/228. ... Throws right, bats right. ... Full name: Brandon T. Webb. ... High school: Ashland (Ky.). ... College: Kentucky.

TRANSACTIONS/CAREER NOTES: Selected by Arizona Diamondbacks organization in eighth round of 2000 free-agent draft.

CAREER HITTING: 11-for-114 (.096), 5 R, 1 2B, 0 3B, 0 HR, 4 RBI.

Year Team (League)	W	L	Pct.	ERA	WHIP	G	GS	CG	ShO	Hld.	Sv.-Opp.	IP	H	R	ER	HR	BB-IBB	SO	Avg.
2000— Ariz. D'backs (Ariz.)	0	0	...	9.00	2.00	1	1	0	0		0-...	1.0	2	1	1	0	0-0	3	.400
— South Bend (Mid.)	0	0	...	3.24	1.14	12	0	0	0		2-...	16.2	10	7	6	0	9-1	18	.172
2001— Lancaster (Calif.)	6	10	.375	3.99	1.34	29	28	0	0		0-...	162.1	174	90	72	9	44-0	158	.276
2002— Tucson (PCL)	0	1	.000	3.86	1.29	1	1	0	0		0-...	7.0	5	3	3	0	4-0	5	.200

Year	Team (League)	W	L	Pct.	ERA	WHIP	G	GS	CG	ShO	Hld.	Sv.-Opp.	IP	H	R	ER	HR	BB-IBB	SO	Avg.
—	El Paso (Texas)	10	6	.625	3.14	1.32	26	25	1	1	...	0-...	152.0	141	66	53	4	59-1	122	.247
2003—	Tucson (PCL)	1	1	.500	6.00	1.50	3	3	0	0	...	0-...	18.0	18	17	12	0	9-0	17	.257
—	Arizona (N.L.)	10	9	.526	2.84	1.15	29	28	1	1	0	0-0	180.2	140	65	57	12	68-4	172	.212
2004—	Arizona (N.L.)	7	* 16	.304	3.59	1.50	35	• 35	1	0	0	0-0	208.0	194	111	83	17 *	119-11	164	.248
Major League totals (2 years)		17	25	.405	3.24	1.34	64	63	2	1	0	0-0	388.2	334	176	140	29	187-15	336	.232

WEBB, JOHN   P

PERSONAL: Born May 23, 1979, in Pensacola, Fla. ... 6-3/220. ... Throws right, bats right. ... Full name: John Floyd Webb. ... High school: Pensacola (Fla.). ... College: West Florida.

TRANSACTIONS/CAREER NOTES: Selected by Chicago Cubs organization in 19th round of 1999 free-agent draft. ... Claimed on waivers by Tampa Bay Devil Rays (February 24, 2004).

CAREER HITTING: 0-for-0 (.000), 0 R, 0 2B, 0 3B, 0 HR, 0 RBI.

Year	Team (League)	W	L	Pct.	ERA	WHIP	G	GS	CG	ShO	Hld.	Sv.-Opp.	IP	H	R	ER	HR	BB-IBB	SO	Avg.
1999—	Ariz. Cubs (Ariz.)	0	0	...	3.58	1.26	18	0	0	0	...	3-...	32.2	33	20	13	0	8-0	39	.246
—	Eugene (N'west)	1	0	1.000	0.00	0.50	2	0	0	0	...	1-...	4.0	1	0	0	0	1-0	3	.077
2000—	Lansing (Midw.)	7	6	.538	2.47	1.23	21	21	1	1	...	0-...	134.2	125	53	37	4	40-0	108	.250
—	Daytona (Fla. St.)	1	1	.500	4.76	1.18	4	2	0	0	...	1-...	17.0	17	11	9	1	3-0	18	.250
2001—	Daytona (Fla. St.)	1	1	.500	5.40	1.50	5	4	0	0	...	0-...	20.0	23	13	12	0	7-1	20	.280
2002—	Daytona (Fla. St.)	5	3	.625	3.43	1.14	10	10	1	1	...	0-...	57.2	43	23	22	3	23-0	65	.207
—	West Tenn. (Sou.)	4	5	.444	4.52	1.20	11	11	0	0	...	0-...	61.2	52	33	31	5	22-0	45	.231
2003—	West Tenn. (Sou.)	5	8	.385	4.50	1.42	30	22	0	0	...	1-...	132.0	135	74	66	11	52-1	85	.270
2004—	Montgomery (Sou.)	2	1	.667	4.10	1.29	9	3	0	0	...	0-...	26.1	26	12	12	3	8-0	12	.263
—	Durham (Int'l)	1	3	.250	3.27	1.36	6	6	0	0	...	0-...	33.0	31	19	12	5	14-0	22	.246
—	Tampa Bay (A.L.)	0	0	...	7.00	2.11	4	0	0	0	0	0-0	9.0	12	7	7	2	7-0	9	.324
Major League totals (1 year)		0	0	...	7.00	2.11	4	0	0	0	0	0-0	9.0	12	7	7	2	7-0	9	.324

WEBER, BEN   P

PERSONAL: Born November 17, 1969, in Port Arthur, Texas. ... 6-4/205. ... Throws right, bats right. ... Full name: Benjamin Edward Weber. ... Name pronounced: webb-er. ... High school: Port Neches-Groves (Port Neches, Texas). ... College: Houston.

TRANSACTIONS/CAREER NOTES: Selected by Toronto Blue Jays organization in 20th round of 1991 free-agent draft. ... Released by Blue Jays (March 24, 1996). ... Signed by San Francisco Giants organization (October 30, 1998). ... Claimed on waivers by Anaheim Angels (August 30, 2000). ... Released by Angels (September 8, 2004).

CAREER HITTING: 0-for-0 (.000), 0 R, 0 2B, 0 3B, 0 HR, 0 RBI.

Year	Team (League)	W	L	Pct.	ERA	WHIP	G	GS	CG	ShO	Hld.	Sv.-Opp.	IP	H	R	ER	HR	BB-IBB	SO	Avg.
1991—	St. Catharines (NY-Penn.) .	6	3	.667	3.24	1.33	16	14	1	0	...	0-...	97.1	105	43	35	3	24-2	60	.274
1992—	Myrtle Beach (SAL)	4	7	.364	1.64	1.14	41	1	0	0	...	6-...	98.2	83	27	18	1	29-3	65	.227
1993—	Dunedin (Fla. St.)	8	3	.727	2.92	1.34	55	0	0	0	...	12-...	83.1	87	36	27	4	25-5	45	.278
1994—	Dunedin (Fla. St.)	3	2	.600	2.73	1.14	18	0	0	0	...	3-...	26.1	25	8	8	1	5-3	19	.255
—	Knoxville (Southern)	4	3	.571	3.76	1.24	25	10	0	0	...	0-...	95.2	103	49	40	8	16-0	55	.272
1995—	Syracuse (Int'l)	4	5	.444	5.40	1.51	25	15	0	0	...	1-...	91.2	111	62	55	10	27-1	38	.300
—	Knoxville (Southern)	4	1	.800	3.91	1.26	12	1	0	0	...	0-...	25.1	26	12	11	3	6-0	16	.268
1996—	Salinas (West.)	12	6	.667	3.47	1.22	22	22	2	...	...	0-...	148.0	138	68	57	11	42-1	102	.248
1997—	Taipei (Taiwan)	7	3	.700	0.00	1.19	40		0	0	...	5-...	99.0	85				33-...	78	...
1998—	Taipei (Taiwan)	12	7	.632	0.00	1.40	56		0	0	...	7-...	144.0	150				52-...	122	...
1999—	Fresno (PCL)	2	4	.333	3.34	1.23	51	0	0	0	...	8-...	86.1	78	34	32	6	28-2	67	.245
2000—	San Francisco (N.L.)	0	1	.000	14.63	2.50	9	0	0	0	1	0-2	8.0	16	13	13	0	4-0	6	.400
—	Fresno (PCL)	4	8	.333	2.42	1.18	38	3	0	0	...	7-...	78.0	72	31	21	7	20-0	66	.245
—	Erie (East.)	0	1	.000	16.20	3.00	2	0	0	0	...	0-...	1.2	3	5	3	1	2-0	2	.333
—	Anaheim (A.L.)	1	0	1.000	1.84	0.95	10	0	0	0	1	0-0	14.2	12	6	3	0	2-1	8	.214
2001—	Anaheim (A.L.)	6	2	.750	3.42	1.42	56	0	0	0	6	0-1	68.1	66	28	26	4	31-8	40	.251
2002—	Anaheim (A.L.)	7	2	.778	2.54	1.18	63	0	0	0	18	7-11	78.0	70	25	22	4	22-3	43	.249
2003—	Anaheim (A.L.)	5	1	.833	2.69	1.32	62	0	0	0	11	0-2	80.1	84	26	24	7	22-7	46	.275
2004—	Anaheim (A.L.)	0	2	.000	8.06	2.33	15	0	0	0	2	0-1	22.1	37	24	20	4	15-0	11	.363
—	Ariz. Angels (Ariz.)	0	0	...	0.00	0.00	1	1	0	0	...	0-...	1.0	0	0	0	0	0-0	2	.000
—	Salt Lake (PCL)	0	2	.000	8.64	2.16	15	0	0	0	...	1-...	16.2	27	25	16	3	9-1	18	.346
American League totals (5 years)		19	7	.731	3.24	1.37	209	0	0	0	38	7-15	263.2	269	109	95	19	92-19	148	.267
National League totals (1 year)		0	1	.000	14.63	2.50	9	0	0	0	1	0-2	8.0	16	13	13	0	4-0	6	.400
Major League totals (5 years)		19	8	.704	3.58	1.40	218	0	0	0	39	7-17	271.2	285	122	108	19	96-19	154	.272

DIVISION SERIES RECORD

Year	Team (League)	W	L	Pct.	ERA	WHIP	G	GS	CG	ShO	Hld.	Sv.-Opp.	IP	H	R	ER	HR	BB-IBB	SO	Avg.
2002—	Anaheim (A.L.)	0	1	.000	18.00	4.00	2	0	0	0	2	0-0	1.0	2	2	2	0	2-0	0	.400

CHAMPIONSHIP SERIES RECORD

Year	Team (League)	W	L	Pct.	ERA	WHIP	G	GS	CG	ShO	Hld.	Sv.-Opp.	IP	H	R	ER	HR	BB-IBB	SO	Avg.
2002—	Anaheim (A.L.)	0	0	...	3.38	1.13	3	0	0	0	0	0-0	2.2	3	1	1	0	0-0	3	.300

WORLD SERIES RECORD

Year	Team (League)	W	L	Pct.	ERA	WHIP	G	GS	CG	ShO	Hld.	Sv.-Opp.	IP	H	R	ER	HR	BB-IBB	SO	Avg.
2002—	Anaheim (A.L.)	0	0	...	13.50	2.57	4	0	0	0	0	0-0	4.2	10	7	7	1	2-1	5	.455

WELLEMEYER, TODD   P

PERSONAL: Born August 30, 1978, in Louisville, Ky. ... 6-3/205. ... Throws right, bats right. ... Full name: Todd Allen Wellemeyer. ... Name pronounced: WELL-my-er. ... High school: Eastern (Louisville, Ky.). ... College: Bellarmine (Ky.) College.

TRANSACTIONS/CAREER NOTES: Selected by Chicago Cubs organization in fourth round of 2000 free-agent draft. ... On disabled list (May 22-July 16, 2004); included rehabilitation assignment to Iowa.

CAREER HITTING: 0-for-1 (.000), 0 R, 0 2B, 0 3B, 0 HR, 0 RBI.

Year	Team (League)	W	L	Pct.	ERA	WHIP	G	GS	CG	ShO	Hld.	Sv.-Opp.	IP	H	R	ER	HR	BB-IBB	SO	Avg.
2000—	Eugene (N'west)	4	4	.500	3.67	1.25	15	15	0	0	...	0-...	76.0	62	35	31	3	33-2	85	.225
2001—	Lansing (Midw.)	13	9	.591	4.16	1.63	27	27	1	0	...	0-...	147.0	165	85	68	14	74-0	167	.288
2002—	Daytona (Fla. St.)	2	4	.333	3.79	1.11	14	14	0	0	...	0-...	73.2	63	33	31	7	19-1	87	.230

W

Year	Team (League)	W	L	Pct.	ERA	WHIP	G	GS	CG	ShO	Hld.	Sv.-Opp.	IP	H	R	ER	HR	BB-IBB	SO	Avg.
	—West Tenn (Sou.)	3	3	.500	4.70	1.11	8	8	1	1	...	0-...	46.0	33	25	24	2	18-0	37	.204
2003—	West Tenn (Sou.)	1	1	.500	5.48	1.36	4	4	0	0	...	0-...	21.1	19	13	13	1	10-0	34	.238
	—Iowa (PCL)	5	5	.500	5.18	1.53	13	12	0	0	...	0-...	66.0	68	39	38	7	33-4	56	.272
	—Chicago (N.L.)	1	1	.500	6.51	1.59	15	0	0	0	1	1-1	27.2	25	22	20	5	19-1	30	.245
2004—	Iowa (PCL)	1	1	.500	3.91	1.57	14	4	0	0	...	0-...	23.0	24	11	10	2	12-0	23	.273
	—Chicago (N.L.)	2	1	.667	5.92	1.93	20	0	0	0	0	0-0	24.1	27	16	16	1	20-2	30	.287
Major League totals (2 years)		3	2	.600	6.23	1.75	35	0	0	0	1	1-1	52.0	52	38	36	6	39-3	60	.265

WELLS, DAVID — P

PERSONAL: Born May 20, 1963, in Torrance, Calif. ... 6-4/248. ... Throws left, bats left. ... Full name: David Lee Wells. ... High school: Point Loma (San Diego).

TRANSACTIONS/CAREER NOTES: Selected by Toronto Blue Jays organization in second round of June 1982 free-agent draft. ... Released by Blue Jays (March 30, 1993). ... Signed by Detroit Tigers (April 3, 1993). ... On disabled list (August 1-20, 1993). ... On disabled list (April 19-June 6, 1994); included rehabilitation assignment to Lakeland. ... Traded by Tigers to Cincinnati Reds for Ps C.J. Nitkowski and David Tuttle and a player to be named (July 31, 1995); Tigers acquired IF Mark Lewis to complete deal (November 16, 1995). ... Traded by Reds to Baltimore Orioles for OFs Curtis Goodwin and Trovin Valdez (December 26, 1995). ... Signed as a free agent by New York Yankees (December 24, 1996). ... Traded by Yankees with P Graeme Lloyd and 2B Homer Bush to Blue Jays for P Roger Clemens (February 18, 1999). ... Traded by Blue Jays with P Matt DeWitt to Chicago White Sox for Ps Mike Sirotka, Kevin Beirne and Mike Williams and OF Brian Simmons (January 14, 2001). ... On disabled list (July 2, 2001-remainder of season). ... Signed as a free agent by Yankees (January 17, 2002). ... Signed as a free agent by San Diego Padres (January 6, 2004). ... On disabled list (May 17-June 7, 2004).

CAREER HITTING: 13-for-113 (.115), 4 R, 1 2B, 0 3B, 0 HR, 3 RBI.

Year	Team (League)	W	L	Pct.	ERA	WHIP	G	GS	CG	ShO	Hld.	Sv.-Opp.	IP	H	R	ER	HR	BB-IBB	SO	Avg.
1982—	Medicine Hat (Pio.)	4	3	.571	5.18	1.60	12	12	1	0	...	0-...	64.1	71	42	37	5	32-1	53	...
1983—	Kinston (Caro.)	6	5	.545	3.73	1.35	25	25	5	0	...	0-...	157.0	141	81	65	13	71-2	115	.238
1984—	Kinston (Caro.)	1	6	.143	4.71	1.67	7	7	0	0	...	0-...	42.0	51	29	22	1	19-1	44	.302
	—Knoxville (Southern)	3	2	.600	2.59	1.27	8	8	3	1	...	0-...	59.0	58	22	17	3	17-0	34	.262
1985—	Syracuse (Int'l)			Did not play.																
1986—	Florence (S. Atl.)	0	0	...	3.55	1.26	4	1	0	0	...	0-...	12.2	7	6	5	1	9-0	14	.159
	—Ventura (Calif.)	2	1	.667	1.89	0.89	5	2	0	0	...	0-...	19.0	13	5	4	0	4-0	26	.200
	—Knoxville (Southern)	1	3	.250	4.05	1.50	10	7	1	0	...	0-...	40.0	42	24	18	1	18-0	32	.280
	—Syracuse (Int'l)	0	1	.000	9.82	1.91	3	0	0	0	...	0-...	3.2	6	4	4	0	1-0	2	.400
1987—	Syracuse (Int'l)	4	6	.400	3.87	1.23	43	12	0	0	...	6-...	109.1	102	49	47	9	32-0	106	.248
	—Toronto (A.L.)	4	3	.571	3.99	1.67	18	2	0	0	2	1-2	29.1	37	14	13	0	12-0	32	.311
1988—	Toronto (A.L.)	3	5	.375	4.62	1.49	41	0	0	0	8	4-6	64.1	65	36	33	12	31-9	56	.269
	—Syracuse (Int'l)	0	0	...	0.00	1.59	6	0	0	0	...	3-...	5.2	7	1	0	0	2-1	8	.269
1989—	Toronto (A.L.)	7	4	.636	2.40	1.09	54	0	0	0	8	2-9	86.1	66	25	23	5	28-7	78	.207
1990—	Toronto (A.L.)	11	6	.647	3.14	1.11	43	25	0	0	3	3-3	189.0	165	72	66	14	45-3	115	.235
1991—	Toronto (A.L.)	15	10	.600	3.72	1.19	40	28	2	0	3	1-2	198.1	188	88	82	24	49-1	106	.252
1992—	Toronto (A.L.)	7	9	.438	5.40	1.45	41	14	0	0	3	2-4	120.0	138	84	72	16	36-6	62	.289
1993—	Detroit (A.L.)	11	9	.550	4.19	1.20	32	30	0	0	1	0-0	187.0	183	93	87	26	42-6	139	.254
1994—	Detroit (A.L.)	5	7	.417	3.96	1.23	16	16	5	1	0	0-0	111.1	113	54	49	13	24-6	71	.260
	—Lakeland (Fla. St.)	0	0	...	0.00	0.83	2	2	0	0	...	0-...	6.0	5	1	0	0	0-0	3	.217
1995—	Detroit (A.L.)	10	3	.769	3.04	1.20	18	18	3	0	0	0-0	130.1	120	54	44	17	37-5	83	.242
	—Cincinnati (N.L.)	6	5	.545	3.59	1.24	11	11	3	0	0	0-0	72.2	74	34	29	6	16-4	50	.265
1996—	Baltimore (A.L.)	11	14	.440	5.14	1.33	34	34	3	0	0	0-0	224.1	247	132	128	32	51-7	130	.285
1997—	New York (A.L.)	16	10	.615	4.21	1.30	32	32	5	2	0	0-0	218.0	239	109	102	24	45-0	156	.278
1998—	New York (A.L.)	18	4	.818	3.49	1.05	30	30	8	* 5	0	0-0	214.1	195	86	83	29	29-0	163	.239
1999—	Toronto (A.L.)	17	10	.630	4.82	1.33	34	34	* 7	1	0	0-0	* 231.2	* 246	132	124	32	62-2	169	.271
2000—	Toronto (A.L.)	• 20	8	.714	4.11	1.29	35	• 35	* 9	1	0	0-0	229.2	* 266	115	105	23	31-0	166	.289
2001—	Chicago (A.L.)	5	7	.417	4.47	1.40	16	16	1	0	0	0-0	100.2	120	55	50	12	21-1	59	.297
2002—	New York (A.L.)	19	7	.731	3.75	1.24	31	31	2	1	0	0-0	206.1	210	100	86	21	45-2	137	.259
2003—	New York (A.L.)	15	7	.682	4.14	1.23	31	30	4	1	0	0-0	213.0	242	101	98	24	20-0	101	.286
2004—	San Diego (N.L.)	12	8	.600	3.73	1.14	31	31	0	0	0	0-0	195.2	203	85	81	23	20-1	101	.266
American League totals (17 years)		194	123	.612	4.07	1.25	546	375	49	12	28	13-26	2754.0	2840	1350	1245	324	608-55	1823	.266
National League totals (2 years)		18	13	.581	3.69	1.17	42	42	3	0	0	0-0	268.1	277	119	110	29	36-5	151	.266
Major League totals (18 years)		212	136	.609	4.03	1.24	588	417	52	12	28	13-26	3022.1	3117	1469	1355	353	644-60	1974	.266

DIVISION SERIES RECORD

Year	Team (League)	W	L	Pct.	ERA	WHIP	G	GS	CG	ShO	Hld.	Sv.-Opp.	IP	H	R	ER	HR	BB-IBB	SO	Avg.
1995—	Cincinnati (N.L.)	1	0	1.000	0.00	1.11	1	1	0	0	0	0-0	6.1	6	1	0	0	1-0	8	.231
1996—	Baltimore (A.L.)	1	0	1.000	4.61	1.39	2	2	0	0	0	0-0	13.2	15	7	7	1	4-1	6	.288
1997—	New York (A.L.)	1	0	1.000	1.00	0.56	1	1	1	0	0	0-0	9.0	5	1	1	0	0-0	1	.152
1998—	New York (A.L.)	1	0	1.000	0.00	0.75	1	1	0	0	0	0-0	8.0	5	0	0	0	1-0	9	.172
2002—	New York (A.L.)	0	1	.000	15.43	2.14	1	1	0	0	0	0-0	4.2	10	8	8	1	0-0	0	.435
2003—	New York (A.L.)	1	0	1.000	1.17	1.04	1	1	0	0	0	0-0	7.2	8	1	1	0	0-0	5	.258
Division series totals (6 years)		5	1	.833	3.10	1.11	7	7	1	0	0	0-0	49.1	49	18	17	2	6-1	29	.253

CHAMPIONSHIP SERIES RECORD

Year	Team (League)	W	L	Pct.	ERA	WHIP	G	GS	CG	ShO	Hld.	Sv.-Opp.	IP	H	R	ER	HR	BB-IBB	SO	Avg.
1989—	Toronto (A.L.)	0	0	...	0.00	2.00	1	0	0	0	0	0-0	1.0	0	1	0	0	2-0	1	.000
1991—	Toronto (A.L.)	0	0	...	2.35	1.04	4	0	0	0	0	0-0	7.2	6	2	2	0	2-1	9	.207
1992—	Toronto (A.L.)			Did not play.																
1995—	Cincinnati (N.L.)	0	1	.000	4.50	1.67	1	1	0	0	0	0-0	6.0	8	3	3	1	2-0	3	.320
1996—	Baltimore (A.L.)	1	0	1.000	4.05	1.65	1	1	0	0	0	0-0	6.2	8	3	3	0	3-0	6	.308
1998—	New York (A.L.)	2	0	1.000	2.87	0.89	2	2	0	0	0	0-0	15.2	12	5	5	3	2-0	18	.218
2003—	New York (A.L.)	1	0	1.000	2.35	0.91	2	1	0	0	0	0-0	7.2	5	2	2	2	2-0	5	.179
Champ. series totals (6 years)		4	1	.800	3.02	1.16	11	5	0	0	0	0-0	44.2	39	16	15	6	13-1	42	.235

WORLD SERIES RECORD

Year	Team (League)	W	L	Pct.	ERA	WHIP	G	GS	CG	ShO	Hld.	Sv.-Opp.	IP	H	R	ER	HR	BB-IBB	SO	Avg.
1992—	Toronto (A.L.)	0	0	...	0.00	0.69	4	0	0	0	0	1	0-0	4.1	1	0	0	0	2-0	3	.083
1998—	New York (A.L.)	1	0	1.000	6.43	1.29	1	1	0	0	0	0-0	7.0	7	5	5	3	2-0	4	.269
2003—	New York (A.L.)	0	1	.000	3.38	1.00	2	2	0	0	0	0-0	8.0	6	3	3	0	2-0	1	.222
World series totals (3 years)		1	1	.500	3.72	1.03	7	3	0	0	0	0-0	19.1	14	8	8	3	6-0	8	.215

ALL-STAR GAME RECORD

Year	Team (League)	W	L	Pct.	ERA	WHIP	G	GS	CG	ShO	Hld.	Sv.-Opp.	IP	H	R	ER	HR	BB-IBB	SO	Avg.
All-Star Game totals (3 years)		0	0	...	0.00	0.69	3	2	0	0	0	0-0	4.1	2	0	0	0	1-0	4	.143

W

WELLS, KIP   P

PERSONAL: Born April 21, 1977, in Houston, Texas. ... 6-3/200. ... Throws right, bats right. ... Full name: Robert Kip Wells. ... High school: Elkins (Fort Bend, Texas). ... College: Baylor.

TRANSACTIONS/CAREER NOTES: Selected by Milwaukee Brewers organization in 58th round of 1995 free-agent draft; did not sign. ... Selected by Chicago White Sox organization in first round (16th pick overall) of 1998 free-agent draft. ... Traded by White Sox with Ps Sean Lowe and Josh Fogg to Pittsburgh Pirates for P Todd Ritchie and C Lee Evans (December 13, 2001). ... On disabled list (August 14-September 5, 2004).

CAREER HITTING: 34-for-182 (.187), 17 R, 8 2B, 1 3B, 2 HR, 10 RBI.

Year	Team (League)	W	L	Pct.	ERA	WHIP	G	GS	CG	ShO	Hld.	Sv.-Opp.	IP	H	R	ER	HR	BB-IBB	SO	Avg.
1999—	Winston-Salem (Caro.)	5	6	.455	3.57	1.31	14	14	0	0	...	0-...	85.2	78	39	34	4	34-1	95	.252
—	Birmingham (Southern)	8	2	.800	2.94	1.14	11	11	0	0	...	0-...	70.1	49	24	23	5	31-0	44	.198
—	Chicago (A.L.)	4	1	.800	4.04	1.35	7	7	0	0	0	0-0	35.2	33	17	16	2	15-0	29	.248
2000—	Chicago (A.L.)	6	9	.400	6.02	1.86	20	20	0	0	0	0-0	98.2	126	76	66	15	58-4	71	.312
—	Charlotte (Int'l)	5	3	.625	5.37	1.52	12	12	2	1	...	0-...	62.0	67	38	37	10	27-1	38	.272
2001—	Charlotte (Int'l)	2	1	.667	3.55	1.34	4	4	0	0	...	0-...	25.1	26	11	10	2	8-0	24	.260
—	Chicago (A.L.)	10	11	.476	4.79	1.55	40	20	0	0	6	0-2	133.1	145	80	71	14	61-5	99	.281
2002—	Pittsburgh (N.L.)	12	14	.462	3.58	1.35	33	33	1	1	0	0-0	198.1	197	92	79	21	71-11	134	.261
2003—	Pittsburgh (N.L.)	10	9	.526	3.28	1.25	31	31	1	0	0	0-0	197.1	171	77	72	24	76-7	147	.233
2004—	Pittsburgh (N.L.)	5	7	.417	4.55	1.53	24	24	0	0	0	0-0	138.1	145	71	70	14	66-4	116	.270
	American League totals (3 years)	20	21	.488	5.14	1.64	67	47	0	0	6	0-2	267.2	304	173	153	31	134-9	199	.289
	National League totals (3 years)	27	30	.474	3.72	1.36	88	88	2	1	0	0-0	534.0	513	240	221	59	213-22	397	.253
	Major League totals (6 years)	47	51	.480	4.20	1.45	155	135	2	1	6	0-2	801.2	817	413	374	90	347-31	596	.265

WELLS, VERNON   OF

PERSONAL: Born December 8, 1978, in Shreveport, La. ... 6-1/225. ... Bats right, throws right. ... Full name: Vernon III Wells. ... High school: Bowie (Arlington, Texas).

TRANSACTIONS/CAREER NOTES: Selected by Toronto Blue Jays organization in first round (fifth pick overall) of 1997 free-agent draft. ... On disabled list (June 16-July 16, 2004).

HONORS: Won A.L. Gold Glove as outfielder (2004).

2004 GAMES PLAYED BY POSITION (MLB): OF—131, DH—3.

										BATTING										FIELDING	
Year	Team (League)	Pos.	G	AB	R	H	2B	3B	HR	RBI	BB	SO	HBP	GDP	SB-CS	Avg.	OBP	SLG	OPS	E	Avg.
1997—	St. Catharines (NY-Penn.)	OF	66	264	52	81	20	1	10	31	30	44	1	2	8-6	.307	.377	.504	.881	7	.953
1998—	Hagerstown (SAL)	OF	134	509	86	145	35	2	11	65	49	84	1	8	13-8	.285	.348	.426	.774	5	.980
1999—	Dunedin (Fla. St.)	OF-DH	70	265	43	91	16	2	11	43	26	34	1	6	13-2	.343	.403	.543	.946	1	.993
—	Knoxville (Southern)	OF	26	106	18	36	6	2	3	17	12	15	0	0	6-2	.340	.400	.519	.919	0	1.000
—	Syracuse (Int'l)	OF	33	129	20	40	8	1	4	21	10	22	1	3	5-1	.310	.357	.481	.837	2	.976
—	Toronto (A.L.)	OF	24	88	8	23	5	0	1	8	4	18	0	6	1-1	.261	.293	.352	.646	0	1.000
2000—	Syracuse (Int'l)	OF	127	493	76	120	31	7	16	66	48	88	4	8	23-4	.243	.313	.432	.745	4	.990
—	Toronto (A.L.)	OF	3	2	0	0	0	0	0	0	0	0	0	0	0-0	.000	.000	.000	.000	0	1.000
2001—	Syracuse (Int'l)	OF	107	413	57	116	27	4	12	52	29	68	4	3	15-11	.281	.333	.453	.785	5	.978
—	Toronto (A.L.)	OF	30	96	14	30	8	0	1	6	5	15	1	0	5-0	.313	.350	.427	.777	2	.969
2002—	Toronto (A.L.)	OF	159	608	87	167	34	4	23	100	27	85	3	15	9-4	.275	.305	.457	.762	3	.992
2003—	Toronto (A.L.)	OF	161	678	118	* 215	• 49	5	33	117	42	80	7	21	4-1	.317	.359	.550	.909	4	.990
2004—	Toronto (A.L.)	OF-DH	134	536	82	146	34	2	23	67	51	83	2	17	9-2	.272	.337	.472	.809	1	.997
	Major League totals (6 years)		511	2008	309	581	130	11	81	298	129	281	13	59	28-8	.289	.333	.486	.820	10	.992

		ALL-STAR GAME RECORD																
	G	AB	R	H	2B	3B	HR	RBI	BB	SO	HBP	GDP	SB-CS	Avg.	OBP	SLG	OPS	E	Avg.
All-Star Game totals (1 year)	1	2	1	1	1	0	0	1	0	0	0	0	0-0	.500	.500	1.000	1.500	0	1.000

WENDELL, TURK   P

PERSONAL: Born May 19, 1967, in Pittsfield, Mass. ... 6-2/205. ... Throws right, bats left. ... Full name: Steven John Wendell. ... Name pronounced: WEN-del. ... High school: Wahconah Regional (Dalton, Mass.). ... College: Quinnipiac.

TRANSACTIONS/CAREER NOTES: Selected by Atlanta Braves organization in fifth round of 1988 free-agent draft. ... Traded by Braves with P Yorkis Perez to Chicago Cubs for P Mike Bielecki and C Damon Berryhill (September 29, 1991). ... On disabled list (April 16-May 27, 1995); included rehabilitation assignments to Daytona and Orlando. ... Traded by Cubs with OF Brian McRae and P Mel Rojas to New York Mets for OF Lance Johnson and two players to be named (August 8, 1997); Cubs acquired P Mark Clark (August 11, 1997) and IF Manny Alexander (August 14, 1997) to complete deal. ... Traded by Mets with P Dennis Cook to Philadelphia Phillies for Ps Bruce Chen and Adam Walker (July 27, 2001). ... On disabled list (March 30, 2002-entire season). ... On disabled list (March 21-April 14, 2003); included rehabilitation assignment to Clearwater. ... Signed as a free agent by Colorado Rockies organization (January 14, 2004). ... On disabled list (May 14-July 21, 2004); included rehabilitation assignment to Colorado Springs. ... Released by Rockies (July 27, 2004).

CAREER HITTING: 3-for-43 (.070), 1 R, 0 2B, 0 3B, 0 HR, 0 RBI.

Year	Team (League)	W	L	Pct.	ERA	WHIP	G	GS	CG	ShO	Hld.	Sv.-Opp.	IP	H	R	ER	HR	BB-IBB	SO	Avg.
1988—	Pulaski (Appalachian)	3	8	.273	3.83	1.14	14	14	6	1	...	0-...	101.0	85	50	43	3	30-0	87	.228
1989—	Burlington (Midw.)	9	11	.450	2.21	1.06	22	22	9	5	...	0-...	159.0	127	63	39	7	41-1	153	.213
—	Greenville (Sou.)	0	0	...	9.82	2.18	1	1	0	0	...	0-...	3.2	7	5	4	3	1-0	3	.389
—	Durham (Caro.)	2	0	1.000	1.13	0.79	3	3	1	0	...	0-...	24.0	13	4	3	0	6-0	27	.157
1990—	Greenville (Sou.)	4	9	.308	5.74	1.68	36	13	1	1	...	2-...	91.0	105	70	58	5	48-2	85	.288
—	Durham (Caro.)	1	3	.250	1.86	1.01	6	5	1	0	...	0-...	38.2	24	10	8	3	15-1	26	.175
1991—	Greenville (Sou.)	11	3	.786	2.56	1.23	25	20	1	1	...	0-...	147.2	130	47	42	4	51-5	122	.236
—	Richmond (Int'l)	0	2	.000	3.43	1.71	3	3	1	0	...	0-...	21.0	20	9	8	3	16-0	18	.260
1992—	Iowa (Am. Assoc.)	2	0	1.000	1.44	1.28	4	4	0	0	...	0-...	25.0	17	7	4	3	15-0	12	.191
1993—	Iowa (Am. Assoc.)	10	8	.556	4.60	1.31	25	25	3	0	...	0-...	148.2	148	88	76	9	47-0	110	.257
—	Chicago (N.L.)	1	2	.333	4.37	1.41	7	4	0	0	0	0-0	22.2	24	13	11	0	8-1	15	.273
1994—	Iowa (Am. Assoc.)	11	6	.647	2.95	1.01	23	23	6	3	...	0-...	168.0	141	58	55	12	28-1	118	.230
—	Chicago (N.L.)	0	1	.000	11.93	2.23	6	2	0	0	0	0-0	14.1	22	20	19	3	10-1	9	.349
1995—	Daytona (Fla. St.)	0	0	...	1.17	0.78	4	2	0	0	...	0-...	7.2	5	2	1	0	1-0	8	.179
—	Orlando (Sou.)	1	0	1.000	3.86	1.43	5	0	0	0	...	1-...	7.0	6	3	3	0	4-0	7	.250
—	Chicago (N.L.)	3	1	.750	4.92	1.57	43	0	0	0	3	0-0	60.1	71	35	33	11	24-4	50	.298
1996—	Chicago (N.L.)	4	5	.444	2.84	1.29	70	0	0	0	6	18-21	79.1	58	26	25	8	44-4	75	.201
1997—	Chicago (N.L.)	3	5	.375	4.20	1.53	52	0	0	0	2	4-5	60.0	53	32	28	4	39-5	54	.238
—	New York (N.L.)	0	0	...	4.96	1.78	13	0	0	0	1	1-2	16.1	15	10	9	4	14-1	9	.250

W

Year Team (League)	W	L	Pct.	ERA	WHIP	G	GS	CG	ShO	Hld.	Sv.-Opp.	IP	H	R	ER	HR	BB-IBB	SO	Avg.
1998— New York (N.L.)	5	1	.833	2.93	1.24	66	0	0	0	11	4-8	76.2	62	25	25	4	33-9	58	.221
1999— New York (N.L.)	5	4	.556	3.05	1.37	80	0	0	0	21	3-6	85.2	80	31	29	9	37-8	77	.245
2000— New York (N.L.)	8	6	.571	3.59	1.22	77	0	0	0	16	1-5	82.2	60	36	33	9	41-7	73	.206
2001— New York (N.L.)	4	3	.571	3.51	1.25	49	0	0	0	6	1-3	51.1	42	23	20	8	22-6	41	.223
— Philadelphia (N.L.)	0	2	.000	7.47	2.11	21	0	0	0	2	0-0	15.2	21	13	13	4	12-3	15	.323
2002— Philadelphia (N.L.)	Did not play.																		
2003— Clearwater (Fla. St.)	0	0	...	0.00	0.50	5	5	0	0	...	0-...	6.0	3	0	0	0	0	5	.143
— Philadelphia (N.L.)	3	3	.500	3.38	1.28	56	0	0	0	8	1-5	64.0	54	24	24	6	28-5	27	.235
2004— Colorado (N.L.)	0	0	...	7.02	1.98	12	0	0	0	0	0-1	16.2	21	13	13	4	12-1	11	.328
— Colo. Springs (PCL)	0	1	.000	5.79	1.64	12	8	0	0	0	0-...	14.0	19	10	9	2	4-0	8	.328
Major League totals (11 years)	36	33	.522	3.93	1.40	552	6	0	0	75	33-56	645.2	583	301	282	73	324-55	515	.242

DIVISION SERIES RECORD

Year Team (League)	W	L	Pct.	ERA	WHIP	G	GS	CG	ShO	Hld.	Sv.-Opp.	IP	H	R	ER	HR	BB-IBB	SO	Avg.
1999— New York (N.L.)	1	0	1.000	0.00	1.00	2	0	0	0	0	0-0	2.0	0	0	0	0	2-0	5	.000
2000— New York (N.L.)	0	0	...	0.00	0.50	2	0	0	0	0	0-0	2.0	0	0	0	0	1-0	5	.000
Division series totals (2 years)	1	0	1.000	0.00	0.75	4	0	0	0	0	0-0	4.0	0	0	0	0	3-0	5	.000

CHAMPIONSHIP SERIES RECORD

Year Team (League)	W	L	Pct.	ERA	WHIP	G	GS	CG	ShO	Hld.	Sv.-Opp.	IP	H	R	ER	HR	BB-IBB	SO	Avg.
1999— New York (N.L.)	1	0	1.000	4.76	1.06	5	0	0	0	0	0-0	5.2	2	3	3	0	4-2	5	.111
2000— New York (N.L.)	1	0	1.000	0.00	1.50	2	0	0	0	0	0-1	1.1	1	0	0	0	1-1	2	.200
Champ. series totals (2 years)	2	0	1.000	3.86	1.14	7	0	0	0	0	0-1	7.0	3	3	3	0	5-3	7	.130

WORLD SERIES RECORD

Year Team (League)	W	L	Pct.	ERA	WHIP	G	GS	CG	ShO	Hld.	Sv.-Opp.	IP	H	R	ER	HR	BB-IBB	SO	Avg.
2000— New York (N.L.)	0	1	.000	5.40	3.00	2	0	0	0	0	0-0	1.2	3	1	1	0	2-1	2	.375

WERTH, JAYSON — OF

PERSONAL: Born May 20, 1979, in Springfield, Ill. ... 6-5/215. ... Bats right, throws right. ... Full name: Jayson Richard Werth. ... High school: Chatham Glenwood (Chatham, Ill.). ... Stepson of Dennis Werth, outfielder/first baseman with two major league teams (1979-82); nephew of Dick Schofield, infielder with four major league teams (1983-96); grandson of Dick Schofield, infielder/outfielder with six major league teams (1953-71).

TRANSACTIONS/CAREER NOTES: Selected by Baltimore Orioles organization in first round (22nd pick overall) of 1997 free-agent draft. ... Traded by Orioles to Toronto Blue Jays for P John Bale (December 11, 2000). ... On disabled list (March 21-April 13, 2003); included rehabilitation assignment Dunedin. ... Recalled from Syracuse by Toronto (July 9, 2003). ... Optioned to Syracuse by Toronto (July 25, 2003). ... Traded by Blue Jays to Los Angeles Dodgers for P Jason Frasor (March 29, 2004). ... On disabled list (April 6-June 4, 2004); included rehabilitation assignment to Las Vegas.

2004 GAMES PLAYED BY POSITION (MLB): OF—79, DH—1.

Year Team (League)	Pos.	G	AB	R	H	2B	3B	HR	RBI	BB	SO	HBP	GDP	SB-CS	Avg.	OBP	SLG	OPS	E	Avg.
1997— GC Orioles (GCL)	C-1B	32	88	16	26	6	0	1	8	22	22	0	0	7-1	.295	.432	.398	.830	9	.958
1998— Delmarva (S. Atl.)	C	120	408	71	108	20	3	8	53	50	92	15	14	21-6	.265	.364	.387	.751	9	.991
— Bowie (East.)	C	5	19	2	3	2	0	0	1	2	6	0	0	1-0	.158	.238	.263	.501	0	1.000
1999— Frederick (Carolina)	C-OF	66	236	41	72	10	1	3	30	37	37	3	4	16-3	.305	.403	.394	.797	10	.981
— Bowie (East.)	C-OF	35	121	18	33	5	1	1	11	17	26	2	1	7-1	.273	.364	.355	.719	1	.996
2000— Bowie (East.)	C-OF	85	276	47	63	16	2	5	26	54	50	4	10	9-3	.228	.361	.355	.716	7	.988
— Frederick (Carolina)	C	24	83	16	23	3	0	2	18	10	15	0	3	5-1	.277	.347	.386	.733	2	.985
2001— Dunedin (Fla. St.)	C	21	70	9	14	3	0	2	14	17	19	0	2	1-1	.200	.356	.329	.685	0	1.000
— Tennessee (Sou.)	C-1B	104	369	51	105	23	1	18	69	63	93	3	5	12-3	.285	.387	.499	.886	7	.988
2002— Syracuse (Int'l)	OF-C	127	443	65	114	25	2	18	82	67	125	4	7	24-7	.257	.354	.445	.798	5	.985
— Toronto (A.L.)	OF	15	46	4	12	2	1	0	6	6	11	0	4	1-0	.261	.340	.348	.687	0	1.000
2003— Dunedin (Fla. St.)	OF-DH	18	62	10	23	5	0	4	18	3	14	0	2	1-0	.371	.388	.645	1.033	0	1.000
— Toronto (A.L.)	OF-DH	26	48	7	10	4	0	2	10	3	22	0	0	1-0	.208	.255	.417	.672	0	1.000
— Syracuse (Int'l)	OF-DH	64	236	37	56	19	1	9	34	15	68	2	7	11-1	.237	.285	.441	.726	7	.954
2004— Las Vegas (PCL)	OF-DH	14	51	13	21	2	1	5	20	8	10	1	2	2-0	.412	.500	.784	1.284	0	1.000
— Los Angeles (N.L.)	OF-DH	89	290	56	76	11	3	16	47	30	85	4	1	4-1	.262	.338	.486	.825	4	.974
American League totals (2 years)		41	94	11	22	6	1	2	16	9	33	0	4	2-0	.234	.298	.383	.681	0	1.000
National League totals (1 year)		89	290	56	76	11	3	16	47	30	85	4	1	4-1	.262	.338	.486	.825	4	.974
Major League totals (3 years)		130	384	67	98	17	4	18	63	39	118	4	5	6-1	.255	.329	.461	.790	4	.982

DIVISION SERIES RECORD

Year Team (League)	Pos.	G	AB	R	H	2B	3B	HR	RBI	BB	SO	HBP	GDP	SB-CS	Avg.	OBP	SLG	OPS	E	Avg.
2004— Los Angeles (N.L.)	OF	4	14	3	4	1	0	2	3	3	4	0	0	0-0	.286	.412	.786	1.197	0	1.000

WESTBROOK, JAKE — P

PERSONAL: Born September 29, 1977, in Athens, Ga. ... 6-3/185. ... Throws right, bats right. ... Full name: Jacob Cauthen Westbrook. ... High school: Madison County (Danielsville, Ga.).

TRANSACTIONS/CAREER NOTES: Selected by Colorado Rockies organization in first round (21st pick overall) of 1996 free-agent draft. ... Traded by Rockies with P John Nicholson and OF Mark Hamlin to Montreal Expos for 2B Mike Lansing (December 16, 1997). ... Traded by Expos with two players to be named to New York Yankees for P Hideki Irabu (December 22, 1999); Yankees acquired Ps Ted Lilly (March 17, 2000) and Christian Parker (March 22, 2000) to complete deal. ... Traded by Yankees with P Zach Day to Cleveland Indians (July 25, 2000), completing deal in which Indians traded OF Dave Justice to Yankees for OF Ricky Ledee and two players to be named (June 29, 2000). ... On disabled list (September 1, 2000-remainder of season). ... On disabled list (March 30-July 11 and August 26, 2002-remainder of season); included rehabilitation assignments to Akron and Buffalo.

CAREER HITTING: 0-for-4 (.000), 0 R, 0 2B, 0 3B, 0 HR, 0 RBI.

Year Team (League)	W	L	Pct.	ERA	WHIP	G	GS	CG	ShO	Hld.	Sv.-Opp.	IP	H	R	ER	HR	BB-IBB	SO	Avg.
1996— Ariz. Rockies (Ariz.)	4	2	.667	2.87	1.28	11	11	0	0	...	0-...	62.2	66	33	20	0	14-0	57	.269
— Portland (N'west)	1	1	.500	2.55	1.09	4	4	0	0	...	0-...	24.2	22	8	7	1	5-0	19	.237
1997— Asheville (S. Atl.)	14	11	.560	4.82	1.36	28	27	3	2	...	0-...	170.0	176	93	91	16	55-0	92	.269
1998— Jupiter (FSL)	11	6	.647	3.26	1.34	27	27	2	0	...	0-...	171.0	169	70	62	11	60-0	79	.264
1999— Harrisburg (Eastern)	11	5	.688	3.92	1.39	27	27	2	2	...	0-...	174.2	180	88	76	14	63-1	90	.274
2000— Columbus (Int'l)	5	7	.417	4.65	1.48	16	15	2	0	...	0-...	89.0	94	53	46	3	38-0	61	.272
— New York (A.L.)	0	2	.000	13.50	2.85	3	2	0	0	...	0-0	6.2	15	10	10	1	4-1	1	.469
2001— Buffalo (Int'l)	8	1	.889	3.20	1.28	12	12	0	0	...	0-...	64.2	60	27	23	2	23-0	45	.249

Year Team (League)	W	L	Pct.	ERA	WHIP	G	GS	CG	ShO	Hld.	Sv.-Opp.	IP	H	R	ER	HR	BB-IBB	SO	Avg.
— Cleveland (A.L.)	4	4	.500	5.85	1.56	23	6	0	0	5	0-0	64.2	79	43	42	6	22-4	48	.306
2002— Akron (East.)	0	1	.000	4.80	0.93	3	3	0	0	...	0-...	15.0	13	8	8	0	1-0	8	.228
— Buffalo (Int'l)	1	0	1.000	6.00	1.33	1	1	0	0	...	0-...	6.0	8	4	4	1	0-0	2	.333
— Cleveland (A.L.)	1	3	.250	5.83	1.49	11	4	0	0	1	0-2	41.2	50	30	27	6	12-1	20	.296
2003— Buffalo (Int'l)	1	0	1.000	5.00	0.40	2	2	0	0	...	0-...	10.0	0	0	0	0	4-0	7	.000
— Cleveland (A.L.)	7	10	.412	4.33	1.49	34	22	1	0	1	0-0	133.0	142	70	64	9	56-1	58	.281
2004— Cleveland (A.L.)	14	9	.609	3.38	1.25	33	33	•5	1	0	0-0	215.2	208	95	81	19	61-3	116	.255
Major League totals (5 years)	26	28	.481	4.37	1.41	104	64	6	1	7	0-2	461.2	494	248	224	41	155-10	243	.277

WHEELER, DAN — P

PERSONAL: Born December 10, 1977, in Providence, R.I. ... 6-3/222. ... Throws right, bats right. ... Full name: Daniel Michael Wheeler. ... High school: Pilgrim (Warwick, R.I.). ... Junior college: Central Arizona.

TRANSACTIONS/CAREER NOTES: Selected by Tampa Bay Devil Rays organization in 34th round of 1996 free-agent draft. ... Released by Devil Rays (December 13, 2001). ... Signed by Atlanta Braves organization (January 10, 2002). ... Signed as a free agent by New York Mets organization (January 27, 2003). ... Traded by Mets to Houston Astros for P Adam Seuss (August 27, 2004). ... On suspended list (September 24-27, 2004).

CAREER HITTING: 1-for-7 (.143), 1 R, 0 2B, 0 3B, 0 HR, 0 RBI.

Year Team (League)	W	L	Pct.	ERA	WHIP	G	GS	CG	ShO	Hld.	Sv.-Opp.	IP	H	R	ER	HR	BB-IBB	SO	Avg.
1997— Hudson Valley (NY-Penn.)	6	7	.462	3.00	1.10	15	15	0	0	...	0-...	84.0	75	38	28	2	17-0	81	.228
1998— Char., S.C. (SAL)	12	14	.462	4.43	1.30	29	29	3	1	...	0-...	181.0	206	96	89	16	29-0	136	.290
1999— Orlando (Sou.)	3	0	1.000	3.26	1.10	9	9	0	0	...	0-...	58.0	56	27	21	7	8-0	53	.252
— Durham (Int'l)	7	5	.583	4.92	1.55	14	14	2	1	...	0-...	82.1	103	59	45	16	25-0	58	.307
— Tampa Bay (A.L.)	0	4	.000	5.87	1.57	6	6	0	0	0	0-0	30.2	35	20	20	7	13-1	32	.287
2000— Tampa Bay (A.L.)	1	1	.500	5.48	1.74	11	2	0	0	1	0-1	23.0	29	14	14	2	11-2	17	.302
— Durham (Int'l)	5	11	.313	5.63	1.50	26	26	0	0	...	0-...	150.1	183	109	94	35	42-1	91	.300
2001— Durham (Int'l)	3	5	.375	5.23	1.27	18	10	0	0	...	0-...	65.1	72	51	38	11	11-0	39	.271
— Tampa Bay (A.L.)	1	0	1.000	8.66	1.98	13	0	0	0	...	0-...	17.2	30	17	17	3	5-0	12	.375
— Orlando (Sou.)	0	2	.000	2.81	1.31	3	3	0	0	...	0-...	16.0	15	5	5	2	6-1	12	.242
2002— Richmond (Int'l)	9	6	.600	4.65	1.32	27	25	0	0	...	0-...	155.0	163	87	80	23	42-0	110	.268
2003— Norfolk (Int'l)	4	2	.667	3.94	1.40	22	5	0	0	...	4-...	45.2	48	20	20	4	16-3	44	.265
— New York (N.L.)	1	3	.250	3.71	1.29	35	0	0	0	...	2-3	51.0	49	23	21	6	17-4	35	.253
2004— Norfolk (Int'l)	1	0	1.000	2.46	1.36	5	0	0	0	...	0-...	7.1	8	2	2	0	2-0	10	.276
— New York (N.L.)	3	1	.750	4.80	1.62	32	1	0	0	3	0-0	50.2	65	29	27	9	17-2	46	.307
— Houston (N.L.)	0	0	...	2.51	0.98	14	0	0	0	2	0-0	14.1	11	4	4	1	3-0	9	.216
American League totals (3 years)	2	5	.286	6.43	1.72	30	8	0	0	1	0-1	71.1	94	51	51	12	29-3	61	.315
National League totals (2 years)	4	4	.500	4.03	1.40	81	1	0	0	5	2-3	116.0	125	56	52	16	37-6	90	.274
Major League totals (5 years)	6	9	.400	4.95	1.52	111	9	0	0	6	2-4	187.1	219	107	103	28	66-9	151	.290

DIVISION SERIES RECORD

Year Team (League)	W	L	Pct.	ERA	WHIP	G	GS	CG	ShO	Hld.	Sv.-Opp.	IP	H	R	ER	HR	BB-IBB	SO	Avg.
2004— Houston (N.L.)	0	0	...	0.00	0.00	1	0	0	0	0	0-0	1.0	0	0	0	0	0-0	0	.000

CHAMPIONSHIP SERIES RECORD

Year Team (League)	W	L	Pct.	ERA	WHIP	G	GS	CG	ShO	Hld.	Sv.-Opp.	IP	H	R	ER	HR	BB-IBB	SO	Avg.
2004— Houston (N.L.)	1	0	1.000	0.00	0.57	4	0	0	0	0	0-0	7.0	4	0	0	0	0-0	9	.160

WHITE, GABE — P

PERSONAL: Born November 20, 1971, in Sebring, Fla. ... 6-2/205. ... Throws left, bats left. ... Full name: Gabriel Allen White. ... High school: Sebring (Fla.).

TRANSACTIONS/CAREER NOTES: Selected by Montreal Expos organization in supplemental round ("sandwich pick" between first and second rounds, 28th pick overall) of 1990 free-agent draft; pick received as part of compensation for California Angels signing Type A free-agent P Mark Langston. ... Traded by Expos to Cincinnati Reds for 2B Jhonny Carvajal (December 15, 1995). ... On disabled list (September 17, 1996-remainder of season). ... Traded by Reds to Colorado Rockies for P Manny Aybar (April 7, 2000). ... Traded by Rockies with P Luke Hudson to Reds for 2B Pokey Reese and P Dennys Reyes (December 18, 2001). ... On disabled list (July 12-31 and August 29, 2002-remainder of season). ... On disabled list (June 21-August 26, 2003); included rehabilitation assignments to Louisville, GCL Yankees, Tampa and Trenton. ... Traded by Reds to New York Yankees for a player to be named (July 31, 2003). ... Traded by Yankees to Reds for P Charlie Manning, a player to be named and cash (June 18, 2004).

RECORDS: Shares N.L. record for most consecutive home runs allowed in one inning—3 (July 7, 1995, second inning).

CAREER HITTING: 4-for-38 (.105), 1 R, 0 2B, 0 3B, 1 HR, 3 RBI.

Year Team (League)	W	L	Pct.	ERA	WHIP	G	GS	CG	ShO	Hld.	Sv.-Opp.	IP	H	R	ER	HR	BB-IBB	SO	Avg.
1990— GC Expos (GCL)	4	2	.667	3.14	1.08	11	11	1	0	...	0-...	57.1	50	21	20	3	12-0	41	.231
1991— Sumter (S. Atl.)	6	9	.400	3.26	1.21	24	24	5	0	...	0-...	149.0	127	73	54	7	53-0	140	.229
1992— Rockford (Midwest)	14	8	.636	2.84	1.12	27	27	7	0	...	0-...	187.0	148	73	59	10	61-0	176	.215
1993— Harrisburg (Eastern)	7	2	.778	2.16	1.08	16	16	2	1	...	0-...	100.0	80	30	24	4	28-0	80	.221
— Ottawa (Int'l)	2	1	.667	3.12	1.09	6	6	1	1	...	0-...	40.1	38	15	14	3	6-0	28	.242
1994— W.P. Beach (FSL)	1	0	1.000	1.50	0.50	1	1	0	0	...	0-...	6.0	2	2	1	0	1-0	4	.105
— Ottawa (Int'l)	8	3	.727	5.05	1.44	14	14	0	0	...	0-...	73.0	77	49	41	11	28-2	63	.270
— Montreal (N.L.)	1	1	.500	6.08	1.48	7	5	0	0	...	1-1	23.2	24	16	16	4	11-0	17	.261
1995— Ottawa (Int'l)	2	3	.400	3.90	1.20	12	12	0	0	...	0-...	62.1	58	31	27	10	17-0	37	.244
— Montreal (N.L.)	1	2	.333	7.01	1.36	19	1	0	0	...	0-0	25.2	26	21	20	7	9-0	25	.260
1996— Indianapolis (A.A.)	6	3	.667	2.77	1.14	11	11	0	0	...	0-...	68.1	69	25	21	6	9-3	51	.266
1997— Indianapolis (A.A.)	7	4	.636	2.82	1.16	20	19	0	0	...	0-...	118.0	119	46	37	10	18-0	62	.257
— Cincinnati (N.L.)	2	2	.500	4.39	1.15	12	6	0	0	3	1-1	41.0	39	20	20	6	8-1	25	.253
1998— Cincinnati (N.L.)	5	5	.500	4.01	1.15	69	3	0	0	6	9-13	98.2	86	46	44	17	27-6	83	.231
1999— Cincinnati (N.L.)	1	2	.333	4.43	1.34	50	0	0	0	5	0-1	61.0	68	31	30	13	14-1	61	.281
2000— Cincinnati (N.L.)	0	0	...	18.00	3.00	1	0	0	0	0	0-0	1.0	2	2	2	1	1-0	2	.400
— Colorado (N.L.)	11	2	.846	2.17	0.92	67	0	0	0	19	5-9	83.0	62	21	20	5	14-2	82	.208
2001— Colorado (N.L.)	1	7	.125	6.25	1.42	69	0	0	0	8	0-2	67.2	70	47	47	18	26-5	47	.270
2002— Cincinnati (N.L.)	6	1	.857	2.98	1.09	62	0	0	0	19	0-1	54.1	49	19	18	3	10-2	41	.239
2003— Cincinnati (N.L.)	3	0	1.000	3.93	1.22	34	0	0	0	6	0-1	34.1	36	15	15	5	6-3	23	.275
— Louisville (Int'l)	0	0	...	9.00	3.00	1	1	0	0	...	0-...	1.0	2	1	1	0	1-0	0	.400
— GC Yankees (GCL)	0	0	...	0.00	1.00	1	1	0	0	...	0-...	1.0	1	0	0	0	1-0	1	.000
— Tampa (FSL)	0	0	...	0.00	1.50	1	1	0	0	...	0-...	.2	1	0	0	0	0-0	0	.333
— Trenton (East.)	0	0	...	7.71	1.30	2	2	0	0	...	0-...	2.1	3	2	2	1	0-0	2	.300
— New York (A.L.)	2	1	.667	4.38	0.81	12	0	0	0	1	0-1	12.1	8	7	6	2	2-1	6	.182
2004— New York (A.L.)	0	1	.000	8.27	1.94	24	0	0	0	3	0-2	20.2	33	19	19	2	7-4	8	.355
— Cincinnati (N.L.)	1	2	.333	6.23	1.13	40	0	0	0	9	1-3	39.0	39	27	27	12	5-0	33	.257
American League totals (2 years)	2	2	.500	6.82	1.52	36	0	0	0	9	0-3	33.0	41	26	25	4	9-5	14	.299
National League totals (10 years)	32	24	.571	4.40	1.19	430	15	0	0	73	17-32	529.1	501	265	259	91	131-20	439	.249
Major League totals (10 years)	34	26	.567	4.55	1.21	466	15	0	0	82	17-35	562.1	542	291	284	95	140-25	453	.252

W

DIVISION SERIES RECORD

Year	Team (League)	W	L	Pct.	ERA	WHIP	G	GS	CG	ShO	Hld.	Sv.-Opp.	IP	H	R	ER	HR	BB-IBB	SO	Avg.
2003— New York (A.L.)		0	0	...	0.00	0.75	1	0	0	0	0	0-0	1.1	1	0	0	0	0-0	1	.200

CHAMPIONSHIP SERIES RECORD

Year	Team (League)	W	L	Pct.	ERA	WHIP	G	GS	CG	ShO	Hld.	Sv.-Opp.	IP	H	R	ER	HR	BB-IBB	SO	Avg.
2003— New York (A.L.)		0	0	...	4.50	2.00	2	0	0	0	0	0-0	2.0	4	1	1	1	0-0	1	.444

WHITE, RICK — P

PERSONAL: Born December 23, 1968, in Springfield, Ohio. ... 6-4/230. ... Throws right, bats right. ... Full name: Richard Allen White. ... High school: Kenton Ridge (Springfield, Ohio). ... Junior college: Paducah (Ky.).

TRANSACTIONS/CAREER NOTES: Selected by Pittsburgh Pirates organization in 15th round of 1990 free-agent draft. ... On disabled list (April 14-May 17, 1995); included rehabilitation assignment to GCL Pirates. ... Signed as a free agent by Tampa Bay Devil Rays organization (February 4, 1997). ... Loaned by Devil Rays organization to Chicago Cubs organization (April 3-September 11, 1997). ... Traded by Devil Rays with OF Bubba Trammell to New York Mets for OF Jason Tyner and P Paul Wilson (July 28, 2000). ... On disabled list (March 31-April 21, 2001 and May 1-17, 2001). ... Signed as a free agent by Colorado Rockies (January 10, 2002). ... On disabled list (May 27-June 18, 2002); included rehabilitation assignment to Colorado Springs. ... Released by Rockies (August 12, 2002). ... Signed St. Louis Cardinals organization (August 17, 2002). ... Signed as a free agent by Chicago White Sox (January 22, 2003). ... Released by White Sox (August 11, 2003). ... Signed by Houston Astros (August 14, 2003). ... Signed as a free agent by Los Angeles Dodgers organization (January 16, 2004). ... Traded by Dodgers to Cleveland Indians for OF Trey Dyson (April 25, 2004).

CAREER HITTING: 4-for-40 (.100), 1 R, 1 2B, 0 3B, 0 HR, 1 RBI.

Year	Team (League)	W	L	Pct.	ERA	WHIP	G	GS	CG	ShO	Hld.	Sv.-Opp.	IP	H	R	ER	HR	BB-IBB	SO	Avg.
1990— GC Pirates (GCL)		3	1	.750	0.76	0.84	7	6	0	0	...	0-...	35.2	26	11	3	0	4-0	27	.194
— Welland (N.Y.-Penn)		1	4	.200	3.26	1.37	9	5	1	0	...	0-...	38.2	39	19	14	2	14-2	43	.265
1991— Augusta (S. Atl.)		4	4	.500	3.00	1.37	34	0	0	0	...	6-...	63.0	68	26	21	2	18-2	52	.264
— Salem (Caro.)		2	3	.400	4.66	1.08	13	5	1	0	...	1-...	46.1	41	27	24	2	9-3	36	.233
1992— Salem (Caro.)		7	9	.438	3.80	1.16	18	18	5	0	...	0-...	120.2	116	58	51	15	24-1	70	.255
— Carolina (Southern)		1	7	.125	4.21	1.34	10	10	1	0	...	0-...	57.2	59	32	27	8	18-1	45	.265
1993— Carolina (Southern)		4	3	.571	3.50	1.02	12	12	1	0	...	0-...	69.1	59	29	27	5	12-0	52	.231
— Buffalo (A.A.)		0	3	.000	3.54	1.18	7	3	0	0	...	0-...	28.0	25	13	11	1	8-0	16	.238
1994— Pittsburgh (N.L.)		4	5	.444	3.82	1.27	43	5	0	0	3	6-9	75.1	79	35	32	9	17-3	38	.280
1995— Pittsburgh (N.L.)		2	3	.400	4.75	1.53	15	9	0	0	0	0-0	55.0	66	33	29	3	18-0	29	.299
— Calgary (PCL)		6	4	.600	4.20	1.35	14	11	1	0	...	0-...	79.1	97	40	37	13	10-0	56	.302
1996— GC Pirates (GCL)		0	0	...	2.25	0.92	3	3	0	0	...	0-...	12.0	8	4	3	0	3-0	8	.205
— Carolina (Southern)		0	1	.000	11.37	1.58	2	1	0	0	...	0-...	6.1	9	8	8	2	1-0	7	.321
1997— Orlando (Sou.)		5	7	.417	4.71	1.34	39	8	0	0	...	12-...	86.0	93	55	45	7	22-2	65	.275
1998— Durham (Int'l)		4	2	.667	4.22	1.39	9	9	1	0	...	0-...	53.1	63	29	25	3	11-0	31	.294
— Tampa Bay (A.L.)		2	6	.250	3.80	1.30	38	3	0	0	2	0-0	68.2	66	32	29	8	23-2	39	.253
1999— Tampa Bay (A.L.)		5	3	.625	4.08	1.57	63	1	0	0	4	0-2	108.0	132	56	49	8	38-5	81	.304
2000— Tampa Bay (A.L.)		3	6	.333	3.41	1.16	44	0	0	0	2	2-5	71.1	57	30	27	7	26-3	47	.220
— New York (N.L.)		2	3	.400	3.81	1.34	22	0	0	0	2	1-2	28.1	26	14	12	2	12-2	20	.232
2001— New York (N.L.)		4	5	.444	3.88	1.26	55	0	0	0	10	2-4	69.2	71	38	30	7	17-4	51	.257
2002— Colorado (N.L.)		2	6	.250	6.20	1.65	41	0	0	0	9	0-0	40.2	49	30	28	4	18-4	27	.310
— Memphis (PCL)		0	0	...	2.45	1.91	3	0	0	0	...	0-...	3.2	4	1	1	0	3-0	4	.286
— St. Louis (N.L.)		3	1	.750	0.82	0.73	20	0	0	0	7	0-0	22.0	13	3	2	0	3-1	14	.169
2003— Chicago (A.L.)		1	2	.333	6.61	1.45	34	0	0	0	3	1-1	47.2	56	39	35	11	13-2	35	.295
— Houston (N.L.)		0	0	...	3.72	1.34	15	0	0	0	1	0-0	19.1	18	9	8	2	8-0	17	.243
2004— Las Vegas (PCL)		0	0	...	0.00	0.43	6	0	0	0	...	2-...	11.2	4	0	0	0	1-0	14	.105
— Cleveland (A.L.)		5	5	.500	5.29	1.49	59	0	0	0	2	1-3	78.1	88	52	46	15	29-7	44	.293
American League totals (5 years)		**16**	**22**	**.421**	**4.48**	**1.41**	**238**	**4**	**0**	**0**	**13**	**4-11**	**374.0**	**399**	**209**	**186**	**49**	**129-19**	**248**	**.276**
National League totals (6 years)		**17**	**23**	**.425**	**4.09**	**1.34**	**211**	**14**	**0**	**0**	**32**	**9-16**	**310.1**	**322**	**162**	**141**	**27**	**93-14**	**196**	**.268**
Major League totals (9 years)		**33**	**45**	**.423**	**4.30**	**1.38**	**449**	**18**	**0**	**0**	**45**	**13-27**	**684.1**	**721**	**371**	**327**	**76**	**222-33**	**444**	**.273**

DIVISION SERIES RECORD

Year	Team (League)	W	L	Pct.	ERA	WHIP	G	GS	CG	ShO	Hld.	Sv.-Opp.	IP	H	R	ER	HR	BB-IBB	SO	Avg.
2000— New York (N.L.)		1	0	1.000	0.00	3.00	2	0	0	0	0	0-0	2.2	6	0	0	0	2-0	4	.429
2002— St. Louis (N.L.)		0	0	...	0.00	1.00	2	0	0	0	1	0-1	2.0	1	1	0	0	1-0	1	.125
Division series totals (2 years)		**1**	**0**	**1.000**	**0.00**	**2.14**	**4**	**0**	**0**	**0**	**1**	**0-1**	**4.2**	**7**	**1**	**0**	**0**	**3-0**	**5**	**.318**

CHAMPIONSHIP SERIES RECORD

Year	Team (League)	W	L	Pct.	ERA	WHIP	G	GS	CG	ShO	Hld.	Sv.-Opp.	IP	H	R	ER	HR	BB-IBB	SO	Avg.
2000— New York (N.L.)		0	0	...	9.00	2.00	1	0	0	0	0	0-0	3.0	5	3	3	0	1-0	1	.385
2002— St. Louis (N.L.)		0	1	.000	4.50	1.00	3	0	0	0	1	0-1	4.0	2	2	2	1	2-1	5	.143
Champ. series totals (2 years)		**0**	**1**	**.000**	**6.43**	**1.43**	**4**	**0**	**0**	**0**	**1**	**0-1**	**7.0**	**7**	**5**	**5**	**1**	**3-1**	**6**	**.259**

WORLD SERIES RECORD

Year	Team (League)	W	L	Pct.	ERA	WHIP	G	GS	CG	ShO	Hld.	Sv.-Opp.	IP	H	R	ER	HR	BB-IBB	SO	Avg.
2000— New York (N.L.)		0	0	...	6.75	1.50	1	0	0	0	0	0-0	1.1	1	1	1	0	1-1	1	.250

WHITE, RONDELL — OF

PERSONAL: Born February 23, 1972, in Milledgeville, Ga. ... 6-1/225. ... Bats right, throws right. ... Full name: Rondell Bernard White. ... High school: Jones County (Gray, Ga.).

TRANSACTIONS/CAREER NOTES: Selected by Montreal Expos organization in first round (24th pick overall) of 1990 free-agent draft; pick received as part of compensation for California Angels signing Type A free-agent P Mark Langston. ... On disabled list (April 28-July 16, 1996); included rehabilitation assignments to West Palm Beach, GCL Expos and Harrisburg. ... On disabled list (July 21, 1998-remainder of season; June 14-29 and July 2-17, 1999). ... On disabled list (July 8-August 6 and August 27, 2000-remainder of season). ... Traded by Expos to Chicago Cubs for P Scott Downs (July 31, 2000). ... On disabled list (June 26-July 12 and July 14-September 1, 2001); included rehabilitation assignment to West Tenn. ... Signed as a free agent by New York Yankees (December 21, 2001). ... Traded by Yankees to San Diego Padres for OF Bubba Trammell, P Mark Phillips and cash (March 19, 2003). ... Traded by Padres to Kansas City Royals for Ps Chris Tierney and Brian Sanches (August 26, 2003). ... Signed as a free agent by Detroit Tigers (December 19, 2003).

2004 GAMES PLAYED BY POSITION (MLB): OF—74, DH—43.

							BATTING												FIELDING	
Year	Team (League)	Pos.	G	AB	R	H	2B	3B	HR	RBI	BB	SO	HBP	GDP	SB-CS	Avg.	OBP	SLG	OPS	E	Avg.
1990— GC Expos (GCL)		OF	57	221	33	66	7	4	5	34	17	33	5	4	10-7	.299	.362	.434	.797	2	.973
1991— Sumter (S. Atl.)		OF	123	465	80	122	23	6	13	68	57	109	8	7	50-17	.262	.351	.422	.772	3	.987
1992— W.P. Beach (FSL)		OF	111	450	80	142	10	12	4	41	46	78	5	7	42-16	.316	.384	.418	.802	3	.984
— Harrisburg (East.)		OF	21	89	22	27	7	1	2	7	6	14	4	3	6-1	.303	.374	.472	.846	2	.938

W

Year Team (League)	Pos.	G	AB	R	H	2B	3B	HR	RBI	BB	SO	HBP	GDP	SB-CS	Avg.	OBP	SLG	OPS	E	Avg.
1993— Harrisburg (East.)	OF	90	372	72	122	16	10	12	52	22	72	5	3	21-6	.328	.371	.522	.892	1	.995
— Ottawa (Int'l)	OF	37	150	28	57	8	2	7	32	12	20	3	4	10-1	.380	.436	.600	1.036	1	.988
— Montreal (N.L.)	OF	23	73	9	19	3	1	2	15	7	16	0	2	1-2	.260	.321	.411	.732	0	1.000
1994— Montreal (N.L.)	OF	40	97	16	27	10	1	2	13	9	18	3	1	1-1	.278	.358	.464	.822	2	.946
— Ottawa (Int'l)	OF	42	169	23	46	7	0	7	18	15	17	4	5	9-2	.272	.344	.438	.782	2	.979
1995— Montreal (N.L.)	OF	130	474	87	140	33	4	13	57	41	87	6	11	25-5	.295	.356	.464	.820	4	.986
1996— Montreal (N.L.)	OF	88	334	35	98	19	4	6	41	22	53	2	11	14-6	.293	.340	.428	.768	2	.990
— W.P. Beach (FSL)	DH-OF	3	10	0	2	1	0	0	2	0	4	0	0	0-1	.200	.200	.300	.500	0	1.000
— GC Expos (GCL)	OF	3	12	3	3	0	0	2	4	0	1	0	1	1-0	.250	.250	.750	1.000	0	1.000
— Harrisburg (East.)	OF	5	20	5	7	1	0	3	6	1	1	0	1	1-1	.350	.381	.850	1.231	0	1.000
1997— Montreal (N.L.)	OF	151	592	84	160	29	5	28	82	31	111	10	18	16-8	.270	.316	.478	.794	3	.992
1998— Montreal (N.L.)	OF-DH	97	357	54	107	21	2	17	58	30	57	7	7	16-7	.300	.363	.513	.875	1	.996
1999— Montreal (N.L.)	OF	138	539	83	168	26	6	22	64	32	85	11	17	10-6	.312	.359	.505	.863	11	.964
2000— Montreal (N.L.)	OF	75	290	52	89	24	0	11	54	28	67	2	4	5-1	.307	.370	.503	.873	1	.994
— Chicago (N.L.)	OF	19	67	7	22	2	0	2	7	5	12	2	0	0-2	.328	.392	.448	.840	0	1.000
2001— Chicago (N.L.)	OF	95	323	43	99	19	1	17	50	26	56	7	14	1-0	.307	.371	.529	.900	3	.979
— West Tenn. (Sou.)	OF	9	28	2	4	1	0	2	4	1	7	2	1	0-0	.143	.226	.393	.619	0	1.000
2002— New York (A.L.)	OF-DH	126	455	59	109	21	0	14	62	25	86	8	11	1-2	.240	.288	.378	.666	0	1.000
2003— San Diego (N.L.)	OF-DH	115	413	49	115	17	3	18	66	25	71	8	11	1-4	.278	.330	.465	.795	4	.978
— Kansas City (A.L.)	OF-DH	22	75	13	26	6	1	4	21	6	8	2	2	0-0	.347	.400	.613	1.013	1	.978
2004— Detroit (A.L.)	OF-DH	121	448	76	121	21	2	19	67	39	77	8	13	1-2	.270	.337	.453	.790	3	.977
American League totals (3 years)		269	978	148	256	48	3	37	150	70	171	18	26	2-4	.262	.320	.430	.750	4	.991
National League totals (10 years)		971	3559	519	1044	203	27	138	507	256	633	58	96	90-42	.293	.348	.482	.830	31	.985
Major League totals (12 years)		1240	4537	667	1300	251	30	175	657	326	804	76	122	92-46	.287	.342	.471	.813	35	.986

DIVISION SERIES RECORD

Year Team (League)	Pos.	G	AB	R	H	2B	3B	HR	RBI	BB	SO	HBP	GDP	SB-CS	Avg.	OBP	SLG	OPS	E	Avg.
2002— New York (A.L.)	DH	1	3	1	1	0	0	1	1	0	0	0	0	0-0	.333	.333	1.333	1.667	0	...

ALL-STAR GAME RECORD

	G	AB	R	H	2B	3B	HR	RBI	BB	SO	HBP	GDP	SB-CS	Avg.	OBP	SLG	OPS	E	Avg.
All-Star Game totals (1 year)	1	1	0	0	0	0	0	0	0	0	0	1	0-0	.000	.000	.000	.000	0	...

WICKMAN, BOB   P

PERSONAL: Born February 6, 1969, in Green Bay, Wis. ... 6-1/240. ... Throws right, bats right. ... Full name: Robert Joe Wickman. ... High school: Oconto Falls (Wis.). ... College: Wisconsin-Whitewater.

TRANSACTIONS/CAREER NOTES: Selected by Chicago White Sox organization in second round of 1990 free-agent draft. ... Traded by White Sox with Ps Melido Perez and Domingo Jean to New York Yankees for 2B Steve Sax and cash (January 10, 1992). ... Traded by Yankees with OF Gerald Williams to Milwaukee Brewers for P Graeme Lloyd and OF Pat Listach (August 23, 1996). ... Traded by Brewers with Ps Steve Woodard and Jason Bere to Cleveland Indians for 1B/OF Richie Sexson, Ps Paul Rigdon and Kane Davis and a player to be named (July 28, 2000); Brewers acquired 2B Marco Scutaro to complete deal (August 30, 2000). ... On disabled list (July 22-August 10 and August 11, 2002-remainder of season). ... On disabled list (March 29, 2003-entire season); included rehabilitation assignments to Akron and Lake County. ... Recalled from minor league rehab assignment (September 2, 2003). ... On disabled list (April 2-July 6, 2004); included rehabilitation assignments to Akron and Buffalo.

CAREER HITTING: 0-for-2 (.000), 0 R, 0 2B, 0 3B, 0 HR, 0 RBI.

Year Team (League)	W	L	Pct.	ERA	WHIP	G	GS	CG	ShO	Hld.	Sv.-Opp.	IP	H	R	ER	HR	BB-IBB	SO	Avg.
1990— GC White Sox (GCL)	2	0	1.000	2.45	0.73	2	2	0	0	...	0-...	11.0	7	4	3	0	1-0	15	.175
— Sarasota (Florida State)	0	1	.000	1.98	1.54	2	2	0	0	...	0-...	13.2	17	7	3	0	4-0	8	.304
— South Bend (Mid.)	7	2	.778	1.38	1.01	9	9	3	0	...	0-...	65.1	50	16	10	1	16-0	50	.212
1991— Sarasota (Florida State)	5	1	.833	2.05	1.23	7	7	1	1	...	0-...	44.0	43	16	10	2	11-0	32	.247
— Birmingham (Southern)	6	10	.375	3.56	1.35	20	20	4	1	...	0-...	131.1	127	68	52	5	50-0	81	.250
1992— Columbus (Int'l)	12	5	.706	2.92	1.18	23	23	2	1	...	0-...	157.0	131	61	51	12	55-0	108	.227
— New York (A.L.)	6	1	.857	4.11	1.41	8	8	0	0	0	0-0	50.1	51	25	23	2	20-0	21	.273
1993— New York (A.L.)	14	4	.778	4.63	1.61	41	19	1	1	2	4-8	140.0	156	82	72	13	69-7	70	.284
1994— New York (A.L.)	5	4	.556	3.09	1.16	53	0	0	0	11	6-10	70.0	54	26	24	3	27-3	56	.213
1995— New York (A.L.)	2	4	.333	4.05	1.38	63	1	0	0	21	1-10	80.0	77	38	36	6	33-3	51	.253
1996— New York (A.L.)	4	1	.800	4.67	1.62	58	0	0	0	6	0-3	79.0	94	41	41	7	34-1	61	.299
— Milwaukee (A.L.)	3	0	1.000	3.24	1.32	12	0	0	0	4	0-1	16.2	12	9	6	3	10-2	14	.200
1997— Milwaukee (A.L.)	7	6	.538	2.73	1.36	74	0	0	0	28	1-5	95.2	89	32	29	8	41-7	78	.252
1998— Milwaukee (N.L.)	6	9	.400	3.72	1.43	72	0	0	0	9	25-32	82.1	79	38	34	5	39-2	71	.262
1999— Milwaukee (N.L.)	3	8	.273	3.39	1.52	71	0	0	0	0	37-45	74.1	75	31	28	6	38-6	60	.262
2000— Milwaukee (N.L.)	2	2	.500	2.93	1.24	43	0	0	0	0	16-20	46.0	37	18	15	1	20-2	44	.215
— Cleveland (A.L.)	1	3	.250	3.38	1.46	26	0	0	0	0	14-17	26.2	27	12	10	0	12-3	11	.270
2001— Cleveland (A.L.)	5	0	1.000	2.39	1.11	70	0	0	0	4	32-35	67.2	61	18	18	4	14-2	66	.240
2002— Cleveland (A.L.)	1	3	.250	4.46	1.51	36	0	0	0	0	20-22	34.1	42	22	17	3	10-0	36	.284
2003— Lake County (S.Atl.)	0	0	...	0.50	2	2	0	0	0	...	0-...	2.0	1	0	0	0	0-0	4	.143
— Akron (East.)	0	0	...	16.20	2.40	2	2	0	0	0	0-...	1.2	3	3	3	0	1-0	2	.429
2004— Akron (East.)	0	0	...	0.00	2.00	1	1	0	0	0	0-...	1.0	1	0	0	0	2-0	1	.000
— Buffalo (Int'l)	1	0	1.000	10.13	1.50	6	1	0	0	0	0-...	5.1	4	6	6	0	4-0	4	.211
— Cleveland (A.L.)	0	2	.000	4.25	1.45	30	0	0	0	4	13-14	29.2	33	14	14	4	10-0	26	.282
American League totals (10 years)	48	28	.632	3.78	1.41	471	28	1	1	80	91-125	690.0	696	319	290	53	280-28	490	.264
National League totals (3 years)	11	19	.367	3.42	1.42	186	0	0	0	9	78-97	202.2	191	87	77	12	97-10	175	.252
Major League totals (12 years)	59	47	.557	3.70	1.42	657	28	1	1	89	169-222	892.2	887	406	367	65	377-38	665	.261

DIVISION SERIES RECORD

Year Team (League)	W	L	Pct.	ERA	WHIP	G	GS	CG	ShO	Hld.	Sv.-Opp.	IP	H	R	ER	HR	BB-IBB	SO	Avg.
1995— New York (A.L.)	0	0	...	0.00	1.67	3	0	0	0	0	0-0	3.0	5	0	0	0	0-0	3	.417
2001— Cleveland (A.L.)	0	0	...	0.00	0.00	1	0	0	0	0	0-0	1.0	0	0	0	0	0-0	2	.000
Division series totals (2 years)	0	0	...	0.00	1.25	4	0	0	0	0	0-0	4.0	5	0	0	0	0-0	5	.333

ALL-STAR GAME RECORD

	W	L	Pct.	ERA	WHIP	G	GS	CG	ShO	Hld.	Sv.-Opp.	IP	H	R	ER	HR	BB-IBB	SO	Avg.
All-Star Game totals (1 year)	0	0	...	0.00	0.00	1	0	0	0	0	0-0	1.0	0	0	0	0	0-0	1	.000

W

WIGGINTON, TY — 3B/2B

PERSONAL: Born October 11, 1977, in San Diego, Calif. ... 6-0/200. ... Bats right, throws right. ... Full name: Ty Allen Wigginton. ... College: UNC-Asheville.

TRANSACTIONS/CAREER NOTES: Selected by New York Mets organization in 17th round of 1998 free-agent draft. ... On disabled list (April 21-May 7, 2004); included rehabilitation assignment to St. Lucie. ... Traded by Mets with IF Jose Bautista and P Matt Peterson to Pittsburgh Pirates for P Kris Benson and IF Jeff Keppinger (July 30, 2004).

2004 GAMES PLAYED BY POSITION (MLB): 3B—122, 2B—25, 1B—5.

Year Team (League)	Pos.	G	AB	R	H	2B	3B	HR	RBI	BB	SO	HBP	GDP	SB-CS	Avg.	OBP	SLG	OPS	E	Avg.
1998— Pittsfield (N.Y.-Penn.)	2B-3B-OF	70	272	39	65	14	4	8	29	16	72	1	4	11-2	.239	.284	.408	.692	14	.949
1999— St. Lucie (Fla. St.)	2B	123	456	69	133	23	5	21	73	56	82	4	5	9-12	.292	.373	.502	.875	16	.974
2000— Binghamton (East.)	2B-3B	122	453	64	129	27	3	20	77	24	107	2	4	5-5	.285	.319	.490	.809	23	.943
2001— St. Lucie (Fla. St.)	2B	3	9	1	3	1	0	0	1	4	2	1	0	0-0	.333	.571	.444	1.016	0	1.000
— Binghamton (East.)	2B-3B	8	28	5	8	3	0	0	0	5	5	0	0	1-0	.286	.394	.393	.787	3	.870
— Norfolk (Int'l)	3-2-1-C-O	78	260	29	65	12	0	7	24	27	66	4	2	3-3	.250	.323	.377	.700	17	.924
2002— Norfolk (Int'l)	3-2-OF-1	104	383	49	115	26	3	6	48	43	50	1	7	5-3	.300	.366	.431	.796	11	.967
— New York (N.L.)	3-1-2-OF	46	116	18	35	8	0	6	18	8	19	2	4	2-1	.302	.354	.526	.880	5	.966
2003— New York (N.L.)	3B	156	573	73	146	36	6	11	71	46	124	9	15	12-2	.255	.318	.396	.714	16	.962
2004— St. Lucie (Fla. St.)	3B	2	8	1	3	0	0	0	0	0	1	0	0	0-0	.375	.375	.375	.750	0	1.000
— New York (N.L.)	3B-2B-1B	86	312	46	89	23	2	12	42	23	48	1	11	6-1	.285	.334	.487	.822	16	.949
— Pittsburgh (N.L.)	3B	58	182	17	40	7	0	5	24	22	34	1	4	1-0	.220	.306	.341	.646	6	.955
Major League totals (3 years)		346	1183	154	310	74	8	34	155	99	225	13	34	21-4	.262	.324	.424	.748	43	.958

WILKERSON, BRAD — 1B/OF

PERSONAL: Born June 1, 1977, in Daviess, Ky. ... 6-0/206. ... Bats left, throws left. ... Full name: Stephen Bradley Wilkerson. ... High school: Apollo (Owensboro, Ky.). ... College: Florida.

TRANSACTIONS/CAREER NOTES: Selected by Los Angeles Dodgers organization in 13th round of 1995 free-agent draft; did not sign. ... Selected by Montreal Expos organization in supplemental round ("sandwich pick" between first and second rounds, 33rd pick overall) of 1998 free-agent draft; pick received as part of compensation for Toronto Blue Jays signing Type A free-agent C Darrin Fletcher. Expos franchise transferred to Washington, D.C., for 2005 season.

HONORS: Named Rookie Player of the Year by THE SPORTING NEWS (2002).

2004 GAMES PLAYED BY POSITION (MLB): 1B—86, OF—80.

Year Team (League)	Pos.	G	AB	R	H	2B	3B	HR	RBI	BB	SO	HBP	GDP	SB-CS	Avg.	OBP	SLG	OPS	E	Avg.
1999— Harrisburg (East.)	1B-OF	138	422	66	99	21	3	8	49	88	100	7	3	3-5	.235	.372	.355	.727	7	.972
2000— Harrisburg (East.)	1B-OF	66	229	53	77	36	2	6	44	42	38	4	4	8-4	.336	.442	.590	1.032	3	.983
— Ottawa (Int'l)	OF	63	212	40	53	11	1	12	35	45	60	3	0	5-4	.250	.387	.481	.868	6	.956
2001— Jupiter (FSL)	DH	6	26	3	6	3	0	0	1	3	10	0	0	0-0	.231	.310	.346	.656	...	...
— Ottawa (Int'l)	OF	69	233	43	63	10	0	12	48	60	68	3	2	12-5	.270	.423	.468	.891	3	.973
— Montreal (N.L.)	OF	47	117	11	24	7	2	1	5	17	41	0	2	2-1	.205	.304	.325	.628	2	.970
2002— Montreal (N.L.)	OF-1B	153	507	92	135	27	8	20	59	81	161	5	5	7-8	.266	.370	.469	.840	7	.984
2003— Montreal (N.L.)	OF-1B	146	504	78	135	34	4	19	77	89	155	4	5	13-10	.268	.380	.464	.844	5	.988
2004— Montreal (N.L.)	1B-OF	160	572	112	146	39	2	32	67	106	152	4	6	13-6	.255	.374	.498	.872	7	.993
Major League totals (4 years)		506	1700	293	440	107	16	72	208	293	509	13	18	35-25	.259	.370	.468	.838	21	.989

WILLIAMS, BERNIE — OF

PERSONAL: Born September 13, 1968, in San Juan, Puerto Rico. ... 6-2/205. ... Bats both, throws right. ... Full name: Bernabe Figueroa Williams. ... High school: Escuela Libre de Musica (San Juan, Puerto Rico). ... College: University of Puerto Rico.

TRANSACTIONS/CAREER NOTES: Signed as a non-drafted free agent by New York Yankees organization (September 13, 1985). ... On disabled list (May 13-June 7, 1993; May 11-May 26, 1996; June 16-July 2 and July 15-August 1, 1997). ... On disabled list (June 11-July 18, 1998); included rehabilitation assignments to Tampa and Norwich. ... On disabled list (May 23-July 9, 2003); included rehabilitation assignment to Trenton.

RECORDS: Shares major league record for most strikeouts, nine-inning game—5 (August 21, 1991).

HONORS: Won A.L. Gold Glove as outfielder (1997-2000).

2004 GAMES PLAYED BY POSITION (MLB): OF—97, DH—50.

Year Team (League)	Pos.	G	AB	R	H	2B	3B	HR	RBI	BB	SO	HBP	GDP	SB-CS	Avg.	OBP	SLG	OPS	E	Avg.
1986— GC Yankees (GCL)	OF	61	230	45	62	5	3	2	25	39	40	1	3	33-12	.270	.374	.343	.717	3	.976
1987— Fort Laud. (FSL)	OF	25	71	11	11	3	0	0	4	18	22	3	1	9-1	.155	.348	.197	.545	0	1.000
— Oneonta (N.Y.-Penn.)	OF	25	93	13	32	4	0	0	15	10	14	1	0	9-3	.344	.410	.387	.797	2	.952
1988— Prince Will. (Car.)	OF	92	337	72	113	16	7	7	45	65	65	4	5	29-11	.335	.447	.487	.934	5	.975
1989— Columbus (Int'l)	OF	50	162	21	35	8	1	2	16	25	38	2	3	11-5	.216	.325	.315	.639	1	.991
— Alb./Colon. (East.)	OF	91	314	63	79	11	8	11	42	60	72	6	9	26-13	.252	.381	.443	.823	5	.974
1990— Alb./Colon. (East.)	OF	134	466	91	131	28	5	8	54	98	97	4	12	39-18	.281	.409	.414	.823	4	.987
1991— Columbus (Int'l)	OF	78	306	52	90	14	6	8	37	38	43	2	5	9-7	.294	.372	.458	.830	1	.994
— New York (A.L.)	OF	85	320	43	76	19	4	3	34	48	57	1	4	10-5	.238	.336	.350	.686	5	.979
1992— New York (A.L.)	OF	62	261	39	73	14	2	5	26	29	36	1	5	7-6	.280	.354	.406	.760	1	.995
— Columbus (Int'l)	OF	95	363	68	111	23	9	8	50	52	61	1	8	20-8	.306	.389	.485	.873	2	.990
1993— New York (A.L.)	OF	139	567	67	152	31	4	12	68	53	106	4	17	9-9	.268	.333	.400	.734	4	.989
1994— New York (A.L.)	OF	108	408	80	118	29	1	12	57	61	54	3	11	16-9	.289	.384	.453	.837	3	.990
1995— New York (A.L.)	OF	144	563	93	173	29	9	18	82	75	98	5	12	8-6	.307	.392	.487	.878	•8	.982
1996— New York (A.L.)	OF-DH	143	551	108	168	26	7	29	102	82	72	0	15	17-4	.305	.391	.535	.926	5	.986
1997— New York (A.L.)	OF	129	509	107	167	35	6	21	100	73	80	1	10	15-8	.328	.408	.544	.952	2	.993
1998— New York (A.L.)	OF-DH	128	499	101	169	30	5	26	97	74	81	1	19	15-9	.339	.422	.575	.997	3	.990
— Tampa (Fla. St.)	OF	1	2	0	1	1	0	0	0	1	0	0	0	0-0	.500	.667	1.000	1.667	0	1.000
— Norwich (East.)	OF	3	11	6	6	2	0	2	5	2	1	0	1	0-0	.545	.571	1.273	1.844	0	1.000
1999— New York (A.L.)	OF-DH	158	591	116	202	28	6	25	115	100	95	1	11	9-10	.342	.435	.536	.971	5	.987
2000— New York (A.L.)	OF-DH	141	537	108	165	37	6	30	121	71	84	6	15	13-5	.307	.391	.566	.957	0	1.000
2001— New York (A.L.)	OF-DH	146	540	102	166	38	0	26	94	78	67	6	15	11-5	.307	.395	.522	.917	2	.994
2002— New York (A.L.)	OF-DH	154	612	102	204	37	2	19	102	83	97	3	19	8-4	.333	.415	.493	.908	5	.986
2003— Trenton (East.)	OF-DH	5	15	4	5	2	0	0	4	4	1	1	1	0-1	.333	.476	.467	.943	0	1.000
— New York (A.L.)	OF-DH	119	445	77	117	19	1	15	64	71	61	3	21	5-0	.263	.367	.411	.778	1	.997
2004— New York (A.L.)	OF-DH	148	561	105	147	29	1	22	70	85	96	2	19	1-5	.262	.360	.435	.795	1	.995
Major League totals (14 years)		1804	6964	1248	2097	401	54	263	1132	983	1084	36	193	144-85	.301	.388	.488	.875	45	.990

DIVISION SERIES RECORD

Year Team (League)	Pos.	G	AB	R	H	2B	3B	HR	RBI	BB	SO	HBP	GDP	SB-CS	Avg.	OBP	SLG	OPS	E	Avg.
1995— New York (A.L.)	OF	5	21	8	9	2	0	2	5	7	3	0	0	1-0	.429	.571	.810	1.381	0	1.000
1996— New York (A.L.)	OF	4	15	5	7	0	0	3	5	2	1	0	0	1-1	.467	.500	1.067	1.567	0	1.000
1997— New York (A.L.)	OF	5	17	3	2	1	0	0	1	4	3	1	1	0-0	.118	.318	.176	.495	0	1.000
1998— New York (A.L.)	OF	3	11	0	0	0	0	0	0	1	4	0	2	0-0	.000	.083	.000	.083	0	1.000
1999— New York (A.L.)	OF	3	11	2	4	1	0	1	6	1	2	1	0	0-0	.364	.462	.727	1.189	0	1.000
2000— New York (A.L.)	OF	5	20	3	5	3	0	0	1	1	4	0	0	0-1	.250	.273	.400	.673	0	1.000
2001— New York (A.L.)	OF	5	18	4	4	3	0	0	5	3	3	0	2	0-1	.222	.333	.389	.722	0	1.000
2002— New York (A.L.)	OF	4	15	4	5	1	0	1	3	3	2	0	0	0-0	.333	.444	.600	1.044	0	1.000
2003— New York (A.L.)	OF	4	15	3	6	2	0	0	3	2	2	0	0	0-0	.400	.444	.533	.978	1	.900
2004— New York (A.L.)	OF	4	18	2	5	1	0	1	3	1	2	0	4	0-0	.278	.316	.500	.816	0	1.000
Division series totals (10 years)		42	161	34	47	14	0	8	32	25	26	2	11	2-3	.292	.387	.528	.915	1	.991

CHAMPIONSHIP SERIES RECORD

Year Team (League)	Pos.	G	AB	R	H	2B	3B	HR	RBI	BB	SO	HBP	GDP	SB-CS	Avg.	OBP	SLG	OPS	E	Avg.
1996— New York (A.L.)	OF	5	19	6	9	3	0	2	6	5	4	0	0	1-0	.474	.583	.947	1.531	0	1.000
1998— New York (A.L.)	OF	6	21	4	8	1	0	0	5	7	4	0	1	1-1	.381	.536	.429	.964	0	1.000
1999— New York (A.L.)	OF	5	20	3	5	1	0	1	2	2	5	0	0	1-0	.250	.318	.450	.768	0	1.000
2000— New York (A.L.)		6	23	5	10	1	0	1	3	2	3	1	1	1-0	.435	.481	.609	1.090	0	1.000
2001— New York (A.L.)	OF	5	17	4	4	0	0	3	5	5	4	0	1	0-1	.235	.409	.765	1.174	1	.900
2003— New York (A.L.)	OF	7	26	5	5	1	0	0	2	4	3	0	0	0-0	.192	.300	.231	.531	0	1.000
2004— New York (A.L.)	OF	7	36	4	11	3	0	2	10	0	5	0	0	0-0	.306	.306	.556	.861	0	1.000
Champ. series totals (7 years)		41	162	31	52	10	0	9	33	25	28	1	3	4-2	.321	.413	.549	.962	1	.991

WORLD SERIES RECORD

Year Team (League)	Pos.	G	AB	R	H	2B	3B	HR	RBI	BB	SO	HBP	GDP	SB-CS	Avg.	OBP	SLG	OPS	E	Avg.
1996— New York (A.L.)	OF	6	24	3	4	0	0	1	4	3	6	0	1	1-0	.167	.259	.292	.551	0	1.000
1998— New York (A.L.)	OF	4	16	2	1	0	0	1	3	2	5	0	0	0-0	.063	.167	.250	.417	0	1.000
1999— New York (A.L.)	OF	4	13	2	3	0	0	0	0	4	2	0	1	0-0	.231	.412	.231	.643	0	1.000
2000— New York (A.L.)	OF	5	18	2	2	0	0	1	1	5	5	0	0	0-0	.111	.304	.278	.582	0	1.000
2001— New York (A.L.)	OF	7	24	2	5	1	0	0	1	4	6	0	0	0-0	.208	.321	.250	.571	0	1.000
2003— New York (A.L.)	OF	6	25	5	10	2	0	2	5	2	2	0	1	0-0	.400	.429	.720	1.149	0	1.000
World series totals (6 years)		32	120	16	25	3	0	5	14	20	26	0	3	2-0	.208	.319	.358	.677	0	1.000

ALL-STAR GAME RECORD

	G	AB	R	H	2B	3B	HR	RBI	BB	SO	HBP	GDP	SB-CS	Avg.	OBP	SLG	OPS	E	Avg.
All-Star Game totals (4 years)	4	5	1	0	0	0	0	0	1	1	0		1-0	.000	.167	.000	.167	0	1.000

WILLIAMS, DAVE — P

PERSONAL: Born March 12, 1979, in Anchorage, Alaska. ... 6-2/219. ... Throws left, bats left. ... Full name: David Aaron Williams. ... Junior college: Delaware Tech & Community College.

TRANSACTIONS/CAREER NOTES: Selected by Pittsburgh Pirates organization in 17th round of 1998 free-agent draft. ... On disabled list (May 28, 2002-remainder of season; March 24-June 3, 2003; and August 13-31, 2004).

CAREER HITTING: 7-for-59 (.119), 2 R, 2 2B, 0 3B, 1 HR, 5 RBI.

Year Team (League)	W	L	Pct.	ERA	WHIP	G	GS	CG	ShO	Hld.	Sv.-Opp.	IP	H	R	ER	HR	BB-IBB	SO	Avg.
1998— Erie (N.Y.-Penn)	2	2	.500	3.23	1.25	22	2	0	0	...	0-...	47.1	45	21	17	6	14-0	38	.245
1999— Williamsport (N.Y.-Penn.) .	4	2	.667	2.56	0.96	7	7	1	1	...	0-...	45.2	33	17	13	2	11-0	47	.198
— Hickory (S. Atl.)	3	1	.750	3.20	0.90	9	9	1	1	...	0-...	59.0	42	22	21	5	11-0	46	.201
2000— Hickory (S. Atl.)	11	9	.550	2.96	1.08	24	24	1	1	...	0-...	170.0	145	66	56	14	39-2	193	.232
— Lynchburg (Carolina)	1	0	1.000	6.55	1.91	2	2	0	0	...	0-...	11.0	18	8	8	2	3-0	8	.383
2001— Altoona (East.)	5	2	.714	2.61	0.97	9	8	1	0	...	0-...	58.2	45	17	17	8	12-0	39	.211
— Nashville (PCL)	1	1	.500	3.38	1.31	2	2	0	0	...	0-...	10.2	9	5	4	3	5-0	6	.231
— Pittsburgh (N.L.)	3	7	.300	3.71	1.27	22	18	0	0	1	0-0	114.0	100	53	47	15	45-4	57	.244
2002— Pittsburgh (N.L.)	2	5	.286	4.98	1.43	9	9	0	0	0	0-0	43.1	38	26	24	9	24-2	33	.232
2003— Nashville (PCL)	7	4	.636	4.19	1.40	16	16	0	0	...	0-...	77.1	78	44	36	7	30-2	56	.260
2004— Nashville (PCL)	6	2	.750	3.47	1.25	21	21	0	0	...	0-...	116.2	113	52	45	10	33-2	103	.252
— Pittsburgh (N.L.)	2	3	.400	4.42	1.14	10	6	0	0	0	0-0	38.2	31	21	19	4	13-2	33	.217
Major League totals (3 years)	7	15	.318	4.13	1.28	41	33	0	0	1	0-0	196.0	169	100	90	28	82-8	123	.236

WILLIAMS, GERALD — OF

PERSONAL: Born August 10, 1966, in New Orleans, La. ... 6-2/187. ... Bats right, throws right. ... Full name: Gerald Floyd Williams. ... High school: East St. John (Reserve, La.). ... College: Grambling State.

TRANSACTIONS/CAREER NOTES: Selected by New York Yankees organization in 14th round of 1987 free-agent draft. ... Traded by Yankees with P Bob Wickman to Milwaukee Brewers for P Graeme Lloyd and OF Pat Listach (August 23, 1996). ... Traded by Brewers to Atlanta Braves for P Chad Fox (December 11, 1997). ... Signed as a free agent by Tampa Bay Devil Rays (December 19, 1999). ... On suspended list (September 22-25, 2000). ... Released by Devil Rays (June 24, 2001). ... Signed by Yankees (June 28, 2001). ... Released by Yankees (June 5, 2002). ... Signed by St. Louis Cardinals organization (June 6, 2002). ... Released by Cardinals (July 8, 2002). ... Signed by Cincinnati Reds organization (July 11, 2002). ... Signed as a free agent by Florida Marlins organization (January 18, 2003). ... Released by Marlins (April 2, 2004). ... Signed by New York Mets organization (April 23, 2004) ... Refused minor league assignment and became a free agent (October 13, 2004).

2004 GAMES PLAYED BY POSITION (MLB): OF—45.

Year Team (League)	Pos.	G	AB	R	H	2B	3B	HR	RBI	BB	SO	HBP	GDP	SB-CS	Avg.	OBP	SLG	OPS	E	Avg.
1987— Oneonta (N.Y.-Penn.)	OF	29	115	26	42	6	2	2	29	16	18	1	3	6-2	.365	.447	.504	.951	3	.959
1988— Prince Will. (Car.)	OF	54	159	20	29	3	0	2	18	15	47	0	4	6-1	.182	.251	.239	.490	3	.961
— Fort Laud. (FSL)	OF	63	212	21	40	7	2	2	17	16	56	3	4	4-3	.189	.255	.269	.524	6	.965
1989— Prince Will. (Car.)	OF	134	454	63	104	19	6	13	69	51	120	7	7	15-10	.229	.316	.383	.699	8	.974
1990— Fort Laud. (FSL)	OF	50	204	25	59	4	5	7	43	16	52	2	1	19-5	.289	.344	.461	.805	3	.975
— Alb./Colon. (East.)	OF	96	324	54	81	17	2	13	58	35	74	2	7	18-8	.250	.324	.435	.759	7	.969
1991— Alb./Colon. (East.)	OF	45	175	28	50	15	0	5	32	18	26	0	5	18-3	.286	.347	.457	.804	3	.974
— Columbus (Int'l)	OF	61	198	20	51	8	3	2	27	16	39	1	3	9-12	.258	.309	.359	.668	3	.977
1992— Columbus (Int'l)	OF	142	547	92	156	31	6	16	86	38	98	5	12	36-14	.285	.334	.452	.786	8	.977
— New York (A.L.)	OF	15	27	7	8	2	0	3	6	0	3	0	0	2-0	.296	.296	.704	1.000	2	.913
1993— Columbus (Int'l)	OF	87	336	53	95	19	6	8	38	20	66	2	7	29-12	.283	.321	.446	.768	3	.985
— New York (A.L.)	OF-DH	42	67	11	10	2	3	0	6	1	14	2	2	2-0	.149	.183	.269	.452	2	.956

Year	Team (League)	Pos.	G	AB	R	H	2B	3B	HR	RBI	BB	SO	HBP	GDP	SB-CS	Avg.	OBP	SLG	OPS	E	Avg.
1994— New York (A.L.)	OF-DH	57	86	19	25	8	0	4	13	4	17	0	6	1-3	.291	.319	.523	.842	2	.957
1995— New York (A.L.)	OF-DH	100	182	33	45	18	2	6	28	22	34	1	4	4-2	.247	.327	.467	.794	1	.993
1996— New York (A.L.)	OF-DH	99	233	37	63	15	4	5	30	15	39	4	7	7-8	.270	.319	.433	.753	3	.978
— Milwaukee (A.L.)	OF	26	92	6	19	4	0	0	4	4	18	1	1	3-1	.207	.247	.250	.497	1	.987
1997— Milwaukee (A.L.)	OF-DH	155	566	73	143	32	2	10	41	19	90	6	9	23-9	.253	.282	.369	.651	3	.992
1998— Atlanta (N.L.)	OF	129	266	46	81	19	2	10	44	17	48	3	5	11-5	.305	.352	.504	.856	5	.970
1999— Atlanta (N.L.)	OF	143	422	76	116	24	1	17	68	33	67	6	8	19-11	.275	.335	.457	.792	3	.985
2000— Tampa Bay (A.L.)	OF-DH	146	632	87	173	30	2	21	89	34	103	3	5	12-12	.274	.312	.427	.739	6	.983
2001— Tampa Bay (A.L.)	OF	62	232	30	48	17	0	4	17	13	42	4	8	10-4	.207	.261	.332	.593	2	.989
— New York (A.L.)	OF-DH	38	47	12	8	1	0	0	2	5	13	1	1	3-1	.170	.264	.191	.456	1	.967
2002— New York (A.L.)	OF-DH	33	17	6	0	0	0	0	0	2	4	0	1	2-0	.000	.105	.000	.105	0	1.000
— Memphis (PCL)	OF	21	73	11	11	3	0	1	3	3	8	1	2	2-0	.151	.195	.233	.428	0	1.000
— Louisville (Int'l)	OF	48	205	29	54	10	3	2	12	11	36	2	4	6-4	.263	.307	.371	.678	1	.992
2003— Albuquerque (PCL)	OF	85	327	59	99	22	5	14	50	24	45	4	2	15-11	.303	.356	.529	.885	6	.972
— Florida (N.L.)	OF	27	31	5	4	1	0	0	3	2	5	0	0	3-0	.129	.182	.161	.343	1	.941
2004— Norfolk (Int'l)	OF-DH	63	246	37	75	10	3	7	28	9	35	3	4	6-9	.305	.335	.455	.790	1	.993
— New York (N.L.)	OF	57	129	17	30	8	2	4	11	8	26	0	2	2-1	.233	.277	.419	.696	1	.982
American League totals (9 years)		773	2181	321	542	129	13	53	236	119	377	22	44	69-40	.249	.292	.392	.684	23	.984
National League totals (4 years)		356	848	144	231	52	5	31	126	60	146	9	15	35-17	.272	.326	.455	.781	10	.977
Major League totals (13 years)		1129	3029	465	773	181	18	84	362	179	523	31	59	104-57	.255	.301	.410	.711	33	.982

DIVISION SERIES RECORD

Year	Team (League)	Pos.	G	AB	R	H	2B	3B	HR	RBI	BB	SO	HBP	GDP	SB-CS	Avg.	OBP	SLG	OPS	E	Avg.
1995— New York (A.L.)	OF	5	5	1	0	0	0	0	0	2	3	0	0	0-0	.000	.286	.000	.286	0	1.000
1998— Atlanta (N.L.)	OF	2	2	1	1	0	0	0	1	0	1	0	0	0-0	.500	.500	.500	1.000	0	1.000
1999— Atlanta (N.L.)	OF	4	18	2	7	1	0	0	3	0	3	0	0	1-0	.389	.389	.444	.833	0	1.000
Division series totals (3 years)		11	25	4	8	1	0	0	4	2	7	0	0	1-0	.320	.370	.360	.730	0	1.000

CHAMPIONSHIP SERIES RECORD

Year	Team (League)	Pos.	G	AB	R	H	2B	3B	HR	RBI	BB	SO	HBP	GDP	SB-CS	Avg.	OBP	SLG	OPS	E	Avg.
1998— Atlanta (N.L.)	OF	5	13	0	2	0	0	0	0	1	6	0	1	1-0	.154	.154	.154	.368	0	1.000
1999— Atlanta (N.L.)	OF	6	28	4	5	2	0	0	1	2	2	1	2	3-1	.179	.258	.250	.508	1	.923
Champ. series totals (2 years)		11	41	4	7	2	0	0	1	3	8	1	2	4-1	.171	.244	.220	.464	1	.938

WORLD SERIES RECORD

Year	Team (League)	Pos.	G	AB	R	H	2B	3B	HR	RBI	BB	SO	HBP	GDP	SB-CS	Avg.	OBP	SLG	OPS	E	Avg.
1999— Atlanta (N.L.)	OF	4	17	2	3	0	1	0	0	4	0	0	1	0-0	.176	.176	.294	.471	0	1.000

WILLIAMS, JEROME   P

PERSONAL: Born December 4, 1981, in Honolulu, Hawaii. ... 6-3/246. ... Throws right, bats right. ... Full name: Jerome Lee Williams. ... High school: Waipahu (Hawaii).

TRANSACTIONS/CAREER NOTES: Selected by San Francisco Giants organization in supplemental round ("sandwich" pick between first and second rounds, 39th pick overall) of 1999 free-agent draft; pick received as compensation for Seattle Mariners signing free-agent P Jose Mesa. ... On disabled list (July 31-September 16, 2004).

CAREER HITTING: 9-for-73 (.123), 2 R, 1 2B, 0 3B, 0 HR, 1 RBI.

Year	Team (League)	W	L	Pct.	ERA	WHIP	G	GS	CG	ShO	Hld.	Sv.-Opp.	IP	H	R	ER	HR	BB-IBB	SO	Avg.
1999— Salem-Keizer (N'west)	1	1	.500	2.19	1.08	7	7	1	1	...	0-...	37.0	29	13	9	1	11-0	34	.213
2000— San Jose (California)	7	6	.538	2.94	1.09	23	19	0	0	...	0-...	125.2	89	53	41	6	48-3	115	.201
2001— Shreveport (Texas)	9	7	.563	3.95	1.15	23	23	2	1	...	0-...	130.0	116	69	57	14	34-0	84	.235
2002— Fresno (PCL)	6	11	.353	3.59	1.18	28	28	0	0	...	0-...	160.2	140	76	64	16	50-1	130	.234
2003— Fresno (PCL)	4	2	.667	2.68	1.19	10	10	1	0	...	0-...	57.0	52	19	17	3	16-0	40	.237
— San Francisco (N.L.)	7	5	.583	3.30	1.26	21	21	2	1	0	0-0	131.0	116	54	48	10	49-3	88	.242
2004— San Francisco (N.L.)	10	7	.588	4.24	1.29	22	22	0	0	0	0-0	129.1	123	69	61	14	44-1	80	.254
Major League totals (2 years)	17	12	.586	3.77	1.28	43	43	2	1	0	0-0	260.1	239	123	109	24	93-4	168	.248

DIVISION SERIES RECORD

Year	Team (League)	W	L	Pct.	ERA	WHIP	G	GS	CG	ShO	Hld.	Sv.-Opp.	IP	H	R	ER	HR	BB-IBB	SO	Avg.
2003— San Francisco (N.L.)	0	0	...	13.50	3.00	1	1	0	0	0	0-0	2.0	5	3	3	0	1-0	1	.455

WILLIAMS, RANDY   P

PERSONAL: Born September 18, 1975, in Harlingen, Texas. ... 6-3/195. ... Throws left, bats left. ... Full name: Randall Duane Williams. ... High school: Buna (Texas). ... College: Lamar.

TRANSACTIONS/CAREER NOTES: Selected by Chicago Cubs organization in 12th round of 1997 free-agent draft. ... Released by Cubs (March 24, 2001). ... Signed as a free agent by Seattle Mariners organization (September 30, 2002).

CAREER HITTING: 0-for-0 (.000), 0 R, 0 2B, 0 3B, 0 HR, 0 RBI.

Year	Team (League)	W	L	Pct.	ERA	WHIP	G	GS	CG	ShO	Hld.	Sv.-Opp.	IP	H	R	ER	HR	BB-IBB	SO	Avg.
1998— Ariz. Cubs (Ariz.)	1	0	1.000	0.00	0.67	2	1	0	0	...	0-...	3.0	0	0	0	0	2-0	6	.000
1999— Daytona (Fla. St.)	3	4	.429	4.75	1.60	14	9	0	0	...	1-...	53.0	55	36	28	5	30-0	47	.266
2003— San Antonio (Texas)	4	1	.800	1.73	0.96	29	0	0	0	...	2-...	41.2	33	9	8	2	7-0	38	.213
— Tacoma (PCL)	2	2	.500	5.26	1.40	18	0	0	0	...	1-...	25.2	25	17	15	3	11-0	19	.253
2004— Tacoma (PCL)	7	2	.778	3.63	1.44	50	0	0	0	...	8-...	79.1	68	37	32	6	46-0	64	.230
— Seattle (A.L.)	0	0	...	5.79	1.93	6	0	0	0	1	0-0	4.2	3	3	3	0	6-0	4	.188
Major League totals (1 year)	0	0	...	5.79	1.93	6	0	0	0	1	0-0	4.2	3	3	3	0	6-0	4	.188

WILLIAMS, TODD   P

PERSONAL: Born February 13, 1971, in Syracuse, N.Y. ... 6-3/210. ... Throws right, bats right. ... Full name: Todd Michael Williams. ... High school: Minoa (East Syracuse, N.Y.). ... Junior college: Onondaga (N.Y.) Community College.

TRANSACTIONS/CAREER NOTES: Selected by Los Angeles Dodgers organization in 54th round of 1990 free-agent draft. ... Traded by Dodgers to Oakland Athletics for P Matt McDonald (September 8, 1995). ... Released by A's (January 16, 1997). ... Signed by Cincinnati Reds organization (February 3, 1997). ... Traded by Reds to Seattle Mariners for OF Kerry Robinson (July 22, 1999). ... Released by Mariners (November 16, 2000). ... Signed by New York Yankees organization (January 3, 2001). ... On disabled list (May 27-July 18, 2001); included rehabilitation assignment to GCL Yankees. ... Signed as a free agent by Dodgers organization (December 27, 2001). ... Released by Dodgers (March 26, 2002). ... Signed by Montreal Expos organization (May 3, 2002). ... Signed as a free agent by Tampa Bay Devil Rays organization (December 23, 2002). ... Signed as a free agent by Texas Rangers organization (December 4, 2003). ... Released by Rangers (June 14, 2004). ... Signed as a free agent by Baltimore Orioles organization (June 15, 2004).

W

CAREER HITTING: 1-for-4 (.250), 0 R, 0 2B, 0 3B, 0 HR, 0 RBI.

Year	Team (League)	W	L	Pct.	ERA	WHIP	G	GS	CG	ShO	Hld.	Sv.-Opp.	IP	H	R	ER	HR	BB-IBB	SO	Avg.
1991—	Great Falls (Pio.)	5	2	.714	2.72	1.40	28	0	0	0	...	8-...	53.0	50	26	16	1	24-1	59	.242
1992—	Bakersfield (California)	0	0	...	2.30	1.15	13	0	0	0	...	9-...	15.2	11	4	4	1	7-1	11	.196
	— San Antonio (Texas)	7	4	.636	3.27	1.59	39	0	0	0	...	13-...	44.0	47	17	16	0	23-6	35	.281
1993—	Albuquerque (PCL)	5	5	.500	4.99	1.68	65	0	0	0	...	21-...	70.1	87	44	39	2	31-6	56	.302
1994—	Albuquerque (PCL)	4	2	.667	3.11	1.31	59	0	0	0	...	13-...	72.1	78	29	25	5	17-3	30	.287
1995—	Los Angeles (N.L.)	2	2	.500	5.12	1.34	16	0	0	0	0	0-1	19.1	19	11	11	3	7-2	8	.264
	— Albuquerque (PCL)	4	1	.800	3.38	1.63	25	0	0	0	...	0-...	45.1	59	21	17	4	15-4	23	.319
1996—	Edmonton (PCL)	5	3	.625	5.50	1.77	35	10	0	0	...	0-...	91.2	125	71	56	4	37-3	33	.329
1997—	Chattanooga (Southern)	3	3	.500	2.10	1.13	48	0	0	0	...	31-...	55.2	38	16	13	1	25-2	45	.186
	— Indianapolis (A.A.)	2	0	1.000	2.13	1.34	12	0	0	0	...	2-...	12.2	11	4	3	0	6-1	11	.239
1998—	Indianapolis (Int'l)	0	3	.000	2.31	1.34	53	0	0	0	...	26-...	58.1	54	19	15	0	24-2	35	.255
	— Cincinnati (N.L.)	0	1	.000	7.71	2.25	6	0	0	0	...	0-0	9.1	15	8	8	1	6-0	4	.341
1999—	Indianapolis (Int'l)	1	3	.250	5.10	1.20	38	0	0	0	...	24-...	42.1	38	24	24	3	13-0	35	.250
	— Tacoma (PCL)	0	0	...	0.00	0.60	1	0	0	0	...	1-...	1.2	1	0	0	0	0-0	0	.200
	— Seattle (A.L.)	0	0	...	4.66	1.86	13	0	0	0	...	0-0	9.2	11	5	5	1	7-0	7	.289
2000—	Tacoma (PCL)	2	3	.400	2.98	1.34	50	0	0	0	...	32-...	51.1	51	20	17	2	18-1	26	.268
2001—	New York (A.L.)	1	0	1.000	4.70	2.02	15	0	0	0	1	0-0	15.1	22	9	8	1	9-2	13	.324
	— GC Yankees (GCL)	0	0	...	0.00	0.50	1	1	0	0	...	0-...	2.0	1	0	0	0	0-0	5	.143
	— Columbus (Int'l)	0	1	.000	7.11	2.11	17	0	0	0	...	2-...	19.0	31	19	15	5	9-3	14	.352
	— Norwich (East.)	1	0	1.000	0.00	0.50	6	0	0	0	...	1-...	8.0	4	0	0	0	0-0	5	.148
2002—	Ottawa (Int'l)	3	5	.375	3.75	1.42	46	0	0	0	...	24-...	48.0	56	26	20	4	12-3	21	.298
2003—	Durham (Int'l)	3	2	.600	1.55	1.00	56	0	0	0	...	4-...	69.2	55	12	12	2	14-2	36	.215
2004—	Oklahoma (PCL)	2	2	.500	3.03	1.48	27	0	0	0	...	9-...	29.2	37	15	10	2	7-2	11	.308
	— Ottawa (Int'l)	1	1	.500	3.05	1.06	14	0	0	0	...	2-...	20.2	19	7	7	0	3-1	11	.250
	— Baltimore (A.L.)	2	0	1.000	2.87	1.12	29	0	0	0	3	0-0	31.1	26	10	10	2	9-0	13	.232
American League totals (3 years)		**3**	**0**	**1.000**	**3.67**	**1.49**	**57**	**0**	**0**	**0**	**4**	**0-0**	**56.1**	**59**	**24**	**23**	**4**	**25-2**	**33**	**.271**
National League totals (2 years)		**2**	**3**	**.400**	**5.97**	**1.64**	**22**	**0**	**0**	**0**	**0**	**0-1**	**28.2**	**34**	**19**	**19**	**4**	**13-2**	**12**	**.293**
Major League totals (5 years)		**5**	**3**	**.625**	**4.45**	**1.54**	**79**	**0**	**0**	**0**	**4**	**0-1**	**85.0**	**93**	**43**	**42**	**8**	**38-4**	**45**	**.278**

WILLIAMS, WOODY   P

PERSONAL: Born August 19, 1966, in Houston, Texas. ... 6-0/200. ... Throws right, bats right. ... Full name: Gregory Scott Williams. ... High school: Cypress-Fairbanks (Houston). ... College: Houston.

TRANSACTIONS/CAREER NOTES: Selected by Toronto Blue Jays organization in 28th round of 1988 free-agent draft. ... On disabled list (July 17, 1995-remainder of season); included rehabilitation assignment to Syracuse. ... On disabled list (March 22-May 31 and June 11-July 26, 1996); included rehabilitation assignments to Dunedin, Syracuse and St. Catharines. ... Traded by Blue Jays with P Carlos Almanzar and OF Peter Tucci to San Diego Padres for P Joey Hamilton (December 13, 1998). ... On disabled list (May 2-July 2, 2000); included rehabilitation assignments to Rancho Cucamonga and Las Vegas. ... Traded by Padres to St. Louis Cardinals for OF Ray Lankford and cash (August 2, 2001). ... On disabled list (April 6-May 15 and July 7-August 29, 2002); included rehabilitation assignment to Memphis.

CAREER HITTING: 81-for-381 (.213), 43 R, 24 2B, 1 3B, 3 HR, 34 RBI.

Year	Team (League)	W	L	Pct.	ERA	WHIP	G	GS	CG	ShO	Hld.	Sv.-Opp.	IP	H	R	ER	HR	BB-IBB	SO	Avg.
1988—	St. Catharines (NY-Penn.)	8	2	.800	1.54	0.91	12	12	2	0	...	0-...	76.0	48	22	13	1	21-0	58	.178
	— Knoxville (Southern)	2	2	.500	3.81	1.38	6	4	0	0	...	0-...	28.1	27	13	12	1	12-0	25	.250
1989—	Dunedin (Fla. St.)	3	5	.375	2.32	1.11	20	9	0	0	...	3-...	81.1	63	26	21	3	27-1	60	.217
	— Knoxville (Southern)	3	5	.375	3.55	1.32	14	12	2	2	...	1-...	71.0	61	32	28	6	33-2	51	.235
1990—	Knoxville (Southern)	7	9	.438	3.14	1.19	42	12	0	0	...	5-...	126.0	111	55	44	7	39-3	74	.236
	— Syracuse (Int'l)	0	1	.000	10.00	2.11	3	0	0	0	...	0-...	9.0	15	10	10	1	4-0	8	.375
1991—	Knoxville (Southern)	3	2	.600	3.59	1.31	18	1	0	0	...	3-...	42.2	42	18	17	1	14-0	37	.261
	— Syracuse (Int'l)	3	4	.429	4.12	1.45	31	0	0	0	...	6-...	54.2	52	27	25	2	27-3	37	.250
1992—	Syracuse (Int'l)	6	8	.429	3.13	1.29	25	16	1	0	...	1-...	120.2	115	46	42	4	41-0	81	.253
1993—	Syracuse (Int'l)	1	1	.500	2.20	1.22	12	0	0	0	...	3-...	16.1	15	5	4	2	5-3	16	.246
	— Toronto (A.L.)	3	1	.750	4.38	1.68	30	0	0	0	4	0-2	37.0	40	18	18	2	22-3	24	.274
	— Dunedin (Fla. St.)	0	0	...	0.00	0.50	2	0	0	0	...	0-...	4.0	0	0	0	0	2-0	2	.000
1994—	Toronto (A.L.)	1	3	.250	3.64	1.30	38	0	0	0	5	0-0	59.1	44	24	24	5	33-1	56	.205
	— Syracuse (Int'l)	0	0	...	0.00	0.00	1	0	0	0	...	1-...	1.2	0	0	0	0	0-0	1	.000
1995—	Toronto (A.L.)	1	2	.333	3.69	1.34	23	3	0	0	1	0-1	53.2	44	23	22	6	28-1	41	.220
	— Syracuse (Int'l)	0	0	...	3.52	1.30	5	1	0	0	...	1-...	7.2	5	3	3	0	5-0	13	.172
1996—	Dunedin (Fla. St.)	0	2	.000	8.22	1.43	2	2	0	0	...	0-...	7.2	9	7	7	1	2-0	11	.281
	— Syracuse (Int'l)	3	1	.750	1.41	0.91	7	7	1	1	...	0-...	32.0	22	5	5	3	7-0	33	.191
	— Toronto (A.L.)	4	5	.444	4.73	1.44	12	10	1	0	0	0-0	59.0	64	33	31	8	21-1	43	.278
	— St. Catharines (NY-Penn.)	0	0	...	3.68	1.50	2	2	0	0	...	0-...	7.1	7	3	3	0	4-0	12	.269
1997—	Toronto (A.L.)	9	14	.391	4.35	1.37	31	31	0	0	0	0-0	194.2	201	98	94	31	66-3	124	.269
1998—	Toronto (A.L.)	10	9	.526	4.46	1.32	32	32	1	1	0	0-0	209.2	196	112	104	36	81-3	151	.245
1999—	San Diego (N.L.)	12	12	.500	4.41	1.37	33	33	0	0	0	0-0	208.1	213	106	102	33	73-5	137	.268
2000—	San Diego (N.L.)	10	8	.556	3.75	1.23	23	23	4	0	0	0-0	168.0	152	74	70	23	54-2	111	.239
	— Rancho Cuca. (Calif.)	0	0	...	0.00	0.60	1	1	0	0	...	0-...	5.0	3	0	0	0	0-0	10	.167
	— Las Vegas (PCL)	0	0	...	1.50	1.17	1	1	0	0	...	0-...	6.0	7	2	1	0	0-0	5	.292
2001—	San Diego (N.L.)	8	8	.500	4.97	1.43	23	23	0	0	0	0-0	145.0	170	88	80	28	37-4	102	.296
	— St. Louis (N.L.)	7	1	.875	2.28	0.97	11	11	3	1	0	0-0	75.0	54	22	19	7	19-1	52	.205
2002—	St. Louis (N.L.)	9	4	.692	2.53	1.05	17	17	1	0	0	0-0	103.1	84	30	29	10	25-2	76	.222
	— Memphis (PCL)	1	0	1.000	1.80	0.40	1	1	0	0	...	0-...	5.0	1	1	1	0	1-0	7	.067
2003—	St. Louis (N.L.)	18	9	.667	3.87	1.25	34	33	0	0	0	0-1	220.2	220	101	95	20	55-2	153	.256
2004—	St. Louis (N.L.)	11	8	.579	4.18	1.32	31	31	0	0	0	0-0	189.2	193	93	88	20	58-3	131	.262
American League totals (6 years)		**28**	**34**	**.452**	**4.30**	**1.37**	**166**	**76**	**2**	**1**	**10**	**0-3**	**613.1**	**589**	**308**	**293**	**88**	**251-12**	**439**	**.262**
National League totals (6 years)		**75**	**50**	**.600**	**3.92**	**1.27**	**172**	**171**	**8**	**1**	**0**	**0-1**	**1110.0**	**1086**	**514**	**483**	**141**	**321-19**	**762**	**.256**
Major League totals (12 years)		**103**	**84**	**.551**	**4.05**	**1.30**	**338**	**247**	**10**	**2**	**10**	**0-4**	**1723.1**	**1675**	**822**	**776**	**229**	**572-31**	**1201**	**.254**

DIVISION SERIES RECORD

Year	Team (League)	W	L	Pct.	ERA	WHIP	G	GS	CG	ShO	Hld.	Sv.-Opp.	IP	H	R	ER	HR	BB-IBB	SO	Avg.
2001—	St. Louis (N.L.)	1	0	1.000	1.29	0.71	1	1	0	0	0	0-0	7.0	4	1	1	0	1-0	9	.160
2004—	St. Louis (N.L.)	1	0	1.000	3.00	1.50	1	1	0	0	0	0-0	6.0	8	2	2	0	1-0	2	.320
Division series totals (2 years)		**2**	**0**	**1.000**	**2.08**	**1.08**	**2**	**2**	**0**	**0**	**0**	**0-0**	**13.0**	**12**	**3**	**3**	**0**	**2-0**	**11**	**.240**

CHAMPIONSHIP SERIES RECORD

Year Team (League)	W	L	Pct.	ERA	WHIP	G	GS	CG	ShO	Hld.	Sv.-Opp.	IP	H	R	ER	HR	BB-IBB	SO	Avg.
2002— St. Louis (N.L.)	0	1	.000	4.50	1.17	1	1	0	0	0	0-0	6.0	6	3	3	2	1-0	7	.261
2004— St. Louis (N.L.)	1	0	1.000	2.77	0.62	2	2	0	0	0	0-0	13.0	5	4	4	2	3-0	9	.114
Champ. series totals (2 years)	1	1	.500	3.32	0.79	3	3	0	0	0	0-0	19.0	11	7	7	4	4-0	16	.164

WORLD SERIES RECORD

Year Team (League)	W	L	Pct.	ERA	WHIP	G	GS	CG	ShO	Hld.	Sv.-Opp.	IP	H	R	ER	HR	BB-IBB	SO	Avg.
2004— St. Louis (N.L.)	0	0	...	27.00	4.71	1	0	0	0	0	0-0	2.1	8	7	7	1	3-0	1	.533

ALL-STAR GAME RECORD

Year Team (League)	W	L	Pct.	ERA	WHIP	G	GS	CG	ShO	Hld.	Sv.-Opp.	IP	H	R	ER	HR	BB-IBB	SO	Avg.
All-Star Game totals (1 year)	0	0	...	18.00	2.00	1	0	0	0	0	0-0	1.0	2	2	2	1	0-0	1	.400

WILLIAMSON, SCOTT   P

PERSONAL: Born February 17, 1976, in Fort Polk, La. ... 6-0/180. ... Throws right, bats right. ... Full name: Scott Ryan Williamson. ... High school: Friendswood (Texas). ... College: Oklahoma State.

TRANSACTIONS/CAREER NOTES: Selected by Cincinnati Reds organization in ninth round of 1997 free-agent draft. ... On disabled list (August 24-September 8, 2000; and April 4, 2001-remainder of season). ... Traded by Reds to Boston Red Sox for P Phil Dumatrait, a player to be named and cash (July 30, 2003). ... On disabled list (May 19-June 11 and July 1-September 9, 2004); included rehabilitation assignment to Pawtucket.

HONORS: Named N.L. Rookie Pitcher of the Year by THE SPORTING NEWS (1999). ... Named N.L. Rookie of the Year by Baseball Writers' Association of America (1999).

CAREER HITTING: 1-for-23 (.043), 1 R, 0 2B, 0 3B, 0 HR, 0 RBI.

Year Team (League)	W	L	Pct.	ERA	WHIP	G	GS	CG	ShO	Hld.	Sv.-Opp.	IP	H	R	ER	HR	BB-IBB	SO	Avg.
1997— Billings (Pio.)	8	2	.800	1.78	1.03	13	13	2	1	...	0-...	86.0	66	25	17	5	23-0	101	.209
1998— Chattanooga (Southern)	4	5	.444	3.78	1.31	18	18	0	0	...	0-...	100.0	85	49	42	4	46-4	105	.234
— Indianapolis (Int'l)	0	0	...	3.48	1.40	5	5	0	0	...	0-...	20.2	20	9	8	2	9-0	17	.260
1999— Cincinnati (N.L.)	12	7	.632	2.41	1.04	62	0	0	0	5	19-26	93.1	54	29	25	8	43-6	107	.171
2000— Cincinnati (N.L.)	5	8	.385	3.29	1.49	48	10	0	0	6	6-8	112.0	92	45	41	7	75-7	136	.224
2001— Cincinnati (N.L.)	0	0	...	0.00	4.50	2	0	0	0	1	0-0	.2	1	0	0	0	2-0	0	.333
2002— Cincinnati (N.L.)	3	4	.429	2.92	1.11	63	0	0	0	8	8-12	74.0	46	27	24	5	36-5	84	.181
2003— Cincinnati (N.L.)	5	3	.625	3.19	1.39	42	0	0	0	0	21-26	42.1	34	15	15	6	25-4	53	.214
— Boston (A.L.)	0	1	.000	6.20	1.43	24	0	0	0	5	0-2	20.1	20	15	14	1	9-2	21	.253
2004— Pawtucket (Int'l)	1	0	1.000	12.27	2.45	4	1	0	0	...	0-...	3.2	3	5	5	0	6-0	6	.231
— Boston (A.L.)	0	1	.000	1.26	1.01	28	0	0	0	3	1-2	28.2	11	6	4	0	18-1	28	.115
American League totals (2 years)	0	2	.000	3.31	1.18	52	0	0	0	8	1-4	49.0	31	21	18	1	27-3	49	.177
National League totals (5 years)	25	22	.532	2.93	1.27	217	10	0	0	20	54-72	322.1	227	116	105	26	181-22	380	.199
Major League totals (6 years)	25	24	.510	2.98	1.25	269	10	0	0	28	55-76	371.1	258	137	123	27	208-25	429	.196

DIVISION SERIES RECORD

Year Team (League)	W	L	Pct.	ERA	WHIP	G	GS	CG	ShO	Hld.	Sv.-Opp.	IP	H	R	ER	HR	BB-IBB	SO	Avg.
2003— Boston (A.L.)	2	0	1.000	0.00	1.00	5	0	0	0	0	0-0	5.0	2	0	0	0	3-0	8	.125

CHAMPIONSHIP SERIES RECORD

Year Team (League)	W	L	Pct.	ERA	WHIP	G	GS	CG	ShO	Hld.	Sv.-Opp.	IP	H	R	ER	HR	BB-IBB	SO	Avg.
2003— Boston (A.L.)	0	0	...	3.00	0.33	3	0	0	0	0	3-3	3.0	1	1	1	0	0-0	6	.100

WILLINGHAM, JOSH   C/OF

PERSONAL: Born February 17, 1979, in Florence, Ala. ... 6-1/200. ... Bats right, throws right. ... Full name: Joshua David Willingham. ... High school: Mars Hill Bible (Florence, Ala.). ... College: Northern Alabama.

TRANSACTIONS/CAREER NOTES: Selected by Florida Marlins organization in third round of 2000 free-agent draft.

2004 GAMES PLAYED BY POSITION (MLB): C—5, OF—3.

Year Team (League)	Pos.	G	AB	R	H	2B	3B	HR	RBI	BB	SO	HBP	GDP	SB-CS	Avg.	OBP	SLG	OPS	E	Avg.
2000— Utica (N.Y.-Penn)	O-2-3-S-1	65	205	37	54	16	0	6	29	39	55	9	2	9-5	.263	.400	.429	.829	2	.982
2001— Kane Co. (Midw.)	3B-OF-2B	97	320	57	83	20	2	7	36	53	85	13	7	24-2	.259	.382	.400	.782	15	.945
2002— Jupiter (FSL)	1B-3B-OF	107	376	72	103	21	4	17	69	63	88	13	7	18-5	.274	.394	.487	.881	9	.975
2003— Jupiter (FSL)	C-1-0-3	59	193	46	51	17	1	12	34	46	42	9	3	9-2	.264	.422	.549	.972	2	.994
— GC Marlins (GCL)		2	7	3	3	1	0	1	3	1	2	0	0	0-0	.429	.500	1.000	1.500	—	—
— Carolina (Southern)	1-C-3-O	22	67	15	20	2	1	5	14	13	20	3	0	0-0	.299	.434	.582	1.016	0	1.000
2004— Florida (N.L.)	C-OF	12	25	2	5	0	0	1	1	4	8	0	1	0-0	.200	.310	.320	.630	1	.955
— Carolina (Southern)	C-1-0-DH-3	112	338	81	95	24	0	24	76	91	87	18	5	6-3	.281	.449	.565	.992	5	.994
Major League totals (1 year)		12	25	2	5	0	0	1	1	4	8	0	1	0-0	.200	.310	.320	.630	1	.955

WILLIS, DONTRELLE   P

PERSONAL: Born January 12, 1982, in Oakland, Calif. ... 6-4/239. ... Throws left, bats left. ... Full name: Dontrelle Wayne Willis. ... High school: Encinal (Alameda, Calif.).

TRANSACTIONS/CAREER NOTES: Selected by Chicago Cubs organization in eighth round of 2000 free-agent draft. ... Traded by Cubs with Ps Julian Tavarez and Jose Cueto and C Ryan Jorgensen to Florida Marlins for Ps Antonio Alfonseca and Matt Clement (March 27, 2002).

HONORS: Named N.L. Rookie Pitcher of the Year by THE SPORTING NEWS (2003). ... Named N.L. Rookie of the Year by Baseball Writers' Association of America (2003).

CAREER HITTING: 29-for-132 (.220), 7 R, 4 2B, 1 3B, 2 HR, 7 RBI.

Year Team (League)	W	L	Pct.	ERA	WHIP	G	GS	CG	ShO	Hld.	Sv.-Opp.	IP	H	R	ER	HR	BB-IBB	SO	Avg.
2000— Ariz. Cubs (Ariz.)	3	1	.750	3.86	1.21	9	1	0	0	...	0-...	28.0	26	15	12	0	8-1	22	.245
2001— Boise (N'west)	8	2	.800	2.98	1.01	15	15	0	0	...	0-...	93.2	76	36	31	1	19-0	77	.217
2002— Kane County (Midwest)	10	2	.833	1.83	0.88	19	19	3	2	...	0-...	127.2	91	29	26	3	21-0	101	.200
— Jupiter (FSL)	2	0	1.000	1.80	0.90	5	5	0	0	...	0-...	30.0	24	7	6	2	3-0	27	.216
2003— Carolina (Southern)	4	0	1.000	1.49	0.91	6	6	0	0	...	0-...	36.1	24	6	6	2	9-0	32	.194
— Florida (N.L.)	14	6	.700	3.30	1.28	27	27	3	2	0	0-0	160.2	148	61	59	13	58-0	142	.245
2004— Florida (N.L.)	10	11	.476	4.02	1.38	32	32	0	0	0	0-0	197.0	210	99	88	20	61-8	139	.273
Major League totals (2 years)	24	17	.585	3.70	1.33	59	59	4	2	0	0-0	357.2	358	160	147	33	119-8	281	.261

DIVISION SERIES RECORD

Year Team (League)	W	L	Pct.	ERA	WHIP	G	GS	CG	ShO	Hld.	Sv.-Opp.	IP	H	R	ER	HR	BB-IBB	SO	Avg.
2003— Florida (N.L.)	0	0	...	7.94	1.59	2	1	0	0	0	0-0	5.2	7	5	5	0	2-0	3	.318

W

CHAMPIONSHIP SERIES RECORD

Year Team (League)	W	L	Pct.	ERA	WHIP	G	GS	CG	ShO	Hld.	Sv.-Opp.	IP	H	R	ER	HR	BB-IBB	SO	Avg.
2003— Florida (N.L.)	0	1	.000	18.90	3.00	2	1	0	0	0	0-0	3.1	4	7	7	1	6-0	4	.308

WORLD SERIES RECORD

Year Team (League)	W	L	Pct.	ERA	WHIP	G	GS	CG	ShO	Hld.	Sv.-Opp.	IP	H	R	ER	HR	BB-IBB	SO	Avg.
2003— Florida (N.L.)	0	0	...	0.00	1.64	3	0	0	0	1	0-0	3.2	4	0	0	0	2-0	3	.267

WILSON, CRAIG — OF/1B

PERSONAL: Born November 30, 1976, in Fountain Valley, Calif. ... 6-2/220. ... Bats right, throws right. ... Full name: Craig Alan Wilson. ... High school: Marina (Huntington Beach, Calif.).

TRANSACTIONS/CAREER NOTES: Selected by Toronto Blue Jays organization in second round of 1995 free-agent draft. ... Traded by Blue Jays to Pittsburgh Pirates (December 11, 1996), completing deal in which Pirates traded 2B Carlos Garcia, 1B Orlando Merced and P Dan Plesac to Blue Jays for Ps Mike Halperin, Jose Pett and Jose Silva, SSs Abraham Nunez and Brandon Cromer and a player to be named (November 14, 1996).

2004 GAMES PLAYED BY POSITION (MLB): OF—100, 1B—65, C—4, DH—2.

										BATTING									FIELDING	
Year Team (League)	Pos.	G	AB	R	H	2B	3B	HR	RBI	BB	SO	HBP	GDP	SB-CS	Avg.	OBP	SLG	OPS	E	Avg.
1995— Medicine Hat (Pio.)	C	49	184	33	52	14	1	7	35	24	44	3	1	8-2	.283	.367	.484	.851	5	.982
1996— Hagerstown (SAL)	C-OF	131	495	66	129	27	5	11	70	32	120	10	12	17-11	.261	.316	.402	.718	9	.986
1997— Lynchburg (Caro.)	C	117	401	54	106	26	1	19	69	39	98	15	3	6-5	.264	.350	.476	.826	12	.985
1998— Lynchburg (Caro.)	C-1B	61	219	26	59	12	2	12	45	22	53	5	3	2-1	.269	.348	.507	.855	6	.986
— Carolina (Southern)	C	45	148	20	49	11	0	5	21	14	32	4	2	4-1	.331	.399	.507	.906	1	.995
1999— Altoona (East.)	C-1B-OF	111	362	57	97	21	3	20	69	40	104	19	8	1-3	.268	.367	.508	.875	9	.978
2000— Nashville (PCL)	C-1B	124	396	83	112	24	1	33	86	44	121	25	7	1-2	.283	.383	.598	.982	13	.982
2001— Nashville (PCL)	1B-C	11	45	4	13	2	1	1	3	2	14	1	1	0-0	.289	.333	.444	.778	2	.976
— Pittsburgh (N.L.) 1B-0-C-DH	88	158	27	49	3	1	13	32	15	53	7	4	3-1	.310	.390	.589	.979	3	.987
2002— Pittsburgh (N.L.) OF-1-C-DH	131	368	48	97	16	1	16	57	32	116	21	10	2-3	.264	.355	.443	.798	5	.988
2003— Pittsburgh (N.L.) OF-1-C-DH	116	309	49	81	15	4	18	48	35	89	13	6	3-1	.262	.360	.511	.872	6	.986
2004— Pittsburgh (N.L.) OF-1-C-DH	155	561	97	148	35	5	29	82	50	169	30	11	2-2	.264	.354	.499	.853	7	.990
Major League totals (4 years)		490	1396	221	375	69	11	76	219	132	427	71	31	10-7	.269	.360	.497	.857	21	.988

WILSON, DAN — C

PERSONAL: Born March 25, 1969, in Barrington, Ill. ... 6-3/215. ... Bats right, throws right. ... Full name: Daniel Allen Wilson. ... High school: Barrington (Ill.). ... College: Minnesota.

TRANSACTIONS/CAREER NOTES: Selected by New York Mets organization in 26th round of 1987 free-agent draft; did not sign. ... Selected by Cincinnati Reds organization in first round (seventh pick overall) of 1990 free-agent draft. ... Traded by Reds with P Bobby Ayala to Seattle Mariners for P Erik Hanson and 2B Bret Boone (November 2, 1993). ... On disabled list (July 21-September 1, 1998). ... On disabled list (June 15-July 14, 2000); included rehabilitation assignments to Everett and Tacoma. ... On disabled list (March 19-April 6, 2003); included rehabilitation assignment to San Antonio.

2004 GAMES PLAYED BY POSITION (MLB): C—103.

										BATTING									FIELDING	
Year Team (League)	Pos.	G	AB	R	H	2B	3B	HR	RBI	BB	SO	HBP	GDP	SB-CS	Avg.	OBP	SLG	OPS	E	Avg.
1990— Char., W.Va. (SAL)	C	32	113	16	28	9	1	2	17	13	17	0	1	0-0	.248	.323	.398	.721	1	.995
1991— Char., W.Va. (SAL)	C	52	197	25	62	11	1	3	29	25	21	2	6	1-1	.315	.396	.426	.822	3	.992
— Chattanooga (Sou.)	C	81	292	32	75	19	2	2	38	21	39	0	10	2-2	.257	.303	.363	.659	4	.993
1992— Nashville (A.A.)	C	106	366	27	92	16	1	4	34	31	58	2	7	1-4	.251	.310	.333	.644	8	.990
— Cincinnati (N.L.)	C	12	25	2	9	1	0	0	3	3	8	0	2	0-0	.360	.429	.400	.829	0	1.000
1993— Cincinnati (N.L.)	C	36	76	6	17	3	0	0	8	9	16	0	2	0-0	.224	.302	.263	.565	1	.994
— Indianapolis (A.A.)	C	51	191	18	50	11	1	1	17	19	31	1	4	1-0	.262	.330	.346	.676	2	.994
1994— Seattle (A.L.)	C	91	282	24	61	14	2	3	27	10	57	1	11	1-2	.216	.244	.312	.556	* 9	.986
1995— Seattle (A.L.)	C	119	399	40	111	22	3	9	51	33	63	2	12	2-1	.278	.336	.416	.752	5	.995
1996— Seattle (A.L.)	C	138	491	51	140	24	1	18	83	32	88	3	15	1-2	.285	.330	.444	.774	4	.996
1997— Seattle (A.L.)	C	146	508	66	137	31	1	15	74	39	72	5	12	7-2	.270	.326	.423	.749	6	.995
1998— Seattle (A.L.)	C	96	325	39	82	17	1	9	44	24	56	5	6	2-1	.252	.308	.394	.702	4	.994
1999— Seattle (A.L.)	C-1B	123	414	46	110	23	2	7	38	29	83	2	10	5-0	.266	.315	.382	.697	4	.995
2000— Seattle (A.L.)	C-3B-1B	90	268	31	63	12	0	5	27	22	51	0	8	1-2	.235	.291	.336	.627	5	.990
— Everett (N'west)	C	1	2	2	1	0	0	1	1	1	0	0	0	0-0	.500	.667	2.000	2.667	0	1.000
— Tacoma (PCL)	DH	1	4	0	1	1	0	0	0	0	1	0	0	0-0	.250	.250	.500	.750	...	...
2001— Seattle (A.L.)	C-1B	123	377	44	100	20	1	10	42	20	69	2	6	3-2	.265	.305	.403	.708	1	.999
2002— Seattle (A.L.)	C-1B	115	359	35	106	16	1	6	44	18	81	2	8	1-2	.295	.326	.396	.721	2	.997
2003— San Antonio (Texas)	C	2	7	0	0	0	0	0	0	3	0	0	0	0-0	.000	.000	.000	.000	1	.941
— Seattle (A.L.)	C	96	316	32	76	15	2	4	43	15	52	0	8	0-0	.241	.272	.339	.611	1	.998
2004— Seattle (A.L.)	C	103	319	23	80	13	0	2	33	26	57	1	8	0-1	.251	.305	.310	.615	2	.997
American League totals (11 years)		1240	4058	431	1066	207	13	88	506	268	729	23	104	23-13	.263	.309	.385	.694	43	.995
National League totals (2 years)		48	101	8	26	4	0	0	11	12	24	0	4	0-0	.257	.333	.297	.630	1	.995
Major League totals (13 years)		1288	4159	439	1092	211	13	88	517	280	753	23	108	23-13	.263	.310	.383	.693	44	.995

DIVISION SERIES RECORD

Year Team (League)	Pos.	G	AB	R	H	2B	3B	HR	RBI	BB	SO	HBP	GDP	SB-CS	Avg.	OBP	SLG	OPS	E	Avg.
1995— Seattle (A.L.)	C	5	17	0	2	0	0	0	1	2	6	0	1	0-0	.118	.211	.118	.328	0	1.000
1997— Seattle (A.L.)	C	4	13	0	0	0	0	0	0	0	9	0	0	0-0	.000	.000	.000	.000	0	1.000
2000— Seattle (A.L.)	C	2	3	0	0	0	0	0	1	1	2	0	0	0-0	.000	.200	.000	.200	1	.833
2001— Seattle (A.L.)	C	5	15	0	3	1	0	0	0	0	5	0	1	0-0	.200	.200	.267	.467	0	1.000
Division series totals (4 years)		16	48	0	5	1	0	0	2	3	22	0	2	0-0	.104	.154	.125	.279	1	.991

CHAMPIONSHIP SERIES RECORD

Year Team (League)	Pos.	G	AB	R	H	2B	3B	HR	RBI	BB	SO	HBP	GDP	SB-CS	Avg.	OBP	SLG	OPS	E	Avg.
1995— Seattle (A.L.)	C	6	16	0	0	0	0	0	0	0	4	0	0	0-0	.000	.000	.000	.000	1	.974
2000— Seattle (A.L.)	C	4	11	0	1	0	0	0	0	1	5	0	0	0-0	.091	.167	.091	.258	1	.960
2001— Seattle (A.L.)	C	4	13	2	2	0	0	0	0	0	1	0	0	0-0	.154	.154	.154	.308	0	1.000
Champ. series totals (3 years)		14	40	2	3	0	0	0	0	1	10	0	0	0-0	.075	.098	.075	.173	2	.977

ALL-STAR GAME RECORD

		G	AB	R	H	2B	3B	HR	RBI	BB	SO	HBP	GDP	SB-CS	Avg.	OBP	SLG	OPS	E	Avg.
All-Star Game totals (1 year)		1	1	0	0	0	0	0	0	0	0	0	0	0-0	.000	.000	.000	.000	...	...

WILSON, ENRIQUE — 2B

PERSONAL: Born July 27, 1973, in Santo Domingo, Dominican Republic. ... 5-11/195. ... Bats both, throws right. ... Full name: Enrique Martes Wilson. ... High school: Liceo Ramon Amelio Jiminez (Santo Domingo, Dominican Republic).

TRANSACTIONS/CAREER NOTES: Signed as a non-drafted free agent by Minnesota Twins organization (April 15, 1992). ... Traded by Twins to Cleveland Indians (February 21, 1994), completing deal in which Twins acquired P Shawn Bryant for a player to be named (February 21, 1994). ... On disabled list (April 4-June 15, 1998); included rehabilitation assignment to Buffalo. ... On disabled list (July 14-August 1, 2000); included rehabilitation assignment to Nashville. ... Traded by Indians with OF Alex Ramirez to Pittsburgh Pirates for 1B/OF Wil Cordero (July 28, 2000). ... Traded by Pirates to New York Yankees for P Damaso Marte (June 13, 2001).

2004 GAMES PLAYED BY POSITION (MLB): 2B—80, SS—16.

Year — Team (League)	Pos.	G	AB	R	H	2B	3B	HR	RBI	BB	SO	HBP	GDP	SB-CS	Avg.	OBP	SLG	OPS	E	Avg.
1992— GC Twins (GCL)	SS	13	44	12	15	1	0	0	8	4	4	4	0	3-0	.341	.434	.364	.798	4	.897
1993— Elizabethton (App.)	3B-SS	58	197	42	57	8	4	13	50	14	18	6	1	5-4	.289	.352	.569	.920	19	.909
1994— Columbus (S. Atl.)	SS	133	512	82	143	28	12	10	72	44	34	6	7	21-13	.279	.341	.439	.780	33	.947
1995— Kinston (Caro.)	2B-SS	117	464	55	124	24	7	6	52	25	38	2	10	18-19	.267	.301	.388	.689	21	.964
1996— Cant./Akr. (Eastern)	SS-2B	117	484	70	147	17	5	5	50	31	46	4	9	23-16	.304	.346	.391	.737	28	.949
— Buffalo (A.A.)	3B-SS	3	8	1	4	1	0	0	0	1	1	0	1	0-2	.500	.556	.625	1.181	1	.750
1997— Buffalo (A.A.)	SS-2B-3B	118	451	78	138	20	3	11	39	42	41	5	7	9-8	.306	.369	.437	.805	20	.965
— Cleveland (A.L.)	SS-2B	5	15	2	5	0	0	1	1	0	2	0	0	0-0	.333	.333	.333	.667	1	.952
1998— Cleveland (A.L.)	2B-SS	32	90	13	29	6	0	2	12	4	8	1	1	2-4	.322	.354	.456	.810	2	.983
— Buffalo (Int'l)	2B-SS	56	221	40	62	13	0	4	23	19	21	0	6	8-3	.281	.335	.394	.728	6	.976
1999— Cleveland (A.L.)	3-S-2-DH	113	332	41	87	22	1	2	24	25	41	1	12	5-4	.262	.310	.352	.663	8	.968
2000— Cleveland (A.L.)	3-DH-2-SS	40	117	16	38	9	0	2	12	7	11	0	2	2-1	.325	.360	.453	.813	1	.985
— Nashville (PCL)	SS	2	7	0	2	0	0	0	1	0	0	0	2	0-0	.286	.286	.286	.571	1	.889
— Pittsburgh (N.L.)	3B-2B-SS	40	122	11	32	6	1	3	15	11	13	0	4	0-1	.262	.321	.402	.723	6	.942
2001— Pittsburgh (N.L.)	SS-2B-3B	46	129	7	24	3	0	1	8	3	23	0	7	0-3	.186	.203	.233	.436	4	.974
— New York (A.L.)	S-3-2-DH	48	99	10	24	5	1	1	12	6	14	0	3	0-2	.242	.283	.343	.626	2	.981
2002— New York (A.L.)	3-S-2-DH-OF	60	105	17	19	2	2	2	11	8	22	0	2	1-1	.181	.239	.295	.534	5	.955
2003— New York (A.L.)	S-3-2-DH	63	135	18	31	9	0	3	15	7	14	2	3	3-1	.230	.276	.363	.639	3	.979
2004— New York (A.L.)	2B-SS	93	240	19	51	9	0	6	31	15	20	0	5	1-2	.213	.254	.325	.579	8	.977
American League totals (8 years)		454	1133	136	284	62	4	18	118	72	132	4	28	14-15	.251	.294	.360	.654	30	.974
National League totals (2 years)		86	251	18	56	9	1	4	23	14	36	0	11	0-4	.223	.262	.315	.577	10	.961
Major League totals (8 years)		540	1384	154	340	71	5	22	141	86	168	4	39	14-19	.246	.288	.352	.640	40	.972

DIVISION SERIES RECORD

Year — Team (League)	Pos.	G	AB	R	H	2B	3B	HR	RBI	BB	SO	HBP	GDP	SB-CS	Avg.	OBP	SLG	OPS	E	Avg.
1998— Cleveland (A.L.)	2B	1	2	0	0	0	0	0	0	0	0	0	0	0-0	.000	.000	.000	.000	0	1.000
1999— Cleveland (A.L.)	2B	3	2	0	0	0	0	0	0	0	0	0	0	0-0	.000	.000	.000	.000	0	1.000
2002— New York (A.L.)		1	0	0	0	0	0	0	0	0	0	0	0	0-0	...	...	...	...	0	...
Division series totals (3 years)		5	4	0	0	0	0	0	0	0	0	0	0	0-0	.000	.000	.000	.000	0	1.000

CHAMPIONSHIP SERIES RECORD

Year — Team (League)	Pos.	G	AB	R	H	2B	3B	HR	RBI	BB	SO	HBP	GDP	SB-CS	Avg.	OBP	SLG	OPS	E	Avg.
1998— Cleveland (A.L.)	2B	5	14	2	3	0	0	0	1	1	3	0	0	0-0	.214	.267	.214	.481	1	.960
2001— New York (A.L.)	SS	1	1	0	1	0	0	0	0	0	0	0	0	0-0	1.000	1.000	1.000	2.000	0	...
2003— New York (A.L.)	3B	2	7	0	1	0	0	0	0	0	1	0	0	0-0	.143	.143	.143	.286	1	.800
Champ. series totals (3 years)		8	22	2	5	0	0	0	1	1	4	0	0	0-0	.227	.261	.227	.488	2	.933

WORLD SERIES RECORD

Year — Team (League)	Pos.	G	AB	R	H	2B	3B	HR	RBI	BB	SO	HBP	GDP	SB-CS	Avg.	OBP	SLG	OPS	E	Avg.
2001— New York (A.L.)	SS	2	3	0	0	0	0	0	0	0	0	0	0	0-0	.000	.000	.000	.000	0	1.000
2003— New York (A.L.)	2B-3B	2	4	0	2	1	0	0	1	1	0	0	1	0-0	.500	.600	.750	1.350	1	.857
World series totals (2 years)		4	7	0	2	1	0	0	1	1	0	0	1	0-0	.286	.375	.429	.804	1	.875

WILSON, JACK — SS

PERSONAL: Born December 29, 1977, in Westlake Village, Calif. ... 6-0/192. ... Bats right, throws right. ... Full name: Jack Eugene Wilson. ... High school: Thousand Oaks (Calif.). ... Junior college: Oxnard (Calif.).

TRANSACTIONS/CAREER NOTES: Selected by St. Louis Cardinals organization in ninth round of 1998 free-agent draft. ... Traded by Cardinals to Pittsburgh Pirates for P Jason Christiansen (July 30, 2000).

2004 GAMES PLAYED BY POSITION (MLB): SS—156.

Year — Team (League)	Pos.	G	AB	R	H	2B	3B	HR	RBI	BB	SO	HBP	GDP	SB-CS	Avg.	OBP	SLG	OPS	E	Avg.
1998— Johnson City (App.)	SS	61	241	50	90	18	4	4	29	18	30	3	4	22-6	.373	.424	.531	.955	16	.940
1999— Peoria (Midw.)	SS	64	251	47	86	22	4	3	28	15	23	2	2	11-5	.343	.384	.498	.882	16	.943
— Potomac (Caro.)	SS	64	257	44	76	10	1	2	18	19	31	1	2	7-4	.296	.345	.366	.711	18	.941
2000— Potomac (Caro.)	SS	13	47	7	13	0	1	2	7	5	10	0	1	2-3	.277	.340	.447	.786	2	.967
— Arkansas (Texas)	SS	88	343	65	101	20	8	6	34	36	59	5	5	2-3	.294	.368	.452	.820	12	.971
— Altoona (East.)	SS	33	139	17	35	7	2	1	16	14	17	2	3	1-3	.252	.325	.353	.677	5	.966
2001— Pittsburgh (N.L.)	SS	108	390	44	87	17	1	3	25	16	70	1	4	1-3	.223	.255	.295	.550	16	.968
— Nashville (PCL)	SS	27	103	20	38	6	1	1	6	9	13	2	1	2-2	.369	.430	.476	.906	3	.974
2002— Pittsburgh (N.L.)	SS	147	527	77	133	22	4	4	47	37	74	4	7	5-2	.252	.306	.332	.638	15	.977
2003— Pittsburgh (N.L.)	SS	150	558	58	143	21	3	9	62	36	74	4	11	5-5	.256	.303	.353	.656	17	.975
2004— Pittsburgh (N.L.)	SS	157	652	82	201	41	*12	11	59	26	71	3	15	8-4	.308	.335	.459	.794	17	.977
Major League totals (4 years)		562	2127	261	564	101	20	27	193	115	289	12	37	19-14	.265	.305	.370	.674	65	.975

ALL-STAR GAME RECORD

		G	AB	R	H	2B	3B	HR	RBI	BB	SO	HBP	GDP	SB-CS	Avg.	OBP	SLG	OPS	E	Avg.
All-Star Game totals (1 year)		1	2	0	0	0	0	0	0	0	0	0	0	0-0	.000	.000	.000	.000	0	1.000

W

WILSON, PAUL — P

PERSONAL: Born March 28, 1973, in Orlando, Fla. ... 6-5/215. ... Throws right, bats right. ... Full name: Paul Anthony Wilson. ... High school: William R. Boone (Orlando). ... College: Florida State.

TRANSACTIONS/CAREER NOTES: Selected by New York Mets organization in first round (first pick overall) of 1994 free-agent draft. ... On disabled list (June 5-July 15, 1996); included rehabilitation assignments to St. Lucie and Binghamton. ... On disabled list (March 27, 1997-entire season); included rehabilitation assignments to GCL Mets and St. Lucie. ... On disabled list (March 13-August 4, 1998); included rehabilitation assignment to St. Lucie. ... On disabled list (April 8, 1999-entire season). ... Traded by Mets with OF Jason Tyner to Tampa Bay Devil Rays for OF Bubba Trammell and P Rick White (July 28, 2000). ... Signed as a free agent by Cincinnati Reds (January 11, 2003). ... On disabled list (August 14-September 1, 2004).

CAREER HITTING: 16-for-167 (.096), 6 R, 3 2B, 0 3B, 1 HR, 7 RBI.

Year Team (League)	W	L	Pct.	ERA	WHIP	G	GS	CG	ShO	Hld.	Sv.-Opp.	IP	H	R	ER	HR	BB-IBB	SO	Avg.
1994— GC Mets (GCL)	0	2	.000	3.00	1.00	3	3	0	0	...	0-...	12.0	8	4	4	0	4-0	13	.190
— St. Lucie (Fla. St.)	0	5	.000	5.06	1.31	8	8	0	0	...	0-...	37.1	32	23	21	3	17-1	37	.230
1995— Binghamton (Eastern)	6	3	.667	2.17	0.94	16	16	4	1	...	0-...	120.1	89	34	29	5	24-2	127	.208
— Norfolk (Int'l)	5	3	.625	2.85	1.19	10	10	4	2	...	0-...	66.1	59	25	21	3	20-0	67	.242
1996— New York (N.L.)	5	12	.294	5.38	1.53	26	26	1	0	0	0-0	149.0	157	102	89	15	71-11	109	.268
— St. Lucie (Fla. St.)	0	1	.000	3.38	1.25	2	2	0	0	...	0-...	8.0	6	5	3	0	4-0	5	.194
— Binghamton (Eastern)	0	1	.000	7.20	2.20	1	1	0	0	...	0-...	5.0	6	4	4	0	5-0	5	.316
1997— GC Mets (GCL)	1	0	1.000	1.45	0.96	4	3	0	0	...	1-...	18.2	14	7	3	0	4-0	18	.203
— St. Lucie (Fla. St.)	0	0	...	2.57	0.86	1	1	0	0	...	0-...	7.0	6	2	2	1	0-0	6	.231
1998— St. Lucie (Fla. St.)	0	1	.000	6.38	1.47	5	5	0	0	...	0-...	18.1	23	13	13	2	4-0	16	.315
— Norfolk (Int'l)	4	1	.800	4.42	1.32	7	7	0	0	...	0-...	38.2	42	19	19	2	9-0	30	.273
1999— Norfolk (Int'l)			Did not play.																
2000— St. Lucie (Fla. St.)	2	0	1.000	1.40	1.01	5	5	0	0	...	0-...	25.2	22	9	4	0	4-0	19	.234
— Norfolk (Int'l)	5	5	.500	4.23	1.33	15	13	0	0	...	0-...	83.0	85	40	39	7	25-1	56	.266
— Tampa Bay (A.L.)	1	4	.200	3.35	1.06	11	7	0	0	1	0-0	51.0	38	20	19	1	16-2	40	.209
2001— Tampa Bay (A.L.)	8	9	.471	4.88	1.43	37	24	0	0	0	0-1	151.1	165	94	82	21	52-2	119	.278
2002— Tampa Bay (A.L.)	6	12	.333	4.83	1.48	30	30	1	0	0	0-0	193.2	219	113	104	29	67-2	111	.287
2003— Cincinnati (N.L.)	8	10	.444	4.64	1.44	28	28	0	0	0	0-0	166.2	190	97	86	24	50-5	93	.285
2004— Cincinnati (N.L.)	11	6	.647	4.36	1.39	29	29	1	0	0	0-0	183.2	192	93	89	26	63-5	117	.271
American League totals (3 years)	15	25	.375	4.66	1.41	78	61	1	0	1	0-1	396.0	422	227	205	51	135-6	270	.274
National League totals (3 years)	24	28	.462	4.76	1.45	83	83	2	0	0	0-0	499.1	539	292	264	65	184-21	319	.275
Major League totals (6 years)	39	53	.424	4.71	1.43	161	144	3	0	1	0-1	895.1	961	519	469	116	319-27	589	.275

WILSON, PRESTON — OF

PERSONAL: Born July 19, 1974, in Bamberg, S.C. ... 6-2/213. ... Bats right, throws right. ... Full name: Preston James Richard Wilson. ... High school: Bamberg Erhardt (Bamberg, S.C.). ... Stepson of Mookie Wilson, first base/outfield coach, New York Mets; and outfielder with Mets (1980-89) and Toronto Blue Jays (1989-91).

TRANSACTIONS/CAREER NOTES: Selected by New York Mets organization in first round (ninth pick overall) of 1992 free-agent draft. ... Traded by Mets with Ps Ed Yarnall and Geoff Goetz to Florida Marlins for C Mike Piazza (May 22, 1998). ... On disabled list (July 2-August 10, 2001); included rehabilitation assignment to Calgary. ... Traded by Marlins with C Charles Johnson, P Vic Darensbourg and 2B Pablo Ozuna to Colorado Rockies for P Mike Hampton, OF Juan Pierre and cash (November 16, 2002). ... On disabled list (April 13-June 18 and August 21, 2004-remainder of season); included rehabilitation assignment to Tulsa.

HONORS: Named N.L. Rookie Player of the Year by THE SPORTING NEWS (1999).

2004 GAMES PLAYED BY POSITION (MLB): OF—52.

								BATTING													FIELDING	
Year Team (League)	Pos.	G	AB	R	H	2B	3B	HR	RBI	BB	SO	HBP	GDP	SB-CS	Avg.	OBP	SLG	OPS		E	Avg.
1993— Kingsport (Appalachian)	3B	66	259	44	60	10	0	16	48	24	75	3	6	6-2	.232	.303	.456	.759		25	.873
— Pittsfield (N.Y.-Penn.)	3B	8	29	6	16	5	1	1	12	2	7	1	0	1-0	.552	.576	.897	1.472		6	.700
1994— Capital City (SAL)	3B	131	474	55	108	17	4	14	58	20	135	3	4	10-10	.228	.262	.369	.631		47	.884
1995— Capital City (SAL)	OF	111	442	70	119	26	5	20	61	19	114	9	4	20-6	.269	.311	.486	.797		8	.961
1996— St. Lucie (Fla. St.)	OF	23	85	6	15	3	0	1	7	8	21	2	3	1-1	.176	.263	.247	.510		2	.956
1997— St. Lucie (Fla. St.)	OF-DH	63	245	32	60	12	1	11	48	8	66	1	4	3-4	.245	.267	.437	.704		3	.973
— Binghamton (East.)	OF-DH-3B	70	259	37	74	12	1	19	47	21	71	2	5	7-1	.286	.340	.560	.900		6	.952
1998— Norfolk (Int'l)	OF	18	73	9	18	5	1	1	9	2	22	1	...	1-1	.247	.273	.384	.656		2	.958
— New York (N.L.)	OF	8	20	3	6	2	0	0	2	1	8	0	0	1-1	.300	.364	.400	.764		1	.909
— Charlotte (Int'l)	OF-DH	94	356	71	99	25	3	25	77	34	121	2	...	14-6	.278	.341	.576	.917		4	.979
— Florida (N.L.)	OF	14	31	4	2	0	0	1	1	4	13	1	0	0-0	.065	.194	.161	.356		0	1.000
1999— Florida (N.L.)	OF	149	482	67	135	21	4	26	71	46	156	9	15	11-4	.280	.350	.502	.852		9	.973
2000— Florida (N.L.)	OF	161	605	94	160	35	3	31	121	55 *	187	8	11	36-14	.264	.331	.486	.817		5	.988
2001— Florida (N.L.)	OF	123	468	70	128	30	2	23	71	36	107	6	14	20-8	.274	.331	.494	.825		2	.993
— Calgary (PCL)	OF	4	10	3	5	2	0	0	1	5	1	0	0	2-0	.500	.667	.700	1.367		0	1.000
2002— Florida (N.L.)	OF	141	510	80	124	22	2	23	65	58	140	9	17	20-11	.243	.329	.429	.759		6	.981
2003— Colorado (N.L.)	OF	155	600	94	169	43	1	36 *	141	54	139	4	23	14-7	.282	.343	.537	.880		7	.980
2004— Tulsa (Texas)	OF-DH	6	17	4	7	1	0	1	2	3	4	1	1	1-1	.412	.524	.647	1.171		0	1.000
— Colorado (N.L.)	OF	58	202	24	50	11	0	6	29	17	49	3	9	2-1	.248	.315	.391	.706		6	.953
Major League totals (7 years)		809	2918	436	774	164	12	146	501	272	799	40	89	104-46	.265	.334	.480	.814		36	.981

ALL-STAR GAME RECORD

	G	AB	R	H	2B	3B	HR	RBI	BB	SO	HBP	GDP	SB-CS	Avg.	OBP	SLG	OPS	E	Avg.
All-Star Game totals (1 year)	1	2	0	1	0	0	0	0	0	1	0	0	0-0	.500	.500	.500	1.000	0	1.000

W

WILSON, TOM　　　　　　　　　　　C

PERSONAL: Born December 19, 1970, in Fullerton, Calif. ... 6-3/220. ... Bats right, throws right. ... Full name: Thomas Leroy Wilson. ... High school: Troy (Fullerton, Calif.). ... Junior college: Fullerton (Calif.).

TRANSACTIONS/CAREER NOTES: Selected by New York Yankees organization in 23rd round of 1990 free-agent draft. ... Traded by Yankees to Cleveland Indians for C Ryan Martindale and OF Marc Marini (April 6, 1996). ... Released by Indians (October 15, 1996). ... Signed by Yankees organization (February 1, 1997). ... Signed as a free agent by Arizona Diamondbacks organization (December 15, 1997). ... Signed as a free agent by Tampa Bay Devil Rays organization (November 23, 1998). ... Signed as a free agent by Yankees organization (November 9, 1999). ... Signed as a free agent by Oakland Athletics organization (November 7, 2000). ... Traded by A's to Toronto Blue Jays for C Mike Kremblas (January 2, 2002). ... Claimed on waivers by San Diego Padres (January 7, 2004). ... Released by Padres (March 29, 2004). ... Signed by Athletics organization (April 3, 2004). ... Released by Athletics (April 23, 2004). ... Signed by New York Mets organization (May 4, 2004). ... Traded by Mets to Los Angeles Dodgers for C Tony Socarras (August 17, 2004).

2004 GAMES PLAYED BY POSITION (MLB): C—10.

Year Team (League)	Pos.	G	AB	R	H	2B	3B	HR	RBI	BB	SO	HBP	GDP	SB-CS	Avg.	OBP	SLG	OPS	E	Avg.
1991— Oneonta (N.Y.-Penn.)	C-OF	70	243	38	59	12	2	4	42	34	72	3	6	4-4	.243	.337	.358	.695	17	.950
1992— Greensboro (S. Atl.)	C-OF	117	395	50	83	22	0	6	48	68	128	3	8	2-1	.210	.325	.311	.636	10	.984
1993— Greensboro (S. Atl.)	C	120	394	55	98	20	1	10	63	91	112	4	5	2-5	.249	.388	.381	.769	13	.986
1994— Albany (East.)	3B-C	123	408	54	100	20	1	7	42	58	100	6	6	4-6	.245	.345	.350	.695	8	.990
1995— Columbus (Int'l)	C	22	62	11	16	3	1	0	9	9	10	0	0	0-0	.258	.352	.339	.691	5	.962
— Norwich (East.)	3B-C	28	84	6	12	4	0	0	4	17	22	0	3	0-0	.143	.287	.190	.478	6	.964
— Tampa (Fla. St.)	C	17	48	3	8	0	0	0	2	11	13	0	0	1-0	.167	.317	.167	.483	0	1.000
1996— Columbus (Int'l)	DH	1	1	0	0	0	0	0	0	1	0	0	0	0-0	.000	.500	.000	.500	...	...
— Buffalo (A.A.)	SS-C	72	208	28	56	14	2	9	30	35	66	6	4	0-1	.269	.390	.486	.875	5	.988
1997— Norwich (East.)	3B-C-1B	124	419	88	124	21	4	21	80	86	126	4	8	1-4	.296	.416	.516	.932	8	.990
— Columbus (Int'l)	C	1	3	0	0	0	0	0	0	1	0	0	0	0-0	.000	.250	.000	.250	0	1.000
1998— Tucson (PCL)	3B-C-1B-O	111	370	59	112	17	3	12	54	41	81	7	10	3-1	.303	.380	.462	.842	16	.978
1999— Durham (Int'l)	C-1B-OF	67	215	41	60	19	0	16	44	49	59	0	9	0-2	.279	.411	.591	1.002	6	.987
— Orlando (South.)	C	30	104	12	30	7	0	2	23	18	34	3	2	0-0	.288	.405	.510	.914	4	.971
2000— Columbus (Int'l)	3B-C-OF	104	330	63	91	20	0	20	71	73	114	3	9	2-2	.276	.410	.518	.929	8	.987
2001— Sacramento (PCL)	C-3B-OF-1	77	259	43	73	15	1	8	48	49	62	4	5	0-1	.282	.394	.440	.834	5	.988
— Oakland (A.L.)	C	9	21	4	4	0	0	2	4	1	5	1	1	0-0	.190	.250	.476	.726	1	.974
2002— Toronto (A.L.)	C-DH-1B	96	265	33	68	10	0	8	37	28	79	5	6	0-0	.257	.334	.385	.719	4	.991
2003— Toronto (A.L.)	C-1-O-DH	96	256	37	66	19	0	5	35	28	80	1	4	0-0	.258	.331	.391	.722	5	.990
2004— Sacramento (PCL)	DH-C-3-1	14	42	6	10	2	0	1	5	15	13	0	0	0-0	.238	.439	.357	.796	1	.974
— New York (N.L.)	C	4	4	0	1	0	0	0	0	1	2	0	0	0-0	.250	.400	.250	.650	0	1.000
— Norfolk (Int'l)	C-DH-1-3	34	115	26	37	10	4	7	22	25	24	0	3	0-1	.322	.443	.591	1.034	7	.961
— Las Vegas (PCL)	C	9	38	10	16	2	0	4	9	4	10	0	0	0-0	.421	.476	.789	1.266	1	.986
— Los Angeles (N.L.)	C	9	8	1	1	0	0	0	0	0	3	0	0	0-0	.125	.125	.125	.250	0	1.000
American League totals (3 years)		201	542	74	138	29	0	15	76	57	164	7	11	0-0	.255	.330	.391	.721	10	.989
National League totals (1 year)		13	12	1	2	0	0	0	0	1	5	0	0	0-0	.167	.231	.167	.397	0	1.000
Major League totals (4 years)		214	554	75	140	29	0	15	76	58	169	7	11	0-0	.253	.327	.386	.714	10	.990

DIVISION SERIES RECORD

Year Team (League)	Pos.	G	AB	R	H	2B	3B	HR	RBI	BB	SO	HBP	GDP	SB-CS	Avg.	OBP	SLG	OPS	E	Avg.
2004— Los Angeles (N.L.)	C	2	1	1	1	0	0	1	1	0	0	0	0	0-0	1.000	1.000	4.000	5.000	0	1.000

WILSON, VANCE　　　　　　　　　　　C

PERSONAL: Born March 17, 1973, in Mesa, Ariz. ... 5-11/190. ... Bats right, throws right. ... Full name: Vance Allen Wilson. ... High school: Red Mountain (Mesa, Ariz.). ... Junior college: Mesa (Ariz.) Community College.

TRANSACTIONS/CAREER NOTES: Selected by New York Mets organization in 44th round of 1993 free-agent draft. ... On disabled list (September 8, 1998-remainder of season; and August 28, 1999-remainder of season). ... On disabled list (June 16-July 7 and September 14, 2004-remainder of season); included rehabilitation assignments to Binghamton and Norfolk.

2004 GAMES PLAYED BY POSITION (MLB): C—69.

Year Team (League)	Pos.	G	AB	R	H	2B	3B	HR	RBI	BB	SO	HBP	GDP	SB-CS	Avg.	OBP	SLG	OPS	E	Avg.
1994— Pittsfield (N.Y.-Penn.)	C	44	166	22	51	12	0	2	20	5	27	5	1	4-1	.307	.343	.416	.758	6	.977
1995— Capital City (SAL)	C	91	324	34	81	11	0	6	32	19	45	8	4	4-3	.250	.306	.340	.645	14	.981
1996— St. Lucie (Fla. St.)	C	93	311	29	76	14	2	6	44	31	41	6	7	2-4	.244	.321	.360	.681	8	.987
1997— Binghamton (East.)	C	92	322	46	89	17	0	15	40	20	46	5	6	2-5	.276	.328	.469	.797	11	.984
1998— Norfolk (Int'l)	C	46	154	18	40	3	0	4	16	9	29	1	5	0-3	.260	.305	.357	.662	4	.990
— GC Mets (GCL)	C	10	28	5	10	5	0	2	9	0	0	1	2	0-1	.357	.367	.750	1.117	2	.957
— St. Lucie (Fla. St.)	C	4	16	0	1	0	0	0	0	0	5	0	0	0-0	.063	.063	.063	.125	0	1.000
1999— Norfolk (Int'l)	C	15	53	10	14	3	0	3	5	4	8	1	4	1-0	.264	.328	.491	.818	1	.991
— New York (N.L.)	C	1	0	0	0	0	0	0	0	0	0	0	0	0-0	...	...	...	...	0	1.000
2000— Norfolk (Int'l)	C	111	400	47	104	23	1	16	62	24	65	12	12	11-6	.260	.319	.443	.761	3	.996
— New York (N.L.)	C	4	4	0	0	0	0	0	0	0	2	0	0	0-0	.000	.000	.000	.000	0	1.000
2001— Norfolk (Int'l)	C	65	228	24	56	14	0	6	31	12	34	9	7	0-1	.246	.306	.386	.692	8	.984
— New York (N.L.)	C	32	57	3	17	3	0	0	6	2	16	2	1	0-1	.298	.339	.351	.690	1	.993
2002— New York (N.L.)	C-1B	74	163	19	40	7	0	5	26	5	32	8	4	0-1	.245	.301	.380	.682	6	.983
2003— New York (N.L.)	C	96	268	28	65	9	1	8	39	15	56	5	5	1-2	.243	.293	.373	.666	5	.990
2004— Binghamton (East.)	C	1	3	2	1	0	0	1	1	0	0	1	0	0-0	.333	.500	1.333	1.833	0	1.000
— Norfolk (Int'l)	C	1	4	1	2	0	0	1	1	0	0	0	0	0-0	.500	.500	1.250	1.750	0	1.000
— New York (N.L.)	C	79	157	18	43	10	1	4	21	11	24	5	5	1-0	.274	.335	.427	.762	2	.993
Major League totals (6 years)		286	649	68	165	29	2	17	92	33	130	20	16	2-4	.254	.308	.384	.692	14	.989

WINN, RANDY — OF

PERSONAL: Born June 9, 1974, in Los Angeles, Calif. ... 6-2/197. ... Bats both, throws right. ... Full name: Dwight Randolph Winn. ... High school: San Ramon Valley (Danville, Calif.). ... College: Santa Clara.

TRANSACTIONS/CAREER NOTES: Selected by Florida Marlins organization in third round of 1995 free-agent draft. ... Selected by Tampa Bay Devil Rays in third round (58th pick overall) of expansion draft (November 18, 1997). ... Traded by Devil Rays to Seattle Mariners for SS Antonio Perez (October 28, 2002).

2004 GAMES PLAYED BY POSITION (MLB): OF—154, DH—2.

Year Team (League)	Pos.	G	AB	R	H	2B	3B	HR	RBI	BB	SO	HBP	GDP	SB-CS	Avg.	OBP	SLG	OPS	E	Avg.
1995— Elmira (N.Y.-Penn)	OF	51	213	38	67	7	4	0	22	15	31	3	1	19-7	.315	.365	.385	.750	5	.954
1996— Kane Co. (Midw.)	OF	130	514	90	139	16	3	0	35	47	115	8	3	30-18	.270	.340	.313	.654	8	.970
1997— Brevard County (FSL)	OF	36	143	26	45	8	2	0	15	16	28	5	3	16-8	.315	.400	.399	.799	0	1.000
— Portland (East.)	OF	96	384	66	112	15	6	8	36	42	92	7	4	35-20	.292	.371	.424	.795	4	.979
1998— Durham (Int'l)	OF	29	123	25	35	5	2	1	16	15	24	0	1	10-4	.285	.362	.382	.744	2	.966
— Tampa Bay (A.L.)	OF-DH	109	338	51	94	9	9	1	17	29	69	1	2	26-12	.278	.337	.367	.704	4	.980
1999— Tampa Bay (A.L.)	OF	79	303	44	81	16	4	2	24	17	63	1	3	9-9	.267	.307	.366	.673	1	.995
— Durham (Int'l)	OF	46	207	38	73	20	3	3	30	16	27	1	2	9-6	.353	.402	.522	.924	4	.966
2000— Tampa Bay (A.L.)	OF	79	303	67	100	24	5	7	40	48	53	3	5	18-5	.330	.425	.512	.937	7	.960
— Tampa Bay (A.L.)	OF-DH	51	159	28	40	5	0	1	16	26	25	2	2	6-7	.252	.362	.302	.664	1	.990
2001— Tampa Bay (A.L.)	OF-DH	128	429	54	117	25	6	6	50	38	81	6	10	12-10	.273	.339	.401	.740	5	.981
2002— Tampa Bay (A.L.)	OF-DH	152	607	87	181	39	14	14	75	55	109	6	9	27-8	.298	.360	.461	.821	3	.993
2003— Seattle (A.L.)	OF	157	600	103	177	37	4	11	75	41	108	8	9	23-5	.295	.346	.425	.771	3	.992
2004— Seattle (A.L.)	OF-DH	157	626	84	179	34	6	14	81	50	98	8	16	21-7	.286	.346	.427	.772	4	.991
Major League totals (7 years)		833	3062	451	869	165	38	49	338	259	553	32	51	124-58	.284	.344	.411	.754	21	.989

ALL-STAR GAME RECORD

	G	AB	R	H	2B	3B	HR	RBI	BB	SO	HBP	GDP	SB-CS	Avg.	OBP	SLG	OPS	E	Avg.
All-Star Game totals (1 year)	1	2	1	1	1	0	0	0	1	1	0	0	1-0	.500	.667	1.000	1.667	0	1.000

WISE, DEWAYNE — OF

PERSONAL: Born February 24, 1978, in Columbia, S.C. ... 6-1/180. ... Bats left, throws left. ... Full name: Larry Dewayne Wise. ... High school: Chapin (S.C.).

TRANSACTIONS/CAREER NOTES: Selected by Cincinnati Reds organization in fifth round of 1997 free-agent draft. ... Selected by Toronto Blue Jays from Reds organization in Rule 5 major league draft (December 13, 1999). ... On disabled list (June 6-September 1, 2000); included rehabilitation assignment to Tennessee. ... Refused minor league assignment and became a free agent (September 30, 2003). ... Signed by Atlanta Braves organization (November 18, 2003). ... On disabled list (June 23-July 15, 2004); included rehabilitation assignments to Rome and Myrtle Beach. ... Claimed on waivers by Detroit Tigers (October 15, 2004).

2004 GAMES PLAYED BY POSITION (MLB): OF—56.

Year Team (League)	Pos.	G	AB	R	H	2B	3B	HR	RBI	BB	SO	HBP	GDP	SB-CS	Avg.	OBP	SLG	OPS	E	Avg.
1997— Billings (Pio.)	OF	62	268	53	84	13	9	7	41	9	47	2	2	18-8	.313	.337	.507	.844	13	.907
1998— Burlington (Midw.)	OF	127	496	61	111	15	9	2	44	41	111	1	4	27-17	.224	.280	.302	.582	7	.972
1999— Rockford (Midwest)	OF	131	502	70	127	20	13	11	81	42	81	7	6	35-13	.253	.312	.410	.722	8	.975
2000— Toronto (A.L.)	OF-DH	28	22	3	3	0	0	0	0	1	5	1	0	1-0	.136	.208	.136	.345	0	1.000
— Tennessee (Sou.)	OF	15	56	10	14	5	2	2	8	7	13	0	1	3-2	.250	.333	.518	.851	4	.882
2001— Tennessee (Sou.)	OF	87	351	44	84	13	6	8	44	21	58	1	6	13-5	.239	.283	.379	.662	5	.976
— Syracuse (Int'l)	OF	3	13	1	3	0	0	0	0	0	8	0	0	0-1	.231	.231	.231	.462	0	1.000
— Dunedin (Fla. St.)	OF	25	103	9	23	3	1	2	16	5	13	0	1	5-0	.223	.252	.330	.582	0	1.000
2002— Tennessee (Sou.)	OF	86	340	59	101	21	4	10	49	29	49	1	4	15-8	.297	.350	.471	.821	4	.981
— Toronto (A.L.)	OF-DH	42	112	14	20	4	1	3	13	4	15	0	0	5-0	.179	.207	.313	.519	0	1.000
2003— Syracuse (Int'l)	OF-DH	80	285	37	62	11	4	10	37	17	72	1	10	11-3	.218	.262	.389	.651	5	.974
2004— Myrtle Beach (Caro.)	OF-DH	4	16	1	4	0	1	0	0	0	6	0	0	0-0	.250	.250	.375	.625	0	1.000
— Rome (S. Atl.)	DH-OF	5	15	4	5	0	0	2	4	1	5	1	0	1-0	.333	.412	.733	1.145	0	1.000
— Richmond (Int'l)	OF	34	118	18	37	4	6	5	16	5	19	0	1	5-0	.314	.341	.576	.918	1	.986
— Atlanta (N.L.)	OF	77	162	24	37	9	4	6	17	9	28	1	1	6-1	.228	.272	.444	.716	0	1.000
American League totals (2 years)		70	134	17	23	4	1	3	13	5	20	1	0	6-0	.172	.207	.284	.491	0	1.000
National League totals (1 year)		77	162	24	37	9	4	6	17	9	28	1	1	6-1	.228	.272	.444	.716	0	1.000
Major League totals (3 years)		147	296	41	60	13	5	9	30	14	48	2	1	12-1	.203	.243	.372	.614	0	1.000

DIVISION SERIES RECORD

Year Team (League)	Pos.	G	AB	R	H	2B	3B	HR	RBI	BB	SO	HBP	GDP	SB-CS	Avg.	OBP	SLG	OPS	E	Avg.
2004— Atlanta (N.L.)	OF	5	5	1	1	1	0	0	0	0	2	0	0	0-0	.200	.200	.400	.600	0	...

WISE, MATT — P

PERSONAL: Born November 18, 1975, in Montclair, Calif. ... 6-4/200. ... Throws right, bats right. ... Full name: Matthew John Wise. ... Name pronounced: WIZE. ... High school: Bonita (Calif.). ... College: Cal State Fullerton.

TRANSACTIONS/CAREER NOTES: Selected by Seattle Mariners organization in 54th round of 1993 free-agent draft; did not sign. ... Selected by Anaheim Angels organization in sixth round of 1997 free-agent draft. ... On disabled list (March 18, 2003-entire season). ... Released by Angels (October 6, 2003). ... Signed by Milwaukee Brewers organization (January 20, 2004).

CAREER HITTING: 0-for-4 (.000), 0 R, 0 2B, 0 3B, 0 HR, 0 RBI.

Year Team (League)	W	L	Pct.	ERA	WHIP	G	GS	CG	ShO	Hld.	Sv.-Opp.	IP	H	R	ER	HR	BB-IBB	SO	Avg.
1997— Boise (N'west)	9	1	.900	3.25	1.40	15	15	0	0	...	0-...	83.0	82	37	30	5	34-0	86	.269
1998— Midland (Texas)	9	10	.474	5.42	1.45	27	27	3	1	...	0-...	167.2	195	111	101	23	48-0	131	.289
1999— Erie (East.)	8	5	.615	3.77	1.29	16	16	3	0	...	0-...	98.0	102	48	41	10	24-0	72	.268
2000— Edmonton (PCL)	9	6	.600	3.69	1.19	19	19	2	1	...	0-...	124.1	122	54	51	10	26-0	82	.258

W

Year	Team (League)	W	L	Pct.	ERA	WHIP	G	GS	CG	ShO	Hld.	Sv.-Opp.	IP	H	R	ER	HR	BB-IBB	SO	Avg.
—	Anaheim (A.L.)	3	3	.500	5.54	1.42	8	6	0	0	0	0-0	37.1	40	23	23	7	13-1	20	.272
2001—	Anaheim (A.L.)	1	4	.200	4.38	1.32	11	9	0	0	0	0-0	49.1	47	27	24	11	18-1	50	.250
—	Salt Lake (PCL)	9	9	.500	5.04	1.22	21	21	0	0	...	0-...	123.1	134	79	69	19	17-0	111	.271
2002—	Salt Lake (PCL)	3	4	.429	5.42	1.50	16	16	0	0	...	0-...	78.0	102	51	47	12	15-0	76	.324
—	Anaheim (A.L.)	0	0	...	3.24	0.96	7	0	0	0	0	0-0	8.1	7	3	3	0	1-0	6	.233
2004—	Indianapolis (Int'l)	1	0	1.000	1.80	0.80	7	1	0	0	...	0-...	20.0	12	4	4	3	4-0	20	.176
—	Milwaukee (N.L.)	1	2	.333	4.44	1.25	30	3	0	0	3	0-0	52.2	51	27	26	3	15-1	30	.252
American League totals (3 years)		4	7	.364	4.74	1.33	26	15	0	0	0	0-0	95.0	94	53	50	18	32-2	76	.258
National League totals (1 year)		1	2	.333	4.44	1.25	30	3	0	0	3	0-0	52.2	51	27	26	3	15-1	30	.252
Major League totals (4 years)		5	9	.357	4.63	1.30	56	18	0	0	3	0-0	147.2	145	80	76	21	47-3	106	.256

WITASICK, JAY — P

PERSONAL: Born August 28, 1972, in Baltimore, Md. ... 6-4/235. ... Throws right, bats right. ... Full name: Gerald Alphonse Witasick. ... Name pronounced: wi-TASS-ik. ... High school: C. Milton Wright (Bel Air, Md.). ... College: Maryland-Baltimore County.

TRANSACTIONS/CAREER NOTES: Selected by St. Louis Cardinals organization in second round of 1993 free-agent draft. ... Traded by Cardinals with OF Allen Battle and Ps Bret Wagner and Carl Dale to Oakland Athletics for P Todd Stottlemyre (January 9, 1996). ... On disabled list (March 31-June 14, 1997); included rehabilitation assignment to Modesto. ... Traded by A's to Kansas City Royals for a player to be named and cash (March 30, 1999); A's acquired P Scott Chiasson to complete deal (June 10, 1999). ... Traded by Royals to San Diego Padres for P Brian Meadows (July 31, 2000). ... Traded by Padres to New York Yankees for IF D'Angelo Jimenez (June 23, 2001). ... Traded by Yankees to San Francisco Giants for OF John Vander Wal (December 13, 2001). ... On disabled list (July 27-August 15, 2002); included rehabilitation assignment to Fresno. ... Signed as a free agent by Padres (December 24, 2002). ... On disabled list (March 21-June 9, 2003); included rehabilitation assignments to Lake Elsinore and Portland. ... On disabled list (August 16-September 18, 2004); included rehabilitation assignment to Portland. ... Released by Padres (October 7, 2004).

CAREER HITTING: 3-for-42 (.071), 0 R, 0 2B, 0 3B, 0 HR, 3 RBI.

Year	Team (League)	W	L	Pct.	ERA	WHIP	G	GS	CG	ShO	Hld.	Sv.-Opp.	IP	H	R	ER	HR	BB-IBB	SO	Avg.
1993—	Johnson City (App.)	4	3	.571	4.12	1.24	12	12	0	0	...	0-...	67.2	65	42	31	8	19-0	74	.246
—	Savannah (S. Atl.)	1	0	1.000	4.50	1.50	1	1	0	0	...	0-...	6.0	7	3	3	0	2-0	8	.280
1994—	Madison (Midw.)	10	4	.714	2.32	1.03	18	18	2	0	...	0-...	112.1	74	36	29	5	42-0	141	.189
1995—	St. Pete. (FSL)	7	7	.500	2.74	1.10	18	18	1	1	...	0-...	105.0	80	39	32	4	36-1	109	.208
—	Arkansas (Texas)	2	4	.333	6.88	1.82	7	7	0	0	...	0-...	34.0	46	29	26	4	16-1	26	.317
1996—	Huntsville (Southern)	0	3	.000	2.30	1.10	25	6	0	0	...	4-...	66.2	47	21	17	3	26-2	63	.195
—	Oakland (A.L.)	1	1	.500	6.23	1.31	12	0	0	0	0	0-1	13.0	12	9	9	5	5-0	12	.245
—	Edmonton (PCL)	0	0	...	4.15	1.73	6	0	0	0	0	2-...	8.2	9	4	4	1	6-0	9	.300
1997—	Modesto (Calif.)	0	1	.000	4.15	1.21	9	2	0	0	...	1-...	17.1	16	9	8	1	5-0	29	.232
—	Edmonton (PCL)	3	2	.600	4.28	1.46	13	1	0	0	...	0-...	27.1	25	13	13	3	15-3	17	.243
—	Oakland (A.L.)	0	0	...	5.73	1.82	8	0	0	0	1	0-0	11.0	14	7	7	2	6-0	8	.304
1998—	Edmonton (PCL)	11	7	.611	3.87	1.17	27	26	2	1	...	0-...	149.0	126	74	64	19	49-0	155	.226
—	Oakland (A.L.)	1	3	.250	6.33	1.89	7	3	0	0	0	0-0	27.0	36	24	19	9	15-1	29	.310
1999—	Kansas City (A.L.)	9	12	.429	5.57	1.73	32	28	1	1	0	0-0	158.1	191	108	98	23	83-1	102	.304
2000—	Kansas City (A.L.)	3	8	.273	5.94	1.65	22	14	2	0	0	0-0	89.1	109	65	59	15	38-0	67	.301
—	San Diego (N.L.)	3	2	.600	5.64	1.71	11	11	0	0	0	0-0	60.2	69	42	38	9	35-5	54	.284
2001—	San Diego (N.L.)	5	2	.714	1.86	1.19	31	0	0	0	5	1-3	38.2	31	14	8	3	15-3	53	.218
—	New York (A.L.)	3	0	1.000	4.69	1.61	32	0	0	0	5	0-1	40.1	47	27	21	5	18-1	53	.283
2002—	San Francisco (N.L.)	1	0	1.000	2.37	1.16	44	0	0	0	4	0-0	68.1	58	19	18	3	21-3	54	.234
—	Fresno (PCL)	0	0	...	4.50	1.00	2	2	0	0	...	0-...	2.0	1	1	1	0	1-0	2	.143
2003—	Lake Elsinore (Calif.)	0	0	...	5.79	1.30	4	0	0	0	...	0-...	4.2	6	4	3	0	0-0	7	.300
—	Portland (PCL)	0	0	...	3.00	0.80	5	0	0	0	...	1-...	6.0	4	2	2	0	1-0	8	.182
—	San Diego (N.L.)	3	7	.300	4.53	1.47	46	0	0	0	12	2-7	45.2	42	24	23	6	25-4	42	.244
2004—	San Diego (N.L.)	0	1	.000	3.21	1.35	44	0	0	0	2	1-3	61.2	57	28	22	8	26-2	57	.244
American League totals (6 years)		17	24	.415	5.65	1.69	113	45	3	1	6	0-2	339.0	409	240	213	59	165-3	271	.299
National League totals (5 years)		12	12	.500	3.57	1.38	176	11	0	0	23	4-13	275.0	257	127	109	29	122-17	260	.247
Major League totals (9 years)		29	36	.446	4.72	1.55	289	56	3	1	29	4-15	614.0	666	367	322	88	287-20	531	.277

DIVISION SERIES RECORD

Year	Team (League)	W	L	Pct.	ERA	WHIP	G	GS	CG	ShO	Hld.	Sv.-Opp.	IP	H	R	ER	HR	BB-IBB	SO	Avg.
2001—	New York (A.L.)	0	0	...	13.50	3.00	1	0	0	0	0	0-0	.2	1	1	1	0	1-0	0	.500
2002—	San Francisco (N.L.)	0	0	...	0.00	0.00	2	0	0	0	0	0-0	2.1	0	0	0	0	0-0	1	.000
Division series totals (2 years)		0	0	...	3.00	0.67	3	0	0	0	0	0-0	3.0	1	1	1	0	1-0	1	.111

CHAMPIONSHIP SERIES RECORD

Year	Team (League)	W	L	Pct.	ERA	WHIP	G	GS	CG	ShO	Hld.	Sv.-Opp.	IP	H	R	ER	HR	BB-IBB	SO	Avg.
2001—	New York (A.L.)	0	0	...	9.00	2.00	1	0	0	0	0	0-0	3.0	6	3	3	1	0-0	2	.375
2002—	San Francisco (N.L.)	0	1	.000	9.00	1.00	1	0	0	0	0	0-0	1.0	1	1	1	1	0-0	0	.250
Champ. series totals (2 years)		0	1	.000	9.00	1.75	2	0	0	0	0	0-0	4.0	7	4	4	2	0-0	2	.350

WORLD SERIES RECORD

Year	Team (League)	W	L	Pct.	ERA	WHIP	G	GS	CG	ShO	Hld.	Sv.-Opp.	IP	H	R	ER	HR	BB-IBB	SO	Avg.
2001—	New York (A.L.)	0	0	...	54.00	7.50	1	0	0	0	0	0-0	1.1	10	9	8	0	0-0	4	.714
2002—	San Francisco (N.L.)	0	0	...	54.00	15.00	2	0	0	0	0	0-0	.1	3	2	2	0	2-0	1	.750
World series totals (2 years)		0	0	...	54.00	9.00	3	0	0	0	0	0-0	1.2	13	11	10	0	2-0	5	.722

W

WOLF, RANDY — P

PERSONAL: Born August 22, 1976, in Canoga Park, Calif. ... 6-0/200. ... Throws left, bats left. ... Full name: Randall Christopher Wolf. ... High school: El Camino Real (Woodland Hills, Calif.). ... College: Pepperdine.

TRANSACTIONS/CAREER NOTES: Selected by Los Angeles Dodgers organization in 25th round of 1994 free-agent draft; did not sign. ... Selected by Philadelphia Phillies organization in second round of 1997 free-agent draft. ... On disabled list (August 2-September 1, 2001); included rehabilitation assignments to Scranton/Wilkes-Barre and Reading. ... On disabled list (March 25-April 12, 2002); included rehabilitation assignment to Clearwater. ... On disabled list (June 3-26 and August 29, 2004-remainder of season); included rehabilitation assignment to Reading.

CAREER HITTING: 60-for-306 (.196), 30 R, 15 2B, 0 3B, 4 HR, 29 RBI.

Year Team (League)	W	L	Pct.	ERA	WHIP	G	GS	CG	ShO	Hld.	Sv.-Opp.	IP	H	R	ER	HR	BB-IBB	SO	Avg.
1997— Batavia (N.Y.-Penn.)	4	0	1.000	1.58	0.93	7	7	0	0	...	0-...	40.0	29	8	7	1	8-0	53	.204
1998— Reading (East.)	2	0	1.000	1.44	0.76	4	4	0	0	...	0-...	25.0	15	4	4	0	4-0	33	.172
—Scran./W.B. (I.L.)	9	7	.563	4.62	1.45	24	23	1	0	...	0-...	148.0	167	88	76	16	48-4	118	.285
1999—Scran./W.B. (I.L.)	4	5	.444	3.61	1.32	12	12	0	0	...	0-...	77.1	73	36	31	8	29-1	72	.247
—Philadelphia (N.L.)	6	9	.400	5.55	1.59	22	21	0	0	...	0-0	121.2	126	78	75	20	67-0	116	.266
2000— Philadelphia (N.L.)	11	9	.550	4.36	1.42	32	32	1	0	...	0-0	206.1	210	107	100	25	83-2	160	.269
2001— Philadelphia (N.L.)	10	11	.476	3.70	1.23	28	25	4	2	0	0-0	163.0	150	74	67	15	51-4	152	.248
—Scran./W.B. (I.L.)	0	1	.000	5.00	1.67	2	2	0	0	...	0-...	9.0	10	6	5	2	5-0	7	.286
—Reading (East.)	0	0	...	4.50	1.17	1	1	0	0	...	0-...	6.0	5	3	3	0	2-0	7	.208
2002— Philadelphia (N.L.)	11	9	.550	3.20	1.12	31	31	3	2	0	0-0	210.2	172	77	75	23	63-5	172	.223
—Clearwater (Fla. St.)	0	0	...	0.00	0.40	1	1	0	0	...	0-...	5.0	1	0	0	0	1-0	8	.071
2003— Philadelphia (N.L.)	16	10	.615	4.23	1.27	33	33	2	2	0	0-0	200.0	176	101	94	27	78-4	177	.233
2004— Reading (East.)	0	0	...	2.25	1.25	1	1	0	0	...	0-...	4.0	5	1	1	0	4-0	4	.333
—Philadelphia (N.L.)	5	8	.385	4.28	1.32	23	23	1	1	0	0-0	136.2	145	73	65	20	36-4	89	.271
Major League totals (6 years)	59	56	.513	4.13	1.31	169	165	11	7	0	0-0	1038.1	979	510	476	130	378-19	866	.250

ALL-STAR GAME RECORD

	W	L	Pct.	ERA	WHIP	G	GS	CG	ShO	Hld.	Sv.-Opp.	IP	H	R	ER	HR	BB-IBB	SO	Avg.
All-Star Game totals (1 year)	0	0	...	9.00	2.00	1	0	0	0	0	0-0	1.0	1	1	1	0	1-0	2	.250

WOMACK, TONY — 2B

PERSONAL: Born September 25, 1969, in Danville, Va. ... 5-9/170. ... Bats left, throws right. ... Full name: Anthony Darrell Womack. ... Name pronounced: WO-mack. ... High school: Gretna (Va.). ... College: Guilford (N.C.).

TRANSACTIONS/CAREER NOTES: Selected by Pittsburgh Pirates organization in seventh round of 1991 free-agent draft. ... Traded by Pirates to Arizona Diamondbacks for OF Paul Weichard and a player to be named (February 26, 1999); Pirates acquired P Jason Boyd to complete deal (August 25, 1999). ... On disabled list (March 26-April 12, 1999); included rehabilitation assignment to Tucson. ... On disabled list (July 23-August 6, 2001); included rehabilitation assignment to Tucson. ... On disabled list (June 29-July 18, 2003); included rehabilitation assignment to El Paso. ... Traded by Diamondbacks to Colorado Rockies for P Mike Watson (July 18, 2003). ... Traded by Rockies to Chicago Cubs for P Enmanuel Ramires (August 19, 2003). ... Signed by Boston Red Sox organization (January 24, 2004). ... Traded by Red Sox to St. Louis Cardinals for P Matt Duff (March 21, 2004).

2004 GAMES PLAYED BY POSITION (MLB): 2B—133.

Year Team (League)	Pos.	G	AB	R	H	2B	3B	HR	RBI	BB	SO	HBP	GDP	SB-CS	Avg.	OBP	SLG	OPS	E	Avg.
1991— Welland (N.Y.-Penn.)	2B-SS	45	166	30	46	3	0	1	8	17	39	0	1	26-5	.277	.344	.313	.658	16	.921
1992— Augusta (S. Atl.)	2B-SS	102	380	62	93	8	3	0	18	41	59	5	2	50-25	.245	.325	.282	.606	40	.923
1993— Salem (Caro.)	SS	72	304	41	91	11	3	2	18	13	34	2	2	28-14	.299	.331	.375	.706	28	.927
—Carolina (Southern)	SS	60	247	41	75	7	2	0	23	17	34	1	3	21-6	.304	.346	.348	.694	11	.961
—Pittsburgh (N.L.)	SS	15	24	5	2	0	0	0	3	3	3	0	0	2-0	.083	.185	.083	.269	1	.971
1994— Buffalo (A.A.)	SS-2B	106	421	40	93	9	2	0	18	19	76	0	0	41-10	.221	.253	.252	.505	22	.957
—Pittsburgh (N.L.)	2B-SS	5	12	4	4	0	0	0	1	2	3	0	0	0-0	.333	.429	.333	.762	2	.818
1995— Calgary (PCL)	2B-SS	30	107	12	30	3	1	0	6	12	11	0	1	7-5	.280	.353	.327	.680	5	.963
—Carolina (Southern)	SS-2B	82	332	52	85	9	4	1	19	19	36	2	2	27-10	.256	.300	.316	.617	18	.953
1996— Calgary (PCL)	S-2-O-DH	131	506	75	151	19	11	1	47	31	79	3	3	37-12	.298	.339	.385	.725	24	.961
—Pittsburgh (N.L.)	OF-2B	17	30	11	10	3	1	0	7	6	1	1	0	2-0	.333	.459	.500	.959	2	.905
1997— Pittsburgh (N.L.)	2B-SS	155	641	85	178	26	9	6	50	43	109	3	6	* 60-7	.278	.326	.374	.700	‡ 20	.975
1998— Pittsburgh (N.L.)	2B-OF-SS	159	655	85	185	26	7	3	45	38	94	0	4	* 58-8	.282	.319	.357	.677	17	.978
1999— Tucson (PCL)	OF	4	16	1	4	1	0	1	3	2	3	0	2	0-1	.250	.333	.500	.833	0	1.000
—Arizona (N.L.)	OF-2B-SS	144	614	111	170	25	10	4	41	52	68	2	4	* 72-13	.277	.332	.370	.702	5	.987
2000— Arizona (N.L.)	SS-OF	146	617	95	167	21	* 14	7	57	30	74	5	6	45-11	.271	.307	.384	.692	18	.970
2001— Arizona (N.L.)	SS-OF	125	481	66	128	19	5	3	30	23	54	6	4	28-7	.266	.307	.345	.652	22	.955
—Tucson (PCL)	SS	4	13	1	5	0	1	0	1	0	1	0	0	0-1	.385	.385	.538	.923	2	.846
2002— Arizona (N.L.)	SS-OF	153	590	90	160	23	5	2	57	46	80	4	9	29-12	.271	.325	.353	.678	20	.964
2003— Arizona (N.L.)	SS	61	219	30	52	10	3	2	15	8	27	2	6	8-3	.237	.270	.338	.607	7	.966
—El Paso (Texas)	SS	4	17	3	5	0	0	0	2	2	2	0	0	3-0	.294	.368	.294	.663	1	.923
—Colorado (N.L.)	SS-2B-OF	21	79	9	15	2	0	0	5	0	9	1	1	3-1	.190	.200	.215	.415	2	.974
—Chicago (N.L.)	2B-SS	21	51	4	12	2	1	0	2	1	11	0	0	2-1	.235	.250	.314	.564	0	1.000
2004— St. Louis (N.L.)	2B	145	553	91	170	22	3	5	38	36	60	3	6	26-5	.307	.350	.385	.735	15	.976
Major League totals (11 years)		1167	4566	686	1253	179	58	35	348	288	593	27	46	335-68	.274	.319	.362	.681	131	.972

DIVISION SERIES RECORD

Year Team (League)	Pos.	G	AB	R	H	2B	3B	HR	RBI	BB	SO	HBP	GDP	SB-CS	Avg.	OBP	SLG	OPS	E	Avg.
1999— Arizona (N.L.)	SS-OF	4	18	2	2	0	1	0	0	0	6	0	0	0-0	.111	.111	.222	.333	2	.833
2001— Arizona (N.L.)	SS	5	17	1	5	1	0	0	1	3	2	0	0	0-1	.294	.400	.353	.753	2	.905

W

Year Team (League)	Pos.	G	AB	R	H	2B	3B	HR	RBI	BB	SO	HBP	GDP	SB-CS	Avg.	OBP	SLG	OPS	E	Avg.
2002—Arizona (N.L.)	SS	3	13	1	2	0	0	0	0	1	1	0	0	0-0	.154	.214	.154	.368	1	.941
2004—St. Louis (N.L.)	2B	4	19	2	3	0	1	0	1	0	2	0	0	1-0	.158	.158	.263	.421	0	1.000
Division series totals (4 years)		16	67	6	12	1	2	0	2	4	11	0	0	1-1	.179	.225	.254	.479	5	.919

CHAMPIONSHIP SERIES RECORD

Year Team (League)	Pos.	G	AB	R	H	2B	3B	HR	RBI	BB	SO	HBP	GDP	SB-CS	Avg.	OBP	SLG	OPS	E	Avg.
2001—Arizona (N.L.)	SS	4	20	4	4	1	0	0	0	0	0	0	0	0-1	.200	.200	.250	.450	0	1.000
2004—St. Louis (N.L.)	2B	7	26	5	7	1	0	0	1	1	3	0	0	2-0	.269	.296	.308	.604	0	1.000
Champ. series totals (2 years)		11	46	9	11	2	0	0	1	1	5	0	0	2-1	.239	.255	.283	.538	0	1.000

WORLD SERIES RECORD

Year Team (League)	Pos.	G	AB	R	H	2B	3B	HR	RBI	BB	SO	HBP	GDP	SB-CS	Avg.	OBP	SLG	OPS	E	Avg.
2001—Arizona (N.L.)	SS	7	32	3	8	3	0	0	3	1	7	1	1	1-1	.250	.294	.344	.638	1	.968
2004—St. Louis (N.L.)	2B	4	11	1	2	0	0	0	0	1	2	0	0	0-0	.182	.250	.182	.432	0	1.000
World series totals (2 years)		11	43	4	10	3	0	0	3	2	9	1	1	1-1	.233	.283	.302	.585	1	.978

ALL-STAR GAME RECORD

	G	AB	R	H	2B	3B	HR	RBI	BB	SO	HBP	GDP	SB-CS	Avg.	OBP	SLG	OPS	E	Avg.
All-Star Game totals (1 year)	1	1	0	0	0	0	0	0	0	0	0	0	0-0	.000	.000	.000	.000	0	1.000

WOOD, KERRY — P

PERSONAL: Born June 16, 1977, in Irving, Texas. ... 6-5/225. ... Throws right, bats right. ... Full name: Kerry Lee Wood. ... High school: Grand Prairie (Texas).

TRANSACTIONS/CAREER NOTES: Selected by Chicago Cubs organization in first round (fourth pick overall) of 1995 free-agent draft. ... On disabled list (March 31, 1999-entire season). ... On disabled list (March 25-May 2 and July 30-August 22, 2000); included rehabilitation assignments to Daytona and Iowa. ... On suspended list (September 8-11, 2000). ... On disabled list (August 4-September 7, 2001). ... On suspended list (May 14-20, 2004). ... On disabled list (May 20-July 11, 2004); included rehabilitation assignment to Iowa. ... On suspended list (August 16-22, 2004).

RECORDS: Shares major league record for most strikeouts, nine-inning game—20 (May 6, 1998).

HONORS: Named N.L. Rookie Pitcher of the Year by THE SPORTING NEWS (1998). ... Named N.L. Rookie of the Year by Baseball Writers' Association of America (1998).

CAREER HITTING: 54-for-320 (.169), 23 R, 3 2B, 0 3B, 7 HR, 28 RBI.

Year Team (League)	W	L	Pct.	ERA	WHIP	G	GS	CG	ShO	Hld.	Sv.-Opp.	IP	H	R	ER	HR	BB-IBB	SO	Avg.
1995—GC Cubs (GCL)	0	0	...	0.00	0.33	1	1	0	0	...	0-...	3.0	0	0	0	0	1-0	2	.000
—Williamsport (N.Y.-Penn.)	0	0	...	10.38	2.31	2	2	0	0	...	0-...	4.1	5	8	5	0	5-0	5	.278
1996—Daytona (Fla. St.)	10	2	.833	2.91	1.24	22	22	0	0	...	0-...	114.1	72	51	37	6	70-0	136	.179
1997—Orlando (Sou.)	6	7	.462	4.50	1.46	19	19	0	0	...	0-...	94.0	58	49	47	2	79-2	106	.181
—Iowa (Am. Assoc.)	4	2	.667	4.68	1.51	10	10	0	0	...	0-...	57.2	35	35	30	2	52-0	80	.181
1998—Iowa (PCL)	1	0	1.000	0.00	0.60	1	1	0	0	...	0-...	5.0	1	0	0	0	2-0	11	.067
—Chicago (N.L.)	13	6	.684	3.40	1.21	26	26	1	1	0	0-0	166.2	117	69	63	14	85-1	233	.196
1999—Chicago (N.L.)	Did not play.																		
2000—Daytona (Fla. St.)	2	0	1.000	1.50	0.67	2	2	0	0	...	0-...	12.0	3	2	2	0	5-0	17	.081
—Iowa (PCL)	0	0	...	2.57	1.14	1	1	0	0	...	0-...	7.0	4	2	2	1	4-0	7	.174
—Chicago (N.L.)	8	7	.533	4.80	1.45	23	23	1	0	0	0-0	137.0	112	77	73	17	87-0	132	.226
2001—Chicago (N.L.)	12	6	.667	3.36	1.26	28	28	1	1	0	0-0	174.1	127	70	65	16	92-3	217	.202
2002—Chicago (N.L.)	12	11	.522	3.66	1.24	33	33	4	1	0	0-0	213.2	169	92	87	22	97-5	217	.221
2003—Chicago (N.L.)	14	11	.560	3.20	1.19	32	32	4	2	0	0-0	211.0	152	77	75	24	100-2	* 266	.203
2004—Iowa (PCL)	1	0	1.000	0.00	0.60	1	1	0	0	...	0-...	5.0	2	0	0	0	1-0	4	.111
—Chicago (N.L.)	8	9	.471	3.72	1.27	22	22	0	0	0	0-0	140.1	127	62	58	16	51-0	144	.244
Major League totals (6 years)	67	50	.573	3.63	1.26	164	164	11	5	0	0-0	1043.0	804	447	421	109	512-11	1209	.214

DIVISION SERIES RECORD

Year Team (League)	W	L	Pct.	ERA	WHIP	G	GS	CG	ShO	Hld.	Sv.-Opp.	IP	H	R	ER	HR	BB-IBB	SO	Avg.
1998—Chicago (N.L.)	0	1	.000	1.80	1.40	1	1	0	0	0	0-0	5.0	3	1	1	0	4-1	5	.167
2003—Chicago (N.L.)	2	0	1.000	1.76	0.91	2	2	0	0	0	0-0	15.1	7	3	3	1	7-0	18	.132
Division series totals (2 years)	2	1	.667	1.77	1.03	3	3	0	0	0	0-0	20.1	10	4	4	1	11-1	23	.141

CHAMPIONSHIP SERIES RECORD

Year Team (League)	W	L	Pct.	ERA	WHIP	G	GS	CG	ShO	Hld.	Sv.-Opp.	IP	H	R	ER	HR	BB-IBB	SO	Avg.
2003—Chicago (N.L.)	0	1	.000	7.30	1.70	2	2	0	0	0	0-0	12.1	14	10	10	1	7-0	13	.280

ALL-STAR GAME RECORD

	W	L	Pct.	ERA	WHIP	G	GS	CG	ShO	Hld.	Sv.-Opp.	IP	H	R	ER	HR	BB-IBB	SO	Avg.
All-Star Game totals (1 year)	0	0	...	0.00	1.00	1	0	0	0	0	0-0	1.0	1	0	0	0	0-0	2	.250

WOOD, MIKE — P

PERSONAL: Born April 26, 1980, in West Palm Beach, Fla. ... 6-3/210. ... Throws right, bats right. ... Full name: Michael Burton Wood. ... High school: Forest Hill Community (West Palm Beach, Fla.). ... College: North Florida.

TRANSACTIONS/CAREER NOTES: Selected by Oakland Athletics organization in 10th round of 2001 free-agent draft. ... Traded by Oakland Athletics with 3B Mark Teahen to Kansas City Royals as part of three-team deal in which Royals acquired C John Buck from Houston Astros, Athletics acquired P Octavio Dotel from Astros and Astros acquired OF Carlos Beltran from Royals (June 24, 2004).

CAREER HITTING: 0-for-2 (.000), 0 R, 0 2B, 0 3B, 0 HR, 0 RBI.

Year Team (League)	W	L	Pct.	ERA	WHIP	G	GS	CG	ShO	Hld.	Sv.-Opp.	IP	H	R	ER	HR	BB-IBB	SO	Avg.
2001—Vancouver (N'west)	2	0	1.000	1.25	0.97	5	2	0	0	...	0-...	21.2	17	4	3	0	4-0	24	.210
—Modesto (Calif.)	4	3	.571	3.09	0.96	10	9	0	0	...	0-...	58.1	46	22	20	6	10-3	52	.211
2002—Modesto (Calif.)	3	3	.500	3.48	1.14	7	7	0	0	...	0-...	41.1	41	17	16	4	6-0	50	.265
—Midland (Texas)	11	3	.786	3.15	1.25	17	17	0	0	...	0-...	105.2	103	41	37	8	29-0	63	.259

W

Year Team (League)	W	L	Pct.	ERA	WHIP	G	GS	CG	ShO	Hld.	Sv.-Opp.	IP	H	R	ER	HR	BB-IBB	SO	Avg.
2003—Sacramento (PCL)	9	3	.750	3.05	1.20	16	16	0	0	...	0-...	91.1	87	34	31	5	23-1	59	.257
—Oakland (A.L.)	2	1	.667	10.54	2.27	7	1	0	0	0	0-0	13.2	24	17	16	1	7-2	15	.387
2004—Sacramento (PCL)	11	3	.786	2.80	1.19	15	15	1	0	...	0-...	90.0	83	42	28	8	24-1	66	.241
—Kansas City (A.L.)	3	8	.273	5.94	1.40	17	17	0	0	0	0-0	100.0	112	67	66	16	28-3	54	.286
Major League totals (2 years)	5	9	.357	6.49	1.50	24	18	0	0	0	0-0	113.2	136	84	82	17	35-5	69	.300

WOODWARD, CHRIS — SS

PERSONAL: Born June 27, 1976, in Covina, Calif. ... 6-0/185. ... Bats right, throws right. ... Full name: Christopher Michael Woodward. ... High school: Northview (Covina, Calif.). ... Junior college: Mt. San Antonio (Calif.). ... College: Mt. San Antonio (Calif.).

TRANSACTIONS/CAREER NOTES: Selected by Toronto Blue Jays organization in 54th round of 1994 free-agent draft. ... On disabled list (July 1-26, 2001); included rehabilitation assignment to Syracuse. ... On disabled list (June 21-July 11, 2002); included rehabilitation assignment to Dunedin. ... On disabled list (May 12-June 8, 2004); included rehabilitation assignment to Dunedin. ... Refused minor league assignment and became a free agent (October 15, 2004).

2004 GAMES PLAYED BY POSITION (MLB): SS—64, DH—2.

Year Team (League)	Pos.	G	AB	R	H	2B	3B	HR	RBI	BB	SO	HBP	GDP	SB-CS	Avg.	OBP	SLG	OPS	E	Avg.
1995—Medicine Hat (Pio.)	SS	72	241	44	56	8	0	3	21	33	41	6	1	9-4	.232	.336	.303	.639	30	.911
1996—Hagerstown (S. Atl.)	SS	123	424	41	95	24	2	1	48	43	70	5	3	11-3	.224	.300	.297	.597	30	.951
1997—Dunedin (Fla. St.)	SS	91	314	38	92	13	4	1	38	52	52	5	3	4-8	.293	.397	.369	.767	12	.972
1998—Knoxville (Southern)	SS	73	253	36	62	12	0	3	27	26	47	3	4	3-5	.245	.319	.328	.647	11	.971
—Syracuse (Int'l)	SS	25	85	9	17	6	0	2	6	7	20	0	4	1-1	.200	.261	.341	.602	4	.961
1999—Toronto (A.L.)	SS-2B	75	281	46	82	20	3	1	20	38	49	1	5	4-1	.292	.378	.395	.773	11	.966
—Toronto (A.L.)	SS-3B	14	26	1	6	1	0	0	2	2	6	0	1	0-0	.231	.276	.269	.545	2	.944
2000—Toronto (A.L.)	S-3-2-1	37	104	16	19	7	0	3	14	10	28	0	1	1-0	.183	.254	.337	.591	5	.963
—Syracuse (Int'l)	2B-3B-SS	37	143	23	46	13	2	5	25	11	30	0	2	2-0	.322	.370	.545	.916	2	.988
2001—Toronto (A.L.)	2-3-S-1-DH	37	63	9	12	3	2	2	5	1	14	0	1	0-1	.190	.203	.397	.600	8	.933
—Syracuse (Int'l)	3-S-2-1	51	193	29	59	14	3	11	31	16	40	1	4	0-0	.306	.360	.580	.941	9	.950
2002—Toronto (A.L.)	S-2-1-3-DH	90	312	48	86	13	4	13	45	26	72	3	8	3-0	.276	.330	.468	.797	15	.964
—Dunedin (Fla. St.)	SS	2	6	1	2	0	0	0	0	0	0	1	0	0-0	.333	.429	.333	.762	0	1.000
2003—Toronto (A.L.)	SS	104	349	46	91	22	2	7	45	28	72	3	6	1-2	.261	.316	.395	.711	17	.964
2004—Dunedin (Fla. St.)	SS	6	16	2	5	2	0	1	3	1	2	0	0	0-0	.313	.333	.625	.958	0	1.000
—Toronto (A.L.)	SS-DH	69	213	21	50	13	4	1	24	14	46	1	3	1-2	.235	.283	.347	.630	5	.981
Major League totals (6 years)		351	1067	144	264	59	12	26	135	81	238	7	20	6-5	.247	.300	.398	.699	52	.964

WOOTEN, SHAWN — 1B/3B

PERSONAL: Born July 24, 1972, in Glendora, Calif. ... 5-10/220. ... Bats right, throws right. ... Full name: William Shawn Wooten. ... High school: South Hills (Covina, Calif.). ... Junior college: Mt. San Antonio (Calif.). ... College: Mt. San Antonio (Calif.).

TRANSACTIONS/CAREER NOTES: Selected by Detroit Tigers organization in 18th round of 1993 free-agent draft. ... Released by Tigers (June 19, 1995). ... Signed by California Angels organization (February 26, 1997). ... Angels franchise renamed Anaheim Angels for 1997 season. ... On disabled list (March 21-July 11, 2002); included rehabilitation assignment to Salt Lake and Rancho Cucamonga. ... Signed as a free agent by Philadelphia Phillies (December 23, 2003). ... Refused minor league assignment and became a free agent (October 12, 2004).

2004 GAMES PLAYED BY POSITION (MLB): 1B—11, 3B—4.

Year Team (League)	Pos.	G	AB	R	H	2B	3B	HR	RBI	BB	SO	HBP	GDP	SB-CS	Avg.	OBP	SLG	OPS	E	Avg.
1993—Bristol (Appal.)	3B-1B-OF	52	177	26	62	12	2	8	39	24	20	3	7	1-2	.350	.432	.576	1.008	10	.956
—Fayetteville (S. Atl.)	3B-1B	5	16	2	4	0	0	1	5	3	3	0	1	0-0	.250	.368	.438	.806	0	1.000
1994—Fayetteville (S. Atl.)	3B-1B	121	439	45	118	25	4	3	61	27	84	11	11	1-3	.269	.324	.364	.689	24	.938
1995—Jacksonville (Sou.)	3B	20	70	4	9	1	0	2	7	1	17	1	3	0-0	.129	.151	.229	.379	5	.921
—Lakeland (Fla. St.)	3B	38	135	11	31	10	1	2	11	10	28	2	2	0-1	.230	.291	.363	.654	7	.942
—Moose Jaw (PRA)		52	201	38	75	12	2	11	55	18	26	...		3-...	.373	...	.617	...	...	...
1996—Moose Jaw (PRA)		77	292	44	89	17	0	12	57	18	46	2	8	2-0	.305	.348	.486	.835	...	...
1997—Cedar Rap. (Midw.)	C-1B	108	353	43	102	23	1	15	75	49	71	6	8	0-1	.289	.379	.487	.866	0	1.000
1998—Lake Elsinore (Calif.)	2B-3B-1B	105	395	56	116	31	0	16	74	38	82	3	9	0-2	.294	.357	.494	.850	1	.999
—Midland (Texas)	1B	8	28	3	9	4	0	1	6	3	4	0	0	0-0	.321	.387	.571	.959	1	.967
1999—Erie (East.)	3B-C-1B	137	518	70	151	27	1	19	88	50	102	10	12	3-1	.292	.360	.458	.818	22	.940
2000—Erie (East.)	C-3B	51	191	32	56	12	2	9	35	17	30	2	3	4-1	.293	.350	.518	.869	9	.970
—Edmonton (PCL)	C-3B-1B	66	252	43	89	21	3	11	42	18	38	3	4	0-0	.353	.401	.591	.993	7	.982
—Anaheim (A.L.)	C-1B	7	9	2	5	1	0	0	1	0	0	0	0	0-0	.556	.556	.667	1.222	0	1.000
2001—Anaheim (A.L.)	DH-1B-3B	79	221	24	69	8	1	8	32	5	42	3	5	2-0	.312	.332	.466	.798	2	.992
2002—Salt Lake (PCL)	1B-3B-C	10	42	2	11	2	0	0	7	0	11	1	1	0-0	.262	.279	.310	.589	1	.976
—Anaheim (A.L.)	DH-1B-C-3B	49	113	13	33	8	0	3	19	6	24	1	3	2-0	.292	.331	.442	.773	0	1.000
—Rancho Cuca. (Calif.)	1B	6	18	2	4	0	0	3	4	4	4	0	1	0-0	.222	.348	.389	.737	0	1.000
2003—Anaheim (A.L.)		98	272	25	66	8	0	7	32	24	45	1	7	0-4	.243	.303	.349	.653	2	.994
2004—Scran./W.B. (I.L.)	3B-DH-1B	61	225	28	66	22	0	4	34	24	29	4	11	0-1	.293	.370	.444	.815	8	.941
—Philadelphia (N.L.)	1B-3B	33	53	2	9	3	0	0	2	2	9	2	0	0-0	.170	.228	.226	.454	0	1.000
American League totals (4 years)		233	615	64	173	25	1	18	84	35	111	5	15	4-4	.281	.322	.413	.735	4	.994
National League totals (1 year)		33	53	2	9	3	0	0	2	2	9	2	4	0-0	.170	.228	.226	.454	0	1.000
Major League totals (5 years)		266	668	66	182	28	1	18	86	37	120	7	19	4-4	.272	.314	.398	.713	4	.995

DIVISION SERIES RECORD

Year Team (League)	Pos.	G	AB	R	H	2B	3B	HR	RBI	BB	SO	HBP	GDP	SB-CS	Avg.	OBP	SLG	OPS	E	Avg.
2002—Anaheim (A.L.)	DH	3	9	4	6	0	0	1	2	0	1	0	0	0-0	.667	.667	1.000	1.667	0	...

W

Year Team (League)	Pos.	G	AB	R	H	2B	3B	HR	RBI	BB	SO	HBP	GDP	SB-CS	Avg.	OBP	SLG	OPS	E	Avg.
2002—Anaheim (A.L.)	DH	3	8	1	2	0	0	0	1	0	3	0	0	0-0	.250	.250	.250	.500	0	...

WORLD SERIES RECORD

Year Team (League)	Pos.	G	AB	R	H	2B	3B	HR	RBI	BB	SO	HBP	GDP	SB-CS	Avg.	OBP	SLG	OPS	E	Avg.
2002—Anaheim (A.L.)	1B	3	2	0	1	0	0	0	0	0	0	0	0	0-0	.500	.500	.500	1.000	0	1.000

WORRELL, TIM — P

PERSONAL: Born July 5, 1967, in Pasadena, Calif. ... 6-4/230. ... Throws right, bats right. ... Full name: Timothy Howard Worrell. ... Name pronounced: wor-RELL. ... High school: Maranatha (Sierra Madre, Calif.). ... College: Biola (Calif.). ... Brother of Todd Worrell, pitcher with two major league teams (1985-97).

TRANSACTIONS/CAREER NOTES: Selected by San Diego Padres organization in 20th round of 1989 free-agent draft. ... On disabled list (April 19, 1994-remainder of season). ... On disabled list (April 24-September 1, 1995); included rehabilitation assignments to Rancho Cucamonga and Las Vegas. ... Traded by Padres with OF Trey Beamon to Detroit Tigers for Ps Dan Miceli and Donne Wall and 3B Ryan Balfe (November 19, 1997). ... Traded by Tigers with OF David Roberts to Cleveland Indians for OF Geronimo Berroa (June 24, 1998). ... Traded by Indians to Oakland Athletics for a player to be named (July 12, 1998); Indians acquired SS Adam Robinson to complete deal (July 27, 1998). ... On disabled list (July 20-August 8, 1999); included rehabilitation assignment to Modesto. ... Signed as a free agent by Baltimore Orioles organization (February 4, 2000). ... Released by Orioles (May 1, 2000). ... Signed by Chicago Cubs organization (May 8, 2000). ... Traded by Cubs to San Francisco Giants for 3B Bill Mueller (November 19, 2000). ... On disabled list (July 9-26, 2001); included rehabilitation assignment to AZL Giants. ... Signed as a free agent by Philadelphia Phillies (December 10, 2003).

CAREER HITTING: 8-for-79 (.101), 6 R, 1 2B, 0 3B, 0 HR, 4 RBI.

Year Team (League)	W	L	Pct.	ERA	WHIP	G	GS	CG	ShO	Hld.	Sv.-Opp.	IP	H	R	ER	HR	BB-IBB	SO	Avg.
1990—Char., S.C. (S. Atl.)	5	8	.385	4.64	1.34	20	19	3	0	...	0-...	110.2	120	65	57	6	28-2	68	.272
1991—Waterloo (Midw.)	8	4	.667	3.34	1.19	14	14	3	2	...	0-...	86.1	70	36	32	5	33-0	83	.217
—High Desert (Calif.)	5	2	.714	4.24	1.54	11	11	2	0	...	0-...	63.2	65	32	30	2	33-0	70	.267
1992—Wichita (Texas)	8	6	.571	2.86	1.17	19	19	1	1	...	0-...	125.2	115	46	40	8	32-0	109	.245
—Las Vegas (PCL)	4	2	.667	4.26	1.26	10	10	1	1	...	0-...	63.1	61	32	30	4	19-0	32	.253
1993—Las Vegas (PCL)	5	6	.455	5.48	1.47	15	14	2	0	...	0-...	87.0	102	61	53	13	26-1	89	.294
—San Diego (N.L.)	2	7	.222	4.92	1.46	21	16	0	0	1	0-0	100.2	104	63	55	11	43-5	52	.269
1994—San Diego (N.L.)	0	1	.000	3.68	0.95	3	3	0	0	0	0-0	14.2	9	7	6	0	5-0	14	.170
1995—Rancho Cuca. (Calif.)	0	2	.000	5.16	1.37	9	3	0	0	0	1-...	22.2	25	17	13	2	6-1	17	.266
—Las Vegas (PCL)	0	2	.000	6.00	1.83	10	3	0	0	0	0-...	24.0	27	21	16	1	17-0	18	.273
—San Diego (N.L.)	1	0	1.000	4.73	1.65	9	0	0	0	0	0-0	13.1	16	7	7	2	6-0	13	.291
1996—San Diego (N.L.)	9	7	.563	3.05	1.22	50	11	0	0	10	1-2	121.0	109	45	41	9	39-1	99	.236
1997—San Diego (N.L.)	4	8	.333	5.16	1.56	60	10	0	0	16	3-7	106.1	116	67	61	14	50-2	81	.280
1998—Detroit (A.L.)	2	6	.250	5.98	1.38	15	9	0	0	0	0-1	61.2	66	42	41	11	19-2	47	.270
—Cleveland (A.L.)	0	0	...	5.06	1.50	3	0	0	0	0	0-0	5.1	6	3	3	0	2-0	2	.300
—Oakland (A.L.)	0	1	.000	4.00	1.17	25	0	0	0	6	0-2	36.0	34	17	16	5	8-1	33	.241
1999—Oakland (A.L.)	2	2	.500	4.15	1.49	53	0	0	0	5	0-5	69.1	69	38	32	6	34-1	62	.256
—Modesto (Calif.)	0	0	...	0.00	0.00	1	1	0	0	0	0-...	2.0	0	0	0	0	0-0	5	.000
2000—Baltimore (A.L.)	2	2	.500	7.36	2.32	5	0	0	0	0	0-0	7.1	12	6	6	3	5-3	5	.353
—Iowa (PCL)	2	0	1.000	5.06	1.31	6	0	0	0	0	0-...	10.2	9	6	6	3	5-1	7	.237
—Chicago (N.L.)	3	4	.429	2.47	1.35	54	0	0	0	12	3-6	62.0	60	20	17	7	24-8	52	.252
2001—San Francisco (N.L.)	2	5	.286	3.45	1.33	73	0	0	0	13	0-3	78.1	71	33	30	4	33-4	63	.240
—Ariz. Giants (Ariz.)	0	0	...	0.00	0.67	1	1	0	0	...	0-...	3.0	1	0	0	0	1-0	2	.125
2002—San Francisco (N.L.)	8	2	.800	2.25	1.18	80	0	0	0	23	0-1	72.0	55	21	18	3	30-2	55	.212
2003—San Francisco (N.L.)	4	4	.500	2.87	1.30	76	0	0	0	1	38-45	78.1	74	35	25	5	28-6	65	.246
2004—Philadelphia (N.L.)	5	6	.455	3.68	1.23	77	0	0	0	20	19-27	78.1	75	36	32	10	21-4	64	.254
American League totals (3 years)	6	11	.353	4.91	1.42	101	9	0	0	11	0-8	179.2	187	106	98	25	68-7	149	.264
National League totals (10 years)	38	44	.463	3.62	1.34	503	40	0	0	96	64-91	725.0	689	334	292	65	279-32	558	.250
Major League totals (12 years)	44	55	.444	3.88	1.35	604	49	0	0	107	64-99	904.2	876	440	390	90	347-39	707	.253

DIVISION SERIES RECORD

Year Team (League)	W	L	Pct.	ERA	WHIP	G	GS	CG	ShO	Hld.	Sv.-Opp.	IP	H	R	ER	HR	BB-IBB	SO	Avg.
1996—San Diego (N.L.)	0	0	...	2.45	1.36	2	0	0	0	0	0-1	3.2	4	1	1	0	1-0	2	.286
2002—San Francisco (N.L.)	0	0	...	12.00	3.00	3	0	0	0	1	0-0	3.0	7	6	4	2	2-0	3	.438
2003—San Francisco (N.L.)	0	1	.000	0.00	2.25	2	0	0	0	0	0-0	2.2	3	2	0	0	3-1	0	.273
Division series totals (3 years)	0	1	.000	4.82	2.14	7	0	0	0	1	0-1	9.1	14	9	5	2	6-1	5	.341

CHAMPIONSHIP SERIES RECORD

Year Team (League)	W	L	Pct.	ERA	WHIP	G	GS	CG	ShO	Hld.	Sv.-Opp.	IP	H	R	ER	HR	BB-IBB	SO	Avg.
2002—San Francisco (N.L.)	2	0	1.000	2.08	0.46	4	0	0	0	0	0-0	4.1	2	1	1	1	0-0	3	.133

WORLD SERIES RECORD

Year Team (League)	W	L	Pct.	ERA	WHIP	G	GS	CG	ShO	Hld.	Sv.-Opp.	IP	H	R	ER	HR	BB-IBB	SO	Avg.
2002—San Francisco (N.L.)	1	1	.500	3.18	0.88	6	0	0	0	2	0-0	5.2	4	3	2	1	1-0	4	.190

WRIGHT, DAN — P

W

PERSONAL: Born December 14, 1977, in Longview, Texas. ... 6-5/240. ... Throws right, bats right. ... Full name: Jonathan Daniel Wright. ... High school: Sullivan South (Kingsport, Tenn.). ... College: Arkansas.

TRANSACTIONS/CAREER NOTES: Selected by Cleveland Indians organization in 19th round of 1996 free-agent draft; did not sign. ... Selected by Chicago White Sox organization in second round of 1999 free-agent draft; choice received as part of compensation for Baltimore Orioles signing Type A free-agent OF Albert Belle. ... On disabled list (March 25-May 5, 2003); included rehabilitation assignment to Charlotte.

CAREER HITTING: 0-for-6 (.000), 0 R, 0 2B, 0 3B, 0 HR, 0 RBI.

Year Team (League)	W	L	Pct.	ERA	WHIP	G	GS	CG	ShO	Hld.	Sv.-Opp.	IP	H	R	ER	HR	BB-IBB	SO	Avg.
1999—Bristol (Appalachian)	2	0	1.000	1.00	1.28	10	0	0	0	...	1-...	18.0	14	8	2	1	9-1	18	.203
—Burlington (Midw.)	0	0	...	6.00	1.33	2	0	0	0	...	0-...	6.0	5	4	4	1	3-0	3	.227
2000—Winston-Salem (Caro.)	9	8	.529	3.74	1.40	21	21	1	0	...	0-...	132.1	135	64	55	4	50-0	106	.266

Year Team (League)	W	L	Pct.	ERA	WHIP	G	GS	CG	ShO	Hld.	Sv.-Opp.	IP	H	R	ER	HR	BB-IBB	SO	Avg.
—Birmingham (Southern) ...	2	4	.333	2.49	1.20	7	7	0	0	...	0-...	43.1	28	15	12	3	24-0	31	.187
2001—Birmingham (Southern) ...	7	7	.500	2.82	1.14	20	20	0	0	...	0-...	134.0	112	54	42	6	41-0	128	.229
—Chicago (A.L.)	5	3	.625	5.70	1.76	13	12	0	0	0	0-0	66.1	78	45	42	12	39-1	36	.300
2002—Chicago (A.L.)	14	12	.538	5.18	1.38	33	33	1	1	0	0-0	196.1	200	124	113	32	71-1	136	.263
2003—Charlotte (Int'l)	1	3	.250	4.64	1.10	8	7	1	0	...	0-...	33.0	25	18	17	5	10-0	25	.212
—Chicago (A.L.)	1	7	.125	6.15	1.59	20	15	0	0	0	1-1	86.1	91	63	59	16	46-2	47	.277
2004—Chicago (A.L.)	0	4	.000	8.15	1.98	4	4	0	0	0	0-0	17.2	24	17	16	5	11-1	6	.320
—Charlotte (Int'l)	0	2	.000	28.69	4.31	2	2	0	0	...	0-...	5.1	17	19	17	4	6-0	3	.515
Major League totals (4 years)	20	26	.435	5.65	1.53	70	64	1	1	0	1-1	366.2	393	249	230	65	167-5	225	.276

WRIGHT, DAVID — 3B

PERSONAL: Born December 20, 1982, in Norfolk, Va. ... 6-0/200. ... Bats right, throws right. ... Full name: David Allen Wright. ... High school: Hickory (Chesapeake, Va.).

TRANSACTIONS/CAREER NOTES: Selected by New York Mets organization in supplemental round ("sandwich pick" between first and second rounds, 38th pick overall) of 2001 free-agent draft; pick acquired as compensation for Colorado Rockies signing Type A free-agent P Mike Hampton.

2004 GAMES PLAYED BY POSITION (MLB): 3B—69.

Year Team (League)	Pos.	G	AB	R	H	2B	3B	HR	RBI	BB	SO	HBP	GDP	SB-CS	Avg.	OBP	SLG	OPS	E	Avg.
2001—Kingsport (Appalachian) ..	3B	36	120	27	36	7	0	4	17	16	30	2	3	9-1	.300	.391	.458	.850	5	.939
2002—Capital City (S. Atl.)	3B	135	496	85	132	30	2	11	93	76	114	5	4	21-5	.266	.367	.401	.768	19	.942
2003—St. Lucie (Fla. St.)	3B	133	466	69	126	39	2	15	75	72	98	4	8	19-5	.270	.369	.459	.828	16	.951
2004—Binghamton (East.)	3B-DH	60	223	44	81	27	0	10	40	39	41	7	5	20-6	.363	.467	.619	1.072	8	.943
—Norfolk (Int'l)	3B	31	114	18	34	8	0	8	17	16	19	2	3	2-4	.298	.388	.579	.958	7	.933
—New York (N.L.)	3B	69	263	41	77	17	1	14	40	14	40	3	7	6-0	.293	.332	.525	.857	11	.942
Major League totals (1 year)		69	263	41	77	17	1	14	40	14	40	3	7	6-0	.293	.332	.525	.857	11	.942

WRIGHT, JAMEY — P

PERSONAL: Born December 24, 1974, in Oklahoma City, Okla. ... 6-6/235. ... Throws right, bats right. ... Full name: Jamey Alan Wright. ... High school: Westmoore (Moore, Okla.).

TRANSACTIONS/CAREER NOTES: Selected by Colorado Rockies organization in first round (28th pick overall) of 1993 free-agent draft. ... On disabled list (May 15-June 8, 1997); included rehabilitation assignment to Salem. ... Traded by Rockies with C Henry Blanco to Milwaukee Brewers as part of three-team deal in which Rockies acquired 3B Jeff Cirillo, P Scott Karl and cash from Brewers, Oakland Athletics acquired P Justin Miller and cash from Rockies and Brewers acquired P Jimmy Haynes from A's (December 13, 1999). ... On disabled list (March 28-May 23, 2000); included rehabilitation assignments to Huntsville and Indianapolis. ... On disabled list (May 25-June 10, 2001). ... On disabled list (April 11-May 24, 2002); included rehabilitation assignment to Indianapolis. ... Traded by Brewers with cash to St. Louis Cardinals for OF Chris Morris and a player to be named (August 29, 2002); Brewers acquired P Mike Matthews to complete deal (September 11, 2002). ... Signed as a free agent by Seattle Mariners organization (January 24, 2003). ... Released by Mariners (March 18, 2003). ... Signed by Milwaukee Brewers organization (March 26, 2003). ... Released by Brewers (April 28, 2003). ... Signed by Texas Rangers organization (May 7, 2003). ... Released by Rangers (June 15, 2003). ... Signed by Kansas City Royals (June 20, 2003). ... Signed as a free agent by Chicago Cubs organization (December 29, 2003). ... Released by Cubs. ... Signed by Royals organization (March 27, 2004). ... Released by Royals (July 21, 2004). ... Signed by Rockies (July 22, 2004).

CAREER HITTING: 44-for-333 (.132), 20 R, 12 2B, 1 3B, 1 HR, 13 RBI.

Year Team (League)	W	L	Pct.	ERA	WHIP	G	GS	CG	ShO	Hld.	Sv.-Opp.	IP	H	R	ER	HR	BB-IBB	SO	Avg.
1993—Ariz. Rockies (Ariz.)	1	3	.250	4.00	1.22	8	8	0	0	...	0-...	36.0	35	19	16	1	9-0	26	.243
1994—Asheville (S. Atl.)	7	14	.333	5.97	1.72	28	27	2	0	...	0-...	143.1	188	107	95	6	59-1	103	.329
1995—Salem (Caro.)	10	8	.556	2.47	1.36	26	26	2	1	...	0-...	171.0	160	74	47	7	72-3	95	.251
—New Haven (East.)	0	1	.000	9.00	3.00	1	1	0	0	...	0-...	3.0	6	6	3	0	3-0	0	.375
1996—New Haven (East.)	5	1	.833	0.81	0.87	7	7	1	1	...	0-...	44.2	27	7	4	0	12-0	54	.180
—Colo. Springs (PCL)	4	2	.667	2.72	1.26	9	9	0	0	...	0-...	59.2	53	20	18	3	22-0	40	.240
—Colorado (N.L.)	4	4	.500	4.93	1.60	16	15	0	0	1	0-0	91.1	105	60	50	8	41-1	45	.298
1997—Colorado (N.L.)	8	12	.400	6.25	1.80	26	26	1	0	0	0-0	149.2	198	113	104	19	71-3	59	.327
—Salem (Caro.)	0	1	.000	9.00	2.00	1	1	0	0	...	0-...	1.0	1	1	1	0	1-0	1	.250
—Colo. Springs (PCL)	1	0	1.000	1.64	1.27	2	2	0	0	...	0-...	11.0	9	3	2	1	5-0	11	.231
1998—Colorado (N.L.)	9	14	.391	5.67	1.60	34	34	1	0	0	0-0	206.1	235	143	130	24	95-3	86	.294
1999—Colorado (N.L.)	4	3	.571	4.87	1.74	16	16	0	0	0	0-0	94.1	110	52	51	10	54-3	49	.308
—Colo. Springs (PCL)	5	7	.417	6.46	1.70	17	16	2	0	...	0-...	100.1	133	87	72	13	38-2	75	.324
2000—Huntsville (Southern)	2	0	1.000	0.00	0.97	2	2	0	0	...	0-...	12.1	7	0	0	0	5-0	10	.175
—Indianapolis (Int'l)	0	0	...	1.80	2.20	1	1	0	0	...	0-...	5.0	8	5	1	0	3-0	7	.364
—Milwaukee (N.L.)	7	9	.438	4.10	1.49	26	25	0	0	0	0-0	164.2	157	81	75	12	88-5	96	.261
2001—Milwaukee (N.L.)	11	12	.478	4.90	1.54	33	33	1	1	0	0-0	194.2	201	115	106	26	98-10	129	.272
2002—Milwaukee (N.L.)	5	13	.278	5.35	1.56	19	19	1	1	0	0-0	114.1	115	72	68	15	63-8	69	.270
—Indianapolis (Int'l)	1	1	.500	4.11	1.37	3	3	0	0	...	0-...	15.1	16	7	7	3	5-0	13	.271
—St. Louis (N.L.)	2	0	1.000	4.80	1.80	4	3	0	0	0	0-0	15.0	15	8	8	2	12-1	8	.259
2003—Indianapolis (Int'l)	1	3	.250	7.36	1.90	7	4	0	0	...	0-...	22.0	32	21	18	5	10-0	17	.344
—Oklahoma (PCL)	2	1	.667	4.12	1.50	7	7	2	1	...	0-...	39.1	38	18	18	1	21-0	40	.260
—Omaha (PCL)	3	5	.375	3.64	1.40	13	12	1	0	...	0-...	76.2	70	35	31	10	38-0	65	.246
—Kansas City (A.L.)	1	2	.333	4.26	1.34	4	4	2	1	0	0-0	25.1	23	14	12	1	11-0	19	.245
2004—Omaha (PCL)	8	6	.571	4.21	1.39	18	18	1	0	...	0-...	104.2	111	58	49	13	35-0	70	.273
—Colorado (N.L.)	2	3	.400	4.12	1.61	14	14	0	0	0	0-0	78.2	82	39	36	8	45-3	41	.266
American League totals (1 year)	1	2	.333	4.26	1.34	4	4	2	1	0	0-0	25.1	23	14	12	1	11-0	19	.245
National League totals (8 years)	52	70	.426	5.10	1.61	188	185	4	2	1	0-0	1109.0	1218	683	628	124	567-37	582	.287
Major League totals (9 years)	53	72	.424	5.08	1.60	192	189	6	3	1	0-0	1134.1	1241	697	640	125	578-37	601	.286

WRIGHT, JARET — P

PERSONAL: Born December 29, 1975, in Anaheim, Calif. ... 6-2/230. ... Throws right, bats right. ... Full name: Jaret Samuel Wright. ... High school: Katella (Anaheim, Calif.). ... Son of Clyde Wright, pitcher with three major league teams (1966-75).

TRANSACTIONS/CAREER NOTES: Selected by Cleveland Indians organization in first round (10th pick overall) of 1994 free-agent draft. ... On suspended list (May 10-16, 1999). ... On disabled list (July 19-August 3 and August 9-September 10, 1999); included rehabilitation assignments to Buffalo and Akron. ... On disabled list (May

W

12-27 and June 3, 2000-remainder of season); included rehabilitation assignments to Buffalo and Akron. ... On disabled list (March 31-May 19 and September 1, 2001-remainder of season); included rehabilitation assignments to Buffalo and Akron. ... On disabled list (March 30-July 20, 2002); included rehabilitation assignment to Buffalo. ... Refused minor league assignment and became a free agent (October 16, 2002). ... Signed by San Diego Padres (December 10, 2002). ... Claimed on waivers by Atlanta Braves (August 29, 2003).

CAREER HITTING: 11-for-75 (.147), 6 R, 2 2B, 0 3B, 1 HR, 5 RBI.

Year Team (League)	W	L	Pct.	ERA	WHIP	G	GS	CG	ShO	Hld.	Sv.-Opp.	IP	H	R	ER	HR	BB-IBB	SO	Avg.
1994—Burlington (Appalachian) .	0	1	.000	5.40	1.65	4	4	0	0	...	0-...	13.1	13	10	8	1	9-0	16	.260
1995—Columbus (S. Atl.)	5	6	.455	3.00	1.33	24	24	0	0	...	0-...	129.0	93	55	43	9	79-0	113	.205
1996—Kinston (Caro.)	7	4	.636	2.50	1.19	19	19	0	0	...	0-...	101.0	65	32	28	1	55-0	109	.190
1997—Akron (East.)	3	3	.500	3.67	1.22	8	8	1	0	...	0-...	54.0	43	26	22	4	23-2	59	.223
—Buffalo (A.A.)	4	1	.800	1.80	1.09	7	7	1	1	...	0-...	45.0	30	16	9	4	19-0	47	.185
—Cleveland (A.L.)	8	3	.727	4.38	1.28	16	16	0	0	0	0-0	90.1	81	45	44	9	35-0	63	.238
1998—Cleveland (A.L.)	12	10	.545	4.72	1.53	32	32	1	1	0	0-0	192.2	207	109	101	22	87-4	140	.277
1999—Cleveland (A.L.)	8	10	.444	6.06	1.65	26	26	0	0	0	0-0	133.2	144	99	90	18	77-1	91	.277
—Buffalo (Int'l)	0	0	...	0.00	0.00	1	1	0	0	0	0-...	3.0	0	0	0	0	0-0	4	.000
—Akron (East.)	1	0	1.000	0.00	0.80	1	1	0	0	0	0-...	5.0	3	0	0	0	1-0	6	.167
2000—Cleveland (A.L.)	3	4	.429	4.70	1.39	9	9	1	1	0	0-0	51.2	44	27	27	6	28-0	36	.235
—Buffalo (Int'l)	0	0	...	0.00	0.50	1	1	0	0	0	0-...	2.0	0	0	0	0	1-0	1	.000
—Akron (East.)	0	0	...	3.38	0.88	2	2	0	0	0	0-...	8.0	4	3	3	0	3-0	5	.133
2001—Buffalo (Int'l)	3	1	.750	4.71	1.33	7	7	0	0	0	0-...	28.2	25	18	15	3	13-0	28	.234
—Akron (East.)	0	0	...	1.29	0.29	1	1	0	0	0	0-...	7.0	2	1	1	1	0-0	4	.087
—Cleveland (A.L.)	2	2	.500	6.52	2.00	7	7	0	0	0	0-0	29.0	36	22	21	2	22-0	18	.313
2002—Cleveland (A.L.)	2	3	.400	15.71	3.22	8	6	0	0	0	0-0	18.1	40	34	32	3	19-0	12	.435
—Buffalo (Int'l)	5	3	.625	3.88	1.46	10	10	1	0	0	0-...	55.2	57	27	24	5	24-0	43	.268
2003—Portland (PCL)	2	1	.667	1.42	1.20	12	1	0	0	0	0-...	19.0	16	7	3	0	7-0	21	.222
—San Diego (N.L.)	1	5	.167	8.37	2.05	39	0	0	0	1	2-4	47.1	69	44	44	9	28-2	41	.348
—Atlanta (N.L.)	1	0	1.000	2.00	1.11	11	0	0	0	3	0-1	9.0	7	2	2	0	3-0	9	.226
2004—Atlanta (N.L.)	15	8	.652	3.28	1.28	32	32	0	0	0	0-0	186.1	168	79	68	11	70-5	159	.242
American League totals (6 years)	35	32	.522	5.50	1.59	98	96	2	2	0	0-0	515.2	552	336	315	60	268-5	360	.276
National League totals (2 years)	17	13	.567	4.23	1.42	82	32	0	0	4	2-5	242.2	244	125	114	20	101-7	209	.264
Major League totals (8 years)	52	45	.536	5.09	1.54	180	128	2	2	4	2-5	758.1	796	461	429	80	369-12	569	.272

DIVISION SERIES RECORD

Year Team (League)	W	L	Pct.	ERA	WHIP	G	GS	CG	ShO	Hld.	Sv.-Opp.	IP	H	R	ER	HR	BB-IBB	SO	Avg.
1997—Cleveland (A.L.)	2	0	1.000	3.97	1.59	2	2	0	0	0	0-0	11.1	11	6	5	0	7-1	10	.256
1998—Cleveland (A.L.)	0	1	.000	12.46	2.08	1	1	0	0	0	0-0	4.1	7	6	6	2	2-0	6	.350
1999—Cleveland (A.L.)	0	1	.000	22.50	2.50	1	0	0	0	0	0-0	2.0	4	5	5	1	1-0	1	.444
2003—Atlanta (N.L.)	0	0	...	0.00	0.50	4	0	0	0	1	0-0	4.0	0	0	0	0	2-0	4	.000
2004—Atlanta (N.L.)	0	2	.000	9.31	1.55	2	2	0	0	0	0-0	9.2	14	10	10	5	1-0	7	.350
Division series totals (5 years)	2	4	.333	7.47	1.56	10	5	0	0	1	0-0	31.1	36	27	26	8	13-1	28	.290

CHAMPIONSHIP SERIES RECORD

Year Team (League)	W	L	Pct.	ERA	WHIP	G	GS	CG	ShO	Hld.	Sv.-Opp.	IP	H	R	ER	HR	BB-IBB	SO	Avg.
1997—Cleveland (A.L.)	0	0	...	15.00	2.67	1	1	0	0	0	0-0	3.0	6	5	5	3	2-0	3	.400
1998—Cleveland (A.L.)	0	1	.000	8.10	2.25	2	1	0	0	0	0-0	6.2	7	6	6	1	8-0	4	.304
Champ. series totals (2 years)	0	1	.000	10.24	2.38	3	2	0	0	0	0-0	9.2	13	11	11	4	10-0	7	.342

WORLD SERIES RECORD

Year Team (League)	W	L	Pct.	ERA	WHIP	G	GS	CG	ShO	Hld.	Sv.-Opp.	IP	H	R	ER	HR	BB-IBB	SO	Avg.
1997—Cleveland (A.L.)	1	0	1.000	2.92	1.38	2	2	0	0	0	0-0	12.1	7	4	4	2	10-0	12	.167

WUERTZ, MICHAEL   P

PERSONAL: Born December 15, 1978, in Austin, Minn. ... 6-3/205. ... Throws right, bats right. ... Full name: Michael James Wuertz. ... High school: Austin (Minn.).

TRANSACTIONS/CAREER NOTES: Selected by Chicago Cubs organization in 11th round of 1997 free-agent draft.

CAREER HITTING: 0-for-1 (.000), 0 R, 0 2B, 0 3B, 0 HR, 0 RBI.

Year Team (League)	W	L	Pct.	ERA	WHIP	G	GS	CG	ShO	Hld.	Sv.-Opp.	IP	H	R	ER	HR	BB-IBB	SO	Avg.
1998—Williamsport (N.Y.-Penn.)	7	5	.583	3.44	1.14	14	14	1	0	...	0-...	86.1	79	36	33	4	19-0	59	.236
1999—Lansing (Midw.)	11	12	.478	4.80	1.46	28	28	1	0	...	0-...	161.1	191	104	86	11	44-0	127	.290
2000—Daytona (Fla. St.)	12	7	.632	3.78	1.34	28	28	3	2	...	0-...	171.1	166	79	72	15	64-1	142	.253
2001—West Tenn (Sou.)	4	9	.308	3.99	1.36	27	27	1	1	...	0-...	160.0	160	80	71	20	58-2	135	.260
2002—Iowa (PCL)	9	5	.643	5.55	1.65	28	27	0	0	...	0-...	154.0	185	109	95	24	69-3	131	.295
2003—Iowa (PCL)	3	9	.250	4.57	1.41	43	16	0	0	...	1-...	124.0	140	70	63	16	35-8	92	.288
2004—Iowa (PCL)	1	1	.500	2.42	1.01	37	0	0	0	...	19-...	44.2	30	13	12	4	15-2	59	.186
—Chicago (N.L.)	1	0	1.000	4.34	1.34	31	0	0	0	1	1-1	29.0	22	14	14	4	17-1	30	.218
Major League totals (1 year)	1	0	1.000	4.34	1.34	31	0	0	0	1	1-1	29.0	22	14	14	4	17-1	30	.218

WUNSCH, KELLY   P

PERSONAL: Born July 12, 1972, in Houston, Texas. ... 6-5/225. ... Throws left, bats left. ... Full name: Kelly Douglas Wunsch. ... Name pronounced: wunch. ... High school: Bellaire (Texas). ... College: Texas A&M.

TRANSACTIONS/CAREER NOTES: Selected by Atlanta Braves organization in 54th round of 1990 free-agent draft; did not sign. ... Selected by Milwaukee Brewers organization in first round (26th pick overall) of 1993 free-agent draft; pick received as compensation for Toronto Blue Jays signing Type-A free-agent DH Paul Molitor. ... Signed as a free agent by Chicago White Sox organization (November 15, 1999). ... On disabled list (June 18, 2001-remainder of season). ... On disabled list (March 27-May 18, 2002); included rehabilitation assignments to Charlotte. ... On disabled list (June 12-July 25, 2003); included rehabilitation assignment to Charlotte. ... On disabled list (March 31-May 9, 2004); included rehabilitation assignment to Charlotte.

CAREER HITTING: 0-for-0 (.000), 0 R, 0 2B, 0 3B, 0 HR, 0 RBI.

Year Team (League)	W	L	Pct.	ERA	WHIP	G	GS	CG	ShO	Hld.	Sv.-Opp.	IP	H	R	ER	HR	BB-IBB	SO	Avg.
1993—Beloit (Midw.)	1	5	.167	4.83	1.53	12	12	0	0	...	0-...	63.1	58	39	34	5	39-1	61	.245
1994—Beloit (Midw.)	3	10	.231	6.16	1.62	17	17	0	0	...	0-...	83.1	88	69	57	11	47-1	77	.264
—Helena (Pio.)	4	2	.667	5.12	1.61	9	9	1	0	...	0-...	51.0	52	39	29	7	30-0	57	.267
1995—Beloit (Midw.)	4	7	.364	4.20	1.48	14	14	3	1	...	0-...	85.2	90	47	40	7	37-0	66	.280
—Stockton (Calif.)	5	6	.455	5.33	1.72	14	13	1	1	...	0-...	74.1	89	51	44	4	39-0	62	.303
1996—				Did not play.															
1997—Stockton (Calif.)	7	9	.438	3.46	1.42	24	22	2	2	...	0-...	143.0	141	65	55	11	62-0	98	.263
1998—El Paso (Texas)	5	6	.455	5.95	1.56	17	17	1	1	...	0-...	101.1	127	81	67	11	31-0	70	.301
—Louisville (Int'l)	3	1	.750	3.83	1.32	9	8	0	0	...	0-...	51.2	53	23	22	6	15-0	36	.264
1999—Huntsville (Southern)	4	1	.800	1.95	1.24	22	3	0	0	...	1-...	50.2	40	13	11	1	23-1	35	.229
—Louisville (Int'l)	2	1	.667	4.75	1.58	16	2	0	0	...	0-...	41.2	52	23	22	4	14-0	20	.311
2000—Chicago (A.L.)	6	3	.667	2.93	1.29	83	0	0	0	25	1-5	61.1	50	22	20	4	29-1	51	.221
2001—Chicago (A.L.)	2	1	.667	7.66	1.34	33	0	0	0	3	0-2	22.1	21	19	19	4	9-1	16	.247
2002—Charlotte (Int'l)	1	0	1.000	2.25	1.50	10	2	0	0	...	0-...	12.0	13	3	3	0	5-0	9	.295
—Chicago (A.L.)	2	1	.667	3.41	1.42	50	0	0	0	9	0-1	31.2	26	12	12	3	19-1	22	.230
2003—Charlotte (Int'l)	0	1	.000	5.40	1.80	3	0	0	0	...	0-...	3.1	6	3	2	1	0-0	4	.429
—Chicago (A.L.)	0	0	...	2.75	1.17	43	0	0	0	5	0-0	36.0	17	13	11	1	25-4	33	.139
2004—Chicago (A.L.)	0	0	...	0.00	1.50	3	0	0	0	0	0-0	2.0	2	0	0	0	1-0	1	.286
—Charlotte (Int'l)	1	0	1.000	2.93	1.19	27	0	0	0	...	2-...	27.2	21	9	9	1	12-0	29	.216
Major League totals (5 years)	10	5	.667	3.64	1.30	212	0	0	0	42	1-8	153.1	116	66	62	12	83-7	123	.210

DIVISION SERIES RECORD

Year Team (League)	W	L	Pct.	ERA	WHIP	G	GS	CG	ShO	Hld.	Sv.-Opp.	IP	H	R	ER	HR	BB-IBB	SO	Avg.
2000—Chicago (A.L.)	0	1	.000	0.00	3.00	3	0	0	0	0	0-0	.2	2	1	0	0	0-0	0	.500

YAN, ESTEBAN   P

PERSONAL: Born June 22, 1975, in Campina del Seibo, Dominican Republic. ... 6-4/255. ... Throws right, bats right. ... Full name: Esteban Luis Yan. ... Name pronounced: YAHN. ... High school: Escuela Hicayagua (Dominican Republic).

TRANSACTIONS/CAREER NOTES: Signed as a non-drafted free agent by Atlanta Braves organization (November 21, 1990). ... Traded by Braves with OFs Roberto Kelly and Tony Tarasco to Montreal Expos for OF Marquis Grissom (April 6, 1995). ... Traded by Expos to Baltimore Orioles for cash (April 6, 1996). ... Selected by Tampa Bay Devil Rays in first round (18th pick overall) of expansion draft (November 18, 1997). ... On disabled list (June 17-July 15, 1999); included rehabilitation assignment to St. Petersburg. ... On disabled list (June 22-July 12, 2001); included rehabilitation assignment to Orlando. ... Signed as a free agent by Texas Rangers (December 26, 2002). ... Traded by Rangers to St. Louis Cardinals for OF Rick Asadoorian (May 27, 2003). ... Released by Cardinals (August 23, 2003). ... Signed by Detroit Tigers organization (January 20, 2004). ... Released by Tigers (March 30, 2004). ... Re-signed by Tigers (April 2, 2004).

CAREER HITTING: 2-for-2 (1.000), 1 R, 0 2B, 0 3B, 1 HR, 1 RBI.

Year Team (League)	W	L	Pct.	ERA	WHIP	G	GS	CG	ShO	Hld.	Sv.-Opp.	IP	H	R	ER	HR	BB-IBB	SO	Avg.
1991—San Pedro (DSL)	4	1	.800	3.63	1.21	18	11	0	0	...	0-...	72.0	61	36	29	...	26-...	34	...
1992—San Pedro (DSL)	12	3	.800	1.32	0.93	16	16	7	4	...	0-...	115.2	85	37	17	1	23-...	86	...
1993—Danville (Appalachian)	4	7	.364	3.03	1.36	14	14	0	0	...	0-...	71.1	73	46	24	4	24-1	50	.253
1994—Macon (S. Atl.)	11	12	.478	3.27	1.11	28	28	4	3	...	0-...	170.2	155	85	62	15	34-1	121	.242
1995—W.P. Beach (FSL)	6	8	.429	3.07	1.25	24	21	1	0	...	1-...	137.2	139	63	47	3	33-0	89	.265
1996—Bowie (East.)	0	2	.000	5.63	1.63	9	1	0	0	...	0-...	16.0	18	12	10	2	8-0	15	.277
—Baltimore (A.L.)	0	0	...	5.79	1.71	4	0	0	0	0	0-0	9.1	13	7	6	3	3-1	7	.333
—Rochester (Int'l)	5	4	.556	4.27	1.30	22	10	0	0	...	1-...	71.2	75	37	34	6	18-0	61	.269
1997—Rochester (Int'l)	11	5	.688	3.10	1.21	34	12	0	0	...	2-...	119.0	107	54	41	13	37-0	131	.243
—Baltimore (A.L.)	0	1	.000	15.83	2.79	3	2	0	0	0	0-0	9.2	20	18	17	3	7-0	4	.417
1998—Tampa Bay (A.L.)	5	4	.556	3.86	1.34	64	0	0	0	8	1-5	88.2	78	41	38	11	41-2	77	.236
1999—Tampa Bay (A.L.)	3	4	.429	5.90	1.59	50	1	0	0	7	0-3	61.0	77	41	40	8	32-4	46	.326
—St. Pete. (FSL)	0	0	...	0.00	1.00	2	2	0	0	...	0-...	4.0	3	1	0	0	1-0	0	.214
2000—Tampa Bay (A.L.)	7	8	.467	6.21	1.45	43	20	0	0	3	0-2	137.2	158	98	95	26	42-0	111	.285
2001—Tampa Bay (A.L.)	4	6	.400	3.90	1.20	54	0	0	0	0	22-31	62.1	64	34	27	7	11-1	64	.262
—Orlando (Sou.)	0	0	...	3.00	1.00	2	2	0	0	...	0-...	3.0	3	1	1	0	0-0	4	.250
2002—Tampa Bay (A.L.)	7	8	.467	4.30	1.43	55	0	0	0	0	19-27	69.0	70	35	33	10	29-1	53	.259
2003—Texas (A.L.)	0	1	.000	6.94	1.63	15	0	0	0	1	0-0	23.1	31	19	18	5	7-1	25	.307
—St. Louis (N.L.)	2	0	1.000	6.02	1.59	39	0	0	0	3	1-1	43.1	53	29	29	8	16-4	28	.308
2004—Detroit (A.L.)	3	6	.333	3.83	1.43	69	0	0	0	11	7-17	87.0	92	43	37	8	32-5	69	.274
American League totals (9 years)	29	38	.433	5.11	1.47	357	23	0	0	30	49-85	548.0	603	336	311	81	204-15	456	.279
National League totals (1 year)	2	0	1.000	6.02	1.59	39	0	0	0	3	1-1	43.1	53	29	29	8	16-4	28	.308
Major League totals (9 years)	31	38	.449	5.17	1.48	396	23	0	0	33	50-86	591.1	656	365	340	89	220-19	484	.281

YATES, TYLER   P

PERSONAL: Born August 7, 1977, in Lihue, Hawaii. ... 6-4/220. ... Throws right, bats right. ... Full name: Tyler Kali Yates. ... High school: Kauai High (Lihue Kauai, Hawaii). ... College: Hawaii-Hilo.

TRANSACTIONS/CAREER NOTES: Selected by Oakland Athletics organization in 23rd round of 1998 free-agent draft. ... Traded by Athletics with P Mark Guthrie to New York Mets for OF David Justice (December 14, 2001). ... On disabled list (March 21-April 6, 2003); included rehabilitation assignment to St. Lucie.

CAREER HITTING: 1-for-11 (.091), 0 R, 0 2B, 0 3B, 0 HR, 0 RBI.

Year Team (League)	W	L	Pct.	ERA	WHIP	G	GS	CG	ShO	Hld.	Sv.-Opp.	IP	H	R	ER	HR	BB-IBB	SO	Avg.
1998—Ariz. A's (Ariz.)	0	0	...	3.91	1.83	15	0	0	0	...	2-...	23.0	28	12	10	0	14-0	20	.304
—S. Oregon (N'west)	0	0	...	0.00	0.86	2	0	0	0	...	1-...	2.1	2	0	0	0	0-0	1	.222
1999—Visalia (Calif.)	2	5	.286	5.47	1.62	47	1	0	0	...	4-...	82.1	98	64	50	12	35-3	74	.290
2000—Modesto (Calif.)	4	2	.667	2.86	1.29	30	0	0	0	...	1-...	56.2	50	23	18	2	23-4	61	.237
—Midland (Texas)	1	1	.500	6.15	1.63	22	0	0	0	...	0-...	26.1	28	20	18	2	15-3	24	.275
2001—Midland (Texas)	4	6	.400	4.31	1.48	56	0	0	0	...	17-...	62.2	66	39	30	4	27-8	61	.261

Y

Year	Team (League)	W	L	Pct.	ERA	WHIP	G	GS	CG	ShO	Hld.	Sv.-Opp.	IP	H	R	ER	HR	BB-IBB	SO	Avg.
—Sacramento (PCL)		1	0	1.000	0.00	0.75	4	0	0	0	...	1-...	5.1	3	0	0	0	1-0	3	.167
2002—Norfolk (Int'l)		2	2	.500	1.32	1.24	24	0	0	0	...	6-...	34.0	29	10	5	1	13-1	34	.227
2003—St. Lucie (Fla. St.)		1	2	.333	4.31	1.35	14	11	0	0	...	0-...	48.0	41	28	23	5	24-0	49	.232
—Binghamton (Eastern)		1	2	.333	4.35	1.27	8	8	0	0	...	0-...	39.1	33	21	19	4	17-0	36	.223
—Norfolk (Int'l)		1	2	.333	4.05	1.55	4	4	0	0	...	0-...	20.0	22	9	9	1	9-0	15	.289
2004—Norfolk (Int'l)		6	2	.750	3.18	1.26	30	1	0	0	...	4-...	39.2	28	18	14	2	22-0	43	.194
—New York (N.L.)		2	4	.333	6.36	1.84	21	7	0	0	2	0-0	46.2	61	36	33	6	25-3	35	.311
Major League totals (1 year)		2	4	.333	6.36	1.84	21	7	0	0	2	0-0	46.2	61	36	33	6	25-3	35	.311

YOUKILIS, KEVIN — 3B/1B

PERSONAL: Born March 15, 1979, in Cincinnati, Ohio. ... 6-1/220. ... Bats right, throws right. ... Full name: Kevin E. Youkilis. ... High school: Sycamore High (Cincinnati). ... College: Cincinnati.

TRANSACTIONS/CAREER NOTES: Selected by Boston Red Sox organization in eighth round of 2001 free-agent draft. ... On disabled list (August 16-September 1, 2004); included rehabilitation assignment to Lowell.

2004 GAMES PLAYED BY POSITION (MLB): 3B—65, DH—2.

									BATTING										FIELDING	
Year	Team (League)	Pos.	G	AB	R	H	2B	3B	HR	RBI	BB	SO	HBP	GDP	SB-CS	Avg.	OBP	SLG	OPS	E	Avg.
2001—Lowell (NY-Penn)		3B	59	183	52	58	14	2	3	28	70	28	5	0	4-3	.317	.512	.464	.976	12	.936
—Augusta (S. Atl.)		3B	5	12	0	2	0	0	0	0	3	3	1	0	0-0	.167	.375	.167	.542	0	1.000
2002—Augusta (S. Atl.)		3B	15	53	5	15	5	0	0	6	13	8	1	0	0-0	.283	.433	.377	.810	4	.913
—Sarasota (Fla. St.)		1B-3B	76	268	45	79	16	0	3	48	49	37	15	5	0-2	.295	.422	.388	.810	12	.974
—Trenton (East.)		3B	44	160	34	55	10	0	5	26	31	18	5	1	5-4	.344	.462	.500	.962	11	.916
2003—Portland (East.)		3B	94	312	74	102	23	1	6	37	86	40	15	7	7-0	.327	.487	.465	.952	20	.925
—Pawtucket (Int'l)		3B	32	109	9	18	3	0	2	15	18	21	3	2	0-1	.165	.295	.248	.543	4	.952
2004—Pawtucket (Int'l) 3B-1B-DH			38	154	25	41	12	0	3	18	19	28	2	1	2-0	.266	.350	.403	.745	5	.955
—Lowell (NY-Penn)		3B	2	4	1	3	1	1	0	0	2	0	1	0	0-0	.750	.857	1.500	2.333	0	1.000
—Boston (A.L.)		3B-DH	72	208	38	54	11	0	7	35	33	45	4	1	0-1	.260	.367	.413	.780	5	.968
Major League totals (1 year)			72	208	38	54	11	0	7	35	33	45	4	1	0-1	.260	.367	.413	.780	5	.968

DIVISION SERIES RECORD

									BATTING											
Year	Team (League)	Pos.	G	AB	R	H	2B	3B	HR	RBI	BB	SO	HBP	GDP	SB-CS	Avg.	OBP	SLG	OPS	E	Avg.
2004—Boston (A.L.)		3B	1	2	0	0	0	0	0	0	0	1	0	0	0-0	.000	.000	.000	.000	0	...

YOUNG, CHRIS — P

PERSONAL: Born May 25, 1979, in Dallas, Texas. ... 6-10/250. ... Throws right, bats right. ... Full name: Christopher Ryan Young. ... High school: Highland Park (Dallas). ... College: Princeton.

TRANSACTIONS/CAREER NOTES: Selected by Pittsburgh Pirates organization in third round of 2000 free-agent draft. ... Traded by Pirates with P Jon Searles to Montreal Expos for P Matt Herges (December 20, 2002). ... Traded by Expos with OF Josh McKinley to Texas Rangers for C Einar Diaz and P Justin Echols (April 3, 2004).

CAREER HITTING: 0-for-0 (.000), 0 R, 0 2B, 0 3B, 0 HR, 0 RBI.

Year	Team (League)	W	L	Pct.	ERA	WHIP	G	GS	CG	ShO	Hld.	Sv.-Opp.	IP	H	R	ER	HR	BB-IBB	SO	Avg.
2001—Hickory (S. Atl.)		5	3	.625	4.12	1.33	12	12	2	0	...	0-...	74.1	79	39	34	6	20-0	72	.269
2002—Hickory (S. Atl.)		11	9	.550	3.11	1.11	26	26	1	0	...	0-...	144.2	127	57	50	11	34-1	136	.234
2003—Brevard County (FSL)		5	2	.714	1.62	0.62	8	8	0	0	...	0-...	50.0	26	9	9	3	5-0	39	.150
—Harrisburg (Eastern)		4	4	.500	4.01	1.27	15	15	0	0	...	0-...	83.0	83	39	37	9	22-0	64	.259
2004—Frisco (Texas)		6	5	.545	4.48	1.42	18	18	0	0	...	0-...	81	94	48	44	9	31-1	75	.269
—Oklahoma (PCL)		3	0	1.000	1.48	0.96	5	5	1	0	...	0-...	30.1	20	7	5	2	9-0	34	.189
—Texas (A.L.)		3	2	.600	4.71	1.27	7	7	0	0	0	0-0	36.1	36	21	19	7	10-0	27	.250
Major League totals (1 year)		3	2	.600	4.71	1.27	7	7	0	0	0	0-0	36.1	36	21	19	7	10-0	27	.250

YOUNG, DMITRI — 1B/OF

PERSONAL: Born October 11, 1973, in Vicksburg, Miss. ... 6-2/245. ... Bats both, throws right. ... Full name: Dmitri Dell Young. ... High school: Rio Mesa (Oxnard, Calif.).

TRANSACTIONS/CAREER NOTES: Selected by St. Louis Cardinals organization in first round (fourth pick overall) of 1991 free-agent draft. ... On disabled list (May 11-29, 1997); included rehabilitation assignment to Louisville. ... Traded by Cardinals to Cincinnati Reds for P Jeff Brantley (November 10, 1997). ... Selected by Tampa Bay Devil Rays in first round (16th pick overall) of expansion draft (November 18, 1997). ... Traded by Devil Rays to Reds (November 18, 1997), completing deal in which Reds traded OF Mike Kelly to Devil Rays for a player to be named (November 11, 1997). ... Traded by Reds to Detroit Tigers for OF Juan Encarnacion and P Luis Pineda (December 11, 2001). ... On disabled list (April 23-May 14 and July 6, 2002-remainder of season). ... On disabled list (April 7-May 31, 2004); included rehabilitation assignment to Toledo.

2004 GAMES PLAYED BY POSITION (MLB): DH—74, 1B—25, OF—2, 3B—1.

									BATTING										FIELDING	
Year	Team (League)	Pos.	G	AB	R	H	2B	3B	HR	RBI	BB	SO	HBP	GDP	SB-CS	Avg.	OBP	SLG	OPS	E	Avg.
1991—Johnson City (App.)		3B	37	129	22	33	10	0	2	22	21	28	2	1	2-1	.256	.364	.380	.743	5	.932
1992—Springfield (Midw.)		3B	135	493	74	153	36	6	14	72	51	94	5	9	14-13	.310	.378	.493	.871	42	.879
1993—St. Pete. (FSL)		3B-1B	69	270	31	85	13	3	5	43	24	28	2	7	3-4	.315	.369	.441	.810	10	.972
—Arkansas (Texas)		3B-1B	45	166	13	41	11	2	3	21	9	29	2	5	4-4	.247	.294	.392	.685	7	.982
1994—Arkansas (Texas)		1B-OF	125	453	53	123	33	2	8	54	36	60	5	6	0-3	.272	.330	.406	.736	16	.971
1995—Arkansas (Texas)		OF-DH	97	367	54	107	18	6	10	62	30	46	3	11	2-4	.292	.347	.455	.802	9	.931
—Louisville (A.A.)		OF	7	7	3	2	0	0	0	0	1	1	0	0	0-0	.286	.375	.286	.661	1	.750
1996—Louisville (A.A.)		1B	122	459	90	153	31	8	15	64	34	67	1	5	16-5	.333	.378	.534	.912	8	.993
—St. Louis (N.L.)		1B	16	29	3	7	0	0	0	2	4	5	1	1	0-1	.241	.353	.241	.594	1	.976
1997—St. Louis (N.L.) 1B-OF-DH			110	333	38	86	14	3	5	34	38	63	2	8	6-5	.258	.335	.363	.698	13	.981
—Louisville (A.A.)		OF-1B	24	84	10	23	7	0	4	14	13	15	0	1	1-1	.274	.371	.500	.871	1	.985

Y

Year Team (League)	Pos.	G	AB	R	H	2B	3B	HR	RBI	BB	SO	HBP	GDP	SB-CS	Avg.	OBP	SLG	OPS	E	Avg.
1998—Cincinnati (N.L.)	OF-1B	144	536	81	166	48	1	14	83	47	94	2	16	2-4	.310	.364	.481	.846	12	.976
1999—Cincinnati (N.L.)	OF-1B-DH	127	373	63	112	30	2	14	56	30	71	2	11	3-1	.300	.352	.504	.856	4	.982
2000—Cincinnati (N.L.)	OF-1B-DH	152	548	68	166	37	6	18	88	36	80	3	16	0-3	.303	.346	.491	.837	8	.981
2001—Cincinnati (N.L.)	OF-1B-3B	142	540	68	163	28	3	21	69	37	77	5	22	8-5	.302	.350	.481	.832	16	.967
2002—Detroit (A.L.)	DH-1-3-O	54	201	25	57	14	0	7	27	12	39	2	12	2-0	.284	.329	.458	.786	4	.972
2003—Detroit (A.L.)	DH-O-3-1	155	562	78	167	34	7	29	85	58	130	11	16	2-1	.297	.372	.537	.909	10	.947
2004—Toledo (Int'l)	DH	2	10	1	5	1	1	1	5	1	0	0	0	0-0	.500	.545	1.100	1.645	0	...
—Detroit (A.L.)	DH-1-O-3	104	389	72	106	23	2	18	60	33	71	6	8	0-1	.272	.336	.481	.816	0	1.000
American League totals (3 years)		313	1152	175	330	71	9	54	172	103	240	19	36	4-2	.286	.352	.504	.857	14	.975
National League totals (6 years)		691	2359	321	700	157	15	72	332	192	390	15	74	19-19	.297	.351	.468	.818	54	.977
Major League totals (9 years)		1004	3511	496	1030	228	24	126	504	295	630	34	110	23-21	.293	.351	.480	.831	68	.977

DIVISION SERIES RECORD

Year Team (League)	Pos.	G	AB	R	H	2B	3B	HR	RBI	BB	SO	HBP	GDP	SB-CS	Avg.	OBP	SLG	OPS	E	Avg.
1996—St. Louis (N.L.)	Did not play.																			

CHAMPIONSHIP SERIES RECORD

Year Team (League)	Pos.	G	AB	R	H	2B	3B	HR	RBI	BB	SO	HBP	GDP	SB-CS	Avg.	OBP	SLG	OPS	E	Avg.
1996—St. Louis (N.L.)	1B	4	7	1	2	0	1	0	2	0	2	0	0	0-0	.286	.286	.571	.857	0	1.000

YOUNG, ERIC   OF

PERSONAL: Born May 18, 1967, in New Brunswick, N.J. ... 5-8/186. ... Bats right, throws right. ... Full name: Eric Orlando Young. ... High school: New Brunswick (N.J.). ... College: Rutgers.

TRANSACTIONS/CAREER NOTES: Selected by Los Angeles Dodgers organization in 43rd round of 1989 free-agent draft. ... Selected by Colorado Rockies organization in first round (11th pick overall) of expansion draft (November 17, 1992). ... On disabled list (March 22-April 22, 1996); included rehabilitation assignments to New Haven, Salem and Colorado Springs. ... Traded by Rockies to Dodgers for P Pedro Astacio (August 19, 1997). ... On disabled list (July 13-31, 1998). ... On disabled list (July 24-August 13, 1999); included rehabilitation assignment to San Bernardino. ... Traded by Dodgers with P Ismael Valdes to Chicago Cubs for Ps Terry Adams and Chad Ricketts and a player to be named (December 12, 1999); Dodgers acquired P Brian Stephenson to complete deal (December 16, 1999). ... Signed as a free agent by Milwaukee Brewers (January 17, 2002). ... Traded by Brewers to San Francisco Giants for P Greg Bruso (August 19, 2003). ... Signed as a free agent by Texas Rangers (January 6, 2004).

2004 GAMES PLAYED BY POSITION (MLB): OF—53, DH—23, 2B—20, SS—8, 3B—1.

							BATTING												FIELDING	
Year Team (League)	Pos.	G	AB	R	H	2B	3B	HR	RBI	BB	SO	HBP	GDP	SB-CS	Avg.	OBP	SLG	OPS	E	Avg.
1989—GC Dodgers (GCL)	2B	56	197	53	65	11	5	2	22	33	16	3	1	41-10	.330	.432	.467	.899	15	.939
1990—Vero Beach (FSL)	2B-OF	127	460	101	132	23	7	2	50	69	35	6	4	76-16	.287	.384	.380	.764	25	.937
1991—San Antonio (Texas)	2B-OF	127	461	82	129	17	4	3	35	67	36	2	13	70-26	.280	.373	.354	.726	13	.974
—Albuquerque (PCL)	2B	1	5	0	2	0	0	0	0	0	0	0	0	0-0	.400	.400	.400	.800	0	1.000
1992—Albuquerque (PCL)	2B	94	350	61	118	16	5	3	49	33	18	4	10	28-11	.337	.393	.437	.831	20	.961
—Los Angeles (N.L.)	2B	49	132	9	34	1	0	1	11	8	9	0	3	6-1	.258	.300	.288	.588	9	.957
1993—Colorado (N.L.)	2B-OF	144	490	82	132	16	8	3	42	63	41	4	9	42-19	.269	.355	.353	.708	18	.964
1994—Colorado (N.L.)	OF-2B	90	228	37	62	13	1	7	30	38	17	2	3	18-7	.272	.378	.430	.808	2	.981
1995—Colorado (N.L.)	2B-OF	120	366	68	116	21	•9	6	36	49	29	5	4	35-12	.317	.404	.473	.876	§ 11	.974
1996—New Haven (East.)	2B	3	15	0	1	0	0	0	0	0	3	0	0	0-0	.067	.067	.067	.133	0	1.000
—Salem (Caro.)	2B	3	10	2	3	3	0	0	0	3	1	0	0	2-0	.300	.462	.600	1.062	2	.875
—Colo. Springs (PCL)	2B	7	23	4	6	1	1	0	3	5	1	0	1	0-0	.261	.393	.391	.784	3	.917
—Colorado (N.L.)	2B	141	568	113	184	23	4	8	74	47	31	21	9	* 53-19	.324	.393	.421	.814	12	.985
1997—Colorado (N.L.)	2B	118	468	78	132	29	6	6	45	57	37	5	16	32-12	.282	.363	.408	.771	15	.978
—Los Angeles (N.L.)	2B	37	154	28	42	4	2	2	16	14	17	4	2	13-2	.273	.347	.364	.710	3	.979
1998—Los Angeles (N.L.)	2B-DH	117	452	78	129	24	1	8	45	45	32	5	4	42-13	.285	.355	.396	.751	13	.976
1999—Los Angeles (N.L.)	2B	119	456	73	128	24	2	2	41	63	26	5	12	51-21	.281	.371	.355	.726	9	.984
—San Bern. (Calif.)	2B	3	12	0	3	0	0	0	0	0	2	0	0	0-0	.250	.250	.250	.500	2	.833
2000—Chicago (N.L.)	2B	153	607	98	180	40	2	6	47	63	39	8	12	54-7	.297	.368	.399	.766	15	.979
2001—Chicago (N.L.)	2B	149	603	90	168	43	4	6	42	42	45	9	15	31-14	.279	.333	.393	.726	12	.981
2002—Milwaukee (N.L.)	2B-DH-OF	138	496	57	139	29	3	3	28	39	38	6	14	31-11	.280	.338	.369	.707	12	.979
2003—Milwaukee (N.L.)	2B-DH	109	404	71	105	18	1	15	31	48	34	4	9	25-7	.260	.344	.421	.764	15	.967
—San Francisco (N.L.)	2B-OF	26	71	9	14	2	0	0	3	9	10	1	3	3-5	.197	.293	.225	.518	1	.989
2004—Texas (A.L.)	O-DH-2-S-3	104	344	55	99	25	2	1	27	43	28	8	9	14-9	.288	.377	.381	.758	9	.952
American League totals (1 year)		104	344	55	99	25	2	1	27	43	28	8	9	14-9	.288	.377	.381	.758	9	.952
National League totals (12 years)		1510	5495	899	1565	287	43	73	489	585	405	79	115	436-151	.285	.360	.393	.752	147	.977
Major League totals (13 years)		1614	5839	954	1664	312	45	74	516	628	433	87	124	450-160	.285	.361	.392	.753	156	.976

DIVISION SERIES RECORD

Year Team (League)	Pos.	G	AB	R	H	2B	3B	HR	RBI	BB	SO	HBP	GDP	SB-CS	Avg.	OBP	SLG	OPS	E	Avg.
1995—Colorado (N.L.)	2B	4	16	3	7	1	0	1	2	2	2	0	0	1-0	.438	.500	.688	1.188	3	.875

ALL-STAR GAME RECORD

		G	AB	R	H	2B	3B	HR	RBI	BB	SO	HBP	GDP	SB-CS	Avg.	OBP	SLG	OPS	E	Avg.
All-Star Game totals (1 year)		1	1	0	0	0	0	0	0	0	0	0	0	0-0	.000	.000	.000	.000	0	1.000

YOUNG, ERNIE   OF

PERSONAL: Born July 8, 1969, in Chicago, Ill. ... 6-1/230. ... Bats right, throws right. ... Full name: Ernest Wesley Young. ... High school: Mendel Catholic (Chicago). ... College: Lewis (Ill.) University.

TRANSACTIONS/CAREER NOTES: Selected by Oakland Athletics organization in 10th round of 1990 free-agent draft. ... Traded by A's to Kansas City Royals for cash (March 17, 1998). ... On disabled list (May 22-June 15, 1998); included rehabilitation assignment to Omaha. ... Signed as a free agent by Arizona Diamondbacks organization (December 17, 1998). ... Released by Diamondbacks (November 22, 1999). ... Signed by St. Louis Cardinals organization (January 19, 2000). ... Signed as a

Y

free agent by San Diego Padres organization (November 20, 2000). ... Signed as a free agent by Cardinals organization (November 21, 2001). ... Traded by Cardinals to Diamondbacks for cash (March 24, 2002). ... Released by Diamondbacks (June 3, 2002). ... Signed as a free agent by Detroit Tigers organization (November 29, 2002). ... Signed as a free agent by Cleveland Indians organization (November 19, 2003).

2004 GAMES PLAYED BY POSITION (MLB): DH—2.

Year Team (League)	Pos.	G	AB	R	H	2B	3B	HR	RBI	BB	SO	HBP	GDP	SB-CS	Avg.	OBP	SLG	OPS	E	Avg.
1990—S. Oregon (N'west)	OF	50	168	34	47	6	2	6	23	29	53	3	2	4-4	.280	.391	.446	.838	2	.971
1991—Madison (Midw.)	OF	114	362	75	92	19	2	15	71	58	115	9	4	20-9	.254	.366	.442	.808	7	.968
1992—Modesto (California)	OF	74	253	55	63	12	4	11	33	47	74	6	5	11-3	.249	.378	.459	.836	6	.958
1993—Modesto (California)	OF	85	301	83	92	18	6	23	71	72	92	4	2	23-7	.306	.442	.635	1.077	3	.984
—Huntsville (Sou.)	OF	45	120	26	25	5	0	5	15	24	36	2	1	8-5	.208	.345	.375	.720	4	.963
1994—Huntsville (Sou.)	OF-DH	72	257	45	89	19	4	14	55	37	45	2	6	5-6	.346	.427	.615	1.041	2	.982
—Oakland (A.L.)	OF-DH	11	30	2	2	1	0	0	3	1	8	0	1	0-0	.067	.097	.100	.197	1	.958
—Tacoma (PCL)	OF-DH	29	102	19	29	4	0	6	16	13	27	2	3	0-5	.284	.370	.500	.870	2	.965
1995—Edmonton (PCL)	OF-DH	95	347	70	96	21	4	15	72	49	73	3	5	2-2	.277	.365	.490	.854	6	.971
—Oakland (A.L.)	OF	26	50	9	10	3	0	2	5	8	12	0	1	0-0	.200	.310	.380	.690	2	.946
1996—Oakland (A.L.)	OF	141	462	72	112	19	4	19	64	52	118	7	13	7-5	.242	.326	.424	.750	1	.997
1997—Oakland (A.L.)	OF	71	175	22	39	7	0	5	15	19	57	2	6	1-3	.223	.303	.349	.652	4	.972
—Edmonton (PCL)	OF-DH	54	195	39	63	10	0	9	45	37	46	6	7	5-2	.323	.442	.554	.954	1	.991
1998—Kansas City (A.L.)	OF	25	53	2	10	3	0	1	3	2	9	1	3	2-1	.189	.232	.302	.534	0	1.000
—Omaha (PCL)	OF-DH	79	297	58	97	13	1	22	55	29	68	5	8	6-4	.327	.395	.599	.994	2	.989
1999—Arizona (N.L.)	OF	6	11	1	2	0	0	0	0	3	2	1	0	0-0	.182	.400	.182	.582	0	1.000
—Tucson (PCL)	OF-DH	126	453	78	133	25	1	30	95	57	129	5	9	4-1	.294	.374	.552	.926	2	.987
2000—Memphis (PCL)	OF-DH	124	453	76	119	16	0	35	98	66	117	4	17	11-1	.263	.359	.530	.888	2	.990
2001—Portland (PCL)	OF	116	409	66	112	21	2	20	67	38	115	14	13	0-3	.274	.355	.482	.837	4	.974
2002—Tucson (PCL)	OF	48	160	29	52	9	1	14	48	24	33	5	5	0-3	.325	.426	.656	1.083	1	.988
2003—Detroit (A.L.)	DH	5	11	0	2	0	0	0	0	4	5	0	1	0-2	.182	.400	.182	.582	0	...
—Toledo (Int'l) DH-OF-1B		128	454	56	120	22	0	21	84	50	119	6	10	10-6	.264	.342	.452	.793	3	.979
2004—Buffalo (Int'l) DH-1B-OF		115	441	71	132	26	2	27	100	40	104	12	7	2-2	.299	.368	.551	.919	2	.993
—Cleveland (A.L.)	DH	3	4	0	2	0	0	0	0	1	2	0	0	0-0	.500	.600	.500	1.100	0	...
American League totals (7 years)		282	785	107	177	33	4	27	90	87	211	10	25	10-11	.225	.309	.381	.689	8	.987
National League totals (1 year)		6	11	1	2	0	0	0	0	3	2	1	0	0-0	.182	.400	.182	.582	0	1.000
Major League totals (8 years)		288	796	108	179	33	4	27	90	90	213	11	25	10-11	.225	.310	.378	.688	8	.987

YOUNG, JASON   P

PERSONAL: Born September 28, 1979, in Oakland, Calif. ... 6-5/214. ... Throws right, bats right. ... Full name: Jason Kariya Young. ... High school: Berkeley (Calif.). ... College: Stanford.

TRANSACTIONS/CAREER NOTES: Selected by Texas Rangers organization in 29th round of 1997 free-agent draft; did not sign. ... Selected by Colorado Rockies organization in second round of 2000 free-agent draft. ... On disabled list (May 22, 2004-remainder of season).

CAREER HITTING: 2-for-9 (.222), 1 R, 1 2B, 0 3B, 0 HR, 1 RBI.

Year Team (League)	W	L	Pct.	ERA	WHIP	G	GS	CG	ShO	Hld.	Sv.-Opp.	IP	H	R	ER	HR	BB-IBB	SO	Avg.
2001—Salem (Caro.)	6	7	.462	3.44	1.26	17	17	2	1	...	0-...	104.2	104	47	40	8	28-0	91	.259
2002—Carolina (Southern)	7	4	.636	2.64	1.14	14	14	1	1	...	0-...	88.2	71	30	26	1	30-0	76	.219
—Colo. Springs (PCL)	6	5	.545	4.97	1.57	13	13	0	0	...	0-...	79.2	87	52	44	10	38-0	74	.272
2003—Colo. Springs (PCL)	6	7	.462	3.95	1.42	23	21	2	1	...	0-...	116.1	128	63	51	10	37-0	99	.272
—Colorado (N.L.)	0	2	.000	8.44	2.02	8	3	0	0	0	0-0	21.1	34	22	20	8	9-0	18	.354
2004—Colo. Springs (PCL)	5	2	.714	4.73	1.65	7	7	0	0	...	0-...	40.0	54	26	21	6	12-0	20	.340
—Colorado (N.L.)	0	1	.000	12.96	2.40	2	2	0	0	0	0-0	8.1	15	12	12	3	5-1	7	.385
Major League totals (2 years)	0	3	.000	9.71	2.12	10	5	0	0	0	0-0	29.2	49	34	32	11	14-1	25	.363

YOUNG, MICHAEL   SS

PERSONAL: Born October 19, 1976, in Covina, Calif. ... 6-1/190. ... Bats right, throws right. ... Full name: Michael Brian Young. ... High school: Bishop Amat (La Puente, Calif.). ... College: UC-Santa Barbara.

TRANSACTIONS/CAREER NOTES: Selected by Baltimore Orioles organization in 25th round of 1994 free-agent draft; did not sign. ... Selected by Toronto Blue Jays organization in fifth round of 1997 free-agent draft. ... Traded by Blue Jays with P Darwin Cubillan to Texas Rangers for P Esteban Loaiza (July 19, 2000).

2004 GAMES PLAYED BY POSITION (MLB): SS—158, DH—2.

Year Team (League)	Pos.	G	AB	R	H	2B	3B	HR	RBI	BB	SO	HBP	GDP	SB-CS	Avg.	OBP	SLG	OPS	E	Avg.
1997—St. Catharines (NY-Penn.)	2B-SS	74	276	49	85	18	3	9	48	33	59	7	6	9-5	.308	.392	.493	.885	18	.946
1998—Hagerstown (S. Atl.) 2B-SS-OF		140	522	86	147	33	5	16	87	55	96	7	12	16-8	.282	.354	.456	.810	13	.977
1999—Dunedin (Fla. St.)	2B-SS	129	495	86	155	36	3	5	83	61	78	4	10	30-6	.313	.389	.428	.818	22	.961
2000—Tennessee (Sou.)	2B-SS	91	345	50	95	24	5	6	47	36	72	1	5	16-5	.275	.340	.426	.766	16	.965
—Tulsa (Texas)	SS	43	188	30	60	13	5	1	32	17	28	0	4	9-3	.319	.368	.457	.826	7	.965
—Texas (A.L.)	2B	2	2	0	0	0	0	0	0	0	1	0	0	0-0	.000	.000	.000	.000	0	...
2001—Oklahoma (PCL)	2B-SS	47	189	28	55	8	0	8	28	20	34	1	6	3-3	.291	.358	.460	.819	6	.968
—Texas (A.L.)	2B	106	386	57	96	18	4	11	49	26	91	3	9	3-1	.249	.298	.402	.699	8	.984
2002—Texas (A.L.) 2-S-3-DH		156	573	77	150	26	8	9	62	41	112	0	14	6-7	.262	.308	.382	.690	9	.988
2003—Texas (A.L.)	2B-SS	160	666	106	204	33	9	14	72	36	103	1	14	13-2	.306	.339	.446	.785	10	.987
2004—Texas (A.L.)	SS-DH	160	690	114	216	33	9	22	99	44	89	1	11	12-3	.313	.353	.483	.836	19	.972
Major League totals (5 years)		584	2317	354	666	110	30	56	282	147	396	5	48	34-13	.287	.328	.433	.762	46	.983

ALL-STAR GAME RECORD

	G	AB	R	H	2B	3B	HR	RBI	BB	SO	HBP	GDP	SB-CS	Avg.	OBP	SLG	OPS	E	Avg.
All-Star Game totals (1 year)	1	2	0	0	0	0	0	0	0	0	0	0	0-0	.000	.000	.000	.000	0	1.000

ZAMBRANO, CARLOS   P

PERSONAL: Born June 1, 1981, in Puerto Cabello, Venezuela. ... 6-5/255. ... Throws right, bats both. ... Full name: Carlos Alberto Zambrano. ... Name pronounced: zam-BRAH-no.

TRANSACTIONS/CAREER NOTES: Signed as a non-drafted free agent by Chicago Cubs organization (July 12, 1997). ... On disabled list (May 10-June 7, 2002); included rehabilitation assignment to Iowa. ... On suspended list (August 3-9, 2002; and August 5-11, 2004).

CAREER HITTING: 35-for-177 (.198), 17 R, 7 2B, 0 3B, 3 HR, 11 RBI.

Year Team (League)	W	L	Pct.	ERA	WHIP	G	GS	CG	ShO	Hld.	Sv.-Opp.	IP	H	R	ER	HR	BB-IBB	SO	Avg.
1998—Ariz. Cubs (Ariz.)	0	1	.000	3.15	1.60	14	2	0	0	...	1-...	40.0	39	17	14	0	25-3	36	.257
1999—Lansing (Midw.)	13	7	.650	4.17	1.38	27	24	2	1	...	0-...	153.1	150	87	71	9	62-1	98	.258
2000—West Tenn (Sou.)	3	1	.750	1.34	0.99	9	9	0	0	...	0-...	60.1	39	14	9	2	21-0	43	.181
—Iowa (PCL)	2	5	.286	3.97	1.66	34	0	0	0	...	6-...	56.2	54	30	25	3	40-2	46	.260
2001—Iowa (PCL)	10	5	.667	3.88	1.27	26	25	1	0	...	0-...	150.2	124	73	65	9	68-1	155	.226
—Chicago (N.L.)	1	2	.333	15.26	2.48	6	1	0	0	0	0-1	7.2	11	13	13	2	8-0	4	.355
2002—Iowa (PCL)	0	0	...	0.00	0.89	3	3	0	0	0	0-0	9.0	2	0	0	0	6-0	11	.069
—Chicago (N.L.)	4	8	.333	3.66	1.45	32	16	0	0	0	0-0	108.1	94	53	44	9	63-2	93	.235
2003—Chicago (N.L.)	13	11	.542	3.11	1.32	32	32	3	1	0	0-0	214.0	188	88	74	9	94-12	168	.239
2004—Chicago (N.L.)	16	8	.667	2.75	1.22	31	31	1	1	0	0-0	209.2	174	73	64	14	81-4	188	.225
Major League totals (4 years)	34	29	.540	3.25	1.32	101	80	4	2	0	0-1	539.2	467	227	195	34	246-18	453	.235

DIVISION SERIES RECORD

Year Team (League)	W	L	Pct.	ERA	WHIP	G	GS	CG	ShO	Hld.	Sv.-Opp.	IP	H	R	ER	HR	BB-IBB	SO	Avg.
2003—Chicago (N.L.)	0	0	...	4.76	1.94	1	1	0	0	0	0-0	5.2	11	3	3	0	0-0	4	.407

CHAMPIONSHIP SERIES RECORD

Year Team (League)	W	L	Pct.	ERA	WHIP	G	GS	CG	ShO	Hld.	Sv.-Opp.	IP	H	R	ER	HR	BB-IBB	SO	Avg.
2003—Chicago (N.L.)	0	1	.000	5.73	1.73	2	2	0	0	0	0-0	11.0	14	8	7	4	5-0	8	.311

ALL-STAR GAME RECORD

	W	L	Pct.	ERA	WHIP	G	GS	CG	ShO	Hld.	Sv.-Opp.	IP	H	R	ER	HR	BB-IBB	SO	Avg.
All-Star Game totals (1 year)	0	0	...	9.00	2.00	1	0	0	0	0	0-0	1.0	1	1	1	0	1-0	1	.250

ZAMBRANO, VICTOR   P

PERSONAL: Born August 6, 1975, in Los Teques, Venezuela. ... 6-0/203. ... Throws right, bats both. ... Full name: Victor Manuel Zambrano. ... High school: Manve Maria Billolobo (Los Teques, Venezuela).

TRANSACTIONS/CAREER NOTES: Signed as a non-drafted free agent by New York Yankees organization (August 19, 1993). ... Played infield in Yankees organization (1994-95). ... Released by Yankees (February 7, 1996). ... Signed by Tampa Bay Devil Rays organization (March 14, 1996). ... Traded by Devil Rays with P Bartolome Fortunato to New York Mets for Ps Scott Kazmir and Jose Diaz (July 30, 2004). ... On disabled list (August 18, 2004-remainder of season).

CAREER HITTING: 2-for-15 (.133), 1 R, 1 2B, 0 3B, 0 HR, 1 RBI.

Year Team (League)	W	L	Pct.	ERA	WHIP	G	GS	CG	ShO	Hld.	Sv.-Opp.	IP	H	R	ER	HR	BB-IBB	SO	Avg.
1996—GC Devil Rays (GCL)	0	0	...	8.10	1.20	1	0	0	0	...	0-...	3.1	4	4	3	0	0-0	6	.250
1997—GC Devil Rays (GCL)	0	0	...	0.00	0.33	2	0	0	0	...	0-...	3.0	1	0	0	0	0-0	2	.100
—Princeton (Appalachian)	0	2	.000	1.82	0.91	20	0	0	0	...	0-...	29.2	18	13	6	1	9-1	36	.159
1998—Char., S.C. (S. Atl.)	6	4	.600	3.38	1.19	48	2	0	0	...	0-...	77.1	72	32	29	5	20-1	89	.246
1999—St. Pete. (FSL)	0	2	.000	4.00	1.67	7	0	0	0	...	0-...	9.0	10	6	4	1	5-0	15	.278
—Orlando (Sou.)	7	2	.778	4.59	1.58	40	4	0	0	...	1-...	82.1	92	55	42	5	38-2	81	.280
2000—Durham (Int'l)	0	6	.000	5.03	1.61	53	0	0	0	...	8-...	62.2	72	38	35	9	29-2	55	.285
2001—Durham (Int'l)	1	2	.333	2.08	1.25	29	0	0	0	...	12-...	30.1	26	10	7	2	12-1	29	.232
—Tampa Bay (A.L.)	6	2	.750	3.16	1.09	36	0	0	0	5	2-6	51.1	38	21	18	6	18-0	58	.201
2002—Tampa Bay (A.L.)	8	8	.500	5.53	1.65	42	11	0	0	6	1-3	114.0	120	77	70	15	68-5	73	.278
—Durham (Int'l)	0	1	.000	1.93	0.93	10	0	0	0	...	1-...	14.0	9	4	3	2	4-0	15	.180
2003—Durham (Int'l)	0	1	.000	4.50	1.50	1	1	0	0	...	0-...	4.0	4	6	2	0	2-0	6	.222
—Tampa Bay (A.L.)	12	10	.545	4.21	1.44	34	28	1	0	2	0-0	188.1	165	97	88	21	* 106-2	132	.237
2004—Tampa Bay (A.L.)	9	7	.563	4.43	1.59	23	22	0	0	1	0-0	128.0	107	68	63	13	• 96-2	109	.230
—New York (N.L.)	2	0	1.000	3.86	1.29	3	3	0	0	0	0-0	14.0	12	9	6	0	6-0	14	.222
American League totals (4 years)	35	27	.565	4.47	1.49	135	61	1	0	14	3-9	481.2	430	263	239	55	288-9	372	.241
National League totals (1 year)	2	0	1.000	3.86	1.29	3	3	0	0	0	0-0	14.0	12	9	6	0	6-0	14	.222
Major League totals (4 years)	37	27	.578	4.45	1.48	138	64	1	0	14	3-9	495.2	442	272	245	55	294-9	386	.240

ZAUN, GREGG   C

PERSONAL: Born April 14, 1971, in Glendale, Calif. ... 5-10/190. ... Bats both, throws right. ... Full name: Gregory Owen Zaun. ... Name pronounced: ZAHN. ... High school: St. Francis (La Canada, Calif.). ... Nephew of Rick Dempsey, coach, Baltimore Orioles, and catcher with six major league teams (1969-92).

TRANSACTIONS/CAREER NOTES: Selected by Baltimore Orioles organization in 17th round of 1989 free-agent draft. ... Traded by Orioles to Florida Marlins (August 23, 1996), completing deal in which Marlins traded P Terry Mathews to Orioles for a player to be named (August 21, 1996). ... Traded by Marlins to Texas Rangers for cash (November 23, 1998). ... Traded by Rangers with OF Juan Gonzalez and P Danny Patterson to Detroit Tigers for Ps Justin Thompson, Francisco Cordero and Alan Webb, OF Gabe Kapler, C Bill Haselman and 2B Frank Catalanotto (November 2, 1999). ... Traded by Tigers to Kansas City Royals for a player to be named or cash (March 7, 2000). ... On disabled list (April 15-May 29, 2000); included rehabilitation assignment to Omaha. ... On disabled list (March 31-July 23, 2001); included rehabilitation assignments to GCL Royals and Omaha. ... Signed as a free agent by Houston Astros (December 11, 2001). ... Released by Astros (August 21, 2003). ... Signed by Colorado Rockies (August 26, 2003). ... Signed as a free agent by Montreal Expos organization (January 13, 2004). ... Released by Expos. ... Signed by Toronto Blue Jays organization (April 10, 2004).

2004 GAMES PLAYED BY POSITION (MLB): C—97, DH—6.

Year Team (League)	Pos.	G	AB	R	H	2B	3B	HR	RBI	BB	SO	HBP	GDP	SB-CS	Avg.	OBP	SLG	OPS	E	Avg.
1990—Wausau (Midw.)	C	37	100	3	13	0	1	1	7	7	17	1	2	0-0	.130	.194	.180	.374	3	.990
—Bluefield (Appal.)	P	61	184	29	55	5	2	2	21	23	15	1	2	5-5	.299	.378	.380	.758	10	.980
1991—Kane Co. (Midw.)	C	113	409	67	112	17	5	4	51	50	41	2	10	4-4	.274	.353	.369	.722	16	.980
1992—Frederick (Carolina)	2B-C	108	383	54	96	18	6	6	52	42	45	3	10	3-5	.251	.324	.376	.700	18	.979

Year Team (League)	Pos.	G	AB	R	H	2B	3B	HR	RBI	BB	SO	HBP	GDP	SB-CS	Avg.	OBP	SLG	OPS	E	Avg.
1993—Bowie (East.)	C-P	79	258	25	79	10	0	3	38	27	26	1	7	4-7	.306	.373	.380	.753	10	.979
—Rochester (Int'l)	C	21	78	10	20	4	2	1	11	6	11	0	1	0-0	.256	.302	.397	.700	4	.975
1994—Rochester (Int'l)	C	123	388	61	92	16	4	7	43	56	72	4	5	4-2	.237	.337	.353	.690	9	.989
1995—Rochester (Int'l)	C-DH	42	140	26	41	13	1	6	18	14	21	3	0	0-3	.293	.367	.529	.896	3	.989
—Baltimore (A.L.)	C	40	104	18	27	5	0	3	14	16	14	0	2	1-1	.260	.358	.394	.753	3	.987
1996—Baltimore (A.L.)	C	50	108	16	25	8	1	1	13	11	15	2	3	0-0	.231	.309	.352	.661	3	.987
—Rochester (Int'l)	C-DH	14	47	11	15	2	0	0	4	11	6	0	0	0-2	.319	.441	.362	.802	2	.965
—Florida (N.L.)	C	10	31	4	9	1	0	1	2	3	5	0	2	1-0	.290	.353	.419	.772	0	1.000
1997—Florida (N.L.)	C-1B	58	143	21	43	10	2	2	20	26	18	2	3	1-0	.301	.415	.441	.856	9	.978
1998—Florida (N.L.)	C-2B	106	298	19	56	12	2	5	29	35	52	1	7	5-2	.188	.274	.292	.566	8	.986
1999—Texas (A.L.)	C-DH	43	93	12	23	2	1	1	12	10	7	0	2	1-0	.247	.314	.323	.637	3	.984
2000—Kansas City (A.L.)	C-2B-1B	83	234	36	64	11	0	7	33	43	34	3	4	7-3	.274	.390	.410	.800	5	.988
—Omaha (PCL)	C	9	25	7	7	3	0	0	3	4	3	0	1	1-1	.280	.379	.400	.779	0	1.000
2001—GC Royals (GCL)	C	6	18	3	1	0	0	0	1	7	5	0	1	0-0	.056	.320	.056	.376	0	1.000
—Omaha (PCL)	C	11	43	5	12	4	0	1	8	3	3	1	2	0-0	.279	.333	.442	.775	1	.985
—Kansas City (A.L.)	C-DH	39	125	15	40	9	0	6	18	12	16	0	2	1-2	.320	.377	.536	.913	5	.975
2002—Houston (N.L.)	C	76	185	18	41	7	1	3	24	12	36	2	4	1-0	.222	.275	.319	.594	5	.985
2003—Houston (N.L.)	C	59	120	9	26	7	0	1	13	14	14	1	5	1-0	.217	.299	.300	.599	4	.976
—Colorado (N.L.)	C	15	46	6	12	1	0	3	8	5	7	0	0	0-1	.261	.333	.478	.812	2	.973
2004—Syracuse (Int'l)	C-DH	7	23	4	7	1	0	0	2	2	5	0	1	1-0	.304	.346	.348	.694	0	1.000
—Toronto (A.L.)	C-DH	107	338	46	91	24	0	6	36	47	61	6	7	0-2	.269	.367	.393	.761	8	.987
American League totals (6 years)		362	1002	143	270	59	2	24	126	139	147	11	20	10-8	.269	.362	.404	.766	27	.985
National League totals (5 years)		324	823	77	187	38	5	15	96	95	132	6	21	9-3	.227	.310	.340	.650	27	.983
Major League totals (10 years)		686	1825	220	457	97	7	39	222	234	279	17	41	19-11	.250	.339	.375	.714	54	.984

DIVISION SERIES RECORD

Year Team (League)	Pos.	G	AB	R	H	2B	3B	HR	RBI	BB	SO	HBP	GDP	SB-CS	Avg.	OBP	SLG	OPS	E	Avg.
1997—Florida (N.L.)						Did not play.														

CHAMPIONSHIP SERIES RECORD

Year Team (League)	Pos.	G	AB	R	H	2B	3B	HR	RBI	BB	SO	HBP	GDP	SB-CS	Avg.	OBP	SLG	OPS	E	Avg.
1997—Florida (N.L.)	C	1	0	0	0	0	0	0	0	0	0	0	0	0-0	...	...	...	...	0	1.000

WORLD SERIES RECORD

Year Team (League)	Pos.	G	AB	R	H	2B	3B	HR	RBI	BB	SO	HBP	GDP	SB-CS	Avg.	OBP	SLG	OPS	E	Avg.
1997—Florida (N.L.)	C	2	2	0	0	0	0	0	0	0	0	0	0	0-0	.000	.000	.000	.000	0	1.000

ZEILE, TODD   3B/1B

PERSONAL: Born September 9, 1965, in Van Nuys, Calif. ... 6-1/200. ... Bats right, throws right. ... Full name: Todd Edward Zeile. ... Name pronounced: ZEAL. ... High school: Hart (Newhall, Calif.). ... College: UCLA. ... Husband of Julianne McNamara, Olympic gold-medal gymnast (1984).

TRANSACTIONS/CAREER NOTES: Selected by Kansas City Royals organization in 30th round of June 1983 free-agent draft; did not sign. ... Selected by St. Louis Cardinals organization in supplemental round ("sandwich pick" between second and third rounds, 55th pick overall) of June 1986 free-agent draft; pick received as compensation for New York Yankees signing Type C free-agent IF Ivan DeJesus. ... On disabled list (April 23-May 9, 1995); included rehabilitation assignment to Louisville. ... Traded by Cardinals with cash to Chicago Cubs for P Mike Morgan, 3B/OF Paul Torres and C Francisco Morales (June 16, 1995). ... Signed as a free agent by Philadelphia Phillies (December 22, 1995). ... Traded by Phillies with OF Pete Incaviglia to Baltimore Orioles for two players to be named (August 29, 1996); Phillies acquired P Calvin Maduro and P Garrett Stephenson to complete deal (September 4, 1996). ... Signed as a free agent by Los Angeles Dodgers (December 8, 1996). ... Traded by Dodgers with C Mike Piazza to Florida Marlins for OFs Gary Sheffield and Jim Eisenreich, 3B Bobby Bonilla, C Charles Johnson and P Manuel Barrios (May 15, 1998). ... Traded by Marlins to Texas Rangers for 3B Jose Santos and P Dan DeYoung (July 31, 1998). ... Signed as a free agent by New York Mets (December 11, 1999). ... Traded by Mets with OF Benny Agbayani, IF/OF Lenny Harris and cash to Colorado Rockies as part of three-team deal in which Mets acquired 1B/OF Ross Gload and P Craig House from Rockies and P Jeff D'Amico, OF Jeromy Burnitz, OF/1B Mark Sweeney, IF Lou Collier and cash from Milwaukee Brewers, and Brewers acquired P Glendon Rusch from Mets and OF Alex Ochoa from Rockies (January 21, 2002). ... Signed as a free agent by New York Yankees (December 18, 2002). ... Released by Yankees (August 18, 2003). ... Signed by Montreal Expos (August 20, 2003). ... Signed as a free agent by Mets (February 8, 2004). ... Career major league pitching: 0-0, 22.50 ERA, 2 G, 2.0 IP, 5 H, 5 R, 5 ER, 2 BB, 1 SO.

2004 GAMES PLAYED BY POSITION (MLB): 1B—67, 3B—46, C—2, P—1.

Year Team (League)	Pos.	G	AB	R	H	2B	3B	HR	RBI	BB	SO	HBP	GDP	SB-CS	Avg.	OBP	SLG	OPS	E	Avg.
1986—Erie (N.Y.-Penn)	C	70	248	40	64	14	1	14	63	37	52	2	3	5-1	.258	.352	.492	.843	8	.983
1987—Springfield (Midw.)	3B-C	130	487	94	142	24	4	25	106	70	85	1	10	1-3	.292	.380	.511	.891	14	.985
1988—Arkansas (Texas)	C-1B-OF	129	430	95	117	33	2	19	75	83	64	1	11	6-5	.272	.388	.491	.879	10	.987
1989—Louisville (A.A.)	3B-C-1B	118	453	71	131	26	3	19	85	45	78	1	10	0-1	.289	.350	.486	.835	6	.991
—St. Louis (N.L.)	C	28	82	7	21	3	1	1	8	9	14	0	1	0-0	.256	.326	.354	.680	4	.971
1990—St. Louis (N.L.) ...	3-C-1-OF	144	495	62	121	25	3	15	57	67	77	2	11	2-4	.244	.333	.398	.731	15	.980
1991—St. Louis (N.L.)	3B	155	565	76	158	36	3	11	81	62	94	5	15	17-11	.280	.353	.412	.765	* 25	.943
1992—St. Louis (N.L.)	3B	126	439	51	113	18	4	7	48	68	70	0	11	7-10	.257	.352	.364	.717	13	.960
—Louisville (A.A.)	3B	21	74	11	23	4	1	5	13	9	13	0	4	0-0	.311	.381	.595	.976	5	.918
1993—St. Louis (N.L.)	3B	157	571	82	158	36	1	17	103	70	76	0	15	5-4	.277	.352	.433	.785	33	.923
1994—St. Louis (N.L.)	3B	113	415	62	111	25	1	19	75	52	56	3	13	1-3	.267	.348	.470	.818	12	.960
1995—Louisville (A.A.)	1B	2	8	0	1	0	0	0	0	0	2	0	0	0-0	.125	.125	.125	.250	1	.923
—St. Louis (N.L.)	1B	34	127	16	37	6	0	5	22	18	23	1	2	1-0	.291	.378	.457	.835	7	.980
—Chicago (N.L.)	3B-OF-1B	79	299	34	68	16	0	9	30	16	53	3	11	0-0	.227	.271	.371	.642	12	.939
1996—Philadelphia (N.L.)	3B-1B	134	500	61	134	24	0	20	80	67	88	1	16	1-1	.268	.353	.436	.789	14	.972
—Baltimore (A.L.)	3B	29	117	17	28	8	0	5	19	15	16	0	2	0-0	.239	.326	.436	.762	3	.964
1997—Los Angeles (N.L.)	3B	160	575	89	154	17	0	31	90	85	112	6	18	8-7	.268	.365	.459	.824	* 26	.931
1998—Los Angeles (N.L.)	3B-1B	40	158	22	40	6	1	7	27	10	24	1	5	1-1	.253	.300	.437	.737	6	.930
—Florida (N.L.)	3B	66	234	37	68	12	1	6	39	31	34	2	4	2-3	.291	.374	.427	.801	5	.971
—Texas (A.L.)	3B	52	180	26	47	14	1	6	28	28	32	1	3	1-0	.261	.358	.450	.808	12	.915
1999—Texas (A.L.)	3B-DH-1B	156	588	80	172	40	1	24	98	56	94	4	20	1-2	.293	.354	.488	.842	§ 25	.941

Year Team (League)	Pos.	G	AB	R	H	2B	3B	HR	RBI	BB	SO	HBP	GDP	SB-CS	Avg.	OBP	SLG	OPS	E	Avg.
2000—New York (N.L.)	1B	153	544	67	146	36	3	22	79	74	85	2	15	3-4	.268	.356	.467	.823	10	.992
2001—New York (N.L.)	1B	151	531	66	141	25	1	10	62	73	102	6	15	1-0	.266	.359	.373	.732	11	.992
2002—Colorado (N.L.)	3B	144	506	61	138	23	0	18	87	66	92	1	27	1-1	.273	.353	.425	.778	* 21	.942
2003—New York (A.L.) 3B-1B-DH	66	186	29	39	8	0	6	23	24	36	0	3	0-0	.210	.294	.349	.644	7	.974
—Montreal (N.L.)	3B	34	113	11	29	2	2	5	19	10	18	3	3	1-0	.257	.331	.442	.773	5	.947
2004—New York (N.L.) 1B-3B-C-P	137	348	30	81	16	0	9	35	44	83	1	13	0-0	.233	.319	.356	.675	10	.982
American League totals (4 years)		303	1071	152	286	71	2	41	168	123	178	5	28	2-2	.267	.341	.452	.793	47	.949
National League totals (15 years)		1855	6502	834	1718	326	21	212	942	822	1101	37	195	51-49	.264	.347	.419	.766	229	.970
Major League totals (16 years)		2158	7573	986	2004	397	23	253	1110	945	1279	42	223	53-51	.265	.346	.423	.769	276	.968

DIVISION SERIES RECORD

Year Team (League)	Pos.	G	AB	R	H	2B	3B	HR	RBI	BB	SO	HBP	GDP	SB-CS	Avg.	OBP	SLG	OPS	E	Avg.
1996—Baltimore (A.L.)	3B	4	19	2	5	1	0	0	0	2	5	0	2	0-0	.263	.333	.316	.649	2	.867
1998—Texas (A.L.)	3B	3	9	0	3	0	0	0	0	0	2	0	0	0-1	.333	.333	.333	.667	0	1.000
1999—Texas (A.L.)	3B	3	10	0	1	0	0	0	0	2	1	0	0	0-0	.100	.250	.100	.350	2	.714
2000—New York (N.L.)	1B	4	14	0	1	1	0	0	0	4	3	0	0	0-0	.071	.278	.143	.421	0	1.000
Division series totals (4 years)		14	52	2	10	2	0	0	0	8	11	0	2	0-1	.192	.300	.231	.531	4	.933

CHAMPIONSHIP SERIES RECORD

Year Team (League)	Pos.	G	AB	R	H	2B	3B	HR	RBI	BB	SO	HBP	GDP	SB-CS	Avg.	OBP	SLG	OPS	E	Avg.
1996—Baltimore (A.L.)	3B	5	22	3	8	0	0	3	5	2	1	0	0	0-0	.364	.417	.773	1.189	1	.909
2000—New York (N.L.)	1B	5	19	1	7	3	0	1	8	2	4	0	0	0-0	.368	.409	.684	1.093	0	1.000
Champ. series totals (2 years)		10	41	4	15	3	0	4	13	4	5	0	0	0-0	.366	.413	.732	1.145	1	.980

WORLD SERIES RECORD

Year Team (League)	Pos.	G	AB	R	H	2B	3B	HR	RBI	BB	SO	HBP	GDP	SB-CS	Avg.	OBP	SLG	OPS	E	Avg.
2000—New York (N.L.)	1B	5	20	1	8	2	0	0	1	1	5	0	0	0-0	.400	.429	.500	.929	0	1.000

ZINTER, ALAN   1B

PERSONAL: Born May 19, 1968, in El Paso, Texas. ... 6-2/195. ... Bats both, throws right. ... Full name: Alan Michael Zinter. ... High school: J.M. Hanks (El Paso, Texas). ... College: Arizona.

TRANSACTIONS/CAREER NOTES: Selected by San Diego Padres organization in 23rd round of June 1986 free-agent draft; did not sign. ... Selected by New York Mets organization in first round (24th pick overall) of 1989 free-agent draft. ... Traded by Mets to Detroit Tigers for 1B Rico Brogna (March 31, 1994). ... Signed as a free agent by Boston Red Sox organization (December 13, 1995). ... Signed as a free agent by Seattle Mariners organization (December 11, 1996). ... Signed by Chicago Cubs organization (December 4, 1997). ... Contract sold by Cubs to Seibu of the Japan Pacific League (April 28, 1999). ... Signed as a free agent by Cubs organization (November 7, 1999). ... Traded by Cubs to Arizona Diamondbacks for cash (August 23, 2000). ... Signed as a free agent by Houston Astros organization (January 8, 2001). ... Signed as a free agent by Arizona Diamondbacks organization (November 12, 2003). ... On disabled list (June 20-August 19, 2004); included rehabilitation assignment to Tucson.

2004 GAMES PLAYED BY POSITION (MLB): 1B—8, DH—2.

Year Team (League)	Pos.	G	AB	R	H	2B	3B	HR	RBI	BB	SO	HBP	GDP	SB-CS	Avg.	OBP	SLG	OPS	E	Avg.
1989—Pittsfield (NYP)	C	12	41	11	15	2	1	2	12	12	4	0	0	0-1	.366	.500	.610	1.110	0	1.000
—St. Lucie (Fla. St.)	C-1B-OF	48	159	17	38	10	0	3	32	18	31	1	5	0-1	.239	.311	.358	.670	8	.964
1990—St. Lucie (Fla. St.)	C	98	333	63	97	19	6	7	63	54	70	1	10	8-1	.291	.386	.447	.833	11	.981
—Jackson (Texas)	C	6	20	2	4	1	0	0	1	3	11	0	1	1-0	.200	.304	.250	.554	0	1.000
1991—Williamsport (East.)	C	124	422	44	93	13	6	9	54	59	106	3	10	3-3	.220	.319	.344	.663	10	.983
1992—Binghamton (East.)	1B	128	431	63	96	13	5	16	50	70	117	4	7	0-0	.223	.337	.387	.724	12	.988
1993—Binghamton (East.) 1-OF-C-3	134	432	68	113	24	4	24	87	90	105	1	4	1-0	.262	.386	.502	.889	11	.986
1994—Toledo (Int'l) 1-DH-OF-C	134	471	66	112	29	5	21	58	69	185	7	3	13-5	.238	.344	.454	.798	8	.989
1995—Toledo (Int'l) 1-DH-OF-C	101	334	42	74	15	4	13	48	36	102	2	5	4-1	.222	.297	.407	.704	5	.991
1996—Pawtucket (Int'l) 1-DH-C-3	108	357	78	96	19	5	26	69	58	123	4	3	5-1	.269	.373	.569	.941	6	.990
1997—Tacoma (PCL) 1-DH-1-O	104	404	69	116	19	4	20	70	64	113	3	7	3-1	.287	.388	.502	.890	9	.986
1998—Iowa (PCL) 1-C-3-DH-O	129	419	82	130	23	1	23	81	75	116	3	10	3-5	.310	.416	.535	.951	10	.987
1999—Iowa (PCL)	1B-C	14	51	7	13	2	0	3	8	5	13	0	0	0-0	.255	.321	.471	.792	0	1.000
—Seibu (Jp. East.)		18	61	15	19	5	0	5	11	17	17	...	...	1-...	.311	...	.639	...	...	...
—Seibu (Jp. Pac.)	C	61	173	20	35	8	0	8	28	35	59	...	...	2-0	.202	...	.387	...	...	...
2000—Iowa (PCL)	1-C-O-3	90	233	27	53	12	2	14	35	39	78	2	3	0-0	.227	.339	.476	.816	7	.981
—Tucson (PCL)	1B-OF	11	36	9	13	5	1	1	5	8	8	0	1	0-0	.361	.477	.639	1.116	0	1.000
2001—New Orleans (PCL)	1-DH-C-OF	104	332	58	88	16	0	19	65	33	85	3	13	1-1	.265	.334	.485	.819	4	.993
2002—New Orleans (PCL)	1B	63	225	30	52	14	0	11	39	22	64	0	3	0-0	.231	.298	.440	.738	1	.998
—Houston (N.L.)	1B-C	39	44	5	6	2	0	2	3	0	19	0	0	0-0	.136	.136	.318	.455	0	1.000
2003—New Orleans (PCL) 1-C-DH-3	114	342	48	87	17	0	17	57	36	77	5	10	1-0	.254	.333	.453	.786	3	.994
2004—Tucson (PCL) 1-3-DH-C	54	179	28	60	12	2	7	39	24	33	1	3	0-0	.335	.403	.542	.945	4	.985
—Arizona (N.L.)	1B-DH	28	34	2	7	2	0	1	6	5	15	0	0	0-0	.206	.300	.353	.653	1	.978
Major League totals (2 years)		67	78	7	13	4	0	3	9	5	34	0	0	0-0	.167	.214	.333	.548	1	.986

ZITO, BARRY   P

PERSONAL: Born May 13, 1978, in Las Vegas, Nev. ... 6-4/215. ... Throws left, bats left. ... Full name: Barry William Zito. ... Name pronounced: ZEE-toe. ... High school: University (San Diego). ... College: USC.

TRANSACTIONS/CAREER NOTES: Selected by Seattle Mariners organization in 59th round of 1996 free-agent draft; did not sign. ... Selected by Texas Rangers organization in third round of 1998 free-agent draft; did not sign. ... Selected by Oakland Athletics organization in first round (ninth pick overall) of 1999 free-agent draft.

HONORS: Named A.L. Pitcher of the Year by THE SPORTING NEWS (2002). ... Named A.L. Cy Young Award winner by Baseball Writers' Association of America (2002).

CAREER HITTING: 0-for-19 (.000), 0 R, 0 2B, 0 3B, 0 HR, 0 RBI.

Year Team (League)	W	L	Pct.	ERA	WHIP	G	GS	CG	ShO	Hld.	Sv.-Opp.	IP	H	R	ER	HR	BB-IBB	SO	Avg.
1999—Visalia (Calif.)	3	0	1.000	2.45	1.07	8	8	0	0	...	0-...	40.1	21	13	11	3	22-0	62	.157
—Midland (Texas)	2	1	.667	4.91	1.50	4	4	0	0	...	0-...	22.0	22	15	12	1	11-0	29	.253
—Vancouver (PCL)	1	0	1.000	1.50	1.17	1	1	0	0	...	0-...	6.0	5	1	1	0	2-0	6	.227

Year	Team (League)	W	L	Pct.	ERA	WHIP	G	GS	CG	ShO	Hld.	Sv.-Opp.	IP	H	R	ER	HR	BB-IBB	SO	Avg.
2000—Sacramento (PCL)		8	5	.615	3.19	1.31	18	18	0	0	...	0-...	101.2	88	44	36	4	45-0	91	.230
—Oakland (A.L.)		7	4	.636	2.72	1.18	14	14	1	1	0	0-0	92.2	64	30	28	6	45-2	78	.195
2001—Oakland (A.L.)		17	8	.680	3.49	1.23	35	• 35	3	2	0	0-0	214.1	184	92	83	18	80-0	205	.230
2002—Oakland (A.L.)	* 23	5	.821	2.75	1.13	35	* 35	1	0	0	0-0	229.1	182	79	70	24	78-2	182	.218
2003—Oakland (A.L.)		14	12	.538	3.30	1.18	35	35	4	1	0	0-0	231.2	186	98	85	19	88-3	146	.219
2004—Oakland (A.L.)		11	11	.500	4.48	1.39	34	34	0	0	0	0-0	213.0	216	116	106	28	81-2	163	.263
Major League totals (5 years)		72	40	.643	3.41	1.23	153	153	9	4	0	0-0	981.0	832	415	372	95	372-9	774	.229

DIVISION SERIES RECORD

Year	Team (League)	W	L	Pct.	ERA	WHIP	G	GS	CG	ShO	Hld.	Sv.-Opp.	IP	H	R	ER	HR	BB-IBB	SO	Avg.
2000—Oakland (A.L.)		1	0	1.000	1.59	1.59	1	1	0	0	0	0-0	5.2	7	1	1	0	2-0	5	.304
2001—Oakland (A.L.)		0	1	.000	1.13	0.38	1	1	0	0	0	0-0	8.0	2	1	1	1	1-0	6	.077
2002—Oakland (A.L.)		1	0	1.000	4.50	1.50	1	1	0	0	0	0-0	6.0	5	3	3	0	4-0	8	.217
2003—Oakland (A.L.)		1	1	.500	3.46	1.00	2	2	0	0	0	0-0	13.0	9	5	5	2	4-0	13	.191
Division series totals (4 years)		3	2	.600	2.76	1.04	5	5	0	0	0	0-0	32.2	23	10	10	3	11-0	32	.193

ALL-STAR GAME RECORD

		W	L	Pct.	ERA	WHIP	G	GS	CG	ShO	Hld.	Sv.-Opp.	IP	H	R	ER	HR	BB-IBB	SO	Avg.
All-Star Game totals (1 year)		0	0	...	0.00	0.00	1	0	0	0	0	0-0	.1	0	0	0	0	0-0	0	.000

Z

ALOU, FELIPE — GIANTS

PERSONAL: Born May 12, 1935, in Haina, Dominican Republic. ... Full name: Felipe Rojas Alou. ... College: University of Santo Domingo (Dominican Republic). ... Father of Moises Alou, outfielder with Chicago Cubs in 2004; brother of Jesus Alou, outfielder with four major league teams (1965-75 and 1978-79); brother of Matty Alou, outfielder with six major league teams (1960-74).

RECORD AS PLAYER

	G	AB	R	H	2B	3B	HR	RBI	Avg.	BB	SO	SB	PO	A	E	Avg.
Major League totals (17 years)	2082	7339	985	2101	359	49	206	852	.286	423	706	107	6537	322	96	.986

RECORD AS MANAGER

BACKGROUND: Spring training instructor, Montreal Expos (1976). ... Coach, Expos (1979-80, 1984 and 1991-92).

HONORS: Named Florida State League Manager of the Year (1990). ... Named N.L. Manager of the Year by THE SPORTING NEWS (1994). ... Named N.L. Manager of the Year by Baseball Writers' Association of America (1994).

Year Team (League)	W	L	Pct.	Pos	Year Team (League)	W	L	Pct.	Pos
1977—West Palm Beach (FSL)	77	65	.542	1S	1991—West Palm Beach (FSL)	33	31	.516	4E
1978—Memphis (Sou.)	71	73	.493	2W	—Second half	39	28	.582	2E
1981—Denver (A.A.)	76	60	.559	2W	1992—Montreal (N.L.)	70	55	.560	2E
1982—Wichita (A.A.)	70	67	.511	2W	1993—Montreal (N.L.)	94	68	.580	2E
1983—Wichita (A.A.)	65	71	.478	3W	1994—Montreal (N.L.)	74	40	.649	—
1985—Indianapolis (A.A.)	61	81	.430	4E	1995—Montreal (N.L.)	66	78	.458	5E
1986—West Palm Beach (FSL)	80	55	.593	1S	1996—Montreal (N.L.)	88	74	.543	2E
1987—West Palm Beach (FSL)	75	63	.543	2S	1997—Montreal (N.L.)	78	84	.481	4E
1988—West Palm Beach (FSL)	41	27	.603	2E	1998—Montreal (N.L.)	65	97	.401	4E
—Second half	30	36	.455	3E	1999—Montreal (N.L.)	68	94	.420	4E
1989—West Palm Beach (FSL)	39	31	.557	2E	2000—Montreal (N.L.)	67	95	.414	4E
—Second half	35	33	.515	2E	2001—Montreal (N.L.)	21	32	.396	—
1990—West Palm Beach (FSL)	49	19	.721	1E	2003—San Francisco (N.L.)	100	61	.621	1W
—Second half	43	21	.672	1E	2004—San Francisco (N.L.)	91	71	.562	2W
					Major League totals (12 years)	882	849	.510	

NOTES:
1977—Lost to St. Petersburg, 2-1, in semifinals....**1978**—Memphis tied one game....**1981**—Defeated Omaha, 4-0, in league championship....**1986**—Defeated Winter Haven, 2-0, in semifinals; lost to St. Petersburg, 3-1, in league championship....**1988**—Defeated Vero Beach, 2-0, in first round; lost to Osceola, 2-0, in semifinals....**1990**—Defeated Lakeland, 2-1, in semifinals; lost to Vero Beach, 2-1, in league championship....**1991**—Defeated Vero Beach, 2-1, in first round; defeated Lakeland, 2-0, in semifinals; defeated Clearwater, 2-0, in league championship....**1992**—Replaced Tom Runnells as Montreal manager with club in fourth place and record of 17-20 (May 22)....**1994**—Montreal was in first place in N.L. East at time of season-ending strike (August 12)....**2003**—Lost to Florida, 3-1, in N.L. Division Series....Career major league postseason record: 1-3.

BAKER, DUSTY — CUBS

PERSONAL: Born June 15, 1949, in Riverside, Calif. ... Full name: Johnnie B. Baker Jr.. ... High school: Del Campo (Fair Oaks, Calif.). ... College: American River College (Calif.).

RECORD AS PLAYER

	G	AB	R	H	2B	3B	HR	RBI	Avg.	BB	SO	SB	PO	A	E	Avg.
Major League totals (19 years)	2039	7117	964	1981	320	23	242	1013	.278	762	926	137	4073	136	59	.986

RECORD AS MANAGER

BACKGROUND: Coach, San Francisco Giants (1988-92). ... Manager, Scottsdale Scorpions, Arizona Fall League (1992).

HONORS: Named N.L. Manager of the Year by Baseball Writers' Association of America (1993, 1997 and 2000). ... Named N.L. Manager of the Year by The Sporting News (1997 and 2000).

Year Team (League)	W	L	Pct.	Pos	Year Team (League)	W	L	Pct.	Pos
1993—San Francisco (N.L.)	103	59	.636	2W	1999—San Francisco (N.L.)	86	76	.531	2W
1994—San Francisco (N.L.)	55	60	.478	—	2000—San Francisco (N.L.)	97	65	.599	1W
1995—San Francisco (N.L.)	67	77	.465	4W	2001—San Francisco (N.L.)	90	72	.556	2W
1996—San Francisco (N.L.)	68	94	.420	4W	2002—San Francisco (N.L.)	95	66	.590	2W
1997—San Francisco (N.L.)	90	72	.555	1W	2003—Chicago (N.L.)	88	74	.543	1C
1998—San Francisco (N.L.)	89	74	.546	2W	2004—Chicago (N.L.)	89	73	.549	3C
					Major League totals (12 years)	1017	862	.541	

NOTES:
1994—San Francisco was in second place in N.L. West at time of season-ending strike (August 12)....**1997**—Lost to Florida, 3-0, in N.L. Division Series....**2000**—Lost to New York Mets, 3-1, in N.L. Division Series....**2002**—Defeated Atlanta, 3-2, in N.L. Division Series; defeated St. Louis, 4-1, N.L. Championship Series; lost to Anaheim, 4-3, in World Series....**2003**—Defeated Atlanta, 3-2, in N.L. Division Series; lost to Florida, 4-3, in N.L. Championship Series....Career postseason record: 17-19.

BOCHY, BRUCE — PADRES

PERSONAL: Born April 16, 1955, in Landes de Boussac, France. ... Full name: Bruce Douglas Bochy. ... Name pronounced: BO-chee. ... High school: Melbourne (Fla.). ... Junior college: Brevard Community College (Fla.). ... College: Florida State.

RECORD AS PLAYER

	G	AB	R	H	2B	3B	HR	RBI	Avg.	BB	SO	SB	PO	A	E	Avg.
Major League totals (9 years)	358	802	75	192	37	2	26	93	.239	67	177	1	1220	130	29	.979

RECORD AS MANAGER

BACKGROUND: Player/coach, Las Vegas, San Diego Padres organization (1988). ... Coach, Padres (1993-94).

HONORS: Named N.L. Manager of the Year by Baseball Writers' Association of America (1996). ... Named N.L. Manager of the Year by THE SPORTING NEWS (1996).

Year Team (League)	W	L	Pct.	Pos
1989—Spokane (NW)	41	34	.547	1N
1990—Riverside (Calif.)	35	36	.493	4S
—Second half	29	42	.408	5S
1991—High Desert (Calif.)	31	37	.456	3S
—Second half	42	26	.618	1S
1992—Wichita (Texas)	39	29	.574	1W
—Second half	31	37	.456	4W
1995—San Diego (N.L.)	70	74	.486	3W
1996—San Diego (N.L.)	91	71	.562	1W

Year Team (League)	W	L	Pct.	Pos
1997—San Diego (N.L.)	76	86	.469	4W
1998—San Diego (N.L.)	98	64	.605	1W
1999—San Diego (N.L.)	74	88	.457	4W
2000—San Diego (N.L.)	76	86	.469	5W
2001—San Diego (N.L.)	79	83	.488	4W
2002—San Diego (N.L.)	66	96	.407	5W
2003—San Diego (N.L.)	64	98	.395	5W
2004—San Diego (N.L.)	87	75	.537	3W
Major League totals (10 years)	781	821	.488	

NOTES:
1989—Defeated Southern Oregon, 2-1, in league championship....**1991**—Defeated Bakersfield, 3-0, in semifinals; defeated Stockton, 3-2, in league championship....**1992**—Defeated El Paso, 2-1, in semifinals; defeated Shreveport, 4-0, in league championship....**1996**—Lost to St. Louis, 3-0, in N.L. Division Series....**1998**—Defeated Houston, 3-1, in N.L. Division Series; defeated Atlanta, 4-2, in N.L. Championship Series; lost to New York Yankees, 4-0, in World Series....Career major league postseason record: 7-10.

COX, BOBBY — BRAVES

PERSONAL: Born May 21, 1941, in Tulsa, Okla. ... Full name: Robert Joseph Cox. ... High school: Selma (Calif.). ... Junior college: Reedley Junior College (Calif.).

RECORD AS PLAYER

				BATTING									FIELDING			
	G	AB	R	H	2B	3B	HR	RBI	Avg.	BB	SO	SB	PO	A	E	Avg.
Major League totals (2 years)	220	628	50	141	22	2	9	58	.225	75	126	3	148	426	28	.953

RECORD AS MANAGER

BACKGROUND: Minor league instructor, New York Yankees (October 28, 1970-March 24, 1971). ... Player/manager, Fort Lauderdale, Yankees organization (1971). ... Coach, Yankees (1977). ... General manager, Braves (October 1985-October 1990).
HONORS: Named Major League Manager of the Year by THE SPORTING NEWS (1985). ... Named N.L. Manager of the Year by THE SPORTING NEWS (1991, 1993, 1999, 2003 and 2004). ... Named A.L. Manager of the Year by Baseball Writers' Association of America (1985). ... Named N.L. Manager of the Year by Baseball Writers' Association of America (1991 and 2004).

Year Team (League)	W	L	Pct.	Pos
1971—Fort Lauderdale (FSL)	71	70	.504	4E
1972—West Haven (East.)	84	56	.600	1A
1973—Syracuse (I.L.)	76	70	.521	3A
1974—Syracuse (I.L.)	74	70	.514	2N
1975—Syracuse (I.L.)	72	64	.529	3rd
1976—Syracuse (I.L.)	82	57	.590	2nd
1978—Atlanta (N.L.)	69	93	.426	6W
1979—Atlanta (N.L.)	66	94	.413	6W
1980—Atlanta (N.L.)	81	80	.503	4W
1981—Atlanta (N.L.)	25	29	.463	4W
—Second half	25	27	.481	5W
1982—Toronto (A.L.)	78	84	.481	6E
1983—Toronto (A.L.)	89	73	.549	4E
1984—Toronto (A.L.)	89	73	.549	2E
1985—Toronto (A.L.)	99	62	.614	1E
1990—Atlanta (N.L.)	40	57	.412	6W

Year Team (League)	W	L	Pct.	Pos
1991—Atlanta (N.L.)	94	68	.580	1W
1992—Atlanta (N.L.)	98	64	.605	1W
1993—Atlanta (N.L.)	104	58	.642	1W
1994—Atlanta (N.L.)	68	46	.596	—
1995—Atlanta (N.L.)	90	54	.625	1E
1996—Atlanta (N.L.)	96	66	.593	1E
1997—Atlanta (N.L.)	101	61	.623	1E
1998—Atlanta (N.L.)	106	56	.654	1E
1999—Atlanta (N.L.)	103	59	.636	1E
2000—Atlanta (N.L.)	95	67	.586	1E
2001—Atlanta (N.L.)	88	74	.543	1E
2002—Atlanta (N.L.)	101	59	.631	1E
2003—Atlanta (N.L.)	101	61	.623	1E
2004—Atlanta (N.L.)	96	66	.593	1E
American League totals (4 years)	355	292	.549	
National League totals (19 years)	1647	1239	.571	
Major League totals (23 years)	2002	1531	.567	

NOTES:
1972—Defeated Three Rivers in league championship, 3-0....**1976**—Defeated Memphis, 3-0, in semifinals; defeated Richmond, 3-1, in league championship....**1985**—Lost to Kansas City, 4-3, in A.L. Championship Series....**1990**—Replaced Russ Nixon as Atlanta manager [Atlanta manager Russ Nixon with club in sixth place and record of 25-40] (June 22)....**1991**—Defeated Pittsburgh, 4-3, in N.L. Championship Series; lost to Minnesota, 4-3, in World Series....**1992**—Defeated Pittsburgh, 4-3, in N.L. Championship Series; lost to Toronto, 4-2, in World Series....**1993**—Lost to Philadelphia, 4-2, in N.L. Championship Series....**1994**—Atlanta was in second place in N.L. East at time of season-ending strike (August 12)....**1995**—Defeated Colorado, 3-1, in N.L. Division Series; defeated Cincinnati, 4-0, in N.L. Championship Series; defeated Cleveland, 4-2, in World Series....**1996**—Defeated Los Angeles, 3-0, in N.L. Division Series; defeated St. Louis, 4-3, in N.L. Championship Series; lost to New York Yankees, 4-2, in World Series....**1997**—Defeated Houston, 3-0, in N.L. Division Series; lost to Florida, 4-2, in N.L. Championship Series....**1998**—Defeated Chicago Cubs, 3-0, in N.L. Division Series; lost to San Diego, 4-2, in N.L. Championship Series....**1999**—Defeated Houston, 3-1, in N.L. Division Series; defeated New York Mets, 4-2, in N.L. Championship Series; lost to New York Yankees, 4-0, in World Series....**2000**—Lost to St. Louis, 3-0, in N.L. Division Series....**2001**—Defeated Houston, 3-0, in N.L. Division Series; lost to Arizona, 4-1, in N.L. Championship Series....**2002**—Lost to San Francisco, 3-2, in N.L. Division Series....**2003**—Lost to Chicago Cubs, 3-2, in N.L. Division Series....**2004**—Lost to Houston, 3-2, in N.L. Division Series....Major league postseason record: 65-63.

FRANCONA, TERRY — RED SOX

PERSONAL: Born April 22, 1959, in Aberdeen, S.D. ... Full name: Terry Jon Francona. ... High school: New Brighton (Pa.). ... College: Arizona. ... Son of Tito Francona, outfielder/first baseman with nine major league teams (1956-70).

RECORD AS PLAYER

				BATTING									FIELDING			
	G	AB	R	H	2B	3B	HR	RBI	Avg.	BB	SO	SB	PO	A	E	Avg.
Major League totals (10 years)	708	1731	163	474	74	6	16	143	.274	65	119	12	2032	188	22	.990

RECORD AS MANAGER

BACKGROUND: Manager, Scottsdale Scorpions, Arizona Fall League (1994). ... Coach, Detroit Tigers (1996). ... Coach, Texas Rangers (2002). ... Coach, Oakland Athletics (2003).
HONORS: Named Southern League Manager of the Year (1993).

Year Team (League)	W	L	Pct.	Pos
1992—South Bend (Midw.)	35	33	.515	3rd
—Second half	38	31	.551	2nd
1993—Birmingham (Sou.)	35	36	.493	2nd
—Second half	43	28	.606	1st
1994—Birmingham (Sou.)	31	38	.449	4th
—Second half	34	36	.486	5th
1995—Birmingham (Sou.)	33	39	.458	4th
—Second half	47	25	.653	2nd

Year Team (League)	W	L	Pct.	Pos
1997—Philadelphia (N.L.)	68	94	.420	5E
1998—Philadelphia (N.L.)	75	87	.463	3E
1999—Philadelphia (N.L.)	77	85	.475	3E
2000—Philadelphia (N.L.)	65	97	.401	5E
2004—Boston (A.L.)	98	64	.605	2E
American League totals (1 year)	98	64	.605	
National League totals (4 years)	285	363	.440	
Major League totals (5 years)	383	427	.473	

NOTES:
1993—Defeated Nashville, 3-0, in semifinals; defeated Knoxville, 3-1, in league championship....**2004**—Defeated Anaheim, 3-0, in A.L. Division Series; defeated New York Yankees, 4-3, in A.L. Championship Series; defeated St. Louis, 4-0, in World Series....Career major league postseason record: 11-3.

GARDENHIRE, RON — TWINS

PERSONAL: Born October 24, 1957, in Butzbach, West Germany. ... Full name: Ronald Clyde Gardenhire. ... High school: Okmulgee (Okla.) High School ... Junior college: Paris (Texas) ... College: Texas

RECORD AS PLAYER

	G	AB	R	H	2B	3B	HR	RBI	Avg.	BB	SO	SB	PO	A	E	Avg.
						BATTING								FIELDING		
Major League totals (5 years)..........	285	710	57	165	27	3	4	49	.232	46	122	13	395	665	47	.958

RECORD AS MANAGER

BACKGROUND: Coach, Minnesota Twins (1991-2001).
HONORS: Named co-A.L. Manager of the Year by THE SPORTING NEWS (2004).

Year Team (League)	W	L	Pct.	Pos	Year Team (League)	W	L	Pct.	Pos
1988—Kenosha (Midw.)	41	27	.603	1N	—Second half	43	29	.597	2E
—Second half	40	32	.556	2N	2002—Minnesota (A.L.)	94	67	.584	1C
1989—Orlando (Sou.)	40	31	.563	1E	2003—Minnesota (A.L.)	90	72	.556	1C
—Second half	39	34	.534	4E	2004—Minnesota (A.L.)	92	70	.568	1C
1990—Orlando (Sou.)	42	30	.583	1E	Major League totals (3 years)	276	209	.569	

NOTES:
1988—Defeated Rockford, 2-0, in semifinals; lost to Cedar Rapids, 3-1, in league championship....**1989**—Lost to Greenville, 3-1, in semifinals....**1990**—Defeated Jacksonville, 3-1, in semifinals; lost to Memphis, 3-2, in league championship....**2002**—Defeated Oakland, 3-2, in A.L. Division Series; lost to Anaheim, 4-1, in A.L. Championship Series....**2003**—Lost to New York Yankees, 3-1, in A.L. Division Series....**2004**—Lost to New York Yankees, 3-1, in A.L. Division Series....Career major league postseason record: 6-12.

GARNER, PHIL — ASTROS

PERSONAL: Born April 30, 1949, in Jefferson City, Tenn. ... Full name: Philip Mason Garner. ... High school: Beardon (Knoxville, Tenn.). ... College: Tennessee.

RECORD AS PLAYER

	G	AB	R	H	2B	3B	HR	RBI	Avg.	BB	SO	SB	PO	A	E	Avg.
						BATTING								FIELDING		
Major League totals (16 years).........	1860	6136	780	1594	299	82	109	738	.260	564	842	225	2746	4356	259	.965

RECORD AS MANAGER

BACKGROUND: Coach, Houston Astros (1989-91).

Year Team (League)	W	L	Pct.	Pos	Year Team (League)	W	L	Pct.	Pos
1992—Milwaukee (A.L.)	92	70	.567	2E	2000—Detroit (A.L.)	79	83	.487	3C
1993—Milwaukee (A.L.)	69	93	.425	7E	2001—Detroit (A.L.)	66	96	.407	4C
1994—Milwaukee (A.L.)	53	62	.460	—	2002—Detroit (A.L.)	0	6	.000	—
1995—Milwaukee (A.L.)	65	79	.451	4C	2004—Houston (N.L.)	48	26	.648	2C
1996—Milwaukee (A.L.)	80	82	.493	3C	American League totals (9 years)	582	654	.471	
1997—Milwaukee (A.L.)	78	83	.484	3C	National League totals (3 years)	174	174	.500	
1998—Milwaukee (N.L.)	74	88	.456	5C	Major League totals (12 years)	756	828	.477	
1999—Milwaukee (N.L.)	52	60	.464						

NOTES:
1993—On suspended list (September 24-27)....**1994**—Milwaukee was in fifth place in A.L. Central at time of season-ending strike (August 12)....**1995**—On suspended list (July 27-31)....**2002**—Replaced as Tigers manager by interim manager Luis Pujols with club in fifth place (April 8)....**2004**—Replaced Houston manager Jimy Williams on an interim basis with club in fifth place and record of 44-44 (July 14); on suspended list (August 13); defeated Atlanta, 3-2, in N.L. Division Series; lost to St. Louis, 4-3, in N.L. Championship Series....Career major league postseason record: 6-6.

GIBBONS, JOHN — BLUE JAYS

PERSONAL: Born June 8, 1962... Full name: John Michael Gibbons. ... High school: MacArthur (Great Falls)

RECORD AS PLAYER

	G	AB	R	H	2B	3B	HR	RBI	Avg.	BB	SO	SB	PO	A	E	Avg.
						BATTING								FIELDING		
Major League totals (2 years)..........	18	50	5	11	4	0	1	2	.220	6	16	0	87	10	1	.990

RECORD AS MANAGER

BACKGROUND: Minor league instructor, New York Mets (1991-93). ... Minor league coach, Mets (1994). ... Coach, Toronto Blue Jays (2002-August 8, 2004).

Year Team (League)	W	L	Pct.	Pos	Year Team (League)	W	L	Pct.	Pos
1995—Kingsport (Appl.)	48	18	.727	1st	1999—Norfolk (I.L.)	77	63	.550	3rd
1996—St. Lucie (FSL)	32	34	.485	3rd	2000—Norfolk (I.L.)	65	79	.451	3rd
—Second half	39	28	.582	1st	2001—Norfolk (I.L.)	85	57	.599	1st
1997—St. Lucie (FSL)	28	39	.418	4th	2003—Toronto (A.L.)	3	0	1.000	—
—Second half	26	42	.382	6th	2004—Toronto (A.L.)	20	30	.400	5E
1998—Binghamton (East.)	82	60	.577	2nd	Major League totals (2 years)	23	30	.433	

NOTES:
1995—Defeated Bluefield, 2-1, in league championship....**1996**—Defeated Vero Beach, 2-0, in semifinals; defeated Clearwater, 3-1, in league championship....**1998**—Lost to New Britain, 3-1, in semifinals....**2001**—Lost to Louisville, 3-2, in semifinals....**2003**—Managed Blue Jays on an interim basis for three games (May 2-3 and September 5)....**2004**—Replaced Toronto manager Carlos Tosca on an interim basis with club in fifth place and record of 47-64 (August 9).

GUILLEN, OZZIE — WHITE SOX

PERSONAL: Born January 20, 1964, in Ocumare del Tuy, Miranda, Venezuela. ... 5-11/165. ... Bats left, throws right. ... Full name: Oswaldo Jose Barrios Guillen. ... Name pronounced: GHEE-un.

RECORD AS PLAYER

	G	AB	R	H	2B	3B	HR	RBI	Avg.	BB	SO	SB	PO	A	E	Avg.
						BATTING								FIELDING		
Major League totals (16 years).........	1993	6686	773	1764	275	69	28	619	.264	239	511	169	2935	5376	222	.974

RECORD AS MANAGER

BACKGROUND: Coach, Montreal Expos (2001). ... Coach, Florida Marlins (2002-03).

Year Team (League)	W	L	Pct.	Pos
2004—Chicago (A.L.)	83	79	.512	2C
Major League totals (1 year)	83	79	.512	

HARGROVE, MIKE — MARINERS

PERSONAL: Born October 26, 1949, in Perryton, Texas. ... Full name: Dudley Michael Hargrove. ... High school: Perryton (Texas) ... College: Northwestern State (Okla.)

RECORD AS PLAYER

	G	AB	R	H	2B	3B	HR	RBI	Avg.	BB	SO	SB	PO	A	E	Avg.
					BATTING								**FIELDING**			
Major League totals (12 years).........	1666	5564	783	1614	266	28	80	686	.290	965	550	24	11603	1027	123	.990

RECORD AS MANAGER

BACKGROUND: Minor league coach, Cleveland Indians organization (1986). ... Coach, Indians (1990-91).

HONORS: Named Carolina League Manager of the Year (1987). ... Named Pacific Coast League Manager of the Year (1989). ... Named A.L. Manager of the Yera by The Sporting News (1995).

Year Team (League)	W	L	Pct.	Pos	Year Team (League)	W	L	Pct.	Pos
1987—Kinston (Caro.)	33	37	.471	T3S	1996—Cleveland (A.L.)	99	62	.615	1C
—Second half	42	28	.600	1S	1997—Cleveland (A.L.)	86	75	.534	1C
1988—Williamsport (East.)	66	73	.475	6th	1998—Cleveland (A.L.)	89	73	.549	1C
1989—Colorado Springs (PCL)	44	26	.629	1S	1999—Cleveland (A.L.)	97	65	.599	1C
—Second half	34	38	.472	3S	2000—Baltimore (A.L.)	74	88	.457	4E
1991—Cleveland (A.L.)	32	53	.376	7E	2001—Baltimore (A.L.)	63	98	.391	4E
1992—Cleveland (A.L.)	76	86	.469	4E	2002—Baltimore (A.L.)	67	95	.414	4E
1993—Cleveland (A.L.)	76	86	.469	6E	2003—Baltimore (A.L.)	71	91	.438	4E
1994—Cleveland (A.L.)	66	47	.584	—					
1995—Cleveland (A.L.)	100	44	.694	1C	**Major League totals (13 years)**	996	963	.508	

NOTES:
1987—Defeated Winston-Salem, 2-0, in playoffs; lost to Salem, 3-1, in league championship....**1989**—Lost to Albuquerque, 3-2, in semifinals....**1991**—Replaced Cleveland manager John McNamara with club in seventh place and record of 25-52 (July 6)....**1994**—Cleveland was in second place in A.L. Central at time of season-ending strike (August 12)....**1995**—Defeated Boston, 3-0, in A.L. Division Series; defeated Seattle, 4-2, in A.L. Championship Series; lost to Atlanta, 4-2, in World Series....**1996**—Lost to Baltimore, 3-1, in A.L. Division Series....**1997**—Defeated New York Yankees, 3-2, in A.L. Division Series; defeated Baltimore, 4-2, in A.L. Championship Series; lost to Florida, 4-3, in World Series....**1998**—Defeated Boston, 3-1, in A.L. Division Series; lost to New York Yankees, 4-2, in A.L. Championship Series....**1999**—Lost to Boston, 3-2, in A.L. Division Series....Career major league postseason record: 27-25.

HURDLE, CLINT — ROCKIES

PERSONAL: Born July 30, 1957, in Big Rapids, Mich. ... Full name: Clinton Merrick Hurdle. ... High school: Merritt Island (Fla.)

RECORD AS PLAYER

	G	AB	R	H	2B	3B	HR	RBI	Avg.	BB	SO	SB	PO	A	E	Avg.
					BATTING								**FIELDING**			
Major League totals (10 years).........	515	1391	162	360	81	12	32	193	.259	176	261	1	1384	96	34	.978

RECORD AS MANAGER

BACKGROUND: Roving hitting instructor, Colorado Rockies (1994-96). ... Coach, Rockies (1997-2002).

HONORS: Named Texas League Manager of the Year (1990).

Year Team (League)	W	L	Pct.	Pos	Year Team (League)	W	L	Pct.	Pos
1988—St. Lucie (FSL)	36	34	.514	4E	1991—Williamsport (East.)	60	79	.432	7th
—Second half	38	31	.551	1E	1992—Tidewater (I.L.)	56	86	.394	4W
1989—St. Lucie (FSL)	42	28	.600	1E	1993—Norfolk (I.L.)	70	71	.496	4W
—Second half	37	27	.578	1E	2002—Colorado (N.L.)	67	73	.479	4W
1990—Jackson (Texas)	35	32	.522	2E	2003—Colorado (N.L.)	74	88	.457	4W
—Second half	38	30	.559	1E	2004—Colorado (N.L.)	68	94	.420	4W
					Major League totals (3 years)	209	255	.450	

NOTES:
1988—Defeated Lakeland, 2-1, in first round; defeated Tampa, 2-0, in semifinals; defeated Osceola, 2-0, in league championship....**1989**—Lost to Port Charlotte, 2-1, in first round....**1990**—Lost to Shreveport, 2-0, in semifinals....**2002**—Replaced Buddy Bell as Colorado manager (April 26).

LA RUSSA, TONY — CARDINALS

PERSONAL: Born October 4, 1944, in Tampa, Fla. ... Full name: Anthony La Russa Jr.. ... High school: Jefferson (Tampa). ... College: University of Tampa, then South Florida, then Florida State.

RECORD AS PLAYER

	G	AB	R	H	2B	3B	HR	RBI	Avg.	BB	SO	SB	PO	A	E	Avg.
					BATTING								**FIELDING**			
Major League totals (6 years)...........	132	176	15	35	5	2	0	7	.199	23	37	0	112	127	10	.960

RECORD AS MANAGER

BACKGROUND: Coach, St. Louis Cardinals organization (June 20-September 29, 1977). ... Coach, Chicago White Sox (July 3, 1978-remainder of season).

HONORS: Named A.L. Manager of the Year by Baseball Writers' Association of America (1983, 1988 and 1992). ... Named N.L. Manager of the Year by Baseball Writers' Association of America (2002). ... Named Major League Manager of the Year by The Sporting News (1983). ... Named A.L. Manager of the Year by The Sporting News (1988 and 1992). ... [Coach, A.L. All-Star team (1984 and 1987).]

Year Team (League)	W	L	Pct.	Pos	Year Team (League)	W	L	Pct.	Pos
1978—Knoxville (Sou.)	49	21	.700	1st	1990—Oakland (A.L.)	103	59	.635	1W
—Second half	4	4	.500	—	1991—Oakland (A.L.)	84	78	.519	4W
1979—Iowa (A.A.)	54	52	.509	—	1992—Oakland (A.L.)	96	66	.593	1W
—Chicago (A.L.)	27	27	.500	5W	1993—Oakland (A.L.)	68	94	.420	7W
1980—Chicago (A.L.)	70	90	.438	5W	1994—Oakland (A.L.)	51	63	.447	—
1981—Chicago (A.L.)	31	22	.585	3W	1995—Oakland (A.L.)	67	77	.465	4W
—Second half	23	30	.434	6W	1996—St. Louis (N.L.)	88	74	.543	1C
1982—Chicago (A.L.)	87	75	.537	3W	1997—St. Louis (N.L.)	73	89	.451	4C
1983—Chicago (A.L.)	99	63	.611	1W	1998—St. Louis (N.L.)	83	79	.512	3C
1984—Chicago (A.L.)	74	88	.457	5W	1999—St. Louis (N.L.)	75	86	.466	4C
1985—Chicago (A.L.)	85	77	.525	3W	2000—St. Louis (N.L.)	95	67	.586	1C
1986—Chicago (A.L.)	26	38	.406	—	2001—St. Louis (N.L.)	93	69	.574	2C
1986—Oakland (A.L.)	45	34	.570	3W	2002—St. Louis (N.L.)	97	65	.599	1C
1987—Oakland (A.L.)	81	81	.500	3W	2003—St. Louis (N.L.)	85	77	.525	3C
1988—Oakland (A.L.)	104	58	.642	1W	2004—St. Louis (N.L.)	105	57	.648	1C
1989—Oakland (A.L.)	99	63	.611	1W					
					American League totals (17 years)	1320	1183	.527	
					National League totals (9 years)	794	663	.543	
					Major League totals (26 years)	2114	1846	.534	

NOTES:
1978—Became Chicago White Sox coach and replaced as Knoxville manager by Joe Jones, with club in third place (July 3)....**1979**—Replaced as Iowa manager by Joe Sparks, with club in second place (August 3); replaced Chicago manager Don Kessinger with club in fifth place and record of 46-60 (August 3)....**1983**—Lost to Baltimore, 3-1, in A.L. Championship Series....**1985**—On suspended list (August 10-11)....**1986**—Replaced as White Sox manager by interim manager Doug RadeR, with club in sixth place (June 20); replaced Oakland manager Jackie Moore (record of 29-44) and interim manager Jeff Newman (record of 2-8) with club in seventh place and record of 31-52 (July 7)....**1988**—Defeated Boston, 4-0, in A.L. Championship Series; lost to Los Angeles, 4-1, in World Series....**1989**—Defeated Toronto, 4-1, in A.L. Championship Series; defeated San Francisco, 4-0, in World Series....**1990**—Defeated Boston, 4-0, in A.L. Championship Series; lost to Cincinnati, 4-0, in World Series....**1992**—Lost to Toronto, 4-2, in A.L. Championship Series....**1993**—On suspended list (October 1-remainder of season)....**1994**—Oakland was in second place in A.L. West at time of season-ending strike (August 12)....**1996**—Defeated San Diego, 3-0, in N.L. Division Series; lost to Atlanta, 4-3, in N.L. Championship Series....**2000**—Defeated Atlanta, 3-0, in N.L. Division Series; lost to New York Mets, 4-1, in N.L. Championship Series....**2001**—Lost to Arizona, 3-2, in N.L. Division Series....**2002**—Defeated Arizona, 3-0, in N.L. Division Series; lost to San Francisco, 4-1, in N.L. Championship Series....**2003**—On suspended list (September 26-27)....**2004**—Defeated Los Angeles, 3-1, in N.L. Division Series; defeated Houston, 4-3, in N.L. Championship Series; lost to Boston, 4-0, in World Series....Career major league postseason record: 43-39.

MACHA, KEN — ATHLETICS

PERSONAL: Born September 29, 1950, in Monroeville, Pa. ... Full name: Kenneth Edward Macha. ... High school: Gateway (Pittsburgh) ... College: Pittsburgh ... Brother of Mike Macha, third baseman/catcher with two major league teams (1978 and 1980).

RECORD AS PLAYER

	G	AB	R	H	2B	3B	HR	RBI	Avg.	BB	SO	SB	PO	A	E	Avg.
														FIELDING		
Major League totals (6 years)...........	180	380	30	98	16	3	1	35	.258	39	68	4	237	143	13	.967

RECORD AS MANAGER

BACKGROUND: Coach, Montreal Expos (1986-89). ... Coach, California Angels (1992-94). ... Coach, Oakland Athletics (1999-2002).

Year Team (League)	W	L	Pct.	Pos	Year Team (League)	W	L	Pct.	Pos
1995—Trenton (East.)	73	69	.514	1st	1998—Pawtucket (I.L.)	77	64	.546	3rd
1996—Trenton (East.)	86	56	.606	1st	2003—Oakland (A.L.)	96	66	.593	1W
1997—Pawtucket (I.L.)	81	60	.574	2nd	2004—Oakland (A.L.)	91	71	.562	2W
					Major League totals (2 years)	187	137	.577	

NOTES:
1995—Lost to Reading, 3-0, in semifinals....**1996**—Lost to Harrisburg, 3-2, in semifinals....**1997**—Lost to Rochester, 3-1, in semifinals. **2003**—Lost to Boston, 3-2, in A.L. Division Series. Career major league postseason record: 2-3.

MANUEL, CHARLIE — PHILLIES

PERSONAL: Born January 4, 1944, in North Fork, W. Va.. ... Full name: Charles Fuqua Manuel. High school: Parry McCluer (Buena Vista, W. Va.).

RECORD AS PLAYER

	G	AB	R	H	2B	3B	HR	RBI	Avg.	BB	SO	SB	PO	A	E	Avg.
														FIELDING		
Major League totals (6 years)...........	239	384	25	76	12	0	4	43	.198	40	77	1	103	6	3	.973

RECORD AS MANAGER

BACKGROUND: Scout, Minnesota Twins (1982). ... Coach, Cleveland Indians (1988-89 and 1994-99).

HONORS: Named International League Manager of the Year (1993).

Year Team (League)	W	L	Pct.	Pos	Year Team (League)	W	L	Pct.	Pos
1983—Wisconsin (Midw.)	71	67	.518	2N	1991—Colorado Springs (PCL)	30	41	.422	5S
1984—Orlando (Southern)	34	35	.493	3E	—Second half	42	26	.617	1S
—Second half	45	30	.600	2E	1992—Colorado Springs (PCL)	36	33	.521	2S
1985—Orlando (Southern)	29	35	.453	5E	—Second half	48	24	.667	1S
—Second half	43	36	.544	2E	1993—Charlotte (International)	86	55	.610	1W
1986—Toledo (International)	62	77	.446	6th	2000—Cleveland (A.L.)	90	72	.556	2C
1987—Portland (PCL)	20	49	.290	5N	2001—Cleveland (A.L.)	91	71	.562	1C
—Second half	25	47	.347	5N	2002—Cleveland (A.L.)	39	47	.530	—
1990—Colorado Springs (PCL)	37	34	.521	2S	Major League totals (3 years)	220	190	.537	
—Second half	39	33	.541	3S					

NOTES:
1984—Lost to Charlotte in 1-game playoff. ... **1991**—Lost to Tucson, 3-1, in semfinals.... **1992**—Defeated Las Vegas, 3-2, in semifinals; lost to Vancouver, 3-0, in leagie championship. **1993**—Defeated Richmond, 3-1, in semifinals; defeated Rochester, 3-2, in league championship. **2001**—Lost to Seattle, 3-2, in A.L. Division Series. 2002—Replaced as Cleveland manager by Joel Skinner with club in third place. Career major league postseason record: 2-3.

MAZZILLI, LEE — ORIOLES

PERSONAL: Born March 25, 1955... Full name: Lee Louis Mazzilli. ... High school: Lincoln (Brooklyn, N.Y.).

RECORD AS PLAYER

	G	AB	R	H	2B	3B	HR	RBI	Avg.	BB	SO	SB	PO	A	E	Avg.
														FIELDING		
Major League totals (14 years).........	1475	4124	571	1068	191	24	93	460	.259	642	672	197	3425	131	51	.986

RECORD AS MANAGER

BACKGROUND: Coach, New York Yankees (2000-03).

Year Team (League)	W	L	Pct.	Pos	Year Team (League)	W	L	Pct.	Pos
1997—Tampa (FSL)	41	26	.612	2nd	—Second half	46	23	.667	1st
—Second half	29	40	.420	6th	1999—Norwich (East.)	78	64	.549	2nd
1998—Tampa (FSL)	26	44	.371	8th	2004—Baltimore (A.L.)	78	84	.481	3rd
					Major League totals (1 year)	78	84	.481	

NOTES:
1998—Defeated Charlotte, 2-0, in semifinals; lost to St. Lucie, 3-2, in league championship....**1999**—Defeated Trenton, 3-1, in semifinals; lost to Harrisburg, 3-2, in league championship.

MCCLENDON, LLOYD   PIRATES

PERSONAL: Born January 11, 1959, in Gary, Ind. ... Full name: Lloyd Glenn McClendon. ... High school: Roosevelt (Gary, Ind.). ... College: Valparaiso.

RECORD AS PLAYER

					BATTING								FIELDING		
	G	AB	R	H	2B	3B	HR	RBI	Avg.	BB	SO	SB	PO	A	E	Avg.
Major League totals (8 years)...........	570	1204	150	294	54	3	35	154	.244	143	165	15	1150	73	23	.982

RECORD AS MANAGER

BACKGROUND: Minor league hitting instructor, Pittsburgh Pirates (1996). ... Coach, Pirates (1997-2000).

Year Team (League)	W	L	Pct.	Pos	Year Team (League)	W	L	Pct.	Pos
2001—Pittsburgh (N.L.)	62	100	.383	6th	2003—Pittsburgh (N.L.)	75	87	.463	4th
2002—Pittsburgh (N.L.)	72	89	.447	4th	2004—Pittsburgh (N.L.)	72	89	.447	5th
					Major League totals (4 years)	281	365	.435	

MCKEON, JACK   MARLINS

PERSONAL: Born November 23, 1930, in South Amboy, N.J. ... Full name: John Aloysius McKeon. ... High school: St. Mary's (South Amboy, N.J.). ... College: Holy Cross, then Seton Hall, then Elon (N.C.) College. ... Father-in-law of Greg Booker, pitcher with two major league teams (1983-89).

RECORD AS PLAYER

					BATTING								FIELDING		
	G	AB	R	H	2B	3B	HR	RBI	Avg.	BB	SO	SB	PO	A	E	Avg.
Career Playing Record					Did not play in major leagues										

RECORD AS MANAGER

BACKGROUND: Scout, Minnesota Twins (1965-67). ... Coach, Oakland Athletics (April 7-May 22, 1978). ... Scout/assistant to general manager, San Diego Padres (1980). ... Vice-president of baseball operations, Padres (1980-90). ... Senior adviser/player personnel, Cincinnati Reds (Janury 6, 1993-July 25, 1997).
HONORS: Named N.L. Manager of the Year by Baseball Writers' Association of America (1999 and 2003).

Year Team (League)	W	L	Pct.	Pos	Year Team (League)	W	L	Pct.	Pos
1955—Fayetteville (Caro.)	70	67	.511	3rd	1972—Omaha (A.A.)	71	69	.507	2nd
1956—Missoula (Pio.)	61	71	.462	7th	1973—Kansas City (A.L.)	88	74	.543	2W
1957—Missoula (Pio.)	26	35	.426	6th	1974—Kansas City (A.L.)	77	85	.475	5W
—Second half	36	29	.554	3rd	1975—Kansas City (A.L.)	50	46	.521	—
1958—Missoula (Pio.)	34	29	.540	4th	1976—Richmond (I.L.)	69	71	.493	4th
—Second half	36	30	.545	3rd	1977—Oakland (A.L.)	26	27	.491	—
1959—Fox Cities (I.I.I.)	26	39	.400	7th	1978—Oakland (A.L.)	45	78	.366	4W
—Second half	33	28	.541	4th	1980—Denver (A.A.)	62	73	.459	3rd
1960—Walla Walla (NW)	36	34	.514	3rd	1988—San Diego (N.L.)	67	48	.583	3W
—Second half	37	31	.544	2nd	1989—San Diego (N.L.)	89	73	.549	2W
1961—Walla Walla (NW)	41	28	.594	1st	1990—San Diego (N.L.)	37	43	.463	—
—Second half	42	28	.600	1st	1997—Cincinnati (N.L.)	33	30	.524	3C
1962—Vancouver (PCL)	72	79	.477	7th	1998—Cincinnati (N.L.)	77	85	.475	4C
1963—Dallas//Fort Worth (A.A.)	79	79	.500	3rd	1999—Cincinnati (N.L.)	96	67	.589	2C
1964—Atlanta (I.L.)	19	42	.311	—	2000—Cincinnati (N.L.)	85	77	.525	2C
1968—High Point-Thomasville (Caro.)	69	71	.493	2nd	2003—Florida (N.L.)	75	49	.605	2E
1969—Omaha (A.A.)	85	55	.607	1st	2004—Florida (N.L.)	83	79	.512	3E
1970—Omaha (A.A.)	73	65	.529	1st					
1971—Omaha (A.A.)	69	70	.496	3rd	American League totals (5 years)	286	310	.480	
					National League totals (9 years)	642	551	.538	
					Major League totals (14 years)	928	861	.519	

NOTES:
1955—Replaced Fayetteville manager Aaron Robinson (June 11). Replaced as Fayetteville manager by John Sanford (August 6) [because of hand injury with team tied for first place (record is for full season)]....**1964**—Replaced as Atlanta manager by Peter Appleton with club in eighth place (June 21)....**1968**—Defeated Greensboro, 1-0, in quarterfinals; defeated Lynchburg, 2-0 in semifinals; defeated Raleigh-Durham, 2-0, in championship....**1970**—Defeated Denver, 4-1, in championship; lost to Syracuse, 4-1, in Junior World Series....**1975**—Replaced as Kansas City manager by Whitey Herzog with club in second place (July 24)....**1977**—Replaced as Oakland manager by Bobby Winkles with club tied for fifth place (June 10)....**1978**—Replaced Oakland manager Bobby Winkles with club in first place and record of 24-15 (May 23)....**1988**—Replaced San Diego manager Larry Bowa with club in fifth place and record of 16-30 (May 28)....**1997**—Replaced Cincinnati manager Ray Knight with club in fourth place and record of 43-56 (July 25)....**2003**—Replaced Florida manager Jeff Torborg with club in fourth place and record of 16-22 (May 11); defeated San Francisco, 3-1, in N.L. Division Series; defeated Chicago Cubs, 4-3, in N.L. Championship Series; defeated New York Yankees, 4-2, in World Series. Career major league postseason record: 11-6.

MELVIN, BOB   DIAMONDBACKS

PERSONAL: Born October 28, 1961, in Palo Alto, Calif. ... Full name: Robert Paul Melvin. ... High school: Menlo-Atherton (Menlo Park, Calif.). ... Junior college: Canada College (Calif.). ... College: California.

RECORD AS PLAYER

					BATTING								FIELDING		
	G	AB	R	H	2B	3B	HR	RBI	Avg.	BB	SO	SB	PO	A	E	Avg.
Major League totals (10 years).........	692	1955	174	456	85	6	35	212	.233	98	396	4	2961	253	24	.993

RECORD AS MANAGER

BACKGROUND: Scout, Milwaukee Brewers (1996). ... Roving fielding instructor, Brewers (1997). ... Assistant to general manager, Brewers (1998). ... Coach, Brewers (1999). ... Coach, Detroit Tigers (2000). ... Coach, Arizona Diamondbacks (2001-02).

Year Team (League)	W	L	Pct.	Pos
2003—Seattle (A.L.)	93	69	.574	2W
2004—Seattle (A.L.)	63	99	.388	4W
Major League totals (2 years)	156	168	.481	

MILEY, DAVE   REDS

PERSONAL: Born April 3, 1962... High school: Chamberlain (Tampa, Fla.).

RECORD AS PLAYER

					BATTING								FIELDING		
	G	AB	R	H	2B	3B	HR	RBI	Avg.	BB	SO	SB	PO	A	E	Avg.
Career Playing Record					Did not play in major leagues										

RECORD AS MANAGER

BACKGROUND: Coach, Cincinnati Reds (1993). ... Assistant minor league field coordinator, Reds (1994).

HONORS: Named Southern League Manager of the Year (1995). ... Named Class AA Manager of the Year (1995). ... Named International League Manager of the Year (1997).

Year Team (League)	W	L	Pct.	Pos	Year Team (League)	W	L	Pct.	Pos
1988—Greensboro (West. Car.)	37	33	.529	2nd	—Second half	47	24	.662	1st
—Second half	42	27	.609	1st	1996—Indianapolis (A.A.)	78	66	.542	2nd
1989—Cedar Rapids (Midw.)	41	27	.603	1st	1997—Indianapolis (A.A.)	85	59	.590	2nd
—Second half	39	30	.565	3rd	1998—Indianapolis (A.A.)	76	67	.531	2nd
1990—Cedar Rapids (Midw.)	45	21	.682	1st	1999—Indianapolis (A.A.)	75	69	.520	2nd
—Second half	43	25	.632	2nd	2000—Louisville (A.A.)	71	73	.493	3rd
1991—Charleston, W.Va. (I.L.)	46	26	.639	1st	2001—Louisville (A.A.)	84	60	.583	1st
—Second half	46	24	.657	1st	2002—Louisville (A.A.)	79	65	.549	2nd
1992—Chattanooga (Sou.)	46	25	.648	1st	2003—Louisville (A.A.)	62	47	.569	—
—Second half	5	1	.833	—	—Cincinnati (N.L.)	22	35	.386	5C
—Nashville (Sou.)	32	36	.471	4th	2004—Cincinnati (N.L.)	76	86	.469	4C
1995—Chattanooga (Sou.)	36	36	.500	2nd	**Major League totals (2 years)**	**98**	**121**	**.447**	

NOTES:
1988—Lost to Spartanburg, 2-0, in semifinals....**1989**—Lost to Springfield, 2-0, in semifinals....**1990**—Lost to Quad City, 2-0, in semifinals....**1991**—Lost to Columbia, 3-0, in semifinals....**1992**—Replaced Nashville manager Pete Mackanin with team in fourth place and record of 35-41 (June 28); replaced as Chattanooga manager by interim manager Tom Nieto with club in first place and second-half record of 5-1 (June 26)....**1995**—Defeated Memphis, 3-2, in semifinals; lost to Carolina, 3-2, in league championship....**1996**—Defeated Buffalo, 3-2, in semifinals; lost to Oklahoma City, 3-1, in league championship....**1997**—Lost to Buffalo, 3-2, in semifinals....**2001**—Defeated Norfolk, 3-2, in semifinals; was leading Scranton/Wilkes-Barre, 1-0, in league championship when Louisville declared league champion due to stoppage of play in professional baseball....**2003**—Replaced Cincinnati manager Bob Boone (46-58) and interim manager Ray Knight (1-0) on an interim basis with team in fifth place and record of 47-58 (July 28).

PENA, TONY — ROYALS

PERSONAL: Born June 4, 1957, in Monte Cristi, Dominican Republic. ... Full name: Antonio Francisco Padilla Pena. ... High school: Liceo Marti (Monte Cristi, Dominican Republic). ... Brother of Ramon Pena, pitcher, Detroit Tigers (1989).

RECORD AS PLAYER

	G	AB	R	H	2B	3B	HR	RBI	Avg.	BB	SO	SB	PO	A	E	Avg.
						BATTING								FIELDING		
Major League totals (18 years)	1988	6489	667	1687	298	27	107	708	.260	455	846	80	11260	1049	118	.991

RECORD AS MANAGER

BACKGROUND: Coach, Houston Astros (2002).

HONORS: Named A.L. Manager of the Year by Baseball Writers' Association of America (2003). ... Named A.L. Manager of the Year by The Sporting News (2003).

Year Team (League)	W	L	Pct.	Pos	Year Team (League)	W	L	Pct.	Pos
1999—New Orleans (PCL)	55	85	.393	4th	2002—Kansas City (A.L.)	49	77	.389	4th
2000—New Orleans (PCL)	68	74	.479	3rd	2003—Kansas City (A.L.)	83	79	.512	3rd
2001—New Orleans (PCL)	82	57	.590	1st	2004—Kansas City (A.L.)	58	104	.358	5th
					Major League totals (3 years)	**190**	**260**	**.422**	

NOTES:
2001—Defeated Iowa, 3-0, in playoffs. Shared league championship due to stoppage in professional baseball....**2002**—Replaced Kansas City manager Tony Muser (record of 8-15) and interim manager John Mizerock (record of 5-8) with club in fourth place and record of 13-23 (May 15).

PINIELLA, LOU — DEVIL RAYS

PERSONAL: Born August 28, 1943, in Tampa. ... Full name: Louis Victor Piniella. ... Name pronounced: pin-ELL-uh. ... High school: Jesuit (Tampa). ... College: Tampa. ... Cousin of Dave Magadan, first baseman//third baseman, San Diego Padres.

RECORD AS PLAYER

	G	AB	R	H	2B	3B	HR	RBI	Avg.	BB	SO	SB	PO	A	E	Avg.
						BATTING								FIELDING		
Major League totals (18 years)	1747	5867	651	1705	305	41	102	766	.291	368	541	33	2546	106	52	.981

RECORD AS MANAGER

BACKGROUND: Coach, New York Yankees (June 25, 1984-85). ... Vice-president/general manager, Yankees (beginning of 1988 season-June 22, 1988). ... Special adviser, Yankees (1989).

HONORS: Named A.L. Manager of the Year by Baseball Writers' Association of America (1995).

Year Team (League)	W	L	Pct.	Pos	Year Team (League)	W	L	Pct.	Pos
1986—New York (A.L.)	90	72	.556	2nd	1997—Seattle (A.L.)	90	72	.556	1st
1987—New York (A.L.)	89	73	.549	4th	1998—Seattle (A.L.)	76	85	.472	3rd
1988—New York (A.L.)	45	48	.484	5th	1999—Seattle (A.L.)	79	83	.488	3rd
1990—Cincinnati (N.L.)	91	71	.562	1st	2000—Seattle (A.L.)	91	71	.562	2nd
1991—Cincinnati (N.L.)	74	88	.457	5th	2001—Seattle (A.L.)	116	46	.716	1st
1992—Cincinnati (N.L.)	90	72	.556	2nd	2002—Seattle (A.L.)	93	69	.574	3rd
1993—Seattle (A.L.)	82	80	.506	4th	2003—Tampa Bay (A.L.)	63	99	.389	5th
1994—Seattle (A.L.)	49	63	.438	—	2004—Tampa Bay (A.L.)	70	91	.435	4th
1995—Seattle (A.L.)	79	66	.545	1st	**American League totals (15 years)**	**1197**	**1094**	**.522**	
1996—Seattle (A.L.)	85	76	.528	2nd	**National League totals (3 years)**	**255**	**231**	**.525**	
					Major League totals (18 years)	**1452**	**1325**	**.523**	

NOTES:
1988—Replaced New York manager Billy Martin [with club in second place and record of 40-28] (June 23)....**1990**—Defeated Pittsburgh, 4-2, in N.L. Championship Series; defeated Oakland, 4-0, in World Series....**1994**—Seattle was in third place in A.L. West at time of season-ending strike (August 12)....**1995**—Defeated New York Yankees, 3-2, in A.L. Division Series; lost to Cleveland, 4-2, in A.L. Championship Series....**1997**—Lost to Baltimore, 3-1, in A.L. Division Series....**2000**—Defeated Chicago White Sox, 3-0, in A.L. Division Series; lost to New York Yankees, 4-2, in A.L. Championship Series....**2001**—Defeated Cleveland, 3-1, in A.L. Division Series; lost to New York Yankees, 4-1, in A.L. Championship Series....Career major league postseason record: 23-21.

RANDOLPH, WILLIE

PERSONAL: Born July 6, 1954, in Holly Hill, SC. ... 5-11/171. ... Bats right, throws right. ... Full name: William Larry Randolph Jr.. ... High school: Tilden (Brooklyn, N.Y.). ... Brother of Terry Randolph, defensive back, Green Bay Packers (1977).

RECORD AS PLAYER

	G	AB	R	H	2B	3B	HR	RBI	Avg.	BB	SO	SB	PO	A	E	Avg.
							BATTING							FIELDING		
Major League totals (18 years).........	2202	8018	1239	2210	316	65	54	687	.276	1243	675	271	4859	6339	237	.979

RECORD AS MANAGER

BACKGROUND: Assistant general manager, New York Yankees (1993). ... Coach, New York Yankees (1994-2004).

ROBINSON, FRANK

PERSONAL: Born August 31, 1935, in Beaumont, Texas. ... High school: McClymonds (Oakland). ... College: Xavier.

RECORD AS PLAYER

	G	AB	R	H	2B	3B	HR	RBI	Avg.	BB	SO	SB	PO	A	E	Avg.
							BATTING							FIELDING		
Major League totals (21 years).........	2808	10006	1829	2943	528	72	586	1812	.294	1420	1532	204	6346	333	106	.984

RECORD AS MANAGER

BACKGROUND: Player/manager, Indians (1975). ... Coach, California Angels (1977). ... Coach, Baltimore Orioles (1978-80 and 1985-87). ... Coach, Milwaukee Brewers (1984). ... Special assistant to the president, Orioles (1988). ... Assistant general manager, Orioles (1991-95). ... Vice president of on-field operations for Major League Baseball (1999-2001).

HONORS: Named A.L. Manager of the Year by The Sporting News (1989).

Year Team (League)	W	L	Pct.	Pos	Year Team (League)	W	L	Pct.	Pos
1975—Cleveland (A.L.)	79	80	.497	4E	1988—Baltimore (A.L.)	54	101	.348	7E
1976—Cleveland (A.L.)	81	78	.509	4E	1989—Baltimore (A.L.)	87	75	.537	2E
1977—Cleveland (A.L.)	26	31	.456	—	1990—Baltimore (A.L.)	76	85	.472	5E
1978—Rochester (I.L.)	58	64	.475	6th	1991—Baltimore (A.L.)	13	24	.351	—
1981—San Francisco (N.L.)	27	32	.458	5W	2002—Montreal (N.L.)	83	79	.512	2E
—Second half	29	23	.558	3W	2003—Montreal (N.L.)	83	79	.512	4E
1982—San Francisco (N.L.)	87	75	.537	3W	2004—Montreal (N.L.)	67	95	.414	5E
1983—San Francisco (N.L.)	79	83	.488	5W	**American League totals (7 years)**	416	474	.467	
1984—San Francisco (N.L.)	42	64	.396	—	**National League totals (7 years)**	497	530	.483	
					Major League totals (14 years)	913	1004	.476	

NOTES:
1977—Replaced as Cleveland manager by Jeff Torborg with club in sixth place (June 19).... **1978**—Replaced Rochester interim manager Al Widmar and manager Ken Boyer (May 8) ...**1984**—Replaced as San Francisco manager by Jim Davenport with club in sixth place (August 4)....**1988**—Replaced Baltimore manager Cal Ripken (April 12)....**1991**—Replaced as Baltimore manager by Johnny Oates (May 23).

SCIOSCIA, MIKE

PERSONAL: Born November 27, 1958, in Upper Darby, Pa. ... Full name: Michael Lorri Scioscia. ... Name pronounced: SO-sha. ... High school: Springfield (Pa.). ... College: Penn State.

RECORD AS PLAYER

	G	AB	R	H	2B	3B	HR	RBI	Avg.	BB	SO	SB	PO	A	E	Avg.
							BATTING							FIELDING		
Major League totals (13 years).........	1441	4373	398	1131	198	12	68	446	.259	567	307	29	8335	737	114	.988

RECORD AS MANAGER

BACKGROUND: Minor league catching coordinator, Dodgers organization (1995-96). ... Coach, Dodgers (1997-98). ... Manager, Peoria Javelinas, Arizona Fall League (1997).

HONORS: Named A.L. Manager of the Year by Baseball Writers' Association of America (2002). ... Named A.L. Manager of the Year by The Sporting News (2002).

Year Team (League)	W	L	Pct.	Pos	Year Team (League)	W	L	Pct.	Pos
1999—Albuquerque (PCL)	65	74	.468	3rd	2002—Anaheim (A.L.)	99	63	.611	2W
2000—Anaheim (A.L.)	82	80	.506	3W	2003—Anaheim (A.L.)	77	85	.475	3W
2001—Anaheim (A.L.)	75	87	.463	3W	2004—Anaheim (A.L.)	92	70	.568	1W
					Major League totals (5 years)	425	385	.525	

NOTES:
2002—Defeated New York Yankees, 3-1, in A.L. Division Series; defeated Minnesota, 4-1, in A.L. Championship Series; defeated San Francisco, 4-3, in World Series....**2004**—Lost to Boston, 3-0, in A.L. Division Series....Career major league postseason record: 11-8.

SHOWALTER, BUCK

PERSONAL: Born May 23, 1956, in DeFuniak Springs, Fla. ... Full name: William Nathaniel Showalter III. ... High school: Century (Fla.). ... Junior college: Chipola Junior College (Fla.). ... College: Mississippi State (degree in education).

RECORD AS PLAYER

BATTING	FIELDING
Career Playing Record	Did not play in major leagues.

RECORD AS MANAGER

BACKGROUND: Minor league coach, New York Yankees organization (1984). ... Coach, Yankees (1990-91).

HONORS: Named New York-Penn League Manager of the Year (1985). ... Named Eastern League Manager of the Year (1989). ... Named A.L. Manager of the Year by Baseball Writers' Association of America (1994 and 2004). ... Named A.L. Manager of the Year by The Sporting News (1994).

Year	Team (League)	W	L	Pct.	Pos		Year	Team (League)	W	L	Pct.	Pos
1985—Oneonta (NY-P)		55	23	.705	1st		1995—New York (A.L.)		79	65	.548	2nd
1986—Oneonta (NY-P)		59	18	.766	1st		1998—Arizona (N.L.)		65	97	.401	5th
1987—Fort Lauderdale (FSL)		85	53	.616	1st		1999—Arizona (N.L.)		100	62	.617	1st
1988—Fort Lauderdale (FSL)		39	29	.574	3rd		2000—Arizona (N.L.)		85	77	.524	3rd
—Second half		30	36	.455	3rd		2003—Texas (A.L.)		71	91	.438	4th
1989—Albany (East.)		92	48	.657	1st		2004—Texas (A.L.)		89	73	.549	3rd
1992—New York (A.L.)		76	86	.469	4E		American League totals (6 years)		473	432	.522	
1993—New York (A.L.)		88	74	.543	2E		National League totals (3 years)		250	236	.514	
1994—New York (A.L.)		70	43	.619	—		Major League totals (9 years)		723	668	.519	

NOTES:
1985—Defeated Geneva, 1-0, in semifinals; defeated Auburn, 2-0, in league championship....**1986**—Lost to Newark, 1-0, in semifinals....**1987**—Defeated Lakeland, 2-0, in semifinals; defeated Osceola, 3-1, in league championship....**1989**—Defeated Reading, 3-1, in semifinals; defeated Harrisburg, 3-1, in league championship....**1994**—New York was in first place in A.L. East at time of season-ending strike (August 12)....**1995**—Lost to Seattle, 3-2, in A.L. Division Series....**1999**—Lost to New York Mets, 3-1, in N.L. Division Series....Career major league postseason record: 3-6.

TORRE, JOE — YANKEES

PERSONAL: Born July 18, 1940, in Brooklyn, NY. ... Full name: Joseph Paul Torre. ... Name pronounced: TORE-ee. ... High school: St. Francis Prep (Brooklyn, N.Y.). ... Brother of Frank Torre, first baseman, Milwaukee Braves and Philadelphia Phillies (1956-60, 1962-63).

RECORD AS PLAYER

		BATTING												FIELDING			
	G	AB	R	H	2B	3B	HR	RBI	Avg.	BB	SO	SB	PO	A	E	Avg.
Major League totals (18 years)	2209	7874	996	2342	344	59	252	1185	.297	779	1094	23	11618	1731	169	.987

RECORD AS MANAGER

BACKGROUND: Player/manager, New York Mets (May 31-June 18, 1977).

HONORS: Named Sportsman of the Year by THE SPORTING NEWS (1996). ... Named co-A.L. Manager of the Year by Baseball Writers' Association of America (1996). ... Named A.L. Manager of the Year by THE SPORTING NEWS (1998). ... Named A.L. Manager of the Year by Baseball Writers' Association of America (1998).

Year	Team (League)	W	L	Pct.	Pos		Year	Team (League)	W	L	Pct.	Pos
1977—New York (N.L.)		49	68	.419	6E		1994—St. Louis (N.L.)		53	61	.465	—
1978—New York (N.L.)		66	96	.407	6E		1995—St. Louis (N.L.)		20	27	.426	4C
1979—New York (N.L.)		63	99	.389	6E		1996—New York (A.L.)		92	70	.568	1E
1980—New York (N.L.)		67	95	.414	5E		1997—New York (A.L.)		96	66	.593	2E
1981—New York (N.L.)		17	34	.333	5E		1998—New York (A.L.)		114	48	.704	1E
—Second half		24	28	.462	4E		1999—New York (A.L.)		98	64	.605	1E
1982—Atlanta (N.L.)		89	73	.549	1W		2000—New York (A.L.)		87	74	.540	1E
1983—Atlanta (N.L.)		88	74	.543	2W		2001—New York (A.L.)		95	65	.594	1E
1984—Atlanta (N.L.)		80	82	.494	2W		2002—New York (A.L.)		103	58	.640	1E
1990—St. Louis (N.L.)		24	34	.414	6E		2003—New York (A.L.)		101	61	.623	1E
1991—St. Louis (N.L.)		84	78	.519	2E		2004—New York (A.L.)		101	61	.623	1E
1992—St. Louis (N.L.)		83	79	.512	3E		American League totals (9 years)		887	567	.610	
1993—St. Louis (N.L.)		87	75	.537	3E		National League totals (14 years)		894	1003	.471	
							Major League totals (23 years)		1781	1570	.531	

NOTES:
1977—Replaced New York manager Joe Frazier with club in sixth place and record of 15-30 (May 31); served as player/manager (May 31-June 18, when released as player)....**1982**—Lost to St. Louis, 3-0, in N.L. Championship Series....**1990**—Replaced St. Louis manager Whitey Herzog (33-47) and interim manager Red Schoendienst (13-11) with club in sixth place and record of 46-58 (August 1)....**1994**—St. Louis was tied for third place in N.L. Central at time of season-ending strike (August 12)....**1995**—Replaced as Cardinals manager by interim manager Mike Jorgensen[, with club in fourth place] (June 16)....**1996**—Defeated Texas, 3-1, in A.L. Division Series; defeated Baltimore, 4-1, in A.L. Championship Series; defeated Atlanta, 4-2, in World Series....**1997**—Lost to Cleveland, 3-2, in A.L. Division Series....**1998**—Defeated Texas, 3-0, in A.L. Division Series; defeated Cleveland, 4-2, in A.L. Championship Series; defeated San Diego, 4-0, in World Series....**1999**—Defeated Texas, 3-0, in A.L. Division Series; defeated Boston, 4-1, in A.L. Championship Series; defeated Atlanta, 4-0, in World Series....**2000**—Defeated Oakland, 3-2, in A.L. Division Series; defeated Seattle, 4-2, in A.L. Championship Series; defeated New York Mets, 4-1, in World Series....**2001**—Defeated Oakland, 3-2, in A.L. Division Series; defeated Seattle, 4-1, in A.L. Championship Series; lost to Arizona, 4-3, in World Series....**2002**—Lost to Anaheim, 3-1, in A.L. Division Series....**2003**—Defeated Minnesota, 3-1, in A.L. Division Series; defeated Boston, 4-3, in A.L. Championship Series; lost to Florida, 4-2, in World Series....**2004**—Defeated Minnesota, 3-1, in A.L. Division Series; lost to Boston, 4-3, in A.L. Championship Series...Career major league postseason record: 72-41.

TRACY, JIM — DODGERS

PERSONAL: Born December 31, 1955, in Hamilton, Ohio. ... Full name: James Edwin Tracy. ... High school: Badin (Hamilton, Ohio) ... College: Marietta College (Ohio)

RECORD AS PLAYER

		BATTING												FIELDING			
	G	AB	R	H	2B	3B	HR	RBI	Avg.	BB	SO	SB	PO	A	E	Avg.
Major League totals (2 years)	87	185	18	46	5	4	3	14	.249	25	51	3	60	0	2	.968

RECORD AS MANAGER

BACKGROUND: Minor league field coordinator, Cincinnati Reds (1992). ... Coach, Montreal Expos (1995-98). ... Coach, Los Angeles Dodgers (1999-2000).

HONORS: Named Minor League Manager of the Year by THE SPORTING NEWS (1993).

Year	Team (League)	W	L	Pct.	Pos		Year	Team (League)	W	L	Pct.	Pos
1987—Peoria (Midw.)		71	69	.507	2nd		—Second half		38	39	.494	3rd
1988—Peoria (Midw.)		29	40	.420	6th		1993—Harrisburg (East.)		94	44	.681	1st
—Second half		41	30	.577	3rd		1994—Ottawa (I.L.)		70	72	.493	3rd
1989—Chattanooga (Sou.)		33	38	.465	4th		2001—Los Angeles (N.L.)		86	76	.531	3W
—Second half		25	43	.368	5th		2002—Los Angeles (N.L.)		92	70	.568	3W
1990—Chattanooga (Sou.)		35	36	.493	4th		2003—Los Angeles (N.L.)		85	77	.525	2W
—Second half		31	42	.425	4th		2004—Los Angeles (N.L.)		93	69	.574	1W
1991—Chattanooga (Sou.)		35	32	.522	2nd		Major League totals (4 years)		356	292	.549	

MAJOR LEAGUE MANAGERS

1993—Defeated Albany, 3-1, in semifinals; defeated Canton-Akron, 3-2, in league championship....**2004**—Lost to St. Louis, 3-1, in N.L. Division Series....Career major league postseason record: 1-3.

TRAMMELL, ALAN   TIGERS

PERSONAL: Born February 21, 1958, in Garden Grove, Calif. ... Full name: Alan Stuart Trammell. ... Name pronounced: TRAM-ull. ... High school: Kearney (San Diego).

RECORD AS PLAYER

					BATTING								FIELDING			
	G	AB	R	H	2B	3B	HR	RBI	Avg.	BB	SO	SB	PO	A	E	Avg.
Major League totals (20 years)..........	2293	8288	1231	2365	412	55	185	1003	.285	850	874	236	3448	6265	235	.976

RECORD AS MANAGER

BACKGROUND: Assistant director of baseball operations, Detroit Tigers (1997-98). ... Coach, Tigers (1999). ... Coach, San Diego Padres (2000-02)

Year Team (League)	W	L	Pct.	Pos
2003—Detroit (A.L.)	43	119	.265	5C
2004—Detroit (A.L.)	72	90	.444	4C
Major League totals (2 years)	115	209	.355	

WEDGE, ERIC   INDIANS

PERSONAL: Born January 27, 1968, in Fort Wayne, Ind. ... Full name: Eric Michael Wedge. ... High school: Northrop (Fort Wayne, Ind.). ... College: Wichita State.

RECORD AS PLAYER

					BATTING								FIELDING			
	G	AB	R	H	2B	3B	HR	RBI	Avg.	BB	SO	SB	PO	A	E	Avg.
Major League totals (4 years)...........	39	86	13	20	2	0	5	12	.233	14	25	0	25	3	0	1.000

RECORD AS MANAGER

HONORS: Named Carolina League Manager of the Year (1999). ... Named International League Manager of the Year (2001).

Year Team (League)	W	L	Pct.	Pos	Year Team (League)	W	L	Pct.	Pos
1998—Columbus (S.Atl.)	28	42	.400	4th	2001—Buffalo (I.L.)	91	51	.641	1st
—Second half	31	39	.443	3rd	2002—Buffalo (I.L.)	87	57	.604	2nd
1999—Kinston (Caro.)	37	32	.536	1st	2003—Cleveland (A.L.)	68	94	.420	4C
—Second half	42	26	.618	2nd	2004—Cleveland (A.L.)	80	82	.494	3C
2000—Akron (East.)	75	68	.524	3rd	Major League totals (2 years)	148	176	.457	

NOTES:
1999—Lost to Myrtle Beach, 2-1, in semifinals....**2001**—Lost to Scranton/Wilkes-Barre, 3-2, in semifinals....**2002**—Defeated Scranton/Wilkes-Barre, 3-0, in semifinals; lost to Durham, 3-0, in league championship.

YOST, NED   BREWERS

PERSONAL: Born August 19, 1955, in Eureka, Calif. ... Full name: Edgar Frederick Yost. ... Junior college: Chabot Junior College

RECORD AS PLAYER

					BATTING								FIELDING			
	G	AB	R	H	2B	3B	HR	RBI	Avg.	BB	SO	SB	PO	A	E	Avg.
Major League totals (6 years)...........	219	605	54	128	15	4	16	64	.212	21	117	5	843	54	16	.982

RECORD AS MANAGER

BACKGROUND: Coach, Altanta Braves (1991-02).

Year Team (League)	W	L	Pct.	Pos	Year Team (League)	W	L	Pct.	Pos
1988—Sumter (S.Atl.)	29	40	.420	6th	1990—Sumter (S.Atl.)	38	34	.527	4th
—Second half	35	33		4th	—Second half	35	35		4th
1989—Sumter (S.Atl.)	30	40	.428	5th	2003—Milwaukee (N.L.)	68	94	.419	5th
—Second half	30	41		6th	2004—Milwaukee (N.L.)	67	94	.416	6th
					Major League totals (2 years)	135	188	.417	

MAJOR LEAGUE MANAGERS

OFFENSE

				STOLEN BASES								SACRIFICE BUNTS				HIT & RUN	
				Pitchout	2nd	3rd	Home	Dbl	— Out Percentage —					Suc.	Fav.			Suc.
	G	Att.	SB%	Rn Mv	SB-CS	SB-CS	SB-CS	Stls	0	1	2	Att.	%	Inn.	Sqz.	Att.	%
AL Managers																	
Francona, Terry, Bos	162	98	69.4	1	64-27	4-2	0-1	2	20.4	35.7	43.9	20	70.0	7	1	33	21.2
Gardenhire, Ron, Min	162	162	71.6	2	97-39	19-6	0-1	7	16.7	43.2	40.1	68	80.9	6	4	81	23.5
Gibbons, John, Tor	50	34	64.7	1	19-10	3-2	0-0	0	14.7	41.2	44.1	2	100.0	5	0	16	31.3
Guillen, Ozzie, CWS	162	129	60.5	4	71-46	7-5	0-0	2	16.3	35.7	48.1	90	78.9	1	6	73	34.2
Macha, Ken, Oak	162	69	68.1	1	41-20	6-2	0-0	2	10.1	37.7	52.2	34	82.4	8	1	25	28.0
Mazzilli, Lee, Bal	162	142	71.1	7	82-35	19-5	0-1	6	23.9	33.8	42.3	58	84.5	7	3	83	36.1
Melvin, Bob, Sea	162	152	72.4	2	92-33	18-9	0-0	8	16.4	38.2	45.4	59	86.4	1	1	96	40.6
Pena, Tony, KC	162	115	58.3	7	55-40	12-3	0-5	2	18.3	41.7	40.0	59	79.7	2	1	96	42.7
Piniella, Lou, TB	161	174	75.9	11	110-33	21-8	1-1	4	24.1	35.6	40.2	46	80.4	3	0	69	37.7
Scioscia, Mike, Ana	162	189	75.7	6	123-42	19-3	1-1	8	18.5	37.0	44.4	75	82.7	5	7	131	38.9
Showalter, Buck, Tex	162	105	65.7	2	64-32	5-4	0-0	0	13.3	29.5	57.1	32	71.9	2	1	55	43.6
Torre, Joe, NYY	162	117	71.8	4	67-25	16-8	1-0	7	12.0	49.6	38.5	50	82.0	1	1	47	42.6
Tosca, Carlos, Tor	111	55	65.5	1	30-19	5-0	1-0	2	18.2	38.2	43.6	23	82.6	7	1	55	49.1
Trammell, Alan, Det	162	136	63.2	5	75-46	11-4	0-0	3	17.6	33.8	48.5	69	85.5	5	11	68	38.2
Wedge, Eric, Cle	162	149	63.1	7	83-46	11-7	0-2	3	8.1	32.9	59.1	57	93.0	9	3	78	29.5
NL Managers																	
Alou, Felipe, SF	162	66	65.2	0	36-20	7-2	0-1	0	19.7	43.9	36.4	107	88.8	5	5	69	50.7
Baker, Dusty, ChC	162	94	70.2	4	64-24	2-4	0-0	0	23.4	41.5	35.1	110	80.0	2	2	48	33.3
Bochy, Bruce, SD	162	77	67.5	5	45-21	7-4	0-0	2	22.1	31.2	46.8	75	77.3	3	3	56	44.6
Bowa, Larry, Phi	160	127	78.7	4	94-24	6-2	0-1	1	15.7	31.5	52.8	78	83.3	5	5	50	40.0
Brenly, Bob, Ari	79	40	57.5	0	21-15	2-2	0-0	2	25.0	35.0	40.0	36	75.0	3	1	47	42.6
Cox, Bobby, Atl	162	118	72.9	1	83-27	3-3	0-2	0	25.4	30.5	44.1	105	79.0	3	4	49	32.7
Garner, Phil, Hou	74	78	82.1	0	46-14	17-0	1-0	8	15.4	42.3	42.3	45	80.0	7	3	38	39.5
Howe, Art, NYM	162	130	82.3	3	95-19	12-4	0-0	1	20.0	36.9	43.1	95	75.8	3	0	63	36.5
Hurdle, Clint, Col	162	77	57.1	2	36-31	8-2	0-0	0	24.7	31.2	44.2	133	80.5	5	6	51	35.3
La Russa, Tony, StL	162	158	70.3	7	96-41	15-5	0-1	3	19.0	39.9	41.1	92	85.9	5	10	116	37.9
McClendon, Lloyd, Pit	161	103	61.2	7	57-32	6-4	0-4	1	21.4	33.0	45.6	102	81.4	3	1	98	32.7
McKeon, Jack, Fla	162	139	69.1	6	81-41	14-2	1-0	3	18.0	35.3	46.8	107	80.4	3	7	72	38.9
Miley, Dave, Cin	162	102	75.5	3	70-23	6-2	1-0	1	22.5	41.2	36.3	80	77.5	5	3	46	37.0
Pedrique, Al, Ari	83	45	66.7	1	25-14	5-1	0-0	0	11.1	33.3	55.6	46	69.6	3	4	18	16.7
Robinson, Frank, Mon	162	147	74.1	7	88-34	21-3	0-1	3	14.3	42.9	42.9	124	89.5	2	8	83	38.6
Tracy, Jim, LA	162	143	71.3	1	91-35	10-3	1-3	2	23.1	37.8	39.2	90	77.8	5	10	47	36.2
Varsho, Gary, Phi	2	0	-	0	0-0	0-0	0-0	0	-	-	-	2	100.0	2	0	0	-
Williams, Jimy, Hou	88	41	61.0	1	24-14	1-1	0-1	0	31.7	34.1	34.1	73	87.7	1	6	27	37.0
Yost, Ned, Mil	161	178	77.5	10	124-35	14-2	0-3	2	23.0	35.4	41.6	84	72.6	7	9	76	38.2

DEFENSE

		PITCHOUT			Non-PO	INTENTIONAL BB			DEFENSIVE SUBS				
			Runners				Pct. of	Fav. Score			Favorite		
	G	Total	Moving	CS%	CS%	IBB	Situations	Diff.	Total	Inning	Pos. 1	Pos. 2	Pos. 3
AL Managers													
Francona, Terry, Bos	162	28	6	66.7	18.2	22	3.2	0	53	8	1b-18	rf-17	lf-12
Gardenhire, Ron, Min	162	16	4	75.0	36.3	21	3.7	0	24	8	c-7	2b-7	1b-3
Gibbons, John, Tor	50	19	0	-	25.0	5	2.5	-2	1	3	c-1	-	-
Guillen, Ozzie, CWS	162	19	2	100.0	33.8	20	3.7	0	13	9	1b-5	c-3	2b-1
Macha, Ken, Oak	162	2	0	-	39.8	42	6.4	-1	6	9	2b-2	rf-2	1b-1
Mazzilli, Lee, Bal	162	34	5	20.0	32.8	29	4.8	0	12	8	cf-6	rf-3	2b-1
Melvin, Bob, Sea	162	29	4	75.0	35.7	25	3.9	-2	16	9	1b-7	cf-7	3b-1
Pena, Tony, KC	162	8	1	0.0	29.7	33	5.1	-2	12	8	rf-6	lf-4	c-1
Piniella, Lou, TB	161	17	6	0.0	34.4	29	4.7	-1	25	9	3b-8	lf-6	cf-4
Scioscia, Mike, Ana	162	35	7	85.7	30.6	18	2.8	-2	31	8	3b-16	lf-6	2b-5
Showalter, Buck, Tex	162	3	1	0.0	35.8	22	3.5	1	17	9	rf-5	2b-4	lf-3
Torre, Joe, NYY	162	35	6	66.7	24.1	26	4.1	-2	36	9	1b-20	cf-5	rf-5
Tosca, Carlos, Tor	111	42	8	50.0	31.8	23	4.8	0	10	9	ss-2	lf-2	rf-2
Trammell, Alan, Det	162	9	2	50.0	36.4	21	3.1	-2	18	8	3b-7	cf-3	2b-2
Wedge, Eric, Cle	162	31	4	50.0	24.5	33	4.6	0	13	8	1b-9	3b-2	cf-2

		PITCHOUT				INTENTIONAL BB			DEFENSIVE SUBS				
			Runners		Non-PO		Pct. of	Fav. Score		Favorite			
NL Managers	G	Total	Moving	CS%	CS%	IBB	Situations	Diff.	Total	Inning	Pos. 1	Pos. 2	Pos. 3
Alou, Felipe, SF	162	3	1	100.0	24.2	29	4.5	0	29	9	ss-15	1b-4	c-3
Baker, Dusty, ChC	162	68	13	46.2	24.6	24	3.7	0	6	7	3b-3	cf-2	2b-1
Bochy, Bruce, SD	162	12	4	75.0	24.4	25	4.3	-1	26	7	lf-15	3b-4	c-2
Bowa, Larry, Phi	160	25	4	50.0	19.4	48	7.1	4	14	8	lf-5	cf-5	2b-2
Brenly, Bob, Ari	79	30	5	80.0	37.5	24	7.1	-2	0	0	-	-	-
Cox, Bobby, Atl	162	25	2	100.0	22.9	34	5.9	-1	11	7	1b-5	lf-4	c-1
Garner, Phil, Hou	74	6	1	0.0	26.3	19	6.6	-1	13	9	lf-6	c-4	3b-2
Howe, Art, NYM	162	26	8	62.5	26.0	55	8.6	0	22	9	c-9	lf-5	1b-3
Hurdle, Clint, Col	162	16	2	0.0	22.7	65	8.9	-1	22	8	lf-12	cf-5	rf-4
La Russa, Tony, StL	162	8	3	66.7	34.2	21	3.5	-2	23	6	lf-10	rf-9	c-2
McClendon, Lloyd, Pit	161	64	4	50.0	34.0	46	7.1	0	27	9	3b-14	2b-8	rf-3
McKeon, Jack, Fla	162	18	5	60.0	23.2	41	6.1	-1	18	7	lf-6	rf-6	ss-3
Miley, Dave, Cin	162	13	5	60.0	28.6	38	5.4	-2	25	8	3b-11	ss-9	rf-2
Pedrique, Al, Ari	83	16	1	0.0	28.6	22	7.3	-2	4	9	1b-2	ss-1	lf-1
Robinson, Frank, Mon	162	1	0	-	41.4	57	9.9	0	16	8	rf-7	ss-2	lf-2
Tracy, Jim, LA	162	5	2	50.0	29.1	30	5.0	-1	9	8	2b-5	1b-2	3b-1
Varsho, Gary, Phi	2	0	0	-	0.0	0	0.0	0	0	0	-	-	-
Williams, Jimy, Hou	88	22	3	33.3	30.0	25	7.0	-2	10	8	cf-4	rf-3	1b-1
Yost, Ned, Mil	161	9	2	50.0	24.1	19	2.9	-2	13	7	rf-10	1b-2	3b-1

LINEUPS

		STARTING LINEUP				SUBSTITUTIONS					
		Lineups	%LHB	%RHB		Percent					PR
CS	G	Used	vs. RHSP	vs. LHSP	#PH	PH Platoon	PH BA	PH HR	#PR	SB-	
AL Managers											
Francona, Terry, Bos	162	141	57.2	80.0	116	66.4	.263	2	65	6-2	
Gardenhire, Ron, Min	162	130	51.0	75.1	126	71.4	.257	6	45	2-0	
Gibbons, John, Tor	50	36	63.0	80.2	42	83.3	.229	3	3	0-0	
Guillen, Ozzie, CWS	162	134	38.5	87.1	132	82.6	.283	4	35	1-0	
Macha, Ken, Oak	162	119	56.1	68.8	122	82.8	.182	3	13	1-1	
Mazzilli, Lee, Bal	162	104	55.0	68.0	89	79.8	.195	2	44	5-1	
Melvin, Bob, Sea	162	151	50.0	78.7	109	70.6	.271	4	66	7-1	
Pena, Tony, KC	162	140	46.0	83.9	53	66.0	.174	1	27	1-0	
Piniella, Lou, TB	161	137	57.8	74.2	97	82.5	.209	1	25	1-2	
Scioscia, Mike, Ana	162	126	48.1	74.9	94	67.0	.260	2	32	3-2	
Showalter, Buck, Tex	162	120	53.3	86.2	86	72.1	.167	1	15	0-0	
Torre, Joe, NYY	162	116	58.2	80.8	86	91.9	.308	5	35	1-0	
Tosca, Carlos, Tor	111	92	49.3	80.6	60	78.3	.220	1	15	0-0	
Trammell, Alan, Det	162	131	60.6	77.2	105	77.1	.174	1	29	2-3	
Wedge, Eric, Cle	162	114	71.4	73.2	91	69.2	.264	4	34	0-2	
NL Managers											
Alou, Felipe, SF	162	138	56.3	80.9	239	57.7	.295	4	47	3-1	
Baker, Dusty, ChC	162	113	30.8	84.4	254	74.4	.237	4	16	0-0	
Bochy, Bruce, SD	162	96	42.4	75.6	261	76.2	.203	5	28	5-2	
Bowa, Larry, Phi	160	105	44.7	76.1	258	58.1	.239	9	21	2-0	
Brenly, Bob, Ari	79	48	55.8	70.4	124	77.4	.171	3	12	0-0	
Cox, Bobby, Atl	162	101	55.1	88.1	243	53.9	.277	5	57	4-0	
Garner, Phil, Hou	74	31	39.1	95.7	141	66.7	.282	3	19	2-0	
Howe, Art, NYM	162	136	35.3	88.1	273	57.1	.218	6	47	2-0	
Hurdle, Clint, Col	162	131	47.0	76.4	288	77.1	.254	11	19	0-2	
La Russa, Tony, StL	162	119	42.3	76.6	275	79.6	.263	6	25	0-2	
McClendon, Lloyd, Pit	161	114	39.6	82.9	278	80.2	.217	5	13	2-0	
McKeon, Jack, Fla	162	90	32.5	84.9	224	63.4	.174	4	27	0-0	
Miley, Dave, Cin	162	132	50.8	72.8	264	66.7	.192	7	25	3-0	
Pedrique, Al, Ari	83	77	47.2	84.0	118	81.4	.250	1	14	0-0	
Robinson, Frank, Mon	162	131	61.3	68.7	253	70.4	.190	2	16	0-1	
Tracy, Jim, LA	162	94	64.6	75.6	295	74.6	.211	9	25	0-0	
Varsho, Gary, Phi	2	2	44.4	-	4	75.0	.333	0	1	0-0	
Williams, Jimy, Hou	88	52	25.4	98.8	132	76.5	.241	2	2	0-0	
Yost, Ned, Mil	161	132	54.3	63.5	283	69.3	.205	7	24	3-2	

PITCHING

		STARTERS					RELIEVERS					
	G	Slow Hooks	Quick Hooks	> 120 Pitches	> 140 Pitches	3 Days Rest	Relief App	Mid-Inning Change	Save > 1 IP	1st Batter Platoon Pct	1-Batter App	3 Pit. (<=2run)
AL Managers												
Francona, Terry, Bos...............	162	25	11	3	0	0	437	174	8	60.6	37	29
Gardenhire, Ron, Min	162	11	20	1	0	1	435	163	4	60.0	26	35
Gibbons, John, Tor	50	3	9	2	0	1	130	47	1	41.5	4	4
Guillen, Ozzie, CWS...............	162	22	8	5	0	4	399	177	8	60.2	24	21
Macha, Ken, Oak...................	162	19	12	9	0	1	414	161	5	60.6	46	33
Mazzilli, Lee, Bal	162	22	29	2	0	2	452	194	4	61.3	27	32
Melvin, Bob, Sea	162	17	16	12	0	2	414	180	5	62.8	45	17
Pena, Tony, KC	162	21	20	3	0	1	409	168	5	55.0	28	12
Piniella, Lou, TB	161	13	21	8	0	0	401	207	15	65.1	27	23
Scioscia, Mike, Ana	162	14	19	4	0	5	343	102	11	47.5	5	32
Showalter, Buck, Tex...............	162	11	30	3	0	3	468	241	10	68.2	33	27
Torre, Joe, NYY	162	13	17	3	0	4	436	190	10	58.9	36	29
Tosca, Carlos, Tor	111	9	12	3	0	1	301	112	7	51.5	13	20
Trammell, Alan, Det...............	162	16	28	3	0	1	432	201	6	62.4	33	20
Wedge, Eric, Cle...................	162	10	21	2	0	1	479	169	0	55.6	39	24
NL Managers												
Alou, Felipe, SF	162	7	19	13	1	0	521	247	8	70.2	95	30
Baker, Dusty, ChC	162	7	14	13	0	1	460	154	8	62.4	39	33
Bochy, Bruce, SD	162	9	24	2	0	6	437	133	3	53.0	23	35
Bowa, Larry, Phi	160	7	23	2	0	2	472	118	5	54.1	24	27
Brenly, Bob, Ari	79	10	10	2	0	0	242	98	5	60.3	26	8
Cox, Bobby, Atl	162	12	15	4	0	3	483	125	16	61.3	29	40
Garner, Phil, Hou	74	4	20	3	0	0	241	76	4	61.0	19	12
Howe, Art, NYM	162	10	25	8	0	1	474	153	5	62.0	27	43
Hurdle, Clint, Col	162	22	23	3	0	4	473	148	1	64.3	31	27
La Russa, Tony, StL...................	162	16	19	6	0	0	469	186	16	68.7	54	37
McClendon, Lloyd, Pit	161	15	20	4	0	1	464	145	1	62.0	29	38
McKeon, Jack, Fla...................	162	7	18	2	0	5	404	136	12	60.4	31	29
Miley, Dave, Cin	162	20	20	2	0	0	497	156	2	56.7	35	27
Pedrique, Al, Ari...................	83	10	8	4	0	0	229	82	0	57.6	20	9
Robinson, Frank, Mon	162	14	30	13	2	0	462	154	4	61.9	41	31
Tracy, Jim, LA	162	10	20	4	0	0	459	141	16	62.5	46	27
Varsho, Gary, Phi...................	2	0	1	0	0	1	5	1	0	40.0	0	0
Williams, Jimy, Hou	88	2	13	3	0	1	252	84	6	57.9	16	23
Yost, Ned, Mil.........................	161	8	19	9	0	1	423	124	2	58.4	20	31

One of the things about baseball which appeals to many of us is the game's endless opportunity for analysis. . . and few things are analyzed more than managerial decisions. Major league skippers may not have batting averages and slugging percentages to point to at the end of the season, but when it comes time to judge their performance and production, there's no reason we can't take a look at their statistics.

Which manager posted the best stolen-base success rate?

Which skippers were constantly tinkering with their lineups?

Which managers wore out a path to the pitching mound?

It's questions like these that get our second-guessing juices going, and it's questions like these that inspired the following pages, which look at managerial tendencies in a number of situations. Once again, the skippers are compared based on offense, defense, lineups and pitching use. We don't rank the managers; there is plenty of room for argument on whether certain moves are good or bad. We are simply providing fodder for the discussion.

Offensively, managers have control over bunting, stealing and the timing of hit-and-runs. This section looks at the quantity, timing and success of these moves.

Defensively, this section looks at the success of pitchouts, the frequency of intentional walks, and the pattern of defensive substitutions.

Most managers spend large amounts of their time devising lineups. Here you'll find the number of lineups used, as well as the platoon percentage. The use of pinch-hitters and pinch-runners also is explored.

Finally, how does the manager use pitchers? For starters, this section shows slow and quick hooks, along with the number of times a starter was allowed to throw more than 120 and 140 pitches. For relievers, we look at the number of relief appearances, mid-inning changes and how often a pitcher gets a save going more than one inning (a rare occurrence these days).

For the purposes of this section, it is assumed that a coach filling in for his manager will make his decisions based on what the manager would do in a given situation.

The categories include:

Stolen Base Success Percentage: Stolen bases divided by attempts.

Pitchout Runners Moving: The number of times the opposition is running when a manager calls a pitchout.

Double Steals: The number of double steals attempted in 2004.

Out Percentage: The proportion of stolen bases with that number of outs.

Sacrifice Bunt Attempts: A bunt is considered a sac attempt if no runner is on third, there are no outs, or the pitcher attempts a bunt.

Sacrifice Bunt Success %: A bunt that results in a sacrifice or a hit, divided by the number of attempts.

Favorite Inning: The most common inning in which an event occurred.

Hit-and-Run Success: The hit-and-run results in baserunner advancement with no double play.

Intentional Walk Situation: Runners on base, first base open, and anyone but the pitcher up. The teams must be within two runs of each other, or the tying run must be on base, at bat or on deck.

Defensive Substitutions: Straight defensive substitutions, with the team leading by four runs or less.

Number of Lineups: Based on batting order, 1-8 for National Leaguers, 1-9 for American Leaguers.

Percent LHB vs. RHSP and RHB vs. LHSP: A measure of platooning. A batter is considered to always have the platoon advantage if he is a switch-hitter.

Percent PH platoon: Frequency the manager gets his pinch-hitter the platoon advantage. Switch-hitters always have the advantage.

Score Diff: The most common score differential on which an intentional walk is called for.

Slow and Quick Hooks: A quick hook is the removal of a pitcher who has pitched fewer than six innings and given up three runs or less. A slow hook occurs when a pitcher pitches more than nine innings, or allows seven or more runs, or whose combined innings pitched and runs allowed totals 13 or more.

Mid-Inning Change: The number of times a manager changed pitchers in the middle of an inning.

1-Batter Appearances: The number of times a pitcher was brought in to face only one batter. Called the "Tony La Russa special" because of his penchant for trying to orchestrate specific matchups for specific situations.

3 Pitchers (2 runs or less): The club gives up two runs or less in a game, but uses at least three pitchers.

2004 STATISTICAL LEADERS

American League leaders

National League leaders

Active career leaders

2004 AMERICAN LEAGUE LEADERS

BATTING

Batting Average
(minimum 502 PA)

Player, Team	AB	H	Avg.
I Suzuki, Sea.	704	262	.372
M Mora, Bal.	550	187	.340
V Guerrero, Ana.	612	206	.337
I Rodriguez, Det.	527	176	.334
E Durazo, Oak.	511	164	.321
C Guillen, Det.	522	166	.318
J Lopez, Bal.	579	183	.316
M Kotsay, Oak.	606	190	.314
M Young, Tex.	690	216	.313
T Hafner, Cle.	482	150	.311

On-Base Percentage
(minimum 502 PA; *AB+BB+HBP+SF)

Player, Team	*PA	OB	OBP
M Mora, Bal.	630	264	.419
I Suzuki, Sea.	760	315	.414
T Hafner, Cle.	573	235	.410
J Posada, N.Y.	547	219	.400
E Chavez, Oak.	577	229	.397
M Ramirez, Bos.	663	263	.397
E Durazo, Oak.	578	229	.396
G Sheffield, N.Y.	684	269	.393
V Guerrero, Ana.	680	266	.391
J Varitek, Bos.	536	209	.390

Slugging Percentage
(minimum 502 PA)

Player, Team	AB	TB	Slg.
M Ramirez, Bos.	568	348	.613
D Ortiz, Bos.	582	351	.603
V Guerrero, Ana.	612	366	.598
T Hafner, Cle.	482	281	.583
M Mora, Bal.	550	309	.562
M Teixeira, Tex.	545	305	.560
A Rowand, Chi.	487	265	.544
C Guillen, Det.	522	283	.542
C Delgado, Tor.	458	245	.535
P Konerko, Chi.	563	301	.535

Games

H Matsui, N.Y.	162
M Tejada, Bal.	162
I Suzuki, Sea.	161
M Young, Tex.	160
2 tied with	159

Plate Appearances

I Suzuki, Sea.	762
M Young, Tex.	739
B Roberts, Bal.	736
M Tejada, Bal.	725
D Jeter, N.Y.	721

At-Bats

I Suzuki, Sea.	704
M Young, Tex.	690
M Tejada, Bal.	653
D Jeter, N.Y.	643
B Roberts, Bal.	641

Hits

I Suzuki, Sea.	262
M Young, Tex.	216
V Guerrero, Ana.	206
M Tejada, Bal.	203
M Kotsay, Oak.	190

Singles

I Suzuki, Sea.	225
M Young, Tex.	152
M Kotsay, Oak.	135
C Crawford, T.B.	129
D Eckstein, Ana.	129

Doubles

B Roberts, Bal.	50
R Belliard, Cle.	48
D Ortiz, Bos.	47
D Jeter, N.Y.	44
M Ramirez, Bos.	44

Triples

C Crawford, T.B.	19
C Figgins, Ana.	17
C Guillen, Det.	10
O Infante, Det.	9
M Young, Tex.	9

Home Runs

M Ramirez, Bos.	43
P Konerko, Chi.	41
D Ortiz, Bos.	41
V Guerrero, Ana.	39
M Teixeira, Tex.	38

Total Bases

V Guerrero, Ana.	366
D Ortiz, Bos.	351
M Tejada, Bal.	349
M Ramirez, Bos.	348
M Young, Tex.	333

Runs Scored

V Guerrero, Ana.	124
J Damon, Bos.	123
G Sheffield, N.Y.	117
M Young, Tex.	114
A Rodriguez, N.Y.	112

Runs Batted In

M Tejada, Bal.	150
D Ortiz, Bos.	139
M Ramirez, Bos.	130
V Guerrero, Ana.	126
G Sheffield, N.Y.	121

GDP

J Posada, N.Y.	24
M Tejada, Bal.	24
T Hunter, Min.	23
P Konerko, Chi.	23
2 tied with	21

Sacrifice Hits

O Vizquel, Cle.	20
D Jeter, N.Y.	16
B Roberts, Bal.	15
D Eckstein, Ana.	14
C Guzman, Min.	13

Sacrifice Flies

M Tejada, Bal.	14
C Delgado, Tor.	11
R Palmeiro, Bal.	9
8 tied with	8

Stolen Bases

C Crawford, T.B.	59
I Suzuki, Sea.	36
C Figgins, Ana.	34
B Roberts, Bal.	29
A Rodriguez, N.Y.	28

Caught Stealing

C Crawford, T.B.	15
C Crisp, Cle.	13
C Figgins, Ana.	13
A Sanchez, Det.	13
B Roberts, Bal.	12

Walks

E Chavez, Oak.	95
G Sheffield, N.Y.	92
M Bellhorn, Bos.	88
H Matsui, N.Y.	88
J Posada, N.Y.	88

Intentional Walks

I Suzuki, Sea.	19
R Palmeiro, Bal.	15
M Ramirez, Bos.	15
V Guerrero, Ana.	14
2 tied with	12

Hit by Pitch

T Hafner, Cle.	17
K Millar, Bos.	17
J Guillen, Ana.	15
M Cairo, N.Y.	14
D Jeter, N.Y.	14

Strikeouts

M Bellhorn, Bos.	177
H Blalock, Tex.	149
C Pena, Det.	146
B Crosby, Oak.	141
2 tied with	139

2004 NATIONAL LEAGUE LEADERS

BATTING

Batting Average
(minimum 502 PA)

Player, Team	AB	H	Avg.
B Bonds, S.F.	373	135	.362
T Helton, Col.	547	190	.347
M Loretta, S.D.	620	208	.335
A Beltre, L.A.	598	200	.334
A Pujols, St.L.	592	196	.331
J Pierre, Fla.	678	221	.326
S Casey, Cin.	571	185	.324
J Kendall, Pit.	574	183	.319
A Ramirez, Chi.	547	174	.318
L Berkman, Hou.	544	172	.316

On-Base Percentage
(minimum 502 PA; *AB+BB+HBP+SF)

Player, Team	*PA	OB	OBP
B Bonds, S.F.	617	376	.609
T Helton, Col.	683	320	.469
L Berkman, Hou.	687	309	.450
J Drew, Atl.	644	281	.436
B Abreu, Phi.	713	305	.428
J Edmonds, St.L.	612	256	.418
A Pujols, St.L.	692	287	.415
S Rolen, St.L.	592	242	.409
J Kendall, Pit.	657	262	.399
J Thome, Phi.	618	245	.396

Slugging Percentage
(minimum 502 PA)

Player, Team	AB	TB	Slg.
B Bonds, S.F.	373	303	.812
A Pujols, St.L.	592	389	.657
J Edmonds, St.L.	498	320	.643
A Beltre, L.A.	598	376	.629
T Helton, Col.	547	339	.620
S Rolen, St.L.	500	299	.598
J Thome, Phi.	508	295	.581
A Ramirez, Chi.	547	316	.578
J Drew, Atl.	518	295	.569
A Dunn, Cin.	568	323	.569

Games

S Finley, Ari.-L.A.	162
J Pierre, Fla.	162
A Dunn, Cin.	161
D Lee, Chi.	161
3 tied with	160

Plate Appearances

J Pierre, Fla.	748
C Izturis, L.A.	728
J Rollins, Phi.	725
B Abreu, Phi.	713
S Podsednik, Mil.	713

At-Bats

J Pierre, Fla.	678
C Izturis, L.A.	670
J Rollins, Phi.	657
J Wilson, Pit.	652
S Podsednik, Mil.	640

Hits

J Pierre, Fla.	221
M Loretta, S.D.	208
J Wilson, Pit.	201
A Beltre, L.A.	200
A Pujols, St.L.	196

Singles

J Pierre, Fla.	184
C Izturis, L.A.	148
J Kendall, Pit.	148
L Castillo, Fla.	143
M Loretta, S.D.	143

Doubles

L Overbay, Mil.	53
A Pujols, St.L.	51
T Helton, Col.	49
3 tied with	47

Triples

J Pierre, Fla.	12
J Rollins, Phi.	12
J Wilson, Pit.	12
C Izturis, L.A.	9
4 tied with	8

Home Runs

A Beltre, L.A.	48
A Dunn, Cin.	46
A Pujols, St.L.	46
B Bonds, S.F.	45
2 tied with	42

Total Bases

A Pujols, St.L.	389
A Beltre, L.A.	376
T Helton, Col.	339
M Alou, Chi.	335
A Dunn, Cin.	323

Runs Scored

A Pujols, St.L.	133
B Bonds, S.F.	129
J Rollins, Phi.	119
B Abreu, Phi.	118
J Drew, Atl.	118

Runs Batted In

V Castilla, Col.	131
S Rolen, St.L.	124
A Pujols, St.L.	123
A Beltre, L.A.	121
M Cabrera, Fla.	112

GDP

A Pierzynski, S.F.	27
A Ramirez, Chi.	25
A Jones, Atl.	24
J Kent, Hou.	23
3 tied with	22

Sacrifice Hits

R Clayton, Col.	24
A Everett, Hou.	22
K Benson, Pit.-N.Y.	15
L Hernandez, Mon.	15
J Pierre, Fla.	15

Sacrifice Flies

M Loretta, S.D.	16
J Kent, Hou.	11
T Batista, Mon.	10
E Renteria, St.L.	10
2 tied with	9

Stolen Bases

S Podsednik, Mil.	70
J Pierre, Fla.	45
B Abreu, Phi.	40
R Freel, Cin.	37
D Roberts, L.A.	33

Caught Stealing

J Pierre, Fla.	24
S Podsednik, Mil.	13
M Bradley, L.A.	11
E Renteria, St.L.	11
R Freel, Cin.	10

Walks

B Bonds, S.F.	232
B Abreu, Phi.	127
L Berkman, Hou.	127
T Helton, Col.	127
J Drew, Atl.	118

Intentional Walks

B Bonds, S.F.	120
J Thome, Phi.	26
T Helton, Col.	19
L Berkman, Hou.	14
M Piazza, N.Y.	14

Hit by Pitch

C Wilson, Pit.	30
J LaRue, Cin.	24
J Kendall, Pit.	19
A Cora, L.A.	18
2 tied with	15

Strikeouts

A Dunn, Cin.	195
C Wilson, Pit.	169
C Patterson, Chi.	168
G Jenkins, Mil.	152
B Wilkerson, Mon.	152

Earned Run Average
(minimum 162 IP)

Pitcher, Team	IP	ER	ERA
J Santana, Min. 228.0		66	2.61
C Schilling, Bos................226.2		82	3.26
J Westbrook, Cle...............215.2		81	3.38
B Radke, Min. 219.2		85	3.48
T Hudson, Oak. 188.2		74	3.53
R Lopez, Bal. 170.2		68	3.59
F Garcia, Sea.-Chi............210.0		89	3.81
M Buehrle, Chi.................245.1		106	3.89
P Martinez, Bos. 217.0		94	3.90
K Escobar, Ana................208.1		91	3.93

Won-Lost Percentage
(minimum 15 decisions)

Pitcher, Team	W	L	Pct.
C Schilling, Bos....................21		6	.778
J Santana, Min. 20		6	.769
M Mulder, Oak. 17		8	.680
K Rogers, Tex. 18		9	.667
T Hudson, Oak. 12		6	.667
J Rincon, Min. 11		6	.647
P Martinez, Bos. 16		9	.640
C Lee, Cle. 14		8	.636
J Lieber, N.Y. 14		8	.636
C Silva, Min. 14		8	.636

Opponents' Batting Average
(minimum 162 IP)

Pitcher, Team	AB	H	Avg.
J Santana, Min. 812		156	.192
T Lilly, Tor. 744		171	.230
P Martinez, Bos. 812		193	.238
C Schilling, Bos..................861		206	.239
F Garcia, Sea.-Chi..............795		192	.242
R Harden, Oak. 708		171	.242
J Bonderman, Det...............695		168	.242
K Escobar, Ana...................786		192	.244
B Arroyo, Bos......................688		171	.249
C Sabathia, Cle. 699		176	.252

Games

P Quantrill, N.Y. 86
T Gordon, N.Y. 80
J Rincon, Min. 77
B Ryan, Bal.....................................76
M Timlin, Bos. 76

Games Started

M Buehrle, Chi. 35
K Rogers, Tex. 35
5 tied with 34

Complete Games

M Mulder, Oak. 5
S Ponson, Bal. 5
J Westbrook, Cle................................5
M Buehrle, Chi. 4
3 tied with 3

Games Finished

M Rivera, N.Y. 69
F Cordero, Tex. 63
J Nathan, Min. 63
K Foulke, Bos. 61
D Baez, T.B. 59

Wins

C Schilling, Bos. 21
J Santana, Min. 20
B Colon, Ana. 18
K Rogers, Tex. 18
M Mulder, Oak. 17

Losses

D May, K.C. 19
R Franklin, Sea. 16
M Hendrickson, T.B. 15
J Johnson, Det. 15
S Ponson, Bal. 15

Saves

M Rivera, N.Y. 53
F Cordero, Tex. 49
J Nathan, Min. 44
T Percival, Ana. 33
K Foulke, Bos. 32

Shutouts

J Bonderman, Det..............................2
T Hudson, Oak. 2
S Ponson, Bal. 2
27 tied with 1

Hits Allowed

S Ponson, Bal. 265
M Buehrle, Chi. 257
C Silva, Min. 255
K Rogers, Tex. 248
M Maroth, Det. 244

Doubles Allowed

K Rogers, Tex. 59
D May, K.C. 58
B Anderson, K.C. 54
C Schilling, Bos.................................54
M Redman, Oak. 51

Triples Allowed

D May, K.C. 9
P Martinez, Bos. 8
K Rogers, Tex. 8
J Johnson, Det. 7
M Maroth, Det. 7

Home Runs Allowed

J Moyer, Sea.....................................44
B Colon, Ana.....................................38
D May, K.C. 38
J Garland, Chi....................................34
4 tied with 33

Batters Faced

M Buehrle, Chi. 1016
S Ponson, Bal. 954
M Mulder, Oak. 952
K Rogers, Tex. 935
M Maroth, Det. 928

Innings Pitched

M Buehrle, Chi..................................245.1
J Santana, Min. 228.0
C Schilling, Bos.................................226.2
M Mulder, Oak..................................225.2
B Radke, Min....................................219.2

Runs Allowed

D Lowe, Bos. 138
S Ponson, Bal. 136
D May, K.C. 130
K Lohse, Min. 128
J Moyer, Sea.....................................127

Strikeouts

J Santana, Min. 265
P Martinez, Bos. 227
C Schilling, Bos. 203
K Escobar, Ana.................................191
F Garcia, Sea.-Chi............................184

Walks Allowed

M Batista, Tor. 96
V Zambrano, T.B. 96
D Cabrera, Bal. 89
T Lilly, Tor. 89
J Contreras, N.Y.-Chi.........................84

Hit Batsmen

B Arroyo, Bos. 20
P Martinez, Bos. 16
T Wakefield, Bos................................16
V Zambrano, T.B. 16
C Park, Tex. 13

Wild Pitches

J Contreras, N.Y.-Chi..........................17
K Gregg, Ana.....................................13
M Batista, Tor. 12
D Cabrera, Bal. 12
J Vazquez, N.Y. 12

Balks

T Lilly, Tor. 4
J Affeldt, K.C......................................3
R Franklin, Sea. 3
R Ortiz, Ana. 3
12 tied with 2

Earned Run Average
(minimum 162 IP)

Pitcher, Team	IP	ER	ERA
J Peavy, S.D.	166.1	42	2.27
R Johnson, Ari.	245.2	71	2.60
B Sheets, Mil.	237.0	71	2.70
C Zambrano, Chi.	209.2	64	2.75
R Clemens, Hou.	214.1	71	2.98
O Perez, Pit.	196.0	65	2.98
C Pavano, Fla.	222.1	74	3.00
J Schmidt, S.F.	225.0	80	3.20
A Leiter, N.Y.	173.2	62	3.21
O Perez, L.A.	196.1	71	3.25

Won-Lost Percentage
(minimum 15 decisions)

Pitcher, Team	W	L	Pct.
R Clemens, Hou.	18	4	.818
C Carpenter, St.L.	15	5	.750
J Lima, L.A.	13	5	.722
J Schmidt, S.F.	18	7	.720
J Peavy, S.D.	15	6	.714
E Milton, Phi.	14	6	.700
C Pavano, Fla.	18	8	.692
T Jones, Cin.-Phi.	11	5	.688
J Marquis, St.L.	15	7	.682
2 tied with			.667

Opponents' Batting Average
(minimum 162 IP)

Pitcher, Team	AB	H	Avg.
R Johnson, Ari.	898	177	.197
J Schmidt, S.F.	817	165	.202
O Perez, Pit.	701	145	.207
R Clemens, Hou.	778	169	.217
A Leiter, N.Y.	632	138	.218
C Zambrano, Chi.	773	174	.225
B Sheets, Mil.	891	201	.226
M Clement, Chi.	677	155	.229
J Peavy, S.D.	619	146	.236
J Wright, Atl.	694	168	.242

Games

J Brower, S.F.	89
R King, St.L.	86
R Cormier, Phi.	84
C Reitsma, Atl.	84
S Torres, Pit.	84

Games Started

L Hernandez, Mon.	35
R Johnson, Ari.	35
R Oswalt, Hou.	35
B Webb, Ari.	35
8 tied with	34

Complete Games

L Hernandez, Mon.	9
C Lidle, Cin.-Phi.	5
B Sheets, Mil.	5
R Johnson, Ari.	4
J Schmidt, S.F.	4

Games Finished

J Isringhausen, St.L.	66
J Mesa, Pit.	65
J Smoltz, Atl.	61
S Chacon, Col.	60
B Looper, N.Y.	60

Wins

R Oswalt, Hou.	20
R Clemens, Hou.	18
C Pavano, Fla.	18
J Schmidt, S.F.	18
4 tied with	16

Losses

B Webb, Ari.	16
C Fossum, Ari.	15
L Hernandez, Mon.	15
5 tied with	14

Saves

A Benitez, Fla.	47
J Isringhausen, St.L.	47
E Gagne, L.A.	45
J Smoltz, Atl.	44
J Mesa, Pit.	43

Shutouts

C Lidle, Cin-Phi.	3
J Schmidt, S.F.	3
6 tied with	2

Hits Allowed

J Jennings, Col.	241
L Hernandez, Mon.	234
R Oswalt, Hou.	233
B Lawrence, S.D.	226
K Rueter, S.F.	225

Doubles Allowed

R Oswalt, Hou.	57
B Sheets, Mil.	57
W Williams, St.L.	53
K Rueter, S.F.	52
J Acevedo, Cin.	51

Triples Allowed

R Johnson, Ari.	9
S Estes, Col.	8
J Jennings, Col.	8
B Tomko, S.F.	8
4 tied with	7

Home Runs Allowed

E Milton, Phi.	43
G Maddux, Chi.	35
M Morris, St.L.	35
J Lima, L.A.	33
I Valdez, S.D.-Fla.	33

Batters Faced

L Hernandez, Mon.	1053
R Oswalt, Hou.	983
R Johnson, Ari.	964
B Sheets, Mil.	937
J Weaver, L.A.	935

Innings Pitched

L Hernandez, Mon.	255.0
R Johnson, Ari.	245.2
R Oswalt, Hou.	237.0
B Sheets, Mil.	237.0
J Schmidt, S.F.	225.0

Runs Allowed

S Estes, Col.	133
J Jennings, Col.	125
C Lidle, Cin.-Phi.	123
M Morris, St.L.	116
2 tied with	113

Strikeouts

R Johnson, Ari.	290
B Sheets, Mil.	264
J Schmidt, S.F.	251
O Perez, Pit.	239
R Clemens, Hou.	218

Walks Allowed

B Webb, Ari.	119
R Ortiz, Atl.	112
S Estes, Col.	105
J Jennings, Col.	101
K Ishii, L.A.	98

Hit Batsmen

C Zambrano, Chi.	20
J Williams, S.F.	17
J Weaver, L.A.	14
S Kim, Mon.	13
M Clement, Chi.	12

Wild Pitches

B Webb, Ari.	17
M Clement, Chi.	14
W Williams, St.L.	12
J Brower, S.F.	10
B Tomko, S.F.	10

Balks

C Pavano, Fla.	3
7 tied with	2

Scoring-Position Average†
(minimum 100 PA)

Player, Team	AB	H	Avg.
I Suzuki, Sea.	121	45	.372
I Rodriguez, Det.	133	48	.361
S Stewart, Min.	92	33	.359
J Damon, Bos.	155	55	.355
D Ortiz, Bos.	160	56	.350
D Newhan, Bal.	99	34	.343
H Blalock, Tex.	143	49	.343
M Young, Tex.	161	55	.342
B Surhoff, Bal.	94	32	.340
M Ramirez, Bos.	156	53	.340

Leadoff OBP†
(minimum 150 PA; *AB+BB+HBP+SF)

Player, Team	*PA	OB	OBP
I Suzuki, Sea.	718	300	.418
J Damon, Bos.	688	265	.385
R Belliard, Cle.	250	96	.384
M Lawton, Cle.	397	151	.380
S Stewart, Min.	429	163	.380
D DeJesus, K.C.	370	139	.376
B Williams, N.Y.	224	83	.371
A Rowand, Chi.	179	66	.369
E Byrnes, Oak.	182	67	.368
M Young, Tex.	424	156	.368

Cleanup Slugging†
(minimum 150 PA)

Player, Team	AB	TB	Slg.
M Ramirez, Bos.	380	236	.621
M Tejada, Bal.	328	194	.591
D Ortiz, Bos.	186	106	.570
C Lee, Chi.	164	93	.567
V Guerrero, Ana.	164	92	.561
C Delgado, Tor.	458	245	.535
M Teixeira, Tex.	283	150	.530
F Thomas, Chi.	128	67	.523
J Morneau, Min.	258	134	.519
G Anderson, Ana.	304	150	.493

Avg. vs. LHP
(minimum 125 PA)

I Suzuki, Sea.	.404
J Varitek, Bos.	.350
A Sanchez, Det.	.348
E Byrnes, Oak.	.344
I Rodriguez, Det.	.343

Avg. vs. RHP
(minimum 377 PA)

I Suzuki, Sea.	.359
M Mora, Bal.	.352
T Hafner, Cle.	.344
E Durazo, Oak.	.340
V Guerrero, Ana.	.335

Avg. at Home
(minimum 251 PA)

M Mora, Bal.	.356
I Rodriguez, Det.	.354
K Millar, Bos.	.350
M Young, Tex.	.346
M Kotsay, Oak.	.346

Avg. on Road
(minimum 251 PA)

I Suzuki, Sea.	.405
V Guerrero, Ana.	.335
H Matsui, N.Y.	.327
M Mora, Bal.	.327
E Durazo, Oak.	.325

OBP vs. LHP
(minimum 125 PA)

M Ramirez, Bos.	.446
I Suzuki, Sea.	.444
V Guerrero, Ana.	.434
J Varitek, Bos.	.426
G Sheffield, N.Y.	.423

OBP vs. RHP
(minimum 377 PA)

T Hafner, Cle.	.433
M Mora, Bal.	.419
E Durazo, Oak.	.419
D Ortiz, Bos.	.411
J Posada, N.Y.	.407

Late & Close Avg.†
(minimum 50 PA)

I Suzuki, Sea.	.393
H Matsui, N.Y.	.378
C Gomez, Tor.	.370
K Harvey, K.C.	.358
R Winn, Sea.	.347

Bases Loaded Avg.
(minimum 10 PA)

C Guillen, Det.	.667
B Broussard, Cle.	.636
R Gload, Chi.	.615
S Hatteberg, Oak.	.615
I Suzuki, Sea.	.583

Slg. vs. LHP
(minimum 125 PA)

V Guerrero, Ana.	.723
A Rodriguez, N.Y.	.659
K Mench, Tex.	.646
M Ramirez, Bos.	.631
J Phelps, Tor.-Cle.	.618

Slg. vs. RHP
(minimum 377 PA)

T Hafner, Cle.	.690
D Ortiz, Bos.	.671
M Ramirez, Bos.	.605
H Matsui, N.Y.	.572
M Mora, Bal.	.567

AB per Home Run
(minimum 502 PA)

M Ramirez, Bos.	13.2
P Konerko, Chi.	13.7
D Ortiz, Bos.	14.2
C Delgado, Tor.	14.3
M Teixeira, Tex.	14.3

Times on Base*
(*H+BB+HBP)

I Suzuki, Sea.	315
G Sheffield, N.Y.	269
J Damon, Bos.	267
V Guerrero, Ana.	266
H Matsui, N.Y.	265

Pitches Seen

B Roberts, Bal.	2908
J Damon, Bos.	2893
C Blake, Cle.	2844
H Blalock, Tex.	2807
A Rodriguez, N.Y.	2747

Pitches per PA
(minimum 502 PA)

C Blake, Cle.	4.26
J Dye, Oak.	4.25
B Crosby, Oak.	4.17
M Bellhorn, Bos.	4.15
J Damon, Bos.	4.12

Pct. of Pitches Taken
(minimum 1500 pitches)

J Olerud, Sea.-N.Y.	64.7
S Hatteberg, Oak.	63.9
B Higginson, Det.	62.5
E Chavez, Oak.	62.2
B Williams, N.Y.	62.2

Ground/Fly Ratio†
(minimum 502 PA)

I Suzuki, Sea.	3.31
R Johnson, Tor.	2.12
L Bigbie, Bal.	2.08
D Erstad, Ana.	2.07
C Guzman, Min.	1.95

GDP/GDP Opp.†
(minimum 50 PA)

E Munson, Det.	0.02
G Matthews Jr., Tex.	0.02
D Brown, K.C.	0.02
C Crawford, T.B.	0.02
B Roberts, Bal.	0.03

SB Success Pct.
(minimum 20 SB attempts)

L Ford, Min.	90.9
A Rodriguez, N.Y.	87.5
J DaVanon, Ana.	85.7
D Jeter, N.Y.	85.2
R Baldelli, T.B.	81.0

Steals of Third

D Jeter, N.Y.	12
C Figgins, Ana.	10
C Crawford, T.B.	9
R Winn, Sea.	8
J Lugo, T.B.	7

Pct. CS by Catchers
(minimum 50 SB attempts)

H Blanco, Min.	44.6
B Inge, Det.	37.5
I Rodriguez, Det.	28.6
D Miller, Oak.	28.1
T Hall, T.B.	27.9

†**Scoring-Position Average** denotes batting average when a runner is at second and/or third base. **Leadoff OBP** denotes OBP for a player batting in the first position of the batting order. **Cleanup Slugging** denotes slugging percentage for a player batting in the fourth position of the batting order. **Late & Close Avg.** refers to batting average when the game is in the seventh inning or later and the batting team is either leading by one run, tied, or has the potential tying run on base, at bat or on deck (a batting situation coming close to a pitcher's save situation). **Ground/Fly Ratio** denotes ground balls hit divided by fly balls hit. All batted balls except line drives and bunts are included. **GDP/GDP Opp.** denotes the ratio of times grounding into double plays per opportunities to do so (any situation with a runner on first and less than two out).

Scoring-Position Average†
(minimum 100 PA)

Player, Team	AB	H	Avg.
B Bonds, S.F.	71	28	.394
J Snow, S.F.	83	30	.361
S Rolen, St.L.	151	54	.358
J Franco, Atl.	95	33	.347
J Kendall, Pit.	107	37	.346
A Pujols, St.L.	143	49	.343
J Estrada, Atl.	139	47	.338
T Sledge, Mon.	95	32	.337
A Ramirez, Chi.	122	41	.336
D Cruz, S.F.	105	35	.333

Leadoff OBP†
(minimum 150 PA; *AB+BB+HBP+SF)

Player, Team	*PA	OB	OBP
J Kendall, Pit.	542	219	.404
R Freel, Cin.	478	186	.389
J Pierre, Fla.	641	245	.382
B Wilkerson, Mon.	490	187	.382
T Walker, Chi.	262	97	.370
R Durham, S.F.	531	194	.365
J Rollins, Phi.	547	197	.360
T Womack, St.L.	577	203	.352
S Burroughs, S.D.	460	158	.343
R Furcal, Atl.	615	211	.343

Cleanup Slugging†
(minimum 150 PA)

Player, Team	AB	TB	Slg.
B Bonds, S.F.	371	303	.817
A Beltre, L.A.	353	232	.657
M Alou, Chi.	363	222	.612
S Rolen, St.L.	386	233	.604
J Thome, Phi.	459	265	.577
A Dunn, Cin.	323	182	.563
V Castilla, Col.	517	286	.553
M Lowell, Fla.	268	145	.541
M Piazza, N.Y.	223	119	.534
L Overbay, Mil.	184	98	.533

Avg. vs. LHP
(minimum 125 PA)

A Pujols, St.L.	.379
E Renteria, St.L.	.366
M Loretta, S.D.	.352
M Lowell, Fla.	.344
R Durham, S.F.	.333

Avg. vs. RHP
(minimum 377 PA)

B Bonds, S.F.	.395
T Helton, Col.	.360
A Beltre, L.A.	.347
J Pierre, Fla.	.334
S Casey, Cin.	.332

Avg. at Home
(minimum 251 PA)

B Bonds, S.F.	.412
T Helton, Col.	.368
S Hillenbrand, Ari.	.347
M Alou, Chi.	.339
J Pierre, Fla.	.338

Avg. on Road
(minimum 251 PA)

M Loretta, S.D.	.368
S Casey, Cin.	.361
J Estrada, Atl.	.351
S Rolen, St.L.	.346
A Beltre, L.A.	.342

OBP vs. LHP
(minimum 125 PA)

B Bonds, S.F.	.524
A Pujols, St.L.	.465
P Nevin, S.D.	.431
M Loretta, S.D.	.431
2 tied with	.429

OBP vs. RHP
(minimum 377 PA)

B Bonds, S.F.	.652
T Helton, Col.	.492
L Berkman, Hou.	.463
J Drew, Atl.	.450
B Abreu, Phi.	.438

Late & Close Avg.†
(minimum 50 PA)

M Grudzielanek, Chi.	.457
D Bautista, Ari.	.386
M Ensberg, Hou.	.383
J Wilson, Pit.	.379
S Burroughs, S.D.	.377

Bases Loaded Avg.
(minimum 10 PA)

S Rolen, St.L.	.583
P Lo Duca, L.A.-Fla.	.563
P Nevin, S.D.	.556
4 tied with	.500

Slg. vs. LHP
(minimum 125 PA)

A Pujols, St.L.	.741
M Lowell, Fla.	.672
J Hernandez, L.A.	.627
D Lee, Chi.	.595
P Nevin, S.D.	.582

Slg. vs. RHP
(minimum 377 PA)

B Bonds, S.F.	.957
A Beltre, L.A.	.672
T Helton, Col.	.669
J Edmonds, St.L.	.651
J Thome, Phi.	.641

AB per Home Run
(minimum 502 PA)

B Bonds, S.F.	8.3
J Edmonds, St.L.	11.9
J Thome, Phi.	12.1
A Dunn, Cin.	12.3
A Beltre, L.A.	12.5

Times on Base*
(*H+BB+HBP)

B Bonds, S.F.	376
T Helton, Col.	320
L Berkman, Hou.	309
B Abreu, Phi.	305
A Pujols, St.L.	287

Pitches Seen

B Abreu, Phi.	3077
B Wilkerson, Mon.	2954
A Dunn, Cin.	2888
S Podsednik, Mil.	2837
J Bagwell, Hou.	2819

Pitches per PA
(minimum 502 PA)

B Abreu, Phi.	4.32
B Wilkerson, Mon.	4.29
A Dunn, Cin.	4.24
J Edmonds, St.L.	4.23
J Kendall, Pit.	4.21

Pct. of Pitches Taken
(minimum 1500 pitches)

B Bonds, S.F.	71.9
T Zeile, N.Y.	66.4
D Jimenez, Cin.	65.1
B Abreu, Phi.	64.8
J Kendall, Pit.	64.7

Ground/Fly Ratio†
(minimum 502 PA)

L Castillo, Fla.	3.63
J Pierre, Fla.	2.36
R Clayton, Col.	2.34
S Burroughs, S.D.	2.18
T Redman, Pit.	1.96

GDP/GDP Opp.†
(minimum 50 PA)

J Werth, L.A.	0.01
T Sledge, Mon.	0.03
R Mackowiak, Pit.	0.03
J Edmonds, St.L.	0.03
B Abreu, Phi.	0.03

SB Success Pct.
(minimum 20 SB attempts)

C Beltran, Hou.	100.0
D Roberts, L.A.	97.1
J Reyes, N.Y.	90.5
B Abreu, Phi.	88.9
S Podsednik, Mil.	84.3

Steals of Third

C Beltran, Hou.	11
S Podsednik, Mil.	10
J Pierre, Fla.	8
J Reyes, N.Y.	6
R Sanders, St.L.	6

Pct. CS by Catchers
(minimum 50 SB attempts)

B Schneider, Mon.	47.8
J Kendall, Pit.	32.3
J LaRue, Cin.	29.6
P Bako, Chi.	29.4
M Matheny, St.L.	28.3

†**Scoring-Position Average** denotes batting average when a runner is at second and/or third base. **Leadoff OBP** denotes OBP for a player batting in the first position of the batting order. **Cleanup Slugging** denotes slugging percentage for a player batting in the fourth position of the batting order. **Late & Close Avg.** refers to batting average when the game is in the seventh inning or later and the batting team is either leading by one run, tied, or has the potential tying run on base, at bat or on deck (a batting situation coming close to a pitcher's save situation). **Ground/Fly Ratio** denotes ground balls hit divided by fly balls hit. All batted balls except line drives and bunts are included. **GDP/GDP Opp.** denotes the ratio of times grounding into double plays per opportunities to do so (any situation with a runner on first and less than two out).

Baserunners per 9 IP
(minimum 162 IP)

Pitcher, Team	IP	BR	BR/9
J Santana, Min.	228.0	219	8.64
C Schilling, Bos.	226.2	246	9.77
B Radke, Min.	219.2	261	10.69
P Martinez, Bos.	217.0	270	11.20
F Garcia, Sea.-Chi.	210.0	263	11.27
J Westbrook, Cle.	215.2	274	11.43
M Buehrle, Chi.	245.1	316	11.59
R Lopez, Bal.	170.2	220	11.60
K Escobar, Ana.	208.1	275	11.88
T Hudson, Oak.	188.2	250	11.93

Strikeouts per 9 IP
(minimum 162 IP)

Pitcher, Team	IP	SO	SO/9
J Santana, Min.	228.0	265	10.46
P Martinez, Bos.	217.0	227	9.41
K Escobar, Ana.	208.1	191	8.25
J Bonderman, Det.	184.0	168	8.22
C Lee, Cle.	179.0	161	8.09
C Schilling, Bos.	226.2	203	8.06
J Contreras, N.Y.-Chi.	170.1	150	7.93
R Harden, Oak.	189.2	167	7.92
F Garcia, Sea.-Chi.	210.0	184	7.89
T Lilly, Tor.	197.1	168	7.66

Run Support per 9 IP†
(minimum 162 IP)

Pitcher, Team	IP	R	RS/9
C Schilling, Bos.	226.2	190	7.54
D Lowe, Bos.	182.2	148	7.29
B Colon, Ana.	208.1	162	7.00
K Rogers, Tex.	211.2	161	6.85
J Lieber, N.Y.	176.2	134	6.83
M Buehrle, Chi.	245.1	181	6.64
M Mulder, Oak.	225.2	164	6.54
J Westbrook, Cle.	215.2	155	6.47
N Robertson, Det.	196.2	139	6.36
J Contreras, N.Y.-Chi.	170.1	120	6.34

Opposition OBP
(minimum 162 IP)

J Santana, Min.	.249
C Schilling, Bos.	.271
B Radke, Min.	.291
P Martinez, Bos.	.301
F Garcia, Sea.-Chi.	.303

Opposition SLG
(minimum 162 IP)

J Santana, Min.	.315
R Harden, Oak.	.366
T Hudson, Oak.	.366
J Westbrook, Cle.	.386
C Schilling, Bos.	.387

Hits per 9 IP
(minimum 162 IP)

J Santana, Min.	6.16
T Lilly, Tor.	7.80
P Martinez, Bos.	8.00
R Harden, Oak.	8.11
C Schilling, Bos.	8.18

Home Runs per 9 IP
(minimum 162 IP)

T Hudson, Oak.	0.38
R Drese, Tex.	0.69
D Lowe, Bos.	0.74
R Harden, Oak.	0.76
J Westbrook, Cle.	0.79

Avg. vs. LHB
(minimum 125 BFP)

J Rincon, Min.	.148
K Foulke, Bos.	.185
T Gordon, N.Y.	.185
S Elarton, Cle.	.190
J Santana, Min.	.196

Avg. vs. RHB
(minimum 225 BFP)

J Santana, Min.	.191
V Zambrano, T.B.	.219
J Bonderman, Det.	.223
R Bell, T.B.	.226
B Arroyo, Bos.	.227

Avg. Allowed Sc. Pos.†
(minimum 125 BFP)

V Zambrano, T.B.	.157
J Santana, Min.	.165
P Martinez, Bos.	.197
R Lopez, Bal.	.197
F Garcia, Sea.-Chi.	.218

OBP Leading off Inn.
(minimum 150 BFP)

C Schilling, Bos.	.223
J Vazquez, N.Y.	.255
J Santana, Min.	.264
B Arroyo, Bos.	.275
R Lopez, Bal.	.275

SO/BB Ratio
(minimum 162 IP)

C Schilling, Bos.	5.80
J Lieber, N.Y.	5.67
B Radke, Min.	5.50
J Santana, Min.	4.91
P Martinez, Bos.	3.72

Grd/Fly Ratio Off†
(minimum 162 IP)

D Lowe, Bos.	2.87
J Westbrook, Cle.	2.72
T Hudson, Oak.	2.53
R Drese, Tex.	2.20
M Mulder, Oak.	2.05

Pitches per Start
(minimum 30 games started)

B Zito, Oak.	108.5
C Schilling, Bos.	106.6
F Garcia, Sea.-Chi.	106.1
P Martinez, Bos.	105.8
M Buehrle, Chi.	105.6

Pitches per Batter
(minimum 162 IP)

C Silva, Min.	3.33
J Lieber, N.Y.	3.40
R Drese, Tex.	3.46
M Mulder, Oak.	3.46
S Ponson, Bal.	3.47

Stolen Bases Allowed

D Lowe, Bos.	34
T Wakefield, Bos.	33
J Contreras, N.Y.-Chi.	29
K Escobar, Ana.	24
2 tied with	19

Caught Stealing Off

M Mulder, Oak.	13
M Batista, Tor.	11
J Contreras, N.Y.-Chi.	11
M Maroth, Det.	11
A Sele, Ana.	11

SB Pct. Allowed
(minimum 162 IP)

B Anderson, K.C.	20.0
K Rogers, Tex.	28.6
J Vazquez, N.Y.	28.6
B Colon, Ana.	33.3
2 tied with	38.5

Pickoffs

M Buehrle, Chi.	10
M Mulder, Oak.	9
M Redman, Oak.	9
K Rogers, Tex.	6
S Schoeneweis, Chi.	6

PkOf Throw/Runner†
(minimum 162 IP)

R Franklin, Sea.	1.06
K Escobar, Ana.	0.73
D May, K.C.	0.67
B Zito, Oak.	0.66
M Redman, Oak.	0.62

GDP Induced

M Mulder, Oak.	37
S Ponson, Bal.	36
M Buehrle, Chi.	33
J Westbrook, Cle.	29
2 tied with	28

GDP per 9 IP
(minimum 162 IP)

S Ponson, Bal.	1.5
M Mulder, Oak.	1.5
D Lowe, Bos.	1.4
C Silva, Min.	1.2
N Robertson, Det.	1.2

Quality Starts†

J Santana, Min.	25
B Radke, Min.	24
M Buehrle, Chi.	23
P Martinez, Bos.	22
C Schilling, Bos.	22

†**Run Support per 9 IP** denotes the number of runs scored by a pitcher's team while he was still in the game times nine divided by his innings pitched. **Avg. Allowed Sc. Pos.** denotes batting average allowed when a runner is at second and/or third base. **Grd/Fly Ratio Off** denotes ground balls allowed divided by fly balls allowed. All batted balls except line drives and bunts are included. **PkOf Throw/Runner** denotes the number of pickoff throws made by a pitcher divided by the number of runners on first base. **Quality Starts** denote the number of outings in which a starting pitcher works at least six innings and allows three or fewer earned runs.

Baserunners per 9 IP
(minimum 162 IP)

Pitcher, Team	IP	BR	BR/9
R Johnson, Ari.	245.2	231	8.46
B Sheets, Mil.	237.0	237	9.00
J Schmidt, S.F.	225.0	245	9.80
D Wells, S.D.	195.2	225	10.35
O Perez, L.A.	196.1	227	10.41
C Carpenter, St.L.	182.0	215	10.63
R Clemens, Hou.	214.1	254	10.67
O Perez, Pit.	196.0	235	10.79
G Maddux, Chi.	212.2	260	11.00
C Pavano, Fla.	222.1	272	11.01

Strikeouts per 9 IP
(minimum 162 IP)

Pitcher, Team	IP	SO	SO/9
O Perez, Pit.	196.0	239	10.97
R Johnson, Ari.	245.2	290	10.62
J Schmidt, S.F.	225.0	251	10.04
B Sheets, Mil.	237.0	264	10.03
M Clement, Chi.	181.0	190	9.45
J Peavy, S.D.	166.1	173	9.36
R Clemens, Hou.	214.1	218	9.15
C Zambrano, Chi.	209.2	188	8.07
R Oswalt, Hou.	237.0	206	7.82
J Wright, Atl.	186.1	159	7.68

Run Support per 9 IP†
(minimum 162 IP)

Pitcher, Team	IP	R	RS/9
K Ishii, L.A.	172.0	128	6.70
S Estes, Col.	202.0	147	6.55
E Milton, Phi.	201.0	146	6.54
J Peavy, S.D.	166.1	119	6.44
B Myers, Phi.	176.0	121	6.19
C Zambrano, Chi.	209.2	141	6.05
R Oswalt, Hou.	237.0	159	6.04
B Tomko, S.F.	194.0	129	5.98
J Marquis, St.L.	201.1	133	5.95
J Thomson, Atl.	198.1	130	5.90

Opposition OBP
(minimum 162 IP)

R Johnson, Ari.	.241
B Sheets, Mil.	.255
J Schmidt, S.F.	.272
D Wells, S.D.	.285
C Carpenter, St.L.	.291

Opposition SLG
(minimum 162 IP)

R Johnson, Ari.	.315
J Schmidt, S.F.	.323
R Clemens, Hou.	.329
J Wright, Atl.	.337
C Zambrano, Chi.	.338

Hits per 9 IP
(minimum 162 IP)

R Johnson, Ari.	6.48
J Schmidt, S.F.	6.60
O Perez, Pit.	6.66
R Clemens, Hou.	7.10
A Leiter, N.Y.	7.15

Home Runs per 9 IP
(minimum 162 IP)

J Wright, Atl.	0.53
C Zambrano, Chi.	0.60
D Davis, Mil.	0.61
R Clemens, Hou.	0.63
R Oswalt, Hou.	0.65

Avg. vs. LHB
(minimum 125 BFP)

R King, St.L.	.150
L Vizcaino, Mil.	.163
R Johnson, Ari.	.163
S Linebrink, S.D.	.178
J Kennedy, Col.	.184

Avg. vs. RHB
(minimum 225 BFP)

J Beckett, Fla.	.192
R Johnson, Ari.	.204
O Perez, Pit.	.204
A Pettitte, Hou.	.208
A Burnett, Fla.	.211

Avg. Allowed Sc. Pos.†
(minimum 125 BFP)

A Leiter, N.Y.	.173
C Zambrano, Chi.	.179
O Perez, Pit.	.180
J Schmidt, S.F.	.180
J Peavy, S.D.	.185

OBP Leading off Inn.
(minimum 150 BFP)

R Johnson, Ari.	.200
B Sheets, Mil.	.218
C Carpenter, St.L.	.250
D Wells, S.D.	.260
E Milton, Phi.	.266

SO/BB Ratio
(minimum 162 IP)

B Sheets, Mil.	8.25
R Johnson, Ari.	6.59
D Wells, S.D.	5.05
G Maddux, Chi.	4.58
C Carpenter, St.L.	4.00

Grd/Fly Ratio Off†
(minimum 162 IP)

B Webb, Ari.	3.55
J Marquis, St.L.	2.17
M Hampton, Atl.	2.01
C Carpenter, St.L.	1.93
B Lawrence, S.D.	1.82

Pitches per Start
(minimum 30 games started)

J Schmidt, S.F.	112.8
L Hernandez, Mon.	112.2
C Zambrano, Chi.	111.9
A Leiter, N.Y.	108.3
B Sheets, Mil.	105.4

Pitches per Batter
(minimum 162 IP)

G Maddux, Chi.	3.36
J Lima, L.A.	3.44
C Lidle, Cin.-Phi.	3.44
C Pavano, Fla.	3.47
B Lawrence, S.D.	3.47

Stolen Bases Allowed

B Webb, Ari.	31
J Schmidt, S.F.	28
G Maddux, Chi.	26
R Clemens, Hou.	23
G Mota, L.A.-Fla.	21

Caught Stealing Off

G Maddux, Chi.	12
R Clemens, Hou.	10
R Johnson, Ari.	10
B Webb, Ari.	10
2 tied with	9

SB Pct. Allowed
(minimum 162 IP)

C Carpenter, St.L.	0.0
K Rueter, S.F.	25.0
T Glavine, N.Y.	46.7
O Perez, Pit.	50.0
P Wilson, Cin.	50.0

Pickoffs

C Capuano, Mil.	6
5 tied with	5

PkOf Throw/Runner†
(minimum 162 IP)

A Leiter, N.Y.	0.98
S Trachsel, N.Y.	0.90
R Clemens, Hou.	0.80
P Wilson, Cin.	0.73
R Ortiz, Atl.	0.64

GDP Induced

S Estes, Col.	34
J Fogg, Pit.	27
M Morris, St.L.	26
O Perez, L.A.	25
K Rueter, S.F.	25

GDP per 9 IP
(minimum 162 IP)

S Estes, Col.	1.5
J Fogg, Pit.	1.4
K Rueter, S.F.	1.2
M Morris, St.L.	1.2
O Perez, L.A.	1.1

Quality Starts†

R Johnson, Ari.	26
J Weaver, L.A.	25
D Davis, Mil.	24
B Sheets, Mil.	24
2 tied with	23

†**Run Support per 9 IP** denotes the number of runs scored by a pitcher's team while he was still in the game times nine divided by his innings pitched. **Avg. Allowed Sc. Pos.** denotes batting average allowed when a runner is at second and/or third base. **Grd/Fly Ratio Off** denotes ground balls allowed divided by fly balls allowed. All batted balls except line drives and bunts are included. **PkOf Throw/Runner** denotes the number of pickoff throws made by a pitcher divided by the number of runners on first base. **Quality Starts** denote the number of outings in which a starting pitcher works at least six innings and allows three or fewer earned runs.

Saves

Pitcher, Team	Saves
M Rivera, N.Y.	53
F Cordero, Tex.	49
J Nathan, Min.	44
T Percival, Ana.	33
K Foulke, Bos.	32
D Baez, T.B.	30
O Dotel, Oak.	22
J Julio, Bal.	22
U Urbina, Det.	21
S Takatsu, Chi.	19

Save Percentage
(minimum 20 save opportunities)

Pitcher, Team	Opp.	Sv.	Pct.
S Takatsu, Chi.	20	19	95.0
J Nathan, Min.	47	44	93.6
M Rivera, N.Y.	57	53	93.0
D Baez, T.B.	33	30	90.9
F Cordero, Tex.	54	49	90.7
U Urbina, Det.	24	21	87.5
T Percival, Ana.	38	33	86.8
J Julio, Bal.	26	22	84.6
K Foulke, Bos.	39	32	82.1
O Dotel, Oak.	28	22	78.6

Relief ERA
(minimum 50 relief IP)

Pitcher, Team	IP	ER	ERA
J Nathan, Min.	72.1	13	1.62
F Rodriguez, Ana.	84.0	17	1.82
M Rivera, N.Y.	78.2	17	1.94
F Cordero, Tex.	71.2	17	2.13
K Foulke, Bos.	83.0	20	2.17
T Gordon, N.Y.	89.2	22	2.21
B Ryan, Bal.	87.0	22	2.28
S Takatsu, Chi.	62.1	16	2.31
R Mahay, Tex.	67.0	19	2.55
J Rincon, Min.	82.0	24	2.63

Relief Wins

J Rincon, Min.	11
T Gordon, N.Y.	9
S Shields, Ana.	8
5 tied with	7

Relief Losses

J Speier, Tor.	8
C Bradford, Oak.	7
J Grimsley, K.C.-Bal.	7
J Jimenez, Cle.	7
9 tied with	6

Holds†

T Gordon, N.Y.	36
F Rodriguez, Ana.	27
P Quantrill, N.Y.	22
3 tied with	21

Blown Saves†

E Yan, Det.	10
J Grimsley, K.C.-Bal.	9
6 tied with	7

Relief Games

P Quantrill, N.Y.	86
T Gordon, N.Y.	80
J Rincon, Min.	77
B Ryan, Bal.	76
M Timlin, Bos.	76

Games Finished

M Rivera, N.Y.	69
F Cordero, Tex.	63
J Nathan, Min.	63
K Foulke, Bos.	61
D Baez, T.B.	59

Relief Innings

S Shields, Ana.	105.1
J Duchscherer, Oak.	96.1
P Quantrill, N.Y.	95.1
T Gordon, N.Y.	89.2
K Gregg, Ana.	87.2

Pct. Inherited Scored†
(minimum 30 inherited runners)

N Field, K.C.	14.3
D Brocail, Tex.	15.2
T Gordon, N.Y.	16.2
B Shouse, Tex.	16.7
J Cerda, K.C.	17.4

Opposition Avg.
(minimum 50 relief IP)

F Rodriguez, Ana.	.172
T Gordon, N.Y.	.180
J Rincon, Min.	.181
S Takatsu, Chi.	.182
J Nathan, Min.	.187

Opposition OBP
(minimum 50 relief IP)

T Gordon, N.Y.	.237
K Foulke, Bos.	.254
F Rodriguez, Ana.	.256
J Nathan, Min.	.259
S Takatsu, Chi.	.259

Opposition SLG
(minimum 50 relief IP)

F Rodriguez, Ana.	.226
J Nathan, Min.	.257
J Rincon, Min.	.265
B Ryan, Bal.	.272
M Rivera, N.Y.	.280

First Batter Avg.
(minimum 40 first BFP)

R Villone, Sea.	.093
S Takatsu, Chi.	.143
C Bradford, Oak.	.145
M Miller, Cle.	.163
D Marte, Chi.	.169

Avg. vs. LHB
(minimum 50 relief IP)

B Ryan, Bal.	.094
D Marte, Chi.	.143
J Rincon, Min.	.148
K Foulke, Bos.	.185
T Gordon, N.Y.	.185

Avg. vs. RHB
(minimum 50 relief IP)

F Rodriguez, Ana.	.127
S Takatsu, Chi.	.150
J Nathan, Min.	.160
F Francisco, Tex.	.165
T Gordon, N.Y.	.174

Avg., Runners On†
(minimum 50 relief IP)

S Takatsu, Chi.	.155
J Nathan, Min.	.159
T Gordon, N.Y.	.162
F Rodriguez, Ana.	.164
O Dotel, Oak.	.176

Avg., Scoring Pos.†
(minimum 50 relief IP)

M Rivera, N.Y.	.139
T Gordon, N.Y.	.153
D Marte, Chi.	.161
F Francisco, Tex.	.167
J Nathan, Min.	.172

Easy Saves†

M Rivera, N.Y.	36
F Cordero, Tex.	27
J Nathan, Min.	24
T Percival, Ana.	23
K Foulke, Bos.	20

Regular Saves†

F Cordero, Tex.	20
J Nathan, Min.	19
M Rivera, N.Y.	15
D Baez, T.B.	13
K Foulke, Bos.	12

Tough Saves†

E Guardado, Sea.	4
F Rodriguez, Ana.	4
J Affeldt, K.C.	3
4 tied with	2

Pitches per Batter
(minimum 50 relief IP)

S Camp, K.C.	3.35
C Almanzar, Tex.	3.44
B Groom, Bal.	3.48
P Quantrill, N.Y.	3.51
J Walker, Det.	3.52

†Holds denote the number of times a relief pitcher enters the game in a save situation, records at least one out and leaves the game never having relinquished the lead. A pitcher cannot finish the game and receive credit for a hold, nor can he earn a hold and a save in the same game. **Blown Saves** denote the number of times a relief pitcher enters a game in a save situation and allows the tying or go-ahead run to score. **Pct. Inherited Scored** denotes the percent of inherited runners (those on base when a reliever enters the game) that score. **Avg., Runners On** denotes batting average allowed when runners are on base. **Avg., Scoring Pos.** denotes batting average allowed when a runner is at second and/or third base. **Easy Saves** denote saves in which the first batter faced doesn't represent the tying run and the reliever pitches one inning or less. **Regular Saves** denote those saves that are not Easy Saves or Tough Saves. **Tough Saves** denote saves which occur after the reliever enters with the tying run anywhere on base.

Saves

Pitcher, Team	Saves
A Benitez, Fla.	47
J Isringhausen, St.L.	47
E Gagne, L.A.	45
J Smoltz, Atl.	44
J Mesa, Pit.	43
D Graves, Cin.	41
T Hoffman, S.D.	41
D Kolb, Mil.	39
S Chacon, Col.	35
2 tied with	29

Save Percentage
(minimum 20 save opportunities)

Pitcher, Team	Opp.	Sv.	Pct.
E Gagne, L.A.	47	45	95.7
A Benitez, Fla.	51	47	92.2
T Hoffman, S.D.	45	41	91.1
J Smoltz, Atl.	49	44	89.8
J Mesa, Pit.	48	43	89.6
D Kolb, Mil.	44	39	88.6
B Lidge, Hou.	33	29	87.9
J Isringhausen, St.L.	54	47	87.0
B Looper, N.Y.	34	29	85.3
D Hermanson, S.F.	20	17	85.0

Relief ERA
(minimum 50 relief IP)

Pitcher, Team	IP	ER	ERA
A Benitez, Fla.	69.2	10	1.29
R Madson, Phi.	76.1	14	1.65
A Otsuka, S.D.	77.1	15	1.75
S Kline, St.L.	50.1	10	1.79
B Lidge, Hou.	94.2	20	1.90
S Linebrink, S.D.	84.0	20	2.14
G Carrara, L.A.	53.2	13	2.18
E Gagne, L.A.	82.1	20	2.19
E Dessens, Ari.-L.A.	60.0	15	2.25
T Hoffman, S.D.	54.2	14	2.30

Relief Wins

T Jones, Cin-Phi.	11
R Madson, Phi.	9
G Mota, LA-Fla.	9
7 tied with	7

Relief Losses

L Ayala, Mon.	12
S Chacon, Col.	9
G Mota, LA-Fla.	8
S Reed, Col.	8
F Rodriguez, S.F.-Phi.	8

Holds†

A Otsuka, S.D.	34
R King, St.L.	31
C Reitsma, Atl.	31
G Mota, L.A.-Fla.	30
S Torres, Pit.	30

Blown Saves†

S Chacon, Col.	9
D Graves, Cin.	9
L Hawkins, Chi.	9
M Herges, S.F.	8
T Worrell, Phi.	8

Relief Games

J Brower, S.F.	89
R King, St.L.	86
R Cormier, Phi.	84
C Reitsma, Atl.	84
S Torres, Pit.	84

Games Finished

J Isringhausen, St.L.	66
J Mesa, Pit.	65
J Smoltz, Atl.	61
S Chacon, Col.	60
B Looper, N.Y.	60

Relief Innings

G Mota, L.A.-Fla.	96.2
B Lidge, Hou.	94.2
J Brower, S.F.	93.0
S Torres, Pit.	92.0
L Ayala, Mon.	90.1

Pct. Inherited Scored†
(minimum 30 inherited runners)

B Lidge, Hou.	6.7
J Lopez, Col.	13.0
S Eyre, S.F.	15.6
M Perisho, Fla.	20.6
W Franklin, S.F.	20.9

Opposition Avg.
(minimum 50 relief IP)

A Benitez, Fla.	.152
B Lidge, Hou.	.174
E Gagne, L.A.	.181
S Randolph, Ari.	.191
R King, St.L.	.197

Opposition OBP
(minimum 50 relief IP)

A Benitez, Fla.	.220
T Hoffman, S.D.	.242
E Gagne, L.A.	.248
B Lidge, Hou.	.254
J Isringhausen, St.L.	.265

Opposition SLG
(minimum 50 relief IP)

R King, St.L.	.257
A Benitez, Fla.	.257
E Gagne, L.A.	.263
R Madson, Phi.	.284
B Lidge, Hou.	.290

First Batter Avg.
(minimum 40 first BFP)

J Horgan, Mon.	.100
K Calero, St.L.	.108
B Lidge, Hou.	.113
J Isringhausen, St.L.	.116
E Gagne, L.A.	.123

Avg. vs. LHB
(minimum 50 relief IP)

S Kline, St.L.	.143
R King, St.L.	.150
L Vizcaino, Mil.	.163
A Benitez, Fla.	.168
S Linebrink, S.D.	.178

Avg. vs. RHB
(minimum 50 relief IP)

E Gagne, L.A.	.129
A Benitez, Fla.	.140
B Lidge, Hou.	.155
T Hoffman, S.D.	.161
K Mercker, Chi.	.170

Avg., Runners On†
(minimum 50 relief IP)

B Lidge, Hou.	.141
A Benitez, Fla.	.148
T Hoffman, S.D.	.158
S Linebrink, S.D.	.177
J Cruz, Atl.	.186

Avg., Scoring Pos.†
(minimum 50 relief IP)

T Hoffman, S.D.	.087
B Lidge, Hou.	.101
K Mercker, Chi.	.148
J Cruz, Atl.	.159
R Madson, Phi.	.159

Easy Saves†

D Graves, Cin.	31
A Benitez, Fla.	29
J Mesa, Pit.	29
S Chacon, Col.	28
J Isringhausen, St.L.	27

Regular Saves†

E Gagne, L.A.	23
J Smoltz, Atl.	20
T Hoffman, S.D.	17
A Benitez, Fla.	15
J Isringhausen, St.L.	15

Tough Saves†

J Smoltz, Atl.	6
J Isringhausen, St.L.	5
M Herges, S.F.	4
B Lidge, Hou.	4
2 tied with	3

Pitches per Batter
(minimum 50 relief IP)

S Kim, Mon.	3.28
D Graves, Cin.	3.34
R Stone, Hou.-S.D.	3.38
B Meadows, Pit.	3.44
C Reitsma, Atl.	3.53

†**Holds** denote the number of times a relief pitcher enters the game in a save situation, records at least one out and leaves the game never having relinquished the lead. A pitcher cannot finish the game and receive credit for a hold, nor can he earn a hold and a save in the same game. **Blown Saves** denote the number of times a relief pitcher enters a game in a save situation and allows the tying or go-ahead run to score. **Pct. Inherited Scored** denotes the percent of inherited runners (those on base when a reliever enters the game) that score. **Avg., Runners On** denotes batting average allowed when runners are on base. **Avg., Scoring Pos.** denotes batting average allowed when a runner is at second and/or third base. **Easy Saves** denote saves in which the first batter faced doesn't represent the tying run and the reliever pitches one inning or less. **Regular Saves** denote those saves that are not Easy Saves or Tough Saves. **Tough Saves** denote saves which occur after the reliever enters with the tying run anywhere on base.

2004 ACTIVE CAREER LEADERS

BATTING

Batting Average
(minimum 1000 PA)

Rk.	Player	AB	H	Avg.
1	Ichiro Suzuki	2722	924	.339
2	Todd Helton	4051	1372	.339
3	Albert Pujols	2363	787	.333
4	Vladimir Guerrero	4375	1421	.325
5	Nomar Garciaparra	4133	1330	.322
6	Manny Ramirez	5572	1760	.316
7	Mike Piazza	5805	1829	.315
8	Derek Jeter	5513	1734	.315
9	Larry Walker	6592	2069	.314
10	Juan Pierre	2755	859	.312
11	Edgar Martinez	7213	2247	.312
12	Frank Thomas	6851	2113	.308
13	Magglio Ordonez	3807	1167	.307
14	Ivan Rodriguez	6694	2051	.306
15	Jason Kendall	4606	1409	.306
16	Alex Rodriguez	5590	1707	.305
17	Bobby Abreu	4140	1264	.305
18	Mike Sweeney	3717	1132	.305
19	Jose Vidro	3485	1061	.304
20	Sean Casey	3488	1060	.304
21	Chipper Jones	5616	1705	.304
22	Lance Berkman	2683	814	.303
23	Shannon Stewart	4098	1242	.303
24	Mark Loretta	3871	1172	.303
25	Bernie Williams	6964	2097	.301

On-Base Percentage
(minimum 1000 PA; *AB+BB+HBP+SF)

Rk.	Player	*PA	OB	OBP
1	Barry Bonds	11580	5125	.443
2	Todd Helton	4796	2070	.432
3	Frank Thomas	8478	3634	.429
4	Edgar Martinez	8662	3619	.418
5	Lance Berkman	3247	1352	.416
6	Albert Pujols	2727	1126	.413
7	Bobby Abreu	4958	2042	.412
8	Brian Giles	4982	2049	.411
9	Jason Giambi	5782	2376	.411
10	Manny Ramirez	6573	2701	.411
11	Jim Thome	7038	2885	.410
12	Jeff Bagwell	9305	3799	.408
13	Larry Walker	7656	3070	.401
14	Chipper Jones	6631	2656	.401
15	Gary Sheffield	8710	3487	.400
16	John Olerud	8859	3536	.399
17	Carlos Delgado	6018	2362	.392
18	J.D. Drew	2852	1114	.391
19	Vladimir Guerrero	4900	1912	.390
20	Bernie Williams	8035	3116	.388
21	Jason Kendall	5273	2040	.387
22	Erubiel Durazo	2124	821	.387
23	Tim Salmon	6795	2623	.386
24	Mike Piazza	6535	2519	.385
25	Derek Jeter	6194	2385	.385

Slugging Percentage
(minimum 1000 PA)

Rk.	Player	AB	TB	Slg.
1	Albert Pujols	2363	1474	.624
2	Todd Helton	4051	2497	.616
3	Barry Bonds	9098	5556	.611
4	Manny Ramirez	5572	3339	.599
5	Vladimir Guerrero	4375	2577	.589
6	Alex Rodriguez	5590	3207	.574
7	Jim Thome	5726	3259	.569
8	Larry Walker	6592	3746	.568
9	Frank Thomas	6851	3887	.567
10	Lance Berkman	2683	1511	.563
11	Mike Piazza	5805	3260	.562
12	Juan Gonzalez	6555	3676	.561
13	Ken Griffey Jr.	7379	4131	.560
14	Carlos Delgado	5008	2786	.556
15	Brian Giles	4111	2259	.550
16	Nomar Garciaparra	4133	2269	.549
17	Sammy Sosa	8021	4368	.545
18	Jim Edmonds	5090	2767	.544
19	Jeff Bagwell	7697	4175	.542
20	Jason Giambi	4757	2568	.540
21	Chipper Jones	5616	3014	.537
22	Richie Sexson	3065	1618	.528
23	Gary Sheffield	7302	3854	.528
24	Magglio Ordonez	3807	1998	.525
25	Mark Teixeira	1074	559	.520

Hits

Player	
Rafael Palmeiro	2922
Barry Bonds	2730
Roberto Alomar	2724
Craig Biggio	2639
Fred McGriff	2490
Julio Franco	2457
Barry Larkin	2340
Steve Finley	2336
Andres Galarraga	2333
Jeff Bagwell	2289
B.J. Surhoff	2248
Edgar Martinez	2247
Marquis Grissom	2222
Sammy Sosa	2220
John Olerud	2189
Gary Sheffield	2175
Ken Griffey Jr.	2156
Omar Vizquel	2147
Frank Thomas	2113
Ruben Sierra	2108

Home Runs

Player	
Barry Bonds	703
Sammy Sosa	574
Rafael Palmeiro	551
Ken Griffey Jr.	501
Fred McGriff	493
Jeff Bagwell	446
Frank Thomas	436
Juan Gonzalez	434
Jim Thome	423
Gary Sheffield	415
Andres Galarraga	399
Manny Ramirez	390
Alex Rodriguez	381
Mike Piazza	378
Larry Walker	368
Ellis Burks	352
Carlos Delgado	336
Tino Martinez	322
Chipper Jones	310
Edgar Martinez	309

Runs Batted In

Player	
Barry Bonds	1843
Rafael Palmeiro	1775
Fred McGriff	1550
Sammy Sosa	1530
Jeff Bagwell	1510
Ken Griffey Jr.	1444
Frank Thomas	1439
Andres Galarraga	1425
Juan Gonzalez	1404
Gary Sheffield	1353
Ruben Sierra	1289
Manny Ramirez	1270
Edgar Martinez	1261
Larry Walker	1259
Tino Martinez	1222
Jeff Kent	1207
Ellis Burks	1206
John Olerud	1193
Robin Ventura	1182
Luis Gonzalez	1172

Stolen Bases

Player	
Kenny Lofton	545
Barry Bonds	506
Roberto Alomar	474
Eric Young	450
Marquis Grissom	428
Craig Biggio	396
Barry Larkin	379
Tom Goodwin	369
Tony Womack	335
Omar Vizquel	318
Steve Finley	305
Reggie Sanders	283
Mark McLemore	272
Luis Castillo	271
Julio Franco	269
Johnny Damon	263
Ray Lankford	258
Ray Durham	242
Edgar Renteria	237
Sammy Sosa	233

Seasons Played

Roger Clemens	21
John Franco	20
Julio Franco	20
Barry Bonds	19
Andres Galarraga	19
Barry Larkin	19
Greg Maddux	19
Fred McGriff	19
Mark McLemore	19
Rafael Palmeiro	19
Benito Santiago	19

Games

Rafael Palmeiro	2721
Barry Bonds	2716
Fred McGriff	2460
Craig Biggio	2409
Roberto Alomar	2379
Steve Finley	2289
Julio Franco	2269
Andres Galarraga	2257
B.J. Surhoff	2222
Barry Larkin	2180

At-Bats

Rafael Palmeiro	10103
Craig Biggio	9221
Barry Bonds	9098
Roberto Alomar	9073
Fred McGriff	8757
Steve Finley	8471
Julio Franco	8189
Marquis Grissom	8138
Andres Galarraga	8096
Sammy Sosa	8021

Runs Scored

Barry Bonds	2070
Rafael Palmeiro	1616
Craig Biggio	1603
Roberto Alomar	1508
Jeff Bagwell	1506
Sammy Sosa	1383
Fred McGriff	1349
Barry Larkin	1329
Steve Finley	1327
Ken Griffey Jr.	1320

Doubles

Rafael Palmeiro	572
Craig Biggio	564
Barry Bonds	563
Edgar Martinez	514
Roberto Alomar	504
John Olerud	493
Jeff Bagwell	484
Luis Gonzalez	458
Larry Walker	451
2 tied with	444

Triples

Steve Finley	109
Kenny Lofton	93
Roberto Alomar	80
Barry Bonds	77
Barry Larkin	76
Johnny Damon	74
Jose Offerman	71
Ray Durham	70
Ellis Burks	63
Luis Gonzalez	63

AB per HR
(minimum 1000 AB)

Barry Bonds	12.9
Jim Thome	13.5
Sammy Sosa	14.0
Manny Ramirez	14.3
Adam Dunn	14.6
Alex Rodriguez	14.7
Ken Griffey Jr.	14.7
Albert Pujols	14.8
Carlos Delgado	14.9
Juan Gonzalez	15.1

AB per RBI
(minimum 1000 AB)

Manny Ramirez	4.4
Juan Gonzalez	4.7
Albert Pujols	4.7
Carlos Delgado	4.7
Frank Thomas	4.8
Todd Helton	4.8
Jim Thome	4.9
Barry Bonds	4.9
Richie Sexson	5.0
Mike Piazza	5.0

Total Bases

Barry Bonds	5556
Rafael Palmeiro	5223
Fred McGriff	4458
Sammy Sosa	4368
Jeff Bagwell	4175
Ken Griffey Jr.	4131
Andres Galarraga	4038
Roberto Alomar	4018
Craig Biggio	4007
Frank Thomas	3887

Walks

Barry Bonds	2302
Frank Thomas	1450
Jeff Bagwell	1383
Rafael Palmeiro	1310
Fred McGriff	1305
Edgar Martinez	1283
John Olerud	1259
Jim Thome	1212
Gary Sheffield	1202
Robin Ventura	1075

Intentional Walks

Barry Bonds	604
Ken Griffey Jr.	207
Fred McGriff	171
Rafael Palmeiro	168
Frank Thomas	162
John Olerud	155
Jeff Bagwell	154
Sammy Sosa	148
Vladimir Guerrero	144
Mike Piazza	138

Hit by Pitch

Craig Biggio	256
Andres Galarraga	178
Jason Kendall	177
Fernando Vina	157
Larry Walker	129
Jeff Bagwell	127
Carlos Delgado	122
Damion Easley	111
Gary Sheffield	110
Jeff Kent	97

Strikeouts

Sammy Sosa	2110
Andres Galarraga	2003
Fred McGriff	1882
Jim Thome	1703
Ray Lankford	1550
Jeff Bagwell	1537
Craig Biggio	1467
Reggie Sanders	1438
Barry Bonds	1428
Ellis Burks	1340

SO/BB Ratio
(minimum 1000 AB)

Barry Bonds	620
Eric Young	689
Brian Giles	724
Gary Sheffield	731
Frank Thomas	782
John Olerud	791
Orlando Palmeiro	798
Todd Helton	813
Barry Larkin	870
Matt Lawton	875

Sacrifice Hits

Tom Glavine	186
Omar Vizquel	185
Greg Maddux	152
Roberto Alomar	148
Mark McLemore	105
Jose Vizcaino	104
Curt Schilling	102
Shane Reynolds	97
Royce Clayton	93
John Smoltz	92

Sacrifice Flies

Ruben Sierra	117
Rafael Palmeiro	111
Frank Thomas	106
B.J. Surhoff	100
Jeff Bagwell	98
Roberto Alomar	97
Gary Sheffield	96
John Olerud	93
Jeff Kent	88
Barry Bonds	87

SB Success Pct.
(minimum 100 SB attempts)

Carlos Beltran	89.3
Pokey Reese	84.7
Tony Womack	83.1
Barry Larkin	83.1
Scott Podsednik	83.1
Doug Glanville	82.4
Dave Roberts	80.8
Roberto Alomar	80.6
Carl Crawford	80.4
Alex Rodriguez	80.4

Caught Stealing

Eric Young	160
Kenny Lofton	145
Barry Bonds	141
Omar Vizquel	129
Mark McLemore	119
Craig Biggio	118
Tom Goodwin	118
Ray Lankford	117
Marquis Grissom	115
2 tied with	114

GDP

Julio Franco	289
Fred McGriff	226
John Olerud	226
Rafael Palmeiro	223
Todd Zeile	223
Ivan Rodriguez	220
Jeff Bagwell	219
Roberto Alomar	206
Benito Santiago	203
Vinny Castilla	201

AB per GDP
(minimum 1000 AB)

Dave Roberts	258.8
Carl Crawford	216.4
Rob Mackowiak	180.6
Greg Maddux	166.3
Ichiro Suzuki	136.1
Peter Bergeron	122.6
Joe McEwing	121.6
Russell Branyan	114.7
Rafael Furcal	105.7
Tony Womack	99.3

Wins

Roger Clemens	328
Greg Maddux	305
Tom Glavine	262
Randy Johnson	246
David Wells	212
Mike Mussina	211
Kevin Brown	207
Jamie Moyer	192
Curt Schilling	184
Pedro Martinez	182

Losses

Greg Maddux	174
Tom Glavine	171
Roger Clemens	164
Jamie Moyer	145
Terry Mulholland	140
Kevin Appier	137
Kevin Brown	137
David Wells	136
Scott Erickson	132
Steve Trachsel	131

Won-Lost Percentage
(minimum 100 decisions)

Pedro Martinez	.705
Tim Hudson	.702
Roger Clemens	.667
Mark Mulder	.659
Randy Johnson	.658
Andy Pettitte	.654
Barry Zito	.643
Mike Mussina	.639
Greg Maddux	.637
Roy Halladay	.632

ERA
(minimum 750 IP)

Pedro Martinez	2.71
Trevor Hoffman	2.74
John Franco	2.84
Greg Maddux	2.95
Randy Johnson	3.07
Roger Clemens	3.18
Kevin Brown	3.20
John Smoltz	3.27
Tim Hudson	3.30
Rod Beck	3.30

Games

John Franco	1088
Mike Jackson	1005
Mike Stanton	968
Jose Mesa	832
Roberto Hernandez	825
Mike Timlin	812
Steve Reed	803
Paul Quantrill	791
Todd Jones	744
Jeff Nelson	743

Games Started

Roger Clemens	639
Greg Maddux	604
Tom Glavine	570
Randy Johnson	479
Kevin Brown	463
Jamie Moyer	453
David Wells	417
Mike Mussina	413
Kevin Appier	402
2 tied with	370

Innings Pitched

Roger Clemens	4493.0
Greg Maddux	4181.1
Tom Glavine	3740.1
Randy Johnson	3368.0
Kevin Brown	3183.0
David Wells	3022.1
Jamie Moyer	2939.2
Mike Mussina	2833.1
Curt Schilling	2812.2
John Smoltz	2699.2

Batters Faced

Roger Clemens	18531
Greg Maddux	16989
Tom Glavine	15725
Randy Johnson	13864
Kevin Brown	13196
David Wells	12615
Jamie Moyer	12473
Mike Mussina	11548
Kenny Rogers	11546
Curt Schilling	11399

Complete Games

Roger Clemens	117
Greg Maddux	105
Randy Johnson	92
Curt Schilling	82
Kevin Brown	72
Mike Mussina	54
Tom Glavine	53
David Wells	52
Scott Erickson	51
John Smoltz	47

Complete Game Pct.
(minimum 100 games started)

Curt Schilling	0.22
Randy Johnson	0.19
Roger Clemens	0.18
Greg Maddux	0.17
Livan Hernandez	0.16
Kevin Brown	0.16
Mark Mulder	0.15
Scott Erickson	0.14
Terry Mulholland	0.14
Sidney Ponson	0.14

Shutouts

Roger Clemens	46
Randy Johnson	37
Greg Maddux	35
Tom Glavine	23
Mike Mussina	21
Curt Schilling	19
Kevin Brown	17
Scott Erickson	17
Pedro Martinez	16
John Smoltz	14

Quality Start Pct.†
(minimum 100 games started)

Pedro Martinez	70.4
Randy Johnson	70.4
Roy Oswalt	68.2
Curt Schilling	68.1
Greg Maddux	67.9
Kevin Brown	67.0
Tim Hudson	66.1
Barry Zito	66.0
Mark Buehrle	65.5
Roger Clemens	65.3

Strikeouts

Roger Clemens	4317
Randy Johnson	4161
Greg Maddux	2916
Curt Schilling	2745
Pedro Martinez	2653
John Smoltz	2398
Kevin Brown	2347
Mike Mussina	2258
Tom Glavine	2245
Kevin Appier	1994

Walks Allowed

Roger Clemens	1458
Randy Johnson	1302
Tom Glavine	1276
Al Leiter	1065
Kenny Rogers	964
Kevin Appier	933
Tom Gordon	893
Kevin Brown	882
Greg Maddux	871
Hideo Nomo	853

Strikeouts per 9 IP
(minimum 750 IP)

Randy Johnson	11.12
Kerry Wood	10.43
Pedro Martinez	10.40
Trevor Hoffman	10.13
Hideo Nomo	8.93
Mike Remlinger	8.81
Arthur Rhodes	8.80
Curt Schilling	8.78
Roger Clemens	8.65
Darren Dreifort	8.27

Walks per 9 IP
(minimum 750 IP)

Brad Radke	1.68
Jon Lieber	1.76
Greg Maddux	1.87
David Wells	1.92
Brian Anderson	1.98
Mike Mussina	2.02
Curt Schilling	2.04
Ramiro Mendoza	2.05
Jose Lima	2.10
Ben Sheets	2.10

†**Quality Starts** denote the number of outings in which a starting pitcher works at least six innings and allows three or fewer earned runs.

SO/BB Ratio
(minimum 750 IP)

Pedro Martinez	4.31
Curt Schilling	4.30
Trevor Hoffman	3.83
Jon Lieber	3.72
Ben Sheets	3.55
Mike Mussina	3.54
Rod Beck	3.37
Shane Reynolds	3.35
Greg Maddux	3.35
Brad Radke	3.25

Hits per 9 IP
(minimum 750 IP)

Trevor Hoffman	6.77
Pedro Martinez	6.84
Kerry Wood	6.94
Randy Johnson	6.98
Mike Jackson	7.44
Barry Zito	7.63
Roger Clemens	7.70
John Smoltz	7.76
Mike Remlinger	7.83
Hideo Nomo	7.84

Baserunners per 9 IP
(minimum 750 IP)

Trevor Hoffman	9.49
Pedro Martinez	9.71
Curt Schilling	10.16
Greg Maddux	10.40
Mike Mussina	10.63
John Smoltz	10.65
Rod Beck	10.71
Randy Johnson	10.88
Roger Clemens	10.92
Kevin Brown	11.27

Home Runs per 9 IP
(minimum 750 IP)

Kevin Brown	0.57
Greg Maddux	0.58
John Franco	0.59
Terry Adams	0.63
Bob Wickman	0.66
Derek Lowe	0.66
Roger Clemens	0.67
Tim Hudson	0.68
Julian Tavarez	0.68
Pedro Martinez	0.69

Opposition Avg.
(minimum 750 IP)

Trevor Hoffman	.206
Pedro Martinez	.209
Randy Johnson	.213
Kerry Wood	.214
Mike Jackson	.226
Barry Zito	.229
Roger Clemens	.230
John Smoltz	.232
Hideo Nomo	.235
Mike Remlinger	.235

Opposition OBP
(minimum 750 IP)

Trevor Hoffman	.264
Pedro Martinez	.271
Curt Schilling	.281
Greg Maddux	.288
Rod Beck	.292
Mike Mussina	.292
John Smoltz	.292
Randy Johnson	.296
Roger Clemens	.296
Kevin Brown	.304

Opposition Slg.
(minimum 750 IP)

Pedro Martinez	.323
Trevor Hoffman	.337
Randy Johnson	.337
John Franco	.342
Roger Clemens	.343
Greg Maddux	.345
Kevin Brown	.346
John Smoltz	.352
Kerry Wood	.353
Barry Zito	.354

Home Runs Allowed

Jamie Moyer	358
David Wells	353
Roger Clemens	336
Randy Johnson	301
Mike Mussina	300
Steve Trachsel	290
Tom Glavine	288
Terry Mulholland	286
Curt Schilling	286
Kenny Rogers	271

Hit Batsmen

Randy Johnson	156
Roger Clemens	147
Kevin Brown	132
Tim Wakefield	125
Greg Maddux	118
Pedro Martinez	115
Pedro Astacio	108
Chan Ho Park	106
Al Leiter	105
Aaron Sele	103

Wild Pitches

Roger Clemens	130
John Smoltz	128
Kevin Appier	106
Hideo Nomo	105
Kevin Brown	102
Tom Gordon	101
David Wells	96
Randy Johnson	95
Jason Grimsley	94
Matt Clement	85

GDP Induced

Greg Maddux	354
Tom Glavine	353
Kevin Brown	321
Scott Erickson	301
Roger Clemens	294
Kenny Rogers	267
Terry Mulholland	257
Mike Hampton	251
Jamie Moyer	239
David Wells	222

GDP per 9 IP
(minimum 750 IP)

Shawn Estes	1.28
Scott Erickson	1.18
Julian Tavarez	1.17
Jamey Wright	1.17
Bob Wickman	1.16
Mike Hampton	1.13
Jon Garland	1.12
Derek Lowe	1.07
Danny Graves	1.06
Andy Pettitte	1.04

Saves

John Franco	424
Trevor Hoffman	393
Mariano Rivera	336
Roberto Hernandez	320
Troy Percival	316
Jose Mesa	292
Rod Beck	286
Billy Wagner	246
Armando Benitez	244
Ugueth Urbina	227

Save Percentage
(minimum 50 save opportunities)

Eric Gagne	96.2
John Smoltz	91.7
Trevor Hoffman	89.1
Mariano Rivera	87.5
Joe Nathan	86.5
Troy Percival	86.3
Armando Benitez	86.2
Dan Kolb	85.9
Jose Mesa	85.9
Billy Wagner	85.4

Games Finished

John Franco	770
Roberto Hernandez	608
Trevor Hoffman	578
Jose Mesa	538
Rod Beck	519
Mariano Rivera	474
Troy Percival	466
Armando Benitez	441
Mike Jackson	422
2 tied with	417

SB Pct. Allowed
(minimum 750 IP)

Kirk Rueter	35.1
Mark Buehrle	35.4
Terry Mulholland	41.0
Chris Carpenter	41.0
Kenny Rogers	41.8
Mark Redman	48.6
Brian Anderson	49.1
Wilson Alvarez	49.7
Jeff Weaver	51.2
Chan Ho Park	51.2

2004 LEFTY/RIGHTY STATISTICS

Batters versus lefthanded and righthanded pitchers

Pitchers versus lefthanded and righthanded batters

BATTERS VS. LEFTHANDED AND RIGHTHANDED PITCHERS

Batter	vs.	Avg.	AB	H	2B	3B	HR	RBI	BB	SO	OBP	Slg.	Batter	vs.	Avg.	AB	H	2B	3B	HR	RBI	BB	SO	OBP	Slg.
Abreu, Bobby	L	.267	187	50	15	0	7	26	43	43	.408	.460	Bautista, Jose	L	.208	53	11	1	0	0	0	1	24	.222	.226
Bats Left	R	.318	387	123	32	1	23	79	84	73	.438	.584	Bats Right	R	.200	35	7	2	0	0	2	6	16	.317	.257
Adams, Russ	L	.100	10	1	0	0	0	1	0	0	.182	.100	Bay, Jason	L	.265	83	22	3	0	7	17	11	25	.367	.554
Bats Left	R	.339	62	21	2	1	4	9	5	5	.388	.597	Bats Right	R	.287	328	94	21	4	19	65	30	104	.355	.549
Aguila, Chris	L	.056	18	1	1	0	0	1	0	5	.056	.111	Bell, David	L	.296	125	37	11	0	2	16	14	10	.379	.432
Bats Right	R	.333	27	9	1	1	3	4	2	7	.379	.778	Bats Right	R	.289	408	118	22	1	16	61	43	65	.357	.466
Alexander, M	L	.267	15	4	1	0	0	2	1	4	.313	.333	Bellhorn, Mark	L	.298	181	54	16	2	7	33	20	61	.374	.525
Bats Right	R	.167	6	1	1	0	0	1	0	3	.167	.333	Bats Both	R	.246	342	84	21	1	10	49	68	116	.373	.401
Alfaro, Jason	L	.143	7	1	0	0	0	0	0	3	.143	.143	Belliard, R	L	.319	204	65	20	1	7	23	26	33	.398	.529
Bats Right	R	.250	4	1	0	0	0	0	0	2	.250	.250	Bats Right	R	.263	395	104	28	0	5	47	34	65	.322	.372
Alfonzo, E	L	.318	154	49	8	0	5	27	25	1	.412	.468	Beltran, C	L	.276	174	48	13	0	11	33	18	23	.347	.540
Bats Right	R	.277	365	101	18	1	6	50	21	39	.321	.381	Bats Both	R	.264	425	112	23	9	27	71	74	78	.375	.551
Allen, Chad	L	.243	37	9	3	0	0	3	2	7	.282	.324	Beltre, Adrian	L	.291	134	39	7	0	6	17	19	14	.381	.478
Bats Right	R	.238	21	5	1	0	0	3	0	6	.227	.381	Bats Right	R	.347	464	161	25	0	42	104	34	73	.390	.672
Alomar, R	L	.286	42	12	1	0	1	9	3	12	.326	.381	Bennett, Gary	L	.256	39	10	4	0	1	5	5	5	.333	.436
Bats Both	R	.256	129	33	5	2	3	15	11	19	.319	.395	Bats Right	R	.217	180	39	10	0	2	15	17	27	.289	.306
Alomar Jr., S	L	.200	35	7	0	0	2	4	1	2	.216	.371	Berg, Dave	L	.241	79	19	1	0	1	10	3	10	.277	.291
Bats Right	R	.252	111	28	4	0	0	10	10	11	.323	.288	Bats Right	R	.267	75	20	3	0	2	13	1	17	.278	.387
Alou, Moises	L	.298	114	34	6	2	4	10	10	15	.355	.491	Berger, B	L	.278	18	5	2	0	0	2	0	2	.278	.389
Bats Right	R	.292	487	142	30	1	35	96	58	65	.363	.573	Bats Right	R	.118	17	2	0	0	0	0	0	5	.118	.118
Alvarez, Tony	L	.318	22	7	2	0	1	7	4	4	.407	.545	Bergeron, P	L	.188	16	3	0	0	0	0	1	4	.235	.188
Bats Right	R	.063	16	1	0	0	0	1	0	3	.111	.063	Bats Left	R	.231	26	6	0	0	0	1	1	12	.259	.231
Amezaga, A	L	.200	35	7	0	0	1	6	0	8	.200	.286	Berkman, Lance	L	.272	125	34	8	0	4	21	24	21	.404	.432
Bats Both	R	.138	58	8	2	0	1	5	3	16	.219	.224	Bats Both	R	.329	419	138	32	3	26	85	103	80	.463	.606
Anderson, G	L	.262	149	39	5	0	2	27	4	32	.277	.336	Berroa, Angel	L	.259	139	36	9	1	2	12	7	19	.318	.381
Bats Left	R	.321	293	94	15	1	12	48	25	43	.375	.502	Bats Right	R	.263	373	98	18	5	6	31	16	68	.304	.386
Anderson, M	L	.160	25	4	1	0	0	1	2	2	.222	.200	Betemit, W	L	.333	9	3	0	0	0	2	1	2	.364	.333
Bats Left	R	.246	228	56	11	0	8	27	10	36	.275	.399	Bats Both	R	.132	38	5	0	0	0	1	3	14	.195	.132
Ardoin, Danny	L	.000	0	0	0	0	0	0	0	0	.000	.000	Bigbie, Larry	L	.216	148	32	5	0	6	22	17	36	.299	.372
Bats Right	R	.125	8	1	0	0	0	1	3	2	.364	.125	Bats Left	R	.309	330	102	18	1	9	46	28	77	.360	.452
Atkins, G	L	.333	15	5	1	0	0	3	3	1	.444	.400	Biggio, Craig	L	.303	119	36	7	0	6	12	11	7	.385	.513
Bats Right	R	.385	13	5	1	0	1	5	1	2	.400	.692	Bats Right	R	.276	514	142	40	0	18	51	29	87	.326	.459
Aurilia, Rich	L	.257	136	35	8	1	3	19	11	22	.325	.397	Blake, Casey	L	.243	189	46	5	0	11	25	27	44	.341	.444
Bats Right	R	.240	263	63	13	1	3	25	26	49	.308	.331	Bats Right	R	.284	398	113	31	3	17	63	41	95	.360	.505
Ausmus, Brad	L	.308	78	24	3	0	2	12	10	8	.382	.423	Blalock, Hank	L	.282	195	55	13	1	5	29	17	56	.344	.436
Bats Right	R	.234	325	76	11	1	3	19	23	48	.287	.302	Bats Left	R	.273	429	117	25	2	27	81	58	93	.360	.529
Baerga, Carlos	L	.500	8	4	0	0	0	2	3	0	.636	.500	Blanco, Andres	L	.412	17	7	2	0	0	1	4	1	.545	.529
Bats Both	R	.208	77	16	2	0	2	9	3	12	.265	.312	Bats Both	R	.279	43	12	0	2	0	4	1	5	.295	.372
Bagwell, Jeff	L	.149	101	15	1	0	4	10	24	22	.312	.277	Blanco, Henry	L	.204	98	20	5	0	5	13	14	16	.307	.408
Bats Right	R	.291	471	137	28	2	23	79	72	109	.392	.505	Bats Right	R	.207	217	45	14	1	5	24	7	40	.237	.350
Bako, Paul	L	.095	21	2	0	0	1	1	0	9	.095	.238	Bloomquist, W	L	.281	89	25	7	0	2	10	6	22	.326	.427
Bats Left	R	.222	117	26	8	0	0	9	15	20	.319	.291	Bats Right	R	.212	99	21	3	0	0	8	4	26	.243	.242
Baldelli, R	L	.331	124	41	9	0	6	19	10	18	.382	.548	Blum, Geoff	L	.288	80	23	6	0	3	15	9	14	.360	.475
Bats Right	R	.264	394	104	18	3	10	55	20	70	.308	.401	Bats Both	R	.193	259	50	15	0	5	20	15	44	.236	.309
Barajas, Rod	L	.248	101	25	7	0	4	19	5	14	.284	.436	Bocachica, H	L	.400	30	12	3	0	1	2	7	3	.514	.600
Bats Right	R	.249	257	64	19	1	11	39	8	49	.272	.459	Bats Right	R	.167	60	10	2	0	2	4	5	24	.239	.300
Bard, Josh	L	.429	7	3	1	0	1	2	0	0	.375	1.000	Bonds, Barry	L	.307	140	43	9	2	8	23	59	16	.524	.571
Bats Both	R	.417	12	5	1	0	0	2	3	0	.533	.500	Bats Left	R	.395	233	92	18	1	37	78	173	25	.652	.957
Barmes, Clint	L	.345	29	10	1	0	1	3	2	3	.406	.483	Boone, Bret	L	.257	148	38	10	0	8	24	23	30	.355	.486
Bats Right	R	.238	42	10	2	1	1	7	1	7	.256	.405	Bats Right	R	.249	445	111	20	0	16	59	33	105	.304	.402
Barrett, M	L	.248	105	26	7	1	3	12	9	14	.307	.419	Borchard, Joe	L	.177	96	17	0	1	3	8	8	21	.240	.292
Bats Right	R	.299	351	105	25	5	13	53	24	50	.345	.510	Bats Both	R	.171	105	18	4	0	6	12	11	36	.256	.381
Bartlett, J	L	.000	2	0	0	0	0	0	0	0	.000	.000	Borders, Pat	L	.318	22	7	1	0	1	4	0	3	.318	.500
Bats Right	R	.100	10	1	0	0	0	1	1	1	.182	.100	Bats Right	R	.205	73	15	5	0	0	6	1	19	.227	.274
Batista, Tony	L	.230	165	38	6	0	13	25	9	22	.268	.503	Bowen, Rob	L	.111	9	1	0	0	1	2	1	3	.200	.444
Bats Right	R	.245	441	108	24	2	19	85	17	56	.274	.438	Bats Both	R	.111	18	2	0	0	0	0	3	7	.238	.111
Bautista, D	L	.279	154	43	6	0	1	14	14	13	.339	.338	Bradley, M	L	.295	146	43	9	0	4	21	13	24	.356	.438
Bats Right	R	.288	385	111	21	1	10	51	21	53	.329	.426	Bats Both	R	.257	370	95	15	0	15	46	58	99	.364	.419

Batter	vs.	Avg.	AB	H	2B	3B	HR	RBI	BB	SO	OBP	Slg.
Bragg, Darren	L	.235	17	4	0	0	0	2	2	7	.316	.235
Bats Left	R	.179	84	15	3	1	4	7	8	24	.250	.381
Branyan, R	L	.167	30	5	0	0	1	3	2	17	.212	.267
Bats Left	R	.250	128	32	11	1	10	24	18	51	.349	.586
Brazell, Craig	L	1.000	1	1	0	0	1	1	0	0	1.000	4.000
Bats Left	R	.242	33	8	2	0	0	2	1	7	.265	.303
Brito, Juan	L	.182	44	8	2	0	2	5	3	5	.229	.364
Bats Right	R	.213	127	27	5	0	1	7	6	36	.252	.276
Broussard, Ben	L	.362	69	25	7	2	3	22	6	18	.429	.652
Bats Left	R	.258	349	90	21	3	14	60	46	77	.359	.456
Brown, Adrian	L	.333	9	3	0	0	0	0	0	1	.333	.333
Bats Both	R	.000	2	0	0	0	0	0	0	1	.000	.000
Brown, Dee	L	.234	47	11	1	0	1	5	2	13	.265	.319
Bats Left	R	.257	148	38	6	0	3	19	9	37	.302	.358
Bruntlett, E	L	.250	16	4	0	0	2	5	4	2	.381	.625
Bats Right	R	.250	36	9	2	0	2	3	3	11	.300	.472
Buchanan, B	L	.205	44	9	2	0	1	5	6	14	.294	.318
Bats Right	R	.158	19	3	0	0	1	1	1	6	.238	.316
Buck, John	L	.222	72	16	4	0	3	10	2	25	.243	.403
Bats Right	R	.241	166	40	5	0	9	20	13	54	.294	.434
Burke, Chris	L	.000	2	0	0	0	0	0	1	0	.333	.000
Bats Right	R	.067	15	1	0	0	0	0	2	3	.176	.067
Burke, Jamie	L	.311	61	19	6	0	0	5	7	8	.377	.410
Bats Right	R	.356	59	21	3	0	0	10	3	5	.397	.407
Burks, Ellis	L	.176	17	3	0	0	1	1	1	6	.222	.353
Bats Right	R	.188	16	3	0	0	0	2	2	2	.316	.188
Burnitz, J	L	.279	136	38	8	1	10	28	11	28	.344	.574
Bats Left	R	.285	404	115	22	3	27	82	47	96	.360	.554
Burrell, Pat	L	.271	96	26	5	0	3	17	23	27	.407	.417
Bats Right	R	.253	352	89	12	0	21	67	55	103	.353	.466
Burroughs, S	L	.269	130	35	1	2	0	16	3	9	.307	.308
Bats Left	R	.308	393	121	22	1	2	31	28	43	.362	.384
Bush, Homer	L	.000	1	0	0	0	0	0	0	1	.000	.000
Bats Right	R	.000	6	0	0	0	0	0	0	1	.143	.000
Byrd, Marlon	L	.213	75	16	4	2	1	8	4	10	.250	.360
Bats Right	R	.232	271	63	9	0	4	25	18	58	.297	.310
Byrnes, Eric	L	.344	157	54	15	2	7	23	17	21	.406	.599
Bats Right	R	.260	412	107	24	1	13	50	29	90	.324	.417
Cabrera, J	L	.286	126	36	9	1	2	17	10	24	.338	.421
Bats Right	R	.262	233	61	10	1	4	30	6	46	.298	.365
Cabrera, M	L	.262	126	33	8	0	7	27	22	27	.373	.492
Bats Right	R	.302	477	144	23	1	26	85	46	121	.365	.518
Cabrera, O	L	.295	193	57	14	2	3	15	15	9	.352	.435
Bats Right	R	.249	425	106	24	1	7	47	24	45	.285	.360
Cairo, Miguel	L	.336	128	43	7	2	1	15	7	17	.377	.445
Bats Right	R	.267	232	62	10	3	5	27	11	32	.329	.401
Calloway, Ron	L	.000	14	0	0	0	0	1	1	7	.067	.000
Bats Left	R	.200	70	14	2	0	1	9	4	15	.240	.271
Cameron, Mike	L	.216	102	22	5	0	5	12	15	29	.316	.412
Bats Right	R	.235	391	92	25	1	25	64	42	114	.320	.496
Cantu, Jorge	L	.373	51	19	9	0	0	2	2	10	.396	.549
Bats Right	R	.270	122	33	11	1	2	15	7	34	.318	.426
Carroll, Jamey	L	.250	76	19	5	1	0	5	10	7	.333	.342
Bats Right	R	.310	142	44	9	1	0	11	22	14	.401	.387
Casey, Sean	L	.306	183	56	9	0	10	35	16	13	.372	.519
Bats Left	R	.332	388	129	35	2	14	64	30	23	.385	.541
Cash, Kevin	L	.213	75	16	5	0	2	11	6	21	.280	.360
Bats Right	R	.179	106	19	4	0	2	10	4	38	.226	.274
Castilla, V	L	.267	161	43	8	2	9	29	17	33	.337	.509
Bats Right	R	.273	422	115	35	1	26	102	34	80	.330	.545

Batter	vs.	Avg.	AB	H	2B	3B	HR	RBI	BB	SO	OBP	Slg.
Castillo, A	L	.222	27	6	1	0	0	0	5	6	.344	.259
Bats Right	R	.290	62	18	5	0	1	11	9	4	.375	.419
Castillo, Jose	L	.267	90	24	5	1	1	8	9	21	.327	.378
Bats Right	R	.253	293	74	10	1	7	31	14	71	.289	.365
Castillo, Luis	L	.308	143	44	5	6	1	9	14	18	.369	.448
Bats Both	R	.285	421	120	7	1	1	38	61	50	.374	.314
Castro, Juan	L	.238	80	19	6	1	1	9	1	11	.247	.375
Bats Right	R	.247	219	54	15	1	4	17	13	40	.288	.379
Castro, Ramon	L	.143	14	2	0	0	0	1	1	2	.250	.143
Bats Right	R	.134	82	11	3	0	3	7	10	28	.228	.280
Castro, R	L	.000	3	0	0	0	0	0	1	0	.250	.000
Bats Right	R	.167	12	2	1	0	0	3	0	3	.167	.250
Catalanotto, F	L	.227	44	10	2	0	0	4	0	8	.222	.273
Bats Left	R	.307	205	63	17	1	1	22	17	25	.368	.415
Cedeno, Roger	L	.194	36	7	0	0	1	5	4	6	.275	.278
Bats Both	R	.280	164	46	9	2	2	18	15	35	.339	.396
Cepicky, Matt	L	.250	4	1	0	0	1	1	0	1	.250	1.000
Bats Left	R	.214	56	12	4	0	0	2	1	17	.228	.286
Chavez, Endy	L	.241	137	33	5	1	2	12	3	12	.259	.336
Bats Left	R	.290	365	106	15	5	3	22	27	28	.339	.384
Chavez, Eric	L	.306	183	56	5	0	9	28	31	47	.412	.481
Bats Left	R	.257	292	75	15	0	20	49	64	52	.388	.514
Chavez, Raul	L	.139	36	5	1	0	0	5	2	8	.184	.167
Bats Right	R	.230	126	29	7	0	0	18	8	30	.276	.286
Chen, C	L	.000	5	0	0	0	0	0	0	2	.000	.000
Bats Right	R	.000	3	0	0	0	0	0	2	1	.400	.000
Choi, Hee Seop	L	.167	36	6	1	0	1	4	3	13	.268	.278
Bats Left	R	.261	307	80	20	1	14	42	60	83	.381	.469
Church, Ryan	L	.167	12	2	0	0	0	1	1	3	.231	.167
Bats Left	R	.176	51	9	1	0	1	5	6	13	.263	.255
Cintron, Alex	L	.295	156	46	5	3	1	11	6	9	.321	.385
Bats Both	R	.250	408	102	26	4	3	38	25	50	.294	.355
Cirillo, Jeff	L	.207	29	6	0	0	1	6	3	4	.273	.310
Bats Right	R	.217	46	10	3	0	0	1	2	10	.250	.283
Clark, Brady	L	.250	92	23	4	0	1	12	15	9	.368	.326
Bats Right	R	.291	261	76	14	1	6	34	38	39	.391	.421
Clark, Howie	L	.125	8	1	0	0	0	2	0	3	.111	.125
Bats Left	R	.224	107	24	6	0	3	10	13	12	.306	.364
Clark, J	L	.000	4	0	0	0	0	0	1	2	.333	.000
Bats Left	R	.154	26	4	1	0	0	2	0	6	.185	.192
Clark, Tony	L	.196	92	18	5	0	3	13	6	23	.242	.348
Bats Both	R	.236	161	38	7	0	13	36	20	69	.326	.522
Clayton, Royce	L	.288	146	42	10	0	1	11	18	25	.366	.377
Bats Right	R	.276	428	118	26	4	7	43	30	100	.328	.404
Closser, J.D.	L	.346	26	9	1	0	0	1	2	5	.393	.385
Bats Both	R	.310	87	27	5	0	1	9	4	17	.355	.402
Colbrunn, Greg	L	.200	15	3	0	0	0	1	0	1	.200	.200
Bats Right	R	.000	12	0	0	0	0	0	1	4	.077	.000
Collier, Lou	L	.200	10	2	0	0	0	2	3	3	.385	.500
Bats Right	R	.308	26	8	1	0	0	2	2	7	.379	.346
Conine, Jeff	L	.275	109	30	9	0	5	21	17	13	.370	.495
Bats Right	R	.282	412	116	26	1	9	62	31	65	.331	.415
Conti, Jason	L	.200	5	1	0	0	0	0	0	3	.200	.200
Bats Left	R	.180	50	9	3	0	0	4	5	16	.255	.240
Cora, Alex	L	.239	46	11	2	0	2	8	4	3	.345	.413
Bats Left	R	.267	359	96	7	4	8	39	43	38	.367	.376
Cordero, Wil	L	.280	25	7	2	0	0	4	0	2	.269	.360
Bats Right	R	.146	41	6	1	0	1	2	3	17	.239	.244
Cota, Humberto	L	.188	16	3	0	0	1	4	1	3	.278	.375
Bats Right	R	.240	50	12	1	1	4	4	2	17	.269	.540

Batter	vs.	Avg.	AB	H	2B	3B	HR	RBI	BB	SO	OBP	Slg.
Counsell, C	L	.184	87	16	2	2	0	4	9	19	.260	.253
Bats Left	R	.254	386	98	17	3	2	19	50	69	.345	.329
Crawford, Carl	L	.295	146	43	7	4	1	11	12	24	.346	.418
Bats Left	R	.296	480	142	19	15	10	44	23	57	.326	.460
Crede, Joe	L	.256	164	42	9	0	4	20	14	25	.311	.384
Bats Right	R	.230	326	75	16	0	17	49	20	56	.292	.436
Crespo, Cesar	L	.154	13	2	0	0	0	0	0	6	.154	.154
Bats Both	R	.167	66	11	2	1	0	2	0	14	.167	.227
Crisp, Coco	L	.311	177	55	10	1	8	32	12	24	.353	.514
Bats Both	R	.290	314	91	14	1	7	39	24	45	.339	.408
Crosby, Bobby	L	.194	139	27	6	1	6	13	18	28	.287	.381
Bats Right	R	.254	406	103	28	0	16	51	40	113	.330	.441
Crosby, Bubba	L	.063	16	1	0	0	0	1	1	4	.167	.063
Bats Left	R	.189	37	7	2	0	2	6	1	9	.211	.405
Crozier, Eric	L	.333	3	1	1	0	0	0	0	2	.333	.667
Bats Left	R	.133	30	4	1	0	2	4	6	17	.278	.367
Cruz, Deivi	L	.259	108	28	10	0	2	14	2	10	.283	.407
Bats Right	R	.304	289	88	20	2	5	41	15	22	.335	.439
Cruz, Jacob	L	.000	3	0	0	0	0	0	0	2	.000	.000
Bats Left	R	.229	144	33	8	0	3	28	16	41	.323	.347
Cruz Jr., Jose	L	.264	159	42	10	2	6	22	26	24	.364	.465
Bats Both	R	.233	386	90	15	6	15	56	50	93	.320	.420
Cuddyer, M	L	.293	123	36	8	1	4	17	16	29	.379	.472
Bats Right	R	.245	216	53	14	0	8	28	21	45	.317	.421
Cummings, M	L	.000	2	0	0	0	0	0	0	1	.000	.000
Bats Left	R	.288	52	15	4	0	2	7	5	11	.373	.481
Cust, Jack	L	.000	0	0	0	0	0	0	0	0	.000	.000
Bats Left	R	.000	1	0	0	0	0	0	0	1	.000	.000
Dallimore, B	L	.429	14	6	2	0	1	5	2	3	.529	.786
Bats Right	R	.207	29	6	0	0	0	2	2	4	.250	.207
Damon, Johnny	L	.278	223	62	15	2	3	29	19	26	.339	.404
Bats Left	R	.319	398	127	20	4	17	65	57	45	.403	.518
Daubach, Brian	L	.000	3	0	0	0	0	0	0	3	.000	.000
Bats Left	R	.236	72	17	8	0	2	8	10	18	.337	.431
DaVanon, Jeff	L	.136	22	3	0	0	0	0	3	8	.240	.136
Bats Both	R	.289	263	76	11	4	7	34	43	46	.383	.441
Davis, Ben	L	.172	58	10	1	0	1	5	4	16	.222	.241
Bats Both	R	.222	135	30	8	0	5	13	8	33	.271	.393
Davis, J.J.	L	.190	21	4	1	0	0	1	3	3	.292	.238
Bats Right	R	.071	14	1	0	0	0	2	1	7	.125	.071
DeJesus, David	L	.224	98	22	2	0	0	8	6	18	.283	.245
Bats Left	R	.309	265	82	13	3	7	31	27	35	.388	.460
Delgado, C	L	.271	177	48	14	0	9	37	20	39	.348	.503
Bats Left	R	.267	281	75	12	0	23	62	49	76	.386	.555
Delgado, W	L	.240	25	6	0	0	0	2	3	1	.321	.240
Bats Both	R	.305	105	32	4	1	2	11	12	28	.376	.419
Dellucci, D	L	.107	28	3	0	0	0	2	3	9	.212	.107
Bats Left	R	.254	303	77	13	1	17	59	44	79	.354	.472
DeRosa, Mark	L	.233	86	20	2	0	1	6	7	11	.292	.291
Bats Right	R	.242	223	54	14	0	2	25	16	42	.294	.332
DeVore, Doug	L	.176	17	3	0	0	2	5	0	5	.176	.529
Bats Left	R	.233	90	21	3	2	1	8	7	26	.289	.344
Diaz, Einar	L	.210	81	17	5	0	1	7	8	5	.290	.309
Bats Right	R	.241	58	14	1	1	0	4	3	5	.297	.293
Diaz, Matt	L	.267	15	4	1	1	1	3	0	4	.353	.667
Bats Right	R	.000	6	0	0	0	0	0	1	2	.143	.000
Diaz, Victor	L	.273	11	3	2	0	0	2	1	4	.333	.455
Bats Right	R	.300	40	12	1	0	3	6	0	11	.317	.550
DiFelice, Mike	L	.200	10	2	0	1	0	1	1	3	.273	.400
Bats Right	R	.067	15	1	0	0	0	1	2	1	.176	.067
Dobbs, Greg	L	.750	4	3	1	0	0	3	0	1	.750	1.000
Bats Left	R	.184	49	9	0	0	1	6	1	13	.212	.245
Dominique, A	L	.333	3	1	0	0	0	1	0	0	.333	.333
Bats Right	R	.125	8	1	0	0	0	0	0	3	.125	.125
Dransfeldt, K	L	.214	14	3	0	0	0	2	0	3	.214	.214
Bats Right	R	.438	16	7	0	0	0	2	0	3	.438	.438
Drew, J.D.	L	.287	167	48	13	4	6	31	34	39	.408	.521
Bats Left	R	.313	351	110	15	4	25	62	84	77	.450	.593
Dubois, Jason	L	.125	8	1	0	0	0	1	0	3	.111	.125
Bats Right	R	.267	15	4	0	1	1	4	1	4	.313	.600
Duncan, Jeff	L	.167	6	1	0	0	0	1	0	1	.167	.167
Bats Left	R	.000	9	0	0	0	0	0	1	4	.100	.000
Dunn, Adam	L	.256	180	46	8	0	10	21	29	68	.362	.467
Bats Left	R	.271	388	105	26	0	36	81	79	127	.399	.616
Durazo, E	L	.278	158	44	9	0	5	28	13	49	.343	.430
Bats Left	R	.340	353	120	26	1	17	60	43	55	.419	.564
Durham, Ray	L	.333	132	44	9	2	4	23	11	11	.386	.523
Bats Both	R	.263	339	89	19	6	13	42	46	49	.356	.469
Durrington, T	L	.379	29	11	0	1	2	3	1	5	.400	.655
Bats Right	R	.151	53	8	2	2	0	1	3	18	.196	.264
Dye, Jermaine	L	.280	161	45	6	2	8	30	26	28	.376	.491
Bats Right	R	.259	371	96	23	2	15	50	23	100	.307	.453
Easley, Damion	L	.149	87	13	4	1	2	10	9	6	.245	.287
Bats Right	R	.294	136	40	16	0	7	33	15	30	.384	.566
Eckstein, D	L	.279	179	50	7	0	2	12	15	13	.345	.352
Bats Right	R	.274	387	106	17	1	0	23	27	36	.336	.323
Edmonds, Jim	L	.330	106	35	15	0	5	23	13	33	.400	.613
Bats Left	R	.293	392	115	23	3	37	88	88	117	.423	.651
Ellison, Jason	L	.500	2	1	0	0	0	2	0	1	.500	2.000
Bats Right	R	.500	2	1	0	0	0	1	0	0	.500	.500
Encarnacion, J	L	.217	115	25	5	0	1	7	15	19	.313	.287
Bats Right	R	.241	369	89	25	2	15	55	23	67	.295	.442
Ensberg, M	L	.282	103	29	8	1	1	13	11	14	.351	.408
Bats Right	R	.273	308	84	12	2	9	53	25	32	.323	.412
Erickson, Matt	L	.000	1	0	0	0	0	0	0	0	.000	.000
Bats Left	R	.200	5	1	0	0	0	0	0	1	.200	.200
Erstad, Darin	L	.253	166	42	10	0	2	23	9	25	.298	.349
Bats Left	R	.316	329	104	19	1	5	46	28	49	.370	.426
Escalona, F	L	.000	0	0	0	0	0	0	0	0	.000	.000
Bats Right	R	.000	8	0	0	0	0	0	0	2	.111	.000
Escobar, Alex	L	.200	50	10	3	0	1	6	11	9	.344	.320
Bats Right	R	.216	102	22	5	2	0	6	12	33	.304	.304
Estalella, B	L	.188	16	3	0	0	1	3	3	7	.316	.375
Bats Right	R	.182	11	2	0	0	1	1	0	4	.250	.455
Estrada, J	L	.272	125	34	7	0	3	14	6	15	.311	.400
Bats Both	R	.329	337	111	29	0	6	62	33	51	.401	.469
Everett, Adam	L	.235	68	16	4	1	2	9	4	11	.278	.412
Bats Right	R	.282	316	89	11	1	6	22	13	45	.326	.380
Everett, Carl	L	.233	90	21	6	0	0	10	3	14	.293	.300
Bats Both	R	.272	191	52	11	1	7	25	13	31	.332	.450
Feliz, Pedro	L	.291	172	50	13	0	7	31	7	31	.313	.488
Bats Right	R	.269	331	89	20	3	15	53	16	54	.301	.483
Fick, Robert	L	.111	18	2	0	0	1	2	2	3	.238	.278
Bats Left	R	.207	208	43	5	2	5	24	20	33	.280	.322
Figgins, Chone	L	.314	169	53	5	5	1	18	22	38	.393	.420
Bats Both	R	.289	408	118	17	12	4	42	27	56	.332	.419
Finley, Steve	L	.245	192	47	7	0	11	29	19	30	.311	.453
Bats Left	R	.282	436	123	21	1	25	65	42	52	.342	.507
Flaherty, John	L	.310	29	9	3	0	1	3	1	5	.333	.517
Bats Right	R	.235	98	23	6	0	5	13	4	20	.272	.449

Batter	vs.	Avg.	AB	H	2B	3B	HR	RBI	BB	SO	OBP	Slg.	Batter	vs.	Avg.	AB	H	2B	3B	HR	RBI	BB	SO	OBP	Slg.
Flores, Jose	L	.000	1	0	0	0	0	0	0	1	.000	.000	Gomes, Jonny	L	.000	6	0	0	0	0	0	1	3	.143	.000
Bats Right	R	.333	3	1	0	0	0	0	1	1	.500	.333	Bats Right	R	.125	8	1	0	0	0	1	0	3	.125	.125
Floyd, Cliff	L	.239	113	27	8	0	1	14	7	30	.296	.336	Gomez, Alexis	L	.250	8	2	0	0	0	0	0	4	.250	.250
Bats Left	R	.269	283	76	18	0	17	49	40	73	.373	.512	Bats Left	R	.286	21	6	1	0	0	4	2	4	.348	.333
Ford, Lew	L	.293	174	51	9	0	8	24	20	19	.367	.483	Gomez, Chris	L	.300	100	30	2	0	2	15	16	7	.397	.380
Bats Right	R	.301	395	119	22	4	7	48	47	56	.387	.430	Bats Right	R	.274	241	66	9	1	1	22	12	34	.310	.332
Fordyce, Brook	L	.037	27	1	1	0	0	0	3	6	.133	.074	Gonzalez, A	L	.000	7	0	0	0	0	0	0	0	.000	.000
Bats Right	R	.242	124	30	5	0	2	9	6	28	.288	.331	Bats Left	R	.286	35	10	3	0	1	7	2	6	.324	.457
Fox, Andy	L	.111	9	1	0	0	0	0	1	2	.200	.111	Gonzalez, Alex	L	.278	115	32	10	2	5	21	10	24	.333	.530
Bats Left	R	.087	46	4	0	0	1	1	0	17	.087	.152	Bats Right	R	.220	446	98	20	1	18	58	17	102	.253	.390
Franco, Julio	L	.306	134	41	7	0	2	20	15	21	.368	.403	Gonzalez, A	L	.180	61	11	4	1	2	11	5	15	.242	.377
Bats Right	R	.312	186	58	11	3	4	37	21	47	.385	.468	Bats Right	R	.237	224	53	14	0	5	16	9	49	.269	.366
Freel, Ryan	L	.235	115	27	4	1	1	5	22	18	.362	.313	Gonzalez, Juan	L	.297	37	11	2	0	3	5	3	4	.350	.595
Bats Right	R	.290	390	113	17	7	2	23	45	70	.379	.385	Bats Right	R	.267	90	24	2	1	2	12	6	15	.316	.378
Freeman, Choo	L	.205	39	8	1	1	0	5	6	6	.311	.282	Gonzalez, Luis	L	.244	127	31	8	1	9	21	21	21	.353	.535
Bats Right	R	.176	51	9	2	1	1	6	8	15	.288	.314	Bats Left	R	.266	252	67	20	4	8	27	47	37	.382	.472
Fullmer, Brad	L	.278	36	10	4	0	2	6	3	3	.333	.556	Gonzalez, L	L	.268	97	26	6	1	9	9	4	20	.297	.443
Bats Left	R	.225	222	50	15	1	9	27	24	27	.307	.423	Bats Right	R	.302	225	68	11	1	9	31	11	47	.344	.480
Furcal, Rafael	L	.276	163	45	9	1	6	18	18	23	.352	.454	Gonzalez, Raul	L	.167	6	1	0	0	0	0	0	1	.167	.167
Bats Both	R	.280	400	112	15	4	8	41	40	48	.342	.398	Bats Right	R	.000	5	0	0	0	0	0	0	3	.000	.000
Galarraga, A	L	.500	4	2	0	0	0	1	0	2	.500	.500	Goodwin, Tom	L	.118	17	2	2	0	0	1	1	5	.167	.235
Bats Right	R	.167	6	1	0	0	1	1	0	1	.286	.667	Bats Left	R	.216	88	19	6	0	0	2	7	17	.271	.284
Garcia, Danny	L	.067	30	2	0	0	1	4	6	13	.222	.167	Gotay, Ruben	L	.250	40	10	0	0	1	4	4	13	.333	.325
Bats Right	R	.278	108	30	7	1	2	13	16	21	.410	.417	Bats Both	R	.277	112	31	7	3	0	12	5	23	.308	.393
Garcia, Jesse	L	.278	36	10	0	0	0	1	0	3	.278	.278	Grabowski, J	L	.286	14	4	0	0	1	2	0	3	.286	.500
Bats Right	R	.241	79	19	4	1	1	9	1	13	.259	.354	Bats Left	R	.214	159	34	7	0	6	18	19	47	.298	.371
Garcia, Karim	L	.281	32	9	0	1	1	5	2	4	.324	.375	Graffanino, T	L	.265	68	18	2	0	0	6	9	3	.351	.294
Bats Left	R	.221	226	50	7	2	9	28	12	46	.257	.389	Bats Right	R	.262	210	55	9	0	3	20	18	35	.326	.348
Garciaparra, N	L	.240	75	18	4	0	2	9	3	11	.266	.373	Granderson, C	L	.000	1	0	0	0	0	0	0	1	.000	.000
Bats Right	R	.329	246	81	17	3	7	32	21	19	.394	.508	Bats Left	R	.250	24	6	1	1	0	0	3	7	.333	.375
Gathright, J	L	.400	5	2	0	0	0	0	1	1	.500	.400	Green, Andy	L	.182	55	10	2	0	0	1	1	8	.196	.218
Bats Left	R	.234	47	11	0	0	0	1	1	13	.294	.234	Bats Right	R	.222	54	12	0	1	1	3	4	9	.283	.315
German, E	L	.167	12	2	0	0	0	1	1	2	.231	.167	Green, Nick	L	.354	82	29	5	2	0	6	5	20	.400	.463
Bats Right	R	.271	48	13	1	1	0	6	3	11	.314	.333	Bats Right	R	.236	182	43	10	1	3	20	7	43	.271	.352
Gerut, Jody	L	.208	149	31	7	1	2	15	21	26	.326	.309	Green, Shawn	L	.232	181	42	6	0	8	31	18	42	.305	.398
Bats Left	R	.271	332	90	24	4	9	36	33	33	.338	.449	Bats Left	R	.281	409	115	22	1	20	55	53	72	.372	.487
Gettis, Byron	L	.176	17	3	1	0	0	0	7	9	.417	.235	Greene, Khalil	L	.291	127	37	5	2	7	21	15	15	.378	.528
Bats Right	R	.182	22	4	0	1	0	1	1	5	.240	.273	Bats Right	R	.266	357	95	26	2	8	44	38	79	.338	.417
Giambi, Jason	L	.263	80	21	4	0	6	17	12	19	.385	.538	Greene, Todd	L	.366	71	26	5	0	7	20	7	9	.423	.732
Bats Left	R	.185	184	34	5	0	6	23	35	43	.323	.310	Bats Right	R	.234	124	29	9	0	3	15	6	29	.267	.379
Gibbons, Jay	L	.257	109	28	8	0	2	14	4	24	.289	.385	Grieve, Ben	L	.308	26	8	3	0	1	5	4	12	.400	.538
Bats Left	R	.241	237	57	6	1	8	33	25	40	.309	.376	Bats Left	R	.254	224	57	14	0	7	30	35	58	.356	.411
Gil, Geronimo	L	.364	11	4	2	0	0	2	2	2	.462	.545	Griffey Jr., K	L	.198	111	22	8	0	5	13	12	27	.276	.405
Bats Right	R	.238	21	5	0	0	0	2	1	3	.273	.238	Bats Left	R	.286	189	54	10	0	15	47	32	40	.391	.577
Gil, Jerry	L	.200	35	7	1	1	0	4	0	10	.200	.286	Grissom, M	L	.315	149	47	6	0	11	34	10	19	.356	.577
Bats Right	R	.157	51	8	1	0	0	4	0	23	.170	.176	Bats Right	R	.266	413	110	20	2	11	56	27	64	.311	.404
Giles, Brian	L	.237	211	50	7	1	5	25	16	31	.286	.351	Gross, Gabe	L	.091	11	1	1	0	0	0	4	5	.333	.182
Bats Left	R	.309	398	123	26	6	18	69	73	49	.417	.540	Bats Left	R	.220	118	26	3	0	3	16	15	26	.308	.322
Giles, Marcus	L	.402	92	37	8	1	5	18	15	12	.486	.674	Grudzielanek, M	L	.220	82	18	5	0	0	4	7	11	.281	.280
Bats Right	R	.282	287	81	14	1	3	30	21	58	.341	.369	Bats Right	R	.349	175	61	7	1	6	19	8	21	.378	.503
Ginter, Keith	L	.325	80	26	6	0	6	13	13	22	.426	.625	Guerrero, V	L	.342	155	53	12	1	15	32	24	17	.434	.723
Bats Right	R	.245	306	75	17	2	13	47	24	78	.307	.441	Bats Right	R	.335	457	153	27	1	24	94	28	57	.376	.556
Gipson, C	L	.000	1	0	0	0	0	0	0	0	.000	.000	Guerrero, W	L	.250	8	2	0	0	0	0	0	0	.250	.250
Bats Right	R	.667	3	2	0	0	0	0	0	1	.667	.667	Bats Both	R	.208	24	5	0	1	0	1	0	4	.208	.292
Glanville, D	L	.255	47	12	1	0	0	4	4	7	.308	.277	Guiel, Aaron	L	.171	41	7	1	0	1	8	5	14	.277	.268
Bats Right	R	.191	115	22	0	1	2	10	4	14	.217	.261	Bats Left	R	.149	94	14	3	0	4	5	12	28	.257	.309
Glaus, Troy	L	.242	62	15	4	0	5	15	9	16	.347	.548	Guillen, C	L	.269	197	53	13	3	6	35	12	32	.316	.457
Bats Right	R	.255	145	37	7	1	13	27	22	36	.359	.586	Bats Both	R	.348	325	113	24	7	14	62	40	55	.416	.594
Gload, Ross	L	.425	40	17	3	0	2	6	2	3	.452	.650	Guillen, Jose	L	.299	144	43	7	0	7	31	9	22	.346	.493
Bats Left	R	.299	194	58	13	0	5	38	18	34	.359	.443	Bats Right	R	.292	421	123	21	3	20	73	28	70	.353	.499

Batter	vs.	Avg.	AB	H	2B	3B	HR	RBI	BB	SO	OBP	Slg.
Gutierrez, R	L	.226	31	7	1	0	0	4	2	3	.273	.258
Bats Right	R	.208	72	15	2	0	0	4	6	11	.278	.236
Guzman, C	L	.326	184	60	10	0	3	11	7	19	.351	.429
Bats Both	R	.250	392	98	21	4	5	35	23	45	.290	.362
Guzman, Freddy	L	.286	21	6	1	0	0	1	1	1	.348	.333
Bats Both	R	.182	55	10	2	0	0	4	2	12	.211	.218
Hafner, Travis	L	.244	156	38	9	0	3	24	18	38	.364	.359
Bats Left	R	.344	326	112	32	3	25	85	50	73	.433	.690
Hairston, S	L	.307	101	31	3	3	6	9	8	15	.358	.574
Bats Right	R	.223	238	53	12	3	7	20	13	73	.265	.387
Hairston Jr., J	L	.316	98	31	5	1	0	6	10	6	.376	.388
Bats Right	R	.296	189	56	14	0	2	18	19	23	.379	.402
Hall, Bill	L	.190	105	20	6	0	3	17	7	29	.239	.333
Bats Right	R	.256	285	73	14	3	6	36	13	90	.290	.389
Hall, Toby	L	.294	102	30	5	0	3	14	8	15	.339	.431
Bats Right	R	.242	302	73	16	0	5	46	16	26	.287	.344
Halter, Shane	L	.152	46	7	2	0	3	7	2	13	.188	.391
Bats Right	R	.235	68	16	3	0	1	6	5	17	.288	.324
Hammock, R	L	.253	79	20	5	1	3	8	8	14	.322	.456
Bats Right	R	.233	116	27	11	1	1	10	5	25	.262	.371
Hammonds, J	L	.231	39	9	2	0	2	3	10	7	.388	.436
Bats Right	R	.196	56	11	3	0	1	3	5	15	.297	.304
Hansen, Dave	L	.000	4	0	0	0	0	0	1	2	.200	.000
Bats Left	R	.255	102	26	5	0	2	12	20	19	.374	.363
Harris, B	L	.071	14	1	1	0	0	0	1	3	.133	.143
Bats Right	R	.200	45	9	2	0	1	3	2	9	.250	.311
Harris, Lenny	L	.000	2	0	0	0	0	0	0	1	.000	.000
Bats Left	R	.215	93	20	5	0	1	17	3	7	.237	.301
Harris, Willie	L	.181	72	13	3	0	1	4	4	19	.224	.264
Bats Left	R	.279	337	94	12	2	1	23	47	60	.366	.335
Hart, Bo	L	.000	6	0	0	0	0	1	0	0	.000	.000
Bats Right	R	.286	7	2	0	0	0	1	1	3	.375	.286
Hart, Corey	L	.000	1	0	0	0	0	0	0	1	.000	.000
Bats Right	R	.000	0	0	0	0	0	0	0	0	.000	.000
Harvey, Ken	L	.273	128	35	7	0	3	17	6	29	.309	.398
Bats Right	R	.293	328	96	13	1	10	38	22	60	.349	.430
Hatteberg, S	L	.285	172	49	7	0	4	25	14	21	.351	.395
Bats Left	R	.283	378	107	23	0	11	57	58	27	.374	.431
Hawpe, Brad	L	.154	13	2	1	0	0	0	1	8	.267	.231
Bats Left	R	.261	92	24	2	2	3	9	10	26	.330	.424
Helms, Wes	L	.306	72	22	5	1	1	6	11	14	.398	.444
Bats Right	R	.248	202	50	8	0	3	22	13	46	.306	.332
Helton, Todd	L	.320	172	55	10	1	7	27	26	26	.413	.512
Bats Left	R	.360	375	135	39	1	25	69	101	46	.492	.669
Hermansen, C	L	.000	5	0	0	0	0	0	0	2	.000	.000
Bats Right	R	.000	2	0	0	0	0	0	0	1	.000	.000
Hernandez, J	L	.310	126	39	5	1	11	20	15	29	.383	.627
Bats Right	R	.259	85	22	7	0	2	9	11	32	.351	.412
Hernandez, R	L	.310	100	31	10	0	7	19	17	17	.415	.620
Bats Right	R	.264	284	75	13	0	11	44	18	28	.313	.426
Hessman, Mike	L	.148	27	4	1	0	1	3	1	9	.179	.296
Bats Right	R	.119	42	5	2	0	1	2	0	15	.140	.238
Hidalgo, R	L	.265	102	27	2	1	7	17	15	31	.350	.510
Bats Right	R	.233	421	98	24	2	18	65	29	98	.288	.428
Hietpas, Joe	L	.000	0	0	0	0	0	0	0	0	.000	.000
Bats Right	R	.000	0	0	0	0	0	0	0	0	.000	.000
Higginson, B	L	.233	116	27	5	2	0	16	24	27	.377	.310
Bats Left	R	.250	332	83	19	0	12	48	46	57	.345	.416
Hill, Bobby	L	.222	18	4	1	0	0	1	2	1	.333	.278
Bats Both	R	.270	215	58	6	2	2	26	18	38	.355	.344
Hill, Koyie	L	.286	7	2	0	0	0	1	0	1	.286	.286
Bats Both	R	.241	29	7	1	0	1	5	2	5	.290	.379
Hillenbrand, S	L	.323	158	51	12	1	6	27	10	18	.366	.525
Bats Right	R	.304	404	123	24	2	9	53	14	31	.340	.441
Hinch, A.J.	L	.000	2	0	0	0	0	0	0	2	.000	.000
Bats Right	R	.222	9	2	1	0	0	0	0	2	.222	.333
Hinske, Eric	L	.268	168	45	11	0	4	26	12	34	.321	.405
Bats Left	R	.236	402	95	12	3	11	43	42	75	.309	.363
Hocking, Denny	L	.190	21	4	0	0	0	0	1	6	.227	.190
Bats Both	R	.205	73	15	2	0	0	4	6	14	.266	.233
Hollandsworth, T	L	.353	17	6	0	0	1	3	0	3	.353	.529
Bats Left	R	.313	131	41	6	2	7	19	17	23	.396	.550
Holliday, Matt	L	.237	97	23	8	1	2	10	13	17	.333	.402
Bats Right	R	.307	303	93	23	2	12	47	18	69	.355	.515
Hollins, Damon	L	.400	10	4	2	0	0	2	0	1	.400	.600
Bats Right	R	.333	12	4	0	0	0	3	0	3	.333	.333
House, J.R.	L	.000	0	0	0	0	0	0	0	0	.000	.000
Bats Right	R	.111	9	1	1	0	0	0	0	2	.111	.222
Howard, Ryan	L	.111	9	1	0	0	0	0	0	5	.111	.111
Bats Left	R	.333	30	10	5	0	2	5	2	8	.394	.700
Huckaby, Ken	L	.158	19	3	1	0	0	0	4	4	.304	.211
Bats Right	R	.129	31	4	2	0	0	0	1	8	.156	.194
Hudson, O	L	.262	122	32	9	2	4	19	13	25	.326	.467
Bats Both	R	.272	367	100	23	5	8	39	38	73	.346	.428
Huff, Aubrey	L	.304	184	56	5	1	8	39	14	23	.358	.473
Bats Left	R	.293	416	122	22	1	21	65	42	51	.361	.502
Hummel, Tim	L	.238	42	10	2	0	1	2	0	4	.267	.357
Bats Right	R	.206	68	14	2	0	0	5	8	13	.289	.235
Hunter, Torii	L	.255	157	40	9	0	8	27	10	32	.299	.465
Bats Right	R	.278	363	101	28	0	15	54	30	69	.343	.479
Hyzdu, Adam	L	.500	4	2	2	0	0	1	0	1	.500	1.000
Bats Right	R	.167	6	1	0	0	1	1	1	1	.286	.667
Ibanez, Raul	L	.295	146	43	9	0	4	16	10	33	.342	.438
Bats Left	R	.307	335	103	22	1	12	46	26	39	.358	.487
Infante, Omar	L	.277	188	52	8	5	5	20	14	39	.320	.452
Bats Both	R	.257	315	81	19	4	11	35	26	73	.315	.448
Inge, Brandon	L	.327	168	55	5	4	7	27	16	27	.386	.530
Bats Right	R	.258	240	62	10	3	6	37	16	45	.308	.400
Izturis, Cesar	L	.269	182	49	6	2	1	12	9	15	.304	.341
Bats Both	R	.295	488	144	26	7	3	50	34	55	.339	.395
Izturis, M	L	.111	18	2	1	0	0	2	2	4	.200	.167
Bats Both	R	.225	89	20	4	2	1	2	8	16	.303	.348
Jackson, D	L	.111	18	2	1	0	1	1	3	5	.238	.333
Bats Right	R	.083	12	1	1	0	0	2	1	7	.154	.167
Jacobsen, B	L	.340	50	17	3	0	4	12	5	11	.400	.640
Bats Right	R	.245	110	27	6	0	5	16	9	36	.306	.436
Jenkins, Geoff	L	.215	158	34	6	1	6	24	10	55	.286	.380
Bats Left	R	.281	459	129	30	5	21	69	36	97	.338	.505
Jeter, Derek	L	.314	156	49	14	1	6	17	13	20	.378	.532
Bats Right	R	.285	487	139	30	0	17	61	33	79	.343	.452
Jimenez, D	L	.240	154	37	6	0	0	11	16	18	.312	.279
Bats Both	R	.281	409	115	22	3	12	56	66	81	.382	.438
Johnson, C	L	.233	73	17	2	0	5	10	13	23	.349	.466
Bats Right	R	.237	232	55	18	0	8	37	36	68	.350	.418
Johnson, Mark	L	.000	2	0	0	0	0	0	0	0	.000	.000
Bats Left	R	.111	9	1	0	0	0	2	3	2	.308	.111
Johnson, Nick	L	.323	62	20	3	0	1	9	17	13	.488	.419
Bats Left	R	.228	189	43	13	0	6	24	23	45	.310	.392
Johnson, Reed	L	.301	173	52	7	1	5	21	13	26	.351	.439
Bats Right	R	.255	364	93	18	1	5	40	15	72	.304	.352

Batter	vs.	Avg.	AB	H	2B	3B	HR	RBI	BB	SO	OBP	Slg.
Jones, Andruw	L	.265	151	40	11	2	7	24	22	36	.358	.503
Bats Right	R	.260	419	109	23	2	22	67	49	111	.340	.482
Jones, Chipper	L	.268	149	40	5	1	12	35	31	28	.396	.557
Bats Both	R	.238	323	77	15	0	18	61	53	68	.345	.452
Jones, Jacque	L	.245	155	38	7	0	2	18	13	34	.328	.329
Bats Left	R	.258	400	103	15	1	22	62	27	83	.310	.465
Jordan, Brian	L	.259	85	22	10	0	3	13	8	10	.316	.482
Bats Right	R	.197	127	25	3	1	2	10	8	25	.246	.283
Kapler, Gabe	L	.317	126	40	9	1	4	16	4	23	.333	.500
Bats Right	R	.238	164	39	5	0	2	17	11	26	.294	.305
Karros, Eric	L	.210	62	13	2	0	2	8	5	8	.265	.339
Bats Right	R	.171	41	7	4	0	0	3	2	8	.209	.268
Kata, Matt	L	.189	53	10	2	0	1	2	2	10	.218	.283
Bats Both	R	.275	109	30	7	2	1	11	11	19	.339	.404
Kearns, Austin	L	.213	47	10	1	1	2	7	13	16	.383	.404
Bats Right	R	.235	170	40	9	1	7	25	15	55	.301	.424
Kelton, David	L	.200	5	1	1	0	0	0	0	1	.200	.400
Bats Right	R	.000	5	0	0	0	0	0	0	2	.000	.000
Kendall, Jason	L	.291	103	30	5	0	0	5	15	8	.393	.340
Bats Right	R	.325	471	153	27	0	3	46	45	33	.400	.401
Kennedy, Adam	L	.250	108	27	3	2	2	11	12	27	.349	.370
Bats Left	R	.286	360	103	17	3	8	37	29	65	.352	.417
Kent, Jeff	L	.284	109	31	4	0	7	19	13	20	.358	.514
Bats Right	R	.290	431	125	30	8	20	88	36	76	.346	.536
Keppinger, J	L	.394	33	13	1	0	2	2	1	0	.412	.606
Bats Right	R	.241	83	20	1	0	1	7	5	7	.281	.289
Kielty, Bobby	L	.259	116	30	1	0	6	18	14	16	.338	.491
Bats Both	R	.172	122	21	5	1	1	13	21	31	.306	.254
Klesko, Ryan	L	.325	114	37	9	1	1	18	13	26	.392	.447
Bats Left	R	.278	288	80	23	1	8	48	60	41	.401	.448
Knoedler, J	L	.000	1	0	0	0	0	0	0	0	.000	.000
Bats Right	R	.000	0	0	0	0	0	0	0	0	.000	.000
Knott, Jon	L	.200	10	2	1	0	0	1	0	3	.200	.300
Bats Right	R	.250	4	1	1	0	0	0	1	2	.400	.500
Konerko, Paul	L	.288	163	47	8	0	13	38	23	32	.372	.577
Bats Right	R	.273	400	109	14	0	28	79	46	75	.354	.518
Koskie, Corey	L	.233	133	31	4	1	5	19	13	43	.322	.391
Bats Left	R	.260	289	75	20	1	20	52	36	60	.351	.543
Kotchman, C	L	.000	7	0	0	0	0	0	0	2	.222	.000
Bats Left	R	.239	109	26	6	0	0	15	7	9	.294	.294
Kotsay, Mark	L	.336	152	51	5	1	4	21	17	16	.401	.461
Bats Left	R	.306	454	139	32	2	11	42	38	54	.359	.458
Kroeger, Josh	L	.333	3	1	0	0	0	0	0	2	.333	.333
Bats Left	R	.157	51	8	3	0	0	2	1	19	.173	.216
Krynzel, Dave	L	.000	5	0	0	0	0	0	1	2	.375	.000
Bats Left	R	.250	36	9	1	0	0	3	2	13	.308	.278
Kubel, Jason	L	.333	6	2	0	0	0	0	0	3	.333	.333
Bats Left	R	.296	54	16	2	0	2	7	6	6	.361	.444
Labandeira, J	L	.000	5	0	0	0	0	0	0	0	.000	.000
Bats Right	R	.000	9	0	0	0	0	0	0	4	.000	.000
Laird, Gerald	L	.317	41	13	4	0	0	4	6	7	.380	.415
Bats Right	R	.189	106	20	2	0	1	12	6	28	.246	.236
Laker, Tim	L	.333	51	17	1	0	1	10	2	13	.364	.412
Bats Right	R	.121	66	8	1	0	2	7	5	15	.183	.227
Lamb, Mike	L	.349	43	15	4	0	2	13	5	12	.417	.581
Bats Left	R	.277	235	65	10	3	12	45	26	51	.345	.498
Lane, Jason	L	.280	50	14	4	0	2	7	5	11	.345	.480
Bats Right	R	.267	86	23	6	2	2	12	11	22	.350	.453
Lankford, Ray	L	.200	25	5	2	1	0	3	2	9	.241	.360
Bats Left	R	.263	175	46	12	0	6	19	27	46	.364	.434

Batter	vs.	Avg.	AB	H	2B	3B	HR	RBI	BB	SO	OBP	Slg.
Larkin, Barry	L	.207	92	19	3	1	4	14	10	9	.279	.391
Bats Right	R	.319	254	81	12	2	4	30	24	30	.379	.429
LaRoche, Adam	L	.250	20	5	1	0	1	2	6	6	.423	.450
Bats Left	R	.280	304	85	26	1	12	43	21	72	.326	.490
Larson, B	L	.071	28	2	1	0	0	1	1	11	.100	.107
Bats Right	R	.256	90	23	5	0	3	13	13	24	.362	.411
LaRue, Jason	L	.274	95	26	4	1	4	11	9	30	.346	.463
Bats Right	R	.244	295	72	20	1	10	44	17	78	.330	.420
Lawton, Matt	L	.262	191	50	9	0	6	25	24	32	.355	.403
Bats Left	R	.285	400	114	16	0	14	45	50	52	.372	.430
LeCroy, M	L	.322	90	29	7	0	4	13	7	15	.367	.533
Bats Right	R	.241	174	42	7	0	5	26	9	45	.296	.368
Ledee, Ricky	L	.286	14	4	1	0	1	3	4	5	.444	.571
Bats Left	R	.228	162	37	8	0	6	27	23	42	.326	.389
Lee, Carlos	L	.308	156	48	8	0	10	24	19	24	.385	.551
Bats Right	R	.303	435	132	29	0	21	75	35	62	.359	.515
Lee, Derrek	L	.306	111	34	5	0	9	23	17	20	.408	.595
Bats Right	R	.271	494	134	34	1	23	75	51	108	.344	.484
Lee, Travis	L	.000	6	0	0	0	0	0	0	1	.000	.000
Bats Left	R	.154	13	2	1	0	0	2	1	2	.214	.231
Leon, Jose	L	.222	45	10	2	0	2	6	2	9	.255	.400
Bats Right	R	.095	21	2	0	0	0	2	0	10	.091	.095
Leone, Justin	L	.222	27	6	1	0	3	6	2	5	.276	.593
Bats Right	R	.213	75	16	4	0	3	7	7	27	.306	.387
Lieberthal, M	L	.284	102	29	6	1	4	13	9	9	.354	.480
Bats Right	R	.267	374	100	25	0	13	48	28	60	.330	.439
Liefer, Jeff	L	.000	3	0	0	0	0	0	1	3	.000	.000
Bats Left	R	.240	25	6	2	0	1	4	2	5	.296	.440
Linden, Todd	L	.000	15	0	0	0	0	0	4	6	.211	.000
Bats Both	R	.294	17	5	1	0	0	1	1	1	.368	.353
Little, Mark	L	.364	11	4	0	0	0	2	0	4	.385	.364
Bats Right	R	.000	9	0	0	0	0	0	0	3	.100	.000
Lo Duca, Paul	L	.314	137	43	7	0	2	15	9	13	.354	.409
Bats Right	R	.276	398	110	22	2	11	65	27	36	.333	.425
Lofton, Kenny	L	.308	26	8	2	0	0	2	3	6	.400	.385
Bats Left	R	.272	250	68	8	7	3	16	28	21	.340	.396
Logan, Nook	L	.395	43	17	2	0	0	4	0	4	.395	.442
Bats Both	R	.222	90	20	3	2	0	6	13	20	.317	.300
Long, Terrence	L	.231	39	9	3	1	0	1	0	12	.231	.359
Bats Left	R	.305	249	76	16	3	3	27	19	39	.350	.430
Lopez, Felipe	L	.292	65	19	7	1	2	12	3	18	.333	.523
Bats Both	R	.226	199	45	11	1	5	19	22	63	.308	.367
Lopez, Javy	L	.313	150	47	10	1	8	20	18	15	.385	.553
Bats Right	R	.317	429	136	23	2	15	66	29	82	.365	.485
Lopez, Jose	L	.214	56	12	2	0	0	3	2	5	.241	.250
Bats Right	R	.238	151	36	11	0	5	19	6	26	.270	.411
Lopez, Luis	L	.216	37	8	4	0	1	2	1	6	.237	.405
Bats Both	R	.157	51	8	1	0	0	6	2	14	.193	.176
Lopez, Luis	L	.200	20	4	0	0	0	0	0	6	.238	.200
Bats Right	R	.000	6	0	0	0	0	0	0	3	.000	.000
Lopez, Mendy	L	.158	19	3	0	0	1	3	1	6	.238	.316
Bats Right	R	.053	19	1	0	0	0	1	3	3	.182	.053
Lopez, Mickey	L	.000	1	0	0	0	0	0	0	0	.000	.000
Bats Both	R	.333	3	1	0	0	0	0	1	0	.600	.333
Loretta, Mark	L	.352	182	64	13	0	5	25	28	11	.431	.505
Bats Right	R	.329	438	144	34	2	11	51	30	34	.373	.491
Lowell, Mike	L	.344	128	44	9	0	11	19	12	19	.429	.672
Bats Right	R	.279	470	131	35	1	16	56	45	65	.347	.460
Ludwick, Ryan	L	.188	32	6	1	0	2	2	0	8	.212	.406
Bats Right	R	.278	18	5	1	0	0	2	2	6	.381	.333

Batter	vs.	Avg.	AB	H	2B	3B	HR	RBI	BB	SO	OBP	Slg.
Lugo, Julio	L	.300	150	45	9	1	0	19	17	27	.371	.373
Bats Right	R	.267	431	115	32	3	7	56	37	79	.326	.404
Luna, Hector	L	.240	75	18	3	0	2	8	6	23	.298	.360
Bats Right	R	.255	98	25	4	2	1	14	7	14	.308	.367
Mabry, John	L	.333	54	18	2	0	3	15	7	16	.403	.537
Bats Left	R	.285	186	53	9	0	10	25	19	47	.351	.495
Machado, A	L	.000	4	0	0	0	0	0	2	2	.333	.000
Bats Both	R	.288	52	15	5	1	0	4	8	24	.383	.423
Machado, R	L	.143	21	3	1	0	0	1	3	1	.250	.190
Bats Right	R	.154	52	8	2	0	1	2	1	17	.170	.250
Macias, Jose	L	.238	63	15	1	1	2	9	0	9	.238	.381
Bats Both	R	.282	131	37	5	2	1	13	5	29	.317	.374
Mackowiak, R	L	.164	61	10	0	2	0	5	1	13	.188	.230
Bats Left	R	.258	430	111	22	4	17	70	49	101	.337	.447
Magruder, C	L	.333	36	12	3	0	2	3	4	4	.400	.583
Bats Both	R	.170	53	9	3	1	0	7	4	17	.250	.264
Majewski, Val	L	.000	0	0	0	0	0	0	0	0	.000	.000
Bats Left	R	.154	13	2	1	0	0	1	0	1	.154	.231
Marrero, Eli	L	.415	106	44	10	1	5	21	9	16	.462	.670
Bats Right	R	.250	144	36	8	0	5	19	14	34	.311	.410
Martinez, E	L	.300	130	39	11	0	4	18	25	24	.413	.477
Bats Right	R	.250	356	89	12	0	8	45	33	83	.315	.351
Martinez, R	L	.243	70	17	5	1	0	4	11	12	.354	.343
Bats Right	R	.247	190	47	10	0	3	26	15	28	.297	.347
Martinez, S	L	.000	3	0	0	0	0	0	0	1	.000	.000
Bats Left	R	.000	3	0	0	0	0	0	0	2	.000	.000
Martinez, Tino	L	.246	126	31	5	0	9	29	18	21	.356	.500
Bats Left	R	.268	332	89	15	1	14	47	48	51	.365	.446
Martinez, V	L	.282	170	48	11	1	6	28	25	26	.380	.465
Bats Both	R	.283	350	99	27	0	17	80	35	43	.348	.506
Mateo, Henry	L	.154	13	2	1	0	0	0	0	5	.154	.231
Bats Both	R	.323	31	10	1	0	0	0	1	4	.344	.355
Mateo, Ruben	L	.184	49	9	0	2	3	9	5	14	.259	.449
Bats Right	R	.221	77	17	4	1	0	5	3	12	.277	.299
Matheny, Mike	L	.247	93	23	7	1	2	17	6	12	.297	.409
Bats Right	R	.247	292	72	15	0	3	33	17	71	.291	.329
Matos, Luis	L	.133	105	14	3	0	2	7	7	20	.191	.219
Bats Right	R	.267	225	60	15	0	4	21	12	40	.315	.387
Matsui, Hideki	L	.265	189	50	7	2	6	30	26	32	.358	.418
Bats Left	R	.314	395	124	27	0	25	78	62	71	.405	.572
Matsui, Kazuo	L	.306	98	30	8	0	3	11	11	16	.376	.480
Bats Both	R	.262	362	95	24	2	4	33	29	81	.319	.373
Matthews Jr., G	L	.244	90	22	2	0	4	10	11	23	.324	.400
Bats Both	R	.289	190	55	15	1	7	26	22	41	.363	.489
Mauer, Joe	L	.182	33	6	1	0	0	4	3	6	.263	.212
Bats Left	R	.365	74	27	7	1	6	13	8	8	.417	.730
Mayne, Brent	L	.406	32	13	3	0	0	1	4	7	.472	.500
Bats Left	R	.184	158	29	3	1	0	14	23	34	.283	.215
McCarty, Dave	L	.259	58	15	2	1	1	5	5	12	.317	.379
Bats Right	R	.258	93	24	6	0	3	12	9	28	.333	.419
McCracken, Q	L	.231	39	9	3	0	0	2	1	9	.244	.308
Bats Both	R	.285	137	39	8	1	2	11	14	18	.351	.401
McDonald, D	L	.200	25	5	1	0	0	1	1	4	.231	.240
Bats Right	R	.000	7	0	0	0	0	0	1	2	.125	.000
McDonald, John	L	.176	34	6	0	1	1	4	4	1	.263	.324
Bats Right	R	.220	59	13	5	0	1	3	0	10	.220	.356
McEwing, Joe	L	.250	44	11	1	1	0	2	6	11	.340	.318
Bats Right	R	.255	94	24	2	0	1	14	3	21	.276	.309
McGriff, Fred	L	.200	5	1	0	0	0	0	0	4	.200	.200
Bats Left	R	.179	67	12	3	0	2	7	9	15	.276	.313
McKay, Cody	L	.222	9	2	0	0	0	0	1	1	.300	.222
Bats Left	R	.231	65	15	2	0	0	6	1	13	.265	.262
McLemore, M	L	.130	23	3	1	0	0	1	5	3	.286	.174
Bats Both	R	.260	227	59	13	0	2	20	36	30	.362	.344
McMillon, B	L	.200	5	1	0	0	0	0	0	2	.200	.200
Bats Left	R	.184	87	16	4	0	3	11	8	20	.258	.333
McPherson, D	L	.083	12	1	0	0	0	0	2	6	.214	.083
Bats Left	R	.286	28	8	1	0	3	6	1	11	.310	.643
Melhuse, Adam	L	.120	25	3	0	0	1	5	5	9	.267	.240
Bats Both	R	.275	189	52	11	0	10	26	11	38	.315	.492
Mench, Kevin	L	.319	144	46	17	0	10	28	15	12	.390	.646
Bats Right	R	.259	294	76	13	3	16	43	18	51	.306	.486
Menechino, F	L	.315	108	34	5	2	6	15	15	17	.398	.565
Bats Right	R	.248	161	40	8	2	3	11	22	35	.353	.379
Merloni, Lou	L	.327	113	37	9	1	4	23	9	27	.379	.531
Bats Right	R	.234	77	18	3	0	0	5	5	14	.291	.273
Michaels, J	L	.286	84	24	1	0	5	14	12	22	.371	.476
Bats Right	R	.270	215	58	11	0	5	26	30	58	.361	.391
Mientkiewicz, D	L	.220	123	27	8	1	1	10	12	23	.304	.325
Bats Left	R	.246	268	66	16	0	5	25	36	33	.336	.362
Miles, Aaron	L	.267	120	32	3	0	2	13	12	15	.336	.342
Bats Both	R	.301	402	121	12	3	4	34	17	38	.327	.376
Millar, Kevin	L	.299	154	46	14	0	3	17	16	26	.369	.448
Bats Right	R	.297	354	105	22	0	15	57	41	65	.388	.486
Miller, Corky	L	.000	2	0	0	0	0	0	2	1	.667	.000
Bats Right	R	.027	37	1	0	0	0	3	4	11	.140	.027
Miller, Damian	L	.290	124	36	6	0	2	11	12	24	.358	.387
Bats Right	R	.264	273	72	19	0	7	47	27	63	.330	.410
Minor, Damon	L	.200	10	2	1	0	0	2	2	5	.429	.300
Bats Left	R	.250	48	12	1	0	0	4	10	13	.400	.271
Mirabelli, D	L	.311	45	14	4	0	3	9	8	9	.415	.600
Bats Right	R	.270	115	31	8	0	6	23	11	37	.349	.496
Moeller, Chad	L	.242	62	15	3	0	2	8	4	16	.288	.387
Bats Right	R	.200	255	51	10	1	3	19	17	58	.260	.282
Mohr, Dustan	L	.243	115	28	10	1	2	10	16	30	.338	.400
Bats Right	R	.297	148	44	10	0	5	18	30	34	.433	.466
Molina, Bengie	L	.252	103	26	6	0	3	11	6	14	.291	.398
Bats Right	R	.286	234	67	7	0	7	43	12	21	.323	.406
Molina, Jose	L	.339	59	20	4	2	1	9	3	13	.371	.525
Bats Right	R	.229	144	33	6	0	2	16	7	39	.265	.313
Molina, Yadier	L	.250	32	8	2	0	0	1	3	4	.314	.313
Bats Right	R	.272	103	28	4	0	2	14	10	16	.333	.369
Mondesi, Raul	L	.240	25	6	0	0	1	2	2	4	.296	.360
Bats Right	R	.241	108	26	9	0	2	13	11	27	.317	.380
Monroe, Craig	L	.256	160	41	11	1	5	21	9	26	.291	.431
Bats Right	R	.314	287	90	16	2	13	51	20	53	.362	.519
Mora, Melvin	L	.303	132	40	8	0	8	27	24	20	.418	.545
Bats Right	R	.352	418	147	33	0	19	77	42	75	.419	.567
Mordecai, Mike	L	.238	21	5	1	0	0	0	5	4	.385	.286
Bats Right	R	.222	63	14	2	0	1	5	1	14	.234	.302
Morneau, J	L	.240	75	18	5	0	3	18	4	20	.289	.427
Bats Left	R	.283	205	58	12	0	16	40	24	34	.358	.576
Mottola, Chad	L	.250	8	2	1	0	1	3	1	0	.333	.750
Bats Right	R	.000	6	0	0	0	0	0	1	3	.143	.000
Mueller, Bill	L	.255	137	35	9	0	4	18	7	21	.301	.409
Bats Both	R	.298	262	78	18	1	8	39	44	35	.395	.466
Munson, Eric	L	.227	66	15	1	0	5	13	5	16	.282	.470
Bats Left	R	.208	255	53	13	2	14	36	24	74	.291	.439
Murphy, Donnie	L	.222	9	2	2	0	0	1	0	3	.222	.444
Bats Right	R	.167	18	3	1	0	0	2	0	4	.167	.222

Batter	vs.	Avg.	AB	H	2B	3B	HR	RBI	BB	SO	OBP	Slg.
Murray, Calvin	L	.000	1	0	0	0	0	0	0	0	.000	.000
Bats Right	R	.250	4	1	0	0	0	1	1	0	.400	.250
Myers, Greg	L	.000	0	0	0	0	0	0	1	0	1.000	.000
Bats Left	R	.222	18	4	2	0	0	1	1	4	.263	.333
Nady, Xavier	L	.344	32	11	1	0	2	4	3	4	.417	.563
Bats Right	R	.178	45	8	3	0	1	5	2	9	.213	.311
Navarro, D	L	1.000	1	1	0	0	0	1	0	0	1.000	1.000
Bats Both	R	.333	6	2	0	0	0	0	0	0	.333	.333
Nevin, Phil	L	.324	170	55	12	1	10	28	31	31	.431	.582
Bats Right	R	.273	377	103	19	0	16	77	35	90	.337	.451
Newhan, David	L	.297	101	30	4	2	1	10	4	20	.345	.406
Bats Left	R	.316	272	86	11	5	7	44	23	52	.367	.471
Nivar, Ramon	L	.286	14	4	0	0	0	4	0	6	.267	.286
Bats Right	R	.000	4	0	0	0	0	0	0	1	.000	.000
Nix, Laynce	L	.176	74	13	2	1	1	7	3	30	.218	.270
Bats Left	R	.266	297	79	18	3	13	39	20	83	.312	.478
Nixon, Trot	L	.133	15	2	0	0	0	0	0	3	.188	.133
Bats Left	R	.336	134	45	9	1	6	23	15	21	.397	.552
Norton, Greg	L	.182	44	8	1	0	1	1	3	11	.234	.273
Bats Both	R	.167	42	7	0	0	1	1	9	10	.314	.238
Nunez, Abraham	L	.221	86	19	2	0	4	17	7	21	.277	.384
Bats Both	R	.211	199	42	8	1	2	17	27	48	.305	.291
Nunez, A	L	.158	19	3	0	0	0	1	2	2	.238	.158
Bats Both	R	.245	163	40	9	0	2	12	8	34	.279	.337
Offerman, Jose	L	.176	51	9	3	0	0	4	9	12	.300	.235
Bats Both	R	.289	121	35	11	2	2	18	20	19	.390	.463
Ojeda, Augie	L	.000	7	0	0	0	0	0	1	0	.125	.000
Bats Both	R	.385	52	20	1	0	2	7	9	3	.468	.519
Ojeda, Miguel	L	.351	37	13	0	0	5	12	6	5	.432	.757
Bats Right	R	.227	119	27	3	0	3	14	9	29	.285	.328
Olerud, John	L	.250	92	23	5	0	2	8	12	13	.355	.370
Bats Left	R	.261	333	87	15	1	7	40	49	48	.360	.375
Olivo, Miguel	L	.322	87	28	7	0	6	23	7	17	.368	.609
Bats Right	R	.196	214	42	8	4	7	17	13	67	.252	.369
Olmedo, Ray	L	.000	1	0	0	0	0	0	0	0	.000	.000
Bats Both	R	.000	0	0	0	0	0	0	1	0	1.000	.000
Olson, Tim	L	.244	45	11	4	0	1	2	6	4	.333	.400
Bats Right	R	.135	52	7	3	0	1	3	10	14	.274	.250
Ordonez, M	L	.339	59	20	2	2	2	7	2	7	.371	.542
Bats Right	R	.273	143	39	6	0	7	30	14	15	.344	.462
Ordonez, Rey	L	.222	9	2	1	0	0	2	1	1	.300	.333
Bats Right	R	.154	52	8	2	0	1	3	1	13	.170	.250
Ortiz, David	L	.250	196	49	13	0	10	43	17	46	.315	.469
Bats Left	R	.326	386	126	34	3	31	96	58	87	.411	.671
Osik, Keith	L	.125	8	1	0	0	0	0	0	1	.125	.125
Bats Right	R	.059	17	1	0	0	0	0	0	6	.059	.059
Overbay, Lyle	L	.298	151	45	17	1	5	20	13	30	.357	.523
Bats Left	R	.301	428	129	36	0	11	67	68	98	.394	.463
Palmeiro, O	L	.167	12	2	1	0	0	1	2	4	.286	.250
Bats Left	R	.248	121	30	4	0	3	11	16	15	.350	.355
Palmeiro, R	L	.189	159	30	3	0	5	20	15	15	.254	.302
Bats Left	R	.286	391	112	26	0	18	68	71	46	.399	.491
Pascucci, Val	L	.212	33	7	1	0	1	3	7	13	.341	.333
Bats Right	R	.138	29	4	0	0	1	3	3	9	.242	.241
Patterson, C	L	.289	173	50	7	2	8	26	8	43	.328	.491
Bats Left	R	.258	458	118	26	4	16	46	37	125	.317	.437
Paul, Josh	L	.316	19	6	3	0	1	5	2	5	.364	.632
Bats Right	R	.216	51	11	0	0	1	5	5	12	.286	.275
Payton, Jay	L	.283	152	43	5	2	3	23	20	14	.369	.401
Bats Right	R	.248	306	76	12	2	5	32	23	42	.303	.350
Pellow, Kit	L	.182	55	10	2	1	1	2	6	22	.262	.309
Bats Right	R	.288	66	19	3	0	1	8	2	21	.347	.379
Pena, Carlos	L	.245	147	36	5	3	8	30	13	50	.315	.483
Bats Left	R	.240	334	80	17	1	19	52	57	96	.348	.467
Pena, Wily Mo	L	.302	86	26	3	0	9	22	9	30	.388	.651
Bats Right	R	.244	250	61	7	1	17	44	13	78	.289	.484
Peralta, J	L	.222	9	2	1	0	0	2	1	2	.300	.333
Bats Right	R	.250	16	4	0	0	0	0	2	4	.333	.250
Perez, Antonio	L	.167	6	1	0	0	0	0	0	2	.286	.167
Bats Right	R	.286	7	2	1	0	0	0	0	3	.286	.429
Perez, Eddie	L	.250	68	17	4	0	1	6	3	10	.282	.353
Bats Right	R	.216	102	22	8	0	2	7	8	19	.289	.353
Perez, Eduardo	L	.185	27	5	1	0	1	5	4	6	.290	.333
Bats Right	R	.273	11	3	1	0	0	2	0	3	.273	.364
Perez, Neifi	L	.252	115	29	8	0	3	15	8	15	.298	.400
Bats Both	R	.256	266	68	9	1	1	24	16	26	.295	.308
Perez, Timo	L	.140	43	6	1	0	0	1	3	4	.196	.163
Bats Left	R	.264	250	66	11	0	5	39	12	25	.301	.368
Perez, Tomas	L	.213	47	10	4	1	2	7	3	12	.260	.468
Bats Both	R	.217	129	28	9	1	4	14	6	32	.255	.395
Perry, Herbert	L	.231	91	21	1	1	4	14	11	13	.327	.396
Bats Right	R	.209	43	9	1	0	1	3	3	6	.261	.302
Phelps, Josh	L	.309	152	47	11	0	12	32	11	38	.358	.618
Bats Right	R	.210	219	46	8	2	5	29	11	55	.267	.333
Phillips, Andy	L	.000	0	0	0	0	0	0	0	0	.000	.000
Bats Right	R	.250	8	2	0	0	1	2	0	1	.250	.625
Phillips, B	L	.167	6	1	0	0	0	0	0	2	.167	.167
Bats Right	R	.188	16	3	2	0	0	1	2	3	.278	.313
Phillips, J	L	.224	85	19	6	0	2	12	7	11	.274	.365
Bats Right	R	.217	277	60	12	0	5	22	28	31	.305	.314
Phillips, Paul	L	.000	2	0	0	0	0	0	0	1	.000	.000
Bats Right	R	.333	3	1	0	0	0	0	0	0	.500	.333
Piazza, Mike	L	.303	89	27	5	0	4	15	18	16	.421	.494
Bats Right	R	.257	366	94	16	0	16	39	50	62	.347	.432
Pickering, C	L	.214	42	9	1	0	1	3	2	15	.250	.310
Bats Left	R	.263	80	21	7	1	6	23	16	27	.378	.600
Piedra, Jorge	L	.308	13	4	3	0	0	2	0	4	.308	.538
Bats Left	R	.295	78	23	5	0	3	8	5	15	.345	.474
Pierre, Juan	L	.305	187	57	8	2	0	9	9	10	.361	.369
Bats Left	R	.334	491	164	14	10	3	40	36	25	.379	.422
Pierzynski, A	L	.227	97	22	3	0	2	14	0	7	.224	.320
Bats Left	R	.283	374	106	25	2	9	63	19	20	.341	.433
Podsednik, S	L	.224	147	33	4	3	3	14	13	32	.294	.354
Bats Left	R	.249	493	123	23	4	9	25	45	73	.319	.367
Polanco, P	L	.327	147	48	5	0	7	18	8	11	.354	.503
Bats Right	R	.287	356	102	16	0	10	37	19	28	.341	.416
Pond, Simon	L	.000	5	0	0	0	0	0	0	0	.000	.000
Bats Left	R	.182	44	8	2	0	1	6	5	11	.275	.295
Porter, Colin	L	1.000	1	1	0	0	0	0	0	0	1.000	1.000
Bats Left	R	.294	34	10	1	0	1	2	0	13	.294	.412
Posada, Jorge	L	.275	142	39	12	0	8	28	26	28	.385	.528
Bats Both	R	.270	307	83	19	0	13	53	62	64	.407	.459
Pratt, Todd	L	.318	22	7	3	0	0	2	7	4	.467	.455
Bats Right	R	.245	106	26	2	0	3	14	11	34	.322	.349
Pride, Curtis	L	.500	4	2	0	0	0	0	0	1	.600	.500
Bats Left	R	.222	36	8	3	0	0	3	0	10	.222	.306
Prieto, Alex	L	.364	11	4	0	0	1	2	1	3	.417	.636
Bats Right	R	.190	21	4	1	0	0	2	2	6	.250	.238
Pujols, Albert	L	.379	116	44	13	1	9	34	21	7	.465	.741
Bats Right	R	.319	476	152	38	1	37	89	63	45	.401	.637

Batter	vs.	Avg.	AB	H	2B	3B	HR	RBI	BB	SO	OBP	Slg.
Punto, Nick	L	.250	32	8	0	0	1	4	4	6	.333	.344
Bats Both	R	.254	59	15	0	0	1	8	8	13	.343	.305
Quinlan, Robb	L	.390	59	23	6	0	3	7	8	4	.456	.644
Bats Right	R	.317	101	32	8	0	2	16	6	22	.367	.455
Quintero, H	L	.360	25	9	2	0	1	4	0	4	.360	.560
Bats Right	R	.191	47	9	1	0	1	6	5	12	.264	.277
Quiroz, G	L	.217	23	5	0	0	0	0	1	4	.280	.217
Bats Right	R	.207	29	6	2	0	0	6	1	4	.250	.276
Raburn, Ryan	L	.188	16	3	1	0	0	1	2	8	.278	.250
Bats Right	R	.077	13	1	0	0	0	0	0	7	.077	.077
Raines Jr., T	L	.250	52	13	4	0	0	2	2	8	.278	.327
Bats Right	R	.262	42	11	2	0	0	3	2	8	.311	.310
Ramirez, A	L	.267	90	24	4	0	6	14	10	12	.333	.511
Bats Right	R	.328	457	150	28	1	30	89	39	50	.381	.591
Ramirez, Manny	L	.306	160	49	13	0	13	41	39	30	.446	.631
Bats Right	R	.309	408	126	31	0	30	89	43	94	.375	.605
Randa, Joe	L	.299	144	43	8	1	3	16	9	19	.340	.431
Bats Right	R	.282	341	96	23	1	5	40	31	58	.345	.399
Ransom, Cody	L	.500	16	8	3	0	1	4	3	5	.600	.875
Bats Right	R	.173	52	9	3	0	0	7	3	15	.218	.231
Redman, Tike	L	.266	109	29	4	1	1	13	5	12	.302	.349
Bats Left	R	.284	437	124	15	3	7	38	18	40	.312	.380
Redmond, Mike	L	.179	56	10	2	0	1	2	2	8	.258	.268
Bats Right	R	.279	190	53	13	0	1	23	12	20	.332	.363
Reed, Jeremy	L	.200	5	1	1	0	0	2	1	1	.429	.400
Bats Left	R	.415	53	22	3	0	0	3	6	3	.475	.472
Reese, Pokey	L	.224	85	19	3	2	1	13	4	16	.258	.341
Bats Right	R	.220	159	35	4	0	2	16	13	44	.277	.283
Relaford, Desi	L	.216	102	22	5	0	1	8	17	20	.341	.294
Bats Both	R	.223	278	62	9	0	5	26	17	36	.277	.309
Renteria, E	L	.366	131	48	12	0	4	20	14	17	.429	.550
Bats Right	R	.264	455	120	25	0	6	52	25	61	.297	.358
Restovich, M	L	.368	19	7	1	0	1	2	2	5	.429	.579
Bats Right	R	.179	28	5	2	0	1	4	2	5	.233	.357
Reyes, Jose	L	.326	43	14	7	0	1	3	0	4	.326	.558
Bats Both	R	.237	177	42	9	2	1	11	5	27	.258	.328
Reyes, Rene	L	.100	10	1	1	0	0	0	2	5	.250	.200
Bats Both	R	.157	51	8	1	0	0	1	3	12	.204	.176
Riggs, Adam	L	.333	15	5	3	0	0	2	0	0	.333	.533
Bats Right	R	.095	21	2	0	0	0	1	1	10	.136	.095
Rios, Alexis	L	.287	101	29	7	1	0	6	14	22	.374	.376
Bats Right	R	.286	325	93	17	6	1	22	17	62	.326	.385
Rivas, Luis	L	.291	103	30	7	1	4	14	3	10	.306	.495
Bats Right	R	.240	233	56	12	4	6	20	10	43	.273	.403
Rivera, Carlos	L	.000	0	0	0	0	0	0	0	0	.000	.000
Bats Left	R	.200	15	3	0	0	0	1	1	3	.250	.200
Rivera, Juan	L	.276	156	43	11	0	6	21	10	13	.323	.462
Bats Right	R	.328	235	77	13	1	6	28	24	32	.390	.468
Rivera, Rene	L	.000	0	0	0	0	0	0	0	0	.000	.000
Bats Right	R	.000	3	0	0	0	0	0	0	1	.000	.000
Roberts, Brian	L	.215	200	43	18	1	0	15	25	29	.301	.315
Bats Both	R	.299	441	132	32	1	4	38	46	66	.363	.404
Roberts, Dave	L	.179	56	10	2	1	0	3	5	12	.242	.250
Bats Left	R	.270	263	71	12	6	4	32	33	36	.356	.407
Robinson, K	L	.167	12	2	0	0	0	0	1	0	.231	.167
Bats Left	R	.313	80	25	4	0	0	5	4	8	.345	.363
Rodriguez, A	L	.311	132	41	4	0	14	28	25	27	.422	.659
Bats Right	R	.279	469	131	20	2	22	78	55	104	.361	.471
Rodriguez, I	L	.343	175	60	11	0	5	30	24	31	.420	.491
Bats Right	R	.330	352	116	21	2	14	56	17	60	.363	.520
Rolen, Scott	L	.371	89	33	8	1	6	27	28	19	.525	.685
Bats Right	R	.302	411	124	24	3	28	97	44	73	.379	.579
Rollins, Jimmy	L	.303	165	50	11	1	5	26	15	12	.365	.473
Bats Both	R	.285	492	140	32	11	9	47	42	61	.342	.449
Rolls, Damian	L	.152	66	10	4	0	0	5	3	18	.186	.212
Bats Right	R	.176	51	9	1	0	0	4	7	18	.283	.196
Romano, Jason	L	.188	16	3	0	0	1	4	0	6	.188	.375
Bats Right	R	.111	18	2	0	0	0	0	2	6	.200	.111
Rose, Mike	L	.000	0	0	0	0	0	0	0	0	.000	.000
Bats Both	R	.000	2	0	0	0	0	0	0	2	.000	.000
Ross, David	L	.125	64	8	1	0	1	1	8	29	.233	.188
Bats Right	R	.198	101	20	2	1	4	14	7	33	.265	.356
Rowand, Aaron	L	.302	179	54	16	0	11	27	18	30	.371	.575
Bats Right	R	.315	308	97	22	2	13	42	12	61	.355	.526
Ryan, Michael	L	.350	20	7	1	1	0	1	0	5	.350	.500
Bats Left	R	.196	51	10	1	0	0	6	4	11	.255	.216
Sadler, Donnie	L	.167	6	1	1	0	0	0	0	3	.167	.333
Bats Right	R	.118	17	2	1	0	0	0	1	4	.167	.176
Saenz, Olmedo	L	.338	65	22	1	0	6	13	10	18	.427	.631
Bats Right	R	.196	46	9	0	0	2	9	2	15	.245	.326
Salmon, Tim	L	.147	75	11	2	0	0	5	4	15	.195	.173
Bats Right	R	.324	111	36	5	0	2	18	10	26	.379	.423
Sanchez, Alex	L	.348	141	49	4	1	1	15	1	22	.350	.411
Bats Left	R	.304	191	58	5	2	1	11	6	28	.325	.366
Sanchez, F	L	.000	2	0	0	0	0	0	0	1	.000	.000
Bats Right	R	.176	17	3	0	0	0	2	0	2	.176	.176
Sanchez, Rey	L	.289	83	24	4	2	0	10	6	6	.337	.386
Bats Right	R	.228	202	46	10	1	2	16	6	22	.257	.317
Sanders, R	L	.230	113	26	9	0	3	14	17	33	.333	.389
Bats Right	R	.270	333	90	18	3	19	53	16	85	.308	.514
Santiago, B	L	.250	44	11	3	0	1	5	1	6	.267	.386
Bats Right	R	.282	131	37	7	0	5	18	7	26	.326	.450
Santiago, R	L	.200	10	2	1	0	0	0	1	2	.273	.300
Bats Both	R	.172	29	5	0	0	0	2	2	1	.250	.172
Schneider, B	L	.244	86	21	0	2	2	8	4	12	.286	.360
Bats Left	R	.260	350	91	20	1	10	41	38	51	.334	.409
Scutaro, Marco	L	.276	145	40	12	1	6	19	9	15	.316	.497
Bats Right	R	.271	310	84	20	0	1	24	7	43	.287	.345
Segui, David	L	.353	17	6	1	0	0	2	3	7	.450	.412
Bats Both	R	.333	42	14	2	0	1	5	2	6	.378	.452
Sexson, Richie	L	.222	18	4	2	0	0	1	7	5	.440	.333
Bats Right	R	.236	72	17	2	0	9	22	7	16	.304	.639
Sheffield, G	L	.314	140	44	9	0	8	30	26	16	.423	.550
Bats Right	R	.282	433	122	21	1	28	91	66	67	.384	.529
Shelton, Chris	L	.208	24	5	0	0	1	3	7	7	.375	.333
Bats Right	R	.182	22	4	1	0	0	0	2	7	.250	.227
Sierra, Ruben	L	.243	136	33	7	1	5	24	9	25	.284	.419
Bats Both	R	.246	171	42	5	0	12	41	16	30	.305	.485
Simon, Randall	L	.235	17	4	0	0	0	1	0	4	.235	.235
Bats Left	R	.183	175	32	6	0	3	13	18	15	.269	.269
Sizemore, G	L	.178	45	8	0	0	0	2	5	8	.296	.178
Bats Left	R	.280	93	26	6	2	4	22	9	26	.352	.516
Sledge, T	L	.241	87	21	3	1	2	16	4	15	.275	.368
Bats Left	R	.277	311	86	17	5	13	46	36	51	.352	.489
Smith, Jason	L	.242	33	8	0	1	0	4	2	9	.286	.303
Bats Left	R	.238	122	29	7	3	5	15	6	28	.279	.467
Snead, Esix	L	.000	0	0	0	0	0	0	0	0	.000	.000
Bats Both	R	.000	0	0	0	0	0	0	0	0	.000	.000
Snow, J.T.	L	.255	47	12	4	0	1	9	9	10	.379	.404
Bats Left	R	.338	299	101	28	1	11	51	49	51	.437	.548

Batter	vs.	Avg.	AB	H	2B	3B	HR	RBI	BB	SO	OBP	Slg.
Snyder, Chris	L	.250	32	8	1	0	3	4	3	8	.314	.563
Bats Right	R	.234	64	15	5	0	2	11	10	17	.333	.406
Snyder, Earl	L	.000	0	0	0	0	0	0	0	0	.000	.000
Bats Right	R	.250	4	1	0	0	0	0	0	1	.250	.250
Soriano, A	L	.266	158	42	9	2	9	31	16	38	.335	.519
Bats Right	R	.284	450	128	23	2	19	60	17	83	.319	.471
Sosa, Sammy	L	.253	95	24	6	0	4	12	22	34	.393	.442
Bats Right	R	.253	383	97	15	0	31	68	34	99	.315	.535
Spencer, Shane	L	.228	57	13	1	0	1	8	5	12	.290	.298
Bats Right	R	.305	128	39	9	1	3	18	8	25	.350	.461
Spiezio, Scott	L	.203	74	15	4	0	1	8	6	9	.263	.297
Bats Both	R	.218	293	64	8	3	9	33	30	51	.294	.358
Spivey, Junior	L	.279	43	12	3	0	3	5	10	9	.426	.558
Bats Right	R	.270	185	50	10	0	4	23	15	39	.341	.389
Stairs, Matt	L	.223	94	21	3	0	4	16	11	28	.318	.383
Bats Left	R	.278	345	96	18	3	14	50	38	64	.352	.470
Stewart, S	L	.257	113	29	5	0	3	10	18	17	.356	.381
Bats Right	R	.325	265	86	12	2	8	37	29	27	.391	.475
Stinnett, K	L	.167	18	3	0	0	0	2	2	7	.286	.167
Bats Right	R	.366	41	15	0	0	3	5	3	9	.422	.585
Stynes, Chris	L	.190	58	11	3	0	1	8	4	8	.254	.293
Bats Left	R	.231	104	24	7	0	0	8	5	15	.273	.298
Surhoff, B.J.	L	.333	99	33	6	0	1	14	6	13	.377	.424
Bats Left	R	.299	244	73	8	1	7	36	24	33	.361	.418
Sutton, Larry	L	.000	0	0	0	0	0	0	0	0	.000	.000
Bats Left	R	.200	5	1	0	0	0	1	1	2	.333	.200
Suzuki, Ichiro	L	.404	208	84	9	1	5	21	15	19	.444	.529
Bats Left	R	.359	496	178	15	4	3	39	34	44	.402	.423
Sweeney, Mark	L	.556	9	5	2	0	1	3	1	1	.600	1.111
Bats Left	R	.250	168	42	10	2	8	37	31	50	.366	.476
Sweeney, Mike	L	.221	113	25	5	0	4	8	8	15	.276	.372
Bats Right	R	.312	298	93	18	0	18	71	25	29	.374	.554
Swisher, Nick	L	.500	10	5	2	0	0	0	5	2	.667	.700
Bats Both	R	.200	50	10	2	0	2	8	3	9	.268	.360
Taguchi, So	L	.266	94	25	4	0	2	10	6	11	.311	.372
Bats Right	R	.318	85	27	6	2	1	15	6	12	.366	.471
Taveras, Willy	L	.000	0	0	0	0	0	0	0	0	.000	.000
Bats Right	R	.000	1	0	0	0	0	0	0	1	.000	.000
Teixeira, Mark	L	.313	163	51	11	0	10	34	18	38	.395	.564
Bats Both	R	.267	382	102	23	2	28	78	50	79	.359	.558
Tejada, Miguel	L	.327	159	52	13	0	11	40	19	16	.396	.616
Bats Right	R	.306	494	151	27	2	23	110	29	57	.348	.508
Terrero, Luis	L	.268	56	15	2	0	3	7	9	15	.379	.464
Bats Right	R	.237	173	41	12	0	1	7	11	63	.298	.324
Thames, M	L	.284	81	23	5	0	6	17	10	15	.363	.568
Bats Right	R	.226	84	19	7	0	4	16	6	27	.290	.452
Thomas, C	L	.281	32	9	0	2	1	8	3	10	.395	.500
Bats Left	R	.289	204	59	8	2	6	23	18	35	.364	.436
Thomas, Frank	L	.200	50	10	2	0	3	7	18	10	.420	.420
Bats Right	R	.289	190	55	14	0	15	42	46	47	.438	.600
Thome, Jim	L	.239	188	45	9	0	12	34	23	55	.324	.479
Bats Left	R	.294	320	94	19	1	30	71	81	89	.435	.641
Thompson, Rich	L	.000	0	0	0	0	0	0	0	0	.000	.000
Bats Left	R	.000	1	0	0	0	0	0	0	0	.000	.000
Thurston, Joe	L	.500	2	1	0	0	0	0	0	0	.500	.500
Bats Left	R	.133	15	2	1	1	0	1	0	5	.125	.333
Tiffee, Terry	L	.158	19	3	1	0	2	5	2	2	.273	.526
Bats Both	R	.360	25	9	3	0	0	3	1	1	.385	.480
Tonis, Mike	L	.000	2	0	0	0	0	0	1	0	.333	.000
Bats Right	R	.000	4	0	0	0	0	0	0	0	.000	.000

Batter	vs.	Avg.	AB	H	2B	3B	HR	RBI	BB	SO	OBP	Slg.
Torcato, Tony	L	.000	1	0	0	0	0	0	0	0	.000	.000
Bats Left	R	.625	8	5	0	0	0	2	1	0	.636	.625
Torrealba, Y	L	.286	84	24	4	2	5	17	6	13	.344	.560
Bats Right	R	.170	88	15	3	1	1	6	11	18	.263	.261
Torres, Andres	L	.000	0	0	0	0	0	0	0	0	.000	.000
Bats Both	R	.000	0	0	0	0	0	0	0	0	.000	.000
Tracy, Andy	L	.000	0	0	0	0	0	0	0	0	.000	.000
Bats Left	R	.188	16	3	1	0	0	1	1	8	.235	.250
Tracy, Chad	L	.215	107	23	4	1	1	10	7	15	.261	.299
Bats Left	R	.305	374	114	25	2	7	43	38	45	.365	.439
Treanor, Matt	L	.182	11	2	0	0	0	0	0	4	.182	.182
Bats Right	R	.250	44	11	2	0	0	1	4	9	.340	.295
Tremie, Chris	L	.000	0	0	0	0	0	0	0	0	.000	.000
Bats Right	R	.000	0	0	0	0	0	0	0	0	.000	.000
Tucker, M	L	.234	64	15	1	2	1	8	7	18	.311	.359
Bats Left	R	.260	400	104	20	4	12	54	63	88	.360	.420
Upton, B.J.	L	.410	61	25	6	0	1	3	5	15	.455	.557
Bats Right	R	.163	98	16	2	2	3	9	10	31	.245	.316
Uribe, Juan	L	.264	178	47	7	4	12	34	10	37	.302	.551
Bats Right	R	.293	324	95	24	2	11	40	22	59	.340	.481
Utley, Chase	L	.200	45	9	1	0	1	3	2	6	.234	.289
Bats Left	R	.279	222	62	10	2	12	54	13	34	.322	.505
Valdez, Wilson	L	.273	22	6	1	0	1	3	1	3	.304	.455
Bats Right	R	.190	21	4	0	0	0	1	1	2	.227	.190
Valent, Eric	L	.100	10	1	0	0	0	0	2	3	.250	.100
Bats Left	R	.273	260	71	15	2	13	34	26	58	.340	.496
Valentin, J	L	.109	46	5	0	0	0	2	1	11	.146	.109
Bats Both	R	.269	156	42	10	1	6	18	16	25	.333	.462
Valentin, Jose	L	.191	136	26	6	1	7	16	13	53	.262	.404
Bats Left	R	.226	314	71	14	2	23	54	30	86	.298	.503
Vander Wal, J	L	.000	0	0	0	0	0	0	0	0	.000	.000
Bats Left	R	.118	51	6	2	0	2	4	4	20	.182	.275
Varitek, Jason	L	.350	137	48	10	1	6	26	16	30	.426	.569
Bats Both	R	.273	326	89	20	0	12	47	46	96	.375	.445
Vazquez, R	L	.143	14	2	0	0	0	2	1	3	.188	.143
Bats Left	R	.248	101	25	3	2	1	11	10	21	.313	.347
Ventura, Robin	L	.286	7	2	1	0	0	1	1	1	.375	.429
Bats Left	R	.241	145	35	2	0	5	27	21	30	.335	.359
Vidro, Jose	L	.267	131	35	5	0	2	13	15	17	.338	.351
Bats Both	R	.306	281	86	19	0	12	47	34	26	.381	.502
Vina, Fernando	L	.182	33	6	2	0	0	0	5	3	.325	.242
Bats Left	R	.244	82	20	3	0	0	7	4	6	.300	.280
Vizcaino, Jose	L	.250	68	17	0	0	1	8	4	9	.288	.294
Bats Both	R	.279	290	81	21	3	2	25	16	30	.316	.393
Vizquel, Omar	L	.258	190	49	14	1	1	23	14	16	.306	.358
Bats Both	R	.308	377	116	14	2	6	36	43	46	.377	.403
Walker, Larry	L	.316	76	24	7	1	1	12	14	22	.447	.474
Bats Right	R	.291	182	53	9	3	16	35	35	35	.414	.637
Walker, Todd	L	.268	41	11	0	1	0	2	7	7	.423	.317
Bats Left	R	.275	331	91	19	3	15	48	36	45	.342	.486
Ward, Daryle	L	.296	54	16	5	0	1	7	3	14	.333	.444
Bats Left	R	.238	239	57	12	2	14	50	19	31	.299	.481
Wells, Vernon	L	.287	150	43	11	1	10	24	19	22	.371	.573
Bats Right	R	.267	386	103	23	1	13	43	32	61	.324	.433
Werth, Jayson	L	.290	93	27	5	1	8	19	13	30	.377	.624
Bats Right	R	.249	197	49	6	2	8	28	17	55	.320	.421
White, Rondell	L	.293	157	46	9	2	3	19	17	20	.367	.433
Bats Right	R	.258	291	75	12	0	16	48	22	57	.321	.464
Wigginton, Ty	L	.222	108	24	8	0	4	11	11	15	.292	.407
Bats Right	R	.272	386	105	22	2	13	55	34	67	.333	.440

Batter	vs.	Avg.	AB	H	2B	3B	HR	RBI	BB	SO	OBP	Slg.
Wilkerson, B	L	.278	176	49	12	1	9	21	22	47	.366	.511
Bats Left	R	.245	396	97	27	1	23	46	84	105	.377	.492
Williams, B	L	.265	166	44	6	0	9	26	32	24	.384	.464
Bats Both	R	.261	395	103	23	1	13	44	53	72	.350	.423
Williams, G	L	.275	51	14	3	1	2	6	5	13	.339	.490
Bats Right	R	.205	78	16	5	1	2	5	3	13	.235	.372
Willingham, J	L	.333	3	1	0	0	1	1	2	1	.600	1.333
Bats Right	R	.182	22	4	0	0	0	0	2	7	.250	.182
Wilson, Craig	L	.259	108	28	8	2	6	14	16	25	.375	.537
Bats Right	R	.265	453	120	27	3	23	68	34	144	.349	.490
Wilson, Dan	L	.203	79	16	2	0	2	12	8	12	.270	.304
Bats Right	R	.267	240	64	11	0	0	21	18	45	.317	.313
Wilson, E	L	.299	67	20	6	0	1	6	1	6	.304	.433
Bats Both	R	.179	173	31	3	0	5	25	14	14	.236	.283
Wilson, Jack	L	.261	115	30	5	3	5	12	8	10	.315	.487
Bats Right	R	.318	537	171	36	9	6	47	18	61	.340	.453
Wilson, P	L	.290	69	20	5	0	2	13	5	12	.338	.449
Bats Right	R	.226	133	30	6	0	4	16	12	37	.304	.361
Wilson, Tom	L	.000	5	0	0	0	0	0	0	2	.000	.000
Bats Right	R	.286	7	2	0	0	0	0	1	3	.375	.286
Wilson, Vance	L	.200	40	8	2	0	0	3	0	4	.214	.250
Bats Right	R	.299	117	35	8	1	4	18	11	20	.373	.487
Winn, Randy	L	.257	191	49	6	3	3	17	15	31	.316	.366
Bats Both	R	.299	435	130	28	3	11	64	38	67	.359	.453
Wise, Dewayne	L	.250	24	6	1	0	2	3	2	5	.296	.542
Bats Left	R	.225	138	31	8	4	4	14	7	23	.267	.428
Womack, Tony	L	.285	123	35	4	0	0	8	9	15	.338	.317
Bats Left	R	.314	430	135	18	3	5	30	27	45	.353	.405

Batter	vs.	Avg.	AB	H	2B	3B	HR	RBI	BB	SO	OBP	Slg.
Woodward, C	L	.254	59	15	2	1	0	6	7	18	.343	.322
Bats Right	R	.227	154	35	11	3	1	18	7	28	.258	.357
Wooten, Shawn	L	.071	14	1	0	0	0	1	0	4	.133	.071
Bats Right	R	.205	39	8	3	0	0	1	2	5	.262	.282
Wright, David	L	.309	55	17	3	0	1	5	0	7	.309	.418
Bats Right	R	.288	208	60	14	1	13	35	14	33	.338	.553
Youkilis, K	L	.250	72	18	4	0	3	14	16	12	.386	.431
Bats Right	R	.265	136	36	7	0	4	21	17	33	.356	.404
Young, Dmitri	L	.248	137	34	10	0	8	23	8	26	.293	.496
Bats Both	R	.286	252	72	13	2	10	37	25	45	.358	.472
Young, Eric	L	.329	164	54	17	0	1	15	22	13	.413	.451
Bats Right	R	.250	180	45	8	2	0	12	21	15	.344	.317
Young, Ernie	L	.333	3	1	0	0	0	0	1	2	.500	.333
Bats Right	R	1.000	1	1	0	0	0	0	0	0	1.000	1.000
Young, Michael	L	.330	188	62	11	1	7	29	17	21	.383	.511
Bats Right	R	.307	502	154	22	8	15	70	27	68	.341	.472
Zaun, Gregg	L	.272	81	22	6	0	0	6	6	14	.322	.346
Bats Both	R	.268	257	69	18	0	6	30	41	47	.380	.409
Zeile, Todd	L	.241	87	21	5	0	2	7	13	17	.337	.368
Bats Right	R	.230	261	60	11	0	7	28	31	66	.313	.352
Zinter, Alan	L	.000	7	0	0	0	0	0	3	3	.300	.000
Bats Both	R	.259	27	7	2	0	1	6	2	12	.300	.444
AL	L	.271	...	...	...	...	...	...	...	...	.340	.436
	R	.270	...	...	...	...	...	...	...	...	.337	.432
NL	L	.259	...	...	...	...	...	...	...	...	.333	.419
	R	.264	...	...	...	...	...	...	...	...	.333	.424
MLB	L	.265	...	...	...	...	...	...	...	...	.336	.427
	R	.266	...	...	...	...	...	...	...	...	.335	.428

Pitcher	vs.	Avg.	AB	H	2B	3B	HR	RBI	BB	SO	OBP	Slg.
Aardsma,David	L	.474	19	9	3	0	0	5	4	3	.560	.632
Throws Right	R	.379	29	11	2	0	1	6	6	2	.500	.552
Abbott,Paul	L	.261	203	53	8	0	10	31	41	23	.386	.448
Throws Right	R	.288	184	53	11	0	12	32	17	23	.358	.543
Acevedo,Jose	L	.342	278	95	26	1	13	42	18	41	.378	.583
Throws Right	R	.254	366	93	25	0	17	57	27	76	.311	.462
Adams,Mike	L	.241	87	21	4	0	2	10	4	14	.283	.356
Throws Right	R	.252	115	29	5	0	3	15	10	25	.313	.374
Adams,Terry	L	.228	158	36	6	1	3	17	21	39	.319	.335
Throws Right	R	.400	120	48	5	0	7	34	7	17	.427	.617
Adkins,Jon	L	.327	107	35	3	0	8	15	13	20	.397	.579
Throws Right	R	.288	139	40	7	0	5	21	7	24	.327	.446
Affeldt,J	L	.271	70	19	6	0	4	12	8	12	.354	.529
Throws Left	R	.312	231	72	21	2	2	33	24	37	.375	.446
Ainsworth,K	L	.313	64	20	3	1	4	22	13	12	.439	.578
Throws Right	R	.328	58	19	4	1	2	10	7	8	.418	.534
Alfonseca,A	L	.248	117	29	1	0	3	9	12	12	.315	.333
Throws Right	R	.261	161	42	10	0	2	16	16	33	.328	.360
Almanza,A	L	.192	26	5	0	0	3	5	3	9	.276	.538
Throws Left	R	.211	19	4	2	1	0	2	4	4	.360	.421
Almanzar,C	L	.228	114	26	4	0	2	14	11	18	.302	.316
Throws Right	R	.256	156	40	11	0	6	19	8	26	.299	.442
Alvarez,Abe	L	.200	10	2	1	0	0	0	0	2	.200	.300
Throws Left	R	.600	10	6	3	0	2	5	5	0	.733	1.500
Alvarez,W	L	.307	114	35	6	0	6	22	9	19	.362	.518
Throws Left	R	.222	333	74	11	1	6	29	22	83	.274	.315
Anderson,B	L	.337	169	57	15	0	8	25	15	25	.390	.568
Throws Left	R	.314	510	160	39	0	25	88	38	45	.358	.537
Anderson,J	L	.000	2	0	0	0	0	2	3	1	.600	.000
Throws Right	R	.500	2	1	0	0	1	4	1	0	.667	2.000
Anderson,J	L	.294	17	5	1	1	0	5	2	3	.400	.471
Throws Left	R	.311	45	14	3	0	0	4	4	3	.380	.378
Ankiel,Rick	L	.222	18	4	2	0	0	2	1	1	.300	.333
Throws Left	R	.286	21	6	1	0	2	4	0	8	.318	.619
Appier,Kevin	L	.308	13	4	1	0	0	1	2	2	.400	.385
Throws Right	R	.500	6	3	1	0	0	4	1	0	.571	.667
Aquino,Greg	L	.167	66	11	3	1	1	6	14	15	.313	.288
Throws Right	R	.224	58	13	2	1	3	10	3	11	.277	.448
Armas,Tony	L	.231	108	25	6	0	5	12	23	21	.370	.426
Throws Right	R	.258	159	41	8	1	8	22	22	33	.355	.472
Arroyo,B	L	.269	357	96	23	2	10	40	30	52	.341	.429
Throws Right	R	.227	331	75	24	2	7	42	17	90	.283	.375
Ashby,Andy	L	.167	6	1	0	0	0	0	0	2	.167	.167
Throws Right	R	.000	1	0	0	0	0	0	0	0	.000	.000
Astacio,Pedro	L	.348	23	8	3	0	0	3	2	4	.400	.478
Throws Right	R	.333	15	5	0	0	2	6	3	3	.444	.733
Atchison,S	L	.209	43	9	3	0	2	6	7	14	.320	.419
Throws Right	R	.274	73	20	2	0	2	11	7	22	.333	.384
Ayala,Luis	L	.246	134	33	6	1	3	14	6	18	.277	.373
Throws Right	R	.282	209	59	12	1	3	36	9	45	.326	.392
Backe,Brandon	L	.347	101	35	7	0	4	10	14	25	.426	.535
Throws Right	R	.253	158	40	9	1	6	18	13	29	.312	.437
Bacsik,Mike	L	.350	20	7	2	0	1	4	0	0	.381	.600
Throws Left	R	.225	40	9	3	0	1	4	1	6	.262	.375
Baek,C	L	.303	66	20	4	1	3	12	7	11	.378	.530
Throws Right	R	.250	60	15	6	0	2	9	4	9	.308	.450
Baez,Danys	L	.252	123	31	7	0	3	18	12	25	.328	.382
Throws Right	R	.223	130	29	4	1	3	11	17	27	.333	.338
Bajenaru,Jeff	L	.278	18	5	0	1	0	5	2	6	.350	.389
Throws Right	R	.526	19	10	2	0	0	1	4	2	.609	.632
Baldwin,James	L	.444	9	4	0	1	2	4	3	0	.583	1.333
Throws Right	R	.450	20	9	2	1	1	4	2	1	.522	.800
Balfour,Grant	L	.183	60	11	1	1	2	6	9	23	.290	.333
Throws Right	R	.276	87	24	0	0	2	13	12	19	.376	.345
Bartosh,Cliff	L	.286	42	12	4	0	2	15	9	15	.412	.524
Throws Left	R	.263	38	10	3	0	2	5	2	10	.300	.500
Batista,M	L	.264	432	114	16	4	11	56	67	63	.362	.396
Throws Right	R	.285	323	92	27	1	11	50	29	41	.345	.477
Bauer,Rick	L	.293	92	27	6	0	2	18	13	16	.387	.424
Throws Right	R	.193	114	22	3	0	2	11	7	21	.258	.272
Bautista,D	L	.348	69	24	5	0	2	16	11	12	.432	.507
Throws Right	R	.357	56	20	6	0	1	9	2	7	.410	.518
Beck,Rod	L	.318	44	14	0	2	5	9	7	7	.412	.750
Throws Right	R	.245	53	13	4	0	3	8	2	8	.263	.491
Beckett,Josh	L	.281	285	80	18	5	10	41	32	80	.354	.484
Throws Right	R	.192	297	57	14	0	6	26	22	72	.258	.300
Bedard,Erik	L	.277	112	31	5	2	2	16	22	27	.406	.411
Throws Left	R	.269	439	118	27	1	11	58	49	94	.345	.410
Beimel,Joe	L	.500	6	3	1	0	1	5	2	2	.625	1.167
Throws Left	R	.714	7	5	1	0	0	3	0	0	.714	.857
Bell,Heath	L	.161	31	5	1	0	0	2	3	9	.235	.194
Throws Right	R	.304	56	17	2	0	5	10	3	18	.339	.607
Bell,Rob	L	.282	227	64	19	1	7	34	29	24	.365	.467
Throws Right	R	.226	252	57	9	1	9	28	12	33	.270	.377
Beltran,F	L	.250	72	18	3	0	6	13	11	13	.345	.542
Throws Right	R	.254	114	29	8	0	5	17	16	35	.353	.456
Beltran,Rigo	L	.500	2	1	0	0	0	0	0	0	.500	.500
Throws Left	R	.000	1	0	0	0	0	0	0	0	.000	.000
Benitez,A	L	.168	101	17	3	0	3	7	17	23	.288	.287
Throws Right	R	.140	136	19	4	0	3	12	4	39	.163	.235
Bennett,Jeff	L	.291	117	34	7	1	6	21	17	24	.380	.521
Throws Left	R	.268	164	44	8	4	6	26	9	21	.305	.476
Benoit,J	L	.249	209	52	8	3	7	29	17	51	.300	.416
Throws Right	R	.311	196	61	10	2	12	34	14	44	.371	.566
Benson,Kris	L	.276	362	100	20	4	8	46	37	54	.347	.420
Throws Right	R	.251	407	102	25	2	7	44	24	80	.300	.373
Bentz,Chad	L	.283	46	13	2	0	3	6	8	13	.411	.522
Throws Left	R	.182	55	10	1	0	2	9	15	5	.357	.309
Bergman,Dusty	L	.333	3	1	0	0	0	1	1	1	.400	.333
Throws Left	R	.500	6	3	1	0	0	4	0	0	.500	.667
Bernero,Adam	L	.305	59	18	3	0	4	12	14	6	.427	.559
Throws Right	R	.265	68	18	5	0	3	9	3	15	.292	.471
Betancourt,R	L	.272	136	37	7	2	4	16	13	33	.333	.441
Throws Right	R	.264	129	34	5	1	3	18	5	43	.289	.388
Biddle,Rocky	L	.307	137	42	7	2	6	28	11	21	.366	.518
Throws Right	R	.308	182	56	9	1	9	36	20	30	.389	.516
Bierbrodt,N	L	.188	16	3	0	0	1	2	3	0	.316	.375
Throws Left	R	.268	41	11	0	0	3	7	16	10	.483	.488
Blackley,T	L	.296	27	8	1	0	2	8	7	3	.457	.556
Throws Left	R	.329	82	27	4	0	7	13	15	13	.429	.634
Blanton,Joe	L	.167	12	2	0	0	1	4	2	2	.286	.417
Throws Right	R	.250	16	4	2	0	0	0	0	4	.250	.375
Boehringer,B	L	.304	23	7	1	0	0	2	12	6	.543	.348
Throws Right	R	.290	69	20	5	1	2	12	5	14	.333	.478
Bonderman,J	L	.255	404	103	21	4	16	64	51	89	.339	.446
Throws Right	R	.223	291	65	13	0	8	27	22	79	.294	.351
Bong,J	L	.294	17	5	1	0	0	2	0	5	.294	.353
Throws Left	R	.261	46	12	3	0	3	9	10	6	.393	.522
Borkowski,D	L	.270	111	30	10	1	3	13	10	23	.333	.459
Throws Right	R	.307	114	35	7	0	3	17	5	22	.344	.447

Pitcher	vs.	Avg.	AB	H	2B	3B	HR	RBI	BB	SO	OBP	Slg.
Borland,Toby	L	.321	28	9	1	1	1	2	4	5	.406	.536
Throws Right	R	.209	43	9	3	0	2	6	8	13	.327	.419
Borowski,Joe	L	.344	32	11	0	1	3	11	12	6	.511	.688
Throws Right	R	.281	57	16	4	1	0	7	3	11	.317	.386
Bottalico,R	L	.205	78	16	5	0	0	7	19	12	.373	.269
Throws Right	R	.220	173	38	8	0	3	18	15	49	.283	.318
Boyd,Jason	L	.429	14	6	3	0	2	6	4	3	.556	1.071
Throws Right	R	.194	36	7	2	0	2	2	4	9	.326	.417
Bradford,Chad	L	.298	57	17	0	0	2	5	18	9	.467	.404
Throws Right	R	.211	161	34	3	0	3	22	6	25	.260	.286
Brazelton,D	L	.250	252	63	20	1	5	26	29	43	.330	.397
Throws Right	R	.272	213	58	16	0	7	31	24	21	.364	.446
Brazoban,Y	L	.224	49	11	3	0	0	2	13	11	.387	.286
Throws Right	R	.215	65	14	1	0	2	7	2	16	.239	.323
Brocail,Doug	L	.190	79	15	3	0	1	12	8	16	.270	.266
Throws Right	R	.320	122	39	9	0	1	16	12	27	.396	.418
Brooks,Frank	L	.083	24	2	1	0	0	1	2	6	.154	.125
Throws Left	R	.275	40	11	1	0	5	11	7	12	.383	.675
Brower,Jim	L	.333	132	44	11	3	2	22	20	15	.422	.508
Throws Right	R	.213	216	46	3	0	4	20	16	48	.275	.282
Brown,Jamie	L	.611	18	11	3	0	1	4	4	0	.682	.944
Throws Right	R	.222	18	4	1	0	0	4	0	6	.211	.278
Brown,Kevin	L	.261	280	73	22	0	9	26	18	47	.301	.436
Throws Right	R	.263	224	59	14	0	5	31	17	36	.317	.393
Bruney,Brian	L	.214	42	9	1	0	2	8	14	11	.411	.381
Throws Right	R	.172	64	11	2	0	0	4	13	23	.321	.203
Buehrle,Mark	L	.287	202	58	9	1	6	25	8	41	.333	.431
Throws Left	R	.267	745	199	31	3	27	83	43	124	.307	.426
Bukvich,Ryan	L	.200	10	2	0	0	0	2	4	3	.429	.200
Throws Right	R	.167	12	2	1	0	0	0	3	4	.333	.250
Bullinger,K	L	.326	46	15	5	0	0	8	6	4	.415	.435
Throws Right	R	.263	80	21	4	0	5	14	4	7	.294	.500
Bump,Nate	L	.282	117	33	6	0	3	13	15	20	.373	.410
Throws Right	R	.306	173	53	8	0	4	35	17	24	.368	.422
Burba,Dave	L	.264	121	32	9	0	5	15	13	20	.341	.463
Throws Right	R	.224	170	38	6	1	2	20	13	30	.278	.306
Burnett,A.J.	L	.247	243	60	11	1	4	25	17	60	.304	.350
Throws Right	R	.211	199	42	8	1	5	19	21	53	.286	.337
Burnett,Sean	L	.324	71	23	3	0	1	8	9	7	.407	.408
Throws Left	R	.293	215	63	8	0	8	29	19	23	.349	.442
Bush,David	L	.289	218	63	7	1	9	26	20	38	.351	.454
Throws Right	R	.206	155	32	9	0	2	19	5	26	.247	.303
Bynum,Mike	L	.500	2	1	0	0	0	0	2	0	.750	.500
Throws Left	R	.000	1	0	0	0	0	0	1	0	.500	.000
Byrd,Paul	L	.329	213	70	15	2	7	22	11	18	.364	.516
Throws Right	R	.219	242	53	6	1	11	27	8	61	.244	.388
Cabrera,D	L	.249	293	73	8	3	10	47	44	43	.347	.399
Throws Right	R	.270	267	72	12	1	4	35	45	33	.371	.367
Cabrera,F	L	.083	12	1	0	0	0	2	1	4	.143	.083
Throws Right	R	.333	6	2	1	0	0	2	0	2	.333	.500
Calero,Kiko	L	.175	57	10	3	0	3	8	4	17	.230	.386
Throws Right	R	.177	96	17	4	0	2	6	6	30	.233	.281
Cali,Carmen	L	.333	12	4	2	0	0	1	3	2	.467	.500
Throws Left	R	.429	21	9	2	0	1	3	3	6	.480	.667
Callaway,M	L	.290	31	9	3	0	1	5	6	5	.410	.484
Throws Right	R	.500	18	9	2	0	1	5	1	4	.526	.778
Camp,Shawn	L	.287	115	33	5	1	6	18	5	19	.331	.504
Throws Right	R	.283	145	41	7	0	4	18	11	32	.368	.414
Capellan,Jose	L	.167	12	2	1	0	0	1	4	3	.375	.250
Throws Right	R	.522	23	12	2	0	2	9	1	1	.520	.870
Capuano,Chris	L	.207	58	12	5	0	0	4	6	20	.292	.293
Throws Left	R	.282	280	79	18	0	18	48	31	60	.361	.539

Pitcher	vs.	Avg.	AB	H	2B	3B	HR	RBI	BB	SO	OBP	Slg.
Carpenter,C	L	.268	310	83	13	0	16	49	18	57	.316	.465
Throws Right	R	.226	381	86	15	1	8	23	20	95	.269	.333
Carrara,G	L	.182	77	14	3	0	0	2	10	18	.276	.221
Throws Right	R	.256	125	32	6	2	1	13	10	30	.316	.360
Carrasco,D.J.	L	.323	62	20	2	0	2	10	10	7	.411	.452
Throws Right	R	.259	81	21	2	0	3	15	5	15	.326	.395
Carter,Lance	L	.276	156	43	10	1	7	27	14	14	.329	.487
Throws Right	R	.227	150	34	7	1	5	12	9	22	.272	.387
Castillo,F	L	.000	0	0	0	0	0	0	1	0	1.000	.000
Throws Right	R	.333	3	1	0	0	0	1	0	0	.333	.333
Cerda,Jaime	L	.185	65	12	2	0	0	6	10	17	.308	.215
Throws Left	R	.282	103	29	4	0	1	11	20	16	.397	.350
Chacin,G	L	.143	14	2	1	0	0	1	2	3	.294	.214
Throws Left	R	.176	34	6	3	0	0	0	1	3	.200	.265
Chacon,Shawn	L	.236	123	29	5	2	6	25	32	32	.409	.455
Throws Right	R	.326	129	42	8	1	6	20	20	20	.420	.543
Chen,Bruce	L	.200	45	9	1	0	2	4	5	8	.280	.356
Throws Right	R	.227	132	30	4	2	5	14	11	24	.285	.402
Choate,Randy	L	.280	100	28	9	0	1	20	11	31	.359	.400
Throws Left	R	.253	95	24	5	0	0	11	17	18	.374	.305
Christiansen,J	L	.243	70	17	2	0	2	13	13	14	.379	.357
Throws Left	R	.258	66	17	2	0	1	11	13	8	.375	.333
Chulk,Vinnie	L	.308	117	36	5	2	5	21	17	15	.393	.513
Throws Right	R	.228	101	23	6	0	1	9	10	29	.304	.317
Claussen,B	L	.375	56	21	4	1	3	13	11	8	.485	.643
Throws Left	R	.278	212	59	13	1	6	29	24	37	.350	.434
Clemens,Roger	L	.218	395	86	15	4	5	29	46	102	.300	.314
Throws Right	R	.217	383	83	19	0	10	38	33	116	.283	.345
Clement,Matt	L	.234	329	77	14	0	13	42	51	100	.342	.395
Throws Right	R	.224	348	78	14	1	10	34	26	90	.292	.356
Colome,Jesus	L	.245	53	13	3	0	3	9	11	12	.375	.472
Throws Right	R	.163	92	15	3	0	1	9	7	28	.230	.228
Colon,Bartolo	L	.273	455	124	28	1	22	69	43	97	.333	.484
Throws Right	R	.256	355	91	21	1	16	46	28	61	.312	.456
Colon,Roman	L	.344	32	11	3	0	0	4	2	5	.382	.438
Throws Right	R	.179	39	7	1	0	0	4	6	10	.277	.205
Colyer,Steve	L	.255	55	14	6	1	2	9	10	20	.379	.509
Throws Left	R	.284	67	19	7	1	6	16	14	11	.407	.687
Contreras,J	L	.251	366	92	14	2	14	52	46	81	.337	.415
Throws Right	R	.254	291	74	13	1	17	47	38	69	.348	.481
Cook,Aaron	L	.267	202	54	13	3	4	23	26	17	.358	.421
Throws Right	R	.324	179	58	6	0	3	18	13	23	.383	.408
Cooper,Brian	L	.348	23	8	3	0	4	9	4	2	.444	1.000
Throws Right	R	.241	29	7	1	0	0	3	1	5	.281	.276
Corcoran,Roy	L	.429	7	3	0	1	0	3	1	1	.500	.714
Throws Right	R	.250	16	4	1	0	0	3	4	3	.400	.313
Cordero,Chad	L	.243	136	33	6	0	4	13	31	37	.385	.375
Throws Right	R	.205	171	35	5	0	4	12	12	46	.253	.304
Cordero,F	L	.235	149	35	8	0	0	19	19	44	.321	.289
Throws Right	R	.216	116	25	4	0	1	8	13	30	.298	.276
Corey,Mark	L	.250	52	13	0	0	0	5	9	8	.355	.250
Throws Right	R	.289	90	26	4	0	3	20	10	20	.373	.433
Cormier,Lance	L	.387	75	29	6	2	8	22	11	8	.471	.840
Throws Right	R	.297	111	33	5	0	5	19	14	16	.372	.477
Cormier,Rheal	L	.250	108	27	4	3	1	13	11	23	.336	.370
Throws Left	R	.230	187	43	9	1	6	24	15	23	.293	.385
Cornejo,Nate	L	.371	62	23	6	0	4	10	7	8	.443	.661
Throws Right	R	.380	50	19	3	1	0	8	4	4	.426	.480
Correia,Kevin	L	.467	30	14	5	0	2	8	2	4	.500	.833
Throws Right	R	.244	45	11	3	0	1	11	8	10	.351	.378
Cotts,Neal	L	.269	104	28	5	0	7	26	9	29	.342	.519
Throws Left	R	.231	143	33	4	1	6	14	21	29	.329	.399

Pitcher	vs.	Avg.	AB	H	2B	3B	HR	RBI	BB	SO	OBP	Slg.		Pitcher	vs.	Avg.	AB	H	2B	3B	HR	RBI	BB	SO	OBP	Slg.
Crain,Jesse	L	.211	38	8	2	0	0	6	8	3	.362	.263		Dreifort,D	L	.209	67	14	1	0	4	11	17	23	.365	.403
Throws Right	R	.158	57	9	1	0	2	9	4	11	.213	.281		Throws Right	R	.246	118	29	6	1	1	17	19	40	.348	.339
Cressend,Jack	L	.308	26	8	1	0	2	6	5	3	.406	.577		Drese,Ryan	L	.279	452	126	23	3	13	53	42	62	.349	.429
Throws Right	R	.350	40	14	2	0	2	3	5	5	.422	.550		Throws Right	R	.293	365	107	18	3	3	34	16	36	.326	.384
Crowell,Jim	L	.333	6	2	0	0	0	1	0	0	.333	.333		Drew,Tim	L	.360	25	9	2	0	1	2	3	3	.429	.560
Throws Left	R	.333	12	4	1	0	0	1	0	1	.333	.417		Throws Right	R	.293	41	12	3	0	1	7	2	4	.341	.439
Cruceta,F	L	.278	18	5	1	0	0	3	3	7	.381	.333		Driskill,T	L	.467	15	7	2	0	0	4	2	2	.529	.600
Throws Right	R	.333	15	5	2	0	1	5	1	2	.389	.667		Throws Right	R	.286	21	6	0	0	0	3	1	4	.318	.286
Cruz,Juan	L	.239	109	26	3	0	3	11	16	22	.344	.349		DuBose,Eric	L	.167	60	10	5	0	2	5	11	14	.292	.350
Throws Right	R	.214	154	33	9	0	4	15	14	48	.280	.351		Throws Left	R	.288	229	66	15	1	10	42	33	34	.385	.493
Cubillan,D	L	.375	16	6	2	0	1	4	2	4	.444	.688		Duchscherer,J	L	.247	170	42	4	1	5	18	17	37	.319	.371
Throws Right	R	.259	27	7	0	0	2	7	5	4	.375	.481		Throws Right	R	.235	183	43	4	2	8	22	15	22	.305	.410
Cunnane,Will	L	.333	18	6	0	0	0	3	3	6	.391	.333		Duckworth,B	L	.377	77	29	4	1	5	12	10	13	.443	.649
Throws Right	R	.353	34	12	3	0	3	6	1	5	.389	.706		Throws Right	R	.302	86	26	4	1	6	18	3	10	.326	.581
Daigle,Casey	L	.341	88	30	8	2	4	15	18	7	.453	.614		Dunn,Scott	L	.636	11	7	1	0	0	4	1	0	.667	.727
Throws Right	R	.303	109	33	9	0	5	20	9	10	.364	.523		Throws Right	R	.000	5	0	0	0	0	0	0	2	.000	.000
D'Amico,Jeff	L	.314	70	22	5	2	2	14	3	10	.338	.529		Durbin,Chad	L	.287	115	33	5	1	6	21	14	27	.376	.504
Throws Right	R	.354	65	23	5	0	4	11	3	6	.386	.615		Throws Right	R	.295	132	39	9	0	5	26	21	21	.397	.477
Darensbourg,V	L	.556	9	5	3	0	0	0	2	1	.636	.889		Durbin,J.D.	L	.400	20	8	1	0	0	5	5	5	.500	.450
Throws Left	R	.353	17	6	0	0	1	5	1	0	.350	.529		Throws Right	R	.364	11	4	1	0	0	1	1	1	.417	.455
Davis,Doug	L	.259	143	37	8	0	2	15	12	25	.335	.357		Eaton,Adam	L	.260	384	100	20	0	11	40	31	71	.320	.398
Throws Left	R	.244	635	155	31	4	12	54	67	141	.316	.362		Throws Right	R	.272	383	104	20	3	17	66	21	82	.316	.473
Davis,Jason	L	.305	233	71	6	1	8	29	37	37	.401	.442		Eischen,Joey	L	.167	24	4	1	0	1	5	4	9	.310	.333
Throws Right	R	.317	243	77	20	0	5	39	14	35	.360	.461		Throws Left	R	.267	45	12	1	0	1	5	4	8	.320	.356
Dawley,Joe	L	.294	17	5	1	0	1	5	3	3	.400	.529		Elarton,Scott	L	.226	318	72	19	4	16	46	40	63	.311	.462
Throws Right	R	.154	13	2	0	0	0	0	4	5	.353	.154		Throws Right	R	.306	301	92	20	1	17	55	22	40	.356	.548
Day,Zach	L	.279	190	53	15	2	8	26	31	21	.386	.505		Eldred,Cal	L	.271	96	26	3	0	5	15	5	24	.307	.458
Throws Right	R	.254	252	64	13	1	5	20	14	40	.297	.373		Throws Right	R	.280	161	45	10	1	6	20	12	30	.330	.466
DeJean,Mike	L	.319	94	30	5	1	1	19	19	23	.458	.426		Embree,Alan	L	.240	104	25	1	0	4	14	2	22	.257	.365
Throws Right	R	.272	147	40	7	1	1	23	14	37	.341	.354		Throws Left	R	.247	97	24	8	2	3	12	9	15	.311	.464
de la Rosa,J	L	.231	13	3	0	0	0	1	3	1	.389	.231		Ennis,John	L	.270	37	10	4	0	0	3	4	7	.341	.378
Throws Left	R	.321	81	26	8	1	1	15	11	4	.394	.481		Throws Right	R	.313	32	10	1	0	3	11	1	6	.324	.625
de los Santos,V	L	.227	22	5	2	1	0	4	3	7	.308	.409		Erickson,S	L	.328	67	22	2	2	2	10	14	5	.434	.507
Throws Left	R	.273	22	6	3	0	0	3	7	3	.448	.409		Throws Right	R	.348	46	16	4	0	1	9	6	4	.415	.500
Dempster,Ryan	L	.222	27	6	1	0	1	3	8	6	.417	.370		Escobar,K	L	.252	405	102	23	0	6	38	48	98	.334	.353
Throws Right	R	.200	50	10	1	0	0	1	5	12	.286	.220		Throws Right	R	.236	381	90	23	2	15	43	28	93	.292	.425
Denney,Kyle	L	.395	43	17	4	0	3	8	7	6	.480	.698		Estes,Shawn	L	.280	168	47	7	2	6	30	17	28	.371	.452
Throws Right	R	.455	33	15	2	1	0	9	1	7	.457	.576		Throws Left	R	.294	599	176	33	6	24	91	88	89	.383	.489
DePaula,Jorge	L	.571	7	4	1	0	1	3	1	0	.625	1.143		Estrella,Leo	L	1.000	1	1	1	0	0	1	0	0	1.000	2.000
Throws Right	R	.200	25	5	2	0	1	4	3	2	.267	.400		Throws Right	R	.700	10	7	1	0	0	3	1	0	.667	.800
Dessens,Elmer	L	.316	187	59	13	1	10	31	15	32	.363	.556		Eyre,Scott	L	.200	100	20	5	1	4	11	6	28	.243	.390
Throws Right	R	.264	242	64	14	2	5	32	16	41	.312	.401		Throws Left	R	.240	96	23	3	0	4	12	21	21	.370	.396
Diaz,Felix	L	.347	98	34	4	2	7	22	11	18	.420	.643		Falkenborg,B	L	.292	24	7	0	0	1	3	5	5	.414	.417
Throws Right	R	.275	102	28	5	0	6	15	5	15	.309	.500		Throws Right	R	.343	35	12	3	0	1	12	4	6	.452	.514
Dickey,R.A.	L	.281	221	62	12	1	11	40	21	29	.348	.493		Farnsworth,K	L	.267	105	28	5	1	3	19	9	29	.336	.419
Throws Right	R	.343	216	74	16	0	6	32	12	28	.378	.500		Throws Right	R	.255	153	39	2	2	7	19	24	49	.356	.431
DiNardo,Lenny	L	.314	35	11	2	0	0	1	6	6	.419	.371		Fassero,Jeff	L	.336	146	49	6	1	3	23	9	17	.377	.452
Throws Left	R	.291	79	23	6	0	1	17	6	15	.349	.405		Throws Left	R	.288	302	87	16	0	6	43	35	43	.360	.401
Dingman,Craig	L	.243	37	9	2	1	3	8	9	7	.417	.595		Feliciano,P	L	.128	39	5	1	0	0	3	6	11	.244	.154
Throws Right	R	.320	75	24	7	2	0	13	13	9	.424	.467		Throws Left	R	.321	28	9	0	0	2	10	6	3	.444	.536
Dohmann,Scott	L	.211	76	16	6	0	3	7	8	20	.279	.408		Fernandez,J	L	.500	4	2	1	0	0	2	4	0	.750	.750
Throws Right	R	.255	98	25	9	0	5	25	11	29	.327	.500		Throws Right	R	1.000	4	4	0	0	0	4	1	0	.833	1.000
Dominguez,J	L	.159	44	7	1	0	1	3	2	12	.191	.250		Fetters,Mike	L	.370	27	10	3	1	1	5	8	2	.486	.667
Throws Right	R	.400	45	18	4	0	1	6	3	2	.460	.556		Throws Right	R	.260	50	13	2	0	1	8	6	12	.351	.360
Donnelly,B	L	.211	76	16	3	0	2	7	11	27	.318	.329		Field,Nate	L	.216	74	16	3	1	3	13	9	9	.301	.405
Throws Right	R	.237	76	18	1	0	3	12	4	29	.368	.368		Throws Right	R	.261	92	24	7	0	2	13	10	21	.340	.402
Dotel,Octavio	L	.245	159	39	8	3	9	25	18	57	.326	.503		Figueroa,N	L	.357	42	15	4	1	2	10	5	3	.426	.643
Throws Right	R	.188	154	29	6	1	4	14	15	65	.269	.318		Throws Right	R	.266	64	17	3	2	2	11	6	7	.329	.469
Douglass,Sean	L	.269	78	21	2	1	5	13	20	22	.424	.513		Fikac,Jeremy	L	.325	40	13	2	1	3	15	9	6	.449	.650
Throws Right	R	.232	69	16	2	0	1	12	8	14	.313	.304		Throws Right	R	.236	55	13	1	0	2	8	4	16	.283	.364
Downs,Scott	L	.286	42	12	1	0	0	4	2	9	.318	.310		File,Bob	L	.308	78	24	6	0	3	14	8	10	.360	.500
Throws Left	R	.315	213	67	9	1	9	35	21	29	.382	.493		Throws Right	R	.362	58	21	4	0	1	8	4	5	.415	.483

Pitcher table (left half):

Pitcher	vs.	Avg.	AB	H	2B	3B	HR	RBI	BB	SO	OBP	Slg.
Flores,Randy	L	.235	17	4	1	0	0	1	0	4	.316	.294
Throws Left	R	.281	32	9	3	0	0	1	3	3	.351	.375
Floyd,Gavin	L	.289	45	13	2	0	1	6	5	15	.360	.400
Throws Right	R	.203	59	12	2	1	0	4	11	9	.373	.271
Fogg,Josh	L	.282	326	92	26	3	8	34	49	32	.377	.454
Throws Right	R	.285	355	101	24	0	9	51	17	50	.325	.428
Foppert,Jesse	L	.500	2	1	0	0	0	0	0	0	.500	.500
Throws Right	R	.000	2	0	0	0	0	0	0	2	.000	.000
Ford,Ben	L	.275	40	11	2	0	2	5	2	4	.318	.475
Throws Right	R	.264	53	14	2	0	2	14	8	9	.371	.415
Fortunato,B	L	.139	36	5	0	1	1	4	4	12	.225	.278
Throws Right	R	.311	61	19	4	1	2	8	11	13	.417	.508
Fossum,Casey	L	.257	136	35	1	1	4	15	12	33	.325	.368
Throws Left	R	.316	431	136	23	1	27	81	51	84	.396	.561
Foulke,Keith	L	.185	168	31	6	0	3	8	10	44	.235	.274
Throws Right	R	.232	138	32	7	1	5	17	5	35	.276	.406
Fox,Chad	L	.222	18	4	2	0	1	2	5	9	.391	.500
Throws Right	R	.227	22	5	1	0	0	3	3	8	.346	.273
Francis,Jeff	L	.308	26	8	1	0	0	2	2	2	.357	.346
Throws Left	R	.281	121	34	10	0	8	19	11	30	.343	.562
Francisco,F	L	.247	73	18	2	0	2	7	14	22	.375	.356
Throws Right	R	.165	109	18	3	0	2	9	14	38	.270	.248
Franco,John	L	.173	75	13	2	0	3	10	6	13	.241	.320
Throws Left	R	.320	103	33	5	2	3	13	18	23	.418	.495
Franklin,Ryan	L	.275	433	119	25	2	13	49	46	61	.344	.432
Throws Right	R	.297	353	105	25	4	20	56	15	43	.335	.561
Franklin,W	L	.250	80	20	2	0	6	15	7	23	.326	.500
Throws Left	R	.302	116	35	5	2	5	29	15	17	.381	.509
Frasor,Jason	L	.232	142	33	8	0	4	19	20	36	.325	.373
Throws Right	R	.274	113	31	7	0	0	12	16	18	.369	.336
Frederick,K	L	.258	66	17	3	2	1	14	12	13	.370	.409
Throws Right	R	.319	47	15	4	0	3	6	4	9	.365	.596
Fuentes,Brian	L	.213	61	13	2	1	1	10	2	12	.284	.328
Throws Left	R	.300	110	33	8	0	4	16	17	36	.394	.482
Fultz,Aaron	L	.212	85	18	2	0	1	15	10	24	.293	.271
Throws Left	R	.314	102	32	7	0	4	16	13	13	.388	.500
Gagne,Eric	L	.233	146	34	7	0	2	15	14	50	.309	.322
Throws Right	R	.129	147	19	2	0	3	8	8	64	.188	.204
Gallo,Mike	L	.286	112	32	5	3	5	21	12	26	.367	.518
Throws Left	R	.280	82	23	3	1	7	14	8	8	.366	.598
Garcia,Freddy	L	.236	420	99	24	0	14	43	40	86	.305	.393
Throws Right	R	.248	375	93	25	1	8	39	24	98	.300	.384
Garcia,Jairo	L	.100	10	1	0	0	1	1	4	2	.357	.400
Throws Right	R	.333	12	4	0	0	2	7	5	3	.556	.833
Garcia,Rosman	L	.429	14	6	1	0	0	2	2	2	.471	.500
Throws Right	R	.200	15	3	0	0	1	2	3	3	.333	.400
Garland,Jon	L	.262	446	117	20	1	19	69	46	56	.334	.439
Throws Right	R	.277	383	106	24	3	15	50	30	57	.329	.473
Gaudin,Chad	L	.403	62	25	7	0	0	5	10	7	.486	.516
Throws Right	R	.301	113	34	10	1	4	27	6	23	.346	.513
Geary,Geoff	L	.326	86	28	5	2	5	15	5	8	.363	.605
Throws Right	R	.261	92	24	5	2	3	16	11	22	.352	.457
George,Chris	L	.317	41	13	6	0	0	10	4	6	.370	.463
Throws Left	R	.336	140	47	9	1	1	27	21	9	.422	.436
German,F	L	.240	25	6	0	1	2	5	3	0	.321	.560
Throws Right	R	.306	36	11	1	0	2	11	8	8	.432	.500
Germano,J	L	.383	47	18	4	1	1	14	9	5	.474	.574
Throws Right	R	.295	44	13	6	0	1	6	5	11	.367	.500
Ginter,Matt	L	.316	133	42	10	1	7	22	12	17	.377	.564
Throws Right	R	.265	151	40	5	0	1	15	8	21	.317	.318
Gissell,Chris	L	.391	23	9	1	0	1	7	2	8	.423	.565
Throws Right	R	.550	20	11	1	1	3	9	1	3	.571	1.150

Pitcher table (right half):

Pitcher	vs.	Avg.	AB	H	2B	3B	HR	RBI	BB	SO	OBP	Slg.
Glavine,Tom	L	.242	223	54	12	3	6	18	22	25	.309	.404
Throws Left	R	.255	588	150	29	0	14	70	48	84	.307	.376
Glover,Gary	L	.273	33	9	1	1	1	5	5	3	.359	.455
Throws Right	R	.257	35	9	1	0	1	4	3	5	.341	.371
Glynn,Ryan	L	.261	46	12	2	0	2	6	7	7	.386	.435
Throws Right	R	.233	30	7	1	0	2	4	1	7	.258	.467
Gobble,Jimmy	L	.317	145	46	9	1	7	20	11	16	.361	.538
Throws Left	R	.255	436	111	25	2	17	64	32	33	.307	.438
Gonzalez,D	L	.091	11	1	0	0	0	0	2	5	.231	.091
Throws Right	R	.444	18	8	3	0	1	7	0	2	.421	.778
Gonzalez,E	L	.415	94	39	7	0	10	30	12	15	.486	.809
Throws Right	R	.314	105	33	6	2	5	17	6	16	.368	.552
Gonzalez,J	L	.427	89	38	13	0	5	25	8	8	.469	.742
Throws Right	R	.286	119	34	8	1	4	13	12	14	.360	.471
Gonzalez,Mike	L	.213	61	13	2	0	0	3	3	19	.262	.246
Throws Left	R	.194	98	19	1	0	2	10	3	36	.218	.265
Good,Andrew	L	.264	72	19	5	1	4	11	8	10	.354	.528
Throws Right	R	.279	86	24	4	1	4	15	5	16	.319	.488
Gordon,Tom	L	.185	162	30	9	1	1	9	14	53	.249	.272
Throws Right	R	.174	149	26	5	1	4	14	9	43	.225	.302
Gosling,Mike	L	.194	31	6	1	0	2	4	2	5	.242	.419
Throws Left	R	.313	64	20	5	1	3	8	11	9	.429	.563
Grabow,John	L	.327	113	37	3	2	4	15	7	33	.364	.496
Throws Left	R	.319	138	44	9	0	4	21	21	31	.409	.471
Gracesqui,F	L	.333	6	2	0	0	0	1	2	1	.500	.333
Throws Left	R	.333	12	4	0	0	0	3	1	0	.467	.333
Graman,Alex	L	.571	7	4	2	0	0	3	0	1	.571	.857
Throws Left	R	.476	21	10	4	1	1	7	2	3	.500	.905
Graves,Danny	L	.267	116	31	6	1	5	20	7	17	.309	.466
Throws Right	R	.293	157	46	11	0	7	23	6	23	.323	.497
Gregg,Kevin	L	.260	173	45	10	3	2	20	13	49	.321	.384
Throws Right	R	.250	164	41	8	1	4	25	15	35	.306	.384
Greinke,Zack	L	.251	311	78	17	1	9	22	18	50	.295	.399
Throws Right	R	.262	248	65	14	0	17	39	8	50	.300	.524
Greisinger,S	L	.283	99	28	3	2	8	20	10	24	.354	.596
Throws Right	R	.351	114	40	7	1	4	17	5	12	.378	.535
Griffiths,J	L	.286	7	2	0	0	1	3	2	2	.444	.714
Throws Right	R	.200	10	2	0	0	0	0	1	3	.273	.200
Grilli,Jason	L	.292	96	28	4	1	7	24	16	16	.395	.573
Throws Right	R	.296	81	24	2	1	4	13	4	10	.345	.494
Grimsley,J	L	.314	102	32	4	0	2	18	17	8	.412	.412
Throws Right	R	.206	141	29	3	1	2	18	18	31	.307	.284
Groom,Buddy	L	.333	93	31	4	2	4	14	3	16	.361	.548
Throws Left	R	.290	124	36	4	0	2	16	13	16	.353	.371
Gryboski,K	L	.309	68	21	3	0	1	14	16	8	.440	.397
Throws Right	R	.264	125	33	2	1	1	20	7	16	.303	.320
Guardado,E	L	.109	46	5	1	0	1	5	0	14	.125	.196
Throws Left	R	.228	114	26	2	0	7	12	14	31	.313	.430
Guerrier,Matt	L	.298	47	14	2	0	4	13	4	8	.365	.596
Throws Right	R	.286	28	8	1	0	1	4	2	3	.333	.429
Guthrie,J	L	.160	25	4	1	0	0	1	4	5	.276	.200
Throws Right	R	.294	17	5	1	0	1	2	2	2	.400	.529
Halama,John	L	.266	139	37	8	2	2	16	6	29	.325	.396
Throws Left	R	.291	333	97	18	1	15	47	21	30	.338	.486
Halladay,Roy	L	.285	281	80	11	0	8	29	28	46	.348	.409
Throws Right	R	.258	233	60	6	0	5	30	11	49	.291	.348
Halsey,Brad	L	.143	28	4	3	0	0	5	2	8	.219	.250
Throws Left	R	.349	106	37	8	0	4	17	12	17	.417	.538
Hammond,Chris	L	.282	71	20	4	0	0	7	1	11	.292	.338
Throws Left	R	.275	131	36	11	0	4	19	12	23	.342	.450
Hampton,Mike	L	.253	146	37	4	0	3	15	9	15	.295	.342
Throws Left	R	.300	537	161	29	2	12	57	56	72	.366	.428

Pitcher	vs.	Avg.	AB	H	2B	3B	HR	RBI	BB	SO	OBP	Slg.
Hancock,Josh	L	.265	132	35	2	2	7	18	18	18	.351	.470
Throws Right	R	.299	127	38	8	0	10	20	10	18	.353	.598
Harang,Aaron	L	.262	267	70	19	2	10	26	27	55	.328	.461
Throws Right	R	.292	366	107	22	3	16	51	26	70	.344	.500
Harden,Rich	L	.254	382	97	17	4	8	40	50	92	.339	.382
Throws Right	R	.227	326	74	15	0	8	37	31	75	.296	.347
Haren,Danny	L	.190	79	15	3	1	1	4	10	15	.281	.291
Throws Right	R	.330	91	30	9	1	3	18	7	17	.382	.549
Harikkala,Tim	L	.243	103	25	5	1	7	21	15	13	.336	.515
Throws Right	R	.229	131	30	7	0	3	19	8	17	.277	.351
Harper,Travis	L	.233	116	27	6	0	4	21	16	23	.331	.388
Throws Right	R	.235	179	42	6	1	4	21	7	36	.283	.346
Harville,Chad	L	.259	85	22	6	1	3	23	11	17	.351	.459
Throws Right	R	.256	133	34	5	0	5	19	16	29	.340	.406
Hasegawa,S	L	.265	113	30	6	0	2	20	15	20	.344	.372
Throws Right	R	.255	145	37	14	2	3	18	16	26	.335	.441
Hawkins,L	L	.230	135	31	12	1	5	12	10	35	.291	.444
Throws Right	R	.236	174	41	6	0	5	18	4	34	.251	.356
Haynes,Jimmy	L	.238	21	5	0	0	2	9	4	2	.385	.524
Throws Right	R	.457	46	21	4	0	1	8	3	6	.500	.609
Heilman,Aaron	L	.232	56	13	3	1	2	7	5	9	.295	.429
Throws Right	R	.286	49	14	3	0	2	8	8	13	.386	.469
Hendrickson,B	L	.291	79	23	9	1	1	7	13	13	.404	.468
Throws Right	R	.324	108	35	6	0	5	21	7	16	.370	.519
Hendrickson,M	L	.249	169	42	6	0	5	27	5	19	.279	.373
Throws Left	R	.295	572	169	42	3	16	73	41	68	.345	.463
Hennessey,B	L	.297	74	22	8	0	2	15	7	9	.354	.486
Throws Right	R	.290	69	20	7	0	0	7	8	16	.364	.391
Hensley,Matt	L	.333	51	17	2	0	2	6	6	14	.404	.490
Throws Right	R	.259	58	15	3	0	3	7	1	16	.290	.466
Hentgen,Pat	L	.274	168	46	8	2	7	28	20	16	.345	.470
Throws Right	R	.293	150	44	6	1	9	29	22	17	.388	.527
Heredia,Felix	L	.216	74	16	5	0	3	16	11	15	.333	.405
Throws Left	R	.333	84	28	6	1	2	15	9	10	.394	.500
Herges,Matt	L	.366	112	41	5	3	3	23	13	15	.422	.545
Throws Right	R	.318	154	49	11	0	5	27	8	24	.361	.487
Hermanson,D	L	.285	239	68	19	1	10	33	28	43	.354	.498
Throws Right	R	.242	265	64	10	3	5	29	18	59	.294	.358
Hernandez,A	L	.333	27	9	1	0	0	3	4	4	.419	.370
Throws Right	R	.268	41	11	3	0	1	11	10	10	.404	.415
Hernandez,C	L	.324	37	12	2	0	4	9	5	7	.419	.703
Throws Left	R	.297	128	38	8	0	7	20	18	19	.392	.523
Hernandez,L	L	.258	450	116	21	3	16	49	50	82	.337	.424
Throws Right	R	.238	495	118	25	1	10	38	33	104	.292	.354
Hernandez,O	L	.255	188	48	7	0	6	17	21	36	.341	.388
Throws Right	R	.194	129	25	8	1	3	10	15	48	.283	.341
Hernandez,R	L	.278	90	25	3	1	3	15	16	19	.387	.433
Throws Right	R	.311	132	41	5	1	6	26	13	25	.374	.500
Hill,Shawn	L	.412	17	7	1	1	0	8	2	5	.476	.588
Throws Right	R	.417	24	10	3	0	1	6	5	5	.500	.667
Hitchcock,S	L	.300	10	3	1	0	1	2	4	1	.500	.700
Throws Left	R	.260	73	19	6	0	4	9	4	13	.299	.507
Hoffman,T	L	.255	106	27	10	1	3	7	6	28	.295	.453
Throws Right	R	.161	93	15	4	0	2	7	2	25	.179	.269
Horgan,Joe	L	.235	51	12	3	0	1	6	7	13	.361	.353
Throws Left	R	.228	101	23	8	0	4	13	15	17	.328	.426
Howard,Ben	L	.250	64	16	2	1	4	13	11	16	.360	.500
Throws Right	R	.269	78	21	5	0	2	11	10	17	.352	.410
Howry,Bob	L	.291	79	23	5	0	2	9	7	18	.360	.430
Throws Right	R	.169	83	14	2	0	3	5	5	21	.216	.301
Hudson,Luke	L	.160	81	13	2	0	2	10	20	16	.253	.259
Throws Right	R	.250	92	23	10	0	1	9	15	18	.360	.391

Pitcher	vs.	Avg.	AB	H	2B	3B	HR	RBI	BB	SO	OBP	Slg.
Hudson,Tim	L	.298	403	120	27	4	5	49	31	42	.354	.422
Throws Right	R	.229	323	74	13	0	3	30	13	61	.271	.297
Hughes,Travis	L	.250	4	1	0	0	0	0	1	3	.400	.250
Throws Right	R	.750	4	3	1	0	0	2	1	1	.800	1.000
Huisman,J	L	.372	43	16	4	0	1	5	5	5	.438	.535
Throws Right	R	.313	64	20	2	0	2	13	3	8	.353	.438
Ishii,K	L	.264	163	43	3	2	6	24	27	29	.376	.417
Throws Left	R	.240	467	112	26	5	15	63	71	70	.338	.413
Isringhausen,J	L	.205	122	25	7	1	2	14	9	35	.265	.328
Throws Right	R	.195	154	30	9	0	3	17	14	36	.265	.312
Jackson,Edwin	L	.308	52	16	2	0	3	6	7	4	.390	.519
Throws Right	R	.306	49	15	2	1	4	10	4	12	.358	.633
Jackson,Mike	L	.354	82	29	8	0	3	19	9	11	.419	.561
Throws Right	R	.248	105	26	7	0	4	19	6	15	.296	.429
Jarvis,Kevin	L	.407	27	11	5	0	4	11	8	2	.543	1.037
Throws Right	R	.366	41	15	4	1	1	2	1	5	.381	.585
Jennings,J	L	.340	391	133	27	8	15	66	70	50	.442	.565
Throws Right	R	.261	414	108	20	0	12	50	31	83	.319	.396
Jimenez,Jose	L	.343	70	24	6	0	4	18	8	9	.418	.600
Throws Right	R	.256	82	21	2	0	2	8	6	12	.330	.354
Johnson,Jason	L	.281	430	121	27	5	10	56	36	73	.333	.437
Throws Right	R	.286	353	101	14	2	12	47	24	52	.337	.439
Johnson,Randy	L	.163	147	24	5	1	2	9	7	46	.235	.252
Throws Left	R	.204	751	153	29	8	16	64	37	244	.243	.328
Johnston,Mike	L	.357	42	15	4	0	1	7	5	7	.438	.524
Throws Left	R	.280	50	14	3	1	1	10	10	11	.410	.440
Jones,B	L	.400	5	2	0	0	1	2	1	1	.500	1.000
Throws Left	R	.167	6	1	0	0	0	0	7	2	.615	.167
Jones,Todd	L	.250	132	33	5	0	3	13	17	24	.357	.356
Throws Right	R	.290	176	51	9	1	4	27	16	35	.342	.420
Julio,Jorge	L	.234	137	32	4	0	6	20	23	36	.346	.394
Throws Right	R	.221	122	27	4	0	5	16	16	34	.317	.377
Karsay,Steve	L	.154	13	2	0	0	1	2	1	2	.200	.385
Throws Right	R	.300	10	3	0	0	1	2	1	2	.333	.600
Kazmir,Scott	L	.400	25	10	1	0	0	3	6	7	.516	.440
Throws Left	R	.221	104	23	7	1	4	14	15	34	.331	.423
Kennedy,Joe	L	.184	141	26	1	1	4	13	13	31	.258	.291
Throws Left	R	.289	474	137	39	2	13	50	54	86	.366	.462
Kensing,Logan	L	.320	25	8	2	0	1	4	7	2	.455	.520
Throws Right	R	.367	30	11	2	0	4	10	2	5	.424	.833
Kershner,J	L	.368	38	14	1	0	1	7	1	4	.385	.474
Throws Left	R	.281	57	16	4	1	2	12	7	11	.359	.491
Kida,Masao	L	.292	24	7	1	1	0	2	4	5	.414	.417
Throws Right	R	.353	34	12	3	0	1	5	2	5	.405	.529
Kieschnick,B	L	.275	80	22	4	1	3	8	6	13	.326	.463
Throws Right	R	.250	88	22	5	0	3	17	7	15	.305	.409
Kim,B	L	.308	39	12	4	1	1	7	4	1	.383	.538
Throws Right	R	.185	27	5	2	0	0	1	3	5	.267	.259
Kim,Sun-Woo	L	.301	229	69	12	3	6	35	29	33	.388	.459
Throws Right	R	.255	298	76	14	1	11	39	26	54	.331	.419
King,Ray	L	.150	113	17	2	0	0	4	12	27	.236	.168
Throws Left	R	.248	105	26	6	1	1	11	12	13	.336	.352
Kinney,Matt	L	.413	155	64	13	2	5	30	14	23	.462	.619
Throws Right	R	.229	175	40	11	1	6	32	16	50	.299	.406
Kline,Steve	L	.143	84	12	1	0	1	8	10	21	.263	.190
Throws Left	R	.269	93	25	5	0	2	9	7	14	.320	.387
Knotts,Gary	L	.215	270	58	12	1	11	37	26	39	.284	.389
Throws Right	R	.322	261	84	15	2	9	38	32	42	.402	.498
Koch,Billy	L	.236	89	21	5	0	4	13	24	23	.400	.427
Throws Right	R	.245	98	24	5	0	2	14	12	27	.327	.357
Kolb,Dan	L	.256	90	23	1	1	0	5	9	6	.323	.289
Throws Right	R	.218	124	27	2	0	3	15	6	15	.269	.306

Pitcher	vs.	Avg.	AB	H	2B	3B	HR	RBI	BB	SO	OBP	Slg.
Koplove,Mike	L	.315	143	45	5	1	4	25	30	26	.440	.448
Throws Right	R	.232	177	41	6	1	3	15	7	29	.271	.328
Kroon,Marc	L	.333	12	4	1	0	0	4	5	2	.500	.417
Throws Right	R	.375	8	3	1	0	1	2	5	1	.615	.875
Lackey,John	L	.303	419	127	17	3	13	50	36	68	.362	.451
Throws Right	R	.248	355	88	23	3	9	45	24	76	.301	.406
Lawrence,B	L	.301	405	122	20	2	17	58	35	54	.357	.486
Throws Right	R	.272	382	104	30	2	9	38	20	67	.312	.432
League,B	L	.182	11	2	0	0	0	0	0	1	.182	.182
Throws Right	R	.167	6	1	0	0	0	0	1	1	.286	.167
Ledezma,W	L	.227	44	10	3	0	0	8	2	7	.286	.295
Throws Left	R	.285	158	45	6	0	3	20	16	22	.347	.380
Lee,Cliff	L	.231	143	33	8	1	2	15	19	31	.333	.343
Throws Left	R	.277	559	155	35	3	28	88	62	130	.354	.501
Lee,Dave	L	.250	8	2	0	0	0	1	3	2	.455	.250
Throws Right	R	.400	15	6	2	1	0	7	1	2	.438	.667
Lehr,Justin	L	.310	58	18	4	0	1	6	9	9	.403	.431
Throws Right	R	.254	67	17	4	0	2	14	5	7	.316	.403
Leicester,Jon	L	.373	51	19	0	0	4	9	11	12	.484	.608
Throws Right	R	.200	105	21	3	0	3	9	4	23	.225	.314
Leiter,Al	L	.204	137	28	6	1	2	10	20	25	.308	.307
Throws Left	R	.222	495	110	30	0	14	52	77	92	.338	.368
Leskanic,C	L	.268	82	22	2	1	4	15	11	17	.347	.463
Throws Right	R	.291	86	25	4	1	4	14	19	20	.425	.500
Levine,Al	L	.299	107	32	6	1	4	20	15	11	.387	.486
Throws Right	R	.293	174	51	7	1	6	27	9	21	.326	.448
Lewis,Colby	L	.267	30	8	1	0	0	1	5	5	.389	.300
Throws Right	R	.185	27	5	2	0	1	5	8	6	.371	.370
Lidge,Brad	L	.191	173	33	5	1	3	9	13	67	.263	.283
Throws Right	R	.155	155	24	1	3	5	14	17	90	.244	.297
Lidle,Cory	L	.278	345	96	19	1	15	53	32	47	.345	.470
Throws Right	R	.269	475	128	29	6	12	62	29	79	.317	.432
Lieber,Jon	L	.346	382	132	20	3	14	52	11	28	.361	.524
Throws Right	R	.250	336	84	15	0	6	35	7	74	.266	.348
Ligtenberg,K	L	.309	97	30	8	0	4	21	17	23	.422	.515
Throws Right	R	.316	136	43	8	0	2	21	8	26	.354	.419
Lilly,Ted	L	.196	148	29	6	0	4	14	26	31	.324	.318
Throws Left	R	.238	596	142	30	4	22	69	63	137	.314	.413
Lima,Jose	L	.278	324	90	16	1	16	36	24	36	.329	.481
Throws Right	R	.264	333	88	12	1	17	38	10	57	.286	.459
Lincoln,Mike	L	.130	23	3	1	0	0	2	1	6	.167	.174
Throws Right	R	.184	38	7	2	0	1	5	5	8	.283	.316
Linebrink,S	L	.178	135	24	5	0	3	15	19	36	.278	.281
Throws Right	R	.236	157	37	10	0	5	17	7	47	.277	.395
Liriano,Pedro	L	.276	29	8	2	0	1	5	1	2	.300	.448
Throws Right	R	.206	34	7	2	1	2	5	2	8	.270	.500
Loaiza,E	L	.298	409	122	20	5	15	54	51	69	.376	.482
Throws Right	R	.293	324	95	17	0	17	58	20	48	.330	.503
Loe,Kameron	L	.250	12	3	0	1	0	2	4	1	.438	.417
Throws Right	R	.300	10	3	1	0	0	0	2	2	.462	.400
Lohse,Kyle	L	.290	448	130	30	0	17	65	54	73	.367	.471
Throws Right	R	.324	339	110	16	1	11	45	22	38	.370	.475
Looper,Braden	L	.311	151	47	7	0	3	20	9	22	.352	.417
Throws Right	R	.227	172	39	3	0	2	12	7	38	.264	.279
Lopez,A	L	.382	34	13	4	0	4	10	8	6	.512	.853
Throws Right	R	.178	45	8	3	0	1	3	5	7	.269	.311
Lopez,Javier	L	.221	77	17	4	0	0	9	14	9	.355	.273
Throws Left	R	.350	80	28	3	2	1	14	12	11	.441	.475
Lopez,Rodrigo	L	.258	337	87	15	2	7	25	39	48	.333	.377
Throws Right	R	.245	314	77	7	1	14	36	15	73	.284	.408
Lowe,Derek	L	.305	413	126	24	1	7	61	40	53	.371	.419
Throws Right	R	.293	335	98	17	3	8	53	31	52	.357	.433
Lowry,Noah	L	.338	71	24	4	1	3	14	5	12	.382	.549
Throws Left	R	.238	281	67	16	2	7	25	23	60	.295	.384
MacDougal,M	L	.304	23	7	2	1	1	4	6	7	.448	.609
Throws Right	R	.321	28	9	2	0	1	4	3	7	.406	.500
Maddux,Greg	L	.271	362	98	13	2	22	52	20	68	.316	.500
Throws Right	R	.268	447	120	17	2	13	41	13	83	.291	.403
Madritsch,B	L	.220	91	20	3	1	1	10	13	23	.317	.308
Throws Left	R	.237	228	54	13	1	2	17	20	37	.310	.329
Madson,Ryan	L	.252	123	31	5	1	1	8	12	24	.321	.333
Throws Right	R	.227	163	37	3	0	5	15	7	31	.276	.337
Mahay,Ron	L	.227	110	25	3	0	2	13	10	25	.303	.309
Throws Left	R	.241	145	35	5	1	3	22	19	29	.329	.352
Maine,John	L	.444	9	4	0	0	1	3	2	1	.545	.778
Throws Right	R	.429	7	3	1	0	0	0	1	0	.500	.571
Majewski,Gary	L	.419	31	13	4	0	1	5	1	5	.455	.645
Throws Right	R	.273	55	15	0	0	1	8	4	7	.328	.327
Malaska,Mark	L	.188	32	6	1	0	0	2	4	7	.297	.219
Throws Left	R	.319	47	15	4	2	2	15	8	5	.418	.617
Mantei,Matt	L	.263	19	5	0	0	3	8	5	5	.400	.789
Throws Right	R	.414	29	12	2	0	2	8	1	8	.433	.690
Manzanillo,J	L	.340	53	18	3	0	3	8	11	9	.453	.566
Throws Right	R	.260	77	20	3	1	3	11	4	18	.318	.442
Maroth,Mike	L	.267	195	52	9	2	4	13	15	41	.319	.395
Throws Left	R	.294	652	192	33	5	21	79	44	67	.344	.457
Marquis,Jason	L	.278	363	101	16	3	14	44	38	66	.346	.455
Throws Right	R	.271	420	114	20	1	12	38	32	72	.334	.410
Marsonek,Sam	L	.000	2	0	0	0	0	0	0	0	.000	.000
Throws Right	R	.500	4	2	1	0	0	0	0	0	.500	.750
Marte,Damaso	L	.143	98	14	1	0	2	10	13	29	.259	.214
Throws Left	R	.263	160	42	5	0	8	20	21	39	.341	.444
Martin,Tom	L	.310	100	31	6	1	3	20	10	22	.377	.480
Throws Left	R	.247	73	18	3	0	4	13	9	8	.329	.452
Martinez,A	L	.211	19	4	1	0	0	3	3	2	.318	.263
Throws Right	R	.346	26	9	2	0	2	8	3	3	.433	.654
Martinez,P	L	.236	449	106	21	3	15	43	34	128	.302	.396
Throws Right	R	.240	363	87	16	5	11	47	27	99	.299	.402
Mateo,Julio	L	.275	80	22	5	0	7	13	12	17	.362	.600
Throws Right	R	.238	143	34	10	0	4	27	4	26	.279	.392
Matthews,Mike	L	.282	39	11	1	0	3	8	6	7	.391	.538
Throws Left	R	.256	78	20	6	1	4	16	10	8	.344	.513
Maurer,Dave	L	.333	3	1	0	0	1	4	2	1	.600	1.333
Throws Left	R	.714	7	5	2	0	0	2	3	0	.800	1.000
May,Darrell	L	.296	186	55	14	2	7	28	7	37	.320	.505
Throws Left	R	.310	578	179	44	7	31	94	48	83	.360	.571
McConnell,Sam	L	.435	23	10	1	0	0	3	1	3	.458	.478
Throws Left	R	.067	15	1	1	0	0	1	3	1	.263	.133
McLeary,Marty	L	.286	7	2	0	1	1	3	0	2	.286	1.000
Throws Right	R	.556	9	5	1	0	1	3	2	2	.583	1.000
Meadows,Brian	L	.226	93	21	5	0	3	16	7	18	.272	.376
Throws Right	R	.275	200	55	11	1	4	25	12	28	.313	.400
Meche,Gil	L	.269	297	80	19	1	14	42	30	59	.336	.481
Throws Right	R	.278	212	59	19	1	7	26	17	40	.342	.476
Mecir,Jim	L	.236	89	21	1	2	3	11	11	24	.340	.393
Throws Right	R	.242	99	24	2	0	2	8	8	25	.306	.323
Mendoza,R	L	.216	51	11	1	0	1	5	5	6	.286	.294
Throws Right	R	.233	60	14	2	0	2	6	2	7	.270	.367
Mercker,Kent	L	.240	96	23	4	1	3	11	9	26	.312	.396
Throws Left	R	.170	94	16	3	0	1	9	18	25	.307	.234
Mesa,Jose	L	.331	127	42	6	1	4	11	11	18	.381	.488
Throws Right	R	.255	141	36	9	0	2	15	9	19	.303	.362
Meyer,Dan	L	.500	2	1	1	0	0	0	0	0	.500	1.000
Throws Left	R	.200	5	1	0	0	0	0	1	1	.333	.200

Pitcher	vs.	Avg.	AB	H	2B	3B	HR	RBI	BB	SO	OBP	Slg.
Miceli,Dan	L	.307	150	46	6	1	7	22	12	37	.360	.500
Throws Right	R	.188	149	28	4	1	3	14	15	46	.263	.289
Miller,Justin	L	.367	166	61	12	2	10	34	24	15	.447	.645
Throws Right	R	.260	154	40	11	1	4	25	18	32	.341	.422
Miller,Matt	L	.255	55	14	2	2	1	9	14	12	.431	.418
Throws Right	R	.201	139	28	7	1	0	12	9	43	.263	.266
Miller,Trever	L	.214	98	21	6	0	2	17	7	29	.280	.337
Throws Left	R	.303	89	27	5	2	1	14	8	14	.367	.438
Miller,Wade	L	.212	151	32	7	1	3	10	24	33	.318	.331
Throws Right	R	.242	182	44	6	1	8	16	20	41	.317	.418
Millwood,K	L	.309	269	83	24	1	6	38	29	68	.381	.472
Throws Right	R	.250	288	72	17	1	8	35	22	57	.311	.399
Milton,Eric	L	.252	119	30	10	2	6	16	15	23	.338	.521
Throws Left	R	.256	649	166	36	2	37	84	60	138	.317	.488
Mitre,Sergio	L	.408	98	40	6	1	4	16	10	13	.468	.612
Throws Right	R	.261	119	31	9	0	2	14	10	24	.333	.387
Moreno,Orber	L	.200	55	11	2	0	0	3	7	13	.290	.236
Throws Right	R	.237	76	18	1	0	0	11	4	16	.301	.250
Morris,Matt	L	.259	347	90	14	1	18	60	29	58	.317	.461
Throws Right	R	.272	423	115	24	1	17	52	27	73	.321	.454
Moss,Damian	L	.111	9	1	0	0	0	2	4	1	.429	.111
Throws Left	R	.429	28	12	2	0	2	12	1	5	.448	.714
Mota,G	L	.196	153	30	3	2	3	13	18	34	.282	.301
Throws Right	R	.236	191	45	5	0	5	21	19	51	.313	.340
Moyer,Jamie	L	.293	229	67	8	0	9	30	19	43	.370	.445
Throws Left	R	.263	570	150	25	1	35	90	44	82	.315	.495
Mulder,Mark	L	.269	167	45	7	0	3	21	19	25	.347	.365
Throws Left	R	.263	677	178	41	3	22	87	64	115	.334	.430
Mulholland,T	L	.284	141	40	3	0	5	21	12	20	.340	.411
Throws Left	R	.344	358	123	19	2	12	42	21	40	.383	.508
Munoz,Arnie	L	.320	25	8	1	0	0	2	5	6	.452	.360
Throws Left	R	.353	34	12	5	1	4	16	7	5	.442	.912
Munro,Pete	L	.337	184	62	18	2	8	24	16	21	.393	.587
Throws Right	R	.272	213	58	10	3	4	23	10	42	.325	.404
Mussina,Mike	L	.254	338	86	18	3	8	33	23	93	.303	.396
Throws Right	R	.299	308	92	15	1	14	46	17	39	.334	.490
Myers,Brett	L	.278	338	94	21	0	12	42	34	56	.342	.447
Throws Right	R	.283	360	102	28	2	19	63	28	60	.344	.531
Myers,Mike	L	.233	103	24	5	0	2	13	12	24	.325	.340
Throws Left	R	.344	61	21	5	0	3	14	11	8	.438	.574
Myers,Rodney	L	.000	2	0	0	0	0	0	0	1	.000	.000
Throws Right	R	.250	4	1	0	0	0	0	0	0	.250	.250
Myette,Aaron	L	.286	7	2	1	0	0	0	5	2	.615	.429
Throws Right	R	.111	9	1	1	0	0	2	3	4	.385	.222
Nageotte,C	L	.307	75	23	1	0	0	11	16	11	.435	.320
Throws Right	R	.342	73	25	3	0	3	15	11	13	.438	.507
Nakamura,Mike	L	.233	43	10	2	0	4	11	3	8	.306	.558
Throws Right	R	.283	60	17	4	2	3	8	4	16	.328	.567
Nance,Shane	L	.419	31	13	2	0	1	5	3	5	.471	.581
Throws Left	R	.261	23	6	3	0	1	4	9	4	.514	.522
Narron,Sam	L	.375	8	3	1	0	1	2	0	0	.375	.875
Throws Left	R	.400	5	2	0	0	2	2	4	1	.667	1.600
Nathan,Joe	L	.212	132	28	5	0	2	10	13	42	.293	.295
Throws Right	R	.160	125	20	4	0	1	4	10	47	.222	.216
Neal,Blaine	L	.250	68	17	3	0	2	11	7	12	.333	.382
Throws Right	R	.327	98	32	7	1	4	15	4	24	.350	.541
Nelson,Jeff	L	.167	24	4	0	0	1	3	8	4	.375	.292
Throws Right	R	.224	58	13	1	0	2	7	11	18	.343	.345
Nelson,Joe	L	.500	2	1	0	0	0	0	2	0	.833	.500
Throws Right	R	.333	9	3	1	0	0	1	1	5	.400	.444
Neu,Mike	L	.300	10	3	1	0	0	0	2	1	.417	.400
Throws Right	R	.333	6	2	0	1	1	2	0	1	.333	1.167
Nitkowski,C	L	.266	64	17	4	0	1	13	7	16	.373	.375
Throws Left	R	.324	71	23	7	0	3	16	9	10	.405	.549
Nomo,Hideo	L	.338	139	47	8	0	7	26	26	18	.449	.547
Throws Right	R	.293	198	58	14	0	12	43	16	36	.347	.545
Norton,Phil	L	.273	99	27	9	1	0	12	16	21	.373	.384
Throws Left	R	.291	151	44	7	1	5	26	22	27	.385	.450
Novoa,Roberto	L	.333	33	11	2	0	4	10	3	4	.368	.758
Throws Right	R	.292	48	14	2	0	0	8	3	11	.345	.333
Nunez,F	L	.316	19	6	1	0	0	4	3	5	.458	.368
Throws Right	R	.227	22	5	0	1	1	5	4	9	.345	.455
Nunez,V	L	.281	32	9	1	0	3	10	7	9	.390	.594
Throws Right	R	.279	61	17	3	1	3	15	7	13	.347	.508
Obermueller,W	L	.284	218	62	15	4	6	24	25	26	.354	.472
Throws Right	R	.296	257	76	18	2	9	40	17	33	.344	.486
Ohka,Tomo	L	.278	162	45	5	2	5	11	12	19	.328	.426
Throws Right	R	.298	178	53	15	0	6	26	8	19	.328	.483
Oliver,Darren	L	.321	78	25	3	2	5	11	7	11	.368	.603
Throws Left	R	.300	207	62	14	1	9	35	14	35	.345	.507
Oropesa,Eddie	L	.235	17	4	1	0	1	2	6	3	.435	.471
Throws Left	R	.133	15	2	0	1	0	3	7	3	.409	.267
Ortiz,Ramon	L	.305	259	79	16	0	15	39	23	34	.364	.541
Throws Right	R	.253	237	60	17	1	3	22	15	48	.302	.371
Ortiz,Russ	L	.254	382	97	15	1	11	42	60	67	.357	.385
Throws Right	R	.262	382	100	22	0	12	42	52	76	.347	.414
Osborne,D	L	.500	24	12	4	0	1	7	3	3	.571	.792
Throws Left	R	.271	48	13	2	0	2	10	2	7	.314	.438
Osuna,Antonio	L	.215	65	14	4	0	1	6	7	20	.288	.323
Throws Right	R	.247	73	18	5	0	2	12	4	16	.295	.397
Oswalt,Roy	L	.257	460	118	29	1	7	44	39	110	.319	.370
Throws Right	R	.264	435	115	28	1	10	49	23	96	.310	.402
Otsuka,A	L	.214	140	30	5	2	1	9	17	40	.299	.300
Throws Right	R	.183	142	26	3	0	5	12	9	47	.232	.310
Padilla,Juan	L	.333	51	17	4	1	2	9	4	6	.382	.569
Throws Right	R	.373	59	22	5	0	5	13	8	11	.456	.712
Padilla,V	L	.289	242	70	15	3	10	34	27	39	.366	.500
Throws Right	R	.241	203	49	12	2	6	27	9	43	.291	.409
Park,Chan Ho	L	.277	184	51	10	2	11	27	21	27	.360	.533
Throws Right	R	.284	190	54	5	0	11	29	12	36	.352	.484
Parra,Jose	L	.200	25	5	1	0	1	3	1	8	.231	.360
Throws Right	R	.300	30	9	1	0	1	1	5	6	.400	.433
Parrish,John	L	.243	103	25	5	2	3	20	21	24	.375	.417
Throws Left	R	.235	183	43	7	0	1	22	34	47	.351	.290
Patterson,D	L	.284	67	19	4	0	2	9	9	9	.385	.433
Throws Right	R	.281	89	25	3	0	5	15	7	15	.354	.483
Patterson,J	L	.228	162	37	6	1	2	13	26	38	.344	.315
Throws Right	R	.283	223	63	14	1	16	38	20	61	.353	.570
Pavano,Carl	L	.267	393	105	23	2	11	40	28	62	.322	.420
Throws Right	R	.240	445	107	23	3	5	32	21	77	.283	.339
Pearce,Josh	L	.500	2	1	0	0	0	0	0	0	.500	.500
Throws Right	R	.333	6	2	1	0	0	1	0	0	.333	.500
Peavy,Jake	L	.234	312	73	16	3	7	25	31	85	.318	.372
Throws Right	R	.238	307	73	11	2	6	23	22	88	.290	.345
Penny,Brad	L	.242	273	66	14	1	7	19	30	63	.317	.377
Throws Right	R	.243	263	64	19	2	5	29	15	48	.288	.388
Percival,Troy	L	.218	101	22	3	0	5	13	15	19	.331	.396
Throws Right	R	.244	86	21	1	1	2	10	4	14	.278	.349
Perez,Odalis	L	.277	173	48	8	2	8	23	9	41	.321	.486
Throws Left	R	.241	548	132	27	3	18	49	35	87	.286	.400
Perez,Oliver	L	.220	132	29	7	0	3	10	6	59	.259	.341
Throws Left	R	.204	569	116	20	7	19	56	75	180	.303	.364
Perisho,Matt	L	.207	87	18	3	0	4	12	13	28	.317	.379
Throws Left	R	.284	95	27	6	0	2	15	13	14	.373	.411

Pitcher	vs.	Avg.	AB	H	2B	3B	HR	RBI	BB	SO	OBP	Slg.
Peterson,Adam	L	.417	12	5	1	0	1	5	1	2	.462	.750
Throws Right	R	.667	3	2	1	0	0	1	2	0	.800	1.000
Pettitte,Andy	L	.290	69	20	6	0	3	8	4	17	.329	.507
Throws Left	R	.208	245	51	15	0	5	27	27	62	.287	.331
Phelps,Tommy	L	.263	38	10	2	3	2	7	5	8	.349	.632
Throws Left	R	.270	89	24	2	0	4	14	7	20	.316	.427
Phelps,Travis	L	.333	12	4	0	0	2	4	2	2	.429	.833
Throws Right	R	.250	16	4	1	0	0	1	1	1	.294	.313
Pineiro,Joel	L	.209	258	54	9	0	7	28	25	65	.277	.326
Throws Right	R	.316	285	90	20	2	14	45	18	46	.361	.547
Politte,Cliff	L	.351	74	26	4	1	4	15	12	14	.442	.595
Throws Right	R	.208	125	26	5	1	2	15	10	34	.273	.312
Ponson,Sidney	L	.321	455	146	26	3	12	70	50	49	.391	.470
Throws Right	R	.288	413	119	20	2	11	50	19	66	.326	.426
Pote,Lou	L	.333	6	2	1	0	0	3	1	3	.429	.500
Throws Right	R	.167	6	1	0	0	0	0	0	2	.167	.167
Powell,Brian	L	.323	62	20	4	2	2	12	11	8	.410	.548
Throws Right	R	.238	80	19	6	1	3	16	5	16	.279	.450
Powell,Jay	L	.226	31	7	2	1	1	6	6	7	.351	.452
Throws Right	R	.288	59	17	2	0	2	6	5	10	.338	.424
Pratt,Andy	L	.000	2	0	0	0	0	0	2	1	.500	.000
Throws Left	R	.000	3	0	0	0	0	0	5	0	.667	.000
Prinz,Bret	L	.150	40	6	0	1	3	7	11	12	.333	.425
Throws Right	R	.324	68	22	6	0	2	15	3	10	.356	.500
Prior,Mark	L	.258	194	50	18	0	7	15	24	54	.336	.459
Throws Right	R	.245	253	62	11	2	7	30	24	85	.316	.387
Proctor,Scott	L	.255	51	13	1	0	1	6	8	12	.350	.333
Throws Right	R	.314	51	16	5	0	4	16	6	9	.379	.647
Puffer,B	L	.242	33	8	0	0	2	4	8	6	.390	.424
Throws Right	R	.381	42	16	5	0	1	9	3	6	.435	.571
Pulido,Carlos	L	.238	21	5	1	0	1	6	0	4	.261	.429
Throws Left	R	.407	27	11	4	0	1	9	4	5	.469	.667
Putz,J.J.	L	.234	111	26	4	0	8	19	11	24	.315	.486
Throws Right	R	.308	130	40	8	1	2	25	13	23	.378	.431
Qualls,Chad	L	.264	53	14	3	0	2	7	5	13	.339	.434
Throws Right	R	.267	75	20	4	0	1	6	3	11	.317	.360
Quantrill,P	L	.292	185	54	12	1	4	28	14	16	.345	.432
Throws Right	R	.337	208	70	11	1	1	29	6	21	.358	.413
Radke,Brad	L	.254	468	119	14	2	15	47	19	67	.287	.389
Throws Right	R	.281	391	110	18	2	8	35	7	76	.296	.399
Rakers,Aaron	L	.250	8	2	0	0	0	0	0	2	.250	.250
Throws Right	R	.300	10	3	0	0	0	2	1	1	.364	.300
Ramirez,E	L	.241	29	7	2	0	1	2	2	5	.290	.414
Throws Right	R	.323	31	10	5	0	2	5	3	4	.389	.677
Ramirez,E	L	.290	62	18	2	1	2	13	4	8	.353	.452
Throws Left	R	.219	73	16	2	0	3	11	3	13	.256	.370
Ramirez,H	L	.220	50	11	2	0	2	5	7	6	.310	.380
Throws Left	R	.227	176	40	7	2	5	16	23	25	.317	.375
Randolph,S	L	.243	103	25	4	1	2	16	16	30	.339	.359
Throws Left	R	.232	207	48	10	0	9	40	60	32	.404	.411
Rauch,Jon	L	.321	53	17	6	1	0	6	8	6	.410	.472
Throws Right	R	.203	64	13	2	0	1	3	3	16	.235	.281
Redding,Tim	L	.345	171	59	11	1	8	38	28	21	.433	.561
Throws Right	R	.283	233	66	14	0	7	24	15	35	.337	.433
Redman,Mark	L	.286	175	50	13	1	6	21	16	30	.351	.474
Throws Left	R	.294	571	168	38	2	22	79	52	72	.354	.483
Reed,Steve	L	.282	103	29	5	0	2	11	13	19	.378	.388
Throws Right	R	.281	153	43	8	0	5	22	4	19	.315	.431
Regilio,Nick	L	.270	37	10	2	0	2	9	10	3	.438	.486
Throws Right	R	.286	35	10	2	0	1	7	5	9	.381	.429
Reith,Brian	L	.382	34	13	3	0	3	7	8	3	.512	.735
Throws Right	R	.243	70	17	5	2	2	12	11	21	.361	.457

Pitcher	vs.	Avg.	AB	H	2B	3B	HR	RBI	BB	SO	OBP	Slg.
Reitsma,Chris	L	.310	145	45	6	0	4	19	10	24	.356	.434
Throws Right	R	.262	168	44	9	0	5	15	10	36	.302	.405
Remlinger,M	L	.303	66	20	2	1	3	18	6	12	.351	.500
Throws Left	R	.191	68	13	1	0	0	8	10	23	.296	.206
Reyes,Al	L	.105	19	2	1	0	0	0	0	6	.105	.158
Throws Right	R	.056	18	1	0	0	0	3	2	5	.150	.056
Reyes,Dennys	L	.316	133	42	5	1	4	20	12	33	.376	.459
Throws Left	R	.254	284	72	18	2	8	36	38	58	.343	.415
Reynolds,S	L	.333	3	1	1	0	0	2	2	0	.600	.667
Throws Right	R	.556	9	5	5	0	0	4	0	0	.556	1.111
Rhodes,Arthur	L	.314	51	16	3	0	2	10	7	11	.397	.490
Throws Left	R	.283	106	30	7	0	7	15	14	23	.364	.547
Riedling,John	L	.291	117	34	7	2	6	22	18	16	.382	.538
Throws Right	R	.283	198	56	16	0	4	38	22	30	.363	.424
Riley,Matt	L	.318	44	14	1	0	3	12	11	11	.455	.545
Throws Left	R	.228	202	46	6	0	8	22	33	49	.339	.376
Rincon,Juan	L	.148	122	18	2	0	3	13	14	54	.239	.238
Throws Right	R	.206	165	34	5	1	2	20	18	52	.285	.285
Rincon,R	L	.200	90	18	4	0	1	10	5	24	.250	.278
Throws Left	R	.314	86	27	4	0	2	14	17	16	.423	.430
Riske,David	L	.224	143	32	9	0	7	24	24	41	.335	.434
Throws Right	R	.255	145	37	8	0	4	17	17	37	.337	.393
Ritchie,Todd	L	.235	17	4	0	0	1	2	5	2	.435	.412
Throws Right	R	.444	18	8	0	1	3	4	1	2	.474	1.056
Rivera,M	L	.234	154	36	2	0	2	8	12	40	.289	.286
Throws Right	R	.215	135	29	5	0	1	13	8	26	.284	.274
Roa,Joe	L	.342	120	41	7	3	4	12	16	21	.423	.550
Throws Right	R	.264	163	43	8	0	5	32	8	26	.311	.405
Robbins,Jake	L	.500	4	2	0	0	1	2	0	0	.500	1.250
Throws Right	R	.250	4	1	0	0	0	0	0	0	.250	.250
Roberts,Grant	L	.636	11	7	2	0	2	9	2	0	.692	1.364
Throws Right	R	.200	10	2	0	0	0	1	4	1	.400	.200
Roberts,W	L	.385	13	5	1	0	0	3	7	3	.600	.462
Throws Right	R	.233	30	7	2	0	0	7	2	4	.306	.300
Robertson,J	L	.571	21	12	1	1	2	10	2	1	.609	1.000
Throws Left	R	.238	42	10	2	0	3	9	7	5	.365	.500
Robertson,N	L	.252	143	36	2	1	2	21	7	35	.291	.322
Throws Left	R	.279	623	174	33	2	28	87	59	120	.343	.474
Rodriguez,E	L	.194	67	13	4	0	1	10	15	17	.349	.299
Throws Right	R	.258	89	23	7	0	4	14	15	20	.385	.472
Rodriguez,F	L	.192	99	19	1	1	1	6	17	34	.310	.253
Throws Right	R	.278	151	42	13	0	7	22	12	25	.349	.503
Rodriguez,F	L	.213	155	33	5	0	1	12	19	55	.301	.265
Throws Right	R	.127	142	18	5	0	1	12	14	68	.205	.183
Rodriguez,R	L	.235	51	12	3	1	0	4	8	8	.339	.333
Throws Right	R	.286	56	16	4	0	1	5	4	7	.333	.411
Rogers,Kenny	L	.294	194	57	10	1	3	15	19	47	.372	.402
Throws Left	R	.292	654	191	49	7	21	96	47	79	.341	.485
Romero,J.C.	L	.261	111	29	1	0	3	15	11	26	.344	.351
Throws Left	R	.199	161	32	9	0	1	25	27	43	.319	.273
Rueter,Kirk	L	.277	188	52	11	0	4	22	11	17	.318	.399
Throws Left	R	.302	572	173	41	6	17	77	55	39	.362	.484
Rusch,Glendon	L	.225	120	27	2	1	1	12	10	25	.288	.283
Throws Left	R	.265	377	100	24	2	9	42	23	65	.312	.411
Ryan,B.J.	L	.094	106	10	1	0	2	7	8	46	.165	.160
Throws Left	R	.252	214	54	8	1	2	24	27	76	.333	.327
Saarloos,Kirk	L	.294	51	15	6	0	2	5	10	7	.410	.529
Throws Right	R	.273	44	12	0	0	2	8	2	3	.327	.409
Sabathia,C.C.	L	.265	151	40	11	0	7	22	13	24	.324	.477
Throws Left	R	.248	548	136	33	4	13	63	59	115	.326	.394
Saenz,Chris	L	.200	5	1	0	0	0	0	1	0	.333	.200
Throws Right	R	.067	15	1	0	0	0	0	2	7	.222	.067

Pitcher	vs.	Avg.	AB	H	2B	3B	HR	RBI	BB	SO	OBP	Slg.
Sanchez,D	L	.276	123	34	8	0	4	13	10	11	.336	.439
Throws Right	R	.260	181	47	5	0	5	23	17	33	.335	.370
Sanchez,Jesus	L	.200	15	3	0	0	1	1	1	1	.250	.400
Throws Left	R	.341	44	15	4	0	3	11	8	7	.442	.636
Santana,Johan	L	.196	194	38	6	1	5	16	10	52	.238	.314
Throws Left	R	.191	618	118	16	2	19	39	44	213	.253	.316
Santos,Victor	L	.244	250	61	11	3	6	34	31	42	.328	.384
Throws Right	R	.303	357	108	24	0	12	48	26	73	.355	.471
Schilling,C	L	.238	462	110	30	2	6	39	18	105	.267	.351
Throws Right	R	.241	399	96	24	0	17	40	17	98	.276	.429
Schmidt,Jason	L	.191	398	76	13	5	6	35	44	116	.271	.294
Throws Right	R	.212	419	89	18	2	12	43	33	135	.273	.351
Schoeneweis,S	L	.244	86	21	3	0	0	7	7	19	.305	.279
Throws Left	R	.303	357	108	21	1	17	60	42	50	.378	.510
Seanez,Rudy	L	.256	82	21	5	3	0	10	13	22	.354	.390
Throws Right	R	.202	89	18	5	0	3	19	6	24	.247	.360
Seay,Bobby	L	.200	35	7	3	1	0	7	2	5	.282	.343
Throws Left	R	.264	53	14	2	0	2	8	3	12	.304	.415
Seibel,Phil	L	.000	6	0	0	0	0	0	0	1	.143	.000
Throws Left	R	.000	6	0	0	0	0	1	5	0	.455	.000
Sele,Aaron	L	.296	267	79	12	1	6	32	31	29	.368	.416
Throws Right	R	.324	259	84	12	2	10	47	20	22	.374	.502
Seo,Jae Weong	L	.273	209	57	11	2	7	24	26	29	.354	.445
Throws Right	R	.322	236	76	20	1	10	29	24	25	.384	.542
Serrano,Jimmy	L	.359	64	23	5	1	2	8	8	9	.432	.563
Throws Right	R	.197	61	12	3	0	3	9	4	16	.239	.393
Service,Scott	L	.211	38	8	2	1	0	7	6	7	.318	.316
Throws Right	R	.348	46	16	3	0	5	16	4	10	.415	.739
Sheets,Ben	L	.232	427	99	21	3	15	39	17	131	.266	.400
Throws Right	R	.220	464	102	36	1	10	41	15	133	.244	.366
Sherrill,G	L	.239	46	11	3	0	2	11	0	11	.250	.435
Throws Left	R	.277	47	13	2	0	1	6	9	5	.393	.383
Shields,Scot	L	.235	200	47	5	0	1	19	30	52	.335	.275
Throws Right	R	.242	207	50	10	2	5	25	10	57	.283	.382
Shouse,Brian	L	.188	96	18	6	0	2	11	7	25	.245	.313
Throws Left	R	.277	65	18	5	1	1	4	11	9	.382	.431
Silva,Carlos	L	.328	442	145	27	3	15	52	23	38	.365	.505
Throws Right	R	.289	381	110	21	1	8	34	12	38	.314	.412
Simontacchi,J	L	.250	20	5	1	0	0	1	2	1	.318	.300
Throws Right	R	.333	36	12	1	0	5	14	5	2	.419	.778
Simpson,Allan	L	.315	54	17	4	1	2	10	11	11	.418	.537
Throws Right	R	.276	98	27	10	0	2	19	9	35	.354	.439
Small,Aaron	L	.333	30	10	1	0	1	4	6	5	.444	.467
Throws Right	R	.350	40	14	4	0	4	16	1	3	.366	.750
Smith,Travis	L	.221	77	17	3	0	3	8	4	18	.268	.377
Throws Right	R	.356	87	31	5	0	9	22	8	8	.411	.724
Smoltz,John	L	.255	145	37	4	0	5	20	5	40	.280	.386
Throws Right	R	.236	161	38	6	1	3	7	8	45	.272	.342
Snare,Ryan	L	.286	7	2	0	0	1	2	1	0	.375	.714
Throws Left	R	.375	8	3	1	0	2	3	1	0	.444	1.250
Snell,Ian	L	.333	15	5	1	1	1	3	5	4	.500	.733
Throws Right	R	.281	32	9	1	0	1	6	4	5	.361	.406
Soriano,R	L	.429	7	3	1	0	0	1	0	0	.429	.571
Throws Right	R	.462	13	6	3	0	0	1	3	3	.563	.692
Sosa,Jorge	L	.283	191	54	10	1	14	43	26	36	.368	.565
Throws Right	R	.236	195	46	10	1	3	15	28	58	.329	.344
Sparks,Steve	L	.348	210	73	14	2	6	37	24	22	.413	.519
Throws Right	R	.241	274	66	15	2	12	38	21	35	.301	.442
Speier,Justin	L	.258	132	34	6	1	7	22	14	26	.342	.477
Throws Right	R	.220	123	27	3	0	1	13	11	26	.288	.268
Springer,Russ	L	.240	25	6	2	1	0	2	4	6	.355	.400
Throws Right	R	.310	29	9	0	1	1	6	2	3	.355	.483
Standridge,J	L	.318	22	7	0	0	4	7	3	6	.400	.864
Throws Right	R	.333	21	7	3	0	1	4	1	1	.348	.619
Stanford,J	L	.125	8	1	0	0	0	1	1	2	.300	.125
Throws Left	R	.314	35	11	2	0	0	0	4	3	.385	.371
Stanton,Mike	L	.269	108	29	5	0	4	18	18	28	.373	.426
Throws Left	R	.219	187	41	5	2	2	22	15	30	.283	.299
Stark,Denny	L	.468	62	29	7	0	6	19	11	2	.541	.871
Throws Right	R	.387	62	24	3	1	3	19	7	8	.431	.613
Stewart,Josh	L	.273	11	3	0	0	0	1	1	3	.333	.273
Throws Left	R	.520	25	13	5	1	3	12	2	2	.517	1.160
Stewart,Scott	L	.411	56	23	7	0	0	14	4	17	.435	.536
Throws Left	R	.345	58	20	3	1	5	20	8	9	.418	.690
Stone,Ricky	L	.333	90	30	6	2	6	24	12	17	.417	.644
Throws Right	R	.288	125	36	6	1	5	16	4	21	.333	.472
Sturtze,T	L	.261	153	40	13	0	6	24	21	22	.352	.464
Throws Right	R	.246	142	35	10	2	3	20	12	34	.327	.408
Sullivan,S	L	.359	92	33	9	2	6	18	17	14	.469	.696
Throws Right	R	.276	145	40	6	0	2	27	7	31	.321	.359
Suppan,Jeff	L	.272	309	84	16	1	13	40	34	48	.347	.456
Throws Right	R	.260	416	108	25	0	12	45	31	62	.317	.406
Sweeney,Brian	L	.188	32	6	2	0	1	2	1	6	.212	.344
Throws Right	R	.483	29	14	4	1	0	7	1	4	.500	.690
Szuminski,J	L	.059	17	1	0	0	0	3	8	4	.385	.059
Throws Right	R	.440	25	11	1	0	3	6	3	1	.517	.840
Tadano,K	L	.222	90	20	7	0	3	12	6	20	.278	.400
Throws Right	R	.313	112	35	7	0	3	16	12	19	.389	.455
Takatsu,S	L	.215	107	23	5	0	5	15	11	19	.294	.402
Throws Right	R	.150	113	17	1	0	1	3	10	31	.226	.186
Tankersley,D	L	.230	74	17	6	1	2	7	11	17	.329	.419
Throws Right	R	.281	64	18	2	1	1	10	6	12	.352	.391
Tavarez,J	L	.253	83	21	2	2	1	8	11	12	.347	.361
Throws Right	R	.231	156	36	7	1	0	14	8	36	.288	.288
Taylor,Aaron	L	.300	10	3	0	0	1	3	2	4	.417	.600
Throws Right	R	.333	6	2	0	0	1	4	1	0	.429	.833
Tejera,M	L	.278	18	5	1	0	1	6	4	6	.435	.500
Throws Left	R	.435	23	10	0	0	0	4	5	4	.552	.435
Telemaco,A	L	.267	90	24	2	0	6	12	11	18	.347	.489
Throws Right	R	.235	115	27	8	1	6	12	8	14	.285	.478
Thomas,Brad	L	.800	5	4	1	1	0	6	1	0	.833	1.400
Throws Left	R	.333	9	3	0	0	0	0	0	0	.333	.333
Thomson,John	L	.274	339	93	14	4	9	38	36	67	.342	.419
Throws Right	R	.277	422	117	19	0	11	50	16	66	.312	.400
Thornton,Matt	L	.300	40	12	3	0	1	3	7	16	.404	.450
Throws Left	R	.225	80	18	5	0	1	10	18	14	.364	.325
Timlin,Mike	L	.269	134	36	10	0	3	20	9	24	.319	.410
Throws Right	R	.247	158	39	14	0	5	26	10	32	.306	.430
Tomko,Brett	L	.294	333	98	21	2	9	39	37	40	.364	.450
Throws Right	R	.233	420	98	22	6	10	49	27	68	.280	.386
Torres,S	L	.254	126	32	5	0	2	17	9	15	.299	.341
Throws Right	R	.257	214	55	9	0	4	21	13	47	.316	.355
Towers,Josh	L	.312	276	86	18	1	8	27	18	26	.355	.471
Throws Right	R	.308	201	62	14	0	8	34	8	25	.355	.498
Trachsel,S	L	.245	380	93	19	1	8	34	39	55	.319	.363
Throws Right	R	.279	394	110	29	2	17	56	44	62	.349	.492
Tsao,Chin-hui	L	.286	14	4	1	0	2	3	0	5	.286	.786
Throws Right	R	.143	21	3	1	0	0	4	1	6	.182	.190
Tucker,T.J.	L	.282	103	29	5	2	1	11	9	19	.348	.398
Throws Right	R	.272	162	44	6	0	4	20	8	25	.312	.383
Turnbow,D	L	.125	8	1	0	0	0	0	3	0	.364	.125
Throws Right	R	.091	11	1	0	0	0	0	4	3	.333	.091
Urbina,Ugueth	L	.191	89	17	5	0	2	15	20	17	.339	.315
Throws Right	R	.196	107	21	4	0	5	14	12	39	.289	.374

Pitcher	vs.	Avg.	AB	H	2B	3B	HR	RBI	BB	SO	OBP	Slg.
Urdaneta,Lino	L	1.000	3	3	0	0	0	5	1	0	1.000	1.000
Throws Right	R	1.000	2	2	0	0	0	1	0	0	1.000	1.000
Valdez,Ismael	L	.294	350	103	25	5	18	50	24	24	.341	.549
Throws Right	R	.295	336	99	18	1	15	45	25	43	.342	.484
Valdez,Merkin	L	.600	5	3	1	0	1	6	1	1	.667	1.400
Throws Right	R	.250	4	1	1	0	0	1	2	1	.500	.500
Valentine,Joe	L	.067	45	3	1	0	1	5	15	16	.311	.156
Throws Right	R	.313	64	20	6	1	3	10	10	13	.413	.578
Valverde,Jose	L	.152	46	7	3	0	1	4	10	13	.304	.283
Throws Right	R	.258	62	16	3	0	6	18	7	25	.333	.597
Van Benschoten,J	L	.391	46	18	6	0	0	10	10	6	.491	.522
Throws Right	R	.234	64	15	4	0	3	15	9	12	.342	.438
Van Poppel,T	L	.311	193	60	19	1	11	33	17	26	.370	.591
Throws Right	R	.288	264	76	21	2	11	46	15	46	.326	.508
Vargas,C	L	.301	196	59	16	1	11	38	32	37	.403	.561
Throws Right	R	.239	255	61	11	0	15	38	32	52	.331	.459
Vasquez,Jorge	L	.167	6	1	0	0	0	0	1	0	.286	.167
Throws Right	R	.333	9	3	1	0	1	3	0	4	.400	.778
Vazquez,J	L	.253	395	100	16	5	20	57	39	76	.326	.471
Throws Right	R	.256	371	95	18	0	13	42	21	74	.303	.410
Venafro,Mike	L	.200	20	4	0	0	1	4	2	5	.333	.350
Throws Left	R	.438	16	7	3	0	0	3	1	1	.471	.625
Villacis,E	L	.286	7	2	0	0	1	4	4	0	.545	.714
Throws Right	R	.444	9	4	0	0	0	1	0	0	.444	.444
Villafuerte,B	L	.556	27	15	1	0	1	3	9	2	.676	.704
Throws Right	R	.189	53	10	2	0	1	4	5	11	.259	.283
Villarreal,O	L	.250	28	7	3	1	0	6	3	7	.323	.429
Throws Right	R	.400	45	18	4	0	3	15	4	10	.460	.689
Villone,Ron	L	.203	143	29	3	0	3	20	16	29	.314	.287
Throws Left	R	.247	296	73	16	2	9	39	48	57	.357	.405
Vizcaino,Luis	L	.163	129	21	3	1	6	21	14	36	.245	.341
Throws Right	R	.290	138	40	14	0	6	20	10	27	.333	.522
Vogelsong,R	L	.276	239	66	19	2	10	41	34	43	.368	.498
Throws Right	R	.293	280	82	21	1	12	46	33	49	.378	.504
Waechter,Doug	L	.279	154	43	6	0	17	33	24	16	.381	.649
Throws Right	R	.216	116	25	7	2	3	14	9	20	.281	.388
Wagner,Billy	L	.103	29	3	0	0	0	0	6	13	.133	.103
Throws Left	R	.197	142	28	4	1	5	15	6	53	.235	.345
Wagner,Ryan	L	.224	58	13	2	0	1	5	14	7	.365	.310
Throws Right	R	.307	150	46	9	0	6	36	13	30	.367	.487
Wakefield,Tim	L	.225	347	78	13	2	10	44	32	60	.295	.360
Throws Right	R	.298	399	119	23	3	19	62	31	56	.364	.514
Walker,Jamie	L	.200	115	23	5	0	1	12	7	30	.252	.270
Throws Left	R	.313	147	46	9	1	7	24	5	23	.333	.531
Walker,Kevin	L	.500	2	1	1	0	0	1	1	1	.667	1.000
Throws Left	R	.400	5	2	0	0	1	3	1	0	.571	1.000
Walker,Tyler	L	.287	101	29	6	2	4	11	9	19	.348	.505
Throws Right	R	.288	139	40	7	3	4	22	15	29	.344	.468
Wasdin,John	L	.319	144	46	5	0	10	25	16	13	.396	.563
Throws Right	R	.289	128	37	6	0	8	24	7	23	.324	.523
Washburn,J	L	.225	142	32	5	0	6	21	10	32	.277	.387
Throws Right	R	.283	448	127	34	2	14	54	30	54	.331	.462
Watkins,Steve	L	.227	22	5	1	0	1	3	4	2	.370	.409
Throws Right	R	.333	36	12	5	1	2	11	0	5	.351	.694
Wayne,Justin	L	.349	43	15	1	1	2	5	11	6	.491	.558
Throws Right	R	.247	81	20	3	1	4	15	7	14	.304	.457
Weathers,D	L	.241	116	28	5	0	2	6	20	30	.355	.336
Throws Right	R	.294	194	57	7	2	10	46	15	31	.355	.505
Weaver,Jeff	L	.291	405	118	28	3	13	57	44	61	.371	.472
Throws Right	R	.231	437	101	22	2	6	36	23	92	.274	.332
Webb,Brandon	L	.268	429	115	19	4	11	58	85	77	.390	.408
Throws Right	R	.223	354	79	12	1	6	32	34	87	.304	.314
Webb,John	L	.467	15	7	1	0	1	5	5	3	.600	.733
Throws Right	R	.227	22	5	0	0	1	2	2	6	.320	.364
Weber,Ben	L	.383	47	18	5	0	2	17	12	4	.508	.617
Throws Right	R	.345	55	19	4	0	2	6	3	7	.379	.527
Wellemeyer,T	L	.302	43	13	2	0	1	6	11	15	.449	.419
Throws Right	R	.275	51	14	2	0	0	8	9	15	.371	.314
Wells,David	L	.275	149	41	8	0	10	21	5	19	.297	.530
Throws Left	R	.263	615	162	29	2	13	54	15	82	.282	.380

Pitcher	vs.	Avg.	AB	H	2B	3B	HR	RBI	BB	SO	OBP	Slg.
Wells,Kip	L	.300	247	74	8	1	6	31	34	43	.378	.413
Throws Right	R	.244	291	71	12	4	8	31	32	73	.330	.395
Wendell,Turk	L	.318	22	7	0	1	1	7	7	3	.467	.545
Throws Right	R	.333	42	14	3	1	3	6	5	8	.420	.667
Westbrook,J	L	.262	428	112	30	0	12	55	46	54	.331	.416
Throws Right	R	.247	389	96	18	1	7	29	15	62	.281	.352
Wheeler,Dan	L	.380	108	41	6	0	7	22	11	18	.437	.630
Throws Right	R	.226	155	35	8	0	3	20	9	37	.271	.335
White,Gabe	L	.288	104	30	6	1	6	20	2	14	.306	.538
Throws Left	R	.298	141	42	13	1	8	30	10	27	.344	.574
White,Rick	L	.243	136	33	8	1	8	28	14	25	.309	.493
Throws Right	R	.335	164	55	14	1	7	26	15	19	.396	.512
Wickman,Bob	L	.354	65	23	4	1	3	9	5	13	.400	.585
Throws Right	R	.192	52	10	1	1	1	4	5	13	.288	.308
Williams,Dave	L	.282	39	11	3	1	1	6	3	7	.349	.487
Throws Left	R	.192	104	20	6	0	3	17	10	26	.274	.337
Williams,J	L	.274	234	64	11	3	6	34	35	27	.365	.423
Throws Right	R	.235	251	59	16	1	8	26	9	53	.299	.402
Williams,R	L	.000	7	0	0	0	0	0	3	4	.300	.000
Throws Left	R	.333	9	3	1	0	0	2	0		.500	.444
Williams,Todd	L	.256	43	11	2	0	1	7	3	6	.319	.372
Throws Right	R	.217	69	15	1	0	1	10	6	7	.316	.275
Williams,W	L	.223	337	75	18	2	9	35	33	71	.298	.368
Throws Right	R	.296	399	118	35	1	11	55	25	60	.343	.471
Williamson,S	L	.120	50	6	2	0	0	6	12	10	.288	.160
Throws Right	R	.109	46	5	2	0	0	2	6	18	.241	.152
Willis,D	L	.205	127	26	4	3	1	13	15	42	.294	.307
Throws Left	R	.287	641	184	35	2	19	75	46	97	.341	.437
Wilson,Paul	L	.282	301	85	17	2	11	41	37	48	.361	.462
Throws Right	R	.262	408	107	20	1	15	47	26	69	.312	.426
Wise,Matt	L	.244	90	22	3	0	0	7	4	15	.274	.278
Throws Right	R	.259	112	29	8	0	3	19	11	15	.333	.411
Witasick,Jay	L	.327	101	33	7	1	5	16	15	18	.410	.564
Throws Right	R	.180	133	24	6	0	3	12	11	39	.247	.293
Wolf,Randy	L	.254	122	31	9	0	5	8	8	21	.298	.451
Throws Left	R	.276	413	114	25	2	15	51	28	68	.328	.455
Wood,Kerry	L	.262	248	65	12	5	10	32	30	63	.351	.472
Throws Right	R	.227	273	62	11	1	6	28	21	81	.292	.341
Wood,Mike	L	.326	224	73	18	2	7	29	18	27	.379	.518
Throws Right	R	.234	167	39	8	1	9	33	10	27	.293	.455
Worrell,Tim	L	.310	129	40	8	2	1	16	11	25	.359	.426
Throws Right	R	.211	166	35	7	0	9	26	10	39	.260	.416
Wright,Dan	L	.302	43	13	0	0	4	8	6	3	.412	.581
Throws Right	R	.344	32	11	3	0	1	6	5	3	.432	.531
Wright,Jamey	L	.253	162	41	9	1	4	15	32	22	.383	.395
Throws Right	R	.281	146	41	7	1	4	21	13	19	.354	.425
Wright,Jaret	L	.259	347	90	14	2	8	40	44	68	.343	.380
Throws Right	R	.225	347	78	15	0	3	26	26	91	.280	.294
Wuertz,M	L	.212	33	7	2	0	3	13	9	10	.364	.545
Throws Right	R	.221	68	15	6	0	1	5	8	20	.303	.353
Wunsch,Kelly	L	1.000	1	1	0	0	0	1	1	0	1.000	1.000
Throws Left	R	.167	6	1	0	0	0	1	0	1	.167	.167
Yan,Esteban	L	.255	165	42	9	1	1	18	19	32	.332	.339
Throws Right	R	.292	171	50	10	2	7	31	13	37	.351	.497
Yates,Tyler	L	.330	88	29	7	2	2	14	12	12	.422	.523
Throws Right	R	.296	108	32	5	0	4	18	13	23	.371	.454
Young,Chris	L	.153	72	11	0	0	1	5	5	15	.218	.194
Throws Right	R	.347	72	25	2	0	6	16	5	12	.397	.625
Young,Jason	L	.350	20	7	1	0	2	7	2	2	.409	.700
Throws Right	R	.421	19	8	6	0	1	4	3	5	.500	.895
Zambrano,C	L	.232	370	86	17	2	7	31	43	82	.325	.346
Throws Right	R	.218	403	88	16	4	7	35	38	106	.302	.330
Zambrano,V	L	.241	257	62	11	2	7	31	55	47	.374	.381
Throws Right	R	.217	263	57	16	1	6	32	47	76	.358	.354
Zito,Barry	L	.323	167	54	9	1	5	25	24	34	.419	.479
Throws Left	R	.248	653	162	37	1	23	85	57	129	.309	.413
AL	L	.268	...	...	...	...	...	...	...	...	.344	.430
	R	.270	...	...	...	...	...	...	...	...	.332	.432
NL	L	.270	...	...	...	...	...	...	...	...	.349	.437
	R	.259	...	...	...	...	...	...	...	...	.322	.417
MLB	L	.269	...	...	...	...	...	...	...	...	.347	.433
	R	.264	...	...	...	...	...	...	...	...	.326	.424

These dollar values are based on the Sporting News Ultimate Fantasy Baseball salary cap game. To learn more about Sporting News games, go to http://fantasygames.sportingnews.com. To see a different ranking system for a traditional league style game, check out STATS Fantasy Baseball at http://www.stats.com.

PITCHERS

Rank		Team	$ Value	Points
1.	Johan Santana	MIN	6,570,000	3096
2.	Randy Johnson	ARI	9,240,000	3068
3.	Jason Schmidt	SF	9,000,000	2698
4.	Ben Sheets	MIL	5,540,000	2679
5.	Curt Schilling	BOS	9,070,000	2579
6.	Eric Gagne	LA	9,590,000	2546
7.	Roger Clemens	HOU	6,010,000	2539
8.	Mariano Rivera	NYY	6,720,000	2493
9.	Armando Benitez	FLA	4,650,000	2328
10.	Roy Oswalt	HOU	6,560,000	2319
11.	Brad Lidge	HOU	2,190,000	2273
12.	Joe Nathan	MIN	3,940,000	2269
13.	Carlos Zambrano	CHC	7,560,000	2256
14.	Jason Isringhausen	STL	3,430,000	2253
15.	Francisco Cordero	TEX	3,850,000	2243
16.	Oliver Perez	PIT	1,840,000	2222
17.	Carl Pavano	FLA	5,420,000	2192
18.	Pedro Martinez	BOS	7,500,000	2145
19.	John Smoltz	ATL	6,410,000	2121
20.	Jake Peavy	SD	5,300,000	2032
21.	Livan Hernandez	MON	5,080,000	2019
22.	Octavio Dotel	OAK	4,120,000	2015
23.	Mark Buehrle	CHW	4,960,000	1983
24.	Keith Foulke	BOS	6,620,000	1969
25.	Trevor Hoffman	SD	2,550,000	1880
26.	Chris Carpenter	STL	2,570,000	1878
27.	Freddy Garcia	CHW	4,420,000	1874
28.	Jaret Wright	ATL	1,380,000	1863
29.	Jose Mesa	PIT	2,950,000	1858
30.	Brad Radke	MIN	4,270,000	1843
31.	Jake Westbrook	CLE	2,030,000	1826
32.	Greg Maddux	CHC	5,940,000	1792
33.	Doug Davis	MIL	800,000	1780
34.	Kelvim Escobar	ANA	2,920,000	1729
35.	Odalis Perez	LA	4,250,000	1698
36.	Mark Mulder	OAK	7,920,000	1685
37.	Ted Lilly	TOR	2,610,000	1644
38.	Jason Marquis	STL	1,130,000	1644
39.	Jeff Weaver	LA	2,350,000	1636
40.	John Thomson	ATL	2,410,000	1630
41.	LaTroy Hawkins	CHC	3,190,000	1629
42.	Rich Harden	OAK	2,500,000	1624
43.	David Wells	SD	3,740,000	1587
44.	Danny Graves	CIN	1,990,000	1585
45.	Matt Clement	CHC	5,650,000	1578
46.	Francisco Rodriguez	ANA	3,120,000	1567
47.	Eric Milton	PHI	500,000	1560
48.	Tom Glavine	NYM	3,690,000	1552
49.	Braden Looper	NYM	3,400,000	1548
50.	Russ Ortiz	ATL	5,730,000	1544
51.	Tim Hudson	OAK	8,150,000	1541
52.	Rodrigo Lopez	BAL	1,360,000	1540
53.	Dan Kolb	MIL	3,460,000	1539
54.	Bartolo Colon	ANA	6,610,000	1502
55.	Al Leiter	NYM	4,330,000	1492
56.	Danys Baez	TB	740,000	1458
57.	Matt Morris	STL	4,190,000	1452
58.	Jeff Suppan	STL	3,090,000	1446
59.	Javier Vazquez	NYY	7,530,000	1442
60.	C.C. Sabathia	CLE	5,420,000	1440
61.	Barry Zito	OAK	6,610,000	1439
62.	Josh Beckett	FLA	6,860,000	1421
63.	Brett Tomko	SF	670,000	1417
64.	Bronson Arroyo	BOS	820,000	1415
65.	Troy Percival	ANA	4,110,000	1408
66.	Kris Benson	NYM	2,100,000	1404
67.	Woody Williams	STL	4,000,000	1402
68.	Brian Lawrence	SD	2,980,000	1402
69.	Brandon Webb	ARI	3,830,000	1392
70.	Tom Gordon	NYY	1,760,000	1391
71.	Jose Lima	LA	1,090,000	1384
72.	Steve Trachsel	NYM	2,100,000	1377
73.	Kenny Rogers	TEX	3,960,000	1373
74.	Dontrelle Willis	FLA	5,330,000	1370
75.	Dustin Hermanson	SF	560,000	1359
76.	Shingo Takatsu	CHW	720,000	1346
77.	Billy Wagner	PHI	4,990,000	1343
78.	Adam Eaton	SD	2,360,000	1343
79.	Ryan Drese	TEX	720,000	1337
80.	Chad Cordero	MON	500,000	1332
81.	Nate Robertson	DET	760,000	1325
82.	John Lackey	ANA	1,180,000	1323
83.	Jeremy Bonderman	DET	890,000	1310
84.	Brad Penny	LA	5,190,000	1304
85.	Paul Wilson	CIN	2,900,000	1283
86.	Juan Rincon	MIN	500,000	1276
87.	Jon Lieber	NYY	2,100,000	1266
88.	Mike Maroth	DET	1,910,000	1256
89.	Jon Garland	CHW	1,140,000	1254
90.	Joe Kennedy	COL	550,000	1251
91.	Kerry Wood	CHC	7,680,000	1241
92.	Scot Shields	ANA	840,000	1238
93.	Carlos Silva	MIN	1,750,000	1236
94.	Mike Mussina	NYY	6,840,000	1235
95.	Cory Lidle	PHI	1,250,000	1235
96.	Tim Worrell	PHI	1,740,000	1233
97.	Cliff Lee	CLE	1,620,000	1172
98.	Glendon Rusch	CHC	500,000	1169
99.	Kazuhisa Ishii	LA	3,920,000	1166
100.	Miguel Batista	TOR	1,930,000	1160
101.	Tim Wakefield	BOS	4,570,000	1156
102.	Akinori Otsuka	SD	500,000	1153
103.	Guillermo Mota	FLA	750,000	1147
104.	B.J. Ryan	BAL	500,000	1143
105.	A.J. Burnett	FLA	2,590,000	1133
106.	Jorge Julio	BAL	970,000	1119
107.	Jose Contreras	CHW	3,760,000	1114
108.	Zack Greinke	KC	500,000	1093
109.	Mike Hampton	ATL	2,580,000	1093
110.	Victor Zambrano	NYM	3,070,000	1085
111.	Mark Prior	CHC	8,860,000	1084
112.	Scott Linebrink	SD	500,000	1082
113.	Wilson Alvarez	LA	1,040,000	1073
114.	Ugueth Urbina	DET	1,190,000	1073
115.	Kevin Brown	NYY	8,020,000	1065
116.	Eddie Guardado	SEA	2,560,000	1045
117.	Aaron Harang	CIN	520,000	1026
118.	Shawn Chacon	COL	500,000	1025
119.	Jarrod Washburn	ANA	3,480,000	1011
120.	Mark Redman	OAK	2,570,000	1009
121.	Josh Fogg	PIT	500,000	994
122.	Jason Frasor	TOR	500,000	983
123.	Jerome Williams	SF	2,190,000	967
124.	Ryan Madson	PHI	500,000	963
125.	Kevin Millwood	PHI	4,980,000	961
126.	Roy Halladay	TOR	6,890,000	960
127.	Jamie Moyer	SEA	3,640,000	943
128.	Shawn Estes	COL	1,710,000	938
129.	Orlando Hernandez	NYY	2,570,000	934
130.	Matt Herges	SF	750,000	930
131.	Damaso Marte	CHW	870,000	923
132.	Victor Santos	MIL	500,000	918
133.	David Riske	CLE	500,000	915
134.	Jason Johnson	DET	860,000	915
135.	Paul Byrd	ATL	1,070,000	914
136.	Ron Villone	SEA	500,000	895
137.	Daniel Cabrera	BAL	670,000	895
138.	Ismael Valdez	FLA	500,000	893
139.	Mark Hendrickson	TB	500,000	892
140.	Brett Myers	PHI	1,870,000	889
141.	Salomon Torres	PIT	500,000	882
142.	Joel Pineiro	SEA	2,560,000	867
143.	Sidney Ponson	BAL	2,800,000	859
144.	Justin Duchscherer	OAK	500,000	856
145.	Randy Wolf	PHI	3,080,000	849
146.	Julian Tavarez	STL	500,000	849
147.	Noah Lowry	SF	650,000	847
148.	Derek Lowe	BOS	4,300,000	838
149.	Bobby Madritsch	SEA	1,720,000	834
150.	Juan Cruz	ATL	500,000	829
151.	Kip Wells	PIT	2,690,000	827
152.	Esteban Loaiza	NYY	5,780,000	824
153.	Wade Miller	HOU	3,370,000	815
154.	Luis Ayala	MON	500,000	814
155.	Todd Jones	PHI	500,000	810
156.	Jason Jennings	COL	500,000	805
157.	Jim Brower	SF	500,000	799
158.	Dan Miceli	HOU	500,000	797
159.	Andy Pettitte	HOU	5,770,000	794
160.	Kirk Rueter	SF	1,170,000	787
161.	Esteban Yan	DET	500,000	784
162.	Kevin Gregg	ANA	500,000	784
163.	Rob Bell	TB	500,000	783
164.	David Bush	TOR	500,000	779
165.	Ryan Franklin	SEA	1,540,000	774
166.	Erik Bedard	BAL	500,000	774
167.	J.C. Romero	MIN	500,000	773
168.	Vicente Padilla	PHI	2,430,000	768

#	Name	Team	Salary		#	Name	Team	Salary		#	Name	Team	Salary	
169.	Gary Knotts	DET	500,000	767	234.	Jesus Colome	TB	500,000	513	299.	Erasmo Ramirez	TEX	500,000	333
170.	Greg Aquino	ARI	500,000	761	235.	Joaquin Benoit	TEX	500,000	513	300.	Jeff Fassero	ARI	500,000	326
171.	Ramon Ortiz	ANA	500,000	760	236.	Kyle Farnsworth	CHC	500,000	499	301.	Buddy Groom	BAL	500,000	325
172.	Gil Meche	SEA	1,140,000	756	237.	Tomo Ohka	MON	520,000	496	302.	Ryan Vogelsong	PIT	500,000	325
173.	John Parrish	BAL	500,000	734	238.	Brandon Backe	HOU	500,000	493	303.	Sean Burnett	PIT	500,000	323
174.	Jeremy Affeldt	KC	770,000	732	239.	Horacio Ramirez	ATL	1,670,000	493	304.	Nate Bump	FLA	500,000	322
175.	Travis Harper	TB	500,000	732	240.	Jose Valverde	ARI	500,000	490	305.	Francis Beltran	MON	500,000	322
176.	Rafael Betancourt	CLE	500,000	718	241.	Bob Howry	CLE	500,000	490	306.	Ricardo Rincon	OAK	500,000	321
177.	Jimmy Gobble	KC	500,000	714	242.	Arthur Rhodes	OAK	900,000	484	307.	Scott Dohmann	COL	500,000	320
178.	Antonio Alfonseca	ATL	500,000	711	243.	Brian Shouse	TEX	500,000	480	308.	Danny Haren	STL	500,000	319
179.	Kyle Lohse	MIN	1,250,000	709	244.	Jae Weong Seo	NYM	500,000	466	309.	Curtis Leskanic	BOS	500,000	318
180.	Giovanni Carrara	LA	500,000	706	245.	Rudy Seanez	FLA	500,000	466	310.	Cliff Politte	CHW	500,000	317
181.	Ray King	STL	500,000	694	246.	Joe Horgan	MON	500,000	465	311.	Matt Wise	MIL	500,000	314
182.	Zach Day	MON	950,000	691	247.	Dan Wheeler	HOU	500,000	462	312.	Tim Redding	HOU	680,000	314
183.	Carlos Almanzar	TEX	500,000	688	248.	Scott Eyre	SF	500,000	461	313.	Steve Sparks	ARI	500,000	311
184.	Sun-Woo Kim	MON	500,000	687	249.	Yhency Brazoban	LA	500,000	461	314.	Mike Wood	KC	500,000	310
185.	Justin Speier	TOR	500,000	686	250.	Bruce Chen	BAL	500,000	453	315.	Jon Adkins	CHW	500,000	309
186.	Chris Reitsma	ATL	500,000	681	251.	Rocky Biddle	MON	2,120,000	446	316.	Amaury Telemaco	PHI	500,000	309
187.	Luis Vizcaino	MIL	500,000	679	252.	Trever Miller	TB	500,000	445	317.	Dave Borkowski	BAL	500,000	306
188.	Mike Gonzalez	PIT	500,000	679	253.	Tim Harikkala	OAK	500,000	443	318.	Jeff Bennett	MIL	500,000	306
189.	Dave Burba	SF	500,000	676	254.	Kevin Gryboski	ATL	500,000	443	319.	Brooks Kieschnick	MIL	500,000	305
190.	Ron Mahay	TEX	500,000	674	255.	Scott Schoeneweis	CHW	690,000	441	320.	Matt Ginter	NYM	500,000	304
191.	Matt Miller	CLE	500,000	669	256.	Chad Bradford	OAK	500,000	430	321.	Dave Williams	PIT	500,000	301
192.	John Halama	TB	500,000	666	257.	Mike Adams	MIL	500,000	429	322.	Stephen Randolph	ARI	500,000	300
193.	Kiko Calero	STL	500,000	648	258.	Wes Obermueller	MIL	500,000	422	323.	Randy Choate	ARI	500,000	298
194.	Mike Koplove	ARI	500,000	639	259.	Pete Munro	HOU	500,000	421	324.	Todd Williams	BAL	500,000	297
195.	Ricky Bottalico	NYM	500,000	639	260.	Rick White	CLE	500,000	419	325.	Joe Valentine	CIN	500,000	296
196.	Mike Timlin	BOS	500,000	636	261.	Jason Grimsley	BAL	500,000	418	326.	Ryan Wagner	CIN	500,000	294
197.	Rheal Cormier	PHI	510,000	635	262.	Brian Anderson	KC	500,000	413	327.	John Grabow	PIT	500,000	293
198.	Darrell May	SD	1,730,000	634	263.	Todd Van Poppe	CIN	500,000	411	328.	Scott Sullivan	KC	500,000	292
199.	Steve Kline	STL	500,000	632	264.	Antonio Osuna	SD	500,000	407	329.	Darren Oliver	HOU	500,000	292
200.	Dewon Brazelton	TB	500,000	625	265.	Terry Mulholland	MIN	500,000	406	330.	Kazuhito Tadano	CLE	500,000	289
201.	Frank Francisco	TEX	500,000	622	266.	Alan Embree	BOS	500,000	405	331.	Mike Gallo	HOU	500,000	289
202.	Aaron Sele	ANA	860,000	620	267.	R.A. Dickey	TEX	500,000	400	332.	Doug Waechter	TB	500,000	287
203.	Claudio Vargas	MON	500,000	614	268.	Matt Perisho	FLA	500,000	397	333.	Michael Wuertz	CHC	500,000	284
204.	Duaner Sanchez	LA	500,000	603	269.	Chan Ho Park	TEX	500,000	396	334.	Ricardo Rodriguez	TEX	500,000	284
205.	David Weathers	FLA	500,000	598	270.	Orber Moreno	NYM	500,000	395	335.	Jason Davis	CLE	500,000	280
206.	Cal Eldred	STL	500,000	598	271.	Jamey Wright	COL	500,000	395	336.	Chris Young	TEX	500,000	280
207.	Elmer Dessens	LA	500,000	593	272.	Neal Cotts	CHW	500,000	390	337.	Blaine Neal	SD	500,000	279
208.	Lance Carter	TB	1,060,000	591	273.	Grant Balfour	MIN	500,000	387	338.	Scott Atchison	SEA	500,000	276
209.	Dennys Reyes	KC	500,000	591	274.	Nate Field	KC	500,000	387	339.	Eddy Rodriguez	BAL	500,000	276
210.	Brian Meadows	PIT	500,000	591	275.	John Riedling	CIN	500,000	386	340.	Ramiro Mendoza	BOS	500,000	275
211.	Kent Mercker	CHC	500,000	588	276.	Chad Qualls	HOU	500,000	381	341.	Brian Bruney	ARI	500,000	273
212.	Jamie Walker	DET	500,000	575	277.	Julio Mateo	SEA	500,000	381	342.	Joe Borowski	CHC	2,190,000	271
213.	Felix Rodriguez	PHI	500,000	575	278.	Chad Harville	HOU	500,000	376	343.	Phil Norton	CIN	500,000	269
214.	John Patterson	MON	500,000	575	279.	Darren Dreifort	LA	500,000	376	344.	Matt Kinney	KC	500,000	262
215.	Mike Stanton	NYM	500,000	574	280.	Tony Armas	MON	500,000	375	345.	Tom Martin	ATL	500,000	259
216.	J.J. Putz	SEA	500,000	564	281.	Steve Reed	COL	500,000	372	346.	Roberto Hernandez	PHI	500,000	257
217.	Billy Koch	FLA	1,660,000	561	282.	Josh Hancock	CIN	500,000	371	347.	Allan Simpson	CIN	500,000	256
218.	Brendan Donnelly	ANA	500,000	560	283.	Scott Williamson	BOS	500,000	371	348.	Bartolome Fortunato	NYM	500,000	250
219.	Jose Acevedo	CIN	1,020,000	556	284.	Jon Rauch	MON	500,000	368	349.	Wayne Franklin	SF	500,000	250
220.	Scott Elarton	CLE	500,000	556	285.	Wilfredo Ledezma	DET	500,000	367	350.	Mike Jackson	CHW	500,000	249
221.	Chris Capuano	MIL	500,000	554	286.	Rick Bauer	BAL	500,000	364	351.	Jeff Francis	COL	500,000	244
222.	Chris Hammond	OAK	500,000	554	287.	Shigetoshi Hasegawa	SEA	500,000	364	352.	Eric DuBose	BAL	500,000	243
223.	Terry Adams	BOS	500,000	548	288.	Jim Mecir	OAK	500,000	363	353.	Mike DeJean	NYM	500,000	237
224.	Tanyon Sturtze	NYY	500,000	546	289.	Mike Remlinger	CHC	500,000	359	354.	Brian Fuentes	COL	500,000	235
225.	Tyler Walker	SF	500,000	544	290.	Jesse Crain	MIN	500,000	353	355.	Casey Fossum	ARI	500,000	232
226.	Paul Quantrill	NYY	500,000	544	291.	Mike Myers	BOS	500,000	351	356.	Scott Downs	MON	500,000	231
227.	Jorge Sosa	TB	500,000	542	292.	Jaime Cerda	KC	500,000	350	357.	Ryan Dempster	CHC	500,000	224
228.	Bob Wickman	CLE	500,000	542	293.	Joe Roa	MIN	500,000	349	358.	Tommy Phelps	FLA	500,000	223
229.	Josh Towers	TOR	500,000	538	294.	Vinnie Chulk	TOR	500,000	348	359.	Ben Howard	FLA	500,000	213
230.	Aaron Cook	COL	500,000	537	295.	Al Levine	DET	500,000	336	360.	Bobby Seay	TB	500,000	205
231.	T.J. Tucker	MON	500,000	529	296.	Matt Riley	BAL	500,000	335	361.	Matt Thornton	SEA	500,000	205
232.	Jay Witasick	SD	500,000	525	297.	Jason Christiansen	SF	500,000	334	362.	Geoff Geary	PHI	500,000	203
233.	Shawn Camp	KC	500,000	520	298.	Aaron Fultz	PHI	500,000	334	363.	Justin Miller	TOR	500,000	200

No.	Name	Team	Salary	Val	No.	Name	Team	Salary	Val	No.	Name	Team	Salary	Val
364.	George Sherrill	SEA	500,000	198	429.	Byung-Hyun Kim	BOS	500,000	91	494.	Jorge DePaula	NYY	500,000	19
365.	Heath Bell	NYM	500,000	198	430.	Ryan Bukvich	SD	500,000	90	495.	Javier Lopez	COL	500,000	18
366.	Brian Powell	PHI	500,000	196	431.	Rick Ankiel	STL	500,000	88	496.	Jesse Foppert	SF	500,000	16
367.	Danny Patterson	STL	500,000	194	432.	Felix Diaz	CHW	500,000	87	497.	Mike Neu	FLA	500,000	15
368.	Scott Kazmir	TB	2,260,000	194	433.	Tyler Yates	NYM	500,000	86	498.	Rosman Garcia	TEX	500,000	15
369.	Mike Lincoln	STL	500,000	191	434.	Jason Boyd	PIT	500,000	83	499.	Lou Pote	SD	500,000	12
370.	Roman Colon	ATL	500,000	191	435.	Ben Ford	MIL	500,000	83	500.	Juan Padilla	CIN	500,000	12
371.	Andrew Good	ARI	500,000	185	436.	Jung Keun Bong	CIN	500,000	83	501.	Josh Pearce	STL	500,000	10
372.	Jay Powell	TEX	500,000	183	437.	Russ Springer	HOU	500,000	81	502.	Ben Hendrickson	MIL	500,000	10
373.	Al Reyes	STL	500,000	182	438.	Armando Almanza	ATL	500,000	80	503.	Sam Marsonek	NYY	500,000	10
374.	Mark Corey	PIT	500,000	181	439.	Aquilino Lopez	TOR	500,000	79	504.	Casey Daigle	ARI	500,000	9
375.	Jimmy Serrano	KC	500,000	181	440.	Brian Sweeney	SD	500,000	79	505.	Travis Driskill	COL	500,000	9
376.	Chad Durbin	ARI	500,000	179	441.	Sergio Mitre	CHC	500,000	79	506.	Jim Crowell	PHI	500,000	8
377.	John Franco	NYM	500,000	178	442.	Mike MacDougal	KC	500,000	77	507.	Frank Castillo	BOS	500,000	7
378.	D.J. Carrasco	KC	500,000	177	443.	Jason Stanford	CLE	500,000	77	508.	Shane Nance	ARI	500,000	7
379.	Josias Manzanillo	FLA	500,000	177	444.	Edwin Jackson	LA	500,000	75	509.	Turk Wendell	COL	500,000	6
380.	Bret Prinz	NYY	500,000	176	445.	Jimmy Anderson	CHC	500,000	74	510.	Roy Corcoran	MON	500,000	2
381.	Brad Hennessey	SF	500,000	175	446.	Derrick Turnbow	MIL	500,000	73	511.	Oscar Villarreal	ARI	500,000	2
382.	Gabe White	CIN	500,000	171	447.	Sam McConnell	ATL	500,000	72	512.	Jeremy Griffiths	HOU	500,000	1
383.	Jeff Nelson	TEX	500,000	169	448.	Elizardo Ramirez	CIN	500,000	69	513.	Steve Parris	TB	500,000	0
384.	Kerry Ligtenberg	TOR	500,000	166	449.	Jason Grilli	CHW	500,000	69	514.	Scott Randall	KC	500,000	0
385.	Cliff Bartosh	CLE	500,000	157	450.	Donovan Osborne	SD	500,000	69	515.	Jason Bere	CLE	500,000	0
386.	Jose Jimenez	CLE	500,000	154	451.	Brian Reith	CIN	500,000	66	516.	Mario Ramos	OAK	500,000	0
387.	Ricky Stone	CIN	500,000	153	452.	Steve Karsay	NYY	500,000	61	517.	Jason Pearson	FLA	500,000	0
388.	Justin Wayne	FLA	500,000	150	453.	Fernando Cabrera	CLE	500,000	60	518.	Jason Roach	NYM	500,000	0
389.	Gary Glover	MIL	500,000	149	454.	Carlos Hernandez	HOU	500,000	59	519.	Denny Neagle	COL	500,000	0
390.	Scott Proctor	NYY	500,000	146	455.	Tim Drew	ATL	500,000	58	520.	Chad Paronto	STL	500,000	0
391.	Chad Gaudin	TB	500,000	145	456.	Brad Halsey	NYY	500,000	57	521.	Brady Raggio	ARI	500,000	0
392.	Todd Wellemeyer	CHC	500,000	145	457.	Nick Bierbrodt	CIN	500,000	57	522.	Ruben Quevedo	BAL	500,000	0
393.	Jose Parra	NYM	500,000	144	458.	Scott Service	ARI	500,000	55	523.	Manny Aybar	SF	500,000	0
394.	Travis Smith	ATL	500,000	144	459.	Craig Dingman	DET	500,000	55	524.	Charles Nagy	SD	500,000	0
395.	Kirk Saarloos	OAK	500,000	143	460.	Chad Bentz	MON	500,000	54	525.	John Rocker	TB	500,000	0
396.	C.J. Nitkowski	NYY	500,000	142	461.	Matt Guerrier	MIN	500,000	52	526.	Fernando Rodney	DET	500,000	0
397.	Juan Dominguez	TEX	500,000	141	462.	Justin Huisman	KC	500,000	47	527.	Jason C. Phillips	CLE	500,000	0
398.	Justin Lehr	OAK	500,000	140	463.	Kevin Frederick	TOR	500,000	45	528.	Dan Plesac	PHI	500,000	0
399.	Matt Hensley	ANA	500,000	138	464.	Brandon Duckworth	HOU	500,000	45	529.	Scott Mullen	LA	500,000	0
400.	Brian Boehringer	PIT	500,000	136	465.	Chad Fox	FLA	500,000	44	530.	Rich Rodriguez	ANA	500,000	0
401.	Lenny DiNardo	BOS	500,000	136	466.	Mike Venafro	LA	500,000	43	531.	Tony Mounce	TEX	500,000	0
402.	Steve Colyer	DET	500,000	133	467.	Joe Dawley	CLE	500,000	43	532.	Mike Porzio	CLE	500,000	0
403.	Adam Bernero	COL	500,000	132	468.	Mike Johnston	PIT	500,000	43	533.	Rick Reed	PIT	500,000	0
404.	Mike Gosling	ARI	500,000	132	469.	Rod Beck	SD	500,000	43	534.	Shane Loux	DET	500,000	0
405.	Kirk Bullinger	HOU	500,000	130	470.	Jason Kershner	TOR	500,000	41	535.	Chris Spurling	DET	500,000	0
406.	Aaron Heilman	NYM	500,000	127	471.	Valerio de los Santos	TOR	500,000	40	536.	Matt Roney	DET	500,000	0
407.	Chin-hui Tsao	COL	500,000	125	472.	Mike Nakamura	TOR	500,000	40	537.	Rodrigo Rosario	HOU	500,000	0
408.	Jeremy Fikac	MON	500,000	122	473.	Jason Simontacchi	STL	500,000	40	538.	Tim Spooneybarger	FLA	500,000	0
409.	Cha Seung Baek	SEA	500,000	121	474.	Willis Roberts	PIT	500,000	38	539.	Nate Bland	CHC	500,000	0
410.	Mike Matthews	CIN	500,000	121	475.	Nelson Figueroa	PIT	500,000	37	540.	Sean Lowe	KC	500,000	0
411.	Gary Majewski	MON	500,000	120	476.	Franklyn German	DET	500,000	36	541.	Gabe Molina	CHC	500,000	0
412.	Frank Brooks	PIT	500,000	117	477.	Masao Kida	SEA	500,000	36	542.	Brandon Lyon	ARI	500,000	0
413.	Seth Greisinger	MIN	500,000	117	478.	Brandon Villafuerte	ARI	500,000	34	543.	Brian Moehler	ATL	500,000	0
414.	Joey Eischen	MON	500,000	114	479.	Anastacio Martinez	BOS	500,000	34	544.	Robert Person	CHW	500,000	0
415.	Felix Heredia	NYY	500,000	114	480.	Sterling Hitchcock	SD	500,000	33	545.	Carl Sadler	CLE	500,000	0
416.	Pedro Feliciano	NYM	500,000	113	481.	Matt Mantei	ARI	1,530,000	31	546.	Jason Middlebrook	ANA	500,000	0
417.	Sean Douglass	TOR	500,000	113	482.	Andy Ashby	SD	500,000	31	547.	Pat Mahomes	PIT	500,000	0
418.	Toby Borland	FLA	500,000	108	483.	Dicky Gonzalez	TB	500,000	30	548.	Bart Miadich	TEX	500,000	0
419.	Pedro Liriano	MIL	500,000	108	484.	Darwin Cubillan	BAL	500,000	28	549.	Felix Sanchez	DET	500,000	0
420.	Dennis Tankersley	KC	500,000	108	485.	Will Cunnane	ATL	500,000	28	550.	Jose Mercedes	MON	500,000	0
421.	Mark Malaska	BOS	500,000	107	486.	Rodney Myers	NYM	500,000	28	551.	David Sanders	CHW	500,000	0
422.	John Wasdin	TEX	500,000	105	487.	Scott Stewart	LA	500,000	27	552.	Hector Mercado	PHI	500,000	0
423.	Brandon Claussen	CIN	500,000	104	488.	Brian Falkenborg	LA	500,000	27	553.	Jose Santiago	CHW	500,000	0
424.	Colby Lewis	DET	500,000	101	489.	Brandon Puffer	BOS	500,000	25	554.	Chris Mears	DET	500,000	0
425.	Vladimir Nunez	COL	500,000	101	490.	Pat Hentgen	TOR	500,000	21	555.	Ryan Rupe	BOS	500,000	0
426.	Mike Bacsik	TEX	500,000	99	491.	John Van Benschoten	PIT	580,000	21	556.	Scott Sauerbeck	CLE	500,000	0
427.	Paul Abbott	PHI	500,000	97	492.	Kelly Wunsch	CHW	500,000	20	557.	Dan Reichert	MIL	500,000	0
428.	Roberto Novoa	DET	500,000	96	493.	Eddie Oropesa	SD	500,000	19	558.	Kevin Olsen	FLA	500,000	0

#	Player	Team	Salary	Value	#	Player	Team	Salary	Value	#	Player	Team	Salary	Value
559.	Carlos Reyes	NYY	500,000	0	624.	Rick DeHart	KC	500,000	0	689.	Kevin Correia	SF	500,000	-16
560.	Lance Painter	STL	500,000	0	625.	Matt Anderson	DET	500,000	0	690.	Franklyn Gracesqui	FLA	500,000	-17
561.	Seth McClung	TB	500,000	0	626.	Juan Acevedo	PIT	500,000	0	691.	Dusty Bergman	ANA	500,000	-20
562.	Matt Belisle	CIN	500,000	0	627.	Runelvys Hernandez	KC	500,000	0	692.	Ryan Snare	TEX	500,000	-21
563.	Jose Paniagua	CHW	500,000	0	628.	John Bale	CIN	500,000	0	693.	Vic Darensbourg	NYM	500,000	-21
564.	Kevin Ohme	ANA	500,000	0	629.	Albie Lopez	KC	500,000	0	694.	Aaron Small	FLA	500,000	-22
565.	Dan Serafini	CIN	500,000	0	630.	Troy Brohawn	LA	500,000	0	695.	Dave Lee	CLE	500,000	-25
566.	Jerrod Riggan	NYM	500,000	0	631.	Aaron Looper	SEA	500,000	0	696.	Kevin Walker	SF	500,000	-26
567.	Luis Martinez	COL	500,000	0	632.	Garrett Stephenson	STL	500,000	0	697.	Jesus Sanchez	TOR	500,000	-28
568.	Jason Shiell	BOS	500,000	0	633.	Hector Carrasco	BAL	500,000	0	698.	Joe Nelson	BOS	500,000	-30
569.	Brian Schmack	DET	500,000	0	634.	Chad Zerbe	SF	500,000	0	699.	Shane Reynolds	ARI	500,000	-31
570.	Paul Shuey	LA	500,000	0	635.	Carlton Loewer	SD	500,000	0	700.	Mickey Callaway	TEX	500,000	-32
571.	Jim Parque	ARI	500,000	0	636.	Bryan Hebson	BOS	500,000	0	701.	Pedro Astacio	BOS	500,000	-32
572.	Julio Manon	MON	500,000	0	637.	Graeme Lloyd	KC	500,000	0	702.	Brian Cooper	SF	500,000	-32
573.	Britt Reames	OAK	500,000	0	638.	Rick Helling	TEX	500,000	0	703.	Marty McLeary	SD	500,000	-34
574.	Dan Smith	MON	500,000	0	639.	Doug Linton	KC	500,000	0	704.	Travis Phelps	MIL	500,000	-35
575.	David Manning	CHC	500,000	0	640.	Chris Bootcheck	ANA	500,000	0	705.	Chris George	KC	500,000	-35
576.	Jim Mann	PIT	500,000	0	641.	Pat Strange	NYM	500,000	0	706.	Jairo Garcia	OAK	500,000	-35
577.	Alan Benes	STL	500,000	0	642.	Steve Woodard	STL	500,000	0	707.	Justin Germano	SD	500,000	-39
578.	Kyle Snyder	KC	500,000	0	643.	Scott Strickland	NYM	500,000	0	708.	Adrian Hernandez	MIL	500,000	-40
579.	Randy Keisler	NYM	500,000	0	644.	Kris Wilson	KC	500,000	0	709.	Scott Erickson	TEX	500,000	-48
580.	Juan Alvarez	FLA	500,000	0	645.	Mike Williams	TB	500,000	0	710.	Merkin Valdez	SF	500,000	-48
581.	Reynaldo Garcia	BOS	500,000	0	646.	Allen Levrault	SEA	500,000	0	711.	Brad Thomas	BOS	500,000	-48
582.	Ben Kozlowski	CIN	500,000	0	647.	Pedro Borbon	MON	500,000	0	712.	Adam Peterson	TOR	500,000	-48
583.	Miguel Asencio	KC	500,000	0	648.	Alex Herrera	COL	500,000	0	713.	Jason Anderson	NYY	500,000	-49
584.	Jimmy Journell	STL	500,000	0	649.	Jon Switzer	TB	500,000	0	714.	Andy Pratt	MIL	500,000	-51
585.	Eric Junge	PHI	500,000	0	650.	Matt White	KC	500,000	0	715.	Kevin Appier	KC	500,000	-53
586.	Victor Alvarez	PHI	500,000	0	651.	Jeremy Hill	NYM	500,000	0	716.	Hideo Nomo	LA	3,470,000	-56
587.	Robb Nen	SF	670,000	0	652.	Brian Tallet	CLE	500,000	0	717.	Eduardo Villacis	CHW	500,000	-57
588.	Jason Gilfillan	COL	500,000	0	653.	Jeff Tam	COL	500,000	0	718.	Mike Bynum	SD	500,000	-59
589.	David Cortes	DET	500,000	0	654.	Trey Hodges	ATL	500,000	0	719.	Todd Ritchie	TB	500,000	-59
590.	Nick Neugebauer	MIL	500,000	0	655.	Corey Thurman	MON	500,000	0	720.	Kevin Jarvis	PIT	500,000	-61
591.	Edwin Almonte	BOS	500,000	0	656.	Darren Holmes	ATL	500,000	0	721.	Leo Estrella	SF	500,000	-63
592.	David Cone	NYM	500,000	0	657.	Kevin Tolar	CHC	500,000	0	722.	Arnie Munoz	CHW	500,000	-66
593.	Clay Condrey	PHI	500,000	0	658.	Brian Tollberg	COL	500,000	0	723.	Clint Nageotte	SEA	500,000	-71
594.	John Foster	CHC	500,000	0	659.	Steve Avery	DET	500,000	0	724.	Jeremi Gonzalez	TB	500,000	-73
595.	Doug Creek	STL	500,000	0	660.	Brian Bowles	COL	500,000	0	725.	Jason Young	COL	500,000	-79
596.	Matt Ford	MIL	500,000	0	661.	Mark Watson	CIN	500,000	0	726.	Lance Cormier	ARI	500,000	-79
597.	Tony Fiore	BAL	500,000	0	662.	Les Walrond	KC	500,000	0	727.	Nate Cornejo	DET	500,000	-80
598.	Bud Smith	PHI	500,000	0	663.	Billy Traber	CLE	500,000	0	728.	Grant Roberts	NYM	500,000	-80
599.	Anthony Ferrari	MON	500,000	0	664.	Pete Walker	TOR	500,000	0	729.	Lino Urdaneta	DET	500,000	-88
600.	Hector Almonte	COL	500,000	0	665.	Ryan Jensen	SF	500,000	0	730.	Jared Fernandez	HOU	500,000	-90
601.	John Stephens	BOS	500,000	0	666.	Micah Bowie	OAK	500,000	0	731.	Jeriome Robertson	MON	500,000	-90
602.	Ben Diggins	MIL	500,000	0	667.	Eric Knott	LA	500,000	0	732.	Rafael Soriano	SEA	500,000	-90
603.	Dave Coggin	PHI	500,000	0	668.	Adam Johnson	MIN	500,000	0	733.	Ben Weber	ANA	500,000	-92
604.	Seth Etherton	OAK	500,000	0	669.	Jonathan Johnson	HOU	500,000	0	734.	Michael Tejera	TEX	500,000	-93
605.	Nelson Cruz	FLA	500,000	0	670.	Brad Voyles	KC	500,000	0	735.	Kurt Ainsworth	BAL	500,000	-95
606.	Jayson Durocher	TOR	500,000	0	671.	Cory Vance	TEX	500,000	0	736.	Joe Beimel	MIN	500,000	-95
607.	Adam Wainwright	STL	500,000	0	672.	Greg Jones	ANA	500,000	0	737.	Dan Wright	CHW	500,000	-96
608.	Jason Arnold	TOR	500,000	0	673.	Dave Veres	SF	500,000	0	738.	Alex Graman	NYY	500,000	-99
609.	Jeff Zimmerman	TEX	500,000	0	674.	Aaron Myette	CIN	500,000	-2	739.	Chris Gissell	COL	500,000	-101
610.	Joe Mays	MIN	500,000	0	675.	Mike Fetters	ARI	500,000	-3	740.	Dave Maurer	TOR	500,000	-102
611.	Robert Ellis	PHI	500,000	0	676.	Jamie Brown	BOS	500,000	-4	741.	Shawn Hill	MON	500,000	-104
612.	Jeff Austin	CIN	500,000	0	677.	Rigo Beltran	MON	500,000	-5	742.	Josh Stewart	CHW	500,000	-104
613.	Mark Guthrie	PIT	500,000	0	678.	Ian Snell	PIT	500,000	-5	743.	Denny Bautista	KC	500,000	-106
614.	Juan Cerros	CIN	500,000	0	679.	Jack Cressend	CLE	500,000	-6	744.	Damian Moss	CIN	500,000	-110
615.	Luther Hackman	PIT	500,000	0	680.	Marc Kroon	COL	500,000	-6	745.	Travis Blackley	SEA	500,000	-111
616.	Dave Elder	NYY	500,000	0	681.	Aaron Taylor	SEA	500,000	-7	746.	Jimmy Haynes	DET	500,000	-113
617.	Omar Daal	BAL	500,000	0	682.	Jeff D'Amico	CLE	500,000	-8	747.	James Baldwin	DET	500,000	-120
618.	Eric Eckenstahler	CHC	500,000	0	683.	Carlos Pulido	MIN	500,000	-8	748.	Edgar Gonzalez	ARI	500,000	-256
619.	Josh Hall	CIN	500,000	0	684.	David Aardsma	SF	500,000	-11	749.	Denny Stark	COL	500,000	-299
620.	John Burkett	BOS	500,000	0	685.	Jason Standridge	TB	500,000	-11					
621.	Joey Hamilton	SD	500,000	0	686.	Jason Szuminski	CHC	500,000	-14					
622.	Mike Crudale	PIT	500,000	0	687.	Bobby M. Jones	BOS	500,000	-15					
623.	Roger Deago	SD	500,000	0	688.	Nick Regilio	TEX	500,000	-15					

HITTERS

Rank		Team	$ Value	Points
1.	Barry Bonds	SF	10,690,000	2926
2.	Albert Pujols	STL	9,620,000	2684
3.	Bobby Abreu	PHI	6,320,000	2528
4.	Vladimir Guerrero	ANA	8,070,000	2509
5.	Carlos Beltran	HOU	8,420,000	2488
6.	Todd Helton	COL	8,770,000	2384
7.	Adrian Beltre	LA	4,950,000	2347
8.	Manny Ramirez	BOS	8,260,000	2284
9.	Miguel Tejada	BAL	6,500,000	2266
10.	Lance Berkman	HOU	6,990,000	2211
11.	David Ortiz	BOS	6,070,000	2210
12.	Jim Edmonds	STL	5,370,000	2202
13.	J.D. Drew	ATL	4,320,000	2173
14.	Alex Rodriguez	NYY	8,280,000	2171
15.	Scott Rolen	STL	6,060,000	2164
16.	Gary Sheffield	NYY	7,400,000	2152
17.	Melvin Mora	BAL	4,680,000	2110
18.	Moises Alou	CHC	5,730,000	2039
19.	Adam Dunn	CIN	4,020,000	2015
20.	Johnny Damon	BOS	4,550,000	2014
21.	Hideki Matsui	NYY	5,030,000	1990
22.	Mark Teixeira	TEX	4,810,000	1958
23.	Michael Young	TEX	5,510,000	1933
24.	Travis Hafner	CLE	2,770,000	1930
25.	Aramis Ramirez	CHC	3,880,000	1928
26.	Ichiro Suzuki	SEA	6,040,000	1922
27.	Jim Thome	PHI	7,040,000	1911
28.	Carlos Lee	CHW	4,870,000	1910
29.	Sean Casey	CIN	4,590,000	1905
30.	Vinny Castilla	COL	4,400,000	1888
31.	Jimmy Rollins	PHI	2,930,000	1883
32.	Miguel Cabrera	FLA	4,650,000	1872
33.	Carl Crawford	TB	5,000,000	1865
34.	Hank Blalock	TEX	5,670,000	1850
35.	Carlos Guillen	DET	4,440,000	1843
36.	Derek Jeter	NYY	5,950,000	1841
37.	Jeromy Burnitz	COL	3,880,000	1841
38.	Brian Giles	SD	4,490,000	1827
39.	Paul Konerko	CHW	3,520,000	1824
40.	Mark Loretta	SD	5,010,000	1815
41.	Jeff Kent	HOU	5,620,000	1806
42.	Derrek Lee	CHC	5,840,000	1786
43.	Aubrey Huff	TB	5,240,000	1773
44.	Brad Wilkerson	MON	2,450,000	1746
45.	Steve Finley	LA	4,730,000	1713
46.	Mike Lowell	FLA	5,770,000	1695
47.	Jeff Bagwell	HOU	5,400,000	1676
48.	Juan Pierre	FLA	4,150,000	1665
49.	Lew Ford	MIN	1,470,000	1662
50.	Jose Guillen	ANA	5,120,000	1661
51.	Aaron Rowand	CHW	1,100,000	1642
52.	Matt Lawton	CLE	3,480,000	1642
53.	Alfonso Soriano	TEX	7,480,000	1607
54.	Erubiel Durazo	OAK	2,510,000	1592
55.	Casey Blake	CLE	2,830,000	1575
56.	Phil Nevin	SD	3,550,000	1574
57.	Corey Patterson	CHC	4,020,000	1571
58.	Victor Martinez	CLE	1,780,000	1570
59.	Javy Lopez	BAL	5,380,000	1570
60.	Eric Byrnes	OAK	2,600,000	1562
61.	Eric Chavez	OAK	4,890,000	1562
62.	Lyle Overbay	MIL	2,150,000	1561
63.	Craig Wilson	PIT	3,150,000	1550
64.	Carlos Delgado	TOR	5,800,000	1546
65.	Scott Podsednik	MIL	4,440,000	1542
66.	Shawn Green	LA	4,040,000	1542
67.	Rafael Furcal	ATL	3,870,000	1529
68.	Andruw Jones	ATL	3,830,000	1526
69.	Randy Winn	SEA	1,810,000	1526
70.	Ivan Rodriguez	DET	5,250,000	1524
71.	Craig Biggio	HOU	3,610,000	1521
72.	Tony Batista	MON	1,900,000	1512
73.	Torii Hunter	MIN	2,520,000	1502
74.	Geoff Jenkins	MIL	2,860,000	1497
75.	Ray Durham	SF	3,230,000	1473
76.	Chipper Jones	ATL	4,690,000	1448
77.	Chone Figgins	ANA	3,040,000	1441
78.	Mike Cameron	NYM	2,960,000	1424
79.	Brian Roberts	BAL	3,330,000	1424
80.	Mark Bellhorn	BOS	2,010,000	1422
81.	Mark Kotsay	OAK	1,720,000	1419
82.	Bernie Williams	NYY	2,220,000	1417
83.	Carlos Pena	DET	1,140,000	1398
84.	Scott Hatteberg	OAK	1,960,000	1395
85.	Rafael Palmeiro	BAL	2,920,000	1394
86.	Vernon Wells	TOR	4,420,000	1386
87.	Jorge Posada	NYY	5,700,000	1385
88.	Jack Wilson	PIT	3,050,000	1374
89.	Juan Uribe	CHW	3,660,000	1374
90.	Kevin Millar	BOS	3,710,000	1367
91.	Jermaine Dye	OAK	580,000	1354
92.	Julio Lugo	TB	2,500,000	1354
93.	Marquis Grissom	SF	1,670,000	1351
94.	Cesar Izturis	LA	1,360,000	1345
95.	Shea Hillenbrand	ARI	1,890,000	1343
96.	Jason Varitek	BOS	3,930,000	1338
97.	Coco Crisp	CLE	790,000	1332
98.	Rocco Baldelli	TB	2,080,000	1325
99.	Jose Cruz Jr.	TB	1,700,000	1321
100.	Sammy Sosa	CHC	6,710,000	1307
101.	David Bell	PHI	1,360,000	1303
102.	Kevin Mench	TEX	860,000	1302
103.	Pedro Feliz	SF	1,980,000	1296
104.	Jason Kendall	PIT	2,200,000	1289
105.	Jason Bay	PIT	1,010,000	1289
106.	Edgar Renteria	STL	4,180,000	1276
107.	Omar Vizquel	CLE	2,260,000	1273
108.	Bret Boone	SEA	4,110,000	1269
109.	Tino Martinez	TB	1,120,000	1264
110.	Ronnie Belliard	CLE	2,790,000	1263
111.	Corey Koskie	MIN	1,950,000	1261
112.	Ben Broussard	CLE	520,000	1254
113.	D'Angelo Jimenez	CIN	2,830,000	1251
114.	Reggie Sanders	STL	2,710,000	1248
115.	Milton Bradley	LA	1,860,000	1237
116.	Tony Womack	STL	670,000	1236
117.	Darin Erstad	ANA	2,060,000	1236
118.	Pat Burrell	PHI	2,930,000	1234
119.	J.T. Snow	SF	1,020,000	1233
120.	Mike Sweeney	KC	2,940,000	1222
121.	Luis Castillo	FLA	2,740,000	1220
122.	Jacque Jones	MIN	2,420,000	1211
123.	Paul Lo Duca	FLA	3,060,000	1202
124.	Ryan Freel	CIN	630,000	1179
125.	Placido Polanco	PHI	2,370,000	1177
126.	Craig Monroe	DET	1,060,000	1167
127.	Orlando Cabrera	BOS	2,920,000	1167
128.	Royce Clayton	COL	2,320,000	1163
129.	Rob Mackowiak	PIT	1,500,000	1159
130.	Jeff Conine	FLA	3,220,000	1157
131.	Raul Ibanez	SEA	2,250,000	1155
132.	Khalil Greene	SD	970,000	1155
133.	Edgardo Alfonzo	SF	1,170,000	1150
134.	Johnny Estrada	ATL	590,000	1150
135.	Richard Hidalgo	NYM	5,290,000	1147
136.	Larry Bigbie	BAL	1,180,000	1142
137.	Rondell White	DET	3,530,000	1140
138.	Orlando Hudson	TOR	1,580,000	1133
139.	Ryan Klesko	SD	1,640,000	1125
140.	Jose Valentin	CHW	2,670,000	1123
141.	Luis Gonzalez	ARI	3,960,000	1120
142.	Omar Infante	DET	690,000	1116
143.	Bobby Crosby	OAK	570,000	1115
144.	Michael Tucker	SF	1,580,000	1113
145.	Ty Wigginton	PIT	1,250,000	1109
146.	Michael Barrett	CHC	1,730,000	1105
147.	Bill Mueller	BOS	3,810,000	1097
148.	Jody Gerut	CLE	2,060,000	1094
149.	Cliff Floyd	NYM	2,310,000	1080
150.	Marcus Giles	ATL	4,530,000	1078
151.	Dmitri Young	DET	2,910,000	1070
152.	Dave Roberts	BOS	2,580,000	1070
153.	Larry Walker	STL	4,190,000	1062
154.	Adam Kennedy	ANA	1,690,000	1059
155.	Matt Holliday	COL	690,000	1057
156.	David Newhan	BAL	2,070,000	1057
157.	Garret Anderson	ANA	4,840,000	1057
158.	Danny Bautista	ARI	1,560,000	1056
159.	Mike Lieberthal	PHI	2,080,000	1046
160.	Jose Vidro	MON	2,630,000	1037
161.	Endy Chavez	MON	500,000	1037
162.	Eric Hinske	TOR	1,320,000	1030
163.	Alex Gonzalez	FLA	500,000	1028
164.	Cristian Guzman	MIN	500,000	1025
165.	Bobby Higginson	DET	500,000	1016
166.	David Eckstein	ANA	500,000	1004
167.	Joe Crede	CHW	720,000	1003
168.	Keith Ginter	MIL	660,000	994
169.	Matt Stairs	KC	500,000	991
170.	Tike Redman	PIT	500,000	990
171.	Ramon Hernandez	SD	1,410,000	984
172.	Mike Piazza	NYM	5,120,000	979
173.	Frank Thomas	CHW	3,740,000	978
174.	David Dellucci	TEX	580,000	966
175.	Joe Randa	KC	1,270,000	966
176.	Juan Rivera	MON	500,000	963
177.	A.J. Pierzynski	SF	1,290,000	959
178.	Wily Mo Pena	CIN	500,000	958
179.	Aaron Miles	COL	660,000	957
180.	Todd Walker	CHC	1,740,000	954
181.	Reed Johnson	TOR	1,350,000	948
182.	Ken Griffey Jr.	CIN	5,980,000	948
183.	Terrmel Sledge	MON	500,000	945
184.	Juan Encarnacion	FLA	1,690,000	944
185.	Kazuo Matsui	NYM	3,930,000	939
186.	Brandon Inge	DET	540,000	937
187.	Morgan Ensberg	HOU	1,870,000	936
188.	Sean Burroughs	SD	1,230,000	934
189.	Shannon Stewart	MIN	2,580,000	929
190.	Angel Berroa	KC	1,830,000	922

#	Player	Team	Salary		#	Player	Team	Salary		#	Player	Team	Salary	
191.	Nomar Garciaparra	CHC	6,370,000	881	256.	Doug Mientkiewicz	BOS	1,540,000	604	321.	Calvin Pickering	KC	1,220,000	368
192.	Brady Clark	MIL	500,000	880	257.	Gabe Kapler	BOS	500,000	595	322.	Roger Cedeno	STL	500,000	367
193.	Justin Morneau	MIN	600,000	869	258.	Charles Thomas	ATL	500,000	589	323.	Mark McLemore	OAK	500,000	367
194.	Hee Seop Choi	LA	3,130,000	866	259.	Nick Johnson	MON	2,340,000	580	324.	Mark DeRosa	ATL	1,300,000	365
195.	Chad Tracy	ARI	500,000	862	260.	Jay Gibbons	BAL	1,780,000	579	325.	Joe Mauer	MIN	840,000	364
196.	Josh Phelps	CLE	580,000	853	261.	Mark Sweeney	COL	500,000	576	326.	Jose Offerman	MIN	500,000	363
197.	Ken Harvey	KC	580,000	844	262.	Magglio Ordonez	CHW	4,450,000	574	327.	Miguel Ojeda	SD	500,000	362
198.	Jayson Werth	LA	520,000	844	263.	Scott Hairston	ARI	500,000	573	328.	Richie Sexson	ARI	3,800,000	358
199.	Edgar Martinez	SEA	2,490,000	842	264.	Chris Gomez	TOR	500,000	559	329.	Jorge Cantu	TB	500,000	357
200.	Miguel Cairo	NYY	500,000	832	265.	Jose Castillo	PIT	500,000	550	330.	Willie Bloomquist	SEA	500,000	353
201.	Mike Lamb	HOU	550,000	829	266.	Scott Spiezio	SEA	920,000	549	331.	Jose Molina	ANA	500,000	348
202.	Jay Payton	SD	2,330,000	827	267.	Kevin Youkilis	BOS	500,000	548	332.	Jason Lane	HOU	500,000	345
203.	Deivi Cruz	SF	500,000	821	268.	Jason Giambi	NYY	4,320,000	545	333.	Hector Luna	STL	500,000	343
204.	Jeff DaVanon	ANA	680,000	814	269.	Ben Grieve	CHC	500,000	538	334.	Yorvit Torrealba	SF	500,000	340
205.	Barry Larkin	CIN	500,000	814	270.	Junior Spivey	MIL	1,230,000	536	335.	Vance Wilson	NYM	500,000	336
206.	Adam Everett	HOU	1,250,000	809	271.	Terrence Long	KC	500,000	523	336.	Pokey Reese	BOS	1,420,000	336
207.	B.J. Surhoff	BAL	500,000	808	272.	Carl Everett	CHW	2,390,000	512	337.	Brian Jordan	TEX	500,000	331
208.	Alex Cora	LA	500,000	808	273.	Tony Graffanino	KC	500,000	512	338.	Danny Garcia	NYM	500,000	327
209.	Julio Franco	ATL	500,000	806	274.	Jose Vizcaino	HOU	500,000	511	339.	Luis Terrero	ARI	500,000	326
210.	David DeJesus	KC	500,000	795	275.	Todd Greene	COL	500,000	506	340.	Olmedo Saenz	LA	500,000	324
211.	Eric Young	TEX	500,000	795	276.	Doug Mirabelli	BOS	500,000	505	341.	Jose Macias	CHC	500,000	324
212.	David Wright	NYM	1,690,000	794	277.	Neifi Perez	CHC	500,000	503	342.	Mike Redmond	FLA	500,000	322
213.	Jason LaRue	CIN	500,000	793	278.	Matthew LeCroy	MIN	500,000	497	343.	Dan Wilson	SEA	500,000	316
214.	Rod Barajas	TEX	510,000	792	279.	Mark Grudzielanek	CHC	900,000	495	344.	Robin Ventura	LA	500,000	315
215.	Ruben Sierra	NYY	500,000	791	280.	Timo Perez	CHW	500,000	490	345.	Robby Hammock	ARI	500,000	314
216.	Troy Glaus	ANA	3,300,000	785	281.	Robb Quinlan	ANA	500,000	487	346.	Benito Santiago	KC	500,000	314
217.	Michael Cuddyer	MIN	500,000	783	282.	Todd Hollandsworth	CHC	500,000	486	347.	Rey Sanchez	TB	500,000	307
218.	Adam LaRoche	ATL	500,000	778	283.	Desi Relaford	KC	600,000	483	348.	Dave McCarty	BOS	500,000	304
219.	John Olerud	NYY	740,000	776	284.	Jose Reyes	NYM	2,770,000	481	349.	Jose Lopez	SEA	500,000	303
220.	Alex Cintron	ARI	2,500,000	773	285.	Jamey Carroll	MON	500,000	478	350.	Roberto Alomar	CHW	660,000	297
221.	Daryle Ward	PIT	550,000	765	286.	Felipe Lopez	CIN	500,000	473	351.	Quinton McCracken	ARI	500,000	297
222.	Willie Harris	CHW	570,000	763	287.	Luis Matos	BAL	1,860,000	470	352.	Tomas Perez	PHI	500,000	290
223.	Alexis Rios	TOR	500,000	760	288.	Marcus Thames	DET	500,000	466	353.	Jamie Burke	CHW	500,000	290
224.	Luis Rivas	MIN	500,000	757	289.	Mike Matheny	STL	500,000	465	354.	Jacob Cruz	CIN	500,000	289
225.	Eli Marrero	ATL	500,000	752	290.	Todd Zeile	NYM	500,000	463	355.	Enrique Wilson	NYY	500,000	287
226.	Chase Utley	PHI	500,000	744	291.	Ray Lankford	STL	500,000	460	356.	Jason Smith	DET	500,000	284
227.	Laynce Nix	TEX	500,000	739	292.	Henry Blanco	MIN	500,000	456	357.	Javier Valentin	CIN	500,000	283
228.	Damian Miller	OAK	500,000	738	293.	Marlon Byrd	PHI	1,310,000	455	358.	B.J. Upton	TB	2,580,000	281
229.	Brian Schneider	MON	500,000	734	294.	Karim Garcia	BAL	500,000	454	359.	Juan Gonzalez	KC	2,520,000	272
230.	Charles Johnson	COL	2,880,000	720	295.	Brad Ausmus	HOU	910,000	453	360.	Chris Woodward	TOR	500,000	268
231.	Craig Counsell	MIL	1,630,000	691	296.	Austin Kearns	CIN	1,580,000	452	361.	Gary Bennett	MIL	500,000	260
232.	Marco Scutaro	OAK	500,000	688	297.	Jason Phillips	NYM	1,400,000	446	362.	Dee Brown	KC	500,000	259
233.	Gary Matthews Jr.	TEX	500,000	687	298.	Adam Melhuse	OAK	500,000	443	363.	Jason Grabowski	LA	500,000	257
234.	Luis A. Gonzalez	COL	500,000	684	299.	Bobby Kielty	OAK	500,000	443	364.	Joe Borchard	CHW	500,000	251
235.	Jolbert Cabrera	SEA	500,000	678	300.	John Buck	KC	510,000	442	365.	Kerry Robinson	SD	500,000	250
236.	Jerry Hairston Jr.	BAL	500,000	677	301.	Nick Green	ATL	500,000	441	366.	Matt Kata	ARI	500,000	246
237.	Dustan Mohr	SF	500,000	676	302.	So Taguchi	STL	500,000	440	367.	Orlando Palmeiro	HOU	500,000	242
238.	Jason Michaels	PHI	500,000	668	303.	Marlon Anderson	STL	500,000	440	368.	Robert Fick	SD	760,000	237
239.	Gregg Zaun	TOR	500,000	666	304.	Frank Catalanotto	TOR	1,490,000	438	369.	Chad Moeller	MIL	500,000	234
240.	Bengie Molina	ANA	500,000	662	305.	Trot Nixon	BOS	3,310,000	435	370.	Nick Punto	MIN	500,000	231
241.	Eric Munson	DET	500,000	654	306.	Ricky Ledee	SF	500,000	427	371.	Tim Salmon	ANA	1,530,000	229
242.	Bill Hall	MIL	500,000	650	307.	Geoff Blum	TB	500,000	427	372.	Nook Logan	DET	500,000	226
243.	Toby Hall	TB	620,000	649	308.	Juan Castro	CIN	500,000	424	373.	Gerald Williams	NYM	500,000	225
244.	Miguel Olivo	SEA	500,000	646	309.	Russell Branyan	MIL	500,000	421	374.	Ben Davis	CHW	500,000	224
245.	John Mabry	STL	500,000	640	310.	Shane Spencer	NYY	500,000	417	375.	Todd Pratt	PHI	500,000	224
246.	Eric Valent	NYM	500,000	640	311.	Lou Merloni	CLE	500,000	410	376.	John Flaherty	NYY	500,000	223
247.	Rich Aurilia	SD	790,000	630	312.	Abraham Nunez	KC	500,000	405	377.	Ruben Gotay	KC	500,000	220
248.	Alex Sanchez	DET	2,780,000	621	313.	Bucky Jacobsen	SEA	1,010,000	391	378.	Justin Leone	SEA	500,000	219
249.	Jose Hernandez	LA	500,000	620	314.	Alex S. Gonzalez	SD	500,000	389	379.	Herbert Perry	TEX	500,000	219
250.	Ross Gload	CHW	520,000	616	315.	Preston Wilson	COL	3,730,000	382	380.	Doug Glanville	PHI	500,000	217
251.	Kenny Lofton	NYY	1,570,000	614	316.	Wes Helms	MIL	500,000	373	381.	Eric Bruntlett	HOU	500,000	215
252.	Damion Easley	FLA	500,000	610	317.	Dewayne Wise	DET	500,000	372	382.	Chris Snyder	ARI	500,000	213
253.	Tony Clark	NYY	500,000	608	318.	Grady Sizemore	CLE	500,000	371	383.	Wilson Delgado	NYM	500,000	212
254.	Brad Fullmer	TEX	2,050,000	604	319.	Bobby Hill	PIT	500,000	370	384.	Jorge Piedra	COL	500,000	211
255.	Frank Menechino	TOR	500,000	604	320.	Ramon Martinez	CHC	500,000	369	385.	Augie Ojeda	MIN	500,000	207

#	Player	Team	Salary	Value	#	Player	Team	Salary	Value	#	Player	Team	Salary	Value
386.	Joe McEwing	NYM	500,000	204	451.	Humberto Quintero	SD	500,000	101	516.	Charles Gipson	TB	500,000	20
387.	Dave Hansen	SD	500,000	202	452.	Tom Goodwin	CHC	500,000	99	517.	Jeff Duncan	NYM	500,000	20
388.	Gabe Gross	TOR	500,000	202	453.	Josh Bard	CLE	500,000	97	518.	Henry Mateo	MON	500,000	20
389.	Dave Berg	TOR	500,000	196	454.	Tim Hummel	BOS	500,000	91	519.	Adam Riggs	ANA	500,000	20
390.	Yadier Molina	STL	500,000	191	455.	Lou Collier	PHI	500,000	91	520.	Josh Willingham	FLA	500,000	19
391.	Alex Escobar	CHW	500,000	190	456.	Dallas McPherson	ANA	500,000	90	521.	Brendan Harris	MON	500,000	17
392.	Howie Clark	TOR	500,000	189	457.	Brook Fordyce	TB	500,000	89	522.	Willy Taveras	HOU	500,000	17
393.	Eddie Perez	ATL	500,000	186	458.	Damon Minor	SF	500,000	89	523.	Mike Hessman	ATL	500,000	17
394.	Sandy Alomar Jr.	CHW	500,000	174	459.	Jeff Cirillo	SD	500,000	88	524.	Jhonny Peralta	CLE	500,000	16
395.	Alberto Castillo	KC	500,000	172	460.	Alfredo Amezaga	ANA	500,000	88	525.	Andres Torres	CHW	500,000	15
396.	Brandon Larson	CIN	500,000	172	461.	Adrian Gonzalez	TEX	500,000	86	526.	Jermaine Clark	CIN	500,000	14
397.	Ruben Mateo	KC	500,000	172	462.	Bubba Crosby	NYY	500,000	81	527.	Ramon A. Castro	OAK	500,000	14
398.	Jeff Keppinger	NYM	500,000	170	463.	Freddy Guzman	SD	500,000	79	528.	Rich Thompson	PIT	500,000	13
399.	Clint Barmes	COL	500,000	170	464.	Michael Ryan	MIN	500,000	78	529.	Mendy Lopez	KC	500,000	13
400.	Kevin Cash	TOR	500,000	169	465.	Jason Ellison	SF	500,000	75	530.	Val Majewski	BAL	500,000	12
401.	Raul Mondesi	ANA	1,120,000	169	466.	Esteban German	OAK	500,000	74	531.	Jon Knott	SD	500,000	11
402.	Fernando Vina	DET	500,000	165	467.	Fred McGriff	TB	500,000	70	532.	Damian Jackson	KC	500,000	11
403.	Brad Hawpe	COL	500,000	164	468.	Val Pascucci	MON	500,000	69	533.	Jason Conti	TEX	500,000	11
404.	Gerald Laird	TEX	500,000	164	469.	Brian Buchanan	NYM	500,000	67	534.	Mike DiFelice	CHC	500,000	11
405.	Jeffrey Hammonds	SF	500,000	162	470.	Ricky Gutierrez	BOS	500,000	66	535.	Jason Romano	CIN	500,000	11
406.	Hiram Bocachica	SEA	500,000	161	471.	Andy Green	ARI	500,000	62	536.	Greg Myers	TOR	500,000	9
407.	Tim Raines Jr.	BAL	500,000	159	472.	Damon Hollins	ATL	500,000	58	537.	Danny Ardoin	TEX	500,000	8
408.	Cody Ransom	SF	500,000	159	473.	Wil Cordero	FLA	840,000	55	538.	Ernie Young	CLE	500,000	7
409.	Chris Stynes	PIT	670,000	156	474.	Eduardo Perez	TB	500,000	53	539.	Joe Thurston	LA	500,000	7
410.	Kit Pellow	COL	500,000	154	475.	Adam Hyzdu	BOS	500,000	52	540.	Homer Bush	NYY	500,000	7
411.	Trent Durrington	MIL	500,000	153	476.	Ellis Burks	BOS	500,000	50	541.	Mark Johnson	MIL	500,000	7
412.	Midre Cummings	TB	500,000	151	477.	Ramon Castro	FLA	500,000	50	542.	Darnell McDonald	BAL	500,000	6
413.	Abraham O. Nunez	PIT	500,000	151	478.	Chad Allen	TEX	500,000	50	543.	Denny Hocking	CHC	500,000	6
414.	Einar Diaz	MON	500,000	149	479.	Mike Mordecai	FLA	500,000	50	544.	Esix Snead	NYM	500,000	5
415.	Brent Mayne	LA	500,000	149	480.	Matt Diaz	TB	500,000	49	545.	Rey Ordonez	CHC	500,000	5
416.	Chris Magruder	MIL	500,000	148	481.	Chris Shelton	DET	500,000	49	546.	Larry Sutton	FLA	500,000	3
417.	Josh Paul	ANA	500,000	148	482.	Kelly Dransfeldt	CHW	500,000	49	547.	John Vander Wal	CIN	500,000	2
418.	J.D. Closser	COL	720,000	148	483.	Bobby Estalella	TOR	500,000	47	548.	Ray Olmedo	CIN	500,000	1
419.	Ramon Vazquez	SD	500,000	148	484.	Curtis Pride	ANA	500,000	47	549.	Carlos Rivera	PIT	500,000	1
420.	Humberto Cota	PIT	500,000	145	485.	Alex Prieto	MIN	500,000	47	550.	Jarrod Patterson	KC	500,000	0
421.	Choo Freeman	COL	500,000	145	486.	Ryan Ludwick	CLE	500,000	46	551.	Lance Niekro	SF	500,000	0
422.	Kelly Stinnett	KC	500,000	143	487.	Alan Zinter	ARI	500,000	46	552.	Michael Rivera	OAK	500,000	0
423.	Casey Kotchman	ANA	500,000	142	488.	Craig Brazell	NYM	500,000	46	553.	Ruben Rivera	BAL	500,000	0
424.	Tim Laker	CLE	500,000	137	489.	Jason Dubois	CHC	500,000	45	554.	Julio Ramirez	ARI	500,000	0
425.	Randall Simon	TB	500,000	137	490.	Jeff Liefer	MIL	500,000	44	555.	Marvin Benard	TOR	500,000	0
426.	Brian Daubach	BOS	500,000	136	491.	Cody McKay	STL	500,000	44	556.	Ben Petrick	SD	500,000	0
427.	Darren Bragg	CIN	500,000	135	492.	Luis Lopez	BAL	500,000	43	557.	Adam Piatt	CLE	500,000	0
428.	Aaron Guiel	KC	500,000	135	493.	Damian Rolls	TB	500,000	41	558.	Tom Prince	KC	500,000	0
429.	John McDonald	CLE	500,000	133	494.	Wilton Guerrero	KC	500,000	41	559.	Warren Morris	DET	500,000	0
430.	Shane Halter	ANA	500,000	129	495.	Colin Porter	STL	500,000	39	560.	Chris Singleton	PIT	500,000	0
431.	Xavier Nady	SD	500,000	129	496.	Simon Pond	TOR	500,000	39	561.	Jose Morban	BAL	500,000	0
432.	Jesse Garcia	ATL	500,000	128	497.	Jose Leon	BAL	500,000	39	562.	Mandy Romero	COL	500,000	0
433.	Juan Brito	ARI	500,000	127	498.	Tony Torcato	SF	500,000	38	563.	Cody Ross	LA	500,000	0
434.	David Segui	BAL	500,000	127	499.	Geronimo Gil	BAL	500,000	38	564.	Trey Lunsford	SF	500,000	0
435.	Andres Blanco	KC	500,000	125	500.	Ron Calloway	MON	500,000	38	565.	Wilkin Ruan	KC	500,000	0
436.	Paul Bako	CHC	500,000	122	501.	Greg Norton	DET	500,000	38	566.	Eric Owens	DET	500,000	0
437.	Doug DeVore	ARI	500,000	119	502.	Ryan Church	MON	500,000	36	567.	Pablo Ozuna	PHI	500,000	0
438.	Chris Aguila	FLA	500,000	114	503.	Matt Treanor	FLA	500,000	36	568.	Chad Meyers	DET	500,000	0
439.	Michael Restovich	MIN	500,000	112	504.	Matt Cepicky	MON	500,000	36	569.	Jay Bell	NYM	500,000	0
440.	Lenny Harris	FLA	500,000	111	505.	Ramon Santiago	SEA	500,000	35	570.	Freddy Sanchez	PIT	500,000	0
441.	Pat Borders	MIN	500,000	110	506.	Byron Gettis	DET	500,000	34	571.	Zach Sorensen	ANA	500,000	0
442.	Carlos Baerga	ARI	500,000	110	507.	Chad Mottola	BAL	500,000	34	572.	Jared Sandberg	TB	500,000	0
443.	Billy McMillon	OAK	500,000	105	508.	Antonio Perez	LA	500,000	33	573.	Orlando Merced	PIT	500,000	0
444.	Eric Karros	OAK	500,000	104	509.	Andres Galarraga	ANA	500,000	31	574.	Donaldo Mendez	PIT	500,000	0
445.	David Ross	LA	500,000	104	510.	Manny Alexander	TEX	500,000	29	575.	Carlos Mendez	BAL	500,000	0
446.	Garrett Atkins	COL	500,000	103	511.	J.J. Davis	PIT	500,000	27	576.	Angel Santos	CLE	500,000	0
447.	Joey Gathright	TB	500,000	103	512.	Alexis Gomez	DET	500,000	26	577.	Francisco Santos	SF	500,000	0
448.	Tim Olson	ARI	500,000	102	513.	Ramon Nivar	TEX	500,000	25	578.	Dane Sardinha	CIN	500,000	0
449.	Brian Dallimore	SF	500,000	101	514.	Brandon Berger	KC	500,000	22	579.	Dean Palmer	DET	500,000	0
450.	Raul Chavez	HOU	500,000	101	515.	Todd Linden	SF	500,000	22	580.	Todd Sears	SD	500,000	0

#	Player	Team	Salary	Value		#	Player	Team	Salary	Value		#	Player	Team	Salary	Value
581.	Fernando Seguignol	NYY	500,000	0		646.	Mark Ellis	OAK	500,000	0		711.	Shawn Wooten	PHI	500,000	-5
582.	Chris Richard	COL	500,000	0		647.	Aaron Boone	CLE	1,320,000	0		712.	Andy Dominique	BOS	500,000	-6
583.	Bill Selby	CHC	500,000	0		648.	Victor Hall	ARI	500,000	0		713.	Matt Erickson	MIL	500,000	-6
584.	Dave Matranga	HOU	500,000	0		649.	George Lombard	BOS	500,000	0		714.	David Kelton	CHC	500,000	-6
585.	Julius Matos	TOR	500,000	0		650.	Brent Butler	ATL	500,000	0		715.	Cesar Crespo	BOS	500,000	-7
586.	Troy O'Leary	CHC	500,000	0		651.	Pete Zoccolillo	TEX	500,000	0		716.	Tom Wilson	LA	500,000	-7
587.	Luis Sojo	NYY	500,000	0		652.	Bill Haselman	BAL	500,000	0		717.	Chin-Feng Chen	LA	500,000	-8
588.	Prentice Redman	NYM	500,000	0		653.	Kevin Young	MIN	500,000	0		718.	Mike Tonis	KC	500,000	-9
589.	Al Martin	TB	500,000	0		654.	Keith Lockhart	SD	500,000	0		719.	Felix Escalona	NYY	500,000	-10
590.	Tsuyoshi Shinjo	NYM	500,000	0		655.	Rickey Henderson	LA	500,000	0		720.	Chris Burke	HOU	500,000	-11
591.	Craig Paquette	STL	500,000	0		656.	Drew Henson	NYY	500,000	0		721.	Ken Huckaby	TEX	500,000	-13
592.	Terry Shumpert	PIT	500,000	0		657.	Jamal Strong	SEA	500,000	0		722.	Donnie Sadler	CHW	500,000	-14
593.	Jeff Reboulet	PIT	500,000	0		658.	Jason Childers	MON	500,000	0		723.	Sandy Martinez	BOS	500,000	-15
594.	Mark Smith	PHI	500,000	0		659.	Mike Hinckley	MON	500,000	0		724.	Chad Hermansen	TOR	500,000	-17
595.	Stephen Smitherman	CIN	500,000	0		660.	Kevin Witt	STL	500,000	0		725.	Jose Bautista	PIT	500,000	-19
596.	Armando Rios	STL	500,000	0		661.	Pedro Swann	BAL	500,000	0		726.	Raul Gonzalez	CLE	500,000	-19
597.	Chris Mabeus	OAK	500,000	0		662.	Michel Hernandez	PHI	500,000	0		727.	Jonny Gomes	TB	500,000	-19
598.	Adam Loewen	BAL	500,000	0		663.	Chris Widger	STL	500,000	0		728.	Brandon Phillips	CLE	500,000	-19
599.	Felix Jose	ARI	500,000	0		664.	Ryan Langerhans	ATL	500,000	0		729.	Peter Bergeron	MIL	500,000	-21
600.	Mark Budzinski	PHI	500,000	0		665.	Barry Wesson	ANA	500,000	0		730.	Rene Reyes	CHC	500,000	-21
601.	Marty Cordova	BAL	500,000	0		666.	Larry Barnes	LA	500,000	0		731.	Wilson Betemit	ATL	500,000	-22
602.	Ron Gant	OAK	500,000	0		667.	Reggie Taylor	CHW	500,000	0		732.	Greg Colbrunn	ARI	500,000	-25
603.	Corwin Malone	CHW	500,000	0		668.	Jeremy Lambert	BOS	500,000	0		733.	Luis Lopez	ATL	500,000	-30
604.	Ron Coomer	LA	500,000	0		669.	Tyler Houston	NYY	500,000	0		734.	Corky Miller	MIN	500,000	-31
605.	Jorge Velandia	ATL	500,000	0		670.	Andy Abad	PIT	500,000	0		735.	Keith Osik	TB	500,000	-43
606.	D.J. Mattox	CIN	500,000	0		671.	Trenidad Hubbard	CHC	500,000	0		736.	Andy Fox	TEX	500,000	-51
607.	Rett Johnson	SEA	500,000	0		672.	Chris Latham	NYY	500,000	0						
608.	Nic Jackson	CHC	500,000	0		673.	Rickie Weeks	MIL	500,000	0						
609.	Jeremy Giambi	LA	500,000	0		674.	Greg LaRocca	CLE	500,000	0						
610.	Pat Meares	PIT	500,000	0		675.	Todd Hundley	LA	500,000	0						
611.	Benji Gil	DET	500,000	0		676.	Brian L. Hunter	STL	500,000	0						
612.	Tim Hamulack	BOS	500,000	0		677.	Mark Teahen	KC	500,000	0						
613.	Josh Hamilton	TB	500,000	0		678.	Pete LaForest	TB	500,000	0						
614.	Joe Girardi	NYY	500,000	0		679.	Cory Sullivan	COL	500,000	0						
615.	Matt Franco	ATL	500,000	0		680.	Matt Watson	OAK	500,000	0						
616.	Mike Glavine	NYM	500,000	0		681.	Chad Kreuter	TEX	500,000	0						
617.	Talley Haines	TOR	500,000	0		682.	Mike Bordick	TOR	500,000	0						
618.	Alfredo Gonzalez	LA	500,000	0		683.	Graham Koonce	OAK	500,000	0						
619.	Erick Almonte	COL	500,000	0		684.	Bubba Trammell	TB	500,000	0						
620.	Dave Parrish	NYY	500,000	0		685.	Chris Truby	PIT	500,000	0						
621.	Jason Ryan	KC	500,000	0		686.	Brent Abernathy	CLE	500,000	0						
622.	Tripp Cromer	HOU	500,000	0		687.	Jason Tyner	CLE	500,000	0						
623.	Jerome Gamble	BOS	500,000	0		688.	Matt Walbeck	DET	500,000	0						
624.	Henri Stanley	LA	500,000	0		689.	Danny Klassen	DET	500,000	0						
625.	Wiki Gonzalez	SEA	500,000	0		690.	Mike Kinkade	LA	500,000	0						
626.	Morgan Burkhart	CHW	500,000	0		691.	Gene Kingsale	BAL	500,000	0						
627.	Enrique Cruz	MIL	500,000	0		692.	Luis Ugueto	SEA	500,000	0						
628.	Carlos Febles	BOS	500,000	0		693.	Joe Vitiello	DET	500,000	0						
629.	Ryan Christenson	FLA	500,000	0		694.	Rontrez Johnson	ATL	500,000	0						
630.	Derek Thompson	LA	500,000	0		695.	Carlos Valderrama	SF	500,000	0						
631.	Steve Cox	STL	500,000	0		696.	Greg Vaughn	STL	500,000	0						
632.	Tom Gregorio	ANA	500,000	0		697.	Gary Johnson	ANA	500,000	0						
633.	Mike Bumatay	COL	500,000	0		698.	Jason Jones	TEX	500,000	0						
634.	Brian Banks	FLA	500,000	0		699.	Shane Victorino	LA	500,000	0						
635.	Danny Borrell	NYY	500,000	0		700.	Rob Bowen	MIN	500,000	-1						
636.	Colter Bean	NYY	500,000	0		701.	Bo Hart	STL	500,000	-2						
637.	Alec Zumwalt	ATL	500,000	0		702.	Jerry Gil	ARI	500,000	-2						
638.	Travis Chapman	KC	500,000	0		703.	A.J. Hinch	PHI	500,000	-2						
639.	Jim Chamblee	CIN	500,000	0		704.	Earl Snyder	BOS	500,000	-2						
640.	Edwards Guzman	BAL	500,000	0		705.	Adrian Brown	KC	500,000	-3						
641.	Fernando Tatis	TB	500,000	0		706.	Jack Cust	BAL	500,000	-3						
642.	Mike Edwards	OAK	500,000	0		707.	Mark Little	CLE	500,000	-3						
643.	Gookie Dawkins	CHC	500,000	0		708.	Corey Hart	MIL	500,000	-3						
644.	Jovanny Cedeno	TEX	500,000	0		709.	Travis Lee	NYY	1,370,000	-4						
645.	Joe DePastino	ATL	500,000	0		710.	Robert Machado	BAL	500,000	-5						